# FEATURES AND BENEFITS
## *MathMatters 2* ©2006

**See page(s):**

| | | |
|---|---|---|
| **Student-Friendly** | . . . real-life application and career features build excitement for and understanding of mathematics. | |
| | • Chapter openers incorporate high-interest themes for both individual and group investigations. | 146–147 |
| | • Each lesson begins with an easy-to-do activity that helps build understanding. | 192 |
| | • Problem-solving lessons engage the student in the learning process to build their confidence. | 274–275 |
| | • **Math***Works* **Careers** feature helps students apply their knowledge to see the usefulness of math in their lives. | 323 |
| **Reading/Writing/ Communicating Mathematics** | . . . strategies and activities are essential for student success in mathematics. | |
| | • Key concepts are included in highlighted rectangles for quick reference and emphasis. | 86 |
| | • Frequent **Reading Math** and **Check Understanding** notes appear at the point of need. | 126–127, 133 |
| | • Frequent **Writing Math** practice problems help students build strong math communication skills. | 204, 209 |
| | • Lesson opener activities require students to communicate their results or observations. | 248 |
| **Intervention and Student Help** | • **Are You Ready?** feature at the beginning of each chapter refreshes skills needed throughout the chapter. | 294–295 |
| | • Homework exercises include a generous balance of applications, concepts, and skills to ensure students receive the practice that best suits their needs. | 312–313 |
| | • **Review and Practice Your Skills** feature covers the previous two lessons' content to provide more help with newly introduced concepts. | 394–395 |
| | • Extensive **Chapter Reviews** include both Vocabulary and individual lesson practice. | 464–466 |
| | • A wide variety of Online Study Tools are provided at **www.mathmatters2.com**. | 489, 491, 503, 513, 516 |
| **Test Preparation and Assessment** | . . . provide targeted practice for local, state, and national tests. | |
| | • **Mid-Chapter Quiz** includes lesson references for quick reviews. | 167 |
| | • **Chapter Assessment** includes a link for additional assessment at **www.mathmatters2.com/chapter_assessment**. | 185 |
| | • Every chapter concludes with a two-page **Standardized Test Practice** covering multiple-choice, short-response/grid-in, and extended-response assessment formats. Additional standardized test practice problems are available at **www.mathmatters2.com/standardized_test**. | 328–329 |
| | • A special **Preparing for Standardized Tests** section provides test-taking tips, examples, and practice covering four types of assessment formats: multiple choice, gridded response, short response, and extended response. | 627–644 |
| **Staff Development** | . . . features are available to assist new teachers and teachers new to teaching *MathMatters 2*. | |
| | • The **Teacher's Handbook** located at the front of the **Annotated Teacher's Edition** provides detailed information about student learning, assessment, technology, and course planning. | vii–xvi |
| | • The **Resource Manager** located at the beginning of each chapter in the Annotated Teacher's Edition includes suggested pacing, assessment options, information on Glencoe technology, and a lot more. | 292A–292D |

*"Sticky Notes" in Chapter 1 provide a "walk-through" of key features. pp. 2–47*

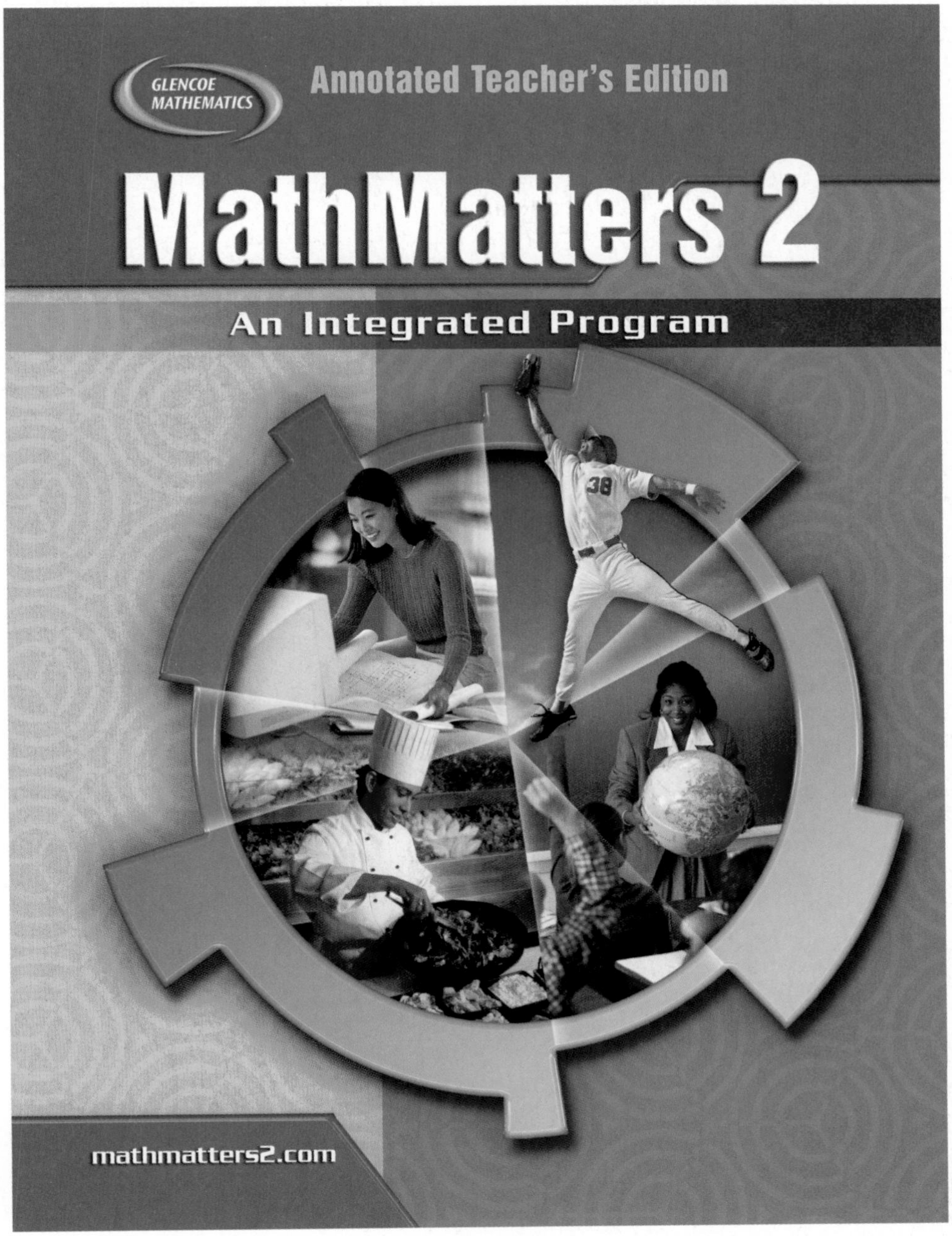

GLENCOE MATHEMATICS

Annotated Teacher's Edition

# MathMatters 2

## An Integrated Program

mathmatters2.com

**Lynch**

**Olmstead**

**De Forest-Davis**

McGraw Hill Glencoe

New York, New York
Columbus, Ohio
Chicago, Illinois
Peoria, Illinois
Woodland Hills, California

The McGraw-Hill Companies

Send all inquiries to:
Glencoe/McGraw-Hill
8787 Orion Place
Columbus, OH 43240-4027

ISBN: 0-07-868176-6   (Student Edition)
ISBN: 0-07-868177-4   (Annotated Teacher's Edition)

Printed in the United States of America

2 3 4 5 6 7 8 9 10 058/111 10 09 08 07

# Contents in Brief

**Chapter 1 Sample and Display Data** ....................................2
Theme: Market Research

**2 Foundations of Algebra** ..............................48
Theme: Population

**3 Equations and Inequalities** ....................100
Theme: Physics

**4 Probability** ........................................146
Theme: Games

**5 Logic and Geometry** ..............................188
Theme: Navigation

**6 Graphing Functions** ..............................240
Theme: Business

**7 Coordinate Graphing and Transformations** ..............292
Theme: Architecture

**8 Systems of Equations and Inequalities** ..................330
Theme: Sports

**9 Polynomials** ........................................372
Theme: Geography

**10 Three-Dimensional Geometry** ....................418
Theme: History

**11 Right Triangle Trigonometry** ....................470
Theme: Photography

**12 Logic and Sets** ....................................516
Theme: Music

# Authors

**Chicha Lynch** currently teaches Honors Advanced Algebra II at Marin Catholic High School in Kentfield, California. She is a graduate of the University of Florida. She was a state finalist in 1988 for the Presidential Award for Excellence in mathematics teaching. Currently, Ms. Lynch is a participating member of the National Council of Teachers of Mathematics as well as a long-time member of California Math Council North.

**Eugene Olmstead** is a mathematics teacher at Elmira Free Academy in Elmira, New York. He earned his B.S. in Mathematics at State University College at Geneseo in New York. In addition to teaching high school, Mr. Olmstead is an instructor for $T^3$, Teachers Teaching with Technology, and has participated in writing several of the $T^3$ Institutes. In 1991 and 1992, Mr. Olmstead was selected as a state finalist for the Presidential Award for Excellence in mathematics teaching.

**Kenneth De Forest-Davis** is the mathematics department chairperson at Beloit Memorial High School in Beloit, Wisconsin. Mr. De Forest-Davis earned his B.A. in Mathematics and Computer Science from Beloit College in Wisconsin. He later completed his M.A.T from Beloit College, where he received the Von-Eschen-Steele Excellence in Teaching Award.

# Reviewers and Consultants

These educators reviewed every chapter and gave suggestions for improving the effectiveness of the mathematics instruction.

**Tamara L. Amundsen**
Teacher
Windsor Forest High School
Savannah, Georgia

**Kyle A. Anderson**
Mathematics Teacher
Waiakea High School
Milo, Hawaii

**Murney Bell**
Mathematics and Science
   Teacher
Anchor Bay High School
New Baltimore, Michigan

**Fay Bonacorsi**
High School Math Teacher
Lafayette High School
Brooklyn, New York

**Boon C. Boonyapat**
Mathematics Department
   Chairman
Henry W. Grady High School
Atlanta, Georgia

**Peggy A. Bosworth**
Retired Math Teacher
Plymouth-Canton High School
Canton, Michigan

**Sandra C. Burke**
Mathematics Teacher
Page High School
Page, Arizona

**Jill Conrad**
Math Teacher
Crete Public Schools
Crete, Nebraska

**Nancy S. Cross**
Math Educator
Merritt High School
Merritt Island, Florida

**Mary G. Evangelista**
Chairperson, Mathematics
   Department
Grove High School
Garden City, Georgia

**Timothy J. Farrell**
Teacher of Mathematics and
   Physical Science
Perth Amboy Adult School
Perth Amboy, New Jersey

**Greg A. Faulhaber**
Mathematics and Computer
   Science Teacher
Winton Woods High School
Cincinnati, Ohio

**Leisa Findley**
Math Teacher
Carson High School
Carson City, Nevada

**Linda K. Fiscus**
Mathematics Teacher
New Oxford High School
New Oxford, Pennsylvania

**Louise M. Foster**
Teacher and Mathematics
   Department Chairperson
Frederick Douglass High School
Altanta, Georgia

**Darleen L. Gearhart**
Mathematics Curriculum
   Specialist
Newark Public Schools
Newark, New Jersey

**Faye Gunn**
Teacher
Douglass High School
Atlanta, Georgia

**Dave Harris**
Math Department Head
Cedar Falls High School
Cedar Falls, Iowa

**Barbara Heinrich**
Teacher
Wauconda High School
Wauconda, Illinois

**Margie Hill**
District Coordinating Teacher
   Mathematics, K-12
Blue Valley School District
   USD229
Overland Park, Kansas

**Suzanne E. Hills**
Mathematics Teacher
Halifax Area High School
Halifax, Pennsylvania

**Robert J. Holman**
Mathematics Department
St. John's Jesuit High School
Toledo, Ohio

**Eric Howe**
Applied Math Graduate Student
Air Force Institute of Technology
Dayton, Ohio

**Daniel R. Hudson**
Mathematics Teacher
Northwest Local School District
Cincinnati, Ohio

**Susan Hunt**
Math Teacher
Del Norte High School
Albuquerque, New Mexico

**Todd J. Jorgenson**
Secondary Mathematics
    Instructor
Brookings High School
Brookings, South Dakota

**Susan H. Kohnowich**
Math Teacher
Hartford High School
White River Junction, Vermont

**Mercedes Kriese**
Chairperson, Mathematics
    Department
Neenah High School
Neenah, Wisconsin

**Kathrine Lauer**
Mathematics Teacher
Decatur High School
Federal Way, Washington

**Laurene Lee**
Mathematics Instructor
Hood River Valley High School
Hood River, Oregon

**Randall P. Lieberman**
Math Teacher
Lafayette High School
Brooklyn, New York

**Scott Louis**
Mathematics Teacher
Elder High School
Cincinnati, Ohio

**Dan Lufkin**
Mathematics Instructor
Foothill High School
Pleasanton, California

**Gary W. Lundquist**
Teacher
Macomb Community College
Warren, Michigan

**Evelyn A. McDaniel**
Mathematics Teacher
Natrona County High School
Casper, Wyoming

**Lin McMullin**
Educational Consultant
Ballston Spa, New York

**Margaret H. Morris**
Mathematics Instructor
Saratoga Springs Senior High
    School
Saratoga Springs, New York

**Tom Muchlinski**
Mathematics Resource Teacher
Wayzata Public Schools
Plymouth, Minnesota

**Andy Murr**
Mathematics
Wasilla High School
Wasilla, Alaska

**Janice R. Oliva**
Mathematics Teacher
Maury High School
Norfolk, Virginia

**Fernando Rendon**
Mathematics Teacher
Tucson High Magnet
    School/Tucson Unified
    School District #1
Tucson, Arizona

**Candace Resmini**
Mathematics Teacher
Belfast Area High School
Belfast, Maine

**Kathleen A. Rooney**
Chairperson, Mathematics
    Department
Yorktown High School
Arlington, Virginia

**Mark D. Rubio**
Mathematics Teacher
Hoover High School—GUSD
Glendale, California

**Tony Santilli**
Chairperson, Mathematics
    Department
Godwin Heights High School
Wyoming, Michigan

**Michael Schlomer**
Mathematics Department Chair
Elder High School
Cincinnati, Ohio

**Jane E. Swanson**
Math Teacher
Warren Township High School
Gurnee, Illinois

**Martha Taylor**
Teacher
Jesuit College Preparatory School
Dallas, Texas

**Cheryl A. Turner**
Chairperson, Mathematics
    Department
LaQuinta High School
LaQuinta, California

**Linda Wadman**
Instructor, Mathematics
Cut Bank High School
Cut Bank, Montana

**George K. Wells**
Coordinator of Mathematics
Mt. Mansfield Union
    High School
Jericho, Vermont

# Teacher Handbook

## Table of Contents

Integrated Instructional Approach .................................. viii

Reading and Writing ................................................... x

Intervention ............................................................... xi

Assessment .............................................................. xii

Time-Saving Teacher Resources ................................. xiii

Scope and Sequence ................................................. xiv

Pacing ..................................................................... xvi

# Motivate Students by Integrating

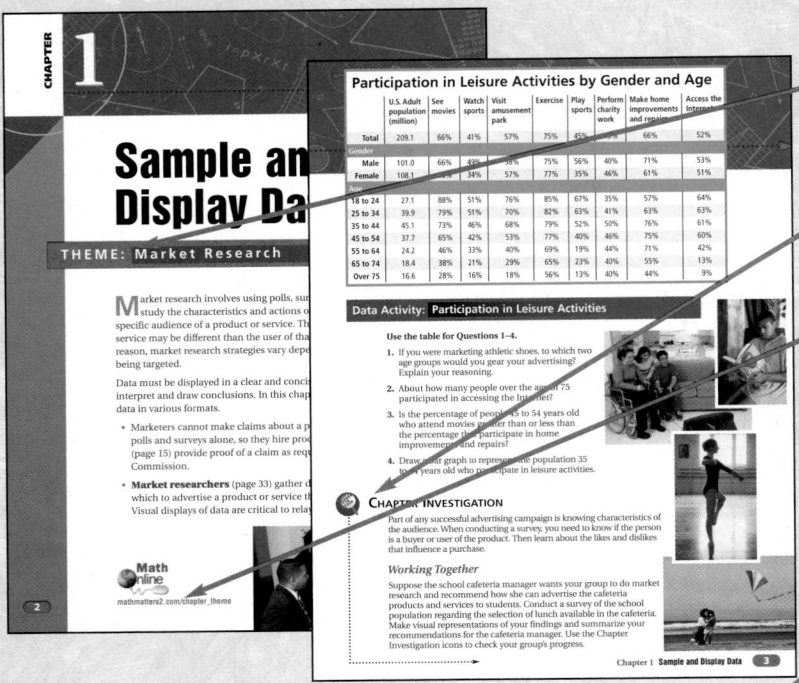

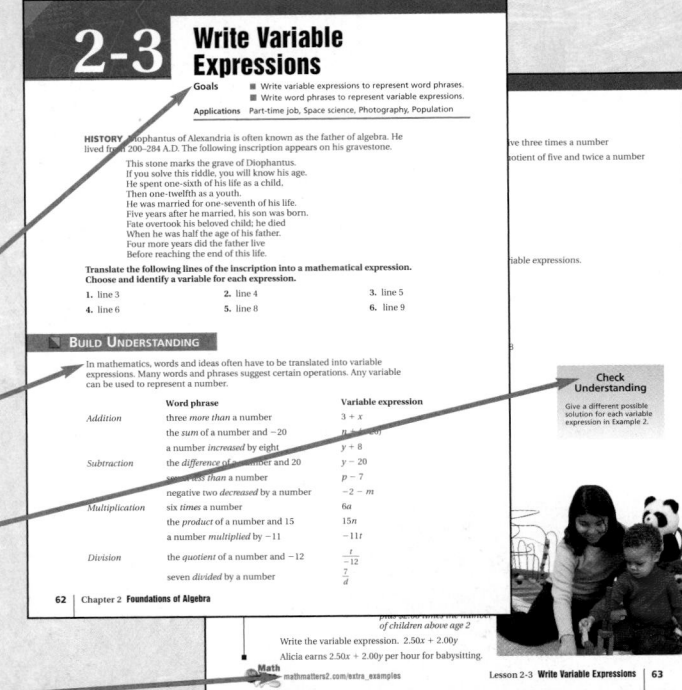

A **theme**, such as travel, sports, or architecture, introduces each chapter, reinforcing the importance of mathematics in real life.

The **Chapter Investigation** presents a project related to the theme that is completed throughout the course of the chapter.

**mathmatters2.com/chapter_theme** features links that enhance the chapter theme and relate math to the real world.

**Goals** and **Applications** are clearly stated at the beginning of each lesson.

**Build Understanding** sections provide clear and concise explanations of concepts followed by detailed examples.

**Sidebar boxes** appear throughout each chapter, offering problem-solving and estimation strategies, introducing technology, providing help with reading mathematics, and offering assessment activities.

**mathmatters2.com/extra_examples** features additional fully worked-out examples.

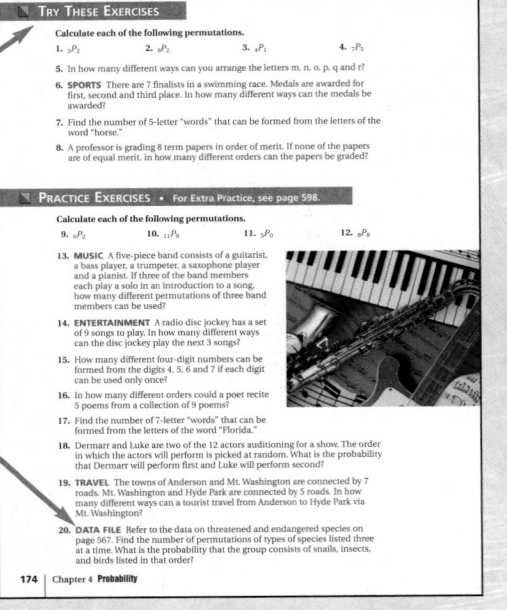

**Try These Exercises** can be used as guided in-class practice.

**Practice Exercises** offer students both skills practice and real-life problem solving.

**Data File Exercises** provide students with practice solving problems that involve interpreting data from a variety of visual displays in the Data File.

# Mathematics with Real Life.

**Extended Practice Exercises** take students one step further in developing their critical thinking skills and applying the concepts to real-life problems.

**Mixed Review Exercises** review the skills and concepts taught in previous lessons.

**mathmatters2.com/self_check_quiz** allows students to check their progress in each lesson.

**MathWorks** features a career related to the chapter theme. Students learn how knowledge of mathematics is instrumental in a broad spectrum of careers.

**mathmatters2.com/mathworks** offers more information about the featured career.

The **Data File** provides students with real-life statistics presented through a variety of graphical displays.

A two-page **Problem Solving Skills** lesson appears in each chapter and focuses on one problem solving strategy.

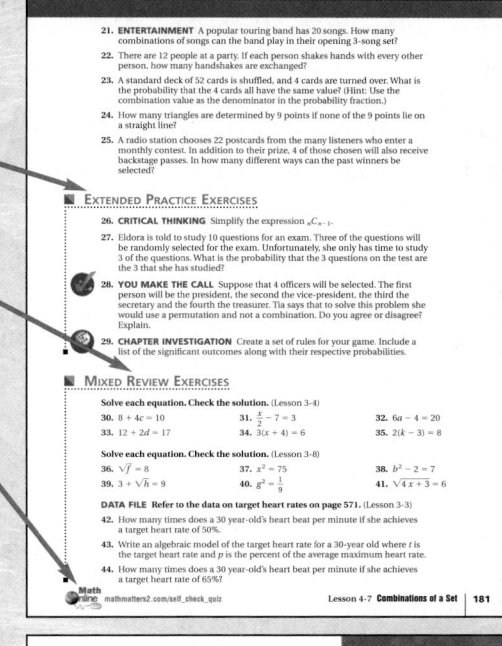

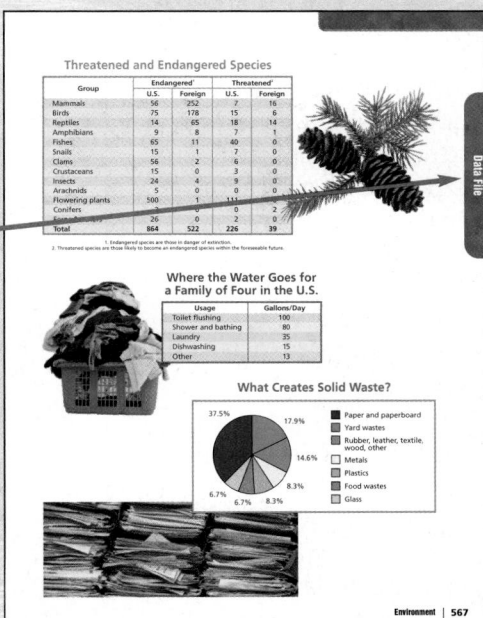

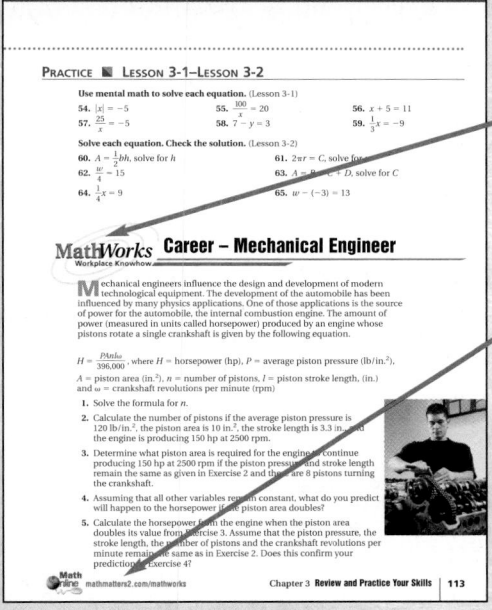

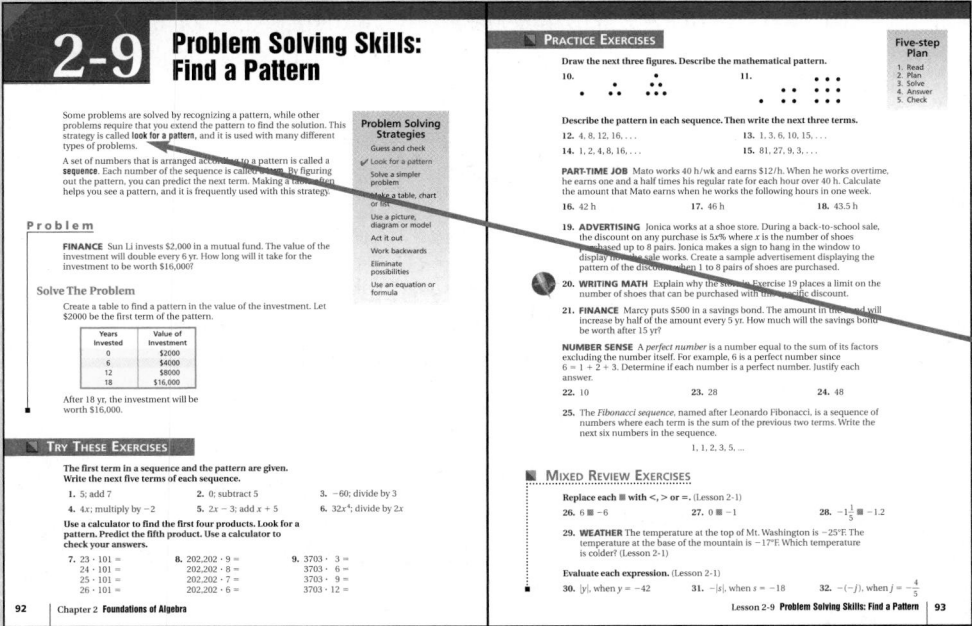

# Help Students Become Fluent in the
# Language of Mathematics.

Glencoe's *MathMatters* makes it easy for you to incorporate constructive reading and writing strategies into every class you teach.

## Student Edition

**Reading Math** sidebars help students learn and use the language of math.

**Chapter Investigations** give students the chance to work through long-term projects to develop their research and creative writing skills.

**Vocabulary terms** are printed in bold type when defined. The **Vocabulary** section in each Chapter Review summarizes and reviews key terms.

**ESL/LEP** features suggest ways to help English as a Second Language/Limited English Proficiency students grasp content.

and 9 adults. How much does the class need t

### Teaching Tip

**ESL/LEP** Have students write the five-step plan i
Provide them with a note card and have them wri
English on one side and in their native language c
them to use the card regularly until they become
solving plan.

**Writing Math** questions give students opportunities to define, describe, and explain the mathematical concepts they've just learned.

**You Make The Call** and **Error Alert** questions invite students to take on the role of an evaluator by reviewing the work of others to check for possible errors. In doing so, students must use the language of mathematics to explain their reasoning.

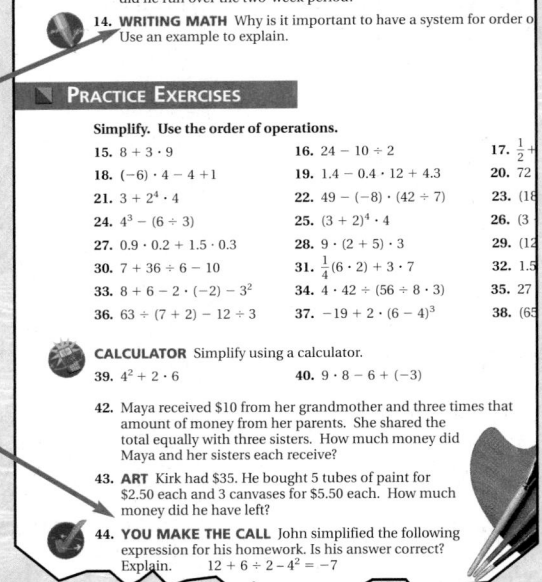

did he run over the two-week period?

**14. WRITING MATH** Why is it important to have a system for order o
Use an example to explain.

**PRACTICE EXERCISES**

Simplify. Use the order of operations.

15. $8 + 3 \cdot 9$
16. $24 - 10 \div 2$
17. $\frac{1}{2} +$
18. $(-6) \cdot 4 - 4 + 1$
19. $1.4 - 0.4 \cdot 12 + 4.3$
20. $72$
21. $3 + 2^4 \cdot 4$
22. $49 - (-8) \cdot (42 \div 7)$
23. (18
24. $4^3 - (6 \div 3)$
25. $(3 + 2)^4 \cdot 4$
26. (3
27. $0.9 \cdot 0.2 + 1.5 \cdot 0.3$
28. $9 \cdot (2 + 5) \cdot 3$
29. (12
30. $7 + 36 \div 6 - 10$
31. $\frac{1}{4}(6 \cdot 2) + 3 \cdot 7$
32. 1.5
33. $8 + 6 - 2 \cdot (-2) - 3^2$
34. $4 \cdot 42 \div (56 \div 8 \cdot 3)$
35. 27
36. $63 \div (7 + 2) - 12 \div 3$
37. $-19 + 2 \cdot (6 - 4)^3$
38. (65

**CALCULATOR** Simplify using a calculator.

39. $4^2 + 2 \cdot 6$
40. $9 \cdot 8 - 6 + (-3)$

42. Maya received $10 from her grandmother and three times that amount of money from her parents. She shared the total equally with three sisters. How much money did Maya and her sisters each receive?

43. **ART** Kirk had $35. He bought 5 tubes of paint for $2.50 each and 3 canvases for $5.50 each. How much money did he have left?

44. **YOU MAKE THE CALL** John simplified the following expression for his homework. Is his answer correct? Explain.  $12 + 6 \div 2 - 4^2 = -7$

**Differentiated Instruction** features help students at all points on the learning spectrum develop their reading, writing, and comprehension skills.

## Technology Support

**StudentWorks™**, Glencoe's backpack solution, includes the entire text formatted like the hardbound book, so students can study from just about anywhere—no book required. Students can also print their own lesson worksheet pages and get instant access to interactive web resources.

## Additional Resources

- **Vocabulary Builder** in the Chapter Resource Masters helps students locate and define key vocabulary words from the chapter.

- **Quick Review Math Handbook: Hot Words, Hot Topics** is Glencoe's mathematical handbook for students. The Hot Words section includes a glossary of terms while the Hot Topics section consists of an explanation of key mathematical concepts.

## Annotated Teacher's Edition

**Alternative Assessment** features offer additional suggestions on how to allow students to express what they have learned.

**Flexible Grouping** features outline opportunities for using heterogeneous groups for instruction or intervention. Working together often helps students solidify their understanding of mathematical terminology and concepts.

# Know who needs Extra Help,
## And Be Able To Deliver It.

Whether you need daily intervention resources integrated right into the program, or supplemental materials for after school and summer school programs, Glencoe's *MathMatters* puts it all right at your fingertips!

## Prerequisite Skills

Students often struggle in mathematics because they have not mastered the prerequisite skills needed to be successful. Glencoe's *MathMatters* provides the opportunity to check student skills to determine if they need additional review and practice.

- The **Are You Ready?** section at the beginning of every chapter helps students identify and practice skills they'll need for each new concept.

- Additional **Prerequisite Skills** practice is provided at the back of the Student Edition.

- The **Basic Mathematics Review** masters provide extra practice on basic skills needed for success in mathematics.

The **Annotated Teacher's Edition** contains teaching suggestions to help you determine which students need intervention and allows you to develop strategies for giving students the help they need.

- **Differentiated Instruction** features are keyed to three commonly accepted learning styles: auditory, visual, and tactile/kinesthetic.

- **Chalkboard Examples** provide students further opportunities to practice concepts and skills in a classroom setting.

- **Teaching Tips** include suggestions for English as a Second Language/Limited English Proficiency (ESL/LEP) students and suggestions on how to connect new concepts to students' prior mathematical knowledge.

## Daily Intervention Opportunities

The **Student Edition** contains additional problems in the Extra Practice section in the back of the book to help students master the concepts of each lesson. These problems include both skills and problem solving practice.

The **Chapter Resource Masters** include worksheets that can be used for daily intervention in each lesson. *For a description of each worksheet, see page xiii.*

- **Reteaching**
- **Extra Practice**

Each of these worksheets is available as a **consumable workbook**.

## Online Resources for Intervention

In addition to print resources, Glencoe's **Online Study Tools** include comprehensive review and intervention tools that are available anytime, anyplace simply by logging on to

 **mathmatters2.com**

Self-check quizzes are available for nearly every lesson, and immediate feedback helps students check their progress and find specific pages and examples in the Student Edition whenever they need extra review. These Online Study Tools also include extra examples, chapter assessments, and standardized test practice.

# Give Assessment
## Extra Attention
## Without Extra Preparation.

**Glencoe's *MathMatters* gives you all the tools you need to prepare students for success.**

## Student Edition

**Review and Practice Your Skills** appear after every other lesson allowing students to practice the concepts they have just learned.

A **Mid-Chapter Quiz** gives students the opportunity to assess their progress in learning the material presented to that point in the chapter.

The **Chapter Review** provides vocabulary and concept review at the point of use for students.

A **Chapter Assessment** provides practice questions students need to succeed on the chapter assessment.

**Standardized Test Practice** for each chapter provides a variety of practice questions and test-taking tips to help students succeed on standardized tests.

## Online Study Tools

- Self-Check Quizzes
- Chapter Assessment Practice
- Standardized Test Practice

## Technology Support

 Use the networkable **ExamView® Pro TestMaker CD-ROM** to:
- Create **multiple versions** of tests.
- Create **modified** tests for *inclusion* students with one mouse click.
- **Edit** existing questions and **add** your own questions.
- Build tests aligned with **state standards** using built-in **state curriculum correlations**.
- Change **English** tests to **Spanish** with one mouse click and vice versa.

## Annotated Teacher's Edition

**Quick Assessment** question(s) are provided in each lesson in the margin of the Annotated Teacher's Edition.

## Teacher Classroom Resources

**Warm-Ups and Color Transparencies** provide full-size transparencies with questions that allow you to gauge student readiness and provide a springboard for discussion of the next lesson.

## Assessment Options in the Chapter Resource Masters

These assessment resources are available for each chapter.
- 2 Chapter Assessments
- 3-page Standardized Test Practice with multiple-choice, short-answer/grid-in, and extended-response questions.

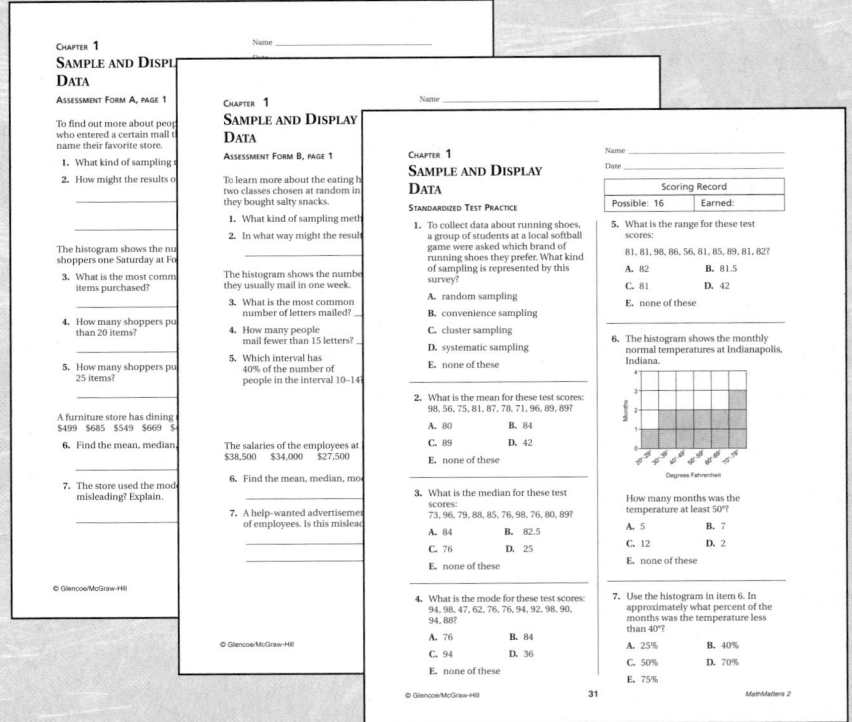

# Accomplish More...
## In Less Time.

Glencoe's *MathMatters* provides the resources for creating a complete, customized course in mathematics quickly...and easily.

## Start Here

In addition to teaching suggestions, additional examples, and answers, the **Annotated Teacher's Edition** provides a guide for all of the print and software materials available for each lesson.

**Chapter Resource Masters** contain all of the core supplements you'll need to begin teaching a chapter of Glencoe's *MathMatters*.

**FAST FILE**

- **Vocabulary Builder** helps students locate and define key vocabulary words from the chapter.

- **Reteaching** summarizes key concepts, offers additional examples, and provides practice.

- **Extra Practice** provides ample exercises, both computational and verbal, to help students master mathematical concepts, lesson by lesson.

- **Enrichment** goes beyond the scope of the student text to give students interesting and challenging hands-on activities to further their knowledge of mathematics.

- **Assessment** options for each chapter include two forms of chapter assessments and standardized test practice, which includes multiple-choice, short-answers/grid-in, and extended-response questions.

## Applications

**Technology Activities** incorporate scientific and graphing calculators and computer software into your mathematics classroom.

 **What's Math Got To Do With It?** Real-Life Math Videos connect mathematics to real life in an exciting, student-friendly format.

## Assessment and Intervention

**Warm-ups and Color Transparencies** contain 5-minute warm-up transparencies that provide a brief assessment of the prerequisite skills needed for each lesson.

**Basic Mathematics Review** includes worksheets for reviewing prerequisite mathematics skills.

**Practice Workbook** is a consumable version of the Extra Practice found in the Chapter Resource Masters.

## Technology Support for Teachers

**TeacherWorks** **TeacherWorks All-in-One Lesson Planner and Resource Center** CD-ROM includes a lesson planner and interactive Teacher Edition, so you can customize lesson plans and reproduce classroom resources quickly and easily, from just about anywhere.

 **Answer Key Maker** CD-ROM allows you to customize answer keys for your assignments from the Student Edition exercises.

# Connect Algebra and Geometry

Glencoe's *MathMatters* provides the equivalent of first-year algebra and geometry over three years. A truly integrated curriculum, it also covers content from the number and operation and probability and statistics strands. Problem-solving strategies are woven throughout the series.

| | MathMatters 1 | MathMatters 2 | MathMatters 3 |
|---|---|---|---|
| **Algebra** | | | |
| Basic concepts | 3-5 | 2-2 | 1-1 |
| Exponents | 3-7, 3-8 | 2-7, 2-8 | 1-7 |
| Monomials | 9-3 | 9-2 | 11-2 |
| Polynomials | 9-1 | | 11-1 |
| Polynomial Operations | 9-2, 9-4, 9-6 | 9-1, 9-3, 9-4, 9-5 | 11-1 |
| Solve Equations | 5-1 to 5-6 | 3-1, 3-2, 3-4 | 2-4, 2-5 |
| Solve Inequalities | 5-9 | 3-7 | 2-6 |
| Write Linear Equations | | 6-3 | 6-3 |
| Graph Linear Equations | 7-4 | 6-3 | 2-3 |
| Functions | 7-3 | 6-5 to 6-7 | 2-2 |
| Graph Systems | | 8-2 | 6-4 |
| Solve Systems | | 8-3, 8-4 | 6-5, 6-6 |
| Quadratic and Polynomial Equations | | 6-6 | 11-6, 12-1, 12-2, 12-5 |
| Conics | | | 13-1 to 13-4 |
| Radical Expressions and Equations | | 3-8 | |
| Matrices | | 1-8 | 6-7, 8-5 to 8-8 |
| **Geometry** | | | |
| Constructions | 8-2 | | 3-4, 10-7 |
| Points, Lines, and Planes | 4-1 | 5-1 | 3-1 |
| Angles | 8-1 | 5-2 | 3-2, 3-3 |
| Polygons | 4-2 | 5-7 | 4-7 |
| Area | 2-4, 2-9 | | 5-2 |
| Triangles | 4-2 | 5-4, 5-5 | 4-1, 4-3 |
| Right Triangles and Trigonometry | 7-7 | 11-3  11-4 to 11-7 | 10-2  10-3 |
| Pythagorean Theorem | 7-7 | 11-3 | 10-2, 12-6 |
| Quadrilaterals | 4-2 | 5-6 | 4-8, 4-9 |
| Similarity and Proportion | 2-8 | 11-1, 11-2 | 7-1, 7-2 |

KEY: **Introduction** **Development** Reinforcement

# While Developing
# Problem-Solving Skills.

| | MathMatters 1 | MathMatters 2 | MathMatters 3 |
|---|---|---|---|
| Circles | 2-7 | 5-8 | 10-4, 10-6 |
| Solids and Space | 4-3 | 10-1 | 5-5 |
| Transformations | 8-5 to 8-7 | 7-1 to 7-6 | 8-1 to 8-3 |
| Surface Area | 4-9 | 10-2 to 10-3 | 5-6 |
| Volume | 4-7, 4-8 | 10-7 to 10-8 | 5-7 |
| Coordinate Geometry | 7-2 | 6-1 | |
| Proofs | | 12-7 | 3-7, 4-3 |
| **Number and Operation** | | | |
| Ratios | 2-6 | 11-4 | 5-1, 7-1 |
| Proportion | 6-1 | 3-5 | 7-1, 7-3  7-5, 7-6 |
| Percent | 6-1 to 6-7 | 1-6 | 9-1 |
| Whole Numbers, Integers, and Rational Numbers | 3-1, 3-2, 3-4 | 2-1 | |
| Irrational Numbers | 3-4 | 2-1 | 10-1 |
| Properties | 3-1 | 2-1 | |
| Computation | 3-1, 3-2, 3-3 | 2-2 | 1-4, 1-5 |
| **Probability and Statistics** | | | |
| Constructing and Interpreting Graphs | 1-1 to 1-8 | 1-1 to 1-8 | 9-6 |
| Interpreting Data | 1-1 | 1-7 | 9-2 |
| Probability | 10-1, 10-2 | 4-1 to 4-7 | 9-1 |
| **Problem Solving** | | | |
| Guess and Check | 10-6 | 1-5, 12-3 | 4-5 |
| Look for a Pattern | 3-6 | 7-6 | 11-8 |
| Solve a Simpler Problem | 1-4 | | 5-4 |
| Make a Table, Chart, or List | 3-6, 6-8 | 2-9, 6-7 | 2-9, 8-8, 10-5 |
| Use a Picture, Diagram, or Model | 4-4, 9-7 | 3-3, 5-9, 8-6 | 7-7 |
| Act it Out | 7-1, 8-4 | 4-2 | 9-2 |
| Work Backwards | 5-7 | 9-6 | 12-7 |
| Eliminate Possibilities | 11-6 | 11-8 | 3-8 |
| Use an Equation or Formula | 2-5 | 10-9 | 1-6, 6-7 |

# Plan Your Mathematics Course
## To Meet Your Needs.

Glencoe's *MathMatters* and the accompanying support materials allow you to create a mathematics course that meets the needs of all the students in your class.

The charts shown on this page offer general suggestions for pacing your students through this book. Pacing for both standard class periods (45 minutes) and block schedule class periods (90 minutes) is given. The total number of days in each level of pacing is less than the typical 180-day school year and 90-day semester to allow for flexibility in planning due to testing, school cancellation, or shortened class periods.

## Year-Long Schedule
### 45-minute periods

| Grading Period | Chapter | Days |
|---|---|---|
| **1** | 1 | 15 |
| | 2 | 16 |
| | 3 | 14 |
| **2** | 4 | 13 |
| | 5 | 16 |
| | 6 | 16 |
| **3** | 7 | 11 |
| | 8 | 13 |
| | 9 | 14 |
| **4** | 10 | 16 |
| | 11 | 14 |
| | 12 | 13 |
| | Total | 171 |

## Block Schedule
### 90-minute periods

| Chapter | Days |
|---|---|
| 1 | 9 |
| 2 | 9 |
| 3 | 9 |
| 4 | 8 |
| 5 | 9 |
| 6 | 9 |
| 7 | 7 |
| 8 | 8 |
| 9 | 9 |
| 10 | 9 |
| 11 | 8 |
| 12 | 8 |
| Total | 102 |

## Daily Planning

**TeacherWorks** **All-in-One Lesson Planner and Resource Center**
This CD-ROM includes a lesson planner and an interactive teacher's edition that enables you to customize an entire course of study to meet your students' needs.

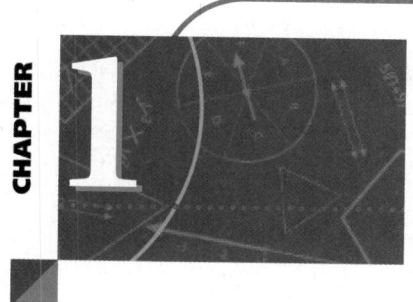

**CHAPTER 1**

# Sample and Display Data

**Are You Ready?** .................................................4

**1-1** Surveys and Sampling Methods ...................................6

**1-2** Measures of Central Tendency and Range.................10

**Review and Practice Your Skills**
Lessons 1-1 through 1-2 .........................................14

**1-3** Histograms and Stem-and-Leaf Plots ......................16

**1-4** Scatter Plots and Lines of Best Fit ...........................20

**Review and Practice Your Skills**
Lessons 1-1 through 1-4 ..........................................24

**Mid-Chapter Quiz** .........................................................25

**1-5** Problem Solving Skills: Coefficient of Correlation.....26

**1-6** Quartiles and Percentiles .......................................28

**Review and Practice Your Skills**
Lessons 1-1 through 1-6 .........................................32

**1-7** Misleading Graphs and Statistics ............................34

**1-8** Use Matrices to Organize Data ...............................38

**Assessment**

**Chapter 1 Review** ......................................................42

**Chapter 1 Assessment** ..............................................45

**Chapter 1 Standardized Test Practice** .......................46

**Theme: Market Research**

**Math*Works* Career**
Product Tester 15
Market Researcher 33

**Applications**
advertising 35
business 34, 40, 41
economics 23
education 12, 28
entertainment 7, 18, 37
fitness 17
food service 8, 36
manufacturing 7
market research 19, 23, 36
medicine 21
music 11, 36
political science 9
recreation 8, 41
retail 8, 17, 26, 41
sports 19, 31
weather 36

**Standardized Test Practice**
Multiple Choice 46
Short Response/Grid In 47
Extended Response 47

Page 2

# Foundations of Algebra

Are You Ready? ...........................................................50

2-1 Real Numbers...............................................................52

2-2 Order of Operations.......................................................56

**Review and Practice Your Skills**
Lessons 2-1 through 2-2 ...........................................60

2-3 Write Variable Expressions...........................................62

2-4 Add and Subtract Variable Expressions .....................66

**Review and Practice Your Skills**
Lessons 2-1 through 2-4 ...........................................70

**Mid-Chapter Quiz** ........................................................71

2-5 Multiply and Divide Variable Expressions ................72

2-6 Simplify Variable Expressions ....................................76

**Review and Practice Your Skills**
Lessons 2-1 through 2-6 ...........................................80

2-7 Properties of Exponents ..............................................82

2-8 Zero and Negative Exponents...................................86

**Review and Practice Your Skills**
Lessons 2-1 through 2-8 ...........................................90

2-9 Problem Solving Skills: Find a Pattern ......................92

**Assessment**

**Chapter 2 Review** .......................................................94

**Chapter 2 Assessment** ..............................................97

**Chapter 2 Standardized Test Practice** ......................98

**Theme: Population**

**Math*Works* Career**

Concession Stand Operator 61
Commercial Aircraft
Designer 81

**Applications**

advertising 93
astronomy 89
biology 82
computers 85
detective work 69
engineering 75
entertainment 59
fashion 78
finance 78, 84, 92, 93
fitness 58, 59
history 62
hobbies 65
industry 65
part-time job 58, 63, 74, 93
photography 65, 78
physics 88, 89
population 55, 59, 65, 69, 79, 85, 88
recycling 55, 69
space science 64
sports 55, 77
weather 54, 74, 79, 93

**Standardized Test Practice**

Multiple Choice 98
Short Response/Grid In 99
Extended Response 99

# Equations and Inequalities

**Are You Ready?** .......................................... 102

**3-1** Equations and Formulas ............................................ 104

**3-2** One-Step Equations.................................................. 108

**Review and Practice Your Skills**
Lessons 3-1 through 3-2 ........................................ 112

**3-3** Problem Solving Skills: Model Algebra ................... 114

**3-4** Equations with Two or More Operations.................. 116

**Review and Practice Your Skills**
Lessons 3-1 through 3-4 ......................................... 120

**Mid-Chapter Quiz** .................................................... 121

**3-5** Proportions.............................................................. 122

**3-6** Graph Inequalities on a Number Line ...................... 126

**Review and Practice Your Skills**
Lessons 3-1 through 3-6 ......................................... 130

**3-7** Solve Inequalities......................................................... 132

**3-8** Equations with Squares and Square Roots.............. 136

**Assessment**

**Chapter 3 Review** ....................................................... 140

**Chapter 3 Assessment** ............................................... 143

**Chapter 3 Standardized Test Practice** ..................... 144

**Theme: Physics**

**Math*Works* Career**
Mechanical Engineer 113
Automobile Designer 131

**Applications**
art 122
business 124, 126, 135
communications 132
engineering 139
entertainment 115
finance 111, 120
fitness 115, 134
geography 129
government 127
health 134
hobbies 135
machinery 123
manufacturing 124
mechanics 119, 139
packaging 111
part-time job 115
physics 107, 110, 114, 119, 125,
  129, 136, 138
retail 125
safety 107, 135, 138
sports 119, 128
transportation 120
travel 106

**Standardized Test Practice**
Multiple Choice 144
Short Response/Grid In 145
Extended Response 145

Page 138

# Probability

**Are You Ready?** .........................................148

4-1 Experiments and Probabilities .................150

4-2 Problem Solving Skills: Simulations ........154

**Review and Practice Your Skills**
Lessons 4-1 through 4-2 ........................156

4-3 Sample Spaces and Theoretical Probability .............158

4-4 Probability of Compound Events .............162

**Review and Practice Your Skills**
Lessons 4-1 through 4-4 ........................166

**Mid-Chapter Quiz** .................................167

4-5 Independent and Dependent Events .......168

4-6 Permutations of a Set ..............................172

**Review and Practice Your Skills**
Lessons 4-1 through 4-6 ........................176

4-7 Combinations of a Set ..............................178

**Assessment**

**Chapter 4 Review** ...................................182

**Chapter 4 Assessment** ...........................185

**Chapter 4 Standardized Test Practice** ..................186

**Theme: Games**

**Math*Works* Career**
Baseball Player  157
Board Game Designer  177

**Applications**
cooking  173
entertainment  174, 181
food service  159
games  161, 163, 164, 171,
   175, 180
government  170
health  170
landscaping  180
market research  150, 151
medicine  155
music  160, 174
part-time job  154
retail  152, 159
safety  180
sports  155, 160, 171, 174, 180
travel  174

**Standardized Test Practice**
Multiple Choice  186
Short Response/Grid In  187
Extended Response  187

Page 172

# Logic and Geometry

| | Are You Ready? | 190 |
|---|---|---|
| **5-1** | Elements of Geometry | 192 |
| **5-2** | Angles and Perpendicular Lines | 196 |
| | Review and Practice Your Skills Lessons 5-1 through 5-2 | 200 |
| **5-3** | Parallel Lines and Transversals | 202 |
| **5-4** | Properties of Triangles | 206 |
| | Review and Practice Your Skills Lessons 5-1 through 5-4 | 210 |
| | Mid-Chapter Quiz | 211 |
| **5-5** | Congruent Triangles | 212 |
| **5-6** | Quadrilaterals and Parallelograms | 216 |
| | Review and Practice Your Skills Lessons 5-1 through 5-6 | 220 |
| **5-7** | Diagonals and Angles of Polygons | 222 |
| **5-8** | Properties of Circles | 226 |
| | Review and Practice Your Skills Lessons 5-1 through 5-8 | 230 |
| **5-9** | Problem Solving Skills: Circle Graphs | 232 |

**Assessment**

| | |
|---|---|
| **Chapter 5 Review** | 234 |
| **Chapter 5 Assessment** | 237 |
| **Chapter 5 Standardized Test Practice** | 238 |

**Theme: Navigation**

**Math*Works* Career**
Cattle Rancher  201
Ship Captain  221

**Applications**
art  195, 215, 229
civil engineering  218
construction  194, 204, 217
engineering  214
entertainment  232
food service  228
health  199
hobbies  224
industry  233
interior design  209
market research  227
music  205
nature  224
navigation  194, 199, 205, 209, 219, 229, 233
photography  194
physics  198
recreation  214, 229
retail  219
safety  205, 224
travel  208

**Standardized Test Practice**
Multiple Choice  238
Short Response/Grid In  239
Extended Response  239

# Graphing Functions

| | | |
|---|---|---|
| | **Are You Ready?** | 242 |
| 6-1 | Distance in the Coordinate Plane | 244 |
| 6-2 | Slope of a Line | 248 |
| | **Review and Practice Your Skills** Lessons 6-1 through 6-2 | 252 |
| 6-3 | Write and Graph Linear Equations | 254 |
| 6-4 | Write and Graph Linear Inequalities | 258 |
| | **Review and Practice Your Skills** Lessons 6-1 through 6-4 | 262 |
| | **Mid-Chapter Quiz** | 263 |
| 6-5 | Linear and Nonlinear Functions | 264 |
| 6-6 | Graph Quadratic Functions | 268 |
| | **Review and Practice Your Skills** Lessons 6-1 through 6-6 | 272 |
| 6-7 | Problem Solving Skills: Patterns and Functions | 274 |
| 6-8 | Direct Variation | 276 |
| | **Review and Practice Your Skills** Lessons 6-1 through 6-8 | 280 |
| 6-9 | Inverse Variation | 282 |

**Assessment**

| | |
|---|---|
| **Chapter 6 Review** | 286 |
| **Chapter 6 Assessment** | 289 |
| **Chapter 6 Standardized Test Practice** | 290 |

**Theme: Business**

**Math*Works* Career**
Music Store Owner 253
Restaurateur 273

**Applications**
agriculture 270, 278
business 260, 261, 267, 275, 285
business travel 251
community service 247
economics 275
engineering 284
finance 278
geography 244
industry 284
market research 245, 261
music 282, 284
part-time job 278
physics 269, 270, 272, 276, 277, 278, 283, 285
recreation 264
retail 257
science 257
space 278
sports 270
travel 284

**Standardized Test Practice**
Multiple Choice 290
Short Response/Grid In 291
Extended Response 291

Page 273

# Coordinate Graphing and Transformations

Are You Ready? ...........................................294

**7-1** Translations in the Coordinate Plane.......................296

**7-2** Reflections in the Coordinate Plane.........................300

Review and Practice Your Skills
Lessons 7-1 through 7-2 ........................................304

**7-3** Rotations in the Coordinate Plane ...........................306

**7-4** Line Symmetry and Rotational Symmetry ..............310

Review and Practice Your Skills
Lessons 7-1 through 7-4 ........................................314

Mid-Chapter Quiz ......................................................315

**7-5** Dilations in the Coordinate Plane ...........................316

**7-6** Problem Solving Skills: Tessellations........................320

Review and Practice Your Skills
Lessons 7-1 through 7-6 ........................................322

## Assessment

Chapter 7 Review ........................................................324

Chapter 7 Assessment .................................................327

Chapter 7 Standardized Test Practice ....................328

**Theme: Architecture**

**Math*Works* Career**
Campus Facilities Manager 305
Architect 323

## Applications
architecture 299, 303, 309,
   312, 318
art 301, 309, 313, 321
entertainment 318
gardening 319
hobbies 321
industry 311
landscaping 303
machinery 307
music 298
nature 320
navigation 302
photography 299, 317, 318
weather 312

## Standardized Test Practice
Multiple Choice 328
Short Response/Grid In 329
Extended Response 329

Page 309

# 8

# Systems of Equations and Inequalities

**Theme: Sports**

**Math*Works* Career**
Runner 343
Coach 361

**Applications**
business 358
construction 345, 351, 357
economics 341
entertainment 359, 362
finance 365
landscaping 350
movies 356
recreation 346
retail 364
safety 341
sports 337, 340, 347, 356, 357, 362
transportation 344, 359, 360
travel 337, 360

**Standardized Test Practice**
Multiple Choice 370
Short Response/Grid In 371
Extended Response 371

Are You Ready? ...........................................................332

8-1 Parallel and Perpendicular Lines..............................334

8-2 Solve Systems of Equations Graphically..................338

Review and Practice Your Skills
Lessons 8-1 through 8-2 ..........................................342

8-3 Solve Systems by Substitution ..................................344

8-4 Solve Systems by Adding, Subtracting, and
Multiplying ................................................................348

Review and Practice Your Skills
Lessons 8-1 through 8-4 ..........................................352

Mid-Chapter Quiz .......................................................353

8-5 Matrices and Determinants.......................................354

8-6 Problem Solving Skills: Directed Graphs .................358

Review and Practice Your Skills
Lessons 8-1 through 8-6 ..........................................360

8-7 Systems of Inequalities...............................................362

Assessment

Chapter 8 Review ........................................................366

Chapter 8 Assessment ................................................369

Chapter 8 Standardized Test Practice ....................370

Page 330

# Polynomials

Are You Ready? ........................................................374

9-1 Add and Subtract Polynomials ...............................376

9-2 Multiply Monomials .............................................380

**Review and Practice Your Skills**
Lessons 9-1 through 9-2 .........................................384

9-3 Divide by a Monomial .........................................386

9-4 Multiply a Polynomial by a Monomial....................390

**Review and Practice Your Skills**
Lessons 9-1 through 9-4 .........................................394

**Mid-Chapter Quiz** ................................................395

9-5 Multiply Binomials .............................................396

9-6 Problem Solving Skills: Work Backwards ................400

**Review and Practice Your Skills**
Lessons 9-1 through 9-6 .........................................402

9-7 Factor Using Greatest Common Factor (GCF) .........404

9-8 Perfect Squares and Difference of Squares..............408

**Assessment**

**Chapter 9 Review** ................................................412

**Chapter 9 Assessment** ..........................................415

**Chapter 9 Standardized Test Practice** ...................416

**Theme: Geography**

**Math*Works* Career**
Truck Driver 385
Air Traffic Controller 403

**Applications**
finance 393, 399, 406
geography 379, 382, 389, 393, 399, 401, 406, 411
interior design 389
landscaping 388
manufacturing 383
money 401
part-time job 379, 392
photography 383, 399
physics 401, 406
recreation 398
retail 388
sports 382, 392
travel 379, 391, 392, 401, 411

**Standardized Test Practice**
Multiple Choice 416
Short Response/Grid In 417
Extended Response 417

Page 406

# Three-Dimensional Geometry

| | Are You Ready? | 420 |
| 10-1 | Visualize and Represent Solids | 422 |
| 10-2 | Nets and Surface Area | 426 |
| | Review and Practice Your Skills Lessons 10-1 through 10-2 | 430 |
| 10-3 | Surface Area of Three-Dimensional Figures | 432 |
| 10-4 | Perspective Drawings | 436 |
| | Review and Practice Your Skills Lessons 10-1 through 10-4 | 440 |
| | Mid-Chapter Quiz | 441 |
| 10-5 | Isometric Drawings | 442 |
| 10-6 | Orthogonal Drawings | 446 |
| | Review and Practice Your Skills Lessons 10-1 through 10-6 | 450 |
| 10-7 | Volume of Prisms and Pyramids | 452 |
| 10-8 | Volume of Cylinders, Cones, and Spheres | 456 |
| | Review and Practice Your Skills Lessons 10-1 through 10-8 | 460 |
| 10-9 | Problem Solving Skills: Length, Area, and Volume | 462 |

**Assessment**

| Chapter 10 Review | 464 |
| Chapter 10 Assessment | 467 |
| Chapter 10 Standardized Test Practice | 468 |

**Theme: History**

**Math*Works* Career**
Urban Planner 431
Exhibit Designer 451

**Applications**
architecture 428, 437, 439, 443
astronomy 457
construction 462
Earth science 455
engineering 447
fitness 456
food service 435
geography 433
history 425, 428, 435, 438, 445, 449, 455, 459
hobbies 455
horticulture 458
interior design 438, 449
landscaping 463
machinery 424, 429, 455
packaging 435, 454, 463
recreation 424, 444, 453
retail 427
safety 449
sports 458

**Standardized Test Practice**
Multiple Choice 468
Short Response/Grid In 469
Extended Response 469

Page 433

# Right Triangle Trigonometry

| | Are You Ready? | 472 |
| **11-1** | Similar Polygons | 474 |
| **11-2** | Indirect Measurement | 478 |
| | Review and Practice Your Skills<br>Lessons 11-1 through 11-2 | 482 |
| **11-3** | The Pythagorean Theorem | 484 |
| **11-4** | Sine, Cosine, and Tangent Ratios | 488 |
| | Review and Practice Your Skills<br>Lessons 11-1 through 11-4 | 492 |
| | Mid-Chapter Quiz | 493 |
| **11-5** | Find Lengths of Sides in Right Triangles | 494 |
| **11-6** | Find Measures of Angles in Right Triangles | 498 |
| | Review and Practice Your Skills<br>Lessons 11-1 through 11-6 | 502 |
| **11-7** | Special Right Triangles | 504 |
| **11-8** | Problem Solving Skills: Reasonable Solutions | 508 |

**Assessment**

| Chapter 11 Review | 510 |
| Chapter 11 Assessment | 513 |
| Chapter 11 Standardized Test Practice | 514 |

**Theme: Photography**

**Math*Works* Career**
Aerial Photographer 483
Camera Designer 503

**Applications**

advertising 480
archaeology 496
architecture 476, 505
art 477
astronomy 501
business 509
construction 496
Earth science 481
engineering 495
entertainment 506
fitness 486, 508
geography 509
health 478
history 484
hobbies 487
monuments 481
nature 478, 506
navigation 491
photography 477, 481, 487,
  490, 497, 501, 506
recreation 480, 485, 496
safety 500
sports 475, 486, 506
travel 491, 500, 501

**Standardized Test Practice**

Multiple Choice 514
Short Response/Grid In 515
Extended Response 515

# Logic and Sets

Are You Ready? .................................................................... 518

**12-1** Properties of Sets ................................................... 520

**12-2** Union and Intersection of Sets ............................ 524

**Review and Practice Your Skills**
Lessons 12-1 through 12-2 ................................... 528

**12-3** Problem Solving Skills: Conditional Statements ...... 530

**12-4** Converse, Inverse, and Contrapositive .................. 532

**Review and Practice Your Skills**
Lessons 12-1 through 12-4 ................................... 536

**Mid-Chapter Quiz** ............................................... 537

**12-5** Inductive and Deductive Reasoning ...................... 538

**12-6** Patterns of Deductive Reasoning .......................... 542

**Review and Practice Your Skills**
Lessons 12-1 through 12-6 ................................... 546

**12-7** Logical Reasoning and Proof ................................ 548

**Assessment**

**Chapter 12 Review** ............................................... 552

**Chapter 12 Assessment** ...................................... 555

**Chapter 12 Standardized Test Practice** ................ 556

**Student Handbook** ..................................................... 559

Data File .................................................................. 560

Prerequisite Skills .................................................. 576

Extra Practice ......................................................... 585

Preparing for Standardized Tests ........................... 627

Technology Reference Guide .................................... 646

English-Spanish Glossary ....................................... 650

Selected Answers .................................................... 672

Photo Credits .......................................................... 699

Index ....................................................................... 700

**Theme: Music**

**Math*Works* Career**
Symphony Orchestra
Conductor 529
Research Professor of Music
History 547

**Applications**
advertising 534, 545
biology 525, 540
cooking 526
food service 523, 540
geography 534
history 522
hobbies 524
horticulture 543
landscaping 550
machinery 526
music 522, 527, 535, 544, 551
physics 531
retail 544
safety 550
travel 540, 549
weather 533

**Standardized Test Practice**
Multiple Choice 556
Short Response/Grid In 557
Extended Response 557

Page 527

# How to Use Your MathMatters Book

Welcome to *MathMatters*! This textbook is different from other mathematics books you have used because *MathMatters* combines mathematics topics and themes into an integrated program. The following are recurring features you will find in your textbook.

**Chapter Opener** This introduction relates the content of the chapter and a theme. It also presents a question that will be answered as part of the ongoing chapter investigation.

**Are You Ready?** The topics presented on these two pages are skills that you will need to understand in order to be successful in the chapter.

**Build Understanding** The section presents the key points of the lesson through examples and completed solutions.

**Try These Exercises** Completing these exercises in class are an excellent way for you to determine if you understood the key points in the lesson.

**Practice Exercises** These exercises provide an excellent way to practice and apply the concepts and skills you learned in the lesson.

**Extended Practice Exercises** Critical thinking, advanced connections, and chapter investigations highlight this section.

**Mixed Review Exercises** Practicing what you have learned in previous lessons helps you prepare for tests at the end of the year.

**MathWorks** This feature connects a career to the theme of the chapter.

**Problem Solving Skills** Each chapter focuses on one problem-solving skill to help you become a better problem solver.

## Look for these icons that identify special types of exercises.

 **CHAPTER INVESTIGATION** Alerts you to the on-going search to answer the investigation question in the chapter opener.

 **WRITING MATH** Identifies where you need to explain, describe, and summarize your thinking in writing.

 **MANIPULATIVES** Shows places where the use of a manipulative can help you complete the exercise.

 **TECHNOLOGY** Notifies you that the use of a scientific or graphing calculator or spreadsheet software is needed to complete the exercise.

 **ERROR ANALYSIS** Allows you to review the work of others or your own work to check for possible errors.

# Sample and Display Data

| Lesson | Lesson Objectives | Pacing (days) | NCTM Standards | State/Local Objectives |
|--------|-------------------|---------------|----------------|------------------------|
| 1-1 | **Surveys and Sampling Methods** *(pp. 6–9)*<br>• Identify sampling methods.<br>• Recognize biased surveys. | 1 | 5, 8, 9 | |
| 1-2 | **Measures of Central Tendency and Range** *(pp. 10–13)*<br>• Calculate the mean, median, and mode of data.<br>• Find the range of a set of data. | 2 | 5, 8, 9 | |
| 1-3 | **Histograms and Stem-and-Leaf Plots** *(pp. 16–19)*<br>• Use and create histograms to solve problems.<br>• Use and create stem-and-leaf plots to solve problems. | 2 | 5, 8, 9, 10 | |
| 1-4 | **Scatter Plots and Lines of Best Fit** *(pp. 20–23)*<br>• Use scatter plots to solve problems.<br>• Use a graphing utility to determine a line of best fit. | 2 | 5, 8, 9, 10 | |
| 1-5 | **Problem Solving Skills: Coefficient of Correlation** *(pp. 26–27)*<br>• Solve a problem using coefficient of correlation.<br>• Guess and check. | 1 | 1, 5, 6, 9 | |
| 1-6 | **Quartiles and Percentiles** *(pp. 28–31)*<br>• Identify quartiles and calculate percentiles.<br>• Create a box-and-whisker plot. | 2 | 5, 8, 9, 10 | |
| 1-7 | **Misleading Graphs and Statistics** *(pp. 34–37)*<br>• Recognize how a graph can be misleading.<br>• Identify the misleading use of the word "average." | 2 | 5, 8, 9, 10 | |
| 1-8 | **Use Matrices to Organize Data** *(pp. 38–41)*<br>• Organize and display data in matrices.<br>• Perform basic operations using matrices. | 1 | 1, 5, 9, 10 | |
| Review | | 1 | | |
| Testing | | 1 | | |

**Key to NCTM Standards:**

*1=Number & Operations, 2=Algebra, 3=Geometry,
4=Measurement, 5=Data Analysis & Probability,
6=Problem Solving, 7=Reasoning & Proof,
8=Communication, 9=Connections, 10=Representation*

**Pacing:** Suggestions for the year can be found on page xvi.

# Chapter Resource Manager

## Chapter 1 Resource Masters

FAST FILE

| Reteaching Activities | Extra Practice | Enrichment | Assessment | Basic Mathematics Review | Study Skills Activities | Lesson Warm-Ups Transparencies | Teaching Transparencies | Technology Activities | Materials Needed |
|---|---|---|---|---|---|---|---|---|---|
| 1 | 2 | 3 | | 1–2 | | 1 | | | |
| 4 | 5 | 6 | | 2 | | 1 | RF-2 | 1-2 | calculator |
| 7 | 8 | 9 | | 2 | | 1 | TK-1 TK-2 TK-9 | | graphing calculator, graph paper |
| 10 | 11 | 12 | | | 3 | 2 | TK-9 | | graphing calculator, graph paper, toothpicks |
| 13 | 14 | 15 | | 2, 3 | | 2 | RF-1 | | graphing calculator |
| 16 | 17 | 18 | | | 4–5 | 2 | TK-9, RF-3 | 1-6 | graphing calculator graph paper |
| 19 | 20 | 21 | | | | 3 | TK-9 | 1-7 | graph paper, graph calculator |
| 22 | 23 | 24 | 27–33 | | | 3 | TK-3 | | graphing calculator, graph paper |

## Quick Review Math Handbook, Book 2

hot words
hot topics

| MathMatters 2 Lesson(s) | Hot Topic Lesson(s) |
|---|---|
| 1-1 | 4-1 |
| 1-2 | 4-4 |
| 1-3, 1-6 | 4-2 |
| 1-4, 1-5 | 4-3 |
| 1-7 | 4-1, 4-3 |
| 1-8 | 4-1 |

# Content and Connections

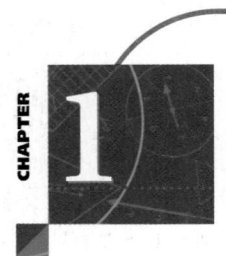

## Connections to the Past

**MM1 (Ch. 1):** Choose a sampling procedure.

**MM1 (Ch. 1):** Use measures of central tendency.

**PC:** Interpret and create bar graphs.

**MM1 (Ch. 1):** Read stem-and-leaf plots.

**MM1 (Ch. 1):** Read and create scatter plots, and use lines of best fit to identify trends.

**PC:** Identify trends in data.

**MM1 (Ch. 1):** Read and create box-and-whisker plots.

**PC:** Choose appropriate scales for a graph.

**PC:** Use tables to organize and display data.

### Key

| | |
|---|---|
| PC | = Previous Course |
| MM1 | = *MathMatters 1* |
| MM2 | = *MathMatters 2* |
| MM3 | = *MathMatters 3* |

## MathMatters 2 Chapter 1 Highlights

Identify sampling methods and recognize biased surveys. (1-1)

Calculate the mean, median, and mode of data and find the range of a set of data. (1-2)

Use and create histograms to solve problems. (1-3)

Use and create stem-and-leaf plots to solve problems. (1-3)

Use a graphing calculator to determine a line of best fit. (1-4)

Solve a problem using a coefficient of correlation. (1-5)

Identify quartiles, calculate percentiles, and create a box-and-whisker plot. (1-6)

Recognize how a graph and the word "average" can be misleading. (1-7)

Use matrices to organize and display data and perform basic operations. (1-8)

## Connections to the Future

**MM2 (Ch. 4):** Use experiments to collect data.
**MM3 (Ch. 2):** Construct frequency tables for data.

**MM3 (Ch. 9):** Find the variance, standard deviation, and 2-scores for a set of data.

**MM3 (Ch. 2):** Construct histograms for a data set.

**MM3 (Ch. 2):** Construct stem-and-leaf plots.

**MM3 (Ch. 9):** Interpret and make scatter plots.

**MM3 (Ch. 9:** Interpret and make scatter plots.

**MM3 (Ch. 9):** Interpret and make box-and-whisker plots.

**MM3 (Ch. 2):** Solve a problem with misleading graphs.

**MM3 (Ch. 6):** Solve a problem with determinants and matrices.

## Connecting the Strands

| NCTM Strand | Lesson(s) |
|---|---|
| Number & Operations | 1-5, 1-8 |
| Data Analysis & Probability | 1-1, 1-2, 1-3, 1-4, 1-5, 1-6, 1-7, 1-8 |
| Problem Solving | 1-5 |
| Communication | 1-1, 1-2, 1-3, 1-4, 1-6, 1-7 |
| Connections | 1-1, 1-2, 1-3, 1-4, 1-5, 1-6, 1-7, 1-8 |
| Representation | 1-3, 1-4, 1-6, 1-7, 1-8 |

# Ongoing Assessment and Intervention

<table>
<tr><th></th><th>Type</th><th>Student Edition</th><th>Teacher Resources</th><th>Technology/Internet</th></tr>
<tr><td rowspan="3">INTERVENTION</td><td>Ongoing</td><td>Are You Ready?, pp. 4–5<br>Check Understanding, pp. 7, 11, 29<br>Review and Practice Your Skills, pp. 14–15, 24–25, 32–33<br>Mid-Chapter Quiz, p. 25</td><td>Lesson Warm-Ups Transparencies, pp. WU-1, WU-2, WU-3<br>Quick Assessment, ATE pp. 3, 8, 12, 18, 22, 27, 30, 36, 40</td><td>mathmatters2.com/extra_ examples<br>mathmatters2.com/self_check_quiz</td></tr>
<tr><td>Mixed Review</td><td>pp. 9, 13, 19, 23, 27, 31, 37, 41</td><td></td><td></td></tr>
<tr><td>Error Analysis</td><td>Talk About It, p. 9<br>You Make the Call, p. 13</td><td>Teaching Tip, ATE pp. 12, 24, 42</td><td></td></tr>
<tr><td rowspan="3">ASSESSMENT</td><td>Standardized Test Practice</td><td>pp. 46–47<br>Preparing for Standardized Tests, pp. 627–644</td><td>Standardized Test Practice, CRM pp. 31–33</td><td>mathmatters2.com/standardized_test</td></tr>
<tr><td>Open-Ended Assessment</td><td>Chapter Investigation, pp. 5, 9, 31, 37, 44</td><td>Chapter Investigation, ATE p. 44<br>Alternative Assessment, ATE p. 45</td><td></td></tr>
<tr><td>Chapter Assessment</td><td>Chapter Review, pp. 42–44<br>Chapter Assessment, p. 45</td><td>Multiple-Choice Tests (Forms A and B), CRM pp. 27–30</td><td>mathmatters2.com/chapter_assessment</td></tr>
</table>

**Key to Abbreviations:** *ATE* = Annotated Teacher's Edition, *CRM* = Chapter Resource Masters

## Additional Intervention

***Basic Mathematics Review*** includes 80 lessons, consisting of an instructional page and a test page. This workbook also features a pretest, posttest, table of measurement equivalents, and calculator appendices.

### ExamView® Pro

Use ExamView® Pro Testmaker CD-ROM to:
- Create **multiple versions** of tests.
- Create **modified** tests for *inclusion* students with one mouse click.
- **Edit** existing questions and **add** your own questions.
- Build tests aligned with **state standards** using built-in **state curriculum correlations**.
- Change **English** tests to **Spanish** with one mouse click and vice versa.

## Chapter Opener

### NCTM Standards/Strands
- Data Analysis & Probability
- Representation
- Communication

### Vocabulary

| | |
|---|---|
| market research | poll |
| survey | statistical data |

### Theme Connections
Public opinion is shaped both by relatively permanent circumstances and by temporary influences. The systematic measurement of public attitudes was a 20th-century development. Opinion polls are generally accepted as useful tools by business, political organizations, the mass media, and government, as well as in academic research.

*Statistics* is the branch of mathematics that involves the collection, organization, and analysis of numerical data. Since decision making is often based on data analysis, appropriate and accurate display of data is essential.

### Career Opportunities
Many careers require understanding of data collection, presentation, and analysis. Two such careers are highlighted in the MathWorks features. Others include: sales coordinator, advertising campaign manager, political operative, political strategist, consumer analyst, product developer.
- Product tester, page 15
- Market researcher, page 33

## Internet Connection

### Theme Activities
Mathmatters2.com/chapter_theme provides links to the Internet that will help students gather information about the use of math in the real world, particularly data and measures. To search for additional addresses, begin a search of *market research*. Then within that search, use key words that will call up specific aspects of the topic, such as *opinion poll*, *audience research*, *focus group*, *research techniques*,

# Sample and Display Data

## THEME: Market Research

**M**arket research involves using polls, surveys, and statistical data to study the characteristics and actions of a market. A market is the specific audience of a product or service. The purchaser of a product or service may be different than the user of that product or service. For this reason, market research strategies vary depending on the type of audience being targeted.

Data must be displayed in a clear and concise way for the reader to easily interpret and draw conclusions. In this chapter you will learn to present data in various formats.

- Marketers cannot make claims about a product or service based on polls and surveys alone, so they hire product testers. **Product testers** (page 15) provide proof of a claim as required by the Federal Trade Commission.

- **Market researchers** (page 33) gather data and then decide a format in which to advertise a product or service that will reach a targeted market. Visual displays of data are critical to relaying messages.

mathmatters2.com/chapter_theme

and *statistical methods*. In small groups, students can brainstorm other key words.

### Chapter Investigation
Use the Internet and other resources to locate additional information about market research.

### ADDITIONAL ANSWER

4.

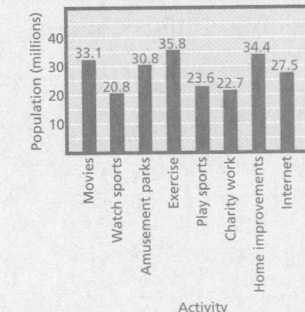

Participation in Leisure Activities for 35-44 Year Olds

## Participation in Leisure Activities by Gender and Age

| | U.S. Adult population (million) | See movies | Watch sports | Visit amusement park | Exercise | Play sports | Perform charity work | Make home improvements and repairs | Access the Internet |
|---|---|---|---|---|---|---|---|---|---|
| **Total** | 209.1 | 66% | 41% | 57% | 75% | 45% | 43% | 66% | 52% |
| **Gender** | | | | | | | | | |
| Male | 101.0 | 66% | 49% | 58% | 75% | 56% | 40% | 71% | 53% |
| Female | 108.1 | 65% | 34% | 57% | 77% | 35% | 46% | 61% | 51% |
| **Age** | | | | | | | | | |
| 18 to 24 | 27.1 | 88% | 51% | 76% | 85% | 67% | 35% | 57% | 64% |
| 25 to 34 | 39.9 | 79% | 51% | 70% | 82% | 63% | 41% | 63% | 63% |
| 35 to 44 | 45.1 | 73% | 46% | 68% | 79% | 52% | 50% | 76% | 61% |
| 45 to 54 | 37.7 | 65% | 42% | 53% | 77% | 40% | 46% | 75% | 60% |
| 55 to 64 | 24.2 | 46% | 33% | 40% | 69% | 19% | 44% | 71% | 42% |
| 65 to 74 | 18.4 | 38% | 21% | 29% | 65% | 23% | 40% | 55% | 13% |
| Over 75 | 16.6 | 28% | 16% | 18% | 56% | 13% | 40% | 44% | 9% |

## Data Activity: Participation in Leisure Activities

**Use the table for Questions 1–4.**

1. If you were marketing athletic shoes, to which two age groups would you gear your advertising? Explain your reasoning. 18 to 24 and 25–34; They exercise and play sports most.

2. About how many people over the age of 75 participated in accessing the Internet? 150,000

3. Is the percentage of people 45 to 54 years old who attend movies greater than or less than the percentage that participate in home improvements and repairs? less than

4. Draw a bar graph to represent the population 35 to 44 years old who participate in leisure activities. See additional answers.

### CHAPTER INVESTIGATION

Part of any successful advertising campaign is knowing characteristics of the audience. When conducting a survey, you need to know if the person is a buyer or user of the product. Then learn about the likes and dislikes that influence a purchase.

*Working Together*

Suppose the school cafeteria manager wants your group to do market research and recommend how she can advertise the cafeteria products and services to students. Conduct a survey of the school population regarding the selection of lunch available in the cafeteria. Make visual representations of your findings and summarize your recommendations for the cafeteria manager. Use the Chapter Investigation icons to check your group's progress.

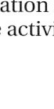
Each chapter opens with a Data Activity and Chapter Investigation. Students will continue their work on the Chapter Investigation each time they see the Chapter Investigation icon.

Chapter 1 **Sample and Display Data**    3

## Project Planning Calendar

Name _____  Date _____
**CHAPTER 1 PROJECT PLANNING CALENDAR**

Benchmarks
a. Suppose the school cafeteria manager asks your group to do market research and recommend how she can advertise the cafeteria products and services to students and hopefully increase sales. Choose a sampling method for your survey. Determine the method of delivery and how to eliminate polling the same students more than once. Write a summary of your plan. Write your survey questions and execute your plan. (*Lesson 1-1*)
b. Organize your data to determine the information to highlight about the cafeteria. Calculate the mean, median, mode, range and percentiles that ~~~~~~~ your claims. (*Lesson 1-6*)

PROJECT GOAL
To plan an advertising campaign for the school cafeteria.

## Group Project Planner

Name _____  Date _____
**CHAPTER 1 GROUP PROJECT PLANNER**

Assignment _____    Objective _____
_____    _____
_____    _____
_____    _____

Group Members        Assigned Roles
1) _____    _____
2) _____    _____
3) _____    _____
4) _____    _____
5) _____    _____

## Refresher Skills

The skills on these two pages are skills that have been presented in previous math courses. Continuous review of basic math skills will make stronger math students. These skills are identified as necessary to be successful in Chapter 1.

### Skills Correlation Chart

| Skill | Lesson Number |
|-------|---------------|
| Reading Graphs | 1-1, 1-3, 1-7 |
| Rounding | 1-2, 1-3, 1-5 |
| Estimation | 1-5 |

## Vocabulary

rounding
front-end estimation
circle graph     pictograph
bar graph     line graph

## Chalkboard Examples

### Rounding
A school group of 308 is to be transported by buses to a field day. The maximum bus load is 42. How many buses are needed?
**Solution: Dividing 308 by 42 gives 7.333 . . . Mathematically, the number rounds to 7; but, in such a case, it is necessary to round up. So, 8 buses are needed.**

### Estimation
Here's a way to adjust a front-end estimate to get a better approximation.

| Add the digits in the greatest place. | Estimate the sum of the digits in the next place. |
|---|---|
| 1547 | 1547 ⎫ |
| 419 | 419 ⎬ about 900 |
| 544 | 544 ⎫ |
| 2680 | 2680 ⎬ about 1100 |
| **estimate 3000** | **about: 2000** |

Add 2000 to the estimate.
adjusted estimate = 5000

Note that the adjusted estimate of 5000 is closer to the actual value, 5190, than is the original front-end estimate.

---

# Are You Ready?
## Refresh Your Math Skills for Chapter 1

Are You Ready? pages offer prerequisite skills practice in the chapter. The Additional Practice list on the next page shows where to find more prerequisite skills practice.

The skills on these two pages are ones you have already learned. Use the examples to refresh your memory and complete the exercises. For additional practice on these and more prerequisite skills, see pages 576-584.

## READING GRAPHS

In this chapter it will be useful to be able to interpret graphs such as circle graphs, pictographs, bar graphs and line graphs.

**Refer to the circle graph for Exercises 1–4.**

1. How many chose red as their favorite color? 140
2. What percentage chose blue as their favorite color? 25%
3. How many chose black as their favorite color? 30
4. What percentage chose purple as their favorite color? 16%

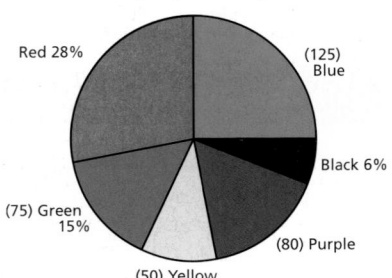

Favorite Colors
500 people surveyed

Red 28%    (125) Blue    Black 6%    (80) Purple    (50) Yellow    (75) Green 15%

**Refer to the pictograph for Exercises 5–8.**

5. What is the value of half a football? 2 touchdowns
6. How many more touchdowns were scored by the Bengals than by the Jets this season? 19
7. How many touchdowns did the Broncos and Rams score in all? 46
8. How many more touchdowns did the Steelers score than the Broncos? 6

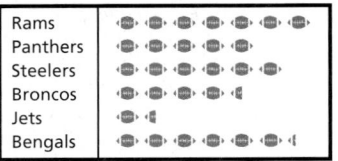

Touchdowns Scored in One Season

| Rams | |
| Panthers | |
| Steelers | |
| Broncos | |
| Jets | |
| Bengals | |

= 4 touchdowns

**Refer to the bar graph for Exercises 9–12.**

9. Which of these cities has the greatest projected population in 2015? Tokyo
10. Which of these cities has a projected population of 23 million for 2015? Shanghai
11. What is the projected population of Bombay and Sao Paulo altogether? 48 million
12. How many more people are projected to be living in Mexico City than in Los Angeles? 5 million

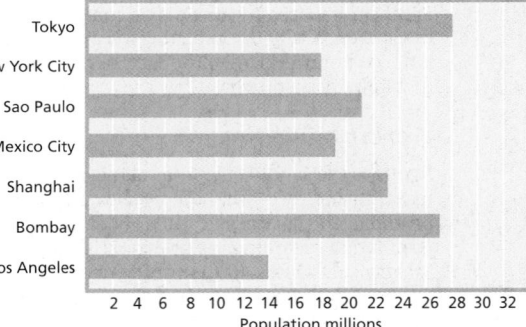

Projected Population of Selected Cities for 2015

Tokyo, New York City, Sao Paulo, Mexico City, Shanghai, Bombay, Los Angeles
Population millions

 Chapter 1 **Sample and Display Data**

---

## Teaching Tip

After using the second Chalkboard Example to demonstrate how to adjust a front-end estimation in addition, you might have students apply the process to a subtraction.

| Subtract the digits in the greatest place. | Adjust by subtracting the digits in the next greatest place. |
|---|---|
| 7.53 | 7.53 |
| − 2.32 | − 2.32   Think: 0.5 − 0.3 = 0.2 |
| **estimate 5** | **adjusted estimate = 5.2** |

## Refer to the line graph for Exercises 13–16.

**Monthly Normal Temperature for Pittsburgh, PA**

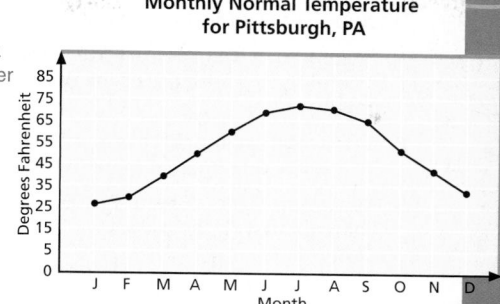

13. Is the normal temperature for Pittsburgh greater in March or November?  November

14. For what month is the normal temperature in Pittsburgh the highest?
July

15. What is the difference between the normal temperature in August and the normal temperature in December?
≈39°

16. Which month has the lowest normal temperature?  January

## ROUNDING

**Example**  Round 467,376 to the nearest thousand.
The digit in the thousands place is 7. The number to the right of 7 is less than 5, so don't change 7. The rounded number is 467,000.

**Round each number to the place of the underlined digit.**

17. 438,160  440,000

18. 718,760  719,000

19. 483.0967  483.10

20. 1.987052  1.987

21. 953,187  1,000,000

22. 185,438  185,000

23. 27.84827  27.85

24. 18.69328  19

25. 761,825  762,000

26. 521,618  520,000

27. 51.8535  51.9

28. 0.83715  1

## ESTIMATION

Front-end estimation is a way to estimate an answer or check an answer.

**Examples**  Estimate the sum.

```
  6849
+8164
```

Estimate the difference.

```
  8953
-4729
```

Mentally round each number to the place to the far left. Then add or subtract.

```
 6849  ⟶   7000
+8164  ⟶  +8000
          15,000
```

```
 8953  ⟶   9000
-4729  ⟶  -5000
           4000
```

**Estimate each sum or difference.**

29. 
```
  4618
+3904
```
9000

30. 
```
  7183
-2468
```
5000

31. 
```
  5679
+1538
```
8000

32. 
```
  2871
+5062
```
8000

33. 
```
  3894
+2156
```
6000

34. 
```
  9297
-5564
```
3000

35. 
```
  7428
-2986
```
4000

36. 
```
  8310
+1938
```
10,000

37. 
```
  6498
-3781
```
2000

38. 
```
  1368
+5632
```
7000

39. 
```
  8488
-6541
```
1000

40. 
```
  5277
-1409
```
4000

Chapter 1  **Are You Ready?**  5

## Extend the Lesson

**CHALLENGE**  Have students refer to this double line graph.
a. What does the graph compare?   the cost of electricity generated by wind to the cost of electricity generated by oil over the time interval 1980–2010
b. In what year did oil production costs for oil and wind become equivalent?  about 1997
c. What is the current difference between the cost of electricity generated by wind and by oil?
Answers vary depending on year of comparison. In 2000, oil-generated electricity is 2¢ more.

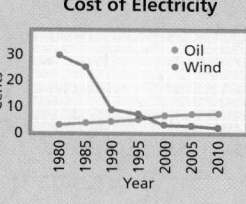

**Cost of Electricity**

## Reading Graphs

**Petroleum and Natural Gas Production**

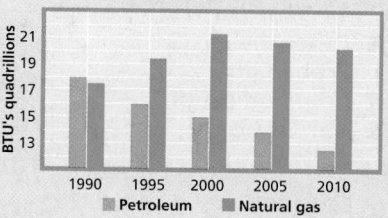

**Refer to the bar graph shown.**
a. What does the graph compare?
the production of petroleum to the production of natural gas over the time interval 1990–2010
b. In what year was the production of the two fuels about the same?
1990
c. In what year was the production ratio of the two fuels about 7 : 5?   2000
d. What is the trend in the production of petroleum?   steadily declining

## Refresher Wrap-up

### QUICK ASSESSMENT

Ask the following questions to determine if students have mastered the basic skills reviewed on these pages.

**Consider the number 3827.**
1. Which two thousands is the number between?  between 3000 and 4000
2. To which thousand is the number closer?   4000

**Match the type of graph named in 3–5 with the primary manner in which it is used (A–C).**

3. circle graph  C     4. line graph  A     5. bar graph  B

A. show changes in data over time
B. compare data at a given point in time
C. represent data as portions of a whole

### ADDITIONAL PRACTICE

Refer to the Prerequisite Skills lessons beginning on page 576 for more practice. The following lesson references are to *Basic Mathematics Review*.
- Rounding: Lesson 2
- Estimation: Lesson 3

# Surveys and Sampling Methods

**Goals**
- Identify sampling methods.
- Recognize biased surveys.

**Applications** Manufacturing, Research, Marketing, Politics

**Work in groups of three to five students.**
For 1–3, answers will vary.
1. Brainstorm a list of at least five ways to find out which recording groups or artists are most popular among teens.

2. Review the list and discuss any methods that may not be feasible due to time, money or people limitations.

3. As a group, select the four best methods discussed. Share them with the class.

### ■ BUILD UNDERSTANDING

One way to make a decision about an entire group, or **population**, is to collect data from members of that population. To do this, you need to conduct a survey or poll. Tools used to collect data include questionnaires, interviews and records of events.

Since surveying all members of a population can be costly and time-consuming, a more efficient way is to survey a representative part, or **sample**, of the population.

The first step in collecting data from a sample of a population is to choose an appropriate method of sampling. The following table explains four different methods of sampling.

| Method | Explanation | Example |
|---|---|---|
| **Random sampling** | Each member of the population has an equal chance of being selected. | The names of all students in a school are placed in a box. Fifty names are drawn and only those students are surveyed. |
| **Cluster sampling** | Members of the population are randomly selected from particular parts of the population and surveyed in clusters. | A number of classrooms in a school are selected at random. All students who have classes in those rooms during the first period of the day are surveyed. |
| **Convenience sampling** | Members of a population are selected because they are readily available, and all are surveyed. | All students in the school bookstore before the school opens are surveyed. |
| **Systematic sampling** | Members of a population that have been organized in some way are selected according to a pattern. | As students in your school pass through the cafeteria line during one day, every tenth person is surveyed. |

**6** | Chapter 1 **Sample and Display Data**

## Example 1

**ENTERTAINMENT** A concert organizer wants to identify the type of music most popular with adults in her city. Listed below are three ideas for collecting the data. Which type of sampling method is represented by each?

**a.** Ask the first 30 adults who arrive for a concert at Symphony Hall one evening.

**b.** Ask all adults who shop in randomly selected music stores in the city.

**c.** Ask all adults living in the city whose phone numbers end with the digit 3.

### Solution

**a.** convenience sampling

**b.** cluster sampling

**c.** random sampling

Sometimes survey findings are **biased**, or not truly representative of the entire population. A biased survey can be a result of the sampling method used. For example, if the only adults surveyed about their favorite type of music are those attending a country music concert, the survey findings are likely to indicate that country music is the type of music most popular with adults.

Survey findings may also be biased because some people do not respond to surveys, and some do not tell the truth on surveys. For example, suppose your teacher gives all students in your class a questionnaire to fill out about the time spent on homework each night. Some students may not fill out the questionnaire. Others may say they spend more time on homework than they actually do.

> **Check Understanding**
>
> Give reasons why you think Example 1, parts b and c, may or may not return biased results.
>
> *Answers will vary.*

## Example 2

**MANUFACTURING** A cereal manufacturer wants to identify the most popular type of breakfast food. The manufacturer decides to include a questionnaire in every tenth box of cereal that it packages.

**a.** What method of sampling does this represent?

**b.** Explain whether or not the results are likely to be biased.

### Solution

**a.** This method is systematic sampling. The members of the population have been selected according to a pattern. Every tenth box of cereal contains a questionnaire.

**b.** The survey results are likely to be biased. The only people who will be polled are those who eat one particular type of breakfast food, cereal.

Some people may not return the questionnaire, and others may not fill it out accurately.

 mathmatters2.com/extra_examples

Lesson 1-1 **Surveys and Sampling Methods** 7

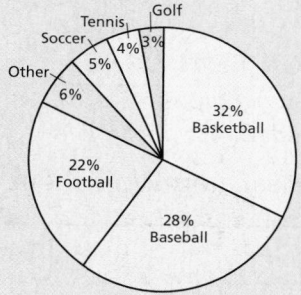
## Extend the Lesson

**REAL WORLD CONNECTION** In connection with Example 1 and Supplementary Example 1, ask students to discuss why a surveyor might use the methods of sampling suggested. For example, by using method c of Example 1, the concert organizer would collect results from people who liked all different types of music, regardless of whether or not they shopped in music stores.

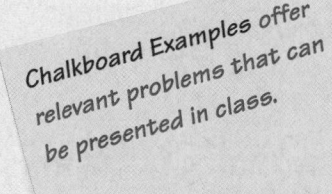

*Chalkboard Examples offer relevant problems that can be presented in class.*

## Lesson Wrap-up

### QUICK ASSESSMENT

Ask the following question to determine if students understand the content presented in this lesson.

Describe what makes each sampling method unique.
a. random sample   Each person in the population has an equal chance of being surveyed.
b. cluster sample   Only one part of the population is surveyed.
c. convenience sample   Only the most readily available people are surveyed.
d. systematic sample   People are selected to be surveyed according to a pattern.

Practice Exercises may be used for homework or seatwork.

### ASSIGNMENT GUIDE

**Basic:** 1–25, 30–45
**Enriched:** 1–45

### Reteaching Worksheet 1-1

Name _____ Date _____

RETEACHING  **1-1**
**SURVEYS AND SAMPLING METHODS**
In **random sampling** members of a population are selected in such a way that each member of the population has an equal chance of being selected. In **cluster sampling** members of the population are selected randomly from a particular portion of the group. In **convenience sampling** members of a group are selected because they are easy to locate, and all selected are surveyed. In **systematic sampling** members of a population that has been ordered according to some pattern are selected.

**Example**
The owners of a coffee shop want to find out which of the 9 types of coffee served is the most popular. What kind of sampling method is represented by each of these possible ways that the owners have considered using?

**a.** Ask the first 50 customers who arrive after the shop opens.
**b.** Ask all the customers who are seated at tables 3, 4, and 9.
**c.** Ask every tenth customer throughout the day.

**Solution**
a. convenience sampling   b. cluster sampling   c. systematic sampling

**EXERCISES**
A local bookstore owner is planning to introduce a line of home repair manuals and wants to find out if there is a potential market for such books. Which sampling technique is represented by each of the following methods?

**1.** Ask the first 30 customers who enter the bookstore each day.
convenience sampling

**2.** Ask every sixth customer who enters the bookstore each day.
systematic sampling

Suppose that you want to find out which is the most popular computer game among the students in your school. Name the sampling method represented by each description. Give one reason why the results obtained from each method could be biased.

**3.** Ask every teenager in 9 homerooms out of a total of 50.
Cluster sampling; students in those rooms might not necessarily own a computer game or be interested in computer games.

**4.** Ask every tenth student in band and chorus.
Systematic sampling; students sampled may or may not have an interest in computer games.

---

### TRY THESE EXERCISES

**FOOD SERVICE** The owners of a restaurant are planning a new menu and want to know the type of sandwich customers like best. What sampling method is represented by each possibility that the owners are considering?

**1.** Ask every fifth customer who arrives at the restaurant during one day.   systematic

**2.** Ask all customers seated at the table closest to the cashier between 11:30 A.M. and 2:30 P.M. on one day.   convenience

**3.** Ask all customers served during one day by a waiter chosen at random.   cluster

**4.** Randomly select numbers beforehand, and ask customers with those numbers on their receipts.   random

To identify the time most parents set as a curfew for their teenagers on Friday nights, all teenagers attending the 9:00 P.M. show at one movie theater are surveyed.

**5.** What method of sampling does this represent?   convenience

**6.** Are the results of this survey likely to be biased? Explain.
See additional answers.

**7.** Explain how the survey can be altered so that it represents systematic sampling.   Answers will vary, but a possible answer is to ask every fifth teenager in line at the cafeteria.

**8.** Explain how the survey can be altered so that it represents cluster sampling.
Answers will vary, but a possible answer is to take a random sample of teenagers in your class.

### PRACTICE EXERCISES • For Extra Practice, see page 585.

**Name the sampling method represented. Then give one reason why the results from each method can be biased.**   For 9–16, see additional answers.

**RECREATION** You conduct a survey to find out the favorite sport among teenagers in your town.

**9.** Ask every eighth teenager who enters a stadium for one particular game.

**10.** Ask eight teenagers whose names are drawn from all students in your town.

**11.** Ask the first eight teenagers who arrive at a party.

**12.** Randomly select a team from eight teams and poll the members of the team.

**RETAIL** A local radio station conducts a survey to determine the most popular brand of pizza in the area.

**13.** Have people call into the radio station with their responses.

**14.** Ask people who exit the Pizza Palace.

**15.** Call ten people selected randomly from a local phone book.

**16.** Ask every tenth person entering the supermarket.

**17.** Describe a sampling procedure that you believe will provide the most accurate results for the survey in Exercises 9–12. Explain your choice.   Answers will vary.

**18.** Describe a sampling procedure that you believe will provide the most accurate results for the survey in Exercises 13–16. Explain your choice.   Answers will vary.

### ADDITIONAL ANSWERS

**6.** Yes. If you know the movie is at least 2 h long, then all students at the 9 P.M. movie must have a curfew past 11 P.M.

**9.** Systematic. People who attend a sporting event usually have a greater interest in that sport than another.

**10.** Random. Because of your town's success in one sport, the favorite sport named may not be representative of the favorite of teenagers in general.

**11.** Convenience. Teenagers at the same party are most likely friends, and a common interest of friends can be the sport they participate in or enjoy watching.

**12.** Cluster. Teenagers who play a particular sport will most likely name that sport as their favorite sport.

**13.** Convenience. Only people with a strong opinion are likely to call in.

**14.** Convenience. People at Pagliaro's Pizza Palace will likely state that as their favorite pizza.

**15.** Random. The people may not be home or may not eat pizza.

19. **DATA FILE** Refer to the data on teen attendance at various events on page 562. How do you think the data were collected? *Answers will vary.*

20. **TALK ABOUT IT** Jamie says that a random sampling is always the best. Do you agree with Jamie? Explain your answer. *No. It is not always easy to get a random sample, and it can be expensive.*

**POLITICAL SCIENCE** A town council is considering a law that requires citizens to recycle all glass and plastic containers. The town holds a public meeting to discuss the proposed law. Before the meeting begins, a council member asks the 50 citizens who arrive first if they are in favor of the recycling law. *For 22–24, see additional answers.*

21. What sampling method is the town council using? *convenience*

22. How might the results of their survey be biased?

23. How can the sampling method be changed to produce a convenience sample that is definitely biased in favor of the proposed law?

24. How can the sampling method be changed to produce a convenience sample that is definitely biased against the proposed law?

The Writing Math icon identifies exercises in which students can practice their communication skills.

25. **WRITING MATH** Set up a table that lists the four types of sampling with advantages and disadvantages of each type. *Answers will vary.*

### ■ EXTENDED PRACTICE EXERCISES

26. How can the sampling method used in Exercises 21–24 be changed to produce a cluster sample that is less biased? *See additional answers.*

27. How can the sampling method used in Exercises 21–24 be changed to produce a random sample? *See additional answers.*

28. **CRITICAL THINKING** Would the results of the random survey in Exercise 27 likely be biased? *No, not if the survey is truly random.*

29. **CHAPTER INVESTIGATION** Choose a sampling method for your survey. Determine the method of delivery and how to eliminate polling the same students more than once. Write a summary of your plan. Write your survey questions and execute your plan. *Answers will vary.*

### ■ MIXED REVIEW EXERCISES

**Add.** (Basic math skills)

| | | | |
|---|---|---|---|
| 30. $4839$ $+2763$   7602 | 31. $2096$ $+3887$   5983 | 32. $460.76$ $+915.8$   1376.56 | 33. $118.37$ $+537.86$   656.23 |
| 34. $8763$ $+9031$   17,794 | 35. $7318$ $+4555$   11,873 | 36. $62.904$ $+56.72$   119.624 | 37. $1048.3$ $+392.144$   1440.444 |

**Subtract.** (Basic math skills)

| | | | |
|---|---|---|---|
| 38. $7618$ $-4296$   3322 | 39. $6100$ $-4629$   1471 | 40. $5394$ $-1625$   3769 | 41. $8461$ $-2996$   5465 |
| 42. $8000$ $-3917$   4083 | 43. $6432$ $-5981$   451 | 44. $3056$ $-2967$   89 | 45. $5306$ $-3198$   2108 |

**Math Online** mathmatters2.com/self_check_quiz

---

16. Systematic. The people may not eat pizza.

22. People who attend the meeting probably feel more strongly in favor of or opposed to the proposed law than citizens who did not attend.

23. A possible method is to survey fifty people at a recycling center.

24. A possible method is to survey residents of fifty homes that have more trash cans set out on trash pick-up day than their neighbors.

26. A possible method is to randomly select blocks throughout the town and survey all residents of these blocks.

27. A possible method is to survey all citizens whose phone number ends with a particular digit.

Every effort is made to show the Answers to exercises (1) on the reduced Student Edition page, or (2) in the margin of the Annotated Teacher's Edition. Odd answers to all exercises can be found in the Selected Answers at the back of the book.

---

## Extra Practice Worksheet 1-1

Name _____ Date _____

EXTRA PRACTICE **1-1**
## SURVEYS AND SAMPLING METHODS

### ✍ EXERCISES

Name the sampling method represented. Then give one reason why the results from each sample can be biased.

A local mall conducts a survey to determine the most popular store in the area.

1. Ask people who exit the mall. *Convenience sampling; the only people who will be polled are those who visit the mall, and they are likely to choose a store in the mall.*

2. Call ten people randomly selected from the phone book. *Random sampling; some people called may not want to participate in the survey.*

3. Ask every tenth person who enters the mall. *Systematic sampling; the only people who will be polled are those who visit the mall, and they are likely to choose a store in the mall.*

An internet provider conducts a survey to find out the favorite feature of web browsers among all internet users.

4. Call 30 people signed up for any internet service. *Cluster sampling; some people called may not want to participate in the survey.*

5. Have people call a toll-free number with their response. *Convenience sampling; the people most likely to call are those who have a strong like or dislike for certain browser features.*

6. Send an e-mail to 30 people selected at random. *Random sampling; some people e-mailed may not want to participate in the survey.*

7. Ask all customers who sign on to their service between 10 AM and 11 AM on one day. *Convenience sampling; some people may not want to participate in the survey or may not tell the truth.*

---

## Enrichment Worksheet 1-1

Name _____ Date _____

ENRICHMENT **1-1**
## CLEVER CATCHES

A sampling method sometimes used by life scientists is called the **capture–recapture method**. In this method, certain animals are captured, tagged, and then released. Later, another sample from the same population is captured, and the number of tagged animals is counted. Researchers estimate the size of the entire population based on the assumption that when the sample is chosen randomly, the fraction of tagged animals in the sample is about the same as the fraction of tagged animals in the entire population.

$$\frac{\text{number of tagged animals in sample}}{\text{number of animals in sample}} = \frac{\text{number of tagged animals in population}}{\text{total animal population } (P)}$$

**Example**

From a variety of locations in the forest, a researcher catches 100 owls, tags them, and returns them to the forest. Two weeks later, 50 owls are caught in the same locations. Exactly 5 of the 50 have tags. Assuming that both catches are made randomly, estimate the owl population.

**Solution**

The researcher found that $\frac{5}{50}$ of the sample had tags. So, the researcher estimates that $\frac{5}{50}$ of *all* the owls in the forest were originally tagged. Let $P$ be the total owl population of the forest.

$\frac{5}{50} = \frac{100}{P}$, so $P = 1000$

There are about 1000 owls in the forest.

### ✍ EXERCISES

1. From randomly chosen spots in a lake, biologists catch, tag, and release 275 trout. A week later, 80 trout are caught and exactly 16 of them have tags. Estimate the trout population. *1375*

2. Suppose wildlife managers randomly caught, tagged, and released 24 deer on an island. Two weeks later, another 24 deer were caught and exactly 2 of them had tags. Estimate the deer population of the island. *288*

3. You can simulate a capture–recapture experiment. Work with a partner. Use identical objects of two different colors, such as black and red jellybeans.
   a. Fill a container that you cannot see through with a large number of the black jellybeans. This is the population for the experiment.
   b. Select a sample by taking a handful. Instead of tagging your sample, replace each black jellybean with a red one. Mix all the jellybeans well.
   c. Select a second sample. Use it to estimate the size of the entire population. Record your answer on a separate sheet of paper.
   d. Repeat the experiment four more times. Record your answers.
   e. Use your results from steps c–d to estimate the actual size of the population. *Answers may vary.*

### Vocabulary

measures of central tendency
mean            median
mode            range

### Tools/Materials Needed

calculator

### Lesson Resources

Warm-up Transparency 1
Transparency RF-2
Reteaching 1-2
Extra Practice 1-2
Enrichment 1-2
Technology Activity 1–2

## Getting Started

### 5-Minute Warm-up

Write four 3-digit numbers.
Order the numbers from least to greatest.
Find the sum of the two middle numbers and divide that sum by 2.   See students' work.

### Introduction to Lesson 1-2
After students have determined "average" scores for Ana and Stefan, have them consider Odilla's scores on 5 quizzes: 10, 10, 10, 10, 1. Ask students if they think that adding the 5 scores and dividing by 5 is the fairest way of describing the data for Odilla. Ask them to suggest a number that would be a better "average" score for Odilla rather than the score of 8.2 obtained by adding the 5 scores and dividing by 5.

---

# 1-2 Measures of Central Tendency and Range

**Goals**
- Calculate the mean, median, and mode of data.
- Find the range of a set of data.

**Applications**  Statistics, Sports, Measurement, Education

**Use the table for Questions 1–3.**

1. Which score did Ana receive most often? Which score did Stefan receive most often?
   9; 8
2. Whose average score do you think is higher? Why?
   Answers will vary.
3. Verify your prediction in Question 2 by dividing the total of the quiz scores by 10 for both Ana and Stefan.
   Ana: 8.1; Stefan: 8.4

| Quiz | 1 | 2 | 3 | 4 | 5 | 6 | 7 | 8 | 9 | 10 |
|------|---|---|---|---|---|---|---|---|---|----|
| Ana | 9 | 7 | 10 | 9 | 8 | 8 | 9 | 10 | 2 | 9 |
| Stefan | 9 | 8 | 10 | 10 | 7 | 7 | 8 | 9 | 8 | 8 |

### ◼ BUILD UNDERSTANDING

The **mean**, or *arithmetic average*, is the sum of the values in the data set divided by the number of data. The mean is most appropriate to use when there are no extreme values in the data. The mean may or may not be an actual number in the set.

The **median** is the middle value of the data when the data are arranged in numerical order. The median is the most appropriate measure to use when there are extreme values in the data. If the number of data is odd, the median is a number in the set. If the number of data is even, the median is the average of the two middle numbers. It may not be an actual number in the set.

The **mode** is the number that occurs most often in a set of data. A set of data may have one mode, more than one mode, or no mode. Use the mode to describe the most characteristic value of the data. The mode is an actual number in the set.

The mean, median, and mode are **measures of central tendency** because they represent the average value of a data set. Statisticians report the measures that explain the data most appropriately.

> **Technology Note**
>
> Most scientific and graphing calculators have a statistics menu for computing measures of central tendency. Many use the symbol $\bar{x}$ for the mean.

### Example 1

**Find the mean, median, and mode.**

| 4 | 12 | 21 | 33 | 9 | 4 | 78 |

**Solution**

**Mean:** $(4 + 12 + 21 + 33 + 9 + 4 + 78) \div 7 = 23$   Divide by 7 since there are 7 items in the set.

**Median:** 4 4 9 [12] 21 33 78    Write the data in numerical order from least to greatest.

**Mode:** The number 4 appears twice.

The mean is 23. The median is 12. The mode is 4.

---

## Alternative Assessment

**STUDENT PORTFOLIO** After completing Example 1, have students use the same data set and consider the following questions. Ask them to make conjectures and check the conjectures with appropriate calculations.

1. a. What happens to the mean if every data value is doubled?   The mean is doubled.
   b. Are the median and mode similarly affected?   yes
2. a. What happens to the mean if the data set is doubled—that is, if the new data set is {4, 12, 21, 33, 9, 4, 78, 4, 12, 21, 33, 9, 4, 78}   The mean remains the same.
   b. Are the median and mode similarly affected?   Both remain the same.

Another number useful in describing a set of data is the range. The **range** is the difference between the greatest and least values in a set.

## Example 2

**MUSIC** South Central High School's band and flag corp scored the following number of points during its performances this past season.

27  32  6  24  29  30  8  26  30  32

**Find each of the following. Use a calculator for parts a–b.**

**a.** mean      **b.** median      **c.** mode      **d.** range

**e.** Which measure of central tendency is the best indicator of the typical number of points scored per game?

### Solution

**a.** Enter the data into list L1, as shown. Return to the main menu by pressing [2nd] **[Quit]**. Then press [2nd] **[List]** [▶] [▶] 3 [2nd] **[List]** 1 [ ) ] [ENTER] to find that the mean is 24.4.

**b.** Repeat the same process as in part a to find the median, however, choose 4 in the menu for median. The median score is 28.

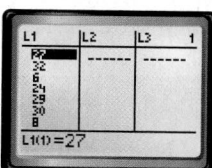

**c.** The data has two modes, 30 and 32, since both occur twice.

**d.** Subtract the lowest value, 6, from the highest value, 32. The range (32 − 6) is 26 points.

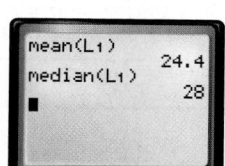

**e.** The best indicator of points scored per game is the median score since it is not affected by the extreme values 6 and 8.

> ### Check Understanding
> Describe how to solve Example 2, parts a and b, without a calculator.
>
> Answers will vary.

## Example 3

**EDUCATION** Joanie has scores of 78, 99, 78, 85, and 95 on math tests this grading period. She needs an average of at least 88 to receive a B in the class. She has one more test. What is the minimum score she can get to earn a B for the grading period if all the tests are of equal value?

### Solution

Find the total of Joanie's test scores.    $78 + 99 + 78 + 85 + 95 = 435$

If her desired average is 88 and there are 6 tests, find the total points she needs by multiplying 88 and 6.    $88 \cdot 6 = 528$

Find the score she must earn on the last test by subtracting the points already earned from the required points to get a B.    $528 - 435 = 93$

Joanie must score at least 93 on the last test to earn a B for the grading period.

> *Check Understanding features allow students to practice the main concept of the lesson.*

Math Online   mathmatters2.com/extra_examples      **Lesson 1-2 Measures of Central Tendency and Range**   |   **11**

## Extend the Lesson

**CHALLENGE** To determine the median of a given data set, first arrange the data in order and then count to the "middle" number.

**1.** Tell which item of an ordered data set the median is if the set contains:
   **a.** 5 data items   3rd
   **b.** 15 data items   8th
   **c.** 39 data items   20th
   **d.** $N$ data items ($N$ odd)   $\frac{N+1}{2}$

**2.** Tell which items of an ordered data set are averaged to obtain the median if the set contains:
   **a.** 8 values   4th and 5th
   **b.** 18 values   9th and 10th
   **c.** 42 values   21st and 22nd
   **d.** $N$ data items ($N$ even)   $\frac{N}{2}$ and $\frac{N}{2}+1$

## QUICK ASSESSMENT

Ask the following questions to determine if students understand the content presented in this lesson.

1. Explain the meaning of *measure of central tendency*. **value that is typical of a data set**
2. Why is there more than one type of measure of central tendency? **to best measure sets that have extreme values or are very spread out**
3. Which of the measures of central tendency is always a member of the data set? **the mode**
4. What information about a data set does the *range* give? **how the data is spread out**

## ASSIGNMENT GUIDE

**Basic:** 1–24, 29–44
**Enriched:** 1–44

### Reteaching Worksheet 1-2

Name _____ Date _____

RETEACHING **1-2**

#### MEASURES OF CENTRAL TENDENCY AND RANGE

**Measures of central tendency** are useful in representing central, or middle, values in a set of data. The **mean**, or arithmetic average, is the sum of the data divided by the number of items. The **median** is the middle value of the data, when they are arranged in numerical order. For even numbers of items, the median is the average of the two middle numbers. The **mode** is the number that occurs most frequently in a set of data. A set of data may have one, more than one, or no mode. The **range** of a set of data is the difference between the least and greatest values in the set.

**Example**

Beverly's quiz scores in second-year Latin were as follows:
72  73  83  79  92  98  96  79  92  86

a. Find the mean.   b. Find the median.   c. Find the mode.

**Solution**

a. Add the numerical values of the data and average them.
72 + 73 + 83 + 79 + 92 + 98 + 96 + 79 + 92 + 86 = 850
850 ÷ 10 = 85
The mean of the data is 85.

b. Rewrite the data in numerical order.
72  73  79  79  83  86  92  92  96  98
The number of items is even. The median is halfway between 83 and 86.
(83 + 86) ÷ 2 = 84.5
The median is 84.5.

c. The scores 79 and 92 occur twice. So, the set of data has two modes, 79 and 92.

**EXERCISES**

Here are Rundel High School's basketball team's scores for February and March.
77  58  77  91  68  63  69  86  85  45  77  74

1. Find the mean. __72.5__   2. Find the median. __75.5__
3. Find the mode. __77__   4. Find the range. __46__

Craig jogged every day during his semester break. The number of miles he jogged each day is given below.
4.4   2.7   3.7   3.4   2.9   4.1   3.8

5. Find the mean. __3.6__   6. Find the median. __3.7__
7. Find the mode. __no mode__   8. Find the range. __1.7__

9. Which measure best indicates the typical distance jogged?
__mean or median__

**Find the mean, median, mode, and range for each set of data. Round answers to the nearest hundredth.**

1. Davon biked the following number of miles on each day of his trip.

   12.3  12.8  12.4  18.4  27.1  14.9  17.5  12.7  11.4  13.5
   mean = 15.3 mi; median = 13.15 mi; no mode; range = 15.7 mi

2. Juanita spent the following on restaurant meals last month.

   $4.32  $5.16  $3.59  $6.18  $15.87  $8.81  $7.49  $10.00  $2.88
   mean = $7.14; median = $6.18; no mode; range = $12.99

3. In Exercise 1, which measure of central tendency is the best indicator of the typical number of miles Davon biked each day? **mean**

4. In Exercise 2, which measure of central tendency is the best indicator of the typical amount of money Juanita spent on lunch? **median**

5. **WRITING MATH** Explain how removing the $15.87 meal from the data in Exercise 2 affects the mean, median, mode, and range. By how much is each affected? Round answers to the nearest cent. See additional answers.

**Find each of the following.**

**Number of Glasses of Water
Consumed Daily**

| Number of glasses | 3 | 4 | 5 | 6 | 7 |
|---|---|---|---|---|---|
| Frequency | 12 | 18 | 9 | 15 | 6 |

6. mean  4.75
7. median  4.5
8. any modes  4
9. range  4

10. Which measure of central tendency best indicates the amount of water the average person drinks daily? **Answers will vary.**

11. **WRITING MATH** If your teacher were to allow you to choose the measure of central tendency that is used to determine your grade, which measure would you choose? Why? Answers will vary. Have students experiment with their grades. Different students' grades will benefit from different measures.

**EDUCATION** Mrs. Jones returned to college to finish her degree. She must have an average of 85% for her employer to reimburse 85% of the tuition fees. She has scored 84, 75, 87, 96 and 75 on her exams. All exam scores are given in percents.

12. Will she receive an 85% if her professor uses the median to determine her grade? Explain. No. Her median is 84.

13. If her professor uses the mean, what score must she receive on the last exam to raise her average to 85%? Assume all exams have equal value. 93

14. If Mrs. Jones can earn a 90%, her employer will reimburse 90% of her tuition fees. If her professor uses the mean, can Mrs. Jones score enough points to receive a 90% average on six exams? If not, what is her highest possible average? Round to the nearest tenth. no; 86.2

15. **DATA FILE** Refer to the data on sleep times of animals on page 561. Explain whether you think "average" refers to the mean, median, or mode. Mean. Some animals hibernate or are more dormant at certain times of the year than they are at other times.

*Try These Exercises allow students to practice concepts in a classroom setting.*

### Teaching Tip

For Exercises 19–22, remind students that finding one example and one counterexample is all that is necessary to determine that a statement is *sometimes* true. However, to determine that a statement is *always* true or *never* true requires justifying that it is true for every example or not true for every example.

**Find the unknown number in each data set so that the mean of the set is the value given.**

**16.** 6, 14, 18, 22, 11, ■   19
mean = 15

**17.** 22, 22, 45, 98, ■   13
mean = 40

**18.** 105, 168, 197, ■   306
mean = 194

**Determine whether each statement is *sometimes*, *always*, or *never* true. If the answer is *sometimes* or *never*, create sample data that supports your answer.**

**19.** If you change one number in a set of data, the mean of the data will change.   always

**20.** If you change one number in a set of data, the median of the data will change.
Sometimes; change 8 to 4 in 4, 5, 6, 8, 10.

**21.** If you change one number in a set of data, the mode of the data will change.
Sometimes; change 1 to 4 in 1, 1, 2, 4.

**22.** If you change one number in a set of data, the range of the data will change.
Sometimes; change 7 to 10 in 7, 11, 12, 15, 20.

**23. YOU MAKE THE CALL** Meiying received a 70 on the first test and a 90 on the second test, for a test average of 80. On the third test, she received a 100. She reasoned that her average is 90. Is she correct? Explain.   No. She needs to average all test scores, not just the previous average. Her average is 86.7.

**24. DATA FILE** Refer to the data about the coldest U.S. temperatures recorded on page 577. Find the mean, median, mode, and range of the record coldest temperatures.
mean = −63.4°; median = −60.5°; mode = −60°; range = 26°

### ■ EXTENDED PRACTICE EXERCISES

To give greater emphasis to the grades students make as a semester progresses, Ricardo's teacher uses a *weighted mean* to assign grades. The first test counts as one grade. The second test counts as two grades. The third test counts as three grades and the fourth test as four grades. Due to the weighting, it is as if there is a total of 10 grades.

**25.** Ricardo's test scores are 60, 70, 80 and 90, in that order. Find his weighted total.   800

**26.** What number must you divide by to find Ricardo's weighted mean? What is his weighted mean?   10; 80

**27.** Lamesha is in the same math class as Ricardo. Her test scores are 90, 80, 70 and 60 in that order. Find her weighted mean.   70

**28. CRITICAL THINKING** When does a weighted mean have the same value as the arithmetic mean of a set of data?   See additional answers.

### ■ MIXED REVIEW EXERCISES

**Multiply.** (Prerequisite skills)

**29.** 372 × 58   21,576

**30.** 976 × 42   40,992

**31.** 522 × 77   40,194

**32.** 861 × 19   16,359

**33.** 187 × 65   12,155

**34.** 318 × 65   20,670

**35.** 855.6 × 17.52   14,990.112

**36.** 412.13 × 80.09   33,007.4917

**Divide. Round answers to the nearest thousandth.** (Prerequisite skills)

**37.** 9286 ÷ 52   178.577

**38.** 8104 ÷ 96   84.417

**39.** 7328 ÷ 60   122.133

**40.** 1053 ÷ 64   16.453

**41.** 5000 ÷ 43   116.279

**42.** 6218 ÷ 24   259.083

**43.** 382.4 ÷ 9.685   39.484

**44.** 50.562 ÷ 19.7   2.567

Math Online   mathmatters2.com/self_check_quiz

---

## ADDITIONAL ANSWERS

**5.** Removing the $15.87 meal will affect the measures of central tendency except for the mode, since in this case there is no mode. The mean decreases by $1.09, the median decreases by $0.51, and the range decreases by $5.87.

**28.** This can occur in an infinite number of ways. A possible answer is that if a data set has an even number of elements and their values are symmetrical about the mean. This is especially clear when all of the data values are the same.
For example,
$$\frac{80 + 2(80) + 3(80) + 4(80)}{10} = 80.$$

---

## Extra Practice Worksheet 1-2

Name _____   Date _____

EXTRA PRACTICE   **1-2**
**MEASURES OF CENTRAL TENDENCY AND RANGE**

**✔ EXERCISES**

Find the mean, median, mode, and range for each set of data. Round answers to the nearest tenth.

1. Micael ran the following number of miles on each day last week.
6.5   4.2   5.3   6.8   2.9   3.6   5.8
mean = 5.0; median = 5.3; no mode; range = 3.9

2. Jamiel worked the following number of hours each week for the last 2 months.
38.6   40.5   32.8   36.5   40.5   32.8   42.5   25.5
mean = 36.2; median = 37.6; mode = 32.8; range = 17

3. In Exercise 1, which measure of central tendency is the best indicator of the typical number of miles Micael ran each day? Why? Answers may vary.
Possible answer: The mode because it is in the middle of the data.

4. In Exercise 2, which measure of central tendency is the best indicator of the number of hours Jamiel worked each week for the last 2 months? Why? Answers may vary
Possible answer: The mean because it is the average number of hours she worked.

Ricardo earns a base salary of $500 a week plus a weekly commission. He has earned a commission of $325, $460, $280, $400, $380, and $250 each week for the last six weeks.

5. Find the mean, median, mode, and range for the commission Ricardo earned during these six weeks. Round answers to the nearest tenth.
$349.20; $352.50; none; $210

6. Find the mean, median, mode, and range the total amount Ricardo earned during these six weeks. Round answers to the nearest tenth. $849.20; $852.50; none; $210

7. What commission must Ricardo earn during the seventh week to raise his mean weekly commission to $370.70? $500

8. What commission must Ricardo earn during the seventh week to raise his mean weekly earnings to $850? $355

---

## Enrichment Worksheet 1-2

Name _____   Date _____

ENRICHMENT   **1-2**
**FINDING THE SPREAD**

Measures of central tendency tell something about a "typical" value, but they tell little about how the data are spread out. Statistics that describe how the data are distributed are called **measures of spread**. One measure of spread is the **range**, which is the difference between the greatest and least values. Two others, which describe how spread out the scores are in relation to the mean, are the **variance** and the **standard deviation**. To find these statistics, follow these steps.

1. Find the mean of the data, $m$.
2. For each number $x$, find the difference between the number and the mean, that is, $x - m$.
3. Square each difference in Step 2, that is $(x - m)^2$.
4. Add all the squares from Step 3 and divide by $n$. This is the **variance**.
5. Find the square root of the variance. This is the **standard deviation**.

In general, the greater the variance and the standard deviation, the more the data items are spread out.

**✔ EXERCISES**

Use the following set of test scores for the exercises below.
76   80   81   82   83   84   77   78   90   89

1. Find the mean of the test scores. $m$ = _____ 82

2. Use the value for $m$ you just found. Complete the table above.

| Test Score | Step 1 $m$ | Step 2 $x - m$ | Step 3 $(x - m)^2$ |
|---|---|---|---|
| 76 | | −6 | 36 |
| 80 | 82 | −2 | 4 |
| 81 | 82 | −1 | 1 |
| 82 | 82 | 0 | 0 |
| 83 | 82 | 1 | 1 |
| 84 | 82 | 2 | 4 |
| 77 | 82 | −5 | 25 |
| 78 | 82 | −4 | 16 |
| 90 | 82 | 8 | 64 |
| 89 | 82 | 7 | 49 |

3. Find the sum of the squares in the column for Step 3. _____ 200
Divide this sum by $n$ to find the variance. _____ 20

4. Use the square root key √ on a calculator. To the nearest tenth, find the standard deviation, the square root of the variance you found in Exercise 3. _____ 4.5

### Vocabulary Review

**Lesson 1-1**
population      sample
random sampling
cluster sampling
systematic sampling
convenience sampling
biased

**Lesson 1-2**
measures of central tendency
mean           median
mode           range

*Vocabulary Review features list terms introduced in the previous two lessons.*

## ASSIGNMENT GUIDE

**All students:** 1–24

## Chalkboard Examples

### Lesson 1-1
**POLITICAL SCIENCE** During her re-election campaign, the mayor of Lockwood decided to conduct a popularity poll. Her staff gave a questionnaire to everyone stopping at the mayor's campaign head-quarters.
a. What method of sampling does this represent?   convenience sampling
b. Explain if the results are likely to be biased and why.   Biased; people stopping in at her campaign headquarters are likely to be strong supporters of the mayor.

### PRACTICE ■ LESSON 1-1

A pretzel manufacturer wants to identify the most popular type of snack food. Name the sampling method represented by each of the following.

1. Place a questionnaire in every sixth package of pretzels produced.   systematic

2. Place a questionnaire in every package of pretzels sold in a certain state.   cluster

3. Give a questionnaire to all of the people who tour the plant where the pretzels are processed and packaged.   convenience

4. Dial phone numbers around the country and ask to speak with someone over age 18.   random

A major city wants to build a new sports stadium. The decision on where to build the stadium is controversial. A survey will be given. Name the sampling method represented by each of the following.

5. Choose a city building and survey everyone entering on a particular day.   cluster

6. A survey is given to every fifth commuter going over the bridge into downtown.   systematic

7. Give a survey to everyone at the baseball game.   convenience

8. Which sampling method above would have the most bias. Why?   See additional answers.

### PRACTICE ■ LESSON 1-2

Find the mean, median, mode, and range for each set of data. Round answers to the nearest tenth.

9. Yearly incomes
   $22,000     $26,000     $27,000     $29,000     $22,000     $35,000     $30,000
   mean = $27,285.70; median = $27,000; mode = $22,000; range = $13,000
10. Heights of students
   57 in.     49 in.     57 in.     60 in.     48 in.     58 in.     55 in.     57 in.
   mean = 55.1 in.; median = 57 in.; mode = 57 in.; range = 12 in.
11. Price of a hotel room
   $65     $71     $89     $105     $155     $80     $105
   mean = $95.70; median = $89; mode = $105; range = $90
12. Pupils in a class
   22     23     21     24     23     19     23     20     24
   mean = 22.1; median = 23; mode =23; range = 5
13. Airfare prices
   $275     $325     $410     $260     $305
   mean = $315; median = $305; no mode; range = $150
14. Weight of athletes
   199 lb     189 lb     170 lb     192 lb     202 lb     192 lb     160 lb     189 lb
   mean = 186.6 lb; median = 190.5 lb; mode = 192 lb; range = 42 lb

Find the unknown number in each data set so that the mean of the set is the given value.

15. 75, 87, 90, 99, 72, ■   57
    mean = 80

16. 11, 8, 6, 7, 9, 12, ■   10
    mean = 9

17. 220, 250, 325, ■   225
    mean = 255

## ADDITIONAL ANSWERS

8. The convenience sampling at the base-ball game would likely have the most bias because the people in the sample group are more likely to be sports fans who would support a new stadium and a growth of the sport in their city. Another possibility is that these people would be biased against a new stadium because they like the old stadium and want to preserve it for nostalgia.

**A community wants to know if the residents would support an increase in property taxes to pay for a community swimming pool.** (Lesson 1-1)

18. How can a random sample of 50 residents be selected?
    Sample answer: Send a survey to 50 random addresses.
19. How can a clustered sampling of 50 residents be selected?
    Sample answer: Send a survey to 50 random addresses of one neighborhood within the community.
20. How can a convenience sampling of 50 residents be selected?
    Sample answer: Take a survey of 50 people who come to town hall on a given day.
21. How can a systematic sampling of 50 residents be identified?
    Sample answer: Send a survey in every tenth water bill, with a total of 50 surveys sent in all.

**Find the mean, median, mode, and range for each set of data. Round answers to the nearest tenth.** (Lesson 1-2)

22. Test scores
    88    92    81    88    95    70
    mean = 85.7; median = 88; mode = 88; range = 25
23. Miles run each day
    6 mi    8 mi    7 mi    6 mi    5 mi    5.5 mi    6.4 mi    9 mi    6 mi    7 mi
    mean = 6.6 mi; median = 6.2 mi; mode = 6; range = 4 mi
24. Create a set of data with six numbers whose range is 70. (Lesson 1-2)
    Answers will vary.

## MathWorks    Career – Product Tester
Workplace Knowhow

**A** product tester evaluates claims that a manufacturer makes about its products. He or she must decide what population or sample of the population to survey, what method to use, and concisely report the survey results. The table lists the stopping distances on wet pavement for the same car using two different brands of tires.

| Brand X | 36 ft | 34 ft | 37 ft | 40 ft | 32 ft | 38 ft |
|---------|-------|-------|-------|-------|-------|-------|
| Brand Y | 33 ft | 42 ft | 35 ft | 34 ft | 38 ft | 34 ft |

1. Calculate the mean stopping distance for each tire brand.
   mean X = 36.2 ft; mean Y = 36 ft
2. Find the mode for Brand X. Find the mode for Brand Y.
   mode X = none; mode Y = 34 ft
3. Determine the median stopping distance for the two brands of tires. median X = 36.5 ft; median Y = 34.5 ft

4. Calculate the range of stopping distances for Brands X and Y.
   range X = 8 ft; range Y = 9 ft
5. Which measure of central tendency most accurately represents the stopping distance data for each brand of tire?
   Answers will vary since all measures are similar.
6. Which brand of tire appears to have a shorter stopping distance? Justify your answer. Y. Its measures of central tendency are lower in general.

 Math Online   mathmatters2.com/mathworks
                                     Chapter 1   **Review and Practice Your Skills**    **15**

### Lesson 1-2
**FOOD SERVICE** The number of customers at a frozen yogurt stand each day during one week were 61, 52, 92, 84, 155, 240, and 184.
a. Determine the measures of central tendency and the range for the data. **mean = 124, median = 92, no mode, range = 188**
b. Which measure of central tendency is the best indicator of the typical number of customers per day? Explain. **Mean; possible reason: the data shows two groupings: Mon.–Thurs. and Fri.–Sun. where, as might be expected, the weekend group has more customers. The higher mean value reflects this better than does the lower median value.**

## MathWorks

Before the advertising industry became well organized, the sharp and unethical practices of some advertisers prompted the passing of many laws and legal restrictions by the federal, state, and municipal governments. At present, advertising is one of the most strictly regulated industries in the U.S.

Students should answer Questions 1–6 to better understand how a product tester might apply data analysis to evaluate performance and quality.

Students who are interested in learning more about this career choice can go to mathmatters2.com/mathworks. School Guidance Counselors are another resource for information about training requirements and appropriate schools.

## Teaching Tip

Ask students to tell how they can check their results for Exercises 15–17 in which they are to supply a value to complete a data set so that a certain mean value may be achieved. **Use the completed data set and find the mean value.**

*MathWorks features highlight two careers per chapter.*

# Histograms and Stem-and-Leaf Plots

**Goals**
- Use and create histograms to solve problems.
- Use and create stem-and-leaf plots to solve problems.

**Applications** Education, Statistics, Inventory, Sports, Entertainment

## Lesson Planning

### NCTM Standards/Strands
- Data Analysis & Probability
- Representation
- Communication
- Connections

*Applications appear at the beginning of each lesson and list subject areas related to problems from the lesson.*

### Vocabulary

frequency table
histogram
stem-and-leaf plot
stem
leaf
outliers
clusters
gaps

### Tools/Materials Needed

graphing calculator   graph paper

### Lesson Resources

Warm-up Transparency 1
Transparency TK-1, 2, 9
Reteaching 1-3
Extra Practice 1-3
Enrichment 1-3

## Getting Started

### 5-Minute Warm-up

**Sort these numbers into three groups based on their tens digit. Order each group.**
32, 23, 35, 41, 30, 31, 32, 35, 40, 41, 42   **23, 25; 30, 31, 32, 35; 40, 41, 42**

### Introduction to Lesson 1-3

Elicit that a *frequency table* is a record of the number of items in a category. Discuss the nature of the given tables. In Table 1, the items are recorded in intervals of 5, where every number from 1 through 20 is represented. In Table 2, the items are recorded by actual score (not every number from 1 through 20 is represented).

**EDUCATION** For each math test, Mr. Lyons makes a frequency table of the class results. Marissa's test paper for one test is missing, but Mr. Lyons knows that he graded it and recorded it in the table.

1. If he uses a table like Table 1, can he identify the missing score? Explain.
No, the table does not give enough detail to identify the missing score.
2. If he uses a table like Table 2, can he identify the missing score? Explain.
Yes, the table gives enough detail to identify the range of scores the missing score could be.

| Test Scores (max. score = 20) | Frequency |
|---|---|
| 0 - 5 | II |
| 6 - 10 | II |
| 11 - 15 | ЖЖ ЖЖ III |
| 16 - 20 | ЖЖ ЖЖ I |

Table 1

| Test Scores (max. score = 20) | Frequency |
|---|---|
| 3 | I |
| 4 | I |
| 6 | I |
| 8 | II |
| 11 | III |
| 12 | ЖЖ |
| 13 | I |
| 14 | IIII |
| 16 | III |
| 17 | II |
| 18 | IIII |
| 19 | I |
| 20 | I |

Table 2

### BUILD UNDERSTANDING

It is difficult to see a pattern or trend in data that is not organized. The manner in which the data is organized affects its usefulness. A **frequency table** records the number of times a response occurs but does not offer a visual display.

Frequencies can be shown in a bar graph called a histogram. A **histogram** differs from other bar graphs in that no space is between the bars and the bars usually represent numbers grouped by intervals.

Most graphing utilities can display a histogram. With technology you do not have to make a frequency table first. The calculator does the organizing for you. The intervals are determined by the *x*-scale in the window setting.

### Example 1

**TECHNOLOGY** Use a graphing utility to display the data below in a histogram. For each bar, name the interval and its frequency.

12   15   22   36   45   10   51   12   20   42   16   33

14   23   40   37   15   54   16   22   18   47   50   11

### Solution

Enter the data into a list, L1. Choose *histogram* in the statistics plot menu. Set the viewing window as follows.

Xmin = 10   Xmax = 55   Xscl = 5
Ymin = 0   Ymax = 10   Yscl = 1

Intervals and frequencies:   10 to 15: 5   15 to 20: 5   20 to 25: 4
25 to 30: 0   30 to 35: 1   35 to 40: 2
40 to 45: 2   45 to 50: 2   50 to 55: 3

## Teaching Tip

Students may find it helpful to make stem-and-leaf plots on graph paper, writing one stem or leaf in each box. Have students rotate the horizontal arrangement of a stem-and-leaf plot a quarter turn counterclockwise to note the physical resemblance to a histogram. The diagram at the right shows the outline of the histogram that would result from rotating the stem-and-leaf plot of Supplementary Example 2. In this diagram, the stems have been redistributed to the leaves. Elicit that in a stem-and-leaf plot, the actual data entries are visible and that they are in order, while all that would be visible in a histogram of the same data are blank bars with no actual data entries but with interval values written below each bar.

| | | 48 | |
| | 39 | 46 | |
| | 39 | 46 | |
| | 37 | 45 | |
| 29 | 36 | 45 | |
| 29 | 35 | 44 | |
| 26 | 35 | 44 | 54 |
| 25 | 33 | 42 | 52 |
| 25 | 31 | 40 | 51 |
| 22 | 30 | 40 | 50 |

## Example 2

**FITNESS** A gym teacher tested the number of sit-ups students in two classes could do in 1 min. The results are shown.

a. Make a histogram of the data. Title the histogram.

b. How many students were able to do 25–29 sit-ups in 1 min?

c. How many students were unable to do 10 sit-ups in 1 min?

d. Between which two consecutive intervals does the greatest increase in frequency occur? What is the increase?

**Sit-Ups Done in 1 Minute**

| Number of sit-ups | Frequency |
|---|---|
| 0 - 4 | 8 |
| 5 - 9 | 12 |
| 10 - 14 | 15 |
| 15 - 19 | 6 |
| 20 - 24 | 18 |
| 25 - 29 | 10 |

### Solution

a. Use the same intervals as those in the frequency table on the horizontal axis. Label the vertical axis with a scale that includes the frequency numbers from the table.

b. Ten students were able to do 25–29 sit-ups in 1 min.

c. Add the students who did 0–4 sit-ups and 5–9 sit-ups. So 8 + 12, or 20, students were unable to do 10 sit-ups in 1 min.

d. The greatest increase is between intervals 15–19 and 20–24. These frequencies are 6 and 18. So the increase is 18 − 6 = 12.

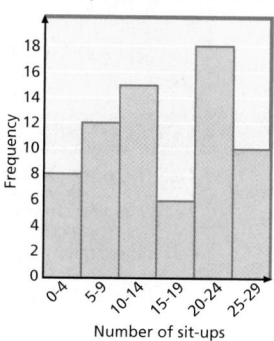

**Sit-Ups Done in 1 Minute**

Another method for organizing and displaying data is a **stem-and-leaf plot**. One is shown in Example 3. Each number of the data set is represented by a *leaf* and a *stem*. A leaf is the digit(s) in the place farthest to the right in the number. A stem is the digit(s) that remain when the leaf is dropped. A vertical line separates the stems and leaves.

**Outliers** are values much greater or less than most of the other values. **Clusters** are isolated groups of values. **Gaps** are large spaces between values. A stem-and-leaf plot helps you notice outliers, clusters and gaps. The plot must include a key.

## Example 3

**RETAIL** The stem-and-leaf plot gives the number of shirts sold daily for 2 wk at Nims department store. Find the following:

a. outliers, clusters, and gaps

b. median     c. mode     d. range

**Number of Shirts Sold Daily For 2 Weeks at Nims**

```
 4 | 3
 7 | 2 3 4 5 5 5 9 9
 8 | 0 0 3 4
10 | 2
```

4 | 3 represents 43 shirts.

### Solution

a. Since 43 is much less than the other data and 102 is much greater than the other data, both are possible outliers. Clusters of data are in the low to middle 70s and around 79 and 80. The greatest gaps occur between the outliers and the rest of the data and between 75 and 79.

b. The median is the mean of 75 and 79. The median is 77 shirts.

c. Since 75 appears most often, the mode is 75 shirts.

d. The range is the difference between 102 and 43. The range is 59 shirts.

mathmatters2.com/extra_examples     Lesson 1-3 **Histograms and Stem-and-Leaf Plots**  **17**

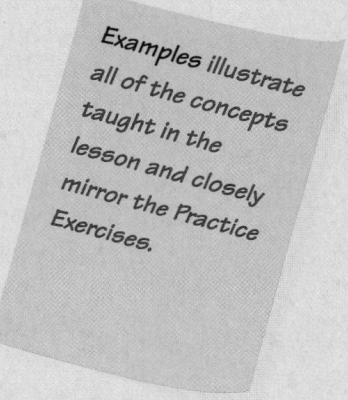
*Examples illustrate all of the concepts taught in the lesson and closely mirror the Practice Exercises.*

---

# Chalkboard Examples

## Supplementary Example 1
**Refer to the following histogram.**

a. What is the length of each interval?   **4 units**

b. How many students took the test? Explain your method.
**140; add all the frequencies**

c. Which interval has the highest frequency?  **70–74**   the lowest frequency?  **55–59**

d. If 65% is passing, how many students passed? Explain your method.   **110; Add the frequencies beginning with the interval 65–69, or subtract 30 from 140.**

e. What percent of the students failed?  $\frac{10 + 20}{140} \approx 21.4\%$

f. What percent of the students had grades of at least 90%?
$\frac{10 + 5}{140} \approx 10.7\%$

## Supplementary Example 2
**WEATHER** The Weather Bureau in Baltimore, MD recorded these daily high temperatures in °F for the month of November.
46 31 33 39 25 29 37 44 35 36
35 40 52 48 35 39 40 42 51 29
45 30 26 52 44 54 46 50 45 22
Make a stem-and-leaf plot of the data.

To determine the stems, note that the data can be arranged in four groups: the 20's, the 30's, the 40's, and the 50's.
Read through the data to put on the leaves.

```
2 |
3 |
4 |
5 |
```

First, use the order that appears in the data.

```
2 | 5 9 9 6 2
3 | 1 3 9 7 5 6 5 5 9 0
4 | 6 4 0 8 0 2 5 4 6 5
5 | 2 1 2 4 0
```

Then, order the leaves from least to greatest.

**November Temperatures**

```
2 | 2 5 6 9 9
3 | 0 1 3 5 5 5 6 7 9 9
4 | 0 0 2 4 4 5 5 6 6 8
5 | 0 1 2 2 4
```

2 | 6 represents 26°F.

# Example 4

Display the data in a stem-and-leaf plot. Include a key that explains the plot.

**a.** Miles ran each day: 3.5, 4.6, 3.9, 4.1, 2.7, 3.4

**b.** Price of stereos: $121, $129, $125, $117, $124, $119, $110, $117, $120

## Solution

**a.** Use 2, 3 and 4 for the stems.

```
2 | 7
3 | 4 5 9
4 | 1 6
```

2|7 represents 2.7 mi.

**b.** Use 11 and 12 for the stems.

```
11 | 0 7 7 9
12 | 0 1 4 5 9
```

11|0 represents $110.

## Lesson Wrap-up

### QUICK ASSESSMENT

Ask the following question to determine if students understand the content presented in this lesson.

How are histograms and stem-and-leaf plots the same? How are they different? **Same: both are visual displays of data and both show the frequency of data within certain intervals. Different: histograms show only the intervals within which data items fall, while stem-and-leaf plots show individual data items.**

### ASSIGNMENT GUIDE

**Basic:** 1–25, 29–32
**Enriched:** 1–32

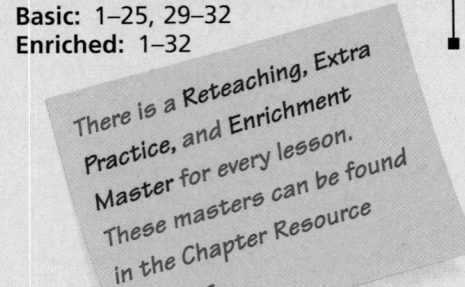

There is a Reteaching, Extra Practice, and Enrichment Master for every lesson. These masters can be found in the Chapter Resource Masters.

**Reteaching Worksheet 1-3**

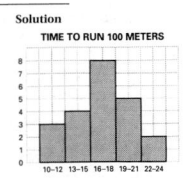

Name _____ Date _____

RETEACHING **1-3**

**HISTOGRAMS AND STEM-AND-LEAF PLOTS**

Frequencies of values in a set of data can be shown in a bar graph known as a **histogram**. In a histogram, there is no space between the bars.

**Example 1**

Twenty-two students tried out for the track team. The track coach recorded the number of seconds it took the students to run the 100-meter dash. The results are shown in this frequency table. Make a histogram of the data.

| TIME TO RUN 100 METERS | |
|---|---|
| Time (s) | Frequency |
| 10–12 | 3 |
| 13–15 | 4 |
| 16–18 | 8 |
| 19–21 | 5 |
| 22–24 | 2 |

**Solution**

TIME TO RUN 100 METERS

A **stem-and-leaf** plot is another way to visualize data. Each number is represented by a **leaf**, the digit in the rightmost place of the number, and a **stem**, the digit or digits that are left when the leaf is dropped. Stem-and-leaf plots help you spot **outliers**, values in the data that are much greater or less than the rest of the values, and to note **clusters** of values or **gaps** between values.

**Example 2**

Organize this data into a stem-and-leaf plot.

| 18 | 40 | 9 | 38 |
| 23 | 35 | 41 | 20 |
| 12 | 72 | 23 | 15 |
| 39 | 32 | 22 | 39 |

**Solution**
Let the tens digits be the stems and the ones digits be the leaves.

| Stems | Leaves |
|---|---|
| 0 | 9 |
| 1 | 2 5 8 |
| 2 | 0 2 3 3 |
| 3 | 2 5 8 9 9 |
| 4 | 0 1 |
| 7 | 2 |

**EXERCISES**

Use the histogram in Example 1 to answer these questions.

1. How many students ran the distance in 13–15 s? ___4___

2. How many students finished the run in 15 s or under? ___7___

Use the stem-and-leaf plot in Example 2 to answer these questions.

3. Find any outliers in the data. ___72___

4. Find any clusters or gaps. **Clusters occur in the low 20's and around 40; gaps occur between 23 and 32 and between 41 and 72.**

### TRY THESE EXERCISES

**Use the data shown for Exercises 1–5.**

**Number of Pets Per Family**

| 1 | 2 | 3 | 1 | 0 | 2 | 1 | 0 |
| 1 | 0 | 1 | 4 | 1 | 2 | 0 | 0 |
| 0 | 1 | 1 | 2 | 2 | 5 | 1 | 0 |

1. Use a frequency table to make a histogram of the data. See additional answers.

2. How many families own two to three pets? 6

3. How many families own more than three pets? 2

4. To the nearest percent, what percent of families own no pets? 29%

5. Name the median, mode, and range of the data. median = 1; mode = 1; range = 5

**ENTERTAINMENT** Tickets for a rock concert were sold each day as follows: 149, 253, 366, 169, 297, 421, 183, 256, 303, 427, 189, 229, 367, 520, 147, 168, 253, 146, 182, 305, 412, 277

6. Make a stem-and-leaf plot. See additional answers.

7. Name any outliers, clusters, or gaps. outlier: 520; clusters: 146–189, 229–305, 412–427; gaps: 189–229, 305–366, 367–412, 427–520

8. Find the median. 254.5

9. Find the mode. 253

10. Find the range. 374

**Make a stem-and-leaf plot of each set of data.**
For 11–12, see additional answers.

11. Miles biked each day: 12.8, 11.6, 14.8, 15.0, 15.1, 11.6, 13.0, 16.8, 11.6, 10.5

12. Age of Stella's grandchildren: 4, 9, 12, 16, 23, 14, 7, 1, 16, 14, 19, 22, 20, 13, 5, 29, 6, 2, 1, 17

### PRACTICE EXERCISES • For Extra Practice, see page 586.

**Use the histogram for Exercises 13–16.**

13. Which interval contains the most evergreen seedlings? 120–129

14. Which intervals contain an equal number of trees? 90–99 and 150–159; 100–109 and 130–139

15. Which intervals contain 95% of the data? 100–109, 110–119, 120–129, 130–139, 140–149

**Height of Evergreens in Reforestation Project**

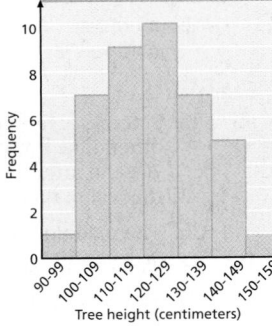

## ADDITIONAL ANSWERS

**1.**

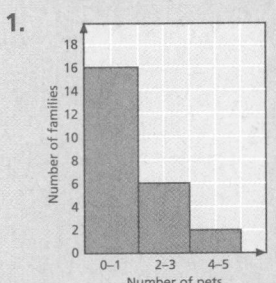

**6.**

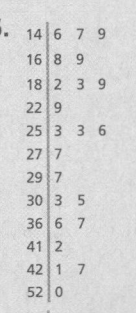

```
14 | 6 7 9
16 | 8 9
18 | 2 3 9
22 | 9
25 | 3 3 6
27 | 7
29 | 7
30 | 3 5
36 | 6 7
41 | 2
42 | 1 7
52 | 0
```

14|6 represents 146 tickets.

**11.**

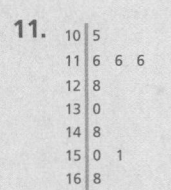

```
10 | 5
11 | 6 6 6
12 | 8
13 | 0
14 | 8
15 | 0 1
16 | 8
```

10|5 represents 10.5 mi.

**12.**

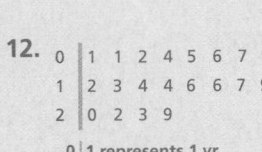

```
0 | 1 1 2 4 5 6 7 9
1 | 2 3 4 4 6 6 7 9
2 | 0 2 3 9
```

0|1 represents 1 yr.

**16. WRITING MATH** Explain how the histogram on page 18 changes if intervals of 20, instead of 10, are used. *Answers will vary.*

**SPORTS** The data are the percents of free throws Alan made during the basketball games he played.

| 55 | 59 | 56 | 46 | 43 |
|----|----|----|----|----|
| 79 | 53 | 60 | 39 | 57 |
| 86 | 45 | 66 | 72 | 46 |
| 24 | 64 | 47 | 43 | 41 |

**17.** Organize the data into a stem-and-leaf plot.
*See additional answers.*
**18.** Make a histogram of the data in intervals of 10.
*See additional answers.*
**19.** In how many games did Alan make at least 60% of his free throws? 6

**20.** What is the median percent of scoring free throws Alan made per game? 54%

**21.** Is the median the best indicator of Alan's successful free throws during the season? If yes, explain. If not, name the best indicator and explain.
*The mean and median are almost equal in this case.*

**22. WRITING MATH** When given data organized in a stem-and-leaf plot, explain the process of identifying the mean, median, and mode.
*See additional answers.*

**23.** Measure the lengths of your fingers in centimeters. Make a stem-and-leaf plot. *Answers will vary.*

**24. DATA FILE** Refer to the data about how often earthquakes occur on page 564. Make a histogram of the data. *See additional answers.*

**25. MARKET RESEARCH** A civil engineer is studying traffic patterns. She counts the number of cars that make it through one rush-hour green-light cycle. Organize her data into a frequency table, and then make a histogram.
*See additional answers.*

| 15 | 16 | 10 | 8 | 8 | 14 | 9 | 7 | 6 | 9 | 10 | 11 | 14 | 10 | 7 | 8 | 9 | 11 | 14 | 10 |
|----|----|----|---|---|----|---|---|---|---|----|----|----|----|---|---|---|----|----|----|

## EXTENDED PRACTICE EXERCISES

A value must meet certain criteria to be named an *outlier*. Follow this process:

   a. Locate the median of a set of data.
   b. Find the median of the lower half of the data. Name it $Q_1$.
   c. Find the median of the upper half of the data. Name it $Q_3$.
   d. Subtract $Q_1$ from $Q_3$. Name this value IQR since it is the interquartile range.
   e. An **outlier** is any data in the set that is less than $Q_1 - 1.5$ (IQR) or that is greater than $Q_3 + 1.5$ (IQR).

**26.** Refer to Example 3. Use steps a through e to determine if the possible outliers are indeed outliers. *The data values 43 and 102 are indeed outliers.*

**27.** Refer to Exercise 7. Use steps a through e to determine if the possible outliers are indeed outliers. *The data has no outliers.*

**28. CRITICAL THINKING** Describe why histograms are not used to identify mean, median, and mode. *Answers will vary, but may include that individual data values are not given.*

## MIXED REVIEW EXERCISES

**Find the mean of each set of data. Round to the nearest tenth.** (Lesson 1-2)

**29.** Cost of dinner: $12, $16, $19, $27, $32, $15, $17, $18, $21, $13, $14, $12 $18

**30.** Miles driven: 37, 42, 47, 38, 40, 29, 34, 36, 44, 45, 43, 46 40.1 mi

**31. DATA FILE** Refer to the data on the ways people get to work on page 575. If there are 657,688 people in Austin, Texas, how many commute to work in a carpool? (Prerequisite Skill) 80,238 people

Math Online mathmatters2.com/self_check_quiz

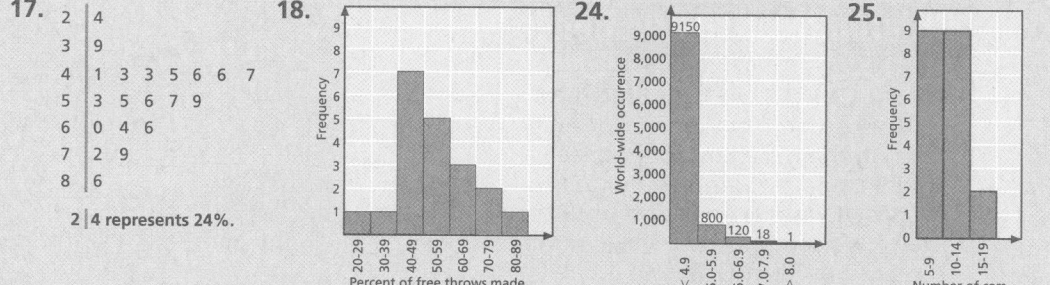

**17.**
```
2 | 4
3 | 9
4 | 1 3 3 5 6 6 7
5 | 3 5 6 7 9
6 | 0 4 6
7 | 2 9
8 | 6
```
2 | 4 represents 24%.

**18.** [histogram: Frequency vs Percent of free throws made; intervals 20-29, 30-39, 40-49, 50-59, 60-69, 70-79, 80-89]

**24.** [histogram: World-wide occurrence vs Richter scale; 9150, 800, 120, 18, 1]

**25.** [histogram: Frequency vs Number of cars; 5-9, 10-14, 15-19]

**22.** For the mean, the values must be added and divided by the total number of values. For the median, count to the middle value on the stem-and-leaf plot. For the mode, identify any values that repeat and choose the one that repeats the most.

---

## Extra Practice Worksheet 1-3

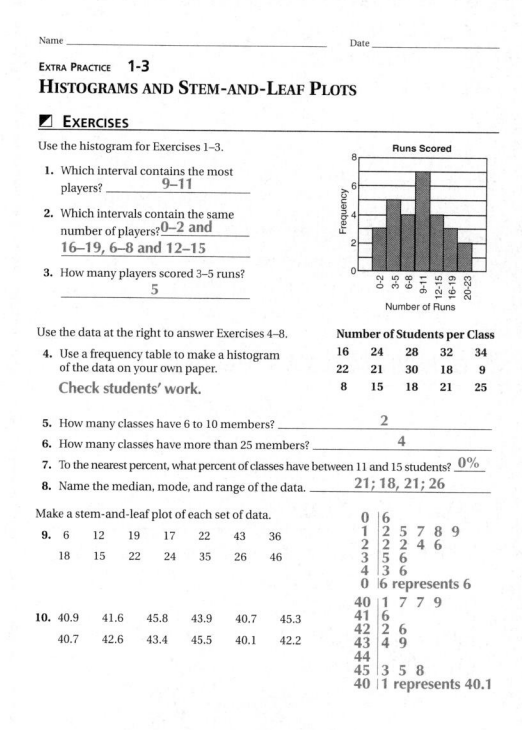

Name _____ Date _____

**EXTRA PRACTICE 1-3**
**HISTOGRAMS AND STEM-AND-LEAF PLOTS**

### EXERCISES

Use the histogram for Exercises 1–3.

**1.** Which interval contains the most players? 9–11

**2.** Which intervals contain the same number of players? 0–2 and 16–19, 6–8 and 12–15

**3.** How many players scored 3–5 runs? 5

Use the data at the right to answer Exercises 4–8.

**Number of Students per Class**

| 16 | 24 | 28 | 32 | 34 |
|----|----|----|----|----|
| 22 | 21 | 30 | 18 | 9 |
| 8 | 15 | 18 | 21 | 25 |

**4.** Use a frequency table to make a histogram of the data on your own paper.
Check students' work.

**5.** How many classes have 6 to 10 members? 2

**6.** How many classes have more than 25 members? 4

**7.** To the nearest percent, what percent of classes have between 11 and 15 students? 0%

**8.** Name the median, mode, and range of the data. 21; 18, 21; 26

Make a stem-and-leaf plot of each set of data.

**9.** 6  12  19  17  22  43  36
18  15  22  24  35  26  46
```
0 | 6
1 | 2 5 7 8 9
2 | 2 2 4 6
3 | 5 6
4 | 3 6
0 | 6 represents 6
```

**10.** 40.9  41.6  45.8  43.9  40.7  45.3
40.7  42.6  43.4  45.5  40.1  42.2
```
40 | 1 7 7 9
41 | 6
42 | 2 6
43 | 4 9
44 |
45 | 3 5 8
40 | 1 represents 40.1
```

---

## Enrichment Worksheet 1-3

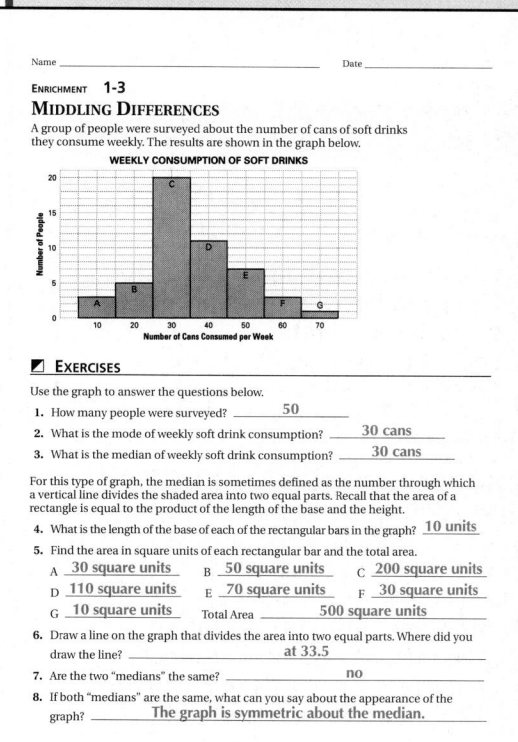

Name _____ Date _____

**ENRICHMENT 1-3**
**MIDDLING DIFFERENCES**

A group of people were surveyed about the number of cans of soft drinks they consume weekly. The results are shown in the graph below.

[graph: WEEKLY CONSUMPTION OF SOFT DRINKS; Number of People vs Number of Cans Consumed per Week]

### EXERCISES

Use the graph to answer the questions below.

**1.** How many people were surveyed? 50

**2.** What is the mode of weekly soft drink consumption? 30 cans

**3.** What is the median of weekly soft drink consumption? 30 cans

For this type of graph, the median is sometimes defined as the number through which a vertical line divides the shaded area into two equal parts. Recall that the area of a rectangle is equal to the product of the length of the base and the height.

**4.** What is the length of the base of each of the rectangular bars in the graph? 10 units

**5.** Find the area in square units of each rectangular bar and the total area.
A 30 square units  B 50 square units  C 200 square units
D 110 square units  E 70 square units  F 30 square units
G 10 square units  Total Area 500 square units

**6.** Draw a line on the graph that divides the area into two equal parts. Where did you draw the line? at 33.5

**7.** Are the two "medians" the same? no

**8.** If both "medians" are the same, what can you say about the appearance of the graph? The graph is symmetric about the median.

## Lesson Planning

### NCTM Standards/Strands
- Data Analysis & Probability
- Representation
- Communication
- Connections

### Vocabulary

scatter plot      correlation
positive correlation
negative correlation
line of best fit (trend line)

### Tools/Materials Needed

graphing calculator   graph paper
toothpicks

### Lesson Resources

Warm-up Transparency 2
Transparency TK-9
Reteaching 1-4
Extra Practice 1-4
Enrichment 1-4

*All of the resources available for the lesson, including transparencies, are listed under Lesson Resources.*

## Getting Started

### 5-MINUTE WARM-UP

In these ordered pairs, look for a pattern between the *x*-coordinate and *y*-coordinate.
(3, 10), (4, 9), (6, 7), (9, 4)   As the *x*-coordinate increases, the *y*-coordinate decreases.

### Introduction to Lesson 1-4
In addition to finding the mean of the distances and the mean of the times for the data they have collected, have students identify other measures of central tendency (the median and any existing modes). Also, have students note the range of their data.

**Goals**
- Use scatter plots to solve problems.
- Use a graphing utility to determine a line of best fit.

**Applications**   Retail, Education, Sports, Statistics, Insurance

**Work as a class to answer Questions 1–5.**
For 1–5, answers will vary.
1. Record the number of miles each student lives from school and the number of minutes it takes to get from home to school.

2. Display these data in a graph using one axis for distance and the other for time. Plot a point on the graph to represent each student.

3. Find the mean of the distances. Find the mean of the times.

4. Plot the point (*a*, *b*) where *a* is the mean of the distances and *b* is the mean of the times.

5. What patterns do you see in your graph? Explain.

### BUILD UNDERSTANDING

This type of visual display for data is a **scatter plot,** which shows the relationship of two sets of data. The data are grouped as ordered pairs and graphed as points on a grid. There can be more than one point for any number on either axis.

### Example 1

**Use the scatter plot.**

a. How many people were at the pool on the day the high temperature was 91°F?

b. Find the mode of the high temperatures.

c. Find the range of the daily attendance.

d. Find the median of the daily attendance.

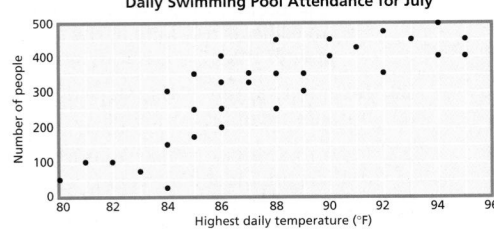

*Daily Swimming Pool Attendance for July*

### Solution

a. Locate 91 on the horizontal axis. Move up to the point, then left to the vertical axis. The day the temperature reached 91°F, 425 people were at the pool.

b. Find the temperature with the greatest number of points above it. The mode of the high temperatures is 86°F.

c. Find the difference between the greatest attendance (500) and the lowest attendance (25). 500 − 25 = 475. The range of the daily attendance is 475.

d. Since there are 31 days in July, count to the sixteenth point on the graph, starting with the least number of people in attendance. The median of the daily attendance is 350.

## Differentiated Instruction

### TACTILE/KINESTHETIC LEARNERS
To assist students in drawing trend lines on their scatter plots, have students place toothpicks on their graphs in various positions, until they are convinced that they have found the position for the line that will be closest to the most points.

*Differentiated Instruction suggestions are keyed to three commonly accepted learning styles.*

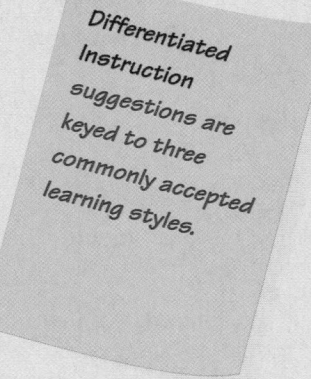

To create a scatter plot, you must choose a scale for each axis and arrange the data into ordered pairs. To display a scatter plot on a graphing utility, enter the data into lists. The scales are determined by the setting for the viewing window.

## Example 2

**MEDICINE** The list below shows the age and weight of 15 children who visit Dr. Warren's office during one week for their well-child checkup.

**Use a graphing calculator to display a scatter plot of the data.**

| | | | | |
|---|---|---|---|---|
| 1 year old, 20 lb | 12 year old, 108 lb | 5 year old, 60 lb | 10 year old, 120 lb | 2 year old, 38 lb |
| 3 year old, 35 lb | 9 year old, 87 lb | 2 year old, 30 lb | 4 year old, 45 lb | 6 year old, 50 lb |
| 5 year old, 50 lb | 7 year old, 64 lb | 10 year old, 84 lb | 7 year old, 70 lb | 11 year old, 90 lb |

### Solution

Enter the age data into a list, L1, and the weight that corresponds to each age into another list, L2. Turn on Plot 1. Select *scatter plot* as the type of plot to display. Set the viewing window as follows:

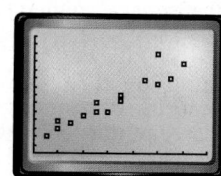

Xmin = 0   Xmax = 14   Xscl = 2
Ymin = 0   Ymax = 140   Yscl = 10

The relationship that a scatter plot displays is a *correlation*. A correlation can be positive or negative and weak or strong. Some scatter plots show no correlation.

A **positive correlation** means that as the horizontal axis values increase, so do the vertical axis values. A **negative correlation** means that as the horizontal axis values increase, the vertical axis values decrease.

When a scatter plot shows a correlation, a straight line can be drawn that best fits the set of data. This line, called a **line of best fit**, approximates a trend for the data in the scatter plot. For this reason, this line is often called a **trend line**. To find the best approximation for a line of best fit, use a graphing calculator.

## Example 3

**Graph a line of best fit for the scatter plot in Example 2.**

### Solution

The line of best fit is called a *linear regression*, which can be shown as an equation in $y = mx + b$ form. Since the data from Example 2 is already entered into your calculator in L1 and L2, you can find the equation from the home screen. Press STAT ▶ 4 2nd [L1] , 2nd [L2] ENTER to find the equation of the linear regression to be $y = 7.88x + 14.02$.

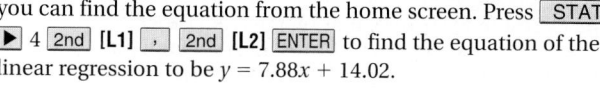

**Math Online** mathmatters2.com/extra_examples

Lesson 1-4 **Scatter Plots and Lines of Best Fit** 21

---

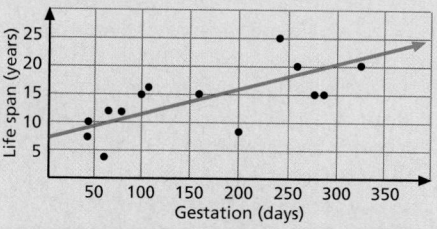
---

# Extend the Lesson

**REAL WORLD CONNECTION** After students have completed the Supplementary Example, they may research:

a. the longest known gestation period for an animal and its corresponding life expectancy   An Asian elephant has a gestation period of 20 to 22 months, with an average life expectancy of 70 years.   Elicit that these findings are consistent with the trend line of the scatter plot—the longer the gestation period, the longer the life span

b. the change in life expectancy for a human   The average life expectancy for people in the U.S. rose from about 50 years at the beginning of the 20th century to about 76 years at the end of the 20th century, with predictions of longer life spans.

To graph the line on the scatterplot, enter the equation into Y1. You can also have the calculator enter the full equation automatically. Press Y= and clear any stored equations. Then press VARS 5 ▶ ▶ ENTER. The full equation is then entered. Press GRAPH to graph both the scatter plot and line of best fit.

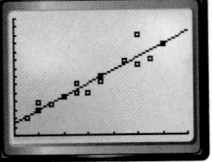

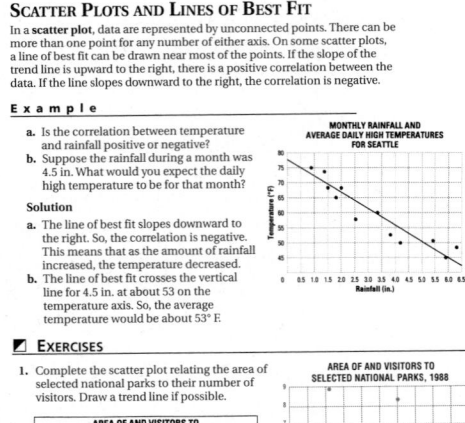
## Example 4

**Use Examples 2 and 3 to answer the following.**

a. Predict the weight of an eight-year-old child visiting Dr. Warren for a checkup.

b. Name the type of correlation between age and weight. Explain.

c. Which point lies farthest from the trend line? What could account for this?

### Solution

a. Locate age eight on the vertical axis. Move across to the line, then down to the horizontal axis. The weight is about 77 lb.

b. The trend line slopes upward to the right, so there is a positive correlation. As a child gets older, the child's weight increases.

c. The point farthest from the trend line represents a ten-year-old child who weighs 120 lb. This is a ten-year-old who is unusually tall or who is overweight.

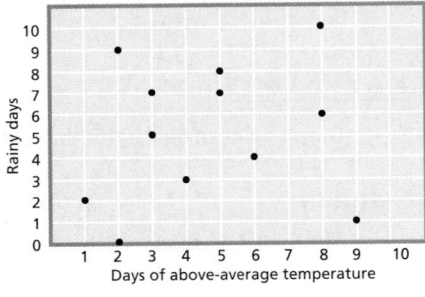

### ▰ TRY THESE EXERCISES

**Use the scatter plot for Exercises 1–4.**

1. During the month that had six days of rain, how many days had above-average temperatures?  8

2. Find the range of days with above-average temperatures.  8

3. Find the mode of the number of rainy days each month.  7

4. Find the median number of days with above-average temperatures.  4.5

5. Collect data from your classmates about the amount of time each studied for the last test and the grade each received. Display the data in a scatter plot.   Answers will vary.

6. **GRAPHING** Graph a line of best fit for your scatter plot in Exercise 5. Describe any correlation and draw a conclusion. Write a recommendation for your classmates about time spent studying and expected grades.
Answers will vary.

**Above-Average Temperatures and Rainy Days Each Month**

### ADDITIONAL ANSWERS

9. There are two points that are farthest from the trendline. One point reflects that the student only watched one hour of TV, but scored only a 50. This suggests that perhaps the student participates in other activities that take away from study time. The other point reflects that a student did not watch any TV, but only scored a 64. Answers will vary as to why for both points.

10.

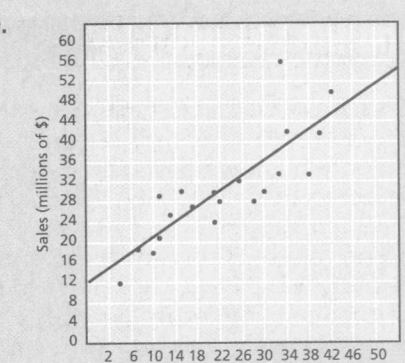

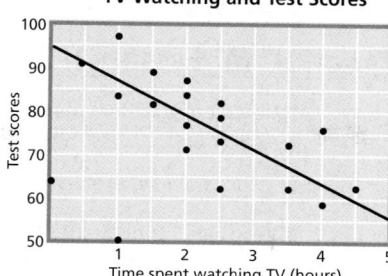

**TV Watching and Test Scores**

**Use the scatter plot for Exercises 7–9.**

7. Predict the test score of a student who watched 3 h of television.   72

8. Does the graph show positive or negative correlation? Explain.   Negative. The slope of the line of best fit is negative.

9. Which point lies farthest from the trend line? What could account for this?   See additional answers.

**MARKET RESEARCH** Advertising is a major factor in a company's annual budget. The table shows several months' commercial time purchased and sales in millions of dollars.

| | | | | |
|---|---|---|---|---|
| 5 min, 12.0 sales | 40 min, 39.0 sales | 21 min, 24.0 sales | 10 min, 18.0 sales | 30 min, 30.0 sales |
| 42 min, 50.0 sales | 33 min, 34.0 sales | 7 min, 19.0 sales | 11 min, 29.0 sales | 21 min, 31.0 sales |
| 13 min, 25.0 sales | 38 min, 33.0 sales | 15 min, 29.5 sales | 17 min, 27.5 sales | 22 min, 28.0 sales |
| 25 min, 32.0 sales | 28 min, 28.0 sales | 33 min, 56.5 sales | 34 min, 41.2 sales | 11 min, 21.5 sales |

10. Draw a scatter plot and line of best fit for the data.   See additional answers.

11. Is there a positive or negative correlation between commercial time and sales?   positive

12. Predict the company's sales if they have 50 min of commercials in 1 mo.   $50 million

13. **WRITING MATH** Describe a relationship of data that shows a positive correlation. Describe another relationship that shows a negative correlation and another that shows no correlation. Provide sample data for each.   Answers will vary.

14. **DATA FILE** Refer to the data on cricket chirps/min on page 560. Make a scatter plot of the data, and show a trend line. Is there a correlation between the number of chirps a minute and temperature? Plot the chirps per minute on the horizontal axis.   See additional answers. Yes. Higher temperature correlates with more chirps.

## EXTENDED PRACTICE EXERCISES

15. **ECONOMICS** Work with a partner. Choose Topic A or B. Research data to make a scatter plot. Explain any correlation and draw a conclusion.   Answers will vary.

Topic A—prices for new cars and expected highway mileage (mi/gal)
Topic B—population of a country and literacy rate (expressed as %)

16. **WRITING MATH** Write three paragraphs explaining when it is best to use a stem-and-leaf plot, a histogram and a scatter plot to display data.   Answers will vary.

## MIXED REVIEW EXERCISES

**Complete.** (Basic math skills)

17. 4 m = __?__ mm   4000

18. 80 cm = __?__ m   0.8

19. 45 ft = __?__ yd   15

20. 12 c = __?__ qt   3

21. 2 L = __?__ mL   2000

22. 16 gal = __?__ qt   64

23. 2 km = __?__ m   2000

24. 8 yd = __?__ ft   24

25. 300 dm = __?__ m   30

26. 2 yd = __?__ in.   72

27. 6,000 g = __?__ kg   6

28. 96 in. = __?__ ft   8

---

### Extra Practice Worksheet 1-4

Name _____     Date _____

ExTRA PRACTICE  **1-4**

**SCATTER PLOTS AND LINES OF BEST FIT**

**EXERCISES**

Use the scatter plot for Exercises 1–3.

**Study Time and Final Grade**

1. Predict the final grade of a student who spends an average of 2 hours a week studying.   67

2. Predict the final grade of a student who spends an average of 9 hours a week studying.   90

3. Does the graph show positive or negative correlation? Explain.   positive; The more time a student studies, the higher the final grade.

The amount of time spent exercising each week and the resting heart rates in beats per minute of members of an aerobics class are listed below.

| | | | |
|---|---|---|---|
| 4 h, 60 bpm | 3 h, 62 bpm | 3.5 h, 67 bpm | 4 h, 55 bpm |
| 2 h, 70 bpm | 2.5 h, 65 bpm | 3 h, 60 bpm | 5 h, 50 bpm |
| 4.5 h, 60 bpm | 5 h, 65 bpm | 4.5 h, 50 bpm | 3 h, 70 bpm |
| 5 h, 55 bpm | 1 h, 75 bpm | 3 h, 55 bpm | 4 h, 57 bpm |

**Exercise Time and Heart Rate**

4. Draw a scatter plot and line of best fit for the data.

5. Is there a positive or negative correlation between amount of time spent exercising each week and resting heart rate?   negative

6. Predict the resting heart rate of a person who exercises 7 hours a week.   45 bpm

---

### Enrichment Worksheet 1-4

Name _____     Date _____

ENRICHMENT  **1-4**

**LINE OF BEST FIT**

Each point on the graph shows the relation between the number of people attending the Roxy Cinema and the number of cars in the parking lot.

A line is drawn that appears to lie close to most of the points. This is called the *line of best fit.* Here is how to find the equation of this line.

The line passes through (100, 40) and (300, 120). Use the slope-intercept form.

**Attendance and Parking**

$m = \dfrac{y_2 - y_1}{x_2 - x_1}$   Definition of slope        $y = mx + b$   Slope-intercept form

$m = \dfrac{120 - 40}{300 - 100}$   $(x_1, y_1) = (100, 40)$ $(x_2, y_2) = (300, 120)$        $40 = \dfrac{2}{5}(100) + b$   Replace $(x, y)$ with $(100, 40)$ and $m$ with $\frac{2}{5}$.

$= \dfrac{80}{200}$ or $\dfrac{2}{5}$   Simplify.        $0 = b$   Simplify.

So an equation for the line is $y = \dfrac{2}{5}x + 0$ or $y = \dfrac{2}{5}x$.

**EXERCISES**

Solve each problem.

1. Suppose the owner of the Roxy decides to increase the seating capacity of the theater to 1000. How many cars should the parking lot be prepared to accommodate?   **400 cars**

2. The points (240, 60) and (340, 120) lie on the scatter plot. Write an equation for the line through these points.   $y = \dfrac{3}{5}x - 84$

3. Do you think the equation in Exercise 2 is a good representation of the relationship in this problem? Explain.   No; The graph of the equation does not appear to go through the center of the data points.

4. Suppose the equation for the relationship between attendance at the theater and cars in the parking lot is $y = 2x + 20$. What might you suspect about the users of the parking lot?   Many people are parking in the lot who are not going to the Roxy.

---

14.

*Mixed Review Exercises provide an opportunity to review concepts from previous lessons.*

## Vocabulary Review

**Lesson 1-3**
frequency table          histogram
stem-and-leaf plot       stem
leaf                     outliers
clusters                 gaps

**Lesson 1-4**
scatter plot             correlation
positive correlation
negative correlation
line of best fit         trend line

## ASSIGNMENT GUIDE

**All students: 1–25**

## Chalkboard Examples

### Lesson 1-3

**TRAVEL** This stem-and-leaf plot shows the daily commuting time, in minutes, of the employees at AtaCo.

| 4 | 2 2 5 8 |
| 5 | 2 4 6 8 8 |
| 6 | 0 0 5 8 8 |
| 7 | 0 3 4 5 5 6 |
| 8 | |
| 9 | 0 2 2 2 5 6 7 |
| 10 | 1 2 5 5 7 8 |

4|2 represents 42 min

**a.** Find the range of the data.
$108 - 42 = 66$

**b.** Determine the number of employees for whom the commuting time is:
**(1)** at most 1 hr   **11**
**(2)** at least $1\frac{3}{4}$ hr   **4**

### Lesson 1-4

**NATURE** This scatter plot relates weekly rainfall to the growth of a tree seedling.

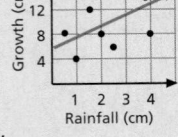

**a.** How much did the seedling grow in the week that had 1 cm of rain?   **4 cm**
**b.** How much rain was there in the week in which there was the most growth?   **3 cm**
**c.** What type of correlation is shown for these data?   **positive; more rain, more growth**
**d.** Use the trend line to predict the growth for 3.5 cm of rainfall.   **about 12 cm**

---

## PRACTICE ■ LESSON 1-3

**Make a stem-and-leaf plot of each set of data.**
For 1–3, see additional answers.
1. Price of tickets: $23, $34, $27, $35, $31, $29, $42, $38

2. Miles traveled each day: 26 mi, 52 mi, 37 mi, 43 mi, 57 mi, 28 mi, 33 mi, 40 mi

3. The ages of the first 15 Presidents of the U.S. at the time of their first inauguration are listed below. Make a stem-and-leaf plot of the data.

57   61   57   57   58   57   61   54   68   51   49   64   50   48   65

4. What was the most common age of the Presidents?   57

5. What is the median age of the Presidents?   57

6. What is the range in age of the Presidents?   20

**Use the frequency table for Exercises 7–9.**

**Television Use**

| Number of hours | Frequency |
|---|---|
| 0-9 | 1 |
| 10-19 | 6 |
| 20-29 | 15 |
| 30-39 | 12 |
| 40-49 | 2 |
| 50-59 | 4 |

7. Construct a histogram to display the data of TV use.
See additional answers.
8. Which interval has the greatest frequency?   20–29

9. Which interval contains 10% of the data?   50–59

## PRACTICE ■ LESSON 1-4

**Use the table of a basketball player's scoring average.**

10. Make a scatter plot of the data. Plot the ages on the vertical axis.
See additional answers.
11. What is the range of the players scoring average?   10

12. Does the scatter plot show a positive correlation, a negative correlation or no correlation?   no correlation

| Age | Scoring average |
|---|---|
| 23 | 18 |
| 24 | 17.5 |
| 25 | 22.5 |
| 26 | 24 |
| 27 | 21.5 |
| 28 | 26 |
| 29 | 23.5 |
| 30 | 22.5 |
| 31 | 27.5 |
| 32 | 20.5 |

**Tell which of the following scatter plots would show a *positive correlation*, a *negative correlation* or *no correlation*.**

13. price of a product, amount of tax on the product   positive

14. height in inches, weight in pounds   positive

15. population of a city, amount of rain   none

16. car speed, time needed to reach destination   negative

**Use the scatter plot of home runs and runs batted in (RBI's).**

17. Do players who hit a lot of home runs drive in a lot of runs?   yes

18. Describe the correlation of the data?   positive

19. If a player hit 25 home runs, about how many RBI's would they expect to have?   80

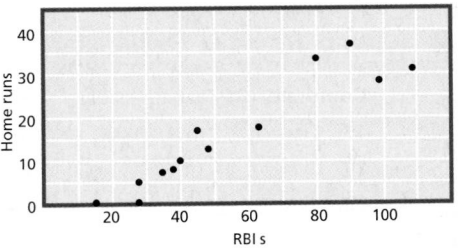

Review and Practice Your Skills pages occur after every other lesson, allowing students to practice the concepts they have just learned.

### Teaching Tip

When students are making stem-and-leaf plots, encourage them to verify that no data has been left out by making it a point to check that the number of entries in their plot equals the number of data items listed in the problem.

## PRACTICE ■ LESSON 1-1–LESSON 1-4

**DATA FILE** For Exercises 20–23, refer to the data on recent noteable earthquakes on page 564. 20. See additional answers.

20. Organize the magnitude data into a stem-and-leaf plot.

21. Find the mode(s) of the data. 6.9, 8.1

22. Find the median of the data. 7.25

23. Find the mean of the data. 7.2

| Stem | Leaf |
|------|------|
| 6 | 1 8 9 9 |
| 7 | 0 1 4 5 6 9 |
| 8 | 1 1 |

7|1 = 7.1

**Teenagers were polled about the number of evening meals they ate at home in a 4-wk period.**

18   20   16   28   31   23   25   24   33   35   17   14

24. Organize the data into a stem-and-leaf plot. (Lesson 1-3)  See additional answers.

25. What is the median number of meals eaten at home? (Lesson 1-2)  23.5

# Mid-Chapter Quiz

**POLITICAL SCIENCE** A politician is running for reelection to Congress. She wants to know if people are likely to vote for her. What kind of sampling method is represented by each of these possibilities. (Lesson 1-1)

1. Ask all delegates at a political convention.  convenience

2. Ask all registered voters who live on randomly selected streets in her Congressional district.  cluster

3. Ask every tenth adult arriving at the county fair in her Congressional district.
   systematic

**Use the table for Exercises 4–8.** (Lessons 1-2 through 1-4)

4. Find the mean, median, and mode of the data.
   mean = 7.5; median = 7; mode = 9
5. Make a frequency table for the data with intervals 1-3, 4-6, and so on.  See additional answers.

6. How many families spent 10–14 days on vacation?
   3
7. Organize the data in a stem-and-leaf plot.
   See additional answers.
8. Name any outliers, clusters or gaps in the data.
   outliers: none; clusters: 3–9; gaps: 10–14, 14–17

**Number of Days Families Spend on Vacation per Year**

| 7 | 10 | 4 | 5 | 9 | 14 | 18 | 9 | 6 | 3 |
|---|----|---|---|---|----|----|---|---|---|
| 2 | 8 | 3 | 1 | 4 | 17 | 7 | 14 | 1 | 9 |

**Write** *positive correlation, negative correlation* **or** *no correlation* **for each.** (Lesson 1-4)

9. As a person's age increases, the hours of sleep per night decreases.  negative correlation

10. As a person's age increases, the number of vacation days per year increases.
    positive correlation

Chapter 1 **Review and Practice Your Skills** | 25

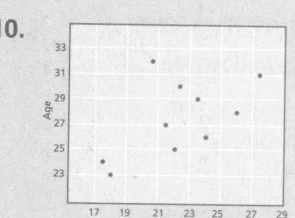

**10.**

**20.**

| 1 | 6 |
|---|---|
| 2 | 7 8 8 |
| 3 | 2 3 4 8 8 8 |
| 4 | 0 |
| 5 | 0 2 5 6 6 7 9 |
| 6 | 0 0 1 2 5 6 9 |
| 7 | 1 1 4 5 |
| 8 | 6 |

1|6 represents a score of 16.

**24.**

| 1 | 4 6 7 8 |
|---|---------|
| 2 | 0 3 4 5 8 |
| 3 | 1 3 5 |

1|4 represents 14 meals.

## MID-CHAPTER QUIZ

**5.**

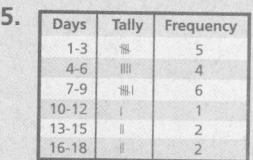

| Days | Tally | Frequency |
|------|-------|-----------|
| 1-3 | 卌 | 5 |
| 4-6 | IIII | 4 |
| 7-9 | 卌I | 6 |
| 10-12 | I | 1 |
| 13-15 | II | 2 |
| 16-18 | II | 2 |

**7.**

| 0 | 0 1 2 3 3 4 4 5 6 7 7 8 9 9 9 |
|---|-------------------------------|
| 1 | 0 4 4 7 8 |

0|1 represents 1 day.

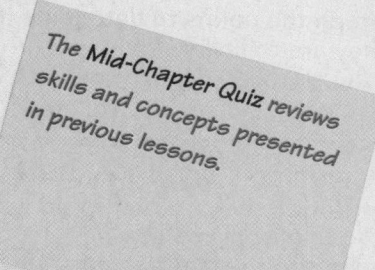

The Mid-Chapter Quiz reviews skills and concepts presented in previous lessons.

## ADDITIONAL ANSWERS

**1.**

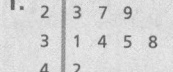

| 2 | 3 7 9 |
|---|-------|
| 3 | 1 4 5 8 |
| 4 | 2 |

2|3 represents $23.

**3.**

| 4 | 8 9 |
|---|-----|
| 5 | 0 1 4 7 7 7 7 8 |
| 6 | 1 1 4 5 8 |

4|8 represents 48 yr.

**2.**

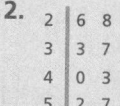

| 2 | 6 8 |
|---|-----|
| 3 | 3 7 |
| 4 | 0 3 |
| 5 | 2 7 |

2|6 represents 26 mi.

**7.**

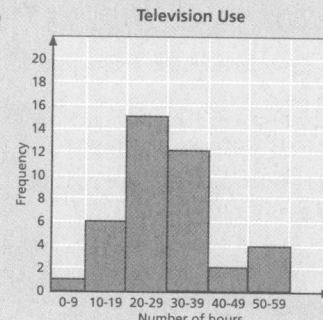

Television Use

(histogram: Frequency vs. Number of hours; intervals 0-9, 10-19, 20-29, 30-39, 40-49, 50-59)

# 1-5 Problem Solving Skills: Coefficient of Correlation

### NCTM Standards
- Data Analysis & Probability
- Connections
- Number & Operations
- Problem Solving

### Vocabulary
coefficient of correlation
guess and check

### Tools/Materials Needed
graphing calculator

### Lesson Resources
Warm-up Transparency 2
Transparency RF-1
Reteaching 1-5
Extra Practice 1-5
Enrichment 1-5

## ASSIGNMENT GUIDE
**Basic:** 1–25
**Enriched:** 1–25

## Getting Started

### 5-MINUTE WARM-UP

**Graph the points to determine if they are collinear.**
1. (1, 1), (2, 3), (4, 6)  not collinear
2. (1, 1), (2, 4), (3, 7)  collinear

**THE FIVE-STEP PLAN Read**—ask questions to help students understand the problem. **Plan**—guide students to related problems and previously mastered skills and strategies. **Solve**—students solve problem on their own. **Answer**—write the solution in a format that answers the question. **Check**—review work, check for reasonableness, and review strategy used.
**THE STRATEGY** *Guess and check*—this strategy helps students understand the process of refinement. While even wild guesses can be gradually refined, suggest that students try to start with an "educated guess," based on the data.

The arrangement of points on a scatter plot provides a visual idea of the *degree of correlation* between two variables. This means you can tell if the relationship is positive or negative, strong or weak. Another way to tell the characteristics of a relationship is a **coefficient of correlation,** a statistical measure of how closely data fits a line.

A coefficient of correlation, $r$, is between 1 and $-1$. The closer a coefficient of correlation is to 1 or $-1$, the stronger the relationship between $x$ and $y$. Visually, the points almost form a line. The closer a coefficient of correlation is to 0, the weaker the relationship is between $x$ and $y$.

You can predict a coefficient of correlation by looking at data or a scatter plot. To be precise or confirm your prediction, use a graphing calculator to calculate linear regression and the coefficient. This strategy is **guess and check**.

### Problem Solving Strategies
- ✔ Guess and check
- Look for a pattern
- Solve a simpler problem
- Make a table, chart or list
- Use a picture, diagram or model
- Act it out
- Work backwards
- Eliminate possibilities
- Use an equation or formula

### Problem

**RETAIL** The manager of a concession stand orders bottled water and juice based on the daily temperature and number of bottles sold.

a. Is the correlation between temperature and combined sales positive or negative, strong or weak?

b. Predict the drink with a stronger correlation to temperature.

c. Use a graphing calculator to identify the coefficient of correlation for temperature and bottled water sales and the coefficient of correlation for temperature and juice sales.

d. Were your predictions in parts a and b correct?

| Daily high temperature | Bottled water sales | Fruit juice sales |
|---|---|---|
| 66°F | 141 | 142 |
| 70°F | 149 | 138 |
| 74°F | 159 | 133 |
| 78°F | 165 | 114 |
| 82°F | 175 | 146 |
| 86°F | 180 | 166 |
| 90°F | 193 | 160 |
| 94°F | 195 | 158 |
| 98°F | 210 | 178 |

### Solve the Problem

a. As temperature increases, sales of drinks increase. The correlation is strong and positive, so the coefficient of correlation will be close to 1.

b. As temperature increases, sales of bottled water increase the most.

c. Enter temperatures in a list, L1; water sales in a second list, L2; and juice sales in a third list, L3. To find the coefficient for temperature and water, use L1 and L2. Use L1 and L3 to find the coefficient for temperature and fruit juice. The screens at the right show that $r \approx 0.995$ for water sales and $r \approx 0.732$ for juice sales.

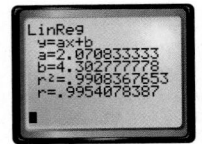 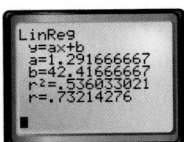

d. The correlation is strong and positive. The coefficient $r$ is positive and close to 1 for both. However, bottled water sales show a stronger relationship.

## ADDITIONAL ANSWERS

7. Negative. As temperature rises, snow ski sales will fall.
8. Zero. No correlation exists between shoe size and salary.
9. Negative. In general, as a car experiences wear and tear, gas mileage will suffer.
10. Positive. In general, it is likely that as a person grows taller, their weight will increase also.

### Teaching Tip

To obtain the correlation coefficient, $r$, on some graphing calculators, it is necessary to first put the calculator into Diagnostics Display Mode. Do this by selecting Diagnostics On from the Catalog menu.

## TRY THESE EXERCISES

**Match each scatter plot with a possible description. Describe its correlation.**

**1.** *x*-value: hours of daylight
*y*-value: hours after dark
B; negative

Graph A

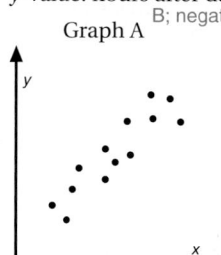

**2.** *x*-value: amount of rainfall
*y*-value: levels of area rivers
A; positive

Graph B

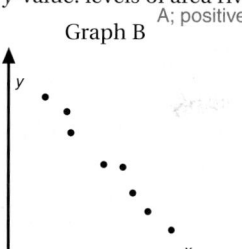

**3.** *x*-value: heart rate
*y*-value: reading speed
C; no correlation

Graph C

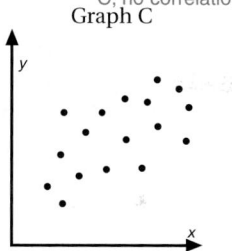

## PRACTICE EXERCISES

**Five-step Plan**
1 Read
2 Plan
3 Solve
4 Answer
5 Check

**Predict the characteristics of the correlation between the two variables. Find the coefficient of correlation to check your prediction.**

**4.**

| x | 1.0 | 2.0 | 2.5 | 3.1 | 4.2 | 5.0 | 7.0 | 8.3 |
|---|---|---|---|---|---|---|---|---|
| y | 1.1 | 3.9 | 5.4 | 7.1 | 10.6 | 13.2 | 19.1 | 22.1 |

$r \approx 0.999$

**5.**

| Year | 1993 | 1994 | 1995 | 1996 | 1997 | 1998 | 1999 | 2000 | 2001 |
|---|---|---|---|---|---|---|---|---|---|
| Number of evening papers | 954 | 935 | 891 | 846 | 816 | 781 | 760 | 727 | 704 |

$r \approx -0.996$

**6.**

| Year | 1984 | 1986 | 1988 | 1990 | 1992 | 1994 | 1996 | 1998 | 2000 |
|---|---|---|---|---|---|---|---|---|---|
| Average MPG | 17.4 | 17.4 | 18.8 | 20.3 | 21.0 | 20.8 | 21.2 | 21.6 | 22.0 |

$r \approx 0.944$

 **WRITING MATH** State whether you think each of the following sets of variables would show a *positive*, *negative*, or *zero* correlation. Explain your reasoning.
For 7–10, see additional answers.

**7.** outside temperature and snow ski sales

**8.** an adult shoe size and annual salary

**9.** miles a car is driven and its gas mileage

**10.** a person's height and weight from birth to age 20

## MIXED REVIEW EXERCISES

**Write three equivalent ratios.** (Basic math skills)

**11.** $\frac{3}{12}, \frac{1}{4}, \frac{2}{8}, \frac{4}{16}$ **12.** $\frac{5}{15}, \frac{1}{3}, \frac{2}{6}, \frac{4}{9}$ **13.** $\frac{20}{25}, \frac{4}{5}, \frac{8}{10}, \frac{12}{15}$ **14.** $\frac{1}{2}, \frac{2}{4}, \frac{3}{6}, \frac{4}{8}$ **15.** $\frac{7}{8}, \frac{14}{16}, \frac{21}{24}, \frac{28}{32}$ **16.** $\frac{4}{20}, \frac{1}{5}, \frac{2}{10}, \frac{3}{15}$

**Simplify.** (Basic math skills)

**17.** $-4 - (-6) + 12$   14

**18.** $13 + (-6) - 14$   $-7$

**19.** $-3 + (-7) - 8 + 6$   $-12$

**20.** $7 - (-4) - 16 + (-2)$   $-7$

**21.** $-6 - (-5) - (-8)$   7

**22.** $15 - 8 - (-3) + (-9)$   1

**23.** $5 + (-8) - (-9) + 4$   10

**24.** $-9 + (-9) - (-9) + 9$   0

**25.** $8 - 7 - 6 - (-5) + 4$   4

---

## Chalkboard Examples

### Supplementary Problem

**NATURE**
Scientists have monitored the number of chirps per minute made by crickets and the corresponding air temperature. One set of observations is shown in the table at the right.

| Temperature (in °C) | Chirps per min |
|---|---|
| 17 | 105 |
| 18 | 110 |
| 19 | 110 |
| 20 | 126 |
| 21 | 126 |
| 22 | 130 |
| 23 | 130 |
| 24 | 152 |
| 24 | 156 |
| 25 | 169 |
| 26 | 170 |
| 27 | 171 |
| 28 | 175 |
| 29 | 196 |
| 30 | 212 |

**a.** State whether you think the correlation between temperature and cricket chirps is positive or negative, strong or weak.
positive, strong

**b.** Verify your prediction by using a graphing utility to identify the coefficient of correlation.
$r \approx 0.975$

## Lesson Wrap-up

### QUICK ASSESSMENT

Ask the following questions to determine if students understand the content presented in this lesson.

**1.** What does a *coefficient of correlation* measure?   how closely data fit a line

**2.** What does it mean if a coefficient of correlation is 1 or −1?
The plot of the data is a straight line and shows a perfect positive correlation ($r = 1$) or a perfect negative correlation ($r = -1$).

---

## Extend the Lesson

**REAL WORLD CONNECTION** Have students research a recent study that has found a correlation between intake of a given substance and the onset of a disease, such as smoke from cigarettes and lung cancer.

Note with students that a statistically strong linear correlation does not necessarily imply a cause-and-effect relationship. For example, the variables *x* = the price of tea in China and *y* = the price of bagels in New York may be strongly positively correlated. That does not mean, however, that raising the price of tea in China causes the price of bagels in New York to increase, or vice versa. It means that there is one force at work, perhaps worldwide inflation, that tends to have a similar effect.

*Extend the Lesson suggestions provide a variety of ways to further students' understanding of the concepts discussed in the lesson through real-world connections, challenge problems, interdisciplinary connections, and historical notes.*

## Lesson Planning

### NCTM Standards/Strands
- ■ Data Analysis & Probability
- ■ Representation
- ■ Connections
- ■ Communication

### Vocabulary

quartiles
first quartile
second quartile
third quartile
interquartile range
box-and-whisker plot
whiskers
outliers
percentile

*Reading Math features help students learn and use the language of mathematics.*

### Tools/Materials Needed

graphing calculator  graph paper

### Lesson Resources

Warm-up Transparency 2
Transparency TK-9, RF-3
Reteaching 1-6
Extra Practice 1-6
Enrichment 1-6
Technology Activity 1-6

## Getting Started

### 5-MINUTE WARM-UP

**Find the median for each data set.**
1. 10, 6, 13, 15, 12   **12**
2. 4, 9, 1, 3, 2, 4   **3.5**

### Introduction to Lesson 1-6
After students have decided in answer to Question 2 that the median is not a good indicator of how well the class in the problem did as a whole on their test, ask if any other measure of central tendency would be a better indicator.   **No. Measures of central tendency give a typical score for a data set but they do not allow for observation of dispersion.**

**Goals**
- ■ Identify quartiles and calculate percentiles.
- ■ Create a box-and-whisker plot.

**Applications**   Education, Market research, Statistics

**EDUCATION**  The test scores for students in one class are given.

58  84  72  40  95  78  92  98  82  50
67  90  75  93  87  55  84  86  62  67

1. Find the median of the scores.  80

2. Is the median a good indicator of how well the class did on this test? Explain.  Yes. The values 40 and 50 affect the mean too much for the mean to be a good indicator.

3. Find the median of all the scores below the median class score and the median of all the scores above the median class score.  64.5; 88.5

4. How can using the three medians from Questions 1 and 3 give a better indication of how well the class did on the test?  Answers will vary but may include that they help reveal the distribution.

5. Into how many equal parts do the three medians separate the scores?  4

### ■ BUILD UNDERSTANDING

Another way to analyze data is by **quartiles**, three numbers that group the data into four equal parts. To find the quartiles, first determine the median, also called the *second quartile*. The *third quartile* is the median of the data above the second quartile. The *first quartile* is the median of the data below the second quartile.

Data that are greater than the third quartile are in the top quarter of the data set. Data that are less than the first quartile are in the bottom quarter. The **interquartile range** is the difference between the first and third quartiles.

**Reading Math**

The abbreviations $Q_1$, $Q_2$ and $Q_3$ are used to represent the first, second and third quartiles.

### Example 1

**Find the following for the data.**

Age of employees: 18   29   56   42   58   31   40   28   37   46

**a.** median        **b.** first quartile        **c.** third quartile        **d.** interquartile range

**Solution**

Write the ages in order from least to greatest.

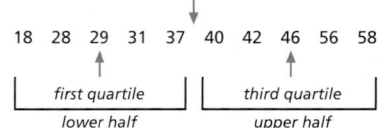

median of all data, or *second quartile*

18   28   29   31   37   40   42   46   56   58

first quartile          third quartile

lower half          upper half

28  |  Chapter 1  **Sample and Display Data**

### Teaching Tip

**ESL/LEP**  Have students make a list of words containing the prefix *quart*. Discuss how each word relates to the number 4.

*ESL/LEP suggestions offer ways to assist students for whom English is a second language.*

**a.** The median age is 38.5, halfway between the two middle ages. So the second quartile is 38.5.

**b.** There are five ages below 38.5. The middle of these is 29. So the first quartile is 29.

**c.** There are five ages above 38.5. The middle of these is 46. So the third quartile is 46.

**d.** The interquartile range is the difference between the first quartile and the third quartile, $46 - 29 = 17$. So the interquartile range is 17.

**Check Understanding**

In Example 1, suppose the lowest score, 18, is not listed in the data. Find the first quartile, median and third quartile.

$Q_1 = 31, Q_2 = 40, Q_3 = 46$

Some graphs show the distribution of data related to measures in a data set. One such graph is a **box-and-whisker plot** that uses quartiles and a box to illustrate the interquartile range. Box-and-whisker plots are drawn using a number line; however, the number line does not have to be part of the completed plot.

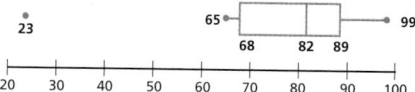

The lines that are drawn from the ends of boxes to the least and greatest values of the data are called **whiskers**. **Outliers**, which are marked with only a point, are data that are at least 1.5 times the interquartile range above the third quartile or at least 1.5 times the interquartile range below the first quartile.

## Example 2

**Make a box-and-whisker plot for the data.**

**Prices of Microwave Ovens (dollars)**

225 257 175 300 265 185 229 235 299

### Solution

175  185  225  229  235  257  265  299  300   Write in order from least to greatest.

Find the quartile values.

$Q_2$: The median of the data is 235.

$Q_1$: The median of the lower half of the data is midway between 185 and 225.

$$185 + 225 = 410$$
$$410 \div 2 = 205$$

$Q_3$: The median of the upper half of the data is midway between 265 and 299.

$$265 + 299 = 564$$
$$564 \div 2 = 282$$

Use points to mark these values below a number line. Complete the box and whiskers. No data is far from the rest of the data, so there are no outliers.

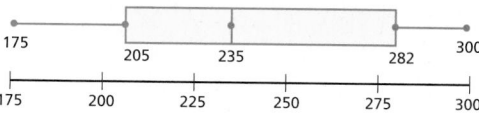

**Prices of Microwave Ovens (dollars)**

**Technology Note**

You can use a graphing calculator to create a box-and-whisker plot, which is also called a boxplot. Enter the data into a list, and select *boxplot* as the statistical plot to display.

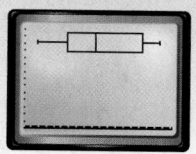

## Chalkboard Examples

### Supplementary Examples 1 & 2

**NATURE** Here is an alphabetic list of the highest waterfalls in the world.

| Name of Falls | Height (ft) |
| --- | --- |
| Angel | 3212 |
| Cuquenán | 2000 |
| Great | 1600 |
| Mardalsfoss | 2149 |
| Ribbon | 1612 |
| Sutherland | 1904 |
| Tugela | 2014 |
| Yosemite | 2425 |

**a.** Find the quartile values.

From lowest to highest, the data values are:

1600 1612 1904 2000 2014 2149 2425 3212

$Q_1 = 1758$   $Q_2 = 2007$   $Q_3 = 2287$

**b.** Make a box-and-whisker plot for the data.

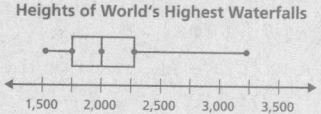

Heights of World's Highest Waterfalls

### Supplementary Example 3

Serena is ranked 75th in her senior class of 200 students. Lucas is in the same senior class and has a percentile rank of 75. Who has the higher standing in the class, Serena or Lucas?   Lucas has the higher standing. To find Serena's percentile rank, calculate $\frac{126}{200} = 0.63$. Her percentile is 63, which is lower than Lucas's percentile.

Technology Note features offer students helpful information about how to use technology to explore the concepts they are studying.

## Extend the Lesson

**REAL WORLD CONNECTION** If your school participated in a state-wide or national standardized testing program, obtain overall school results from a recent test and discuss what the percentiles indicate. If your school provides parents with individual reports of these test results, provide a sample report to the students and discuss how to interpret it.

When you take a standardized test, your score is often reported in terms of percentiles. Your **percentile** indicates the percent of those who took the test who achieved at or below your score.

For example, if your score is in the 83rd percentile, approximately 83% of those who took the test had a score less than or equal to yours. Only 17% of those who took the test had a score greater than yours. So a percentile is a measure of a rank, or standing, within a group.

| Percentile | $\dfrac{\text{number of scores less than or equal to given score}}{\text{total number of scores}} \cdot 100$ |
|---|---|

## Example 3

**EDUCATION** Bernardo took a placement test in order to be accepted into a computer course. His score is 48th from the highest out of the 760 students who took the test. Find the percentile rank that Bernardo achieved.

## Solution

The total number of students who took the test was 760. Bernardo was 48th. So there were 47 students who had higher scores than he did. The number of students who scored equal to or less than he did, was 760 − 47, or 713.

$$\frac{\text{number of scores less than or equal to given score}}{\text{total number of scores}} = \frac{713}{760} \approx 0.938$$

So, Bernardo's ranking is in the 94th percentile.

### TRY THESE EXERCISES

1. The interquartile range is the difference of which quartiles?
   $Q_3 - Q_1$

2. Find the first quartile, the median and the third quartile of the science test scores shown. Then find the interquartile range.
   73.5, 80, 87; 13.5

3. Draw a box-and-whisker plot for the data in Exercise 2.
   See additional answers.

4. On a test, Cheung has the ninth highest test score. If there are 28 students who take the test, what is Cheung's percentile rank?
   71st

5. If you score in the 90th percentile on a test, how many people scored above you out of 20 students?  2

**Science Test Scores**

| 84 | 89 | 76 | 65 | 74 |
| 73 | 85 | 89 | 91 | 74 |
| 93 | 82 | 68 | 76 | 94 |
| 63 | 83 | 80 | 80 | 70 |

### PRACTICE EXERCISES • For Extra Practice, see page 587.

**For each set of data, find the first quartile, the median and the third quartile.**

6. Test scores: 71, 86, 92, 53, 87, 76, 75, 84, 83   73, 83, 86.5

7. Points scored: 20, 16, 15, 13, 12, 19, 18, 20, 18, 10, 12, 14   12.5, 15.5, 18.5

8. Miles biked: 4.6, 8.3, 9.3, 7.2, 5.8, 8.7, 3.2, 5.9, 11.6   5.2, 7.2, 9.0

9. Bowling scores: 200, 114, 162, 260, 149, 140, 146, 125, 172   132.5, 149, 186

**30** | Chapter 1  **Sample and Display Data**

### ADDITIONAL ANSWERS

3.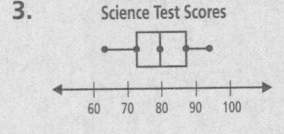
Science Test Scores

10.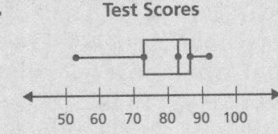
Test Scores

11.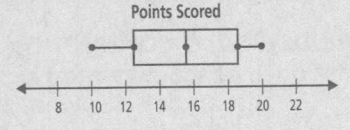
Points Scored

12.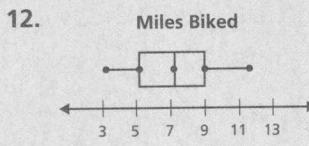
Miles Biked

13.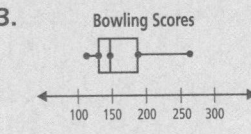
Bowling Scores

14.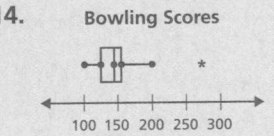
Bowling Scores

**10–13.** Create a box-and-whisker plot for each set of data in Exercises 6–9.
For 10–13, see additional answers.

**14. SPORTS** Make a box-and-whisker plot for these bowling scores.

200 101 162 273 149 153 146
125 118 129 135 142 111 156

See additional answers.

**15.** Exercise 9 gives Mario's bowling scores and Exercise 14 gives Shannon's bowling scores. Use their box-and-whisker plots to compare their scores. Write a statement that describes Mario's scores in terms of Shannon's scores.
See additional answers.

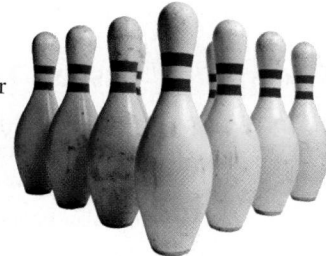

**16. DATA FILE** Refer to the data on the ten hottest U.S. temperatures on record on page 577. Make a box-and-whisker plot to show the distribution of temperatures.
See additional answers.

**Find the percentile ranks for each of the following students' science midterm exam taken from the science test scores on the previous page.**

|  | Test 1 |
|---|---|
| Apple, Felicia | 93 |
| Bean, Jamal | 91 |
| Carrot, Robert | 76 |
| Ditto, Bethany | 68 |
| Ever, Mark | 80 |
| Floor, Martha | 70 |

**17.** Felicia 95th   **18.** Martha 20th   **19.** Mark 55th

**20.** Bethany 15th   **21.** Robert 45th   **22.** Jamal 90th

**23. WRITING MATH** Explain step-by-step how to solve the following problem. If there is any information not needed, explain how you know it is not needed.

*Bly took a history exam and received a score of 27 out of 50. If out of 32 students in the class he ranked 19th, what is his percentile rank?*
See additional answers.

**24.** If you score at the 96th percentile on a test, how many people scored above you out of 25 students? 1

**25.** Explain the difference between the 90th percentile and the 10th percentile.
See additional answers.

## EXTENDED PRACTICE EXERCISES

**26.** If your score on a test is equal to the median of the scores, in what percentile rank is your score?   If the median is not also the mode, you scored in the 50th percentile.

**27.** If exactly one-quarter of your class scored higher than you did on a test, what is your percentile ranking? 75th

**28. CRITICAL THINKING** If your score on a test is equal to the mean of all the scores, can you determine your percentile ranking? Explain.   No. To find the percentile rank you must know how many scored below your score.

**29. CHAPTER INVESTIGATION** Organize your data to determine the information to highlight about the cafeteria. Calculate the mean, median, mode, range and percentiles that you can use to support your claims.
Answers will vary.

## MIXED REVIEW EXERCISES

**Multiply or divide.** (Basic math skills)

**30.** −72 ÷ (−4)  18   **31.** 4(−3)  −12   **32.** 81 ÷ (−9)  −9

**33.** −7(13)  −91   **34.** −70 ÷ (−5)  14   **35.** −108 ÷ 12  −9

**36.** 5(−6)(4)  −120   **37.** −96 ÷ (−2)  48   **38.** 7(−6)(−5)  210

Math Online   mathmatters2.com/self_check_quiz

**15.** The range for Mario's was less than the range for Shannon's scores. However, the interquartile range was greater for Mario than for Shannon.

**16.**

**Hottest U.S. Temperatures on Record**

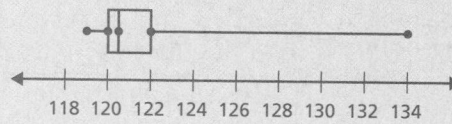

118 120 122 124 126 128 130 132 134

**23.** If Bly ranked 19th in the class then 18 students scored higher and 13 scored lower on the history exam. The percentile rank is the number of scores less than or equal to Bly's, 14, divided by the total number of students, 32. His percentile rank is 44. The information about his score of 27 out of 50 is not needed.

**25.** To be ranked in the 90th percentile means that 90% of the scores were equal or less than yours. To be ranked in the 10th percentile means that 90% of the scores were greater than yours.

---

## Extra Practice Worksheet 1-6

Name _____   Date _____

EXTRA PRACTICE **1-6**

**QUARTILES AND PERCENTILES**

☑ **EXERCISES**

For each set of data, find the first quartile, the median, and the third quartile.

1. 15 18 24 18 12 20 28 19 30 36 _____ 18; 19.5; 28

2. 2.5 3.8 4.2 7.5 1.9 6.4 2.8 4.9 9.1 2.7 _____ 2.7; 4; 6.4

3. 45 65 37 49 50 39 48 66 32 54 68 _____ 39; 49; 65

4. 120 125 154 127 200 210 110 105 150 _____ 115; 127; 177

5. 98 76 88 90 80 70 66 76 82 64 72 _____ 70; 76; 88

6. Make a box-and-whisker plot for these golf scores.

76  88  80  70  75  90  85  86  75  92

**Golf Scores**

70    75    82.5    88    92

70 72 74 76 78 80 82 84 86 88 90 92

7. Make a box-and-whisker plot for the data.

**Prices of Televisions (dollars)**

250   175   180   290   350   325   160
190   200   300   310   210   260   270

**Prices of Televisions (dollars)**

160   190   255   300   350

150  200  250  300  350

8. If you scored at the 80th percentile on a test, how many people scored above you out of 20 students? _____ 4

9. If you scored at the 90th percentile on a test, how many people scored below you out of 30 students? _____ 27

10. On a test, Kylie has the tenth highest score. If there are 25 students who take the test, what is Kylie's percentile rank? _____ 64th

---

## Enrichment Worksheet 1-6

Name _____   Date _____

ENRICHMENT **1-6**

**DOGGIE DATA**

The table below shows the number of kennel club registrations for 25 breeds of dogs. The data are sequenced in descending order, that is, from highest to lowest.

**25 KENNEL CLUB REGISTRATIONS**

| Rank | Breed | Number | Rank | Breed | Number |
|---|---|---|---|---|---|
| 1 | Cocker Spaniel | 111,636 | 14 | Pomeranian | 32,109 |
| 2 | Labrador Retriever | 91,107 | 15 | Lhasa Apso | 28,810 |
| 3 | Poodle | 78,600 | 16 | Chihuahua | 24,917 |
| 4 | Golden Retriever | 64,296 | 17 | Pekingese | 22,966 |
| 5 | German Shepherd | 58,422 | 18 | Boxer | 22,037 |
| 6 | Rottweiler | 51,291 | 19 | Siberian Huskie | 21,875 |
| 7 | Chow Chow | 50,150 | 20 | Doberman Pinscher | 21,782 |
| 8 | Dachshund | 44,305 | 21 | Basset Hound | 21,517 |
| 9 | Beagle | 43,314 | 22 | English Springer Spaniel | 20,911 |
| 10 | Miniature Schnauzer | 42,175 | 23 | Collie | 18,227 |
| 11 | Shetland Sheepdog | 39,665 | 24 | Dalmatian | 17,488 |
| 12 | Yorkshire Terrier | 39,268 | 25 | Boston Terrier | 15,355 |
| 13 | Shih Tzu | 38,131 | | | |

☑ **EXERCISES**

Use the table to solve the problems below.

Find each of the following. Round to the nearest whole number if necessary.

1. median _____ 38,131   2. upper quartile _____ 50,721

3. lower quartile _____ 21,829   4. range _____ 96,281

5. interquartile range (IQR) _____ 28,892

6. Multiply the interquartile range by 1.5 _____ 43,338

7. Determine if there are any outliers in the data set. If there are, name the breed(s). _____ cocker spaniel

8. To the nearest percent, what is the percentile rank of Labrador Retrievers? _____ 92nd percentile

9. Which breed is approximately the 12th percentile? _____ collies

10. The *interdecile range* is the difference between the values for the 90th and 10th percentiles (or the percentiles closest to those values). What is the interdecile range for the set of data above? _____ 72,880

11. The average value of the upper and lower quartiles is sometimes called the *midquartile*. What is the midquartile for the set of data above? _____ 36,275

12. Is the midquartile necessarily equal to the median? _____ no

## Vocabulary Review

**Lesson 1-5**
coefficient of correlation
guess and check

**Lesson 1-6**

| | |
|---|---|
| quartiles | first quartile |
| second quartile | third quartile |
| whiskers | outliers |
| interquartile range | percentile |
| box-and-whisker plot | |

## ASSIGNMENT GUIDE

All students: 1–22

## Chalkboard Examples

### Lesson 1-5

**POPULATION** The first coordinate in each ordered pair below is the age of a randomly selected married woman, and the second coordinate is the age of her husband.

(29, 34) (37, 38) (19, 20) (57, 57) (34, 32)
(23, 25) (51, 54) (72, 81) (29, 29) (70, 70)
(45, 54) (39, 37) (58, 56) (64, 71) (35, 35)
(42, 50) (25, 24) (37, 48) (36, 36) (27, 32)
(56, 42) (17, 24) (28, 28) (57, 26) (41, 39)
(47, 47) (16, 18) (24, 27) (84, 87) (55, 59)

a. Predict the characteristic of the correlation between the two variables. **positive, strong**
b. Verify your prediction by finding the coefficient of correlation.
   $r \approx 0.908$

### Lesson 1-6

**EDUCATION** To be accepted into the college of her choice, LuAnn must achieve a percentile rank of at least 85 on the standardized test that the college uses as an admission factor. LuAnn's score is 113th from the highest out of the 810 students who took the test. Is LuAnn eligible for admission?

$$\frac{\text{number of scores} \le \text{given score}}{\text{total number of scores}} = \frac{810 - 112}{810} \approx 0.862$$

LuAnn's ranking is in the 86th percentile; so, she is eligible for admission.

# Review and Practice Your Skills

## PRACTICE ■ LESSON 1-5

Predict the characteristics of the correlation between the two variables. Find the coefficient of correlation to check your prediction.

1.

| Years since 1900 | 10 | 20 | 30 | 40 | 50 | 60 | 70 | 80 | 90 | 100 |
|---|---|---|---|---|---|---|---|---|---|---|
| U.S. Population (millions) | 92.2 | 106.0 | 123.2 | 132.2 | 151.3 | 179.3 | 203.3 | 226.5 | 248.7 | 281.4 |

$r = 0.991$

2.

| Average monthly temperature (°F) | 8 | 14 | 29 | 37 | 45 | 52 |
|---|---|---|---|---|---|---|
| Average monthly snowfall (inches) | 22 | 17 | 12 | 6 | 2 | 0 |

negative; $r \approx -0.99$

State whether each of the following sets of variables would show a *positive*, *negative*, or *zero* correlation.

3. hours of TV watched per week, GPA   negative

4. your age, the number of letters in your name   zero

5. age of a car, the value of the car   negative

6. height of a cylinder, the volume of the cylinder   positive

## PRACTICE ■ LESSON 1-6

For each set of data, find the first quartile, the median, and the third quartile.

7. Number of sit-ups: 12   14   20   21   25   29   30   30   31   32   59   46
   20.5, 29.5, 31.5
8. Number of vacation trips: 5   7   1   3   5   4   5   4   6   2   6   4
   3.5, 4.5, 5.5

Make a box-and-whisker plot for these exam scores. Label $Q_1$, $Q_2$, and $Q_3$.
See additional answers.
9. 70   65   85   72   93   97   89   94   88

**DATA FILE** For Exercises 10–14, use the data on page 575 to make a box-and-whisker plot of the birth years of the states.

10. What is the median year?   1836, 6 mo

11. What is $Q_1$, $Q_2$, and $Q_3$?   $Q_1 = 1790$, $Q_2 = 1836$, 6 mo, $Q_3 = 1876$

12. What is the interquartile range?   86 yr

13. Does the birth of Texas fall between $Q_1$ and $Q_3$?   yes

14. Does the birth of North Carolina fall between $Q_1$ and $Q_3$?   no

Find the percentile ranks for each of the following students' English final exam. Round to the nearest percent.

15. Arnold   27th

16. Lynn   64th

17. Bo   91st

18. Kavita   36th

| Arnold | 77 |
|---|---|
| Bo | 90 |
| Ciana | 100 |
| Deb | 68 |
| Eduardo | 80 |
| Gayle | 81 |
| Kavita | 78 |
| Jose | 61 |
| Lynn | 84 |
| Mika | 90 |
| Naomi | 89 |

## Differentiated Instruction

**AUDITORY LEARNERS** When reviewing the material of Lesson 1-6, elicit that *quartiles* are equivalent to particular *percentiles*:
   the first quartile, $Q_1$ = 25th percentile
   the second quartile, $Q_2$ = 50th percentile
   the third quartile, $Q_3$ = 75th percentile

**19.** Find the mean, median, and mode of the following test scores. (Lesson 1-2)

89  76  76  90  93  97  80  78  90  82  85
mean = 85.1; median = 85; mode = 76, 90

**Use the box-and-whisker plot to answer the following questions.** (Lesson 1-6)

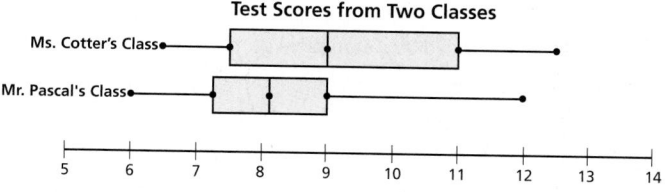

Test Scores from Two Classes

Ms. Cotter's Class

Mr. Pascal's Class

5  6  7  8  9  10  11  12  13  14

**20.** Which class had the higher median score?  Ms. Cotter's

**21.** Which class had its scores grouped more closely around its median?  Mr. Pascal's

**22.** Which class, as a whole, scored better on the test?  Ms. Cotter's

## MathWorks  Career – Market Researcher
Workplace Knowhow

A market researcher plays a key role in a company's decisions. The results of the studies that a market researcher performs determine what new merchandise will be sold in different locations. It is critical that the data collected by a market researcher be accurate and easily interpreted. The table records the shirt sizes (collar and sleeve length) and pant sizes (waist and inseam) of ten men. The market researcher plans to use this data to recommend how many of each size of shirts and pants that a men's specialty shop should keep in stock.

**1.** Construct a frequency table of the collar size data listed in the table. What are the median and the mode for this data?  See additional answers. median = 16.5; mode = 16.5

**2.** Draw a scatter plot to determine whether there is a positive or negative correlation between the waist size data ($x$-axis) and inseam data ($y$-axis). Is the coefficient of correlation closer to 1 or −1?  See additional answers. positive; 1

**3.** Design a stem-and-leaf plot of the data for collar size. Be sure to include a key that explains the plot.
See additional answers.

**4.** Construct a box-and-whisker plot of the sleeve length data. Calculate the first, second and third quartiles as well as the range and the interquartile range.  34, 34.5, 36, 5, 2

| Collar size (inches) | Sleeve length (inches) | Waist size (inches) | Inseam (inches) |
|---|---|---|---|
| 15.5 | 35 | 34 | 32 |
| 16.0 | 34 | 33 | 30 |
| 17.0 | 36 | 36 | 35 |
| 17.0 | 36 | 37 | 38 |
| 14.5 | 32 | 32 | 33 |
| 16.5 | 36 | 35 | 34 |
| 15.5 | 34 | 35 | 33 |
| 16.5 | 34 | 36 | 35 |
| 16.5 | 33 | 35 | 35 |
| 17.5 | 37 | 38 | 37 |

4. See additional answers for plot.

Math Online  mathmatters2.com/mathworks

## MathWorks

Knowing the needs and buying habits of its potential customers is crucial to the success of a local retail shop.

Students should answer Questions 1–4 to better understand how the findings of a market researcher might be of use to the owner of a local retail shop.

Because of the nature of advertising, depending as it does on psychological and other variables difficult to ascertain precisely, the whole field of audience research is complex and controversial. Researchers have found it necessary to consistently refine their techniques and make them increasingly reliable.

Students who are interested in learning more about this career choice can go to mathmatters2.com/mathworks. School Guidance Counselors are another resource for information about training requirements and appropriate schools.

**2.**

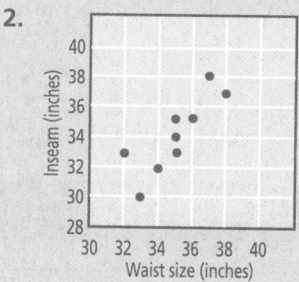

**3.**

```
14 | 5
15 | 5 5
16 | 0 5 5 5
17 | 0 0 5
```

14 | 5 represents 14.5 collar size.

**4.**

Sleeve Length

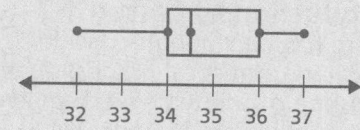

32  33  34  35  36  37

## ADDITIONAL ANSWERS

**9.**

Exam Scores

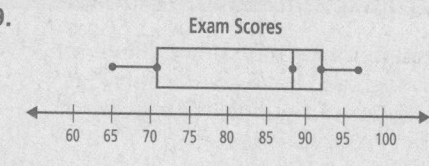

60  65  70  75  80  85  90  95  100

**10–13.**

Birth Years of the States

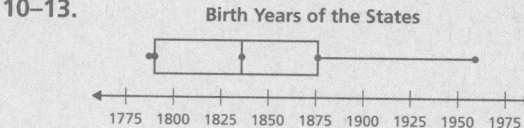

1775  1800  1825  1850  1875  1900  1925  1950  1975

## MATHWORKS

**1.**

| Collar Size | Frequency |
|---|---|
| 14.5 | I |
| 15.0 | |
| 15.5 | II |
| 16.0 | I |
| 16.5 | III |
| 17.0 | II |
| 17.5 | I |

- ■ Data Analysis & Probability
- ■ Communication
- ■ Representation
- ■ Connections

### Vocabulary

misleading data

### Tools/Materials Needed

graph paper    graphing calculator

*New Vocabulary words are boldface at point of use.*

### Lesson Resources

Warm-up Transparency 3
Transparency TK-9
Reteaching 1-7
Extra Practice 1-7
Enrichment 1-7
Technology Activity 1-7

## Getting Started

### 5-MINUTE WARM-UP

**Find the measures of central tendency (mean, median, and mode) for these data sets.**
1. $150, $200, $160, $150, $80
   $148; $150; $150
2. $600, $600, $600, $600, $2000
   $880; $600, $600

### Introduction to Lesson 1-7

Before having students consider misleading statistical graphs, open a discussion of printed advertisements and how they are intended to attract attention. For example, the use of the word "free" in an ad. If possible, have some ads to show. Include ads for "free" computer software that depend on receiving a rebate after first paying for the item when purchased.

---

# 1-7 Misleading Graphs and Statistics

**Goals**
- ■ Recognize how a graph can be misleading.
- ■ Identify the misleading use of the word "average."

**Applications**    Insurance, Business, Advertising, Market research

One advantage of a statistical graph is that it can provide information at a glance. But sometimes this can be a disadvantage. There are ways to change the appearance of a graph to create different impressions.
For 1–3, answers will vary.
1. Explain a time when you were convinced by a statistical graph.
2. Did you later find out that the graph was misleading?
3. How was the data presented that led you to misunderstand?

### ■ BUILD UNDERSTANDING

Data is presented in many different formats. People see displays of data in the news, on television, in magazines, on financial reports, and in medical records. Much of this data is presented so that a judgement will be formed quickly without a lot of attention to detail.

**Misleading data** representation is data representation that leads to a false perception. One way to present correct data so that it is misinterpreted is to alter a scale or show only a certain segment of the results.

### Example 1

**BUSINESS** Admissions data for a waterpark is shown.

a. Make a line graph of the data using a vertical scale from 500,000 to 530,000 with each unit equal to 5000.

b. Make a line graph of the same data using a vertical scale from 515,000 to 527,000 with each unit equal to 2000.

c. If you are a manager planning to include a graph in a report for investors, which graph would you use? Explain.

| Month | Admissions |
|---|---|
| May | 516,633 |
| June | 519,312 |
| July | 521,654 |
| August | 523,809 |
| September | 525,248 |

**Solution**

a.

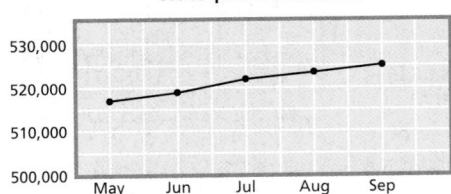

Waterpark Admissions

---

## Alternative Assessment

**MATH JOURNAL** Have students find newspaper ads that they believe may involve the misleading use of statistics. For each ad, have them tell what other information they would like to have before they decide whether or not to patronize a certain business or buy a certain product.

**b.**

**Waterpark Admissions**

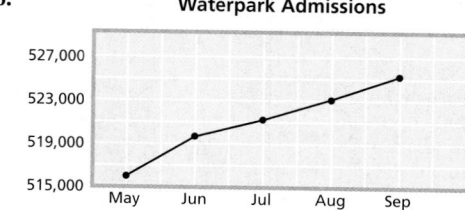

**c.** A manager would show the graph created in part b. This graph makes it appear that admissions have increased dramatically.

It is not uncommon for the word "average" to be used in place of any of the three measures of central tendency. However, when people read the word "average," they often think of *arithmetic average*. In these cases, the word "average" is used correctly, but the misleading aspect comes from the interpretation by the reader.

### Example 2

**ADVERTISING** Furniture World has seven salespeople. The commissions they earned last week were $493, $283, $301, $299, $366, $304 and $299. The owner of the store places an ad in the newspaper for additional salespeople.

**a.** Which measure of central tendency does the owner use in the ad?

**b.** Does this ad give a fair picture of the salespeople's weekly commissions? Explain.

**c.** Which measure(s) of central tendency would be useful to a person considering a sales position at Furniture World? Explain.

> **EXPERIENCED SALESPEOPLE**
> wanted for furniture store.
> Earn an average weekly commission of $335.
> Apply in person at
>
> **FURNITURE WORLD**
> 219 Plainfield Tpke.

### Solution

**a.** Determine the three measures of central tendency. Arranging the data in order simplifies finding the median and the mode.

$283   $299   $299   $301   $304   $366   $493

median: The middle commission of the seven is $301.

mode: The commission of $299 is the mode since it appears twice.

mean: Add the commissions and divide by 7.

$283 + $299 + $299 + $301 + $304 + $366 + $493 = $2345
2345 ÷ 7 = $335

The measure of central tendency used in the ad is the mean.

**b.** No. Only two of the seven commissions are greater than or equal to the mean. The other five commissions are not close to the mean.

**c.** The median and mode are useful because four commissions are equal to or near these measures.

> **Math: Who, Where, When**
>
> The Latin expression *caveat emptor* means "let the buyer beware." Remember this rule when making a decision based on survey data that has been interpreted for you.

 **Math Online** mathmatters2.com/extra_examples

---

### Extend the Lesson

**INTERDISCIPLINARY CONNECTION** After students have completed Exercises 3–5, have them write a statement for the resort's brochure that would be attractive to the potential tourist but not misleading.

---

## Chalkboard Examples

### Supplementary Example
**FINANCE** Since Paul was saving to buy a car, his family gave him cash for his birthday on August 2nd. The deposit of his birthday money doubled the balance in Paul's savings account, as represented by the graphs below.

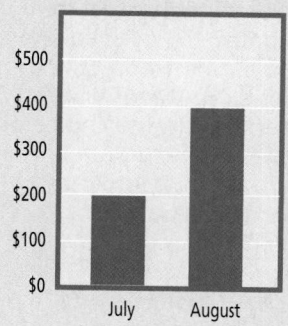

Which of the two graphs suggests a bigger increase in savings? Explain. **Although both graphs show the same height difference, the bar graph increases in only the one dimension (height). The other graph shows an increase in area, enlarging the picture in two dimensions, thereby suggesting a larger overall increase.**

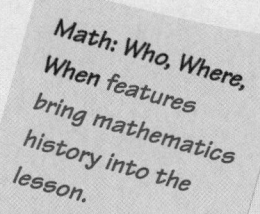

Math: Who, Where, When features bring mathematics history into the lesson.

## Lesson Wrap-up

### QUICK ASSESSMENT

Ask the following questions to determine if students understand the content presented in this lesson.

1. Why might different people consider different measures of central tendency to be the best indicator of the typical item in a set of data?  *They want to use the same data to present or emphasize different viewpoints.*

2. What effect can the choice of vertical scale have on a line graph?  *Using a scale that just accommodates the data is comparable to a "zoom" view, more sharply emphasizing an increase or decrease.*

### ASSIGNMENT GUIDE

**Basic:** 1–17, 21–32
**Enriched:** 1–32

*One or more Quick Assessment questions accompany every lesson. The Assignment Guide provides suggestions for the exercises that are appropriate for a basic course or an enriched course.*

### Reteaching Worksheet 1-7

Name _____ Date _____

RETEACHING  **1-7**

**MISLEADING GRAPHS AND STATISTICS**

Depending on which measure of central tendency is used to interpret a set of data, the mean, median, or mode can either offer an accurate picture of the data or distort them.

**Example**

The owner of a gift shop wants to sell her business. In her classified advertisement, monthly sales were stated as $30,000 or better. Here are the monthly sales figures for the past year.

J-$14,000  M-$18,000  M-$20,000  J-$30,000  S-$17,000  N-$37,000
F-$11,000  A-$19,000  J-$22,000  A-$30,000  O-$31,000  D-$45,000

a. Which measure of central tendency was used to arrive at the wording used in the advertisement?
b. Does the statement about monthly sales give a fair picture of monthly sales over the year?
c. If you were a prospective buyer, which measure would give you a more accurate picture of monthly sales?

**Solution**

a. Arrange the data in numerical order in thousands of dollars. Determine the three measures of central tendency.
11 + 14 + 17 + 18 + 19 + 20 + 22 + 30 + 30 + 31 + 37 + 45
mean: $\frac{294,000}{12}$ = 24,500    median: 21,000    mode: 30,000
The measure of central tendency used in the ad is the mode.

b. No; seven of the twelve figures are below the mode, and six are below the median and mean.
c. Either the median or the mean would be more accurate.

**☑ EXERCISES**

In a new housing subdivision, seven different styles of house are available. Prices are $91,000, $110,000, $127,000, $98,000, $110,000, $95,000, and $92,000. The developer advertised the average price of a home as $98,000.

1. Which measure of the central tendency did the developer use in the advertisement?
   the median
2. Does the advertisement give a fair picture of the range of prices?
   No; the median does not accurately reflect the upper prices in the data.
3. Which measure would have been least misleading to potential home buyers? Explain.
   The mean would more accurately reflect the range of prices.

**36** Chapter 1  **Sample and Display Data**

---

### ▨ TRY THESE EXERCISES

**FOOD SERVICE** The number of pizzas sold by the Pizza Tunnel chain for each of the three years since it opened is as follows: 2002–100,000; 2003–200,000; 2004–300,000. To show the sales, the chain's president made the graph shown.

Pizza Tunnel Sales

1. Is the president justified in claiming the graph presents the data accurately? How might the graph be misleading?
   No. By tripling the diameter, the area is increased 9 times.
2. How can the graph be drawn to avoid misleading anyone?
   Use a bar graph.

**WEATHER** The monthly rainfall, in centimeters, at Mountain Valley Resort last year is shown. A part of the resort's brochure is also shown.

| J | F | M | A | M | J | J | A | S | O | N | D |
|---|---|---|---|---|---|---|---|---|---|---|---|
| 0 | 2 | 7 | 12 | 18 | 24 | 25 | 25 | 22 | 6 | 3 | 0 |

3. Which measure of central tendency was used in the brochure?  median
4. Does the statement about rainfall in the brochure give a fair picture of weather conditions? Explain.
   No. All of the summer months had rainfall much greater than 10 cm.
5. Which measure of central tendency would be a better indicator?  The mean would be a little better (12); however, since the data varies greatly, only the summer month data should be used.

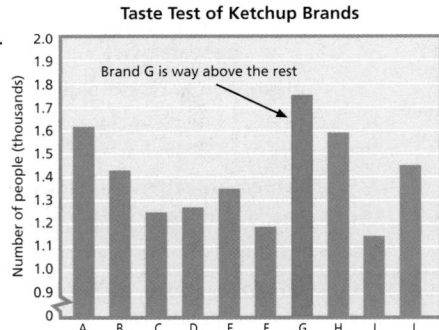

**BEAUTIFUL SUMMER WEATHER**
Average monthly rainfall less than 10 cm!

### ▨ PRACTICE EXERCISES • For Extra Practice, see page 587.

**MUSIC** A songwriter earned the following yearly totals in royalties over a 4-yr period.

    1996—$35,000   1997—$35,800   1998—$37,250   1999—$38,000
For 6–7, see additional answers.

6. Draw a graph that shows the actual trend in the writer's earnings.

7. Draw a graph so that the writer's earnings appear to be growing substantially.

**MARKET RESEARCH** The bar graph shows the average ratings from a taste test for ten brands of ketchup. This information is used by the makers of Brand G.

8. Approximately how many times as high is the tallest bar than the shortest bar?  4

9. Make a list of the ten brands of ketchup and the number of people who favored each brand. For example, 1600 people chose Brand A as their favorite.  See additional answers.

10. Based on your numbers, how does the most favored brand compare with the least favored.
    1.5 times greater (much less than double)
11. What caused the distortion in the graph?
    Only portions of the complete bars are shown.
12. Suppose Brands C and D want to speak out against Brand G's advertisement that included the bar graph above. Redraw the graph so that it is about the same overall size but gives a more accurate picture of the situation.
    See additional answers.

Taste Test of Ketchup Brands
Brand G is way above the rest

**36** | Chapter 1  **Sample and Display Data**

### ADDITIONAL ANSWERS

6.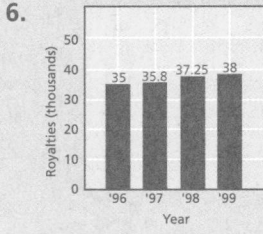

7.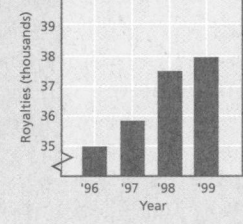

9. A → 1625
   B → 1425
   C → 1250
   D → 1275
   E → 1350
   F → 1200
   G → 1750
   H → 1600
   I → 1150
   J → 1450

12.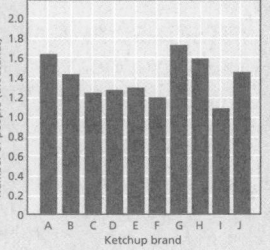

**ENTERTAINMENT** A movie theater charges $7 for a ticket. The theater manager is considering raising the ticket prices and asked 25 people to name the greatest amount they would be willing to pay to see a movie. The results are shown in the table.

**Greatest Amount People Would Pay to See a Movie**

| Amount | Frequency |
|--------|-----------|
| $20.00 | 3 |
| 15.00 | 4 |
| 12.00 | 3 |
| 10.00 | 5 |
| 8.00 | 7 |
| 7.00 | 1 |
| 5.00 | 1 |
| 2.00 | 1 |

13. In order to justify a large increase in the ticket price, which measure of central tendency might the theater manager use? Explain. He should use the mean to justify the largest increase.

14. If the theater patrons saw this survey, which measure of central tendency might they point out to the manager to keep the price increase low? Explain. They should use the mode to justify the lowest increase.

15. Do you think the results of the manager's survey are biased? Yes. Answers will vary.

16. How would you conduct your own survey differently to show the theater manager that the ticket price should not be increased? Survey your friends who don't often go to see a movie.

17. **WRITING MATH** Write a short paragraph explaining what to look for to be sure that you are drawing correct conclusions about data presented in a line graph. Answers will vary.

### ■ EXTENDED PRACTICE EXERCISES

18. Use the data to create two graphs. In one, make it appear that sales fluctuated greatly from month to month. In the second, make it appear that sales varied little from month to month. See additional answers.

**Gloria's Gloves Sales**

| Month | 1 | 2 | 3 | 4 | 5 | 6 |
|-------|---|---|---|---|---|---|
| Sales (hundreds) | 72 | 65 | 81 | 84 | 75 | 79 |

19. **CRITICAL THINKING** Name a reason why a marketer would use each of the graphs in Exercise 18 in different advertisements. See additional answers.

20. **CHAPTER INVESTIGATION** Compare the different types of visual displays and your data. Choose the statistical graphs and the statistical measures that best represent your recommendations. Prepare the visuals and the summary of your market research. Answers will vary.

### ■ MIXED REVIEW EXERCISES

**Find the perimeter of each figure.** (Basic geometry skills)

21. 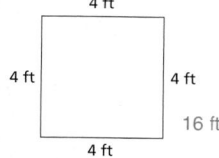 16 ft

22. 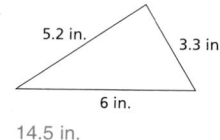 14.5 in.

23. 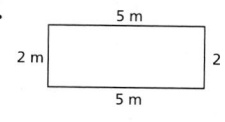 14 m

**Determine whether each equation is *true* or *false*.** (Basic math skills)

24. $3 \cdot 12 = 36$ true

25. $(-2)(6) = 12$ false

26. $\frac{-48}{12} = -4$ true

27. $(-5)(-9) = 45$ true

28. $72 \div 4 = 18$ true

29. $28 \div (-7) = -3$ false

30. $(-5)(-8) = 40$ true

31. $(-6)(-3) = -18$ false

32. $\frac{-81}{9} = -9$ true

Math
Online mathmatters2.com/self_check_quiz

## ADDITIONAL ANSWERS

18.
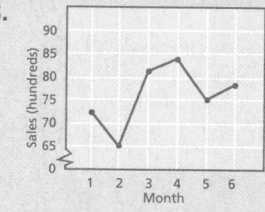

19. A marketer may use the first graph to advertise for a potential new trend to fad buyers. The second graph could be used to advertise the reliability and consistency of its product line.

*Extended Practice Exercises offer students the opportunity to extend their learning.*

---

## Extra Practice Worksheet 1-7

Name _____ Date _____

EXTRA PRACTICE **1-7**
**MISLEADING GRAPHS AND STATISTICS**

### ☑ EXERCISES

The bar graph shows the number of calories per serving of four different brands of chocolate ice cream. This information is used by the makers of Brand A.

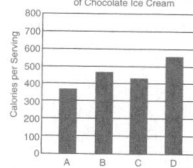

Number of Calories per Serving of Chocolate Ice Cream

1. Approximately how many times as high is the tallest bar than the shortest bar? **2**

2. Make a list of the four brands of ice cream and the number of calories per serving for each.
   Brand A: 375 calories; Brand B: 475 calories; Brand C: 425 calories; Brand D: 550 calories

3. Based on your numbers, how does the brand with the least calories per serving compare to the brand with the most calories per serving? It has 175 fewer calories per serving.

4. What caused the distortion in the graph? The broken vertical scale.

5. Suppose Brands B and D want to speak out against Brand A's advertisement that included the bar graph above. Redraw the graph so that it is about the same overall size but gives a more honest picture of the situation. Answers may vary. Possible graph is given.

Number of Calories per Serving of Chocolate Ice Cream

---

## Enrichment Worksheet 1-7

Name _____ Date _____

ENRICHMENT **1-7**
**NUMBERS DON'T LIE—DO THEY?**

Statistical data can be used in misleading ways. The exercises below illustrate a statistical reversal paradox. In a statistical reversal paradox, one conclusion is drawn when sets of data are analyzed individually. When the sets of data are combined and analyzed in the same way, the opposite conclusion can be drawn.

### ☑ EXERCISES

Suppose you want to decide if employment agencies are more successful in finding jobs for women or for men. Consider the following situation at two employment agencies, Great Jobs and Perfect Positions.

At Great Jobs, 96 out of 120 women who registered with the agency were placed in jobs. Out of 180 men who registered, the agency found jobs for 117 of them.

1. What percent of registered women were placed in jobs? **80%**
2. What percent of registered males were placed in jobs? **65%**

At Perfect Positions, 25 out of 125 women who registered with the agency were placed in jobs. Out of 40 men who registered, the agency found jobs for 6 of them.

3. What percent of registered women were placed in jobs? **20%**
4. What percent of registered men were placed in jobs? **15%**
5. Based on the percent above, what conclusion would you draw about whether employment agencies are more successful in finding jobs for women or men? Agencies are more successful in finding jobs for women.

Combine the data for Great Jobs and Perfect Positions to answer the questions. If necessary, round answers to the nearest percent.

6. How many women in all registered for jobs? **245**
7. How many women were placed? **121**
8. What percent of registered women were placed? **49%**
9. How many men in all registered for jobs? **220**
10. How many men were placed? **123**
11. What percent of registered men were placed? **56%**
12. Based on your answers to Exercises 8 and 11, what conclusions would you draw about whether employment agencies are more successful in finding jobs for women or men? Agencies are more successful in finding jobs for men.

# Use Matrices to Organize Data

**Goals**
■ Organize and display data in matrices.
■ Peform basic operations using matrices.

**Applications** Business, Retail, Food service, Recreation

## Lesson Planning

### NCTM Standards/Strands
■ Data Analysis & Probability
■ Representation
■ Connections
■ Number & Operations

### Vocabulary

matrix                    element
dimensions of a matrix
square matrix
corresponding elements

### Tools/Materials Needed

graphing calculator   graph paper

### Lesson Resources

Warm-up Transparency 3
Transparency TK-3
Reteaching 1-8
Extra Practice 1-8
Enrichment 1-8

## Getting Started

### 5-MINUTE WARM-UP

**Display the information in a table.**
The Reds won 8 games and lost 2 games.
The Blues won 6 games and lost 4 games.

|       | Number of Games | |
|-------|-----|------|
| Team  | Won | Lost |
| Reds  | 8   | 2    |
| Blues | 6   | 4    |

### Introduction to Lesson 1-8
Students should understand that the nature of their display is to serve two purposes: (1) make it easy to identify the hair color and shirt color of each group member and (2) make it easy for compatible data to be merged with it.

**Divide the class into two groups. Answer Questions 1 and 2 in your group and Questions 3 and 4 as a class.**
For 1–4, answers will vary.
1. For all members of your group, record their hair color and the color of their shirt.

2. Decide how to organize the data so that it can be combined easily with the data collected by the other group. Do not discuss your ideas with the other group. Display your organized data.

3. Compare the sets of data, and discuss how compatible the displays are. Will it be simple to add the corresponding data together? Will it be simple to determine how many people are wearing red?

4. Discuss methods for organizing and displaying data that may make it simple to add data or to quickly identify a single fact.

### ◤ BUILD UNDERSTANDING

Data can be displayed in many different ways. A table and a spreadsheet are two common ways to organize and display data.

|          | Store 1 | Store 2 | Store 3 |
|----------|---------|---------|---------|
| Cam Plus | 77      | 15      | 42      |
| Easy-Cam | 19      | 89      | 21      |

Table

If you remove the labels from a table or spreadsheet, you have a rectangular array of numbers. By placing brackets around the numbers, you create a matrix. A **matrix** is a rectangular arrangement of data in rows and columns and enclosed by brackets.

|   | A  | B  | C  |
|---|----|----|----|
| 1 | 77 | 15 | 42 |
| 2 | 19 | 89 | 21 |

Spreadsheet

Each number in a matrix is an **element**, or *entry*. The sample matrix has elements 77, 15, 42, 19, 89 and 21.

The number of rows and columns in a matrix determine its dimensions. Since the sample matrix has 2 rows and 3 columns, its dimensions are $2 \times 3$, read 2 by 3.

$$\begin{bmatrix} 77 & 15 & 42 \\ 19 & 89 & 21 \end{bmatrix}$$

Matrix

### Example 1

**Give the dimensions of matrix $A$.**   $A = \begin{bmatrix} 3 & 1 & 16 & 4 \\ 0 & 1 & 3 & 2 \\ 21 & 3 & 6 & 0 \end{bmatrix}$

**Solution**

The matrix has 3 rows and 4 columns, so its dimensions are $3 \times 4$.

**Reading Math**

The plural of matrix is *matrices*.

Capital letters are used to name matrices so that they can be referred to easily.

### Teaching Tip

Some students may find it easier to write their matrices on grid paper. To emphasize that matrix addition or subtraction can take place only when the matrices have the same dimensions, present students with several matrices of different dimensions and ask them to list all the additions and subtractions that could possibly take place.

$$J = \begin{bmatrix} 8 & 5 & 9 & 12 \\ -2 & 6 & 0 & 12 \end{bmatrix} \quad K = \begin{bmatrix} -5 & 8 & -1 \\ -3 & 5 & 4 \\ -4 & 3 & 10 \end{bmatrix} \quad M = \begin{bmatrix} 0.7 & 6 & 2 & 5 \\ 3.1 & 5 & 1 & 4 \end{bmatrix} \quad N = \begin{bmatrix} 7 & 0 & -6 \\ 1 & 6 & 9 \\ 0 & 2 & -7 \end{bmatrix}$$

$J + M, M + J, K + N, N + K, J - M, M - J, K - N, N - K$
*Note:* In Exercise 23, students consider whether or not matrix addition is commutative.

A matrix with the same number of rows and columns is a **square matrix**. When two matrices have equal dimensions, *corresponding elements* are the elements in the same position of each matrix. To find the sum or difference of two matrices with the same dimensions, add or subtract corresponding elements.

# Example 2

Use matrices $A$ and $B$.

$$A = \begin{bmatrix} 14 & 7 \\ 21 & 19 \\ 35 & 12 \end{bmatrix} \qquad B = \begin{bmatrix} 11 & 0 \\ 9 & 18 \\ 25 & 5 \end{bmatrix}$$

**a.** Find $A + B$.  **b.** Find $A - B$.

## Solution

**a.** $A + B = \begin{bmatrix} 14 + 11 & 7 + 0 \\ 21 + 9 & 19 + 18 \\ 35 + 25 & 12 + 5 \end{bmatrix} = \begin{bmatrix} 25 & 7 \\ 30 & 37 \\ 60 & 17 \end{bmatrix}$

**b.** $A - B = \begin{bmatrix} 14 - 11 & 7 - 0 \\ 21 - 9 & 19 - 18 \\ 35 - 25 & 12 - 5 \end{bmatrix} = \begin{bmatrix} 3 & 7 \\ 12 & 1 \\ 10 & 7 \end{bmatrix}$

**Math: Who, Where, When**

In 1850, British mathematician James Sylvester (1814–1897) coined the term "matrix" from the Hebrew word "gematria," an ancient system that assigned numbers to the letters in Hebrew words. Sylvester and Arthur Cayley (1821–1895) developed the theory of matrices.

You can add and subtract matrices on a graphing calculator. First define the dimensions and the elements for each matrix. You can perform the basic operations at the home screen. The left and center figures below show the defining screens, and the right figure shows the home-screen operations.

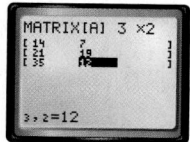 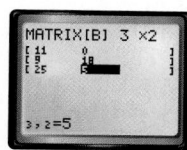 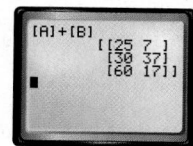 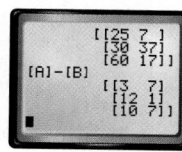

# Example 3

Use a graphing calculator to find the sum and the difference of matrices $A$ and $B$.

$$A = \begin{bmatrix} 5 & 5 \\ 55 & 19 \end{bmatrix} \qquad B = \begin{bmatrix} 3 & 19 \\ 13 & 2 \end{bmatrix}$$

## Solution

Use the matrix feature to enter matrix A and matrix B. At the home screen calculate the sum and difference.

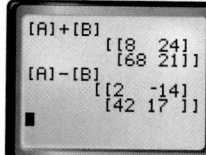

 mathmatters2.com/extra_examples

Lesson 1-8  **Use Matrices to Organize Data**  **39**

# Extend the Lesson

**REAL WORLD CONNECTION** After students have worked through Example 4, ask them how matrices $A$, $B$, and $C$ could be used to find the store inventories on any given day.  $A$ is the starting inventory for a day. Deliveries and sales for the day are entered in $B$ and $C$. The matrix that results from calculating $A + B - C$ becomes the matrix $A$ for the next day.

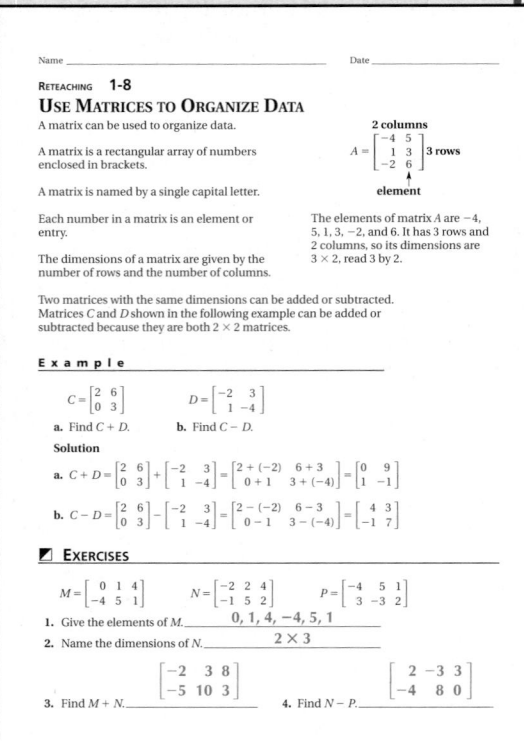

### Example 4

| | Brown | Black |
|---|---|---|
| Deck shoes | 38 | 52 |
| Sandals | 49 | 70 |
| Penny loafers | 25 | 41 |

**BUSINESS** The spreadsheet shows the inventory levels at the Gold-n-Sole for two colors of three styles of shoes on May 1. During May, the manufacturer delivers the following quantities of brown and black shoes in each style.

deck shoes (25, 32)   sandals (30, 35)   penny loafers (18, 12)

During May, customers purchased brown and black shoes in the following quantities.

deck shoes (31, 19)   sandals (39, 43)   penny loafers (11, 17)

a. Write inventory matrix A.     b. Write delivery matrix B.
c. Write purchase matrix C.      d. Calculate $A + B - C$. What does this matrix represent?

**Solution**

a. $A = \begin{bmatrix} 38 & 52 \\ 49 & 70 \\ 25 & 41 \end{bmatrix}$   b. $B = \begin{bmatrix} 25 & 32 \\ 30 & 35 \\ 18 & 12 \end{bmatrix}$   c. $C = \begin{bmatrix} 31 & 19 \\ 39 & 43 \\ 11 & 17 \end{bmatrix}$

d. $A + B - C = \begin{bmatrix} 38+25-31 & 52+32-19 \\ 49+30-39 & 70+35-43 \\ 25+18-11 & 41+12-17 \end{bmatrix} = \begin{bmatrix} 32 & 65 \\ 40 & 62 \\ 32 & 36 \end{bmatrix}$

This matrix represents the inventory levels for each color shoe in each style at the end of May.

### TRY THESE EXERCISES

**Write each set of data as a matrix. Name its dimensions.** For 1–3, see additional answers.

1.
| | A | B | C |
|---|---|---|---|
| 1 | | Adult | Child |
| 2 | Friday | 106 | 255 |
| 3 | Saturday | 348 | 491 |
| 4 | Sunday | 196 | 304 |

2.
| Age | A | B | C |
|---|---|---|---|
| Under 18 | 15 | 72 | 44 |
| 18-40 | 91 | 60 | 29 |
| Over 40 | 17 | 19 | 88 |

3.
| Distance | Number of parks | Distance | Number of parks |
|---|---|---|---|
| 390 | 1 | 404 | 3 |
| 400 | 5 | 410 | 3 |
| 402 | 1 | 440 | 1 |

4. Can any of the matrices from Exercises 1–3 be added together? If so, find their sum. If not, explain why. No. They all have different dimensions.

5. **WRITING MATH** Make a list of all the new terms presented in this lesson, and associate them to the matrix and its elements in Exercise 3.
   Check students' work.

### PRACTICE EXERCISES • For Extra Practice, see page 588.

**Use matrices E, F, G and H for Exercises 6–11.**

6. Give the elements of E.  12, 8, 20, 9, 6, 13

7. Name the dimensions of H.  2 × 2
   For 8–11, see additional answers.

8. Find $E + G$.              9. Find $G + F$.

10. Find $F - G$.             11. Find $F + G - E$.

$E = \begin{bmatrix} 12 & 9 \\ 8 & 6 \\ 20 & 13 \end{bmatrix}$   $F = \begin{bmatrix} 9 & 5 \\ 8 & 0 \\ 16 & 7 \end{bmatrix}$

$G = \begin{bmatrix} 26 & 14 \\ 9 & 12 \\ 5 & 25 \end{bmatrix}$   $H = \begin{bmatrix} -1 & 6 \\ 2 & -7 \end{bmatrix}$

### ADDITIONAL ANSWERS

3. $\begin{bmatrix} 390 & 1 \\ 400 & 5 \\ 402 & 1 \\ 404 & 3 \\ 410 & 3 \\ 440 & 1 \end{bmatrix}$ $6 \times 2$

8. $\begin{bmatrix} 38 & 23 \\ 17 & 18 \\ 25 & 38 \end{bmatrix}$   9. $\begin{bmatrix} 35 & 19 \\ 17 & 12 \\ 21 & 32 \end{bmatrix}$   10. $\begin{bmatrix} -17 & -9 \\ -1 & -12 \\ 11 & -18 \end{bmatrix}$   11. $\begin{bmatrix} 23 & 10 \\ 9 & 6 \\ 9 & 6 \end{bmatrix}$

12. $\begin{bmatrix} 117 & 88 \\ 91 & 95 \end{bmatrix}$   13. $\begin{bmatrix} 38 & 35 \\ 25 & 40 \end{bmatrix}$   14. $\begin{bmatrix} 13 & 9 \\ 6 & 10 \end{bmatrix}$   15. $\begin{bmatrix} 142 & 114 \\ 110 & 125 \end{bmatrix}$   18. $\begin{bmatrix} 255 & 462 & 164 \\ 582 & 203 & 170 \end{bmatrix}$

**RECREATION** The 1999 membership in the CC Astronomy Club is listed by grade level and gender.

| At beginning of year: | seniors (117 males, 88 females) | juniors (91 males, 95 females) |
| Joined during the year: | seniors (38 males, 35 females) | juniors (25 males, 40 females) |
| Stopped attending: | seniors (13 males, 9 females) | juniors (6 males, 10 females) |

For 12–15, see additional answers.

**12.** Write initial membership matrix $A$.     **13.** Write new member matrix $B$.

**14.** Write stopped attending matrix $C$.     **15.** Calculate $A + B - C$.

**16.** What does the matrix in Exercise 15 represent? Explain. current membership; initial memberships + new memberships − terminated memberships = current memberships

**BUSINESS** Matrix $W$ represents the inventories of three models of handheld vacuums in two warehouses at the beginning of April. Matrix $V$ represents the number of vacuums received from the manufacturer during the month. Matrix $Z$ represents vacuums shipped out during the same month.

$$W = \begin{bmatrix} 317 & 490 & 166 \\ 555 & 207 & 181 \end{bmatrix} \quad V = \begin{bmatrix} 52 & 70 & 48 \\ 88 & 86 & 66 \end{bmatrix} \quad Z = \begin{bmatrix} 114 & 98 & 50 \\ 61 & 90 & 77 \end{bmatrix}$$

**17.** At the beginning of April, how many vacuums, all models combined, were in stock in both warehouses? 1916

**18.** Write a matrix that represents inventory of the three models at month's end. See additional answers.

**RETAIL** The matrix summarizes the sticker price of four car models at three automobile dealerships. Each dealer will add 8% in taxes to the sticker price.
For 19–20, see additional answers.
**19.** Write a matrix giving the tax on each car.

**20.** Add the matrices to show the total prices.

$$\begin{bmatrix} 12{,}400 & 12{,}600 & 12{,}000 \\ 11{,}100 & 11{,}400 & 11{,}500 \\ 14{,}800 & 14{,}100 & 14{,}400 \\ 10{,}200 & 10{,}900 & 10{,}300 \end{bmatrix}$$

## ■ EXTENDED PRACTICE EXERCISES

**CRITICAL THINKING** Find the matrix $M$ that makes each equation true. For 21–22, see additional answers.

**21.** $\begin{bmatrix} 19 & 44 & 30 \\ 62 & 91 & 55 \end{bmatrix} - M = \begin{bmatrix} 8 & 29 & 6 \\ 43 & 60 & 27 \end{bmatrix}$     **22.** $M + \begin{bmatrix} 29 & 63 \\ 77 & 49 \end{bmatrix} = \begin{bmatrix} 81 & 83 \\ 115 & 62 \end{bmatrix}$

**23. WRITING MATH** Is the addition of matrices commutative? (Hint: Does $A + B = B + A$ if $A$ and $B$ have the same dimensions?) Justify your answer. Yes. Addition of each element is commutative.

## ■ MIXED REVIEW EXERCISES

**Find the area of each figure.** (Basic geometry skills)

**24.** 6 m, 4 m, 4 m, 6 m   24 m²

**25.** 1.4 ft, 1.4 ft, 1.4 ft, 1.4 ft   1.96 ft²

**26.** 7 cm, 8 cm   28 cm²

**DATA FILE** Refer to the data on top concert tours on page 563. (Lesson 1-3)

**27.** Make a histogram of the data in intervals of $10 million. See additional answers.

**28.** Which concert is closest to the mean? Backstreet Boys, 2001

Math Online mathmatters2.com/self_check_quiz

## ADDITIONAL ANSWERS

**19.** $\begin{bmatrix} 992 & 1008 & 960 \\ 888 & 912 & 920 \\ 1184 & 1128 & 1152 \\ 816 & 872 & 824 \end{bmatrix}$   **20.** $\begin{bmatrix} 13{,}392 & 13{,}608 & 12{,}960 \\ 11{,}988 & 12{,}312 & 12{,}420 \\ 15{,}984 & 15{,}228 & 15{,}552 \\ 11{,}016 & 11{,}772 & 11{,}124 \end{bmatrix}$

**21.** $\begin{bmatrix} 11 & 15 & 24 \\ 19 & 31 & 28 \end{bmatrix}$   **22.** $\begin{bmatrix} 52 & 20 \\ 38 & 13 \end{bmatrix}$   **27.**

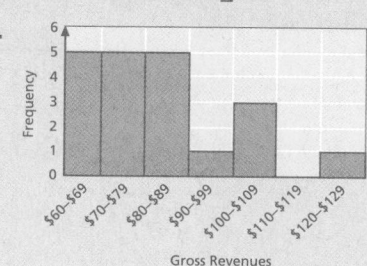

---

Name _____ Date _____

ExTRA PRACTICE **1-8**
**USE MATRICES TO ORGANIZE DATA**

☑ **EXERCISES**

Use matrices $A$–$E$ for Exercises 1–7.

$$A = \begin{bmatrix} -2 & 5 \\ 8 & 1 \end{bmatrix} \quad B = \begin{bmatrix} 0 & -8 \\ 5 & -5 \end{bmatrix} \quad C = \begin{bmatrix} 3 & 4 & 1 \\ -1 & -2 & 2 \end{bmatrix}$$

$$D = \begin{bmatrix} -9 & 4 & -2 \\ -1 & 0 & 7 \end{bmatrix} \quad E = \begin{bmatrix} 25 & 20 & -10 \\ 4 & -15 & 16 \end{bmatrix}$$

**1.** Give the elements of $C$.   3, 4, 1, −1, −2, 2

**2.** Name the dimensions of $B$. 2 × 2   **3.** Name the dimensions of $E$. 2 × 3

**4.** Find $A + B$. $\begin{bmatrix} -2 & -3 \\ 13 & -4 \end{bmatrix}$   **5.** Find $D - E$. $\begin{bmatrix} -34 & -16 & 8 \\ -5 & 15 & -9 \end{bmatrix}$

**6.** Find $C + D + E$. $\begin{bmatrix} 19 & 28 & -11 \\ 2 & -17 & 25 \end{bmatrix}$   **7.** Find $C + E - D$. $\begin{bmatrix} 37 & 20 & -7 \\ 4 & -17 & 11 \end{bmatrix}$

The inventory of white and gray T-shirts during the month of June at *Only Ts* is listed by size and color.

| | | | |
|---|---|---|---|
| In stock: | M (10 white, 15 gray) | L (15 white, 20 gray) | XL (10 white, 25 gray) |
| Sold: | M (9 white, 8 gray) | L (7 white, 5 gray) | XL (2 white, 15 gray) |
| New stock: | M (5 white, 5 gray) | L (3 white, 8 gray) | XL (8 white, 10 gray) |

**8.** Write in stock matrix $A$. $\begin{bmatrix} 10 & 15 \\ 15 & 20 \\ 10 & 25 \end{bmatrix}$   **9.** Write sold matrix $B$. $\begin{bmatrix} 9 & 8 \\ 7 & 5 \\ 2 & 15 \end{bmatrix}$

**10.** Write new stock matrix $C$. $\begin{bmatrix} 5 & 5 \\ 3 & 8 \\ 8 & 10 \end{bmatrix}$   **11.** Calculate $A - B + C$. $\begin{bmatrix} 6 & 12 \\ 11 & 23 \\ 16 & 20 \end{bmatrix}$

**12.** What does the matrix in Exercise 11 represent? Explain. The inventory at the end of the month of June.

---

Name _____ Date _____

ENRICHMENT **1-8**
**GEOMETRIC SERIES**

The terms of this polynomial form a geometric series.

$$a + ar + ar^2 + ar^3 + ar^4$$

The first term is the constant $a$. Then each term after that is found by multiplying by a constant multiplier $r$.

☑ **EXERCISES**

Use the equation $S = a + ar + ar^2 + ar^3 + ar^4$ for Exercises 1–3.

**1.** Multiply each side of the equation by $r$.

$rS = ar + ar^2 + ar^3 + ar^4 + ar^5$

**2.** Subtract the original equation from your result in Exercise 1.

$rS - S = ar^5 - a$

**3.** Solve the result from Exercise 2 for the variable $S$.

$S = \dfrac{a(r^5 - 1)}{r - 1}$

Use the polynomial $a + ar + ar^2 + ar^3 + ar^4 + \ldots + ar^{n-1}$ for Exercises 4–8.

**4.** Write the 10th term of the polynomial.

$ar^9$

**5.** If $a = 5$ and $r = 2$, what is the 8th term?

$ar^7 = 640$

**6.** Follow the steps in Exercises 1–3 to write a formula for the sum of this polynomial $S$.

$S = \dfrac{a(r^n - 1)}{r - 1}$

**7.** If the 3rd term is 20 and the 6th term is 160, write a division expression to solve for $r^3$ and then find $r$. Then solve $ar^2 = 20$ for $a$ and find the value of the first six terms of the polynomial.

$\dfrac{ar^5}{ar^2} = \dfrac{160}{20}$, $r^3 = 8$, $r = 2$; $ar^2 = 20$; $a = 5$; 5, 10, 20, 40, 80, 160

**8.** Find the sum of the first six terms of the geometric series that begins 3, 6, 12, 24, …. First write the values for $a$ and $r$.

$a = 3$, $r = 2$; $S = \dfrac{3(2^6 - 1)}{2 - 1} = 3 \times 63 = 189$

---

### Vocabulary Assessment

- A matching section checks for student understanding of the new vocabulary introduced in this chapter.
- A vocabulary review/test for Chapter 1 is available on pp. vii–viii of the *Chapter 1 Resource Masters*.

### Lesson-by-Lesson Review

For each lesson,

- the main ideas are summarized, and
- practice exercises are provided.

## EXAMVIEW® PRO

Use the networkable **ExamView® Pro** to:

- Create **multiple versions** of tests.
- Create **modified tests** for *inclusion* students.
- **Edit** existing questions and **add** your own questions.
- Use built-in **state curriculum correlations** to create tests aligned with state standards.
- Change **English** tests to **Spanish** and vice versa.

*The Chapter Review contains key concepts and practice problems from each lesson. The Vocabulary exercises are intended to give students practice using terms and definitions presented throughout the chapter.*

---

# Chapter 1 Review

## VOCABULARY

**Choose the word from the list that best completes each statement.**

1. A number that is much greater or much less than the other values in a set of data is known as a(n) ___?___.  h
2. ___?___ divide a set of data arranged in numerical order into four equal parts.  j
3. ___?___ are isolated groups of values in a set of data.  c
4. The mean, median and mode are ___?___ that represent a middle value of a data set.  g
5. A(n) ___?___ records the number of times a response occurs.  d
6. A(n) ___?___ uses a number line to show the distribution of data.  b
7. A rectangular arrangement of data in rows and columns enclosed in brackets is called a(n) ___?___.  f
8. A(n) ___?___ is a representative part of a population.  k
9. The relationship of two sets of data can be shown using a(n) ___?___.  l
10. Survey results that do not truly represent the population are ___?___.  a

| a. | biased |
|----|--------|
| b. | box-and-whisker plot |
| c. | clusters |
| d. | frequency table |
| e. | interquartile range |
| f. | matrix |
| g. | measures of central tendency |
| h. | outlier |
| i. | percentile |
| j. | quartiles |
| k. | sample |
| l. | scatter plot |

### LESSON 1-1 ■ Surveys and Sampling Methods, p. 6

▶ **Random**, **cluster**, **convenience**, and **systematic** sampling are methods of collecting data that can be used to make decisions about a population.

**To identify the most popular current movie among teenagers, seven students seated at the same table in the school cafeteria were asked to name the most recent movie they had seen.**

11. What kind of sampling method is this?
convenience
12. How might the results be biased?
Some may have seen them together.

### LESSON 1-2 ■ Measures of Central Tendency and Range, p. 10

▶ The **mean** is the sum of the values in a data set divided by the number of data. The **median** is the middle value of the data when the data are arranged in numerical order. The **mode** is the number that occurs most often in a set of data. There may be no mode or more than one mode.

▶ The **range** is the difference between the greatest and least values in a set of data.

**Price of Shoes Sold at Shoe Mart**

| $49 | $34 | $37 | $28 | $39 | $44 | $34 | $49 |
|-----|-----|-----|-----|-----|-----|-----|-----|
| $52 | $34 | $37 | $37 | $49 | $39 | $34 | $39 |

13. Find the mean, median, mode, and range of the data.
mean = $39.69; median = $38; mode = $34; range = $24
14. Would an ad stating "Most styles priced at $34" be misleading? Explain.
Yes. Most styles are not priced at $34.

## Teaching Tip

Remind students that to determine the median or other quartiles of a data set, it is necessary to first put a data set in order.
Elicit that to draw a box-and-whisker plot, students must first calculate the 1st, 2nd, and 3rd quartiles.

## LESSON 1-3 ■ Histograms and Stem-and-Leaf Plots, p. 16

▶ The frequency of data can be displayed in a **histogram**, a type of bar graph.

▶ Individual data items can be displayed in **stem-and-leaf plots**.

**Daily High Temperature (°F)**

| 80 | 91 | 68 | 92 | 86 | 69 | 71 | 75 | 90 | 86 |
|----|----|----|----|----|----|----|----|----|----|
| 70 | 91 | 83 | 81 | 79 | 78 | 99 | 76 | 80 | 86 |
| 90 | 71 | 79 | 86 | 90 | 76 | 84 | 78 | 88 | 81 |

**15.** Use a frequency table to make a histogram of the data using intervals of 5 starting with 65. See additional answers.

**16.** Make a stem-and-leaf plot of the data. See additional answers.

**17.** Locate the greatest gap in the data. between 92 and 99

**18.** How many days had a high temperature below 80°? 12 days

## LESSON 1-4 ■ Scatter Plots and Lines of Best Fit, p. 20

▶ A **scatter plot** shows data grouped as ordered pairs and graphed as points on a grid. The points are not connected.

▶ A **line of best fit**, or **trend line**, on a scatter plot indicates either a **positive**, **negative**, or **no correlation** between items of data.

**19.** In the scatter plot, what is the correlation between points scored and minutes played? positive

**20.** Predict how many points Carrie would score if she played 24 min in one game. 16

**21.** Predict how many points Carrie would score if she played 30 minutes. 25

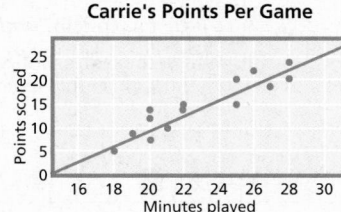

**Carrie's Points Per Game**

## LESSON 1-5 ■ Problem Solving Skills: Coefficient of Correlation, p. 26

▶ The coefficient of correlation is a statistical measure of how closely data fits a line.

**Predict the characteristics of the correlation between the two variables. Find the coefficient of correlation to check your prediction.**

**22.**

| $x$ | 1.5 | 2.6 | 3 | 4 | 4.3 | 5 | 1 | 1 | 2 | 2 | 3.4 | 5.7 | 6 | 6 |
|-----|-----|-----|---|---|-----|---|---|---|---|---|-----|-----|---|---|
| $y$ | 0.5 | 1.5 | 2.5 | 3 | 4 | 4 | 1 | 2 | 2 | 3.5 | 4 | 6 | 6 | 5.8 |

positive; $r = 0.91$

**23.**

| $x$ | 4 | 7 | 8 | 5 | 3 | 1 | 6 | 9 | 2 | 10 |
|-----|---|---|---|---|---|---|---|---|---|----|
| $y$ | 5 | 3 | 1 | 7 | 5 | 6 | 2 | 3 | 7 | 1 |

negative; $r = -0.83$

**State whether each of the following sets of variables would show a positive, negative, or zero correlation.**

**24.** your height and month of your birth zero

**25.** temperature and the cost of heating bill negative

## ADDITIONAL ANSWERS

**15.**

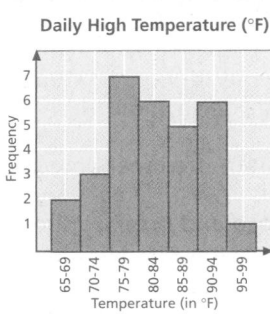

Daily High Temperature (°F)

**16.** **Daily High Temperature (°F)**

```
6 | 8  9
7 | 0  1  1  5  6  6  6  8  8  9  9
8 | 0  0  1  1  3  4  6  6  6  6  8
9 | 0  0  0  1  1  2  9
```

6 | 8 represents 68°F.

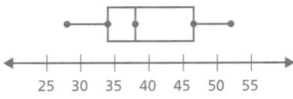
## LESSON 1-6 ■ Quartiles and Percentiles, p. 28

▶ **Box-and-whisker-plots** are used to display the distribution of data.

▶ A **percentile** represents the percent of scores at or below a particular score by dividing the number of scores less than or equal to a given score by the total number of scores.

26. Make a box-and-whisker plot of the data for Exercises 13–14.   See additional answers.

27. What is the interquartile range of the data for Exercises 13–14?   12.5

28. Out of 30 students who took a test, Darius had the fifth highest score. What is his percentile rank?   87

## LESSON 1-7 ■ Misleading Graphs and Statistics, p. 34

▶ **Misleading data** is data that leads to a false perception.

**Average Monthly Temp. (°F) at Sand City Resort**

| J | F | M | A | M | J | J | A | S | O | N | D |
|---|---|---|---|---|---|---|---|---|---|---|---|
| 45° | 50° | 70° | 82° | 88° | 97° | 98° | 95° | 80° | 50° | 50° | 40° |

29. Which measure(s) of central tendency would make this beach resort seem a little too cold for swimming?   mode

30. Which measure(s) of central tendency would the beach resort use to encourage people to come to the resort to swim?   median

## LESSON 1-8 ■ Use Matrices to Organize Data, p. 38

▶ A **matrix** is a rectangular arrangement of data in rows and columns enclosed by brackets.

$$A = \begin{bmatrix} 3 & 10 \\ 5 & 6 \\ 11 & 4 \\ 8 & 1 \\ 0 & 5 \end{bmatrix} \quad B = \begin{bmatrix} 7 & 13 \\ 6 & 6 \\ 9 & 2 \\ 0 & 3 \\ 7 & 2 \end{bmatrix}$$

31. Give the elements of $A$.   3, 10, 5, 6, 11, 4, 8, 1, 0, 5

32. Name the dimensions of $A$.   $5 \times 2$

33. Find $A + B$.   For 33–34, see additional answers.

34. Find $A - B$.

## CHAPTER INVESTIGATION

**EXTENSION** Present to the class your recommendations to the manager. Be sure to include advertisement suggestions, what to offer, and claims that the cafeteria can use to support your findings. After all groups have presented, as a class, discuss the differences and similarities in the findings and recommendations among the groups. What did each group do to get different results? How could the statistical graphs and measures have been used to mislead the students? How would the presentation differ if the class unites the data from each group and makes visual displays and recommendations?

### THEME: Market Research

The benchmarks and expectations for this extension are as follows.
• Students choose a sampling method for a survey to advertise cafeteria products and services to students. They determine the method of delivery and how to eliminate polling the same students more than once. They write a summary, write survey questions, and execute the plan.
• Students determine the information to highlight about the cafeteria. They calculate the mean, median, mode, range, and percentiles.
• Students compare the different types of visual displays and their data. They choose and prepare the statistical graphs and measures that best represent their recommendations.
• Students present to the class recommendations for the cafeteria.

# Chapter 1 Assessment

To find out the most popular breed of dog, every tenth person who entered a pet shop one Saturday was asked to name one favorite breed.

1. What kind of sampling method is being used? systematic, convenience

2. How might the results of this survey be biased? Answers will vary.

**The histogram shows the number of hours worked each week by part-time employees.**

3. What is the most common number of hours worked? 30–34

4. How many employees work less than 20 h? 14

5. How many part-time employees are there? 47

**Hours Worked by Employees**

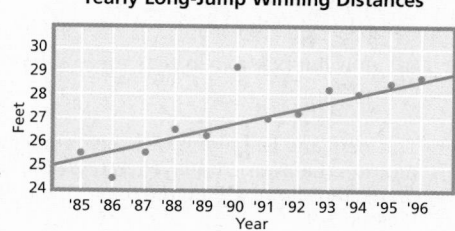

**A hotel charges the following daily rates for its different types of rooms.**

$75    $120    $65    $84    $150    $79

6. Find the mean, median, mode, and range of these data. mean = $95.50; median = $81.50; no mode; range = $85

7. The hotel used the median to advertise its average room rate. Is this misleading? Explain. Yes. No room costs $81.50 and most rooms cost more.

**The number of games won by a certain baseball team during the past eleven seasons is shown in the stem-and-leaf plot.**

| 4 | 7 8 9 9 |
| 5 | 0 1 8 9 |
| 6 | 1 2 |
| 8 | 3 |

4 | 8 represents 48 games.

8. During how many seasons did the team win 50 or fewer games? 5

9. What is the range of the number of games won? 36

10. During how many seasons did the team win more than 60 games? 3

**Use the scatter plot for Exercises 11–12.**

11. Is there a positive or negative correlation between the year and distance? positive

12. Predict the winning distance for the 1996 long-jump. ≈ 29 ft

13. On a test, Susan had the fourth highest score. If there were 30 students who took the test, what is Susan's percentile rank? 90

14. Predict the characteristics of the correlation between the two variables. Find the coefficient of correlation to check your prediction. negative; $r = -0.98$

**Yearly Long-Jump Winning Distances**

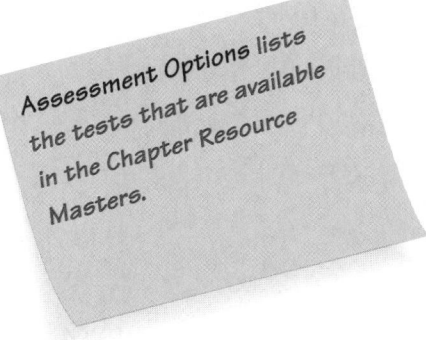

| x | 1 | 6 | 3 | 1 | 2 | 4 | 3 | 2 | 5 | 6 |
| y | 8 | 1 | 4 | 9 | 6 | 3 | 5 | 7 | 2 | 0 |

**Use matrices A and B for Exercises 15–18.**

15. Give the elements of A. 10, 3, 8, 9, 3, 7

16. Give the dimensions of B. $3 \times 2$

17. Find $A + B$.

18. Find $A - B$.

For 17–18, see additional answers.

$$A = \begin{bmatrix} 10 & 3 \\ 8 & 9 \\ 3 & 7 \end{bmatrix} \quad B = \begin{bmatrix} 4 & -3 \\ -1 & 0 \\ 7 & 3 \end{bmatrix}$$

Math Online mathmatters2.com/chapter_assessment

## ADDITIONAL ANSWERS

17. $\begin{bmatrix} 14 & 0 \\ 7 & 9 \\ 10 & 10 \end{bmatrix}$    18. $\begin{bmatrix} 6 & 6 \\ 9 & 9 \\ -4 & 4 \end{bmatrix}$

Assessment Options lists the tests that are available in the Chapter Resource Masters.

## Assessment Options

Chapter 1 Test A, pages 27–28
Chapter 1 Test B, pages 29–30

## ALTERNATIVE ASSESSMENT

**GRAPHING RESULTS** Have students create their own marketing survey around a question such as "What brand of soap do you prefer?" Students should then survey at least 100 people, noting their sex and age as well as their responses. Students can use a computer graphing program to compile their results. They should show results by both sex and age in at least two different formats. If a graphing program is not available, the graphs can be drawn by hand. Encourage students to include color in their graphs to emphasize their results.

**RUBRIC** The following rubric is a sample scoring guide.

| Points | Description |
|--------|-------------|
| 4 | Conducts survey with appropriate questions. Gives **very convincing report** using measures of central tendency and one or more graphs. |
| 3 | Conducts survey with appropriate questions. Gives **fairly convincing report** using measure of central tendency and one graph. |
| 2 | Conducts survey with some appropriate questions. Makes **minor errors in fairly convincing report** using measure of central tendency and one graph. |
| 1 | Conducts survey with some appropriate questions. Makes **several errors in report** using measure of central tendency and one graph. |
| 0 | Makes **no attempt** to conduct a survey. |

## Standardized Test Practice

These two pages contain practice questions in the various formats that can be found on the most frequently given standardized tests.

A student recording sheet for these two pages can be found on p. A1 of the *Chapter 1 Resource Masters*.

### Standardized Test Practice Student Recording Sheet

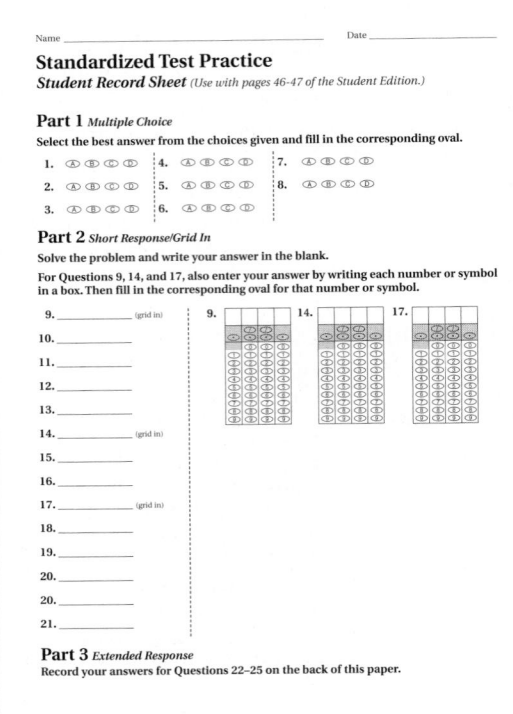

### Additional Practice

See pp. 31–33 in the *Chapter 1 Resource Masters* for additional standardized test practice.

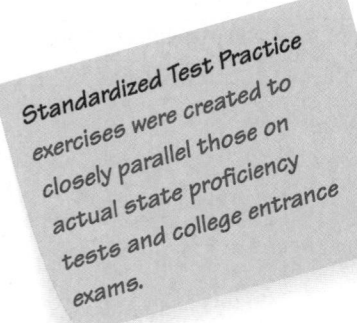

Standardized Test Practice exercises were created to closely parallel those on actual state proficiency tests and college entrance exams.

---

# Standardized Test Practice

### Part 1   Multiple Choice

**Record your answers on the answer sheet provided by your teacher or on a sheet of paper.**

1. You will be collecting information on how athletes at your school view good sportsmanship. Each of the coaches have sent you a roster. You plan to write the names on pieces of paper and select 20 names out of a hat to choose the students you will interview. What type of sampling is this method?   (Lesson 1-1)  C
   - Ⓐ cluster sampling
   - Ⓑ convenience sampling
   - Ⓒ random sampling
   - Ⓓ systematic sampling

2. What measure of central tendency is determined by finding the middle value when the data are arranged in numerical order? (Lesson 1-2)  B
   - Ⓐ mean
   - Ⓑ median
   - Ⓒ mode
   - Ⓓ range

3. You have test scores of 86, 87, and 90. You would like a mean score of 90 for the end of the semester. If all your tests are weighted the same and the highest score is 100, what is the lowest score you must get on the fourth and final test? (Lesson 1-2)  B
   - Ⓐ 95
   - Ⓑ 97
   - Ⓒ 99
   - Ⓓ It is not possible to get a mean score of 90.

4. The stem and leaf plot shows the number of minutes that music is played in one hour on nine radio stations. Find the range of the data. (Lesson 1-3)  B

   | 3 | 2 |
   |---|---|
   | 4 | 1 1 2 2 4 9 9 |
   | 5 | 0 |

   3|2 represents 32 min.

   - Ⓐ 9
   - Ⓑ 18
   - Ⓒ 42
   - Ⓓ 50

**Use the scatter plot for Questions 5–7.**

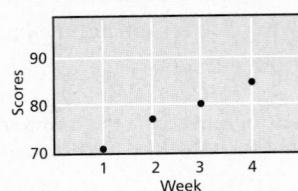

John's Quiz Scores

5. What kind of correlation does the data in the scatter plot show? (Lesson 1-4)  A
   - Ⓐ positive
   - Ⓑ negative
   - Ⓒ no correlation
   - Ⓓ cannot be determined

6. On a quiz, John's score was fifth from the highest in a class of 30 students. Find the percentile rank that John achieved. (Lesson 1-6)  C
   - Ⓐ 20th
   - Ⓑ 83rd
   - Ⓒ 87th
   - Ⓓ 95th

7. Which part of the graph is misleading? (Lesson 1-7)  B
   - Ⓐ x-axis
   - Ⓑ y-axis
   - Ⓒ title
   - Ⓓ The graph is not misleading.

8. Find the second quartile in the data. (Lesson 1-6)  D

   14.1, 16.4, 12.3, 10.9, 12.0, 9.2, 15.5

   - Ⓐ 10.9
   - Ⓑ 12.0
   - Ⓒ 12.2
   - Ⓓ 12.3

**Test-Taking Tip**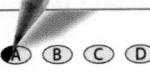

**Question 6**
If you don't know how to solve a problem, eliminate the answer choices you know are incorrect and then guess from the remaining choices. Even eliminating one answer choice greatly increases your chance of guessing the correct answer.

---

## ADDITIONAL ANSWERS

19. $\begin{bmatrix} 9 & -10 \\ 8 & 3 \\ -9 & 10 \end{bmatrix}$

20. $\begin{bmatrix} 1 & -10 \\ 8 & 3 \\ -9 & 10 \end{bmatrix}$

22.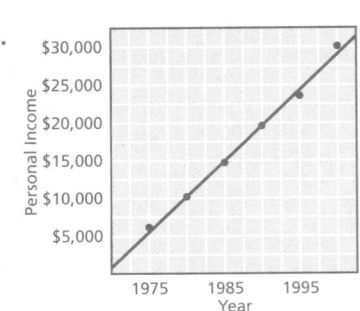

## Part 2 | Short Response/Grid In

Record your answers on the answer sheet provided by your teacher or on a sheet of paper.

The graph shows the number of heads that resulted from 10 tosses of a coin for each student in a group of 30 students. Use the graph for Questions 9-14. (Lesson 1-2)

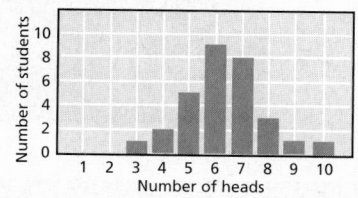

**9.** How many students got 4 heads in 10 coin tosses? 2

**10.** How many students got 2 tails in 10 coin tosses? 8

**11.** What is the mean of the data? 6.3

**12.** What is the mode of the data? 6

**13.** What is the median of the data? 6

**14.** What is the range of the data? 7

**15.** The table shows the average cost of a loaf of bread from 1960–2000. What type of relationship is shown from the data? (Lesson 1-4) positive

| Year | 1960 | 1970 | 1980 | 1990 | 2000 |
|------|------|------|------|------|------|
| Cents | 20 | 24 | 52 | 72 | 99 |

South Central High School's band and flag corps scored the following number of points during its performances this past season. Use the data for Questions 16–18. (Lesson 1-6)

27, 32, 6, 24, 29, 30, 8, 26, 30, 32

**16.** Find the first, second, and third quartiles of the data. $Q_1 = 24$, $Q_2 = 28$, $Q_3 = 30$

**17.** What is the interquartile range? 6

**18.** Name any outliers? 6, 8

 **Math Online** mathmatters2.com/standardized_test

Use matrices $A$ and $B$ for Questions 19 and 20. (Lesson 1-8) 19–20. See additional answers.

$$A = \begin{bmatrix} 5 & -3 \\ 8 & 2 \\ -1 & 5 \end{bmatrix} \quad B = \begin{bmatrix} 4 & 7 \\ 0 & -1 \\ 8 & -5 \end{bmatrix}$$

**19.** Find $A + B$.

**20.** Find $A - B$.

**21.** Name the dimensions of matrix $K$. (Lesson 1-8) $2 \times 3$

$$K = \begin{bmatrix} 2 & 7 & -10 \\ -9 & 3 & 6 \end{bmatrix}$$

## Part 3 | Extended Response

Record your answers on a sheet of paper. Show your work.

The table shows the personal income of individuals from 1975 to 2000. Use the data for Questions 22 and 23.

| Year | Income |
|------|--------|
| 1975 | $6,166 |
| 1980 | $10,205 |
| 1985 | $14,738 |
| 1990 | $19,614 |
| 1995 | $23,571 |
| 2000 | $30,069 |

**22.** Make a scatter plot of the data. Sketch a trend line on your scatter plot. (Lesson 1-4) See additional answers.

**23.** Does the data show a positive or negative correlation? Find the coefficient of correlation. (Lesson 1-5) positive; $r = 0.997$

**24.** Describe a relationship that would show a negative correlation. (Lesson 1-5) See additional answers.

**25.** A music group has designed a new marketing campaign. Attendances at their recent concerts are 125, 55, 65, 98, and 112. They also opened for a big name band at the state fair where the attendance was 55,000. In their new brochure, the band claims that "Average attendance at concerts is over 9,000 people. Evaluate this claim. (Lesson 1-7) See additional answers.

## Rubrics

The following rubrics are sample scoring guides for short response and extended response questions.

### Short Response

| Points | Description |
|--------|-------------|
| 2 | The student demonstrates a **thorough understanding** of the mathematics of the task. The response may contain minor flaws that do not detract from the demonstration of a thorough understanding. |
| 1 | The student has provided a response that is only **partially correct.** |
| 0 | The student has provided a **completely incorrect** solution or no response at all. |

### Extended Response

| Points | Description |
|--------|-------------|
| 4 | The student demonstrates a **thorough understanding** of the mathematics of the task. The response contains minor flaws that do not detract from the demonstration of a thorough understanding. |
| 3 | The student demonstrates an **understanding** of the mathematics of the task. The response is essentially correct and demonstrates an essential but less than thorough understanding of the mathematics. |
| 2 | The student has demonstrated only a **partial understanding** of the mathematics of the task. Although the student may have used the correct approach to a solution or may have provided a correct solution, the work lacks an essential understanding of the underlying mathematical concepts. |
| 1 | The student has demonstrated a **very limited understanding** of the mathematics of the task. The response is incomplete and exhibits many flaws. |
| 0 | The student has provided a **completely incorrect** solution or no response at all. |

## ADDITIONAL ANSWERS

24. Sample answer: time spent studying, questions missed on test
25. Sample answer: The claim is misleading. The attendance at the state fair is driving up the mean. The median, 105, is a better measure of the average attendance.

# 2 Foundations of Algebra

| Lesson | Lesson Objectives | Pacing (days) | NCTM Standards | State/Local Objectives |
|--------|-------------------|---------------|----------------|------------------------|
| 2-1 | **Real Numbers** *(pp. 52–55)*<br>• Graph sets of numbers on a number line.<br>• Evaluate expressions with absolute value. | 1 | 1, 8, 10 | |
| 2-2 | **Order of Operations** *(pp. 56–59)*<br>• Evaluate numerical expressions using order of operations. | 2 | 1, 8, 10 | |
| 2-3 | **Write Variable Expressions** *(pp. 62–65)*<br>• Write variable expressions to represent word phrases.<br>• Write word phrases to represent variable expressions. | 1 | 8, 9, 10 | |
| 2-4 | **Add and Subtract Variable Expressions** *(pp. 66–69)*<br>• Simplify variable expressions.<br>• Evaluate variable expressions. | 2 | 8, 9, 10 | |
| 2-5 | **Multiply and Divide Variable Expressions** *(pp. 72–75)*<br>• Simplify variable expressions.<br>• Evaluate variable expressions. | 2 | 8, 9, 10 | |
| 2-6 | **Simplify Variable Expressions** *(pp. 76–79)*<br>• Add, subtract, multiply, and divide to simplify variable expressions. | 2 | 8, 9, 10 | |
| 2-7 | **Properties of Exponents** *(pp. 82–85)*<br>• Choose appropriate units of measure.<br>• Evaluate variable expressions. | 2 | 2, 8, 9, 10 | |
| 2-8 | **Zero and Negative Exponents** *(pp. 86–89)*<br>• Write numbers using zero and negative integers as exponents.<br>• Write numbers in scientific notation. | 1 | 8, 9, 10 | |
| 2-9 | **Problem Solving Skills: Find a Pattern** *(pp. 92–93)*<br>• Describe and extend sequences to solve problems. | 1 | 1, 2, 6, 9 | |
| Review | | 1 | | |
| Testing | | 1 | | |

**Key to NCTM Standards:**

*1=Number & Operations, 2=Algebra, 3=Geometry,*
*4=Measurement, 5=Data Analysis & Probability,*
*6=Problem Solving, 7=Reasoning & Proof,*
*8=Communication, 9=Connections, 10=Representation*

**Pacing:** Suggestions for the year can be found on page xvi.

# Chapter Resource Manager

**Chapter 2 Resource Masters**

FAST FILE

| Reteaching Activities | Extra Practice | Enrichment | Assessment | Basic Mathematics Review | Study Skills Activities | Lesson Warm-Ups Transparencies | Teaching Transparencies | Technology Activities | Materials Needed |
|---|---|---|---|---|---|---|---|---|---|
| 35 | 36 | 37 | | 45–49, 57, 59 | 6–7 | 4 | RF-7 | | ruler |
| 38 | 39 | 40 | | 41–44, 57, 59 | | 4 | TK-4, TK-5, RF-8 | 2-2 | calculator, toothpicks, Algeblocks and Basic Mat |
| 41 | 42 | 43 | | | | 5 | | | |
| 44 | 45 | 46 | | 41–44, 45–49, 57, 59 | | 5 | TK-4, TK-5, RF-8 | | Algeblocks and Basic Mat |
| 47 | 48 | 49 | | 41–44, 45–49 | 8–9 | 6 | TK-4, TK-6, RF-8 | | Algeblocks and Basic Mat |
| 50 | 51 | 52 | | | | 6 | RF-6, RF-8 | | |
| 53 | 54 | 55 | | 45–49 | | 7 | RF-9 | 2-7, 2-8 | calculator |
| 56 | 57 | 58 | | | 16 | 8 | RF-9, RF-10 | 2-7, 2-8 | grid paper, calculator |
| 59 | 60 | 61 | 65–71 | | | 8 | RF-1 | 2-9 | calculator |

## Quick Review Math Handbook, Book 2

*hot* **words**
*hot* **topics**

| MathMatters 2 Lesson(s) | Hot Topic Lesson(s) | MathMatters 2 Lesson(s) | Hot Topic Lesson(s) |
|---|---|---|---|
| 2-1 | 1-5 | 2-6 | 6-2 |
| 2-2 | 1-3 | 2-7 | 3-1 |
| 2-3 | 6-1 | 2-8 | 3-1, 3-3 |
| 2-4, 2-5 | 6-2, 6-3 | 2-9 | 4-2 |

# Content and Connections

## Connections to the Past

**MM1 (Ch 3):** Categorize numbers according to sets.

**MM1 (Ch. 3):** Evaluate expressions with absolute value.

**MM1 (Ch. 3):** Use order of operations to evaluate expressions.

**MM1 (Ch. 3):** Write and evaluate variable expressions.

**MM1 (Ch. 3):** Add and subtract signed numbers.

**MM1 (Ch. 3):** Multiply and divide signed numbers.

**MM1 (Ch. 3):** Use order of operations to evaluate expressions.

**MM1 (Ch. 3):** Apply the laws of exponents.

**MM1 (Ch. 3):** Express numbers in exponential form.

**MM1 (Ch. 3):** Make a table and look for a pattern to solve a problem.

## MathMatters 2 Chapter 2 Highlights

Graph sets of numbers on a number line. (2-1)

Evaluate expressions with absolute value. (2-1)

Evaluate numerical expressions using order of operations. (2-2)

Write variable expressions to represent word phrases. (2-3)

Simplify and evaluate variable expressions using addition and subtraction. (2-4)

Simplify and evaluate variable expressions using multiplication and division. (2-5)

Add, subtract, multiply, and divide to simplify variable expressions. (2-6)

Choose appropriate units of measure and evaluate variable expressions. (2-7)

Write numbers using zero and negative integers as exponents.(2-8)

Describe and extend sequences to solve problems. (2-9)

## Connections to the Future

**MM2 (Ch. 6) and MM3 (Ch. 2):** Graph a linear inequality with two variables.

**MM3 (Ch. 2):** Evaluate absolute value functions.

**MM3 (Ch. 1):** Multiply and divide rational numbers.

**MM2 (Ch. 3) and MM3 (Ch. 3):** Solve one-step equations.

**MM2 (Ch. 9) and MM3 (Ch. 11):** Simplify polynomials after applying arithmetic operations.

**MM2 (Ch. 9) and MM3 (Ch. 11):** Multiply binomials and factor polynomials.

**MM2 (Ch. 8) and MM3 (Ch. 6):** Solve systems of equations by adding, subtracting, and multiplying.

**MM2 (Ch. 9) and MM3 (Ch. 11):** Use rules of exponents to multiply monomials.

**MM3 (Ch. 1):** Simplify and evaluate variable expressions with negative exponents.

**MM3 (Ch. 2):** Identify the rule in an iterative process.

## Key

| | |
|---|---|
| PC | = Previous Course |
| MM1 | = *MathMatters 1* |
| MM2 | = *MathMatters 2* |
| MM3 | = *MathMatters 3* |

## Connecting the Strands

| NCTM Strand | Lesson(s) |
|---|---|
| Number & Operations | 2-1, 2-2, 2-9 |
| Algebra | 2-7, 2-9 |
| Problem Solving | 2-9 |
| Communication | 2-1, 2-2, 2-3, 2-4, 2-5, 2-6, 2-7 |
| Connections | 2-3, 2-4, 2-5, 2-6, 2-7, 2-8, 2-9 |
| Representation | 2-1, 2-2, 2-3, 2-4, 2-5, 2-6, 2-7, 2-8 |

# Ongoing Assessment and Intervention

| Type | Student Edition | Teacher Resources | Technology/Internet |
|---|---|---|---|
| **INTERVENTION** | | | |
| Ongoing | Are You Ready?, pp. 50–51<br>Check Understanding,<br>  pp. 63, 67, 86<br>Review and Practice Your Skills,<br>  pp. 60–61, 70–71, 80–81<br>Mid-Chapter Quiz, p. 71 | Lesson Warm-Ups<br>  Transparencies, pp. WU-4,<br>  WU-5, WU-6, WU-7, WU-8<br>Quick Assessment, *ATE* pp. 51,<br>  54, 58, 64, 68, 74, 78, 84,<br>  88, 93 | mathmatters2.com/extra_examples<br>mathmatters2.com/self_check_quiz |
| Mixed Review | pp. 55, 59, 65, 69, 75, 79,<br>  85, 89 | | |
| Error Analysis | You Make the Call, p. 79<br>Error Alert, p. 75 | Predictable Error, *ATE* pp. 62, 83<br>Teaching Tip, *ATE* pp. 53, 81 | |
| **ASSESSMENT** | | | |
| Standardized<br>Test Practice | pp. 98–99<br>Preparing for Standardized<br>  Tests, pp. 627–644 | Standardized Test Practice,<br>  *CRM* pp. 69–71 | mathmatters2.com/standardized_test |
| Open-Ended<br>Assessment | Chapter Investigation, pp. 49,<br>  59, 75, 89, 96 | Chapter Investigation, *ATE*<br>  p. 96<br>Alternative Assessment, *ATE*<br>  p. 97 | |
| Chapter<br>Assessment | Chapter Review, pp. 94–96<br>Chapter Assessment, p. 97 | Multiple-Choice Tests (Forms<br>  A and B), *CRM* pp. 65–68 | mathmatters2.com/chapter_assessment |

**Key to Abbreviations:** *ATE* = Annotated Teacher's Edition, *CRM* = Chapter Resource Masters

## Additional Intervention

***Basic Mathematics Review*** includes 80 lessons, consisting of an instructional page and a test page. This workbook also features a pretest, posttest, table of measurement equivalents, and calculator appendices.

## ExamView® Pro

Use ExamView® Pro Testmaker CD-ROM to:
- Create **multiple versions** of tests.
- Create **modified** tests for *inclusion* students with one mouse click.
- **Edit** existing questions and **add** your own questions.
- Build tests aligned with **state standards** using built-in **state curriculum correlations**.
- Change **English** tests to **Spanish** with one mouse click and vice versa.

# Foundations of Algebra

## THEME: Population

In all aspects of life, algebra is the foundation for expressing known and unknown quantities. You have been using algebraic concepts since you first started learning mathematics. These concepts continue to be used throughout life in both personal and professional situations.

Expressions, variables, and exponents are a few of the many algebra topics that are used when studying population data. Although the term population refers to the organisms that live in a specific area, population is usually connected with the number of people that live in the world, a country, a state, or a city.

- The attendance at a sporting event is a population. **Concession stand operators** (page 61) use the buying patterns of the population that regularly attend events to make decisions about inventory and product availability.

- **Commercial aircraft designers** (page 81) use data about the average weight of passengers and cargo to establish size and weight restrictions of airplanes.

Math Online
mathmatters2.com/chapter_theme

### Chapter Investigation
Use the internet and other resources to locate additional information about population density.

## Area and Populations of Ten Countries

| Country | Capital | Area (square kilometers) | Population |
|---|---|---|---|
| Bangladesh | Dhaka | 144,000 | 138,448,210 |
| Brazil | Brasilia | 8,511,965 | 182,032,604 |
| China, People's Republic of | Beijing | 9,596,960 | 1,286,975,468 |
| India | New Delhi | 3,287,590 | 1,049,700,118 |
| Indonesia | Jakarta | 1,919,440 | 234,893,453 |
| Japan | Tokyo | 377,835 | 127,214,499 |
| Nigeria | Abuja | 923,768 | 133,881,703 |
| Pakistan | Islamabad | 803,940 | 150,694,740 |
| Russia | Moscow | 17,075,200 | 144,526,278 |
| United States | Washington, D.C. | 9,629,091 | 290,342,554 |

## Data Activity: Area and Population of Ten Countries

**Use the table for Questions 1–5.**

1. How many countries in the table have a population less than Russia?  4

2. In the table, what is the capital of the country with the largest population?  Beijing

3. In the table, what is the capital of the country with the smallest population?  Abuja

4. What is the approximate area per person in the United States?
   $\approx 0.033 \text{ km}^2$ per person

5. Russia's population would have to increase by how many people to become ranked fifth most populous in the table?
   37,506,327

## CHAPTER INVESTIGATION

Population density is the number of people per square mile or square kilometer that live in a given location, such as a town, county, city, state, or country. For example, the population density of Indiana is 155. This means that for every square mile of Indiana, approximately 155 people live there.

### Working Together

The population density of a state is not necessarily the same as the population density of a city within that state. Choose a state and a city within that state to compare population densities. Use the Chapter Investigation icons to guide your group.

Chapter 2  **Foundations of Algebra**  49

## Project Planning Calendar

Name _____ Date _____

**CHAPTER 2 PROJECT PLANNING CALENDAR**

Benchmarks
a. Use an almanac or the internet to find the population and number of square miles or square kilometers of any state and a city in that state. *(Lesson 2-2)*
b. Calculate the population density of the state and city by dividing the population by its area in square miles or kilometers. *(Lesson 2-5)*
c. Compare the population density of the state and city. Explain similarities and differences. *(Lesson 2-8)*
d. Find the population density of your town or city. Compare the population, number of square miles and population density of your city with that of _____ population. *(Chapter*

PROJECT GOAL
To find the population density of your town or city and compare it to that of a city similar in population.

## Group Project Planner

Name _____ Date _____

**CHAPTER 2 GROUP PROJECT PLANNER**

Assignment _____ Objective _____

Group Members          Assigned Roles
1) _____        _____
2) _____        _____
3) _____        _____
4) _____        _____
5) _____        _____

_____ Done

# Refresher Skills

The skills on these two pages are skills that have been presented in previous math courses. Continuous review of basic math skills will make stronger math students. These skills are identified as necessary to be successful in Chapter 2.

## Skills Correlation Chart

| Skill | Lesson Number |
|---|---|
| Adding and Subtracting Fractions | 2-2, 2-4, 2-5 |
| Multiplying and Dividing Fractions | 2-1, 2-4, 2-5, 2-7 |
| Operations with Decimals | 2-1, 2-2, 2-4 |
| Absolute Value | 2-1 |
| Operations with Integers | 2-4, 2-5, 2-6 |

## Vocabulary

fraction
common denominator
reciprocal
multiple of 10

# Chalkboard Examples

## Adding and Subtracting Fractions

$$5\frac{1}{8} = 5\frac{1}{8} = 4\frac{9}{8}$$
$$-2\frac{3}{4} = 2\frac{6}{8} = 2\frac{6}{8}$$
$$\overline{\qquad\qquad\qquad 2\frac{3}{8}}$$

## Multiplying and Dividing Fractions

$$\frac{2}{15} \cdot \frac{5}{8} = \frac{\overset{1}{\cancel{2}}}{\underset{3}{\cancel{15}}} \cdot \frac{\overset{1}{\cancel{5}}}{\underset{4}{\cancel{8}}} = \frac{1 \cdot 1}{3 \cdot 4} = \frac{1}{12}$$

---

The skills on these two pages are ones you have already learned. Use the examples to refresh your memory and complete the exercises. For additional practice on these and more prerequisite skills, see pages 576–584.

## ADDING AND SUBTRACTING FRACTIONS

You will perform many computations in this chapter. Remember when adding and subtracting fractions, you must find a common denominator.

**Examples**

$$3\frac{1}{4} = 3\frac{3}{12}$$
$$+ 1\frac{5}{6} = 1\frac{10}{12}$$
$$\overline{\qquad 4\frac{13}{12} = 5\frac{1}{12}}$$

$$16\frac{2}{5} = 16\frac{8}{20} = 15\frac{28}{20}$$
$$- 7\frac{3}{4} = 7\frac{15}{20} = 7\frac{15}{20}$$
$$\overline{\qquad\qquad\qquad 8\frac{13}{20}}$$

**Add or subtract.**

1. $\frac{1}{3} + \frac{3}{8}$   $\frac{17}{24}$
2. $\frac{6}{7} + \frac{2}{9}$   $1\frac{5}{63}$
3. $2\frac{4}{5} + 6\frac{8}{9}$   $9\frac{31}{45}$
4. $3\frac{7}{8} + 1\frac{3}{4}$   $5\frac{5}{8}$
5. $\frac{5}{8} - \frac{1}{3}$   $\frac{7}{24}$
6. $\frac{7}{9} - \frac{1}{2}$   $\frac{5}{18}$
7. $6\frac{2}{3} - 5\frac{8}{9}$   $\frac{7}{9}$
8. $3\frac{1}{2} - \frac{6}{7}$   $2\frac{9}{14}$
9. $8\frac{4}{5} + 3\frac{1}{2}$   $12\frac{3}{10}$

## MULTIPLYING AND DIVIDING FRACTIONS

Common denominators are not needed when multiplying and dividing fractions. When multiplying fractions remember to find the product of all the denominators and the product of all the numerators.

Division problems are changed to multiplication problems by finding the reciprocal of the divisor.

**Examples**

$$2\frac{3}{8} \cdot \frac{5}{6} = \frac{19}{8} \cdot \frac{5}{6}$$
$$= \frac{95}{48}$$
$$= 1\frac{47}{48}$$

$$6\frac{2}{3} \div 1\frac{1}{2} = \frac{20}{3} \div \frac{3}{2}$$
$$= \frac{20}{3} \cdot \frac{2}{3}$$
$$= \frac{40}{9} = 4\frac{4}{9}$$

**Multiply or divide.**

10. $2\frac{1}{8} \cdot \frac{1}{4}$   $\frac{17}{32}$
11. $1\frac{6}{7} \cdot 1\frac{5}{6}$   $3\frac{17}{42}$
12. $5\frac{2}{3} \cdot 4\frac{3}{5}$   $26\frac{1}{15}$
13. $1\frac{1}{3} \div \frac{5}{6}$   $1\frac{3}{5}$
14. $2\frac{3}{4} \div 1\frac{7}{8}$   $1\frac{7}{15}$
15. $8\frac{3}{4} \div 4\frac{4}{9}$   $1\frac{31}{32}$
16. $6\frac{2}{3} \cdot 1\frac{5}{8} \div 3\frac{1}{2}$   $3\frac{2}{21}$
17. $4\frac{3}{4} \div 8\frac{2}{3} \cdot 7\frac{1}{5}$   $3\frac{123}{130}$
18. $4\frac{2}{3} + \left(6\frac{1}{8} \cdot 1\frac{1}{2}\right)$   $13\frac{41}{48}$

---

# Teaching Tip

Students should understand that when working with a common denominator, it is convenient to use the *least* common denominator so that they are working with smaller numbers.

Use the first Chalkboard Example to show how to handle a subtraction situation in which the fraction in the subtrahend is greater than the fraction in the minuend: rewrite the fraction in the minuend by borrowing one whole unit from the integer portion of the mixed number.

Use the second Chalkboard Example to show students that they can divide numerator and denominator by common factors ("cancel") before they multiply—thus, again, working with smaller numbers and avoiding the need for future simplification.

## OPERATIONS WITH DECIMALS

You will also be working with decimals in this chapter. Refresh your memory of how to work with decimals.

**Examples**

$$\begin{array}{r} 5.6 \\ + 0.034 \\ \hline 5.634 \end{array}$$

$$\begin{array}{r} 10.95 \\ - 4.063 \\ \hline 6.887 \end{array}$$

$$\begin{array}{r} 6.4 \\ \times 0.07 \\ \hline 0.448 \end{array}$$

$$\begin{array}{r} 2.6 \\ 4.6\overline{)11.96} \\ \underline{92} \\ 276 \\ \underline{276} \\ 0 \end{array}$$

**Simplify.**

**19.** $6.5 + 11.84$  18.34

**20.** $4 - 3.23$  0.77

**21.** $1.25 \cdot 0.9$  1.125

**22.** $0.088 \div 1.1$  0.08

**23.** $3.27 + 18.9$  22.17

**24.** $14.75 + 8.125$  22.875

**25.** $0.076 \cdot 1.5$  0.114

**26.** $0.1035 \div 0.23$  0.45

## ABSOLUTE VALUE

The *absolute value* of a number is the distance the number is from zero on a number line.

**Find each absolute value.**

**27.** $|-3|$  3

**28.** $|7|$  7

**29.** $|0|$  0

**30.** $\left|-\dfrac{1}{3}\right|$  $\dfrac{1}{3}$

**31.** $|0.7|$  0.7

**32.** $|-4|$  4

**33.** $|1|$  1

**34.** $|-47|$  47

## OPERATIONS WITH INTEGERS

The set $\{\ldots, -3, -2, -1, 0, 1, 2, 3, \ldots\}$ is the set of *integers*. Addition, subtraction, multiplication and division can be applied to integers.

To add numbers with the same signs, add their absolute values. The sign of the sum is the same sign as the numbers. To add numbers with different signs, subtract their absolute values. The sign of the sum is the sign of the number with the greater absolute value. To subtract a number, add its opposite.

The product or quotient of two numbers with the same sign is positive. The product or quotient of two numbers with different signs is negative.

**Examples**

$$4 + (-3) = 1 \qquad -3 - 8 = -3 + (-8) = -11 \qquad -4 \cdot 6 = -24 \qquad \dfrac{-18}{-6} = 3$$

**Perform the indicated operation.**

**35.** $5 + 7$  12

**36.** $17 - 20$  −3

**37.** $8 - (-3)$  11

**38.** $6 + (-2)$  4

**39.** $-7 \cdot 5$  −35

**40.** $\dfrac{-15}{3}$  −5

**41.** $-11.7 - 3.9$  −15.6

**42.** $\dfrac{-120}{-4}$  30

**43.** $12 - (-8) + 6$  26

**44.** $-3 \cdot (-3) \cdot 9$  81

**45.** $15 - 9 + (-27)$  −21

**46.** $4 \cdot (-8) \cdot 12$  −384

Chapter 2  **Are You Ready?**  51

---

Divide and round the quotient to the nearest tenth.

$$3.58\overline{)14.9}$$

$$\begin{array}{r} 4.16 \approx 4.2 \\ 3.58\overline{)14.90.00} \\ \underline{1432} \\ 580 \\ \underline{358} \\ 2220 \\ \underline{2148} \\ 72 \end{array}$$

**Mental Math**
Use the distributive property to find each value.

$$937 \cdot 0.8 + 937 \cdot 0.2 = 937(0.8 + 0.2)$$
$$= 937(1)$$
$$= 937$$

$$36\left(\dfrac{1}{3} + \dfrac{1}{4}\right) = 36 \cdot \dfrac{1}{3} + 36 \cdot \dfrac{1}{4}$$
$$= 12 + 9$$
$$= 21$$

## Refresher Wrap-up

### QUICK ASSESSMENT

Ask the following questions to determine if students have mastered the basic skills reviewed on these pages.

1. In which operations with fractions must you first get a common denominator?  **addition and subtraction**
2. How do you determine the number of decimal places in a product?  **Add the number of decimal places in the multiplier and the multiplicand.**

### ADDITIONAL PRACTICE

Refer to the Prerequisite Skills lessons beginning on page 576 for more practice. The following lesson references are to *Basic Mathematics Review*.

■ Adding and Subtracting Fractions: Lessons 41-44
■ Multiplying and Dividing Fractions: Lessons 45-49
■ Operations with Decimals: Lessons 57, 59

---

## Extend the Lesson

**CONNECTING TO PRIOR KNOWLEDGE** When adding or subtracting decimals, students should understand that they first align numbers on the decimal point. You may wish to have students use zeros as placeholders so that they equalize the number of places in the addends or between minuend and subtrahend.

From the third Chalkboard Example, point out that the number of decimal places in the divisor determines how many places the decimal point should be moved. As needed, zeros may be added after the decimal point in the dividend.

When an answer is to be rounded, note with students that the division should be carried to one place more than the place required for the answer.

**NCTM Standards/Strands**
- Number & Operations
- Representation
- Connections

## Vocabulary

integers      opposites
rational numbers
terminating decimal
repeating decimal
irrational numbers
real numbers
coordinate of a point
graph of a number
absolute value
opposite of the opposite property

## Tools/Materials Needed

ruler

## Lesson Resources

Warm-up Transparency 4
Transparency RF-7
Reteaching 2-1
Extra Practice 2-1
Enrichment 2-1

## Getting Started

### 5-Minute Warm-up

Select a type of number appropriate to represent the situations
described below. More than one
selection is possible for a
situation.
**A.** fraction      **B.** decimal
**C.** negative number
**D.** whole number
1. the number of people in a
room  **D**
2. the length of a line segment
**A, B, D**

### Introduction to Lesson 2-1
After students have answered Questions 1–4, emphasize the usefulness
of a number line to represent a
situation and how the numbers
involved dictate the labels that go
on the number line.

---

# 2-1 Real Numbers

**Goals**
- Graph sets of numbers on a number line.
- Evaluate expressions with absolute value.

**Applications**    Weather, Sports, Population

**Work in a group of two or three students.**

**Joe's Family**

| Family member | Birth year |
|---|---|
| Father | 1957 |
| Mother | 1959 |
| Joe | 1984 |
| Sister | 1988 |
| Brother | 1992 |

1. Copy the number line. Place a point on the birth year of each
family member. Label each point with the person's name.
See additional answers.

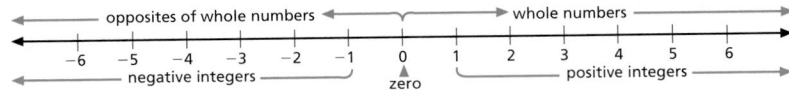

2. If Joe's birth year were equal to 0, what numbers would
correspond with the following events?

    **a.** mother's birth    **b.** father's birth    **c.** brother's birth    **d.** sister's birth
    &minus;25        &minus;27        8        4

3. Redraw the time line using positive and negative numbers.  See additional answers.

4. Construct two time lines using you and your family's birth years. One should
use the actual years and another should use positive and negative numbers.
Answers will vary.

### ▮ BUILD UNDERSTANDING

The set of **integers** consists of the whole numbers and their opposites. **Opposites** of
whole numbers are the same distance from zero but in the opposite direction.

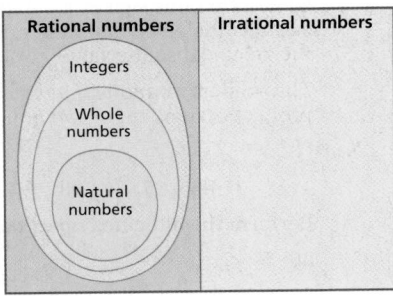

Positive integers are greater than zero. Negative integers are less than zero. Zero
is neither positive nor negative. Zero is its own opposite.

A **rational number** is a number that can be expressed as a ratio of two integers $a$
and $b$, where $b$ is not equal to zero. This is usually written $\frac{a}{b}$, $b \neq 0$. The symbol $\neq$
means "is not equal to."

**Real Numbers**

All rational numbers can be expressed as **terminating
decimals** or **repeating decimals**. Some numbers, such as
$\pi$ (pi) and $\sqrt{2}$, are non-terminating and non-
repeating decimals. Such numbers are called **irrational
numbers**. Together the set of rational and irrational
numbers make up the set of **real numbers**.

| Rational numbers | Irrational numbers |
|---|---|
| Integers | |
| Whole numbers | |
| Natural numbers | |

The number that corresponds to a point on a number
line is called the **coordinate of the point**. Each real
number corresponds to exactly one point on a
number line. The point that corresponds to a number
is called the **graph of the number** and is indicated on the
number line by a solid dot. Each point on a number
line corresponds to exactly one real number.

**52**    Chapter 2  **Foundations of Algebra**

---

### ADDITIONAL ANSWERS

1.
Mother, 1959    Joe, 1984    Brother, 1992
1950  1960  1970  1980  1990
Father, 1957    Sister, 1988

3.  Father  Mother    Joe  Sister  Brother
  &minus;27  &minus;25    0  4  8

### Teaching Tip

In the Examples and Supplementary Examples, the number lines
are displayed horizontally. Remind
students that number lines can
also be drawn in a vertical position. The Fahrenheit and Celsius
temperature scales are generally
shown in a vertical display.

## Example 1

Graph the set of numbers $\{0.25, -1, -2\frac{3}{4}, -4\}$ on a number line.

### Solution

Draw a number line. Use a solid dot to graph each number.

### Reading Math

A **set** is a collection of objects, such as a set of integers or the set of whole numbers. Objects in the set are called **members**, or **elements**, of the set.

A set is indicated by braces { } enclosing the names of set members.

## Example 2

Use a number line to compare numbers. Replace each ■ with <, > or =.

a. $-3$ ■ $1$    b. $2$ ■ $0$    c. $\frac{1}{4}$ ■ $-\frac{3}{4}$

### Solution

Draw a number line and graph each number.

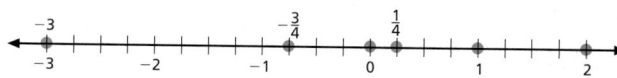

a. $-3$ is to the left of 1, so $-3 < 1$.

b. $2$ is to the right of 0, so $2 > 0$.

c. $\frac{1}{4}$ is to the right of $-\frac{3}{4}$, so $\frac{1}{4} > -\frac{3}{4}$.

## Example 3

Graph each set of numbers on a number line.

a. the integers from $-3$ to $2$     b. the real numbers from $-3$ to $2$

c. all real numbers less than or equal to $2$     d. all real numbers greater than $-1$

### Solution

a. The set consists of $-3, -2, -1, 0, 1,$ and $2$. To graph the set, put a solid dot at each of these points on the number line.

b. The set consists of $-3$ and $2$ and all real numbers between. Graph the set by drawing solid dots at $-3$ and $2$ and connecting the two points.

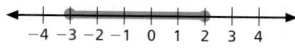

c. The set consists of $2$ and all real numbers less than 2. Graph the set by drawing an arrow beginning at 2 and pointing to the left. To indicate that 2 is part of the set, draw a solid dot at 2.

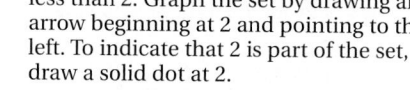

d. The set consists of all real numbers greater than $-1$. Graph the set by drawing an arrow beginning at $-1$ and pointing to the right. To indicate that $-1$ is not part of the set, draw an open circle at $-1$.

## Chalkboard Examples

### Supplementary Example 1

On a number line, graph:
$$\left\{-\frac{1}{2}, \frac{5}{6}, \frac{2}{3}, -\frac{1}{6}\right\}$$

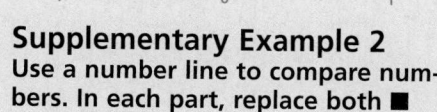

### Supplementary Example 2

Use a number line to compare numbers. In each part, replace both ■ with either > or <.

a. $-4$ ■ $0$ ■ $2$   $-4 < 0 < 2$

b. $-1$ ■ $-3$ ■ $-6$   $-1 > -3 > -6$

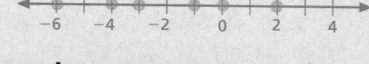

### Supplementary Example 3

Graph each set of numbers on a number line.

a. the real numbers that are greater than 2 or less than $-1$

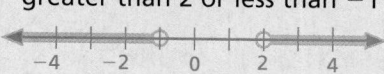

b. the real numbers that are greater than $-3$ and less than 2

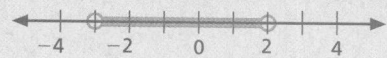

### Supplementary Example 4

Evaluate each expression.

a. $|m - 4|$ when $m = -3$
$|-3 - 4| = |-7| = 7$

b. $9 - |1 - k|$ when $k = 4$
$9 - |1 - 4| = 9 - |-3| = 9 - 3 = 6$

## Teaching Tip

From Supplementary Example 1, note with students that to compare fractions, the fractions must be expressed with a common denominator. When using a number line to compare fractions, the subdivisions represent the common denominator chosen. Here is another place to note the convenience of using the least common denominator rather than just any common denominator.

A **variable** is a symbol used to represent a number. Letters such as $a$ and $n$ can be used as variables.

The distance a number is from zero on the number line is the **absolute value** of the number. The absolute value of an integer $a$ is written as $|a|$.

The **opposite of the opposite** property states if $n$ is a real number then $-(-n) = n$.

### Example 4

Evaluate each expression.
a. $-t$, when $t = 2.7$
b. $-(-d)$, when $d = -\frac{1}{3}$
c. $|k|$, when $k = -6.5$
d. $-|-n|$, when $n = 12$

**Solution**
a. Since $t = 2.7$, $-t = -2.7$.
b. Since $d = -\frac{1}{3}$, $-(-d) = -\left[-\left(-\frac{1}{3}\right)\right] = -\frac{1}{3}$.
c. Since $k = -6.5$, $|k| = |-6.5| = 6.5$.
d. Since $n = 12$, $-|-n| = -|-12| = -12$.

### ■ TRY THESE EXERCISES

Graph the given sets of numbers on a number line.   For 1–3, see additional answers.

1. $\{2.5, 0.5, -1, -2\}$
2. $\left\{2\frac{2}{3}, 1\frac{1}{3}, -1\frac{2}{3}, -2\frac{1}{3}\right\}$
3. $\{-3.75, -2.5, 0, 2.25, 5.75\}$

Use a number line to compare numbers.   Replace each ■ with $<$, $>$, or $=$.

4. $2 \; \blacksquare \; -2$   $>$
5. $0 \; \blacksquare \; 3$   $<$
6. $-2\frac{2}{3} \; \blacksquare \; 1\frac{1}{3}$   $<$

Graph each set of numbers on a number line.   For 7–9, see additional answers.

7. whole numbers from 1 to 5
8. the integers from $-5$ to 1
9. all real numbers less than 4

Evaluate each expression.

10. $|n|$, when $n = 79$   79
11. $|x|$, when $x = 0$   0
12. $|w|$, when $w = -212$   212
13. $-r$, when $r = 3$   $-3$
14. $-|-k|$, when $k = -2$   $-2$
15. $-(-y)$, when $y = \frac{3}{4}$   $\frac{3}{4}$

### ■ PRACTICE EXERCISES  •  For Extra Practice, see page 588.

Graph each set of numbers on a number line.   For 16–21, see additional answers.

16. $\{-2, -0.75, 0, 1, 3\}$
17. $\left\{-5, -\frac{1}{2}, 0.25, 3\frac{1}{3}, 4.5\right\}$
18. the integers from $-7$ to $-2$
19. all real numbers greater than 6
20. all real numbers less than or equal to $-6\frac{1}{2}$
21. all real numbers between $-3$ and 3

22. **WRITING MATH** Explain what your graph looks like for Exercise 21. Did you use open or closed circles?   open circles with a solid line between

23. **WEATHER** In January the average temperature in Barrow, Alaska, is $-13°F$. In Fairbanks, Alaska, the average temperature in January is $-10°F$. Which place is warmer in January? Explain.   Fairbanks; $-10°F > -13°F$

**54** | Chapter 2 **Foundations of Algebra**

## ADDITIONAL ANSWERS

1.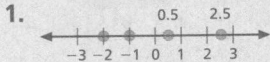

2.

3.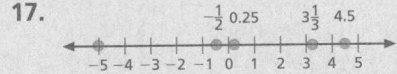

7.

8.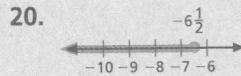

9.

16.

17.

18. 19.

20.

21.

**Replace each ■ with <, >, or =.**

24. $-3.5$ ■ $-2.8$  <
25. $|-9|$ ■ $9$  =
26. $5\frac{1}{3}$ ■ $5\frac{2}{5}$  <

27. $-4$ ■ $|-4|$  <
28. $|16|$ ■ $-|-20|$  >
29. $-|3|$ ■ $3$  <

**Evaluate each expression when $a = -4$, $b = 2\frac{1}{2}$, and $c = -8$.**

30. $-a$  4
31. $-|-b|$  $-2\frac{1}{2}$
32. $-(-c)$  $-8$
33. $-|a|$  $-4$

34. $-\left(\dfrac{c}{a}\right)$  $-2$
35. $-bc$  20
36. $|-ab|$  10
37. $-|abc|$  $-80$

38. **POPULATION** Between 1990 to 2002, the population changed $-5.9\%$ in Philadelphia, $4.4\%$ in Austin, and $-4.7$ in New Orleans. Which city had the greatest population decrease over the 12-yr period?  Philadelphia

**SPORTS** Golf scores are based on a number called par. The object is to score as far under par as possible. So a score of $-2$ is two strokes under par. The table shows four players' scores for a round of golf.

| Player | Final score |
|--------|-------------|
| Marcus | $-3$ |
| Darnesha | $+4$ |
| Joelle | $-1$ |
| Garrett | $+7$ |

39. Graph the set of scores on a number line.  See additional answers.

40. Which golfer had the best score?  Marcus

**Draw a number line for each situation.**  For 41–43, see additional answers.

41. Jamar's test scores were 76, 79, 80, 90 and 82.

42. Raja's GPA (grade point average) ranges from 3.25 to 3.6.

43. The temperature in Wisconsin ranges from $-15°$F to $105°$F.

■ **EXTENDED PRACTICE EXERCISES**

44. **CRITICAL THINKING** Explain what is meant by the statement "Every real number can be matched with a point on a number line."  Answers will vary but may include that the number line is the set of all real numbers.

**Write *true* or *false* for each statement. For any false statement, give an example that proves the statement is false.**

45. Between any two integers there is another integer.  False; there are no integers between 3 and 4.

46. Between any two rational numbers there is another rational number.  true

47. All negative numbers are rational numbers.  false; $-\pi$

48. For any real number $n$ where $n < 0$, $|n| = n$.  False; if $n > 0$, then $|n| = -n$.

 ■ **MIXED REVIEW EXERCISES**

**RECYCLING** A condominium association is considering making recycling bins available to the home owners. They want to know if the residents will recycle. They conducted a survey by asking all the owners who attended a home owner's meeting one evening. (Lesson 1-1)

49. What method of sampling did they use?  convenience sampling

50. Could the results of this survey be biased? How?  Yes. The responsible and concerned residents who are most likely to recycle are also the residents most likely to attend a home owner's meeting.

**Math Online** mathmatters2.com/self_check_quiz

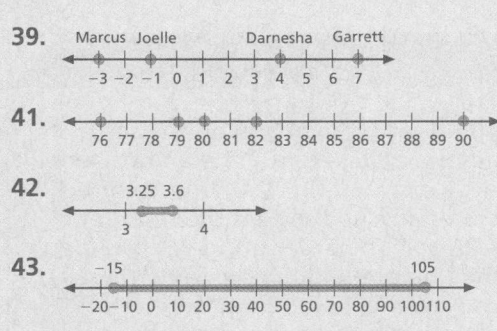

39.
Marcus  Joelle      Darnesha  Garrett
$-3$ $-2$ $-1$  0  1  2  3  4  5  6  7

41.
76 77 78 79 80 81 82 83 84 85 86 87 88 89 90

42.
3.25  3.6
3        4

43.
$-15$                    105
$-20$ $-10$  0  10 20 30 40 50 60 70 80 90 100 110

Name _____  Date _____

EXTRA PRACTICE  **2-1**
**REAL NUMBERS**

☑ **EXERCISES**

Graph each set of numbers on a number line.

1. $\{3.5, -1, 4.5, 0\}$
$-7$ $-6$ $-5$ $-4$ $-3$ $-2$ $-1$ 0 1 2 3 4 5 6 7

2. $\left\{-6, 2\frac{1}{2}, \frac{3}{4}, 1.25, -0.75\right\}$
$-7$ $-6$ $-5$ $-4$ $-3$ $-2$ $-1$ 0 1 2 3 4 5 6 7

3. all real numbers greater than $-2$
$-7$ $-6$ $-5$ $-4$ $-3$ $-2$ $-1$ 0 1 2 3 4 5 6 7

4. all integers from $-3$ to 7
$-7$ $-6$ $-5$ $-4$ $-3$ $-2$ $-1$ 0 1 2 3 4 5 6 7

Replace each __ with <, >, or =.

5. $-2.6$  >  $-5$
6. $|-7|$  >  $-7$
7. $4\frac{3}{5}$  >  $4\frac{7}{12}$

8. $8$  =  $|-8|$
9. $-|5|$  <  $-|-5|$
10. $-1\frac{4}{7}$  <  $3\frac{1}{8}$

Evaluate each expression when $a = -6$, $b = 3\frac{1}{3}$, and $c = -9$.

11. $-a$  _____ 6
12. $-|-c|$  _____ $-9$
13. $-|b|$  _____ $-3\frac{1}{3}$

14. $-(-a)$  _____ $-6$
15. $bc$  _____ $-30$
16. $-\left(\frac{a}{c}\right)$  _____ $-\frac{2}{3}$

Name _____  Date _____

ENRICHMENT  **2-1**
**DECIMAL EQUIVALENTS OF FRACTIONS**

To find the decimal equivalent to $\frac{1}{5}$, divide 1 by 5.

$$\begin{array}{r} 0.20 \\ 5\overline{)1.00} \\ \underline{1\,0} \\ 00 \\ \underline{00} \\ 0 \end{array}$$

Since the remainder is 0, the division process ends. The decimal equivalent to $\frac{1}{5}$ is a **terminating decimal**.

$$\frac{1}{5} = 0.2$$

To find the decimal equivalent to $\frac{1}{9}$, divide 1 by 9.

$$\begin{array}{r} 0.111 \\ 9\overline{)1.0000} \\ \underline{9} \\ 10 \\ \underline{9} \\ 10 \\ \underline{9} \\ 10 \end{array}$$

The remainder is not 0. The digit 1 repeats in the quotient. The decimal equivalent to $\frac{1}{9}$ is a **repeating decimal**.

$$\frac{1}{9} = 0.111\ldots \text{ or } 0.\overline{1}$$

☑ **EXERCISES**

Find the decimal equivalent of each fraction.

1. $\frac{3}{8}$
2. $\frac{5}{6}$
3. $\frac{2}{20}$
4. $\frac{2}{11}$
5. $\frac{1}{16}$
6. $\frac{5}{9}$

_0.375_  _$0.8\overline{3}$_  _0.35_  _$0.\overline{18}$_  _0.0625_  _$0.\overline{5}$_

7. Look at the denominators of the fractions that are equivalent to terminating decimals. What do you notice about the prime factors of these denominators?
__The prime factors are either 2 or 5.__

8. Look at the denominators of those fractions equivalent to repeating decimals. Are the prime factors the same as for fractions equivalent to terminating decimals?
__No; the prime factors are neither 2 nor 5, or there are factors in addition to 2 and 5.__

9. What conjecture can you use to determine whether a fraction has a terminating or repeating decimal as its equivalent?
__If the denominator has only 2 or 5 as prime factors, the decimal equivalent of the fraction terminates. If the denominator does not contain 2 or 5 as prime factors, or contains prime factors in addition to 2 or 5, the decimal will repeat.__

### Vocabulary

numerical expression
value                          simplify
order of operations            variable
variable expression            evaluate

### Tools/Materials Needed

calculator
Algeblocks and Basic Mat
toothpicks

### Lesson Resources

Warm-up Transparency 4
Transparency TK-4, 5, RF-8
Reteaching 2-2
Extra Practice 2-2
Enrichment 2-2
Technology Activity 2-2

## Getting Started

### 5-MINUTE WARM-UP

Perform the indicated operations.
1. $(-3)(2)$ **−6**    2. $6 + (-2)$ **4**
3. $-7 - 1$ **−8**    4. $-16 \div (-2)$ **8**

### Introduction to Lesson 2-2

Students should come away from
the activity with an understanding
that parentheses are a symbol of
grouping. When parentheses are
used in an expression such as
$(8 + 3) \cdot 5$, it is clear that 55 is the
only possible result.

---

# 2-2 | Order of Operations

**Goals**   ■ Evaluate numerical expressions using order of operations.

**Applications**   Part-time job, Fitness, Entertainment, Population

**Determine where the symbols $+$, $-$, $\times$, and $(\ )$ should be placed to make each sentence true.**

1. $8 \blacksquare 3 \blacksquare 5 = 55$   $(8 + 3) \times 5 = 55$
2. $5 \blacksquare 7 \blacksquare 6 \blacksquare 5 = 65$   $(5 \times 7) + (6 \times 5) = 65$
3. $6 \blacksquare 9 \blacksquare 7 = 96$   $6 \times (9 + 7) = 96$
4. Did you use parentheses in any of the above questions? If so, were they necessary to make the sentence true? Explain. Yes; they are needed to show the order of operations that makes the statement true.

### ■ BUILD UNDERSTANDING

A **numerical expression** is two or more numbers joined by operations such as addition, subtraction, multiplication, and division. Parentheses also can be used in a numerical expression.

$$2 + 7 - 4 \qquad\qquad 2 \div 7 + 4 \qquad\qquad 5 + 2(7 - 4)$$

The number represented by the numerical expression is called its **value**. When you find the value of the numerical expression, you **simplify** the expression.

### Example 1

**Simplify each numerical expression.**

**a.** $9.64 - 3.2$       **b.** $\frac{1}{2}(12) + 7$       **c.** $(60 \div 3) \cdot 4$

**Solution**

**a.** $9.64 - 3.2 = 6.44$       **b.** $\frac{1}{2}(12) + 7 = 6 + 7$       **c.** $(60 \div 3) \cdot 4 = 20 \cdot 4$
$\qquad\qquad\qquad\qquad\qquad\qquad\qquad\qquad = 13 \qquad\qquad\qquad\qquad\qquad = 80$

Without parentheses or rules, it is possible to get two different answers for the same expression. For this reason, it is important to follow the **order of operations**.

| **Order of Operations** | 1. First, perform all calculations within parentheses and brackets. |
| | 2. Then perform all calculations involving exponents. |
| | 3. Next, multiply or divide in order from left to right. |
| | 4. Finally, add or subtract in order from left to right. |

---

### Teaching Tip

After completing Supplementary Example 1, ask students to do the same
calculations but with no given parentheses. So, for $12 + 3 \cdot 4$, some students
may offer $15 \cdot 4 = 60$ as an answer and others $12 + 12 = 24$. Who is correct?
Emphasize that an *order of operations* is established so that the result of a
calculation is *unique*, only one correct answer. The order of operations speci-
fies that multiplication is to be performed before addition; so, now there is
a correct answer to $12 + 3 \cdot 4$, and that answer is $12 + 12 = 24$.
Emphasize that in the order of operations, a left-to-right order does apply,
but only when dealing with strings of multiplications and divisions or with
strings of additions and subtractions.

An **exponent** tells how many times a number is used as a factor. The small number written to the upper right of the factor is the exponent.

## Example 2

**Simplify each numerical expression.**

**a.** $(4 + 3) \cdot 5^2$  **b.** $55 - 7 - 12 \div 4$  **c.** $2^3 \cdot (6 - 3)$

### Solution

**a.** $(4 + 3) \cdot 5^2 = 7 \cdot 5^2$  **b.** $55 - 7 - 12 \div 4 = 55 - 7 - 3$  **c.** $2^3 \cdot (6 - 3) = 2^3 \cdot 3$

$= 7 \cdot 25$  $= 48 - 3$  $= 8 \cdot 3$

$= 175$  $= 45$  $= 24$

An expression containing one or more variables is called a **variable expression**.

Variable expressions that involve multiplication can be written with or without the $\times$ sign, with the symbol $\cdot$ or with parentheses. Each of the variable expressions below represents the product of 6 and the variable $m$.

$6 \times m$  $6 \cdot m$  $6(m)$  $6m$

Similarly, the following expressions all represent division.

$n \div 6$  $6\overline{)n}$  $\dfrac{n}{6}$  $n/6$

To **evaluate** a variable expression, substitute a given number for each variable. Then simplify the numerical expression.

**Reading Math**

Read the expression $9y^2 \div 15$ as "nine y squared divided by 15."

Read the expression $\frac{1}{2}(x - 5)$ as "one-half times the quantity x minus 5."

## Example 3

**Evaluate each variable expression when $n = 1.8$.**

**a.** $7 + n^2$  **b.** $\frac{1}{3}n + 2.7$  **c.** $(4.6 - n) \div 4$  **d.** $n \cdot 3^2 + 45 \div 9$

### Solution

In each expression, substitute 1.8 for $n$.

**a.** $7 + n^2 = 7 + (1.8)^2$  **b.** $\frac{1}{3}n + 2.7 = \frac{1}{3}(1.8) + 2.7$

$= 7 + 3.24$  $= 0.6 + 2.7$

$= 10.24$  $= 3.3$

**c.** $(4.6 - n) \div 4 = (4.6 - 1.8) \div 4$  **d.** $n \cdot 3^2 + 45 \div 9 = 1.8 \cdot 3^2 + 45 \div 9$

$= 2.8 \div 4$  $= 1.8 \cdot 9 + 45 \div 9$

$= 0.7$  $= 16.2 + 5$

$= 21.2$

Algeblocks are models that can be used to represent variable expressions.

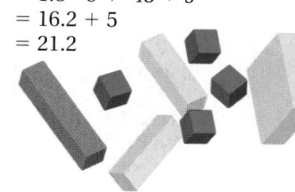

Math Online  mathmatters2.com/extra_examples

---

## Chalkboard Examples

**Supplementary Example 1**
Simplify each numerical expression.
a. $12 + (3 \cdot 4)$  $12 + 12 = 24$
b. $16 - (5 \cdot |-2|)$  $16 - 5 \cdot 2 =$
   $16 - 10 = 6$

**Supplementary Example 2**
Simplify each numerical expression.
a. $-5 \cdot 4^2 - (-3)$  $-5 \cdot 16 + 3 =$
   $-80 + 3 = -77$
b. $-(10 - 8)^2 - 2^3$  $-(2)^2 - 8 =$
   $-4 - 8 = -12$

**Supplementary Example 3**
Evaluate each variable expression when $k = \frac{2}{3}$.
a. $\frac{1}{2}k^2$  $\frac{1}{2}\left(\frac{2}{3}\right)^2 = \frac{1}{2} \cdot \frac{4}{9} = \frac{2}{9}$
b. $\frac{1}{3}k - k^2$  $\frac{1}{3} \cdot \frac{2}{3} - \left(\frac{2}{3}\right)^2 =$
   $\frac{2}{9} - \frac{4}{9} = -\frac{2}{9}$

**Supplementary Example 4**
Write the variable expression shown in each of the Algeblocks models.
a.
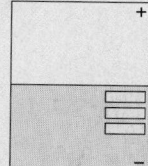
$-3x$

b.
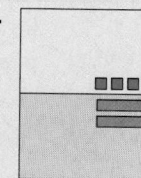
$-2y + 4$

---

## Extend the Lesson

**CHALLENGE** Demonstrate that using only the number 2 and parentheses, exponents, the order of operations, and the zero power, you can write expressions equal to each of the whole numbers from 1 through 10.

$2^0 = 1$  $2 \cdot 2 + 2 - 2^2 = \mathbf{2}$  $2^2 - 2^0 = \mathbf{3}$  $2^2 = \mathbf{4}$

$2 \cdot 2 + 2^0 = \mathbf{5}$  $2 + 2 \cdot 2 = \mathbf{6}$  $2 \cdot 2 \cdot 2 - 2^0 = \mathbf{7}$  $2^2 + 2^2 = \mathbf{8}$

$(2^2)^2 - (2 \cdot 2 \cdot 2) + 2^0 = \mathbf{9}$  $2(2)^2 + 2(2^0) = \mathbf{10}$

Have students try this exercise using only 3, only 4, only 5, only 8, and only 9.

## Example 4

**MODELING** Use Algeblocks to represent each variable expression.

**a.** $x + 4$      **b.** $3y$      **c.** $2x^2 - 3$      **d.** $-4x + y^2$

**Solution**

**a.**     **b.** 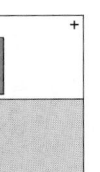    **c.** 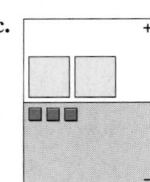    **d.**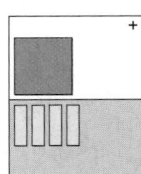

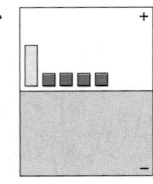

## ▰ TRY THESE EXERCISES

**Simplify each numerical expression.**

**1.** $8 - 2 \cdot 3$   2     **2.** $(102 + 42) \div 6^2$   4     **3.** $1.3 + (2.5 \div 1.25)$   3.3

**4.** $(14 - 4) \cdot 4 + 4^2$   56     **5.** $80 \div (3 + 7) - 1^5$   7     **6.** $10 + 8 \div 2 \cdot 5$   30

**Evaluate each variable expression when $b = 25$.**

**7.** $b + 4$   29     **8.** $\frac{1}{2}(b - 1)$   12     **9.** $10b + 20 \div 2^2$   255   **10.** $b + 5b$   150

 **11.** **CALCULATOR** Some calculators follow order of operations, and some do not. Does your calculator follow order of operations? Use Exercise 6 to test your calculator. Explain your results.   Answers will vary depending on calculator function.

**12.** **PART-TIME JOB** Ana works $3\frac{1}{2}$ h/day on Monday, Wednesday and Friday and 5 h on Saturday. Write and simplify a numerical expression for the number of hours that Ana works per week.   $3\left(3\frac{1}{2}\right) + 5 = 15.5$ h

## ▰ PRACTICE EXERCISES • For Extra Practice, see page 589.

**Simplify each numerical expression.**

**13.** $4 \cdot 9 - 9 + 7$   34     **14.** $(20 + 8) \div 7 \cdot 6$   24     **15.** $1^3 \cdot 1 + 5 \cdot 2$   11

**16.** $\frac{1}{2}\left(\frac{1}{2} + \frac{5}{8}\right)$   $\frac{9}{16}$     **17.** $6.9 - 3.2 \cdot (10 \div 5)$   0.5     **18.** $[20 + (2 \cdot 8)] \div 3^2$   4

**19.** $7^2 + 81 \div 9 + 3$   61     **20.** $(120 + 42.5) \div (4^3 + 1)$   2.5   **21.** $14 - (6 + 3) \div 3 + 10$   21

**Evaluate each expression when $w = 16$.**

**22.** $30 - w$   14     **23.** $(w^2 + 0) + 7$   263     **24.** $\frac{w}{4} - w \div 8$   2     **25.** $\frac{1}{4}w \cdot (w \div 2)$   32

 **26.** **WRITING MATH** Do the expressions $12(4 + 3)$ and $12 \cdot 4 + 3$ equal the same value? Explain why or why not.   No. They are different expressions as defined by the order of operations.

**27.** **FITNESS** On Saturday Rosa rode her bike 15 mi. On Sunday she rode 6 mi less than she did on Saturday. Write and simplify a numerical expression to determine the number of miles she rode on both days.   $15 + (15 - 6) = 24$ mi

---

## Lesson Wrap-up

### QUICK ASSESSMENT

Ask the following questions to determine if students understand the content presented in this lesson.

**For each expression, tell which operation you must do first.**

**1.** $7 + 5 \cdot 2$   multiplication
**2.** $6 \cdot 3^2 + 9$   square
**3.** $22 - 12 \div 3 + 1$   division
**4.** $10 \cdot (6 - 4)^3$   subtraction

**Choose the correct answer.**
**5.** Which is the value of the expression $-ab^2c$ when $a = -2$, $b = 4$, and $c = 5$?   **D**
    **A.** $-320$ **B.** $320$ **C.** $-160$ **D.** $160$

### ASSIGNMENT GUIDE

**Basic:** 1–34, 44–46
**Enriched:** 1–46

### Reteaching Worksheet 2-2

Name _____    Date _____

RETEACHING **2-2**
**ORDER OF OPERATIONS**
When you perform calculations to simplify or evaluate expressions involving numbers or variables, use the correct order of operations.

- Perform calculations with parentheses or brackets first.
- Multiply or divide *in order*, from left to right.
- Add or subtract *in order*, from left to right.

**Example 1**      **Example 2**

Simplify the numerical expression.    Evaluate the expression when $x = 2$,
$4(8 - 2) \div 12 + 1$      $y = 6$, and $r = 1$.
                       $2y\left(4 - \frac{x}{2}\right) + 2r$

**Solution**            **Solution**

$4(8 - 2) \div 12 + 1$       $2y\left(4 - \frac{x}{2}\right) + 2r$
$= 4(6) \div 12 + 1$       $= 2 \cdot 6\left(4 - \frac{2}{2}\right) + 2 \cdot 1$
$= 24 \div 12 + 1$        $= 2 \cdot 6(4 - 1) + 2$
$= 2 + 1$             $= 12(3) + 2 = 36 + 2 = 38$
$= 3$

☑ **EXERCISES**

Simplify each numerical expression.

**1.** $25 - 6 + 2 \cdot 8$     **2.** $8 \cdot 7 - 5(2 + 1)$     **3.** $7.5 - (0.6 + 8) \div 2$
       35                41                 3.2
**4.** $3[(3.6 \div 1.2) + 2]$    **5.** $\frac{1}{3}(8 + 4 - 6)$     **6.** $\frac{7}{8} + 1 - 3\frac{5}{8}$
       15                2                 0

Evaluate each expression when $a = 2$, $b = 3.5$, and $c = 1$.

**7.** $abc$         **8.** $b(a + 3c)$       **9.** $\frac{1.5(a + c)}{a - c}$
      7              17.5              4.5
**10.** $b - ac$      **11.** $c(2b + a)$     **12.** $3b - 2c$
      1.5             9                8.5

## Flexible Grouping

After completing Example 4 and Supplementary Example 4, have students work in pairs. One student models a variable expression using Algeblocks and gives a value for the expression. The other student has to write the expression that has been modeled and decide whether, to obtain the given value, the expression can be true for a whole number value of the variable. For example, if the expression modeled is $3x + 9$ and the value set is 26, then $x$ cannot be a whole number.

**28. ENTERTAINMENT** Carla is selling tickets for the school play. Floor seats cost $5 and bleacher seats cost $4. She sold 46 floor tickets and 79 bleacher tickets. Write and simplify a numerical expression for the amount of money that Carla collected for the tickets. $5(46) + 4(79) = \$546$

**29. FITNESS** Javier ran for $x$ miles on Monday, $y$ miles on Tuesday and $z$ miles on Wednesday. Write a variable expression for the average number of miles Javier ran Monday through Wednesday. $(x + y + z) \div 3$

**30. POPULATION** The population of Wyoming, the least-populated U.S. state, can be represented by the variable expression $5x - 20,000 + (2800 \div 2)$ where $x = 100,000$. Evaluate the expression to find the population of Wyoming. 481,400

**MODELING** Write the variable expression represented by each Basic Mat. Find the value of each expression if each $x$-block equals 2 and each $y$-block equals 4.

**31.**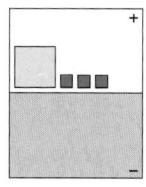

$x^2 + 3$; 7

**32.**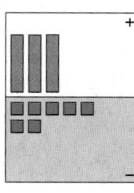

$3y - 7$; 5

**33.**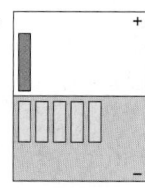

$y - 5x$; $-6$

**34.**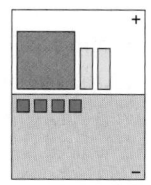

$y^2 + 2x - 4$; 16

## EXTENDED PRACTICE EXERCISES

Evaluate each expression when $n = 10.2, p = 6$ and $r = 0.8$.

**35.** $n \div p^2$  0.28$\overline{3}$
**36.** $p(n + r)$  66
**37.** $n \cdot (p - r)$  53.04
**38.** $rp + n^3$  1066.008

**39.** $\dfrac{n + p + r}{3p}$  $\dfrac{17}{18}$
**40.** $\dfrac{2}{3}n + \dfrac{1}{4}p$  8.3
**41.** $2n - 6r$  15.6
**42.** $8p \div (3r + n)$  $\approx 3.8$

**43. CHAPTER INVESTIGATION** Use an almanac or the Internet to find the population and number of square miles or square kilometers of any state and a city in that state. Answers will vary.

## MIXED REVIEW EXERCISES

Use the data in the table to answer the following questions. (Lesson 1-2)

| Name | Test 1 | Test 2 | Test 3 | Test 4 | Final |
|------|--------|--------|--------|--------|-------|
| Carol Jenn | 89 | 76 | 90 | 85 | 92 |
| Michael Sand | 79 | 54 | 87 | 88 | 91 |
| Morgan Tate | 86 | 95 | 89 | 92 | 95 |

**44.** What is the range of the student's grades?  41

**45.** What is the overall average test score for these three students?  $\approx 86$

**46.** Which student would benefit the most if the teacher decides to weight the final test as twice the value of the other four tests? Explain.
Michael Sand's average score would increase from 79.8 to 81.7.

**Math Online**  mathmatters2.com/self_check_quiz

## Alternative Assessment

**STUDENT PORTFOLIO** Students arrange toothpicks into a row of triangles, as shown. Students create and complete a table showing the number of toothpicks it takes to make each number of triangles. Students write a variable expression to represent the number of toothpicks it takes to make $t$ triangles. $3t - (t - 1)$  Use the expression to find the number of toothpicks needed to make 20 triangles.  41

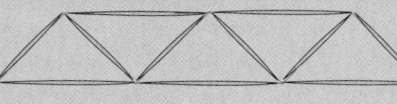

| Number of triangles | Number of toothpicks |
|---------------------|----------------------|
| 1 | 3 |
| 2 | 5 |
| 3 | 7 |
| 4 | 9 |

---

### Extra Practice Worksheet 2-2

Name _____  Date _____

EXTRA PRACTICE **2-2**

## ORDER OF OPERATIONS

**EXERCISES**

Simplify each numerical expression.

**1.** $3 \cdot 6 - 2 \cdot 8$ ___2___
**2.** $(4 + 8) \div 2 - 6$ ___0___

**3.** $2^3 \cdot 1 - 6 + 4$ ___6___
**4.** $\frac{1}{4}\left(\frac{3}{8} + \frac{1}{2}\right)$ ___$\frac{7}{32}$___

**5.** $\frac{2}{5}(4 \cdot 5 - 10)$ ___4___
**6.** $8.5 - 4.6 \cdot (12 \div 4)$ ___$-5.3$___

**7.** $[24 + (8 \div 2)] \div 2^2$ ___7___
**8.** $15 - 8 \cdot 2 + (7 \cdot 4)$ ___27___

**9.** $18 - 3^2 + (4 \cdot 3) \div 2$ ___15___
**10.** $16 + 4 \div 4 - 6 + 4$ ___15___

Evaluate each expression when $m = 12$.

**11.** $15 - m$ ___3___
**12.** $m^2 \div (m \div 2)$ ___24___

**13.** $m \div 4 \cdot \left(\frac{m}{2}\right)$ ___18___
**14.** $\frac{1}{3}m \div 2 + (m + 2)$ ___16___

**15.** $m + 0.5m - 10$ ___8___
**16.** $\frac{4m - 6}{m - 5}$ ___6___

**17.** On Monday, Mona drove 6 hours. On Tuesday, she drove 2 hours more than half the time she drove on Monday. Write and simplify a numerical expression to determine the number of hours she drove on both days.
$6 + (6 \div 2 + 2) = 11$ hr

**18.** Leon bought tickets for a concert. He bought 6 tickets for $15.50 and 4 for $12.50. Write and simplify a numerical expression for the amount of money Leon paid for the tickets.
$6 \cdot 15.50 + 4 \cdot 12.50 = \$143.00$

**19.** Ned worked $12\frac{1}{4}$ hours each of the last 4 weeks. Write and simplify an expression for the number of hours that Ned worked during the last 4 weeks.
$4\left(12\frac{1}{4}\right) = 49$ hr

**20.** Rita studied for $a$ hours on Monday, $b$ hours on Tuesday, and $c$ hours each on Wednesday and Thursday. Write a variable expression for the average number of hours Rita studied Monday through Thursday.
$\dfrac{a + b + 2c}{4}$

---

### Enrichment Worksheet 2-2

Name _____  Date _____

ENRICHMENT **2-2**

## EXPRESSIONS OF VALUE

Write numerical expressions that have given values using each of the numbers 3, 4, 5, and 6 only once. You may use the grouping and operation symbols as many times as necessary.

**Example**

Write a numerical expression with a value of 5, using each of the numbers 3, 4, 5, and 6 only once and any grouping and operation symbols.

**Solution**

$\dfrac{6 + 4 + 5}{3} = \dfrac{15}{3} = 5$

**EXERCISES**

Write a numerical expression that has the given value using each of the numbers 3, 4, 5, and 6 only once.  Answers may vary. Possible answers are given.

**1.** 26  $4(3 + 5) - 6$
**2.** 40  $6 \cdot 5 \cdot 4 \div 3$
**3.** 15  $3[(6 - 5) + 4]$
**4.** 36  $4(3 \cdot 5 - 6)$

**5.** 19  $3 \cdot 6 + 5 - 4$
**6.** 16  $(6 - 4)(3 + 5)$
**7.** 18  $6 \cdot 5 - 4 \cdot 3$
**8.** 77  $6 \cdot 4 \cdot 3 + 5$

**9.** 8  $3 + 4 + 6 - 5$
**10.** 0  $6 - 5 - 4 + 3$
**11.** 7  $(6 - 5)(4 + 3)$
**12.** 6  $3 + 4 + 5 - 6$

**13.** Write three different expressions, each of which has a value of 10.
Possible answers: $3 + 5 + 6 - 4$; $3 \cdot 4 \cdot 5 \div 6$; $(6 + 5) - (4 - 3)$

**14.** Write three different expressions, each of which has a value of 9.
Possible answers: $3(4 + 5 - 6)$; $4 \cdot 6 - 3 \cdot 5$; $3(5 - 4) + 6$

**15.** Find two different ways to write expressions having each of these values: 1, 2, 3, 4.
Possible answers: $(6 - 5)(4 - 3) = 1$   $(6 - 5) \div (4 - 3) = 1$

$4 \cdot 5 - 3 \cdot 6 = 2$   $3 \cdot 6 \div (5 + 4) = 2$   $(6 - 3)(5 - 4) = 3$

$\dfrac{6}{3} + 5 - 4 = 3$   $(6 - 4)(5 - 3) = 4$   $(6 - 4) + (5 - 3) = 4$

If $a = 3$, $b = 4$, $c = 5$, and $d = 6$, write an expression using variables to find the following numbers.

**16.** 360  $abcd$
**17.** 81  $(a + d)(b + c)$
**18.** 117  $bcd - a$
**19.** 22.5  $\dfrac{acd}{b}$

**Lesson 2-1**
integers                          opposites
rational numbers
terminating decimal
repeating decimal
irrational numbers
real numbers
coordinate of a point
graph of a number
absolute value
opposite of the opposite property

**Lesson 2-2**
numerical expression
value                          simplify
order of operations          variable
variable expression          evaluate

## ASSIGNMENT GUIDE

**All students: 1–64**

## Chalkboard Examples

**Lesson 2-1**
On a number line, graph the set
$\left\{\frac{1}{5}, -1.4, 0.6, -0.8, 1\frac{2}{5}\right\}$.

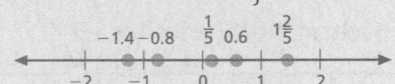

**Lesson 2-2**
Simplify each numerical expression.
a. $20 - 12 \div 2 + 4$   $20 - 6 + 4 =$
   $14 + 4 = 18$
b. $14 + 5 \cdot 3^2 - 8$   $14 + 5 \cdot 9 - 8 =$
   $14 + 45 - 8 = 59 - 8 = 51$

## ADDITIONAL ANSWERS

1.

1.5
−5 −4 −3 −2 −1 0 1 2 3 4

2.

−4 −3 −2 −1 0 1 2 3 4

3.

$-2\frac{1}{2}$ $-1\frac{1}{2}$   $\frac{1}{2}$   $2\frac{1}{2}$
−3 −2 −1 0 1 2 3

4.

π
−5 −4 −3 −2 −1 0 1 2 3 4 5

5.

−5.25   −2.25      1.75   4.5
−6 −5 −4 −3 −2 −1 0 1 2 3 4 5

6.

0 1 2 3 4 5 6 7 8

# Review and Practice Your Skills

## PRACTICE ◢ LESSON 2-1

**Graph the given sets of numbers on a number line.** For 1–6, see additional answers.

1. $\{4, 1.5, 0, -1, -5\}$
2. $\{-4, -2, 0, 2, 4\}$
3. $\left\{2\frac{1}{2}, \frac{1}{2}, 0, -1\frac{1}{2}, -2\frac{1}{2}\right\}$
4. $\{\sqrt{4}, \pi, \sqrt{25}\}$
5. $\{-5.25, -2.25, 1.75, 4.5\}$
6. even single digit numbers

**Use a number line to compare numbers. Replace each ■ with <, > or = .**

7. $0$ ■ $-3$  $>$
8. $|-6|$ ■ $6$  $=$
9. $-2$ ■ $-1$  $<$
10. $\frac{1}{3}$ ■ $\frac{1}{2}$  $<$
11. $0.5$ ■ $1.5$  $<$
12. $-7$ ■ $-10$  $>$

**Graph each set of numbers on a number line.** For 13–18, see additional answers.

13. all real numbers greater than 5
14. the integers between 0 and $|-3|$
15. the integers from $-4$ to 4
16. the odd numbers between 10 and 18
17. all real numbers less than $-2$
18. the number 5 and its opposite

**Evaluate each expression.**

19. $|x|$, when $x = 17$  17
20. $|y|$, when $y = -2$  2
21. $|r|$, when $r = -111$  111
22. $-w$, when $w = -4$  4
23. $-|d|$, when $d = 4$  $-4$
24. $-(-n)$, when $n = \frac{2}{3}$  $\frac{2}{3}$

## PRACTICE ◢ LESSON 2-2

**Simplify each numerical expression.**

25. $6 + 3 \cdot 7$  27
26. $3^2 \div (9 - 6)$  3
27. $6 \cdot 2 - 4 \cdot 2$  4
28. $5^2 - 4 \cdot 4 + 5^2$  34
29. $3^4 - 3^3 \div 3^3 - 3^2$  71
30. $2(34 - 19)$  30

**Evaluate each expression when $x = 8$.**

31. $x - 2$  6
32. $3x + x \cdot 3^2$  96
33. $x^2 + x + 1$  73

**Evaluate each variable expression when $a = 6$, $b = 4$ and $c = 3$.**

34. $5(a - b)$  10
35. $5a - 5b$  10
36. $(5b - 2c) + c^2$  23
37. $\frac{1}{b}(6c - a)$  3
38. $b^3 - \frac{1}{3}c^3$  55
39. $10c \div a + b^2$  21

**Evaluate each expression when $w = 2$, $x = 3$, $y = 12$ and $z = -10$.**

40. $7(y - x)$  63
41. $y + x \cdot 5$  27
42. $16x - (4x + y)$  24
43. $w^2 + x \cdot y$  40
44. $[x + w\,(y)]x$  81
45. $y^2 - 2w + y$  152
46. $x(3 + w^2)$  21
47. $3\,|y|$  36
48. $3\,|z|$  30

## Teaching Tip

In preparation for questions concerning graphs on a number line, such as those found in Exercises 13–18 and 55–58, remind students that it is essential for them to be aware of the type of number with which they are working. On a graph, individual numbers are represented by individual points. Entire intervals of real numbers are shown by shading entire parts of the number line. Students must know whether endpoints are to be "closed holes" (included in the set) or "open holes" (excluded from the set).

## PRACTICE ◼ LESSON 2-1–LESSON 2-2

**Replace each ◼ with <, > or =.** (Lesson 2-1)

**49.** $-3$ ◼ $|-3|$  $<$

**50.** $|3|$ ◼ $|-3|$  $=$

**51.** $\frac{1}{2}$ ◼ $\frac{1}{4}$  $>$

**52.** $0.2$ ◼ $.02$  $>$

**53.** $-1$ ◼ $-\frac{4}{4}$  $=$

**54.** $\frac{1}{4}$ ◼ $0.25$  $=$

**Graph each set of numbers on a number line.** (Lesson 2-1) For 55–58, see additional answers.

**55.** the integers from $-6$ to $-1$

**56.** all real numbers less than or equal to $3\frac{1}{2}$

**57.** $\left\{-4, -2.5, -\frac{3}{4}, 2\frac{2}{3}, 3.5\right\}$

**58.** the integers between $|-2|$ and $-4$

**Simplify each numerical expression.** (Lesson 2-2)

**59.** $(15 \cdot 2) \div (5 \cdot 3)$  $2$

**60.** $16 \div 2 \cdot 8 + 4 - 4$  $64$

**61.** $3[2 + 4(4)]$  $54$

**62.** $7 \div 7 - 7 \cdot 7$  $-48$

**63.** $2 \cdot 2 + 2 \div 2 - 2$  $3$

**64.** $|-2| - 2$  $0$

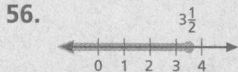 **Career – Concession Stand Operator**

**C**oncession stands provide refreshments for sports fans and participants. Concession stand operators strive to provide the highest quality food products as well as efficient service. As a concession stand operator plans for a homecoming football game, he or she must order appropriate quantities of food, drinks, utensils, and other supplies.

**Use the table at the right for Exercises 1–3.**
For 1–3, see additional answers.

**1.** Complete the table below, indicating which years had increases and which years had decreases in the numbers of men, women, and youth attending the games.

**Projected Attendance**

| Year | Men | Women | Youth (under 18) |
|------|-----|-------|------------------|
| 2000 - 2001 | 240 | 113 | 147 |
| 2001 - 2002 | 244 | 58 | 226 |
| 2002 - 2003 | 291 | 76 | 193 |
| 2003 - 2004 | 302 | 94 | 193 |
| 2004 - 2005 | 257 | 125 | 122 |

**Increases and Decreases in Attendance**

| Year | Men | Women | Youth | Total |
|------|-----|-------|-------|-------|
| 2001 - 2002 | +4 | −55 | +79 | +28 |
| 2002 - 2003 | +47 | +18 | −33 | +32 |
| 2003 - 2004 | ◼ | ◼ | ◼ | ◼ |
| 2004 - 2005 | ◼ | ◼ | ◼ | ◼ |

**2.** Between which years was there an increase in the total population of those attending the games? Between how many years was there a decrease?

**3.** Is there a correlation between the increases and decreases of the individual groups and the total population? What factors might influence the increases or decreases?

 **Math Online** mathmatters2.com/mathworks

## ADDITIONAL ANSWERS

**13.** (number line: 4 5 6 7 8, point at 6)

**14.** (number line: 0 1 2 3, points at 1 and 2)

**15.** (number line: −4 −3 −2 −1 0 1 2 3 4, multiple points)

**16.** (number line: 10 11 12 13 14 15 16 17 18, points)

**17.** (number line: −5 −4 −3 −2 −1 0, open point at −1)

**18.** (number line: −5 −4 −3 −2 −1 0 1 2 3 4 5, points)

**55.** (number line: −6 −5 −4 −3 −2 −1 0, points from −6 to −1)

**56.** (number line: 0 1 2 3 4 with $3\frac{1}{2}$ marked)

**57.** (number line: −4 −3 −2 −1 0 1 2 3 4 with −2.5, $-\frac{3}{4}$, $2\frac{2}{3}$, 3.5 marked)

**58.** (number line: −4 −3 −2 −1 0 1 2)

## MathWorks

Not only do Americans eat from concession stands found at special events, they also regularly eat fast foods found in every shopping mall and along many highways. Vendors on busy city streets often offer food served from a variety of vehicles that are moved away at night. Wherever Americans go, refreshments are offered for sale.

Concession stands are often *franchised operations*, involving individual ownership of many units carrying a single trade name. Some widely known fast-food establishments operate internationally under a franchise arrangement.

Students should answer Questions 1–3 to better understand that food providers at an event must be aware of how big their potiential audience will be so that they can have adequate provisions.

Whatever their location and length of duration, refreshment providers must plan for the size of their operation. Those in a permanent location must be especially concerned with quality and service since their success depends on repeat customers.

Students who are interested in learning more about this career choice can go to mathmatters2.com/mathworks. School Guidance Counselors are another resource for information about training requirements and appropriate schools.

## MathWorks

**1.**

| Year | Men | Women | Youth | Total |
|------|-----|-------|-------|-------|
| 2003 - 2004 | +11 | +18 | 0 | +29 |
| 2004 - 2005 | −45 | +31 | −71 | −85 |

**2.** Population increased between 2000–2001 and 2001–2002, 2001–2002 and 2002–2003, and 2002–2003 and 2003–2004. Population decreased one time between 2003–2004 and 2004–2005.

**3.** There is no correlation between the women and the total population. Nor is there one between youth and the total. However, there is a correlation between the number of men attending and the total population. Factors will vary.

## Lesson Planning

### NCTM Standards/Strands
- Representation
- Connections
- Communication

### Vocabulary

translate expressions

### Lesson Resources

Warm-up Transparency 5
Reteaching 2-3
Extra Practice 2-3
Enrichment 2-3

## Getting Started

### 5-MINUTE WARM-UP

Evaluate each expression.
1. $-3 \cdot 2 - 1 \cdot 3$   $-6 - 3 = -9$
2. $1 + 12 \div 2 - 7$   $1 + 6 - 7 =$
   $7 - 7 = 0$
3. $3 \cdot 4^2 \div 6$   $3 \cdot 16 \div 6 =$
   $48 \div 6 = 8$

### Introduction to Lesson 2-3
Before beginning the activity, ask students if they are studying another language, such as Spanish or French, or if English is a second language for them.

Elicit that when working between two languages, words and phrases are *translated*.

Point out that mathematics has a language of its own, consisting of symbols. The words and phrases of a language such as English are translated into mathematical symbols. Conversely, expressions written in mathematical symbols can be translated into the words and phrases of English.

**Goals**
- Write variable expressions to represent word phrases.
- Write word phrases to represent variable expressions.

**Applications**   Part-time job, Space science, Photography, Population

**HISTORY**  Diophantus of Alexandria is often known as the father of algebra. He lived from 200–284 A.D. The following inscription appears on his gravestone.

> This stone marks the grave of Diophantus.
> If you solve this riddle, you will know his age.
> He spent one-sixth of his life as a child,
> Then one-twelfth as a youth.
> He was married for one-seventh of his life.
> Five years after he married, his son was born.
> Fate overtook his beloved child; he died
> When he was half the age of his father.
> Four more years did the father live
> Before reaching the end of this life.

**Translate the following lines of the inscription into a mathematical expression. Choose and identify a variable for each expression.**

1. line 3   $\frac{1}{6}x$; $x$ = age at death
2. line 4   $\frac{1}{12}x$; $x$ = age at death
3. line 5   $\frac{1}{7}x$; $x$ = age at death
4. line 6   $y + 5$; $y$ = age when married
5. line 8   $\frac{1}{2}z$; $z$ = father's age when son died
6. line 9   $z + 4$; $z$ = father's age when son died

### BUILD UNDERSTANDING

In mathematics, words and ideas often have to be translated into variable expressions. Many words and phrases suggest certain operations. Any variable can be used to represent a number.

| | Word phrase | Variable expression |
|---|---|---|
| Addition | three *more than* a number | $3 + x$ |
| | the *sum* of a number and $-20$ | $n + (-20)$ |
| | a number *increased* by eight | $y + 8$ |
| Subtraction | the *difference* of a number and 20 | $y - 20$ |
| | seven *less than* a number | $p - 7$ |
| | negative two *decreased* by a number | $-2 - m$ |
| Multiplication | six *times* a number | $6a$ |
| | the *product* of a number and 15 | $15n$ |
| | a number *multiplied* by $-11$ | $-11t$ |
| Division | the *quotient* of a number and $-12$ | $\frac{t}{-12}$ |
| | seven *divided* by a number | $\frac{7}{d}$ |

## Predictable Error

When writing a variable expression to represent a word phrase such as "seven less than a number," students often mistakenly write $7 - n$. To help students avoid making this mistake, which disregards the fact that subtraction is not commutative, encourage them to *always add or subtract <u>at the end</u>*. So, write $n + 7$ for "seven more than a number" rather than $7 + n$, even though, in the case of addition, $7 + n$ is equivalent to $n + 7$.

## Example 1

**Write each phrase as a variable expression.**

**a.** a number increased by 33

**b.** negative three times a number

**c.** the difference of 15 and a number

**d.** the quotient of five and twice a number

### Solution

Let $n$ = a number.

**a.** $n + 33$

**b.** $-3n$

**c.** $15 - n$

**d.** $\dfrac{5}{2n}$

This process can be reversed to write word phrases for variable expressions.

## Example 2

**Translate each variable expression into a word phrase.**

**a.** $4 + y$

**b.** $\dfrac{x}{20}$

**c.** $-\dfrac{1}{2}m$

**d.** $2n - 8$

### Solution

**a.** the sum of four and a number

**b.** the quotient of a number and 20

**c.** negative one half times a number

**d.** twice a number decreased by eight

> **Check Understanding**
>
> Give a different possible solution for each variable expression in Example 2.
>
> Answers will vary.

## Example 3

**PART-TIME JOB** When Alicia babysits, she charges $2.50/h for each child age 2 and under and $2.00/h for each child above age 2. Write a variable expression to represent the amount of money Alicia earns each hour of babysitting.

### Solution

Let $x$ = the number of children age 2 and under. Let $y$ = the number of children above age 2.

Think of a word phrase. *$2.50 times the number of children age 2 and under plus $2.00 times the number of children above age 2*

Write the variable expression. $2.50x + 2.00y$

Alicia earns $2.50x + 2.00y$ per hour for babysitting.

Math online   mathmatters2.com/extra_examples

Lesson 2-3  **Write Variable Expressions** | **63**

Lesson 2-3  **Write Variable Expressions**  **63**

---

## Chalkboard Examples

### Supplementary Example 1
Write each phrase as a variable expression.
**a.** twice the sum of a number and three   **2(n + 3)**
**b.** six less than the product of a number and ten   **10n − 6**

### Supplementary Example 2
Translate each variable expression into a word phrase.
**a.** **3(x + 10)**   three times the sum of a number and ten
**b.** **8n + 5**   five more than the product of a number and eight

### Supplementary Example 3
**BUSINESS** Ms. Munro makes and sells candles. For her medium-size pillar candles, she charges $5.50 each for the unscented ones and $7.00 each for the scented ones. Write a variable expression to show how much Ms. Munro takes in when she sells her medium-size pillar candles.   Let $u$ = the number of unscented, medium-size pillar candles. Let $s$ = the number of scented, medium-size pillar candles. Ms. Munro takes in **5.50u + 7.00s** when she sells medium-size pillar candles.

### Reteaching Worksheet 2-3

Name _____ Date _____

RETEACHING  **2-3**
**WRITE VARIABLE EXPRESSIONS**
When you are translating words into variable expressions, you need to look for certain phrases to determine which operation to use.

| Operation | Phrases | Examples |
|---|---|---|
| Addition | more than | four **more than** a number $4 + n$ |
| | sum of | the **sum of** a number and six $n + 6$ |
| | increased by | eight **increased by** a number $8 + n$ |
| Subtraction | less than | seven **less than** a number $n - 7$ |
| | difference of | the **difference of** six and a number $6 - n$ |
| | decreased by | a number **decreased by** three $n - 3$ |
| Multiplication | times | four **times** a number $4n$ |
| | product of | the **product of** six and a number $6n$ |
| | multiplied by | negative two **multiplied by** a number $-2n$ |
| Division | quotient of | the **quotient of** a number and five $\dfrac{n}{5}$ |
| | divided by | negative nine **divided by** a number $\dfrac{-9}{n}$ |

**✓ EXERCISES**

Write each phrase as a variable expression.

1. two more than a number   $2 + n$

2. a number divided by eight   $\dfrac{n}{8}$

3. six less than a number   $n - 6$

4. the product of four and a number   $4n$

5. the sum of one and a number   $1 + n$

6. negative three times a number   $-3n$

---

## Teaching Tip

**ESL/LEP** When translating from a variable expression into a word phrase, students should be aware that different translations may be possible. Have students write as many different translations as they can for the variable expressions given in Example 2 and Supplementary Example 2.
For example, some ways in which the variable expression $4 + y$ can be translated are: "four more than a number", "four increased by a number", "a number increased by four", "the sum of four and a number".

## QUICK ASSESSMENT

Ask the following questions to determine if students understand the content presented in this lesson.

**Match each word phrase in 1–4 with a variable expression chosen from A–F below.**

1. nine more than a number   C
2. nine less than a number   E
3. the product of a number and nine   F
4. twice a number increased by nine   B

**A.** $\frac{2}{n} + 9$   **B.** $2n + 9$   **C.** $9 + n$

**D.** $9 - n$   **E.** $n - 9$   **F.** $9n$

## ASSIGNMENT GUIDE

**Basic:** 1–53, 61–64
**Enriched:** 1–64

## ADDITIONAL ANSWERS

7. the product of eight and a number
8. the sum of a number and negative five
9. the quotient of −20 and a number
10. the difference of a number and three
11. half of a number
12. ten decreased by six times a number
30. a number increased by 17
31. six decreased by a number
32. negative six times a number
33. the sum of one-half and a number
34. the difference of −12 and a number
35. a number divided by 25
36. six more than twice a number
37. −21 divided by three times a number
38. a number multipled by 0.8
39. 12 less than three times a number
40. the sum of one-third and 11 times a number
41. the quotient of negative five times a number and negative 11
42. three times a number decreased by four
43. the product of a number and three
44. negative two times twice the opposite of a number

---

### ◤ TRY THESE EXERCISES

**Write each phrase as a variable expression.**

1. the product of seven and a number   $7x$
2. one-half less than a number   $x - \frac{1}{2}$
3. negative two increased by a number   $-2 + x$
4. the quotient of 16 and a number   $\frac{16}{x}$
5. a number decreased by 22   $x - 22$
6. four more than three times a number   $3x + 4$

**Translate each variable expression into a word phrase.**   For 7–12, see additional answers.

7. $8x$
8. $-5 + y$
9. $\frac{-20}{x}$
10. $z - 3$
11. $\frac{1}{2}x$
12. $10 - 6m$

13. **SPACE SCIENCE** The time that a space shuttle is to blast off is referred to as $t$. For this situation, what does the expression $t - 9$ sec refer to?   9 sec before blastoff

### ◤ PRACTICE EXERCISES   •   For Extra Practice, see page 589.

**Write each phrase as a variable expression.**

14. five more than a number   $x + 5$
15. the difference of a number and 101   $x - 101$
16. negative ten times a number   $-10x$
17. the quotient of negative six and a number   $\frac{-6}{x}$
18. a number decreased by two   $x - 2$
19. the sum of 32 and twice a number   $32 + 2x$
20. one-third more than a number   $x + \frac{1}{3}$
21. the product of a number and 16   $16x$
22. nine less than a number times six   $6x - 9$
23. five tenths increased by a number   $\frac{5}{10} + x$
24. the sum of 11 and five times a number   $5x + 11$
25. negative four decreased by a number   $-4 - x$
26. seven times a number divided by $-13$   $\frac{7x}{-13}$
27. the difference of eight and a number   $8 - x$
28. one-half a number multiplied by 22   $22\left(\frac{1}{2}x\right)$
29. 30 times a number divided by $-62$   $\frac{30x}{-62}$

**Translate each variable expression into a word phrase.**   For 30–41, see additional answers.

30. $m + 17$
31. $6 - f$
32. $-6y$
33. $\frac{1}{2} + n$
34. $-12 - v$
35. $\frac{y}{25}$
36. $2x + 6$
37. $\frac{-21}{3y}$
38. $0.8w$
39. $3x - 12$
40. $11s + \frac{1}{3}$
41. $\frac{-5x}{-11}$

 **MODELING** Write a word phrase for each variable expression that is represented by Algeblocks.   For 42–44, see additional answers.

42.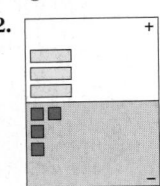
43.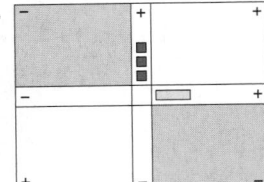
44.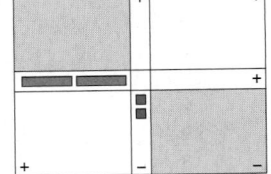

**DATA FILE** Refer to the data on the top ten national parks on page 566. Let *n* equal the acreage of the Grand Canyon. Write a variable expression and a word phrase in terms of *n* for the acreage of the following parks.
For 45–48, see additional answers.

**45.** Yellowstone Park

**46.** Gates of the Arctic

**47.** the Everglades

**48.** Katmai

**Write each phrase as a variable expression.**

**49. PHOTOGRAPHY** Two more than half the number of pictures remain on the roll of film. $\frac{1}{2}x + 2$

**50. INDUSTRY** Eight less than six times the number of boxes of books remain in stock. $6x - 8$

**51. POPULATION** The approximate population of Montana is 101,000 less than twice the population of Wyoming. $2x - 101{,}000$

**52. HOBBIES** To rent a paddle boat, it costs $10 the first hour and $3 for each additional half hour. $10 + 6(x - 1) = 6x + 4$

**53.** If a polygon has *n* sides, the sum of the measures of its interior angles is 180° times two less than the number of sides. $180(n - 2)$

Yellowstone Park

### ■ EXTENDED PRACTICE EXERCISES

For 54–57, answers will vary.
 **WRITING MATH** Write a real-life situation to represent each variable expression.

**54.** $y + 12$     **55.** $\frac{3n}{5}$     **56.** $\frac{1}{2}(b - 9)$     **57.** $5x$

**58.** Write a variable expression for the phrase *seven times the difference of four and twice a number.* $7(4 - 2x)$

**59.** Write a word phrase for the expression $-12(3x + 9)$. See additional answers.

**60. CRITICAL THINKING** Write two phrases that are stated differently but equal the same value. Answers will vary.

### ■ MIXED REVIEW EXERCISES

**Use the data for Exercises 61–64.**

| 48 | 64 | 26 | 39 | 22 | 45 | 56 | 67 | 43 | 26 |
|----|----|----|----|----|----|----|----|----|----|
| 41 | 35 | 39 | 42 | 68 | 65 | 52 | 58 | 48 | 33 |

**61.** Make a stem-and-leaf plot to display the data. (Lesson 1-3) See additional answers.

**62.** Name any outliers, clusters or gaps in the data. (Lesson 1-3) outliers: none; clusters: none; gaps: 26–33, 58–64

**63.** Find the interquartile range of the data. (Lesson 1-4) 20

**64.** Suppose a data set includes the 20 elements above plus one more. The mean of this set is 46. What is the value of the 21st element? (Lesson 1-2) 49

 **Math Online** mathmatters2.com/self_check_quiz

### ADDITIONAL ANSWERS

**45.** $n + 1{,}000{,}000$, a number increased by one million

**46.** $n + 5{,}800{,}000$, a number increased by 5.8 million

**47.** $n + 200{,}000$, a number increased by 200 thousand

**48.** $n + 2{,}300{,}000$, a number increased by 2.3 million

**59.** −12 multiplied by the sum of three times a number and nine

**61.**
```
2 | 2 6 6
3 | 3 5 9 9
4 | 1 2 3 5 8 8
5 | 2 6 8
6 | 4 5 7 8
```
3 | 5 represents 35

---

---

## NCTM Standards/Strands
- Representation
- Connections
- Communication

## Vocabulary
like terms
unlike terms
simplify a variable expression
combining like terms
zero pairs

## Tools/Materials Needed
Algeblocks and Basic Mat

## Lesson Resources
Warm-up Transparency 5
Transparency TK-4, 5, RF-8
Reteaching 2-4
Extra Practice 2-4
Enrichment 2-4

## Getting Started

### 5-MINUTE WARM-UP

**Evaluate each expression for**
$a = 4$ and $b = 2.5$.
1. $2a - b$   5.5
2. $a + 4b$   14
3. $\dfrac{a+b}{b}$   2.6
4. $\dfrac{2b}{a}$   1.25

### Introduction to Lesson 2-4
Before students attempt to write the required variable expressions, you might suggest they first organize the given information in a table.

|        | CD's ($c$) | movies ($m$) |
|--------|------------|--------------|
| Marcus | 1          | 2            |
| Rob    | 3          | 1            |
| Jiro   | 2          | 0            |

---

# 2-4 Add and Subtract Variable Expressions

**Goals**
- Simplify variable expressions.
- Evaluate variable expressions

**Applications**   Sports, Recycling, Population, Detective work

Marcus, Rob and Jiro went to a media store. Marcus bought 1 CD and 2 movies, Rob bought 3 CDs and 1 movie, and Jiro bought 2 CDs. Write a variable expression for the total amount spent on CDs and movies by each of the following. Let $c =$ the price for each CD and $m =$ the price for each movie.

1. Marcus
   $c + 2m$
2. Rob
   $3c + m$
3. Jiro
   $2c$
4. Marcus and Rob
   $4c + 3m$
5. Rob and Jiro
   $5c + m$
6. Marcus, Rob, and Jiro
   $6c + 3m$

## ■ BUILD UNDERSTANDING

The parts of a variable expression separated by addition or subtraction signs are called **terms** of the expression.

one term: $2x$   two terms: $3x + 6y$   three terms: $-4a + 5b - 7$

Terms that have identical variable parts are called **like terms**. Terms that have different variable parts are called **unlike terms**.

like terms: $2x$ and $4.5x$     unlike terms: $2a$ and $2\frac{1}{2}b$

$3st$ and $-\dfrac{1}{3}st$          $7xy$ and $7xz$

$2a^3b$ and $-9a^3b$       $8x^4y^2$ and $4x^3y^4$

To **simplify** a variable expression, perform as many of the indicated operations as possible. Use the distributive property in reverse order to simplify an expression that contains like terms. This process is called **combining like terms**. An expression is simplified when only unlike terms remain.

> **Think Back**
>
> The distributive property states that each factor outside parentheses is multiplied by each term within the parentheses.
>
> $a(b + c) = ab + ac$

### Example 1

**Simplify.**

a. $3x + 2x$
b. $-9n + n + 3m$
c. $12xy + 8xz + (-15xy)$

**Solution**

a. $3x + 2x = (3 + 2)x$     Use the distributive property.
   $= 5x$

Another way to solve this example is in expanded form.

$3x + 2x = x + x + x + x + x$
$= 5x$

66    Chapter 2 **Foundations of Algebra**

## Teaching Tip

Guide students to connect the concept of like terms back to operations with fractions. Fractions must have a common denominator before they can be combined by the operations of addition or subtraction.

**b.** $-9n + n + 3m = (-9 + 1)n + 3m$
               $= -8n + 3m$

**c.** $12xy + 8xz + (-15xy) = 12xy + (-15xy) + 8xz$     Rewrite using the commutative property.
                       $= [12 + (-15)]xy + 8xz$     Use the distributive property.
                       $= -3xy + 8xz$

By applying the distributive property, the resulting sum inside the parentheses is the sum of the coefficients of the like terms. To simplify an expression involving subtraction, change subtraction to *addition of the opposite*.

## Example 2

**Simplify.**

**a.** $\frac{1}{3}a - \frac{2}{3}a$           **b.** $-3x + 8y - 6y$           **c.** $2.4st - (-7.1sy) - 10.8st$

**Solution**

**a.** $\frac{1}{3}a - \frac{2}{3}a = \frac{1}{3}a + \left(-\frac{2}{3}a\right)$     Change subtraction to addition of the opposite.
             $= \left[\frac{1}{3} + \left(-\frac{2}{3}\right)\right]a$     Use the distributive property.
             $= -\frac{1}{3}a$

**b.** $-3x + 8y - 6y = -3x + 8y + (-6y)$     Change subtraction to addition of the opposite.
                  $= -3x + [8 + (-6)]y$
                  $= -3x + 2y$

**c.** $2.4st - (-7.1sy) - 10.8st = 2.4st + 7.1sy + (-10.8st)$
                             $= 2.4st + (-10.8st) + 7.1sy$
                             $= [2.4 + (-10.8)]st + 7.1sy$
                             $= -8.4st + 7.1sy$

### Supplementary Example 1
Simplify.
**a.** $3\sqrt{x} + 8\sqrt{x}$    $11\sqrt{x}$
**b.** $2x + 4x^2 + (-3x) + (-10x^2)$
     $-x - 6x^2$
**c.** $7(x + y) + 4(x + y)$    $11(x + y)$

### Supplementary Example 2
Simplify.
**a.** $0.1m - 1.1m$    $-m$
**b.** $7y + 4x - 7y - 3x$    $x$
**c.** $12x^2 + 3y - 6x^2 - 2y - 6x^2$    $y$

### Supplementary Example 3
Evaluate each expression when $x = 2$ and $y = -3$.
**a.** $6x^2 + 3x^2$
     $9x^2 = 9 \cdot 2^2 = 9 \cdot 4 = 36$
**b.** $3x^2 - y - x^2$   $2x^2 - y = 2 \cdot 2^2 - (-3) = 2 \cdot 4 + 3 = 8 + 3 = 11$
**c.** $x^2 - 4y - 2x^2 + y$   $-x^2 - 3y = -(2)^2 - 3(-3) = -4 + 9 = 5$

### Supplementary Example 4
Use Algeblocks to simplify the expression $4x + 3y - 2x - y$.

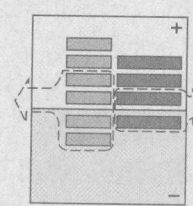

$2x + 2y$

## Example 3

**Evaluate each expression when $m = -7$ and $p = 12$.**

**a.** $m + 2m$          **b.** $m - p + 3p$          **c.** $7m - 5m - p + 3p$

**Check Understanding**

Describe how to combine like terms without using the words "distributive property."

Answers will vary.

**Solution**

First, simplify each variable expression. Then substitute the appropriate value for each variable. Finally, simplify the expression using the order of operations.

**a.** $m + 2m = 3m$      **b.** $m - p + 3p = m + 2p$      **c.** $7m - 5m - p + 3p = 2m + 2p$
       $= 3(-7)$                     $= -7 + 2(12)$                     $= 2(-7) + 2(12)$
       $= -21$                         $= -7 + 24$                         $= -14 + 24$
                               $= 17$                                 $= 10$

Simplifying expressions can be modeled by Algeblocks. When equal numbers of the same block are on opposite sides of the mat, they are called **zero pairs**. To simplify an expression, remove zero pairs from the mat.

 **Math Online** mathmatters2.com/extra_examples         Lesson 2-4 **Add and Subtract Variable Expressions** | **67**

## Teaching Tip

In Example 2b, $-3x + 8y - 6y$, note with students the different meanings of the symbol $-$. In front of the first term, that symbol means that the coefficient of $x$ is negative 3. Point out that in the printed display, there is no space between the symbol and 3. Now, in conjunction with the third term, that symbol means the operation of subtraction. Point out the space between the symbol and $6y$. Before considering Supplementary Example 2, ask students what they think the coefficient of a term such as $x$ is. Some students may think the missing coefficient is 0. Point out that this could not be so since the product of 0 and any number is 0. Students should conclude that in a term such as $x$, where the coefficient does not appear, it is understood that the coefficient is 1. And, in the term $-x$, the coefficient is understood to be $-1$. Tell students that, in a simplification problem, when they arrive at an answer with a coefficient of 1, such as $7x - 6x = 1x$, they should write the result as simply $x$. Also, an answer with a coefficient of $-1$, such as $3y - 4y = -1y$ should be written as $-y$.

## Example 4

**MODELING** Use Algeblocks to simplify each expression.

**a.** $-3x + 7x$

**b.** $2y - 4y + 2$

**Solution**

**a.**

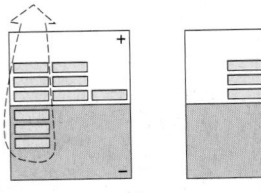

$-3x + 7x = 4x$

**b.**

$2y - 4y + 2 = -2y + 2$

---

### TRY THESE EXERCISES

**Simplify.**

1. $5t + 2t$  $7t$
2. $-3r + r$  $-2r$
3. $-6t - 6t$  $-12t$
4. $-0.9m + 1.3n - 4.6m$
   $1.3n - 5.5m$
5. $\frac{3}{5}x - \frac{1}{10}x + \frac{1}{5}y$  $\frac{1}{2}x + \frac{1}{5}y$
6. $7xy - xy + xz$  $6xy + xz$
7. $-3ab - 9ac + 11ab$  $8ab - 9ac$
8. $pq - 6rs - 3pq + 6rs$  $-2pq$

**Evaluate each expression when $a = -4$ and $b = 11$.**

9. $a - 6a$  $20$
10. $-b + 3b$  $22$
11. $a - b + 2b - 9a$  $43$
12. $\frac{1}{2}a + (-b) + \frac{1}{4}a$  $-14$

13. **MODELING** Use Algeblocks to simplify $-3x + 6x + 5 - 1$.  $3x + 4$; See additional answers.

14. **SPORTS** A football team completed a pass for a gain of $5x$ yards. On the next play, they were penalized $2x$ yards. Write and simplify an expression for the yardage gained after these two plays.  $5x - 2x = 3x$

---

### PRACTICE EXERCISES  •  For Extra Practice, see page 590.

**Simplify.**

15. $8s + 6s$  $14s$
16. $-2r + 7r$  $5r$
17. $18k - 25k$  $-7k$
18. $4b - (-5b)$  $9b$
19. $-\frac{1}{3}m + \frac{4}{9}m$  $\frac{1}{9}m$
20. $3g - 11g + 16g$  $8g$
21. $-7c - (-7c) + 7c$  $7c$
22. $2.1x - 3.5y - 1.5x$  $0.6x - 3.5y$
23. $11xy - 3xy + x$  $8xy + x$
24. $-36pq + 9pq - 3$  $-27pq - 3$
25. $15a - 2b + 3a - 6b$  $18a - 8b$
26. $-7jk - (-9jk) + 8j$  $2jk + 8j$
27. $\frac{2}{3}d - \frac{5}{6}d + \frac{1}{3}d$  $\frac{1}{6}d$
28. $ab - 22ab - 9ab$  $-30ab$
29. $-0.7st + 9.4st - 0.4t$  $8.7st - 0.4t$
30. $8m - 2n + 3m - 3n$  $11m - 5n$
31. $a - 7b - a + b$  $-6b$
32. $3r - 6rs + 6r + r$  $10r - 6rs$
33. $\frac{7}{8}xy - \frac{1}{4}x + \frac{3}{4}xy$  $\frac{13}{8}xy - \frac{1}{4}x$
34. $-c + 16cd - 12c + cd$  $-13c + 17cd$
35. $7wz + 7w - wz - 3w + 11w$  $6wz + 15w$

**Evaluate each expression when $x = -5$, $y = 4$ and $z = \frac{1}{2}$.**

36. $2y - 6y$  $-16$
37. $-5x + 11x$  $-30$
38. $-3z - (-9z)$  $3$
39. $-3x + 4y - 2x$  $41$
40. $\frac{1}{2}y - \frac{3}{4}y - \frac{1}{2}z$  $-1\frac{1}{4}$
41. $4z + 4x - 6z - x$  $-16$
42. $7y - 2x + 9y - x$  $79$
43. $3xy - 6xy + 2y$  $68$

---

### QUICK ASSESSMENT

Ask the following questions to determine if students understand the content presented in this lesson.

**Tell if the terms are like or unlike. If they are not like terms, explain why not.**

1. $3x$ and $3y$  unlike; variables are different
2. $7x$ and $-14.1x$  like
3. $6x$ and $3x^2$  unlike; variable parts are different

**Explain how you would simplify each expression.**

4. $2x + 5y + 7x + 9y$  add the $x$-terms, add the $y$-terms
5. $5x + 7y - (-2x)$  change the subtraction to addition of the opposite; add the $x$-terms

### ASSIGNMENT GUIDE

**Basic:** 1–55, 59–60
**Enriched:** 1–60

---

**Reteaching Worksheet 2-4**

Name _____  Date _____

RETEACHING  **2-4**

**ADD AND SUBTRACT VARIABLE EXPRESSIONS**

Terms are the parts of a variable expression that are separated by addition or subtraction signs. Terms are called **like terms** if their variable parts are identical. Terms that are not like terms are called **unlike terms.** An expression that contains like terms can be simplified by combining the like terms. An expression that contains all unlike terms cannot be simplified.

**Example 1**

Simplify $5y + 4y$.

**Solution**

$5y$ and $4y$ are like terms because their variable parts, namely $y$, are identical. Use the distributive property to combine the terms.

$5y + 4y = (5 + 4)y$
$= 9y$

**Example 2**

Simplify $-6r + 3r + (-2t)$.

**Solution**

$-6r$ and $3r$ are like terms because their variable parts, namely $r$, are identical. $-2t$ is unlike the other terms because its variable part is different. Use the distributive property to combine the like terms.

$-6r + 3r + (-2t) = (-6 + 3)r + (-2t)$
$= -3r - 2t$

**EXERCISES**

Name the like terms in each expression.

1. $6r + 5t + 4r$  $6r, 4r$
2. $8p + (-6p) + 6m$  $8p, -6p$
3. $9a + 4a - 6b - 4a$  $9a, 4a, -4a$
4. $7x + 3y - 2z + 2y$  $3y, 2y$

Simplify.

5. $7w + 4w$  $11w$
6. $9q + (-4q)$  $5q$
7. $-7c + 5c$  $-2c$
8. $8g - 2g$  $6g$
9. $-8v - 4v$  $-12v$
10. $2b + 4b + 5b$  $11b$
11. $7z - 5z - 4z$  $-2z$
12. $9w + 10w - 8w$  $11w$
13. $6r + 5t + 4r$  $10r + 5t$
14. $8p + (-6p) + 6m$  $2p + 6m$
15. $9a + 4a - 6b - 4a$  $9a - 6b$
16. $7x + 3y - 2z + 2y$  $7x + 5y - 2z$

---

---

## Teaching Tip

For Example 3, the text indicates that students should simplify the given expressions before evaluating. To emphasize how this is a work-saver, have students work out part c by doing the substitution and evaluation first and then simplifying.

Also, for Example 3, you may wish to have students use a calculator to evaluate these expressions after they have been simplified. Students working with an advanced calculator can enter variables and use the store feature.

**44. RECYCLING** During a recycling drive, the eighth grade collected $(2h + 9t)$ newspapers, the ninth grade collected $(h + 7t)$ newspapers and the tenth grade collected $4h$ newspapers. Write and simplify an expression for the total number of newspapers collected. $7h + 16t$

**45. WRITING MATH** Write a short paragraph explaining how to simplify a variable expression. Include examples.
Answers will vary.

**46. POPULATION** There are approximately $(1.7x + 0.2)$ million Americans between the ages of 15 and 19. There are approximately $(2x + 0.6)$ million Americans between the ages of 35 and 39. Find the difference in the population of these two age groups. $(0.3x + 0.4)$ million

**47. DETECTIVE WORK** When part of a skeleton is found, detectives determine the height of the victim to help find the identity. If the victim is male and the length of the femur (large thigh bone) is known, the expression $69.089 + 2.238F$ can be used to find the height, where $F$ is the length of the femur. Find the height of a male victim whose femur measures 41 cm. $160.847$ cm

**MODELING** Use Algeblocks to simplify each expression. For 48–50, see additional answers.

**48.** $5x - 2x$
$3x$

**49.** $-2y + y - 3$
$-y - 3$

**50.** $3x - y - 6x + 2y$
$-3x + y$

**DATA FILE** For Exercises 51–54, use the data on sleep times on page 561. Let $x$ equal the average hours of sleep per day for a human adult. Write a variable expression for the sleep time of the following creatures.

**51.** elephant $x - 5$ **52.** armadillo $x + 11$ **53.** sheep $x - 2$ **54.** pig $x + 5$

**55.** Write and simplify an expression in terms of $x$ for the combined sleep time per day of the creatures in Exercises 51–54. $4x + 9$

## ■ EXTENDED PRACTICE EXERCISES

**56.** Subtract $(4a + b) + (3a + 2b)$ from $6a + 8b + (-4b + 7a)$. $6a + b$

**57.** Find the sum of $4a - 3b$, $a - b$ and $a - 5b$. $6a - 9b$

**58. CRITICAL THINKING** On Monday Kaz did $n$ sit-ups, on Tuesday he did $(n + 2)$ sit-ups, on Wednesday he did $(n + 5)$ sit-ups and on Thursday he did $(n + 9)$ sit-ups. If Kaz exercises every day and the pattern continues, how many sit-ups will he have done in all for the seven-day week? $7n + 77$

## ■ MIXED REVIEW EXERCISES

**Use the data for Exercises 59 and 60.** (Lesson 1-4)

| 15 | 37 | 23 | 39 | 34 | 26 | 11 | 23 | 18 | 29 |
|----|----|----|----|----|----|----|----|----|----|
| 26 | 34 | 19 | 12 | 15 | 28 | 21 | 36 | 29 | 35 |

**59.** Create a box-and-whisker plot to display the data. See additional answers.

**60.** Find the interquartile range of the data. $15.5$

 Math Online mathmatters2.com/self_check_quiz

## ADDITIONAL ANSWERS

**13.** 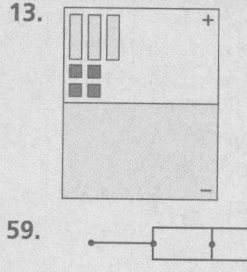  **48.** 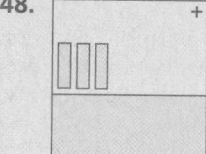  **49.** 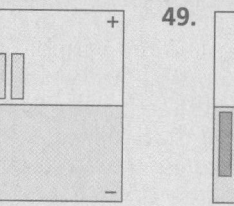  **50.**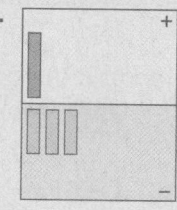

**59.**
$$\begin{array}{c}\hline 12\ \ 16\ \ 20\ \ 24\ \ 28\ \ 32\ \ 36\ \ 40\end{array}$$

---

Name _____ Date _____

EXTRA PRACTICE **2-4**
**ADD AND SUBTRACT VARIABLE EXPRESSIONS**

☑ **EXERCISES**

Simplify.

1. $7t + 4t$ _____ $11t$
2. $-4f + 5f$ _____ $f$
3. $15b - 24b$ _____ $-9b$
4. $3y - (-9y)$ _____ $12y$
5. $4w - 5w + 2w$ _____ $w$
6. $-\frac{1}{4}n - \frac{3}{4}n$ _____ $-n$
7. $-8d - (-2d) - 6d$ _____ $-12d$
8. $4.5x + 4.2y - 3x$ _____ $1.5x + 4.2y$
9. $12rs - 2rs + 4t$ _____ $10rs + 4t$
10. $\frac{3}{5}w - \frac{3}{10}z + \frac{2}{5}w$ _____ $w - \frac{3}{10}z$
11. $-0.9x + xy - 0.8y + 2y$ _____ $-0.9x + xy + 1.2y$
12. $9v + 4w - 10v + 3w$ _____ $-v + 7w$
13. $-j + 4k + jk - 5jk + 5j$ _____ $4j + 4k - 4jk$
14. $mn - 4mn + 7mn + m - n$ _____ $4mn + m - n$
15. $6rs + 5r + 8s - rs - r - s$ _____ $5rs + 4r + 7s$

Evaluate each expression when $x = -4$, $y = 6$, and $z = -\frac{1}{2}$.

16. $4x + 3x$ _____ $-28$
17. $-8z + 2y$ _____ $16$
18. $-4z + y + x$ _____ $4$
19. $-3y + 2x$ _____ $-26$
20. $\frac{1}{4}x - \frac{2}{3}y + z$ _____ $-5\frac{1}{2}$
21. $4xz + 4z - 2z$ _____ $7$
22. $\frac{1}{3}y + 2z + y$ _____ $7$
23. $5y - 3x + 2y - 4x$ _____ $70$

24. A basketball team scored $8x$ two-point baskets and $2x$ three-point baskets. Write and simplify an expression for the number of two-point and three-point baskets the team scored.
$8x + 2x = 10x$

---

Name _____ Date _____

ENRICHMENT **2-4**
**WHAT IS THE EXPRESSION?**

☑ **EXERCISES**

Fill in the blanks to find the expression that has been simplified. Answers may vary. Possible answers are given.

1. $\underline{6}x + \underline{2}x = 8x$
2. $\underline{10}y - \underline{5}y = 5y$
3. $\underline{6}m + \underline{6}m - \underline{(-4)}n = 12m + 4n$
4. $\underline{4}r - \underline{(-5)}s + \underline{(-2)}r = 2r + 5s$
5. $\underline{6}a - \underline{2}a - \underline{(-1)}b = 4a + b$
6. $\underline{5}z + \underline{2}y + \underline{5}z - \underline{17}y = 10z - 15y$
7. $\underline{14}ab - \underline{10}bc - \underline{2}ab = 12ab - 10bc$
8. $\underline{2}t - \underline{\frac{3}{2}}t = \frac{1}{2}t$
9. $\underline{\left(-\frac{1}{2}\right)}q + \underline{\left(-\frac{1}{2}\right)}q - \underline{\frac{1}{4}}q = -\frac{3}{4}q$
10. $\underline{2}h + \underline{0.5}h = 2.5h$
11. $\underline{2}m - \underline{(-1.5)}n + \underline{1.2}m = 3.2m + 1.5n$
12. $\underline{2}a + \underline{2}b - \underline{7}b + \underline{2}a = 4a - 5b$
13. $\underline{8}xy + \underline{4}yz + \underline{(-7)}yz - \underline{3}xy = 5xy - 3yz$
14. $\underline{1.2}t - \underline{0.2}tv + \underline{1.6}t - \underline{0.2}tv = 2.8t - 0.4tv$
15. $\underline{\frac{8}{1}}yz + \underline{\frac{6}{5}}z + \underline{\frac{1}{1}}yz = \frac{3}{8}yz + \frac{5}{6}z$
16. $\underline{\frac{2}{3}}st + \underline{\frac{3}{5}}s + \underline{\frac{1}{5}}s = \frac{4}{5}s - \frac{2}{3}st$

17. Can you write more than one answer for any of the exercises above? Why or why not?
Yes; many of them have more than one answer because there are many possible terms to combine to get the answer given.

---

**Lesson 2-3**
translate expressions

**Lesson 2-4**
like terms          unlike terms
simplify a variable expression
combining like terms
zero pairs

## Assignment Guide

**All students:** 1–90

## Chalkboard Examples

**Lesson 2-3**
Write each phrase as a variable expression.
a. a number decreased by four
   $n - 4$
b. the sum of twice a number and ten   $2n + 10$
c. the product of negative five and a number   $-5n$
d. the quotient of six and three times a number   $\frac{6}{3n}$

**Lesson 2-4**
Use Algeblocks to simplify the expression $x + 4 - 2x - 6$.
Solution:

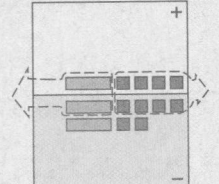

# Review and Practice Your Skills

## Practice ■ Lesson 2-3

**Write each phrase as a variable expression.**

1. eight increased by a number   $8 + x$
2. the sum of 11 and a number   $11 + x$
3. five less than a number   $x - 5$
4. some number less 19   $x - 19$
5. the product of eight and $y$   $8y$
6. the quotient of 15 and a number   $\frac{15}{x}$
7. four times a number decreased by seven   $4x - 7$
8. a number divided by three   $\frac{x}{3}$
9. one-half a number increased by six   $\frac{1}{2}x + 6$
10. a number increased by itself   $x + x$
11. two-thirds a number minus 14   $\frac{2}{3}x - 14$
12. the quotient of 45 and a number   $\frac{45}{x}$

**Translate each variable expression into a word phrase.**   For 13–28, see additional answers.

13. $b - 6$
14. $3a + 4$
15. $-4 - k$
16. $\frac{1}{3}x$
17. $-7x$
18. $\frac{t}{8}$
19. $\frac{5x}{10}$
20. $\frac{x}{y}$
21. $6x - 11$
22. $\frac{3}{x}$
23. $n + (-15)$
24. $4x$
25. $2x - 7$
26. $x - 9$
27. $5xy$
28. $\frac{1}{2}x + 10$

## Practice ■ Lesson 2-4

**Simplify.**

29. $x + x$   $2x$
30. $4x - x$   $3x$
31. $2y - 4y$   $-2y$
32. $3b - 5b + 10b$   $8b$
33. $7c - (-4c)$   $11c$
34. $x + 2y - x$   $2y$
35. $\frac{1}{2}t - \left(-\frac{1}{2}t\right) + \frac{1}{4}t$   $\frac{5}{4}t$
36. $6c - 2d + 7c - 5d$   $13c - 7d$
37. $3xy - xy + 4x$   $2xy + 4x$
38. $7ab + 9bc + (-4ab)$   $3ab + 9bc$
39. $5.2r - 3.1r + 7.5t$   $2.1r + 7.5t$
40. $p + p - q - q$   $2p - 2q$
41. $2z - 4y - 2z - 4y$   $-8y$
42. $\frac{1}{2}a - \frac{1}{4}a + \frac{2}{3}b$   $\frac{1}{4}a + \frac{2}{3}b$
43. $-3cd + 4d - 7d + 6cd$   $3cd - 3d$
44. $0.3x - 1.7y + 2.3y - 4.1x$   $-3.8x + 0.6y$
45. $n - 2m + 2n - m$   $3n - 3m$
46. $\frac{3}{7}p - \frac{1}{14}p + \frac{2}{3}q - \frac{1}{6}q$   $\frac{5}{14}p + \frac{1}{2}q$
47. $7a + \frac{1}{3}b + \frac{2}{3}a - \frac{2}{3}b$   $7\frac{2}{3}a - \frac{1}{3}b$
48. $\frac{11}{15}x + \frac{2}{9}z + \frac{2}{5}z - \frac{1}{3}x$   $\frac{2}{5}x + \frac{28}{45}z$
49. $19.3x - 17.7x - 3.7t + 5.9t$   $1.6x + 2.2t$
50. $17x - (-23x) - 2y + 14y$   $40x + 12y$
51. $2.6j - 4.8k - 4.3k - 0.2j$   $2.4j - 9.1k$
52. $\frac{1}{3}x + \frac{3}{4}y + \frac{2}{5}x - \frac{1}{y}$   $\frac{11}{15}x + \frac{8}{5}y$

**Evaluate each expression when $w = 2$, $x = 3$, $y = 4$ and $z = 6$.**

53. $-7x - y$   $-25$
54. $-5z - (-3y)$   $-18$
55. $-9w + 2y + 4w$   $-2$
56. $\frac{1}{2}y + \frac{2}{3}z$   $6$
57. $y - x + 6z$   $37$
58. $4x - 3w + x - 2w$   $5$
59. $4w + 2y$   $16$
60. $z - 2w$   $2$
61. $-x - x$   $-6$
62. $-\frac{1}{2}w + y$   $3$
63. $w + x - y + z$   $7$
64. $-w - x - y - z$   $-15$
65. $4z + 4w - 4x$   $20$
66. $\frac{1}{3}(z + x)$   $3$
67. $\frac{1}{4}w + \frac{2}{3}z$   $4\frac{1}{2}$
68. $2x - 4y + 7w - z$   $-2$
69. $\frac{2}{7}x + \frac{z}{7} + \frac{w}{7}$   $2$
70. $1.2z + 7.9w - 0.7z$   $-2.9w$   $13$

## Teaching Tip

Remind students that when translating a variable expression into a word phrase, there is more than one possible answer. For Exercises 13–28, have students use two different word phrases as translations for each variable expression. For example, some translations for $b - 6$ (Exercise 13) are: "a number decreased by six", "six less than a number", "the difference of a number and 6".

13. the difference of a number and six
14. three times a number increased by four
15. negative four decreased by a number
16. one-third of a number
17. the product of negative seven and a number
18. the quotient of a number and eight
19. the product of five and a number divided by ten
20. a number divided by a number
21. six times a number decreased by 11
22. three divided by a number
23. the sum of a number and $-15$
24. four times a number
25. twice a number decreased by seven
26. a number decreased by nine
27. a product of five and two other numbers
28. one-half of a number increased by ten
75. the difference of 8.7 and a number
76. a number decreased by 270.5
77. the quotient of a number and three
78. the product of two and the sum of a number and five

## PRACTICE ◼ LESSON 2-1–LESSON 2-4

**Write each phrase as a variable expression.** (Lesson 2-3)

**71.** the sum of five and twice a number  $5 + 2x$  **72.** seven less than a number  $x - 7$

**73.** 12 divided by a number  $\dfrac{12}{y}$  **74.** a number multiplied by $-13$  $-13y$

**Translate each variable expression into a word phrase.** (Lesson 2-3)
For 75–78, see additional answers.

**75.** $8.7 - z$  **76.** $x - 270.5$  **77.** $\dfrac{x}{3}$  **78.** $2(x + 5)$

**Simplify.** (Lesson 2-4)

**79.** $-5x - (-5x) + 5x$  $5x$  **80.** $-3xy - 4xy - 7xy$  $-14xy$  **81.** $-2x + 2x$  $0$

**82.** $9x + 12 + x$  $10x + 12$  **83.** $15 + 14z - z$  $15 + 13z$  **84.** $6n + 7m + 16n$  $22n + 7m$

**Evaluate each expression when $a = 3$, $b = 8$ and $c = 5$.** (Lesson 2-1–Lesson 2-4)

**85.** $-3a + 2a + 4b$  $29$  **86.** $4b - 5b$  $-8$  **87.** $\dfrac{1}{5}c - \dfrac{1}{3}a + \dfrac{1}{2}b$  $4$

**88.** $-b + a - (-c)$  $0$  **89.** $2ab - c$  $43$  **90.** $-2a + 5c + c$  $24$

# Mid-Chapter Quiz

**Graph the given sets of numbers on a number line.** (Lesson 2-1) For 1–4, see additional answers.

**1.** $\left\{-\dfrac{1}{2}, 0, \dfrac{1}{2}, \dfrac{3}{2}\right\}$  **2.** $\{-3.25, -1.5, -0.75, 1.75\}$

**3.** all real numbers greater than $-2$  **4.** integers between $-2$ and $7$

**Simplify each numerical expression.** (Lesson 2-2)

**5.** $(7 + 21) \div 2^2$  $7$  **6.** $4 \cdot 6 - 3 + 11$  $32$  **7.** $3.4 - 2(0.8 - 1.3)$  $4.4$

**8.** $3 \cdot 5 - 2 \div 4$  $14\frac{1}{2}$  **9.** $(5^2 \div 5) + 5 \cdot 2^3$  $45$  **10.** $\dfrac{2}{3} \cdot 3^2 - 6$  $0$

**Write each word phrase as a variable expression.** (Lesson 2-3)

**11.** seven more than a number  $x + 7$  **12.** the quotient of a number and 11  $\dfrac{x}{11}$

**13.** one-third of a number  $\dfrac{1}{3}x$  **14.** the difference of $-44$ and a number  $-44 - x$

**Evaluate each variable expression when $x = -4$, $y = -10$ and $z = 3.5$.** (Lesson 2-4)

**15.** $2y - 10$  $-30$  **16.** $-|x|$  $-4$  **17.** $\dfrac{yz}{x}$  $\dfrac{35}{4}$  **18.** $(x + y) - z$  $-17.5$

**19.** $(x - y)z$  $21$  **20.** $-4z - \left(\dfrac{2y}{x}\right)$  $-19$  **21.** $x - 2y$  $16$  **22.** $|y + 3z|$  $0.5$

**Simplify.** (Lesson 2-4)

**23.** $4x + 8x$  $12x$  **24.** $7y - 15y$  $-8y$  **25.** $-\dfrac{2}{3}b + \dfrac{1}{6}b$  $-\dfrac{1}{2}b$

**26.** $1.6a - 3.5b + 2.7a$  $4.3a - 3.5b$  **27.** $-4x - (-4x) + 4x$  $4x$  **28.** $5ab - 7a - 11ab + b$  $-7a - 6ab + b$

## MID-CHAPTER QUIZ

**1.**

**2.**

**3.**

**4.**

## Lesson Planning

### NCTM Standards/Strands
- Representation
- Connections
- Communication

### Vocabulary
property of the opposite of a sum

### Tools/Materials Needed
Algeblocks and Quadrant Mat

### Lesson Resources
Warm-up Transparency 6
Transparency TK-4, 6, RF-8
Reteaching 2-5
Extra Practice 2-5
Enrichment 2-5

## Getting Started

### 5-MINUTE WARM-UP

**Simplify each expression.**
1. $3 \cdot (2 + 4)$    **18**
2. $-4 \cdot (5 - 3)$    **−8**
3. $-2 \cdot (-7 - 1)$    **16**
4. $\frac{1}{3} \cdot (6 - 18)$    **−4**

### Introduction to Lesson 2-5
Remind students that when "forming rectangular areas" in the quadrants bounded by Algeblocks, the "union" of two unit blocks is a unit block and the "union" of a unit block and an $x$-block is an $x$-block.

---

# 2-5 Multiply and Divide Variable Expressions

**Goals**
- Simplify variable expressions.
- Evaluate variable expressions.

**Applications**   Part-time job, Weather, Engineering, Spreadsheets

**Use Algeblocks to multiply the variable expression $2(x - 3)$.**
For 1–3, see additional answers.
1. On a Quadrant Mat, place 2 unit blocks on the positive part of the horizontal axis.

2. Place 1 $x$-block in the positive part of the vertical axis and 3 unit blocks in the negative part of the vertical axis.

3. Form rectangular areas in all the quadrants that are bounded by Algeblocks.

4. Read the answer from the Quadrant Mat. $2x - 6$

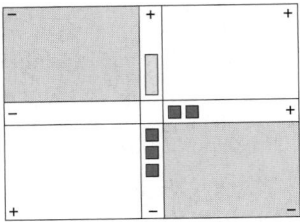

### ▶ BUILD UNDERSTANDING

To multiply variable expressions, use the distributive property.

### Example 1

**Simplify.**

**a.** $4(m + 7)$        **b.** $-8(4.5 - rs)$        **c.** $-(2x + y)$

**Solution**

**a.** $4(m + 7) = 4m + 4(7)$          Use the distributive property.
$\qquad\qquad = 4m + 28$

**b.** $-8(4.5 - rs) = -8(4.5) - (-8)(rs)$     Use the distributive property.
$\qquad\qquad = -36 - (-8rs)$        To subtract, add the opposite.
$\qquad\qquad = -36 + 8rs$

**c.** $-(2x + y) = (-1)(2x + y)$        Apply the multiplication property of $-1$.
$\qquad\qquad = (-1)(2x) + (-1)(y)$     Use the distributive property.
$\qquad\qquad = -2x + (-y) = -2x - y$

Example 1, part c, is an illustration of the **property of the opposite of a sum**. The negative sign on the outside of parentheses indicates you are to multiply each term by $-1$.

| **Property of the Opposite of a Sum** | For all real numbers $a$ and $b$, $-(a + b) = -1(a + b)$ $= -a + (-b)$ |
|---|---|

72 | Chapter 2 **Foundations of Algebra**

---

## Teaching Tip

Have students explain different ways of doing the calculations in the Warm-up Exercises. *Example:* $3 \cdot (2 + 4)$

Method 1—*First work in parentheses.*
$$3 \cdot (2 + 4)$$
$$= 3 \cdot (6)$$
$$= 18$$

Method 2—*Apply the distributive property.*
$$3 \cdot (2 + 4)$$
$$= 3 \cdot 2 + 3 \cdot 4$$
$$= 6 + 12$$
$$= 18$$

Students should conclude that when a product containing parentheses is all numerical, the calculation is easier if the work within the parentheses is done first.

To divide a variable expression, divide each term in the numerator by the denominator.

## Example 2

**Simplify.**

**a.** $\dfrac{2x + 6}{2}$

**b.** $\dfrac{-7y - 16}{-4}$

**c.** $\dfrac{3.6 + 1.2rs}{0.6}$

### Solution

**a.** $\dfrac{2x + 6}{2} = \dfrac{2x}{2} + \dfrac{6}{2}$

$= x + 3$

**b.** $\dfrac{-7y - 16}{-4} = \dfrac{-7y}{-4} - \dfrac{16}{-4}$

$= \dfrac{7}{4}y + 4$

**c.** $\dfrac{3.6 + 1.2rs}{0.6} = \dfrac{3.6}{0.6} + \dfrac{1.2rs}{0.6}$

$= 6 + 2rs$

> **Think Back**
>
> Recall division of signed numbers.
>
> $\dfrac{12}{4} = 3$ $\qquad$ $\dfrac{-12}{4} = -3$
>
> $\dfrac{12}{-4} = -3$ $\qquad$ $\dfrac{-12}{-4} = 3$

## Example 3

Evaluate each expression when $a = 6$, $b = -5$, and $c = \dfrac{1}{3}$.

**a.** $-2(a + 7)$

**b.** $\dfrac{4b - 12}{-4}$

**c.** $9c(a - 10)$

### Solution

First substitute the appropriate value for each variable. Then simplify the expression using the order of operations.

**a.** $-2(a + 7) = -2(6 + 7)$

$= -2(13)$

$= -26$

**b.** $\dfrac{4b - 12}{-4} = \dfrac{4(-5) - 12}{-4}$

$= \dfrac{-20 - 12}{-4}$

$= \dfrac{-32}{-4}$

$= 8$

**c.** $9c(a - 10) = 9\left(\dfrac{1}{3}\right)(6 - 10)$

$= 3(-4)$

$= -12$

## Example 4

**PART-TIME JOB** Katie works $(9x + 6)$ hours every week. She works 3 days for the same amount of time each day. How many hours does Katie work in one day?

### Solution

$\dfrac{9x + 6}{3} = \dfrac{9x}{3} + \dfrac{6}{3}$ $\qquad$ $\dfrac{\text{number of hours per week}}{\text{number of days per week}}$

$= 3x + 2$

Katie works $(3x + 2)$ hours in one day.

**Math Online** mathmatters2.com/extra_examples

Lesson 2-5 **Multiply and Divide Variable Expressions** 73

---

## Chalkboard Examples

**Supplementary Example 1**
**Simplify.**

**a.** $-2(n - 5)$ $\quad -2n + 10$

**b.** $0.3(x + 0.7)$ $\quad 0.3x + 0.21$

**c.** $-(2ab + 9ac)$ $\quad -2ab - 9ac$

**Supplementary Example 2**
**Simplify.**

**a.** $\dfrac{6x + 3}{3}$ $\quad \dfrac{6x}{3} + \dfrac{3}{3} = 2x + 1$

**b.** $\dfrac{10y - 5}{2}$ $\quad \dfrac{10y}{2} - \dfrac{5}{2} = 5y - \dfrac{5}{2}$

**c.** $\dfrac{1.6 - 0.8z}{-8}$ $\quad \dfrac{1.6}{-8} - \dfrac{0.8z}{-8} =$
$-0.2 + 0.1z$

**Supplementary Example 3**
Evaluate each expression when $x = 2$ and $y = -4$.

**a.** $-3(x^2 + 1)$ $\quad -3(2^2 + 1) =$
$-3(4 + 1) = -3(5) = -15$

**b.** $-4|6 - y|$
$-4|6 - (-4)| = -4|10| = -40$

**c.** $\dfrac{|y - x|}{|x - y|}$ $\quad \dfrac{|-4 - 2|}{|2 - (-4)|} = \dfrac{|-6|}{|6|} = \dfrac{6}{6} = 1$

**Supplementary Example 4**
**TRAVEL** Moesha covered a distance of $(55x + 110)$ miles while driving at the rate of 55 miles per hour. How many hours did she drive?
Solution:
Since $D = R \cdot T$, $T = \dfrac{D}{R}$.

$\dfrac{55x + 110}{55} = \dfrac{55x}{55} + \dfrac{110}{55} = x + 2$

Moesha drove for $(x + 2)$ hours.

---

## ADDITIONAL ANSWERS

1.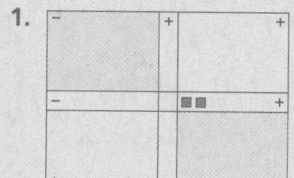

2.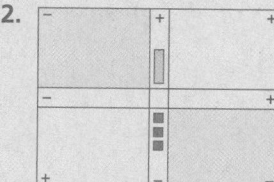

3.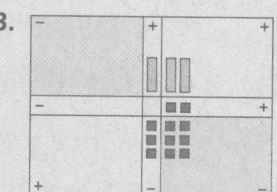

## Lesson Wrap-up

### QUICK ASSESSMENT

Ask the following questions to determine if students understand the content presented in this lesson.

**Choose the correct answer for each simplification.**

1. $-2(3x - 6)$ **C**
   A. $-6x - 6$  B. $-6x - 12$
   C. $-6x + 12$  D. $6x + 12$

2. $\dfrac{8x - 4}{-4}$ **D**
   A. $-2x$  B. $-2x + 0$
   C. $-2x - 1$  D. $-2x + 1$

3. $\dfrac{10 - y}{-5}$ **C**
   A. $-2 + y$  B. $-2 - y$
   C. $-2 + \dfrac{y}{5}$  D. $-2 - \dfrac{y}{5}$

### ASSIGNMENT GUIDE

**Basic:** 1–59, 66–68
**Enriched:** 1–68

---

### Reteaching Worksheet 2-5

Name _____  Date _____

RETEACHING  **2-5**
**MULTIPLY AND DIVIDE VARIABLE EXPRESSIONS**
The distributive property is used to multiply variable expressions.
Sometimes you can use the property of the opposite of a sum to simplify.

| Property of the Opposite of a Sum | For all real numbers $a$ and $b$, $-(a + b) = -a + (-b)$. |
|---|---|

**Example 1**
Simplify $3(r + 6)$.
**Solution**
Distribute 3 to $r$ and 6.
$3(r + 6) = 3r + 3(6)$
$= 3r + 18$

**Example 2**
Simplify $-(5a + c)$.
**Solution**
Use the property of the opposite of a sum.
$-(5a + c) = -5a + (-c)$
$= -5a - c$

Each term in the numerator is divided by the denominator to divided variables expressions.

**Example 3**
Simplify $\dfrac{4y + 8}{4}$.
**Solution**
Divide 4y by 4 and divide 8 by 4.
$\dfrac{4y + 8}{4} = \dfrac{4y}{4} + \dfrac{8}{4}$
$= y + 2$

**Example 4**
Simplify $\dfrac{5x - 9}{3}$.
**Solution**
Divide 5x by 3 and divide −9 by 3.
$\dfrac{5x - 9}{3} = \dfrac{5x}{3} - \dfrac{9}{3}$
$= \dfrac{5}{3}x - 3$

■ **EXERCISES**

Simplify each variable expression.

1. $2(c + 2)$  $2c + 4$
2. $4(r - 4)$  $4r - 16$
3. $-(5 + w)$  $-5 - w$
4. $-8(3 - a)$  $-24 + 8a$
5. $2(a + b)$  $2a + 2b$
6. $-4(2x + y)$  $-8x - 4y$
7. $\dfrac{3r - 6}{3}$  $r - 2$
8. $\dfrac{10t - 15}{5}$  $2t - 3$
9. $\dfrac{5d + 12}{4}$  $\dfrac{5}{4}d + 3$

---

### ■ TRY THESE EXERCISES

**Simplify.**

1. $2(5 + s)$  $10 + 2s$
2. $-3\left(x + \dfrac{1}{6}\right)$  $-3x - \dfrac{1}{2}$
3. $6(3.1 - 4b)$  $18.6 - 24b$
4. $-8(x - y)$  $-8x + 8y$
5. $\dfrac{2d - 6}{2}$  $d - 3$
6. $\dfrac{-15j + 30}{5}$  $-3j + 6$
7. $\dfrac{-4.2w - 3.5}{0.7}$  $-6w - 5$
8. $\dfrac{12x + 15y}{-3}$  $-4x - 5y$

**Evaluate each expression when $x = -3$, $y = 7$, and $z = 0.5$.**

9. $3(z - 0.7)$  $-0.6$
10. $-\dfrac{1}{2}(11 - y)$  $-2$
11. $\dfrac{2x - 9}{3}$  $-5$
12. $\dfrac{3y + x}{-9}$  $-2$

13. **MODELING** Use Algeblocks to find the product $-4(y + 2)$.  $-4y - 8$; See additional answers.

14. **PART-TIME JOB** Tim earns \$3.50/h plus tips as a waiter after school. Write and simplify an expression for the amount of money he earns in 5 h.  \$17.50 + t

15. **WRITING MATH** Describe how you would simplify $-7(x + y)$.
Answers will vary but may include to distribute $-7$ over the expression $(x + 4)$.

### ■ PRACTICE EXERCISES • For Extra Practice, see page 590.

**Simplify.**

16. $3(a + 11)$  $3a + 33$
17. $-5(m + 3)$  $-5m - 15$
18. $16(rs - 5)$  $16rs - 80$
19. $\dfrac{1}{4}(-36 - x)$  $-9 - \dfrac{1}{4}x$
20. $-17(2a + b)$  $-34a - 17b$
21. $0.4(0.8h - 0.6k)$  $0.32h - 0.24k$
22. $-2(-5n + 8p)$  $10n - 16p$
23. $-3(-3q - 4r)$  $9q + 12r$
24. $-8(-7h + 5j)$  $56h - 40j$
25. $7(-8q - 7r)$  $-56q - 49r$
26. $11(-10s - 11t)$  $-110s - 121t$
27. $-\dfrac{7}{8}(-16c + 40d)$  $14c - 35d$
28. $\dfrac{-6a + 42}{6}$  $-a + 7$
29. $\dfrac{24b + 8}{-4}$  $-6b - 2$
30. $\dfrac{14x - 84}{-7}$  $-2x + 12$
31. $\dfrac{3.5 - 4.0p}{0.5}$  $7 - 8p$
32. $\dfrac{-36r - 48s}{12}$  $-3r - 4s$
33. $\dfrac{-20m + 50n}{-5}$  $4m - 10n$
34. $\dfrac{56j - 48k}{8}$  $7j - 6k$
35. $\dfrac{-9q + 9r}{-3}$  $3q - 3r$
36. $\dfrac{2.7c - 3.3d}{-0.3}$  $-9c + 11d$
37. $\dfrac{-6d - 3g}{-3}$  $2d + g$
38. $-17s + \dfrac{16t}{4}$  $-17s + 4t$
39. $\dfrac{169w - 39v}{-11}$  $-\dfrac{169}{11}w + \dfrac{39}{11}v$

**Evaluate each expression when $a = \dfrac{1}{3}$, $b = -5$ and $c = 6$.**

40. $-9(a - 27)$  $240$
41. $8(-b - 6)$  $-8$
42. $\dfrac{c - 21}{3}$  $-5$
43. $\dfrac{6a + 14}{2}$  $8$
44. $a(-9 + c)$  $-1$
45. $-0.5(b - 2c)$  $8.5$
46. $\dfrac{-9a - b}{5}$  $\dfrac{2}{5}$
47. $\dfrac{3c - 2b}{7}$  $4$

**MODELING** Use Algeblocks to find each product. For 48–51, see additional answers.

48. $3(x - 4)$  $3x - 12$
49. $-2(y + 1)$  $-2y - 2$
50. $2(x - y)$  $2x - 2y$
51. $-1(2x + 3)$  $-2x - 3$

52. Write and simplify an expression for the area of the figure shown.  $30x + 45$

2x + 3

15

53. Most movie screens in movie theaters have a length of $(x + 14)$ feet and a height of $x$ feet. Find the area of a movie screen if $x = 19$.  627 ft²

54. **WEATHER** The formula $C = \dfrac{5}{9}(F - 32)$ relates Celsius and Fahrenheit temperatures. The temperature in Celsius is $C$, and the degrees in Fahrenheit is $F$. Find the number of degrees Celsius that is equal to a temperature of 50°F.  10°C

### ADDITIONAL ANSWERS

13.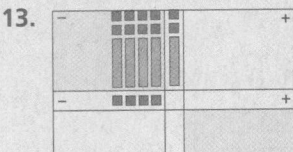
48.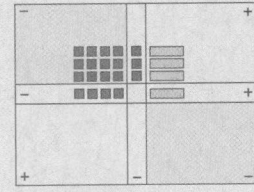
49.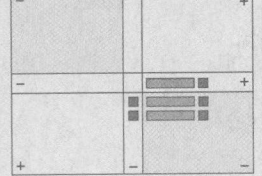

To divide a variable expression, divide each term in the numerator by the denominator.

## Example 2

**Simplify.**

**a.** $\dfrac{2x + 6}{2}$

**b.** $\dfrac{-7y - 16}{-4}$

**c.** $\dfrac{3.6 + 1.2rs}{0.6}$

### Solution

**a.** $\dfrac{2x + 6}{2} = \dfrac{2x}{2} + \dfrac{6}{2}$

$\quad = x + 3$

**b.** $\dfrac{-7y - 16}{-4} = \dfrac{-7y}{-4} - \dfrac{16}{-4}$

$\quad = \dfrac{7}{4}y + 4$

**c.** $\dfrac{3.6 + 1.2rs}{0.6} = \dfrac{3.6}{0.6} + \dfrac{1.2rs}{0.6}$

$\quad = 6 + 2rs$

> **Think Back**
>
> Recall division of signed numbers.
>
> $\dfrac{12}{4} = 3 \qquad \dfrac{-12}{4} = -3$
>
> $\dfrac{12}{-4} = -3 \qquad \dfrac{-12}{-4} = 3$

## Example 3

**Evaluate each expression when $a = 6$, $b = -5$, and $c = \dfrac{1}{3}$.**

**a.** $-2(a + 7)$

**b.** $\dfrac{4b - 12}{-4}$

**c.** $9c(a - 10)$

### Solution

First substitute the appropriate value for each variable. Then simplify the expression using the order of operations.

**a.** $-2(a + 7) = -2(6 + 7)$

$\quad = -2(13)$

$\quad = -26$

**b.** $\dfrac{4b - 12}{-4} = \dfrac{4(-5) - 12}{-4}$

$\quad = \dfrac{-20 - 12}{-4}$

$\quad = \dfrac{-32}{-4}$

$\quad = 8$

**c.** $9c(a - 10) = 9\left(\dfrac{1}{3}\right)(6 - 10)$

$\quad = 3(-4)$

$\quad = -12$

## Example 4

**PART-TIME JOB** Katie works $(9x + 6)$ hours every week. She works 3 days for the same amount of time each day. How many hours does Katie work in one day?

### Solution

$\dfrac{9x + 6}{3} = \dfrac{9x}{3} + \dfrac{6}{3}$ $\qquad$
number of hours per week / number of days per week

$\quad = 3x + 2$

Katie works $(3x + 2)$ hours in one day.

---

**Chalkboard Examples**

**Supplementary Example 1**
Simplify.
**a.** $-2(n - 5)$  $-2n + 10$
**b.** $0.3(x + 0.7)$  $0.3x + 0.21$
**c.** $-(2ab + 9ac)$  $-2ab - 9ac$

**Supplementary Example 2**
Simplify.
**a.** $\dfrac{6x + 3}{3}$  $\dfrac{6x}{3} + \dfrac{3}{3} = 2x + 1$
**b.** $\dfrac{10y - 5}{2}$  $\dfrac{10y}{2} - \dfrac{5}{2} = 5y - \dfrac{5}{2}$
**c.** $\dfrac{1.6 - 0.8z}{-8}$  $\dfrac{1.6}{-8} - \dfrac{0.8z}{-8} = -0.2 + 0.1z$

**Supplementary Example 3**
Evaluate each expression when $x = 2$ and $y = -4$.
**a.** $-3(x^2 + 1)$  $-3(2^2 + 1) = -3(4 + 1) = -3(5) = -15$
**b.** $-4|6 - y|$
$-4|6 - (-4)| = -4|10| = -40$
**c.** $\dfrac{|y - x|}{|x - y|}$  $\dfrac{|-4 - 2|}{|2 - (-4)|} = \dfrac{|-6|}{|6|} = \dfrac{6}{6} = 1$

**Supplementary Example 4**
**TRAVEL** Moesha covered a distance of $(55x + 110)$ miles while driving at the rate of 55 miles per hour. How many hours did she drive?
Solution:
Since $D = R \cdot T$, $T = \dfrac{D}{R}$.
$\dfrac{55x + 110}{55} = \dfrac{55x}{55} + \dfrac{110}{55} = x + 2$
Moesha drove for $(x + 2)$ hours.

---

## ADDITIONAL ANSWERS

1.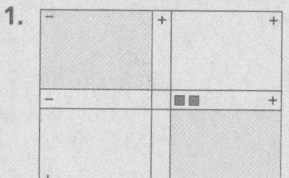

2.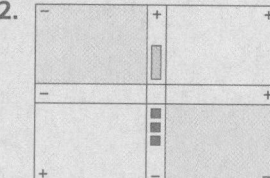

3.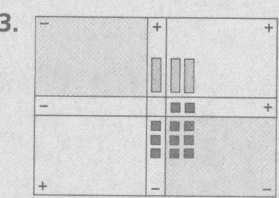

# Lesson Wrap-up

## QUICK ASSESSMENT

Ask the following questions to determine if students understand the content presented in this lesson.

**Choose the correct answer for each simplification.**

1. $-2(3x - 6)$ **C**
   A. $-6x - 6$      B. $-6x - 12$
   C. $-6x + 12$     D. $6x + 12$

2. $\dfrac{8x - 4}{-4}$ **D**
   A. $-2x$       B. $-2x + 0$
   C. $-2x - 1$    D. $-2x + 1$

3. $\dfrac{10 - y}{-5}$ **C**
   A. $-2 + y$      B. $-2 - y$
   C. $-2 + \dfrac{y}{5}$    D. $-2 - \dfrac{y}{5}$

## ASSIGNMENT GUIDE

**Basic:** 1–59, 66–68
**Enriched:** 1–68

---

### Reteaching Worksheet 2-5

Name _____ Date _____

RETEACHING **2-5**

**MULTIPLY AND DIVIDE VARIABLE EXPRESSIONS**

The distributive property is used to multiply variable expressions. Sometimes you can use the property of the opposite of a sum to simplify.

| Property of the Opposite of a Sum | For all real numbers $a$ and $b$, $-(a + b) = -a + (-b)$. |
|---|---|

**Example 1**

Simplify $3(r + 6)$.

**Solution**

Distribute 3 to $r$ and 6.

$3(r + 6) = 3r + 3(6)$
$= 3r + 18$

**Example 2**

Simplify $-(5a + c)$.

**Solution**

Use the property of the opposite of a sum.

$-(5a + c) = -5a + (-c)$
$= -5a - c$

Each term in the numerator is divided by the denominator to divided variables expressions.

**Example 3**

Simplify $\dfrac{4y + 8}{4}$.

**Solution**

Divide $4y$ by 4 and divide 8 by 4.

$\dfrac{4y + 8}{4} = \dfrac{4y}{4} + \dfrac{8}{4}$
$= y + 2$

**Example 4**

Simplify $\dfrac{5x - 9}{3}$.

**Solution**

Divide $5x$ by 3 and divide $-9$ by 3.

$\dfrac{5x - 9}{3} = \dfrac{5x}{3} - \dfrac{9}{3}$
$= \dfrac{5}{3}x - 3$

☑ **EXERCISES**

Simplify each variable expression.

1. $2(c + 2)$   $2c + 4$    2. $4(r - 4)$   $4r - 16$    3. $-(5 + w)$   $-5 - w$

4. $-8(3 - a)$   $-24 + 8a$    5. $2(a + b)$   $2a + 2b$    6. $-4(2x + y)$   $-8x - 4y$

7. $\dfrac{3r - 6}{3}$   $r - 2$    8. $\dfrac{10t - 15}{5}$   $2t - 3$    9. $\dfrac{5d + 12}{4}$   $\dfrac{5}{4}d + 3$

---

## ▸ TRY THESE EXERCISES

**Simplify.**

1. $2(5 + s)$   $10 + 2s$     2. $-3\left(x + \dfrac{1}{6}\right)$   $-3x - \dfrac{1}{2}$     3. $6(3.1 - 4b)$   $18.6 - 24b$     4. $-8(x - y)$   $-8x + 8y$

5. $\dfrac{2d - 6}{2}$   $d - 3$     6. $\dfrac{-15j + 30}{5}$   $-3j + 6$     7. $\dfrac{-4.2w - 3.5}{0.7}$   $-6w - 5$     8. $\dfrac{12x + 15y}{-3}$   $-4x - 5y$

**Evaluate each expression when $x = -3$, $y = 7$, and $z = 0.5$.**

9. $3(z - 0.7)$   $-0.6$     10. $-\dfrac{1}{2}(11 - y)$   $-2$     11. $\dfrac{2x - 9}{3}$   $-5$     12. $\dfrac{3y + x}{-9}$   $-2$

13. **MODELING** Use Algeblocks to find the product $-4(y + 2)$.   $-4y - 8$; See additional answers.

14. **PART-TIME JOB** Tim earns \$3.50/h plus tips as a waiter after school. Write and simplify an expression for the amount of money he earns in 5 h.   $\$17.50 + t$

15. **WRITING MATH** Describe how you would simplify $-7(x + y)$.
   Answers will vary but may include to distribute $-7$ over the expression $(x + 4)$.

## ▸ PRACTICE EXERCISES  •  For Extra Practice, see page 590.

**Simplify.**

16. $3(a + 11)$   $3a + 33$    17. $-5(m + 3)$   $-5m - 15$    18. $16(rs - 5)$   $16rs - 80$    19. $\dfrac{1}{4}(-36 - x)$   $-9 - \dfrac{1}{4}x$

20. $-17(2a + b)$   $-34a - 17b$    21. $0.4(0.8h - 0.6k)$   $0.32h - 0.24k$    22. $-2(-5n + 8p)$   $10n - 16p$    23. $-3(-3q - 4r)$   $9q + 12r$

24. $-8(-7h + 5j)$   $56h - 40j$    25. $7(-8q - 7r)$   $-56q - 49r$    26. $11(-10s - 11t)$   $-110s - 121t$    27. $-\dfrac{7}{8}(-16c + 40d)$   $14c - 35d$

28. $\dfrac{-6a + 42}{6}$   $-a + 7$    29. $\dfrac{24b + 8}{-4}$   $-6b - 2$    30. $\dfrac{14x - 84}{-7}$   $-2x + 12$    31. $\dfrac{3.5 - 4.0p}{0.5}$   $7 - 8p$

32. $\dfrac{-36r - 48s}{12}$   $-3r - 4s$    33. $\dfrac{-20m + 50n}{-5}$   $4m - 10n$    34. $\dfrac{56j - 48k}{8}$   $7j - 6k$    35. $\dfrac{-9q + 9r}{-3}$   $3q - 3r$

36. $\dfrac{2.7c - 3.3d}{-0.3}$   $-9c + 11d$    37. $\dfrac{-6d - 3g}{-3}$   $2d + g$    38. $-17s + \dfrac{16t}{4}$   $-17s + 4t$    39. $\dfrac{169w - 39v}{-11}$   $-\dfrac{169}{11}w + \dfrac{39}{11}v$

**Evaluate each expression when $a = \dfrac{1}{3}$, $b = -5$ and $c = 6$.**

40. $-9(a - 27)$   $240$    41. $8(-b - 6)$   $-8$    42. $\dfrac{c - 21}{3}$   $-5$    43. $\dfrac{6a + 14}{2}$   $8$

44. $a(-9 + c)$   $-1$    45. $-0.5(b - 2c)$   $8.5$    46. $\dfrac{-9a - b}{5}$   $\dfrac{2}{5}$    47. $\dfrac{3c - 2b}{7}$   $4$

**MODELING** Use Algeblocks to find each product. For 48–51, see additional answers.

48. $3(x - 4)$   $3x - 12$    49. $-2(y + 1)$   $-2y - 2$    50. $2(x - y)$   $2x - 2y$    51. $-1(2x + 3)$   $-2x - 3$

52. Write and simplify an expression for the area of the figure shown.   $30x + 45$

[Figure: rectangle with top labeled $2x + 3$ and left side labeled 15]

53. Most movie screens in movie theaters have a length of $(x + 14)$ feet and a height of $x$ feet. Find the area of a movie screen if $x = 19$.   $627 \text{ ft}^2$

54. **WEATHER** The formula $C = \dfrac{5}{9}(F - 32)$ relates Celsius and Fahrenheit temperatures. The temperature in Celsius is $C$, and the degrees in Fahrenheit is $F$. Find the number of degrees Celsius that is equal to a temperature of 50°F.   $10°C$

## ADDITIONAL ANSWERS

13.

48.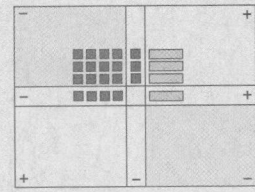

49.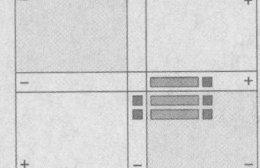

**SPREADSHEET** Cells of a spreadsheet can include variable expressions. Cell A2 contains the number of people that are registered to play basketball.

| | A | B | C | D |
|---|---|---|---|---|
| 1 | number of players | uniform costs | number of teams | |
| 2 | | | | |
| 3 | | | | |
| 4 | | | | |
| 5 | | | | |

**55.** Write an expression for cell B2 that will compute the total cost of uniforms at $21/uniform. A2 · 21

**56.** Write an expression for cell C2 that will compute the number of teams that can be formed if each team must include at least 10 people. A2 ÷ 10

**57.** Suppose the value in cell A2 is 127. Find the total cost of uniforms. $2667

**58.** Find the number of teams that can be formed with 127 total players. Will there be exactly 10 members on each team? 12; no

**59. ERROR ALERT** Ermano simplified the expression $-5(2x - 3y + 4xy)$. His work is shown. Is he correct? Explain.

$$-5(2x - 3y + 4xy) = -10x + 15y + 4xy$$
$$= 5xy + 4xy$$
$$= 9xy$$

No; he did not multiply $-5$ and $4xy$, and he combined unlike terms $-10x$ and $15y$.

## ■ EXTENDED PRACTICE EXERCISES

Simplify.

**60.** $-\frac{2}{5}(10xy + 25x - 15y)$     **61.** $41(-9a + 25b - c + 12d)$     **62.** $\dfrac{-21f - 49g + 7h - 21k}{-7}$
$-4xy - 10x + 6y$           $-369a + 1025b - 41c + 492d$
                                                           $3f + 7g - h + 3k$

**63. ENGINEERING** Before building a house, an engineer calculates the amount of material to be removed from the ground in order to pour the foundation. The formula to find the amount of earth to remove for the shape shown is $\frac{d(a + b)}{2} \cdot L$. Find the amount of earth to be removed when $a = 43$ m, $b = 39$ m, $d = 7$ m and $L = 32$ m. 9184 m³

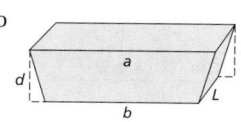

**64. CRITICAL THINKING** If $3(x + y) = 3x + 3y$, is $3 + (x \cdot y) = (3 + x)(3 + y)$ true? Experiment by substituting values for $x$ and $y$. Explain your conclusion.
No; both sides of the equation have different values for each $x$ and $y$.

**65. CHAPTER INVESTIGATION** Calculate the population density of the state and city you chose by dividing the population by its area in square miles or kilometers. Answers will vary.

## ■ MIXED REVIEW EXERCISES

Refer to the histogram to answer the questions. (Lesson 1-3)

**66.** Which interval contains the heights of the greatest number of people? 63–67

**67.** Name an interval that contains about 25% of the people. 58–62

**68.** How many sixteen-year-olds are between 5 ft 3 in. and 5 ft 7 in. tall? 7

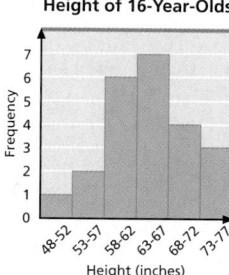
**Height of 16-Year-Olds**

## ADDITIONAL ANSWERS

**50.** 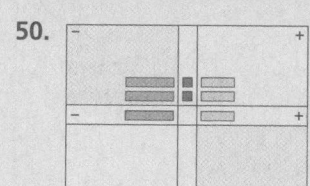      **51.**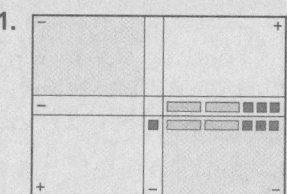

---

Name _____ Date _____

EXTRA PRACTICE 2-5
**MULTIPLY AND DIVIDE VARIABLE EXPRESSIONS**

### ☑ EXERCISES

Simplify each variable expression.

1. $4(r + 10)$   $4r + 40$     2. $-3(2r - 4)$   $-6r + 12$
3. $\frac{1}{3}(-n - 12)$   $-\frac{1}{3}n - 4$     4. $-15(2 - 3x)$   $-30 + 45x$
5. $0.2(0.5f + 0.3)$   $0.1f + 0.06$     6. $-2(-8d - 6)$   $16d + 12$
7. $10(-5t - 10)$   $-50t - 100$     8. $-\frac{5}{6}(12w + 18)$   $-10w - 15$
9. $\frac{-5w - 10}{5}$   $-w - 2$     10. $\frac{16 - 8a}{-2}$   $-8 + 4a$
11. $\frac{9t - 15}{3}$   $3t - 5$     12. $\frac{2.5 - 4d}{0.5}$   $5 - 8d$
13. $\frac{121r - 66}{-11}$   $-11r + 6$     14. $\frac{8.1f - 2.7}{-0.9}$   $-9f + 3$

Evaluate each expression when $m = \frac{1}{4}$, $n = -8$, and $p = -4$.

15. $-2(n + p)$   $24$     16. $4(m - p)$   $17$
17. $\frac{4 + p}{6}$   $0$     18. $\frac{3n + 6}{-3}$   $6$
19. $m(n + p)$   $-3$     20. $-1.5(p - 2n)$   $-18$
21. $\frac{4m + p}{n}$   $\frac{3}{8}$     22. $\frac{5p + n}{2}$   $-14$

23. Write and simplify an expression for the area of the figure shown.
$12(3x + 1) = 36x + 12$

---

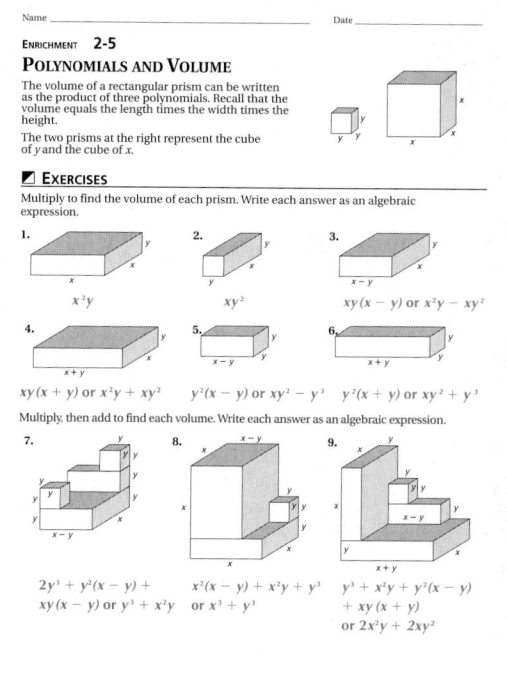

Name _____ Date _____

ENRICHMENT 2-5
**POLYNOMIALS AND VOLUME**

The volume of a rectangular prism can be written as the product of three polynomials. Recall that the volume equals the length times the width times the height.

The two prisms at the right represent the cube of $y$ and the cube of $x$.

### ☑ EXERCISES

Multiply to find the volume of each prism. Write each answer as an algebraic expression.

1. $x^2y$     2. $xy^2$     3. $xy(x - y)$ or $x^2y - xy^2$

4. $xy(x + y)$ or $x^2y + xy^2$     5. $y^2(x - y)$ or $xy^2 - y^3$     6. $y^2(x + y)$ or $xy^2 + y^3$

Multiply, then add to find each volume. Write each answer as an algebraic expression.

7. $2y^3 + y^2(x - y) +$
$xy(x - y)$ or $y^3 + x^2y$

8. $x^2(x - y) + x^2y + y^3$
or $x^3 + y^3$

9. $y^3 + x^2y + y^2(x - y)$
$+ xy(x + y)$
or $2x^2y + 2xy^2$

# Simplify Variable Expressions

**Goals** ■ Add, subtract, multiply and divide to simplify variable expressions.

**Applications** Sports, Finance, Photography, Fashion, Population

---

For each step below, list the rule from the order of operations or the property that is used to simplify the expression.

**Rule or Property**

1. $4(x + 6) + 2^3 = 4(x + 6) + 8$ — exponents
2. $= 4(x) + 4(6) + 8$ — distributive property
3. $= 4x + 24 + 8$ — multiplication
4. $= 4x + 32$ — addition
5. Use order of operations to simplify $6(3 - y) - 4^2$.  $2 - 6y$

---

### Think Back

Recall the **order of operations.**

1. Perform all operations within parentheses and brackets.

2. Then perform all calculations involving exponents.

3. Multiply or divide in order from left to right.

4. Add or subtract in order from left to right.

---

### ◨ BUILD UNDERSTANDING

In Lesson 2-4, variable expressions were simplified by addition and subtraction. In Lesson 2-5, variable expressions were simplified by multiplication and division. Together these four operations can be combined to simplify a variable expression. Recall the order of operations when simplifying a variable expression with more than one operation.

### Example 1

Simplify.

**a.** $3x + 2(5x - 1)$   **b.** $9 - 4(x - 4)$

### Solution

**a.** $3x + 2(5x - 1) = 3x + 2(5x) + 2(-1)$   Use the distributive property.

$= 3x + 10x + (-2)$   Simplify.

$= 13x - 2$   Combine like terms.

**b.** $9 - 4(x - 4) = 9 + (-4)[x + (-4)]$   Rewrite subtraction as addition of the opposite.

$= 9 + (-4)(x) + (-4)(-4)$   Use the distributive property.

$= 9 - 4x + 16$   Simplify.

$= (9 + 16) - 4x$   Use the associative property to combine like terms.

$= 25 - 4x$   Simplify.

---

---

## Teaching Tip

As students become skilled in handling signs when dealing with the distributive property, they may be able to write a solution for Example 1b as follows, without first rewriting the subtraction as an addition.

$9 - 4(x - 4)$
$= 9 - 4(x) - 4(-4)$   Write out the distributive property to avoid errors in multiplication.

$= 9 - 4x + 16$
$= 25 - 4x$   Combine like terms.

## Example 2

Simplify.

**a.** $2(x + 3) + 3(x - 4)$

**b.** $3(ab - a) - 3(b + a)$

### Solution

**a.** $2(x + 3) + 3(x - 4) = 2(x) + 2(3) + 3(x) + 3(-4)$   Use the distributive property.

$\qquad = 2x + 6 + 3x + (-12)$

$\qquad = (2x + 3x) + [6 + (-12)]$   Use the associative property to combine like terms.

$\qquad = 5x + (-6)$

$\qquad = 5x - 6$

**b.** $3(ab - a) - 3(b + a) = 3(ab) + 3(-a) - 3(b) - 3(a)$   Use the distributive property.

$\qquad = 3ab + (-3a) - 3b - 3a$

$\qquad = 3ab + [(-3a) - 3a] - 3b$   Combine like terms.

$\qquad = 3ab + (-6a) - 3b$

$\qquad = 3ab - 6a - 3b$

In Lesson 2-3, you translated word phrases into variable expressions. This skill is useful when solving real-life problems.

## Example 3

**SPORTS** A baseball team buys 12 bats. Some are wooden and some are aluminum. Wooden bats cost $36 each, and aluminum bats cost $43 each. Write and simplify a variable expression for the total cost of the baseball bats.

### Solution

Let $n =$ the number of wooden bats. If $n$ of the 12 bats are wooden, then $12 - n$ are aluminum. Write an expression for the amount spent on each type of bat.

wooden: $36(n)$

aluminum: $43(12 - n)$

Find the total cost.

$36n + 43(12 - n) = 36n + 43(12) + 43(-n)$

$\qquad = 36n + 516 + (-43n)$

$\qquad = -7n + 516$

The total cost of the baseball bats is $(-7n + 516)$ dollars.

 Math Online   mathmatters2.com/extra_examples   Lesson 2-6 **Simplify Variable Expressions**   77

---

### Supplementary Example 1
Simplify.

**a.**   $5(x + 3) + 2x$
$= 5(x) + 5(3) + 2x$
$= 5x + 15 + 2x$
$= (5x + 2x) + 15$
$= 7x + 15$

**b.**   $2x - 5(x - 1)$
$= 2x - 5[x + (-1)]$
$= 2x - 5(x) + (-5)(-1)$
$= 2x - 5x + 25$
$= -3x + 25$

### Supplementary Example 2
Simplify.

**a.**   $4(x + y) - 7(x - y)$
$= 4(x) + 4(y) - 7(x) - 7(-y)$
$= 4x + 4y - 7x + 7y$
$= (4x - 7x) + (4y + 7y)$
$= -3x + 11y$

**b.**   $2(mn + m) - 5(mn - n)$
$= 2(mn) + 2(m) - 5(mn) - 5(-n)$
$= 2mn + 2m - 5mn + 5n$
$= (2mn - 5mn) + 2m + 5n$
$= -3mn + 2m + 5n$

### Supplementary Example 3
**ENTERTAINMENT** The ticket prices at a movie theater are $8.00 for regular admission and $5.50 for students or seniors. For Saturday's first show, 350 tickets were sold.

Write and simplify a variable expression for the total admission fees of the tickets for that show.
Solution:
Let $r =$ the number of regular admissions.
Then $350 - r =$ the number of students and seniors.
total admission fees
$= 8.00r + 5.50(350 - r)$
$= 8.00r + 5.50(350) + 5.50(-r)$
$= 8.00r + 1925.00 - 5.50r$
$= 2.50r + 1925.00$
The total admission fees were $(2.50r + 1925.00)$ dollars.

---

## Differentiated Instruction

**AUDITORY LEARNERS** Before students start writing out the steps of a simplification problem, ask them to verbalize the nature of the operations in a problem, looking for a global view.
For example, in Example 2a, the expression $2(x + 3) + 3(x - 4)$ is the sum of two products.
In Example 2b, the expression $3(ab - a) - 3(b + a)$ is the difference of two products.
Elicit a general two-step procedure.
(1) Simplify each product. (Apply the distributive property to eliminate parentheses.)
(2) Combine like terms. (Apply the associative property to regroup.)

Lesson 2-6 **Simplify Variable Expressions**   77

## Lesson Wrap-up

### QUICK ASSESSMENT

Ask the following questions to determine if students understand the content presented in this lesson.

**There is an error in each simplification. Write the correct line. Then complete the simplification.**

1. $-3(y + 2) + 4(y - 1)$
   $= -3y - 6 + 4y - 1$
   $-3y - 6 + 4y - 4$
   $= y - 10$

2. $-2(x - 1) - 3(x + 2)$
   $= -2x + 2 - 3x + 6$
   $-2x + 2 - 3x - 6$
   $= -5x - 4$

### ASSIGNMENT GUIDE

**Basic:** 1–46, 52–56
**Enriched:** 1–56

### Reteaching Worksheet 2-6

Name _____ Date _____

RETEACHING **2-6**
**SIMPLIFY VARIABLE EXPRESSIONS**
To simplify a variable expression, perform as many of the indicated operations as possible.

**Example**

Simplify.
$5st - 2st + 4(s + t)$

**Solution**

$5st - 2st + 4(s + t) = 5st - 2st + 4s + 4t$     Use the distributive property.
$= 3st + 4s + 4t$     Add like terms.

**EXERCISES**

Simplify.

1. $5c - 3c$
   $2c$

2. $-8m - 2m$
   $-10m$

3. $12(r - s)$
   $12r - 12s$

4. $-(2p + 3q) + q$
   $-2p - 2q$

5. $4(c + 12.5)$
   $4c + 50$

6. $9m - 7n + 2m$
   $11m - 7n$

7. $(9b + 17) + (-3b - 8)$
   $6b + 9$

8. $(15x + y) - (5y + x)$
   $14x - 4y$

9. $3(ab + b) + 2(-a + ab)$
   $5ab + 3b - 2a$

10. $-3(4s + 5) + 2s$
    $-10s - 15$

11. $-(m + n) + 18(m + n)$
    $17m + 17n$

12. $c - 5 + (-3c) + 5d$
    $-2c - 5 + 5d$

### TRY THESE EXERCISES

**Simplify.**

1. $5x + 7(-2x + 3)$
   $-9x + 21$

2. $7y - 2(8 + 3x)$
   $7y - 16 - 6x$

3. $-3n + 3(-n + 2m)$
   $-6n + 6m$

4. $15u + \frac{1}{3}(12u - 9n)$
   $19u - 3n$

5. $6(c - 9) - (2c + 30)$
   $4c - 84$

6. $2(6x - 2y) + 3(x + y)$
   $15x - y$

7. $(a - 2) - 1.5(a + b)$
   $-0.5a - 1.5b - 2$

8. $7(gh + 8g) - 4(g + 5.2)$
   $7gh + 52g - 20.8$

9. $8(3x + y) - (-x + 21)$
   $25x + 8y - 21$

10. **WRITING MATH** Explain how you used the order of operations in Exercise 9.
    Answers will vary.

11. **FINANCE** A cellular phone company sells stock for $83 a share. A cable company sells stock for $56 a share. Between the two companies, Felipe buys 15 shares of stock. Write and simplify a variable expression for the total amount that Felipe spent on the stocks. $83x + 56(15 - x) = 27x + 840$
    or $56x + 83(15 - x) = 1245 - 27x$

### PRACTICE EXERCISES • For Extra Practice, see page 591.

**Simplify.**

12. $6x + 12(10 - x)$   $120 - 6x$

13. $m + 5(m - 1)$   $6m - 5$

14. $8y - (2y - 3)$   $6y + 3$

15. $-3(x - 1) + 9$   $-3x + 12$

16. $\frac{3}{4}(4n - 8) + 6n$   $9n - 6$

17. $6(x + 4) - 2x$   $4x + 24$

18. $\frac{1}{3}(6b + 9) + b$   $3b + 3$

19. $2(1.5d + 4) - 3.7$
    $3d + 4.3$

20. $(n - 6) - 2(3n + 4)$   $-5n - 14$

21. $3(x - 4) + 6(2x + 7)$
    $15x + 30$

22. $-4(3w - 9) + 9(w - 2)$
    $-3w + 18$

23. $-\frac{1}{2}(y + 6) + \frac{2}{3}(6y - 9)$ $3\frac{1}{2}y - 9$

24. $5(3 - 2.1x) - 5(2 + 0.9x)$
    $5 - 15x$

25. $11(2f - 8) - 10(-f + 6)$
    $32f - 148$

26. $3.5(6a - 6) + 9(3a - 2)$
    $48a - 39$

27. $-9(3t - 2) + 5(-4t + 8)$
    $-47t + 58$

28. $6(2n + 7) - 3(-7n - 4)$
    $33n + 54$

29. $\frac{2}{3}(9 - 6w) + 7(2 - w)$
    $20 - 11w$

30. $2(12a - b) + (-a + b)$
    $23a - b$

31. $6(p + 3q) - (7p + 4q)$
    $-p + 14q$

32. $4(ab - 5a) - (9ab - 6a)$
    $-5ab - 14a$

33. $-3(r + 2s) + 2(-3r - s)$
    $-9r - 8s$

34. $7(wz + w) - 2(wz + z)$
    $5wz + 7w - 2z$

35. $16(-c - \frac{1}{4}cd) - (cd + 12d)$
    $-16c - 5cd - 12d$

36. **PHOTOGRAPHY** Queisha used a roll of 25 pictures at her family reunion. Some of the pictures were panoramic, and the rest were standard size. It costs $0.19 to develop standard size and $0.32 to develop panoramic. Write and simplify a variable expression for the total cost of developing the film.
    See additional answers.

37. **FASHION** Phoebe is the buyer for women's clothing at a department store. This month she buys 200 women's jeans. Some are slim fit, and the rest are relaxed fit. The manufacturer cost of the slim fit jeans is $18, and the manufacturer cost of the relaxed fit jeans is $21. Write and simplify an expression for the total amount spent on the jeans.
    See additional answers.

38. Find the perimeter of a rectangle with a length of $(3x - 2)$ in. and a width of $(x + 7)$ in.   $(8x + 10)$ in.

**Match each expression with the equivalent expression in simplified form.**

39. $5(a + b) - 6(a - b)$   e

40. $2(6a + b) - (a + 3b)$   c

41. $3(a + 2b) + 7(a + b)$   a

42. $-7(3a + 2b) - 5(-2a - 3b)$   b

43. $4(4a - 6b) - 3(a - 9b)$   d

**a.** $10a + 13b$

**b.** $-11a + b$

**c.** $11a - b$

**d.** $13a + 3b$

**e.** $-a + 11b$

### ADDITIONAL ANSWERS

36. $0.32x + 0.19(25 - x) = 4.75 + 0.13x$ or $0.19x + 0.32(25 - x) = 8 - 0.13x$

37. $18x + 21(200 - x) = 4200 - 3x$ or $21x + 18(200 - x) = 3x + 3600$

44. $4x + 8.7(90 - x) = 783 - 4.7x$ or $8.7x + 4(90 - x) = 360 + 4.7x$

44. **DATA FILE** Refer to the data on calories spent per minute on page 568. Twice a week Kuan goes to the gym to walk around the track and then swim. He spends 90 minutes working out. Kuan weighs about 150 lb. Write and simplify a variable expression for the number of calories that Kuan burns each day that he works out at the gym. See additional answers.

45. **POPULATION** In 1970 the population of New Jersey was approximately $10a + 1.7b$. From 1970 to 1980, the population of New Jersey increased by 28.1%. From 1980 to 1990, the population increased by 16.2%. Write and simplify a variable expression for the population of New Jersey in 1990. $14.9a + 2.5b$

46. **YOU MAKE THE CALL** Alicia and Frank each simplified the variable expression $3(-4g + 6f) - 3(g + 2f)$. Explain where Alicia and Frank each made a mistake. Then simplify and write the variable expression correctly.

| Alicia's work | Frank's work |
|---|---|
| $3(-4g + 6f) - 3(g + 2f)$ | $3(-4g + 6f) - 3(g + 2f)$ |
| $= -12g + 6f - 3g - 6f$ | $= 12g + 18f - 3g + 6f$ |
| $= -15g$ | $= -9g + 24f$ |
| She didn't distribute 3 over $6f$. | He did not distribute the negative sign in the second expression; $-15g + 12f$. |

## Extended Practice Exercises

**Simplify.**

47. $3(-4a + 7b) - 9(8a - 3b) + 4(-a - 4b)$ $\quad -88a + 32b$

48. $\frac{1}{3}(6p - 18q) - \frac{3}{4}(-24q - 16p) + \frac{3}{5}(15p - 40q)$ $\quad 23p - 12q$

49. $-11(ab - 3a + 7b) + 3(-13ab + 6b - 8a) - 4(-12ab - 14a + 6b)$ $\quad -2ab + 65a - 83b$

50. **SPORTS** Kashauna made 11 baskets at the basketball game. Some were 3-point baskets, some were 2-point baskets and the rest were 1-point free throws. Write and simplify a variable expression for the total number of points that Kashauna had in the basketball game. $3x + 2y + 1(11 - x - y) = 11 + 2x + y$

51. **CRITICAL THINKING** Simplify the expression $-4[3[2(x + 1)]]$. $\quad -24x - 24$

## Mixed Review Exercises

**Use the scatter plot to answer the following questions.** (Lesson 1-4)

Average Scores on Weekly Quizes

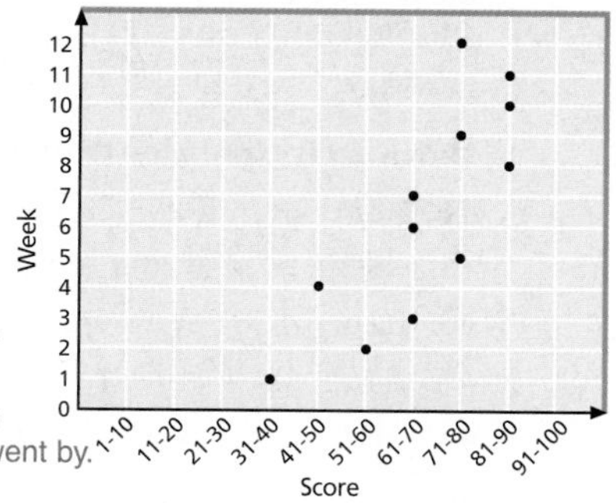

Week
12
11
10
9
8
7
6
5
4
3
2
1
0
1-10
11-20
21-30
31-40
41-50
51-60
61-70
71-80
81-90
91-100
Score


52. How many weekly quizzes were given? 12

53. What is the least possible range of the average scores? 41

54. What is the greatest possible range of the average scores? 59

55. Is there a positive or negative correlation between the scores and the number of quizzes given? positive

56. Using one sentence, describe the trend in the data. Sample answer: The average score on weekly quizzes increased as the weeks went by.

57. In what scoring group is the median weekly average score? 61–70

Math Online mathmatters2.com/self_check_quiz



## Extend the Lesson

**CHALLENGE** Ask students this question: If a page in a book is numbered $n$, what is the number of the next page? $n + 1$ Then have students write sentences with variable expressions and use guess-and-check to solve.

1. Two consecutive pages have a sum of 175. What are the pages?
$n + (n + 1) = 175$
$2n + 1 = 175$
$n = 87$
$n + 1 = 88$

2. Three consecutive pages have a sum of 768. What are the pages?
$n + (n + 1) + (n + 2) = 768$
$3n + 3 = 768$
$n = 255$
$n + 1 = 256$
$n + 2 = 257$

## Extra Practice Worksheet 2-6

Name ______________ Date ______________

EXTRA PRACTICE 2-6

**SIMPLIFY VARIABLE EXPRESSIONS**

**EXERCISES**

Simplify.

1. $5y + 2(5 - y)$ $\quad 3y + 10$
2. $n + 8(n - 2)$ $\quad 9n - 16$
3. $5t - (4t - 1)$ $\quad t + 1$
4. $-2(x - 4) + 6$ $\quad -2x + 14$
5. $\frac{2}{3}(6d - 9) + d$ $\quad 5d - 6$
6. $(h - 1) + 2(3 - h)$ $\quad -h + 5$
7. $2(0.5 - 2c) + 2.8$ $\quad 3.8 - 4c$
8. $-\frac{2}{5}(5w - 10) - 4w$ $\quad -6w + 4$
9. $4(x - 3) - 5(x + 3)$ $\quad -x - 27$
10. $10(3d + 2) - 6(3 - d)$ $\quad 36d + 2$
11. $(r - 3) - (4 - 2r)$ $\quad 3r - 7$
12. $\frac{3}{8}(4r - 24) - (3r + 3)$ $\quad -1\frac{1}{2}r - 12$
13. $4(8r - 2) - 3(5 - 3r)$ $\quad 41r - 23$
14. $6(2p + 5) - (4p - 2)$ $\quad 8p + 32$
15. $15\left(-w - \frac{2}{5}\right) - (w + 4)$ $\quad -16w - 10$
16. $5(p + q) - (4p - 8q)$ $\quad p + 13q$
17. $-2(m - 2n) + 5(-2m + 4n)$ $\quad -12m + 24n$
18. $8(xy + x) - 4(xy - y)$ $\quad 4xy + 8x + 4y$
19. $15\left(-a - \frac{1}{3}bc\right) - (bc + 4a)$ $\quad -19a + 4bc$

Match each expression with the equivalent expression in simplified form.

20. $6(n + m) - (m + 4n)$ a
21. $6(m + n) - 4(m - n)$ d
22. $-3(2m - 4n) - (8m - 7n)$ e
23. $8(m - 2n) - 3(m + n)$ b
24. $5(2m - 2n) - 2(4m + 2n)$ c

a. $2n + 5m$
b. $5m - 19n$
c. $2m - 14n$
d. $2m + 10n$
e. $-14m + 19n$

## Enrichment Worksheet 2-6

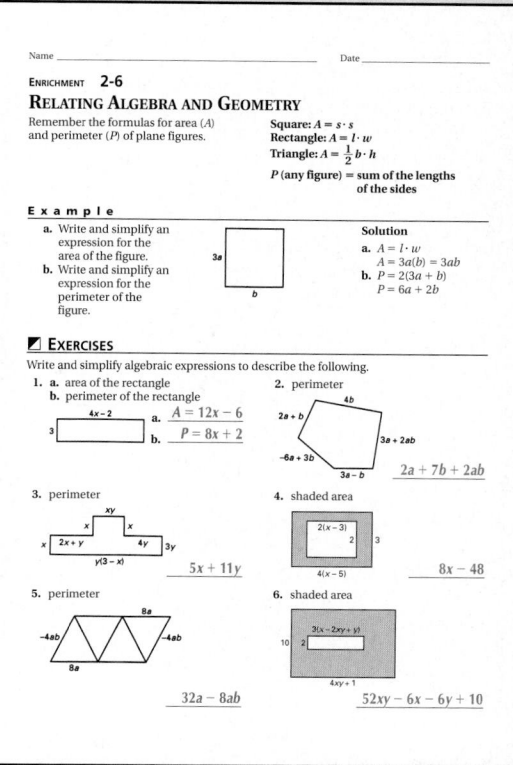

Name ______________ Date ______________

ENRICHMENT 2-6

**RELATING ALGEBRA AND GEOMETRY**

Remember the formulas for area ($A$) and perimeter ($P$) of plane figures.

**Square:** $A = s \cdot s$
**Rectangle:** $A = l \cdot w$
**Triangle:** $A = \frac{1}{2} b \cdot h$
$P$ **(any figure) = sum of the lengths of the sides**

**Example**

a. Write and simplify an expression for the area of the figure.
b. Write and simplify an expression for the perimeter of the figure.

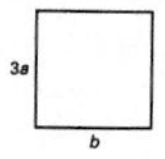

3a
b


**Solution**

a. $A = l \cdot w$
$A = 3a(b) = 3ab$
b. $P = 2(3a + b)$
$P = 6a + 2b$

**EXERCISES**

Write and simplify algebraic expressions to describe the following.

1. a. area of the rectangle
b. perimeter of the rectangle

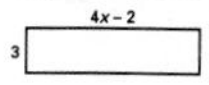

4x - 2
3


a. $A = 12x - 6$
b. $P = 8x + 2$

2. perimeter

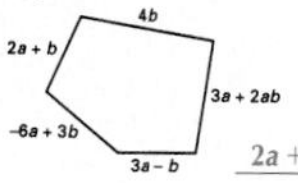

4b
2a + b
3a + 2ab
-6a + 3b
3a - b


$2a + 7b + 2ab$

3. perimeter

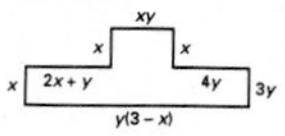

xy
x
x
x
2x + y
4y
3y
y(3 - x)


$5x + 11y$

4. shaded area

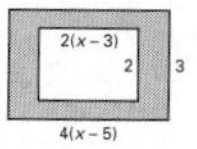

2(x - 3)
2
3
4(x - 5)


$8x - 48$

5. perimeter

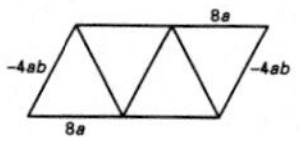

8a
-4ab
-4ab
8a


$32a - 8ab$

6. shaded area

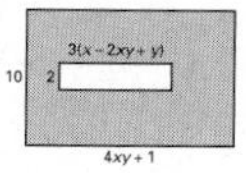

3(x - 2xy + y)
10
2
4xy + 1


$52xy - 6x - 6y + 10$

## PRACTICE ◼ LESSON 2-5

Simplify each variable expression.

1. $-(6c - d)$  $-6c + d$
2. $\dfrac{3x + 12}{3}$  $x + 4$
3. $\dfrac{-3y - 16}{-2}$  $\dfrac{3}{2}y + 8$
4. $-7(y - 4z)$  $-7y + 28z$
5. $\dfrac{-5}{6}(-12e + 36f)$  $10e - 30f$
6. $\dfrac{1.6 - 3.2w}{0.8}$  $2 - 4w$
7. $\dfrac{4x - 8}{4}$  $x - 2$
8. $\dfrac{21w + 14y}{-7}$  $-3w - 2y$
9. $-(a + 2b)$  $-a - 2b$
10. $\dfrac{-(7w - 4)}{3}$  $-\dfrac{7}{3}w + \dfrac{4}{3}$
11. $-3(6bc - 7)$  $-18bc + 21$
12. $\dfrac{1}{5}(-x - 25)$  $-\dfrac{1}{5}x - 5$
13. $\dfrac{-44s - 66t}{11}$  $-4s - 6t$
14. $\dfrac{-8(x + 1.5)}{3}$  $-\dfrac{8}{3}x - 4$
15. $\dfrac{132c - 60}{12}$  $11c - 5$

Evaluate each expression when $x = 7$, $y = 4$, and $z = -1$.

16. $x - (y - z)$  2
17. $x^2 + 2x + y$  67
18. $(x + y)(y - z)$  55
19. $3(x - y)$  9
20. $\dfrac{5x - 21}{2}$  7
21. $\dfrac{12z + 10y}{7}$  4
22. $\dfrac{-16z + 20}{-y}$  $-9$
23. $\dfrac{-6x - 5y}{2}$  $-31$
24. $\dfrac{1}{2} - (7z + x)$  $\dfrac{1}{2}$
25. $\dfrac{3(x - y)}{z^2}$  9
26. $\dfrac{4z - 4y}{y}$  $-5$
27. $\dfrac{x^2 - y}{9z}$  $-5$

## PRACTICE ◼ LESSON 2-6

Simplify.

28. $3(a + b) + b$
$3a + 4b$
29. $8(x + 2y) - x$
$7x + 16y$
30. $5(x + y) + 4(x + y)$
$9x + 9y$
31. $5(a + 2) + 10(a + 3)$
$15a + 40$
32. $12(m - 3) - (4m - 2)$
$8m - 34$
33. $9(b + 3) - 4(a - 2)$
$9b - 4a + 35$
34. $3 + 2(8 + 4c) - 2c$
$19 + 6c$
35. $-\dfrac{1}{5}(25x - 5y) + (-x + y)$
$-6x + 2y$
36. $-8(3 + a) + 7(6 + 2a)$
$6a + 18$
37. $0.4(4 - 2x) - 5(2 + 0.1x)$
$-1.3x - 8.4$
38. $\dfrac{3}{4}(16x - 8y) + (-x - 2y)$
$11x - 8y$
39. $4(2x + 3) + 5(x - 1)$
$13x + 7$
40. $9(xy + x) - 3(xy + x)$
$6xy + 6x$
41. $-(a - b) - a$
$-2a + b$
42. $\dfrac{1}{3}(6x - 9y) + \dfrac{1}{4}(16x - 8y)$
$6x - 5y$

43. Find the perimeter of a rectangle with a length of $\left(\dfrac{1}{4}x + 6z\right)$ cm and a width of $\left(x - \dfrac{1}{3}z\right)$ cm.  $\left(2\dfrac{1}{2}x + 11\dfrac{1}{3}z\right)$ cm

Match each expression with the equivalent expression in simplified form.

44. $3(3p + q) - 3(2p - 3q)$  b
45. $-5(3p + 2q) + 2(6p - q)$  d
46. $4(2p + q) - (-6p + q)$  e
47. $2(4p - 3q) + (4p + 3q)$  a
48. $-6(p + 2q) + 3(-2p + 3q)$  c

a. $12p - 3q$
b. $3p + 12q$
c. $-12p - 3q$
d. $-3p - 12q$
e. $14p + 3q$

## PRACTICE ◤ LESSON 2-1–LESSON 2-6

**Simplify.** (Lesson 2-1–Lesson 2-6)

**49.** $-(3x - 5) + x$   $-2x + 5$

**50.** $(c + 7) + 8(2c - 1)$   $17c - 1$

**51.** $(r + 3) - 2(7 - r)$   $3r - 11$

**52.** $\frac{1}{4}t - \left(-\frac{1}{2}t\right) + t^2$   $t^2 + \frac{3}{4}t$

**53.** $(5b - 7) - (5b - 7)$   $0$

**54.** $9 + 4(y - 3) - y$   $3y - 3$

**55.** $-3(x - 7)$   $-3x + 21$

**56.** $\frac{1}{3}(-15x - 5)$   $-5x - \frac{5}{3}$

**57.** $4(4t + 6)$   $16t + 24$

**58.** $\frac{14r + 12}{-2}$   $-7r - 6$

**59.** $\frac{100ab - 10}{10}$   $10ab - 1$

**60.** $\frac{-81 - 9x}{9}$   $-9 - x$

**Evaluate each expression when** $a = \frac{1}{2}, b = -3,$ **and** $c = 6.$ (Lesson 2-1–Lesson 2-6)

**61.** $a(8b + 10)$   $-7$

**62.** $b^2 + (3c - b)$   $30$

**63.** $a(c - b)$   $\frac{9}{2}$

**64.** $\frac{7c - 12}{b}$   $-10$

**65.** $\frac{-7b - c}{a}$   $30$

**66.** $\frac{-c|b|}{a}$   $-36$

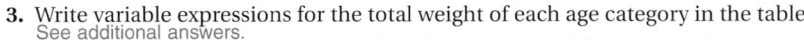 **Career – Commercial Aircraft Designer**

Workplace Knowhow

**C**ommercial aircraft designers must consider many factors when engineering a safe airplane. One of the most critical factors is the amount of weight that will be carried. This influences everything from the types of seats that will be installed, to the material used to construct the floor of the passenger seating area, to the amount of thrust required from the engines.

**Airline Travelers**

| Age Group (years) | Average Weight (pounds) | Percent of Travelers |
|---|---|---|
| 0 - 9 | 35 | 7% |
| 10 - 14 | 85 | 8% |
| 15 - 19 | 125 | 12% |
| 20 - 39 | 135 | 28% |
| 40 and above | 155 | 45% |

**Use the table for Exercises 1–5.**

1. If $x$ number of people board an airplane, write a variable expression for the number of people 20–39 years old who board the flight.   $0.28x$

2. Using the answer from Exercise 1, write an expression for the total weight of the 20–39 year-old passengers on this flight.   $135(0.28x) = 37.8x$

3. Write variable expressions for the total weight of each age category in the table.
   See additional answers.

4. Combine the variable expressions from Exercises 2 and 3 to express the total weight of all persons on board the aircraft in simplified form.   $131.8x$

5. If the maximum capacity of a Boeing B-777 is 279 people, what is the total passenger weight?   36,772.2 lb

 Math Online   mathmatters2.com/mathworks

---

## MathWorks

Centuries of dreaming, study, speculation, and experimentation preceded the first successful flight. The first form of aircraft made was the *kite*, about the 5th century BC. Today, people fly routinely, for business and for pleasure, making air travel an essential part of modern life.

Students may be interested in researching some aspects in the history of aviation, or might do research in the science of aerodynamics.

There are four primary forces that act upon an airplane: lift, weight, thrust, and drag. Managing the balance between these four forces is the challenge of flight. Modern airplanes also have to contend with the phenomenon of the sound barrier.

Students should answer Questions 1–5 to better understand how weight and capacity are considered in flight preparation.

Designers of commercial aircraft, concerned with efficiency and safety, must have a keen understanding of algebra and other branches of mathematics to accomplish their goals.

Students who are interested in learning more about this career choice can go to mathmatters2.com/mathworks. School Guidance Counselors are another resource for information about training requirements and appropriate schools.

## MathWorks

3. 0–9 years: $35(0.07x) = 2.45x$
   10–14 years: $85(0.08x) = 6.8x$
   15–19 years: $125(0.12x) = 15x$
   40 and above: $155(0.45x) = 69.75x$

---

## Teaching Tip

When simplifying expressions that contain division, suggest that students show the intended divisions as a separate step. This will help to ensure that every term of the numerator gets divided and will be especially useful in a case such as Exercise 59 (shown below) to ensure that a second term appears in the answer.

$$\frac{100ab - 10}{10} = \frac{100ab}{10} - \frac{10}{10}$$
$$= 10ab - 1 \longleftarrow$$

Writing the intended division helps to ensure the inclusion of this second term.

# Properties of Exponents

Goals
- Choose appropriate units of measure.
- Evaluate variable expressions.

Applications   Biology, Finance, Computers, Population

**BIOLOGY** During a lab experiment, Kayla observes that a single-cell organism divides into two organisms every hour.

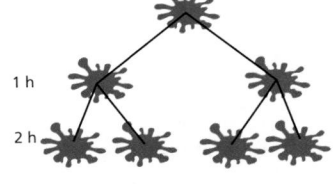

1. Copy and complete the table to determine the number of organisms after 5 h.

| Hours | 1 | 2 | 3 | 4 | 5 |
|-------|---|---|---|---|---|
| Numbers of organisms | 2 | 4 | 8 | 16 | 32 |

2. What pattern do you notice every hour?  The number of organisms doubles.

3. Rewrite the number of organisms each hour by repeatedly multiplying by the same number. What pattern do you notice?  For each hour that passes another 2 is multiplied.

4. Predict the number of organisms in the sixth, seventh and eighth hours. 64, 128, 256

5. How many hours will it take until the number of organisms is more than 2000?  11

## BUILD UNDERSTANDING

A shortcut to writing a number that is repeatedly multiplied by itself is called **exponential form**. A number written in exponential form has a base and an exponent.

$$a \cdot a \cdot a \cdot a \cdot a = a^5$$

The **base** tells what factor is being multiplied. The **exponent** tells how many equal factors there are. The expression $a^5$ is read as "$a$ to the fifth power." Any number raised to the first power is that number.

$$n^1 = n, \text{ so } 8^1 = 8$$

### Reading Math

Read $xy^2$ as '$x$ times $y$ squared.'

Read $(xy)^2$ as 'the quantity $x$ times $y$, squared.'

### Example 1

Evaluate each expression. Let $x = 4$ and $y = -3$.

a. $x^2$          b. $y^3$          c. $xy^2$

**Solution**

a. $x^2 = 4^2$
   $= 4 \cdot 4$
   $= 16$

b. $y^3 = (-3)^3$
   $= (-3)(-3)(-3)$
   $= -27$

c. $xy^2 = (4)(-3)^2$
   $= (4)(-3)(-3)$
   $= (4)(9) = 36$

To find the product of $3^2 \cdot 3^4$, you can write out the factors for each term and then write the product using exponents.

$$3^2 \cdot 3^4 = 3 \cdot 3 \cdot 3 \cdot 3 \cdot 3 \cdot 3 = 3^6$$

A shorter method is to use the **product rule**. To multiply numbers with the same base, write the base raised to the sum of the exponents.

$$a^m \cdot a^n = a^{m+n}$$
$$3^2 \cdot 3^4 = 3^{2+4} = 3^6$$

Apply the product rule to an exponential number raised to an exponent.

$$(5^2)^4 = 5^2 \cdot 5^2 \cdot 5^2 \cdot 5^2 = 5^{2+2+2+2} = 5^8$$

This relationship is described by the **power rule**. To raise an exponential number to an exponent, multiply exponents.

$$(a^m)^n = a^{mn}$$
$$(5^2)^4 = 5^{2 \cdot 4} = 5^8$$

When a product is raised to an exponent, each factor is raised to that exponent.

$$(2y^2)^3 = (2y^2)(2y^2)(2y^2) = (2)(2)(2)(y^2)(y^2)(y^2) = 8y^6$$

The result is described by the **power of a product rule**. To find the power of a product, find the power of each factor and multiply.

$$(ab)^m = a^m b^m$$
$$(2y^2)^3 = (2^3)(y^2)^3 = 8y^6$$

| Properties of Exponents for Multiplication | For all real numbers $a$ and $b$, if $m$ and $n$ are integers, then |
|---|---|
| | $a^m \cdot a^n = a^{m+n}$ $\qquad (a^m)^n = a^{mn}$ $\qquad (ab)^m = a^m b^m$ |

## Example 2

**Simplify.**

**a.** $x^3 \cdot x^5$

**b.** $(5r^4)^2$

**c.** $(u^3 v)^4$

### Solution

**a.** $x^3 \cdot x^5 = x^{3+5}$
$\qquad = x^8$

**b.** $(5^2)(r^4)^2 = 25r^{4 \cdot 2}$
$\qquad = 25r^8$

**c.** $(u^3 v)^4 = u^{3 \cdot 4} v^{1 \cdot 4}$
$\qquad = u^{12} v^4$

Study the following examples.

$$3^4 \div 3^2 = \frac{3^4}{3^2} = \frac{3 \cdot 3 \cdot 3 \cdot 3}{3 \cdot 3} = 3^2 \qquad\qquad \left(\frac{2}{5}\right)^3 = \frac{2}{5} \cdot \frac{2}{5} \cdot \frac{2}{5} = \frac{2^3}{5^3}$$

These examples illustrate two properties of exponents for division. One property is the **quotient rule**. To divide numbers with the same base, write the base with the difference of the exponents.

$$a^m \div a^n = \frac{a^m}{a^n} = a^{m-n}, a \neq 0 \qquad\qquad \frac{3^4}{3^2} = 3^{4-2} = 3^2$$

Another property is the **power of a quotient rule**. To find the power of a quotient, find the power of each number and divide.

$$\left(\frac{a}{b}\right)^m = \frac{a^m}{b^m}, b \neq 0 \qquad\qquad \left(\frac{2}{5}\right)^3 = \frac{2^3}{5^3}$$

**Supplementary Example 1**
Evaluate each expression. Let $x = 0.8$ and $y = 1.2$.

**a.** $3x^2 y$
$= 3(0.8)^2(1.2)$
$= 3(0.64)(1.2)$
$= 2.304$

**b.** $(4x)^3 y^2$
$= (4 \cdot 0.8)^3 (1.2)^2$
$= (3.2)^3 \cdot (1.2)^2$
$= 32.768 \cdot 1.44$
$= 47.18592$

**Supplementary Example 2**
Simplify.

**a.** $3^2 \cdot 3^5$
$= 3^{2+5}$
$= 3^7$

**b.** $6(m^4)^2$
$= 6 \cdot m^{4 \cdot 2}$
$= 6m^8$

**Supplementary Example 3**
Evaluate each expression.
Let $x = \frac{1}{2}$ and $y = \frac{2}{3}$.

**a.** $x^2 y$
$= \left(\frac{1}{2}\right)^2 \left(\frac{2}{3}\right)$
$= \frac{1^2}{2^2} \cdot \frac{2}{3}$
$= \frac{1}{4} \cdot \frac{2}{3}$
$= \frac{1}{\overset{2}{4}} \cdot \frac{\overset{1}{2}}{3}$
$= \frac{1 \cdot 1}{2 \cdot 3}$
$= \frac{1}{6}$

**b.** $3x^3 y^2$
$= 3\left(\frac{1}{2}\right)^3 \left(\frac{2}{3}\right)^2$
$= 3 \cdot \frac{1^3}{2^3} \cdot \frac{2^2}{3^2}$
$= \frac{3}{1} \cdot \frac{1}{8} \cdot \frac{4}{9}$
$= \frac{\overset{1}{3}}{1} \cdot \frac{1}{\overset{2}{8}} \cdot \frac{\overset{1}{4}}{\overset{3}{9}}$
$= \frac{1 \cdot 1 \cdot 1}{1 \cdot 2 \cdot 3}$
$= \frac{1}{6}$

## Predictable Error

Students may readily accept that $x^2 \cdot x^5 = x^7$ (primarily because they don't know what else to do with the $x$'s), but still will want to do more with $3^2 \cdot 3^5$ (they think "3 times 3" and often erroneously write $9^7$).
To help students avoid this type of error, point out that when they are multiplying powers with like bases, they are simply counting how many times *that base* is used as a factor, not actually performing a computation.

## Lesson Wrap-up

### QUICK ASSESSMENT
Ask the following questions to determine if students understand the content presented in this lesson.

1. a. When do you add exponents?
   when multiplying powers of the same base
   b. Give a numerical example.
   $4^5 \cdot 4^3 = 4^8$
   c. Give a similar example using variables.  $x^5 \cdot x^3 = x^8$

2. a. When do you subtract exponents?  when dividing powers of the same base
   b. Give a numerical example.
   $\dfrac{4^5}{4^3} = 4^2$

3. a. When do you multiply exponents?  when raising a power to a power
   b. Give an example using variables.  $(x^5)^3 = x^{15}$

### ASSIGNMENT GUIDE

**Basic:** 1–48, 55–62
**Enriched:** 1–62

### Reteaching Worksheet 2-7

Name _____   Date _____

RETEACHING  **2-7**
**PROPERTIES OF EXPONENTS**
For all real numbers $a$ and $b$, if $m$ and $n$ are integers:

The product rule         The power rule         The power of a product rule
$a^m \cdot a^n = a^{m+n}$   $(a^m)^n = a^{mn}$      $(ab)^m = a^m b^m$

**Example 1**

Simplify.
a. $y^4 \cdot y^3$          b. $(s^2)^5$          c. $(ab^3)^2$

Solution
a. $y^4 \cdot y^3 = y^{4+3}$     b. $(s^2)^5 = s^{2 \cdot 5}$     c. $(ab^3)^2 = a^2 b^{3 \cdot 2}$
$= y^7$                     $= s^{10}$                 $= a^2 b^6$

For all real numbers $a$ and $b$, if $m$ and $n$ are integers:

The quotient rule          The power of a quotient rule
$a^m \div a^n = a^{m-n}$, if $a \neq 0$   $\left(\dfrac{a}{b}\right)^m = \dfrac{a^m}{b^m}$, if $b \neq 0$

**Example 2**

Simplify.                            Solution
a. $\dfrac{m^6}{m^2}$, $m \neq 0$    b. $\left(\dfrac{r}{3}\right)^2$    a. $\dfrac{m^6}{m^2} = m^{6-2}$   b. $\left(\dfrac{r}{3}\right)^2 = \dfrac{r^2}{3}$
                                                                            $= m^4$                             $= \dfrac{r^2}{9}$

✔ **EXERCISES**

Simplify.
1. $p^2 \cdot p^7$   2. $(c^5)^3$   3. $(uv^2)^7$   4. $x^4 \cdot x^5$   5. $(r^2t)^4$
   $p^9$               $c^{15}$       $u^7 v^{14}$    $x^9$               $r^8 t^4$

6. $\dfrac{v^9}{v^2}$, $v \neq 0$   7. $(m^8)^2$   8. $\left(\dfrac{z}{5}\right)^3$   9. $\dfrac{w^5}{w}$, $w \neq 0$   10. $\dfrac{30b^2}{5b}$, $b \neq 0$
   $v^7$                              $m^{16}$        $\dfrac{z^3}{125}$                 $w^4$                           $6b$

11. $(g^3 h)^2$   12. $\left(\dfrac{1}{a}\right)^5$, $a \neq 0$   13. $(n^3)(n)(n^5)$   14. $8(q^2)^3$   15. $\left(\dfrac{x}{3}\right)^4$
    $g^{10} h^2$     $\dfrac{1}{a^5}$                               $n^9$                  $8q^6$             $\dfrac{x^4}{81}$

---

| Properties of Exponents for Division | For all real numbers $a$ and $b$, if $m$ and $n$ are integers, then |
|---|---|
| | $\dfrac{a^m}{a^n} = a^{m-n}$, if $a \neq 0$ $\qquad$ $\left(\dfrac{a}{b}\right)^m = \dfrac{a^m}{b^m}$, if $b \neq 0$ |

## Example 3

Simplify.

a. $\dfrac{t^5}{t^2}$, $t \neq 0$    b. $\left(\dfrac{d}{2}\right)^3$    c. $\left(\dfrac{x^3}{x^2}\right)^4$, $x \neq 0$

**Solution**

a. $\dfrac{t^5}{t^2} = t^{5-2}$    b. $\left(\dfrac{d}{2}\right)^3 = \dfrac{d^3}{2^3}$    c. $\left(\dfrac{x^3}{x^2}\right)^4 = (x^{3-2})^4$

$= t^3$                                 $= \dfrac{d^3}{8}$                              $= (x^1)^4$

$\qquad\qquad\qquad\qquad\qquad\qquad\qquad\qquad\qquad\qquad\qquad\qquad\qquad\qquad = x^4$

### ▶ TRY THESE EXERCISES

Evaluate each expression when $x = 5$ and $y = -2$.

1. $y^2$  4     2. $x^4$  625     3. $x^2 y$  $-50$     4. $xy^3$  $-40$

Simplify.

5. $c^4 \cdot c^7$  $c^{11}$     6. $x \cdot x^9$  $x^{10}$     7. $(d^5)^2$  $d^{10}$     8. $(gh^2)^3$  $g^3 h^6$

9. $\dfrac{v^7}{v^3}$, $v \neq 0$  $v^4$     10. $\left(\dfrac{c}{3}\right)^3$  $\dfrac{c^3}{27}$     11. $z^5 \div z$, $z \neq 0$  $z^4$     12. $\left(\dfrac{t^6}{t^4}\right)^3$, $t \neq 0$  $t^6$

 13. **WRITING MATH** Explain why it is necessary to include $v \neq 0$ in Exercise 9.
    It is impossible to divide by 0.

### ▶ PRACTICE EXERCISES • For Extra Practice, see page 591.

Evaluate each expression when $a = 3$ and $b = -4$.

14. $a^3$  27     15. $a^2 - b^2$  $-7$     16. $b^4$  256     17. $\left(\dfrac{b}{7}\right)^2$  $\dfrac{16}{49}$

18. $4a^2 b$  $-144$     19. $\dfrac{a^8}{a^7}$  3     20. $(2 + b)^3$  $-8$     21. $(a^2 - 5)^2$  16

Simplify.

22. $c^4 \cdot c^3$  $c^7$     23. $(x^3)^5$  $x^{15}$     24. $\dfrac{y^9}{y^4}$, $y \neq 0$  $y^5$     25. $g(g^5)$  $g^6$

26. $\dfrac{r^{10}}{r^9}$, $r \neq 0$  $r$     27. $j^{10} \cdot j^2$  $j^{12}$     28. $(z^4)^4$  $z^{16}$     29. $\left(\dfrac{0}{d}\right)^6$, $d \neq 0$  0

30. $\left(\dfrac{m}{4}\right)^3$  $\dfrac{m^3}{64}$     31. $\dfrac{15w^7}{3w^5}$, $w \neq 0$  $5w^2$     32. $3(y^3)^4$  $3y^{12}$     33. $(d^2)(d^3)(d^4)$  $d^9$

34. **FINANCE** If $500 is invested in a savings account at 5% interest, it will take a little more than 14 years to double (with no deposits or withdrawals). What is the value of the account in 70 years?  $15,200

### Alternative Assessment

**MATH JOURNAL** Have students use a calculator to evaluate the expression $(9^9)^9$.
$(9^9)^9 = (387,420,489)^9 \approx 1.966270505 \cdot 10^{77}$
Remind students that scientific notation is used to express very large numbers. In scientific notation, a number is expressed as the product of two factors. The first factor is greater than or equal to 1 and less than 10, and the second factor is a power of 10. A calculator shows the value of the first factor and then tells the power of 10. Have students tell how their calculators indicate the power of 10.

**COMPUTERS** A byte is the amount of memory in a computer needed to store a single character. A kilobyte (K) is equivalent to $2^{10}$ or 1024 bytes. A megabyte (MB) is equivalent to $2^{20}$ or 1,048,576 bytes. A gigabyte (GB) is equivalent to $2^{30}$ bytes.

**35.** If a computer disk has 800K of memory, how many bytes does it contain? 819,200 bytes

**36.** A word processing program requires 2500K of memory to run. How many megabytes does it require? 2.44 MB

**37.** How many times larger is a megabyte than a kilobyte? $2^{10}$ or 1024 times

**Simplify. You may need to use more than one of the properties.**

**38.** $(x^2y)^3$ $x^6y^3$

**39.** $\left(\dfrac{x^8}{x^2}\right)^3$, $x \neq 0$ $x^{18}$

**40.** $m^2(m^3n^4)$ $m^5n^4$

**41.** $\dfrac{f^2g^2}{f}$, $f \neq 0$ $fg^2$

**42.** $\dfrac{25z^8}{50z^6}$, $z \neq 0$ $\dfrac{z^2}{2}$

**43.** $\left(\dfrac{r}{s^2}\right)^5$, $s \neq 0$ $\dfrac{r^5}{s^{10}}$

**44.** $(b^3 \cdot b^4)^3$ $b^{21}$

**45.** $\dfrac{v^2(v^5)}{v^3}$, $v \neq 0$ $v^4$

**POPULATION** In 1994 the population of the U. S. was about 250 million people. The expression $250(1.01)^x$ can be used to represent the U.S. population where $x$ represents the number of years since 1994. Determine the approximate U.S. population in the following years. Round to the nearest tenth.

**46.** 1998 260 million

**47.** 2002 271 million

**48.** 2005 279 million

## ■ EXTENDED PRACTICE EXERCISES

**Find each missing exponent.**

**49.** $a^? \cdot a^2 = a^6$ 4

**50.** $\dfrac{c^?}{c^4} = c^3$, $c \neq 0$ 7

**51.** $\dfrac{x^7y^?}{x^2y^3} = x^5y^9$, $x \neq 0$ and $y \neq 0$ 12

**Write *true* or *false*. Give examples to support your answer.**

**52.** If $a$ and $b$ are integers and $a < b$, then $a^2 < b^2$. False; $a$ is negative, $b$ is positive.

**53.** If $a$ and $b$ are integers and $a < b$, then $a^3 < b^3$. true

**54. CRITICAL THINKING** A certain type of bacteria doubles in number every 35 min. At 10:00 A.M. there were 16,384 bacteria. At what time had there been exactly half that amount? 9:25 A.M.

## ■ MIXED REVIEW EXERCISES

**Simplify each numerical expression.** (Lesson 2-2)

**55.** $18 - 5 \cdot 3$ 3

**56.** $14 \cdot (28 - 4^2)$ 168

**57.** $6.4 + 9.6 \div 0.3$ 38.4

**58.** $26 - 12 \div 2^2 + 16$ 39

**59.** $10 + 8 - 16 \div 2$ 10

**60.** $81 \div (3 + 9) - 6$ 3

**Draw a number line for each situation.** (Lesson 2-1) For 61–62, see additional answers.

**61.** The number of miles Antjuan walked each day this week is 3.5, 1.4, 2.6, 3.7, 4, 2.8 and 2.

**62.** Mitch was thinking of a number. Five people made guesses. They were off by $-2$, 3, 7, $-5$ and $-1$.

Math
nline mathmatters2.com/self_check_quiz

## ADDITIONAL ANSWERS

**61.**

A number line from 0 to 4 with marks at 1.4, 2.6, 2.8, 3.5, 3.7

**62.**

A number line from $-5$ to 7 with marks at $-5$, $-2$, $-1$, 3, 7

---

Name _____ Date _____

EXTRA PRACTICE **2-7**
**PROPERTIES OF EXPONENTS**

**☑ EXERCISES**

Evaluate each expression when $x = 2$ and $y = -3$.

**1.** $x^3$ ____ 8

**2.** $y^2$ ____ 9

**3.** $x^2 - y^3$ ____ 31

**4.** $\left(\frac{x}{2}\right)^2$ ____ 1

**5.** $5x^2y$ ____ $-60$

**6.** $\frac{x^2}{y^4}$, $x \neq 0$ ____ $\frac{4}{81}$

**7.** $(2 - x)^2$ ____ 0

**8.** $(y^2 + 2)^2$ ____ 121

**9.** $(4 + y)^3$ ____ 1

**10.** $\left(\frac{4}{y}\right)^2$, $y \neq 0$ ____ $\frac{16}{9}$

Simplify.

**11.** $\frac{w^{12}}{w^3}$, $w \neq 0$ ____ $w^9$

**12.** $r^8 \cdot r^6$ ____ $r^{14}$

**13.** $m(m^3)$ ____ $m^4$

**14.** $\frac{t^5}{t^9}$, $t \neq 0$ ____ $\frac{1}{t^4}$

**15.** $\left(\frac{1}{a}\right)^7$, $a \neq 0$ ____ $\frac{1}{a^7}$

**16.** $\left(\frac{n}{3}\right)^4$ ____ $\frac{n^4}{81}$

**17.** $\frac{16p^5}{8p^4}$, $p \neq 0$ ____ $2p$

**18.** $(s^3)(s^4)(s^2)$ ____ $s^9$

**19.** $(x^3y^2)^3$ ____ $x^9y^6$

**20.** $\left(\frac{x^3}{x^2}\right)^4$, $x \neq 0$ ____ $x^{12}$

**21.** $\frac{5d^5}{25d^8}$, $d \neq 0$ ____ $\frac{1}{5d^3}$

**22.** $(v^4 \cdot v^5)^4$ ____ $v^{36}$

**23.** $\frac{q^3(q^5)}{q^4}$, $q \neq 0$ ____ $q^4$

**24.** $(mnp^2)^5$ ____ $m^5n^5p^{10}$

**25.** $\frac{c^6d^2}{c}$, $c \neq 0$ ____ $c^4d^2$

**26.** $(rs^4)(r^2s^3)$ ____ $r^3s^7$

---

Name _____ Date _____

ENRICHMENT **2-7**
**EXPONENTIAL ADVENTURE**

Algebraic expressions involving variables, exponents, and equal signs are equations that are true for some values of the variables. A well-known exponential equation studied by the Greek mathematician Diophantus (c. 245 A.D.) is $x^2 + y^2 = z^3$.

**Example 1**

$x^2 + y^2 = z^3$

**Solution**
You cannot solve by isolating any of the variables. Guess and check.
Try $x = 2$, $y = 2$, $z = 2$.
$2^2 + 2^2 = 2^3$
$4 + 4 = 8$
$8 = 8$   So, $(2, 2, 2)$ is a solution.

Explore solutions for this equation when the variables $x$, $y$, and $z$ represent rational numbers.

**Example 2**

$x^2 + y^2 = z^3$

**Solution**
Try $x = \frac{1}{2}$, $y = \frac{1}{2}$, $z = \frac{1}{2}$.
$\left(\frac{1}{2}\right)^2 + \left(\frac{1}{2}\right)^2 = \left(\frac{1}{2}\right)^3$
$\frac{1}{4} + \frac{1}{4} = \frac{1}{8}$
$\frac{2}{4} \neq \frac{1}{8}$
No solution possible.

**Solution**
Try $x = \frac{1}{4}$, $y = \frac{1}{4}$, $z = \frac{1}{2}$.
$\left(\frac{1}{4}\right)^2 + \left(\frac{1}{4}\right)^2 = \left(\frac{1}{2}\right)^3$
$\frac{1}{16} + \frac{1}{16} = \frac{1}{8}$
$\frac{2}{16} = \frac{1}{8}$
So, $\left(\frac{1}{4}, \frac{1}{4}, \frac{1}{2}\right)$ is a solution.

**☑ EXERCISES**

**1.** Find eight other solutions for $x^2 + y^2 = z^3$ when $x$, $y$, and $z$ are integers. Is there a pattern in your search? Discuss and compare your search strategy with your classmates.
Answers may vary. Possible answers: (0, 1, 1) (0, 8, 4) (2, 11, 5) (5, 10, 5) (16, 16, 8) (0, 27, 9) (10, 30, 10) (18, 26, 10) (0, 64, 16)

**2.** Can you find a solution when $x$, $y$, and $z$ are all negative integers?
No; the sum of two squares will always be positive and the cube of a negative will be negative.

# Zero and Negative Exponents

**Goals**
- Write numbers using zero and negative integers as exponents
- Write numbers in scientific notation.

**Applications** Physics, Astronomy, Population

---

**Lesson Planning**

## NCTM Standards/Strands
- Representation
- Connections
- Communication

## Vocabulary
zero property of exponents
property of negative exponents
standard form
scientific notation

## Tools/Materials Needed
grid paper          calculator

## Lesson Resources
Warm-up Transparency 8
Transparency RF-9, 10
Reteaching 2-8
Extra Practice 2-8
Enrichment 2-8
Technology Activity 2-7 and 2-8

## Getting Started

### 5-MINUTE WARM-UP

**Simplify each expression.**
1. $x^8 \cdot x^4$   $x^{12}$     2. $3^8 \cdot 3^4$   $3^{12}$
3. $(x^8)^4$   $x^{32}$     4. $(3^8)^4$   $3^{32}$
5. $\frac{x^8}{x^4}$   $x^4$     6. $\frac{3^8}{3^4}$   $3^4$

### Introduction to Lesson 2-8
Elicit that the area of a plane figure is the number of square units contained in its interior, and that the area of a rectangle is calculated from $l \cdot w$.

After students have concluded that $2^{-n} = \frac{1}{2^n}$, ask them to make a conjecture about an equivalent expression for $10^{-n}$. Have them verify their conjecture by writing out powers of 10. **See the Teaching Tip.**

---

**Use grid paper. Copy and label the figures shown.**

1. Describe the relationship between $2^4$ and $2^3$.   $2^4$ is twice the size of $2^3$.
2. How are $2^3$ and $2^2$ related? How are $2^3$ and $2^1$ related?   $2^3$ is twice the size of $2^2$ and quadruple the size of $2^1$.
3. Write a statement summarizing the pattern.
   With increase of the exponent by 1 the size doubles.
4. What repeating pattern of shapes do you notice in the figures?
   square, rectangle, square, rectangle
5. Following the pattern, draw the next figure after the 2 by 1 rectangle.
   See additional answers.
6. What is the area of the figure you drew? What power of 2 do you think this figure represents?   1, $2^0$
7. Draw the next three figures in the pattern that represent $2^{-1}$, $2^{-2}$ and $2^{-3}$.
   See additional answers.
8. What is the area of each figure?   $\frac{1}{2}, \frac{1}{4}, \frac{1}{8}$
9. Complete: $2^{-n} = \frac{\blacksquare}{\blacksquare}$   $\frac{1}{2^n}$

Area = 16 units
$2^4 = 16$

Area = 8 units
$2^3 = 8$

Area = 4 units
$2^2 = 4$

Area = 2 units
$2^1 = 2$

### ▉ BUILD UNDERSTANDING

Any nonzero real number raised to the zero power has a value that is equal to 1.

| **Zero Property of Exponents** | For any nonzero real number $a$, $$a^0 = 1$$ |
|---|---|

Exponents can be negative numbers. The quotient property of exponents can help you understand the meaning of negative exponents.

$$\frac{4^3}{4^5} = \frac{\overset{1}{\cancel{4}} \cdot \overset{1}{\cancel{4}} \cdot \overset{1}{\cancel{4}}}{\underset{1}{\cancel{4}} \cdot \underset{1}{\cancel{4}} \cdot \underset{1}{\cancel{4}} \cdot 4 \cdot 4} = \frac{1}{4 \cdot 4} = \frac{1}{4^2}$$

Using the quotient property, $\frac{4^3}{4^5} = 4^{3-5} = 4^{-2} = \frac{1}{4^2}$.

| **Property of Negative Exponents** | For any nonzero real number $a$, if $n$ is a positive integer, $$a^{-n} = \frac{1}{a^n}$$ |
|---|---|

**Check Understanding**

Write each expression as a fraction.

a. $5^{-2}$     b. $7^{-5}$

c. $(-2)^{-4}$     d. $x^{-3}$

a. $\frac{1}{5^2}$     b. $\frac{1}{7^5}$

c. $\frac{1}{(-2)^4}$     d. $\frac{1}{x^3}$

---

## Teaching Tip

Have students complete a table of powers of 10, from $10^5$ through $10^{-5}$, as shown. As they work, students will note that a logical value for $10^0$ is 1.
Based on their experiences with powers of 2 and powers of 10, have students generalize the base.
From $2^0 = 1$ and $10^0 = 1$, then $a^0 = 1$
                    (where $a$ is any nonzero real number).
From $2^{-n} = \frac{1}{2^n}$ and $10^{-n} = \frac{1}{10^n}$, then $a^{-n} = \frac{1}{a^n}$
                    (where $a$ is any nonzero real number).

| **Powers of 10** |
|---|
| $10^5 = 100,000$ |
| $10^4 = 10,000$ |
| $10^3 = 1000$ |
| $10^2 = 100$ |
| $10^1 = 10$ |
| $10^0 = 1$ |
| $10^{-1} = 0.1 = \frac{1}{10}$ |
| $10^{-2} = 0.01 = \frac{1}{100}$ |
| $10^{-3} = 0.001 = \frac{1}{1000}$ |
| $10^{-4} = 0.0001 = \frac{1}{10,000}$ |
| $10^{-5} = 0.00001 = \frac{1}{100,000}$ |

# Example 1

Simplify each expression.

**a.** $x^7 \div x^{-3}$   **b.** $c^5 \cdot c^{-2}$   **c.** $(y^3)^{-4}$

## Solution

**a.** $x^7 \div x^{-3} = x^{7-(-3)}$   **b.** $c^5 \cdot c^{-2} = c^{5+(-2)}$   **c.** $(y^3)^{-4} = y^{3(-4)}$

$= x^{10}$   $= c^3$   $= y^{-12}$ or $\dfrac{1}{y^{12}}$

# Example 2

Evaluate each expression when $m = 2$ and $s = -3$.

**a.** $m^{-5}$   **b.** $(s^2)^{-3}$   **c.** $m^3 s^{-2}$

## Solution

**a.** $m^{-5} = (2)^{-5}$   **b.** $(s^2)^{-3} = s^{-6} = (-3)^{-6}$   **c.** $m^3 s^{-2} = m^3 \cdot \dfrac{1}{s^2} = \dfrac{m^3}{s^2}$

$= \dfrac{1}{2^5} = \dfrac{1}{32}$   $= \dfrac{1}{(-3)^6} = \dfrac{1}{729}$   $= \dfrac{(2)^3}{(-3)^2} = \dfrac{8}{9}$

Any number in decimal form such as 26.376, 0.0067 or 200,000,000 is in **standard form**. In order to be able to write and compute with very large and small numbers, the number can be written in **scientific notation**. A number written in scientific notation has two factors. The first factor is greater than or equal to 1 and less than 10. The second factor is a power of 10.

| standard form | scientific notation |
|---|---|
| 0.0000268 | $2.68 \cdot 10^{-5}$ |
| 370,000,000 | $3.7 \cdot 10^8$ |

Calculators use scientific notation to display very large and very small numbers. On some calculators you can convert between scientific notation and standard form by changing the mode.

> ### Mental Math Tip
>
> To multiply by $10^n$ when $n$ is a positive integer, move the decimal point $n$ places to the right.
>
> $5.18 \cdot 10^7 = 51,800,000$
>
> To multiply by $10^n$ when $n$ is a negative integer, move the decimal point $n$ places to the left.
>
> $9.2 \cdot 10^{-4} = 0.00092$

# Example 3

**a.** Write 2,674,000 in scientific notation.

**b.** Write $6.3 \cdot 10^{-5}$ in standard form.

## Solution

**a.** $2,674,000 = 2,674,000.$

2.674000   Move the decimal point so the first factor is between 1 and 10.

$= 2.674 \cdot 10^6$   The exponent of 10 is the number of places that the decimal point moved.

**b.** $6.3 \cdot 10^{-5} = 0.000063$   Move the decimal point to the left 5 places.

$= 0.000063$

 mathmatters2.com/extra_examples

Lesson 2-8 **Zero and Negative Exponents** 87

---

### Supplementary Example 1
Simplify each expression. Write the answer with a positive exponent.

**a.** $\dfrac{x^2}{x^8}$   **b.** $y^3 \cdot \dfrac{1}{y^4}$   **c.** $(z^{-3})^2$

$= x^{2-8}$   $= \dfrac{y^3}{y^4}$   $= z^{-3(2)}$

$= x^{-6}$   $= y^{3-4}$   $= z^{-6}$

$= \dfrac{1}{x^6}$   $= y^{-1}$   $= \dfrac{1}{z^6}$

$= \dfrac{1}{y}$

### Supplementary Example 2
Evaluate each expression when $m = -2$ and $n = 4$.

**a.** $6m^4$   **b.** $(n^3)^{-2}$   **c.** $m^5 n^{-3}$

$= 6(-2)^4$   $= n^{-6}$   $= (-2)^5 \cdot 4^{-3}$

$= 6 \cdot 16$   $= 4^{-6}$   $= -32 \cdot \dfrac{1}{4^3}$

$= 96$   $= \dfrac{1}{4^6}$   $= \dfrac{-32}{1} \cdot \dfrac{1}{64}$

$= \dfrac{1}{4096}$   $= -\dfrac{1}{2}$

### Supplementary Example 3
**a.** Write 0.0000013 in scientific notation.   $1.3 \cdot 10^{-6}$

**b.** Write $7.2 \cdot 10^6$ in standard form.   7,200,000

### Supplementary Example 4
**CHEMISTRY** The mass of one hydrogen atom is $1.67 \cdot 10^{-24}$ gram. Find the mass of 2,700,000,000,000,000 hydrogen atoms.

Solution:
Write 2,700,000,000,000,000 in scientific notation.
$2.70 \cdot 10^{15}$   For the exponent, use the number of places the decimal point was moved.

Find the product.
$(2.70 \cdot 10^{15})(1.67 \cdot 10^{-24})$
$= (2.70 \cdot 1.67)(10^{15} \cdot 10^{-24})$
$= 4.509 \cdot 10^{-9}$   Round: $4.51 \cdot 10^{-9}$
The total mass is $4.51 \cdot 10^{-9}$ gram.

---

## ADDITIONAL ANSWERS

5.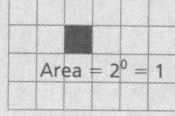

Area = $2^0$ = 1

7.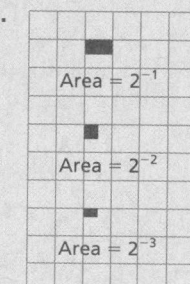

Area = $2^{-1}$

Area = $2^{-2}$

Area = $2^{-3}$

## Lesson Wrap-up

### QUICK ASSESSMENT

Ask the following questions to determine if students understand the content presented in this lesson.

**Choose the correct answer.**

1. Which number is equivalent to $119^0$?  **D**
   A. 119         B. −119
   C. 0           D. 1
2. Which number is equivalent to $46^{-1}$?  **B**
   A. $-\frac{1}{46}$      B. $\frac{1}{46}$
   C. −46          D. −4.6
3. Which number is equivalent to $2.4 \cdot 10^7$?  **D**
   A. 0.000000024   B. 0.00000024
   C. 240,000,000   D. 24,000,000
4. Which number is equivalent to $3.58 \cdot 10^{-5}$?  **A**
   A. 0.0000358     B. 0.00000358
   C. 358,000       D. 35,800,000

### ASSIGNMENT GUIDE

**Basic:** 1–50, 57–66
**Enriched:** 1–66

### Reteaching Worksheet 2-8

Name _____  Date _____

RETEACHING  **2-8**
**ZERO AND NEGATIVE EXPONENTS**
Any nonzero number raised to the zero power has a value equal to 1.
   $a^0 = 1$, for $a \neq 0$
for every nonzero real number $a$, if $n$ is an integer, then
   $a^{-n} = \frac{1}{a^n}$
So, for any nonzero real number $a$, $a^{-n}$ is the reciprocal of $a^n$.
All of the properties of exponents defined for real numbers with positive exponents can be extended to real numbers with negative exponents.

**Example 1**

| Simplify each expression. | Solution |
|---|---|
| **a.** $c^8 \cdot c^{-2}$  **b.** $x^7 \div x^{-4}$ | **a.** $c^8 \cdot c^{-2} = c^{8 + (-2)}$  **b.** $x^7 \div x^{-4} = x^{7-(-4)}$ |
| | $= c^6$    $= x^{11}$ |

**Example 2**

| Evaluate each expression for $r = 3$ and $s = -2$. | Solution |
|---|---|
| **a.** $r^1 s^{-2}$   **b.** $r^3 s^0$ | **a.** $r^1 s^{-2} = \frac{r}{s^2}$  **b.** $r^3 s^0 = (3)^2 \cdot 1$ |
| | $= \frac{3}{(-2)^2} = \frac{3}{4}$    $= 9$ |

**EXERCISES**
Simplify each expression.

1. $x^5 \cdot x^{-3}$  $x^2$
2. $(p^{-2})^4$  $p^{-8}$
3. $z^4 \div z^{10}$  $z^{-6}$
4. $x^{-10} \cdot x^7$  $x^{-3}$
5. $(r^5)^{-2}$  $r^{-10}$
6. $y^{-4} \cdot y^{-5}$  $y^{-9}$
7. $(q^{-3})^{-4}$  $q^{12}$
8. $s^{-9} \div s^4$  $s^{-13}$

Evaluate each expression for $a = -5$ and $b = 2$.

9. $(b)^{-2}$  $\frac{1}{4}$
10. $a^0 b$  2
11. $a^{-4}$  $\frac{1}{625}$
12. $ab^{-3}$  $-\frac{5}{8}$
13. $(b^{-2})^{-3}$  64
14. $(ab)^{-2}$  $\frac{1}{100}$
15. $a^{-2}b^2$  $\frac{4}{25}$
16. $b^5 \cdot b^{-3}$  4

---

## Example 4

**PHYSICS** The speed of light is $3.00 \cdot 10^5$ km/sec. How far does light travel in 1 h? Write the answer in scientific notation.

**Solution**

Find the number of seconds in 1 h.

   $1 \text{ h} = 60 \text{ min} = 60(60) \text{ sec} = 3600 \text{ sec} = (3.6 \cdot 10^3) \text{ sec}$

To find the distance light travels in 1 h, multiply.

$(3.00 \cdot 10^5)(3.6 \cdot 10^3) = (3.00 \cdot 3.6)(10^5 \cdot 10^3)$

$= (10.8)(10^{5+3})$

$= 10.8 \cdot 10^8$

$= 1.08 \cdot 10^9$  Remember that the first factor must be less than 10.

Light travels $1.08 \cdot 10^9$ km in 1 h.

### Technology Note

The first three lines of the calculator screen show Example 4 in normal mode.

The last three lines show it in scientific mode.

```
(3.00*10^5)(3.6*
10^3)
        1080000000
(3.00*10^5)(3.6*
10^3)
          1.08E9
```

### ◼ TRY THESE EXERCISES

**Simplify.**

1. $x^4 \div x^7$  $x^{-3}$ or $\frac{1}{x^3}$
2. $b^{-5} \cdot b^9$  $b^4$
3. $(w^5)^{-4}$  $w^{-20}$ or $\frac{1}{w^{20}}$
4. $d^3 \cdot d^{-8}$  $d^{-5}$ or $\frac{1}{d^5}$

**Evaluate each expression when $m = -4$ and $n = 5$.**

5. $m^{-2}$  $\frac{1}{16}$
6. $n^{-4}$  $\frac{1}{625}$
7. $m^0 n^{-2}$  $\frac{1}{25}$
8. $n^3 \cdot n^{-6}$  $\frac{1}{125}$

**Write each number in scientific notation.**

9. 29,000,000  $2.9 \cdot 10^7$
10. 0.0039  $3.9 \cdot 10^{-3}$
11. 0.0000808  $8.08 \cdot 10^{-5}$

**Write each number in standard form.**

12. $7.6 \cdot 10^8$  760,000,000
13. $9.5 \cdot 10^{-3}$  0.0095
14. $4.03 \cdot 10^{-6}$  0.00000403

15. **POPULATION** The most highly populated city in the world is Tokyo, Japan. Its population is about 27,000,000. Express the population of Tokyo in scientific notation.  $2.7 \cdot 10^7$

### ◼ PRACTICE EXERCISES  •  For Extra Practice, see page 592.

**Simplify.**

16. $z^{-10} \div z^2$  $z^{-12}$ or $\frac{1}{z^{12}}$
17. $y^{-4} \cdot y^{-6}$  $y^{-10}$ or $\frac{1}{y^{10}}$
18. $(w^3)^{-3}$  $w^{-9}$ or $\frac{1}{w^9}$
19. $a^8 \cdot a^{-8}$  $a^0 = 1$
20. $x^5 \div x^8$  $x^{-3}$ or $\frac{1}{x^3}$
21. $b^{-3} \cdot b^3$  $b^0 = 1$
22. $\frac{p^2}{p^5}$  $p^{-3}$ or $\frac{1}{p^3}$
23. $\left(\frac{a}{a^3}\right)^6$  $\frac{1}{a^{12}}$ or $a^{-12}$

**Evaluate each expression when $s = -1$ and $t = 4$.**

24. $s^{-3}$  −1
25. $t^{-5}$  $\frac{1}{1024}$
26. $(st)^{-2}$  $\frac{1}{16}$
27. $t^6 \cdot t^{-4}$  16
28. $\frac{s^2}{s^7}$  −1
29. $(t^2)^{-1}$  $\frac{1}{16}$
30. $\frac{t^{-3}}{t^{-2}}$  $\frac{1}{4}$
31. $\left(\frac{s^2}{s^7}\right)^3$  −1

## Alternative Assessment

**STUDENT PORTFOLIO** Have students use a calculator.
The Sahara is a desert about 16,896,000 ft long and about 5,808,000 ft wide, and its sand is on average 12 ft deep. The volume of a single grain of sand is about $1.3 \cdot 10^{-9}$ ft³. About how many grains of sand make up the Sahara?

Volume of sand in the Sahara = length · width · height
$\approx 1.6896 \cdot 10^7 \cdot 5.808 \cdot 10^6 \cdot 12$
$\approx 117.758 \cdot 10^{13} \approx 1.17758 \cdot 10^{15} \approx 1.18 \cdot 10^{15}$

Number of grains of sand = $\frac{\text{volume of sand}}{\text{volume per grain}} \approx \frac{1.18 \cdot 10^{15}}{1.31 \cdot 10^{-9}} \approx 9.01 \cdot 10^{23}$

There are about $9.01 \cdot 10^{23}$ grains of sand in the Sahara desert.

**Write each number in scientific notation.**

**32.** 8450  $8.45 \cdot 10^3$     **33.** 0.04658  $4.658 \cdot 10^{-2}$     **34.** 0.0000317  $3.17 \cdot 10^{-5}$

**35.** 15,000,000  $1.5 \cdot 10^7$     **36.** 0.0096  $9.6 \cdot 10^{-3}$     **37.** 3,658,000  $3.658 \cdot 10^6$

**Write each number in standard form.**

**38.** $2.01 \cdot 10^{-4}$  0.000201     **39.** $5.3 \cdot 10^8$  530,000,000     **40.** $8.6 \cdot 10^{-6}$  0.0000086

**41.** $3.907 \cdot 10^3$  3907     **42.** $9.98 \cdot 10^{-5}$  0.0000998     **43.** $6.0046 \cdot 10^7$  60,046,000

**DATA FILE** For Exercises 44–46, refer to the data on American pet ownership on page 560. Write the number of each pet in scientific notation.

**44.** reptiles     **45.** dogs     **46.** cats
$9.0 \cdot 10^5$          $3.46 \cdot 10^7$     $2.92 \cdot 10^7$

**47. ASTRONOMY** Mercury travels around the sun at a speed of approximately $1.72 \cdot 10^5$ km/h. At this rate, how far does Mercury travel in 30 days?
123,840,000 km = $1.2384 \cdot 10^8$ km

**48. PHYSICS** The wavelength of red light is about $6.5 \cdot 10^{-5}$ cm. Express this distance in meters.
$6.5 \cdot 10^{-7}$ m

**Write in order from least to greatest.**

**49.** $2^3 \cdot 2^{-2}$; $(6 \cdot 3)^0$; $\left(\frac{1}{3}\right)^{-1}$  $(6 \cdot 3)^0, 2^3 \cdot 2^{-2}, \left(\frac{1}{3}\right)^{-1}$

**50.** $(-4)^{-2}(-4)$; $(-5)^2(-5)$; $(-5)(-5)^{-2}$
$(-5)^2(-5), (-4)^{-2}(-4), (-5)(-5)^{-2}$

## ■ EXTENDED PRACTICE EXERCISES

**51. CRITICAL THINKING** You know that $2^2 = 4$ and $2^{-2} = \frac{1}{4}$. What do you think is the value of $\frac{1}{2^{-2}}$? If $a$ is a nonzero real number and $n$ is an integer, what does $\frac{1}{a^{-n}}$ represent?  $4; a^n$

**Use the results of Exercise 51. Rewrite each with positive exponents.**

**52.** $\frac{1}{m^{-3}}$  $m^3$     **53.** $\frac{x^{-2}}{y^{-2}}$  $\frac{y^2}{x^2}$     **54.** $\frac{a^4}{b^{-3}}$  $a^4b^3$     **55.** $\frac{m^{-7}}{n^3}$  $\frac{1}{m^7n^3}$

 **56. CHAPTER INVESTIGATION** Compare the population density of the state and city you chose. Explain similarities and differences.  Answers will vary.

## ■ MIXED REVIEW EXERCISES

**Simplify.** (Lessons 2-4 and 2-5)

**57.** $-5v + 6w - 8w$  $-5v - 2w$   **58.** $\frac{1s}{2} - 9s + 6s$  $-2.5s$   **59.** $-11tw - (6w)$  $-11tw - 6w$

**60.** $1.4x + 0.69x$  $2.09x$    **61.** $\frac{3}{4}(-8r + 16)$  $-6r + 12$    **62.** $\frac{28f + 16g}{-4}$  $-7f - 4g$

**63.** $-0.5(17v - 8)$  $-8.5v + 4$    **64.** $\frac{32q + 14r}{8}$  $4q - 1.75r$    **65.** $\frac{1}{4}(8x - 6y + 12)$  $2x - \frac{3}{2}y + 3$

**66. DATA FILE** Refer to the data on record transportation speeds on page 573. Find the record speed of the combat jet fighter in ft/s. (Hint: 1 mi = 5280 ft) (Prerequisite Skill)  3095 ft/s

 Math Online   mathmatters2.com/self_check_quiz

---

## Extra Practice Worksheet 2-8

Name _____ Date _____

EXTRA PRACTICE **2-8**
**ZERO AND NEGATIVE EXPONENT**

### ☑ EXERCISES

Simplify.

**1.** $x^{-9} \div x^4$ _____ $\frac{1}{x^{13}}$     **2.** $w^{-2} \cdot w^{-4}$ _____ $\frac{1}{w^6}$

**3.** $(a^4)^{-2}$ _____ $\frac{1}{a^8}$     **4.** $s^5 \cdot s^{-7}$ _____ $\frac{1}{s^2}$

**5.** $\frac{r^6}{r^4}$ _____ $r^2$     **6.** $\frac{c^2}{c^8}$ _____ $\frac{1}{c^6}$

**7.** $\left(\frac{m}{m^3}\right)^2$ _____ $\frac{1}{m^4}$     **8.** $\left(\frac{t^5}{t^3}\right)^5$ _____ $t^{10}$

Evaluate each expression when $d = -2$ and $f = 3$.

**9.** $d^{-4}$ _____ $\frac{1}{16}$     **10.** $f^{-2}$ _____ $\frac{1}{9}$

**11.** $(df)^{-2}$ _____ $\frac{1}{36}$     **12.** $d^2 \cdot f^{-3}$ _____ $\frac{4}{27}$

**13.** $\frac{d^2}{d^4}$ _____ $\frac{1}{4}$     **14.** $(f^{-1})^2$ _____ $\frac{1}{9}$

**15.** $\frac{f^{-4}}{f^{-5}}$ _____ $3$     **16.** $\left(\frac{d^3}{d^6}\right)^2$ _____ $\frac{1}{64}$

Write each number in scientific notation.

**17.** 9630 _____ $9.63 \cdot 10^3$     **18.** 0.0875 _____ $8.75 \cdot 10^{-2}$

**19.** 0.00000918 _____ $9.18 \cdot 10^{-6}$     **20.** 1,600,000 _____ $1.6 \cdot 10^6$

**21.** 0.00058 _____ $5.8 \cdot 10^{-4}$     **22.** 16,450,000 _____ $1.645 \cdot 10^7$

**23.** 0.0001298 _____ $1.298 \cdot 10^{-4}$     **24.** 458,900 _____ $4.589 \cdot 10^5$

Write each number in standard form.

**25.** $4.03 \cdot 10^{-5}$ _____ 0.0000403     **26.** $6.3 \cdot 10^7$ _____ 63,000,000

**27.** $8.702 \cdot 10^3$ _____ 8702     **28.** $7.8 \cdot 10^{-4}$ _____ 0.00078

**29.** $8.76 \cdot 10^7$ _____ 87,600,000     **30.** $7.0003 \cdot 10^6$ _____ 7,000,300

---

## Enrichment Worksheet 2-8

Name _____ Date _____

ENRICHMENT **2-8**
**MORE MAGIC**

A multiplicative magic square can be created from any additive magic square. For any number $x$ in the additive magic square, the corresponding number in a multiplicative magic square is $2^x$.

**E x a m p l e**

Create a multiplicative magic square from the given additive magic square.

**Solution**

| 3 | -4 | 1 |
|---|---|---|
| -2 | 0 | 2 |
| -1 | 4 | -3 |

→

| $2^3$ | $2^{-4}$ | $2^1$ |
|---|---|---|
| $2^{-2}$ | $2^0$ | $2^2$ |
| $2^{-1}$ | $2^4$ | $2^{-3}$ |

→

| 8 | $\frac{1}{16}$ | 2 |
|---|---|---|
| $\frac{1}{4}$ | 1 | 4 |
| $\frac{1}{2}$ | 16 | $\frac{1}{8}$ |

This is a magic square with magic product = 1.

### ☑ EXERCISES

Create a multiplicative magic square from the given additive magic square. Check by finding the magic product.

**1.**

| 0 | -7 | -2 |
|---|---|---|
| -5 | -3 | -1 |
| -4 | 1 | -6 |

→

| $2^0$ | $2^{-7}$ | $2^{-2}$ |
|---|---|---|
| $2^{-5}$ | $2^{-3}$ | $2^{-1}$ |
| $2^{-4}$ | $2^1$ | $2^{-6}$ |

→

| 1 | $\frac{1}{128}$ | $\frac{1}{4}$ |
|---|---|---|
| $\frac{1}{32}$ | $\frac{1}{8}$ | $\frac{1}{2}$ |
| $\frac{1}{16}$ | 2 | $\frac{1}{64}$ |

Magic product is $\frac{1}{512}$.

**2.**

| 4 | -10 | 0 |
|---|---|---|
| -6 | -2 | 2 |
| -4 | 6 | -8 |

→

| $2^4$ | $2^{-10}$ | $2^0$ |
|---|---|---|
| $2^{-6}$ | $2^{-2}$ | $2^2$ |
| $2^{-4}$ | $2^6$ | $2^{-8}$ |

→

| 16 | $\frac{1}{1024}$ | 1 |
|---|---|---|
| $\frac{1}{64}$ | $\frac{1}{4}$ | 4 |
| $\frac{1}{16}$ | 64 | $\frac{1}{256}$ |

Magic product is $\frac{1}{64}$.

**3.** Can you create another multiplicative magic square by multiplying each number by a constant? How will it affect the magic product? Explain your reasoning.
Yes; the magic product will be the cube of the constant factor times the original product.

### Vocabulary Review

**Lesson 2-7**
exponential form    base
exponent    product rule
power rule
power of a product rule
quotient rule
power of a quotient rule

**Lesson 2-8**
zero property of exponents
property of negative exponents
standard form
scientific notation

## ASSIGNMENT GUIDE

**All students:** 1–112

## Chalkboard Examples

**Example from Lesson 2-7**
Evaluate each expression for $x = -3$
and $y = 4$.

a. $-2xy^3$
$= -2(-3)(4)^3$
$= -2(-3)64$
$= 6(64)$
$= 384$

b. $(-3x)^2 y$
$= [-3(-3)]^2(4)$
$= 9^2 \cdot 4$
$= 81 \cdot 4$
$= 324$

**Example from Lesson 2-8**
Evaluate each expression when
$u = 3$ and $v = -2$.

a. $4uv^4$
$= 4 \cdot 3(-2)^4$
$= 4 \cdot 3 \cdot 16$
$= 12 \cdot 16$
$= 192$

b. $(v^{-3})^3$
$= v^{-9}$
$= \dfrac{1}{v^9}$
$= \dfrac{1}{(-2)^9}$
$= -\dfrac{1}{512}$

c. $u^{-4}v^3$
$= 3^{-4}(-2)^3$
$= \dfrac{1}{3^4} \cdot (-8)$
$= \dfrac{1}{81} \cdot \dfrac{-8}{1}$
$= -\dfrac{8}{81}$

### PRACTICE ◼ LESSON 2-7

Evaluate each expression when $x = 2$ and $y = -3$.

1. $(x^2 y)^2$   144
2. $5xy^2$   90
3. $\left(\dfrac{y}{4}\right)^2$   $\dfrac{9}{16}$
4. $4x^2 y$   $-48$
5. $y^4 - x^3$   73
6. $-x^3$   $-8$
7. $\dfrac{x^5}{x^4}$   2
8. $(5 + y)^5$   32
9. $\dfrac{x^3}{y^2}$   $\dfrac{8}{9}$
10. $x^3 - y^2$   $-1$
11. $2\left(\dfrac{y^5}{y^3}\right)$   18
12. $(x + 4)^3$   216

Simplify.

13. $a^2 \cdot a^5$   $a^7$
14. $(c^2)^4$   $c^8$
15. $(c^4 d)^2$   $c^8 d^2$
16. $\dfrac{g^7}{g^3}$, $g \neq 0$   $g^4$
17. $4(x^3)^2$   $4x^6$
18. $f^5 \cdot f^3$   $f^8$
19. $\left(\dfrac{2}{y}\right)^4$, $y \neq 0$   $\dfrac{16}{y^4}$
20. $(3r^3)^3$   $27r^9$
21. $x \cdot x$   $x^2$
22. $y^4 \div y$, $y \neq 0$   $y^3$
23. $\left(\dfrac{m^3}{m}\right)^4$, $m \neq 0$   $m^8$
24. $(-2x^2)^3$   $-8x^6$
25. $\left(\dfrac{a^4}{a}\right)^3$, $a \neq 0$   $a^9$
26. $b^3 \cdot b^8$   $b^{11}$
27. $(4x^2)^3$   $64x^6$
28. $(x^2 y^4)^5$   $x^{10} y^{20}$
29. $-3(d^2 e)^3$   $-3d^6 e^3$
30. $\left(\dfrac{-2}{n}\right)^3$, $n \neq 0$   $\dfrac{-8}{n^3}$

### PRACTICE ◼ LESSON 2-8

Simplify.

31. $y^{-3} \cdot y^{-5}$   $y^{-8}$ or $\dfrac{1}{y^8}$
32. $b^{-4} \cdot b^4$   1
33. $r^0 \cdot b^{-2}$   $b^{-2}$ or $\dfrac{1}{b^2}$
34. $x^3 \div x^9$   $x^{-6}$ or $\dfrac{1}{x^6}$
35. $\dfrac{m^2}{m^7}$, $m \neq 0$   $m^{-5}$ or $\dfrac{1}{m^5}$
36. $(p^{-3})^{-2}$   $p^6$

Evaluate each expression when $f = 2$ and $g = -4$.

37. $f^{-4}$   $\dfrac{1}{16}$
38. $(f^3)^{-2}$   $\dfrac{1}{64}$
39. $g^0 \cdot f^3$   8
40. $\dfrac{f^{-2}}{f^{-4}}$   4
41. $(g^2)^{-1}$   $\dfrac{1}{16}$
42. $g^4 \cdot f^{-4}$   16

Write each number in scientific notation.

43. 1,000,000   $1 \cdot 10^6$
44. 45,000   $4.5 \cdot 10^4$
45. 3334   $3.334 \cdot 10^3$
46. 0.00505   $5.05 \cdot 10^{-3}$
47. 0.00013   $1.3 \cdot 10^{-4}$
48. 0.0147   $1.47 \cdot 10^{-2}$

Write each number in standard form.

49. $7.2 \cdot 10^{-3}$   0.0072
50. $9.45 \cdot 10^6$   9,450,000
51. $1.2 \cdot 10^{-5}$   0.000012
52. $3.03 \cdot 10^{-2}$   0.0303
53. $5.5 \cdot 10^4$   55,000
54. $7.1 \cdot 10^7$   71,000,000

**90**   Chapter 2   **Foundations of Algebra**

## Teaching Tip

Remind students that when evaluating an expression, they should decide
whether to do some simplification before substitution, or to substitute
immediately and then simplify. Discuss both methods for Exercise 1, as
shown below.

**Method 1** *Do some simplification first.*
$(x^2 y)^2$
$= x^4 y^2$
$= 2^4(-3)^2$
$= 16 \cdot 9$
$= 144$

**Method 2** *Substitute first.*
$(x^2 y)^2$
$= [2^2(-3)]^2$
$= [4(-3)]^2$
$= [-12]^2$
$= 144$

## PRACTICE ◾ LESSON 2-1–LESSON 2-8

**Graph the given sets of numbers on a number line.** (Lesson 2-1)

For 55–60, see additional answers.

**55.** $\left\{-\dfrac{2}{3}, 0, \dfrac{1}{2}, \dfrac{3}{2}\right\}$

**56.** $\{-1.5, -0.5, 0, 2.5\}$

**57.** the integers from $-3$ to $5$

**58.** all real numbers less than 2

**59.** all real numbers between $-4$ and $4$

**60.** all real numbers greater than 6.

**Simplify each numerical expression.** (Lesson 2-2)

**61.** $3 \cdot 4 - 7$   5

**62.** $4(7 - 9) + 6$   $-2$

**63.** $-\dfrac{1}{2} + \dfrac{4}{3} \cdot 3^2$   $11\dfrac{1}{2}$

**64.** $7 - 6 \div 2 + 11$   15

**65.** $6^2 \div 2 + 14$   32

**66.** $11 - (7 - 3) \div 2^2$   10

**Translate each variable expression into a word phrase.** (Lesson 2-3)

For 67–72, see additional answers.

**67.** $x + 7$

**68.** $\dfrac{4}{a}$

**69.** $-3y$

**70.** $\dfrac{1}{2}x + 15$

**71.** $-0.5 - y$

**72.** $\dfrac{4x}{3}$

**Simplify.** (Lesson 2-4–Lesson 2-8)

**73.** $b + b$   $2b$

**74.** $b \cdot b$   $b^2$

**75.** $(2ab)(a^2b)$   $2a^3b^2$

**76.** $4(x - 10) + 2(x + 4)$   $6x - 32$

**77.** $\dfrac{10(x + 3)}{5}$   $2x + 6$

**78.** $-7a - 5 - 2a$   $-9a - 5$

**79.** $-(a - 3) - 2a - 11$   $-3a - 8$

**80.** $8 + 2^3 \div 4$   10

**81.** $5 + 3 \cdot 3^2$   32

**82.** $(2ab)^2 + 3a^2b^2$   $7a^2b^2$

**83.** $(2a^2b)^3$   $8a^6b^3$

**84.** $x^4 \cdot x^{-3}$   $x$

**85.** $7(x - 4) - 6(2x + 8) + 3(-4x + 1)$   $-17x - 73$

**86.** $-4(2a - b) + 6(4a + 2b) - 3(-a + 7b)$   $19a - 5b$

**True or False.** (Lesson 2-1–Lesson 2-8)

**87.** $|-3| = -3$   false

**88.** $2x^2 = (2x)^2$   false

**89.** $\dfrac{f^6}{f^4} = f^{-2}$   false

**90.** $4.28 \cdot 10^4 = 42,800$   true

**91.** $2x^2 + 2x^2 = 4x^2$   true

**92.** $2f^{-2} = \dfrac{1}{2f^2}$   false

**93.** $9^0 = 1$   true

**94.** $0.0000714 = 7.14 \cdot 10^5$   false

**95.** $(4x^2)^3 = 64x^5$   false

**96.** "six less than a number" is the expression $6 - x$.   false

**97.** "a number squared times two" is the expression $2x^2$.   true

**Evaluate each expression when $x = 2$, $y = -5$ and $z = 3$.** (Lesson 2-1–Lesson 2-8)

**98.** $xy - z$   $-13$

**99.** $6(z - x) + y^2$   31

**100.** $2x - 3y + z$   22

**101.** $z^2 + 2x - y$   18

**102.** $2|y| - z$   7

**103.** $\dfrac{1}{2}(2y - 4z)$   $-11$

**104.** $\dfrac{1}{5}y - \dfrac{2}{3}z + \dfrac{3}{2}x$   0

**105.** $-9(x + y) - 3z$   18

**106.** $-6|x| - 4z$   $-24$

**107.** $\dfrac{-(xy - z)}{26}$   $\dfrac{1}{2}$

**108.** $\dfrac{12z + 20x}{4}$   19

**109.** $0.4x - 1.5y + 0.2z$   8.9

**110.** $-4x^3$   $-32$

**111.** $\dfrac{(-2z)^4}{18z^0}$   72

**112.** $4x^2 \cdot (x^3)^2$   1024

Chapter 2  **Review and Practice Your Skills**  |  91

**ADDITIONAL ANSWERS**

**55.**

**56.**

**57.**

**58.**

**59.**

**60.**

**67.** the sum of a number and seven

**68.** the quotient of four and a number

**69.** the product of negative three and a number

**70.** one-half of a number added to 15

**71.** $-0.5$ decreased by a number

**72.** four times a number divided by three

---

**Teaching Tip**

Remind students that to write a number in scientific notation, they can obtain the first factor by locating a decimal point between the first two significant digits of the standard form. Then, to obtain the necessary power of 10, they count from the newly-located decimal point to the originally-located decimal point. If the direction of the count is to the right, the power of 10 is positive; if the direction of the count is to the left, the power of 10 is negative.

## Lesson Planning

### NCTM Standards/Strands
- Algebra
- Connections
- Problem Solving
- Number & Operations

### Vocabulary
look for a pattern    sequence
term of a sequence

### Tools/Materials Needed
calculator

### Lesson Resources
Warm-up Transparency 8
Transparency RF-1
Reteaching 2-9
Extra Practice 2-9
Enrichment 2-9
Technology Activities 2-9

### ASSIGNMENT GUIDE
**Basic:** 1–32
**Enriched:** 1–32

## Getting Started

### 5-MINUTE WARM-UP
Write each set of numbers in order.
1. the multiples of 3 between 40 and 65   42, 45, 48, 51, 54, 57, 60, 63
2. in standard form, the powers of 10 from $10^0$ to $10^4$   1, 10, 100, 1000, 10,000

**THE FIVE-STEP PLAN Read**—ask questions to help students understand the problem. **Plan**—guide students to related problems and previously mastered skills and strategies. **Solve**—students solve problem on their own. **Answer**—write the solution in a format that answers the question. **Check**—review work, check for reasonableness, and review strategy used. Students will benefit from the experience of verbalizing their methods.

---

Some problems are solved by recognizing a pattern, while other problems require that you extend the pattern to find the solution. This strategy is called **look for a pattern**, and it is used with many different types of problems.

A set of numbers that is arranged according to a pattern is called a **sequence**. Each number of the sequence is called a **term**. By figuring out the pattern, you can predict the next term. Making a table often helps you see a pattern, and it is frequently used with this strategy.

### Problem

**FINANCE** Sun Li invests $2,000 in a mutual fund. The value of the investment will double every 6 yr. How long will it take for the investment to be worth $16,000?

### Solve The Problem

Create a table to find a pattern in the value of the investment. Let $2000 be the first term of the pattern.

| Years Invested | Value of Investment |
|---|---|
| 0 | $2000 |
| 6 | $4000 |
| 12 | $8000 |
| 18 | $16,000 |

After 18 yr, the investment will be worth $16,000.

### TRY THESE EXERCISES

The first term in a sequence and the pattern are given. Write the next five terms of each sequence.
For 1–6, see additional answers.

1. 5; add 7
2. 0; subtract 5
3. −60; divide by 3
4. $4x$; multiply by −2
5. $2x − 3$; add $x + 5$
6. $32x^4$; divide by $2x$

Use a calculator to find the first four products. Look for a pattern. Predict the fifth product. Use a calculator to check your answers.

7. 23 · 101 =   2323
   24 · 101 =   2424
   25 · 101 =   2525
   26 · 101 =   2626
              2727

8. 202,202 · 9 =   1,819,818
   202,202 · 8 =   1,617,616
   202,202 · 7 =   1,415,414
   202,202 · 6 =   1,213,212
                   1,011,010

9. 3703 ·  3 =   11,109
   3703 ·  6 =   22,218
   3703 ·  9 =   33,327
   3703 · 12 =   44,436
                 55,545

---

**THE STRATEGY** *Look for a pattern*—this strategy helps students understand underlying structure. When a problem can be resolved into a numerical, algebraic, or diagrammatic representation, the structure of the pattern leads to the solution.

### ADDITIONAL ANSWERS

1. 12, 19, 26, 33, 40
2. −5, −10, −15, −20, −25
3. −20, $-\frac{20}{3}$, $-\frac{20}{9}$, $-\frac{20}{27}$, $-\frac{20}{81}$
4. $-8x$, $16x$, $-32x$, $64x$, $-128x$
5. $3x + 2$, $4x + 7$, $5x + 12$, $6x + 17$, $7x + 22$
6. $16x^3$, $8x^2$, $4x$, $2$, $\frac{1}{x}$

### Problem Solving Strategies
Guess and check
✓ Look for a pattern
Solve a simpler problem
Make a table, chart or list
Use a picture, diagram or model
Act it out
Work backwards
Eliminate possibilities
Use an equation or formula

**Five-step Plan**
1. Read
2. Plan
3. Solve
4. Answer
5. Check

**Draw the next three figures. Describe the mathematical pattern.**
For 10–11, see additional answers.

10.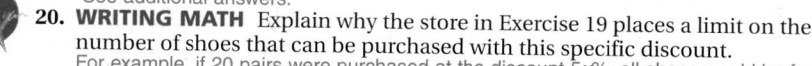

11.

**Describe the pattern in each sequence. Then write the next three terms.**

12. 4, 8, 12, 16, . . .  add 4; 20, 24, 28

13. 1, 3, 6, 10, 15, . . .  add 2, 3, 4, . . . ; 21, 28, 36

14. 1, 2, 4, 8, 16, . . .  multiply by 2; 32, 64, 128

15. 81, 27, 9, 3, . . .  divide by 3; 1, $\frac{1}{3}$, $\frac{1}{9}$

**PART-TIME JOB** Mato works 40 h/wk and earns $12/h. When he works overtime, he earns one and a half times his regular rate for each hour over 40 h. Calculate the amount that Mato earns when he works the following hours in one week.

16. 42 h  $516

17. 46 h  $588

18. 43.5 h  $543

19. **ADVERTISING** Jonica works at a shoe store. During a back-to-school sale, the discount on any purchase is $5x\%$ where $x$ is the number of shoes purchased up to 8 pairs. Jonica makes a sign to hang in the window to display how the sale works. Create a sample advertisement displaying the pattern of the discount when 1 to 8 pairs of shoes are purchased.
See additional answers.

20. **WRITING MATH** Explain why the store in Exercise 19 places a limit on the number of shoes that can be purchased with this specific discount.
For example, if 20 pairs were purchased at the discount 5x%, all shoes would be free.

21. **FINANCE** Marcy puts $500 in a savings bond. The amount in the bond will increase by half of the amount every 5 yr. How much will the savings bond be worth after 15 yr?  $1687.50

**NUMBER SENSE** A *perfect number* is a number equal to the sum of its factors excluding the number itself. For example, 6 is a perfect number since $6 = 1 + 2 + 3$. Determine if each number is a perfect number. Justify each answer.

22. 10  no; $10 \neq 1 + 2 + 5$

23. 28  yes; $28 = 1 + 2 + 4 + 7 + 14$

24. 48  no; $48 \neq 1 + 2 + 3 + 4 + 6 + 8 + 12 + 16 + 24$

25. The *Fibonacci sequence*, named after Leonardo Fibonacci, is a sequence of numbers where each term is the sum of the previous two terms. Write the next six numbers in the sequence.

1, 1, 2, 3, 5, ...  8, 13, 21, 34, 55, 89

## ■ MIXED REVIEW EXERCISES

**Replace each ■ with <, > or =.** (Lesson 2-1)

26. 6 ■ −6  >

27. 0 ■ −1  >

28. $-1\frac{1}{5}$ ■ −1.2  =

29. **WEATHER** The temperature at the top of Mt. Washington is −25°F. The temperature at the base of the mountain is −17°F. Which temperature is colder? (Lesson 2-1)  −25°F

**Evaluate each expression.** (Lesson 2-1)

30. $|y|$, when $y = -42$  42

31. $-|s|$, when $s = -18$  −18

32. $-(-j)$, when $j = -\frac{4}{5}$  $-\frac{4}{5}$

Lesson 2-9 **Problem Solving Skills: Find a Pattern**  93

10.

11.

Add on a bottom row that has one more dot than the current bottom row.

Increase the number of rows and columns of dots by 1.

19. 1—5%
2—10%
3—15%
4—20%
5—25%
6—30%
7—35%
8—40%

## Vocabulary Assessment

- A matching section checks for student understanding of the new vocabulary introduced in this chapter.
- A vocabulary review/test for Chapter 2 is available on pp. vii–viii of the *Chapter 2 Resource Masters*.

## Lesson-by-Lesson Review

For each lesson,

- the main ideas are summarized, and
- practice exercises are provided.

 **EXAMVIEW® PRO**

Use the networkable **ExamView® Pro** to:

- Create **multiple versions** of tests.
- Create **modified** tests for *inclusion* students.
- **Edit** existing questions and **add** your own questions.
- Use built-in **state curriculum correlations** to create tests aligned with state standards.
- Change **English** tests to **Spanish** and vice versa.

---

# Chapter 2 Review

## VOCABULARY ◣

**Choose the word from the list that best completes each statement.**

| | |
|---|---|
| **a.** | absolute value |
| **b.** | base |
| **c.** | coordinate |
| **d.** | exponent |
| **e.** | numerical expression |
| **f.** | opposites |
| **g.** | order of operations |
| **h.** | scientific notation |
| **i.** | sequence |
| **j.** | simplify |
| **k.** | standard form |
| **l.** | variable |

1. Two different integers that are the same distance from zero on the number line but in the opposite direction are ___?___. f

2. A(n) ___?___ is a symbol used to represent a number. l

3. The distance a number is from zero on the number line is the ___?___ of the number. a

4. The number that corresponds to a point on a number line is called the ___?___ of the point. c

5. A(n) ___?___ is two or more numbers joined by operations such as addition, subtraction, multiplication and division. e

6. To ___?___ a variable expression, perform as many of the indicated operations as possible. j

7. The ___?___ of a number written in exponential form tells how many equal factors are being multiplied. d

8. The ___?___ are a set of rules that specify which operations must precede other operations in order to properly evaluate expression. g

9. The ___?___ of $1.2 \cdot 10^5$ is 120,000. k

10. A set of numbers arranged according to a pattern is called a(n) ___?___. i

## LESSON 2-1 ◣ Real Numbers, p. 52

▶ The set of **integers** consists of the whole numbers and their **opposites**.

▶ The set of **rational** and **irrational numbers** make up the set of **real numbers**.

**Graph each set of numbers on a number line.** For 11–12, see additional answers.

11. real numbers less than 1          12. real numbers greater than or equal to $-4$

**Replace each ■ with $<$, $>$, or $=$.**

13. $2\frac{3}{8}$ ■ $2\frac{2}{5}$  $<$          14. $-5.3$ ■ $3.1$  $>$          15. $|7|$ ■ $-7$  $>$

16. Evaluate $-|x|$, when $x = -8$.  $-8$

## LESSON 2-2 ◣ Order of Operations, p. 56

▶ When you find the **value** of a **numerical expression**, you **simplify** the expression.

▶ An expression containing one or more **variables** is called a **variable expression**. To **evaluate** a variable expression, substitute a given number for each variable, then simplify the numerical expression.

**94** Chapter 2 **Foundations of Algebra**

---

## ADDITIONAL ANSWERS

11.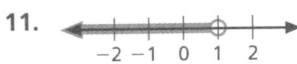

12.

**Simplify each numerical expression.**

**17.** $42 - 2 \cdot 5 + (8 - 2)$   12

**18.** $2[18 - (5 + 3^2) \div 7]$   32

**Evaluate each expression when $x = 12$.**

**19.** $x + 5$   17
**20.** $\frac{1}{3}x - 1$   3
**21.** $6x - 7$   65
**22.** $\frac{x}{2} + 10$   16
**23.** $(x)(x)$   144

## LESSON 2-3 ◼ Write Variable Expressions, p. 62

▶ Many words and phrases suggest certain operations. Any variable can be used to represent a number.

**Write each phrase as a variable expression.**

**24.** six more than a number   $n + 6$
**25.** nine less than a number   $n - 9$

**26.** the product of a number and eight   $8n$
**27.** the difference of four and twice a number
   $4 - 2n$

**Translate each variable expression into a word phrase.**   28–31. See additional answers.

**28.** $5 - x$
**29.** $\frac{w}{3}$
**30.** $3n + 4$
**31.** $6x - 1$

## LESSON 2-4 ◼ Add and Subtract Variable Expressions, p. 66

▶ To **simplify** a variable expression, use the properties and **combine like terms**.

▶ An expression is simplified when only like terms remain.

**Simplify.**

**32.** $6rs + rs - rt$
   $7rs - rt$
**33.** $-2 - mn + 3.2mn + 3$
   $2.2mn + 1$
**34.** $-2cd - (-3cd)$
   $cd$
**35.** $\frac{1}{2}xy + \frac{1}{2}xy - 3xy - x$
   $-2xy - x$

**Evaluate each expression when $x = -2$, $y = 5$, and $z = \frac{1}{3}$.**

**36.** $-3x + 7x$   $-8$
**37.** $-11y - (-9y)$   $-10$
**38.** $6y - 7y + 15z$   0
**39.** $9z - 2y - 3z + 5y$   17

## LESSON 2-5 ◼ Multiply and Divide Variable Expressions, p. 72

▶ To multiply variable expressions, use the distributive property.

▶ To divide variable expressions, divide each term in the numerator by the denominator.

**Simplify.**

**40.** $-2(mn + 3.2)$
   $-2mn - 6.4$
**41.** $-(c + 3d)$   $-c - 3d$
**42.** $2(xy + y)$   $2xy + 2y$
**43.** $-3(2y - 4x)$   $-6y + 12x$

**44.** $\frac{12x - 16}{2}$   $6x - 8$
**45.** $\frac{-9y + 9x}{-3}$   $3y - 3x$
**46.** $\frac{25n - 15m}{-5}$   $-5n + 3m$
**47.** $\frac{4x + y}{2}$   $2x + \frac{1}{2}y$

**48.** Evaluate $\frac{-2x - y}{5}$ when $x = 5$ and $y = -6$.   $-\frac{4}{5}$

## LESSON 2-6 ◼ Simplify Variable Expressions, p. 76

▶ Use the **order of operations** when simplifying variable expressions.

**Simplify.**

**49.** $2x + 3(4x - 1)$
   $14x - 3$
**50.** $8 - 2(x - 5)$
   $18 - 2x$
**51.** $8(x - 1) - 5x$
   $3x - 8$
**52.** $3(2x - 5) - 4(3x - 7)$
   $-6x + 13$

## Teaching Tip

When simplifying variable expressions, encourage students to work neatly and in a line-by-line fashion arranged in a vertical display.
Suggest that students always devote a line to indicate:
• the intended multiplications that will remove parentheses, as in Exercises 40–43.
• the intended divisions that will break a fraction into two fractions, as in Exercises 44–48.
Lines may be consolidated when the same type of operation appears more than once in an expression, as in Exercise 52, where only one line is necessary to indicate the multiplications that are intended each time the distributive property is to be used.

**Simplify.**

**53.** $4(x + 5) + 2(x - 1)$   $6x + 18$

**54.** $-(x - 9) - 2(-3x + 8)$   $5x - 7$

**55.** $\frac{1}{3}(6x + 21) - \frac{3}{4}(4x - 12)$   $-x + 16$

**56.** $4(xy - 6x) - 4(x - xy)$   $8xy - 28x$

**57.** Find the perimeter of a rectangle with a length of $(2x - 7)$ ft and a width of $(x + 3)$ ft. $(6x - 8)$ in.

## LESSON 2-7 ■ Properties of Exponents, p. 82

▶ A number written in exponential form has a **base** and an **exponent**.

▶ Use the properties of exponents for multiplication and division to simplify expressions.

**Evaluate each expression when $m = 5$ and $n = -2$.**

**58.** $m^3$   125

**59.** $m^2 - n^3$   33

**60.** $\left(\frac{m}{8}\right)^2$   $\frac{25}{64}$

**61.** $mn^2$   20

**Simplify.**

**62.** $x^2 \cdot x^5$   $x^7$

**63.** $(a^2)^4$   $a^8$

**64.** $\frac{27a^3}{9a}$   $3a^2$

**65.** $\left(\frac{27w^3}{9w}\right)^2$, $w \neq 0$   $9w^4$

## LESSON 2-8 ■ Zero and Negative Exponents, p. 86

▶ For every nonzero real number $a$, $a^0 = 1$ and $a^{-n} = \frac{1}{a^n}$.

▶ A number written in **scientific notation** has two factors. The first factor is greater than or equal to 1 and less than 10. The second factor is a power of 10.

**Evaluate each expression when $r = -2$ and $s = 2$.**

**66.** $r^0$   1

**67.** $r^{-2}$   $\frac{1}{4}$

**68.** $r^0 s^{-3}$   $\frac{1}{8}$

**69.** $s^2 \cdot s^{-5}$   $\frac{1}{8}$

**70.** Write 3,500,000 in scientific notation. $3.5 \cdot 10^6$ **71.** Write $7.5 \cdot 10^{-4}$ in standard form.   0.00075

**72.** Write $2.4 \cdot 10^8$ in standard form. 240,000,000   **73.** Write 0.0000546 in scientific notation. $5.46 \cdot 10^{-5}$

## LESSON 2-9 ■ Problem Solving Skills: Find a Pattern, p. 92

▶ A set of numbers that is arranged according to a pattern is called a **sequence**. Each number of the sequence is called a **term**.

▶ Some problems are solved by recognizing a pattern, and then extending the pattern to find the solution.

**Write the next three terms in each sequence.**

**74.** 95, 91, 87, 83, ■, ■, ■   79, 75, 71

**75.** $1, \frac{1}{3}, \frac{1}{9}, \frac{1}{27}$, ■, ■, ■   $\frac{1}{81}, \frac{1}{243}, \frac{1}{729}$

**76.** $-4, 8, -16, 32$, ■, ■, ■   $-64, 128, -256$

**77.** 7, 18, 16, 27, 25, ■, ■, ■   36, 34 45

### CHAPTER INVESTIGATION

**EXTENSION** Find the population density of your town or city. Compare the population, number of square miles, and population density of your city with those of a city similar in population. Write a paragraph explaining the similarities and differences of these two cities. Include possible reasons for any differences in population density.

## THEME: Population

The benchmarks and expectations for this extension are as follows.

• Students use an almanac or the internet to find the population and number of square miles or square kilometers of any state and a city in that state.

• Students calculate the population density of the state and city by dividing the population by its area in square miles or kilometers.

• Students compare the population density of the state and city. Explain similarities and differences.

• Students find the population density of your own town or city. Compare the population, number of square miles and population density of your city with that of a city similar in population.

# Chapter 2 Assessment

**Graph each set of numbers on a number line.** For 1–2, see additional answers.

**1.** all real numbers greater than $-5$   **2.** all real numbers less than or equal to $-2$

**Evaluate each expression when $r = -4$.**

**3.** $|r|$  4   **4.** $-|-r|$  $-4$   **5.** $-r$  4

**Simplify each numerical expression.**

**6.** $20 + 8 \times 2$  24   **7.** $(300 + 42) \div 3^2$  38   **8.** $(18 - 2) \cdot 2 + 4^2$  48

**Evaluate each variable expression when $c = 25$.**

**9.** $2c - 15$  35   **10.** $\frac{1}{2}(c + 13)$  19   **11.** $100c \div 5^2$  100

**Write each phrase as a variable expression.**

**12.** the quotient of six and three times a number  $6 \div (3n)$

**13.** a number decreased by 18  $n - 18$

**Translate each variable phrase into a word phrase.**

**14.** $5x$  five times a number   **15.** $12 + 2x$  twelve added to twice a number   **16.** $\frac{2}{-7}$  a number divided by negative seven

**Simplify.**

**17.** $5x + 7x$  $12x$   **18.** $5mn + 3mn + (-2mn)$  $6mn$   **19.** $-3x - 5x + 8y$  $-8x + 8y$

**20.** $2(x + 4)$  $2x + 8$   **21.** $-4(2 - xy)$  $-8 + 4xy$   **22.** $\frac{14x + 7}{7}$  $2x + 1$

**23.** $\frac{-6y + 24}{-3}$  $2y - 8$   **24.** $5(rs + s) - 3(rs + r)$  $2rs + 5s - 3r$   **25.** $6(y - 3) - 4y$  $2y - 18$

**Simplify.**

**26.** $x^3 x^5$  $x^8$   **27.** $(n^2)^3$  $n^6$   **28.** $\frac{16b^6}{4b^2}, b \neq 0$  $4b^4$   **29.** $(3y^2)^3$  $27y^6$

**30.** $x^{-8} \div x^5$  $x^{-13}$   **31.** $y^{-2} \cdot y^{-5}$  $y^{-7}$   **32.** $\frac{a^{-3}}{a^{-6}}$  $a^3$   **33.** $d^5 \div d^9$  $d^{-4}$

**Evaluate each expression when $a = 2$ and $b = 24$.**

**34.** $b^0$  1   **35.** $a^{-3}$  $\frac{1}{8}$   **36.** $(a^3)^{-2}$  $\frac{1}{64}$

**Write each number in scientific notation.**

**37.** 0.00385  $3.85 \cdot 10^{-3}$   **38.** 9,380,000,000  $9.38 \cdot 10^9$   **39.** 0.0543  $5.43 \cdot 10^{-2}$

**Write the next three terms in each sequence.**

**40.** 101, 100, 98, 95, 91, ■, ■, ■  86, 80, 73   **41.** $x, 2x + 1, 3x + 2, 4x + 3$, ■, ■, ■  $5x + 4, 6x + 5, 7x + 6$

**42.** David won $4000 in a contest. If the first day he spends half of this amount and then each day there after spends half of what is left, how long will it take before he only has about $4.00 left? 10 days

Math Online  mathmatters2.com/chapter_assessment

## Assessment Options

Chapter 2 Test A, pages 65–66
Chapter 2 Test B, pages 67–68

## ALTERNATIVE ASSESSMENT

**SCIENTIFIC NOTATION** Exponents are used in scientific notation to make it easier to record very large and very small numbers. Have students research scientific data to find numbers that can be written in scientific notation.

Students should then write at least five word problems that use the data they have found. Solutions to these problems should use operations with scientific notation.

**RUBRIC** The following rubric is a sample scoring guide.

| Points | Description |
|---|---|
| 4 | Writes and **accurately solves five or more complex word problems** involving scientific data in scientific notation. |
| 3 | Writes and **accurately solves five word problems** involving scientific data in scientific notation. |
| 2 | Writes and **solves with minor errors five word problems** involving scientific data in scientific notation. |
| 1 | Writes and **solves with major errors some word problems** involving scientific data in scientific notation. |
| 0 | Makes **no attempt to write problems** or **writes but does not solve problems** involving scientific data in scientific notation. |

## ADDITIONAL ANSWERS

**1.**
$-6\ -5\ -4\ -3\ -2\ -1\ \ 0\ \ 1$

**2.**
$-5\ -4\ -3\ -2\ -1\ \ 0$

## Standardized Test Practice

These two pages contain practice questions in the various formats that can be found on the most frequently given standardized tests.

A student recording sheet for these two pages can be found on p. A1 of the *Chapter 2 Resource Masters*.

### Standardized Test Practice Student Recording Sheet

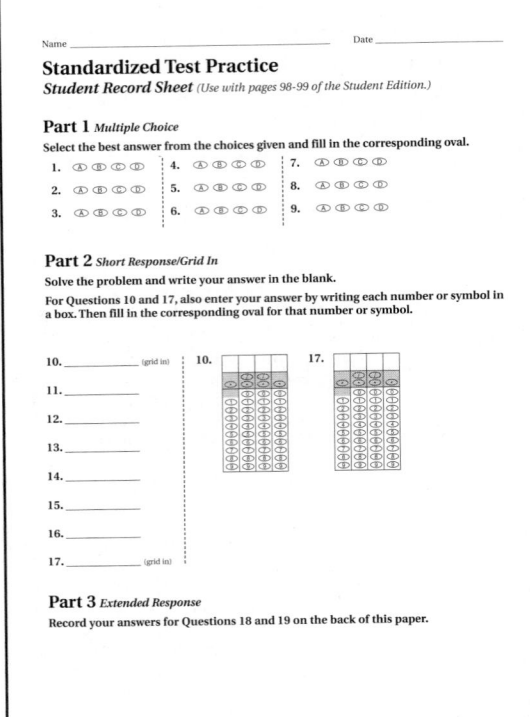

### Additional Practice

See pp. 69–71 in the *Chapter 2 Resource Masters* for additional standardized test practice.

### Part 1 Multiple Choice

**Record your answers on the answer sheet provided by your teacher or on a sheet of paper.**

1. The data shows the heights, in inches, of plants grown for a science experiment. What is the median height of the plants? (Lesson 1-2) C

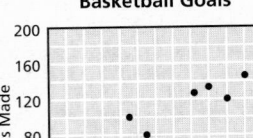

   29, 22, 27, 31, 19, 25, 22, 28

   (A) 22 in.      (B) 25 in.
   (C) 26 in.      (D) 29 in.

2. Kayla took last year's shot statistics for her school's basketball team and created the scatter plot below. What type of relationship do the data show? (Lesson 1-4) A

   **Basketball Goals**

   (A) positive
   (B) negative
   (C) even
   (D) odd

3. Use the box-and-whisker plot to determine what percent of the highest recorded wind speeds in the U.S. range from 40 to 70 mph. (Lesson 1-6) C

   **Highest Recorded Wind Speeds (mph) in the U.S.**

   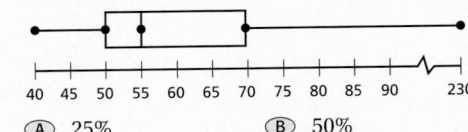

   (A) 25%      (B) 50%
   (C) 75%      (D) 100%

4. If $a = -3$ and $b = 3$, then which of the following statements is *false*? (Lesson 2-1) C
   (A) $|a| > 2$
   (B) $|a| = |b|$
   (C) $|b| < 2$
   (D) $|a| = b$

5. The Rockies scored four more runs than the Cubs scored. Which expression represents the number of runs the Cubs scored if the Rockies scored n runs? (Lesson 2-3) D
   (A) $n + 4$
   (B) $4n$
   (C) $4 - n$
   (D) $n - 4$

6. Simplify $\frac{40x - 16}{-8}$. (Lesson 2-5) B
   (A) $32x + 8$
   (B) $-5x + 2$
   (C) $-5x - 16$
   (D) $5x - 2$

7. Which expression is equivalent to $2(y + 7) - 3(y + 7)$? (Lesson 2-6) A
   (A) $-y - 7$
   (B) $2y + 7$
   (C) $-y + 7$
   (D) $-y + 14$

8. Simplify $\left(\frac{n^7}{n^5}\right)^4$, $n \neq 0$. (Lesson 2-7) B
   (A) $n^6$        (B) $n^8$
   (C) $n^{13}$     (D) $n^{23}$

9. A human blinks about $6.25 \cdot 10^6$ times a year. What is this number in standard notation? (Lesson 2-8) B
   (A) 625,000
   (B) 6,250,000
   (C) 62,500,000
   (D) 625,000,000

## Part 2 Short Response/Grid In

Record your answers on the answer sheet provided by your teacher or on a sheet of paper.

**10.** The stem-and-leaf plot shows the number of points scored by the Grizzlies in each of their basketball games this season. In how many games did they score at least 30 points? (Lesson 1-3)  1

| Stem | Leaf |
|---|---|
| 1 | 8 9 |
| 2 | 0 2 3 3 6 8 8 9 |
| 3 | 0 1 4 4 5 6 8 9 |
| 4 | 0 1 2 |

1|8 represents 18 points.

**11.** Find $A - B$ if $A = \begin{bmatrix} -2 & 1 \\ 5 & -3 \end{bmatrix}$ and

$B = \begin{bmatrix} 4 & 6 \\ -1 & 2 \end{bmatrix}$. (Lesson 1-8)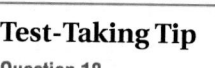

**12.** Write an algebraic expression for the phrase *three times the difference of m and n increased by twice p*. (Lesson 2-3)  $3(m - n) + 2p$

**13.** Write an expression in simplest form for the perimeter of the figure. (Lesson 2-4)  $12x + 6$

$$4x$$
$$x + 3 \qquad 4x + 3$$
$$6x$$

**14.** What is the area of a triangle with a base of 8 and a height of $3x - 6$? (Lesson 2-5)  $12x - 24$

**15.** Simplify the expression $(7y^3)^2$. (Lesson 2-7)  $49y^6$

### Test-Taking Tip Ⓐ Ⓑ Ⓒ Ⓓ

**Question 18**
If a problem seems difficult, don't panic. Reread the question slowly and carefully. Always ask yourself, "What have I been asked to find?" and "What information will help me find the answer?"

 **Math Online** mathmatters2.com/standardized_test

**16.** Evaluate $\dfrac{a^2}{b^{-3}}$ if $a = 3$ and $b = -2$. (Lesson 2-8)  $-72$

**17.** What is the eighth term in the sequence 8, 7, 14, 13, 26, …? (Lesson 2-9)  49

## Part 3 Extended Response

Record your answers on a sheet of paper. Show your work.

**18.** Anthony wants to change his cellular phone carrier. Before he signs an agreement, he compares the different service plans available.

| Plan | Monthly Fee | Cost per minute |
|---|---|---|
| A | $5.95 | $0.30 |
| B | $12.95 | $0.10 |

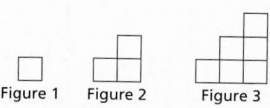

  **a.** Suppose $x$ represents the monthly fee, and $y$ represents the number of minutes. Write an algebraic expression cost per month for any one of these phone plans. (Lesson 2-3)

  **b.** Which plan should Anthony pick if he makes an average of 150 minutes worth of calls each month? Explain. (Lesson 2-2)
  See additional answers.

**19.** The figures are formed using toothpicks. If each toothpick is a unit, then the perimeter of the first figure is 4 units.

Figure 1  Figure 2  Figure 3

  **a.** Copy and complete the table below. (Lesson 2-9)

| Figure Number | 1 | 2 | 3 | 4 | 5 | 6 |
|---|---|---|---|---|---|---|
| Perimeter | 4 | 8 | 12 | 16 | 20 | 24 |

  **b.** Write an expression for the perimeter of figure $n$? (Lesson 2-3)  $4n$

  **c.** Use the expression you wrote in part b to find the perimeter of Figure 20. (Lesson 2-1)  80

**Chapter 2 Standardized Test Practice** 99

## Rubrics

The following rubrics are sample scoring guides for short response and extended response questions.

### Short Response

| Points | Description |
|---|---|
| 2 | The student demonstrates a **thorough understanding** of the mathematics of the task. The response may contain minor flaws that do not detract from the demonstration of a thorough understanding. |
| 1 | The student has provided a response that is only **partially correct.** |
| 0 | The student has provided a **completely incorrect** solution or no response at all. |

### Extended Response

| Points | Description |
|---|---|
| 4 | The student demonstrates a **thorough understanding** of the mathematics of the task. The response contains minor flaws that do not detract from the demonstration of a thorough understanding. |
| 3 | The student demonstrates an **understanding** of the mathematics of the task. The response is essentially correct and demonstrates an essential but less than thorough understanding of the mathematics. |
| 2 | The student has demonstrated only a **partial understanding** of the mathematics of the task. Although the student may have used the correct approach to a solution or may have provided a correct solution, the work lacks an essential understanding of the underlying mathematical concepts. |
| 1 | The student has demonstrated a **very limited understanding** of the mathematics of the task. The response is incomplete and exhibits many flaws. |
| 0 | The student has provided a **completely incorrect** solution or no response at all. |

## ADDITIONAL ANSWERS

**18b.** Plan B; using Plan B, his average monthly cellular phone bill will be $12.95 + 0.1(150)$ or $27.95. Under Plan A, this cost would be $50.95 and under Plan C, the cost would be $31.99.

# 3

# Equations and Inequalities

| Lesson | Lesson Objectives | Pacing (days) | NCTM Standards | State/Local Objectives |
|--------|-------------------|---------------|----------------|------------------------|
| 3-1 | **Equations and Formulas** *(pp. 104–107)* <br> • Determine if a number is a solution of an equation. <br> • Solve an equation or formula. | 1 | 1, 2, 10 | |
| 3-2 | **One-Step Equations** *(pp. 108–111)* <br> • Solve one-step equations. <br> • Solve formulas for a given variable. | 1 | 1, 2, 7, 10 | |
| 3-3 | **Problem Solving Skills: Model Algebra** *(pp. 114–115)* <br> • Use algebra to model and solve a problem. <br> • Use a picture, diagram, or model to solve a problem. | 1 | 2, 6, 9, 10 | |
| 3-4 | **Equations with Two or More Operations** *(pp. 116–119)* <br> • Solve two-step equations and formulas. | 2 | 1, 2, 7, 10 | |
| 3-5 | **Proportions** *(pp. 122–125)* <br> • Write and solve proportions. | 2 | 1, 2, 7, 10 | |
| 3-6 | **Graph Inequalities on a Number Line** *(pp. 126–129)* <br> • Determine if a number is a solution of an inequity. <br> • Graph the solution of an inequality on a number line. | 1 | 1, 2, 9, 10 | |
| 3-7 | **Solve Inequalities** *(pp. 132–135)* <br> • Solve and graph inequalities on a number line. <br> • Solve problems involving inequalities. | 2 | 1, 2, 9, 10 | |
| 3-8 | **Equations with Squares and Square Roots** *(pp. 136–139)* <br> • Solve equations involving squares. <br> • Solve equations involving square roots. | 2 | 1, 2, 6, 9 | |
| Review | | 2 | | |
| Testing | | 2 | | |

**Key to NCTM Standards:**

*1=Number & Operations, 2=Algebra, 3=Geometry,*
*4=Measurement, 5=Data Analysis & Probability,*
*6=Problem Solving, 7=Reasoning & Proof,*
*8=Communication, 9=Connections, 10=Representation*

**Pacing:** Suggestions for the year can be found on page xvi.

**Real-Life Math Videos**

*What's Math Got To Do With It?* Real-Life Math Videos engage students, showing them how math is used in everyday situations. Use *Algebra 1* Video 1 with this chapter.

# Chapter Resource Manager

## FAST FILE — Chapter 3 Resource Masters

| Reteaching Activities | Extra Practice | Enrichment | Assessment | Basic Mathematics Review | Study Skills Activities | Lesson Warm-Ups Transparencies | Teaching Transparencies | Technology Activities | Materials Needed |
|---|---|---|---|---|---|---|---|---|---|
| 73 | 74 | 75 | | 28, 29 | 17–18 | 9 | | 3-1 | blank cards |
| 76 | 77 | 78 | | 28, 29 | | 9 | TK-4 RF-11 | | Algeblocks with Sentence Mat |
| 79 | 80 | 81 | | 28, 29 | | 10 | TK-4 TK-7 RF-1 | | Algeblocks with Sentence Mat |
| 82 | 83 | 84 | | 28, 29 | 25 | 11 | | 3-4 | Algeblocks with Sentence Mat |
| 85 | 86 | 87 | | 28, 29 | | 12 | RF-12 | 3-5 | centimeter rule |
| 88 | 89 | 90 | | 28, 29 | | 12 | TK-8 RF-13 | | ruler, number lines |
| 91 | 92 | 93 | | 28, 29 | 26 | 13 | TK-8 RF-14 | | ruler, number lines |
| 94 | 95 | 96 | 99–105 | 28, 29 | | 14 | TK-7 | 3-8 | ruler, string, weight, calculator, Algeblocks with Sentence Mat |

## Quick Review Math Handbook, Book 2

### hot words hot topics

| MathMatters 2 Lesson(s) | Hot Topic Lesson(s) |
|---|---|
| 3-1 | 6-3, 6-4 |
| 3-2, 3-4 | 6-4 |
| 3-3 | 6-1 |
| 3-5 | 6-4, 6-5 |
| 3-6, 3-7 | 6-6 |
| 3-8 | 3-2, 6-4 |

# Content and Connections

## Connections to the Future

**MM2 (Ch. 8):** Determine if an ordered pair is included in a solution to an equation.

**MM3 (Ch. 2):** Solve multi-step linear equations.

**MM2 (Ch. 6) and MM3 (Ch. 2):** Graph linear equations.

**MM2 (Ch. 8) and MM3 (Ch. 6):** Solve systems of linear equations using substitution.

**MM2 (Ch. 5) and MM3 (Ch. 10):** Create and solve problems with circle graphs.

**MM2 (Ch. 6) and MM3 (Ch. 6):** Graph linear inequalities in two variables on the coordinate plane.

**MM2 (Ch. 8) and MM3 (Ch. 2):** Solve a linear inequality with two variables.

**MM3 (Ch. 10):** Solve equations involving squares and square roots.

## MathMatters 2 Chapter 3 Highlights

Determine if a number is a solution of an equation. (3-1)

Solve one-step equations and formulas for a give variable. (3-2)

Use algebra to model and solve a problem. (3-3)

Solve two-step equations and formulas. (3-4)

Write and solve proportions. (3-5)

Graph the solution of an inequality on a number line. (3-6)

Solve problems involving inequalities. (3-7)

Solve equations involving squares and square roots. (3-8)

## Connections to the Past

**MM1 (Ch. 5):** Understand equations and find their solutions.

**MM1 (Ch. 5):** Solve equations using addition, subtraction, multiplication, or division.

**MM1 (Ch. 5):** Write and solve simple equations.

**MM1 (Ch. 5):** Solve two-step equations.

**MM1 (Ch. 6):** Use a proportion to solve problems involving percent.

**MM1 (Ch. 5):** Graph open sentences on a number line.

**MM1 (Ch. 5):** Solve inequalities with one variable.

**MM1 (Ch. 3):** Calculate squares and square roots of rational numbers.

Key

PC = Previous Course
MM1 = MathMatters 1
MM2 = MathMatters 2
MM3 = MathMatters 3

## Connecting the Strands

| NCTM Strand | Lesson(s) |
|---|---|
| Number & Operations | 3-1, 3-2, 3-4, 3-5, 3-6, 3-7, 3-8 |
| Algebra | 3-1, 3-2, 3-3, 3-4, 3-5, 3-6, 3-7, 3-8 |
| Problem Solving | 3-3, 3-8 |
| Reasoning & Proof | 3-2, 3-4, 3-5 |
| Connections | 3-3, 3-6, 3-7, 3-8 |
| Representation | 3-1, 3-2, 3-3, 3-4, 3-5, 3-6, 3-7 |

| Type | Student Edition | Teacher Resources | Technology/Internet |
|------|-----------------|-------------------|---------------------|
| **INTERVENTION** Ongoing | Are You Ready?, pp. 102–103<br>Check Understanding, pp. 104, 122, 133, 137<br>Review and Practice Your Skills, pp. 112–113, 120–121, 130–131<br>Mid-Chapter Quiz, p.121 | Lesson Warm-Ups<br>Transparencies, pp. WU-9, WU-10, WU-11, WU-12, WU-13, WU-14<br>Quick Assessment, *ATE* pp. 103, 106, 110, 115, 124, 128, 134, 138 | mathmatters2.com/extra_ examples<br>mathmatters2.com/self_check_quiz |
| Mixed Review | pp. 107, 111, 115, 125, 129, 135, 139 | | |
| **ASSESSMENT** Error Analysis | You Make the Call, pp. 111, 124 | Predictable Error, *ATE* p. 123<br>Teaching Tip, *ATE* pp. 130, 144 | |
| Standardized Test Practice | pp. 144–145<br>Preparing for Standardized Tests, pp. 627–644 | Standardized Test Practice, *CRM* pp. 103–105 | mathmatters2.com/standardized_test |
| Open-Ended Assessment | Chapter Investigation, pp. 101, 107, 119, 139, 142 | Chapter Investigation, *ATE* p. 142<br>Alternative Assessment, *ATE* p. 143 | |
| Chapter Assessment | Chapter Review, pp. 140–142<br>Chapter Assessment, p. 143 | Multiple-Choice Tests (Forms A and B), *CRM* pp. 99–102 | mathmatters2.com/chapter_assessment |

**Key to Abbreviations:** *ATE* = Annotated Teacher's Edition, *CRM* = Chapter Resource Masters

## Additional Intervention

***Basic Mathematics Review*** includes 80 lessons, consisting of an instructional page and a test page. This workbook also features a pretest, posttest, table of measurement equivalents, and calculator appendices.

### ExamView® Pro

Use ExamView® Pro Testmaker CD-ROM to:

- Create **multiple versions** of tests.
- Create **modified** tests for *inclusion* students with one mouse click.
- **Edit** existing questions and **add** your own questions.
- Build tests aligned with **state standards** using built-in **state curriculum correlations**.
- Change **English** tests to **Spanish** with one mouse click and vice versa.

## Chapter Opener

### NCTM Standards/Strands
- Representation
- Data Analysis & Probability
- Number & Operations

### Vocabulary

| | |
|---|---|
| phenomena | relationships |
| physics | algebra |
| equations | inequalities |

### Theme Connections
In the 17th and 18th centuries, the rise of rationalist philosophy and empirical science unseated theology as "queen of the sciences." It is often said that mathematics became the reigning monarch. In its most general form, algebra may be described as the language of mathematics—the language that gives voice to the science of physics, which emerged as a separate science only in the early 19th century.

Classical algebra is concerned with solving equations. Many problems in physics can be modeled by algebraic equations and many of its laws are expressed as algebraic equations.

### Career Opportunities
Many careers require understanding of the laws of physics. Two such careers are highlighted in the Math-Works features. Others include: seismologist, astronomer, cryogenicist, electrical engineer, mining engineer, petroleum engineer, optic lens designer, air conditioning designer.
- Mechanical engineer, page 113
- Automobile designer, page 131

## Internet Connection

### Theme Activities
Mathmatters2.com/chapter_theme provides links to the Internet that will help students gather information about the use of math in the real world, particularly data and measures. To search for additional addresses, begin a search of *physics*. Then within that search, use key words that will call up specific fields, such as *mechanics*, *fluid dynamics*,

optics, *nuclear physics*, *thermodynamics*. In small groups, students can brainstorm other key words.

### Chapter Investigation
Use the Internet and other resources to locate additional information about market research.

# Equations and Inequalities

## THEME: Physics

**A**ny time you are dealing with relationships, you can use equations and inequalities to describe and study the interactions of cause-and-effect connections.

When you hear the word "physics" you may think of simple machines, acoustics, gravity, movement, or other natural and material phenomena, but it should also make you think of mathematics, especially algebra. Physics is the science of matter and energy and how they interact. These interactions can be expressed using equations and inequalities.

- **Mechanical engineers** (page 113) design and develop equipment. Much of their work involves using formulas associated with physics, or discovering formulas that can be applied to the physical world.

- Passenger safety is one of the primary goals of **automobile designers** (page 131). They study the physical principles that relate to acceleration, force, and mass to determine how cars react when a collision occurs.

**Math Online**

mathmatters2.com/chapter_theme

## Planet Table

| Planet | Length of year (Earth days) | Length of day (Earth hours) | Approximate mass (kilograms) |
|---|---|---|---|
| Mercury | 87.969 | 1,407.6 | $3.30 \cdot 10^{23}$ kg |
| Venus | 224.7 | 8,532.5 | $4.87 \cdot 10^{24}$ kg |
| Earth | 365.26 | 23.934 | $5.97 \cdot 10^{24}$ kg |
| Moon | | 7.35 $\cdot 10^{22}$ kg | $7.35 \cdot 10^{22}$ kg |
| Mars | 686.98 | 24.62 | $6.42 \cdot 10^{23}$ kg |
| Jupiter | 4,330.6 | 9.92 | $1.90 \cdot 10^{27}$ kg |
| Saturn | 10,747 | 10.5 | $5.69 \cdot 10^{26}$ kg |
| Uranus | 30,588 | 17.24 | $8.69 \cdot 10^{25}$ kg |
| Neptune | 59,800 | 16.11 | $1.02 \cdot 10^{26}$ kg |
| Pluto | 90,591 | 153.3 | $1.25 \cdot 10^{22}$ kg |

## Data Activity: Planet Table

Newton's Universal Law of Gravitation states that all objects in the universe attract all other objects. It also states that the strength of the force of attraction depends on the masses of the two objects. The mass of an object is a measure of how much material it contains.

**Use the table for Questions 1–4.**

1. Which planet exerts the greatest force of attraction?  Jupiter

2. About how many times greater is the force of attraction on Saturn than on Earth?  About 95 times

3. Which planet has a year that is about 84 times as long as a year on Earth?  Uranus

4. About how many more hours are there in a Mars year than in an Earth year?  About 8171 h

### CHAPTER INVESTIGATION

Gravity is the force of attraction between any two pieces of matter. The force of attraction between you and the Earth is what allows you to stand still and not float away. The gravitational field strength of the Earth is the force of gravity exerted on an object with a mass of 1 kg. So a more massive object will have a greater gravity force acting on it.

#### *Working Together*

In the 1800's, scientists measured the strength of the Earth's gravity field with a simple pendulum. The pendulum was a heavy ball suspended on a long wire string. This procedure produced some of the most accurate measurements of the Earth's gravity field. Use the Chapter Investigation icons to measure the strength of the Earth's gravity field using a pendulum.

Chapter 3  **Equations and Inequalities**   **101**

## Project Planning Calendar

Name _____ Date _____
CHAPTER 3 PROJECT PLANNING CALENDAR

Benchmarks
a. Set up a pendulum as shown on page 113. Measure the length *L* of the string. (*Lesson 3-1*)
b. Set the ball of the pendulum swinging through an arc of about 5°. Find the time *t* it takes the pendulum to make 50 swings. A swing is counted each time the ball completely moves back and forth. (*Lesson 3-4*)
c. Calculate the strength of the Earth's gravity using the formula $g = \frac{4\pi^2 L}{t^2}$, where *L* is the length of the pendulum string and *t* is the time for 50 swings. (*Lesson 3-8*)
d. Do the investigation one more time, but this ... ndulum string

PROJECT GOAL
To use the results of a pendulum experiment to calculate and compare the strength of the Earth's gravity.

## Group Project Planner

Name _____ Date _____
CHAPTER 3 GROUP PROJECT PLANNER

Assignment _____ Objective _____
_____ _____
_____ _____

Group Members       Assigned Roles
1) _____       _____
2) _____       _____
3) _____       _____
4) _____       _____
5) _____       _____

Deadlines       Done
                    □

## Data Activity

Sir Isaac Newton (1642–1727), English physicist, mathematician, and natural philosopher, is considered one of the most important scientists of all time. Newton's place in scientific history rests on his application of mathematics to the study of nature and his explanation of a wide range of natural phenomena with one general principle—the law of gravity.

### Extend the Data Activity
**Student Portfolio** Students can research Newton's laws of motion—laws that explain how objects move on Earth as well as through the heavens. Or, students may research the Foucault Pendulum—a type of pendulum that demonstrates the rotation of the earth.

## Chapter Investigation

### As an Overarching Problem
Open this investigation with a discussion about gravity. Ask students what they know about gravity. Encourage them to ask any questions they have about gravity too. Students will continue to work on the investigation as they complete the exercises identified by the Investigation icon that is found throughout the chapter. These exercises will guide students through the task described in *Working Together*. Encourage students to keep all of their work on the Investigation together. Have students use the suggestions in the Chapter Investigation Extension to summarize their work.

### As a Chapter Project
The goal of this project is for students to use the results of their pendulum experiment to calculate and compare the strength of the Earth's gravity. Students can use the Team Project Planner on page 97 and the Project Planning Calendar on page 98 in the *Chapter 3 Resource Masters* to complete the project. Benchmarks **a**, **b**, and **c** should be completed after the lesson listed in parentheses has been studied. Benchmark **d** should be completed at the end of the chapter.

Chapter 3   **Opener**   **101**

### Skills Correlation Chart

| Skill | Lesson Number |
|-------|---------------|
| Signed Numbers | All lessons |
| Ratios and Rates | 3-2, 3-5 |
| Squares and Square Roots | 3-1, 3-8 |

### Vocabulary

| | |
|---|---|
| signed numbers | ratio |
| positive number | proportion |
| negative number | square root |
| unit rate | square |

## Chalkboard Examples

### Signed Numbers
Add a negative number and a positive number:
$-5 + 4 = -1$

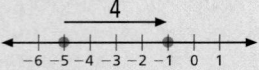

Subtract a positive number from a negative number:

$-1 - 5 = -6$

### Ratios and Rates
In a kindergarten class of 20 students, there are 9 boys. What is the ratio of boys to girls? **9 : 11**

Marissa typed her 1500-word report in half an hour. What is her unit typing rate in words per minute?
**50 words/min**

Is $\frac{9}{4} = \frac{3}{2}$ a proportion? Explain.

$\frac{9}{4} = \frac{3}{2}$ is not a proportion since

$9 \cdot 2 \neq 4 \cdot 3.$

### Squares and Square Roots
$\left(\frac{3}{5}\right)^2 = \frac{3^2}{5^2} = \frac{9}{25}$    $(0.8)^2 = 0.64$

$\sqrt{\frac{16}{81}} = \frac{\sqrt{16}}{\sqrt{81}} = \frac{4}{9}$    $\sqrt{2.25} = 1.5$

---

The skills on these two pages are ones you have already learned. Use the examples to refresh your memory and complete the exercises. For additional practice on these and more prerequisite skills, see pages 576–584.

## SIGNED NUMBERS

In this chapter you will solve equations that include signed numbers. It is important to understand how these numbers affect the final solution of the equation.

**Examples**    Add a positive and negative number:

$5 + (-8) = -3$

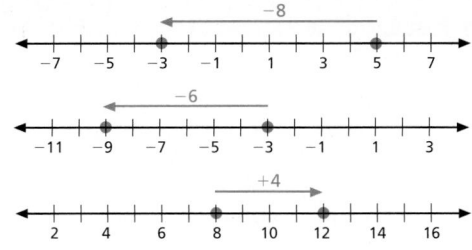

Add two negative numbers:

$-3 + (-6) = -9$

Subtract a negative number from a positive number:

$8 - (-4) = 8 + 4 = 12$

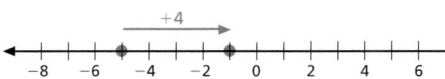

Subtract a negative number from a negative number:

$-5 - (-4) = -5 + 4 = -1$

**Add or subtract.**

1. $-4 + 6$  2
2. $-7 - 9$  $-16$
3. $5 - (-12)$  17
4. $-13 + (-3)$  $-16$
5. $7 - (-4)$  11
6. $-8 + 15$  7
7. $-\frac{4}{5} - \frac{3}{15}$  $-1$
8. $\frac{1}{2} - \frac{5}{8}$  $-\frac{1}{8}$
9. $-\frac{3}{4} - \left(-\frac{7}{16}\right)$  $-\frac{5}{16}$
10. $3.2 + (-0.5)$  2.7
11. $-2.8 + (-1.4)$  $-4.2$
12. $4 - (-7.8)$  11.8
13. $-3 + (-5) + 6$  $-2$
14. $5 - (-8) + (-3)$  10
15. $-4 - 7 + (-2)$  $-13$

## RATIOS AND RATES

Ratios and rates are found in many formulas.

**Examples**    A **ratio** compares two quantities by division:

$$\frac{\text{number of flowers picked}}{\text{total number of flowers in the garden}}$$

A **rate** is a special ratio that compares different units:

$$\frac{\text{number of cans of soup}}{\text{cost of soup can}}$$

## Teaching Tip

In Exercises 1–15, as students work with addition and subtraction of signed numbers, they experience fractions and decimals as well as integers. Before students work on Exercises 7–9, elicit the procedure for adding or subtracting fractions, which requires finding the least common denominator.
For work with equations and inequalities, students will need to be familiar with all operations involving signed numbers. Lessons 28 and 29 in *Basic Mathematics Review* also include a review of multiplication and division of signed numbers.

A **unit rate** is a comparison to 1 unit:

$$\frac{\text{number of miles traveled}}{1\ h} \quad \text{(miles per hour)}$$

A **proportion** is an equation stating that two ratios are equal. You can use cross products to check if the ratios are equal.

$$\frac{5}{10} = \frac{3}{6}$$
$$5 \cdot 6 = 10 \cdot 3$$
$$30 = 30$$

**Identify each relation as a ratio, rate, or unit rate. Be as specific as possible.**

**16.** $\dfrac{\text{number of questions answered correctly}}{\text{total number of questions}}$ ratio

**17.** $\dfrac{\text{number of miles traveled}}{1\ \text{gal of gas}}$ unit rate

**18.** $\dfrac{\text{number of pages printed}}{90\ \text{sec}}$ rate

**19.** $\dfrac{\text{number of sticks of gum}}{\$0.50}$ rate

**20.** $\dfrac{\text{number of words typed}}{1\ \text{min}}$ unit rate

**21.** $\dfrac{\text{number of pages for the index}}{\text{total number of pages in book}}$ ratio

**Determine if each pair of ratios form a proportion. Write = or ≠.**

**22.** $\dfrac{5}{6} \ \blacksquare\ \dfrac{25}{30}$  =

**23.** $\dfrac{3}{16} \ \blacksquare\ \dfrac{9}{48}$  =

**24.** $\dfrac{46}{60} \ \blacksquare\ \dfrac{4}{5}$  ≠

**25.** $\dfrac{17}{38} \ \blacksquare\ \dfrac{68}{152}$  =

**26.** $\dfrac{19}{26} \ \blacksquare\ \dfrac{38}{54}$  ≠

**27.** $\dfrac{7}{12} \ \blacksquare\ \dfrac{56}{96}$  =

**28.** $\dfrac{58}{104} \ \blacksquare\ \dfrac{29}{52}$  =

**29.** $\dfrac{4}{14} \ \blacksquare\ \dfrac{7}{17}$  ≠

## SQUARES AND SQUARE ROOTS

Squares and square roots are found in many equations and formulas.

**Examples**    **Find the square.**

**a.** $7^2 = 7 \cdot 7 = 49$

**b.** $(-6)^2 = (-6) \cdot (-6) = 36$

**Find the square roots.**

**a.** $\sqrt{64} = 8$    $8 \cdot 8 = 64$

**b.** $-\sqrt{25} = -5$    $5 \cdot 5 = 25$

**Find each square.**

**30.** $9^2$ 81

**31.** $(-4)^2$ 16

**32.** $12^2$ 144

**33.** $(-18)^2$ 324

**34.** $22^2$ 484

**35.** $(-15)^2$ 225

**36.** $13^2$ 169

**37.** $(-25)^2$ 625

**Find each square root. Use a calculator or table of squares. If necessary, round to the nearest ten-thousandth.**

**38.** $\sqrt{196}$ 14

**39.** $\sqrt{58}$ 7.6158

**40.** $\sqrt{96}$ 9.7980

**41.** $\sqrt{74}$ 8.6023

**42.** $\sqrt{1024}$ 32

**43.** $\sqrt{67}$ 8.1854

**44.** $\sqrt{295}$ 17.1756

**45.** $\sqrt{430}$ 20.7364

## Refresher Wrap-up

### QUICK ASSESSMENT

Ask the following questions to determine if students have mastered the basic skills reviewed on these pages.

**Answer *always true, sometimes true,* or *never true*. Justify your answers.**

**1.** The sum of two negative numbers is positive.   never true; the sum of two negative numbers is always negative

**2.** The sum of a positive number and a negative number is positive.   sometimes true; the sum is positive when the number with the larger absolute value is positive

**3.** Subtracting a negative number is equivalent to adding a positive number.   always true; subtraction is equivalent to addition of an opposite

### ADDITIONAL PRACTICE

Refer to the Prerequisite Skills lessons beginning on page 576 for more practice. The following lesson references are to *Basic Mathematics Review*.
■ Signed Numbers: Lessons 28, 29

## Teaching Tip

In Exercises 22–29, students may check cross products to determine if the given ratios form a proportion. You might also demonstrate the following as an alternative method that encourages the use of mental math.

To determine if the ratios $\dfrac{58}{104}$ and $\dfrac{29}{52}$ (Exercise 28) form a proportion, suggest that students look at the numerators. Here, if 58 is divided by 2, the result is 29. Does the same operation take place in the denominators? Yes, if 104 is divided by 2, the result is 52. So, the two ratios form a proportion.

## NCTM Standards/Strands
- Algebra
- Number & Operations
- Representation

## Vocabulary

equation
solution of an equation
solve an equation
formula

## Tools/Materials Needed

blank cards

## Lesson Resources

Warm-up Transparency 9
Reteaching 3-1
Extra Practice 3-1
Enrichment 3-1
Technology Activity 3-1

## Getting Started

### 5-MINUTE WARM-UP

**Compute, using mental math.**
1. $-2(6) - 3$ **−15**
2. $48 \div (-6) + 5$ **−3**
3. $-15(-2) + (-9)$ **21**
4. $-24 \div (-8) - 10$ **−7**

### Introduction to Lesson 3-1

When students are making their own expression cards, encourage them to write expressions that have several operations.

After students have made their own sets of cards and completed playing a second game, have each partner list all of the matches he or she has collected. Have volunteers state one match from their list and allow the class to decide if the match is correct.

---

# 3-1 Equations and Formulas

**Goals**
- Determine if a number is a solution of an equation.
- Solve an equation or formula.

**Applications** Travel, Safety, Physics

**Work with a partner.** For 1–5, observe students' work.

1. Make a set of ten number cards by writing one of these numbers on each card.

   $-30 \quad -15 \quad -10 \quad 4 \quad 21 \quad 36 \quad 48 \quad 60 \quad 75 \quad 100$

2. Make a set of ten expression cards by writing each expression on a card.

   $16 - 12 \qquad 40 \div (-4) \qquad -20 + 5 \qquad 16 + 5 \qquad -3 \cdot 10$

   $40 - 4 \qquad 12 \cdot 4 \qquad 30 + 30 \qquad 100 - 25 \qquad -60 + 160$

3. Shuffle the two sets of cards together; then arrange the cards face down in four rows of five cards.

4. The first player turns two cards face up and determines if the expressions are equal. If they are equal, the player keeps the cards. If the expressions on the cards are not equal, they are placed face down in their original position. The next player takes a turn. Play continues until all cards have been taken. The player with the greatest number of cards wins.

5. Work with your partner to make different sets of number and expression cards. Then play the new game.

## ◤ BUILD UNDERSTANDING

An **equation** is a statement in which two numbers or expressions are equal. Equations can be true, false or open. If both sides of an equation have the same numerical expression, the equation is *true*. If the numerical expressions on both sides of an equation are not equal, the equation is *false*.

true: $-8 + 2 = -6$     false: $-8 + 2 = -10$

$-6 = -6$        $-6 \neq -10$

An equation that contains one or more variables is a type of *open sentence*. An open sentence can be true or false depending upon the values that are substituted for the variables. The value that makes the equation true is called the **solution of the equation**.

equation: $x - 3 = 11$

solution:    $x = 14$

### Check Understanding

Tell whether each equation is true, false or open.

1. $x + 9 = 5$
2. $16 + 23 = 39$
3. $7y = 40$
4. $8(-6) = -54$

Answers:
1. open
2. true
3. open
4. false

---

Determine if 2 is a solution of each equation.

**a.** $7w + 4 = 18$

**b.** $8x - 1 = 4x + 3$

**c.** $y^2 + 5 = 9$

**d.** $-6a^2 = 12a$

**Solution**

Substitute 2 for the variable in each equation.

**a.** $7w + 4 = 18$

$7(2) + 4 \stackrel{?}{=} 18$

$14 + 4 \stackrel{?}{=} 18$

$18 = 18$  So 2 is a solution.

**b.** $8x - 1 = 4x + 3$

$8(2) - 1 \stackrel{?}{=} 4(2) + 3$

$16 - 1 \stackrel{?}{=} 8 + 3$

$15 \neq 11$  So 2 is not a solution.

**c.** $y^2 + 5 = 9$

$(2)^2 + 5 \stackrel{?}{=} 9$

$4 + 5 \stackrel{?}{=} 9$

$9 = 9$  So 2 is a solution.

**d.** $-6a^2 = 12a$

$-6(2^2) \stackrel{?}{=} 12(2)$

$-6(4) \stackrel{?}{=} 24$

$-24 \neq 24$  So 2 is not a solution.

To **solve an equation**, find all the values of the variable that make the equation true.

**E x a m p l e  2**

Use mental math to solve each equation.

**a.** $p + 3 = 7$

**b.** $3w = 24$

**Solution**

**a.** $p + 3 = 7$   *What number added to 3 equals 7?*

You know that $4 + 3 = 7$, so $p = 4$.

**b.** $3w = 24$   *Three times what number equals 24?*

You know that $3 \cdot 8 = 24$, so $w = 8$.

A **formula** is an equation stating a relationship between two or more quantities. For example, the distance that you travel is equal to your average speed, or rate, multiplied by the time you spend traveling at that rate.

$$distance = rate \cdot time$$
$$d = rt$$

Often you can evaluate a variable in a formula using given information. For example, suppose a car travels at 55 mi/h for 3 h.

$$d = rt$$
$$d = 55 \text{ mi/h} \cdot 3h$$
$$= 165 \text{ mi}$$

The distance traveled is 165 mi.

 **Math nline** mathmatters2.com/extra_examples

---

## Chalkboard Examples

**Supplementary Example 1**
Using only numbers from $\{-2, -1, 0, 1, 2\}$, determine the solution of each equation.
**a.** $16x + 4 = 10x + 16$  2
**b.** $x^2 = 4$  2, −2
**c.** $2x + 4 = 10$  no solution from the given set

**Supplementary Example 2**
Use mental math to solve each equation.
**a.** $w - 8 = 11$
Since $19 - 8 = 11$, the solution is 19.
**b.** $\dfrac{h}{3} = 12$

Since $\dfrac{36}{3} = 12$, the solution is 36.

**Supplementary Example 3**
**WEATHER** The formula for converting from degrees Celsius to degrees Fahrenheit is $F = \dfrac{9}{5}C + 32$. Convert 20°C to °F.

$$F = \dfrac{9}{5}C + 32$$
$$F = \dfrac{9}{5}(20) + 32$$
$$F = 36 + 32$$
$$F = 68$$

So, 20°C is equivalent to 68°F.

## Reteaching Worksheet 3-1

Name _____  Date _____

RETEACHING  **3-1**
**EQUATIONS AND FORMULAS**

An **equation** is a statement that two numbers or expressions are equal.
An **open sentence** is an equation that contains one or more variables.
A **solution of an equation** is the value of the variable that makes the sentence true.

**E x a m p l e  1**

Tell whether 3 is a solution of the equation.
**a.** $2x + 5 = 11$   **b.** $2y + 3 = 4y - 7$

**Solution**

Substitute 3 for the variable in each equation.
**a.** $2(3) + 5 = 11$
$6 + 5 = 11$
$11 = 11$
So, 3 is a solution.

**b.** $2(3) + 3 = 4(3) - 7$
$6 + 3 = 12 - 7$
$9 \neq 5$
So, 3 is not a solution.

**E x a m p l e  2**

Use mental math to solve the equation $x + \dfrac{2}{3} = 1$.

**Solution**

Think: What number added to $\dfrac{2}{3}$ equals 1? You know that $\dfrac{1}{3} + \dfrac{2}{3} = 1$, so $x = \dfrac{1}{3}$.

**✏ EXERCISES**

Which of the given values is a solution of the equation?

**1.** $7m - 5 = 23$; −4, 5, 4
4

**2.** $c^2 + 5 = 69$; −8, 7, 8
−8 or 8

**3.** $6w - 2 = 7$; 0.5, 1.5, 2
1.5

**4.** $3x^2 - 9 = 39$; −4, 3, 4
−4 or 4

**5.** $-\dfrac{1}{5} + y = \dfrac{3}{5}$; $\dfrac{2}{5}, \dfrac{3}{5}, \dfrac{4}{5}$
$\dfrac{4}{5}$

**6.** $0.1a^2 - 10 = 0$; 10, 1, −10
10 or −10

Use mental math to solve the following equations.

**7.** $-6 + x = -3$
3

**8.** $\dfrac{1}{3}m = 12$
36

**9.** $2t = 17 - 9$
4

**10.** $b - 4.5 = 10$
14.5

**11.** $-x = -7$
7

**12.** $\dfrac{1}{6}b = 7$
42

**13.** $-y = 4.3$
−4.3

**14.** $t - 48 = 48$
96

## Teaching Tip

In Supplementary Example 3, students see the formula for converting from degrees Celsius to degrees Fahrenheit and in the direction for Exercises 25–27, they see the formula for converting from degrees Fahrenheit to degrees Celsius. Have students compare the two formulas, noting the inverses. Have them use both formulas on one set of temperatures to verify the conversion.

*Example:* 59°F is equivalent to 15°C

$F = \dfrac{9}{5}C + 32$

$F = \dfrac{9}{5}(15) + 32$

$F = 27 + 32$

$F = 59$

$C = \dfrac{5}{9}(F - 32)$

$C = \dfrac{5}{9}(59 - 32)$

$C = \dfrac{5}{9}(27)$

$C = 15$

Ask the following questions to determine if students understand the content presented in this lesson.

1. How can you check if a solution to an equation is correct? **Substitute the value for the variable into the equation and see if the numerical equation is true.**

**Match the equations in 2–4 with their solutions chosen from A–D.**

2. $|x| = -5$   D
3. $x^2 = 25$   A
4. $3x - 1 = 14$   C

A. 5, −5
B. −5 only
C. 5 only
D. There is no solution.

## ASSIGNMENT GUIDE

**Basic:** 1–31, 40–52
**Enriched:** 1–52

---

## Example 3

a. **TRAVEL** Mitch traveled for 120 mi in 2 h. What was his average speed?

b. The formula for the perimeter of a triangle is $P = a + b + c$, where $a$, $b$ and $c$ are the lengths of the sides. The perimeter of a triangle is 25 cm. The length of one side is 5 cm, and another side is 10 cm. What is the length of the third side?

### Solution

a. $d = rt$

$120 = r \cdot 2$      *Two times what number is 120?*

Since $60 \cdot 2 = 120$, then $r = 60$.

Mitch's average speed was 60 mi/h.

b. $P = a + b + c$

$25 = 5 + 10 + c$      *What number added to 10 and 5 is 25?*

Since $5 + 10 + 10 = 25$, $c = 10$.

The length of the third side is 10 cm.

### ■ TRY THESE EXERCISES

**Determine if −1, 1, or 4 is a solution of each equation.**

1. $y + 7 = 6$   −1
2. $2x - 5 = 3$   4
3. $8m - 4 = 4$   1

**Use mental math to solve each equation.**

4. $t - 1 = \dfrac{1}{2}$   $\dfrac{3}{2}$
5. $6w = 36$   6
6. $\dfrac{1}{3}b = 7$   21

7. The perimeter of a triangle is 1.8 m. The length of one side is 0.4 m, and another side is 0.8 m. Find the length of the third side.   0.6 m

8. The area of a rectangle is 18 ft$^2$, and the width is 3 ft. Use the formula $A = lw$ to find the length.   6 ft

9. Caroline traveled for 67.5 mi in $2\dfrac{1}{2}$ h. Find her average speed.   27 mi/h

### ▶ PRACTICE EXERCISES • For Extra Practice, see page 592.

**Which of the given values is a solution of the equation?**

10. $c + 4 = 2$; −4, −2, 2   −2
11. $8x - 3 = 21$; −3, 2, 3   3
12. $m^2 - 8 = 41$; −7, −6, 7   −7, 7
13. $3x = 2\dfrac{1}{4}$; $\dfrac{1}{2}, \dfrac{2}{3}, \dfrac{3}{4}$   $\dfrac{3}{4}$
14. $2w + 2 = 3$; 0.1, 0.5, 1.5   0.5
15. $\dfrac{2}{5}k = 14$; 28, 35, 70   35
16. $3x^2 - 1 = 26$; −4, −3, 3   −3, 3
17. $10a + 10 = 10$; −2, 0, 1   0
18. $-\dfrac{2}{3} + m = -\dfrac{1}{2}$; $\dfrac{1}{3}, \dfrac{1}{6}, -\dfrac{1}{6}$   $\dfrac{1}{6}$
19. $0.5c^2 + 1 = 9$; −4, 8, 4   −4, 4

20. **WRITING MATH** Are all equations formulas? Are all formulas equations? Use an example to explain.   No; yes; for example, $3x + 2 = 12$ is not a formula.

106 | Chapter 3 **Equations and Inequalities**

---

## Extend the Lesson

**CONNECTING TO PRIOR KNOWLEDGE** Have students show the solutions to some equations on a number line.

$3x - 1 = 14$
*Solution:* 5

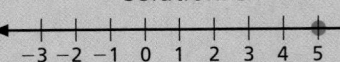

$|x| = 3$
*Solutions:* 3, −3

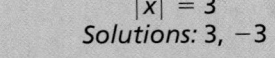

**Use mental math to solve each equation.**

**21.** $a - 2.5 = 0$  2.5    **22.** $\frac{1}{4}x = 12$  48    **23.** $8r = -48$  −6    **24.** $-10 + w = -6$  4

**DATA FILE** Refer to the data on cricket chirps in relation to temperature on page 560. Use the formula $C = \frac{5}{9}(F - 32)$, where $C$ is degrees Celsius and $F$ is degrees Fahrenheit, to find the temperature in degrees Celsius for the following number of cricket chirps.

**25.** 64 chirps/min  13.3°C    **26.** 160 chirps/min  26.7°C    **27.** 98 chirps/sec  17.8°C

**SAFETY** The formula $d = \frac{s + s^2}{20}$ is used to determine the approximate stopping distance ($d$) in feet for a car traveling $s$ mi/h on a dry road. Find the approximate stopping distance for each car traveling at the following speeds.

**28.** 20 mi/h  21 ft    **29.** 35 mi/h  63 ft    **30.** 40 mi/h  82 ft    **31.** 55 mi/h  154 ft

## ■ EXTENDED PRACTICE EXERCISES

**Solve each equation. If no solution exists, explain why.**

∅, absolute values are positive.

**32.** $-x = 13$  −13    **33.** $|b| = 8$  8, −8    **34.** $-p = -1$  1    **35.** $|x| = -3$

**PHYSICS** The formula for the amount of energy used by an appliance is $E = P \cdot T$, where $E$ is energy used in kilowatt-hours (kWh), $P$ is the power usage in watts/hour and $T$ is the number of hours the appliance is used. (Hint: 1 kilowatt-hour = 1000 watts)

| Appliance | Power usage (watts per hour) |
|---|---|
| Hair dryer | 1000 |
| Microwave | 700 |
| Television | 200 |
| Refrigerator | 620 |
| Stereo | 110 |
| 100-watt bulb | 100 |

**36.** The Changs watch their color TV an average of 4 h/day. Approximately how many kilowatt-hours of energy do they use each day watching TV?  0.8 kWh

**37.** Mario listens to his stereo an average of 2 h/day. Approximately how many kilowatt-hours of energy does Mario use each day listening to his stereo?  0.22 kWh

**38.** If the rate charged for electricity is $0.11/kWh, what is the cost of operating a refrigerator for the month of April? Assume the refrigerator is always running.  $49.10

**39. CHAPTER INVESTIGATION** Set up a pendulum as shown. Measure the length $L$ of the string.  Answers will vary.

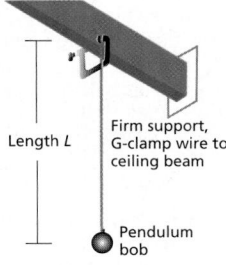

Length L

Firm support, G-clamp wire to ceiling beam

Pendulum bob

## ■ MIXED REVIEW EXERCISES

**Identify each of these numbers as an integer, a rational number, or an irrational number.** (Lesson 2-1)

**40.** $-34$  integer, rational    **41.** 3.101001...  irrational    **42.** $\sqrt{7}$  irrational    **43.** $\frac{5}{16}$  rational

**Simplify each numerical expression.** (Lesson 2-2)

**44.** $16 - (4 + 3) \cdot 2$  2    **45.** $8^2 - (3 \cdot 4) \div 2$  58    **46.** $84 \div 6 \cdot \frac{2}{3}$  $9\frac{1}{3}$

**47.** $(9 - 2)^2 - (5 \cdot 3)$  34    **48.** $6 + 3 \cdot 2 - 8$  4    **49.** $\frac{1}{2}(7 - 3) \cdot 8 \div 4$  4

**50.** $[36 - (2 + 4)] \div 3$  10    **51.** $7.2 - (3 + 8) + 12.3$  8.5    **52.** $(180 \div 9) \div 4 + 2^3$  13

Math Online  mathmatters2.com/self_check_quiz

Lesson 3-1 **Equations and Formulas**  107

Name _____  Date _____

EXTRA PRACTICE  **3-1**
**EQUATIONS AND FORMULAS**

**☑ EXERCISES**

Which of the given values is a solution of the equation?

**1.** $m + 5 = 3$; −7, −2, 2 ____−2    **2.** $4x + 2 = 6$; −2, −1, 1 ____1

**3.** $5a - 1 = 9$; −2, 2, 4 ____2    **4.** $r^2 + 2 = 11$; −3, 3, 9 ____−3,3

**5.** $4d = 16$; −4, 4, 8 ____4    **6.** $4t - 5 = 7$; −3, 2, 3 ____3

**7.** $\frac{3}{4}h = 12$; 12, 16, 24 ____16    **8.** $\frac{1}{2} + m = \frac{3}{4}$; $-\frac{1}{4}, \frac{1}{4}, \frac{1}{2}$ ____$\frac{1}{4}$

**9.** $12s + 12 = 12$; −1, 0, 1 ____0    **10.** $2x = 1\frac{1}{2}$; $\frac{1}{2}, \frac{1}{4}, \frac{3}{4}$ ____$\frac{3}{4}$

**11.** $2t^2 + 2 = 34$; −4, 2, 4 ____−4,4    **12.** $5n^2 - 9 = 11$; −2, 2, 4 ____−2, 2

Use mental math to solve each equation.

**13.** $b - 1.5 = 0$ ____1.5    **14.** $\frac{1}{2}c = 7$ ____14

**15.** $9w = 81$ ____9    **16.** $m + 2 = \frac{2}{3}$ ____$-1\frac{1}{3}$

**17.** $p - \frac{3}{4} = 4$ ____$4\frac{3}{4}$    **18.** $-15 + q = -10$ ____5

**19.** $x - 3 = -4$ ____−1    **20.** $-4 + y = 8$ ____12

Find the unknown side of each rectangle. Use the formula $A = lw$.

**21.** The area of the rectangle is 16 ft$^2$ and the width is 2 ft. Find the length. ____8 ft
**22.** The area of the rectangle is 24 m$^2$ and the width is 4 m. Find the length. ____6 m
**23.** The area of the rectangle is 100 cm$^2$ and the length is 20 cm. Find the width. ____5 cm
**24.** The area of the rectangle is 48 in$^2$ and the length is 8 in. Find the width. ____6 in.

Find the rate in miles per hour for each distance and time given. Use the formula $d = rt$.

**25.** The distance is 80 miles and the time is 1.5 hours. ____$53\frac{1}{3}$ mph
**26.** The distance is 120 miles and the time is 2 hours. ____60 mph
**27.** The distance is 200 miles and the time is 2.25 hours. ____$88\frac{8}{9}$ mph
**28.** The distance is 350 miles and the time is 5 hours. ____70 mph

Name _____  Date _____

ENRICHMENT  **3-1**
**FIND THE NUMBER PAIRS**

Solutions of open sentences such as $x + y = 7$ will be pairs of values for $x$ and for $y$ that make the open sentence true. One such pair of whole-number values is $x = 4$ and $y = 3$.

$x + y = 7$
$4 + 3 = 7$    Substitute 4 for x and 3 for y.
$7 = 7$

So, the whole-number values $x = 4$ and $y = 3$ make the sentence true. This can be written as $(4, 3)$.

**☑ EXERCISES**

**1.** Find all the other pairs of the whole numbers 1 through 10 that make $x + y = 7$ true.
5 solutions: (1, 6), (2, 5), (3, 4), (5, 2), (6, 1)

Find all pairs of whole numbers 1 through 10 that make each equation true.

**2.** $x + y + 6 = 15$
8 solutions: (1, 8), (2, 7), (3, 6), (4, 5), (5, 4), (6, 3), (7, 2), (8, 1)

**3.** $9 - x + y = 7$
8 solutions: (3, 1), (4, 2), (5, 3), (6, 4), (7, 5), (8, 6), (9, 7), (10, 8)

**4.** $x - 3 = y + 5$
2 solutions: (9, 1), (10, 2)

**5.** $x + y = 7 - y$
3 solutions: (5, 1), (3, 2), (1, 3)

**6.** $x - (y + 1) = 6$
3 solutions: (8, 1), (9, 2), (10, 3)

**7.** $(x - y) + 2 = 9$
3 solutions: (8, 1), (9, 2), (10, 3)

**8.** $x + y = x - y$
no solutions

**9.** $x + y = 18 - y$
5 solutions: (10, 4), (8, 5), (6, 6), (4, 7), (2, 8)

**10.** $x - (y + 3) = y + 2$
2 solutions: (7, 1), (9, 2)

**11.** $x + (y - 1) = 2y + x$
no solutions

Write an open sentence that has the given number of solution pairs. Use only the numbers 1 through 10 to replace each variable. Show each pair of values that make the sentence true.

**12.** 3 solutions
Answers may vary.

**13.** 5 solutions
Answers may vary.

## Extend the Lesson

**INTERDISCIPLINARY CONNECTION** The Law of Universal Gravitation between any two objects is stated by the formula $F = \frac{Gm_1m_2}{r^2}$, where $G$ represents the universal gravitational constant, $m_1$ and $m_2$ are the masses of the objects, and $r$ is the distance between the objects. Use the formula to find the gravitational pull exerted by the moon on Earth.
Use $G = 6.67 \cdot 10^{-11}$ N · m$^2$/kg$^2$, mass of Earth = $6.0 \cdot 10^{24}$ kg, mass of the moon = $6.0 \cdot 10^{22}$ kg, Earth-moon distance = $3.7 \cdot 10^7$ m
$$F \approx \frac{(6.7 \cdot 10^{-11})(6.0 \cdot 10^{24})(6.0 \cdot 10^{22})}{(3.7 \cdot 10^7)^2} \approx \frac{241.2 \cdot 10^{35}}{13.69 \cdot 10^{14}} \approx 17.6 \cdot 10^{21} \approx 2.0 \cdot 10^{22} \text{ Newtons}$$

### NCTM Standards/Strands
- Algebra
- Number & Operations
- Representation
- Reasoning & Proof

### Vocabulary
addition property of equality
multiplication property of equality

### Tools/Materials Needed
Algeblocks and Sentence Mat

### Lesson Resources
Warm-up Transparency 9
Transparency TK-4, RF-11
Reteaching 3-2
Extra Practice 3-2
Enrichment 3-2

## Getting Started

### 5-Minute Warm-up

**Name the inverse operation.**
1. $r - 17$  addition
2. $\frac{e}{8}$  multiplication
3. $3w$  division
4. $t + 9$  subtraction

### Introduction to Lesson 3-2
Elicit that a *zero pair*, as its name implies, is a pair of numbers that has a sum of zero. So, a zero pair consists of a number and its opposite.

After students have used models to solve the equations, ask them how they can check that their solutions are correct. Use the value obtained to replace the variable in the original equation, and show that the resulting numerical equation is true.

---

# 3-2 One-Step Equations

**Goals**
- Solve one-step equations.
- Solve formulas for a given variable.

**Applications**  Physics, Packaging, Finance

**Use Algeblocks and a Sentence Mat to solve the equation $x + 3 = 7$.**
For 1–3, 5, see additional answers.
1. Sketch or show the equation on a Sentence Mat.
2. To isolate the $x$-block, create a zero pair by adding the opposite of 3, or $-3$, to each side of the Mat.
3. Simplify each side of the Mat by removing zero pairs.
4. Read the answer from what remains on the Mat. $x = 4$
5. Use Algeblocks and a Sentence Mat to solve the equation $x - 2 = 3$. Sketch or show each step. $x = 5$

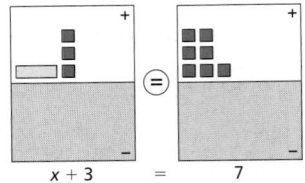

$x + 3$     $=$     $7$

### ◣ BUILD UNDERSTANDING

When two expressions are equal, if you add the same number to each expression, the resulting sums will be equal. This is called the **addition property of equality**.

| Addition Property of Equality | If $a = b$, then $a + c = b + c$ and $c + a = c + b$. |
|---|---|

For example, if $x + 1 = 4$, then $x + 1 + 5 = 4 + 5$.

You can also multiply two equal expressions by the same number. The resulting products will be equal. This is called the **multiplication property of equality**.

| Multiplication Property of Equality | If $a = b$, then $a \cdot c = b \cdot c$ and $c \cdot a = c \cdot b$. |
|---|---|

For example, if $2x = 10$, then $3(2x) = 3(10)$.

If you cannot solve an equation mentally, use these properties to perform the same operations on both sides of the equation. When the variable is alone on one side, you have solved the equation.

### Example 1

**Solve each equation. Check the solution.**

a. $x - 3 = 5$  b. $y + 2.7 = 6.1$  c. $6 - z = 14$

> **Think Back**
>
> The sum of a number and its opposite is 0.
>
> $-5 + 5 = 0$
> $\frac{2}{3} + \left(-\frac{2}{3}\right) = 0$

**108** | Chapter 3 **Equations and Inequalities**

---

## ADDITIONAL ANSWERS

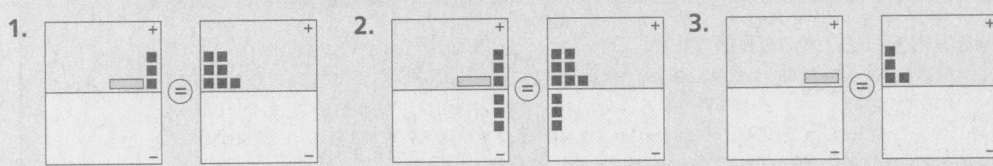

## Solution

Since the sum of a number and its opposite is zero, use the Addition Property of Equality. To check each solution, substitute the solution into the original equation.

**a.**  $x - 3 = 5$

$x - 3 + 3 = 5 + 3$    To isolate $x$, add 3 to both sides.

$x + 0 = 8$

$x = 8$

**Check** $x - 3 = 5$

$8 - 3 \stackrel{?}{=} 5$

$5 = 5$ ✔

**b.** $y + 2.7 = 6.1$

$y + 2.7 + (-2.7) = 6.1 + (-2.7)$    Add the opposite of 2.7 to both sides.

$y + 0 = 3.4$

$y = 3.4$

**Check** $y + 2.7 = 6.1$

$3.4 + 2.7 \stackrel{?}{=} 6.1$

$6.1 = 6.1$ ✔

**c.** $6 - z = 14$

$6 + (-6) - z = 14 + (-6)$

$0 + (-z) = 8$

$-z = 8$    The opposite of what number is 8?

$z = -8$    The opposite of 8 is $-8$.

**Check** $6 - z = 14$

$6 - (-8) \stackrel{?}{=} 14$

$6 + 8 \stackrel{?}{=} 14$

$14 = 14$ ✔

To solve an equation involving multiplication or division of a variable, perform the inverse operation.

## Example 2

Solve each equation. Check the solution.

**a.** $\dfrac{x}{4} = 2.5$      **b.** $-7s = |-35|$

## Solution

**a.** $\dfrac{x}{4} = 2.5$    $\dfrac{x}{4}$ means $\left(\dfrac{1}{4}\right)x$.

$4\left(\dfrac{x}{4}\right) = (2.5)4$    Multiply both sides by 4, the reciprocal of $\frac{1}{4}$.

$1x = 10$

$x = 10$

**Check** $\dfrac{x}{4} = 2.5$

$\dfrac{10}{4} \stackrel{?}{=} 2.5$

$2.5 = 2.5$ ✔

**b.** $-7s = |-35|$    The absolute value of $-35$ is 35.

$\dfrac{-7s}{-7} = \dfrac{35}{-7}$    Divide both sides by $-7$.

$1s = -5$

$s = -5$

**Check** $-7s = |-35|$

$-7(-5) \stackrel{?}{=} 35$

$35 = 35$ ✔

Sometimes you must solve for a variable in a formula. To do so, solve for the indicated variable by performing opposite operations. Addition and subtraction are opposite operations, as are multiplication and division.

**Math Online** mathmatters2.com/extra_examples

Lesson 3-2 **One-Step Equations** | **109**

5.
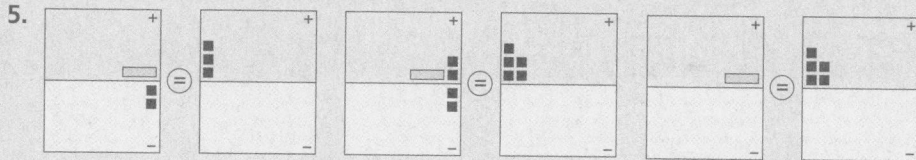

# Chalkboard Examples

## Supplementary Example 1
Solve the equation. Check the solution.

$x + \dfrac{2}{3} = 4$

$x + \dfrac{2}{3} - \dfrac{2}{3} = 4 - \dfrac{2}{3}$

$x + 0 = \dfrac{12}{3} - \dfrac{2}{3}$

$x = \dfrac{10}{3}$

**Check**

$x + \dfrac{2}{3} = 4$

$\dfrac{10}{3} + \dfrac{2}{3} \stackrel{?}{=} 4$

$\dfrac{12}{3} \stackrel{?}{=} 4$

$4 = 4$ ✓

## Supplementary Example 2
Solve the equation. Check the solution.

$\dfrac{x}{\frac{1}{2}} = 18$

$\dfrac{1}{2}\left(\dfrac{x}{\frac{1}{2}}\right) = (18)\dfrac{1}{2}$

$x = 9$

**Check**

$\dfrac{x}{\frac{1}{2}} = 18$

$9 \div \dfrac{1}{2} \stackrel{?}{=} 18$

$9 \cdot 2 \stackrel{?}{=} 18$

$18 = 18$ ✓

## Supplementary Example 3
Solve the formula $E = \dfrac{360}{n}$ for $n$.

$n \cdot E = \dfrac{360}{n} \cdot n$    Multiply each side by $n$.

$nE = 360$

$\dfrac{nE}{E} = \dfrac{360}{E}$    Divide each side by $E$.

$n = \dfrac{360}{E}$

## Reteaching Worksheet 3-2

Name _____ Date _____

RETEACHING **3-2**

## ONE-STEP EQUATIONS

To solve equations involving addition or subtraction, use the addition property of equality to get the variable alone on one side of the equation. To solve problems involving multiplication or division, use the multiplication property of equality to isolate the variable on one side of the equation.

**Addition Property of Equality**
If $a = b$, then $a + c = b + c$ and $c + a = c + b$.

**Multiplication Property of Equality**
If $a = b$, then $ac = bc$ and $ca = cb$.

### Example 1

Solve the equation. Check the solution.
$x + 2 = 11$

**Solution**

$x + 2 = 11$    Think: The opposite of 2 is $-2$.

$x + 2 + (-2) = 11 + (-2)$    Use the addition property of equality.

$x + 0 = 9$

$x = 9$

**Check:** $9 + 2 = 11$    Substitute 9 in the original equation.

$11 = 11$

### Example 2

Solve the equation. Check the solution.
$3x = 15$

**Solution**

$3x = 15$    Think: The reciprocal of 3 is $\frac{1}{3}$.

$\left(\dfrac{1}{3}\right)3x = 15\left(\dfrac{1}{3}\right)$    Use the multiplication property of equality.

$x = 5$

**Check:** $3(5) = 15$    Substitute 5 in the original equation.

$15 = 15$

☑ **EXERCISES**

Solve each equation. Check the solution.

1. $x - 13 = 25$ __38__    2. $10c = 90$ __9__    3. $-3 + y = 12$ __15__

4. $6 + s = -2$ __$-8$__    5. $r - 0.07 = 0.32$ __0.39__    6. $4m = 0.8$ __0.2__

7. $\dfrac{a}{2} = 5$ __10__    8. $\dfrac{m}{6} = 7$ __42__    9. $m + \dfrac{3}{8} = \dfrac{7}{8}$ __$\frac{4}{8}$ or $\frac{1}{2}$__

10. $1.5x = 0.45$ __0.3__    11. $-1.5 + q = -2.4$ __$-0.9$__    12. $\dfrac{2}{3}m = \dfrac{4}{9}$ __$\frac{2}{3}$__

Example 3

**Solve each formula for the indicated variable.**

**a.** $d = rt$, solve for $t$          **b.** $P = a + b + c$, solve for $c$

**Solution**

**a.** $d = rt$

$\dfrac{d}{r} = \dfrac{rt}{r}$     Divide both sides by $r$.

$\dfrac{d}{r} = t$

**b.**     $P = a + b + c$

$P - a = a - a + b + c$     Subtract $a$ from both sides.

$P - a = b + c$     Simplify.

$P - a - b = b - b + c$     Subtract $b$ from both sides.

$P - a - b = c$     Simplify.

## ◤ TRY THESE EXERCISES

**State the operation and number you would use to solve each equation.**

**1.** $3x = 12$   divide by 3

**2.** $m - 17 = 20$   add 17

**3.** $\dfrac{m}{8} = 1.6$   multiply by 8

**4.** $y + 2 = 1$   subtract 2

**5.** $n + 3 = 0$   subtract 3

**6.** $7 - w = 12$   subtract 7, then multiply by $-1$

**Solve each equation.  Check the solution.**

**7.** $4x = 48$   12

**8.** $x + 5 = 14$   9

**9.** $\dfrac{1}{2}c = 2.3$   4.6

**10.** $8 - z = 2$   6

**11.** $\dfrac{2}{3} + g = \dfrac{1}{10}$   $-\dfrac{17}{30}$

**12.** $1.5d = 30$   20

**13.** $P = 4s$, solve for $s$
$s = \dfrac{P}{4}$

**14.** $A = bh$, solve for $h$
$h = \dfrac{A}{b}$

**15.** $I = prt$, solve for $r$   $r = \dfrac{I}{pt}$

## ◤ PRACTICE EXERCISES  •  For Extra Practice, see page 593.

**Solve each equation.  Check the solution.**

**16.** $6w = 12$   2

**17.** $b + 8 = 29$   21

**18.** $\dfrac{3}{4}b = -8$   $-\dfrac{32}{3}$

**19.** $2.5 - t = 3.4$   $-0.9$

**20.** $z - 16 = 5$   21

**21.** $12k = 1.44$   0.12

**22.** $-4d = 1$   $-\dfrac{1}{4}$

**23.** $5n = -45$   $-9$

**24.** $1.5 - c = 3$   $-1.5$

**25.** $p - 3.5 = 10$   13.5

**26.** $\dfrac{5}{8}n = 15$   24

**27.** $-52 = 13h$   $-4$

**28.** $-\dfrac{x}{7} = -4$   28

**29.** $-8c = 100$   $-\dfrac{25}{2}$

**30.** $\dfrac{2}{3}n = -6$   $-9$

**31.** $3.5 - x = 6$   $-2.5$

**32.** $-8 = 4y$   $-2$

**33.** $11 + c = 4\dfrac{1}{2}$   $-6\dfrac{1}{2}$

**34.** $-1 = \dfrac{3}{4}x$   $-\dfrac{4}{3}$

**35.** $-\dfrac{x}{2} = 1\dfrac{1}{4}$   $-2.5$

**36.** $12 + 22 + n = 10$   $-24$

**37.** $-\dfrac{r}{5} = -13$   65

**38.** $-3.9q = -0.3$   $\dfrac{1}{13}$

**39.** $-\dfrac{4}{5}w = |-16|$   $-20$

**40.** $e - 7 = |-12|$   19

**41.** $-\dfrac{2}{5} = \dfrac{3}{7}d$   $-\dfrac{14}{15}$

**42.** $t + 3 = |-4|$   1

**43. WRITING MATH** Write a paragraph explaining the different ways you know to solve an equation. Use examples.   Check students' work.

**44. PHYSICS** The formula $F = ma$ is used to find the force applied to an object, where $F$ is the force, $m$ is the mass and $a$ is the acceleration of the object. Solve the equation for $m$. Then solve the equation for $a$.   $m = \dfrac{F}{a}, a = \dfrac{F}{m}$

---

## Lesson Wrap-up

### QUICK ASSESSMENT

Ask the following questions to determine if students understand the content presented in this lesson.

**Match the equations in 1–4 with the operation you would use to solve for $x$, chosen from A–E.**

**1.** $\dfrac{x}{2} = 20$   E

**2.** $x - 2 = 20$   C

**3.** $x + 2 = 20$   B

**4.** $2x = 20$   D

**A.** Square each side.

**B.** Add $(-2)$ to each side.

**C.** Add 2 to each side.

**D.** Multiply both sides by $\dfrac{1}{2}$.

**E.** Multiply both sides by 2.

### ASSIGNMENT GUIDE

**Basic:** 1–54, 60–68
**Enriched:** 1–68

### ADDITIONAL ANSWERS

**48.**

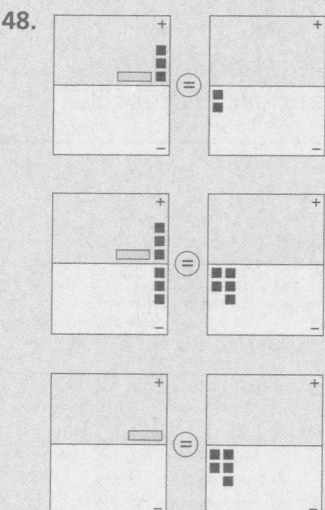

**49.**

**45. YOU MAKE THE CALL** Kenny solved the equation $-\frac{2}{5}x = 14$. His work is shown. Is he correct? Explain why or why not.

$$-\frac{2}{5}x = 14$$

No; he needs to multiply both sides by $-\frac{5}{2}$.

$$\frac{5}{2}\left(-\frac{2}{5}\right)x = (14)\frac{5}{2}$$

$$x = 35$$

**46. PACKAGING** A case of canned pineapples weighs 18 lb and contains 24 cans. A store manager wrote the equation $24x = 18$. What does $x$ represent? Solve the equation.  weight of each can, 0.75 lb

**47. FINANCE** The formula $I = prt$ is used to calculate the simple interest on money in a savings account. The amount of interest is represented by $I$, $p$ is the principal or amount of money in the account, $r$ is the interest rate, and $t$ is the time in years that the money is in the account. Find the interest rate if $500 earns $162.50 in interest after 5 yr.  6.5%

**MODELING** Use Algeblocks to model and solve each equation.
For 48–50, see additional answers.

**48.** $x + 3 = -2$  $x = -5$   **49.** $y - 4 = 3$  $y = 7$   **50.** $x - 6 = -3$  $x = 3$

**Translate each word phrase into an equation. Then solve the equation.**

**51.** A number increased by six is ten.
$x + 6 = 10; 4$

**52.** Three times a number is $-21$.
$3x = -21; 7$

**53.** One-third of a number is 24.
$\frac{1}{3}x = 24; 72$

**54.** Eight decreased by a number is 13.
$8 - x = 13; -5$

## EXTENDED PRACTICE EXERCISES

**Complete.**

**55.** If $3a + 4 = 10$, then $6a + 8 = \underline{\quad?\quad}$.
20

**56.** If $8w - 6 = 9$, then $4w - 3 = \underline{\quad?\quad}$.
4.5

**57. CRITICAL THINKING** Suppose $x + a = b$. What happens to $x$ if $a$ increases and $b$ remains the same?  The value of $x$ decreases.

**58.** If $x + 8 = 17$, find the value of $5x$.  45

**59.** If $w - 3 = 21$, find the value of $3w - 100$.
$-28$

## MIXED REVIEW EXERCISES

Refer to the histogram for Exercises 60–62. (Lesson 1-3)

**60.** People of which age interval use their membership for emergency service most often?  66–75

**61.** Which intervals show equal frequencies?  16–25 and 36–45; 26–35 and 46–55

**62.** Name the interval that contains 5% of the drivers.  16–25, 36–45

**Evaluate each expression.** (Lesson 2-1)

**63.** $|g|$ when $g = 4$  4

**64.** $|f|$ when $f = -6$  6

**65.** $|r|$ when $r = -3.8$  3.8

**66.** $|q|$ when $q = 7.146$  7.146

**67.** $|h|$ when $h = 85$  85

**68.** $|m|$ when $m = -\frac{3}{4}$  $\frac{3}{4}$

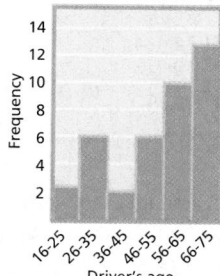

**Drivers Using Car Club Membership for Emergency Service**

Frequency (vertical axis) vs. Driver's age (horizontal axis: 16-25, 26-35, 36-45, 46-55, 56-65, 66-75)

Math Online  mathmatters2.com/self_check_quiz

Lesson 3-2  **One-Step Equations**  111

50.

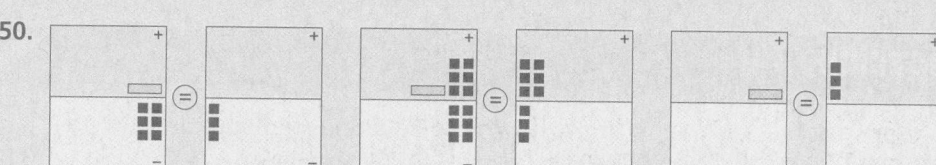

---

### Vocabulary Review

**Lesson 3-1**
equation
solve an equation
solution of an equation
formula

**Lesson 3-2**
addition property of equality
multiplication property of equality

## Assignment Guide

**All students: 1–65**

## Chalkboard Examples

**Lesson 3-1**
Use mental math to solve each equation.

a. $16 - z = 20$
   Since $16 + 4 = 20$,
   then $16 - (-4) = 20$, and $z = -4$.

b. $\frac{t}{-4} = 4$
   Since $\frac{-16}{-4} = 4$, then $t = -16$.

**Lesson 3-2**
Solve the equation. Check the solution.

$$\frac{3}{4} - x = 4$$

$$\frac{3}{4} + \left(-\frac{3}{4}\right) - x = 4 + \left(-\frac{3}{4}\right)$$

$$0 + (-x) = \frac{16}{4} + \left(-\frac{3}{4}\right)$$

$$-x = \frac{13}{4}$$

$$x = -\frac{13}{4}$$

Check

$$\frac{3}{4} - x = 4$$

$$\frac{3}{4} - \left(-\frac{13}{4}\right) \overset{?}{=} 4$$

$$\frac{3}{4} + \frac{13}{4} \overset{?}{=} 4$$

$$\frac{16}{4} \overset{?}{=} 4$$

$$4 = 4 \checkmark$$

# Review and Practice Your Skills

## PRACTICE ■ LESSON 3-1

**Which of the given values is a solution of the equation?**

1. $x + 5 = 3$; $-4, 2, -2$  $-2$
2. $w + 0.9 = 8.3$; $17.3, 7.4, 9.2$  $7.4$
3. $b^2 - 7 = 29$; $-6, 7, 6$  $-6, 6$
4. $3x + 5 = 26$; $7, 8, 9$  $7$
5. $y - 2\frac{3}{4} = 9$; $6\frac{1}{4}, 12\frac{1}{4}, 11\frac{3}{4}$  $11\frac{3}{4}$
6. $1.5c = 45$; $3, 0.3, 30$  $30$
7. $\frac{m}{8} = 0$; $0, 1, 8$  $0$
8. $d^2 - 7 = 9$; $-4, 0, 4$  $-4, 4$

**Find the unknown side of each triangle. Use the formula $A = \frac{1}{2}bh$.**

9. The area of the triangle is 24 in.$^2$ and the base is 12 in. Find the height.  4 in.
10. The area of the triangle is 40 m$^2$ and the height is 4 m. Find the base.  20 m
11. The area of the triangle is 27 ft$^2$ and the base is 9 ft. Find the height.  6 ft

**Use mental math to solve each equation.**

12. $3m = -24$  $-8$
13. $\frac{24}{x} = 12$  $2$
14. $-2 + y = -11$  $-9$
15. $7b = 1$  $\frac{1}{7}$
16. $x + 4 = 9$  $5$
17. $4a = 48$  $12$
18. $\frac{x}{3} = 3$  $9$
19. $11 - y = 2$  $9$

## PRACTICE ■ LESSON 3-2

**Solve each equation. Check the solution.**

20. $m + 3 = -5$  $-8$
21. $3x = -21$  $-7$
22. $-\frac{3}{4}y = 9$  $-12$
23. $\frac{b}{4} = -8$  $-32$
24. $a - 9 = -2$  $7$
25. $-4 + n = -3$  $1$
26. $x + 5 = -\frac{2}{3}$  $-5\frac{2}{3}$
27. $13b = -143$  $-11$
28. $9x = -207$  $-23$
29. $-\frac{4}{5} = -\frac{5}{4}P$  $\frac{16}{25}$
30. $a - 2.7 = -4.32$  $-1.62$
31. $-60 = \frac{2}{3}x$  $-90$
32. $-5x = 75$  $-15$
33. $\frac{2}{3}v = 24$  $36$
34. $\frac{f}{-9} = 207$  $-1863$
35. $r - 17 = 15$  $32$
36. $x + 11 = 3$  $-8$
37. $-\frac{1}{4} = 8c$  $-\frac{1}{32}$
38. $-18 = 3y$  $-6$
39. $5.2 - a = 3$  $2.2$
40. $\frac{x}{-9} = -3$  $27$
41. $2 = 4y$  $\frac{1}{2}$
42. $b - 6 = |-13|$  $19$
43. $\frac{3}{5}a = -\frac{2}{5}$  $-\frac{2}{3}$
44. $-\frac{x}{6} = -15$  $90$
45. $0.7y = -4.9$  $-7$
46. $|15| = -3a$  $-5$
47. $-\frac{x}{2} = 2\frac{1}{2}$  $-5$
48. $R = 3v$, solve for $v$  $v = \frac{R}{3}$
49. $I = prt$, solve for $t$  $t = \frac{I}{pr}$

**Translate each word phrase into an equation. Then solve the equation.**

50. A number decreased by four is ten.
    $x - 4 = 10$; $14$
51. Seven times a number is $-35$.
    $7x = -35$; $-5$
52. One-fourth of a number is $-16$.
    $\frac{1}{4}x = -16$; $-64$
53. Ten increased by a number is 27.
    $10 + x = 27$; $17$

**112** Chapter 3 **Equations and Inequalities**

## Teaching Tip

After Lesson 3-2, students know how to solve a one-step equation. So, to work on Exercises 1–8, they may choose solution over substitution. However, in Exercises 3 and 8, where the variable is to the second power, students must use substitution. In such cases, students see that there are two solutions. Remind students that an equation may have more than one solution or there may be no solution.

## PRACTICE ▮ LESSON 3-1–LESSON 3-2

**Use mental math to solve each equation.** (Lesson 3-1)

**54.** $|x| = -5$  no solution

**55.** $\dfrac{100}{x} = 20$  5

**56.** $x + 5 = 11$  6

**57.** $\dfrac{25}{x} = -5$  −5

**58.** $7 - y = 3$  4

**59.** $\dfrac{1}{3}x = -9$  −27

**Solve each equation. Check the solution.** (Lesson 3-2)

**60.** $A = \dfrac{1}{2}bh$, solve for $h$  $h = \dfrac{2A}{b}$

**61.** $2\pi r = C$, solve for $r$  $r = \dfrac{C}{2\pi}$

**62.** $\dfrac{w}{4} = 15$  60

**63.** $A = B + C + D$, solve for $C$  $C = A - B - D$

**64.** $\dfrac{1}{4}x = 9$  36

**65.** $w - (-3) = 13$  10

## Math*Works* Career – Mechanical Engineer
Workplace Knowhow

**M**echanical engineers influence the design and development of modern technological equipment. The development of the automobile has been influenced by many physics applications. One of those applications is the source of power for the automobile, the internal combustion engine. The amount of power (measured in units called horsepower) produced by an engine whose pistons rotate a single crankshaft is given by the following equation.

$H = \dfrac{PAnl\omega}{396,000}$, where $H$ = horsepower (hp), $P$ = average piston pressure (lb/in.²),

$A$ = piston area (in.²), $n$ = number of pistons, $l$ = piston stroke length, (in.) and $\omega$ = crankshaft revolutions per minute (rpm)

1. Solve the formula for $n$.  $n = \dfrac{396,000H}{PAl\omega}$

2. Calculate the number of pistons if the average piston pressure is 120 lb/in.², the piston area is 10 in.², the stroke length is 3.3 in., and the engine is producing 150 hp at 2500 rpm.  6

3. Determine what piston area is required for the engine to continue producing 150 hp at 2500 rpm if the piston pressure and stroke length remain the same as given in Exercise 2 and there are 8 pistons turning the crankshaft.  7.5 in.²

4. Assuming that all other variables remain constant, what do you predict will happen to the horsepower if the piston area doubles?  When all other variables are constant, $H$ and $A$ are directly proportional, and if $A$ doubles so will $H$.

5. Calculate the horsepower from the engine when the piston area doubles its value from Exercise 3. Assume that the piston pressure, the stroke length, the number of pistons and the crankshaft revolutions per minute remain the same as in Exercise 2. Does this confirm your prediction in Exercise 4? 300 hp; yes

**Math Online** mathmatters2.com/mathworks

Chapter 3  **Review and Practice Your Skills** | **113**

**MathWorks**

*One horsepower* was originally defined as the amount of power required to lift 33,000 pounds 1 foot in 1 minute, or 550 foot-pounds per second. Scottish engineer and inventor James Watt established this value for the horsepower after determining in practical tests that horses could haul coal at the average rate of 22,000 foot-pounds per minute. He then arbitrarily raised this figure by a factor of one-half to establish the current value.

Students should answer Questions 1–5 to better understand how the unit *horsepower* is used in a formula.

As they design, test, build, and operate machinery of all types; mechanical engineers use many different units of measure.

Students who are interested in learning more about this career choice can go to mathmatters2.com/mathworks. School Guidance Counselors are another resource for information about training requirements and appropriate schools.

## Teaching Tip

In preparation for Exercises 9–11, note with students that the formula $A = \dfrac{1}{2}bh$ has three variables: $A$, $b$, and $h$. Elicit that to find a value for any one variable, values for the other two variables must be known. Note also that although the variables in this formula take on different values, the number $\dfrac{1}{2}$ remains *constant*. After students have completed Exercises 9–11, you may wish to ask them to solve the formula $A = \dfrac{1}{2}bh$ for $b$ and then for $h$.

## Lesson Planning

### NCTM Standards/Strands
- Algebra
- Representation
- Problem Solving
- Connections

### Vocabulary
model
mathematical model
algebraic model

### Tools/Materials Needed
Algeblocks and Sentence Mat

### Lesson Resources
Warm-up Transparency 10
Transparency TK-4, 7, RF-1
Reteaching 3-3
Extra Practice 3-3
Enrichment 3-3

### ASSIGNMENT GUIDE

**Basic:** 1–35
**Enriched:** 1–35

## Getting Started

### 5-MINUTE WARM-UP

**Solve and check.**
1. $m - 16 = 16$   $m = 32$
2. $\frac{t}{3} = 9$   $t = 27$
3. $8 - n = 12$   $n = -4$

**THE FIVE-STEP PLAN Read**—ask questions to help students understand the problem. **Plan** guide students to related problems and previously mastered skills and strategies. **Solve**—students solve problem on their own. **Answer**—write the solution in a format that answers the question. **Check**—review work, check for reasonableness, and review strategy used. Students will benefit from the experience of verbalizing their methods.

**THE STRATEGY** *Make a model*—with this strategy, students have a concrete visualization of the circumstances of a problem, thus leading to solution.

---

A **model** is a physical or numerical representation of a real-life situation. There are various types of models. Algeblocks are a type of physical model in which blocks are used to represent variables and numbers. A **mathematical model** uses numbers, usually in a table or list, to describe a situation. An **algebraic model** is a mathematical model that includes a variable and is often written as an expression. A **rule** is an equation or a formula that represents a model.

### Problem Solving Strategies
- Guess and check
- Look for a pattern
- Solve a simpler problem
- Make a table, chart or list
- ✔ Use a picture, diagram or model
- Act it out
- Work backwards
- Eliminate possibilities
- Use an equation or formula

### Problem

**COMMUNICATIONS** A phone company charges $7.00 each month plus $0.10 per call.

**a.** Make a mathematical model of the billing system.

**b.** Write an algebraic model of the billing system.

**c.** Write a rule for the billing system.

### Solve the Problem

**a.** Make a table to represent a mathematical model of this situation. Numbers are used to represent the billing system.

| Number of calls | 0 | 10 | 20 | 30 | 40 | 50 |
|---|---|---|---|---|---|---|
| Monthly bill | $7.00 | $8.00 | $9.00 | $10.00 | $11.00 | $12.00 |

**b.** To write an algebraic model, choose a variable to represent an element of the situation. Let $c$ represent the number of calls per month. The algebraic model of the billing system is $7 + 0.10c$.

**c.** To write a rule, choose another variable to represent the entire situation. Let $m$ represent a monthly bill. The rule for the billing system is $m = 7 + 0.10c$.

### ▶ TRY THESE EXERCISES

 **MODELING** Use Algeblocks to model each equation. Do not solve.
For 1–4, see additional answers.
1. $2x - 6 = 4$　　2. $4x + 2 = 10$　　3. $9 = 3 - 3y$　　4. $-8 - 2x = -6$

**PHYSICS** On Pluto the weight of an object is $\frac{1}{25}$ the weight of an object on Earth.

5. Make a mathematical model by using five different weights on Earth, $E$, to find the corresponding weight on Pluto, $P$.   See additional answers.

6. Write an algebraic model.   $\frac{1}{25}E$

7. Write a rule.   $P = \frac{1}{25}E$

**114** | Chapter 3  **Equations and Inequalities**

---

## ADDITIONAL ANSWERS

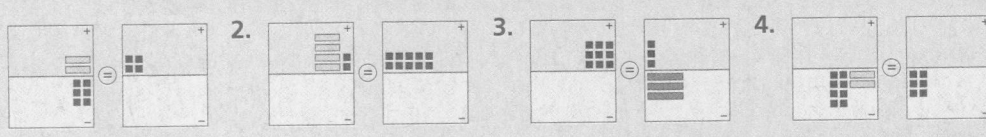

1.　2.　3.　4.

5.

| Weight on Earth | 100 | 125 | 150 | 175 | 200 |
|---|---|---|---|---|---|
| Weight on Pluto | 4 | 5 | 6 | 7 | 8 |

8.

| Number of movies rented | 0 | 1 | 2 | 3 | 4 | 5 |
|---|---|---|---|---|---|---|
| Total cost | $10.00 | $12.00 | $14.00 | $16.00 | $18.00 | $20.00 |

9.

| Week | 1 | 2 | 3 | 4 | 5 | 6 | 7 |
|---|---|---|---|---|---|---|---|
| Distance of run (miles) | 1 | $1\frac{1}{2}$ | 2 | $2\frac{1}{2}$ | 3 | $3\frac{1}{2}$ | 4 |

10.

| Number of 8 x 10 sheets | 1 | 2 | 3 | 4 |
|---|---|---|---|---|
| Total cost | $45 | $55 | $65 | $75 |

**For each situation, set up a mathematical model (table), write an algebraic model and a rule.** See additional answers for tables in Exercises 8–12.

8. **ENTERTAINMENT** It costs $10 to become a member at a movie rental store and $2 to rent a movie. $10 + 2m$, $c = 10 + 2m$

9. **FITNESS** Elonzo starts a jogging program. He begins by running 1 mi and adds $\frac{1}{2}$ mi each week for the next 6 wk. $1 + \frac{1}{2}(w - 1)$; $d = 1 + \frac{1}{2}(w - 1)$

10. A photographer charges $35 for a sitting and $10 for each 8 × 10 sheet produced. $35 + 10s$, $C = 35 + 10s$

11. Barry opens a savings account with a deposit of $300. He puts $50 of each bi-weekly paycheck in this savings account. $300 + 50w$, $A = 300 + 50w$

12. Mika designs and sells quilts to schools with the school name, logo and mascot. She charges an initial fee of $650, which includes creating the design and the first 20 quilts. Each additional quilt costs $15. $650 + 15q$, $q = \{21, 22, 23, \ldots\}$, $C = 650 + 15q$, $q = \{21, 22, 23, \ldots\}$

**PART-TIME JOB** During the summer, Kristen runs a day camp at her house for neighborhood kids. She charges each family $15/day plus $5 for each child in the family that attends the camp.

13. Make a mathematical model for the amount each family pays per day. See additional answers.

14. Write an algebraic model for the amount each family pays per day. $15 + 5n$

15. Write a rule for the amount each family pays per day. $C = 15 + 5n$

16. If 3 families attend her camp, set up a mathematical model for the amount that Kristen earns each day. See additional answers.

17. Write an algebraic model for Exercise 16. $45 + 5n$

18. Write a rule for Exercise 16. $e = 45 + 5n$

19. Do you think the method of payment that Kristen uses is fair? Explain why or why not. Answers will vary, but should include a discussion of the flat rate and cost per child.

20. **WRITING MATH** Write a paragraph explaining the differences among a mathematical model, an algebraic model and a rule. Use examples to support your explanation. See additional answers.

■ **MIXED REVIEW EXERCISES**

**Simplify.** (Lesson 2-4)

21. $15a - 7a$  $8a$

22. $4n - (-2n)$  $6n$

23. $-17k + 31k$  $14k$

24. $4.8x + 3.5x - 2x$  $6.3x$

25. $-\frac{2}{3}b + \frac{5}{8}b + \frac{1}{2}b$  $\frac{11}{24}b$

26. $5d(6) - 22d$  $8d$

27. $3.1g + 1.2h - 1.8g + 2.7h$  $1.3g + 3.9h$

28. $\frac{1}{2}(6x + 14y + 3x - 2y)$  $4\frac{1}{2}x + 6y$

29. $8s - 4t + 7t - 9s$  $3t - s$

**Simplify.** (Lesson 2-7)

30. $g^3 \cdot g^6$  $g^9$

31. $(h^4)^3$  $h^{12}$

32. $\frac{z^9}{z^5}$, $z \neq 0$  $z^4$

33. $2(f^3)^7$  $2f^{21}$

34. $\frac{q^5}{q^2}$, $q \neq 0$  $q^3$

35. $m^2\left(\frac{m^6}{m^3}\right)$, $m \neq 0$  $m^5$

Lesson 3-3  **Problem Solving Skills: Model Algebra**  115

---

**Chalkboard Examples**

**Supplementary Problem**
**TRAVEL** A taxi charges $2.50 plus $0.75 for each quarter-mile.
a. Make a mathematical model.

| Number of miles | 1 | 2 | 3 | 5 |
|---|---|---|---|---|
| Fare | $5.50 | $8.50 | $11.50 | $17.50 |

b. Write an algebraic model of the fare system. Let $q$ represent the number of quarter-miles traveled. Then the fare is $2.50 + 0.75q$.

c. Write a rule for the fare system. Let $F$ represent the fare for a taxi ride. Then $F = 2.50 + 0.75q$.

**Lesson Wrap-up**

**QUICK ASSESSMENT**

What is the form of an algebraic rule that can be used to represent the circumstances of a problem? an equation

**Reteaching Worksheet 3-3**

Name _____  Date _____

RETEACHING  3-3
**PROBLEM SOLVING SKILLS: MODEL ALGEBRA**

An **algebraic model** provides an equation or formula to describe a situation. You can use an algebraic model to help solve a problem.

**E x a m p l e**

Compare vacation packages offered at two beach resorts. The Royal Surf resort offers a family package of $500 for 4 days with a charge of $75 for each additional day. The Sun and Sand resort offers a similar plan of $350 for 3 days with a charge of $100 for each additional day. Which resort is less expensive for a 12-day stay?

**Solution**

To stay at the Royal Surf resort for $n$ days, you pay a fixed cost for the first 4 days, then pay for each additional day. If $c$ represents the cost of the package, the equation is $c = 500 + 75(n - 4)$.
To find the cost for 12 days, let $n = 12$.
$c = 500 + 75(12 - 4) = 500 + 75(8) = 1100$
To stay at the Sun and Sand for $n$ days, you pay a fixed cost for the first 3 days, then pay for each additional day. The equation is $c = 350 + 100(n - 3)$.
To find the cost for 12 days, let $n = 12$.
$c = 350 + 100(12 - 3) = 350 + 100(9) = 1250$
To stay at the Royal Surf for 12 days would cost $1100. To stay at the Sun and Sand for 12 days would cost $1250. The Royal Surf is less expensive for a 12-day stay.

☑ **EXERCISES**

A bank offers two checking plans. The Easy Go plan costs $0.25 a check. The Deluxe plan costs $0.10 a check plus a monthly fee of $4.00.

1. Which plan is less expensive if you write 8 checks a month?  the Easy Go plan

2. For each plan, write an equation for the cost of writing $n$ checks a month. Then find the cost of writing 35 checks a month.
Easy Go plan $c = 0.25n$, $8.75$ for 35 checks;
Deluxe plan $c = 4 + 0.1n$, $7.50$ for 35 checks

3. Paul can buy a surfboard for $255, or he can rent the same surfboard for $11.50 per day. Paul plans to surf 3 days each week during his 4 weeks of summer vacation. Compare the cost of buying the surfboard to the cost of renting it during the 4 weeks of Paul's vacation.
Cost to rent = $138; Cost to buy = $225; Renting is $87 cheaper.

---

**11.**

| Number of biweekly checks | 0 | 1 | 2 | 3 | 4 | 5 |
|---|---|---|---|---|---|---|
| Amount in savings account | $300 | $350 | $400 | $450 | $500 | $550 |

**12.**

| Number of quilts purchased | 20 | 21 | 22 | 23 | 24 | 25 |
|---|---|---|---|---|---|---|
| Total cost | $650 | $665 | $680 | $695 | $710 | $725 |

**13.**

| Number of children at camp | 1 | 2 | 3 | 4 | 5 |
|---|---|---|---|---|---|
| Total cost | $20 | $25 | $30 | $35 | $40 |

**16.**

| Charge for 3 families | $45 | $45 | $45 | $45 | $45 | $45 | $45 |
|---|---|---|---|---|---|---|---|
| Number of children | 3 | 4 | 5 | 6 | 7 | 8 | 9 |
| Total earned per day | $60 | $65 | $70 | $75 | $80 | $85 | $90 |

**20.** A mathematical model is a physical or numeric representation of data, for example with tables and numbers and Algeblocks. An algebraic model is an expression with a variable. A rule is a formula or equation.

### Vocabulary

two-step equations

### Tools/Materials Needed

Algeblocks and Sentence Mat

### Lesson Resources

Warm-up Transparency 11
Reteaching 3-4
Extra Practice 3-4
Enrichment 3-4
Technology Activity 3-4

## Getting Started

### 5-MINUTE WARM-UP

**Solve and check.**
1. $x - 17 = -3$   $x = 14$
2. $-6y = 42$   $y = -7$
3. $t - (-9) = 15$   $t = 6$
4. $\frac{3}{5}g = 12$   $g = 20$

### Introduction to Lesson 3-4
Extend the activity by asking students to create a verbal problem that can be modeled by the given equation.
Example: Sue and Jon have each started a collection of racing cars. So far, Sue has 3 cars more than Jon and, together, they have 21 cars. How many cars does Jon have?

---

# 3-4 Equations with Two or More Operations

**Goals** ■ Solve two-step equations and formulas.

**Applications** Physics, Mechanics, Sports, Modeling

In Figure A, each bag contains the same unknown weight of nails. Each single nail weighs 1 oz. The two bags with the three additional nails weigh 21 oz.

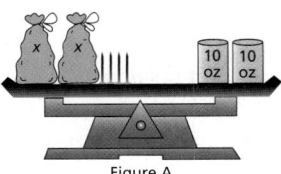

**Figure A**

1. Estimate the weight of each bag of nails. Check your estimate. Continue until you find the value of $x$.   8 oz

2. If the bags are combined into one larger bag weighing the same as the two bags, will the scale remain balanced? Explain.
Yes; the weight is the same.

3. Write an equation to describe the scale in Figure B.
$2x + 4 = 20$

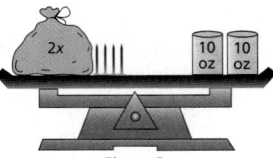

**Figure B**

4. Test the solution you found in Question 1 in this equation. Does it satisfy the equation?   yes

### ◢ BUILD UNDERSTANDING

Some equations involve multiplication or division and addition or subtraction. To solve these **two-step equations**, use the addition property of equality first. Then use the multiplication property.

### Example 1

Solve each equation. Check the solution.

**a.** $\frac{x}{3} + 4 = 9$          **b.** $5a - 15 = 5$

**Solution**

**a.**

$$\frac{x}{3} + 4 = 9$$

$$\frac{x}{3} + 4 + (-4) = 9 + (-4) \qquad \text{Add } -4 \text{ to both sides.}$$

$$\frac{x}{3} = 5$$

$$3\left(\frac{x}{3}\right) = 3(5) \qquad \text{Multiply both sides by 3.}$$

$$x = 15$$

**Check** $\frac{x}{3} + 4 = 9$

$$\frac{15}{3} + 4 \stackrel{?}{=} 9$$

$$5 + 4 \stackrel{?}{=} 9$$

$$9 = 9 \ ✔$$

**b.**

$$5a - 15 = 5$$

$$5a - 15 + 15 = 5 + 15 \qquad \text{Add 15 to both sides.}$$

$$5a = 20$$

$$\frac{5a}{5} = \frac{20}{5} \qquad \text{Divide both sides by 5.}$$

$$a = 4$$

**Check** $5a - 15 = 5$

$$5(4) - 15 \stackrel{?}{=} 5$$

$$20 - 15 \stackrel{?}{=} 5$$

$$5 = 5 \ ✔$$

**116** Chapter 3 **Equations and Inequalities**

---

## Differentiated Instruction

**VISUAL LEARNERS** When solving equations, you may wish to demonstrate a vertical arrangement for additions and subtractions. Students may find it useful to then strike through a zero pair.

**Using Example 1b**

$$5a - 15 = 5$$
$$\underline{+ 15 = +15}$$
$$\frac{5a}{5} = \frac{20}{5}$$
$$a = 4$$

**Using Example 2b**

$$2(x + 7) = 4(x - 1) \rightarrow$$

$$2x + 14 = 4x - 4$$
$$\underline{-2x \qquad = -2x}$$
$$14 = 2x - 4$$
$$\underline{+ 4 = \qquad + 4}$$
$$\frac{18}{2} = \frac{2x}{2}$$
$$9 = x$$

Sometimes it is necessary to simplify the equation before you can solve it. To simplify, combine like terms or distribute over parentheses.

## Example 2

**Solve each equation. Check the solution.**

**a.** $7x + 6 - 2x + 3 = 34$

**b.** $2(x + 7) = 4(x - 1)$

### Solution

**a.**

$$7x + 6 - 2x + 3 = 34$$
$$(7x - 2x) + (6 + 3) = 34 \qquad \text{Combine like terms.}$$
$$5x + 9 = 34$$
$$5x + 9 - 9 = 34 - 9 \qquad \text{Subtract 9 from both sides.}$$
$$5x = 25$$
$$\frac{5x}{5} = \frac{25}{5} \qquad \text{Divide both sides by 5.}$$
$$x = 5$$

**Check** $7x + 6 - 2x + 3 = 34$
$$7(5) + 6 - 2(5) + 3 \overset{?}{=} 34$$
$$35 + 6 - 10 + 3 \overset{?}{=} 34$$
$$34 = 34 \quad ✔$$

**b.**

$$2(x + 7) = 4(x - 1)$$
$$2x + 14 = 4x - 4 \qquad \text{Distribute 2 and 4.}$$
$$2x - 2x + 14 = 4x - 2x - 4 \qquad \text{Subtract } 2x \text{ from both sides.}$$
$$14 = 2x - 4$$
$$14 + 4 = 2x - 4 + 4 \qquad \text{Add 4 to both sides.}$$
$$18 = 2x$$
$$\frac{18}{2} = \frac{2x}{2} \qquad \text{Divide both sides by 2.}$$
$$9 = x$$

**Check** $2(x + 7) = 4(x - 1)$
$$2(9 + 7) \overset{?}{=} 4(9 - 1)$$
$$2(16) \overset{?}{=} 4(8)$$
$$32 = 32 \quad ✔$$

Formulas that involve two operations can be solved in a similar manner.

## Example 3

**Solve the formula $T = \frac{n}{4} + 40$ for $n$.**

### Solution

$$T = \frac{n}{4} + 40$$
$$T - 40 = \frac{n}{4} + 40 - 40 \qquad \text{Subtract 40 from both sides.}$$
$$T - 40 = \frac{n}{4}$$
$$4(T - 40) = 4\left(\frac{n}{4}\right) \qquad \text{Multiply both sides by 4.}$$
$$4(T - 40) = n$$

 **Math Online** mathmatters2.com/extra_examples

---

## Extend the Lesson

You can extend the use of equations into classroom discussion by occasionally referring to times, distances, or other measures algebraically. For example, "The number of minutes for this quiz will be 5 minutes less than twice the number of questions" or "In 2 days more than 3 times the number of days in a week, we will go on a trip."

---

## Chalkboard Examples

### Supplementary Example 1
Solve the equation. Check the solution.
$$4x + 9 = -3$$
$$4x + 9 + (-9) = -3 + (-9)$$
$$4x + 0 = -12$$
$$\frac{4x}{4} = \frac{-12}{4}$$
$$x = -3$$

**Check**
$$4x + 9 = -3$$
$$4(-3) + 9 \overset{?}{=} -3$$
$$-12 + 9 \overset{?}{=} -3$$
$$-3 = -3 \checkmark$$

### Supplementary Example 2
Solve the equation. Check the solution.
$$-5(x - 4) = 2(x - 0.5)$$
$$-5(x) - 5(-4) = 2(x) + 2(-0.5)$$
$$-5x + 20 = 2x - 1$$
$$-5x + 5x + 20 = 2x + 5x - 1$$
$$20 = 7x - 1$$
$$20 + 1 = 7x - 1 + 1$$
$$21 = 7x$$
$$\frac{21}{7} = \frac{7x}{7}$$
$$3 = x$$

**Check**
$$-5(x - 4) = 2(x - 0.5)$$
$$-5(3 - 4) \overset{?}{=} 2(3 - 0.5)$$
$$-5(-1) \overset{?}{=} 2(2.5)$$
$$5 = 5 \checkmark$$

### Supplementary Example 3
Solve the formula $S = \frac{n}{2}(a + \ell)$ for $\ell$.

$$\frac{2}{n} \cdot S = \frac{2}{n} \cdot \frac{n}{2}(a + \ell)$$

Multiply each side by $\frac{2}{n}$.

$$\frac{2S}{n} = a + \ell$$

$$\frac{2S}{n} - a = a - a + \ell$$

Subtract $a$ from each side.

$$\frac{2S}{n} - a = \ell$$

Alternately, students may first multiply both sides by 2, giving $2S = n(a + \ell)$. Then distribute $n$, giving $2S = na + n\ell$. Next subtract $na$, giving $2S - na = n\ell$. Finally, divide by $n$, to set $\frac{2S - na}{n} = \ell$, which is equivalent to $\frac{2S}{n} - a = \ell$.

Example 4

## Lesson Wrap-up

### QUICK ASSESSMENT

Ask the following questions to determine if students understand the content presented in this lesson.

1. In general, why should you use the addition property of equality before the mutliplication property when solving two-step equations. **Possible answer: Often, fractions can be avoided.**

2. When there are variable terms on both sides of an equation, on which side would you collect them? **Possible answer: On whichever side would result in a positive coefficient.**

### ASSIGNMENT GUIDE

**Basic:** 1–50, 57–62
**Enriched:** 1–62

---

**MODELING** Solve the equation $2y - 1 = 5$ using Algeblocks.

**Solution**

*Step 1* Model the equation on a Sentence Mat.

*Step 2* Add 1 to both sides of the Mat. Then remove zero pairs.

*Step 3* There are two $y$-blocks. Make the 6 unit blocks into two equal groups.

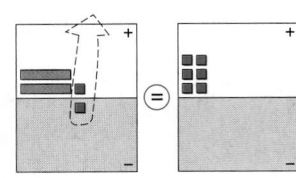 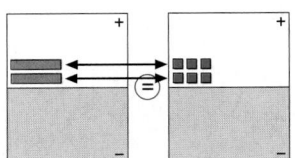 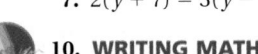  

Read the answer for $1y$ from the Mat, $y = 3$.

### ▶ TRY THESE EXERCISES

**Solve each equation. Check the solution.**

1. $3x + 2 = 14$   4
2. $\frac{m}{2} - 4 = 8$   24
3. $2w - 7 = 25$   16
4. $-\frac{1}{4}n + 5 = 2$   12
5. $3(t - 2) = 15$   7
6. $-6x + 8 = 4x - 42$   5
7. $2(y + 7) = 3(y - 1)$   17
8. $P = 2l + 2w$, solve for $w$   $w = \frac{P - 2l}{2}$
9. $y = mx + b$, solve for $x$   $x = \frac{y - b}{m}$

10. **WRITING MATH** When solving two-step equations, why do you undo addition and subtraction before multiplication and division? Explain. You want to reverse the order of operations to simplify the computation.

11. In a circle graph, all sections or percentages must add up to 100%. Write an equation for the circle graph shown. Solve the equation to determine the percent of each section.
$n + 16 + n + 32 + 34 = 100$; $n = 9$, $n + 16 = 25$

12. **MODELING** Use Algeblocks to model and solve $3x + 4 = -2$.
$x = -2$; See additional answers.

*(circle graph: $n\%$, $32\%$, $(n + 16)\%$, $34\%$)*

### ▶ PRACTICE EXERCISES • For Extra Practice, see page 593.

**Solve each equation. Check the solution.**

13. $8m - 1 = 31$   4
14. $\frac{w}{3} + 4 = 10$   18
15. $-6g + 8 = -46$   9
16. $\frac{x}{2} - 4 = 5$   18
17. $3p - p + 1 = -9$   -5
18. $5a - 10 = 0$   2
19. $5q + 3q - 1 = -33$   -4
20. $\frac{3}{4}n + 2 = 8$   8
21. $-4m - 10 = -6$   -1
22. $7 = \frac{3}{8}t - 2$   24
23. $4r - 2.5 = 6.3$   2.2
24. $-2y - 2y + 3 = -13$   4
25. $4(b + 6) = -20$   -11
26. $1.5z - 7 - 3.5z = 3$   -5
27. $-12g + 8 + 3g + 3 = 29$   -2
28. $6c - 2 = c + 13$   3
29. $8(x - 1) = 0$   1
30. $3(2w + 5) = 4$   $-\frac{11}{6}$
31. $4(c + 3) = -3(c - 2)$   $-\frac{6}{7}$
32. $2(9 - d) = 4$   7
33. $\frac{1}{2}(14k - 8) = 10$   2
34. $y = \frac{x}{3} - 20$, solve for $x$   $x = 3(y + 20)$
35. $p = \frac{7}{8}r + 20$, solve for $r$   $r = \frac{8}{7}(p - 20)$
36. $4(w - 2) = 16v$, solve for $w$   $w = 4v + 2$

**118** Chapter 3 **Equations and Inequalities**

---

### Reteaching Worksheet 3-4

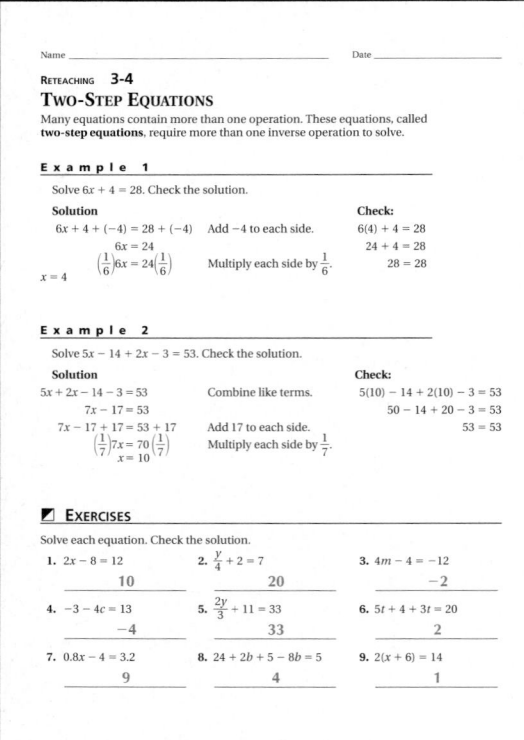

Name _____ Date _____

RETEACHING **3-4**

**TWO-STEP EQUATIONS**

Many equations contain more than one operation. These equations, called **two-step equations**, require more than one inverse operation to solve.

**Example 1**

Solve $6x + 4 = 28$. Check the solution.

| Solution | | Check: |
|---|---|---|
| $6x + 4 + (-4) = 28 + (-4)$ | Add $-4$ to each side. | $6(4) + 4 = 28$ |
| $6x = 24$ | | $24 + 4 = 28$ |
| $\left(\frac{1}{6}\right)6x = 24\left(\frac{1}{6}\right)$ | Multiply each side by $\frac{1}{6}$. | $28 = 28$ |
| $x = 4$ | | |

**Example 2**

Solve $5x - 14 + 2x - 3 = 53$. Check the solution.

| Solution | | Check: |
|---|---|---|
| $5x + 2x - 14 - 3 = 53$ | Combine like terms. | $5(10) - 14 + 2(10) - 3 = 53$ |
| $7x - 17 = 53$ | | $50 - 14 + 20 - 3 = 53$ |
| $7x - 17 + 17 = 53 + 17$ | Add 17 to each side. | $53 = 53$ |
| $\left(\frac{1}{7}\right)7x = 70\left(\frac{1}{7}\right)$ | Multiply each side by $\frac{1}{7}$. | |
| $x = 10$ | | |

■ **EXERCISES**

Solve each equation. Check the solution.

1. $2x - 8 = 12$   10
2. $\frac{y}{4} + 2 = 7$   20
3. $4m - 4 = -12$   -2
4. $-3 - 4c = 13$   -4
5. $\frac{2y}{3} + 11 = 33$   33
6. $5t + 4 + 3t = 20$   2
7. $0.8x - 4 = 3.2$   9
8. $24 + 2b + 5 - 8b = 5$   4
9. $2(x + 6) = 14$   1

---

### ADDITIONAL ANSWERS

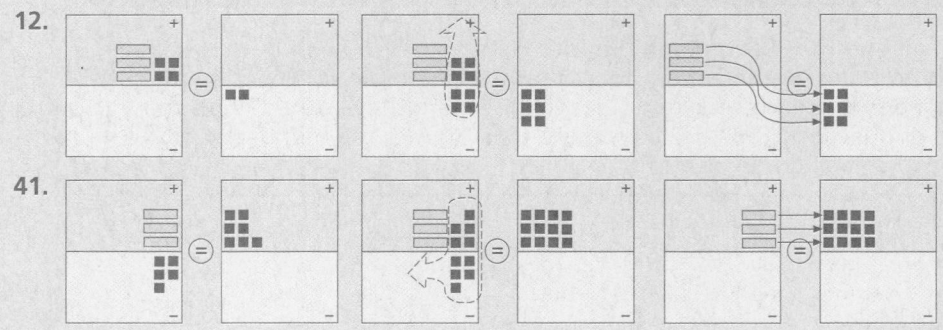

12.

41.

**PHYSICS** The formula $F = \frac{9}{5}C + 32$ is used to convert a temperature in Celsius to Fahrenheit. Round to the nearest tenth.

**37.** Solve the equation for $C$. $\quad C = \frac{5}{9}(F - 32)$    **38.** Convert 27°C to Fahrenheit. 80.6°F

**39.** Convert 82°F to Celsius. 27.8°C    **40.** Convert −5°C to Fahrenheit. 23°F

**MODELING** Use Algeblocks to model and solve each equation.
For 41–43, see additional answers.

**41.** $3x - 5 = 7$   $x = 4$    **42.** $4y - 2 = 2$   $y = 1$    **43.** $2x + 3 = -3$   $x = -3$

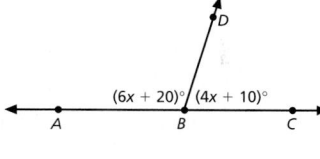

**44.** In the figure shown, $\angle ABD$ and $\angle CBD$ are supplementary angles, so $m\angle ABD + m\angle CBD = 180°$. Write and solve an equation to find the measure of each angle.
$6x + 20 + 4x + 10 = 180$; 15; $m\angle ABD = 110°$, $m\angle CBD = 70°$

**45.** Complementary angles are angles whose sum is 90°. The $m\angle EFG$ is $(10x + 1)°$ and $m\angle GFH$ is $(8x - 1)°$. Find the measure of each angle if $\angle EFG$ and $\angle GFH$ are complementary angles. $\quad m\angle EFG = 51°$, $m\angle GFH = 39°$

**46. MECHANICS** Jontay had his car repaired, and the bill was $235. The cost for parts was $127. The cost of labor was $27/h. Write and solve an equation to find the total number of hours spent on repairing Jontay's car.
$235 = 127 + 27h$; 4

**47. SPORTS** The length of a football field is 67 yd greater than the width. The perimeter of the field is 346 yd. Find the length and width of a football field.
$l = 120$ yd, $w = 53$ yd

**Translate each sentence into an equation. Then solve the equation.**

**48.** Twice a number increased by four is 20.    **49.** Half a number decreased by five is −12.
$2n + 4 = 20$, $n = 8$                               $\frac{1}{2}x - 5 = -12$, $x = -14$

**50.** Three more than half a number is two less than the number.
$3 + \frac{1}{2}y = y - 2$, $y = 10$

## EXTENDED PRACTICE EXERCISES

**51.** Find the measure of each angle of the triangle shown.
24°, 54°, 102°

**Solve each equation. Check the solution.**

**52.** $\frac{1}{2}(6t - 20) + 15 = -5 + 2(t + 3)$   −4    **53.** $2(3 - k) = 3(2 + k)$   0

**54.** $4[1 - 3(x + 2)] + 2x = 2(x + 2)$   −2    **55.** $2[3(g+3) - (g + 2)] = 5(g + 1) + 4$   5

**56. CHAPTER INVESTIGATION** Set the ball of the pendulum swinging through an arc of about 5°. Find the time $t$ it takes the pendulum to make 50 swings. A swing is counted each time the ball moves back and forth completely.
Answers will vary.

## MIXED REVIEW EXERCISES

**Use the stem-and-leaf plot for Exercises 57–62.** (Lesson 1-3)

**57.** Find any outliers in the data.
43, 45, 50, 129

**58.** Find the median. 91

**59.** Find any clusters or gaps.
clusters: high 80s/low 90s; gaps: 50–82, 108–129

**60.** Find the mode. 91

**61.** Find the range. 86

**62.** Find the mean. 89.2

| 4 | 3 5 |
|---|---|
| 5 | 0 |
| 8 | 2 3 3 5 7 9 9 |
| 9 | 0 1 1 1 2 5 6 8 9 |
| 10 | 1 2 5 5 8 |
| 12 | 9 |

4 | 3 represents 43.

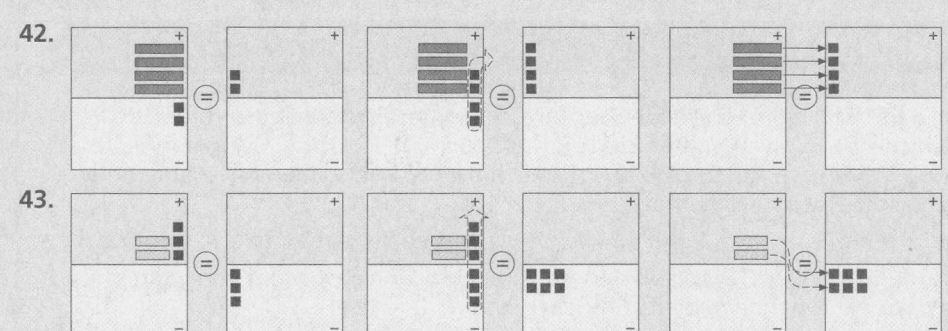

**42.**

**43.**

---

### Extra Practice Worksheet 3-4

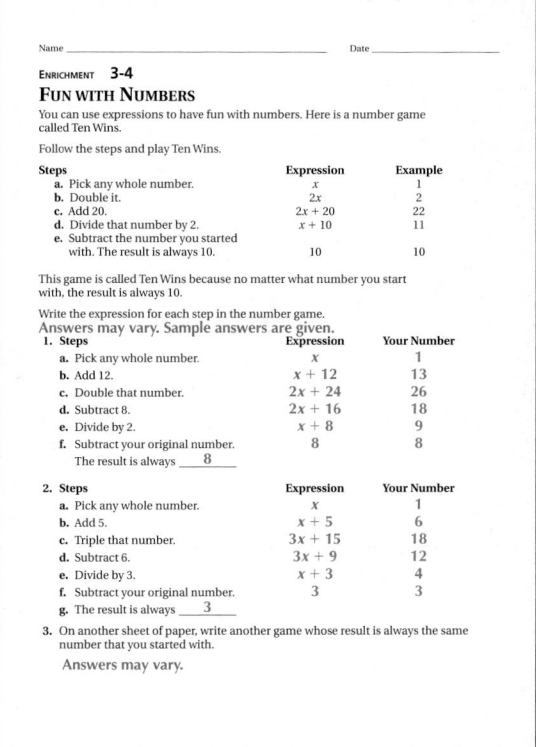

Name _____ Date _____

EXTRA PRACTICE **3-4**
**TWO-STEP EQUATIONS**

☑ **EXERCISES**

Solve each equation. Check the solution.

**1.** $4m + 2 = 10$   2       **2.** $-5w - 2 = 13$   −3

**3.** $\frac{p}{2} - 6 = 1$   14       **4.** $4s - 15 = 5$   5

**5.** $4a - a + 1 = 19$   6       **6.** $\frac{2}{3}r + 4 = 12$   12

**7.** $3w - 4w + 5 = -4$   9       **8.** $-3x - 3x - 4 = 8$   −2

**9.** $5 = \frac{4}{5}d - 3$   10       **10.** $5y - 1.5 = 8.5$   2

**11.** $2.6 - 4r = -2.2$   1.2       **12.** $2(h + 4) = 9$   $\frac{1}{2}$

**13.** $-10h + 2 + 4h - 6 = -16$   2       **14.** $5(x - 1) = -15$   −2

**15.** $5r - 3 = 4r$   3       **16.** $\frac{1}{3}(12c - 9) = -7$   $-\frac{1}{3}$

**17.** $2(m + 1) = 4(m + 2)$   −3       **18.** $4(8 - w) = 29$   $\frac{3}{4}$

**19.** $y = \frac{x}{2} + 10$; solve for $x$   $x = 2y - 20$

**20.** $m = \frac{4}{5}n - 6$; solve for $n$   $n = \frac{5}{4}m + \frac{15}{2}$

**21.** $5(r - 4) = 20s$; solve for $r$   $r = 4s + 4$

**22.** $V = lwh$; solve for $w$   $w = \frac{V}{lh}$

**23.** $y = -\frac{2}{3}x - 2$; solve for $x$   $x = -\frac{3}{2}y - 3$

Translate each sentence into an equation. Then solve the equation.

**24.** Four times a number increased by six is negative six.   $4x + 6 = -6$; −3

**25.** One fourth of a number decreased by four is negative one.   $\frac{1}{4}x - 4 = -1$; 12

**26.** Eight less than twice a number is two.   $2x - 8 = 2$; 5

---

### Enrichment Worksheet 3-4

Name _____ Date _____

ENRICHMENT **3-4**
**FUN WITH NUMBERS**

You can use expressions to have fun with numbers. Here is a number game called Ten Wins.

Follow the steps and play Ten Wins.

| Steps | Expression | Example |
|---|---|---|
| **a.** Pick any whole number. | $x$ | 1 |
| **b.** Double it. | $2x$ | 2 |
| **c.** Add 20. | $2x + 20$ | 22 |
| **d.** Divide that number by 2. | $x + 10$ | 11 |
| **e.** Subtract the number you started with. The result is always 10. | 10 | 10 |

This game is called Ten Wins because no matter what number you start with, the result is always 10.

Write the expression for each step in the number game.
Answers may vary. Sample answers are given.

**1.**
| Steps | Expression | Your Number |
|---|---|---|
| **a.** Pick any whole number. | $x$ | 1 |
| **b.** Add 12. | $x + 12$ | 13 |
| **c.** Double that number. | $2x + 24$ | 26 |
| **d.** Subtract 8. | $2x + 16$ | 18 |
| **e.** Divide by 2. | $x + 8$ | 9 |
| **f.** Subtract your original number. The result is always ___ 8 | 8 | 8 |

**2.**
| Steps | Expression | Your Number |
|---|---|---|
| **a.** Pick any whole number. | $x$ | 1 |
| **b.** Add 5. | $x + 5$ | 6 |
| **c.** Triple that number. | $3x + 15$ | 18 |
| **d.** Subtract 6. | $3x + 9$ | 12 |
| **e.** Divide by 3. | $x + 3$ | 4 |
| **f.** Subtract your original number. | 3 | 3 |
| **g.** The result is always ___ 3 | | |

**3.** On another sheet of paper, write another game whose result is always the same number that you started with.

Answers may vary.

**Lesson 3-3**
model
mathematical model
algebraic model

**Lesson 3-4**
two-step equations

## ASSIGNMENT GUIDE

**All students:** 1–46

## Chalkboard Examples

### Lesson 3-3
**BUSINESS** A mailing service charges a handling fee of $3.50 plus $1.50 per half-pound.
**a.** Make a mathematical model.

| Number of pounds | 1 | 2 | 3 | 5 |
|---|---|---|---|---|
| Charge | $5.00 | $6.50 | $8.00 | $11.00 |

**b.** Write an algebraic model of the fee system.
   Let $h$ represent the number of half-pounds of weight. Then the charge is $3.50 + 1.50h$.
**c.** Write a rule for the fee system. Let $C$ represent the charge for a package. Then $C = 3.50 + 1.50h$.

### Lesson 3-4
Solve the formula $A = \frac{h}{2}(b_1 + b_2)$ for $b_1$.

$$\frac{2}{h} \cdot A = \frac{2}{h} \cdot \frac{h}{2}(b_1 + b_2)$$

    Multiply each side by $\frac{2}{h}$.

$$\frac{2A}{h} = b_1 + b_2$$

$$\frac{2A}{h} - b_2 = b_1 + b_2 - b_2$$

    Subtract $b^2$ from each side.

$$\frac{2A}{h} - b_2 = b_1$$

# Review and Practice Your Skills

## PRACTICE ■ LESSON 3-3

**FINANCE** Luis opens a savings account with a deposit of $90. He puts $30 in each week from tips he has earned as a waiter.

1. Make a mathematical model for the amount he has in the bank for 1, 2, 3, 4, 5, and 6 weeks after opening his account.   See additional answers.

2. Write an algebraic model for the amount he has in the bank.   $90 + 30w$

3. Write a rule for the amount he has in the bank after a certain number of weeks.   $A = 90 + 30w$

**TRANSPORTATION** Car Rental Company A charges $45/day plus $0.10/mi. A competitor, Company B, charges $35/day plus $0.12/mi. Answer Exercises 4–9 based on a one day rental.

4. Make a mathematical model for Company A.   See additional answers.

5. Make a mathematical model for Company B.   See additional answers.

6. Write an algebraic model for Company A.   $45 + 0.10m$

7. Write an algebraic model for Company B.   $35 + 0.12m$

8. Write a rule for Company A.   $A = 45 + 0.10m$

9. Write a rule for Company B.   $B = 35 + 0.12m$

10. If you were going to travel about 300 mi each day which company would you prefer to use? Why?   You will save money by using Company B unless you are going to travel over 500 mi each day.

## PRACTICE ■ LESSON 3-4

**Solve each equation. Check the solution.**

11. $7r + 5 = 26$   3
12. $4t - 6 = 14$   5
13. $-8 - 2w = 11$   $-\frac{19}{2}$
14. $5(x - 5) = 10$   7
15. $12 - 3m = 24$   $-4$
16. $-2(r + 9) = -28$   5
17. $-8 = 12 - 4x$   5
18. $\frac{x}{4} - 6 = 13$   76
19. $112 = 12 + 8y$   12.5
20. $(w - 3)5 + 7 = 2$   2
21. $\frac{b}{13} + 6 = 15$   117
22. $-1 = \frac{h}{11} - 14$   143
23. $-m + 3(m + 1) = 11$   4
24. $\left(\frac{1}{4}\right)x - 9 = 5$   56
25. $-9 = \frac{w}{4} - 2$   $-28$

**Translate each sentence into an equation. Then solve the equation.**

26. Twice a number decreased by three is 21.   $2x - 3 = 21$, $x = 12$
27. Two more than three-fourths a number is eight.   $\frac{3}{4}x + 2 = 8$, $x = 8$
28. Four more than a number divided by three is ten.   $\frac{x}{3} + 4 = 10$, $x = 18$
29. Five times a number decreased by ten is zero.   $5x - 10 = 0$, $x = 2$
30. Twice a number decreased by seven is 25.   $2x - 7 = 25$, $x = 16$

## Teaching Tip

In Exercises 1–6 of the Mid-Chapter Quiz, where students are to decide which of the given values are solutions to each equation, ask students to scan the equations to pick out those that they know must have only one solution. Recognizing that
$m - 3 = 6$, $\frac{1}{3}b = -3$, $2.4y = 14.4$, $\frac{5}{6}r - \frac{1}{6} = 4$ each have only one solution, students may prefer to solve these to decide which of the given values works, rather than substituting each of the given values.
Students should use mental math to solve the equation containing absolute value in Exercise 9. Elicit that $|30| = |-30| = 30$.

## PRACTICE ■ LESSON 3-1–LESSON 3-4

**Solve each equation. Check the solution.** (Lessons 3-1 and 3-2)

**31.** $\frac{1}{3}x = 10$  30

**32.** $7r = -49$  $-7$

**33.** $3.1 + b = 0$  $-3.1$

**34.** $-9 + x = -4$  5

**35.** $\frac{a}{4} = -2$  $-8$

**36.** $-25 = 5c$  $-5$

**37.** Igashu has a lawn mowing business. He deposited $200 in a savings account and adds $50 a week. Set up a mathematical model, write an algebraic model and a rule. (Lesson 3-3)  See additional answers. $200 + 50w$, $A = 200 + 50w$

**Solve the equation. Check the solution.** (Lesson 3-4)

**38.** $3x - 7 = 11$  6

**39.** $\frac{a}{2} - 3 = 12$  30

**40.** $4y - 2 = 14$  4

**41.** $3(y + 2) = 18$  4

**42.** $-3y - 4y + 6 = -8$  2

**43.** $11b - 5b + 7 = 19$  2

**44.** $-2x - 9 = 3$  $-6$

**45.** $5(c + 4) = -(c + 4)$  $-4$

**46.** $4(x + 3) = -3(x - 2)$  $-\frac{6}{7}$

# Mid-Chapter Quiz

**Which of the given values is a solution of the equation?** (Lesson 3-1)

**1.** $m - 3 = 6$; $-3, 3, 9$  9

**2.** $2x^2 + 1 = 33$; $-4, 4, 8$  $-4, 4$

**3.** $\frac{1}{3}b = -3$; $-9, -6, 3, 9$  $-9$

**4.** $2.4y = 14.4$; $1.2, 2.4, 6.0$  6.0

**5.** $\frac{5}{6}r - \frac{1}{6} = 4$; $1, 2, 3, 4, 5$  5

**6.** $|x + 3| = 7$; $-10, -4, 4, 10$  $-10, 4$

**7.** A rectangle has an area of 70 ft$^2$ and width of 7 ft. Find its length.
10 ft

**Solve each equation. Check the solution.** (Lessons 3-2 and 3-4)

**8.** $3x = 36$  12

**9.** $|5p| = 30$  $-6, 6$

**10.** $12p = -72$  $-6$

**11.** $\frac{3}{5} - n = \frac{1}{3}$  $\frac{4}{15}$

**12.** $-4b = -38$  $\frac{19}{2}$

**13.** $-1.7n = -51$  30

**14.** $2\frac{1}{2}x = 7\frac{1}{2}$  3

**15.** $9y = 171$  19

**16.** $\frac{m}{5} - 7 = -2$  25

**17.** $26 - 17z = -8$  2

**18.** $13(y + 6) = 39$  $-3$

**19.** $5x - 2 = -20 + 7x$  9

**20.** $-4(z - 1) = 6z$  $\frac{2}{5}$

**21.** $0.9x - 8.1 = 2.7$  12

**22.** $\frac{1}{2}x + 3 = x - 2$  10

**23.** $4c + 9c + 5 = 18$  1

**Translate each word phrase into an equation. Then solve the equation.** (Lesson 3-2)

**24.** The difference between a number and seven is negative four.  $x - 7 = -4$, $x = 3$

**25.** The product of 2.5 and a number is 20.  $2.5x = 20$, $x = 8$

**MUSIC** Two weeks before a concert, a piano player begins to practice his repertoire 2 h/day plus $\frac{1}{2}$ h more each day until the day of the concert. (Lesson 3-3)

**26.** Make a mathematical model for the amount the pianist practices per day.
See additional answers.

**27.** Write an algebraic model for the amount the pianist practices per day.  $2 + \frac{1}{2}d$

**28.** Write a rule for the amount the pianist practices per day.  $h = 2 + \frac{1}{2}d$

Chapter 3 **Review and Practice Your Skills**   |   **121**

**1.**

| Week | 1 | 2 | 3 | 4 | 5 | 6 |
|---|---|---|---|---|---|---|
| Amount in bank | $120 | $150 | $180 | $210 | $240 | $270 |

**4.**

| Miles | 100 | 200 | 300 | 400 | 500 | 600 |
|---|---|---|---|---|---|---|
| Charge per day | $55 | $65 | $75 | $85 | $95 | $105 |

**5.**

| Miles | 100 | 200 | 300 | 400 | 500 | 600 |
|---|---|---|---|---|---|---|
| Charge per day | $47 | $59 | $71 | $83 | $95 | $107 |

**37.**

| Week | 1 | 2 | 3 | 4 | 5 | 6 |
|---|---|---|---|---|---|---|
| Amount in savings account | $250 | $300 | $350 | $400 | $450 | $500 |

## Teaching Tip

For Exercise 24, where students are to express a difference, remind them that it is customary to write the terms in the given order. So, in this case, the difference would be $n - 7$, which in the equation $n - 7 = -4$ yields a result of $n = 3$. Since subtraction is not commutative, if students had written $7 - n$ for the difference, they would have obtained a different result ($7 - n = -4$ yields $n = 11$).

## MID-CHAPTER QUIZ

**26.**

| Day | 1 | 2 | 3 | 4 | 5 | 6 | 7 | 8 | 9 | 10 | 11 | 12 | 13 | 14 |
|---|---|---|---|---|---|---|---|---|---|---|---|---|---|---|
| Hours of practice | $2\frac{1}{2}$ | 3 | $3\frac{1}{2}$ | 4 | $4\frac{1}{2}$ | 5 | $5\frac{1}{2}$ | 6 | $6\frac{1}{2}$ | 7 | $7\frac{1}{2}$ | 8 | $8\frac{1}{2}$ | 9 |

### Vocabulary

| | |
|---|---|
| proportion | means |
| extremes | cross-products |

### Tools/Materials Needed

centimeter ruler

### Lesson Resources

Warm-up Transparency 12
Transparency RF-12
Reteaching 3-5
Extra Practice 3-5
Enrichment 3-5
Technology Activity 3-5

## Getting Started

### 5-Minute Warm-up

**Determine if the two fractions are equivalent.**

1. $\frac{4}{25}$ and $\frac{2}{5}$   no

2. $\frac{15}{20}$ and $\frac{18}{24}$   yes

3. $\frac{72}{108}$ and $\frac{50}{75}$   yes

4. $\frac{11}{15}$ and $\frac{121}{225}$   no

### Introduction to Lesson 3-5

Discuss how students found their answers to Questions 3 and 4. Did they use equivalent fractions? Did they write a proportion?

Have students write different word patterns that could be used as proportions for this problem, such as those shown below.

$$\frac{\text{actual length}}{\text{length in drawing}} = \frac{\text{actual width}}{\text{width in drawing}}$$

$$\frac{\text{actual length}}{\text{actual width}} = \frac{\text{length in drawing}}{\text{width in drawing}}$$

# 3-5 Proportions

**Goals** ■ Write and solve proportions.

**Applications** Art, Machinery, Manufacturing, Business, Physics, Retail

**ART** Artists often create scale drawings in order to portray a real-life object. A *scale drawing* is a drawing that represents an object. The *scale* of the drawing is the ratio of the size of the drawing to the actual size of the object.

1. Use a centimeter ruler to measure the length of the car.
   6 cm
2. Use a centimeter ruler to measure the height of the car.
   3 cm
3. The scale of this drawing is 1 cm : 2 ft. This means that each centimeter of the drawing represents 2 ft of the actual object. Find the actual length of the car.
   12 ft
4. Find the actual height of the car.   6 ft
5. Explain how you can use an equation for Questions 3 and 4.   Set up a proportion.

### ▨ BUILD UNDERSTANDING

Recall that a **proportion** is an equation stating that two ratios are equivalent. There are three different ways to write a proportion.

$a$ is to $b$ as $c$ is to $d$          $a : b = c : d$          $\frac{a}{b} = \frac{c}{d}$

In any of these forms, $b$ and $c$ are called the **means** of the proportion and $a$ and $d$ are called the **extremes**. In a proportion, the **cross-products** are equal. You can use cross-products to solve a proportion.

$$\frac{a}{b} = \frac{c}{d}, \text{ so } ad = bc$$

### Example 1

**Solve the proportion $\frac{9}{12} = \frac{21}{n}$; $n \neq 0$. Check the solution.**

**Solution**

$\frac{9}{12} = \frac{21}{n}$

$9 \cdot n = 12 \cdot 21$   Find the cross-products.

$9n = 252$

$\frac{9n}{9} = \frac{252}{9}$   Divide both sides by 9.

$n = 28$

**Check**

$\frac{9}{12} = \frac{21}{n}$

$\frac{9}{12} \stackrel{?}{=} \frac{21}{28}$   Reduce each ratio.

$\frac{3}{4} = \frac{3}{4}$ ✔

> **Check Understanding**
>
> Explain how you would set up and solve the following proportions:
>
> 1. 25 is to $x$ as 40 is to 16
>
> 2. $-36 : 24 = 27 : x$
>
> 1. $x = 10$    2. $x = -18$

## Teaching Tip

After students have reviewed the terms *means* and *extremes*, have them examine a specific proportion and determine if there are other ways to arrange the four terms so that the equation is still a proportion.

*Example:* In the proportion $\frac{2}{10} = \frac{1}{5}$, the extremes are 2 and 5, and the means are 1 and 10.

If the means of the proportion are interchanged, $\frac{2}{1} = \frac{10}{5}$, the equation is still a proportion.

If the extremes of the proportion are interchanged, $\frac{5}{10} = \frac{1}{2}$, the equation is still a proportion.

If the means and extremes are interchanged, $\frac{10}{2} = \frac{5}{1}$, the equation is still a proportion.

## Example 2

**MACHINERY** A machine produces 45 hinges in 6 min. How many minutes does it take the machine to produce 75 hinges?

### Solution

Set up a proportion. Let $x =$ the amount of time to produce 75 hinges.

$$\frac{\text{number of hinges}}{\text{time}} \quad \frac{45}{6} = \frac{75}{x} \quad \frac{\text{number of hinges}}{\text{time}}$$

$$45 \cdot x = 6 \cdot 75 \quad \text{Find the cross-products.}$$

$$45x = 450$$

$$\frac{45x}{45} = \frac{450}{45}$$

$$x = 10$$

It takes the machine 10 min to produce 75 hinges.

Some proportions involve variable expressions as the terms of the ratios. To solve these equations, find the cross-products. Then solve for the variable.

**Problem Solving Tip**

When solving a word problem that requires you to write a proportion, checking the solution by substitution will only tell you if you solved the proportion correctly.

Check your answer for reasonableness. Since 45 hinges are produced in 6 min, 90 hinges would be produced in 12 min. So 75 hinges in 10 min is reasonable.

## Example 3

Solve each proportion. Check the solution.

**a.** $\dfrac{36}{n+2} = 4;\ n + 2 \neq 0$

**b.** $\dfrac{3y+3}{6} = \dfrac{2y-1}{2}$

### Solution

**a.**
$$\frac{36}{n+2} = 4$$

$$\frac{36}{n+2} = \frac{4}{1} \quad \text{Write 4 as } \tfrac{4}{1}.$$

$$36 \cdot 1 = 4(n+2) \quad \text{Find the cross-products.}$$

$$36 = 4n + 8$$

$$36 - 8 = 4n + 8 - 8 \quad \text{Subtract 8 from both sides.}$$

$$28 = 4n$$

$$\frac{28}{4} = \frac{4n}{4}$$

$$7 = n$$

**Check** $\dfrac{36}{n+2} = 4$

$$\frac{36}{7+2} \overset{?}{=} 4$$

$$\frac{36}{9} \overset{?}{=} 4$$

$$4 = 4 \ \checkmark$$

**b.**
$$\frac{3y+3}{6} = \frac{2y-1}{2}$$

$$2(3y+3) = 6(2y-1) \quad \text{Find the cross-products.}$$

$$6y + 6 = 12y - 6$$

$$6y - 6y + 6 = 12y - 6y - 6$$

$$6 = 6y - 6$$

$$6 + 6 = 6y - 6 + 6$$

$$12 = 6y$$

$$\frac{12}{6} = \frac{6y}{6}$$

$$2 = y$$

**Check** $\dfrac{3y+3}{6} = \dfrac{2y-1}{2}$

$$\frac{3 \cdot 2 + 3}{6} \overset{?}{=} \frac{2 \cdot 2 - 1}{2}$$

$$\frac{6+3}{6} \overset{?}{=} \frac{4-1}{2}$$

$$\frac{9}{6} \overset{?}{=} \frac{3}{2} \quad \text{Reduce each ratio.}$$

$$\frac{3}{2} = \frac{3}{2} \ \checkmark$$

 mathmatters2.com/extra_examples

---

## Chalkboard Examples

**Supplementary Example 1**
Solve the proportion and check your solution.

$$\frac{x}{18} = \frac{25}{30}$$

$$30 \cdot x = 18 \cdot 25$$

$$30x = 450$$

$$\frac{30x}{30} = \frac{450}{30}$$

$$x = 15$$

**Check**

$$\frac{x}{18} = \frac{25}{30}$$

$$\frac{15}{18} \overset{?}{=} \frac{25}{30}$$

$$\frac{5}{6} = \frac{5}{6} \ \checkmark$$

**Supplementary Example 2**
**NUTRITION** The cheese that Reggie bought contains about 90 calories in 20 g. Reggie ate 70 g of the cheese. About how many calories was that?

Let $x =$ the number of calories in 70 g.

$$\frac{\text{calories}}{\text{grams}} \quad \frac{x}{70} = \frac{90}{20} \quad \frac{\text{calories}}{\text{grams}}$$

$$20 \cdot x = 70 \cdot 90$$

$$20x = 6300$$

$$\frac{20x}{20} = \frac{6300}{20}$$

$$x = 315$$

There were about 315 calories in the 70 g of cheese that Reggie ate.

**Supplementary Example 3**
Solve the proportion and check your solution.

$$\frac{12}{x-2} = \frac{32}{x+8}$$

$$12(x+8) = 32(x-2)$$

$$12x + 96 = 32x - 64$$

$$12x - 12x + 96 = 32x - 12x - 64$$

$$96 = 20x - 64$$

$$96 + 64 = 20x - 64 + 64$$

$$160 = 20x$$

$$\frac{160}{20} = \frac{20x}{20}$$

$$8 = x$$

**Check**

$$\frac{12}{x-2} = \frac{32}{x+8}$$

$$\frac{12}{8-2} \overset{?}{=} \frac{32}{8+8}$$

$$\frac{12}{6} \overset{?}{=} \frac{32}{16}$$

$$2 = 2 \ \checkmark$$

---

## Predictable Error

From Example 1, note with students that in the check, the sides are simplified separately to show that both sides reduce to the same ratio.

Emphasize that in the check, it is important not to reproduce the original procedure. The following will demonstrate that if an error occurs in the original procedure and that same error is made in the check, then the incorrect value will appear to check as a solution.

For $\dfrac{9}{12} = \dfrac{21}{n}$, suppose you incorrectly use these products: $9 \cdot 12 = 21 \cdot n \rightarrow n = 5.14$.

Then, checking 5.14 by reproducing the procedure: $9 \cdot 12 = 21 \cdot 5.14$ appears to confirm that 5.14 is the correct solution. Point out that the products used were not the cross-products.

## Lesson Wrap-up

### QUICK ASSESSMENT

Ask the following questions to determine if students understand the content presented in this lesson.

**Tell whether each statement is *true* or *false*. If the statement is false, rewrite it so that it is true.**

1. In a proportion, the sum of the means is equal to the sum of the extremes.   **False. In a proportion, the product of the means is equal to the product of the extremes.**

2. To determine an unknown term of a proportion, you cross-multiply.   **True.**

3. To check a solution to a proportion, you cross-multiply.   **False. To check a solution to a proportion, you show that both sides reduce to the same ratio.**

### ASSIGNMENT GUIDE

**Basic:** 1–47, 52–60
**Enriched:** 1–60

---

**Reteaching Worksheet 3-5**

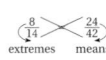

Name _____   Date _____

RETEACHING  **3-5**
### MORE TWO-STEP EQUATIONS

A **proportion** is an equation stating that two ratios are equivalent. Proportions may be written in three different ways. The numbers of a proportion are called **terms**. The first and fourth terms are called the **extremes** of the proportion. The second and third terms are called **means** of the proportion.

means | means
$8 : 14 = 24 : 42$   $8$ is to $14$ as $24$ is to $42$   $\frac{8}{14} \diagup\!\!\!\diagdown \frac{24}{42}$
extremes | extremes | extremes  means

The cross-products of the terms of a proportion are equal. You can use this fact to solve for an unknown term.

**Example**

A stack of 8 concrete blocks weighs 212 lb. How much would a stack of 18 blocks weigh?

**Solution**
Write a proportion.   number of blocks → $\frac{8}{212} = \frac{18}{m}$ ← number of blocks, weight

Find the cross-products.   $8m = 18 \cdot 212$
$8m = 3816$
$m = 477$

A stack of 18 blocks would weigh 477 lb.

**EXERCISES**

Use cross-products to solve each proportion.

1. $\frac{26}{n} = \frac{4}{10}$ ___ 65   2. $\frac{d}{7} = \frac{15}{21}$ ___ 5   3. $\frac{35}{30} = \frac{14}{b}$ ___ 12

4. $\frac{8}{12} = \frac{40}{n}$ ___ 60   5. $\frac{1}{7} = \frac{n}{56}$ ___ 8   6. $\frac{2.5}{7.5} = \frac{n}{21}$ ___ 7

7. Four out of every seven people attending a conference are engineers. If there are 68 engineers at the conference, how many people are there in all? ___ 119

8. Bill works for 15 h and earns $114.30. How much money would he earn for working 22 h?
$167.64

**124** Chapter 3   **Equations and Inequalities**

---

### TRY THESE EXERCISES

**Solve each proportion. Assume no denominator is 0. Check the solution.**

1. $\frac{16}{n} = \frac{36}{27}$   12

2. $\frac{x}{9} = \frac{50}{15}$   30

3. $11 : 6 = m : 18$   33

4. $\frac{15}{r-3} = 3$   8

5. $\frac{x+4}{-5} = 10$   −54

6. $\frac{-4z}{z+4} = -3$   12

7. $\frac{x}{x+2} = \frac{3}{5}$   3

8. $\frac{x+6}{3} = \frac{5x}{9}$   9

9. $\frac{b-4}{4} = \frac{b+4}{8}$   12

10. **WRITING MATH** Explain why it is necessary in Exercises 1–9 to assume that the denominator can't be zero.   The expression would be undefined and the equation would have no solution.

11. A company produced 260 turbine engines. Of these, 15% are for motor boats. How many engines are for the motor boats? (Hint: The ratio represented by 15% is 15 to 100.)   39

12. **MANUFACTURING** Of all computer chips manufactured, 3% are defective. If a company produces 367 chips, approximately how many are defective?   11

### PRACTICE EXERCISES  •  For Extra Practice, see page 594.

**Solve each proportion. Assume no denominator is 0. Check the solution.**

13. $\frac{18}{48} = \frac{12}{n}$   32

14. $\frac{21}{z} = \frac{77}{33}$   9

15. $85 : 100 = c : 20$   17

16. $96 : 69 = 32 : x$   23

17. $\frac{f}{44} = \frac{24}{66}$   16

18. 21 is to $k$ as 15 is to 25   35

19. $\frac{99}{18} = \frac{p}{8}$   44

20. $38 : g = 57 : 18$   12

21. $\frac{7.5}{21.2} = \frac{y}{106}$   37.5

22. $-6 = \frac{p+9}{11}$   −75

23. $\frac{9}{w+3} = \frac{1}{6}$   51

24. $\frac{k-13}{9} = 2$   31

25. $\frac{u-3}{u} = \frac{2}{5}$   5

26. $\frac{9}{5} = \frac{3n}{8-n}$   3

27. $\frac{36}{t+2} = \frac{4}{3}$   25

28. $\frac{22}{a+3} = \frac{11}{12}$   21

29. $\frac{x}{-9} = \frac{x-6}{-27}$   −3

30. $\frac{4}{5} = \frac{3}{m-2}$   $\frac{23}{4}$

31. $\frac{3y+4}{y} = 11$   $\frac{1}{2}$

32. $\frac{c-2}{3} = \frac{5c-2}{3}$   0

33. $\frac{20}{4} = \frac{n}{n-4}$   5

34. $\frac{t+3}{2} = \frac{t-3}{3}$   −15

35. $\frac{2m+1}{9} = \frac{12-7m}{6}$   $\frac{34}{25}$

36. $\frac{6a-8}{7} = \frac{-40+4a}{-4}$   6

37. **YOU MAKE THE CALL** Erica and Jenisa solved the proportion $\frac{t-4}{-6} = \frac{3}{2}$. Erica's solution is $t = 5$, and Jenisa solution is $t = -5$. Who is correct? Explain Erica's or Jenisa's possible mistake.   Jenisa; Erica added 8 to −18 and received an answer of 10. Dividing 2 into 10 resulted in 5.

38. An automobile manufacturer employs 21,550 people. Of these, 68% are production workers. How many production workers does the company employ?   14,654

39. **BUSINESS** For one year, a company's income was $820,650. The company's expenses for that year were $754,998. What percent of the company's income was profit? (Hint: income − expenses = profit)   8%

### Teaching Tip

From Supplementary Example 1, you can demonstrate how working with factors produces smaller numbers in the calculation.

$\frac{x}{18} = \frac{25}{30}$

$30 \cdot x = 18 \cdot 25$   Cross-multiply

$\frac{30x}{30} = \frac{18 \cdot 25}{30}$   Leave the product in factored form. Divide both sides by 30.

$x = \frac{3 \cdot 6 \cdot 5 \cdot 5}{6 \cdot 5}$   Factor numerator and denominator. Cancel common factors.

$x = 15$

**40. PHYSICS** A cylindrical water tank is 10-ft high. When the water is 4-ft deep, the volume of water is 75 ft³. How much water is there in a full tank?  187.5 ft³

**41. WRITING MATH** When solving a proportion involving a percent, explain how to set up each ratio. $\frac{\text{part}}{\text{whole}} = \frac{x}{100}$

**DATA FILE** For Exercises 42–44, refer to the data on the leading causes of death for men and women on page 569.

**42.** Approximately what percent of people who die from heart disease are men?  about 50%

**43.** Approximately what percent of people who die from cancer are women?  about 48%

**44.** Approximately what percent of people who die from accidents are women?  about 35%

**Use the scale drawing of a bus for Exercises 45–47. The scale is 1 cm : 2 m.**

**45.** Find the actual height of the bus.  3 m

**46.** Find the actual length of the bus.  11 m

**47.** How many buses of this size could be parked along one side of a street that is 78 m long?  7

1.5 cm
5.5 cm

■ **EXTENDED PRACTICE EXERCISES**

**Solve each proportion. Check the solution.**

**48.** $\frac{-9h - 17}{2} = -3h + 5$  −9     **49.** $\frac{5(x + 3)}{4} = \frac{3(x + 8)}{2}$  −33

**50. RETAIL** The manager of a clothing store is having no success selling a particular shirt at $35.99. She decides to lower the price to $23.39. Write and solve a proportion to determine the percent of the discount. (Hint: Find the amount of the discount first.)  ≈ 35%

**51.** Keandre deposits $540 in a bank account paying simple interest. Exactly one year later, he closes the account and withdraws $564.30. At what percent is interest paid on his account during the year?  4.5%

■ **MIXED REVIEW EXERCISES**

**52.** Find the median, mode, mean and range of the time that 15 students spent studying for a math test. Round to the nearest hundredth. (Lesson 1-2)
median = 2.8, mode = 3.1 mean = 2.71, range = 3.8

**Hours Spent Studying for Math Test**

| | | | | |
|---|---|---|---|---|
| 4.3 | 2.8 | 3.1 | 1.9 | 2.0 |
| 0.5 | 3.6 | 4.2 | 2.3 | 2.1 |
| 3.1 | 2.5 | 1.8 | 3.4 | 3.1 |

**Graph each set of numbers on a number line.**
(Lesson 2-1)  For 53–60, see additional answers.

**53.** integers from −4 to 3

**54.** real numbers from −2 to 5

**55.** integers from −3 to 8

**56.** real numbers from −4 to 0

**57.** real numbers greater than or equal to −3

**58.** real numbers less than or equal to 2

**59.** real numbers less than 3

**60.** real numbers greater than −4

**Math Online** mathmatters2.com/self_check_quiz

Lesson 3-5 **Proportions** | **125**

**ADDITIONAL ANSWERS**

**53.**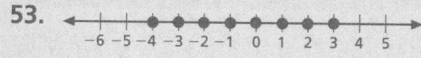

**54.**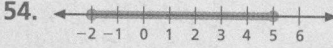

**55.**

**56.**

**57.**

**58.**

**59.**

**60.**

Name _____  Date _____

EXTRA PRACTICE **3-5**
**MORE TWO-STEP EQUATIONS**

☑ **EXERCISES**

Solve each proportion. Check the solution.

1. $\frac{6}{8} = \frac{n}{20}$  15     2. $\frac{24}{c} = \frac{36}{12}$  8

3. $25 : 150 = r : 75$  12.5     4. $90 : 45 = 80 : m$  40

5. $\frac{w}{30} = \frac{15}{40}$  11.25     6. 32 is to $n$ as 12 is to 15  40

7. $39 : h = 3 : 7$  91     8. $-5 = \frac{x + 1}{2}$  −11

9. $\frac{1.5}{5} = \frac{j}{10}$  3     10. $\frac{f + 5}{6} = 7$  37

11. $w + \frac{1}{3} = \frac{4}{5}$  $\frac{7}{15}$     12. $\frac{14}{k + 2} = \frac{1}{2}$  26

13. $\frac{y}{-4} = \frac{y + 1}{2}$  $-\frac{2}{3}$     14. $\frac{16}{12} = \frac{j}{j + 2}$  −8

15. $\frac{a + 5}{3} = \frac{a - 5}{2}$  25     16. $\frac{3x - 2}{4} = \frac{4 - 2x}{3}$  $1\frac{5}{17}$

17. $\frac{3d - 5}{4} = \frac{-10 + 2d}{2}$  15     18. $\frac{1 - 8f}{2} = \frac{2 - f}{6}$  $\frac{1}{23}$

19. A factory employs 2500 people. Of these, 15% work overtime every week. How many people work overtime every week? _____  375

20. Hannah makes $36,000 a year. She spends 26% of her yearly income on her house. How much does she spend each year on her house? _____  $9360

21. On Saturday, Luke planted 42 of the 96 flowers he bought. What percent of the flowers did he plant? _____  43.75%

22. Jason spends 15% of each day studying. How many hours does he study in each 24-hour day? _____  3.6 hours

23. Lila paid $45.25 for a pair of jeans. If she spent 8% of that amount in sales tax, how much tax did she pay? _____  $3.62

Name _____  Date _____

ENRICHMENT **3-5**
**ANGLES OF A TRIANGLE**

In geometry, many statements about physical space are proven to be true. Such statements are called **theorems**. Here are two examples of geometric theorems.

**a.** The sum of the measures of the angles of a triangle is 180°.
**b.** If two sides of a triangle have equal measure, then the two angles opposite those sides also have equal measure.

☑ **EXERCISES**

For each of the triangles, write an equation and then solve for x. (A tick mark on two or more sides of a triangle indicates that the sides have equal measure.)

1. 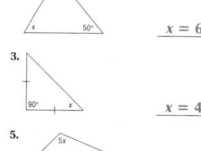  $x = 60°$     2. 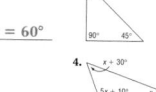  $x = 45°$

3.   $x = 45°$     4. 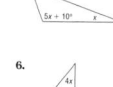  $x = 20°$

5.  $x = 22.5°$     6.   $x = 10°$

7. 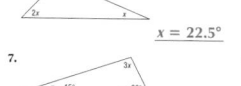  $x = 33°$     8. 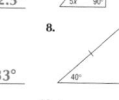  $x = 100°$

9.   $x = 60°$     10. 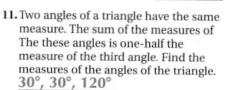  $x = 50°$

11. Two angles of a triangle have the same measure. The sum of the measures of The these angles is one-half the measure of the third angle. Find the measures of the angles of the triangle.
30°, 30°, 120°

12. The measure of one angle of a triangle is twice the measure of a second angle. The measure of the third angle is 12 less than the sum of the other two. Find the measures of the angles of the triangle.
64°, 32°, 84°

**53.** 
-6 -5 -4 -3 -2 -1 0 1 2 3 4 5

**54.** 
-2 -1 0 1 2 3 4 5 6

**55.** 
-4 -3 -2 -1 0 1 2 3 4 5 6 7 8 9

**56.** 
-4 -3 -2 -1 0 1 2 3

**57.** 
-4 -3 -2 -1 0 1 2 3 4

**58.** 
-4 -3 -2 -1 0 1 2 3 4

**59.** 
-4 -3 -2 -1 0 1 2 3 4

**60.** 
-4 -3 -2 -1 0 1 2 3 4

# Graph Inequalities on a Number Line

**Goals**
- Determine if a number is a solution of an inequality.
- Graph the solution of an inequality on a number line.

**Applications** Business, Government, Sports, Physics, Geography

---

## Lesson Planning

### NCTM Standards/Strands
- Representation
- Algebra
- Number & Operations
- Connections

### Vocabulary

inequality
solution of an inequality

### Tools/Materials Needed

ruler          number lines

### Lesson Resources

Warm-up Transparency 12
Transparency TK-8, RF-13
Reteaching 3-6
Extra Practice 3-6
Enrichment 3-6

---

## Getting Started

### 5-MINUTE WARM-UP

**Determine if each statement is *true* or *false*.**

1. $-3 + 12 < -12 + 13$   false
2. $-5(6 + 2) > 30$   false
3. $\frac{20}{-5} > -5$   true
4. $-8 + 4 + 2 < -1 + 1$   true

### Introduction to Lesson 3-6

When naming numbers less than or greater than 1,000,000, students should note that, in either case, there are infinitely many answers. In this application, only positive numbers qualify; but still there are infinitely many numbers between 0 and 1,000,000.

---

**BUSINESS** In a company meeting, Kiesha presented the number line shown.

1. Kiesha said that sales this year are less than last year's sales. Name a possible amount of this year's sales.
   any amount less than 1,000,000

2. She said that she expects next year's sales to be better than last year's. Name a possible amount of what Kiesha expects for next year's sales.   any amount greater than 1,000,000

**Last Year's Sales (dollars)**

3. In Question 1, could you have named other amounts? How many others? Where are the points corresponding to these amounts located on the number line shown?   yes; 999,998; to the left of 1,000,000

4. In Question 2, could you have named other amounts? How many others? Where are the points corresponding to these amounts located on the number line shown?   yes; several that would show a reasonable increase in sales; to the right of 1,000,000

### ◣ BUILD UNDERSTANDING

An **inequality** is a mathematical sentence containing one of these symbols: $<$ , $>$ , $\neq$, $\leq$, or $\geq$. Like an equation, an inequality may be true, or false, or an open sentence.

$$\textit{true: } -4 \leq -4 \qquad \textit{false: } -4 < -4 \qquad \textit{open sentence: } m < -4$$

An inequality is an open sentence that is neither true nor false until the variables are replaced by specific values. A value of the variable that makes such an inequality true is called a **solution of the inequality**. Inequalities like these often have an infinite number of solutions.

$$\textit{Inequality}: x \leq -3$$

$$\textit{Solution}: \text{any real number less than or equal to } -3$$

### Example 1

**Determine whether $-7$ is a solution of $x = 10, x < 10$ or $x > 10$.**

**Solution**

Substitute $-7$ for $x$ in each equation and inequality.

| | | |
|---|---|---|
| $x = 10$ | $-7 = 10$ | false |
| $x < 10$ | $-7 < 10$ | true |
| $x > 10$ | $-7 > 10$ | false |

So $-7$ is a solution of $x < 10$.

### Reading Math

Read the following inequality symbols as:

| | |
|---|---|
| $<$ | "is less than" |
| $>$ | "is greater than" |
| $\leq$ | "is less than or equal to" |
| $\geq$ | "is greater than or equal to." |
| $\neq$ | "is not equal to" |

---

## Teaching Tip

When reading a statement such as $-4 \leq -4$, emphasize that the symbol $\leq$ is read "is less than *or* equal to." Ask students what other symbol could be used to replace ? in $-4 \,?\, -4$ to make a true statement.   $=$ or $\geq$ Have students use two different symbols to replace ? in each of the following to make true statements.

1. $-7 \,?\, -6$   $-7 \leq -6, -7 < -6$
2. $0 \,?\, -5$   $0 \geq -5, 0 > -5$
3. $0.11 \,?\, 0.111$   $0.11 \leq 0.111, 0.11 < 0.111$
4. $\frac{1}{3} \,?\, \frac{1}{4}$   $\frac{1}{3} \geq \frac{1}{4}, \frac{1}{3} > \frac{1}{4}$
5. $-\frac{1}{3} \,?\, -\frac{1}{4}$   $-\frac{1}{3} \leq -\frac{1}{4}, -\frac{1}{3} < -\frac{1}{4}$

Besides −7, there are many other numbers that are solutions of $x < 10$. In fact, the solution of $x < 10$ includes all real numbers less than 10.

The solution of an inequality can be represented on a number line. Graph points using a solid circle. To show that a point is not included, use an open circle. Then shade the number line to include all other solutions of the inequality.

**Reading Math**

Words such as "at least," "at most," "greater than," "less than," "maximum" and "minimum" often indicate that an inequality will be used in solving a problem.

## Example 2

**Graph the solution of each inequality on a number line.**

**a.** $x < 5$                    **b.** $n \geq -3$

### Solution

**a.** Place an open circle on 5 to indicate that 5 is not a solution. Then shade to the left of 5 to show that all real numbers less than 5 are solutions of the inequality.

**b.** Place a solid circle on −3 to indicate that −3 is a solution of the inequality. Then shade to the right of −3 to show that all real numbers greater than −3 are also solutions of the inequality.

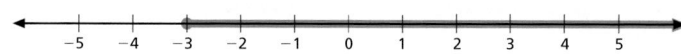

Inequalities can be used to model real-world situations. Choose a variable to represent the solution. Then express the situation as an inequality.

## Example 3

**GOVERNMENT** To vote in the U.S., a citizen must be 18 years of age or older.

**a.** Write an inequality that describes the age in years of voters in the U.S.

**b.** Graph the solution of the inequality on a number line.

### Solution

**a.** Let $a =$ the age of U.S. voters. The inequality $a \geq 18$ represents the age of U.S. voters.

**b.** Place a solid circle on 18 to show that 18 is a solution. Shade to the right to show that all ages greater than or equal to 18 are solutions of the inequality.

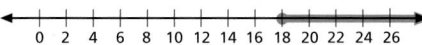

---

## Chalkboard Examples

**Supplementary Example 1**
Name all of the inequalities chosen from A–F for which 0 is a solution.
A, C, E, F
**A.** $x \leq 0$              **B.** $x < 0$
**C.** $-3 < x < 3$           **D.** $-3 < x < 0$
**E.** $-3 < x \leq 0$        **F.** $-0.5 \leq x \leq 0.5$

**Supplementary Example 2**
Graph the solution of each inequality on a number line.
**a.** $x \leq -1$

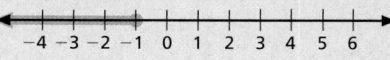

**b.** $x > -1$

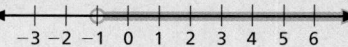

**Supplementary Example 3**
**SAFETY** By order of their fire commisioner, the capacity of a local diner is not to exceed 75 people.
**a.** Write an inequality that describes the capacity of the diner.
Let $p =$ the number of people. Then $0 \leq p \leq 75$ represents the capacity of the diner.
**b.** Graph the solution of the inequality on a number line.

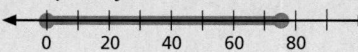

---

## Teaching Tip

Note that when a number is greater than 3 *and* less than 7, the number is *between* 3 and 7. Suppose both 3 and 7 are to be included in the values. Then, such an inequality may be written as $3 \leq x \leq 7$ or $7 \geq x \geq 3$.
Have students write two different inequalities to express each of the following statements, and give an example of a number that satisfies the inequality.

1. A number is between –5 and 0, inclusive.    $-5 \leq x \leq 0$ or $0 \geq x \geq -5$; a number that satisfies is –4
2. A number is between –6 and –7, including –6 but not including –7.
$-7 < x \leq -6$ or $-6 \geq x > -7$; a number that satisfies is –6.5

Example 4

**State the inequality that is represented on each number line.**

a.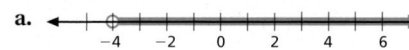

b.

**Solution**

a. Since the circle on −4 is open, −4 is not a solution. The line is shaded to the right; therefore, all real numbers greater than −4 are solutions of the inequality. So $x > -4$.

b. Since the circle on 12 is closed, 12 is a solution. The line is shaded to the left; therefore, all real numbers less than or equal to 12 are solutions of the inequality. So $y \le 12$.

## TRY THESE EXERCISES

**Determine whether each number is a solution of $y = 2.8$, $y < 2.8$ or $y > 2.8$.**

1. 2.5  $y < 2.8$
2. 3.1  $y > 2.8$
3. 2.8  $y = 2.8$
4. −2.8  $y < 2.8$

**Graph the solution of each inequality on a number line.**   For 5–8, see additional answers.

5. $x > 4$
6. $b \le -1$
7. $n > \dfrac{1}{2}$
8. $-8 \ge z$

**State the inequality that is represented on each number line.**

9.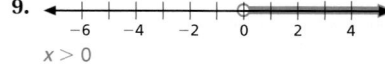
   $x > 0$

10.
    $x \le -11$

**SPORTS** In every basketball game this season, Colin has scored at least 13 points.

11. Write an inequality to describe the number of points Colin scored each game.  $p \ge 13$

12. Graph the solution on a number line.  See additional answers.

## PRACTICE EXERCISES  •  For Extra Practice, see page 594.

**Determine whether each number is a solution of $d = -\dfrac{1}{3}$, $d < -\dfrac{1}{3}$ or $d > -\dfrac{1}{3}$.**

13. $-\dfrac{1}{2}$  $d < -\dfrac{1}{3}$
14. $\dfrac{1}{3}$  $d > -\dfrac{1}{3}$
15. $-\dfrac{1}{3}$  $d = -\dfrac{1}{3}$
16. $-1$  $d < -\dfrac{1}{3}$

17. **WRITING MATH** Describe two different ways you can show that your answers for Exercises 13–16 are correct.  substitution and number line

**Graph the solution of each inequality on a number line.**   For 18–33, see additional answers.

18. $a \ge 6$
19. $g < -2$
20. $m \le 2.5$
21. $n > 0$
22. $b \le -\dfrac{3}{4}$
23. $d > -4.5$
24. $6 \ge x$
25. $h < 3$
26. $\dfrac{3}{2} < y$
27. $h \ge 0.8$
28. $-1 \le k$
29. $9 > t$
30. $h \ge 18$
31. $-20 < x$
32. $r \le -\dfrac{1}{4}$
33. $2.2 > n$

---

# Lesson Wrap-up

## QUICK ASSESSMENT

Ask the following questions to determine if students understand the content presented in this lesson.

1. Explain why a ray rather than a series of dots is used to represent the graph of $x < 5$.
   **Every number less than 5 makes $x < 5$ true.**

2. Write an inequality that is represented by the graph shown below.  $x \ge -3$

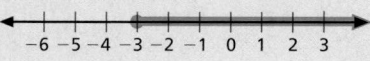

## ASSIGNMENT GUIDE

**Basic:** 1–43, 49–68
**Enriched:** 1–68

---

### Reteaching Worksheet 3-6

Name _____ Date _____

RETEACHING  **3-6**

**GRAPH INEQUALITIES ON A NUMBER LINE**

An **inequality** is an mathematical sentence that contains one of the following symbols.

less than: <                greater than: >
less than or equal to: ≤      greater than or equal to: ≥

An inequality that contains a variable is an open sentence that may be true or false. The solution of an inequality is all values of the variable that make the inequality true.

**Example 1**

Graph the solution of the inequality $x < 2$ on a number line.

**Solution**

Since the < sign is used, 2 is not a solution of the inequality. Place an open dot to indicate that 2 is not a solution. Then shade to the left of the open dot.

−7 −6 −5 −4 −3 −2 −1 0 1 2 3 4 5 6 7

**Example 2**

Graph the solution of the inequality $x \ge 2$ on a number line.

**Solution**

Since the ≥ sign is used, 2 is a solution of the inequality. Place a solid dot to indicate that 2 is not a solution. Then shade to the right of the solid dot.

−7 −6 −5 −4 −3 −2 −1 0 1 2 3 4 5 6 7

**EXERCISES**

Graph the solution of each inequality on a number line.

1. $m < 4$      −7 −6 −5 −4 −3 −2 −1 0 1 2 3 4 5 6 7

2. $m \ge 4$    −7 −6 −5 −4 −3 −2 −1 0 1 2 3 4 5 6 7

3. $m < -4$     −7 −6 −5 −4 −3 −2 −1 0 1 2 3 4 5 6 7

4. $m \ge -4$   −7 −6 −5 −4 −3 −2 −1 0 1 2 3 4 5 6 7

## ADDITIONAL ANSWERS

5. 3 4 5 6 7

6. −4 −3 −2 −1 0

7. 0 $\frac{1}{2}$ 1 $\frac{3}{2}$ 2

8. −11 −10 −9 −8 −7

12. 12 13 14 15 16

18. 5 6 7 8 9

19. −5 −4 −3 −2 −1

20. 1.0 1.5 2.0 2.5 3.0

21. −1 0 1 2 3

22. $-\frac{3}{2}$ $-\frac{5}{4}$ −1 $-\frac{3}{4}$ $-\frac{1}{2}$

**State the inequality that is represented on each number line.**

**34.**
$x \geq 10$

**35.**
$x < 13$

**36.**
$x > -\frac{1}{2}$

**37.**
$x \leq \frac{2}{3}$

**38.** To get an A in math class for the semester, Natasha must score at least 94% on the exam. Write an inequality that describes the score she must receive.   $x \geq 94\%$

**39. PHYSICS** Water boils at 212°F. Write an inequality that describes the temperature of water that is not boiling.
$x < 212$

**GEOGRAPHY** The Dead Sea, located in both Israel and Jordan, has the lowest continental altitude. It is 1312 ft below sea level.

**40.** Write an inequality that describes the elevations in feet of all other places in the world.   $x > -1312$

**41.** Graph the solution on a number line.
See additional answers.

**DATA FILE** Refer to the data on the ten largest lakes of the world on page 565.

**42.** Write an inequality that describes the area in square miles of all the lakes in the world in relation to the Caspian Sea.
$x < 152{,}239$

**43.** Write an inequality that describes the length in kilometers of all the lakes in the world in relation to the Caspian Sea.
$x < 1199$

Satellite image of the Dead Sea

### ■ EXTENDED PRACTICE EXERCISES

**State whether each statement is *always*, *sometimes*, or *never* true for real numbers *a*, *b* and *c*. Justify each *sometimes* or *never* answer.**

**44.** $a < a + 1$   always

**45.** $b > b - 1$   always

**46.** If $a < b$, then $b < a$   Never; if $a = 1$ and $b = 2$, $a$ will always be less than 2.

**47.** If $a \leq b$, then $b \leq a$   sometimes; true when $a = b$

**48. CRITICAL THINKING** If $a > 0$ and $b > -2$, is it true that $a > b$? Explain.
No; it is possible for $b > a$.

### ■ MIXED REVIEW EXERCISES

 **Use a calculator. Identify each number as a repeating decimal, terminating decimal, or an irrational number.** (Lesson 2-1)

**49.** 3.846   terminating

**50.** 5.989898. . .   repeating

**51.** 0.2222   terminating

**52.** 1.632632. . .   repeating

**53.** $\frac{3}{7}$   repeating

**54.** $\sqrt{54}$   irrational

**55.** $\sqrt{33.64}$   terminating

**56.** $\frac{9}{15}$   terminating

**Simplify.** (Lessons 2-7 and 2-8)

**57.** $z^{-5} \cdot z^2$   $z^{-3}$

**58.** $(t^{-4})^5$   $t^{-20}$

**59.** $r^4 \cdot r^{-2}$   $r^2$

**60.** $\frac{x^4}{x}$   $x^3$

**61.** $p^5 \div p^4$   $p$

**62.** $\left(\frac{c^3}{c^5}\right)^4$   $c^{-8}$

**63.** $(v^{-5})^5$   $v^{-25}$

**64.** $y^4 \cdot y^5$   $y^9$

**65. DATA FILE** Refer to the data on weekly time spent traveling on page 574. How much time is spent shopping and visiting friends and family during the week? Express your answer in minutes. (Prerequisite Skills)   93 min

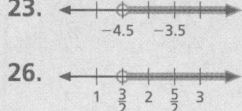

mathmatters2.com/self_check_quiz

Lesson 3-6   **Graph Inequalities on a Number Line**   **129**

**23.**   $-4.5$   $-3.5$

**24.**   3 4 5 6 7

**25.**   0 1 2 3 4

**26.**   1  $\frac{3}{2}$  2  $\frac{5}{2}$  3

**27.**   0.6 0.8 1.0 1.2 1.4

**28.**   $-2$ $-1$ 0 1 2

**29.**   6 7 8 9 10

**30.**   17 18 19 20 21

**31.**   $-20$   $-18$

**32.**   $-1$  $-\frac{3}{4}$  $-\frac{1}{2}$  $-\frac{1}{4}$  0

**33.**   1.6 1.8 2.0 2.2 2.4

**41.**   $-1313$ $-1312$ $-1311$ $-1310$ $-1309$

---

## Skills Practice

### Vocabulary Review

**Lesson 3-5**
proportion   means
extremes   cross-products

**Lesson 3-6**
inequality
solution of an inequality

## Assignment Guide

**All students: 1–50**

## Chalkboard Examples

### Lesson 3-5

Solve the proportion and check.

$$\frac{x}{12-x} = \frac{10}{30}$$
$$30(x) = 10(12-x)$$
$$30x = 120 - 10x$$
$$30x + 10x = 120 - 10x + 10x$$
$$40x = 120$$
$$\frac{40x}{40} = \frac{120}{40}$$
$$x = 3$$

**Check**
$$\frac{x}{12-x} = \frac{10}{30}$$
$$\frac{3}{12-3} \stackrel{?}{=} \frac{10}{30}$$
$$\frac{3}{9} \stackrel{?}{=} \frac{10}{30}$$
$$\frac{1}{3} = \frac{1}{3} \checkmark$$

### Lesson 3-6

Graph the solution of the inequality on a number line.

$$x \le 0$$

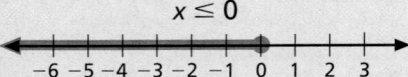

# Review and Practice Your Skills

## PRACTICE ◼ LESSON 3-5

Solve each proportion. Assume no denominator is 0. Check the solution.

1. $\frac{21}{27} = \frac{x}{18}$   14

2. $\frac{3}{x} = \frac{5}{9}$   5.4

3. $\frac{10}{b} = \frac{20}{28}$   14

4. $\frac{5}{4} = \frac{10}{c}$   8

5. 4 is to $x$ as 8 is to 24   12

6. $\frac{9}{16} = \frac{b}{32}$   18

7. $\frac{4}{9} = \frac{36}{x}$   81

8. $\frac{215}{5} = \frac{y}{8}$   344

9. $\frac{7}{1} = \frac{y}{7}$   49

10. $\frac{6}{14} = \frac{7}{x-3}$   $19\frac{1}{3}$

11. $y:5 = 22:10$   11

12. $\frac{14}{10} = \frac{5+x}{x-3}$   23

13. $\frac{5}{x+3} = \frac{3}{2x-8}$   7

14. $\frac{3}{3a+2} = \frac{3}{8}$   2

15. $\frac{8}{z-5} = \frac{3}{4}$   $15\frac{2}{3}$

16. $\frac{x-4}{4} = \frac{x+4}{8}$   12

17. $\frac{y-13}{9} = 2$   31

18. $\frac{a}{9} = \frac{a-6}{27}$   -3

19. $\frac{b-2}{3} = \frac{5b-2}{3}$   0

20. $\frac{a+4}{-1} = \frac{a+4}{5}$   -4

21. $\frac{c}{c+2} = \frac{3}{5}$   3

22. **BUSINESS** For one month, a company's income was $12,450. The company's expenses for that month were $7,470. What percent of the company's income was profit? (Hint: income − expenses = profit).   40%

23. **RETAIL** A shoe store advertises a running shoe on sale for $38.40. The regular price on the running shoes is $48.00. What is the discount percent on the running shoes?   20%

## PRACTICE ◼ LESSON 3-6

Graph the solution of each inequality on a number line.   For 24–35, see additional answers.

24. $x < 5$

25. $a \ge -6$

26. $g < -1$

27. $-10 < y$

28. $h > -6$

29. $x \le 10$

30. $-2 > b$

31. $\frac{5}{2} \le y$

32. $t < 6$

33. $t \ge -4$

34. $a \ge 0$

35. $3.2 > n$

State the inequality that is represented on each number line.

36.    $x \ge 5$

37.   $x > -8$

38.   $x < 17$

## Teaching Tip

To help students remember which way to draw rays for graphs of inequalities, elicit that the ray representing a graph corresponding to "greater than, >" 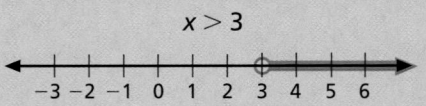 generally goes in the same direction as the symbol >, as shown for $x > 3$. But caution students that this generalization is true only for those cases where the variable is on the left. If the inequality reads $3 > x$, students must first think of this with $x$ on the left, $x < 3$, in which case the ray follows the direction of the "less than" symbol, <, and goes to the left.

## PRACTICE ■ LESSON 3-1–LESSON 3-6

**Solve each equation. Check the solution.** (Lessons 3-2 and 3-4)

**39.** $\frac{6}{5}y = 36$  30

**40.** $n - 3 = -11$  −8

**41.** $3 + d = 7.5$  4.5

**42.** $3y - 8 = 43$  17

**43.** $\frac{2}{5} + x = \frac{3}{4}$  $\frac{7}{20}$

**44.** $-4 + 6w = 38$  7

**Solve each proportion. Assume no denominator is 0. Check the solution.** (Lesson 3-5)

**45.** $\frac{2}{8} = \frac{x}{40}$  10

**46.** $\frac{17}{4} = \frac{17}{y}$  4

**47.** $\frac{3}{5} = \frac{6}{y - 4}$  14

**Graph the solution to the inequality on a number line.** (Lesson 3-6) For 48–50, see additional answers.

**48.** $x > |-5|$

**49.** $x \le -2$

**50.** $x \ge 6.5$

 **MathWorks Career – Automobile Designer**
Workplace Knowhow

**A**utomobile design requires the application of many physical principles. For passenger safety, one of the most important principles to understand is how automobiles respond when they collide. To prevent serious injury, the air bag acts as a cushion of air between the passenger and the dashboard, steering wheel, and door.

The following exercises analyze a situation in which an automobile strikes a stationary object head on and a passenger in the front seat is thrown toward the dashboard. The following equations will be useful in this analysis.

Force = mass · acceleration

Acceleration = $\frac{[\text{final velocity} - \text{initial velocity}]}{\text{time}}$

Force is measured in newtons (N), mass is measured in kilograms (kg), acceleration is measured in meters per second per second (m/sec²), velocity is measured in meters per second (m/sec), and time is measured in seconds (sec).

**1.** A car traveling 13.4 m/sec (30 mi/h) strikes a utility pole and comes to rest in 2 sec. With how much force does a 54.4-kg (120-lb) person in the car strike the dashboard in the absence of an airbag? −364.5 N

**2.** If there are 4.448 N per pound of force, how many pounds of force were exerted on the person in Exercise 1? 81.9 lb

**3.** An airbag is to be deployed in 1 sec to prevent the passenger described in Exercise 1 from striking the dashboard. The force exerted by the airbag against the passenger must be equivalent to or greater than the force with which the passenger would strike the dashboard. Assuming that the airbag weighs 2.3 kg (5 lb), what is the velocity of the airbag when it reaches the force calculated in Exercise 1? $V_f = 158.5$ m/sec

**4.** Convert the velocity value in Exercise 3 from m/sec to mi/h. (1 mi/h = 0.4470 m/sec) 354.6 mi/h

Math Online mathmatters2.com/mathworks

Chapter 3 **Review and Practice Your Skills** | **131**

## MathWorks

During the design process of an automobile, many features related to safety are considered. Among the physical phenomena that impact on safety are force and motion.

Students should answer Questions 1–3 to better understand how force and velocity/acceleration are modeled by algebraic equations.

In addition to being knowledgeable about force and motion, automobile designers must be knowledgeable about other aspects of the science of physics, such as mechanics and thermodynamics.

Students who are interested in learning more about this career choice can go to mathmatters2.com/mathworks. School Guidance Counselors are another resource for information about training requirements and appropriate schools.

## ADDITIONAL ANSWERS

**24.**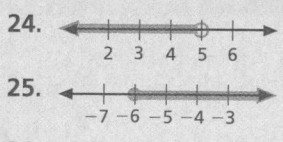

**25.**

**26.**

**27.**

**28.**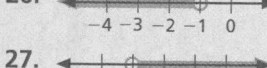

**29.**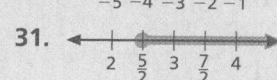

**30.**

**31.**

**32.**

**33.**

**34.**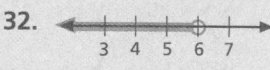

**35.**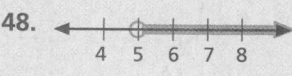

**48.**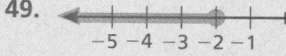

**49.**

**50.**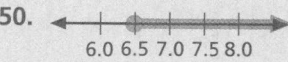

### NCTM Standards/Strands
- Algebra
- Number & Operations
- Representation
- Connections

### Vocabulary

solve an inequality
addition property of inequality
multiplication and division
properties of inequality

### Tools/Materials Needed

ruler                number lines

### Lesson Resources

Warm-up Transparency 13
Transparency TK-8, RF-14
Reteaching 3-7
Extra Practice 3-7
Enrichment 3-7

## Getting Started

### 5-MINUTE WARM-UP

Solve and check each equation.
1. $3x + 4 = 10$   $x = 2$
2. $15 - 2x = 31$   $x = -8$
3. $\frac{x}{-5} = -5$   $x = 25$
4. $\frac{x}{3} + 1 = 13$   $x = 36$

### Introduction to Lesson 3-7
To connect this activity to prior knowledge, have students consider ways of displaying the data of the completed tables. See the Extend the Lesson at the bottom of this page for a double-bar graph that displays the data.

---

# 3-7 Solve Inequalities

**Goals**
- Solve and graph inequalities on a number line.
- Solve problems involving inequalities.

**Applications**   Communications, Health, Fitness, Hobbies, Safety, Business

**COMMUNICATIONS** Two competing telephone companies offer two different plans. National Telephone Company charges $4.95/mo plus $0.10/call. American Long Distance charges $6.50/mo and $0.05/call.

1. Copy and complete the tables for each company.   See additional answers.

2. For what number of calls is National a better deal than American?   30 or fewer

3. Write an algebraic expression to represent the monthly charge for each phone company.  Let $c =$ the number of calls.   $4.95 + 0.10c$
$6.50 + 0.05c$

4. Compare the two expressions from Question 3 using $<$ or $>$ if a customer makes 25 calls/mo.
$4.95 + 0.10c < 6.50 + 0.05c, c = 25$

**National Telephone Company**

| Number of calls | Monthly charge |
|---|---|
| 5 | |
| 10 | |
| 15 | |
| 20 | |
| 30 | |
| 40 | |

**American Long Distance**

| Number of calls | Monthly charge |
|---|---|
| 5 | |
| 10 | |
| 15 | |
| 20 | |
| 30 | |
| 40 | |

## ▶ BUILD UNDERSTANDING

To **solve an inequality**, find all values of the variable that make the inequality true. You can use techniques similar to those used to solve an equation.  For example, if you add the same number to each side of an inequality, the order of the inequality remains the same.  This is called the **addition property of inequality**.

| Addition Property of Inequality | If $a < b$, then $a + c < b + c$ and $c + a < c + b$. |
|---|---|
| | If $a > b$, then $a + c > b + c$ and $c + a > c + b$. |

### Example 1

Solve and graph $n + 5 \geq 8$.

**Solution**

$$n + 5 \geq 8$$
$$n + 5 + (-5) \geq 8 + (-5) \qquad \text{Add } -5 \text{ to both sides.}$$
$$n \geq 3$$

Graph the solution. Use a closed circle to show that 3 is a solution.

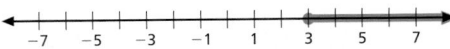

132 | Chapter 3  **Equations and Inequalities**

## Extend the Lesson

**REAL WORLD CONNECTION** This double-bar graph displays the data for the two competing telephone companies in the opening activity.

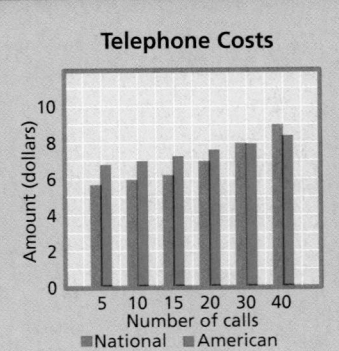

**Telephone Costs**

You can also multiply or divide each side of an inequality by the same number, but it is very important to be aware of the sign of the number. The **multiplication and division properties of inequality** state the following:

If you multiply or divide each side of an inequality by the same positive number, the order of the inequality remains the same.

If you multiply or divide each side of an inequality by the same negative number, the order of the inequality is reversed.

| **Multiplication and Division Properties of Inequality** | For all real numbers $a$, $b$ and $c$: <br><br> If $a > b$ and $c > 0$, then $ac > bc$ and $\dfrac{a}{c} > \dfrac{b}{c}$. <br><br> If $a < b$ and $c > 0$, then $ac < bc$ and $\dfrac{a}{c} < \dfrac{b}{c}$. <br><br> If $a > b$ and $c < 0$, then $ac < bc$ and $\dfrac{a}{c} < \dfrac{b}{c}$. <br><br> If $a < b$ and $c < 0$, then $ac > bc$ and $\dfrac{a}{c} > \dfrac{b}{c}$. |
|---|---|

## Example 2

**Solve and graph each inequality.**

**a.** $3x \le 9$

**b.** $-\dfrac{1}{4}y < 2$

### Solution

**a.** $3x \le 9$

$\dfrac{3x}{3} \le \dfrac{9}{3}$     Divide both sides by 3.

$x \le 3$

Graph $x \le 3$.

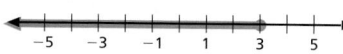

**b.** $-\dfrac{1}{4}y < 2$

$-4\left(-\dfrac{1}{4}y\right) > 2(-4)$     Multiply both sides by $-4$ and reverse the inequality.

$y > -8$

Graph $y > -8$.

## Example 3

**Solve and graph $-2x - 3 < -1$.**

### Solution

$-2x - 3 < -1$

$-2x - 3 + 3 < -1 + 3$     Add 3 to both sides.

$-2x < 2$

$\dfrac{-2x}{-2} > \dfrac{2}{-2}$     Divide both sides by $-2$ and reverse the order of the inequality.

$x > -1$

Graph $x > -1$.

> **Check Understanding**
>
> In the inequality $-\dfrac{r}{3} > -1$, do you reverse the inequality for the solution? Why or why not?
>
> Yes. You multiply both sides by $-3$ to solve. For 1–9, see

mathmatters2.com/extra_examples

Lesson 3-7 **Solve Inequalities** | **133**

### Supplementary Example 1
Solve and graph the inequality.

$5 - n \le 3$

$5 - n + n \le 3 + n$

$\quad\quad 5 \le 3 + n$

$5 - 3 \le 3 - 3 + n$

$\quad\quad 2 \le n$

$\quad\quad n \ge 2$

### Supplementary Example 2
Solve and graph the inequality.

$-3x \ge 12$

$\dfrac{-3x}{-3} \le \dfrac{12}{-3}$    Divide by $-3$ and reverse the inequality.

$x \le -4$

### Supplementary Example 3
Solve and graph the inequality.

$-3x + 1 \ge -5$

$-3x + 1 - 1 \ge -5 - 1$    Subtract 1 from each side.

$-3x \ge -6$

$\dfrac{-3x}{-3} \ge \dfrac{-6}{-3}$    Divide by $-3$ and reverse the inequality.

$x \ge 2$

### Supplementary Example 4
**TRAVEL** A car rental agency charges $49 per day, plus $0.35 per mile driven. If Gladys rents a car for one day, what distance can she drive and keep her total rental charge to a maximum of $80?

Let $m$ = number of miles Gladys will drive. Then $49 + 0.35m \le 80$. Solving gives $m \le 88.57$. Rounding down, she can go a maximum of about 88 mi.

## ADDITIONAL ANSWERS

**1.**

**National Telephone Company**

| Number of calls | Monthly charge |
|---|---|
| 5 | $5.45 |
| 10 | $5.95 |
| 15 | $6.45 |
| 20 | $6.95 |
| 30 | $7.95 |
| 40 | $8.95 |

**American Long Distance**

| Number of calls | Monthly charge |
|---|---|
| 5 | $6.75 |
| 10 | $7.00 |
| 15 | $7.25 |
| 20 | $7.50 |
| 30 | $8.00 |
| 40 | $8.50 |

## QUICK ASSESSMENT

Ask the following questions to determine if students understand the content presented in this lesson.

1. Compare the processs of solving an equation with the process of solving an inequality.   **You always perform identical operations on both sides of either an equation or an inequality. But, in an inequality, if you multiply or divide by a negative number, you must reverse the order of the inequality.**

## ASSIGNMENT GUIDE

**Basic:** 1–45, 51–62
**Enriched:** 1–62

### Reteaching Worksheet 3-7

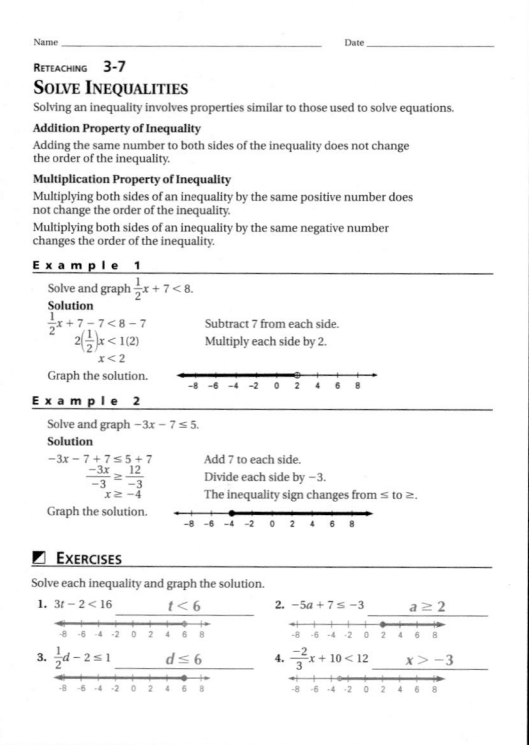

Name _____ Date _____

RETEACHING  **3-7**

**SOLVE INEQUALITIES**

Solving an inequality involves properties similar to those used to solve equations.

**Addition Property of Inequality**

Adding the same number to both sides of the inequality does not change the order of the inequality.

**Multiplication Property of Inequality**

Multiplying both sides of an inequality by the same positive number does not change the order of the inequality.

Multiplying both sides of an inequality by the same negative number changes the order of the inequality.

**Example 1**

Solve and graph $\frac{1}{2}x + 7 < 8$.

**Solution**

$\frac{1}{2}x + 7 - 7 < 8 - 7$   Subtract 7 from each side.

$2(\frac{1}{2})x < 1(2)$   Multiply each side by 2.

$x < 2$

Graph the solution.

**Example 2**

Solve and graph $-3x - 7 \le 5$.

**Solution**

$-3x - 7 + 7 \le 5 + 7$   Add 7 to each side.

$\frac{-3x}{-3} \ge \frac{12}{-3}$   Divide each side by $-3$.

$x \ge -4$   The inequality sign changes from $\le$ to $\ge$.

Graph the solution.

**EXERCISES**

Solve each inequality and graph the solution.

1. $3t - 2 < 16$      $t < 6$

2. $-5a + 7 \le -3$      $a \ge 2$

3. $\frac{1}{2}d - 2 \le 1$      $d \le 6$

4. $\frac{-2}{3}x + 10 < 12$      $x > -3$

---

## Example 4

**FITNESS** Nita is training for a bike race.  She plans to ride at least 100 mi/wk. One wheel broke on Monday, so she only rode 7 mi that day. What is the least number of miles she must average daily for the next 6 days to reach her goal?

### Solution

Write and solve an inequality that represents the situation. Let $m$ = number of miles Nita rides each day. Let $6m$ = number of miles for the next 6 days.

$$6m + 7 \ge 100$$
$$6m + 7 - 7 \ge 100 - 7$$
$$6m \ge 93$$
$$\frac{6m}{6} \ge \frac{93}{6}$$
$$m \ge 15.5$$

Nita must average at least 15.5 mi each day for the next 6 days.

## TRY THESE EXERCISES

**Solve and graph each inequality.**  See additional answers.

1. $z - 4 \le -2$   $z \le 2$
2. $3m \ge 12$   $m \ge 4$
3. $y + 9 < 3$   $y < -6$
4. $\frac{x}{4} > -3$   $x > -12$
5. $-\frac{2}{3}t \le -8$   $t \ge 12$
6. $8 - 2p \le 10$   $p \ge -1$
7. $-9 > 4n + 7$   $n < -4$
8. $3x - 14 < 7$   $x < 7$
9. $-\frac{w}{3} + 5 \ge -1$   $w \le 18$

10. **WRITING MATH**  Explain each step you used to solve and graph the inequality in Exercise 9.   See additional answers.

11. **HEALTH**  Julio is on an 1800-calorie-a-day diet. He consumed 450 calories at breakfast. What must Julio's average caloric intake be for lunch and dinner in order for him to maintain his diet?   He can consume at most 675 calories.

## PRACTICE EXERCISES • For Extra Practice, see page 595.

**Solve and graph each inequality.**   For 12–38, see additional answers.

12. $2 - c > -2$   $c < 4$
13. $2 \ge -\frac{1}{2}x$   $x \ge -4$
14. $d - 9 < -7$   $d < 2$
15. $-4x \le -12$   $x \ge 3$
16. $5 > b + 11$   $b < -6$
17. $\frac{3}{4}h \le -6$   $h \le -8$
18. $-14 + p > -21$   $p > -7$
19. $14 \le -4r$   $r \le -\frac{7}{2}$
20. $6n + 5 < -25$   $n < -5$
21. $7k + 4 \ge -10$   $k \ge -2$
22. $4z + 8 > -2$   $z > -\frac{5}{2}$
23. $5 + 4y < 37$   $y < 8$
24. $14 < 5e + 4$   $e > 2$
25. $4 - 3q > 13$   $q < -3$
26. $16 \ge 3c + 7$   $c \le 3$
27. $\frac{2}{3}b - 3 \le 1$   $b \le 6$
28. $10 \le -2x + 5$   $x \le -\frac{5}{2}$
29. $0.8x - 7 \le 0.2$   $x \le 9$
30. $3 - 9t \ge 30$   $t \le -3$
31. $2 - \frac{1}{4}a \ge 4$   $a \le -8$
32. $17 \ge 5 - 6x$   $x \ge -2$
33. $3x - 6x \ge 12$   $x \le -4$
34. $4(c + 1) > -3$   $c > -\frac{7}{4}$
35. $2p + 3.7 < p - 1.5$   $p < -5.2$
36. $1 + m \le 3 - 2m$   $m \le \frac{2}{3}$
37. $5x + 4 \ge 3x + 2$   $x \ge -1$
38. $2(x + 1) < 4(x + 3)$   $x > -5$

## ADDITIONAL ANSWERS

1.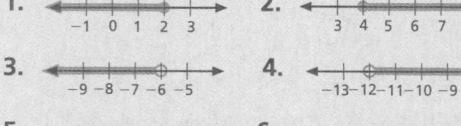
2. 
3. 
4. 

5.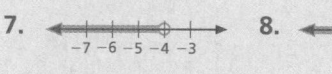
6. 

7. 

8. 

9. 

10. Step 1   Subtract 5 from each side.
    Step 2   Multiply each side by $-3$.
    Step 3   Change $\ge$ to $\le$ because of sign change.
    Step 4   Draw a number line with a closed circle on 18 and shade to the left.

12.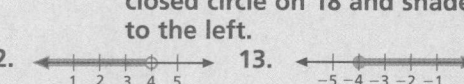
13. 

14.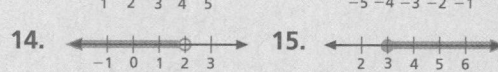
15.

**39. HOBBIES** Parker wants to read a 150-page book over 5 days. He plans to read 30 pages each day. However, on the first day he read 38 pages. What is the least number of pages Parker must average for the next 4 days to reach his goal?  28

**40. SAFETY** The maximum load for an elevator is 2400 lb. A crate weighing 300 lb is put on the elevator. Suppose the average weight of a passenger is 150 lb. How many passengers can get on the elevator with the crate?  14

**Write and solve an inequality for each statement.** $-6 < 18x,$

**41.** Negative six is less than 18 times a number.   $x > -\frac{1}{3}$

**42.** A number decreased by seven is at least negative nine.
$x - 7 \geq -9,\ x \geq -2$

**43.** Eight increased by four times a number is at most $-12$.
$8 + 4x \leq -12,\ x \leq -5$

**44.** Three-fourths of a number, decreased by 11, is greater than 4.   $\frac{3}{4}x - 11 > 4,\ x > 20$

**45.** Sara can afford no more than 36 yd of fencing for her yard. What is the largest length of $x$?
12.5 yd

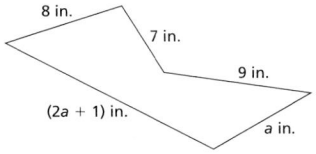

## ■ EXTENDED PRACTICE EXERCISES

**46. BUSINESS** Hoshi begins her own company selling music CDs. The start-up cost of her business is \$4500. It costs Hoshi \$8.50 for each CD, which she will sell for \$15.00. Write and solve an inequality to show the number of CDs she must sell to earn a profit of at least \$500.   $15c - (8.5c + 4500) \geq 500;$
$c \geq 770$

**47.** In order for the perimeter of the polygon shown to be no more than 50 in., what values can $a$ have?   $a < 8\frac{1}{3}$

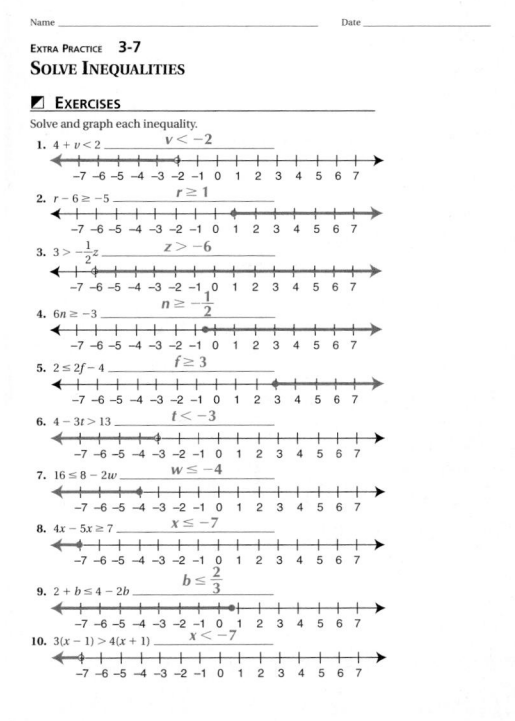

8 in.

7 in.

9 in.

(2a + 1) in.

a in.

**48. WRITING MATH** Write a problem that could be solved using $3c + 25 \leq 100$.   Answers will vary.

**49. CRITICAL THINKING** If $a > b$ and $c > d$, then is $a - c > b - d$ *sometimes*, *always* or *never* true? Use examples to justify your answer.

Sometimes; for example if $a = 0$, $b = 2$, $c = 4$, and $d = 1$, then $2 > 1$, or if $a = 1$, $b = 0$, $c = 4$, and $d = 1$, then $-3 < -1$.

**50.** If $m \geq n$ and $-m \geq -n$, what do you think is true about $m$ and $n$?
They are equal.

## ■ MIXED REVIEW EXERCISES

**Write each number in scientific notation.** (Lesson 2-8)

**51.** 7,382,047   $7.382047 \cdot 10^6$
**52.** 0.00826   $8.26 \cdot 10^{-3}$
**53.** 38,471,900   $3.84719 \cdot 10^7$

**Write each number in standard form.** (Lesson 2-8)

**54.** $3.2 \cdot 10^5$   320,000
**55.** $5.697 \cdot 10^{-4}$   0.0005697
**56.** $3.2168 \cdot 10^8$   321,680,000

**Simplify each variable expression.** (Lesson 2-5)

**57.** $5(2z + 8)$   $10z + 40$
**58.** $-3(3b + 1)$   $-9b - 3$
**59.** $\frac{1}{2}(2f - 6g)$   $f - 3g$
**60.** $\frac{(5 - 12x)}{3}$   $\frac{5}{3} - 4x$
**61.** $\frac{(-4a - 12)}{2}$   $-2a - 6$
**62.** $\frac{(6j - 30k)}{3}$   $2j - 10k$

**Math Online** mathmatters2.com/self_check_quiz

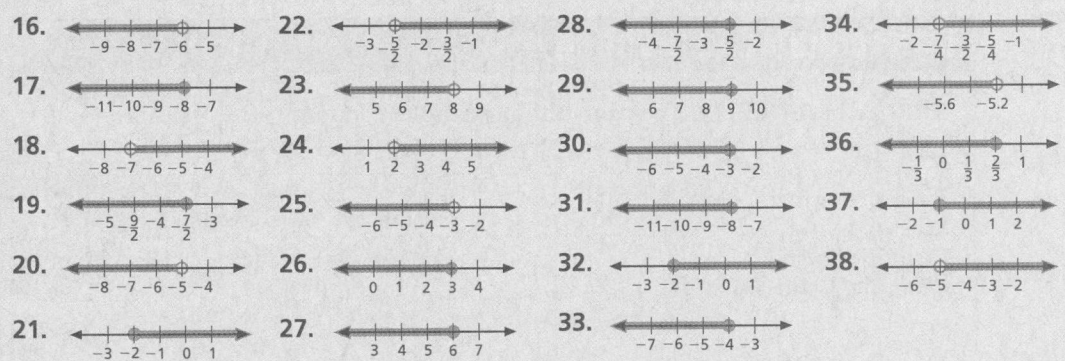

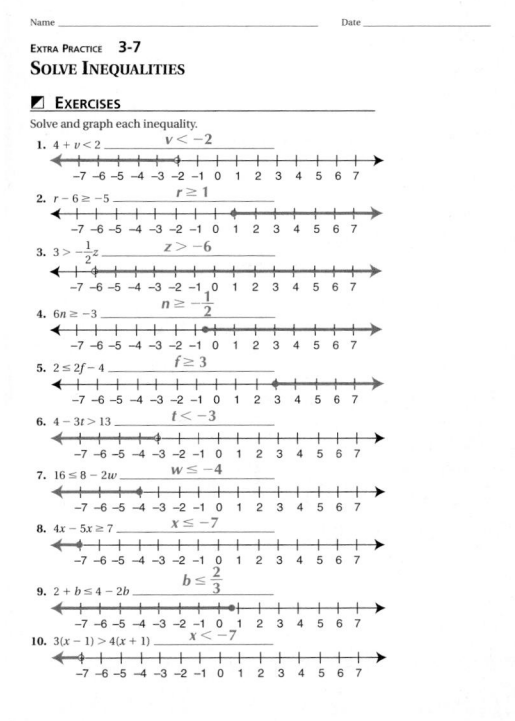

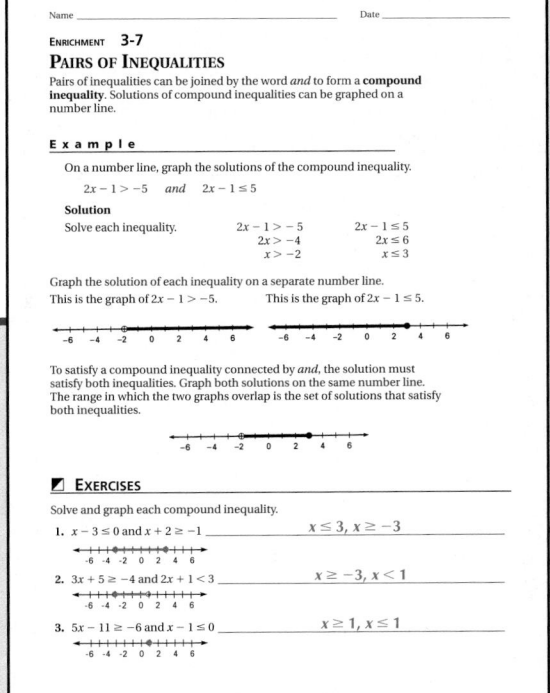

### Tools/Materials Needed

ruler
string
calculator
weight (washer, ring,
    or binder clip)
Algeblocks and Sentence Mat

### Lesson Resources

Warm-up Transparency 14
Transparency TK-7
Reteaching 3-8
Extra Practice 3-8
Enrichment 3-8
Technology Activity 3-8

## Getting Started

### 5-Minute Warm-Up

**Simplify each expression.**
1. $8^2$   64       2. $4^2 + 3^2$   25
3. $13^2$   169     4. $(7.5)^2$   56.25

### Introduction to Lesson 3-8

After students have completed
Question 2, have them consider
the units of measure used in this
formula and guide them through
dimensional analysis to see how
the units work out. ($g$, the force
of acceleration due to gravity, is
$981 \frac{cm}{sec^2}$ .)

$$T = 2\pi \cdot \sqrt{\frac{L}{g}}$$

$$sec = \text{no unit} \cdot \sqrt{\frac{cm}{\frac{cm}{sec^2}}}$$

$$sec = \sqrt{\frac{cm}{1} \div \frac{cm}{sec^2}}$$

$$= \sqrt{\frac{cm}{1} \cdot \frac{sec^2}{cm}}$$

$$= \sqrt{sec^2}$$

$$= sec$$

---

# 3-8 Equations with Squares and Square Roots

**Goals**  ■ Solve equations involving squares.
          ■ Solve equations involving square roots.

**Applications**  Physics, Safety, Engineering, Mechanics

**PHYSICS**  The period of a pendulum is the time it takes the pendulum to
complete a full swing (back and forth). The period is found using the formula
$T = 2\pi \cdot \sqrt{\frac{L}{981}}$, where $T$ is the period and $L$ is the length of the pendulum.

1. Use a ruler, a piece of string and a weight (such as a washer, ring or binder
   clip) to construct a pendulum similar to the one shown.
   Observe students' work.
2. Copy and complete the table. Use the formula to find the period.

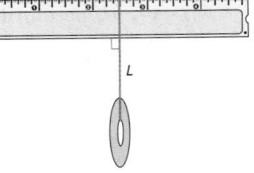

| Length of pendulum (centimeters) | 10 | 20 | 30 | 40 | 50 |
|---|---|---|---|---|---|
| Period (seconds) | | | | | |

0.6   0.9   1.1   1.3   1.4
3. Determine the length of the pendulum if the period is 1 sec.
   $\approx 24.8$ cm

### ▶ BUILD UNDERSTANDING

To solve an equation, perform the inverse of the operation that is
applied to the variable to both sides of the equation. The inverse of
squaring a number is taking its square root. The inverse of taking
the square root of a number is squaring that number.

Recall that when you multiply two radical expressions with the
same radicand, the product is the radicand.

$$\sqrt{x} \cdot \sqrt{x} = x \qquad \sqrt{2x} \cdot \sqrt{2x} = 2x \qquad \sqrt{x+5} \cdot \sqrt{x+5} = x+5 \qquad \sqrt{\frac{2}{5}} \cdot \sqrt{\frac{2}{5}} = \frac{2}{5}$$

To solve an equation with $x^2$ on one side of the equation and a non-negative real
number on the other side take the square root of both sides. Recall that every
positive real number has a positive square root and a negative square root.

To solve an equation with $\sqrt{x}$ on one side of the equation and a real number on
the other side, square both sides of the equation.

**Think Back**

An expression such as
$\sqrt{36}$ is called a **radical**.

$\sqrt{}$ is the **radical symbol**.

The number under the
radical symbol is the
**radicand**.

### Example 1

Solve each equation. Check the solutions.

a. $x^2 = 36$                          b. $\sqrt{x} = 4$

**Solution**                                               **Check**

a.   $x^2 = 36$                                    $x^2 = 36$         $x^2 = 36$
     $\sqrt{x^2} = \sqrt{36}$         Find each square root.         $6^2 = 36$     $(-6)^2 = 36$
     $x = 6$  or  $x = -6$   Include the positive and negative solutions.   $36 = 36$ ✔   $36 = 36$ ✔

**136**  Chapter 3 **Equations and Inequalities**

---

## Differentiated Instruction

**VISUAL LEARNERS** To reinforce the concept of square roots, have students
build squares for several whole numbers using unit Algeblocks. For each
square they build, have students record the following information. An
example is shown.

| Number $(n)$ | Picture of square with side $n$ | Number of tiles used $(t)$ | $\sqrt{t} = n$ |
|---|---|---|---|
| 10 | | 100 | $\sqrt{100} = 10$ |

**b.** $\sqrt{x} = 4$

$(\sqrt{x})^2 = 4^2$    Square both sides.

$x = 16$

**Check**

$\sqrt{x} = 4$

$\sqrt{16} = 4$ ✔

## Example 2

Solve each equation. Check the solutions.

**a.** $x^2 = 1.21$

**b.** $\sqrt{x} = \dfrac{3}{4}$

**Check Understanding**

Explain why part a of Example 1 has two solutions and part b has only one solution.

See additional answers.

### Solution

**a.**   $x^2 = 1.21$

$\sqrt{x^2} = \sqrt{1.21}$    Find each square root.

$x = 1.1$ or $x = -1.1$

**Check**

$x^2 = 1.21$      $x^2 = 1.21$

$(1.1)^2 \stackrel{?}{=} 1.21$    $(-1.1)^2 \stackrel{?}{=} 1.21$

$1.21 = 1.21$ ✔    $1.21 = 1.21$ ✔

**b.**   $\sqrt{x} = \dfrac{3}{4}$

$(\sqrt{x})^2 = \left(\dfrac{3}{4}\right)^2$    Square both sides.

$x = \dfrac{9}{16}$

**Check**

$\sqrt{x} = \dfrac{3}{4}$

$\sqrt{\dfrac{9}{16}} \stackrel{?}{=} \dfrac{3}{4}$    $\sqrt{\dfrac{9}{16}} = \dfrac{\sqrt{9}}{\sqrt{16}}$

$\dfrac{3}{4} = \dfrac{3}{4}$ ✔

Often equations with squares or square roots require more than one step. First isolate the term or expression with the variable. Then perform the inverse operation.

## Example 3

Solve each equation. Check the solutions.

**a.** $x^2 - 6 = 19$

**b.** $\sqrt{g + 4} = 5$

### Solution

**a.**   $x^2 - 6 = 19$

$x^2 - 6 + 6 = 19 + 6$    Add 6 to both sides.

$x^2 = 25$

$\sqrt{x^2} = \sqrt{25}$    Find each square root.

$x = \pm 5$

**Check**

$x^2 - 6 = 19$      $x^2 - 6 = 19$

$5^2 - 6 \stackrel{?}{=} 19$    $(-5)^2 - 6 \stackrel{?}{=} 19$

$25 - 6 \stackrel{?}{=} 19$    $25 - 6 \stackrel{?}{=} 19$

$19 = 19$ ✔      $19 = 19$ ✔

**b.**   $\sqrt{g + 4} = 5$

$(\sqrt{g + 4})^2 = 5^2$    Square both sides.

$g + 4 = 25$

$g + 4 - 4 = 25 - 4$    Subtract 4 from both sides.

$g = 21$

**Check**

$\sqrt{g + 4} = 5$

$\sqrt{21 + 4} \stackrel{?}{=} 5$

$\sqrt{25} \stackrel{?}{=} 5$

$5 = 5$ ✔

## ADDITIONAL ANSWERS

**Check Understanding**

Taking the square root of a number results in a positive answer and a negative answer. Squaring a number results in only one answer.

---

# Chalkboard Examples

### Supplementary Example 1

Solve the equation. Check the solution.

$x^2 = \dfrac{4}{9}$

$\sqrt{x^2} = \sqrt{\dfrac{4}{9}}$    Take the square root of each side.

$x = \pm \dfrac{2}{3}$    $x = \dfrac{2}{3}$ or $x = -\dfrac{2}{3}$

### Supplementary Example 2

Solve the equation. Check the solution.

$x^2 - 225 = 0$

$x^2 - 225 + 225 = 0 + 225$    Add 225 to each side.

$x^2 = 225$

$\sqrt{x^2} = \sqrt{225}$    Take the square root of each side.

$x = \pm 15$    $x = 15$ or $x = -15$

### Supplementary Example 3

Solve the equation. Check the solution.

$3\sqrt{x} + 1 = 3$

$3\sqrt{x} + 1 - 1 = 3 - 1$

$3\sqrt{x} = 2$

$(3\sqrt{x})^2 = 2^2$

$9x = 4$

$x = \dfrac{4}{9}$

> **Check**
>
> $3\sqrt{x} + 1 = 3$
>
> $3\sqrt{\dfrac{4}{9}} + 1 \stackrel{?}{=} 3$
>
> $3 \cdot \dfrac{2}{3} + 1 \stackrel{?}{=} 3$
>
> $2 + 1 \stackrel{?}{=} 3$
>
> $3 = 3$ ✔

### Supplementary Example 4

**ASTRONOMY** The velocity, $v$, of a satellite moving in a circular orbit near the surface of Earth is given by the formula $v = \sqrt{gr}$ where $g$ represents the acceleration due to gravity and $r$ represents the radius of Earth. Given that $g = 9.81$ m/sec$^2$ and $v = 7.91 \cdot 10^3$ m/sec, determine the radius of Earth to the nearest meter.

$v = \sqrt{gr}$

$7.91 \cdot 10^3 = \sqrt{9.81r}$

$(7.91 \cdot 10^3)^2 = (\sqrt{9.81r})^2$

$62{,}568{,}100 = 9.81r$

$\dfrac{62{,}568{,}100}{9.81} = \dfrac{9.81r}{9.81}$

$6{,}377{,}992 \text{ m} \approx r$

Ask the following questions to determine if students understand the content presented in this lesson.

**1.** What is the inverse operation of squaring?   taking the square root

**2.** Why does every positive number have two square roots?   because both a positive times a positive and a negative times a negative give a positive product

**3.** If $x^2 = 9$, what numbers are solutions of the equation?   C
   **A.** 81 or $-81$     **B.** 81 only
   **C.** 3 and $-3$     **D.** 3 only

**4.** If $\sqrt{x} = 25$, what numbers are solutions of the equation?   D
   **A.** 5 and $-5$     **B.** 5 only
   **C.** 625 and $-625$   **D.** 625 only

## ASSIGNMENT GUIDE

**Basic:** 1–52, 59–66
**Enriched:** 1–66

### Reteaching Worksheet 3-8

Name _____ Date _____

RETEACHING **3-8**
**EQUATIONS WITH SQUARES AND SQUARE ROOTS**
Some equations contain squares. Here are some examples.
   $x^2 = 2.25$        $y^2 + 17 = 186$
Recall that all positive numbers have two square roots.

**Example 1**

Solve $x^2 = 2.25$. Check the solutions.
**Solution**
$x^2 = 2.25$        Think: The square of what number equals 2.25?
$x = 1.5$ or $x = -1.5$
$x = \pm 1.5$

The solutions are 1.5 and $-1.5$.
**Check:** $x^2 = 2.25$        $(1.5)^2 = 2.25$        $(-1.5)^2 = 2.25$
                           $2.25 = 2.25$        $2.25 = 2.25$

**Example 2**

Solve $y^2 + 17 = 186$. Check the solutions.
**Solution**
$y^2 + 17 + (-17) = 186 + (-17)$        Add $-17$ to each side.
$y^2 = 169$
$\sqrt{y^2} = \sqrt{169}$        Find the square root of each side.
$y = 13$ or $-13$
$y = \pm 13$

The solutions are 13 and $-13$.
**Check:** $y^2 + 17 = 186$        $13^2 + 17 = 186$        $(-13)^2 + 17 = 186$
                           $169 + 17 = 186$        $169 + 17 = 186$
                           $186 = 186$        $186 = 186$

**■ EXERCISES**

Solve each equation. Check the solutions.
**1.** $x^2 = 196$   **2.** $y^2 = \frac{49}{256}$   **3.** $z^2 = 0.25$   **4.** $c^2 = \frac{1}{16}$
   $\pm 14$       $\pm \frac{7}{16}$       $\pm 0.5$       $\pm \frac{1}{4}$

**5.** $s^2 = 35$   **6.** $b^2 - 1 = 48$   **7.** $x^2 = 23$   **8.** $5n^2 = 845$
   $\pm \sqrt{35}$   $\pm 7$       $\pm \sqrt{23}$   $\pm 13$

**9.** $4w^2 = 2.56$   **10.** $2m^2 - 6 = 156$   **11.** $5x^2 - 7 = 173$   **12.** $10s^2 = 1000$
   $\pm 0.8$       $\pm 9$       $\pm 6$       $\pm 10$

---

### Example 4

**PHYSICS** In the formula $d = 16t^2$, $d$ is the distance in feet traveled by a freely falling object dropped from a resting position. The time of the fall in seconds is $t$. Find the time in seconds for an object to fall 484 ft.

**Solution**

$d = 16t^2$
$484 = 16t^2$        Substitute 484 for $d$.
$\dfrac{484}{16} = \dfrac{16t^2}{16}$
$30.25 = t^2$
$\sqrt{30.25} = \sqrt{t^2}$
$\pm 5.5 = t$

Since $t$ represents time, the solution cannot be negative. So it takes 5.5 sec for an object to fall 484 ft.

### TRY THESE EXERCISES

Solve each equation. Check the solutions.

**1.** $x^2 = 25$  $\pm 5$     **2.** $\sqrt{x} = 9$  81     **3.** $y^2 = 7$  $\pm\sqrt{7}$     **4.** $n^2 = 2.25$  $\pm 1.5$

**5.** $z^2 = \dfrac{49}{100}$  $\pm\dfrac{7}{10}$     **6.** $\sqrt{m} = \dfrac{1}{4}$  $\dfrac{1}{16}$     **7.** $\sqrt{d+3} = 2$  1     **8.** $89 = x^2 + 8$  $\pm 9$

**9.** $2w^2 = 288$  $\pm 12$     **10.** $\sqrt{2x+1} = 5$  12     **11.** $0 = 2.4b^2$  0     **12.** $\sqrt{j} - 3 = 1$  16

**13. WRITING MATH** Explain the difference between Exercises 7 and 12. What did you do differently in solving each?  See additional answers.

**14.** Using the formula $d = 16t^2$, find the time in seconds for an object to fall 96 ft.
   2.45 sec

### PRACTICE EXERCISES • For Extra Practice, see page 595.

Solve each equation. Check the solutions.

**15.** $\sqrt{x} = 9$  81     **16.** $\sqrt{m} = -11$  $\varnothing$     **17.** $y^2 = 64$  $\pm 8$     **18.** $h^2 = 169$  $\pm 13$

**19.** $\sqrt{a} = 2$  4     **20.** $\sqrt{b} = 0.3$  0.09     **21.** $59 = c^2$  $\pm\sqrt{59}$     **22.** $d^2 = \dfrac{1}{4}$  $\pm\dfrac{1}{2}$

**23.** $m^2 = -1.8$  $\varnothing$     **24.** $6 = \sqrt{n-3}$  39     **25.** $a^2 - 1 = 15$  $\pm 4$     **26.** $\sqrt{m-4} = 0$  4

**27.** $279 = x^2 + 23$  $\pm 16$     **28.** $3n^2 = 300$  $\pm 10$     **29.** $5\sqrt{p} = 30$  36     **30.** $\sqrt{s+9} = 5$  16

**31.** $\sqrt{2k} - 5 = 7$  72     **32.** $2w^2 = 1.62$  $\pm 0.9$     **33.** $4y^2 = 200$  $\pm\sqrt{50}$     **34.** $\sqrt{3h} = \dfrac{1}{3}$  $\dfrac{1}{27}$

**35.** $\sqrt{3t-5} = 5$  10     **36.** $5 = \sqrt{2(x+1)}$  $\dfrac{23}{2}$     **37.** $x^2 - 3 = 102$  $\pm\sqrt{105}$     **38.** $9 + 3n^2 = 21$  $\pm 2$

**39. SAFETY** In the formula $b = 0.06v^2$, $b$ is the distance in feet needed to stop a car after the brakes are applied. The speed at which a car is traveling when the brakes are applied in miles per hour is $v$. If a car traveled 96 ft after the brakes were applied, how fast was the car going when the driver applied the brakes?   40 mi/h

### Extend the Lesson

**CHALLENGE** After students have worked numerically with the formulas of this lesson, you may wish to have them solve for one variable in terms of the other variables. At the right, the pendulum formula is solved for $L$, the length of the pendulum.

$T = 2\pi \cdot \sqrt{\dfrac{L}{g}}$

$(T)^2 = \left(2\pi \cdot \sqrt{\dfrac{L}{g}}\right)^2$

$T^2 = 4\pi^2 \cdot \dfrac{L}{g}$

$\dfrac{g}{4\pi^2} \cdot T^2 = \dfrac{g}{4\pi^2} \cdot \dfrac{4\pi^2}{g} \cdot L$

$\dfrac{gT^2}{4\pi^2} = L$

**40.** The perimeter of the rectangle shown is 42 yd. Find the value of $x$.
218

6 yd
$\sqrt{x} + 7$ yd

**41.** Heta has three identical square pieces of fabric with a total area of 588 in.$^2$ Write and solve an equation to find the dimensions of each piece of fabric. $3x^2 = 588$; 14 in. by 14 in.

**42. ENGINEERING** A circular pipe has an inner radius of $r$ and a cross-sectional area of $A$. The outer radius $R$ of the pipe is given by $R = \sqrt{\frac{A}{\pi} + r^2}$. Find the inner radius of a pipe with an outer radius of 2 cm and a cross-sectional area of $1.75\pi$ cm$^2$. 1.5 cm

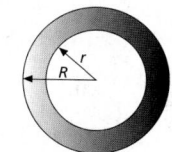

**43.** Solve the equation $T = 2\pi \cdot \sqrt{\frac{L}{981}}$ for $L$. $\left(\frac{T}{2\pi}\right)^2 \cdot 981 = L$

**CALCULATOR** Solve each equation. Then use a calculator to approximate the solutions to the nearest thousandth.

**44.** $a^2 = \frac{49}{10,000}$  ±0.07     **45.** $k^2 = 0.0144$ ±0.12  **46.** $67 = c^2$ ±8.185     **47.** $7f^2 = 1.75$  ±0.5

**48.** $x^2 - 8 = 30$         **49.** $328 = 4p^2$             **50.** $3m^2 + 2 = 50$ ±4  **51.** $117 = 6y^2 - 9$
±6.164                ±9.055                                                        ±4.583

**52. MODELING** What equation is modeled on the Sentence Mat? Solve for $x$.  $3x^2 = 12$, $x = ±2$

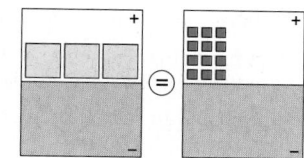

## ■ EXTENDED PRACTICE EXERCISES

Solve each radical equation.

**53.** $\sqrt{x + 7} = \sqrt{3x - 19}$ 13

**54.** $\sqrt{5n + 2} = \sqrt{-2n + 23}$ 3

**55. MECHANICS** An engine piston is acted on by a force $F$ producing pressure $P$. The diameter $d$ of the piston is given by $d = \sqrt{\frac{5F}{4P}}$. Find the force in pounds that produces a pressure 80 lb/in.$^2$ on a piston with a diameter of 3 in.  576 lb

**56.** Use the formula $d = 16t^2$ to find the time in seconds ($t$) for an object to fall 200 ft, 400 ft and 600 ft. Round each answer to the nearest hundredth.  3.54, 5.00, 6.12

**57. CRITICAL THINKING** Compare your results for Exercise 56. Does it take twice as long for an object to fall twice as far? Is the difference in time between 600 ft and 400 ft the same as the difference between 400 ft and 200 ft? What conclusions can you draw?  No. No. An object's velocity increases the further it falls.

**58. CHAPTER INVESTIGATION** Calculate the acceleration due to Earth's gravity using the formula $g = \frac{4\pi^2 L}{t}$, where $L$ is the length of the pendulum string in feet and $t$ is the time in seconds for 50 complete swings.  Answers will vary, but should be approximately 32 ft/sec$^2$.

## ■ MIXED REVIEW EXERCISES

Write each phrase as a variable expression. (Lesson 2-3)

**59.** seven more than a number  $x + 7$

**60.** the difference between a number and 143  $x - 143$

**61.** five times a number divided by $-12$  $\frac{5x}{-12}$

**62.** the product of 14 and a number  $14x$

Evaluate each expression when $x = 3$, $y = -4$, and $z = \frac{1}{4}$. (Lesson 2-4)

**63.** $5x + 3y$  3      **64.** $2(x + y)^2$  2      **65.** $z(3y - 4x)$  −6      **66.** $2xy + 8z$  −22

## ADDITIONAL ANSWERS

**13.** In Exercise 7 the entire expression $d + 3$ is under the radical and both sides of the equation can be easily squared immediately. In Exercise 12, you can add 3 to both sides before squaring them.

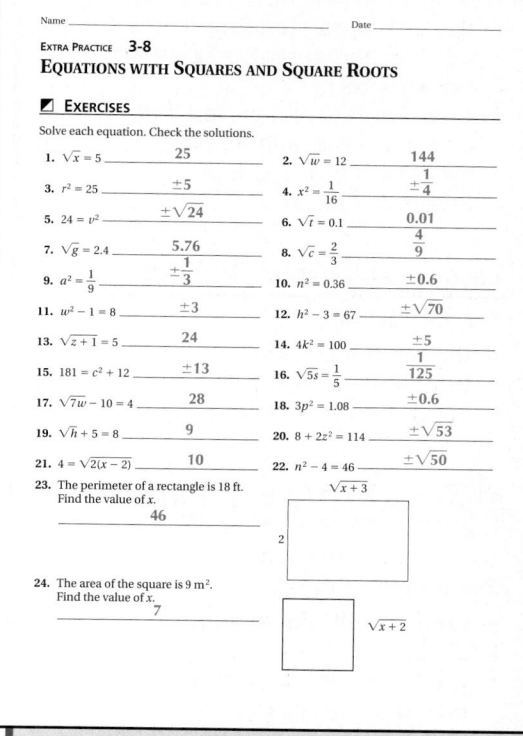

### Extra Practice Worksheet 3-8

Name _____  Date _____

EXTRA PRACTICE  **3-8**
**EQUATIONS WITH SQUARES AND SQUARE ROOTS**

☑ **EXERCISES**

Solve each equation. Check the solutions.

1. $\sqrt{x} = 5$    25          2. $\sqrt{w} = 12$    144
3. $r^2 = 25$    ±5            4. $x^2 = \frac{1}{16}$    ±$\frac{1}{4}$
5. $24 = v^2$    ±$\sqrt{24}$        6. $\sqrt{t} = 0.1$    0.01
7. $\sqrt{g} = 2.4$    5.76        8. $\sqrt{c} = \frac{2}{3}$    $\frac{4}{9}$
9. $a^2 = \frac{1}{9}$    ±$\frac{1}{3}$        10. $n^2 = 0.36$    ±0.6
11. $w^2 - 1 = 8$    ±3        12. $h^2 - 3 = 67$    ±$\sqrt{70}$
13. $\sqrt{z + 1} = 5$    24        14. $4k^2 = 100$    ±5
15. $181 = c^2 + 12$    ±13        16. $\sqrt{5s} = \frac{1}{5}$    $\frac{1}{125}$
17. $\sqrt{7w} - 10 = 4$    28        18. $3p^2 = 1.08$    ±0.6
19. $\sqrt{h} + 5 = 8$    9        20. $8 + 2z^2 = 114$    ±$\sqrt{53}$
21. $4 = \sqrt{2(x - 2)}$    10        22. $n^2 - 4 = 46$    ±$\sqrt{50}$

23. The perimeter of a rectangle is 18 ft. Find the value of $x$.    46
$\sqrt{x + 3}$
2

24. The area of the square is 9 m$^2$. Find the value of $x$.    7
$\sqrt{x + 2}$

### Enrichment Worksheet 3-8

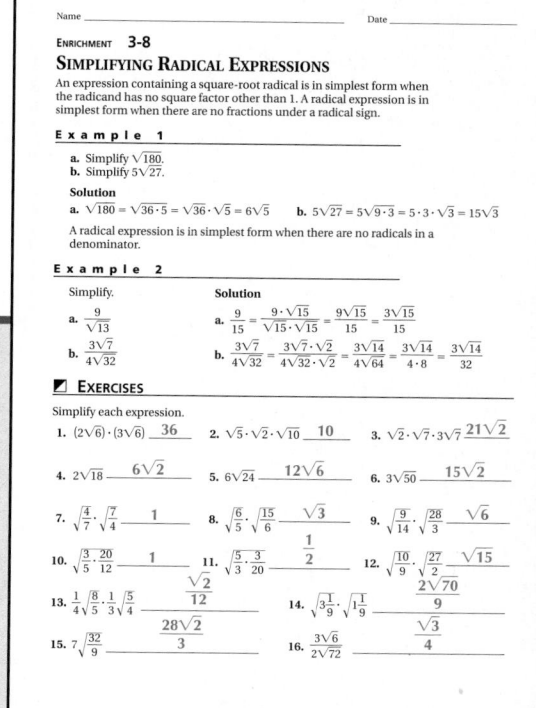

Name _____  Date _____

ENRICHMENT  **3-8**
**SIMPLIFYING RADICAL EXPRESSIONS**

An expression containing a square-root radical is in simplest form when the radicand has no square factor other than 1. A radical expression is in simplest form when there are no fractions under a radical sign.

**Example 1**

a. Simplify $\sqrt{180}$.
b. Simplify $5\sqrt{27}$.

**Solution**

a. $\sqrt{180} = \sqrt{36 \cdot 5} = \sqrt{36} \cdot \sqrt{5} = 6\sqrt{5}$    b. $5\sqrt{27} = 5\sqrt{9 \cdot 3} = 5 \cdot 3 \cdot \sqrt{3} = 15\sqrt{3}$

A radical expression is in simplest form when there are no radicals in a denominator.

**Example 2**

Simplify.            Solution
a. $\frac{9}{\sqrt{13}}$        a. $\frac{9}{15} = \frac{9 \cdot \sqrt{15}}{\sqrt{15} \cdot \sqrt{15}} = \frac{9\sqrt{15}}{15} = \frac{3\sqrt{15}}{15}$
b. $\frac{3\sqrt{7}}{4\sqrt{32}}$        b. $\frac{3\sqrt{7}}{4\sqrt{32}} = \frac{3\sqrt{7} \cdot \sqrt{2}}{4\sqrt{32} \cdot \sqrt{2}} = \frac{3\sqrt{14}}{4\sqrt{64}} = \frac{3\sqrt{14}}{4 \cdot 8} = \frac{3\sqrt{14}}{32}$

☑ **EXERCISES**

Simplify each expression.

1. $(2\sqrt{6}) \cdot (3\sqrt{6})$  36    2. $\sqrt{5} \cdot \sqrt{2} \cdot \sqrt{10}$  10    3. $\sqrt{2} \cdot \sqrt{7} \cdot 3\sqrt{7}$  $21\sqrt{2}$
4. $2\sqrt{18}$  $6\sqrt{2}$    5. $6\sqrt{24}$  $12\sqrt{6}$    6. $3\sqrt{50}$  $15\sqrt{2}$
7. $\sqrt{\frac{4}{7}} \cdot \sqrt{\frac{7}{4}}$  1    8. $\sqrt{\frac{6}{5}} \cdot \sqrt{\frac{15}{6}}$  $\sqrt{3}$    9. $\sqrt{\frac{9}{14}} \cdot \sqrt{\frac{28}{3}}$  $\sqrt{6}$
10. $\sqrt{\frac{3}{5}} \cdot \sqrt{\frac{20}{12}}$  1    11. $\sqrt{\frac{5}{3}} \cdot \sqrt{\frac{3}{20}}$  $\frac{1}{2}$    12. $\sqrt{\frac{10}{9}} \cdot \sqrt{\frac{27}{25}}$  $\frac{\sqrt{15}}{2}$
13. $\frac{1}{4}\sqrt{\frac{8}{5}} \cdot \frac{1}{3}\sqrt{\frac{5}{4}}$  $\frac{\sqrt{2}}{12}$    14. $\sqrt{3\frac{1}{9}} \cdot \sqrt{1\frac{1}{9}}$  $\frac{2\sqrt{70}}{9}$
15. $7\sqrt{\frac{32}{9}}$  $\frac{28\sqrt{2}}{3}$    16. $\frac{3\sqrt{6}}{2\sqrt{72}}$  $\frac{\sqrt{3}}{4}$

## Vocabulary Assessment

- A matching section checks for student understanding of the new vocabulary introduced in this chapter.
- A vocabulary review/test for Chapter 3 is available on pp. vii–viii of the *Chapter 3 Resource Masters.*

## Lesson-by-Lesson Review

For each lesson,

- the main ideas are summarized, and
- practice exercises are provided.

 EXAMVIEW® PRO

Use the networkable **ExamView® Pro** to:

- Create **multiple versions** of tests.
- Create **modified** tests for *inclusion* students.
- **Edit** existing questions and **add** your own questions.
- Use built-in **state curriculum correlations** to create tests aligned with state standards.
- Change **English** tests to **Spanish** and vice versa.

# Chapter 3 Review

## VOCABULARY ◼

**Choose the word from the list that best completes each statement.**

1. A value of the variable that makes an equation true is called a(n) __?__ of the equation.  l
2. When you add the same number to each side of an inequality, the result is a(n) __?__ inequality.  e
3. An equation stating the relationship between two or more variable quantities is called a(n) __?__.  g
4. Squaring a number and finding that number's square root are __?__ operations.  i
5. In the equation $\frac{a}{b} = \frac{c}{d}$, *a* and *d* are called the __?__.  f
6. A mathematical sentence that states that "*a* is greater than or equal to $-6$" is an example of a(n) __?__.  h
7. One way to solve a proportion is to write an equation using the __?__.  c
8. A(n) __?__ uses a variable or variables to describe a real-life situation.  b
9. The statement $-8 + 2 = 6$ is an example of a false __?__.  d
10. The statement "1 is to 2 as 5 is to 10" is an example of a(n) __?__.  k

| | |
|---|---|
| **a.** | addition property of equality |
| **b.** | algebraic model |
| **c.** | cross products |
| **d.** | equation |
| **e.** | equivalent |
| **f.** | extremes |
| **g.** | formula |
| **h.** | inequality |
| **i.** | inverse |
| **j.** | means |
| **k.** | proportion |
| **l.** | solution |

## LESSON 3-1 ◼ Equations and Formulas, p. 104

▶ An **equation** is a statement that two numbers or expressions are equal.

▶ To **solve an equation**, find all the values of the variable that make the equation true.

▶ A **formula** is an equation stating a relationship between two or more variable quantities.

**Determine if 7, 12, or 21.5 are solutions of each equation.**

11. $2p - 3 = 11$  7
12. $-4x = 6$  $-1.5$
13. $9 = \frac{z}{3} + 5$  12

14. What is the weight ($F$) of a man of 100-kg mass on a mountain near the equator where $g = 9.76$ m/s²? Use the formula $F = mg$.  976 kg · m/s²

**For Exercises 15–16, use the cylinder at the right.**

15. The formula for the volume of a cylinder is $V = \pi r^2 h$. In this formula, $V$ is the volume of the cylinder, $r$ is the radius of the base, and $h$ is the height of the cylinder. Find the volume of the cylinder.  282.7 cm³

16. The formula for the surface area of a cylinder is $SA = 2\pi rh + 2\pi r^2$. In this formula, $SA$ is the surface area, $r$ is the radius of the base, and $h$ is the height of the cylinder. Find the surface area of the cylinder.  245.0 cm²

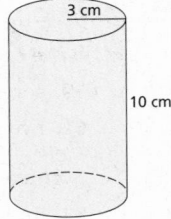
3 cm
10 cm

## LESSON 3-2 ◾ One-Step Equations, p. 108

▶ When two expressions are equal, if you add or multiply the same number to each expression the resulting expressions will be equal.

**Solve each equation. Check the solution.**

**17.** $x + 7 = 3$   −4       **18.** $-4m = 3.2$   −0.8       **19.** $\frac{2}{3}y = 6$   9

**Translate each word sentence into an equation. Then solve the equation.**

**20.** A number decreased by −12 is two.   $x - (-12) = 2$, $x = -10$

**21.** One-fourth a number is −15.   $\frac{1}{4}x = -15$, $x = -60$

## LESSON 3-3 ◾ Problem Solving Skills: Model Algebra, p. 114

▶ An **algebraic model** is a variable representation of a situation.

▶ A **mathematical model** uses numbers to describe a situation.

▶ A **rule** is an equation or formula that represents a model.

**For each situation, set up a mathematical model (table), write an algebraic model and a rule.**   For 22–25, see additional answers.

**22.** Nicole starts a savings program. She begins by saving $10 and adds $5 each week for 8 weeks.

**23.** When an American alligator is hatched, it is about 8 in. long. It grows about 12 in. each year.

**24.** The cost of renting a car is $25 per day plus $0.10/mi.

**25.** Devin owes the library $1.80 for a previous overdue book. If he does not return the book today, he will be fined an additional $0.30 per day.

## LESSON 3-4 ◾ Equations With Two or More Operations, p. 116

▶ To solve **multi-step equations**, first use the addition property of equality. Then use the multiplication property.

**Solve each equation. Check the solution.**

**26.** $\frac{c}{2} + 8 = 21$   −18       **27.** $25 = 40n + 5$  0.5       **28.** $2z - 11 + 9z = 11$  2

**29.** $\frac{a}{8} + 21 = 14$   −56       **30.** $10y - 2 = 8y - 1$  0.5       **31.** $4(2a - 1) = -10(a - 5)$  3

## LESSON 3-5 ◾ Proportions, p. 122

▶ A **proportion** is an equation stating that two ratios are equivalent.

▶ In a proportion, the **cross-products** are equal.

**Solve each proportion. Assume no denominator is 0. Check the solution.**

**32.** $\frac{12}{22} = \frac{30}{x}$   55       **33.** $\frac{y}{8} = \frac{65}{52}$   10       **34.** $\frac{(n - 2)}{3} = \frac{(n + 2)}{6}$   6

**35.** The Harrisons' car requires 4 gal to travel 120 mi. How many gallons will they need to travel 300 mi?   10 gal

## ADDITIONAL ANSWERS

**22.**

| Number of weeks | 0 | 1 | 2 | 3 | 4 | 5 | 6 | 7 | 8 |
|---|---|---|---|---|---|---|---|---|---|
| Amount saved | $10 | $15 | $20 | $25 | $30 | $35 | $40 | $45 | $50 |

Let $w$ = number of weeks; $10 + 5w$
Let $s$ = amount saved; $s = 10 + 5w$

**24.**

| Miles driven | 0 | 1 | 2 | 3 | 4 | 5 |
|---|---|---|---|---|---|---|
| Cost of renting car | $25.00 | $25.10 | $25.20 | $25.30 | $25.40 | $25.50 |

Let $m$ = miles driven; $25.00 + 0.10m$
Let $c$ = cost of renting car; $c = 25.00 + 0.10m$

**23.**

| Age of alligator (years) | 0 | 1 | 2 | 3 | 4 | 5 |
|---|---|---|---|---|---|---|
| Length of alligator (inches) | 8 | 20 | 32 | 44 | 56 | 68 |

Let $a$ = age in years; $8 + 12a$
Let $\ell$ = length of alligator; $\ell = 8 + 12a$

**25.**

| Days overdue | 0 | 1 | 2 | 3 | 4 | 5 |
|---|---|---|---|---|---|---|
| Amount owed | $1.80 | $2.10 | $2.40 | $2.70 | $3.00 | $3.30 |

Let $d$ = days overdue; $1.80 + 0.30d$
Let $a$ = amount owed; $a = 1.80 + 0.30d$

**36.**
$-6\ -5\ -4\ -3\ -2$

**37.** 
$0\ 1\ 2\ 3\ 4$

**38.** 
$-7\ -6\ -5\ -4\ -3$

**39.** 
$0\ 1\ 2\ 3\ 4$

**40.** 
$-4\ -3\ -2\ -1\ 0$

**41.** 
$0\ 1\ 2\ 3\ 4$

**42.** 
$-3\ -2\ -1\ 0\ 1$

**43.** 
$0\ 1\ 2\ 3\ 4$

**44.** 
$-12\quad -10$

**45.** 
$2\ 3\ 4\ 5\ 6$

**46.** 
$2\ 3\ 4\ 5\ 6$

**47.** 
$10\ 11\ 12\ 13\ 14$

---

## LESSON 3-6 ▪ Graph Inequalities on a Number Line, p. 126

▶ An **inequality** is a mathematical sentence that contains one of these symbols: $\neq, <, >, \leq,$ or $\geq$.

▶ The **solution of an inequality** can be represented on a number line.

▶ An open circle on the graph indicates that the number is not part of the solution. A solid circle on the graph indicated that the number is part of the solution.   See additional answers.

**Graph the solution of each inequality on a number line.**

**36.** $m < -3$      **37.** $4 \geq z$      **38.** $-5.2 \leq x$

**39.** $t > 3$      **40.** $-3.8 > h$      **41.** $a \leq 2.3$

## LESSON 3-7 ▪ Solve Inequalities, p. 132

▶ To solve an inequality, find all the values of the variable that make the inequality true.

▶ Use the addition, multiplication, and division properties to solve inequalities.

**Graph the solution of each inequality on a number line.**  For 42–47, see additional answers.

**42.** $3m \leq -3$  $m \leq -1$     **43.** $4z - 4 > 4$  $z > 2$     **44.** $-5 \leq \frac{x}{2} + 1$  $-12 \leq x$

**45.** $-7t + 19 < -16$  $t > 5$     **46.** $-2 - \frac{d}{5} \leq -3$  $d \geq 5$     **47.** $3(s - 7) + 9 < 21$  $s < 11$

## LESSON 3-8 ▪ Equations with Squares and Square Roots, p. 136

▶ The inverse of squaring a number is finding the square root.

▶ The inverse operation of taking the square root of a number is squaring that number.

**Solve each equation. Check the solutions.**

**48.** $y^2 = 49$  $\pm 7$     **49.** $\sqrt{x} = 25$  625     **50.** $m^2 + 3 + 19$  $\pm 4$

**51.** $\sqrt{x} + 2 = 10$  64     **52.** $4 = \sqrt{4(x - 5)}$  9     **53.** $4 + y^2 = 40$  $\pm 6$

**54.** Using the formula $d = 16t^2$, find the time in seconds for an object to fall 144 ft.  3 sec

**55.** Meterologists can use the formula $t = \frac{d^3}{216}$ to estimate the amount of time $t$ a storm of diameter $d$ will last. Suppose the eye of a hurricane, which causes the greatest amount of destruction, is 9 mi in diameter. How long will the worst part of the hurricane last? Round to the nearest tenth of an hour.  1.8 h

### CHAPTER INVESTIGATION

**EXTENSION** The weight of an object is the measure of the gravitational force on an object. The formula $F = mg$ represents the weight of object ($F$) as a product of its mass ($m$) and the strength of the Earth's gravity ($g$). Find three different objects of varying weights. Measure the weight of each object. Use the formula $F = mg$ to find the mass of each object.

## THEME: Physics

The benchmarks and expectations for this extension are as follows.
- Students set up a pendulum. They measure the length of the string.
- Students set the ball of the pendulum swinging through an arc of about 5°. They find the time it takes the pendulum to make 20 swings.
- Students calculate the acceleration due to Earth's gravity using the formula $g = \frac{4\pi^2 L}{t}$.
- Students do the investigation one more time, but this time they change the length of the pendulum string and use a ball with a different mass. They calculate the acceleration due to Earth's gravity. They compare the values of $g$ for both investigations.

# Chapter 3 Assessment

**Which of the given values is a solution of the equation?**

1. $-3x = 12$; 2, $-4$, $-2$   $-4$

2. $11 = 3 + \dfrac{c}{2}$; 16, 18, 20   16

3. $-\dfrac{b}{6} = 6$; 236, 26, 36   $-36$

**Solve each equation. Check the solution.**

4. $d - 9 = 9$   18

5. $48 = -8n$   $-6$

6. $w - 7.3 = -6.2$   1.1

7. $\dfrac{x}{6} = -2$   $-12$

8. $5g - 13 = 32$   9

9. $-\dfrac{2}{3}n + 10 = 24$   $-21$

10. $0 = 0.5t - 1$   2

11. $8g - 10 + g = 71$   9

12. $35 = 3x + 1 - 5x$   $-17$

**Solve each proportion. Assume no denominator is 0. Check the solution.**

13. $\dfrac{6}{21} = \dfrac{28}{x}$   98

14. $\dfrac{t}{45} = \dfrac{8}{40}$   9

15. $\dfrac{y - 5}{7} = \dfrac{y + 11}{3}$   $-23$

**Solve and graph each inequality.** For 16–21, see additional answers.

16. $7d \geq 21$   $d \geq 3$

17. $3f - 2 < 4$   $f < 2$

18. $\dfrac{-x}{2} + 1 < 3$   $x > -4$

19. $-10 \leq 3k + 8$   $k \geq -6$

20. $-x < 2$   $x > -2$

21. $-5 \geq -z$   $z \geq 5$

**Solve.**

22. If it is 95° Fahrenheit, what is the temperature in Celsius? Use the formula $F = \dfrac{9}{5}C + 32$.   35°C

23. Use the formula $p = \dfrac{a}{2} + 110$ to find the value of $p$ when $a = 32$.   $p = 126$

**Solve each equation. Check the solutions.**

24. $x^2 = 100$   $\pm 10$

25. $m^2 = 0.36$   $\pm 0.6$

26. $w^2 = \dfrac{9}{196}$   $\pm\dfrac{3}{14}$

27. $\sqrt{y} = 225$   50,625

28. $\sqrt{4n} = 8$   16

29. $\sqrt{y + 9} = 3$   0

30. $\sqrt{3(w - 2)} = 1$   $\dfrac{7}{3}$

31. $\sqrt{y} - 7 = 2$   81

32. $11 + 9j^2 = 15$   $\pm\dfrac{2}{3}$

**Set up a mathematical model, then write an algebraic model and a rule for each situation.** For 33–35, see additional answers.

33. Karl has been adding 12 cards to his baseball card collection each week for the past 5 weeks. He started with 60 cards.

34. A long distance phone call from the motel costs $3.50 plus $0.25 for each minute.

35. Kendra began with $20 worth of animal feed. Every minute for 5 minutes she gave $1.50 worth of feed to the animals.

 **Math Online** mathmatters2.com/chapter_assessment

Chapter 3 **Assessment**   **143**

## Chapter 3 Assessment

### Assessment Options

Chapter 3 Test A, pages 99–100
Chapter 3 Test B, pages 101–102

## ALTERNATIVE ASSESSMENT

**SPORTS PAGE** Sports statistics are used to predict who will win the next Super Bowl and World Series. Have students look up some of the statistics and determine which can be given as ratios. For instance, a baseball player's batting average can be given as: $\dfrac{\text{number of hits}}{\text{number of times at bat}}$.

Students should compile a list of at least 7 such statistics and demonstrate how each final statistic is calculated.

**RUBRIC** The following rubric is a sample scoring guide.

| Points | Description |
| --- | --- |
| 4 | Finds at least 7 sports ratios, explains them clearly, and **correctly shows** how each is calculated. |
| 3 | Finds 7 sports ratios, explains them clearly, but **makes a minor error** when showing how they are calculated. |
| 2 | Finds some sports ratios, explains them clearly, but **makes errors** when showing how they are calculated. |
| 1 | Finds a few sports ratios, explains them poorly, and gives **no sample calculations.** |
| 0 | Makes **no attempt** to find or explain sports ratios. |

## ADDITIONAL ANSWERS

16.

17.

18.

19.

20.

21.

33.

| Number of weeks | 0 | 1 | 2 | 3 | 4 | 5 |
| --- | --- | --- | --- | --- | --- | --- |
| Number of cards | 60 | 72 | 84 | 96 | 108 | 120 |

Let $w$ = the number of weeks; $60 + 12w$
Let $c$ = the number of cards; $c = 60 + 12w$

34.

| Number of minutes | 0 | 1 | 2 | 3 | 4 |
| --- | --- | --- | --- | --- | --- |
| Cost of phone call | $3.50 | $3.75 | $4.00 | $4.25 | $4.50 |

Let $m$ = the number of minutes; $3.50 + 0.25m$
Let $c$ = the cost of the phone call; $c = 3.50 + 0.25m$

35.

| Number of minutes | 0 | 1 | 2 | 3 | 4 | 5 |
| --- | --- | --- | --- | --- | --- | --- |
| Amount of money remaining | $20 | $18.50 | $17 | $15.50 | $14 | $12.50 |

Let $m$ = the number of minutes; $20 - 1.50m$
Let $a$ = the amount of money remaining; $a = 20 - 1.50m$

## Standardized Test Practice

These two pages contain practice questions in the various formats that can be found on the most frequently given standardized tests.

A student recording sheet for these two pages can be found on p. A1 of the *Chapter 3 Resource Masters*.

### Standardized Test Practice Student Recording Sheet

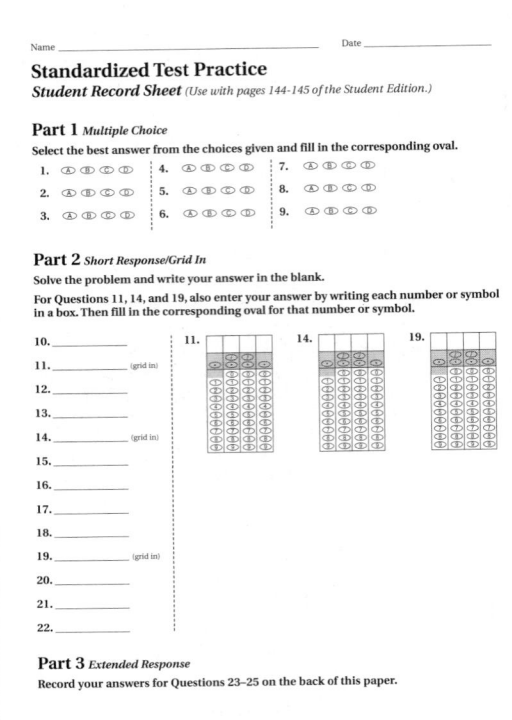

### Additional Practice

See pp. 103–105 in the *Chapter 3 Resource Masters* for additional standardized test practice.

# Standardized Test Practice

**Record your answers on the answer sheet provided by your teacher or on a sheet of paper.**

1. The stem-and-leaf plot below lists the cost of various bicycle helmets. Which statement about the data is true? (Lesson 1-3)  B

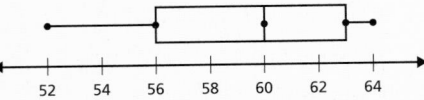

   | 2 | 1 3 4 4 5 7 |
   | 3 | 0 0 0 1 5 9 |
   | 4 | 3 9 9 |

   2|1 represents $21.

   Ⓐ The median and mean are equal.
   Ⓑ The median and mode are equal.
   Ⓒ The median is greater than the mode.
   Ⓓ The mode is greater than the mean.

2. The box-and-whisker plot below represents the high temperatures in degrees Fahrenheit for various cities. Which statement about the data is true? (Lesson 1-6)  A

   [box-and-whisker plot with scale 52 54 56 58 60 62 64]

   Ⓐ The median is 60°.
   Ⓑ The first quartile is 52°.
   Ⓒ The interquartile range is 12°.
   Ⓓ 64° is an outlier.

3. Which statement is *not* true? (Lesson 2-1)  C
   Ⓐ $|-3| > -3$
   Ⓑ $-\frac{3}{2} < -1$
   Ⓒ $\frac{1}{4} > \frac{1}{3}$
   Ⓓ $-2\frac{2}{3} < 1\frac{3}{4}$

4. What is the value of $(14 - 4) \div 2 + 3^2$? (Lesson 2-2)  A
   Ⓐ 14      Ⓑ 19
   Ⓒ 35      Ⓓ 64

5. Which expression is equivalent to $3(2x - y) + 4(x + 2y) - 3(x + y)$? (Lesson 2-6)  B
   Ⓐ $7x + 8y$      Ⓑ $7x + 2y$
   Ⓒ $9x$            Ⓓ $9y$

6. An online music store charges $12 for each CD and $5 per order for shipping and handling. If $c$ represents the number of CDs ordered, which rule can be used to determine the cost of the order? (Lesson 3-3)  A
   Ⓐ $12c + 5$
   Ⓑ $5c + 12$
   Ⓒ $12c - 5$
   Ⓓ $5c - 12$

7. What is the solution of $\frac{2x + 3}{6} = \frac{x - 4}{4}$? (Lesson 3-5)  D
   Ⓐ 18   Ⓑ $\frac{1}{2}$   Ⓒ $-\frac{1}{2}$   Ⓓ $-18$

8. Which graph represents the solution of $-2x + 3 \le 5$? (Lesson 3-7)  C

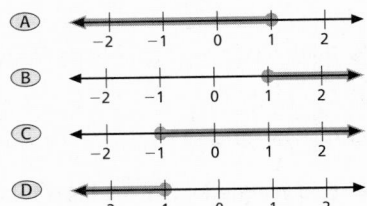

9. What is the solution of $\sqrt{x + 4} = 6$? (Lesson 3-8)  B
   Ⓐ 2      Ⓑ 32      Ⓒ 36      Ⓓ 40

**Test-Taking Tip**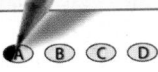

**Questions 7 and 9**
Some multiple-choice questions ask you to solve an equation or inequality. You can check your solution by replacing the variable in the equation or inequality with your answer. The answer choice that results in a true statement is the correct answer.

## Teaching Tip

Be sure students understand that the scatterplot given for Questions 10–12 relates two measures for each male student in the sample: the length of his foot and his height. When calculating measures of central tendency and other statistical measures, it is important to know the total number of items in a data set. Ask students to consider the way in which they find the total number of items in a data set when reading a scatterplot as opposed to the way in which they find the total number of items in a data set when reading a frequency table.   **For a scatter plot, count the number of points. For a frequency table, add all of the frequencies.**

## Part 2   Short Response/Grid In

Record your answers on the answer sheet provided by your teacher or on a sheet of paper.

The scatter plot shows the relationship between the foot length and the height of a sample of male students in the 11th grade. Use the scatter plot for Questions 10–12.

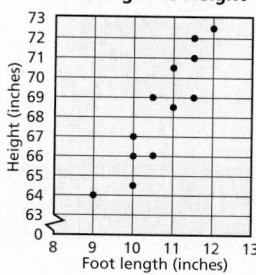

**Foot Length vs Height**

10. What is the median of the heights of the males? (Lesson 1-2)  68.75 in.

11. What is the mode of the foot lengths? (Lesson 1-2)  10 in. and 11.5 in.

12. Does the scatter plot show a positive correlation, a negative correlation, or no correlation? (Lesson 1-4)  positive

13. Write four less than half of a number as a variable expression. (Lesson 2-3)  $\frac{x}{2} - 4$

14. Evaluate $2.5x + 7y - 3z$ when $x = 3$, $y = 4$, and $z = -9$. (Lesson 2-4)  47.5

15. Simplify $(p^3)^2 \cdot p^{11}$. (Lesson 2-7)  $p^{17}$

16. The diameter of a red blood cell is about $7.4 \cdot 10^{-4}$ cm. Write this number in standard form. (Lesson 2-8)  0.00074 cm

17. What is the next term in the sequence? (Lesson 2-9)  $-10$

$$10, 6, 2, -2, -6, \ldots$$

**Math Online** mathmatters2.com/standardized_test

18. The formula that can be used to change degrees Celsius to degrees Fahrenheit is $F = \frac{9}{5}C + 32$. What is the Fahrenheit temperature that is equivalent to 30°C? (Lesson 3-1)  86°F

19. If $x + 2 = 6$, what is the value of $4x$? (Lesson 3-2)  16

20. Autumn withdrew an amount of money from her bank account. She spent one fourth for gasoline and had $90 left. How much money did she withdraw? (Lesson 3-4)  $120

21. Mr. Rollins drove 174 mi in 3 h. At that rate, how long will it take him to travel 290 mi? (Lesson 3-5)  5 hr

22. Write an inequality represented by the number line. (Lesson 3-6)  $x < 2$

## Part 3   Extended Response

Record your answers on a sheet of paper.
Show your work. 23–25. See additional answers.

23. Mrs. Anderson and her family are going to the zoo. She buys the same number of adult tickets as child tickets. Adult tickets cost $12 and child tickets cost $8. She also buys a T-shirt for $15. She spends $75 altogether. Write an equation for this situation. Solve the equation showing your work. Explain the meaning of the solution. (Lesson 3-4)

24. Leon is driving his car at a rate of 7 mi every 10 min. Hana is driving her car at a rate of 20 mi every 25 min. Who is driving his or her car faster? If the speed limit is 50 mi/h, is either vehicle exceeding the speed limit? Explain. (Lesson 3-5)

25. Explain why $x^2 = -4$ has no solution. (Lesson 3-8)

## Rubrics

The following rubrics are sample scoring guides for short response and extended response questions.

### Short Response

| Points | Description |
|--------|-------------|
| 2 | The student demonstrates a **thorough understanding** of the mathematics of the task. The response may contain minor flaws that do not detract from the demonstration of a thorough understanding. |
| 1 | The student has provided a response that is only **partially correct.** |
| 0 | The student has provided a **completely incorrect** solution or no response at all. |

### Extended Response

| Points | Description |
|--------|-------------|
| 4 | The student demonstrates a **thorough understanding** of the mathematics of the task. The response contains minor flaws that do not detract from the demonstration of a thorough understanding. |
| 3 | The student demonstrates an **understanding** of the mathematics of the task. The response is essentially correct and demonstrates an essential but less than thorough understanding of the mathematics. |
| 2 | The student has demonstrated only a **partial understanding** of the mathematics of the task. Although the student may have used the correct approach to a solution or may have provided a correct solution, the work lacks an essential understanding of the underlying mathematical concepts. |
| 1 | The student has demonstrated a **very limited understanding** of the mathematics of the task. The response is incomplete and exhibits many flaws. |
| 0 | The student has provided a **completely incorrect** solution or no response at all. |

## ADDITIONAL ANSWERS

23. 
$$12x + 8x + 15 = 75$$
$$20x + 15 = 75 \qquad \text{Combine like terms.}$$
$$20x + 15 - 15 = 75 - 15 \qquad \text{Subtract 15 from both sides.}$$
$$20x = 60$$
$$\frac{20x}{20} = \frac{60}{20} \qquad \text{Divide both sides by 20.}$$
$$x = 3$$

The solution 3 means that Mrs. Anderson bought 3 adult tickets and 3 child tickets.

24. 20 mi every 25 min is the same as 4 mi every 5 min or 8 mi every 10 min. Since 8 mi in 10 min is more than 7 mi in 10 min, Hana is driving faster. 7 mi every 10 min is the same as 42 mi every 60 min or 42 mi/h. 4 mi every 5 min is the same as 48 mi every 60 min or 48 mi/h. Neither of the drivers is driving above the speed limit.

25. Answers will vary. Since $x$ is being squared, the resulting sign must be positive. Therefore, it cannot equal $-4$.

# Chapter Overview

## Probability

| Lesson | Lesson Objectives | Pacing (days) | NCTM Standards | State/Local Objectives |
|---|---|---|---|---|
| 4-1 | **Experiments and Probabilities** *(pp. 150–153)*<br>• Use experiments to collect data.<br>• Use data to find experimental probabilities. | 1 | 5, 6, 9, 10 | |
| 4-2 | **Problem Solving Skills: Simulations** *(pp. 154–155)*<br>• Solve a problem using simulations.<br>• Solve a problem by acting it out. | 1 | 5, 6, 9, 10 | |
| 4-3 | **Sample Spaces and Theoretical Probability** *(pp. 158–161)*<br>• Determine sample spaces using various methods.<br>• Find theoretical probabilities. | 1 | 5, 6, 9, 10 | |
| 4-4 | **Probability of Compound Events** *(pp. 162–165)*<br>• Find probabilities of compound events.<br>• Explore mutually exclusive compound events. | 2 | 5, 6, 9, 10 | |
| 4-5 | **Independent and Dependent Events** *(pp. 168–171)*<br>• Find probabilities of dependent events.<br>• Find the probability of independent events. | 2 | 5, 6, 9, 10 | |
| 4-6 | **Permutations of a Set** *(pp. 172–175)*<br>• Find the number of permutations of a set. | 2 | 5, 6, 9, 10 | |
| 4-7 | **Combinations of a Set** *(pp. 178–181)*<br>• Find the number of combinations of a set. | 2 | 5, 6, 9, 10 | |
| Review | | 1 | | |
| Testing | | 1 | | |

**Key to NCTM Standards:**

*1=Number & Operations, 2=Algebra, 3=Geometry,*
*4=Measurement, 5=Data Analysis & Probability,*
*6=Problem Solving, 7=Reasoning & Proof,*
*8=Communication, 9=Connections, 10=Representation*

**Pacing:** Suggestions for the year can be found on page xvi.

## What's MATH Got To Do With It? Real-Life Math Videos

*What's Math Got To Do With It?* Real-Life Math Videos
engage students, showing them how math is used
in everyday situations. Use *Algebra 1* Video 4 with
this chapter.

# Chapter Resource Manager

Timesaving Tools
**TeacherWorks**™
**All-In-One Planner
and Resource Center**
See page xiii.

**FAST FILE** — Chapter 4 Resource Masters

| Reteaching Activities | Extra Practice | Enrichment | Assessment | Basic Mathematics Review | Study Skills Activities | Lesson Warm-Ups Transparencies | Teaching Transparencies | Technology Activities | Materials Needed |
|---|---|---|---|---|---|---|---|---|---|
| 107 | 108 | 109 | | | 10 | 15 | | | thumbtacks, calculator |
| 110 | 111 | 112 | | | | 15 | | 4-2 | coin, standard deck of playing cards, graphing calculator |
| 113 | 114 | 115 | | | 13 | 16 | RF-17 | | calculator |
| 116 | 117 | 118 | | | | 16 | RF-18 | | calculator |
| 119 | 120 | 121 | | | | 17 | RF-18 | | calculator |
| 122 | 123 | 124 | | | 19 | 17 | RF-19 | 4-6 | coins (penny, nickel, dime, quarter), calculator |
| 125 | 126 | 127 | 131–137 | | | 18 | RF-20 | 4-7 | calculator |

**Quick Review Math Handbook, Book 2**

hot **words**
hot **topics**

| *MathMatters 2* Lesson(s) | Hot Topic Lesson(s) |
|---|---|
| 4-1 | 4-1, 4-6 |
| 4-2 | 4-1 |
| 4-3 | 4-5, 4-6 |
| 4-4, 4-5 | 4-6 |
| 4-6, 4-7 | 4-5 |

# Content and Connections

## MathMatters 2
## Chapter 4 Highlights

Use experiments to collect data. (4-1)

Use data to find experimental probabilities. (4-1)

Solve a problem using simulations. (4-2)

Determine sample spaces using various methods. (4-3)

Find theoretical probabilities. (4-3)

Find probabilities of compound events. (4-4)

Find the probabilities of independent and dependent events. (4-5)

Find the number of permutations of a set. (4-6)

Find the number of combinations of a set. (4-7)

## Connections to the Past

**MM1 (Ch. 1):** Choose a sampling procedure and interpret survey results.

**MM1 (Ch. 10):** Find experimental probabilities.

**MM1 (Ch. 10):** Simulate an experiment using a graphing calculator.

**MM1 (Ch. 10):** Use a tree diagram to find possible outcomes in a sample space.

**MM1 (Ch. 10):** Find the probability of an event.

**MM1 (Ch. 10):** Find the probability of an event.

**MM1 (Ch. 10):** Find the probabilities of independent and dependent events.

**MM1 (Ch. 10):** Use the counting principle to find the number of outcomes.

**MM1 (Ch. 10):** Use the counting principle to find the number of outcomes.

## Connections to the Future

**MM3 (Ch. 9):** Find experimental probabilities.

**MM3 (Ch. 9):** Find experimental probabilities.

**MM3 (Ch. 9):** Solve a problem using simulations.

**MM3 (Ch. 9):** Determine sample spaces using various methods.

**MM3 (Ch. 9):** Find theoretical probabilities.

**MM3 (Ch. 9):** Find the probabilities of compound events.

**MM3 (Ch. 9):** Find the probabilities of independent and dependent events.

**MM3 (Ch. 9):** Find the number of permutations of a set.

**MM3 (Ch. 9):** Find the number of combinations of a set.

Key

| | |
|---|---|
| PC | = Previous Course |
| MM1 | = *MathMatters 1* |
| MM2 | = *MathMatters 2* |
| MM3 | = *MathMatters 3* |

## Connecting the Strands

| NCTM Strand | Lesson(s) |
|---|---|
| Data Analysis & Probability | 4-1, 4-2, 4-3, 4-4, 4-5, 4-6, 4-7 |
| Problem Solving | 4-1, 4-2, 4-3, 4-4, 4-5, 4-6, 4-7 |
| Connections | 4-1, 4-2, 4-3, 4-4, 4-5, 4-6, 4-7 |
| Representation | 4-1, 4-2, 4-3, 4-4, 4-5, 4-6, 4-7 |

# Ongoing Assessment and Intervention

| | Type | Student Edition | Teacher Resources | Technology/Internet |
|---|---|---|---|---|
| **INTERVENTION** | Ongoing | Are You Ready?, pp. 148–149 Check Understanding, pp. 151, 159, 163, 169 Review and Practice Your Skills, pp. 156–157, 166–167, 176–177 Mid-Chapter Quiz, p. 167 | Lesson Warm-Ups Transparencies, pp. WU-15, WU-16, WU-17, WU-18 Quick Assessment, *ATE* pp. 149, 152, 155, 160, 164, 170, 180 | mathmatters2.com/extra_ examples mathmatters2.com/self_check_quiz |
| | Mixed Review | pp. 153, 155, 161, 165, 171, 175, 181 | | |
| **ASSESSMENT** | Error Analysis | You Make the Call, pp. 155, 165, 181 Error Alert, p. 175 | Teaching Tip, *ATE* pp. 176, 182 | |
| | Standardized Test Practice | pp. 186–187 Preparing for Standardized Tests, pp. 627–644 | Standardized Test Practice, *CRM* pp. 135–137 | mathmatters2.com/standardized_test |
| | Open-Ended Assessment | Chapter Investigation, pp. 147, 161, 171, 181, 184 | Chapter Investigation, *ATE* p. 184 Alternative Assessment, *ATE* p. 185 | |
| | Chapter Assessment | Chapter Review, pp. 182–184 Chapter Assessment, p. 185 | Multiple-Choice Tests (Forms A and B), *CRM* pp. 131–134 | mathmatters2.com/chapter_assessment |

**Key to Abbreviations:** *ATE* = Annotated Teacher's Edition, *CRM* = Chapter Resource Masters

## Additional Intervention

***Basic Mathematics Review*** includes 80 lessons, consisting of an instructional page and a test page. This workbook also features a pretest, posttest, table of measurement equivalents, and calculator appendices.

## ExamView® Pro

Use ExamView® Pro Testmaker CD-ROM to:
- Create **multiple versions** of tests.
- Create **modified** tests for *inclusion* students with one mouse click.
- **Edit** existing questions and **add** your own questions.
- Build tests aligned with **state standards** using built-in **state curriculum correlations**.
- Change **English** tests to **Spanish** with one mouse click and vice versa.

# Chapter Opener

## NCTM Standards/Strands
■ Algebra
■ Data Analysis & Probability

## Vocabulary
probability          outcome

## Theme Connections
*Game Theory* is a mathematical analysis of any situation involving a conflict of interest, with the intent of indicating the optimal choices that, under given conditions, will lead to a desired outcome. Although game theory has roots in the study of such amusements as checkers or ticktacktoe, it also involves more serious conflicts of interest arising in such fields as sociology and military science.

In game theory, a *move* is the way in which the game progresses. A number cube or number wheel often determine a given move, the probabilities of which are calculable. *Payoff* refers to what happens at the end of a game. If money is the payoff, its amount may be predetermined by percentages calculated on the odds of winning.

## Career Opportunities
Many careers require understanding of the principles of probability. Two such careers are highlighted in the MathWorks features. Others include: electronic-game designer, game theorist, economist, political scientist, military strategist.
■ Baseball player, page 157
■ Board game designer, page 177

## Internet Connection

### Theme Activities
Mathmatters2.com/chapter_theme provides links to the Internet that will help students gather information about the use of math in the real world, particularly data and measures. To search for additional addresses, begin a search of *games*. Then within that search, use key words that will call up specific types of games, such as *electronic games,*

# Probability

## THEME: Games

**A**t some point during the last week, have you said, "Chances are...?" Chances are the answer to that question is yes. Chance, also referred to as "likelihood," means the probability something will occur. Many events in your life are affected by probability.

People often find taking a chance as a form of entertainment. From children to adults, people enjoy playing card games, board games, electronic games, and sports games. Knowing the probability of winning a game makes game play exciting.

- **Baseball players** (page 157) are successful based on their game statistics. Coaches use the calculated probability of getting a hit to help establish a batting lineup.

- **Board Game designers** (page 177) use probability to build games of strategy, knowledge and nonsense. The board layout, game pieces and winning strategy must come together using sample spaces, permutations and probability.

**Math Online**
mathmatters2.com/chapter_theme

board games, card games, lotteries. In small groups, students can brainstorm other key words.

### Chapter Investigation
Use the Internet and other resources to locate additional information about games.

### As a Chapter Project
The goal of this project is for students to design a game of chance and calculate the probabilities of various outcomes within the game. Students can use the Group Project Planner on page 129 and the Project Planning Calendar on page 130 in the Chapter 4 Resource Masters to complete the project. Benchmarks **a**, **b**, and **c** should be completed after the lesson listed in parentheses has been studied. Benchmark **d** should be completed at the end of the chapter.

# Nested Shapes

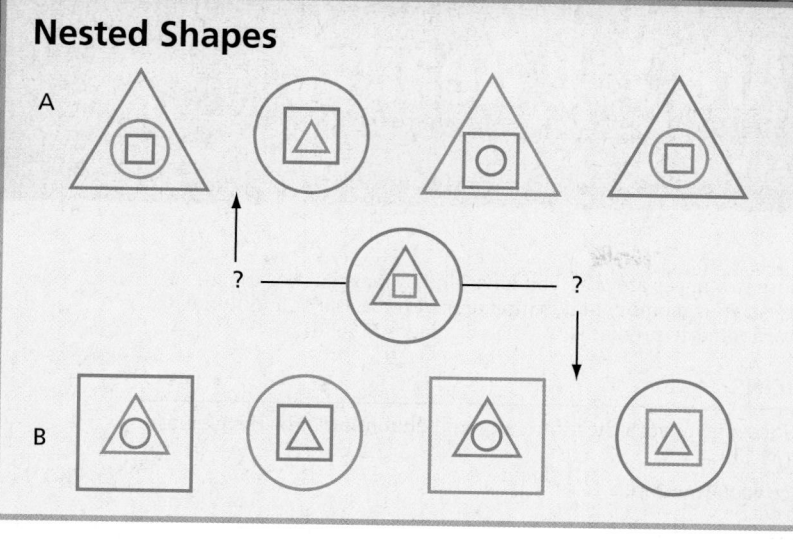

A

B

## Data Activity: Nested Shapes

**Use the figures above for Questions 1–5.**

1. Identify the three shapes, colors and sizes that make up each nested figure.  *Shapes: square, triangle, circle; colors: red, green, blue; sizes: small, medium, large.*

2. Explain any similarities among the figures in group A.
*Sample answer: Each figure contains a triangle, circle, and square.*

3. Explain any similarities among the figures in group B.
*Sample answer: All red figures lie within the green figure.*

4. Does the figure in the middle belong in group A or in group B?
*Group A*

5. Name some board games you have played. How was the game board marked? Did geometric shapes appear on the board or on the playing pieces? Did geometric shapes affect the way in which the game was played?  *Answers will vary.*

## CHAPTER INVESTIGATION

Many popular games rely on the principles of probability and chance to determine outcomes. For example, in card games, being dealt a particular hand can be thought of as an event. As such, that event has a certain likelihood of occurring, which is its probability.

### *Working Together*

Design your own game of chance and calculate the probabilities of various outcomes within the game. Use the Chapter Investigation icons throughout the chapter to guide you in the design of your game.

Chapter 4 **Probability** 147

# Data Activity

Board games are among favored forms of small-group entertainment.

Applications of game theory are wide-ranging and account for steadily growing interest in the subject. Aspects of game theory were first explored by the French mathematician Émile Borel, who wrote several papers on games of chance and theories of play. The acknowledged father of game theory, however, is the Hungarian-American mathematician John von Neumann, who in a series of papers in the 1920s and '30s established the mathematical framework for all subsequent theoretical developments.

## Extend the Data Activity
**Student Portfolio** Students may research how game theory distinguishes different varieties of games, depending on the number of players and the circumstances of play in the game itself. Or, students can research how game theory is used in a specialized area. For example, game theory has been applied to studying the distribution of power in legislative procedures.

# Chapter Investigation

## As an Overarching Problem
Display examples of several games of chance. Include the rules or a brief description with each game, as well as the items needed to play the game. Discuss the rules for different games and ask students how they think the rules were created. Students will continue to work on the investigation as they complete the exercises identified by the Chapter Investigation icon that is found throughout the chapter. These exercises will guide students through the task described in *Working Together*. Encourage students to keep all of their work on the Investigation together. Have students use the suggestions in the Chapter Investigation Extension to summarize their work.

See page 146 for Chapter Investigation as a Chapter Project.

## Project Planning Calendar

Name _____ Date _____

**CHAPTER 4 PROJECT PLANNING CALENDAR**

Benchmarks
a. Choose a format for your chance game. This may include drawing cards from a deck, rolling a number cube, spinning a spinner or some other event. Your game should include at least two events. *(Lesson 4-3)*
b. Determine how the turns of your game are played and assign point values to possible outcomes. The less likely an outcome is to occur, the more valuable it should be. Decide how the game will begin and be won, if there are free turns, if there are penalties and other aspects of the game. *(Lesson 4-5)*
c. Create a set of rules for your game. Include a list ...

PROJECT GOAL
To design a game of chance and calculate the probabilities of various outcomes.

## Group Project Planner

Name _____ Date _____

**CHAPTER 4 GROUP PROJECT PLANNER**

Assignment _____ Objective _____
_____ _____
_____ _____

Group Members          Assigned Roles
1) _____
2) _____
3) _____
4) _____
5) _____

Chapter 4 **Opener** 147

# Refresher Skills

The skills on these two pages are skills that have been presented in earlier chapters of this book or in previous math courses. Continuous review of basic math skills will make stronger math students. These skills are identified as necessary to be successful in Chapter 4.

## Skills Correlation Chart

| Skill | Lesson Number |
|---|---|
| Reducing Fractions | 4-1, 4-2, 4-3, 4-4, 4-5 |
| Area | 4-1 |
| Sets and Venn Diagrams | 4-4, 4-5 |

## Vocabulary

set
subset, ⊆
roster notation, { }
complement of a set
union of two sets, ∪
intersection of two sets, ∩
the null set, ∅
Venn diagram

## Chalkboard Examples

### Reducing Fractions

Reduce $\frac{56}{84}$.

$\frac{56}{84} = \frac{56 \div 28}{84 \div 28}$ or $\frac{2}{3}$

### Area
Find the area of each figure.

a.
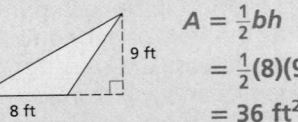

$A = \frac{1}{2}bh$
$= \frac{1}{2}(8)(9)$
$= 36 \text{ ft}^2$

b.
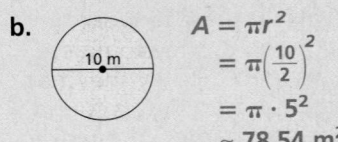

$A = \pi r^2$
$= \pi\left(\frac{10}{2}\right)^2$
$= \pi \cdot 5^2$
$\approx 78.54 \text{ m}^2$

---

# 4 Are You Ready?

### Refresh Your Math Skills for Chapter 4

The skills on these two pages are ones you have already learned. Use the examples to refresh your memory and complete the exercises. For additional practice on these and more prerequisite skills, see pages 576–584.

## REDUCING FRACTIONS

To reduce fractions, divide both the numerator and denominator by the greatest common factor (GCF).

**Examples**    Reduce each fraction.

$\frac{18}{32} = \frac{9}{16}$    The GCF is 2.      $\frac{20}{32} = \frac{5}{8}$    The GCF is 4.

Reduce each fraction.

1. $\frac{9}{12}$   $\frac{3}{4}$    2. $\frac{24}{32}$   $\frac{3}{4}$    3. $\frac{28}{32}$   $\frac{7}{8}$    4. $\frac{28}{56}$   $\frac{1}{2}$

5. $\frac{25}{80}$   $\frac{5}{16}$    6. $\frac{15}{48}$   $\frac{5}{16}$    7. $\frac{28}{64}$   $\frac{7}{16}$    8. $\frac{18}{30}$   $\frac{3}{5}$

9. $\frac{27}{72}$   $\frac{3}{8}$    10. $\frac{35}{42}$   $\frac{5}{6}$    11. $\frac{15}{60}$   $\frac{1}{4}$    12. $\frac{91}{156}$   $\frac{7}{12}$

## AREA

**Examples**    Use the following formulas to find the area of a figure.

| Figure | Area formula |
|---|---|
| square | $A = s^2$ |
| rectangle | $A = b \cdot h$ |
| triangle | $A = \frac{1}{2}b \cdot h$ |
| parallelogram | $A = b \cdot h$ |
| circle | $A = \pi r^2$ |

Find the area of each figure. Round to the nearest hundredth.

13.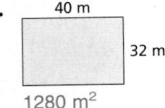
40 m   32 m
1280 m²

14.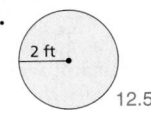
2 ft
12.57 ft²

15.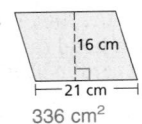
16 cm   21 cm
336 cm²

16.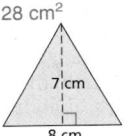
28 cm²
7 cm
8 cm

Find the area of each figure with the given dimensions. Round to the nearest hundredth.

17. square: $s = 5$ ft   25 ft²

18. triangle: $b = 6.2$ cm, $h = 3.2$ cm   9.92 cm²

19. circle: $r = 3$ in.   28.27 in.²

20. parallelogram: $b = 2$ m, $h = 6$ m   12 m²

21. rectangle: $b = \frac{2}{3}$ yd, $h = \frac{3}{4}$ yd   $\frac{1}{2}$ yd²

22. circle: $d = 6$ cm   28.27 cm²

## SETS AND VENN DIAGRAMS

It will be helpful to review sets and Venn diagrams so that you can use them to compute probability.

**Examples**   The following lists several symbols used as set notation.

| U | Universal set, or all the elements. | $U = \{1, 2, 3, 4, 5, 6\}$ |
|---|---|---|
| { } | Roster notation | $\{1, 2, 3, 4, 5, 6\}$ |
| $\in$ | "is an element of" | $3 \in \{1, 2, 3\}$ |
| $\notin$ | "is not an element of" | $8 \notin \{1, 2, 3, 4\}$ |
| $\subseteq$ | "is a subset of" | $\{1, 2, 3\} \subseteq \{1, 2, 3, 4, 5, 6\}$ |
| $\not\subseteq$ | "is not a subset of" | $\{1, 2, 3\} \not\subseteq \{1, 2, 4, 6\}$ |
| $\varnothing$ | the null set, which has no elements | $\{ \}$ |

**Venn diagrams** can help you see the sets and their relationships more clearly.

*Complement of a set:* The subset of all elements of a universal set that are not elements of subset *A*.

$A = \{1, 2, 3, 4\}$        $A' = \{5, 6\}$

*Union of two sets:* All the elements of two sets.

$A = \{1, 2, 3, 4\}, B = \{4, 5, 6\}$

$A \cup B = \{1, 2, 3, 4, 5, 6\}$

*Intersection of two sets:* The elements that two sets have in common.

$A = \{1, 2, 3, 4\}, B = \{4, 5, 6\}$

$A \cap B = \{4\}$

**Use roster notation to represent the sets named when $U = \{1, 2, 3, 4, 5, 6, 7, 8, 9\}$, $A = \{1, 4, 5, 7\}, B = \{2, 3, 5, 8\}$, and $C = \{5, 7, 8, 9\}$.**

**23.** $A \cup B$
{1, 2, 3, 4, 5, 7, 8}

**24.** $A \cup C$
{1, 4, 5, 7, 8, 9}

**25.** $B \cup C$
{2, 3, 5, 7, 8, 9}

**26.** $A \cap B$  {5}

**27.** $A \cap C$  {5, 7}

**28.** $B \cap C$
{5, 8}

**29.** $A'$  {2, 3, 6, 8, 9}

**30.** $B'$  {1, 4, 6, 7, 9}

**31.** $C'$
{1, 2, 3, 4, 6}

**Use the diagram to find the set named. List the elements in roster notation.**   For 32–40, see additional answers.

**32.** $A \cup B$

**33.** $A \cup C$

**34.** $A'$

**35.** $B \cup C$

**36.** $A \cap B$

**37.** $B'$

**38.** $A \cap C$

**39.** $B \cap C$

**40.** $(A \cup B)'$

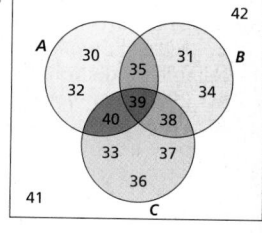

---

## Sets and Venn Diagrams

Use roster notation to represent the sets named when $A = \{$nonnegative even integers$\}$ and $B = \{$nonnegative multiples of 3$\}$.

**a.** $A \cap B$          **b.** $A \cup B$

First write a roster of each set.

$A = \{0, 2, 4, 6, 8, 10, 12, 14, 16, 18, 20, 22, 24, \ldots\}$

$B = \{0, 3, 6, 9, 12, 15, 18, 21, 24, \ldots\}$

$A \cap B = \{0, 6, 12, 18, 24, \ldots\}$ or {nonnegative even multiples of 3}

$A \cup B = \{0, 2, 3, 4, 6, 8, 9, 10, 12, 14, 15, \ldots\}$ or {0, positive even integers, and positive odd multiples of 3}

## Refresher Wrap-up

### QUICK ASSESSMENT

Ask the following questions to determine if students have mastered the basic skills reviewed on these pages.

**If you know the elements of two sets, describe how you would list the elements in each of the following.**

1. the intersection of the two sets   list only those elements that are in both sets

2. the union of the two sets   list all the elements in each set, writing only once the elements that are common to both sets

### ADDITIONAL PRACTICE

Refer to the Prerequisite Skills lessons beginning on page 576 for more practice.

### ADDITIONAL ANSWERS

**32.** {30, 31, 32, 34, 35, 38, 39, 40}

**33.** {30, 32, 33, 35, 36, 37, 38, 39, 40}

**34.** {31, 33, 34, 36, 37, 38, 41, 42}

**35.** {31, 33, 34, 35, 36, 37, 38, 39, 40}

**36.** {35, 39}

**37.** {30, 32, 33, 36, 37, 40, 41, 42}

**38.** {39, 40}

**39.** {38, 39}

**40.** {33, 36, 37, 41, 42}

---

## Differentiated Instruction

**VISUAL LEARNERS** To assist in understanding and remembering the meanings of *intersection, union,* and *complement* as applied to sets, some students may find it helpful to view diagrams such as those below.

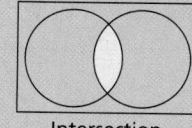

Intersection of sets

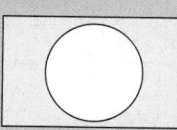

Union of sets          The complement of a set

### Vocabulary

experiment
relative frequency
experimental probability

### Tools/Materials Needed

thumbtack          calculator

### Lesson Resources

Warm-up Transparency 15
Reteaching 4-1
Extra Practice 4-1
Enrichment 4-1

## Getting Started

### 5-MINUTE WARM-UP

**Evaluate each expression. Express each answer as a decimal and as a percent.**

1. $\frac{147}{245}$   0.6 or 60%

2. $\frac{609}{609 + 116}$   0.84 or 84%

3. $\frac{12 + 28 + 15}{250}$   0.22 or 22%

### Introduction to Lesson 4-1

After students have calculated

the ratio $\frac{\text{tack landed point down}}{\text{total number of times}}$, have

them calculate $\frac{\text{tack landed point up}}{\text{total number of times}}$.

Ask students to draw a conclusion about the two ratios.   **Their sum is 1.**

---

# 4-1 Experiments and Probabilities

**Goals**
- Use experiments to collect data.
- Use data to find experimental probabilities.

**Applications**   Music, Market research, Games, Statistics, Probability

**When a coin is tossed, it will either land heads up or tails up. Prepare a table to tally the number of times a coin lands heads up and tails up.**   For 1–3, answers will vary.

| Event | Tally | Results |
|-------|-------|---------|
| Heads up | ■ | ■ |
| Tails up | ■ | ■ |

1. Toss a coin 20 times. Record the results in the table.

2. Find the ratio of the number of times the coin lands tails up to the total number of times tossed. How does your ratio compare with the ratios of other groups?

3. Find the total number of times a coin lands tails up for your entire class, and divide by the total number of times a coin was tossed. What is the ratio? Is it more likely that a tossed coin will land heads up or tails up?

## ■ BUILD UNDERSTANDING

Most real-world situations involve more than one possible outcome. Often these outcomes are not equally likely. While you cannot be sure of the outcome in advance, an experiment can help you find the likelihood of one particular outcome occurring.

An **experiment** is an activity that is used to produce data that can be observed and recorded. The **relative frequency** of an outcome compares the number of times the outcome occurs to the total number of observations.

The **experimental probability** represents an estimate of the likelihood of an event, $E$, or desired outcome.

**Experimental Probability**   $P(E) = \dfrac{\text{number of observations favorable to } E}{\text{total number of observations}}$

Suppose you want to find whether a music department will be a successful addition to a store. If you ask 10 of the store's customers about the proposed music department, you would not have enough data to make a reliable prediction. But if you ask 2000 customers each week for a month, your prediction will be more accurate.

| | Number of positive responses | Total number questioned | Relative frequency of positive responses |
|---|---|---|---|
| Week 1 | 384 | 2000 | $\frac{384}{2000} = 0.192$ |
| Week 2 | 420 | 2000 | $\frac{420}{2000} = 0.21$ |
| Week 3 | 396 | 2000 | $\frac{396}{2000} = 0.198$ |
| Week 4 | 412 | 2000 | $\frac{412}{2000} = 0.206$ |

## Differentiated Instruction

**AUDITORY LEARNERS** Have students verbalize the meaning of ratio and explain why probability is a ratio.   A *ratio* is a comparison of two numbers by division. Using division, *probability* compares the number of successful outcomes to the total number of outcomes.

From the results in the table, the experimental probability that a customer will shop at the music department is about 0.20, or 1 out of 5.

## Example 1

**MARKET RESEARCH** The table shows the number of customers and skate rentals at a roller-skating rink during a week of summer vacation.

| | Customers | Pairs of skates rented |
|---|---|---|
| Monday | 192 | 130 |
| Tuesday | 328 | 212 |
| Wednesday | 296 | 222 |
| Thursday | 325 | 195 |
| Friday | 456 | 292 |

**a.** What is the experimental probability that a customer will rent skates on a Wednesday?

**b.** What is the experimental probability that a customer will rent skates on a Thursday?

### Solution

For both parts a and b, use the experimental probability formula.

$$P(\text{customers renting skates}) = \frac{\text{pairs of skates rented}}{\text{number of customers}}$$

**a.** $P(\text{customers renting skates on Wednesday}) = \frac{222}{296} = 0.75$
The probability of a customer renting skates on Wednesday is 0.75, or $\frac{3}{4}$. This means that for every four customers on a given Wednesday, three of them will probably rent skates.

**b.** $P(\text{customers renting skates on Thursday}) = \frac{195}{325} = 0.6$
The probability of a customer renting skates on Thursday is 0.6, or $\frac{3}{5}$.

**Check Understanding**

Relative frequencies allow you to make statements that estimate probabilities.

What can you conclude if the relative frequency of an outcome is 1? 0?

1: all the observations had that outcome;
0: none of the observations had that outcome

## Example 2

According to the table, what is the probability that a July customer is over 40 years old?

**Customers by Age**

| | 12-18 | 19-25 | 26-40 | 41-55 | Over 55 |
|---|---|---|---|---|---|
| June | 961 | 930 | 749 | 711 | 220 |
| July | 812 | 748 | 819 | 507 | 164 |
| August | 645 | 702 | 736 | 499 | 217 |

### Solution

To find the experimental probability, find the total number of July customers and the number of July customers over 40 years old.

$$P(\text{July customers over 40}) = \frac{\text{July customers over 40 years old}}{\text{total number of July customers}}$$

$$= \frac{507 + 164}{812 + 748 + 819 + 507 + 164}$$

$$= \frac{671}{3050}$$

$$= 0.22$$

The probability that a customer is over 40 years old in July is 0.22.

Some probability problems can be solved by using an *area model*. Suppose that a region $A$ contains a smaller region $B$. The probability ($P$) that a randomly chosen point in $A$ is in $B$ is given by:

$$P = \frac{\text{area of } B}{\text{area of } A}$$

**Math Online** mathmatters2.com/extra_examples

Lesson 4-1 **Experiments and Probabilities** | 151

---

## Chalkboard Examples

### Supplementary Example 1
**MARKET RESEARCH** A manufacturer gave samples of a new lipstick and asked the women who received the samples to rate the lipstick according to certain standards of appeal. The results of the survey are displayed in the histogram below.

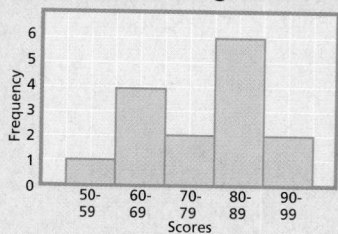

What is the experimental probability that a woman who received a lipstick sample gave it a rating of at least 80?

$$P(\geq 80) = \frac{\text{Number of ratings} \geq 80}{\text{total number of ratings}}$$

$$= \frac{6 + 2}{15} = \frac{8}{15}$$

$$\approx 0.53$$

The probability that a woman who received a lipstick sample gave it a rating of at least 80 is about 0.53. This means that about 53% (just over half) of the women surveyed gave the lipstick a rating of 80 or more.

### Supplementary Example 2
What is the probability that a dart thrown at this board will land in the "bull's-eye"?

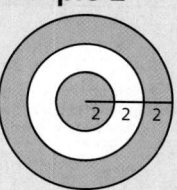

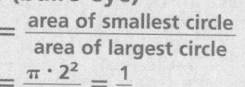

$P(\text{bull's-eye})$

$$= \frac{\text{area of smallest circle}}{\text{area of largest circle}}$$

$$= \frac{\pi \cdot 2^2}{\pi \cdot 6^2} = \frac{1}{9}$$

The probability that the dart will land in the bull's-eye is $\frac{1}{9}$.

---

## Teaching Tip

In Example 1, make sure the students understand that the number of customers for the day specified is the total number of observations in the experiment.

As an extension of Example 2, ask students to tell how they would find the probability that a summer customer is 18 years old or younger. Add the number of customers in the age group 12–18 for the three months and divide by the total number of customers for the three months.

Example 3

**What is the probability that a thrown dart will hit the yellow region?**

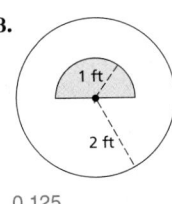

4 ft

1 ft

**Solution**

Find the areas of the yellow region and the entire region and divide.

$$P(\text{yellow}) = \frac{\text{area of yellow region}}{\text{area of entire region}}$$

$$= \frac{\pi \cdot 1^2}{\pi \cdot 4^2} = \frac{\cancel{\pi} \cdot 1}{\cancel{\pi} \cdot 16} = \frac{1}{16} \qquad \text{Use the formula for area of a circle, } A = \pi r^2.$$

The probability that the dart will hit the yellow region is $\frac{1}{16}$.

## TRY THESE EXERCISES

1. At a fork in a hiking trail, 82 people take the lake trail while 43 people take the mountain trail. What is the probability of a hiker taking the lake trail? ≈ 0.66

2. **RETAIL** In June, 243 customers at an optician's office buy contact lenses and 207 buy glasses. Find the probability that a customer will buy glasses. 0.46

3. The ratio of boys to girls in a high school is 2 : 3. What is the probability that the first student to arrive at school one day is a boy? a girl? 0.4, 0.6

4. What is the probability of a correct answer if 54 are correct out of 180? 0.3

**Find the probability that a point selected at random lies in the shaded region. Round to the nearest hundredth.**

5.

5 m
2 m
5 m
5 m

0.71

6.

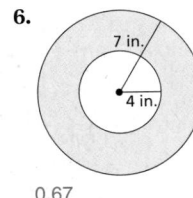

7 in.
4 in.

0.67

7.

3 m
5 m
7 m
2 m
7 m

0.31

8.

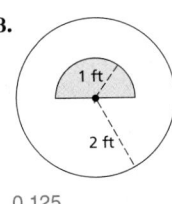

1 ft
2 ft

0.125

## PRACTICE EXERCISES • For Extra Practice, see page 596.

9. In a poll conducted to find students' favorite sports, 119 vote for football, 135 vote for baseball, 126 vote for volleyball and 160 vote for other sports. What is the probability that a student chooses baseball? 0.25

10. **STATISTICS** A survey of 500 students shows that the probability that a student's birthday is in April is 0.15. Of the boys surveyed, 29 have April birthdays. How many girls surveyed have April birthdays? 46

11. **WRITING MATH** In Example 2, the manager can use probability to plan a promotional campaign targeted at the age of the customer who visits the store the most in July. Choose either Example 1 or 3, and describe a benefit of knowing the probability. Answers will vary.

12. A circle with a 7-cm radius lies within a rectangle that is 22 cm by 21 cm. What is the probability that a point in the rectangle lies within the circle? ≈ 0.33

---

## Lesson Wrap-up

### QUICK ASSESSMENT

Ask the following question to determine if students understand the content presented in this lesson.

Explain how an experiment designed to predict probability works. **Possible answer: The experiment is performed many times, records of the results are kept, and then the results are analyzed.**

### ASSIGNMENT GUIDE

**Basic:** 1–20, 24
**Enriched:** 1–24

---

### Reteaching Worksheet 4-1

Name _____ Date _____

RETEACHING **4-1**

**EXPERIMENTS AND PROBABILITIES**

The **experimental probability** of an event $E$ can be estimated using this formula.

$$P(E) = \frac{\text{number of observations favorable to } E}{\text{total number of observations}}$$

Probabilities can be written as fractions, decimals or percents.

**Example**

The table at the right shows the number of customers at Terrific Travel Agency who booked cruises for their summer vacations.

What is the experimental probability that a customer will book a cruise in May?

| TERRIFIC TRAVEL AGENCY | | |
|---|---|---|
| Month | Customers | Cruises Booked |
| May | 510 | 102 |
| June | 564 | 151 |
| July | 406 | 140 |
| August | 458 | 109 |

**Solution**

$P(\text{customers booking cruises in May}) = \frac{\text{number of cruises booked in May}}{\text{number of customers in May}}$

$= \frac{102}{510} = \frac{1}{5} = 0.2$

In May, the experimental probability of a customer booking a cruise is $\frac{1}{5}$ or 0.2.

**✓ EXERCISES**

The table at the right shows the sales at Smartee's Department Store. Use the table for Exercises 1–6. Round answers to the nearest hundredth.

| SALES AT SMARTEE'S | | | | |
|---|---|---|---|---|
| Day of Week | Under $10 | $10–$29.99 | $30–$49.99 | over $50 |
| Wednesday | 65 | 162 | 76 | 47 |
| Thursday | 83 | 205 | 91 | 75 |
| Friday | 89 | 184 | 187 | 66 |
| Saturday | 115 | 170 | 258 | 101 |

1. On Friday, what is the probability that a customer at Smartee's will spend $30–$49.99? 0.36

2. On Wednesday, what is the probability that a customer will spend over $50? 0.13

3. On Thursday, what is the probability that a customer will spend at least $10? 0.82

4. On Saturday, what is the probability that a customer will spend less than $50? 0.84

5. Which is more likely, that a customer on Wednesday will spend over $50 or that a customer on Saturday will spend less than $10? less than $10 on Saturday

6. On which day is it most likely that a customer will spend $10–$29.99? Wednesday

---

## ADDITIONAL ANSWERS

24.

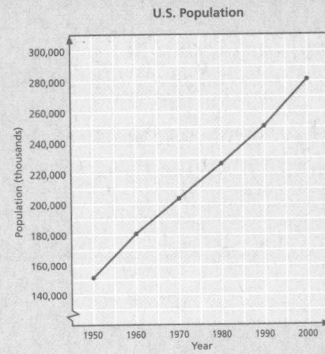

U.S. Population

Population (thousands)
300,000
280,000
260,000
240,000
220,000
200,000
180,000
160,000
140,000
1950 1960 1970 1980 1990 2000
Year

25.

Wind Speeds

| Miles per hour | Tally | Frequency |
|---|---|---|
| 1-3 | I | 1 |
| 4-7 | IIII | 4 |
| 8-12 | IIII III | 8 |
| 13-18 | III | 3 |
| 19-24 | III | 3 |
| 25-31 | II | 2 |
| 32-38 | III | 3 |
| 39-46 | | 0 |
| 47-54 | III | 3 |
| 55-63 | | 0 |
| 64-75 | | 0 |
| 775 | | 0 |

**Use the table for Exercises 13–15.**

**People Using the College Library**

| | Undergraduate students | Graduate students | Professors |
|---|---|---|---|
| Friday | 737 | 105 | 33 |
| Saturday | 588 | 132 | 30 |
| Sunday | 448 | 91 | 36 |

13. On Friday what is the probability that a person in the library is a graduate student? 0.12

14. On Saturday what is the probability that a person using the library is a professor? 0.04

15. On Sunday what is the probability that a person using the library is a professor? ≈ 0.06

**Find the probability that a point selected at random lies in the shaded region.**

16.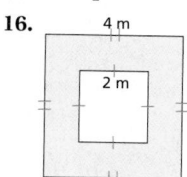
4 m
2 m
0.75

17.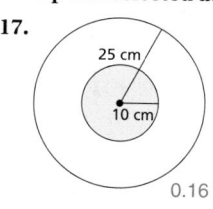
25 cm
10 cm
0.16

18.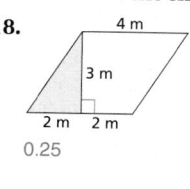
4 m
3 m
2 m  2 m
0.25

19.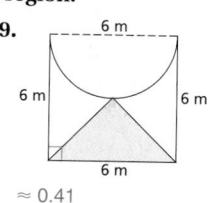
6 m
6 m  6 m
6 m
≈ 0.41

20. **MUSIC** Of the first 1200 people to buy tickets to a concert, 840 do not want the most expensive seats. What is the probability that the next ticket buyer wants one of the most expensive seats? 0.3

## ■ EXTENDED PRACTICE EXERCISES

21. **DATA FILE** Refer to the data on pet ownership on page 561. What is the probability of a household not owning a cat or a dog? ≈ 0.91

22. **WRITING MATH** Write a probability problem that can be solved by using an area model. Include a solution. Answers will vary.

23. At a picnic, a man loses his wallet in a square field that is 50 m on each side. Each person at the picnic searches an area 10 m². Assuming someone finds the wallet, what is the probability that the man who lost the wallet will be the one who finds it? 0.004

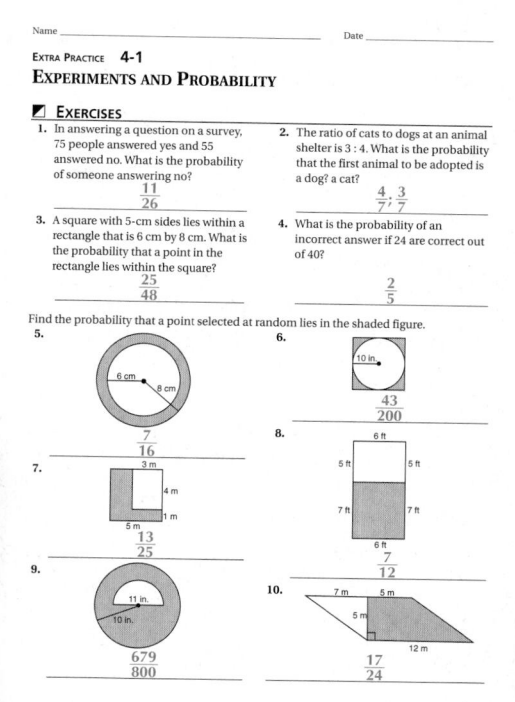

## ■ MIXED REVIEW EXERCISES

24. **DATA FILE** Refer to the U.S. population data on page 574. Make a line graph of only the census years and make it appear that the population varied greatly from decade to decade. (Lesson 1-7) See additional answers.

25. **DATA FILE** Refer to the data on wind speed on page 565. Make a frequency table for the following wind speeds (in miles per hour) using the Beaufort Scale intervals. (Lesson 1-3) See additional answers.

| | | | |
|---|---|---|---|
| 11 | 4 | 10 | 8 |
| 6 | 34 | 14 | 6 |
| 15 | 23 | 33 | 51 |
| 36 | 9 | 8 | 9 |
| 30 | 5 | 49 | 12 |
| 2 | 22 | 17 | 10 |

## Alternative Assessment

**STUDENT PORTFOLIO** Have students consider the following diagrams. Each has a shaded area drawn on a grid. For each case, ask students to find the probability that any point within the grid lies in the shaded area.

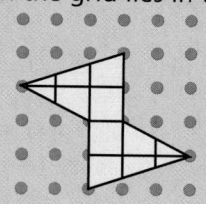

$P(\text{shaded area}) = \frac{7}{25}$

$P(\text{shaded area}) = \frac{7}{25}$

---

### Extra Practice Worksheet 4-1

Name _____ Date _____

EXTRA PRACTICE **4-1**
### EXPERIMENTS AND PROBABILITY

☑ **EXERCISES**

1. In answering a question on a survey, 75 people answered yes and 55 answered no. What is the probability of someone answering no? $\frac{11}{26}$

2. The ratio of cats to dogs at an animal shelter is 3 : 4. What is the probability that the first animal to be adopted is a dog? a cat? $\frac{4}{7}; \frac{3}{7}$

3. A square with 5-cm sides lies within a rectangle that is 6 cm by 8 cm. What is the probability that a point in the rectangle lies within the square? $\frac{25}{48}$

4. What is the probability of an incorrect answer if 24 are correct out of 40? $\frac{2}{5}$

**Find the probability that a point selected at random lies in the shaded figure.**

5. 6 cm 8 cm $\frac{7}{16}$

6. 10 in $\frac{43}{200}$

7. 3 m 4 m 1 m 5 m $\frac{13}{25}$

8. 6 ft 5 ft 5 ft 7 ft 7 ft 6 ft $\frac{7}{12}$

9. 11 in. 10 in. $\frac{679}{800}$

10. 7 m 5 m 5 m 12 m $\frac{17}{24}$

---

### Enrichment Worksheet 4-1

Name _____ Date _____

ENRICHMENT **4-1**
### TRIPLE TOSS

The table below summarizes the results when two number cubes are tossed.

| Sum of two number cubes | 2 | 3 | 4 | 5 | 6 | 7 | 8 | 9 | 10 | 11 | 12 |
|---|---|---|---|---|---|---|---|---|---|---|---|
| Number of ways | 1 | 2 | 3 | 4 | 5 | 6 | 5 | 4 | 3 | 2 | 1 |

Think about the sums and the number of ways to get each sum when you toss three number cubes.

☑ **EXERCISES**

1. How many different outcomes can there be when three number cubes are tossed? 216

2. Use the table above for two number cubes. Suppose the third number cube shows 1 with each of the sums in that table. Complete the table below.

| Third cube shows 1 | Sum of three number cubes | 3 | 4 | 5 | 6 | 7 | 8 | 9 | 10 | 11 | 12 | 13 |
|---|---|---|---|---|---|---|---|---|---|---|---|---|
| | Number of ways | 1 | 2 | 3 | 4 | 5 | 6 | 5 | 4 | 3 | 2 | 1 |

3. Suppose the third number cube shows 2 with each of the sums for two cubes. Complete the table below.

| Third cube shows 2 | Sum of three number cubes | 4 | 5 | 6 | 7 | 8 | 9 | 10 | 11 | 12 | 13 | 14 |
|---|---|---|---|---|---|---|---|---|---|---|---|---|
| | Number of ways | 1 | 2 | 3 | 4 | 5 | 6 | 5 | 4 | 3 | 2 | 1 |

4. Complete the table below to show the results for all the possible numbers on the third cube. Show the number of ways to get each sum.

| Number on third cube | | | | | | | Sum of all three number cubes | | | | | | | | | | |
|---|---|---|---|---|---|---|---|---|---|---|---|---|---|---|---|---|---|
| | 3 | 4 | 5 | 6 | 7 | 8 | 9 | 10 | 11 | 12 | 13 | 14 | 15 | 16 | 17 | 18 |
| 1 | 1 | 2 | 3 | 4 | 5 | 6 | 5 | 4 | 3 | 2 | 1 | | | | | |
| 2 | | 1 | 2 | 3 | 4 | 5 | 6 | 5 | 4 | 3 | 2 | 1 | | | | |
| 3 | | | 1 | 2 | 3 | 4 | 5 | 6 | 5 | 4 | 3 | 2 | 1 | | | |
| 4 | | | | 1 | 2 | 3 | 4 | 5 | 6 | 5 | 4 | 3 | 2 | 1 | | |
| 5 | | | | | 1 | 2 | 3 | 4 | 5 | 6 | 5 | 4 | 3 | 2 | 1 | |
| 6 | | | | | | 1 | 2 | 3 | 4 | 5 | 6 | 5 | 4 | 3 | 2 | 1 |
| Total number of ways → | 1 | 3 | 6 | 10 | 15 | 21 | 25 | 27 | 27 | 25 | 21 | 15 | 10 | 6 | 3 | 1 |

5. What is the sum of the *total number of ways*? 216

6. How do the number of ways of getting sums of 7 and 14 compare? The number of ways of getting the sums are the same.

7. What is the probability of getting a sum of 11? $\frac{1}{8}$

## Lesson Planning

### NCTM Standards/Strands
- Representation
- Data Analysis & Probability
- Problem Solving
- Connections

### Vocabulary

act it out          simulation

### Tools/Materials Needed

coin          graphing calculator
standard deck of playing cards

### Lesson Resources

Warm-up Transparency 15
Reteaching 4-2
Extra Practice 4-2
Enrichment 4-2
Technology Activities 4-2

## ASSIGNMENT GUIDE

**Basic:** 1–26
**Enriched:** 1–26

## Getting Started

### 5-MINUTE WARM-UP

**Solve for $n$ and check.**

1. $\frac{n}{150} = 0.22$   33

2. $0.06 = \frac{n}{1850}$   111

3. $\frac{4}{n} = \frac{27}{486}$   72

4. $\frac{64}{13} = \frac{1216}{n}$   247

**THE FIVE-STEP PLAN Read**—ask questions to help students understand the problem. **Plan**—guide students to related problems and previously mastered skills and strategies. **Solve**—students solve problem on their own. **Answer**—write the solution in a format that answers the question. **Check**—review work, check for reasonableness, and review strategy used.
**THE STRATEGY** *Act it out*—this strategy enables students to establish the given, recognize the constraints, and create an appropriate simulation.

---

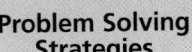

When you physically go through the motions described in a problem or you use objects to represent elements of the problem, you are using the **act it out** problem solving strategy.

In many cases, you can act out a complex probability problem through a simulation. A **simulation** is a model of a situation in which you carry out the trials, collect data and calculate probabilities. Simulations can be done using coins, number cubes, spinners or any method that involves random outcomes.

The manipulative you use should have the same number of outcomes as the number of possible outcomes. Computers and graphing utilities are useful when you need to produce many random numbers in a short amount of time.

### Problem Solving Strategies

Guess and check

Look for a pattern

Solve a simpler problem

Make a table, chart or list

Use a picture, diagram or model

✔ Act it out

Work backwards

Eliminate possibilities

Use an equation or formula

### Problem

**PART-TIME JOB** Two-thirds of the seniors at Central High School have part-time jobs. If three seniors are polled, what is the probability that at least one of them has a part-time job?

**a.** Design an experiment to simulate the situation.

**b.** Preform 20 trials of the experiment, and calculate the probability.

### Solve the Problem

**a.** To model a ratio of $\frac{2}{3}$, use a number cube. Since there are six outcomes on a number cube, write a ratio equivalent to $\frac{2}{3}$ with a denominator of 6.

$$\frac{2}{3} = \frac{4}{6}$$

Let 1, 2, 3 and 4 represent having a part-time job.
Let 5 and 6 represent not having a part-time job.
Since there are three seniors polled, roll three number cubes at a time.

**b.** The following results indicate the three numbers rolled for each trial. The asterisk (*) indicates trials containing at least one of the numbers 1, 2, 3, or 4.

| *251 | *213 | *264 | 556 | *343 | *422 | *152 | *125 | 555 | *562 |
|------|------|------|-----|------|------|------|------|-----|------|
| *361 | *661 | *242 | *354 | *246 | *265 | *445 | *546 | *221 | *345 |

Since 18 of the 20 trials resulted in at least one student that works part-time,

$$P(\text{at least 1 student works part-time}) = \frac{18}{20} = \frac{9}{10} = 90\%.$$

The simulation shows that if three seniors are polled at Central High School, the probability that at least one of them has a part-time job is 90%.

---

## ADDITIONAL ANSWERS

1. Use a coin to model gender. Let heads represent a girl and tails represent a boy. Since the family is planning to have 4 children, flip 4 coins at a time.

2. Use a number cube to model a students' chance of returning. Let an outcome of 1 represent a student not returning. Let outcomes of 2, 3, 4, or 5 represent a student returning. Disregard an outcome of 6. Since 5 freshman are polled at a time, throw 5 number cubes together.

4. Use a standard deck of cards to model a batting average of 0.250 $\left(\frac{250}{1000} = \frac{1}{4}\right)$.

Since the ratio of the number of clubs to the number of cards in a full deck is $\frac{1}{4}$, let drawing a club represent getting a hit. Drawing a card of any other suit represents getting no hit. Draw 10 cards, to simulate the players next 10 at-bats. Note whether these 10 cards contain exactly 3 clubs. Replace all 10 cards, shuffle, and repeat drawing 10 cards.

5. Use a number cube to model the chance for a cure. Let the outcomes 1, 3, and 5 to represent that the drug works. Let the outcomes 2 and 4 represent that the drug does not work. Disregard the outcome 6. Toss 2 number cubes at a time to represent the 2 patients chosen randomly.

**Describe a model that could be used to simulate each situation.**
For 1–2, models will vary. See additional answers for possible simulations.

1. The Bowers family is planning to have 4 children. Find the probability that there will be 2 boys and 2 girls.

2. At one university, a freshman has a 4 in 5 chance of returning his sophomore year. If 5 freshman are polled, what is the probability that 4 will return?

3. **CALCULATOR** Use a random number generator to find the probability in Exercise 2. Answers will vary.

**Describe a model for each situation. Perform 25 trials of the simulation and find the indicated probability.** For 4–8, models and experimental probabilities will vary. See additional answer for possible simulations.

4. **SPORTS** Gordon has a batting average of .250. In his next 10 times at bat, what is the probability that he gets exactly 3 hits?

5. **MEDICINE** A medicine has a 3 in 5 chance of curing the condition for which it is prescribed. If 2 patients are chosen at random to use the medicine, what is the probability that it will cure their condition?

6. A litter has 6 solid-colored kittens who are either black or white. What is the probability that there are 3 black and 3 white kittens?

7. **SPORTS** The likelihood that Tia will make a free throw in a basketball game is $\frac{2}{3}$. In her next 5 free throws, what is the probability that she will make 3?

8. At a stable, $\frac{1}{2}$ of the horses are brown and $\frac{1}{6}$ of the horses have braided manes. Design a model that uses two simulations to find the probability that a given horse is brown and has a braided mane.

9. **YOU MAKE THE CALL** To simulate a situation with two equally likely outcomes, Alex said you could only use a device with two outcomes, such as a coin. Jolon said you could also use a device that has more than two outcomes, such as a number cube. With whom do you agree? Explain. See additional answers.

10. **WRITING MATH** Explain an advantage of using the act it out strategy to solve a problem. See additional answers.

■ **MIXED REVIEW EXERCISES**

**Evaluate each expression when $a = \frac{1}{3}$, $b = -2$, and $c = 3$.** (Lesson 2-5)

11. $6a + 5b$  $-8$

12. $-2(4a - 3b)$  $-\frac{44}{3}$

13. $\frac{(0.4a - 0.2b)}{0.2c}$  $0.8\overline{8}$

14. $3(4b - 4c)$  $-60$

15. $\frac{(-5b - 2c)}{-4a}$  $-3$

16. $\frac{(3c + 5b)}{2}$  $-\frac{1}{2}$

17. $-2(a + b + c)$  $-\frac{8}{3}$

18. $\frac{(4.8c - 2.4b)}{1.2a}$  $48$

**Write each number in standard form.** (Lesson 2-8)

19. $4.08 \cdot 10^4$  40,800

20. $6.22 \cdot 10^8$  622,000,000

21. $9.17 \cdot 10^{-5}$  0.0000917

22. $2.01 \cdot 10^4$  20,100

23. $3.2987 \cdot 10^6$  3,298,700

24. $1.7803 \cdot 10^{-5}$  0.000017803

25. $6.59 \cdot 10^{-4}$  0.000659

26. $7.668 \cdot 10^7$  76,680,000

Lesson 4-2 **Problem Solving Skills: Simulations** 155

**Five-step Plan**
1 Read
2 Plan
3 Solve
4 Answer
5 Check

**Chalkboard Examples**

**Supplementary Problem**
**SPORTS** Yolanda has a batting average of 0.250. In her next 10 times at bat, what is the probability that she gets exactly 3 hits?

To model a batting average of 0.250 (that is, $\frac{250}{1000}$ or $\frac{1}{4}$), use a device that has outcomes in the ratio $\frac{1}{4}$. A simulation could be drawing a particular suit from a standard deck of playing cards. Since the ratio of the number of hearts, 13, to the number of cards in a full deck, 52, is $\frac{1}{4}$, let drawing a heart represent getting a hit and drawing a card of any other suit represent getting no hit. Since the player has 10 times at bat, draw 10 cards, with replacement of all 10 cards each time.

**Lesson Wrap-up**

**QUICK ASSESSMENT**
Ask the following questions to determine if students understand the contents presented in this lesson.

Name a device that could be used to model a situation for which the ratio is given.
1. 1 : 2  coin
2. 1 : 4  standard deck of playing cards
3. 1 : 6  a number cube

6. Toss 6 coins at once, letting heads represent black and tails represent white.

7. Use a spinner divided into three equal sections labeled 1, 2, and 3. Let 1 and 2 represent a made free throw and 3 represent a missed free throw. Spin 5 spinners at a time to model 5 free throws shot by Tia.

8. Toss a coin and roll a number cube at the same time. A head on the coin represents a brown horse and a 1 on the cube represents a horse with a braided mane.

9. Jolon is correct. Any device, such as a number cube, that has an even number of outcomes can be used since the outcomes can be separated into two equal categories.

10. Problems such as finding theoretical probabilities may be impossible or may require extremely long and complicated computations. Finding an experimental probability may be more feasible and much quicker.

## Vocabulary Review

**Lesson 4-1**
experiment
relative frequency
experimental probability

**Lesson 4-2**
act it out        simulation

## ASSIGNMENT GUIDE

**All students:** 1–22

## Chalkboard Examples

### Lesson 4-1

**SPORTS** In a poll conducted to find high school students' favorite sports, 119 voted for football, 135 voted for baseball, 126 voted for basketball, and 160 voted for other sports. What is the experimental probability that a high school student's favorite sport is baseball?

*P*(baseball)

$$= \frac{135}{119 + 135 + 126 + 160} = 0.25$$

### Lesson 4-2

Describe a model that would be used to similate the following situation.

**MEDICAL RESEARCH** A medicine has a 3 in 5 chance of curing the condition for which it is prescribed. If two patients are chosen at random to use the medicine, what is the probability it will cure their condition?

Using a number cube, let the outcomes 1, 3, 5 represent "the drug works" and the outcomes 2, 4 represent the "drug does not work." Disregard the outcome 6. In this way, you simulate the 3 in 5 chance of cure.

Since two patients are chosen, one trial in the simulation is to roll one cube twice.

---

### PRACTICE ◼ LESSON 4-1

**Find the probability that a point selected at random lies in the shaded region.**

**1.**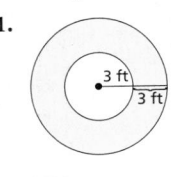

0.75

**2.**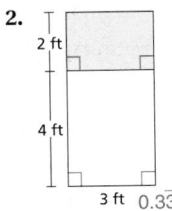

0.33

**3.**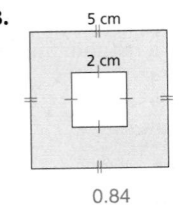

0.84

**4.**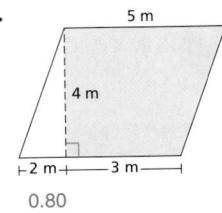

0.80

**Use the table for Exercises 5–7.**

**5.** On Thursday what is the probability that a person using the gym is not a freshman? ≈ 0.48

**6.** On Saturday what is the probability that a person using the gym is a freshman? ≈ 0.23

**7.** On Sunday what is the probability that a person using the gym is a sophomore? ≈ 0.46

**People Using Gym**

|          | Freshmen | Sophomores | Others |
|----------|----------|------------|--------|
| Tuesday  | 53       | 30         | 15     |
| Thursday | 62       | 37         | 21     |
| Saturday | 21       | 45         | 25     |
| Sunday   | 19       | 41         | 30     |

**8.** There are 22 marbles in a bag. Fifteen are red and 7 are blue. What is the probability that a red marble will be selected? ≈ 0.68

**9.** In a poll conducted to find a student's favorite fruit juice, 107 vote for orange juice, 91 vote for apple juice, 120 vote for grape juice and 61 vote for pineapple juice. What is the probability that a randomly-chosen student chose apple juice? ≈ 0.24

**10.** A circle with an 8-cm radius lies within a rectangle that is 18 cm by 22 cm. What is the probability that a point in the rectangle lies within the circle? ≈ 0.51

### PRACTICE ◼ LESSON 4-2

**Describe a model for each situation. Perform 25 trials of the simulation and find the indicated probability.** For 11–14, models and experimental probabilities will vary. See additional answers for possible simulations.

**11.** Each box of pancake mix contains 1 of 6 different baseball cards. Assuming that the company has evenly distributed the cards among the boxes, what is the probability that you will find all 6 cards if you buy 6 boxes of pancake mix?

**12.** A litter has 5 puppies. What is the probability that there are 3 female puppies and 2 male puppies?

**13.** A husband and wife want to have 3 children. Find the probability that they will have 3 boys or 3 girls.

**14.** A baseball player has a batting average of 0.333. This means that he has a hit approximately 33.3% of the time that he is at bat. In his next 10 at bats, what is the probability that he gets exactly 3 hits?

## PRACTICE ■ LESSON 4-1–LESSON 4-2

Find the probability that a point selected at random lies in the shaded area. (Lesson 4-1)

**15.**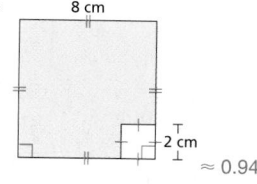
≈ 0.94

**16.**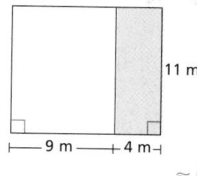
≈ 0.31

**17.**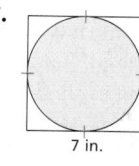
≈ 0.79

Use the graph for Exercises 18–22. (Lessons 4-1 and 4-2).

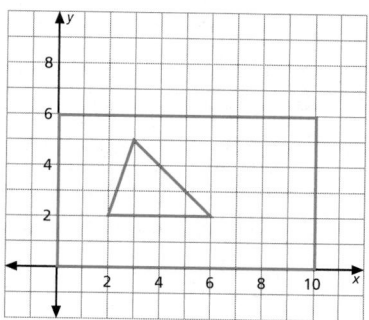

**18.** What is the area of the triangle?  6

**19.** What is the area of the rectangle?  60

**20.** What is the probability that a point selected at random inside the rectangle is in the triangle?  0.10

**21.** What is the probability that a point selected at random inside the rectangle is not in the triangle?  0.90

**22.** What do you notice about your answer to Exercises 20 and 21?  Their sum is 1.

## MathWorks Career – Baseball Player
Workplace Knowhow

On average, a baseball player receives 20 pitches in four at bats during each game. During spring training a certain player swings and hits the ball every 40 out of 100 pitches. Of the pitches he hits, 13 are fly outs or ground outs, 20 are foul balls and 7 are base hits. Of these base hits, two are home runs. Use the spring training statistics to answer the following questions concerning the player's regular season.

1. What is the probability the player will hit a fly out or a ground out on a pitch?  $\frac{13}{100}$ or 0.13

2. Predict how many foul balls the player will hit per game. 4

3. Predict how many base hits the player will hit during the regular 162-game season.
approximately 227

4. At the All-Star break (after 81 games), the player has hit 34 home runs. By how many home runs is he exceeding or falling short of his expected number of home runs at this point in the season based on his spring training statistics? Are his spring training home run statistics an accurate prediction of the number of home runs he will hit in the regular season? Explain.
Exceeding by 2; yes; his actual number of home runs is close to what would have been predicted.

 Math
nline  mathmatters2.com/mathworks

---

In addition to personal charisma and audience appeal, the success and quality of a professional baseball player are measured against the numerous statistics that are collected.

Students should answer Questions 1–4 to better understand the role of probability in expected performance that will impact on the statistic known as *batting average*, which is calculated each season for each player by dividing the total number of base hits by the total number of times at bat.

Students may be interested in researching other statistics that are collected about baseball players and find out how these statistics are compiled. For example, the *slugging percentage* is calculated by dividing the total number of bases for all hits by the total number of at bats, where the total number of bases = (home runs × 4) + (triples × 3) + (doubles × 2) + singles.

A professional baseball player's contract negotiations are much influenced by the statistical record he has achieved.

Students who are interested in learning more about this career choice can go to mathmatters2.com/mathworks. School Guidance Counselors are another resource for information about training requirements and appropriate schools.

## ADDITIONAL ANSWERS

11. Use a number cube with each number representing a different baseball card. Roll 6 cubes at once to represent 6 boxes.

12. Toss 5 coins at once, letting heads represent female and tails represent male.

13. Use a coin to model gender. Let heads represent a girl and tails represent a boy. Since the family wants to have 3 children, flip 3 coins at a time.

14. Use a spinner divided into 3 equal sections to model a batting average of 0.333. Let 1 represent a hit. Spin the spinner 10 times or spin 10 spinners at once.

## NCTM Standards/Strands
- Data Analysis & Probability
- Representation
- Problem Solving
- Connections

## Vocabulary

event        sample space
tree diagram
theoretical probability
fundamental counting principle

## Tools/Materials Needed

calculator

## Lesson Resources

Warm-up Transparency 16
Transparency RF-17
Reteaching 4-3
Extra Practice 4-3
Enrichment 4-3

# Getting Started

### 5-Minute Warm-Up

**Write each fraction in lowest terms.**

1. $\frac{27}{42}$    $\frac{9}{14}$     2. $\frac{110}{143}$    $\frac{10}{13}$

3. $\frac{135}{165}$    $\frac{9}{11}$     4. $\frac{180}{204}$    $\frac{15}{17}$

## Introduction to Lesson 4-3

Discuss the meaning of *organized list* in the context of trying to list all the possibilities for the 3 places to be filled by red (R), blue (B), green (G).

R B G   With R in the 1st place,
R G B   do all possibilities for 2nd
         and 3rd places.

B R G   With B in the 1st place,
B G R   do all possibilities for 2nd
         and 3rd places.

G R B   With G in the 1st place,
G B R   do all possibilities for 2nd
         and 3rd places.

   With 3 places, the list shows 6 possibilities.

---

# 4-3 Sample Spaces and Theoretical Probability

**Goals**
- Determine sample spaces using various methods.
- Find theoretical probabilities.

**Applications**    Sports, Food service, Games, Number theory

**A game has cards marked with either a circle or a square.**

1. If the shapes can be colored red, blue or green, how many different kinds of cards can there be?   6

2. If the shapes can be colored red, blue, green or yellow, how many different kinds of cards can there be?   8

3. How can you be sure that you have counted each kind of card?
Carefully examine the cards and make a list of all possible combinations.

## ▍ BUILD UNDERSTANDING

When evaluating probability, you must know all the different things that can happen in, or outcomes of, a situation. Any one of the possible outcomes or combination of possible outcomes of an experiment is considered an **event**.

The **sample space** for a probability experiment is the set of all possible outcomes of the experiment. Often ordered pairs are used to organize and show a sample space.

### Example 1

**In an experiment, a coin is tossed and a number cube is rolled. How many possible outcomes are there?**

**Solution**

The sample space can be shown as a set of ordered pairs. For the coin, let $H$ represent heads and $T$ represent tails. For the number cube, use the number for each face: 1, 2, 3, 4, 5, 6. Then list the possible outcomes.

| | | | | | |
|---|---|---|---|---|---|
| $(H, 1)$ | $(H, 2)$ | $(H, 3)$ | $(H, 4)$ | $(H, 5)$ | $(H, 6)$ |
| $(T, 1)$ | $(T, 2)$ | $(T, 3)$ | $(T, 4)$ | $(T, 5)$ | $(T, 6)$ |

There are 12 possible outcomes.

Another way to organize and show a sample space is with a diagram. One common diagram used is a **tree diagram**. It is called a tree diagram since you list one part of an event and then add branches to show all the outcomes involving that part of the event. When the entire sample space is complete, the diagram looks similar to a tree.

---

## Teaching Tip

After students have written an organized list for the 3-color arrangements of the opening activity, have them try an organized list now with 4 places to be filled by the colors red (R), blue (B), green (G), and yellow (Y). In all, there are 24 possibilities.

| with R in 1st place | with B in 1st place | with G in 1st place | with Y in 1st place |
|---|---|---|---|
| R B G Y | B R G Y | G R B Y | Y R B G |
| R B Y G | B R Y G | G R Y B | Y R G B |
| R G B Y | B G R Y | G B R Y | Y B R G |
| R G Y B | B G Y R | G B Y R | Y B G R |
| R Y B G | B Y R G | G Y R B | Y G R B |
| R Y G B | B Y G R | G Y B R | Y G B R |

After introducing *tree diagrams*, have students draw a tree diagram for this sample space of 4-color arrangements and compare the results with those of the organized list.

## Example 2

**FOOD SERVICE** A pizza parlor offers three sizes of pizza: large (L), medium (M), and small (S). It also offers three toppings: cheese (C), peppers (P), and onions (O). How many different pizzas with one topping are available? Use a tree diagram to solve the problem.

### Solution

Use the tree diagram to count the total number of combinations.

The pizza parlor sells nine different one-topping pizzas.

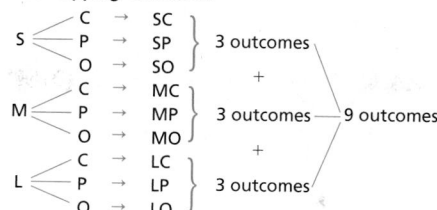

In many problems, the sample space is too large to list as a set of ordered pairs or to show as a tree diagram. According to the **fundamental counting principle**, if there are two or more stages of an activity, the total number of possible outcomes is the product of the number of possible outcomes for each stage of the activity.

## Example 3

**RETAIL** A retail store sells shirts in 8 different sizes. For each size, there is a choice of 5 colors. For each color, there is a choice of 6 patterns. How many different kinds of shirts does the store have?

### Solution

You must consider size, color, and pattern. Multiply the number of possible outcomes for each stage.

$$\boxed{\text{size}} \cdot \boxed{\text{color}} \cdot \boxed{\text{pattern}} = \boxed{\text{possible outcomes}}$$
$$8 \cdot 5 \cdot 6 = 240$$

The store has 240 different shirts.

Probability is not always determined from the observed outcomes of an experiment. The **theoretical probability** of an event, $E$, can be assigned using the formula below.

You may think of theoretical probabilities of events in a sample space as representing the results of an *ideal* experiment.

> **Check Understanding**
>
> What is the theoretical probability of getting heads on one toss of a coin? $\frac{1}{2}$
>
> What is the experimental probability of getting heads if heads comes up 60 times in 100 tosses? $\frac{3}{5}$

| **Theoretical Probability** | $P(E) = \dfrac{\text{number of favorable outcomes}}{\text{number of possible outcomes}}$ |
| --- | --- |

In Example 3, the number of different kinds of shirts represents the number of possible outcomes. If the store has exactly one of each kind and you are calculating the theoretical probability of selling a particular kind of shirt, the denominator would equal 240.

 **Math Online** mathmatters2.com/extra_examples

Lesson 4-3 **Sample Spaces and Theoretical Probability** | 159

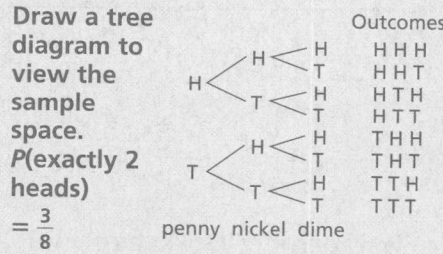

## Example 4

A card is picked at random from a set of twelve marked with the numbers 1 through 12. Find $P$(odd number greater than 5).

### Solution

There are twelve possible outcomes: 1, 2, 3, 4, 5, 6, 7, 8, 9, 10, 11, 12.
There are six odd numbers: 1, 3, 5, 7, 9, 11.
Only three odd numbers are greater than 5: 7, 9 and 11.
So there are three favorable outcomes.

$$P(\text{odd number greater than 5}) = \frac{3}{12} \quad \frac{\text{favorable outcomes}}{\text{total possible outcomes}}$$

$$= \frac{1}{4} = 0.25$$

So the probability of drawing an odd number greater than 5 is 0.25.

### QUICK ASSESSMENT

Ask the following questions to determine if students understand the content presented in this lesson.
1. What is another name for the set of all possible outcomes in a situation?  the sample space
2. What is a convenient way to get a list of a sample space?  Draw a tree diagram.
3. If you just want to know how many outcomes there are in a sample space, do you need a tree diagram?  No
4. What operation do you use in the counting principle?  multiplication
5. What numbers are you multiplying in the counting principle?  the number of choices for each stage of the event

### ▣ TRY THESE EXERCISES

1. **SPORTS** A store sells baseball bats in 3 different weights and 4 different lengths. The bats can be either wooden or aluminum. How many different types of bats does the store sell?  24

2. Show the sample space when a nickel and a dime are tossed. Use ordered pairs.
   (nickel, dime) → (H, H), (H, T), (T, H), (T, T)

**A number cube is rolled, and a spinner labeled A through D is spun.**

3. Use a tree diagram to show the sample space.
   See additional answers.
4. How many possible outcomes are there?  24
5. Find $P$(1, A).  $\frac{1}{24}$
6. Find $P$(odd number, D).  $\frac{1}{8}$

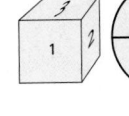 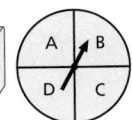

**Use the spinner for Exercises 7 and 8.**

7. In the spinner, what is $P$(multiple of 6)?  $\frac{1}{4}$
8. What is $P$(multiple of 10, less than 50)?  $\frac{3}{8}$

### ASSIGNMENT GUIDE

**Basic:** 1–22, 29–40
**Enriched:** 1–40

### ▣ PRACTICE EXERCISES  •  For Extra Practice, see page 596.

9. **MUSIC** At an audition for a three-piece band, there are 8 guitarists, 4 bass players and 5 drummers. How many different ways can a guitarist, bass player and a drummer be selected?  160

10. A spinner with four equal sections labeled 1 through 4 is spun, and a coin is tossed. Show the sample space using ordered pairs and a tree diagram.
    See additional answers.

**Use both spinners for Exercises 11–15.**

11. How many possible outcomes are there?  64
12. Find $P$(number less than 4, vowel).  $\frac{3}{32}$
13. Find $P$(number greater than or equal to six, G).  $\frac{3}{64}$
14. Find $P$(3, D).  $\frac{1}{64}$
15. Find $P$(odd number, B).  $\frac{1}{16}$

 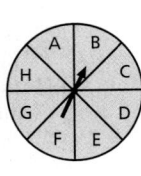

### Reteaching Worksheet 4-3

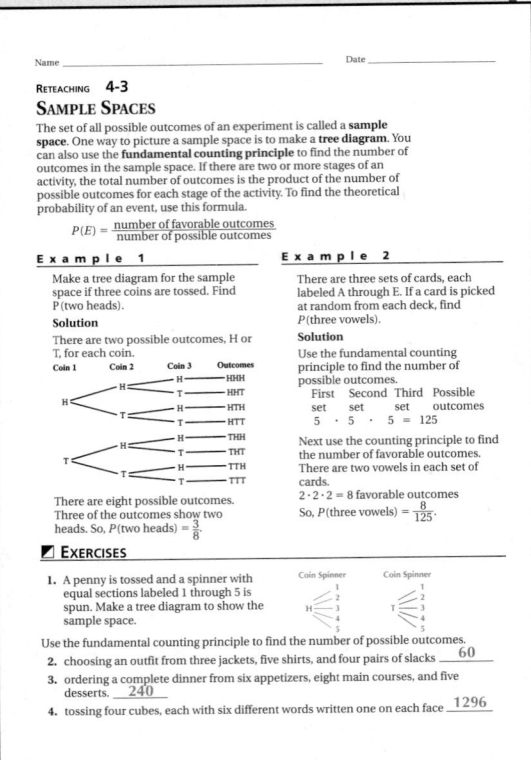

Name _____  Date _____

RETEACHING **4-3**

**SAMPLE SPACES**

The set of all possible outcomes of an experiment is called a **sample space**. One way to picture a sample space is to make a **tree diagram**. You can also use the **fundamental counting principle** to find the number of outcomes in the sample space. If there are two or more stages of an activity, the total number of outcomes is the product of the number of possible outcomes for each stage of the activity. To find the theoretical probability of an event, use this formula.

$$P(E) = \frac{\text{number of favorable outcomes}}{\text{number of possible outcomes}}$$

**Example 1**

Make a tree diagram for the sample space if three coins are tossed. Find P(two heads).

**Solution**

There are two possible outcomes, H or T, for each coin.

There are eight possible outcomes. Three of the outcomes show two heads. So, $P(\text{two heads}) = \frac{3}{8}$.

**Example 2**

There are three sets of cards, each labeled A through E. If a card is picked at random from each deck, find P(three vowels).

**Solution**

Use the fundamental counting principle to find the number of possible outcomes.

| First set | Second set | Third set | Possible outcomes |
|---|---|---|---|
| 5 | · 5 | · 5 | = 125 |

Next use the counting principle to find the number of favorable outcomes. There are two vowels in each set of cards.
2 · 2 · 2 = 8 favorable outcomes
So, $P(\text{three vowels}) = \frac{8}{125}$.

**▣ EXERCISES**

1. A penny is tossed and a spinner with equal sections labeled 1 through 5 is spun. Make a tree diagram to show the sample space.

Use the fundamental counting principle to find the number of possible outcomes.
2. choosing an outfit from three jackets, five shirts, and four pairs of slacks  60
3. ordering a complete dinner from six appetizers, eight main courses, and five desserts.  240
4. tossing four cubes, each with six different words written one on each face  1296

### ADDITIONAL ANSWERS

3. **Number Cube / Spinner / Outcomes**

| Cube | Spinner | Outcomes |
|---|---|---|
| 1 | A | 1A |
| | B | 1B |
| | C | 1C |
| | D | 1D |
| 2 | A | 2A |
| | B | 2B |
| | C | 2C |
| | D | 2D |
| 3 | A | 3A |
| | B | 3B |
| | C | 3C |
| | D | 3D |
| 4 | A | 4A |
| | B | 4B |
| | C | 4C |
| | D | 4D |
| 5 | A | 5A |
| | B | 5B |
| | C | 5C |
| | D | 5D |
| 6 | A | 6A |
| | B | 6B |
| | C | 6C |
| | D | 6D |

10.

| Spinner | Coin | Outcomes |
|---|---|---|
| 1 | H | 1H |
| | T | 1T |
| 2 | H | 2H |
| | T | 2T |
| 3 | H | 3H |
| | T | 3T |
| 4 | H | 4H |
| | T | 4T |

20. It is helpful to list the outcomes when the probability of a certain outcome is desired. The fundamental counting principle is best when only the total number of outcomes is desired.

**16. WRITING MATH** Explain the similarities and differences between using ordered pairs and tree diagrams to list the sample space of an experiment. Answers will vary.

**17.** A menu has a choice of 2 soups, 5 main dishes and 3 desserts. How many different three-course meals are possible? 30

**18.** A combination lock has 3 dials, each numbered from 1 to 8. How many different ways can the lock be set? 512

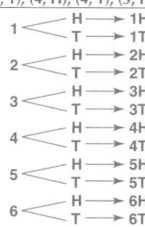

**19. GAMES** A card is picked at random from a full deck of 52 playing cards. What is the probability that it will have a value greater than nine? (Assume that aces are worth more than nines.) $\frac{5}{13}$

**20. WRITING MATH** Describe when it is helpful to list the outcomes in a sample space and when it is more convenient to use the fundamental counting principle without identifying the outcomes. See additional answers.

**21.** A store sells both oil-based and latex house paints. Each type of paint is available in 12 colors and in 3 different can sizes. How many different choices of paint does the store carry? 72

**22. DATA FILE** Refer to the data on popular symphony orchestras on page 562. How many ways can a trio of trombonists be selected so that each orchestra is represented? 24

## ▇ EXTENDED PRACTICE EXERCISES

**CRITICAL THINKING** A number cube is rolled three times.

**23.** Find P(all sixes). $\frac{1}{216}$   **24.** Find P(all even numbers). $\frac{1}{8}$   **25.** Find P(no sixes). $\frac{125}{216}$

**26.** How many five-digit numbers can be made using the digits 1, 2, 3, 4 and 5? (Assume that a digit can be used more than once.) 3125

**27. NUMBER THEORY** A number cube is tossed twice, and each outcome is written down in order as a two-digit number. What is the probability that the two-digit number is a perfect square? $\frac{1}{9}$

**28. CHAPTER INVESTIGATION** Choose a format for your chance game. This may include drawing cards from a deck, rolling a number cube, spinning a spinner, or some other event. Your game should include at least two events. Answers will vary.

## ▇ MIXED REVIEW EXERCISES

**Solve each equation. Check the solution.** (Lesson 3-2)

**29.** $4z = 28$  7

**30.** $\frac{1}{3}d = -6$  −18

**31.** $-3a = 18$  −6

**32.** $\frac{f}{8} = -6$  −48

**33.** $-2.5g = -5$  2

**34.** $\frac{y}{0.4} = -3.2$  −1.28

**Solve each proportion. Check the solution.** (Lesson 3-5)

**35.** $\frac{15}{45} = \frac{n}{30}$  10

**36.** $\frac{g}{8} = \frac{7}{2}$  28

**37.** $\frac{3.6}{5.4} = \frac{h}{0.9}$  0.6

**38.** $\frac{4u}{8} = \frac{24}{16}$  3

**39.** $\frac{6x}{9} = \frac{24}{18}$  2

**40.** $\frac{25}{6 + b} = \frac{10}{2}$  −1

Math Online mathmatters2.com/self_check_quiz

---

## Extra Practice Worksheet 4-3

Name _____ Date _____

ExTRA PRACTICE **4-3**

**SAMPLE SPACES**

☑ **EXERCISES**

**1.** A sandwich shop sells packaged sandwiches with three different types of bread and four different types of meat. There is only one type of bread and one type of meat used on each sandwich. How many different packaged sandwiches does the shop sell? 12

**2.** A spinner with six equal sections, labeled 1–6, is spun and a coin is tossed. Show the sample space using ordered pairs and a tree diagram. (1, H), (1, T), (2, H), (2, T), (3, H), (3, T), (4, H), (4, T), (5, H), (5, T), (6, H), (6, T)

```
      H ──→ 1H
1 <
      T ──→ 1T
      H ──→ 2H
2 <
      T ──→ 2T
      H ──→ 3H
3 <
      T ──→ 3T
      H ──→ 4H
4 <
      T ──→ 4T
      H ──→ 5H
5 <
      T ──→ 5T
      H ──→ 6H
6 <
      T ──→ 6T
```

Both spinners are spun for Exercises 3–6.

**3.** How many outcomes are there? 32

**4.** Find P(number greater than 4, B). $\frac{1}{8}$

**5.** Find P(6, A). $\frac{1}{32}$

**6.** Find P(even number, consonant). $\frac{3}{8}$

---

## Enrichment Worksheet 4-3

Name _____ Date _____

ENRICHMENT **4-3**

**WHAT TO EXPECT**

The concept of **mathematical expectation** or **expected value** is used in a wide variety of probability situations dealing with such things as fairness of games, insurance premiums and decision making in business ventures. The examples below illustrate what is meant by mathematical expectation.

A contractor estimates a probability of 0.5 of making a profit of $20,000 on a building project, a probability of 0.3 of breaking even on the same project, and a probability of 0.2 of losing $10,000 on the project. The contractor's mathematical expectation of income from the project is

$$E = 0.5(20,000) + 0.3(0) + 0.2(-10,000)$$
$$= 10,000 - 2000$$
$$= 8000$$

The contractor's expected income is $8000.

☑ **EXERCISES**

**1.** A player rolls a number cube and receives points equal to ten times the number that comes up.

What is the player's mathematical expectation? 35 points

**2.** The table at the right shows a breakdown of yearly dental claims for people aged 20 through 25. How much should the insurance company charge as its average annual premium in order to break even on its cost for claims? $1060

| Amount of Claim | Probability |
|---|---|
| 0 | 0.65 |
| $2000 | 0.25 |
| $4000 | 0.05 |
| $6000 | 0.03 |
| $8000 | 0.01 |
| $10,000 | 0.01 |

A photographer is considering entering two contests. Contest A offers a prize of $5000 and Contest B offers a prize of $20,000. The photographer will incur costs of $50 in entering Contest A and $100 in entering Contest B. The probability of winning Contest A is 0.05. The probability of winning Contest B is 0.01.

**3.** What is the photographer's mathematical expectation in entering Contest A? $200

**4.** What is the photographer's mathematical expectation in entering Contest B? $100

**5.** If the photographer can enter only one contest, which should it be? Contest A

---

## Teaching Tip

Explain to students that the 52 cards in a standard deck of playing cards are divided into 4 equal *suits*, called *hearts, diamonds, spades,* and *clubs*. Two of the suits, hearts and diamonds, are red and the other two suits, clubs and spades, are black.
The 13 cards in each suit are ace, 2, 3, 4, 5, 6, 7, 8, 9, 10, jack, queen, king. The jack, queen, and king are known as *face cards*.

## Lesson Planning

### NCTM Standards/Strands
- Data Analysis & Probability
- Representation
- Problem Solving
- Connections

### Vocabulary

compound event
mutually exclusive

### Tools/Materials Needed

calculator

### Lesson Resources

Warm-up Transparency 16
Transparency RF-18
Reteaching 4-4
Extra Practice 4-4
Enrichment 4-4

## Getting Started

### 5-MINUTE WARM-UP

Evaluate each expression. Write your answer as a fraction in lowest terms.

1. $\frac{1}{4} + \frac{7}{52}$    $\frac{5}{13}$

2. $\frac{4}{52} + \frac{12}{52} - \frac{3}{52}$    $\frac{1}{4}$

3. $\frac{1}{6} + \frac{1}{9} - \frac{1}{12}$    $\frac{7}{36}$

4. $\frac{1}{4} + \frac{2}{5} - \frac{3}{20}$    $\frac{1}{2}$

### Introduction to Lesson 4-4

To begin, make sure students understand that the Venn diagram shown is just a reminder of how to draw a Venn diagram involving an intersection of two sets.

---

# 4-4 Probability of Compound Events

**Goals**
- Find probabilities of compound events.
- Explore mutually exclusive compound events.

**Applications**   Games, Probability, Number sense

---

**The Venn diagram shows even numbers and multiples of 5.**

1. Draw a Venn diagram showing {numbers greater than 12} and {prime numbers} for whole numbers 1 through 20.
   See additional answers.

2. Draw a Venn diagram showing {multiples of 4} and {prime numbers} for the numbers 1 through 20.
   See additional answers.

3. What is the difference between your two Venn diagrams?
   The first overlaps, but the second has no intersection.

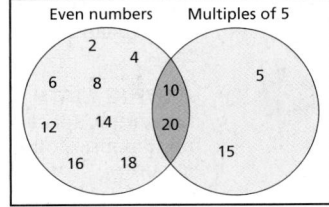

### ◤ BUILD UNDERSTANDING

A **compound event** is made up of two or more simpler events. Problems dealing with compound events ask for the probability of one event *and* another event occurring. The probability of event A and event B is written P(A and B). Other problems ask for the probability of one event *or* another event occurring. The probability of event A or event B is written P(A or B).

Sometimes two events are mutually exclusive. Events that are **mutually exclusive** are events that cannot occur at the same time. When two events A and B are mutually exclusive, the probability of A or B can be found using the formula $P(A \text{ or } B) = P(A) + P(B)$.

### Example 1

**Two number cubes are rolled. Find P(the sum is 7 or 11).**

**Solution**

List the sample space for the experiment. There are 36 possible outcomes.

| | |
|---|---|
| (1, 1) (1, 2) (1, 3) (1, 4) (1, 5) (1, 6) | (2, 1) (2, 2) (2, 3) (2, 4) (2, 5) (2, 6) |
| (3, 1) (3, 2) (3, 3) (3, 4) (3, 5) (3, 6) | (4, 1) (4, 2) (4, 3) (4, 4) (4, 5) (4, 6) |
| (5, 1) (5, 2) (5, 3) (5, 4) (5, 5) (5, 6) | (6, 1) (6, 2) (6, 3) (6, 4) (6, 5) (6, 6) |

Six outcomes have a sum of 7: (1, 6); (2, 5); (3, 4); (4, 3); (5, 2); (6, 1).

$$P(\text{sum of 7}) = \frac{6}{36}$$

Two outcomes have a sum of 11: (5, 6); (6, 5).

$$P(\text{sum of 11}) = \frac{2}{36}$$

Since the sum cannot be 7 and 11 at the same time, both sums are mutually exclusive.

$$P(\text{sum of 7 or 11}) = \frac{6}{36} + \frac{2}{36} = \frac{8}{36} = \frac{2}{9}$$

**162**   Chapter 4   **Probability**

---

### ADDITIONAL ANSWERS

1.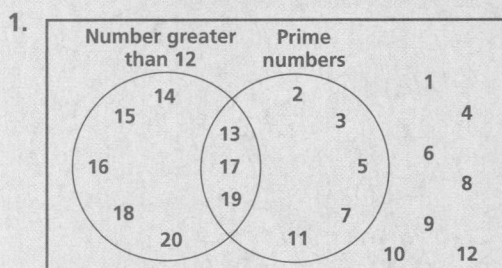

2.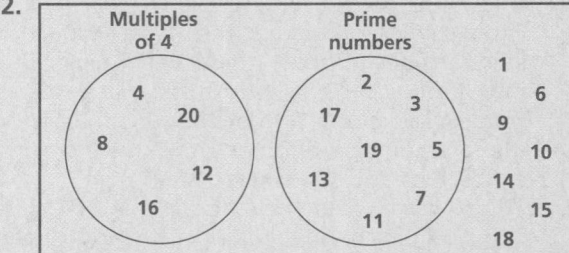

Events that are not mutually exclusive can happen at the same time. The next example shows how to find the probability of two such events.

# Example 2

**Two number cubes are rolled. Find the probability that the sum of the numbers rolled is even or a multiple of 3.**

## Solution

Refer to the sample space of Example 1. The events are not mutually exclusive because a sum can be both even and a multiple of 3. Of the 36 possible outcomes, 18 are even sums.

$$P(\text{even}) = \frac{18}{36} = \frac{1}{2}$$

Sums of 3, 6, 9 and 12 are multiples of 3. There are 12 sums that are multiples of 3.

$$P(\text{multiple of } 3) = \frac{12}{36} = \frac{1}{3}$$

However, sums that are even and a multiple of 3 have been counted twice. These are 6 and 12. There are six pairs with these sums.

$$P(\text{even and multiple of } 3) = \frac{6}{36} = \frac{1}{6}$$

Subtract the probability of the sums that have been counted twice.

$$P(\text{even or multiple of } 3) = \frac{1}{2} + \frac{1}{3} - \frac{1}{6} = \frac{3}{6} + \frac{2}{6} - \frac{1}{6} = \frac{4}{6} = \frac{2}{3}$$

The probability of an even sum or a sum that is a multiple of 3 is $\frac{2}{3}$.

When two events $A$ and $B$ are not mutually exclusive, the probability of $A$ or $B$ can be found using the formula: $P(A \text{ or } B) = P(A) + P(B) - P(A \text{ and } B)$.

> ### Problem Solving Tip
> When listing the outcomes in a sample space, double check them to make sure you have accounted for all possibilities and that none of them have been repeated.

# Example 3

**GAMES** A card is drawn at random from a standard deck of 52 playing cards. Find the probability that the card is a heart or an ace.

## Solution

The events are not mutually exclusive. A card can be both a heart and an ace.

$$P(\text{heart or ace}) = P(\text{heart}) + P(\text{ace}) - P(\text{heart and ace})$$

Of the 52 cards, there are 13 hearts; so $P(\text{heart}) = \frac{13}{52}$.

Of the 52 cards, there are 4 aces; so $P(\text{ace}) = \frac{4}{52}$.

There is 1 heart that is an ace, so $P(\text{heart and ace}) = \frac{1}{52}$.

$$P(\text{heart or ace}) = \frac{13}{52} + \frac{4}{52} - \frac{1}{52}$$
$$= \frac{16}{52}$$
$$= \frac{4}{13}$$

The probability that the card drawn is a heart or an ace is $\frac{4}{13}$.

> ### Check Understanding
> A card is drawn at random from a standard deck of 52 cards. Find $P(\text{red and 5})$.
>
> $\frac{2}{52}$

 **Math Online** mathmatters2.com/extra_examples

Lesson 4-4 **Probability of Compound Events** | **163**

---

## Chalkboard Examples

### Supplementary Example 1
Two number cubes are rolled. Is $P(\text{sum is at least 8})$ less than or greater than 50%?

There are 36 outcomes in all, as shown in the text under Example 1. Fifteen of the outcomes have a sum of 8 or more:

(2, 6), (3, 5), (3, 6), (4, 4), (4, 5), (4,6), (5, 3), (5, 4), (5, 5), (5, 6), (6, 2), (6, 3), (6, 4), (6, 5), (6, 6)

$P(\text{sum is at least 8}) = \frac{15}{36}$, which is less than 50%.

### Supplementary Example 2
From nine students—Max, Neil, Oprah, Pam, Raul, Rita, Tom, Will, and Zoe, the teacher will choose a student at random to work a problem at the chalkboard. What is the probability that the student is a girl or has a name that begins with R?

Of the 9 students, there are 4 girls and 5 boys. Two of the students (1 girl and 1 boy) have names beginning with R.

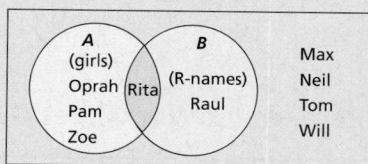

$P(\text{girl or R-name})$
$= P(\text{girl}) + P(R) - P(\text{girl and R})$
$= \frac{4}{9} + \frac{2}{9} - \frac{1}{9}$
$= \frac{5}{9}$

The probability that the teacher calls on a student who is a girl or has a name beginning with R is $\frac{5}{9}$.

# Extend the Lesson

**CHALLENGE** Have students consider the following problem.
A box contains 7 red marbles and 41 marbles of other colors.
If a marble is picked at random, the probability that it is red or green is $\frac{1}{4}$.
How many green marbles are in the box?
Let $g$ = the number of green marbles in the box

$P(\text{red or green}) = \frac{7 + g}{48} = \frac{1}{4}$   Cross-multiplying: $4(7 + g) = 48(1)$

Solving: $g = 5$
So, there are 5 green marbles in the box.

## QUICK ASSESSMENT

Ask the following questions to determine if students understand the content presented in this lesson.

**Classify the event as *simple* or *compound*.**

1. rolling a number cube   simple
2. rolling a number cube and tossing a coin   compound
3. tossing a coin twice   compound

**Classify the events as *mutually exclusive* or *not mutually exclusive*.**

4. having black hair and wearing glasses   not mutually exclusive
5. having blue eyes and having brown eyes   mutually exclusive
6. rolling a number cube and tossing a coin   mutually exclusive
7. being an even number and being a multiple of 3   not mutually exclusive

## ASSIGNMENT GUIDE

**Basic:** 1–26, 32–48
**Enriched:** 1–48

### Reteaching Worksheet 4-4

---

Name _____    Date _____

RETEACHING   **4-4**

### PROBABILITY OF COMPOUND EVENTS

A **compound event** is one made up of two or more simpler events. The probability of event $A$ and event $B$ occurring is written $P(A \text{ and } B)$. The probability of event $A$ or event $B$ occurring is written $P(A \text{ or } B)$. Events that cannot occur at the same time are **mutually exclusive**. When two events $A$ and $B$ are mutually exclusive, $P(A \text{ or } B) = P(A) + P(B)$. When two events $A$ and $B$ are *not* mutually exclusive, $P(A \text{ or } B) = P(A) + P(B) - P(A \text{ and } B)$.

**Example 1**

A box contains five red, two black, and three green balls. Find the probability that a ball picked at random will be red or green.

**Solution**

The events of picking a red ball and picking a green ball cannot occur at the same time, so the events are mutually exclusive.
$P(\text{red}) = \frac{5}{10}$   $P(\text{green}) = \frac{3}{10}$
So, $P(\text{red } or \text{ green}) = \frac{5}{10} + \frac{3}{10} = \frac{8}{10} = \frac{4}{5}$.

**Example 2**

A card is drawn at random from a set of cards marked 1 through 10. Find the probability that the card drawn is an odd-numbered card or a card with a number less than 5.

**Solution**

Since a number can be both odd and less than 5, the events are not mutually exclusive. The odd numbers are 1, 3, 5, 7 and 9. The numbers less than 5 are 1, 2, 3 and 4. The numbers that are odd and less than 5 are 1 and 3.
$P(\text{odd}) = \frac{5}{10}$   $P(\text{less than } 5) = \frac{4}{10}$
$P(\text{odd } and \text{ less than } 5) = \frac{2}{10}$
$P(\text{odd } or \text{ less than } 5) = \frac{5}{10} + \frac{4}{10} - \frac{2}{10} = \frac{7}{10}$

☑ **EXERCISES**

A single card is drawn from a set of alphabet cards marked A to Z. Tell whether or not the events are mutually exclusive. Find each probability.

1. $P(\text{K or P})$ _____   mutually exclusive; $\frac{1}{13}$
2. $P(\text{a letter before E or a letter after W})$ _____   mutually exclusive; $\frac{7}{26}$
3. $P(\text{a vowel or a letter before M})$ _____   not mutually exclusive; $\frac{7}{13}$
4. $P(\text{a consonant or a letter after S})$ _____   not mutually exclusive; $\frac{11}{13}$
5. $P(\text{a vowel or a consonant})$ _____   mutually exclusive; 1
6. $P(\text{C or a letter after J})$ _____   mutually exclusive; $\frac{17}{26}$

---

## TRY THESE EXERCISES

1. Two coins are tossed. Find the probability that the coins show 2 tails or 2 heads.   $\frac{1}{2}$
2. Two number cubes are rolled. Find the probability that the numbers rolled are doubles and have a sum that is a multiple of 4.   $\frac{1}{12}$
3. Two number cubes are rolled. Find the probability that the numbers rolled are doubles or have a sum of 4.   $\frac{2}{9}$
4. A card is drawn from a standard deck of 52 cards. Find the probability that it is a red card or a jack.   $\frac{7}{13}$

**A card is drawn from a standard deck of 52 cards. Find each probability.**

5. $P(\text{red and face card})$   $\frac{3}{26}$   6. $P(\text{black or face card})$   $\frac{8}{13}$   7. $P(\text{red or club})$   $\frac{3}{4}$

8. **WRITING MATH** Explain why it is necessary to involve subtraction when finding the probability of two events that are not mutually exclusive.
This avoids counting a single outcome two times.

## PRACTICE EXERCISES  •  For Extra Practice, see page 597.

9. Two number cubes are rolled. Find the probability that the sum of the numbers is 5 or 6.   $\frac{1}{4}$
10. A card is drawn at random from a standard deck of 52 cards. Find the probability that the card is a 10 or a jack.   $\frac{2}{13}$
11. Two number cubes are rolled. Find the probability that the sum of the numbers is odd and less than 6.   $\frac{1}{6}$
12. A card is drawn from a standard deck of 52 cards. Find the probability that the card is a diamond or a face card.   $\frac{11}{26}$

**The spinner shown is spun one time. Find each probability.**

13. $P(\text{blue or 7})$   $\frac{5}{8}$
14. $P(\text{blue and an even number})$   $\frac{1}{4}$
15. $P(\text{green or less than 6})$   $\frac{7}{8}$
16. $P(\text{yellow or greater than 5})$   $\frac{1}{2}$

17. **GAMES** While playing a board game, Yasuhiro's piece is seven blocks away from landing on the home space. What is the probability that he will miss the home space on his next turn if two number cubes are rolled?   $\frac{5}{6}$

18. **DATA FILE** Refer to the data on trips to foreign destinations on page 574. What is the probability that an American visited Mexico or Asia?   31.2%

19. Three coins are tossed. Draw a tree diagram of the outcomes, and find the probability that the coins show three heads or three tails.   See additional answers.   $\frac{1}{4}$

20. **NUMBER SENSE** Six coins are tossed. Use the fundamental counting principle to find the probability of all heads or all tails.   $\frac{1}{32}$

---

## ADDITIONAL ANSWERS

19.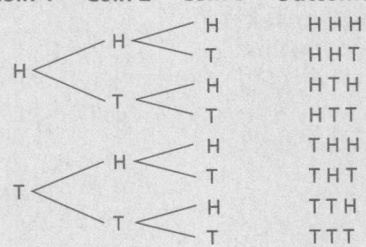

| Coin 1 | Coin 2 | Coin 3 | Outcomes |
|---|---|---|---|
| | | H | H H H |
| | H | T | H H T |
| H | | H | H T H |
| | T | T | H T T |
| | | H | T H H |
| | H | T | T H T |
| T | | H | T T H |
| | T | T | T T T |

25. Mary is probably incorrect because the results of the survey are most likely not mutually exclusive. In other words, just because a voter lies about voting on one county position does not exclude them from lying about voting for the other position.

A box contains 9 ball-point pens and 6 felt-tip pens. Of the ball-point pens, 4 are blue, 2 are red and 3 are black. Of the felt-tip pens, 3 are blue, 1 is red and 2 are black. A pen is picked at random from the box. Find each probability.

**21.** $P$(ball-point pen or blue)  $\frac{4}{5}$

**22.** $P$(felt-tip pen or red)  $\frac{8}{15}$

**23.** $P$(black ball-point pen)  $\frac{1}{5}$

**24.** $P$(red or ball-point pen)  $\frac{2}{3}$

**25. YOU MAKE THE CALL**  In a recent county election, 70% of the voters surveyed said they voted for a county auditor, but only 61% actually did. On the same survey, 50% of the voters surveyed said they voted for a county clerk, but only 43% actually did. Mary says that the probability of someone lying on this survey is 9% + 7% = 16%. Do you agree or disagree? Explain.
See additional answers.

**26. WRITING MATH**  Describe the difference between events that are mutually exclusive and events that are not mutually exclusive. Give an example of each type, and describe how the probability of each can be found.
See additional answers.

## ■ EXTENDED PRACTICE EXERCISES

**CRITICAL THINKING**  A photo album contains pictures of Joe or Catina, or both Joe and Catina. Joe is in 25 of the pictures, and Catina is in 30 of them. Joe and Catina are together in 15 of the pictures.

**27.** How many pictures are in the photo album?  40

**28.** If a picture is selected at random, what is the probability that it shows only Joe or only Catina?  $\frac{5}{8}$

The **complement** of the event $A$ is the event *not A*. For example, if you roll two number cubes, the event *the sum is 3* has the complement *the sum is not 3*.

**29.** Does $P(A$ or complement of $A) = P(A) + P$(complement of $A$)? Explain.
Yes; they are mutually exclusive.

**30.** What does $P(A) + P$(complement of $A$) equal?  1

**31.** Two number cubes are rolled. Find the probability that the sum of the numbers is neither a multiple of 3 nor a multiple of 4.  $\frac{4}{9}$

## ■ MIXED REVIEW EXERCISES

**Find the mean, median, and mode of each set of numbers. Round to the nearest tenth.** (Lesson 1-2)

**32.** 4, 8, 12, 16, 15, 13, 7, 9, 12, 15, 14  mean: 11.4; median: 12; mode: 12, 15

**33.** 1, 2, 1, 2, 1, 2, 3, 2, 1, 2, 3  mean: 1.8; median: 2; mode: 2

**34.** 26, 28, 31, 42, 37, 26, 28, 31, 26, 19, 24  mean: 28.9; median: 28; mode: 26

**35.** 6, 8, 12, 6, 12, 7, 9, 10, 12, 8, 6  mean: 8.7; median: 8; mode: 6, 12

**36.** 52, 54, 56, 57, 54, 53, 51, 50, 58, 59, 55  mean: 54.5; median: 54; mode: 54

**Simplify each numerical expression.** (Lesson 2-2)

**37.** $5 + 3 \cdot 9$  32

**38.** $3(8 - 6) \div 2$  3

**39.** $2^3 - (8 - 3) \div 5$  7

**40.** $\frac{2}{3}(6^2 + 3)$  26

**41.** $12 \cdot 8 + 2$  98

**42.** $12(8 + 2)$  120

**43.** $16 \div 4 + 1 - 3^2$  −4

**44.** $(2 + 3)^2 - 8 \cdot 7$  −31

**45.** $35 \div 3^2 + 4 - 7$  $0.8\overline{8}$

**46.** $5^2 + 64 \div 8 - 2$  31

**47.** $2.1 \cdot 3.4 \div 1.5$  4.76

**48.** $6^2 - 32 \div 8 + 6$  38

 **Math Online**  mathmatters2.com/self_check_quiz

---

## Extra Practice Worksheet 4-4

Name _____  Date _____

EXTRA PRACTICE  **4-4**
### PROBABILITY OF COMPOUND EVENTS

**■ EXERCISES**

1. Two coins are tossed. Find the probability that the coins show one tail and one head, or two heads.  $\frac{3}{4}$

2. Two six-sided number cubes are rolled. Find the probability that the sum of the numbers rolled is 2 or 3.  $\frac{1}{12}$

3. Two six-sided number cubes are rolled. Find the probability that the sum of the numbers rolled is even and is less than 5.  $\frac{1}{9}$

A card is drawn from a standard deck of 52 cards. Find each probability.

4. $P$(black or heart)  $\frac{3}{4}$

5. $P$(red or spade)  $\frac{3}{4}$

6. $P$(black and an ace)  $\frac{1}{26}$

7. $P$(club or heart)  $\frac{1}{2}$

8. $P$(heart or face card)  $\frac{25}{52}$

9. $P$(red or an 8)  $\frac{7}{13}$

The spinner is spun one time. Find each probability.

10. $P$(gray or 5)  $\frac{5}{8}$

11. $P$(white or 1)  $\frac{5}{8}$

12. $P$(white and 6)  $\frac{1}{8}$

13. $P$(gray and an odd number)  $\frac{1}{4}$

14. $P$(gray or a multiple of 3)  $\frac{5}{8}$

15. $P$(white and a number greater than 5)  $\frac{3}{8}$

A box contains ten colored pencils and five markers. Of the pencils, two are red, five are blue, and three are green. Of the markers, one is red, two are blue, and two are green. A pencil or marker is picked at random from the box. Find each probability.

16. $P$(pencil or red)  $\frac{11}{15}$

17. $P$(marker or blue)  $\frac{2}{3}$

18. $P$(green pencil)  $\frac{1}{5}$

19. $P$(green or pencil)  $\frac{4}{5}$

---

## Enrichment Worksheet 4-4

Name _____  Date _____

ENRICHMENT  **4-4**
### HAPPY BIRTHDAY

The probabilities that an event will happen and that it will not happen are called **complementary**. The sum of two complementary probabilities is always 1. Assume that a year has 365 days. Round answers to the nearest thousandth.

**■ EXERCISES**

1. What is the probability that in a group of just two people, both will have the same birthday month and date? Let the first person's birthday be any day. The probability the second person's birthday is *not* the same is $\frac{364}{365}$. So, $P$(two have the same birthday) = 1 − $P$(do not have the same birthday). Find $P$(two have the same birthday).
$1 − 0.997 = 0.003$

2. What is the probability that in a group of three people, two will have the same birthday? To find out, answer these questions.
   **a.** What is the probability that the third person will not have the same birthday as the other two?  $\frac{363}{365} = 0.995$
   **b.** What is the probability that both the second and third persons' birthdays will be different from that of the first?  $\frac{364}{365} \cdot \frac{363}{365} = 0.992$
   **c.** Use complementary probabilities to find the probability that two of the three people have the same birthday.  $1 − 0.992 = 0.008$

3. Using the same reasoning as in Exercise 2, find the probability that two people in a group of four have the same birthday.  0.016

The graph shows the probability of coinciding birthdays for two people in groups of different sizes. Use the graph to answer the following questions.

4. What is the probability that two people in a group of 20 have the same birthday?  about 0.43

5. How many people must there be in a group for the probability that two have the same birthday to be about 0.7?  about 30

6. How many people would have to be in a group to be sure that two have the same birthday? (Don't ignore leap years.)  367 people

7. Use the members of your class to test the results shown in the graph. Or, test the results by going to an almanac or encyclopedia and using the birthdates of 40 people selected at random.  Answers may vary.

---

## ADDITIONAL ANSWERS

26. Events that are mutually exclusive cannot occur together in a single outcome. For example, finding the probability of randomly selecting a girl with red hair or a boy with brown hair in your class is simply a matter of adding the number of girls with red hair and the number of boys with brown hair and dividing by the total number of students in the class. Events that are not mutually exclusive can occur together in a single outcome, and therefore another step in computing probability is required. For example, finding the probability of randomly selecting a girl with red hair and a girl with long hair in your class also requires that you add the number of girls with red hair and the number of girls with long hair, but also requires that you subtract from that total the number of girls with long, red hair, so they are not counted twice, before dividing by the total number of students in the class.

## Vocabulary Review

**Lesson 4-3**
event                    sample space
tree diagram
theoretical probability
fundamental counting principle

**Lesson 4-4**
compound event
mutually exclusive

## Assignment Guide

**All students: 1–30**

## Chalkboard Examples

### Lesson 4-3

**TRAVEL** Use the map below to determine how many different routes are possible when traveling from West Pike to East Pike through Pike.

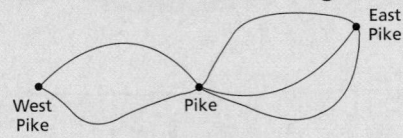

$$\underset{\substack{\uparrow \\ \text{W. Pike} \\ \text{to Pike}}}{2} \cdot \underset{\substack{\uparrow \\ \text{Pike to} \\ \text{E. Pike}}}{3} = 6 \text{ possibilities}$$

### Lesson 4-4

In one spin on the board shown, what is the probability of getting an even number or the number 5?

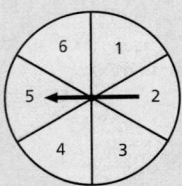

These events are mutually exclusive.
Of the 6 numbers on the spinner, there are 3 ways to get an even number, {2, 4, 6} and 1 way to get the number 5.

$P(\text{even or 5}) = \dfrac{3}{6} + \dfrac{1}{6}$

$\qquad\qquad\qquad = \dfrac{4}{6} \text{ or } \dfrac{2}{3}$

---

# Review and Practice Your Skills

## PRACTICE ◼ LESSON 4-3

**A number cube is rolled and a spinner with sections A, B, C, D and E is spun. Each section of the spinner is the same size.**

1. How many possible outcomes are there?  30
2. Find $P(C, 2)$.  $\dfrac{1}{30}$
3. Find $P(B, \text{even number})$.  $\dfrac{1}{10}$
4. Find $P(\text{number less than 4, consonant})$.  $\dfrac{3}{10}$
5. Find $P(\text{vowel, factor of 4})$.  $\dfrac{1}{5}$

6. At an audition for a brass trio there are 7 trumpets, 5 french horns and 4 trombones. How many different ways can a trumpeter, french hornist and a trombonist be selected?  140

7. Find the probability of drawing a red 9 from a standard deck of playing cards.  $\dfrac{1}{26}$

8. A combination lock has 4 dials, each numbered from 1 to 9. How many different ways can the lock be set?  6561

9. A spinner with 5 equal sections labeled 1 through 5 is spun and a coin is tossed. Show the sample space using ordered pairs and a tree diagram.
See additional answers.

10. A menu has a choice of 2 soups, 4 main dishes and 3 desserts. How many different three-course meals are possible?  24

**A number cube is rolled two times.**

11. Find $P(\text{all fours})$.  $\dfrac{1}{36}$
12. Find $P(\text{all odd numbers})$.  $\dfrac{1}{4}$
13. Find $P(\text{no fours})$.  $\dfrac{25}{36}$

## PRACTICE ◼ LESSON 4-4

**A card is drawn at random from a standard deck of 52 cards.**

14. Find the probability that the card is a 2, 3 or 4.  $\dfrac{3}{13}$
15. Find the probability that the card is a heart or a face card.  $\dfrac{11}{26}$
16. Find the probability that the card is a spade and an even number.  $\dfrac{5}{52}$

**A box contains 8 regular marbles and 7 shooter marbles. Of the regular marbles, 3 are blue, 2 are green and 3 are yellow. Of the shooter marbles, 2 are blue, 4 are green and 1 is yellow. Find each probability.**

17. $P(\text{regular marble or green})$  $\dfrac{4}{5}$
18. $P(\text{shooter marble or blue})$  $\dfrac{2}{3}$
19. $P(\text{green shooter marble})$  $\dfrac{4}{15}$
20. $P(\text{yellow or regular marble})$  $\dfrac{3}{5}$

**Two number cubes are rolled.**

21. Find the probability that the sum of the numbers is 10 or 11.  $\dfrac{1}{12}$
22. Find the probability that the sum is odd and greater than 5.  $\dfrac{1}{3}$
23. Find the probability that the number cubes rolled are doubles and the sum is greater than 4.  $\dfrac{1}{9}$

## Teaching Tip

Remind students that it is not always necessary to draw a tree diagram when working with sample spaces. Elicit that a tree diagram is effective if a listing of a sample space is required, as in Exercises 29 and 30. Students will, of course, draw a tree diagram if that is the requirement, as in Exercise 9. Otherwise, if it is necessary to know only the number of elements in the sample space, students can get that information in various ways.
The number of elements in the sample space:
   may be given (as in Exercises 14–16),
   may be easily determined (as in Exercises 17–20), or
   may be remembered from previous experience (as in Exercises 21–23).

## PRACTICE ◼ LESSON 4-1–LESSON 4-4

**Find the probability that a point selected at random is in the shaded region. Round to the nearest hundredth.** (Lesson 4-1)

**24.** 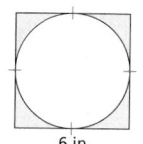 0.21
6 in.

**25.** 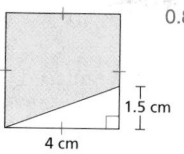 0.81
1.5 cm
4 cm

**26.** 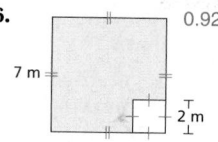 0.92
7 m
2 m

**List all the elements of the sample space as ordered pairs for each of the following experiments.** (Lesson 4-3)
For 27–28, see additional answers.

**27.** You flip a dime and a nickel.

**28.** You spin each of these spinners once.

**Find each probability.** (Lesson 4-4)

**29.** Guessing incorrectly on a multiple-choice question with 5 choices. $\frac{4}{5}$

**30.** Rolling 2 number cubes and getting a multiple of 3. $\frac{1}{3}$

# Mid-Chapter Quiz

**Find the probability that a point selected at random lies in the shaded region.** (Lesson 4-1)

**1.**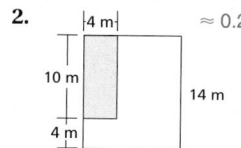
4 ft   0.25
2 ft

**2.**  ≈ 0.24
4 m
10 m
14 m
4 m
12 m

**3.** 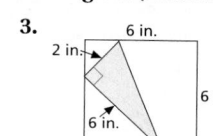 $\frac{1}{6}$
6 in.
2 in.
6 in.
6 in.

**4.** A box contains 12 tennis balls, 15 golf balls, 9 ping-pong balls and 6 baseballs. What is the probability that a golf ball is chosen? (Lesson 4-1)  ≈ 0.36

**5.** A glass has a 5 in 6 chance of breaking if dropped onto a wooden floor. If 3 glasses are dropped, what is the probability that just one of them breaks? Describe a model and perform 25 trials of the simulation. (Lesson 4-1)
$\frac{5}{72}$, or about 0.07; use three number cubes for the simulation.

**6.** A family wants to adopt 1 puppy and 1 kitten from an animal shelter. They have narrowed their choices down to 6 puppies and 4 kittens. How many possible different dog and cat duos are possible? (Lesson 4-2)  24

**A number cube is rolled and a letter from the alphabet is randomly selected.** (Lesson 4-3)

**7.** How many possible outcomes are there?  156

**8.** Find $P(6, Z)$. $\frac{1}{156}$

**9.** Find $P$(even number, vowel). $\frac{5}{52}$

**10.** Find $P$(number less than 4, B). $\frac{1}{52}$

Chapter 4 **Review and Practice Your Skills** | **167**

---

**ADDITIONAL ANSWERS**

**9.**

| Spinner | Coin | Outcomes |
|---|---|---|
| 1 | H | 1H |
|   | T | 1T |
| 2 | H | 2H |
|   | T | 2T |
| 3 | H | 3H |
|   | T | 3T |
| 4 | H | 4H |
|   | T | 4T |
| 5 | H | 5H |
|   | T | 5T |

**27.** (dime, nickel) → (H, H), (H, T), (T, H), (T, T)

**28.** (A, 1), (A, 2), (A, 3), (B, 1), (B, 2), (B, 3), (C, 1), (C, 2), (C, 3)

---

## Extend the Lesson

Students should be aware that when two events are mutually exclusive, a Venn diagram that models the events would show two sets that do not intersect (called *disjoint sets*).

For example, this Venn diagram models the two mutually exclusive events of getting an even number or getting a 5 on a spinner divided into 6 equal portions that are numbered 1–6.

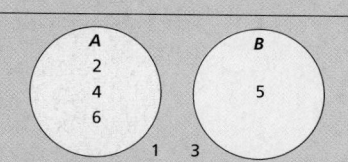

## NCTM Standards/Strands
■ Data Analysis & Probability
■ Representation
■ Problem Solving
■ Connections

## Vocabulary
independent    dependent

## Tools/Materials Needed
calculator

## Lesson Resources
Warm-up Transparency 17
Transparency RF-18
Reteaching 4-5
Extra Practice 4-5
Enrichment 4-5

# Getting Started

## 5-MINUTE WARM-UP

**Multiply. Write your answer as a fraction in lowest terms.**

1. $\dfrac{8}{15} \cdot \dfrac{7}{14}$    $\dfrac{4}{15}$

2. $\dfrac{15}{21} \cdot \dfrac{4}{20}$    $\dfrac{1}{7}$

3. $\dfrac{8}{58} \cdot \dfrac{10}{24}$    $\dfrac{5}{87}$

4. $\dfrac{18}{28} \cdot \dfrac{7}{27}$    $\dfrac{1}{6}$

## Introduction to Lesson 4-5
Elicit that the tree diagram for Questions 1 and 2 results in some outcomes that are repeating pairs of letters such as (B, B), while the tree diagram for Questions 3 and 4 has no outcomes with repeats.

---

# 4-5 Independent and Dependent Events

**Goals**  ■ Find probabilities of dependent events.
　　　　　■ Find the probability of independent events.

**Applications**  Government, Health, Sports, Games

**Refer to the set of cards. Assume they are placed face down.**

1. A card is selected at random, then replaced. Another card is selected. Make a tree diagram of the sample space. See additional answers.

2. Use the tree diagram to find $P(\text{B, then L})$.  $\dfrac{1}{8}$

3. A card is selected at random, but it is not replaced. Then another card is selected. Make a tree diagram for the sample space.  See additional answers.

4. Use the tree diagram to find $P(\text{B, then L})$.  $\dfrac{1}{6}$

5. Compare your results from Questions 2 and 4. What do you notice?
The probability of finding $P(\text{B, then L})$ is higher for Question 4.

## ◢ BUILD UNDERSTANDING

Two events are **independent** if the result of the second event is not affected by the result of the first event.

If $A$ and $B$ are independent events, the probability of both events occurring is the product of the probabilities of the individual events.

$$P(A \text{ and } B) = P(A) \cdot P(B)$$

Sometimes $P(A \text{ and } B)$ is written $P(A, \text{ then } B)$ to emphasize that $A$ and $B$ do not characterize a single event.

### Example 1

A bag contains 3 red marbles, 4 green marbles and 5 blue marbles. One marble is taken at random and then replaced. Then another marble is taken at random.

**Find the probability that the first marble is red and the second marble is blue.**

### Solution

Because the first marble is replaced, the sample space of 12 marbles does not change for each event. The two events are independent.

$$P(\text{red, then blue}) = P(\text{red}) \cdot P(\text{blue}) \qquad \frac{\text{red marbles}}{\text{total marbles}} \cdot \frac{\text{blue marbles}}{\text{total marbles}}$$

$$= \frac{3}{12} \cdot \frac{5}{12}$$

$$= \frac{15}{144} = \frac{5}{48}$$

The probability of picking red, then blue is $\dfrac{5}{48}$.

## ADDITIONAL ANSWERS

**1.**

| Card 1 | Card 2 | Outcomes |
|---|---|---|
| B | B | BB |
|   | E | BE |
|   | L | BL |
|   | L | BL |
| E | B | EB |
|   | E | EE |
|   | L | EL |
|   | L | EL |
| L | B | LB |
|   | E | LE |
|   | L | LL |
|   | L | LL |
| L | B | LB |
|   | E | LE |
|   | L | LL |
|   | L | LL |

**3.**

| Card 1 | Card 2 | Outcomes |
|---|---|---|
| B | E | BE |
|   | L | BL |
|   | L | BL |
| E | B | EB |
|   | L | EL |
|   | L | EL |
| L | B | LB |
|   | E | LE |
|   | L | LL |
| L | B | LB |
|   | E | LE |
|   | L | LL |

Two events are **dependent** if the result of one event *is* affected by the result of another event. If A and B are dependent,

$$P(A \text{ and } B) = P(A) \cdot P(B, \text{ given that } A \text{ occurred}).$$

## Example 2

A bag contains 3 red marbles, 4 green marbles, and 5 blue marbles. One marble is taken at random from the bag. It is not replaced. Then another marble is taken at random.

**Find the probability that the first marble is red and the second marble is blue.**

### Solution

Because the first marble is not replaced, the second event is dependent on the first event. Find the probability of the first event.

$$P(\text{red}) = \frac{3}{12} = \frac{1}{4} \qquad \frac{\text{red marbles}}{\text{total marbles}}$$

On the next selection, there are only 11 marbles. Assuming that a red marble was removed, there are still 5 marbles in the bag.

$$P(\text{blue after red}) = \frac{5}{11} \qquad \frac{\text{blue marbles}}{\text{remaining marbles}}$$

Multiply the two probabilities together.

$$P(\text{red, then blue}) = \frac{1}{4} \cdot \frac{5}{11}$$
$$= \frac{5}{44}$$

The probability of picking red, then blue is $\frac{5}{44}$.

## Example 3

A bag contains 3 red marbles, 4 green marbles, and 5 blue marbles. Two marbles are taken at random from the bag.

**Find the probability that both marbles are blue.**

### Solution

Consider that one of the marbles must be taken before the other. Since the first marble is not replaced, the second event is dependent on the first event.

$$P(\text{first blue marble}) = \frac{5}{12} \qquad \frac{\text{blue marbles}}{\text{total marbles}}$$

$$P(\text{second blue marble}) = \frac{5-1}{12-1} = \frac{4}{11} \qquad \frac{\text{remaining blue marbles}}{\text{remaining marbles}}$$

Multiply the two probabilities together.

$$P(\text{blue, then blue}) = \frac{5}{12} \cdot \frac{4}{11} = \frac{20}{132} = \frac{5}{33}$$

The probability of picking blue, then blue is $\frac{5}{33}$.

mathmatters2.com/extra_examples

Lesson 4-5 **Independent and Dependent Events** 169

## Chalkboard Examples

### Supplementary Examples

1. A card is drawn at random from a standard deck of playing cards. The card is identified and then returned to the deck. A second card is drawn. Find the probability that both cards will be black. Since the first card is replaced before the second card is drawn, the two stages of the event are independent—meaning that the sample space is the same for the second draw as it was for the first.

$P(\text{black, then black})$
$= P(\text{black}) \cdot P(\text{black})$
$= \frac{26}{52} \cdot \frac{26}{52}$
$= \frac{1}{4}$

So, when the first card is replaced before the second card is drawn, the probability that both cards will be black is 1 : 4.

2. A card is drawn at random from a standard deck of playing cards. The card is identified and not returned to the deck. A second card is drawn. Find the probability that both cards will be black. Since the first card is not replaced before the second card is drawn, the second stage of the event is dependent on the first—meaning that the sample space for the second draw is less than it was for the first draw.

$P(\text{black, then black})$
$= P(\text{black}) \cdot P(\text{black})$
$= \frac{26}{52} \cdot \frac{25}{51}$
$= \frac{25}{102}$

So, when the first card is not replaced before the second card is drawn, the probability that both cards will be black is 25 : 102.

## Extend the Lesson

**CHALLENGE** Ed has two quarters and one nickel in his pocket. The pocket has a hole in it, and one coin drops out. Ed picks up the coin and puts it back in his pocket. A few minutes later, a coin drops out of his pocket again.
Find the probability that:
a. the two coins that fell have a total value of 30 cents
   $\frac{4}{9}$; the 4 favorable outcomes are marked • in the tree diagram.
b. a quarter fell out at least once $\frac{8}{9}$

| | | Outcomes |
|---|---|---|
| $Q_1$ → $Q_1$ | | $Q_1$ $Q_1$ |
| $Q_1$ → $Q_2$ | | $Q_1$ $Q_1$ |
| → N | | $Q_1$ N • |
| $Q_2$ → $Q_1$ | | $Q_2$ $Q_1$ |
| $Q_2$ → $Q_2$ | | $Q_2$ $Q_2$ |
| → N | | $Q_2$ N • |
| N → $Q_1$ | | N $Q_1$ • |
| N → $Q_2$ | | N $Q_2$ • |
| → N | | N N |

## Lesson Wrap-up

### QUICK ASSESSMENT

Ask the following questions to determine if students understand the content presented in this lesson.

**Classify the events as *independent* or *dependent*.**

1. rolling a number cube twice
   **independent**
2. drawing two cards from a deck, replacing the first card before the second is drawn **independent**
3. drawing two marbles from a bag, not replacing the first marble before drawing the second **dependent**

**Tell the number of possible outcomes in the sample space for each stage of the event.**

4. tossing a coin twice **There are 2 possible outcomes for each toss.**
5. rolling four number cubes **There are 6 possible outcomes for each cube.**

### ASSIGNMENT GUIDE

**Basic:** 1–25, 31–45
**Enriched:** 1–45

---

### Reteaching Worksheet 4-5

Name _____ Date _____

RETEACHING **4-5**

**INDEPENDENT AND DEPENDENT EVENTS**

Two events are **independent** if the result of the first event does not affect the result of the second event. If $A$ and $B$ are independent events, then $P(A \text{ and } B) = P(A) \cdot P(B)$.

If the result of one event is affected by the result of another event, then the events are **dependent**. If $A$ and $B$ are dependent events, then $P(A \text{ and } B) = P(A) \cdot P(B, \text{ given that } A \text{ has occurred})$. Often, $P(A \text{ and } B)$ is written $P(A, \text{ then } B)$.

**Example**

A box contains four blue, five red, and six yellow balls.
**a.** A ball is picked at random and replaced. Then another ball is picked. Find the probability that the first ball is yellow and the second ball is red.
**b.** A ball is picked at random, but it is not replaced. Then another ball is picked. Find the probability that the first ball is yellow and the second ball is red.

**Solution**
**a.** Because the ball is replaced, the sample space of 15 balls does not change the events. The events are independent.
$P(\text{yellow}) = \frac{6}{15} = \frac{2}{5}$   $P(\text{red}) = \frac{5}{15} = \frac{1}{3}$
$P(\text{yellow, then red}) = P(\text{yellow}) \cdot P(\text{red}) = \frac{2}{5} \cdot \frac{1}{3} = \frac{2}{15}$
The probability of picking yellow, then red is $\frac{2}{15}$.
**b.** Because the ball is not replaced, the sample space is reduced to 14 balls for the second pick. The events are dependent.
$P(\text{yellow}) = \frac{6}{15} = \frac{2}{5}$   $P(\text{red after yellow}) = \frac{5}{14}$
$P(\text{yellow, then red}) = \frac{2}{5} \cdot \frac{5}{14} = \frac{10}{70} = \frac{1}{7}$
In this case, the probability of picking yellow, then red is $\frac{1}{7}$.

**✔ EXERCISES**

Tell if the events are independent or dependent. Then find each probability.

1. You toss a coin twice. Find $P$(two heads).   **independent; $\frac{1}{4}$**

2. Your drawer contains two black socks and two blue ones. Without looking, you take a sock out, hold onto it, then take another sock. Find $P$(two black socks).
   **dependent; $\frac{1}{6}$**

3. You toss a coin and roll a number cube marked 1 to 6. Find $P$(H, odd number).
   **independent; $\frac{1}{4}$**

---

---

A box contains ten 1998 pennies, four 2001 pennies and six 2004 pennies. Pennies are taken at random from the box one at a time and then put back. Find each probability.

1. $P$(1998, then 2001) $\frac{1}{10}$   2. $P$(2004, then 1998) $\frac{3}{20}$   3. $P$(2001, then 2001) $\frac{1}{25}$

A bag contains 5 blue, 3 red, and 2 green marbles. Marbles are taken at random and not replaced. Find each probability.

4. $P$(red, then blue) $\frac{1}{6}$   5. $P$(red, then red) $\frac{1}{15}$   6. $P$(blue, then green) $\frac{1}{9}$

7. A mail carrier is delivering 6 bills and 3 letters to the Jensen family. The wind blows two of the envelopes away. What is the probability that both of the envelopes are bills? $\frac{5}{12}$

8. **WRITING MATH** Describe how to find the probability of dependent events. See additional answers.

### ◣ PRACTICE EXERCISES • For Extra Practice, see page 597.

A group of numbered cards contains one 1, two 2s, three 3s and four 4s. Cards are picked one at a time, then replaced. Find each probability.

9. $P$(1, then 2) $\frac{1}{50}$   10. $P$(3, then 4) $\frac{3}{25}$   11. $P$(4, then 4) $\frac{4}{25}$

12. A farmer buys individual letters to make a sign saying NO TRESPASSING. On the way home, the farmer loses three of the letters. What is the probability that he loses all three S's? $\frac{1}{286}$

13. **GOVERNMENT** For the 108th Congress (2004), 62 women served in the House and 14 women served in the Senate. If you select a member from each body, what is the probability that they are both women? (The Senate has 100 members and the House has 435 members.) $\frac{868}{43,500} \approx 0.02$

14. Yasu has two $1 bills, three $5 bills and four $10 bills in her pocket. Without looking, she pulls two bills out. What is the probability that she pulls out a total of $15? $\frac{1}{3}$

15. Five chicken sandwiches, six cheese sandwiches, and four egg sandwiches are packed in identical bags. If the bags are picked at random, find the probability that the first three picks include one of each kind. $\frac{4}{91}$

16. A child is playing with letter blocks. There is one letter on each block, and the letters are A, B, C, D, O, P, R, S, and T. What is the probability of the child selecting three blocks and placing them side by side to spell CAT? $\frac{1}{504}$

**HEALTH** For a given population, 43% of the people have Type A blood, 32% have Type O, 17% have Type B and 8% have Type AB. If two people are selected at random, find each probability.

17. $P$(they both have Type O blood)  0.1024   18. $P$(one Type A and one Type B)  0.0731

19. $P$(one Type O and one AB, or both A)   20. $P$(they have the same blood type)  0.3226
    0.2105

---

### Teaching Tip

**ESL/LEP** Point out that the terms *dependent* and *independent* have the same meanings when they are used in probability as they have in everyday use. *Dependent* means *relying on another* or *influenced by another*, while *independent* has the opposite meaning: *not influenced or controlled by another*. Have students consider the following compound events to discuss the difference between *mutually exclusive* and *independent* events.

rolling a number cube and tossing a coin **mutually exclusive; neither stage of the event could have an effect on the other**

rolling a number cube twice **independent; the second roll is not influenced by the first**

21. **WRITING MATH** Write a short paragraph explaining the difference between dependent events and independent events. Give an example of each by using a standard deck of 52 cards. See additional answers.

22. There are four true-false questions on a quiz. A student has not studied and guesses at each of the questions. What is the probability of the student answering all four questions correctly? $\frac{1}{16}$

23. **DATA FILE** Refer to the data on physician office visits on page 568. What is the probability that two randomly selected people visiting a physician will see one who specializes in internal medicine? 0.013

24. A drawer of unmatched socks contains 11 blue socks and 22 red socks. If two socks are taken at random, what is the probability that both are blue? What is the probability that one is blue and one is red? $\frac{5}{48}$, $\frac{11}{48}$

25. **GAMES** In a game of chance, there are 52 spaces on a spinning board. Of the 52 spaces, 25 are red, 25 are black and 2 are green. What is the probability of spinning a green space, then a red space? $\frac{25}{1352}$

## ■ EXTENDED PRACTICE EXERCISES

**SPORTS** The Bears and the Pumas are playing a "three-out-of-five" series to determine a league champion. The Bears have an estimated $\frac{2}{3}$ probability of winning any game.

26. What is the probability that the Bears win the series in three straight games? $\frac{8}{27}$

27. The Bears can win the series in four games, losing one and winning three. In how many ways can this happen? What is the probability that the Bears win the series in four games? $3$; $\frac{8}{81}$

28. The series can go to five games. How many ways can the Bears win a five-game series? What is the probability of the Bears winning a five-game series? $6$; $\frac{8}{243}$

29. **CRITICAL THINKING** Two number cubes are rolled. If the sum of the numbers rolled is a multiple of 3, Player A scores a point. If the sum rolled is a multiple of 4, Player B scores a point. Is this a *fair* game? That is, does each player have an equal chance of scoring a point? No; there are 12 ways to get a multiple of 3 and 9 ways to get a multiple of 4.

30. **CHAPTER INVESTIGATION** Determine how the turns of your game are played, and assign point values to possible outcomes. The less likely an outcome is to occur, the more valuable it should be. Decide how the game will begin and be won, if there are free turns, if there are penalties and other aspects of the game. Answers will vary.

## ■ MIXED REVIEW EXERCISES

Evaluate each expression when $a = -2$ and $b = 3$. (Lesson 2-7)

31. $b^2$ 9
32. $3a^2b$ 36
33. $4(a^2 + b^2)$ 52
34. $(3 + b)^2$ 36
35. $\frac{a^5}{a^2}$ −8
36. $(-2 - a)^3$ 0
37. $\frac{b^7}{b^5}$ 9
38. $(a + b^2)^2$ 49
39. $\frac{1}{a^2}(3b^3)$ $\frac{81}{4}$

Simplify each expression. (Lesson 2-4)

40. $6g - (-3g)$ 9g
41. $2ab - 4a - 6ab$ −4ab − 4a
42. $-8c - (-4c)$ −4c
43. $6k + 4m - 3k - 7m$ 3k − 3m
44. $3.5r - 7.2r + 4.6r$ 0.9r
45. $-7c + 3b - 4c - 2b$ −11c + b

mathmatters2.com/self_check_quiz

## ADDITIONAL ANSWERS

8. Find the probability of the first event. Then be sure to adjust the possible number of outcomes in the sample space. Then find the probability of the dependent event and multiply that probability times the probability of the first event.

21. Independent events are events whose outcomes do not affect one another. For example, when a card is drawn from a deck of cards it is then replaced and reshuffled before drawing the second card. Dependent events are events for which the outcome of one can affect the other. When a card is drawn from a deck of cards and not replaced, the probability of the next card drawn is different than if the card were replaced and the deck reshuffled.

---

### Extra Practice Worksheet 4-5

Name _____ Date _____

**EXTRA PRACTICE** 4-5
**INDEPENDENT AND DEPENDENT EVENTS**

☑ **EXERCISES**

A box contains eight blue index cards, four yellow index cards, and two pink index cards. Two cards are taken at random from the box, one at a time, and then put back. Find each probability.

1. P(blue, then pink) $\frac{4}{49}$
2. P(yellow, then blue) $\frac{8}{49}$
3. P(yellow, then pink) $\frac{2}{49}$
4. P(pink, then yellow) $\frac{2}{49}$
5. P(blue, then yellow) $\frac{8}{49}$
6. P(pink, then blue) $\frac{4}{49}$
7. P(both yellow) $\frac{4}{49}$
8. P(both blue) $\frac{16}{49}$

A bag contains three red buttons, six black buttons, and eight white buttons. Two buttons are taken at random and not replaced. Find each probability.

9. P(red, then black) $\frac{9}{136}$
10. P(black, then white) $\frac{3}{17}$
11. P(white, then black) $\frac{3}{17}$
12. P(white, then red) $\frac{3}{34}$
13. P(red, then white) $\frac{3}{34}$
14. P(black, then red ) $\frac{9}{136}$
15. P(both red) $\frac{3}{136}$
16. P(both black) $\frac{15}{136}$

Four white socks, six blue socks, and eight gray socks are in a drawer. Without looking, two socks are pulled from the drawer. Find each probability.

17. P(both white) $\frac{2}{51}$
18. P(both gray) $\frac{28}{153}$
19. P(both blue) $\frac{5}{51}$
20. P(blue and white) $\frac{4}{51}$
21. P(gray and white) $\frac{16}{153}$
22. P(blue and gray) $\frac{8}{51}$

---

### Enrichment Worksheet 4-5

Name _____ Date _____

**ENRICHMENT** 4-5
**CHANGING CONDITIONS**

Sometimes you are given additional information about an experiment that may reduce the size of the sample space. Because the information changes the number of possible outcomes, it therefore affects the probability.

**Example**

Three coins are tossed.
a. What is the probability that all three coins come up heads?
b. What is the probability that all three coins come up heads, given that the first coin came up heads?

**Solution**

a. When you toss three coins, there are eight outcomes.

HHH HHT HTH HTT THH TTH THT TTT

Only one outcome is three heads. So, P(all heads) = $\frac{1}{8}$.

b. Suppose that the first coin comes up heads. The new sample space then consists of only those outcomes with a head for the first coin. There are four such outcomes.

HHH HHT HTH HTT

So, P(all heads, given first coin is heads) = $\frac{1}{4}$.

When the probability of an event A is adjusted, based on information about another event B, the result is called **conditional probability**.

☑ **EXERCISES**

1. What is the probability that the spinner lands on 5? $\frac{1}{6}$
2. If you are told that the spinner landed on an odd number, what is the probability that it landed on 5? $\frac{1}{3}$
3. If you are told that the spinner landed on an even number, what is the probability that it landed on 5? 0

A number cube is tossed. What is the probability that it shows 4 if you know the following?

4. It shows an even number. $\frac{1}{3}$
5. It shows a number less than 5. $\frac{1}{4}$
6. It does not show a 1. $\frac{1}{5}$
7. It shows an even number less than 5. $\frac{1}{2}$

## NCTM Standards/Strands
- Data Analysis & Probability
- Representation
- Problem Solving
- Connections

## Vocabulary

permutation     factorial

## Tools/Materials Needed

coins (a penny, a nickel, a dime, a quarter)
calculator

## Lesson Resources

Warm-up Transparency 17
Transparency RF-19
Reteaching 4-6
Extra Practice 4-6
Enrichment 4-6
Technology Activity 4-6

# Getting Started

## 5-MINUTE WARM-UP

**Use mental math to evaluate each expression.**

1. $\dfrac{7 \cdot 6 \cdot 5 \cdot 4 \cdot 3 \cdot 2 \cdot 1}{5 \cdot 4 \cdot 3 \cdot 2 \cdot 1}$  42

2. $\dfrac{6 \cdot 5 \cdot 4 \cdot 3 \cdot 2 \cdot 1}{3 \cdot 2 \cdot 1 \cdot 3 \cdot 2 \cdot 1}$  20

## Introduction to Lesson 4-6
Students should consider a tree diagram to view the sample space for

 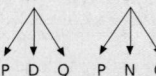 

Question 1.
Of the 12 possible outcomes, have students identify and eliminate those that give the same amount of money: for example, P N = N P = 6¢. Then, there are only 6 outcomes that are different amounts of money: P N, P D, P Q, N D, N Q, D Q.

---

# 4-6 Permutations of a Set

**Goals**     ■ Find the number of permutations of a set.
**Applications**   Cooking, Travel, Music, Sports, Games

**Work with a partner. Use coins to help you answer Questions 1–3.**

1. Suppose you have a penny, nickel, dime and quarter in your pocket. If you take out two coins, how many different amounts of money might you have in your hand?  6

2. How can you be sure you have listed all the different amounts of money?   The best way is to make a tree diagram.

3. Suppose you have the same coins as in Question 1. In how many different ways could you take out two coins and give one each to two friends?  12

### ■ BUILD UNDERSTANDING

A word is a set of letters arranged in a definite order. For example, *charm* and *march* are different words even though they contain the same letters. An arrangement of items in a particular order is called a **permutation**. Order is important in permutations.

You can use the fundamental counting principle to find the number of possible permutations of a set of items. Each time you pick an item for a position in a permutation, there will be one less item to pick from for the next position of the permutation.

| *n!* (*n* factorial) | The number of permutations of *n* different items is $n(n-1)(n-2) \ldots (2)(1)$ and is written as *n!* |
|---|---|

### Example 1

**How many different "words" can be made with the letters a, b, c, d, and e if all the letters are used?**

(The "words" do not have to make sense in English or any other language.)

**Technology Note**

Most advanced calculators have a factorial function key. You can often find it in the probability menu.

### Solution

Find the number of permutations of five letters.

number of permutations $= 5! = 5 \cdot 4 \cdot 3 \cdot 2 \cdot 1 = 120$

There are 120 different "words" that can be made using five letters.

---

## Teaching Tip

From the Warm-up Exercises, students should note that common strings of factors can be cancelled before multiplying. After introducing *factorial notation*, have students consider the calculations with factorials shown below.

1. $\dfrac{10!}{2! \cdot 4!} = \dfrac{10 \cdot 9 \cdot 8 \cdot 7 \cdot 6 \cdot 5 \cdot 4 \cdot 3 \cdot 2 \cdot 1}{2 \cdot 1 \cdot 4 \cdot 3 \cdot 2 \cdot 1} = 75{,}600$

2. $3 \cdot (5 - 2)! = 3 \cdot 3! = 3 \cdot 3 \cdot 2 \cdot 1 = 18$

3. $\dfrac{7!}{(7 - 3)!} = \dfrac{7!}{4!} = \dfrac{7 \cdot 6 \cdot 5 \cdot 4 \cdot 3 \cdot 2 \cdot 1}{4 \cdot 3 \cdot 2 \cdot 1} = 210$

Sometimes you may want to use only part of a set. The number of permutations of $n$ different items taken $r$ items at a time and with no repetitions, is written $_nP_r$. This is read as "the number of permutations of $n$ items taken $r$ at a time." You can use the formula below to find the number of permutations when only part of the set is used.

$$_nP_r \qquad _nP_r = \frac{n!}{(n-r)!}$$
where $n$ is the number of different items and $r$ is the number of items taken at a time.

By definition, $n!$ is the number of permutations of $n$ items taken $n$ at a time, so
$$_nP_n = \frac{n!}{(n-n)!} = \frac{n!}{0!}.$$

This means that $0! = 1$.

## Example 2

**How many different "words" can be made with the letters a, b, c, d and e if only three different letters are used in each word?**

### Solution

There are five letters to be taken three at a time. So $n = 5$ and $r = 3$ in the permutation formula.

$$_nP_r = \frac{n!}{(n-r)!} \qquad _5P_3 = \frac{5!}{(5-3)!}$$
$$= \frac{5 \cdot 4 \cdot 3 \cdot \cancel{2} \cdot \cancel{1}}{\cancel{2} \cdot \cancel{1}} \qquad \text{Cancel common factors to simplify.}$$
$$= 60$$

There are 60 "words" that can be made.

**Technology Note**

Most advanced calculators have a permutation function key. It is usually symbolized as $_nP_r$.

For example, entering the sequence 5 $_nP_r$ 3 calculates $\frac{5!}{2!} = 60$.

## Example 3

**COOKING** A sandwich shop offers 6 toppings for their submarine sandwiches: ham, turkey, cheese, lettuce, tomatoes and onions. How many different ways can the ingredients of a sandwich be arranged if exactly 2 ingredients are chosen from the menu?

### Solution

There are six different menu items to be taken two at a time. So $n = 6$ and $r = 2$ in the permutation formula.

$$_nP_r = \frac{n!}{(n-r)!} \qquad _6P_2 = \frac{6!}{(6-2)!}$$
$$= \frac{6 \cdot 5 \cdot \cancel{4} \cdot \cancel{3} \cdot \cancel{2} \cdot \cancel{1}}{\cancel{4} \cdot \cancel{3} \cdot \cancel{2} \cdot \cancel{1}} \qquad \text{Cancel common factors to simplify.}$$
$$= 30$$

There are 30 different ways that the ingredients can be arranged.

mathmatters2.com/extra_examples

Lesson 4-6 **Permutations of a Set** **173**

## Lesson Wrap-up

### QUICK ASSESSMENT

Ask the following questions to determine if students understand the content presented in this lesson.

1. What is a short way of indicating $6 \cdot 5 \cdot 4 \cdot 3 \cdot 2 \cdot 1$? **6!**

2. Is $2! \cdot 3!$ equivalent to $6!$ ? Explain. **no; $2! \cdot 3! = 2 \cdot 1 \cdot 3 \cdot 2 \cdot 1 = 12$ and $6! = 6 \cdot 5 \cdot 4 \cdot 3 \cdot 2 \cdot 1 = 720$**

3. Which of the following is the value of $0!$? **B**
   A. 0  B. 1  C. $-1$  D. $\pm 1$

4. Which of the following situations are examples of *permutations*? **A and B**
   A. arranging 5 people on a bench that seats 5
   B. choosing 4 letters from 6 and writing all possible arrangements of the choices
   C. selecting a committee of 3 from 10 women

### ASSIGNMENT GUIDE

**Basic:** 1–26, 32–55
**Enriched:** 1–55

### Reteaching Worksheet 4-6

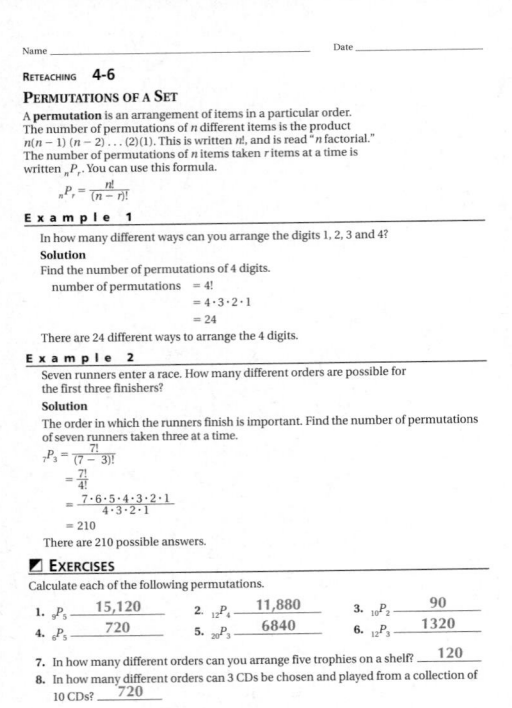

**Calculate each of the following permutations.**

1. $_5P_2$  20      2. $_8P_2$  56      3. $_4P_1$  4      4. $_7P_5$  2520

5. In how many different ways can you arrange the letters m, n, o, p, q and r?  720

6. **SPORTS** There are 7 finalists in a swimming race. Medals are awarded for first, second and third place. In how many different ways can the medals be awarded?  210

7. Find the number of 5-letter "words" that can be formed from the letters of the word "horse."  120

8. A professor is grading 8 term papers in order of merit. If none of the papers are of equal merit, in how many different orders can the papers be graded?  40,320

▧ PRACTICE EXERCISES • For Extra Practice, see page 598.

**Calculate each of the following permutations.**

9. $_6P_2$  30      10. $_{11}P_9$  19,958,400      11. $_5P_0$  1      12. $_8P_8$  40,320

13. **MUSIC** A five-piece band consists of a guitarist, a bass player, a trumpeter, a saxophone player and a pianist. If three of the band members each play a solo in an introduction to a song, how many different permutations of three band members can be used?  60

14. **ENTERTAINMENT** A radio disc jockey has a set of 9 songs to play. In how many different ways can the disc jockey play the next 3 songs?  504

15. How many different four-digit numbers can be formed from the digits 4, 5, 6 and 7 if each digit can be used only once?  24

16. In how many different orders could a poet recite 5 poems from a collection of 9 poems?  15,120

17. Find the number of 7-letter "words" that can be formed from the letters of the word "Florida."  5040

18. Dermarr and Luke are two of the 12 actors auditioning for a show. The order in which the actors will perform is picked at random. What is the probability that Dermarr will perform first and Luke will perform second?  $\frac{1}{132}$

19. **TRAVEL** The towns of Anderson and Mt. Washington are connected by 7 roads. Mt. Washington and Hyde Park are connected by 5 roads. In how many different ways can a tourist travel from Anderson to Hyde Park via Mt. Washington?  35

20. **DATA FILE** Refer to the data on threatened and endangered species on page 567. Find the number of permutations of types of species listed three at a time. What is the probability that the group consists of snails, insects, and birds listed in that order?  1716, $\frac{1}{1716}$

**21.** How many 5-digit zip codes can be formed using odd digits if digits can be reused? How many can be formed if digits cannot be reused? **3125; 120**

**22.** How many different ways can 6 classes be scheduled in a 6-period day? **720**

 **23. GAMES** Nakeisha selects seven tiles from the group of letters to begin a Scrabble® game. How many different ways can she arrange her 7 tiles? **5040**

 **24. WRITING MATH** Describe a situation in which the number of outcomes is given by $_6P_3$. Sample answer: There are six people in a contest. How many ways can the first, second, and third prizes be awarded?

**25.** The lunch menu at a school cafeteria lists 3 soups, 6 sandwiches and 4 fruits. In how many different ways can a student choose a lunch that consists of a soup, a sandwich, and a fruit? **72**

**26. ERROR ALERT** Manuel is asked to determine how many different 2-digit numbers can be formed from the digits 3, 4, 5 and 6 if a digit can appear only once. He reasons that since there are 4 numbers, there are $4 \cdot 4 = 16$ possible 2-digit numbers. What mistake has Manuel made, and what is the correct answer? He used the calculation that would be appropriate if digits could be used more than once; 12.

## ■ EXTENDED PRACTICE EXERCISES

**27.** In how many ways can the five CD-ROMs of an encyclopedia be placed next to each other on a shelf if the first CD-ROM is always on the extreme left? **24**

**28.** Damon needs to name the vertices of a triangle and wants to use the letters of his name. In how many ways can he do this? **60**

**29.** Krystal wants to collect all 5 prizes given in a box of cereal. If her parents buy a box of cereal a week, what is the probability that she will get all five prizes in five weeks? $\frac{24}{625}$

**30. CRITICAL THINKING** If the digits 1–9 are equally likely to be selected, what is the probability that a 3-digit number is a palindrome? A *palindrome* is a word or number that reads the same backwards and forwards. $\frac{1}{9}$

**31.** How many even numbers can be formed from the digits 1, 2, 3, 4 and 5 if each digit is used once in each number? **48**

## ■ MIXED REVIEW EXERCISES

**Graph the solution of each inequality on a number line.** (Lesson 3-6)
For 32–43, see additional answers.

**32.** $b \leq 7$     **33.** $a > -3.5$     **34.** $c < 1.5$

**35.** $3 \leq h$     **36.** $2 \geq g$     **37.** $l \leq 3$

**38.** $p \geq -3$     **39.** $r < -2.5$     **40.** $m < -4$

**41.** $d \geq -2$     **42.** $-3 < e$     **43.** $4 > j$

**Solve each inequality.** (Lesson 3-7)

**44.** $4 + c > -2$   $c > -6$     **45.** $-3x \leq -12$   $x \geq 4$     **46.** $10 \geq g + 4$   $g \leq 6$

**47.** $\frac{r}{2} - 6 < -2$   $r < 8$     **48.** $7k + 8 > 3$   $k > -\frac{5}{7}$     **49.** $1.4f - 3 < -0.2$   $f < 2$

**50.** $3 + \frac{1}{4}g \geq 7$   $g \geq 16$     **51.** $3r - 5 \leq 4$   $r \leq 3$     **52.** $3(2.5h - 1) \geq 12$   $h \geq 2$

**53.** $8 \geq 0.3s - 7$   $s \leq 50$     **54.** $4(3h + 1) < 6h - 4$   $h < -\frac{4}{3}$    **55.** $2(8 + a) > 3(4 + a)$   $a < 4$

**32.** 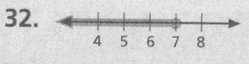    **33.** 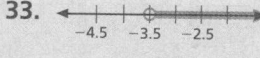    **34.**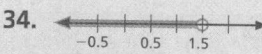

**35.** 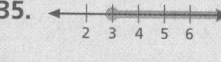    **36.** 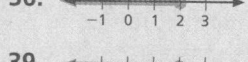    **37.**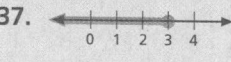

**38.** 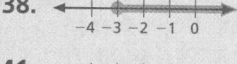    **39.**    **40.**

**41.**    **42.**    **43.**

---

## Extra Practice Worksheet 4-6

Name _____ Date _____

EXTRA PRACTICE **4-6**
**PERMUTATIONS OF A SET**

### ✎ EXERCISES

Calculate each of the following permutations.

**1.** $_6P_2$ ___30___    **2.** $_8P_4$ ___1680___    **3.** $_9P_1$ ___9___

**4.** $_7P_4$ ___840___    **5.** $_7P_6$ ___20,160___    **6.** $_{10}P_7$ ___604,800___

**7.** $_{15}P_3$ ___2730___    **8.** $_{13}P_9$ ___259,459,200___    **9.** $_{20}P_5$ ___1,860,480___

**10.** In how many different ways can you arrange the letters r, s, t, u and v? ___120___

**11.** Find the number of "words" that can be formed from the letters of the word "center." ___720___

**12.** How many different four-digit numbers can be formed by the digits 1, 2, 3, 4 and 5 if each digit can be used only once? ___120___

**13.** In how many different orders can six dogs be chosen from a group of ten dogs? ___151,200___

**14.** How many different ways can 6 classes be scheduled in a 6-period day? ___720___

**15.** In how many different orders can 12 e-mail messages be read? ___479,001,600___

**16.** There are six finalists in a spelling bee. Trophies are awarded for first, second and third place. In how many different ways can the trophies be awarded? ___120___

**17.** In how many ways can six different books be placed next to each other on a shelf if the books on the ends do not change? ___24___

**18.** The breakfast menu at a cafeteria lists 3 juices, 4 cereals and 2 breads. In how many different ways may someone choose a breakfast that consists of a juice, a cereal, and a bread? ___24___

**19.** Find the number of "words" that can be formed from the letters of the word "dictionary." ___3,628,800___

**20.** How many different six-digit numbers can be formed by the digits 1, 2, 3, 4, 5, 6, and 7 if each digit can be used only once? ___5040___

---

## Enrichment Worksheet 4-6

Name _____ Date _____

ENRICHMENT **4-6**
**SITTING IN CIRCLES**

Permutations are usually assumed to be along a line. However, consider the permutations of seating people at a circular table. The different places at the table are assumed to be indistinguishable and only relative positions of the people are significant.

### ✎ EXERCISES

Use a circular region to represent a table and identify people with the letters A, B, C, and so on. Sketch each of the possible arrangements for seating the given number of people at a circular table with equally spaced chairs.

**1.** one person        **2.** two people

**3.** three people        **4.** four people

Look for a pattern in your answers for Exercises 1–4. Use the pattern to predict the number of arrangements for seating the given number of people at a circular table.

**5.** five people ___24___ arrangements    **6.** six people ___120___ arrangements

**7.** How many arrangements are possible for seating $N$ people at a circular table? Write your answer using factorial notation. ___$(N-1)!$___

Unlike the seating of people around a table, the position of keys on a circular key ring varies because a key ring can be turned over. What effect does this have on the number of distinguishable permutations of keys on the key ring?

**8.** How many arrangements are possible for four keys on a circular key ring? ___3___

**9.** How many arrangements are possible for five keys on a circular key ring? ___12___

**10.** How many arrangements are possible for eight keys on a circular key ring? ___2520___

**11.** How many arrangements are possible for $N$ keys on a circular key ring? Write your answer using factorial notation. ___$\frac{(N-1)!}{2}$___

## Vocabulary Review

**Lesson 4-5**
independent        dependent

**Lesson 4-6**
permutation

## ASSIGNMENT GUIDE

All students: 1–45

## Chalkboard Examples

### Lesson 4-5
A stack of mail consists of 8 bills, 10 letters, and 6 advertisements. One piece of mail is drawn at random from the stack and put aside; then a second piece of mail is drawn at random from the stack. Find the probability that:
a. both pieces of mail are letters
b. the first piece of mail is either a letter or a bill and the second piece is an advertisement

a. $P$(letter, then letter)
$= \dfrac{10}{24} \cdot \dfrac{9}{23}$ or $\dfrac{15}{92}$

b. $P$(letter or bill, then advertisement) $= \dfrac{8+10}{24} \cdot \dfrac{6}{23}$ or $\dfrac{9}{46}$

### Lesson 4-6
In the 4 periods before lunch, Kim will take Math, French, Biology, and English. In how many ways can Kim's morning program be arranged?
Find the number of permutations of 4 subjects.
$4! = 4 \cdot 3 \cdot 2 \cdot 1 = 24$
So, Kim's morning program can be arranged in 24 different ways.

# Review and Practice Your Skills

## PRACTICE ■ LESSON 4-5

A bag contains 5 quarters, 4 dimes and 3 nickels. Coins are taken at random and then replaced. Find each probability.

1. $P$(quarter, then dime) $\dfrac{5}{36}$
2. $P$(dime, then dime) $\dfrac{1}{9}$
3. $P$(nickel, then quarter) $\dfrac{5}{48}$
4. $P$(nickel, then dime) $\dfrac{1}{12}$
5. $P$(quarter, then quarter) $\dfrac{25}{144}$
6. $P$(dime, then quarter) $\dfrac{5}{36}$

A box contains 6 yellow, 4 purple and 3 pink marbles. Marbles are taken at random and not replaced. Find each probability.

7. $P$(yellow, then pink) $\dfrac{3}{26}$
8. $P$(purple, then yellow) $\dfrac{2}{13}$
9. $P$(pink, then purple) $\dfrac{1}{13}$
10. $P$(yellow, then yellow) $\dfrac{5}{26}$
11. $P$(pink, then pink) $\dfrac{1}{26}$
12. $P$(purple, then purple) $\dfrac{1}{13}$

A drawer contains 3 pairs of black socks, 2 pairs of brown socks and 4 pairs of white socks. One sock is taken at a time at random and not replaced. Find each probability.

13. $P$(black, then black) $\dfrac{5}{51}$
14. $P$(white, then black) $\dfrac{8}{51}$
15. $P$(brown, then brown) $\dfrac{2}{51}$
16. $P$(brown, then white) $\dfrac{16}{153}$
17. $P$(white, then white) $\dfrac{28}{153}$
18. $P$(black, then brown) $\dfrac{4}{51}$

## PRACTICE ■ LESSON 4-6

Calculate each of the following permutations.

19. $_7P_3$  210
20. $_8P_4$  1680
21. $_5P_2$  20
22. $_3P_2$  6
23. $_9P_3$  504
24. $_5P_3$  60
25. $_5P_1$  5
26. $_8P_6$  20,160
27. $_{11}P_6$  332,640

28. How many different 4-digit numbers can be formed from the digits, 2, 3, 4 and 5 if each digit can be used only once?  24

29. The art club will select 4 of 10 students to be on a committee for the positions of president, vice president, secretary and treasurer. How many different committees are possible?  5040

30. A school fair will have a snack bar with items from Brazil, Ethiopia, Greece, Haiti, Italy, Korea, Mexico and Thailand. How many ways can the flags of 4 of these nations be displayed in a circular arrangement around the snack bar?  1680

31. A store owner received a shipment of picture frames in 7 new styles. How many different ways can the owner display 3 of the new styles on a shelf?  210

32. How many different ways can you arrange the letters l, m, n, o and p?  120

## Teaching Tip

In preparation for Exercises 1–18, remind students to pay careful attention to whether or not the first stage of the event ends in *replacement* or *no replacement*. Elicit that if there is replacement after the first stage, then the number of elements in the sample space remains unchanged for the second stage. However, if there is no replacement after the first stage, then the number of elements in the sample space for the second stage is decreased.

**A number cube is rolled and a spinner labeled A through H is spun.** (Lesson 4-3)

**33.** How many possible outcomes are there?  48

**34.** Find $P(6, H)$.  $\frac{1}{48}$

**35.** Find $P(\text{even, vowel})$.  $\frac{1}{8}$

**36.** Find $P(\text{number less than 3, C})$.  $\frac{1}{24}$

**37.** Find $P(\text{number greater than or equal to 2, G})$.  $\frac{5}{48}$

**A card is drawn at random from a standard deck of 52 cards.** (Lesson 4-4)

**38.** Find the probability that the card drawn is a face card.  $\frac{3}{13}$

**39.** Find the probability that the card drawn is a diamond or a face card.  $\frac{11}{26}$

**40.** Find the probability that the card drawn is a club and not a face card.  $\frac{5}{26}$

**41.** A bag of marbles contains 4 green marbles, 5 red marbles and 7 yellow marbles. Find the probability that when three marbles are taken and not replaced you get one of each color. (Lesson 4-5)  $\frac{1}{24}$

**Calculate each of the following permutations.** (Lesson 4-6)

**42.** $_5P_3$  60

**43.** $_6P_3$  120

**44.** $_7P_5$  2520

**45.** $_4P_2$  12

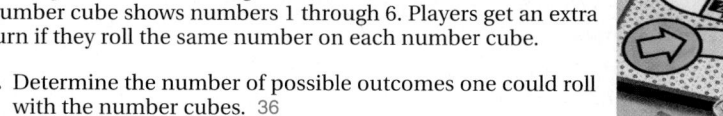

## MathWorks — Career – Board Game Designer

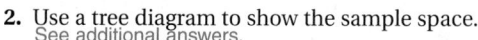
Workplace Knowhow

**B**oard game designers must decide the logic behind the game, the layout, the pieces to be included and the possible ways to win the game. When a board game is created, the designer must know the probability of certain events occurring. Finding these probabilities will determine the rules of the game. A new board game has two number cubes. Each number cube shows numbers 1 through 6. Players get an extra turn if they roll the same number on each number cube.

**1.** Determine the number of possible outcomes one could roll with the number cubes.  36

**2.** Use a tree diagram to show the sample space.
See additional answers.

**3.** What is the probability of getting an extra turn by rolling the same number on both number cubes?  $\frac{1}{6}$

**4.** What is the probability of rolling a 3 or 5 on one of the number cubes?  $\frac{5}{9}$

**5.** What is the probability of rolling a 3 and a 5?  $\frac{1}{18}$

Math Online   mathmatters2.com/mathworks

## MathWorks

There are thousands of different games, and they can be classified in many ways. Games can be grouped according to the kind of people who usually play them, as in children's games, or according to the number of players they require, as in solitaire games. Games may also be grouped according to the object of the game, as in cooperative games. Games are most commonly grouped by the kind of equipment used to play them. The major game groups are board games, card games, tile games, target games, dice games, table games, paper and pencil games, and electronic games.

Board games probably have the greatest variety. Each year, hundreds of new board games appear on the market in the United States alone.

Students should answer Questions 1–5 to better understand the role of probability in determining how a board-game designer might plan the device chosen to control the moves in a game.

Students may be interested in researching the history of board games and learn about some of the earliest. For example, one of the oldest known board games was found at Ur, a city of ancient Sumer (now in Iraq). Archaeologists believe the board is about 4,500 years old. The game was probably a race game in which players threw dice and moved pieces around a track.

Students who are interested in learning more about this career choice can go to www.math.glencoe.com. School Guidance Counselors are another resource for information about training requirements and appropriate schools.

## ADDITIONAL ANSWERS

**2.**

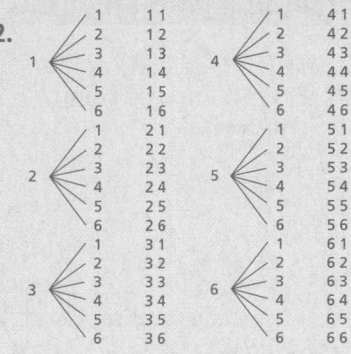

| 1 | 1 1 | | 4 | 4 1 |
|---|-----|---|---|-----|
|   | 1 2 | | | 4 2 |
|   | 1 3 | | | 4 3 |
|   | 1 4 | | | 4 4 |
|   | 1 5 | | | 4 5 |
|   | 1 6 | | | 4 6 |
| 2 | 2 1 | | 5 | 5 1 |
|   | 2 2 | | | 5 2 |
|   | 2 3 | | | 5 3 |
|   | 2 4 | | | 5 4 |
|   | 2 5 | | | 5 5 |
|   | 2 6 | | | 5 6 |
| 3 | 3 1 | | 6 | 6 1 |
|   | 3 2 | | | 6 2 |
|   | 3 3 | | | 6 3 |
|   | 3 4 | | | 6 4 |
|   | 3 5 | | | 6 5 |
|   | 3 6 | | | 6 6 |

## Lesson Planning

### NCTM Standards/Strands
- Data Analysis & Probability
- Representation
- Problem Solving
- Connections

### Vocabulary

combination

### Tools/Materials Needed

calculator

### Lesson Resources

Warm-up Transparency 18
Transparency RF-20
Reteaching 4-7
Extra Practice 4-7
Enrichment 4-7
Technology Activity 4-7

## Getting Started

### 5-MINUTE WARM-UP

**Evaluate each expression.**

1. $5!$   120
2. $6!$   720
3. $\dfrac{7!}{3!}$   840
4. $\dfrac{8! \cdot 5!}{4!}$   201,600

### Introduction to Lesson 4-7

In order to make a list of the 24 different ways in which 3 students can be selected from the group of 4 (call these students A, B, C, D) and assigned to the 3 offices, students should consider a tree diagram to view the sample space. (See the Teaching Tip at the bottom of this page.)

In order to determine the number of ways to simply select 3 students from the group, students must recognize that there are far fewer ways since, now, arrangements are not important. In fact, there are only 4 ways: ABC, ABD, ACD, BCD.

# 4-7 Combinations of a Set

**Goals**   ■   Find the number of combinations of a set

**Applications**   Safety, Sports, Games, Probability, Landscaping

**Work in groups of four. Record your answers.**

1. From your group of four, select three officers: a president, a vice president and a treasurer. List all the different possibilities.
   24 possibilities

2. From your group of four, select a committee of three. List all possibilities.   4 possibilities

3. Are your lists the same for Questions 1 and 2? Can you find a relationship between the two lists? Explain.
   No. Yes; in one list the order is not important.

4. From a group of five, how many ways can you select three officers?
   60

### ■ BUILD UNDERSTANDING

In the last lesson, you learned how to use the fundamental counting principle to find the number of possible permutations of a set of items. In this case, the order of the items is important. Sometimes, however, the order of items is *not* important. A set of items in which order is not important is called a **combination**. For example, *acb* and *bac* are both combinations of the letters *a*, *b* and *c*.

The number of combinations of *n* items taken *r* items at a time is written $_nC_r$. You can use the formula below to find the number of possible combinations when only part of a set is used.

$$_nC_r \qquad _nC_r = \frac{n!}{(n-r)! \, r!}$$

where *n* is the number of different items and *r* is the number of items taken at time.

### Example 1

**Calculate the combinations.**

a. $_4C_2$

b. $_6C_4$

**Solution**

a. $_4C_2 = \dfrac{4!}{(4-2)! \, 2!}$

$= \dfrac{4 \cdot 3 \cdot 2 \cdot 1}{(2 \cdot 1)(2 \cdot 1)}$

$= \dfrac{12}{2}$

$= 6$

b. $_6C_4 = \dfrac{6!}{(6-4)! \, 4!}$

$= \dfrac{6 \cdot 5 \cdot 4 \cdot 3 \cdot 2 \cdot 1}{(2 \cdot 1)(4 \cdot 3 \cdot 2 \cdot 1)}$

$= \dfrac{30}{2}$

$= 15$

**Technology Note**

Many calculators have a combination function key symbolized $_nC_r$.

For example, entering the sequence 5 MATH ►

► ► 3 1 will calculate $\dfrac{5!}{4! \, 1!} = 5$.

**178**   Chapter 4   **Probability**

### Teaching Tip

To accompany Question 1 of the opening activity, here is a tree diagram for selecting 3 members from a group of 4 students (A, B, C, D) and assigning them to one of 3 offices (President, Vice President, Treasurer).

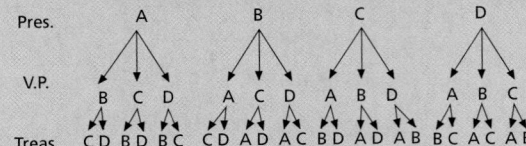

So, there are 24 possible ways to choose 3 students from the group of 4 and assign them as the 3 officers: ABC, ABD, ACB, ACD, ADB, ADC, BAC, BAD, BCA, BCD, BDA, BDC, CAB, CAD, CBA, CBD, CDA, CDB, DAB, DAC, DBA, DBC, DCA, DCB.

## Example 2

**How many different ways can a 2-person committee be chosen from 8 people if there are no restrictions?**

**Solution**

So $n = 8$ and $r = 2$ in the combination formula.

$$_nC_r = \frac{n!}{(n-r)!\, r!}$$

$$_8C_2 = \frac{8!}{6!2!}$$

$$= \frac{8 \cdot 7 \cdot \cancel{6} \cdot \cancel{5} \cdot \cancel{4} \cdot \cancel{3} \cdot \cancel{2} \cdot \cancel{1}}{(\cancel{6} \cdot \cancel{5} \cdot \cancel{4} \cdot \cancel{3} \cdot \cancel{2} \cdot \cancel{1})(2 \cdot 1)}$$

Cancel common factors to simplify.

$$= \frac{56}{2}$$

$$= 28$$

There are 28 ways to select the committee.

> **Reading Math**
>
> Read the combination $_8C_2$ in Example 2 as "combinations of eight, taken two at a time."

## Example 3

**A random drawing is held to determine which 2 of the 6 members of the math club will be sent to a regional math contest.**

**a.** How many different pairs of two could be sent to the contest?

**b.** If the members of the club are James, Dontae, Colin, Daphne, Nashota and Nicole, what is the probability that James and Nashota will be picked?

**Solution**

**a.** There are six people to be picked two at a time, and the order is not important. So $n = 6$ and $r = 2$ in the combination formula.

$$_nC_r = \frac{n!}{(n-r)!r!}$$

$$_6C_2 = \frac{6!}{(6-2)!2!}$$

$$= \frac{6 \cdot 5 \cdot \cancel{4} \cdot \cancel{3} \cdot \cancel{2} \cdot \cancel{1}}{(\cancel{4} \cdot \cancel{3} \cdot \cancel{2} \cdot \cancel{1})(2 \cdot 1)}$$

Cancel common factors to simplify.

$$= \frac{30}{2}$$

$$= 15$$

There are 15 different groups of two members.

**b.** The group of James and Nashota is one of the 15 possible combinations.

$$P(\text{James and Nashota}) = \frac{\text{favorable outcomes}}{\text{possible outcomes}}$$

$$= \frac{1}{15}$$

The probability that James and Nashota will be picked is $\frac{1}{15}$.

 **Math Online** mathmatters2.com/extra_examples

Lesson 4-7 **Combinations of a Set** | 179

## Extend the Lesson

**CONNECTING TO PRIOR KNOWLEDGE** Guide students to note the relationship between the formula for combinations and the formula for permutations.

$$_nC_r = \frac{n!}{(n-r)! \cdot r!} = \frac{_nP_r}{r!}$$

The number of combinations of $n$ items taken $r$ at a time is the number of permutations of $n$ items taken $r$ at a time divided by $r!$.

↑ This is the permutations formula.

Have students use a calculator to verify that, for example, $_7C_4 = \frac{_7P_4}{4!}$.

## QUICK ASSESSMENT

Ask the following questions to determine if students understand the content presented in this lesson.

1. Which of the choices below has more possible outcomes? Explain.
   A. After selection, if arrangement is considered, then A B C is different from B A C. But, if only selection is considered, then A B C is the same as B A C.
   A. selecting 3 people from a group of 5 and then arranging them in a line
   B. simply selecting 3 people from a group of 5

2. a. Evaluate $_7P_4$.   **840**
   b. Using the result of $_7P_4$, how would you find the value of $_7C_4$?   **divide by 4!**
   c. How could you express $_nC_r$ in terms of $_nP_r$?   $_nC_r = {_nP_r} \div r!$

## ASSIGNMENT GUIDE

**Basic:** 1–25, 30–50
**Enriched:** 1–50

### Reteaching Worksheet 4-7

Name _____   Date _____

RETEACHING **4-7**

**COMBINATIONS OF A SET**

A set of items in which order is not important is called a **combination**. The number of combinations of $n$ different items taken $r$ items at a time is written $_nC_r$. You can use this formula.

$_nC_r = \frac{n!}{(n-r)!r!}$

**Example 1**

Calculate the combination $_8C_4$.

**Solution**

$_8C_4 = \frac{8!}{(8-4)!4!}$

$= \frac{8\cdot7\cdot6\cdot5\cdot4\cdot3\cdot2\cdot1}{(4\cdot3\cdot2\cdot1)(4\cdot3\cdot2\cdot1)}$

$= \frac{40,320}{576}$

$= 70$

**Example 2**

A committee of three people will be chosen from a group of seven people. How many different committees are possible?

**Solution**

Since the order of the people on the committee is not important, find the number of combinations of seven people taken three at a time.

$_7C_3 = \frac{7!}{(7-3)!3!}$

$= \frac{7!}{4!3!}$

$= \frac{7\cdot6\cdot5\cdot4\cdot3\cdot2\cdot1}{(4\cdot3\cdot2\cdot1)(3\cdot2\cdot1)}$

$= 35$

There are 35 possible committees.

**EXERCISES**

Calculate each combination.

1. $_{10}C_6$ __**210**__
2. $_{12}C_8$ __**495**__
3. $_5C_1$ __**5**__
4. $_9C_6$ __**84**__
5. $_{20}C_{12}$ __**125,970**__
6. $_{15}C_3$ __**455**__

7. There are eight books on a shelf. How many different sets of four books can be chosen? __**70**__

8. A team of three students is to be chosen from a group of nine students. In how many ways can the three students be chosen? __**84**__

### TRY THESE EXERCISES

Calculate each combination.

1. $_5C_3$   10
2. $_8C_4$   70
3. $_5C_5$   1
4. $_7C_5$   21

5. **SPORTS** A doubles team is to be picked at random from the 9 members of a tennis team. If Marciann and Leah are two of the members, what is the probability that they will both be picked?   $\frac{1}{36}$

6. There are 7 different points on a circle. How many straight lines can be drawn through pairs of these points?   21

7. There are six 1-qt cans, each containing a different fruit juice. How many different types of fruit punch could be obtained by mixing 3 full containers together?   20

8. **LANDSCAPING** How many different flower arrangements can be made from 6 different types of flowers if each arrangement contains 3 types?   20

### PRACTICE EXERCISES • For Extra Practice, see page 598.

Calculate each combination.

9. $_{11}C_8$   165
10. $_4C_2$   6
11. $_3C_0$   1
12. $_9C_1$   9

13. A deck of 26 alphabet cards marked A through Z is shuffled, and 2 cards are dealt. What is the probability that the cards are X and Y?   $\frac{1}{325}$

14. A committee of three people is to be selected at random from a group of 24 people that includes Santiago, Tina, and Rashad. Find the probability that the committee will consist of Santiago, Tina, and Rashad.   $\frac{1}{2024}$

15. A basketball coach wants to know how many different 5-member teams she can play from a roster of 10 team members.   252

16. Each of five friends gives Mary his or her favorite book. Mary only has time to read 3 of the books. In how many ways can she select 3 of the 5 books? If you are one of the friends, then what is the probability that your book will be one of the three books read? (Hint: To help you find the probability, list the sample space.)   $10; \frac{3}{5}$

17. **SAFETY** In how many ways can a 6-person neighborhood nightwatch be selected from 12 men and 8 women who are on the safety patrol?   38,760

18. There are 5 points in a plane, no 3 of which are collinear. If 2 noncollinear points determine a line, how many lines are determined?   10

19. **WRITING MATH** Explain the differences and similarities between permutations and combinations of a set of items. Give an example of each.   Answers will vary. An insightful answer will note that a combination is equal to the permutation divided by $r!$.

20. **GAMES** In the game of *bridge*, a hand has 13 cards. Determine the number of bridge hands possible from a standard deck of 52 cards. Write the answer in scientific notation.   $6.350135596 \cdot 10^{11}$

NEIGHBORHOOD CRIME WATCH

We immediately report all SUSPICIOUS PERSONS and activities to our Police Dept.

### Extend the Lesson

**CHALLENGE** Have students use a calculator to evaluate each of the following pairs of combinations.

a. $_8C_3$ and $_8C_5$   $_8C_3 = {_8C_5} = 56$

b. $_{12}C_5$ and $_{12}C_7$   $_{12}C_5 = {_{12}C_7} = 792$

c. $_{100}C_{97}$ and $_{100}C_3$   $_{100}C_{97} = {_{100}C_3} = 161,700$

Ask students to look for a pattern and generalize the results in terms of $n$ and $r$. Discuss why this result is logical.

$$_nC_r = {_nC_{n-r}}$$

When you choose, for example, 3 people from 8 to be on a committee, you are automatically making another selection: the 5 people from the 8 who are *not* to be on the committee.

**21. ENTERTAINMENT** A popular touring band has 20 songs. How many combinations of songs can the band play in their opening 3-song set? 1140

**22.** There are 12 people at a party. If each person shakes hands with every other person, how many handshakes are exchanged? 66

**23.** A standard deck of 52 cards is shuffled, and 4 cards are turned over. What is the probability that the 4 cards all have the same value? (Hint: Use the combination value as the denominator in the probability fraction.) $\frac{1}{20,825}$

**24.** How many triangles are determined by 9 points if none of the 9 points lie on a straight line? 84

**25.** A radio station chooses 22 postcards from the many listeners who enter a monthly contest. In addition to their prize, 4 of those chosen will also receive backstage passes. In how many different ways can the past winners be selected? 7315

### ■ EXTENDED PRACTICE EXERCISES

**26. CRITICAL THINKING** Simplify the expression $_nC_{n-1}$. $_nC_{n-1} = n$

**27.** Eldora is told to study 10 questions for an exam. Three of the questions will be randomly selected for the exam. Unfortunately, she only has time to study 3 of the questions. What is the probability that the 3 questions on the test are the 3 that she has studied? $\frac{1}{120}$

**28. YOU MAKE THE CALL** Suppose that 4 officers will be selected. The first person will be the president, the second the vice-president, the third the secretary and the fourth the treasurer. Tia says that to solve this problem she would use a permutation and not a combination. Do you agree or disagree? Explain. agree; order is important

**29. CHAPTER INVESTIGATION** Create a set of rules for your game. Include a list of the significant outcomes along with their respective probabilities. Answers will vary.

### ■ MIXED REVIEW EXERCISES

**Solve each equation. Check the solution.** (Lesson 3-4)

**30.** $8 + 4c = 10$  $\frac{1}{2}$

**31.** $\frac{x}{2} - 7 = 3$  20

**32.** $6a - 4 = 20$  4

**33.** $12 + 2d = 17$  2.5

**34.** $3(x + 4) = 6$  −2

**35.** $2(k - 3) = 8$  7

**Solve each equation. Check the solution.** (Lesson 3-8)

**36.** $\sqrt{f} = 8$  −64

**37.** $x^2 = 75$  $\pm 5\sqrt{3}$

**38.** $b^2 - 2 = 7$  $\pm 3$

**39.** $3 + \sqrt{h} = 9$  36

**40.** $g^2 = \frac{1}{9}$  $\pm\frac{1}{3}$

**41.** $\sqrt{4x + 3} = 6$  $\frac{33}{4}$

**DATA FILE  Refer to the data on target heart rates on page 571.** (Lesson 3-3)

**42.** How many times does a 30 year-old's heart beat per minute if she achieves a target heart rate of 50%? 95 bpm

**43.** Write an algebraic model of the target heart rate for a 30-year old where $t$ is the target heart rate and $p$ is the percent of the average maximum heart rate. $t = 190p$

**44.** How many times does a 30 year-old's heart beat per minute if she achieves a target heart rate of 65%? 123.5

---

## Extend the Lesson

**CHALLENGE** Have students find $n$ in each of the following cases and explain how they got their answers.

1. $_nP_2 = 20$   $n = 5$
2. $_nC_2 = 10$   $n = 5$
3. $_nP_2 = 342$   $n = 19$
4. $_nC_2 = 171$   $n = 19$

**Solution:** Working with $_nP_2$ means using the first two factors of $n!$, that is, $n(n - 1)$. So, to find $n$ in $_nP_2 = 20$, guess and check to find $n$ in $n(n - 1) = 20$.

Working with $_nC_2$ is the same as working with $\frac{_nP_2}{2!}$. So, to find $n$ in $_nC_2 = 10$, guess and check to find $n$ in $\frac{n(n - 1)}{2} = 10$ or in $n(n - 1) = 20$.

---

## Extra Practice Worksheet 4-7

Name _____  Date _____

EXTRA PRACTICE **4-7**
### COMBINATIONS OF A SET

**■ EXERCISES**

Calculate each combination.

1. $_5C_4$ __5__
2. $_9C_3$ __84__
3. $_5C_1$ __5__
4. $_{10}C_8$ __45__
5. $_{12}C_8$ __495__
6. $_7C_4$ __35__
7. $_{15}C_7$ __6435__
8. $_{10}C_9$ __10__
9. $_{13}C_5$ __1287__
10. $_{18}C_3$ __816__
11. $_{24}C_2$ __276__
12. $_{15}C_{10}$ __3003__

**13.** A committee of four people is to be selected at random from a group of 30 people that includes Maria, Rita, Ricardo, and Miquel. Find the probability that the committee will consist of Maria, Rita, Ricardo, and Miquel. $\frac{1}{27,405}$

**14.** There are 10 people at a party. If each person shakes hands with every other person, how many handshakes are exchanged? 45

**15.** In how many ways can a 5-student advisory council be selected from the 10 girls and 6 boys who have volunteered to be on the council? 4368

**16.** How many different ways can two captains be chosen from a team of 15 people? 105

A random drawing is held to determine the class representatives. Two students will be chosen from a class of 15 students.

**17.** How many different pairs of students can be chosen? 105

**18.** Tia and Gregory are two students in the class. What is the probability that Tia and Gregory will be chosen as class representatives? $\frac{1}{105}$

**19.** Beth needs to choose two books from a list of eight to read for her English class. How many different ways can she choose the two books? 28

## Enrichment Worksheet 4-7

Name _____  Date _____

ENRICHMENT **4-7**
### LATIN SQUARES

In designing a statistical experiment, it is important to try to randomize the variables. For example, suppose 4 different motor oils are being compared to see which give the best gasoline mileage. An experimenter might then choose 4 different drivers and four different cars. To test-drive all the possible combinations, the experimenter would need 64 test-drives.

To reduce the number of test drives, a statistician might use an arrangement called a Latin Square.

|       | $D_1$ | $D_2$ | $D_3$ | $D_4$ |
|-------|-------|-------|-------|-------|
| $C_1$ | A | B | C | D |
| $C_2$ | B | A | D | C |
| $C_3$ | C | D | A | B |
| $C_4$ | D | C | B | A |

For this example, the four motor oils are labeled A, B, C, and D and are arranged as shown. Each oil must appear exactly one time in each row and column of the square.

The drivers are labeled $D_1$, $D_2$, $D_3$, and $D_4$; the cars are labeled $C_1$, $C_2$, $C_3$, and $C_4$.

Now, the number of test-drives is just 16, one for each cell of the Latin Square.

**■ EXERCISES**

Create two 4-by-4 Latin Squares that are different from the example.

1.

|       | $D_1$ | $D_2$ | $D_3$ | $D_4$ |
|-------|-------|-------|-------|-------|
| $C_1$ | B | C | A | D |
| $C_2$ | D | A | C | B |
| $C_3$ | C | D | B | A |
| $C_4$ | A | B | D | C |

2.

|       | $D_1$ | $D_2$ | $D_3$ | $D_4$ |
|-------|-------|-------|-------|-------|
| $C_1$ | D | C | B | A |
| $C_2$ | A | B | C | D |
| $C_3$ | B | D | A | C |
| $C_4$ | C | A | D | B |

Answers will vary. Sample answers are given.

Make three different 3-by-3 Latin Squares.

3.

|       | $D_1$ | $D_2$ | $D_3$ |
|-------|-------|-------|-------|
| $C_1$ | A | B | C |
| $C_2$ | B | C | A |
| $C_3$ | C | A | B |

4.

|       | $D_1$ | $D_2$ | $D_3$ |
|-------|-------|-------|-------|
| $C_1$ | A | C | B |
| $C_2$ | C | B | A |
| $C_3$ | B | A | C |

5.

|       | $D_1$ | $D_2$ | $D_3$ |
|-------|-------|-------|-------|
| $C_1$ | B | C | A |
| $C_2$ | C | A | B |
| $C_3$ | A | B | C |

### Vocabulary Assessment

- A matching section checks for student understanding of the new vocabulary introduced in this chapter.
- A vocabulary review/test for Chapter 4 is available on pp. vii–viii of the *Chapter 4 Resource Masters*.

### Lesson-by-Lesson Review

For each lesson,
- the main ideas are summarized, and
- practice exercises are provided.

## ExamView® Pro

Use the networkable **ExamView® Pro** to:

- Create **multiple versions** of tests.
- Create **modified** tests for *inclusion* students.
- **Edit** existing questions and **add** your own questions.
- Use built-in **state curriculum correlations** to create tests aligned with state standards.
- Change **English** tests to **Spanish** and vice versa.

---

# Chapter 4 Review

## VOCABULARY ◣

**Choose the word from the list that best completes each statement.**

1. A(n) __?__ is an activity that is used to produce data that can be observed and recorded.  g

2. When you use objects to represent elements of the problem, you are using the __?__ strategy.  a

3. A(n) __?__ contains all the possible outcomes of an experiment.  k

4. Any outcome or combination of possible outcomes of an experiment is considered a(n) __?__.  f

5. Problems dealing with __?__ may ask for the probability of one event *and/or* another occurring.  d

6. Two events that cannot occur at the same time are called __?__.  i

7. When one event affects the outcome of another event, the events are called __?__.  e

8. The number of ways a group of children can stand in line is an example of a(n) __?__.  j

9. The fundamental counting principle uses __?__ to determine the number of possibilities.  h

10. A(n) __?__ can be used to systematically list all possible outcomes.  l

| | |
|---|---|
| **a.** | act it out |
| **b.** | addition |
| **c.** | combination |
| **d.** | compound events |
| **e.** | dependent |
| **f.** | event |
| **g.** | experiment |
| **h.** | multiplication |
| **i.** | mutually exclusive |
| **j.** | permutation |
| **k.** | sample space |
| **l.** | tree diagram |

## LESSON 4-1 ◣ Experiments and Probabilities, p. 150

▶ An **experimental probability** is an estimate of the likelihood of an event, $E$, or desired outcome. It can be expressed using the formula

$$P(E) = \frac{\text{number of observations favorable to } E}{\text{total number of observations}}.$$

11. Last month a music store sold 1178 cassette tapes, 2574 CDs and 1968 DVDs. What is the relative frequency of cassette tape sales?  ≈ 0.21

12. In a random survey of 240 students, 168 said they would vote for Maria for class president. What is the probability that a student will vote for Maria?  0.7

**The enrollment at Washington High School is given below.**

### Washington High School Enrollment

| | Freshmen | Sophomores | Juniors | Seniors |
|---|---|---|---|---|
| Male | 55 | 50 | 48 | 62 |
| Female | 43 | 62 | 47 | 53 |

13. What is the probability that a student picked at random is a junior?  0.23

14. What is the probability that a student picked at random is a male?  0.51

---

### Teaching Tip

In preparation for Exercises 21–27, review the following terms as "opposite pairs," asking students to tell the feature that sets them apart and how that affects the probability calculation.

**mutually exclusive vs. not mutually exclusive**  Mutually exclusive events have no overlapping outcomes. The probability of the overlapping outcomes of events that are not mutually exlcusive has to be subtracted from the sum of the individual probabilities.

**independent vs. dependent**  The sample space for the second of two independent events is the same as the sample space for the first of the two events. The sample space for the second of two dependent events is diminished from that of the first.

## LESSON 4-2 ◼ Problem Solving Skills: Simulations, p. 154

▶ A **simulation** is a model of a problem that is easier to implement than the actual problem.

15. At a grocery store, $\frac{1}{3}$ of all the bread is whole wheat and $\frac{1}{2}$ of all the bread is dated to be sold by the middle of the week. Design a simulation using a number cube and a coin to find the probability that a given loaf of bread is whole wheat and dated to be sold by the middle of the week. See additional answers.

16. Victor has 6 ties. He works at the mall every Friday, Saturday and Sunday. Each work day he chooses a tie at random to wear for his job. Design a simulation to find the probability that Victor will wear a different tie each of the three work days. See additional answers.

17. A restaurant chain gives one of three action figures at random with every child's meal. Design a simulation to find the probability that a child will get all three action figures if he or she buys five of these meals. See additional answers.

## LESSON 4-3 ◼ Sample Spaces and Theoretical Probability, p 158

▶ The **sample space** for a probability is the set of all possible outcomes of the experiment.

▶ The **fundamental counting principle** states that to find the number of possible outcomes for an activity, multiply the number of possible outcomes for each stage of the activity.

▶ The **theoretical probability** of an event, $E$, can be assigned using the formula
$P(E) = \dfrac{\text{number of favorable outcomes}}{\text{number of possible outcomes}}$.

18. A company has printed eleven new books about American artists. Each book is available in hardcover or paperback and in regular type or large type. How many different books were printed? 44

19. A car comes in two or four doors, a four or six-cylinder engine, and eight exterior colors. How many of these cars are available? 32 cars

20. A spinner with six equal sections marked A through F is spun and a number cube is rolled. Find $P$(vowel, number greater than 3). $\frac{1}{6}$

## LESSON 4-4 ◼ Probability of Compound Events, p. 162

▶ If $A$ and $B$ are **mutually exclusive events**, they cannot occur at the same time. $P(A \text{ or } B) = P(A) + P(B)$.

▶ If $A$ and $B$ are **not mutually exclusive events**, they can occur at the same time. $P(A \text{ or } B) = P(A) + P(B) - P(A \text{ and } B)$.

21. Two number cubes are rolled. Find the probability that the sum of the numbers rolled is 7 or greater than 10. $\frac{1}{4}$

22. A card is drawn at random from a standard deck of 52 cards. Find the probability that it is a red card or a king. $\frac{7}{13}$

23. The numbers 1 through 30 are each written on a separate piece of paper. If one piece of paper is picked at random, what is the probability that the number is divisible by 2 or 3? $\frac{2}{3}$

## ADDITIONAL ANSWERS

15. Answers will vary. Sample answer: Use the numbers 1 and 2 on a number cube to represent whole wheat bread. Use heads on a coin to represent bread dated to be sold by the middle of the week. Roll the number cube and flip the coin. Record whether or not the number cube shows 1 or 2 and the coin shows heads. Repeat the simulation 30 times and determine the experimental probability.

16. Answers will vary. Sample answer: Let the different ties be represented by a different number from 1 to 6. Roll three number cubes and record whether or not the number cubes all have different numbers. Repeat the simulation 30 times and determine the experimental probability.

17. Answers will vary. Sample answer: Let 1 and 2 represent one action figure, 3 and 4 represent another action figure, and 5 and 6 represent the third action figure. Roll a number cube five times and record the result. Determine whether all 3 action figures are represented. Repeat the simulation 30 times and determine the experimental probability.

## LESSON 4-5 ◼ Independent and Dependent Events, p. 168

▶ Two events are **independent** if the outcome of one does not affect the outcome of the other. If $A$ and $B$ are independent events, $P(A \text{ and } B) = P(A) \cdot P(B)$.

▶ Two events are **dependent** if the outcome of one affects the outcome of the other. If $A$ and $B$ are dependent events, $P(A \text{ and } B) = P(A) \cdot P(B, \text{ given } A)$.

**A box contains 2 green cards, 3 red cards and 5 blue cards. Cards are picked one at a time, then replaced. Find each probability.**

**24.** $P$(blue, then red)  $\frac{3}{20}$

**25.** $P$(green, then blue)  $\frac{1}{10}$

**Two cards are drawn from a deck of ten cards numbered 1 through 10. Once a card is selected, it is not replaced. Find each probability.**

**26.** $P$(two even numbers)  $\frac{2}{9}$

**27.** $P$(two numbers greater than 4)  $\frac{1}{3}$

## LESSON 4-6 ◼ Permutations of a Set, p. 172

▶ A **permutation** is an arrangement of items in a particular order.

**$n!$ ($n$ factorial)**  The number of permutations of $n$ different items is $n(n-1)(n-2)\ldots(2)(1)$ and is written as $n!$

**$_nP_r$**  $_nP_r = \frac{n!}{(n-r)!}$ where $n$ is the number of different items and $r$ is the number of items taken at a time.

**28.** In how many different ways can 8 paintings be awarded first, second, and third prizes? 336

**29.** How many ways can you arrange the letters in the word *math*? 24 ways

**30.** There are 9 players on a baseball team. How many ways can the coach pick the first 4 batters? 3,024 ways

## LESSON 4-7 ◼ Combinations of a Set, p. 178

▶ A **combination** is a set of items in which order is not important.

**$_nC_r$**  $_nC_r = \frac{n!}{(n-r)!r!}$, where $n$ is the number of different items and $r$ is the number of items taken at a time.

**31.** How many different pairs of students can be chosen from a class of 28? 378

**32.** How many ways can you choose 3 CDs out of 10 CDs to take on a trip? 120 ways

**33.** Pizza Palace offers 8 different toppings for its pizza. How many four-topping pizzas does the Pizza Palace offer? 70 pizzas

## CHAPTER INVESTIGATION

**EXTENSION** Present your game to the rest of the class and play a few rounds as a demonstration. Explain your reasoning for the assignment of point values to the various outcomes as well as why you have chosen the particular format. Discuss how probability plays a key role in the outcome of your game.

## THEME: Games

The benchmarks and expectations for this extension are as follows.
- Students choose a format for their game which may include drawing cards from a deck, rolling a number cube, spinning a spinner or some other event.
- Students determine how the turns of their game are played and assign point values to possible outcomes. They decide how the game will begin and be won, if there are free turns, if there are penalties and other aspects of the game.
- Students create a set of rules for their game. They include a list of the significant outcomes along with their respective probabilities.
- Students present their game to the rest of the class and play a few rounds as a demonstration. They explain their reasoning for the assignment of point values to the various outcomes as well as why you have chosen the particular format. They discuss how probability plays a key role in the outcome of their game.

# Chapter 4 Assessment

**Answer each question.**

1. In a random survey of students, 152 students could swim and 48 could not. What is the probability that a student can swim? 0.76

2. Suppose you spin two spinners, one marked 1 through 4 and the other marked A through E. How many possible outcomes are there? 20

3. In a random sample of 1,000 voters in Kerr City, 525 said they would vote for Higgins for mayor. If there are 122,680 voters in the city, how many might be expected to vote for Higgins? 64,407

4. An ice cream store sells 24 different flavors and offers a choice of 3 sizes of cones and 5 types of sprinkles. How many choices of a cone with sprinkles are there? 360

5. Each card in a set is marked with a letter, a number, and a shape. The letters that can be used are A, B, C, D; the numbers that can be used are 1 to 5; and the shapes are a square, circle, and triangle. A card is selected at random from a box that contains one of each possible card. Find the probability that the card shows an even number and a circle. $\frac{2}{15}$

6. Find the probability that a point selected at random lies in the shaded region. $\frac{1}{3}$

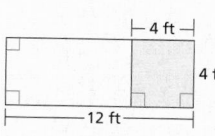

The spinners are both spun for Exercises 7–10.

7. Find $P(D, 1)$. $\frac{1}{48}$

8. Find $P(\text{not E, 4 or 5})$. $\frac{7}{24}$

9. Find $P(D, \text{odd number})$. $\frac{1}{16}$

10. Find $P(\text{vowel, number greater than 2})$. $\frac{1}{6}$

11. Two number cubes are rolled. Find the probability that the sum of the numbers rolled is 6 or 10. $\frac{2}{9}$

12. Find the probability that the sum of the numbers rolled on two number cubes is less than 6 or a multiple of 3. $\frac{5}{9}$

**A bag contains 7 green marbles, 3 red marbles and 5 yellow marbles.**

13. Find $P(\text{yellow, then green})$ if you take one marble, replace it, and then take another marble. $\frac{7}{45}$

14. Find $P(\text{red, then green})$ if you take one marble and then take another marble without replacing the first. $\frac{1}{10}$

15. How many ways can a group of 5 books be lined up on a shelf if there are 9 books to choose from? 15,120

16. How many ways can 5 runners be chosen from a track team that has 10 members? 252

 Math Online mathmatters2.com/chapter_assessment

Chapter 4 **Assessment** | **185**

## ALTERNATIVE ASSESSMENT

**YOUR GAME** Have students design a game of their own whose outcome is mostly dependent on chance. Students should make any necessary items, such as game boards, cards, or pieces. They should thoroughly describe the items in a few paragraphs, explain the rules of the game, and tell why they think the outcome will depend mostly on chance. If a player's ability will have an influence on the outcome, students should include that in their explanation as well. Students should give an example of how they might calculate the probability of a player winning the game. If possible, arrange for some students to play the game and test these theories.

**RUBRIC** The following rubric is a sample scoring guide.

| Points | Description |
|--------|-------------|
| 4 | Designs an original game whose outcome is **mostly dependent on chance, clearly defines the rules**, and makes and describes in detail the components of the game. |
| 3 | Designs a game whose outcome has **aspects of chance, defines the rules**, and makes and describes the component of the game. |
| 2 | Designs a game that has aspects of chance, defines the rules, but **does not make or describe the game's components**. |
| 1 | Attempts to design a game, but **does not define the rules or make or describe the game's components**. |
| 0 | Makes **no attempt** to design a game. |

## Standardized Test Practice

These two pages contain practice questions in the various formats that can be found on the most frequently given standardized tests.

A student recording sheet for these two pages can be found on p. A1 of the *Chapter 4 Resource Masters*.

### Standardized Test Practice Student Recording Sheet

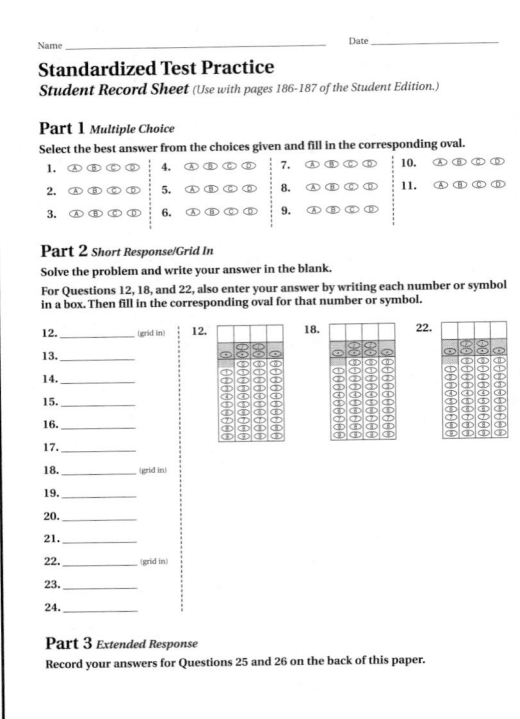

### Additional Practice

See pp. 135–137 in the *Chapter 4 Resource Masters* for additional standardized test practice.

---

### Part 1 | Multiple Choice

**Record your answers on the answer sheet provided by your teacher or on a sheet of paper.**

1. Joannie works for a marketing research company. The company acquires names and phone numbers by purchasing a list of all subscribers to a certain magazine. Then the telemarketers call everyone on the list. This is an example of what type of sampling? (Lesson 1-1) A
   - Ⓐ convenience
   - Ⓑ random
   - Ⓒ systematic
   - Ⓓ none of these

**Use the scatter plot for Exercises 2 and 3.**

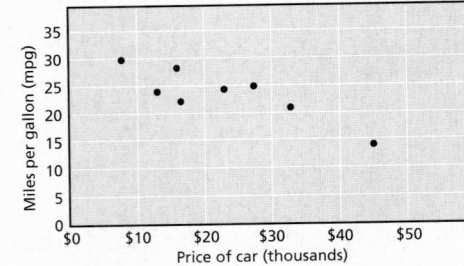

Price of Cars and Miles per Gallon

2. What kind of correlation does the data represent? (Lesson 1-4) B
   - Ⓐ positive correlation
   - Ⓑ negative correlation
   - Ⓒ no correlation
   - Ⓓ cannot be determined

3. Estimate the coefficient of correlation. (Lesson 1-5) D
   - Ⓐ 0.90
   - Ⓑ 0.50
   - Ⓒ 0
   - Ⓓ −0.90

4. A dust particle has a mass of 0.00000081 g. What is this number in scientific notation? (Lesson 2-8) D
   - Ⓐ $81 \cdot 10^8$
   - Ⓑ $8.1 \cdot 10^7$
   - Ⓒ $81 \cdot 10^{-8}$
   - Ⓓ $8.1 \cdot 10^{-7}$

5. Find the next term in the sequence. (Lesson 2-9) D
   $$2, -6, 18, -54, \ldots$$
   - Ⓐ −162
   - Ⓑ −90
   - Ⓒ 90
   - Ⓓ 162

6. The perimeter of a rectangle can be found using the formula $P = 2l + 2w$. Solve the formula for $l$. (Lesson 3-4) C
   - Ⓐ $l = P - w$
   - Ⓑ $l = w - P$
   - Ⓒ $z = \frac{1}{2}P - w$
   - Ⓓ $l = \frac{P - w}{2}$

7. Solve $\frac{2x - 3}{3} = \frac{3x + 1}{4}$. (Lesson 3-5) C
   - Ⓐ $x = 17$
   - Ⓑ $x = 15$
   - Ⓒ $x = -15$
   - Ⓓ $x = -17$

8. The square root of a number is 4. What is the number? (Lesson 3-8) A
   - Ⓐ 16
   - Ⓑ 2
   - Ⓒ −2
   - Ⓓ −16

9. How many outcomes are there for rolling a number cube and spinning the spinner at the right? (Lesson 4-3) B

   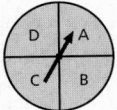

   - Ⓐ 36
   - Ⓑ 24
   - Ⓒ 12
   - Ⓓ 10

10. What is the probability of drawing a club or an ace out of a standard deck of 52 cards? (Lesson 4-4) B
    - Ⓐ $\frac{1}{13}$
    - Ⓑ $\frac{4}{13}$
    - Ⓒ $\frac{17}{52}$
    - Ⓓ 0

11. The forecast predicts a 40% chance of rain on Wednesday and a 60% chance of rain on Thursday. If these probabilities are independent, what is the chance that it will rain on both days? (Lesson 4-5) C
    - Ⓐ 2.4%
    - Ⓑ 20%
    - Ⓒ 24%
    - Ⓓ 100%

## Part 2  Short Response/Grid In

Record your answers on the answer sheet provided by your teacher or on a sheet of paper.

**Use the following data for Questions 12–14.**

**Number of Daily Service Calls by Town and Country Heating in November**

| | | | | | |
|---|---|---|---|---|---|
| 20 | 1 | 20 | 45 | 32 | 31 |
| 41 | 24 | 3 | 20 | 32 | 37 |
| 48 | 51 | 37 | 36 | 4 | 6 |
| 29 | 54 | 44 | 28 | 3 | 38 |
| 20 | 8 | 38 | 27 | 29 | 30 |

**12.** Find the range of the data. (Lesson 1-2)  53

**13.** Find the mean of the data. (Lesson 1-2)  27.9

**14.** Find the first, second, and third quartiles of the data. (Lesson 1-6)  20; 29.5; 38

**15.** Trevor scored 12 points less than half Emma's total in Laser tag. If Emma scored $x$ points, what expression can be used to describe Trevor's points? (Lesson 2-3)  $\frac{x}{2} - 12$

**16.** Simplify: $4(x - 2) + \frac{1}{2}(2x - 6)$. (Lesson 2-6)  $5x - 11$

**17.** The sum of twice a number and 6 is 10. What is the number? (Lesson 3-4)  2

**18.** The time it takes for a falling object to travel a certain distance $d$ is given by the equation $t = \sqrt{\frac{d}{16}}$, where $t$ is in seconds and $d$ is in feet. If you dropped a ball from a window 28 ft above the ground, how long will it take for the ball to reach the ground? (Lesson 3-8)  1.32 s

Two cubes are rolled. The numbers on the number cube are multiplied. Use this information to answer Questions 19–22.

**19.** How many outcomes are there in a sample space? (Lesson 4-3)  36 outcomes

 **Math Online** mathmatters2.com/standardized_test

**20.** What is the probability of rolling a product of 2? (Lesson 4-3)  $\frac{1}{18}$

**21.** Is the probability of an odd product less than, equal to, or greater than the probability of an even product? (Lesson 4-3)  less than

**22.** What is the probability of getting an odd or an even product? (Lesson 4-4)  1

**23.** The pentatonic scale has five notes: C#, D#, F#, G#, and A#. These are the black keys on a piano. How many different five-note sequences can be written if each note is used only once? (Lesson 4-6)  120 sequences

**24.** How many different two-topping pizzas can be made with the toppings sausage, hamburger, ham, peppers, onions, mushrooms, olives, and pineapple? (Lesson 4-7)  28 pizzas

## Part 3  Extended Response

Record your answers on a sheet of paper. Show your work.

**25.** Design a spinner with four sections so that no two sections have an equal probability. Explain your answer. (Lesson 4-1)  See additional answers.

**26.** Jasmine usually makes $\frac{1}{3}$ of her free-throw shots. Devise a simulation to determine the probability that Jasmine will make her next two free-throw shots. (Lesson 4-2)  See additional answers.

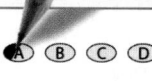

**Test-Taking Tip**
Ⓐ Ⓑ Ⓒ Ⓓ

**Questions 23 and 24**
If you have time at the end of a test, go back to check your calculations and answers. If the test allows you to use a calculator, use it to check your calculations.

Chapter 4  **Standardized Test Practice**  **187**

## Rubrics

The following rubrics are sample scoring guides for short response and extended response questions.

### Short Response

| Points | Description |
|---|---|
| 2 | The student demonstrates a **thorough understanding** of the mathematics of the task. The response may contain minor flaws that do not detract from the demonstration of a thorough understanding. |
| 1 | The student has provided a response that is only **partially correct.** |
| 0 | The student has provided a **completely incorrect** solution or no response at all. |

### Extended Response

| Points | Description |
|---|---|
| 4 | The student demonstrates a **thorough understanding** of the mathematics of the task. The response contains minor flaws that do not detract from the demonstration of a thorough understanding. |
| 3 | The student demonstrates an **understanding** of the mathematics of the task. The response is essentially correct and demonstrates an essential but less than thorough understanding of the mathematics. |
| 2 | The student has demonstrated only a **partial understanding** of the mathematics of the task. Although the student may have used the correct approach to a solution or may have provided a correct solution, the work lacks an essential understanding of the underlying mathematical concepts. |
| 1 | The student has demonstrated a **very limited understanding** of the mathematics of the task. The response is incomplete and exhibits many flaws. |
| 0 | The student has provided a **completely incorrect** solution or no response at all. |

## ADDITIONAL ANSWERS

**25.** The spinner should have four sections, no two being alike. Students should explain that if none of the sections are the same size, the probability for each section will be different.

**26.** Answers will vary. Sample answer: Let 1 and 2 on a number cube represent a made free-throw shot. Roll two number cubes. Record whether or not both cubes show either 1 or 2. Repeat the simulation 30 times and determine the experimental probability.

# Chapter Overview

## Logic and Geometry

| Lesson | Lesson Objectives | Pacing (days) | NCTM Standards | State/Local Objectives |
|--------|-------------------|---------------|----------------|------------------------|
| 5-1 | **Elements of Geometry** *(pp. 192–195)*<br>• Identify fundamental geometric concepts.<br>• Identify and use basic geometric postulates. | 1 | 3, 4, 7, 9 | |
| 5-2 | **Angles and Perpendicular Lines** *(pp. 196–199)*<br>• Identify and use perpendicular lines.<br>• Identify and use angle relationships. | 2 | 3, 4, 7, 9 | |
| 5-3 | **Parallel Lines and Transversals** *(pp. 202–205)*<br>• Identify angles formed by parallel lines and transversals.<br>• Identify and use properties of parallel lines. | 2 | 3, 4, 7, 9 | |
| 5-4 | **Properties of Triangles** *(pp. 206–209)*<br>• Classify triangles according to their sides and angles.<br>• Identify and use properties of triangles. | 1 | 3, 4, 7, 9 | |
| 5-5 | **Congruent Triangles** *(pp. 212–215)*<br>• Use postulates to identify congruent triangles. | 2 | 3, 4, 7, 9 | |
| 5-6 | **Quadrilaterals and Parallelograms** *(pp. 216–219)*<br>• Classify different types of quadrilaterals.<br>• Identify and use properties of parallelograms. | 2 | 3, 4, 7, 9 | |
| 5-7 | **Diagonals and Angles of Polygons** *(pp. 222–225)*<br>• Classify polygons according to their sides.<br>• Find the sum of the angle measures of polygons. | 2 | 3, 4, 7, 9 | |
| 5-8 | **Properties of Circles** *(pp. 226–229)*<br>• Understand relationships among parts of a circle.<br>• Identify and use properties of circles. | 1 | 3, 4, 7, 9 | |
| 5-9 | **Problem Solving Skills: Circle Graphs** *(pp. 232–233)*<br>• Solve a problem using a circle graph.<br>• Use a picture, diagram, or model. | 1 | 6, 8, 9, 10 | |
| **Review** | | 1 | | |
| **Testing** | | 1 | | |

**Key to NCTM Standards:**

*1=Number & Operations, 2=Algebra, 3=Geometry,*
*4=Measurement, 5=Data Analysis & Probability,*
*6=Problem Solving, 7=Reasoning & Proof,*
*8=Communication, 9=Connections, 10=Representation*

**Pacing:** Suggestions for the year can be found on page xvi.

# Chapter Resource Manager

## FAST FILE Chapter 3 Resource Masters

| Reteaching Activities | Extra Practice | Enrichment | Assessment | Basic Mathematics Review | Study Skills Activities | Lesson Warm-Ups Transparencies | Teaching Transparencies | Technology Activities | Materials Needed |
|---|---|---|---|---|---|---|---|---|---|
| 139 | 140 | 141 | | | 11 | 19 | RF-21 | 5-1 | ruler |
| 142 | 143 | 144 | | | | 19 | RF-22 | | file folder, paper plate, straightedge, scissors |
| 145 | 146 | 147 | | | | 20 | RF-23 | | compass, straightedge |
| 148 | 149 | 150 | | | 14 | 20 | RF-25 | 5-4 | protractor, centimeter paper |
| 151 | 152 | 153 | | | | 21 | RF-26 | | compass, straws (5", 7", 9") plus "connectors" (clay, pipe cleaners, etc.), straightedge |
| 154 | 155 | 156 | | | | 21 | RF-27, RF-28 | | protractor, compass, straws plus connectors, ruler, straightedge |
| 157 | 158 | 159 | | | | 21 | RF-29 | 5-7 | compass, straightedge, protractor |
| 160 | 161 | 162 | | | 27 | 22 | RF-30 | | compass, calculator, ruler, string |
| 163 | 164 | 165 | 169–175 | | | 22 | RF-1 | | compass, protractor, ruler |

### Quick Review Math Handbook, Book 2 — hot words hot topics

| MathMatters 2 Lesson(s) | Hot Topic Lesson(s) |
|---|---|
| 5-1, 5-2, 5-4, 5-5 | 7-1 |
| 5-3, 5-6 | 7-2 |
| 5-8 | 7-8 |
| 5-9 | 4-2, 7-8 |

**CHAPTER 5**

## Connections to the Past

**MM1 (Ch. 4):** Identify and classify geometric figures.

**MM1 (Ch. 8):** Construct perpendicular bisectors.

**MM1 (Ch. 4):** Use a protractor to measure and draw angles.

**MM1 (Ch. 8):** Explore the relationship between transversals and angles.

**MM1 (Ch. 4):** Identify and classify polygons.

**MM1 (Ch. 8):** Measure and classify angles.

**MM1 (Ch. 2):** Find the area of parallelograms using a formula.

**MM1 (Ch. 8):** Explore the sum of the interior angles in a polygon.

**MM1 (Ch. 2):** Find the circumference and area of circles.

**MM1 (Ch. 1):** Solve a problem with circle graphs.

## MathMatters 2 Chapter 5 Highlights

Identify fundamental geometric concepts and basic postulates. (5-1)

Identify and use perpendicular lines. (5-2)

Identify and use angle relationships. (5-2)

Identify angles formed by parallel lines and transversals. (5-3)

Identify and use properties of triangles based on their sides and angles. (5-4)

Use postulates to identify congruent triangles. (5-5)

Identify and use properties of parallelograms. (5-6)

Find the sum of the angle measures of polygons. (5-7)

Understand relationships among parts of a circle. (5-8)

Solve a problem using a circle graph. (5-9)

## Connections to the Future

**MM3 (Ch. 3):** Apply postulates about points, lines, and planes, and write geometric proofs in a two-column format.

**MM2 (Ch. 8):** Write equations of parallel and perpendicular lines.
**MM3 (Ch. 3):** Identify perpendicular lines.

**MM2 (Ch. 11):** Identify similar polygons.
**MM3 (Ch. 3):** Apply theorems about midpoints, angle bisectors, and vertical angles.

**MM3 (Ch. 3):** Identify congruent angles formed by parallel lines and a transversal.

**MM3 (Ch. 4):** Classify triangles according to their sides or angles.

**MM3 (Ch. 4):** Prove triangles are congruent.

**MM3 (Ch. 4):** Apply properties of parallelograms to find missing lengths and angle measures.

**MM3 (Ch. 4):** Find the measures of interior and exterior angles of polygons.

**MM3 (Ch. 13):** Write equations for circles.

**MM3 (Ch. 10):** Solve a problem with circle graphs.

### Key
PC    = Previous Course
MM1 = *MathMatters 1*
MM2 = *MathMatters 2*
MM3 = *MathMatters 3*

## Connecting the Strands

| NCTM Strand | Lesson(s) |
|---|---|
| Geometry | 5-1, 5-2, 5-3, 5-4, 5-5, 5-6, 5-7, 5-8 |
| Measurement | 5-1, 5-2, 5-3, 5-4, 5-5, 5-6, 5-7, 5-8 |
| Problem Solving | 5-1, 5-2, 5-3, 5-4, 5-5, 5-6, 5-7, 5-8 |
| Reasoning & Proof | 5-9 |
| Communication | 5-9 |
| Connections | 5-1, 5-2, 5-3, 5-4, 5-5, 5-6, 5-7, 5-8, 5-9 |
| Representation | 5-9 |

# Ongoing Assessment and Intervention

| Type | | Student Edition | Teacher Resources | Technology/Internet |
|---|---|---|---|---|
| **INTERVENTION** | Ongoing | Are You Ready?, pp. 190–191<br>Check Understanding, pp. 193<br>Review and Practice Your Skills,<br>pp. 200–201, 210–211,<br>220–221, 230–231<br>Mid-Chapter Quiz, p. 211 | Lesson Warm-Ups<br>Transparencies, pp. WU-19,<br>WU-20, WU-21, WU-22<br>Quick Assessment, *ATE* pp. 191,<br>194, 198, 204, 208, 214, 218,<br>224, 228, 233 | mathmatters2.com/extra_ examples<br>mathmatters2.com/self_check_quiz |
| | Mixed Review | pp. 195, 199, 205, 209, 215,<br>219, 225, 229, 233 | | |
| **ASSESSMENT** | Error Analysis | You Make the Call, pp. 215, 218<br>Error Alert, p. 224 | Teaching Tip, *ATE* pp. 211, 230 | |
| | Standardized<br>Test Practice | pp. 238–239<br>Preparing for Standardized<br>Tests, pp. 627–644 | Standardized Test Practice,<br>*CRM* pp. 173–175 | mathmatters2.com/standardized_test |
| | Open-Ended<br>Assessment | Chapter Investigation, pp. 189,<br>195, 209, 229, 236 | Chapter Investigation, *ATE*<br>p. 236<br>Alternative Assessment, *ATE*<br>p. 237 | |
| | Chapter<br>Assessment | Chapter Review, pp. 234–236<br>Chapter Assessment, p. 237 | Multiple-Choice Tests<br>(Forms A and B),<br>*CRM* pp. 169–172 | mathmatters2.com/chapter_assessment |

**Key to Abbreviations:** *ATE* = Annotated Teacher's Edition, *CRM* = Chapter Resource Masters

## Additional Intervention

***Basic Mathematics Review*** includes 80 lessons, consisting of an instructional page and a test page. This workbook also features a pretest, posttest, table of measurement equivalents, and calculator appendices.

### ExamView® Pro

Use ExamView® Pro Testmaker CD-ROM to:
- Create **multiple versions** of tests.
- Create **modified** tests for *inclusion* students with one mouse click.
- **Edit** existing questions and **add** your own questions.
- Build tests aligned with **state standards** using built-in **state curriculum correlations**.
- Change **English** tests to **Spanish** with one mouse click and vice versa.

## Chapter Opener

### NCTM Standards/Strands
- Representation
- Measurement

### Vocabulary

| | |
|---|---|
| navigation | point |
| line | angle |
| plane | solid |

### Theme Connections
Humans use navigation to find their way from place to place and to know where they are going along the way. By perfecting navigation skills, humans have found their way from ocean to ocean and continent to continent, from the Stone Age to the Space Age.

The relationships among lines, planes, and angles are associated with the physical characteristics of *direction* and *distance*, the primary focuses of navigation.

### Career Opportunities
Many careers require understanding of the elements of plane geometry. Two such careers are highlighted in the MathWorks features. Others include: surveyor, cartographer, tour guide, astronaut, flight engineer, air traffic controller.
- Cattle rancher, page 201
- Ship captain, page 221

## Internet Connection

### Theme Activities
Mathmatters2.com/chapter_theme provides links to the Internet that will help students gather information about the use of math in the real world, particularly data and measures. To search for additional addresses, begin a search of *navigation*. Then within that search, use key words that will call up specific systems, such as *Loran* (*long range navigation*), *VOR* (*very high frequency omnidirectional range*), *GPS* (*global positioning system*), or specific tools such as *compass*, *sextant*, *octant*, *transit*. In small groups, students can brainstorm other key words.

# LOGIC AND GEOMETRY

## THEME: Navigation

The study of geometry involves the properties, measurements, and relationships of points, lines, angles, planes, and solids. Navigation combines these geometric elements together with geography and logical reasoning. Think back to the last time you read a map or gave someone directions to your home. You used geometry, measurement, and logic. Not only is navigation used by people to get from here to there, but it is also used by many in their professions.

- **Cattle ranchers** (page 201) use navigation to herd their cattle to the best grazing and watering locations. They must do this without crossing land that is treacherous to the animals.

- **Ship captains** (page 221) determine course, speed, and effects of the weather to transport their cargo. Ship captains use compasses and anemometers that measure relationships among the geometric elements found in nature and the location of the stars.

mathmatters2.com/chapter_theme

### Chapter Investigation
Use the Internet and other resources to locate additional information about a compass.

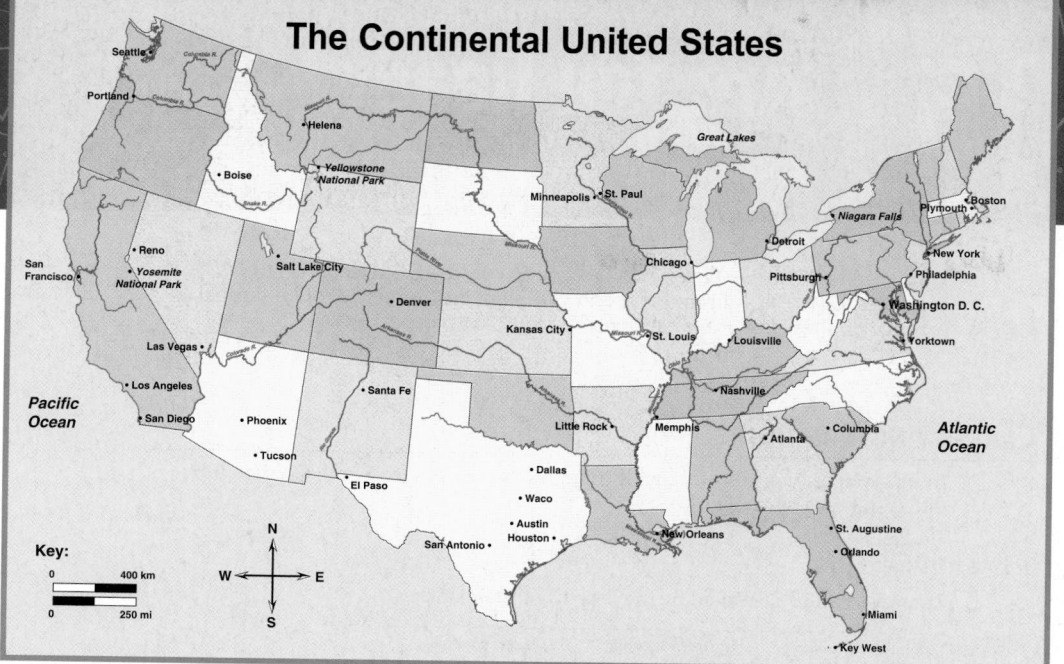

## The Continental United States

Key:
0 ——— 400 km
0 ——— 250 mi

N W E S

Pacific Ocean

Atlantic Ocean

**Use the map for Questions 1–4.**

1. On this map, 250 mi is equal to how many inches? about $\frac{5}{8}$ in.

2. What is the approximate distance in miles between New York and Kansas City? 1050 mi

3. Pedro took a trip from Chicago to El Paso. He drove at a rate of 65 mi/h. To the nearest hour, how long was the trip? 18 h

4. What direction would you travel from Salt Lake City to Yosemite National Park? southwest

## CHAPTER INVESTIGATION

A compass is a navigational tool that works in conjunction with the Earth's magnetic fields, particularly the *magnetic north pole*. A compass is a mechanical device that has a magnetic needle, which pivots from its center and points toward magnetic north.

### *Working Together*

If a compass is not available, the sun and a stick can be used to identify which direction is north, south, east and west. Use the Chapter Investigation icons to build a compass to use in nature.

Chapter 5 **Logic and Geometry** (189)

## Data Activity

A *map* is a representation of a geographic area, usually a portion of the earth's surface, drawn or printed on a flat surface. In most instances, a map is a diagrammatic rather than a pictorial representation of the terrain.

Maps may be used for a variety of purposes and, as a result, a number of specialized types of maps have been developed.

### Extend the Data Activity
**Student Portfolio** Students may research specialized types of maps. *Hydrographic charts* are used for the navigation of ships. These charts cover the surface of the oceans, other large bodies of water, and their shores. *Aviation charts* are used for navigation over land.

## Chapter Investigation

### As an Overarching Problem
Bring several magnetic compasses to class and allow students to study them. Discuss how a compass works and what it is used for. Students will continue to work on the investigation as they complete the exercises identified by the Investigation icon that is found throughout the chapter. These exercises will guide students through the task described in *Working Together*. Encourage students to keep all of their work on the Investigation together. Have students use the suggestions in the Chapter Investigation Extension to summarize their work.

### As a Chapter Project
The goal of this project is for students to design a game of chance and calculate the probabilities of various outcomes within the game. Students can use the Group Project Planner on page 167 and the Project Planning Calendar on page 168 in the *Chapter 5 Resource Masters* to complete the project. Benchmarks **a**, **b**, and **c** should be completed after the lesson listed in parentheses has been studied. Benchmark **d** should be completed at the end of the chapter.

## Project Planning Calendar

## Group Project Planner

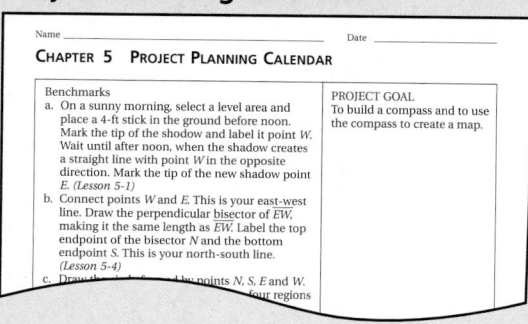

The skills on these two pages are skills that have been presented in earlier chapters of this book or in previous math courses. Continuous review of basic math skills will make stronger math students. These skills are identified as necessary to be successful in Chapter 5.

### Skills Correlation Chart

| Skill | Lesson Number |
|---|---|
| Classifying Triangles | 5-4, 5-5 |
| Sum of Angles | 5-4 |
| Parallelograms | 5-6 |

### Vocabulary

equilateral triangle
isosceles triangle
scalene triangle     acute triangle
right triangle       obtuse triangle

## Chalkboard Examples

### Classifying Triangles

The sides and angles of an *isosceles triangle* have special names, as shown.
In a *right triangle*, the side opposite the right angle is called the *hypotenuse*. It is the longest side of the triangle. The other two sides are the legs, which are not usually the same length. When the legs are of equal length, the triangle is an *isosceles right triangle*.

### Sum of Angles

The three angle measures of $\triangle ABC$ are in the ratio 1 : 2 : 3. Find the measure of each angle.
Let $x$, $2x$, and $3x$ represent the measures.
Then
$$x + 2x + 3x = 180$$
$$6x = 180$$
$$\frac{6x}{6} = \frac{180}{6}$$
$$x = 30$$
$$2x = 2(30) = 60$$
$$3x = 3(30) = 90$$
So, the measures of the three angles of $\triangle ABC$ are 30°, 60°, and 90°.

The skills on these two pages are ones you have already learned. Use the examples to refresh your memory and complete the exercises. For additional practice on these and more prerequisite skills, see pages 576–584.

## CLASSIFYING TRIANGLES

In this chapter you will work with triangles. It is helpful to be able to recognize different types of triangles.

### Examples

Triangles can be classified by the lengths of their sides.

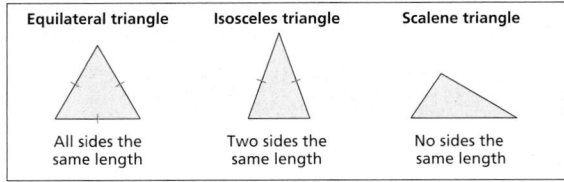

Triangles can also be classified by the measure of their angles.

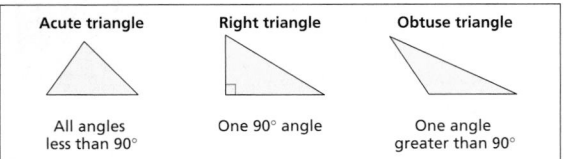

**Classify each triangle both by side and by angle measurements.**

1.
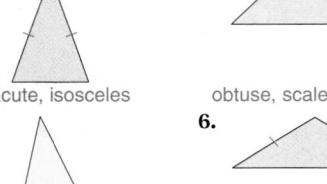
acute, isosceles

2.
obtuse, scalene

3.
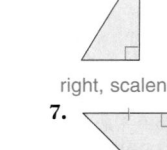
right, scalene

4.
acute, equilateral, isosceles

5.
acute, scalene

6.
obtuse, isosceles

7.

right, isosceles

8.
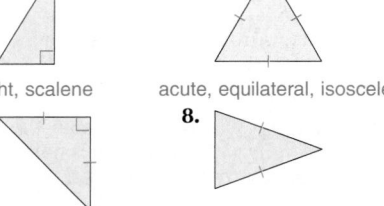
acute, isosceles

## Teaching Tip

**CONNECTING TO PRIOR KNOWLEDGE** Before discussing the Chalkboard Example about angles whose measures are in a given ratio, have students give examples of numbers that are in the given ratios.
numbers in the ratio 1 : 2   5 : 10, 6 : 12, 30 : 60, 100 : 200, $x : 2x$
numbers in the ratio 1 : 2 : 3   2 : 4 : 6, 3 : 6 : 9, 10 : 20 : 30, 50 : 100 : 150, $x : 2x : 3x$

## SUM OF ANGLES

In working with triangles and other polygons, it is helpful to know that the sum of the angles of any triangle is always 180°.

**Examples** Find the measure of the missing angle measure.

$$45 + 78 + x = 180$$
$$123 + x = 180$$
$$x = 57$$

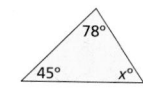

**Find the measure of each missing angle.**

**9.** 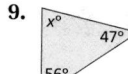  77°

**10.** 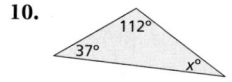  31°

**11.** 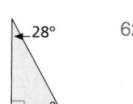  62°

**12.** What are the measures of the angles in an equilateral triangle?  60°, 60°, 60°

**13.** What are the measures of the angles in a right isosceles triangle?  90°, 45°, 45°

**14.** If one angle of a right triangle measures 30°, what are the measures of the other two angles?  90°, 60°

## PARALLELOGRAMS

**Examples** Parallelograms that have unique characteristics are known by specific names.

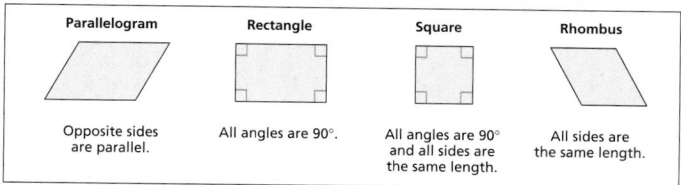

| Parallelogram | Rectangle | Square | Rhombus |
|---|---|---|---|
| Opposite sides are parallel. | All angles are 90°. | All angles are 90° and all sides are the same length. | All sides are the same length. |

**Write the most common name of each shape—parallelogram, rectangle, square or rhombus.**

**15.** 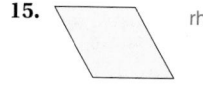  rhombus

**16.** 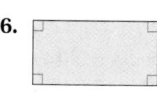  rectangle

**17.** 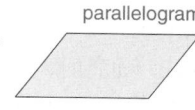  parallelogram

**18.**   parallelogram

**19.** square

**20.** rhombus

---

## Differentiated Instruction

**VISUAL LEARNERS** As an initial review of quadrilaterals, ask students to put the following terms in logical sequence: square, parallelogram, quadrilateral, rectangle. quadrilateral, parallelogram, rectangle, square
Then elicit a relationship diagram, such as the one shown here. A more comprehensive pictorial diagram is available as a transparency.

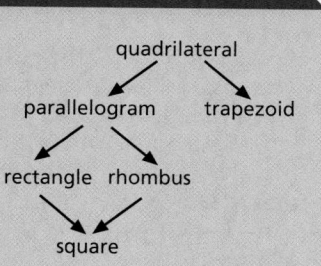

---

## Refresher Wrap-up

### QUICK ASSESSMENT

Ask the following questions to determine if students have mastered the basic skills reviewed on these pages.

**Write a fact about the angles of a triangle that follows from the given fact. Classify the triangle.**
1. Triangle *ABC* has two sides that are equal in measure.  Triangle *ABC* has two angles that are equal in measure; triangle *ABC* is an isosceles triangle.
2. Triangle *NOM* has three sides that are equal in measure.  Triangle *MNO* has three angles that are equal in measure. Triangle *MNO* is an equilateral triangle.
3. The legs of right triangle *RST* are equal in measure.  The measures of the three angles of triangle *RST* are 45°, 45°, 90°. Triangle *RST* is an isosceles right triangle.

**Explain why the given figure cannot exist.**
4. equilateral right triangle  This would mean three right angles, with a sum of measures = 270°; but the sum of the measures of the angles of any triangle = 180°.
5. a parallelogram with exactly two right angles  Since opposite angles of a parallelogram are equal in measure, if a parallelogram contains two consecutive right angles, it must contain four right angles.
6. an equilateral trapezoid  An equilateral quadrilateral is a rhombus, which has both pairs of opposite sides parallel. A trapezoid has only one pair of parallel sides.

### ADDITIONAL PRACTICE

Refer to the Prerequisite Skills lessons beginning on page 576 for more practice.

# Elements of Geometry

**Goals**
■ Identify fundamental geometric concepts.
■ Identify and use basic geometric postulates.

**Applications** Construction, Art, Photography, Navigation

## Lesson Planning

### NCTM Standards/Strands
■ Geometry
■ Measurement
■ Reasoning & Proof
■ Connections

### Vocabulary

geometry    point
line    plane
space    collinear points
coplanar    noncoplanar
intersection
noncollinear points
congruent line segments
midpoint of a segment
bisector of a segment

### Tools/Materials Needed

ruler

### Lesson Resources

Warm-up Transparency 19
Transparency RF-21
Reteaching 5-1
Extra Practice 5-1
Enrichment 5-1
Technology Activity 5-1

## Getting Started

### 5-MINUTE WARM-UP

**For each term, give an example that can be found in your class-room.** **Possible answers shown.**
1. point   a doorknob
2. line segment   an edge of a desktop
3. angle   the figure formed by two adjacent edges of a desktop
4. plane   a desktop

### Introduction to Lesson 5-1
Recognize that line *BC* is the same as line *CB*, reinforcing the concept that through any two points, only one line can be drawn.

---

Draw three dots spread apart that do not lie in a straight line. Label them points *A*, *B*, and *C*.

1. How many straight lines can be drawn through point *A*?   infinitely many

2. How many straight lines can be drawn that will pass through both points *B* and *C*?   1

3. How many straight lines can be drawn that will pass through all three points?   0

### ► BUILD UNDERSTANDING

**Geometry** (from the Greek words *geo*, meaning "earth," and *metria*, meaning "measurement") is the study of points in space. In geometry, *point*, *line*, and *plane* are basic terms.

A **point** (*P*) is a location in space having no dimensions. Every other geometric figure is composed of sets of points. A **line** ($\overleftrightarrow{TB}$) is a set of points that extends infinitely in two opposite directions. A **plane** (*M*) is a flat surface that extends endlessly in all directions. **Space** is the set of all points.

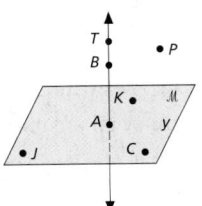

**Collinear points** (*T*, *B*, and *A*) lie on the same line, while **noncollinear points** (*A*, *K*, and *C*) do not lie on the same line. **Coplanar points** (*J*, *K*, and *C*) lie in the same plane, while **noncoplanar points** (*J*, *K*, *C*, and *B*) do not lie in the same plane.

### Example 1

**In the figures shown, name the following.**
**a.** two collinear points   **b.** three noncollinear points
**c.** three coplanar points   **d.** four noncoplanar points

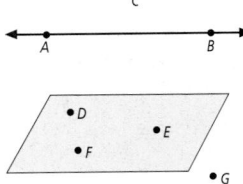

**Solution**

**a.** *A* and *B* lie on the same line, so they are collinear.

**b.** *A*, *B*, and *C* are noncollinear since there is no line that contains all three points.

**c.** *D*, *E*, and *F* lie in the same plane, so they are coplanar.

**d.** *D*, *E*, *F*, and *G* are noncoplanar since they do not lie in the same plane.

**192** Chapter 5 **Logic and Geometry**

---

### Extend the Lesson

**REAL WORLD CONNECTION** Geographers call the point on the opposite side of Earth from another point an *antipode*. In theory, the antipode of a point can be found by using a line segment through the center of a globe. Students can estimate the location of different antipodes. For example, the antipodes of both New York City, NY and Los Angeles, CA are in the Indian Ocean.

The **intersection** of two figures is the set of points that both figures share. Two lines intersect in a point. A plane and a line can intersect in a point or a line. A plane and a line may not intersect at all.

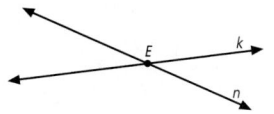 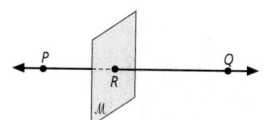

A **line segment** is a part of a line consisting of two endpoints and all points that lie between these two endpoints. **Congruent line segments** have the same measure. The **midpoint of a segment** is the point that divides the segment into two congruent segments. The symbol ≅ means "is congruent to." A **bisector of a segment** is any line, segment, ray, or plane that intersects the segment at its midpoint.

**Check Understanding**

Describe the intersection of plane $M$ and $\overleftrightarrow{PQ}$. Draw a figure to represent the other two possible intersections of a plane and a line.

Check students' work.

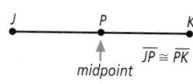

$\overline{JP} \cong \overline{PK}$

midpoint

## Example 2

**In the figure, $\overleftrightarrow{XY}$ bisects $\overline{MN}$. Name two congruent line segments.**

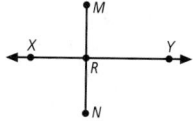

### Solution

Since $\overleftrightarrow{XY}$ bisects $\overline{MN}$, point $R$ is the midpoint of $\overline{MN}$. Therefore, segments $\overline{MR}$ and $\overline{RN}$ have the same length, or $\overline{MR} \cong \overline{RN}$.

There are certain statements about the relationships between *points*, *lines* and *planes* that are assumed to be true. These assumptions are called **postulates**.

| | |
|---|---|
| **Point, Line and Plane Postulates** | *Postulate 1* Through any two points, there is exactly one line.<br><br>*Postulate 2* Through any three noncollinear points, there is exactly one plane.<br><br>*Postulate 3* If two points lie in a plane, then the line joining them lies in that plane.<br><br>*Postulate 4* If two planes intersect, then their intersection is a line. |

## Example 3

**State which postulate is illustrated in each figure.**

a.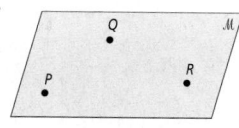

b.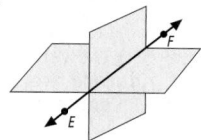

### Solution

a. Points $P$, $Q$ and $R$ are noncollinear and are all contained in plane $M$, so the first figure illustrates *Postulate 2*.

b. The second figure shows two planes intersecting at $\overleftrightarrow{EF}$, which illustrates *Postulate 4*.

 **Math Online** mathmatters2.com/extra_examples

Lesson 5-1 **Elements of Geometry** 193

## Chalkboard Examples

### Supplementary Example 1

Refer to the diagram at the right to name the types of points indicated.

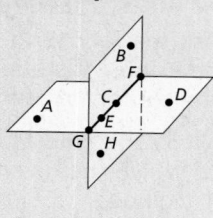

a. three collinear points   any 3 of *G, E, C, F*

b. all the points that are coplanar with point *B, C,* and *F*   *G, E, H*

c. all points that are not coplanar with points *A, F,* and *D*   *B* and *H*

### Supplementary Example 2

In the figure, $\overline{MN}$ and $\overline{AB}$ bisect each other at *Q*. Name congruent segments.
$\overline{MQ} \cong \overline{QN}, \overline{BQ} \cong \overline{QA}$

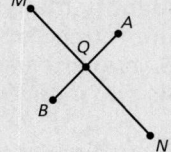

### Supplementary Example 3

Identify the intersection of the two planes.   $\overleftrightarrow{XY}$

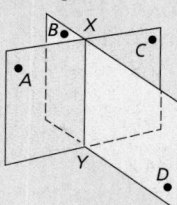

## Teaching Tip

**ESL/LEP** These students may benefit from making a vocabulary list of the terms present in this chapter, including an illustration of each term. They should keep the list handy to refer to when reading the lessons and working on exercises.

# Lesson Wrap-up

## QUICK ASSESSMENT

Ask the following questions to determine if students understand the content presented in this lesson.

**Name the kind of geometric figures to which the given term can apply.**
1. collinear   points
2. coplanar   points or lines

**Tell how many points are necessary so that the given geometric figure is *determined* (exactly one can be drawn).**
3. a line   2 points
4. a plane   3 noncollinear points

**Identify the type of geometric figure formed by the given figures.**
5. two intersecting lines   a point
4. two intersecting planes   a line

## ASSIGNMENT GUIDE

**Basic:** 1–29, 35–38
**Enriched:** 1–38

### Reteaching Worksheet 5-1

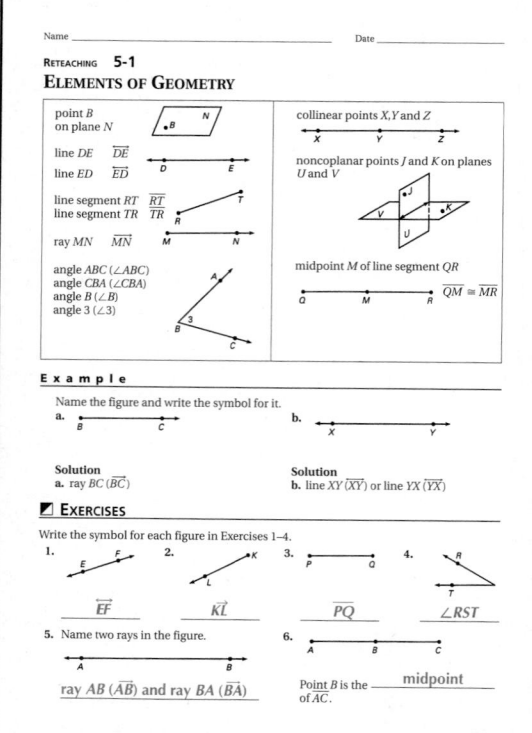

---

**Refer to the figure.**

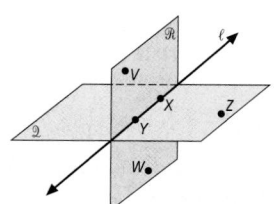

1. Name three points that determine plane 𝒥.
   any three of *A, B, X* and *Y*
2. Name the intersection of planes 𝒥 and 𝒦.
   $\overline{XY}$
3. How many lines do points *A* and *B* determine?   1
4. In how many planes shown is $\overrightarrow{XY}$ contained?   2
5. Does $\overleftrightarrow{AC}$ lie on plane 𝒥 or plane 𝒦?   neither

**Draw a figure to illustrate each situation.**
For 6–9, see additional answers.
6. Points *A, B,* and *C* are noncollinear.
7. Points *W, X, Y,* and *Z* are noncoplanar.
8. Line *m* intersects plane 𝒵 at point *Q*.
9. Planes *J* and *K* intersect at line *t*.

10. **PHOTOGRAPHY** Photographers often use tripods, three-legged stands, to hold their cameras steady. Which postulate does this illustrate? Why do you think they do not use stands with four legs?   See additional answers.

◼ **PRACTICE EXERCISES** • **For Extra Practice, see page 599.**

**Refer to the figure.**

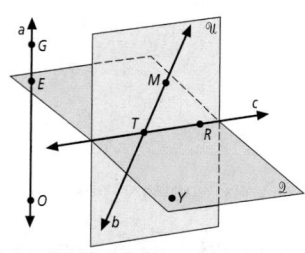

11. Name two points that determine line *l*.   *X* and *Y*
12. Name three points that determine plane ℛ.
    any three of *V, W, X* and *Y*
13. Name the intersection of plane ℛ and plane 𝒬.
    line *l*
14. Name three lines that lie in plane 𝒬.
    ∠*BGC*, ∠*CGE*, ∠*FGB*

**State whether each statement is *true* or *false*. If the statement is false, explain why.**

15. Points *G* and *O* determine line *a*.   true
16. Points *M* and *T* determine plane 𝒰.
    False; three points are needed to determine a plane.
17. The intersection of lines *b* and *c* is point *T*.   true
18. The intersection of planes 𝒰 and 𝒬 is points *R* and *T*.
    False; the intersection of two planes is a line.
19. Points *G, E,* and *O* are collinear.   true
20. Points *M, T, R,* and *E* are coplanar.   False; point *E* is not in plane 𝒰.

21. **CONSTRUCTION** To make sure a wall being built is straight, a mason will place two sticks in the ground flush with the wall and pull a rope tight between the sticks. Which postulate does the mason apply to this situation?   Postulate 1

22. **NAVIGATION** A forest ranger is leading a group of hikers through the woods to visit three noncollinear locations. Describe the plane that contains these three points. Is the ground a good model for a plane? Explain.
    See additional answers.

---

## ADDITIONAL ANSWERS

6.
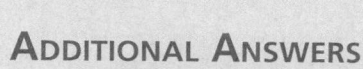

7.
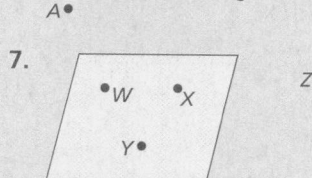

8.
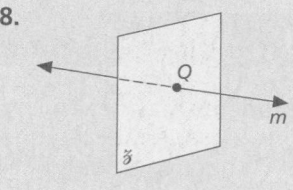

9.
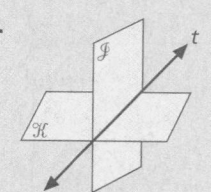

**Refer to the figure. Point *E* is not in plane *M*.**

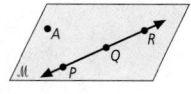

**23.** Which postulate states that exactly one plane contains *A*, *P*, and *Q*?
Postulate 2

**24.** Which postulate states that exactly one line contains *A* and *R*?
Postulate 1

**25.** If points *A* and *P* are in plane *M*, which postulate states that $\overrightarrow{AP}$ is in plane *M*?  Postulate 3

**ART**  Many works of artist Piet Mondrian consist only of rectangles and parts of rectangles. Refer to the geometric representation of one of his works in the figure shown.

**26.** Name all the points that are collinear with points *A* and *D*.
G, F, E

**27.** Identify the intersection of $\overline{LN}$ and $\overline{RM}$.  U

**28.** Identify the intersection of $\overline{KQ}$ and $\overline{EP}$.  $\overline{QP}$

**29.** Name all segments shown for which point *L* is one endpoint.  $\overline{LB}, \overline{LC}, \overline{LU}, \overline{LN}, \overline{LP}$

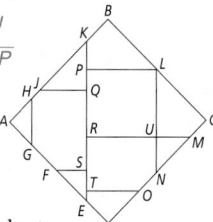

## ■ EXTENDED PRACTICE EXERCISES

**30. MODELING**  Use a sheet of paper and a cube to demonstrate how the intersection of a plane and a cube could be a point, a line segment, or a square region.
See additional answers.

**31. CRITICAL THINKING**  What do you think the intersection of three planes might look like? Think of a corner of a room to help you visualize the answer.
It would most likely be a point, but it could be a line.

**32. WRITING MATH**  Explain why it is important to include the word *noncollinear* in the statement of *Postulate 2*.  See additional answers.

**33. DATA FILE**  Refer to the data on road congestion at ten major cities on page 575. Use an atlas to locate three of these cities that are approximately collinear. List the three cities.  Atlanta, New York, Boston

**34. CHAPTER INVESTIGATION**  On a sunny morning, select a level area and place a 4-ft stick in the ground before noon. Mark the tip of the shadow and label it point *W*. Wait until after noon when the shadow creates a straight line with point *W* in the opposite direction. Mark the tip of the new shadow point *E*.  The points *W* and *E* represent West and East, respectively. The line connecting the two points is orientated in an East-West direction.

## ■ MIXED REVIEW EXERCISES

**Use the frequency table for Exercises 35–38.** (Lesson 1-3).

**35.** How many more flights head to Chicago than to Boston each day?  24

**36.** The number of flights to Los Angeles each day is the same as the combined number of flights to which two cities?
Boston and Baltimore or Boston and St. Louis

**37.** How many fewer flights are there to Denver than to St. Louis each day?  4

**38.** Suppose you took a random survey of people in this airport asking each person to what city they were flying. The results showed that more people were flying to Los Angeles than Chicago. Would you consider the survey to be invalid? Explain.
(Lesson 1-1)  No. The survey is of passengers and the table is of flights.

| Departing flights by destination | Tally | Frequency |
|---|---|---|
| Boston | 卌 卌 卌 卌 III | 23 |
| Los Angeles | 卌 卌 卌 卌 卌 卌 卌 IIII | 39 |
| Chicago | 卌 卌 卌 卌 卌 卌 卌 卌 卌 II | 47 |
| Baltimore | 卌 卌 卌 I | 16 |
| Cincinnati | 卌 III | 8 |
| Denver | 卌 卌 II | 12 |
| St. Louis | 卌 卌 卌 I | 16 |

---

## ADDITIONAL ANSWERS

**10.** Postulate 2: Only three legs are necessary to balance the tripod on a surface; and furthermore, a four-legged stand would be difficult to balance on a non-flat surface.

**22.** The plane is flat and contains the three points. Since the shape of the ground is not perfectly flat, it is not a perfect model for a plane.

**30.** The intersection is a point when just a corner of the cube is contained in the plane, a line segment when an edge of the cube but no other part of the cube is contained in the plane, and a plane when a face of the cube is contained in the plane.

**32.** If the points were collinear, then they would be on a single line. That line would be a part of an infinite number of planes, so a single plane would not be determined by the three points.

---

## Extra Practice Worksheet 5-1

## Enrichment Worksheet 5-1

# Lesson Planning

## NCTM Standards/Strands
- Geometry
- Measurement
- Reasoning & Proof
- Connections

## Vocabulary

| | |
|---|---|
| ray | opposite rays |
| angle | vertex (vertices) |
| degree | |
| complementary angles | |
| supplementary angles | |
| adjacent angles | |
| congruent angles | |
| perpendicular lines | |
| vertical angles | |
| bisector of an angle | |

## Tools/Materials Needed

| | |
|---|---|
| file folder | straightedge |
| paper plate | scissors |

## Lesson Resources

Warm-up Transparency 19
Transparency RF-22
Reteaching 5-2
Extra Practice 5-2
Enrichment 5-2

# Getting Started

## 5-Minute Warm-up

**Solve for *x* and check.**
1. $4x + 5x = 90$   $x = 10$
2. $2x + 7x - 90 = 180$   $x = 30$
3. $8x - 4 = 3x + 11$   $x = 3$
4. $x + 2(x - 30) = 90$   $x = 50$

## Introduction to Lesson 5-2

As an alternative to the file folder, students can work with angles constructed from two strips of cardboard and a paper fastener. Whatever device, as students obtain angles of different measures, elicit the terms *acute angle*, *right angle*, *obtuse angle*, and *straight angle*.

---

# 5-2 Angles and Perpendicular Lines

**Goals**
- Identify and use perpendicular lines.
- Identify and use angle relationships.

**Applications**   Health, Physics, Paper folding, Navigation

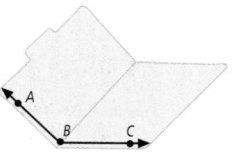

**Use a file folder or a piece of paper, a straightedge and a pencil.**
For 1–4, observe student's work
1. Draw ∠*ABC* on the file folder or paper.
2. Position the folder so *m*∠*ABC* is 0°, 90°, and then 180°.
3. Position the folder so *m*∠*ABC* is greater than 0° but less than 90°.
4. Work with a partner. Position your two papers so the sum of the measures of the angles together is 90°, then 180°.

## BUILD UNDERSTANDING

A **ray** is part of a line that begins at one endpoint and extends without end in one direction. If point *B* is between points *A* and *C*, then $\overrightarrow{BA}$ and $\overrightarrow{BC}$ are **opposite rays**.

An **angle** is the figure formed by two rays that have a common endpoint. The endpoint is called the **vertex** (plural: *vertices*) of the angle. Each ray forms a *side* of the angle. The size of an angle is measured in units called **degrees**.

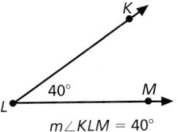

$m\angle KLM = 40°$

Two angles whose measures have a sum of 90° are called **complementary angles**. Two angles whose measures have a sum of 180° are called **supplementary angles**.

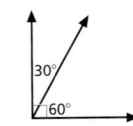

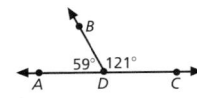

### Think Back

Recall that *acute angles* measure less than 90°, *right angles* measure exactly 90°, *obtuse angles* measure between 90° and 180° and *straight angles* measure exactly 180°.

### Example 1

**Use the three angles shown to name:**
a. two complementary angles
b. two supplementary angles

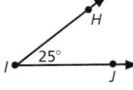
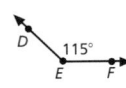
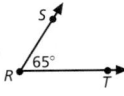

### Solution

a. $m\angle HIJ + m\angle SRT = 25° + 65° = 90°$, so the angles are complementary.

b. $m\angle SRT + m\angle DEF = 65° + 115° = 180°$, so the angles are supplementary.

## Teaching Tip

Students should be familiar with the *protractor* and its use for measuring angles. As a quick review, have students determine the measure of ∠*POQ* shown.   Using the outer scale, $115 - 25 = 90°$. Using the inner scale, $|65 - 155| = |-90| = 90°$
You may wish to have students make their own simple protractor as a handy device for judging the reasonableness of answers. Here's how: Have students cut a half circle from a paper plate. Mark the center of the diameter, to be used as the vertex point. Then mark 0°, 45°, 90°, 135°, and 180°.

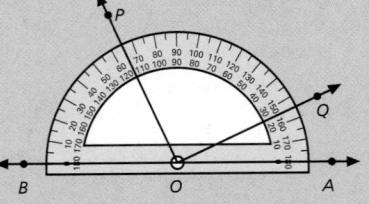

Two angles that have a common vertex and share a common side, but do not overlap are called **adjacent angles**, such as ∠1 and ∠2.

**Congruent angles** have the same angle measure.

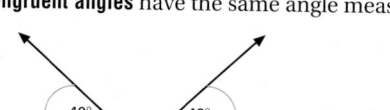

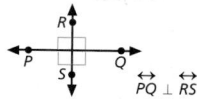

40° A    B 40°    ∠A ≅ ∠B

**Perpendicular lines** are two lines that intersect to form right angles.

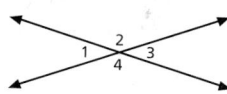

When two lines intersect, the angles that are not adjacent to each other are called **vertical angles**. Vertical angles are congruent. In the figure, ∠1 and ∠3 are vertical and ∠2 and ∠4 are vertical.

## Example 2

In the figure, $\overline{AD} \perp \overline{CF}$ and ∠FGE and ∠BGC are vertical angles.

**a.** Name all right angles.    **b.** Find m∠AGB.    **c.** Find m∠EGF.

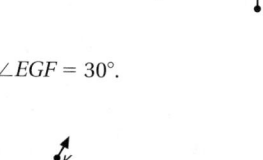

### Solution

**a.** $\overline{AD} \perp \overline{CF}$. So ∠AGF, ∠AGC, ∠CGD, and ∠DGF are all right angles.

**b.** ∠AGB and ∠BGC are complementary angles. So
m∠AGB = 90° − m∠BGC = 90° − 30° = 60°.

**c.** ∠BGC and ∠EGF are vertical angles, so m∠BGC = m∠EGF = 30°.

The **bisector of an angle** is a ray that divides the angle into two congruent adjacent angles. $\overrightarrow{LN}$ is the bisector of ∠KLM.

∠KLN ≅ ∠NLM

## Example 3

**GEOMETRY SOFTWARE** Use geometry software to bisect an angle and verify that the bisector divides the angle into two congruent adjacent angles.

### Solution

*Step 1* Construct an angle and display the measure of the angle.

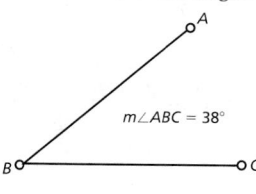

m∠ABC = 38°

*Step 2* Using the construct option, bisect the angle.

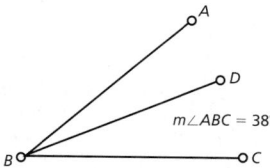

m∠ABC = 38°

**Math Online** mathmatters2.com/extra_examples

Lesson 5-2 **Angles and Perpendicular Lines** | **197**

---

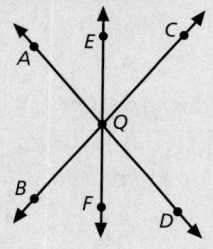
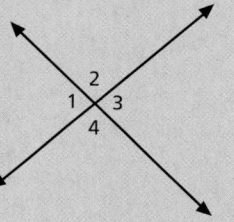
---

## Lesson Wrap-up

### QUICK ASSESSMENT

Ask the following questions to determine if students understand the content presented in this lesson.

**1.** If $m\angle A = 20°$, $m\angle B = 60°$, and $m\angle B = 100°$, are angles $A$, $B$, and $C$ supplementary angles? Explain.
No; even though the sum of the measures of the three angles is 180°, only *two* angles can be supplementary.

**2.** Are angles 1 and 2 adjacent angles? Explain.
No; even though they have the same vertex, they do not have a common side.

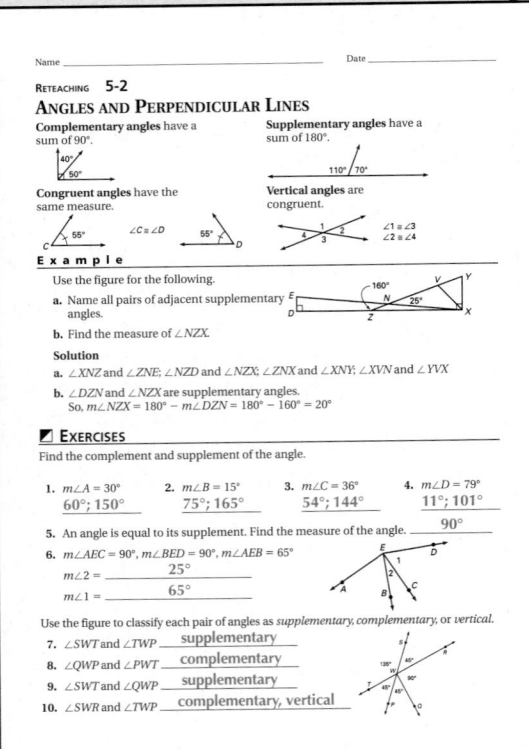

**3.** Are angles $APB$ and $CPD$ vertical angles? Explain.
No; $A$, $P$, and $D$ are noncollinear, and so are $A$, $P$, and $C$.

### ASSIGNMENT GUIDE

**Basic:** 1–27, 33–42
**Enriched:** 1–42

### Reteaching Worksheet 5-2

Name _____ Date _____

RETEACHING **5-2**

**ANGLES AND PERPENDICULAR LINES**

Complementary angles have a sum of 90°.

Supplementary angles have a sum of 180°.

Congruent angles have the same measure.

Vertical angles are congruent.

$\angle 1 \cong \angle 3$
$\angle 2 \cong \angle 4$

**Example**

Use the figure for the following.
**a.** Name all pairs of adjacent supplementary angles.
**b.** Find the measure of $\angle NZX$.

**Solution**
**a.** $\angle XNZ$ and $\angle ZNE$; $\angle NZD$ and $\angle NZX$; $\angle ZNX$ and $\angle XNY$; $\angle XVN$ and $\angle YVX$
**b.** $\angle DZN$ and $\angle NZX$ are supplementary angles.
So, $m\angle NZX = 180° - m\angle DZN = 180° - 160° = 20°$

**EXERCISES**

Find the complement and supplement of the angle.
**1.** $m\angle A = 30°$   60°; 150°
**2.** $m\angle B = 15°$   75°; 165°
**3.** $m\angle C = 36°$   54°; 144°
**4.** $m\angle D = 79°$   11°; 101°
**5.** An angle is equal to its supplement. Find the measure of the angle.   90°
**6.** $m\angle AEC = 90°$, $m\angle BED = 90°$, $m\angle AEB = 65°$
$m\angle 2 =$   25°
$m\angle 1 =$   65°

Use the figure to classify each pair of angles as *supplementary, complementary,* or *vertical.*
**7.** $\angle SWT$ and $\angle TWP$   supplementary
**8.** $\angle QWP$ and $\angle PWT$   complementary
**9.** $\angle SWT$ and $\angle QWP$   supplementary
**10.** $\angle SWR$ and $\angle TWP$   complementary, vertical

---

**Step 3** Display the measures of the newly created adjacent angles. Notice they have the same measure.

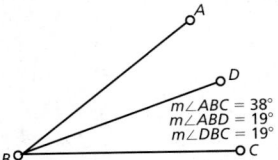

$m\angle ABC = 38°$
$m\angle ABD = 19°$
$m\angle DBC = 19°$

**Step 4** Keep all of the measures displayed and move the original angle. Observe how the angle measurements change.

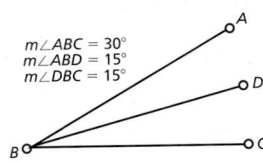

$m\angle ABC = 30°$
$m\angle ABD = 15°$
$m\angle DBC = 15°$

### TRY THESE EXERCISES

Find the measure of the complement and supplement of each angle.

**1.** $m\angle A = 14°$   76°, 166°
**2.** $m\angle B = 47°$   43°, 133°
**3.** $m\angle 1 = 30°$   60°, 150°
**4.** $m\angle DEG = 89°$   1°, 91°

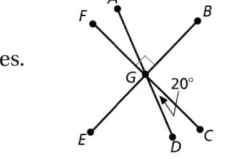

In the figure shown, $\overline{FG} \perp \overline{BE}$.

**5.** Name all right angles.
$\angle BGC$, $\angle CGE$, $\angle EGF$, $\angle FGB$
**6.** Name a pair of vertical angles.
See additional answers.
**7.** Find $m\angle AGB$.
70°
**8.** Find $m\angle BGC$.
90°

Find the value of $x$ in each figure. Justify your answer.
For 9–12, see additional answers.

**9.**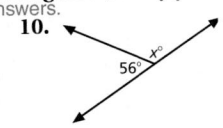
**10.**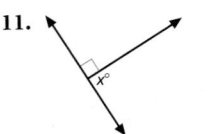
**11.**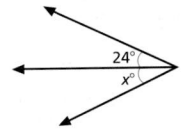
**12.**

### PRACTICE EXERCISES • For Extra Practice, see page 599.

For Exercises 13–15, use the figure shown.

**13.** Name a pair of perpendicular segments.
$TO \perp RO$; $TO \perp OS$
**14.** Name two adjacent complementary angles.
$\angle ROP$ and $\angle POT$
**15.** Name two pairs of vertical angles.
$\angle ROP$ and $\angle QOS$, $\angle ROQ$ and $\angle POS$

In the figures shown, $\overrightarrow{OX}$ and $\overrightarrow{OY}$ are opposite rays. Find $m\angle XOZ$.

**16.** 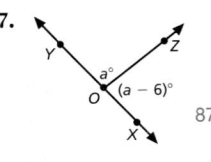 47°
**17.** 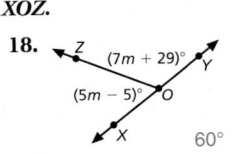 87°
**18.** 60°

**19. PHYSICS** According to the *law of reflection*, when a ray of light is reflected from a plane surface, the *angle of incidence* is congruent to the *angle of reflection.* Copy the figure shown, and give as many angle measures as you can.   See additional answers.

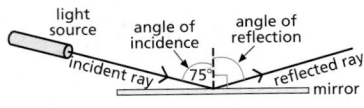

---

### ADDITIONAL ANSWERS

**6.** $\angle FGA$ and $\angle CGD$, $\angle BGA$ and $\angle EGD$, $\angle AGE$ and $\angle BGD$, $\angle AGC$ and $\angle FGD$, $\angle FGB$ and $\angle EGC$, $\angle FGE$ and $\angle BGC$
**9.** 37° since the two angles are complementary and $90° - 53° = 37°$.
**10.** 124° since the two angles are supplementary and $180° - 56° = 124°$.
**11.** 90° since the supplement of a right angle is a right angle.
**12.** 24° since the angles are congruent.

**19.**

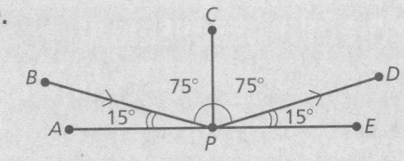

$m\angle APC = m\angle EPC = 90°$
$m\angle APD = m\angle EPB = 165°$
$m\angle BPD = 150°$
$m\angle APE = 180°$

**In the figures shown, $\angle RST$ is a right angle. Find $m\angle RSP$.**

**20.**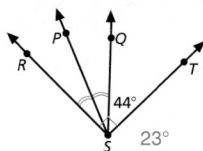
44°
23°

**21.**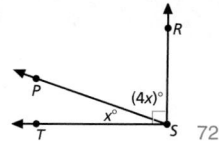
$(4x)°$
$x°$
72°

**22.**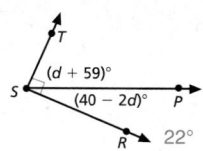
$(d + 59)°$
$(40 - 2d)°$
22°

**23. PAPER FOLDING** Draw an angle of any size on a sheet of paper. Fold the paper so one side of the angle lies directly on top of the other. Unfold the paper. What does the crease in the paper represent? the bisector of the angle

**24. WRITING MATH** Look up the words *complementary* and *supplementary* in a dictionary. Describe why you think they are used in reference to angles. See additional answers.

**HEALTH** An orthopedist adjusts the position of a patient's crutch handles so that the hand pieces allow a 30° elbow angle.

**25.** Measure the indicated elbow angle with a protractor. 90°

**26.** Find the supplement of this angle. 90°

**27.** Should the hand piece be lowered or raised to obtain the proper elbow angle? lowered

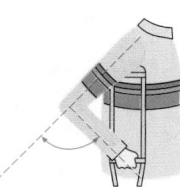

## ■ EXTENDED PRACTICE EXERCISES

**NAVIGATION** Submarines use a periscope to see above the water.

**28.** Describe any perpendicular lines if $\angle 2$ and $\angle 5$ are right angles. The horizontal pieces are perpendicular to the vertical piece.

**29.** If $\angle 2$ and $\angle 5$ are right angles, estimate $m\angle 4$, $m\angle 1$ and $m\angle 3$. $m\angle 4 = 45°$, $m\angle 1 = 45°$, $m\angle 3 = 45°$

**CRITICAL THINKING** Classify each statement as *true* or *false*. If the statement is false, explain why.

**30.** Two vertical angles may also be adjacent. false; by definition of vertical angles

**31.** The complement of an acute angle is an obtuse angle. false; the complement of an acute angle is an acute angle

**32.** Two vertical angles may be complementary. true

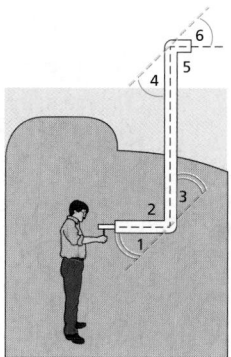

## ■ MIXED REVIEW EXERCISES

**Solve each inequality. Graph each solution on a number line.**
(Lessons 3-6 and 3-7) For 33–38, see additional answers for graphs.

**33.** $4x < -12$ $\quad x < -3$
**34.** $v + -18 \geq -5$ $\quad v \geq 13$
**35.** $4 - w \leq 36$ $\quad w \geq -32$
**36.** $\frac{3}{5}y > 21$ $\quad y > 35$
**37.** $3d - 9 \geq -15$ $\quad d \geq -2$
**38.** $16 - \frac{1}{5}f > -1$ $\quad f < 85$

**39.** Miranda spent at least 120 min on homework this week. She spent the same amount of time on her homework Monday, Tuesday, Wednesday and Thursday. She did not study on Friday or Saturday, but she spent 60 min on homework on Sunday. Find the least amount of time Miranda spent on her homework on Monday. (Lesson 3-7) 15 min.

**Add.** (Basic Math Skills)

**40.** $\frac{2}{3} + \frac{1}{3}$ $\quad 1$
**41.** $\frac{3}{5} + \frac{7}{10}$ $\quad \frac{13}{10}$
**42.** $8 + \frac{1}{4} + 6\frac{1}{3}$ $\quad 14\frac{7}{12}$

**Math Online** mathmatters2.com/self_check_quiz

**24.** Both words mean to fill up or complete, and both complementary and supplementary angles fill up or complete an angle to 90° and 180°, which are important angle measures in many real-world applications.

**33.**
$-6$ $-5$ $-4$ $-3$ $-2$ $-1$

**34.**
11 12 13 14 15 16

**35.**
$-34$ $-32$ $-30$

**36.**
33 34 35 36 37 38

**37.**
$-4$ $-3$ $-2$ $-1$ $\ 0$ $\ 1$

**38.**
82 83 84 85 86 87

---

## Extra Practice Worksheet 5-2

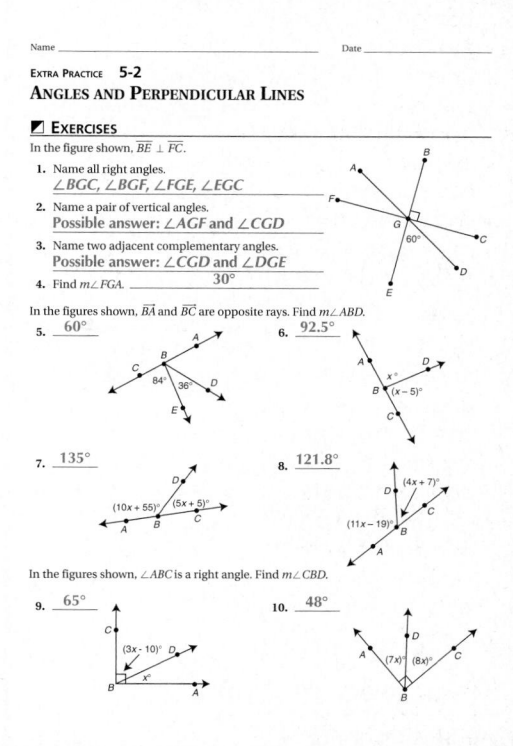

Name _____ Date _____

EXTRA PRACTICE **5-2**
**ANGLES AND PERPENDICULAR LINES**

**☑ EXERCISES**

In the figure shown, $\overline{BE} \perp \overline{FC}$.

**1.** Name all right angles.
$\angle BGC$, $\angle BGF$, $\angle FGE$, $\angle EGC$

**2.** Name a pair of vertical angles.
Possible answer: $\angle AGF$ and $\angle CGD$

**3.** Name two adjacent complementary angles.
Possible answer: $\angle CGD$ and $\angle DGE$

**4.** Find $m\angle FGA$. _____ 30°

In the figures shown, $\overline{BA}$ and $\overline{BC}$ are opposite rays. Find $m\angle ABD$.

**5.** _____ 60°
**6.** _____ 92.5°

**7.** _____ 135°
**8.** _____ 121.8°

In the figures shown, $\angle ABC$ is a right angle. Find $m\angle CBD$.

**9.** _____ 65°
**10.** _____ 48°

---

## Enrichment Worksheet 5-2

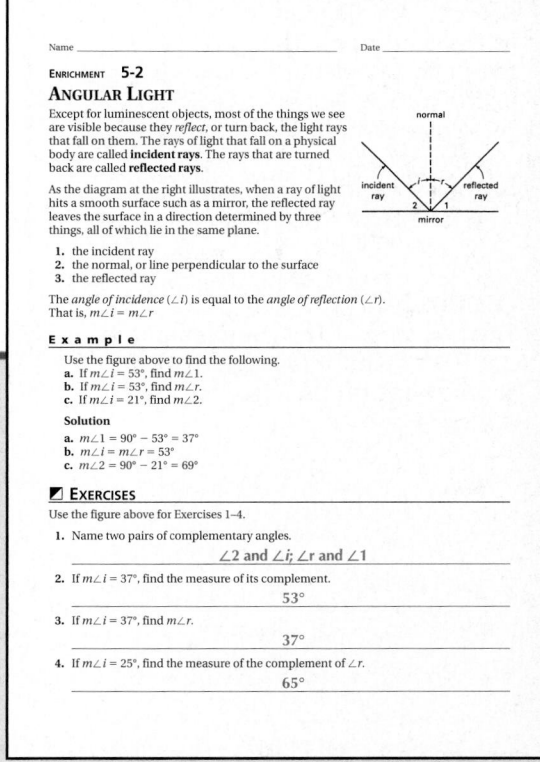

Name _____ Date _____

ENRICHMENT **5-2**
**ANGULAR LIGHT**

Except for luminescent objects, most of the things we see are visible because they *reflect*, or turn back, the light rays that fall on them. The rays of light that fall on a physical body are called **incident rays**. The rays that are turned back are called **reflected rays**.

As the diagram at the right illustrates, when a ray of light hits a smooth surface such as a mirror, the reflected ray leaves the surface in a direction determined by three things, all of which lie in the same plane.

1. the incident ray
2. the normal, or line perpendicular to the surface
3. the reflected ray

The *angle of incidence* ($\angle i$) is equal to the *angle of reflection* ($\angle r$). That is, $m\angle i = m\angle r$.

**E x a m p l e**

Use the figure above to find the following.
**a.** If $m\angle i = 53°$, find $m\angle 1$.
**b.** If $m\angle i = 53°$, find $m\angle r$.
**c.** If $m\angle i = 21°$, find $m\angle 2$.

**Solution**
**a.** $m\angle 1 = 90° - 53° = 37°$
**b.** $m\angle r = m\angle i = 53°$
**c.** $m\angle 2 = 90° - 21° = 69°$

**☑ EXERCISES**

Use the figure above for Exercises 1–4.

**1.** Name two pairs of complementary angles.
$\angle 2$ and $\angle i$; $\angle r$ and $\angle 1$

**2.** If $m\angle i = 37°$, find the measure of its complement.
53°

**3.** If $m\angle i = 37°$, find $m\angle r$.
37°

**4.** If $m\angle i = 25°$, find the measure of the complement of $\angle r$.
65°

### Vocabulary Review

**Lesson 5-1**

| | |
|---|---|
| geometry | point |
| line | plane |
| space | collinear points |

noncollinear points
coplanar
noncoplanar    intersection
congruent line segments
midpoint of a segment
bisector of a segment

**Lesson 5-2**

| | |
|---|---|
| ray | opposite rays |
| angle | vertex (vertices) |

degree
complementary angles
supplementary angles
adjacent angles
congruent angles
perpendicular lines
vertical angles
bisector of an angle

## ASSIGNMENT GUIDE

**All students:** 1–38

## Chalkboard Examples

**Lesson 5-1**
Refer to the diagram at the right to name the indicated elements.
a. the intersection of plane $\mathcal{M}$ and plane $\mathcal{N}$   line $\ell$
b. three noncollinear points that are in plane $\mathcal{M}$   P and any 2 of R, S, T

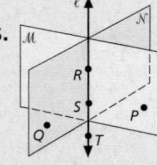

**Lesson 5-2**
The measure of the complement of $\angle A$ is 70°. Find the measure of the supplement of $\angle A$.
$m\angle A + 70 = 90$; so, $m\angle A = 20°$ and the measure of the supplement of $\angle A$ is 160°.

# Review and Practice Your Skills

## PRACTICE ◼ LESSON 5-1

1. How many points determine a plane?   3
2. Name three undefined terms.   point, line, plane

**Refer to the figure for Exercises 3–10.**

3. Name two points coplanar with $H$, $D$, and $E$.   F and C
4. Name three points on plane $\mathcal{I}$.   A, B, D, E, F or G
5. Name the intersection of planes $\mathcal{I}$ and $\mathcal{J}$.   $\overrightarrow{DE}, \overrightarrow{EF}, \overrightarrow{DF}$ or line $\ell$

**Tell whether each statement is *true* or *false*.**

6. $\overrightarrow{BA}$ is a bisector of $\overline{DF}$.   false
7. $\overrightarrow{BA}$ intersects $\overline{DF}$.   true
8. $A$, $C$, and $B$ are coplanar.   true
9. Three points determine a line.   false
10. If $\overline{BE} \cong \overline{EG}$, then $E$ is the midpoint of $\overline{BG}$.   true

**Draw a figure to illustrate each situation.**
For 11–12, see additional answers.
11. Line $m$ intersects plane $\mathcal{X}$ at point $B$.
12. The midpoint of $\overline{AB}$ is $C$. Line $CD$ bisects $\overleftrightarrow{AB}$.

## PRACTICE ◼ LESSON 5-2

**Use the figure shown for Exercises 13–17.**

13. Find $m\angle ABF$ if $m\angle ABE = 140°$ and $\overrightarrow{BF}$ bisects $\angle ABE$.   70°
14. Name the angle vertical to $\angle ABD$.   $\angle EBC$
15. Name all right angles.   none
16. Name two angles supplementary to $\angle EBC$.   $\angle ABE, \angle DBC$
17. Find the measure of $\angle ABD$.   40°

**Find the measures of the complement and supplement of each angle.**

| | |
|---|---|
| 18. $m\angle 1 = 23°$   67°, 157° | 19. $m\angle 2 = 77°$   13°, 103° |
| 20. $m\angle 3 = 89°$   1°, 91° | 21. $m\angle 4 = 59°$   31°, 121° |
| 22. $m\angle 5 = 13°$   77°, 167° | 23. $m\angle 6 = 60°$   30°, 120° |
| 24. $m\angle 7 = 12°$   78°, 168° | 25. $m\angle 8 = 45°$   45°, 135° |
| 26. $m\angle 9 = 70°$   20°, 110° | 27. $m\angle 10 = 31°$   59°, 149° |
| 28. $m\angle 11 = 55°$   35°, 125° | 29. $m\angle 12 = 5°$   85°, 175° |

### Teaching Tip

In preparation for Exercises 1 and 9, elicit the meaning of *determine* (that exactly one of the indicated elements can be drawn).
For Exercise 12, students should recognize that the number of bisectors of a line segment is infinite. (Since the midpoint is the only required point, no one line is determined.) However, there is only one bisector that is also perpendicular to the line segment. (Since now there are two required conditions—the midpoint and the right angle, one line is determined.) This special bisector is called the *perpendicular bisector*.

## PRACTICE ■ LESSON 5-1–LESSON 5-2

**Use the figure to match each term with the correct symbol.** (Lessons 5-1 and 5-2)

30. midpoint  e
31. bisector  b
32. plane  a
33. collinear points  c
34. $f$ ■ $\overline{AB}$  d

a. $\mathcal{P}$
b. $f$
c. $A, M, B$
d. $\perp$
e. $M$

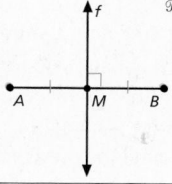

**Find the value of $x$ in each figure. List a vocabulary word to justify each answer.** (Lessons 5-1 and 5-2)

35.

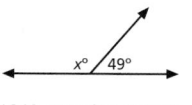

131°, supplementary

36.

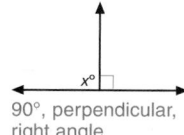

90°, perpendicular, right angle

37.

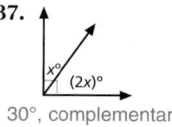

30°, complementary

38.

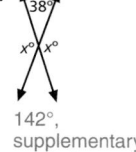

142°, supplementary, vertical

## Career – Cattle Rancher

Workplace Knowhow

A cattle rancher is responsible for the well-being of the cattle he or she is raising. Part of providing for the animals requires knowing the best grazing and watering locations. In the mountains it can be difficult to move animal herds, as certain areas are too steep or treacherous for cattle to negotiate. In the diagram, the ranch is at point $A$. The best grazing fields are at point $C$. However, because a straight path from $A$ to $C$ is too steep, they travel first to point $B$ at an angle of 70° to the vertical line. At point $B$, they turn 50° to the left and head up the mountain to point $C$. After grazing, they walk down the mountain, reaching the river at point $D$.

**Refer to the diagram for Exercises 1–4.**

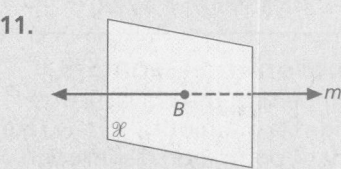

1. What acute angle is formed by the herd's path approaching the river and the river's shore?  55°

2. If the herd retraces its path on the way home, it moves from $D$ to $C$, turns left and continues to $B$, and turns right at $B$ and returns toward $A$. At what angle must the herd turn right at $B$ in order to head directly home?  130°

3. Point $G$ is the midpoint of $\overline{AF}$. If $GF = 2DF$, find $AF$.  5.6 mi

4. The length of $CD$ is 3.7 mi and $AB = 1.8$ mi. Find the length of the entire trip.  15 mi

---

## MathWorks

It is believed that cattle were domesticated about 8500 years ago in southeastern Europe, with Southeast Asia a probable second center of domestication. World cattle population is more than 1 billion, with half concentrated in South America, Europe, countries of the former USSR, the U.S., and India.

People on every continent raise cattle. Cattle live in cold lands and in hot lands. Wherever they live, cattle need to be moved, often in large herds, from place to place.

Students should answer Questions 1–4 to better understand the role of geometry in the process of moving a herd of cattle.

Another branch of mathematics that plays an important role in cattle ranching is probability, as related to the breeding of specific types of cattle. Cattle ranchers know that by analyzing breeding results it is possible to predict which traits will occur, and in what proportions, in the next generation.

Students who are interested in learning more about this career choice can go to mathmatters2.com/mathworks. School Guidance Counselors are another resource for information about training requirements and appropriate schools.

## ADDITIONAL ANSWERS

11.

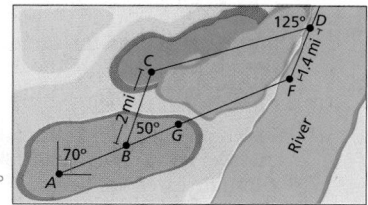

12.

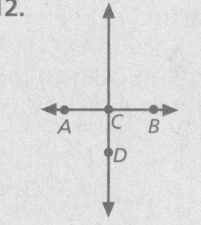

---

## Teaching Tip

In Exercises 35–38, you might have students write some sentences to explain their thoughts. For example, a series of sentences is shown below for Exercise 38.

Since two lines intersect, four angles are formed.
The 38°-angle is the supplement of each of the $x$°-angles.
The sum of the measures of two supplementary angles is 180°.
So, $38 + x = 180$ and $x° = 142°$.

### Vocabulary

| | |
|---|---|
| parallel lines | parallel planes |
| skew lines | transversal |
| interior angles | exterior angles |
| alternate interior angles | |
| same-side interior angles | |
| alternate exterior angles | |
| corresponding angles | |

### Tools/Materials Needed

compass       straightedge

### Lesson Resources

Warm-up Transparency 20
Transparency RF-23
Reteaching 5-3
Extra Practice 5-3
Enrichment 5-3

## Getting Started

### 5-MINUTE WARM-UP

Two lines intersect.
List as many facts as you can
about the angles.
$\angle 1 \cong \angle 3; \angle 2 \cong \angle 4;$
supplements: 1, 2;
2, 3; 3, 4; 4, 1; $m\angle 1 +$
$m\angle 2 + m\angle 3 + m\angle 4 = 360°.$

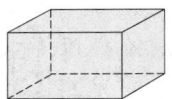

### Introduction to Lesson 5-3

After completing the construction,
have students do another. Draw line
$\ell$, and mark point $P$ on it. Through
$P$, construct (or draw if necessary)
line $m$ perpendicular to $\ell$. Then
mark point $Q$ on $m$. Through $Q$,
construct line $n$ perpendicular to $m$.
What is true about lines $\ell$ and $n$?
parallel

## Parallel Lines and Transversals

**Goals**
- Identify angles formed by parallel lines and transversals.
- Identify and use properties of parallel lines.

**Applications** Construction, Safety, Navigation, Music

**Use line $m$ and point $P$ to construct congruent angles.**
For 1–2, check students' work.
1. Draw line $m$ and point $P$ as shown. Through $P$ draw any line $n$ that intersects line $m$. Label $\angle 1$.

2. At $P$, using line $n$ as one side, construct $\angle 2$ so that $\angle 2 \cong \angle 1$. Label the intersection of the two arcs point $X$.

3. Draw and label $\overrightarrow{PX}$. What seems to be true about the relationship between $\overrightarrow{PX}$ and line $m$? They are parallel.

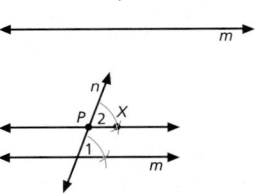

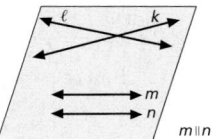

### BUILD UNDERSTANDING

Coplanar lines may intersect in a point. Coplanar lines that do not intersect are called **parallel lines**. In the figure, lines $k$ and $l$ intersect. Lines $m$ and $n$ have no points in common, so they are parallel lines.

Planes that do not intersect are called **parallel planes**. The top and bottom of a cube are contained in two parallel planes. Noncoplanar lines that do not intersect and are not parallel are called **skew lines**.

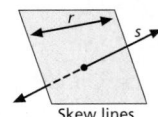

Skew lines

A **transversal** is a line that intersects each of two other coplanar lines in different points to produce **interior** and **exterior angles**. In the figure, transversal $t$ intersects lines $j$ and $k$.

Two nonadjacent interior angles on opposite sides of a transversal are called **alternate interior angles**. The two pairs of alternate interior angles are $\angle 1$ and $\angle 4$, and $\angle 2$ and $\angle 3$.

Interior angles on the same side of a transversal are called **same-side interior angles**. In the figure, the two pairs of same-side interior angles are $\angle 1$ and $\angle 3$, and $\angle 2$ and $\angle 4$.

Two nonadjacent exterior angles on opposite sides of the transversal are called **alternate exterior angles**. The two pairs of alternate exterior angles are $\angle 5$ and $\angle 8$, and $\angle 6$ and $\angle 7$.

Two angles in corresponding positions relative to two lines cut by a transversal are called **corresponding angles**. In the figure, the four pairs of corresponding angles are $\angle 1$ and $\angle 7$, $\angle 2$ and $\angle 8$, $\angle 3$ and $\angle 5$, and $\angle 4$ and $\angle 6$.

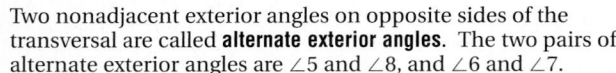
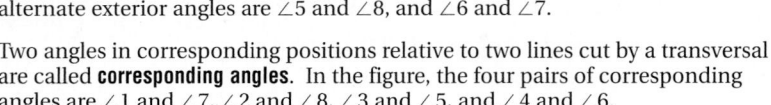

**202** | Chapter 5 **Logic and Geometry**

## Extend the Lesson

**CHALLENGE** At the right, a diagram (without construction arcs) is shown for the suggested extension to the opening activity. Ask students how lines $\ell$ and $n$ relate to line $m$. Lines $\ell$ and $n$ are each perpendicular to $m$. Guide students to conclude that lines perpendicular to the same line are parallel to each other.

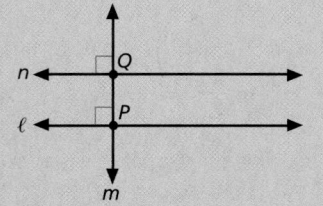

## Example 1

**Refer to the figure to name the following.**

a. all pairs of alternate interior angles

b. all pairs of alternate exterior angles

c. all pairs of same-side interior angles

d. all pairs of corresponding angles

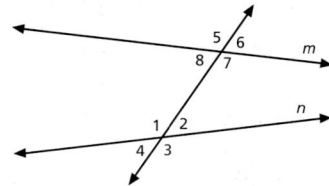

### Solution

a. $\angle 1$ and $\angle 7$, $\angle 2$ and $\angle 8$    b. $\angle 5$ and $\angle 3$, $\angle 6$ and $\angle 4$

c. $\angle 2$ and $\angle 7$, $\angle 1$ and $\angle 8$    d. $\angle 1$ and $\angle 5$, $\angle 2$ and $\angle 6$, $\angle 3$ and $\angle 7$, $\angle 4$ and $\angle 8$

When a transversal intersects two parallel lines, the angles formed have special relationships, which are postulates in geometry.

| **Parallel Line Postulates** | *Postulate 5* If two parallel lines are cut by a transversal, then corresponding angles are congruent. |
| --- | --- |
| | *Postulate 6* If two lines are cut by a transversal so that corresponding angles are congruent, then the lines are parallel. |

From these postulates, it can be shown that the following statements are true.

*Statement 5A* If two parallel lines are cut by a transversal, then alternate interior angles are congruent.

*Statement 5B* If two parallel lines are cut by a transversal, then alternate exterior angles are congruent.

*Statement 6A* If two lines are cut by a transversal so that alternate interior angles are congruent, then the lines are parallel.

*Statement 6B* If two lines are cut by a transversal so that alternate exterior angles are congruent, then the lines are parallel.

## Example 2

**In the figure, $\overrightarrow{AB} \parallel \overrightarrow{CD}$. Name the postulate or statement that gives the reason why each statement is true.**

a. $\angle 2 \cong \angle 6$     b. $\angle 4 \cong \angle 5$     c. $\angle 1 \cong \angle 8$

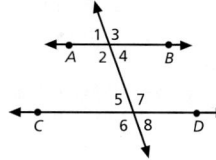

### Solution

a. $\angle 2$ and $\angle 6$ are corresponding angles, so *Postulate* 5 says that they are congruent angles.

b. $\angle 4$ and $\angle 5$ are alternate interior angles, so *Statement 5A* says that they are congruent angles.

c. $\angle 1$ and $\angle 8$ are alternate exterior angles, so *Statement 5B* says that they are congruent angles.

 **Math Online** mathmatters2.com/extra_examples     Lesson 5-3 **Parallel Lines and Transversals**    **203**

---

## Chalkboard Examples

### Supplementary Example 1

In the figure, $\overrightarrow{AB} \parallel \overrightarrow{CD}$.

Find $m\angle AEF$.

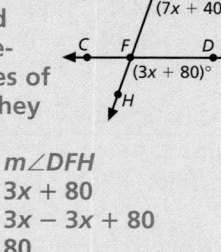

Since $\angle AEF$ and $\angle EFD$ are alternate interior angles of parallel lines, they are congruent.

$$m\angle AEF = m\angle EFD$$
$$4x - 10 = 2x + 20$$
$$4x - 2x - 10 = 2x - 2x + 20$$
$$2x - 10 = 20$$
$$2x - 10 + 10 = 20 + 10$$
$$2x = 30$$
$$\frac{2x}{2} = \frac{30}{2}$$
$$x = 15$$

So, $m\angle AEF = 4(15) - 10 = 60 - 10 = 50°$.

### Supplementary Example 2

In the figure, $\overrightarrow{AB} \parallel \overrightarrow{CD}$.

Find $m\angle BEF$.

Since $\angle BEF$ and $\angle DFH$ are corresponding angles of parallel lines, they are congruent.

$$m\angle BEF = m\angle DFH$$
$$7x + 40 = 3x + 80$$
$$7x - 3x + 40 = 3x - 3x + 80$$
$$4x + 40 = 80$$
$$4x + 40 - 40 = 80 - 40$$
$$\frac{4x}{4} = \frac{40}{4}$$
$$4x = 40$$
$$x = 10$$

So, $m\angle BEF = 7(10) + 40 = 70 + 40 = 110°$.

---

## Differentiated Instruction

**VISUAL LEARNERS** To assist students in identifying alternate interior angles formed by two parallel lines and a transversal, have them look for a pattern. Alternate interior angles suggest a Z pattern.

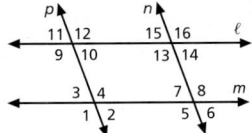

**Refer to the figure to name a pair of each type of angle.**

1. alternate interior angles
   ∠6 and ∠3, ∠5 and ∠4
2. alternate exterior angles
   ∠8 and ∠1, ∠7 and ∠2
3. same-side interior angles
   ∠5 and ∠3, ∠6 and ∠4
4. corresponding angles
   See additional answers.

**In the figure, line *PQ* ∥ line *RS*. Justify each statement.**

5. ∠5 ≅ ∠1
   corresponding
6. ∠8 ≅ ∠1
   alternate exterior
7. ∠4 ≅ ∠5
   alternate interior
8. ∠2 ≅ ∠6
   corresponding

**In the figure, *m*∠5 = 120°. Find each measure.**

9. *m*∠4  120°
10. *m*∠2  60°
11. *m*∠6  60°
12. *m*∠7  60°

## PRACTICE EXERCISES • For Extra Practice, see page 600.

**Refer to the figure to classify each pair of angles.**

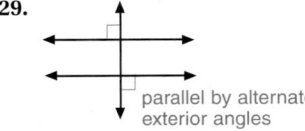
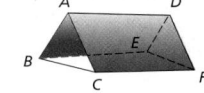

13. ∠1 and ∠9
    corresponding
14. ∠9 and ∠3
    same-side interior
15. ∠1 and ∠5
    corresponding
16. ∠3 and ∠10
    alternate interior
17. ∠15 and ∠6
    alternate exterior
18. ∠8 and ∠13
    alternate interior
19. ∠5 and ∠16
    alternate exterior
20. ∠7 and ∠13
    same-side interior

**In the figure, $\overrightarrow{PQ}$ ∥ $\overrightarrow{RS}$ and *m*∠5 = 105°. Find each measure.**

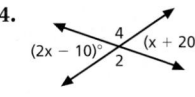

21. *m*∠1  105°
22. *m*∠2  75°
23. *m*∠4  105°
24. *m*∠6  75°
25. *m*∠7  75°
26. *m*∠8  105°

**State whether the lines cut by the transversal are parallel, not parallel or if there is not enough information. Justify your answer if they are not parallel.**

27.
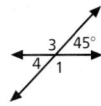
parallel by alternate interior angles

28.
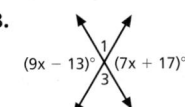
not parallel

29.
parallel by alternate exterior angles

30. **CONSTRUCTION** The top of a house is shown. Use the figure to name all skew line segments, parallel line segments, and parallel planes.   See additional answers.

31. **WRITING MATH** Describe an object or objects that model each of the following: parallel lines, parallel planes, and skew lines.
    Answers will vary.

**Find each unknown angle measure.**   For 32–34, see additional answers.

32.
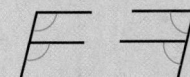

33.

(9x − 13)° (7x + 17)°

34.
(2x − 10)°  (x + 20)°

204 | Chapter 5  **Logic and Geometry**

---

# Lesson Wrap-up

## QUICK ASSESSMENT

Ask the following questions to determine if students understand the content presented in this lesson.

Visualize two lines cut by a transversal. You do not know if the lines are parallel.

1. What kinds of angle pairs can you be certain are formed at the intersection of each line with the transversal?   adjacent, vertical and supplementary angles

2. What must be true about the vertical angles and the adjacent angles at both intersections? vertical angles must be congruent; these adjacent angles must be supplementary

Suppose now that you have two *parallel* lines cut by a transversal.

3. Name the additional types of angle pairs that must be congruent.   alternate interior, alternate exterior and corresponding angles

## ASSIGNMENT GUIDE

**Basic:** 1–39, 44–49
**Enriched:** 1–49

### Reteaching Worksheet 5-3

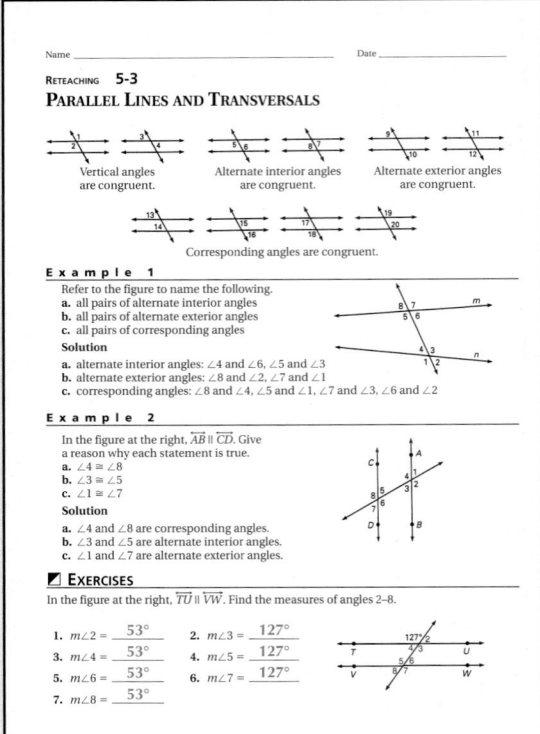

RETEACHING  **5-3**
**PARALLEL LINES AND TRANSVERSALS**

Vertical angles are congruent. Alternate interior angles are congruent. Alternate exterior angles are congruent.

Corresponding angles are congruent.

**Example 1**
Refer to the figure to name the following.
a. all pairs of alternate interior angles
b. all pairs of alternate exterior angles
c. all pairs of corresponding angles
**Solution**
a. alternate interior angles: ∠4 and ∠6, ∠5 and ∠3
b. alternate exterior angles: ∠8 and ∠2, ∠7 and ∠1
c. corresponding angles: ∠8 and ∠4, ∠5 and ∠1, ∠7 and ∠3, ∠6 and ∠2

**Example 2**
In the figure at the right, $\overline{AB}$ ∥ $\overline{CD}$. Give a reason why each statement is true.
a. ∠4 ≅ ∠8
b. ∠3 ≅ ∠5
c. ∠1 ≅ ∠7
**Solution**
a. ∠4 and ∠8 are corresponding angles.
b. ∠3 and ∠5 are alternate interior angles.
c. ∠1 and ∠7 are alternate exterior angles.

**EXERCISES**
In the figure at the right, $\overline{TU}$ ∥ $\overline{VW}$. Find the measures of angles 2–8.

1. *m*∠2 = 53°
2. *m*∠3 = 127°
3. *m*∠4 = 53°
4. *m*∠5 = 127°
5. *m*∠6 = 53°
6. *m*∠7 = 127°
7. *m*∠8 = 53°

---

## Differentiated Instruction

**VISUAL LEARNERS** To assist students in identifying corresponding angles formed by two parallel lines and a transversal, have them look for a pattern. Corresponding angles suggest an F pattern.

**35. SAFETY** To avoid possible collisions, airplanes headed eastbound are assigned an altitude level that is an odd number of thousands of feet while westbound planes fly at an even number of thousands of feet. What type of lines are modeled? skew

**36. GEOMETRY SOFTWARE** Use geometry software to draw three lines that are all parallel to each other. Then draw a transversal that cuts each of the three lines. Use the measure tool to find the measurements of the angles created. What do you notice about corresponding, alternate interior, and alternate exterior angles?
The angles are congruent.

**NAVIGATION** Sailboats cannot sail directly into the wind. Instead, sailors use a technique called *tacking*, where the boat sails a series of short paths. In the figure, the boat is tacking first 45° left of the wind, then 45° right of the wind and so on.

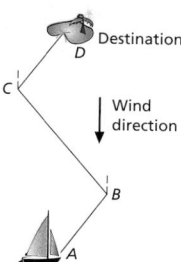

**37.** What appears to be true of the relationship between $\overline{AB}$ and $\overline{CD}$?
They are parallel.

**38.** If the relationship in Exercise 37 is true, what does $\overline{BC}$ represent?
a transversal

**39.** What type of angles are represented by ∠DCB and ∠ABC?
alternate interior angles

## EXTENDED PRACTICE EXERCISES

Classify each statement as *true* or *false*. If the statement is false, explain why.

**40.** Two skew lines never intersect.   true

**41.** Two lines in the same plane are sometimes skew lines.
False, by definition, skew lines do not lie in the same plane.

**42.** If a transversal is perpendicular to one of two parallel lines, then it is perpendicular to the other line.   true

**43. MUSIC** The word *parallel* is used in music to describe songs that have consistency, such as harmony with parallel voices. Describe two other uses of the word *parallel* in real world applications.
Answers will vary, but one idea is parallel lines in poetry.

## MIXED REVIEW EXERCISES

A bag contains 3 white marbles, 6 blue marbles, 2 green marbles and 1 red marble. Find the probability of the following events. (Lessons 4-1 and 4-5)

**44.** $P$(drawing one red marble)   $\frac{1}{12}$

**45.** $P$(drawing 1 green marble, then a second green marble without replacement)   $\frac{1}{66}$

**46.** $P$(drawing 1 green marble, then a second green marble with replacement)   $\frac{1}{36}$

**47.** Describe an event in relation to this bag of marbles that has the probability of 1.   $P$(white or blue or green or red)

**48.** Describe an event in relation to this bag of marbles that has the probability of 0.   Answers will vary. Sample answer: $P$(purple)

**Math Online** mathmatters2.com/self_check_quiz

## ADDITIONAL ANSWERS

**4.** ∠7 and ∠3, ∠5 and ∠1, ∠8 and ∠4, ∠6 and ∠2

**30.** Skew line segments: $\overline{AB}$ and $\overline{DF}$, $\overline{AB}$ and $\overline{EF}$, $\overline{AB}$ and $\overline{CF}$, $\overline{AC}$ and $\overline{EF}$, $\overline{AC}$ and $\overline{BE}$, $\overline{AC}$ and $\overline{DE}$, $\overline{CF}$ and $\overline{ED}$, $\overline{BE}$ and $\overline{DF}$, $\overline{DE}$ and $\overline{BC}$, $\overline{DF}$ and $\overline{BC}$
parallel line segments: $\overline{AC}$ and $\overline{DF}$; $\overline{AB}$ and $\overline{ED}$; $\overline{BC}$ and $\overline{EF}$; $\overline{BE}$, $\overline{CF}$, and $\overline{AD}$
parallel planes: plane $ABC$ and plane $DEF$

**32.** $m\angle 1 = 135°$
$m\angle 3 = 135°$
$m\angle 4 = 45°$

**33.** $m\angle 1 = 58°$
$m\angle 3 = 58°$
$(9x - 13)° = 122°$
$(7x + 17)° = 122°$

**34.** $m\angle 2 = 130°$
$m\angle 4 = 130°$
$(2x - 10)° = 50°$
$(x + 20)° = 50°$

---

### Extra Practice Worksheet 5-3

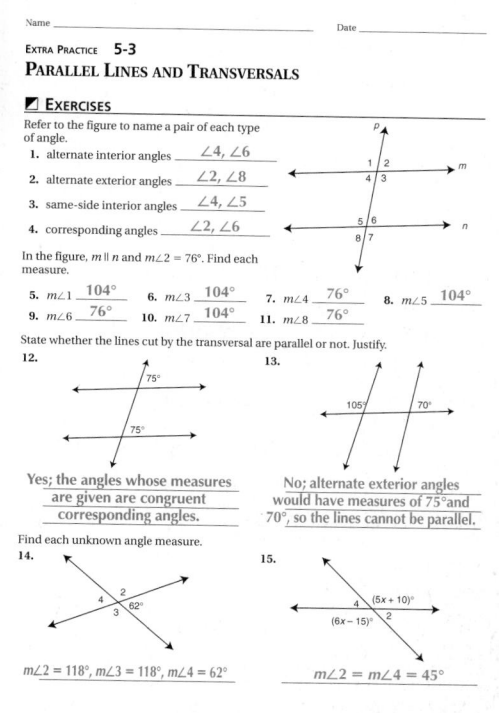

Name _____   Date _____

**EXTRA PRACTICE  5-3**
**PARALLEL LINES AND TRANSVERSALS**

**EXERCISES**

Refer to the figure to name a pair of each type of angle.

1. alternate interior angles   ∠4, ∠6
2. alternate exterior angles   ∠2, ∠8
3. same-side interior angles   ∠4, ∠5
4. corresponding angles   ∠2, ∠6

In the figure, $m \parallel n$ and $m\angle 2 = 76°$. Find each measure.

5. $m\angle 1$  104°    6. $m\angle 3$  104°    7. $m\angle 4$  76°    8. $m\angle 5$  104°
9. $m\angle 6$  76°    10. $m\angle 7$  104°    11. $m\angle 8$  76°

State whether the lines cut by the transversal are parallel or not. Justify.

12.
Yes; the angles whose measures are given are congruent corresponding angles.

13.
No; alternate exterior angles would have measures of 75° and 70°, so the lines cannot be parallel.

Find each unknown angle measure.

14.
$m\angle 2 = 118°, m\angle 3 = 118°, m\angle 4 = 62°$

15.
$m\angle 2 = m\angle 4 = 45°$

---

### Enrichment Worksheet 5-3

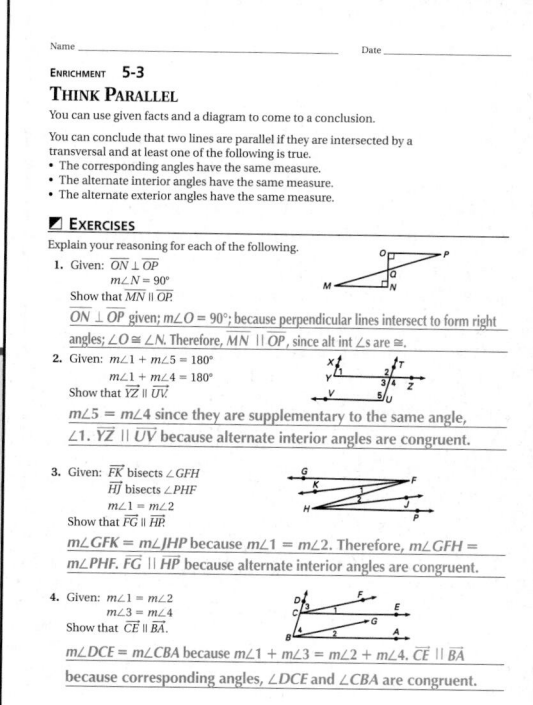

Name _____   Date _____

**ENRICHMENT  5-3**
**THINK PARALLEL**

You can use given facts and a diagram to come to a conclusion.

You can conclude that two lines are parallel if they are intersected by a transversal and at least one of the following is true.
• The corresponding angles have the same measure.
• The alternate interior angles have the same measure.
• The alternate exterior angles have the same measure.

**EXERCISES**

Explain your reasoning for each of the following.

1. Given: $\overline{ON} \perp \overline{OP}$
$m\angle N = 90°$
Show that $\overline{MN} \parallel \overline{OP}$.
$\overline{ON} \perp \overline{OP}$ given; $m\angle O = 90°$; because perpendicular lines intersect to form right angles; $\angle O \cong \angle N$. Therefore, $\overline{MN} \parallel \overline{OP}$, since alt int ∠s are ≅.

2. Given: $m\angle 1 + m\angle 5 = 180°$
$m\angle 1 + m\angle 4 = 180°$
Show that $\overline{YZ} \parallel \overline{UV}$.
$m\angle 5 = m\angle 4$ since they are supplementary to the same angle, $\angle 1$. $\overline{YZ} \parallel \overline{UV}$ because alternate interior angles are congruent.

3. Given: $\overrightarrow{FK}$ bisects $\angle GFH$
$\overrightarrow{HJ}$ bisects $\angle PHF$
$m\angle 1 = m\angle 2$
Show that $\overline{FG} \parallel \overline{HP}$.
$m\angle GFK = m\angle JHP$ because $m\angle 1 = m\angle 2$. Therefore, $m\angle GFH = m\angle PHF$. $\overline{FG} \parallel \overline{HP}$ because alternate interior angles are congruent.

4. Given: $m\angle 1 = m\angle 2$
$m\angle 3 = m\angle 4$
Show that $\overline{CE} \parallel \overline{BA}$.
$m\angle DCE = m\angle CBA$ because $m\angle 1 + m\angle 3 = m\angle 2 + m\angle 4$. $\overline{CE} \parallel \overline{BA}$ because corresponding angles, $\angle DCE$ and $\angle CBA$ are congruent.

## Lesson Planning

### NCTM Standards/Strands
- Geometry
- Measurement
- Reasoning & Proof
- Connections

### Vocabulary

triangle  vertex of a triangle
angle of a triangle
side of a triangle
congruent sides
congruent angles
exterior angle of a triangle

### Tools/Materials Needed

protractor  centimeter ruler

### Lesson Resources

Warm-up Transparency 20
Transparency RF-25
Reteaching 5-4
Extra Practice 5-4
Enrichment 5-4
Technology Activity 5-4

## Getting Started

### 5-MINUTE WARM-UP

**Solve using mental math.**
1. $180 - 34 = a$  $a = 146$
2. $180 - b = 79$  $b = 101$
3. $180 - (55 + 45) = c$  $c = 80$
4. $65 + 30 + d = 180$  $d = 85$

### Introduction to Lesson 5-4

After completing the activity, have students draw a line segment and mark a point on it; then cut out the triangle they had previously traced and tear off the three corners. Tell them to place the three corners around the point on the line segment, angles facing the point. Discuss what they see and draw a conclusion. **The three corners exactly "fit" around the point, forming a straight angle. So, the sum of the measures of the three angles of a triangle = 180°.**

# 5-4 Properties of Triangles

**Goals**
- Classify triangles according to their sides and angles.
- Identify and use properties of triangles.

**Applications** Travel, Interior design, Navigation

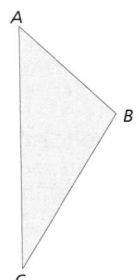

**On a sheet of paper, trace the triangle shown.**

1. Use a protractor to find the measure of each angle of the triangle. What is the sum of the three angles?  48°, 100°, 32°; sum = 180°

2. Which side is longest? Which angle is largest?  $\overline{AC}$, $\angle B$

3. Which side is shortest? Which angle is smallest?  $\overline{AB}$, $\angle C$

4. Based on these results, describe what you think are some properties of triangles. Do you think they apply to all triangles?  The sum of angles is 180°. The longest/shortest sides are opposite largest/smallest angles. Yes.

5. Draw a triangle of your own, and test these properties.  Check students' work.

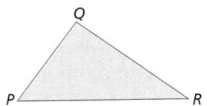

### BUILD UNDERSTANDING

A **triangle** is a closed plane figure formed by three line segments joining three noncollinear points. Each point is called a **vertex**. Each vertex corresponds to an angle of the triangle. Each of the line segments that joins the vertices is called a side.

> **Think Back**
> Equal number of tick marks on the sides of a figure indicate congruence.

Vertices: Points $P$, $Q$ and $R$

Sides: $\overline{PQ}$, $\overline{QR}$ and $\overline{RP}$

Angles: $\angle P$, $\angle Q$ and $\angle R$

A triangle is named by its vertices. The figure is named triangle $PQR$, usually written $\triangle PQR$.

Two sides of a triangle that have the same length are **congruent sides**. Two angles of a triangle that have the same measure are **congruent angles**.

A triangle may be classified by its number of congruent sides.

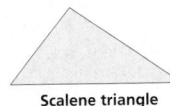
**Scalene triangle**
no congruent sides

**Isosceles triangle**
at least two congruent sides

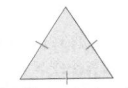
**Equilateral triangle**
all three sides congruent

A triangle may also be classified by its angles.

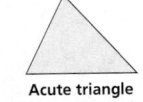
**Acute triangle**
three acute angles

**Obtuse triangle**
one obtuse angle

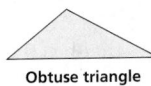
**Right triangle**
one right angle

**Isosceles triangle**
at least two congruent angles

**Equiangular triangle**
all three angles congruent

## Extend the Lesson

**REAL WORLD CONNECTION** Have students find examples of structures—such as bicycles, bridges, TV and cell towers, automobile chassis—that use triangular construction in their supports.
Explain that a triangular brace is particularly strong since a triangle is the only polygon that is *rigid*; once the sides are formed, they cannot be moved. Have students construct a triangle and a quadrilateral from paper strips and fasteners to demonstrate that a triangle retains its shape, but a quadrilateral can be moved and formed into different shapes.

The following properties are true for all triangles.

| **Properties of Triangles** | *Property 1* The sum of the angles of a triangle is 180°. |
| | *Property 2* The sum of the lengths of any two sides is greater than the length of the third side. |
| | *Property 3* The longest side is opposite the largest angle, and the shortest side is opposite the smallest angle. |

## Example 1

**State whether it is possible to have a triangle with sides of the given lengths.**

**a.** 14, 9, 6                 **b.** 8, 5, 3

### Solution

**a.** It is possible because $14 + 9 = 23$, $9 + 6 = 15$ and $14 + 6 = 20$. In each case, the sum of any two sides is greater than the third side.

**b.** It is not possible because $3 + 5 = 8$, which is not greater than the length of the remaining side, which is 8.

**Check Understanding**

For example 1, part b, use a centimeter ruler to illustrate the truth of Property 2.

In the figure, $\angle LMR$ is called an **exterior angle** of $\triangle LMN$. Notice that $m\angle LMR = m\angle L + m\angle N$.

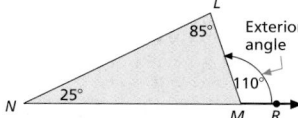

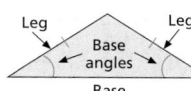

For isosceles triangles, the two angles opposite the congruent sides, called **base angles**, are congruent.

These two properties are summarized below.

| **More Properties of Triangles** | *Property 4* If one side of a triangle is extended, then the exterior angle formed is equal to the sum of the two remote interior angles of the triangle. |
| | *Property 5* If two sides of a triangle are congruent, then the angles opposite those sides are congruent. |

## Example 2

**Find the values of $a$ and $b$.**

**a.**

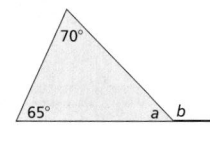

**b.**

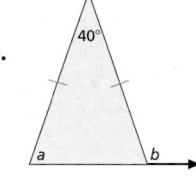

**Math Online** mathmatters2.com/extra_examples

Lesson 5-4 **Properties of Triangles** | **207**

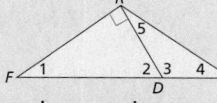
## Teaching Tip

To emphasize the reasonableness of Triangle Property 2 (the sum of the lengths of any two sides is greater than the length of the third side), have students consider three noncollinear points: *A, B, C*. Ask students to tell how to get from point *A* to point *B* by the shortest way. The shortest distance between two points is a straight segment. So, $AC + BC$ must be greater than *AB*. Likewise, $BA + AC > CB$ and $CB + BA > AC$.

Note with students that when the length of a line segment is represented, the segment symbol is omitted. So, for example, *AB* represents the length of $\overline{AB}$.

### Solution

a. According to *Property 1*, $a + 70° + 65° = 180°$.
$$a = 180° − 70° − 65° = 45°$$

Using *Property 4*, $b = 70° + 65° = 135°$.

b. Since the triangle is isosceles, the base angles are congruent.

$$a + a + 40° = 180° \qquad b = 40° + 70°$$
$$2a = 140° \qquad b = 110°$$
$$a = 70°$$

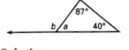
### TRY THESE EXERCISES

**State whether it is possible to have a triangle with sides of the given lengths.**

1. 12, 7, 6  yes
2. 13, 7, 5  no
3. 11, 14, 16  yes
4. 1, 2, 3  no

**Find the unknown angle measures in each figure.**

5.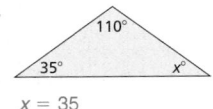
$x = 35$

6.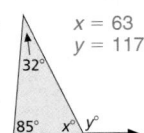
$x = 63$
$y = 117$

7.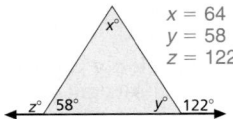
$x = 64$
$y = 58$
$z = 122$

8. **WRITING MATH** Explain how to find the measure of one angle of a triangle when you are given the other two angle measures.
   Subtract the sum of the two known angle measures from 180°.

### PRACTICE EXERCISES • For Extra Practice, see page 600.

**State whether it is possible to have a triangle with sides of the given lengths.**

9. 11, 32, 21  no
10. 0.2, 0.3, 0.5  no
11. 3, 6, 8  yes
12. 56, 32, 85  yes

**Use the figure to classify each triangle by its sides.**

13. △ABC  scalene
14. △BDC  scalene
15. △AEB  equilateral
16. △BCE  isosceles

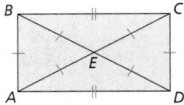

**Find the unknown angle measures in each figure.**

17.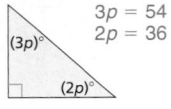
$3p = 54$
$2p = 36$

18.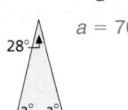
$a = 76$

19.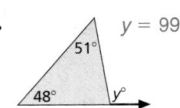
$y = 99$

20. A triangle has angle measures of $4x°$, $(2x − 30)°$ and $(2x − 30)°$. Classify the triangle, and find its angle measures.   obtuse isosceles triangle $(4x) = 120$, $(2x − 30) = 30$

21. **TRAVEL** At what angle (opposite McDonald Blvd.) do Jasmine Ave. and Rogers Rd. intersect? What property of triangles does this model?
   123°; The sum of angles is 180°.

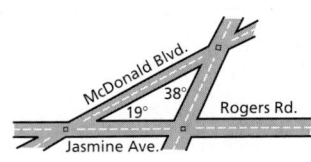

## Alternative Assessment

**STUDENT PORTFOLIO** Have students use Triangle Property 2 (the sum of the lengths of two side of a triangle is greater than the length of the third side) to determine the range of possible values for the third side.

In △STU, $ST = 10$, $TU = 14$ and $US = x$. Determine the range of possible values for US.

Use Triangle Property 2 to write three inequalities in terms of $x$.

$$10 + 14 > x \qquad 10 + x > 14 \qquad 14 + x > 10$$
$$24 > x \qquad x > 4 \qquad x > −4$$

So, $4 < US < 24$.

**In the figure, $\overrightarrow{AB} \parallel \overrightarrow{CD}$. Find each measure.**

**22.** $m\angle 1$   140°

**23.** $m\angle 2$   40°

**24.** $m\angle 3$   50°

**25.** $m\angle 4$   90°

**26.** $m\angle 5$   140°

**27.** $m\angle 6$   40°

**28.** $m\angle 7$   40°

**29.** $m\angle 8$   140°

**30.** $m\angle 9$   50°

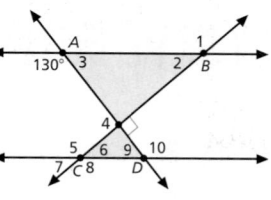

**31. WRITING MATH** Briefly describe the different types of triangles in this lesson. Draw a right isosceles triangle, and explain how you know it is both isosceles and right.   Check students' work.

**32. INTERIOR DESIGN** Felicity is redesigning her kitchen and wishes to have a large window installed that is in the shape of an isosceles triangle. If two of the sides of the window are 8 ft long, can the base be 18 ft long? Explain.   No. The sum of the length of any two sides of a triangle is greater than the third side.

**33. NAVIGATION** The Bermuda Triangle is the area of the Atlantic Ocean famous for causing navigational difficulties. It is an equilateral triangle formed by Bermuda, Puerto Rico and Ft. Lauderdale, Florida. The distance between vertices is about 1000 mi. Since the Bermuda Triangle is equilateral, is it necessarily equiangular? Explain.   Yes. The angles opposite of congruent sides are congruent.

Bermuda Triangle

### EXTENDED PRACTICE EXERCISES

**34. CRITICAL THINKING** Explain why a triangle cannot have more than one obtuse angle.   The sum of two obtuse angles is greater than 180°.

**35.** An exterior angle of a triangle measures $(14x + 43)°$, and the remote interior angles both measure $(13x - 11.5)°$. Classify the triangle, and find the measure of the angles.   equilateral; interior angles: 60°; exterior angle: 120°

**Complete each statement with *always*, *sometimes*, or *never*.**

**36.** An isosceles triangle is __?__ scalene.   never

**37.** An exterior angle of a triangle is __?__ acute.   sometimes

**38.** In a right triangle, the acute angles are __?__ complementary.   always

**39. CHAPTER INVESTIGATION** Connect points $W$ and $E$. This is your east-west line. Draw the perpendicular bisector of $\overline{EW}$, making it the same length as $EW$. Label the top endpoint of the bisector $N$ and the bottom endpoint $S$. This is your north-south line.   Check students' work.

### MIXED REVIEW EXERCISES

**Simplify.** (Lessons 2-7 and 2-8)

**40.** $3x^2 + 7x - x^2$
$2x^2 + 7x$

**41.** $5(7t^5)$   $35t^5$

**42.** $2(r^2)^3$   $2r^6$

**43.** $5s(s - 5)$
$5s^2 - 25s$

**44.** $\dfrac{14v^3}{7v}$   $2v^2$

**45.** $\dfrac{(36s - 21s^2t)}{3s}$   $-7st + 12$

**46.** $3t(4t^4)^2$   $48t^9$

**47.** $\dfrac{x^2(3x - x^3)}{x}$   $-x^4 + 3x^2$

**48.** $(3x^8)(2x^{-4})(x^{-4})$   6

## Extend the Lesson

**CONNECTING TO PRIOR KNOWLEDGE** Have students consider the following algebraic representation of a geometric situation.

The sides of $\triangle STU$ are represented in terms of $x$ by $US = x + 2$, $ST = x$, and $TU = x - 2$. Which angle of $\triangle STU$ has the least measure? Justify your answer.

Since you are looking for the smallest angle of the triangle, identify the shortest side. Since $x - 2 < x < x + 2$, $TU$ is the shortest side of the triangle. So, $\angle S$, which lies opposite $TU$, must be the smallest angle of the triangle.

---

### Extra Practice Worksheet 5-4

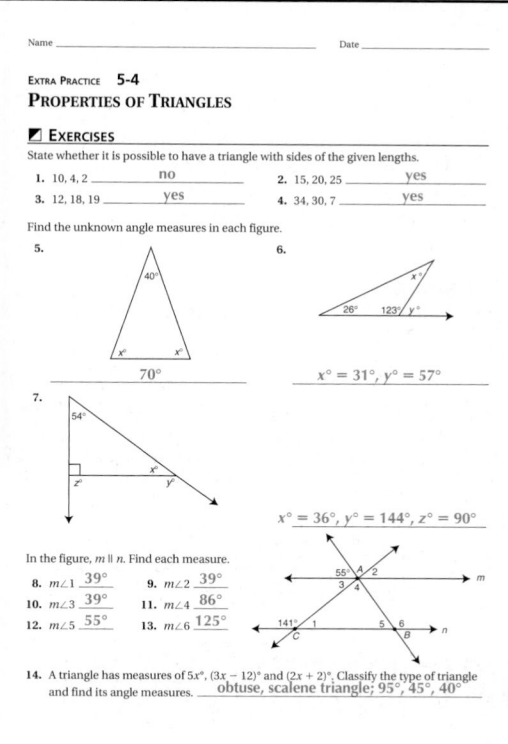

Name _____   Date _____

EXTRA PRACTICE **5-4**
**PROPERTIES OF TRIANGLES**

**EXERCISES**

State whether it is possible to have a triangle with sides of the given lengths.

1. 10, 4, 2 ____no____   2. 15, 20, 25 ____yes____

3. 12, 18, 19 ____yes____   4. 34, 30, 7 ____yes____

Find the unknown angle measures in each figure.

5. (40°, x°, x°)   70°

6. (26°, 123°, x°, y°)   $x° = 31°, y° = 57°$

7. (54°, x°, y°, z°)   $x° = 36°, y° = 144°, z° = 90°$

In the figure, $m \parallel n$. Find each measure.

8. $m\angle 1$  __39°__   9. $m\angle 2$  __39°__

10. $m\angle 3$  __39°__   11. $m\angle 4$  __86°__

12. $m\angle 5$  __55°__   13. $m\angle 6$  __125°__

14. A triangle has measures of $5x°$, $(3x - 12)°$ and $(2x + 2)°$. Classify the type of triangle and find its angle measures.   obtuse, scalene triangle; 95°, 45°, 40°

---

### Enrichment Worksheet 5-4

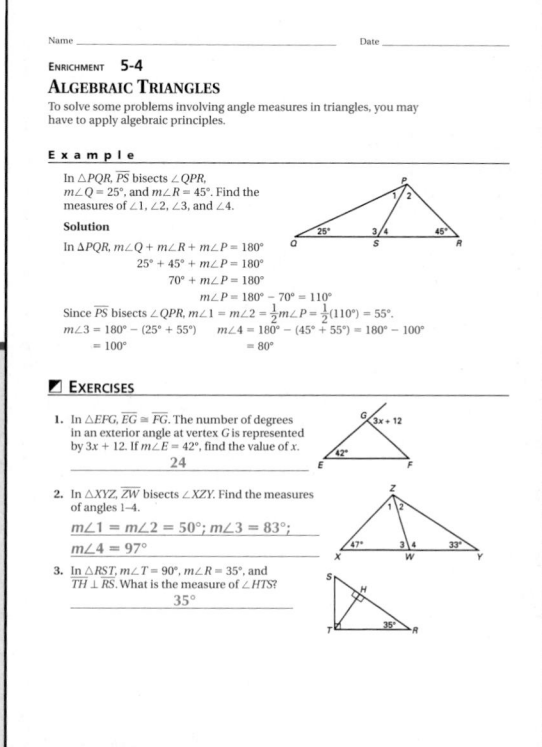

Name _____   Date _____

ENRICHMENT **5-4**
**ALGEBRAIC TRIANGLES**
To solve some problems involving angle measures in triangles, you may have to apply algebraic principles.

**Example**

In $\triangle PQR$, $\overline{PS}$ bisects $\angle QPR$, $m\angle Q = 25°$, and $m\angle R = 45°$. Find the measures of $\angle 1$, $\angle 2$, $\angle 3$, and $\angle 4$.

**Solution**

In $\triangle PQR$, $m\angle Q + m\angle R + m\angle P = 180°$
$25° + 45° + m\angle P = 180°$
$70° + m\angle P = 180°$
$m\angle P = 180° - 70° = 110°$

Since $\overline{PS}$ bisects $\angle QPR$, $m\angle 1 = m\angle 2 = \frac{1}{2}m\angle P = \frac{1}{2}(110°) = 55°$.
$m\angle 3 = 180° - (25° + 55°)$   $m\angle 4 = 180° - (45° + 55°) = 180° - 100°$
$= 100°$   $= 80°$

**EXERCISES**

1. In $\triangle EFG$, $\overline{EG} \cong \overline{FG}$. The number of degrees in an exterior angle at vertex $G$ is represented by $3x + 12$. If $m\angle E = 42°$, find the value of $x$.   24

2. In $\triangle XYZ$, $\overline{ZW}$ bisects $\angle XZY$. Find the measures of angles 1-4.
$m\angle 1 = m\angle 2 = 50°; m\angle 3 = 83°;$
$m\angle 4 = 97°$

3. In $\triangle RST$, $m\angle T = 90°$, $m\angle R = 35°$, and $\overline{TH} \perp \overline{RS}$. What is the measure of $\angle HTS$?   35°

## Vocabulary Review

**Lesson 5-3**
parallel lines    parallel planes
skew lines    transversal
interior angles    exterior angles
alternate interior angles
same-side interior angles
alternate exterior angles
corresponding angles

**Lesson 5-4**
triangle    vertex of a triangle
angle of a triangle
side of a triangle
congruent sides
congruent angles
exterior angle of a triangle

## ASSIGNMENT GUIDE

**All students:** 1–47

## Chalkboard Examples

### Lesson 5-3
Find the measure of the eight angles in the figure.

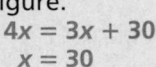

$$4x = 3x + 30$$
$$x = 30$$
$$4x = 120°$$
$$3x + 30 = 120°$$
$$m\angle 1 = m\angle 3 = m\angle 6 = m\angle 8 = 60°$$
$$m\angle 2 = m\angle 5 = 120°$$

### Lesson 5-4
Find $m\angle C$.
Since $\triangle ABC$ is isosceles, the base angles are congruent, $m\angle CAB = x$. Then

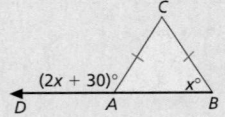

$$m\angle DAC + m\angle CAB = 180°$$
$$(2x + 30) + x = 180 \rightarrow x = 50°$$
Finally,
$$m\angle C + m\angle CAB + m\angle CAB = 180°$$
$$m\angle C + 50° + 50° = 180°$$
So, $m\angle C = 80°$.

---

### PRACTICE ■ LESSON 5-3

**Assume line $\ell \parallel$ line $m$ and line $n \parallel$ line $p$. Classify each pair of angles.**

1. $\angle 1$ and $\angle 4$
  vertical
2. $\angle 1$ and $\angle 7$
  supplementary, exterior
3. $\angle 3$ and $\angle 6$
  alternate, interior
4. $\angle 11$ and $\angle 15$
  corresponding
5. $\angle 2$ and $\angle 10$
  corresponding
6. $\angle 12$ and $\angle 13$
  alternate, interior
7. $\angle 11$ and $\angle 13$
  supplementary, same-side interior
8. $\angle 14$ and $\angle 16$
  adjacent, supplementary
9. $\angle 2$ and $\angle 7$
  alternate, exterior
10. $\angle 8$ and $\angle 13$
  alternate, interior

**In the figure, line $\ell \parallel$ line $m$ and $m\angle 3 = 120°$. Find each measure.**

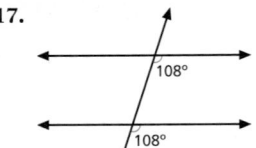

11. $m\angle 1$   60°
12. $m\angle 2$   120°
13. $m\angle 4$   60°
14. $m\angle 6$   120°
15. $m\angle 7$   120°
16. $m\angle 8$   60°

**State whether the lines cut by the transversal are parallel, not parallel or if there is not enough information. Justify your answer if they are parallel.**

17.

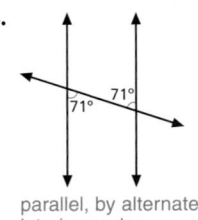

108°
108°

parallel, by corresponding angles

18.

71° 71°

parallel, by alternate interior angles

19.

87°
87°

not enough information

### PRACTICE ■ LESSON 5-4

**State whether it is possible to have a triangle with sides of the given lengths.**

20. 7, 11, 14   yes
21. 10, 10, 10   yes
22. 0.4, 0.5, 0.9   no
23. 1, 3, 6   no
24. 30, 40, 50   yes
25. 30, 30, 60   no

**In the figure, $\overrightarrow{EF} \parallel \overrightarrow{GH}$.**

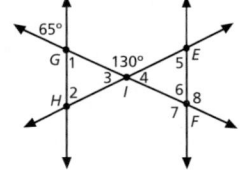

26. $m\angle 1$   65°
27. $m\angle 2$   65°
28. $m\angle 3$   50°
29. $m\angle 4$   50°
30. $m\angle 5$   65°
31. $m\angle 6$   65°
32. $m\angle 7$   115°
33. $m\angle 8$   115°

**Draw a figure to illustrate each triangle.** (Lesson 5-4)
For 34–37, see additional answers.
34. Draw an acute triangle.
35. Draw an obtuse triangle.
36. Draw an isosceles right triangle.
37. Draw an equilateral triangle.

---

## Teaching Tip

In preparation for Exercises 1–10, remind students to look for:
  an F pattern to identify corresponding angles formed by two lines and a transversal, and a Z pattern to identify alternate interior angles formed by two lines and a transversal.
Other hints are:
  Use a light shading (colored if possible) to separate interior from exterior.
  Remember that corresponding angles are the only angle pairs consisting of one interior angle and one exterior angle.
  All others are either both interior angles (alternate interior angles or same-side interior) or both exterior angles (alternate sexterior angles).

## PRACTICE ◾ LESSON 5-1–LESSON 5-4

**Use the figure to determine whether each statement is *true* or *false*.**
(Lessons 5-1 and 5-3)

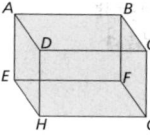

**38.** $\overleftrightarrow{AD} \parallel \overrightarrow{FG}$   true

**39.** $\overleftrightarrow{AD}$ and $\overleftrightarrow{CG}$ are skew lines.   true

**40.** Plane *ABCD* and plane *BCGF* are parallel.   false

**Find the measure of the complement and supplement of each angle.** (Lesson 5-2)

**41.** $m\angle 1 = 41°$   49°, 139°   **42.** $m\angle 2 = 60°$   30°, 120°   **43.** $m\angle 3 = 14°$   76°, 166°

**44.** $m\angle 4 = 10°$   80°, 170°   **45.** $m\angle 5 = 82°$   8°, 98°   **46.** $m\angle 6 = 33°$   57°, 147°

**Find the unknown angle measures in each figure.** (Lesson 5-4)

**47.**

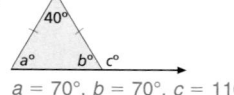

$a = 70°, b = 70°, c = 110°$

**48.**

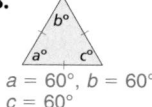

$a = 60°, b = 60°,$
$c = 60°$

**49.**

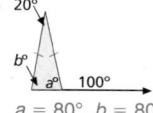

$a = 80°, b = 80°$

**50.**

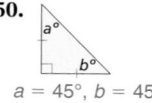

$a = 45°, b = 45°$

# Mid-Chapter Quiz

**For exercises 1–6, use the figure shown.** (Lesson 5-1)

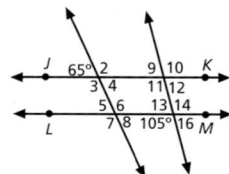

1. Name two points that determine line $\ell$.   D, H

2. Name three points that determine plane $\mathcal{P}$.
   any 3 of B, C, D, E, H except {C, D, E}
3. Name two collinear points on line $m$.   F, G

4. Name three coplanar points in plane $\mathcal{Q}$.
   any 3 of A, C, D, E, F
5. Name the intersection of planes $\mathcal{P}$ and $\mathcal{Q}$.   $\overleftrightarrow{CE}$

6. How many lines do points *A* and *B* determine?   1

**Use the figure shown to find the measure of the angles and make an observation about their relation to each other.** (Lesson 5-2)

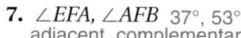

**7.** $\angle EFA, \angle AFB$   37°, 53°
adjacent, complementary
**8.** $\angle EFB, \angle BFC$   90°, 90°
right, adjacent, supplementary

**In the figure, $\overleftrightarrow{JK} \parallel \overleftrightarrow{LM}$. Classify each pair of angles and find their measures.** (Lessons 5-2 and 5-3)

**9.** $\angle 10$ and $\angle 14$   105°, 105°
corresponding
**10.** $\angle 6$ and $\angle 7$   115°, 115°
vertical
**11.** $\angle 12$ and $\angle 13$   75°, 75°
alternate interior
**12.** $\angle 9$ and $\angle 16$   75°, 75°
alternate exterior

**State whether it is possible to have a triangle with sides of the given lengths.** (Lesson 5-3)

**13.** 10, 9, 8   yes   **14.** 21, 4, 6   no   **15.** 7, 7, 7   yes   **16.** 100, 51, 49   no

Chapter 5 **Review and Practice Your Skills** | **211**

---

34.

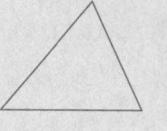

35.

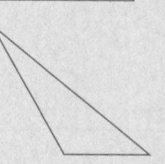

36.

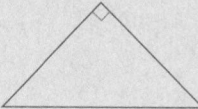

37.

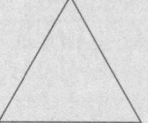

---

## Teaching Tip

In preparation for Exercises 20–25, remind students that they must test three different inequalities to be sure that a triangle exists. However, as soon as one inequality fails, students may conclude that the given measures do not give a triangle.

### Vocabulary

congruent triangles
corresponding sides
corresponding angles of
congruent triangles
included side

### Tools/Materials Needed

compass          straightedge
straws (5 in., 7 in., 9 in.) plus
"connectors" (clay, pipe cleaners,
etc.)

### Lesson Resources

Warm-up Transparency 21
Transparency RF-26
Reteaching 5-5
Extra Practice 5-5
Enrichment 5-5

## Getting Started

### 5-MINUTE WARM-UP

**Classify each triangle.**
1. no congruent sides   scalene
   triangle
2. two 45° angles   isosceles
   right triangle
3. three 60° angles
   equiangular/equilateral

### Introduction to Lesson 5-5

After completing the construction,
supply each student with three
straws (5 in., 7 in., 9 in.). Have students use clay (or other material)
to connect the straws in any order
to form a triangle. Display triangles
that were assembled in different
orders and lead a discussion on why,
regardless of the order of assembly,
the triangles can all be made to fit
each other exactly.

---

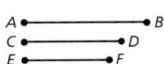

# 5-5 Congruent Triangles

**Goals**  ■  Use postulates to identify congruent triangles.

**Applications**   Engineering, Art, Recreation

**Use the three line segments to construct a triangle.**
For 1–5, check students' work.

1. With a straightedge, draw line $m$.

2. Choose point $X$ on line $m$. Set a compass for the length of $\overline{AB}$. With $X$ as the center, draw an arc that intersects line $m$. Label that point $Z$.

3. Set the compass for the length of $\overline{CD}$. With $X$ as the center, draw an arc above line $m$.

4. Set the compass for the length of $\overline{EF}$. With $Z$ as the center, draw an arc that intersects the arc drawn in Step 3. Label that intersection point $Y$.

5. Connect points $X$ and $Y$ and points $Z$ and $Y$.

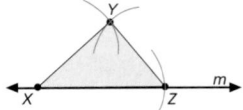

### ◣ BUILD UNDERSTANDING

If you trace $\triangle KLM$ and slide it over $\triangle PQR$, the vertices of one triangle match, or correspond to, the vertices of the other triangle. The angles and sides of one triangle match, or correspond to, the angles and sides of the other.

| Corresponding sides | Corresponding angles |
|---|---|
| $\overline{LK}$ and $\overline{QP}$ | $\angle K$ and $\angle P$ |
| $\overline{LM}$ and $\overline{QR}$ | $\angle L$ and $\angle Q$ |
| $\overline{KM}$ and $\overline{PR}$ | $\angle M$ and $\angle R$ |

Corresponding parts have equal measures and, therefore, are congruent.

Two triangles are **congruent** if their vertices can be matched so that corresponding parts of the triangles are congruent.

#### Example 1

**Name the congruent sides and angles of $\triangle KLM$ and $\triangle PQR$ shown above.**

**Solution**

$$\overline{LK} \cong \overline{QP} \qquad \angle K \cong \angle P$$
$$\overline{LM} \cong \overline{QR} \qquad \angle L \cong \angle Q$$
$$\overline{KM} \cong \overline{PR} \qquad \angle M \cong \angle R$$

Triangles $KLM$ and $PQR$ are congruent, written $\triangle KLM \cong \triangle PQR$.

> **Problem Solving Tip**
>
> To name two congruent triangles, match the vertices of one triangle to the corresponding vertices of the other triangle.

**212** | Chapter 5 **Logic and Geometry**

---

### Differentiated Instruction

**VISUAL LEARNERS** To assist students in identifying corresponding sides and angles of congruent triangles, you may introduce *prime notation* so that vertex $A'$ corresponds to vertex $A$, $B'$ to $B$, and $C'$ to $C$.

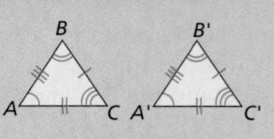

$$\triangle ABC \cong \triangle A'B'C'$$

Also, have students use tick marks and arcs as shown, marking their diagrams to indicate congruent corresponding sides and congruent corresponding angles. Note how this scheme reminds students that corresponding angles are found opposite corresponding sides.

To show that two triangles are congruent, you need only show that certain combinations of at least three of the corresponding parts are congruent.

| **Side-Side-Side Postulate (SSS)** | If three sides of one triangle are congruent to three corresponding sides of another triangle, then the triangles are congruent. |
| --- | --- |

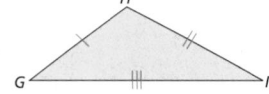

$\triangle GHI \cong \triangle JKL$ by the Side-Side-Side Postulate.

| **Side-Angle-Side Postulate (SAS)** | If two sides and the included angle of one triangle are congruent to two corresponding sides and the included angle of another triangle, then the triangles are congruent. |
| --- | --- |

The **included angle** for the two sides of a triangle is the angle formed by the two sides.

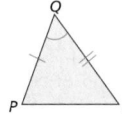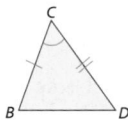

$\triangle PQR \cong \triangle BCD$ by the Side-Angle-Side Postulate.

| **Angle-Side-Angle Postulate (ASA)** | If two angles and the included side of one triangle are congruent to two corresponding angles and the included side of another triangle, then the triangles are congruent. |
| --- | --- |

The **included side** for two angles of a triangle is the side whose endpoints are the vertices of the angles.

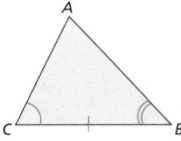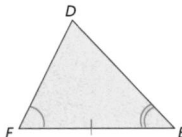

$\triangle ABC \cong \triangle DEF$ by the Angle-Side-Angle Postulate.

## Example 2

State whether each pair of triangles is congruent. If a pair is congruent, name the congruence and the appropriate postulate.

**a.** 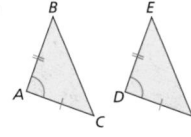  **b.** 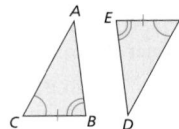  **c.**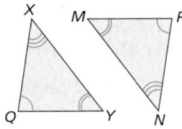

### Solution

**a.** $\triangle ABC \cong \triangle DEF$ by the Side-Angle-Side Postulate (SAS)

**b.** $\triangle CAB \cong \triangle FDE$ by the Angle-Side-Angle Postulate (ASA)

**c.** not necessarily congruent

The order of the vertices in naming a triangle congruence is not important as long as the corresponding vertices match. For example, stating that $\triangle ABC \cong \triangle DEF$ is the same as stating $\triangle BCA \cong \triangle EFD$.

 **Math Online** mathmatters2.com/extra_examples

Lesson 5-5 **Congruent Triangles** | **213**

Lesson 5-5 **Congruent Triangles** **213**

---

## Chalkboard Examples

**Supplementary Example 1**
For the congruent triangles shown, name the congruent sides and congruent angles.

$\overline{AB} \cong \overline{RS}$
$\overline{BC} \cong \overline{ST}$
$\overline{CA} \cong \overline{TR}$
$\angle C \cong \angle T$
$\angle A \cong \angle R$
$\angle B \cong \angle S$

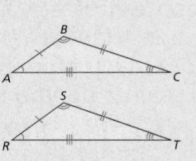

**Supplementary Example 2**
According to the markings shown, tell which of the two pairs of triangles is congruent. Name the congruence and the appropriate postulate.

**a.**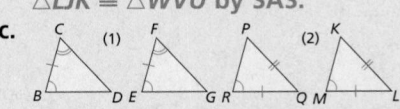

Pair (2) is the congruent pair.
$\triangle MNO \cong \triangle PQR$ by SSS.

**b.**

Pair (1) is the congruent pair.
$\triangle LJK \cong \triangle WVU$ by SAS.

**c.**

Pair (1) is the congruent pair.
$\triangle DBC \cong \triangle GEF$ by ASA.

---

## Teaching Tip

Students can investigate the congruences stated in the postulates (SSS, SAS, ASA) by using small cutouts of angles and lengths of straws. For example, students can be given an angle cutout measuring 37° and two lengths of straws measuring 8 in. and 10 in. Students should lay the angle between the straws and draw the resulting triangle. Comparing results, students will see that all the triangles drawn are congruent.

Remind students of the word *determine*, as in "two points determine a line" and "three points determine a plane." Discuss the word *determine* with respect to the congruence postulates. For example, "SSS determines a triangle" in the sense that all triangles constructed with the same three given lengths will be congruent.

## Lesson Wrap-up

### QUICK ASSESSMENT

Ask the following questions to determine if students understand the content presented in this lesson.
1. If two triangles are congruent, how many pairs of congruent elements do you know there are? **6 pairs: 3 pairs of congruent corresponding sides and 3 pairs of congruent corresponding angles**
2. If you know which are the corresponding sides of two congruent triangles, how do you locate the corresponding angles? **Corresponding angles lie opposite corresponding sides.**
3. What does the representation of the postulate SAS require about the location of the angle? **The angle is included between the two sides.**

### ASSIGNMENT GUIDE

**Basic:** 1–33, 40–51
**Enriched:** 1–51

### Reteaching Worksheet 5-5

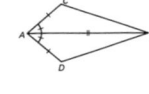
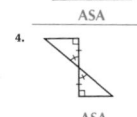 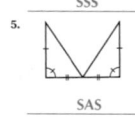 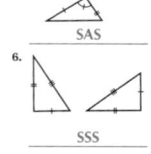
---

### TRY THESE EXERCISES

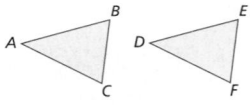

1. In the figure, $\triangle ABC \cong \triangle DEF$. Name the corresponding, congruent parts. $\overline{AB} \cong \overline{DE}$, $\overline{AC} \cong \overline{DF}$, $\overline{BC} \cong \overline{EF}$, $\angle A \cong \angle D$, $\angle B \cong \angle E$, $\angle C \cong \angle F$

**State whether each pair of triangles is congruent. If a pair is congruent, name the congruence and the appropriate postulate.**

2.
$\triangle DEF \cong \triangle GHJ$ by SAS

3.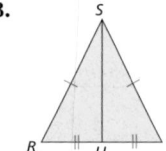
$\triangle USR \cong \triangle UST$ by SSS

4.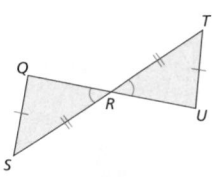
not necessarily congruent

**For Exercises 5–8, use $\triangle ABC$.**

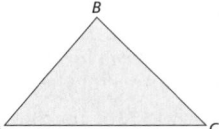

5. Which angle is included between $\overline{AB}$ and $\overline{BC}$?   $\angle B$
6. Which angle is included between $\overline{AC}$ and $\overline{AB}$?   $\angle A$
7. Which side is included between $\angle A$ and $\angle B$?   $\overline{AB}$
8. Which side is included between $\angle B$ and $\angle C$?   $\overline{BC}$

### PRACTICE EXERCISES • For Extra Practice, see page 601.

9. If $\triangle RST \cong \triangle XYZ$, name all the corresponding congruent parts. $\overline{RS} \cong \overline{XY}$, $\overline{ST} \cong \overline{YZ}$, $\overline{RT} \cong \overline{XZ}$, $\angle R \cong \angle X$, $\angle S \cong \angle Y$, $\angle T \cong \angle Z$

**State whether the pair of triangles is congruent by SAS, ASA or SSS.**

10.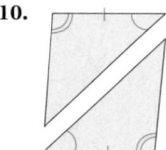
ASA

11.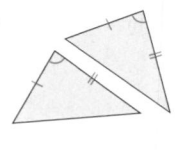
SAS

12.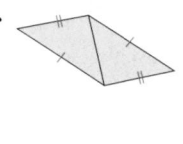
SSS

13.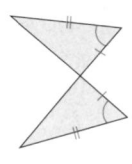
SAS or ASA

14. **ENGINEERING** The bridge shown uses a triangular truss design. In the figure, $\triangle RSU \cong \triangle TSU$. Name the corresponding congruent parts. $\overline{RS} \cong \overline{TS}$, $\overline{SU} \cong \overline{SU}$, $\overline{RU} \cong \overline{TU}$, $\angle R \cong \angle T$, $\angle RSU \cong \angle TSU$, $\angle SUR \cong \angle SUT$

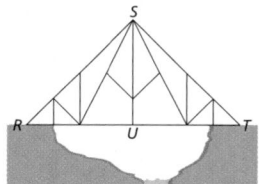

**Use the figure of the bridge to answer the following.**

15. Which angle is included between $\overline{SR}$ and $\overline{RU}$?   $\angle R$
16. Which angle is included between $\overline{SU}$ and $\overline{UT}$?   $\angle SUT$
17. Which side is included between $\angle SRU$ and $\angle RUS$?   $\overline{RU}$
18. Which side is included between $\angle UST$ and $\angle STU$?   $\overline{ST}$

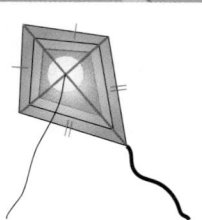

19. **RECREATION** Are the two halves of the kite congruent triangles? If so, which postulate guarantees their congruence?   yes; by SSS

### Extend the Lesson

**CONNECTING TO PRIOR KNOWLEDGE** Have students explain why the triangles in the following diagrams must be congruent.

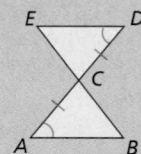

$\angle ECD \cong \angle BCA$   vertical angles
$\triangle ECD \cong \triangle BCA$   ASA

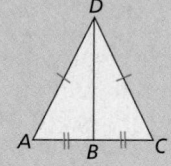

$\angle DAC \cong \angle DCA$   base angles of isosceles $\triangle ACD$
$\triangle ADB \cong \triangle CDB$   SAS

**20. WRITING MATH** To apply the Angle-Side-Angle Postulate, what information do you need to know?   See additional answers.

**21. ART** In the design pattern, quadrilateral *ABCD* is a square and points *W, X, Y* and *Z* are the midpoints of the sides. Can you use this information to conclude that △*WAX* ≅ △*YCZ*? If so, which postulate allows you to draw this conclusion?   yes; by SAS, SSS and ASA

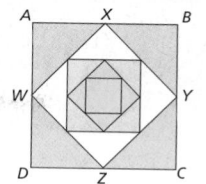

**Find the value of *x* for each pair of congruent triangles.**

**22.** 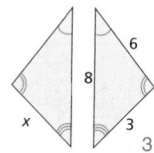  **23.** 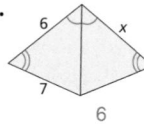  **24.**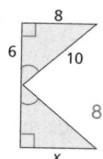

**25. YOU MAKE THE CALL** Gabe claims that the two triangles in the figure are not congruent because the side marked is not included between the two congruent angles. Latravis says that since the sum of the angles of a triangle is 180°, the triangles are congruent by ASA. Who is correct and why?
See additional answers.

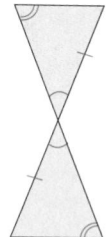

## ■ EXTENDED PRACTICE EXERCISES

**26. WRITING MATH** Compare and contrast the Side-Side-Side, Side-Angle-Side and Angle-Side-Angle Triangle Congruence Postulates.
See additional answers.

**27. CRITICAL THINKING** If three angles of a triangle are congruent to three corresponding angles of another triangle, are the two triangles necessarily congruent? Explain.   No. The sides of the two triangles are not necessarily congruent.

**28. GEOMETRY SOFTWARE** Use geometry software to determine if SSA is a valid method of proving triangle congruence. Fix the lengths of two sides, and then fix the size of one of the two angles that is not included between your two fixed sides. Does this result in only one triangle, or could you have more than one triangle? Is SSA a valid Triangle Congruence Postulate?
could have more than one; no

Boston, Massachusetts

**29. DATA FILE** Refer to the data on the ten windiest U.S. cities on page 577. Use an atlas to find which of the cities creates an isosceles triangle with Dodge City, KS, and Goodland, KS. (Hint: The base is 143 mi, and the sides are about 580 mi.)   Rochester, MN

## ■ MIXED REVIEW EXERCISES

**Find the next three terms for each sequence.** (Lesson 2-9)

**30.** $-32, -16, -8, -4, -2, \ldots$ **31.** $5, -25, 125, -625, 3125, \ldots$   $-15,625, 78,125, -390,625$ **32.** $\frac{3}{4}, \frac{1}{2}, \frac{1}{3}, \frac{2}{9}, \ldots$   $\frac{4}{27}, \frac{8}{81}, \frac{16}{243}$

**33.** $1, 1, 2, 3, 5, -1, \ldots$, $-\frac{1}{2}, \frac{1}{4}$   8, 13, 21 **34.** $-2, -2, -4, -6, -10, \ldots$   $-16, -26, -42$ **35.** $4, 8, 13, 19, 26, \ldots$   34, 43, 53

**Find the 100th term for each sequence.** (Lesson 2-9)

**36.** $0, 3, 6, 9, 12, \ldots$ 297 **37.** $-\frac{1}{2}, \frac{1}{2}, -\frac{1}{4}, \frac{1}{4}, -\frac{1}{6}, \frac{1}{6}, \ldots$   $\frac{1}{100}$ **38.** $x^2, 2x^3, 3x^4, 4x^5, 5x^6, \ldots$   $100x^{101}$

---

## ADDITIONAL ANSWERS

**20.** You need to know that two angles and the included side of one triangle are congruent to two corresponding angles and the included side of another triangle.

**25.** Latravis is correct. Since two angles of one triangle are congruent to two angles of another triangle, their third angles must also be congruent. This is because the sum of the angles in every triangle is 180°. The triangles then are congruent by ASA.

**26.** Side-Side-Side requires that all three pairs of corresponding sides are known to be congruent. Side-Angle-Side requires that two pairs of corresponding sides and their included angles are known to be congruent. Angle-Side-Angle requires that two pairs of corresponding angles and their included sides are known to be congruent.

---

**Lesson 5-5 Congruent Triangles 215**

### Extra Practice Worksheet 5-5

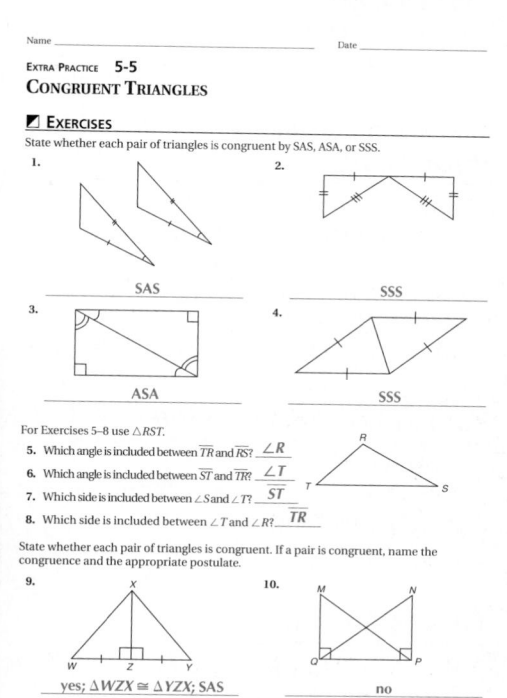

Name _____ Date _____

EXTRA PRACTICE **5-5**
**CONGRUENT TRIANGLES**

☑ **EXERCISES**

State whether each pair of triangles is congruent by SAS, ASA, or SSS.

1.                                 2.

SAS                               SSS

3.                                 4.

ASA                               SSS

For Exercises 5–8 use △*RST*.

**5.** Which angle is included between $\overline{TR}$ and $\overline{RS}$?   ∠R
**6.** Which angle is included between $\overline{ST}$ and $\overline{TR}$?   ∠T
**7.** Which side is included between ∠*S* and ∠*T*?   $\overline{ST}$
**8.** Which side is included between ∠*T* and ∠*R*?   $\overline{TR}$

State whether each pair of triangles is congruent. If a pair is congruent, name the congruence and the appropriate postulate.

9.                                 10.

yes; △*WZX* ≅ △*YZX*; SAS       no

### Enrichment Worksheet 5-5

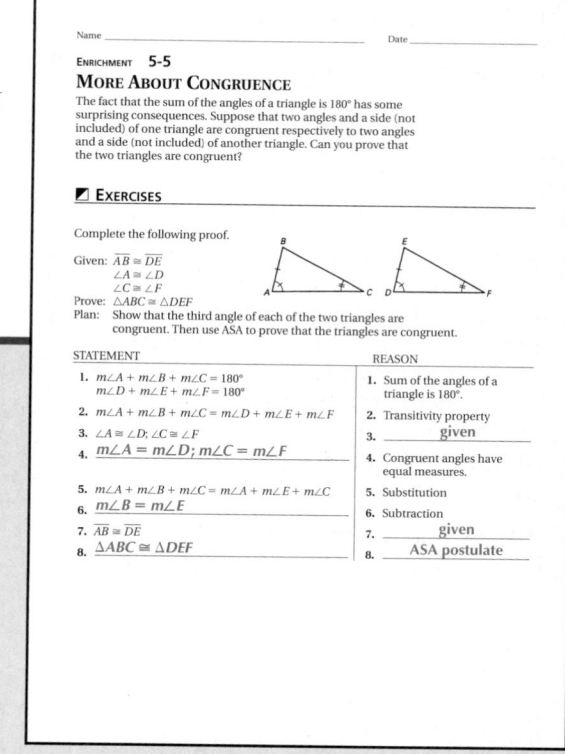

Name _____ Date _____

ENRICHMENT **5-5**
**MORE ABOUT CONGRUENCE**

The fact that the sum of the angles of a triangle is 180° has some surprising consequences. Suppose that two angles and a side (not included) of one triangle are congruent respectively to two angles and a side (not included) of another triangle. Can you prove that the two triangles are congruent?

☑ **EXERCISES**

Complete the following proof.

Given: $\overline{AB} \cong \overline{DE}$
∠*A* ≅ ∠*D*
∠*C* ≅ ∠*F*
Prove: △*ABC* ≅ △*DEF*
Plan:   Show that the third angle of each of the two triangles are congruent. Then use ASA to prove that the triangles are congruent.

| STATEMENT | REASON |
|---|---|
| 1. $m\angle A + m\angle B + m\angle C = 180°$  $m\angle D + m\angle E + m\angle F = 180°$ | 1. Sum of the angles of a triangle is 180°. |
| 2. $m\angle A + m\angle B + m\angle C = m\angle D + m\angle E + m\angle F$ | 2. Transitivity property |
| 3. ∠*A* ≅ ∠*D*; ∠*C* ≅ ∠*F* | 3. _____ given |
| 4. $m\angle A = m\angle D$; $m\angle C = m\angle F$ | 4. Congruent angles have equal measures. |
| 5. $m\angle A + m\angle B + m\angle C = m\angle A + m\angle E + m\angle C$ | 5. Substitution |
| 6. $m\angle B = m\angle E$ | 6. Subtraction |
| 7. $\overline{AB} \cong \overline{DE}$ | 7. _____ given |
| 8. △*ABC* ≅ △*DEF* | 8. _____ ASA postulate |

# Quadrilaterals and Parallelograms

**Goals**
- Classify different types of quadrilaterals.
- Identify and use properties of parallelograms.

**Applications** Construction, Civil engineering, Navigation

## Lesson Planning

**NCTM Standards/Strands**
- Geometry
- Measurement
- Reasoning & Proof
- Connections

### Vocabulary

| | |
|---|---|
| quadrilateral | trapezoid |
| parallelogram | rectangle |
| rhombus | square |
| opposite angles | |
| consecutive angles | |
| opposite sides | consecutive sides |

### Tools/Materials Needed

| | |
|---|---|
| protractor | ruler |
| compass | straightedge |
| straws plus "connectors" | |
| (pipe cleaners, clay) | |

### Lesson Resources

Warm-up Transparency 21
Transparency RF-27, 28
Reteaching 5-6
Extra Practice 5-6
Enrichment 5-6

## Getting Started

### 5-Minute Warm-up

**Solve each equation.**
1. $x + 70 = 180$   110
2. $360 - y = 210$   150
3. $125 = 180 - z$   55
4. $4m = 360$   90

### Introduction to Lesson 5-6

Have students construct a parallelogram from straws. Have students move the sides of the straw parallelogram until they form a rectangle. Ask students to reconsider Questions 1–4 for the rectangle to speculate about the relationship between a parallelogram and a rectangle.

For a compass construction of a parallelogram, see the Teaching Tip at the bottom of this page.

**Refer to parallelogram _ABCD_.**

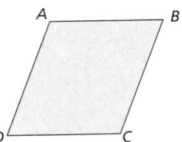

1. Use a protractor to measure each of the angles of _ABCD_.
   Observe students' work.
2. What do you notice about the relationship between ∠_A_ and ∠_C_ and the relationship between ∠_B_ and ∠_D_?
   They are congruent.
3. Use a ruler to measure the length of each side of _ABCD_.
   Observe students' work.
4. What do you notice about the relationship between the different sides? $\overline{AD} \cong \overline{BC}$, $\overline{AB} \cong \overline{DC}$

### ■ BUILD UNDERSTANDING

A **quadrilateral** is a closed plane figure that has four sides. A **parallelogram** is a quadrilateral with two pairs of parallel sides. The relationships between different kinds of quadrilaterals are shown in the diagram.

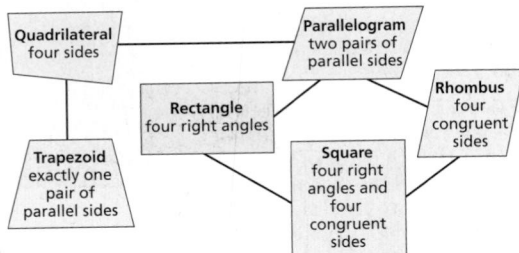

The parts of a quadrilateral have special names. In parallelogram _ABCD_, angles such as ∠_A_ and ∠_C_ are **opposite angles**. Angles such as ∠_A_ and ∠_B_ are **consecutive angles**. Sides such as $\overline{AB}$ and $\overline{CD}$ are **opposite sides**. Sides such as $\overline{AB}$ and $\overline{BC}$ are **consecutive sides**.

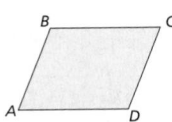

There are several important properties of parallelograms.

| | |
|---|---|
| **Properties of Parallelograms** | *Property 1* The opposite sides of a parallelogram are congruent. |
| | *Property 2* The opposite angles of a parallelogram are congruent. |
| | *Property 3* The consecutive angles of a parallelogram are supplementary. |
| | *Property 4* The sum of the angle measures of a parallelogram is 360°. |

## Extend the Lesson

Given two segments of different lengths, construct a parallelogram with these lengths as sides.

Segment a ●———● Segment b ●———●

1. Draw line _m_. Choose point _A_ on line _m_ and construct $\overline{AB}$ congruent to segment _a_.
2. Through _A_, draw line _n_ intersecting _m_ at _A_ at any convenient angle. Through _B_, construct line _p_ parallel to line _n_.
3. On _p_, construct $\overline{BC}$ congruent to segment _b_.
4. On _n_, construct $\overline{AD} \cong \overline{BC}$. Draw $\overline{DC}$.

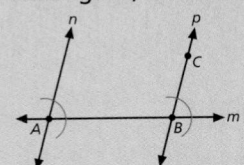

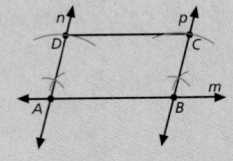

## Example 1

In parallelogram *DEFG*, $m\angle D = 60°$. Find $m\angle E$, $m\angle F$, and $m\angle G$.

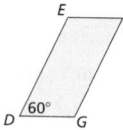

### Solution

$\angle E$ and $\angle D$ are consecutive angles, so they are supplementary.

$$m\angle E + m\angle D = 180°$$
$$m\angle E + 60° = 180°$$
$$m\angle E = 180° - 60° = 120°$$

$\angle F$ and $\angle D$ are opposite angles, so they are congruent.
$\angle F \cong \angle D$, so $m\angle F = 60°$

$\angle E$ and $\angle G$ are opposite angles, so they are also congruent.
$\angle E \cong \angle G$, so $m\angle G = 120°$

Another group of properties of parallelograms involves diagonals.

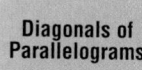

**Diagonals of Parallelograms**

*Property 5* The diagonals of a parallelogram bisect each other.

*Property 6* The diagonals of a rectangle are congruent.

*Property 7* The diagonals of a rhombus are perpendicular.

## Example 2

Figure *ABCD* is a square. Name all the pairs of congruent segments.

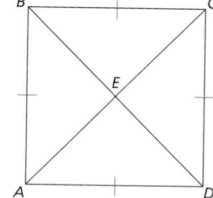

### Solution

Since *ABCD* is a square, by definition $\overline{AB} \cong \overline{BC} \cong \overline{CD} \cong \overline{DA}$.

Since a square is also a rectangle, by *Property 6*, $\overline{AC}$ and $\overline{BD}$ are congruent.

Since the figure is parallelogram, by *Property 5*, $\overline{AE} \cong \overline{CE}$ and $\overline{BE} \cong \overline{DE}$.

For $\overline{AB}$, the notation *AB* (no segment bar) means the measure of $\overline{AB}$. When you state that two segments are congruent, write $\overline{AB} \cong \overline{CD}$. Use an equal symbol to state that the measure of two segments are equal, $AB = CD$.

## Example 3

**CONSTRUCTION** A builder is adding a handrail to a staircase. The handrail is supported by vertical posts called *balusters* and must be constructed so that $\overline{PQ} \parallel \overline{SR}$. If the baluster at the bottom step is 3 ft high, what should be the height of the other balusters?

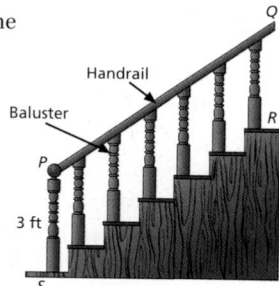

### Solution

Since all of the balusters must be vertical, $\overline{PS} \parallel \overline{QR}$. It is given that $\overline{PQ} \parallel \overline{SR}$, so *PQRS* is a parallelogram. *Property 1* says that opposite sides of a parallelogram are congruent. Since $PS = 3$ ft, $QR = 3$ ft. By similar reasoning, the height of each other baluster also must be 3 ft.

**Math Online** mathmatters2.com/extra_examples

Lesson 5-6 **Quadrilaterals and Parallelograms** | **217**

---

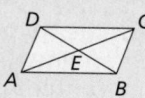
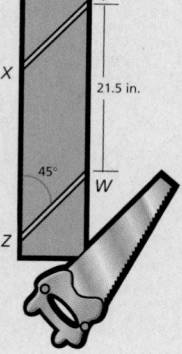
---

## QUICK ASSESSMENT

Ask the following questions to determine if students understand the content presented in this lesson.

**Use the quadrilateral tree on page 216 to answer *true* or *false*.**

1. All rectangles are parallelograms.
   true
2. All quadrilaterals are either trapezoids or parallelograms.
   false
3. All rhombuses are squares.   false
4. All trapezoids are quadrilaterals.
   true
5. All squares are both rhombuses and rectangles.   true

## ASSIGNMENT GUIDE

**Basic:** 1–45, 50–62
**Enriched:** 1–62

### Reteaching Worksheet 5-6

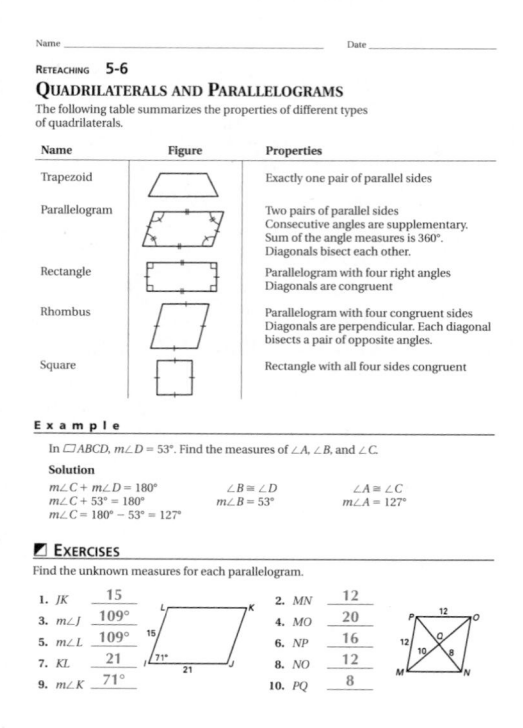

Name _____  Date _____

RETEACHING **5-6**
**QUADRILATERALS AND PARALLELOGRAMS**
The following table summarizes the properties of different types of quadrilaterals.

| Name | Figure | Properties |
|---|---|---|
| Trapezoid | | Exactly one pair of parallel sides |
| Parallelogram | | Two pairs of parallel sides. Consecutive angles are supplementary. Sum of the angle measures is 360°. Diagonals bisect each other. |
| Rectangle | | Parallelogram with four right angles. Diagonals are congruent |
| Rhombus | | Parallelogram with four congruent sides. Diagonals are perpendicular. Each diagonal bisects a pair of opposite angles. |
| Square | | Rectangle with all four sides congruent |

**Example**

In □ABCD, m∠D = 53°. Find the measures of ∠A, ∠B, and ∠C.

**Solution**

m∠C + m∠D = 180°      ∠B ≅ ∠D      ∠A ≅ ∠C
m∠C + 53° = 180°       m∠B = 53°    m∠A = 127°
m∠C = 180° − 53° = 127°

**EXERCISES**
Find the unknown measures for each parallelogram.

1. JK ___15___   2. MN ___12___
3. m∠J ___109°___  4. MO ___20___
5. m∠L ___109°___  6. NP ___16___
7. KL ___21___   8. NO ___12___
9. m∠K ___71°___  10. PQ ___8___

**218**   Chapter 5   **Logic and Geometry**

---

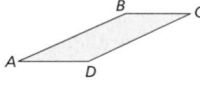

In □ABCD, m∠A = 42°. Find each measure.

1. m∠B  138°      2. m∠C  42°      3. m∠D  138°

4. Name all the pairs of congruent segments in □EFGH. Justify each answer. $\overline{EH} \cong \overline{HG} \cong \overline{GF} \cong \overline{EF}$ by Property 1, $\overline{HD} \cong \overline{DF}$ and $\overline{ED} \cong \overline{DG}$ by Property 5

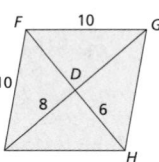

**Find the length of each segment.**

5. $\overline{EH}$  10      6. $\overline{HG}$  10      7. $\overline{DG}$  8
8. $\overline{EG}$  16      9. $\overline{FD}$  6      10. $\overline{FH}$  12

**Find the unknown angle measures in each parallelogram.**

11. m∠D  122°      12. m∠M  119°
13. m∠B  122°      14. m∠N  61°
15. m∠C  58°      16. m∠L  61°

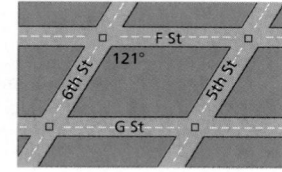

**Find each unknown measure in □ABCD.**

17. BC  18
18. CD  12
19. m∠B  106°
20. m∠C  74°
21. m∠D  106°

**Name all the types of quadrilaterals with the following properties.**

22. Opposite sides are congruent.
    parallelogram, rectangle, rhombus, square
23. Consecutive sides are perpendicular.
    rectangle, square
24. Diagonals bisect each other.
    parallelogram, rectangle, rhombus, square
25. Opposite angles are congruent.
    parallelogram, rectangle, rhombus, square
26. Diagonals are congruent.
    rectangle, square
27. Diagonals are perpendicular.
    rhombus, square
28. Consecutive angles are congruent.
    rectangle, square
29. All four angles are congruent.
    rectangle, square

30. **YOU MAKE THE CALL** A rectangle is defined as a quadrilateral with four right angles. Sying says this means that a rectangle is not a parallelogram, but Hal says a rectangle is a parallelogram. Who is correct and why?
    See additional answers.

31. **CIVIL ENGINEERING** In Center City, all lettered streets are parallel to each other, and all numbered streets are parallel to each other. The corner of F Street and 6th Street has an angle measure of 121°. What are the angle measures at the other three corners bounded?  59°, 59°, 121°

32. **WRITING MATH** Given that quadrilateral RSTU is a parallelogram, list as many facts about the angles, sides and diagonals of quadrilateral RSTU as you can.
    See additional answers.

**218**   Chapter 5   **Logic and Geometry**

## ADDITIONAL ANSWERS

30. Hal is correct. A rectangle is a parallelogram since it is a quadrilateral with two pairs of parallel sides.

32. Answers will vary. $\overline{RS} \cong \overline{UT}$, $\overline{RU} \cong \overline{ST}$, m∠R + m∠S + m∠T + m∠U = 360°, ∠R ≅ ∠T, ∠U ≅ ∠S, ∠R and ∠U are supplementary. ∠S and ∠T are supplementary, ∠R and ∠S are supplementary. ∠U and ∠T are supplementary. $\overline{RT}$ bisects $\overline{US}$ and $\overline{SU}$ bisects $\overline{RT}$.

49. The legs represent the diagonals of a quadrilateral where $\overline{AB}$ and $\overline{DC}$ are opposite sides. Since $\overline{AO} \cong \overline{OC}$ and $\overline{BO} \cong \overline{OD}$, these diagonals bisect each other. Thus, the quadrilateral ABCD is a parallelogram and $\overline{AB} \parallel \overline{DC}$.

**Refer to ▱ABCD to answer the following.**

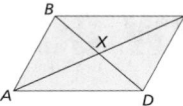

33. If $AB = 10$, then $DC =$ __?__.  10

34. If $AC = 15$, then $AX =$ __?__.  7.5

35. If $m\angle CBA = 111°$, then $m\angle ADC =$ __?__.  111°

36. If $m\angle BAD = 69°$, then $m\angle BCD =$ __?__.  69°

**Quadrilateral *PARK* is a parallelogram. Tell if each statement is justified.**

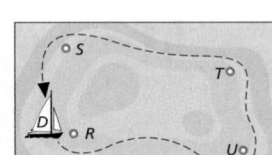

37. $\overline{PS} \cong \overline{KS}$  no

38. $\overline{PK} \cong \overline{RA}$  yes

39. $\overline{PA} \perp \overline{AR}$  no

40. $\overline{PK} \parallel \overline{AR}$  yes

41. $SR = \frac{1}{2}PR$  yes

42. $m\angle ARP = \frac{1}{2}m\angle ARK$  no

43. $\angle KPA \cong \angle RAP$  no

44. $\angle PAR \cong \angle RKP$  yes

45. **NAVIGATION** Four buoys have been placed at the vertices of a parallelogram to outline the course for a yacht race. If the boats start northwest of buoy *R*, what is the sum of angle measures of the four turns they will have to make? Do you think turn *T* or turn *U* will be more difficult? Explain. 360°; Turn *U* will be more difficult because it is a sharper turn.

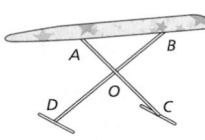

## ■ EXTENDED PRACTICE EXERCISES

**Use the properties you have learned to complete each statement.**

46. If a quadrilateral is a parallelogram, then __?__.  Answers will vary.

47. If __?__, then the quadrilateral is a parallelogram.  a quadrilateral has two pairs of parallel sides

48. Show why a parallelogram having four angles of equal measure must be a rectangle. (Hint: Let $x =$ the measure of any angle.)  $x + x + x + x = 360° \rightarrow 4x = 360° \rightarrow x = 90°$

49. **CRITICAL THINKING** The adjustable ironing board is built so that when open, $\overline{AO} \cong \overline{OC} \cong \overline{BO} \cong \overline{OD}$. Explain why the ironing surface is parallel to the floor.  See additional answers.

## ■ MIXED REVIEW EXERCISES

**Solve each equation. Check the solution.** (Lesson 3-4)

50. $3x + 12 = -9$  $-7$

51. $4d - 19 = 28$  $\frac{47}{4}$

52. $\frac{2}{5} - \frac{1}{10}s = 3\frac{1}{2}$  $-31$

53. $\frac{f}{5} - 9 = -4$  25

54. $-\frac{1}{2}g + 15 = 13$  4

55. $-4t + -12 = -20$  2

56. $2y - 17 = 212$  114.5

57. $\frac{3}{4}x = 7.5$  10

58. $-5 - 4a = 27$  $-8$

59. $\frac{2}{3}x - 9 = 7 + \frac{1}{3}x$  48

60. $7t + 110 = 319$  $\approx 29.86$

61. $-y + 0.55 = 3.75$  $-3.2$

62. **RETAIL** Maska has a scratch card for a clothing store. The sales clerk will scratch the card to reveal the discount Maska can take on his purchases. Maska wants to buy a coat that regularly costs $175. He can only afford to pay $125. What is the least discount Maska needs in order to buy the coat? Round to the nearest tenth of a percent. (Lesson 3-7)  28.6%

**Math Online** mathmatters2.com/self_check_quiz

## Extend the Lesson

Tell students that a parallelogram can be determined by the lengths of its diagonals and one side.
Given diagonal $AC = 3$ in., diagonal $BD = 2$ in., and side $AB = 2.5$ in.
To construct parallelogram *ABCD*, have students follow these instructions:
1. Start with diagonal $\overline{AC}$. Find its midpoint.
2. Using the midpoint of $\overline{AC}$ as center, draw a circle with $\overline{BD}$ as diameter. Find point *B* on the circle at distance $\overline{AB}$ from *A*.
3. Complete the figure by drawing *AB*, *BC*, *CD*, *DA*.

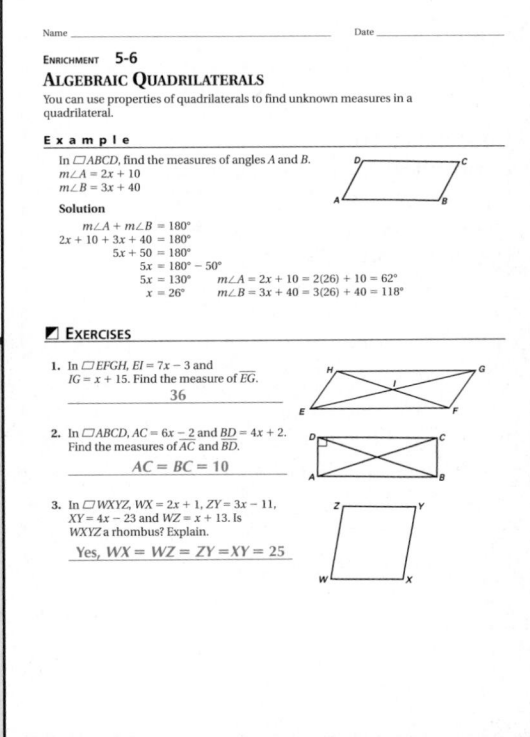

### Extra Practice Worksheet 5-6

Name _____   Date _____

EXTRA PRACTICE → **5-6**
**QUADRILATERALS AND PARALLELOGRAMS**

▮ **EXERCISES**

Find the unknown angle measures in the parallelogram.

1. $m\angle M$ ___120°___
2. $m\angle N$ ___60°___
3. $m\angle Q$ ___60°___

Find each unknown measure in parallelogram *XYZW*.

4. $m\angle Y$ ___114°___
5. $m\angle Z$ ___66°___
6. $m\angle W$ ___114°___
7. $WX$ ___6___

Find the length of each segment.

8. $\overline{HK}$ ___12___
9. $\overline{KJ}$ ___14___
10. $\overline{HL}$ ___7___
11. $\overline{IL}$ ___11___

Refer to parallelogram *DEFG* to answer the following.

12. If $DE = 12$, then $GF =$ ___12___
13. If $DH = 5$, then $DF =$ ___10___
14. If $m\angle DEF = 100°$, then $m\angle EFG =$ ___80°___
15. If $m\angle GDE = 75°$, then $m\angle FGD =$ ___105°___

### Enrichment Worksheet 5-6

Name _____   Date _____

ENRICHMENT **5-6**
**ALGEBRAIC QUADRILATERALS**
You can use properties of quadrilaterals to find unknown measures in a quadrilateral.

**E x a m p l e**
In ▱*ABCD*, find the measures of angles *A* and *B*.
$m\angle A = 2x + 10$
$m\angle B = 3x + 40$

**Solution**
$m\angle A + m\angle B = 180°$
$2x + 10 + 3x + 40 = 180°$
$5x + 50 = 180°$
$5x = 180° - 50°$
$5x = 130°$   $m\angle A = 2x + 10 = 2(26) + 10 = 62°$
$x = 26°$   $m\angle B = 3x + 40 = 3(26) + 40 = 118°$

▮ **EXERCISES**

1. In ▱*EFGH*, $EI = 7x - 3$ and $IG = x + 15$. Find the measure of $\overline{EG}$.
   ___36___

2. In ▱*ABCD*, $AC = 6x - 2$ and $BD = 4x + 2$. Find the measures of $\overline{AC}$ and $\overline{BD}$.
   $AC = BC = 10$

3. In ▱*WXYZ*, $WX = 2x + 1$, $ZY = 3x - 11$, $XY = 4x - 23$ and $WZ = x + 13$. Is *WXYZ* a rhombus? Explain.
   Yes, $WX = WZ = ZY = XY = 25$

## Vocabulary Review

**Lesson 5-5**
congruent triangles
corresponding sides
corresponding angles of
    congruent triangles
included side

**Lesson 5-6**
quadrilateral    trapezoid
parallelogram    rectangle
rhombus          square
opposite angles
consecutive angles
opposite sides
consecutive sides

## ASSIGNMENT GUIDE

All students: 1–35

## Chalkboard Examples

**Lesson 5-5**
According to the markings shown, which pair of triangles is not necessarily congruent? **B**

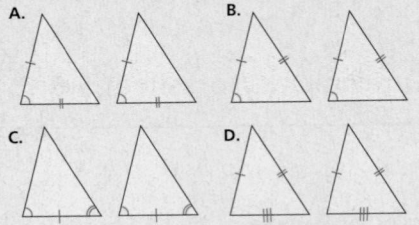

**Lesson 5-6**
In parallelogram $ABCD$, $m\angle A = 2x + 40$ and $m\angle C = 6x - 100$.
Find the measure of each angle of the parallelogram.
$A$ and $C$ are opposite angles, which are congruent.
$2x + 40 = 6x - 100$
$\phantom{2x+}140 = 4x$
$\phantom{2x+4}35 = x$
$m\angle A = 2x + 40 = 2(35) + 40 = 110°$
$m\angle C = 6x - 100 = 6(35) - 100 = 110°$
So, $m\angle B = m\angle D = 70°$

### PRACTICE ◼ LESSON 5-5

State whether each pair of triangles is congruent by SAS, SSS, or ASA.

1. 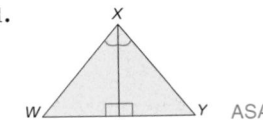   ASA

2. 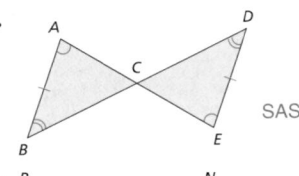   SAS

3. 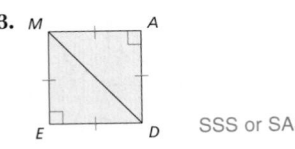   SSS or SAS

4. 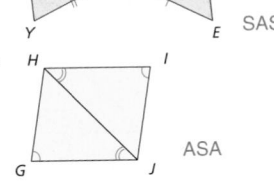   SAS

5. 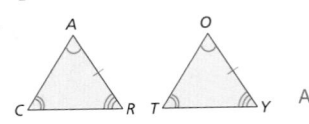   ASA

6. 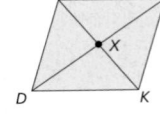   ASA

$\triangle MNO \cong \triangle STU$.  Fill in the blanks.

7. $\angle M \cong$ __?__  $\angle S$

8. $\angle O \cong$ __?__  $\angle U$

9. $\angle N \cong$ __?__  $\angle T$

10. $\overline{MN} \cong$ __?__  $\overline{ST}$

11. $\overline{NO} \cong$ __?__  $\overline{TU}$

12. $\overline{MO} \cong$ __?__  $\overline{SU}$

### PRACTICE ◼ LESSON 5-6

Refer to parallelogram DARK.

13. If $DA = 8$, then $RK =$ __?__ .  8

14. If $DR = 18$, then $DX =$ __?__ .  9

15. If $m\angle RAD = 81°$, then $m\angle DKR =$ __?__ .  81°

16. If $m\angle ADK = 60°$, then $m\angle DKR =$ __?__ .  120°

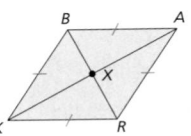

Fill in the blanks for each parallelogram.

17. If $m\angle KRA = 128°$, then $m\angle ABK =$ __?__ .  128°

18. If $BARK$ is a rhombus, then $m\angle KXB =$ __?__ .  90°

19. If $m\angle KBA = 128°$, then $m\angle BAR =$ __?__ .  52°

20. If $BR = 12$, then $BX =$ __?__ .  6

21. $\overline{FI} \cong$ __?__    $\overline{DN}$

22. $\overline{FY} \cong$ __?__    $\overline{YN}$

23. $\angle FDN \cong$ __?__    $\angle NIF$

24. __?__ and __?__ are supplementary to $\angle DFI$.
    $\angle FDN$ and $\angle FIN$

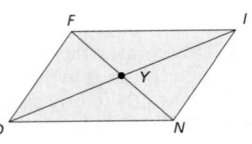

## Teaching Tip

As a review of properties of the family of parallelograms, have students copy and complete the following table about sides and angles. See the Teaching Tip on page 221 for a table to be presented as a second part to this table.

| Properties | Parallelogram | Rectangle | Rhombus | Square |
|---|---|---|---|---|
| Both pairs of opposite sides are parallel. | ✓ | ✓ | ✓ | ✓ |
| Both pairs of opposite sides are congruent. | ✓ | ✓ | ✓ | ✓ |
| All four sides are congruent. | | | ✓ | ✓ |
| Sum of measures of interior angles is 360°. | ✓ | ✓ | ✓ | ✓ |
| Both pairs of opposite angles are congruent. | ✓ | ✓ | ✓ | ✓ |
| Consecutive angles are supplementary. | ✓ | ✓ | ✓ | ✓ |
| All four angles are right angles. | | ✓ | | ✓ |

## PRACTICE ■ LESSON 5-1–LESSON 5-6

State whether each pair of triangles is congruent by SSS, SAS, or ASA. (Lesson 5-5)

25.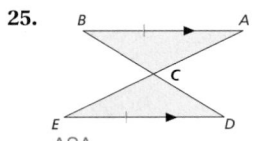
ASA

26.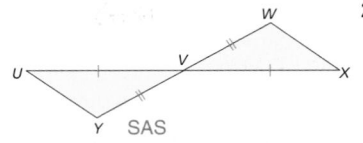
SAS

27.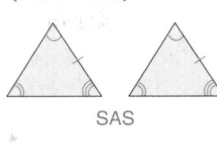
SAS

In the figure, $\overline{YN} \parallel \overline{ED}$ and $m\angle 4 = 82°$. Find each measure. (Lesson 5-3)

28. $m\angle 1$  98°
29. $m\angle 2$  82°
30. $m\angle 3$  98°
31. $m\angle 5$  82°
32. $m\angle 6$  98°
33. $m\angle 7$  82°
34. $m\angle 8$  98°

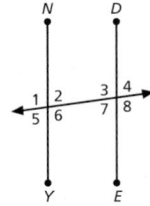

## Math*Works*
Workplace Knowhow
### Career – Ship Captain

**S**hip captains are in command of a water vessel, such as a deep-sea merchant ship, tugboat, ferry, yacht, cruise ship or other waterborne craft. The captain determines the course and speed, monitors the vessel's position, directs the crew and maintains logs of the ship's movements and cargo. When a ship sails from Cape Verde, Africa, to Cape Hatteras, North Carolina, to the southern coast of Newfoundland, to Lisbon, Spain, and back to Cape Verde, it sails approximately in the shape of a parallelogram.

**Refer to the diagram for Exercises 1–5.**

1. Through what angle must the ship's captain turn the ship when arriving at the south coast of Newfoundland from Cape Hatteras to head toward Lisbon?  110°

2. If the boat is headed toward Lisbon from Newfoundland and at Lisbon turns north to travel toward Iceland, through what angle must he turn the ship at Lisbon?  51°

3. What is the approximate distance between Cape Verde and Cape Hatteras?  3000 mi

4. What is the maximum distance in miles between Iceland and Lisbon?  5849 mi

5. There is a very tiny island located at the intersection of the diagonals of the parallelogram formed by Cape Verde, Cape Hatteras, Newfoundland, and Lisbon. What is the distance between Newfoundland and this island?  1650 mi

Math Online  mathmatters2.com/mathworks

When planning the course of a ship, the captain and navigator use *directed distances*, which involve angles as well as length.

Students should answer Questions 1–5 to better understand how directed distances are used with parallelograms.

An important instrument of navigation is the *compass*, two fundamental types of which are the *magnetic compass*, which in a crude form was used as early as the 10th century; and the *gyrocompass*, a device developed at the beginning of the 20th century.

Students can learn more about how to accurately use a magnetic compass by researching the corrections needed for *variation* (which takes into consideration the angle between the direction of magnetic north and the true North Pole at any location) and *deviation* (the angle that is formed between magnetic north and the direction the compass points).

Students can research other instruments of navigation that make use of angle measure. The *sextant* and the *octant* are optical instruments that measure the altitude of celestial bodies to assist a captain in determining a ship's position.

Students who are interested in learning more about this career choice can go to mathmatters2.com/mathworks. School Guidance Counselors are another resource for information about training requirements and appropriate schools.

## Teaching Tip

This table about diagonals can be presented as a second part to the table shown in the Teaching Tip at the bottom of page 220.

| Properties | Parallelogram | Rectangle | Rhombus | Square |
|---|---|---|---|---|
| Diagonals bisect each other. | ✓ | ✓ | ✓ | ✓ |
| Diagonals are congruent. | | ✓ | | ✓ |
| Diagonals are perpendicular. | | | ✓ | ✓ |

You might mention that an additional property of the rhombus and square is that the diagonals bisect the opposite angles of the figure.

## Lesson Planning

### NCTM Standards/Strands
- Geometry
- Measurement
- Reasoning & Proof
- Connections

### Vocabulary

polygon      side of a polygon
convex polygon    concave polygon
vertex of a polygon
regular polygon
diagonal of a polygon

### Tools/Materials Needed

compass      protractor
straightedge

### Lesson Resources

Warm-up Transparency 21
Transparency RF-29
Reteaching 5-7
Extra Practice 5-7
Enrichment 5-7
Technology Activity 5-7

## Getting Started

### 5-MINUTE WARM-UP

Classify each triangle and find the measure of the third angle.
1. 30°, 48° obtuse, 102°
2. 32°, 58° right, 90°
3. 40°, 40° isosceles obtuse, 100°

### Introduction to Lesson 5-7

Emphasize that only one compass setting is used for the entire construction. Ask what type of figure would be formed if the students connected every other point. **an equilateral triangle**

If lines are drawn from the center of the circle to each of the six vertices of the regular hexagon, what is the measure of each angle formed by consecutive radii? **60°** of the sum of all these angles? **360°** Find these same angle measures for the equilateral triangle. **each 120°, all 360°**

---

**Goals**
- Classify polygons according to their sides.
- Find the sum of the angle measures of polygons.

**Applications**   Safety, Hobbies, Nature

With a compass, protractor and straightedge, you can construct a **regular hexagon.** For 1–4, see additional answers.

1. Use the compass to construct a circle on a sheet of paper.

2. With the same setting from Step 1, set the point of the compass on the circle and strike an arc on the circle.

3. Place the point of the compass on your arc and strike a new arc. Repeat this around the circle until you reach your first arc.

4. Use the straightedge to connect the points where the arcs intersect the sides of the circle. The resulting figure is a regular hexagon.

### ◼ BUILD UNDERSTANDING

A **polygon** is a simple, closed plane figure formed by joining three or more line segments at their endpoints. Each segment, or **side**, of the polygon intersects exactly two other segments, one at each endpoint. The point at which the endpoints meet is called a **vertex** of the polygon. Polygons are named by their number of sides.

A polygon is **convex** if each line containing a side has no points in the interior of the polygon. A polygon in which a line that contains a side of the polygon also contains a point in its interior, is called **concave**.

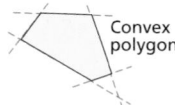 Convex polygon       Concave polygon

A polygon that has all sides congruent and all angles congruent is called a **regular polygon**.

| Name of polygon | Number of sides |
|---|---|
| Triangle | 3 |
| Quadrilateral | 4 |
| Pentagon | 5 |
| Hexagon | 6 |
| Heptagon | 7 |
| Octagon | 8 |
| Nonagon | 9 |
| Decagon | 10 |
| $n$-gon | $n$ |

### Check Understanding

How are the number of sides and the number of vertices of a polygon related? See additional answers.

### Example 1

Classify each polygon by its number of sides. State whether it is convex or concave, regular or not regular.

a.     b.     c.     d.

**222**   Chapter 5 **Logic and Geometry**

---

### ADDITIONAL ANSWERS

1–4.

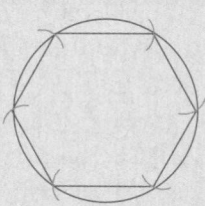

### Check Understanding

A polygon has the same number of vertices as sides (a $n$-sided polygon has $n$ vertices).

## Solution

**a.** The figure has four sides, so it is a quadrilateral. It is convex, but since not all sides and angles are congruent, it is not regular.

**b.** The figure has eight congruent sides and eight congruent angles. It is a convex, regular octagon.

**c.** The figure has five sides of unequal length. There are two lines containing sides with points in the interior, so it is a concave pentagon that is not regular.

**d.** The figure has six congruent sides and six congruent angles. It is a convex, regular hexagon.

A **diagonal** of a polygon is a segment that joins two vertices but is not a side. You can find the sum of the angles of any convex polygon by drawing the diagonals from any vertex. The diagonals separate the interior of the polygon into nonoverlapping triangular regions.

The sum of the measures of the interior angles of the polygon is the product of the number of triangles formed and 180°.

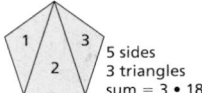
5 sides
3 triangles
sum = 3 • 180°

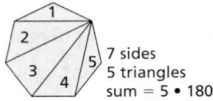
7 sides
5 triangles
sum = 5 • 180°

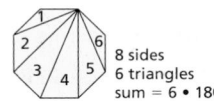
8 sides
6 triangles
sum = 6 • 180°

The number of triangles is two less than the number of sides of the polygon.

| **Angle Sum of a Polygon** | The sum of the interior angle measures of a convex polygon with $n$ sides is $(n-2)180°$. |
|---|---|

## Example 2

**Find the sum of the interior angles of each convex polygon.**

**a.** pentagon

**b.** heptagon

### Solution

**a.** A pentagon has 5 sides.
$(n-2)180°$      Substitute 5 for $n$.
$(5-2)180° = 3 \cdot 180°$
$= 540°$

**b.** A heptagon has 7 sides.
$(n-2)180°$      Substitute 7 for $n$.
$(7-2)180° = 5 \cdot 180°$
$= 900°$

You can find the measure of each interior angle of a regular polygon when you know the number of sides. A regular polygon of $n$ sides has $n$ angles of equal measure. Divide the sum of the angles by the number of angles.

| **Angle Measure of a Regular Polygon** | The measure of each interior angle of a regular polygon with $n$ sides is given by the formula $\frac{(n-2)180°}{n}$. |
|---|---|

**Math Online** mathmatters2.com/extra_examples

Lesson 5-7 **Diagonals and Angles of Polygons** | **223**

---

## Extend the Lesson

**CHALLENGE** Students know that a triangle has no diagonals and a quadrilateral has two diagonals. Have students draw a pentagon and a hexagon and determine the number of diagonals in each. Then ask students to make a table to find a formula for the total number of diagonals in an $n$-gon. $\frac{n(n-3)}{2}$

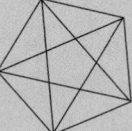
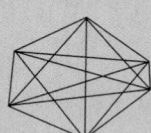

| Number of sides | Diagonals from one vertex | Total number of diagonals |
|---|---|---|
| 3 | 0 | 0 |
| 4 | 1 | 2 |
| 5 | 2 | 5 |
| 6 | 3 | 9 |

---

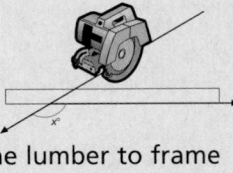

# Lesson Wrap-up

## QUICK ASSESSMENT

Ask the following questions to determine if students understand the content presented in this lesson.

1. Explain how to tell whether a polygon is convex or concave. **When connecting two points inside the polygon, the polygon is convex if the connecting segment is always inside the polygon. Otherwise, the polygon is concave.**

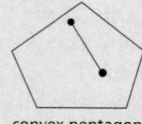 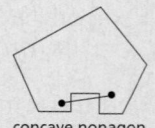

convex pentagon     concave nonagon

2. Explain how to find the measure of each interior angle of a regular pentagon. **Calculate (5 − 2)180°. Divide the result by 5.**

## ASSIGNMENT GUIDE

**Basic:** 1–33, 38–41
**Enriched:** 1–41

### Reteaching Worksheet 5-7

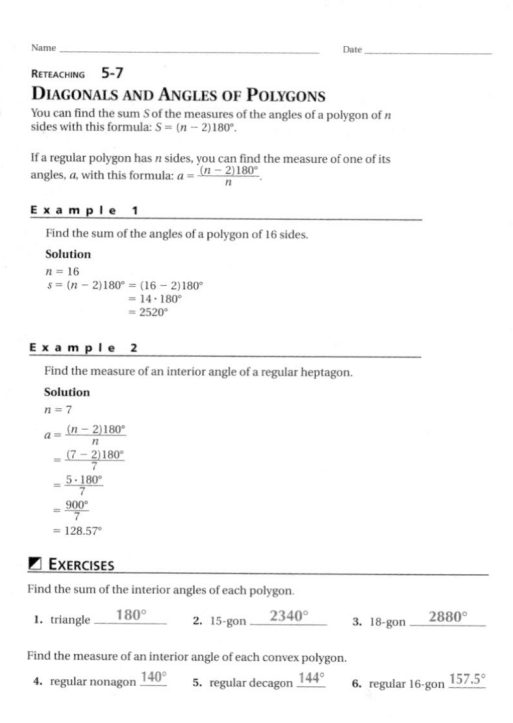

Name _____ Date _____

RETEACHING **5-7**

**DIAGONALS AND ANGLES OF POLYGONS**

You can find the sum $S$ of the measures of the angles of a polygon of $n$ sides with this formula: $S = (n − 2)180°$.

If a regular polygon has $n$ sides, you can find the measure of one of its angles, $a$, with this formula: $a = \frac{(n − 2)180°}{n}$.

**Example 1**

Find the sum of the angles of a polygon of 16 sides.

**Solution**
$n = 16$
$s = (n − 2)180° = (16 − 2)180°$
$\quad = 14 \cdot 180°$
$\quad = 2520°$

**Example 2**

Find the measure of an interior angle of a regular heptagon.

**Solution**
$n = 7$
$a = \frac{(n − 2)180°}{n}$
$\quad = \frac{(7 − 2)180°}{7}$
$\quad = \frac{5 \cdot 180°}{7}$
$\quad = \frac{900°}{7}$
$\quad = 128.57°$

**EXERCISES**

Find the sum of the interior angles of each polygon.

1. triangle __180°__     2. 15-gon __2340°__    3. 18-gon __2880°__

Find the measure of an interior angle of each convex polygon.

4. regular nonagon __140°__    5. regular decagon __144°__    6. regular 16-gon __157.5°__

---

## Example 3

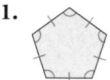

**NATURE** A beehive is a large array of regular hexagons. Find the measure of an interior angle of each regular hexagon.

### Solution

Use the formula for the interior angle measure of a regular hexagon.

$$\frac{(n − 2)180°}{n} = \frac{(6 − 2)180°}{6} = \frac{4 \cdot 180°}{6} = \frac{720°}{6} = 120°$$

### ▍ TRY THESE EXERCISES

Classify each polygon by its number of sides. Tell whether it is convex or concave, regular or not regular.

1.  convex regular pentagon
2.  convex not regular quadrilateral
3.  concave not regular hexagon

Find the sum of the interior angles of each convex polygon.

4. octagon   1080°    5. decagon   1440°    6. nonagon   1260°    7. 13-gon   1980°

Find the measure of an interior angle of each regular polygon.

8. pentagon   108°    9. decagon   144°    10. triangle   60°    11. 15-gon   156°

### ▍ PRACTICE EXERCISES • For Extra Practice, see page 602.

**Sketch each polygon.** For 12–14, see additional answers.

12. a regular triangle    13. a convex quadrilateral    14. a concave quadrilateral

**For each convex polygon, find the sum of the interior angles.**

15. quadrilateral 360°    16. triangle 180°    17. 20-gon 3240°    18. heptagon 900°

19. Find the measure of an interior angle of a regular 24-sided polygon.   165°

20. What is the measure of an interior angle of a regular 45-gon?   172°

21. **HOBBIES** Masaru is designing a quilt that will contain the pattern shown. Classify the polygon containing the cloth pattern.   convex, not regular, 12-gon

22. **ERROR ALERT** Angela calculates the sum of the interior angles of a regular 13-gon by multiplying 13 by 180° to arrive at 2340°. What mistake has Angela made, and what is the correct answer?   See additional answers.

**SAFETY** Name the shape of each sign. Is it a polygon?

23. 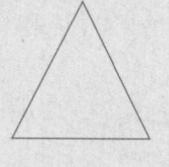 quadrilateral, yes
24. 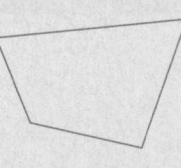 circle, no
25. HELP STOP DRINKING AND DRIVING   octagon, yes
26. CAUTION WET FLOOR    triangle, yes

---

## ADDITIONAL ANSWERS

12.

13.

14.

22. Angela forgot to subtract 2 from 13 before multiplying by 180°. The correct answer is (13 − 2)180° = 1980°.

31.

32.    33.

**Classify each statement as *true* or *false*. If the statement is false, explain why.**

27. The sum of the measures of the interior angles of an 11-gon is 1820°.   false; the sum is 1620°

28. The measure of an interior angle of a regular 18-gon is 160°.   true

29. An interior angle of a regular polygon cannot have a measure of 148°.   true

30. The sum of the interior angle measures of a polygon cannot be 1500°.   true

**Sketch the polygon described by each set of characteristics.**   For 31–33, see additional answers.

31. A quadrilateral with both pairs of opposite sides lying along parallel lines.

32. A concave hexagon with at least three sides the same length.

33. A convex pentagon with exactly two right angles.

## ■ EXTENDED PRACTICE EXERCISES

**CRITICAL THINKING** At each vertex of any convex polygon, there is a pair of supplementary angles. So a convex polygon of $n$ vertices has $n$ pairs of supplementary angles, one interior angle and one exterior angle at each vertex.

34. Write an expression for the sum of all the interior and exterior angles of a polygon with $n$ sides.   $n(180°)$

35. Show that the sum of the exterior angles of a convex polygon is 360° by solving the equation:

    (sum of interior angles) + (sum of exterior angles) = $n(180°)$.
    See additional answers.

36. **WRITING MATH** Sketch a concave heptagon and a convex heptagon. Describe in your own words the difference between a concave and a convex polygon.   See additional answers.

37. If the measure of an interior angle of a regular polygon is 168°, how many sides does the polygon have?   30

## ■ MIXED REVIEW EXERCISES

**Gina's Pizzeria offers the following toppings for pizzas: pepperoni, bacon, hamburger, sausage, peppers, onions, and tomatoes.** (Lessons 4-3 and 4-7)

38. How many unique pizzas can be created using three toppings? None of the toppings are duplicated.   35

39. How many unique two-topping pizzas can be created?   21

40. How many unique four-topping pizzas can be created?   35

41. Of all the three-topping pizzas possible, what is the probability of a customer ordering a pizza with pepperoni and tomatoes?   $\frac{1}{7}$

42. If Gina's only allows up to five toppings on each pizza, how many different five-topping pizzas can be created?   21

   Lesson 5-7 **Diagonals and Angles of Polygons**   **225**

35. (sum of interior angles) + (sum of exterior angles) = $n(180°)$
    the sum of interior angles = $(n - 2)180°$
    So, $(n - 2)180° + $ (sum of exterior angles) = $n(180°)$
    $(180°n - 360°) + $ (sum of exterior angles) = $180°n$
    sum of exterior angles = $360°$

36.

**Descriptions of differences will vary.**

---

### Extra Practice Worksheet 5-7

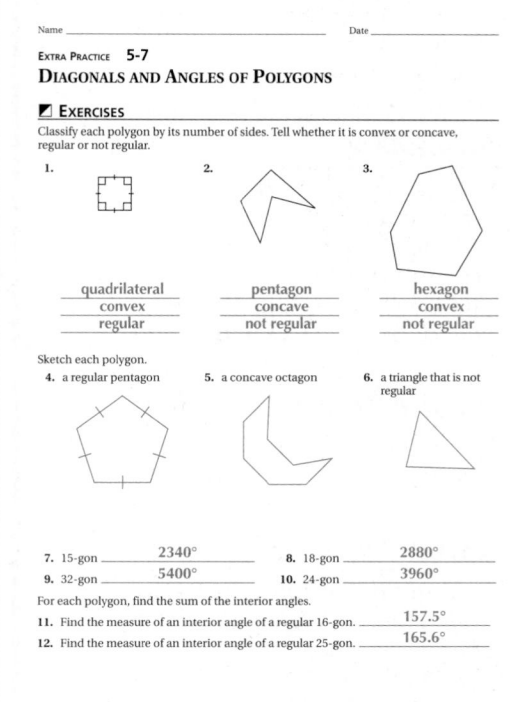

### Enrichment Worksheet 5-7

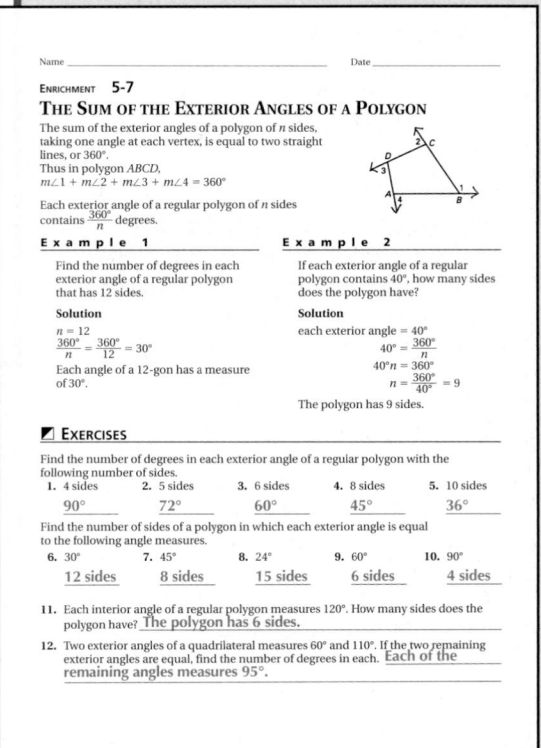

## Lesson Planning

### NCTM Standards/Strands
- Geometry
- Measurement
- Reasoning & Proof
- Connections

### Vocabulary

| | |
|---|---|
| circle | center |
| radius (radii) | chord |
| diameter | central angle |
| circumference | arc |
| semicircle | minor arc |
| major arc | inscribed angle |

### Tools/Materials Needed

| | |
|---|---|
| compass | ruler |
| calculator | string |

### Lesson Resources

Warm-up Transparency 22
Transparency RF-30
Reteaching 5-8
Extra Practice 5-8
Enrichment 5-8

## Getting Started

### 5-MINUTE WARM-UP

Solve each equation.
1. $360 - x = 275$    85
2. $2y = 98$    49
3. $m + 109 = 360$    251
4. $\frac{z}{2} = 76$    152

### Introduction to Lesson 5-8
Pass out string so that students can verify their conjectures for Question 2 by measuring the circumferences of the two circles.

## ADDITIONAL ANSWERS

4. circle with 2-in. radius: $A = 4\pi \approx 12.56$ in.$^2$
$C = 4\pi \approx 12.56$ in.
   circle with 4-in. radius: $A = 16\pi \approx 50.24$ in.$^2$
$C = 8\pi \approx 25.12$ in.

---

# 5-8 Properties of Circles

**Goals**
- Understand relationships among parts of a circle.
- Identify and use properties of circles.

**Applications** Market research, Food service, Art, Recreation, Navigation

**Use a compass, a ruler and a calculator.**

1. On a sheet of paper, draw a circle with a radius of 2 in. Then keeping the same center, draw a circle with a radius of 4 in.
Check students' work.
2. Study the two circles. How do you think the circumferences of the two circles compare?   The larger circle has a circumference two times greater than the smaller.
3. How do you think the areas of the two circles compare?
The larger circle has an area four times greater than the smaller.
4. Recall that the formulas for the area and circumference of a circle are $A \approx 3.14 \cdot r^2$ and $C \approx 3.14 \cdot d$. Use a calculator to find the areas and circumferences of the two circles.
See additional answers.
5. How do the circles compare in terms of area and circumference? Was your guess correct?   Answers will vary.

## ■ BUILD UNDERSTANDING

A **circle** is the set of all points in a plane that are a given distance from a fixed point in the plane. The fixed point is called the **center** of the circle. The given distance is the **radius** (plural: *radii*). A radius is a segment that has one endpoint at the center and one on the circle.

A **chord** is a segment with both endpoints on the circle.

A **diameter** is a chord that passes through the center of the circle. The length of a diameter is twice the length of a radius.

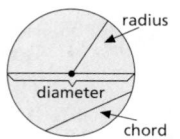

### Example 1

Use letters to name the parts of circle *P*.

**a.** three radii    **b.** a diameter    **c.** two chords

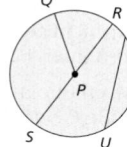

### Solution

**a.** $\overline{PQ}$ or $\overline{QP}$
$\overline{RP}$ or $\overline{PR}$
$\overline{SP}$ or $\overline{PS}$

**b.** $\overline{RS}$ or $\overline{SR}$

**c.** $\overline{TU}$ or $\overline{UT}$
$\overline{RS}$ or $\overline{SR}$

> ### Reading Math
>
> The symbol ⊙ is used to name a circle by its center.
> The expression "⊙*P*" is read "circle *P*."

226 | Chapter 5 **Logic and Geometry**

---

## Extend the Lesson

**CONNECTING TO PRIOR KNOWLEDGE** Note with students that as the number of sides of a regular polygon inscribed in a circle is increased from 3 to 6 to 12 to 24, the polygon resembles the circle more and more. Yet, no matter how large the number of sides of the polygon may become, the polygon never really becomes the circle. But, as the number of sides continues to increase, the polygon is approaching the circle as a *limit*.

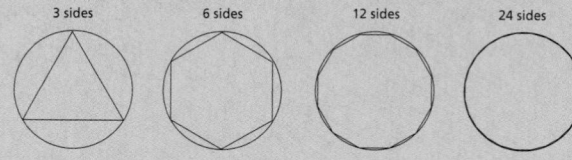

3 sides    6 sides    12 sides    24 sides

A **central angle** of a circle is an angle with its vertex at the center of a circle. In ⊙D, ∠ADB is a central angle.

An **arc** is a section of the circumference of a circle.

A **semicircle** is an arc of a circle with endpoints that are the endpoints of a diameter. Three letters are used to name a semicircle. Read $\overset{\frown}{ABC}$ as "arc ABC" or "semicircle ABC."

A **minor arc** is an arc that is smaller than a semicircle. A minor arc is named by its two endpoints. Read $\overset{\frown}{AB}$ as "arc AB."

A **major arc** is an arc that is larger than a semicircle. A major arc is named by three points, the first and last being its endpoints. Read $\overset{\frown}{ACB}$ as "arc ACB."

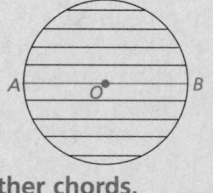

## Example 2

Identify the following parts of ⊙G.

**a.** a minor arc

**b.** a major arc

**c.** a semicircle

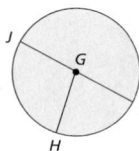

### Solution

**a.** $\overset{\frown}{JH}$ or $\overset{\frown}{HJ}$, $\overset{\frown}{HI}$ or $\overset{\frown}{IH}$

**b.** $\overset{\frown}{HJI}$ or $\overset{\frown}{IJH}$, $\overset{\frown}{HIJ}$ or $\overset{\frown}{JIH}$

**c.** $\overset{\frown}{IHJ}$ or $\overset{\frown}{JHI}$

Each minor arc is associated with a central angle that is said to intercept the minor arc. The measure of a minor arc is defined to be the same as the measure of its central angle. In ⊙N, $m\angle LNM = m\overset{\frown}{LM} = 75°$.

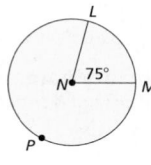

The measure of a major arc is found by subtracting the measure of its related minor arc from 360°. In ⊙N, $m\overset{\frown}{LPM} = 360° - m\overset{\frown}{LM} = 360° - 75° = 285°$.

The measure of a semicircle, or half of a circle, is 180°.

## Example 3

**MARKET RESEARCH** The results of a survey on favorite types of music are shown. Find the measure of the arc for the part of the circle representing each type of music.

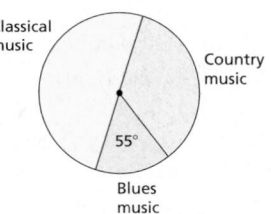

### Solution

The arc for classical music is a semicircle, so it measures 180°.

The arc for blues measures 55°.

The arc for country measures 180° − 55°, or 125°.

 **Math Online** mathmatters2.com/extra_examples

## Extend the Lesson

**HISTORICAL NOTE** The division of the circle into 360° comes from the Babylonians, who lived in what is now Iraq. Babylonian scholars observed that a year was about 365 days long, and that stars appeared to move about $\frac{1}{365}$ of the way around the sky each day. They decided to work with 360, an easier number than 365 because it has many factors. The factors of 360 that are less than 20 are : 2, 3, 4, 5, 6, 8, 9, 10, 12, 15, 18. So, by splitting the circle into 360 equal parts, one part of which has been defined as *one degree*, each part was approximately the same as the change in the position of a star from one night to the next.

## Chalkboard Examples

### Supplementary Example 1

Draw ⊙O with diameter $\overline{AOB}$. Then draw, on either side of $\overline{AOB}$, a **series** of chords that are parallel to $\overline{AOB}$.

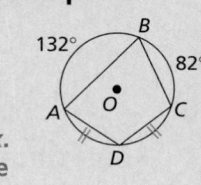

**a.** How does the length of the diameter compare to that of other chords? The diameter is longer than other chords.

**b.** Make a statement about the lengths of chords of a circle with respect to their location in the circle. The closer to the center, the longer the chord; the farther away from the center, the shorter the chord.

**c.** What do you think would be true about congruent chords with respect to their location in the circle? Congruent chords are the same distance from the center.

### Supplementary Example 2

In ⊙O, $\overset{\frown}{AD} \cong \overset{\frown}{CD}$. Find the measures of the angles of quadrilateral ABCD.

Let $m\overset{\frown}{AD} = m\overset{\frown}{CD} = x$.
There are 360° in the whole circle:
$x + x + 132 + 82 = 360 \rightarrow x = 73$
Each angle of the quadrilateral is an inscribed angle of the circle, measured by $\frac{1}{2}$ its intercepted arc.

$m\angle ADC = \frac{1}{2}(m\overset{\frown}{AB} + m\overset{\frown}{BC})$

$= \frac{1}{2}(132 + 82) = 107°$

$m\angle DCB = \frac{1}{2}(m\overset{\frown}{AD} + m\overset{\frown}{AB})$

$= \frac{1}{2}(73 + 132) = 102.5°$

$m\angle CBA = \frac{1}{2}(m\overset{\frown}{CD} + m\overset{\frown}{AD})$

$= \frac{1}{2}(73 + 73) = 73°$

$m\angle BAD = \frac{1}{2}(m\overset{\frown}{BC} + m\overset{\frown}{CD})$

$= \frac{1}{2}(82 + 73) = 77.5°$

Check: The sum of the measures of the quadrilateral should be 360°.
107° + 102.5° + 73° + 77.5° = 360° ✓

## Lesson Wrap-up

An **inscribed angle** is an angle whose vertex lies on the circle and whose sides contain chords of the circle. In the figure, $\angle ACB$ is an inscribed angle. The measure of an inscribed angle is one-half the measure of the arc it intercepts.

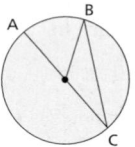

## Quick Assessment

Ask the following questions to determine if students understand the content presented in this lesson.

**In any circle:**
1. What is the longest chord that can be drawn?   **the diameter**
2. What do you call an angle formed by two noncollinear radii?   **a central angle**

**The radius of ⊙O is 3 in. and the radius of ⊙P is 6 in.**
3. How does the circumference of ⊙P compare to the circumference of ⊙O?   **The circumference of ⊙P is twice that of ⊙O.**

### Example 4

Identify the following for ⊙N.

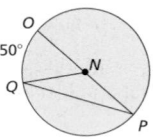

**a.** an inscribed angle       **b.** a central angle

**c.** $m\angle ONQ$              **d.** $m\angle OPQ$

**Solution**

**a.** $\angle OPQ$              **b.** $\angle ONQ$ or $\angle QNP$

**c.** $50°$                     **d.** $25°$

## Assignment Guide

**Basic:** 1–28, 33–37
**Enriched:** 1–37

### Try These Exercises

Identify the following for ⊙L.
For 3 and 4, see additional answers.

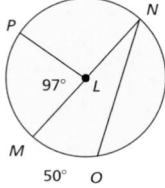

1. a radius
   *LP, LN, LM*
2. a chord
   *ON, MN*
3. a major arc
4. a minor arc
5. $m\widehat{MPN}$
   180°
6. $m\widehat{PN}$
   83°
7. $m\widehat{POM}$
   263°
8. $m\widehat{MON}$
   180°
9. an inscribed angle
   $\angle MNO$
10. $m\angle MNO$
    25°

## Reteaching Worksheet 5-8

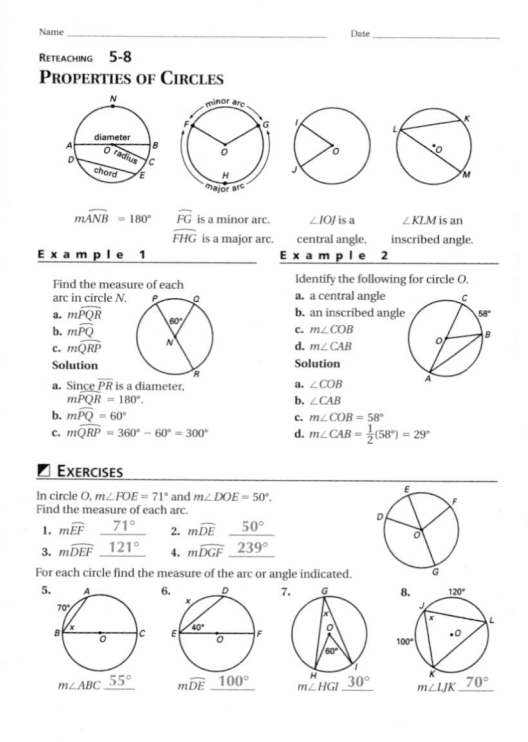

### Practice Exercises • For Extra Practice, see page 602.

In the figure, $m\angle KHJ = 60°$ and $m\angle JHI = 45°$.
Find each measure.

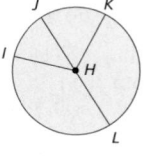

11. $m\widehat{JK}$  60°
12. $m\widehat{IJ}$  45°
13. $m\widehat{IK}$  105°
14. $m\widehat{ILK}$  255°

In ⊙M, $\overline{NO}$ and $\overline{PQ}$ are diameters. Identify the following.

15. four semicircles
    See additional answers.
16. four central angles
    $\angle PMO, \angle OMQ,$
    $\angle NMQ, \angle PMN$
17. $m\widehat{NQ}$  110°
18. $m\widehat{PNQ}$  180°

19. How do you know that $\overline{PM}$ has the same length as $\overline{MO}$?   Both are radii.

20. How do you know that $\overline{NO}$ is twice the length of $\overline{MO}$?
    A diameter is twice the length of a radius.

21. **WRITING MATH** Discuss how an arc of a circle is similar to a line segment and how it is different.   Answers will vary.

22. **FOOD SERVICE** A pizza company cuts each pizza into six approximately-equal sized slices. Find the measure of the arc formed by the crust of a piece of pizza. Does this measure depend on the size of the pizza? Explain.
    See additional answers.

**228**   Chapter 5  **Logic and Geometry**

## Extend the Lesson

**CONNECTING TO PRIOR KNOWLEDGE** Have students draw ⊙O with two parallel chords, $AB \parallel CD$. Ask students what appears to be true about the arcs intercepted between the chords.  **appear congruent** Have students justify their conclusion.  **As alternate interior angles of parallel lines, $\angle BAD \cong \angle CDA$. Since these angles are inscribed angles of the circle, the arcs they intercept are twice their measures. Since the angles are of equal measure, the arcs are of equal measure.**
Have students generalize the result.  **In a circle, parallel chords intercept congruent arcs between them.**

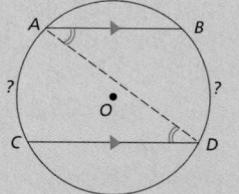

**23. ART** An artist's design for a floor display is shown. What is the measure of a central angle formed by two consecutive outer points on the large star?   60°

**Classify each statement as *true* or *false*. If the statement is false, explain why.**

**24.** A chord of a circle contains exactly two points on the circle.   true

**25.** The measure of a radius is always one-half the measure of a chord.
True; the measure of a radius is one half the measure of a diameter.

**26.** If a central angle and an inscribed angle are congruent, their arcs are congruent.
False; the measure of the arc for the inscribed angle is twice that of the arc for the central angle.

**GEOMETRY SOFTWARE** Use geometry software to draw a circle and construct two chords to form an inscribed angle.

**27.** Use the measure tools to verify the relationship between the intercepted arc and the measure of the inscribed angle.   Check students' work.

**28.** Do you think the measure of the inscribed angle will increase if the size of the circle is increased? Explain why or why not, and use the software to check.   no

## ■ EXTENDED PRACTICE EXERCISES

**29. NAVIGATION** A *compass rose* is used to determine the heading, or direction, of a boat at sea. Find the measure of the minor arc formed by the headings 212° SSW and 12° NNE.   160°

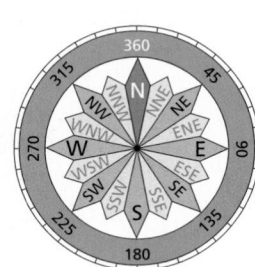

**30. CRITICAL THINKING** If you double the measure of a minor arc, will the measure of the related major arc be doubled? Will the measure of the central angle be doubled? Explain.
No. Yes. Doubling a minor arc decreases the size of the major arc.

**31. RECREATION** The Jones family is having a circular pool installed that has a radius of 14 ft. The pool will have a wooden deck hanging over the edge as shown in the figure. What is the length of the arc covered by the deck? Round your answer to the nearest tenth. (Hint: Find the pool's circumference and set up a proportion.)   26.4 ft

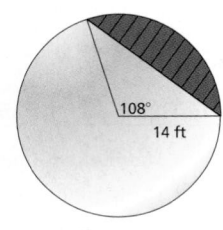

**32. CHAPTER INVESTIGATION** Draw the circle formed by points *N*, *S*, *E* and *W*. Draw four radii to bisect each of the four regions of your compass. Label the endpoints of the radii *NE*, *SE*, *SW* and *NW* as appropriate to complete your compass.   See additional answers.

## ■ MIXED REVIEW EXERCISES

**Use the spinner shown and a number cube.** (Lessons 4-4 and 4-5)

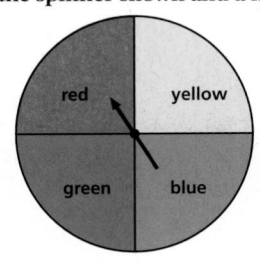

**33.** *P*(spinning blue, then red)   $\frac{1}{16}$

**34.** *P*(spinning green and rolling an even number)   $\frac{1}{8}$

**35.** *P*(spinning blue and rolling an odd number)   $\frac{1}{8}$

**36.** *P*(spinning red or green and rolling a prime number)   $\frac{1}{4}$

**37.** *P*(spinning blue or green and rolling a 6)   $\frac{1}{12}$

**38.** *P*(spinning yellow and rolling a number less than 7)   $\frac{1}{4}$

## ADDITIONAL ANSWERS

**3.** $\overset{\frown}{PMN}, \overset{\frown}{PNM}, \overset{\frown}{NOP}, \overset{\frown}{MPO}, \overset{\frown}{PNO}$

**4.** $\overline{PN}, \overline{NO}, \overline{OM}, \overline{MP}, \overline{PO}$

**15.** $\overset{\frown}{POQ}, \overset{\frown}{PNQ}, \overset{\frown}{NQO}, \overset{\frown}{OPN}$

**22.** 60°; no; although the segments that determine the angle will be longer, the measure of the angle does not change and nor does the measure of the arc.

**32.**

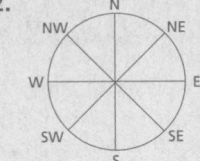

---

### Extra Practice Worksheet 5-8

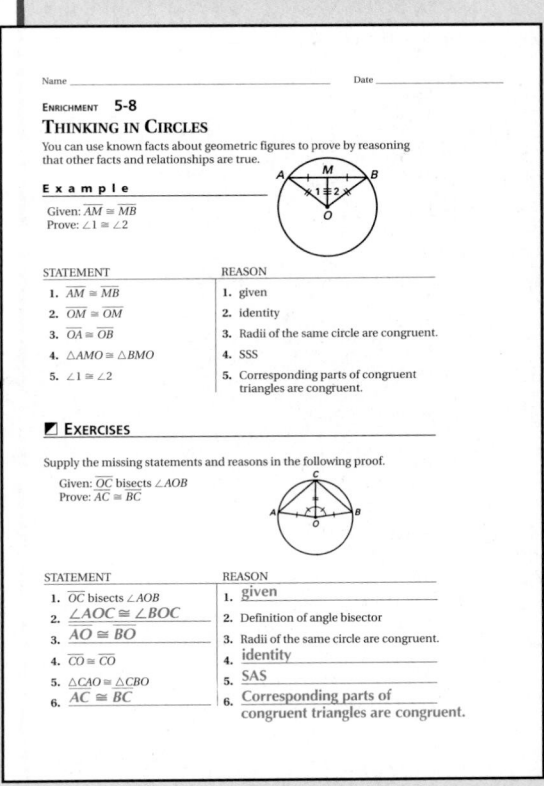

### Enrichment Worksheet 5-8

## Vocabulary Review

**Lesson 5-7**
polygon                    side of a polygon
vertex of a polygon
convex polygon
concave polygon    regular polygon
diagonal of a polygon

**Lesson 5-8**
circle               center
radius (radii)    chord
diameter         central angle
circumference  arc
semicircle       minor arc
major arc        inscribed angle

## ASSIGNMENT GUIDE

All students: 1–54

## Chalkboard Examples

**Lesson 5-7**
Identify each figure as one of the following: *convex polygon, concave polygon, not a polygon*. If the figure is a polygon, tell how many sides it has.

a.

not a polygon

b.
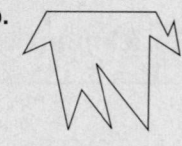
concave 13-gon

c.
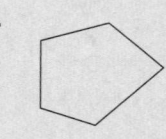
convex pentagon

d.

not a polygon

### PRACTICE ◼ LESSON 5-7

**Sketch each polygon.**  For 1–4, see additional answers.

1. a regular quadrilateral
2. a concave pentagon
3. a regular pentagon
4. a concave hexagon

**For each regular polygon, find the sum of the interior angles and the measure of an interior angle.**

5. 12-gon   1800°, 150°
6. heptagon   900°, 128.6°
7. 40-gon   6840°, 171°
8. octagon   1080°, 135°

**Classify each polygon by its number of sides.  Tell whether it is convex or concave, regular or not regular.**

9.
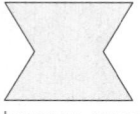
hexagon, concave, not regular

10.

hexagon, convex, not regular

11.
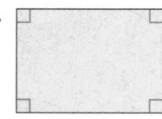
rectangle, convex, not regular

12.

nonagon, concave, not regular

### PRACTICE ◼ LESSON 5-8

**Match the following for circle *P*.**

13. a minor arc   b
14. a chord   d or f
15. a radius   g
16. an inscribed angle   e
17. a major arc   c
18. a central angle   a
19. a diameter   f

a. $\angle QPR$
b. $\overparen{QS}$
c. $\overparen{RSQ}$
d. $\overline{QS}$
e. $\angle QSR$
f. $\overline{SR}$
g. $\overline{QP}$

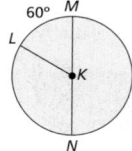

**In circle *K*, find each measure.**

20. $m\angle LKM$   60°
21. $m\overparen{LNM}$   300°
22. $m\overparen{MLN}$   180°
23. $m\overparen{LN}$   120°
24. $m\angle LKN$   120°
25. $m\angle MKN$   180°

## Teaching Tip

Remind students that, when they know the number of sides of a convex polygon, they can always determine the sum of the measures of all the angles of the polygon, whether the polygon is a regular polygon or not a regular polygon. However, to determine the measure of each interior angle of a polygon from the number of its sides, the polygon must be a regular polygon.

**Fill in the blanks. In the figure, $\overleftrightarrow{AB}$ bisects $\overline{CD}$.** (Lesson 5-1)

26. __?__ ≅ __?__   $\overline{DE}, \overline{EC}$

27. The intersection of two lines is a __?__, and the intersection of two planes is a __?__.   point, line

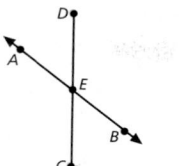

**In the figure, $\ell \parallel m$, classify each pair of angles as congruent, supplementary, or neither.** (Lessons 5-3)

28. ∠1 and ∠2   congruent
29. ∠7 and ∠12   congruent
30. ∠3 and ∠7   supplementary
31. ∠4 and ∠12   congruent
32. ∠11 and ∠14   neither
33. ∠11 and ∠7   supplementary
34. ∠6 and ∠9   congruent
35. ∠2 and ∠5   neither

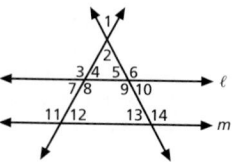

**State whether it is possible to have a triangle with sides of the given lengths.** (Lesson 5-4)

36. 1, 2, 3   no
37. 7, 8, 11   yes
38. $\frac{1}{2}, \frac{2}{3}, \frac{3}{4}$   yes
39. 14, 17, 25   yes
40. 2, 4, 6   no
41. 37, 49, 90   no

**Find the value of $x$ in each figure.** (Lesson 5-4)

42.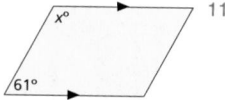
43.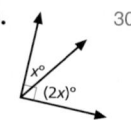
44.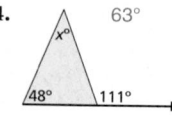

**State whether each pair of triangles is congruent by SSS, SAS, or ASA.** (Lesson 5-5)

45. 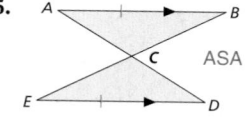   ASA
46. 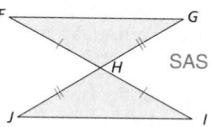   SAS
47. 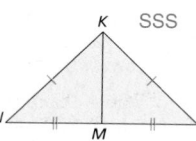   SSS

**Classify each statement as *true* or *false*.** (Lessons 5-2, 5-7 and 5-8)

48. A diameter in a circle is a chord.   true
49. A radius is a chord.   false
50. An inscribed angle is equal to the measure of the arc it intercepts.   false
51. The diagonals of a rectangle are congruent.   true
52. A rhombus is a square.   false
53. A square is a rhombus.   true
54. Two angles whose measures have a sum of 180° are called complementary angles.   false

Chapter 5 **Review and Practice Your Skills** | 231

**Lesson 5-8**
Find $m\angle BOC$.
Central $\angle BOC$ intercepts the same arc as does inscribed $\angle BAC$. Since an inscribed angle is measured by $\frac{1}{2}$ its intercepted arc, $m\widehat{BC} = 50°$. The measure of a central angle is the same as the measure of its intercepted arc. So, $m\angle BOC = 50°$.

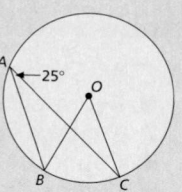

**ADDITIONAL ANSWERS**

1.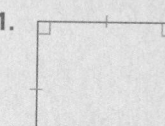

2.

3.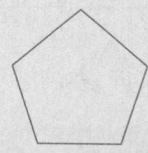

4.

**Teaching Tip**

In preparation for Exercises 13–25, have students explain, without looking at a diagram, the differences among a line segment that is a radius of a circle, a line segment that is a diameter of a circle, and a line segment that is a chord of a circle. For a radius, one endpoint of the line segment is at the center of the circle and the other endpoint is on the circle. For a diameter, the center of the circle is the midpoint of the line segment and both endpoints are on the circle. For a chord, both endpoints of the line segment are on the circle.
Again, without looking at a diagram, ask students to explain the difference between how a central angle and an inscribed angle of a circle are formed, the location of each vertex, and the difference in how they are measured. A central angle is formed by two radii; its vertex is at the center of the circle; it has the same measure as its intercepted arc. An inscribed angle is formed by two chords; its vertex is on the circle; it has half the measure of its intercepted arc.

## Lesson Planning

### NCTM Standards/Strands
- Representation
- Problem Solving
- Connections
- Communication

### Vocabulary

use a picture, diagram, or model
circle graph      sector

### Tools/Materials Needed

compass        ruler
protractor

### Lesson Resources

Warm-up Transparency 22
Transparency RF-1
Reteaching 5-9
Extra Practice 5-9
Enrichment 5-9

### ASSIGNMENT GUIDE

**Basic:** 1–16
**Enriched:** 1–16

## Getting Started

### 5-MINUTE WARM-UP

**Find each percent.**
1. 24% of 360   86.4
2. 78% of 200   156
3. 9% of 58   5.22
4. 1.5% of 186   2.79

**THE FIVE-STEP PLAN Read**—ask questions to help students understand the problem. **Plan**—guide students to related problems and previously mastered skills and strategies. **Solve**—students solve problem on their own. **Answer**—write the solution in a format that answers the question. **Check**—review work, check for reasonableness, and review strategy used. **THE STRATEGY** *Use a picture, diagram, or model*—this strategy enables students to present a visual interpretation of a problem situation, thereby clarifying the details of the circumstance.

---

An effective problem solving strategy is to **use a picture, diagram or model**. A **circle graph** is one way to display data to make comparisons. The whole circle represents 100% of the data. Each part, or percent of the data, is represented by a **sector**. Since there are 360° in a circle, the sum of the measures of the central angles for the sectors is 360°.

### Problem Solving Strategies

Guess and check

Look for a pattern

Solve a simpler problem

Make a table, chart or list

✓ Use a picture, diagram or model

Act it out

Work backwards

Eliminate possibilities

Use an equation or formula

### Problem

**ENTERTAINMENT** A recent poll surveyed students about their favorite form of entertainment. Of the 950 students surveyed, 229 chose movies, 209 said music, 176 liked TV, 155 said sports, 73 said video games, 61 chose the Internet, and 47 said dancing. Make a circle graph of the data.

### Solve the Problem

*Step 1* Write each response as a percent of the entire survey, 950.

*Step 2* Find the number of degrees in the central angle by multiplying by 360°.

| | | |
|---|---|---|
| Movies | $229 \div 950 \approx 24\%$ | $0.24 \cdot 360° \approx 86°$ |
| Music | $209 \div 950 = 22\%$ | $0.22 \cdot 360° \approx 79°$ |
| Watching TV | $176 \div 950 \approx 19\%$ | $0.19 \cdot 360° \approx 68°$ |
| Sports | $155 \div 950 \approx 16\%$ | $0.16 \cdot 360° \approx 58°$ |
| Video games | $73 \div 950 \approx 8\%$ | $0.08 \cdot 360° \approx 29°$ |
| Internet | $61 \div 950 \approx 6\%$ | $0.06 \cdot 360° \approx 22°$ |
| Dancing | $47 \div 950 \approx 5\%$ | $0.05 \cdot 360° = 18°$ |

*Step 3* Draw a circle with a compass. To construct the central angles for the sectors, draw any radius. Place a protractor along the radius with 0 at the circle's center. Measure and mark 86°. Draw another radius from the center to this point.

*Step 4* Place the protractor along the new radius. Measure and mark 79°. Draw another radius to this point. Draw the rest of the central angles this way. Label each sector and title the graph.

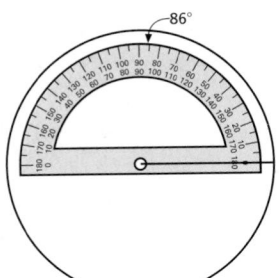

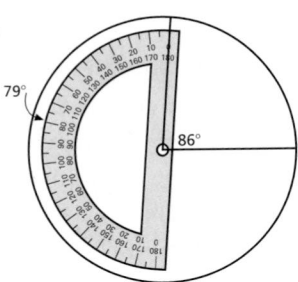

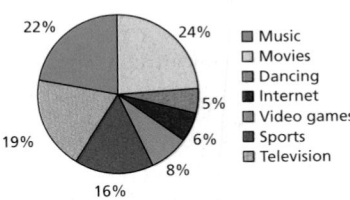

**Favorite Forms of Entertainment**

22%  24%
5%
19%  6%
8%
16%

- ■ Music
- □ Movies
- ■ Dancing
- ■ Internet
- □ Video games
- ■ Sports
- □ Television

---

## ADDITIONAL ANSWERS

**1.**
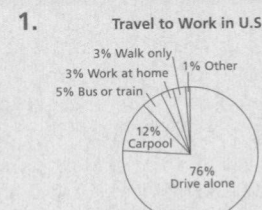
Travel to Work in U.S.
3% Walk only
3% Work at home    1% Other
5% Bus or train
12% Carpool
76% Drive alone

**2.**
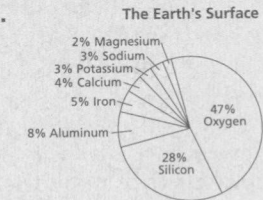
The Earth's Surface
2% Magnesium
3% Sodium
3% Potassium
4% Calcium
5% Iron
8% Aluminum
47% Oxygen
28% Silicon

**3.**
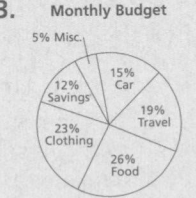
Monthly Budget
5% Misc.
15% Car
12% Savings
19% Travel
23% Clothing
26% Food

**4.**
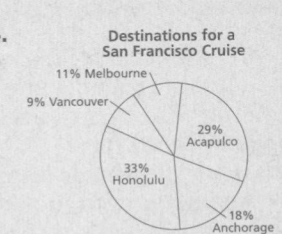
Destinations for a San Francisco Cruise
11% Melbourne
9% Vancouver
29% Acapulco
33% Honolulu
18% Anchorage

**Make a circle graph for each set of data. Write a title for your graph.**
For 1–3, see additional answers.

**1. Travel to Work in U.S.**

| Means of travel | % |
|---|---|
| Drive alone | 76 |
| Carpool | 12 |
| Bus or train | 5 |
| Walk only | 3 |
| Work at home | 3 |
| Other | 1 |

**2. The Earth's Surface**

| Element | % |
|---|---|
| Oxygen | 47 |
| Silicon | 28 |
| Aluminum | 8 |
| Iron | 5 |
| Calcium | 4 |
| Potassium | 3 |
| Sodium | 3 |
| Magnesium | 2 |

**3. Monthly Budget**

| Expenses | % |
|---|---|
| Car | 15 |
| Travel | 19 |
| Food | 26 |
| Clothing | 23 |
| Savings | 12 |
| Miscellaneous | 5 |

**Five-step Plan**
1. Read
2. Plan
3. Solve
4. Answer
5. Check

■ **PRACTICE EXERCISES**

**Make a circle for each set of data. Begin by finding each sector's percent.**
For 4–5, see additional answers.

**4. Cruise Line Destinations**

| Destination | Number of cruises |
|---|---|
| Acapulco, Mexico | 47 |
| Anchorage, Alaska | 28 |
| Honolulu, Hawaii | 53 |
| Vancouver, Canada | 14 |
| Melbourne, Australia | 18 |

**5. University Degrees**

| Major | Number of students |
|---|---|
| Education | 822 |
| Computers | 650 |
| Engineering | 510 |
| Psychology | 423 |
| Math | 119 |
| Law | 100 |

**6. INDUSTRY** A car manufacturer produces 735 cars in one month. Of these, 215 are economy cars, 190 sports cars, 145 minivans, 130 luxury cars and 55 full-size vans. Make a circle graph representing the information.  See additional answers.

**7. NAVIGATION** In Pierre Mondrin's career in exploration, he sailed to Antarctica 12 times, the South China Sea 9 times, Alaska 8 times and the Mediterranean Sea 2 times. Make a circle graph representing Pierre's favorite places to explore.  See additional answers.

**8. WRITING MATH** Describe the advantages of using a circle graph to represent data. How does it make comparing information easier?  Answers will vary, but should include benefit of visually comparing a part to the whole.

**9. DATA FILE** Refer to the data on water usage for a family on page 567. Make a circle graph of the information presented. Round each percent to the nearest tenth.  See additional answers.

■ **MIXED REVIEW EXERCISES**

**Simplify.** (Lesson 2-6)

**10.** $14g - 5(g - 7)$  $9g + 35$
**11.** $\frac{3}{4}(d + 21)$  $\frac{3}{4}d + 15\frac{3}{4}$
**12.** $\frac{3}{5}(15j - 3)$  $9j - 1\frac{4}{5}$
**13.** $-3(n - 1) + 6(4 - n)$  $-9n + 27$
**14.** $4(2.5k + 1.7) - 3.6k$  $6.4k + 6.8$
**15.** $3.5(6 + 6a) + 0.5(4 + 9a)$  $23 + 25.5a$

**16.** Jamesha has measured phone service. She pays \$0.06/call for the first 60 calls and \$0.05/call for any additional calls. Her base fee is \$5.40. Write and simplify a variable expression for the total cost of 150 calls.
$5.40 + 0.60 (60) + 0.05 (c - 60)$, $6 + 0.05c$; \$13.50

---

**Chalkboard Examples**

**Supplementary Problem**

**AGRICULTURE** Miranda has a circular flower bed of radius 8 ft. that she has divided into four congruent sectors. She has planted the area bounded by the arc of one sector and the chord joining the endpoints of the radii of that sector in pink. What amount of area has she planted in pink?

The area described is called a *segment* of the circle, shown shaded.

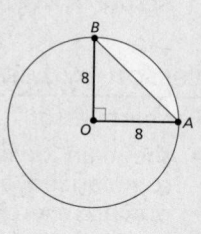

Area of segment $AB$ = Area of sector $AOB$ − Area of right $\triangle AOB$

Area of sector $AOB = \frac{1}{4}$ Area of

$\odot O = \frac{1}{4}(\pi \cdot 8^2) = 16\pi \text{ft}^2$

Area of right $\triangle AOB = \frac{1}{2} \cdot 8 \cdot 8 = 32 \text{ ft}^2$

Area of segment $AB = (16\pi - 32)\text{ft}^2 \approx 18 \text{ ft}^2$

**Lesson Wrap-up**

**QUICK ASSESSMENT**

Ask the following question to determine if students understand the contents presented in this lesson.

How is a sector of a circle formed?
A sector is the region bounded by an arc of the circle and the two radii to the endpoints of the arc.

---

**ADDITIONAL ANSWERS**

**5.**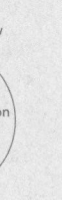
University Degrees
5% Math  4% Law
16% Psychology
31% Education
19% Engineering
25% Computers

**6.**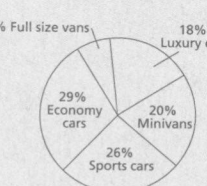
Car Production
7% Full size vans
18% Luxury cars
29% Economy cars
20% Minivans
26% Sports cars

**7.**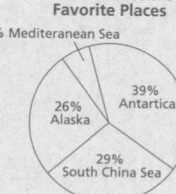
Pierre Mondrin's Favorite Places
6% Mediteranean Sea
39% Antartica
26% Alaska
29% South China Sea

**9.**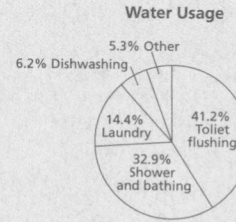
Water Usage
5.3% Other
6.2% Dishwashing
14.4% Laundry
41.2% Toilet flushing
32.9% Shower and bathing

### Vocabulary Assessment

- A matching section checks for student understanding of the new vocabulary introduced in this chapter.
- A vocabulary review/test for Chapter 5 is available on pp. vii–x of the *Chapter 5 Resource Masters*.

### Lesson-by-Lesson Review

For each lesson,

- the main ideas are summarized, and
- practice exercises are provided.

 EXAMVIEW® PRO

Use the networkable **ExamView® Pro** to:

- Create **multiple versions** of tests.
- Create **modified tests** for *inclusion* students.
- **Edit** existing questions and **add** your own questions.
- Use built-in **state curriculum correlations** to create tests aligned with state standards.
- Change **English** tests to **Spanish** and vice versa.

# Chapter 5 Review

## VOCABULARY ▮

**Choose a word from the list to complete each statement.**

1. Two lines that intersect to form right angles are called ___?___. h
2. A(n) ___?___ is a quadrilateral with two pairs of parallel sides. g
3. A(n) ___?___ is a line that intersects two other coplanar lines in different points. l
4. A(n) ___?___ is formed by two rays that have a common endpoint. a
5. A segment with both endpoints on a circle is called a(n) ___?___. c
6. A triangle with all three sides congruent is called ___?___. f
7. A ray that divides an angle into two congruent adjacent angles is the ___?___ of the angle. b
8. If the line containing a side of a polygon contains points in the interior of the polygon, the polygon is called ___?___. e
9. A(n) ___?___ is a statement that is assumed to be true. i
10. If two adjacent angles form a right angle, the angles are called ___?___. d

a. angle
b. bisector
c. chord
d. complementary
e. concave
f. equilateral
g. parallelogram
h. perpendicular
i. postulate
j. skew
k. supplementary
l. transversal

## LESSON 5-1 ▮ Elements of Geometry, p. 192

▶ The **midpoint** of a segment is the point that divides the segment into two **congruent segments**. A **bisector** of a segment is any line, segment, ray, or plane that intersects the segment at its midpoint.

**Draw a figure to illustrate each situation.** For 11–14, check students' drawings.

11. Points $C$, $D$, and $E$ are noncollinear.
12. Points $P$, $Q$, $R$ and $S$ are noncoplanar.
13. Line $t$ intersects plane $\mathcal{H}$ at point $R$.
14. Planes $\mathcal{P}$ and $\mathcal{Q}$ intersect at line $m$.

15. You can think of your classroom as a model of six planes: the ceiling, the floor, and the four walls. Find two planes that do *not* intersect. Answers will vary.
Sample answer: the floor and the ceiling

## LESSON 5-2 ▮ Angles and Perpendicular Lines, p. 196

▶ Two angles whose measures have a sum of 90° are called **complementary angles**. Two angles whose measures have a sum of 180° are called **supplementary angles**.

**Find the measure of the complement and supplement of each angle.**

16. $m\angle A = 34°$  56°, 146°
17. $m\angle B = 49°$  41°, 131°
18. $m\angle C = 87°$  3°, 93°
19. $m\angle D = 12°$  78°, 168°
20. If $\overline{BD}$ is the bisector of $\angle ABC$, what is the value of $x$? 10

## LESSON 5-3 ■ Parallel Lines and Transversals, p. 202

► When two parallel lines are cut by a **transversal**, pairs of **corresponding angles**, **alternate interior angles**, and **alternate exterior angles** formed are congruent.

**Refer to the figure to name two pairs of each type of angle.**

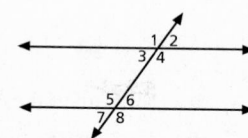

**21.** corresponding angles
∠1 and ∠5; ∠2 and ∠6; ∠3 and ∠7; ∠4 and ∠8

**22.** alternate interior angles
∠3 and ∠6; ∠4 and ∠5

**23.** alternate exterior angles
∠1 and ∠8; ∠2 and ∠7

**24.** same-side interior angles
∠3 and ∠5; ∠4 and ∠6

**25.** Refer to the figure. If $m\angle 1 = 120°$ and $m\angle 8 = 120°$, are the lines cut by the transversal parallel? Justify your answer.
The lines are parallel because the angles are alternate exterior angles.

## LESSON 5-4 ■ Properties of Triangles, p. 206

► The sum of the **angles** of a **triangle** is 180°. The sum of the lengths of any two **sides** of a triangle is greater than the length of the third side.

**State whether it is possible to have a triangle with sides of the given lengths.**

**26.** 13, 19, 8  yes

**27.** 9, 5, 4  no

**28.** 11, 22, 33  no

**Find the unknown angle measures in each figure.**

**29.**
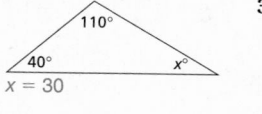
$x = 30$

**30.**
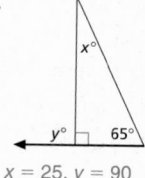
$x = 25, y = 90$

**31.**
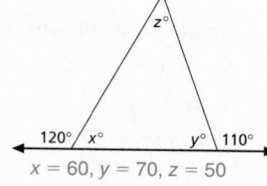
$x = 60, y = 70, z = 50$

## LESSON 5-5 ■ Congruent Triangles, p. 212

► To show that two triangles are **congruent** you can use the SSS, SAS, or ASA postulates.

**State whether △ABC ≅ △DEF. If so, name the appropriate postulate.**

**32.**
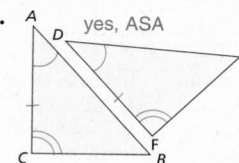
yes, ASA

**33.**
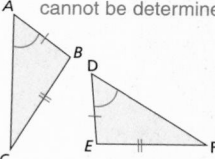
cannot be determined

**34.**
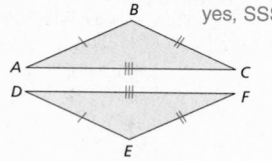
yes, SSS

## LESSON 5-6 ■ Quadrilaterals and Parallelograms, p. 216

► A **quadrilateral** is a closed plane figure that has four sides.

► **Parallelograms** have pairs of congruent opposite sides and opposite angles.

**Use ▱ABCD to find each unknown measure.**

**35.** $\overline{AD}$  10

**36.** $m\angle A$  80°

**37.** $m\angle D$  100°

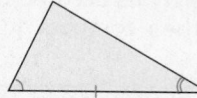

**50.**

Possible Points on a Test

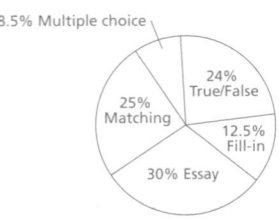

8.5% Multiple choice
24% True/False
25% Matching
12.5% Fill-in
30% Essay

**51. Ocean Surface Areas**

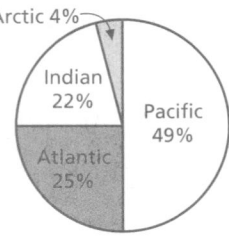

Arctic 4%
Indian 22%
Pacific 49%
Atlantic 25%

---

Tell whether each statement is *true* or *false*.

**38.** All squares are parallelograms. true

**39.** All parallelograms are rectangles. false

**40.** A trapezoid can never be a parallelogram. true

## LESSON 5-7 ◼ Diagonals and Angles of Polygons, p. 222

▶ The sum of the angle measures of a polygon with $n$ sides is $(n - 2)180°$.

▶ The measure of each interior angle of a regular $n$-gon is $\frac{(n - 2)180°}{n}$.

**41.** Find the sum of the interior angle measures of an 11-gon. 1620°

**42.** Find the sum of the interior angles of a polygon with 15 sides. 2340°

**43.** Find the measure of each interior angle of a regular octagon. 135°

## LESSON 5-8 ◼ Properties of Circles, p. 226

▶ An **arc** is an unbroken part of a **circle**. A **central angle** has its vertex at the center of a circle. An **inscribed angle** has its vertex on the circle.

**Identify the following for ⊙$N$.**

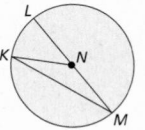

**44.** a central angle ∠KNL, ∠KNM

**45.** an inscribed angle ∠KML

**46.** major arc $\overarc{KML}$

**47.** minor arc $\overarc{KL}$, $\overarc{KM}$

**48.** a radius $\overline{NL}$, $\overline{NM}$, $\overline{NK}$

**49.** a chord $\overline{KM}$, $\overline{LM}$

## LESSON 5-9 ◼ Problem Solving Skills: Circle Graphs, p. 232

▶ In a circle graph the whole circle represents 100% of the data.

▶ Each percent of the data is represented by a sector of the circle.

50–51. See additional answers.

**Make a circle graph of each set of data.**

**50.** Possible Points on a Test

| Section | Number of points |
|---|---|
| True/False | 48 |
| Fill-in | 25 |
| Essay | 60 |
| Matching | 50 |
| Multiple choice | 17 |

**51.** Ocean Surface Areas

| Ocean | Area (square miles) |
|---|---|
| Pacific | 64,186,300 |
| Atlantic | 33,420,000 |
| Indian | 28,350,500 |
| Arctic | 5,105,700 |

## CHAPTER INVESTIGATION

**EXTENSION** Notice the objects and landmarks that surround your compass. Create a map of the area. Include at least four objects or landmarks, a scale and a directional key (N-S-E-W). Present your map to the class. Note geometric properties, such as collinear and noncollinear points, polygons and parallel lines.

---

# THEME: Navigation

The benchmarks and expectations for this extension are as follows.
- Students select a level area and place a 4-ft stick in the ground before noon. They mark the tip of the shadow and label it point *W*. Then wait until after noon, when the shadow creates a straight line with point *W* in the opposite direction. They mark the tip of the new shadow point *E*.
- Students connect the points *W* and *E*. They draw the perpendicular bisector of $\overline{EW}$, making it the same length as $\overline{EW}$.
- Students draw the circle formed by points *N, S, E* and *W*. They draw four radii to bisect each of the four regions of their compass. They use a magnetic compass to verify its accuracy.
- Students create a map of the objects that surround their compass. Include at least four objects, a scale and a directional key (N-S-E-W).

# Chapter 5 Assessment

**Refer to the figure.**

1. Name three points that determine plane $\mathcal{M}$. *F, B, E*

2. Name the intersection of planes $\mathcal{M}$ and $\mathcal{N}$. $\ell$

3. Name three lines that lie in plane $\mathcal{N}$. $\overleftrightarrow{AB}, \overleftrightarrow{AD}, \overleftrightarrow{BD}$

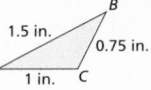

**For exercises 4–8, use the figure shown to name each.**

4. a pair of perpendicular segments $\overline{BE} \perp \overline{DE}; \overline{DE} \perp \overline{EF}; \overline{BF} \perp \overline{DE}$

5. two adjacent complementary angles $\angle BEC, \angle CED$

6. two pairs of vertical angles $\angle BEC, \angle GEF; \angle CEF, \angle BEG$

7. two pairs of adjacent supplementary angles  See additional answers.

8. the measure of the complement of $\angle CDE$ 65°

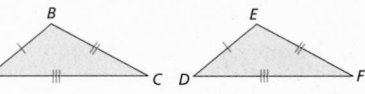

**In the figure, $k \parallel m$ and $m\angle 4 = 125°$. Find each measure.**

9. $m\angle 1$ 125°        10. $m\angle 2$ 55°        11. $m\angle 3$ 55°

12. $m\angle 5$ 125°       13. $m\angle 6$ 55°        14. $m\angle 7$ 55°

15. Order the angles of $\triangle ABC$ from smallest to largest. $\angle A, \angle B, \angle C$

16. If $m\angle A = 32°$ and $m\angle B = 45°$, what is the measure of $\angle C$? 103°

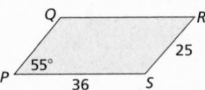

17. If $\triangle RST \cong \triangle ABC$, name all the corresponding, congruent parts.  See additional answers.

18. State whether the pair of triangles is congruent by SSS, SAS, or ASA.  SSS

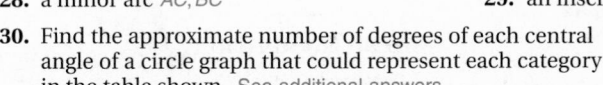

**Find each unknown measure of the parallelogram.**

19. $\overline{QR}$ 36                  20. $\overline{PQ}$ 25

21. $\angle S$ 125°                  22. $\angle R$ 55°

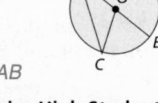

23. Sketch a concave pentagon.  Check students' work.

24. Find the sum of the interior angles of a 14-gon. 2160°

25. Find the measure of an interior angle of a regular 36-gon. 170°

**Refer to the figure to name the following.**

26. a diameter $\overline{AB}$              27. a chord $\overline{AC}, \overline{AB}$

28. a minor arc $\overparen{AC}, \overparen{BC}$         29. an inscribed angle $\angle CAB$

30. Find the approximate number of degrees of each central angle of a circle graph that could represent each category in the table shown.  See additional answers.

**Craven Junior High Students**

| Grade | Percent |
|---|---|
| Sixth | 18% |
| Seventh | 25% |
| Eighth | 27% |
| Ninth | 30% |

---

## ADDITIONAL ANSWERS

7. $\angle BEC, \angle CEF; \angle BED, \angle DEF; \angle CED,$ $\angle DEG; \angle CEF, \angle FEG; \angle FEG, \angle BEG;$ $\angle ABE, \angle CBE; \angle BCE, \angle DCE$

17. $\angle R, \angle A; \angle S, \angle B; \angle T, \angle C; \overline{RS}, \overline{AB};$ $\overline{ST}, \overline{BC}; \overline{RT}, \overline{AC}$

30. Sixth = 65°; Seventh: 90°; Eighth = 97°; Ninth: 108°

---

## Chapter 5 Assessment

**Assessment Options**

Chapter 5 Test A, pages 169–170
Chapter 5 Test B, pages 171–172

## ALTERNATIVE ASSESSMENT

**GEOMETRIC DICTIONARY**  Have students create their own dictionary of geometric terms. They should choose at least one principle to illustrate from each lesson in this chapter and include a word explanation or definition with each illustration. Students should try to write explanations in their own words, rather than simply transcribing definitions given in the text.

**RUBRIC**  The following rubric is a sample scoring guide.

| Points | Description |
|---|---|
| 4 | Creates a geometric dictionary that <u>accurately illustrates and describes more than nine</u> geometric principles taken from all nine lessons of the chapter. |
| 3 | Creates a geometric dictionary that <u>accurately illustrates and describes nine</u> geometric principles taken from all nine lessons of the chapter. |
| 2 | Creates a geometric dictionary that <u>accurately illustrates and describes seven or eight</u> geometric principles take from different lessons of the chapter. |
| 1 | Creates a geometric dictionary that, <u>with some errors, illustrates and describes a few</u> geometric principles take from the chapter. |
| 0 | Makes <u>no attempt</u> to create a geometric dictionary. |

## Standardized Test Practice

These two pages contain practice questions in the various formats that can be found on the most frequently given standardized tests.

A student recording sheet for these two pages can be found on p. A1 of the *Chapter 5 Resource Masters*.

## Standardized Test Practice Student Recording Sheet

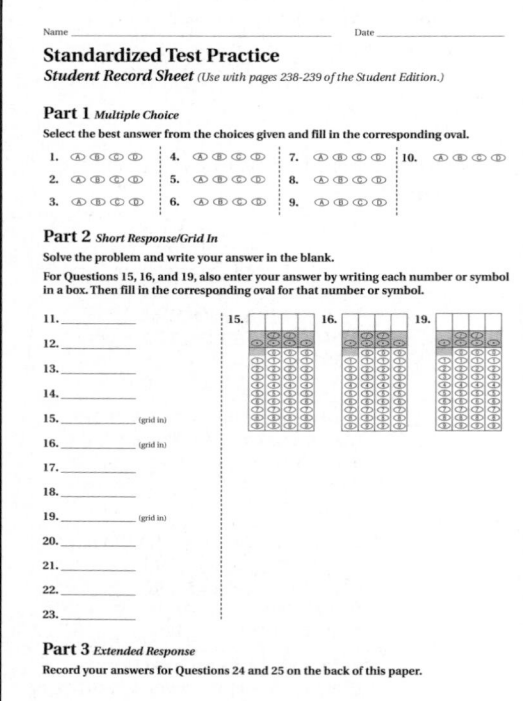

## Additional Practice

See pp. 173–175 in the *Chapter 5 Resource Masters* for additional standardized test practice.

# Standardized Test Practice

**Part 1 Multiple Choice**

Record your answers on the answer sheet provided by your teacher or on a sheet of paper.

**1.** According to the box-and-whisker plot, between which two numbers will you find half of the data? (Lesson 1-6)  C

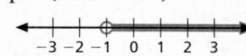

| | |
|---|---|
| 10 and 15 | Ⓑ 10 and 30 |
| Ⓒ 15 and 30 | Ⓓ 20 and 30 |

**2.** The student council of South High School is planning to sell school T-shirts. They hire a company to make the T-shirts. The company charges $40 to prepare the design and $8 for each T-shirt. If $t$ represents the number of T-shirts, which expression represents the total cost to make the T-shirts? (Lesson 2-3)  A

- Ⓐ $8t + 40$
- Ⓑ $40t + 8$
- Ⓒ $40 + 8 + t$
- Ⓓ $t(40 + 8)$

**3.** Which expression is equivalent to $\dfrac{-45t + 60s}{-15}$? (Lesson 2-5)  B

- Ⓐ $-3t + 4s$
- Ⓑ $3t - 4s$
- Ⓒ $-3t + 60s$
- Ⓓ $3t - 60s$

**4.** Which equation has a solution that is equivalent to the solution of $4x + 6 = -18$? (Lesson 3-4)  A

- Ⓐ $4x = -24$
- Ⓑ $4x = -12$
- Ⓒ $x + 6 = -4.5$
- Ⓓ $x + 6 = 4.5$

**5.** Which inequality has the solution represented on the graph? (Lesson 3-7)  A

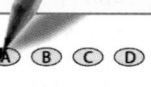

- Ⓐ $-2x - 4 < -2$
- Ⓑ $-2x - 4 > -2$
- Ⓒ $-2x + 4 < 2$
- Ⓓ $-2x + 4 > 2$

**6.** Brian has 10 rock CDs, 5 jazz CDs, and 8 country CDs. If Brian picks one CD at random to play, what is the probability that he will choose a CD that is *not* jazz? (Lesson 4-3)  D

- Ⓐ $\dfrac{5}{23}$
- Ⓑ $\dfrac{5}{18}$
- Ⓒ $\dfrac{5}{15}$
- Ⓓ $\dfrac{18}{23}$

**7.** Tomaso drops a penny in a pond, and then he drops a nickel in the pond. What is the probability that both coins land with tails showing? (Lesson 4-4)  B

- Ⓐ $\dfrac{1}{8}$
- Ⓑ $\dfrac{1}{4}$
- Ⓒ $\dfrac{1}{2}$
- Ⓓ $\dfrac{3}{4}$

**8.** An ice cream store has 20 flavors. Abigail wants to buy three different flavors of ice cream to take home for a birthday party. Which expression can be used to determine how many ways she can choose the flavors of ice cream? (Lesson 4-7)  B

- Ⓐ $\dfrac{17!}{20!\,3!}$
- Ⓑ $\dfrac{20!}{17!\,3!}$
- Ⓒ $\dfrac{17!}{3!}$
- Ⓓ $\dfrac{20!}{17!}$

**9.** Point $C$ is the midpoint of $\overline{AB}$. Point $D$ is the midpoint of $\overline{AC}$. Which of the following segments is the longest? (Lesson 5-1)  C

Ⓐ $\overline{AC}$  Ⓑ $\overline{AD}$  Ⓒ $\overline{BD}$  Ⓓ $\overline{CD}$

**10.** Which is *not* a postulate that can be used to prove two triangles are congruent? (Lesson 5-5)  A

- Ⓐ Angle-Angle-Side
- Ⓑ Angle-Side-Angle
- Ⓒ Side-Angle-Side
- Ⓓ Side-Side-Side

**Test-Taking Tip**  Ⓐ Ⓑ Ⓒ Ⓓ

**Question 6**
Read each question carefully. Be sure you understand what the question asks. Look for words like *not*, *estimate*, and *approximately*.

## ADDITIONAL ANSWERS

**11.** $\begin{bmatrix} -6 & 12 & -5 \\ -7 & 4 & 6 \end{bmatrix}$

**24.**

Since the transversal is perpendicular to both lines, all angles are 90°. Therefore corresponding angles are congruent and the two lines are parallel. Since all angles are 90°, same side interior angles are congruent.

Preparing for the Standardized Tests
For test-taking strategies and more
practice, see pages 627–644.

## Part 2   Short Response/Grid In

Record your answers on the answer sheet
provided by your teacher or on a sheet of paper.

**11.** Find $R + S$. (Lesson 1-8)
$$R = \begin{bmatrix} -2 & 5 & 0 \\ -8 & -1 & 4 \end{bmatrix} \quad S = \begin{bmatrix} -4 & 7 & -5 \\ 1 & -3 & 2 \end{bmatrix}$$
See additional answers.

**12.** Simplify $4(q + 2p) - (8q + 3p)$.
(Lesson 2-6)  $-4q + 5p$

**13.** What is the value of $(-1)^{21}$? (Lesson 2-8)  $-1$

**14.** The day after a hurricane, the barometric
pressure in a coastal town had risen to 29.7 in.
of mercury, which is 2.9 in. of mercury higher
than the pressure when the eye of the
hurricane passed over. Write an equation
to represent the situation.
(Lesson 3-2)  $b + 2.9 = 29.7$

**15.** When 2000 lb of paper are recycled, 17 trees
are saved. How many trees would be saved if
5000 lb of paper are recycled?  (Lesson 3-5)
42.5 trees

**16.** Solve $\sqrt{4x + 1} = 5$. (Lesson 3-8)  6

**17.** A poll is taken to determine whether
registered voters plan to vote for the school
levy. The results of the poll are given below.
What is the experimental probability that a
registered voter is undecided?
(Lesson 4-1)  0.384

| Response | Yes | No | Undecided |
|----------|-----|-----|-----------|
| Men | 83 | 70 | 92 |
| Women | 103 | 52 | 100 |

**18.** There are 17 floats in the Founder's Day
Parade. If the queen's float must be last, how
many ways can the organizer pick the first
two floats in the parade? (Lesson 4-6)  240 ways

**19.** Find the value of $y$ in the figure.
(Lesson 5-4)  120

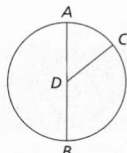

 mathmatters2.com/standardized_test

**20.** Suppose $\triangle DEF \cong \triangle JKL$. Name the congruent
sides of the two triangles. (Lesson 5-5)
$\overline{DE} \cong \overline{JK}, \overline{EF} \cong \overline{KL}, \overline{FD} \cong \overline{LJ}$

**21.** In quadrilateral $MNOP$, $m\angle M = 73°$,
$m\angle N = 101°$, and $m\angle O = 84°$. Find the
measure of $\angle P$. (Lesson 5-6)  102°

**22.** What is the sum of the interior angles of a
convex hexagon? (Lesson 5-7)  720°

**23.** $\overline{AD}$ is a diameter of circle $D$. If the measure of
$\angle ADC$ equals 45°, what is the measure of $\overarc{BC}$?
(Lesson 5-8)  135°

## Part 3   Extended Response

Record your answers on a sheet of paper.
Show your work.

**24.** Draw a set of parallel lines and a transversal
where the same side interior angles are
congruent. Explain why the lines are parallel
and why the same side interior angles are
congruent. (Lesson 5-2)  See additional answers.

**25.** Write six true statements about parallelogram
$ABCD$. (Lesson 5-6)

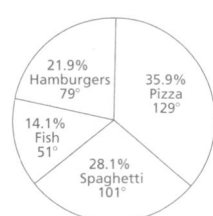

See additional answers.

**26.** The results of a student survey about favorite
foods are as follows: 23 chose pizza, 14 chose
hamburgers, 18 chose spaghetti, and 9 chose
fish. Make a circle graph that reflects the data.
Label each sector with the favorite food, the
percentage of students the sector represents,
and the measure of the central angle.
(Lesson 5-9)  See additional answers.

Chapter 5 **Standardized Test Practice**  **239**

## Rubrics

The following rubrics are sample
scoring devices for short response
and extended response questions.

### Short Response

| Points | Description |
|--------|-------------|
| 2 | The student demonstrates a **thorough understanding** of the mathematics of the task. The response may contain minor flaws that do not detract from the demonstration of a thorough understanding. |
| 1 | The student has provided a response that is only **partially correct.** |
| 0 | The student has provided a **completely incorrect** solution or no response at all. |

### Extended Response

| Points | Description |
|--------|-------------|
| 4 | The student demonstrates a **thorough understanding** of the mathematics of the task. The response contains minor flaws that do not detract from the demonstration of a thorough understanding. |
| 3 | The student demonstrates an **understanding** of the mathematics of the task. The response is essentially correct and demonstrates an essential but less than thorough understanding of the mathematics. |
| 2 | The student has demonstrated only a **partial understanding** of the mathematics of the task. Although the student may have used the correct approach to a solution or may have provided a correct solution, the work lacks an essential understanding of the underlying mathematical concepts. |
| 1 | The student has demonstrated a **very limited understanding** of the mathematics of the task. The response is incomplete and exhibits many flaws. |
| 0 | The student has provided a **completely incorrect** solution or no response at all. |

**25.** Answers will vary. Sample answer: $\angle A \cong \angle C$, $\angle B \cong \angle D$, $\angle A$ is supplementary to $\angle B$,
$\angle B$ is supplementary to $\angle C$, $\overline{AB} \cong \overline{DC}$, $\overline{AD} \cong \overline{BC}$

**26.** Favorite Foods of Students

21.9% Hamburgers 79°
35.9% Pizza 129°
14.1% Fish 51°
28.1% Spaghetti 101°

# 6 Graphing Functions

| Lesson | Lesson Objectives | Pacing (days) | NCTM Standards | State/Local Objectives |
|---|---|---|---|---|
| 6-1 | **Distance in the Coordinate Plane** *(pp. 244–247)*<br>• Use the distance formula to find the distance between two points.<br>• Use the midpoint formula. | 2 | 2, 4, 6, 9 | |
| 6-2 | **Slope of a Line** *(pp. 248–251)*<br>• Find the slope of a line.<br>• Identify horizontal and vertical lines. | 2 | 2, 4, 9, 10 | |
| 6-3 | **Write and Graph Linear Equations** *(pp. 254–257)*<br>• Write equations of lines using slope, intercepts, and points.<br>• Graph a line given the equation. | 2 | 2, 9, 10 | |
| 6-4 | **Write and Graph Linear Inequalities** *(pp. 258–261)*<br>• Write linear inequalities in two variables.<br>• Graph linear inequalities in two variables on the coordinate plane. | 1 | 2, 9, 10 | |
| 6-5 | **Linear and Nonlinear Functions** *(pp. 264–267)*<br>• Graph linear functions.<br>• Identify the domain and range of a function. | 2 | 2, 6, 9, 10 | |
| 6-6 | **Graph Quadratic Functions** *(pp. 268–271)*<br>• Identify points given the graph of a quadratic function.<br>• Graph simple quadratic functions. | 2 | 2, 6, 9, 10 | |
| 6-7 | **Problem Solving Skills: Patterns and Functions** *(pp. 274–275)*<br>• Use a function table to recognize a function rule. | 1 | 2, 6, 8, 9 | |
| 6-8 | **Direct Variation** *(pp. 276–279)*<br>• Solve problems involving direct variation functions.<br>• Solve problems involving direct square variation functions. | 1 | 2, 6, 9, 10 | |
| 6-9 | **Inverse Variation** *(pp. 282–285)*<br>• Solve problems involving inverse variation functions.<br>• Solve problems involving inverse square variation functions. | 1 | 2, 6, 9, 10 | |
| Review | | 1 | | |
| Testing | | 1 | | |

**Key to NCTM Standards:**

*1=Number & Operations, 2=Algebra, 3=Geometry,*
*4=Measurement, 5=Data Analysis & Probability,*
*6=Problem Solving, 7=Reasoning & Proof,*
*8=Communication, 9=Connections, 10=Representation*

**Pacing:** Suggestions for the year can be found on page xvi.

**What's MATH Got To Do With It?** Real-Life Math Videos

*What's Math Got To Do With It?* Real-Life Math Videos engage students, showing them how math is used in everyday situations. Use *Algebra 1* Video 3 with this chapter.

# Chapter Resource Manager

**Timesaving Tools**
**TeacherWorks**™
All-In-One Planner
and Resource Center
See page xiii.

**FAST FILE** Chapter 6 Resource Masters

| Reteaching Activities | Extra Practice | Enrichment | Assessment | Basic Mathematics Review | Study Skills Activities | Lesson Warm-Ups Transparencies | Teaching Transparencies | Technology Activities | Materials Needed |
|---|---|---|---|---|---|---|---|---|---|
| 177 | 178 | 179 | | 12 | 23 | TK-9–TK-12, RF-31, RF-32 | 6-1, | | graph paper |
| 180 | 181 | 182 | | | 23 | TK-3, TK-9–TK-12, RF-33 | 6-2 | | spreadsheet, graph paper |
| 183 | 184 | 185 | | | 24 | TK-9–TK-12, RF-34 | 6-3, 6-6 | | graph paper |
| 186 | 187 | 188 | | | 24 | TK-9–TK-13, RF-35 | | | graph paper |
| 189 | 190 | 191 | | 20 | 25 | TK-9–TK-12 | | | graph paper |
| 192 | 193 | 194 | | | 25 | TK-9–TK-12 | 6-3, 6-6 | | graph paper |
| 195 | 196 | 197 | | | 26 | RF-1 | | | calculator |
| 198 | 199 | 200 | | 24 | 26 | TK-9–TK-12, RF-36 | | | graph paper, calculator |
| 201 | 202 | 203 | 207–213 | | 27 | TK-9, RF-36 | | | graph paper, identical coins, calculator, 12" ruler plus pivot |

## *Quick Review Math Handbook, Book 2*

hot words hot topics

| *MathMatters 2* Lesson(s) | Hot Topic Lesson(s) | *MathMatters 2* Lesson(s) | Hot Topic Lesson(s) |
|---|---|---|---|
| 6-1 | 7-9 | 6-5 | 6-4, 6-7 |
| 6-2 | 6-8 | 6-6, 6-7 | 6-7 |
| 6-3 | 6-7, 6-8 | 6-8 | 6-5 |
| 6-4 | 6-6 | 6-9 | 6-5 |

# Content and Connections

## Connections to the Past

**MM1 (Ch. 7):** Use the distance formula to find the distance between two points.

**MM1 (Ch. 7):** Identify slopes of lines as positive, negative, zero, or undefined.

**MM1 (Ch. 7):** Write an equation using slope-intercept form.

**MM1 (Ch. 7):** Graph an equation using slope-intercept form.

**MM1 (Ch. 5):** Graph open sentences on a number line and solve simple inequalities.

**MM1 (Ch. 7):** State the domain, range, and whether a relation is a function.

**MM1 (Ch. 7):** Graph functions.

**MM1 (Ch. 5):** Write one- and two-step equations to solve problems.

**MM1 (Ch. 5):** Solve equations using multiplication and division.

**MM1 (Ch. 6):** Solve a proportion.

## MathMatters 2 Chapter 6 Highlights

Use the distance formula to find the distance between two points. (6-1)

Find the slope of a line and identify horizontal and vertical lines. (6-2)

Write equations of lines using slope, intercepts, and points. (6-3)

Graph a line given its equation. (6-3)

Write and graph linear inequalities in two variables. (6-4)

Graph and identify the domain and range of linear functions. (6-5)

Graph simple quadratic functions. (6-6)

Use a function table to recognize a function rule. (6-7)

Solve problems involving direct variation and direct square variation. (6-8)

Solve problems involving inverse variation and inverse square variation. (6-9)

## Connections to the Future

**MM2 (Ch. 11) and MM3 (Ch. 10):** Use the Pythagorean Theorem to find unknown lengths and solve problems involving right triangles.

**MM3 (Ch. 6):** Use slope to determine whether two lines are parallel or perpendicular.

**MM3 (Ch. 6):** Write equations of lines using slope-intercept and point-slope form.

**MM3 (Ch. 6):** Solve a system of equations by graphing.

**MM3 (Ch. 6):** Use graphing to solve systems of linear inequalities.

**MM3 (Ch. 2):** Identify relations and their domains and ranges.

**MM3 (Ch. 12):** Graph quadratic functions given in standard form.

**MM3 (Ch. 2):** Identify and evaluate functions.

**MM3 (Ch. 13):** Solve problems involving direct variation and direct square variation.

**MM3 (Ch. 13):** Solve problems involving inverse variation and inverse square variation.

### Key

PC = Previous Course
MM1 = *MathMatters 1*
MM2 = *MathMatters 2*
MM3 = *MathMatters 3*

### Connecting the Strands

| NCTM Strand | Lesson(s) |
|---|---|
| Algebra | 6-1, 6-2, 6-3, 6-4, 6-5, 6-6, 6-7, 6-8, 6-9 |
| Measurement | 6-1, 6-2 |
| Problem Solving | 6-1, 6-5, 6-6, 6-7, 6-8, 6-9 |
| Communication | 6-7 |
| Connections | 6-1, 6-2, 6-3, 6-4, 6-5, 6-6, 6-7, 6-8, 6-9 |
| Representation | 6-2, 6-3, 6-4, 6-5, 6-6, 6-8, 6-9 |

| Type | Student Edition | Teacher Resources | Technology/Internet |
|---|---|---|---|
| **INTERVENTION** | | | |
| Ongoing | Are You Ready?, pp. 242–243<br>Check Understanding, pp. 245, 248, 277, 283<br>Review and Practice Your Skills, pp. 252–253, 262–263, 272–273, 280–281<br>Mid-Chapter Quiz, p. 263 | Lesson Warm-Ups Transparencies, pp. WU-23, WU-24, WU-25, WU-26, WU-27<br>Quick Assessment, *ATE* pp. 243, 246, 250, 256, 260, 266, 270, 275, 278, 284 | mathmatters2.com/extra_ examples<br>mathmatters2.com/self_check_quiz |
| Mixed Review | pp. 247, 251, 257, 261, 267, 271, 275, 279 | | |
| Error Analysis | You Make the Call, p. 246 | Teaching Tip, *ATE* p. 280 | |
| **ASSESSMENT** | | | |
| Standardized Test Practice | pp. 290–291<br>Preparing for Standardized Tests, pp. 627–644 | Standardized Test Practice, *CRM* pp. 211–213 | mathmatters2.com/standardized_test |
| Open-Ended Assessment | Chapter Investigation, pp. 241, 247, 257, 261, 271, 279, 285, 288 | Chapter Investigation, *ATE* p. 288<br>Alternative Assessment, *ATE* p. 289 | |
| Chapter Assessment | Chapter Review, pp. 286–288<br>Chapter Assessment, p. 289 | Multiple-Choice Tests (Forms A and B), *CRM* pp. 207–210 | mathmatters2.com/chapter_assessment |

**Key to Abbreviations:** *ATE* = Annotated Teacher's Edition, *CRM* = Chapter Resource Masters

## Additional Intervention

***Basic Mathematics Review*** includes 80 lessons, consisting of an instructional page and a test page. This workbook also features a pretest, posttest, table of measurement equivalents, and calculator appendices.

## ExamView® Pro

Use ExamView® Pro Testmaker CD-ROM to:
- Create **multiple versions** of tests.
- Create **modified** tests for *inclusion* students with one mouse click.
- **Edit** existing questions and **add** your own questions.
- Build tests aligned with **state standards** using built-in **state curriculum correlations**.
- Change **English** tests to **Spanish** with one mouse click and vice versa.

# 6

## Chapter Opener

### NCTM Standards/Strands
- Data Analysis & Probability
- Representation

### Vocabulary

function        graph
coordinate grid system

### Theme Connections
The main objective of most businesses—ranging from small shops owned by one person to huge organizations owned by thousands of stockholders—is to provide goods or services with the ultimate goal of making a profit. To this end, a business owner must monitor and analyze a variety of cost relationships, many of which can be represented graphically in the coordinate plane.

### Career Opportunities
Many careers require understanding of relations and, often, their graphs. Two such careers are highlighted in the MathWorks features. Others include: beauty shop owner, clothing store owner, travel agency owner, jewelry store owner, furniture shop owner, garden nursery owner, construction contractor, plumbing service provider, day care center provider, and landscaping service provider.
- Music store owner, page 253
- Restaurateur, page 273

## Internet Connection

### Theme Activities
Mathmatters2.com/chapter_theme provides links to the Internet that will help students gather information about the use of math in the real world, particularly data and measures. To search for additional addresses, begin a search of *business*. Then within that search, use key words that will call up specific forms of ownership such as *sole proprietorship*, *partnership*, *corporation*, *syndicate*, *franchise*, or help organizations, such as *Small Business Administration* or *National Alliance of Business*. Students can brainstorm other key words.

# Graphing Functions

### THEME: Business

Have you ever thought of someday owning your own business and being your own boss? Business owners must understand how to solve equations that represent relationships between factors such as cost and profit, cost and reliability, and time and quantity. Businesses often use graphs to visually represent these relationships. As a business owner, an analysis of financial information each year will help you plan for future income and spending.

- One responsibility of **music store owners** (page 253) is to display product on the store floor so that customers are encouraged to make purchases.

- **Restaurateurs** (page 273) use previous sales and inventory costs to place orders for supplies, determine staffing needs, and estimate weekly profits.

**Math Online**
mathmatters2.com/chapter_theme

240

### Chapter Investigation
Use the Internet and other resources to locate additional information about a corporate annual report.

## Sales of Cars in the U.S., 1995-2001

| Year | Sales (thousands) |
|------|-------------------|
| 1995 | 8687 |
| 1996 | 8527 |
| 1997 | 8273 |
| 1998 | 8142 |
| 1999 | 8697 |
| 2000 | 8852 |
| 2001 | 8422 |

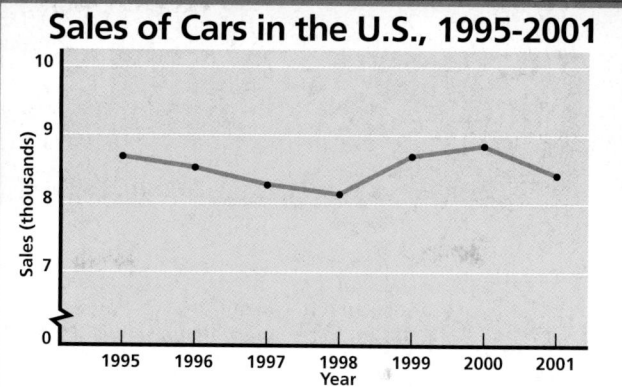

**Sales of Cars in the U.S., 1995-2001**

---

## Data Activity: Sales of Cars in the U.S., 1995 -2001

**Use the table and graph for Questions 1–5.**

1. Describe the change in car sales from 1995-2001.
   decreasing, then increasing, then decreasing
2. Did you look to the table or graph first to answer Question 1? Why?
   Answers will vary.
3. Which year had the greatest sales? Which year had the least sales?
   2000        1998
4. Use the graph to predict the sales for the year 2006, 2007, and 2008.
   Answers will vary.
5. If possible, check the accuracy of your predictions by using current data available. Check students' work.

### CHAPTER INVESTIGATION

Most companies, especially those that have stockholders or investors, compile an annual report of profit and loss information. This report includes financial statements, graphs, and other data for the past year, as well as any significant plans for the future. It is important to understand the language used in a business plan. Two terms frequently used are *sales revenue* and *operating costs*. *Sales revenue* is the amount of money received for products or services sold to customers. Sales revenue can also be referred to as income. *Operating cost* is the amount of money that is needed to run the business. This amount includes all monies used to produce, market, and sell a product or service.

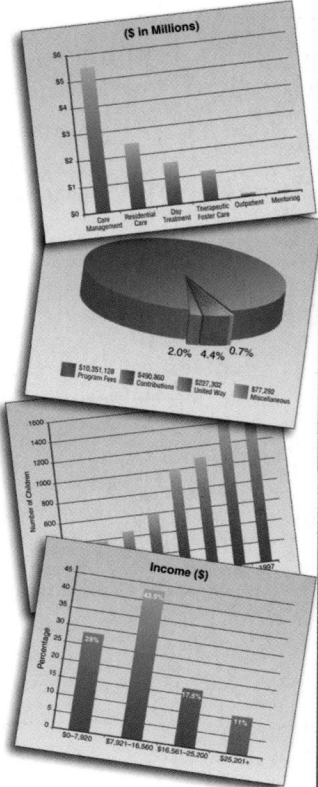

#### *Working Together*

Use the library or the Internet to get an annual report of a company. Locate information in the report about the company's operating costs, sales revenue and operating profit/loss. Draw graphs that illustrate the finances of your selected company. Use the Chapter Investigation icons to guide your group through the analysis of the annual report.

Chapter 6 **Graphing Functions** 241

---

## Data Activity

The annual results obtained by an entire industry, such as the U.S. automobile industry, is but one of the many economic statistics generated for public knowledge. Students should answer Questions 1–5 to better understand how statistics gathered annually are used for comparison purposes.

### Extend the Data Activity
**Student Portfolio** Students may research other types of economic statistics that are reported annually by U.S. industry, such as steel production or advertising expenditures listed by business category.

## Chapter Investigation

### As an Overarching Problem
Display data and graphs that show the operating costs and sales revenue for a few companies. Discuss the display and ask students if they have any questions about what is shown. Students will continue to work on the investigation as they complete the exercises identified by the Investigation icon that is found throughout the chapter. These exercises will guide students through the task described in *Working Together*. Encourage students to keep all of their work on the Investigation together. Have students use the suggestions in the Chapter Investigation Extension to summarize their work.

### As a Chapter Project
The goal of this project is for students to generate graphs and equations to analyze and describe the finances of a selected company. Students can use the Group Project Planner on page 205 and the Project Planning Calendar on page 206 in the *Chapter 6 Resource Masters* to complete the project. Benchmarks **a, b, c, d, e,** and **f** should be completed after the lesson listed in parentheses has been studied. Benchmark **g** should be completed at the end of the chapter.

---

## Project Planning Calendar

Name _____ Date _____

**CHAPTER 6   PROJECT PLANNING CALENDAR**

| Benchmarks | PROJECT GOAL |
|------------|--------------|
| a. Set up two coordinate planes where the horizontal axis represents the quarter and the vertical axis represents dollar amounts. *(Lesson 6-1)*<br>b. Find the data on your company's operating costs for each quarter of the year. Plot four ordered pairs, and describe the operating costs by quarters and by the entire year. *(Lesson 6-3)*<br>c. Find the data on your company's sales revenue for each quarter of the year. Plot four ordered pairs, and describe the sales by quarters and by the entire year. *(Lesson 6-4)*<br>d. Use your graphs to determine which quarters were profitable and which had a loss. | To draw graphs and write equations to analyze and describe the finances of a selected company. |

## Group Project Planner

Name _____ Date _____

**CHAPTER 6   GROUP PROJECT PLANNER**

Assignment _____   Objective _____

Group Members         Assigned Roles
1) _____    _____
2) _____    _____
3) _____    _____
4) _____    _____
5) _____    _____

Benchmark         Deadlines  Done

## Refresher Skills

The skills on these two pages are skills that have been presented in earlier chapters of this book or in previous math courses. Continuous review of basic math skills will make stronger math students. These skills are identified as necessary to be successful in Chapter 6.

### Skills Correlation Chart

| Skill | Lesson Number |
|---|---|
| The Coordinate Plane | 6-1, 6-2, 6-3, 6-4, 6-5, 6-6, 6-7, 6-8 |
| Evaluate Expressions | 6-2, 6-3, 6-4, 6-5, 6-6, 6-7, 6-8, 6-9 |
| Use Multiplication and Division to Solve Equations | 6-3, 6-5, 6-8, 6-9 |
| Patterns and Sequences | 6-7 |

### Vocabulary

coordinate plane
coordinates of a point
expression
solve an equation
sequence

## Chalkboard Examples

### The Coordinate Plane
**Name the point with coordinates that are the opposites of the coordinates of the given point.**
a. point $C$   $F$
b. point $A$   $G$
c. point $E$   $B$

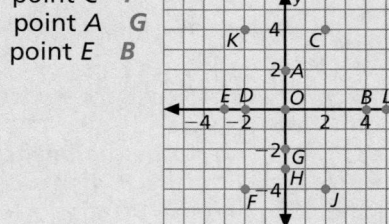

### Evaluate Expressions
Evaluate $-y^x$ when $x = 2$ and $y = -3$.
$-y^x = -(-3)^2 = -(-3)(-3) = -9$

---

# Are You Ready?

**Refresh Your Math Skills for Chapter 6**

The skills on these two pages are ones you have already learned. Use the examples to refresh your memory and complete the exercises. For additional practice on these and more prerequisite skills, see pages 576–584.

## THE COORDINATE PLANE

In this chapter you will learn to graph equations of several types. It is helpful to review the basics of graphing on a coordinate plane.

### Example

Give the coordinates $(x, y)$ of point $L$ and two points in Quadrant I.

The coordinates of point $L$ are $(-6, -4)$. Points $E$ and $F$ are both in Quadrant I.

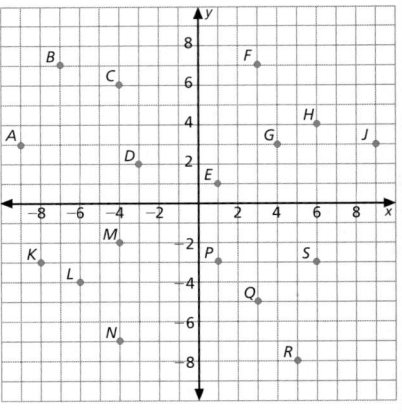

**Give the coordinates of the indicated points.**

1. point $A$   $(-9, 3)$
2. two points in Quadrant II
   $(-9, 3), (-7, 7), (-4, 6)$ or $(-3, 2)$
3. point $S$   $(6, -3)$
4. two points in Quadrant III
   $(-8, -3), (-6, -4), (-4, -2)$ or $(-4, -7)$

**Name each point.**

5. the point at $(-4, 6)$   $C$
6. the point at $(3, -5)$   $Q$
7. the point at $(3, 7)$   $F$
8. the point at $(-4, -2)$   $M$

## EVALUATE EXPRESSIONS

To evaluate an expression, substitute the given value for each variable and then follow the order of operations.

### Example

Evaluate the expression $3x + 5$ when $x = 4$.   $3x + 5$
$$3 \cdot 4 + 5 = 12 + 5 = 17$$

**Evaluate each expression for the given value of the variable.**

9. $1 + 7a$, when $a = 2$   15
10. $-4t$, when $t = -10$   40
11. $\dfrac{x - 8}{2}$, when $x = -4$   $-6$
12. $\dfrac{-10 + y}{-4}$, when $y = -6$   4
13. $2(p + 9)$, when $p = 12$   42
14. $3(r - 20)$, when $r = 15$   $-15$
15. $x^2 + 14$, when $x = 3$   23
16. $16 - d^2$, when $d = 5$   $-9$
17. $8y - y^2$, when $y = 2$   12
18. $\dfrac{24 + b}{3b}$, when $b = 3$   3
19. $\dfrac{4 - x}{x - 4}$, when $x = -1$   $-1$
20. $k(2k - 7)$, when $k = -5$   85
21. $\dfrac{7v - 6}{-v}$, when $v = 2$   $-4$
22. $c^2 - 4c$, when $c = 9$   45
23. $4x - x^2 + 21$, when $x = -7$   $-56$

## Teaching Tip

**ESL/LEP** As part of the discussion of the coordinate plane, elicit the meanings of associated vocabulary: *horizontal, vertical, coordinate axes, origin, quadrants.*

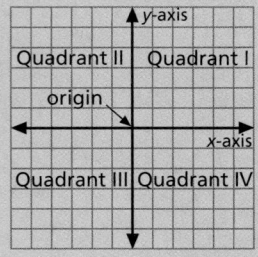

## USE MULTIPLICATION AND DIVISION TO SOLVE EQUATIONS

Recall that to solve an equation, you must isolate the variable on one side of the equal symbol. Use inverse operations to make 1 the variable. If the operation on the variable is multiplication, then divide to solve the equation. If the operation on the variable is division, then multiply to solve the equation.

**Example**

Solve each equation.

$$7y = -35 \qquad\qquad \frac{x}{4} = 5$$

$$\frac{7y}{7} = \frac{-35}{7} \quad \text{Divide both} \qquad 4 \cdot \frac{x}{4} = 5 \cdot 4 \quad \text{Multiply both}$$
$$\qquad\qquad\qquad \text{sides by 7.} \qquad\qquad\qquad\qquad \text{sides by 4.}$$
$$y = -5 \qquad\qquad\qquad\qquad x = 20$$

**Solve each equation. Check the solution.**

**24.** $-5x = 5$  $-1$

**25.** $32b = 192$  $6$

**26.** $\frac{a}{7} = 2$  $14$

**27.** $\frac{3}{5}t = 6$  $10$

**28.** $-24h = 120$  $-5$

**29.** $17x = 51$  $3$

**30.** $\frac{z}{12} = -4$  $-48$

**31.** $8 = -\frac{2}{3}x$  $-12$

**32.** $18k = 90$  $5$

**33.** $96y = 288$  $3$

**34.** $\frac{d}{-13} = 5$  $-65$

**35.** $\frac{2}{9}x = -6$  $-27$

**36.** $-43t = 86$  $-2$

**37.** $\frac{r}{9} = -11$  $-99$

**38.** $63c = -7$  $-\frac{1}{9}$

## PATTERNS AND SEQUENCES

In this chapter, you will learn how to write a function rule from a table of $x$- and $y$-values. To do this, it will be important to recognize the pattern in the $x$-values and $y$-values.

**Example**

State the next three numbers in the sequence.    $1, 2, 4, 8, 16, \ldots$

To get the next number in the sequence, you must multiply each number by 2.

The next three numbers in the sequence are 32, 64, and 128.

**Explain each pattern and state the next three numbers in the sequence.**

**39.** $6, 12, 18, 24, 30, \ldots$  add 6; 36, 42, 48

**40.** $1, 4, 9, 16, 25, \ldots$
square integers; 36, 49, 64

**41.** $-6, -3, 0, 3, 6, 9, \ldots$  add 3; 12, 15, 18

**42.** $5, 6, 9, 10, 13, 14, \ldots$
add 1 then add 3; 17, 18, 21

**43.** $1, \frac{1}{2}, \frac{1}{4}, \frac{1}{8}, \frac{1}{16}, \ldots$  multiply by $\frac{1}{2}$; $\frac{1}{32}, \frac{1}{64}, \frac{1}{128}$

**44.** $4, 12, 36, 108, 324, \ldots$
multiply by 3; 972, 2916, 8748

**45.** $1, 3, 6, 10, 15, 21, \ldots$
add 1 more than before; 28, 36, 45

**46.** $0.2, 0.4, 0.8, 1.4, 2.2, 3.2, \ldots$
add 0.2, then 0.4, etc.; 4.4, 5.8, 7.4

**47.** $1, 1, 2, 3, 5, 8, 13, \ldots$
sum of 2 preceding terms (Fibonacci sequence); 21, 34, 55

**48.** $4, 7, 13, 25, 49, \ldots$
add 2 times more than before; 97, 193, 385

**Patterns and Sequences**
Explain the pattern and state the next three numbers in the sequence $1, 3, 6, 10, \ldots$. If $n$ represents the number of the term, then the pattern for getting a term is $\frac{n(n + 1)}{2}$.
5th term is $\frac{5 \cdot 6}{2}$ or 15, 6th term is $\frac{6 \cdot 7}{2}$ or 21, and 7th term is $\frac{7 \cdot 8}{2}$ or 28.

## Refresher Wrap-up

### QUICK ASSESSMENT

Ask the following questions to determine if students have mastered the basic skills reviewed on these pages.

1. To plot a point, from which point in the coordinate plane do you start counting?   From the *origin*, the point at which the axes intersect.

2. Explain the difference between $A(5, -2)$ and $B(-5, 2)$.   From the origin, $A$ is right 5 and down 2, in Quadrant IV; from the origin, $B$ is left 5 and up 2, in Quadrant II.

3. If $x = -4$ and $y = 3$, which of the following is the value of $-xy^2$?
   D
   A. $-24$        B. 24
   C. $-36$        D. 36

4. For the equation $-\frac{2}{3}x = -12$, which of the following is the solution?   B
   A. 8        B. 18
   C. $-8$        D. $-18$

5. For the sequence
   $\frac{1 \cdot 2}{3}, \frac{2 \cdot 3}{3}, \frac{3 \cdot 4}{3}, \frac{4 \cdot 5}{3}, \ldots,$
   which of the following is the next term?   C
   A. 5        B. $-5$
   C. 10        D. $-10$

### ADDITIONAL PRACTICE

Refer to the Prerequisite Skills lessons beginning on page 576 for more practice.

## Teaching Tip

In preparation for Exercises 27 and 35, discuss with students that although in an equation such as $7y = -35$, the most commonly used approach would be to divide each side by 7, an alternate thought is to multiply each side by $\frac{1}{7}$, the *reciprocal* of 7. Then present an equation such as $\frac{2}{3}x = 12$, for which students should suggest that you multiply each side by $\frac{3}{2}$, the reciprocal of $\frac{2}{3}$.

# Distance in the Coordinate Plane

**Goals**
- Use the distance formula to find the distance between two points.
- Use the midpoint formula.

**Applications** Geography, Market research, Community service, Architecture

## Lesson Planning

### NCTM Standards/Strands
- Measurement
- Algebra
- Problem Solving
- Connections

### Vocabulary

| | |
|---|---|
| coordinate plane | quadrant |
| *x*-axis | *y*-axis |
| ordered pair | origin |

### Tools/Materials Needed

graph paper

### Lesson Resources

Warm-up Transparency 23
Transparency TK-9–12, RF-31, 32
Reteaching 6-1
Extra Practice 6-1
Enrichment 6-1
Technology Activity 6-1

## Getting Started

### 5-MINUTE WARM-UP

**Evaluate.**
1. $-9 + 8$   $-1$   2. $12 + (-7)$   5
3. $\dfrac{-18}{2}$   $-9$   4. $\dfrac{-21}{-3}$   7

### Introduction to Lesson 6-1

After students have located the various attractions in Four-World Fun Park, have them write a short description of a visit to the park that contains directions between attractions and ends at the main gate. For example, if students enter the park and go directly to Rocket Ride, they might write that they walked east 2 units and south 4 units. They could continue by walking west 9 units and south 1 unit to Glacier Climb, and so on. Have volunteers read their descriptions aloud, calling on other students to name the attraction visited at each stop.

**GEOGRAPHY** Directions on the map of Four-World Fun Park are provided by first giving the units to move east or west and then the units to move north or south.

Four-World Fun Park

1. Give directions from the main gate to Tiger Trek.
   go 6 units east and 7 units north
2. Give directions from the main gate to Glacier Climb.
   go 7 units west and 5 units south
3. If you walk east 2 units from the main gate and then south 4 units, where are you?  Rocket Ride
4. Between which two regions do you travel if you walk directly from the restaurant to Lion's Lair?
   from Old America to Safari Land

### ◼ BUILD UNDERSTANDING

On the **coordinate plane**, two number lines are drawn perpendicular to each other and form four **quadrants**. The **x-axis** is the horizontal number line, and the **y-axis** is the vertical number line. Points in the plane are **ordered pairs**. It is important that the order of the coordinates is stated as $(x, y)$. The point $(0, 0)$ is the **origin**, which is where the *x*-axis and the *y*-axis intersect.

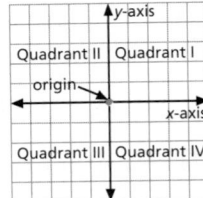

When two points lie on a line that is parallel to the *x*-axis or *y*-axis, find the distance between the points by calculating the absolute value of the difference between the *x*-coordinates or the *y*-coordinates, whichever is appropriate.

### Example 1

**Use the graph to calculate the length of each line segment.**

a. *BC*          b. *PQ*

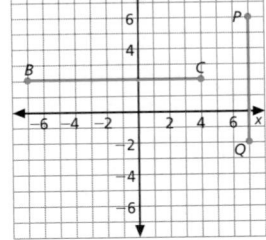

**Solution**

a. Points $B(-7, 2)$ and $C(4, 2)$ are on a line parallel to the *x*-axis. So use the *x*-coordinates.

   $$|-7 - 4| = |-11| = 11$$
   The distance between *B* and *C* is 11 units.

b. Points $P(7, 6)$ and $Q(7, -2)$ are on a line parallel to the *y*-axis. So use the *y*-coordinates.

   $$|6 - (-2)| = |8| = 8$$
   The distance between *P* and *Q* is 8 units.

## Extend the Lesson

**REAL WORLD CONNECTION** Display a map of the world or a globe. Point out the coordinate system of latitude and longitude.  Latitude, which gives the location of a place north or south of the equator, is expressed by angular measurements ranging from 0° at the equator to 90° at the poles. Longitude, the location of a place east or west of a north-south line called the prime meridian passing through Greenwich, England, is measured in angles ranging from 0° at the prime meridian to 180° at the International Date Line.  Have students point out characteristics of the latitude/longitude system that are different from the coordinate plane system.  In a coordinate plane, east-west lines are parallel and so are north-south lines, but longitude lines meet at the poles.

To find the distance between two points that do not lie on a line parallel to the *x*-axis or the *y*-axis, use the coordinates of the ordered pairs in the distance formula.

| Distance Formula | $d = \sqrt{(x_2 - x_1)^2 + (y_2 - y_1)^2}$ for any points $(x_1, y_1)$ and $(x_2, y_2)$. |
|---|---|

## Example 2

**Find the distance between $M(4, -6)$ and $N(-2, 3)$. Round to the nearest tenth.**

### Solution

$$MN = \sqrt{(x_2 - x_1)^2 + (y_2 - y_1)^2}$$
$$MN = \sqrt{(-2 - 4)^2 + (3 - (-6))^2} \quad \text{\small $x_2 = -2, x_1 = 4, y_2 = 3, y_1 = -6$}$$
$$= \sqrt{(-6)^2 + (9)^2} \qquad \text{\small Simplify.}$$
$$= \sqrt{36 + 81}$$
$$= \sqrt{117} \approx 10.817 \qquad \text{\small Approximate.}$$

The distance between $M$ and $N$ is approximately 10.8 units.

The midpoint of a segment is the point halfway between the endpoints of that segment. To find the coordinates of a midpoint, use the midpoint formula.

| Midpoint Formula | $M = \left(\dfrac{x_1 + x_2}{2}, \dfrac{y_1 + y_2}{2}\right)$ for any points $(x_1, y_1)$ and $(x_2, y_2)$. |
|---|---|

**Check Understanding**

Does it make a difference in the distance formula which ordered pair is used for $(x_1, y_1)$? What order is important when you substitute the coordinates?

No. The *x* element used first must correspond to the *y* element used first.

## Example 3

**MARKET RESEARCH** In marketing class, Chris tracks the constant rise in gasoline prices. He uses a coordinate plane to represent his data. Find the midpoint of his results.

### Solution

Use the midpoint formula to find midpoint $M$ of $\overline{AB}$. The endpoints of $\overline{AB}$ are $(1, 1)$ and $(9, 5)$.

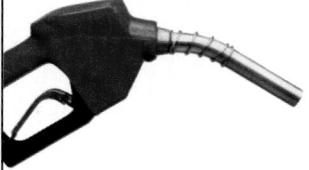

$$M = \left(\frac{1 + 9}{2}, \frac{1 + 5}{2}\right)$$
$$= \left(\frac{10}{2}, \frac{6}{2}\right)$$
$$= (5, 3)$$

So $M(5, 3)$ is the midpoint of $\overline{AB}$.

**Gasoline Prices**

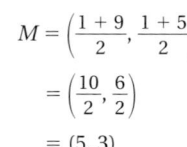

**Math Online** mathmatters2.com/extra_examples

Lesson 6-1 **Distance in the Coordinate Plane** | 245

---

## Chalkboard Examples

### Supplementary Example 1
$A(-2, -2)$, $B(4, -2)$, $C(4, 5)$, $D(-2, 5)$ are the vertices of rectangle *ABCD*. Find the area of *ABCD*.

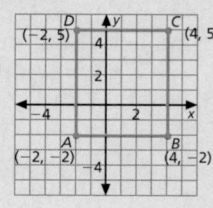

base $AB =$
$|4 - (-2)| =$
$|4 + 2| = |6| = 6$
height $AD =$
$|5 - (-2)| =$
$|5 + 2| = |7| = 7$
Area of *ABCD* =
$\frac{1}{2}(AB)(AD) = \frac{1}{2}(6)(7) =$
**21 square units**

### Supplementary Example 2
The vertices of $\triangle ABC$ are $A(0, 4)$ $B(0, 0)$, $C(4, 0)$.
a. Classify $\triangle ABC$.
   **isosceles right $\triangle$**
b. Find the length of hypotenuse $AC$. $\sqrt{32}$
c. Find the coordinates of the ___ midpoint of $\overline{AC}$.
   **(2, 2)**

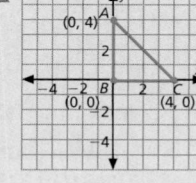

### Supplementary Example 3
The vertices of quadrilateral *ABCD* are $A(2, 4)$, $B(-5, 2)$, $C(-2, -1)$, $D(5, 1)$.
a. What kind of quadrilateral does *ABCD* appear to be?
   **parallelogram**
b. Use distances to justify the type of quadrilateral *ABCD* is.
   $AB = DC = \sqrt{53}$
   $AD = BC = \sqrt{18}$

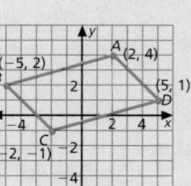

c. Explain how you could have used midpoint to justify the type of quadrilateral *ABCD* is. __Find the midpoint of diagonal *BD*: (0, 1.5). Find the midpoint of diagonal *AC*: (0, 1.5). Since the diagonals have the same midpoint, they bisect each other; so, the quadrilateral is a parallelogram.

---

## Extend the Lesson

**CONNECTING TO PRIOR KNOWLEDGE** Have students mark off a length of 13 units on graph paper and use this length to draw a diagonal line, $\overline{AC}$, somewhere on another coordinate plane. Tell students that $\overline{AC}$ is to be the hypotenuse of a right triangle, $\triangle ABC$. Have students complete the right triangle by drawing the legs. Tell students to find the length of one of the legs from the graph and use the Pythagorean Theorem to determine the length of the other leg. Then confirm this result by finding the length of the other leg from the graph.

## Lesson Wrap-up

### QUICK ASSESSMENT

Ask the following questions to determine if students understand the content presented in this lesson.

1. Explain the difference in locations between the graphs of the points (7, −8) and (−7, 8)
   (7, −8) is in Quadrant IV and (−7, 8) is in Quadrant II.

2. Describe the location of any point whose *x*-coordinate is 0.   on the *y*-axis

3. a. Find the mean value of 4 and −2.   1
   b. Find the mean value of −7 and −1.   −4
   c. Explain how the results of parts a and b relate to the points (4, −7) and (−2, −1).
      The mean value of the *x*-coordinates and the mean value of the *y*-coordinates are the coordinates of the midpoint.

### ASSIGNMENT GUIDE

**Basic:** 1–36, 41–45
**Enriched:** 1–45

### Reteaching Worksheet 6-1

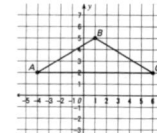

Name _____     Date _____

RETEACHING  **6-1**
**DISTANCE IN THE COORDINATE PLANE**
The distance between two endpoints of a line segment on the *x*-axis or on a line parallel to it is the absolute value of the difference between the *x*-coordinates of the endpoints. The distance between two endpoints of a line segment on the *y*-axis or on a line parallel to it is the absolute value of the difference between the *y*-coordinates of the endpoints.

To find the distance between two points not on an axis or on a line parallel to an axis, use the distance formula.
For any points $A(x_1, y_1)$ and $B(x_2, y_2)$, the length of $\overline{AB}$ is given by the formula $d = \sqrt{(x_2 - x_1)^2 + (y_2 - y_1)^2}$.

**Example 1**
Find the distance between points $A(-2, 3)$ and $B(5, 3)$.
**Solution**
The points have the same *y*-coordinates. So, the line segment joining them is parallel to the *x*-axis. The distance from $A$ to $B$ is the absolute value of the difference of the *x*-coordinates.
$|5 - (-2)| = 7$
The distance between $A$ and $B$ is 7.

**Example 2**
Find the distance between $F(-3, 4)$ and $G(5, 2)$ to the nearest tenth.
**Solution**
Substitute the values of *x* and *y* in the distance formula.
$d = \sqrt{(x_2 - x_1)^2 + (y_2 - y_1)^2}$
$= \sqrt{[5 - (-3)]^2 + (2 - 4)^2}$
$= \sqrt{(8)^2 + (-2)^2}$
$= \sqrt{64 + 4} = \sqrt{68} = 8.2$
The distance between $F$ and $G$ is 8.2.

**EXERCISES**

Find the length of each segment shown on the graph at the right.

1. $\overline{AB}$ ___4___      2. $\overline{CD}$ ___6___
3. $\overline{EF}$ ___7___      4. $\overline{GH}$ ___3___

Use the distance formula to calculate the distance between each pair of points. Round answers to the nearest tenth.

5. $P(4, 1)$, $Q(8, -2)$ ___5___
6. $T(-2, -4)$, $U(4, 8)$ ___13.4___
7. $R(-3, 9)$, $S(2, 5)$ ___6.4___
8. $V(-3, 5)$, $W(4, -2)$ ___9.9___

---

The distance and midpoint formulas can be used with geometric figures that are drawn in the coordinate plane.

### Example 4

The endpoints of a diameter of $\odot P$ are (−1, 10) and (4, 6).

**a.** Find the length of the diameter.    **b.** Find the center of the circle.

**Solution**

**a.** Use the distance formula.
$d = \sqrt{(x_2 - x_1)^2 + (y_2 - y_1)^2}$
$d = \sqrt{(-1 - 4)^2 + (10 - 6)^2}$
$d = \sqrt{(-5)^2 + (4)^2}$
$d = \sqrt{25 + 16}$
$= \sqrt{41} \approx 6.403$

**b.** Use the midpoint formula.
$M = \left( \dfrac{x_1 + x_2}{2}, \dfrac{y_1 + y_2}{2} \right)$
$M = \left( \dfrac{-1 + 4}{2}, \dfrac{10 + 6}{2} \right)$
$M = \left( \dfrac{3}{2}, \dfrac{16}{2} \right)$
$M = \left( \dfrac{3}{2}, 8 \right)$

The diameter of $\odot P$ is approximately 6.4 units.    The center of $\odot P$ is (1.5, 8).

### TRY THESE EXERCISES

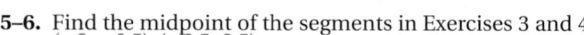

Use the graph to calculate the length of each segment.

1. $\overline{AB}$   8       2. $\overline{PQ}$   7

Find the distance between the points. Round to the nearest tenth.

3. $D(-8, -3)$, $E(4, 2)$   13      4. $X(-5, 2)$, $Y(-2, 5)$   4.2

5–6. Find the midpoint of the segments in Exercises 3 and 4.
   (−2, −0.5); (−3.5, 3.5)
7. A circle has a diameter with endpoints (4, 7) and (10, 11). Find the length of the diameter, length of the radius and coordinates of the center.
   7.2; 3.6; (7, 9)
8. The vertices of a triangle are $A(2, 3)$, $B(5, 7)$ and $C(8, 3)$. Find the length of each side. What type of triangle is $\triangle ABC$?
   $AB = 5$; $BC = 5$; $AC = 6$; isosceles
9. Name the midpoints of each side of the triangle in Exercise 8.
   (3.5, 5); (6.5, 5); (5, 3)

### PRACTICE EXERCISES    • For Extra Practice, see page 603.

Use the graph to calculate the length of each segment.

10. $\overline{AB}$   4       11. $\overline{BD}$   10       12. $\overline{DE}$   5       13. $\overline{CF}$   7

14–17. Find the midpoints of the segments in Exercises 10–13.
   (−4, 7); (−2, 2); (−4.5, −3); (3, 3.5)
18. **YOU MAKE THE CALL** Su says to double the length of a line segment on a coordinate plane, double the coordinates of each endpoint. Do you agree or disagree? Explain.
   Agree. Answers will vary.

**246** | Chapter 6  **Graphing Functions**

### Alternative Assessment

**MATH JOURNAL** Guide students through a justification of the distance formula. Locate points $P_1(x_1, y_1)$ and $P_2(x_2, y_2)$ in a plane without an actual grid.
Have students determine the coordinates of $Q$ (where horizontal and vertical lines meet).
Have students tell how to find a horizontal distance and a vertical distance.
Apply the Pythagorean Theorem:
$\text{hypotenuse}^2 = \text{leg}^2 + \text{leg}^2$

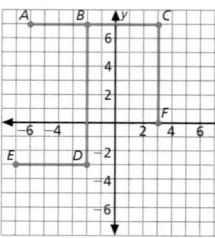

**Find the distance between the points. Round to the nearest tenth.**

**19.** $A(6, 2)$, $B(5, -1)$ 3.2

**20.** $C(-2, -1)$, $D(-2, 9)$ 10

**21.** $E(-8, 3)$, $F(4, -2)$ 13

**22.** $G\left(\frac{2}{3}, -5\right)$, $H(0, 6)$ 11

**23.** $A(2, 6)$, $B(-1, 5)$ 3.2

**24.** $C(-1, -2)$, $D(9, -2)$ 10

**25.** $E(3, 3)$, $F(4, 5)$ 2.2

**26.** $G(2, 8)$, $H(10, -6)$ 16.1

**27.** $X(0, 0)$, $Z\left(\frac{-1}{2}, \frac{6}{7}\right)$ 1.0

**Use the given endpoints of each circle's diameter. Find each circle's center and the lengths of its diameter and radius.** For 28–33, see additional answers.

**28.** $(0, 0)$, $(0, -8)$

**29.** $(10, -2)$, $(8, -8)$

**30.** $(1, 1)$, $(6, 6)$

**31.** $(-2, -4)$, $(10, 5)$

**32.** $(12, -3)$, $(0, -8)$

**33.** $(11, -2)$, $(1, -10)$

**34.** The vertices of a quadrilateral are $S(2, 3)$, $T(5, 7)$, $U(11, 8)$ and $V(8, 4)$. Find the length of each side. What type of quadrilateral is this?
$ST = 5$; $TU = 6.1$; $UV = 5$; $VS = 6.1$; parallelogram

**35. COMMUNITY SERVICE** The layout of the Fairlands Park can be represented by the coordinates $M(4, 1)$, $N(4, 22)$ and $O(17, 22)$. Assume that each square unit of the coordinate plane represents 1 mi². How much land does the clean-up committee need to cover if they clean the entire park?
136.5 mi²

**36. WRITING MATH** The midpoint formula uses the basic math skill of calculating an average. Compare and contrast the average of a set of numbers to the midpoint of a segment. Each coordinate of the midpoint is the average of two numbers, which is equivalent to half of their sum.

## EXTENDED PRACTICE EXERCISES

**37.** Ramón is a meteorologist tracking a storm system over the western U.S. On a coordinate grid over a U.S. map, the straight path of the storm is from $(-190, 47)$ in Washington to $(-17, 31)$ in Nevada. Ramón divides the path into four equal sections. Name the coordinates of the three points that divide the storm into four equal sections.
$(-146.75, 43)$, $(-103.5, 39)$, $(-60.25, 35)$

**38. WRITING MATH** Three points are marked on the coordinate plane: $P(-3, -5)$, $Q(-2, 2)$, and $R(6, 4)$. Name the point that is closer to $Q$. Explain step-by-step how to determine if point $P$ or $R$ is closer to $Q$. $P$; $PQ < RQ$

**39. CRITICAL THINKING** The center of $\odot S$ is at $(-2, 6)$. A diameter of that circle has an endpoint at $(4, -2)$. Find the other endpoint of that diameter. $(-8, 14)$

**40. CHAPTER INVESTIGATION** Draw a diagram that shows only the first and fourth quadrants of a coordinate plane. Label four intervals on the horizontal axis as 1st Q, 2nd Q, 3rd Q and 4th Q. Q stands for Quarter. The first quarter of a year is January–March, the second quarter is April–June and so on. Label the vertical axis as dollar amounts. Answers will vary.

## MIXED REVIEW EXERCISES

**41. DATA FILE** Refer to the data on shopping day preferences on page 571. Make a circle graph representing the information. (Lesson 5-9)
See additional answers.

**Solve each equation. Check the solution.** (Lesson 3-4)

**42.** $6b + 8 = -4$ $-2$

**43.** $\frac{q}{3} + 6 = 5$ $-3$

**44.** $12r - 7 = -20$ $-\frac{13}{12}$

**45.** $12 - 5z = 17$ $-1$

 **Math Online** mathmatters2.com/self_check_quiz

---

Name _____ Date _____

EXTRA PRACTICE **6-1**
**DISTANCE IN THE COORDINATE PLANE**

### ✓ EXERCISES

Use the graph to calculate the length of each segment.

**1.** $\overline{PN}$ __6__

**2.** $\overline{MR}$ __11__

**3.** $\overline{PR}$ __10__

**4.** $\overline{PQ}$ __3__

**5.** $\overline{QS}$ __7__

**6.** $\overline{RT}$ __5__

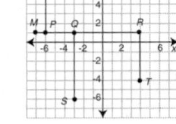

Find the midpoint of each segment shown in the graph above.

**7.** $\overline{PN}$ __$(-6, 4)$__

**8.** $\overline{QS}$ __$\left(-3, -2\frac{1}{2}\right)$__

**9.** $\overline{QR}$ __$\left(\frac{1}{2}, 1\right)$__

**10.** $\overline{RT}$ __$\left(4, -1\frac{1}{2}\right)$__

**11.** $\overline{MQ}$ __$(-5, 1)$__

**12.** $\overline{PQ}$ __$\left(-4\frac{1}{2}, 1\right)$__

Find the distance between the points. Round to the nearest tenth.

**13.** $A(5, 3)$, $B(2, 6)$ __4.2__

**14.** $C(-1, 4)$, $D(-3, -2)$ __6.3__

**15.** $Z(0, -6)$, $W(8, 2)$ __11.3__

**16.** $M\left(\frac{1}{2}, 3\right)$, $N(1, 0)$ __3.0__

**17.** $R(7, 7)$, $S(2, -2)$ __10.3__

**18.** $G\left(\frac{2}{3}, \frac{1}{4}\right)$, $H(0, -1)$ __1.4__

**19.** $L(-3, 4)$, $K(-5, -2)$ __2.8__

**20.** $F(-5, 2)$, $G(-3, 8)$ __6.3__

Use the given endpoints of each circle's diameter. Find each circle's center and the lengths of its diameter and radius.

**21.** $(2, 2)$, $(-2, -2)$ __$(0, 0)$; 5.7; 2.9__

**22.** $(5, -7)$, $(-1, 7)$ __$(2, 0)$; 15.2; 7.6__

---

Name _____ Date _____

ENRICHMENT **6-1**
**USING THE DISTANCE FORMULA**

When the vertices of a geometric figure are given as ordered pairs, the distance formula can be used to identify the figures or to investigate the properties of the figures.

**Example**

Triangle $ABC$ has vertices $A(-4, 2)$, $B(1, 5)$ and $C(6, 2)$. What type of triangle is $\triangle ABC$?

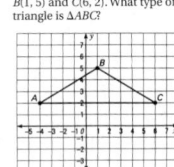

**Solution**

Use the distance formula to find the length of each side.

$d = \sqrt{(x_2 - x_1)^2 + (y_2 - y_1)^2}$
$AB = \sqrt{[1 - (-4)]^2 + (5 - 2)^2}$
$= \sqrt{(5)^2 + (3)^2} = \sqrt{25 + 9} \approx 5.8$
$BC = \sqrt{(6 - 1)^2 + (2 - 5)^2}$
$= \sqrt{(5)^2 + (-3)^2} = \sqrt{25 + 9} \approx 5.8$
$AC = |-4 - 6| = |-10| = 10$

Two sides of $\triangle ABC$ have the same length. The triangle is isosceles.

### ✓ EXERCISES

Rectangle $SEND$ has vertices $S(-1, 5)$, $E(3, 5)$, $N(3, -2)$ and $D(-1, -2)$.

**1.** Find the length of diagonal $\overline{SN}$. __8.1__

**2.** Find the length of diagonal $\overline{ED}$. __8.1__

**3.** Find the coordinates of the midpoint of $\overline{SN}$. __$(1, 1.5)$__

**4.** Find the coordinates of the midpoint of $\overline{ED}$. __$(1, 1.5)$__

**5.** What observations can you make about the diagonals of this rectangle? The diagonals are congruent, have the same midpoint, and bisect each other.

Parallelogram $PARK$ has vertices $P(-3, 4)$, $A(5, 4)$, $R(7, -2)$ and $K(-1, -2)$.

**6.** Find the length of diagonal $\overline{PR}$. __11.7__

**7.** Find the length of diagonal $\overline{AK}$. __8.5__

**8.** Find the coordinates of the midpoint of $\overline{PR}$. __$(2, 1)$__

**9.** Find the coordinates of the midpoint of $\overline{AK}$. __$(2, 1)$__

**10.** What observations can you make? The diagonals are not equal in length. The diagonals bisect each other.

---

## ADDITIONAL ANSWERS

**28.** $C(0, -4)$; $d = 8$; $r = 4$

**29.** $C(9, -5)$; $d \approx 6.3$; $r \approx 3.2$

**30.** $C(3.5, 3.5)$; $d \approx 7.1$; $r \approx 3.5$

**31.** $C(4, 0.5)$; $d = 15$; $r = 7.5$

**32.** $C(6, -5.5)$; $d = 13$; $r = 6.5$

**33.** $C(6, -6)$; $d \approx 12.8$; $r \approx 6.4$

**41. Shopping Day Preference**

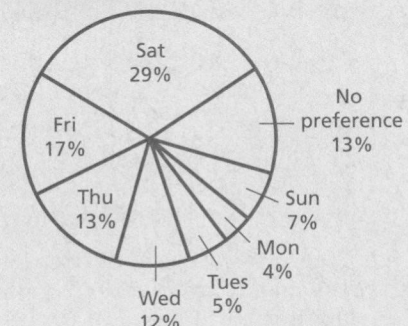

Sat 29%
No preference 13%
Fri 17%
Sun 7%
Thu 13%
Mon 4%
Tues 5%
Wed 12%

# Lesson Planning

## NCTM Standards/Strands
- Measurement
- Algebra
- Representation
- Connections

## Vocabulary

slope      rise / run

## Tools/Materials Needed

spreadsheet      graph paper

## Lesson Resources

Warm-up Transparency 23
Transparency TK-3, 9–12; RF-33
Reteaching 6-2
Extra Practice 6-2
Enrichment 6-2
Technology Activity 6-2

# Getting Started

## 5-MINUTE WARM-UP

**Evaluate each expression.**

1. $\sqrt{3^2 + 4^2}$   5
2. $\sqrt{[6 - (-2)]^2}$   8
3. $\sqrt{[-7 - (-3)]^2}$   4

## Introduction to Lesson 6-2

After students have answered Questions 1–6, have them examine their results as a class to determine the range of values obtained for *ratio of change*. **The value of the ratio can be any real number.**

Have students select one row from their spreadsheet and graph the ordered pair of that row. Ask students to tell what they think the value in Column G represents on the graph. **the vertical distance between the two points divided by the horizontal distance between the two points**

---

## 6-2 Slope of a Line

**Goals**
- Find the slope of a line.
- Identify horizontal and vertical lines.

**Applications**   Business, Science, Transportation

 **Create a spreadsheet like the one shown.**

1. Write ten sets of two ordered pairs. Choose a variety of values including zero, fractions and decimals for both the *x*- and *y*-elements. Include one set where the *x*-elements of both ordered pairs are equal. Include another set where the *y*-elements are equal.
*For 1–2, answers will vary.*

2. Enter your ordered pairs from Question 1 into the spreadsheet so that each set of ordered pairs fills Columns A through D.

3. Format Column E to find the difference of the data in Columns A and C.
*A − C*

4. Format Column F to find the difference of the data in Columns B and D.
*B − D*

5. Format Column G to divide Column F by Column E.
*F ÷ E*

6. Does any data cause a formula error? Describe the cause of the errors.
*division by zero*

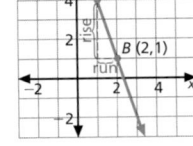

| | A | B | C | D | E | F | G |
|---|---|---|---|---|---|---|---|
| | $x_1$ | $y_1$ | $x_2$ | $y_2$ | change in x | change in y | ratio of change |
| 1 | | | | | | | |
| 2 | | | | | | | |
| 3 | | | | | | | |

### ■ BUILD UNDERSTANDING

Often the meaning of a math term is related to the meaning of the word in everyday life. This is the case with the concept of slope as it refers to the steepness or slant of a line. The **slope** of a segment is the ratio of its change in vertical distance compared to its change in horizontal distance. The variable *m* is usually used to represent slope.

$$m = \frac{rise}{run} = \frac{change\ in\ y\text{-}coordinates}{change\ in\ x\text{-}coordinates}$$

Using a plane, count the units of rise and run between any two points on a line to find its slope. Conversely, given a point on a line and the slope of that line, you can locate other points on the line.

### Example 1

**Find the slope of $\overleftrightarrow{AB}$.**

**Solution**

$$m = \frac{rise}{run} = \frac{down\ 6}{right\ 4} = \frac{-6}{4} = -\frac{3}{2}$$

The slope of $\overleftrightarrow{AB}$ is $-\frac{3}{2}$.

**248**   Chapter 6   **Graphing Functions**

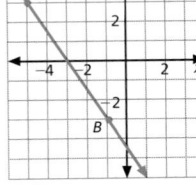

### Check Understanding

Name another point on $\overleftrightarrow{AB}$ that is not shown in the graph for Example 1.

*Answers will vary, but may include (3, −9) or (−7, 6).*

---

## Teaching Tip

From the text of Example 1, students see that from *A* to *B*, they go down 6 and right 4. Ask them to describe how to get from *B* to *A*. **go up 6 and left 4** So students should conclude that a slope of $\frac{-6}{4}$ is equivalent to a slope of $\frac{6}{-4}$, both of which reduce to $-\frac{3}{2}$. Have students start at point *A* and use the slope $\frac{-3}{2}$ to tell the coordinates of another point on the line.

Students should understand that they can begin counting at any point on the line. It is, however, convenient to start at points where the coordinates are both integers.

# Example 2

Graph the line that passes through the point (2, 1) and has a slope of $\frac{5}{4}$.

## Solution

First plot the point (2, 1). Since the slope is $\frac{5}{4}$, the change of rise over run equals a positive ratio.

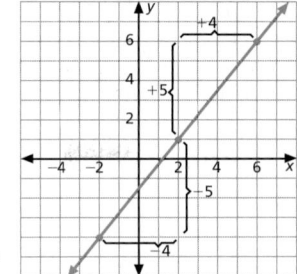

To locate another point, place your pencil at (2, 1). Rise 5 units up and run 4 units right.

To locate a third point on the line, you can rise 5 units and run 4 units again. Or go back to the point (2,1), and rise 5 units down and run 4 units left.

You can also find the slope of a line algebraically by using the following formula.

| **Slope of a Line** | $m = \dfrac{y_2 - y_1}{x_2 - x_1}$, given two points $(x_1, y_1)$ and $(x_2, y_2)$ on a line. |
|---|---|

All points on a horizontal line have equal $y$-coordinates. The numerator of the slope formula simplifies to zero. So a *horizontal line has a slope of 0.* You can describe a horizontal line by the equation $y = b$. The value of $b$ is the value of all $y$-coordinates of points on the horizontal line.

| **Horizontal Line** | A horizontal line containing the point $(a, b)$ is described by the equation $y = b$. |
|---|---|

All points on a vertical line have equal $x$-coordinates. So the denominator of the slope simplifies to zero. Since division by 0 is undefined, the *slope of a vertical line is undefined.* You can describe a vertical line by the equation $x = c$. The value of $c$ is the value of every $x$-coordinate of points on the vertical line.

| **Vertical Line** | A vertical line containing the point $(c, d)$ is described by the equation $x = c$. |
|---|---|

# Example 3

Is the line containing the given points horizontal or vertical? Name the slope.

**a.** $(6, -2)$ and $(-1, -2)$  **b.** $(3, -5)$ and $(3, 0)$  **c.** $\left(0, \frac{1}{2}\right)$ and $\left(\frac{1}{2}, \frac{1}{2}\right)$

## Solution

**a.** The $y$-coordinates are equal, so it is a horizontal line that has a slope of 0.

**b.** The $x$-coordinates are equal, so it is a vertical line that has an undefined slope.

**c.** The $y$-coordinates are equal, so it is a horizontal line that has a slope of 0.

 mathmatters2.com/extra_examples

---

### Supplementary Example 1

Find the slope of $\overleftrightarrow{CD}$ with $C(-4, 0)$ and $D(2, 3)$.

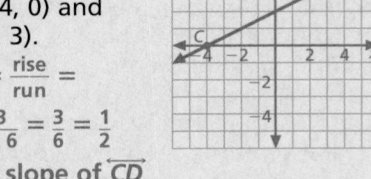

$m = \dfrac{\text{rise}}{\text{run}} =$

$\dfrac{\text{up } 3}{\text{right } 6} = \dfrac{3}{6} = \dfrac{1}{2}$

The slope of $\overleftrightarrow{CD}$ is $\dfrac{1}{2}$.

### Supplementary Example 2

Graph the line that passes through $P(-1, 1)$ and has a slope of $-2$. Express the slope as equivalent fractions.

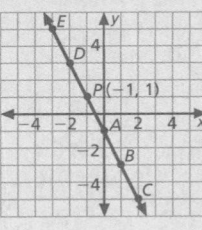

$m = -2 = \dfrac{-2}{1} = \dfrac{2}{-1}$

Begin at $(-1, 1)$ and follow the directions of $\dfrac{-2}{1}$; that is go down 2 and right 1, to arrive at $A$. Continue with these directions to get additional points.
Return to $(-1, 1)$ and follow the directions of $\dfrac{2}{-1}$; that is go up 2 and left 1, to arrive at $D$. Continue with these directions to get additional points.

### Supplementary Example 3

**a.** Find the slope of $\overleftrightarrow{AB}$ with $A(0, -1)$ and $B(2, 2)$.

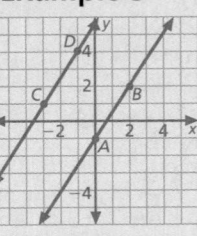

slope of $\overleftrightarrow{AB} = \dfrac{3}{2}$

**b.** Find the slope of $\overleftrightarrow{CD}$ with $C(-3, 1)$ and $D(-1, 4)$.   slope of $\overleftrightarrow{CD} = \dfrac{3}{2}$

**c.** Make an observation from the results.   Lines that have the same slope are parallel.

## QUICK ASSESSMENT

Ask the following questions to determine if students understand the content presented in this lesson.

1. When finding the slope of $\overrightarrow{AB}$ that contains $A(2, -4)$ and $B(-3, 1)$, if you calculate the difference in the $y$-coordinates from $1 - (-4)$, how must you calculate the difference in the $x$-coordinates?   $-3 - 2$

The slope of is $\overrightarrow{PQ}$ is $-\frac{3}{5}$. Starting at any point on $\overrightarrow{PQ}$, to reach another point on $\overrightarrow{PQ}$:

2. you can go down 3 and __right__ 5;

3. or, you can go __up__ 3 and __left__ 5.

## ASSIGNMENT GUIDE

**Basic:** 1–35, 41–44
**Enriched:** 1–44

### Reteaching Worksheet 6-2

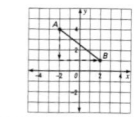
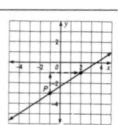

Name _____ Date _____

RETEACHING **6-2**
### SLOPE OF A LINE

The **slope** of a line segment is the ratio of its *rise*, or vertical distance, to its *run*, or horizontal distance.

$$\text{slope} = \frac{\text{rise}}{\text{run}} = \frac{\text{change in } y\text{-coordinates}}{\text{change in } x\text{-coordinates}}$$

**Example 1**

Find the slope of line segment $AB$.

**Solution**

The number of units of vertical change in moving from $A$ to $B$ is 3 units down, or $-3$. Draw a vertical line to show this change. The number of units of horizontal change in moving from $A$ to $B$ is 4 units to the right, or 4. Draw a horizontal line to show this change.

The slope of line segment $AB$ is $\frac{-3}{4}$ or $-\frac{3}{4}$.

You can graph a line, given a point on the line and the slope of the line.

**Example 2**

Graph the line that passes through $P(-1, -3)$ and has a slope of $\frac{2}{3}$.

**Solution**

Graph $P$. Then move up 2 units and to the right 3 units. The ordered pair for the new point on the line is $(2, -1)$. Graph this point and draw a line through both points.

### EXERCISES

Find the slope of each line segment.

Graph the line with the given point and the given slope.

5. $P(2, 5)$; slope $= \frac{1}{3}$

6. $P(-1, 3)$; slope $= \frac{-3}{5}$

1. $\overline{RT}$  $-1$      2. $\overline{PQ}$  $\frac{3}{2}$
3. $\overline{GE}$  $2$      4. $\overline{HK}$  $-\frac{1}{2}$

---

## Example 4

Find the slope of a line that passes through the given points. Graph each line.

**a.** $(0, 0)$ and $(3, 4)$     **b.** $(-2, 3)$ and $(4, 0)$     **c.** $(1, -1)$ and $(-3, -1)$     **d.** $(2, 0)$ and $(2, 5)$

### Solution

Substitute the coordinates in the slope formula.

**a.** $m = \dfrac{4 - 0}{3 - 0} = \dfrac{4}{3}$        $m = \dfrac{y_2 - y_1}{x_2 - x_1}$

**b.** $m = \dfrac{0 - 3}{4 - (-2)} = \dfrac{-3}{6} = -\dfrac{1}{2}$

**c.** $m = \dfrac{-1 - (-1)}{-3 - 1} = \dfrac{0}{-4} = 0$

**d.** $m = \dfrac{5 - 0}{2 - 2} = \dfrac{5}{0}$  Slope is undefined.

To graph each line, plot both points. Use the slope to verify other points on each line.

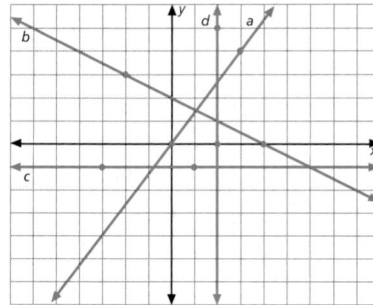

### ■ TRY THESE EXERCISES

Find the slope of each line shown. Note that each graph contains two lines.

**1.**
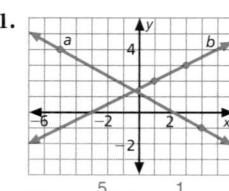
$m_a = -\dfrac{5}{9}$; $m_b = \dfrac{1}{2}$

**2.**
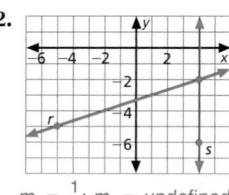
$m_r = \dfrac{1}{3}$; $m_s =$ undefined

**3.**
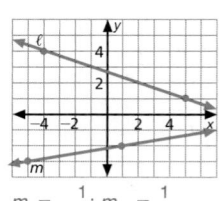
$m_l = -\dfrac{1}{3}$; $m_m = \dfrac{1}{6}$

Graph the line that passes through the given point and has the given slope.
For 4–9, see additional answers.

**4.** $(3, 5)$, $m = -\dfrac{4}{5}$     **5.** $(-2, 1)$, $m = \dfrac{3}{4}$     **6.** $(4, -1)$, $m = 2$

**7.** $(1, -3)$, $m = -3$     **8.** $(3, 9)$, $m$ is undefined     **9.** $(1, -1)$, $m = 0$

Find the slope of the line containing the given points. Name any vertical and horizontal lines.

**10.** $(2, 3)$, $(8, 6)$  $\dfrac{1}{2}$     **11.** $(-4, 3)$, $(-8, 6)$  $-\dfrac{3}{4}$     **12.** $(2, 2)$, $(2, -1)$  undefined vertical line

### ■ PRACTICE EXERCISES • For Extra Practice, see page 603.

Find the slope of each line segment.

**13.** $\overline{AB}$  $\dfrac{2}{5}$      **14.** $\overline{CD}$  $-\dfrac{1}{3}$

**15.** $\overline{EF}$  $\dfrac{2}{5}$      **16.** $\overline{GH}$  $-\dfrac{1}{5}$

**17.** $\overline{IJ}$  $-2$      **18.** $\overline{KL}$  $\dfrac{3}{2}$

**19.** $\overline{MN}$  $\dfrac{2}{3}$      **20.** $\overline{OP}$  $-2$

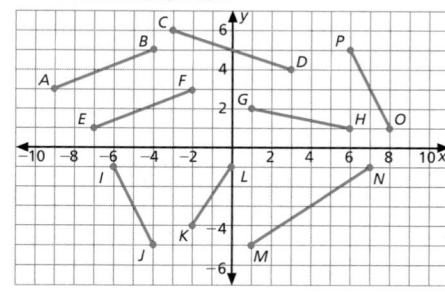

## ADDITIONAL ANSWERS

**4.**

**6.**

**8.**

**21.**

For Exercises 5, 7, 9, 23, 25, 27 and 29, see Selected Answers on page 682.

**Graph a line using the given information.** For 21–29, see additional answers.

**21.** $(1, -3)$, $m = -\dfrac{1}{3}$  **22.** $(-2, -3)$, $m = \dfrac{2}{3}$  **23.** $(5, 0)$, $m$ is undefined

**24.** $(0, 0)$, $m = 0.5$  **25.** $(0, 0)$, $m = -4$  **26.** $\left(\dfrac{1}{2}, \dfrac{1}{2}\right)$, $m$ is undefined

**27.** $(3, -1)$, $m = \dfrac{-5}{3}$  **28.** $(-5, -5)$, $m = 0$  **29.** $(-4, 1)$, $m = \dfrac{1}{4}$

**30.** Find the slope of the line passing through points $(-1, 2)$ and $(3, -2)$.
  −1

**31.** What equation describes a vertical line that passes through $P(4, 0)$?
  $x = 4$

**32.** What equation describes a horizontal line that passes through $P(-4, 2)$?
  $y = 2$

**33. WRITING MATH** Explain how you can tell just from the coordinates of points on a line whether the line is horizontal or vertical.
  The coordinates have the same x- or y-value.

**Find the slope of each line.**

**34.**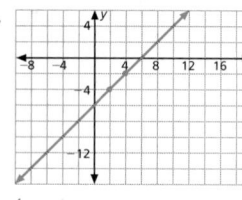

1

**35.**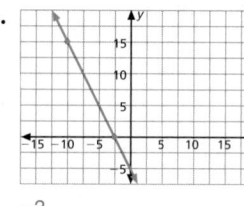

−2

## ■ EXTENDED PRACTICE EXERCISES

**BUSINESS TRAVEL** Kerrie drove from her home to a business meeting and returned in one day. The graph plots her time against her distance from home. The trip is divided into five parts as shown in the graph.

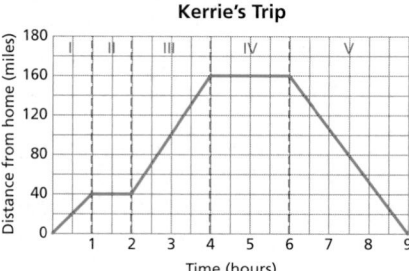

Kerrie's Trip

**36.** What does the slope of each part represent?
  speed

**37.** Find the average speed of section I and section III?  40 mph; 60 mph

**38.** Explain which section of the graph represents Kerrie's time in the meeting.  IV

**39. CRITICAL THINKING** What does the negative slope in section V represent?
  returning home

**40.** Give one possible situation that explains the graph in section II.
  She stopped for some reason, perhaps to eat.

## ■ MIXED REVIEW EXERCISES

**Use the histogram.** (Lesson 1-3)

**41.** How many students read 7–9 books?  12

**42.** How many students read 13–15 books?  10

**43.** How many more students read 0–3 books than read 16–18 books?  6

**44.** How many fewer students read 4–6 books than read 10–12 books?  6

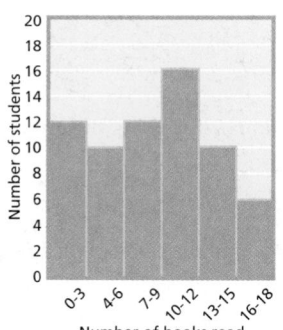

 mathmatters2.com/self_check_quiz

Lesson 6-2 **Slope of a Line**   251

---

## Additional Answers

**22.** 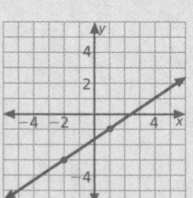  **24.** 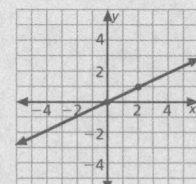  **26.** 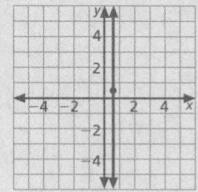  **28.**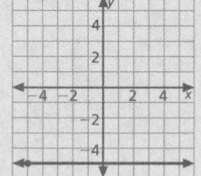

---

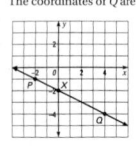

## Vocabulary Review

**Lesson 6-1**
coordinate plane    quadrant
x-axis / y-axis
ordered pair    origin

**Lesson 6-2**
slope    rise / run

## ASSIGNMENT GUIDE

**All students: 1–55**

## Chalkboard Examples

### Lesson 6-1
The vertices of $\triangle ABC$ are $A(1, 6)$, $B(6, 7)$, and $C(5, -2)$. Plot the triangle and find the length of the segment from vertex $B$ that bisects side $AC$.

midpoint $M$
of $\overline{AC}$
$= \left(\dfrac{1 + 5}{2}, \dfrac{6 + (-2)}{2}\right)$
$= (3, 2)$

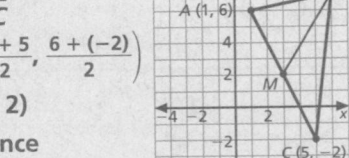

distance between $B(6, 7)$ and $M(3, 2)$
$= \sqrt{(6 - 3)^2 + (7 - 2)^2} = \sqrt{3^2 + 5^2}$
$= \sqrt{9 + 25} = \sqrt{34}$
So, the length of the segment from vertex $B$ that bisects side $AC =$
$\sqrt{34} \approx 5.8$ units.

### Lesson 6-2
Graph the line that intersects the y-axis at $-2$ and has a slope of $-\dfrac{1}{3}$.

$m = -\dfrac{1}{3} = \dfrac{-1}{3} = \dfrac{1}{-3}$

Begin at $(0, -2)$
and follow the
directions of $\dfrac{-1}{3}$
(down 1, right 3) to
get some points.
For additional
points, return to
$(0, -2)$ and follow the directions
of $\dfrac{1}{-3}$ (up 1, left 3).

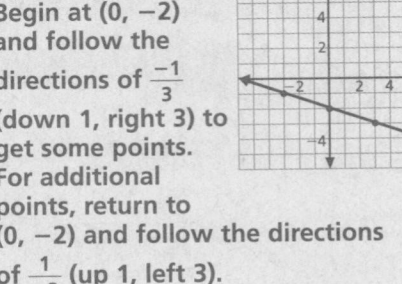

---

## PRACTICE ◼ LESSON 6-1

**Find the distance between the points. Round to the nearest tenth.**

1. $C(-5, -6)$, $D(7, -1)$  13
2. $T(2, 9)$, $W(15, 1)$  15.3
3. $E(-4, 0)$, $F(12, -3)$  16.3
4. $A(-2, 8)$, $B(5, -6)$  15.7
5. $X(10, 3)$, $Y(1, -9)$  15
6. $G\left(-\dfrac{1}{2}, \dfrac{3}{4}\right)$, $H(6, -8)$  10.9

**7–12.** Find the midpoints of the segments in Exercises 1–6.
For 7–12, see additional answers.

**Use the graph to calculate the length of each segment.**

13. $\overline{XY}$  11.3
14. $\overline{YZ}$  8
15. $\overline{XZ}$  8
16. What kind of a triangle is $\triangle XYZ$?  isosceles right triangle

**17–19.** Find the coordinate of the midpoint of the segments in Exercises 13–15.    17. $(2, 0)$  18. $(2, -4)$  19. $(-2, 0)$

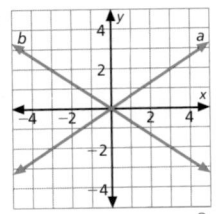

**Use the given endpoints of each circle's diameter. Find each circle's center and the lengths of its diameter and radius.**
For 20–25, see additional answers.
20. $(-5, 2)$, $(7, 2)$
21. $(3, 12)$, $(3, -2)$
22. $(-10, 4)$, $(3, -9)$
23. $(4, 0)$, $(-4, 4)$
24. $(4, 9)$, $(-6, 9)$
25. $(5, -3)$, $(5, 6)$

## PRACTICE ◼ LESSON 6-2

**Find the slope of each line shown. Note that each graph contains two lines.**

26.
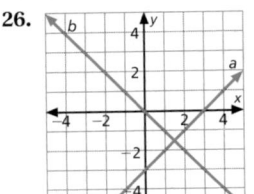

27.
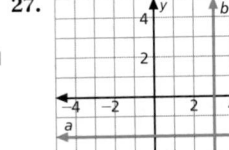
$m_a = 1$
$m_b = -1$

28.
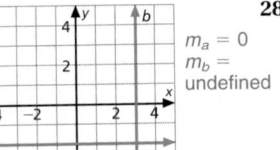
$m_a = 0$
$m_b =$ undefined

$m_a = \dfrac{2}{3}$
$m_b = -\dfrac{2}{3}$

**Graph a line using the given information.**  For 29–34, see additional answers.
29. $(1, 3)$, $m = \dfrac{3}{4}$
30. $(0, 2)$, $m = -2$
31. $(3, 0)$, $m = -\dfrac{1}{3}$
32. $(-1, 2)$, $m = -3$
33. $(1, 2)$, $m$ is undefined
34. $(-2, -2)$, $m = 0$

35. Find the slope of the line passing through points $(-2, 4)$ and $(5, 10)$.  $\dfrac{6}{7}$
36. What equation describes a vertical line that passes through $P(2, 5)$?  $x = 2$
37. What equation describes a horizontal line that passes through $P(-3, 4)$?  $y = 4$

---

## ADDITIONAL ANSWERS

7. $\left(1, -3\dfrac{1}{2}\right)$
8. $\left(8\dfrac{1}{2}, 5\right)$
9. $\left(4, -1\dfrac{1}{2}\right)$
10. $\left(1\dfrac{1}{2}, 1\right)$
11. $\left(5\dfrac{1}{2}, -3\right)$
12. $\left(2\dfrac{3}{4}, -3\dfrac{5}{8}\right)$
20. $C(1, 2)$; $d = 12$; $r = 6$

21. $C(3, 5)$; $d = 14$, $r = 7$
22. $C\left(-3\dfrac{1}{2}, -2\dfrac{1}{2}\right)$; $d \approx 18.4$; $r \approx 9.2$
23. $C(0, 2)$; $d \approx 8.9$; $r \approx 4.5$
24. $C(-1, 9)$; $d = 10$; $r = 5$
25. $C\left(5, 1\dfrac{1}{2}\right)$; $d = 9$; $r = 4\dfrac{1}{2}$

29.
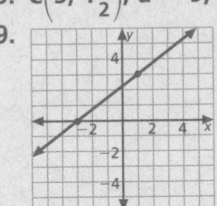

30.
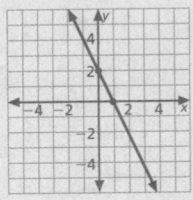

**Use the given endpoints of each circle's diameter. Find each circle's center and the length of its diameter and radius.** (Lesson 6-1) For 38–43, see additional answers.

**38.** $(0, 0)$, $(-8, 8)$

**39.** $\left(\frac{1}{2}, -\frac{2}{3}\right)$, $(0, 0)$

**40.** $(4.5, -6)$, $(-1, 0.5)$

**41.** $(-2, -7)$, $(-1, 4)$

**42.** $(-6, 3)$, $(14, 3)$

**43.** $(-8, 3)$, $(-7, 5)$

**Find the distance between the points. Round to the nearest tenth.** (Lesson 6-1)

**44.** $A(0, -4)$, $B(2, 8)$ 12.2

**45.** $C(5, 10)$, $D(-3, -7)$ 18.8

**46.** $E(0, -7)$, $F(-1, -1)$ 6.1

**47.** $G(0, -4)$, $H(2, -2)$ 2.8

**48.** $I(2, 1)$, $J(7, 9)$ 9.4

**49.** $K\left(\frac{4}{3}, \frac{6}{5}\right)$, $L(-9, 15)$ 17.2

**Graph a line using the given information.** (Lesson 6-2)
For 50–55, see additional answers.

**50.** $(-1, 2)$, $m = -1$

**51.** $(-2, -3)$, $m = \frac{2}{5}$

**52.** $(0, -4)$, $m = -\frac{1}{3}$

**53.** $(1, 0)$, $m = -2$

**54.** $(2, 2)$, $m = \frac{1}{3}$

**55.** $(4, -3)$, $m = 0$

## MathWorks Career – Music Store Owner
Workplace Knowhow

Owners of specialty stores purchase merchandise, manage employees, prepare and evaluate financial documents and determine the layout of the store. The layout of the merchandise can affect the store's success. The owner of a music store needs to determine the best layout for the various sections of music on the showroom floor. The figure shows the general layout for the showroom, but more specific information is needed to determine exactly where the center of each section should be located. The center of the store is at (0 ft, 0 ft). The center of the rock music section is at (0 ft, −45 ft). The center of the classical music section should be 30 ft from the back wall of the store, along the $y$-axis. The central point in the New Age section is at (−37.5 ft, 0 ft).

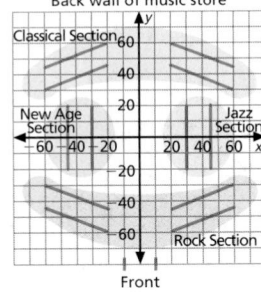

1. What is the distance from the Rock section center to the Classical section center? 95 ft

2. The centers of the New Age and Jazz sections will be on the $x$-axis. The centers of both sections are equidistant from the center of the Rock section, with the Jazz and New Age on opposite sides of the store. Give the coordinates of the center of the Jazz section. (37.5 ft, 0 ft)

3. The slanted lines located in the Classical and Rock sections represent shelves. What is the slope of the shelves on the left-hand side of the Classical section? How does this slope compare to the slope of the shelves on the right-hand side of the Rock section? $\frac{3}{8}$, equal

4. What is the slope of the lines representing the shelves in the New Age and Jazz sections? undefined

Math Online mathmatters2.com/mathworks

Chapter 6 **Review and Practice Your Skills** 253

A music store will generally offer music to the public in a variety of media: compact disc (CD), audio tape, video tape, sheet music, and, for collectors of memorabilia, old phonograph records. In addition, a music store will often sell related equipment, such as CD players, and even some musical instruments and books related to the field of music.

Students should answer Questions 1–4 to better understand the role of coordinate geometry in the process of planning the layout of a music store.

Students may be interested in researching the history of sound recording, which was first accomplished by Thomas Edison in 1876.

Music store owners, keeping pace with rapidly changing innovations, offer increasingly greater varieties of items.

Students who are interested in learning more about this career choice can go to mathmatters2.com/mathworks. School Guidance Counselors are another resource for information about training requirements and appropriate schools.

**50.**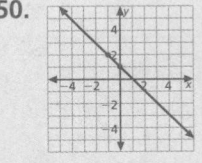

**51.**

**52.**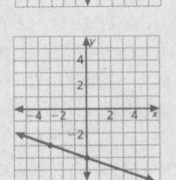

**53.**

**54.**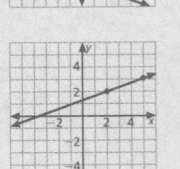

**55.**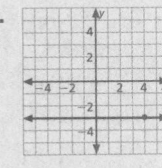

**31.**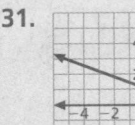

**32.**

**33.**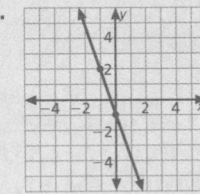

**34.**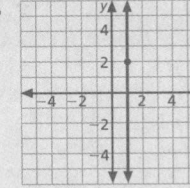

**38.** $C(-4, 4)$; $d \approx 11.3$; $r \approx 5.7$

**39.** $C\left(\frac{1}{4}, -\frac{1}{3}\right)$; $d = \frac{5}{6}$; $r = \frac{5}{12}$

**40.** $C(1.75, -2.75)$; $d \approx 8.5$; $r \approx 4.3$

**41.** $C\left(-1\frac{1}{2}, -1\frac{1}{2}\right)$; $d \approx 11.0$; $r \approx 5.5$

**42.** $C(4, 3)$; $d = 20$; $r = 10$

**43.** $C\left(-7\frac{1}{2}, 4\right)$; $d \approx 2.2$; $r \approx 1.1$

### Vocabulary

*y*-intercept
slope-intercept form of a line
point-slope form of a line

### Tools/Materials Needed

graph paper

### Lesson Resources

Warm-up Transparency 24
Transparency TK-9–12, RF-34
Reteaching 6-3
Extra Practice 6-3
Enrichment 6-3
Technology Activity 6-3 and 6-6

## Getting Started

### 5-MINUTE WARM-UP

**Rewrite each equation with *y* alone on one side.**
1. $3x - y = 14$    $y = 3x - 14$
2. $2x + y = -10$    $y = -2x - 10$
3. $-x - y = -9$    $y = -x + 9$
4. $4x + 3y = 6$    $y = -\frac{4}{3}x + 2$

### Introduction to Lesson 6-3

After students have answered Questions 1 and 2, have them trace one of the graphs and slide the tracing any distance parallel to the original graph. Ask students to compare the slopes of the original line and the parallel tracing as well as the points where these graphs cross the *y*-axis. The slopes of the original line and the parallel tracing are the same but the places at which they cross the *y*-axis are different.

---

# 6-3 Write and Graph Linear Equations

**Goals**
- Write equations of lines using slope, intercepts and points.
- Graph a line given the equation.

**Applications**    Finance, Sports, Transportation, Recreation

**Work with a partner.**

1. Study the graphs at the right and their corresponding equations.

2. Find the slope of each line.  $\frac{1}{2}, -3, -\frac{3}{2}, 1$

3. Find the point where each line crosses the *y*-axis.  2, −1, 1, 0

4. Compare these with the equations for the lines. What do you notice?
   The slope is the number before the *x*, and the *y*-intercept is the last number.

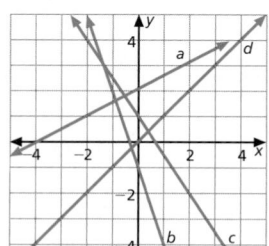

a. $y = \frac{1}{2}x + 2$

b. $y = -3x - 1$

c. $y = -\frac{3}{2}x + 1$

d. $y = x$

### ◼ BUILD UNDERSTANDING

A **linear equation** is an equation whose graph is a straight line. If the line intersects the *y*-axis, the point of intersection is the **y-intercept**.

When the equation of a line is written in the form $y = mx + b$, you can quickly determine the slope and *y*-intercept of a line. Then you can use this information to graph the line.

| Slope-Intercept Form | $y = mx + b$ |
|---|---|
| | where *m* is the slope and *b* is the *y*-intercept. |

### Example 1

**Name the slope and *y*-intercept for the line with the given equation. Graph each line on a coordinate plane.**

a. $y = 3x - 2$            b. $3x + 2y = 6$

**Solution**

Rewrite the equation so that the operation sign is addition.

$$y = 3x + (-2)$$

a. The slope is the coefficient of the *x*-term. The *y*-intercept is the constant. So the slope is 3 and the *y*-intercept is −2.

To graph the line, plot the point (0, −2). Then use the slope as $\frac{3}{1}$ to plot two or three additional points.

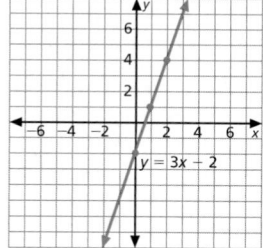

---

## Teaching Tip

When students are trying to identify the slope and *y*-intercept of a line from its equation, be sure they understand that they must first isolate the *y*-term and get it with a coefficient of 1. Then when the equation is in slope-intercept form, $y = mx + b$, the coefficient of the *x*-term is the slope (the *x* is not to be included) and the entire constant term (including sign) is the *y*-intercept.

For example, solving the equation $3y + 2x = -6$ for *y* yields $y = -\frac{2}{3}x - 2$.

So, the slope of this line is $-\frac{2}{3}$ (not $-\frac{2}{3}x$, a common error) and the

*y*-intercept is −2 (not 2, a common error). The coordinates of the *y*-intercept are (0, −2).

**b.** Rewrite the equation in slope-intercept form. Solve for $y$.

$$3x + 2y = 6$$

$$3x - 3x + 2y = -3x + 6 \qquad \text{Subtract } 3x \text{ from both sides.}$$
$$2y = -3x + 6$$
$$\frac{2y}{2} = \frac{-3x + 6}{2} \qquad \text{Divide each term by 2.}$$
$$y = -\frac{3}{2}x + 3$$

The slope is $-\frac{3}{2}$ and the $y$-intercept is 3.

To graph the line, plot the point $(0, 3)$. Then use the slope, $-\frac{3}{2}$, to plot two or three additional points.

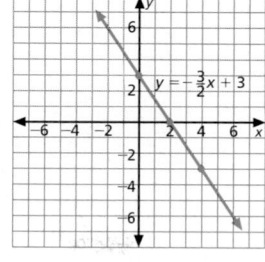

To write the equation of a line when given two points, first calculate the slope. To find the value of $b$, substitute the slope and the coordinates of one point into $y = mx + b$. Then use slope-intercept form to write the equation of the line.

**Problem Solving Tip**

Since the $x$-coordinate for every point on the $y$-axis is 0, the coordinates of the $y$-intercept are $(0, b)$.

### Example 2

**Write an equation of a line using the information given.**

**a.** $(7, 1)$, $y$-intercept is $-1$     **b.** $m = 3$, point on line is $(4, -1)$

**Solution**

**a.** The $y$-intercept coordinates are $(0, -1)$. Use ordered pairs to calculate the slope.

$$m = \frac{1 - (-1)}{7 - 0} = \frac{2}{7} \qquad \text{Use slope formula.}$$

Substitute $m = \frac{2}{7}$ and $b = -1$. The equation of the line is $y = \frac{2}{7}x - 1$.

**b.** To find the value of $b$, use the slope and the point given in $y = mx + b$

$$y = mx + b \qquad \text{Use slope-intercept form.}$$
$$-1 = 3(4) + b \qquad m = 3, x = 4, y = -1$$
$$-1 - 12 = b$$
$$-13 = b$$

Substitute $m = 3$ and $b = -13$. The equation of the line is $y = 3x - 13$.

To write the equation for a line given the graph of the line, use the graph to get information that will help you find the slope and $y$-intercept.

### Example 3

**Use the graph to write the equation of lines $a$ and $b$.**

**Solution**

**a.** Choose two points on the line, and count rise units and run units. $m = \frac{1}{2}$. The line crosses the $y$-axis at $(0, 3)$. The equation is $y = \frac{1}{2}x + 3$.

**b.** The rise is $-4$ units and the run is 3 units, so $m = -\frac{4}{3}$. The line crosses the $y$-axis at $(0, 0)$. The equation is $y = -\frac{4}{3}x$.

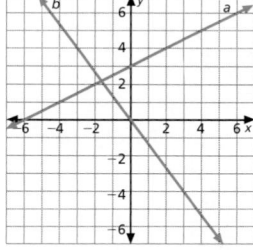

 **Math Online** mathmatters2.com/extra_examples          Lesson 6-3 **Write and Graph Linear Equations**  | **255**

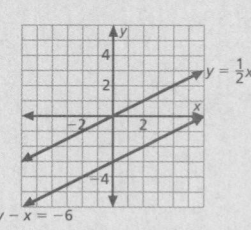
## Extend the Lesson

**CONNECTING TO PRIOR KNOWLEDGE** Have students graph the following four lines on the same set of coordinate axes: $y = x + 3$, $y = x - 5$, $x = -2$, $x = 4$. Then ask students to determine if the figure formed by the lines is a parallelogram. Discuss different methods of approach. **The figure is a parallelogram. Method 1: Use slopes to show both pairs of opposite sides are parallel. Method 2: Use slope and distance formula to show that one pair of opposite sides is both parallel and congruent. Method 3: Use the midpoint formula to show that the diagonals bisect each other.**

### QUICK ASSESSMENT

Ask the following questions to determine if students understand the content presented in this lesson.

1. Is 3 the slope of the line whose equation is $2y = 3x + 4$? Explain. No; in $y = mx + b$ form, the equation is $y = \frac{3}{2}x + 2$. So, the slope of the line is $\frac{3}{2}$.

2. If you know the slope of a line, what other information do you need to write an equation of the line? the $y$-intercept or the coordinates of a point on the line

3. If you know the coordinates of a point on a line, what other information do you need to write an equation of the line? the slope or the coordinates of another point on the line

### ASSIGNMENT GUIDE

Basic: 1–37, 41–52
Enriched: 1–52

**Reteaching Worksheet 6-3**

Name _____  Date _____

RETEACHING  6-3

**WRITE AND GRAPH LINEAR EQUATIONS**

When an equation is written in the form $y = mx + b$, the slope of the line is $m$ and the $y$-intercept (the $y$-coordinate where the line crosses the $y$-axis) is $b$. This form is called the **slope–intercept form** of an equation of a line.

Example

Graph $2x + 3y = 9$.

**Solution**

Rewrite the equation in slope–intercept form.
$3y = -2x + 9$
$y = \frac{-2}{3}x + 3$  Divide both sides of the equation by 3.

The slope of the line is $\frac{-2}{3}$; the $y$-intercept is 3.

To graph the equation, graph the $y$-intercept. Use the slope to find another point on the line. From $(0, 3)$, move 2 units down and 3 units to the right. Connect the two points with a line.

**EXERCISES**

Graph each line.

1. $y = -2x + 1$
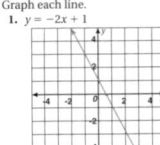

2. $y = \frac{3}{4}x - 2$
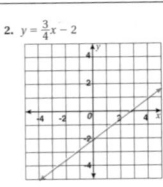

3. $3x + 2y = -4$
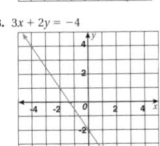

4. $x + y = -3$
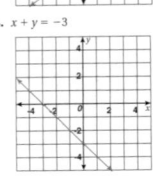

---

You can write the equation of a line using point-slope form if you know the slope and the coordinates of any point on the line. You can also use this form if you know any two points on the line.

| Point-Slope Form | $y - y_1 = m(x - x_1)$ where $m$ is the slope and $(x_1, y_1)$ is a point on the line. |
|---|---|

## Example 4

**Write the equation of the line using the given information.**

a. slope is $\frac{4}{5}$, point on line is $(3, 0)$

b. points on line are $(-1, 5)$ and $(1, -3)$

**Solution**

a. Use $m = \frac{4}{5}$, $x_1 = 3$ and $y_1 = 0$.
$y - y_1 = m(x - x_1)$
$y - 0 = \frac{4}{5}(x - 3)$
$y = \frac{4}{5}x - \frac{12}{5}$

b. Find the slope.
$m = \frac{-3 - 5}{1 - (-1)} = -\frac{8}{2} = -4$
Select either point to use. Substitute.

Use $m = -4$, $x_1 = 1$ and $y_1 = -3$.
$y - y_1 = m(x - x_1)$
$y - (-3) = -4(x - 1)$
$y + 3 = -4x + 4$
$y + 3 - 3 = -4x + 4 - 3$
$y = -4x + 1$

### TRY THESE EXERCISES

**Use the graph to write an equation for each line $a$–$f$.**

1. line $d$  $y = \frac{1}{2}x - 2$
2. line $e$  $x = -5$
3. line $f$  $y = -\frac{1}{3}x + 5$
4. line $a$  $y = 3$
5. line $b$  $y = -x$
6. line $c$  $y = 2x - 6$

7. Graph $y = -2x + 5$ using the slope and $y$-intercept.
See additional answers.

**Write the equation of each line using the given information.**

8. $m = 3$, $(1, 5)$  $y = 3x + 2$
9. $(3, -6)$, $(1, -4)$  $y = -x - 3$
10. $m = 0$, $(0, 0)$  $y = 0$

### PRACTICE EXERCISES  •  For Extra Practice, see page 604.

**Identify the slope and $y$-intercept for each line. Graph each line.**
For 11–14, see additional answers.

11. $-5x + 4y = -8$  $\frac{5}{4}$; $-2$
12. $y = -x + 1$  $-1$; $1$
13. $y = 5x + 3$  $5$; $3$
14. $y = -8$  $0$; $-8$

15. **WRITING MATH** Explain how to use the slope and the $y$-intercept of a line to graph the line. Explain what to do if the line is in the form $ax + by = c$.
See additional answers.

### ADDITIONAL ANSWERS

7.
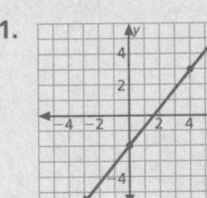

11.
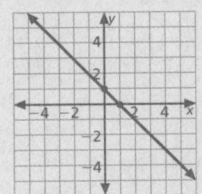

12.
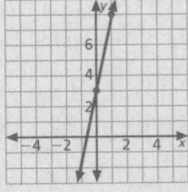

13.
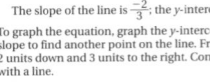

**Write the equation of each line using the given information.**

16. $m = -4$, $(6, 2)$  $y = -4x + 26$ 
17. $(9, 3)$, $(-2, -2)$  $y = \frac{5}{11}x - \frac{12}{11}$ 
18. $(1, 1)$, $b = 5$  $y = -4x + 5$

19. $(9, 5)$, $(5, 6)$  $y = -\frac{1}{4}x + \frac{29}{4}$ 
20. $m = -\frac{5}{2}$, $(3, 0)$  $y = -\frac{5}{2}x + \frac{15}{2}$ 
21. $m$ is undefined, $(0, 0)$  $x = 0$

22. $m = 4$, $(-1, 2)$  $y = 4x + 6$ 
23. $m = -1$, $(3, -4)$  $y = -x - 1$ 
24. $(-1, 1)$, $(1, 5)$  $y = 2x + 3$

25. $(4, 2)$, $(-1, 7)$  $y = -x + 6$ 
26. $m = -\frac{1}{3}$, $(1, 5)$  $y = -\frac{1}{3}x + \frac{16}{3}$ 
27. $m = 0$, $(3, -4)$  $y = -4$

28. $(2, 3)$, $(1, 1)$  $y = 2x - 1$ 
29. $(3, -6)$, $(1, -4)$  $y = -x - 3$ 
30. $(-1, 0)$, $b = 3$  $y = 3x + 3$

31. $m = \frac{1}{2}$, $(-2, -7)$  $y = \frac{1}{2}x - 6$ 
32. $(0, -1)$, $(1, 2)$  $y = 3x - 1$ 
33. $m = \frac{5}{2}$, $(0, -3)$  $y = \frac{5}{2}x - 3$

34. **RETAIL** Bulk dog food sells for \$1.50/lb. Write an equation to represent the cost in terms of the number of pounds purchased. Find the cost of 3.5 lb of food. Explain the meaning of slope for this problem.
$y = 1.50x$; \$5.25; cost per pound

**SCIENCE** An approximate formula for a barometric reading is $p = 760 - 0.09h$, where $p$ is measured in millimeters and $h$ is the altitude and is measured in meters. The formula is for altitudes less than 500 m.

35. What does the slope represent? What is implied by the slope being negative? The change in barometric pressure. Pressure decreases as altitude increases.

36. Explain the meaning of slope for this problem. The barometric reading for 0 m is 760 mm.

37. If there is a change of altitude from 100 m to 250 m, what is the change in the barometric reading? $-13.5$ mm

■ **EXTENDED PRACTICE EXERCISES**

38. Write the equation of a line that passes through all points where the $x$-coordinate equals the $y$-coordinate. $y = x$

39. **CRITICAL THINKING** A linear equation is in *standard form* when it is written as $Ax + By = C$ where $A$, $B$ and $C$ are real numbers and $A$ and $B$ are not both zero. Use the standard form and solve for $y$. Make a general statement that summarizes how to find the slope and $y$-intercept for an equation in the form $Ax + By = C$. $y = -\frac{A}{B}x + \frac{C}{B}$; $m = -\frac{A}{B}$; $y$-int $= \frac{C}{B}$

40. **CHAPTER INVESTIGATION** Find the data on your company's operating costs for each quarter of the year. Plot four ordered pairs, (Quarter, Operating cost). Draw a line connecting each quarter to represent the increase, decrease or steady pace of the operating costs. Describe the operating costs by quarters and by the entire year. Answers will vary.

■ **MIXED REVIEW EXERCISES**

**Graph the solution of each inequality on a number line.** (Lesson 3-6)
For 41–48, see additional answers.
41. $a \le -4$ 
42. $b > -2$ 
43. $c < 3$ 
44. $d \le 2$

45. $e > 4$ 
46. $f \ge 1$ 
47. $g \le -1$ 
48. $h > -5$

**Find the measure of the complement and the supplement of each angle.** (Lesson 5-2)

49. $m\angle 18°$ 72°, 162° 
50. $m\angle 71°$ 19°, 109° 
51. $m\angle 83°$ 7°, 97° 
52. $m\angle 50°$ 40°, 130°

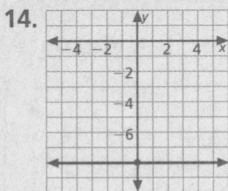

---

Name _____ Date _____

EXTRA PRACTICE  **6-3**
**WRITE AND GRAPH LINEAR EQUATIONS**

■ **EXERCISES**

Use the graph to write an equation for each line *a–f*.
1. line $a$  $y = \frac{1}{4}x + 6$
2. line $b$  $y = -3$
3. line $c$  $y = \frac{2}{3}x - 4$
4. line $d$  $x = 5$
5. line $e$  $y = -2x + 2$
6. line $f$  $y = x + 1$

Identify the slope and $y$-intercept for each line. Graph each line on your own paper.
7. $x + y = 2$  $-1, 2$ 
8. $2x - y = 4$  $2; -4$
9. $4x + 2y = 1$  $-2; \frac{1}{2}$ 
10. $-x + 3y = 6$  $\frac{1}{3}; 2$
11. $-4x + y = 5$  $4; 5$ 
12. $-2x - 3y = 9$  $-\frac{2}{3}; -3$
13. $5x + 2y = 4$  $-\frac{5}{2}; 2$ 
14. $-8x - 2y = 0$  $-4; 0$

Write the equation of each line using the given information.
15. $m = -2$, $(3, -7)$  $y = -2x - 1$ 
16. $m = \frac{1}{4}$, $(4, 3)$  $y = \frac{1}{4}x + 2$
17. $(-1, 0)$, $b = 3$  $y = 3x + 3$ 
18. $m = 0$, $(2, -1)$  $y = -1$
19. $m = -\frac{2}{3}$, $(6, -3)$  $y = -\frac{2}{3}x + 1$ 
20. $m$ is undefined, $(3, 2)$  $x = 3$
21. $(0, 4)$, $(4, 7)$  $y = \frac{3}{4}x + 4$ 
22. $\left(\frac{1}{2}, 3\right)$, $\left(1, \frac{11}{2}\right)$  $y = 5x + \frac{1}{2}$

---

Name _____ Date _____

ENRICHMENT  **6-3**
**CHESS MOVES**

In chess, some of the pieces can move any distance along a line. The rook can move vertically and horizontally, the bishop can move diagonally, and the queen can move vertically, horizontally or diagonally.

**Example**

The 64 positions on a chess board can be represented by 64 ordered pairs, as shown at the right. The bishop is on the square that has coordinates (3, 4). Along which lines can the bishop move?

**Solution**

The bishop can move diagonally. To find the equations for the lines, sketch the lines and examine their slopes and $y$-intercepts. The bishop can move along these lines.
$y = -x + 7$
$y = x + 1$

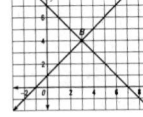

■ **EXERCISES**

Write the equations for all the lines along which each piece can move from its given position.
1. rook at $(4, 2)$  $x = 4$ ; $y = 2$ 
2. rook at $(3, 1)$  $x = 3$ ; $y = 1$
3. bishop at $(5, 3)$  $y = x - 2$ ; $y = -x + 8$ 
4. bishop at $(7, 2)$  $y = x - 5$ ; $y = -x + 9$
5. queen at $(4, 5)$  $x = 4$ ; $y = 5$ ; $y = x + 1$ ; $y = -x + 9$ 
6. queen at $(2, 8)$  $x = 2$ ; $y = 8$ ; $y = x + 6$ ; $y = -x + 10$

---

## ADDITIONAL ANSWERS

14.

41. (number line: $-6$ $-5$ $-4$ $-3$)
42. (number line: $-3$ $-2$ $-1$ $0$)
43. (number line: $5$ $4$ $3$ $2$)
44. (number line: $0$ $1$ $2$ $3$)
45. (number line: $3$ $4$ $5$ $6$)
46. (number line: $0$ $1$ $2$ $3$)
47. (number line: $-3$ $-2$ $-1$ $0$)
48. (number line: $-6$ $-5$ $-4$ $-3$)

15. First, plot the $y$-intercept. Then use the slope to locate one or more other points. Next draw the line. If $ax + by = c$ is the form, first solve for $y$.

## Lesson Planning

### NCTM Standards/Strands
- Algebra
- Representation
- Connections

### Vocabulary

open half-plane
closed half-plane
boundary line
graph of a linear inequality
graphic solution of a linear
  inequality

### Tools/Materials Needed

graph paper

### Lesson Resources

Warm-up Transparency 24
Transparency TK-9–13, RF-35
Reteaching 6-4
Extra Practice 6-4
Enrichment 6-4

## Getting Started

### 5-MINUTE WARM-UP

Rewrite each equation in
slope-intercept form.
1. $-y = 2x + 8$   $y = -2x - 8$
2. $2x - y = -3$   $y = 2x + 3$
3. $3y + 4x = 6$   $y = -\frac{4}{3}x + 2$
4. $4 - y = 3x$   $y = -3x + 4$

### Introduction to Lesson 6-4

When discussing Question 1, emphasize that the equation of a line tells the relationship between the coordinates of every point on that line. So, for example, the point $(-1000, -1000)$ must be on the line whose equation is $y = x$ since its coordinates exhibit the relationship specified by the equation. However, the point $(2, -2)$ is not on the line $y = x$ since its coordinates do not satisfy the specified relationship.

---

# 6-4 Write and Graph Linear Inequalities

**Goals**
- Write linear inequalities in two variables.
- Graph linear inequalities in two variables on the coordinate plane.

**Applications**   Business, Market research, Inventory

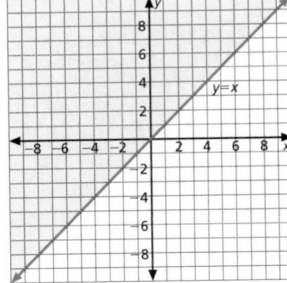

Use the graph to answer Questions 1–3.

1. What is the relationship between the $x$- and $y$-coordinate for each point on the line? Write the equation of the line.
   The $x$-coordinate is equal to the $y$-coordinate. $y = x$
2. What is the relationship between the $x$-coordinate and the $y$-coordinate for each point in the blue region?
   The $y$-coordinate is greater than the $x$-coordinate.
3. What is the relationship between the $x$-coordinate and the $y$-coordinate for each point in the unshaded region?
   The $y$-coordinate is less than the $x$-coordinate.

## ◣ BUILD UNDERSTANDING

The graphed line above separates the coordinate plane into two regions. The region on either side of a line is called an **open half-plane**. The line separating the half-planes forms the **boundary**, or edge, of each half-plane.

When the equal symbol in a linear equation is replaced with an inequality symbol $(>, <, \geq, \leq, \neq)$ the result is a **linear inequality**. Any ordered pair of real numbers that makes an inequality true is a **solution of the inequality**. The graph of all the solutions is the **graph of an inequality** and shows the boundary, with either a solid line or dashed line, along with a shaded region.

To determine if an ordered pair is a solution, substitute its values into the linear inequality. When the simplified inequality is true, the ordered pair is a solution and thus part of the shaded region. When the simplified inequality is false, the ordered pair is not part of the solution and thus not part of the shaded region.

### Example 1

Tell whether the ordered pair is a solution of the inequality.

   **a.** $(2, 6); y \geq 2x - 1$          **b.** $(-2, 4); y < 2x - 1$

**Solution**

**a.** Substitute 2 for $x$ and 6 for $y$ in the inequality.

$$y \geq 2x - 1$$
$$6 \overset{?}{\geq} 2(2) - 1$$
$$6 \geq 3$$

Since the inequality is true, the ordered pair $(2, 6)$ is a solution of $y \geq 2x - 1$.

**b.** Substitute $-2$ for $x$ and 4 for $y$ in the inequality.

$$y < 2x - 1$$
$$4 \overset{?}{<} 2(-2) - 1$$
$$4 < -5$$

Since the inequality is false, the ordered pair $(-2, 4)$ is not a solution of $y < 2x - 1$.

## Teaching Tip

**CONNECTING TO PRIOR KNOWLEDGE** To make sure students understand the meaning of *above* and *below* with respect to a line on a graph, first emphasize that a graph is read from left to right. Then have students consider a horizontal line, for which *above* and *below* are very clear. Next have students look at a vertical line, for which *left* and *right* is a more appropriate description.

Then direct attention to the graph shown in the text (Build Understanding) with the boundary line $y = 2x - 1$. For this line, ask students whether they prefer to think of *above* and *below* or *left* and *right*.

The graph at the right shows the solution of $y \geq 2x - 1$. The solution includes the blue shaded half-plane and the line $y = 2x - 1$. Whether the line is included in the solution depends on the inequality symbol. A solution that includes the line is called a **closed half-plane**.

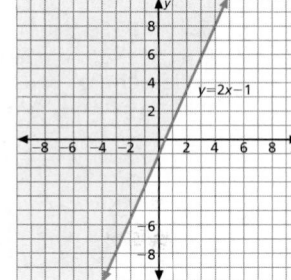

The symbols $>$ and $<$ mean the boundary is not part of the solution and the line is graphed as a dashed line. The symbols $\geq$ and $\leq$, mean the boundary is part of the solution and the line is graphed as a solid line.

To graph an inequality with two variables, first graph the equation related to the inequality. Determine if the line is graphed as a solid or dashed rule. Use a *test point* to determine which region is shaded.

A **test point** is a point that does not lie on the boundary, but rather above or below it. Substitute the coordinates of the ordered pair into the inequality. If the simplified inequality is true, shade the half-plane where the test point lies. If the simplified inequality is false, shade the other half-plane. If $(0, 0)$ is not on the boundary, use it as a test point.

## Example 2

Graph $2x + y \leq -4$.

## Solution

Graph the equation $2x + y = -4$ as the boundary.

Rewrite the equation in slope-intercept form.

$$2x + y = -4$$
$$2x - 2x + y = -2x + (-4)$$
$$y = -2x + (-4)$$

The slope is $-2$ and the $y$-intercept is $-4$.

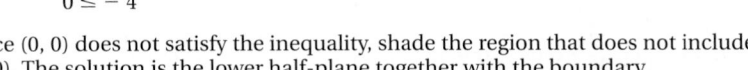

Since the inequality symbol includes "equal to," use a solid line. Then choose and test a point: $(0, 0)$.

$$2x + y \leq -4$$
$$2(0) + 0 \overset{?}{\leq} -4 \quad \text{Use } x = 0 \text{ and } y = 0.$$
$$0 \leq -4$$

Since $(0, 0)$ does not satisfy the inequality, shade the region that does not include $(0, 0)$. The solution is the lower half-plane together with the boundary.

The statements in the box below summarize the shading of open and closed half-planes.

| Forms of Inequalities | Shade the region above a dashed line if $y > mx + b$. |
| | Shade the region above a solid line if $y \geq mx + b$. |
| | Shade the region below a dashed line if $y < mx + b$. |
| | Shade the region below a solid line if $y \leq mx + b$. |

 **Math Online** mathmatters2.com/extra_examples

### Supplementary Example 1
Tell whether the coordinates of the origin satisfy each inequality.
**a.** $2x - 3y < 0$    **b.** $4y - x \geq -6$
Substitute $(0, 0)$ into each inequality.

$$2x - 3y < 0 \qquad 4y - x \geq -6$$
$$2(0) - 3(0) \overset{?}{<} 0 \qquad 4(0) - 0 \overset{?}{\geq} -6$$
$$0 < 0 \text{ false} \qquad 0 \geq -6 \text{ true}$$

So, $(0, 0)$ is not a solution of $2x - 3y < 0$, but $(0, 0)$ is a solution of $4y - x \geq -6$.

### Supplementary Example 2
Rectangle *ABCD* has a perimeter of at least 30 cm.
**a.** Write a linear inequality that represents the situation.
Let $x$ = the length of the rectangle and $y$ = the width of the rectangle. perimeter $\geq 30$
$$2x + 2y \geq 30$$
**b.** Graph the solution of that inequality.
Using a solid line, graph the boundary line $2x + 2y = 30$. Use $(0, 0)$ as a test point in the inequality.

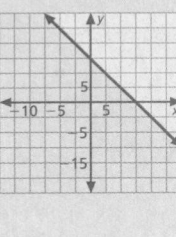

$$2x + 2y \geq 30$$
$$2(0) + 2(0) \overset{?}{\geq} 30$$
$$0 \geq 30 \text{ false}$$

Since $(0, 0)$ does not satisfy the inequality, shade the half-plane that does not contain $(0, 0)$.
**c.** Use the graph to name three possible combinations of length and width for rectangle *ABCD*.
Since the dimensions of a rectangle must be positive, only the ordered pairs in the part of the shaded region that is within Quadrant I represent possible combinations.
Some possible dimensions of rectangle *ABCD* are:
1 cm × 20 cm, 4 cm × 16 cm, and 16.2 cm × 20.5 cm.

## Teaching Tip

After selecting the *shade feature* from the Draw menu on a graphing calculator, students must enter lower and upper bounds for the shading. Here is how for the graph shown in:
1. the **opening activity** where the boundary line is $y = x$
   Window: $-10 \leq x \leq 10$ Xscl = 1
   $-10 \leq y \leq 10$ Yscl = 1
   Shade $(x, 10)$
2. **Example 3** where the boundary line is $y = 0.32x$
   Window: $-10 \leq x \leq 10$ Xscl = 1
   $-10 \leq y \leq 10$ Yscl = 1
   Shade $(-10, .32x)$

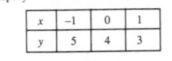
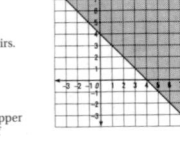
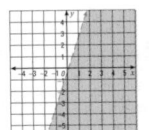
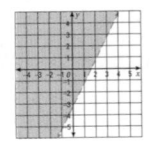
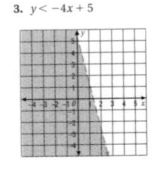
## Example 3

**BUSINESS** A company pays 32% of sales in taxes. The amount of taxes paid is modeled by the equation $y = 0.32x$, where $x$ is the amount of sales and $y$ is the amount of taxes. Determine when taxes are less than or equal to 32% of sales.

### Solution

A graphing calculator can help you graph the equation. Enter the equation $y = 0.32x$ and graph the line.

Since the problem is stated *less than or equal to*, the inequality is $y \leq 0.32x$ and the line is displayed as a solid line.

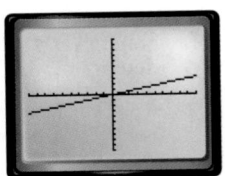

Choose a test point: $(1, 0)$.      $y < 0.32x$
                                    $0 \overset{?}{<} 0.32(1)$   Use $x = 1$ and $y = 0$.
Determine if $(1, 0)$ is           $0 < 0.32$
a solution.

Since $(1, 0)$ is below the line, shade the lower half-plane.

The line and the shaded region of the graph show when taxes are less than or equal to 32% of sales.

### ▰ TRY THESE EXERCISES

Tell if each ordered pair is a solution of the inequality.

1. $(4, 1)$; $y > x - 5$   yes
2. $(-1, 5)$; $y \leq 4x - 3$   no
3. $(-3, -1)$; $y \geq x + 4$   no
4. $(1, 1)$; $y < 3x$   yes

Determine whether solutions of the inequality are *above* or *below* the boundary. State if the boundary line is included.

5. $y - x < 0$
   below; not included
6. $y > 3x - 2$
   above; not included
7. $2x - y \geq 4$
   below; included
8. $-2y > x + 1$
   below; not included
9. $2x + y \geq 4$
   above; included
10. $3y - x > 4$
   above; not included

**Graph each inequality.**
For 11–14, see additional answers.
11. $y < x + 4$
12. $y \geq 3x - 1$
13. $2x - y \leq 2$
14. $x + y < 6$

### ▰ PRACTICE EXERCISES • For Extra Practice, see page 604.

Determine whether solutions of the inequality are *above* or *below* the boundary. State if the boundary line is included.

15. $y + x < 0$
    below; not included
16. $2x + y \leq 4$
    below; included
17. $3y - x > 6$
    above; not included
18. $-2y < x + 3$
    above; not included

**Graph each inequality.**   For 19–30, see additional answers.

19. $y < 4$
20. $x \geq -1$
21. $y < -x$
22. $y > 0.5x + 1$
23. $y > -x + 2$
24. $x + y \geq 3$
25. $2x + y \leq 1$
26. $y \leq 4x + 2$
27. $y \leq \frac{1}{2}x + 1$
28. $y < -\frac{1}{3}x - 1$
29. $y < -\frac{3}{2}x$
30. $y - \frac{2}{3}x > 3$

11.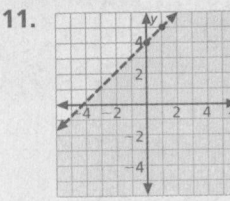
12.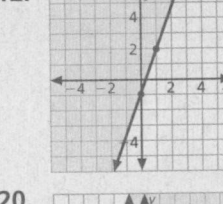
13.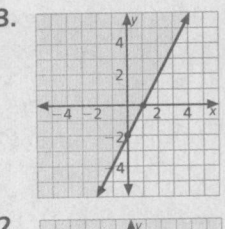
14.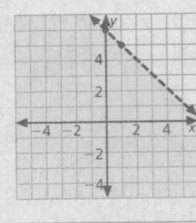

19.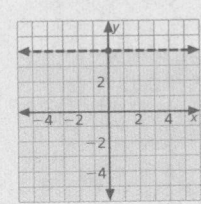
20.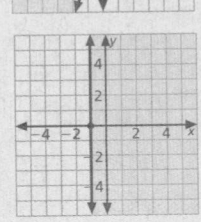
22.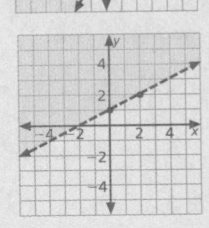
24.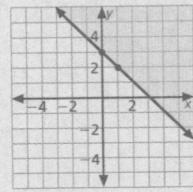

**Write each statement as an inequality. Then graph the inequality.**
For 31–33, see additional answers.

**31.** The $y$-coordinate of a point is at most 3 more than the $x$-coordinate. $y \leq x + 3$

**32.** The sum of the $x$-coordinate and the $y$-coordinate is less than 8. $x + y < 8$

**33.** The $y$-coordinate of a point less 3 times the $x$-coordinate is at least 2. $y - 3x \geq 2$

**Write an inequality for each graph.**

**34.** 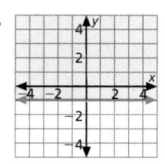 $y \geq -1$

**35.** 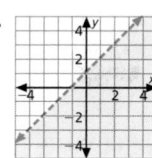 $y < x + 1$

**36.** 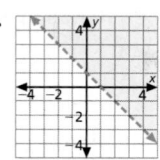 $y > -x + 1$

**37. MARKET RESEARCH** Suppose a company plans to increase sales by $125,000 each year for the next ten years. Sales are now at $1 million. Write and graph an inequality that represents the future sales for the company if sales increase by at least $125,000/yr. Use an appropriate scale for the $y$-axis.
$y \geq 125,000x + 1,000,000$; See additional answers.

**38. WRITING MATH** Use an example to explain the steps you would use to check a solution for an inequality. Answers will vary.

## ■ EXTENDED PRACTICE EXERCISES

**39.** Use a graphing calculator to graph $y = |x|$. See additional answers.

**Use your graph from Exercise 39 to determine which ordered pairs are solutions to the inequality $y \geq |x|$.**

**40.** $(0, 1)$ yes

**41.** $(-2, 5)$ yes

**42.** $(3, -3)$ no

**43.** $(2, 10)$ yes

**44. BUSINESS** A company wants to have sales such that the exports are half of the imports. Write an equation that represents the number of exports in terms of the number of imports. Make a graph to show when the number of exports is not more than half the imports. See additional answers.

**45. CHAPTER INVESTIGATION** Create a coordinate plane like the one you created in Lesson 6-1. Find the data on your company's sales revenue for each quarter of the year. Plot four ordered pairs as (Quarter, Sales revenue). Draw a line connecting each quarter to represent the increase, decrease or steady pace of sales. Describe the sales by quarters and by the entire year. Answers will vary.

## ■ MIXED REVIEW EXERCISES

**A group of lettered cards contains one A, two Q's, three K's and four Z's. Cards are picked one at a time, then replaced. Find each probability.** (Lesson 4-5)

**46.** $P(Q, \text{ then } K)$ $\frac{3}{50}$

**47.** $P(A, \text{ then } Q)$ $\frac{1}{50}$

**48.** $P(K, \text{ then } A)$ $\frac{3}{100}$

**Simplify.** (Lesson 2-8)

**49.** $p^{12} \div p^3$ $p^9$

**50.** $\left(\dfrac{z}{z^4}\right)^3$ $\dfrac{1}{z^9}$ or $z^{-9}$

**51.** $\dfrac{m^{-2}}{m^{-6}}$ $m^4$

**52.** $\dfrac{k^3}{k^8}$ $\dfrac{1}{k^5}$ or $k^{-5}$

**53.** $\dfrac{f^{-3}}{f^{-4}}$ $f$

**54.** $a^{-6} \cdot a^{-3}$ $a^{-9}$ or $\dfrac{1}{a^9}$

**55.** $(r^2)^{-4}$ $\dfrac{1}{r^8}$ or $r^{-8}$

**56.** $\left(\dfrac{x}{x^4}\right)^5$ $\dfrac{1}{x^{15}}$ or $x^{-15}$

**26.**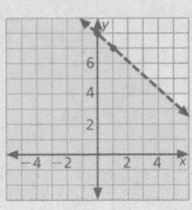

**28.**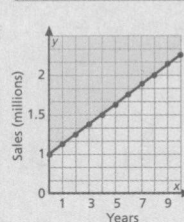

**30.**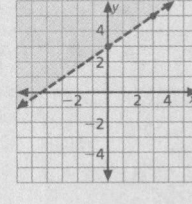

**31.**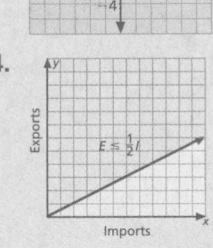

**32.**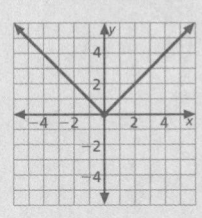

**37.**

**39.**

**44.**

---

## Extra Practice Worksheet 6-4

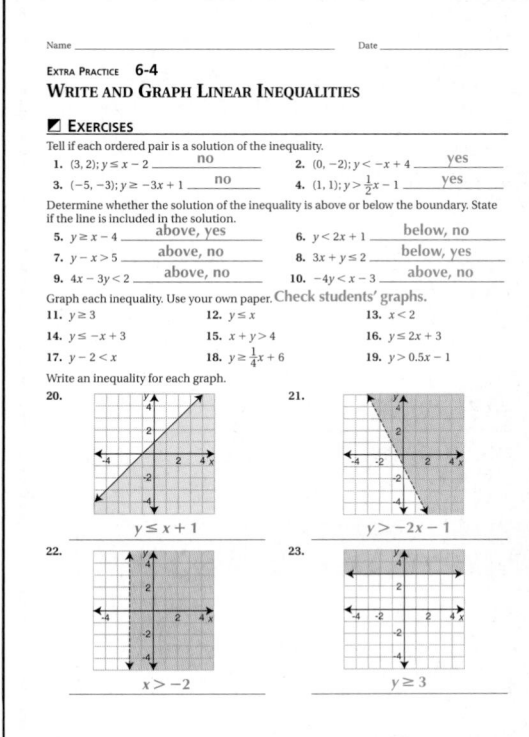

Name _____  Date _____

EXTRA PRACTICE **6-4**
WRITE AND GRAPH LINEAR INEQUALITIES

**☑ EXERCISES**

Tell if each ordered pair is a solution of the inequality.

**1.** $(3, 2); y \leq x - 2$ ___no___

**2.** $(0, -2); y < -x + 4$ ___yes___

**3.** $(-5, -3); y \geq -3x + 1$ ___no___

**4.** $(1, 1); y > \frac{1}{2}x - 1$ ___yes___

Determine whether the solution of the inequality is above or below the boundary. State if the line is included in the solution.

**5.** $y \geq x - 4$ ___above, yes___

**6.** $y < 2x + 1$ ___below, no___

**7.** $y - x > 5$ ___above, no___

**8.** $3x + y \leq 2$ ___below, yes___

**9.** $4x - 3y < 2$ ___above, no___

**10.** $-4y < x - 3$ ___above, no___

Graph each inequality. Use your own paper. Check students' graphs.

**11.** $y \geq 3$  **12.** $y \leq x$  **13.** $x < 2$

**14.** $y \leq -x + 3$  **15.** $x + y > 4$  **16.** $y \leq 2x + 3$

**17.** $y - 2 < x$  **18.** $y \geq \frac{1}{4}x + 6$  **19.** $y > 0.5x - 1$

Write an inequality for each graph.

**20.** $y \leq x + 1$

**21.** $y > -2x - 1$

**22.** $x > -2$

**23.** $y \geq 3$

---

## Enrichment Worksheet 6-4

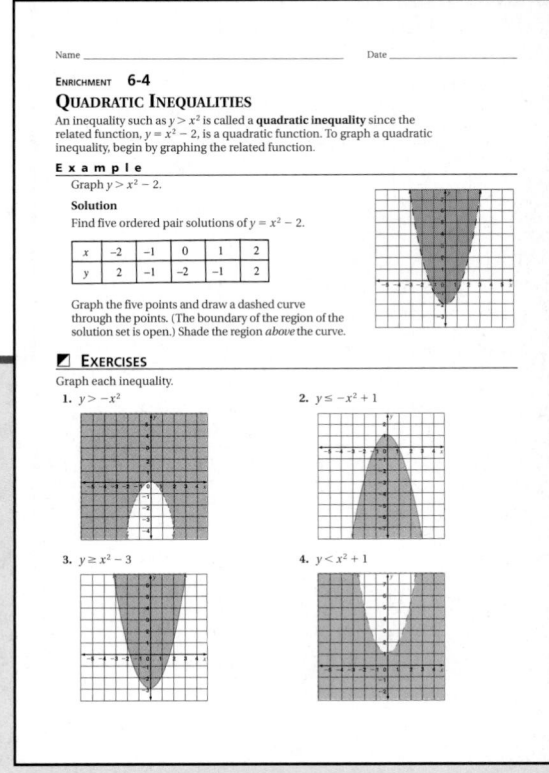

Name _____  Date _____

ENRICHMENT **6-4**
QUADRATIC INEQUALITIES

An inequality such as $y > x^2$ is called a **quadratic inequality** since the related function, $y = x^2 - 2$, is a quadratic function. To graph a quadratic inequality, begin by graphing the related function.

**E x a m p l e**
Graph $y > x^2 - 2$.

**Solution**
Find five ordered pair solutions of $y = x^2 - 2$.

| $x$ | $-2$ | $-1$ | $0$ | $1$ | $2$ |
|---|---|---|---|---|---|
| $y$ | $2$ | $-1$ | $-2$ | $-1$ | $2$ |

Graph the five points and draw a dashed curve through the points. (The boundary of the region of the solution set is open.) Shade the region *above* the curve.

**☑ EXERCISES**

Graph each inequality.

**1.** $y > -x^2$

**2.** $y \leq -x^2 + 1$

**3.** $y \geq x^2 - 3$

**4.** $y < x^2 + 1$

## Vocabulary Review

**Lesson 6-3**
$y$-intercept
slope-intercept form of a line
point-slope form of a line

**Lesson 6-4**
open half-plane
closed half-plane
boundary line
graph of a linear inequality
graphic solution of a linear
   inequality

## ASSIGNMENT GUIDE

**All students:** 1–65

## Chalkboard Examples

**Lesson 6-3**
a. Consider the line $3y = x - 2$.
   Which of the following is the
   value of the slope?   **D**

   **A.** 1   **B.** $x$   **C.** $\frac{1}{3}x$   **D.** $\frac{1}{3}$

b. Consider the line $3x + 4y + 7 = 0$.
   Which of the following is the
   value of the $y$-intercept?   **C**

   **A.** $-\frac{3}{4}$   **B.** $\frac{3}{4}$   **C.** $-\frac{7}{4}$   **D.** $\frac{7}{4}$

**Lesson 6-4**
Match each graph with an inequality.
a.

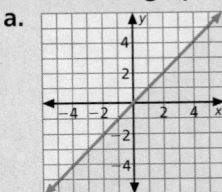

   **A**
   **A.** $y \ge x$
   **B.** $x \ge y$
   **C.** $x \ge 0$
   **D.** $y \ge 0$

b.

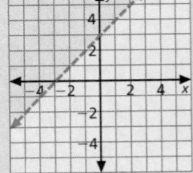

   **B**
   **A.** $y < 3$
   **B.** $y < x + 3$
   **C.** $y > x + 3$
   **D.** $y < 3x + 3$

### PRACTICE ■ LESSON 6-3

**Identify the slope and $y$-intercept for each line.**

1. $y = x + 2$   1; 2
2. $y = -2$   0; $-2$
3. $y = 2x$   2; 0
4. $-3x + 6y = -18$   $\frac{1}{2}$; $-3$
5. $2y = 10x - 12$   5; $-6$
6. $y = \frac{x}{3} + 1$   $\frac{1}{3}$; 1

**Write the equation of each line using the given information.**

7. $(0, 4)$, $m = \frac{2}{3}$   $y = \frac{2}{3}x + 4$
8. $(2, 3)$, $m = 0$   $y = 3$
9. $(2, -2)$, $(-4, 6)$   $y = -\frac{4}{3}x + \frac{2}{3}$
10. $(1, 2)$, $(-2, 5)$   $y = -x + 3$
11. $(5, -1)$, $(-3, 3)$   $y = -\frac{1}{2}x + \frac{3}{2}$
12. $(3, 3)$, $(3, 7)$   $x = 3$
13. $m = 1$, $(3, -5)$   $y = x - 8$
14. $(-2, 5)$, $(10, 6)$   $y = \frac{1}{12}x + \frac{31}{6}$
15. $(0, -1)$, $(-1, -7)$   $y = 6x - 1$
16. $m = \frac{2}{3}$, $(2, -4)$   $y = \frac{2}{3}x - \frac{16}{3}$
17. $m = 0$, $(-5, 5)$   $y = 5$
18. $(-3, 8)$, $(-1, -3)$   $y = -\frac{11}{2}x - \frac{17}{2}$
19. $(-1, 3)$, $b = 4$   $y = x + 4$
20. $(0, -4)$, $(11, 3)$   $y = \frac{7}{11}x - 4$
21. $m = \frac{1}{3}$, $(6, -2)$   $y = \frac{1}{3}x - 4$
22. $(-1, -1)$, $(-5, -5)$   $y = x$
23. $m = -1$, $(-6, 1)$   $y = -x - 5$
24. $(0, 3)$, $(-4, 0)$   $y = \frac{3}{4}x + 3$
25. $(12, -2)$, $(9, 3)$   $y = -\frac{5}{3}x + 18$
26. $m = \frac{3}{2}$, $(5, 0)$   $y = \frac{3}{2}x - \frac{15}{2}$
27. $(4, -3)$, $b = -1$   $y = -\frac{1}{2}x - 1$

### PRACTICE ■ LESSON 6-4

**Tell if each ordered pair is a solution of the inequality.**

28. $(5, -2)$; $y \le 4x + 1$   yes
29. $(4, 1)$; $y \ge 3x - 4$   no
30. $(0, -3)$; $x + y \ge -2$   no
31. $(-1, -4)$; $y < -\frac{1}{2}x - 3$   yes
32. $(-7, 3)$; $2x - y < 2$   yes
33. $\left(-\frac{1}{2}, \frac{1}{3}\right)$; $4x - 3y \ge -3$   yes

**Determine whether solutions of the inequality are *above* or *below* the boundary. State if the boundary line is included.**

34. $y < 3x + 4$   below; not included
35. $2y \ge -3x + 12$   above; included
36. $y > 4$   above; not included
37. $-y - x \le -7$   above; included
38. $9y > 12x - 3$   above; not included
39. $-2y \ge 3x + 3$   below; included

**Graph each inequality.**   For 40–45, see additional answers.

40. $y < 2x - 1$
41. $y \le -3x - 3$
42. $y > 2x$
43. $y > \frac{1}{3}x$
44. $x < -1$
45. $2x + 2y \ge 4$

**Write an inequality for each graph.**

46.

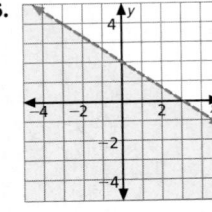

$y < -\frac{2}{3}x + 2$

47.

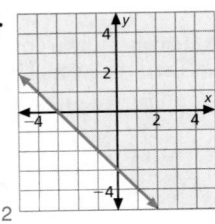

$y \ge -x - 3$

48.

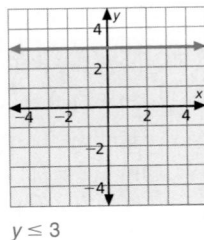

$y \le 3$

262   Chapter 6   **Graphing Functions**

## ADDITIONAL ANSWERS

40.

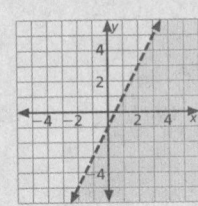

41.

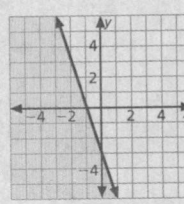

42.

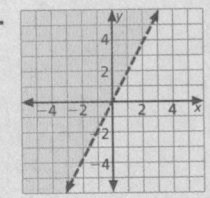

43.

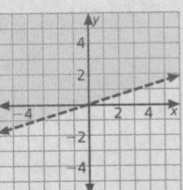

## PRACTICE ◼ LESSON 6-1–LESSON 6-4

**Find the distance between the points. Round to the nearest tenth.** (Lesson 6-1)

**49.** $A(1, 5)$, $B(-1, -5)$  10.2     **50.** $X(8, 2)$, $Y(-3, 2)$  11     **51.** $M(0, 0)$, $N(5, 12)$  13

**52.** Find the slope of a line passing through $(-1, 4)$ and $(5, 12)$. (Lesson 6-2)  $\frac{4}{3}$

**Write the equation of a line using the given information.** (Lesson 6-3)

**53.** $(2, -2)$, $m = -2$     **54.** $(-1, 1)$, $m = \frac{1}{2}$  $y = \frac{1}{2}x + \frac{3}{2}$     **55.** $(-2, 4)$, $(0, -6)$
$y = -2x + 2$                                                                                    $y = -5x - 6$

**Identify the slope and y-intercept for each line. Graph each line.** (Lesson 6-3)
For 56–58, see additional answers.

**56.** $y = \frac{x}{2} - 3$  $\frac{1}{2}$; $-3$     **57.** $y = x + 1$  1; 1     **58.** $y = -2x$  $-2$; 0

**Graph each inequality.** (Lesson 6-4)  For 59–61, see additional answers.

**59.** $y < 2x - 4$     **60.** $y \geq x + 2$     **61.** $2x - 3y \leq 12$

**The vertices of a triangle are $A(1, 7)$, $B(7, 9)$ and $C(9, 3)$. Find the following.** (Lesson 6-4)

**62.** $AB = $ ? .  6.3     **63.** $BC = $ ? .  6.3     **64.** $AC = $ ? .  8.9

**65.** What type of triangle is $\triangle ABC$?  isosceles

# Mid-Chapter Quiz

**Find the distance between the points. Round to the nearest tenth.** (Lesson 6-1)

**1.** $P(-4, 2)$, $Q(-1, 6)$  5     **2.** $A(3, 7)$, $B(10, 2)$  8.6     **3.** $F(-1, -2)$, $G(0, 3)$  5.1

**4.** $X(-8, -4)$, $Y(2, 9)$  16.4     **5.** $H(0, 11)$, $I(12, -4)$  19.2     **6.** $C(5, -1)$, $D(-5, 3)$  10.8

**Find the slope and y-intercept of a line using the information given.
Identify any vertical or horizontal lines.** (Lessons 6-2 and 6-3)

**7.** $(-1, 3)$, $(7, 5)$  $\frac{1}{4}, \frac{13}{4}$     **8.** $(4, 4)$, $(4, -2)$  slope undefined, vertical line     **9.** $(2.9, 7.2)$, $(5.4, 12.2)$  $2, \frac{7}{5}$

**10.** $2x + 5y = 25$  $-\frac{2}{5}, 5$     **11.** $-x = -2y + 6$  $\frac{1}{2}, 3$     **12.** $\frac{3}{4} = \frac{1}{8}y - \frac{3}{2}x$  12, 6

**Graph each line using the given information.** (Lesson 6-3)  For 13–18, see additional answers.

**13.** $(1, 2)$, $m = 4$     **14.** $(7, -2)$, $m = -1$     **15.** $(3, 12)$, $(-2, 2)$

**16.** $\left(\frac{3}{2}, 2\right)$, $m = -2$     **17.** $(1, 10)$, $(-2, 1)$     **18.** $(-6, 4)$, $(3, 1)$

**Determine whether solutions of the inequality are *above* or *below* the
boundary. State if the boundary line is included.** (Lesson 6-3)

**19.** $y + 2x \leq 4$  below; included     **20.** $y > \frac{1}{3}x - 4$  above; not included     **21.** $y \geq -\frac{3}{4}x + 2$  above; included

**Graph each inequality.** (Lesson 6-4)  For 22–24, see additional answers.

**22.** $y < 5$     **23.** $y \geq -x - 1$     **24.** $x - y > 3$

**13.** 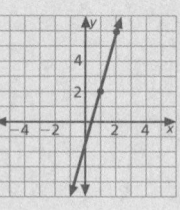     **14.**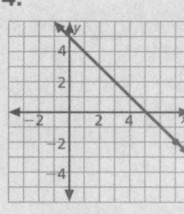

**15.** 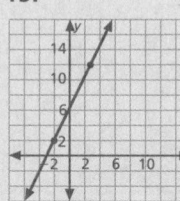     **16.**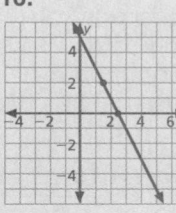

**17.** 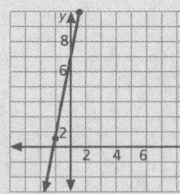     **18.**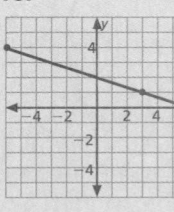

**22.** 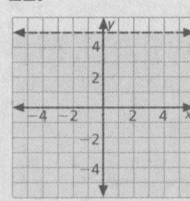     **23.**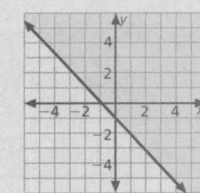

**24.**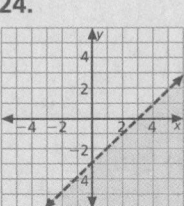

**44.** 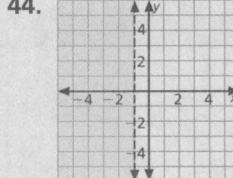     **45.** 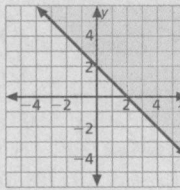     **56.** 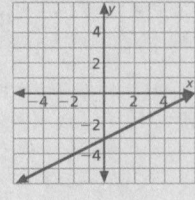     **57.**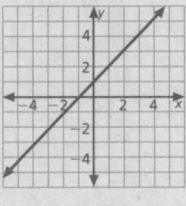

**58.** 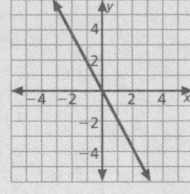     **59.** 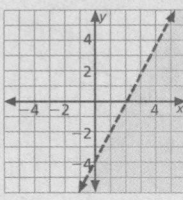     **60.** 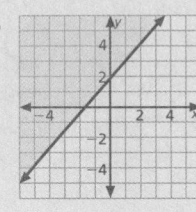     **61.**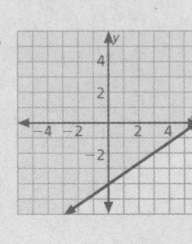

# Linear and Nonlinear Functions

**Goals**
- Graph linear functions.
- Identify the domain and range of a function.

**Applications**   Machinery, Travel, Temperature

### NCTM Standards/Strands
- Algebra
- Representation
- Connections
- Problem Solving

### Vocabulary

| | |
|---|---|
| function | function notation |
| domain | range |
| continuous | linear function |
| vertical line test | |

### Tools/Materials Needed

graph paper

### Lesson Resources

Warm-up Transparency 25
Transparency TK 9-12
Reteaching 6-5
Extra Practice 6-5
Enrichment 6-5

## Getting Started

### 5-MINUTE WARM-UP

Evaluate each expression when
$x = 3$, $y = 2$, $z = 4$.
1. $-4x - y$   $-14$   2. $xz + 3y$   18
3. $\frac{z}{y} - 2x$   $-4$   4. $y^2 - x^2$   $-5$

### Introduction to Lesson 6-5
You may wish to describe a situation for which the graph could be a model. For example, the function $y = 2x + 3$ could represent the cost ($y$) of a visit to a country fair where the admission is $3 and each ride costs $2. The total cost is then a function of the number of rides taken ($x$). Ask the class to speculate about which points on the graph make sense as possible solutions to this situation.   Only whole numbers of rides are possible.

**Use the graph for Questions 1–4.**

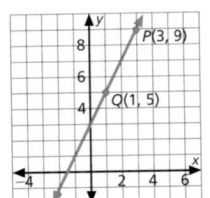

1. Determine whether the coordinates of $P$ and $Q$ are solutions of the equation $y = 2x + 3$.   yes

2. Give the coordinate pairs for three other points that are solutions of $y = 2x + 3$.   Sample answer: (0, 3), (−1, 1), (2, 7)

3. Do you think there are points on the line that are not solutions of $y = 2x + 3$? Explain.   No. All the points on the line are solutions to the equation of the line.

4. Are there any breaks in the line? Explain.
   No. The line is continuous.

### ▮ BUILD UNDERSTANDING

When an equation in two variables has a relationship where each $x$-coordinate is paired with exactly one $y$-coordinate, the equation represents a **function**. You can represent functions using a mapping, a function table or a function rule written in **function notation**, $f(x)$.

An example of a function rule is $x - 3$. Its function notation is $f(x) = x - 3$. However, you can use the equation $y = x - 3$ to represent the function. This equation expresses $y$ as a function of $x$. The set of all possible values of $x$ is called the **domain** of the function. The set of all possible values of $y$ is called the **range**, or *values of the function.*

**Think Back**

A mapping is a visual representation of how the $x$ elements and $f(x)$ elements are paired.

A function table is a table of $x$ and $f(x)$ values.

### Example 1

**RECREATION**   A block-party association needs 12 packages of buns for a party. Write an equation where $h$ is the number of hotdog bun packages and $r$ is the number of hamburger bun packages. Make a function table. Graph the data.

**Solution**

The relationship of the number of each package is a function, written $f(r) = 12 - r$. As an equation, it is written $h = 12 - r$. Select domain values for a function table. Find the range.

Use the horizontal axis to represent hotdog buns and the vertical axis to represent hamburger buns.

The graph shows 13 possible combinations.

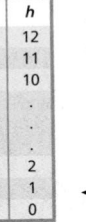

| r | h |
|---|---|
| 0 | 12 |
| 1 | 11 |
| 2 | 10 |
| . | . |
| . | . |
| . | . |
| 10 | 2 |
| 11 | 1 |
| 12 | 0 |

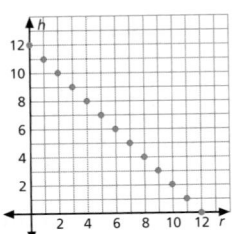

264   Chapter 6   **Graphing Functions**

## Alternative Assessment

**MATH JOURNAL** After students have completed Example 1, have them create their own functions, such as a function that relates their age in years to that of a relative. Such a function can either be in the form $y = x + c$ or $y = x - c$, where c is the constant difference between the ages.
Have students graph the age function they created, and write several questions that can be answered from the graph. Have students work in pairs, asking their questions of their partners.

In the situation in Example 1, the domain is whole numbers from 0 to 12. Negative and fractional values do not make sense when purchasing packages of buns.

In other mathematical situations the domain is not restricted. In such cases, the domain of the function is all real numbers. Ordered pairs are graphed and the points are connected to show that the graph is **continuous**. This shows that for all real numbers, *every point* on the line is a solution of the equation.

All functions can be graphed using a function table. Set up a table. Choose a value for $x$, and find the corresponding $f(x)$ value. Once you have a function table, you are able to graph the function.

## Example 2

**Graph each function when the domain is the set of real numbers.**

**a.** $f(x) = 4x - 3$ **b.** $f(x) = -4$ **c.** $2x + y = 4$

### Solution

**a.** Make a table to show the ordered pairs. Choose at least three values of $x$ from the domain. Calculate $f(x)$. Then graph the points that correspond to the ordered pairs, $(x, f(x))$. Draw a line to connect the points.

| x | f(x) |
|---|------|
| 1 | 1 |
| 0 | -3 |
| -1 | -7 |

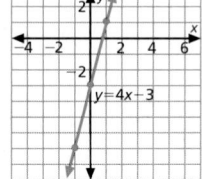

You can also think of the function as $y = 4x - 3$. Draw the graph using the slope and $y$-intercept.

**b.** This function is written as $y = -4$. Recall that the graph of an equation in this form is a horizontal line. In this case, graph the horizontal line $y = -4$.

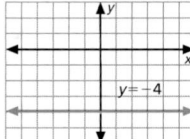

**c.** Make a function table or solve the equation for $y$. Then graph using the slope and $y$-intercept.

$$2x + y = 4$$
$$2x - 2x + y = -2x + 4$$
$$y = -2x + 4$$

The slope is $-2$ and the $y$-intercept is 4.

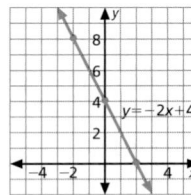

A function that can be represented by a linear equation, where the domain is all real numbers, is called a **linear function**. Not all functions are linear functions. You can tell from looking at a graph whether the function is linear or nonlinear. Recall that the word linear means straight line.

To test whether a graph is a function, use the **vertical line test**. The vertical line test states that if a vertical line drawn anywhere on the graph crosses the graph no more than once, then the graph represents a function.

Math Online mathmatters2.com/extra_examples     Lesson 6-5 **Linear and Nonlinear Functions** | 265

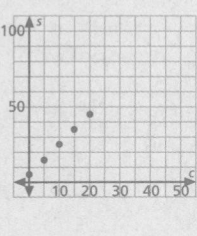
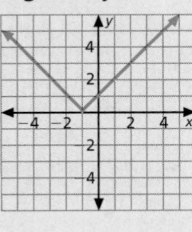

**266** Chapter 6 **Graphing Functions**

## Lesson Wrap-up

### QUICK ASSESSMENT

Ask the following questions to determine if students understand the content presented in this lesson. Consider the relation $y = -x$.

1. Categorize this relation as *a function* or *not a function*, and as *linear* or *not linear*. Explain.   **linear function; passes vertical line test**
2. If the domain is the set of all real numbers, is the relation a *continuous function*? Explain.   **yes; there are no breaks in the line**
3. Through which quadrants does the graph pass?   **Quadrants II and IV**

### ASSIGNMENT GUIDE

**Basic:** 1–23, 27–35
**Enriched:** 1–35

### Reteaching Worksheet 6-5

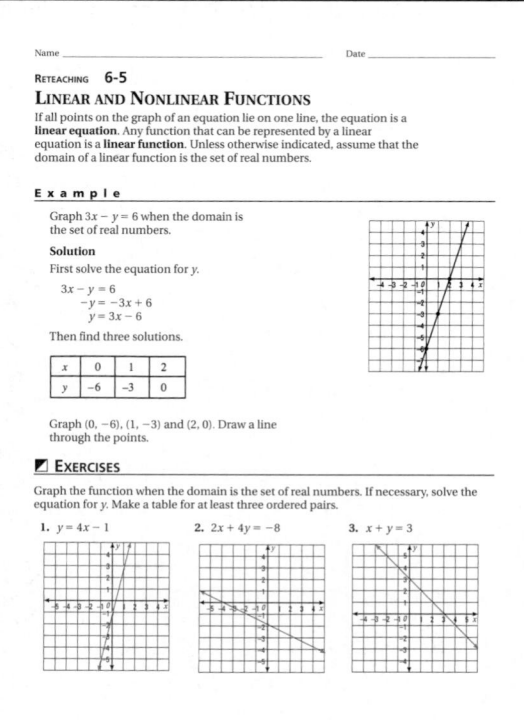

Name _____ Date _____

RETEACHING  **6-5**
**LINEAR AND NONLINEAR FUNCTIONS**
If all points on the graph of an equation lie on one line, the equation is a **linear equation**. Any function that can be represented by a linear equation is a **linear function**. Unless otherwise indicated, assume that the domain of a linear function is the set of real numbers.

**Example**

Graph $3x - y = 6$ when the domain is the set of real numbers.

**Solution**
First solve the equation for $y$.

$3x - y = 6$
$-y = -3x + 6$
$y = 3x - 6$

Then find three solutions.

| x | 0 | 1 | 2 |
|---|---|---|---|
| y | -6 | -3 | 0 |

Graph $(0, -6)$, $(1, -3)$ and $(2, 0)$. Draw a line through the points.

**EXERCISES**

Graph the function when the domain is the set of real numbers. If necessary, solve the equation for $y$. Make a table for at least three ordered pairs.

**1.** $y = 4x - 1$   **2.** $2x + 4y = -8$   **3.** $x + y = 3$

**266** Chapter 6 **Graphing Functions**

---

## Example 3

Determine if each graph represents a function. Explain.

a. 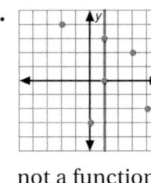   b. 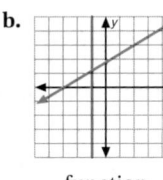   c.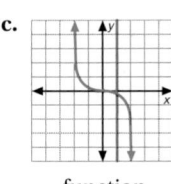

### Solution

a. 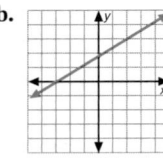   b.   c.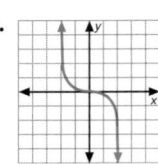

not a function          function          function

## Example 4

Make a table or use your graphing utility to graph the nonlinear function $f(x) = x^3 - 1$.

### Solution

To use your graphing utility, enter $y = x^3 - 1$ at the equation screen and then graph. Notice the graph is a curve.

Set up a table that includes positive and negative values for $x$. Substitute each $x$-value into the equation and solve for the $f(x)$ value.

| x | 0 | -1 | 1 | 2 | -2 |
|---|---|----|----|----|----|
| f(x) | -1 | -2 | 0 | 7 | -9 |

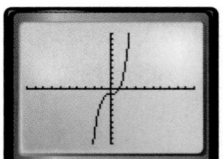

Plot each point on a coordinate plane. Since there are no values for which the function is not defined, the domain is the set of real numbers. The function is continuous.

### ◤ TRY THESE EXERCISES

Determine if each is a function.

**1.**

| x | 1 | 1 | 0 | 2 | 10 |
|---|---|---|---|---|----|
| y | 5 | -4 | -2 | 0 | 10 |

no

**2.** $f(x) = 3x$   yes

**3.** 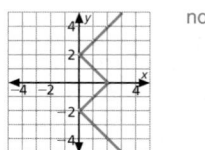   no

**4.**

| x | 0 | -1 | 2 | 12 | -1 |
|---|---|----|----|----|----|
| y | 5 | 0 | -2 | 1 | 5 |

no

**5.** $y = x^2 + 1$   yes

**6.** The area of a circle is a function of the length of the radius. Let $y$ represent the area and $r$ the length of the radius. Graph the area function $y = \pi r^2$ when the domain is $\{1, 2, 3, 4, 5\}$. Round $y$-values to the nearest whole number.   See additional answers.

**266** | Chapter 6 **Graphing Functions**

## ADDITIONAL ANSWERS

**6.**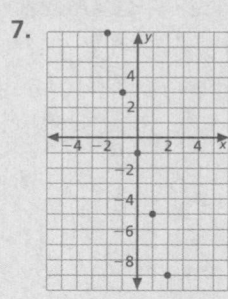

**7.**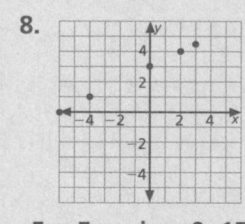

**8.**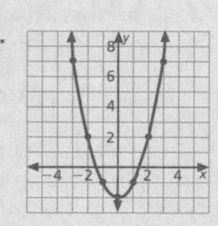

**10.**

For Exercises 9, 15, 17, 19, and 21, see Selected Answers on page 684.

**Graph each function for the given domain.** For 7–10, see additional answers.

**7.** $y = -4x - 1$; $\{-2, -1, 0, 1, 2\}$

**8.** $f(x) = \frac{1}{2}x + 3$; $\{-6, -4, 0, 2, 3\}$

**9.** $f(x) = -3$; {all real numbers}

**10.** $y = x^2 - 2$; {all real numbers}

**Determine if each graph represents a function. Explain.**

**11.**

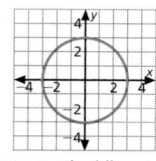

no; vertical line test fails

**12.**

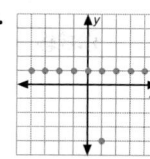

no; vertical line test at $x = 1$

**13.**

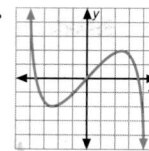

yes; vertical line test passes

**Graph each function.**
For 14–21, see additional answers.

**14.** $y = |x| + 3$

**15.** $y = x^2 - 1$

**16.** $y = \frac{3}{2}x - 2$

**17.** $y = \sqrt{x}$

**18.** $y = -x - 5$

**19.** $2\sqrt{x} + y = 0$

**20.** $y = -0.5x^2$

**21.** $x - y = 2$

 **22. WRITING MATH** Explain the difference between "$y$ as a function of $x$" and "$x$ as a function of $y$." Include examples to show the difference. See additional answers.

**23. BUSINESS** In Jawaun's computer repair business, he charges \$20 for making a house call and \$12 per hour. Write a function for Jawaun's total charges, $c$, in terms of time, $t$. Is this a linear or nonlinear function? $c = 12t + 20$; linear function

**EXTENDED PRACTICE EXERCISES**

**24. CHEMISTRY** According to a scientific supply catalog, the cost of a chemical in cents $C$ is represented by the equation $C = 3V$, where $V$ is the amount of liquid in milliliters. Graph the function to determine the cost of 15 mL and 60 mL of the chemical. \$0.45, \$1.80; See additional answers.

**25.** Use the graph from Exercise 24 to find how much of the chemical can be purchased for \$0.39. 13 mL

**26.** The greatest integer function is another type of nonlinear function that models real-world situations, such as postage rates. The function notation for the *greatest integer function* is $f(x) = [x]$, and it means $f(x)$ equals the greatest integer that does not exceed the value of $x$. For example, when $x = 11.23$, $f(x) = 11$; when $x = 0.346$, $f(x) = 0$. Make a table of at least 12 ordered pairs. Graph the function $f(x) = [x]$ when the domain is greater than 0.
See additional answers. Answers will vary.

**MIXED REVIEW EXERCISES**

**Which of the given values is a solution of the equation?** (Lesson 3-1)

**27.** $5d + 6 = -9$; $-5, -3, 3$  $-3$

**28.** $12r - 3 = 21$; $2, 3, 7$  $2$

**29.** $e^2 - 4 = 12$; $-4, -3, 4$  $-4, 4$

**Solve each inequality.** (Lesson 3-7)

**30.** $5 + d > 3$  $d > -2$

**31.** $3 + 4z < 27$  $z < 6$

**32.** $4p \geq -18$  $p \geq -\frac{9}{2}$

**33.** $2a + 4.7 \leq a - 1.3$  $a \leq -6$

**34.** $12c - 6 > 6c + 9$  $c > \frac{5}{2}$

**35.** $5r - 3 < 3r + 8$  $r < \frac{11}{2}$

 **Math Online** mathmatters2.com/self_check_quiz

---

**Extra Practice Worksheet 6-5**

Name _____ Date _____

Extra Practice **6-5**
**LINEAR AND NONLINEAR FUNCTIONS**

**EXERCISES**
Determine if each is a function.

**1.**

| x | 2 | 4 | −1 | 2 | 4 |
|---|---|---|----|---|---|
| y | 6 | 3 | 1 | 8 | 7 |

no

**2.**

| x | 6 | 5 | −2 | −3 | 4 |
|---|---|---|----|----|---|
| y | 3 | 3 | 3 | 2 | 1 |

yes

**3.** $f(x) = 4x - 1$ _____ yes

**4.** $y = -4x^2 - 2$ _____ yes
Check students' graphs.

Graph each function for the given domain. Use your own paper.

**5.** $y = 5x + 1$; $x = -1, 0, 4, 6, 7$

**6.** $f(x) = \frac{1}{3}x - 2$, $x = -4, -3, 1, 3, 6$

**7.** $f(x) = -1$, $x =$ all real numbers

**8.** $y = x^2 + 1$, $x =$ all real numbers

Use the vertical line test to determine if each graph represents a function. If not, explain why not.

**9.**

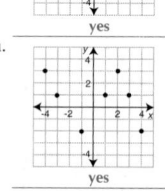

yes

**10.**

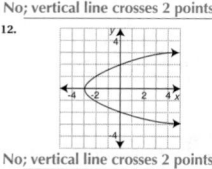

No; vertical line crosses 2 points.

**11.**

yes

**12.**

No; vertical line crosses 2 points.

**26.**

| x | y |
|-----|---|
| 0.4 | 0 |
| 0.7 | 0 |
| 1.3 | 1 |
| 2.7 | 2 |
| 3.1 | 3 |
| 3.2 | 3 |
| 5.9 | 5 |
| 6.01 | 6 |
| 7 | 7 |
| 8.3 | 8 |
| 9.2 | 9 |
| 9.347 | 9 |

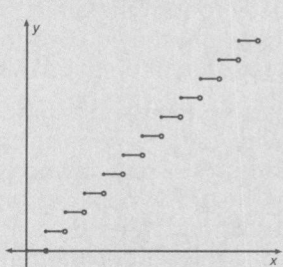

**14.**

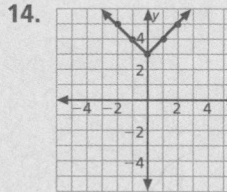

**16.**

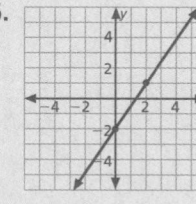

**22.** The statement "$y$ as a function of $x$" gives an equation with $y$ isolated on one side and an expression in terms of $x$ on the other side. For example, $y = x + 2$. "$x$ as a function of $y$" isolates $x$ and gives an expression in terms of $y$ on the other side.

**18.**

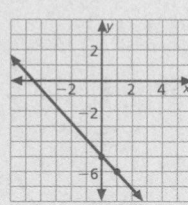

**20.**

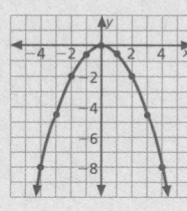

**24.**

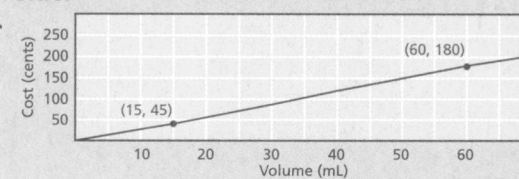

(60, 180)
(15, 45)

Cost (cents): 50, 100, 150, 200, 250
Volume (mL): 10, 20, 30, 40, 50, 60

### NCTM Standards/Strands
- Algebra
- Representation
- Connections
- Problem Solving

### Vocabulary

quadratic function    parabola

### Tools/Materials Needed

graph paper

### Lesson Resources

Warm-up Transparency 25
Transparency TK-9–12
Reteaching 6-6
Extra Practice 6-6
Enrichment 6-6
Technology Activity 6-3 and 6-6

## Getting Started

### 5-MINUTE WARM-UP

Evaluate each expression when $x = -2$.
1. $x^2$   4         2. $(-x)^2$   4
3. $-x^2$   −4       4. $-2x^2 + 3x - 5$
                                    −19

### Introduction to Lesson 6-6

To turn off a particular graph on a graphing calculator (without losing the equation), students should high-light the equals symbol of that equation and press ENTER. When they are ready to turn the graph back on, again highlight the equals symbol of that equation and press ENTER.

When discussing the various graphs of the activity, call attention to the symmetries that exist by having students copy the graph of $y = x^2$ on paper and fold it along the y-axis. After similar explorations, students should conclude that the y-axis is a line of symmetry for each of the three curves $y = x^2$, $y = 3x^2$, and $y = x^2 + 1$.

---

## 6-6 Graph Quadratic Functions

**Goals**
- Identify points given the graph of a quadratic function.
- Graph simple quadratic functions.

**Applications** Sports, Physics, Agriculture

**Use a graphing calculator for Questions 1–7.**

1. Graph $y = x$.   See additional answers.

2. Turn off the graph in Question 1. Graph $y = x^2$.
   See additional answers.

3. Describe the difference between the two graphs?
   The graph for $y = x$ is a line and the graph for $y = x^2$ is a curve.

4. Turn on the graph in Question 1 so that you can view both graphs on the same coordinate plane, and check your answer to Question 3.

5. Look at the form of the following equations. Which equations do you think have a graph similar to the graph in Question 1? Explain your choices.

   $y = x + 3$        $y = x^2 + 1$    $y = 2x,$
   $y = 3x^2$         $y = 2x$         $y = x + 3$

6. Which of the equations above do you think has a graph similar to the graph in Question 2? Explain your choices.   $y = x^2$, $y = 3x^2$

7. Graph the equations in Question 5, and check your answers.
   See additional answers.

### ◼ BUILD UNDERSTANDING

Not all equations with two variables represent linear functions. Linear functions are represented by first-degree equations written in the standard form $Ax + By = C$. A first-degree equation is an equation whose variable terms have only exponents of one.

A **quadratic function** is a nonlinear function that when written in standard form is a second-degree equation, which means that it has one squared term.

| **Quadratic Function** | $y = Ax^2 + Bx + C$, where $A$, $B$, and $C$ are real numbers and $A \neq 0$. |
| --- | --- |

If the domain of a quadratic function is not specified, it is understood that the domain is the set of real numbers. The graph of a quadratic function is a curve known as a *parabola*. Not all parabolas represent functions since parabolas can open upward, downward, to the right or to the left.

To graph quadratic functions, make a table of ordered pairs. Use enough points to get an accurate picture of the graph.

**268**   Chapter 6 **Graphing Functions**

---

## ADDITIONAL ANSWERS

**Check Understanding**

1.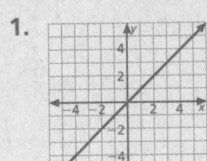
2.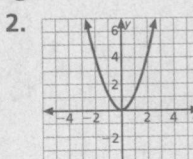
7.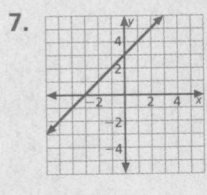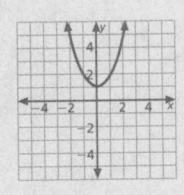

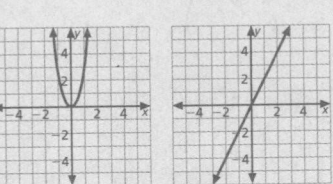

## Example 1

**Graph** $y = x^2 - 2$.

### Solution

Make a table with at least five ordered pairs. Include both positive and negative values for $x$.

| x | -2 | -1 | 0 | 1 | 2 |
|---|----|----|---|---|---|
| y | 2 | -1 | -2 | -1 | 2 |

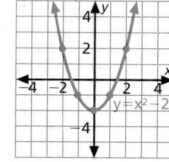

Graph the points that correspond to the ordered pairs in the table.

Draw a smooth curve through the points.

Graphs of quadratic functions are used to solve many types of problems. Use the graph of the function to find maximum or minimum points.

**Technology Note**

If you use a graphing calculator for Example 2 you may need to adjust your viewing window to see the maximum point of the graph.

## Example 2

**PHYSICS** A golf ball is hit into the air with an initial velocity of 144 ft/sec. The height $h$, in feet, of the ball above the ground is modeled by the equation $h = -16t^2 + 144t$ where $t$ is in seconds. Use a graph to find the time when the following occurs.

**a.** the ball reaches 224 ft

**b.** the ball reaches its maximum height

**c.** the ball hits the ground

### Solution

Make a table of ordered pairs. Then draw a graph. Let the horizontal axis represent time and the vertical axis represent height.

| t | 0 | 1 | 2 | 3 | 4 | 5 | 6 | 7 | 8 | 9 |
|---|---|-----|-----|-----|-----|-----|-----|-----|-----|---|
| h | 0 | 128 | 224 | 288 | 320 | 320 | 288 | 224 | 128 | 0 |

**a.** From the table and graph, you see when $t = 2$, $h = 224$ on the way up. On the way down, the ball is 224 ft above the ground when $t = 7$. So, the ball has a height of 224 ft twice, at 2 sec and again at about 7 sec.

**b.** The maximum height of the ball is the $h$-value at the top of the curve. Maximum height occurs at approximately 4.5 sec.

**c.** The ball hits the ground when $h = 0$. So the ball hits the ground after 9 sec.

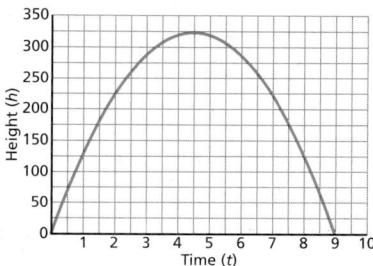

### TRY THESE EXERCISES

**Graph each function for the domain of real numbers.** For 1–3, see additional answers.

**1.** $y = x^2 + 2$

**2.** $y = -2x^2 - 5$

**3.** $y = 3x^2 - x + 3$

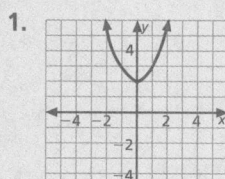

**4. WRITING MATH** Write a few sentences describing the similarities among the graphs of the quadratic equations in Exercises 1–3. Answers will vary.

mathmatters2.com/extra_examples

Lesson 6-6 **Graph Quadratic Functions** 269

## ADDITIONAL ANSWERS

1.
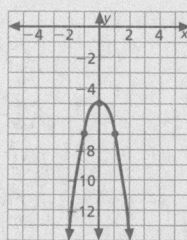

2.

3.
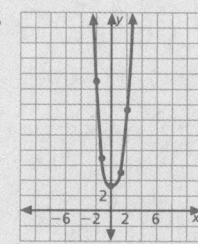

---

**Supplementary Example 1**

**BUSINESS** A stationery supply wholesale chain found that pens that sell for $x$ dollars have a profit, $y$, in thousands of dollars, modeled by the equation $y = -x^2 + 8x - 4$.

**a.** Make a table of ordered pairs to draw a graph.

| x | y |
|---|----|
| 0 | -4 |
| 1 | 3 |
| 2 | 8 |
| 3 | 11 |
| 4 | 12 |
| 5 | 11 |
| 6 | 8 |
| 7 | 3 |
| 8 | -4 |

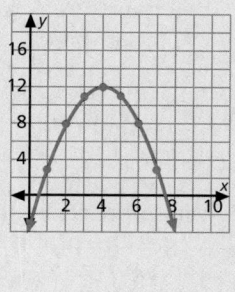

**b.** If the pens sell for $2.00 each, what is the expected profit? $8000

**c.** What is the price of the pens that would yield the maximum profit? $4.00 What is the maximum profit? $12,000

**Supplementary Example 2**

Consider the equation $x = y^2$, which is equivalent to the two equations $y = \pm \sqrt{x}$.

**a.** Make a table of ordered pairs to draw a graph.

| x | y |
|---|-----|
| 0 | 0 |
| 1 | ±1 |
| 4 | ±2 |
| 9 | ±3 |

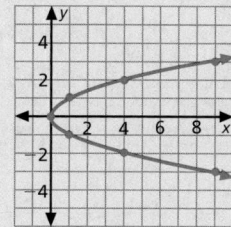

**b.** Is the relation a function? No; except at the origin, vertical lines intersect the graph in two places.

**c.** What are the domain and range of the relation? domain: real numbers $\geq 0$; range: all real numbers

---

Ask the following questions to determine if students understand the content presented in this lesson.

1. Explain how to tell whether the graph of a quadratic equation of the form $y = ax^2 + bx + c$ will have a maximum point or a minimum point.   When $a$, the coefficient of the $x^2$-term, is positive, the curve opens up and has a minimum point; when $a$ is negative, the curve opens down and has a maximum point.

2. When preparing a table of values to get the graph of a parabola, explain how to tell whether your calculations for $y$ are reasonable.   After you have reached a maximum or minimum value for $y$, the values on either side of that number should occur in symmetric pairs.

### ASSIGNMENT GUIDE

Basic: 1–47, 51–60
Enriched: 1–60

### Reteaching Worksheet 6-6

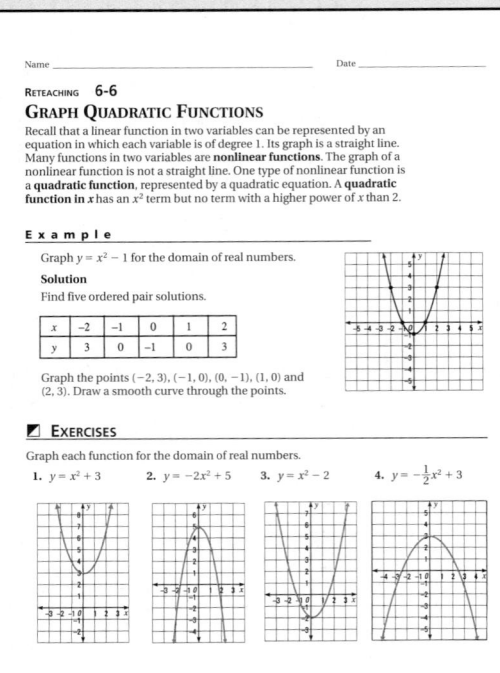

Name _____ Date _____

RETEACHING **6-6**
**GRAPH QUADRATIC FUNCTIONS**
Recall that a linear function in two variables can be represented by an equation in which each variable is of degree 1. Its graph is a straight line. Many functions in two variables are **nonlinear functions**. The graph of a nonlinear function is not a straight line. One type of nonlinear function is a **quadratic function**, represented by a quadratic equation. A **quadratic function in $x$** has an $x^2$ term but no term with a higher power of $x$ than 2.

**Example**

Graph $y = x^2 - 1$ for the domain of real numbers.

**Solution**
Find five ordered pair solutions.

| $x$ | -2 | -1 | 0 | 1 | 2 |
|---|---|---|---|---|---|
| $y$ | 3 | 0 | -1 | 0 | 3 |

Graph the points $(-2, 3)$, $(-1, 0)$, $(0, -1)$, $(1, 0)$ and $(2, 3)$. Draw a smooth curve through the points.

**EXERCISES**

Graph each function for the domain of real numbers.
1. $y = x^2 + 3$  2. $y = -2x^2 + 5$  3. $y = x^2 - 2$  4. $y = -\frac{1}{2}x^2 + 3$

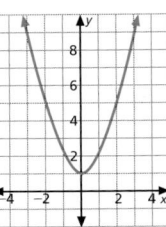

**SPORTS** An arrow is shot into the air. The height of the arrow is a function of the time that the arrow is in the air. The equation that represents this function is $h = -16t^2 + 112t$, where $h$ is the height in feet and $t$ is the seconds the arrow is in the air.

5. Make a table of ordered pairs. Graph the points, and draw a smooth curve through the points.
   See additional answers.
6. When does the arrow reach a height of 96 ft?
   1 sec, 6 sec
7. When does the arrow reach its maximum height?  3.5 sec
8. When does the arrow hit the ground?  7 sec

**Complete each ordered pair so that it corresponds to a point on the graph.**

9. $(-1, ?)$  2
10. $(3, ?)$  9
11. $(?, 1)$  0
12. $(?, 5)$  $-2$ or 2

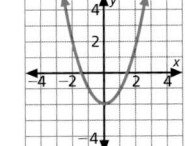

### PRACTICE EXERCISES • For Extra Practice, see page 605.

**Graph each function for the domain of real numbers.** For 13–18, see additional answers.

13. $y = x^2 + 4$
14. $y = 3x^2 - 6$
15. $y = 2x^2$
16. $y = x^2 - 2x + 3$
17. $y = -x^2 - 4$
18. $y = 2x^2 - 1$

**AGRICULTURE** Suppose you have 100 ft of fence for a rectangular garden.

19. Name three possible lengths and widths of the garden to be fenced in.
    Answers will vary but may include 25 × 25, 30 × 20, 35 × 15, 40 × 10, etc.
20. Write an equation for the area.
    $A = (50 - w)w = 50w - w^2$
21. Graph the area as a function of the width.
    See additional answers.
22. What values make sense for the domain?
    $0 \le w \le 50$
23. What is the maximum area possible?
    625 ft²

**Complete each ordered pair so that it corresponds to a point on the graph.**

24. $(1, ?)$  $-1$
25. $(0, ?)$  $-2$
26. $(?, -2)$  0
27. $(?, -1)$  1 or $-1$

**PHYSICS** The height of a softball hit into the air is given by the equation $h = -4.9t^2 + 24t + 3$, where $h$ is the height in feet and $t$ is the time in seconds.

28. Graph the function.   See additional answers.
29. At what time does the disc reach its maximum height? (Remember that time is measured in quarter seconds.)  $\approx$ 2.5 sec
30. How many seconds is the ball in the air?  $\approx$ 5 sec
31. **GRAPHING** Use a graphing utility to graph the equations below on a coordinate plane.   Check students' work.

$y = x^2$     $y = x^2 + 1$     $y = x^2 - 1$     $y = x^2 + 2$     $y = x^2 - 2$

32. Compare the graphs in Exercise 31. What type of changes occur in the graph based on the value of the constant term being positive or negative?
    When the constant is negative, the vertex of the parabola is below the x-axis, and when the constant is positive, the vertex is above the x-axis.

### ADDITIONAL ANSWERS

5.

| $t$ | $h$ |
|---|---|
| 0 | 0 |
| 1 | 96 |
| 2 | 160 |
| 3 | 192 |
| 4 | 192 |
| 5 | 160 |
| 6 | 96 |
| 7 | 0 |

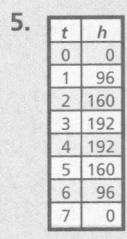

13.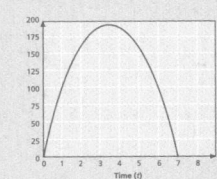

14.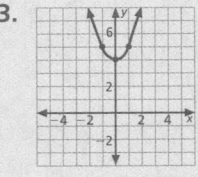

16.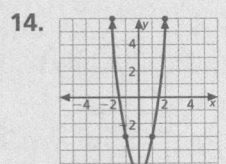

18.

For Exercises 15, 17, 41, 43, 45, and 47, see Selected Answers on page 684.

**33.** Name the function of the graph of $y = x^2$ translated 10 units up. Name the function of the graph of $y = x^2$ translated 10 units down.   $y = x^2 + 10$; $y = x^2 - 10$

**34. GRAPHING** Use a graphing calculator to graph the equations below on the same coordinate plane.   Check students' work.

$y = x^2$ $\qquad$ $y = (x + 1)^2$ $\qquad$ $y = (x - 1)^2$ $\qquad$ $y = (x + 2)^2$ $\qquad$ $y = (x - 2)^2$

**35.** Compare the graphs in Exercise 34. Does it matter whether the value of the constant term is positive or negative?   Yes. Changing the term shifts the graph horizontally.

**36.** What function would a graph the same as the graph of $y = x^2$ but 10 units to the left of it represent? 10 units to the right of it?   $y = (x + 10)^2$; $y = (x - 10)^2$

**37. GRAPHING** Use a graphing calculator to graph the equations below on the same coordinate plane.   Check students' work.

$y = x^2$ $\qquad\qquad$ $y = -x^2$ $\qquad\qquad$ $y = 2x^2$

$y = -2x^2$ $\qquad\qquad$ $y = 0.5x^2$ $\qquad\qquad$ $y = -0.5x^2$

**38.** Compare the graphs in Exercise 37 to others in the form $y = ax^2$. Does it matter if the value of the coefficient of $x$ is positive or negative?
Yes. If $a$ is negative, the parabola opens down, and if $a$ is positive, the parabola opens up.

**39.** Compare the graphs in Exercise 37 to others in the form $y = ax^2$. Does it matter if the value of the coefficient of $x$ is between 0 and 1, or is greater than 1? Yes. If $a$ is between 0 and 1 the parabola opens wider than the graph of $y = x^2$. It is narrower if $a$ is greater than 1.

**Use what you discovered in Exercises 31–39 to graph each quadratic function.**
For 40–47, see additional answers.

**40.** $y = x^2 + 5$ $\qquad$ **41.** $y = 3x^2 - 2$ $\qquad$ **42.** $y = -3x^2$ $\qquad$ **43.** $y = (x - 2)^2$

**44.** $y = x^2 - 4$ $\qquad$ **45.** $y = 2x^2 - 7$ $\qquad$ **46.** $y = -2x^2$ $\qquad$ **47.** $y = 2(x - 2)^2$

## ■ EXTENDED PRACTICE EXERCISES

**48. CRITICAL THINKING** For the graph of a quadratic function $y = ax^2 + bx + c$, find the $x$-coordinate of the vertex in terms of $a$ and $b$.   $x = \dfrac{-b}{2a}$

**49.** Use your answer to Exercise 48. Write the coordinates of the vertex of any quadratic function $y = ax^2 + bx + c$ in terms of $a$ and $b$.   $\left(-\dfrac{b}{2a}, c - \dfrac{b^2}{4a}\right)$

**50. CHAPTER INVESTIGATION** Use your graphs from Lessons 6-3 and 6-4 to determine which quarters were profitable and which had a loss. Brainstorm ideas about business decisions and planning based on similar graphs.
Answers will vary.

## ■ MIXED REVIEW EXERCISES

**Find the unknown angle measures in each parallelogram.** (Lesson 5-6)

**51.** $m\angle A$  128°

**52.** $m\angle B$  52°

**53.** $m\angle C$  128°

**54.** $m\angle Q$  67°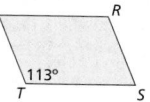

**55.** $m\angle R$  113°

**56.** $m\angle S$  67°

**Write each phrase as a variable expression.** (Lesson 2-3)

**57.** a number multiplied by 27  $27x$

**58.** the quotient of seven and a number  $\dfrac{7}{x}$

**59.** the product of a number and 13  $13x$

**60.** the difference of a number and three.  $x - 3$

## ADDITIONAL ANSWERS

**21.**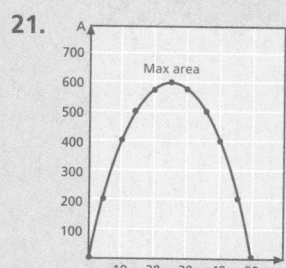

**28.**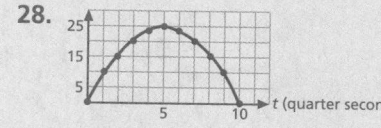

---

**Extra Practice Worksheet 6-6**

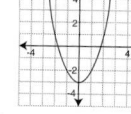
**40.**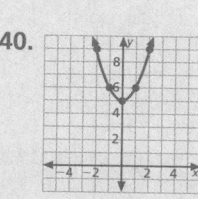

**42.**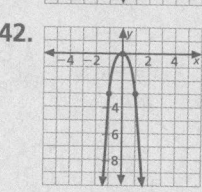

**44.**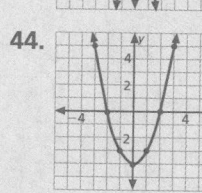

**46.**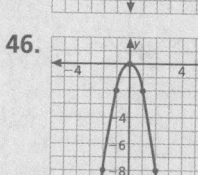

### Vocabulary Review

**Lesson 6-5**
function          function notation
domain            range
continuous        linear function
vertical line test

**Lesson 6-6**
quadratic function    parabola

## ASSIGNMENT GUIDE

All students: 1–38

## Chalkboard Examples

### Lesson 6-5
Graph the relation $y = x^4$ and determine if it is a function.

| $x$ | $y$ |
|-----|-----|
| $-2$ | 16 |
| $-1$ | 1 |
| 0 | 0 |
| 1 | 1 |
| 2 | 16 |

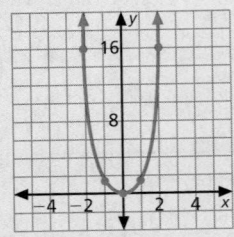

Yes, $y = x^4$ is a function.

### Lesson 6-6
Rectangular plot *ABCD* is to be fenced with 100 ft of fencing. Find the maximum area to the nearest square foot.

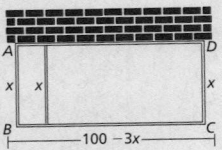

Write a function to represent the area.
Let height $= x$, width $= 100 - 3x$ and *area* $= y$.
$$y = x(100 - 3x) = -3x^2 + 100x$$
Use a graphing calculator to graph the parabola, and read the *y*-coordinate of its maximum point.

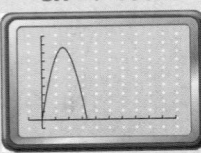

Using 100 ft of fencing, the maximum area of *ABCD* is about 833 ft².

---

# Review and Practice Your Skills

## PRACTICE ▪ LESSON 6-5

**Graph each function for the given domain.**
For 1–4, see additional answers.
1. $y = 2x - 3$; $\{-4, -3, -1, 0, 2\}$
2. $f(x) = -\frac{1}{2}x$; $\{-4, -2, 0, 2, 4\}$
3. $f(x) = -3$; $\{-3, -1, 1, 3\}$
4. $y = -3x^2$; {all real numbers}

**Determine if each graph represents a function. If not, explain why.**

5. 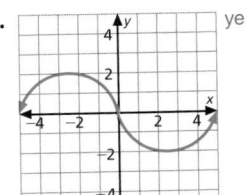 yes

6. 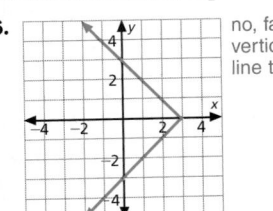 no, fails vertical line test

7. 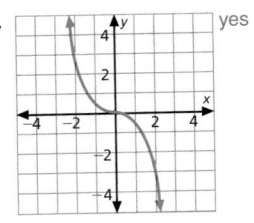 yes

**Graph each function.** For 8–13, see additional answers.

8. $y = |x + 3|$
9. $y = \frac{x}{2} + 2$
10. $y = -|x|$
11. $y = 4\sqrt{x}$
12. $y = x^2 + 2$
13. $x - y = 3$

## PRACTICE ▪ LESSON 6-6

**Graph each function for the domain of real numbers.**
For 14–19, see additional answers.
14. $y = x^2$
15. $y = x^2 - 3$
16. $y = -3x^2$
17. $y = \frac{1}{3}x^2$
18. $y = -x^2 - 3$
19. $y = x^2 + 3$

**Complete each ordered pair so that it corresponds to a point on the graph.**

20. $(?, 0)$  0
21. $(1, ?)$  1
22. $(-2, ?)$  3
23. $(?, 3)$  $-2$ or 2

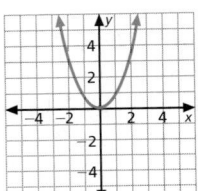

**PHYSICS** A ball is dropped from the top of a building 30-m tall. The height of the ball is a function of the time that the ball is in the air. The equation that represents this function is $h = -4.9t^2 + 30$ where $h$ is the height in meters and $t$ is the time in seconds the ball is in the air.

24. Copy and complete the table of ordered pairs. Round to the nearest tenth.

| $t$ | 0 | 0.5 | 1 | 1.5 | 2 | 2.2 | 2.4 |
|-----|---|-----|---|-----|---|-----|-----|
| $h$ | ■ | ■ | ■ | ■ | ■ | ■ | ■ |

30   28.8   25.1   19.0   10.4   6.3   1.8

25. When does the ball reach a height of 10.4 m?  2 sec

26. When does the ball hit the ground?  2.45 sec

27. Is the ball above or below ground at $t = 3$ sec? Justify your answer.
Above. Although $h$ is negative at $t = 3$ sec, we know from experience that balls bounce.

## ADDITIONAL ANSWERS

1.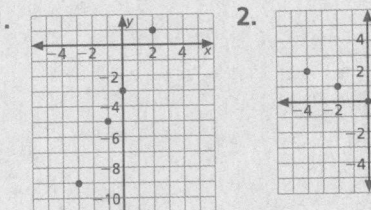

2.

4.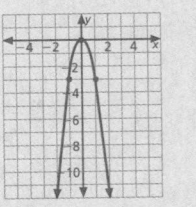

8.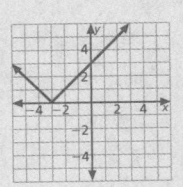

10.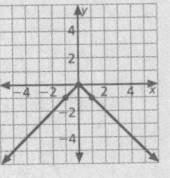

12.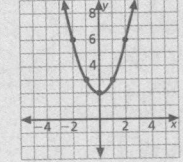

For Exercises 3, 9, 11, 13, 15, 17, and 19, see Selected Answers on page 684-685.

## PRACTICE ■ LESSON 6-1–LESSON 6-6

**Find the midpoints of the segments with the following endpoints.** (Lesson 6-1)

**28.** $A(-7, 3)$, $B(0, -1)$ $\left(-3\frac{1}{2}, 1\right)$ **29.** $C\left(4, \frac{1}{2}\right)$, $D\left(\frac{1}{8}, -6\right)$ $\left(2\frac{1}{16}, -2\frac{3}{4}\right)$ **30.** $F(-1, -1)$, $G(6, -8)$ $\left(2\frac{1}{2}, -4\frac{1}{2}\right)$

**Identify the slope and $y$-intercept of each line.** (Lesson 6-3)

**31.** $y = -x$ $-1; 0$ **32.** $y = \frac{x}{3} - 3$ $\frac{1}{3}; -3$ **33.** $2x - y = 4$ $2; -4$ **34.** $5x - 3y = 15$ $\frac{5}{3}; -5$

**Write an inequality for each graph.** (Lesson 6-4)

**35.**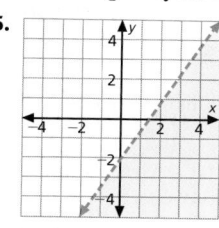

**36.** 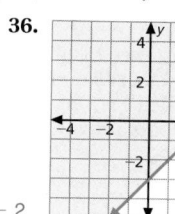 $y < \frac{3}{2}x - 2$

**37.** 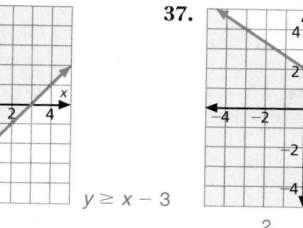 $y \geq x - 3$

$y \leq -\frac{2}{3}x + 2$

**38.** Graph the nonlinear function $y = x^2 + 3$. (Lesson 6-6)
See additional answers.

## MathWorks Career – Restaurateur
Workplace Knowhow

**A** restaurateur sells and serves food to the public. Restaurateurs are responsible for hiring employees, purchasing food, paying bills and satisfying the customers. A restaurateur has determined that the following equation roughly approximates the amount of profit he can make, based on $x$ number of customers.

$$\text{Profit} = 25x - 1000$$

**1.** Graph the profit equation and determine the "break-even" point. The "break-even" point is the minimum number of customers required to obtain a positive profit.
See additional answers. 40

**2.** Suppose that on a given day there were 50 customers and the restaurateur made a profit of $300. This profit is more than what is expected from 50 customers. Shade the region of the graph where the profit is greater than what is normally expected for a given number of customers. What circumstances might occur to allow profits to be higher than expected?
See additional answers. Answers will vary.

**3.** Write the profit equation above using function notation, $f(x)$. What are the domain and range of this profit function? $f(x) = 25x - 1000$; domain: $x \geq 0$; range: $f(x) \geq -1000$

**4.** Suppose that the profit function is $f(x) = 25x^2 - 1000$. Graph this function and determine the break-even point. Plot the graph using $x$-values 0 through 10.
See additional answers. 7

 **Math Online** mathmatters2.com/mathworks

Chapter 6 **Review and Practice Your Skills** | 273

## MathWorks

A person who assumes the responsibility and the risk for a business operation with the expectation of making a profit is called an *entrepreneur*. The entrepreneur generally decides on the product, acquires the facilities, and brings together the labor force, capital, and production materials. If the business succeeds, the entrepreneur reaps the reward of profits; if it fails, he or she takes the loss. Many of our nation's entrepreneurs run small businesses such as restaurants.

Students should answer Questions 1–4 to better understand the role of functions in the process of determining profit.

Many U.S. cities boast a variety of restaurants and are proud of the wide range of ethnic specialties available. Students may be interested in researching the types of restaurants available in their local area. They may even interview a local restaurateur to find out about existing challenges and what the owner deems rewarding about the business in addition to financial gain.

Students who are interested in learning more about this career choice can go to mathmatters2.com/mathworks. School Guidance Counselors are another resource for information about training requirements and appropriate schools.

## MathWorks

1–2.
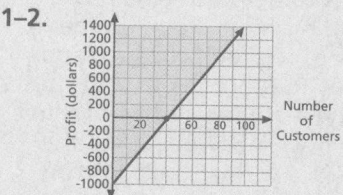

4.
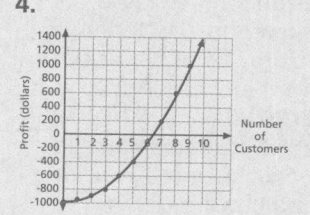

**14.** 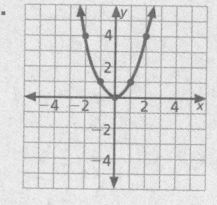 **16.** 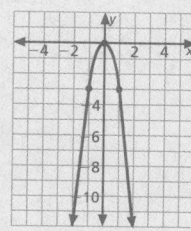 **18.** 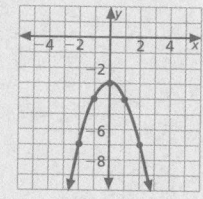 **38.**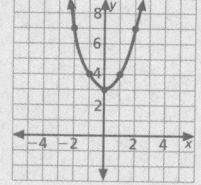

## Lesson Planning

### NCTM Standards/Strands
- Algebra
- Problem Solving
- Connections
- Communication

### Vocabulary
make a table

### Tools/Materials Needed
calculator

### Lesson Resources
Warm-up Transparency 26
Transparency RF-1
Reteaching 6-7
Extra Practice 6-7
Enrichment 6-7

### ASSIGNMENT GUIDE

**Basic:** 1–28
**Enriched:** 1–28

## Getting Started

### 5-MINUTE WARM-UP

Solve each equation.
1. $5a - 14 = 31$   9
2. $13m + 3 = -192$   $-15$
3. $\frac{3x}{4} = 6$   8    4. $\frac{1}{2}y = 12$   24

**THE FIVE-STEP PLAN Read**—ask questions to help students understand the problem. **Plan**—guide students to related problems and previously mastered skills and strategies. **Solve**—students solve problem on their own. **Answer**—write the solution in a format that answers the question. **Check**—review work, check for reasonableness, and review strategy used. Students will benefit from the experience of verbalizing their methods.
**THE STRATEGY** *Make a table*—this strategy enables students to organize data so that they may observe a pattern, leading to a general rule.

---

Functions form patterns that can be summarized using function rules. An equation with two variables is another way to write a function rule. For example, for the function rule $x + 3$, you can write it as $y = x + 3$. An effective strategy to organize and classify the domain and range values is to **make a table**. In this case, a function table can lead you to a function rule.

### Problem Solving Strategies
Guess and check

Look for a pattern

Solve a simpler problem

✓ Make a table, chart or list

Use a picture, diagram or model

Act it out

Work backwards

Eliminate possibilities

Use an equation or formula

### Problem

Darnell is considering a new long-distance telephone provider. The new provider charges $1.10 for placing a call and $0.08 for each minute. His current provider charges $0.12/min, and the cost of his calls range from $2.50 to $7.50. Compare providers' costs.

### Solve the Problem

Use a table to find a pattern or function rule for the new service. The function is $t = 1.10 + 0.08m$. Use the lower price (2.50), and solve for $m$. Then use the upper price (7.50), and solve for $m$.

| | Base charge | Cost of minutes | Total cost |
|---|---|---|---|
| One-minute call | 1.10 | $0.08 \cdot 1 = 0.08$ | 1.18 |
| Two-minute call | 1.10 | $0.08 \cdot 2 = 0.16$ | 1.26 |
| Three-minute call | 1.10 | $0.08 \cdot 3 = 0.24$ | 1.34 |
| Any number of minutes, $m$ | 1.10 | $0.08 \cdot m = 0.08m$ | $1.10 + 0.08m$ |

$2.50 = 1.10 + 0.08m$      $7.50 = 1.10 + 0.08m$
$1.40 = 0.08m$      $6.40 = 0.08m$
$17.5 = m$      $80 = m$

With the new provider, you can talk from 17.5 min to 80 min for the price range.

To find the minutes that Darnell currently talks, divide the cost by the minutes.
$2.50 \div 0.12 = 20.8$      $7.50 \div 0.12 = 62.5$

Currently, Darnell can talk from 20.8 min to 62.5 min. for the price range.

### TRY THESE EXERCISES

Match each function table with the appropriate function rule.

1.   c

| x | 5 | -10 | 0 | 2 | 4 |
|---|---|---|---|---|---|
| y | 3 | 8 | -2 | 0 | 2 |

2.   a

| x | 0 | 6 | -12 | 30 | 3 |
|---|---|---|---|---|---|
| y | 0 | 4 | -8 | 20 | 2 |

a. $f(x) = \frac{2}{3}x$
b. $f(x) = 2x^3$
c. $f(x) = |x| - 2$

**274**   Chapter 6   **Graphing Functions**

---

## ADDITIONAL ANSWERS

7.

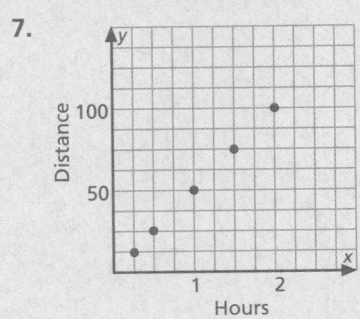

---

**Use each domain to find ordered pair solutions of each equation.**

3. $y = 2x - 1$; {4, −2, 0, 1, 2}
(4, 7), (−2, −5), (0, −1), (1, 1), (2, 3)

4. $y = -3x + 5$; {−5, −3, 0, 2, 4}
(−5, 20), (−3, 14), (0, 5), (2, −1), (4, −7)

**Five-step Plan**
1 Read
2 Plan
3 Solve
4 Answer
5 Check

**Write a function rule for each function table.**

5.

| x | 0 | 1 | 16 | 100 | $\frac{9}{4}$ |
|---|---|---|----|-----|---------------|
| y | 0 | 1 | 4  | 10  | $\frac{3}{2}$ |

$y = \sqrt{x}$

6.

| x | 10 | −6 | −1 | 25 | 0 |
|---|----|----|----|----|----|
| y | −2 | −18 | −13 | 13 | −12 |

$y = x - 12$

7. If a car is moving at a constant speed of 50 mi/h, the function $y = 50x$ gives the distance $y$, in miles, that it travels in $x$ hours. Graph the function when the domain is $\left\{\frac{1}{4}, \frac{1}{2}, 1, 1\frac{1}{2}, 2\right\}$.  See additional answers.

8. **NUMBER SENSE** Is the relationship that matches a number with its positive square root a function? Explain.  Yes. It passes the vertical line test, since no number has two positive square roots.

**Let the domain be the set of real numbers. Give the range of the function.**

9. $y = |x|$  $x \geq 0$

10. $y = -|x|$  $x \leq 0$

11. $y = x$  all real numbers

12. $y = -x$  all real numbers

13. **ECONOMICS** Use the current cost of a loaf of bread. Due to an average rate of inflation of 4% each year, the cost of food increases accordingly. What is the estimated cost of a loaf of bread 10 yr from today?  Answers will vary.

14. **WRITING MATH** Compare *range* as used in this lesson to how it is used in statistics in Chapter 1. How are the meanings alike? How are they different?  Answers will vary.

**BUSINESS** The cost of parking is $1.50 for the first hour and $0.75 for each additional hour.

15. Write a function to represent the cost of parking $x$ hours.
$C(x) = 1.5 + 0.75(x - 1)$

16. What values make sense for the domain?
the set of natural numbers

17. What meaning does the $y$-intercept have for this problem?
If the domain is the set of natural numbers, there is no $y$-intercept.

18. How much will a five-hour stay cost?  $4.50

19. For how long can you park if you have $18.50?  23 hr

20. **DATA FILE** Refer to the data on the age of Internet users on page 571. Write a function that represents the number of Internet users of age 9–17 for a given group of people.  $y = 0.178x$

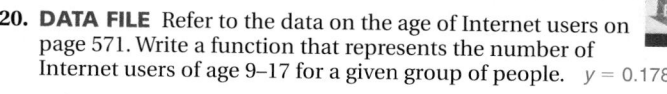

## ■ MIXED REVIEW EXERCISES

**Calculate each of the following permutations.** (Lesson 4-6)

21. $_{12}P_6$  665,280

22. $_{14}P_3$  2184

23. $_8P_3$  336

24. $_{14}P_6$  2,162,160

**Solve each equation. Check the solutions.** (Lesson 3-8)

25. $\sqrt{p} = 6$  36

26. $z^2 = 81$  ±9

27. $b^2 + 4 = 53$  ±7

28. $\sqrt{s + 6} = 8$  58

Lesson 6-7 **Problem Solving Skills: Patterns and Functions** | 275

---

## Chalkboard Examples

### Supplementary Problem
**BUSINESS** An appliance store offers its sales staff a choice of weekly earning plans: a base salary of $200 plus a 7% commission on their sales or 12% commission on their sales. What is the minimum amount of sales for which the strictly-commission plan gives a higher weekly income than the base-salary plan?

Write a function rule for each plan. Let $w$ = the weekly earnings and $s$ = the dollar amount of weekly sales.
base-salary plan: $w = 200 + 0.07s$
strictly-commission plan: $w = 0.12s$

| sales | with salary | without salary |
|-------|-------------|----------------|
| 2000  | 340         | 240            |
| 3000  | 410         | 360            |
| 4000  | 480         | 480            |
| 5000  | 550         | 600            |

A table of values shows that the variable plan earns a salesperson a higher weekly income when the weekly sales are more than $4000.

## Lesson Wrap-up

### QUICK ASSESSMENT
Ask the following question to determine if students understand the content presented in this lesson. Which of the following is the rule for the table shown?  C

| x | 0 | 1 | 2 | 3 | 4 |
|---|---|---|----|----|----|
| y | 0 | 3 | 12 | 27 | 48 |

A. $y = x^3$

B. $y = 2x^3$

C. $y = 3x^2$

D. $y = 3x^3$

### Vocabulary

direct variation
constant of variation

### Tools/Materials Needed

graph paper          calculator

### Lesson Resources

Warm-up Transparency 26
Transparency TK-9–12, RF-36
Reteaching 6-8
Extra Practice 6-8
Enrichment 6-8

## Getting Started

### 5-Minute Warm-Up

Solve for $n$.
1. $72 = 60n$   **1.2**
2. $8n^2 = 98$   **±3.5**
3. $\frac{44}{12} = \frac{n}{15}$   **55**
4. $\frac{n}{8.4} = \frac{4.5}{3.6}$   **10.5**

### Introduction to Lesson 6-8
For Question 4, elicit that the values from any one line of the table can be used to establish the cost ratio needed as one side of the proportion, $\frac{\text{number of muffins}}{\text{cost of muffins}}$. The other side of the proportion will be that ratio applied to 7 muffins.

After students have written the function rule asked for in Question 5, ask them to describe the graph of the equation.   **straight line through the origin ($y$-intercept = 0) and slope = 0.69**

---

# 6-8 Direct Variation

**Goals**
- Solve problems involving direct variation function.
- Solve problems involving direct square variation functions.

**Applications**   Finance, Biology, Physics, Business

**Use the table to answer Questions 1–5.**

| Number of muffins | Cost |
|---|---|
| 5 | $3.45 |
| 10 | $6.90 |
| 12 | $8.28 |
| 20 | $13.80 |
| 24 | $16.56 |

1. Let $m$ = the number of muffins, and let $C$ = the cost. Find the ratio $\frac{C}{m}$ for each pair of entries. What do you discover?   The ratio equals $0.69.
2. As the number of muffins increases, what happens to the cost?   The cost increases.
3. When the number of muffins doubles, what happens to the cost?   The cost also doubles.
4. Use a proportion to find the cost of 7 muffins.   $4.83
5. The cost of the muffins is a function of the number of muffins. Write the function rule using the variables used in Question 1.   $C(m) = 0.69m$

### ■ BUILD UNDERSTANDING

Some linear functions have a relationship that when you divide the range (ouput) value by its corresponding domain (input) value, the quotient is the same. This constant quotient means that "$y$ varies directly as $x$." Such a function is a **direct variation**. The constant $k$ is called the **constant of variation**.

| Direct Variation | $y = kx$, where $k \neq 0$. |
|---|---|

Direct variation problems can be solved by writing and solving an equation or by writing and solving a proportion.

### Example 1

**PHYSICS** The distance a spring stretches varies directly as the weight applied to it. A 12-kg weight stretches the spring 15 cm. How many centimeters will a 20-kg weight stretch the spring?

### Solution

The weight applied is $x$, and the length the spring stretches is $y$.

*Equation Method*         $y = kx \longrightarrow 15 = k(12)$

$$\frac{15}{12} = k$$

$$\frac{5}{4} = k$$

Substitute 20 for $x$ and $\frac{5}{4}$ for $k$ in $y = kx$.

$$y = \frac{5}{4}(20) = 25$$

**276**   Chapter 6  **Graphing Functions**

## Extend the Lesson

**CONNECTING TO PRIOR KNOWLEDGE** Elicit the connection between the equation for direct variation, $y = kx$, and the slope-intercept form of a line, $y = mx + b$. Students should recognize that the graph of a direct variation is a line through the origin (since the $y$-intercept = 0) whose slope is $k$. Using the *equation method* to solve, the two known coordinates of one ordered pair are used to determine the constant of variation. Then that constant along with the known coordinate of the ordered pair with the missing coordinate will result in a value for the missing coordinate. The *proportion method* works directly with the two sets of ordered pairs. Since three of the four elements of the proportion are known, it is easy to solve for the fourth element.

*Proportion Method*

$$\frac{known\ length}{known\ weight} = \frac{new\ length}{new\ weight}$$

$$\frac{15}{12} = \frac{y}{20}$$

$15(20) = 12y$      Cross-products are equal to each other.

$300 = 12y$

$25 = y$      Divide both sides of equation by 12.

The length the spring stretches is 25 cm when 20 kg of weight is applied.

In some cases one quantity varies directly as the square of another. For example, the area of a circle varies directly as the square of the radius, assuming $\pi = 3.14$.

**Area of a Circle**

| Radius | 1 | 2 | 3 | 4 | 5 |
|--------|------|-------|-------|-------|-------|
| Area | 3.14 | 12.56 | 28.26 | 50.24 | 78.50 |

**Area of a Circle**

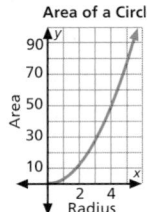

The graph shows that the relationship between the area and the radius is a quadratic function. This is an example of a **direct square variation** stated as "$y$ varies directly as $x^2$," or "$y$ is directly proportional to $x^2$."

| Direct Square Variation | $y = kx^2$, where $k \neq 0$. |
|---|---|

**Check Understanding**

Direct variation is a special case of a linear function $y = mx + b$, where $b = 0$. When a direct variation is graphed, how does the value of the constant of variation relate to the slope of the graph? Through what point on the coordinate plane will the graph of a direct variation always pass?

Their values are equal; the origin.

## Example 2

**PHYSICS** The distance a car rolls down a hill from a stand still position varies directly as the square of the amount of time it is rolling. If the car rolls 15 m downhill in 4 sec, how far will it roll in 10 sec?

**Solution**

Substitute known values of $x$ and $y$ into the equation to find $k$. The time the car is rolling is $x$, and the distance the car rolls is $y$.

$$y = kx^2$$
$$15 = k(4)^2$$
$$15 = 16k$$
$$\frac{15}{16} = k \approx 0.9375$$

Substitute 10 for $x$ and 4.0625 for $k$ into the equation $y = kx^2$.

$$y = 0.9375(10)^2$$
$$= 0.9375(100)$$
$$= 93.75$$

The car will roll approximately 93.75 m in 10 sec.

 mathmatters2.com/extra_examples

## Extend the Lesson

**REAL WORLD CONNECTION** The weight of an object on the moon varies directly as its weight on Earth. An astronaut who weighs 84 kg on Earth would weigh 14.28 kg on the moon.
Ask students to calculate: How much would they weigh on the moon? How much would their math textbook weigh on the moon? Answers will vary; an object's moon weight will be 0.17 times its Earth weight.

# Chalkboard Examples

## Supplementary Example 1

**CHEMISTRY** A law discovered by Jacques Charles, a French scientist of the late 18th and early 19th centuries, states that for a fixed amount of gas at a fixed pressure, the volume varies directly as the temperature in degrees Kelvin. If a gas has a volume of 559 mL at 40°C (313.16°K), what is its volume at 25°C (298.16°K)?

*Equation Method*

$$v = kt$$
$$559 = 40k$$
$$k = \frac{559}{313.16} \approx 1.785$$
$$v \approx 1.785t$$
$$v \approx 1.785(298.16)$$
$$v \approx 532.22 \text{ mL}$$

*Proportion Method*

$$\frac{v_1}{v_2} = \frac{t_1}{t_2}$$
$$\frac{559}{v_2} = \frac{313.16}{298.16}$$
$$313.16v_2 = 559 \cdot 298.16$$
$$v_2 = \frac{559 \cdot 298.16}{313.16}$$
$$v_2 \approx 532.22$$

So, at 25°C, the volume of the gas is 532.22 mL.

## Supplementary Example 2

**PHYSICS** The distance it takes to stop after you have applied the brakes of a car varies directly as the square of the speed of the car. A car going 64 km/h stops in 27 m. If you are going 90 km/h, how far will the car travel after you have applied the brakes?
Use distances expressed in kilometers.

*Equation Method*

$$s = kv^2$$
$$0.027 = k(64)^2$$
$$k = \frac{0.027}{64^2} \approx 6.59 \cdot 10^{-6}$$
$$s \approx (6.59 \cdot 10^{-6})v^2$$
$$s \approx (6.59 \cdot 10^{-6})90^2$$
$$s \approx 0.0534$$

*Proportion Method*

$$\frac{s_1}{s_2} = \frac{(v_1)^2}{(v_2)^2}$$
$$\frac{0.027}{s_2} = \frac{64^2}{90^2}$$
$$4096s_2 = 0.027 \cdot 8100$$
$$s_2 = \frac{0.027 \cdot 8100}{4096}$$
$$s_2 \approx 0.0534$$

So, when a car is traveling at 90 km/h, it takes about 0.0534 km or 53.4 m for it to stop after the brakes have been applied.

## Lesson Wrap-up

### QUICK ASSESSMENT

Ask the following questions to determine if students understand the content presented in this lesson.

1. Describe the graph of a direct variation. **a straight line throught the origin with slope equal to the constant of variation**

2. If $y$ varies directly as $x$, when do $x$ and $y$ have the same value? **when they both equal 0, or when $k = 1$**

3. Express the rate $15 \frac{mi}{hr}$ in the form of a direct variation. **$y = 15x$**

4. If $y$ varies directly as $x^2$, what happens to $y$ when $x$ is doubled? **$y$ is multiplied by 4.**

### ASSIGNMENT GUIDE

**Basic:** 1–24, 33–42
**Enriched:** 1–42

### Reteaching Worksheet 6-8

Name _____  Date _____

RETEACHING **6-8**
**DIRECT VARIATION**
A **direct variation** is a function in which $y$ varies directly as $x$ varies. It can be represented by a rule with the form $y = kx$, where $k$ is a nonzero constant called the **constant of variation**. A **direct square variation** is a function in which $y$ varies directly as $x^2$. It can be represented by a rule with the form $y = kx^2$, where $k$ is a nonzero constant.

**Example 1**

The amount Jane earns varies directly as the number of hours she works. For working 28 h, she is paid $210. How much would she earn for working 40 h?

**Solution**
Write a proportion.
$\frac{210}{28} = \frac{y}{40}$  ←money earned  ←hours worked
$210 \cdot 40 = y \cdot 28$
$8400 = 28y$
$300 = y$
She would earn $300.

**Example 2**

The distance a car needs to stop varies directly as the square of its speed when the brakes are applied. A car traveling at 50 km/h needs 30 m to stop. How many meters does it need to stop when it is traveling at 70 km/h?

**Solution**
Substitute known values for $x$ and $y$ in the equation $y = kx^2$ and solve for $k$.
$30 = k(50^2)$
$\frac{30}{2500} = k$
$0.012 = k$
Write the function rule, using 0.012 for $k$.
$y = 0.012x$
$y = 0.012 \cdot 70^2 = 58.8$
The car needs a distance of 58.8 m to stop.

**EXERCISES**

1. The number of tiles used on a square floor varies directly as the square of the side of the floor. A floor with sides of 24 m requires 2304 tiles. How many tiles would a square floor with sides of 10 m require? **400 tiles**

2. The number of buttons a machine produces varies directly as the time it is running. If the machine produces 688 buttons in 12 min, how many would it produce in 15 min? **860 buttons**

3. The distance traveled by sound varies directly as the time. If a sound travels 62 mi in 5 min, how far does it travel in 60 min? **744 mi**

4. The weight of a circular mirror varies directly as the square of its radius. A mirror with radius 4 in. weighs 6 oz. How much does a mirror with radius 12 in. weigh? **54 oz**

---

### ▰ TRY THESE EXERCISES

1. Assume that $y$ varies directly as $x$. When $x = 24$, $y = 16$. Find $y$ when $x = 42$. **28**

2. Assume that $y$ varies directly as $x$. When $x = 3$, $y = 63$. Find $y$ when $x = 5$. **105**

3. **FINANCE** The annual simple interest on a loan varies directly as the amount of the loan. The interest in one year on a $400 loan is $56. Find the interest in one year on a loan of $650. **$91**

4. **WRITING MATH** Use examples to explain how you know whether the relationship between the area and the radius of a circle is a direct variation or a direct square variation. **The relationship is a direct square variation because $A = \pi r^2$.**

5. **AGRICULTURE** An acre is equivalent to 4840 yd². A chain is a special measure of length equal to 22 yd. How many square chains are equivalent to 1 acre? **10**

6. A map is scaled so that 1 in. = 2.5 mi. How far apart are two cities if they are 6 in. apart on the map? **15 mi**

### ▰ PRACTICE EXERCISES • For Extra Practice, see page 606.

7. Assume that $y$ varies directly as $x$. When $x = 9$, $y = 30$. Find $y$ when $x = 15$. **50**

8. Assume that $y$ varies directly as $x$. When $x = 21$, $y = 12$. Find $y$ when $x = 35$. **20**

9. Assume that $y$ varies directly as $x$. When $x = 6$, $y = 198$. Find $y$ when $x = 2$. **66**

10. Assume that $y$ varies directly as $x$. When $x = 10$, $y = 10$. Find $y$ when $x = 7$. **7**

**Find the constant of variation for each.**

11. $y =$ days, $x =$ weeks **7**   12. $y =$ days, $x =$ hours **$\frac{1}{24}$**

13. $y =$ yards, $x =$ miles **1760**  14. $y =$ in.², $x =$ ft² **144**

15. **SPACE** The weight of an object on the moon varies directly with its weight on Earth. A person who weighs 141 lb on Earth weighs only 23.5 lb on the moon. About how much do you weigh on the moon if you weigh 109 lb on Earth? **18.2 lb**

16. A length of 50 ft is equivalent to a length of 1524 cm. How many centimeters are equivalent to 125 ft? **3810 cm**

17. **PHYSICS** The distance an object falls from a given height varies directly as the square of the time the object falls. A ball falls about 312 m in 8 sec. How far did it fall during the first 4 sec? **78 m**

18. **PART-TIME JOB** For every pound of cherries she picks, Hanna gets paid $1.80. Write a function rule relating her earnings in dollars to the number of pounds she picks. Use $E$ to represent her earnings and $p$ to represent the number of pounds she picks. Draw a graph that shows the relationship. Use it to find how many pounds of cherries Hanna must pick to earn $6. See additional answers. **$E = 1.80p$; $3\frac{1}{3}$ lb.**

**278** | Chapter 6 **Graphing Functions**

### ADDITIONAL ANSWERS

18.
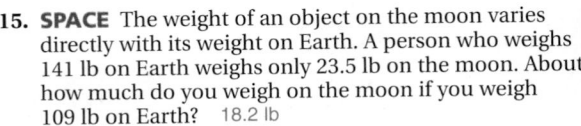
(Graph: Earnings (dollars) vs. Pounds)

27.
$$\frac{y}{x} = \frac{a}{b}$$
$$by = ax$$
$$by + xy = ax + xy$$
$$y(b + x) = x(a + y)$$
$$\frac{y}{x} = \frac{a + y}{b + x}$$

33.
| 0 | 4 8 |
|---|---|
| 1 | 2 5 7 8 8 9 9 |
| 2 | 0 4 7 7 9 |
| 3 | 1 |

0|4 represents 4 calls.

34.
| 4 | 6 8 |
|---|---|
| 5 | 2 8 |
| 6 | 5 5 7 |
| 7 | 3 6 |
| 8 | 1 5 8 |
| 9 | 2 |
| 10 | 3 4 |

4|6 represents 46 shows.

**19. WRITING MATH** Write a problem that involves the relationship between two sets of data that increase or decrease together at a constant rate. Provide a solution to your problem. *Answers will vary.*

**20.** The table shows the cost of operating a refrigerator. Write the rule for the function that describes the relationship of the cost of operating the refrigerator and the amount of time the refrigerator is in operation. What is the constant of variation? $C = 3h; k = 3$

**Refrigerator Operating Costs**

| Cost (cents) | 3 | 6 | 9 | 12 | 15 |
|---|---|---|---|---|---|
| Time (hours) | 1 | 2 | 3 | 4 | 5 |

**Identify each relationship as direct variation, direct square variation or neither.**

**21.** the perimeter of a square and the measure of its side
direct

**22.** the area of a square and the measure of its side
direct square

**23.** the volume of a cube and the measure of its side
neither

**24.** the surface area of a cube and the measure of an edge
direct square

### ■ EXTENDED PRACTICE EXERCISES

**Assume that $y$ varies directly as $x^2$.**

**25.** How is $y$ affected when $x$ is doubled? When $x$ is tripled?
y is quadrupled; y is multiplied by 9

**26.** How is $y$ affected when $x$ is multiplied by $k$?
y is multiplied by $k^2$

**27. CRITICAL THINKING** If $\frac{y}{x} = \frac{a}{b}$, show that $\frac{y}{x} = \frac{y + a}{x + b}$.
See additional answers.

**28.** If $y = kx^2$ and $k < 0$, does $y$ increase or decrease as $x$ increases for $x \geq 0$? decreases

**29.** If $y = kx^2$ and $k > 0$, does $y$ increase or decrease as $x$ increases for $x \geq 0$? increases

**30.** If $y = kx^2$ and $x < 0$, does $y$ increase or decrease as $k$ increases for $k \geq 0$? increases

**31.** If $y = kx^2$ and $x > 0$, does $y$ increase or decrease as $k$ decreases for $k \geq 0$? decreases

**32. CHAPTER INVESTIGATION** Look over your graphs, the list of decision ideas and other information you have about your company. Name as many relationships as you can find that you think are examples of direct variation. Discuss your ideas with the class. *Answers will vary.*

### ■ MIXED REVIEW EXERCISES

**Make a stem-and-leaf plot for each set of data.** (Lesson 1-3)
For 33 and 34, see additional answers.

**33.** Number of long distance calls per month

| 4 | 18 | 29 | 27 | 20 | 31 | 19 | 17 |
|---|---|---|---|---|---|---|---|
| 12 | 18 | 24 | 27 | 19 | 15 | 8 | |

**34.** Number of beagles entered in AKC shows

| 52 | 48 | 65 | 104 | 73 | 81 | 85 | 67 |
|---|---|---|---|---|---|---|---|
| 58 | 65 | 76 | 103 | 88 | 46 | 92 | |

**Simplify each variable expression.** (Lesson 2-5)

**35.** $-3(b + 4)$
$-3b - 12$

**36.** $6(a - 13)$
$6a - 78$

**37.** $\frac{72c - 18d}{9}$
$8c - 2d$

**38.** $\frac{15r + 6t}{-3}$
$-5r - 2t$

**Evaluate each expression when $a = 0.5$, $b = -2$, and $c = 3$.** (Lesson 2-5)

**39.** $-3(a - 2)$ 4.5

**40.** $\frac{6b}{-3}$ 4

**41.** $\frac{-2a + 4b}{6}$ $-\frac{3}{2}$

**42.** $c(6a - 4b)$ 33

Math Online mathmatters2.com/self_check_quiz

Lesson 6-8 **Direct Variation** | **279**

---

## Extra Practice Worksheet 6-8

Name _____  Date _____

EXTRA PRACTICE **6-8**
**DIRECT VARIATION**

**☑ EXERCISES**

1. Assume that $y$ varies directly as $x$. When $x = 10$, $y = 15$. Find $y$ when $x = 15$. $22\frac{1}{2}$

2. Assume that $y$ varies directly as $x$. When $x = 3$, $y = 12$. Find $y$ when $x = 21$. $84$

3. Assume that $y$ varies directly as $x$. When $x = 28$, $y = 14$. Find $y$ when $x = 2$. $1$

4. Assume that $y$ varies directly as $x$. When $x = 2$, $y = 9$. Find $y$ when $x = 16$. $72$

5. Assume that $y$ varies directly as $x$. When $x = 4$, $y = 12$. Find $y$ when $x = 20$. $60$

6. Assume that $y$ varies directly as $x$. When $x = 18$, $y = 3$. Find $y$ when $x = 9$. $1\frac{1}{2}$

7. Assume that $y$ varies directly as $x$. When $x = 14$, $y = 21$. Find $y$ when $x = 7$. $10\frac{1}{2}$

8. Assume that $y$ varies directly as $x$. When $x = 36$, $y = 4$. Find $y$ when $x = 16$. $1\frac{7}{9}$

Find the constant of variation for each.

9. $y =$ years, $x =$ months $\frac{1}{12}$

10. $y =$ centimeters, $x =$ meters $100$

11. $y =$ minutes, $x =$ hours $60$

12. $y =$ cm³, $x =$ mm³ $\frac{1}{1000}$

13. The annual simple interest earned on an account varies directly as the amount invested. The interest earned on $500 is $25. Find the interest earned on an investment of $700. $35

14. The distance an object falls from a given height varies directly as the square of the time the object falls. A ball falls 45 ft in 4 sec. How far did it fall during the first second? 2.8125 ft

Identify each relationship as direct variation, direct square variation, or neither.

15. the circumference of a circle and the measure of its diameter ____ direct

16. the area of a circle and the measure of its radius ____ direct square

17. the perimeter of a rectangle and the measure of one of its sides ____ neither

---

## Enrichment Worksheet 6-8

Name _____  Date _____

ENRICHMENT **6-8**
**HOW BIG IS TOO BIG?**
For any two three-dimensional shapes that are similar, the ratio of the surface areas varies directly as the square of the ratio of their dimensions. That is, if the dimensions of a prism double, the surface area of the larger prism will be $2^2$, or 4, times larger than the surface area of the smaller prism.

Likewise, the ratio of the volumes varies directly as the cube of the ratio of their dimensions. For a prism whose dimensions are twice the size of another prism, the volume will be $2^3$, or 8, times as large.

The weight of a three-dimensional shape is proportional to its volume. For two persons, for example, one of whose measurements are double those of another, the larger person's weight would be $2^3$, or 8, times the weight of the smaller person.

**☑ EXERCISES**

1. Assume that human bones are cylindrical. Suppose that an adult person's leg bone has a diameter of 2 in. What is the cross-sectional area of the bone? 3.14 in²

2. Assume that a 6-ft-tall adult male weighing 200 lb can support a maximum of 500 lb additional weight before the bone breaks. How many pounds per square inch of cross-sectional area can the leg bone support? 223 lb/in²

3. If the person were four times larger than normal, what would be the area of the cross-section of the leg bone? 50.24 in²

4. From Exercise 3, how much weight could this larger leg bone support? 11,204 lb

5. The weight of a person varies directly as that person's volume. If a 6-ft-tall adult weighing 200 lb were four times larger than normal, how much would the person weigh? 12,800 lb

6. Compare your answers to Exercises 4 and 5. What conclusion can you draw? A person whose dimensions were four times larger could not support his or her own weight.

---

## Alternative Assessment

**MATH JOURNAL** Have students suggest an example of direct variation for which the constant of variation would be negative. Height above sea level varies directly as the time taken by a submarine to descend.

Then have students consider if their example were expressed in the form $y = kx$:

how is $y$ affected when $x$ increases? y decreases

how is $y$ affected when $x$ decreases? y increases

## Vocabulary Review

**Lesson 6-7**
make a table

**Lesson 6-8**
direct variation
constant of variation

## ASSIGNMENT GUIDE

**All students:** 1–34

## Chalkboard Examples

**Lesson 6-7**
The table below, which had been distributed by the Highway Code of Great Britain, gives information about three distances, each of which is a function of a car's speed.

| Speed of car (mph) | 10 | 20 | 30 | 40 | 50 | 60 |
|---|---|---|---|---|---|---|
| Thinking distance (ft) | 10 | 20 | 30 | 40 | 50 | 60 |
| Braking distance (ft) | 5 | 20 | 45 | 80 | 125 | 180 |
| Stopping distance (ft) | 15 | 40 | 75 | 120 | 175 | 240 |

Let the car's speed (in mph) be represented by $x$. Write a function rule in terms of $x$ to represent each of the distances mentioned in the table.

**a.** Thinking distance (in ft)    $x$

**b.** Braking distance (in ft)    $\frac{x^2}{20}$

**c.** Stopping distance (in ft)    $x + \frac{x^2}{20}$

---

# Review and Practice Your Skills

## PRACTICE ◼ LESSON 6-7

**Match each function table with the appropriate function rule.**

**1.** $f(x) = x^2$   c

**a.**

| x | 0 | 1 | 2 | 3 | 4 |
|---|---|---|---|---|---|
| y | 0 | $\frac{1}{2}$ | 1 | $\frac{3}{2}$ | 2 |

**2.** $f(x) = \frac{1}{2}x$   a

**b.**

| x | 0 | 1 | 2 | 3 | 4 |
|---|---|---|---|---|---|
| y | −3 | −2 | −1 | 0 | 1 |

**3.** $f(x) = x - 3$   b

**c.**

| x | 0 | 1 | 2 | 3 | 4 |
|---|---|---|---|---|---|
| y | 0 | 1 | 4 | 9 | 16 |

**Use each domain to find ordered pair solutions of each equation.**

**4.** $y = 4x - 1$; $\{-4, -2, 0, 2, 4\}$
$(-4, -17), (-2, -9), (0, -1), (2, 7), (4, 15)$

**5.** $y = x - 5$; $\{-4, -2, 0, 5, 10\}$
$(-4, -9), (-2, -7), (0, -5), (5, 0), (10, 5)$

**6.** $y = \frac{2}{3}x$; $\{-6, -3, 0, 3, 6\}$
$(-6, -4), (-3, -2), (0, 0), (3, 2), (6, 4)$

**7.** $y = -|x| + 2$; $\{-6, -3, 0, 3, 6\}$
$(-6, -4), (-3, -1), (0, 2), (3, -1), (6, -4)$

**Write a function rule for each function table.**

**8.**

| x | 2 | 3 | 4 | 5 | 6 |
|---|---|---|---|---|---|
| y | 8 | 11 | 14 | 17 | 20 |

$f(x) = 3x + 2$

**9.**

| x | 0 | 1 | 2 | 3 | 4 |
|---|---|---|---|---|---|
| y | 0 | 3 | 6 | 9 | 12 |

$f(x) = 3x$

**10.**

| x | 2 | 3 | 4 | 5 | 6 |
|---|---|---|---|---|---|
| y | 2 | 7 | 14 | 23 | 34 |

$f(x) = x^2 - 2$

**11.**

| x | −4 | −2 | 0 | 2 | 4 |
|---|---|---|---|---|---|
| y | 4 | 2 | 0 | 2 | 4 |

$f(x) = |x|$

## PRACTICE ◼ LESSON 6-8

**12.** Assume $y$ varies directly as $x$. When $x = 4$, $y = -12$. Find $y$ when $x = -7$.   21

**13.** Assume $y$ varies directly as $x$. When $x = 5$, $y = 15$. Find $y$ when $x = 8$.   24

**14.** Assume $y$ varies directly as $x$. When $x = 3$, $y = 18$. Find $y$ when $x = 6$.   36

**15.** Assume $y$ varies directly as $x$. When $x = -2$, $y = -13$. Find $y$ when $x = 6$.   39

**16.** Assume $y$ varies directly as $x$. When $x = -3$, $y = -17$. Find $y$ when $x = 4$.   $22\frac{2}{3}$

**17.** Assume $y$ varies directly as the square of $x$. When $x = 4$, $y = -16$. Find $y$ when $x = -2$.   −4

**18.** Assume $y$ varies directly as the square of $x$. When $x = -5$, $y = 75$. Find $y$ when $x = 8$.   192

**19.** Suppose the price of a pizza varies directly with the square of its diameter. At the Pizza Inn an 8 in. pizza cost \$6.00. How much would a 13 in. pizza cost?   \$15.84

**20.** The refund $r$ you get varies directly with the number $n$ of cans you recycle. If you receive a \$6.50 refund for 150 cans, how much should you receive for 500 cans?   \$21.67

## Teaching Tip

In preparation for Exercises 8–11, remind students that a given set of values can have a linear function as its rule only if the ratio $\frac{y_2 - y_1}{x_2 - x_1}$ is constant.

For example, in Exercise 8, the ratio $\frac{y_2 - y_1}{x_2 - x_1}$ between any two points in the table is $\frac{3}{1}$; so, the function rule for this table will be linear (the rule is $y = 3x + 2$). However, in Exercise 10, the ratio $\frac{y_2 - y_1}{x_2 - x_1}$ is not constant; so, the function rule for this table cannot be linear (the rule is $y = x^2 - 2$).

**Match the slope with the graph shown.** (Lesson 6-2)

21. 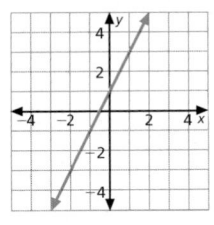 b

22. 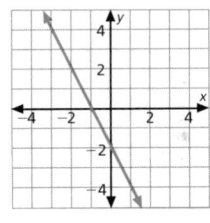 c

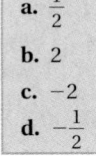
a. $\dfrac{1}{2}$
b. 2
c. $-2$
d. $-\dfrac{1}{2}$

23. 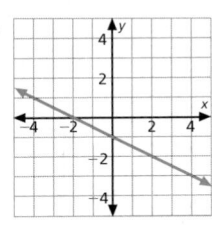 d

24. 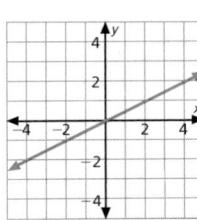 a

**Determine if the following graphs are functions. If not, explain why.** (Lesson 6-5)

25. 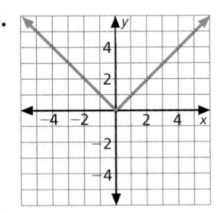 yes

26. 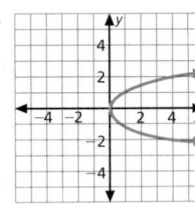 no; fails vertical line test

27. 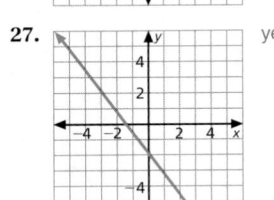 yes

28. 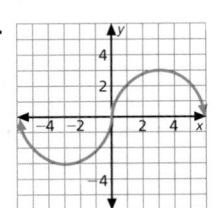 yes

**Make a function table for the following function rules.** (Lesson 6-7)   For 29–30, see additional answers.

29. $y = \dfrac{x}{2} + 3$, {2, 4, 6, 8}

30. $y = x^2 - 3$, {2, 4, 6, 8}

**Use the given endpoints of each circle's diameter. Find each circle's center and the lengths of its diameter and radius.** (Lesson 6-1)   For 31–34, see additional answers.

31. $(-1, 7), (4, -3)$      32. $(0, 1), (-3, 7)$      33. $(10, 7), (-7, 10)$      34. $(4, 6), (-1, 1)$

Chapter 6  **Review and Practice Your Skills**   281

---

**Lesson 6-8**

**CONSTRUCTION** To help consumers compare various insulating materials used in building construction, each material is rated with an $R$-value, which gives the material's rate of resistance to heat flow for 1 cm of thickness. So, the total $R$-value of a material varies directly with its thickness.

If a 6.0-cm space filled with loose foam insulation has an $R$-value of 11.34, find the $R$-value of a 4.0-cm space filled with loose foam insulation.

*Equation Method*

$R = ks$

$11.34 = 6k$

$k = \dfrac{11.34}{6} = 1.89$

$R = 1.89s$

$R = 1.89(4.0)$

$R = 7.56$

*Proportion Method*

$\dfrac{R_1}{R_2} = \dfrac{s_1}{s_2}$

$\dfrac{11.34}{R_2} = \dfrac{6.0}{4.0}$

$6.0R_2 = 11.34 \cdot 4.0$

$R_2 = \dfrac{11.34 \cdot 4.0}{6.0}$

$R_2 = 7.56$

So, a 4.0-cm space filled with loose foam insulation has an $R$-value of 7.56.

**ADDITIONAL ANSWERS**

29.

| x | 2 | 4 | 6 | 8 |
|---|---|---|---|---|
| y | 4 | 5 | 6 | 7 |

30.

| x | 2 | 4 | 6 | 8 |
|---|---|---|---|---|
| y | 1 | 13 | 33 | 61 |

31. $C\left(\dfrac{3}{2}, 2\right)$; $d \approx 11.2$; $r \approx 5.6$

32. $C\left(-\dfrac{3}{2}, 4\right)$; $d \approx 6.7$; $r \approx 3.34$

33. $C\left(\dfrac{3}{2}, \dfrac{17}{2}\right)$; $d = 17.3$; $r = 8.6$

34. $C\left(\dfrac{3}{2}, \dfrac{7}{2}\right)$; $d = 7.1$; $r = 3.4$

---

**Teaching Tip**

For Exercises 19 and 20, some students may find it helpful to first write a word model of the equation.

For example, for Exercise 20, they might write the following:

$y = kx$

$ of refund = (constant)(number of cans)

Some students may prefer to use letters appropriate to the problem.

So, for Exercise 20, thinking of the dollar amount of the refund, $r$, as a function of the number of cans, $c$, they might write $r = kc$ rather than $y = kx$.

### Vocabulary

inverse variation

### Tools/Materials Needed

graph paper      calculator
identical coins
12-in. ruler plus pivot

### Lesson Resources

Warm-up Transparency 27
Transparency TK-9, RF-36
Reteaching 6-9
Extra Practice 6-9
Enrichment 6-9

## Getting Started

### 5-MINUTE WARM-UP

**Solve for $n$.**
1. $13.2n = 59.4$   **4.5**
2. $3.5n^2 = 14$   **±2**
3. $7.5 = \dfrac{n}{2.6}$   **19.5**
4. $\dfrac{1377}{n^2} = 17$   **±9**

### Introduction to Lesson 6-9

After the possible integral dimensions for rectangles of area 80 square units are found, elicit that since the product of $x$ and $y$ is 80, each of these sets of ordered pairs satisfies the equation $xy = 80$.

For Question 3, students plot the points they have obtained, which are only integral values, and connect these points with a continuous curve, signifying that infinitely many values satisfy the requirement. Have students write some nonintegral ordered pairs for dimensions of a rectangle with area 80. **Examples:**
$3, \dfrac{80}{3}; 7, \dfrac{80}{7}; 93, \dfrac{80}{93}$

---

# 6-9 Inverse Variation

**Goals**
- Solve problems involving inverse variation functions.
- Solve problems involving inverse square variation functions.

**Applications**   Music, Physics, Industry, Travel

---

On grid paper, draw as many rectangles as you can that have an area of 80 square units.

1. Copy and complete the table of values for the length $x$ and the width $y$ of your rectangles. Write pairs in order of increasing values of $x$.
   See additional answers.
2. As $x$ increases, does $y$ increase or decrease? Does $x$ vary directly as $y$? Explain.
   Decrease. No; the ratio of $x$ to $y$ is not constant.
3. Draw a graph to show the lengths and widths of all rectangles whose area is 80 square units. Is the graph linear?   See additional answers. No.

**Rectangles with Area of 80**

| length $x$ | | | | |
|---|---|---|---|---|
| width $y$ | | | | |

### ▶ BUILD UNDERSTANDING

Some functions have this relationship: as $x$ increases in value, $y$ decreases in value. This relationship is an **inverse variation** if the product of the two values remain constant. For example, the time it takes to travel a given distance is inversely related to velocity.

| Inverse Variation | $y = \dfrac{k}{x}$ or $xy = k$, where $k \neq 0$ and $x \neq 0$. |
|---|---|

When you describe an inverse variation, you say "$y$ varies inversely as $x$," or "$y$ is inversely proportional to $x$." The constant of variation is $k$.

### Example 1

**MUSIC** If the tension in a guitar string is constant, the frequency of a note varies inversely as the length of the string. When the string is 75 cm, the frequency is 512 hertz (Hz). Find the length of the string that produces a note at a frequency of 640 Hz.

#### Solution

Substitute the length of string for $x$ and the frequency of note for $y$.

$$xy = k$$
$$(75)(512) = k$$
$$38,400 = k$$

Substitute 640 for $y$ and 38,400 for $k$ into the equation $xy = k$.

$$x(640) = 38,400$$
$$x = \frac{38,400}{640} = 60$$

The length of the string that produces a note at a frequency of 640 Hz is 60 cm.

---

## Teaching Tip

Note with students the following contrasts.

| Direct Variation $y = kx$ | Inverse Variation $xy = k$ |
|---|---|
| The dependent variable is a *constant multiple* of the independent variable. | The two variables have a *constant product*. |
| The order of the ratios is the same.   $\dfrac{x_1}{x_2} = \dfrac{y_1}{y_2}$ | The order of the ratios is opposite.   $\dfrac{x_1}{x_2} = \dfrac{y_2}{y_1}$ |

When you stand a certain distance from a light source and then move twice as far away, the intensity of the light is one–fourth as great. If you move three times as far away, the intensity is one–ninth as great. This is an example of **inverse square variation**, stated as "$y$ varies inversely as $x^2$," or "$y$ is inversely proportional to $x^2$."

| Inverse Square Variation | $y = \dfrac{k}{x^2}$ or $x^2 y = k$, where $k \neq 0$ and $x \neq 0$. |
|---|---|

## Example 2

**PHYSICS** The intensity of light varies inversely as the square of the distance from the source. At a distance of 8 ft from the source, a light meter measures 24 units of intensity. How many units of intensity will the light meter measure at a distance of 32 ft from the source?

### Solution

Substitute known values for $x$ and $y$ in the equation to find $k$. The distance from the light is $x$, and the intensity measured by the light meter is $y$.

$$x^2 y = k$$
$$(8)^2(24) = k \qquad x = 8, y = 24$$
$$1536 = k$$

Substitute 32 for $x$ and 1536 for $k$ into the equation $x^2 y = k$.

$$(32)^2(y) = 1536$$
$$1024y = 1536$$
$$y = \frac{1536}{1024} = 1.5$$

The light meter will measure 1.5 units of intensity at 32 ft.

**Check Understanding**

Suppose that $y$ varies inversely as $x$. When $x = n$, $y = m$.

Find $y$ when $x = m$.

$y = n$

## Example 3

**PHYSICS** The force needed to pry open a crate varies inversely as the length of the crowbar used. When the length is 2 m, the force needed is 12 newtons. What force is needed if the crowbar is 1.6 m long?

### Solution

Substitute 2 for $x$ and 12 for $y$.

$$xy = k$$
$$2(12) = k = 24$$

Use $k = 24$ and $x = 1.6$ to find the force needed.

$$xy = k$$
$$1.6y = 24$$
$$y = \frac{24}{1.6} = 15$$

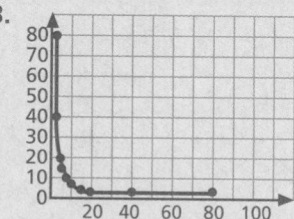

The force needed if the crowbar is 1.6 m long is 15 newtons.

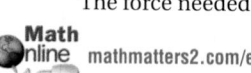

mathmatters2.com/extra_examples

Lesson 6-9 **Inverse Variation** 283

---

## ADDITIONAL ANSWERS

1. Answers will vary but may include:

| Length $x$ | 1 | 2 | 4 | 5 | 8 |
|---|---|---|---|---|---|
| Width $y$ | 80 | 40 | 20 | 16 | 10 |

3.

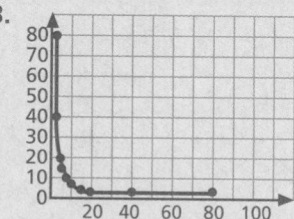

---

## Chalkboard Examples

### Supplementary Example 1
**PHYSICS** The force $f$ of gravitational attraction between two objects varies inversely as the square of the distance between them. If two objects have a gravitational force of 550 newtons (N) when they are 2200 m apart, how far apart are they when their gravitational force is 665.5 N?

*Equation Method*
$$fs^2 = k$$
$$(550)(2200)^2 = k$$
$$2{,}662{,}000{,}000 = k$$

$$fs^2 = 2{,}662{,}000{,}000$$
$$665.5s^2 = 2{,}662{,}000{,}000$$
$$s^2 = \frac{2{,}662{,}000{,}000}{665.5}$$
$$s^2 = 4{,}000{,}000$$
$$s = \sqrt{4{,}000{,}000} \text{ or } 2000$$

*Proportion Method*
$$\frac{f_1}{f_2} = \frac{s_2^2}{s_1^2}$$
$$\frac{555}{665.5} = \frac{s_2^2}{2200^2}$$
$$(665.5)s_2^2 = 550 \cdot 2200^2$$
$$s_2^2 = \frac{550 \cdot 2200^2}{665.5}$$
$$s_2 = \sqrt{\frac{550 \cdot 2200^2}{665.5}} \text{ or } 2000$$

So, when the gravitational force between two objects is 665.5 N, the objects are 2000 m apart.

### Supplementary Example 2
**PHYSICS** The weight of a body is inversely proportional to the square of its distance from the center of the Earth. If a man weighs 147 lb on Earth's surface, what will he weigh 200 mi above Earth? (Assume Earth's radius = 4000 mi.)

*Equation Method*
$$ws^2 = k$$
$$(147)(4000)^2 = k$$
$$2.352 \cdot 10^9 = k$$
$$ws^2 = 2.352 \cdot 10^9$$
$$w \cdot (4200)^2 = 2.352 \cdot 10^9$$
$$w = \frac{2.352 \cdot 10^9}{(4200)^2} \text{ or } 133.3$$

*Proportion Method*
$$\frac{w_1}{w_2} = \frac{(s_2)^2}{(s_1)^2}$$
$$\frac{147}{w_2} = \frac{(4200)^2}{(4000)^2}$$
$$(4200)^2 w_2 = 147 \cdot (4000)^2$$
$$w_2 = \frac{147 \cdot (4000)^2}{(4200)^2} \text{ or } 133.3$$

So, a man who weighs 147 lb on Earth's surface would weigh about 133.3 lb if he were 200 mi above Earth.

## QUICK ASSESSMENT

Ask the following questions to determine if students understand the content presented in this lesson.

**If $y$ varies inversely as $x$, what happens to $y$:**
1. if $x$ is halved?   *y* doubles.
2. if $x$ is doubled?   *y* is halved.
3. if $x$ is divided by 3?   *y* is multiplied by 3.

**In an inverse variation, can 0 be the value of:**
4. the independent variable, $x$?
   No; then the value of $y$ would be $\frac{k}{0}$, which is undefined.
5. the dependent variable, $y$?
   No; then $k$ would be 0; but, by definition, $k$ is nonzero.

## ASSIGNMENT GUIDE

**Basic:** 1–22, 31–40
**Enriched:** 1–40

---

## ▸ TRY THESE EXERCISES

1. Assume that $y$ varies inversely as $x$. When $x = 3$, $y = 8$. Find $y$ when $x = 4$.   6
2. Assume that $y$ varies inversely as $x$. When $x = 9$, $y = 12$. Find $y$ when $x = 6$.   18

**TRAVEL**  The table shows the time taken to travel 100 yd at various speeds. The time taken varies inversely as the speed. If $t$ represents the time in seconds and $r$ represents the rate in yards per second, the function can be represented by the rule $t = \frac{100}{r}$ .

**Time Taken to Travel 100 yd**

| Time (sec) | 2 | 4 | 5 | 8 | 10 | 12.5 | 20 | 25 | 50 |
|---|---|---|---|---|---|---|---|---|---|
| Rate (yd/sec) | 50 | 25 | 20 | 12.5 | 10 | 8 | 5 | 4 | 2 |

3. As the amount of time decreases, does the rate of speed increase or decrease?   increase
4. What amount of time does it take to travel 100 yd at a rate of 8 yd/sec?   12.5 sec
5. What rate of speed is needed if you want to travel 100 yd in 20 sec?   5 yd/sec

**Identify each relationship as a direct variation or an inverse variation.**

6. the area of a circle and its radius   direct square variation
7. the speed of a vehicle and the time it takes to travel 1 mi   inverse variation

8. **WRITING MATH**  Write a paragraph describing the difference between direct variation and inverse variation. Give an example of each.   Answers will vary.

## ▸ PRACTICE EXERCISES • For Extra Practice, see page 606.

9. Assume that $y$ varies inversely as $x$. When $x = 10$, $y = 64$. Find $y$ when $x = 2$.   320
10. Assume that $y$ varies inversely as $x$. When $x = 2.5$, $y = 6$. Find $y$ when $x = 20$.   0.75
11. Assume that $y$ varies inversely as $x$ . When $x = 10$, $y = 1$. Find $y$ when $x = 4$.   2.5
12. Assume that $y$ varies inversely as $x$ . When $x = 4$, $y = 18$. Find $y$ when $x = 3$.   24

13. **ENGINEERING**  The time needed to fill a water tank varies inversely as the square of the diameter of the pipe used to fill it. A pipe with a diameter of 2 cm takes 10 min to fill the tank. How long does it take to fill the tank with a pipe having a diameter of 5 cm?   1.6 min
14. **INDUSTRY**  The volume of gas varies inversely as the pressure applied to it. Air pressure at sea level is 1 atmosphere. If a balloon rises to a point where the air pressure is 0.8 atmosphere, by what percent will its volume increase?   25%
15. **TRAVEL**  The amount paid by each member of a group chartering a bus varies inversely as the number of people in the group. When there are 30 people in the group, the cost per person is $20. What is the cost per person when there are 25 people in the group?   $24
16. **MUSIC**  The frequency of a note varies inversely as the length of a guitar string. When a string is 45 cm long, it produces a frequency of 826 Hz. What frequency will a string produce when it is 70 cm long?   531 Hz

---

## Extend the Lesson

**REAL WORLD CONNECTION**  Have students work in small groups to complete a seesaw experiment, using several identical coins, a 12-in. ruler, and an object that can be used as a pivot for the ruler. The pivot should be at the 6-in. mark on the ruler. Place a coin at the 2-in. mark. Now balance the ruler using two identical coins on the other side. Record the number of coins and the distance from the pivot for each side. Repeat the experiment with different numbers of identical coins at different distances from the pivot, recording the results. Students should observe that the product of the distance and number of coins is equal for each side of the seesaw: $x_1 y_1 = x_2 y_2$
*Problem:* Find the distance needed to balance on the seesaw shown.   about 2.14 yd

72 lb    2.5 yd    ? yd    84 lb

**Identify each relationship as a *direct variation* or an *inverse variation*.**

17. the capacity of a paint can and the number of cans needed to paint a wall
    *inverse*
18. the weight of an object and the force needed to lift it   *direct*

19. the loudness of a sound and the distance from the sound source
    *inverse*
20. the length of a rope and its weight   *direct*

21. **PHYSICS** The force of attraction between two magnets varies inversely as the square of the distance between them. When two magnets are 3 cm apart, the force is 49 newtons. How great is the force when the magnets are 21 cm apart?   *1 newton*

22. **BUSINESS** The manager of a lumber store schedules 6 employees to take inventory in an 8-hr work period. The manager assumes all employees work at the same rate. If 2 employees call in sick, how many hours will 4 employees need to take inventory?   *12 h*

### ■ EXTENDED PRACTICE EXERCISES

**When $x = 4$, $y = 20$. Find $y$ when $x = 100$ for each variation.**

23. $y$ varies directly as $x$   *500*
24. $y$ varies directly as $x^2$   *12,500*

25. $y$ varies inversely as $x$   *0.8*
26. $y$ varies inversely as $x^2$   *0.032*

27. **CRITICAL THINKING** Suppose that $y$ varies inversely as $x$ and $x$ varies inversely as $z^2$. What is the relationship between $y$ and $z$?   *y varies directly as $z^2$.*

28. A triangle has an area of 48 cm$^2$. Write an equation that describes how the length of the base varies in relation to the height of the triangle.   $b = \frac{96}{h}$

29. A cone has a volume of 44 cm$^3$. Write an equation that describes how the height varies in relation to the radius of the cone.   $h = \frac{132}{\pi r^2}$

30. **CHAPTER INVESTIGATION** Look over your graphs, the list of decision ideas and other information you have about your company. Name as many relationships as you can find that you think are examples of indirect variation. Discuss your ideas with the class.   *Answers will vary.*

### ■ MIXED REVIEW EXERCISES

**In the figure, $m\angle ABC = 42°$ and $m\angle CBD = 75°$. Find each measure.** (Lesson 5-8)

31. $m\widehat{AC}$   *42°*
32. $m\widehat{CD}$   *75°*
33. $m\widehat{ACD}$   *117°*
34. $m\widehat{AED}$   *243°*

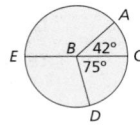

**Find the value of $x$ in each figure.** (Lesson 5-2)

35. *20°*  *70°*  *$x°$*
36. *135°*  *$x°$*  *45°*
37. *33°*  *$x°$*  *57°*

38. *75°*  *$x°$*  *105°*
39. *71°*  *$x°$*  *19°*
40. *68°*  *$x°$*  *112°*

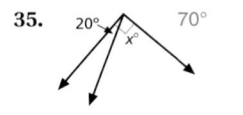

Math
Online   mathmatters2.com/self_check_quiz

---

## Extend the Lesson

**REAL WORLD CONNECTION** When two pulleys are connected, the one with the smaller diameter revolves with the greater speed.

*Law of the Pulley* $n_1 d_1 = n_2 d_2$ or $\frac{n_1}{n_2} = \frac{d_2}{d_1}$

where $d_1$ is the diameter of one pulley and $n_1$ is the number of revolutions it makes per minute (rpm), while $d_2$ and $n_2$ are the corresponding numbers for the other pulley

*Problem* Two pulleys of diameter 6 in. and 10 in. are connected. If the smaller pulley rotates at 150 rpm, what is the speed at which the larger pulley rotates?   **90 rpm**

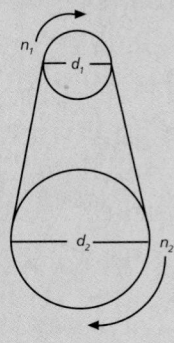

---

## Extra Practice Worksheet 6-9

Name _____   Date _____

EXTRA PRACTICE   **6-9**
## INVERSE VARIATION

### ☑ EXERCISES

1. Assume that $y$ varies inversely as $x$. When $x = 10$, $y = 15$. Find $y$ when $x = 5$.   **30**
2. Assume that $y$ varies inversely as $x$. When $x = 14$, $y = 3$. Find $y$ when $x = 7$.   **6**
3. Assume that $y$ varies inversely as $x$. When $x = 8$, $y = 4$. Find $y$ when $x = 2$.   **16**
4. Assume that $y$ varies inversely as $x$. When $x = 2$, $y = 10$. Find $y$ when $x = 40$.   **$\frac{1}{2}$**
5. Assume that $y$ varies inversely as $x$. When $x = 9$, $y = 3$. Find $y$ when $x = 27$.   **1**
6. Assume that $y$ varies inversely as $x$. When $x = 7$, $y = 2$. Find $y$ when $x = 3$.   **$4\frac{2}{3}$**
7. Assume that $y$ varies inversely as $x$. When $x = 5$, $y = 3$. Find $y$ when $x = 45$.   **$\frac{1}{3}$**
8. Assume that $y$ varies inversely as $x$. When $x = 2$, $y = 6$. Find $y$ when $x = 4$.   **3**
9. The time needed to fill a swimming pool varies inversely as the square of the diameter of the hose used to fill it. A hose with a diameter of $\frac{3}{4}$ in. takes 30 minutes to fill the pool. How long does it take to fill the pool with a hose having a diameter of $1\frac{1}{4}$ in.?   **10.8 min**
10. The amount paid for a gift varies inversely as the number of people paying for the gift. When there are 10 people paying for the gift, the cost per person is $9. What is the cost per person when there are 15 people paying for the gift?   **$6**

Identify each relationship as a direct variation or an inverse variation.

11. the capacity of a watering can and the amount of water needed for each plant   **inverse**
12. the amount of time spent working and the amount earned   **direct**
13. the speed of a car and the time it takes to travel from one place to another   **inverse**

## Enrichment Worksheet 6-9

Name _____   Date _____

ENRICHMENT   **6-9**
## JOINT AND COMBINED VARIATION

When a quantity varies directly as the product of two or more other quantities, the variation is called a **joint variation**. If $y$ varies jointly as $w$ and $x$, then $y = kwx$.

When a quantity varies directly as one quantity and inversely as another, the variation is called a **combined variation**. If $y$ varies directly as $w$ and inversely as $x$, then $y = \frac{kw}{x}$.

**Example 1**

$l$ varies jointly as $m$ and $n$, and $l = 15$ when $m = 3$ and $n = 2$. Find $l$ when $m = 5$ and $n = 12$.

**Solution**
Substitute known values of $l$, $m$, and $n$ in the equation $l = kmn$.
$15 = k \cdot 3 \cdot 2$
$15 = 6k$
$2.5 = k$
Write the rule.
$l = 2.5mn$
$l = 2.5 \cdot 5 \cdot 12$
$l = 150$

**Example 2**

$y$ varies directly as $w$ and inversely as $x$, and $y = 20$ when $w = 2$ and $x = 5$. Find $y$ when $w = 6$ and $x = 12$.

**Solution**
Substitute known values of $y$, $w$, and $x$ in the equation $y = \frac{kw}{x}$.
$20 = \frac{2k}{5}$
$20 \cdot 5 = 2k$
$50 = k$
Write the rule.
$y = \frac{50w}{x}$
$y = \frac{(50 \cdot 6)}{12}$
$y = 25$

### ☑ EXERCISES

1. $f$ varies jointly as $g$ and $h$, and $f = 45$ when $g = 18$ and $h = 10$. Find $f$ when $g = 7$ and $h = 8$.   **14**
2. $x$ varies directly as $y$ and inversely as $z$, and $x = 27$ when $y = 3$ and $z = 7$. Find $x$ when $y = 8$ and $z = 12$.   **42**
3. The weight of a rectangular sheet of metal varies jointly as the length and width of the sheet. A sheet of metal that is 25 cm long and 8 cm wide weighs 70 g. How many grams will a sheet that is 40 cm long and 15 cm wide weigh?   **210 g**
4. The height of a wooden cylinder varies directly as its weight and inversely as its base area. A cylinder with a weight of 200 g and a base area of 12 cm$^2$ has a height of 8 cm. A cylinder made of the same wood weighs 360 g and has a base area of 8 cm$^2$. Find its height.   **21.6 cm**

## Vocabulary Assessment

- A matching section checks for student understanding of the new vocabulary introduced in this chapter.
- A vocabulary review/test for Chapter 6 is available on pp. vii–viii of the *Chapter 6 Resource Masters*.

## Lesson-by-Lesson Review

For each lesson,

- the main ideas are summarized, and
- practice exercises are provided.

 **EXAMVIEW® PRO**

Use the networkable **ExamView® Pro** to:

- Create **multiple versions** of tests.
- Create **modified** tests for *inclusion* students.
- **Edit** existing questions and **add** your own questions.
- Use built-in **state curriculum correlations** to create tests aligned with state standards.
- Change **English** tests to **Spanish** and vice versa.

# Chapter 6 Review

## VOCABULARY ◼

Choose the word from the list that best completes each statement.

1. On a coordinate plane, the horizontal axis is called the __?__.  i
2. A region on one side of a line is called an __?__.  e
3. The __?__ of a segment is the ratio of its change in vertical distance compared to its change in horizontal distance.  f
4. When each *x*-coordinate is paired with exactly one *y*-coordinate, the graph represents a __?__.  c
5. The __?__ is the point where the graph of a line crosses the *y*-axis.  l
6. If the ratio of each member of the range to the corresponding member of the domain is constant, the function is called a __?__.  b
7. The vertical axis on a coordinate plane is called the __?__.  k
8. Use a(n) __?__ to determine which half-plane should be shaded in the graph of a linear inequality.  g
9. The __?__ is used to determine if a graph is a function.  h
10. For the inequality $y < 3x + 4$, the line $y = 3x + 4$ is called the __?__ of each half-plane.  a

| | |
|---|---|
| **a.** | boundary |
| **b.** | direct variation |
| **c.** | function |
| **d.** | inverse variation |
| **e.** | open half-plane |
| **f.** | slope |
| **g.** | test point |
| **h.** | vertical line test |
| **i.** | *x*-axis |
| **j.** | *x*-intercept |
| **k.** | *y*-axis |
| **l.** | *y*-intercept |

### LESSON 6-1 ◼ Distance in the Coordinate Plane, p. 244

▶ To find the distance or midpoint between any two points, $(x_1, y_1)$ and $(x_2, y_2)$, use these formulas: **Distance Formula**, $d = \sqrt{(x_2 - x_1) + (y_2 - y_1)^2}$, and **Midpoint Formula**, $M = \left(\dfrac{x_1 + x_2}{2}, \dfrac{y_1 + y_2}{2}\right)$.

Use the graph to calculate the length of each segment. Round to the nearest tenth if necessary.

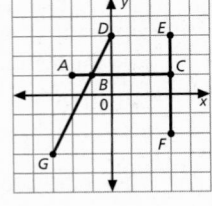

11. $\overline{AB}$  1
12. $\overline{BC}$  4
13. $\overline{AC}$  5
14. $\overline{EF}$  5
15. $\overline{EC}$  2
16. $\overline{CF}$  3
17. $\overline{GB}$  4.5
18. $\overline{GD}$  6.7
19. $\overline{BD}$  2.2

Find the midpoint of each segment. Use the graph.

20. $\overline{EF}$  $(3, \frac{1}{2})$
21. $\overline{GD}$  $(-1\frac{1}{2}, 0)$
22. $\overline{GB}$  $(-2, -1)$

### LESSON 6-2 ◼ Slope of a Line, p. 248

▶ To find the **slope** of a line given two points $(x_1, y_1)$, and $(x_2, y_2)$ on the line, use the formula $m = \dfrac{y_2 - y_1}{x_2 - x_1}$.

23. Find the slope of the line that passes through $A(-3, -1)$ and $B(-5, 7)$.  −4
24. Graph the line that passes through $(-2, -3)$ and has a slope of $\frac{2}{5}$.  See additional answers.

**286** | Chapter 6 **Graphing Functions**

## ADDITIONAL ANSWERS

24.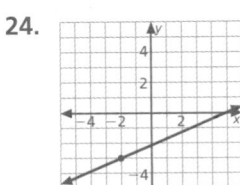

**Find the slope of a line that passes through the given points.**

**25.** $(1, -6), (3, 6)$  6

**26.** $(-2, -4), (3, 6)$  2

**27.** $(0, 5), (-3, 0)$  $\dfrac{5}{3}$

**28.** $(0, 5), (12, -4)$  $-\dfrac{3}{4}$

**29.** $(-5, 8), (-5, -10)$ undefined

**30.** $(-10, -8), (3, 7)$  $\dfrac{15}{13}$

## LESSON 6-3 ◼ Write and Graph Linear Equations, p. 254

▶ **Slope intercept form** of a line is $y = mx + b$, where $m$ = slope and $b$ = $y$-intercept.

▶ **Point-slope form** of a line is $y - y_1 = m(x - x_1)$, where $m$ = slope and $(x_1, y_1)$ is a point on the line.

**Write an equation of each line using the given information.**

**31.** $m = -\dfrac{2}{5}, b = 3$  $y = -\dfrac{2}{5}x + 3$

**32.** $m = -3, (-1, 2)$  $y = -3x - 1$

**33.** $(-6, 1), (-3, 4)$  $y = x + 7$

**34.** $m = 3, (2, -5)$  $y = 3x - 11$

**35.** $(4, 7), (-8, -5)$  $y = x + 4$

**36.** $m = \dfrac{4}{5}, b = -3$  $y = \dfrac{4}{5}x - 3$

**37.** $(7, -3), (2, 7)$  $y = -2x + 11$

**38.** $(2, -4), (-5, 10)$  $y = -2x$

**39.** $m = -\dfrac{1}{2}, b = 2$  $y = -\dfrac{1}{2}x + 2$

**40.** $m = -2, (2, 0)$  $y = -2x + 4$

**41.** $m = \dfrac{2}{3}, b = 4$  $y = \dfrac{2}{3}x + 4$

**42.** $m = \dfrac{3}{2}, (-4, 6)$  $y = \dfrac{3}{2}x + 12$

## LESSON 6-4 ◼ Write and Graph Linear Inequalities, p. 258

▶ The **graph of an inequality** is the set of all ordered pairs that make the inequality true. Any one of these pairs is a solution of the inequality.

**Tell if each ordered pair is a solution of the inequality.**

**43.** $(2, 5); y < 2x + 2$  yes

**44.** $(1, 4); y \le x - 4$  no

**45.** $(0, -3); 2x - y \ge 4$  no

**Write an inequality for each graph.**

**46.**
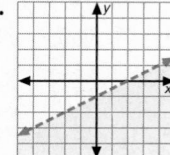
$y < \dfrac{1}{2}x - 1$

**47.**
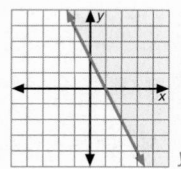
$y \ge -2x + 2$

**48.**
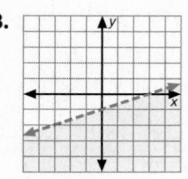
$y < \dfrac{1}{3}x - 1$

## LESSON 6-5 ◼ Linear and Nonlinear Functions, p. 264

▶ A **function** that can be represented by a linear equation where the domain is all real numbers is called a linear function.

**Graph each function for the given domain.**  For 49 and 50, see additional answers.

**49.** $y = x - 1$; all real numbers

**50.** $y = x^2 - 1$; $\{-2, -1, 0, 1, 2\}$

**Determine if each graph represents a function. Explain.**

**51.**
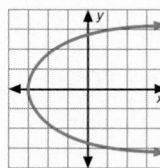
No; vertical line test fails.

**52.**
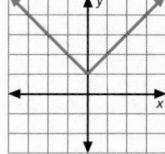
Yes; vertical line test passes.

**53.**
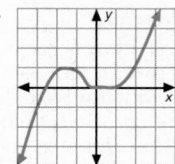
Yes; vertical line test passes.

## ADDITIONAL ANSWERS

**49.**
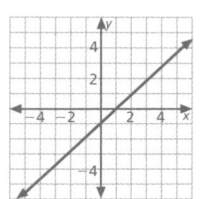

**50.**
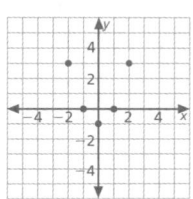

## LESSON 6-6 ◪ Graph Quadratic Functions, p. 268

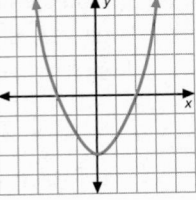

▶ A **quadratic function** is a nonlinear function whose graph is a curve known as a *parabola*. A quadratic function is given by the equation $y = Ax^2 + Bx + C$, where $A$, $B$, and $C$ are real numbers and $A \neq 0$.

**Complete each ordered pair so that it corresponds to a point on the graph.**

**54.** $(1, ?)$  $-2$          **55.** $(2, ?)$  $0$          **56.** $(0, ?)$  $-3$

## LESSON 6-7 ◪ Problem Solving: Patterns and Functions, p. 274

▶ An effective strategy to organize and classify the domain and range values is to **make a table**.

**Use each domain to find ordered pair solutions of each equation.**

**57.** $y = x - 4$; $\{-3, -2, 0, 1, 2\}$
$(-3, -7), (-2, -6), (0, -4), (1, -3), (2, -2)$

**58.** $y = 2x + 2$; $\{-2, -1, 0, 1, 2\}$
$(-2, -2), (-1, 0), (0, 2), (1, 4), (2, 6)$

**Write a function rule for each function table.**

**59.**

| x | -3 | 0 | 2 | 3 |
|---|----|----|----|----|
| y | 18 | 0 | 8 | 18 |

$y = 2x^2$

**60.**

| x | -12 | 0 | 4 | 16 |
|---|----|----|----|----|
| y | -3 | 0 | 1 | 4 |

$y = \frac{1}{4}x$

## LESSON 6-8 ◪ Direct Variation, p. 276

▶ A **direct variation** is a function in the form $y = kx$, where $k \neq 0$.

▶ A **direct square variation** is in the form $y = kx^2$, where $k \neq 0$.

**Assume $y$ varies directly as $x$.**

**61.** When $x = 4.2$, $y = 21$. Find $y$ when $x = 3$. $15$

**62.** When $x = 9$, $y = 54$. Find $y$ when $x = 3.6$.
$21.6$

**63.** When $x = 14$, $y = 49$. Find $y$ when $x = 4$. $14$

**64.** When $x = 5.2$, $y = 20.8$. Find $y$ when $x = 6.4$.
$25.6$

## LESSON 6-9 ◪ Inverse Variation, p. 282

▶ An **inverse variation** is a function in the form $y = \frac{k}{x}$, where $k \neq 0$ and $x \neq 0$.

▶ An **inverse square** variation is in the form $y = \frac{k}{x^2}$ or $x^2y = k$, where $k \neq 0$.

**Assume $y$ varies inversely as $x$.**

**65.** When $x = 15$, $y = 8$. Find $y$ when $x = 16$. $7.5$

**66.** When $x = 5$, $y = 10$. Find $y$ when $x = 25$. $2$

**67.** When $x = \frac{1}{2}$, $y = 6$. Find $y$ when $x = 12$. $\frac{1}{4}$

**68.** When $x = 16$, $y = \frac{7}{8}$. Find $y$ when $x = 2$. $7$

## CHAPTER INVESTIGATION

**EXTENSION** Use your graphs to write equations that model each quarter of the operating costs graph. Also write equations that model each quarter of the sales revenue graph. Select another group that researched a different company than your group. Trade sets of equations. Use the other group's equations for operating costs, and draw a graph that includes all four quarters. Do the same with the sales revenue equations. Compare your group's graphs with the other group's graphs. Discuss reasons for any differences among the graphs.

## THEME: Business

The benchmarks and expectations for this extension are as follows.
- Students find the data on a company's operating costs for each quarter of the year. They plot four ordered pairs, and describe the operating costs by quarters and by the entire year.
- Students find the data on a company's sales revenue for each quarter of the year. They plot four ordered pairs, and describe the operating costs by quarters and by the entire year.
- Students use their graphs to determine which quarters were profitable and which had a loss. They brainstorm ideas about business decisions and planning.
- Students use their graphs to write equations that model each quarter of each graph. They trade equations with other groups and graph their equations. They compare and discuss any differences.

# Chapter 6 Assessment

Use the graph to calculate the length of each segment.

1. $\overline{KL}$  8

2. $\overline{MN}$  8

3. $\overline{OP}$  10

4. Find the slope of each segment in Exercises 1–3.
   0, undefined, $\frac{3}{4}$

5. Find the midpoint of $\overline{OP}$.  (1, 1)

6. Graph the line that passes through $(1, -2)$ and has a slope of 3.  See additional answers.

7. Find the slope of a line containing the points $(0, 5)$ and $(3, -7)$.  $-4$

Identify the slope and y-intercept for each line. Graph each line.  For 8–10, see additional answers.

8. $y = 2x + 1$  2; 1

9. $y = 3x + 2$  3; 2

10. $x + 2y = 4$  $-\frac{1}{2}$; 2

Write an equation of each line from the given information.

11. $m = -6, b = 1$
    $y = -6x + 1$

12. $m = 3, (-2, 4)$
    $y = 3x + 10$

13. $(3, -4), (8, -3)$
    $y = \frac{1}{5}x - \frac{23}{5}$

Tell if each ordered pair is a solution of the inequality.

14. $(1, 4); y > 2x - 2$  yes

15. $(3, 3); y \leq x - 3$  no

16. $(-6, 0); 3x - y - 12$  no

17. Graph the inequality $y > 2x - 4$.  See additional answers.

18. Graph $y = -3$ for the domain of real numbers.  See additional answers.

19. Graph $y = x + 2$ for the domain of real numbers.  See additional answers.

Complete each ordered pair so that it corresponds to a point on the graph.

20. $(-2, ?)$  3

21. $(0, ?)$  $-1$

22. $(?, 8)$  $-3, 3$

23. Graph $y = x^2 - 2$ for the domain of real numbers.
    See additional answers.

Use each domain to find ordered pair solutions of each equation.

24. $y = x - 3; \{-4, -2, 0, 2, 4\}$
    $(-4, -7), (-2, -5), (0, -3), (2, -1), (4, 1)$

25. $y = 2x + 3; \{-2, -1, 0, 1, 2\}$
    $(-2, -1), (-1, 1), (0, 3), (1, 5), (2, 7)$

26. Use the table to write a function rule.  $f(x) = 2x + 1$

| x | 2 | 4 | 6 | 8 | 10 |
|------|---|---|----|----|----|
| f(x) | 5 | 9 | 13 | 17 | 21 |

27. The distance a truck needs to reach a full stop varies directly as the square of its speed. From the speed of 40 mi/h, the truck needs a distance of 86 ft to stop. What distance will it need to stop from a speed of 30 mi/h?  about 48 ft

28. The time it takes to build a wall varies inversely as the number of people doing the job. If it takes 28 h for 12 people, how long would it take 16 people?  21 h

### Assessment Options

Chapter 6 Test A, pages 207–208
Chapter 6 Test B, pages 209–210

## ALTERNATIVE ASSESSMENT

**MUSICAL MATHEMATICS** The frequency of a note from a musical instrument varies inversely as the length of the string. Have students do research to find an instrument whose strings are struck and bowed, another whose strings are plucked and bowed, and another whose strings are strummed and bowed. Students should then compare the strings and frequencies of the instruments. Is the length of the string for each instrument the same for the same note? What other factors influence the pitch of the notes?

**RUBRIC** The following rubric is a sample scoring guide.

| Points | Description |
|--------|-------------|
| 4 | Correctly identifies three musical instruments, compares length of strings, and **draws correct conclusions** about other influencing factors. |
| 3 | Correctly identifies three musical instruments, compares length of strings, but **draws one or more erroneous conclusions.** |
| 2 | Correctly **identifies two musical instruments**, compares length of strings, and draws conclusions. |
| 1 | Correctly **identifies one musical instrument**, compares length of strings, and draws conclusions. |
| 0 | Makes **no attempt** to identify any instruments or compare lengths. |

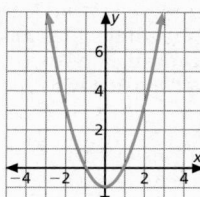

## ADDITIONAL ANSWERS

6.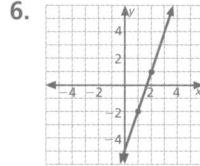

8.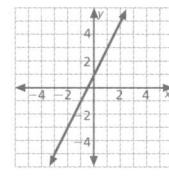

9.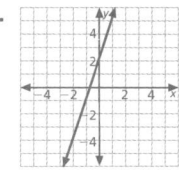

10.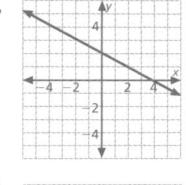

17.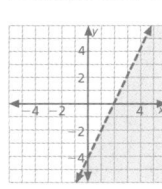

18.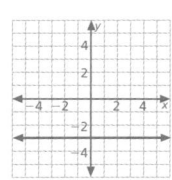

19.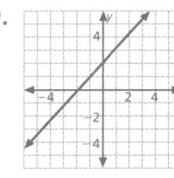

23.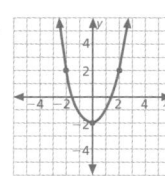

These two pages contain practice questions in the various formats that can be found on the most frequently given standardized tests.

A student recording sheet for these two pages can be found on p. A1 of the *Chapter 6 Resource Masters*.

## Standardized Test Practice Student Recording Sheet

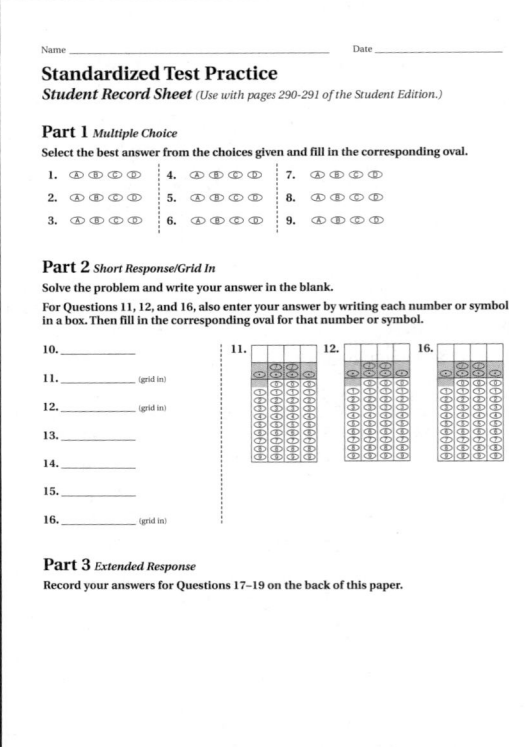

## Additional Practice

See pp. 211–213 in the *Chapter 6 Resource Masters* for additional standardized test practice.

# Standardized Test Practice

1. Which sentence is *not* true? (Lesson 2-1)  B
   - Ⓐ  All natural numbers are whole numbers.
   - Ⓑ  Every whole number is a natural number.
   - Ⓒ  Natural numbers are positive numbers.
   - Ⓓ  Zero is neither positive nor negative.

2. Ms. Lee is planning a business trip for which she needs to rent a car. The car rental company charges $36 per day plus $0.50 per mile over 100 mi. Suppose Ms. Lee rents the car for 5 d and drives 180 mi. Which expression can be used to determine how much Ms. Lee must pay the car rental company? (Lesson 2-2)  D
   - Ⓐ  $0.5(36) + 5(180)$
   - Ⓑ  $5(36) + 0.5(180)$
   - Ⓒ  $0.5(36) + 5(180 - 100)$
   - Ⓓ  $5(36) + 0.5(180 - 100)$

3. There are ten socks in a drawer: 2 yellow, 2 green, 2 blue, 2 white, and 2 red. If you pull out one sock and then another sock without replacing the first, what is the probability of choosing two blue socks? (Lesson 4-5)  A
   - Ⓐ  $\frac{1}{90}$
   - Ⓑ  $\frac{1}{9}$
   - Ⓒ  $\frac{1}{5}$
   - Ⓓ  $\frac{2}{9}$

4. What is the value of $y$? (Lesson 5-4)  C
   - Ⓐ  $35°$
   - Ⓑ  $72.5°$
   - Ⓒ  $107.5°$
   - Ⓓ  $125°$

5. Which theorem or postulate can be used to prove that the two triangles are congruent? (Lesson 5-5)  B
   - Ⓐ  AAS
   - Ⓑ  ASA
   - Ⓒ  SAS
   - Ⓓ  SSS

   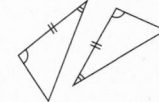

6. What is the value of $a$ in the parallelogram? (Lesson 5-6)  C

   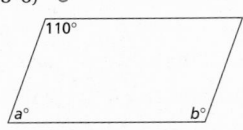

   - Ⓐ  20
   - Ⓑ  45
   - Ⓒ  70
   - Ⓓ  110

7. Find the sum of the interior angles of a 25-gon. (Lesson 5-7)  A
   - Ⓐ  $4140°$
   - Ⓑ  $4320°$
   - Ⓒ  $4500°$
   - Ⓓ  $4680°$

8. Sam plotted his house, school, and library on a coordinate plane. What is the shortest distance from his house to the library? (Lesson 6-1)  B

   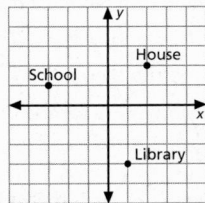

   - Ⓐ  5.8 units
   - Ⓑ  5.1 units
   - Ⓒ  4.9 units
   - Ⓓ  3.2 units

9. Raini is buying chocolate-covered pretzels from a bulk-foods store. The pretzels ($P$) are $1.49 per pound. Which equation represents the cost ($C$)? (Lesson 6-3)  D
   - Ⓐ  $C = 1.49 - P$
   - Ⓑ  $C = 1.49 + 1.49P$
   - Ⓒ  $C = \frac{1.49}{P}$
   - Ⓓ  $C = 1.49P$

 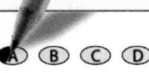

## Part 2 Short Response/Grid In

**Record your answers on the answer sheet provided by your teacher or on a sheet of paper.**

10. The formula for Ohm's Law is $E = IR$, where $E$ represents voltage measured in volts, $I$ represents current measured in amperes, and $R$ represents resistance measured in ohms. Suppose a current of 0.25 ampere flows through a resistor connected to a 12-volt battery. What is the resistance in the circuit? (Lesson 3-1)  48 ohms

11. The expected increase of a population of organisms is directly proportional to the current population. If a sample of 360 organisms increases by 18, by how many will a population of 9,000 increase? (Lesson 3-5)  450

12. If you spin the arrow on the spinner below, what is the probability that the arrow will land on an even number? (Lesson 4-1)  3/8

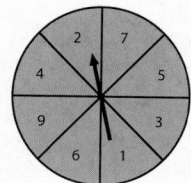

13. The two triangles are congruent. What is the value of *x*? (Lesson 5-5)  40

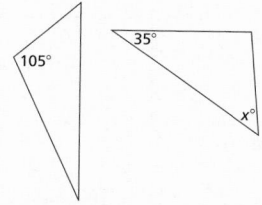

14. The sum of the interior angles of a regular polygon is 900°. Which polygon is it? (Lesson 5-7)  heptagon

15. What is the slope of the line that passes through (3, 5) and (−2, −6)? (Lesson 6-2)  11/5

mathmatters2.com/standardized_test

16. The cost of bananas varies directly with their weight. The cost of $3\frac{1}{2}$ lb of bananas is \$1.12. What is the cost in dollars of $4\frac{1}{4}$ lb of bananas? (Lesson 6-8)  1.36

## Part 3 Extended Response

**Record your answers on a sheet of paper. Show your work.**

17. Pedro wants to construct a triangle. (Lesson 5-4)
    a. He has three pieces of wood. The lengths are 6 in., 8 in., and 16 in. Is it possible for Pedro to form a triangle using these three lengths? Explain.  No; 6 + 8 < 16
    b. Two of the three sides of the triangle are 10 in. and 12 in. long. Write an inequality that expresses the possible lengths of the third side.  x > 22
    c. Pedro constructs a right triangle with a base of 8 in. and a height of 12 in. What is the area of the triangle?  48 in.²

18. In the figure, *B* is the midpoint of $\overline{AE}$. $\overline{AC} \parallel \overline{DE}$. (Lesson 5-5)

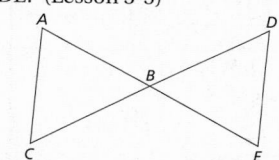

    a. Which pairs of angles are congruent? Explain.  See margin.
    b. Determine whether the two triangles in the figure are congruent. Explain.  △ABC ≅ △EBD by ASA or AAS.

19. The table shows the loss in billions of dollars each year due to computer viruses. Determine whether the data is linear or nonlinear. Explain. (Lesson 6-2)

| Year | 2000 | 2001 | 2002 | 2003 | 2004 |
|------|------|------|------|------|------|
| Loss (billions) | 0.1 | 0.3 | 0.7 | 1.4 | 2.7 |

Nonlinear; the slope of the line segment varies between each data point.

Chapter 6 **Standardized Test Practice** 291

## Rubrics

The following rubrics are sample scoring devices for short response and extended response questions.

### Short Response

| Points | Description |
|--------|-------------|
| 2 | The student demonstrates a **thorough understanding** of the mathematics of the task. The response may contain minor flaws that do not detract from the demonstration of a thorough understanding. |
| 1 | The student has provided a response that is only **partially correct.** |
| 0 | The student has provided a **completely incorrect** solution or no response at all. |

### Extended Response

| Points | Description |
|--------|-------------|
| 4 | The student demonstrates a **thorough understanding** of the mathematics of the task. The response contains minor flaws that do not detract from the demonstration of a thorough understanding. |
| 3 | The student demonstrates an **understanding** of the mathematics of the task. The response is essentially correct and demonstrates an essential but less than thorough understanding of the mathematics. |
| 2 | The student has demonstrated only a **partial understanding** of the mathematics of the task. Although the student may have used the correct approach to a solution or may have provided a correct solution, the work lacks an essential understanding of the underlying mathematical concepts. |
| 1 | The student has demonstrated a **very limited understanding** of the mathematics of the task. The response is incomplete and exhibits many flaws. |
| 0 | The student has provided a **completely incorrect** solution or no response at all. |

## ADDITIONAL ANSWERS

18a. ∠A ≅ ∠E and ∠C ≅ ∠D because if two parallel lines are cut by a transversal alternate interior angles are congruent.
∠ABC ≅ ∠EBD because vertical angles are congruent.

# 7 CHAPTER

# Coordinate Graphing and Transformations

| Lesson | Lesson Objectives | Pacing (days) | NCTM Standards | State/Local Objectives |
|--------|-------------------|---------------|----------------|------------------------|
| 7-1 | **Translations in the Coordinate Plane** *(pp. 296–299)*<br>• Describe and graph translation images on a coordinate plane. | 1 | 3, 4, 7, 10 | |
| 7-2 | **Reflections in the Coordinate Plane** *(pp. 300–303)*<br>• Graph reflection images on a coordinate plane. | 2 | 3, 4, 7, 10 | |
| 7-3 | **Rotations in the Coordinate Plane** *(pp. 306–309)*<br>• Graph rotated images in the coordinate plane.<br>• Identify centers, angles, and directions of rotations. | 2 | 3, 4, 7, 10 | |
| 7-4 | **Line Symmetry and Rotational Symmetry** *(pp. 310–313)*<br>• Identify lines of symmetry.<br>• Identify order of rotational symmetry. | 1 | 3, 4, 7, 10 | |
| 7-5 | **Dilations in the Coordinate Plane** *(pp. 316–319)*<br>• Draw dilation images on a coordinate plane.<br>• Determine the scale factor of dilations. | 2 | 3, 4, 7, 10 | |
| 7-6 | **Problem Solving Skills: Tessellations** *(pp. 320–321)*<br>• Solve a problem using tessellations.<br>• Solve a problem by looking for a pattern. | 1 | 2, 6, 8, 9 | |
| **Review** | | 1 | | |
| **Testing** | | 1 | | |

**Key to NCTM Standards:**

*1=Number & Operations, 2=Algebra, 3=Geometry,*
*4=Measurement, 5=Data Analysis & Probability,*
*6=Problem Solving, 7=Reasoning & Proof,*
*8=Communication, 9=Connections, 10=Representation*

**Pacing:** Suggestions for the year can be found on page xvi.

# Chapter Resource Manager

| | Reteaching Activities | Extra Practice | Enrichment | Assessment | Basic Mathematics Review | Study Skills Activities | Lesson Warm-Ups Transparencies | Teaching Transparencies | Technology Activities | Materials Needed |
|---|---|---|---|---|---|---|---|---|---|---|
| | 215 | 216 | 217 | | | | 28 | TK-9–TK-12, RF-37 | 7-1 | graph paper, scissors, ruler |
| | 218 | 219 | 220 | | | 21 | 28 | TK-9–TK-12, RF-38 | 7-2 | graph paper, ruler, food coloring or paint |
| | 221 | 222 | 223 | | | | 28 | TK-9–TK-12, RF-39 | 7-3 | graph paper, compass, protractor, ruler |
| | 224 | 225 | 226 | | | | 29 | RF-40 | | scissors, mirror |
| | 227 | 228 | 229 | | | 15 | 29 | TK-9–TK-12, RF-41 | 7-5 | ruler |
| | 230 | 231 | 232 | 235–241 | | | 30 | TK-9, TK-15, RF-1, RF-42 | | isometric dot or graph paper, patty paper |

**Chapter 7 Resource Masters**

**FAST FILE**

| Quick Review Math Handbook, Book 2 | |
|---|---|
| *MathMatters 2* Lesson(s) | Hot Topic Lesson(s) |
| 7-1, 7-2, 7-3, 7-4 | 7-3 |
| 7-5 | 7-3, 8-6 |
| 7-6 | 7-3 |

*hot* **words** *hot* **topics**

# Content and Connections

## Connections to the Past

**MM1 (Ch. 8):** Identify and draw translations.

**MM1 (Ch. 8):** Identify and draw reflections.

**MM1 (Ch. 8):** Identify and draw rotations.

**MM1 (Ch. 8):** Identify and use lines of symmetry.

**MM1 (Ch. 2):** Apply and interpret scale drawings.

**MM1 (Ch. 8):** Identify and draw tessellations.

## MathMatters 2 Chapter 7 Highlights

Describe and graph translation images on a coordinate plane. (7-1)

Graph reflection images on a coordinate plane. (7-2)

Graph rotated images on a coordinate plane. (7-3)

Identify lines of symmetry and order of rotational symmetry. (7-4)

Draw dilation images on a coordinate plane. (7-5)

Solve a problem using tessellations. (7-6)

## Connections to the Future

**MM3 (Ch. 8):** Graph translation images on a coordinate plane.

**MM3 (Ch. 8):** Identify and perform transformations with matrices.

**MM3 (Ch. 8):** Graph rotation images and identify center, angles, and directions of rotations.

**MM3 (Ch. 8):** Identify and find composites of transformations.

**MM3 (Ch. 8):** Graph dilation images on a coordinate plane.

**MM3 (Ch. 8):** Represent geometric figures on the coordinate plane using matrices.

### Key

| | |
|---|---|
| PC | = Previous Course |
| MM1 | = *MathMatters 1* |
| MM2 | = *MathMatters 2* |
| MM3 | = *MathMatters 3* |

### Connecting the Strands

| NCTM Strand | Lesson(s) |
|---|---|
| Algebra | 7-6 |
| Geometry | 7-1, 7-2, 7-3, 7-4, 7-5, 7-6 |
| Measurement | 7-1, 7-2, 7-3, 7-4, 7-5, 7-6 |
| Problem Solving | 7-6 |
| Reasoning & Proof | 7-1, 7-2, 7-3, 7-4, 7-5, 7-6 |
| Communication | 7-6 |
| Connections | 7-6 |
| Representation | 7-1, 7-2, 7-3, 7-4, 7-5, 7-6 |

# Ongoing Assessment and Intervention

| | Type | Student Edition | Teacher Resources | Technology/Internet |
|---|---|---|---|---|
| **INTERVENTION** | Ongoing | Are You Ready?, pp. 293–294<br>Check Understanding, pp. 301, 303, 306, 307, 310, 317<br>Review and Practice Your Skills, pp. 304–305, 314–315, 322–323<br>Mid-Chapter Quiz, p. 315 | Lesson Warm-Ups Transparencies, pp. WU-28, WU-29, WU-30<br>Quick Assessment, *ATE* pp. 295, 298, 302, 308, 312, 318, 321 | mathmatters2.com/extra_ examples<br>mathmatters2.com/self_check_quiz |
| | Mixed Review | pp. 299, 303, 309, 313, 319, 321 | | |
| | Error Analysis | Error Alert, p. 299 | Teaching Tip, *ATE* p. 311 | |
| **ASSESSMENT** | Standardized Test Practice | pp. 328–329<br>Preparing for Standardized Tests, pp. 627–644 | Standardized Test Practice, *CRM* pp. 239–241 | mathmatters2.com/standardized_test |
| | Open-Ended Assessment | Chapter Investigation, pp. 293, 299, 313, 319, 326 | Chapter Investigation, *ATE* p. 326<br>Alternative Assessment, *ATE* p. 327 | |
| | Chapter Assessment | Chapter Review, pp. 324–326<br>Chapter Assessment, p. 327 | Multiple-Choice Tests (Forms A and B), *CRM* pp. 235–238 | mathmatters2.com/chapter_assessment |

**Key to Abbreviations:** *ATE* = Annotated Teacher's Edition, *CRM* = Chapter Resource Masters

## Additional Intervention

***Basic Mathematics Review*** includes 80 lessons, consisting of an instructional page and a test page. This workbook also features a pretest, posttest, table of measurement equivalents, and calculator appendices.

## ExamView® Pro

Use ExamView® Pro Testmaker CD-ROM to:
- Create **multiple versions** of tests.
- Create **modified** tests for *inclusion* students with one mouse click.
- **Edit** existing questions and **add** your own questions.
- Build tests aligned with **state standards** using built-in **state curriculum correlations**.
- Change **English** tests to **Spanish** with one mouse click and vice versa.

# Coordinate Graphing and Transformations

## THEME: Architecture

J ust as a map provides directions for travelers, a building blueprint provides instructions for a construction crew. Building a structure requires that architects describe the concept and specifications on paper in an established format. Construction crews interpret the blueprints and build the structure accordingly.

Architects and draftpersons use the coordinate plane to document the measurements and layout of structures and landscaped areas. They create plans for structures such as houses, office complexes, shopping malls, gardens, and monuments.

- **Campus facilities managers** (page 305) use transformations to design the layout of buildings and courtyards. Often they create attractive areas on a campus where the structures and landscaping are of a similar style.

- **Architects** (page 323) incorporate rotations, translations, and dilations of basic geometric shapes to design the interior and exterior of a building.

**Math Online**
mathmatters2.com/chapter_theme

292

### Chapter Investigation
Use the Internet and other resources to locate additional information about blueprints.

## World's Ten Highest Dams

| Name | River, State and Country | Structural Height | | Gross Reservoir Capacity | | Year Completed |
|------|--------------------------|-------------------|--------|--------------------------|----------------------------|----------------|
| | | feet | meters | thousands of acre feet | millions of cubic meters | |
| Rogun | Vakhsh, Tajikistan | 1099 | 335 | 9,404 | 11,600 | 1985 |
| Nurek | Vakhsh, Tajikistan | 984 | 300 | 8,512 | 10,500 | 1980 |
| Grande Dixence | Dixence, Switzerland | 935 | 285 | 324 | 400 | 1962 |
| Inguri | Inguri, Georgia | 892 | 272 | 801 | 1,100 | 1984 |
| Vaiont | Vaiont, Italy | 859 | 262 | 137 | 169 | 1961 |
| Manuel M. Torres | Grijalva, Mexico | 856 | 261 | 1,346 | 1,660 | 1981 |
| Tehri | Bhagirathi, India | 856 | 261 | 2,869 | 3,540 | UC |
| Alvaro Obregon | Mextiquic, Mexico | 853 | 260 | n.a. | n.a. | 1926 |
| Mauvoisn | Drance de Bagnes, Switzerland | 820 | 250 | 146 | 180 | 1957 |
| Alberto Lleras | Orinoca, Columbia | 797 | 243 | 811 | 1,000 | 1989 |

## Data Activity: World's Ten Highest Dams

**Use the table for Questions 1–4.**

1. How old is the highest dam in Switzerland?
   Answers will vary depending on the current year.
2. Replace each ■ with >, ≥, < or ≤ for the structural height of each set of dams.
   a. Nurek ■ Tehri  >
   b. Vaiont ■ Alberto Lleras  >
   c. Alvaro Obregon ■ Rogun  <
   d. Mauvoism ■ Inguri  <
3. When comparing any two dams, would it be correct to assume that the higher dam has the greater reservoir capacity? Explain.
   See additional answers.
4. Is the ratio of feet to meters consistent in the structural height column? Explain.  Yes. There are approximately 3.28 ft in 1 m.

## CHAPTER INVESTIGATION

One of the primary uses of geometry in the real world is architecture. Early in the planning stages of a project, an architect will draw a blueprint showing the layout of the floor plan.

### Working Together

Use grid paper, a straightedge, a compass and any other necessary tools to create a blueprint for the floor plan of your dream house. This will be a diagram showing the size and location of the different rooms in the house. Use the Chapter Investigation icons to guide you in the creation of your blueprint.

## Project Planning Calendar

Name _____ Date _____

**CHAPTER 7 PROJECT PLANNING CALENDAR**

Benchmarks
a. On grid paper, draw the general layout and shape of the main floor of your house. It can be a rectangle, U shape or other design. Make the blueprint large enough to fill most of the page. (Lesson 7-1)
b. Draw the designs of the rooms and hallways of your house on the grid paper. Label the different types of rooms including any special features. Include transformational principles such as two rooms being mirror reflections of each other. (Lesson 7-4)
c. Decide how large your house will be by choosing a scale factor for the blueprint to the actual house. Label the sizes of the rooms and ...

PROJECT GOAL
To create a blueprint for the floor plan of your dream house.

## Group Project Planner

Name _____ Date _____

**CHAPTER 7 GROUP PROJECT PLANNER**

Assignment _____  Objective _____

Group Members        Assigned Roles
1) _____   _____
2) _____   _____
3) _____   _____
4) _____   _____
5) _____   _____

Deadlines        Done

A *dam* is a barrier constructed across a stream or river to impound water and raise its level. A dam may be the effort of a 35-lb beaver or it may result in a 1000-ft structure. The most common reasons that humans build dams are to concentrate the natural fall of a river at a given site, thus making it possible to generate electricity; to direct water from rivers into canals and irrigation and water-supply systems; to increase river depths for navigational purposes; to control water flow during times of flood and drought; and to create artificial lakes for recreational use. Many dams fulfill several of these functions.

Students should answer Questions 1–4 to compare some of the most significant dams that have been created around the world.

## Chapter Investigation

### As an Overarching Problem
Display blueprints of the floor plans of different houses. Have students study the blueprints and record things they like about the floor plans. Students will continue to work on the investigation as they complete the exercises identified by the Investigation icon that is found throughout the chapter. These exercises will guide students through the task described in *Working Together*. Encourage students to keep all of their work on the Investigation together. Have students use the suggestions in the Chapter Investigation Extension to summarize their work.

### As a Chapter Project
The goal of this project is for students to create a blueprint for the floor plan of their dream house. Students can use the Group Project Planner on page 233 and the Project Planning Calendar on page 234 in the *Chapter 7 Resource Masters* to complete the project. Benchmarks **a**, **b**, and **c** should be completed after the lesson listed in parentheses has been studied. Benchmark **d** should be completed at the end of the chapter.

## Refresher Skills

The skills on these two pages are skills that have been presented in earlier chapters of this book or in previous math courses. Continuous review of basic math skills will make stronger math students. These skills are identified as necessary to be successful in Chapter 7.

### Skills Correlation Chart

| Skill | Lesson Number |
|---|---|
| Graphing on the Coordinate Plane | 7-1, 7-2, 7-3, 7-5 |
| Midpoint Formula | 7-2 |
| Draw and Measure Angles | 7-3, 7-4 |

### Vocabulary

coordinate plane
midpoint

## Chalkboard Examples

### Graphing on the Coordinate Plane

$A(1, 1)$, $B(4, 1)$, and $C(2, 4)$ are vertices of parallelogram $CDBA$. What are the coordinates of vertex $D$?
Graph vertices $A$, $B$, and $C$.
Since $\overline{AB}$ is horizontal, $\overline{CD}$ is horizontal and the $y$-coordinate of $D$ is 4.
For the $x$-coordinate of $D$, find the length of $\overline{AB}$, $|4 - 1| = 3$.
So: $D(2 + 3, 4)$ or $D(5, 4)$

### Midpoint Formula

$M(7, 3)$ is the midpoint of $\overline{AB}$, where $A$ has coordinates $(3, 1)$. Find the coordinates of $B$.
Use $B(x, y)$ and apply the formula.

$\frac{3 + x}{2} = 7$      $\frac{1 + y}{2} = 3$
$3 + x = 14$      $1 + y = 6$
$x = 11$      $y = 5$
So $B$ has coordinates $(11, 5)$.

### Draw and Measure Angles

Use a protractor to draw a 145°-angle.

---

# 7 Are You Ready?

## Refresh Your Math Skills for Chapter 7

The skills on these two pages are ones you have already learned. Use the examples to refresh your memory and complete the exercises. For additional practice on these and more prerequisite skills, see pages 576–584.

### GRAPHING ON THE COORDINATE PLANE

In this chapter you will graph lines and figures on the coordinate plane. It is helpful to be able to identify the points on a graph.

**Example**   Graph $\triangle ABC$ with vertices $A(-3, -3)$, $B(-1, 2)$ and $C(8, 3)$.

- Locate point $A$. Start at $(0, 0)$. Go 3 units to the left and 3 units down.
- Locate point $B$. Start at $(0, 0)$. Go 1 unit to the left and 2 units up.
- Locate point $C$. Start at $(0, 0)$. Go 8 units to the right and 3 units up.
- Connect the points.

**Use grid paper to draw each figure.**
For 1–10, see additional answers.

1. rectangle $PRST$ with vertices $P(-1, 2)$, $R(7, 2)$, $S(7, -2)$ and $T(-1, -2)$

2. triangle $FGH$ with vertices $F(-8, 8)$, $G(-2, 7)$ and $H(-7, 4)$

3. parallelogram $ABCD$ with vertices $A(3, 2)$, $B(8, 2)$, $C(6, -1)$ and $D(1, -1)$

4. square $WXYZ$ with vertices $W(1, 3)$, $X(3, 6)$, $Y(6, 4)$ and $Z(4, 1)$

5. triangle $LMN$ with vertices $L(-2, 2)$, $M(5, 8)$ and $N(4, 0)$

6. parallelogram $ABCD$ with vertices $A(-5, 2)$, $B(-4, 7)$, $C(2, 7)$ and $D(1, 2)$

7. trapezoid $MNOP$ with vertices $M(5, -2)$, $N(5, 1)$, $O(8, 2)$ and $P(8, -5)$

8. quadrilateral $STUV$ with vertices $S(-4, 3)$, $T(1, 2)$, $U(3, -5)$ and $V(-6, -1)$

9. rectangle $HIJK$ with vertices $H(-5, 6)$, $I(5, 6)$, $J(5, 4)$ and $K(-5, 4)$

10. triangle $QRS$ with vertices $Q(-3, 0)$, $R(3, 3)$ and $S(1, -5)$

**Write the coordinates for each point on the graph.**

11. $A$ (5, 6)   12. $B$ (2, −3)   13. $C$ (7, 2)   14. $D$ (−6, 4)
15. $E$ (−7, −2)  16. $F$ (−2, 0)   17. $G$ (0, −7)   18. $H$ (−3, −2)

---

## Teaching Tip

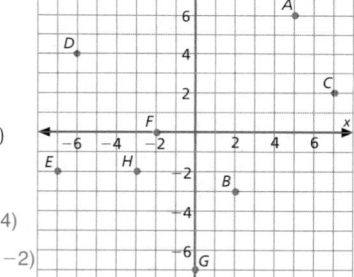

This is a good time to also review the distance formula, $d = \sqrt{(x_2 - x_1)^2 + (y_2 - y_1)^2}$.
Have students apply the formula to show that both pairs of opposite sides of a given parallelogram are congruent. Use parallelogram $ABCD$ with $A(-2, -1)$, $B(3, -2)$, $C(4, 5)$, $D(-1, 6)$.   $AB = DC = \sqrt{26}$, $AD = BC = \sqrt{50}$
Then have students use the midpoint formula to show that the diagonals of the parallelogram bisect each other.   midpoint of $\overline{AC}$ = midpoint of $\overline{BD}$ = (1, 2)

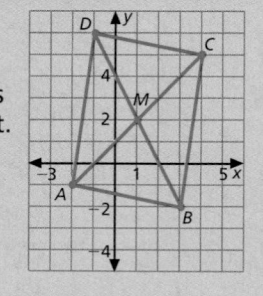

## MIDPOINT FORMULA

Being able to apply the midpoint formula will help you as you learn about reflections across an axis or a given line.

**Example** Find the midpoint of $\overline{ST}$.

The midpoint formula is $M = \left(\dfrac{x_1 + x_2}{2}, \dfrac{y_1 + y_2}{2}\right)$.

The endpoints of $\overline{ST}$ are $(-4, 3)$ and $(3, 8)$.

$M = \left(\dfrac{-4 + 3}{2}, \dfrac{3 + 8}{2}\right) = \left(\dfrac{-1}{2}, \dfrac{11}{2}\right)$

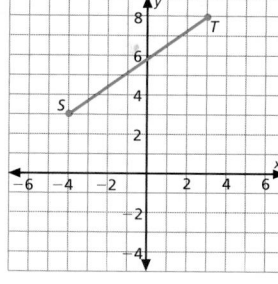

**Find the midpoint of each line segment.**

**19.** 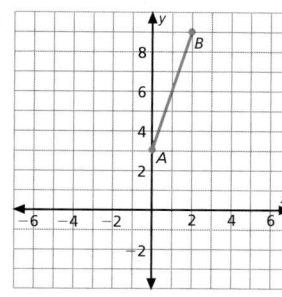 (1, 6)

**20.** 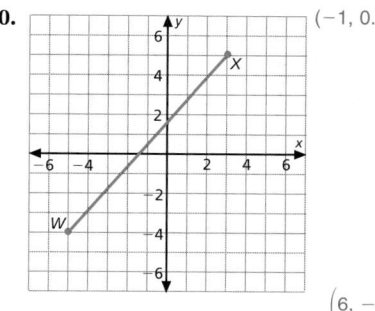 (−1, 0.5)

**21.** $C(8, 4)$, $D(-2, 6)$ (3, 5)  **22.** $R(-3, 5)$, $S(6, -2)$ (1.5, 1.5)  **23.** $K(8, 0)$, $L(4, -1)$ $\left(6, -\dfrac{1}{2}\right)$

**24.** $Y(-7, -4)$, $Z(-8, 5)$ (−7.5, 0.5) **25.** $D(0, 5)$, $E(-4, 9)$ (−2, 7)  **26.** $J(3, -6)$, $K(0, -3)$ (1.5, −4.5)

## DRAW AND MEASURE ANGLES

In this chapter you will use a protractor to rotate figures. It will be helpful to practice using a protractor to draw and measure angles.

**Use a protractor to measure $\angle XYZ$ in each figure.**

**27.** 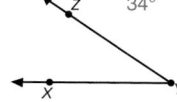 34°  **28.**  115°  **29.** 158°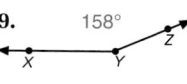

**Use a protractor to draw angles with the given measure.** For 30–34, check students' work.

**30.** 90°  **31.** 35°  **32.** 120°  **33.** 15°  **34.** 160°

## ADDITIONAL ANSWERS

**1.** 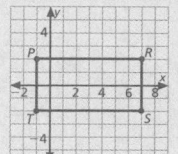  **2.** 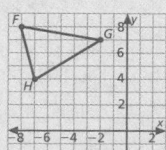  **3.** 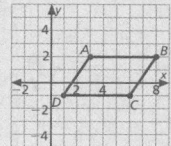  **4.**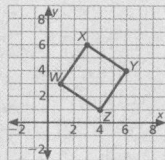

---

### QUICK ASSESSMENT

Ask the following questions to determine if students have mastered the basic skills reviewed on these pages.

1. Explain the difference between $A(-3, 6)$ and $B(3, -6)$.   From the origin, A is left 3 and up 6, in Quadrant II; from the origin, B is right 3 and down 6, in Quadrant IV.
2. Describe the location of $H(0, -5)$. on the negative portion of the y-axis
3. Use words to tell how to find the coordinates of the midpoint of a line segment when you know the coordinates of the endpoints. **Possible answer: Find the mean of the x-coordinates and the mean of the y-coordinates.**

### ADDITIONAL PRACTICE

Refer to the Prerequisite Skills lessons beginning on page 576 for more practice.

### ADDITIONAL ANSWERS

**5.** 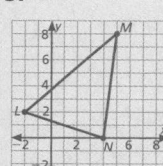  **6.**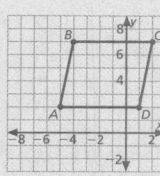

**7.** 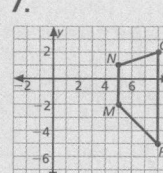  **8.**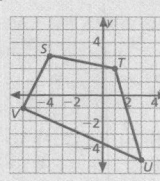

**9.** 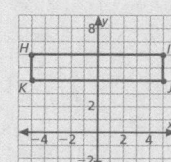  **10.**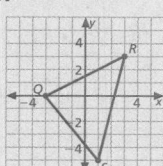

# Translations in the Coordinate Plane

**Goals** ■ Describe and graph translation images on a coordinate plane.

**Applications** Music, Architecture, Sports, Photography

## Lesson Planning

### NCTM Standards/Strands
■ Geometry
■ Representation
■ Measurement
■ Reasoning & Proof

### Vocabulary

translation     image
preimage        transformation

### Tools/Materials Needed

graph paper     ruler
scissors

### Lesson Resources

Warm-up Transparency 28
Transparency TK-9–12, RF-37
Reteaching 7-1
Extra Practice 7-1
Enrichment 7-1
Technology Activity 7-1

## Getting Started

### 5-MINUTE WARM-UP

If $x = -3$ and $y = 2$, find the indicated coordinates.
1. $A(x + 1, y + 2)$   $A(-2, 4)$
2. $B(x - 5, y - 5)$   $B(-8, -3)$
3. $C(x, y + 4)$   $C(-3, 6)$

### Introduction to Lesson 7-1
Have students share their findings for Question 5. Elicit that Triangles 1 and 2 are the same size and shape (congruent), but that they are in different positions in the plane. Ask students to speculate about what would happen to Triangle 1 if they were to slide it elsewhere in the coordinate plane. **Triangle 1 would retain its size and shape, but the coordinates of the vertices would change.**

**Use grid paper, a ruler, and scissors.**
For 1–4, observe students' work.
1. Use the ruler to draw an isosceles triangle on grid paper. Make the base 4 units and the height 5 units. Cut out the triangle and label the vertices *A*, *B* and *C*.

2. Draw a coordinate plane. Label each axis from $-12$ to 12.

3. Place the triangle in the third quadrant so that the coordinates of each vertex are integers. Trace it and label it Triangle 1. Record the coordinates of the vertices.

4. Carefully slide the triangle up 7 units and to the right 8 units. Trace the triangle and label it Triangle 2. Record the coordinates of the vertices.

5. Compare the *x*-coordinates and *y*-coordinates of both triangles. What do you notice? Each *x*-coordinate has increased by 7 and each *y*-coordinate by 8.

### ▧ BUILD UNDERSTANDING

A **translation**, or *slide*, of a figure produces a new figure exactly like the original. The new figure is the **image** of the original figure, and the original figure is the **preimage**. A move like a translation is called a **transformation** of a figure.

As a figure is translated, you can imagine all its points sliding along a plane at once in the same direction and for the same distance. Therefore, the sides and angles of an image are equal in measure to the sides and angles of its preimage. Also, each side of an image is parallel to the corresponding side of its preimage. An image and its preimage are congruent figures.

### Example 1

Graph the image of $\triangle ABC$ with vertices $A(1, -4)$, $B(2, -2)$, and $C(5, -3)$ under a translation of 7 units up and 3 units left.

**Solution**

First graph $\triangle ABC$. To slide the image up 7 units, add 7 to each *y*-coordinate. To slide the image left 3 units, subtract 3 from each *x*-coordinate. Graph $\triangle A'B'C'$.

$$A(1, -4) \rightarrow A'(1 - 3, -4 + 7) = A'(-2, 3)$$
$$B(2, -2) \rightarrow B'(2 - 3, -2 + 7) = B'(-1, 5)$$
$$C(5, -3) \rightarrow C'(5 - 3, -3 + 7) = C'(2, 4)$$

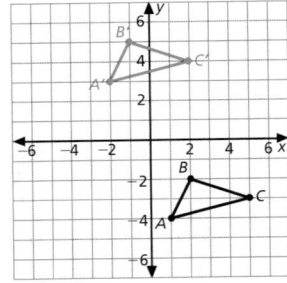

**296** Chapter 7 **Coordinate Graphing and Transformations**

## Teaching Tip

**ESL/LEP** These students may find the terms in this lesson confusing. List the terms translation (slide), transformation (for the purposes of this text, a change to the position, orientation, and/or size of a figure without a change to its shape), preimage (original figure), image (new figure). Draw a diagram to represent each. Have students practice describing the graphs in this lesson using these terms (e.g., the preimage of $\triangle A'B'C'$ is $\triangle ABC$).

A translation can be described by a rule stating the number of units to the left or right and the number of units up or down.

## Example 2

**Write the rule that describes the translation of $\triangle RST$ to $\triangle R'S'T'$.**

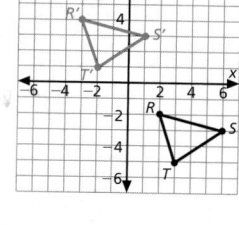

### Solution

Look for a pattern between the $x$-coordinates and $y$-coordinates of each vertex of the preimage ($\triangle RST$) and the $x$-coordinates and $y$-coordinates of each vertex of the image ($\triangle R'S'T'$).

| | | |
|---|---|---|
| $R(2, -2)$ | $S(6, -3)$ | $T(3, -5)$ |
| $R'(-3, 4)$ | $S'(1, 3)$ | $T'(-2, 1)$ |

To find the $x$-coordinate of each image vertex, you must subtract 5 from the $x$-coordinate of each preimage vertex. To find the $y$-coordinate of each image vertex, you must add 6 to the $y$-coordinate of each preimage vertex.

The rule $(x, y) \rightarrow (x - 5, y + 6)$ describes the translation of $\triangle RST$ 5 units to the left and 6 units up.

## Example 3

**SPORTS** Coach Higgins diagrams a play for his basketball team. Each of the five players is represented by the letters $A$, $B$, $C$, $D$ and $E$. Draw the image under the given translations. Which player ends up going to the basket?

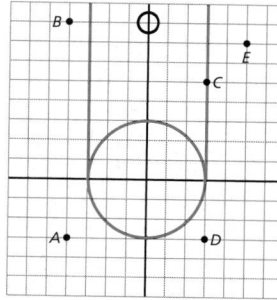

$A(-4, -3)$ under a translation of 5 right and 11 up.

$B(-4, 8)$ under a translation of 0 left or right and 7 down.

$C(3, 5)$ under a translation of 6 left and 7 down.

$D(3, -3)$ under a translation of 3 left and 1 down.

$E(5, 7)$ under a translation of 0 left or right and 0 up or down.

### Solution

Apply each translation to graph the five images.

$$A(-4, -3) \rightarrow A'(-4 + 5, -3 + 11) = A'(1, 8)$$
$$B(-4, 8) \rightarrow B'(-4 + 0, 8 - 7) = B'(-4, 1)$$
$$C(3, 5) \rightarrow C'(3 - 6, 5 - 7) = C'(-3, -2)$$
$$D(3, -3) \rightarrow D'(3 - 3, -3 - 1) = D'(0, -4)$$
$$E(5, 7) \rightarrow E'(5 + 0, 7 + 0) = E'(5, 7)$$

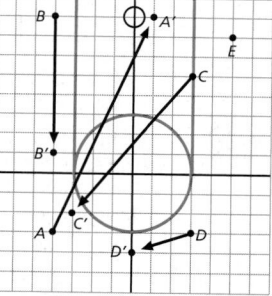

Each player's translation is drawn in the figure. Player $A$ ends up going to the basket.

 **Math Online** mathmatters2.com/extra_examples

### Supplementary Example 1

Graph the image of parallelogram $ABCD$ with vertices $A(1, -4)$, $B(2, -2)$, $C(5, -2)$, $D(4, -4)$ under a translation of 6 units left and 4 units up.

$A(1, -4) \rightarrow A'(1 - 6, -4 + 4) = A'(-5, 0)$

$B(2, -2) \rightarrow B'(2 - 6, -2 + 4) = B'(-4, 2)$

$C(5, -2) \rightarrow C'(5 - 6, -2 + 4) = C'(-1, 2)$

$D(4, -4) \rightarrow D'(4 - 6, -4 + 4) = D'(-2, 0)$

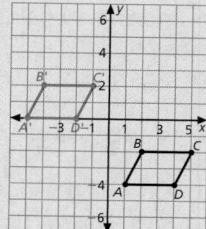

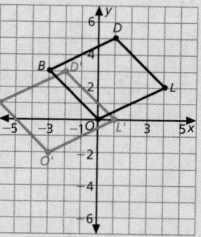

### Supplementary Example 2

Write the rule that describes the translation of parallelogram $BOLD$ to parallelogram $B'O'L'D'$. The rule $(x, y) \rightarrow (x - 3, y - 2)$ describes the translation of parallelogram $BOLD$ 3 units left and 2 units down.

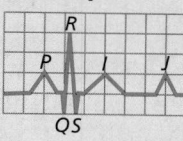

### Supplementary Example 3

**HEALTH** The diagram represents a typical heartbeat over one cycle of pumping. Copy the diagram. Then sketch the next heartbeat.

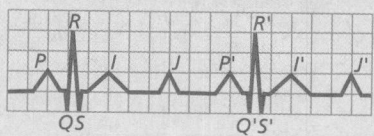

## Extend the Lesson

**CONNECTING TO PRIOR KNOWLEDGE** Have students use a graphing utility to view families of parabolas and describe the relationship in terms of *translation*.

$y = x^2$ is translated 2 units up to $y = x^2 + 2$ or 2 units down to $y = x^2 - 2$.

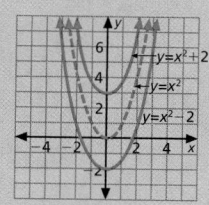

$y = x^2$ is translated 2 units right to $y = (x - 2)^2$ or 2 units left to $y = (x + 2)^2$.

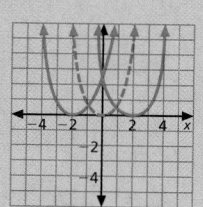

## Lesson Wrap-up

### QUICK ASSESSMENT

Ask the following questions to determine if students understand the content presented in this lesson.

1. Write the coordinates of the image of $P(-2, 5)$ under a translation of 3 units left and 1 unit up.  $P'(-5, 6)$
2. Write the rule that describes the translation of $A(4, -3)$ to $A'(-1, -7)$.  $(x, y) \rightarrow (x - 5, y - 4)$

Describe what happens to each of the following characteristics of a plane figure under a translation in the coordinate plane.

4. the size of the figure  **remains unchanged**
5. the shape of the figure  **remains unchanged**
6. the orientation of the figure (the way the figure is facing)  **remains unchanged**

### ASSIGNMENT GUIDE

**Basic:** 1–23, 28–42
**Enriched:** 1–42

### Reteaching Worksheet 7-1

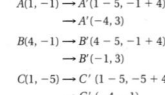
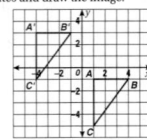
---

### TRY THESE EXERCISES

**Graph the image of rectangle DEFG under the given translations.**
For 1–4, see additional answers.

1. 4 units right
2. 7 units down
3. 1 unit up and 6 units right
4. 5 units right and 5 units down

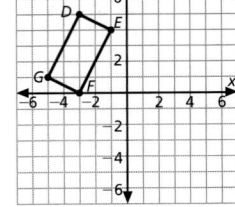

5. What would the coordinates of rectangle DEFG be under a translation of 557 units to the left and 159 units down?
   $D'(-560, -154)$, $E'(-558, -155)$, $F'(-560, -159)$, $G'(-562, -158)$

**Write the rule that describes each translation.**

6.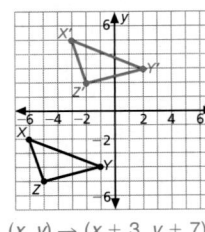
$(x, y) \rightarrow (x + 3, y + 7)$

7.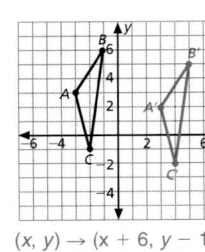
$(x, y) \rightarrow (x + 6, y - 1)$

8.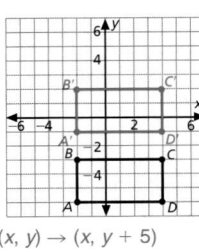
$(x, y) \rightarrow (x, y + 5)$

### PRACTICE EXERCISES  •  For Extra Practice, see page 607.

Pentagon $HIJKL$ has vertices $H(-1, 5)$, $I(2, 6)$, $J(5, 5)$, $K(3, 2)$, and $L(1, 2)$. Graph the pentagon and its image under the given translations.
For 9–14, see additional answers.

9. 4 units left
10. 7 units down
11. 3 units up
12. 5 units right
13. 7 units left and 6 units down
14. 3 units up and 3 units right

15. Is pentagon $HIJKL$ a regular pentagon? Explain.  No; angles are not all congruent, sides are not all congruent.

**Write the rule that describes each translation.**

16.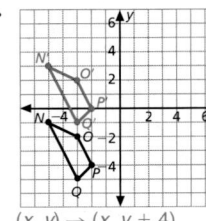
$(x, y) \rightarrow (x, y + 4)$

17.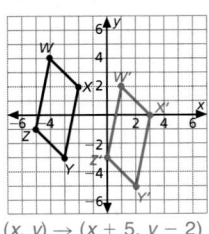
$(x, y) \rightarrow (x + 5, y - 2)$

18.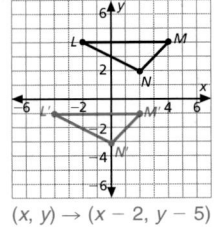
$(x, y) \rightarrow (x - 2, y - 5)$

19. **WRITING MATH** Suppose a preimage is in Quadrant III of the coordinate plane. Describe a translation under which the image is in Quadrant I.
   The image should be translated right and up.

20. **MUSIC** The diagram shows the musical scale that Jontay uses when he practices the flute each day. Copy the diagram, and sketch the next 16 notes that Jontay will play if he repeats what is shown. Describe how this is an example of a translation.  See additional answers.

### ADDITIONAL ANSWERS

1.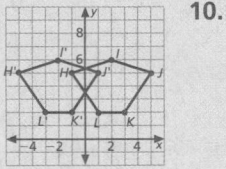
2.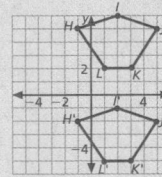
3.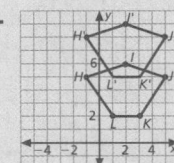
4.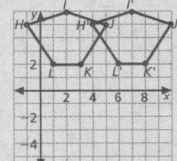

9.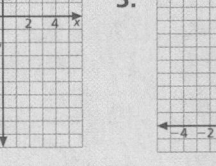
10.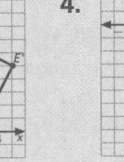
11.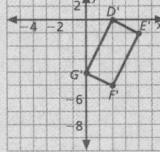
12.

**21. ARCHITECTURE** An architect designs a deck for a client. To access the deck, there is a glass sliding door. Describe how the sliding door is an example of a translation. See additional answers.

**22. PHOTOGRAPHY** When you take a picture with a camera, a shutter opens to expose the film to light. The amount of time that the shutter remains open is known as the *shutter speed*. To illustrate motion in a photograph, a photographer can use a long shutter speed. This suggests a translated image. Sketch a picture that demonstrates a translation in a photograph. See additional answers.

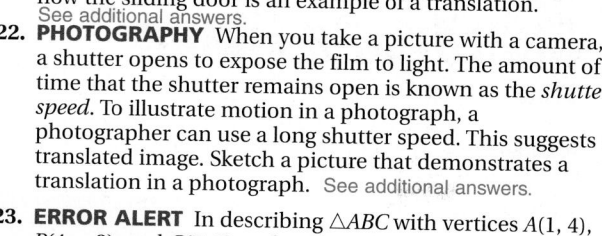

**23. ERROR ALERT** In describing $\triangle ABC$ with vertices $A(1, 4)$, $B(4, -2)$, and $C(7, 9)$ under a translation of 2 units up and 4 units right, Mandy arrives at $\triangle A'B'C'$ with vertices $A'(3, 8)$, $B'(6, 2)$, and $C'(9, 13)$. What mistake has Mandy made, and what are the correct vertices? See additional answers.

### ■ EXTENDED PRACTICE EXERCISES

**24. CRITICAL THINKING** Triangle $QRS$ with vertices $Q(-4, 7)$, $R(-1, 3)$ and $S(-5, 2)$ is translated using the rule $(x, y) \rightarrow (x + 7, y - 1)$ to create $\triangle Q'R'S'$. Triangle $Q'R'S'$ is then translated using the rule $(x, y) \rightarrow (x - 4, y - 7)$ to create $\triangle Q''R''S''$. In words, describe the position of $\triangle Q''R''S''$ in relation to $\triangle QRS$ in the coordinate plane. The image $\triangle Q''R''S''$ is the preimage of $\triangle QRS$ moved 3 units right and 8 units down.

**25.** In the figure shown, is the transformation $\triangle ABC \rightarrow \triangle A'B'C'$ a translation? Explain why or why not.
No; the vertices did not all move the same number of units to the right.

**26. GEOMETRY SOFTWARE** Use geometry software to graph several polygons. Then use the software's transformation functions to translate the images in different directions. Observe students' work.

**27. CHAPTER INVESTIGATION** On grid paper, draw the general layout and shape of the main floor of your house. It can be a rectangle, U shape or any other design. Make the blueprint large enough to fill most of the page. Answers will vary.

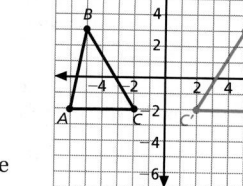

### ■ MIXED REVIEW EXERCISES

**Find each probability.** (Lesson 4-4)

**28.** Two number cubes are tossed. What is the probability that the sum of the numbers is 3 or 4? $\frac{5}{36}$

**29.** One card is drawn at random from a standard deck of 52 cards. What is the probability that the card is a diamond or a king? $\frac{4}{13}$

**30.** Two number cubes are tossed. What is the probability that both cubes show an odd number? $\frac{1}{4}$

**Solve.** (Lesson 3-2)

**31.** $8p = 32$   4    **32.** $6r = 3$   $\frac{1}{2}$    **33.** $z - 8 = 4$   12    **34.** $\frac{1}{2}f = 5$   10

**35.** $k - 6 = |-2|$   8    **36.** $0.3m = 1.8$   6    **37.** $8.2 + n = 4.7$   $-3.5$    **38.** $\frac{t}{4} = 1.6$   6.4

**39.** $g + 3 = |-17|$   14    **40.** $2d = -8$   $-4$    **41.** $-3c = -18$   6    **42.** $k + 3 = 11$   8

Name _____    Date _____

EXTRA PRACTICE **7-1**
**TRANSLATIONS IN THE COORDINATE PLANE**

☑ **EXERCISES**
Write the rule that describes each translation.

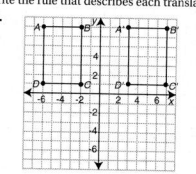
1.

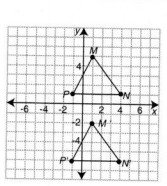
2.

$(x, y) \rightarrow (x + 9, y)$    $(x, y) \rightarrow (x, y - 7)$

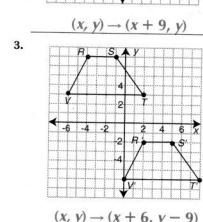
3.

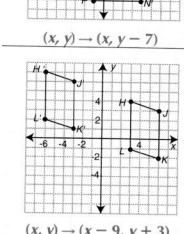
4.

$(x, y) \rightarrow (x + 6, y - 9)$    $(x, y) \rightarrow (x - 9, y + 3)$

Trapezoid $ABCD$ has vertices $A(-1, 4)$, $B(2, 4)$, $C(3, 1)$ and $D(-2, 1)$. Graph the trapezoid and its images under the translations from the original position. Use your own paper. Give the coordinates of the vertices of the images.

**5.** 3 units right    $A'(2, 4)$, $B'(5, 4)$, $C'(6, 1)$, $D'(1, 1)$
**6.** 5 units down    $A'(-1, -1)$, $B'(2, -1)$, $C'(3, -4)$, $D'(-2, -4)$
**7.** 4 units up    $A'(-1, 8)$, $B'(2, 8)$, $C'(3, 5)$, $D'(-2, 5)$
**8.** 2 units left    $A'(-3, 4)$, $B'(0, 4)$, $C'(1, 1)$, $D'(-4, 1)$
**9.** 2 units right and 3 units down    $A'(1, 1)$, $B'(4, 1)$, $C'(5, -2)$, $D'(0, -2)$
**10.** 4 units left and 3 units up    $A'(-5, 7)$, $B'(-2, 7)$, $C'(-1, 4)$, $D'(-6, 4)$

Name _____    Date _____

ENRICHMENT **7-1**
**PROPERTIES OF DETERMINANTS**

The following properties often help when evaluating determinants.

• If all the elements of a row (or column) are zero, the value of the determinant is zero.
$\begin{vmatrix} a & b \\ 0 & 0 \end{vmatrix} = 0 \ (a \cdot 0) - (0 \cdot b) = 0$

• Multiplying all the elements of a row (or column) by a constant is equivalent to multiplying the value of the determinant by the constant.
$3\begin{vmatrix} 4 & -1 \\ 5 & 3 \end{vmatrix} = \begin{vmatrix} 12 & -3 \\ 5 & 3 \end{vmatrix}$   $3[4(3) - 5(-1)] = 51$
$3[12 + 5] = 51$
$12(3) - 5(-3) = 51$

• If two rows (or columns) have equal corresponding elements, the value of the determinant is zero.
$\begin{vmatrix} 5 & 5 \\ -3 & -3 \end{vmatrix} = 0 \ 5(-3) - (-3)(5) = 0$

• The value of a determinant is unchanged if any multiple of a row (or column) is added to corresponding elements of another row (or column).
$\begin{vmatrix} 4 & -3 \\ 2 & 5 \end{vmatrix} = \begin{vmatrix} 6 & 2 \\ 2 & 5 \end{vmatrix}$   $4(5) - 2(-3) =$   $6(5) - 2(2) =$
$20 + 6 = 26$   $30 - 4 = 26$
(Row 2 is added to row 1.)

• If two rows (or columns) are interchanged, the sign of the determinant is changed.
$\begin{vmatrix} 4 & 5 \\ -3 & 8 \end{vmatrix} = \begin{vmatrix} -3 & 8 \\ 4 & 5 \end{vmatrix}$   $4(8) - (-3)(5) =$   $-[(-3)(5) - 4(8)] =$
$32 + 15 = 47$   $-[-15 - 32] = 47$

• The value of the determinant is unchanged if row 1 is interchanged with column 1, and row 2 is interchanged with column 2. The result is called the transpose.
$\begin{vmatrix} 5 & -7 \\ 3 & 4 \end{vmatrix} = \begin{vmatrix} 5 & 3 \\ -7 & 4 \end{vmatrix}$   $5(4) - 3(-7) =$   $5(4) - (-7)(3) =$
$20 + 21 = 41$   $20 + 21 = 41$

☑ **EXERCISES**
**1–6.** Verify each property above by evaluating the given determinants and give another example of the property. Examples will vary.

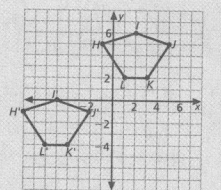
13.

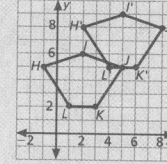
14.

20.

**21.** The sliding door moves horizontally the appropriate number of units to open the door wide enough for a person to access the deck. A move to the right or left depending on the position of the door is a translation.

**22.**

**23.** Mandy translated the preimage 4 units up and 2 units right. The correct vertices are
$A(1, 4) \rightarrow A'(1 + 4, 4 + 2) = A'(5, 6)$
$B(4, -2) \rightarrow B'(4 + 4, -2 + 2) = B'(8, 0)$
$C(7, 9) \rightarrow C'(7 + 4, 9 + 2) = C'(11, 11)$

## Lesson Planning

### NCTM Standards/Strands
- Geometry
- Representation
- Measurement
- Reasoning & Proof

### Vocabulary

reflection          line of reflection

### Tools/Materials Needed

graph paper          ruler
food coloring or paint

### Lesson Resources

Warm-up Transparency 28
Transparency TK-9–12, RF-38
Reteaching 7-2
Extra Practice 7-2
Enrichment 7-2
Technology Activity 7-2

## Getting Started

### 5-MINUTE WARM-UP

If $x = -4$ and $y = 3$, find the indicated coordinates.
1. $E(-x, y)$     $E(4, 3)$
2. $F(x, -y)$     $F(-4, -3)$
3. $G(-x, -y)$     $C(4, -3)$

### Introduction to Lesson 7-2
As students share their answers to Question 4, elicit that the shapes are congruent, are in different positions in the plane, and that the two shapes "face" each other (the *orientation* has changed).

Have students choose a point within the original shape and write its coordinates. Then ask students to tell the coordinates of the point in the image shape that is the image of the chosen point. Students should note that under a reflection across the *y*-axis, a point and its image have opposite *x*-coordinates and the same *y*-coordinate.

**Goals**
- Graph reflection images on a coordinate plane.
- Identify lines of reflection.

**Applications**   Art, Landscaping, Navigation, Architecture

Use grid paper, a ruler and food coloring or paint.
For 1–4, observe students' work.
1. On grid paper, draw a coordinate plane.

2. Place a small drop of food coloring or paint in the Quadrant I. Carefully fold the paper in half along the *y*-axis.

3. Unfold your paper. There should now be a shape on both sides of the *y*-axis.

4. Describe the shapes on each side of the fold line.

### ◣ BUILD UNDERSTANDING

Translations are one type of transformation that can be applied to figures in the coordinate plane to produce an image that is exactly like its preimage. Another type of transformation that yields a congruent figure is a **reflection**, or *flip*. Under a reflection, a figure is *reflected*, or *flipped*, across a *line of reflection*.

When you reflect a point across the *y*-axis, the *y*-coordinate remains the same, but the *x*-coordinate is made its opposite. The reflection of the point $(x, y)$ across the *y*-axis is the point $(-x, y)$.

When you reflect a point across the *x*-axis, the *x*-coordinate remains the same, but the *y*-coordinate is made its opposite. The reflection of the point $(x, y)$ across the *x*-axis is $(x, -y)$.

### Example 1

Graph the image of $\triangle DEF$ with vertices $D(4, 5)$, $E(5, 1)$ and $F(1, 3)$ reflected across the *x*-axis.

#### Solution

First graph $\triangle DEF$. Multiply the *y*-coordinate of each vertex by $-1$.

$$D(4, 5) \rightarrow D'(4, -5)$$

$$E(5, 1) \rightarrow E'(5, -1)$$

$$F(1, 3) \rightarrow F'(1, -3)$$

Graph $\triangle D'E'F'$.

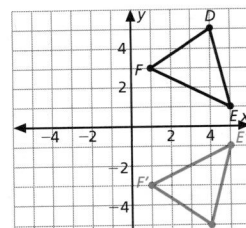

#### Check Understanding

Name the coordinates of $\triangle DEF$ in Example 1 when it is reflected across the *y*-axis.

$D'(-4, 5)$, $E'(-5, 1)$, $F'(-1, 3)$

300   Chapter 7  **Coordinate Graphing and Transformations**

### Extend the Lesson

Have students work in pairs to write secret messages using only parts of letters and lines of reflection, as shown below.

The partner is to decode the message. To decode, students must draw the reflection image of the parts across the given lines.

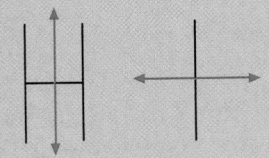

Figures can be reflected over lines other than the $x$-axis or $y$-axis. When a point $(x, y)$ is reflected across the line $y = x$, the image is the point $(y, x)$. When a point is reflected across the line $y = -x$, the image is the point $(-y, -x)$.

## Example 2

**Graph the image of $\triangle JKL$ with vertices $J(-4, 2)$, $K(-2, -1)$, and $L(-5, -3)$ under a reflection across the line $y = x$.**

### Solution

Graph $\triangle JKL$ and the line $y = x$. Transpose the $x$-coordinate and $y$-coordinate of each vertex using the rule $(x, y) \rightarrow (y, x)$.

$$J(-4, 2) \rightarrow J'(2, -4)$$
$$K(-2, -1) \rightarrow K'(-1, -2)$$
$$L(-5, -3) \rightarrow L'(-3, -5)$$

Graph $\triangle J'K'L'$.

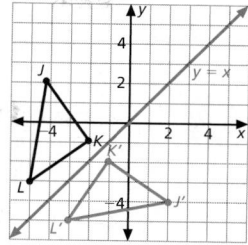

Each point of a reflection image is the same distance from the line of reflection as the corresponding point of its preimage. In other words, the line of reflection lies directly in the middle between the image and its preimage. You can use this fact to help find reflection lines.

## Example 3

**ART** Mani is designing a pattern for a picture she is going to paint. In the pattern, there is a triangle and its reflection image. Triangle $QRS$ has vertices $Q(-7, 1)$, $R(-3, -2)$ and $S(-4, -4)$; and its image has vertices $Q'(5, 1)$, $R'(1, -2)$ and $S'(2, -4)$. Graph the triangles and find the line of reflection.

### Solution

First graph $\triangle QRS$ and $\triangle Q'R'S'$. Imagine line segments connecting each pair of corresponding vertices. Use the midpoint formula to find the midpoint of each of these three line segments. Recall the midpoint formula.

$$M = \left(\frac{x_1 + x_2}{2}, \frac{y_1 + y_2}{2}\right)$$

For $\overline{QQ'}$, $M = \left(\frac{-7 + 5}{2}, \frac{1 + 1}{2}\right) = \left(\frac{-2}{2}, \frac{2}{2}\right) = (-1, 1)$

For $\overline{RR'}$, $M = \left(\frac{-3 + 1}{2}, \frac{-2 + (-2)}{2}\right) = \left(\frac{-2}{2}, \frac{-4}{2}\right) = (-1, -2)$

For $\overline{SS'}$, $M = \left(\frac{-4 + 2}{2}, \frac{-4 + (-4)}{2}\right) = \left(\frac{-2}{2}, \frac{-8}{2}\right) = (-1, -4)$

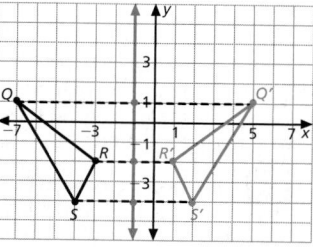

Draw a line through the midpoints. The equation of the line of reflection is $x = -1$.

**Math Online** mathmatters2.com/extra_examples

Lesson 7-2 **Reflections in the Coordinate Plane** | 301

## Extend the Lesson

**CHALLENGE** Have students consider a reflection across a *point*.
Graph the image of $\triangle ABC$ with vertices $A(1, 2)$, $B(5, 5)$, $C(5, 2)$ reflected across the origin.
Under a reflection across the origin, point $(x, y)$ has as its image $(-x, -y)$.
So: $A(1, 2) \rightarrow A'(-1, -2)$    $B(5, 5) \rightarrow B'(-5, -5)$
$C(5, 2) \rightarrow C'(-5, -2)$

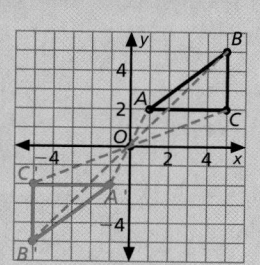

---

## Chalkboard Examples

### Supplementary Example 1
Graph the image of $\triangle KLM$ with vertices $K(-5, 5)$, $L(2, 0)$, and $M(-2, -4)$ reflected across the $y$-axis.
For each vertex, find the point that is the same distance from the $y$-axis, but on the opposite side.
Under a reflection across the $y$-axis, point $(x, y)$ has as its image $(-x, y)$.
$K(-5, 5) \rightarrow K'(5, 5)$
$L(2, 0) \rightarrow L'(-2, 0)$
$M(-2, -4) \rightarrow M'(2, -4)$

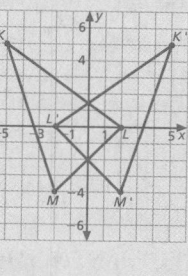

### Supplementary Example 2
Graph the image of $\triangle ABC$ with vertices $A(0, 1)$, $B(2, 6)$, $C(2, 4)$ reflected across the line $y = 2$.
The vertices of the image triangle will have the same $x$-coordinate as the original vertices.
An original vertex and its image will be the same vertical distance from the line $y = 2$ but on opposite sides.
(1 unit below/above $y = 2$)
$A(0, 1) \rightarrow A'(0, 3)$
(4 units above/below $y = 2$)
$B(2, 6) \rightarrow B'(2, -2)$
(2 units above/below $y = 2$)
$C(2, 4) \rightarrow C'(2, 0)$

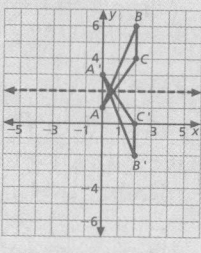

### Supplementary Example 3
**CONSTRUCTION** A power company plans to locate a transformer at a point $P$ along the road between points $A$ and $B$ so that the length of cable from the home at point $C$ to the transformer and then to the home at point $D$ is minimized. Copy the figure at the left below, and locate $P$.

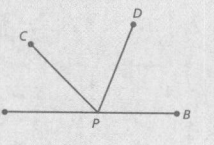
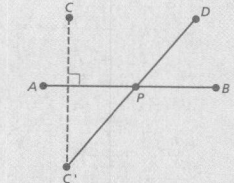

## Lesson Wrap-up

### QUICK ASSESSMENT

Ask the following questions to determine if students understand the content presented in this lesson.

**Write the coordinates of the image of $P(-3, 4)$ after a reflection across the indicated line.**

1. the $x$-axis   $(-3, -4)$
2. the $y$-axis   $(3, 4)$
3. the line $y = -x$   $(-4, 3)$
4. the line $y = x$   $(4, -3)$

**Describe what happens to each of the following characteristics of a plane figure under a line reflection in the coordinate plane.**

5. the size of the figure   remains unchanged
6. the shape of the figure   remains unchanged
7. the orientation of the figure (the way the figure is facing with respect to the line of reflection) is opposite

### ASSIGNMENT GUIDE

Basic: 1–29, 33–44
Enriched: 1–44

### Reteaching Worksheet 7-2

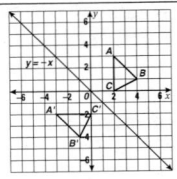

Name _____    Date _____

RETEACHING **7-2**
**REFLECTIONS IN THE COORDINATE PLANE**
The image of a figure under a **reflection** is formed by flipping the figure across **a line of reflection**.

- When a point is reflected across the $x$-axis, $(x, y) \rightarrow (x, -y)$.
- When a point is reflected across the $y$-axis, $(x, y) \rightarrow (-x, y)$.
- When a point is reflected across the line $y = x$, $(x, y) \rightarrow (y, x)$.
- When a point is reflected across the line $y = -x$, $(x, y) \rightarrow (-y, -x)$.

**Example**
Graph the image of $\triangle ABC$ under reflection across the line $y = -x$.

**Solution**
To find the coordinates of a point under reflection across the line $y = -x$, use the rule $(x, y) \rightarrow (-y, -x)$.

$A(2, 3) \rightarrow A'(-3, -2)$
$B(4, 1) \rightarrow B'(-1, -4)$
$C(2, 0) \rightarrow C'(0, -2)$

**EXERCISES**
Give the coordinates of the image of each point under a reflection across the given line.

1. $(3, -2)$; $y$-axis
   $(-3, -2)$
2. $(-5, -6)$; $x$-axis
   $(-5, 6)$
3. $(0, 8)$; $y = x$
   $(8, 0)$
4. Graph the image of $\triangle LMN$ under a reflection across the $x$-axis.
5. Graph the reflection of rectangle $PQRS$ under a reflection across the given line.

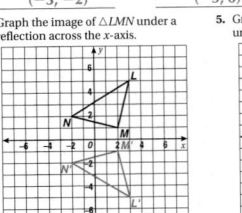
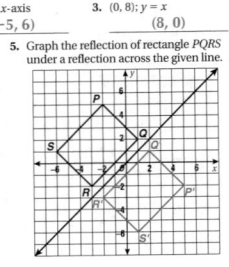

---

### TRY THESE EXERCISES

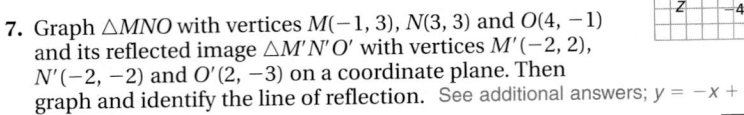

**Graph $\triangle XYZ$ and its image under the given reflection.**
For 1–6, see additional answers.

1. $y$-axis
2. $x$-axis
3. $y = x$
4. $y = -x$
5. $x = 1$
6. $y = 3$

7. Graph $\triangle MNO$ with vertices $M(-1, 3)$, $N(3, 3)$ and $O(4, -1)$ and its reflected image $\triangle M'N'O'$ with vertices $M'(-2, 2)$, $N'(-2, -2)$ and $O'(2, -3)$ on a coordinate plane. Then graph and identify the line of reflection.   See additional answers; $y = -x + 1$

8. The reflected image of $\overline{JK}$ whose endpoints are $J(3, 1)$ and $K(3, -10)$ is $\overline{J'K'}$ with endpoints $J'(-7, 1)$ and $K'(-7, -10)$. What is the line of reflection?
   $x = -2$

9. **WRITING MATH** Suppose a preimage is contained entirely in Quadrant IV. Describe how to graph its reflected image across the $x$-axis. In which quadrant is the image located?   $(x, y) \rightarrow (x, -y)$; Quadrant I

### PRACTICE EXERCISES • For Extra Practice, see page 607.

**Graph quadrilateral $HIJK$ and its image under the given reflection.**
For 10–15, see additional answers.

10. $y$-axis
11. $x$-axis
12. $y = x$
13. $y = -x$
14. $x = 6$
15. $y = -4$

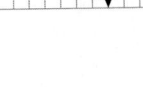

**Give the coordinates of the image of each point under a reflection across the given line.**

16. $(5, -3)$; $x$-axis
    $(5, 3)$
17. $(4, 0)$; $y = -x$
    $(0, -4)$
18. $(-2, -7)$; $y$-axis
    $(2, -7)$
19. $(-6, 8)$; $y = x$
    $(8, -6)$
20. $(0, -6)$; $x$-axis
    $(0, 6)$
21. $(3, -3)$; $y = -x$
    $(3, -3)$

**Copy each figure and its reflected image. Identify the line of reflection.**

22.   $y = 2$

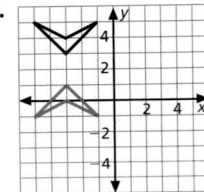

23.   $y = x + 2$

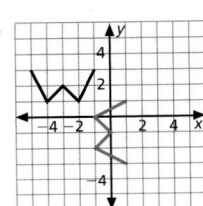

24. **NAVIGATION** A periscope uses two mirrors positioned parallel to each other at $45°$ angles to allow you to see above the line of sight. Explain how a periscope is an example of a reflection.   See additional answers.

25. **WRITING MATH** Suppose you are given $\triangle ABC$ on the left side of a vertical line $m$. Explain how to find the reflection of $\triangle ABC$ across line $m$. Include a diagram with your explanation.   See additional answers.

---

### ADDITIONAL ANSWERS

For Exercises 3, 5, 7, 11, 13, 15, 25, and 29, see Selected Answers on page 686.

1.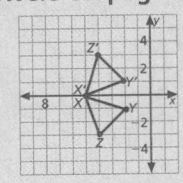

2.

4.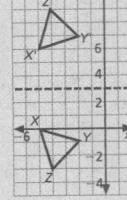

6.

10.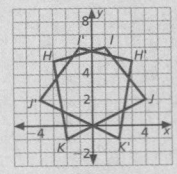

12.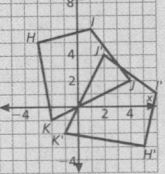

**26. LANDSCAPING** A landscaping company is sketching a preliminary design for a garden that will be on both sides of a trail in a park. The corners of one side are (−3, −4), (−3, 7), (−9, −4) and (−9, 7). It is to be reflected across the y-axis. What are the coordinates of the other side of the garden?
(3, −4), (3, 7), (9, −4), (9, 7)

**Copy each diagram onto grid paper. Then sketch the image of each set of squares under a reflection across line l.** For 27–28, see additional answers.

**27.**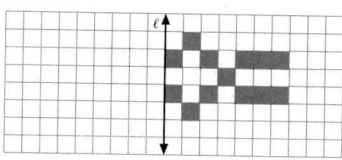

**28.**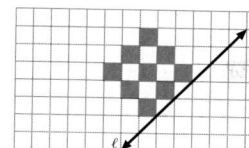

**29. ARCHITECTURE** In designing the twin towers of an office complex, an architect makes a sketch on grid paper. The vertices of one of the towers are (−10, 0), (−5, 0), (−7.5, 14), (−5, 11), and (−10, 11). If he wishes to reflect the tower across the line x = −1, what will the vertices of the image be? Draw both the image and preimage on grid paper. See additional answers.

■ **EXTENDED PRACTICE EXERCISES**

**30. GEOMETRY SOFTWARE** Use geometry software to graph the lines y = −3 and x = 4, on separate coordinate planes. Draw a figure on each plane, and use the software's tools to reflect it across the line. Write a rule for each reflection.
See additional answers.

**31. CRITICAL THINKING** Suppose △ABC is reflected across the y-axis. What does the reflection of this image across the y-axis look like?
It is the same as △ABC.

**32. DATA FILE** Refer to the data on the most visited sites in the National Park System on page 566. Use an atlas to locate three of the parks, and form a triangle by connecting the vertices on a copy of the atlas or map. Draw a line on the copy of the map and reflect the triangle across the line.
Answers will vary.

Blue Ridge Parkway, North Carolina

Name _____ Date _____

EXTRA PRACTICE **7-2**
**REFLECTIONS IN THE COORDINATE PLANE**

■ **EXERCISES**

Graph quadrilateral DEFG and its image under the given reflection. Use your own paper. Give the coordinates of the vertices of the image.
Check students' graphs.
1. y-axis _D′(5, 7), E′(1, 6), F′(−1, 0), G′(7, −5)_
2. x-axis _D′(−5, −7), E′(−1, −6), F(1, 0), G′(−7, 5)_
3. y = x _D′(7, −5), E′(6, −1), F(0, 1), G′(−5, −7)_
4. y = −x _D′(−7, 5), E′(−6, 1), F(0, −1), G′(5, 7)_
5. x = −1 _D′(3, 7), E′(−1, 6), F(−3, 0), G′(5, −5)_
6. y = 2 _D′(−5, −3), E′(−1, −2), F′(1, 4), G′(−7, 9)_

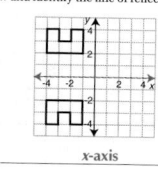

Give the coordinates of the image of each point under a reflection across the given line.

7. (2, −4); y-axis _(−2, −4)_     8. (0, −2); x-axis _(0, 2)_
9. (−5, −8); y = x _(−8, −5)_     10. (−2, 5); y = −x _(−5, 2)_
11. (4, 0); y-axis _(−4, 0)_     12. (−2, 2); y = x _(2, −2)_

Draw and identify the line of reflection for each figure and its reflected image.
13.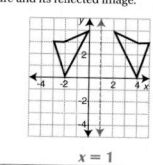

14.

x-axis                x = 1

15. Graph △RST with vertices R(0, 4), S(3, 3), and T(1, −1) and its reflected image R′(−2, 4), S′(−5, 3), and T′(−3, −1) on a coordinate plane on your own paper. Then graph and identify the line of reflection. _x = −1_
Check students' graphs.

■ **MIXED REVIEW EXERCISES**

**Find the mean, median, mode, and range of each set of football data.** (Lesson 1-2)

**33.** Rushing yards (per game)
208   94   132   169   152   145
98   145   152   165   212   mean = 152;
median = 152; mode = 145, 152; range = 118

**34.** Passing yards (per game)
122   138   46   154   92   131   197
119   185   131   182   75   105   mean = 129;
median = 131; mode = 131; range = 151

**35.** Field goals (lengths in yards)
26   26   32   50   43   32   20
35   41   32   18   27   28   39   mean ≈ 32.1;
median = 32; mode = 32; range = 32

**36.** Kickoff returns (lengths in yards)
8   16   9   91   10   12   18   33
6   87   7   13   17   22   26   20   mean ≈ 24.7;
median = 16.5, no mode; range = 85

**Find the measure of the complement and supplement of each angle.** (Lesson 5-2)

**37.** m∠31°   59°, 149°   **38.** m∠15°   75°, 165°   **39.** m∠79°   11°, 101°   **40.** m∠58°   32°, 122°
**41.** m∠22°   68°, 158°   **42.** m∠4°   86°, 176°   **43.** m∠84°   6°, 96°   **44.** m∠61°   29°, 119°

Name _____ Date _____

ENRICHMENT **7-2**
**REBOUND**

You can use a compass to construct the image of a point under a reflection across a line. To construct A′, the reflection of point A across line l, follow these steps.

**Step 1** Place the compass point at A, and draw an arc intersecting line l at B and C.

**Step 2** Keeping the same radius, place the compass point at each point of intersection, and draw two intersecting arcs. Label the point of intersection A′.

**Example**

Figure KLMN represents a squash court. Players can bounce the ball against any combination of walls as long as the ball rebounds against the front wall LM. Balls that hit a corner are hard to hit. At what point should the ball B strike wall LM so that it rebounds off wall NM and hits corner K?

**Solution**

Construct B′, the image of B under reflection across LM. Then construct B″, the image of B′ under reflection across NM (extended). Draw B″K as shown. Label the intersection of B″K and MN as Q. Draw B′Q. Label the intersection of B′Q and LM as P.

The path of the ball can be drawn by connecting points B and P, P and Q, Q and K.

■ **EXERCISES**

Figure PQRS represents a squash court.

1. Construct the path of ball B so that it hits corner P after rebounding off QR and RS.

2. Construct the path of ball B so that it hits corner S after rebounding off PQ and QR.

**14.**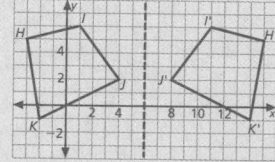

**27.**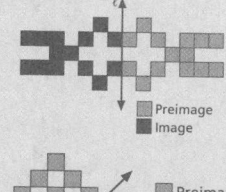
☐ Preimage
☐ Image

**24.** Triangle ABC is reflected over line 1 by mirror 1 which becomes triangle A′B′C′. Then triangle A′B′C′ is reflected over line 2 by mirror 2 which is seen as triangle A″B″C″ by the person using the periscope.

**28.**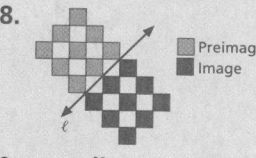
☐ Preimage
☐ Image

**30.** over line y = −3,
(x, y) → (x, −3 + (−3 − y))
over line x = 4, (x, y) → (4 + (4 − x), y)

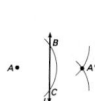
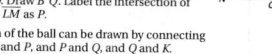
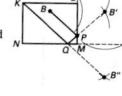
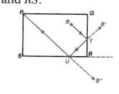
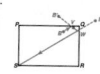

### Vocabulary Review

**Lesson 7-1**
translation    image
preimage    transformation

**Lesson 7-2**
reflection    line of reflection

## ASSIGNMENT GUIDE

**All students:** 1–32

## Chalkboard Examples

### Lesson 7-1

Write the rule that describes the translation of quadrilateral *ABCD* to quadrilateral *A'B'C'D'*.

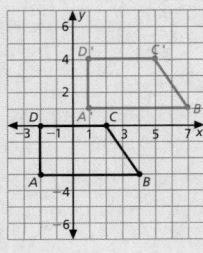

The rule $(x, y) \rightarrow (x + 3, y + 4)$ describes the translation of quadrilateral *ABCD* 3 units right and 4 units up.

### Lesson 7-2

Graph the image of △*ABC* with vertices *A*(0, 1), *B*(2, 6), *C*(2, 4) reflected across the *y*-axis.
For each vertex, find the point that is the same distance from the *y*-axis, but on the opposite side. Points on the *y*-axis remain fixed. Under a reflection across the *y*-axis, point $(x, y)$ has as its image $(-x, y)$.

$A(0, 1) \rightarrow A'(0, 1)$
$B(2, 6) \rightarrow B'(-2, 6)$
$C(2, 4) \rightarrow C'(-2, 4)$

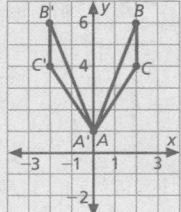

### PRACTICE ◾ LESSON 7-1

**Graph the image of △*LMN* under the given translations.** For 1–4, see additional answers.

1. 3 units right

2. 6 units down

3. 2 units up and 5 units left

4. 3 units right and 3 units down

**Write the rule that describes each translation.**

5.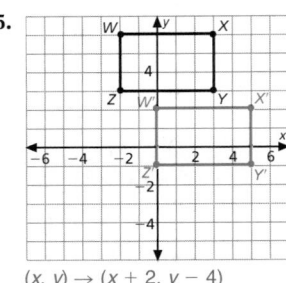

$(x, y) \rightarrow (x + 2, y - 4)$

6.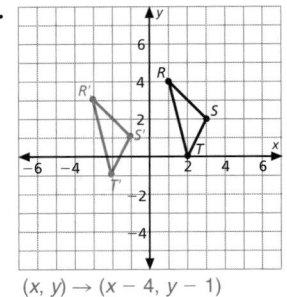

$(x, y) \rightarrow (x - 4, y - 1)$

7.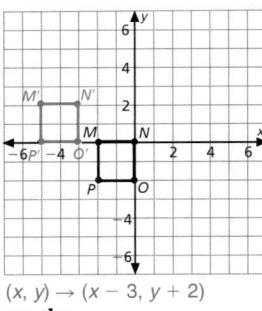

$(x, y) \rightarrow (x - 3, y + 2)$

**Triangle *ABC* has vertices *A* (−2, 1), *B* (−1, 0) and *C* (−3, −3). What are the coordinates of the vertices of the image under each translation?**

8. 5 units right   $A'(3, 1), B'(4, 0), C'(2, -3)$

9. 2 units up   $A'(-2, 3), B'(-1, 2), C'(-3, -1)$

10. 6 units left and 5 units up   $A'(-8, 6), B'(-7, 5), C'(-9, 2)$

11. 4 units right and 9 units down   $A'(2, -8), B'(3, -9), C'(1, -12)$

### PRACTICE ◾ LESSON 7-2

**Graph quadrilateral *WXYZ* and its image under the given reflection.** For 12–17, see additional answers.

12. *y*-axis

13. *x*-axis

14. $y = x$

15. $y = -x$

16. $y = -2$

17. $x = 5$

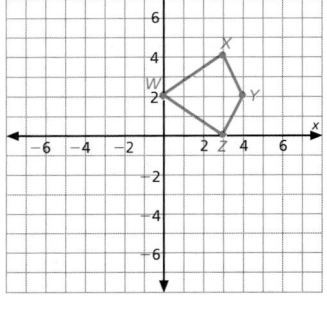

**Give the coordinates of the image of each point under a reflection across the given line.**

18. (4, 1); *x*-axis   (4, −1)

19. (−4, 4); *y*-axis   (4, 4)

20. (5, 2); $y = x$   (2, 5)

21. (1, 6); $y = -x$   (−6, −1)

22. (−2, 2); *x*-axis   (−2, −2)

23. (−3, 0); *y*-axis   (3, 0)

## ADDITIONAL ANSWERS

1.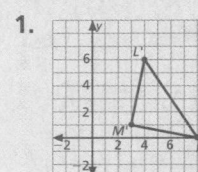

2.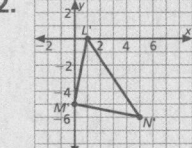

3.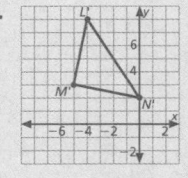

4.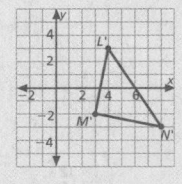

12.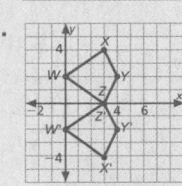

13.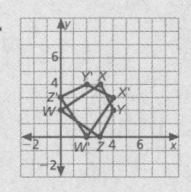

14.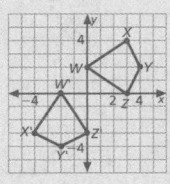

15.

**Write the rule that describes each translation.** (Lesson 7-1)

24.
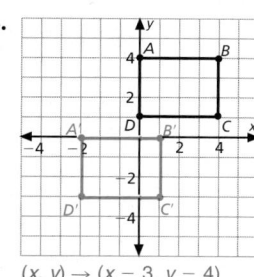

$(x, y) \rightarrow (x - 3, y - 4)$

25.
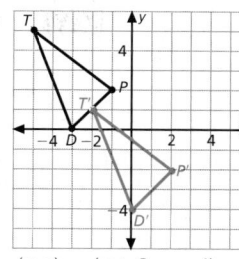

$(x, y) \rightarrow (x + 3, y - 4)$

26.
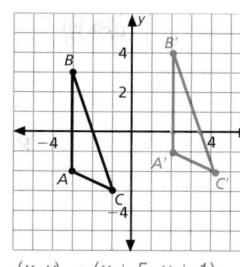

$(x, y) \rightarrow (x + 5, y + 1)$

**Give the coordinates of the image of each point under a reflection across the given line.** (Lesson 7-2)

27. $(5, 4)$; $x$-axis   $(5, -4)$

28. $(-1, -3)$; $y$-axis   $(1, -3)$

29. $(0, -6)$; $y = -x$   $(6, 0)$

30. $(2, -4)$; $y = x$   $(-4, 2)$

31. $(0, 3)$; $y = 1$   $(0, -1)$

32. $(-12, 6)$; $x$-axis   $(-12, -6)$

 **MathWorks**
Workplace Knowhow

# Career – Campus Facilities Manager

**A** campus facilities manager is involved in many aspects of a college or university. They supervise landscaping, maintenance, renovations and new building design. A campus facilities manager is coordinating the design of a new residence complex consisting of four buildings that enclose a courtyard. The campus facilities manager decided to design the four new buildings using the mathematical principles of translation and reflection. The figure shows the location of the first residence building and the courtyard. Complete the following exercises to determine the shapes and locations of the other three buildings. See additional answers.

1. Reflect Building *ABCD* across the line $x = 2$ to determine the location of Building 2, $A'B'C'D'$.
   See additional answers.
2. Across which line would you reflect Building 2 so the majority of Building 3 ($A''B''C''D''$) would be in the first quadrant on the coordinate grid? Reflect Building 2 across that line.
   $y = -1$
3. Describe how you would create Building 4 so that the new residence complexes enclose the courtyard. Create Building 4 through a transformation.   Reflect $A''B''C''D''$ over $x = 2$.
4. Would the reflection of Building 1 across the line $y = -x$ create Building 3? Would the reflection of Building 2 across the line $y = x$ create Building 4? Explain.
   See additional answers.

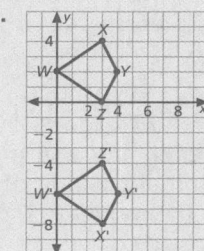

## MATHWORKS

1–3.
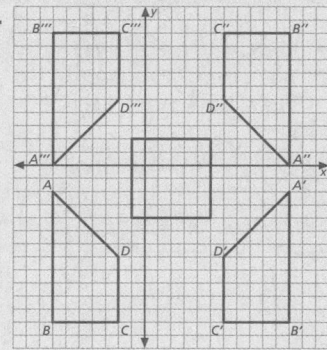

4. No. The reflection across the $y = -x$ or $y = x$ lines are different than a reflection across the $x = 2$ line and a reflection across the $y = -1$ line. The coordinates of vertex *D* of Building 3 are (6, 3) and the coordinates of vertex *D* after a reflection over the $y = -x$ line are (7, 2).

**MathWorks**

*Campus* is typically the land on which a college or university stands. The main buildings on a campus usually include classroom buildings, an administration building, a library, laboratories, a gymnasium, an athletic field and stadium, and dormitories. Many institutions have a building, often called a *union*, where social gatherings, plays, and dances may be held. Many of today's universities and colleges have more than one campus.

Students should answer Questions 1–4 to better understand the role of transformations of the coordinate plane in the process of planning the layout of a college campus.

Students may be interested in researching *campus design* as applied to institutions other than a college. For example, the campus design of a prison resembles a group of small apartment buildings around a town square. It is commonly used for juvenile institutions and may include such facilities as a church, a school, and a library.

A campus facilities manager may also be employed to supervise a large corporate site.

Students who are interested in learning more about this career choice can go to mathmatters2.com/mathworks. School Guidance Counselors are another resource for information about training requirements and appropriate schools.

## ADDITIONAL ANSWERS

16.
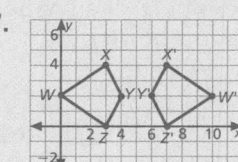

17.

## Lesson Planning

### NCTM Standards/Strands
- Geometry
- Representation
- Measurement
- Reasoning & Proof

### Vocabulary
rotation
center of rotation
angle of rotation

### Tools/Materials Needed
graph paper    protractor
compass        ruler

### Lesson Resources
Warm-up Transparency 28
Transparency TK-9–12, RF-39
Reteaching 7-3
Extra Practice 7-3
Enrichment 7-3
Technology Activity 7-3

## Getting Started

### 5-MINUTE WARM-UP
**Name the number of degrees in the measure of each figure.**
1. a circle    360°
2. a semicircle    180°
3. a quarter-circle    90°

### Introduction to Lesson 7-3
Point out that the base of a Ferris wheel and the part to which the center of the wheel is attached do not rotate. Relate the number of degrees in a turn or fraction of a turn to the number of degrees in a circle or fraction of a circle.

Students can make a model to represent rotation; use large-grid paper, paper fastener, and a strip of cardstock as the initial position of the rotation. Use the model to track various points through different rotations. For example, the image of (4, 0) after a rotation of 90° clockwise is (0, −4).

# 7-3 Rotations in the Coordinate Plane

**Goals**
- Graph rotated images in the coordinate plane.
- Identify centers, angles and directions of rotations.

**Applications**    Machinery, Art, Architecture, Recreation

Refer to the photograph for Questions 1–3.

1. From the side at which the photograph was taken, does this Ferris wheel turn clockwise or counterclockwise around its center? Explain.
   Answers will vary.
2. What fractional part of a turn does it take for a rider to get from the bottom to the top of a Ferris wheel?  $\frac{1}{2}$ turn
3. How many degrees does a Ferris wheel turn while a rider goes completely around one time?  360°

## ▶ BUILD UNDERSTANDING

You have learned about two types of transformations – translations and reflections. A third transformation that produces a new figure exactly like the original is a **rotation**, or *turn*. Under a rotation, a figure is rotated, or turned, about a given point. A complete turn is 360°, a half turn is 180° and a quarter turn is 90°.

The description of a rotation includes three pieces of information.

1. The **center of rotation**, or point about which the figure is rotated
2. The amount of turn expressed as a fractional part of a whole turn, or as the **angle of rotation** in degrees
3. The direction of rotation – clockwise or counterclockwise

When you rotate a point 180° clockwise about (0, 0), both the x-coordinate and the y-coordinate become their opposites.

> **Check Understanding**
>
> How many degrees are in a three-quarter turn? How many degrees are in a full turn?
>
> 270°; 360°

### Example 1

Draw the image of △QRS with vertices Q(2, 4), R(1, 1) and S(4, 1) under a rotation of 180° clockwise about (0, 0).

**Solution**

The rotation is 180°, so the x-coordinate and y-coordinate become their opposites. Multiply each coordinate by −1.

$$Q(2, 4) \rightarrow Q'(2(-1), 4(-1)) = Q'(-2, -4)$$
$$R(1, 1) \rightarrow R'(1(-1), 1(-1)) = R'(-1, -1)$$
$$S(4, 1) \rightarrow S'(4(-1), 1(-1)) = S'(-4, -1)$$

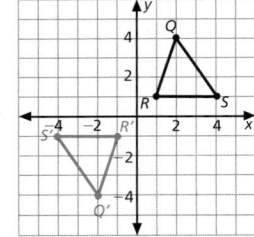

306    Chapter 7  **Coordinate Graphing and Transformations**

## Extend the Lesson

**REAL WORLD CONNECTION** The largest "pleasure wheel" of its time was built by George W. Gale Ferris, a mechanical engineer in Galesburg, Ill., for the World's Columbian Exposition in Chicago in 1893. The wheel was 250 ft in diameter. Each of its 36 cabs could hold 60 people.
Ask students to name other amusement park rides that are examples of rotations, reflections, or translations. Discuss which type of transformation occurs most often among the rides and possible reasons for this.

Use these rules when the angle of rotation is 90°, 180°, and 360° and the center is (0, 0).

| Rules of Rotations about (0, 0) | 90° clockwise $(x, y) \rightarrow (y, -x)$ |
| --- | --- |
| | 90° counterclockwise $(x, y) \rightarrow (-y, x)$ |
| | 180° clockwise or counterclockwise $(x, y) \rightarrow (-x, -y)$ |
| | 360° clockwise or counterclockwise $(x, y) \rightarrow (x, y)$ |

## Example 2

**MACHINERY** A large mechanical shovel is used to move gravel. If the coordinates of the shovel are $A(0, 0)$, $B(-2, 2)$, $C(-4, 4)$, and $D(-4, 2)$ after being rotated clockwise 90° about (0, 0), what were the coordinates in its original position?

### Solution

To find the coordinates of the shovel in its original position, rotate its current image 90° counterclockwise about the origin. Do so by multiplying the $y$-coordinate of each point by $-1$. Then transpose the $x$- and $y$-coordinates.

$A(0, 0) \rightarrow A'(0, 0(-1)) = A'(0, 0)$

$B(-2, 2) \rightarrow B'(-2, 2(-1)) = B'(-2, -2)$

$C(-4, 4) \rightarrow C'(-4, 4(-1)) = C'(-4, -4)$

$D(-4, 2) \rightarrow D'(-4, 2(-1)) = D'(-4, -2)$

**Check Understanding**

What rotation would result in a figure fitting back on itself?

A clockwise or counterclockwise turn of 360°.

To rotate figures when the rules stated above do not apply, use a protractor, compass and ruler. Use a protractor to measure angles where the center of rotation is the vertex. The compass and ruler are used for measuring distances.

## Example 3

**Draw the image of △ABC after a 120° turn clockwise about point P.**

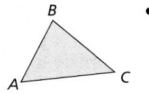

### Solution

Step 1: Draw a segment from vertex $C$ to point $P$.

Step 2: Use a protractor to draw a ray from point $P$ that creates a 120° angle with $\overline{CP}$.

Step 3: Use a compass to measure the length of $\overline{CP}$.

Step 4: Use this measure to locate point $C'$ on the ray drawn in Step 2. Label point $C'$.

Repeat steps 1–4 to locate $A'$ and $B'$. Draw $\overline{A'B'}$, $\overline{B'C'}$, and $\overline{C'A'}$.

The rotated image is △$A'B'C'$.

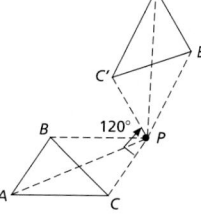

 **Math Online** mathmatters2.com/extra_examples

Lesson 7-3 **Rotations in the Coordinate Plane** | **307**

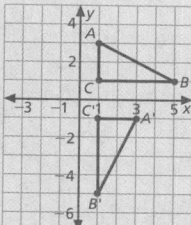
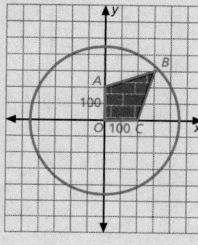
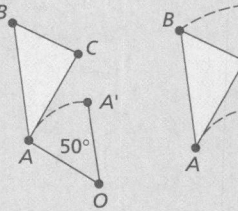
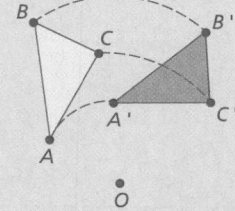
## Extend the Lesson

**CONNECTING TO PRIOR KNOWLEDGE** Have students use geometry software to draw △$XYZ$ and lines $\ell$ and $m$ that intersect at $O$. Reflect △$XYZ$ across line $\ell$ to obtain △$X'Y'Z'$. Then reflect △$X'Y'Z'$ across line $m$ to obtain △$X''Y''Z''$. Ask students to observe how △$X''Y''Z''$ is related to △$XYZ$. When $\ell$ and $m$ intersect at $O$, a reflection in $\ell$ followed by a reflection in $m$ results in a rotation about point $O$. The angle of the rotation is $(2x)°$ where $x°$ is the measure of the acute or right angle between $\ell$ and $m$.

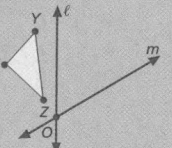 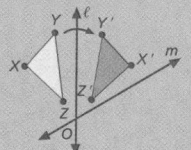 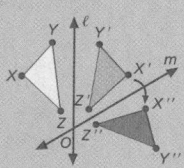

## QUICK ASSESSMENT

Ask the following questions to determine if students understand the content presented in this lesson.

**Write the coordinates of the image of $P(-1, 3)$ after the indicated rotation about (0, 0).**
1. 90° clockwise   **(3, 1)**
2. 90° counterclockwise   **(−3, −1)**
3. 180°   **(1, −3)**

**Describe what happens to each of the following characteristics of a plane figure under a rotation in the coordinate plane.**
4. the size of the figure   **remains unchanged**
5. the shape of the figure   **remains unchanged**
6. the orientation of the figure (the order of the vertices read either clockwise or counterclockwise)   **remains unchanged**

## ASSIGNMENT GUIDE

**Basic:** 1–19, 23–28
**Enriched:** 1–28

### Reteaching Worksheet 7-3

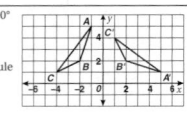
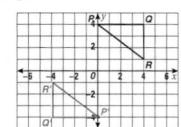
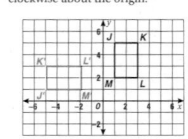

Name _____ Date _____

RETEACHING **7-3**

**ROTATIONS IN THE COORDINATE PLANE**

A **rotation** is the transformation of a figure when it is turned about a point. To draw the image of a figure under rotation, you need to know the center of the rotation, the amount of the rotation expressed in degrees or as a fractional part of a whole turn, and the direction of the rotation, *clockwise* or *counterclockwise*.

Use the following rules for finding the coordinates of the image of a figure rotated about (0, 0).

• When a figure is rotated 180°, $(x, y) \rightarrow (-x, -y)$.
• When a figure is rotated 90° clockwise, $(x, y) \rightarrow (y, -x)$.
• When a figure is rotated 90° counterclockwise, $(x, y) \rightarrow (-y, x)$.

**Example**

Draw the rotation of $\triangle ABC$ under a rotation of 90° clockwise about the origin.

**Solution**

Find the coordinates of $A'$, $B'$ and $C'$ using the rule $(x, y) \rightarrow (y, -x)$.

$A(-1, 5) \rightarrow A'(5, 1)$
$B(-2, 2) \rightarrow B'(2, 2)$
$C(-4, 1) \rightarrow C'(1, 4)$

**EXERCISES**

Find the coordinates of each point under the given rotation about the origin.

1. $(-5, 8)$; 180°
   $(5, -8)$
2. $(0, -2)$; 90° counterclockwise
   $(2, 0)$
3. $(5, -5)$; 90° clockwise
   $(-5, -5)$

4. Graph the image of $\triangle PQR$ under a rotation of 180° clockwise about the origin.
5. Graph the image of rectangle $JKLM$ under a rotation of 90° counterclockwise about the origin.

---

To find the center of rotation, draw segments that join corresponding vertices and find each midpoint. Construct a perpendicular bisector to each segment. Locate the point of intersection of the three perpendicular bisectors.

## Example 4

**For the image of $\triangle XYZ$, identify the center of rotation, the angle of rotation and the direction of rotation.**

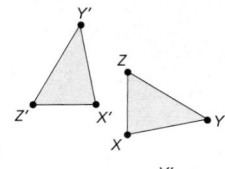

### Solution

Draw a segment connecting each pair of corresponding vertices (shown in red). Construct the perpendicular bisectors of $\overline{XX'}$, $\overline{YY'}$ and $\overline{ZZ'}$ (shown in blue). Label the point where the bisectors intersect as $T$. Draw a segment that connects two corresponding vertices to $T$. Then measure the angle formed by these segments.

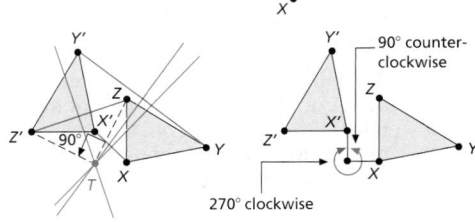

Point $T$ is the center of rotation, and the angle rotation is either 90° counterclockwise or 270° clockwise.

## TRY THESE EXERCISES

**Graph the flag containing points $J$, $K$, $L$ and $M$ on a coordinate plane. Graph its image under the given rotation about zero.**
For 1–4, see additional answers.
1. 90° clockwise
2. 180° counterclockwise
3. 135° counterclockwise
4. 220° counterclockwise

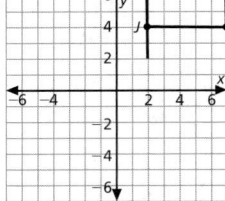

5. **WRITING MATH** Write step-by-step instructions for locating the center of rotation of any image and its preimage.
   See additional answers.

**Copy $\triangle XYZ$ and its rotation image on grid paper.**

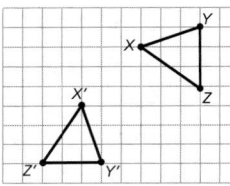

6. Identify the center of rotation of the image. Label it point $T$.
   See additional answers.
7. Identify the angle of rotation and the direction of rotation of the image.   90° clockwise or 270° counterclockwise
8. Identify another angle and direction of rotation of the image.
   270° counterclockwise or 90° clockwise

## PRACTICE EXERCISES  •  For Extra Practice, see page 608.

**On grid paper, graph each figure and its image under the given rotation.**
For 9–12, see additional answers.
9. $A(0, 0)$, $B(1, 2)$, $C(3, 3)$ and $D(2, 1)$; 60° clockwise about (0, 0)
10. $X(-3, 1)$, $Y(-3, 2)$ and $Z(-1, 1)$; 180° counterclockwise about (0, 0)
11. $D(-2, 2)$, $E(2, 2)$, $F(2, -2)$ and $G(-2, -2)$; 100° counterclockwise about (0, 0)
12. $R(-3, 5)$, $S(2, 0)$ and $T(-1, -3)$; 360° clockwise about (0, 0)

**308**   Chapter 7   **Coordinate Graphing and Transformations**

## ADDITIONAL ANSWERS

1.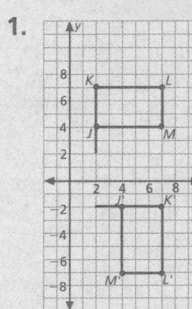

2.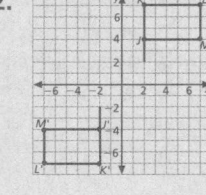

3.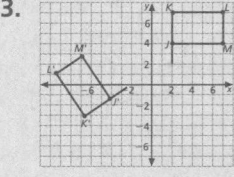

4.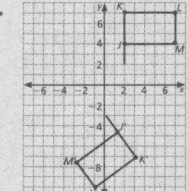

**Trace each figure and its rotation image. Identify the center of rotation, the angle of rotation and the direction of rotation.** For 13–14, see additional answers for center of rotation.

**13.**

90° counterclockwise or 270° clockwise

**14.**

180° clockwise or counterclockwise

**15. ART** Pentagon *OLCEK* represents one-fourth of a finished display space for an art festival. Find the vertices of the rotation image of pentagon *OLCEK* after a 90° clockwise turn about (0, 0). (Each grid block is 100-ft long.)
See additional answers.

**16.** Complete the display in Exercise 15. Draw the preimage and three rotation images of 90° clockwise about (0, 0).
See additional answers.

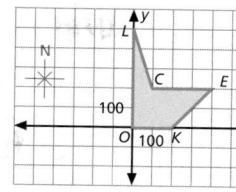

**Refer to the figure shown.**

**17.** Which triangle is the rotation image of △*A* about (−2, 0)? *F*

**18.** Which triangle is the translation image of △*A*? *C*

**19.** Which triangle is the rotation image of △*A* after a turn of 180° clockwise about (0, 0)? *H*

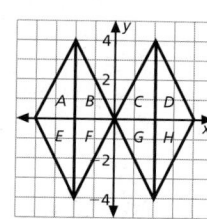

## ■ EXTENDED PRACTICE EXERCISES

**20. CRITICAL THINKING** Does the order that transformations are performed affect the image produced? If it does affect the image, sketch an example.

   **a.** translation, then translation no  **b.** translation, then reflection yes
   **c.** translation, then rotation yes   **d.** reflection, then rotation yes
   Sketches will vary. Check students' work.

**21.** The gondola in an amusement park ride begins its swing at *P* and takes 6 sec to swing counterclockwise from *P* to *Q* and back to *P*. Is the gondola swinging clockwise or counterclockwise after swinging for 43 sec? counterclockwise

**22. ARCHITECTURE** Use a protractor to estimate the angle of rotation that the Tower of Pisa structure has undergone over the years. ≈6°

Tower of Pisa, Italy

## ■ MIXED REVIEW EXERCISES

**State whether the pair of triangles is congruent by SAS, ASA, or SSS. Otherwise, write *not congruent*.** (Lesson 5-5)

**23.**

ASA

**24.**

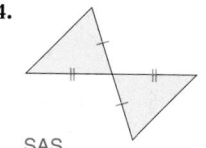

SAS

**25.**

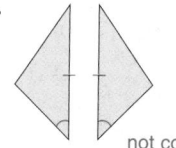

not congruent

**Find the distance between each pair of points. Round to the nearest tenth.** (Lesson 6-1)

**26.** (4, 2) and (3, 6) 4.1    **27.** (2, 1) and (0, 4) 3.6    **28.** (−2, 3) and (−4, 2) 2.2

 mathmatters2.com/self_check_quiz

---

Name _____ Date _____

EXTRA PRACTICE **7-3**
**ROTATIONS IN THE COORDINATE PLANE**

✔ **EXERCISES**

On your own grid paper, graph each figure and its image under the given rotation. Give the coordinates of the vertices of the image. Check students' graphs.
 **1.** *A*(1, 3), *B*(3, 1), *C*(1, 1); 90° clockwise about (0, 0)
       *A*′(3, −1), *B*′(1, −3), *C*′(1, −1)
 **2.** *X*(3, 4), *Y*(6, 4), *Z*(5, 2), *W*(2, 2); 180° counterclockwise about (0, 0)
    *X*′(−3, −4), *Y*′(−6, −4), *Z*′(−5, −2), *W*′(−2, −2)

Identify the center of rotation, the angle of rotation and the direction of rotation.
Answers may vary. Possible answers are given.

**3.**

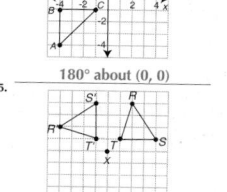

180° about (0, 0)

**4.**

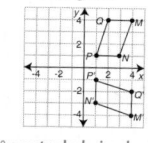

270° counterclockwise about (0, 0)

**5.**

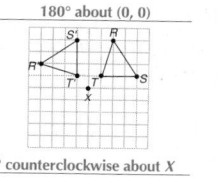

90° counterclockwise about *X*

**6.**

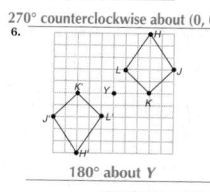

180° about *Y*

Refer to the figure shown.

**7.** Which rectangle is the rotation image of rectangle *M* about (0, −1)? *S*

**8.** Which rectangle is the rotation image of rectangle *P* about (0, 0)? *S*

**9.** Which rectangle is the reflection image of rectangle *V* across the *y*-axis? *R*

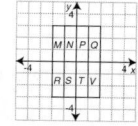

**13.**

**14.**

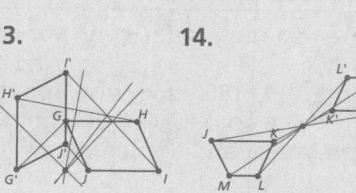

**15.** *L*(0, 500) → *L*′(500, 0)
*C*(100, 200) → *C*′(200, −100)
*E*(400, 200) → *E*′(200, −400)
*K*(200, 0) → *K*′(0, −200)
*O*(0, 0) → *O*′(0, 0)

**16.**

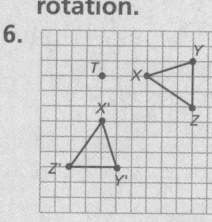

---

**5.** Draw a line segment connecting any two corresponding vertices between the image and the preimage. Construct the perpendicular bisector of the line segment. Repeat for two other corresponding vertices. The intersection of these perpendicular bisectors is the center of rotation.

**6.**

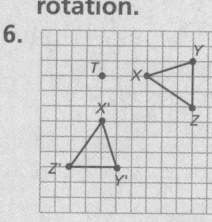

**9.**

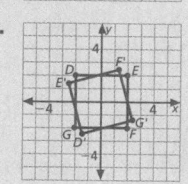

**10.**

**11.**

**12.**

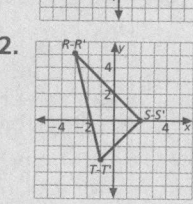

# Line Symmetry and Rotational Symmetry

**Goals** ■ Identify lines of symmetry.
■ Identify order of rotational symmetry.

**Applications** Industry, Weather, Architecture, Number theory, Art

---

## Lesson Planning

### NCTM Standards/Strands
■ Geometry
■ Representation
■ Measurement
■ Reasoning & Proof

### Vocabulary

line symmetry    line of symmetry
rotational symmetry

### Tools/Materials Needed

scissors          mirror

### Lesson Resources

Warm-up Transparency 29
Transparency RF-40
Reteaching 7-4
Extra Practice 7-4
Enrichment 7-4

## Getting Started

### 5-MINUTE WARM-UP

Rotate rectangle *ABCD* with vertices *A*(2, 1), *B*(−2, 1), *C*(−2, −1), and *D*(2, −1) 180° clockwise about (0, 0). Make an observation about the preimage and the image.
**They coincide.**

### Introduction to Lesson 7-4

You may wish to have precut figures on hand (scalene triangle, isosceles triangle, equilateral triangle) for distribution.

After students have shared their findings about the three types of triangles, you may wish to have them work with different quadrilaterals.

See the Extend the Lesson at the bottom of this page for a suggested paper-folding activity involving a square.

---

**Work with a partner. You will need scissors and a mirror.**
For 1–3, observe students' work.
1. Draw and cut out a scalene triangle, an isosceles triangle and an equilateral triangle.

2. Place a mirror on each triangle so that the part in front of the mirror along with the reflection in the mirror forms the original figure. For each you may find one way, more than one way or no way.

3. For each way you found in Step 2 to form the original triangle, have your partner hold the mirror in place while you a draw a line on the triangle along the bottom edge of the mirror.

4. How many lines did you draw on each triangle?
scalene: none; isosceles: 1; equilateral: 3

### ■ BUILD UNDERSTANDING

Many figures are drawn so that a line can divide them exactly into two equal, overlapping parts. A plane figure has **line symmetry** (sometimes called *reflection symmetry*) if you can divide it along a line into two parts that are mirror images of each other. The line is called a **line of symmetry**. Some figures have one line of symmetry. Others have two or more, and still others have none.

> **Check Understanding**
>
> Draw all the types of triangles that have line symmetry. Show the lines of symmetry.

Check students' work. Students should draw an isosceles triangle with 1 line of symmetry and an equilateral triangle with 3 lines of symmetry.

### Example 1

Trace each figure, and draw all its lines of symmetry. If a figure has no lines of symmetry, write *none*.

a.     b.     c.

**Solution**

a.     b.     c.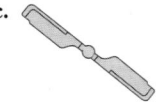

two lines of symmetry    one line of symmetry    none

---

## Extend the Lesson

Have students fold and cut a rectangular sheet of paper as shown below. Tell students to unfold the remaining paper and note its shape. **square** Then ask students to tell the number of

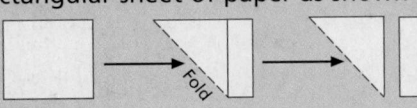

different ways they can fold the square so that one half fits exactly over the other half. **4 ways** Tell students to place the paper square on a flat surface and with a pencil point at the center, turn the paper slowly in a clockwise direction. How many times the square coincides with its original position during one complete turn. **4 times**

## Example 2

**Half of a figure and its line of symmetry is shown. Complete the figure by drawing the other half.**

### Solution

Draw a reflection of the figure across the line of symmetry. The completed figure is the same on each side of the line of symmetry.

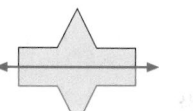

Sometimes a figure does not have line symmetry. However, a figure that has a point about which it is rotated so that it fits exactly over its original position more than once during a complete turn has **rotational symmetry**.

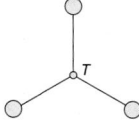

If you rotate the figure shown about point *T* one complete turn, it will fit over the original position of the figure 3 times. Therefore, the figure has rotational symmetry, and its *order of rotational symmetry* is 3.

## Example 3

**Give the order of rotational symmetry for each figure.**

**a.**

**b.**

**c.**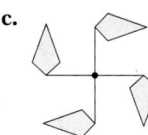

### Solution

**a.** The figure fits over its original position 2 times during a complete turn, so its order of rotational symmetry is 2.

**b.** The figure fits over its original position 5 times during a complete turn, so its order of rotational symmetry is 5.

**c.** The figure fits over its original position 4 times during a complete turn, so its order of rotational symmetry is 4.

## Example 4

**INDUSTRY** Give the order of rotational symmetry for each industrial tool.

**a.** the blade of a circular saw with 100 teeth

**b.** the large wheel of a steamroller

### Solution

**a.** During a complete turn, the blade will fit over its original position 100 times, so its order of rotational symmetry is 100.

**b.** During a complete turn, the wheel will always look like its original position, so its order of rotational symmetry is infinite.

 **Math Online** mathmatters2.com/extra_examples          Lesson 7-4 **Line Symmetry and Rotational Symmetry**   **311**

---

### Extend the Lesson

Use figure c of Example 1 to stress that a figure does not have line symmetry simply because its two halves are identical. Have students redraw this figure so that it does have line symmetry.
For Example 2 and Supplementary Example 2, discuss the relation of corresponding points of a preimage and its reflection image to the line of reflection, and how this is helpful in completing a figure with line symmetry.   **The line of reflection is the perpendicular bisector of the segment determined by a preimage point and its image point.**

---

 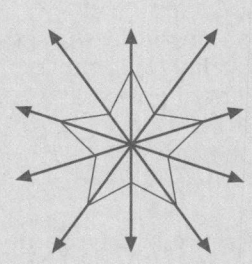
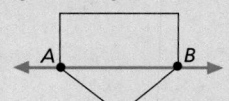
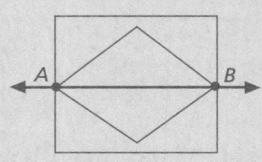

## QUICK ASSESSMENT

Ask the following questions to determine if students understand the content presented in this lesson.

**Consider a figure in Quadrant I that is reflected across the *x*-axis.**

1. In which quadrant will the image figure be? **Quadrant IV**
2. How can you physically show that the *x*-axis is a line of symmetry for the original figure and its image? **Fold the paper along the *x*-axis, and the image in Quadrant IV will exactly fit over the figure in Quadrant I.**
3. Consider a figure in the coordinate plane that has (0, 0) as its center. Explain what it means to say that this figure has rotational symmetry of order 3. **If you rotate the figure about the origin, in one complete turn, it will fit over itself 3 times.**

## ASSIGNMENT GUIDE

**Basic:** 1–21, 33–42
**Enriched:** 1–42

### Reteaching Worksheet 7-4

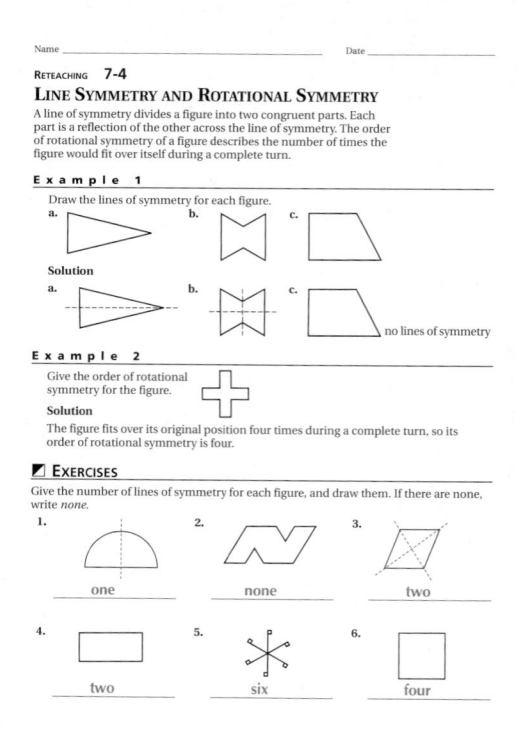

Name _____ Date _____

RETEACHING **7-4**

**LINE SYMMETRY AND ROTATIONAL SYMMETRY**

A line of symmetry divides a figure into two congruent parts. Each part is a reflection of the other across the line of symmetry. The order of rotational symmetry of a figure describes the number of times the figure would fit over itself during a complete turn.

**Example 1**

Draw the lines of symmetry for each figure.
a.       b.       c.

**Solution**
a.       b.       c.
no lines of symmetry

**Example 2**

Give the order of rotational symmetry for the figure.

**Solution**
The figure fits over its original position four times during a complete turn, so its order of rotational symmetry is four.

**EXERCISES**

Give the number of lines of symmetry for each figure, and draw them. If there are none, write *none*.

1. one   2. none   3. two
4. two   5. six   6. four

## TRY THESE EXERCISES

Trace each figure, and draw all lines of symmetry. If applicable, write *none*.
For 1–3, check students' drawings. The number of lines of symmetry is given.

1.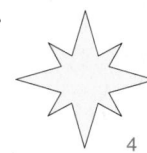
1 line

2.
2 lines

3.
none

**Give the order of rotational symmetry for each figure.**

4.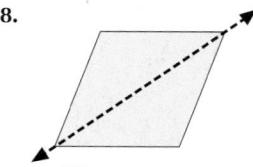
4

5.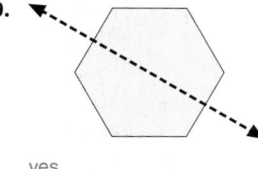
8

6.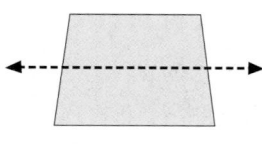
2

7. **WRITING MATH** Is it possible for a figure to have both line symmetry and rotational symmetry? If so, give an example.
Yes. Answers will vary but Exercise 4 is one example.

## PRACTICE EXERCISES • For Extra Practice, see page 608.

Tell whether each dashed line is a line of symmetry. If not, trace the line and one side of the figure. Complete the drawing so that it has line symmetry.

8.
yes

9.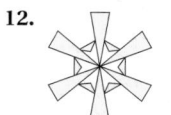
yes

10.
No. Check students' drawings.

**Give the order of rotational symmetry for each figure.**

11.
3

12.
6

13.
5

14. **WEATHER** Describe the symmetries of the snowflake shown. Answers will vary.

15. **WRITING MATH** Explain why every circle has infinitely many lines of symmetry.
See additional answers.

16. **ARCHITECTURE** Draw the front of a building that has line symmetry. Explain the position of the line of symmetry. Observe students' work. The line of symmetry must be at the center of the building.

## Extend the Lesson

**REAL WORLD CONNECTION** Biologists determine an animal's symmetry based on the arrangement of its body parts. Animals, such as sand dollars, with body parts arranged in a circle around a central point have *radial symmetry*. Animals, such as humans, with body parts arranged the same way on both sides of the body have *bilateral symmetry*.

17. **NUMBER THEORY** The numbers 121 and 1221 are called *palindromes* because they read the same forward or backward. Using block numbers, find a palindrome that has line symmetry. Find one with rotational symmetry. Answers will vary. See additional answers.

**ART** Describe the symmetries of each woven basket design. For 18–20, see additional answers.

18.   19.   20.

21. List four capital letters that have a horizontal line of symmetry. List four capital letters that have a vertical line of symmetry. See additional answers.

## ■ EXTENDED PRACTICE EXERCISES

**Draw a polygon with exactly the number of lines of symmetry given.**
For 22–25, answers will vary. Check students' work.

22. 1 line     23. 2 lines     24. 3 lines     25. 4 lines

**Draw a polygon with the order of rotational symmetry given.**
For 26–29, answers will vary. Check students' work.

26. order 2     27. order 3     28. order 4     29. order 5

30. **CRITICAL THINKING** How many lines of symmetry does a regular polygon with *n* sides have? *n*

31. What is the order of rotational symmetry of a regular polygon with *n* sides? *n*

32. **CHAPTER INVESTIGATION** Draw the designs of the rooms and hallways of your house on grid paper. Label the different types of rooms including any special features. Include transformational principles such as two rooms being mirror reflections of each other. Answers will vary.

## ■ MIXED REVIEW EXERCISES

**Calculate each combination.** (Lesson 4-7)

33. $_7C_3$  35     34. $_{14}C_5$  2002     35. $_{12}C_4$  495     36. $_{13}C_6$  1716

37. Eight students are running for Student Council advisors. Three students will be elected. How many different combinations of students can be elected?  56

38. Twelve cards numbered 1 to 12 are placed in a bag. If 5 cards are drawn at random, how many different combinations of cards can be drawn?  792

**Find the measure of an interior angle of each regular polygon.** (Lesson 5-7)

39. 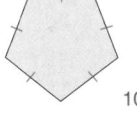     40. 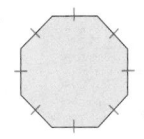     41. 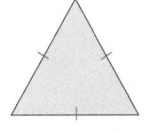     42.
    108°                       135°                        60°                         90°

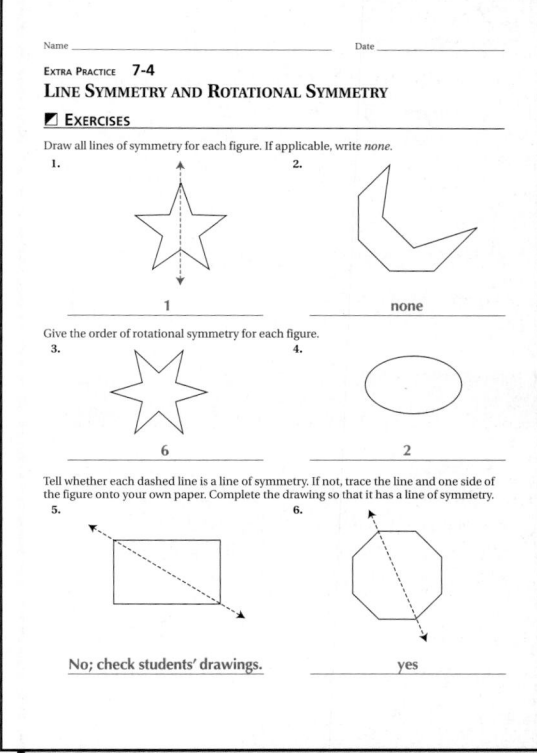
## ADDITIONAL ANSWERS

15. Any line through the center of the circle is a line of symmetry. Since a person can draw an infinite number of lines through a point, a circle would have an infinite number of lines of symmetry.

17. Any palindrome which uses the digits 0, 1, 3, and 8 has line symmetry. A palindrome which uses the digits 0, 1, or 8 has rotational symmetry of order 2.

18. There are 8 lines of symmetry. This figure has order 8 rotational symmetry.

19. There are 6 lines of symmetry. This figure has order 6 rotational symmetry.

20. There are 10 lines of symmetry. This figure has order 10 rotational symmetry.

21. Each of the letters B, C, D, E, H, I, K, O, and X has one horizontal line of symmetry. Each of the letters A, H, I, M, O, T, U, V, W, X, and Y has one vertical line of symmetry.

## Skills Practice

### Vocabulary Review

**Lesson 7-3**
rotation          center of rotation
angle of rotation

**Lesson 7-4**
line symmetry    line of symmetry
rotational symmetry

## ASSIGNMENT GUIDE

**All students:** 1–24

## Chalkboard Examples

### Lesson 7-3
Graph the image of △ABO with
vertices A(3, 0), B(3, 5), and O(0, 0)
under a rotation of 270° clockwise
about point A.
Since point A is
the center of the
rotation, it
remains fixed.
Use distances from
A to determine the
other vertices.

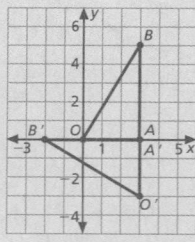

AB = A'B' = 5
AO = A'O' = 3
A(3, 0) → A'(3, 0)
B(3, 5) → B'(−2, 0)
O(0, 0) → O'(3, −3)

### Lesson 7-4

A B C D E F G H I J K L M
N O P Q R S T U V W X Y Z

a. List all the letters that have both
   a vertical and a horizontal line of
   symmetry. **H, I, O, X**
b. List all the letters that have rotation symmetry. **H, I, N, O, S, X, Z**

# Review and Practice Your Skills

## PRACTICE ◼ LESSON 7-3

**On grid paper, graph each figure and its image under the given rotation.**
For 1–4, see additional answers.
1. A(2, 3), B(4, 6), C(8, 6), D(7, 3); 90° clockwise about (0, 0)

2. Q(−6, 2), R(−4, 6), S(−2, 2); 180° clockwise about (0, 0)

3. M(1, −1), N(4, −2), O(4, −5), P(1, −4); 120° clockwise about (0, 0)

4. S(−4, −1), T(−2, −4), U(−5, −7); 60° clockwise about (0, 0)

5. Draw the image of △XYZ after a turn of 120° clockwise
   about point P.  See additional answers.

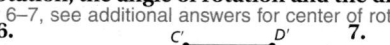

**Trace each figure and its rotated image. Identify the center of
rotation, the angle of rotation and the direction of rotation.**
For 6–7, see additional answers for center of rotation.

6.                                    7.

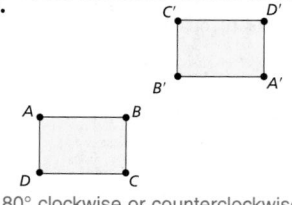     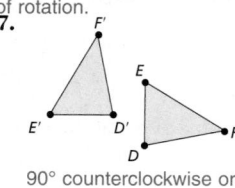

90° counterclockwise or
270° clockwise

180° clockwise or counterclockwise

## PRACTICE ◼ LESSON 7-4

**Trace each figure, and draw all lines of symmetry. If applicable, write *none*.**
For 8–13, check students' drawings. The number of lines of symmetry is given.

8.                          9.                          10.

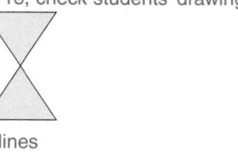     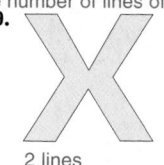     

2 lines                    2 lines                    1 line

11.                        12.                        13.

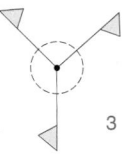         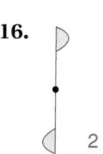

1 line                     1 line                     none

**Give the order of rotational symmetry for each figure.**

14.                        15.                        16.

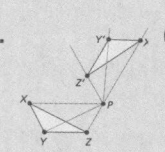    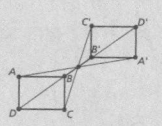    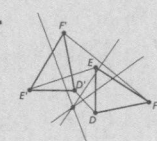

3                          4                          2

## ADDITIONAL ANSWERS

1.                  2.                  3.                  4.

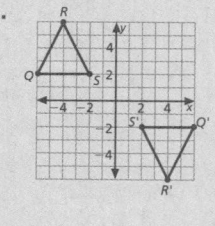

5.          6.          7.

**1.**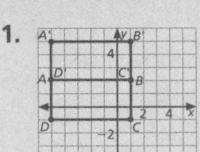

## PRACTICE ■ LESSON 7-1–LESSON 7-4

**Use the figure shown for Exercises 17–21.** (Lesson 7-1–Lesson 7-3)

**17.** Which triangle is the rotation image of triangle 1 about the point $(-3, 0)$?   6

**18.** Which triangle is the reflection image of triangle 1 across the $x$-axis?   5

**19.** Which triangle is the reflection image of triangle 1 across the $y$-axis?   4

**20.** Which triangle is the rotation image of triangle 1 180° clockwise about $(0, 0)$?   8

**21.** Which triangle is the reflection image of triangle 1 across the line $x = -3$?   2

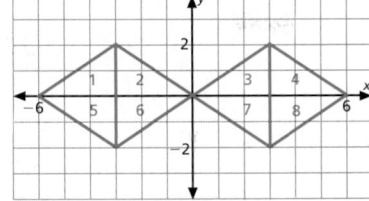

**2.**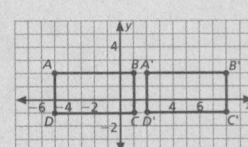

**Trace each figure, and draw all lines of symmetry. If applicable, write *none*.** (Lesson 7-4)
For 22–24, check students' drawings. The number of lines of symmetry is given.

**22.**
3 lines

**23.**
none

**24.**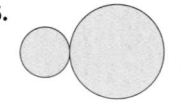
2 lines

**3.** 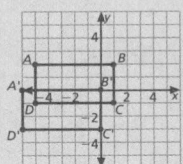     **4.**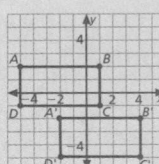

# Mid-Chapter Quiz

**Rectangle $ABCD$ has vertices $A(-5, 2)$, $B(1, 2)$, $C(1, -1)$ and $D(-5, -1)$. Graph the rectangle and its image under the given translations.** (Lesson 7-1)
For 1–4, see additional answers.

**1.** 3 units up

**2.** 7 units right

**3.** 1 unit left and 2 units down

**4.** 4 units down and 3 units right

**5.**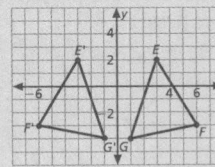

**Triangle $EFG$ has vertices $E(3, 2)$, $F(6, -3)$ and $G(1, -4)$. Graph the triangle and its images under the given reflection from the original position.** (Lesson 7-2)
For 5–10, see additional answers.

**5.** $y$-axis

**6.** $x$-axis

**7.** $y = x$

**8.** $y = -x$

**9.** $y = 2$

**10.** $x = 4$

**6.**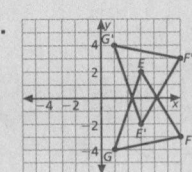

**Graph each figure and its image under the given rotation about $(0, 0)$.** (Lesson 7-3)
For 11–12, see additional answers.

**11.** $H(2, 3)$, $I(4, 3)$, $J(4, 1)$, and $K(2, 1)$; 90° clockwise

**12.** $L(-4, -2)$, $M(-2, 3)$, and $N(-1, -1)$; 180° counterclockwise

**7.**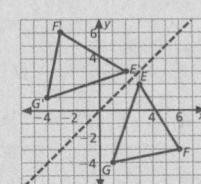

**Draw all lines of symmetry and give the rotational symmetry for each figure.** (Lesson 7-4)
For 13–15, see additional answers.

**13.**
4

**14.**
8

**15.**
1

**8.**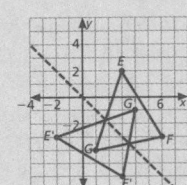

**9.**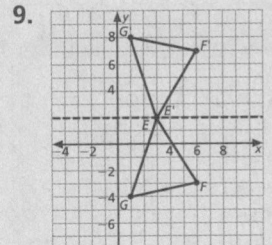

**10.**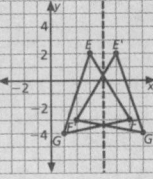

**11.**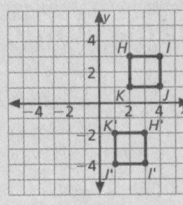

**12.**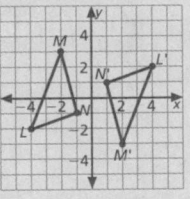

**13.**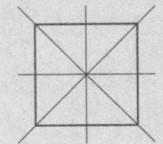

**14.**

**15.**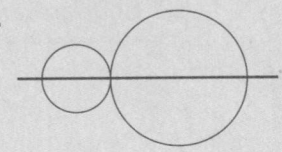

# Dilations in the Coordinate Plane

**Goals**
■ Draw dilation images on a coordinate plane.
■ Determine the scale factor of dilations.

**Applications** Photography, Entertainment, Architecture, Cooking

**Draw △RST and point C nearby the triangle.**

1. Draw $\overrightarrow{CR}$, $\overrightarrow{CS}$, $\overrightarrow{CT}$. Use a ruler to measure $\overline{CR}$, $\overline{CS}$ and $\overline{CT}$ to the nearest millimeter. Observe students' work.

2. Calculate the values $(2 \cdot CR)$, $(2 \cdot CS)$ and $(2 \cdot CT)$. Observe students' work.

3. Use a ruler to find point $R'$ on $\overrightarrow{CR}$ so that $\overline{CR'} = 2 \cdot CR$. Locate points $S'$ and $T'$ in the same manner. Draw △R'S'T'. Observe students' work.

4. Compare corresponding angle measures in △RST and △R'S'T'. What do you notice? They are congruent.

5. Compare the measures of corresponding sides in △RST and △R'S'T'. What do you notice? The sides of △R'S'T' are twice the length of the sides of △RST.

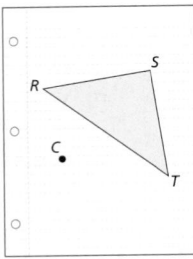

### ◣ BUILD UNDERSTANDING

A transformation that produces an image that is the same shape as the original figure but a different size is a **dilation**. A dilation used to create an image that is larger than the preimage is an **enlargement**, while one that is used to create a smaller figure is a **reduction**. A preimage and its dilation image are similar.

The description of a dilation includes the **scale factor** and the **center of dilation**. Each length in the image is equal to the corresponding length of the preimage multiplied by the scale factor.

The distance from the center of the dilation to each point on the image is equal to the distance from the center of dilation to each corresponding point on the preimage times the scale factor.

### Example 1

Draw the dilation of △ABC with vertices $A(-1, -1)$, $B(0, 2)$ and $C(1, -2)$ with the center of dilation at the origin and a scale factor of 3.

**Solution**

Graph △ABC. Multiply the x-coordinates and y-coordinates of each vertex by the scale factor of 3.

$$A(-1, -1) \rightarrow A'(-1 \cdot 3, -1 \cdot 3) = A'(-3, -3)$$

$$B(0, 2) \rightarrow B'(0 \cdot 3, 2 \cdot 3) = B'(0, 6)$$

$$C(1, -2) \rightarrow C'(1 \cdot 3, -2 \cdot 3) = C'(3, -6)$$

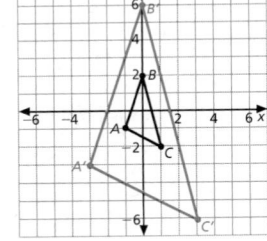

316 | Chapter 7 **Coordinate Graphing and Transformations**

## Differentiated Instruction

**TACTILE/KINESTHETIC LEARNERS** To demonstrate that dilations produce images that are the same shape as the original but may be larger or smaller, use a balloon with printing on it. Inflate and then partially deflate the balloon. You might also move a figure shown on the overhead projector closer to and farther from the screen.

When the center of dilation is a vertex of the preimage, the corresponding vertex of the dilation image is the same point.

## Example 2

**Draw the dilation image of $\triangle EFG$ with the center of dilation at $E$ and a scale factor of $\frac{1}{2}$.**

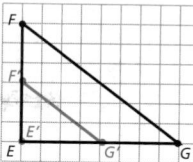

### Solution

The distance from the center of dilation, $E$, to $F$ is 6 units. So the distance from $E$ to $F'$ is $\frac{1}{2} \cdot 6$, or 3 units.

The distance from $E$ to $G$ is 8 units. So the distance from $E$ to $G'$ is $\frac{1}{2} \cdot 8$, or 4 units. Points $E$ and $E'$ coincide.

## Example 3

**PHOTOGRAPHY** Dilations are used when pictures are "blown up" and made larger. Suppose that a film negative is originally $\frac{2}{3}$ in. by 1 in.

a. If the negative makes a 4 in. by 6 in. print, what is the scale factor of the dilation?

b. If a print of the negative is blown up by a scale factor of 24, what are the dimensions of the print?

### Check Understanding

What positive scale factors indicate an enlargement? What positive scale factors indicate a reduction?

Positive scale factors greater than 1; positive scale factors less than 1.

### Solution

a. To determine the scale factor, compare the print length and width to the film negative length and width.

$$\frac{4}{\left(\frac{2}{3}\right)} = 6 \qquad \frac{6}{1} = 6$$

The length and width of the film negative are multiplied by 6 to achieve the print size, so the scale factor is 6.

b. To find the size of the print, multiply the length and width of the negative by the scale factor.

$$\left(\frac{2}{3}\right) \cdot 24 = 16 \qquad 1 \cdot 24 = 24$$

The print is 16 in. by 24 in.

## TRY THESE EXERCISES

**Copy $\triangle TBA$ on grid paper. Draw each dilation.**
For 1–4, see additional answers.
1. scale factor 2, center $(0, 0)$

2. scale factor $\frac{2}{3}$, center $(0, 0)$

3. scale factor 3, center $T$

4. scale factor 2.5, center $A$

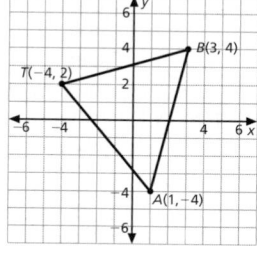

---

### Supplementary Example 1

Draw the dilation of rectangle $ABCD$ with vertices $A(1, 1)$, $B(3, 1)$, $C(3, 2)$, and $D(1, 2)$ with the center of the dilation at the origin and a scale factor of 2.

**Multiply the coordinates of each vertex by the scale factor 2.**

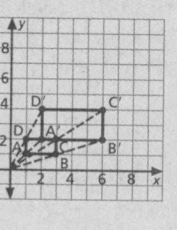

$A(1, 1) \rightarrow A'(2, 2)$
$B(3, 1) \rightarrow B'(6, 2)$
$C(3, 2) \rightarrow C'(6, 4)$
$D(1, 2) \rightarrow D'(2, 4)$

### Supplementary Example 2

The smaller quadrilateral is a reduction of the larger. Find the unknown lengths of the sides of the larger quadrilateral. **Find the scale factor.**

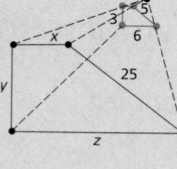

$\dfrac{\text{smaller side}}{\text{larger side}} = \dfrac{5}{25} = \dfrac{1}{5}$

**Use the scale factor to determine the unknown lengths of the larger quadrilateral.**

$\frac{1}{5}x = 2,\ x = 10 \qquad \frac{1}{5}y = 3,\ y = 15$

$\frac{1}{5}z = 6,\ z = 30$

### Supplementary Example 3

**FASHION** Zena has drawn a design on $\frac{1}{4}$-in. graph paper to transfer to a T-shirt. By what scale factor should she enlarge her design to fit an 8 in. by 15 in. rectangle?

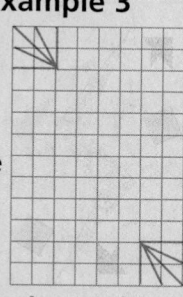

**Count the squares on the graph paper and multiply by $\frac{1}{4}$ to determine the length and width of the design.**

$\text{length} = \frac{1}{4}(8) = 2 \text{ in.}$

$\text{width} = \frac{1}{4}(12) = 3 \text{ in.}$

**The most appropriate scale factor is 4.**

---

## ADDITIONAL ANSWERS

1.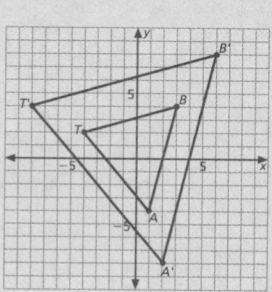

2.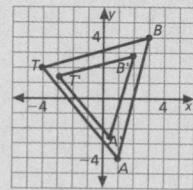

3.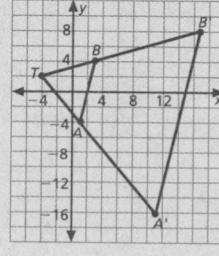

4.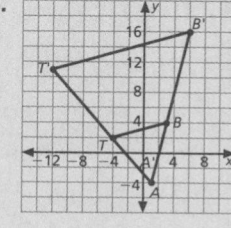

## Lesson Wrap-up

### QUICK ASSESSMENT

Ask the following question to determine if students understand the content presented in this lesson.

How are dilations the same as translations, reflections, and rotations? How are they different? **Same: preimage and image have same shape; preimage and dilation and translation image always face same direction; different: dilations usually produce images that are different in size from the preimages, while the others produce same-size images.**

### ASSIGNMENT GUIDE

**Basic:** 1–21, 29–46
**Enriched:** 1–46

---

**For Exercises 5–8, give the scale factor and center for each dilation.**

5. Triangle $ABC$ has vertices $A(2, 1)$, $B(3, -5)$, and $C(6, 4)$. Its dilation image is $\triangle A'B'C'$ with vertices $A'(6, 3)$, $B'(9, -15)$, and $C'(18, 12)$.   **3; (0, 0)**

6. Rectangle $QRST$ has vertices $Q(2, 1)$, $R(6, 1)$, $S(2, 7)$ and $T(6, 7)$. Its dilation image is rectangle $Q'R'S'T'$ with vertices $Q'(2, 1)$, $R'(4, 1)$, $S'(2, 4)$, and $T'(4, 4)$.   **$\frac{1}{2}$; (2, 1)**

7. 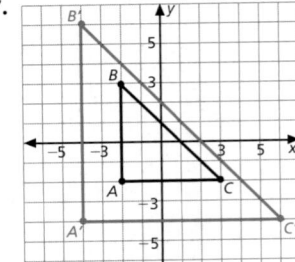   **2; (0, 0)**

8. 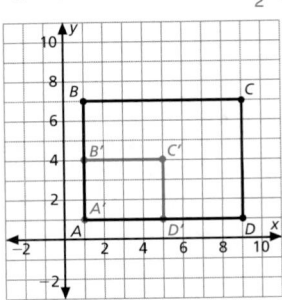   **$\frac{1}{2}$; (1, 1)**

---

### ▉ PRACTICE EXERCISES • For Extra Practice, see page 609.

**Copy parallelogram $ABCD$ on grid paper. Draw each dilation.**
For 9–12, see additional answers.

9. scale factor 2, center (0, 0)    10. scale factor 0.75, center $A$

11. scale factor 1, center (0, 0)    12. scale factor 4, center $C$

13. **PHOTOGRAPHY** If a 0.75 in. by 0.62 in. film negative is blown up to a 10.35 in. by 8.556 in. print, what is the scale factor of the enlargement?   **13.8**

14. An equilateral triangle with 4-in. sides undergoes a dilation with a scale factor of 2.8. In the image, what are the lengths of the sides? What are the measures of the angles of the image?   **11.2 in.; 60°**

15. **ENTERTAINMENT** The projection of a film on a movie screen is a dilation. Most movies are recorded on 35-mm wide film. If the width of a movie screen is 12 m, what is the enlargement scale factor?   **≈ 342.86**

16. **ARCHITECTURE** An architect is designing a shopping center. A shop's dimensions on the blueprint are 19 cm by 25 cm. Using a scale factor of 1 cm : 2 m, what are the shop's dimensions in meters?   **38 m by 50 m**

17. **WRITING MATH** Write a paragraph describing how dilations are similar to translations, reflections and rotations and how they differ.
See additional answers.

**Give the scale factor and center for each dilation represented by the vertices.**

18. $C(0, 0)$, $D(0, 4)$, $E(6, 0)$, and $C'(0, 0)$, $D'(0, 10)$, $E'(15, 0)$   **2.5; (0, 0)**

19. $S(0, 0)$, $T(0, -3)$, $U(-3, -6)$, and $S'(0, 0)$, $T'(0, -1)$, $U'(-1, -2)$   **$\frac{1}{3}$; (0, 0)**

---

### ADDITIONAL ANSWERS

9.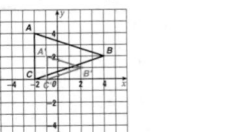

10. 

11.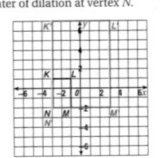

12.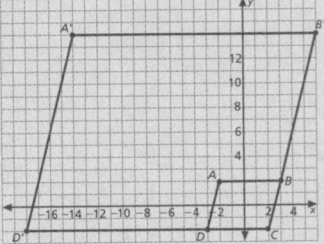

**20.** **CRITICAL THINKING** Is it possible for a scale factor to be a negative number? Explain why or why not. No. A negative scale factor will result in a negative length, which is not possible.

**21.** **GARDENING** Troy made a scale drawing of the plan for his garden. It will be a rectangle measuring 18 ft by 12 ft. On the scaled version, it measures 8 in. on the longer sides. What is the measure of each of the shorter sides? $5\frac{1}{3}$ in.

## ■ EXTENDED PRACTICE EXERCISES

**For each pair of figures, describe the two transformations used to create each image.** For 22–24, answers will vary. See additional answers for possible solutions.

**22.** 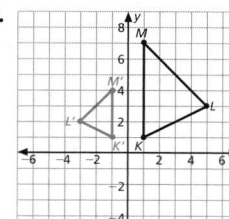  **23.** 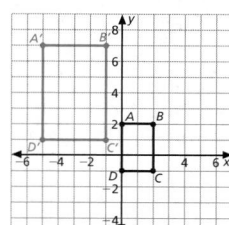  **24.**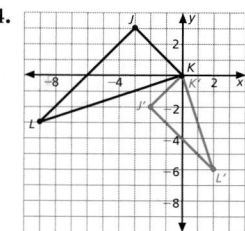

 **25.** **GEOMETRY SOFTWARE** Use Cabri Jr. to draw $\triangle GHI$ with vertices $G(0, 0)$, $H(0, 6)$, and $I(3, 0)$ on a coordinate plane. Use the software's tools to dilate the triangle about the origin with scale factors of 2 and 0.5. Find the area of $\triangle GHI$, its enlargement, and its reduction. 9 square units; 36 square units; 2.25 square units

**26.** Draw rectangle $TUVW$ with vertices $T(1, 1)$, $U(1, 4)$, $V(7, 4)$, and $W(7, 1)$ on a coordinate plane. Draw the dilation images of the rectangle with the center of dilation at $T$ and scale factors of 3 and $\frac{1}{3}$. Find the area of the rectangle, its enlargement and its reduction. 18 square units; 162 square units; 2 square units

**27.** **DATA FILE** Refer to the data on balls used in various sports on page 572. A movie creates large-scale models of certain balls to create the illusion of tiny people. If the scale factor used is 45, what is the height (diameter) of a tennis ball? a baseball? a basketball? tennis ball: 292.5 cm ≈ 3 m; baseball: 343 cm ≈ 3.43 m; basketball: 1080 cm ≈ 10.8 m

 **28.** **CHAPTER INVESTIGATION** Decide how large your house will be by choosing a scale factor for the blueprint to the actual house. Label the sizes of the rooms and halls on the blueprint, and calculate the square footage of the whole floor of your house. Answers will vary.

## ■ MIXED REVIEW EXERCISES

**Simplify each numerical expression.** (Lesson 2-2)

**29.** $5 - 3 \cdot 2 - 4$  $-5$ 
**30.** $3(8 + 2) \div 5$  $6$ 
**31.** $3^2 - 4 + 8 \div 2$  $9$

**32.** $13 - 4 \cdot 9 + 3 \cdot 2$  $-17$ 
**33.** $20 - (4 + 3) \div 2 + 6$  $22.5$ 
**34.** $5 + (3 - 1)^2 \div 3 + 8$  $14\frac{1}{3}$

**35.** $16 \div 4 - (2 + 5)^2$  $-45$ 
**36.** $1 + 6^2 \cdot \frac{1}{4}(9 - 5)^2$  $145$ 
**37.** $6 + (4 - 6)^3 + 2 - 8 \cdot 2$  $-16$

**Identify the slope and $y$-intercept for each line.** (Lesson 6-3)

**38.** $y = 4x - 2$  $4; -2$ 
**39.** $y = 3x + 5$  $3; 5$ 
**40.** $y = \frac{1}{2}x + 2$  $\frac{1}{2}; 2$

**41.** $2x - 2y = 8$  $1; -4$ 
**42.** $-3x + y = 4$  $3; 4$ 
**43.** $5x + 2y = 6$  $-\frac{5}{2}; 3$

**44.** $y = \frac{2}{3}x - 4$  $\frac{2}{3}; -4$ 
**45.** $-x + 2y = 10$  $\frac{1}{2}; 5$ 
**46.** $4x + 5y = -15$  $-\frac{4}{5}; -3$

**Math** online mathmatters2.com/self_check_quiz

---

Name _____  Date _____

EXTRA PRACTICE  **7-5**
## DILATIONS IN THE COORDINATE PLANE

✏ **EXERCISES**

Give the scale factor and center for each dilation.

**1.** Triangle $ABC$ has vertices $A(-2, 1)$, $B(0, 3)$ and $C(2, 1)$. Its dilated image is $\triangle A'B'C'$ with vertices $A'(-4, 2)$, $B'(0, 6)$ and $C'(4, 2)$. 2; origin

**2.** Square $MNPQ$ has vertices $M(-3, 3)$, $N(3, 3)$, $P(3, -3)$ and $Q(-3, -3)$. Its dilated image is square $M'N'P'Q'$ with vertices $M'(-1, 1)$, $N'(1, 1)$, $P'(1, -1)$ and $Q'(-1, -1)$. $\frac{1}{3}$; origin

**3.** 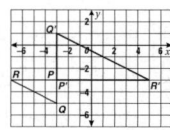 $\frac{1}{2}$; $D$

**4.** $\frac{4}{3}$; origin

Copy parallelogram $MNPQ$ on your own grid paper. Draw each dilation. Give the coordinates of the vertices of the image.

**5.** scale factor 3, center (0, 0)
$M'(-12, 12)$, $N'(6, 12)$, $P'(12, -12)$, $Q'(-6, -12)$

**6.** scale factor 0.5, center $M$
$M'(-4, 4)$, $N'(-1, 4)$, $P'(0, 0)$, $Q'(-3, 0)$

**7.** scale factor 2, center $N$
$M'(-10, 4)$, $N'(2, 4)$, $P'(6, -20)$, $Q'(-6, -20)$

**8.** scale factor 1.5, center $Q$
$M'(-5, 8)$, $N'(4, 8)$, $P'(7, -4)$, $Q'(-2, -4)$

---

Name _____  Date _____

ENRICHMENT  **7-5**
## NEGATIVE DILATIONS

The scale factor for a dilation can be negative. To find the coordinates of a dilation image with center of dilation at the origin and a scale factor of $-n$, use the rule $(x, y) \rightarrow (-nx, -ny)$. To draw a dilation image with a negative scale factor when the center of dilation is *not* at the origin, follow these steps.

**Step 1** Find the distance of a point from the center of dilation by using the absolute value of the scale factor.

**Step 2** Then move that number of units from the center of dilation along the ray opposite to the ray containing that point on the preimage.

**Example**

Draw the dilation image of $\triangle PQR$ with the center of dilation at vertex $P$ and a scale factor of $-2$.

**Solution**

$Q$ is 2 units below $P$, so $Q'$ will be $2 \cdot 2$ or 4 units above $P$ in the direction opposite to $\overline{PQ}$.
$Q(-3, -5) \rightarrow Q'(-3, 1)$

$R$ is 4 units left of $P$, so $R'$ will be $4 \cdot 2$ or 8 units right of $P$ in the direction opposite to $\overline{PR}$.
$R(-7, -3) \rightarrow R'(5, -3)$

✏ **EXERCISES**

**1.** Draw the dilation image of $\triangle ABC$ with the center of dilation at the origin and a scale factor of $-2$.

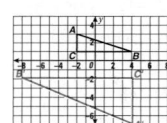

**2.** Draw the dilation image of $\triangle LMN$ with the center of dilation at $L$ and a scale factor of $-3$.

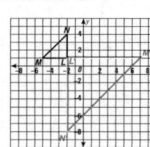

---

**17.** A dilation changes each figure into a similar figure not necessarily congruent to the original figure, while translations, reflections, and rotations change each figure into a congruent figure. All corresponding angles are equal in translations, reflections, rotations, and dilations. Dilations and translations have parallel corresponding sides between the preimage and the image.

**22.** Reflect across the $y$-axis and then a dilation with center at $(-1, 1)$ and a scale factor of $\frac{1}{2}$.

**23.** Translation to the left 3 and up 2. Then use a dilation with center $(-1, 1)$ and a scale factor of 2.

**24.** Rotate 90° counterclockwise about the origin, then use a dilation with center at the origin and a scale factor of $\frac{2}{3}$.

Some problems are solved by recognizing a pattern, while other problems require that you extend the pattern to find the solution. This strategy is called **look for a pattern**, and it is used with many different types of problems. Look for a pattern that is numerical, visual or behavioral. By figuring out the pattern, you can predict the next element or figure out all the elements.

A **tessellation** is a repeating pattern of one or more figures that completely covers a plane without gaps or overlaps. Tessellations are also called *tilings*. A set of figures that can be used to create a tessellation is said to *tessellate*. You can find tessellations in art, nature and everyday life.

### Problem

**Construct a tessellation using regular octagons and squares as tessellating figures.**

### Solve the Problem

*Step* 1 Draw a regular octagon.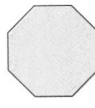

*Step* 2 Draw 4 squares.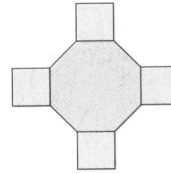

*Step* 3 Complete the tessellation.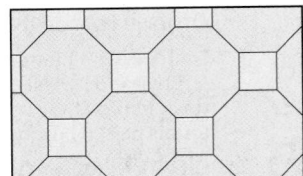

### TRY THESE EXERCISES

**Determine if each polygon can be a tessellating figure. Write *yes* or *no*.**

1. equilateral triangle  yes
2. regular octagon  no
3. regular hexagon  yes
4. isosceles triangle  yes

5. Draw the tessellation for one of the polygons to which you answered "yes" in Exercises 1–4.  Check students' work.

6. **NATURE** Describe the tessellating figure in a honeycomb beehive.  regular hexagons

7. Draw a tessellation whose tessellating figure is composed of regular hexagons, squares, and equilateral triangles.  See additional answers.

**320** | Chapter 7 **Coordinate Graphing and Transformations**

**THE STRATEGY** *Look for a pattern*—this strategy enables students to figure out any element of a sequence, whether the sequence is numerical, algebraic, or diagrammatic.

**Determine if each polygon can be a tessellating figure. Write *yes* or *no*.**

8. regular pentagon  no

9. square  yes

10. circle  no

11. parallelogram  yes

12. **HOBBIES**  Draw a tessellation in which the tessellating figure is a puzzle piece.  See additional answers.

13. **WRITING MATH**  Describe how tessellations are used in everyday life. Sketch some of the examples.  Answers will vary.

**Use each figure to create a tessellation on dot or grid paper.**
For 14–16, see additional answers.

14.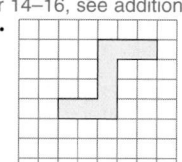
15.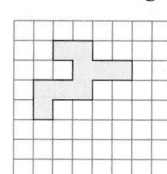
16.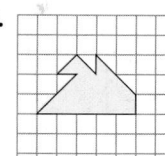

17. **ARCHITECTURE**  The floor of the Taj Mahal in India contains many beautiful tile patterns. Describe the pattern and the tessellation of one of the tile patterns in the Taj Mahal shown at the right.
tessellating rhombuses and four-pointed stars

18. Use isometric grid paper to create a tessellation using large and small equilateral triangles.
See additional answers.

19. **MODELING**  Fold patty paper to create a tessellation design, or fold the paper into a grid and draw a tessellation on it. Name the shapes that appear in the tessellation.  Answers will vary.

20. **CRITICAL THINKING**  Draw a tessellation using a tessellating figure of a quadrilateral that contains no right angles.  Answers will vary.

 **MIXED REVIEW EXERCISES**

**Solve each proportion. Check the solution.** (Lesson 3-5)

21. $\frac{7}{8} = \frac{m}{32}$  28

22. $\frac{6}{5} = \frac{42}{g}$  35

23. $\frac{13}{20} = \frac{r}{4}$  $\frac{13}{5}$

24. $\frac{1}{3} = \frac{f}{21}$  7

25. $\frac{2s}{3} = \frac{24}{12}$  3

26. $\frac{7}{8} = \frac{4p}{56}$  $12\frac{1}{4}$

27. $\frac{15}{25} = \frac{5}{2z}$  $\frac{25}{6}$

28. $\frac{10}{8} = \frac{x}{0.8}$  1

29. During one flight, 32 passengers chose *In Flight* magazine to read, 16 chose a newspaper, 18 chose a book and 8 chose nothing to read. What is the probability that a passenger chose to read *In Flight*? (Lesson 4-1)  $\frac{16}{37}$

30. On the same flight, 24 passengers chose to drink apple juice, 17 chose soda, 19 chose coffee and 14 chose iced tea. What is the probability that a passenger chose iced tea to drink? (Lesson 4-1)  $\frac{7}{37}$

Lesson 7-6  **Problem Solving Skills: Tessellations**  **321**

---

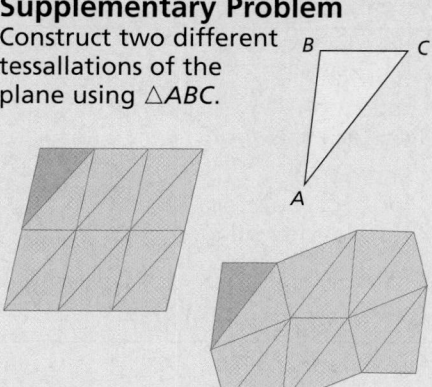
---

**ADDITIONAL ANSWERS**

7. Sample Answer:

12.

14.

15.

16.

18.

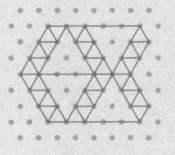

### Vocabulary Review

**Lesson 7-5**
dilation             enlargement
reduction           scale factor
center of dilation

**Lesson 7-6**
look for a pattern
tesselation / tiling

## Assignment Guide

**All students:** 1–20

## Chalkboard Examples

### Lesson 7-5
Point *A* is at (2, 1). Under a dilation with center at the origin, *OA* stretches to *OA'* by a scale factor of 3. Find the length of *OA'*.

$A(2, 1) \rightarrow A'(6, 3)$
Use the distance formula to find the length of *OA'*.

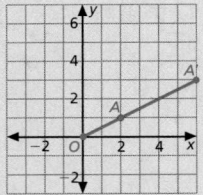

$\sqrt{(6 - 0)^2 + (3 - 0)^2}$
$= \sqrt{45}$
So, $OA' = \sqrt{45}$.

### Lesson 7-6
Construct a tesselation using equilateral triangles and squares. Here are two possible tesselations, with the fundamental pattern for each.

### Practice ■ Lesson 7-5

**Copy △*ABC* on grid paper. Draw each dilation.**
For 1–4, see additional answers.

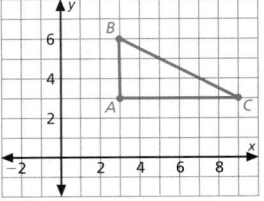

1. scale factor 2, center (0, 0)    2. scale factor $\frac{1}{2}$, center (0, 0)

3. scale factor 2, center *B*    4. scale factor $\frac{2}{3}$, center *A*

**Give the coordinates of each dilated image.**

5. scale factor 4, center (0, 0)    6. scale factor $\frac{1}{2}$, center (0, 0)

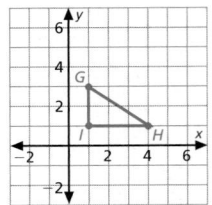 $G'(4,12)$, $H'(16,4)$, $I'(4,4)$

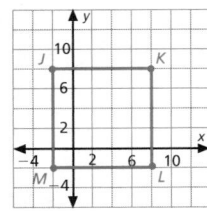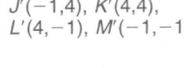 $J'(-1,4)$, $K'(4,4)$, $L'(4,-1)$, $M'(-1,-1)$

7. scale factor 1.5, center (0, 0)    8. scale factor $\frac{1}{2}$, center *S*

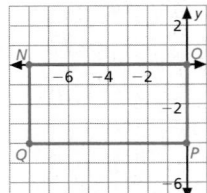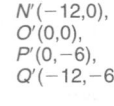 $N'(-12,0)$, $O'(0,0)$, $P'(0,-6)$, $Q'(-12,-6)$

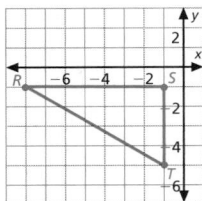 $R'(-4.5,-1)$, $S'(-1,-1)$, $T'(-1,-3)$

### Practice ■ Lesson 7-6

**Determine if each polygon can be a tessellating figure. Write *yes* or *no*.**

9.
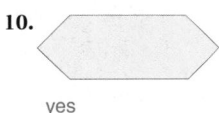
yes

10.

yes

11.
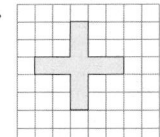
yes

**Determine if each figure can be a tessellating figure. If so, create a tessellation on dot or grid paper.** For 13–14, see additional answers.

12.
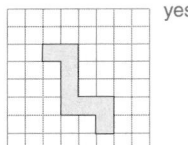
No. This figure alone does not tessellate.

13.
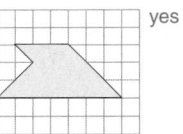
yes

14.
yes

## Additional Answers

1.
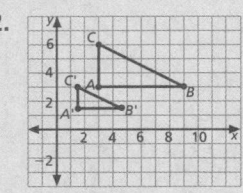

2.
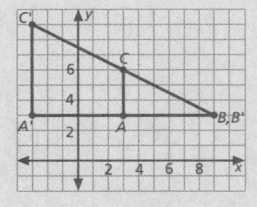

3.

4.
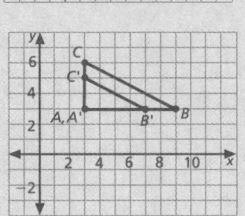

**PRACTICE** ■ **LESSON 7-1–LESSON 7-6**

15. Graph △XYZ with vertices X(0, 0), Y(2, −3) and Z(6, −3) and its reflection over the y-axis. (Lesson 7-2)  See additional answers.

16. Graph △ABC with vertices A(2, −2), B(4, −2) and C(2, −6) and its image with a 180° rotation about (0, 0). (Lesson 7-3)  See additional answers.

**Trace each figure, and draw all lines of symmetry. If applicable, write *none*.**
(Lesson 7-4)  For 17–19, check students' drawings. The number of lines of symmetry is given.

17.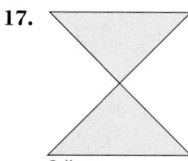

2 lines

18.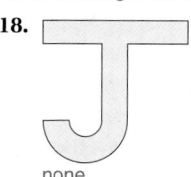

19.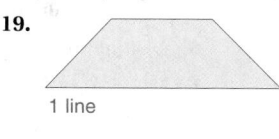

1 line

20. Gayle has a film negative that is 1.25 in. by 1.75 in. To get a print blown up to a 5 in. by 7 in., what is the scale factor of the enlargement? (Lesson 7-5)  4

## MathWorks — Career – Architect
Workplace Knowhow

Architects design buildings and other structures. They are often involved in all phases of development, from the initial discussion with the client through the entire life of the facility. Their duties require skills such as design, engineering, communication and supervision. Architects often begin the design of a group of buildings by choosing a basic geometric shape and repeating it in the design. Rotation, translation and dilation of the chosen shape results in buildings of various shapes and sizes. The steps below outline the process of designing a library. Use one grid to construct all three buildings, allowing both the x- and y-axes to extend from −15 to +15 units.

1. Rotate Building 1 90° counterclockwise around the origin to determine the location of Building 2, A'B'C'D'. What are the coordinates of A', B', C' and D'?
   A'(4, 4), B'(4, 10), C'(8, 10), D'(8, 4)

2. Draw a line of symmetry on Building 1. A flagpole, which is 5 units from Building 1 along the line of symmetry, is located between Buildings 1 and 2. Draw an "x" at the location of the flagpole. What are its coordinates?
   (7, 0)

3. Building 3, figure A"B"C"D" is three times the size of Building 2. To determine its location, draw the dilation of A'B'C'D' with the center of dilation at (11, 10) and translate the dilated figure to the left 3 units. Give the coordinates of A", B", C" and D".
   A"(−13, −8), B"(−13, 10), C"(−1, 10), D"(−1, −8)

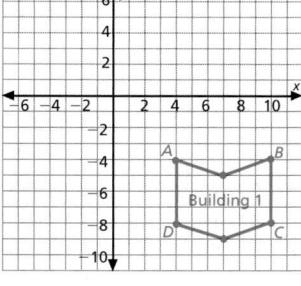

 **Math Online** mathmatters2.com/mathworks

Chapter 7 **Review and Practice Your Skills** | 323

In their work, architects must balance three major elements: function, appearance, and durability.

In designing a building, architects think in terms of *space, planes,* and *openings*. They consider a building as space enclosed by planes—that is, by the surface of walls, floors, and ceilings. Openings include doorways, windows, and archways. An architect's basic task is to "shape" space into appropriate and practical forms through the arrangement of openings and planes.

Students should answer Questions 1–4 to better understand how an architect might use transformations of the coordinate plane in designing a group of buildings.

At various times in history, architects have considered certain shapes more beautiful than others and have emphasized them in their designs.

Students may be interested in researching the *golden rectangle*, a rectangle whose length and width correspond to the approximate ratio 1.61803. Rectangles that look like a golden rectangle are more pleasing to the eye than other rectangles, though no one knows why. Many golden sections and golden rectangles appear in famous paintings, sculpture, and architecture.

Students who are interested in learning more about this career choice can go to mathmatters2.com/mathworks. School Guidance Counselors are another resource for information about training requirements and appropriate schools.

13.

14.

15.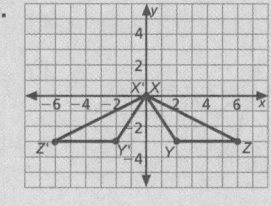

16.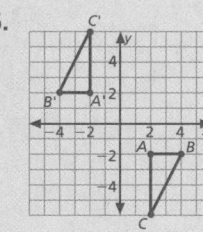

# Chapter 7 Review

## VOCABULARY

Choose the word from the list that best completes each statement.

1. An image produced by a flip across a line is a(n) __?__. f
2. Under a(n) __?__, a figure is turned about a given point. g
3. A transformation that produces an image that is the same shape as the original figure but a different size is a(n) __?__. a
4. A plane figure has __?__ if you can divide it along a line into two parts that are mirror images of each other. c
5. A slide transformation is a(n) __?__. l
6. A(n) __?__ occurs when the image is smaller than the original. e
7. A repeating pattern that covers a plane without gaps or overlaps is called a(n) __?__. j
8. A plane figure has __?__ if you can rotate it so that it fits exactly over its original position more than once in a complete turn. h
9. In an enlargement, the __?__ is greater than one. i
10. In a transformation, the original figure is called a(n) __?__. d

| | |
|---|---|
| **a.** | dilation |
| **b.** | enlargement |
| **c.** | line symmetry |
| **d.** | preimage |
| **e.** | reduction |
| **f.** | reflection |
| **g.** | rotation |
| **h.** | rotational symmetry |
| **i.** | scale factor |
| **j.** | tessellation |
| **k.** | transformation |
| **l.** | translation |

## LESSON 7-1 ■ Translations in the Coordinate Plane, p. 296

▶ A move like a **translation**, or slide, is called a **transformation** of a figure. The original figure is the **preimage**. The new figure is the **image** of the original figure.

▶ A translation can be described by a rule stating the number of units to the left or right and the number of units up or down.

11. Triangle *STU* has vertices $S(-2, 0)$, $T(2, -2)$, and $U(21, 24)$. Graph the image of $\triangle STU$ under a translation 2 units left and 4 units up.
11–12. See additional answers.
12. Triangle *ABC* has vertices $A(-5, -2)$, $B(-2, 3)$, and $C(-2, -3)$. Graph the image of $\triangle ABC$ under a translation 1 unit right and 3 units up.

Write the rule that describes each translation.

13.
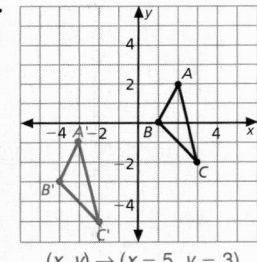
$(x, y) \rightarrow (x - 5, y - 3)$

14.
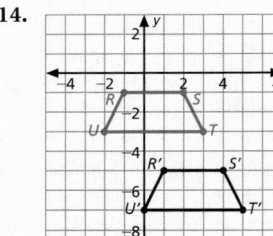
$(x, y) \rightarrow (x + 2, y - 4)$

## Chapter 7 Review (sidebar)

### Vocabulary Assessment

- A matching section checks for student understanding of the new vocabulary introduced in this chapter.
- A vocabulary review/test for Chapter 7 is available on pp. vii–viii of the *Chapter 7 Resource Masters*.

### Lesson-by-Lesson Review

For each lesson,

- the main ideas are summarized, and
- practice exercises are provided.

 EXAMVIEW® PRO

Use the networkable **ExamView® Pro** to:

- Create **multiple versions** of tests.
- Create **modified tests** for *inclusion* students.
- **Edit** existing questions and **add** your own questions.
- Use built-in **state curriculum correlations** to create tests aligned with state standards.
- Change **English** tests to **Spanish** and vice versa.

## ADDITIONAL ANSWERS

11.
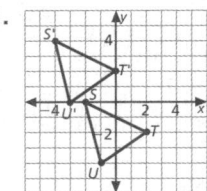

12.
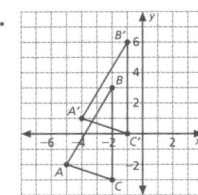

## LESSON 7-2 ◼ Reflections in the Coordinate Plane, p. 300

▶ Under a **reflection**, a figure is reflected, or flipped, across a *line of reflection*. A reflection is a transformation that yields a congruent figure.

15–18. See additional answers.

15. Graph the image of parallelogram *ABCD* under a reflection across the line $y = -x$.

16. Graph the image of parallelogram *ABCD* under a reflection across the *x*-axis.

17. Graph the image of parallelogram *ABCD* under a reflection across the *y*-axis.

18. Graph the image of parallelogram *ABCD* under a reflection across the line $y = x$.

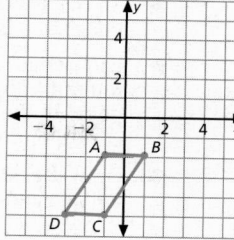

## LESSON 7-3 ◼ Rotations in the Coordinate Plane, p. 306

▶ A rotation is a transformation that includes the following.

   a. The **center of rotation**, or point about which the figure is rotated.

   b. The amount of turn expressed as a fractional part of a whole turn or as the **angle of rotation** in degrees.  19–21. See additional answers.

   c. The direction of rotation—clockwise or counterclockwise.

19. Triangle *FGH* has vertices *F*(0, 0), *G*(5, −2), and *H*(4, −5). Graph the rotation image of △*FGH* under a turn of 90° clockwise about (0, 0).

20. Triangle *VWX* has vertices *V*(−4, 2), *W*(−2, 4), and *X*(2, 1). Graph the rotation image of △*VWX* under a turn of 180° clockwise about (0, 0).

21. Triangle *ABC* has vertices *A*(−5, 3), *B*(−2, 5), and *C*(−3, 2). Graph the rotation image of △*ABC* under a turn of 90° counterclockwise about (0, 0).

## LESSON 7-4 ◼ Line Symmetry and Rotational Symmetry, p. 310

▶ A figure has **line symmetry** if, when you fold it along a line, one side fits exactly over the other side. The line is called a **line of symmetry**.

▶ A figure has **rotational symmetry** if, when you turn it about a point, the figure fits exactly over its original position more than once before the turn is completed.

**Trace each figure, and draw all lines of symmetry. If applicable, write *none*.**

22. 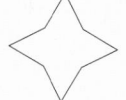    4 lines

23.     2 lines

24.    none

For 22–24, check students' drawings. The number of lines of symmetry is given.

**Give the order of rotational symmetry for each figure.**

25.     6

26.     3

27. 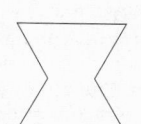    2

15.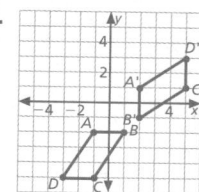

16.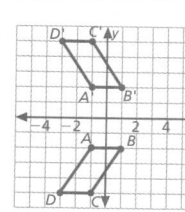

17.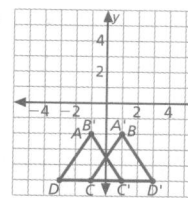

18.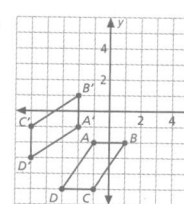

19.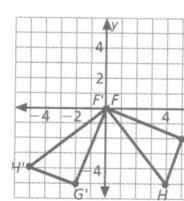

20.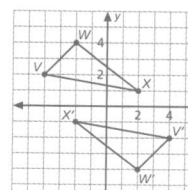

21.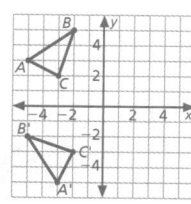

28.

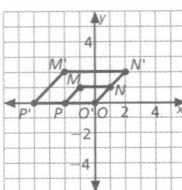

32.

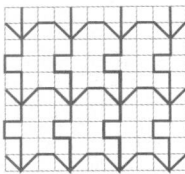

33.

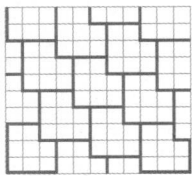

34.

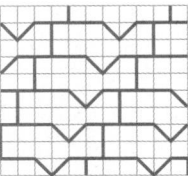

## LESSON 7-5 ◼ Dilations in the Coordinate Plane, p. 316

▶ A **dilation** is a transformation that produces the same shape but a different size image of a figure.

▶ An **enlargement** is an image that is larger than its preimage. A **reduction** is an image that is smaller than its preimage.

▶ Each length in the image is equal to the corresponding side of the preimage multiplied by the **scale factor**. The distance from the **center of dilation** to each point on the image is equal to the distance from the **center of dilation** to each corresponding point on the preimage times the scale factor.

28. Draw the dilation image of parallelogram *MNOP* with the center of dilation at (0, 0) and a scale factor of 2.
See additional answers.

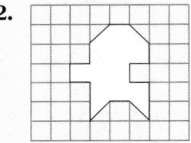

29. Triangle *ABC* has vertices $A(-4, 1)$, $B(-3, 4)$, and $C(-1, 1)$. Its dilation image is $\triangle A'B'C'$ with vertices $A'(-8, 2)$, $B'(-6, 8)$, and $C'(-2, 2)$. What is the scale factor and center of the dilation?   2; (0, 0)

30. A photograph is 8 in. by 10 in. It is being reduced by a scale factor of $\frac{3}{4}$. What are the dimensions of the new photograph?   6 in. by $7\frac{1}{2}$ in.

31. A projector focuses an image from film that is 16 millimeters wide onto a screen that is 1.5 meters wide. What is the scale factor?   93.75

## LESSON 7-6 ◼ Problem Solving Skills: Tessellations, p. 320

▶ A **tessellation**, or **tiling**, is a repeating pattern of figures that completely covers a plane without gaps or overlaps.

**Use each figure to create a tessellation on dot or grid paper.**

32.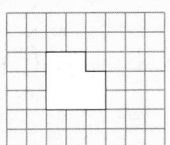

33.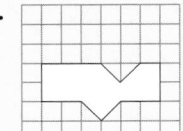

34.

32–34. See additional answers.

## CHAPTER INVESTIGATION

**EXTENSION** Present your blueprint to the class. Describe your reasons for the types of rooms you have included and the way in which they are oriented. Also describe any geometric principles that you have employed in the creation of the blueprint. These may include any transformational principles used, different types of polygons and shapes, a tessellated floor pattern and more.

326 | Chapter 7 **Coordinate Graphing and Transformations**

---

## THEME: Architecture

The benchmarks and expectations for this extension are as follows.
- Students draw the general layout and shape of the main floor of their dream house on grid paper. They make the blueprint large enough to fill most of the page.
- Students draw the designs of the rooms and hallways of their house on the grid paper. They label the different types of rooms including any special features. They include transformational principles such as two rooms mirroring each other.
- Students decide how large their house will be by choosing a scale factor for the blueprint to the actual house. They label the sizes of the rooms and halls on the blueprint and calculate the square footage of the whole floor of their house.
- Students present their blueprint to the class. They describe their reasons for the types of rooms they have included and the way in which the rooms are oriented. They also describe any geometric principles that they have employed in the creation of the blueprint. The geometric principles may include any transformational principles used, different types of polygons and shapes, a tessellated floor pattern and more.

# Chapter 7 Assessment

**Use the figure for Exercises 1–3.**
For 1–3, see additional answers.

1. Graph the image of trapezoid *CDEF* under a translation 3 units to the right and 4 units down.

2. Graph the image of trapezoid *CDEF* under a reflection across the line $y = x$.

3. Graph the rotation image of trapezoid *CDEF* after a 90° turn counterclockwise about (0, 0).

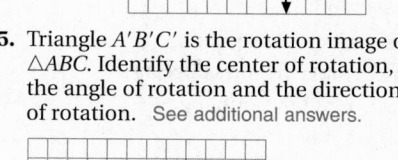

4. Triangle *T′U′V′* is the reflected image of △*TUV*. Graph the line of reflection.
See additional answers.

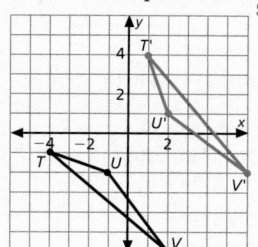

5. Triangle *A′B′C′* is the rotation image of △*ABC*. Identify the center of rotation, *T*, the angle of rotation and the direction of rotation.   See additional answers.

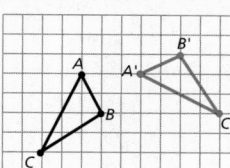

6. How many lines of symmetry does the figure below have?   2

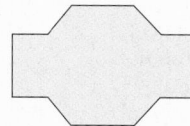

7. What is the order of rotational symmetry of the figure below?   3

8. Write the rule that describes the translation of the black preimage to the blue image.   $(x, y) \rightarrow (x - 4, y - 2)$

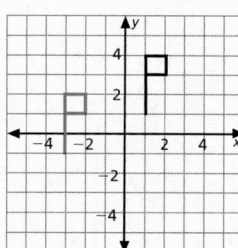

9. Draw the dilation image of △*WXY* with the center of dilation at the origin and a scale factor of $\frac{1}{3}$.   See additional answers.

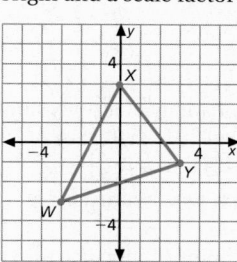

10. Use the figures to create a tessellation on dot or grid paper.
See additional answers.

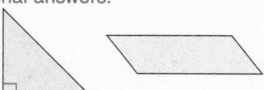

## Chapter 7 Assessment

### Assessment Options

Chapter 7 Test A, pages 235–236
Chapter 7 Test B, pages 237–238

### ALTERNATIVE ASSESSMENT

**BUILDING SYMMETRY** Have students use the library or the Internet to research buildings that demonstrate lines of symmetry. Students can locate pictures in books or print pictures from the Internet. Students should draw all the possible lines of symmetry for each building and determine what architectural period each building represents. Is one period more influenced by symmetry than others?

**RUBRIC** The following rubric is a sample scoring guide.

| Points | Description |
|---|---|
| 4 | Finds many examples of building symmetry, **correctly draws lines** of symmetry, and **correctly identifies** architectural periods, telling influence of symmetry. |
| 3 | Finds examples of building symmetry, **draws most lines** of symmetry, and does **some research** about architectural periods. |
| 2 | Finds examples of building symmetry, **draws some lines** of symmetry, but does **minimal research** about architectural periods. |
| 1 | Finds one example of building symmetry, **draws a line** of symmetry, but does **no research** about architectural periods. |
| 0 | Makes **no attempt** to find building symmetry. |

## ADDITIONAL ANSWERS

**1–3.**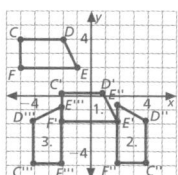

**4.**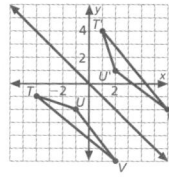

**5.**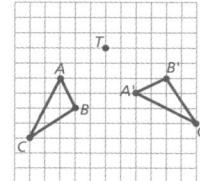

**9.**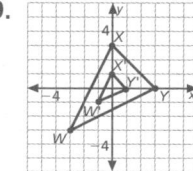

**10.**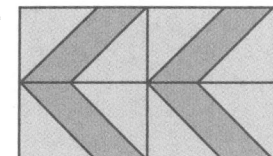

## Standardized Test Practice

These two pages contain practice questions in the various formats that can be found on the most frequently given standardized tests.

A student recording sheet for these two pages can be found on p. A1 of the *Chapter 7 Resource Masters*.

### Standardized Test Practice Student Recording Sheet

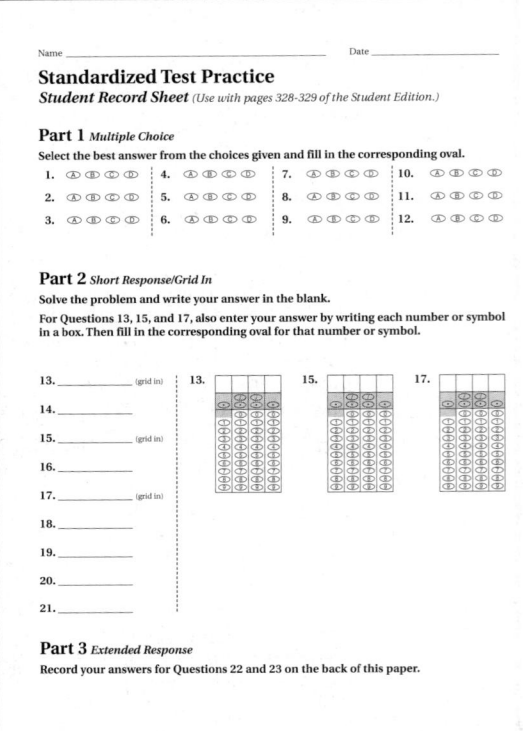

### Additional Practice

See pp. 239–241 in the *Chapter 7 Resource Masters* for additional standardized test practice.

### Part 1 | Multiple Choice

**Record your answers on the answer sheet provided by your teacher or on a sheet of paper.**

1. The staff at a research company is paid to survey shoppers walking past them at the mall. What kind of sampling is this? (Lesson 1-1)  B
   - Ⓐ cluster sampling
   - Ⓑ convenience sampling
   - Ⓒ random sampling
   - Ⓓ systematic sampling

2. Simplify $\frac{-6x + 3}{-3}$. (Lesson 2-5)  B
   - Ⓐ $2x + 1$
   - Ⓑ $2x - 1$
   - Ⓒ $3x + 1$
   - Ⓓ $3x - 1$

3. What is the next term in the sequence? (Lesson 2-9)  D

   $$2, 3, 5, 8, 13, 21, \ldots$$
   - Ⓐ 24
   - Ⓑ 28
   - Ⓒ 30
   - Ⓓ 34

4. If $3a = -6$, what does $2a$ equal? (Lesson 3-2)  B
   - Ⓐ $-6$
   - Ⓑ $-4$
   - Ⓒ 4
   - Ⓓ 6

5. Solve $\sqrt{d} = 4$. (Lesson 3-8)  C
   - Ⓐ $d = 16$ or $-16$
   - Ⓑ $d = 2$ or $-2$
   - Ⓒ $d = 16$
   - Ⓓ $d = 2$

6. What is the probability of an event that is certain to happen? (Lesson 4-1)  C
   - Ⓐ 0
   - Ⓑ 0.5
   - Ⓒ 1
   - Ⓓ depends on the circumstances

7. If you rolled a number cube five times and got a 6 each time, what is the theoretical probability of rolling a 6 on the sixth roll? (Lesson 4-3)  B
   - Ⓐ 1
   - Ⓑ $\frac{1}{6}$
   - Ⓒ $\frac{1}{36}$
   - Ⓓ 0

8. What is the total measure of all the interior angles in a polygon with 14 sides? (Lesson 5-7)  A
   - Ⓐ 2160°
   - Ⓑ 2520°
   - Ⓒ 4320°
   - Ⓓ 5140°

9. $\triangle ABC \cong \triangle DEF$. The vertices of $\triangle ABC$ are $A(-1, 3)$, $B(2, 7)$ and $C(2, -1)$. Find $DF$. (Lesson 6-1)  C
   - Ⓐ $\sqrt{5}$
   - Ⓑ $\sqrt{8}$
   - Ⓒ 5
   - Ⓓ 8

10. The brightness of a light bulb varies inversely as the square of the distance from the source. If a light bulb has a brightness of 300 lumens at 2 ft, what is its brightness at 10 ft? (Lesson 6-7)  C
    - Ⓐ 120 lumens
    - Ⓑ 60 lumens
    - Ⓒ 12 lumens
    - Ⓓ 6 lumens

11. Which of the following figures is *not* a rotation of the figure at the right? (Lesson 7-3)  A

    Ⓐ     Ⓑ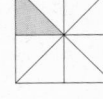

    Ⓒ 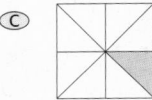    Ⓓ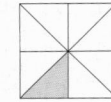

12. Which figure has exactly two lines of symmetry? (Lesson 7-4)  D

    Ⓐ     Ⓑ

    Ⓒ     Ⓓ

## Part 2 | Short Response/Grid In

Record your answers on the answer sheet provided by your teacher or on a sheet of paper.

**13.** The mean of $r$ and $s$ is 25. The mean of $r$, $s$, and $t$ is 30. What is the value of $t$? (Lesson 1-2)  40

**14.** On a car trip, Kwan drove 50 mi more than half the number of miles Molly drove. Together they drove 425 mi. How many miles did Kwan drive? (Lesson 3-4)  175 mi

**15.** A bag contains 2 red, 6 blue, 7 yellow, and 3 orange marbles. Once a marble is selected, it is not replaced. If two marbles are picked at random, what is the probability that both marbles are yellow? (Lesson 4-5)  $\frac{7}{51}$

**16.** Find the value of $x$ in the figure. (Lesson 5-4)  50

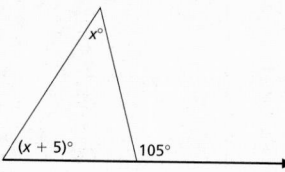

**Use parallelogram $ABCD$ for Exercises 17 and 18.**

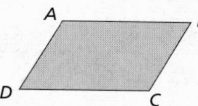

**17.** If $AB = 7$ and $BC = 3$, find $DC$. (Lesson 5-6)  7

**18.** If $m\angle A = 110°$, find $m\angle B$. (Lesson 5-6)  70°

**19.** The weight of an object on the moon varies directly with its weight on Earth. With all of his equipment, an astronaut weighed 420 lb on Earth, but weighed only 70 lb on the moon. Suppose an object weighs 144 lb on Earth. Find its weight on the moon. (Lesson 6-8)  24 lb

mathmatters2.com/standardized_test

**20.** The vertices of $\triangle ABC$ are $A(-2, 3)$, $B(1, 4)$, and $C(2, -3)$. Find the coordinates of $\triangle A'B'C'$ if $\triangle ABC$ is translated 3 units down and 4 units to the right. (Lesson 7-1)
$A'(-5, 7)$, $B'(-2, 8)$, $C'(-1, 1)$

**21.** Which capital letters of the alphabet produce the same letter after being rotated 180°? (Lesson 7-3)  H, I, N, O, S, X, Z

## Part 3 | Extended Response

Record your answers on a sheet of paper. Show your work.

**22.** The drawing shows the pattern for the right half of a shirt. Copy the pattern onto grid paper. Then draw the outline of the pattern after it has been flipped over a vertical line to show the left half of the pattern. Label it "Left Front." Describe the relationship between the right and left fronts of the pattern in mathematical terms. (Lesson 7-2)
See additional answers.

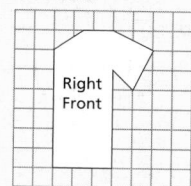

**23.** Jamal is designing a floor for a customer. The customer wants to use three geometrical shapes to tessellate the floor. Create a design that will work and explain how you can use your geometry skills to know that the figures tessellate. (Lesson 7-6)  See additional answers.

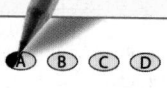

### Test-Taking Tip

**Question 20**
Most standardized tests allow you to write in the test booklet. You may sketch the figure and its translation on a coordinate plane. Doing so will help keep you from making careless errors.

Chapter 7 **Standardized Test Practice** | 329

Preparing for the Standardized Tests
For test-taking strategies and more practice, see pages 627–644.

## Rubrics

The following rubrics are sample scoring guides for short response and extended response questions.

### Short Response

| Points | Description |
|--------|-------------|
| 2 | The student demonstrates a **thorough understanding** of the mathematics of the task. The response may contain minor flaws that do not detract from the demonstration of a thorough understanding. |
| 1 | The student has provided a response that is only **partially correct.** |
| 0 | The student has provided a **completely incorrect** solution or no response at all. |

### Extended Response

| Points | Description |
|--------|-------------|
| 4 | The student demonstrates a **thorough understanding** of the mathematics of the task. The response contains minor flaws that do not detract from the demonstration of a thorough understanding. |
| 3 | The student demonstrates an **understanding** of the mathematics of the task. The response is essentially correct and demonstrates an essential but less than thorough understanding of the mathematics. |
| 2 | The student has demonstrated only a **partial understanding** of the mathematics of the task. Although the student may have used the correct approach to a solution or may have provided a correct solution, the work lacks an essential understanding of the underlying mathematical concepts. |
| 1 | The student has demonstrated a **very limited understanding** of the mathematics of the task. The response is incomplete and exhibits many flaws. |
| 0 | The student has provided a **completely incorrect** solution or no response at all. |

## ADDITIONAL ANSWERS

**22.**

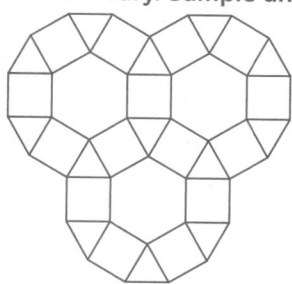

The left front is a reflection of the right front over a vertical line down the middle of the front of the shirt.

**23.** Answers will vary. Sample answer:

The sum of measures of the angles that surround a vertex must equal 180°.

# Systems of Equations and Inequalities

| Lesson | Lesson Objectives | Pacing (days) | NCTM Standards | State/Local Objectives |
|--------|-------------------|---------------|----------------|------------------------|
| 8-1 | **Parallel and Perpendicular Lines** (pp. 334–337)<br>• Use slope to determine if two lines are parallel or perpendicular.<br>• Write equations of parallel and perpendicular lines. | 2 | 2, 7, 9, 10 | |
| 8-2 | **Solve Systems of Equations Graphically** (pp. 338–341)<br>• State if an ordered pair is a solution of a system of equations.<br>• Solve systems of linear equations graphically. | 1 | 2, 7, 9, 10 | |
| 8-3 | **Solve Systems of Equations by Substitution** (pp. 344–347)<br>• Solve systems of equations using substitution. | 2 | 2, 6, 7, 9 | |
| 8-4 | **Solve Systems by Adding, Subtracting, and Multiplying** (pp. 348–351)<br>• Solve systems of equations by adding or subtracting.<br>• Solve systems of equations by adding and multiplying. | 2 | 2, 6, 7, 9 | |
| 8-5 | **Matrices and Determinants** (pp. 354–357)<br>• Find the determinant of a 2 × 2 matrix.<br>• Solve systems of equations using the method of determinants. | 1 | 2, 6, 7, 9 | |
| 8-6 | **Problem Solving Skills: Directed Graphs** (pp. 358–359)<br>• Solve a problem using a directed graph.<br>• Use a picture, diagram, or model to solve a problem. | 1 | 2, 6, 9, 10 | |
| 8-7 | **Systems of Inequalities** (pp. 362–365)<br>• Write a system of linear inequalities for a given graph.<br>• Graph a solution set of a system of linear inequalities. | 2 | 2, 7, 9, 10 | |
| **Review** | | 1 | | |
| **Testing** | | 1 | | |

**Key to NCTM Standards:**

*1=Number & Operations, 2=Algebra, 3=Geometry,*
*4=Measurement, 5=Data Analysis & Probability,*
*6=Problem Solving, 7=Reasoning & Proof,*
*8=Communication, 9=Connections, 10=Representation*

**Pacing:** Suggestions for the year can be found on page xvi.

## What's MATH Got To Do With It? Real-Life Math Videos

*What's Math Got To Do With It?* Real-Life Math Videos engage students, showing them how math is used in everyday situations. Use *Algebra 1* Video 2 with this chapter.

# Chapter Resource Manager

See page xiii.

## Chapter 8 Resource Masters

| Reteaching Activities | Extra Practice | Enrichment | Assessment | Basic Mathematics Review | Study Skills Activities | Lesson Warm-Ups Transparencies | Teaching Transparencies | Technology Activities | Materials Needed |
|---|---|---|---|---|---|---|---|---|---|
| 243 | 244 | 245 | | | 28 | 31 | TK-9– TK-12 | | graph paper, graphing calculator |
| 246 | 247 | 248 | | | | 31 | TK-9– TK-12 | 8-2 | graph paper, graphing calculator |
| 249 | 250 | 251 | | | | 32 | | | graphing calculator |
| 252 | 253 | 254 | | | | 32 | | | |
| 255 | 256 | 257 | | | 29 | 33 | | 8-5 | graph paper, graphing calculator |
| 258 | 259 | 260 | | | | 33 | RF-1 | | graphing calculator |
| 261 | 262 | 263 | 267–273 | | | 34 | TK-9–TK-14, RF-35 | | graph paper, graphing calculator |

### Quick Review Math Handbook, Book 2
**hot words hot topics**

| MathMatters 2 Lesson(s) | Hot Topic Lesson(s) |
|---|---|
| 8-1 | 6-8 |
| 8-2 | 6-7 |
| 8-3, 8-4 | 6-3, 6-4 |
| 8-5 | 6-4 |
| 8-6 | 4-5 |
| 8-7 | 6-7 |

# Content and Connections

## Connections to the Past

**MM1 (Ch. 7):** Find the slopes of lines.

**MM1 (Ch. 7):** Write an equation and graph a line using slope-intercept form.

**MM1 (Ch. 7):** Find solutions and intercepts of equations.

**MM1 (Ch. 5):** Understand equations and find their solutions.

**MM1 (Ch. 1):** Use addition and subtraction to solve equations.

**MM1 (Ch. 5):** Solve multi-step equations.

**MM1 (Ch. 5):** Write open sentences for a given number line graph.

**MM1 (Ch. 5):** Solve inequalities with one variable.

## MathMatters 2 Chapter 8 Highlights

Use slope to determine if two lines are parallel or perpendicular. (8-1)

Write equations of parallel and perpendicular lines. (8-1)

Solve linear equations graphically. (8-2)

Solve systems of equations using substitution. (8-3)

Solve systems of equations by adding or subtracting. (8-4)

Solve systems of equations using determinants. (8-5)

Write a system of linear inequalities for a given graph. (8-7)

Graph a solution set of a system of linear inequalities. (8-7)

## Connections to the Future

**MM3 (Ch. 6):** Use slope to determine whether two lines are parallel or perpendicular.

**MM3 (Ch. 6):** Write equations for lines in slope-intercept and point-slope forms.

**MM3 (Ch. 6):** Solve systems of equations by graphing.

**MM3 (Ch. 6):** Solve systems of equations using substitution.

**MM3 (Ch. 6):** Solve systems of equations by adding, subtracting, and multiplying.

**MM3 (Ch. 6):** Solve a problem with determinants and matrices.

**MM3 (Ch. 6):** Use graphing to solve systems of linear inequalities
**MM3 (Ch. 12):** Use graphs to write equations.

**MM3 (Ch. 6):** Use graphing to solve systems of linear inequalities.

### Key
PC    = Previous Course
MM1 = *MathMatters 1*
MM2 = *MathMatters 2*
MM3 = *MathMatters 3*

## Connecting the Strands

| NCTM Strand | Lesson(s) |
|---|---|
| Algebra | 8-1, 8-2, 8-3, 8-4, 8-5, 8-6, 8-7 |
| Problem Solving | 8-3, 8-4, 8-5, 8-6 |
| Reasoning & Proof | 8-1, 8-2, 8-3, 8-4, 8-5, 8-7 |
| Connections | 8-1, 8-2, 8-3, 8-4, 8-5, 8-6, 8-7 |
| Representation | 8-1, 8-2, 8-6, 8-7 |

# Ongoing Assessment and Intervention

| | Type | Student Edition | Teacher Resources | Technology/Internet |
|---|---|---|---|---|
| **INTERVENTION** | Ongoing | Are You Ready?, pp. 332–333<br>Check Understanding, pp. 339, 345, 348, 349<br>Review and Practice Your Skills, pp. 342–343, 352–353, 360–361<br>Mid-Chapter Quiz, p. 353 | Lesson Warm-Ups Transparencies, pp. WU-31, WU-32, WU-33, WU-34<br>Quick Assessment, *ATE* pp. 333, 336, 340, 346, 350, 356, 359, 364 | mathmatters2.com/extra_ examples<br>mathmatters2.com/self_check_quiz |
| | Mixed Review | pp. 337, 341, 347, 351, 357, 359, 365 | | |
| | Error Analysis | You Make the Call, pp. 341, 357 | Teaching Tip, *ATE* p. 354 | |
| **ASSESSMENT** | Standardized Test Practice | pp. 370–371<br>Preparing for Standardized Tests, pp. 627–644 | Standardized Test Practice, *CRM* pp. 271–273 | mathmatters2.com/standardized_test |
| | Open-Ended Assessment | Chapter Investigation, pp. 331, 347, 351, 357, 368 | Chapter Investigation, *ATE* p. 368<br>Alternative Assessment, *ATE* p. 369 | |
| | Chapter Assessment | Chapter Review, pp. 366–368<br>Chapter Assessment, p. 369 | Multiple-Choice Tests (Forms A and B), *CRM* pp. 267–270 | mathmatters2.com/chapter_assessment |

**Key to Abbreviations:** *ATE* = Annotated Teacher's Edition, *CRM* = Chapter Resource Masters

## Additional Intervention

***Basic Mathematics Review*** includes 80 lessons, consisting of an instructional page and a test page. This workbook also features a pretest, posttest, table of measurement equivalents, and calculator appendices.

## ExamView® Pro

Use ExamView® Pro Testmaker CD-ROM to:
- Create **multiple versions** of tests.
- Create **modified** tests for *inclusion* students with one mouse click.
- **Edit** existing questions and **add** your own questions.
- Build tests aligned with **state standards** using built-in **state curriculum correlations**.
- Change **English** tests to **Spanish** with one mouse click and vice versa.

# Chapter Opener

## NCTM Standards/Strands
- Data Analysis & Probability
- Representation

## Vocabulary
system of equations / inequalities

## Theme Connections
*Sports* are competitions of physical strength, skill, or endurance against opponents or against an objective standard such as time, height, or distance. In addition to players and their coaches, a variety of others are involved with sports, providing information about a particular sport, a player, or a team. Professional sports are financially lucrative to the people directly involved and to the advertisers who wish to capture the attention of vast audiences. In many of these aspects, a "break-even" point is of significance. Such points can be determined mathematically by solving systems of equations.

## Career Opportunities
Many careers require understanding of systems of equations and inequalities. Two such careers are highlighted in the MathWorks features. Others include: sports statistican, sports physician, sports referee, racing-car designer, sports equipment designer, game strategist.
- Runner, page 343
- Coach, page 361

# Internet Connection

## Theme Activities
Mathmatters2.com/chapter_theme provides links to the Internet that will help students gather information about the use of math in the real world, particularly data and measures. To search for additional addresses, begin a search of *sports*. Then within that search, use key words that will call up sporting tests of endurance, such as *marathon* or *decathlon*, or particular sports, such as *baseball* or *soccer,* or special sporting events, such as *Olympic Games* or *Super Bowl*. Students can brainstorm other key words.

# Systems of Equations and Inequalities

## THEME: Sports

The point of intersection in two or more lines signifies a relationship that can indicate where supply equals demand, the location of a ball and a receiver, or number of calories burned equals calories consumed.

Systems of equations and inequalities play an important role in sports. The point or the region of intersection may represent a winning play, a maximum performance, or a dynamic combination of players. Equations and inequalities can represent many aspects of the sports game and the solution to the system is a means to develop the ultimate goal: teamwork and victory.

- Athletes, such as **runners** (page 343), can use equations and systems of equations to monitor their running times so that their performance consistently improves.

- **Coaches** (page 361) can use equations and systems of equations to represent characteristics of individual performers and then plan a winning strategy.

**Math Online**
mathmatters2.com/chapter_theme

## Chapter Investigation
Use the Internet and other resources to locate additional information about sports tournaments.

## All Time Winter Olympics Medal Standings, 1924-2002

| Rank | Nation | Gold | Silver | Bronze | Total |
|------|--------|------|--------|--------|-------|
| 1 | Norway | 94 | 94 | 75 | 263 |
| 2 | Soviet Union (1956-1988) | 78 | 57 | 59 | 194 |
| 3 | United States | 69 | 72 | 52 | 193 |
| 4 | Austria | 41 | 57 | 64 | 162 |
| 5 | Finland | 42 | 51 | 49 | 142 |
| 6 | Germany (1928-36, 1992-) | 47 | 46 | 32 | 125 |
| 7 | East Germany (1956-1988) | 43 | 39 | 36 | 118 |
| 8 | Sweden | 39 | 30 | 39 | 108 |
| 9 | Switzerland | 32 | 33 | 38 | 103 |
| 10 | Canada | 31 | 31 | 27 | 89 |

## Data Activity: Winter Olympics Medal Standings

**Use the table for Questions 1–3.**

1. Let gold = 3 points, silver = 2 points and bronze = 1 point. Who has more points, Switzerland or Sweden?  Sweden

2. Let gold = 5 points, silver = 3 points and bronze = 1 point. Who has more points, the United States or Austria?  United States

3. Draw a bar graph using three of the countries in the table. Use different colors to represent gold, silver and bronze.
Answers will vary.

### CHAPTER INVESTIGATION

In the Central High School League, there are ten football teams. The top four teams advance to the league tournament. To determine the top four teams, points are awarded to each team for a win. Each team also receives points whenever a team it beats wins a game or has already won a game.

#### Working Together

The first table indicates who played each week, and the winning team is circled. Teams are numbered 1 through 10. The second table shows the top four teams and their total points for the year. Use the tables to determine the number of points awarded for winning a game and the number of points awarded whenever a team it beats wins a game or has already won a game. Use the Chapter Investigation icons to guide your group.

| Week 1 | Week 2 |
|--------|--------|
| 1 vs ②  | 1 vs ③ |
| ③ vs 4 | ② vs 4 |
| 5 vs ⑥ | 5 vs ⑦ |
| ⑦ vs 8 | ⑥ vs 9 |
| 9 vs ⑩ | ⑧ vs 10 |

| Week 3 | Week 4 |
|--------|--------|
| ① vs 4 | 1 vs ⑤ |
| ② vs 6 | 3 vs ⑦ |
| 3 vs ⑤ | ② vs 9 |
| ⑦ vs 10 | 4 vs ⑩ |
| ⑧ vs 9 | ⑥ vs 8 |

| Week 5 | Week 6 |
|--------|--------|
| 1 vs ⑧ | 1 vs ⑦ |
| ② vs 10 | ③ vs 8 |
| 3 vs ⑨ | ② vs 5 |
| ④ vs 5 | 4 vs ⑨ |
| 6 vs ⑦ | 6 vs ⑩ |

| Week 7 | Week 8 |
|--------|--------|
| 1 vs ⑥ | ① vs 9 |
| 2 vs ⑦ | 5 vs ⑩ |
| ⑤ vs 9 | ③ vs 6 |
| 3 vs ⑩ | 4 vs ⑦ |
| 4 vs ⑧ | ② vs 8 |

| Week 9 | |
|--------|--------|
| 1 vs ⑩ | |
| ② vs 3 | |
| 4 vs ⑤ | |
| 6 vs ⑧ | |
| ⑦ vs 9 | |

| Team | Total Points |
|------|--------------|
| Team 7 | 198 |
| Team 2 | 160 |
| Team 10 | 104 |
| Team 8 | 86 |

## Data Activity

The *Olympic Games* are an international sports competition, held every four years at a different site, where different nations compete in a variety of sports.

After each individual event, medals are awarded in a ceremony to the first-, second-, and third-place finishers. These winners mount a podium to receive gold (actually gold-plated), silver, and bronze medals. While the national flags of all three competitors are hoisted, the national anthem of the winner's country is played. Citizens of many nations take great pride when their athletes win Olympic medals.

Students should answer Questions 1–3 to compare national medal standings at the Winter Olympics.

## Chapter Investigation

### As an Overarching Problem
Display a football schedule for your school. Be sure the schedule indicates what team all members of the league play each week. Have students study the schedule. Students will continue to work on the investigation as they complete the exercises identified by the Investigation icon that is found throughout the chapter. These exercises will guide students through the task described in *Working Together*. Encourage students to keep all of their work on the Investigation together. Have students use the suggestions in the Chapter Investigation Extension to summarize their work.

### As a Chapter Project
The goal of this project is for students to create a simulation of the outcome of the games during a football season. Students can use the Group Project Planner on page 265 and the Project Planning Calendar on page 266 in the *Chapter 8 Resource Masters* to complete the project. Benchmarks **a**, **b**, and **c** should be completed after the lesson listed in parentheses has been studied. Benchmark **d** should be completed at the end of the chapter.

## Project Planning Calendar

Name _____  Date _____

**CHAPTER 8  PROJECT PLANNING CALENDAR**

Benchmarks
a. Use the information in the Chapter 8 Opener. Choose two of the top four teams in the football league. Write and solve a system of equations using substitution to find the point value of the league standings. *(Lesson 8-3)*
b. Choose two of the top four football teams, other than the pair chosen in Benchmark a. Write and solve a system of equations using addition, subtraction or multiplication. Verify that this is the same answer as that in Benchmark a. *(Lesson 8-4)*
c. Choose both systems of equations in Benchmarks a and b. Set up a matrix and solve each system... check that your answers in ... *(Lesson 8-5)*

PROJECT GOAL
To create a simulation of the outcome of the games during a football season.

## Group Project Planner

Name _____  Date _____

**CHAPTER 8  GROUP PROJECT PLANNER**

Assignment _____   Objective _____

Group Members          Assigned Roles
1) _____
2) _____
3) _____
4) _____
5) _____

Done _____

## Refresher Skills

The skills on these two pages are skills that have been presented in earlier chapters of this book or in previous math courses. Continuous review of basic math skills will make stronger math students. These skills are identified as necessary to be successful in Chapter 8.

### Skills Correlation Chart

| Skill | Lesson Number |
|---|---|
| Reciprocals | 8-1 |
| Slope of a Line | 8-1, 8-2 |
| Graphing Equations | 8-2 |
| Graphing Inequalities | 8-1, 8-7 |

### Vocabulary

slope of a line      y-intercept
slope-intercept form of a line
linear inequality in two variables

## Chalkboard Examples

### Reciprocals
Write the reciprocal of $-4$.  $-\dfrac{1}{4}$

### Slope of a Line
Use slope to determine if the three points $A(-1, 5)$, $B(0, 2)$, $C(1, -1)$ are collinear.

Find the slope of segment $AB$.  $m = \dfrac{2-5}{0-(-1)} = -\dfrac{3}{1}$

Find the slope of segment $BC$.  $m = \dfrac{-1-2}{1-0} = -\dfrac{3}{1}$

Since point $B$ is on both segments and the slopes are equal, the three points are collinear.

### Graphing Equations
Graph $2y + x = 6$.
Put the equation in slope-intercept form.

$y = -\dfrac{1}{2}x + 3$

$m = -\dfrac{1}{2} = \dfrac{-1}{2} = \dfrac{1}{-2}$

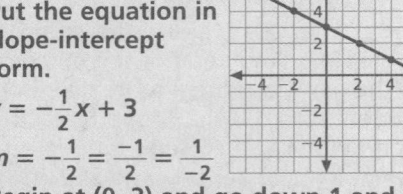

Begin at $(0, 3)$ and go down 1 and then right 2 for more points or go up 1 and then left 2 for more points.

---

The skills on these two pages are ones you have already learned. Use the examples to refresh your memory and complete the exercises. For additional practice on these and more prerequisite skills, see pages 576–584.

### RECIPROCALS

To find the *reciprocal* of a number, switch the numerator and denominator.

**Example**   Write the reciprocal of $\dfrac{2}{3}$.

The reciprocal of $\dfrac{2}{3}$ is $\dfrac{3}{2}$.

**Write the reciprocal of each number.**

1. $\dfrac{1}{2}$  $2$
2. $5$  $\dfrac{1}{5}$
3. $\dfrac{4}{5}$  $\dfrac{5}{4}$
4. $-\dfrac{2}{7}$  $-\dfrac{7}{2}$
5. $\dfrac{4}{3}$  $\dfrac{3}{4}$
6. $-6$  $-\dfrac{1}{6}$
7. $\dfrac{11}{12}$  $\dfrac{12}{11}$
8. $-\dfrac{9}{5}$  $-\dfrac{5}{9}$
9. $12$  $\dfrac{1}{12}$
10. $\dfrac{17}{15}$  $\dfrac{15}{17}$
11. $-\dfrac{1}{8}$  $-8$
12. $\dfrac{99}{100}$  $\dfrac{100}{99}$

### SLOPE OF A LINE

In this chapter you will solve systems of equations by graphing. It is helpful to be able to find the slope of a graphed equation.

**Example**   What is the slope of the line that includes points $A(-3, -2)$ and $B(4, 6)$?

Use the slope formula, $m = \dfrac{y_2 - y_1}{x_2 - x_1}$, where $(x_1, y_1)$ and $(x_2, y_2)$ are points on the line.

$m = \dfrac{y_2 - y_1}{x_2 - x_1}$

$m = \dfrac{6 - (-2)}{4 - (-3)}$

$m = \dfrac{8}{7}$

Since the slope is positive, the line slants upward to the right.

A line with a negative slope runs downward to the right.

The slope of a vertical line is undefined. The slope of a horizontal line is 0.

**Find the slope of a line that passes through the given points.**

13. $(-4, 2), (3, -8)$ $-\dfrac{10}{7}$
14. $(-5, -1), (0, 0)$ $\dfrac{1}{5}$
15. $(6, 2), (1, 4)$ $-\dfrac{2}{5}$
16. $(8, -6), (4, -2)$ $-1$
17. $(1, -5), (4, 0)$ $\dfrac{5}{3}$
18. $(-2, 1), (1, -2)$ $-1$
19. $(3, -1), (3, 5)$ undefined
20. $(4, 4), (-1, -1)$ $1$
21. $(0, 0), (2, 5)$ $\dfrac{5}{2}$
22. $(-2, -4), (-3, 1)$ $-5$
23. $(-4, -6), (-2, 1)$ $\dfrac{7}{2}$
24. $(0, 3), (6, 0)$ $-\dfrac{1}{2}$
25. $(4, -1), (-2, 1)$ $-\dfrac{1}{3}$
26. $(2, 9), (-4, 6)$ $\dfrac{1}{2}$
27. $(2, 5), (-4, 5)$ $0$
28. $(12, -6), (-3, 9)$ $-1$

### ADDITIONAL ANSWERS

29.
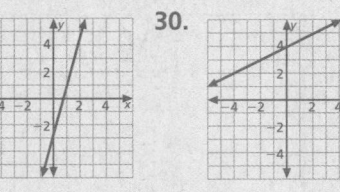

30.
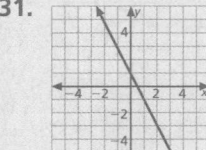

31.
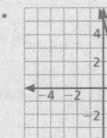

32.

33.
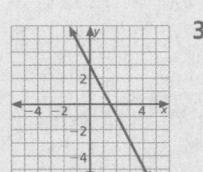

34.
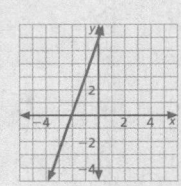

35.
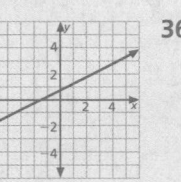

36.
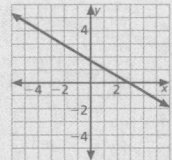

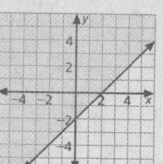
## GRAPHING EQUATIONS

You can graph any linear equation by identifying the slope of the line and the $y$-intercept.

**Example**   Graph the equation $y = 2x - 3$.

The slope is the coefficient of the $x$-term.

$$m = 2$$

The $y$-intercept is the constant term.

$$y\text{-intercept} = -3$$

Plot the point $(0, -3)$. Then use the slope of $\frac{2}{1}$ to plot two or three additional points.

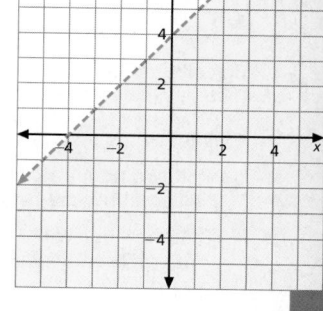

**Identify the slope and the $y$-intercept of each equation. Graph each equation.**   For 29–37, see additional answers.

**29.** $y = 4x - 3$  $4, -3$

**30.** $y = \frac{1}{2}x + 4$  $\frac{1}{2}, 4$

**31.** $y = -2x + 1$  $-2, 1$

**32.** $3x + y = 5$  $-3, 5$

**33.** $4y + 8x = 12$  $-2, 3$

**34.** $-3x + y = 6$  $3, 6$

**35.** $4y - 3 = 2x$  $\frac{1}{2}, \frac{3}{4}$

**36.** $2x - 5 = -3y$  $-\frac{2}{3}, \frac{5}{3}$

**37.** $3x + 2 = 3y$  $1, \frac{2}{3}$

## GRAPHING INEQUALITIES

**Example**   Graph the inequality $y < x + 4$.

To graph the inequality, first graph the equation related to the inequality: $y = x + 4$.

Since the inequality symbol is $<$, the line is not included in the solution. Therefore, the line should be a dashed line.

Choose a test point to determine if you shade above or below the dashed line. Choose $(0, 0)$.

$$y < x + 4$$
$$0 < 0 + 4$$
$$0 < 4$$

Since the test point results in a true statement, shade the half-plane that includes $(0, 0)$ as a solution.

**Graph each inequality.**   For 38–46, see additional answers.

**38.** $y > x - 2$

**39.** $y < 2x + 1$

**40.** $y \geq x - 4$

**41.** $y \leq 3x + 4$

**42.** $x + y > -3$

**43.** $2x \leq y - 4$

**44.** $3x - 4y \geq 8$

**45.** $y < 3 - 4x$

**46.** $3x - 2y > -6$

Chapter 8  **Are You Ready?**  333

## Refresher Wrap-up

### QUICK ASSESSMENT

Ask the following questions to determine if students have mastered the basic skills reviewed on these pages.

1. Consider the points $(-3, 6)$ and $(0, -4)$. If $-4 - 6$ is used in the numerator of the fraction for the slope, what expression should be used in the denominator?
   $0 - (-3)$

2. Consider the equation $3y = 2x - 6$. What are the slope and $y$-intercept of the graph?
   $m = \frac{2}{3}, b = -2$

3. Consider a line whose $y$-intercept is 4 and whose slope is $-2$. Using this slope and $y$-intercept, explain two different ways of getting points for a graph of this line.   **From the $y$-intercept, go down 2-right 1 or up 2-left 1.**

### ADDITIONAL PRACTICE

Refer to the Prerequisite Skills lessons beginning on page 576 for more practice.

**37.**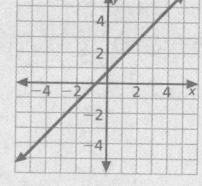

**38.**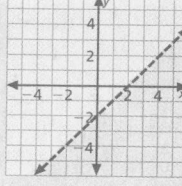

**39.**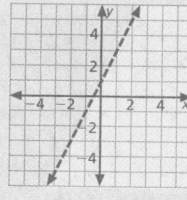

**40.**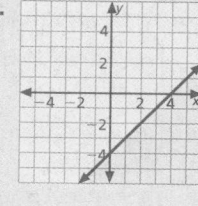

**41.**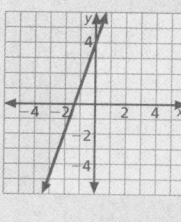

**42.**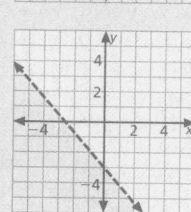

**43.**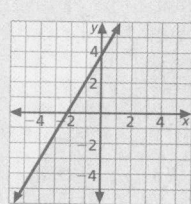

**44.**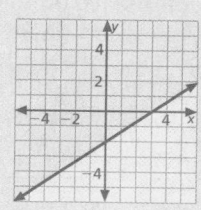

**45.**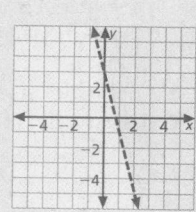

**46.**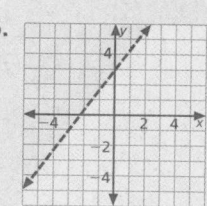

## Vocabulary

negative reciprocals

## Tools/Materials Needed

graph paper    graphing calculator

## Lesson Resources

Warm-up Transparency 31
Transparency TK-9–12
Reteaching 8-1
Extra Practice 8-1
Enrichment 8-1

## Getting Started

### 5-MINUTE WARM-UP

**Find the reciprocal of each number.**

**1.** $\frac{1}{4}$    4    **2.** $-\frac{2}{3}$    $-\frac{3}{2}$

**3.** 2.5    0.4    **4.** $1\frac{3}{4}$    $\frac{4}{7}$

### Introduction to Lesson 8-1

To begin, have students set the "usual" viewing window of $-10 < x < 10$ with x-scale = 1 and $-10 < y < 10$ with y-scale = 1. Students should then work on Questions 1–4. Note that with this viewing window, lines that are perpendicular will not look exactly so on the TI-84 Plus. After students have entered the equation from Question 4 and looked at the result with the original window, have them reset the window using  ZOOM  5. This viewing window gives a better perspective of perpendiculars.

---

# 8-1 Parallel and Perpendicular Lines

**Goals**
- Determine if two lines are parallel or perpendicular.
- Write equations of parallel and perpendicular lines.

**Applications**    Sports, Travel, Safety

**GRAPHING**  Use a graphing calculator for Questions 1–6.

**1.** Enter and graph these linear functions one at a time on your graphing calculator. Graph the functions on the same coordinate plane. Observe students' work.

   **a.** $y = 2x + 5$    **b.** $y = 2x + 1$    **c.** $y = 2x - 1$

**2.** Predict the location of the graph of $y = 2x - 6$.
   Parallel to a, b and c, but lower.
**3.** Use your graphing calculator to check your prediction in Question 2.  Observe students' work.

**4.** Enter and graph $y = -\frac{1}{2}x + 3$ on the same graph as the linear functions in Questions 1 and 2. What appears to be the relationship of this line to the other four lines?
   perpendicular
**5.** Predict the location of the graph of $y = -\frac{1}{2}x - 7$.  5. parallel to but below the graph of $y = -\frac{1}{2}x + 3$

**6.** Use your graphing calculator to check your prediction in Question 5.  Observe students' work.

## ▮ BUILD UNDERSTANDING

The following relationships exist between parallel lines.

   If two nonvertical lines are parallel, they have the same slope.

   If two distinct lines have the same slope, they are parallel.

Recall that two rational numbers that have a product of 1 are called reciprocals. If two rational numbers have a product of $-1$, they are called **negative reciprocals**.

The following relationships exist between perpendicular lines.

   If two nonvertical lines are perpendicular, the product of their slopes is $-1$. The slopes are negative reciprocals of each other.

   If the slopes of two lines are negative reciprocals of each other, then the lines are perpendicular.

### Example 1

For each line identified by two points, state the slope of a line parallel and the slope of a line perpendicular to it.

   **a.** $A(6, 3)$ and $B(4, 6)$    **b.** $C(-1, -5)$ and $D(3, -2)$

   **c.** $E(0, 5)$ and $F(-1, 6)$    **d.** $G(-4, -2)$ and $H(-5, -2)$

**334**    Chapter 8  **Systems of Equations and Inequalities**

## Teaching Tip

Suggest that students begin the study of a particular line by first writing its equation in slope-intercept form. Remind them that a graphing utility requires an equation to be in the form $y = $ (expression in x).

Suggest that students decide before graphing whether to expect that the graph will cross the y-axis above or below the origin. Ask them to tell how. **above if the constant term is positive and below if it is negative**  Students should also decide before graphing whether the graph will slant up or down. Ask them to tell how.  **up if the coefficient of x is positive and down if it is negative**

## Solution

Recall that $m = \dfrac{y_2 - y_1}{x_2 - x_1}$. The slope of the parallel line is $m$, and the slope of the perpendicular line is $\dfrac{-1}{m}$.

| Line | ∥ Line | ⊥ Line |
|---|---|---|
| **a.** $\dfrac{6-3}{4-6} = \dfrac{3}{-2} = -\dfrac{3}{2}$ | $-\dfrac{3}{2}$ | $\dfrac{2}{3}$ |
| **b.** $\dfrac{-2-(-5)}{3-(-1)} = \dfrac{3}{4} = \dfrac{3}{4}$ | $\dfrac{3}{4}$ | $-\dfrac{4}{3}$ |
| **c.** $\dfrac{6-5}{-1-0} = \dfrac{1}{-1} = -1$ | $-1$ | $1$ |
| **d.** $\dfrac{-2-(-2)}{-5-(-4)} = \dfrac{0}{-1} = 0$ | $0$ | undefined |

## Example 2

Determine if the graphs will show parallel or perpendicular lines, or neither.

**a.** $y = \dfrac{1}{3}x - 4$
$y = -3x + 1$

**b.** $y = -2x + \dfrac{1}{2}$
$6x + 3y = 9$

**c.** $y = 5x - 4$
$2x - 4y = 8$

## Solution

**a.** The lines are perpendicular since their slopes are negative reciprocals. $\quad \dfrac{1}{3} \cdot (-3) = -1$

**b.** Write the second equation in slope-intercept form to find the slope.
$6x + 3y = 9$
$y = -2x + 3 \qquad$ Subtract $6x$ and divide by 3.
The lines are parallel since they have the same slope, $m = -2$.

**c.** Write the second equation in slope-intercept form.
$2x - 4y = 8$
$y = \dfrac{1}{2}x - 2 \qquad$ Subtract $2x$ and divide by $-4$.
The lines are neither parallel nor perpendicular since $m = 5$ in the first equation and $m = \dfrac{1}{2}$ in the second equation.

### Technology Note

Use a graphing utility to check the solutions In Example 2. Graph each pair of lines on the same coordinate plane.

## Example 3

Write an equation in slope-intercept form of a line that passes through (2, 4) and is parallel to the line $y = -\dfrac{1}{2}x + 1$.

## Solution

The slope of the line is $-\dfrac{1}{2}$. Substitute $-\dfrac{1}{2}$ for $m$ and the point (2, 4) in slope-intercept form to solve for $b$.

$4 = -\dfrac{1}{2}(2) + b \qquad y = mx + b$
$4 = -1 + b$
$5 = b$

Use the values of $m$ and $b$ to write the equation of the line, $y = -\dfrac{1}{2}x + 5$.

 **Math** online  mathmatters2.com/extra_examples

### Supplementary Example 1

Consider line $\ell$ with a slope of 4.

**a.** Which of the following is the slope of a line that is parallel to line $\ell$?

　**A.** $-4$　**B.** $\dfrac{8}{2}$　**C.** $\dfrac{1}{4}$　**D.** $-\dfrac{1}{4}$

B; since parallel lines have the same slope, look for an expression that is equivalent to 4.

**b.** Which of the following could be the slope of a line that is perpendicular to line $\ell$?

　**A.** $-4$　**B.** 4　**C.** 0.25　**D.** $-0.25$

D; since the slopes of perpendicular lines are negative reciprocals, look for an expression that is equivalent to $-\dfrac{1}{4}$.

### Supplementary Example 2

Write an equation of the line that passes through $(-1, 3)$ and is parallel to the line $3y - 6x = 12$.

To write an equation of a line, you need two pieces of information. So far, you have a point on the line. Since parallel lines have the same slope, you can use the slope of the given line.

To find the slope of the given line, put its equation in slope-intercept form.

$3y - 6x = 12$
$3y - 6x + 6x = 6x + 12$
$3y = 6x + 12$
$y = 2x + 4$
slope $= 2$

To write an equation of the new line, substitute into the point-slope form.

$y - y_1 = m(x - x_1)$
$y - 3 = 2(x - [-1])$
$\qquad$ Use $m = 2$, $x_1 = -1$, $y_1 = 3$.
$y - 3 = 2(x + 1)$
$y - 3 = 2x + 2$
$y = 2x + 5$

So, $y = 2x + 5$ is an equation of the line that passes through $(-1, 3)$ and is parallel to $3y - 6x = 12$.

### Teaching Tip

Remind students that they know two different forms that are helpful in writing an equation when they know the slope and one point on the line: *slope-intercept form* and *point-slope form*.

In Example 3, the text shows how to use the slope-intercept form to write an equation of the line that passes through (2, 4) and is parallel to $y = -\dfrac{1}{2}x + 1$.

You may wish to demonstrate the use of the point-slope form, as shown at the right.

$y - y_1 = m(x - x_1)$
$y - 4 = -\dfrac{1}{2}(x - 2)$
$y - 4 = -\dfrac{1}{2}x + 1$
$y = -\dfrac{1}{2}x + 5$

## QUICK ASSESSMENT

Ask the following questions to determine if students understand the content presented in this lesson.

1. What does it mean to say that two numbers are *reciprocals*? **Their product is 1.** *negative reciprocals*? **Their product is −1.**
2. What is true about the slopes of all horizontal lines? **slope = 0** all vertical lines? **slope is undefined**
3. If you know the coordinates of the four vertices of a quadrilateral, how can you use slope to determine if the figure is a parallelogram? **If each pair of opposite sides has the same slope, both pairs of opposite sides are parallel, and the figure is a parallelogram.**

## ASSIGNMENT GUIDE

**Basic:** 1–39, 45–48
**Enriched:** 1–48

### Reteaching Worksheet 8-1

Name _____ Date _____

RETEACHING **8-1**
**PARALLEL AND PERPENDICULAR LINES**
If two lines are parallel, they have the same slope, or both slopes are undefined.

If two lines are perpendicular, the slope of one is the negative reciprocal of the slope of the other.

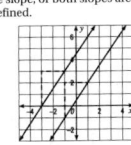

**Example 1**

Points $A(5, 4)$ and $B(-3, 4)$ are on line $AB$. Points $D(-5, 2)$ and $E(3, 2)$ are on line $DE$. Are $\overleftrightarrow{AB}$ and $\overleftrightarrow{DE}$ parallel, perpendicular, or neither?

**Solution**

Find the slope of each line.

slope of $\overleftrightarrow{AB} = \frac{4-4}{-3-5} = 0$

slope of $\overleftrightarrow{DE} = \frac{2-2}{3-(-5)} = 0$

Since $\overleftrightarrow{AB}$ and $\overleftrightarrow{DE}$ have the same slope, they are parallel.

**Example 2**

Points $G(-2, 6)$ and $H(2, 3)$ are on line $GH$. Points $J(2, 7)$ and $K(-1, 3)$ are on line $JK$. Are $\overleftrightarrow{GH}$ and $\overleftrightarrow{JK}$ parallel, perpendicular, or neither?

**Solution**

Find the slope of each line.

slope of $\overleftrightarrow{GH} = \frac{3-6}{2-(-2)} = \frac{-3}{4} = -\frac{3}{4}$

slope of $\overleftrightarrow{JK} = \frac{3-7}{-1-2} = \frac{-4}{-3} = \frac{4}{3}$

Since $-\frac{3}{4}$ and $\frac{4}{3}$ are negative reciprocals, lines $GH$ and $JK$ are perpendicular.

**✓ EXERCISES**

Points $W$ and $X$ are on $\overleftrightarrow{WX}$. $Y$ and $Z$ are on $\overleftrightarrow{YZ}$. Are $\overleftrightarrow{WX}$ and $\overleftrightarrow{YZ}$ parallel, perpendicular, or neither?

1. $W(-2, 4)$ $X(1, 1)$
   $Y(1, 2)$ $Z(5, -2)$
   **parallel**
2. $W(1, 3)$ $X(2, 6)$
   $Y(4, 4)$ $Z(7, 3)$
   **perpendicular**
3. $W(2, 1)$ $X(6, 2)$
   $Y(2, -2)$ $Z(6, -2)$
   **neither**
4. $W(-4, -6)$ $X(-2, -3)$
   $Y(1, -4)$ $Z(4, -6)$
   **perpendicular**
5. $W(-4, -6)$ $X(-2, -3)$
   $Y(-4, -4)$ $Z(-2, -1)$
   **parallel**
6. $W(-6, 4)$ $X(-4, 5)$
   $Y(-5, 5)$ $Z(-4, 3)$
   **perpendicular**

---

## Example 4

Write an equation in slope-intercept form of a line that passes through $(6, 5)$ and is perpendicular to the line $-6x - 2y = 12$.

### Solution

First write the equation in slope-intercept form.

$-6x - 2y = 12$

$y = -3x - 6$     Add $6x$ and divide by $-2$.

The slope is $-3$. The slope of a line perpendicular to this line is $\frac{1}{3}$. Substitute $\frac{1}{3}$ for $m$ and the point $(6, 5)$ in slope-intercept form.

$5 = \frac{1}{3}(6) + b$     $y = mx + b.$

$5 = 2 + b$

$3 = b$

The equation of the line is $y = \frac{1}{3}x + 3$.

### ▮ TRY THESE EXERCISES

For each line identified by two points, state the slope of a line parallel and the slope of a line perpendicular to it.

1. $A(7, 2)$ and $B(5, 7)$   $-\frac{5}{2}, \frac{2}{5}$
2. $C(1, 5)$ and $D(-2, 3)$   $\frac{2}{3}, -\frac{3}{2}$
3. $E(0, -2)$ and $F(-3, -5)$   $1, -1$

Determine if the graphs will show parallel or perpendicular lines, or neither.

4. $y = \frac{2}{3}x - 6$   **parallel**
   $2x - 4 = 3y$
5. $y = \frac{1}{2}x + 4$   **neither**
   $4x - 3y = 12$
6. $2y = 10x - \frac{2}{5}$   **perpendicular**
   $\frac{1}{5}x + y = 3$

Write an equation in slope-intercept form of a line passing through the given point and parallel to the given line.

7. $(2, -7); y = 3x - 1$
   $y = 3x - 13$
8. $(0, -5); 3x - 6y = 15$
   $y = \frac{1}{2}x - 5$
9. $(2, -1); 7y = 5x - 3$
   $y = \frac{5}{7}x - \frac{17}{7}$

Write an equation in slope-intercept form of a line passing through the given point and perpendicular to the given line.

10. $(-3, 1); \frac{1}{3}x + y = 2$
    $y = 3x + 10$
11. $(3, 7); y = \frac{3}{4}x - 1$
    $y = -\frac{4}{3}x + 11$
12. $(4, -3); 2x - 7y = 12$
    $y = -\frac{7}{2}x + 11$

### ▮ PRACTICE EXERCISES • For Extra Practice, see page 609.

For each line identified by two points, state the slope of a line parallel and the slope of a line perpendicular to it.

13. $M(-2, 3)$ and $N(2, 1)$   $-\frac{1}{2}, 2$
14. $P(-7, -3)$ and $Q(0, -1)$   $\frac{2}{7}, -\frac{7}{2}$
15. $F(-3, 3)$ and $G(2, -4)$   $-\frac{7}{5}, \frac{5}{7}$
16. $T(5, -1)$ and $U(-3, 1)$   $-\frac{1}{4}, 4$
17. $E(-4, 1)$ and $F(-4, 3)$   undefined, 0
18. $G(-5, 2)$ and $H(6, 4)$   $\frac{2}{11}, -\frac{11}{2}$

19. **WRITING MATH** Explain how you can tell from the coordinates of two points on a line whether the line is horizontal or vertical? See additional answers.

### Extend the Lesson

**CONNECTING TO PRIOR KNOWLEDGE** Ask students to write equations for two lines that, along with the coordinate axes, divide the plane into eight equal sections. **$y = x$ and $y = -x$** What do students notice about the slopes of these lines? **They are negative reciprocals, 1 and −1, because the lines are perpendicular.** Have students use a graphing utility to view the result to the coordinate plane when $y = x$ and $y = -x$ are graphed, eliciting that $y = x$ bisects Quadrants I and III, and that $y = -x$ bisects Quadrants II and IV. What name would students suggest for eight equal sections of the coordinate plane? *octants*

**Determine if the graphs will show parallel or perpendicular lines, or neither.**

**20.** $y = -7x + 1$  neither
$-7x + y = 1$

**21.** $3x + 4y = 12$  perpendicular
$y = \frac{4}{3}x - 5$

**22.** $y = x + 11$  perpendicular
$x + y = 0$

**23.** $y = -4 - 8x$  parallel
$16x + 2y = 18$

**24.** $y - 3 = 0$  parallel
$y = 6$

**25.** $y = \frac{4}{3}x + \frac{1}{3}$  neither
$3x - 4y = -20$

**Write an equation in slope-intercept form of a line passing through the given point and parallel to the given line.**

**26.** $(2, -1); y = -\frac{1}{2}x + 4$  $y = -\frac{1}{2}x$

**27.** $(-10, -8); 2x + 3y = -1$  $y = -\frac{2}{3}x - \frac{44}{3}$

**28.** $(5, 6); 3y + x = 3$  $y = -\frac{1}{3}x + \frac{23}{3}$

**29.** $(0, -6); -7x + y = 4$
$y = 7x - 6$

**30.** $(1.5, -0.5); x + y = 0$
$y = -x + 1$

**31.** $(-3, 2); 3y = -5x + 15$
$y = -\frac{5}{3}x - 3$

**Write an equation in slope-intercept form of a line passing through the given point and perpendicular to the given line.**

**32.** $(2, -1); 2x - 9y = 5$  $y = -\frac{9}{2}x + 8$

**33.** $(0, -1); 5x - y = 3$  $y = -\frac{1}{5}x - 1$

**34.** $(3, -3); 3x - 2y = -7$  $y = -\frac{2}{3}x - 1$

**35.** $(-4, 0); 7y = -2x - 1$  $y = \frac{7}{2}x + 14$

**36.** $(5, -6); -y = -2x + 4$  $y = -\frac{1}{2}x - \frac{7}{2}$

**37.** $(-1, 0); -\frac{2}{3}x - y = \frac{1}{2}$  $y = \frac{3}{2}x + \frac{3}{2}$

**38. SPORTS** The vertical drop of a ski slope is 1320 ft, and the horizontal distance traveled is 1 mi. What is the slope of the ski slope? (Hint: 1 mi = 5280 ft) $\frac{1}{4}$

**39. TRAVEL** An aircraft takes off following the path shown on the map. Another plane has $y = \frac{1}{3}x + 5$ as the equation of its take-off path. Graph the path of the second plane. Will the planes crash? Explain.  See additional answers. No. The planes will not crash since their paths are parallel.

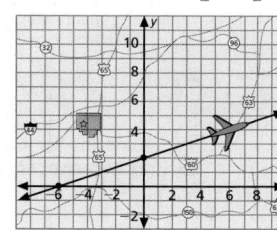

## ■ EXTENDED PRACTICE EXERCISES

**40.** Plot the points $A(1, 2)$, $B(5, 7)$, $C(9, 2)$ and $D(5, -3)$. How many segments do the points determine? Draw the segments and find their slopes. What is true of the opposite sides and diagonals? What type of quadrilateral is this? See additional answers.

**CRITICAL THINKING** Three lines, $l$, $m$, and $n$, lie on the same coordinate plane. Lines $l$ and $m$ are perpendicular and intersect at the point $(0, 3)$. Lines $m$ and $n$ are also perpendicular. Line $n$ is the graph of $y = \frac{3}{2}x + 4$.

**41.** Write the equation of line $m$.  $y = -\frac{2}{3}x + 3$

**42.** Write the equation of line $l$.  $y = \frac{3}{2}x + 3$

**43.** Graph the three lines.
See additional answers.

**44.** Describe the relationship of lines $l$ and $n$.
parallel

## ■ MIXED REVIEW EXERCISES

**Find the value of $y$ in each direct variation.** (Lesson 6-8)

**45.** Assume that $y$ varies directly as $x$. When $x = 3$, $y = 6$. Find $y$ when $x = 7$.  14

**46.** Assume that $y$ varies directly as $x$. When $x = 12$, $y = 7$. Find $y$ when $x = 42$.  24.5

**Find the value of $x$ in each figure.** (Lesson 5-2)

**47.**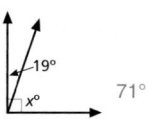
19°
71°
$x°$

**48.**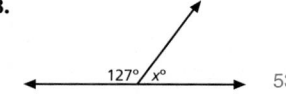
127° $x°$
53°

---

### Extra Practice Worksheet 8-1

Name _____  Date _____

EXTRA PRACTICE  **8-1**
**PARALLEL AND PERPENDICULAR LINES**

### ☑ EXERCISES

For each line identified by two points, state the slope of a line parallel and the slope of a line perpendicular to it.

**1.** $A(3, 2)$ and $B(5, 1)$        parallel: $-\frac{1}{2}$; perpendicular: 2

**2.** $C(-2, 0)$ and $D(-2, -4)$  parallel: undefined; perpendicular: 0

**3.** $M(-4, -3)$ and $N(-8, 8)$  parallel: $-\frac{11}{4}$; perpendicular: $\frac{4}{11}$

**4.** $X(3, -9)$ and $Y(-2, 7)$  parallel: $-\frac{16}{5}$; perpendicular: $\frac{5}{16}$

**5.** $R(4, -4)$ and $S(1, -3)$  parallel: $-\frac{1}{3}$; perpendicular: 3

Determine if the graphs will show parallel or perpendicular lines, or neither.

**6.** $y = -2x + 1$
$2x - 4y = 4$  perpendicular

**7.** $4x = 3y$
$y = -4x + 3$  neither

**8.** $x + y = 3$
$x - y = 5$  perpendicular

**9.** $y + 2 = 0$
$x + 2 = 0$  perpendicular

**10.** $y = \frac{2}{3}x - 1$
$3x - 2y = 2$  parallel

**11.** $x - 5y = 4$
$5x + y = 4$  perpendicular

Write an equation in slope-intercept form of a line passing through the given point and parallel to the given line.

**12.** $(-1, 2); y = 3x + 1$  $y = 3x + 5$

**13.** $(4, 2); x + y = 1$  $y = -x + 6$

**14.** $(0, -4); 2x + y = 3$  $y = -2x - 4$

**15.** $(5, -3); 4x + 5y = 10$  $y = -\frac{4}{5}x + 1$

Write an equation in slope-intercept form of a line passing through the given point and perpendicular to the given line.

**16.** $(-1, 2); y = 3x + 1$  $y = -\frac{1}{3}x + \frac{5}{3}$

**17.** $(4, 2); x + y = 1$  $y = x - 2$

**18.** $(3, 0); x - y = 4$  $y = -x + 3$

**19.** $(-7, -3); 2x + 4y = 8$  $y = 2x + 11$

### Enrichment Worksheet 8-1

Name _____  Date _____

ENRICHMENT  **8-1**
**GEOMETRIC FIGURES ON THE COORDINATE PLANE**
The distance formula and the formula for slope can be used to investigate the properties of figures in the coordinate plane. The slope of a horizontal line is 0. The slope of a vertical line is undefined.

**Example**

What kind of figure is $ABCD$ if its vertices are $A(1, -3)$, $B(4, 0)$, $C(4, 5)$ and $D(1, 2)$?

**Solution**
Begin by finding the slope of all four sides.

slope of $\overline{AB} = \frac{0 - (-3)}{4 - 1} = \frac{3}{3} = 1$

slope of $\overline{BC} = \frac{5 - 0}{4 - 4} = \frac{5}{0}$ = undefined

slope of $\overline{CD} = \frac{2 - 5}{1 - 4} = \frac{-3}{-3} = 1$

slope of $\overline{AD} = \frac{2 - (-3)}{1 - 1} = \frac{5}{0}$ = undefined

The figure has two pairs of parallel sides. It is a parallelogram. It cannot be a rectangle or a square since it does not have perpendicular sides. However, we must check to see whether or not it is a rhombus.

$\overline{AB}$ and $\overline{CD}$ have the same slope. $\overline{BC}$ and $\overline{AD}$ are both vertical.

To check if the figure is a rhombus, find the lengths of two adjacent sides.

$AB = \sqrt{(4 - 1)^2 + (0 - (-3))^2}$
$= \sqrt{9 + 9} = \sqrt{18} = 4.2$
$BC = \sqrt{(4 - 4)^2 + (0 - 5)^2}$
$= \sqrt{0 + 25} = \sqrt{25} = 5$

Since adjacent sides $\overline{AB}$ and $\overline{BC}$ are not congruent, the figure is not a rhombus. So, $ABCD$ is a parallelogram.

### ☑ EXERCISES

Classify each figure.

**1.** $X(-4, -3)$, $Y(0, 4)$, $Z(2, 1)$
$XYZ$ is a ___ right triangle ___

**2.** $G(-1, 3)$, $H(2, 3)$, $I(5, -2)$, $J(-2, -2)$
$GHIJ$ is a ___ trapezoid ___

**3.** $E(2, -1)$, $F(-1, -1)$, $G(-1, 3)$, $H(2, 3)$
$EFGH$ is a ___ rectangle ___

**4.** $P(-1, 3)$, $Q(3, 2)$, $R(2, -2)$, $S(-2, -1)$
$PQRS$ is a ___ square ___

---

## ADDITIONAL ANSWERS

**19.** If the line is a horizontal line, then the $y$-coordinates will be the same in each point. If the line is a vertical line, then the $x$-coordinates will be the same in each point.

**39.**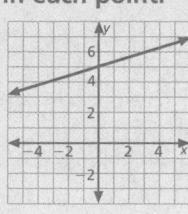

**40.**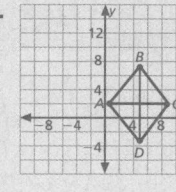

Six segments are determined.
slope of $\overline{AB} = \frac{5}{4}$,
slope of $\overline{BC} = -\frac{5}{4}$,
slope of $\overline{CD} = \frac{5}{4}$,
slope of $\overline{AD} = -\frac{5}{4}$,
slope of $\overline{AC} = 0$, slope of $\overline{BD}$ is undefined Opposite sides are parallel. Diagonals are perpendicular. The quadrilateral is a rhombus.

**43.**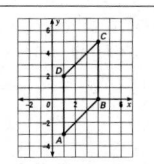

### Vocabulary

system of equations
solution of a system

### Tools/Materials Needed

graph paper    graphing calculator

### Lesson Resources

Warm-up Transparency 31
Transparency TK-9–12
Reteaching 8-2
Extra Practice 8-2
Enrichment 8-2
Technology Activity 8-2

## Getting Started

### 5-MINUTE WARM-UP

**Without graphing, determine if the given point is on the line whose equation is given.**

**1.** $(2, -13)$, $y = -5x - 3$   yes

**2.** $(0, -4)$, $y = -4x + \frac{1}{2}$   no

**3.** $(4, -3)$, $2x - 4y = 20$   yes

### Introduction to Lesson 8-2

The following questions will serve to summarize the key ideas of the completed activity.
Are there any points other than $(2, 3)$ that lie on the graphs of both $x = 2$ and $y = 3$?   no
What ordered pair is a solution to both $x = 2$ and $y = x$?   (2, 2)
What ordered pair is a solution to both $y = 3$ and $y = x$?   (3, 3)
For each pair of lines that intersect, how many solutions do there appear to be?   one

---

## 8-2  Solve Systems of Equations Graphically

**Goals**
- Determine if an ordered pair is a solution of a system of equations.
- Solve systems of linear equations graphically.

**Applications**   Sports, Safety, Economics

**Use the graph.**

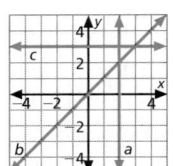

**1.** An equation for line $a$ is $x = 2$. Write three ordered pairs that are on line $a$. What do you notice?
$(2, 0), (2, 1), (2, -3)$; $x$-coordinate is 2

**2.** An equation for line $c$ is $y = 3$. Write three ordered pairs that are on line $c$. What do you notice?
$(1, 3), (0, 3), (-2, 3)$; $y$-coordinate is 3

**3.** Find an ordered pair that is a solution of both equations.   (2, 3)

**4.** An equation for line $b$ is $y = x$. Can you find an ordered pair that is a solution for all three equations? Why or why not?
No. Answers will vary, but may include that they do not all intersect at the same point.

### ▇ BUILD UNDERSTANDING

Two (or more) linear equations with the same two variables form a **system of equations**. A **solution of a system** of equations is an ordered pair that makes both equations true.

### Example 1

Determine whether the ordered pair $(-1, 6)$ is a solution of the system of equations.

$$2x + y = 4$$
$$x - y = -7$$

### Solution

Substitute $-1$ for $x$ and $6$ for $y$ in both equations.

$2x + y = 4$          $x - y = -7$

$2(-1) + 6 \stackrel{?}{=} 4$        $-1 - 6 \stackrel{?}{=} -7$

$-2 + 6 \stackrel{?}{=} 4$           $-7 = -7$ ✔

$4 = 4$ ✔

Since $(-1, 6)$ makes both equations true, it is a solution of the system of equations.

One way to solve a system of equations is to graph both equations on the same coordinate plane. All points of intersection are solutions of the system of equations. If the lines are parallel, there are no solutions.

**338**   Chapter 8  **Systems of Equations and Inequalities**

### Teaching Tip

Have students use a graphing calculator to display the system of Example 2a. Find coordinates for the point of intersection using both the TRACE and CALC feature. To use the CALC feature to find an intersection, select INTERSECT from the CALC menu. The display prompts, **"First curve?"** Students must press ENTER to select the first function. The display then prompts, **"Second curve?"** Students must press ▲ or ▼ and then ENTER to select the second function. Students must then move the cursor close to the location of the point of intersection of the two functions and press ENTER. The coordinates of the solution to the system are displayed at the bottom of the screen.

## Example 2

Solve each system of equations graphically. Check the solution.

a. $y = -2x + 4$
   $y = x - 2$

b. $y = 3x - 1$
   $y = 3x + 2$

### Solution

a. First graph each equation using the slope $m$ and the $y$-intercept $b$. Then read the solution from the graph.

$y = -2x + 4$    $b = 4; m = -2$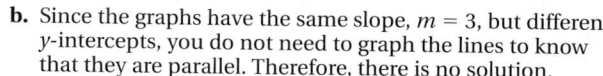

$y = x - 2$    $b = -2; m = 1$

The solution is $(2, 0)$, the point of intersection of the two lines.

To check the solution, substitute $(2, 0)$ in each equation.

$y = -2x + 4$        $y = x - 2$

$0 \stackrel{?}{=} -2(2) + 4$        $0 \stackrel{?}{=} 2 - 2$

$0 = 0$ ✔        $0 = 0$ ✔

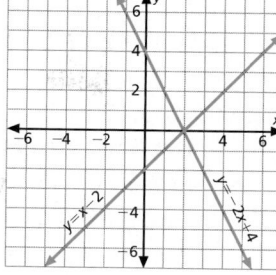

b. Since the graphs have the same slope, $m = 3$, but different $y$-intercepts, you do not need to graph the lines to know that they are parallel. Therefore, there is no solution.

## Example 3

Solve the system of equations.

$x + 3y = 6$
$3x + 2y = 4$

### Solution

First write each equation in slope-intercept form, $y = mx + b$.

$x + 3y = 6$        $3x + 2y = 4$

$3y = -x + 6$        $2y = -3x + 4$

$y = -\frac{1}{3}x + 2$        $y = -\frac{3}{2}x + 2$

Then graph each equation using $m$ and $b$.

$y = -\frac{1}{3}x + 2$        $b = 2$
                              $m = -\frac{1}{3}$

$y = -\frac{3}{2}x + 2$        $b = 2$
                              $m = -\frac{3}{2}$

The solution is $(0, 2)$.

 **Math Online** mathmatters2.com/extra_examples

> **Check Understanding**
>
> Explain how you would check the solution of Example 3.
>
> Substitute $(0, 2)$ into each equation.

### Supplementary Example 1

Tell whether the order pair $(3, 4)$ is a solution of the given system.

$x + y = 7$
$2x - y = 10$

Substitute $(3, 4)$ in both equations.

$x + y = 7$        $2x - y = 10$
$3 + 4 \stackrel{?}{=} 7$        $2(3) - 4 \stackrel{?}{=} 10$
$7 = 7$ ✓        $2 \neq 10$

So $(3, 4)$ is not a solution, since it does not satisfy both equations of the system.

### Supplementary Example 2

Graph the system and determine the area of the triangle formed.

$y = x$
$y = -3$
$y + x = 2$

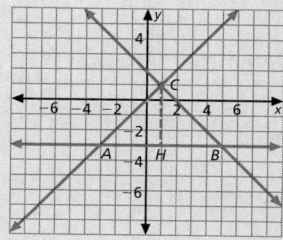

After graphing the three lines of the system, determine the coordinates of the points of intersection, which are the vertices of $\triangle ABC$.

Area of $\triangle ABC = \frac{1}{2}(AB)(CH)$

$= \frac{1}{2}(8)(4)$

$= 16$ square units

## Teaching Tip

Use Example 2 to note the three possibilities for a system of two linear equations and their graphs.

1. **The lines may intersect**, thus producing one ordered pair as the solution of the system (*consistent system*).
2. **The lines may be parallel**, thus producing no solution for the system (*inconsistent system*).
3. **The lines may coincide**, thus producing infinitely many ordered pairs as the solution of the system (*dependent system*).

## Lesson Wrap-up

### QUICK ASSESSMENT

Ask the following question to determine if students understand the content presented in this lesson.

1. If the two equations of a system are in the form $y = mx + b$, how can you tell without graphing if the system has a solution?   If the slopes are different, the lines intersect, and there is one solution to the system. If the slopes are the same and the $y$-intercepts are different, the lines are parallel, and the system has no solution. If the slopes are the same and the $y$-intercepts are the same, the two lines coincide and the system has infinitely many solutions.

### ASSIGNMENT GUIDE

**Basic:** 1–28, 35–38
**Enriched:** 1–38

### Reteaching Worksheet 8-2

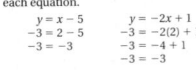

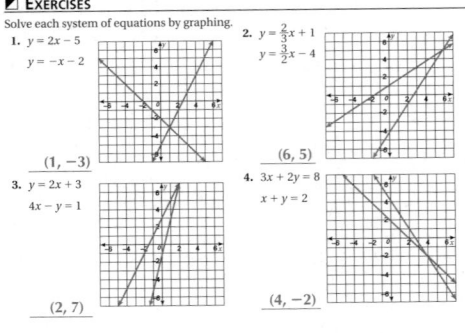

Name _____  Date _____

RETEACHING **8-2**

**SOLVE SYSTEMS OF EQUATIONS GRAPHICALLY**
The solution for a **system of linear equations** is an ordered pair that is a solution for each equation. On a graph, the solution is the point of intersection of the graphs of each of the equations.

**Example**

Solve the system of equations:   $y = x - 5$
                                  $y = -2x + 1$

**Solution**

First, graph each equation, using its slope and $y$-intercept. For the first equation, the slope is 1 and the $y$-intercept is $-5$. For the second equation, the slope is $-2$ and the $y$-intercept is 1.

The point of intersection of the two lines is $(2, -3)$. Check this solution by substituting $x = 2$ and $y = -3$ in each equation.

$$\begin{array}{ll} y = x - 5 & y = -2x + 1 \\ -3 = 2 - 5 & -3 = -2(2) + 1 \\ -3 = -3 & -3 = -4 + 1 \\ & -3 = -3 \end{array}$$

☑ **EXERCISES**

Solve each system of equations by graphing.

1. $y = 2x - 5$
   $y = -x - 2$
   $(1, -3)$

2. $y = \frac{2}{3}x + 1$
   $y = \frac{3}{2}x - 4$
   $(6, 5)$

3. $y = 2x + 3$
   $4x - y = 1$
   $(2, 7)$

4. $3x + 2y = 8$
   $x + y = 2$
   $(4, -2)$

**340**   Chapter 8   **Systems of Equations and Inequalities**

---

Graphing calculators can be used to find or check the solution of a system of equations. You can use the intersection or trace feature to estimate the coordinates of the point of intersection in a graph.

### Example 4

**GRAPHING** Use a graphing calculator to solve the system of equations.

$$2x + y = 3$$
$$x - y = 3$$

### Solution

First write the equations in slope-intercept form, $y = mx + b$.

$$\begin{array}{ll} 2x + y = 3 & x - y = 3 \\ y = -2x + 3 & y = x - 3 \end{array}$$

Then graph both equations on your graphing calculator.

To find the intersection of the two lines,

press 2nd [CALC] 5 ENTER ENTER ENTER .

The point of intersection is $(2, -1)$.

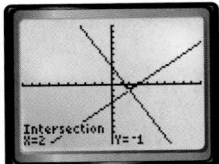

### ◤ TRY THESE EXERCISES

Determine if the given ordered pair is a solution of the system of equations.

1. $(2, 1)$; $3x - 2y = 6$   no
   $x + y = 2$

2. $(2, 5)$; $-4x + y = -3$   yes
   $2x + y = 9$

3. $(-1, 2)$; $y = 4x + 6$   yes
   $y = x + 3$

Solve each system of equations graphically. Check the solution.   For 4–6, see additional answers.

4. $y = 2x - 6$   $(2, -2)$
   $y = x - 4$

5. $2x + 3y = 3$   $(3, -1)$
   $3x + 4y = 5$

6. $y = -x - 1$   $(-2, 1)$
   $y = x + 3$

**SPORTS** Julian and Leticia are in a race together. Julian runs 8 ft/sec and Leticia runs 12 ft/sec. Suppose Leticia starts 10 ft behind Julian in the race.

7. Write an equation for both runners using $d = rt$, where $d =$ distance, $r =$ speed and $t =$ time.
   Julian: $d = 8t$; Leticia: $d = 12t - 10$

8. Graph both equations to determine when Leticia will catch Julian.   See additional answers.

### ▧ PRACTICE EXERCISES • For Extra Practice, see page 610.

Determine if the given ordered pair is a solution of the system of equations.

9. $(2, -3)$; $2x - y = 10$   no
   $x + 2y = -5$

10. $(1, 0)$; $3x + y = 3$   yes
    $x - 4y = 1$

11. $(0, 5)$; $y = 3x + 5$   yes
    $y = -3x + 5$

12. $(3, 5)$; $y = 4x - 7$   yes
    $y = -x + 8$

13. $(-2, 3)$; $y = 3x + 3$   no
    $y = -x + 1$

14. $(0.5, 1)$; $2x + 3y = 4$   yes
    $-8x - 2y = -6$

**340**   Chapter 8   **Systems of Equations and Inequalities**

### ADDITIONAL ANSWERS

4.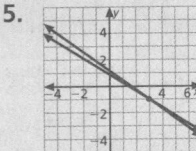

5.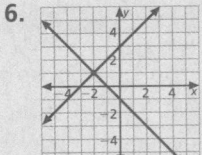

6.

8.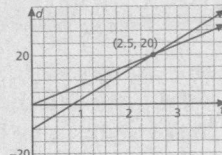

15.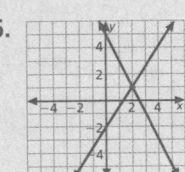

16.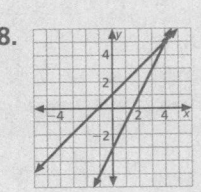

18.

For 17, 19, and 21, see Selected Answers on page 689.

**Solve each system of equations graphically. Check the solution.** For 15–22, see additional answers.

**15.** $y = -x + 7$ (4, 3)
$y = 2x - 5$

**16.** $3x - 2y = 4$ (2, 1)
$2x + y = 5$

**17.** $y = -3x + 4$ (1, 1)
$y = -x + 2$

**18.** $y = x + 1$ (4, 5)
$y = 2x - 3$

**19.** $2x - 2y = 4$ (5, 3)
$x + y = 8$

**20.** $3y - x = 7$ (2, 3)
$y - x = 1$

**21.** $y = -2x + 3$ (2, −1)
$y = 2x - 5$

**22.** $3x - 2y = 4$ (2, 1)
$2x + y = 5$

**GRAPHING** Use a graphing calculator to solve each system of equations. Round to the nearest hundredth, if necessary.

**23.** $y = -x$
$y = -x + 7$
no solution

**24.** $y = -5x - 13$
$y = -4x - 10$
(−3, 2)

**25.** $2x + y = 16$
$x - 3y = 9$
(8.14, −0.29)

**26.** $5x + 6y = 24$
$-7x + y = -29$
(4.21, 0.49)

**27. SAFETY** The position of an accident on a highway is located at $P(4, -6)$ on a map grid. Three emergency vehicles travel on paths given by the following equations. Which of the vehicles will arrive exactly at the site of the accident?
c, the police car
**a.** fire truck: $x - 12 = 2y$　**b.** ambulance: $y = -10 - x$　**c.** police car: $x - 5y = 34$

**28. WRITING MATH** Write a paragraph explaining why the intersection of two lines is the solution of a system of equations. Answers will vary.

## ■ EXTENDED PRACTICE EXERCISES

**Solve each system of equations. State the number of solutions.**

**29.** $y = 4x - 2$　1 solution
$x - 4y = 2$

**30.** $y = 7 - 3x$　infinitely many
$6x + 2y = 14$　solutions

**31.** $y = 2x - 8$　no solution
$2x - y = 10$

**32. CRITICAL THINKING** Use the results in Exercises 29–31 to describe how you can determine the number of solutions for a system of equations by comparing the slopes and the y-intercepts. See additional answers.

**33. YOU MAKE THE CALL** Carla says she can determine the x-value of the point of intersection of any two lines, $y = m_1 x + b_1$ and $y = m_2 x + b_2$. She says that $x = \dfrac{b_2 - b_1}{m_1 - m_2}$. Test her conjecture with the two equations in Exercise 15. See additional answers.

**34. ECONOMICS** When Lorinda graduated from college, she was offered two jobs. One paid an annual salary of $30,000 plus guaranteed increases of $2000/yr. The other job paid an annual salary of $25,000 plus guaranteed increases of $2500/yr. Considering only this information, which job should Lorinda take? Explain why.
Explanations will vary but may include that the salaries are the same in the 11th year.

## ■ MIXED REVIEW EXERCISES

**Find the distance between the points. Round to the nearest tenth.** (Lesson 6-1)

**35.** (−4, 2), (3, 8)　9.2

**36.** (−2, −5), (4, 6)　12.5

**37.** (8, 4), (3, −6)　11.2

**38.** Judges at the county fair judge under a weighted system. Judge 1 has a weight of 1, Judge 2 has a weight of 2, Judge 3 has a weight of 3 and Judge 4 has a weight of 4. There are a total of 10 scores. Pies are scored from 1 to 6, with 6 being the most tasty. Determine the total scores on the score sheet. Which pie won the contest? (Lesson 1-2)
27, 42, 30, 33; Pie B

|  | Pie A | Pie B | Pie C | Pie D |
|---|---|---|---|---|
| Judge 1 | 2 | 5 | 6 | 4 |
| Judge 2 | 4 | 3 | 5 | 3 |
| Judge 3 | 3 | 5 | 2 | 1 |
| Judge 4 | 2 | 4 | 2 | 5 |
| Total score | ■ | ■ | ■ | ■ |

Math Online mathmatters2.com/self_check_quiz

**20.**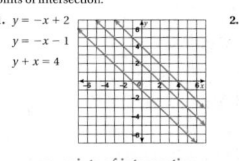

**22.**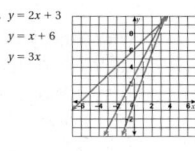

**32.** If the equations yield different slopes, then there is only one solution. If they yield the same slope and the same y-intercept, then there are an infinite number of solutions. If they yield the same slope and different y-intercepts, then the lines are parallel and there are no solutions.

**33.** $y = -x + 7$　$m_1 = -1, b_1 = 7$
$y = 2x - 5$　$m_2 = 2, b_2 = -5$
$x = \dfrac{b_2 - b_1}{m_1 - m_2}$
$x = \dfrac{-5 - 7}{-1 - 2} = \dfrac{-12}{-3} = 4$

---

### Extra Practice Worksheet 8-2

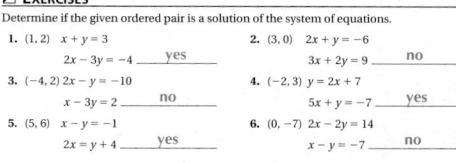

Name _____ Date _____

EXTRA PRACTICE **8-2**
**SOLVE SYSTEMS OF EQUATIONS GRAPHICALLY**

**☑ EXERCISES**

Determine if the given ordered pair is a solution of the system of equations.

**1.** (1, 2)　$x + y = 3$
$2x - 3y = -4$　yes

**2.** (3, 0)　$2x + y = -6$
$3x + 2y = 9$　no

**3.** (−4, 2)　$2x - y = -10$
$x - 3y = 2$　no

**4.** (−2, 3)　$y = 2x + 7$
$5x + y = -7$　yes

**5.** (5, 6)　$x - y = -1$
$2x = y + 4$　yes

**6.** (0, −7)　$2x - 2y = 14$
$x - y = -7$　no

Solve each system of equations graphically. Check the solution.

**7.** $x + y = 5$
$x - y = -1$　(2, 3)

**8.** $y = -3x + 5$
$x - y = 7$　(3, −4)

**9.** $x = y - 4$
$x + 2y = 2$　(−2, 2)

**10.** $2x + 2y = 6$
$3x - y = -7$　(−1, 4)

**11.** $2x - y = -2$
$4x + y = 5$　$\left(\frac{1}{2}, 3\right)$

**12.** $x - y = 5$
$5x + y = -5$　(0, −5)

**13.** $2x - 3y = -3$
$y = x$　(3, 3)

**14.** $x - 2y = -8$
$3x + y = 4$　(0, 4)

**15.** $x = 2y + 1$
$y = 2x - 8$　(5, 2)

**16.** $2x + 6y = -4$
$y = 3x + 6$　(−2, 0)

Use a graphing utility to solve the system of equations.

**17.** $y = -x$
$x = y - 2$　(−1, 1)

**18.** $y = x + 12$
$y = \frac{1}{2}x + 7$　(−10, 2)

**19.** $x + y = 4$
$y = -\frac{2}{3}x + 1$　(9, −5)

**20.** $y = -x + 2$
$x - 2y = 20$　(8, −6)

---

### Enrichment Worksheet 8-2

Name _____ Date _____

ENRICHMENT **8-2**
**GRAPHS OF THREE LINES**

When three linear equations are graphed on the same set of axes, they may intersect at three, two, one, or no points.

**Example**

Graph $y = x + 1$, $y + x = -3$ and $y = 2x$ on the same set of axes. How many points of intersection are there? Name the points of intersection.

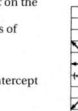

**Solution**

Graph each equation using its slope–intercept form.
$y = x + 1$; $m = 1, b = 1$
$y = -x - 3$; $m = -1, b = -3$
$y = 2x$; $m = 2, b = 0$

The lines intersect in three points, (−2, −1), (−1, −2) and (1, 2).

**☑ EXERCISES**

Graph each set of three equations on the same coordinate plane. Find and name the points of intersection.

**1.** $y = -x + 2$
$y = -x - 1$
$y + x = 4$
no points of intersection

**2.** $y = 2x + 3$
$y = x + 6$
$y = 3x$
1 point; (3, 9)

**3.** Describe the conditions under which three lines would have no points of intersection.
All three lines are parallel.

**4.** Describe the conditions under which three lines would intersect in exactly two points.
Two lines are parallel, and the other intersects them.

### Vocabulary Review

**Lesson 8-1**
negative reciprocals

**Lesson 8-2**
system of equations
solution of a system

## ASSIGNMENT GUIDE

**All students: 1–45**

## Chalkboard Examples

### Lesson 8-1
**a.** Which of the following lines is parallel to the line $y = 4x - 3$?
**C**
A. $4x + y = 9$　　B. $2y = 4x - 7$
C. $4x - y = 2$　　D. $x + 4y = 8$

**b.** Which of the following lines is perpendicular to the line $y = 2x + 4$?　**D**
A. $y = 4x - 2$　　B. $2y = x - 4$
C. $y = 4 - 2x$　　D. $2y = 4 - x$

**c.** Which of the following lines passes through $(0, -4)$ and is parallel to the line $2y = 8x + 1$?　**B**
A. $y = 8x - 3$　　B. $y = 4x - 4$
C. $y = 3 - 8x$　　D. $y = 3x - 4$

### Lesson 8-2
**a.** Which of the following points is the solution of the given system?

$y = x + 1$　　**C**
$2y + x = -4$

A. $(-1, -2)$　　B. $(-2, 1)$
C. $(-2, -1)$　　D. $(0, -2)$

**b.** Which of the following is true about the lines in the given system?　**D**

$x + 2y = 7$
$2x - y = -1$

A. They are parallel.
B. They coincide.
C. They intersect, but are not perpendicular.
D. They are perpendicular.

---

## PRACTICE ▮ LESSON 8-1

For each line identified by two points, state the slope of a line parallel and a slope of a line perpendicular to it.

**1.** $A(1, 2)$ and $B(5, 7)$　$\frac{5}{4}, -\frac{4}{5}$
**2.** $C(-3, -4)$ and $D(-1, 6)$　$5, -\frac{1}{5}$
**3.** $E(1, 1)$ and $F(-2, 3)$　$-\frac{2}{3}, \frac{3}{2}$

**4.** $G(0, 4)$ and $H(-2, 2)$　$1, -1$
**5.** $I(1, 5)$ and $J(-6, 2)$　$\frac{3}{7}, -\frac{7}{3}$
**6.** $K(2, 2)$ and $L(-2, 5)$　$-\frac{3}{4}, \frac{4}{3}$

Determine if the graphs will show parallel or perpendicular lines, or neither.

**7.** $y = 2x - 2$　neither
$2x + y = -5$

**8.** $3x + 2y = 4$　parallel
$y = \frac{-3}{2}x + 1$

**9.** $y - 2 = 0$　parallel
$y = 5$

**10.** $x + y = 12$　perpendicular
$-x + y = -1$

**11.** $3x - 4y = 1$　neither
$y = -3x + 1$

**12.** $y = \frac{1}{2}x$　perpendicular
$y + 2x = 2$

Write an equation in slope-intercept form of a line passing through the given point and parallel to the given line.

**13.** $(3, -2); y - 3x = 2$
$y = 3x - 11$

**14.** $(-3, 3); 2x + y = 4$
$y = -2x - 3$

**15.** $(-1, 3); 2y = 4x - 8$
$y = 2x + 5$

Write an equation in slope-intercept form of a line passing through the given point and perpendicular to the given line.

**16.** $(-3, -2); y = 3x + 2$
$y = -\frac{1}{3}x - 3$

**17.** $(1, 3); x - 3y = 9$
$y = -3x + 6$

**18.** $(-1, 4); y = 7 - 3x$
$y = \frac{1}{3}x + \frac{13}{3}$

## PRACTICE ▮ LESSON 8-2

Determine if the given ordered pair is a solution of the system of equations.

**19.** $(1, 2); 2x + y = 5$　no
$x - 2y = -4$

**20.** $(1, 1); y = x$　yes
$y = 2 - x$

**21.** $(-4, 3); y = \frac{1}{2}x + 5$　yes
$2x + y = -5$

**22.** $(6, 5); y = x - 1$　yes
$x + y = 11$

**23.** $(-3, 2); y = \frac{2}{3}x + 1$　no
$y = 2x - 2$

**24.** $(0, -6); y = x - 6$　no
$y = 4x + 6$

Solve each system of equations graphically. Check the solution.　For 25–30, see additional answers.

**25.** $x - y = 2$　$(3, 1)$
$2x + 3y = 9$

**26.** $y = x$　$(2, 2)$
$x + y = 4$

**27.** $x + y = 6$　$(4, 2)$
$x - y = 2$

**28.** $x + 2y = 7$　$(1, 3)$
$y = 2x + 1$

**29.** $x + y = 3$　$(0, 3)$
$y = x + 3$

**30.** $y = x - 4$　$(3, -1)$
$2x + y = 5$

 **GRAPHING** Use a graphing calculator to solve the system of equations.

**31.** $y = -x + 7$　$(4, 3)$
$y = 2x - 5$

**32.** $3y = x + 7$　$(2, 3)$
$y = x + 1$

**33.** $3x + y = 4$　$(1, 1)$
$x + y = 2$

## Teaching Tip

In Exercises 13–18, students are given the coordinates of a point on a line and information sufficient to determine the slope of the line. Although the requirement is to write a linear equation in slope-intercept form, remind students that they can substitute their information into the point-slope form of a line. Simple manipulation (isolating the $y$-term by adding the relevant constant to each side of the equation) will then put the equation in slope-intercept form.

Running races are the most prominent track-and-field events. They range in length from the indoor 50-meter dash to the outdoor marathon, which is 26.2 mi long.

Students should answer Questions 1–4 to better understand how a runner might use systems of equations in a training program.

Modern track and field traces its origin to the first Olympian Games of Greece, which were staged more than 2,500 years ago. While the rules of 21st-century competition are quite different from those of ancient times, the spirit of the sport remains true to its early Greek roots. The modern Olympic motto *Citius, Altius, Fortius* (faster, higher, stronger) best captures track-and-field competition. Each event determines who can run the fastest, who can jump the highest or the longest, or who can throw the farthest.

Students who are interested in learning more about this career choice can go to mathmatters2.com/mathworks. School Guidance Counselors are another resource for information about training requirements and appropriate schools.

## PRACTICE ■ LESSON 8-1–LESSON 8-2

**Determine if the given ordered pair is a solution of the system of equations.** (Lesson 8-2)

**34.** $(-2, -1)$; $y = 2x + 3$   yes
$\qquad\quad y = -2x - 5$

**35.** $(2, -3)$; $y = 2x - 5$   no
$\qquad\quad x + y = 7$

**36.** $(4, 1)$; $4x + y = 17$   yes
$\qquad\quad 2x + 4y = 12$

**Solve each system of equations graphically. Check the solution.** (Lesson 8-2)   For 37–39, see additional answers.

**37.** $x + y = 5$   $(2, 3)$
$\quad\;\; x - 2y = -4$

**38.** $y = -3x$   $(2, -6)$
$\quad\;\; 4x + y = 2$

**39.** $y = -x$   $(1, -1)$
$\quad\;\; x - y = 2$

**Write an equation in slope-intercept form of a line passing through the given point and parallel to the given line.** (Lesson 8-1)

**40.** $(-3, 1)$; $y = -\frac{1}{2}x + 1$   $y = -\frac{1}{2}x - \frac{1}{2}$

**41.** $(-2, -1)$; $x - y = 0$   $y = x + 1$

**42.** $(1, 1)$; $2x + 3y = -2$   $y = -\frac{2}{3}x + \frac{5}{3}$

**Write an equation in slope-intercept form of a line passing through the given point and perpendicular to the given line.** (Lesson 8-1)

**43.** $(-3, 4)$; $-3x + 2y = 3$   $y = -\frac{2}{3}x + 2$

**44.** $(-6, -1)$; $2x + y = 3$   $y = \frac{1}{2}x + 2$

**45.** $(1, 2)$; $y = \frac{x}{3} - 3$   $y = -3x + 5$

## Career – Runner

A runner has been practicing for an upcoming track and field meet in Europe, trying to improve her time in the mile run by 0.1 min every month. Unfortunately, 8 mo before the event, she sustained an ankle injury that did not allow her to run for 2 mo. When she began running again, she ran the mile in 4.5 min, 0.75 min slower than before her injury. Hoping to still participate in the track and field meet, she set a goal of improving her time by 0.2 min each month for the remaining 6 mo before the meet.   For 1–4, see additional answers.

1. Write an equation in slope-intercept form for her time ($t$) to run 1 mi as a function of the number of months ($m$) of training, beginning with 6 mo before the track and field meet. Write one equation assuming that she did not have an injury and a second equation describing her performance with the injury.

2. Graph each of these equations on the same set of axes. Do these lines intersect? If so, where do they intersect? If not, why don't they intersect?
yes, (7.5, 3)

3. Draw the line $t = 3.75$ min on the graph that was drawn in Exercise 2. Where does this line intersect the line representing the runner's performance after her injury? What does the $x$-value of this point of intersection represent?   (3.75, 3.75)

4. When the track and field meet begins, what speed will she have achieved in the mile run? If she had not injured her ankle, what speed would she have run at the start of the track and field meet?

## MATHWORKS

**1.** $t = 4.5 - 0.2m$; $t = 3.75 - 0.1m$

**2.**
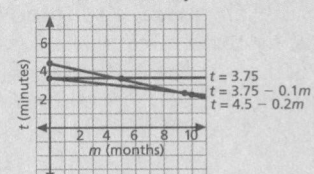

**3.** the number of months it took the runner to achieve the time she would have run a mile 6 mo before the meet if the injury had never occurred

**4.** 1 mi/3.3 min; 1 mi/3.15 min

**39.**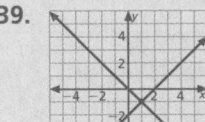

## ADDITIONAL ANSWERS

**25.** 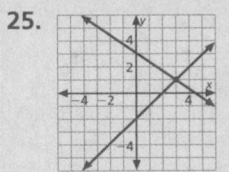   **26.**   **27.** 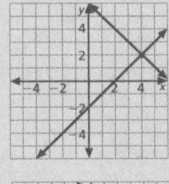   **28.**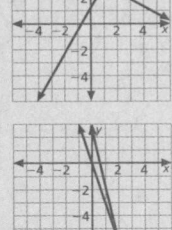

**29.** 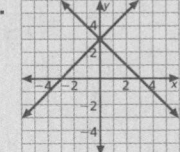   **30.** 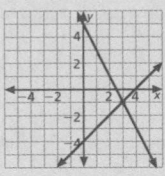   **37.** 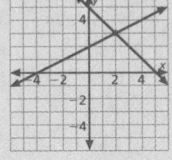   **38.**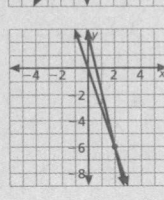

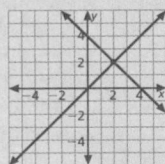

### Vocabulary

substitution

### Tools/Materials Needed

graphing calculator

### Lesson Resources

Warm-up Transparency 32
Reteaching 8-3
Extra Practice 8-3
Enrichment 8-3

## Getting Started

### 5-Minute Warm-up

**Solve each equation for the indicated variable.**

1. $-x - y = 4$ for $y$    $y = -x - 4$

2. $3y - 2x = 0$ for $x$    $x = \frac{3y}{2}$

3. $y = -2x + 4$ for $x$    $x = -\frac{y}{2} + 2$

### Introduction to Lesson 8-3

After students have guessed at the coordinates of the meeting place, have them use what they know about slope and $y$-intercept to estimate an equation for each ship's course. Then students should solve their equations graphically (using a graphing utility) and compare the solution to their guess. If solutions differ greatly from guesses, discuss possible causes of the discrepancy (including the difficulty in estimating slopes and $y$-intercepts).

---

# 8-3 Solve Systems by Substitution

**Goals** ■ Solve systems of equations using substitution.

**Applications** Transportation, Construction, Sports, Recreation

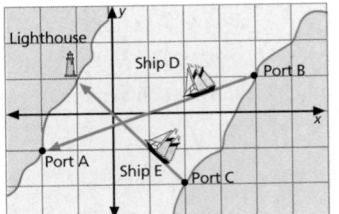

**TRANSPORTATION** The two ships shown on the map will stop in the middle of the strait in order to meet and exchange some cargo.

1. Make a guess at the coordinates of the meeting place.

2. Compare your solutions with those of other classmates.

3. Did you all agree on the coordinates? Why or why not?

For 1–3, answers will vary. Coordinates will probably differ slightly due to difficulty of estimating fractional units on a grid.

### ▶ BUILD UNDERSTANDING

When a system of equations is difficult to solve by reading the graph, you can use algebraic methods to solve it. One of these methods is **substitution**. In any algebraic method, you need to eliminate variables so you have one equation in one variable. Here are the steps to follow when using the substitution method.

1. Solve one of the equations for one variable. It will be in terms of the other.

2. Substitute that expression in the other equation and solve.

3. Substitute that value in one of the original equations and solve.

4. Check the solution in both of the original equations.

### Example 1

Solve the system of equations. Check the solution.

$$x - 2y = 3$$
$$x + y = 6$$

**Solution**

| | |
|---|---|
| $x + y = 6$ | Solve the second equation for $y$ in terms of $x$. |
| $y = -x + 6$ | |
| $x - 2y = 3$ | Write the first equation. |
| $x - 2(-x + 6) = 3$ | Substitute $(-x + 6)$ for $y$. |
| $x + 2x - 12 = 3$ | Solve for $x$. |
| $3x - 12 = 3$ | |
| $3x - 12 + 12 = 3 + 12$ | |
| $\frac{3x}{3} = \frac{15}{3}$ | |
| $x = 5$ | |

**Problem Solving Tip**

When deciding which equation to solve for a variable, use the equation that has a variable with a coefficient of 1.

## Teaching Tip

You may wish to suggest that when students are deciding which equation to use to express one variable in terms of the other, they think about which of the two given equations more easily lends itself to being put into the familiar $y = mx + b$ form. Point out that when an equation is in this form, it does express the variable $y$ in terms of the variable $x$.

Choose one of the original equations.

$$x + y = 6$$

$$5 + y = 6 \qquad \text{Substitute 5 for } x.$$

$$-5 + 5 + y = 6 - 5 \qquad \text{Solve for } y.$$

$$y = 1$$

Check $x = 5$ and $y = 1$ in each original equation.

$$x - 2y = 3 \qquad\qquad x + y = 6$$

$$5 - 2(1) \stackrel{?}{=} 3 \qquad\qquad 5 + 1 \stackrel{?}{=} 6$$

$$3 = 3 \ \checkmark \qquad\qquad 6 = 6 \ \checkmark$$

The solution is (5, 1).

## Example 2

**CONSTRUCTION** M & K Construction Company sends 29 workers out in two crews. One crew has 5 more than twice the number of workers in the other crew. How many workers are in each crew?

### Solution

Define each of the variables. Write and solve a representative system of equations.

Let $n$ = number of workers in larger crew

$s$ = number of workers in smaller crew

There are 29 workers.

$$n + s = 29 \qquad \text{This equation is ready for substitution.}$$

The larger crew has 5 more than twice the smaller.

$$n = 2s + 5$$

$$n + s = 29$$

$$(2s + 5) + s = 29 \qquad \text{Substitute } (2s + 5) \text{ for } n.$$

$$3s + 5 = 29 \qquad \text{Solve for } s.$$

$$3s + 5 - 5 = 29 - 5$$

$$\frac{3s}{3} = \frac{24}{3}$$

$$s = 8$$

$$n + s = 29 \qquad \text{Substitute 8 for } s.$$

$$n + 8 = 29 \qquad \text{Solve for } n.$$

$$n + 8 - 8 = 29 - 8$$

$$n = 21$$

The larger crew has 21 workers.
The smaller crew has 8 workers.

**Check**

$$\begin{array}{ll} n + s = 29 & n = 2s + 5 \\ 21 + 8 \stackrel{?}{=} 29 & 21 \stackrel{?}{=} 2(8) + 5 \\ 29 = 29 \ \checkmark & 21 \stackrel{?}{=} 16 + 5 \\ & 21 = 21 \ \checkmark \end{array}$$

**Check Understanding**

In Example 1, if you solve for $x$ instead of $y$, how does the solution change?

no change

### Supplementary Example 1

Solve the system of equations and check.

$$4x + 3y = 27 \quad \text{A}$$

$$2x - y = 1 \quad \text{B}$$

In equation [B], solve for $y$ in terms of $x$.

$$2x - y = 1$$

$$-y = -2x + 1$$

$$y = 2x - 1 \quad \text{C}$$

Substitute the expression for $y$ into equation [A].

$$4x + 3y = 27$$

$$4x + 3(2x - 1) = 27$$

Solve the resulting equation for $x$.

$$4x + 6x - 3 = 27$$

$$10x - 3 = 27$$

$$10x = 30$$

$$x = 3$$

Substitute 3 for $x$ in equation [C] and solve for $y$.

$$y = 2x - 1$$

$$y = 2(3) - 1$$

$$y = 5$$

Check: (3, 5) in each of the original equations. The solution is (3, 5).

### Supplementary Example 2

**NUMBER SENSE** In a two-digit number, the sum of the digits is 9. The number is 12 times the tens digit. Find the number.

Let $t$ = the tens digit and $u$ = the units digit.

Then $10t + u$ = the number.

The sum of the digits is 9.

$$t + u = 9 \quad \text{A}$$

The number is 12 times the tens digits.

$$10t + u = 12t \quad \text{B}$$

To solve the system, in equation [A], solve for $u$.

$$t + u = 9$$

$$u = 9 - t \quad \text{C}$$

Substitute the expression for $u$ into equation [B].

$$10t + u = 12t$$

$$10t + (9 - t) = 12t$$

Solve the resulting equation for $t$.

$$9t + 9 = 12t$$

$$9 = 3t$$

$$3 = t$$

Substitute 3 for $t$ in equation [C] and solve for $u$.

$$u = 9 - t$$

$$u = 9 - 3$$

$$u = 6$$

Check the result by referring to the problem. The number is 36.

## Teaching Tip

In Example 1, after the value for $x$ has been found, point out to students that they may use the form of the second equation that they have already solved for $y$ to determine the corresponding value of $y$. It is only when checking the system that it is required to go back to the original equations. As shown in Supplementary Examples 1 and 2, a useful technique is to label equations for easy reference during discussion of the solution process.

## Lesson Wrap-up

### QUICK ASSESSMENT

Ask the following questions to determine if students understand the content presented in this lesson.

**1.** What is the relationship between the solution to a system of equations and the graphs of the equations?   The solution is an ordered pair, which are the coordinates of the point of intersection of the graphs.

**2.** Describe how to check the solution to a system of equations. Substitute the values into each original equation of the system.

### ASSIGNMENT GUIDE

**Basic:** 1–34, 40–48
**Enriched:** 1–48

### Reteaching Worksheet 8-3

Name _____ Date _____

RETEACHING **8-3**
**SOLVE SYSTEMS BY SUBSTITUTION**
Algebraic methods can be used to solve systems of equations.
One algebraic method is **substitution**.

**Example 1**

Solve the system of equations.
$x + y = 4$
$2x - y = 5$

**Solution**
Solve one equation for $y$.
$x + y = 4$
$y = -x + 4$

Substitute this expression for $y$ in the other equation.
$2x - (-x + 4) = 5$
$2x + x - 4 = 5$
$3x - 4 = 5$
$3x = 9$
$x = 3$

Substitute 3 for $x$ in the other equation and solve for $y$.
$x + y = 4$
$3 + y = 4$
$y = 1$

The solution is $(3, 1)$.

**Example 2**

Solve the system of equations.
$2x + y = 7$
$4x + 2y = -3$

**Solution**
Solve one equation for $y$.
$2x + y = 7$
$y = -2x + 7$

Substitute this expression for $y$ in the other equation.
$4x + 2(-2x + 7) = -3$
$4x - 4x + 14 = -3$
$14 = -3$

Since $14 = -3$ is a false statement, there is no substitution for this system.

**1.** $y = 8x$
$y - 4x = 12$
$(3, 24)$

**2.** $x = y + 4$
$2x + 3y = -2$
$(2, -2)$

**3.** $x + y = 3$
$5x + 3y = -1$
$(-5, 8)$

**4.** $x + 3y = 5$
$-3x + 2y = 18$
$(-4, 3)$

**5.** $3x + y = 7$
$x - y = 1$
$(2, 1)$

**6.** $y = x - 4$
$y - x = -3$
no solution

**7.** $y = -2x$
$x + 2y = 9$
$(-3, 6)$

**8.** $y = 8 - x$
$4x - 3y = -3$
$(3, 5)$

**9.** $x - y = 7$
$3x - 4y = 16$
$(12, 5)$

---

### Example 3

Solve the system of equations.     $x - 2y = -9$
$-2x + 4y = 13$

**Solution**

$x - 2y = -9$       Solve for $x$.

$x = 2y - 9$

$-2x + 4y = 13$

$-2(2y - 9) + 4y \overset{?}{=} 13$       Substitute $(2y - 9)$ for $x$.

$-4y + 18 + 4y \overset{?}{=} 13$

$18 \overset{?}{=} 13$       The variables cancel and leave a false statement.

Since $18 \neq 13$, the lines are parallel. There is no solution.

> **Check Understanding**
>
> If you solved the system of equations in Example 3 using graphs, what kind of lines would they be?
>
> parallel

### TRY THESE EXERCISES

Solve each system of equations. Check the solution.

**1.** $2x - y = 14$   $(7, 0)$
$x + y = 7$

**2.** $x + 2y = 9$   $(7, 1)$
$x - y = 6$

**3.** $x + y = 7$   $(4, 3)$
$3x - 2y = 6$

**4.** $x - 2y = 7$   infinitely many
$x - 2y = 7$   solutions

**5.** $x - 3y = -4$   $\left(-\frac{1}{4}, \frac{5}{4}\right)$
$2x + 6y = 7$

**6.** $-5x + y = 3$   no solution
$20x - 4y = -2$

**7. RECREATION** During halftime, Joe bought 3 hot dogs and 4 drinks for $10. Cindy paid $5 for 1 hot dog and 3 drinks. Find the cost of each hot dog and each drink.   A hotdog cost $2 and a drink costs $1.

### PRACTICE EXERCISES • For Extra Practice, see page 610.

Solve each system of equations. Check the solution.

**8.** $x + y = 4$   $(2, 2)$
$3x - 2y = 2$

**9.** $-2x + y = 1$   $(0, 1)$
$x + y = 1$

**10.** $2x + y = 2$   $(3, -4)$
$4x - 2y = 20$

**11.** $3x + 2y = 11$   $(3, 1)$
$-2x + y = -5$

**12.** $2x + y = 7$   $(3, 1)$
$x - y = 2$

**13.** $3x - y = 1$   no solution
$-12x + 4y = -3$

**14.** $x + 2y = 4$   $(2, 1)$
$3x + y = 7$

**15.** $4x + y = 17$   $(4, 1)$
$x + 2y = 6$

**16.** $x + y = 5$   $(3, 2)$
$2x - y = 4$

**17.** $x + 5y = 9$   $(-1, 2)$
$3x - 2y = -7$

**18.** $5x + 2y = 10$   $(0, 5)$
$x + y = 5$

**19.** $9x - 6y = 12$   $(2, 1)$
$3x + 2y = 8$

**20.** $2x - 7y = -2$   no solution
$-4x + 14y = 3$

**21.** $-2x + y = -3$   $(9, 15)$
$3x - 3y = -18$

**22.** $-x + 2y = -2$   $\left(\frac{4}{3}, -\frac{1}{3}\right)$
$-2x + y = -3$

**346**   Chapter 8  **Systems of Equations and Inequalities**

### Extend the Lesson

**CHALLENGE** For those students who are successful with Exercises 35–37, in which the system has three equations in three variables, you may wish to present 3-variable systems that are somewhat more difficult, as shown below.

$x + y = 2$
$2x + 3z = 22$
$3y - z = -13$
$(5, -3, 4)$

$2x + 3y = 1$
$6y + z = 6$
$x + z = 4$
$\left(0, \frac{1}{3}, 4\right)$

**23. WRITING MATH** Write an outline explaining the substitution method step-by-step. Use an example with your outline. Answers will vary.

**24. SPORTS** On a cross-country team, there are 14 athletes. Three times the number of males is 2 more than twice the number of females. How many females are on the team?
8 females

**25. DATA FILE** Refer to the data on favorite pastimes on page 570. In a survey on favorite pastimes, $x$ men and $y$ women were surveyed. If the total number of men and women who chose watching TV was 785 and the total number who chose exercise was 160, how many men were surveyed? 1500 men

**26.** The sum of Kelly's and Fernando's ages is 29. Kelly's age exceeds Fernando's by 5 yr. How old is each person?
Kelly is 17 and Fernando is 12.

**Solve each system of equations by substitution.**

**27.** $2x - y = 4$
$-4x + 2y = -8$
infinitely many solutions

**28.** $2x + y = 3$
$-12x - 6y = -18$
infinitely many solutions

**29.** $3x - y = -4$
$-12x + 4y = 8$
no solution

**30.** $-5x + 4y = -12$
$10x - 8y = -16$
no solution

**31–34. GRAPHING** Solve each system of equations in Exercises 27–30 using a graphing calculator. Check students' work.

## ■ EXTENDED PRACTICE EXERCISES

To solve a system of three equations in three variables, try to eliminate one variable and get two equations in two variables. Solve each system of equations.

**35.** $x + y - z = -4$
$x = -2y$
$y - z = -6$
$x = 2, y = -1, z = 5$

**36.** $a + b + c = 1$
$b = 2c$
$-a + c = -5$
$a = 4, b = -2, c = -1$

**37.** $r + s + t = 0$
$r = -3t$
$s + t = 3$
$r = -3, s = 2, t = 1$

**38. CRITICAL THINKING** The sum of the ages of Latifa, Kyle and Luke is 38. Latifa is 6 yr older than Luke. Luke is 2 yr younger than Kyle. Find the age of each.
Latifa is 16, Kyle is 12, and Luke is 10.

**39. CHAPTER INVESTIGATION** Choose two of the top four teams in the football league. Write and solve a system of equations using substitution to find the point value of the league standings. Answers will vary.

## ■ MIXED REVIEW EXERCISES

**Graph each function for the domain of real numbers.** (Lesson 6-6)
For 40–45, see additional answers.

**40.** $y = x^2 - 5$

**41.** $y = 2x^2 + 1$

**42.** $y = 3x^2$

**43.** $y = 2x^2 - 3$

**44.** $y = 3x^2 - 7$

**45.** $y = x^2 + 4$

**46.** A deck of 15 cards lettered A to O is shuffled and 4 cards are dealt. How many different combinations of cards could be dealt? (Lesson 4-7) 1365

**47.** How many different 6-member volleyball teams can be chosen from a roster of 12 players if there are no restrictions? (Lesson 4-7) 924

**48.** Randy has to select a 6-digit number as his computer password. If no digits are repeated, how many possible passwords can he select? (Lesson 4-6) 151,200

## ADDITIONAL ANSWERS

**40.**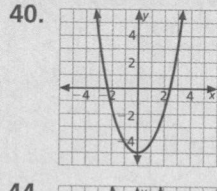

**41.**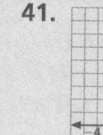

**42.**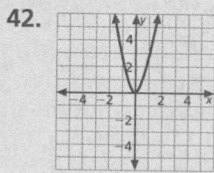

**43.**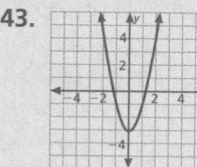

**44.**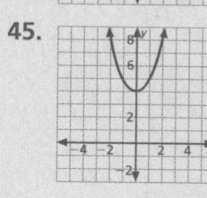

**45.**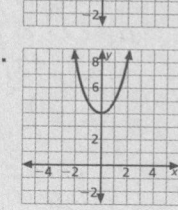

---

## Extra Practice Worksheet 8-3

Name _____ Date _____

EXTRA PRACTICE **8-3**
**SOLVE SYSTEMS BY SUBSTITUTION**

### ■ EXERCISES

Solve each system of equations. Check the solutions.

**1.** $y = 7x - 9$
$y = x + 3$ ____ (2, 5) ____

**2.** $4y + x = -2$
$x = -4y$ ____ no solution

**3.** $2x - y = 2$
$2y - 4x = -4$ infinite solutions

**4.** $2x + 4y = 8$
$x + y = 1$ ____ (-2, 3)

**5.** $x + 3y = 25$
$y - x = -9$ ____ (13, 4)

**6.** $y - x = 3$
$x - y = -3$ infinite solutions

**7.** $y = 2x + 3$
$4x + 2y = 10$ ____ $\left(\frac{1}{2}, 4\right)$

**8.** $3x + 2y = 7$
$x + y = 4$ ____ (-1, 5)

**9.** $x = y + 8$
$2x - 2y = 16$ ____ (2, -6)

**10.** $y = 8x$
$4x - 3 = y$ ____ $\left(-\frac{3}{4}, -6\right)$

**11.** $x - 6 = 9y$
$x - 3y = 10$ $\left(12, \frac{2}{3}\right)$

**12.** $4x - y = -6$
$x + 2y = -6$ ____ (-2, -2)

**13.** Romie paid $22 for 2 pizzas and 3 sandwiches. Rickie paid $12 for 1 pizza and 2 sandwiches. Find the cost of each pizza and sandwich.
$8 for a pizza, $2 for a sandwich

**14.** The sum of Tricia's and Carl's ages is 28. Tricia's age is 4 years less than Carl's. How old is each person? Carl is 16 and Tricia is 12.

**15.** Marc has 45¢ in dimes and nickels. He has 3 more nickels than dimes. How many of each type of coin does Marc have? 5 nickels and 2 dimes

---

## Enrichment Worksheet 8-3

Name _____ Date _____

ENRICHMENT **8-3**
**CHEMICAL SOLUTIONS**

Problems that involve combining chemical mixtures can be solved by writing and solving a system of equations.

**E x a m p l e**

A chemist has a 40% acid solution and a 60% acid solution available. She needs to make 50 L of a 48% acid solution. How much of each solution should she mix together?

**Solution**

Let $x$ = the number of liters of 40% solution. Let $y$ = the number of liters of 60% solution. Write one equation for the total number of liters.
$x + y = 50$
Write another equation for the amount of acid in the mixture.
$0.4x + 0.6y = 0.48(50)$
$0.4x + 0.6y = 24$
Solve the first equation for $x$.
$x = 50 - y$
Substitute for $x$ in the second equation.
$0.4(50 - y) + 0.6y = 24$
$20 - 0.4y + 0.6y = 24$
$20 + 0.2y = 24$
$0.2y = 4$
$y = 20$
Use $y$ to find $x$.
$x + 20 = 50$
$x = 30$

So, the chemist must mix 30 L of the 40% solution with 20 L of the 60% solution to get 50 L of a 48% solution.

### ■ EXERCISES

**1.** A 20% acid solution and a 40% acid solution are available. A chemist needs 64 oz of a solution that is 25% acid. How much of each available solution should be used?
48 oz of 20% solution and 16 oz of 40% solution

**2.** A chemist needs 100 mL of a solution that is 20% sulfuric acid. How much of a 10% sulfuric acid solution should be mixed with a solution that is 60% sulfuric acid?
80 mL of 10% solution and 20 mL of 60% solution

**3.** A chemist needs 80 mL of a solution that is 10% nitric acid. How much of a 5% nitric acid solution should be mixed with a solution that is 25% nitric acid?
60 mL of 5% solution and 20 mL of 25% solution

**Goals**
■ Solve systems of equations by adding or subtracting.
■ Solve systems of equations by adding and multiplying.

**Applications** Landscaping, Construction, Sports

---

## Lesson Planning

### NCTM Standards/Strands
■ Algebra
■ Reasoning & Proof
■ Connections
■ Problem Solving

### Lesson Resources

Warm-up Transparency 32
Reteaching 8-4
Extra Practice 8-4
Enrichment 8-4

---

## Getting Started

### 5-MINUTE WARM-UP

**Solve each system by substitution.**

1. $x + y = 9$
   $y = 2x$
   (3, 6)

2. $x = 5 - y$
   $x - y = 1$
   (3, 2)

### Introduction to Lesson 8-4

Before having students find opposites, review the difference between *additive inverses* (2 and −2) and *multiplicative inverses* $\left(\text{reciprocals } 2 \text{ and } \frac{1}{2}\right)$.

To reinforce the concept of opposites where variables are involved, ask students to find the opposite of $\frac{1}{3}x$. $-\frac{1}{3}x$ Then have them substitute a value for $x$ to verify that the sum is 0.

---

**NUMBER SENSE** The addition property of opposites can help you explore other ways to solve a system of equations. Recall that the sum of opposites is always 0.

$$-x + x = 0 \qquad 5a + (-5a) = 0$$

**For each of the following, explain what you would do to the first term to make the two terms opposites.**

1. $m, -m$  nothing
2. $r, r$  multiply by −1
3. $-2z, -4z$  multiply by −2
4. $5g, -15g$  multiply by 3
5. $3x, x$  multiply by $-\frac{1}{3}$
6. $-q, q$  nothing

---

### ▶ BUILD UNDERSTANDING

When solving a system of equations by an algebraic method, you need to eliminate one of the variables to get one equation in one variable. If the coefficients of one of the variables are opposites, add the equations to eliminate one of the variables. This is the addition method.

### Example 1

**Solve the system of equations. Check the solution.**

$$2x + 3y = 6$$
$$-2x + y = 2$$

#### Solution

$$2x + 3y = 6$$ The $x$-coefficients are opposites.
$$\underline{-2x + \ y = 2}$$ Add the equations.
$$0 + 4y = 8$$ Solve for $y$.
$$\frac{4y}{4} = \frac{8}{4}$$
$$y = 2$$

$$2x + 3y = 6$$ Choose one of the original equations.
$$2x + 3(2) = 6$$ Substitute 2 for $y$.
$$2x + 6 = 6$$ Solve for $x$.
$$2x + 6 - 6 = 6 - 6$$
$$\frac{2x}{2} = \frac{0}{2}$$
$$x = 0$$

The solution is (0, 2).

#### Check Understanding

In Example 1, if $-2x$ is changed to $2x$, what will you have had to multiply the second equation by to eliminate $x$?

−1

**Check**

$$2x + 3y = 6 \qquad\qquad -2x + y = 2$$
$$2(0) + 3(2) \overset{?}{=} 6 \qquad -2(0) + 2 \overset{?}{=} 2$$
$$6 = 6 \ ✔ \qquad\qquad 2 = 2 \ ✔$$

**348** Chapter 8 **Systems of Equations and Inequalities**

---

## Teaching Tip

After students have seen how to use addition to solve the system of Example 1, have them use substitution to solve the system, as shown below. When they compare results, students should be aware that the solution is the same regardless of the method.

If the coefficients of one of the variables are the same, you can use the subtraction method to eliminate that variable.

## Example 2

**Solve the system of equations. Check the solution.**

$$3x + 4y = 14$$
$$x + 4y = 10$$

### Solution

$$
\begin{array}{ll}
3x + 4y = 14 \\
-(x + 4y = 10)
\end{array}
\longrightarrow
\begin{array}{ll}
3x + 4y = \phantom{-}14 \\
-x - 4y = -10
\end{array}
$$

The $y$-coefficients are the same.
Subtract. Distribute the negative over the equation.

$$2x + 0 = 4 \qquad \text{Solve for } x.$$
$$\frac{2x}{2} = \frac{4}{2}$$
$$x = 2$$

Choose one of the original equations.

$$x + 4y = 10 \qquad \text{Substitute 2 for } x.$$
$$2 + 4y = 10 \qquad \text{Solve for } y.$$
$$\frac{4y}{4} = \frac{8}{4}$$
$$y = 2$$

The solution is (2, 2).

**Check**

$$
\begin{array}{ll}
3x + 4y = 14 & x + 4y = 10 \\
3(2) + 4(2) \stackrel{?}{=} 14 & 2 + 4(2) \stackrel{?}{=} 10 \\
6 + 8 \stackrel{?}{=} 14 & 2 + 8 \stackrel{?}{=} 10 \\
14 = 14 \; ✔ & 10 = 10 \; ✔
\end{array}
$$

Sometimes you will need to multiply one or both of the equations by a number to get coefficients of one of the variables to be opposites. This is the multiplication and addition method.

## Example 3

**Solve the system of equations.**

$$2x + 3y = 8$$
$$x + y = -3$$

### Solution

$$
\begin{array}{ll}
2x + 3y = 8 \\
-2(x + y = -3)
\end{array}
\longrightarrow
\begin{array}{ll}
2x + 3y = 8 \\
-2x - 2y = 6
\end{array}
$$

Multiply the second equation by $-2$.

$$0 + y = 14 \qquad \text{Add.}$$
$$y = 14$$

Choose one of the original equations.

$$x + y = -3 \qquad \text{Substitute 14 for } y.$$
$$x + 14 = -3 \qquad \text{Solve for } x.$$
$$x = -17$$

Be sure to check the solution.

The solution is (−17, 14).

---

**Example 4**

Kate has nickels and dimes in her pocket. There are 11 coins. The value of the coins is $0.95. How many of each kind of coin does Kate have?

**Solution**

Let $n$ = the number of nickels and $d$ = the number of dimes. The total number of coins is 11, so $n + d = 11$. The value of the coins is $0.95, so $0.05n + 0.10d = 0.95$.

$$\begin{array}{ll} -0.05(n + d = 11) & -0.05n - 0.05d = -0.55 \quad \text{Multiply the first equation by } -0.05. \\ 0.05n + 0.10d = 0.95 & \underline{\phantom{-}0.05n + 0.10d = \phantom{-}0.95} \quad \text{Add.} \end{array}$$

$$0 + 0.05d = 0.4 \quad \text{Solve for } d.$$
$$\frac{0.05d}{0.05} = \frac{0.4}{0.05}$$
$$d = 8$$

Choose one of the original equations.

$n + d = 11$    Substitute 8 for $d$.
$n + 8 = 11$    Solve for $n$.
$n = 3$

Kate has 3 nickels and 8 dimes.     Check the solution.

## ▶ TRY THESE EXERCISES

**Solve each system of equations. Check the solution.**

1. $3x - y = 15$   $(4, -3)$
   $x + y = 1$

2. $-5a + 4b = -1$   $(1, 1)$
   $7a + 4b = 11$

3. $4x + 3y = 2$   $(-4, 6)$
   $x - y = -10$

4. $5x - y = -23$   $(-4, 3)$
   $3x - y = -15$

5. $j + 3k = 10$   $(1, 3)$
   $j + 2k = 7$

6. $7m - 5n = -2$   $(-1, -1)$
   $-8m - n = 9$

7. **LANDSCAPING** A landscaping firm is designing a flower bed to border a rectangular pool. The perimeter of the pool is 32 m. Three times the width is the same as five times the length. What are the dimensions of the pool?
   length = 6 m; width = 10 m

## ▶ PRACTICE EXERCISES • For Extra Practice, see page 611.

**Solve each system of equations. Check the solution.**

8. $3x + y = 9$   $(2, 3)$
   $-3x + y = -3$

9. $-7x - 8y = 8$   $(0, -1)$
   $7x - 8y = 8$

10. $7a + 2b = 16$   infinitely many
    $8a - 2b = 14$   solutions

11. $2r + 3s = 1$   $(5, -3)$
    $9r - 3s = 54$

12. $r + s = 4$   $(4, 0)$
    $2r + 3s = 8$

13. $2x + 3y = 8$   infinitely many
    $2x + 3y = 8$   solutions

14. $3c - d = 1$   $(1, 2)$
    $c + 5d = 11$

15. $2x + 2y = 2$   $(1, 0)$
    $-3x + y = -3$

16. $-2x - y = 1$   $(-1, 1)$
    $3x + 8y = 5$

17. $c - 2d = 10$   $(8, -1)$
    $2c + 5d = 11$

18. $2x + y = 6$   $(2, 2)$
    $-3x + 2y = -2$

19. $4x - 3y = 12$   $\left(\frac{29}{10}, \frac{-2}{15}\right)$
    $2x + 6y = 5$

20. $5x + 3y = 11$   $(19, -28)$
    $3x + 2y = 1$

21. $2r - 5s = 7$   $(-9, -5)$
    $3r - 2s = -17$

22. $3a + 8b = 1$   $(-5, 2)$
    $2a + 7b = 4$

---

# Lesson Wrap-up

## QUICK ASSESSMENT

Ask the following questions to determine if students understand the content presented in this lesson.

1. When you solve a system of equations, what is the purpose of using any one of the methods in this section?   to eliminate one of the variables and get an equation in one variable

2. When solving a system of equations in which the coefficents of one variable are the same, which operation can you use to eliminate that variable?   subtraction

3. In an effort to get equal or opposite coefficients for one of the variables of a system, you may multiply an equation by a number. Why is it necessary to multiply every term of that equation?
   to get an equivalent equation

**Consider the system shown below.**
$-2x + 4y = 13$
$6x + 4y = 9$

4. Explain how you could eliminate $y$.   Subtract the second equation from the first.

5. Explain how you could eliminate $x$.   Possible answer: Multiply the first equation by 3 and add the result to the second equation.

## ASSIGNMENT GUIDE

**Basic:** 1–27, 35–46
**Enriched:** 1–46

---

# Extend the Lesson

**CHALLENGE** Here are some systems where the coefficients are fractions.

$$\frac{1}{3}x + \frac{1}{4}y = 10$$
$$\frac{1}{3}x - \frac{1}{2}y = 4$$
(24, 8)

$$\frac{2}{3}x + \frac{3}{4}y = 2$$
$$\frac{1}{6}x + \frac{1}{2}y = -2$$
(12, −8)

$$\frac{1}{2}x + \frac{1}{3}y = 8$$
$$\frac{3}{2}x - \frac{4}{3}y = -4$$
(8, 12)

**23. WRITING MATH** Write a brief paragraph explaining how you solved Exercise 22. Answers will vary.

**24.** Yuki pays $5.05 for 3 muffins and 4 coffees. Dave pays $4.90 for 4 muffins and 2 coffees. How much does each item cost? muffins: $0.95, coffee: $0.55

**25. SPORTS** Cara had a combined total of 64 hits during her junior and senior years of fastpitch softball. In her senior year, Cara had 5 fewer than twice as many hits as her junior year. How many hits did Cara have in her senior year? 41 hits

**26. CONSTRUCTION** A work crew of 5 bricklayers and 3 carpenters earns $891 for a job. Another crew of 12 bricklayers and 4 carpenters earns $1748 on the same job. Find the wage of each type of worker. bricklayers: $105, carpenters: $122

**27. DATA FILE** Refer to the data on pizza toppings on page 568. Suppose that John ate $x$ slices of pepperoni pizza and $y$ slices of pizza with extra cheese. If the total number of calories is 576 and the total number of fat grams is 37, how many slices of each type of pizza did John eat? 3 pepperoni and 2 extra cheese

## ◼ EXTENDED PRACTICE EXERCISES

Solve each system of equations.

**28.** $-5x + 2y = 12$  infinitely
$10x - 4y = -24$  many solutions

**29.** $6x - 9y = 36$  infinitely
$-2x + 3y = -12$  many solutions

**30.** $8x - 2y = -10$
$-16x + 4y = 20$
infinitely many solutions

Use the results of Exercises 28–30.

**31.** What do you notice about the relationship between the two equations in each of the systems? What do you notice about the number of solutions? One equation is a multiple of the other. There are infinitely many solutions in each case.

**32.** Solve the systems graphically. What do you notice about the graphs? They are the same line.

**33. CRITICAL THINKING** Write a statement that generalizes your observations. Answers will vary.

**34. CHAPTER INVESTIGATION** Choose two of the top four football teams, other than the pair chosen in Lesson 8-3. Write and solve a system of equations using addition, subtraction or multiplication. Verify that this is the same answer as that in Lesson 8-3. Answers will vary.

## ◼ MIXED REVIEW EXERCISES

Find the slope of the line containing the given points. Identify any vertical or horizontal lines. (Lesson 6-2)

**35.** $(3, 4), (1, -6)$  5

**36.** $(5, -2), (3, 7)$  $-\dfrac{9}{2}$

**37.** $(-3, -2), (5, 3)$  $\dfrac{5}{8}$

**38.** $(6, -1), (-3, -1)$  0, horizontal line

**39.** $(4, -4), (7, 1)$  $\dfrac{5}{3}$

**40.** $(7, -2), (7, 7)$  undefined, vertical line

In the figure, $\overrightarrow{AB} \parallel \overrightarrow{CD}$. Find each measure. (Lesson 5-3)

**41.** $m\angle 1$  138°

**42.** $m\angle 2$  42°

**43.** $m\angle 3$  42°

**44.** $m\angle 5$  138°

**45.** $m\angle 6$  42°

**46.** $m\angle 7$  42°

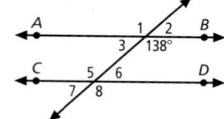

---

**Extra Practice Worksheet 8-4**

Name _____ Date _____

EXTRA PRACTICE **8-4**

**SOLVE SYSTEMS BY ADDING, SUBTRACTING, OR MULTIPLYING**

☑ **EXERCISES**

Solve each system of equations. Check the solutions.

1. $4x - 5y = -17$
$4x + 6y = 38$  (2, 5)

2. $3x + 6y = -15$
$-x - 4y = 13$  (3, -4)

3. $7x + 2y = 9$
$4x - 3y = -28$  (-1, 8)

4. $-2m - 5n = 2$
$5m + 2n = 16$  (4, -2)

5. $2x - 3y = 6$
$4x + 2y = 12$  (3, 0)

6. $3x + 4y = -20$
$2x - 4y = 0$  (-4, -2)

7. $3x + y = 3$
$6x - 2y = -2$  $\left(\dfrac{1}{3}, 2\right)$

8. $r - 2s = 11$
$2r + s = 7$  (5, -3)

9. $3x - y = 8$
$5x + 3y = 4$  (2, -2)

10. $4x - 2y = 3$
$2x + 4y = -1$  $\left(\dfrac{1}{2}, -\dfrac{1}{2}\right)$

11. $16x + 2y = -12$
$4x + y = -9$  $\left(\dfrac{3}{4}, -12\right)$

12. $3x + y = -1$
$5x - 2y = 13$  (1, -4)

13. There were 37 cars and trucks waiting in line to pay a toll. The number of cars was 2 less than twice the number of trucks. How many of each were in line? 24 cars, 13 trucks

14. Melanie scored 24 points in her last basketball game. The number of 2-point goals she scored was 1 more than four times the number of 3-point goals she scored. How many 2-point field goals did she score? 9

15. One week, Juan worked 40 regular hours and 6 overtime hours and made $374. The next week, he worked 40 regular hours and 8 overtime hours and made $392. How much does he make per hour for each overtime hour? $9

**Enrichment Worksheet 8-4**

Name _____ Date _____

ENRICHMENT **8-4**

**THE RIGHT PRICE**

Marketing analysts can help retailers determine the best price at which to sell their merchandise. A price that would be considered acceptable in one neighborhood might be considered too high in another neighborhood.

**Example**

Mr. Sanchez wants to offer a gourmet coffee blend to his customers. A marketing consultant told him that an acceptable price for his customers would be $5.50 per pound. He has coffee beans priced at $4.00 per pound and coffee beans priced at $6.50 per pound. How much of each should he mix together to make 50 pounds of coffee priced at $5.50 per pound?

**Solution**

Let $x$ = the number of pounds of coffee beans at $4.00 per pound and $y$ = the number of pounds of coffee beans at $6.50 per pound. Write an equation for the total number of pounds.
$x + y = 50$
Write an equation for the price of the coffee.
$4.00x + 6.50y = 5.50(50)$ → $4x + 6.5y = 275$
Multiply and subtract.
$4x + 6.5y = 275$           $4x + 6.5y = 275$
$-4(x + y = 50)$    →    $-4x - 4y = -200$
                                    $2.5y = 75$
                                    $y = 30$
Substitute 30 for $y$ in $x + y = 50$ and solve for $x$.
$x + 30 = 50$    $x = 20$
So, there should be 20 pounds of $4 coffee and 30 pounds of $6.50 coffee.
Check. $20 + 30 = 50$
$4(20) + 6.50(30) = $80 + $195 = $275$

☑ **EXERCISES**

1. Walnuts are priced at $1.50 per pound. Pecans are priced at $4.00 per pound. How many pounds of each kind of nut should be used to make 20 pounds of a mixture that sells for $2.50 per pound? 12 lb of walnuts, 8 lb of pecans

2. Dried apples are priced at $3 per pound. Dried apricots are priced at $5 per pound. How much of each should be used to make 10 pounds of a mixture priced at $3.50 per pound? 7.5 lb of apples, 2.5 lb of apricots

3. How many pounds of cashews priced at $3.50 per pound and of peanuts priced at $2.25 per pound should be mixed to make 10 pounds of a nut mix priced at $3 per pound? 4 lb of peanuts, 6 lb of cashews

---

## Flexible Grouping

Have students work in pairs to write and solve a system of equations to find a two-digit number with the following properties. The sum of the digits is 8. If the digits are reversed, the new number is 36 more than the original number. 26

Remind students that if $t$ represents the tens digit and $u$ represents the units digit, then the number is represented by $10t + u$.

## Skills Practice

**Vocabulary Review**

Lesson 8-3
substitution

## ASSIGNMENT GUIDE

**All students:** 1–45

## Chalkboard Examples

### Lesson 8-3

**FINANCE** Ms. Toohey invested some money in a real-estate holding that paid 8% annual interest and twice as much money in a holding that paid 10% annual interest. Her total annual income from these two investments was $420. Find the amount she invested in each holding.

Let $x$ = the amount invested at 8% and $y$ = the amount invested at 10%.

*The amount at 10% is twice the amount at 8%.*          $y = 2x$  A

To calculate interest, multiply principal by rate.

*The total annual income is $420.*      $0.08x + 0.10y = 420$  B

To solve the system, substitute the expression for $y$ from equation [A] into equation [B], clear of decimals, and solve for $x$.

$$0.08x + 0.10y = 420$$
$$0.08x + 0.10(2x) = 420$$
$$8x + 10(2x) = 42,000$$
$$8x + 20x = 42,000$$
$$28x = 42,000$$
$$x = 1500$$

Substitute 1500 for $x$ in equation [A] to find the corresponding value of $y$.

$$y = 2x$$
$$y = 2(1500)$$
$$y = 3000$$

Check:
$$0.08(1500) + 0.10(3000) \stackrel{?}{=} 420$$
$$120 + 300 = 420 \checkmark$$

$$3000 \stackrel{?}{=} 2(1500)$$
$$3000 = 3000 \checkmark$$

So, Ms. Toohey had invested $1500 at 8% and $3000 at 10%.

---

**Use substitution to solve each system of equations. Check the solution.**

1. $y = 2x$  $(2, 4)$
   $2x + y = 8$

2. $y = 3x$  $(-3, -9)$
   $x + 2y = -21$

3. $x = 2y$  $\left(3, \frac{3}{2}\right)$
   $4x + 2y = 15$

4. $x = y + 4$  $(7, 3)$
   $x + 3y = 16$

5. $y = x + 1$  $(2, 3)$
   $2x - 3y = -5$

6. $x = 3 - 2y$  $(3, 0)$
   $2x - 2y = 6$

7. $3x = y + 9$  $(2, -3)$
   $2x - 4y = 16$

8. $-4x + 3y = -16$  $(4, 0)$
   $-x + 2y = -4$

9. $\frac{x}{2} - y = \frac{5}{4}$  $\left(\frac{1}{2}, -1\right)$
   $8x + 3y = 1$

10. $5x + 2y = 1$  $(1, -2)$
    $3x + 4y = -5$

11. $6x - 3y = -9$  $(0, 3)$
    $13x - 5y = -15$

12. $10x - 5y = 65$  $(5, -3)$
    $10y - 5x = -55$

13. $y = -x + 5$  $(3, 2)$
    $2x - y = 4$

14. $-2x = -y - 3$  $(9, 15)$
    $3x = 3y - 18$

15. $y = 2x + 2$  no solution
    $4x - 2y = 3$

16. The sum of Sophia's and Austin's age is 32. Sophia's age exceeds Austin's age by 4 yr. How old is each person?  Sophia is 18 and Austin is 14.

---

**Use addition, subtraction or multiplication to solve each system of equations. Check the solution.**

17. $-x + 2y = 3$  $(-1, 1)$
    $3x + 2y = -1$

18. $x - 5y = 7$  $(2, -1)$
    $-9x - 10y = -8$

19. $-2x + 6y = 10$  $(4, 3)$
    $2x - 9y = -19$

20. $-10x + 6y = 25$  $\left(-\frac{3}{2}, \frac{5}{3}\right)$
    $2x + 9y = 12$

21. $4x - 9y = -1$  $\left(0, \frac{1}{9}\right)$
    $-8x + 9y = 1$

22. $7x + 4y = 6$  $(6, -9)$
    $7x + 5y = -3$

23. $8x + 3y = -4$  $(-2, 4)$
    $6x + 5y = 8$

24. $8x - 3y = 18$  $(0, -6)$
    $8x - 2y = 12$

25. $2x - \frac{1}{2}y = 3$  $(2, 2)$
    $4x + \frac{1}{2}y = 9$

26. $-\frac{1}{2}x + y = 3$  $(-10, -2)$
    $\frac{1}{2}x - 3y = 1$

27. $9a + 7b = 4$  $(2, -2)$
    $6a - 3b = 18$

28. $2x - 5y = -6$  $(7, 4)$
    $6x - 6y = 18$

29. $x - y = 4$  $(10, 6)$
    $-2x + 4y = 4$

30. $4x + 6y = 68$  $\left(\frac{25}{2}, 3\right)$
    $2x - 5y = 10$

31. $4x + 5y = 34$  $\left(4, \frac{18}{5}\right)$
    $-3x + 5y = 6$

32. Samantha paid $6.00 for 3 hotdogs and 2 juices. Damian paid $9.75 for 5 hotdogs and 3 juices. How much does each item cost?  hotdog: $1.50, juice: $0.75

33. The measure of one angle is 15 more than twice the measure of its supplementary angle. Find the measure of each angle.  55°, 125°

Write an equation in slope-intercept form of the line passing through the given point and perpendicular to the given line. (Lesson 8-1)

**34.** $(-2, -3); y = 2x$  $y = -\frac{1}{2}x - 4$  **35.** $(1, 4); x + 3y = 6$  $y = 3x + 1$  **36.** $(3, 1); 2y = 3x - 4$
$y = -\frac{2}{3}x + 3$

**GRAPHING** Use a graphing calculator to solve each system of equations. (Lesson 8-2)

**37.** $y = \frac{2}{3}x$  (3, 2)

$y = -\frac{2}{3}x + 4$

**38.** $y = \frac{1}{2}x - 2$  (6, 1)

$-x + y = -5$

**39.** $-2x + y = 1$  (2, 5)

$y = x + 3$

Use substitution to solve each system of equations. Check the solution. (Lesson 8-3)

**40.** $3x + 2y = 12$  (2, 3)

$y = 2x - 1$

**41.** $2x + y = 6$  (4, −2)

$x - 2y = 8$

**42.** $8x + y = 2$  $\left(\frac{1}{2}, -2\right)$

$6x - 2y = 7$

Use addition, subtraction or multiplication to solve each system of equations. Check the solution. (Lesson 8-4)

**43.** $7x + 5y = 14$  (2, 0)

$4x - 5y = 8$

**44.** $9x - 2y = 5$  $\left(\frac{7}{9}, 1\right)$

$9x + y = 8$

**45.** $12x - y = 7$  (1, 5)

$6x - y = 1$

# Mid-Chapter Quiz

For each line identified by two points, state the slope of a line parallel and the slope of a line perpendicular to it. (Lesson 8-1)

**1.** $A(3, -5)$ and $B(-6, 0)$  $-\frac{5}{9}, \frac{9}{5}$  **2.** $C(11, 4)$ and $D(9, -4)$  $4, -\frac{1}{4}$  **3.** $E(0, 7)$ and $F(-4, -1)$  $2, -\frac{1}{2}$

Determine if the given ordered pair is a solution of the system of equations. (Lesson 8-2)

**4.** $(1, 2);$  $y = -2x + 4$  yes

$y = \frac{3}{2}x + \frac{1}{2}$

**5.** $(-6, 9);$  $y = -2x - 3$  yes

$y + x = 3$

**6.** $(-4, -3);$  $y = x - 7$  no

$x - y = -1$

Solve each system of equations. Check the solution. (Lessons 8-3 and 8-4)

**7.** $y = 7x - 9$  (2, 5)

$y = x + 3$

**8.** $4y + x = -2$  no solution

$x = -4y$

**9.** $2x - y = 2$  infinitely many solutions

$2y - 4x = -4$

**10.** $2x + 4y = 8$  (−2, 3)

$x + y = 1$

**11.** $x + 3y = 25$  (13, 4)

$y - x = -9$

**12.** $4x - 5y = -17$  (2, 5)

$4x + 6y = 38$

**13.** $3x + 6y = -15$  (3, −4)

$-x - 4y = 13$

**14.** $7x + 2y = 9$  (−1, 8)

$4x - 3y = -28$

**15.** $-2m - 5n = 2$  (4, −2)

$5m + 2n = 16$

**16.** There are 37 trucks and cars waiting in line to pay a toll. The number of cars is 2 less than twice the number of trucks. How many cars and trucks are in line? (Lesson 8-4)
24 cars, 13 trucks

---

## Lesson 8-4

**TRAVEL** A motorboat can travel 120 km downstream in 3 h. It requires 5 h to make the return trip against the current. Find the rate of the boat in still water and the rate of the current.

Let $r$ = the rate of the boat in still water and $c$ = the rate of the current.

To calculate distance, multiply rate by time.

downstream  $3(r + c) = 120$  A
upstream  $5(r - c) = 120$  B

To solve the system, simplify in equation [A] and in equation [B].
$3(r + c) = 120$  $5(r - c) = 120$
$r + c = 40$ C  $r - c = 24$ D

Add equations [C] and [D], eliminating $c$.
$$\begin{array}{r} r + c = 40 \\ r - c = 24 \\ \hline 2r \quad = 64 \\ r = 32 \end{array}$$

Substitute 32 for $r$ in equation [C] to find the value of $c$.
$r + c = 40$
$32 + c = 40$
$c = 8$

Check:
downstream  upstream
$3(32 + 8) \stackrel{?}{=} 120$  $5(32 - 8) \stackrel{?}{=} 120$
$120 = 120$ ✓  $120 = 120$ ✓

So, the rate of the boat in still water is 32 km/h and the rate of the current is 8 km/h.

---

## Teaching Tip

Given the context in which they see Question 16 of the Mid-Chapter Quiz, most students will try to write a system of two equations to solve the problem, using different variables to represent the number of trucks and the number of cars. After students complete such a solution, you might have them explore the possiblity of using one variable for this problem, as shown below.

Let $x$ = the number of trucks. Then $2x - 2$ = the number of cars.
The total number of trucks and cars is 37.  $x + 2x - 2 = 37$
$$3x = 39$$
$$x = 13 \text{ trucks}$$
$$2x - 2 = 2(13) - 2 = 24 \text{ cars}$$

### Vocabulary

square matrix  determinant
Cramer's rule

### Tools/Materials Needed

graphing calculator graph paper

### Lesson Resources

Warm-up Transparency 33
Reteaching 8-5
Extra Practice 8-5
Enrichment 8-5
Technology Activity 8-5

## Getting Started

### 5-MINUTE WARM-UP

**Evaluate each expression.**

1. $\dfrac{(3)(6) - (-3)(-3)}{(-3)(4) - (-2)(7)}$ $\dfrac{9}{2}$

2. $\dfrac{(-2)(3) - (-1)(1)}{(1)(4) - (2)(6)}$ $\dfrac{5}{8}$

### Lesson 8-5

When enumerating different methods of solution for a system of two linear equations, you might first summarize the categories as *graphic* or *algebraic*.

In answer to Question 2, you might have student partners work so that one does substitution for $y$ and the other does substitution for $x$; one does elimination of $x$ and the other does elimination of $y$. Then the partners compare methods.

---

# 8-5 Matrices and Determinants

**Goals**
- Find the determinant of a $2 \times 2$ matrix.
- Solve systems of equations using determinants.

**Applications** Sports, Construction, Fitness

**Work with a partner.**

1. In how many ways can you solve a system of equations with two unknowns? Answers will vary, but should include by graphing, by substitution, and by adding, subtracting and using multiplication before adding or subtracting.

2. Solve the system of equations using each method learned in the previous three lessons.

$$2x - 3y = 4 \quad (23, 14)$$
$$-3x + 5y = 1$$

3. Did you arrive at the same solution using each method? yes

4. Which method do you prefer? Why? Answers will vary.

5. Discuss with others the method they prefer. Answers will vary.

### ◣ BUILD UNDERSTANDING

Recall that a matrix is a rectangular array of values. The matrix shown has elements 4, $-1$, 0, 3, 6, and 2, and its dimensions are $2 \times 3$. A matrix of $n$ rows and $m$ columns has dimensions $n \times m$.

$$\begin{bmatrix} 4 & -1 & 0 \\ 3 & 6 & 2 \end{bmatrix}$$

A **square matrix** has the same number of rows and columns. Associated with a $2 \times 2$ square matrix is a number called the determinant. The **determinant** of a matrix is symbolized by using vertical bars in place of the matrix brackets.

The value of a $2 \times 2$ determinant is the difference of the products of the diagonal entries. The determinant of a square matrix $A$ is named det $A$.

**Determinant** $\det A = \begin{vmatrix} a & b \\ c & d \end{vmatrix} = ad - bc$, where $a$, $b$, $c$ and $d$ are real numbers.

### Example 1

Evaluate the determinant of matrix $A = \begin{bmatrix} 1 & 2 \\ -3 & 4 \end{bmatrix}$.

**Solution**

$$\det A = \begin{vmatrix} 1 & 2 \\ -3 & 4 \end{vmatrix}$$

$$= 1(4) - 2(-3) \qquad a = 1, b = 2, c = -3, d = 4$$

$$= 4 + 6$$

$$= 10$$

## Teaching Tip

When demonstrating the first few solutions of systems by determinants, students may find it helpful if you use different colors to represent the $x$-coefficients, the $y$-coefficients, and the constant terms of the equations. Some students may find it easier to organize their work by setting up the three determinants $A$, $A_x$, $A_y$, evaluating them, and substituting the values into and $x = \dfrac{A_x}{A}$ and $y = \dfrac{A_y}{A}$.

One of the important applications of determinants is in solving systems of equations. The method used is called **Cramer's rule**, after the Swiss mathematician Gabriel Cramer (1704–1752). Cramer's rule is demonstrated in Example 2. Notice that to use Cramer's rule, you must first write both equations in standard form, $Ax + By = C$.

**Math: Who, Where, When**

A method of detached coefficients similar to determinants has been traced to twelfth-century Chinese mathematicians. As the Chinese studied patterns involved in solving systems of equations, they discovered that they could arrange numerical coefficients in a square array similar to those on their counting board (the abacus).

## Example 2

**Solve the system of equations using the method of determinants.**

$$2x - 3y = 4$$
$$-3x + 5y = 1$$

**Solution**

Write the coefficients of $x$ and $y$ in a determinant $A$.

$$\det A = \begin{vmatrix} 2 & -3 \\ -3 & 5 \end{vmatrix}$$

*y*-coefficients

*x*-coefficients

Write another determinant. Use $A$ and replace the $x$-column with the constants from the equations. Label it $A_x$.

$$\det A_x = \begin{vmatrix} 4 & -3 \\ 1 & 5 \end{vmatrix}$$

Replace *x*-coefficients with constants.

Write a third determinant. Use $A$ and replace the $y$-column with the constants from the equations. Label it $A_y$.

$$\det A_y = \begin{vmatrix} 2 & 4 \\ -3 & 1 \end{vmatrix}$$

Replace *y*-coefficients with constants.

If $A \neq 0$, the solution of the system is $(x, y)$, where $x = \dfrac{A_x}{A}$ and $y = \dfrac{A_y}{A}$. Solve for $x$ and $y$.

$$x = \frac{A_x}{A} = \frac{\begin{vmatrix} 4 & -3 \\ 1 & 5 \end{vmatrix}}{\begin{vmatrix} 2 & -3 \\ -3 & 5 \end{vmatrix}} = \frac{4(5) - (-3)(1)}{2(5) - (-3)(-3)} = \frac{20 + 3}{10 - 9} = \frac{23}{1} = 23$$

$$y = \frac{A_y}{A} = \frac{\begin{vmatrix} 2 & 4 \\ -3 & 1 \end{vmatrix}}{\begin{vmatrix} 2 & -3 \\ -3 & 5 \end{vmatrix}} = \frac{2(1) - 4(-3)}{2(5) - (-3)(-3)} = \frac{2 + 12}{10 - 9} = \frac{14}{1} = 14$$

Check the solution.

$$2x - 3y = 4$$
$$2(23) - 3(14) \stackrel{?}{=} 4$$
$$46 - 42 \stackrel{?}{=} 4$$
$$4 = 4 \ ✔$$

$$-3x + 5y = 1$$
$$-3(23) + 5(14) \stackrel{?}{=} 1$$
$$-69 + 70 \stackrel{?}{=} 1$$
$$1 = 1 \ ✔$$

The solution is (23, 14).

 **Math Online** mathmatters2.com/extra_examples

**Supplementary Example 1**
Solve the system of equations by the method of determinants.
$$3x - 7y = 26$$
$$x + 2y = 11$$

$$x = \frac{A_x}{A} = \frac{\begin{vmatrix} -6 & -7 \\ 11 & 2 \end{vmatrix}}{\begin{vmatrix} 3 & -7 \\ 1 & 2 \end{vmatrix}} = \frac{(-6)(2) - (-7)(11)}{(3)(2) - (-7)(1)}$$

$$= \frac{65}{13} = 5$$

$$x = \frac{A_y}{A} = \frac{\begin{vmatrix} 3 & -6 \\ 1 & 11 \end{vmatrix}}{\begin{vmatrix} 3 & -7 \\ 1 & 2 \end{vmatrix}} = \frac{(3)(11) - (-6)(1)}{13}$$

$$= \frac{39}{13} = 3$$

**Supplementary Example 2**
**BUSINESS** Workers at Kitchen Industries can assemble an electronic juicer in 3 min and a food procesor in 5 min. Quality control engineers inspect each juicer for 2 min and each food processor for 6 min. The assembly line operates 7 h a day and the quality control department operates 6 h a day. How many juicers and food processors should the company produce daily so that every assembled product is inspected for quality on the day it is made?
Let $x =$ the number of juicers produced and $y =$ the number of food processors produced.
Work in minutes.
*assembly equation* $\quad 3x + 5y = 420$
*quality control*
*equation* $\quad\quad\quad\quad\quad 2x + 6y = 360$

$$x = \frac{A_x}{A} = \frac{\begin{vmatrix} 420 & 5 \\ 360 & 6 \end{vmatrix}}{\begin{vmatrix} 3 & 5 \\ 2 & 6 \end{vmatrix}} = \frac{(420)(6) - (5)(360)}{(3)(6) - (5)(2)}$$

$$= \frac{720}{8} = 90$$

$$x = \frac{A_y}{A} = \frac{\begin{vmatrix} 3 & 420 \\ 2 & 360 \end{vmatrix}}{\begin{vmatrix} 3 & 5 \\ 2 & 6 \end{vmatrix}} = \frac{(3)(360) - (420)(2)}{(3)(6) - (5)(2)}$$

$$= \frac{240}{8} = 30$$

So, the company should produce 90 juicers and 30 food processors daily.

## Extend the Lesson

You may wish to demonstrate the diagonal method for evaluating a 3 × 3 determinant.

To evaluate $\begin{vmatrix} 1 & 2 & 8 \\ 3 & -1 & 6 \\ 5 & 4 & 7 \end{vmatrix}$ , recopy the first two columns: $\begin{vmatrix} 1 & 2 & 8 \\ 3 & -1 & 6 \\ 5 & 4 & 7 \end{vmatrix}\begin{matrix} 1 & 2 \\ 3 & -1 \\ 5 & 4 \end{matrix}$

Find the sums of the products of the diagonals and subtract as shown.

$$\begin{matrix} 1 & 2 & 8 & 1 & 2 \\ 3 & -1 & 6 & 3 & -1 \\ 5 & 4 & 7 & 5 & 4 \end{matrix} = [(1)(-1)(7) + (2)(6)(5) + (8)(3)(4)] - [(8)(-1)(5) + (1)(6)(4) + (2)(3)(7)]$$

$$= [-7 + 60 + 96] - [-40 + 24 + 42] = 123$$

## Lesson Wrap-up

### QUICK ASSESSMENT

Ask the following questions to determine if students understand the content presented in this lesson.

**1.** What is the major difference between a matrix and its determinant? A matrix is an array of numbers; it cannot be evaluated. The determinant of a matrix is a number.

Consider the following system.
$$5x + y = 6$$
$$-3x + 4y = 8$$

**2.** Write the coefficient determinant, A.
$$A = \begin{vmatrix} 5 & 1 \\ -3 & 4 \end{vmatrix}$$

**3.** Using $A$, $A_x$, $A_y$, represent the solution of the system.
$$x = \frac{A_x}{A}, \; y = \frac{A_y}{A}$$

### ASSIGNMENT GUIDE

**Basic:** 1–31, 37–45
**Enriched:** 1–45

### Reteaching Worksheet 8-5

Name _____  Date _____

RETEACHING  **8-5**

#### MATRICES AND DETERMINANTS

A **matrix** is a rectangular array of numbers. A matrix of $n$ rows and $m$ columns has dimensions $n \times m$.

$A = \begin{bmatrix} -1 & 2 \\ 5 & 3 \end{bmatrix}$  Matrix $A$ has 2 rows and 2 columns and thus has dimensions $2 \times 2$.

Since matrix $A$ has same number of rows and columns, it is called a **square matrix**. The value of determinant of a $2 \times 2$ square matrix is the difference of the products of the diagonal entries.

$$\det A = \begin{vmatrix} a & b \\ c & d \end{vmatrix} = ad - bc$$

**Example**

Evaluate the determinant of matrix A.

**Solution**

$\det A = \begin{vmatrix} -1 & 2 \\ 5 & 3 \end{vmatrix}$

$= -1(3) - 2(5)$    $a = -1, b = 2, c = 5, d = 3$

$= -3 - 10$

$= -13$

☑ **EXERCISES**

Evaluate each determinant. Show your work.

**1.** $\begin{vmatrix} 5 & 1 \\ -4 & 0 \end{vmatrix} = \underline{\quad 5(0) \quad} - \underline{\quad 1(-4) \quad} = \underline{\quad 4 \quad}$

**2.** $\begin{vmatrix} -2 & 3 \\ 7 & -1 \end{vmatrix} = \underline{\quad -2(-1) \quad} - \underline{\quad 3(7) \quad} = \underline{\quad -19 \quad}$

**3.** $\begin{vmatrix} 9 & -8 \\ 3 & -2 \end{vmatrix} = \underline{\quad 9(-2) \quad} - \underline{\quad -8(3) \quad} = \underline{\quad 6 \quad}$

**4.** $\begin{vmatrix} 10 & 5 \\ 12 & -8 \end{vmatrix} = \underline{\quad 10(-8) \quad} - \underline{\quad 5(12) \quad} = \underline{\quad -140 \quad}$

---

### Example 3

**MOVIES** Movie tickets to a matinee cost $7.25 for adults and $5.50 for students. A group of friends purchased 8 matinee tickets for $52.75. How many adult tickets and student tickets were purchased?

**Solution**

Let $x$ represent the total number of adult tickets. Let $y$ represent the total number of student tickets.

$$x + y = 8$$
$$7.25x + 5.5y = 52.75$$

Use the method of determinants to find $x$ and $y$.

$$\det A = \begin{vmatrix} 1 & 1 \\ 7.25 & 5.5 \end{vmatrix}, \det A_x = \begin{vmatrix} 8 & 1 \\ 52.75 & 5.5 \end{vmatrix}, \det A_y = \begin{vmatrix} 1 & 8 \\ 7.25 & 52.75 \end{vmatrix}$$

$$x = \frac{A_x}{A} = \frac{\begin{vmatrix} 8 & 1 \\ 52.75 & 5.5 \end{vmatrix}}{\begin{vmatrix} 1 & 1 \\ 7.25 & 5.5 \end{vmatrix}} = \frac{8(5.5) - 1(52.75)}{1(5.5) - 1(7.25)} = \frac{-8.75}{-1.75} = 5$$

$$y = \frac{A_y}{A} = \frac{\begin{vmatrix} 1 & 8 \\ 7.25 & 52.75 \end{vmatrix}}{\begin{vmatrix} 1 & 1 \\ 7.25 & 5.5 \end{vmatrix}} = \frac{1(52.75) - 8(7.25)}{1(5.5) - 1(7.25)} = \frac{-5.25}{-1.75} = 3$$

So, there were 5 adult tickets and 3 student tickets purchased.

### ◼ TRY THESE EXERCISES

Evaluate each determinant.

**1.** $\begin{vmatrix} 0 & 4 \\ -2 & 3 \end{vmatrix}$ 8

**2.** $\begin{vmatrix} -7 & 7 \\ 3 & -3 \end{vmatrix}$ 0

**3.** $\begin{vmatrix} 4.1 & -2.7 \\ 0.1 & -1.2 \end{vmatrix}$ -4.65

**4.** $\begin{vmatrix} 6 & -1 \\ 4 & 0 \end{vmatrix}$ 4

Solve each system of equations using the method of determinants.

**5.** $-4x + 5y = 2$   $(-3, -2)$
$-3x + 6y = -3$

**6.** $-5x + 5y = -5$   $(5, 4)$
$3x - 4y = -1$

**7.** $3x + 5y = 9$   $(-62, 39)$
$-2x - 3y = 7$

**8.** $4x - y = 9$   $(1, -5)$
$x - 3y = 16$

**9.** $3x - 5y = -23$   $(-1, 4)$
$5x + 4y = 11$

**10.** $3x + 2y = 24$   $(4, 6)$
$15x - 2y = 48$

**11. SPORTS** A swim team has 52 members. The number of female athletes is one more than twice the number of male athletes. How many members of the team are female?
35 female members

### ◼ PRACTICE EXERCISES  •  For Extra Practice, see page 611.

Evaluate each determinant.

**12.** $\begin{vmatrix} 0.5 & 1.2 \\ 4 & -3 \end{vmatrix}$ -6.3

**13.** $\begin{vmatrix} 5 & -2 \\ -4 & 8 \end{vmatrix}$ 32

**14.** $\begin{vmatrix} -10 & 9 \\ -8 & 6 \end{vmatrix}$ 12

**15.** $\begin{vmatrix} 12 & 11 \\ 9 & -6 \end{vmatrix}$ -171

---

## Alternative Assessment

**MATH JOURNAL**  If $\begin{vmatrix} a & b \\ c & d \end{vmatrix} = 4$, evaluate each of the following determinants. Explain your answers.

**1.** $\begin{vmatrix} c & d \\ a & b \end{vmatrix}$  -4; since $cb - ad$ is the additive inverse of $ad - bc = 4$

**2.** $\begin{vmatrix} b & a \\ d & c \end{vmatrix}$  -4; since $bc - ad = -(-bc + ad)$

**3.** $\begin{vmatrix} d & c \\ b & a \end{vmatrix}$  4; since $da - bc = ad - bc$

## LESSON 8-3 ◼ Solve Systems by Substitution, p. 344

▶ **Substitution** can be used to solve a system of equations algebraically. Solve one of the equations for one variable. Substitute that expression in the other equation and solve.

▶ When the solution of a system results in a true statement, the lines coincide and there are infinite solutions.

▶ When the solution of a system results in a false statement, the lines are parallel and there are no solutions.

**Solve each system of equations. Check the solution.**

**17.** $x + y = -4$  $(-3, -1)$
$x - y = -2$

**18.** $3x - y = 1$  $(2, 5)$
$y = \frac{1}{2}x + 4$

**19.** $x - 2y = -10$  $(0, 5)$
$7x + 3y = 15$

**20.** The Chess Club wants to order T-shirts for its members. Shirt World will make the shirts for a $30 set-up fee and then $12 per shirt. T-Mania will make the shirts for $70 set-up fee and then $8 per shirt. For how many T-shirts will the cost be the same? What will be the cost?  10 shirts; $150

## LESSON 8-4 ◼ Solve Systems by Adding, Subtracting and Multiplying, p 348

▶ Solving a system of equations by an algebraic method can also be done by eliminating one of the variables using addition, subtraction, or multiplication and addition.

**Solve each system of equations. Check the solution.**

**21.** $3x - 2y = 4$  $(2, 1)$
$-3x + 4y = -2$

**22.** $3x - 5y = -16$  $(3, 5)$
$2x + 5y = 31$

**23.** $2m - 5n = -6$  $(7, 4)$
$2m - 7n = -14$

**24.** $4x - 2y = -10$  $(0, 5)$
$3x - 2y = -10$

**25.** $3x + 8y = -2$  $(2, -1)$
$5x + 3y = 7$

**26.** $4x - 7y = 10$  $(-1, -2)$
$3x + 2y = -7$

## LESSON 8-5 ◼ Matrices and Determinants, p. 354

▶ A **square matrix** has the same number of rows and columns.

▶ The value of a $2 \times 2$ **determinant** is the difference of the products of the diagonal entries in a matrix.

▶ To solve a system of equations using determinants, first write both equations in standard form, $Ax + By = C$.

**Evaluate each determinant.**

**27.** $\begin{vmatrix} 1 & 4 \\ 3 & 6 \end{vmatrix}$  $-6$

**28.** $\begin{vmatrix} -1 & 0 \\ -2 & 4 \end{vmatrix}$  $-4$

**29.** $\begin{vmatrix} 4 & -5 \\ -3 & 2 \end{vmatrix}$  $-7$

**30.** Solve the systems of equations using the method of determinants.
$3x - 5y = -1$
$-2x + 4y = -2$  $(-7, -4)$

$8x + 8y = 3$
$32x - 12y = 1$  $(0.125, 0.25)$

**31.** Play It Again sells used CDs and videos. In its first week, the store sold 40 used CDs and videos, at $4 per CD and $6 per video. The sales for both CDs and videos totalled $180. Use the method of determinants to find the number of CDs and videos the store sold in the first week.  30 CDs, 10 videos

## Teaching Tip

Discuss with students that the method of substitution is most appropriate when one equation of the system already has a variable isolated, as in Exercise 18. But, when both equations are arranged with corresponding terms in columns, unless otherwise instructed, students should first consider using addition or subtraction. For example, Exercise 17 easily lends itself to eliminating the variable $y$ by addition. However, even though the equations of Exercise 19 are arranged in corresponding columns, solving the first equation for $x$ and using substitution is the most efficient method. To use addition or subtraction in this case would require first multiplying each of the original equations by a constant.

**32.**
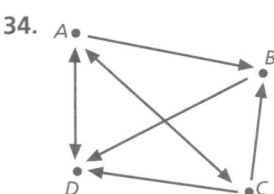

$$\begin{array}{c} \\ A \\ B \\ C \\ D \\ E \end{array}\begin{bmatrix} A & B & C & D & E \\ 0 & 1 & 0 & 1 & 0 \\ 1 & 0 & 0 & 1 & 0 \\ 0 & 1 & 0 & 1 & 0 \\ 0 & 1 & 0 & 0 & 1 \\ 0 & 0 & 1 & 1 & 0 \end{bmatrix}$$

**34.**
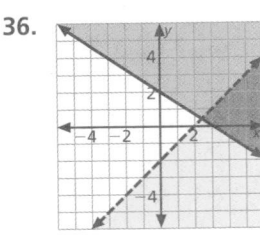

**36.**
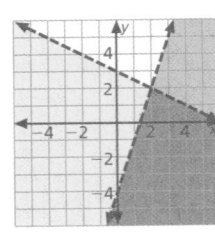

**37.**
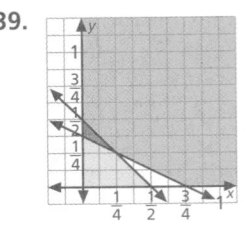

**39.**

---

## LESSON 8-6 ▪ Problem Solving Skills: Directed Graphs, p. 358

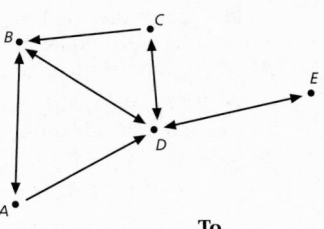

► A **directed graph** is a geometrical representation of a map. It shows locations as points and roads as lines.

**The directed graph represents the number of commuter train runs between cities A, B, C, and D.**

**32.** Create a matrix for the number of runs from one city to another. See additional answers.

**33.** How many ways can you travel by commuter train directly to City C from another city? 1

**34.** The matrix shown represents the number of nonstop bus routes between streets A, B, C and D. Draw a directed graph that corresponds to the matrix. See additional answers.

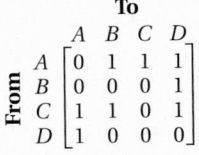

$$\begin{array}{cc} & \text{To} \\ \begin{array}{c}\text{From}\end{array} & \begin{array}{c} A \\ B \\ C \\ D \end{array}\begin{array}{cccc} A & B & C & D \\ \begin{bmatrix} 0 & 1 & 1 & 1 \\ 0 & 0 & 0 & 1 \\ 1 & 1 & 0 & 1 \\ 1 & 0 & 0 & 0 \end{bmatrix} \end{array} \end{array}$$

## LESSON 8-7 ▪ Systems of Inequalities, p. 362

► The solution set of a system of linear inequalities is the intersection of the graphs of the inequalities.

► The slope-intercept form of an inequality indicates the boundary line, whether the boundary line should be solid or dashed, and which part of the plane to shade. $y < x + 1$; $y \le -x + 1$

**35.** Write a system of linear inequalities for the graph shown.

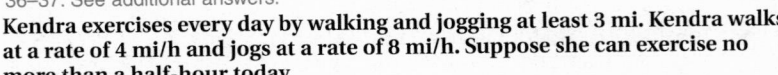

**Graph the solution set of each system of linear inequalities.**

**36.** $-x + y < -2$
$-2x - 3y \le -6$

**37.** $2y + x < 6$
$3x - y > 4$

36–37. See additional answers.

**Kendra exercises every day by walking and jogging at least 3 mi. Kendra walks at a rate of 4 mi/h and jogs at a rate of 8 mi/h. Suppose she can exercise no more than a half-hour today.**

**38.** Write two inequalities to represent the situation. $x + y \le 0.5$; $4x + 8y \ge 3$

**39.** Graph the inequalities. See additional answers.

**40.** Give the coordinates of a point that satisfies the inequalities. Explain the coordinates in terms of the problem. Answers will vary. Sample answer:

A coordinate that satisfies the inequalities is $\left(\frac{1}{10}, \frac{2}{5}\right)$. This means that Kendra can walk for $\frac{1}{10}$ h, or 6 min, and she can jog for $\frac{2}{5}$ h, or 12 min.

## CHAPTER INVESTIGATION

**EXTENSION** Obtain a football schedule for your school. The schedule can be for this year, a past year or the upcoming year. Be sure the schedule indicates whom all members of the league play each week. Work with a partner to create a simulation of the football season. Determine who wins each game by rolling a number cube. Whoever rolls the higher number chooses the winning team of each game. Determine which teams will be the top four to advance to the tournament. Use the point values you found in the Chapter Investigation of this chapter.

---

## THEME: Sports

The benchmarks and expectations for this extension are as follows.
- They choose two of the top four teams in the football league. They write and solve a system of equations using substitution to find the point value.
- Students choose two of the top four football teams. They write and solve a system of equations using addition, subtraction or multiplication.
- Students choose both systems of equations in the first two benchmarks. They verify that their answers in the first two benchmarks are correct.
- Students use a football schedule for their school and work with a partner to create a simulation of the football season. Use a number cube simulation to determine who wins each game and advance. They use the point values they found in the first three benchmarks.

# Chapter 8 Assessment

**For each line identified by two points, state the slope of a line parallel and the slope of a line perpendicular to it.**

**1.** $M(3, -4)$ and $N(8, -3)$ $\frac{1}{5}, -5$  **2.** $A(2, -5)$ and $B(-2, 3)$ $-2, \frac{1}{2}$  **3.** $S(3, 4)$ and $T(3, -5)$ undefined, 0

**Write an equation in slope-intercept form of a line passing through the given point and parallel to the given line.**

$y = -\frac{3}{4}x - \frac{3}{4}$

**4.** $(3, 4); y = -4x + 5$  $y = -4x + 16$  **5.** $(-1, 0); y = -\frac{3}{4}x + 2$  **6.** $(0, 6); x + y = 0$  $y = -x + 6$

**7.** Write an equation in slope-intercept form of a line passing through the given point and perpendicular to the given line in Exercises 4–6. $y = \frac{1}{4}x + \frac{13}{4}; y = \frac{4}{3}x + \frac{4}{3}; y = x + 6$

**Use a graph to solve each system.** For 8–10, see additional answers.

**8.** $3x - y = 2$ $(0, -2)$  **9.** $x + 2y = 6$ no solution  **10.** $x + 3y \geq -3$
$-x + 2y = -4$  $4x + 8y = -8$  $x - 2y < -6$

**Solve each system of equations. Check the solution.**

**11.** $x - y = 7$ $(10, 3)$  **12.** $3x - 4y = 5$ $(-1, -2)$  **13.** $2x - 3y = 4$ $(2, 0)$
$2x - 3y = 11$  $-x + 4y = -7$  $-3x + 4y = -6$

**Evaluate each determinate.**

**14.** $\begin{vmatrix} 5 & 7 \\ -3 & 0 \end{vmatrix}$ 21  **15.** $\begin{vmatrix} 3.1 & -1 \\ 0.5 & -1.2 \end{vmatrix}$ -3.22  **16.** $\begin{vmatrix} 2 & -7 \\ 5 & -1 \end{vmatrix}$ 33  **17.** $\begin{vmatrix} -1 & -2 \\ -1 & -1 \end{vmatrix}$ -1

**Solve each system of equations using the method of determinants.**

**18.** $x - y = 5$ $(8, 3)$  **19.** $5x + 2y = 6$ $(2, -2)$  **20.** $2x + 3y = -3$ $(0.375, -1.25)$
$-x + 2y = -2$  $x + 8y = -14$  $6x - 7y = 11$

**The directed map represents the connections between school buildings in one district.**

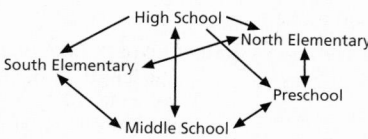

**21.** Create a matrix for the school district that shows the number of direct connections from one school building to another. See additional answers.

**22.** How many ways can you get directly to North Elementary? 3

**23.** Create a matrix for the school district that shows the number of ways a bus could travel between two schools with one stop. See additional answers.

**24.** Jack's and Matt's ages together total 19. Matt is five years older than Jack. How old is each boy? Jack is 7 and Matt is 12.

**25.** Rashida has 16 coins in her pocket that total $2.95. They are dimes and quarters. How many of each coin does she have? 9 quarters, 7 dimes

Math Online mathmatters2.com/chapter_assessment

## ADDITIONAL ANSWERS

**8.** 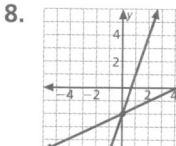  **9.** **10.**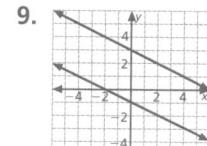

**21.**

To

|      | H | M | N | S | P |
|------|---|---|---|---|---|
| H    | 0 | 1 | 1 | 1 | 1 |
| M    | 1 | 0 | 0 | 1 | 1 |
| N    | 0 | 0 | 0 | 1 | 1 |
| S    | 0 | 1 | 1 | 0 | 0 |
| P    | 0 | 1 | 1 | 0 | 0 |

From

**23.**

To

|      | H | M | N | S | P |
|------|---|---|---|---|---|
| H    | 1 | 2 | 2 | 2 | 2 |
| M    | 0 | 3 | 3 | 1 | 1 |
| N    | 0 | 2 | 2 | 0 | 0 |
| S    | 1 | 0 | 0 | 2 | 2 |
| P    | 1 | 0 | 0 | 2 | 2 |

From

## Standardized Test Practice

These two pages contain practice questions in the various formats that can be found on the most frequently given standardized tests.

A student recording sheet for these two pages can be found on p. A1 of the *Chapter 8 Resource Masters*.

## Standardized Test Practice Student Recording Sheet

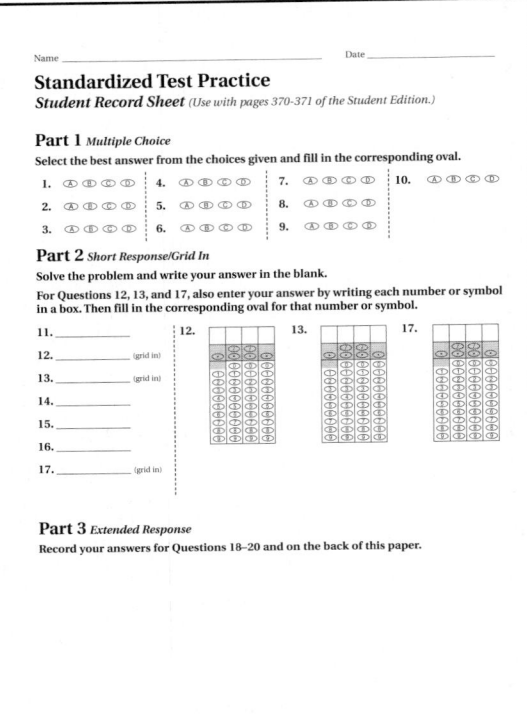

## Additional Practice

See pp. 271–273 in the *Chapter 8 Resource Masters* for additional standardized test practice.

# Standardized Test Practice

### Part 1 Multiple Choice

**Record your answers on the answer sheet provided by your teacher or on a sheet of paper.**

1. Simplify $3x - 4 + (2x - 1) - (3x - 1)$. (Lesson 2-4) A
   - (A) $2x - 4$
   - (B) $2x - 6$
   - (C) $8x - 6$
   - (D) $8x - 2$

2. What is the solution of $\frac{3x - 4}{2} = \frac{7x + 1}{4}$? (Lesson 3-5) B
   - (A) $-10$
   - (B) $-9$
   - (C) $9$
   - (D) $10$

3. If the spinner is spun once, find $P$(gray or odd). (Lesson 4-4) C

   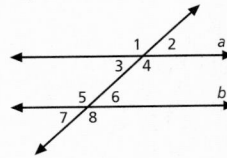

   - (A) $\frac{3}{16}$
   - (B) $\frac{3}{8}$
   - (C) $\frac{5}{8}$
   - (D) $\frac{7}{8}$

4. Luca remembered that the four digits of his locker combination were 4, 9, 15, and 22, but not in that order. What is the maximum number of different attempts Luca can make before his locker opens? (Lesson 4-6) C
   - (A) 4
   - (B) 16
   - (C) 24
   - (D) 256

5. In the figure, $a \parallel b$. Find $m\angle 1$ if $m\angle 7$ is 42°. (Lesson 5-3) D

   - (A) 42°
   - (B) 48°
   - (C) 58°
   - (D) 138°

6. What is the equation of the line? (Lesson 6-3) B
   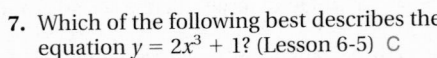
   - (A) $y = -\frac{1}{2}x + 2$
   - (B) $y = -\frac{1}{2}x + 1$
   - (C) $y = \frac{1}{2}x + 1$
   - (D) $y = 2x + 1$

7. Which of the following best describes the equation $y = 2x^3 + 1$? (Lesson 6-5) C
   - (A) not a function
   - (B) a linear function
   - (C) a nonlinear function
   - (D) a quadratic function

8. The coordinates of the vertices of quadrilateral $ABCD$ are $A(-2, 4)$, $B(3, 7)$, $C(4, -2)$, and $D(-5, -3)$. If the quadrilateral is moved up 3 units and left 1 unit, which of these coordinates names a vertex of quadrilateral $A'B'C'D'$? (Lesson 7-1) D
   - (A) $(1, 5)$
   - (B) $(-8, -2)$
   - (C) $(0, 6)$
   - (D) $(7, -3)$

9. Which equation represents a line parallel to the line given by $y - 3x = 6$? (Lesson 8-1) B
   - (A) $y = -3x + 4$
   - (B) $y = 3x - 2$
   - (C) $y = \frac{1}{3}x + 6$
   - (D) $y = \frac{1}{3}x + 4$

10. The perimeter of a rectangular garden is 68 ft. The length of the garden is 4 more than twice the width. Which system of equations will determine the length $\ell$ and the width $w$ of the garden? (Lesson 8-3) A
    - (A) $2\ell + 2w = 68$
      $\ell = 2w + 4$
    - (B) $2\ell + 2w = 68$
      $w = 2\ell + 4$
    - (C) $2 + 2w = 68$
      $2\ell - w = 4$
    - (D) $2\ell + 2w = 68$
      $\ell = 4 - 2w$

## Part 2 | Short Response/Grid In

**Record your answers on the answer sheet provided by your teacher or on a sheet of paper.**

11. On a standardized test, Jenny scored higher than 75 of the 95 people who took the test. In what percentile did she score? (Lesson 1-6)  79th

12. Simplify $2(2x + 3) - 4(x + 2)$. (Lesson 2-6)  $-2$

13. Solve $7 = \sqrt{5x + 2}$ for $x$. (Lesson 3-8)  $\frac{47}{5}$ or 9.4

14. A pair of adjacent, congruent angles are supplementary to each other. What is the measure of each angle? (Lesson 5-2)  90°

15. Triangle $ABC$ is inscribed in a circle. If $m\,\widehat{AB} = 150°$ and $m\,\widehat{AC} = 120°$, what is $m\angle BAC$? (Lesson 5-8)  45°

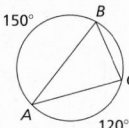

16. Copy the figure. Then shade two squares so that the figure has rotational symmetry. (Lesson 7-4)

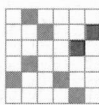

17. The sum of two numbers is 15. The difference between the numbers is 11. Find the value of the greater of the two numbers. (Lesson 8-4)  13

**Test-Taking Tip**
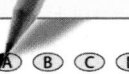  Ⓐ Ⓑ Ⓒ Ⓓ

**Questions 11, 14–16**
Knowing mathematical terms is critical to your success on standardized tests. In preparation, make flash cards of the key terms using the glossary of your textbook.

 **Math Online**  mathmatters2.com/standardized_test

## Part 3 | Extended Response

**Record your answers on a sheet of paper. Show your work.**

18. The capital letter A looks the same after a reflection over a vertical line. It does not look the same after a reflection over a horizontal line.

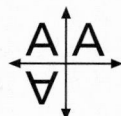

a. Name the other capital letters that look the same after a reflection over a vertical line. (Lesson 7-2)

b. Name the capital letters that look the same after a reflection over a horizontal line. (Lesson 7-2)

c. Which capital letters have line symmetry? (Lesson 7-4)

d. Which capital letters have rotational symmetry? (Lesson 7-4)
18a–d. See additional answers.

19. The manager of a movie theater found that Saturday's sales were $3675. He knew that a total of 650 tickets were sold Saturday. Adult tickets cost $7.50, and children's tickets cost $4.50. (Lesson 8-3)  19b. $7.5A + 4.5C = 3675$

a. Write an equation to represent the number of tickets sold.  $A + C = 650$

b. Write an equation to represent the amount of money collected.

c. How many of each kind of ticket were sold?  250 adult tickets and 400 children tickets

20. Consider the following system of equations. (Lesson 8-5)
$$2x - 3y = -4$$
$$-3x + 2y = 6$$

a. Write determinants $A$, $A_x$, and $A_y$ for this system.

b. Find the value of each determinant and use these values to find the solution of the system.
20a–b. See additional answers.

**Chapter 8  Standardized Test Practice   371**

## Rubrics

The following rubrics are sample scoring devices for short response and extended response questions.

### Short Response

| Points | Description |
|--------|-------------|
| 2 | The student demonstrates a **thorough understanding** of the mathematics of the task. The response may contain minor flaws that do not detract from the demonstration of a thorough understanding. |
| 1 | The student has provided a response that is only **partially correct.** |
| 0 | The student has provided a **completely incorrect** solution or no response at all. |

### Extended Response

| Points | Description |
|--------|-------------|
| 4 | The student demonstrates a **thorough understanding** of the mathematics of the task. The response contains minor flaws that do not detract from the demonstration of a thorough understanding. |
| 3 | The student demonstrates an **understanding** of the mathematics of the task. The response is essentially correct and demonstrates an essential but less than thorough understanding of the mathematics. |
| 2 | The student has demonstrated only a **partial understanding** of the mathematics of the task. Although the student may have used the correct approach to a solution or may have provided a correct solution, the work lacks an essential understanding of the underlying mathematical concepts. |
| 1 | The student has demonstrated a **very limited understanding** of the mathematics of the task. The response is incomplete and exhibits many flaws. |
| 0 | The student has provided a **completely incorrect** solution or no response at all. |

## ADDITIONAL ANSWERS

18a. H, I, M, O, T, U, V, W, X, Y

18b. B, C, D, E, H, I, N, O, X

18c. A, B, C, D, E, H, I, K, M, O, T, U, V, W, X, Y

18d. H, I, N, O, S, X, Z

20a. $A = \begin{vmatrix} 2 & -3 \\ -3 & 2 \end{vmatrix}$, $A_x = \begin{vmatrix} -4 & -3 \\ 6 & 2 \end{vmatrix}$, $A_y = \begin{vmatrix} 2 & -4 \\ -3 & 6 \end{vmatrix}$

20b. $A = \begin{vmatrix} 2 & -3 \\ -3 & 2 \end{vmatrix} = 2 \cdot 2 - (-3 \cdot -3)$
$$= 4 - 9 \text{ or } -5$$

$A_x = \begin{vmatrix} -4 & -3 \\ 6 & 2 \end{vmatrix} = -4 \cdot 2 - (-3 \cdot 6)$
$$= -8 - (-18)$$
$$= -8 + 18 \text{ or } 10$$

$A_y = \begin{vmatrix} 2 & -4 \\ -3 & 6 \end{vmatrix} = 2 \cdot 6 - [-4 \cdot (-3)]$
$$= 12 - 12 \text{ or } 0$$

$x = \frac{A_x}{A}$                    $y = \frac{A_y}{A}$
$\quad = \frac{10}{-5}$ or $-2$          $\quad = \frac{0}{-5}$ or 0

The solution is $(-2, 0)$.

# Polynomials

| Lesson | Lesson Objectives | Pacing (days) | NCTM Standards | State/Local Objectives |
|---|---|---|---|---|
| 9-1 | **Add and Subtract Polynomials** (pp. 376–379)<br>• Write polynomials in standard form.<br>• Add and subtract polynomials. | 1 | 1, 2, 9, 10 | |
| 9-2 | **Multiply Monomials** (pp. 380–383)<br>• Use the rules of exponents to multiply monomials. | 1 | 1, 2, 9, 10 | |
| 9-3 | **Divide by a Monomial** (pp. 386–389)<br>• Divide monomials and polynomials by monomials. | 1 | 1, 2, 9, 10 | |
| 9-4 | **Multiply a Polynomial by a Monomial** (pp. 390–393)<br>• Multiply polynomials by monomials. | 2 | 1, 2, 9, 10 | |
| 9-5 | **Multiply Binomials** (pp. 396–399)<br>• Multiply binomials. | 2 | 1, 2, 9, 10 | |
| 9-6 | **Problem Solving Skills: Work Backwards** (pp. 400–401)<br>• Solve problems by working backwards. | 1 | 1, 2, 6, 10 | |
| 9-7 | **Factor Using Greatest Common Factor (GCF)** (pp. 404–407)<br>• Factor polynomials using the Greatest Common Factor (GCF). | 2 | 1, 2, 9, 10 | |
| 9-8 | **Perfect Squares and Difference of Squares** (pp. 408–411)<br>• Factor perfect square trinomials.<br>• Factor a difference of perfect squares. | 2 | 1, 2, 9, 10 | |
| **Review** | | 1 | | |
| **Testing** | | 1 | | |

**Key to NCTM Standards:**

1=Number & Operations, 2=Algebra, 3=Geometry,
4=Measurement, 5=Data Analysis & Probability,
6=Problem Solving, 7=Reasoning & Proof,
8=Communication, 9=Connections, 10=Representation

**Pacing:** Suggestions for the year can be found on page xvi.

# Chapter Resource Manager

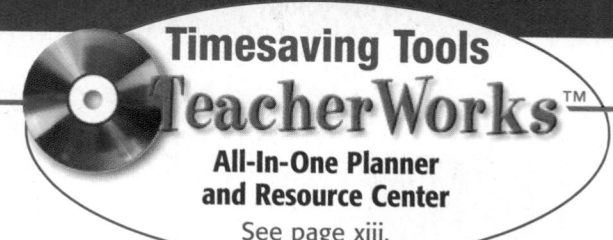

| Reteaching Activities | Extra Practice | Enrichment | Assessment | Basic Mathematics Review | Study Skills Activities | Lesson Warm-Ups Transparencies | Teaching Transparencies | Technology Activities | Materials Needed |
|---|---|---|---|---|---|---|---|---|---|
| 275 | 276 | 277 | | | 22 | 35 | TK-4, TK-5 | 9-1 | Algeblocks with Basic Mat |
| 278 | 279 | 280 | | | | 35 | TK-6 | | Algeblocks with Quadrant Mat |
| 281 | 282 | 283 | | | | 36 | TK-5, TK-6, TK-9 | | graph paper, Algeblocks with Quadrant Mat |
| 284 | 285 | 286 | | | 30 | 36 | TK-5, TK-6 | | Algeblocks with Quadrant Mat, graphing calculator |
| 287 | 288 | 289 | | | | 37 | TK-5, TK-6, TK-16, RF-46 | | Algeblocks with Quadrant Mat |
| 290 | 291 | 292 | | | | 37 | RF-1 | | calculator |
| 293 | 294 | 295 | | | 31 | 38 | TK-5, TK-6 | 9-7 | Algeblocks with Quadrant Map |
| 296 | 297 | 298 | 301–307 | | | 38 | TK-5, TK-6, RF-47 | | Algeblocks with Quadrant Map |

| Quick Review Math Handbook, Book 2 | hot words hot topics |
|---|---|
| **MathMatters 2** Lesson(s) | **Hot Topic** Lesson(s) |
| 9-1 | 6-2 |
| 9-2 | 3-1, 6-2 |
| 9-3 | 2-1, 3-1, 6-2 |
| 9-4, 9-5 | 3-1, 6-2 |
| 9-6 | 1-3, 6-1 |
| 9-7, 9-8 | 1-4 |

# Content and Connections

## MathMatters 2 Chapter 9 Highlights

Add and subtract polynomials. (9-1)

Use rules of exponents to multiply monomials. (9-2)

Divide monomials and polynomials by monomials. (9-3)

Multiply polynomials by monomials. (9-4)

Multiply binomials. (9-5)

Solve problems by working backwards. (9-6)

Factor polynomials using the greatest common factor. (9-7)

Factor perfect square trinomials and differences of perfect squares. (9-8)

## Connections to the Past

**MM1 (Ch. 9):** Add and subtract polynomials.

**MM1 (Ch. 9):** Multiply monomials.

**MM1 (Ch. 9):** Divide monomials and polynomials by monomials.

**MM1 (Ch. 9):** Solve problems by multiplying a polynomial by a monomial.

**MM1 (Ch. 3):** Solve problems by using the distributive property.

**MM1 (Ch. 5):** Solve problems by working backwards.

**MM1 (Ch. 9):** Factor polynomials using the greatest common factor.

**MM1 (Ch. 9):** Solve a problem using Algeblocks and area.

## Connections to the Future

**MM3 (Ch. 11):** Add and subtract polynomials.

**MM3 (Ch. 1):** Use properties of exponents to evaluate and simplify expressions.

**MM3 (Ch. 11):** Factor polynomials into a monomial factor and a polynomial factor.

**MM3 (Ch. 11):** Multiply polynomials by monomials.

**MM3 (Ch. 11):** Use factoring to solve quadratic equations.

**MM3 (Ch. 12):** Solve problems by working backwards.

**MM3 (Ch. 11):** Factor polynomials by grouping.

**MM3 (Ch. 12):** Solve quadratic equations by completing the square.

### Key

| | |
|---|---|
| PC | = Previous Course |
| MM1 | = *MathMatters 1* |
| MM2 | = *MathMatters 2* |
| MM3 | = *MathMatters 3* |

## Connecting the Strands

| NCTM Strand | Lesson(s) |
|---|---|
| Algebra | 9-1, 9-2, 9-3, 9-4, 9-5, 9-6 |
| Geometry | 9-7 |
| Problem Solving | 9-1, 9-2, 9-3, 9-4, 9-5, 9-6, 9-7 |
| Communications | 9-7 |
| Connections | 9-1, 9-2, 9-3, 9-4, 9-5, 9-6 |
| Representation | 9-1, 9-2, 9-3, 9-4, 9-5, 9-6, 9-7 |

| | Type | Student Edition | Teacher Resources | Technology/Internet |
|---|---|---|---|---|
| **INTERVENTION** | Ongoing | Are You Ready?, pp. 374–375<br>Check Understanding, pp. 377, 381, 386, 397, 404, 409<br>Review and Practice Your Skills, pp. 384–385, 394–395, 402–403<br>Mid-Chapter Quiz, p. 395 | Lesson Warm-Ups Transparencies, pp. WU-35, WU-36, WU-37, WU-38<br>Quick Assessment, *ATE* pp. 375, 378, 382, 388, 392, 398, 401, 406, 410 | mathmatters2.com/extra_ examples<br>mathmatters2.com/self_check_quiz |
| | Mixed Review | pp. 379, 383, 389, 393, 399, 401, 407, 411 | | |
| | Error Analysis | You Make the Call, pp. 399, 411<br>Error Alert, p. 382 | Teaching Tip, *ATE* pp. 388, 394 | |
| **ASSESSMENT** | Standardized Test Practice | pp. 416–417<br>Preparing for Standardized Tests, pp. 627–644 | Standardized Test Practice, *CRM* pp. 305–307 | mathmatters2.com/standardized_test |
| | Open-Ended Assessment | Chapter Investigation, pp. 373, 383, 393, 411, 414 | Chapter Investigation, *ATE* p. 414<br>Alternative Assessment, *ATE* p. 415 | |
| | Chapter Assessment | Chapter Review, pp. 412–414<br>Chapter Assessment, p. 415 | Multiple-Choice Tests (Forms A and B), *CRM* pp. 301–304 | mathmatters2.com/chapter_assessment |

**Key to Abbreviations:** *ATE* = Annotated Teacher's Edition, *CRM* = Chapter Resource Masters

## Additional Intervention

***Basic Mathematics Review*** includes 80 lessons, consisting of an instructional page and a test page. This workbook also features a pretest, posttest, table of measurement equivalents, and calculator appendices.

### ExamView® Pro

Use ExamView® Pro Testmaker CD-ROM to:
- Create **multiple versions** of tests.
- Create **modified** tests for *inclusion* students with one mouse click.
- **Edit** existing questions and **add** your own questions.
- Build tests aligned with state standards using built-in **state curriculum correlations**.
- Change **English** tests to **Spanish** with one mouse click and vice versa.

# Polynomials

## THEME: Geography

**P**olynomials are often used in cartography (map making) and other areas of geography.

Whether you are walking to the store, riding your bike to a park, driving to visit relatives, or flying across the country, geography skills are used.

- **Truck drivers** (page 385) drive across the country, delivering goods to manufacturers and retail businesses for consumers to purchase. They must prepare for many unknown possibilities such as changes in weather, changes in road conditions, and the demands of delivery schedules.

- The geographic features of the land play a crucial role in decisions that **air traffic controllers** (page 403) must make on a routine basis. A flight path may vary, depending on the distance of the trip, noise restrictions, weather conditions, and the flight paths of other airplanes.

**Math Online**

mathmatters2.com/chapter_theme

---

## Chapter Opener

### NCTM Standards/Strands
- Data Analysis & Probability
- Representation

### Vocabulary

geography        polynomial

### Theme Connections
The word *geography*, "earth description", was adopted around 200 BC by the Greek scholar Eratosthenes. Geographic study encompasses the environment of the earth's surface and the relationship of humans to this environment, which includes both physical geographic features (climate, land, water, plant life, animal life) and cultural geographic features (artificial entities, such as nations, lines of communication and transportation). Geographers employ mathematics, economics, history, biology, and geology in their work.

### Career Opportunities
Many careers require understanding of polynomials. Two such careers are highlighted in the MathWorks features. Others include: cartographer, geomorphologist, biogeographist, oceanographist, political geographist, military geographist, ethnographist, historical geographist, urban geographist, demographist, linguistic geographist.
- Truck driver, page 385
- Air traffic controller, page 403

## Internet Connection

### Theme Activities
Mathmatters2.com/chapter_theme provides links to the Internet that will help students gather information about the use of math in the real world, particularly data and measures. To search for additional addresses, begin a search of *geography*. Then use key words to call up the two basic branches, *systemic geography* or *regional geography*. Students can brainstorm other key words.

### Chapter Investigation
Use the Internet and other resources to locate additional information about orienteering.

### As a Chapter Project
The goal of this project is for students to use an orienteering map to find the approximate length of an orienteering course. Students can use the Group Project Planner on page 299 and the Project Planning Calendar on page 300 in the *Chapter 9 Resource Masters* to complete the project. Benchmarks **a**, **b**, and **c** should be completed after the lesson listed in parentheses has been studied. Benchmark **d** should be completed at the end of the chapter.

## Extreme Points of the United States (50 States)

| Location | Latitude | Longitude | Distance[1] | |
|---|---|---|---|---|
| | | | miles | kilometers |
| Geographic center: Butte County, SD | 44°58'N | 103°46'W | 0 | 0 |
| Northernmost point: Point Barrow, AK | 71°23'N | 156°29'W | 2507 | 4034 |
| Easternmost point: West Quoddy Head, ME | 44°49'N | 66°57'W | 1788 | 2997 |
| Southernmost point: Ka Lae (South Cape), HI | 18°55'N | 155°41'W | 3463 | 5573 |
| Westernmost point: Cape Wrangell, AK (Attu Island) | 52°55'N | 172°27'E | 3625 | 5833 |

[1] Distance is from geographic center of United States, Butte County, SD.

### Data Activity: Extreme Points in the U.S.

**Use the table for Questions 1–4.**

1. Find the mean distance in miles from the geographic center of the 50 U.S. states to the northernmost point, easternmost point, southernmost point, and westernmost point.
2845.75 mi

2. What extreme location is farthest from Butte County, SD?
Cape Wrangell, AK

3. Why is the distance from the geographic center stated as 0?
The distances are measured from the geographic center.

4. Why do you think all of the longitudes are presented with a west location except Cape Wrangell, AK?
Cape Wrangell, AK is in the eastern hemisphere and therefore has an E for east. All others listed are in the western hemisphere.

### CHAPTER INVESTIGATION

Orienteering is an outdoor sport in which participants (orienteers) use an accurate, detailed map and a compass to find locations on a course, usually in the wilderness. The map's different colors show hills, valleys, streams, trails, fields and other landmarks.

A standard course consists of a start, a series of control sites and a finish. The control sites are marked with circles connected by dashed lines and numbered in the order they are to be visited. On the ground, a flag indicates a control site. To verify a visit to a control site, the orienteer marks the event's control card. To win an orienteering event, you must complete the course in the shortest amount of time.

*Working Together*

Use the orienteering map shown to find the approximate length of the course. Use the Chapter Investigation icons to guide your group.

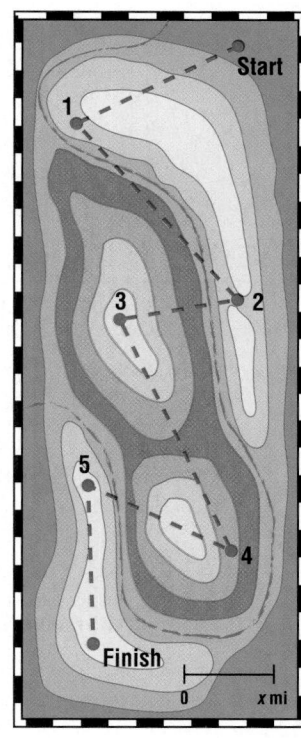

Chapter 9 **Polynomials** 373

---

---

## Data Activity

The *geodetic center* (which takes into account the curvature of the earth's surface) of the continental United States is located at Meades Ranch Triangulation Station in Osborne County in north central Kansas. The station serves as the basic reference point for all government mapping undertaken in the United States (except in Hawaii), Canada, and Mexico. Selected in 1901, it has also served as the geodetic center of North America since 1913.

Students should answer Questions 1-4 to learn more about the extreme points of the 50 United States as measured from the *geographic center* of the United States, located in Butte County, SD.

### Extend the Data Activity
**STUDENT PORTFOLIO** Cartographers have the geometric task of translating the almost spherical surface of Earth to a flat surface. Students can research how cartographers use various types of *projections* to more accurately show true directions, distances, areas, and shapes—which are not accurately shown on a flat map.

## Chapter Investigation

### As an Overarching Problem
Display information about orienteering, including maps of different courses. Have students study the information for class discussion. Students will continue to work on the Investigation as they complete the exercises identified by the Chapter Investigation icon that is found throughout the chapter. These exercises will guide students through the tasks described in *Working Together*. Encourage students to keep all of their work on the Investigation together. Have students use the suggestions in the Chapter Investigation Extension to summarize their work.

See page 372 for Chapter Investigation As a Chapter Project.

# Refresher Skills

The skills on these two pages are skills that have been presented in earlier chapters of this book or in previous math courses. Continuous review of basic math skills will make stronger math students. These skills are identified as necessary to be successful in Chapter 9.

## Skills Correlation Chart

| Skill | Lesson Number |
|---|---|
| **Using Exponents** | 9-2, 9-3, 9-4, 9-5 |
| **Greatest Common Factor (GCF)** | 9-7 |
| **Distributive Property** | 9-4, 9-5 |
| **Perfect Squares** | 9-8 |
| **Like Terms** | 9-1, 9-5 |

## Vocabulary

exponent
greatest common factor
distributive property
perfect square
like terms

## Chalkboard Examples

### Using Exponents

Simplify the expression $\dfrac{[(3m)(4m)]^2}{6m^3}$.

Work within brackets. Multiply, adding exponents of like bases. $\dfrac{[12m^2]^2}{6m^3}$

Raise to the power, multiplying exponents. $\dfrac{144m^4}{6m^3}$

Divide, subtracting exponents of like bases. $24m$

### Greatest Common Factor (GCF)

Find the GCF of $96(a + b)^2$ and $108(a + b)^5$.
$12(a + b)^2$

### Distributive Property

Simplify $-3x^2y(2x - 4y + xy^2)$ using the distributive property.
$-6x^3y + 12x^2y^2 - 3x^3y^3$

---

# 9 Are You Ready?

### Refresh Your Math Skills for Chapter 9

The skills on these two pages are ones you have already learned. Use the examples to refresh your memory and complete the exercises. For additional practice on these and more prerequisite skills, see pages 576–584.

## USING EXPONENTS

Remember the rules of exponents when multiplying and dividing terms with exponents.

**Examples**

$x^3 \cdot x^8 = x^{11}$    Add exponents when terms with like bases are multiplied.

$\dfrac{x^8}{x^3} = x^5$    Subtract exponents when terms with like bases are divided.

$(x^3)^8 = x^{24}$    Mulitply exponents when a power is raised to a power.

**Simplify**

1. $y^4 \cdot y^8$  $y^{12}$
2. $s^6 \cdot 2s^3$  $2s^9$
3. $\dfrac{p^9}{p^3}$  $p^6$
4. $\dfrac{4k^4}{k^3}$  $4k$

5. $(m^2)^3$  $m^6$
6. $(2g^2)^4$  $16g^8$
7. $4x^3 \cdot 3x^5$  $12x^8$
8. $\dfrac{16d^5}{6d^8}$  $\dfrac{8}{3d^3}$

9. $\dfrac{(5w^5)^2}{10w^{10}}$  $\dfrac{5}{2}$
10. $\dfrac{(4x^3 + 2x^3)}{2x}$  $3x^2$
11. $\dfrac{(9x \cdot 2x^3)}{3x^5}$  $\dfrac{6}{x}$
12. $\dfrac{4(y^4)^3}{2y^3}$  $2y^9$

## GREATEST COMMON FACTOR (GCF)

When you compare the factors of one or more numbers, the greatest common factor (GCF) is the greatest factor that is a factor of every number.

**Examples**

The factors of 36 are 1, 2, 3, 4, 6, 9, 12, 18 and 36.

The factors of 16 are 1, 2, 4, 8 and 16.

The GCF of 36 and 16 is 4.

When working with variables, look for the GCF of the constants and each variable.

The factors of $8xy^2$ are 1, 2, 4, 8, $x$, $y$ and $y^2$.

The factors of $28y^3z$ are 1, 2, 4, 7, 14, 28, $y$, $y^2$, $y^3$ and $z$.

The GCF of $8xy^2$ and $28y^3z$ is $4y^2$.

**Find the factors of each number or expression.**

13. 35  1, 5, 7, 35
14. 21  1, 3, 7, 21
15. 81  1, 3, 9, 27, 81
16. 125  1, 5, 25, 125

17. $x^4$  1, $x$, $x^2$, $x^3$, $x^4$
18. $3y^2$  1, 3, $y$, $y^2$
19. $9z^3$  1, 3, 9, $z$, $z^2$, $z^3$
20. $14x^2y^3$
1, 2, 7, 14, $x$, $x^2$, $y$, $y^2$, $y^3$

**Find the GCF of each set of numbers.**

21. 35 and 21  7
22. 21 and 81  3
23. 125 and 200  25

24. $x^4$ and $14x^2y^3$  $x^2$
25. $3y^2$ and $14x^2y^3$  $y^2$
26. $14x^2y^3$ and $12y^2z^3$  $2y^2$

## Teaching Tip

When students are writing numerical factors, encourage them to start with 1, and then work in order to consider if 2, 3, 4, . . . are factors. As possible factors are considered, the "more difficult" factors will appear. Students will know when to stop because factors begin to repeat.
Find all the factors of 108.
1, 108; 2, 54; 3, 36; 4, 27; 5 is not a factor; 6, 18; 7 is not a factor; 8 is not a factor; 9, 12; 10 is not a factor; 11 is not a factor; 12 is a repeat so stop.

When working with the GCF of variable terms, students should look for the lowest exponent of the common variable. The GCF of $x^4$, $x^5$, and $x^2$ is $x^2$.

## DISTRIBUTIVE PROPERTY

You can use the distributive property to simplify an expression. Multiply the expressions inside the parentheses by the factor outside the parentheses.

**Example**
$$4w^2(6w^2 - w + 6) = 4w^2 \cdot 6w^2 - 4w^2 \cdot w + 4w^2 \cdot 6$$
$$= 24w^4 \quad\quad - 4w^3 \quad\quad + 24w^2$$

**Simplify each expression using the distributive property.**

**27.** $9t(3t^2 + 7)$  $27t^3 + 63t$　　**28.** $-4(7y - 15)$  $-28y + 60$　　**29.** $-8x(x^5 + 3x^2)$  $-8x^6 - 24x^3$

**30.** $4y^3(6y^2 + 7y - 12)$　　**31.** $-3w(14w - 12w^2 - 5)$　　**32.** $4y^2z(5y + 6z - 2yz)$
$24y^5 + 28y^4 - 48y^3$　　　　$-42w^2 + 36w^3 + 15w$　　　　$20y^3z + 24y^2z^2 - 8y^3z^2$

## PERFECT SQUARES

It can be easier to recognize factoring patterns if you can recognize perfect squares. A perfect square is the product of a whole number multiplied by itself.

**Examples**

| Base Number | Perfect Square | Base Number | Perfect Square |
|---|---|---|---|
| 4 | 16 | $y$ | $y^2$ |
| 9 | 81 | $y^2$ | $y^4$ |
| 12 | 144 | $3y^3$ | $9y^6$ |

**Determine if each quantity is a perfect square. If so, name the base number.**

**33.** $25$  5　　　　　　　**34.** $116$  no　　　　　　**35.** $256$  16

**36.** $40$  no　　　　　　**37.** $169$  13　　　　　　**38.** $44$  no

**39.** $x^3$  no　　　　　　**40.** $2x^2$  no　　　　　　**41.** $x^2y^2$  $xy$

**42.** $25x^9$  no　　　　　**43.** $100y^{10}$  $10y^5$　　　**44.** $36x^6y^4$  $6x^3y^2$

## LIKE TERMS

When simplifying an expression, you combine like terms. Remember that the variable and exponent must be the same in order to be considered like terms.

**Examples**　　$4x^2y$, $16x^2y$, and $-13x^2y$ are like terms.
　　　　　　　　$12x^2z$, $12x^2$, and $32x^2z^2$ are not like terms.

**Find each pair of like terms.**

**45.** $3vw^3, -4vw, -9vw^3$　　**46.** $-6x^3y, -4x^2y, 19x^2y$　　**47.** $21cs, 7cs^2, cs$  $21cs, cs$
$3vw^3, -9vw^3$　　　　　　　　$-4x^2y, 19x^2y$

**48.** $-\frac{1}{2}x^2y, \frac{1}{2}xy^2, \frac{3}{4}x^2y$　　**49.** $16p^3q^4, 17p^4q^3, 18p^4q^3$　　**50.** $0.8x^2yz^4, 0.5x^2yz^4, 1.5xy^2z^4$
$-\frac{1}{2}x^2y, \frac{3}{4}x^2y$　　　　　　$17p^4q^3, 18p^4q^3$　　　　$0.8x^2yz^4, 0.5x^2yz^4$

---

## Perfect Squares

The quantity $16x^6$ is a perfect square. Its base is $4x^3$. But the quantity $6x^6$ is not a perfect square.

## Like Terms

**Find each pair of like terms.**

**a.** $-2x^3y, -2xy, -3x^3y$
　　$-2x^3y, -3x^3y$

**b.** $3ab^2, 4a^2b^2, 5a^2b^2$
　　$4a^2b^2, 5a^2b^2$

## Refresher Wrap-up

### QUICK ASSESSMENT

Ask the following questions to determine if students have mastered the basic skills reviewed on these pages.

**If each expression were to be simplified, tell what to do with the coefficents and what to do with the exponents.**

**1.** $12x^5 + (-3x^5)$  add the coefficients, keep the exponent

**2.** $(12x^5)(-3x^2)$  multiply the coefficients, add the exponents

**3.** $\frac{12x^5}{-3x^2}$  divide the coefficients, subtract the exponents

**4.** $(4x^5)^3$  cube the coefficient, multiply the exponent by 3

**Simplify if possible.**

**5.** $a^2 \cdot a^3$  $a^5$

**6.** $(xy)^2$  $x^2 \cdot y^2$

**7.** $x^2 + y^2$  in simplest form

### ADDITIONAL PRACTICE

Refer to the Prerequisite Skills lessons beginning on page 576 for more practice.

---

## Extend the Lesson

**CONNECTING TO PRIOR KNOWELDGE** Note with students that the number 6 is a not a perfect square but the number $x^6$ is a perfect square since $x^6 = x^3 \cdot x^3$. With additional examples of this nature, lead students to conclude that although not every even number is a perfect square, every even power is a perfect square.

Emphasize that to determine the base number of a perfect-square term, students are to take the square root of the coefficient and divide the exponent by 2. For example, the base number for $64x^{64}$ is $8x^{32}$.

### Vocabulary

| | |
|---|---|
| monomial | coefficient |
| constant | polynomial |
| term | binomial |
| trinomial | standard form |
| like terms | |

### Tools/Materials Needed

Algeblocks with Basic Mat

### Lesson Resources

Warm-up Transparency 35
Transparency TK-4, 5
Reteaching 9-1
Extra Practice 9-1
Enrichment 9-1
Technology Activity 9-1

## Getting Started

### 5-Minute Warm-up

Simplify each expression.
1. $8a + 5a - 3a$   $10a$
2. $6x^2 - 4x^2 + 2x^2$   $4x^2$
3. $-5y - 6y + 2y$   $-9y$
4. $7b^3 - 6b^3 - 3b^3$   $-2b^3$

### Introduction to Lesson 9-1

Review the Basic Mat, reminding students that they can think of the lower half of the mat in terms of addition of negatives. So, the given model can be written as $2x^2 + (-3x) + 5$. Or, students can think of the lower half of the mat in terms of subtraction, $2x^3 - 3x + 5$.

---

# 9-1 Add and Subtract Polynomials

**Goals**
- Write polynomials in standard form.
- Add and subtract polynomials.

**Applications**  Part-time Job, Travel, Geography, Modeling

**Algeblocks can be used to model variable expressions.**

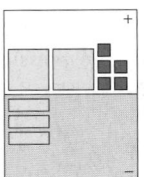

1. What expression is represented on the Basic Mat shown?
   $2x^2 + 5 - 3x$
2. Use Algeblocks and a Basic Mat to model the expression $3x^2 + x + 2$.
   For 2–4, see additional answers.
3. Add three more $x$-blocks to your model. What expression do the Algeblocks now represent?   $3x^2 + 4x + 2$
4. Remove two $x^2$-blocks from your second model. What expression do the remaining Algeblocks represent?   $x^2 + 4x + 2$

## ◼ BUILD UNDERSTANDING

A **monomial** is an expression that is a number, variable, or product of a number and one or more variables with whole number exponents. Each of these expressions is a monomial.

$$-11 \qquad k \qquad \frac{3}{4}mx^4 \qquad 7p^2f$$

The numerical factor of a monomial is the **coefficient**. For example, the coefficient of $-3x^2$ is $-3$. The coefficient of $x$ is 1. A monomial with no variables, such as $-11$, is a **constant**.

A sum or difference of monomials is a **polynomial**. Each monomial is a **term** of the polynomial. A polynomial with two terms is a **binomial**. A polynomial with three terms is a **trinomial**. A monomial is a polynomial with one term.

$$\text{binomial: } \underset{\text{term}}{8n} + \underset{\text{term}}{(-n^2)} \qquad\qquad \text{trinomial: } \underset{\text{term}}{a^2} + \underset{\text{term}}{(-4ab)} + \underset{\text{term}}{4b^2}$$

A polynomial is written in **standard form** when its terms are ordered from the greatest to the least power of one of the variables. This order is referred to as *descending order*.

### Problem Solving Tip

Each term in a polynomial is separated by a plus or minus sign.

### Example 1

Write each polynomial in standard form for the variable $x$.

a. $3x + 5 + 7x^3 - 2x^2$   b. $-8x^2y^3 + 4xy^4 + x^3$

#### Solution

Order the terms from greatest to least powers of $x$.

a. $3x + 5 + 7x^3 - 2x^2 = 7x^3 - 2x^2 + 3x + 5$   b. $-8x^2y^3 + 4xy^4 + x^3 = x^3 - 8x^2y^3 + 4xy^4$

## Extend the Lesson

After students have seen how the definition of *standard form of a polynomial* is applied to the polynomial of Example 1b, $-8x^2y^3 + 4xy^4 + x^3$, with respect to the variable $x$, $x^3 - 8x^2y^3 + 4xy^4$, have students write the given polynomial in standard form with respect to $y$.   $4xy^4 - 8x^2y^3 + x^3$

Terms such as $3xy^2$ and $-7xy^2$ that differ only in their coefficients are called **like terms**. To simplify a polynomial, combine like terms by adding their coefficients. A polynomial is simplified when only unlike terms remain.

### Check Understanding

Sometimes polynomials are written with subtraction signs. How could you write the polynomials below to show that each is really a *sum* of monomials?

**1.** $6b - b^2$　　**2.** $c^2 - 2cd + 3e^2$　　**3.** $4p - 2q + 5$

1. $6b + (-b^2)$　2. $c^2 + (-2cd) + 3e^2$
3. $4p + (-2q) + 5$

## Example 2

**Simplify.**

**a.** $4k^2 - 3k + 5k^2$

**b.** $2x^2y + 4x^2 + 3xy^2 - 7x^2y$

### Solution

**a.** $4k^2 - 3k + 5k^2 = 4k^2 + 5k^2 - 3k$　　Use the commutative property to rearrange like terms.

$\qquad\qquad\qquad = (4 + 5)k^2 - 3k$　　Use the distributive property to combine like terms.

$\qquad\qquad\qquad = 9k^2 - 3k$

**b.** $2x^2y + 4x^2 + 3xy^2 - 7x^2y = 2x^2y - 7x^2y + 4x^2 + 3xy^2$

$\qquad\qquad\qquad = (2 - 7)x^2y + 4x^2 + 3xy^2$

$\qquad\qquad\qquad = -5x^2y + 4x^2 + 3xy^2$

To add polynomials, write the sum and simplify by combining like terms.

## Example 3

**Simplify.**

**a.** $7n + (5 - 3n)$

**b.** $(3x^2y - 7x + 2y) + (5x^2y + 2x - 3y)$

### Solution

To simplify, use the associative and commutative properties as necessary to group like terms. Then use the distributive property to combine like terms.

**a.** $7n + (5 - 3n) = (7n - 3n) + 5$　　Use the commutative and associative properties.

$\qquad\qquad\qquad = (7 - 3)n + 5$　　Use the distributive property to combine like terms.

$\qquad\qquad\qquad = 4n + 5$

**b.** $(3x^2y - 7x + 2y) + (5x^2y + 2x - 3y)$

$\qquad\qquad\qquad = 3x^2y + (-7x) + 2y + 5x^2y + 2x + (-3y)$

$\qquad\qquad\qquad = (3x^2y + 5x^2y) + (-7x + 2x) + [2y + (-3y)]$

$\qquad\qquad\qquad = (3 + 5)x^2y + (-7 + 2)x + (2 - 3)y$

$\qquad\qquad\qquad = 8x^2y + (-5x) + (-y)$

$\qquad\qquad\qquad = 8x^2y - 5x - y$

To subtract one polynomial from another, add the opposite of the polynomial being subtracted.

 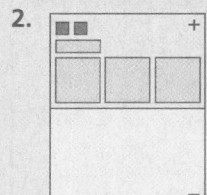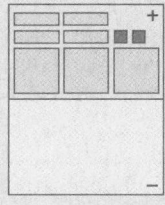
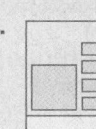

## QUICK ASSESSMENT

Ask the following questions to determine if students understand the content presented in this lesson.

1. How can you tell when one term of a polynomial ends and the next term begins? **Terms are separated by symbols of addition or subtraction.**

2. What are the characteristics of a simplified polynomial in standard form? **All terms are unlike and the terms are ordered from greatest to least power of one variable.**

3. What is the basic principle for addition of polynomials? **Combine like terms.**

4. What is the basic principle for subtraction of polynomials? **Rewrite the subtraction as addition of the opposite of the polynomial to be subtracted.**

## ASSIGNMENT GUIDE

**Basic:** 1–41, 48–54
**Enriched:** 1–54

### Reteaching Worksheet 9-1

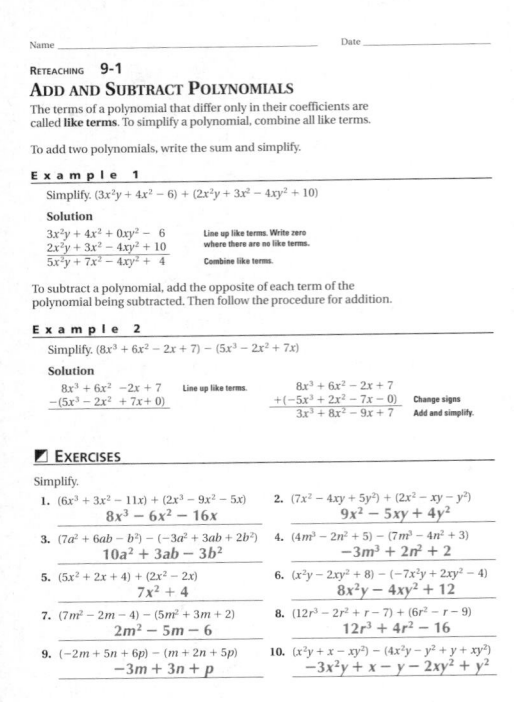

RETEACHING **9-1**

**ADD AND SUBTRACT POLYNOMIALS**

The terms of a polynomial that differ only in their coefficients are called **like terms**. To simplify a polynomial, combine all like terms.

To add two polynomials, write the sum and simplify.

**Example 1**

Simplify. $(3x^2y + 4x^2 - 6) + (2x^2y + 3x^2 - 4xy^2 + 10)$

**Solution**

$3x^2y + 4x^2 + 0xy^2 - 6$   Line up like terms. Write zero
$2x^2y + 3x^2 - 4xy^2 + 10$   where there are no like terms.
$5x^2y + 7x^2 - 4xy^2 + 4$   Combine like terms.

To subtract a polynomial, add the opposite of each term of the polynomial being subtracted. Then follow the procedure for addition.

**Example 2**

Simplify. $(8x^3 + 6x^2 - 2x + 7) - (5x^3 - 2x^2 + 7x)$

**Solution**

$8x^3 + 6x^2 - 2x + 7$   Line up like terms.   $8x^3 + 6x^2 - 2x + 7$
$-(5x^3 - 2x^2 + 7x + 0)$    $+(-5x^3 + 2x^2 - 7x - 0)$   Change signs
              $3x^3 + 8x^2 - 9x + 7$   Add and simplify.

**EXERCISES**

Simplify.

1. $(6x^3 + 3x^2 - 11x) + (2x^3 - 9x^2 - 5x)$    2. $(7x^2 - 4xy + 5y^2) + (2x^2 - xy - y^2)$
   $8x^3 - 6x^2 - 16x$                 $9x^2 - 5xy + 4y^2$

3. $(7a^2 + 6ab - b^2) - (-3a^2 + 3ab + 2b^2)$    4. $(4m^3 - 2m^2 + 5) - (7m^3 - 4m^2 + 3)$
   $10a^2 + 3ab - 3b^2$                $-3m^3 + 2n^2 + 2$

5. $(5x^2 + 2x + 4) + (2x^2 - 2x)$    6. $(x^2y - 2xy^2 + 8) - (-7x^2y + 2xy^2 - 4)$
   $7x^2 + 4$                    $8x^2y - 4xy^2 + 12$

7. $(7m^2 - 2m - 4) - (5m^2 + 3m + 2)$    8. $(12r^3 - 2r^2 + r - 7) + (6r^2 - r - 9)$
   $2m^2 - 5m - 6$                $12r^3 + 4r^2 - 16$

9. $(-2m + 5n + 6p) - (m + 2n + 5p)$    10. $(x^2y + x - xy^2) - (4x^2y - y^2 + y + xy^2)$
   $-3m + 3n + p$             $-3x^2y + x - y - 2xy^2 + y^2$

---

## Example 4

**Simplify.**

**a.** $8y - (5y + 3)$      **b.** $(2xy^2 - 5xy + 6) - (xy^2 + 3xy)$

### Solution

Change each term of the polynomial being subtracted to its opposite. Then follow the same procedure for adding polynomials.

**a.** $8y - (5y + 3) = 8y + [-5y + (-3)] = [8y + (-5y)] + (-3)$
                             $= [8 + (-5)]y + (-3)$
                             $= 3y - 3$

**b.** $(2xy^2 - 5xy + 6) - (xy^2 + 3xy) = (2xy^2 - 5xy + 6) + [-xy^2 + (-3xy)]$
                             $= [2xy^2 + (-xy^2)] + [(-5xy) + (-3xy)] + 6$
                             $= (2 - 1)xy^2 + (-5 - 3)xy + 6$
                             $= 1xy^2 + (-8xy) + 6$
                             $= xy^2 - 8xy + 6$

### TRY THESE EXERCISES

Write each polynomial in standard form for the variable $x$.

1. $9x^2 - 2x + 4 + 3x^3$    2. $-3 - 3x - 3x^2$    3. $x^2y^2 - y^3x$
   $3x^3 + 9x^2 - 2x + 4$       $-3x^2 - 3x - 3$        $x^2y^2 - xy^3$

Simplify.

4. $9p - 4p$   $5p$    5. $k^2 + 2k - 3k - k^3$    6. $5x - 2xy + 3x + 4xy$
                     $-k^3 + k^2 - k$           $8x + 2xy$

7. $(8h^2 - 2h) + (3h^2 + 5h)$    8. $(4a^2b + 8a) - (7a^2b - 3a)$    9. $(-2jk^2 + 6jk) - (5jk^2 + 3jk)$
   $11h^2 + 3h$               $-3a^2b + 11a$            $-7jk^2 + 3jk$

10. **WRITING MATH** Will the sum and difference of two binomials always result in another binomial? Explain. **No; the terms may cancel, or the result may be a trinomial.**

11. Write and simplify an expression for the perimeter of the figure shown.   $3x - 2$    $3x - 2$
   $8x + 5$                                                    $2x + 9$

### PRACTICE EXERCISES • For Extra Practice, see page 612.

Write each polynomial in standard form for the variable $x$.

12. $2 + x^2 + 3x^3$   $3x^3 + x^2 + 2$    13. $3x^3 + 2x^4 + x + x^2$    14. $-x - x^5 + x^3 - 6$
                            $2x^4 + 3x^3 + x^2 + x$       $-x^5 + x^3 - x - 6$

15. $y^3 + 2xy^2 - 3x^2y - 5x^3$    16. $7x - 1 + 3x^2 - 4x^3$    17. $xy^4 + x^2y^2 + x^3y$
   $-5x^3 - 3x^2y + 2xy^2 + y^3$      $-4x^3 + 3x^2 + 7x - 1$      $x^3y + x^2y^2 + xy^4$

Simplify.

18. $3n - 5n$   $-2n$    19. $\frac{1}{4}x^2 + \frac{3}{7}x^2$   $\frac{19}{28}x^2$    20. $7w + 5w - 4w - 8w$   $0$

21. $8y^3 - 4y^2 - 2y^3$   $6y^3 - 4y^2$    22. $-5c + 7d - 3d + 6$    23. $2x^3 + 4x + 7x$   $2x^3 + 11x$
                               $4d - 5c + 6$

24. $e^2 - 4e - 2e^2$   $-e^2 - 4e$    25. $-4n^2 + 2n + 6n + 8n^2$    26. $14a + 9b - 11a - 3b$
                              $4n^2 + 8n$               $3a + 6b$

27. $(1.5x + 2.7) + (3.1x - 4.9)$    28. $(12p + 7) - (8p + 2)$    29. $-8hk + 10k + 3hk + 11hk$
   $4.6x - 2.2$                        $4p + 5$                   $6hk + 10k$

---

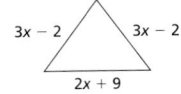
## Teaching Tip

Advise students that they can arrange an addition problem horizontally, as shown in the text, or they can arrange the problem vertically, as shown at the right for Example 3b.

$3x^2y - 7x + 2y$
$+ \; 5x^2y + 2x - 3y$
$\overline{8x^2y - 5x - \; y}$

Note with students that the vertical method is helpful in that it clearly shows like terms. This arrangement is especially helpful when there are more than two polynomials to be added.

Suggest that in a vertical arrangement, students use 0 as a placeholder for a missing term, as in $4x^3 - 3x + 7 = 4x^3 + 0x^2 - 3x + 7$.

**Simplify.**

**30.** $(5r + 3s + t) - (r + 9s + 7t)$
$4r - 6s - 6t$

**31.** $(3x^2y + 2xy - 6) + (9x^2y + 8xy)$
$12x^2y + 10xy - 6$

**32.** $(6k^2 + 7k - 4) - (9k^2 - 11k + 7)$
$-3k^2 + 18k - 11$

**33.** $2.7m + 3.9n - 4.6m + 7.7n + 6.2 - 8.5$
$-1.9m + 11.6n - 2.3$

**DATA FILE** For Exercises 34–36, refer to the data on the size of bird eggs on page 560. Let $x$ represent the length of a grey heron egg. Express the length of the following bird eggs in terms of $x$.

**34.** Arctic tern
$x - 2$

**35.** Partridge
$x - 2.4$

**36.** Chicken (extra large)
$x + 0.3$

**37. PART-TIME JOB** Yesterday Jason earned $(6r + 28t)$ dollars and today he earns $(9r + 18t)$ dollars. Write and simplify an expression for the total amount Jason earns in the two days. $15r + 46t$

**38. TRAVEL** The distance from Alpha City to Betaville on the highway is $(18x^2 + 15x + 13)$ mi. The distance by a shortcut on country roads is $(13x^2 - 11x - 1)$ mi. Write and simplify an expression to show the distance saved by the shortcut. $(5x^2 + 26x + 14)$ mi

**39. GEOGRAPHY** The highest point on Earth above sea level is Mt. Everest, which is $(3x^2 - 9y - 72)$ ft above sea level. The lowest point above water is at the shores of the Dead Sea, which is $(13y - 1)$ ft below sea level. What is the difference in feet between these two points? $(3x^2 - 22y - 71)$ ft

**40. MODELING** Show the sum of $(2x^2 + 4x) + (x^2 - 2x + 3)$ using Algeblocks.
$3x^2 + 2x + 3$; See additional answers.

**41.** Write and simplify an expression for the perimeter of the figure shown. $16x - 10$

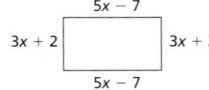

$3x + 2$ ⬚ $3x + 2$
$5x - 7$
$5x - 7$

## ■ EXTENDED PRACTICE EXERCISES

**Simplify.**

**42.** $\frac{3}{4}x^2 - \frac{1}{2}x + \frac{3}{8} - \frac{5}{8}x^2 + \frac{1}{4}x - \frac{1}{2}$
$\frac{1}{8}x^2 - \frac{1}{4}x - \frac{1}{8}$

**43.** $7a^2b^2 + b^3 - b^2 - 4 - 3a^2b^2 + b^2$
$b^3 + 4a^2b^2 - 4$

**44.** $(10a^3 + 8a^2b - 4ab^2 - 7b^3) - (12a^3 - 3a^2b + 5ab^2 + 13b) + (-15a^3 - 9a^2b + ab^2 + 7b^3)$
$-17a^3 + 2a^2b - 8ab^2 - 13b$

**45.** Write two polynomials whose sum is $8p^2 - 6p + 4$. Answers will vary.

**46.** Write two polynomials whose difference is $3x^2 - 5x + 7$. Answers will vary.

**47. CRITICAL THINKING** The perimeter of the end of any box mailed by U.S. parcel post must not exceed 102 in. Find the maximum allowable value of $x$ for the perimeter of the shaded face of this box.
9 in.

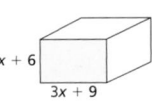

$x + 6$
$3x + 9$

## ■ MIXED REVIEW EXERCISES

**Write each equation in slope-intercept form.** (Lesson 8-3)

**48.** $4x - 3y = -21$
$y = \frac{4}{3}x + 7$

**49.** $-6x + 2y = -5$  $y = 3x - \frac{5}{2}$

**50.** $3x = -5y + 12$
$y = -\frac{3}{5}x + \frac{12}{5}$

**51.** $9x + 3y = 27$
$y = -3x + 9$

**52.** $-15 = 20x - 5y$
$y = 4x + 3$

**53.** $\frac{1}{3}y - 2x = 7$
$y = 6x + 21$

**54.** The formula for finding the area of a trapezoid is $\frac{1}{2}h(b_1 + b_2)$. Find the area of a trapezoid with height $h = 5$ in., base $b_1 = 7$ in. and base $b_2 = 3$ in. (Lesson 3-1) 25 in.$^2$

## ADDITIONAL ANSWERS

**40.**

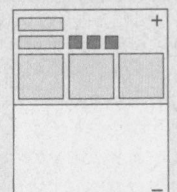

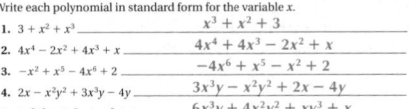

Name _____    Date _____

EXTRA PRACTICE **9-1**
## ADD AND SUBTRACT POLYNOMIALS

☑ **EXERCISES**

Write each polynomial in standard form for the variable $x$.

**1.** $3 + x^2 + x^3$    $x^3 + x^2 + 3$

**2.** $4x^4 - 2x^2 + 4x^3 + x$    $4x^4 + 4x^3 - 2x^2 + x$

**3.** $-x^2 + x^5 - 4x^6 + 2$    $-4x^6 + x^5 - x^2 + 2$

**4.** $2x - x^2y^2 + 3x^3y - 4y$    $3x^3y - x^2y^2 + 2x - 4y$

**5.** $4x^2y^2 + 6x^3y + xy^3 + x$    $6x^3y + 4x^2y^2 + xy^3 + x$

Simplify.

**6.** $4r + 3r$    $7r$

**7.** $\frac{1}{2}g^3 - \frac{3}{10}g^3$    $\frac{1}{5}g^3$

**8.** $5p + 4p - 6p + p$    $4p$

**9.** $9y^4 + 5y^2 - 8y^4$    $y^4 + 5y^2$

**10.** $-4h + 3k - 6k + 7h$    $3h - 3k$

**11.** $-3n^4 + 3n^2 - 5n^2 + 6n^4$    $3n^4 - 2n^2$

**12.** $(2.5z + 1.5) + (1.7z - 4.5)$    $4.2z - 3$

**13.** $(10t + 5) - (8t - 6)$    $2t + 11$

**14.** $-7mn + 14m - 5mn - 6m$    $-12mn + 8m$

**15.** $(7w + 4z - 5x) - (w - 5z + x)$    $6w + 9z - 6x$

**16.** $(5x^2y + 4xy - 7x) + (6x^2y - 6xy - 5)$    $11x^2y - 2xy - 7x - 5$

**17.** $(8q^2 + 2q - 5) - (9q^2 + q - 1)$    $-q^2 + q - 4$

**18.** $3.5a + 4.5b - 4.8a - 5ab + 6.7 - 8.5$    $-1.3a - 5ab + 4.5b - 1.8$

**19.** Write and simplify an expression for the perimeter of the figure shown.
$3x - 2 + 2x - 4 + 3x - 2 + 2x - 4 = 10x - 12$

$3x - 2$
$2x - 4$   ⬚   $2x - 4$
$3x - 2$

Name _____    Date _____

ENRICHMENT **9-1**
## DEGREE OF A MONOMIAL OR A POLYNOMIAL

The **degree of a monomial in a variable** is the number of times the variable occurs as a factor in the monomial. The **degree of a monomial** is the total number of times the variables in the monomial occur as factors. The degree of any nonzero constant monomial is 0.

**E x a m p l e   1**

Find the degree of the monomial $8x^3y^2z$ in each variable. Then find the degree of the monomial.

**Solution**

The degree of the constant 8 is 0. The degree of the monomial in $x$ is 3. The degree in $y$ is 2. The degree in $z$ is 1. The degree of the monomial is $3 + 2 + 1$, or 6.

The **degree of a polynomial** is the greatest of the degrees of its terms after it has been simplified.

**E x a m p l e   2**

Simplify the polynomial. Then find its degree. $6x^4 + 2x^5y^2 - 6x^4 - x^2y^2$

**Solution**

$6x^4 + 2x^5y^2 - 6x^4 - x^2y^2 = 6x^4 + (-6x^4) + 2x^5y^2 - x^2y^2 = 2x^5y^2 - x^2y^2$

The monomial of greatest degree is $2x^5y^2$. Its degree is $5 + 2$, or 7. So, the degree of the polynomial is 7.

☑ **EXERCISES**

Find the degree of the monomial in each variable. Then find the degree of the monomial.

**1.** $6xyz^6$   $1; 1; 6; 8$

**2.** $-12x^3y^3z^2$   $3; 2; 2; 7$

**3.** $2m^5n^6p$   $5; 6; 1; 12$

**4.** $a^{10}b^8c^7d^2$   $10; 8; 7; 2; 27$

Simplify the polynomial. Then find its degree.

**5.** $7x^2 - 7xy^2 + 5xy + 4xy^2 - 4x^2$   $3x^2 - 3xy^2 + 5xy; 3$

**6.** $2a^2 + 3a^4 - 2b + -2a^2 + 8$   $3a^4 - 2b + 8; 4$

**7.** $2x^2y^2z + 6x^2z^2 - xy + xy^2 - 2x^2y^2z$   $6x^2z^2 - xy + xy^2; 4$

**8.** $x^3y^2 - 3x^2y + x - 2x^2y + y$   $x^3y^2 - 5x^2y + x + y; 5$

### Tools/Materials Needed

Algeblocks with Quadrant Mat

### Lesson Resources

Warm-up Transparency 35
Transparency TK-6
Reteaching 9-2
Extra Practice 9-2
Enrichment 9-2

## Getting Started

### 5-MINUTE WARM-UP

Evaluate, writing each answer in
standard form.
1. $3^2 \cdot 3^2$   81     2. $(3^2)^3$   729
3. $3 \cdot 2^3$   24      4. $(3 \cdot 2)^3$   216

### Introduction to Lesson 9-2

After students have answered Questions 1–6, ask them to reconsider a
rectangle of length $\ell$ and width $w$,
with area $\ell w$. If six such rectangles
are fitted together to form one new
rectangle, what is the area of the
new rectangle? $\ell w + \ell w + \ell w + \ell w + \ell w + \ell w = 6\ell w$ How many
$\ell \times w$ rectangles are needed to
model a rectangle of length $3\ell$ and
width $2w$? 6 What is the area of
the $3\ell \times 2w$ rectangle? $6\ell w$

Based on the area result, ask students to find the product of the two
monomials $3a$ and $2b$. 6ab Then
have students find the products of
the following monomials. $a \times 2b$
2ab $4a \times 3b$ 12ab $2a \times 5b$ 10ab
$4a \times 2b$ 8ab Ask students to write
a rule for multiplying monomials.
Multiply the coefficients; multiply
the variable parts.

---

# 9-2 Multiply Monomials

**Goals** ■ Use the rules for exponents to multiply monomials.

**Applications** Manufacturing, Sports, Photography, Modeling

**Draw a rectangle. Label the length 5 cm and label the width 3 cm.**

1. What is the area of the rectangle? 15 cm²

2. If you double both the length and width, what is the area? 60 cm²

3. If you triple both the length and width, what is the area? 135 cm²

4. Draw a new rectangle. Label the length $l$ and label the width $w$.   Check students' work.

5. What is the area of the new rectangle? $lw$

6. If you double both the length and the width, write an expression for the area of the new rectangle.   $4lw$

### ◤ BUILD UNDERSTANDING

The commutative and associative properties of
multiplication can be used to find a product
of two monomials.

### Example 1

**Simplify.**

**a.** $(5x)(7y)$          **b.** $(-2h)(4k)$          **c.** $\left(-\frac{1}{3}mn\right)(-12x)$

**Solution**

**a.** $(5x)(7y) = (5)(7)(x)(y)$
$= 35xy$

**b.** $(-2h)(4k) = (-2)(4)(h)(k)$
$= -8hk$

**c.** $\left(-\frac{1}{3}mn\right)(-12x) = \left(-\frac{1}{3}\right)(-12)(mn)(x)$          $-\frac{1}{3} \cdot -\frac{12}{1} = 4$
$= 4mnx$

Recall the *product rule for exponents*: $a^m \cdot a^n = a^{m+n}$

The product rule for exponents, together with the commutative and associative
properties of multiplication, can be used to find a product of two monomials.

380    Chapter 9  **Polynomials**

---

## Extend the Lesson

**CONNECTING TO PRIOR KNOWLEDGE** After students have found the products of the monomials
in Example 1, ask them to consider how they would add the monomials $5x$ and $7y$ (Example 1a).
Students should then conclude that the sum (or difference) of two monomials is not always a
monomial but the product of two monomials is always a monomial. Compare these operations
with monomials to operations with fractions. The sum or difference of two fractions can be written
as a single fraction only if the fractions to be combined have a common denominator, just as the
sum or difference of two monomials can be written as a monomial only if the monomials have the
same literal factor (like terms). However, the product of two fractions can be written as a single
fraction even if the fractions have different denominators, and the product of two monomials can
be written as a monomial even if the monomials have different little factors (are not like terms).

## Example 2

**MODELING** Use Algeblocks and a Quadrant Mat to find the product $3x(-2x)$.

### Solution

*Step 1* Place three $x$-blocks in the positive part of the horizontal axis.

*Step 2* Place two $x$-blocks in the negative part of the vertical axis.

*Step 3* Use $x^2$-blocks to form the area in the quadrant bounded by the $x$-blocks.

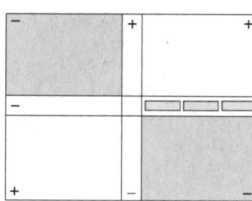 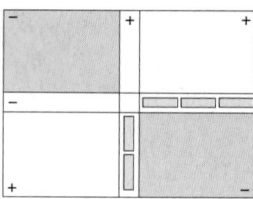 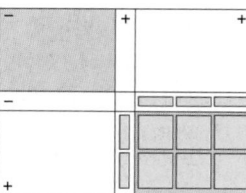

Read the answer from the mat: $-6x^2$.

## Example 3

**Simplify.**

**a.** $(5e^2)(-6e^3)$

**b.** $(4m^2n^3)(-3mn^4p)$

### Solution

**a.** $(5e^2)(-6e^3) = (5)(-6)(e^2 \cdot e^3)$
$= -30e^{2+3}$
$= -30e^5$

**b.** $(4m^2n^3)(-3mn^4p) = (4)(-3)(m^2 \cdot m)(n^3 \cdot n^4)p$
$= -12(m^{2+1})(n^{3+4})p$
$= -12m^3n^7p$

Recall the following rules for exponents.

$$\text{Power rule}: (a^m)^n = a^{mn}$$

$$\text{Power of a product rule}: (ab)^m = a^m b^m$$

Use these rules, with the commutative and associative properties of multiplication, to simplify monomials involving powers.

> **Check Understanding**
>
> In the solution of Example 3, part b, explain why you cannot add the exponents in the expression $-12m^3n^7$.
>
> $m^3$ and $n^7$ do not have the same base.

## Example 4

**Simplify.**

**a.** $(5k^3)^2$

**b.** $(-3w^5y^6)^4$

### Solution

**a.** $(5k^3)^2 = (5)^2(k^3)^2$
$= 25k^{3 \cdot 2}$
$= 25k^6$

**b.** $(-3w^5y^6)^4 = (-3)^4(w^5)^4(y^6)^4$
$= (81w^{5 \cdot 4})(y^{6 \cdot 4})$
$= 81w^{20}y^{24}$

 **Math Online** mathmatters2.com/extra_examples

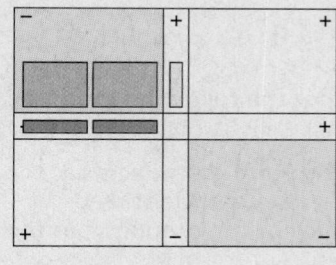
## Differentiated Instruction

**VISUAL LEARNERS** Use Supplementary Example 1 to emphasize that solutions to problems should specify units of measure. Cancellation is a helpful visual device.

$$10x \, \frac{\text{miles}}{\cancel{\text{hour}}} \cdot 4y \, \cancel{\text{hours}} = 40xy \text{ miles}$$

## Lesson Wrap-up

### QUICK ASSESSMENT

Ask the following questions to determine if students understand the content presented in this lesson.

**When multiplying monomials that involve powers, when would you:**

1. add exponents?   when the bases with exponents are the same

2. multiply exponents?   when raising a base with an exponent to a power

3. leave exponents as they are? when the bases with exponents are different

**Consider the following products.**

**A.** $(2x^2)(2x^3)$  **B.** $(2x)^2(2x)^3$  **C.** $(2x^2)^3$

4. Which of the products has the greatest coefficient?   **B**

5. Which of the products has the greatest exponent?   **C**

### ASSIGNMENT GUIDE

**Basic:** 1–59, 66–70
**Enriched:** 1–70

### Reteaching Worksheet 9-2

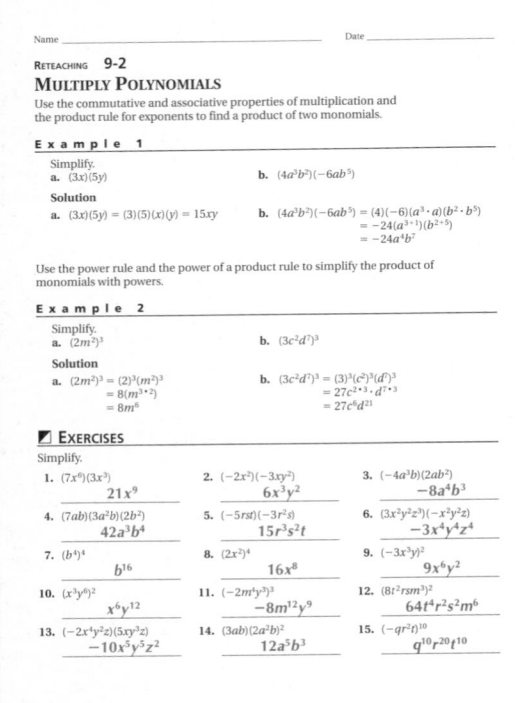

Name _____ Date _____

RETEACHING  **9-2**
**MULTIPLY POLYNOMIALS**
Use the commutative and associative properties of multiplication and the product rule for exponents to find a product of two monomials.

**Example 1**
Simplify.
a. $(3x)(5y)$     b. $(4a^3b^2)(-6ab^5)$

**Solution**
a. $(3x)(5y) = (3)(5)(x)(y) = 15xy$
b. $(4a^3b^2)(-6ab^5) = (4)(-6)(a^3 \cdot a)(b^2 \cdot b^5)$
$= -24(a^{3+1})(b^{2+5})$
$= -24a^4b^7$

Use the power rule and the power of a product rule to simplify the product of monomials with powers.

**Example 2**
Simplify.
a. $(2m^2)^3$     b. $(3c^2d^7)^3$

**Solution**
a. $(2m^2)^3 = (2)^3(m^2)^3$     b. $(3c^2d^7)^3 = (3)^3(c^2)^3(d^7)^3$
$= 8(m^{3\cdot2})$               $= 27c^{2\cdot3} \cdot d^{7\cdot3}$
$= 8m^6$                        $= 27c^6d^{21}$

**EXERCISES**
Simplify.
1. $(7x^6)(3x^3)$  2. $(-2x^2)(-3xy^2)$  3. $(-4a^3b)(2ab^2)$
   $21x^9$            $6x^3y^2$             $-8a^4b^3$
4. $(7ab)(3a^2b)(2b^2)$  5. $(-5rst)(-3r^2s)$  6. $(3x^2y^2z^3)(-x^2y^2z)$
   $42a^3b^4$             $15r^3s^2t$          $-3x^4y^4z^4$
7. $(b^4)^4$  8. $(2x^2)^4$  9. $(-3x^3y)^2$
   $b^{16}$      $16x^8$      $9x^6y^2$
10. $(x^3y^6)^2$  11. $(-2m^4y^6)^3$  12. $(8t^2rsm^3)^2$
    $x^6y^{12}$     $-8m^{12}y^9$       $64t^4r^2s^2m^6$
13. $(-2x^4y^2z)(5xy^3z)$  14. $(3ab)(2a^2b)^2$  15. $(-qr^2t)^{10}$
    $-10x^5y^5z^2$           $12a^5b^3$           $q^{10}r^{20}t^{10}$

---

Simplify.

1. $(9e)(3f)$  $27ef$
2. $(-5x)(8y)$  $-40xy$
3. $\left(\frac{1}{2}a\right)(-16bc)$  $-8abc$
4. $(12n^4)(4n^{12})$  $48n^{16}$
5. $\left(\frac{2}{3}y^2\right)\left(-\frac{2}{5}y^5\right)$  $-\frac{4}{15}y^7$
6. $(-2c^5de^2)(-3c^2d^4)$  $6c^7d^5e^2$
7. $(-2p^5)^4$  $16p^{20}$
8. $(0.6x^3y)^2$  $0.36x^6y^2$
9. $(4a^3b^2c^5)^3$  $64a^9b^6c^{15}$

10. Find the area of a rectangle that is $4ab^2c$ in. by $3a^3b$ in.
    $12a^4b^3c$ in.$^2$

11. **MODELING**  What product is modeled on the Algeblock Mat?
    $2x(-y-x)$

12. Use Algeblocks to find the product in Exercise 11.
    $-2x^2 - 2xy$; See additional answers.

13. **WRITING MATH**  Write a short paragraph explaining the difference between $a^m \cdot a^n$ and $(a^m)^n$.
    See additional answers.

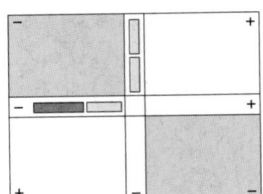

Simplify.

14. $(3p)(7q)$  $21pq$
15. $(-2a)(4b)$  $-8ab$
16. $(6m)(-2n)$  $-12mn$
17. $(-xy)(-5hk)$  $5hkxy$
18. $9(-2a)$  $-18a$
19. $(-16w)\left(-\frac{3}{4}t\right)$  $12tw$
20. $(3.6k)(-2.5e)$  $-9ek$
21. $(2a^5)(5b^6)$  $10a^5b^6$
22. $(-5m^2)(4m)$  $-20m^3$
23. $(8xy)(-3xy)$  $-24x^2y^2$
24. $\left(\frac{2}{3}h^3\right)(-9h^2)$  $-6h^5$
25. $(4.3xy^2)(0.6y^4)$  $2.58xy^6$
26. $(a^5b^2)(a^3b^4)$  $a^8b^6$
27. $(-20x^5y)\left(-\frac{3}{4}x^2y^2\right)$  $15x^7y^3$
28. $8e(-22e^3f)$  $-176e^4f$
29. $(-abc)(abc)$  $-a^2b^2c^2$
30. $(14hkn)(3.5hm)$  $49h^2kmn$
31. $\left(-\frac{2}{5}pq^2\right)\left(\frac{15}{16}p^2q\right)$  $-\frac{3}{8}p^3q^3$
32. $(-3x)^2$  $9x^2$
33. $(2h^3)^3$  $8h^9$
34. $(2ab)^5$  $32a^5b^5$
35. $(-5x^2y)^2$  $25x^4y^2$
36. $(m^2n^5)^4$  $m^8n^{20}$
37. $(-abc^2)^6$  $a^6b^6c^{12}$
38. $(m^3)(m^2)(m^6)$  $m^{11}$
39. $(-2a^5)(2a^4)(-2a^7)$  $8a^{16}$
40. $(2y)(3y)^2$  $18y^3$
41. $(-5x^2)(2x^3)^3$  $-40x^{11}$
42. $(4hk)^3(-h^3k^2)$  $-64h^6k^5$
43. $(-a^2b)^5(a^2b)^4$  $-a^{18}b^9$
44. $(-x^3y^2)(3x^4yz)(-5xy^4z^3)$
    $15x^8y^7z^4$
45. $(4h^2)^2(2h^3)^3$  $128h^{13}$
46. $(-4e^3f)(-e^2f^2)^2\left(\frac{1}{2}ef^4\right)^2$
    $-e^9f^{13}$

**Write and simplify an expression for the area of each figure.**

47.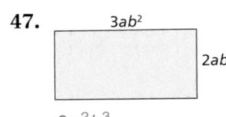
    $3ab^2$
    $2ab$
    $6a^2b^3$

48.
    $3jk^3$
    $8j^2k^2$
    $12j^3k^5$

49.    $x$   $30x^2$
       $2x$
       $5x$  $x$
       $4x$

50. **ERROR ALERT**  Tia says that $10^3 \cdot 10^6 = 100^9$. Explain Tia's mistake.  She multiplied $10 \cdot 10$, but she should have only added the exponents to get $10^3 \cdot 10^6 = 10^9$.

51. **GEOGRAPHY**  On the Earth's surface, there is 3 times as much water as land. Write and simplify an expression to represent the surface area of Earth.   $3x + x = 4x$

52.  **MODELING**  Use Algeblocks to sketch or show the product $-3x$ $(y)$.  $-3xy$; See additional answers.

53.  **SPORTS**  The length of each side of a baseball diamond is $10x^2$ ft. Find the area of a baseball diamond in terms of $x$.   $100x^4$ ft$^2$

### Extend the Lesson

**CONNECTING TO PRIOR KNOWLEDGE**  Have students work on expressions that require multiplication of monomials and also addition or subtraction.

**For each given expression, find an equivalent monomial.**

1. $5x^3 - x(-3x^2)$  $8x^3$
2. $(y^2)(2y) + (y)(y^2)$  $3y^3$
3. $(3x^2y)(2x^2y^3) + (-xy)^4$  $7x^4y^4$
4. $(2z^3)(2z)^4 - (4z)^2(2z^5)$  $0$

**MANUFACTURING** The diagram shows the net of a box that is being manufactured for a new product.

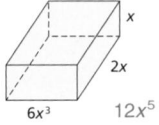

2a²b

54. Find the area of the base of the box. $6a^2b^2$

55. Find the area of each side of the box. $2a^3b$, $3ab$

56. Find the total surface area of the box.
$6a^2b^2 + 4a^3b + 6ab$

57. **PHOTOGRAPHY** Kyree frames a picture from his vacation. Write and simplify an expression to find the area of the frame.
$(2x^2)(3y^2) - (2x)(2xy) = 6x^2y^2 - 4x^2y$

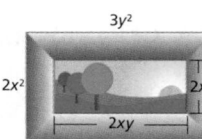

3y²
2x²  2x
2xy

**Write and simplify an expression for the volume of each prism.**

58.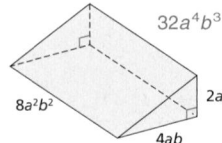
x
2x
6x³   12x⁵

59.
32a⁴b³
8a²b²   2a
4ab

## EXTENDED PRACTICE EXERCISES

**Find the value of $n$ in each equation.**

60. $p^8 \cdot p^n = p^{11}$
3

61. $(k^2)^n = k^6$
3

62. $x^{12} = x^3x^n$
9

63. A rectangle has an area that can be expressed as $64a^6b^9$. When its width is expressed as $4a^2b$, what is its length?
$16a^4b^8$

64. **CRITICAL THINKING** For the product $12x^2$, find nine pairs of monomial factors that have positive integer coefficients. (One possible pair is $3x \cdot 4x$.)
See additional answers.

65. **CHAPTER INVESTIGATION** Write an expression in terms of $x$ for the approximate distance between the following points.

a. start and 1    b. 1 and 2    c. 2 and 3
1.5x mi          2.5x mi        2x mi
d. 3 and 4       e. 4 and 5     f. 5 and finish
3x mi            2.5x mi        2x mi

## MIXED REVIEW EXERCISES

**Use data sets A and B to answer the following questions. Round to the nearest tenth when necessary.**

A: 6, 12, 7, 9, 6, 5, 4, 10, 12, 11, 12

B: 35, 36, 40, 41, 46, 35, 32, 60, 54, 34, 48

66. Find the mean, median and mode for data set A. (Lesson 1-2)
mean = 8.5, median = 9, mode = 12

67. Find the mean, median and mode for data set B. (Lesson 1-2)
mean = 41.9, median = 40, mode = 35

68. Describe the outliers, clusters and gaps for data set B. (Lesson 1-3) no outliers;
clusters = 32−36; gaps = 36−40, 41−46, 48−54, 54−60

69. Create a box-and-whisker plot for data set A. (Lesson 1-6)
See additional answers.

70. What is the greatest number in the first quartile for data set B? (Lesson 1-4) 35

## ADDITIONAL ANSWERS

12.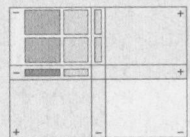

13. Both monomials involve exponents. The monomial $a^m \cdot a^n$ calls for the use of the product rule for exponents where $m$ and $n$ are added to form $a^{m+n}$. The monomial $(a^m)^n$ calls for the use of the power rule for exponents where $m$ and $n$ are multiplied to form $a^{mn}$. The difference to note is that in one case $m$ and $n$ are added and in the other case they are multiplied.

52.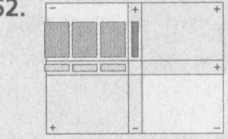

64. $1 \cdot 12x^2$, $2 \cdot 6x^2$, $3 \cdot 4x^2$, $x \cdot 12x$, $2x \cdot 6x$, $3x \cdot 4x$, $x^2 \cdot 12$, $2x^2 \cdot 6$, $3x^2 \cdot 4$

69.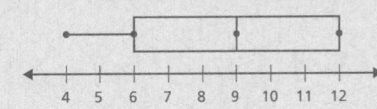
4  5  6  7  8  9  10  11  12

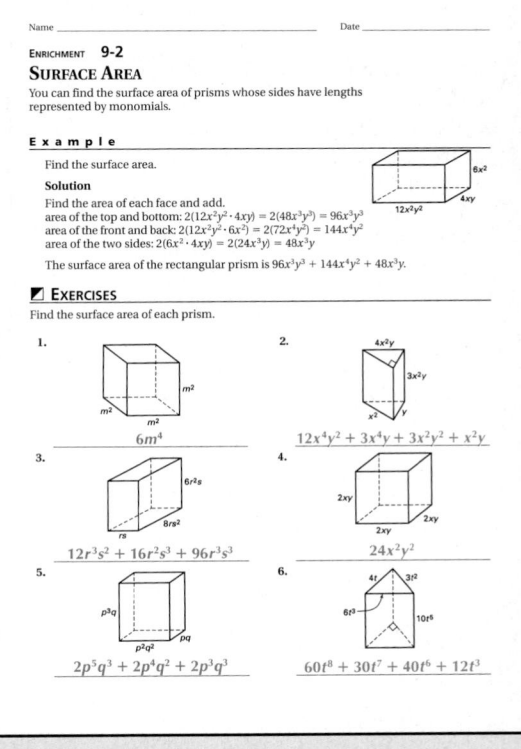

**Extra Practice Worksheet 9-2**

Name _____    Date _____

EXTRA PRACTICE  **9-2**
**MULTIPLY MONOMIALS**

■ **EXERCISES**

Simplify.

1. $(-7h)(-8j)$    $56hj$
2. $(-6a)(4c)$    $-24ac$
3. $(8r)(-4t)$    $-32rt$
4. $7(-4w)$    $-28w$
5. $(-15h)(-\frac{3}{5}k)$    $9hk$
6. $(4.5m)(-1.5n)$    $-6.75mn$
7. $(5x^3)(5x^4)$    $25x^7$
8. $(4c^4)(5d^5)$    $20c^4d^5$
9. $(\frac{4}{5}v^3)(-10v^2)$    $-8v^5$
10. $(9c^4d^2)(-6c^4d)$    $-54c^8d^3$
11. $(3rst)(-3rst)$    $-9r^2s^2t^2$
12. $4r(-11r^5s)$    $-44r^6s$
13. $(-2a)^2$    $4a^2$
14. $(-3b^3)^3$    $-27b^9$
15. $(-2k^4)^3$    $-8k^{12}$
16. $(x^3y^4)^2$    $x^6y^8$
17. $(3s^5tu^3)^2$    $9s^{10}t^2u^6$
18. $(4y)(4y)^3$    $256y^4$
19. $(-4x^3)(3x^2)^3$    $-108x^9$
20. $(-w^3x^5)^2(wx^3)^4$    $w^{10}x^{22}$
21. $(-a^2b^3c^2)(2a^4b^5c)(-7a^2b^3c^5)^2$    $-98a^{10}b^{14}c^{13}$
22. $(5m^2n^3p)(\frac{2}{5}mnp^4)(\frac{1}{2}m^3n^3)^3$    $\frac{1}{10}m^{13}n^{14}p^9$
23. $(\frac{2}{3}hjk^3)(\frac{3}{4}h^2jk)^2(-2h^4j^3k^5)^4$    $6h^{21}j^{15}k^{25}$

Write and simplify an expression for the area of each figure.

24.
5x²y³
4x²y
$(5x^2y^3)(4x^2y) = 20x^4y^4$

25.
4mn²
8m²n²
$\frac{1}{2}(4mn^2)(8m^2n^2) = 16m^3n^4$

**Enrichment Worksheet 9-2**

Name _____    Date _____

ENRICHMENT  **9-2**
**SURFACE AREA**

You can find the surface area of prisms whose sides have lengths represented by monomials.

**E x a m p l e**

Find the surface area.

6x²
12x²y²   4xy

**Solution**

Find the area of each face and add.
area of the top and bottom: $2(12x^2y^2 \cdot 4xy) = 2(48x^3y^3) = 96x^3y^3$
area of the front and back: $2(12x^2y^2 \cdot 6x^2) = 2(72x^4y^2) = 144x^4y^2$
area of the two sides: $2(6x^2 \cdot 4xy) = 2(24x^3y) = 48x^3y$

The surface area of the rectangular prism is $96x^3y^3 + 144x^4y^2 + 48x^3y$.

■ **EXERCISES**

Find the surface area of each prism.

1.
m²
m²
m²
$6m^4$

2.
4x²y
3x²y
x²
y
$12x^4y^2 + 3x^4y + 3x^2y^2 + x^2y$

3.
6r²s
8rs²
rs
$12r^3s^2 + 16r^2s^3 + 96r^3s^3$

4.
2xy
2xy
2xy
$24x^2y^2$

5.
p³q
p²q²
pq
$2p^5q^3 + 2p^4q^2 + 2p^3q^3$

6.
4t
3t²
6t³
10t⁵
$60t^8 + 30t^7 + 40t^6 + 12t^3$

## Vocabulary Review

**Lesson 9-1**

monomial            coefficient
constant            polynomial
term                binomial
trinomial           standard form
like terms

## ASSIGNMENT GUIDE

**All students: 1–62**

## Chalkboard Examples

### Lesson 9-1

a. Which of the choices represents $(3y^3 + 5y) + (-8y^3 - 3y^2 + 8) + (5y^3 - 3y)$?  **B**
   A. $y^3 - 3y^2 + 2y + 8$
   B. $-3y^2 + 2y + 8$
   C. $y^3 - 3y^2 + 10y$
   D. $-3y^2 + 10y$

b. Which of the choices represents the difference of $(3x^3 + 2x)$ and $(-x^3 + 4x^2 - 7)$?  **D**
   A. $2x^3 + 4x^2 + 2x - 7$
   B. $2x^3 - 4x^2 + 2x + 7$
   C. $4x^3 + 4x^2 + 2x - 7$
   D. $4x^3 - 4x^2 + 2x + 7$

### Lesson 9-2

a. Which of the choices represents the product of $(-3a^2b)(-7a^3b)$?
   **C**
   A. $-21a^6b$         B. $-21a^6b^2$
   C. $21a^5b^2$        D. $21a^5b$

b. Which of the choices represents an equivalent expression for $(-5a^2)^3$?  **D**
   A. $-15a^5$          B. $-15a^6$
   C. $-125a^5$         D. $-125a^6$

# Review and Practice Your Skills

## PRACTICE ■ LESSON 9-1

Write each polynomial in standard form for the variable $x$.

1. $4 + 2x^2 + 5x^3$   $5x^3 + 2x^2 + 4$
2. $5x^2 + 2x^3 + x^4 + x$   $x^4 + 2x^3 + 5x^2 + x$
3. $y^3 - xy^2 + 7x^2y - 3x^3$
   $-3x^3 + 7x^2y - xy^2 + y^3$
4. $-2x - 4x^5 + 8 - x^3$   $-4x^5 - x^3 - 2x + 8$
5. $9x - 10 - 4x^2 + 6x^3$
   $6x^3 - 4x^2 + 9x - 10$
6. $x^2y + x^3y^3 + 3xy^3$   $x^3y^3 + x^2y + 3xy^3$

Simplify.

7. $8c - 3c$   $5c$
8. $\frac{1}{3}x^2 + \frac{2}{5}x^2$   $\frac{11}{15}x^2$
9. $9m - 3m - 7m + 5m$   $4m$
10. $5y^2 - 3y^3 - 8y^3$   $-11y^3 + 5y^2$
11. $3b - 6d + 2b + 10d$   $5b + 4d$
12. $7x^3 - 3x - x$   $7x^3 - 4x$
13. $2k + k^2 + 2k - 2k^2$   $-k^2 + 4k$
14. $7x + 8y - 3x - 2y$   $4x + 6y$
15. $(a^2 + ab) + (a^2 - ab)$   $2a^2$
16. $(15p + 11) - (p - 1)$   $14p + 12$
17. $(18.5x - 3.9) - (13.2x + 5.1)$   $5.3x - 9$
18. $(7fg^2 + 3fg) - (-5fg^2 + 6fg)$   $12fg^2 - 3fg$
19. $5x - (3x + 7)$   $2x - 7$
20. $9m - 4n + 4m - 8n$   $13m - 12n$
21. $(3ab^2 - 4ab + 6) - (ab^2 + 3ab)$
    $2ab^2 - 7ab + 6$
22. $14x^2y^3 - 6x^3y^2 - 11x^3y^2 + 3x^2y^3$
    $17x^2y^3 - 17x^3y^2$

## PRACTICE ■ LESSON 9-2

Simplify.

23. $(4a)(9b)$   $36ab$
24. $(5z)(-6x)$   $-30zx$
25. $(-15c)\left(\frac{3}{5}b\right)$   $-9cb$
26. $(xy)(-3xy)$   $-3x^2y^2$
27. $(2c^6)(4b^4c^2)$   $8b^4c^8$
28. $5e(-11e^2g)$   $-55e^3g$
29. $(-stu)(2stu)$   $-2s^2t^2u^2$
30. $7(-3x)$   $-21x$
31. $\left(\frac{2}{5}g^2\right)(25g^5)$   $10g^7$
32. $(-4x)^3$   $-64x^3$
33. $(5g^2)^3$   $125g^6$
34. $(2x^2y)^5$   $32x^{10}y^5$
35. $(x^2)(x^3)(x^5)$   $x^{10}$
36. $(q^2p^3)^3$   $q^6p^9$
37. $(-ef^2g)^4$   $e^4f^8g^4$
38. $(-a^2b^3)(4a^4bc^2)(-3ab^5c)$
    $12a^7b^9c^3$
39. $(5h^4)^2(3h^2)^3$   $675h^{14}$
40. $(-3xy)^2(-x^2y^2)(7xy^3)$   $-63x^5y^7$
41. $(-3p^3)^4$   $81p^{12}$
42. $(-4x^2)(9x^3)^2$   $-324x^8$
43. $(-xy^2z)^4$   $x^4y^8z^4$
44. $(8h^3)(-2h^2)^4$   $128h^{11}$
45. $(-a^2b)(9a^3b^2)(2ab^3)$
    $-18a^6b^6$
46. $\left(-\frac{1}{3}x^3y\right)(9xy)^2$   $-27x^5y^3$

47. Find the area of a rectangle that is $12n^2$ ft by $6n^3$ ft.   $72n^5$ ft²
48. Find the area of a square that has a side measuring $2x^3$ cm.   $4x^6$ cm²
49. Find the area of a triangle that has a base of $9x$ m and a height of $3x^2$ m.   $\frac{27}{2}x^3$ m²
50. Find the area of a parallelogram that has a base of $2.7xy^2$ in. and a height of $1.3x^2y$ in.   $3.51x^3y^3$ in.²

## Differentiated Instruction

**VISUAL LEARNERS** Remind students that they can use a vertical format for both addition and subtraction of polynomials. When using a vertical arrangement for subtraction, suggest that students circle the given signs in the bottom row and write opposite signs above them, thus signifiying that subtraction is the equivalent of adding the opposite of the subtrahend. A vertical format is shown below for the subtraction of Exercise 18.

Rewrite    $7fg^2 + 3fg$    as         $7fg^2 + 3fg$

$-\,-5fg^2 +6fg$         $\ominus\ \ominus 5fg^2 \oplus 6fg$  ← Change the sign of each term of the subtrahend (second polynomial).
                         $12fg^2 - 3fg$

Change subtraction to addition.

**Simplify.** (Lessons 9-1 and 9-2)

**51.** $(-2t - 7) + (6t - 3)$   $4t - 10$

**52.** $(-7x^4)^2$   $49x^8$

**53.** $(5a - 8b) - (4a + b)$   $a - 9b$

**54.** $(3xy^3)^2$   $9x^2y^6$

**55.** $(-3xy^3)^3$   $-27x^3y^9$

**56.** $(a^3b)^3(-ab^2)^2$   $a^{11}b^7$

**57.** $(3p^5)(5p^2) + (4p^3)(4p^4)$   $31p^7$

**58.** $(xy^2)^2 + (xy^3)$   $x^2y^4 + xy^3$

**59.** $(-6a^3)\left(\frac{1}{6}a^3\right)$   $-a^6$

**Write and simplify an expression for the area of each figure.** (Lesson 9-2)

**60.**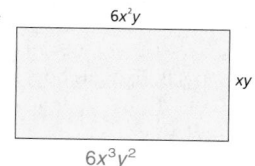
$6x^2y$
$xy$
$6x^3y^2$

**61.**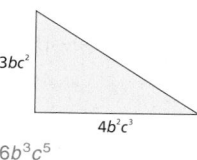
$3bc^2$
$4b^2c^3$
$6b^3c^5$

**62.**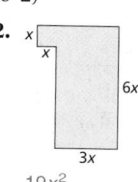
$x$
$x$
$6x$
$3x$
$19x^2$

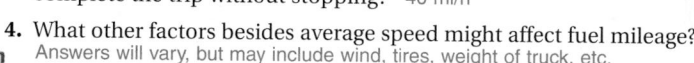

## MathWorks Career – Truck Driver
**Workplace Knowhow**

When truck drivers drive through the Mojave Desert in California, they drive through a very hot, arid, deserted region. Travel from Flagstaff, AZ, to Bakersfield, CA is 300 mi. Because there are few places along this route to refuel, many truck drivers attempt to drive this distance without stopping. They must constantly be aware of their speed, as this is directly proportional to the amount of fuel their vehicles consume. The equation gives the relationship between the fuel consumed in gallons per mile ($f$), average uphill speed in miles per hour ($v_u$) and average downhill speed in miles per hour ($v_d$).

$$f = 0.00001v_u^2 + 0.0002v_d^2$$

1. If the driver averages 40 mi/h uphill and 60 mi/h downhill, how much fuel will be required to travel the 300 mi between Flagstaff and Bakersfield?   221 gal

2. Assuming that the driver has filled his 100-gal tank upon leaving Flagstaff, will the truck need to refuel at some point before arriving in Bakersfield? If so, how many gallons short of completing the trip on one tank of fuel is it? If the trip can be made without stopping, how many gallons of fuel are left in the tank?   yes, 121 gal

3. A truck averages 30 mi/h uphill and has a 100-gal tank. What average speed must the truck maintain downhill in order to complete the trip without stopping?   40 mi/h

4. What other factors besides average speed might affect fuel mileage?
   Answers will vary, but may include wind, tires, weight of truck, etc.

**Math Online** mathmatters2.com/mathworks

Chapter 9  **Review and Practice Your Skills**  385

## Teaching Tip

Ask students to compare Exercise 31, $\left(\frac{2}{5}g^2\right)(25g^5)$, and Exercise 39, $(5h^4)^2(3h^2)^3$, with respect to the order of operations. Note with students that when there is an exponent outside parentheses, as in Exercise 39, that calculation must be done first.

When working with products of monomials, suggest that students first gather the coefficients, then note how many different literal factors there are. For each literal factor, students should scan the monomials, writing down the appropriate exponents in a sum. A systematic approach is especially helpful when there are more than two monomials in a product, as in Exercise 38: $(-a^2b^3)(4a^4bc^2)(-3ab^5c)$.

## MathWorks

Trucking is the predominant means of delivering all types of goods, accounting for four-fifths of all domestic freight value in the United States. Trucks in the mid-1990s hauled 1.4 trillion ton-kilometers of freight annually (a *ton-kilometer* is the movement of one metric ton over the distance of one kilometer). All types of manufacturing are also dependent on trucking for deliveries of parts and for shipping finished goods.

Drivers who work for trucking companies are generally paid by the mile (a typical commercial over-the-road truck is driven over 100,000 mi a year), while owner-operators and commercial carriers charge for freight by weight and distance. An important factor in determining freight charges is fuel consumption.

Students should answer Questions 1–4 to better understand how polynomials might be used in predetermining fuel consumption for an individual trucking trip.

Trucking operations are regulated by state and local agencies to ensure safety on the road. Drivers of over-the-road trucks must have a commercial driver's license, which is obtained by special training and the passing of written and driving examinations. Drivers must also keep written logbooks of their hours and miles traveled, as these are regulated for safety purposes to minimize driver fatigue.

Students who are interested in learning more about this career choice can go to mathmatters2.com/mathworks. School Guidance Counselors are another resource for information about training requirements and appropriate schools.

# Divide by a Monomial

**Goals** ■ Divide monomials and polynomials by monomials.

**Applications** Landscaping, Retail, Interior design, Geography, Modeling

## Lesson Planning

### NCTM Standards/Strands
■ Algebra
■ Representation
■ Number & Operations
■ Connections

### Tools/Materials Needed
graph paper
Algeblocks with Quadrant Mat

### Lesson Resources
Warm-up Transparency 36
Transparency TK-5, 6, 9
Reteaching 9-3
Extra Practice 9-3
Enrichment 9-3

## Getting Started

### 5-Minute Warm-Up

Evaluate each expression.

1. $\frac{18}{24}$  $\frac{3}{4}$          2. $\frac{-22}{28}$  $\frac{-11}{14}$

3. $\frac{3+9}{15}$  $\frac{4}{5}$          4. $\frac{4-12}{8}$  $-1$

### Introduction to Lesson 9-3
To help students understand the meaning of the divisions they will be doing, ask them to model each rectangle on graph paper. Models are shown here and in the Teaching Tip at the bottom of this page.

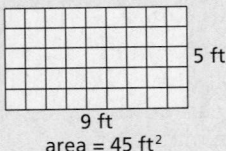

5 ft

9 ft
area = 45 ft²

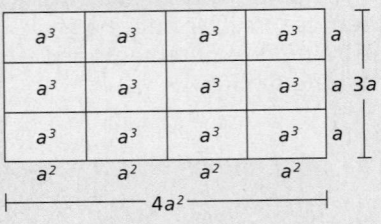

3a

$4a^2$

area = $12a^3$

---

**For Questions 1–5, use the formula for the area of a rectangle.**

1. The area of a rectangle is 45 ft² and the length is 9 ft. What is the width?  5 ft

2. What operation did you use in Question 1?  division

3. The area of a rectangle is $12a^3$ ft² and the width is $3a$ ft. Explain how to find the length.   divide $\frac{12a^3}{3a}$

4. What do you think the length is in Question 3?   $4a^2$

5. The area of a rectangle is $6x^2y + 12xy^2$ ft² and the length is $3xy$ ft. Explain how to find the width.
   divide $\frac{6x^2y + 12xy^2}{3xy}$

### ◤ BUILD UNDERSTANDING

Recall the quotient rule for exponents.

*Quotient rule:* $\frac{a^m}{a^n} = a^{m-n}$

You can use the quotient rule to divide one monomial by another. Since division by zero is undefined, throughout this lesson it is assumed that no denominator has a value of zero.

### Example 1

**Simplify.**

a. $\frac{12mn}{9m}$

b. $\frac{-14h^7k^5}{18hk^3}$

**Solution**

a. $\frac{12mn}{9m} = \frac{2^2 3mn}{3^2 m}$   Write the prime factorization of each coefficient.

$= \frac{4n}{3}$   To simplify, divide the numerator and denominator by any common factors.

b. $\frac{-14h^7k^5}{18hk^3} = \frac{(-1)(2)(7)h^7k^5}{(2)(3^2)hk^3}$   $h^{7-1}, k^{5-3}$

$= \frac{(-1)(7)h^6k^2}{3^2}$   Simplify.

$= \frac{-7h^6k^2}{9}$

#### Check Understanding

In Example 1, part a, what is the GCF of $12mn$ and $9m$? How is dividing a monomial by a monomial like simplifying a fraction?

$3m$; You divide both the numerator and denominator by the GCF.

---

### Differentiated Instruction

**VISUAL LEARNERS** Some students need to see the abstract as a concrete model. A model for the rectangle in Question 5 of the opening activity is shown at the right. The shading indicates like terms.

| $xy^2$ | $xy^2$ | $xy^2$ | $y$ |
|--------|--------|--------|-----|
| $xy^2$ | $xy^2$ | $xy^2$ | $y$ |
| $xy^2$ | $xy^2$ | $xy^2$ | $y$ |
| $xy^2$ | $xy^2$ | $xy^2$ | $y$ |
| $x^2y$ | $x^2y$ | $x^2y$ | $x$ |
| $x^2y$ | $x^2y$ | $x^2y$ | $x$ |
| $xy$   | $xy$   | $xy$   |     |

$2x + 4y$

$3xy$

area = $6x^2y + 12xy^2$

The distributive property is used to multiply each term of a polynomial by a monomial.

$$3n(4n + 7) = 3n(4n) + 3n(7) = 12n^2 + 21n$$

Since division is the inverse of multiplication, you can reverse this process to divide a polynomial by a monomial.

$$3n(4n + 7) = 12n^2 + 21n, \text{ so } \frac{(12n^2 + 21n)}{3n} = 4n + 7.$$

To divide a polynomial by a monomial, divide each term of the polynomial by the monomial. You can use the greatest common factor (GCF) and the quotient rule for exponents to simplify the quotient $(12n^2 + 21n) \div 3n$.

$$\frac{12n^2 + 21n}{3n} = \frac{12n^2}{3n} + \frac{21n}{3n}$$

$$= \frac{12}{3} \cdot \frac{n^2}{n} + \frac{21}{3} \cdot \frac{n}{n} \qquad \text{Divide each pair of coefficients by their GCF, 3.}$$
$$\qquad\qquad\qquad\qquad\qquad \text{Divide each pair of variable parts by their GCF, } n.$$

$$= 4 \cdot n^{2-1} + 7 \cdot 1$$

$$= 4n + 7$$

## Example 2

**Simplify.**

**a.** $\dfrac{8n + 12}{4}$   **b.** $\dfrac{9x^4 - 12x^3 + 15x^2}{3x^2}$   **c.** $\dfrac{3a^2b + 9ab^2}{3ab}$

### Solution

**a.** $\dfrac{8n + 12}{4} = \dfrac{8n}{4} + \dfrac{12}{4} = 2n + 3$

**b.** $\dfrac{9x^4 - 12x^3 + 15x^2}{3x^2} = \dfrac{9x^4}{3x^2} - \dfrac{12x^3}{3x^2} + \dfrac{15x^2}{3x^2} = 3x^2 - 4x + 5$

**c.** $\dfrac{3a^2b + 9ab^2}{3ab} = \dfrac{3a^2b}{3ab} + \dfrac{9ab^2}{3ab} = a + 3b$

> **Think Back**
>
> For any real numbers, $a$, $b$ and $c$, where $c$ is not equal to zero,
> $$\frac{a + b}{c} = \frac{a}{c} + \frac{b}{c}.$$

## Example 3

The area of a rectangle is $(6x^3 + 2x^2 + x)$ cm². The width of the rectangle is $2x^2$ cm. Find the length of the rectangle.

### Solution

Use the formula for the area of a rectangle, $A = l \cdot w$. So, $l = \dfrac{A}{w}$.

$$l = \frac{A}{w} = \frac{6x^3 + 2x^2 + x}{2x^2}$$

$$= \frac{6x^3}{2x^2} + \frac{2x^2}{2x^2} + \frac{x}{2x^2}$$

$$= 3x + 1 + \frac{1}{2x}$$

The area of the rectangle is $\left(3x + 1 + \dfrac{1}{2x}\right)$ cm.

 **Math Online** mathmatters2.com/extra_examples

---

## Chalkboard Examples

### Supplementary Example 1
**MODELING** Use Algeblocks and the Quadrant Mat to divide $2x^2 - 4x$ by $2x$.

Place the divisor, $2x$, on the horizontal axis. Use tiles for $2x^2$ and $-4x$ to form rectangular areas that are $2x$ wide.

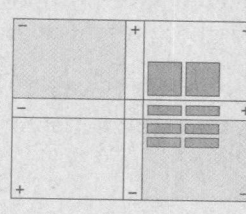

Determine the other dimension of the rectangular area. Read the answer from the vertical axis: $x - 2$.

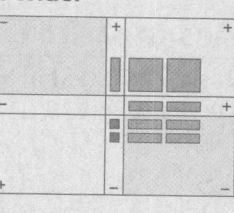

So, $\dfrac{2x^2 - 4x}{2x} = x - 2$.

### Supplementary Example 2
The perimeter of an equilateral triangle is $(45t^4 - 30t^2 + 15t)$ in. Find the length of a side of the triangle. Since the sides of an equilateral triangle are equal in measure, divide the perimeter by 3.

$$\frac{45t^4 - 30t^2 + 15t}{3} = \frac{45t^4}{3} - \frac{30t^2}{3} + \frac{15t}{3}$$

$$= 15t^4 - 10t^2 + 5t$$

So, the length of each side of the equilateral triangle is $(15t^4 - 10t^2 + 5t)$ in.

---

## Teaching Tip

The customary definition of a monomial is $ax^n$ where $a$ denotes a nonzero real number and $n$ denotes a positive integer. As a consequence of the definition, the following single terms are not monomials:

When there is a variable in the denominator, such as $\dfrac{5x}{y}$.

When there is a variable under a radical sign such as $5\sqrt{x}$.

Thus, the quotient of two monomials is not always a monomial.

**Example:** $6y$ and $2x$ are monomials. But $\dfrac{6y}{2x} = \dfrac{3y}{x}$ is not a monomial.

# Lesson Wrap-up

## QUICK ASSESSMENT

Ask the following question to determine if students understand the content presented in this lesson.

Consider the division $\dfrac{9x^3 - 6x^2 + 3x}{3x}$.

Is the result equal to $3x^2 - 2x$? Explain.   No; the result is $3x^2 - 2x + 1$, since $\dfrac{3x}{3x} = 1$ not 0.

## ASSIGNMENT GUIDE

Basic: 1–48, 55–60
Enriched: 1–60

## ADDITIONAL ANSWERS

43.

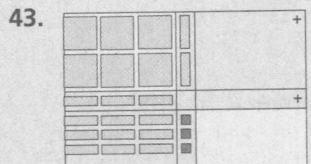

**Reteaching Worksheet 9-3**

---

**Simplify.**

1. $\dfrac{-36ab}{12b}$   $-3a$

2. $\dfrac{24m^5n^6}{30m^2n^6}$   $\dfrac{4m^3}{5}$

3. $\dfrac{-15x^3y^2z}{20x^3y}$   $\dfrac{-3yz}{4}$

4. $\dfrac{64x^2yz^3}{8x^2z^2}$   $8yz$

5. $\dfrac{6p - 12r}{6}$   $p - 2r$

6. $\dfrac{16a^2 + 4ab}{4a}$   $4a + b$

7. $\dfrac{14k^3m^2 - 7km}{7km}$   $2k^2m - 1$

8. $\dfrac{6h^2 - 2h^4 + 10h^3}{2h^3}$   $\dfrac{3}{h} - h + 5$

9. $\dfrac{15c^3d^2 - 5cd + 10c}{-5c}$   $-3c^2d^2 + d - 2$

10. The area of a rectangle is $72mn$ yd$^2$, and the length is $9n$ yd. Find the width.   $8m$ yd

 **MODELING** Use the Quadrant Mat shown for Exercises 11 and 12.

11. What division problem is represented on the Quadrant Mat?   $\dfrac{2xy - 6x}{2x}$

12. What expression should be placed on the vertical axis to complete the Mat?   $y - 3$

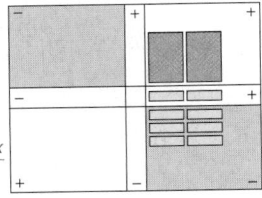

**Simplify.**

13. $\dfrac{8x^2}{2x}$   $4x$

14. $\dfrac{12a^6}{12a^4}$   $a^2$

15. $\dfrac{-20y^3}{14y^3}$   $-\dfrac{10}{7}$

16. $\dfrac{66uv^2}{-11v}$   $-6uv$

17. $\dfrac{6ab}{12ac}$   $\dfrac{b}{2c}$

18. $\dfrac{-16p^2q}{4p}$   $-4pq$

19. $\dfrac{-150x^3y^2}{-10x^2y}$   $15xy$

20. $\dfrac{60x^4yz^2}{-12z}$   $-5x^4yz$

21. $\dfrac{110a^2bc^5}{10ac^2}$   $11abc^3$

22. $\dfrac{-30m^3n}{-6mn}$   $5m^2$

23. $\dfrac{42a^2bc^3}{14a^2bc^3}$   $3$

24. $\dfrac{-24m^7n^9}{16m^3n^6}$   $\dfrac{-3m^4n^3}{2}$

25. $\dfrac{-42a^4b^5c}{7a^4bc}$   $-6b^4$

26. $\dfrac{-81m^3n^3p^3}{-9mn^3p^3}$   $9m^2$

27. $\dfrac{4a + 20}{4}$   $a + 5$

28. $\dfrac{9h - 21}{3}$   $3h - 7$

29. $\dfrac{15a^2 - 10a}{5a}$   $3a - 2$

30. $\dfrac{21n^3 + 35n^2}{-7n}$   $-3n^2 - 5n$

31. $\dfrac{14x^2 - 21x^3}{7x^2}$   $2 - 3x$

32. $\dfrac{4xyz^2 - 4yz^2}{yz^2}$   $4x - 4$

33. $\dfrac{a - 3a^3 + 5a^5}{a}$   $1 - 3a^2 + 5a^4$

34. $\dfrac{36c^6 + 30c^5 - 54c^4}{6c^3}$   $6c^3 + 5c^2 - 9c$

35. $\dfrac{25w^3 - 15w^2 - 30w}{5w}$   $5w^2 - 3w - 6$

36. $\dfrac{-24x^5 + 8x^4 - 64x^3}{-8x^3}$   $3x^2 - x + 8$

37. $\dfrac{-45a^2b^3 + 18a^3b^4 - 9ab^2}{9ab}$   $-5ab^2 + 2a^2b^3 - b$

38. $\dfrac{12m^3n^4 - 20m^4n^3 + 32mn^2}{4mn^2}$   $3m^2n^2 - 5m^3n + 8$

39. $\dfrac{3x^2yz - 4xy^2z + 2xyz^2 - xyz}{xyz}$   $3x - 4y + 2z - 1$

40. $\dfrac{12ab - 21a^2b + 27ab^2 - 6a^2b^2}{-3ab}$   $-4 + 7a - 9b + 2ab$

41. **LANDSCAPING** A rectangular garden has an area of $48pq$ square units. The width is $8q$ units. Write an expression for the length.   $6p$

42. **RETAIL** How many CD's can you buy for \$$48xy^2$ if each CD sells for \$$3y$?   $16xy$

 43. **MODELING** Sketch or show $\dfrac{-6x^2 + 9x}{-3x}$ using Algeblocks.   $2x - 3$; See additional answers.

## Teaching Tip

When dividing a polynomial by a monomial, encourage students to include as a first step each intended division, as demonstrated in Example 2. In this way, students are more likely to include in their answers a term that consists only of 1, as needed in the Quick Assessment question.

**Write an expression for the unknown dimension of each rectangle.**

**44.** area = $36ab$

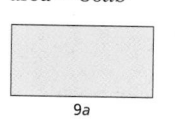

9a

4b

**45.** area = $64mnp$

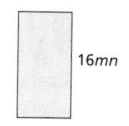

16mn

4p

**46. INTERIOR DESIGN** Carmen is putting a wooden border 3 ft from the floor around the walls of her dining room. The perimeter of the room is $36a^2$ ft. The window and two doorways have a total width of $21a$ ft. To find the total number of yards needed, she can divide the total number of feet needed by 3 ft/yd. Write and simplify an expression for the total number of yards needed for the border. $(12a^2 - 7a)$ yd

**47. GEOGRAPHY** The Great Salt Lake Desert in Utah is rectangular in shape. The area of the desert is approximately $(8x^4 + 4x^3)$ mi$^2$. The width is about $2x^2$ mi. Find the approximate length of the Great Salt Lake Desert. $(4x^2 + 2x)$ mi

**48.** The volume of a rectangular prism is $(135mxy + 45my^2)$ cubic units. The length is $5y$ units and the height is $9m$ units. Write an expression for the width. $3x + y$

Great Salt Lake Desert

### ■ EXTENDED PRACTICE EXERCISES

**49.** The area of a rectangle is $8x^2y^2$. The width of the rectangle is $xy$. Write an expression for the perimeter of the rectangle. $18xy$

**50. CRITICAL THINKING** A square has a perimeter of $28x + 40y$. Express the area using the formula for the area of a square. $A = (7x + 10y)^2$

To divide a polynomial by a polynomial, find two factors of the numerator. Then divide by common factors. Divide the following.

**51.** $\frac{4n + 12}{n + 3}$  4

**52.** $\frac{2x - 12}{x - 6}$  2

**53.** $\frac{5a + xa}{5 + x}$  a

**54.** $\frac{3k^2 - 12k}{k - 4}$  3k

### ■ MIXED REVIEW EXERCISES

**Use the figure for Exercises 55–60.** (Lesson 5-1)

**55.** How many lines go through point $M$?  2

**56.** Name three points that lie on line $CR$. any three of $C, E, G, H, L, R$

**57.** Name all segments shown for which point $I$ is an endpoint.
$\overline{DI}, \overline{GI}, \overline{FI}, \overline{JI}, \overline{OI}, \overline{TI}, \overline{NI}, \overline{SI}, \overline{MI}, \overline{RI}, \overline{HI}$

**58.** Name all the points that are collinear with points $B$ and $Q$.
$A, D, K$

**59.** Identify the intersection of lines $DF$ and $CR$.  $E$

**60.** Line $FS$ bisects line $QU$. Name two congruent line segments made from this bisection.  $\overline{QS}, \overline{SU}$

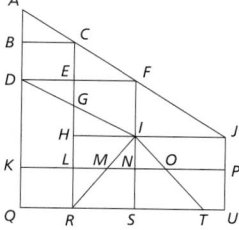

Math nline  mathmatters2.com/self_check_quiz

---

Name _____ Date _____

EXTRA PRACTICE  **9-3**
**DIVIDE BY A MONOMIAL**

**✎ EXERCISES**

Simplify.

1. $\frac{14y^3}{7y}$  $2y^2$

2. $\frac{6t^6}{3t^5}$  $2t$

3. $\frac{9vw}{15v}$  $\frac{3w}{5}$

4. $\frac{-15a^2b^3}{3a}$  $-5ab^3$

5. $\frac{80x^4y^5}{20x^2y^2}$  $4x^2y^3$

6. $\frac{24c^3d^2f^3}{-6cdf^2}$  $-4c^2df$

7. $\frac{30st^2u^3}{25s^3tu^4}$  $\frac{6t}{5s^2u}$

8. $\frac{-18x^3y^2z^5}{-6x^2yz^3}$  $3xyz^2$

9. $\frac{12m - 15}{3}$  $4m - 5$

10. $\frac{8a^2 + 4a}{2a}$  $4a + 2$

11. $\frac{r^3 + 3r^2 - 5r}{r}$  $r^2 + 3r - 5$

12. $\frac{6h^5 + 2h^3 - 8h^2}{2h^2}$  $3h^3 + h - 4$

13. $\frac{-21bc^4 + 14b^3c}{7bc}$  $-3c^3 + 2b^2$

14. $\frac{8a^8 - 6a^5 + 4a^4}{-2a^4}$  $-4a^4 + 3a - 2$

15. $\frac{12x^5y + 8x^3y^3 - 4x^3y^2}{4x^3}$  $3x^2y + 2y^3 - y^2$

16. $\frac{6m^5n^4 - 12mn^7 + 9m^4n^8}{-3mn^2}$  $-2mn^2 + 4n^5 - 3m^3n^6$

17. $\frac{4r^2s^7 - 5r^5s^5 + 10r^4s^3}{rs^3}$  $4rs^4 - 5r^4s^2 + 10r^3$

18. A rectangular dog pen has an area of $64xy$ square units. The width is $4y$. Write an expression for the length.
$\frac{64xy}{4y} = 16x$

19. A rectangular patio has an area of $30x^2y^2$. The length is $6x^2y$. Write an expression for the width.
$\frac{30x^2y^2}{6x^2y} = 5y$

---

### Enrichment Worksheet 9-3

Name _____ Date _____

ENRICHMENT  **9-3**
**OBLIQUE ASYMPTOTES**

The graph of $y = ax + b$, where $a \neq 0$, is called an oblique asymptote of $y = f(x)$ if the graph of $f$ comes closer and closer to the line as $x \to \infty$ or $x \to -\infty$. $\infty$ is the mathematical symbol for **infinity**, which means *endless*.

For $f(x) = 3x + 4 + \frac{2}{x}$, $y = 3x + 4$ is an oblique asymptote because

$f(x) - 3x - 4 = \frac{2}{x}$, and $\frac{2}{x} \to 0$ as $x \to \infty$ or $-\infty$. In other words, as $|x|$

increases, the value of $\frac{2}{x}$ gets smaller and smaller approaching 0.

**Example**

Find the oblique asymptote for $f(x) = \frac{x^2 + 8x + 15}{x + 2}$.

**Solution**

$\begin{array}{r|rrr} -2] & 1 & 8 & 15 \\ & & -2 & -12 \\ \hline & 1 & 6 & 3 \end{array}$  Use synthetic division.

$y = \frac{x^2 + 8x + 15}{x + 2} = x + 6 + \frac{3}{x + 2}$

As $|x|$ increases, the value of $\frac{3}{x + 2}$ gets smaller. In other words, since

$\frac{3}{x + 2} \to 0$ as $x \to \infty$ or $x \to -\infty$, $y = x + 6$ is an oblique asymptote.

**✎ EXERCISES**

Use synthetic division to find the oblique asymptote for each function.

1. $y = \frac{8x^2 - 4x + 11}{x + 5}$  $y = 8x - 44$

2. $y = \frac{x^2 + 3x - 15}{x - 2}$  $y = x + 5$

3. $y = \frac{x^2 - 2x - 18}{x - 3}$  $y = x + 1$

4. $y = \frac{ax^2 + bx + c}{x - d}$  $y = ax + b + ad$

---

## Alternative Assessment

**MATH JOURNAL** Have students consider the following division problems.

1. $\frac{x^{2n} - x^n + x^{n-1}}{x^n}$  $x^n - 1 + \frac{1}{x}$

2. $\frac{2^{2n} - 2^n + 2^{n-1} - 2^{n-2}}{-2^n}$  $-2^n + 1 - \frac{1}{2} + \frac{1}{4}$

### Tools/Materials Needed

Algeblocks with Quadrant Mat graphing calculator

### Lesson Resources

Warm-up Transparency 36
Transparency TK-5, 6
Reteaching 9-4
Extra Practice 9-4
Enrichment 9-4

## Getting Started

### 5-MINUTE WARM-UP

Use multiplication to remove parentheses.
1. $3(a + b)$    $3a + 3b$
2. $4(2c - d)$    $8c - 4d$
3. $\frac{1}{2}(14m + 8n)$    $7m + 4n$

### Introduction to Lesson 9-4

Remind students that they generally read an Algeblocks model by noting the display on the horizontal axis first. So, in the case of Question 1, they would read the product as $(2x + 2)(x)$. By the Commutative Property, this product is equivalent to $x(2x + 2)$.

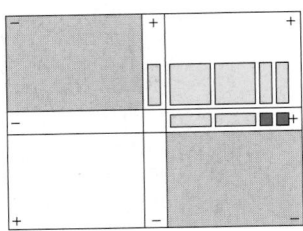

# 9-4 Multiply a Polynomial by a Monomial

**Goals** ■ Multiply polynomials by monomials.

**Applications** Travel, Part-time job, Sports, Finance, Geography, Modeling

**Use Algeblocks for Questions 1–4.**

1. What polynomial expressions are being multiplied on the Quadrant Mat shown?  $x(2x + 2)$

2. What is the product represented by the Algeblocks?  $2x^2 + 2x$

3. Sketch or show $3x(x + 2)$ using Algeblocks.  For 3 and 4, see additional answers.

4. Use Algeblocks to find the product $3x(x + 2)$.  $3x^2 + 6x$

### ▌ BUILD UNDERSTANDING

The distributive property gives a method to multiply a polynomial by a monomial.

*distributive property:* $a(\underset{\uparrow}{\underline{b}} + c) = ab + ac$

$\underset{\text{monomial polynomial}}{}$

$a(\underline{b} - c) = ab - ac$

#### Reading Math

The distributive property states that when a sum or difference of terms is multiplied by a factor, the factor must be *distributed*, through multiplication, over each term.

$a(b + c) = ab + ac$

Factor *a* is *distributed* over both terms, *b* and *c*.

### Example 1

**Simplify.**

a. $5n(2n - 3)$

b. $-6k(-k^2 + 2k + 5)$

**Solution**

a. $5n(2n - 3) = 5n(2n) - 5n(3)$    Use the distributive property.

$= 10n^2 - 15n$    Multiply each pair of monomials.

b. $-6k(-k^2 + 2k + 5) = -6k(-k^2) + (-6k)(2k) + (-6k)(5)$

$= 6k^3 - 12k^2 - 30k$

**390**    Chapter 9  **Polynomials**

## ADDITIONAL ANSWERS

3.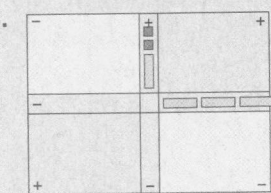

4.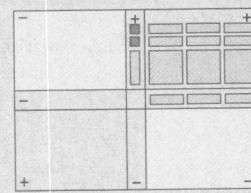

## Example 2

**Show the product $2x(x - 3)$ using Algeblocks.**

### Solution

**Step 1** Use a Quadrant Mat. Place two $x$-blocks on the positive horizontal axis.

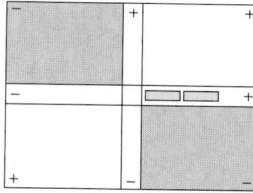

**Step 2** Place one $x$-block on the positive vertical axis, and three unit blocks on the negative vertical axis.

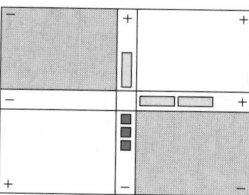

**Step 3** Use $x^2$-blocks and $x$-blocks to form rectangular areas in all quadrants bounded by the pieces.

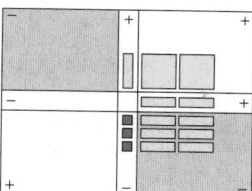

## Example 3

**Simplify.**

**a.** $4(x^2 + xy) - 3(x^2 - xy)$

**b.** $7m(2m - 4) + 2m(2m - 4)$

### Solution

**a.** $4(x^2 + xy) - 3(x^2 - xy)$

$= (4x^2 + 4xy) - (3x^2 - 3xy)$

$= 4x^2 + 4xy - 3x^2 + 3xy$

$= (4x^2 - 3x^2) + (4xy + 3xy)$

$= x^2 + 7xy$

**b.** $7m(2m - 4) + 2m(2m - 4)$

$= [7m(2m) - 7m(4)] + [2m(2m) - 2m(4)]$

$= (14m^2 - 28m) + (4m^2 - 8m)$

$= 14m^2 - 28m + 4m^2 - 8m$

$= (14m^2 + 4m^2) + (-28m - 8m)$

$= 18m^2 - 36m$

## Example 4

**TRAVEL** Renting a four-wheel-drive vehicle at Vacation Rentals costs \$43/day plus \$0.08/mi. The cost $C$ is expressed by the formula $C = 43 + 0.08m$, where $m$ is the number of miles the vehicle is driven.

Wilderness Camp rented a fleet of $v$ vehicles for one day. Write a formula for the total cost of renting all the vehicles. Assume all vehicles travel the same number of miles.

### Solution

total cost = number of vehicles · cost per vehicle

$TC = v(43 + 0.08m)$

$TC = 43v + 0.08mv$

**Math Online** mathmatters2.com/extra_examples

### Problem Solving Tip

In Example 3, part b, the term $(2m - 4)$ appears twice. Think of the binomial $(2m - 4)$ as a "chunk," and use the distributive property to simplify.

$7m(2m - 4) + 2m(2m - 4)$

$= (7m + 2m)(2m - 4)$

$= 9m(2m - 4)$

$= 18m^2 - 36m$

## Chalkboard Examples

### Supplementary Example 1

Show the product $-x(x - 2)$ using Algeblocks.

Place one $x$-block in the negative horizontal axis.

Place one $x$-block in the positive vertical axis and two unit blocks in the negative vertical axis.

Use an $x^2$-block and $x$-blocks to form rectangular areas in all quadrants bounded by the pieces.

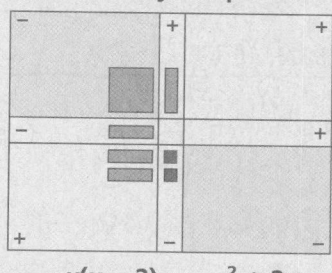

$-x(x - 2) = -x^2 + 2x$

### Supplementary Example 2

**CONSTRUCTION** ABC-Co has hired Dale Construction to build an office building for them. Dale estimates that, for a typical office building, the height of each story is $h$ ft from floor to floor, and the length of a building averages $k$ ft per room. ABC-Co wants a structure that is 5 stories tall and has 11 rooms along the front; but each room is to be 3 ft longer than the standard. Estimate the area of the front wall of the building.

Draw a diagram to model the situation

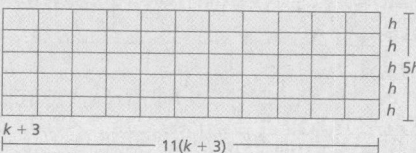

Area = length · width

$= 11(k + 3)$ · $5h$

$= [11 \cdot k + 11 \cdot 3]$ · $5h$

$= (11k + 33)$ · $5h$

$= 5h \cdot 11k + 5h$ · $33$

$= 55hk + 165h$

So, the area of the front wall is $(55hk + 165h)$ ft².

## Teaching Tip

Remind students that they can check the result of operations with polynomials by substituting a value for each variable and noting that this leads to a true numerical statement.

Here is a check for Example 1b.

Let $k = 2$.

$-6k(-k^2 + 2k + 5) \stackrel{?}{=} 6k^3 - 12k^2 - 30k$

$-6 \cdot 2(-2^2 + 2 \cdot 2 + 5) \stackrel{?}{=} 6 \cdot 2^3 - 12 \cdot 2^2 - 30 \cdot 2$

$-12(-4 + 4 + 5) \stackrel{?}{=} 6 \cdot 8 - 12 \cdot 4 - 60$

$-12(5) \stackrel{?}{=} 48 - 48 - 60$

$-60 = -60$ ✓

## Lesson Wrap-up

## QUICK ASSESSMENT

Ask the following question to determine if students understand the content presented in this lesson.

If a polynomial in simplest form is multiplied by a nonzero monomial, how many terms will the product have? **the same number of terms as the polynomial**

## ASSIGNMENT GUIDE

**Basic:** 1–57, 66–75
**Enriched:** 1–75

## ADDITIONAL ANSWERS

1. $6x^2 + 24x$
2. $16n - 2n^3$
3. $12k^5 + 12k^7 + 36k^3$
4. $-35c^7 + 10c^6 - 55c^5$
5. $-4p^3 + 8p^2 - 20p$
6. $4x^3y - 12xy^2$
7. $-3a^2b^2 - 4a^6b$
8. $14x^2 - 7xy$
9. $21a^2 - 18a$

### Reteaching Worksheet 9-4

Name _____ Date _____

RETEACHING **9-4**

**MULTIPLY A POLYNOMIAL BY A MONOMIAL**

The distributive property and the rules of exponents enable you to multiply any polynomial by a monomial.

**Example 1**

Multiply. $-3a(4a^2 - 2a + 1)$

**Solution**

$-3a(4a^2 - 2a + 1) = -3a(4a^2) + (-3a)(-2a) + (-3a)(1)$   Use the distributive property.
$= -12a^3 + 6a^2 - 3a$   Multiply each pair of monomials.

**Example 2**

The cost of renting a two-seat, or tandem, bicycle at Parkland Rentals is given by the formula $C = 12 + 2.25h$, where $h$ represents the number of hours for which the bicycle is used. Write and simplify the formula to express the cost of renting $b$ bicycles for $h$ hours.

**Solution**

$C = b(12 + 2.25h) = 12b + 2.25bh$

**EXERCISES**

1. $2(a + 5)$
   $2a + 10$
2. $5(x - 3)$
   $5x - 15$
3. $t(6t + 2)$
   $6t^2 - 2t$
4. $4(2m - 3n)$
   $8m - 12n$
5. $y(4y^2 + 2y)$
   $4y^3 + 2y^2$
6. $r^2(2r + s)$
   $2r^3 + r^2s$
7. $-2x(3xy - 5y)$
   $-6x^2y + 10xy$
8. $ab(2a^2 + b)$
   $2a^3b + ab^2$
9. $-5x^2y(3x - 2y^3)$
   $-15x^3y + 10x^2y^4$
10. $3(2x^2 - x + 3)$
    $6x^2 - 3x + 9$
11. $4a(a^3b^3 - 2a + 6b^2)$
    $4a^4b^3 - 8a^2 + 24ab^2$
12. $2r^2(r^2 - r + 1)$
    $2r^4 - 2r^3 + 2r^2$
13. $-mn(3m - 2n + 4p)$
    $-3m^2n + 2mn^2 - 4mnp$
14. $-3r^3(2st^2 - 4r^3 + t)$
    $-6st^5 + 12r^3t^3 - 3t^4$
15. The formula $C = 9 + 2.45h$ gives the cost $C$ of renting a rug shampooing machine for $h$ hours. Write and simplify the cost for renting $m$ machines for $h$ hours.
    $9m + 2.45mh$

---

## TRY THESE EXERCISES

**Simplify.**   For 1–9, see additional answers.

1. $6x(x + 4)$
2. $2n(8 - n^2)$
3. $12k^3(k^2 + k^4 + 3)$
4. $-5c^5(7c^2 - 2c + 11)$
5. $-4p(p^2 - 2p + 5)$
6. $4xy(x^2 - 3y)$
7. $-a^2b(3b + 4a^4)$
8. $5(2x^2 + xy) + 4(x^2 - 3xy)$
9. $14a(7a - 6) - 11a(7a - 6)$

10. **WRITING MATH** Explain how you could check your answer for Exercise 6.
    divide the product by either factor to obtain the other factor

11. **TRAVEL** Marcus drives 5 h through the Rocky Mountains at an average rate of 56 mi/h. Write a variable expression in simplest form that represents how far he would drive in the same amount of time if he drives $m$ miles per hour slower.
    $d = 5(56 - m)$

12. **MODELING** What multiplication problem and product are represented on the Quadrant Mat shown?
    $(-y - 2)(-2x) = 2xy + 4x$

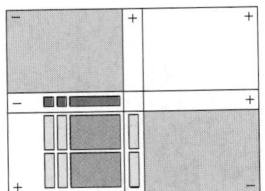

## PRACTICE EXERCISES   •   For Extra Practice, see page 614.

**Simplify.**   For 13–45, see additional answers.

13. $3m(2m + n)$
14. $11x(2x - y)$
15. $2a(3a + 4)$
16. $4k(5k - 7)$
17. $-8p(-3p^2 + 11p)$
18. $-\frac{2}{3}h^2\left(\frac{7}{8}h + \frac{2}{5}\right)$
19. $5x(3x + 2x^2)$
20. $-d^3(4d - 6d^2)$
21. $11n^6(-3n^4 - 12n^2)$
22. $2x(10x^2 - 7x + 13)$
23. $9c(3c + c^2 + 6c^3)$
24. $-4e(3e^2 + 5e - 3)$
25. $7x(1 + 2x + x^2)$
26. $-3y(y^3 - y^2 - y)$
27. $4r(-7r^3 + 2r - 10)$
28. $2a^2b(3a + b)$
29. $-12xy^3(2x^2 - y)$
30. $\frac{3}{7}d^3\left(\frac{1}{2}d^2 - \frac{2}{3}d + \frac{6}{7}\right)$
31. $-k^4(-12k^3 + 3k^2 - k)$
32. $10z^5(-6z^3 + 9z^2 - 5)$
33. $1.3c^4(2.7c^3 + 0.9c^2 - 3.4c)$
34. $-6s(4s^5 - 12s^3 + 9s)$
35. $-8t^3(12 + 5t - t^6)$
36. $4x^2y(3xy + 7xy^2 + 4x^2y^2)$
37. $4m(6m^2 + 3mn + n^2)$
38. $11y(-y^3 + 2y^2 - 8y + 7)$
39. $2(h^2 + 5) + 3(h^2 - 2)$
40. $-3(r^3 - 2) + 9(r^3 + 7)$
41. $8(2x - 3) - 3(2x - 3)$
42. $5x(4x^2 - 12) + 2x(7x^2 - 11)$
43. $14(w^2 - 4) - 9(w^2 - 4)$
44. $6(a - 2b) - 3(a - 2b)$
45. $7xy(2x - 3y) + 3xy(4x + 9y)$

46. **GRAPHING** Use a graphing calculator to graph $y = x(3x - 5)$ and $y = 6x^2 - 10x$ on the same screen. What do you notice about the two graphs? The second graph is dilated by a factor of 3.

47. **PART-TIME JOB** Rose works 16 h/wk and earns \$8.50/h. Write a variable expression in simplest form to represent her weekly earnings if her hourly wage is increased by $d$ dollars per hour.
    $16(8.50 + d) = 136 + 16d$ dollars

48. **TRAVEL** The fare for a cab is \$2 for the first mile and \$0.75 for each additional mile. The fare is expressed by the formula $F = 2 + 0.75m$, where $m$ is the number of miles driven after the first mile. The Smith for President Committee engaged $c$ cabs for a motorcade through the city. Write and simplify a formula for the total fare.
    $F = 2c + 0.75$ cm

49. **SPORTS** The length of a soccer field is 40 m less than twice the width of the field. Write and simplify an expression for the area of the field.
    $w(2w - 40) = (2w^2 - 40w)$ m²

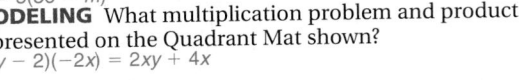

## ADDITIONAL ANSWERS

13. $6m^2 + 3mn$
14. $22x^2 - 11xy$
15. $6a^2 + 8a$
16. $20k^2 - 28k$
17. $24p^3 - 88p^2$
18. $-\frac{7}{12}h^3 - \frac{4}{15}h^2$
19. $15x^2 + 10x^3$
20. $-4d^4 + 6d^5$
21. $-33n^{10} - 132n^8$
22. $20x^3 - 14x^2 + 26x$
23. $27c^2 + 9c^3 + 54c^4$
24. $-12e^3 - 20e^2 + 12e$
25. $7x^3 + 14x^2 + 7x$
26. $-3y^4 + 3y^3 + 3y^2$
27. $-28r^4 + 8r^2 - 40r$
28. $6a^3b + 2a^2b^2$
29. $-24x^3y^3 + 12xy^4$
30. $\frac{3}{14}d^5 - \frac{2}{7}d^4 + \frac{18}{49}d^3$
31. $12k^7 - 3k^6 + k^5$
32. $-60z^8 + 90z^7 - 50z^5$
33. $3.51c^7 + 1.17c^6 - 4.42c^5$
34. $-24s^6 + 72s^4 - 54s^2$
35. $-96t^3 - 40t^4 + 8t^9$
36. $12x^3y^2 + 28x^3y^3 + 16x^4y^3$
37. $24m^3 + 12m^2n + 4mn^2$
38. $-11y^4 + 22y^3 - 88y^2 + 77y$
39. $5h^2 + 4$
40. $6r^3 + 69$
41. $10x - 15$
42. $34x^3 - 82x$
43. $5w^2 - 20$
44. $3a - 6b$
45. $26x^2y + 6xy^2$

**FINANCE** On Monday a share of XYZ stock sold for $x$ dollars. On Tuesday the price rose \$3/share. On Wednesday the price fell \$5/share.

**50.** Akule buys 20 shares of XYZ on Monday, 30 shares on Tuesday, and 40 shares on Wednesday. Write a variable expression in simplest form that represents the total cost of Akule's purchases. $20x + 30(x + 3) + 40(x - 2) = 90x + 10$

**51.** It cost Maria \$225 to buy 9 shares of XYZ on Tuesday and 6 shares on Wednesday. Find the cost of a share of XYZ on Monday. \$14

**Write and simplify an expression for the area of each figure.**

**52.**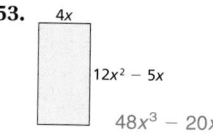
4m
6m + 3
$24m^2 + 12m$

**53.**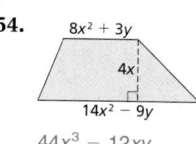
4x
$12x^2 - 5x$
$48x^3 - 20x^2$

**54.**
$8x^2 + 3y$
$4x$
$14x^2 - 9y$
$44x^3 - 12xy$

 **MODELING** Use Algeblocks to find each product.
For 55–57, see additional answers.
**55.** $2x(2x + 2)$  $4x^2 + 4x$
**56.** $-2y(-y - 2)$  $2y^2 + 4y$
**57.** $3x(y + 1)$  $3xy + 3x$

## ■ EXTENDED PRACTICE EXERCISES

**Simplify.**

**58.** $\frac{1}{2}e\left(\frac{2}{3}e^4 - \frac{3}{8}e^3 + \frac{1}{4}e\right)$  $\frac{1}{3}e^5 - \frac{3}{16}e^4 + \frac{1}{8}e^2$

**59.** $(x^3 - 9.2x^2 - 4.6x)2.5x^2$  $2.5x^5 - 23x^4 - 11.5x^3$

**60.** $2y(y^3 + 3y^2 - 5y) - 5y(-3y^3 - 2y^2 + 3y)$  $17y^4 + 16y^3 - 25y^2$

**61.** $5x^3y^2(-x^3y^4 - 2x^6y^2 + y^4 - 3xy)$  $-5x^6y^6 - 10x^9y^4 + 5x^3y^6 - 15x^4y^3$

**62.** Write an expression in simplest form that represents the surface area of the prism. $72k^2 + 32k$
2k
3k + 2
6k

**63.** A picture frame measures 16 in. by 12 in. Write and simplify an expression for the area of the frame if the longer side is increased by $n$ inches. $12(16 + n) = (192 + 12n)$ in.²

**64.** **GEOGRAPHY** Lake Ontario is located in both the U.S. and Canada. It has a width of about $0.5x$ mi, a length of about $(2x - 7)$ mi and a depth of about $8x$ mi. Write and simplify an expression for the volume of Lake Ontario. $(8x^3 - 28x^2)$ mi³

 **65.** **CHAPTER INVESTIGATION** Write an expression in terms of $x$ for the length of the entire course, start to finish. $13.5x$ mi

## ■ MIXED REVIEW EXERCISES

**Solve each equation. Check the solution.** (Lesson 3-2)

**66.** $x + 18 = 23$  5
**67.** $d - 64 = 128$  192
**68.** $s + (-17) = -56$  $-39$
**69.** $15x = 5$  $\frac{1}{3}$
**70.** $\frac{g}{12} = -4$  $-48$
**71.** $-\frac{2}{3}w = -6$  9
**72.** $y - 0.5 = 3.7$  4.2
**73.** $\frac{3}{4}x = 27$  36
**74.** $3.2 = 0.4n$  8

**75.** Kazuo is thinking of a whole number. If you multiply his number by 5 and add 15, the sum is greater than 100. What is the least number Kazuo could be thinking of? (Lesson 3-7)  18

## **ADDITIONAL ANSWERS**

**55.**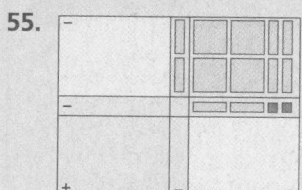
**56.**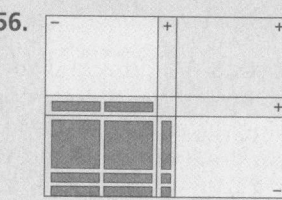
**57.**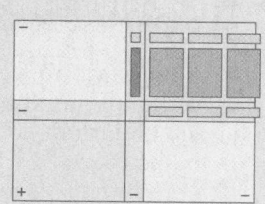

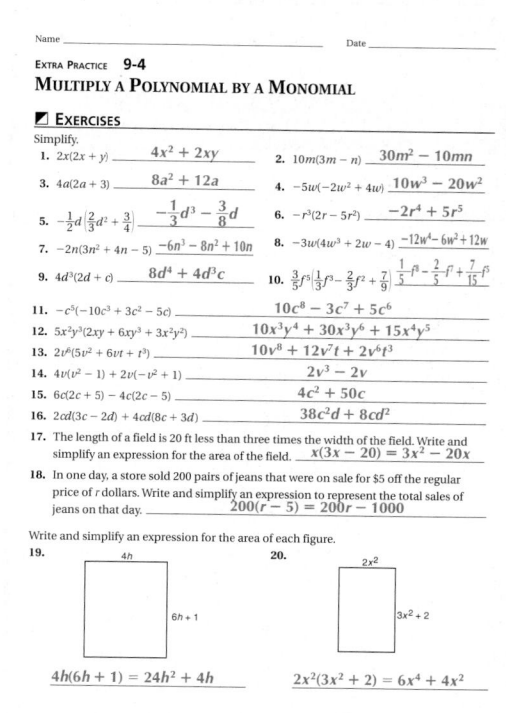
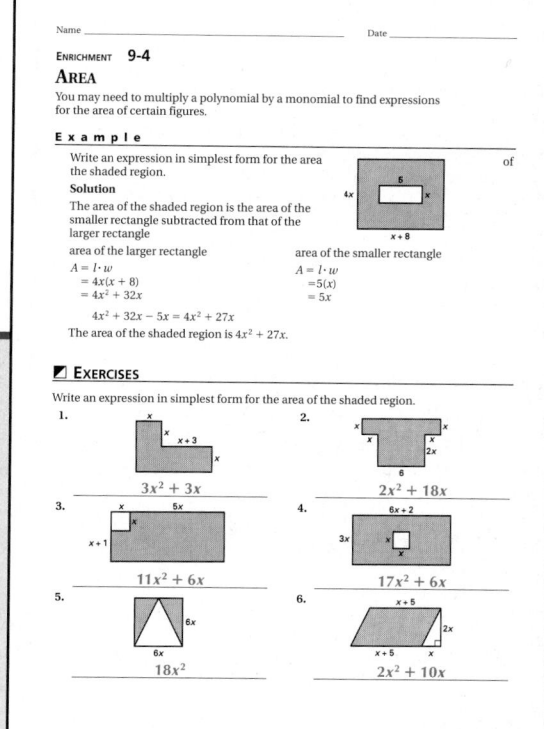

## Chalkboard Examples

### Lesson 9-3
Simplify.

a. $\dfrac{-12xyz}{\frac{1}{3}xy} = \dfrac{-12}{\frac{1}{3}} \cdot \dfrac{x}{x} \cdot \dfrac{y}{y} \cdot z$

$\qquad = -36z$

b. $\dfrac{3m^2n^5}{12m^5n^2} = \dfrac{3}{12} \cdot \dfrac{m^2}{m^5} \cdot \dfrac{n^5}{n^2}$

$\qquad = \dfrac{1}{4} \cdot \dfrac{1}{m^{5-2}} \cdot n^{5-2}$

$\qquad = \dfrac{1}{4} \cdot \dfrac{1}{m^3} \cdot n^3$

$\qquad = \dfrac{n^3}{4m^3}$

c. $\dfrac{6y - 12}{\frac{1}{2}} = \dfrac{6y}{\frac{1}{2}} - \dfrac{12}{\frac{1}{2}}$

$\qquad = 12y - 24$

d. $\dfrac{2.1k^4 - 1.2k^3 + 0.3k}{0.3k} = \dfrac{2.1k^4}{0.3k}$

$\qquad\qquad - \dfrac{1.2k^3}{0.3k} + \dfrac{0.3k}{0.3k}$

$\qquad = 7k^3 - 4k^2 + 1$

# Review and Practice Your Skills

**PRACTICE ◼ LESSON 9-3**

**Simplify.**

1. $\dfrac{12b^2}{3b}$   $4b$

2. $\dfrac{5f^7}{5f^2}$   $f^5$

3. $\dfrac{21x^4}{12x^4}$   $\dfrac{7}{4}$

4. $\dfrac{25a^4b}{-15ab}$   $-\dfrac{5a^3}{3}$

5. $\dfrac{6x - 9x^2 + 12x^3}{x}$   $12x^2 - 9x + 6$

6. $\dfrac{15mn - 25m^2 - 5m^3n^2}{5m}$   $3n - 5m - m^2n^2$

7. $\dfrac{144x^7y^3z^2}{12x^2y^2}$   $12x^5yz^2$

8. $\dfrac{18y^2 - 3y^4 + 15y^3}{3y^3}$   $\dfrac{-y^2 + 5y + 6}{y}$

9. $\dfrac{-49a + 28}{7}$   $-7a + 4$

10. $\dfrac{8abc^2 - 8bc^2}{bc^2}$   $8a - 8$

11. $\dfrac{9x^2y^2}{xy}$   $9xy$

12. $\dfrac{16x^2 - 24x^5}{4x^2}$   $-6x^3 + 4$

13. $\dfrac{8e^2 - 2e^4 + 12e^3}{2e^3}$   $\dfrac{-e^2 + 6e + 4}{e}$

14. $\dfrac{30cd - 50c^2d^3 + 10c}{-10c}$   $5cd^3 - 3d - 1$

15. $\dfrac{(w^4)^3}{(w^5)^2}$   $w^2$

16. The area of a rectangle is $16x^2y$ ft$^2$, and the length is $4x$ ft. Find the width.   $4xy$

17. The area of a rectangle is $36pq^2$, and the width is $9pq$. Find the length.   $4q$

18. How many CD's can you buy for \$$36ab$ if each CD sells for \$$3a$?   $12b$

**PRACTICE ◼ LESSON 9-4**

**Simplify.**

19. $6a(3a + b)$   $18a^2 + 6ab$

20. $5m(2m - n)$   $10m^2 - 5mn$

21. $-7b(4b - 5d^2)$   $-28b^2 + 35bd^2$

22. $-\dfrac{3}{4}k^2\left(\dfrac{5}{6}k + \dfrac{1}{2}\right)$   $-\dfrac{5}{8}k^3 - \dfrac{3}{8}k^2$

23. $-v^3(-10v^2 + 3v^2 - 4v)$   $7v^5 + 4v^4$

24. $-2x(x^3 - 3x - 6x^2)$   $-2x^4 + 12x^3 + 6x^2$

25. $3xy(y^2 - 3x + 1)$   $3xy^3 - 9x^2y + 3xy$

26. $-4xy(x^3 - y^2 - xy)$   $-4x^4y + 4x^2y^2 + 4xy^3$

27. $2m(5m^2 + mn - 4n^2)$   $10m^3 + 2m^2n - 8mn^2$

28. $3a(5a - 4) + 6a(5a - 4)$   $45a^2 - 36a$

29. $\dfrac{1}{2}d^2\left(\dfrac{4}{3}d^2 + \dfrac{1}{5}d + 3\right)$   $\dfrac{2}{3}d^4 + \dfrac{1}{10}d^3 + \dfrac{3}{2}d^2$

30. $8a(-a^3 + 2a^2 - 11a + 2)$   $-8a^4 + 16a^3 - 88a^2 + 16a$

31. $-4(2b + 7) + 9(2b + 7)$   $10b + 35$

32. $7x(4x^3 - 10) + 8x(5x^3 + 5)$   $68x^4 - 30x$

33. $5rs(3r - 2s) - 2rs(r - 3s)$   $13r^2s - 4rs^2$

34. $5x(d - 2) + 7x(d - 2)$   $12xd - 24x$

35. $12x(-x^3 + 2x^2 - 8x + 7)$   $-12x^4 + 24x^3 - 96x^2 + 84x$

36. $5y(y^3 - 2y) + 5y(y - 2y^3)$   $-5y^4 - 5y^2$

37. $-9(n^3 - 4) + 9(n^3 + 7n)$   $63n + 36$

38. $-8x^3(6x^2 - 8x + 11)$   $-48x^5 + 64x^4 - 88x^3$

39. $14b(7b - 6) - 11b(7b - 6)$   $21b^2 - 18b$

40. $3xy(-2x + 4y) + xy(3x - y)$   $-3x^2y + 11xy^2$

**Write and simplify an expression for the area of each figure.**

41. rectangle: $6x$ by $(3x + 9)$   $18x^2 + 54x$

42. rectangle: $3d^2$ by $(4d^3 - 3)$   $12d^5 - 9d^2$

43. triangle: base $= 4y$ and height $= 6y^2 + y$   $12y^3 + 2y^2$

44. triangle: base $= 12xy$ and height $= xy^2 + 3x^2y$   $6x^2y^3 + 18x^3y^2$

## Teaching Tip

In preparation for Exercises 8–14, remind students to write a first step as the intended divsions. In this way, a term that contains only 1 or $-1$ will be included in the answer, as is the case in Exercise 14.

In like manner, when working with multiplication of a polynomial by a monomial, as in Exercises 19–40, suggest that students write a first step showing the intended multiplications. In this way, students will be more likely to remember to multiply every term of the polynomial by the monomial.

## PRACTICE ■ LESSON 9-1–LESSON 9-4

**Write an expression for the unknown dimension of each rectangle.** (Lesson 9-3)

**45.** area = $14a^2b^3$

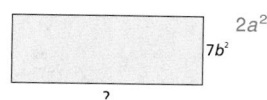

$2a^2b$
$7b^2$
?

**46.** area = $54xyz$

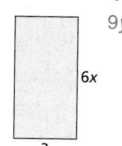

$9yz$
$6x$
?

**Write and simplify an expression for the area of each figure.** (Lesson 9-4)

**47.**

$3a^2b$
$5a + b$
$15a^3b + 3a^2b^2$

**48.**

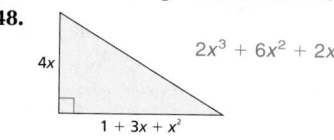

$4x$
$2x^3 + 6x^2 + 2x$
$1 + 3x + x^2$

**Simplify.** (Lessons 9-1 and 9-2)

**49.** $(3xy^3)^3$   $27x^3y^9$

**50.** $(-4a^2b)^2$   $16a^4b^2$

**51.** $5b + b + b^2 - 6b^2$   $-5b^2 + 6b$

**52.** $-(4rs^2)^3$   $-64r^3s^6$

**53.** $4h - (h + 7)$   $3h - 7$

**54.** $x + x + x^3 + x^3$   $2x + 2x^3$

# Mid-Chapter Quiz

**Write each polynomial in standard form for the variable $x$.** (Lesson 9-1)

**1.** $x^2 + 7 + 2x^4 - 9x - 24x^3$
$2x^4 - 24x^3 + x^2 - 9x + 7$

**2.** $2x - x^2y^2 + 3x^3y - 4$
$3x^3y - x^2y^2 + 2x - 4$

**3.** $4y^3x + 6y^2x^2 + yx^3 + x$
$yx^3 + 6y^2x^2 + 4y^3x + x$

**Simplify.** (Lessons 9-1 through 9-4)

**4.** $10w + 3w$   $13w$

**5.** $y^2 - 2y^2 + 4y^2$   $3y^2$

**6.** $\frac{2}{3}x^4 - \frac{1}{6}x^4$   $\frac{1}{2}x^4$

**7.** $11n + n - 9n - 3n$   $0$

**8.** $7a^2 + 17a^3 - 4a^2$
$17a^3 + 3a^2$

**9.** $9p - q + 41q + 11p$
$20p + 40q$

**10.** $6g^2 - 7g^2 - 4g + 3g^2$
$2g^2 - 4g$

**11.** $(3h^2 + 2) + (h^2 + 6h)$
$4h^2 + 6h + 2$

**12.** $(7x^2 + 4x - 3) - (5x^2 - 2x)$
$2x^2 + 6x - 3$

**13.** $(-7h)(-8j)$   $56hj$

**14.** $\left(\frac{1}{4}x^2\right)(-24x^4)$   $-6x^6$

**15.** $(3mn)(2pq)$   $6mnpq$

**16.** $(-8a^2b)(4b^2a)$   $-32a^3b^3$

**17.** $(5x^3)(5x^4)$   $25x^7$

**18.** $(9c^4d^2)(-6c^4d)$   $-54c^8d^3$

**19.** $(-2k^4)^3$   $-8k^{12}$

**20.** $(3s^5ty^3)^2$   $9s^{10}t^2y^6$

**21.** $(4y^2)^3(3yx)^2(x^2)^2$   $576y^8x^6$

**22.** $\frac{9vw}{15v}$   $\frac{3}{5}w$

**23.** $\frac{30st^2(2y^3)}{25s^3tu^4}$   $\frac{12ty^3}{5s^2u^4}$

**24.** $\frac{12m - 15}{3}$   $4m - 5$

**25.** $\frac{6h^5 + 2h^3 - 8h^2}{2h^2}$   $3h^3 + h - 4$

**26.** $\frac{-21bc^4 + 14b^3c}{7bc}$   $-3c^3 + 2b^2$

**27.** $\frac{12b^4 + 2b^2 - 3b}{3b^2}$   $4b^2 + \frac{2}{3} - \frac{1}{b}$

**28.** $5x(4x - 2)$   $20x^2 - 10x$

**29.** $-2n(3n^2 + 4n - 5)$
$-6n^3 - 8n^2 + 10n$

**30.** $\frac{1}{2}y^3\left(\frac{3}{4}y^8 + \frac{5}{8}y^6\right)$   $\frac{3}{8}y^{11} + \frac{5}{16}y^9$

**31.** $2mn(7m - 3n) + 5mn(m + 6n)$

**32.** $4v(v^2 - 1) + 2v(-v^2 + 1)$   $19m^2n +$

## Extend the Lesson

**CONNECTING TO PRIOR KNOWLEDGE** In preparation for Exercise 48, elicit that in a right triangle, the legs of the triangle act as the base and height of the triangle. So, students can still use the formula $A = \frac{1}{2}bh$ for the area of a right triangle.

### Lesson 9-4

**LANDSCAPING** Gary is mowing a rectangular lawn that is 40 ft wide. He has already mowed a 5-ft strip around the entire lawn.

If $x$ represents the length of the lawn, represent the area of the unmowed portion of the lawn as a polynomial in $x$.

**Draw a diagram to model the situation.**

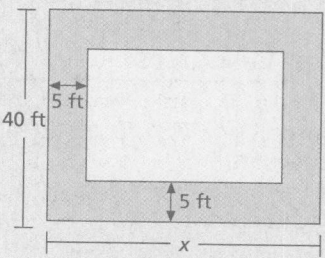

40 ft   5 ft
5 ft
$x$

**Represent the dimensions of the unmowed portion of the lawn.**

For the width of the unmowed portion, subtract the width of the strip from the top and bottom of the width of the lawn.

width = $40 - 10 = 30$ ft

For the length of the unmowed portion, subtract the width of the strip from the left and right of the length of the lawn

length = $(x - 10)$ ft

**Area of the unmowed portion**

= $30(x - 10)$

= $30x - 300$

So, the area of the unmowed portion is $(30x - 300)$ ft².

### Tools/Materials Needed

Algeblocks with Quadrant Mat

### Lesson Resources

Warm-up Transparency 37
Transparency TK-5, 6, 16, RF-46
Reteaching 9-5
Extra Practice 9-5
Enrichment 9-5

## Getting Started

### 5-MINUTE WARM-UP

List the products that can be
added to find the value of each
expression.
1. $3(4 + 8)$    $3(4)$ and $3(8)$
2. $(3 + 2)(4 + 8)$    $3(4)$, $3(8)$, $2(4)$,
and $2(8)$
3. $(7 + 2)(5 + 1)$    $7(5)$, $7(1)$, $2(5)$,
and $2(1)$
4. $(8 - 3)(6 + 2)$    $8(6)$, $8(2)$,
$(-3)(6)$, and $(-3)(2)$

### Introduction to Lesson 9-5

In this activity with Algeblocks, students follow the indicated five steps
to determine that
$(2x + 1)(x - 3) = 2x^2 - 5x - 3$.

Ask students how they think the
model would change if they were to
place $(x - 3)$ in the horizontal axis
and $(2x + 1)$ in the vertical axis.
**The product would be the same but
the rectangular areas would be in
different quadrants: Quadrants I
and II, rather than Quadrants I
and IV.**

Have students verify their conjecture
by completing the model for
$(x - 3)(2x + 1)$, which is shown
in the Teaching Tip.

---

# 9-5 Multiply Binomials

**Goals**   ■ Multiply binomials.

**Applications**   Finance, Geography, Recreation, Photography

You can use Algeblocks to find the product of two
binomials. Use the following steps to sketch or show
the product $(2x + 1)(x - 3)$ on a Quadrant Mat.

For Steps 1–4, see additional answers.

*Step 1*  Place $(2x + 1)$ in the horizontal axis.

*Step 2*  Place $(x - 3)$ in the vertical axis. (Be sure to
put the 3 unit blocks in the negative part of
the axis.)

*Step 3*  Use $x^2$-blocks, $x$-blocks and unit blocks to
form rectangular areas in all quadrants
bounded by the binomials.

*Step 4*  Delete any zero pairs if possible. (Recall, a
*zero pair* is any pair of terms whose sum is
zero. For example, $x^2$ and $-x^2$ are zero
pairs, or opposites.)

*Step 5*  Read the answer from the mat.

$$2x^2 - 5x - 3$$

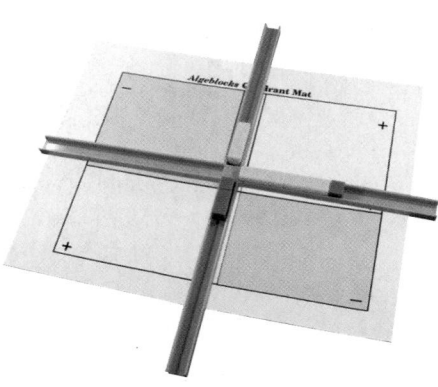

### ■ BUILD UNDERSTANDING

The product of two binomials can be found by applying the distributive property.
The product is a polynomial of four terms that can usually be simplified to a
trinomial or binomial.

### Example 1

**Find the product $(x + 3)(x + 7)$.**

**Solution**

$(x + 3)(x + 7) = (x)(x + 7) + (3)(x + 7)$     Distribute $(x + 3)$ over the binomial $(x + 7)$.

$= x(x) + x(7) + 3(x) + 3(7)$     Use the distributive property twice.

$= x^2 + 7x + 3x + 21$     Combine like terms.

$= x^2 + 10x + 21$

In Example 1, notice that each term in the second step is the product of a
different pair of monomials from the original expression.

This pattern provides a systematic method for multiplying two binomials.
Multiply the *first* term of each binomial, then the *outer* terms, then the *inner*
terms, and finally the *last* terms. Write these four products as a sum and simplify.

---

## Differentiated Instruction

**TACTILE/KINESTHETIC LEARNERS**  Here is an Algeblock model for the
product $(x - 3)(2x + 1) = 2x^2 - 5x - 3$.

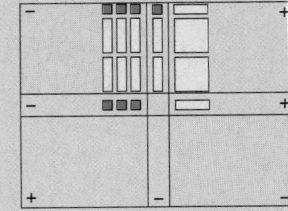
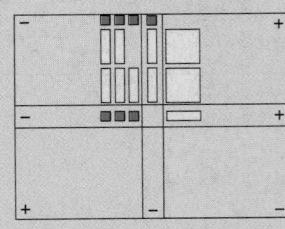

$$\underbrace{(x + 6)}_{\text{first}}\underbrace{(x + 4)}_{\text{last}} = x^2 + 4x + 6x + 24$$
$$= x^2 + 10x + 24$$

Many people use the acronym FOIL as a memory device to remember the order in which to multiply.

$$\begin{array}{cccc} F & O & I & L \\ \uparrow & \uparrow & \uparrow & \uparrow \\ \text{first} & \text{outer} & \text{inner} & \text{last} \end{array}$$

## Example 2

**Simplify.**

**a.** $(x + 5)(x - 8)$          **b.** $(m + 7)(m - 7)$          **c.** $(k - 9)^2$

### Solution

Multiply binomials and use the distributive property.

**a.** $(x + 5)(x - 8) = (x + 5)[x + (-8)]$          Subtracting 8 is the same as adding $-8$.

$$= x(x) + x(-8) + 5(x) + 5(-8)$$
$$= x^2 + (-8x) + 5x + (-40)$$
$$= x^2 - 3x - 40$$

**b.** $(m + 7)(m - 7) = (m + 7)[m + (-7)]$

$$= m(m) + (-7m) + 7m + 7(-7)$$
$$= m^2 + 0m + (-49)$$
$$= m^2 - 49$$

**c.** $(k - 9)^2 = (k - 9)(k - 9)$

$$= [k + (-9)][k + (-9)]$$
$$= k(k) + (-9k) + (-9k) + (-9)(-9)$$
$$= k^2 - 18k + 81$$

### Check Understanding

In Example 2, part b, the sum of the "outer" and "inner" terms is zero, resulting in a product with only two terms $m^2$ and $-49$.

Describe a pattern in the original binomials that will always produce this result.

When you multiply the sum and difference of the same two numbers.

## Example 3

**Simplify.**

$5(n + 3)(n - 4) - 2(n - 6)(n + 5)$

### Solution

$5(n + 3)(n - 4) - 2(n - 6)(n + 5)$          Use FOIL twice.

$= 5[n^2 - 4n + 3n + 3(-4)] + (-2)[n^2 + 5n - 6n - 6(5)]$          Simplify inside parentheses.

$= 5(n^2 - n - 12) + (-2)(n^2 - n - 30)$          Distribute 5 and $-2$.

$= 5n^2 - 5n - 60 + (-2n^2) + 2n + 60$          Simplify.

$= 3n^2 - 3n$

 Math Online    mathmatters2.com/extra_examples

## Supplementary Example 1

**Find each product.**

**a.** $(2x + 4)(3x - 2)$
$$= (2x + 4)[3x + (-2)]$$
$$= 2x(3x) + 2x(-2) + 4(3x)$$
$$+ 4(-2)$$
$$= 6x^2 - 4x + 12x - 8$$
$$= 6x^2 + 8x - 8$$

**b.** $(2x + 3)^2$
$$= (2x + 3)(2x + 3)$$
$$= 2x(2x) + 2x(3) + 3(2x) + 3(3)$$
$$= 4x^2 + 6x + 6x + 9$$
$$= 4x^2 + 12x + 9$$

**c.** $(2x + 3)(2x - 3)$
$$= (2x + 3)[2x + (-3)]$$
$$= 2x(2x) + 2x(-3) + 3(2x)$$
$$+ 3(-3)$$
$$= 4x^2 - 6x + 6x - 9$$
$$= 4x^2 - 9$$

## Supplementary Example 2

The area of the shaded region of the figure shown is 63 ft$^2$. Find the value of $x$.

To determine the area of the shaded region, subtract the area of the square from the area of the larger rectangle.

$$\frac{\text{area of}}{\text{rectangle}} - \frac{\text{area of}}{\text{square}} = 63$$
$$(x + 5)(x + 3) - x^2 = 63$$
$$x(x) + x(3) + 5(x) + 5(3) - x^2 = 63$$
$$x^2 + 8x + 15 - x^2 = 63$$
$$8x + 15 = 63$$
$$8x + 15 - 15 = 63 - 15$$
$$8x = 48$$
$$x = 6$$

**Check:**
If $x = 6$, then the area of the square is $6^2$, or 36, and the area of the rectangle is $(6 + 5)(6 + 3)$, or 99, making the area of the shaded region $99 - 36$, or 63. ✓
So, in the given figure, the value of $x$ is 6.

## ADDITIONAL ANSWERS

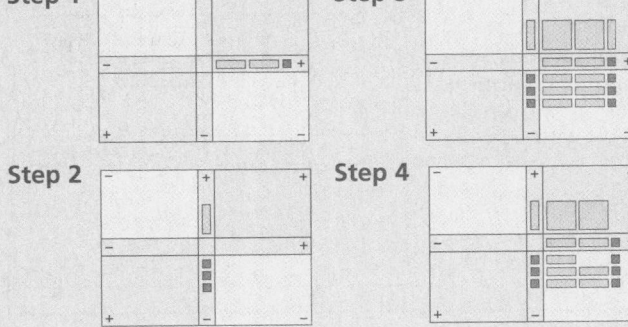

Step 1    Step 2    Step 3    Step 4

## Lesson Wrap-up

### QUICK ASSESSMENT

Ask the following questions to determine if students understand the content presented in this lesson.

**The product of two binomials may be written as a sum of products.**

**1.** How many products are in that sum?  **4**

**2.** How do you get these products for that sum?  **Use the Distributive Property twice or use FOIL.**

**3.** Are there four terms in the final answer? Explain.  **Not necessarily. Frequently, two of the terms can be combined, leaving three terms for the final answer. Sometimes, when the original product has the form $(a + b)(a - b)$, there are only two terms in the final answer.**

### ASSIGNMENT GUIDE

**Basic:** 1–50, 57–60
**Enriched:** 1–60

### Reteaching Worksheet 9-5

Name _____ Date _____

RETEACHING  **9-5**
**MULTIPLY BINOMIALS**

The following shortcut can be used to multiply two binomials.

F  Multiply the first terms of each binomial.
O  Multiply the outer terms.
I  Multiply the inner terms.
L  Multiply the last terms.

This method is called the FOIL (first, outer, inner, last) method for multiplying binomials.

**Example**

Find the product. $(2x + 3)(x - 5)$

**Solution**

Use the FOIL method and combine like terms, using the distributive property.

$(2x + 3)(x - 5)$ $= (2x \cdot x) + (2x \cdot -5) + (3 \cdot x) + (3 \cdot -5)$
$= 2x^2 + (-10x) + 3x - 15$
$= 2x^2 - 7x - 15$

☑ **EXERCISES**

**1.** $(x + 5)(x + 3)$
$x^2 + 8x + 15$
**2.** $(y - 5)(y + 4)$
$y^2 - y - 20$
**3.** $(s + 7)(s - 5)$
$s^2 + 2s - 35$
**4.** $(w - 4)(w - 8)$
$w^2 - 12w + 32$
**5.** $(m - 4)(m + 1)$
$m^2 - 3m - 4$
**6.** $(x + 3)(x - 3)$
$x^2 - 9$
**7.** $(x + 2)(x + 2)$
$x^2 + 4x + 4$
**8.** $(5 + r)(2 - r)$
$10 - 3r - r^2$
**9.** $(y + 5)(y + 5)$
$y^2 + 10y + 25$
**10.** $(3m - 1)(2m + 3)$
$6m^2 + 7m - 3$
**11.** $(2x + 2)(2x - 2)$
$4x^2 - 4$
**12.** $(2b + 3)(b + 1)$
$2b^2 + 5b + 3$
**13.** $(3y - 2)(3y + 2)$
$9y^2 - 4$
**14.** $(2r - 1)(2r - 1)$
$4r^2 - 4r + 1$
**15.** $(4x - 3)(2x - 3)$
$8x^2 - 18x + 9$
**16.** $(5n + 1)(2n - 1)$
$10n^2 - 3n - 1$
**17.** $(3 - t)(5 + 2t)$
$15 + t - 2t^2$
**18.** $(y + 2x)(y - 2x)$
$y^2 - 4x^2$

---

## Example 4

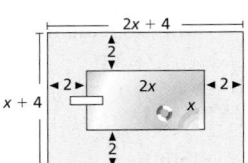

A rectangular swimming pool is twice as long as it is wide. A walkway surrounding the pool is 2 yd wide and has an area of 196 yd². Find the dimensions of the pool.

### Solution

Make a drawing. Let $x$ represent the width of the pool. Label the other dimensions in terms of $x$.

area of walkway = area of pool and walkway − area of pool

$$196 = (2x + 4)(x + 4) - (2x)(x)$$
$$196 = 2x^2 + 8x + 4x + 16 - 2x^2 \quad \text{Combine like terms.}$$
$$196 = 12x + 16$$
$$180 = 12x$$
$$15 = x$$

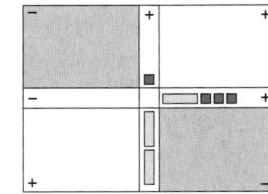

The width of the pool is 15 yd. The length is twice the width, or 30 yd.

### ◣ TRY THESE EXERCISES

**Find the product.**

**1.** $(x + 2)(x + 5)$
$x^2 + 7x + 10$
**2.** $(n - 7)(n + 3)$
$n^2 - 4n - 21$
**3.** $(p - 6)(p + 6)$
$p^2 - 36$
**4.** $(h - 4)^2$
$h^2 - 8h + 16$
**5.** $(y + 12)(y + 11)$
$y^2 + 23y + 132$
**6.** $(b + 4)^2$
$b^2 + 8b + 16$
**7.** $(p + 14)(p - 3)$
$p^2 + 11p - 42$
**8.** $(n - 9)^2$
$n^2 - 18n + 81$

**Simplify.**

**9.** $4(y + 3)(y + 2) + 3(y + 4)(y + 1)$
$7y^2 + 35y + 36$
**10.** $-2(t - 4)(t + 7) + 9(t + 3)(t - 8)$
$7t^2 - 51t - 160$

**11. MODELING** What expressions are being multiplied on the Quadrant Mat shown? Find the product of the binomials.
$(x + 3)(1 - 2x) = -2x^2 - 5x + 3$

**12. RECREATION** A rectangular playground is 4 times as long as it is wide. The area of a 3-ft wide sidewalk around the playground is 1236 ft². Sketch the playground and then find its dimensions.  See additional answers. 40 ft by 160 ft

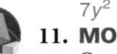

### ◣ PRACTICE EXERCISES  •  For Extra Practice, see page 614.

**Find the product.**

**13.** $(a + 3)(a + 2)$
$a^2 + 5a + 6$
**14.** $(c + 4)(c - 5)$
$c^2 - c - 20$
**15.** $(p - 3)(p + 1)$
$p^2 - 2p - 3$
**16.** $(k + 6)^2$
$k^2 + 12k + 36$
**17.** $(h - 3)(h + 7)$
$h^2 + 4h - 21$
**18.** $(s - 8)(s + 2)$
$s^2 - 6s - 16$
**19.** $(x - 5)(x - 3)$
$x^2 - 8x + 15$
**20.** $(e + 2)^2$
$e^2 + 4e + 4$
**21.** $(c + 5)(c - 5)$
$c^2 - 25$
**22.** $(n + 12)(n - 6)$
$n^2 + 6n - 72$
**23.** $(k - 9)^2$
$k^2 - 18k + 81$
**24.** $(11 + r)(8 - r)$
$-r^2 - 3r + 88$
**25.** $(6 + x)(6 - x)$
$-x^2 + 36$
**26.** $(m - 10)(m + 8)$
$m^2 - 2m - 80$
**27.** $(7 + t)(12 + t)$
$t^2 + 19t + 84$
**28.** $(b + 12)^2$
$b^2 + 24b + 144$
**29.** $(w - 9)(w - 8)$
$w^2 - 17w + 72$
**30.** $(6b + 1)(7b + 3)$
$42b^2 + 25b + 3$
**31.** $(2p + 10)(5p - 6)$
$10p^2 + 38p - 60$
**32.** $(4k - 3)(6k - 7)$
$24k^2 - 46k + 21$
**33.** $(20 + x)(-4 + x)$
$x^2 + 16x - 80$
**34.** $(2x + 3)(3x + 2)$
$6x^2 + 13x + 6$
**35.** $(4k + 4)^2$
$16k^2 + 32k + 16$
**36.** $(5c + 1)(5c - 1)$
$25c^2 - 1$
**37.** $(7y + 3)(7y - 4)$
$49y^2 - 7y - 12$
**38.** $(2x - 3)^2$
$4x^2 - 12x + 9$
**39.** $(6x + 5)(5x + 6)$
$30x^2 + 61x + 30$
**40.** $(3v + 5)(5v - 4)$
$15v^2 + 13v - 20$

**398**  Chapter 9  **Polynomials**

---

## Extend the Lesson

At the top of page 397, students see how to use FOIL to multiply two binomials, $(x + 6)(x + 4)$. Now have them use Alge-blocks to model this product, as shown at the right, and relate FOIL to the blocks:

F → the square block
O → the horizontal rectangles
I → the vertical rectangles
L → the unit blocks

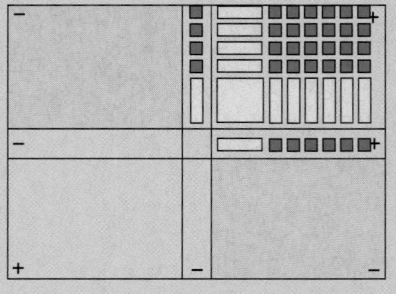

**41. YOU MAKE THE CALL** Ana used FOIL to find the product of $(2y - 7)(5y + 4)$. Her work is shown. Is she correct? If not, explain her error.

$$(2y - 7)(5y + 4) = (2y)(5y) + (2y)(4) + (-7)(5y) + (-7)(4)$$
$$= 10y^2 + 8y - 35y - 28$$
$$= 10y^2 - 27y - 28 \quad \text{Yes, she is correct.}$$

**Simplify.**

**42.** $(y - 4)(y + 6) + (y - 9)(y + 3)$
$2y^2 - 4y - 51$

**43.** $x(x + 1)(x - 3)$  $x^3 - 2x^2 - 3x$

**44.** $3(x + 4)(x + 2) -2(x + 1)(x + 3)$
$x^2 + 10x + 18$

**45.** $n(3n + 3)(5n - 4) + 5n(n - 6)(2n + 3)$
$25n^3 - 42n^2 - 102n$

**46. WRITING MATH** Explain why $(y + 4)^2 \neq y^2 + 16$ for $y \neq 0$.  $(y + 4)^2 = y^2 + 8y + 16$

**47.** Write an expression for the area of a square if the measure of each side is $5 - v$.  $(5 - v)^2 = 25 - 10v + v^2$

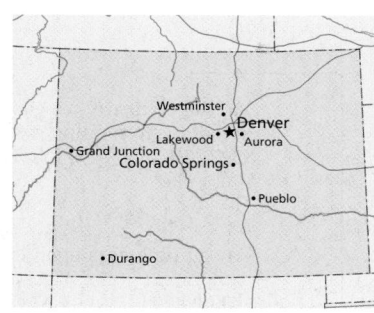

Map of Colorado

**48. GEOGRAPHY** The shape of Colorado is approximately a rectangle. The length is about $(2x^2 + 80)$ mi and the width is about $(3x^2 + 80)$ mi. Find the approximate area of Colorado in terms of $x$.  $(6x^4 + 400x^2 + 6400)$ mi$^2$

**49. PHOTOGRAPHY** A photo is 6 in. longer than it is wide. A $1\frac{1}{2}$ in. frame surrounds the photo. If the area of the frame is 99 in.$^2$, what are the dimensions of the photo?
12 in. by 18 in.

**50. MODELING** Sketch or show $(x + 3)(2x - 1)$ using Algeblocks.  $2x^2 + 5x - 3$; See additional answers.

## ■ EXTENDED PRACTICE EXERCISES

**Simplify.**

**51.** $(3k - 1)(2k + 1) - (k - 1)^2$  $5k^2 + 3k - 2$

**52.** $(5h - 7)^2 - (7 - 5h)^2$  $0$

**53.** $(x + 1)^3$  $x^3 + 3x^2 + 3x + 1$

**54.** $(2c - 3)^3$  $8c^3 - 36c^2 + 54c - 27$

**FINANCE** Compound interest is the interest that is paid on money invested and previously earned interest. The formula for the amount of money $A$ in an account that earns compound interest is $A = p(1 + r)^t$, where $p$ is the amount invested, $r$ is the rate of interest per time period, and $t$ is the number of time periods.

**55.** Find $A$ when $p = \$1000$, $r = 0.06$ and $t = 2$.  $\$1123.60$

**56.** Find $A$ when $p = \$4500$, $r = 0.03$ and $t = 3$.  $\$4917.27$

## ■ MIXED REVIEW EXERCISES

**Solve each system of equations using the substitution method.** (Lesson 8-3)

**57.** $4x + y = 11$  $\left(\frac{3}{2}, 5\right)$
$2x - 4y = -17$

**58.** $x - 3y = 6$  $(0, -2)$
$6x - 6y = 12$

**59.** $3x + 2y = 15$  $(33, -42)$
$x + y = -9$

**60.** Find the equation of the line perpendicular to the line $5x + 2y = 12$ and passing through the point $(-5, 4)$. (Lesson 8-1)  $y = \frac{2}{5}x + 6$

Math Online  mathmatters2.com/self_check_quiz

## ADDITIONAL ANSWERS

**12.**

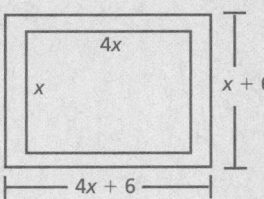

**50.**

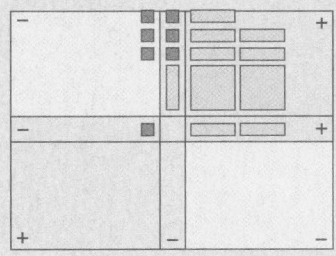

---

# Problem Solving Skills: Work Backwards

When a problem involves a series of steps, you often solve it by working forward from the beginning of the problem to the end. Sometimes, however, you are told what happened at the end and asked to find what happened at the beginning. You can use the strategy **work backwards** to solve this type of problem.

### Problem Solving Strategies

Guess and check

Look for a pattern

Solve a simpler problem

Use a picture, diagram or model

Make a table, chart or list

Act it out

✔ Work backwards

Eliminate possibilities

Use an equation or formula

### Problem

Mr. Bogen drove to a gas station, where he spent $16 on gas. He spent half of his remaining cash for lunch, and then bought a magazine for $2.50. He has $9.50 left. How much cash did he have at the beginning?

### Solve the Problem

The graphic organizer illustrates the steps described in the problem.

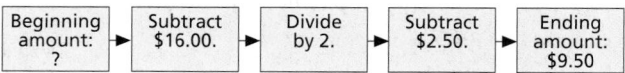

To find the beginning amount, work backwards from the end by reversing each step.

Ending amount: $9.50

*Add* $2.50:   $9.50 + $2.50 = $12.00        Addition is the opposite of subtraction.

*Multiply* by 2:   $12.00 · 2 = $24.00        Multiplication is the opposite of division.

*Add* $16.00:   $24.00 + $16.00 = $40.00

So Mr. Bogen had $40 to begin with.

Check:  $40 − $16.00 = $24.00

$24.00 ÷ 2 = $12.00

$12.00 − $2.50 = $9.50

### TRY THESE EXERCISES

1. A number is multiplied by 2 and then 11 is added to the result. The final number is 37. What is the original number?  13

2. A number is divided by 6, decreased by 10 and then multiplied by 5. The final number is 25. What is the original number?  90

3. Kayla has $5.40. One-third of the money she originally had went to lunch. Then she lent Marcus $3.00. How much money did Kayla originally have?  $12.60

4. If you multiply Keshawn's age by 8, add 8, divide by 8 and then subtract 8, the result is 8. How old is Keshawn?  15

5. **GEOGRAPHY** The smallest U.S. state is Rhode Island. If you double the area of Rhode Island and then subtract 601 mi², the result will be 2489 mi², the number of square miles in Connecticut, the second smallest U.S. state. Find the area of Rhode Island in square miles.   1545 mi²

6. **TRAVEL** After leaving her home in the morning, Gwen drove 25 mi at an average speed of 50 mi/h, then stopped 40 min for breakfast. Resuming her trip, she drove 90 mi at an average speed of 60 mi/h, arriving at 11 A.M. What time did she leave home?   8:20 A.M.

7. Melvern was deciding what time to set his alarm. He has to be at a job interview by 8:30 A.M. He wants to be there 15 min early. It takes him 25 min to drive there. He needs 50 min in the morning to get ready. For what time should Melvern set his alarm?   7:00 A.M.

8. **MONEY** The cash-in receipts in Parker's cash drawer total $823.37, and his cash-out receipts total $734.87. If he currently has $338.40 in his drawer, what was his opening balance?   $250

9. Use the table of the longest highway tunnels in the U.S. Latoya drove at an average rate of 60 mi/h through a tunnel and then 18.85 mi farther to a rest stop. After a 10-min rest she noted that it had been exactly 30 min since she had started through the tunnel. Which tunnel did Latoya drive through?   Allegheny

**Longest Highway Tunnels in the U.S.**

| Name | Length (miles) |
|------|----------------|
| A. Anderson Memorial | 2.52 |
| E. Johnson Memorial | 1.70 |
| Eisenhower Memorial | 1.69 |
| Allegheny | 1.15 |
| Liberty Tubes | 1.12 |
| Zion National Park | 1.09 |
| East River Mountain | 1.03 |
| Tuscarora | 1.02 |

10. Pete is reading a book with 480 pages. When he has read three times as many pages as he already has read, he will be 144 pages from the end. How many pages has he read?   112

11. **PHYSICS** Each time a dropped ball bounces it returns to a height $\frac{2}{3}$ the height of the previous bounce. After the third bounce the ball returns to a height of 4 ft. From what height was it dropped?   13.5 ft

12. **WRITING MATH** Write a problem that can be solved by working backwards. Include the answer to your problem.   Answers will vary.

**Work backwards to find the factors of the given product. Use the distributive property in reverse order.**

13. $x^2 + 5x = x(\blacksquare + \blacksquare)$   $x$, 5

14. $m^2n - m^3 = m^2(\blacksquare - \blacksquare)$   $n$, $m$

15. $7c^2 + 21c - 42 = 7(\blacksquare + \blacksquare - \blacksquare)$   $c^2$, $3c$, 6

16. $9a^3 + 15a^2 - 6a = 3a(\blacksquare + \blacksquare - \blacksquare)$   $3a^2$, $5a$, 2

17. $8w^4y - 10w^3k^2 + 2w^2 = 2w^2(\blacksquare - \blacksquare + \blacksquare)$   $4w^2y$, $5wk^2$, 1

## ◼ MIXED REVIEW EXERCISES

**Simplify.** (Lessons 2-4 and 2-5)

18. $4 + (-7) + (-9) + 12$   0

19. $4x + (-17x) + 21x + (-x)$   $7x$

20. $-41 + 5x + (-11x) + 48$   $-6x + 7$

21. $-8 \cdot 6 \cdot \left(-\frac{3}{4}\right) \cdot 5$   180

22. $6x \cdot 3y \cdot (-2z) \cdot (-x)$   $36x^2yz$

23. $6z \cdot (-2) \cdot (-x) \cdot 4xz \cdot (-7x)$   $-336x^3z^2$

24. $\dfrac{-5 \cdot (-4)}{-2}$   $-10$

25. $\dfrac{-4x^2yz^2}{xyz}$   $-4xz$

26. $\dfrac{7x \cdot (-8z)}{4z}$   $-14x$

## Alternative Assessment

**MATH JOURNAL** Have students discuss games such as tic-tac-toe and checkers in which using the strategy of working backwards is helpful.

---

**Five-step Plan**

1 Read
2 Plan
3 Solve
4 Answer
5 Check

## Chalkboard Examples

**Supplementary Problem**

**TRAVEL** After four pickup stops, every seat in a school bus was taken. Half as many students got on at the second stop as at the first stop, and half as many got on at the third stop as at the second stop. At the fourth stop, five students got on, the same number as at the third stop. How many passenger seats were there on the bus?

*4th stop:* 5 students got on
*3rd stop:* 5 students got on
*2nd stop:* 10 students got on.
*1st stop:* 20 students got on
So, there were 40 seats.

## Lesson Wrap-up

### QUICK ASSESSMENT

What are the characteristics of a problem you would solve by working backwards?   Information about what happened at the end of and during a series of stages is given. The problem asks what happened at the beginning.

### Reteaching Worksheet 9-6

Name _____   Date _____

RETEACHING   **9-6**
**PROBLEM SOLVING SKILLS: WORK BACKWARDS**
Some problems give you the solution and ask you to find the information that led to the solution. To solve such problems, *work backwards.*

**Example**

Elise cashed her paycheck and put half the money into her savings account. Then she bought a skirt for $24.30 and paid $13.50 for gas. After making these transactions, she had $45.50 left. What was the amount of Elise's paycheck?

**Solution**

These are the steps described in the problem.

| Beginning amount | Divide by 2 | Subtract $24.30 | Subtract $13.50 | Ending amount |
|---|---|---|---|---|
| ? | → | → | → | $30.50 |

To find the beginning amount, work backwards from the end, reversing each step.

Ending amount: $45.50
$45.50 + $13.50 = $59.00   Add $13.50.
$59.00 + $24.30 = $83.30   Add $24.30.
$83.30 · 2 = $166.60   Multiply by 2.

The amount of Elise's paycheck was $166.60.

✐ **EXERCISES**

Work backwards to solve.

1. Brandon has $14 in his pocket now. During the day, he spent $27.45 on clothes, $8.62 on food, and $6 on a video. How much money did he begin with?   $56.07

2. After Kelly planted 42 daisies, 32 carnations, and 25 roses in her garden, she had 185 plants in all. How many flower plants were in the garden before she added to them?   86 plants

3. Conner ordered 3 sweatshirts from a mail-order catalog. Each sweatshirt cost the same price. He paid 7% sales tax. He also paid $3.50 shipping and handling charge. The total cost of the order was $51.65. What was the price of each sweatshirt?   $15

**Vocabulary Review**

Lesson 9-6
work backwards

## ASSIGNMENT GUIDE

All students: 1–45

## Chalkboard Examples

### Lesson 9-5

**FINANCE** The formula for the amount of money, $A$, in an account that earns compound interest is $A = p(1 + r)^n$, where $p$ is the principal (the money invested), $r$ is the rate of interest per time period, and $n$ is the number of time periods.

Write the formula for $A$ as a polynomial in $r$, without parentheses, when $p = \$2000$ and $n = 2$.

$A = p(1 + r)^n$
$A = 2000(1 + r)^2$
$A = 2000[(1 + r)(1 + r)]$
$A = 2000[1(1) + 1(r) + r(1) + r(r)]$
$A = 2000(1 + 2r + r^2)$
$A = 2000 + 4000r + 2000r^2$

### Lesson 9-6

**SPORTS** Shaquille scored twice as many points in the second quarter as in the first quarter of a basketball game. He scored 5 points in the third quarter and 2 points in the fourth quarter. If he scored 19 points in the game, how many points did he score in the first quarter?

*4th quarter: 2 points, given*
*3rd quarter: 5 points, given*
*2nd quarter and 1st quarter:* **There are 19 − (2 + 5) or 12 points left for these two quarters. These 12 points are to be divided into two parts, with this part twice as big as the part for the 1st quarter—giving 8 points in the 2nd quarter and 4 points in the 1st quarter. So, Shaquille scored 4 points in the first quarter.**

---

### PRACTICE ■ LESSON 9-5

**Find the product.**

1. $(x + 5)(x + 3)$   $x^2 + 8x + 15$
2. $(a - 2)(a - 4)$   $a^2 - 6a + 8$
3. $(m + 3)(m - 7)$   $m^2 - 4m - 21$
4. $(c - 2)^2$   $c^2 - 4c + 4$
5. $(3 + n)(2 + n)$   $n^2 + 5n + 6$
6. $(e + 6)(e - 8)$   $e^2 - 2e - 48$
7. $(8x + 7)(x - 2)$   $8x^2 - 9x - 14$
8. $(y - 3)(y + 3)$   $y^2 - 9$
9. $(5x - 3)(4x - 2)$   $20x^2 - 22x + 6$
10. $(4d - 8)(4d + 8)$   $16d^2 - 64$
11. $(3x + 3)^2$   $9x^2 + 18x + 9$
12. $(4x - 3)(2x + 1)$   $8x^2 - 2x - 3$
13. $(5y - 12)^2$   $25y^2 - 120y + 144$
14. $5(c - d)(a - b)$   $5ca - 5cb - 5da + 5db$
15. $a(6a - 4)(5a - 3)$   $30a^3 - 38a^2 + 12a$

**Simplify.**

16. $(x - 1)(x + 3) + (x + 1)^2$   $2x^2 + 4x - 2$
17. $5(x - 2)(3x - 1) - (2x + 3)^2$   $11x^2 - 47x + 1$
18. $(y - 3)(y + 2) + (y - 1)(y + 6)$   $2y^2 + 4y - 12$
19. $n(n + 2)(n - 5)$   $n^3 - 3n^2 - 10n$
20. $6(a + 3)(a + 5) - (2a + 6)$   $6a^2 + 46a + 84$
21. $b^2(b - 3)(b + 10)$   $b^4 + 7b^3 - 30b^2$
22. $(x - 9)(x + 11) + (x + 4)(x - 11)$   $2x^2 - 5x - 143$
23. $-4(y + 7)(y - 1) + 8(y + 13)(y - 6)$   $4y^2 + 32y - 596$

### PRACTICE ■ LESSON 9-6

**Use the work backwards strategy to solve.**

24. A number is multiplied by 3 and then increased by 12. The final number is 36. What is the original number?   8

25. Grace is reading a book with 640 pages. When she has read two times as many pages as she has already read, she will be 340 pages from the end. How many pages has she read?   150

26. Carlos rode his bike to his sister's house. He biked 21 mi at an average speed of 7 mi/h, then stopped 30 min for lunch. He finished the trip to his sister's after biking 20 more miles averaging 10 mi/h. What time did he leave home to get to his sister's at 3 P.M.?   9:30 A.M.

27. A number is divided by 3, decreased by 103 and then multiplied by 6. The final number is 48. What is the original number?   333

**Work backwards to find the factors of the given product. Use the distributive property in reverse order.**

28. $x^2 + 10x = x(\blacksquare + \blacksquare)$   $x, 10$

29. $a^2b - a^3 = a^2(\blacksquare - \blacksquare)$   $b, a$

30. $2x^2 + 6x - 12 = 2(\blacksquare + \blacksquare - \blacksquare)$   $x^2, 3x, 6$

31. $3c^3 + 9c^2 + c = c(\blacksquare + \blacksquare + \blacksquare)$   $3c^2, 9c, 1$

32. $4b^2 + 8b + 16 = 4(\blacksquare + \blacksquare + \blacksquare)$   $b^2, 2b, 4$

33. $12x^2y^3 - 9x^2y^2 + 3xy = 3xy(\blacksquare - \blacksquare + \blacksquare)$   $4xy^2, 3xy, 1$

## ADDITIONAL ANSWERS

1.

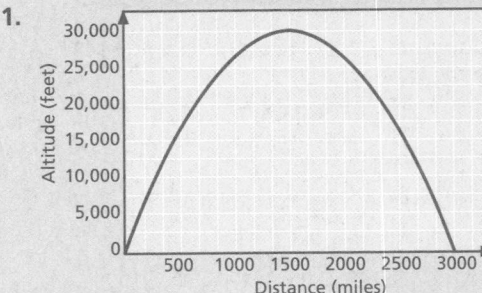

| Distance | Altitude |
|----------|----------|
| 0 | 0 |
| 500 | 16,667 |
| 1000 | 26,667 |
| 1500 | 30,000 |
| 2000 | 26,667 |
| 2500 | 16,667 |
| 3000 | 0 |

**Simplify.** (Lessons 9-2 and 9-3)

**34.** $\dfrac{15x^2y^4}{3xy}$    $5xy^3$     **35.** $(5a^2b)^3$   $125a^6b^3$    **36.** $(-x^4y^3z)^2$   $x^8y^6z^2$    **37.** $\dfrac{27x^3 - 3x}{3xy}$   $\dfrac{9x^2 - 1}{y}$

**Write and simplify an expression for the area of each figure.** (Lesson 9-4)

**38.**
  4x
  $16x^2$
  4x

**39.**
  6m
  $5m - 3$
  $30m^2 - 18m$

**Find the product** (Lesson 9-5)

**40.** $(x - 4)(x - 5)$   $x^2 - 9x + 20$     **41.** $(y - 8)^2$   $y^2 - 16y + 64$     **42.** $(a + 3)(a - 3)$   $a^2 - 9$

**43.** $(3c + 2)(c - 8)$
$3c^2 - 22c - 16$

**44.** $(2a + 5)(3a + 2)$
$6a^2 + 19a + 10$

**45.** $\left(2x + \dfrac{1}{2}\right)^2$   $4x^2 + 2x + \dfrac{1}{4}$

# Math*Works* Career – Air Traffic Controller
### Workplace Knowhow

The landscape and geographical features of the earth partially determine what path an airplane will fly from one city to another. In order for a pilot to fly an airplane safely, an air traffic controller must plan the flight path. In addition, government noise restrictions require airplanes to fly above a minimum distance from the surface of the earth. The distance from New York City to Los Angeles, is 3000 mi. To safely fly this route, a flight path must consider geographical features such as the Rocky Mountains and the Great Salt Lake Desert as well as government restrictions. In the equation, $x$ represents the distance in miles between New York City and Los Angeles, and $y$ is the altitude above sea level in feet at which the airplane will fly at each point along the flight path.

$$y = -\left(\frac{1}{75}\right)x^2 + 40x$$

1. Graph the polynomial above. Among the $x$-values for the graph, use 0, 500, 1000, 1500, 2000, 2500 and 3000 mi.   See additional answers.

2. At what distance from New York City is the airplane located at its highest altitude? What is the plane's altitude at this point?   1500 mi, 30,000 ft

3. The highest point in Utah is at Kings Peak in the Uinta Mountains, at an elevation of 13,528 ft. Assuming that the airplane flies directly over Kings Peak, how high above the Peak is the airplane at this point? (Kings Peak is approximately 2300 mi from New York City.)   7939 ft

4. At what two distances from New York City will the airplane have an altitude of 10,000 ft? Give your answer to the nearest 100 mi.   300 mi, 2700 mi

5. In constructing this equation, two assumptions were made about the elevation of New York City and Los Angeles. What are the assumed elevations of these two cities? Is this accurate or not? Explain why.   See additional answers.

 mathmatters2.com/mathworks

## Teaching Tip

After students have completed Exercise 41, $(y - 8)^2 = y^2 - 16y + 64$, have them collect the results of other problems they did in Lesson 9-6 where they also found the square of a binomial. Ask students to examine all of these results, looking for a pattern. They should conclude that the square of a binomial is a trinominal such that the first term of the trinomial is the square of the first term of the binomial, the last term of the trinomial is the square of the last term of the binomial, and the middle term of the trinomial is twice the product of the terms of the binomial.
In symbols: $(a + b)^2 = a^2 + 2ab + b^2$.

## MathWorks

*Air traffic control* is a combination of three general elements: the basic set of flying rules that pilots follow in the air, the multitude of electronic navigation systems and instruments that pilots use to remain on course, and air traffic controllers with the computer systems they use to track aircraft during takeoff, flight, and landing.

Students should answer Questions 1–4 to better understand how polynomial functions might be used in determining a plane's flight path.

Using radar and radio communication, air traffic controllers monitor and guide all airplanes in the vicinity of their airports. Controllers also track hazardous weather and obstructions to flight, and relay this information to flight crews.

Air traffic controllers work in one of three different types of stations: *Air Route Traffic Control Centers* are located nationwide and track all air traffic within their airspace; *Flight Service Stations* provide weather information to pilots, and are also located nationwide; *Control Towers* are located at airports, and coordinate aircraft landings and takeoffs.

Students who are interested in learning more about this career choice can go to www.mathmatters2.com/mathworks. School Guidance Counselors are another resource for information about training requirements and appropriate schools.

### ADDITIONAL ANSWERS

5. The assumed elevations of New York City and Los Angeles were 0 ft. Answers may vary as to whether or not this assumption is accurate. A possible response might be: The assumption is reasonable, given that the cities are on the coasts of the Atlantic and the Pacific Oceans. However, the actual elevations of John F. Kennedy Airport in New York City is 30 ft and the elevation of Los Angeles International Airport is 140 ft.

### NCTM Standards/Strands
■ Algebra
■ Representation
■ Number & Operations
■ Connections

### Vocabulary

factoring a polynomial

### Tools/Materials Needed

Algeblocks with Quadrant Mat

### Lesson Resources

Warm-up Transparency 38
Transparency TK-5, 6
Reteaching 9-7
Extra Practice 9-7
Enrichment 9-7
Technology Activity 9-7

## Getting Started

### 5-MINUTE WARM-UP

Complete each equation.
1. $12 + 8 = \blacksquare(3 + 2)$   4
2. $10 + 5 = \blacksquare(2 + 1)$   5
3. $20 - 15 = \blacksquare(4 - 3)$   5

### Introduction to Lesson 9-7

Recall that the *surface area* of a 3-dimensional figure is the sum of the areas of all parts of the surface. A *net* for a cylinder has two circular parts and a rectangular region, as shown in its net. The formula for surface area of a cylinder is generally given as $SA = 2\pi r^2 + 2\pi rh$, clearly showing that the surface area is equal to the sum of the areas of the two circular faces (top and bottom) and the rectangle area (the flattened version of the curved surface) of length $2\pi r$ and width $h$.

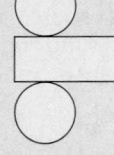

---

# 9-7 Factor Using Greatest Common Factor (GCF)

**Goals**  ■ Factor polynomials using the Greatest Common Factor.
**Applications**  Finance, Geography, Physics, Modeling

The formula for the surface area (*SA*) of a cylinder is usually given as $SA = 2\pi r^2 + 2\pi rh$, where *r* is the radius of the cylinder and *h* is the height. The formula can also be written $SA = 2\pi r(r + h)$.

1. Calculate the surface area of a cylinder with a radius of 3.6 cm and a height of 8.4 cm using each formula. Use 3.14 for π.  ≈ 271.3 cm²

2. Which formula do you like better? Explain.   Answers will vary.

3. What advantage is there in writing a polynomial in a different form?
   Polynomials are sometimes easier to evaluate when written in a different form.

4. The formula for the surface area of a cone is $SA = \pi rs + \pi r^2$, where *s* is the slant height. Can this formula be written differently? Explain.   yes, $SA = \pi r(s + r)$

## ◣ BUILD UNDERSTANDING

In earlier lessons you used the distributive property to simplify expressions.

$$4a(2a + 3) = 4a(2a) + 4a(3) = 8a^2 + 12a$$

In this process you begin with the factors $4a$ and $2a + 3$, then multiply to obtain the polynomial $8a^2 + 12a$.

This process can be reversed. **Factoring** a polynomial means to express it as a product of polynomials. To factor a polynomial like $8a^2 + 12a$, work backwards to find the factors. Begin by finding the greatest common factor (GCF) of its monomial terms.

### Check Understanding

Find the greatest common factor (GCF) of the following.

|  |  |
|---|---|
| 4 | 1. 20, 12 |
| 12 | 2. 84, 120 |
| $6x^2$ | 3. $12x^3$, $18x^2$ |
| $12a^2b$ | 4. $24a^3b^2$, $36a^2b$ |

### Example 1

Factor each polynomial.

a. $10n + 6$
b. $4c^2 - 12c^5$
c. $9h^2k^2 - 12hk^2 + 24h^3k$

### Solution

a. Find the GCF of $10n$ and 6.

$10n = 2 \cdot 5 \cdot n$    $6 = 2 \cdot 3$    The GCF is 2.    Write the prime factorization of each term.

Use the GCF and the distributive property to rewrite the polynomial.

$10n + 6 = 2 \cdot 5n + 2 \cdot 3$    Write each term with 2 as a factor.

$= 2(5n + 3)$

So, $10n + 6 = 2(5n + 3)$.

Check by multiplying.    $2(5n + 3) = 2(5n) + 2(3) = 10n + 6$

---

## Teaching Tip

An extensive presentation of *nets* and *surface area* of three-dimensional figures is given in Chapter 10. However, students have had experience with these concepts in MathMatters Book 1 and, with the suggested recall in the opening activity, should be able to focus on the immediate purpose of examining the surface area formulas for GCF.

**b.** Find the GCF of $4c^2$ and $12c^5$.

$$4c^2 = 2^2c^2 \qquad\qquad 12c^5 = 2^2 \cdot 3 \cdot c^5 \qquad \text{Write the prime factorization of each term.}$$

The GCF is $2^2c^2$, or $4c^2$.

So, $4c^2 - 12c^5 = 4c^2(1 - 3c^3)$

Check: $4c^2(1 - 3c^3) = 4c^2(1) + 4c^2(-3c^3) = 4c^2 - 12c^5$

**c.** Find the GCF for each term.

$$9h^2k^2 = 3^2h^2k^2 \qquad 12hk^2 = 2^2 \cdot 3hk^2 \qquad 24h^3k = 2^3 \cdot 3h^3k$$

The GCF is $3hk$.

So, $9h^2k^2 - 12hk^2 + 24h^3k = 3hk(3hk - 4k + 8h^2)$.

Check: $3hk(3hk - 4k + 8h^2) = 9h^2k^2 - 12hk^2 + 24h^3k$

## Example 2

The formula for the surface area ($SA$) of a rectangular prism with length $l$, width $w$ and height $h$ is $SA = 2lw + 2wh + 2lh$. Rewrite the formula by factoring.

### Solution

The GCF of $2lw$, $2wh$, and $2lh$ is 2.

$2lw + 2wh + 2lh = 2(lw + wh + lh)$

So, $SA = 2(lw + wh + lh)$.

## Example 3

**MODELING** Use Algeblocks to factor $4xy - 2x^2$.

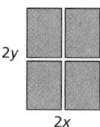 

### Solution

*Step 1* Form rectangular areas of $4xy$ and $2x^2$ having one side as $2x$, the GCF.

*Step 2* Place the GCF, $2x$, on the horizontal axis.

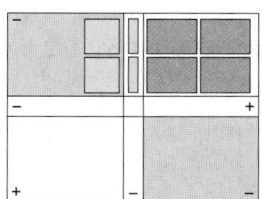

*Step 3* Put the rectangular areas in the proper quadrant with the GCF as a boundary.

*Step 4* Divide by making another boundary. The two boundaries are the factors.

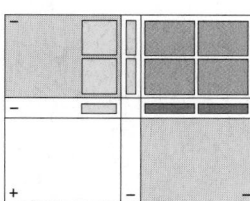

So, $4xy - 2x^2 = 2x(2y - x)$.

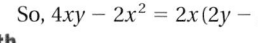

---

### Supplementary Example 1
Since a trapezoid may be divided into two triangles, the formula for the area of a trapezoid is obtained by adding the areas of two triangles.

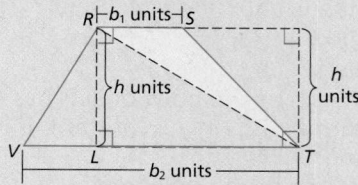

area trapezoid $RSTV$ = area $\triangle RST$ + area $\triangle RTV$

area of trapezoid $= \frac{1}{2}b_1h + \frac{1}{2}b_2h$

Rewrite this formula by factoring.

The GCF of $\frac{1}{2}b_1h$ and $\frac{1}{2}b_2h$ is $\frac{1}{2}h$.

So,
area of trapezoid $= \frac{1}{2}h(b_1 + b_2)$.

### Supplementary Example 2
**MODELING** Use Algeblocks to factor $-4x^2 + 2x$.

Form rectangular areas for $4x^2$ and $2x$.

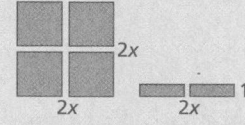

Place the GCF, $2x$, in the horizontal axis.

Place the rectangular areas in the proper quadrants with the GCF as the boundary.

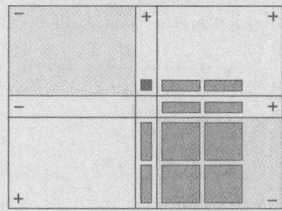

Decide the appropriate boundary for the vertical axis. The two boundaries are the factors.

So, $-4x^2 + 2x = 2x(-2x + 1)$.

---

## Teaching Tip

Suggest that students count the number of terms in the original polynomial and the number of terms in the factored form to make sure they are the same.

This technique is particularly important in a case where the GCF is one of the terms of the polynomial. For example:

$10x^4 + 15x^3 + 5x^2 = 5x^2(2x^2 + 3x + 1)$

↑
Counting terms will help students remember to include this term in the answer.

## Lesson Wrap-up

### QUICK ASSESSMENT

Ask the following questions to determine if students understand the content presented in this lesson.

**Consider these polynomials.**

A. $16x + 32y$

B. $24x^3 + 16x^2$

C. $5x^2y + 3x$

1. Which of the polynomials has terms with only a constant as the GCF?   **A**

2. Which of the polynomials has terms with only a variable as the GCF?   **C**

3. Which of the polynomials has a monomial containing a coefficient and a variable as the GCF of the terms?   **B**

**Suppose the GCF of $x^a$ and $x^b$ is $x^a$.**

4. What does this tell about $a$ and $b$?   $a \le b$

### ASSIGNMENT GUIDE

**Basic:** 1–57, 71–78
**Enriched:** 1–78

### Reteaching Worksheet 9-7

Name _____   Date _____

RETEACHING **9-7**

**FACTOR USING GREATEST COMMON FACTOR (GCF)**
The distributive property is used in multiplying a polynomial by a monomial. To find what factors are multiplied to obtain a polynomial, or to **factor** the polynomial, reverse the process.

**Example**

Factor the polynomial.
**a.** $4m - 2mn$     **b.** $6x^2y - 12xy^2 + 3xy$

**Solution**

**a.** Find the GCF of $4m$ and $2mn$.
$4m = 2 \cdot 2 \cdot m$    $2mn = 2 \cdot m \cdot n$
The GCF is $2m$.
Use the GCF and the distributive property to rewrite the polynomial.
$4m - 2mn = 2m(2 - n)$

**b.** Find the GCF of $6x^2y$, $12xy^2$, and $3xy$.
$6x^2y = 2 \cdot 3 \cdot x^2 \cdot y$    $12xy^2 = 2^2 \cdot 3 \cdot x \cdot y^2$    $3xy = 3 \cdot x \cdot y$
The GCF is $3xy$.
Use the GCF and the distributive property to rewrite the polynomial.
$6x^2y - 12xy^2 + 3xy = 3xy(2x) + 3xy(-4y) + 3xy(1) = 3xy(2x - 4y + 1)$

**✓ EXERCISES**

Factor each polynomial.

1. $3a + 3b$
   $3(a + b)$
2. $7m^2 - 5m$
   $m(7m - 5)$
3. $st + rt$
   $t(s + r)$
4. $18x + 27y$
   $9(2x + 3y)$
5. $12w^2 - 18w^3$
   $6w^2(2 - 3w)$
6. $5x^2y - 10xy^2$
   $5xy(x - 2y)$
7. $3r^2 - 6r + 30$
   $3(r^2 - 2r + 10)$
8. $4m^2n - 6m^4 + 8mn^3$
   $2m(2mn - 3m^3 + 4n^3)$
9. $9xy^2 - 6xy + 3x$
   $3x(3y^2 - 2y + 1)$
10. $28a^4b^2c^3 - 70a^2b^2c^2$
    $14a^2b^2c^2(2a^2c - 5)$
11. $14uwx - 42x^4 + 7w^2x^2$
    $7x(2w - 6x^3 + w^2x)$
12. $2a^5 - 4a^3 + 6a^2$
    $2a^2(a^3 - 2a + 3)$

---

 **TRY THESE EXERCISES**

**Factor each polynomial.**

1. $7w - 21$   $7(w - 3)$

2. $4c^2 + 6c^3$   $2c^2(2 + 3c)$

3. $9a^2 - 6a$   $3a(3a - 2)$

4. $16xy + 12x$   $4x(4y + 3)$

5. $45a^2b - 27ab^2$
   $9ab(5a - 3b)$

6. $25mn^3 - 15mn^2 + 5m$
   $5m(5n^3 - 3n^2 + 1)$

7. **FINANCE** The amount ($A$) in dollars returned after 1 year on a principal of $P$ dollars invested at an annual rate of ($r$) percent is given by the formula $A = P + Pr$. Rewrite the formula by factoring.   $A = P(1 + r)$

8. **MODELING** Use Algeblocks to factor $-2y^2 + y$.   $-y(2y - 1)$; See additional answers.

9. The formula for the perimeter ($P$) of a rectangle with length $l$ and width $w$ is $P = 2l + 2w$. Rewrite the formula by factoring.   $P = 2(l + w)$

 **PRACTICE EXERCISES** • For Extra Practice, see page 615.

**Factor each polynomial.**

10. $8mn - 8mp$   $8m(n - p)$

11. $12k + 15$   $3(4k + 5)$

12. $4x - 20$   $4(x - 5)$

13. $7e^2 + 21e$   $7e(e + 3)$

14. $9p^3 + 27p^2$   $9p^2(p + 3)$

15. $x^2 - xy$   $x(x - y)$

16. $12k^2 - 42k$   $6k(2k - 7)$

17. $5y^4 - 20y^3$   $5y^3(y - 4)$

18. $w^5 - w^4$   $w^4(w - 1)$

19. $100c - 200$   $100(c - 2)$

20. $3xy^2 + 6x$   $3x(y^2 + 2)$

21. $7xy - 56xz$   $7x(y - 8z)$

22. $v^5 - 6v^4 + 3v^3$
    $v^3(v^2 - 6v + 3)$

23. $5n^3 - 30m^2 - 15$
    $5(n^3 - 6m^2 - 3)$

24. $3a^6 - 5a^3 + 2a^2$
    $a^2(3a^4 - 5a + 2)$

25. $xy + xz + 2x$   $x(y + z + 2)$

26. $12x^4y^4 + 3x^3y^2 - 6x^2y^2$
    $3x^2y^2(4x^2y^2 + x - 2)$

27. $2xya - 4xyb + 6xyc$
    $2xy(a - 2b + 3c)$

28. $x^2 + 6xy - x$   $x(x + 6y - 1)$

29. $8h^2 - 16h + 24$
    $8(h^2 - 2h + 3)$

30. $50m^2 + 125mn + 25n^2$
    $25(2m^2 + 5mn + n^2)$

31. $15a^3b + 20a^2b - 10ab$
    $5ab(3a^2 + 4a - 2)$

32. $64x^6 - 48x^4 + 24x^2$
    $8x^2(8x^4 - 6x^2 + 3)$

33. $6m^3n^3 + 3m^3n^2 + m^2n^2$
    $m^2n^2(6mn + 3m + 1)$

**Evaluate each expression. Let $x = 2$ and $y = -3$.**

34. $3xy^2 - 3x^2y$   90

35. $3xy(y - x)$   90

36. **WRITING MATH** What do you notice about your answers in Exercises 34 and 35? Explain.   They are the same. In Exercise 35, the monomial $3xy$ has been factored out.

37. Did Exercise 34 or Exercise 35 require fewer steps?   Exercise 35

38. The formula for the surface area ($SA$) of a cone with radius $r$ and slant height $s$ is $SA = \pi r^2 + \pi rs$. Rewrite the formula by factoring.
    $SA = \pi r(r + s)$

39. The formula for the number of diagonals ($D$) that can be drawn in a polygon with $n$ sides is $D = \frac{1}{2}n^2 - \frac{3}{2}n$. Rewrite the formula by factoring.   $D = \frac{1}{2}n(n - 3)$

40. **GEOGRAPHY** The highest mountain in the U.S. is Mount McKinley, located in Alaska. The height can be expressed as $(2x^4 + 4x^2 - 8x)$ ft. Factor this expression.   $2x(x^3 + 2x - 4)$ ft

41. **PHYSICS** An expression used in connection with certain atomic particles is $\frac{1}{2}Z - \frac{1}{2}N$, where $Z$ is the number of protons and $N$ is the number of neutrons in the nucleus. Factor this expression.
    $\frac{1}{2}(Z - N)$

Mount McKinley, Alaska

### ADDITIONAL ANSWERS

8.

**42.** $2x^2 - 4xy$  $2x(x - 2y)$    **43.** $xy - 3y$  $y(x - 3)$    **44.** $-x^2 + xy - x$  $x(-x + y - 1)$

**Factor each polynomial.** $9m^2n(2mn + 5n^2 + 3m^2 - 6n)$

$5x^2(7x^3y - 8xy^2 + 2 + 9x^2y^3)$

**45.** $18m^3n^2 + 45m^2n^3 + 27m^4n - 54m^2n^2$    **46.** $35x^5y - 40x^3y^2 + 10x^2 + 45x^4y^3$

**47.** $48ab - 40a^3b^2 + 24a^2b^3 + 28a^2b^2$    **48.** $x^2y^3z - x^2y^2z^2 + xy^4z - xy^3z^2$
$4ab(12 - 10a^2b + 6ab^2 + 7ab)$    $xy^2z(xy - xz + y^2 - yz)$

**Write an expression for the perimeter of each figure. Then factor the expression.**

**49.**

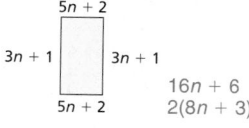

$5n + 2$

$3n + 1$ | $3n + 1$

$5n + 2$

$16n + 6$
$2(8n + 3)$

**50.**

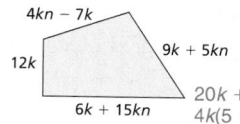

$4kn - 7k$

$12k$        $9k + 5kn$

$6k + 15kn$    $20k + 24kn$
$4k(5 + 6n)$

**51.**

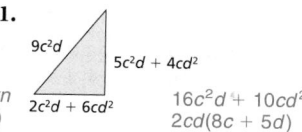

$9c^2d$

$5c^2d + 4cd^2$

$2c^2d + 6cd^2$    $16c^2d + 10cd^2$
$2cd(8c + 5d)$

**If two polynomials have 1 as their greatest common factor, they are *relatively prime*. Tell whether the polynomials are relatively prime.**

**52.** $2, 3x$  yes    **53.** $mn, n^2$  no    **54.** $4ab, 3ab$  no

**55.** $c + c^2, 5c^4$  no    **56.** $k, k + 5$  yes    **57.** $2m + 2, km^2 + km$  no

## ■ EXTENDED PRACTICE EXERCISES

**58. CRITICAL THINKING** The perimeter of a square is $(8t^2 + 36t)$ ft. Find the area of the square.  $(2t^2 + 9t)^2 = (4t^4 + 36t^3 + 81t^2)$ ft$^2$

**Find each product.**

**59.** $(x + 5)(x - 5)$  $x^2 - 25$    **60.** $(n + 7)(n - 7)$  $n^2 - 49$    **61.** $(p + 4)(p - 4)$  $p^2 - 16$

**62.** $(k + 9)(k - 9)$  $k^2 - 81$    **63.** $(y - 11)(y + 11)$  $y^2 - 121$    **64.** $(a + 1.5)(a - 1.5)$
$a^2 - 2.25$

**Study the pattern in the products for Exercise 59–64. Write each polynomial as a product of two binomials.**

**65.** $v^2 - 9$  $(v + 3)(v - 3)$    **66.** $w^2 - 64$  $(w + 8)(w - 8)$    **67.** $m^2 - 36$  $(m + 6)(m - 6)$

**68.** $c^2 - 100$  $(c + 10)(c - 10)$    **69.** $4x^2 - 25$  $(2x + 5)(2x - 5)$    **70.** $36y^2 - 121z^6$
$(6y + 11z^3)(6y - 11z^3)$

## ■ MIXED REVIEW EXERCISES

**Solve each equation. Check the solution.** (Lesson 3-4)

**71.** $5x - 10 = 0$  2    **72.** $\frac{3}{4}y + 4 = 10$  8    **73.** $4a + 10 = 6$  $-1$

**74.** $0.4b - 3.1 = 0.5$  9.0    **75.** $4(x - 6) = -20$  1    **76.** $\frac{w}{5} - 3 = 7$  50

**Translate each sentence into an equation. Then solve the equation.** (Lesson 3-4)

**77.** Three even consecutive numbers have a sum of $-54$. What are the three numbers?  $x + (x + 2) + (x + 4) = -54; -20, -18, -16$

**78.** What is the area of a swimming pool with a length that is 3 times the width and a perimeter of 96 ft.  $2(3w + w) = 96; 432$ ft$^2$

## ADDITIONAL ANSWERS

**42.** 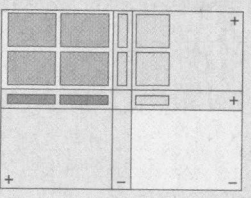    **43.** 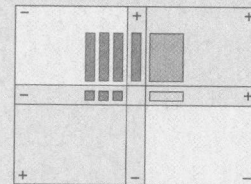    **44.**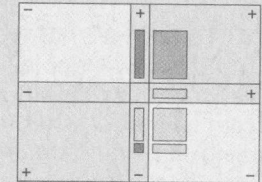

---

### Extra Practice Worksheet 9-7

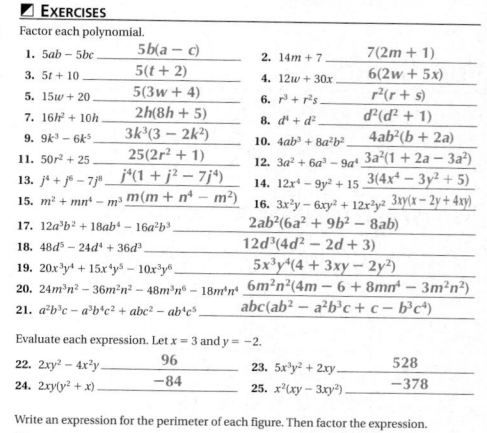

EXTRA PRACTICE  **9-7**
**FACTOR USING GREATEST COMMON FACTOR (GCF)**

**☑ EXERCISES**

Factor each polynomial.

1. $5ab - 5bc$  $5b(a - c)$    2. $14m + 7$  $7(2m + 1)$
3. $5t + 10$  $5(t + 2)$    4. $12w + 30x$  $6(2w + 5x)$
5. $15w + 20$  $5(3w + 4)$    6. $r^3 + r^2s$  $r^2(r + s)$
7. $16h^2 + 10h$  $2h(8h + 5)$    8. $d^4 + d^2$  $d^2(d^2 + 1)$
9. $9k^3 - 6k^5$  $3k^3(3 - 2k^2)$    10. $4ab^3 + 8a^2b^2$  $4ab^2(b + 2a)$
11. $50r^2 + 25$  $25(2r^2 + 1)$    12. $3a^2 + 6a^3 - 9a^4$  $3a^2(1 + 2a - 3a^2)$
13. $j^4 + j^6 - 7j^8$  $j^4(1 + j^2 - 7j^4)$    14. $12x^4 - 9y^2 + 15$  $3(4x^4 - 3y^2 + 5)$
15. $m^2 + mn^4 - m^3$  $m(m + n^4 - m^2)$    16. $3x^2y - 6xy^2 + 12x^2y^2$  $3xy(x - 2y + 4xy)$
17. $12a^3b^2 + 18ab^4 - 16a^2b^3$  $2ab^2(6a^2 + 9b^2 - 8ab)$
18. $48d^5 - 24d^4 + 36d^3$  $12d^3(4d^2 - 2d + 3)$
19. $20x^3y^4 + 15x^4y^5 - 10x^3y^6$  $5x^3y^4(4 + 3xy - 2y^2)$
20. $24m^3n^2 - 36m^2n^2 - 48m^3n^6 - 18m^4n^4$  $6m^2n^2(4m - 6 + 8mn^4 - 3m^2n^2)$
21. $a^2b^3c - a^3b^4c^2 + abc^2 - ab^4c^5$  $abc(ab^2 - a^2b^3c + c - b^3c^4)$

Evaluate each expression. Let $x = 3$ and $y = -2$.

22. $2xy^2 - 4x^2y$  96    23. $5x^3y^2 + 2xy$  528
24. $2xy(y^2 + x)$  $-84$    25. $x^2(xy - 3xy^2)$  $-378$

Write an expression for the perimeter of each figure. Then factor the expression.

26.

$2y + x$

$3y + x$        $2y + 4x$

$5y - 2x$

$12y + 4x = 4(3y + x)$

27.

$2r + 1$

$4r + 2$ | $4r + 2$

$2r + 1$

$12r + 6 = 6(2r + 1)$

---

### Enrichment Worksheet 9-7

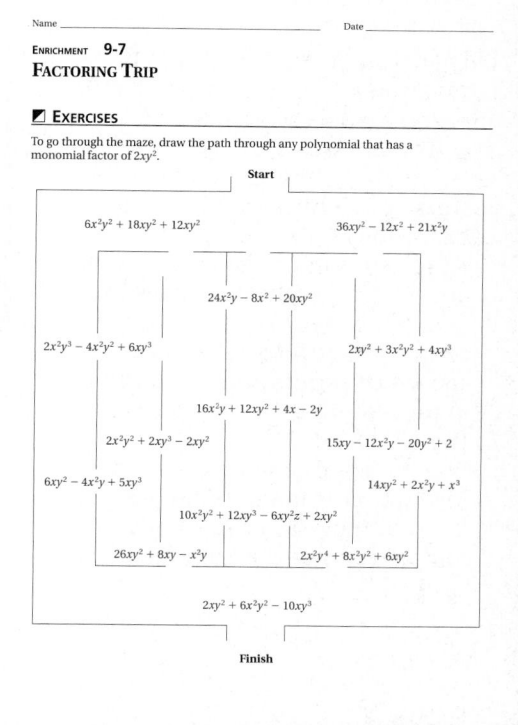

Name _____    Date _____

ENRICHMENT  **9-7**
**FACTORING TRIP**

**☑ EXERCISES**

To go through the maze, draw the path through any polynomial that has a monomial factor of $2xy^2$.

**Start**

$6x^2y^2 + 18xy^2 + 12xy^2$        $36xy^2 - 12x^2 + 21x^2y$

$24x^2y - 8x^2 + 20xy^2$

$2x^2y^3 - 4x^2y^2 + 6xy^3$        $2xy^2 + 3x^2y^2 + 4xy^3$

$16x^2y + 12xy^2 + 4x - 2y$

$2x^2y^2 + 2xy^3 - 2xy^2$        $15xy - 12x^2y - 20y^2 + 2$

$6xy^2 - 4x^2y + 5xy^3$        $14xy^2 + 2x^2y + x^3$

$10x^2y^2 + 12xy^3 - 6xy^2z + 2xy^2$

$26xy^2 + 8xy - x^2y$        $2x^2y^4 + 8x^2y^2 + 6xy^2$

$2xy^2 + 6x^2y^2 - 10xy^3$

**Finish**

### Vocabulary

perfect square trinomial
difference of two squares

### Tools/Materials Needed

Algeblocks with Quadrant Mat

### Lesson Resources

Warm-up Transparency 38
Transparency TK-5, 6, RF-47
Reteaching 9-8
Extra Practice 9-8
Enrichment 9-8

## Getting Started

### 5-MINUTE WARM-UP

**Write two square roots for each number.**
1. 4    2, −2
2. 36    6, −6
3. 81    9, −9
4. 144    12, −12

### Introduction to Lesson 9-8

In Questions 1–4, students establish that the model shows a trinomial and its two factors, $x^2 - 6x + 9 = (x - 3)(x - 3)$, where the two factors are identical. Elicit further observations:

The figures in Quadrants I and III are squares, with the square in Quadrant I representing the first term of the trinomial and the square configuration in Quadrant III representing the last term of the trinomial.

The rectangular configurations in Quadrants II and IV are equal in area; their sum represents the middle term of the trinomial.

---

# 9-8 Perfect Squares and Difference of Squares

**Goals**   ■ Factor perfect square trinomials.
            ■ Factor difference of perfect squares.

**Applications**   Travel, Number sense, Modeling, Geography

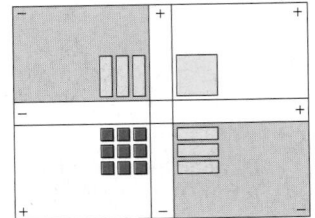

**Use the Quadrant Mat shown for Questions 1–4.**

1. What polynomial expression is represented by the Algeblocks?   $x^2 - 6x + 9$

2. What factor should be placed along the horizontal axis?   $x - 3$

3. What factor should be placed along the vertical axis?   $x - 3$

4. Write an equation to represent the polynomial expression and its factors shown on the Quadrant Mat.   $(x - 3)^2 = x^2 - 6x + 9$

### ■ BUILD UNDERSTANDING

Just as a number can be squared, such as $2^2 = 4$, a binomial can be squared. The result of squaring a binomial is a trinomial, called a **perfect square trinomial**.

$$(w + 6)^2 = (w + 6)(w + 6) = w^2 + 6w + 6w + 36$$
$$= w^2 + 12w + 36$$

Notice the pattern of a perfect square trinomial:

| | |
|---|---|
| The first term is a perfect square. | $w^2 = w \cdot w$ |
| The last term is a perfect square. | $36 = 6 \cdot 6$ |
| The middle term is twice the product of the square roots of the first and last terms. | $12w = 2\,(6 \cdot w)$ |

So, $w^2 + 12w + 36$ fits the pattern. It is a perfect square trinomial.

### Example 1

Tell whether the trinomial is a perfect square trinomial.

a. $n^2 + 10n + 25$         b. $k^2 + 7k + 49$

### Solution

a. 
| | |
|---|---|
| The first term is a perfect square. | $n^2 = n \cdot n$ |
| The last term is a perfect square. | $25 = 5 \cdot 5$ |
| The middle term is twice the product of the square roots of the first and last terms. | $10n = 2(5 \cdot n)$ |

The trinomial is a perfect square trinomial.

> **Think Back**
>
> Recall the following *perfect squares.*
>
> | | |
> |---|---|
> | $1 = 1 \cdot 1$ | $81 = 9 \cdot 9$ |
> | $4 = 2 \cdot 2$ | $100 = 10 \cdot 10$ |
> | $9 = 3 \cdot 3$ | $121 = 11 \cdot 11$ |
> | $16 = 4 \cdot 4$ | $144 = 12 \cdot 12$ |
> | $25 = 5 \cdot 5$ | $169 = 13 \cdot 13$ |
> | $36 = 6 \cdot 6$ | $196 = 14 \cdot 14$ |
> | $49 = 7 \cdot 7$ | $225 = 15 \cdot 15$ |
> | $64 = 8 \cdot 8$ | $256 = 16 \cdot 16$ |

## Differentiated Instruction

**TACTILE/KINESTHETIC LEARNERS** Have students use Algeblocks to model Example 1a, and explain how they can tell from its model whether or not the trinomial is a perfect square.
Then have students explain how an Algeblocks model of Example 1b would show that the trinomial is not a perfect square.

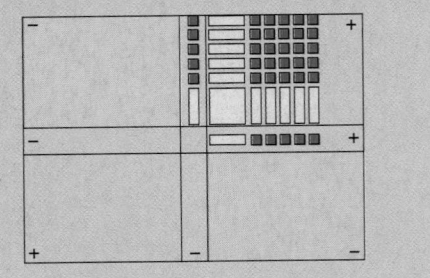

**b.** First term: $k^2 = k \cdot k$       Last term: $49 = 7 \cdot 7$       Middle term: $7k \neq 2(7 \cdot k)$

The trinomial is not a perfect square trinomial.

You can use the patterns in a perfect square trinomial to factor it.

## Example 2

**Factor each polynomial.**

**a.** $n^2 + 10n + 25$

**b.** $y^2 - 20y + 100$

### Solution

**a.** Determine if the trinomial is a perfect square trinomial.

First term: $n^2 = n \cdot n$       Last term: $25 = 5 \cdot 5$       Middle term: $10n = 2(n \cdot 5)$

Then, use the square roots to write the factors.

$$n^2 + 10n + 25 = (n + 5)(n + 5) = (n + 5)^2$$

**b.** Determine if the trinomial is a perfect square trinomial.

First term: $y^2 = y \cdot y$       Last term: $100 = 10 \cdot 10$       Middle term: $20y = 2(y \cdot 10)$

Since the sign of the middle term in the trinomial is negative, use a negative sign in each factor.

$$y^2 - 20y + 100 = (y - 10)(y - 10) = (y - 10)^2$$

A different pattern develops in the product of two binomials that are similar, where one binomial is a sum and the other is a difference.

$$
\begin{array}{cc}
\text{sum of} & \text{difference} \\
y \text{ and } 9 & \text{of } y \text{ and } 9 \\
\downarrow & \downarrow
\end{array}
$$

$$(y + 9)(y - 9) = y^2 - 9y + 9y - 81 = y^2 - 81$$

A polynomial such as $y^2 - 81$ is called the **difference of two squares**. If you recognize that a polynomial is a difference of two perfect squares, you can work backwards to find the factors.

**Check Understanding**

Verify the following:

$k^2 + 9 \neq (k + 3)(k - 3)$

$k^2 + 9 \neq (k + 3)(k + 3)$

Can $k^2 + 9$ be written as a product of two binomials?

no

## Example 3

**Factor $k^2 - 9$.**

### Solution

$$
\begin{array}{c}
k^2 - 9 \\
\swarrow \qquad \searrow \\
k \cdot k \qquad 3 \cdot 3
\end{array}
$$

To factor a difference of two squares, write the two binomials using the square roots of the terms. Make one binomial a sum and the other a difference.

$$k^2 - 9 = (k + 3)(k - 3)$$

 **Math Online** mathmatters2.com/extra_examples

Lesson 9-8 **Perfect Squares and Difference of Squares**   409

## Chalkboard Examples

### Supplementary Example 1
Is $9x^2 + 12x + 4$ a perfect square trinomial?
The first term is a perfect square.   $9x^2 = 3x \cdot 3x$
The last term is a perfect square.       $4 = 2 \cdot 2$
The middle term is twice the product of the square roots of the first and last terms.       $12x = 2(2 \cdot 3x)$
So, $9x^2 + 12x + 4$ is a perfect square trinomial.

### Supplementary Example 2
Factor $4x^2 - 8x + 1$.
Determine if the trinomial is a perfect square.
First term:   $4x^2 = 2x \cdot 2x$
Last term:       $1 = 1 \cdot 1$
Middle term:   $8x = 2(2 \cdot 2x)$
Since $4x^2 - 8x + 1$ is a perfect square trinomial, use the square roots to write the factors.
$4x^2 - 8x + 1 = (2x - 1)(2x - 1) = (2x - 1)^2$

### Supplementary Example 3
Factor each polynomial.
**a.** $\frac{9}{4}x^2 - 81$   $\left(\frac{3}{2}x + 9\right)\left(\frac{3}{2}x - 9\right)$

**b.** $0.64k^2 - 100$
$(0.8k + 10)(0.8k - 10)$

## Extend the Lesson

**CHALLENGE** Introduce students to *square numbers*, those numbers that can be represented as a square array of dots. Note with students that the successive square arrays of dots are also produced by adding consecutive odd numbers of dots, as shown. Have students use these

| 1st | 2nd | 3rd | 4th |
|---|---|---|---|
| 1● | 1● ● ●<br>3●─● | 1● ● ●<br>3●─● ● ●<br>5●─●─● | 1● ● ● ●<br>3●─● ● ●<br>5●─●─● ●<br>7●─●─●─● |
| $1 = 1$ | $1 + 3 = 4$ | $1 + 3 + 5 = 9$ | $1 + 3 + 5 + 7 = 16$ |

patterns to write each of the following square numbers as a sum of consecutive odd numbers:  the 5th square number  $5^2 = 1 + 3 + 5 + 7 + 9$; 5 terms
the 20th square number  $20^2 = 1 + 3 + \ldots + 39$; 20 terms

## Lesson Wrap-up

## Lesson Wrap-up

### QUICK ASSESSMENT

Ask the following questions to determine if students understand the content presented in this lesson.

1. Describe the factors of a perfect square trinomial.   two identical binomials where the first term of each binomial is the square root of the first term of the trinomial and the second term of each binomial is the square root of the last term of the trinomial, with the sign of the second term the same as the sign of the middle term of the trinomial

2. Describe the factors of the difference of two squares.   two binomials with opposite middle signs; the first term of each binomial is the square root of the first square and the second term of each binomial is the square root of the second square

### ASSIGNMENT GUIDE

Basic: 1–57, 66–75
Enriched: 1–75

### Reteaching Worksheet 9-8

Name _____ Date _____

RETEACHING  **9-8**
**FACTORING PERFECT SQUARES AND DIFFERENCES OF SQUARES**
You can factor a **perfect square trinomial** or the **difference of two squares**.

**Example 1**
Factor $x^2 + 8x + 16$.

**Solution**
The first and last terms are perfect squares: $x^2 = x \cdot x$, $16 = 4 \cdot 4$.

The middle term is *twice* the product of the square roots of the first and last terms: $8x = 2(4)(x)$. So, the trinomial is a perfect square trinomial.
$$x^2 + 8x + 16 = (x + 4)(x + 4) = (x + 4)^2$$

**Example 2**
Factor $y^2 - 100$.

**Solution**
The terms of this binomial are both perfect squares.
$y^2 = y \cdot y$     $100 = 10 \cdot 10$

Write the sum and the difference of the square root of each term.
$y^2 - 100 = (y + 10)(y - 10)$

**EXERCISES**

Factor each polynomial.

1. $x^2 - 14x + 49$     $(x - 7)^2$
2. $x^2 + 2x + 1$     $(x + 1)^2$
3. $x^2 + 7x + 14$     not factorable
4. $x^2 + 18x + 81$     $(x + 9)^2$
5. $y^2 - 20y + 100$     $(y - 10)^2$
6. $m^2 - 30m + 225$     $(m - 15)^2$
7. $y^2 + 100$     not factorable
8. $r^2 - 121$     $(r - 11)(r + 11)$
9. $w^2 - 1$     $(w - 1)(w + 1)$
10. $t^2 - 900$     $(t - 30)(t + 30)$
11. $q^2 + 36$     not factorable
12. $h^2 - 144$     $(h - 12)(h + 12)$

---

### TRY THESE EXERCISES

Tell whether the trinomial is a perfect square trinomial.

1. $c^2 - 5c + 25$   no
2. $h^2 + 8h + 16$   yes
3. $s^2 + 6s + 9$   yes

4. **WRITING MATH** Explain why there is a multiple of 2 in the middle term of a perfect square trinomial.   The products of the outer terms and of the inner terms (using FOIL) are identical.

Factor each polynomial if possible.

5. $m^2 + 18m + 81$   $(m + 9)^2$
6. $f^2 - 2f + 1$   $(f - 1)^2$
7. $p^2 + 121$   not factorable
8. $q^2 - 25$   $(q + 5)(q - 5)$
9. $h^2 + 4h + 8$   not factorable
10. $s^2 - 196$   $(s + 14)(s - 14)$

11. **MODELING** For the Quadrant Mat shown, write the trinomial and its factors.   $x^2 - 8x + 16 = (x - 4)^2$

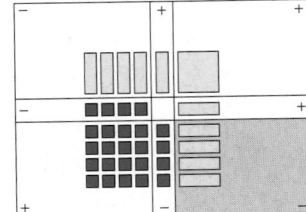

### PRACTICE EXERCISES • For Extra Practice, see page 615.

Tell whether the trinomial is a perfect square trinomial.

12. $x^2 + 6x + 9$   yes
13. $y^2 + 14y + 49$   yes
14. $n^2 + 5n + 25$   no
15. $p^2 - 20p + 40$   no
16. $x^2 + 24x + 144$   yes
17. $m^2 - 40m + 100$   no

Factor each polynomial if possible.

18. $c^2 - 4c + 4$   $(c - 2)^2$
19. $k^2 - 18k + 81$   $(k - 9)^2$
20. $n^2 - 100$   $(n + 10)(n - 10)$
21. $x^2 - 64$   $(x + 8)(x - 8)$
22. $y^2 + 22y + 121$   $(y + 11)^2$
23. $h^2 - 225$   $(h + 15)(h - 15)$
24. $v^2 - 20v + 40$   no
25. $y^2 - 1$   $(y + 1)(y - 1)$
26. $c^2 - 24c + 144$   $(c - 12)^2$
27. $e^2 - 6e + 9$   $(e - 3)^2$
28. $f^2 + 12f + 36$   $(f + 6)^2$
29. $p^2 - 256$   $(p + 16)(p - 16)$
30. $d^2 + 2d + 1$   $(d + 1)^2$
31. $c^2 + 50$   no
32. $w^2 + 49$   no
33. $h^2 + 24h + 144$   $(h + 12)^2$
34. $p^2 - 20p + 100$   $(p - 10)^2$
35. $p^2 - 144$   $(p + 12)(p - 12)$
36. $k^2 - 4$   $(k + 2)(k - 2)$
37. $x^2 - 7x + 49$   no
38. $m^2 + 9$   no
39. $c^2 - 8c + 16$   $(c - 4)^2$
40. $n^2 - 16$   $(n + 4)(n - 4)$
41. $q^2 - q + 1$   no
42. $t^2 - 400$   $(t + 20)(t - 20)$
43. $b^2 + 26b + 169$   $(b + 13)^2$
44. $z^2 - 81$   $(z + 9)(z - 9)$

**GRAPHING** Use a graphing calculator to graph the two curves. Determine whether each equation represents the same graph. If they do not, factor the first polynomial.

45. $y = x^2 + 6x + 9$
$y = (x + 2)^2$
no, $(x + 3)^2$

46. $y = x^2 - 25$
$y = (x - 5)(x + 5)$
yes

Factor each polynomial.

47. $3m^2 - 27$   $3(m + 3)(m - 3)$
48. $n^2p - 25p$   $p(n + 5)(n - 5)$
49. $2m^2 + 32m + 128$   $2(m + 8)^2$
50. $x^2m^2 - 14x^2m + 49x^2$   $x^2(m - 7)^2$
51. $3ak^2 - 300a$   $3a(k + 10)(k - 10)$
52. $4y^2 + 72y + 324$   $4(y + 9)^2$

### ADDITIONAL ANSWERS

53.

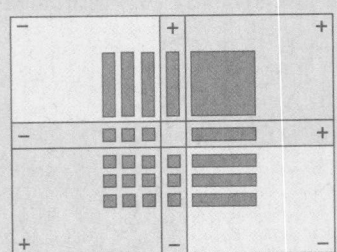

**53. MODELING** Use Algeblocks to find the factors of $y^2 - 6y + 9$.
$(y - 3)^2$; See additional answers.

**54. TRAVEL** Use the table of longest highway tunnels on page 401. The length of the Schelde Tunnel is the square root of the length of the Eisenhower Tunnel in the U. S. How long is the Schelde Tunnel? 1.3 mi

**55. YOU MAKE THE CALL** Eric says the binomial factors of $a^2 - 10a + 25$ are $(a - 5)$ and $(a + 5)$. Sumi says that the binomial factors are $(a - 5)(a - 5)$. Who is correct and why? Sumi is correct. It is a perfect square trinomial.

**NUMBER SENSE** Write a polynomial expression to represent each number trick. Let $x$ equal the original number. Use an equation to check your work.

**56.** Think of a number. Subtract 7. Multiply by 3. Add 30. Divide by 3. Subtract the original number. The result is always 3. $\frac{3(x - 7) + 30}{3} - x$

**57.** Think of any non-zero number. Subtract 6. Multiply by 5. Add 30. Divide by the original number. The result is always 5. $\frac{(x - 6)5 + 30}{x}$

## ▇ EXTENDED PRACTICE EXERCISES

**Factor each polynomial.**

**58.** $9k^2 - 49$  $(3k + 7)(3k - 7)$   **59.** $4n^2 - 25$  $(2n + 5)(2n - 5)$   **60.** $4x^2 + 12x + 9$  $(2x + 3)^2$

**61.** $9m^2 + 30m + 25$  $(3m + 5)^2$   **62.** $49p^2 - 100$  $(7p + 10)(7p - 10)$   **63.** $25x^2 - 40x + 16$  $(5x - 4)^2$

**64. CRITICAL THINKING** Suppose the area measures of these squares are both perfect squares. If the difference in the areas is 32 square units, find the values of $x$ and $y$. 9, 7 or 6, 2

 $x$    $y$

**65. CHAPTER INVESTIGATION** If the average speed of the orienteers is 2.5 mi/h, and the average time it takes to complete the course is 3 h, calculate the total length of the course in miles. $(d = r \cdot t)$ 7.5 mi

## ▇ MIXED REVIEW EXERCISES

**66. GEOGRAPHY** The deepest part of the Pacific Ocean is the Marianna Trench, which is 35,840 ft deep. How many meters is this? How many miles is this? (Basic math skills) ≈ 10,924 m; ≈ 6.8 mi

**67.** Karen ran in a 10 km marathon. How many miles did she run? (Basic math skills) ≈ 6.2 mi

**68.** If Karen can run an average of 10 ft/sec, how long did it take her to complete the marathon? (Basic math skills) ≈ 54.56 min

**69.** A living room measures 15 ft wide by 22 ft long. How many square yards of carpeting is needed to cover the floor? (Basic math skills) $36\frac{2}{3}$ yd$^2$

Moonrise over the Pacific Ocean

**Simplify.** (Lesson 9-4)

**70.** $4y(-3y + 6)$  $-12y^2 + 24y$   **71.** $-9n(11n^2 - 3n)$  $-99n^3 + 27n^2$

**72.** $\frac{1}{3}x(-12x^3 + 6x^2 - 9)$  $-4x^4 + 2x^3 - 3x$   **73.** $4xy(3x^2 - 4y)$  $12x^3y - 16xy^2$

**74.** $7m(m^2 + 3mn - 4n^2)$  $7m^3 + 21m^2n - 28mn^2$   **75.** $12(a - b) + 3(5a - 9b)$  $27a - 39b$

**Math Online** mathmatters2.com/self_check_quiz

---

## Differentiated Instruction

**VISUAL LEARNERS** Have students consider the patterns shown below. Then ask students to draw a diagram showing that $5^2$ can be written as the sum of $4^2$ and two consecutive integers.

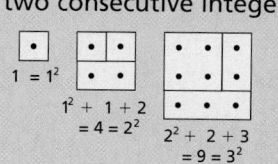
$1 = 1^2$
$1^2 + 1 + 2$
$= 4 = 2^2$

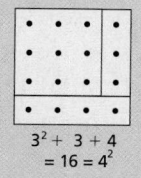
$2^2 + 2 + 3$
$= 9 = 3^2$

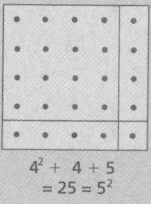
$3^2 + 3 + 4$
$= 16 = 4^2$

$4^2 + 4 + 5$
$= 25 = 5^2$

---

### Extra Practice Worksheet 9-8

Name _____ Date _____

EXTRA PRACTICE **9-8**
**PERFECT SQUARES AND DIFFERENCE OF SQUARES**

✓ **EXERCISES**

Tell whether the trinomial is a perfect square trinomial.

1. $x^2 + 8$ ___ no   2. $r^2 + 10r + 25$ ___ yes
3. $w^2 - 14w + 49$ ___ yes   4. $y^2 - 20y + 20$ ___ no
5. $d^2 - 10d + 100$ ___ no   6. $z^2 + 12z + 36$ ___ yes

Factor each polynomial if possible.

7. $x^2 + 10x + 25$  $(x + 5)^2$   8. $f^2 - 4f + 4$  $(f - 2)^2$
9. $m^2 + 14m + 49$  $(m + 7)^2$   10. $r^2 - 6r + 9$  $(r - 3)^2$
11. $x^2 + 6x + 36$  not factorable   12. $g^2 - 8g + 16$  $(g - 4)^2$
13. $d^2 - 40$  not factorable   14. $a^2 - 49$  $(a - 7)(a + 7)$
15. $x^2 + 28x + 196$  $(x - 14)^2$   16. $m^2 - 100$  $(m - 10)(m + 10)$
17. $r^2 + 36$  not factorable   18. $c^2 + 16c + 64$  $(c + 8)^2$
19. $n^2 + 22n + 121$  $(n + 11)^2$   20. $p^2 + 25$  not factorable
21. $x^2 - 196$  $(x - 14)(x + 14)$   22. $m^2 + 1$  not factorable
23. $d^2 - 625$  $(d - 25)(d + 25)$   24. $a^2 - 32a + 256$  $(a - 16)^2$
25. $x^2 - 14x - 49$  not factorable   26. $n^2 - 2n + 1$  $(n - 1)^2$
27. $t^2 - 25$  $(t - 5)(t + 5)$   28. $b^2 + 8b - 16$  not factorable
29. $x^2 + 28x + 196$  $(x + 14)^2$   30. $m^2 - 100$  $(m - 10)(m + 10)$
31. $2f^2 - 50$  $2(f - 5)(f + 5)$   32. $xy^2 - 4x$  $x(y - 2)(y + 2)$
33. $5t^2 + 20t + 20$  $5(t + 2)^2$   34. $c^4d^2 - 30c^4t + 225c^4$  $c^4(d - 15)^2$
35. $mn^2 - mn + 1$  not factorable   36. $h^2k^2 - 8h^2k + 16h^2$  $h^2(k - 4)^2$
37. $8t^2 - 32$  $8(t - 2)(t + 2)$   38. $3ab^2 - 3ab + 3a$  $3a(b - 1)^2$
39. $x^3y^2 - 4x^3y + 4x^3$  $x^3(y - 2)^2$   40. $5mn^2 + 50mn + 125m$  $5m(n + 5)^2$

---

### Enrichment Worksheet 9-8

Name _____ Date _____

ENRICHMENT **9-8**
**FACTORING QUADRATIC TRINOMIALS**
A polynomial in one variable of degree 2 is called a **quadratic trinomial**. For example, $x^2 + 5x + 6$ is a quadratic trinomial.

The term of degree 2 is called the **quadratic term**. $x^2$
The term of degree 1 is called the **linear term**. $5x$
The numerical term is called the **constant**. 6

You can factor quadratic trinomials of the form $x^2 + bx + c = (x + m)(x + n)$. Follow these steps.

1. Find pairs of factors $m$ and $n$ that have a *product* equal to the constant term.
2. Use the pair of factors in the list that has a *sum* equal to the coefficient of the linear term.

**Example**

Factor. **a.** $x^2 - 5x + 6$   **b.** $y^2 + 4y - 5$

**Solution**

**a.** If $c$ is positive, both factors have to be either positive or negative. Check the middle term to decide.

$x^2 - 5x + 6$   factors of 6: 1, 6, 2, 3
sum of −2   product of −2
and −3   and −3
The factors are $(x - 2)(x - 3)$.
Check by multiplying.
$(x - 2)(x - 3) = x^2 - 5x + 6$

**b.** If $c$ is negative, both factors have opposite signs. The greater factor has the sign of the middle term.

$y^2 + 4y - 5$   factors of 5: 1, 5
sum of −1   product of −1
and 5   and 5
The factors are $(y - 1)(y + 5)$.
Check by multiplying.
$(y - 1)(y + 5) = y^2 + 4y - 5$

✓ **EXERCISES**

Factor. Check your answers by multiplying.

1. $m^2 + 9m + 18$  $(m + 6)(m + 3)$   2. $r^2 - 13r + 42$  $(r - 6)(r - 7)$   3. $y^2 - 2y - 3$  $(y + 1)(y - 3)$
4. $x^2 + 5x - 36$  $(x + 9)(x - 4)$   5. $w^2 - 4w + 3$  $(w - 1)(w - 3)$   6. $b^2 - 10b - 24$  $(b + 2)(b - 12)$
7. $x^2 + 3x - 28$  $(x + 7)(x - 4)$   8. $s^2 - 12s + 20$  $(s - 2)(s - 10)$   9. $r^2 - r - 6$  $(r + 2)(r - 3)$

## Chapter 9 Review

## Vocabulary Assessment

- A matching section checks for student understanding of the new vocabulary introduced in this chapter.
- A vocabulary review/test for Chapter 9 is available on pp. vii–viii of the *Chapter 9 Resource Masters.*

## Lesson-by-Lesson Review

For each lesson,

- the main ideas are summarized, and
- practice exercises are provided.

## EXAMVIEW® PRO

Use the networkable **ExamView® Pro** to:

- Create **multiple versions** of tests.
- Create **modified tests** for inclusion students.
- **Edit** existing questions and **add** your own questions.
- Use built-in **state curriculum correlations** to create tests aligned with state standards.
- Change **English** tests to **Spanish** and vice versa.

# Chapter 9 Review

## VOCABULARY ◼

**Choose the word from the list that best completes each statement.**

1. The __?__ of two or more monomials is the greatest factor that is a factor of every term. g

2. In a polynomial, terms that are exactly alike, or that are alike except for their numerical coefficients, are called __?__. h

3. To __?__ a polynomial means to express it as a product of polynomials. f

4. In a __?__ the first and last terms are perfect squares and the middle term is twice the product of the square roots of the first and last terms. j

5. A __?__ is a polynomial with two terms. a

6. A __?__ is the numerical part of a monomial. b

7. According to the __?__, $3(a + b)$ is equivalent to $3a + 3b$. e

8. A __?__ is a monomial with no variables. c

9. A binomial where one perfect square is subtracted from another perfect square is called a __?__. d

10. A monomial or the sum or difference of two or more monomials is called a __?__. k

| | |
|---|---|
| **a.** | binomial |
| **b.** | coefficient |
| **c.** | constant |
| **d.** | difference of two squares |
| **e.** | distributive property |
| **f.** | factor |
| **g.** | GCF |
| **h.** | like terms |
| **i.** | monomial |
| **j.** | perfect square trinomial |
| **k.** | polynomial |
| **l.** | trinomial |

## LESSON 9-1 ◼ Add and Subtract Polynomials, p. 376

▶ The sum or difference of monomials is a **polynomial**. To simplify a polynomial, combine **like terms** by adding their **coefficients**.

▶ A polynomial is written in **standard form** when its **terms** are arranged in order from greatest to least powers of one of the variables.

**Write each polynomial in standard form for the variable x.**

11. $2x^2 + x^4 - 6$   $x^4 + 2x^2 - 6$

12. $8xy^2 - 7x^2y + 5$   $-7x^2y + 8xy^2 + 5$

13. $6w^3x + 3wx^2 - 10x^6 + 5x^7$   $5x^7 - 10x^6 + 3wx^2 + 6w^3x$

**Simplify.**

14. $7a - 4a$   $3a$

15. $8k^2 - 5k + 8k - 4k^2$   $4k^2 + 3k$

16. $4x + 3y - 6x + 7x - 10y$   $5x - 7y$

## LESSON 9-2 ◼ Multiply Monomials, p. 380

▶ Use the product rule for exponents to find a product of two monomials that have the same base.

▶ Use the power rule for exponents and the power of a product rule for exponents to simplify monomials that involve powers.

**Simplify.**

17. $(-3m)(2m^2n)$   $-6m^3n$

18. $4x(2x^2)^3$   $32x^7$

19. $(3a^2b^3)(-2ab^4c)$   $-6a^3b^7c$

20. $5r^3(4r^4)$   $20r^7$

21. $(10x^3y)(-2xy^2)$   $-20x^4y^3$

22. $3a^3b(5a^4c^2)$   $15a^7bc^2$

## LESSON 9-3 ▨ Divide by a Monomial, p. 386

▶ To simplify the quotient of two monomials, divide both monomials by their GCF.

**Simplify.**

23. $\dfrac{6xy^3}{8xy}$    $\dfrac{3y^2}{4}$

24. $\dfrac{-9c + 21c^3}{3c}$    $7c^2 - 3$

25. $\dfrac{3p^4q + 12p^3q^2 + 15p^2q}{3pq}$    $p^3 + 4p^2q + 5p$

26. $\dfrac{15a^3 - 9ab^3}{3a}$    $5a^2 - 3b^3$

27. $\dfrac{20x^2y^4 + 16x^3y^3 - 4x^4yz}{4x^2y}$    $5y^3 + 4xy^2 - x^2z$

28. $\dfrac{2d^3 - 6d^6f^2 + 2d^7}{-2d^3}$    $-1 + 3d^3f^2 - d^4$

**Write an expression for the unknown dimension of each rectangle.**

29. area $= 24x^5y^3$

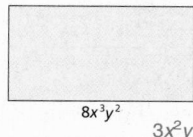

$8x^3y^2$

$3x^2y$

30. area $= 100a^3b$

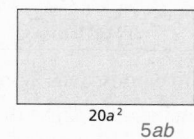

$20a^2$

$5ab$

31. area $= 6x^4 + 12x^2$

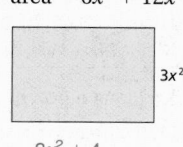

$3x^2$

$2x^2 + 4$

## LESSON 9-4 ▨ Multiply a Polynomial by a Monomial, p. 390

▶ Use the distributive property and the rules for exponents to multiply a polynomial by a monomial.

**Simplify.**

32. $8m(2m^2 + 3m - 4)$
   $16m^3 + 24m^2 - 32m$

33. $3x(2x^2y + xy + 5y^2)$
   $6x^3y + 3x^2y^2 + 15xy^2$

34. $2(h^3 + 6h) + 7(4h^3 - h)$
   $30h^3 + 5h$

35. $d(-2d + 4) + 15d$
   $-2d^2 + 19d$

36. $3w(6w - 4) + 2(5 - 3w)$
   $18w^2 - 18w + 10$

37. $-3c^2(2c + 7) + 2(c^2 - 4)$
   $-6c^3 - 19c^2 - 8$

38. A local business hires employees to stuff envelopes. Employees earn $50 per day plus $0.02 per envelope. Write a variable expression in simplest form that represents the cost to the business if $x$ people each stuff $y$ envelopes.    $50x + 0.02xy$

39. Spencer has $4000 to invest. He puts $x$ dollars of this money into a savings account that earns 2% per year. He uses the rest of the money to buy a certificate of deposit that earns 4% per year. Write an equation for the total amount of money Spencer will earn after one year.    $160 - 0.02x$

## LESSON 9-5 ▨ Multiply Binomials, p. 396

▶ To multiply two binomials, write the products of the *first* terms, the *outer* terms, the *inner* terms and the *last* terms (FOIL), then simplify.

**Find the product.**

40. $(p + 5)(p - 7)$   $p^2 - 2p - 35$

41. $(2t - 4)(t - 1)$   $2t^2 - 6t + 4$

42. $(5y - 3)(5y + 3)$   $25y^2 - 9$

43. $(e + 3)(e + 7)$   $e^2 + 10e + 21$

44. $3(w - 6)(w + 6)$   $3w^2 - 108$

45. $-2(y - 9)(y + 7) + 2(y + 3)(y - 3)$   $4y + 108$

46. A rectangular flower bed is 8 ft longer than it is wide. A walkway surrounding the flower bed is 3 ft wide and has an area of 192 ft². Find the dimensions of the flower bed.   9 ft by 17 ft

## LESSON 9-6 ■ Problem Solving Skills: Work Backwards, p. 400

▶ You can use the strategy **work backwards** to solve some types of problems.

**47.** A number is multiplied by 3 and then 8 is added to the result. The final number is 56. What is the original number?   16

**48.** A bacteria population triples in number every day. If there are 2,187,000 bacteria on the seventh day, how many bacteria were there on the first day?   3000 bacteria

**49.** Kyle and Devin volunteer at the zoo at 9:00 A.M. on Saturdays. It takes 20 min to get from Devin's house to the zoo. Kyle picks up Devin, but it takes him 15 min to get to Devin's house. If it takes Kyle 45 min to get ready in the morning, what is the latest Kyle should get out of bed?   7:40 A.M.

**50.** A store tripled the price it paid for a pair of sandals. After a month, the sandals were marked down $5. Two weeks later, the price was divided in half. Finally, the price was reduced by $3 and the sandals sold for $14.99. How much did the store pay for the pair of sandals?   $13.66

## LESSON 9-7 ■ Factor Using Greatest Common Factor (GCF), p. 404

▶ **Factoring** a polynomial means to express it as a product of polynomials.

▶ To **factor** a polynomial, work backwards to find the factors. Begin by finding the greatest common factor (GCF) of its monomial terms.

**Factor each polynomial.**

**51.** $12x - 16$  $4(3x - 4)$

**52.** $xy^2 - x^2y + xy$  $xy(y - x + 1)$

**53.** $24m^2n - 3m^3n + 15m^4n^3$
$3m^2n(8 - m + 5m^2n^2)$

**54.** $a + a^2b^2 + a^3b^3$  $a(1 + ab^2 + a^2b^3)$

**55.** $3p^3q - 9pq^2 + 36pq$  $3pq(p^2 - 3q + 12)$

**56.** $5x^3y^2 + 10x^2y + 25x$  $5x(x^2y^2 + 2xy + 5)$

**Evaluate each expression. Let $x = -2$ and $y = 3$.**

**57.** $4x^2y + xy$  42

**58.** $xy(4x + 1)$   42

**59.** $2x^2(y - xy)$  72

**60.** $y^3(10x - x^2)$   567

**61.** $8x^3 + x^2y - x$  −50

**62.** $3x^2(x^2y + y)$   180

## LESSON 9-8 ■ Perfect Squares and Difference of Squares, p. 408

▶ Use these patterns to factor **perfect square trinomials** and polynomials that are the **differences of squares**.

$$a^2 + 2ab + b^2 = (a + b)^2 \qquad a^2 - 2ab + b^2 = (a - b)^2 \qquad a^2 - b^2 = (a + b)(a - b)$$

**Factor each polynomial.**

**63.** $k^2 + 12k - 36$  $(k + 6)^2$

**64.** $c^2 - 20c + 100$  $(c - 10)^2$

**65.** $x^2 - 64$  $(x - 8)(x + 8)$

**66.** $r^2 - 49$  $(r + 7)(r - 7)$

**67.** $m^2 - 10m + 25$  $(m - 5)^2$

**68.** $a^2 + 22a + 121$  $(a + 11)^2$

## CHAPTER INVESTIGATION

**EXTENSION** Another type of orienteering is score orienteering, in which the course can be completed in any order. For the map on page 375, how many different ways can the course be completed? Which route is the shortest? Express this distance in terms of $x$.

## THEME: Geography

The benchmarks and expectations for this extension are as follows.
- Students use the orienteering map shown in the Chapter 9 Opener. They write an expression in terms of $x$ for the approximate distance between the points indicated.
- Students write an expression in terms of $x$ for the length of the course.
- Students use the formula $d = r \cdot t$ to calculate the miles in the course given an average speed and the average time to complete the course.
- Students determine the number of different ways the course shown in the given map can be completed. They determine the shortest route and express that distance in terms of $x$.

# Chapter 9 Assessment

**Simplify.**

1. $12x^2y^3 - 4xy^2 + 8xy^2 - 24x^2y^3$
   $-12x^2y^3 + 4xy^2$

2. $(3a^2b - 2a + 3b) + (4a^2b) + (4a^2b - 3a + 2b)$
   $11a^2b - 5a + 5b$

3. $(6r^2s + 2rs - 3) - (4r^2s - 2rs)$
   $2r^2s + 4rs - 3$

4. $(3a^3)(24a^4)$   $-12a^7$

5. $(24a^3b^4)^2$  $16a^6b^8$

6. $-2b(-4b^2 - b + 3)$  $8b^3 + 2b^2 - 6b$

7. $4(x^2 + xy) - 3(x^2 - xy)$  $x^2 + 7xy$

8. $2n(4n - 1) + 3n(4n - 1)$  $20n^2 - 5n$

9. $(b + 4)(b + 2)$  $b^2 + 6b + 8$

10. $(p - 4)(p + 6)$  $p^2 + 2p - 24$

11. $(a + 8)(a - 8)$  $a^2 - 64$

12. $(k - 5)^2$  $k^2 - 10k + 25$

13. $3(x + 3)(x - 2) - 2(x - 1)(x + 4)$  $x^2 - 3x - 10$

**Use the figure for Exercises 14 and 15.**

14. Write an expression for the perimeter of the rectangle.  $12x + 2y$

15. Write an expression for the area of the rectangle.  $8x^2 + 2xy$

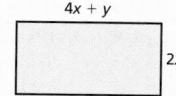

$4x + y$

$2x$

16. If you divide Ana's age by 6, add 5, multiply by 3, and subtract 7, the result is 29. How old is Ana?  42 yr

17. Felix charges customers $25 plus $1.25/h to rent a snow blower. Write a variable expression in simplest form that represents how much Felix will take in if $x$ people rent a snow blower for $y$ hours.  $25x + 1.25xy$

**Factor each polynomial.**

18. $6m + 9$   $3(2m + 3)$

19. $4x^2y - 8x^3y^2$  $4x^2y(1 - 2xy)$

20. $12h^2k^3 + 6hk^2 - 30h^4k$
    $6hk(2hk^2 + k - 5h^3)$

**Evaluate each expression. Let $x = -1$, and $y = 3$.**

21. $14x^2 - xy$  17

22. $-2x^3(y + 24x)$  $-42$

23. $(x - 3)(x + 3)$  $-8$

24. $4y^2(x + 3y)$  288

**Simplify.**

25. $\dfrac{10a^2b^3c}{12a^2b}$  $\dfrac{5b^2c}{6}$

26. $\dfrac{-15p + 20p^2}{25p}$  $\dfrac{-3 + 4p}{5}$

27. $\dfrac{x + x^2 + x^3}{x}$  $1 + x + x^2$

28. $\dfrac{4a^2b + 8a^3b^2}{4a^2}$  $b + 2ab^2$

29. $\dfrac{12x^3y + 3x^2y - 9xy}{3xy}$  $4x^2 + x - 3$

30. $\dfrac{-14a^2b^4 - 21a^3b^5 + 7a^2b^2}{-7a^2b}$  $2b^3 + 3ab^4 - b$

**Factor each polynomial.**

31. $x^2 - 4x + 4$  $(x - 2)^2$

32. $f^2 + 16f + 64$  $(f + 8)^2$

33. $y^2 - 100$  $(y + 10)(y - 10)$

34. $a^2b - 36b$  $b(a + 6)(a - 6)$

35. $t^2 + 25$  not factorable

36. $x^2 - 14x + 49$  $(x - 7)^2$

**Math Online** mathmatters2.com/chapter_assessment

## Assessment Options

Chapter 9 Test A, pages 301–302
Chapter 9 Test B, pages 303–304

## ALTERNATIVE ASSESSMENT

**ALGEBLOCKS** Algeblocks can be used to add, subtract, multiply, or divide polynomials. Have students complete the following activity and record their results on grid paper.

a. Choose one polynomial expression from each set of practice exercises in Lessons 9-1, 9-2, and 9-3.

b. Use Algeblocks to simplify each expression. Draw representations of the Algeblocks on the appropriate mat.

c. Below each drawing, write the numerical and variable expressions for each step.

**RUBRIC** The following rubric is a sample scoring guide.

| Points | Description |
|--------|-------------|
| 4 | Accurately **simplifies three** expressions using both Algeblocks and grid paper, and accurately records steps. |
| 3 | Accurately **simplifies three** expressions using both Algeblocks and grid paper, but makes some **minor errors** when recording steps. |
| 2 | **Simplifies only two** expressions or simplifies three expressions with minor errors using both Algeblocks and grid paper, and makes errors when recording steps. |
| 1 | **Simplifies one** expression using Algeblocks and/or grid paper, and makes errors or does not record steps. |
| 0 | Makes **no attempt** to simplify or model expressions. |

## Teaching Tip

When students are multiplying binomials, as in Exercises 9–13, remind them that there is one special circumstance when the product of two binomials is a binomial, when the binomials differ only in middle sign, as in Exercise 11. Most other times, the product of two binomials will be a trinomial.

## Standardized Test Practice

These two pages contain practice questions in the various formats that can be found on the most frequently given standardized tests.

A student recording sheet for these two pages can be found on p. A1 of the *Chapter 9 Resource Masters.*

## Standardized Test Practice
## Student Recording Sheet

Name _____ Date _____

**Standardized Test Practice**
*Student Record Sheet* (Use with pages 416-417 of the Student Edition.)

**Part 1** *Multiple Choice*
Select the best answer from the choices given and fill in the corresponding oval.

1. Ⓐ Ⓑ Ⓒ Ⓓ   4. Ⓐ Ⓑ Ⓒ Ⓓ   7. Ⓐ Ⓑ Ⓒ Ⓓ   10. Ⓐ Ⓑ Ⓒ Ⓓ
2. Ⓐ Ⓑ Ⓒ Ⓓ   5. Ⓐ Ⓑ Ⓒ Ⓓ   8. Ⓐ Ⓑ Ⓒ Ⓓ   11. Ⓐ Ⓑ Ⓒ Ⓓ
3. Ⓐ Ⓑ Ⓒ Ⓓ   6. Ⓐ Ⓑ Ⓒ Ⓓ   9. Ⓐ Ⓑ Ⓒ Ⓓ   12. Ⓐ Ⓑ Ⓒ Ⓓ

**Part 2** *Short Response/Grid In*
Solve the problem and write your answer in the blank.

For Questions 15, 17, and 23, also enter your answer by writing each number or symbol in a box. Then fill in the corresponding oval for that number or symbol.

13. _____
14. _____
15. _____ (grid in)
16. _____
17. _____ (grid in)
18. _____
19. _____
20. _____
21. _____
22. _____
23. _____ (grid in)
24. _____
25. _____
26. _____
27. _____

**Part 3** *Extended Response*
Record your answers for Question 28 on the back of this paper.

## Additional Practice

See pp. 305–307 in the *Chapter 9 Resource Masters* for additional standardized test practice.

# Standardized Test Practice

**Part 1  Multiple Choice**

**Record your answers on the answer sheet provided by your teacher or on a sheet of paper.**

1. A basketball team scored 70, 65, 75, 70, and 80 points in the first five games of the season. In the sixth game, they scored only 30 points. Which of these measures changed the most as a result of the sixth game? (Lesson 1-2)  A
   Ⓐ mean   Ⓑ median   Ⓒ mode
   Ⓓ They all change the same amount.

2. If 0.00023 is expressed as $2.3 \cdot 10^n$, what is the value of $n$? (Lesson 2-8)  B
   Ⓐ $-5$          Ⓑ $-4$
   Ⓒ $4$           Ⓓ $5$

3. Marcus and Antonio went shopping and spent $122 altogether. Marcus spent $25 less than twice as much as Antonio. How much did Antonio spend? (Lesson 3-4)  A
   Ⓐ $49.00        Ⓑ $73.00
   Ⓒ $73.50        Ⓓ $98.00

4. A company is producing padlocks that operate using a sequence of three different numbers. How many different sequences are there if the numbers can range from 0 through 99? (Lesson 4-6)  C
   Ⓐ 100           Ⓑ 941,094
   Ⓒ 970,200       Ⓓ 1,000,000

5. Which symbol represents the figure? (Lesson 5-2)  D

   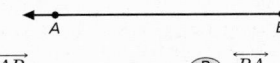

   Ⓐ $\overleftrightarrow{AB}$       Ⓑ $\overrightarrow{BA}$
   Ⓒ $\overrightarrow{AB}$       Ⓓ $\overline{BA}$

6. Find the distance between $R(-3, 2)$ and $S(2, 14)$. (Lesson 6-1)  C
   Ⓐ $\sqrt{13}$       Ⓑ $\sqrt{17}$
   Ⓒ $13$              Ⓓ $17$

7. Which figure has rotational symmetry? (Lesson 7-4)  D
   Ⓐ 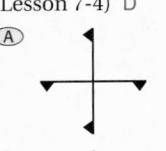      Ⓑ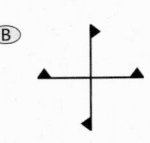
   Ⓒ 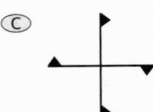      Ⓓ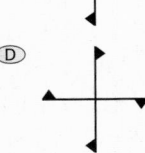

8. What is the slope of a line perpendicular to the line $2x + 3y = 4$? (Lesson 8-1)  D
   Ⓐ $-\dfrac{3}{2}$       Ⓑ $-\dfrac{2}{3}$
   Ⓒ $\dfrac{2}{3}$        Ⓓ $\dfrac{3}{2}$

9. Which graph represents the system of inequalities $y > x + 1$ and $y < -2x - 1$? (Lesson 8-7)  B
   Ⓐ 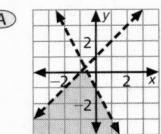      Ⓑ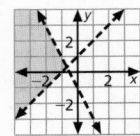
   Ⓒ 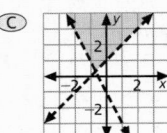      Ⓓ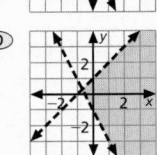

10. What is the product of $(3x^4y^2)^2$ and $4xy^3$? (Lesson 9-2)  A
    Ⓐ $36x^9y^7$        Ⓑ $36x^5y^5$
    Ⓒ $12x^9y^7$        Ⓓ $12x^5y^5$

11. Simplify $\dfrac{y^3z^9}{yz^2}$. (Lesson 9-3)  D
    Ⓐ $y^4z^7$          Ⓑ $y^4z^{11}$
    Ⓒ $y^2z^{11}$       Ⓓ $y^2z^7$

12. Factor $m^2 - 16$. (Lesson 9-8)  C
    Ⓐ $(m - 4)^2$       Ⓑ $(m + 4)^2$
    Ⓒ $(m + 4)(m - 4)$  Ⓓ $4(m - 4)$

## Part 2  Short Response/Grid In

**Record your answers on the answer sheet provided by your teacher or on a sheet of paper.**

13. What is the value of $-18 - (-4) \div 2 + 1$? (Lesson 2-2)  $-15$

14. The length of a side of a square is $6x - 3$. What is the perimeter of the square? (Lesson 2-5)  $24x - 12$

15. What is the least integer that satisfies the inequality $2d + 3 > 2$? (Lesson 3-7)  0

16. What is the least integer that satisfies the equation $x^2 + 3 = 7$? (Lesson 3-8)  $-2$

17. Caroline has 6 nickels, 4 pennies, and 3 dimes in her pocket. She takes one coin from her pocket at random. What is the probability it is a penny or a nickel? (Lesson 4-4)  10/13

18. You are required to read 5 books from a list of 12 great American novels. How many different groups of books can you select? (Lesson 4-7)  792 groups

**Use circle $X$ for Questions 19–21.** (Lesson 5-8)

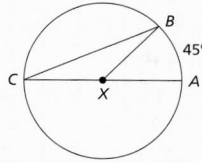

19. Find $m\angle AXB$.  $45°$

20. Find $m\angle ACB$.  $22.5°$

21. Find $m\widehat{ACB}$  $315°$

22. What is the $y$-intercept of the line $5x + 2y = -4$? (Lesson 6-3)  $-2$

23. Assume that $y$ varies directly with $x$. When $x = 6$, $y = 27$. Find $y$ when $x = 10$. (Lesson 6-8)  45

 **Math Online**  mathmatters2.com/standardized_test

24. The current in an electrical circuit varies inversely with the resistance in the circuit. If the current is 1.5 amperes when the resistance is 4 ohms, what is the current when the resistance is 1.2 ohms? (Lesson 6-9)  5 amperes

25. How many lines of symmetry does a square have? (Lesson 7-4)  4 lines of symmetry

26. Simplify $\dfrac{54a^3b^4c^5}{9a^2b^3c^5}$. (Lesson 9-3)  $6ab$

27. In a game show, each question is worth twice as much as the question before it. The fifth question is worth $12,000. How much is the first question worth? (Lesson 9-6)  $750

## Part 3  Extended Response

**Record your answers on a sheet of paper. Show your work.**

28. Tape is placed around a rectangular prism as shown.

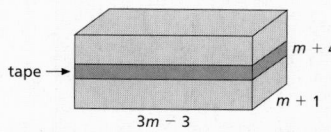

a. Write an expression in simplest form that represents the length of the tape. (Lesson 9-1)  $8m + 2$

b. Write an expression in simplest form that represents the area of the top of the prism. (Lesson 9-5)  $3m^2 - 3$

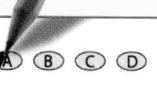

**Test-Taking Tip**

Ⓐ Ⓑ Ⓒ Ⓓ

**Question 28**
When answering open-ended items on standardized tests, follow these steps.
1. Read the item carefully.
2. Show all of your work. You may receive points for items that are only partially correct.
3. Check your work.

## Rubrics

The following rubrics are sample scoring guides for short response and extended response questions

### Short Response

| Points | Description |
|--------|-------------|
| 2 | The student demonstrates a **thorough understanding** of the mathematics of the task. The response may contain minor flaws that do not detract from the demonstration of a thorough understanding. |
| 1 | The student has provided a response that is only **partially correct**. |
| 0 | The student has provided a **completely incorrect** solution or no response at all. |

### Extended Response

| Points | Description |
|--------|-------------|
| 4 | The student demonstrates a **thorough understanding** of the mathematics of the task. The response contains minor flaws that do not detract from the demonstration of a thorough understanding. |
| 3 | The student demonstrates an **understanding** of the mathematics of the task. The response is essentially correct and demonstrates an essential but less than thorough understanding of the mathematics. |
| 2 | The student has demonstrated only a **partial understanding** of the mathematics of the task. Although the student may have used the correct approach to a solution or may have provided a correct solution, the work lacks an essential understanding of the underlying mathematical concepts. |
| 1 | The student has demonstrated a **very limited understanding** of the mathematics of the task. The response is incomplete and exhibits many flaws. |
| 0 | The student has provided a **completely incorrect** solution or no response at all. |

# 10 Three-Dimensional Geometry

| Lesson | Lesson Objectives | Pacing (days) | NCTM Standards | State/Local Objectives |
|--------|-------------------|---------------|----------------|------------------------|
| 10-1 | **Visualize and Represent Solids** *(pp. 422–425)*<br>• Identify properties of three-dimensional figures.<br>• Visualize three-dimensional geometric figures. | 2 | 3, 9, 10 | |
| 10-2 | **Nets and Surface Area** *(pp. 426–429)*<br>• Draw nets for three-dimensional figures.<br>• Use nets to find the surface area of polyhedra. | 2 | 2, 3, 9, 10 | |
| 10-3 | **Surface Area of Three-Dimensional Figures** *(pp. 432–435)*<br>• Find the surface area of three-dimensional figures. | 2 | 2, 3, 9, 10 | |
| 10-4 | **Perspective Drawings** *(pp. 436–439)*<br>• Make one- and two-point perspective drawings.<br>• Locate the vanishing points of perspective drawings. | 1 | 2, 3, 9, 10 | |
| 10-5 | **Isometric Drawings** *(pp. 442–445)*<br>• Visualize and represent objects with isometric drawings. | 1 | 2, 3, 9, 10 | |
| 10-6 | **Orthogonal Drawings** *(pp. 446–449)*<br>• Sketch orthogonal drawings of figures.<br>• Sketch and use foundation drawings. | 1 | 2, 3, 9, 10 | |
| 10-7 | **Volume of Prisms and Pyramids** *(pp. 452–455)*<br>• Use a formula to find the volume of prisms.<br>• Use a formula to find the volume of pyramids. | 2 | 2, 3, 9, 10 | |
| 10-8 | **Volume of Cylinders, Cones, and Spheres** *(pp. 456–459)*<br>• Find the volume of cylinders, cones, and spheres. | 2 | 2, 3, 9, 10 | |
| 10-9 | **Problem Solving Skills: Length, Area, and Volume** *(pp. 462–463)*<br>• Solve a problem using length, area, and volume.<br>• Use an equation or formula to solve a problem. | 1 | 1, 2, 6, 10 | |
| Review | | 1 | | |
| Testing | | 1 | | |

**Key to NCTM Standards:**

*1=Number & Operations, 2=Algebra, 3=Geometry,*
*4=Measurement, 5=Data Analysis & Probability,*
*6=Problem Solving, 7=Reasoning & Proof,*
*8=Communication, 9=Connections, 10=Representation*

**Pacing:** Suggestions for the year can be found on page xvi.

# Chapter Resource Manager

**Chapter 10 Resource Masters**

| Reteaching Activities | Extra Practice | Enrichment | Assessment | Basic Mathematics Review | Study Skills Activities | Lesson Warm-Ups Transparencies | Teaching Transparencies | Technology Activities | Materials Needed |
|---|---|---|---|---|---|---|---|---|---|
| 309 | 310 | 311 | | | | 39 | RF-50, RF-51 | | scissors, tape |
| 312 | 313 | 314 | | | | 39 | TK-9, RF-52 | | grid paper, scissors |
| 315 | 316 | 317 | | 32 | | 40 | RF-52 | 10-3 | box, calculator, ruler, wrapping paper, regulation basketballs |
| 318 | 319 | 320 | | | | 40 | RF-53 | 10-4 | ruler |
| 321 | 322 | 323 | | | | 41 | TK-15, RF-54 | | stacking cubes, isometric grid paper (dot paper) |
| 324 | 325 | 326 | | | | 41 | TK-9 | | stacking cubes |
| 327 | 328 | 329 | | 33 | | 42 | RF-49 | 10-7 | heavy paper, tape, calculator, ruler, dried beans |
| 330 | 331 | 332 | | | | 42 | RF-49 | 10-7 | balloon, tape measure, string, calculator |
| 333 | 334 | 335 | 339–345 | | | 43 | RF-1, RF-49 | | calculator |

**Quick Review Math Handbook, Book 2**

*hot words hot topics*

| *MathMatters 2* Lesson(s) | Hot Topic Lesson(s) |
|---|---|
| **10-1** | **7-1** |
| **10-2, 10-3** | **7-6** |
| **10-4, 10-5, 10-6** | **8-6** |
| **10-7, 10-8** | **7-7** |
| **10-9** | **7-5, 7-7, 8-2, 8-3** |

# Content and Connections

**CHAPTER 10**

## Connections to the Past

**MM1 (Ch. 4):** Identify and classify geometric figures.

**MM1 (Ch. 4):** Use a net to solve a problem.

**MM1 (Ch. 4):** Find the surface area of prisms and cylinders.

**MM1 (Ch. 4):** Make perspective drawings.

**MM1 (Ch. 4):** Visualize and represent shapes with isometric drawings.

**MM1 (Ch. 4):** Make orthogonal drawings.

**MM1 (Ch. 2):** Solve problems using area formulas.

**MM1 (Ch. 4):** Find the volume of prisms, cylinders, pyramids, and cones.

**MM1 (Ch. 2):** Solve problems involving perimeter.

## MathMatters 2 Chapter 10 Highlights

Identify properties of three-dimensional figures. (10-1)

Draw nets and use them to find the surface area of polyhedra. (10-2)

Find the surface area of three-dimensional figures. (10-3)

Make one- and two-point perspective drawings. (10-4)

Visualize and represent objects with isometric drawings. (10-5)

Sketch orthogonal drawings of figures. (10-6)

Use a formula to find the volume of prisms and pyramids. (10-7)

Find the volume of cylinders, cones, and spheres. (10-8)

Solve a problem using length, area, and volume. (10-9)

## Connections to the Future

**MM3 (Ch. 5):** Analyze space figures.

**MM3 (Ch. 7):** Find actual or scale length using scale drawings.

**MM3 (Ch. 5):** Find the surface area of space figures.

**MM3 (Ch. 7):** Use a model or picture.

**MM3 (Ch. 5):** Analyze space figures.

**MM3 (Ch. 7):** Use a model or picture.

**MM3 (Ch. 5):** Apply perimeter, circumference, and area formulas.

**MM3 (Ch. 5):** Find the volume of space figures.

**MM3 (Ch. 5):** Apply perimeter, circumference, and area formulas.

Key

PC  = Previous Course
MM1 = *MathMatters 1*
MM2 = *MathMatters 2*
MM3 = *MathMatters 3*

## Connecting the Strands

| NCTM Strand | Lesson(s) |
|---|---|
| Number & Operations | 10-9 |
| Algebra | 10-2, 10-3, 10-4, 10-5, 10-6, 10-7, 10-8 |
| Geometry | 10-2, 10-3, 10-4, 10-5, 10-6, 10-7, 10-8, 10-9 |
| Problem Solving | 10-9 |
| Connections | 10-1, 10-2, 10-3, 10-4, 10-5, 10-6, 10-7, 10-8 |
| Representation | 10-1, 10-2, 10-3, 10-4, 10-5, 10-6, 10-7, 10-8, 10-9 |

# Ongoing Assessment and Intervention

| | Type | Student Edition | Teacher Resources | Technology/Internet |
|---|---|---|---|---|
| **INTERVENTION** | Ongoing | Are You Ready?, pp. 420–421<br>Check Understanding, pp. 423, 427, 432, 456<br>Review and Practice Your Skills, pp. 430–431, 440–441, 450–451, 460–461<br>Mid-Chapter Quiz, p. 441 | Lesson Warm-Ups Transparencies, pp. WU-39, WU-40, WU-41, WU-42, WU-43<br>Quick Assessment, *ATE* pp. 419, 424, 428, 434, 438, 444, 448, 454, 458, 463 | mathmatters2.com/extra_examples<br>mathmatters2.com/self_check_quiz |
| | Mixed Review | pp. 425, 429, 435, 439, 445, 449, 455, 459, 463 | | |
| | Error Analysis | You Make the Call, pp. 424, 445 | Teaching Tip, *ATE* pp. 452, 462 | |
| **ASSESSMENT** | Standardized Test Practice | pp. 468–469<br>Preparing for Standardized Tests, pp. 627–644 | Standardized Test Practice, *CRM* pp. 343–345 | mathmatters2.com/standardized_test |
| | Open-Ended Assessment | Chapter Investigation, pp. 419, 425, 439, 455, 466 | Chapter Investigation, *ATE* p. 466<br>Alternative Assessment, *ATE* p. 467 | |
| | Chapter Assessment | Chapter Review, pp. 464–466<br>Chapter Assessment, p. 467 | Multiple-Choice Tests (Forms A and B), *CRM* pp. 339–342 | mathmatters2.com/chapter_assessment |

**Key to Abbreviations:** *ATE* = Annotated Teacher's Edition, *CRM* = Chapter Resource Masters

## Additional Intervention

***Basic Mathematics Review*** includes 80 lessons, consisting of an instructional page and a test page. This workbook also features a pretest, posttest, table of measurement equivalents, and calculator appendices.

## ExamView® Pro

Use ExamView® Pro Testmaker CD-ROM to:
- Create **multiple versions** of tests.
- Create **modified** tests for *inclusion* students with one mouse click.
- **Edit** existing questions and **add** your own questions.
- Build tests aligned with **state standards** using built-in **state curriculum correlations**.
- Change **English** tests to **Spanish** with one mouse click and vice versa.

# Three-Dimensional Geometry

## THEME: History

History is a record of significant facts, events, and people. The study of history includes architecture, politics, music, population, language, religion, and mathematics. Specifically, the history of mathematics stretches to every part of the world and spans over thousands of years.

Three-dimensional geometry has been studied since ancient times. Consequently, people from every culture have required three-dimensional geometry to design shelters, clothing, and storage containers.

- **Urban planners** (page 431) supervise the construction of buildings, roads, bridges, and other structures within a city. Because it is important to maintain historically significant elements, while providing for the needs of a city, history plays its part in a city's development.

- **Exhibit designers** (page 451) create images and displays that show a product, historical event, or structure that is pleasing to one's eye.

Math Online

mathmatters2.com/chapter_theme

**418**

### Chapter Investigation

Use the Internet and other resources to locate additional information about a timeline of mathematicians.

## Mathematicians throughout History

| Mathematician | Life span | Accomplishment |
|---|---|---|
| Archimedes | c.298 –212 B.C. | Greatest mathematician of ancient times. Made contributions in geometry. |
| Easley, Annie | 1933– | Developed computer code used to identify energy conversion systems for NASA. |
| Euclid | c.325 –265 B.C. | Wrote *The Elements*, 13 books covering geometry and number theory. |
| Gauss, Carl Friedrich | 1777–1855 | Published treatise on Number Theory. Discovered the asteroid Ceres. |
| Hypatia | c.370–415 | She is considered the first woman of mathematicians. |
| Khayyam, Omar | c.1048–1131 | Persian mathematician, astronomer and poet. Revised the Arabic calendar. Solved cubic equations through geometry. |
| Lovelace, Ada Byron | 1815–1852 | Suggested that Babbage's first "computer" calculate and play music. |
| Pascal, Blaise | 1623–1662 | Invented and sold the first adding machine in 1645. Developed probability theory. |
| Pythagoras of Samos | c.560 –c.480 B.C. | His theorem showed the existence of irrational numbers. |

(c. stands for *circa*, meaning *about* or *approximately*)

### Data Activity: Mathematicians throughout History

**Use the table for Questions 1–4.**

1. How long did Pythagoras live?  80 yr

2. Who is considered the greatest mathematician of ancient times?
Archimedes

3. How many of these mathematicians did work with number theory? Who were they?  2; Euclid and Gauss

4. List the names of mathematicians in the table with whom you are familiar. Discuss with a partner one or two other accomplishments credited to each person on your list.
Answers will vary.

Gauss

### CHAPTER INVESTIGATION

Many people have contributed to the modern understanding of geometry. By studying the work of early mathematicians, you can develop a better understanding of mathematical concepts.

#### *Working Together*

Design a timeline of significant mathematicians who made contributions to geometry. Use the timeline to understand how mathematics influenced life throughout history. Use the Chapter Investigation icons to guide you to a complete timeline.

Pascal

Chapter 10 **Three-Dimensional Geometry**  419

---

## Data Activity

Over recorded time, scholars were often accomplished in many academic areas. Apollonius of Perga (c. 225 BCE) called the Great Geometer, was a mathematician of Ancient Greece who also made contributions to astronomy. Alhazen of Basra (10th century) was an Arab scientist and natural philosopher, who made contributions in optics, astronomy, and mathematics.

Students should answer Questions 1–4 to get a capsule version of the accomplishments of the nine mathematicians of note listed in the table.

### Extend the Data Activity
**Student Portfolio** Students can choose a particular historical era, such as the Renaissance (14th-16th centuries), and research its famed mathematicians. Or, students can choose a particular culture and research its noted mathematicians and their contributions.

## Chapter Investigation

### As an Overarching Problem
Display pictures of and some information about a few famous mathematicians. Discuss their contributions to mathematics and why each contribution was important. Students will continue to work on the investigation as they complete the exercises identified by the Investigation icon that is found throughout the chapter. These exercises will guide students through the task described in *Working Together*.

### As a Chapter Project
The goal of this project is for students to write a report about how the study of mathematics influences history. Students can use the Team Project Planner on page 337 and the Project Planning Calendar on page 338 in the *Chapter 10 Resource Masters* to complete the project. Benchmarks **a, b,** and **c** should be completed after the lesson listed in parentheses has been studied. Benchmark **d** should be completed at the end of the chapter.

---

## Project Planning Calendar

Name _____  Date _____

**CHAPTER 10  PROJECT PLANNING CALENDAR**

Benchmarks
a. Research ten mathematicians. Record the name, accomplishment, dates of birth and death, date of accomplishment and country of birth for each mathematician *(Lesson 10-1)*
b. Draw a line segment about 10 in. long across the center of a piece of paper with an arrowhead at each end. Place the name and accomplishment of each mathematician you researched on the timeline in chronological order. Label appropriately. Be sure the distances between the years recorded on your timeline are in proportion. *(Lesson 10-4)*
c. Research a significant historical event that was _____ on your timeline.

PROJECT GOAL
To write a report about how the study of mathematics influences history.

## Group Project Planner

Name _____  Date _____

**CHAPTER 10  GROUP PROJECT PLANNER**

Assignment _____    Objective _____
_____    _____
_____    _____
_____    _____

Group Members    Assigned Roles
1) _____
2) _____
3) _____
4) _____
5) _____

_____ dlines    Done

## Refresher Skills

The skills on these two pages are skills that have been presented in earlier chapters of this book or in previous math courses. Continuous review of basic math skills will make stronger math students. These skills are identified as necessary to be successful in Chapter 10.

### Skills Correlation Chart

| Skill | Lesson Number |
|---|---|
| Perimeter Formulas | 10-9 |
| Area Formulas | 10-2, 10-3, 10-5, 10-6, 10-7, 10-8 |
| Volume Formulas | 10-7, 10-8 |

### Vocabulary

perimeter     area     volume

## Chalkboard Examples

### Perimeter Formulas
The perimeter of a circle, called *circumference*, *C*, is expressed in terms of the circle's diameter *d*, $C = \pi d$, or radius *r*, $C = 2\pi r$, where $\pi \approx 3.14$.
Find, to the nearest tenth of a foot, the circumference of a circle with radius 4 ft.
$C = 2\pi r$
$\approx 2(3.14)(4)$
$\approx 25.1$ ft

### Area Formulas
The area of a trapezoid is given in terms of its altitude, *h*, and its bases, $b_1$ and $b_2$.
Find the area of the trapezoid shown.
$A = \frac{1}{2}h(b_1 + b_2)$
$= \frac{1}{2}(10)(14 + 21)$
$= 175$ ft$^2$

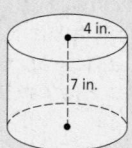

### Volume Formulas
The volume formula $V = B \cdot h$ applies to a right cylinder, which has a circular base.
Find the volume of the cylinder shown.
$V = B \cdot h$
$V = \pi r^2 \cdot h$
$\approx 3.14 \cdot 4^2 \cdot 7$
$\approx 351.7$ in.$^3$

The skills on these two pages are ones you have already learned. Use the examples to refresh your memory and complete the exercises. For additional practice on these and more prerequisite skills, see pages 576–584.

### PERIMETER FORMULAS

In this chapter you will work with three-dimensional solids. Formulas that apply to two-dimensional shapes can be a foundation for understanding solid geometry.

| Perimeter of a square | Perimeter of a rectangle | Perimeter of any polygon |
|---|---|---|
| $P = 4s$, where $s$ = side length | $P = 2l + 2w$, where $l$ = length and $w$ = width | $P$ = sum of the lengths of the sides |

### Examples
**Find the perimeter of each figure.**

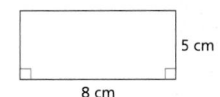

$P = 2(8) + 2(5)$
$P = 16 + 10$
$P = 26$ cm

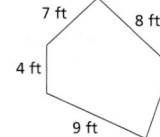

$P = 4 + 7 + 8 + 6 + 9$
$P = 34$ ft

**Find the perimeter of each figure.**

**1.**
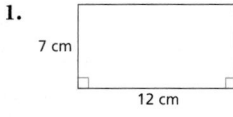
7 cm
12 cm
38 cm

**2.**
5 in.
7 in.     8 in.
5 in.
12 in.     9 in.
46 in.

**3.**
12 m     15 m
18 m
45 m

**4.**
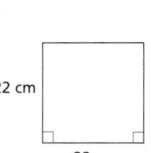
22 cm
22 cm
88 cm

**5.**
6.5 m     6.5 m
6.5 m     6.5 m
6.5 m
32.5 m

**6.**
18 yd
11 yd     9 yd
24 yd
62 yd

### AREA FORMULAS

| Area of a rectangle or square | Area of a parallelogram | Area of a triangle |
|---|---|---|
| $A = l \cdot w$, where $l$ = length and $w$ = width | $A = b \cdot h$, where $b$ = length of the base and $h$ = height | $A = \frac{1}{2}bh$, where $b$ = length of the base and $h$ = height |

## Teaching Tip

When students are working with an area formula that contains the factor $\frac{1}{2}$, such as in the area of a triangle, $A = \frac{1}{2}bh$, elicit that in the calculation, the factor $\frac{1}{2}$ is used exactly once. For example, $\frac{1}{2} \cdot 6 \cdot 10$ can be calculated in either of two ways: take $\frac{1}{2}$ of 6 and multiply the result by 10, or take $\frac{1}{2}$ of 10 and multiply the result by 6. Also, note with students that in a calculation involving $\frac{1}{2}$ where the first dimension is an odd number, such as in $\frac{1}{2} \cdot 5 \cdot 10$, students might do the calculation in either of the following two ways to avoid fractions: multiply 5 by 10 and then take $\frac{1}{2}$ of the product, or first take $\frac{1}{2}$ of the even factor and then multiply the result by the odd factor.

## Examples

**Find the area of each figure.**

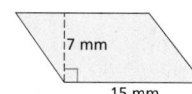

7 mm
15 mm

$A = 15 \cdot 7$

$A = 105 \text{ mm}^2$

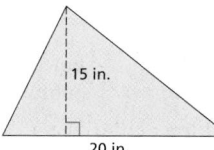

15 in.
20 in.

$A = \frac{1}{2}(20)(15)$

$A = \frac{1}{2}(300)$

$A = 150 \text{ in.}^2$

**Find the area of each figure.**

**7.**

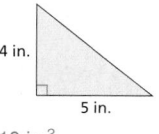

4 in.
5 in.

10 in.²

**8.**

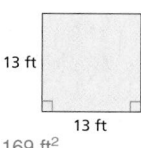

13 ft
13 ft

169 ft²

**9.**

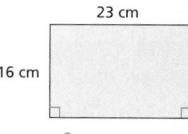

23 cm
16 cm

368 cm²

**10.**

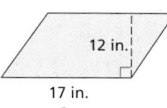

12 in.
17 in.

204 in.²

**11.**

32 m
45 m

720 m²

**12.**

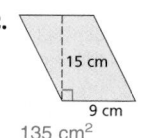

15 cm
9 cm

135 cm²

## VOLUME FORMULAS

| **Volume of a rectangular prism** | **Volume of a triangular prism** |
|---|---|
| $V = B \cdot h$, where $B$ = area of the base and $h$ = height | $V = B \cdot h$, where $B$ = area of the base and $h$ = height |

### Examples

**Find the area of the base and substitute that measure to find the volume.**

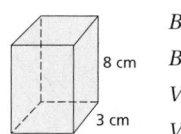

8 cm
3 cm
4 cm

$B = 3 \cdot 4$

$B = 12$

$V = 12 \cdot 8$

$V = 96 \text{ cm}^3$

9 ft
5 ft
8 ft

$B = \frac{1}{2}(5)(8)$

$B = \frac{1}{2}(40)$

$B = 20$

$V = 20 \cdot 9 = 180 \text{ ft}^3$

**Find the volume of each figure.**

**13.**

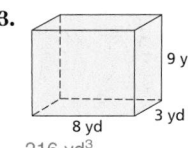

9 yd
8 yd
3 yd

216 yd³

**14.**

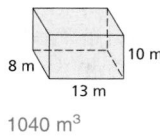

10 m
8 m
13 m

1040 m³

**15.**

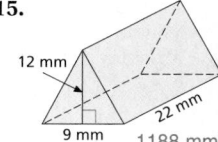

12 mm
22 mm
9 mm

1188 mm³

## QUICK ASSESSMENT

Ask the following questions to determine if students have mastered the basic skills reviewed on these pages.

**If the unit of measure for the dimensions of a two-dimensional figure is *feet*, in what unit is:**

**1.** the perimeter?   feet

**2.** the area?   square feet

**5.** If the unit of measure for the dimensions of a three-dimensional figure is feet, in what unit is the volume?   cubic feet

**6.** Explain why the single formula $V = B \cdot h$ can be used to find the volume of both a rectangular prism and a triangular prism.
The difference between types of prisms is in the shape of the base. Regardless of the shape of the base, the volume of a figure is calculated as the product of the area of the base and the altitude.

## ADDITIONAL PRACTICE

Refer to the Prerequisite Skills lessons beginning on page 576 for more practice.

## Teaching Tip

You might suggest that students use the format shown below when applying the volume formula $V = B \cdot h$.

**Example:** Find the volume of a triangular prism whose altitude is 10 ft and whose triangular base has these dimensions: base = 4 ft and height = 7 ft.

Write the general volume formula.          $V = B \cdot h$

Replace $B$ by the particular area formula.          $V = \left(\frac{1}{2}bh\right)h$

Substitute the known values.          $V = \left(\frac{1}{2} \cdot 4 \cdot 7\right) \cdot 10$

Do the calculations.          $V = (14) \cdot 10 = 140 \text{ ft}^3$

## NCTM Standards/Strands
- Geometry
- Representation
- Connections

## Vocabulary

cylinder: axis, right cylinder,
   oblique cylinder
cone: axis, right cone,
   oblique cone
sphere: center of sphere
polyhedron: faces, edges, vertices
prism: bases
pyramid: faces, vertex, base
lateral face, lateral edge

## Tools/Materials Needed

scissors        tape
large metal washers

## Lesson Resources

Warm-up Transparency 39
Transparency RF-50, 51
Reteaching 10-1
Extra Practice 10-1
Enrichment 10-1

## Getting Started

### 5-MINUTE WARM-UP

**Draw each figure.** See students'
work.
1. right triangle
2. isosceles triangle
3. rectangle      4. hexagon

### Introduction to Lesson 10-1

A way to introduce students to the
idea of oblique solids is to use a tall
stack of large metal washers. Stack
all the washers on a table top to
form a right cylinder. Use a pencil
through the center of the washers
to represent the cylinder's axis. Tilt
the pencil to one side until it makes
about a 60° or 70° angle with the
table top. The washers should shift
to form an oblique cylinder.

---

# 10-1 Visualize and Represent Solids

**Goals**
- Identify properties of three-dimensional figures.
- Visualize three-dimensional geometric figures.

**Applications**    Packaging, History, Sports, Machinery, Recreation

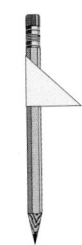

**Use a pencil, paper, tape and scissors.**

1. Cut a small rectangle, a small right triangle and a small semicircle out of the paper.    Observe students' work.

2. Tape the rectangle near the top of the pencil. Spin the pencil on the tip to visualize what solid is created by spinning the rectangle. Describe the solid.   cylinder

3. Repeat Question 2 for the right triangle.    cone

4. Repeat Question 2 for the semicircle.    sphere

### ■ BUILD UNDERSTANDING

Some three-dimensional figures have both flat and curved surfaces.

A **cylinder** has a curved surface and two congruent circular bases that lie in parallel planes. The *axis* is a segment that joins the centers of the bases. If the axis forms a right angle with the bases, it is a *right* cylinder. If not, it is an *oblique* cylinder.

A **cone** has a curved surface and one circular base. The *axis* is a segment that joins the vertex to the center of the base. If the axis forms a right angle with the base, it is a *right* cone. Otherwise, it is an *oblique* cone.

A **sphere** is the set of all points that are a given distance from a given point, called the **center** of the sphere.

A **polyhedron** (plural: *polyhedra*) is a closed, three-dimensional figure made up of polygonal surfaces. The polygonal surfaces are **faces**. Two faces meet, or intersect, at an **edge**. A point at which three or more edges intersect is a **vertex**.

A **prism** is a polyhedron with two identical parallel faces called *bases*. The other faces are parallelograms. A prism is named according to the shape of its base.

A **pyramid** is a polyhedron with only one base. The other faces are triangles that meet at a **vertex**. A pyramid is named by the shape of its base.

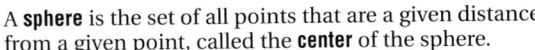

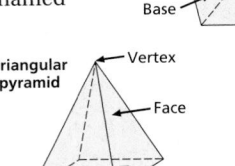

**422**    Chapter 10 **Three-Dimensional Geometry**

---

## Teaching Tip

Have students compare a right circular cylinder and a right circular cone, noting that when the two figures have congruent circular bases and are of equal height, the cone fits inside of the cylinder so that the volume of the cone is one-third of the volume of the corresponding cylinder.
Volume of cylinders and cones will be presented in Lesson 10-8.

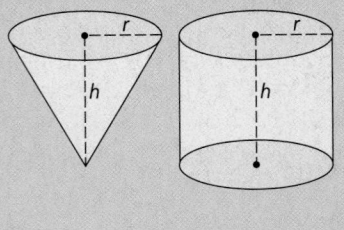

In prisms and pyramids, the faces that are not bases are *lateral faces*. The edges of these faces are *lateral edges*. Lateral faces can be either parallel or intersecting. The lateral edges can be intersecting or parallel. *Skew* edges are noncoplanar.

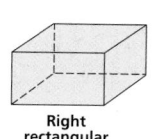

**Right rectangular prism**

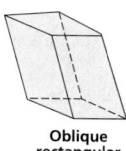

**Oblique rectangular prism**

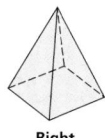

**Right square pyramid**

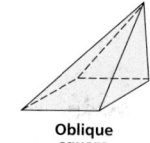

**Oblique square pyramid**

**Check Understanding**

Why is a cube also a rectangular prism?

because a square is a rectangle and a rectangle is a parallelogram

## Example 1

**PACKAGING** Identify each feature of the shoe box.

a. the shape of the shoe box
b. a pair of bases
c. a pair of parallel edges
d. a pair of intersecting edges
e. a pair of skew edges
f. a pair of intersecting faces

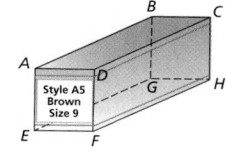

### Solution

a. The shoe box is a right rectangular prism.
b. Two bases are *ADFE* and *BCHG*.
c. $\overline{DC}$ and $\overline{FH}$ are parallel edges.
d. $\overline{GH}$ and $\overline{FH}$ are intersecting edges.
e. $\overline{AD}$ and $\overline{CH}$ are skew edges.
f. *ABCD* and *CDFH* are intersecting faces.

## Example 2

**Draw a right triangular prism.**

### Solution

*Step 1* Draw two congruent triangles.

*Step 2* Draw segments that connect the corresponding vertices of the triangles. Use dashed segments to show the edges that cannot be seen.

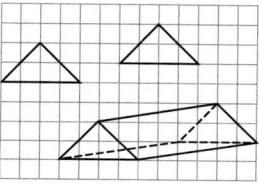

### TRY THESE EXERCISES

**Identify each figure and name its base(s).**

1.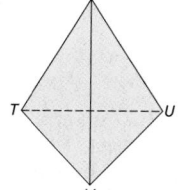

Right rectangular prism; any face can be considered a base.

2. 

triangular pyramid; base △*TUV*

**Math Online** mathmatters2.com/extra_examples

Lesson 10-1 **Visualize and Represent Solids** | 423

## Chalkboard Examples

**Supplementary Example 1**
**Consider the figure shown.**

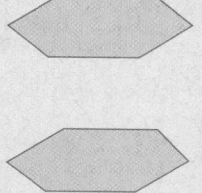

a. Identify the figure.
   triangular prism
b. Name its base(s).
   △*ABC* and △*DEF*
c. If *AD* = 7 cm, name all other edges that measure 7 cm. $\overline{BE}$ and $\overline{CF}$
d. Name a pair of intersecting edges. **Sample answer:** $\overline{AC}$ and $\overline{CF}$
e. Name a pair of skew edges. Sample answer: $\overline{AD}$ and $\overline{EF}$
f. Name a pair of intersecting faces. **Sample answer:** △*ABC* and rectangle *ACFD*

**Supplementary Example 2**
Draw a right hexagonal prism.

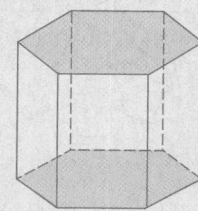

**Step 1**
Draw a hexagon. Then draw a translation of that same hexagon several units straight down.

**Step 2**
Draw segments to connect corresponding vertices of the hexagons. Use dotted segments for hidden edges.

## Teaching Tip

As students consider Example 1, remind them that in order for two lines to be parallel, they must be coplanar. So, coplanar edges $\overline{AB}$ and $\overline{DC}$ are parallel and coplanar edges $\overline{DC}$ and $\overline{FH}$ are parallel, but noncoplanar edges $\overline{AB}$ and $\overline{DF}$ are skew.
Have students give different examples from those given in the text that would satisfy the various requirements.

## QUICK ASSESSMENT

Ask the following questions to determine if students understand the content presented in this lesson.

**1.** How is a right circular cylinder different from an oblique cylinder?  right circular cylinder has circular bases, oblique cylinder has oval (elliptical) bases; axis of right circular cylinder is perpendicular to diameter of circular base, axis of oblique cylinder is not perpendicular to axis of oval base.

**2.** How are the lateral faces of a prism different from those of a pyramid?  lateral faces of a prism are parallelograms, those of a pyramid are triangles

## ASSIGNMENT GUIDE

**Basic:** 1–40, 47–60
**Enriched:** 1–60

### Reteaching Worksheet 10-1

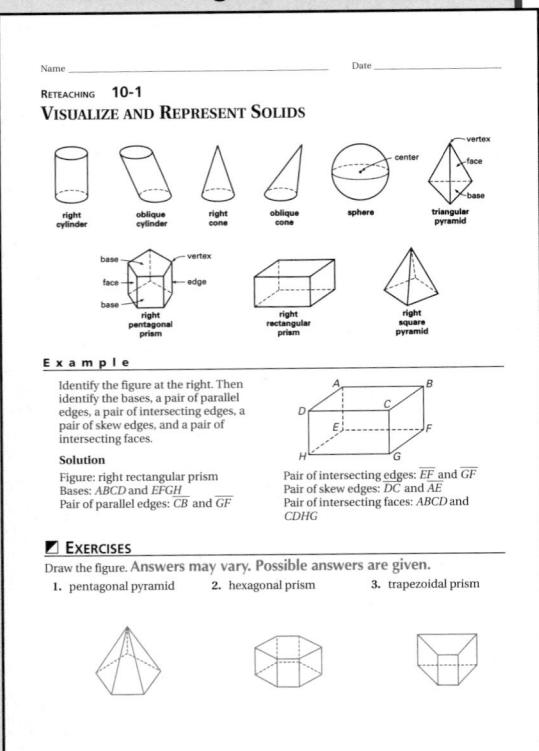

Name _____ Date _____

RETEACHING  **10-1**
**VISUALIZE AND REPRESENT SOLIDS**

**Example**

Identify the figure at the right. Then identify the bases, a pair of parallel edges, a pair of intersecting edges, a pair of skew edges, and a pair of intersecting faces.

**Solution**
Figure: right rectangular prism
Bases: *ABCD* and *EFGH*
Pair of parallel edges: $\overline{CB}$ and $\overline{GF}$

Pair of intersecting edges: $\overline{EF}$ and $\overline{GF}$
Pair of skew edges: $\overline{DC}$ and $\overline{AE}$
Pair of intersecting faces: *ABCD* and *CDHG*

■ **EXERCISES**
Draw the figure. Answers may vary. Possible answers are given.
**1.** pentagonal pyramid  **2.** hexagonal prism  **3.** trapezoidal prism

---

**If possible, identify a pair of parallel faces, parallel edges, intersecting faces, and intersecting edges for each figure.**

**3.** the figure in Exercise 1
For 3–4, answers will vary, but there are no parallel faces or edges for Exercise 4.
**4.** the figure in Exercise 2

**Draw each figure.**
For 5–8, see additional answers.
**5.** right circular cone
**6.** oblique rectangular prism
**7.** right hexagonal prism
**8.** right square pyramid

▰ **PRACTICE EXERCISES** • For Extra Practice, see page 616.

**Identify each figure and name its base(s).**

**9.**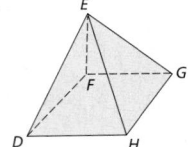
right square pyramid; square *DFGH*

**10.**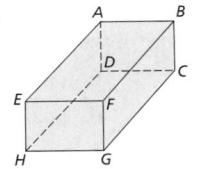
right rectangular prism; any face is a base

**11.**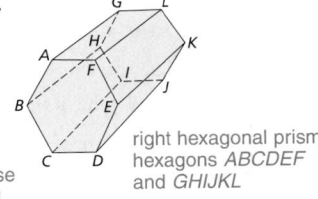
right hexagonal prism
hexagons *ABCDEF* and *GHIJKL*

**Identify a pair of parallel faces, parallel edges, intersecting faces, and intersecting edges for each figure.**  For 12–14, answers will vary, but there are no parallel faces for Exercise 12.

**12.** the figure in Exercise 9
**13.** the figure in Exercise 10
**14.** the figure in Exercise 11

**Draw each figure.**  For 15–20, see additional answers.
**15.** right rectangular prism
**16.** oblique square pyramid
**17.** oblique cone
**18.** right cylinder
**19.** sphere
**20.** right triangular prism

**21. WRITING MATH** Describe ways in which prisms and pyramids are similar. Describe differences between prisms and pyramids.  See additional answers.

**RECREATION** If possible, identify the geometric figure represented and give the number of faces, vertices and edges.
For 22–28, see additional answers.
**22.** tennis ball can
**23.** six-sided number cube
**24.** basketball
**25.** ice cream cone
**26.** rectangular gym
**27.** one-person tent
**28.** Which of the figures in Exercises 22–27 are polyhedra? Explain.

**MACHINERY** A cutting drill uses different bits to cut designs into furniture. Describe the geometric figure cut when using each of the following bits.

**29.**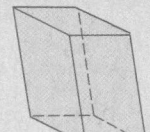
cylinder

**30.**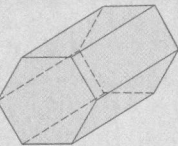
cone

**31.**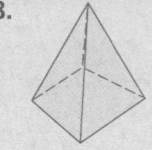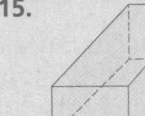
cone with cut-off tip

**32. YOU MAKE THE CALL** Niki says that a right square pyramid is a polyhedron but an oblique square pyramid is not a polyhedron. Daniella says both figures are polyhedra since their faces are polygonal. Who is correct and why?
Daniella. Both are made up of polygons.

## ADDITIONAL ANSWERS

**5.**
**6.**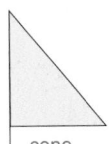
**7.**
**8.**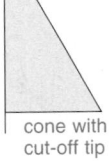
**15.**

**16.**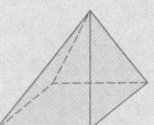
**17.**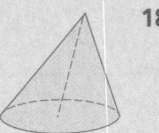
**18.**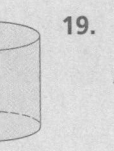
**19.**
**20.**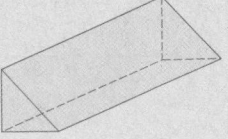

**Decide whether each statement is *true* or *false*. Explain.**
For 33–36, see additional answers.

**33.** A cube is a polyhedron.

**34.** A polyhedron can have exactly three faces.

**35.** A polyhedron can have a circular face.

**36.** A polyhedron can have exactly four faces.

**State whether each solid is a polyhedron. Explain.** For 37–39, see additional answers.

**37.**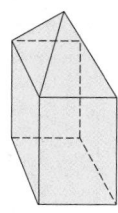

**38.**

**39.**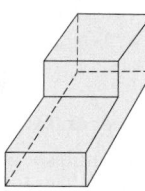

**40. HISTORY** The pyramids of Giza in Egypt are one of the seven wonders of the ancient world. Use the photo on page 433 to sketch the pyramid on paper. Then label the vertices.
See additional answers.

■ **EXTENDED PRACTICE EXERCISES**

 **SPREADSHEET** Create a spreadsheet for the following figures. List figures in Column A, the number of faces ($F$) in Column B, the number of vertices ($V$) in Column C, and the number of edges ($E$) in Column D. In Column E, write a formula to calculate the quantity $F + V - E$.
For 41–44, observe students' work.

**41.** rectangular prism  6, 8, 12; 2

**42.** hexagonal prism  8, 12, 18; 2

**43.** pentagonal pyramid  6, 6, 10; 2

**44.** square pyramid  5, 5, 8; 2

**45.** Compare your results for Exercises 41–44. Make a generalization about the relationship between the numbers of faces, edges and vertices in a polyhedron. The number of edges in a polyhedron is two less than the sum of the faces and vertices.

 **46. CHAPTER INVESTIGATION** Research ten mathematicians. Record the name, accomplishment, dates of birth and death, date of accomplishment and country of birth for each mathematician.  Answers will vary.

■ **MIXED REVIEW EXERCISES**

**Find the slope of the line containing the given points. Identify any vertical or horizontal lines.** (Lesson 6-2)

**47.** (4, 2), (6, 1)  $-\frac{1}{2}$

**48.** (9, 3), (−2, 4)  $-\frac{1}{11}$

**49.** (−1, 3), (2, 8)  $\frac{5}{3}$

**50.** (5, −4), (7, 7)  $\frac{11}{2}$

**51.** (−3, −5), (−3, −2)  vertical line; undefined

**52.** (4, −5), (−2, 3)  $-\frac{4}{3}$

**53.** (−2, 6), (4, 6)  0; horizontal line

**54.** (−1, −1), (−7, −7)  1

**In the figure, $\overleftrightarrow{RS} \parallel \overleftrightarrow{MN}$ and $m\angle 4 = 80°$. Find each measure.** (Lesson 5-3)

**55.** $m\angle 1$  80°

**56.** $m\angle 2$  100°

**57.** $m\angle 3$  100°

**58.** $m\angle 5$  80°

**59.** $m\angle 6$  100°

**60.** $m\angle 7$  100°

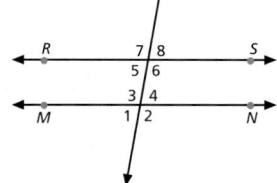

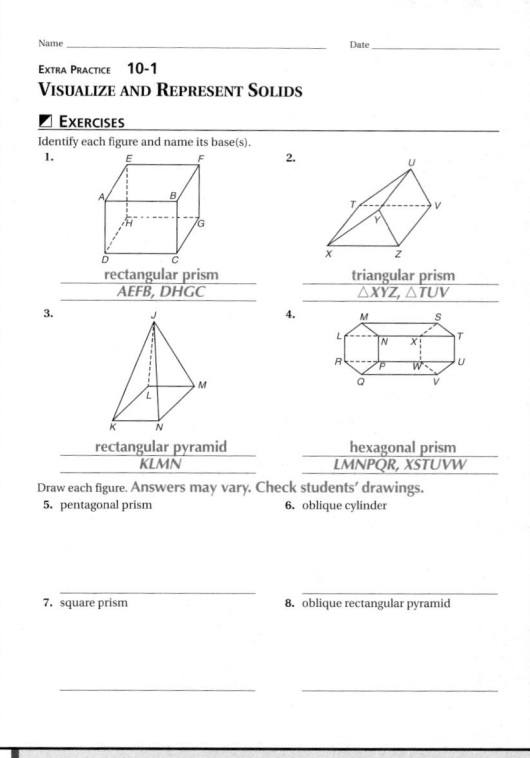
**36.** True. A triangular pyramid has four faces.

**37.** Yes. Every face is polygonal.

**38.** No. Not all faces are polygonal.

**39.** Yes. Every face is polygonal.

**40.**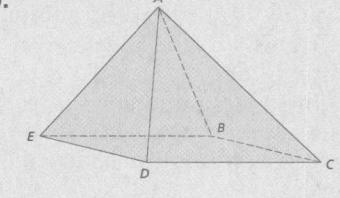

**21.** Prisms and pyramids are both polyhedrons and are both named by the shape of their base. However, prisms have two parallel bases and pyramids have one base. The lateral faces of a prism are parallelograms and the lateral faces of a pyramid are triangles.

**22.** right cylinder; 2 circular faces, vertices or edges

**23.** cube or rectangular prism; 6 faces, 8 vertices, and 12 edges

**24.** sphere; no faces, vertices, or edges

**25.** right cone; no faces, vertices, or edges

**26.** rectangular pyramid; 6 faces, 8 vertices, and 12 edges

**27.** right square pyramid; 5 faces, 5 vertices, and 8 edges

**28.** A six-sided number cube, a rectangular gym, and a square pyramid tent are polyhedra since all of their faces are polygonal.

**33.** True. A cube is a closed three-dimensional figure made up of square faces.

**34.** False. It is impossible for a polyhedron to have only three faces.

**35.** False. The faces must be polygonal.

### Vocabulary

net          surface area

### Tools/Materials Needed

grid paper          scissors

### Lesson Resources

Warm-up Transparency 39
Transparency TK-9, RF-52
Reteaching 10-2
Extra Practice 10-2
Enrichment 10-2

## Getting Started

### 5-MINUTE WARM-UP

**Tell how many faces each figure has. Identify the nature of the faces.**

1. cube    **6 congruent square faces**
2. right rectangular prism    **6 faces: 2 congruent rectangles as bases, 4 rectangles as lateral faces**
3. right square pyramid    **5 faces: one square base, 4 congruent isosceles triangles as lateral faces**

### Introduction to Lesson 10-2

After students have seen that the first given net folds into a cube, ask them if they think relocating one square of the net will also result in a cube. For example, have students consider the configuration shown here, allowing them to discover their own fold lines.    **does make a cube**

---

# 10-2 Nets and Surface Area

**Goals**
- Draw nets for three-dimensional figures.
- Use nets to find the surface area of polyhedra.

**Applications**    Retail, History, Machinery, Architecture

**Use grid paper and scissors.**

1. Copy the figure shown on grid paper, cut it out and fold along the dotted lines.    Observe students' work.

2. What type of polyhedron is formed?    cube

3. Draw a different arrangement of the six squares so when you cut and fold the figure it makes the same solid as the one created in Question 2.
   Answers will vary.

4. Test the figure drawn in Question 3.    Observe students' work.

5. Discuss with your classmates those figures that did create the same solid and those that did not.    Observe students' work.

### BUILD UNDERSTANDING

A **net** is a two-dimensional pattern that can be folded to form a three-dimensional figure. A three-dimensional figure can have more than one net.

### Example 1

**What three-dimensional figure is represented by each net?**

a. 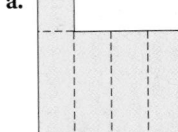    b. 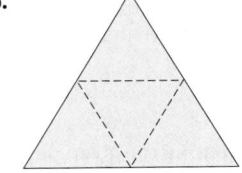    c.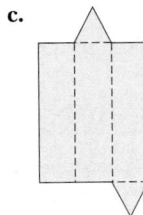

### Solution

Visualize each net being folded to form a three-dimensional figure.

a. This figure will have four rectangular sides and two parallel square bases. It is a rectangular prism.

b. This figure will have three triangular sides and a triangular base. It is a triangular pyramid.

c. This figure will have three rectangular sides and two parallel triangular bases. It is a triangular prism.

## Alternative Assessment

**STUDENT PORTFOLIO** Continuing with the suggested extension of the opening activity, have students consider other configurations of 6 squares and ask if these configurations could be folded into a cube. For example, you might present the configurations shown below.

Yes, folds into a cube 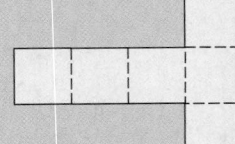    No, does not fold into a cube.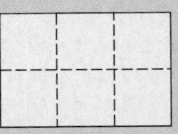

## Example 2

**Draw a net for each three-dimensional figure.**

**a.** right square pyramid

**b.** right cylinder

### Solution

**a.**

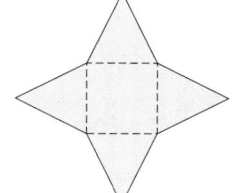

**b.**

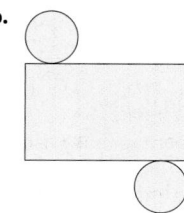

Nets can be used to calculate the surface area of certain three-dimensional figures. The **surface area** of a figure is the sum of the areas of all its bases and faces.

## Example 3

**RETAIL** Find the minimum amount of gift wrapping paper needed to cover a box with dimensions 1 ft by 2 ft by 3 in.

### Solution

Draw the net for the rectangular prism, and calculate the areas of the six sides. Use the formula $A = l \cdot w$.

The top and bottom of the box are rectangles with dimensions 1 ft by 2 ft.

$l \cdot w + l \cdot w$      Find the combined surface area.
$2 \cdot 1 + 2 \cdot 1 = 4 \text{ ft}^2$

The left and right sides of the box are rectangles with dimensions 2 ft by 3 in.

$3 \text{ in.} \cdot \dfrac{1 \text{ ft}}{12 \text{ in.}} = 0.25 \text{ ft}$    Convert 3 in. to feet.
$l \cdot w + l \cdot w$      Find the combined surface area.
$2 \cdot 0.25 + 2 \cdot 0.25 = 1 \text{ ft}^2$

The front and back of the box are rectangles with dimensions 1 ft by 3 in. Use 0.25 ft for 3 in.

$l \cdot w + l \cdot w$
$1 \cdot 0.25 + 1 \cdot 0.25 = 0.5 \text{ ft}^2$

The total surface area is the sum of the areas of the sides.

$4 + 1 + 0.5 = 5.5 \text{ ft}^2$

So the box will require at least 5.5 ft² of gift wrapping paper.

Lesson 10-2 **Nets and Surface Area** | **427**

---

### Problem Solving Tip

If you are unable to figure out the three-dimensional figure a net represents, copy the net, cut it out and fold it to find the answer.

3 in.

2 ft

1 ft

### Check Understanding

In Example 3, why are you asked to find the minimum amount of wrapping paper needed for the box?

The minimum amount represents the surface area of the box.

---

## Chalkboard Examples

### Supplementary Example 1

What three-dimensional figure is represented by the net shown?

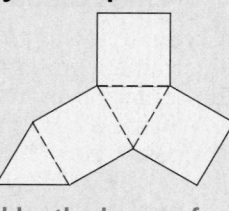

The two congruent equilateral triangles will be the bases of the figure. The congruent squares will be the lateral faces. So, the figure is a triangular prism.

### Supplementary Example 2

Draw a net for the right triangular prism shown.

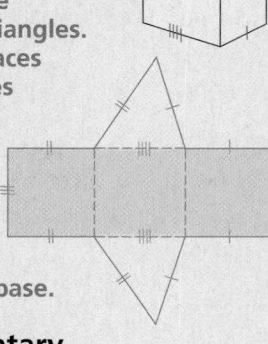

The bases are congruent triangles. The lateral faces are rectangles with one pair of sides the same length as the corresponding sides of the base.

### Supplementary Example 3

**FASHION** A tote bag is to be faced with leather scraps arranged in irregular patches with no overlap. The cost of the leather is $2.50 per ft². The rectangular base of the bag is 7 in. by 12. in., and the height of the bag is 17 in. What is the total cost of leather needed to face the bag? Draw the bag and its net.

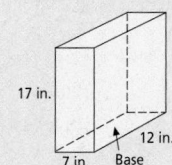

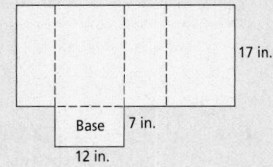

17 in.

17 in.

12 in.

7 in.   Base

Base   7 in.

12 in.

Surface area
= area of base + areas of lateral faces
= $7 \cdot 12$    + ($7 \cdot 17 + 12 \cdot 17 + 7 \cdot 17 + 12 \cdot 17$)
= 730 in.²

So, the bag needs $\dfrac{730 \text{ in.}^2}{144 \text{ in.}^2}$, about 5.1 ft² of leather @ $2.50 per ft²; total cost is about $12.75.

---

## Teaching Tip

Emphasize with students that the two important measures of three-dimensional figures are *surface area* and *volume*. These measures are the counterparts of *perimeter* and *area* in two-dimensional figures. Surface area, like perimeter, is a measure of boundary, the surface of a three-dimensional figure. Volume, like area, is a measure of the space enclosed by the figure.

When students are calculating surface area, as in Example 3, it may be helpful for them to label the faces of the net. They may call the faces according to their locations on the box: Top, Bottom, Left, Right, Front, Back.

### QUICK ASSESSMENT
Ask the following questions to determine if students understand the content presented in this lesson.
1. What is a *net*?   a two-dimensional figure that can be folded on its segments or curved on its boundaries into a three-dimensional figure
2. Explain how a net is useful in calculating the surface area.   Since a net shows all the surfaces, you can add the areas of the parts of the net to find the surface area.

### ASSIGNMENT GUIDE
Basic: 1–23, 30–45
Enriched: 1–45

### ADDITIONAL ANSWERS
5.

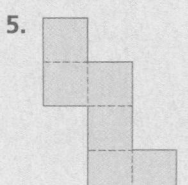

**Reteaching Worksheet 10-2**

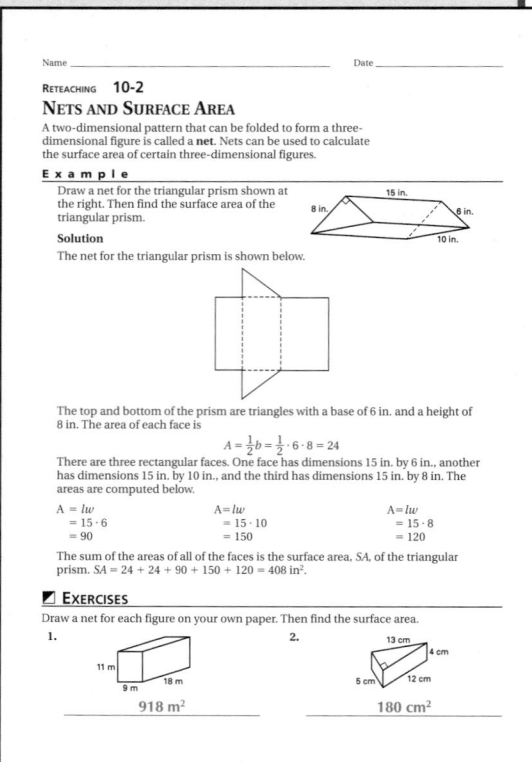

---

### TRY THESE EXERCISES

**Identify the three-dimensional figure for each net.**

1.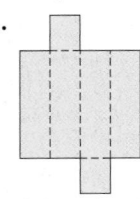
rectangular prism

2.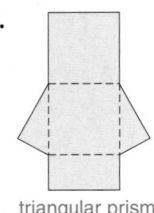
triangular prism

3.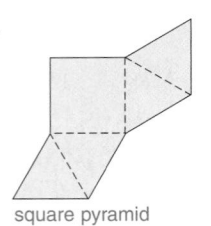
square pyramid

4.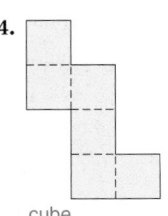
cube

**Draw a net for each three-dimensional figure.**
For 5–7, see additional answers.
5. cube
6. pentagonal prism
7. rectangular prism

**Draw a net for each figure. Then find the surface area. Round each answer to the nearest tenth. Use 3.14 for π.** For 8–10, see additional answers for nets.

8.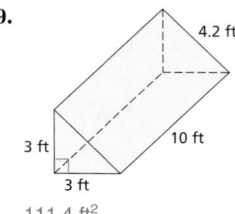
0.5 m    4 m    2 m
22 m²

9.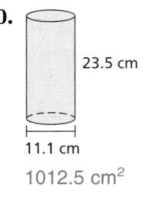
4.2 ft    10 ft    3 ft    3 ft
111.4 ft²

10.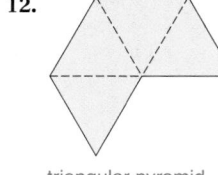
23.5 cm    11.1 cm
1012.5 cm²

### PRACTICE EXERCISES  •  For Extra Practice, see page 616.

**Identify the three-dimensional figure for each net.**

11.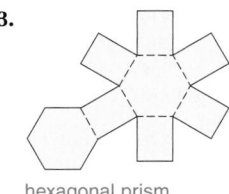
rectangular prism

12.
triangular pyramid

13.
hexagonal prism

**Draw a net for each three-dimensional figure.**
For 14–16, see additional answers.
14. octagonal prism
15. triangular prism
16. right cone

17. **HISTORY**  Design and draw a Native American tepee. Then draw a net for the tepee.
See additional answers.
18. Draw a net of a cube that has a side length of 6 m. Then find the surface area of the cube.
See additional answers. 216 m²
19. **ARCHITECTURE**  What is the total surface area of the glass (including the roof) used to build the greenhouse? Draw a net of the walls and the roof to solve the problem.
See additional answers. 340 ft²

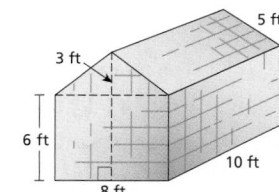
5 ft    3 ft    6 ft    10 ft    8 ft

**428**   |   Chapter 10  **Three-Dimensional Geometry**

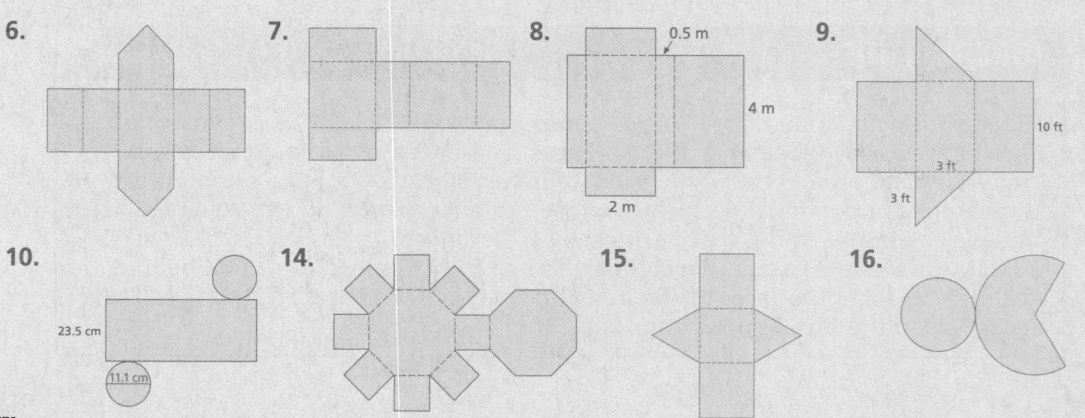

6.   7.   8.  0.5 m   4 m   2 m   9.  10 ft   3 ft   3 ft

10.  23.5 cm   11.1 cm   14.   15.   16.

**Find the area of each net. Use 3.14 for π. Round to the nearest tenth if necessary.**

**20.**

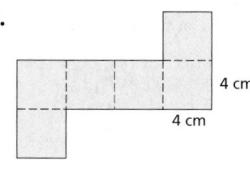

96 cm²

**21.**

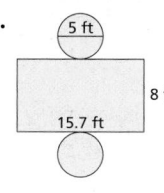

5 ft
8 ft
15.7 ft

164.9 ft²

**22.** The height of each triangle is $\frac{5\sqrt{3}}{3}$.

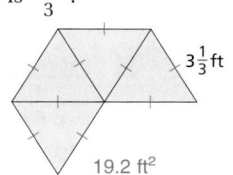

$3\frac{1}{3}$ ft

19.2 ft²

**23. WRITING MATH** How can nets help you find the surface area of three-dimensional figures? What kinds of mistakes do you make when calculating surface area? See additional answers.

## ■ EXTENDED PRACTICE EXERCISES

**Use nets to find the surface area of each prism. Use 3.14 for π.**

**24.**

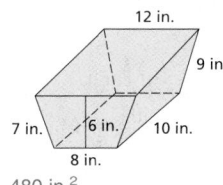

12 in.
9 in.
7 in.  6 in.  10 in.
8 in.

480 in.²

**25.**

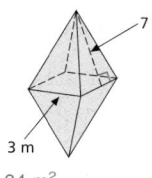

7 m
3 m

84 m²

**26.**

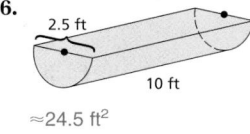

2.5 ft
10 ft

≈24.5 ft²

**27. MACHINERY** The wheel of a steamroller is a cylinder. If the wheel's diameter is 5 ft and its width is 7.2 ft, approximately how much area is covered by one complete wheel revolution? Use a net to visualize and solve the problem. Round the answer to the nearest whole number. 113 ft²

**28. CRITICAL THINKING** There are 11 different nets for a cube. Draw as many of them as you can. Check students' work.

**29.** Refer to exercise 28. To construct 20 cubes out of construction paper, which of the 11 nets would you use? Explain. Answers will vary.

## ■ MIXED REVIEW EXERCISES

**Simplify each numerical expression.** (Lesson 2-2)

**30.** $4 + 3 - 6 \cdot 4$  −17

**31.** $8 \cdot 6 + 4^2 - 3$  61

**32.** $2 + (5 - 2)^2 \div 4$  $\frac{17}{4}$

**33.** $15 \div 3 + (7 - 3) \cdot 2$  13

**34.** $4 + 8(3 + 4) \div 2$  32

**35.** $(6 + 1)^2 - 15 \cdot 3 + 4$  8

**Evaluate each expression when $c = 11$.** (Lesson 2-2)

**36.** $18 - c$  7

**37.** $3(c + 8)$  57

**38.** $(c - 8)^2 + 4$  13

**39.** $9 + c(3c - 2)$  350

**Simplify.** (Lesson 9-2)

**40.** $(4r)(9p)$  $36rp$

**41.** $(6r^2)(4r^3g^2)$  $24r^5g^2$

**42.** $(-3a^2)(5ab^2)^2$  $-75a^4b^4$

**43.** $(5c^3d)(2cd^4)$  $10c^4d^5$

**44.** $(-4k^4f^2)(-6kf^6)$  $24k^5f^8$

**45.** $(3s^3t^2)(-6st^3q)$  $-18s^4t^5q$

---

**17.**

**18.**

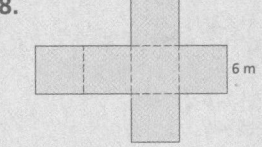

6 m

**19.**

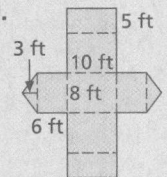

5 ft
3 ft  10 ft
8 ft
6 ft

**23.** Nets help you visualize the three-dimensional object in two dimensions. Nets also help you account for every part of a three-dimensional figure, especially figures with curved surfaces. Nets can transform some curved surfaces into flat surfaces.

---

### Vocabulary Review

**Lesson 10-1**
cylinder: axis, right cylinder,
   oblique cylinder
cone: axis, right cone, oblique
   cone
sphere: center of sphere
polyhedron: faces, edges, vertices
prism: bases
pyramid: faces, vertex, base
lateral face, lateral edge

**Lesson 10-2**
net
surface area

## ASSIGNMENT GUIDE

**All students:** 1–26

## Chalkboard Examples

### Lesson 10-1
**a.** Count the faces, vertices, and edges of each polyhedron.

 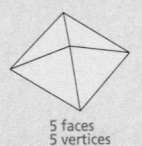 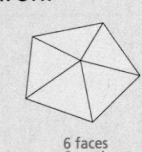

| 4 faces | 5 faces | 6 faces |
| 4 vertices | 5 vertices | 6 vertices |
| 6 edges | 8 edges | 10 edges |

**b.** Express the relationship among the numbers of faces *F*, vertices *V*, and edges *E* of a given polyhedron. $F + V = E + 2$

### Lesson 10-2
The 6 faces of a cube are represented by location as follows: F = front, B = back, U = up, D = down, L = left, R = right
In the given net, the locations of three of the faces of the resulting cube are identified. Where will the other squares of this net end up on the cube? **a. Back, b. Down, c. Left**

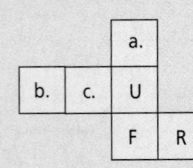

### PRACTICE ▬ LESSON 10-1

**Choose a word from the list to complete each statement.**

1. A __?__ has one square base and triangular faces.   d
2. A __?__ has a curved surface and one circular base.   a
3. A __?__ has two congruent circular bases that lie in parallel planes between a curved surface.   b
4. A __?__ is a figure consisting of the set of all points in space that are a given distance from a given point.   c
5. A __?__ has a triangular base and triangular faces.   f
6. A __?__ has two triangular bases parallel to each other with the faces that are parallelograms.   e

| |
|---|
| **a.** cone |
| **b.** cylinder |
| **c.** sphere |
| **d.** square pyramid |
| **e.** triangular prism |
| **f.** triangular pyramid |

**Identify each figure. State the number of faces, vertices and edges of each.**

7.
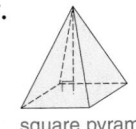
square pyramid; 5, 5, 8

8.
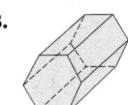
hexagonal prism; 8, 12, 18

9.

pentagonal pyramid; 6, 6, 10

### PRACTICE ▬ LESSON 10-2

**Identify the three-dimensional figure for each net.**

10.
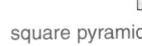
square pyramid

11.
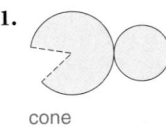
cone

12.
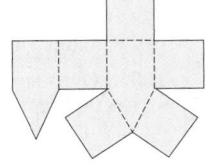
pentagonal prism

**Draw a net for each three-dimensional figure.**
For 13–15, see additional answers.

13.
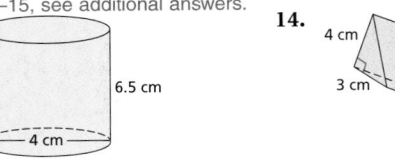
6.5 cm
4 cm

14.
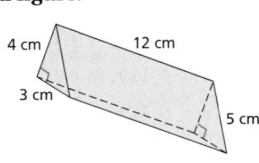
4 cm   12 cm
3 cm   5 cm

15.
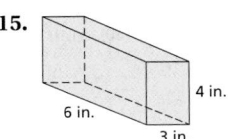
6 in.   4 in.
3 in.

**Find the surface area of each figure.**

16. the figure in Exercise 13   106.76 cm²
17. the figure in Exercise 14   156 cm²
18. the figure in Exercise 15   108 in.²

**430** | Chapter 10 **Three-Dimensional Geometry**

## ADDITIONAL ANSWERS

13.
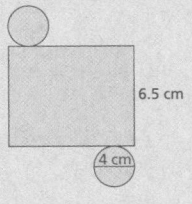
6.5 cm
4 cm

14.
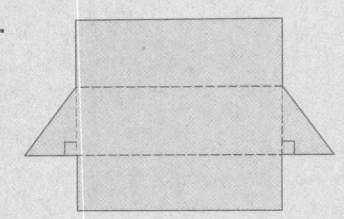

15.
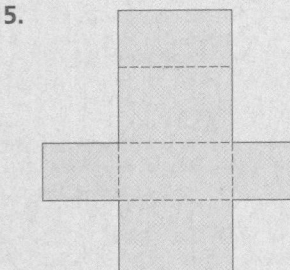

**Draw a net for each three-dimensional figure.** (Lesson 10-2)
For 19–21, see additional answers.

19.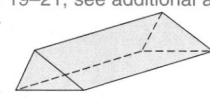

20.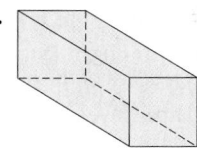

21.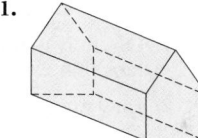

22. Draw a triangular pyramid.   See additional answers.

23. How many vertices, faces and edges does a triangular pyramid have?   4, 4, 6

**Match each pair of edges of the cube with an item in the box.**
(Lesson 10-1)

24. $\overline{AD}$ and $\overline{CG}$   b

25. $\overline{BC}$ and $\overline{EH}$   a

26. $\overline{CG}$ and $\overline{GH}$   c

a. parallel edges

b. skew edges

c. perpendicular edges

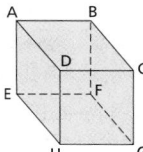

## MathWorks Career – Urban Planner
Workplace Knowhow

An urban planner designs and supervises the construction of roads, buildings, tunnels, bridges, and water supply systems. The city of Berlin, Germany, changed rapidly following the removal of the Berlin Wall. New construction was needed to reconstruct the city and bring its buildings to modern standards. An urban planner in Berlin must decide what types of buildings are most appropriate for the needs of the city while maintaining the historical look and structure. Suppose an urban planner is beginning the design process for a new government building in Berlin.

1. The shape of this new building is a right hexagonal prism. Make a sketch of the new structure, drawing the regular hexagons at the base and the top of the building.
See additional answers.

2. Draw a net (to scale) of the building. The sides of the regular hexagonal bases should have a length of 30 m, and the height of the building should be 60 m.
See additional answers.

3. What is the total surface area of the walls?   10,800 m²

4. How many marble tiles will be required to cover the outside walls if the tiles are 60 cm wide and 10 cm tall?   18,000

## MathWorks

*Urban planning* is the unified development of cities and their environs. For most of its history, city planning dealt primarily with the regulation of land use and the physical arrangement of city structures, as guided by architectural, engineering, and land-development criteria. In the mid-20th century, it broadened to include the comprehensive guidance of the physical, economic, and social environment of a community.

Students should answer Questions 1–4 to better understand how surface area might be considered when an urban planner is working with a new building.

Elements characteristic of city planning include (1) general plans for land development; (2) zoning controls for permissible land uses, densities, and requirements for streets, utility services, and other improvements; (3) plans for traffic flow and public transportation; (4) strategies for economic revitalization of depressed urban and rural areas; (5) strategies for supportive action to help disadvantaged social groups; (6) guidelines for environmental protection and preservation of scarce resources. In carrying out these aspects of their profession, urban planners use a wide variety of geometric concepts and principles.

Students who are interested in learning more about this career choice can go to mathmatters2.com/mathworks. School Guidance Counselors are another resource for information about training requirements and appropriate schools.

19.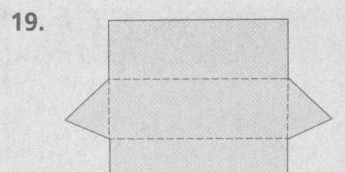

20.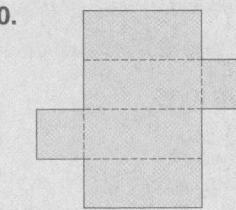

21.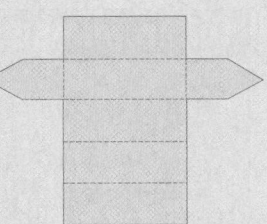

22.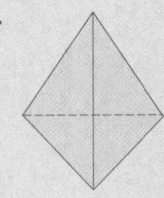

MATHWORKS

1.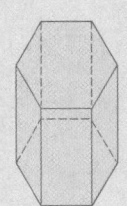

2.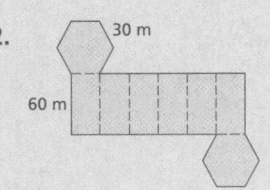

30 m

60 m

# Surface Area of Three-Dimensional Figures

**Goals** ■ Find the surface area of three-dimensional figures.

**Applications** Geography, Food service, Packaging, History

## Getting Started

**Use a box such as a cereal box or a shoe box for the activity.**
For 1–3, answers will vary.
1. Carefully tear the box apart at the edges. Do not keep the tabs that were used to glue the faces of the box together.

2. How many polygons do you now have? Describe them.

3. Use a ruler to measure. Then calculate the area of each of the polygons.

4. Add the area of all the polygons. What does the total area represent?   the surface area of the box (possibly with some overlap)

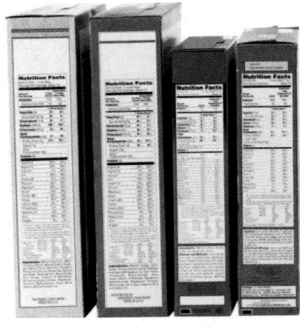

### ▶ BUILD UNDERSTANDING

In the previous lesson, you learned that the surface area of a polyhedron is the sum of the areas of all its bases and faces. You saw how the net of a three-dimensional figure can be used to find the total surface area. In this lesson, you will use formulas to find the surface area of three-dimensional figures.

### Example 1

**Find the surface area of the rectangular prism.**

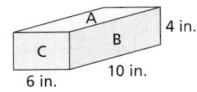

### Solution

A rectangular prism has three pairs of congruent faces. The surface area is the sum of the areas of all the faces. Use the formula $SA = 2(\text{area A}) + 2(\text{area B}) + 2(\text{area C})$, where each area can be found using the formula for the area of a rectangle, $A = lw$.

area of A       $A = 10 \cdot 6$
                $A = 60$

area of B       $A = 10 \cdot 4$
                $A = 40$

area of C       $A = 6 \cdot 4$
                $A = 24$

$$SA = 2 \cdot (\text{area A}) + 2 \cdot (\text{area B}) + 2 \cdot (\text{area C})$$

$$SA = 2 \cdot 60 + 2 \cdot 40 + 2 \cdot 24$$

$$SA = 248$$

The surface area is 248 in.².

**Check Understanding**

How is using the surface area formula similar to using nets to find the surface area of a three-dimensional figure?

The net is a visualization of the formula.

Chapter 10  **Three-Dimensional Geometry**

**432**

## Differentiated Instruction

**TACTILE/KINESTHETIC LEARNERS**
In conjunction with Example 1, you might have students draw a net of the box, as shown here. Students may use the torn box from the opening activity as a guide for placing the rectangular faces in the net.

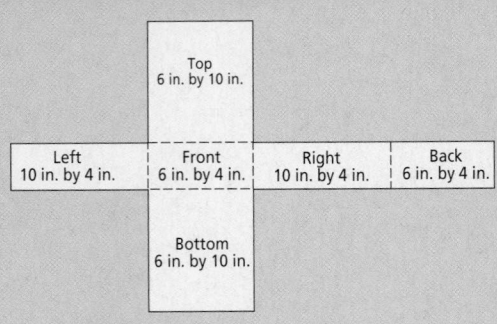

A square pyramid with four congruent triangular faces is called a **regular square pyramid**. If you know the dimensions of just one triangular face, you can calculate the surface area of the pyramid.

## Example 2

**GEOGRAPHY** The Great Pyramid at Giza in Egypt has a square base approximately 756 ft long. The height of each triangular face, called the slant height, is approximately 612 ft. What is the approximate surface area of the faces of the Great Pyramid?

### Solution

The Great Pyramid is a regular square pyramid, so its faces are four congruent triangles. Calculate the surface area of one of the faces and multiply by 4.

$A = \frac{1}{2}bh$    Use the formula for the area of a triangle.

$A = \frac{1}{2} \cdot 756 \cdot 612 = 231,336$

$SA = 4 \cdot 231,336 = 925,344$

The surface area of the faces of the Great Pyramid at Giza is approximately 925,344 ft$^2$.

A cylinder is a figure with two congruent circular bases and a curved surface. To find the surface area, add the areas of the bases to the area of the curved surface.

| Surface Area of a Cylinder | $SA = 2\pi rh + 2\pi r^2$ where $r$ is the radius of a base and $h$ is the height of the cylinder. |
| --- | --- |

## Example 3

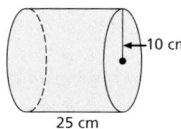

**Find the surface area of the cylinder.**

### Solution

$SA = 2\pi rh + 2\pi r^2$

$SA \approx 2 \cdot 3.14 \cdot 10 \cdot 25 + 2 \cdot 3.14 \cdot 10^2$    $\pi \approx 3.14$

$SA \approx 1570 + 628 \approx 2198$

The surface area of the cylinder is approximately 2198 cm$^2$.

A cone is a three-dimensional figure with a curved surface and one circular base. The height of a cone is the length of a perpendicular segment from its vertex to its base. The **slant height** (*s*) of a cone is the length of a segment from its vertex to its base along the side of the cone.

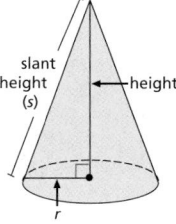

| Surface Area of a Cone | $SA = \pi rs + \pi r^2$ where $r$ is the radius of the base and $s$ is the slant height. |
| --- | --- |

**Math Online** mathmatters2.com/extra_examples       Lesson 10-3 **Surface Area of Three-Dimensional Figures**   | 433

### Supplementary Example 1
**ARCHITECTURE** A skyscraper is 414 m high. The base is a square with sides 64 m. Determine the surface area of the building.
The building is a rectangular prism with 2 square bases and 4 rectangular lateral faces.
$SA = 2(64^2) + 4(64 \cdot 414)$
$\quad = 114,176$
So, the surface area of the building is 114,176 m$^2$.

### Supplementary Example 2
The three lateral faces of this regular pyramid are congruent triangles of base 10 cm and altitude 8 cm. The base is an equilateral triangle of side length 10 cm and altitude 8.66 cm. Find the surface area of this regular triangular pyramid.

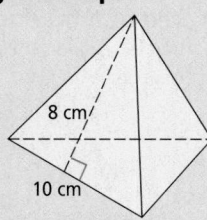

$SA = \begin{array}{c} \text{area of} \\ \text{base} \end{array} + \begin{array}{c} \text{3(area of} \\ \text{lateral face)} \end{array}$

$SA = \frac{1}{2}bh + 3\left(\frac{1}{2}bh\right)$

$\quad = \frac{1}{2}(10)(8.66) + 3\left[\frac{1}{2}(10)(8)\right]$

$\quad = 163.3$

So, the surface area of the regular triangular pyramid is 163.3 cm$^2$.

### Supplementary Example 3
Find the surface area of the right cylinder. Leave answer in terms of $\pi$.

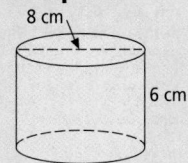

Since $d = 8$ cm, $r = 4$ cm
$SA = 2\pi rh + 2\pi r^2$
$\quad = 2 \cdot \pi \cdot 4 \cdot 6 + 2 \cdot \pi \cdot 4^2$
$\quad = 48\pi + 32\pi$
$\quad = 80\pi$
So, the surface area of the right cylinder is $80\pi$ cm$^2$.

## Teaching Tip

In conjunction with Example 2 and Supplementary Example 2, note with students that the surface area of a regular pyramid is obtained by adding the area of its base and the lateral area, where the lateral area is the sum of the areas of the congruent triangular lateral faces. Emphasize that although the lateral faces are always congruent triangles, the base may take on different shapes (Example 2 shows a square base, Supplementary Example 2 shows a base that is an equilateral triangle).
Have students write a rule for the surface area of a regular pyramid using symbols.   $SA = B + LA$ where $B =$ area of base and $LA =$ lateral area

## Lesson Wrap-up

### QUICK ASSESSMENT

Ask the following questions to determine if students understand the content presented in this lesson.

1. Explain the meaning of surface area of a polyhedron.  **the sum of the areas of all its faces**

2. a. How many congruent faces does a regular square pyramid have?  **4**

   b. What shape are these congruent faces?  **triangular**

3. How would you find the surface area of a triangular prism?  **Add twice the area of a triangular base to the sum of the areas of the three congruent rectangular faces.**

### ASSIGNMENT GUIDE

**Basic:** 1–22, 29–40
**Enriched:** 1–40

### Reteaching Worksheet 10-3

Name _____ Date _____

RETEACHING **10-3**

**SURFACE AREA OF THREE-DIMENSIONAL FIGURES**

The formulas that can be used to find the surface area of some three-dimensional figures are given below.

Surface Area of a Rectangular Prism:  $SA = 2lw + 2lh + 2wh$, where $l$ = length, $w$ = width, $h$ = height

Surface Area of a Cylinder:  $SA = 2\pi rh + 2\pi r^2$ where $r$ = radius of base and $h$ = height

Surface Area of a Cone:  $SA = \pi rs + \pi r^2$ where $r$ = radius of base and $s$ = slant height

**Example**

Find the surface area of the cone at the right

**Solution**

For this cone, $r = 8$ cm and $s = 14$ cm. Substitute these into the formula $SA = \pi rs + \pi r^2$ and simplify to find the surface area.
$SA = \pi rs + \pi r^2$
$SA \approx 3.14 \cdot 8 \cdot 14 + 3.14 \cdot 8^2$
$SA \approx 552.64$
The surface area of the cone is about 553 cm².

**EXERCISES**

Find the surface area of each figure.

1. $SA = 2lw + 2lh + 2wh$
   $= 2 \underline{\quad \cdot 6 \cdot 2 \quad} + 2 \underline{\quad \cdot 6 \cdot 3 \quad} + 2 \underline{\quad \cdot 2 \cdot 3 \quad}$
   $= \underline{\qquad 72 \text{ ft}^2 \qquad}$

2. $SA = 2\pi rh + 2\pi r^2$
   $= 2 \underline{\quad \cdot 3.14 \cdot 13 \cdot 20 \quad} + 2 \underline{\quad \cdot 3.14 \cdot 13^2 \quad}$
   $= \underline{\qquad 2694.12 \text{ cm}^2 \qquad}$

3. $SA = \pi rs \quad + \quad \pi r^2$
   $= \underline{\quad 3.14 \cdot 5 \cdot 8 \quad} + \underline{\quad 3.14 \cdot 5^2 \quad}$
   $= \underline{\qquad 204.1 \text{ in}^2 \qquad}$

---

## Example 4

**Find the surface area of the cone.**

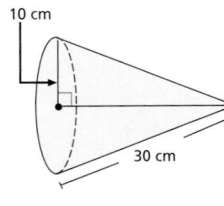

**Solution**

$SA = \pi rs + \pi r^2$

$SA \approx 3.14 \cdot 10 \cdot 30 + 3.14 \cdot 10^2 \qquad \pi \approx 3.14$

$SA \approx 942 + 314$

$SA \approx 1256$

The surface area of the cone is approximately 1256 cm².

### TRY THESE EXERCISES

Find the surface area of each figure. Round to the nearest hundredth.

1.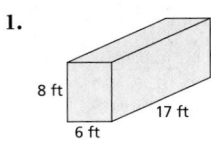
   572 ft²

2.
   2184 m²

3.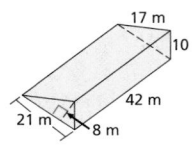
   1752.12 ft²

4.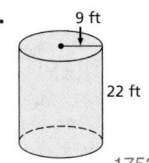
   62.42 m²

5.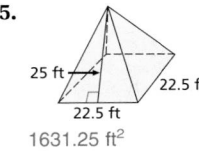
   1631.25 ft²

6.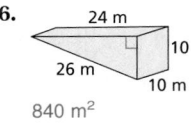
   840 m²

7.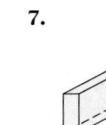
   10.88 cm²

8.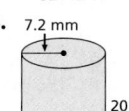
   1229.88 mm²

### PRACTICE EXERCISES • For Extra Practice, see page 617.

Find the surface area of each figure. Round to the nearest hundredth.

9.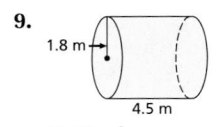
   71.22 m²

10.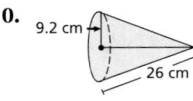
    1016.86 cm²

11.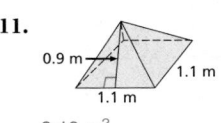
    3.19 m²

12.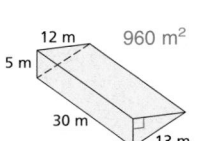
    960 m²

13.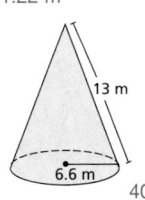
    406.19 m²

14.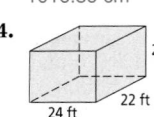
    2896 ft²

15.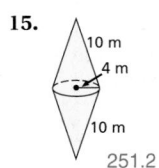
    251.2 m²

16.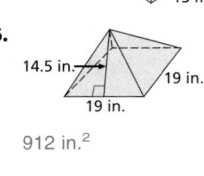
    912 in.²

17. The base of each triangular face of a regular square pyramid is 9 in., and the height of each triangular face is 11 in. Find the surface area of the pyramid.  279 in.²

## Extend the Lesson

**CONNECTING TO PRIOR KNOWLEDGE** In conjunction with Example 3 and Supplementary Example 3, note with students that when a value is substituted for π, the answer obtained for surface area of a cylinder is an approximate value. However, when the value for surface area of a cylinder is left in terms of π, this answer is an exact value for surface area.

Elicit that the answer for the surface area of the cone in Example 4 is approximate since an approximation is used for π.

**18. PACKAGING** Tamara is wrapping a gift. The box is 14 in. by 9 in. by 8 in. What is the minimum amount of wrapping paper she will need to cover the box?   620 in.²

**19. WRITING MATH** Explain why the word "minimum" is used in Exercise 18.
Wrapping a gift requires more paper than just the surface area of the box.

**20. FOOD SERVICE** Find the surface area of a can of cranberry sauce that has a height of 4.2 in. and a radius of 1.5 in.   ≈ 53.69 in.²

**21. SPREADSHEET** Use a spreadsheet to calculate the surface area of cylinders. Enter the formula for the surface area of a cylinder into the first cell. Then evaluate the formula for a cylinder that is 12 cm long with a radius of 3 cm, 6 cm, 12 cm, and 24 cm.   282.6 cm²; 678.24 cm²; 1808.64 cm²; 5425.92 cm²

**22. HISTORY** An ancient Mayan pyramid has a square base. Each side of the base measures 230 m, and the slant height is 179 m tall. Find the area of the faces of the Mayan pyramid.   82,340 m²

## ■ EXTENDED PRACTICE EXERCISES

Find the surface area of each figure.

**23.**
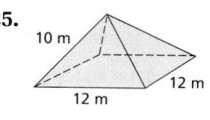
4 m, 4 m, 4 m, 4 m
112 m²

**24.**
6 m, 8 m, 7 m, 12 m
420 m²

**25.**
10 m, 12 m, 12 m
336 m²

**26. CRITICAL THINKING** A cone has a height $h$ and a radius $r$. Find an expression for the slant height. Then write a formula for the surface area of the cone using this expression.   $s = \sqrt{h^2 + r^2}$; $SA = \pi r\sqrt{h^2 + r^2} + \pi r^2$

**27.** A hole is drilled through a solid cube that has edges of 4 cm. The hole is drilled perpendicular to the top face of the cube. The diameter of the hole is 2 cm. To the nearest whole number, what is the total surface area of the resulting solid figure?   115 cm²

**28. DATA FILE** Refer to the data on U.S. shopping centers on page 570. What are possible dimensions of a rectangular prism whose surface area is equal to the area of Tysons Corner Center?   Answers will vary.

## ■ MIXED REVIEW EXERCISES

Write the equation of each line using the given information. (Lesson 6-3)

**29.** $m = 3$, $(1, 4)$
$y = 3x + 1$

**30.** $m = 2$, $(-2, -3)$
$y = 2x + 1$

**31.** $(2, 7)$, $(3, 9)$
$y = 2x + 3$

**32.** $(0, -2)$, $(2, -4)$
$y = -x - 2$

Find each product. (Lesson 9-5)

**33.** $(r + 3)(r - 4)$
$r^2 - r - 12$

**34.** $(z - 1)(z + 4)$
$z^2 + 3z - 4$

**35.** $(b - 4)^2$
$b^2 - 8b + 16$

**36.** $(f - 2)(f - 5)$
$f^2 - 7f + 10$

**37.** $(v + 4)(v - 8)$
$v^2 - 4v - 32$

**38.** $(w - 1)(w - 7)$
$w^2 - 8w + 7$

**39.** $(3k - 1)(2k + 4)$
$6k^2 + 10k - 4$

**40.** $(2c + 3)^2$
$4c^2 + 12c + 9$

---

## Flexible Grouping

Give a group of 3 or 4 students a regulation basketball and some wrapping paper. Allow them 15–20 minutes to find the surface area of the basketball. Students should experiment with wrapping the ball and play with how much paper is necessary to accomplish this task.

The amount of paper needed to cover the ball is the ball's circumference, $2\pi r$, times its diameter, $2r$, or $4\pi r^2$. This is because the paper needed to cover the ball is the same height as the ball's diameter and the same length as its circumference. For a regulation basketball with a 9-in. diameter, the surface area is $4 \cdot \pi \cdot 4.5^2$ or about 254 in.²

---

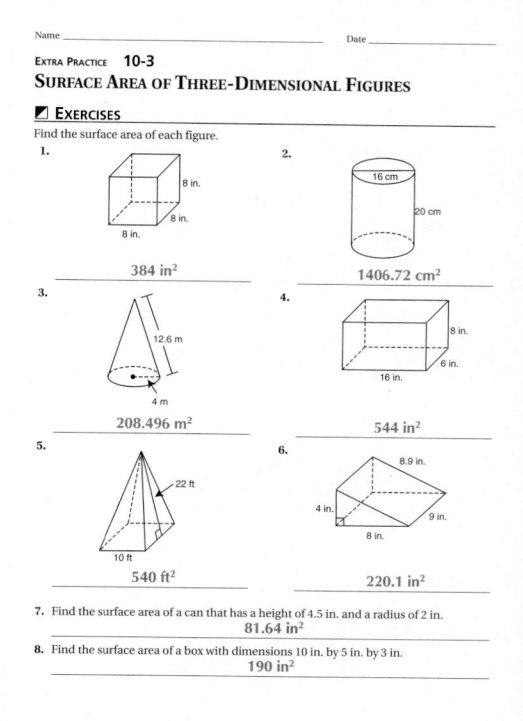
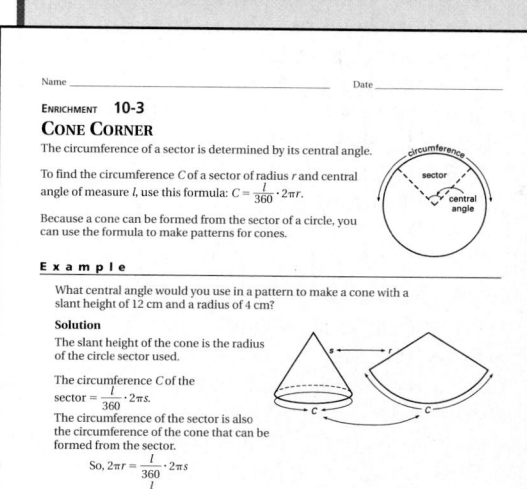

### Vocabulary

perspective drawing
vanishing point
one-point perspective
two-point perspective

### Tools/Materials Needed

ruler

### Lesson Resources

Warm-up Transparency 40
Transparency RF-53
Reteaching 10-4
Extra Practice 10-4
Enrichment 10-4
Technology Activity 10-4

## Getting Started

### 5-MINUTE WARM-UP

A large rectangular billboard stands at ground level in the center of a concrete lot. The front of the billboard faces directly south. Describe the shadow of the billboard at each of the given times.
1. 8:00 A.M.   **parallelogram**
2. 12:00 noon   **rectangle**
3. 4:00 P.M.   **parallelogram**

### Introduction to Lesson 10-4

Have students view one photo at a time (tell them to cover over the others with a piece of paper). Have students tell what about each photo they first noticed. When trying for a fresh view, tell students to close their eyes for a few seconds before looking again at a photo.

---

# 10-4 Perspective Drawings

**Goals**
- Make one- and two-point perspective drawings.
- Locate the vanishing points of perspective drawings.

**Applications**   Art, Interior design, History, Architecture

**Use the three photographs for Questions 1–3.**

1. Can you see depth in each of the photographs?   yes

2. Do you think the photographer was located above, below or at eye level with the subject?   above; eye level; below

3. Does your eye travel to one point or two points in the background of each photograph?   one

### ◢ BUILD UNDERSTANDING

A **perspective drawing** is a way of drawing objects on a flat surface so that they look the same as they appear in real life. The eye and the camera are both constructed so that objects appear progressively smaller the farther away they are. Parallel lines drawn in perspective appear to come together in the distance.

Perspective drawings use vanishing points. A **vanishing point** is a point that lies on the horizon line. The horizon line is a line in the distance where parallel lines appear to come together. Perspective drawings can be made in either **one-point perspective** or **two-point perspective**.

### Example 1

**Draw a cube in one-point perspective.**

### Solution

*Step 1*   Draw a square to show the front surface of the cube. Draw a horizon line *j* and a vanishing point *A* on line *j*.

*Step 2*   Connect the vertices of the square to the vanishing point.

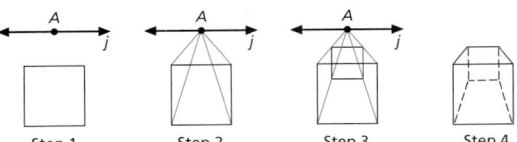

Step 1   Step 2   Step 3   Step 4

*Step 3*   Draw a smaller square whose vertices touch the four line segments.

*Step 4*   Connect the vertices of the two squares. Use a dashed segment to indicate the edges of the cube hidden from view. Remove line *j* and point *A*.

---

## Extend the Lesson

**REAL WORLD CONNECTION** Perspective is based on elementary laws of optics, in particular the fact that distant objects appear smaller and less distinct than near objects. The scientific understanding of perspective is a relatively recent development in human history, not having been accurately formulated until the Italian Renaissance, in the 15th century. Have students find examples in art in which perspective was not used. For example, in drawings of human figures from Ancient Egypt, the head is shown in profile, but the eye, shoulders, and body are viewed frontally, while the legs once again are rendered in profile.

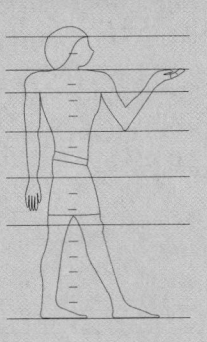

A **two-point perspective** drawing has two vanishing points. If you are looking at the corner of an object in a perspective drawing, then it is probably a two-point perspective drawing.

## Example 2

**ARCHITECTURE** Draw a building shaped like a rectangular prism in two-point perspective.

### Solution

*Step 1* Use a straightedge to draw a vertical line segment to represent the height of the building. Draw a vanishing point (VP) on each side of the segment. Sketch depth lines from the top and bottom of the segment to each point.

*Step 2* Draw two segments parallel to the original segment to represent the height. Draw two segments to complete the top of the building.

*Step 3* Draw two more depth lines from the top corners to the vanishing points.

*Step 4* Erase the unused portions of the depth lines to complete the two-point perspective drawing.

## Example 3

Locate the vanishing point of the perspective drawing.

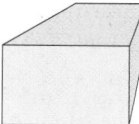

### Solution

To locate the vanishing point, use a straightedge to draw the depth lines from the top edges of the figure. The point of their intersection is the vanishing point of the perspective drawing.

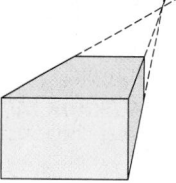

**Sketch each object in one-point perspective.**
For 1–4, see additional answers.
1. cube      2. triangular prism      3. rectangular prism      4. cylinder

5. your first name written in capital block-style letters
   Answers will vary.

**Sketch each object in two-point perspective.**
For 6–8, see additional answers.
6. cube                    7. shoe box                    8. table

Lesson 10-4 **Perspective Drawings** | **437**

## ADDITIONAL ANSWERS

1. 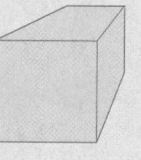   2.

3.

4. 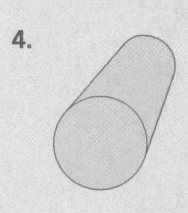   6.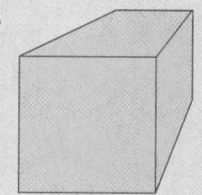

7. 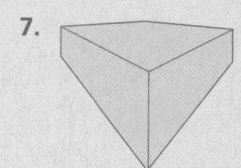   8.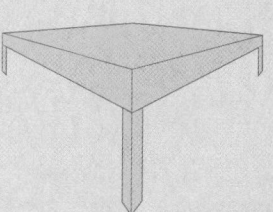

## Chalkboard Examples

### Supplementary Example 1

Locate the vanishing point and horizon line for the drawing of the rectangular prism.

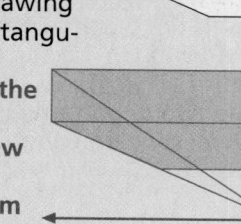

To locate the vanishing point, draw line segments from the four front vertices of the prism until they intersect. Point *Z* is the vanishing point.

Through point *Z*, draw a line, *m*, parallel to the top edge of the prism. Line *m* is the horizon line.

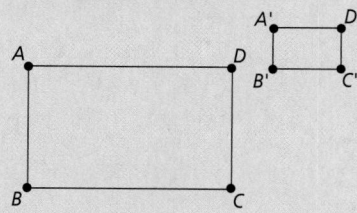

### Supplementary Example 2

**TRANSFORMATIONS** Rectangle $A'B'C'D'$ is a reduction of rectangle $ABCD$ under a dilation.

If $ABCD$ and $A'B'C'D'$ are considered as the front and back of a figure, then the center of dilation is the vanishing point. Locate the center of the dilation.

Draw lines through the vertices until they intersect.

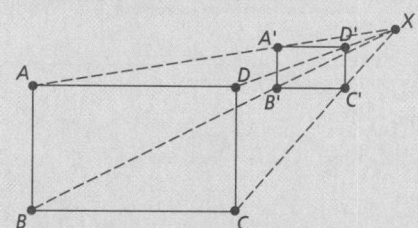

Point *X* is the center of the dilation.

**Trace each perspective drawing to locate the vanishing point(s).**

For 9–11, see additional answers.

9.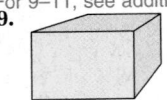

10.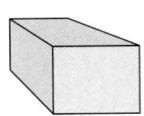

11.

## QUICK ASSESSMENT

Ask the following questions to determine if students understand the content presented in this lesson.

1. What is the purpose of perspective drawings?  **To show objects realistically.**

2. Name two important elements of a perspective drawing.  **the vanishing point(s) and the horizon line**

## ASSIGNMENT GUIDE

**Basic:** 1–34, 41–56
**Enriched:** 1–56

## ADDITIONAL ANSWERS

9.
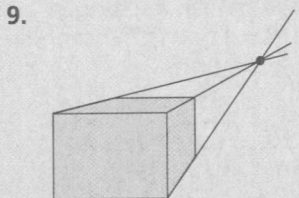

### Reteaching Worksheet 10-4

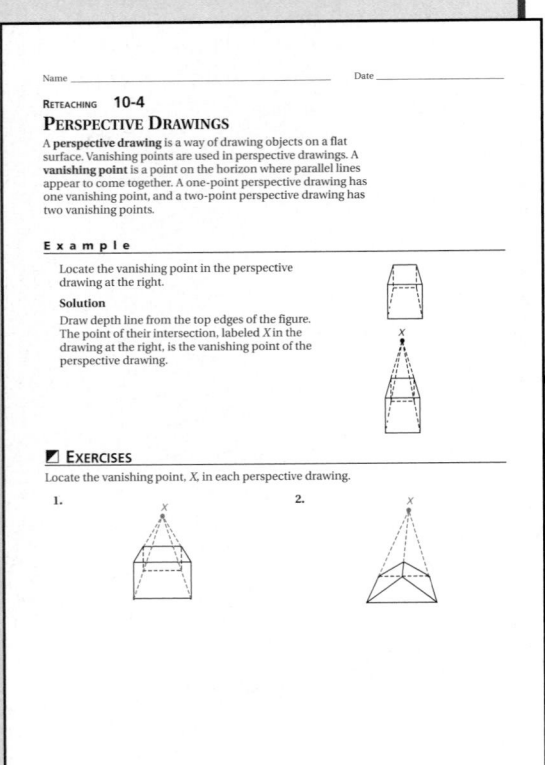

Name _____  Date _____

RETEACHING  **10-4**

**PERSPECTIVE DRAWINGS**

A **perspective drawing** is a way of drawing objects on a flat surface. Vanishing points are used in perspective drawings. A **vanishing point** is a point on the horizon where parallel lines appear to come together. A one-point perspective drawing has one vanishing point, and a two-point perspective drawing has two vanishing points.

**Example**

Locate the vanishing point in the perspective drawing at the right.

**Solution**

Draw depth line from the top edges of the figure. The point of their intersection, labeled *X* in the drawing at the right, is the vanishing point of the perspective drawing.

**EXERCISES**

Locate the vanishing point, *X*, in each perspective drawing.

1.        2.

---

■ **PRACTICE EXERCISES** • **For Extra Practice, see page 617.**

**Sketch each object in one-point perspective.**
For 12–14, see additional answers.

12. window          13. wall of a room          14. couch

**Sketch each object in two-point perspective.**
For 15–17, see additional answers.

15. television          16. street sign          17. school bus

**Trace each perspective drawing to locate the vanishing point(s).**
For 18–20, see additional answers.

18. 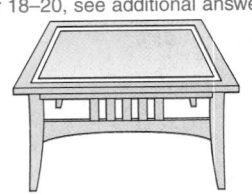          19. 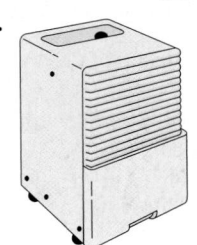          20.

21. **WRITING MATH** Describe the location of the vanishing point when a viewer can see three sides of a box drawn in one-point perspective. anywhere that the box does not obstruct it

22. **HISTORY** The Sears Tower in Chicago is the tallest building in the U.S. Use a picture of the Sears Tower to make the one-point perspective drawing.  Check students' work.

23. **INTERIOR DESIGN** Make a one-point perspective drawing of the square tile pattern of a floor.  See additional answers.

**A square is cut out of cardboard, and a flashlight shines behind it. Decide if it is possible to obtain the indicated shadow.**

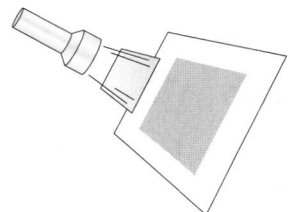

24. square  yes          25. segment  yes
26. triangle  no          27. point  no
28. trapezoid  yes          29. kite  yes
30. pentagon  no          31. parallelogram  yes

**438**   Chapter 10  **Three-Dimensional Geometry**

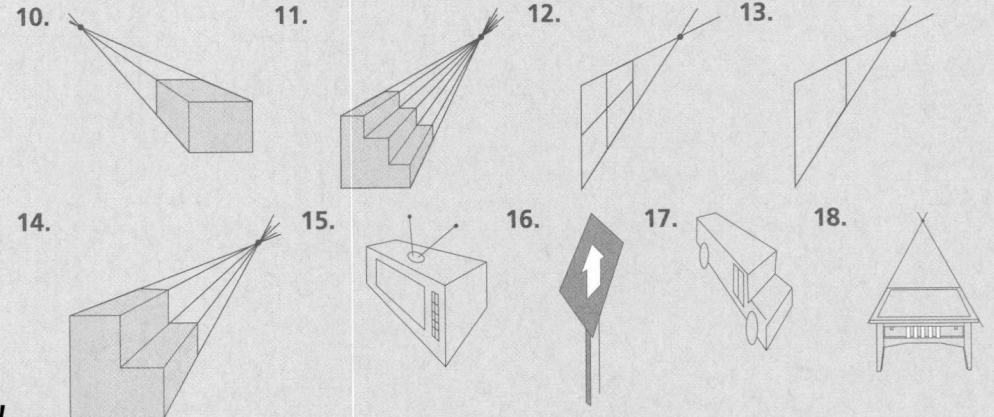

10.   11.   12.   13.

14.   15.   16.   17.   18.

**32. ARCHITECTURE** Describe the perspective used by the architect to create the illusion of a three-dimensional house in her plans.
one-point perspective

**33.** Trace the house on a piece of paper. Locate a vanishing point. Check students' drawings.

**34. GEOMETRY SOFTWARE** Use geometry software to make a one- or two-point perspective drawing. Begin by drawing a figure such as a rectangle and locating one or two vanishing points. Sketch the depth lines, and use them to complete the perspective drawing. Observe students' work.

## ■ EXTENDED PRACTICE EXERCISES

**Determine the number of vanishing points used to draw each cube.**

**35.**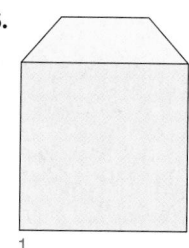
1

**36.**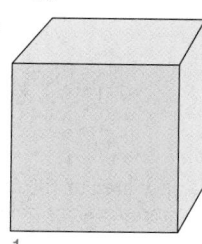
1

**37.**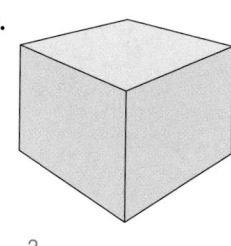
2

**38. RESEARCH** Use your school's library or another resource to find an example of a painting that uses one- and two-point perspectives. Identify the vanishing points used by the artists. Answers will vary.

**39. CRITICAL THINKING** Make a two-point perspective drawing of a rectangular box with a square window cut out of one of the faces. Show that the box has depth or thickness. Drawings will vary. Check students' drawings.

**40. CHAPTER INVESTIGATION** Draw a line segment about 10 in. long across the center of a piece of paper with an arrowhead at each end. Place on the timeline in chronological order the name and accomplishment of each mathematician you researched. Label appropriately. Be sure the distances between the years recorded on your timeline are in proportion. Answers will vary.

## ■ MIXED REVIEW EXERCISES

**State if it is possible to have a triangle with sides of the given lengths.** (Lesson 5-4)

**41.** 8, 5, 4  yes
**42.** 10, 6, 4  no
**43.** 12, 7, 6  yes
**44.** 9, 5, 5  yes

**45.** 16, 14, 12  yes
**46.** 11, 8, 5  yes
**47.** 7, 7, 2  yes
**48.** 12, 6, 5  no

**Factor each polynomial.** (Lesson 9-7)

**49.** $15z^2 + 18z$  $3z(5z + 6)$

**50.** $35r^2 + 60r$  $5r(7r + 12)$

**51.** $8y^5 - 24y^4 + 28$  $4(2y^5 - 6y^4 + 7)$

**52.** $6r^3s + 9r^3s^2 - 18r^2s^2$  $3r^2s(2r + 3rs - 6s)$

**53.** $28b^3c - 84b^2c^5$  $28b^2c(b - 3c^4)$

**54.** $24wx^3 - 12w^2x^2 + 20w^3x^3$  $4wx^2(6x - 3w + 5w^2x)$

**55.** $24g^4h - 40g^2h^2 - 16g^5$
$8g^2(3g^2h - 5h^2 - 2g^3)$

**56.** $30a^3b^2 + 45a^2b^3 - 60a^3b^3$  $15a^2b^2(2a + 3b - 4ab)$

**Math Online** mathmatters2.com/self_check_quiz

Lesson 10-4 **Perspective Drawings**  |  **439**

**19.** 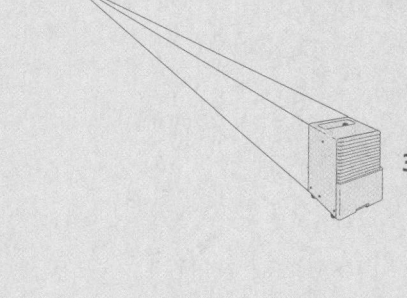  **20.** 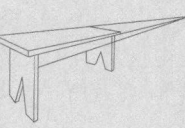  **23.**

**33.**

**Vocabulary Review**

**Lesson 10-3**
regular square pyramid
slant height

**Lesson 10-4**
perspective drawing
vanishing point
one-point perspective
two-point perspective

## ASSIGNMENT GUIDE

**All students: 1–26**

## Chalkboard Examples

### Lesson 10-3
Find the surface area of the right triangular prism.

A triangular prism has two congruent triangular bases—in this case, isosceles right triangles.

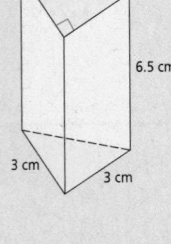
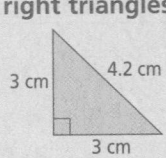

area of
right $\triangle = \frac{1}{2}bh = \frac{1}{2} \cdot 3 \cdot 3 = 4.5 = A_1$

And this triangular prism has two congruent rectangular lateral faces and a third rectangular lateral face.

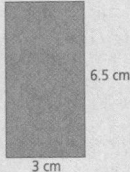

area of rectangle
$= \ell \cdot w$
$= 3 \cdot 6.5$
$= 19.5 = A_2$

area of third rectangle
$= \ell \cdot w$
$= 6.5 \cdot 4.2$
$= 27.3 = A_3$

$SA = 2(A_1) + 2(A_2) + A_3$
$= 2(4.5) + 2(19.5) + 27.3$
$= 75.3$

So, the surface area of this triangular prism is 75.3 cm².

### PRACTICE ■ LESSON 10-3

**Find the surface area of each figure.**

**1.**
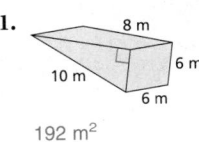
192 m²

**2.**
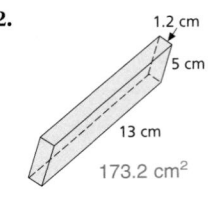
173.2 cm²

**3.**
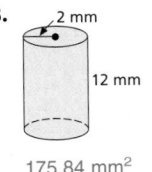
175.84 mm²

**4.**

489.84 cm²

**5.**
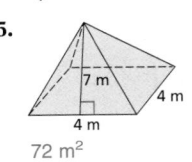
72 m²

**6.**
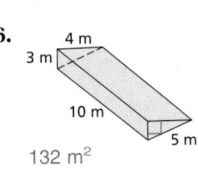
132 m²

**7.** A regular square pyramid has a base area of 100 cm² and a height of 12 cm. What is the surface area? (Hint: Find the slant height *s*.)  360 cm²

**8.** A can of peaches has a height of 5 in. and a diameter of 3 in. How much metal is needed to make the can?  61.23 in.²

### PRACTICE ■ LESSON 10-4

**Sketch each object in one-point perspective.**
For 9–11, see additional answers.
**9.** railroad track  **10.** house  **11.** door

**Sketch each object in two-point perspective.**
For 12–14, see additional answers.
**12.** stereo speaker  **13.** grandfather clock  **14.** building

**Trace each perspective drawing to locate the vanishing point(s).**
For 15–17, see additional answers.

**15.**
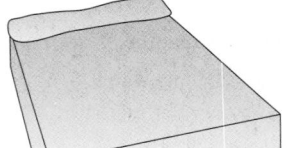

**16.**

**17.**
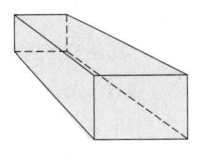

**18.** Explain the difference between a one-point perspective drawing and a two-point perspective drawing.  A one-point has one vanishing point and a two-point has two.

## ADDITIONAL ANSWERS

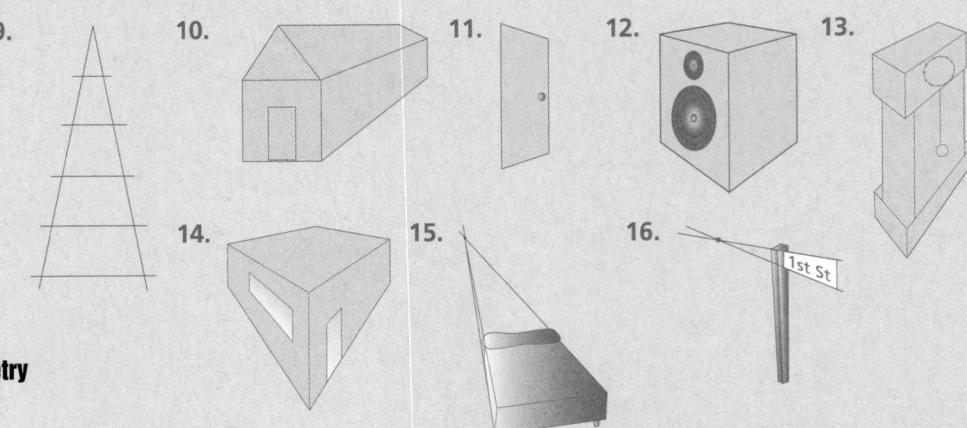

9.  10.  11.  12.  13.

14.  15.  16.

## PRACTICE ■ LESSON 10-1–LESSON 10-4

**Draw a net for each three-dimensional figure.** (Lesson 10-2)
For 19–21, see additional answers.

**19.** 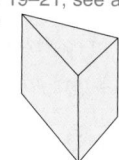  **20.** 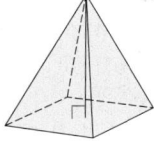  **21.**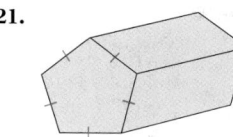

**Refer to the figure.** (Lesson 10-1)

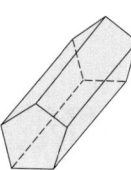

**22.** How many vertices does the figure have?  10

**23.** How many faces does the figure have?  7

**24.** Name the figure.  pentagonal prism

# Mid-Chapter Quiz

**Identify each figure and name its base(s).** (Lesson 10-1)

**1.**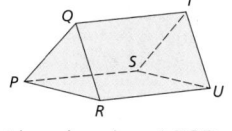
triangular prism; △PQR and △STU

**2.**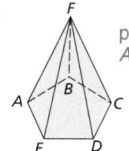
pentagonal pyramid; ABCDE

**3.**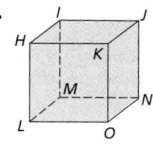
cube; any face

**Identify the three-dimensional figure for each net.** (Lesson 10-2)

**4.**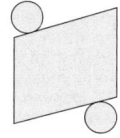
right cylinder

**5.**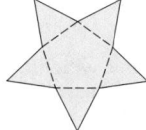
pentagonal pyramid

**6.**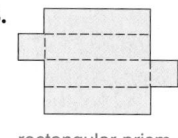
rectangular prism

**Find the surface area of each figure.** (Lesson 10-3)

**7.**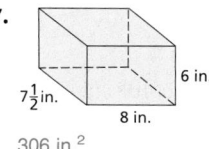
7½ in.    6 in.    8 in.
306 in.²

**8.**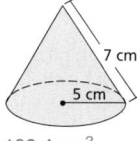
7 cm    5 cm
188.4 cm²

**9.**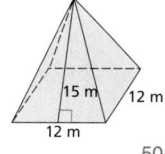
15 m    12 m    12 m
504 m²

**Sketch each object in one-point perspective.** (Lesson 10-4)
For 10–12, see additional answers.

**10.** pentagonal prism   **11.** building   **12.** highway

## MID-CHAPTER QUIZ

**10.** 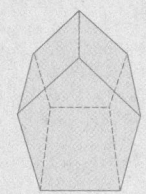   **11.** 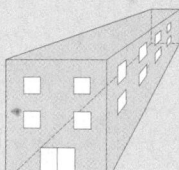   **12.**

### Lesson 10-4
Draw a cube in two-point perspective.

**Step 1** Draw a vertical segment. Choose a horizon line and vanishing point.

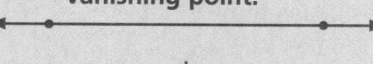

**Step 2** Draw lines from the end-points to the vanishing points. Add lines to complete the two front faces of the cube.

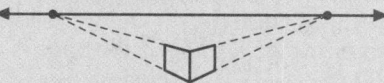

**Step 3** Draw lines from the vertices of the front faces to the vanishing points. Use these lines to complete the cube.

**Step 4** Erase the lines to the van-ishing points. Make hidden lines in the figure dotted.

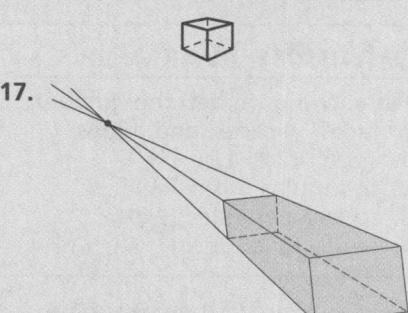

**17.**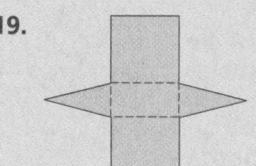

**19.**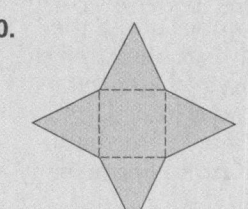

**20.**

**21.**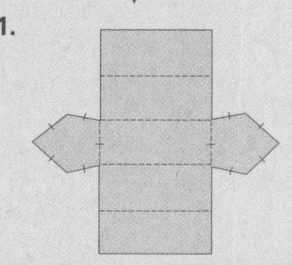

### NCTM Standards/Strands
■ Geometry
■ Representation
■ Connections
■ Algebra

### Vocabulary
isometric drawing

### Tools/Materials Needed
stacking cubes
isometric grid paper (dot paper)

### Lesson Resources
Warm-up Transparency 41
Transparency TK-15, RF-54
Reteaching 10-5
Extra Practice 10-5
Enrichment 10-5

## Getting Started

### 5-MINUTE WARM-UP
**For each figure, tell the number of faces, vertices, and edges.**
**1.** cube   6; 8; 12
**2.** triangular prism   5; 6; 9
**3.** square pyramid   5; 5; 8
**4.** pentagonal prism   7; 10; 14

### Introduction to Lesson 10-5
Before students begin to make their own stacks of cubes, have them look at the configuration shown here (photocopy and enlarge for display), and tell how many cubes are in the stack.   14   Have students tell the method they used to count the cubes. Discuss ways in which this stack could be viewed so that it would be easier to tell how many there are in the stack.

# 10-5 Isometric Drawings

**Goals**  ■  Visualize and represent objects with isometric drawings.

**Applications**  Art, Recreation, History, Architecture

**Work with a partner. Use several cubes, preferably the kind that attach to each other.**
For 1–4, observe students' work.
1. Join or stack the cubes together to build a structure. Hold the structure in your hand, and rotate it to obtain different views.

2. Describe the structure to your partner. Which single view is easiest to describe?

3. Make a new structure. Describe it to your partner so that it is clear how to build the same structure.

4. Have your partner build the new structure based on your description.

### ■ BUILD UNDERSTANDING

In the last lesson, you learned how to reproduce three-dimensional figures on paper using perspective drawings. Another way to show a three-dimensional object is with an isometric drawing. An **isometric drawing** shows an object from a corner view so that three sides of the object can be seen in a single drawing.

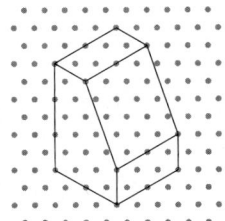

The figure shows an isometric drawing of a structure. In an isometric drawing, all parallel edges of the structure are shown as parallel line segments in the drawing. Perpendicular line segments do not necessarily appear perpendicular.

### Example 1

**Make an isometric drawing of a cube.**

**Solution**

*Step 1* Begin by drawing a vertical line, which will be the front edge of the cube. Then draw the right and left edges of the cube.

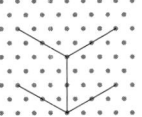

*Step 2* Draw the vertical sides of the cube parallel to the front edge. Complete the isometric drawing by sketching the rear edges of the cube.

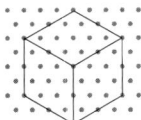

> **Problem Solving Tip**
>
> The length of all edges in an isometric drawing are either the true length or a scaled length. Angle measurements are not preserved in isometric drawings.

**442**  |  Chapter 10  **Three-Dimensional Geometry**

## ADDITIONAL ANSWERS

1.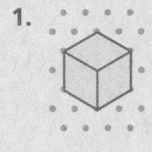

2.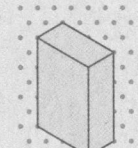

3.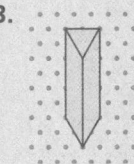

4.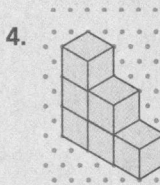

5.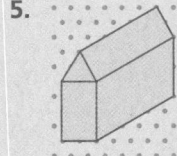

6.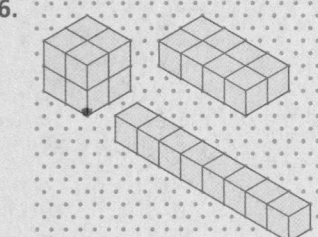

## Example 2

**Make an isometric drawing of a figure containing three cubes that form an L shape.**

### Solution

*Step 1* Begin by drawing the left edges of the figure. Then draw the segments for the right edges of the figure. These segments are parallel to the edges of the left side and shown here in blue.

*Step 2* Complete the isometric drawing by sketching the five remaining segments that outline the cubes.

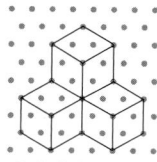

## Example 3

**Use the isometric drawing to answer the questions.**

**a.** How many cubes are used in the drawing?

**b.** How many cube faces are in the figure?

**c.** If each cube face represents 3.5 ft², what is the total surface area of the figure?

### Solution

**a.** Even though there are only three visible cubes, the figure contains four cubes. The top cube is resting on a cube beneath it.

**b.** To count the total number of cube faces, proceed in a logical manner so that you do not miss any sides.

    Cube faces pointing up = 3

    Cube faces pointing to the front = 6

    Cube faces pointing to the back = 6

    Cube faces on the bottom = 3

There are a total of $3 + 6 + 6 + 3 = 18$ cube faces on the figure.

**c.** Since there are 18 cube faces and each face represents $3.5 \text{ ft}^2$, the total surface area of the figure is $18 \cdot 3.5 \text{ ft}^2 = 63 \text{ ft}^2$.

### ▶ TRY THESE EXERCISES

**Create an isometric drawing of each figure.**
For 1–4, see additional answers.

**1.** cube

**2.** rectangular prism

**3.** triangular prism

**4.** staircase composed of cubes

**5. ARCHITECTURE** Using isometric grid paper, design a building using a rectangular prism for the base and a triangular prism for the roof.  See additional answers.

**6.** Use isometric grid paper to draw three different rectangular solids using a total of eight cubes each.  See additional answers.

 mathmatters2.com/extra_examples

---

## Chalkboard Examples

### Supplementary Example 1

Make an isometric drawing of a stack of two cubes.

*Step 1* To draw the bottom cube, begin with a vertical line for the front edge of the cube, deciding upon the length of the edge of the cube. Then draw the right and left edges of the same length.

*Step 2* In like manner, begin the top cube. Complete the top cube by drawing in its upper face, being careful to allow for congruent edges.

### Supplementary Example 2

Make an isometric drawing for the stack of cubes that is shown in the perspective drawing.

*Step 1* Begin a bottom cube.

*Step 2* Add a second cube on top of the first.

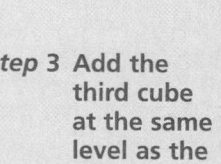
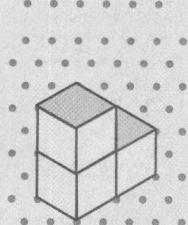

*Step 3* Add the third cube at the same level as the first cube.

---

## Extend the Lesson

**CHALLENGE** Define a *polycube* as a configuration of cubes so that each cube has at least one face exactly meeting a face of another cube.

 This is a polycube

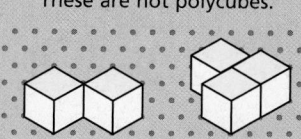 These are not polycubes.

Have students find as many different shapes of four-cube polycubes (*quadracubes*) as possible.

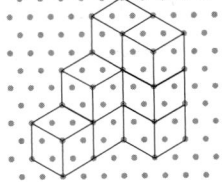

7. How many cubes are used in the drawing? How many are hidden?   9; 2

8. How many cube faces are exposed in the figure?   32

9. If each face represents 1 yd², what is the total surface area of the figure?   32 yd²

## Lesson Wrap-up

### QUICK ASSESSMENT

Ask the following questions to determine if students understand the content presented in this lesson.

1. How is isometric drawing different from one-point or two-point perspective drawing?   In isometric drawing, parallel edges are actually parallel; in perspective drawing, parallel lines meet at a vanishing point.

2. In an isometric drawing of an object, two views, from opposite corners, are often shown. What is the purpose of showing these two views?   Parts of the object that are hidden in one view will be revealed by the other.

### ASSIGNMENT GUIDE

Basic: 1–30, 35–44
Enriched: 1–44

### Reteaching Worksheet 10-5

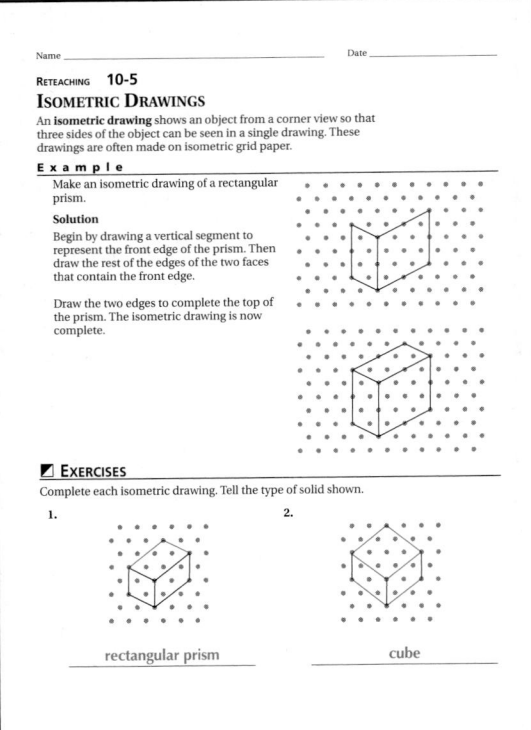

■ **PRACTICE EXERCISES** • For Extra Practice, see page 618.

**Create an isometric drawing of each figure.**
For 10–15, see additional answers.

10. hexagonal prism

11. figure having 14 faces

12. pentagonal prism

13. figure composed of 11 cubes

14. capital block-style letter M

15. cube on top of a rectangular prism

16. Use isometric grid paper to make a sketch of the letters of your first name.
    Answers will vary.

17. Use isometric grid paper to make a sketch of a rectangular prism with 18 faces.
    See additional answers.

**Use the isometric drawing for Exercises 18–20. Assume that no cubes are hidden from view.**

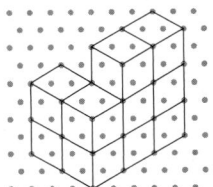

18. How many cubes are used in the drawing?   10

19. How many cube faces are exposed in the figure?   34

20. If the length of an edge of one of the cubes is 3.4 m, what is the total surface area of the figure?   393.04 m²

**Give the number of cubes used to make each figure and the number of cube faces exposed. Be sure to count the cubes that are hidden from view.**

21.
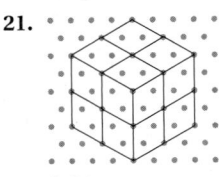
8; 24

22.
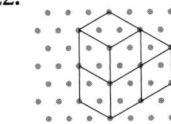
3; 14

23.
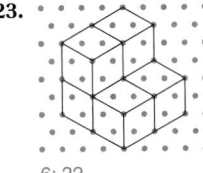
6; 22

24.
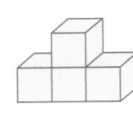
4; 18

25.
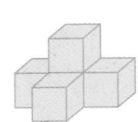
5; 22

26.
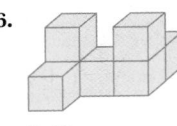
7; 30

27. **RECREATION** Make an isometric drawing of a tent. Use a rectangular prism for the base and a triangular prism for the top of the tent.   See additional answers.

28. **WRITING MATH** Explain the similarities and differences between regular square grid paper and isometric dot paper. Which do you prefer to use for drawing?   Answers will vary.

## ADDITIONAL ANSWERS

10.
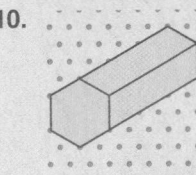

11.
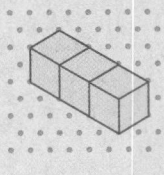

14.
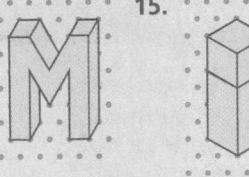

15.
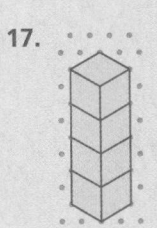

12.
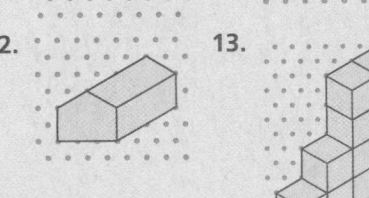

13.
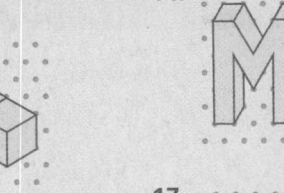

17.
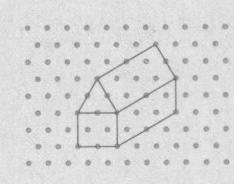

27.

29. **HISTORY** Make an isometric drawing of the ancient Greek Parthenon.
See additional answers.

30. **YOU MAKE THE CALL** Ken says that it is impossible to make an isometric drawing of a rectangular prism containing 6 cubes that has exactly 24 cube faces showing. Brandon says that you can do this by making one long stack of cubes. Who is correct and why?
Ken is correct. Brandon did not count the base faces.

The Parthenon; Athens, Greece

### ■ EXTENDED PRACTICE EXERCISES

**How many cubes are used to make each isometric figure? Be sure to count the cubes that are hidden from view.**

31.
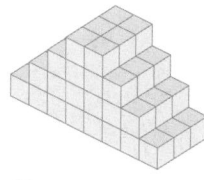
60

32.

48

33.
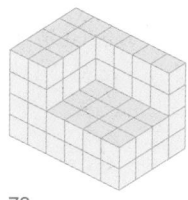
72

34. **ART** Isometric grid paper can be used to make artistic patterns and designs similar to the ones shown. Use isometric grid paper to create two different artistic designs. Color the designs. Answers will vary.

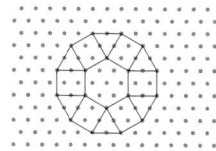 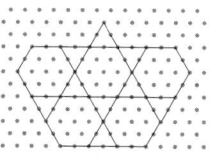

### ■ MIXED REVIEW EXERCISES

**Solve each system of equations graphically.** (Lesson 8-2)

35. $3x - y = 10$ $(3, -1)$
$x + y = 2$

36. $2x + y = 8$ $(2, 4)$
$x - 3y = -10$

37. $x + 2y = 7$ $(-3, 5)$
$4x - 2y = -22$

38. $2x + 2y = -8$ $(-2, -2)$
$2x - 2y = 0$

39. $3x + 2y = 12$ $(2, 3)$
$x - 3y = -7$

40. $x + 3y = 11$ $\left(\frac{1}{5}, \frac{18}{5}\right)$
$x - 2y = -7$

**Show each sample space using ordered pairs.** (Lesson 4-3)
For 41–44, see additional answers.

41. A quarter and a dime are tossed.

42. A six-sided number cube is rolled and a dime is tossed.

43. A six-sided number cube is rolled and a spinner with five different colors is spun. (Use the numbers 1–5 for the colors on the spinner.)

44. Two spinners, one numbered 1–4 and the other lettered A–F, are spun.

 Math Online mathmatters2.com/self_check_quiz

29.
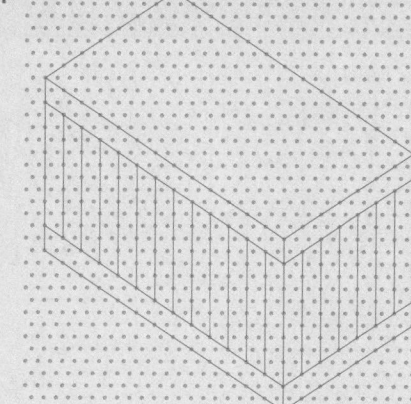

41. HH, HT, TH, TT
42. 1H, 1T, 2H, 2T, 3H, 3T, 4H, 4T, 5H, 5T, 6H, 6T
43. 11, 12, 13, 14, 15, 21, 22, 23, 24, 25, 31, 32, 33, 34, 35, 41, 42, 43, 44, 45, 51, 52, 53, 54, 55, 61, 62, 63, 64, 65
44. 1A, 1B, 1C, 1D, 1E, 1F, 2A, 2B, 2C, 2D, 2E, 2F, 3A, 3B, 3C, 3D, 3E, 3F, 4A, 4B, 4C, 4D, 4E, 4F

## Extra Practice Worksheet 10-5

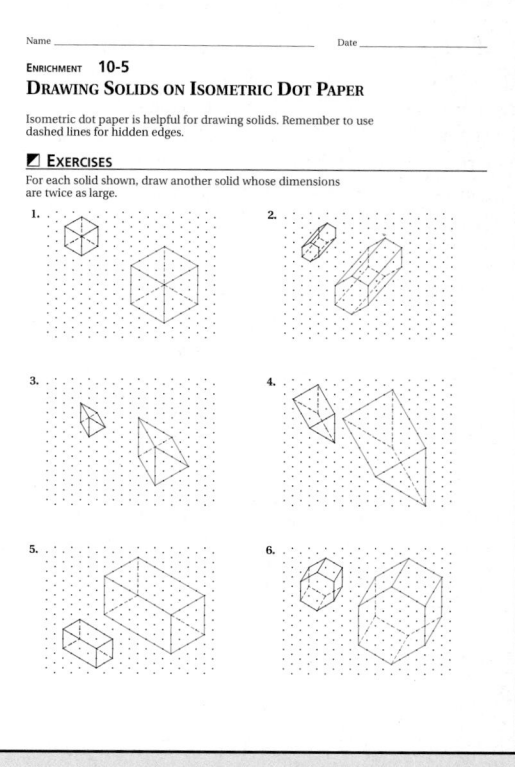

Name _____ Date _____

EXTRA PRACTICE **10-5**
**ISOMETRIC DRAWINGS**

☑ **EXERCISES** Check students' drawings.

Create an isometric drawing of each figure. Use your own paper.

1. a triangular prism
2. a figure composed of 8 cubes
3. a figure composed of 12 cubes
4. two cubes on top of a rectangular prism
5. a bar of soap
6. a cereal box

Use the isometric drawing for Exercises 7–9.

Assume that no cubes are hidden from view.

7. How many cubes are used in the drawing? ___4___
8. How many cube faces are exposed in the figure? ___18___
9. If the length of an edge of one of the cubes is 2.5 m, what is the total surface of the figure to the nearest tenth of a meter? ___112.5 m²___

Give the number of cubes used to make each figure and the number of cube faces exposed.

10.
___4; 18___

11.
___15; 40___

12. Make an isometric drawing of a house. Use a rectangular prism for the base and a rectangular pyramid for the roof. Use your own paper.
Check students' drawings.

## Enrichment Worksheet 10-5

Name _____ Date _____

ENRICHMENT **10-5**
**DRAWING SOLIDS ON ISOMETRIC DOT PAPER**

Isometric dot paper is helpful for drawing solids. Remember to use dashed lines for hidden edges.

☑ **EXERCISES**

For each solid shown, draw another solid whose dimensions are twice as large.

1.
2.
3.
4.
5.
6.

## Lesson Planning

### NCTM Standards/Strands
- Geometry
- Representation
- Connections
- Algebra

### Vocabulary

orthogonal (orthographic) drawing

### Tools/Materials Needed

stacking cubes

### Lesson Resources

Warm-up Transparency 41
Transparency TK-9
Reteaching 10-6
Extra Practice 10-6
Enrichment 10-6

## Getting Started

### 5-MINUTE WARM-UP

How many cubes are in this figure?
**19**

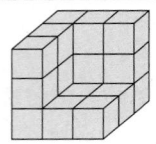

### Introduction to Lesson 10-6

Make sure students understand they are to reproduce the setup within rectangle *ABCD*, using blocks resting on a piece of paper. Students will eventually rotate their paper so that they can view their structure from different corners.

As students examine Figures 1–4 for Question 3, ask them to first tell how many stacks are in each figure and how many cubes are in each stack. **F1: 3 stacks; 2, 3, 1. F2: 3 stacks; 1, 2, 3. F3: 4 stacks; 3, 2, 2, 3. F 4: 5 stacks; 3, 1, 2, 2, 3**

For an activity that reverses this experience, see the Teaching Tip at the bottom of this page.

---

**Goals**
- Sketch orthogonal drawings of figures.
- Sketch and use foundation drawings.

**Applications** Engineering, Interior design, History, Safety

**Use 11 cubes, preferably interlocking ones.**
For 1–2, observe students' work.
1. Label the four corners of a sheet of paper *A*, *B*, *C*, and *D*.

2. Build a structure by stacking the given number of cubes in each position as shown in the figure.

3. Match each figure below with corner views *A*, *B*, *C*, or *D*. Try to visualize the answer in your mind; then check the actual structure to verify.

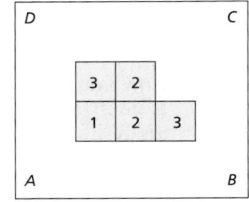

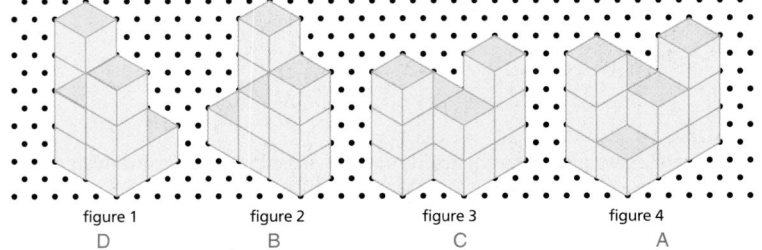

| figure 1 | figure 2 | figure 3 | figure 4 |
| D | B | C | A |

### ◼ BUILD UNDERSTANDING

While perspective drawings and isometric drawings are useful to help visualize a three-dimensional figure, they may not show all the details of an object that you need. An **orthogonal drawing**, or **orthographic drawing**, gives top, front, and side views of a three-dimensional figure as seen from a "straight on" viewpoint. In an orthogonal drawing, solid lines represent any edges that show.

### Example 1

**Make an orthogonal drawing of the figure.**

**Solution**

Draw the front view first.

Draw the top view above it. Make sure it has the same width as the front view.

Draw the right-side view. Make sure it has the same height as the front view and the same depth as the top view.

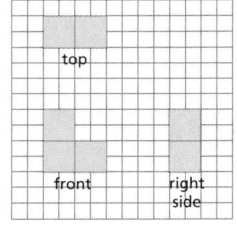

---

## Flexible Grouping

For a reverse experience from that of the opening activity, tell students that some cubes have been arranged on a rectangular sheet labeled *ABCD*. Each of the figures shown represents a view from one of the four corners.
Have students work in pairs to create the structure.

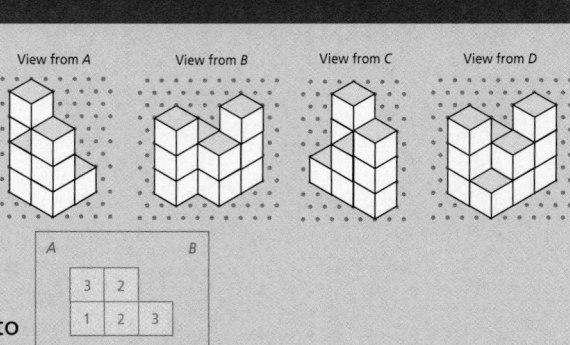

View from A   View from B   View from C   View from D

# Example 2

**ENGINEERING** The isometric drawing shows part of an air-conditioning duct.

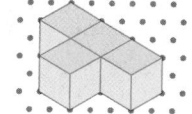

a. Make an orthogonal drawing of the duct showing the front, top, and right-side views.

b. The length of one cube side is 1.6 m. The building engineer needs the surface area of the top to be between 10 m² and 10.5 m². Is the duct within the necessary requirements?

## Solution

a. Think of the duct as a combination of four cubes. Then make each view of the orthogonal drawing.

b. Calculate the surface area of the top of the figure. It is composed of four cube faces.

$1.6 \cdot 1.6 = 2.56$ m²     Calculate the area of one cube.

$2.56 \cdot 4 = 10.24$ m²     Find the total surface area of the top.

The duct is within the given requirements.

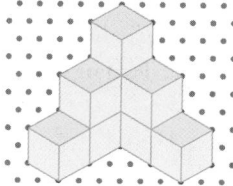

A **foundation drawing** shows the base of a structure and the height of each part. They are often used by architects and design engineers. The figure shows a foundation drawing of the Sears Tower in Chicago. Each number represents how many stories are in each section.

| 54 | 67 | 54 |
|----|----|----|
| 67 | 98 | 67 |
| 41 | 98 | 41 |

# Example 3

**Create a foundation drawing for the isometric drawing. Assume the drawing is viewed from the lower left-hand corner.**

## Solution

First draw the orthogonal top view of the figure.

Then determine how many cubes belong in each section, and write the number to complete the foundation drawing.

| 3 | 2 | 1 |
|---|---|---|
| 2 | | |
| 1 | | |

## ▧ TRY THESE EXERCISES

**Make an orthogonal drawing labeling the front, top, and right-side views.**
For 1–4, see additional answers.

1.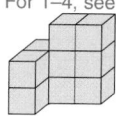
2.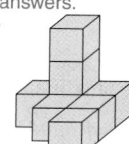
3.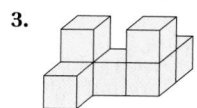
4.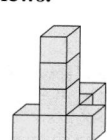

 **Math Online** mathmatters2.com/extra_examples

Lesson 10-6 **Orthogonal Drawings** | **447**

---

## ADDITIONAL ANSWERS

1.
2. 
3.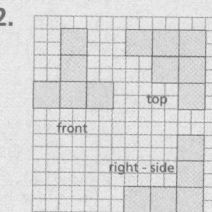
4.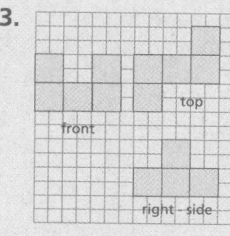
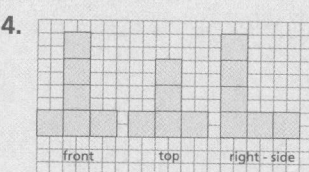

---

# Chalkboard Examples

## Supplementary Example 1

**ARCHITECTURE** Here is an orthogonal drawing of a planned storage building.

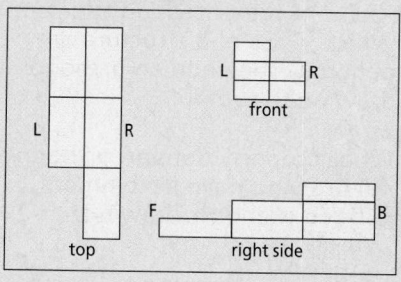

a. How many stories high is the building? **From the front or side view, the building is three stories high.**

b. How many sections long is the building from front to back? **From the top view or right-side view, the building is three sections long.**

c. Where is the highest part of the building located? **From the front view, the highest part is somewhere on the left side; from the right-side view, the highest part is at the back. So, the highest part is at the back left.**

d. Draw a possible shape for the building.

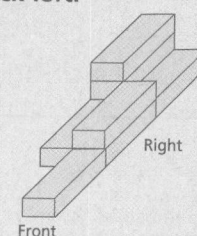

## Supplementary Example 2

A foundation drawing for a building is shown at the right.

| | back | |
|---|---|---|
| 2 | 2 | 3 |
| 1 | 1 | 2 |
| | 3 | |

left      right

front

a. Draw the front orthogonal view and tell how it is related to the back view?

**The front and back views are mirror images.**

b. Draw the left orthogonal view and tell how it is related to the right view. **The left and right views are the same.**

Lesson 10-6 **Orthogonal Drawings**   **447**

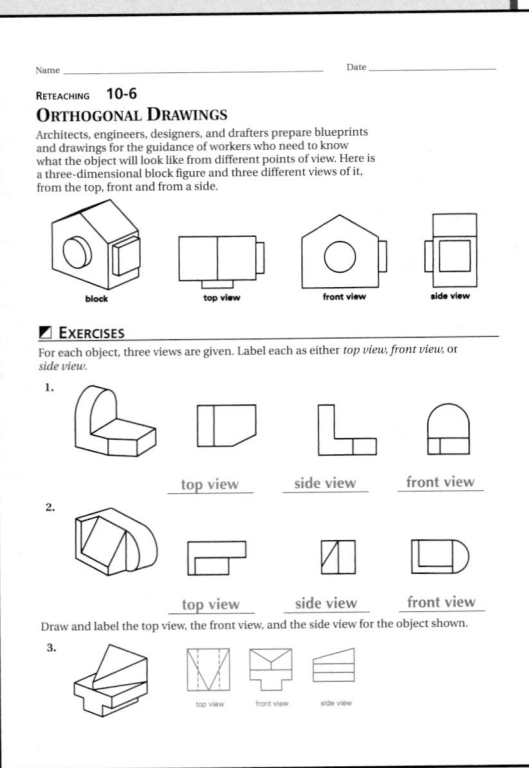
The figure is a cube with a "half cube" on top of it. Tell which view of the figure is shown.

5.  right-side

6.  top

7. front

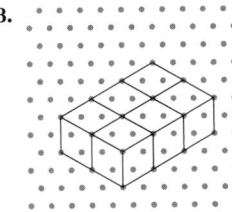

Create a foundation drawing for each figure. Assume the drawing is viewed from the lower left-hand corner. For 8–10, see additional answers.

8.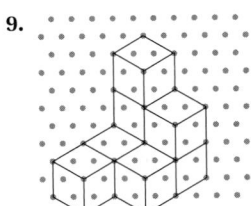

9.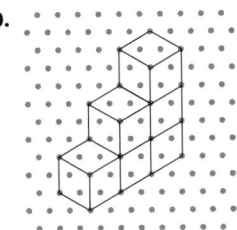

10.

---

### PRACTICE EXERCISES • For Extra Practice, see page 618.

Make an orthogonal drawing labeling the front, top, and right-side views.
For 11–13, see additional answers.

11.
12.
13.

 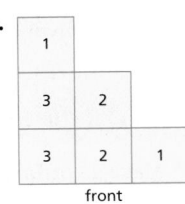

For each foundation drawing, sketch the front and right orthogonal views.
For 14–16, see additional answers.

14.
| 5 | 5 |
|---|---|
| 3 | 1 |

front

15.
| 1 | 2 | 3 |
|---|---|---|
|   | 2 | 1 |

front

16.
| 1 |   |   |
|---|---|---|
| 3 | 2 |   |
| 3 | 2 | 1 |

front

17. **WRITING MATH** Choose an object and describe how the orthogonal drawings of the front, top, and right-side views are different or the same. Answers will vary.

18. Make an orthogonal drawing of a regular six-sided number cube showing a view of each of the six sides. See additional answers.

For Exercises 13, 15, 19, 21, 23, 29, 31, 33 and 35, see Selected Answers on page 694.

11.
top
front
right-side

12.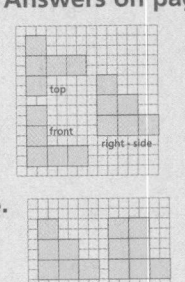
top
front
right-side

14.
front right-side

16.
front right-side

18.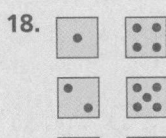

20. The word orthogonal literally means "straight angle" and refers to a relationship of two things that intersect or lie at right angles. The connection to this particular application can be made by the word "straight" in straight-on view.

**19. SAFETY** Most skyscrapers are built using steel girders shaped like the capital letter I. The shape avoids buckling and can support heavy loads. Make an orthogonal drawing of the girder showing the front, top and right-side views. See additional answers.

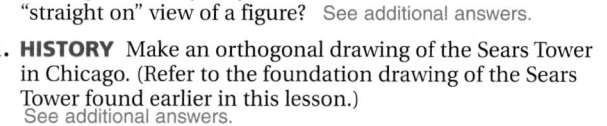

**20. WRITING MATH** Investigate the meaning of the word "orthogonal." Why do you think it is used to describe the "straight on" view of a figure? See additional answers.

**21. HISTORY** Make an orthogonal drawing of the Sears Tower in Chicago. (Refer to the foundation drawing of the Sears Tower found earlier in this lesson.)
See additional answers.

## ■ EXTENDED PRACTICE EXERCISES

**Create an orthogonal drawing for each figure.**
For 22–24, see additional answers.

**22.** 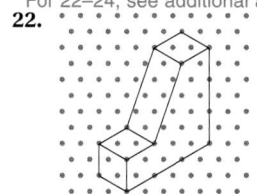   **23.** 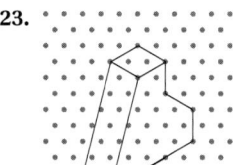   **24.**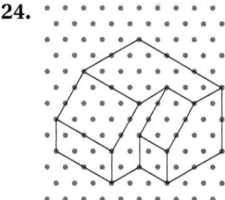

**25. CRITICAL THINKING** The drawing shows top and front views of a building. Draw three possible right-side views of the building.
Answers will vary. Check students' work.

**26.** Make an orthogonal drawing showing the front, top and right-side views of a staircase that is one cube wide and reaches a height of ten cubes. Then make a foundation drawing of the staircase.
See additional answers.

**27. INTERIOR DESIGN** If the height of each cube in Exercise 26 is 8 in., how many square inches of carpeting are needed to completely cover the front and top edges of the staircase? 1280 in.²

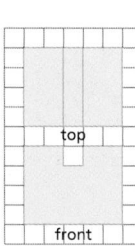

## ■ MIXED REVIEW EXERCISES

**Use grid paper. Graph each function for the domain of real numbers.** (Lesson 6-6)
For 28–36, see additional answers.

**28.** $y = x^2 - 1$     **29.** $y = x^2 - x + 2$     **30.** $y = x^2 + x - 4$

**31.** $y = 2x^2 + 3x + 1$     **32.** $y = 3x^2 - 4$     **33.** $y = 2x^2 - x - 1$

**34.** $y = 2x^2 + 2$     **35.** $y = x^2 - 3x + 4$     **36.** $y = 2x^2 + x - 5$

**Write each phrase as a variable expression.** (Lesson 2-3)

**37.** six times a number divided by three   $\frac{6x}{3}$

**38.** the product of seven and a number   $7x$

**39.** two more than 12 times a number   $12n + 2$

**40.** the quotient of negative six and a number   $-\frac{6}{x}$

**41.** a number less nine   $x - 9$

**42.** negative three times a number   $-3x$

 mathmatters2.com/self_check_quiz

Lesson 10-6 **Orthogonal Drawings** | **449**

Lesson 10-6 **Orthogonal Drawings** 449

**Extra Practice Worksheet 10-6**

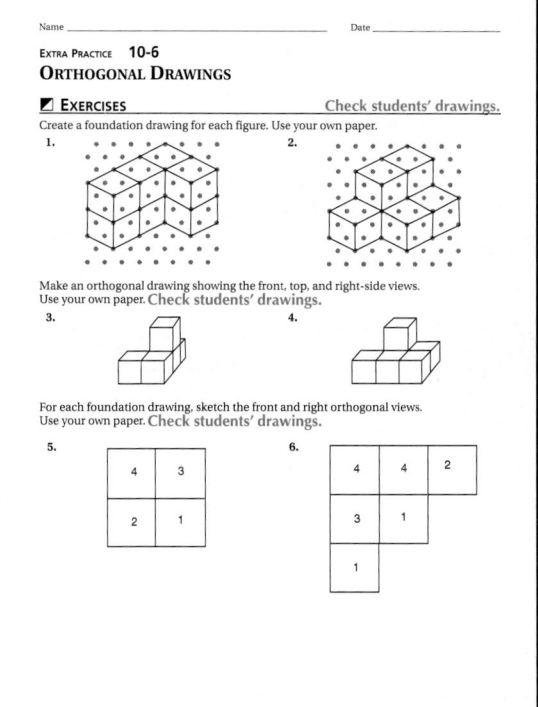

Name _____ Date _____

EXTRA PRACTICE **10-6**
**ORTHOGONAL DRAWINGS**

✎ **EXERCISES**     Check students' drawings.

Create a foundation drawing for each figure. Use your own paper.

1.     2.

Make an orthogonal drawing showing the front, top, and right-side views. Use your own paper. Check students' drawings.

3.     4.

For each foundation drawing, sketch the front and right orthogonal views. Use your own paper. Check students' drawings.

5. 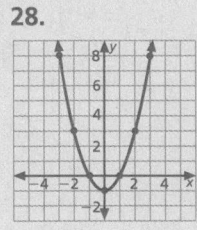     6.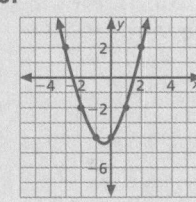

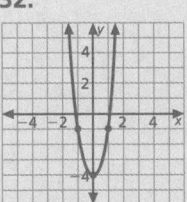    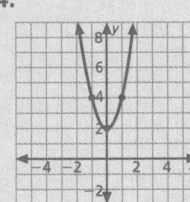

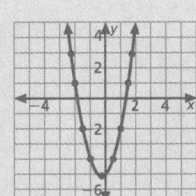

**22.** 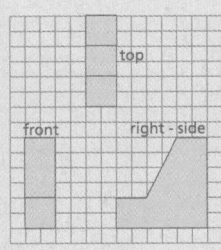     **24.** 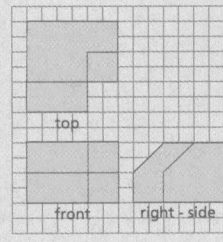     **26.**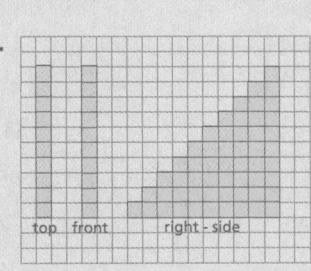

**450** Chapter 10 **Three-Dimensional Geometry**

## Skills Practice

### Vocabulary Review

**Lesson 10-5**
isometric drawing

**Lesson 10-6**
orthogonal (orthographic)
drawing

### ASSIGNMENT GUIDE

**All students: 1–24**

## Chalkboard Examples

### Lesson 10-5

Make two different isometic drawings of four cubes, with three cubes on the first level.

### Lesson 10-6

Which of the choices that follow shows the orthographic views of this isometric drawing? **C**

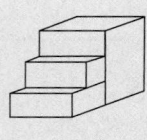

**A.** top

**B.** top

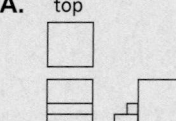

front   right

front   right

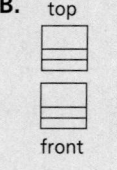

**C.** top

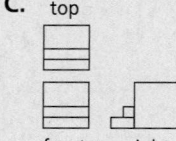

front   right

**450** Chapter 10   **Three-Dimensional Geometry**

# Review and Practice Your Skills

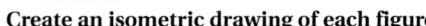

### PRACTICE ◤ LESSON 10-5

**Use the isometric drawing for Exercises 1–3. Assume that no cubes are hidden from view.**

1. How many cubes are used in the drawing?  12

2. How many cube faces are exposed in the figure?  40

3. If the length of one of the cubes is 2.8 in., what is the total surface area of the figure to the nearest tenth of an inch?
313.6 in.²

**Create an isometric drawing of each figure.**
For 4–7, drawings will vary. See additional answers for examples.

4. pentagonal prism

5. figure composed of 10 cubes

6. figure with 7 faces

7. triangular prism

### PRACTICE ◤ LESSON 10-6

**Create a foundation drawing for each isometric drawing. Assume the drawing is viewed from the lower left-hand corner.**
For 8–10, see additional answers.

8.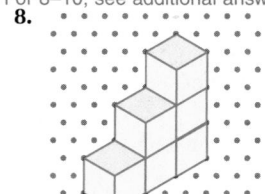

9.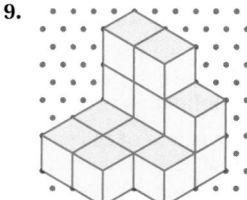

10.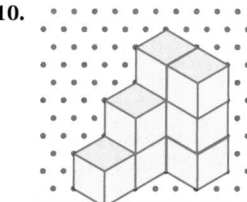

**Make an orthogonal drawing labeling the front, top and right-side views.**
For 11–13, see additional answers.

11.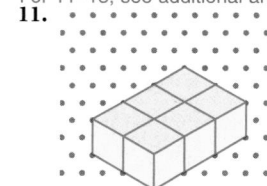

12.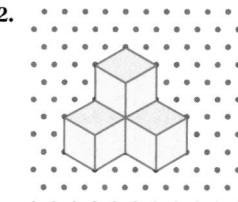

13.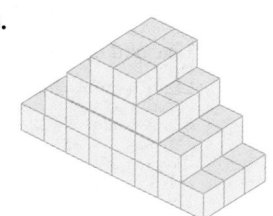

**For each foundation drawing, sketch the front and right orthogonal views.**
For 14–16, see additional answers.

14.

| 3 | 2 |
|---|---|
| 2 | 1 |

front

15.

| 3 | 3 |
|---|---|
| 2 | 2 |
| 1 | 1 |

front

16.

|   | 1 |
|---|---|
| 1 | 2 |
|   | 1 |

front

**450** | Chapter 10 **Three-Dimensional Geometry**

## ADDITIONAL ANSWERS

4.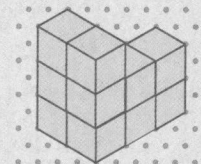

5.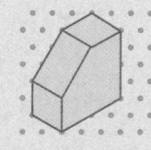

6.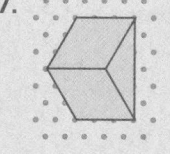

7.

8.

| 3 |
|---|
| 2 |
| 1 |

9.

| 3 | 3 | 2 |
|---|---|---|
| 1 | 1 | 1 |
| 1 | 1 |   |

10.

| 3 | 3 |
|---|---|
| 2 |   |
| 1 |   |

11.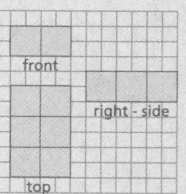

12.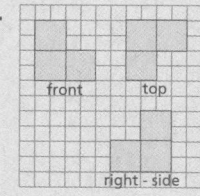

**Draw a rectangular pyramid.** (Lesson 10-1)

17. How many vertices does it have?  5

18. How many faces does it have?  5

19. How many bases does it have?  1

20. What is the surface area of a rectangular prism with dimensions of 2 in. by 6 in. by 4 in.? (Lesson 10-3)  88 in.²

21. Draw a net for a pentagonal prism. (Lesson 10-2)  See additional answers.

**For each foundation drawing, sketch the front and right orthogonal views.** (Lesson 10-6)
For 22–24, see additional answers.

22.

| 3 | 3 | 1 |
|---|---|---|
| 2 | | |
| 1 | | |

front

23.

| 2 | 1 |
|---|---|
| 2 | 1 |

front

24.

| | 1 | 2 | 1 |
|---|---|---|---|
| | | 1 | |

front

---

## Math*Works* Career – Exhibit Designer
Workplace Knowhow

**E**xhibit designers organize and design products and materials so they serve the intended purpose and are visually pleasing. Some exhibit designers work in museums to create, design, install, disassemble and store historical displays. A museum exhibit designer is designing models of notable skyscrapers for a historical exhibit. Accurately communicating the design ideas to the model creator is important. The figure shown is a two-point perspective drawing of the Empire State Building (without the lightning rod) in New York City, NY.

**Refer to the drawing and the table.**
For 1–3, see additional answers.

1. Create an orthogonal drawing of the Empire State Building.

2. Create an isometric drawing of the Empire State Building.

3. Create a one-point perspective drawing of the Empire State Building.

**Empire State Building**

| Section | Width* (feet) | Depth* (feet) | Height* (feet) |
|---|---|---|---|
| 1 | 833 | 375 | 125 |
| 2 | 667 | 292 | 250 |
| 3 | 500 | 208 | 750 |
| 4 | 250 | 125 | 125 |

\* Dimensions are not actual measurements of the Empire State Building

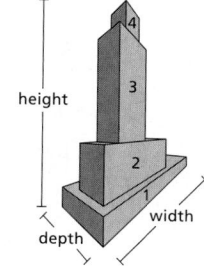

---

## ADDITIONAL ANSWERS

13.
front    top    right - side

14.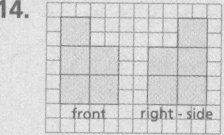
front    right - side

15.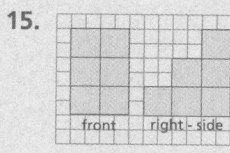
front    right - side

16.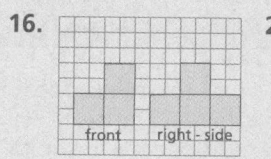
front    right - side

21.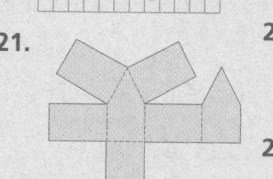

22.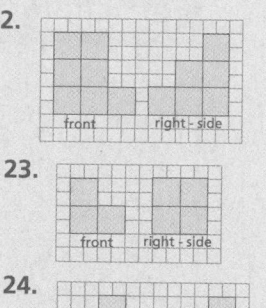
front    right - side

23.
front    right - side

24.
front    right - side

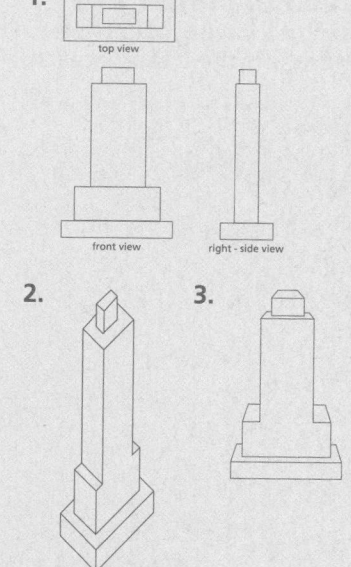

### Vocabulary

volume

### Tools/Materials Needed

heavy paper    ruler
tape            dried beans
calculator

### Lesson Resources

Warm-up Transparency 42
Transparency RF-49
Reteaching 10-7
Extra Practice 10-7
Enrichment 10-7
Technology Activity 10-7 and 10-8

## Getting Started

### 5-Minute Warm-up

**Find the area of each figure.**
1. rectangle: $\ell = 15$ m, $w = 9.6$ m
   **144 m²**
2. triangle: $b = 17$ cm, $h = 22$ cm
   **187 cm²**
3. right triangle: a leg = 12 in.,
   hypotenuse = 37 in.   **210 in.²**
4. square: $s = 11.3$ ft   **127.69 ft²**

### Introduction to Lesson 10-7
You may wish to have students use
a ruler to level off the beans in each
container.

---

# 10-7 Volume of Prisms and Pyramids

**Goals**
- Use a formula to find the volume of prisms.
- Use a formula to find the volume of pyramids.

**Applications**   Earth science, Hobbies, Packaging, History, Machinery

**Use sheets of heavy paper, a ruler, tape and dried beans.**

1. Use the patterns to make a cube and a square pyramid. Both
   shapes should be missing one side.   Observe students' work.

2. Completely fill the cube with dried beans. Record the
   number of beans used.   Answers will vary.

3. Pour the beans directly from the cube to the pyramid.
   Approximately how many times can you fill the pyramid?   3

4. What relationship do you see?   The volume of a cube is
   three times greater than its corresponding pyramid.

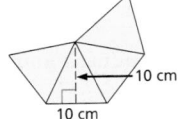

### ◼ BUILD UNDERSTANDING

Recall that **volume** is a measure of the number of cubic units needed to fill a
region of space. To find the volume of any prism, multiply the area of the base
by the height of the prism.

| Volume of a Prism | $V = Bh$ <br> where $B$ is the area of the base and $h$ is the height of the prism. |
|---|---|

### Example 1

**Find the volume of each prism.**

a.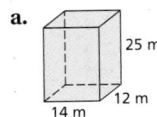

b.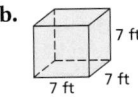

**Problem Solving Tip**

Volume is always
measured in cubic units
since it is found by
multiplying an area
(which is measured in
square units) by a length.

**Solution**

a. The base is a rectangle.

   $B = 14 \cdot 12$     $B = lw$

   $B = 168$

Use the volume formula.

   $V = 168 \cdot 25$    $V = Bh$

   $V = 4200$

The volume is 4200 m³.

b. The base is a square.

   $B = 7^2$      $B = s^2$

   $B = 49$

Use the volume formula.

   $V = 49 \cdot 7$    $V = Bh$

   $V = 343$

The volume is 343 ft³.

---

## Teaching Tip

Emphasize that since volume is obtained by multiplying an area (square
units) by a height (linear units), the unit for volume is *cubic units*. Connect
this situation to multiplication of monomials in which the powers of like
bases are added:
unit² · unit¹ = unit²⁺¹ = unit³
This is also a good place to review
units of measure for all the
geometric measures learned so far.
Have students complete a summary
table, such as the one shown.

| geometric measure | example of unit |
|---|---|
| length | cm |
| area | cm² |
| surface area | cm² |
| lateral area | cm² |
| volume | cm³ |

## Example 2

**Find the volume of the triangular prism.**

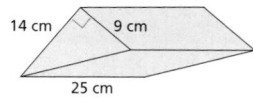

### Solution

The base is a right triangle.

$$B = \frac{1}{2} \cdot 9 \cdot 14 \qquad B = \frac{1}{2}bh$$

$$B = 63$$

Use the volume formula.

$$V = 63 \cdot 25 \qquad V = Bh$$

$$V = 1575$$

The volume is 1575 cm³.

**Problem Solving Tip**

To find the volume of a rectangular prism, use the formula $V = lwh$.

To find the volume of a cube, use the formula $V = s^3$.

## Example 3

**RECREATION** A rectangular swimming pool is filled with 1750 ft³ of water. The pool width is 14 ft and the pool depth is 5 ft. Find the length of the pool.

### Solution

Use the volume formula for a rectangular prism.

$$1750 = l \cdot 14 \cdot 5 \qquad V = lwh$$

$$1750 = 70l \qquad \text{Solve for } l.$$

$$\frac{1750}{70} = \frac{70l}{70}$$

$$25 = l$$

The length of the pool is 25 ft.

The volume of a prism is 3 times the volume of a pyramid. To find the volume of a pyramid, take $\frac{1}{3}$ the product of the area of the base and the height.

> **Volume of a Pyramid**
> $$V = \frac{1}{3}Bh$$
> where $B$ is the area of the base and $h$ is the height.

## Example 4

**Find the volume of the rectangular pyramid.**

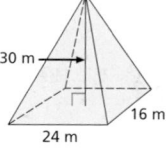

### Solution

Find the area of the rectangle base.

$$B = 24 \cdot 16 \qquad B = lw$$

$$B = 384 \text{ m}^2$$

Use the volume formula.

$$V = \frac{1}{3} \cdot 384 \cdot 30 \qquad V = \frac{1}{3}Bh$$

$$V = 3840$$

The volume of the pyramid is 3840 m³.

 **Math Online** mathmatters2.com/extra_examples

Lesson 10-7 **Volume of Prisms and Pyramids** | **453**

---

## Chalkboard Examples

### Supplementary Example 1

Find the volume of the figure formed when the given net is folded.

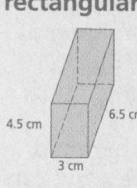

When folded, the net forms a rectangular prism.

The base of the prism is a rectangle. Find its area, $B$.

$$B = 3 \cdot 6.5 = 19.5 \text{ cm}^2$$

height of the prism = 4.5 cm

Apply the volume formula.

$$V = B \cdot h$$
$$= 19.5 \cdot 4.5$$
$$= 87.75$$

So, the volume of the rectangular prism formed by the given net is 87.75 cm³.

### Supplementary Example 2

**FINANCE** The Li family is moving from Connecticut to Arizona. The moving company estimates

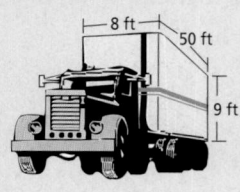

that the Li's belongings weigh an average of 8.5 lb per ft³, and that their belongings will fill about half the van shown. The company charges $750 to ship 1000 lb. About how much should the Li's budget for moving costs? Answer to the nearest hundred dollars.

The van is in the shape of a rectangular prism.

$$V = \ell \cdot w \cdot h = 8 \cdot 50 \cdot 9 = 3600 \text{ ft}^3$$

The Li's belongings will occupy about $\frac{1}{2} \cdot 3600 = 1800$ ft³.

The Li's belongings will weigh about $8.5 \cdot 1800$, or about 15,300 lb. At a cost of $750 per 1000 lb, the Li's cost will be $15.3 \cdot 750 = \$11,475$. So, the Li's moving costs will be about $11,500.

---

## Teaching Tip

Note with students that it may be helpful to subtract volumes, as in Exercise 12, or add volumes, as in Exercise 15.

In Exercise 24, students will need the Pythagorean Theorem to find the altitude of the triangular base. Some students may recognize the Pythagorean triple 3, 4, 5.

In Exercise 25, students will need the formula for the area of a trapezoid, $A = \frac{1}{2}h(b_1 + b_2)$.

## Lesson Wrap-up

### QUICK ASSESSMENT

Ask the following questions to determine if students understand the content presented in this lesson.

1. How can you find the volume of any prism? **Multiply the area of its base by the height of the prism.**

2. How can you find the volume of a rectangular prism? **Multiply the length and width of the base by the height of the prism.**

3. Given the volume of a pyramid and the area of its base, how can you find the height of the pyramid? **Divide the volume by the area of the base, and multiply the result by three.**

### ASSIGNMENT GUIDE

**Basic:** 1–23, 31–42
**Enriched:** 1–42

### Reteaching Worksheet 10-7

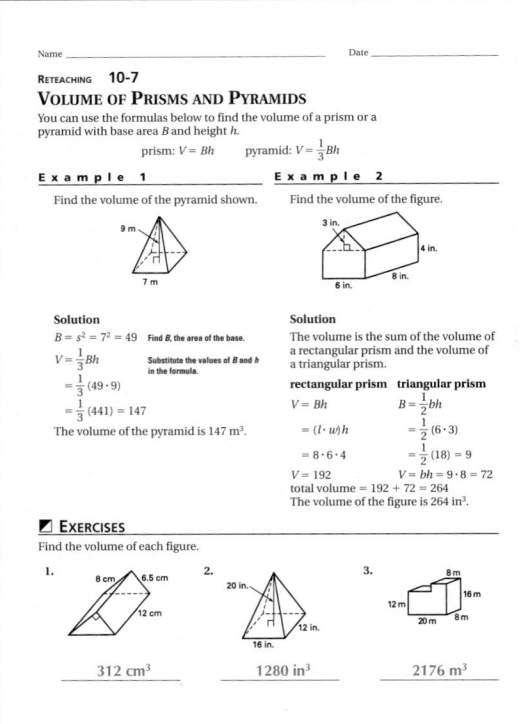

---

**Find the volume of each figure.**

1.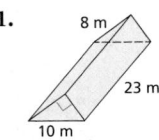
   8 m, 23 m, 10 m
   552 m³

2.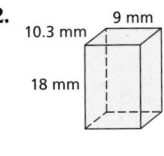
   10.3 mm, 9 mm, 18 mm
   1668.6 mm³

3.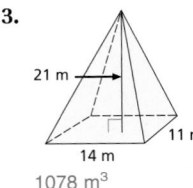
   21 m, 14 m, 11 m
   1078 m³

4.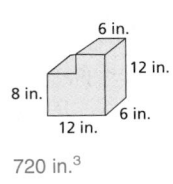
   6 in., 12 in., 8 in., 12 in., 6 in.
   720 in.³

5. **PACKAGING** A gift box that is 15 in. high is a prism with a square base. It has a volume of 540 in.³. What is the length of the sides of its base? **6 in.**

6. Find the volume of a square pyramid if the length of a side of its base is 23 ft and its height is 65 ft. Round the answer to the nearest tenth. **11,461.7 ft³**

7. A triangular prism has a volume of 54 cm³. The triangular base has a height of 4 cm and a base of 6 cm. What is the height of the prism? **4.5 cm**

8. **WRITING MATH** Given the volume of a pyramid and the area of its base, describe how you can find its height. $h = \dfrac{3V}{B}$, where $V$ is the volume of a pyramid and $B$ is the area of its base

---

**Find the volume of each figure.**

9.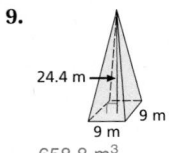
   24.4 m, 9 m, 9 m
   658.8 m³

10.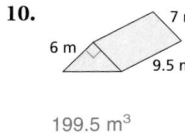
    7 m, 6 m, 9.5 m
    199.5 m³

11.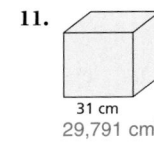
    31 cm
    29,791 cm³

12.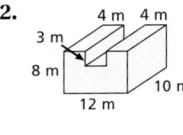
    4 m, 4 m, 3 m, 8 m, 12 m, 10 m
    840 m³

13.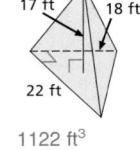
    17 ft, 18 ft, 22 ft
    1122 ft³

14.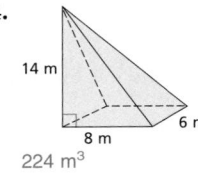
    14 m, 8 m, 6 m
    224 m³

15.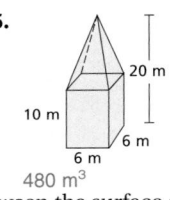
    20 m, 10 m, 6 m, 6 m
    480 m³

16.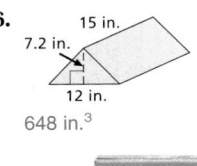
    15 in., 7.2 in., 12 in.
    648 in.³

17. **WRITING MATH** Explain the difference between the surface area and the volume of a three-dimensional figure. **Answers will vary.**

18. A cereal box is 8 in. long and 4 in. wide. Its volume is 368 in.³. What is the height of the box? **11.5 in.**

19. The perimeter of the base of a square prism measures 60 cm. The height of the prism is 25 cm. What is the volume of the prism? **5625 cm³**

20. The base of a prism is an isosceles right triangle with sides measuring $5\sqrt{2}$ cm, $5\sqrt{2}$ cm and 10 cm. The height of the prism is 20 cm. What is the volume of the prism? **500 cm³**

**21. MACHINERY** A dump truck has a bed that is 12 ft long and 8 ft wide. The walls of the bed are 4.5 ft high. When the truck is loaded, no material can be higher than the walls of the bed. If topsoil costs $18/yd³, what is the cost of a full truckload of topsoil?  $288

**22. EARTH SCIENCE** When water freezes, its volume increases by about 10%. A tin container that measures 1 ft by 10 in. by 9 in. is exactly half full of water. It is left outside on a winter day, and all of the water freezes. What is the approximate volume of ice in the tin?  594 in.³

**23. HISTORY** The square base of an Egyptian pyramid is 62 m long. If the height of the pyramid is 78 m, what is its volume?  99,944 m³

## ■ EXTENDED PRACTICE EXERCISES

**Find the volume of each figure.**

**24.**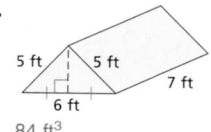
5 ft  5 ft  7 ft  6 ft
84 ft³

**25.**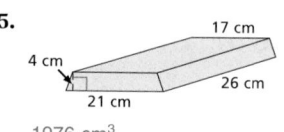
4 cm  17 cm  26 cm  21 cm
1976 cm³

**26.**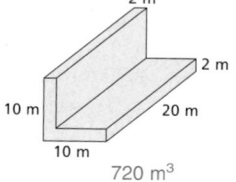
2 m  2 m  10 m  20 m  10 m
720 m³

**27. HOBBIES** An aquarium has a length of 15 in. and a width of 11 in. A rock put into the aquarium causes the water level to rise by 2 in. The rock is completely submerged. What is the volume of the rock?  330 in.³

**28.** Suppose you wish to make a cardboard box with a volume of 1000 cm³. What dimensions would you give to the box in order to use the least amount of cardboard?  Make it a cube with sides 10 cm.

**29. CRITICAL THINKING** The sides of a cube each measure 1 ft. If each side is increased by 1 in., by how many cubic inches would the volume increase?  469 in.³

 **30. CHAPTER INVESTIGATION** Research a significant historical event that was happening at each date on your timeline.  Answers will vary.

## ■ MIXED REVIEW EXERCISES

**Simplify.** (Lesson 9-4)

**31.** $2z(4z + w)$  $8z^2 + 2zw$

**32.** $3d(2d - 3c)$  $6d^2 - 9dc$

**33.** $5rs(3r - 4s)$  $15r^2s - 20rs^2$

**34.** $-6xy(2x - 5y)$  $-12x^2y + 30xy^2$

**35.** $2p(4p + 3r) + 5p(7p - 8r)$  $43p^2 - 34pr$

**36.** $3st(3s - 3t) + 2st(2s - 5t)$  $13s^2t - 19st^2$

**37.** $4yz(y - 3z) + 2yz(6y + 4z)$  $16y^2z - 4yz^2$

**38.** $-5cd(2c + 3d) + 2cd(c - 5d)$  $-8c^2d - 25cd^2$

**Copy quadrilateral *KLMN* on grid paper. Draw each dilation.** (Lesson 7-5)
For 39–42, see additional answers.
**39.** scale factor 2, center (0, 0)

**40.** scale factor $\frac{1}{2}$, center (0, 0)

**41.** scale factor 3, center *L*

**42.** scale factor $\frac{2}{3}$, center *N*

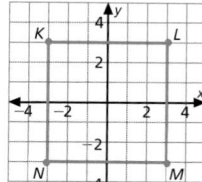

## ADDITIONAL ANSWERS

**39.** 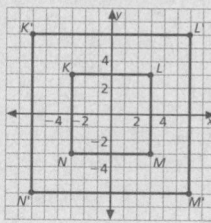  **40.** 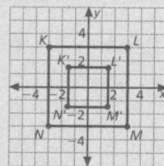  **41.** 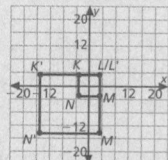  **42.**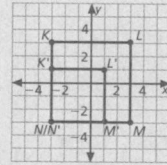

---

### Extra Practice Worksheet 10-7

EXTRA PRACTICE  **10-7**
**VOLUME OF PRISMS AND PYRAMIDS**

**✔ EXERCISES**

Find the volume of each figure.

**1.**  5 ft  4 ft  6 ft
120 ft³

**2.**  3.5 m  5.5 m  7.4 m
71.225 m³

**3.**  12 ft  8 ft  10 ft
160 ft³

**4.**  8 cm
512 cm³

**5.** A box is 10 in. long and 6 in. wide. Its volume is 540 in³. What is the height of the box?  9 in.

**6.** The perimeter of each face of a cube is 72 cm. What is the volume of the cube?  5832 cm³

**7.** The base of a prism is a right triangle with legs of 6 in. and 8 in. The height of the prism is 12 in. What is the volume of the prism?  288 in³

**8.** A rectangular prism a length of 8 cm. The width and height of the prism are the same, and its volume is 128 cm³. What are the width and height of the prism?  4 cm

**9.** The base of a square pyramid has a perimeter of 16 ft. The height of the pyramid is 7 ft. What is the volume of the pyramid?  $37\frac{1}{3}$ ft³

---

### Enrichment Worksheet 10-7

ENRICHMENT  **10-7**
**CUBE CLUB**

**✔ EXERCISES**

Each of the figures below is formed from unit cubes. None of the hidden cubes is missing, so the three faces of each figure that you cannot see are solid. Find the volume, in cubic units, for each figure.

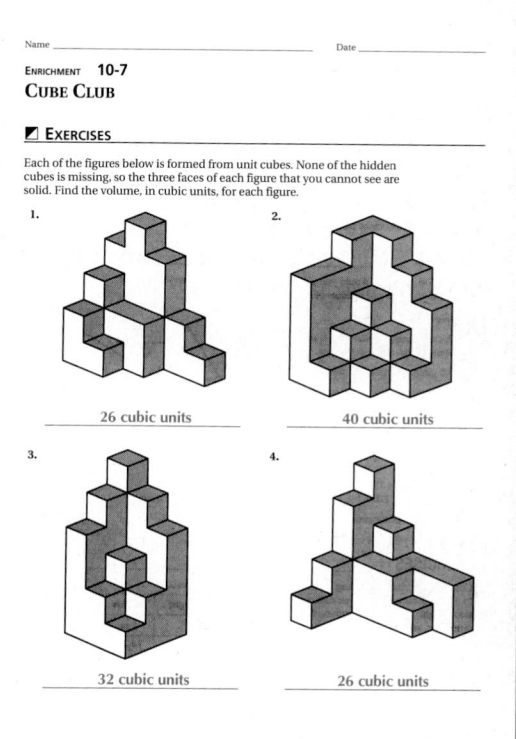

**1.** 26 cubic units

**2.** 40 cubic units

**3.** 32 cubic units

**4.** 26 cubic units

### Vocabulary

vital capacity

### Tools/Materials Needed

| | |
|---|---|
| balloon | string |
| tape measure | calculator |

### Lesson Resources

Warm-up Transparency 42
Transparency RF-49
Reteaching 10-8
Extra Practice 10-8
Enrichment 10-8
Technology Activity 10-7 and 10-8

## Getting Started

### 5-MINUTE WARM-UP

**Find the area of each circle. Use π = 3.14 and round answers to the nearest tenth.**
1. $r = 4.5$ cm    **63.6 cm²**
2. $d = 21$ in.    **346.2 in.²**
3. $C = 56$ ft    **249.7 ft²**

### Introduction to Lesson 10-8

When students have completed the experiment, elicit that the formula for vital capacity measures the volume of a sphere: in the expression for vital capacity, have students substitute $2\pi r$ for $C$ and simplify.

$$VC = \frac{C^3}{6\pi^2} = \frac{(2\pi r)^3}{6\pi^2} = \frac{8\pi^3 r^3}{6\pi^2} = \frac{4}{3}\pi r^3$$

---

# 10-8  Volume of Cylinders, Cones, and Spheres

**Goals**    ■ Find the volume of cylinders, cones, and spheres.

**Applications**    Sports, Horticulture, Astronomy, History, Chemistry

**FITNESS**  A person's **vital capacity** is the measure of the volume of air held in his or her lungs. Take a deep breath, and blow into a balloon as much air as possible. Trap the air by tying off the balloon.
For 1–2, answers will vary.
1. Push on the end of the balloon so that it forms a sphere. Then use a tape measure to find the circumference of the balloon. Let this measure be $C$.

2. Find your vital capacity ($VC$) by using the formula $VC = \frac{C^3}{6\pi^2}$.

### ◼ BUILD UNDERSTANDING

Recall that the general formula for finding the volume of a prism is $V = Bh$, where $B$ is the area of the base. Since the base of a cylinder is circular, replace $B$ in this formula with $\pi r^2$, the formula for the area of a circle.

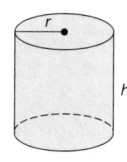

| **Volume of a Cylinder** | $V = \pi r^2 h$ <br> where $r$ is the radius of the base and $h$ is the cylinder's height. |
|---|---|

### Example 1

**Find the volume of the cylinder.**

*4.5 m*
*10 m*

**Solution**

$V = \pi r^2 h$    Use the formula for the volume of a cylinder.

$V \approx 3.14 \cdot (4.5)^2 \cdot 10$    $\pi \approx 3.14$

$V \approx 635.85$

The volume of the cylinder is approximately 635.85 m³.

The volume of a cylinder is 3 times the volume of a cone that has the same radius and height. To find the volume of a cone, take $\frac{1}{3}$ the product of the area of the base and the height of the cone.

| **Volume of a Cone** | $V = \frac{1}{3}\pi r^2 h$ <br> where $r$ is the radius of the base and $h$ is the cone's height. |
|---|---|

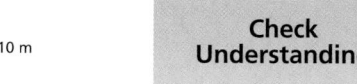

**Check Understanding**

How is the formula for the volume of a cone similar to the formula for the volume of a pyramid?

They are each $\frac{1}{3}$ the volume of corresponding three-dimensional figures.

456    Chapter 10  **Three-Dimensional Geometry**

---

## Teaching Tip

After students have studied Example 1, have them redo the calculation using the π-key on a calculator, and note the difference in the final result: 635.85 when using 3.14 for π versus 636.17 when using the π-key.
Use this difference in results to emphasize that volumes in which a value has been used for π are approximations, while volumes expressed in terms of π are exact values. Students should use the approximation 3.14 for π when completing the exercises in this lesson.

## Example 2

**Find the volume of the cone.**

### Solution

$V = \frac{1}{3}\pi r^2 h$     Use the formula for the volume of a cone.

$V \approx \frac{1}{3} \cdot 3.14 \cdot 4^2 \cdot 6$     $\pi \approx 3.14$

$V \approx 100.48$

The volume of the cone is approximately 100.48 cm³.

There is also a formula for the volume of a sphere.

| **Volume of a Sphere** | $V = \frac{4}{3}\pi r^3$ where $r$ is the radius of the sphere. |
|---|---|

## Example 3

**ASTRONOMY**  The diameter of the planet Mars is approximately 6800 km. What is the volume of Mars?

### Solution

Assume that Mars is a sphere. Mars' radius is half of 6800 km, or 3400 km.

$V = \frac{4}{3}\pi r^3$     Use the formula for the volume of a sphere.

$V \approx \frac{4}{3} \cdot 3.14 \cdot (3400)^3$     $\pi \approx 3.14$

$V \approx 1.6455 \cdot 10^{11} \text{ km}^3$

The volume of Mars is approximately 165,000,000,000 km³.

Mars

## Example 4

**Find the volume of the figure.**

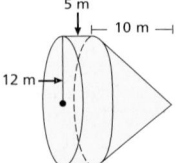

### Solution

The total volume of the figure is the sum of the cylinder's volume and the cone's volume.

Volume of the cylinder

$V = \pi r^2 h$

$V \approx 3.14 \cdot 12^2 \cdot 5$

$V \approx 2260.8$

Volume of the cone

$V = \frac{1}{3}\pi r^2 h$

$V \approx \frac{1}{3} \cdot 3.14 \cdot 12^2 \cdot 10$

$V \approx 1507.2$

Total volume $\approx 2260.8 + 1507.2 \approx 3768$

The volume of the figure is approximately 3768 m³.

 **Math Online** mathmatters2.com/extra_examples

---

## Chalkboard Examples

### Supplementary Example 1
**INTERIOR DESIGN**  A tank used to store home heating oil is in the shape of a right cylinder, as shown in the figure. Find the volume of the oil-storage tank.

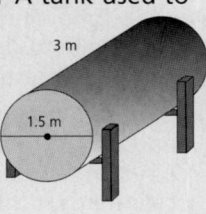

$V = \pi r^2 h$

$\approx 3.14 \cdot (0.75)^2 \cdot 3$

   radius $r = \frac{1}{2}$ diameter $d$

$\approx 5.3$

So, the volume of the cylindrical oil-storage tank is about 5.3 m³.

### Supplementary Example 2
**INDUSTRY**  A water-storage tank is to be shaped as an inverted right cone with a depth of 5 m. The tank is intended to hold 50 m³ of water. What must be the diameter of the tank?

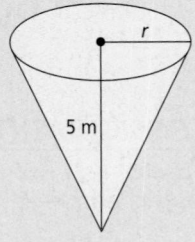

$V = \frac{1}{3}\pi r^2 h$     Use the cone volume formula.

$50 = \frac{1}{3}\pi r^2 (5)$     Substitute 50 for $V$ and 5 for $h$.

$50 = \frac{5}{3}\pi r^2$     Simplify.

$\frac{30}{\pi} = r^2$     Solve for $r^2$.

$\sqrt{\frac{30}{\pi}} = r$     Take the square root of each side.

$2\sqrt{\frac{30}{\pi}} = d$     diameter = twice radius

$2\sqrt{\frac{30}{3.14}} \approx d$     Substitute 3.14 for $\pi$.

$6.18 \approx d$     Simplify and round.

So, to hold 50 m³ of water, the diameter of the conical tank must be at least 6.18 m.

## Lesson Wrap-up

### QUICK ASSESSMENT

Ask the following questions to determine if students understand the content presented in this lesson.

1. Consider cylinder A with $r = 4$ cm and $h = 8$ cm and cylinder B with $r = 8$ cm and $h = 4$ cm. Which cylinder has the greatest volume?
   **cylinder B**

Consider cone C with $r = 10$ cm and $h = 15$ cm.

2. Find the volume of cone C. Answer in terms of $\pi$.   **$500\pi$ cm³**

3. What happens to the volume of cone C if the height is doubled?
   **volume is doubled**

4. What happens to the volume of cone C if the radius is doubled?
   **volume is multipled by 4**

### ASSIGNMENT GUIDE

**Basic:** 1–27, 32–45
**Enriched:** 1–45

### Reteaching Worksheet 10-8

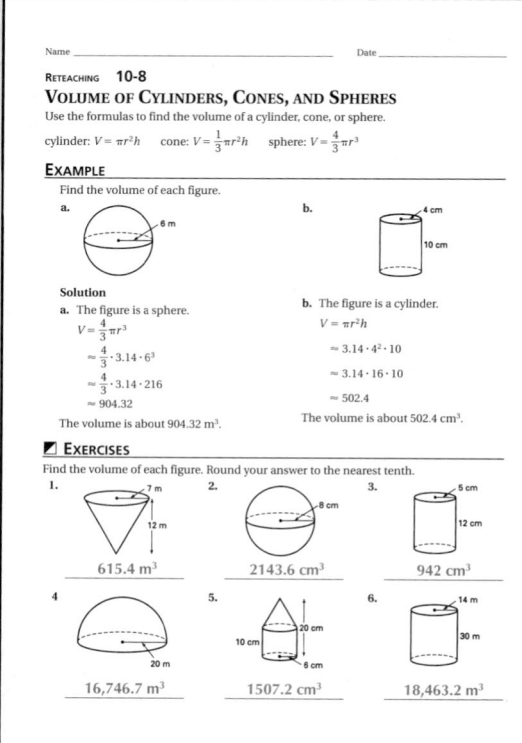

**458   Chapter 10   Three-Dimensional Geometry**

---

**Find the volume of each figure. Round to the nearest whole number.**

1.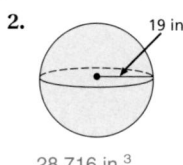
   3151 m³

2.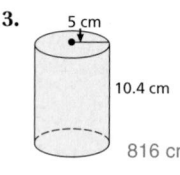
   28,716 in.³

3.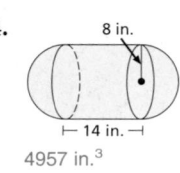
   816 cm³

4.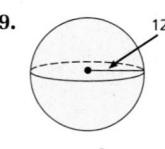
   4957 in.³

5. A cone with a radius of 12 cm has a volume of 753.6 cm³. What is the height of the cone?   5 cm

6. What is the volume of a sphere with a radius of 35 m?   $179{,}503\frac{1}{3}$ m³

7. A cubic foot of sand has a mass of 75 lb. How many pounds of sand would fit into a cylindrical container with a radius of 10 ft and a height of 5 ft?   117,750 lb

8. What is the volume of a hemisphere with a radius $r$?   $V = \frac{2}{3}\pi r^3$

### ◼ PRACTICE EXERCISES • For Extra Practice, see page 619.

**Find the volume of each figure. Round to the nearest whole number.**

9.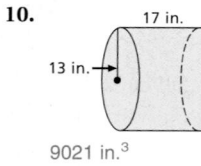
   7235 m³

10.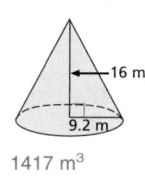
    9021 in.³

11.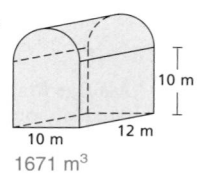
    1417 m³

12.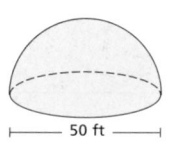
    1671 m³

13. A gasoline storage tank is a cylinder with a radius of 10 ft and a height of 6 ft. How many cubic feet of gasoline will the tank hold?   1884 ft³

14. A sphere has a volume of $523\frac{1}{3}$ in.³. What is the radius of the sphere?   5 in.

15. **SPORTS** Tennis balls are sold in cylindrical cans. Each can holds three tennis balls. If the volume of the can is 150.72 in.³, what is the approximate radius of a tennis ball?   2 in.

16. **HORTICULTURE** The figure at the right is a sketch of a proposed greenhouse that is to be shaped like a hemisphere. To the nearest cubic foot, what is the amount of space inside this greenhouse?   32,708 ft³

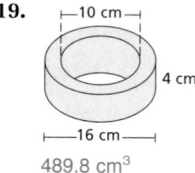

**Find the volume of each figure. Round to the nearest tenth.**

17.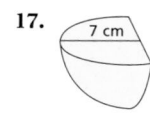
    359.0 cm³

18.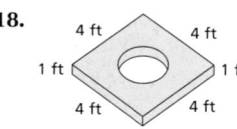
    The radius of the hole is 1 ft.
    12.9 ft³

19.
    489.8 cm³

20. **WRITING MATH** Explain how to find the volume of a cylinder, a cone, and a sphere. Describe the similarities among the three different volume formulas.
    Check students' work.

**458** | Chapter 10 **Three-Dimensional Geometry**

---

## Extend the Lesson

**CONNECTING TO PRIOR KNOWLEDGE** For an informal derivation of the formula for the volume of a sphere, ask students to imagine a sphere and its interior divided into many "pyramids" like those shown. Notice that the height of each pyramid equals the radius $r$ of the sphere. So, the volume of each pyramid is $\frac{1}{3}Br$. Suppose there are $n$ of these pyramids, with volumes $\frac{1}{3}B_1r, \frac{1}{3}B_2r, \frac{1}{3}B_3r \ldots, \frac{1}{3}B_nr$.

Volume of sphere $= \frac{1}{3}B_1r + \frac{1}{3}B_2r + \frac{1}{3}B_3r + \ldots + \frac{1}{3}B_nr$

$= \frac{1}{3}r(B_1 + B_2 + B_3 + \ldots + B_n) = \frac{1}{3}r(4\pi r^2) = \frac{4}{3}\pi r^3$

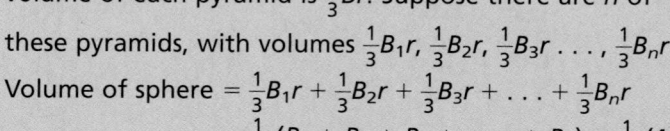

**21. HISTORY** Early astronomers estimated the equatorial radius of the earth to be approximately 520 km. The actual radius is about 6378 km. What is the approximate volume of the earth? How inaccurate was the astronomers' estimate of the earth's volume?
See additional answers.

**22.** A cylinder has a circumference of $12\pi$ m and a height of 4.7 m. What is the volume of the cylinder? Round the answer to the nearest whole number.   531 m³

**23. CHEMISTRY** A chemist pours 188.4 cm³ of a liquid into a glass cylinder that has a radius of 2 cm. How many centimeters deep is the liquid?   15 cm

**DATA FILE** For Exercises 24–27, refer to the data on various balls used in sports on page 571. Find the volume of each sports ball. Round to the nearest tenth.

**24.** baseball
229.7 cm³
**25.** golf ball
41.6 cm³
**26.** volleyball
5496.8 cm³
**27.** croquet ball
332.9 cm³

## ■ EXTENDED PRACTICE EXERCISES

**CRITICAL THINKING** Each of the cans shown in the diagram has a volume of 1000 cm³. (Recall that 1000 cm³ = 1 L.)

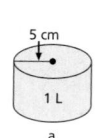 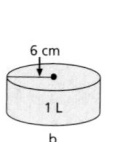 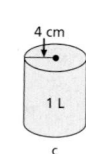 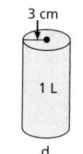 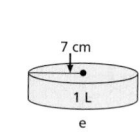 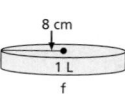

5 cm   6 cm   4 cm   3 cm   7 cm   8 cm
a        b        c        d        e        f

**28.** Find the height of each can rounded to the nearest tenth.
See additional answers.
**29.** Which two cans have the least surface area?   a and b

**30.** If you manufacture one liter cans, what radius would you use so that you save the most material?   5 cm

**31. SPREADSHEET** Write a spreadsheet program to calculate the volume of a sphere. Input the formula in the first cell, and calculate the volumes of spheres with radii 2 m, 4 m, 8 m and 16 m. Do you notice a pattern? Explain.
See additional answers.

## ■ MIXED REVIEW EXERCISES

**Find the value of the determinant of each matrix.** (Lesson 8-5)

**32.** $\begin{vmatrix} 4 & 5 \\ 3 & 6 \end{vmatrix}$  9  **33.** $\begin{vmatrix} 1 & 8 \\ -2 & 5 \end{vmatrix}$  21  **34.** $\begin{vmatrix} -6 & -2 \\ 4 & 7 \end{vmatrix}$  −34  **35.** $\begin{vmatrix} 5 & 6 \\ -12 & 8 \end{vmatrix}$  112  **36.** $\begin{vmatrix} 0 & -1 \\ 2 & 6 \end{vmatrix}$  2

**37.** $\begin{vmatrix} -3 & 3 \\ 4 & -6 \end{vmatrix}$  6  **38.** $\begin{vmatrix} 8 & 13 \\ -10 & -9 \end{vmatrix}$  58  **39.** $\begin{vmatrix} -4 & 7 \\ 2 & -8 \end{vmatrix}$  18  **40.** $\begin{vmatrix} 4 & 9 \\ 2 & 5 \end{vmatrix}$  2  **41.** $\begin{vmatrix} 11 & 4 \\ -9 & -3 \end{vmatrix}$  2

**In the figure, $m\angle MLN = 35°$ and $m\angle NLO = 55°$. Find each measure.** (Lesson 5-8)

**42.** $m\widehat{NO}$  55°  **43.** $m\widehat{MN}$  35°

**44.** $m\widehat{MNO}$  90°  **45.** $m\widehat{MPO}$  270°

## ADDITIONAL ANSWERS

**21.** approximate volume of Earth ≈ 1,086,230,341,000 ≈ 1.086 · 10¹²
early astronomers' estimate ≈ 588,678,827 ≈ 5.887 · 10⁸
The early astronomers were not even close.

**28. a.** 12.7 cm
**b.** 8.8 cm
**c.** 19.9 cm
**d.** 35.4 cm
**e.** 6.5 cm
**f.** 5.0 cm

**31.** 
| radii | volume |
|---|---|
| 2 m | 33.49 m³ |
| 4 m | 267.95 m³ |
| 8 m | 2143.57 m³ |
| 16 m | 17,148.59 m³ |

When the radius is increased by a factor of 2, the volume is increased by a factor of 8.

---

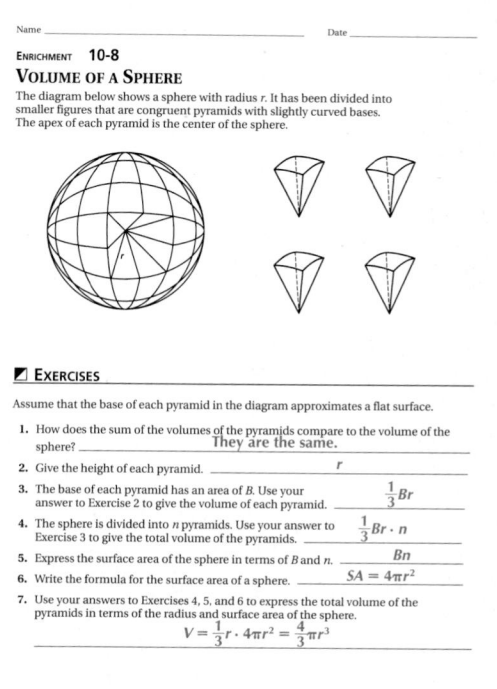

### Extra Practice Worksheet 10-8

Name _____   Date _____

EXTRA PRACTICE   **10-8**
**VOLUME OF CYLINDERS, CONES, AND SPHERES**

■ **EXERCISES**

Find the volume of each figure. Round to the nearest whole number.

1.   10 in. ⟶   12 in.
942 in³

2.   9 m
3052.08 m³

3.   9 cm   3 cm
85 cm³

4.   14 in.   20 in.
1026 in³

5. A cylinder has a volume of 6.28 m³. The height of the cylinder is 2 m. What is the radius of the cylinder?   1 m

6. A cone with a height of 4 in. has a volume of 37.68 in³. What is the radius of the cone?   3 in.

7. What is the volume of a hemisphere with a radius 8 ft?   1072 ft³

8. A sphere has a volume of $4186\frac{2}{3}$ in³. What is the radius of the sphere?   10 in.

9. Two cans are shaped like cylinders. The cans have the same radius, but the height of one can is twice the height of the other can. What is the relationship between their volumes? Be as specific as possible.   The volume of the larger can is twice the volume of the smaller can.

### Enrichment Worksheet 10-8

Name _____   Date _____

ENRICHMENT   **10-8**
**VOLUME OF A SPHERE**
The diagram below shows a sphere with radius $r$. It has been divided into smaller figures that are congruent pyramids with slightly curved bases. The apex of each pyramid is the center of the sphere.

■ **EXERCISES**

Assume that the base of each pyramid in the diagram approximates a flat surface.

1. How does the sum of the volumes of the pyramids compare to the volume of the sphere?   They are the same.

2. Give the height of each pyramid.   $r$

3. The base of each pyramid has an area of $B$. Use your answer to Exercise 2 to give the volume of each pyramid.   $\frac{1}{3}Br$

4. The sphere is divided into $n$ pyramids. Use your answer to Exercise 3 to give the total volume of the pyramids.   $\frac{1}{3}Br \cdot n$

5. Express the surface area of the sphere in terms of $B$ and $n$.   $Bn$

6. Write the formula for the surface area of a sphere.   $SA = 4\pi r^2$

7. Use your answers to Exercises 4, 5, and 6 to express the total volume of the pyramids in terms of the radius and surface area of the sphere.
$V = \frac{1}{3}r \cdot 4\pi r^2 = \frac{4}{3}\pi r^3$

## PRACTICE ◼ LESSON 10-7

Find the volume of each figure. Round to the nearest tenth.

1.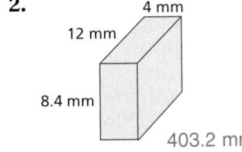
4 m
15 m
5 m
90 m³

2.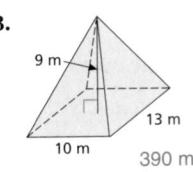
4 mm
12 mm
8.4 mm
403.2 mm³

3.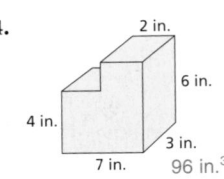
9 m
13 m
10 m
390 m³

4.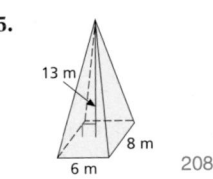
2 in.
6 in.
4 in.
3 in.
7 in.
96 in.³

5.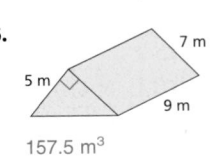
13 m
8 m
6 m
208 m³

6.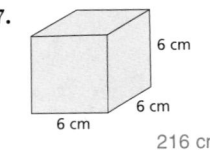
7 m
5 m
9 m
157.5 m³

7.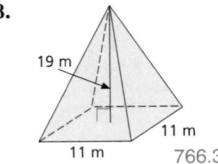
6 cm
6 cm
6 cm
216 cm³

8.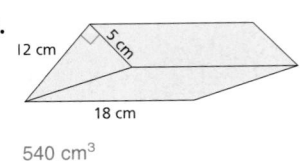
19 m
11 m
11 m
766.3 m³

9. 
12 cm
5 cm
18 cm
540 cm³

10. A triangular prism has a volume of 108 m³. The triangular base has a height of 9 m and a base of 6 m. What is the height of the prism?   4 m

## PRACTICE ◼ LESSON 10-8

Find the volume of each figure. Round to the nearest whole number.

11.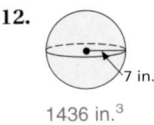
24 m
10 m
2512 m³

12.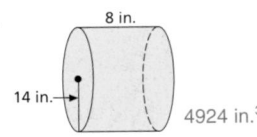
7 in.
1436 in.³

13. 
8 in.
14 in.
4924 in.³

14.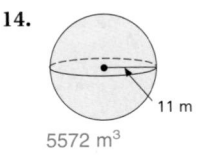
11 m
5572 m³

15.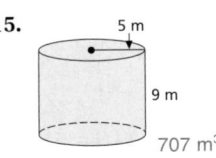
5 m
9 m
707 m³

16.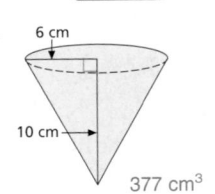
6 cm
10 cm
377 cm³

17. The volume of a cone with a 14-mm diameter is 820 mm³. Find the height.   16 mm

18. The radius of an inflated beach ball is 15 in. What is the amount of air inside?   14,130 in.³

**460** Chapter 10 **Three-Dimensional Geometry**

### Lesson 10-7
Find the volume of the triangular prism.
First find *B*, the area of the triangular base of the prism.

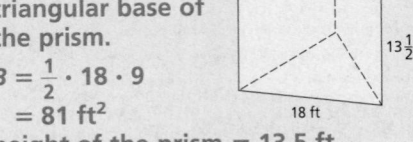
9 ft
13½ ft
18 ft

$B = \frac{1}{2} \cdot 18 \cdot 9$
$= 81 \text{ ft}^2$
height of the prism = 13.5 ft
Apply the volume formula.
$V = B \cdot h$
$= 81 \cdot 13.5$
$= 1093.5$
The volume of the triangular prism is 1093.5 ft³.

## Teaching Tip

To assist students in remembering volume formulas, elicit that the basic formula *V* = *Bh* applies to:
   all prisms—use the appropriate area formula to find the area of the base
   cylinders—use the area formula for circle to find the area of the base
Then, students should remember that, with respect to volume:
   a pyramid is one-third of a prism
   a cone is one-third of a cylinder

19. Find the minimum amount of gift wrap needed to cover a box that measures 2 ft by 3 ft by 6 in. (Lesson 10-2)   17 ft²

20. Sketch a net for the three-dimensional figure. (Lesson 10-2)
    See additional answers.

21. Create an isometric drawing of a triangular prism. (Lesson 10-5)   See additional answers.

22. Create an isometric drawing of a figure composed of six cubes. (Lesson 10-5)   Answers will vary.

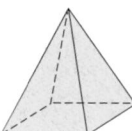

**Find the surface area and volume of each figure. Round to the nearest tenth.**
(Lessons 10-3, 10-7 and 10-8)

23.
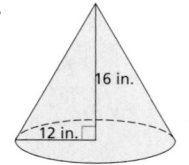
16 in.
12 in.
1205.8 in.²; 2411.5 in.³

24.
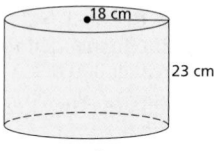
18 cm
23 cm
4634.6 cm²; 23,399.3 cm³

25.
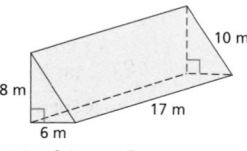
10 m
8 m
6 m
17 m
456 m²; 408 m³

26.
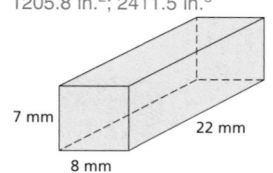
7 mm
22 mm
8 mm
772 mm²; 1232 mm³

27.
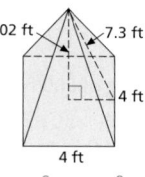
7.02 ft   7.3 ft
4 ft
4 ft
74.4 ft²; 37.4 ft³

28.
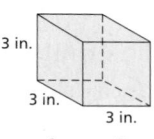
3 in.
3 in.
3 in.
54 in.²; 27 in.³

**Identify each figure and state the number of faces, vertices and edges.**
(Lesson 10-1)

29.
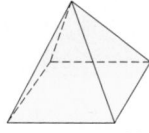
square pyramid; 5, 5, 8

30.
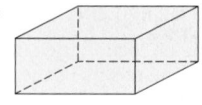
rectangular prism; 6, 8, 12

31.
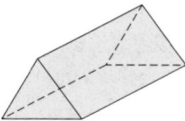
triangular prism; 5, 6, 9

**Trace each perspective drawing to locate the vanishing point(s).** (Lesson 10-4)
For 32–34, see additional answers.

32.
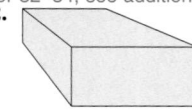

33.
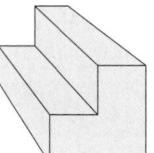

34.
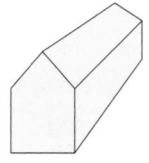

**Lesson 10-8**
**HOBBIES** Sue is making a clay dish shaped like a right cylinder with an indentation shaped like a hemisphere.

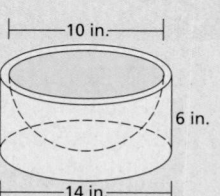
10 in.
6 in.
14 in.

Find the approximate amount of clay Sue needs to make the dish.

The total volume of the dish is the difference between the volume of the cylinder and the volume of the hemisphere.

Volume of cylinder
$V = \pi r^2 h$
$V \approx 3.14 \cdot 7^2 \cdot 6$
$V \approx 923.16$

Volume of sphere
$V = \frac{4}{3}\pi r^3$
$V \approx \frac{4}{3} \cdot 3.14 \cdot 5^3$
$V \approx 523.33$

Volume of hemisphere
= half volume of sphere
$V \approx \frac{1}{2}(523.33)$
$V \approx 261.67$

Volume of dish ≈ 923.16 − 261.67
= 661.49

Sue needs about 661 in.³ of clay to make the dish.

20.
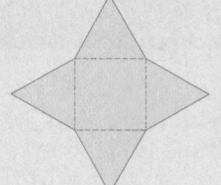

21.
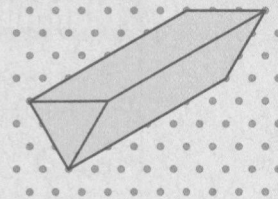

32.

33.
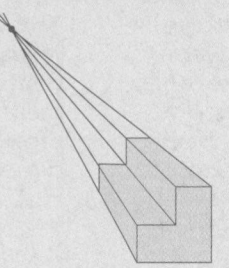

34.
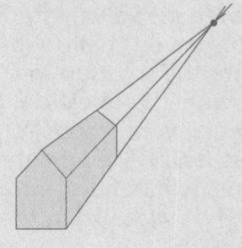

# Problem Solving Skills: Length, Area, and Volume

## Lesson Planning

### NCTM Standards/Strands
- Problem Solving
- Representation
- Number & Operations
- Algebra

### Vocabulary
use an equation or formula

### Tools/Materials Needed
calculator

### Lesson Resources
Warm-up Transparency 43
Transparency RF-49
Reteaching 10-8
Enrichment 10-8

### ASSIGNMENT GUIDE
**Basic:** 1–9, 11–25
**Enriched:** 1–25

## Getting Started

### 5-MINUTE WARM-UP
**Find the volume of each figure. Use π = 3.14 and round answers to nearest tenth.**
1. cylinder: $r = 4.5$ in., $h = 10$ in.
   **635.9 in.$^3$**
2. cone: $r = 4$ ft, $h = 6$ ft
   **100.5 ft$^3$**
3. sphere: $r = 19$ cm
   **28,716.3 cm$^3$**

**THE FIVE-STEP PLAN Read**—ask questions to help students understand the problem. **Plan**—guide students to related problems and previously mastered skills and strategies. **Solve**—students solve problem on their own. **Answer**—write the solution in a format that answers the question. **Check**—review work, check for reasonableness, and review strategy used. Students will benefit from the experience of verbalizing their methods.

---

Formulas are mathematical tools that help guide you to a solution. The strategy, **use an equation or formula**, is appropriate when you have data that can be substituted into a formula or equation. If you do not know the formula, write an equation that states the relationships in the problem. In either case, solve the equation to find the solution.

### Problem Solving Strategies
Guess and check

Look for a pattern

Solve a simpler problem

Make a table, chart or list

Use a picture, diagram or model

Act it out

Work backwards

Eliminate possibilities

✔ Use an equation or formula

### Problem

**CONSTRUCTION** The tank of a raised cylindrical water tower is 26 ft high with a radius of 11 ft. There is a 2-ft-wide walkway around the base of the tank.

a. About how many gallons of paint are needed to paint the exterior of the tank if 1 gal of paint will cover 300 ft$^2$?

b. There is a railing around the walkway. How long is it?

c. How many gallons of water does the tank hold? (The volume of 1 gal is approximately 0.1337 ft$^3$.)

### Solve the Problem

a. Each gallon of paint covers an area of 300 ft$^2$.

$SA = 2\pi r^2 + 2\pi rh$     Use the formula for surface area of a cylinder.
$SA \approx (2 \cdot 3.14 \cdot 11^2) + (2 \cdot 3.14 \cdot 11 \cdot 26)$    $\pi \approx 3.14$
$SA \approx 760 + 1796 \approx 2556$

The surface area is approximately 2556 ft$^2$. Since each gallon of paint covers 300 ft$^2$, divide the surface area by 300 ft.

$2556 \div 300 \approx 8.5$

It will take approximately 8.5 gal of paint.

b. The length of the railing is the circumference of a circle with a radius 2 ft greater than the radius of the tank.

$C = 2\pi r$     Use the formula for the circumference of a circle.
$C \approx 2 \cdot 3.14 \cdot (11 + 2)$    $\pi \approx 3.14$
$C \approx 81.6$

The railing is approximately 81.6 ft long.

c. The number of gallons the tank will hold is the volume of the tank.

$V = \pi r^2 h$     Use the formula for the volume of a cylinder.
$V \approx 3.14 \cdot 11^2 \cdot 26 \approx 9878.4$    $\pi \approx 3.14$

The volume is approximately 9878.4 ft$^3$. Since 1 gal is approximately 0.1337 ft$^3$, the tank holds approximately $9878.4 \div 0.1337 \approx 73,884.8$ gal.

**462**   Chapter 10 **Three-Dimensional Geometry**

---

**THE STRATEGY** Use an equation or formula—this strategy enables students to find various geometric measures (perimeter/circumference, area, surface area, volume) in a direct manner.

### Teaching Tip

Remind students that when they are working with items that are sold only in whole units, they should round up in their estimates at purchase time.
So, for example, in the Problem, the amount of paint needed is 8.5 gal. However, 9 gal of paint would have to be purchased.

**Round answers to the nearest tenth.**

**Five-step Plan**
1 Read
2 Plan
3 Solve
4 Answer
5 Check

1. A cypress tree has a radius of 18.75 ft. If it is fenced in so that there is a border 8 ft wide around the trunk of the tree, how many feet of fencing are needed?  168.0 ft

2. South African ironwood is the world's heaviest wood, weighing about 90 lb/ft³. How much would an 8-in. cube of ironwood weigh?  26.7 lb/ft³

3. **PACKAGING** Find the minimum amount of paper needed for the label of a cylindrical soup can that is 7 in. high with a radius of 2.25 in.  98.9 in.²

4. The windows of a building have a total area of 32.4 m². Each window is a rectangle measuring 1.2 m by 1.8 m. How many windows are in the building?  15

## PRACTICE EXERCISES

**Round answers to the nearest tenth.**

5. **LANDSCAPING** A pound of grass seed covers an area of 250 ft². How many pounds of seed would you need for a rectangular lawn measuring 35 ft by 50 ft?  7 lb

6. The roof of a shed is a square pyramid with sides of 2.4 m. The height of each triangular face is 2 m. How many square meters of tar paper would it take to cover the roof?  9.6 m²

7. A circular swimming pool has a diameter of 17 ft and a depth of 5 ft. If the pool is considered to be full when the water level is 1 ft below the rim of the pool, how many cubic feet of water does it take to fill the pool?  907.5 ft³

8. A cardboard hat is made of a cone with radius 5 in. and slant height 14 in. The circular brim is 4-in. wide. Find the minimum amount of cardboard needed to make the hat.  395.6 in.²

9. **WRITING MATH** Write a problem that can be solved by applying the formula for length, area, or volume. Provide an answer for your problem.
Answers will vary.

10. **CRITICAL THINKING** The names and sizes of wooden boards specify the dimensions before they are dried and planed. For example, a one-by-ten board is actually $\frac{3}{4}$ in. by $9\frac{1}{4}$ in. If a patio is built using 15 one-by-ten boards that are each 12 ft long, what is the area of the patio?  138.75 ft²

## MIXED REVIEW EXERCISES

**Simplify.** (Lesson 9-3)

11. $\frac{14b^2}{2b}$  7b

12. $\frac{51a^2c^3}{3ac}$  17ac²

13. $\frac{27g^3h}{9gh}$  3g²

14. $\frac{7m^3n^4}{m^2n}$  7mn³

15. $\frac{49k^3l^2}{14k^3l^2}$  $\frac{7}{2}$

**Calculate each permutation.** (Lesson 4-6)

16. $_8P_2$  56

17. $_5P_2$  20

18. $_{12}P_4$  11,880

19. $_{10}P_6$  151,200

20. $_9P_4$  3024

21. $_{12}P_8$  19,958,400

22. $_9P_6$  60,480

23. $_{10}P_3$  720

24. $_{14}P_5$  240,240

25. $_{11}P_3$  990

## Teaching Tip

Use the Supplementary Problem to note with students that it is not necessary to memorize a separate surface area formula for a cube.

By using the definition of surface area (sum of the areas of all the faces) and knowing that a cube has six square faces, students can write a formula for the surface area of a cube: $SA = 6e^3$.

Note also that students are writing their own formulas when they show how they are implementing a plan for solution - for example, in the Supplementary Problem, students see that they must subtract volumes: Amount of clear plastic = $V$ cube − $V$ cone

## Chalkboard Examples

### Supplementary Problem
**HOBBIES** Elian is making a decorative paperweight, a colored cone inside a clear cube. If clear plastic costs $0.0125 per in.³ and colored plastic costs $0.02 per in.³, what will be the cost of the paperweight?

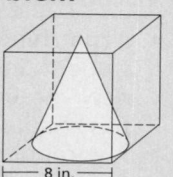
8 in.

$V$ cube = $8^3$ = 512 in.³

$V$ cone = $\frac{1}{3}\pi \cdot 4^2 \cdot 8 \approx 134.0$ in.³

Amount of clear plastic
≈ 512 − 134 ≈ 378 in.³
Cost of clear plastic ≈
378 · 0.0125 ≈ $4.73
Cost of colored plastic ≈
134 · 0.02 ≈ $2.68
Cost of cube ≈ $4.73 + $2.68
= $7.41

## Lesson Wrap-up

### QUICK ASSESSMENT

How would you find the volume of a composite figure?  Add the volumes for all portions of the figure.

### Reteaching Worksheet 10-9

Name _____   Date _____

RETEACHING **10-9**
**PROBLEM SOLVING SKILLS: LENGTH, AREA, AND VOLUME**

Before you can solve a problem that involves a geometric figure, you must choose the appropriate formula. You can choose the correct formula by determining what kind of information the problem asks you to find.

**Example**

A cardboard box has the shape of a rectangular prism, with length 6 in., width 3 in., and height 8 in.
a. Sugar weighs 0.5 oz/in.³. How many ounces of sugar will the box hold?
b. How many square inches of cardboard were needed to make the box?

**Solution**

a. You need to find the volume of the box. Use the formula for the volume of a rectangular prism

$V = lwh$
= 6 · 3 · 8 = 144

The volume of the box is 144 in.³.
A volume of 1 in.³ will hold 0.5 oz.
144 · 0.5 = 72
The box will hold 72 oz of sugar.

b. You need to find the surface area of the box. Use the formula for the surface area of a rectangular prism.

$SA = 2(lw + lh + wh)$
= 2(6 · 3 + 6 · 8 + 3 · 8)
= 2(18 + 48 + 24) = 2(90) = 180
180 in.² of cardboard were needed.

**EXERCISES**

1. A jeweler charges $3/cm² to gold-plate an object. How much would it cost to gold-plate a solid cone with radius 2 cm and slant height 4 cm? _____ $113.04

2. A cylindrical jar has a radius of 10 cm and a height of 20 cm. How many liters of liquid can it hold? (1 L = 1000 cm³) _____ 6.28 L

3. The material used to make a ball weighs 0.3 g/cm³. How many grams does a solid ball with a radius of 10 cm weigh? _____ 1256 g

4. An aquarium measures 22 in. by 14 in. by 12 in. How many gallons of water can it hold? (The volume of 1 gallon is 231 in.³.) _____ 16 gal

# Chapter 10 Review

## Chapter 10 Review

## Vocabulary Assessment

- A matching section checks for student understanding of the new vocabulary introduced in this chapter.
- A vocabulary review/test for Chapter 10 is available on pp. vii–viii of the *Chapter 10 Resource Masters*.

## Lesson-by-Lesson Review

For each lesson,
- the main ideas are summarized, and
- practice exercises are provided.

### EXAMVIEW® PRO

Use the networkable ExamView® Pro to:

- Create **multiple versions** of tests.
- Create **modified** tests for *inclusion* students.
- **Edit** existing questions and **add** your own questions.
- Use built-in **state curriculum correlations** to create tests aligned with state standards.
- Change **English** tests to **Spanish** and vice versa.

## VOCABULARY

**Choose the word from the list that best completes each statement.**

1. A(n) __?__ is a polyhedron with only one base.  g
2. A(n) __?__ is a polyhedron with two identical parallel bases.  f
3. The __?__ of a cone is the length of a segment drawn from its vertex to its base along the side of the cone.  h
4. A(n) __?__ is the set of all points in space that are a given distance from a given point.  i
5. A one-point perspective drawing has one __?__.  k
6. A(n) __?__ is a three-dimensional figure with two congruent circular bases that lie in parallel planes.  b
7. The sum of the areas of all bases and faces of a three-dimensional figure is called its __?__.  j
8. The number of cubic units needed to fill a three-dimensional figure is called its __?__.  l
9. A(n) __?__ drawing shows three sides of a three-dimensional figure.  d
10. A(n) __?__ drawing shows the individual sides of a three-dimensional figure.  e

| |
|---|
| a.  cone |
| b.  cylinder |
| c.  face |
| d.  isometric |
| e.  orthogonal |
| f.  prism |
| g.  pyramid |
| h.  slant height |
| i.  sphere |
| j.  surface area |
| k.  vanishing point |
| l.  volume |

## LESSON 10-1 ■ Visualize and Represent Solids, p. 422

▶ A **polyhedron** is a closed, three-dimensional figure made up of polygonal surfaces called **faces**. A segment that is the intersection of two faces is an **edge**. The point at which three or more edges intersect is a **vertex**.

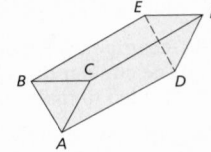

**Use the figure at the right.**

11. Identify the figure.  right triangular prism
12. Identify its base(s).  △ABC, △DEF
13. Identify its lateral face(s).
    rectangles *ACFD*, *BCFE*, and *ABED*
14. State the number of vertices.  6 vertices
15. State the number of edges.  9 edges
16. Identify all edges that are skew to $\overline{CF}$.
    $\overline{AB}, \overline{DE}$

## LESSON 10-2 ■ Nets and Surface Area, p. 426

▶ A net is a two-dimensional pattern that can be folded to form a three-dimensional figure. A net can be used to find surface area.

**Draw a net for each three-dimensional figure. Then find the surface area.**
For 17–19, see additional answers for nets.

17.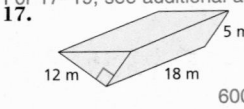
5 m, 12 m, 18 m
600 m²

18.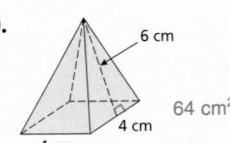
2.4 mm, 4.6 mm
105.6 mm²

19.
6 cm, 4 cm, 4 cm
64 cm²

## ADDITIONAL ANSWERS

17.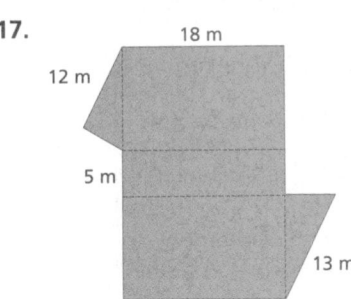
18 m, 12 m, 5 m, 13 m

18.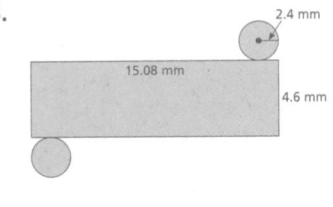
2.4 mm, 15.08 mm, 4.6 mm

19.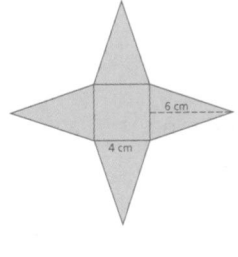
6 cm, 4 cm

## LESSON 10-3 ■ Surface Area of Three-Dimensional Figures, p. 432

▶ **Surface areas** can be found using these formulas.

rectangular prism:
$SA = 2(lw + lh + wh)$

cylinder:
$SA = 2\pi r^2 + 2\pi rh$

cone:
$SA = \pi rs + \pi r^2$

**Find the surface area of each figure. Round to the nearest hundredth.**

**20.**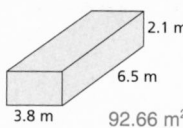
2.1 m
6.5 m
3.8 m
92.66 m²

**21.**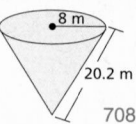
8 m
20.2 m
708.38 m²

**22.**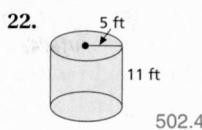
5 ft
11 ft
502.4 ft²

**23.** A soup can has a height of 10 cm and a diameter of 6.5 cm. Find the amount of steel needed to make the can. ≈ 270.43 cm²

**24.** A pet carrier is in the shape of a rectangular prism. It is 2.5 ft long, 1 ft high and 1.25 ft wide. What is the surface area of the carrier? 13.75 ft²

## LESSON 10-4 ■ Perspective Drawings, p. 436

▶ A **perspective drawing** is a way of drawing objects on a flat surface so that they look the same as they appear in real life.

**25.** Sketch a rectangular tissue box in one-point perspective.
See additional answers
**26.** Sketch a rectangular tissue box in two-point perspective.
See additional answers
**27.** Locate the vanishing point in the perspective drawing.
See additional answers

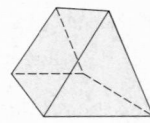

## LESSON 10-5 ■ Isometric Drawings, p. 442

▶ An **isometric drawing** shows an object from a corner view so that three sides of the object can be seen in a single drawing.

**Give the number of cubes used to make each figure and the number of cube faces exposed. Be sure to count the cubes that are hidden from view.**

**28.**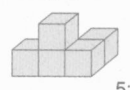
5; 22

**29.**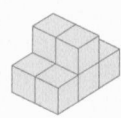
8; 28

**30.**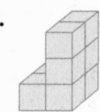
8; 28

## LESSON 10-6 ■ Orthogonal Drawings, p. 446

▶ An **orthogonal drawing** gives top, front and side views of a three-dimensional figure as seen from a "straight on" viewpoint.

**Make an orthogonal drawing labeling the front, top and right-side views.**

**31.**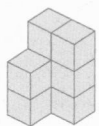

**32.**

**33.**

31–33. See additional answers.

**25.**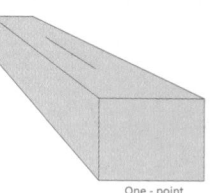
One - point

**26.**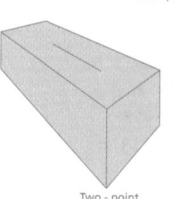
Two - point

**27.**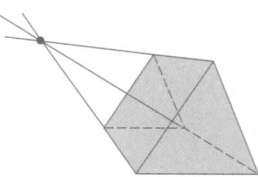

**31.**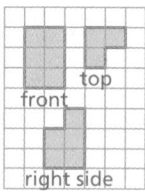
top
front
right side

**32.**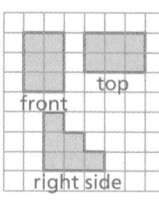
top
front
right side

**33.**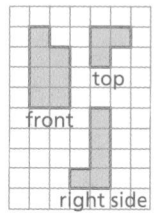
top
front
right side

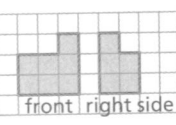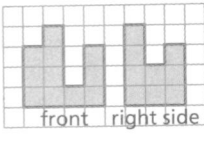
For each foundation drawing, sketch the front and right orthogonal views.

**34.**

| 2 | 1 | 1 |
|---|---|---|
| 1 | 2 | 3 |

**35.**

| | 1 | |
|---|---|---|
| 2 | 1 | |
| 2 | 4 | |

**36.**

| | | 3 |
|---|---|---|
| | | 2 |
| 3 | 4 | 1 | 1 |

34–36. See additional answers.

## LESSON 10-7 ■ Volume of Prisms and Pyramids, p. 452

▶ **Volume** can be found using these formulas.

prism: $V = Bh$        pyramid: $V = \frac{1}{3}Bh$

**37.** Find the volume of a square pyramid if the length of a side of its base is 15 cm and its height is 23 cm.   1725 cm³

**38.** A rectangular prism has a base that measures 5 ft by 3 ft. Its volume is 300 ft³. What is its height?   20 ft

**39.** A rectangular cake pan is 2 in.-by-13 in.-by-9 in. A round cake pan has a diameter of 8 in. and a height of 2 in. Which will hold more cake batter, the rectangular pan or two round pans?   the rectangular pan

## LESSON 10-8 ■ Volume of Cylinders, Cones and Spheres, p. 456

▶ **Volume** can be found using these formulas.

cylinder: $V = \pi r^2 h$        cone: $V = \frac{1}{3}\pi r^2 h$        sphere: $V = \frac{4}{3}\pi r^3$

**Find the volume of each figure. Round to the nearest tenth.**

**40.** cylinder: $r = 6.1$ mm, $h = 3.8$ mm   444.0 mm³   **41.** cone: $r = 4.2$ cm, $h = 11$ cm   203.1 cm³

**42.** sphere: $r = 6$ mm   904.3 mm³        **43.** cone: $r = 5$ in., $h = 15$ in.   392.5 in.³

## LESSON 10-9 ■ Problem Solving Skills: Length, Area and Volume, p. 462

▶ The strategy, **use an equation or formula**, is appropriate when you have data that can be substituted into a formula or equation.

**44.** A rectangular room measures 12 yd by 22 ft. How many square yards of carpet will it take to carpet the entire room?   88 yd²

**45.** A rectangular room is 12 ft-by-21 ft. The walls are 8 ft tall. Paint is sold in 1-gal containers. If a gallon of paint covers 450 ft², how many gallons of paint should be purchased to paint the walls of the room?   2 gal

## CHAPTER INVESTIGATION

**EXTENSION** Write a report about how the study of mathematics influences history. Your report could answer some of the following questions. How did cultural and historical events affect mathematics? How does geography affect the spread of information and new discoveries? How did mathematics help trigger major cultural events like the Industrial Revolution and the Information Age? Have all mathematicians been formally educated? How did computers change the way mathematicians work?

## THEME: History

The benchmarks and expectations for this extension are as follows.
- Students research ten mathematicians. They record the name, accomplishment, dates of birth and death, date of accomplishment and country of birth for each mathematician.
- Students draw a line segment about 10 in. long across the center of a piece of paper with an arrowhead at each end. They place the name and accomplishment of each mathematician they researched on the timeline in chronological order. They label the timeline appropriately.
- Students research a significant historical event that was happening at each date on their timeline.
- Students write a report about how mathematics influences history.

# Chapter 10 Assessment

**Use the figure to name the following.**
For 1, 2 and 4, answers will vary.

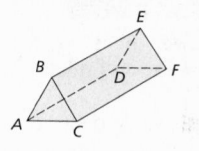

1.  a pair of intersecting edges

2.  a pair of parallel edges

3.  a pair of parallel faces  △ABC, △DEF

4.  a pair of edges that are skew

5.  the bases  △ABC, △DEF

**Draw a net for each figure. Then identify the figure and find its surface area.**
For 6–8, see additional answers for nets.

6.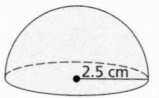
21 ft
3 ft
10 ft

rectangular prism; 606 ft²

7.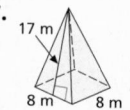
17 m
8 m   8 m

right square pyramid; 336 m²

8.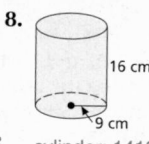
16 cm
9 cm

cylinder; 1413 cm²

9.  Find the surface area of a cone with a radius of 3.1 cm and a slant height of 12.4 cm.   150.9 cm²

10. Find the surface area of the figure.

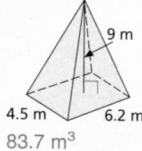
2.5 cm

39.25 cm²

11. Locate the vanishing point of the figure.

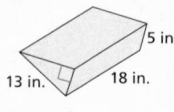

Check students' work.

12. Create an isometric drawing of a figure composed of 5 cubes.
Check students' work.

13. Make an orthogonal drawing of the figure you drew in Exercise 12. Show the front, top and right-side views.   Check students' work.

**Find the volume of each figure. Round to the nearest tenth if necessary.**

14.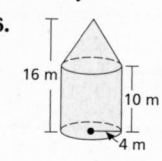
9 m
4.5 m   6.2 m
83.7 m³

15.
5 in.
13 in.   18 in.
540 in.³

16.
16 m
10 m
4 m
602.9 m³

17. To find the number of square feet of wrapping paper needed to cover a box shaped like a rectangular prism, which formula should you use?   c

  **a.**  $P = 2l + 2s$    **b.**  $V = lwh$    **c.**  $SA = 2(lw + lh + wh)$

18. Write a problem that can be solved by applying the formula for the volume of a sphere. Provide an answer for your problem.   Answers will vary.

 **Math Online**
mathmatters2.com/chapter_assessment

Chapter 10  **Assessment**   **467**

## ADDITIONAL ANSWERS

6.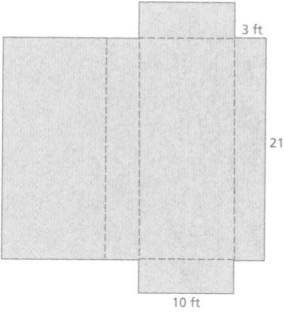
3 ft
21 ft
10 ft

7.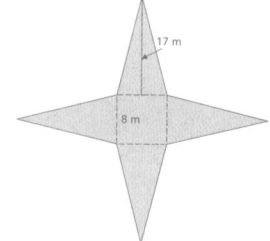
17 m
8 m

8.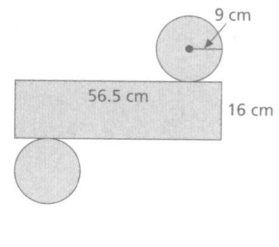
9 cm
56.5 cm
16 cm

---

### Assessment Options

Chapter 10 Test A, pages 339–340
Chapter 10 Test B, pages 341–342

### ALTERNATIVE ASSESSMENT

**CARDBOARD PATTERNS**  Have students select and then carefully dismantle an empty spaghetti box, cake mix box, or other cardboard box. Have students assume that they are a manufacturer who has been asked to produce this box. Cardboard comes in 4-ft, 6-ft, or 10-ft wide rolls. Ask students to determine what roll width they will need and what arrangement of their box pattern will be most cost effective. Students should explain how they made their decision and include a scale drawing of the net of the box shown arranged on one of the cardboard rolls.

**RUBRIC**  The following rubric is a sample scoring guide.

| Points | Description |
|---|---|
| 4 | Creates an **accurate** scale drawing of a net for manufacturing a cardboard box, shows it arranged on an appropriate roll width so that it results in the least amount of waste, and **explains in detail** why this arrangement is most cost effective. |
| 3 | Creates an **accurate** scale drawing, shows it arranged on an appropriate roll width so that it results in the least amount of waste, but **does not explain** why this arrangement is most cost effective. |
| 2 | Creates a **somewhat accurate** scale drawing, shows it arranged on an appropriate roll width so that it results in the least amount of waste, but does not explain why this arrangement is most cost effective. |
| 1 | Creates an **inaccurate** drawing of a net that is not arranged on a roll width so that it will produce the least amount of waste. |
| 0 | Makes **no attempt** to produce a drawing. |

### Standardized Test Practice

These two pages contain practice questions in the various formats that can be found on the most frequently given standardized tests.

A student recording sheet for these two pages can be found on p. A1 of the *Chapter 10 Resource Masters*.

### Standardized Test Practice Student Recording Sheet

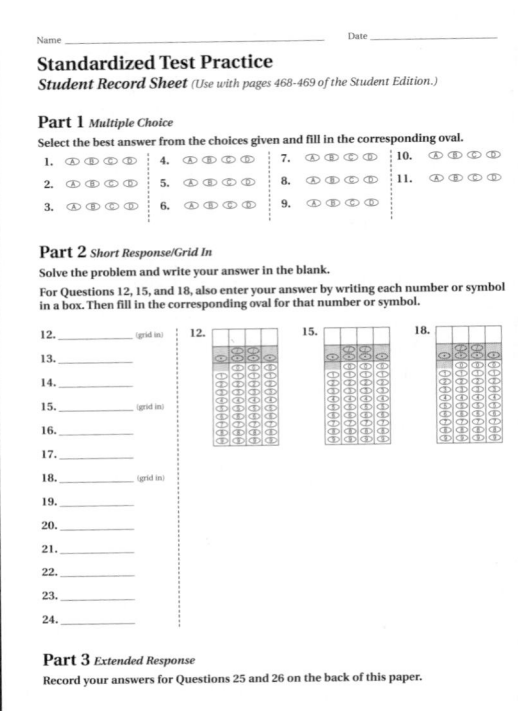

### Additional Practice

See pp. 343–345 in the *Chapter 10 Resource Masters* for additional standardized test practice.

# Standardized Test Practice

### Part 1 | Multiple Choice

Record your answers on the answer sheet provided by your teacher or on a sheet of paper.

1. Desiree's test scores are 83, 75, 86, and 82. If her teacher uses the mean, what score does she need on the fifth test in order to have an average of 85? (Lesson 1-2) C
   - (A) 85
   - (B) 90
   - (C) 99
   - (D) 105

2. Of the people who buy raffle tickets, 500 win nothing, 1 wins $25, and 1 wins $100,000. If you were promoting the raffle and wanted to give a misleading statistic about the average winning, which measure of central tendency would you use? (Lesson 1-7) A
   - (A) mean
   - (B) median
   - (C) mode
   - (D) range

3. Which expression is *not* represented by $2x - 1$? (Lesson 2-3) B
   - (A) twice a number minus one
   - (B) twice a number less than one
   - (C) two times a number decreased by one
   - (D) two times a number minus one

4. Which graph represents the solution of $3t - 5 \geq -2$? (Lesson 3-7) C
   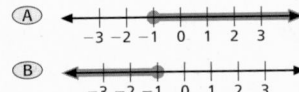
   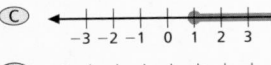

5. What is the measure of each angle of a regular polygon that has 9 sides? (Lesson 5-7) B
   - (A) 126°
   - (B) 140°
   - (C) 150°
   - (D) 180°

6. What is the slope of the line that passes through $A(-3, 2)$ and $B(5, -4)$? (Lesson 6-2) B
   - (A) $-\frac{4}{3}$
   - (B) $-\frac{3}{4}$
   - (C) $\frac{3}{4}$
   - (D) $\frac{4}{3}$

7. Which line is *not* parallel to $2x - 3y = 5$? (Lesson 8-1) D
   - (A) $-2x + 3y = 1$
   - (B) $2x - 3y = 2$
   - (C) $4x - 6y = 5$
   - (D) $3x + 2y = 5$

8. If $2x + y = 3$ and $x + y = 1$, what is the value of $y$? (Lesson 8-4) B
   - (A) $-2$
   - (B) $-1$
   - (C) $1$
   - (D) $2$

9. Factor $x^2 - 4x + 4$. (Lesson 9-8) A
   - (A) $(x - 2)^2$
   - (B) $(x + 2)^2$
   - (C) $x(x - 4)$
   - (D) $(x + 2)(x - 2)$

10. How many faces does a pentagonal pyramid have? (Lesson 10-1) B
    - (A) 5
    - (B) 6
    - (C) 7
    - (D) 8

11. What is the volume of the rectangular pyramid? (Lesson 10-7) A
    - (A) 176 ft³
    - (B) 404 ft³
    - (C) 528 ft³
    - (D) 576 ft³

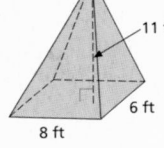

### Test-Taking Tip

(A) (B) (C) (D)

**Question 11**
Most standardized tests include any commonly used formulas at the front of the test booklet, but it will save you time to memorize many of these formulas. For example, you should memorize that the volume of a pyramid is one-third the area of the base times the height of the pyramid.

## ADDITIONAL ANSWERS

25. The figure uses 7 cubes and there are 26 cube faces exposed.
    orthogonal drawing:

    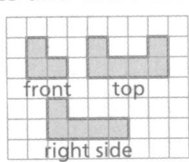

    foundation drawing:

    | 2 |   |   | 1 |
    |---|---|---|---|
    | 1 | 1 | 1 | 1 |

## Part 2  Short Response/Grid In

Record your answers on the answer sheet provided by your teacher or on a sheet of paper.

**12.** What is the value of $t^{-2}$ for $t = 5$? (Lesson 2-8)  $\frac{1}{25}$

**13.** The area of a triangle can be determined by using the formula $A = \frac{1}{2}bh$. Solve this formula for $h$.  (Lesson 3-2)  $h = \frac{2A}{b}$

**14.** Solve $2(3t - 6) = t + 8$.  (Lesson 3-4)  4

**15.** A bag contains 4 red marbles, 3 blue marbles, and 2 white marbles. One marble is chosen without replacement. Then another marble is chosen. What is the probability that the first marble is red and the second marble is blue? (Lesson 4-5)  $\frac{1}{6}$

**16.** Find the value of $x$ in circle $Q$.  (Lesson 5-8)  45

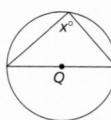

**17.** The center of a circle is located at the origin of a coordinate plane. If $A(5, 12)$ is on the circle, what is the radius of the circle? (Lesson 6-1)  13 units

**18.** The distance a vehicle travels at a given speed is a direct variation of the time it travels. If a vehicle travels 30 mi in 45 min, how far can it travel in 2 h?  (Lesson 6-8)  80 mi

**19.** Triangle $RST$ with vertices $R(5, 4)$, $S(3, -1)$, and $T(0, 2)$ is translated so that $R'$ is at $(3, 1)$. What are the coordinates of $S'$? (Lesson 7-1)  $(1, -4)$

**20.** Solve the system of equations. (Lesson 8-3)  $(-3, -9)$

$$y = 3x$$
$$x + 2y = -21$$

**21.** The perimeter of the rectangle is $16a + 2b$. Write an expression for the length of the rectangle.  (Lessons 9-3 and 9-4)  $3a + 2b$

$5a - b$

**22.** A bowling league has $n$ teams. You can use the expression $\frac{1}{2}n^2 - \frac{1}{2}n$ to find the total number of games that will be played if each team plays each other team exactly once. Factor this expression.  (Lessons 9-7)  $\frac{1}{2}n(n - 1)$

**23.** What is the surface area of a cube with sides of 7 in.?  (Lesson 10-3)  294 in.²

**24.** A can of soup is 12 cm high and has a diameter of 8 cm. A rectangular label is being designed for this can of soup. If the label will cover the surface of the can except for its top and bottom, what is the width and length of the label, to the nearest centimeter?  (Lesson 10-9)  12 cm by 25 cm

## Part 3  Extended Response

Record your answers on a sheet of paper. Show your work.

**25.** Describe the three-dimensional figure. Include the number of cubes needed to make the figure and the number of cube faces exposed. Draw an orthogonal drawing labeling the front, top, and right-side views. Then, draw a foundation drawing. (Lessons 10-5 and 10-6)  See additional answers.

**26.** Draw a cylinder and a cone that have the same volume. Explain your response and calculate the volume and surface area of each figure.  (Lesson 10-8)  See additional answers.

## ADDITIONAL ANSWERS

**26.** Drawings will vary. The easiest way to draw a cone with the same volume as a cylinder is to draw a cone three times the height of the cylinder but keep the same radius.

# Rubrics

The following rubrics are sample scoring guides for short response and extended response questions.

## Short Response

| Points | Description |
|---|---|
| 2 | The student demonstrates a **thorough understanding** of the mathematics of the task. The response may contain minor flaws that do not detract from the demonstration of a thorough understanding. |
| 1 | The student has provided a response that is only **partially correct.** |
| 0 | The student has provided a **completely incorrect** solution or no response at all. |

## Extended Response

| Points | Description |
|---|---|
| 4 | The student demonstrates a **thorough understanding** of the mathematics of the task. The response contains minor flaws that do not detract from the demonstration of a thorough understanding. |
| 3 | The student demonstrates an **understanding** of the mathematics of the task. The response is essentially correct and demonstrates an essential but less than thorough understanding of the mathematics. |
| 2 | The student has demonstrated only a **partial understanding** of the mathematics of the task. Although the student may have used the correct approach to a solution or may have provided a correct solution, the work lacks an essential understanding of the underlying mathematical concepts. |
| 1 | The student has demonstrated a **very limited understanding** of the mathematics of the task. The response is incomplete and exhibits many flaws. |
| 0 | The student has provided a **completely incorrect** solution or no response at all. |

# Right Triangle Geometry

**CHAPTER 11**

| Lesson | Lesson Objectives | Pacing (days) | NCTM Standards | State/Local Objectives |
|---|---|---|---|---|
| 11-1 | **Similar Polygons** (*pp. 474–477*)<br>• Identify similar polygons.<br>• Find measures of similar polygons. | 2 | 2, 3, 4, 9 | |
| 11-2 | **Indirect Measurement** (*pp. 478–481*)<br>• Use similar triangles to find indirect measurements. | 1 | 2, 3, 4, 9 | |
| 11-3 | **The Pythagorean Theorem** (*pp. 484–487*)<br>• Use the Pythagorean Theorem to find unknown lengths. | 2 | 2, 3, 4, 9 | |
| 11-4 | **Sine, Cosine, and Tangent Ratios** (*pp. 488–491*)<br>• Identify the sine, cosine, and tangent ratios in a right triangle.<br>• Compute the sine, cosine, and tangent ratios for different angles. | 2 | 2, 3, 4, 9 | |
| 11-5 | **Find Length of Sides in Right Triangles** (*pp. 494–497*)<br>• Use trigonometric ratios to find the lengths of sides in right triangles. | 1 | 2, 3, 4, 9 | |
| 11-6 | **Find Measures of Angles in Right Triangles** (*pp. 498–501*)<br>• Use trigonometric ratios to find measures of angles in right triangle. | 1 | 2, 3, 4, 9 | |
| 11-7 | **Special Right Triangles** (*pp. 504–507*)<br>• Explore the relationship in 30°-60°-90° right triangles.<br>• Explore the relationship in 45°-45°-90° right triangles. | 2 | 2, 3, 4, 9 | |
| 11-8 | **Problem Solving Skills: Reasonable Solutions** (*pp. 508–509*)<br>• Solve a problem using reasonable solutions.<br>• Solve a problem by eliminating possibilities. | 1 | 1, 4, 6, 10 | |
| **Review** | | 1 | | |
| **Testing** | | 1 | | |

**Key to NCTM Standards:**

*1=Number & Operations, 2=Algebra, 3=Geometry,*
*4=Measurement, 5=Data Analysis & Probability,*
*6=Problem Solving, 7=Reasoning & Proof,*
*8=Communication, 9=Connections, 10=Representation*

**Pacing:** Suggestions for the year can be found on page xvi.

# Chapter Resource Manager

**FAST FILE** — Chapter 11 Resource Masters

| Reteaching Activities | Extra Practice | Enrichment | Assessment | Basic Mathematics Review | Study Skills Activities | Lesson Warm-Ups Transparencies | Teaching Transparencies | Technology Activities | Materials Needed |
|---|---|---|---|---|---|---|---|---|---|
| 347 | 348 | 349 | | | | 44 | TK-17, RF-55 | 11-1 | protractor, ruler |
| 350 | 351 | 352 | | | | 44 | | | calculator |
| 353 | 354 | 355 | | | | 45 | RF-56 | 11-3 | calculator, scissors, centimeter grid paper |
| 356 | 357 | 358 | | 23 | | 45 | RF-57 | | ruler, calculator |
| 359 | 360 | 361 | | | | 46 | | 11-5 | calculator |
| 362 | 363 | 364 | | | | 46 | | | protractor, calculator |
| 365 | 366 | 367 | | | | 47 | TK-9, TK-15, RF-59 | | ruler, calculator, dot paper, protractor, grid paper |
| 368 | 369 | 370 | 373–379 | | | 47 | RF-1 | | calculator |

### Quick Review Math Handbook, Book 2

hot words / hot topics

| MathMatters 2 Lesson(s) | Hot Topic Lesson(s) |
|---|---|
| 11-1 | 7-1, 7-2 |
| 11-2 | 8-6 |
| 11-3 | 7-9 |
| 11-4, 11-5 | 7-10 |
| 11-6 | 7-1, 7-10 |
| 11-7, 11-8 | 7-1, 7-9, 7-10 |

# Content and Connections

## Connections to the Past

**MM1 (Ch. 4):** Identify and classify polygons.

**MM1 (Ch. 2):** Solve problems by writing and solving proportions.

**MM1 (Ch. 7):** Use the Pythagorean Theorem to find distance.

**MM1 (Ch. 2):** Read and write ratios in lowest terms.

**MM1 (Ch. 7):** Use the Pythagorean Theorem to find distance.

**MM1 (Ch. 4)** Use a protractor to measure and draw angles.

**MM1 (Ch. 4):** Identify and classify polygons.

## MathMatters 2 Chapter 11 Highlights

Identify and find measures of similar polygons. (11-1)

Use similar triangles to find indirect measurements. (11-2)

Use the Pythagorean Theorem to find unknown lengths. (11-3)

Identify the sine, cosine, and tangent ratios in a right triangle. (11-4)

Use trigonometric ratios to find the lengths of sides in right triangles. (11-5)

Use trigonometric ratios to find measures of angles in a right triangle. (11-6)

Explore the relationships in special triangles. (11-7)

## Connections to the Future

**MM3 (Ch. 7):** Prove theorems involving similar triangles.

**MM3 (Ch. 7):** Solve a problem involving indirect measurement.

**MM3 (Ch. 10):** Use the Pythagorean Theorem to solve problems involving right triangles.

**MM3 (Ch. 14):** Identify trigonometric ratios in a right triangle.

**MM3 (Ch. 14):** Find the length of sides and the measures of angles in right triangles.

**MM3 (Ch. 14):** Find the lengths of sides and the measures of angles in right triangles.

**MM3 (Ch. 10):** Find the lengths of the sides of special triangles.

Key

| | |
|---|---|
| PC | = Previous Course |
| MM1 | = *MathMatters 1* |
| MM2 | = *MathMatters 2* |
| MM3 | = *MathMatters 3* |

## Connecting the Strands

| NCTM Strand | Lesson(s) |
|---|---|
| Number & Operations | 11-8 |
| Algebra | 11-1, 11-2, 11-3, 11-4, 11-5, 11-6, 11-7 |
| Geometry | 11-1, 11-2, 11-3, 11-4, 11-5, 11-6, 11-7 |
| Measurement | 11-1, 11-2, 11-3, 11-4, 11-5, 11-6, 11-7, 11-8 |
| Problem Solving | 11-8 |
| Connections | 11-1, 11-2, 11-3, 11-4, 11-5, 11-6, 11-7 |
| Representation | 11-8 |

# Ongoing Assessment and Intervention

| | Type | Student Edition | Teacher Resources | Technology/Internet |
|---|---|---|---|---|
| **INTERVENTION** | Ongoing | Are You Ready?, pp. 472–473<br>Check Understanding, pp. 475, 479, 485, 494, 505<br>Review and Practice Your Skills, pp. 482–483, 492–493, 502–503<br>Mid-Chapter Quiz, p. 493 | Lesson Warm-Ups Transparencies, pp. WU-44, WU-45, WU-46, WU-47<br>Quick Assessment, *ATE* pp. 473, 476, 480, 486, 490, 496, 500, 506, 509 | mathmatters2.com/extra_ examples<br>mathmatters2.com/self_check_quiz |
| | Mixed Review | pp. 477, 481, 487, 491, 497, 501, 507, 509 | | |
| | Error Analysis | You Make the Call, pp. 477, 509<br>Error Alert, p. 491 | Teaching Tip, *ATE* p. 483<br>Predictable Error, *ATE*, p. 491 | |
| **ASSESSMENT** | Standardized Test Practice | pp. 514–515<br>Preparing for Standardized Tests, pp. 627–644 | Standardized Test Practice, *CRM* pp. 377–379 | mathmatters2.com/standardized_test |
| | Open-Ended Assessment | Chapter Investigation, pp. 471, 481, 497, 501 | Chapter Investigation, *ATE* p. 512<br>Alternative Assessment, *ATE* p. 513 | |
| | Chapter Assessment | Chapter Review, pp. 510–512<br>Chapter Assessment, p. 513 | Multiple-Choice Tests (Forms A and B), *CRM* pp. 373–376 | mathmatters2.com/chapter_assessment |

**Key to Abbreviations:** *ATE* = Annotated Teacher's Edition, *CRM* = Chapter Resource Masters

## Additional Intervention

***Basic Mathematics Review*** includes 80 lessons, consisting of an instructional page and a test page. This workbook also features a pretest, posttest, table of measurement equivalents, and calculator appendices.

## ExamView® Pro

Use ExamView® Pro Testmaker CD-ROM to:
- Create **multiple versions** of tests.
- Create **modified** tests for *inclusion* students with one mouse click.
- **Edit** existing questions and **add** your own questions.
- Build tests aligned with **state standards** using built-in **state curriculum correlations**.
- Change **English** tests to **Spanish** with one mouse click and vice versa.

# Chapter Opener

## NCTM Standards/Strands
- Communication
- Connections

## Vocabulary
photography
right triangle trigonometry

## Theme Connections
*Optics*, the branch of physical science dealing with the propagation and behavior of light, plays an important role in photograpy. Such principles of optics as the laws of reflection and refraction are described in terms of angle measure. Snell's Law, about the refractive index, involves the trigonometric ratio sine.

## Career Opportunities
Many careers require understanding of the principles of right triangle trigonometry. Two such careers are highlighted in the MathWorks features. Others include: navigator, astronomer, surveyor, cartographer, draftsperson, meteorologist, physicist, geographer, forest ranger, carpenter.
- Aerial photographer, page 483
- Camera designer, page 503

## Internet Connection

### Theme Activities
Mathmatters2.com/chapter_theme provides links to the Internet that will help students gather information about the use of math in the real world, particularly data and measures. To search for additional addresses, begin a search of photography. Then within that search, use such key word adjectives with photography as aerial, satellite, freeze-frame, slow-motion, stop-motion, high-speed, infrared, ultraviolet, kirlian, matte. In small groups, students can brainstorm other key words.

# Right Triangle Trigonometry

## THEME: Photography

**P**hotography is a popular way to record events, capture memories, and create art. The technical process of photography involves light, chemistry, and right triangle trigonometry. Right triangle trigonometry has many other practical applications, including architecture and engineering.

- **Aerial photographers** (page 483) use trigonometry to take images from an elevated location. Real estate developers, cartographers, and transportation engineers use the services of aerial photographers.

- The work of **camera designers** (page 503) is complicated and intense. They use angles, planes, lengths, and proportions to create cameras with unique capabilities.

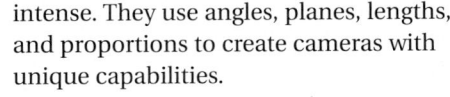

Math Online

mathmatters2.com/chapter_theme

470

## Chapter Investigation
Use the Internet and other resources to locate additional information about "at-an-angle photography."

## As a Chapter Project
The goal of this project is for students to estimate the distance a photographer needs to be from the subject when the angle of the camera is known. Students can use the Group Project Planner on page 371 and the Project Planning Calendar on page 372 in the *Chapter 11 Resource Masters* to complete the project. Benchmarks **a**, **b**, and **c** should be completed after the lesson listed in parentheses has been studied. Benchmark **d** should be completed at the end of the chapter.

# Events in the History of Photography

| Year | Historical Event |
|------|------------------|
| 1558 | Giovanni Battista Porta is the first to describe the concept of the Camera Obscura, or dark chamber. Leonardo da Vinci is also attributed with developing the Camera Obscura. |
| 1826 | During an 8 h process, Joseph Nicephore Niepce produces the first successful picture. |
| 1829 | Louis Daguerre discovers a way to develop film that took 4 h. Deguerre also discovers that an image could be made permanent by immersing it in salt. |
| 1835 | William Henry Fox Talbot develops a paper negative. |
| 1845 | Friederich von Martens introduces a panoramic camera with a lens that moves along an arc of over 150°. |
| 1851 | Frederick Scott Archer introduces a high-quality negative to produce numerous prints. |
| 1861 | Physicist J.C. Maxwell produces the first color photograph. |
| 1873 | Photographs are printed in newspapers for the first time in America. |
| 1925 | The flashbulb is invented. |
| 1963 | Kodak introduces the Instamatic. |
| 1987 | Both Kodak and Fuji introduce the "Quick Snap," the first 35-mm disposable camera. |
| 1991 | The Kodak Professional Digital Camera System is introduced. |
| 1992 | Eastman Kodak Company introduces the Photo CD for the photo-retail market. |
| 1994 | Apple Quick Take 100 was the first mass-market color digital camera. |
| 1996 | Advantix Camera is introduced. |

## Data Activity: Events in the History of Photography

**Use the table for Questions 1–4.**

1. Who invented the first 35-mm disposable camera? Fuji and Kodak

2. How many years passed between the first color photograph and the photo CD? 131 yr

3. Were photographs first printed in newspapers before or after the Civil War? after the Civil War

4. Make a timeline using the information in the table.
   Check students' work.

## CHAPTER INVESTIGATION

The photograph shown at the right was achieved by the photographer being at a different level than the subject of the image. In other words, the picture was taken "at an angle." This technique of having the camera above or below the subject can be used to emphasize a specific characteristic, create a visual effect or produce an abstract view. Even amateur photographers want a variety of photograph styles.

### *Working Together*

The distance from the subject and the angle of the camera are critical for photographers to get their desired results. Determine the distance a photographer needs to be from the subject when the angle of the camera is known. Use the Chapter Investigation icons to guide your group to find the distances for angles whose measures are 15°, 28° and 35°.

Chapter 11 **Right Triangle Trigonometry** 471

From the given list of events, students get a capsule version of the history of photography. Note from the list that although it took more than three centuries to first implement the notion that such a process could happen, the 19th and 20th centuries were active in discovery. Students should answer Questions 1–4 to get a sense of the time frame.

## Extend the Data Activity
**Student Portfolio** Students can research a particular field that came into being due to the existence of photography, such as *photojournalism* or *cinematography*, reporting on its history and noted contributors. Or, students can research popular early uses of photographs, such as *portraiture* or *carte-de-visite*. Or, students can research famous photographers, such as Ansel Adams, Diane Arbus, Mathew Brady, Margaret Bourke-White.

# Chapter Investigation

## As an Overarching Problem
Construct several diagram situations in which a photographer shoots a picture, using different angles between the camera and the object. Discuss the various right triangles that can be formed in the diagrams. Ask students to think about how they can use what they know about right triangles to find the lengths of the sides. Students will continue to work on the Investigation as they complete the exercises identified by the Chapter Investigation icon that is found throughout the chapter. These exercises will guide students through the tasks described in *Working Together*. Encourage students to keep all of their work on the Investigation together. Have student use the suggestions in the Chapter Investigation Extension to summarize their work.

See page 470 for Chapter Investigation As a Chapter Project.

## Project Planning Calendar

Name _____ Date _____

CHAPTER 11 PROJECT PLANNING CALENDAR

Benchmarks
a. The photographer, subject and ground are the vertices of a right triangle. Draw a diagram of the triangle formed by a photographer who is shooting at an upward angle at the subject of the picture. Use the distance between the subject and the ground as one leg of the right triangle. (*Lesson 11-2*)
b. In your diagram label the right angle, the legs of the right triangle and the angle of the camera. What trigonometric ratio will you use to find the distance the photographer is from the subject? (*Lesson 11-5*)
c. Suppose the subject is 5.5 ft from the ground. Use a ___ to write an equation

PROJECT GOAL
To estimate the distance a photographer needs to be from the subject when the angle of the camera is known.

## Group Project Planner

Name _____ Date _____

CHAPTER 11 GROUP PROJECT PLANNER

Assignment _____ Objective _____
_____
_____

Group Members          Assigned Roles
1) _____          _____
2) _____          _____
3) _____          _____
4) _____          _____
5) _____          _____

_____dlines          Done

# 11 Are You Ready?

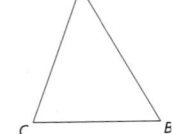

### Refresh Your Math Skills for Chapter 11

---

The skills on these two pages are ones you have already learned. Use the examples to refresh your memory and complete the exercises. For additional practice on these and more prerequisite skills, see pages 576–584.

## MEASURING TRIANGLES

In this chapter you will study trigonometry, which deals with the ratios of sides and angles of triangles. It is helpful to be able to measure the angles of any triangle.

**Example** Measure each angle of $\triangle ABC$.

To measure $\angle A$, line up the protractor's midpoint on point $A$ and the base along $\overline{AB}$. Read the angle measure on the outer edge of the protractor. Measure $\angle B$ the same way. Once you know $m\angle A$ and $m\angle B$, you can calculate $m\angle C$.

$$\angle A = 50° \text{ and } \angle B = 70° \qquad 50° + 70° + \angle C = 180°$$
$$\angle C = 60°$$

**Find the measure of each angle.**

1.

$\angle A = 35°, \angle B = 75°, \angle C = 70°$

2.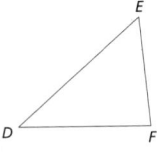

$\angle D = 42°, \angle E = 54°, \angle F = 84°$

3.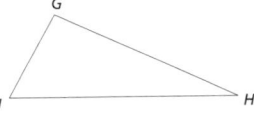

$\angle G = 95°, \angle H = 24°, \angle I = 61°$

## EQUIVALENT RATIOS

Relationships between sides and angles of triangles can be expressed as ratios. It will be helpful to be able to recognize and find equivalent ratios.

**Example** Are the ratios equivalent? $\quad \frac{2}{3}$ and $\frac{8}{12} \qquad \frac{3}{5}$ and $\frac{12}{25}$

Cross-multiply to check. If the products are equal, the ratios are equivalent.

$$\frac{2}{3} \overset{?}{=} \frac{8}{12} \qquad\qquad \frac{3}{5} \overset{?}{=} \frac{12}{25}$$
$$2 \cdot 12 \overset{?}{=} 3 \cdot 8 \qquad\qquad 3 \cdot 25 \overset{?}{=} 5 \cdot 12$$
$$24 = 24 \quad \text{The ratios are equivalent.} \qquad 75 \neq 60 \quad \text{The ratios are not equivalent.}$$

**Example** Find three equivalent ratios. $\quad \dfrac{20}{25}$

Multiply or divide both numbers in the ratio by the same number.

$$\frac{20}{25} \div \frac{5}{5} = \frac{4}{5} \qquad \frac{20}{25} \cdot \frac{3}{3} = \frac{60}{75} \qquad \frac{20}{25} \cdot \frac{4}{4} = \frac{80}{100}$$

$\dfrac{20}{25}$ is equivalent to $\dfrac{4}{5}, \dfrac{60}{75}$ and $\dfrac{80}{100}$.

---

## Refresher Skills

The skills on these two pages are skills that have been presented in earlier chapters of this book or in previous math courses. Continuous review of basic math skills will make stronger math students. These skills are identified as necessary to be successful in Chapter 11.

### Skills Correlation Chart

| Skill | Lesson Number |
|---|---|
| Measuring Triangles | 11-1, 11-2, 11-4, 11-5, 11-6, 11-7 |
| Equivalent Ratios | 11-1, 11-4, 11-7 |
| Solving Radical Equations | 11-3 |

### Vocabulary

trigonometry
equivalent ratios
radical equations

## Chalkboard Examples

### Measuring Triangles

Find the measures of the acute angles of an isosceles right triangle.

Let $x$ = the measure of each acute $\angle$.
$$x + x + 90 = 180$$
$$2x = 90$$
$$x = 45$$

The measure of each acute $\angle$ of isosceles right $\triangle = 45°$.

### Equivalent Ratios

Is $\dfrac{\frac{1}{2}}{3}$ equivalent to $\dfrac{5}{30}$?

Test the cross-products. Since the cross-products are equal, the ratios are equivalent.

$$\frac{\frac{1}{2}}{3} \overset{?}{=} \frac{5}{30}$$
$$\frac{1}{2} \cdot 30 \overset{?}{=} 3 \cdot 5$$
$$15 = 15 \checkmark$$

### Solving Radical Equations

Solve $7 + 2x = \sqrt{\dfrac{42}{5}}$ for $x$. Round to the nearest hundredth.

$$2x \approx -7 + 2.898 \quad \text{Use 3 places.}$$
$$2x \approx -4.102 \quad \text{Truncate, do not round.}$$
$$x \approx -2.05$$

---

## Teaching Tip

When deciding if two ratios are equivalent, students look at the cross-products. You might point out that there are also other ways to make the decision, as demonstrated in the following examples.

Are $\frac{2}{3}$ and $\frac{8}{12}$ equivalent? Look at the relationship between numerators: the first numerator is multiplied by 4 to achieve the second numerator. Since the denominators follow the same pattern, the ratios are equivalent.

Are $\frac{22}{11}$ and $\frac{400}{200}$ equivalent? Look at the relationship between numerator and denominator in the first fraction: the numerator is twice the denominator. Since the pattern is the same in the second fraction, the ratios are equivalent.

**Are the ratios equivalent? Write *yes* or *no*.**

4. $\frac{44}{112}$ and $\frac{11}{28}$   yes

5. $\frac{9}{13}$ and $\frac{27}{39}$   yes

6. $\frac{1}{4}$ and $\frac{17}{69}$   no

7. $\frac{18}{24}$ and $\frac{3}{4}$   yes

8. $\frac{11}{25}$ and $\frac{66}{150}$   yes

9. $\frac{6}{15}$ and $\frac{42}{105}$   yes

10. $\frac{4}{7}$ and $\frac{48}{85}$   no

11. $\frac{38}{120}$ and $\frac{19}{60}$   yes

12. $\frac{7}{11}$ and $\frac{84}{130}$   no

13. $\frac{8}{72}$ and $\frac{1}{9}$   yes

14. $\frac{5}{12}$ and $\frac{22}{48}$   no

15. $\frac{51}{60}$ and $\frac{17}{20}$   yes

16. $\frac{15}{69}$ and $\frac{5}{23}$   yes

17. $\frac{18}{27}$ and $\frac{72}{105}$   no

18. $\frac{14}{17}$ and $\frac{70}{85}$   yes

19. $\frac{31}{84}$ and $\frac{62}{166}$   no

**Find three equivalent ratios.**   For 20–27, answers will vary. Check students' work.

20. $\frac{90}{100}$

21. $\frac{5}{6}$

22. $\frac{12}{16}$

23. $\frac{3}{5}$

24. $\frac{22}{44}$

25. $\frac{75}{100}$

26. $\frac{9}{81}$

27. $\frac{1}{2}$

## SOLVING RADICAL EQUATIONS

Trigonometry frequently involves solving equations that contain radicals.

### Example

Use a calculator to find a decimal approximation for each variable. If necessary, round your answer to the nearest thousandth.

$$y = \sqrt{\frac{37}{4}}$$

$$y \approx 3.041$$

$$7r = \sqrt{\frac{10}{6}}$$

$$\frac{7r}{7} \approx \frac{1.2909}{7}$$

$$r \approx 0.184$$

**Use a calculator to find the decimal approximation for each variable. If necessary, round your answer to the nearest thousandth.**

28. $b = 7\sqrt{16}$   28

29. $r = 4\sqrt{22}$   18.762

30. $\frac{6}{\sqrt{5}} = c$   2.683

31. $\frac{k}{\sqrt{12}} = 5$   17.321

32. $\sqrt{\frac{28}{4}} = g$   2.646

33. $5a = 3\sqrt{42}$   3.888

34. $3z = \sqrt{80}$   2.981

35. $c = 6\sqrt{15}$   23.238

36. $7m = \frac{18}{\sqrt{29}}$   0.478

37. $4n = 9\sqrt{314}$   39.870

38. $y = \frac{(2\sqrt{58})}{6}$   2.539

39. $6d = 2\sqrt{190}$   4.595

40. $p = \frac{(4\sqrt{92})}{3}$   12.789

41. $w = 5\sqrt{34}$   29.155

42. $3g = \frac{\sqrt{55}}{2}$   1.236

43. $4x = \sqrt{\frac{11}{4}}$   0.415

44. $12y = 6\sqrt{21}$   2.291

45. $\frac{\sqrt{17}}{3} = 9a$   0.153

# 11-1 Similar Polygons

**Goals**
- Identify similar polygons.
- Find measures of similar polygons.

**Applications**   Architecture, Sports, Art, Photography

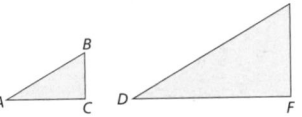

**Refer to the two triangles.**

1. Triangle *ABC* and triangle *DEF* appear to have the same shape, but they are different sizes. Measure each angle of the two triangles. What do you notice?  The corresponding measures are equal. The corresponding angles are congruent.

2. Find the following ratios of the side lengths of each triangle: *AB* : *DE*, *BC* : *EF* and *AC* : *DF*. What do you notice?  All of the ratios are 1 : 2.

3. Describe how the two triangles are similar.  Corresponding angles have equal measures.

4. Describe how the two triangles are different.  Corresponding sides have different lengths.

## ▨ BUILD UNDERSTANDING

**Similar figures** have the same shape, but not necessarily the same size. To indicate that two figures are similar, the symbol ~ is used.

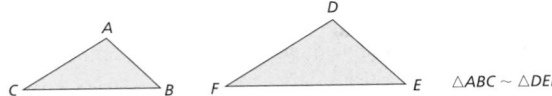

△*ABC* ~ △*DEF*

In similar polygons, vertices can be matched up so that all pairs of corresponding angles are congruent and all pairs of corresponding sides are in proportion.

| Similarity | Congruent angles | Corresponding sides |
|---|---|---|
| △*ABC* ~ △*DEF* | $\angle A \cong \angle D$ | *AB* : *DE* |
| | $\angle B \cong \angle E$ | *BC* : *EF* |
| | $\angle C \cong \angle F$ | *AC* : *DF* |

When identifying two polygons as similar, name their corresponding vertices in the same order. You can show that two triangles are similar if the corresponding angles are congruent or the corresponding sides are in proportion.

### Example 1

**Determine if each pair of triangles is similar.**

a.
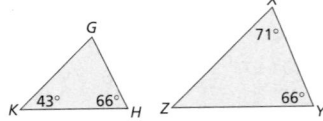

b.
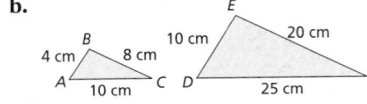

**474**   Chapter 11  **Right Triangle Trigonometry**

## Solution

**a.** Find the missing angle measures.

$m\angle G = 180° - (66° + 43°)$
$= 180° - 109°$
$= 71°$

$m\angle Z = 180° - (66° + 71°)$
$= 180° - 137°$
$= 43°$

So $\angle G \cong \angle X$ and $\angle Z \cong \angle K$. Since corresponding pairs of angles are congruent, $\triangle GHK \sim \triangle XYZ$.

**b.** Find the ratios of corresponding sides.

$\dfrac{AB}{DE} = \dfrac{4}{10} = \dfrac{2}{5}$

$\dfrac{BC}{EF} = \dfrac{8}{20} = \dfrac{2}{5}$

$\dfrac{AC}{DF} = \dfrac{10}{25} = \dfrac{2}{5}$

The ratios are equivalent, so corresponding sides are in proportion and $\triangle ABC \sim \triangle DEF$.

To determine if two polygons that are not triangles are similar, compare *both* their angles and the lengths of their sides.

## Example 2

**Determine if *ABCD* is similar to *PQRS*.**

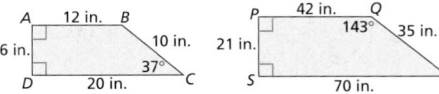

### Solution

Find the missing measures of the angles.

$m\angle B = 360° - (90° + 90° + 37°)$
$= 360° - 217°$
$= 143°$

$m\angle R = 360° - (90° + 90° + 143°)$
$= 360° - 323°$
$= 37°$

Find the ratios of the lengths of corresponding sides.

$\dfrac{AB}{PQ} = \dfrac{12}{42} = \dfrac{2}{7}$  $\dfrac{BC}{QR} = \dfrac{10}{35} = \dfrac{2}{7}$  $\dfrac{CD}{RS} = \dfrac{20}{70} = \dfrac{2}{7}$  $\dfrac{DA}{SP} = \dfrac{6}{21} = \dfrac{2}{7}$

Pairs of corresponding angles are congruent and pairs of corresponding sides are in proportion, so $ABCD \sim PQRS$.

## Example 3

**SPORTS** Miguel is making a model of a basketball court. The dimensions of a basketball court are 84 ft by 50 ft. If the length of Miguel's model is 3.5 ft, how wide is the model?

### Solution

Since Miguel's model is similar to an actual basketball court, the corresponding sides are in proportion. Let $w$ represent the width of Miguel's model.

$\dfrac{84}{3.5} = \dfrac{50}{w}$

$84 \cdot w = 3.5 \cdot 50$        Find the cross-products.

$w = \dfrac{175}{84} = 2\dfrac{7}{84} = 2\dfrac{1}{12}$        Solve for $w$.

So the width of Miguel's model is $2\dfrac{1}{12}$ ft, or 2 ft 1 in.

**Math Online** mathmatters2.com/extra_examples

### Check Understanding

If $\triangle URL \sim \triangle JKT$, what are the congruent angles and corresponding sides?

$\angle U \cong \angle J; \angle R \cong \angle K;$
$\angle L \cong \angle T; UR$ and $JK;$
$RL$ and $KT; UL$ and $JT$

---

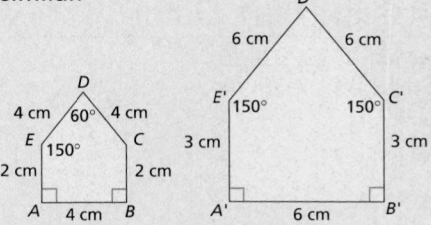
---

## Teaching Tip

From Example 1a and Supplementary Example 1, note with students that it is not necessary to show all three pairs of corresponding angles congruent. If two angles of one triangle are congruent to two angles of another triangle, the remaining angles must also be congruent. Thus, to establish similar triangles, two pairs of congruent angles is sufficient.
From Supplementary Example 1, note also that the acute angles of a right triangle are complementary. So, an alternate computation for $m\angle B$ is $90° - 37° = 53°$.

## Lesson Wrap-up

### QUICK ASSESSMENT

Ask the following questions to determine if students understand the content presented in this lesson.

1. In order to determine if two triangles are similar:
   a. What is the least number of pairs of corresponding angles you need to show congruent?
      two
   b. What is the least number of pairs of corresponding sides you need to show are in proportion?   three
2. Are isosceles right triangles always similar? Explain.   Yes; the measures of the three angles in any isosceles triangle are 45°, 45°, 90°.

### ASSIGNMENT GUIDE

**Basic:** 1–23, 31–36
**Enriched:** 1–36

### Reteaching Worksheet 11-1

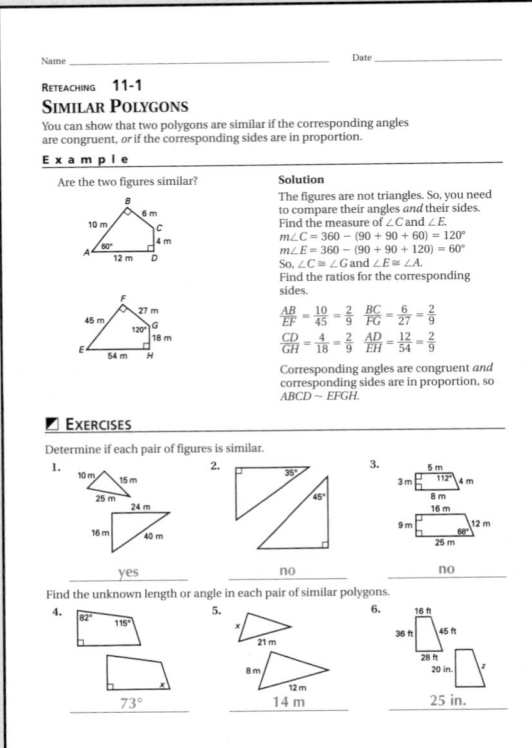

---

**Determine if each pair of polygons is similar.**

1.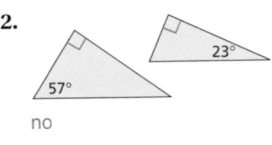
   yes

2.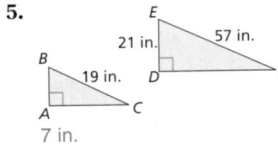
   no

3.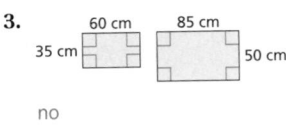
   no

**Find the length of $\overline{AB}$ in each pair of similar figures.**

4.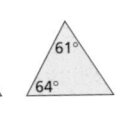
   7.2 cm

5.
   7 in.

6.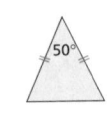
   2 m

7. **WRITING MATH** Write a short paragraph to explain the similarities and differences between the terms "similar" and "congruent." Include examples to illustrate these similarities and differences.   Answers will vary. Check students' work.

8. If $\square ABCD \sim \square RSTU$ and if $AB = 10$, $RS = 8$, and $ST = 4$, what is the length of $\overline{BC}$? 5

---

**■ PRACTICE EXERCISES** • For Extra Practice, see page 620.

**Determine if each pair of polygons is similar.**

9.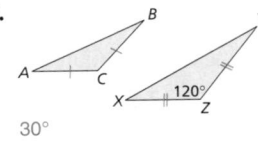
   yes

10. (triangles, 50°, 70°)
    no

11.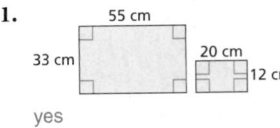
    yes

**Find the length of $\overline{AB}$ in each pair of similar figures.**

12.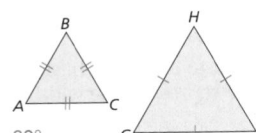
    2 m

13.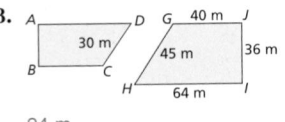
    24 m

14.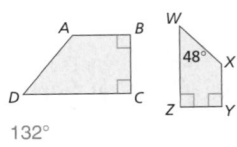
    28 cm

**Find $m\angle A$ in each pair of similar polygons.**

15.
    30°

16.
    60°

17.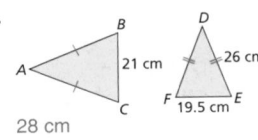
    132°

18. **ARCHITECTURE** An architect draws a blueprint to show the floor plan for a new home. If the scale ratio is 1 cm : 4 m and the master bedroom has dimensions 2.4 cm by 1.7 cm in the blueprint, what are the actual dimensions of the master bedroom?   9.6 m by 6.8 m

---

## Extend the Lesson

**CHALLENGE** Have students work with tangram pieces (shown at the right and provided on a transparency) to make a set of three squares using as many of the tangram pieces as necessary. The set of three squares should fit the following conditions:
One square should have one-half the area of the original tangram.
One square should have one-fourth the area of the original tangram.
One square should have one-eighth the area of the original tangram.

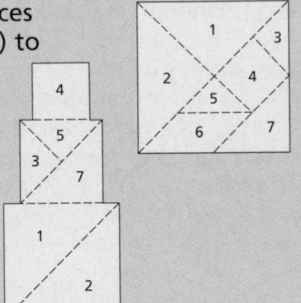

19. **ART** *ABCD* and *EFGH* are similar rectangular picture frames. The length of $\overline{AB}$ is 12 in., and the length of $\overline{BC}$ is 16 in. If $\overline{EF}$ has a length of 21 in., what is the length of $\overline{FG}$?  28 in.

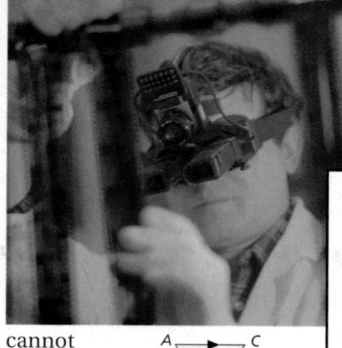

20. **WRITING MATH** Consider this statement: *All squares are similar.* Is this statement true or false? Write a paragraph to support your answer.  See additional answers.

21. Triangle *ABC* is similar to triangle *DEF*. List three equivalent ratios for the sides of the triangles.  *AB* : *DE*, *BC* : *EF*, *CA* : *FD*

22. **PHOTOGRAPHY** Photographers often take a film negative and enlarge the image. Is this an example of similar figures? Explain why or why not.  Yes. Angles are congruent and sides are proportional.

23. **YOU MAKE THE CALL** Tyra claims that in the figure shown, it cannot be determined that the two triangles are similar. Matt says that since $\overline{AC} \parallel \overline{ED}$, $\angle A \cong \angle D$ and $\angle C \cong \angle E$ because they are two pairs of alternate interior angles. Therefore, Matt says that the two triangles can be shown to be similar. Who is correct and why? If you agree with Matt, name the triangle similarity.  Matt; $\triangle ABC \sim \triangle DBE$

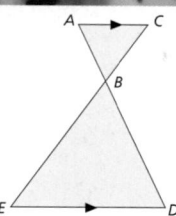

## ■ EXTENDED PRACTICE EXERCISES

**Write *sometimes*, *always* or *never* for each statement.**

24. A rhombus is similar to another rhombus.  sometimes
25. Circles are similar to each other.  always
26. Congruent figures are similar.  always
27. Similar figures are congruent.  sometimes
28. Figures with different numbers of sides can be similar.  never

29. **CRITICAL THINKING** *ABCD* and *MNOP* are similar rectangles. The length of $\overline{AB}$ is 4 cm, and the length of $\overline{MN}$ is 15 cm. If the area of *ABCD* is 48 cm², what is the area of *MNOP*?  675 cm²

30. **GEOMETRY SOFTWARE** Use geometry software to create several different types of triangles. Copy each triangle, and increase or decrease its size to create pairs of similar triangles.  Observe students' work.

## ■ MIXED REVIEW EXERCISES

**Solve. Round answers to the nearest tenth when necessary.** (Lesson 6-9)

31. Assume that *y* varies inversely as *x*. When *x* = 8, *y* = 16. Find *y* when *x* = 2.  64
32. Assume that *y* varies inversely as *x*. When *x* = 5, *y* = 20. Find *y* when *x* = 7.  14.3
33. Assume that *y* varies inversely as *x*. When *x* = 6, *y* = 14. Find *y* when *x* = 2.  42

**State whether each pair of triangles is congruent by SAS, ASA, or SSS. If the pair is not necessarily congruent, write *not congruent*.** (Lesson 5-5)

34.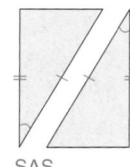
SAS

35.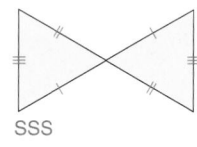
SSS

36.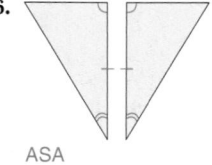
ASA

Math Online  mathmatters2.com/self_check_quiz

Lesson 11-1 **Similar Polygons**  | 477

## ADDITIONAL ANSWERS

20. True. Every angle of every square is 90° so all pairs of corresponding angles are congruent. The sides of a square are the same length so all pairs of corresponding sides are in proportion. Therefore, all squares are similar.

### Vocabulary

indirect measurement

### Tools/Materials Needed

calculator

### Lesson Resources

Warm-up Transparency 44
Reteaching 11-2
Extra Practice 11-2
Enrichment 11-2

## Getting Started

### 5-MINUTE WARM-UP

**Solve each proportion.**

1. $\frac{n}{28} = \frac{6}{7}$   **24**

2. $\frac{5}{7.5} = \frac{13}{n}$   **19.5**

3. $\frac{12}{12 + n} = \frac{18}{42}$   **16**

4. $\frac{200}{n} = \frac{40}{87.6}$   **438**

### Introduction to Lesson 11-2

Encourage students to write a word pattern indicating a proportion appropriate to the situation, noting that different arrangements of the proportion are possible, such as shown below.

$$\frac{\text{short distance (m)}}{\text{short distance (steps)}} = \frac{\text{long distance (m)}}{\text{long distance (steps)}}$$

$$\frac{\text{short distance (m)}}{\text{long distance (m)}} = \frac{\text{short distance (steps)}}{\text{long distance (steps)}}$$

## ADDITIONAL ANSWERS

3. The first approximates distance by the number of steps taken and the second approximates distance by the amount of time taken. Either approximation could be more accurate, but the two are relatively close to each other.

---

# 11-2 Indirect Measurement

**Goals**   ■ Use similar triangles to find indirect measurements.

**Applications**   Nature, Recreation, Advertising, Earth Science, Photography

**HEALTH** Carla is hiking in the woods and wishes to know approximately how far she walks. So she takes a tape measure and marks a distance of 20 m. She walks the 20-m distance several times and finds that she makes on average 26 steps in approximately 14 sec.

1. If Carla takes 5400 steps during her hike walking at a fairly constant rate, approximately how far does she walk?
   4154 m
2. If Carla's hike takes her approximately 50 min to complete, about how far did she hike?   4286 m

3. How can you explain the difference in the approximations? Which do you think is more accurate?
   See additional answers.

### ■ BUILD UNDERSTANDING

In some situations, it is impossible or impractical to find a length by measuring the actual distance. An **indirect measurement** is one in which you take other measurements that allow you to calculate the required measurement.

### Example 1

**NATURE** A tree casts a shadow that is 12 m long. At the same time, a forest ranger 170 cm tall notices that her shadow is 300 cm long. What is the height of the tree?

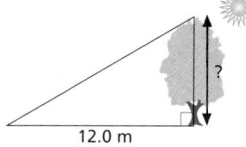

12.0 m

### Solution

The angle at which the sun's rays meet the ground is the same in both right triangles. Since the triangles have corresponding pairs of congruent angles, they are similar. Use this similarity to write and solve a proportion.

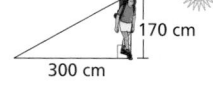

170 cm

300 cm

$$\frac{170}{h} = \frac{300}{12}$$

$$170 \cdot 12 = h \cdot 300 \qquad \text{Find the cross-products.}$$

$$2040 = 300h$$

$$\frac{2040}{300} = \frac{300h}{300} \qquad \text{Divide both sides by 300.}$$

$$6.8 = h$$

The height of the tree is 6.8 m.

## Teaching Tip

Have students write a word pattern for the proportions in Examples 1 and 2, noting that other arrangements are possible, as shown below.

**Example 1**   $\frac{\text{ranger's height}}{\text{tree's height}} = \frac{\text{ranger's shadow}}{\text{tree's shadow}}$ or $\frac{\text{ranger's height}}{\text{ranger's shadow}} = \frac{\text{tree's height}}{\text{tree's shadow}}$

**Example 2**   $\frac{\text{tower's height}}{\text{pole's height}} = \frac{\text{length of } \overline{AB}}{\text{length of } \overline{AC}}$ or $\frac{\text{tower's height}}{\text{length of } \overline{AB}} = \frac{\text{pole's height}}{\text{length of } \overline{CD}}$

## Example 2

The wire supporting a radio transmitting tower touches the top of a 3.6-m pole. What is the height of the tower?

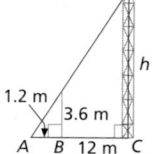

1.2 m
3.6 m
A  B  12 m  C

### Solution

The right triangles share a common acute angle, so they are similar. Use this similarity to write and solve a proportion.

$$\frac{1.2}{1.2 + 12} = \frac{3.6}{h}$$

$1.2 \cdot h = (1.2 + 12)\,3.6$      Find the cross-products.

$$1.2h = 47.52$$

$$h = 39.6$$

The height of the tower is 39.6 m.

The **mirror method** is another means of indirectly measuring the approximate height of an object. Place a mirror on the ground between you and the object you wish to measure. Position yourself so that you can see the top of the object in the mirror. Then the right triangles shown in the diagram are similar since their acute angles that have the mirror as a vertex are congruent.

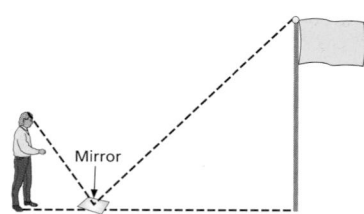

Mirror

The mirror method is useful on a cloudy day when there are no shadows.

### Problem Solving Tip

When you write a proportion, you do not always have to convert measurements to the same units. But the corresponding units of the ratios must be the same.

For example, the proportion $\frac{6\,ft}{34\,in.} = \frac{7\,ft}{x\,in.}$ is suitable to solve for $x$ in inches.

## Example 3

Marty uses the mirror method to find the height of a telephone pole. He places the mirror 33 ft from the pole's base and steps back 6 ft, which allows him to see the top of the telephone pole in the mirror. Marty is 5.5 ft tall. Find the height of the telephone pole.

### Solution

Marty has established a pair of similar triangles. Marty's distance from the mirror corresponds to the pole's distance. His height corresponds to the pole's height.

$$\frac{6}{33} = \frac{5.5}{h}$$

$$6 \cdot h = 33 \cdot 5.5$$

$$6h = 181.5$$

$$h = 30.25$$      The telephone pole is approximately 30.25 ft tall.

### Check Understanding

Explain why the mirror method produces an approximate height of the object being measured.

The mirror method uses your height instead of the distance from the ground to your eyes.

**Math Online** mathmatters2.com/extra_examples

---

## Chalkboard Examples

### Supplementary Example 1
**ENGINEERING** To find the width $AB$ of a river, a surveyor has located points $C$, $D$, and $E$ on land, where $BD$ and $AE$ intersect at $C$. Find the width of the river.

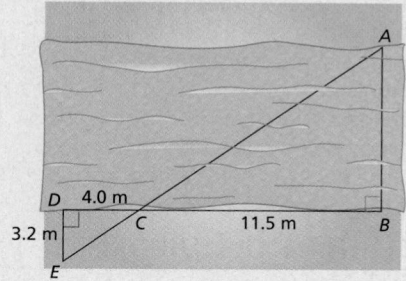

D  4.0 m
3.2 m
E
C
11.5 m
B
A

Since vertical angles are congruent and right angles are congruent, $\triangle CDE \sim \triangle CBA$.
Corresponding sides of similar triangles are in proportion.

$$\frac{AB}{ED} = \frac{BC}{DC}$$

$$\frac{AB}{3.2} = \frac{11.5}{4.0}$$

$$4.0(AB) = 3.2(11.5)$$

$$AB = 9.2$$

So, the width of the river is 9.2 m.

### Supplementary Example 2
Use the information in the diagram to find $DE$, which represents the width of a lake.

E  ?  D
55 m
C
B
120 m
100 m
A

$\triangle ABC \sim \triangle ADE$ since they each contain a right angle and they both contain $\angle A$.

$$\frac{DE}{BC} = \frac{DA}{BA}$$

$$\frac{DE}{55} = \frac{120 + 100}{100}$$

$$100(DE) = 55(220)$$

$$DE = 121 \text{ m}$$

---

## Differentiated Instruction

**VISUAL LEARNERS** Encourage students to draw diagrams for exercises that do not have an accompanying diagram, such as Exercises 5–7, to ensure that they are writing correct proportions.

Discuss with students the placement of certain quantities in a diagram. For example, a right triangle is appropriate when an object (a person, a pole, a tree) is standing on level ground; the vertical leg of the triangle represents the height of the object. The horizontal leg of the right triangle would represent the length of the shadow. A mirror would be placed on the ground.

## QUICK ASSESSMENT

Ask the following questions to determine if students understand the content presented in this lesson.

1. A ruler or similar physical tool is used in *direct measurement*. What algebraic tool is used in *indirect measurement*?   **a pro-portion**

2. If the ratio of the height of two trees is 5 : 6, what is the ratio of the shadows they will cast?   **5 : 6**

## ASSIGNMENT GUIDE

**Basic:** 1–18, 23–28
**Enriched:** 1–28

## ADDITIONAL ANSWERS

8. Direct measurement involves finding the actual size of something by physically measuring it. Indirect measurement is used when it is impractical to measure an actual length, so you use other measurements that allow you to calculate it.

### Reteaching Worksheet 11-2

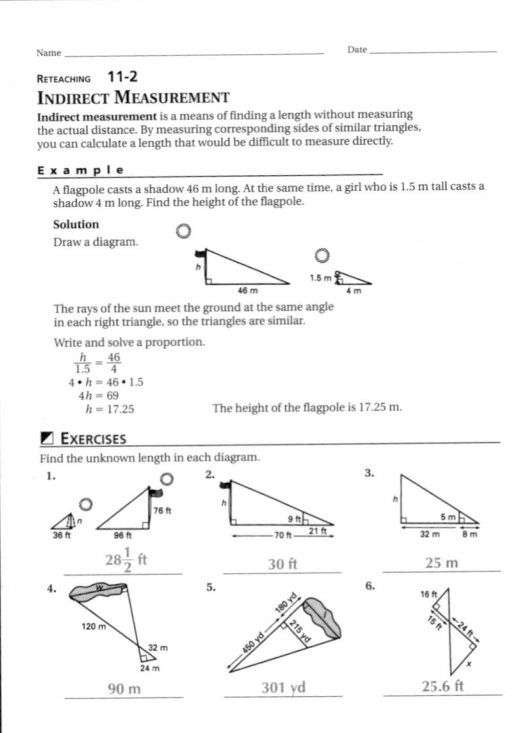

---

### ■ TRY THESE EXERCISES

Use indirect measurement to find the unknown length of *x*.

**1.**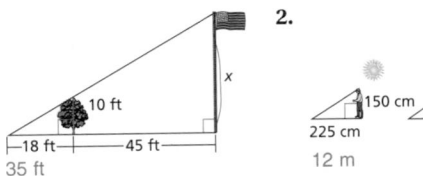

**2.**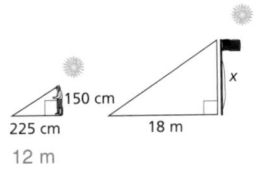

**3.**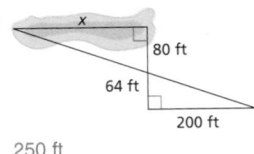

**4.** Find the height of the building in the figure to the right.   53.75 ft

**5. RECREATION** Darnell places a mirror on the ground 48 ft from the base of a rollercoaster hill. He then stands 4 ft from the mirror so that he can see the top of the hill. If Darnell is 5.9 ft tall, how high is the hill?   70.8 ft

**6.** Lian is 5 ft tall. To measure a flagpole that is 60 ft tall, she places a mirror on the ground 4 ft away from her. How far from the flagpole is Lian standing?   52 ft

**7.** A building casts a shadow 72 ft long. At the same time, a 5-ft tall boy casts a shadow 12 ft long. What is the height of the building?   30 ft

**8. WRITING MATH** Write a paragraph describing the difference between direct measurement and indirect measurement. Include examples of each type.
Answers will vary. See additional answers.

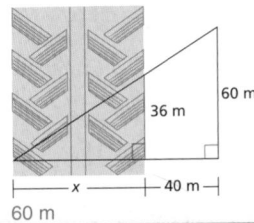

---

### ■ PRACTICE EXERCISES • For Extra Practice, see page 620.

Use indirect measurement to find the unknown length of *x*.

**9.**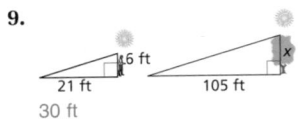

**10.**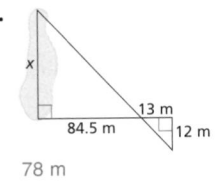

**11.** 

**12.** Mykaela stands 7.5 ft from a mirror she has placed on the ground to measure the height of her house. If the mirror is 23 ft from the house and Mykaela is 5.3 ft tall, how tall is the house?   ≈ 16.3 ft

**13. ADVERTISING** To measure the height of a billboard, Vijay places a mirror on the ground 13 m from the base of the billboard. He then stands 3.7 m away from the mirror so that he can see the reflection of the top of the billboard. If Vijay is 1.9 m tall, how high off the ground is the top of the billboard?   ≈ 6.7 m

---

### Extend the Lesson

The *sight-by-eye* method uses two body measurements to estimate the distance to any object of approximately known size. With one arm straight out in front, elbow straight, and thumb up, close the left eye. Align one thumb edge with one edge of the object. Without moving, switch eyes, now sighting the same edge with the right eye closed. Estimate how many times the object's width the thumb appears to jump and follow the example shown to estimate the object's distance.

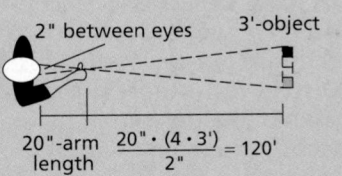

**14.** A tree casts a shadow 26 m long. At the same time, a flagpole 25 m high casts a shadow 32.5 m long. How tall is the tree?  20 m

**15.** A 45-ft tall building casts a shadow 10 yd long. At the same time, Simon casts a shadow that is 3 ft long. How tall is Simon?  4.5 ft

**16.** A lumberjack places a mirror 50 ft from a 100-ft tall tree. If the lumberjack is standing 53 ft from the base of the tree and can see the top of the tree through the mirror, how tall is the lumberjack?  6 ft

**17.** **EARTH SCIENCE** Each time Old Faithful in Yellowstone National Park erupts, rangers can estimate the height of the geyser by comparing it to the height of a tree. The rangers locate a tree of about the same height as the geyser. If the shadow of the tree is 93 ft when the shadow of a 6-ft ranger is 4 ft, what is the height of the tree and the approximate height of the geyser?  139.5 ft

**18.** A 25-ft ladder is leaning against a wall. A rung that is 5 ft from the bottom of the ladder is 4 ft above the ground. How far above the ground does the top of the ladder touch the wall?  20 ft

## ■ EXTENDED PRACTICE EXERCISES

**19.** **MONUMENTS** A monument is 96 ft tall and a tree next to it is 84 ft tall. What is the ratio of the lengths of their shadows? Does the ratio depend on the time of day? Explain.  8 : 7; Yes. This ratio will not exist if the sun is directly over either or both objects or if the sun is not shining.

**20.** **CRITICAL THINKING** Suppose you know the height of a flagpole on the beach of Chesapeake Bay and that it casts a shadow 4 ft long at 4:00 P.M. (EST). You also know the height of a flagpole on the shoreline of Lake Michigan whose shadow is hard to measure at 3:00 P.M. (CST). Since 4:00 (EST) = 3:00 (CST), you propose the following proportion of heights and lengths to find the length of the shadow of the Michigan flagpole. Explain whether this proportion will give an accurate measure.

$$\frac{\text{height of Chesapeake flagpole}}{\text{shadow of Chesapeake flagpole}} = \frac{\text{height of Michigan flagpole}}{\text{shadow of Michigan flagpole}}$$

No; the towns are on different latitudinal lines, so the sun is at a different angle to the two buildings.

**21.** **PHOTOGRAPHY** Annie takes a picture of a pine tree measuring 12.19 m tall. She is 180 cm tall and casts a shadow of 300 cm. What is the greatest distance that Annie can be from the tree if she does not want the lens exposed to direct sunlight?  ≈ 17.3 m

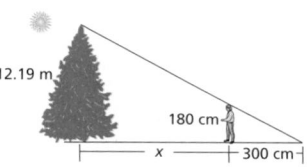
12.19 m
180 cm
x   300 cm

**22.** **CHAPTER INVESTIGATION** The photographer, subject and ground are the vertices of a right triangle. Draw a diagram of the triangle formed by a photographer who is shooting at an upward angle at the subject of the picture. Use the distance between the subject and the ground as one leg of the right triangle.  Answers will vary.

## ■ MIXED REVIEW EXERCISES

Give the coordinates of the image of each point under a reflection across the given axis. (Lesson 7-2)

**23.** (4, 6); y-axis (−4, 6) **24.** (2, −4); x-axis (2, 4) **25.** (−3, 7); x-axis (−3, −7) **26.** (−5, 1); y-axis (5, 1)

**27.** Two number cubes are rolled. Find the probability that the difference of the numbers rolled is 1 or 2. (Lesson 4-4) $\frac{1}{2}$

**28.** One card is drawn from a standard deck of cards. Find the probability that the card drawn is a heart or a queen. (Lesson 4-4) $\frac{4}{13}$

**Math Online** mathmatters2.com/self_check_quiz

## Extend the Lesson

**REAL WORLD CONNECTION** Have students research and report on some of the instruments used by surveyors, such as the *transit, surveyor's compass*, and *theodolite*. Also, ask students to find out about *invar*, the alloy used for surveying tapes.

Surveying is believed to have originated in Egypt, primarily because constructing buildings as massive as the pyramids required an ability to measure angles and calculate long distances. Ask students to research and report on the *groma*, a surveying device used in ancient Egypt.

### Extra Practice Worksheet 11-2

Name _____  Date _____

EXTRA PRACTICE  **11-2**
**INDIRECT MEASUREMENT**

☑ **EXERCISES**

**1.** A tree casts a shadow 25 ft long. At the same time, a lamppost 12 ft high casts a shadow 15 ft long. How tall is the tree?  20 ft

**2.** A 50-ft tall building casts a shadow 20 yd long. At the same time, Niko casts a shadow that is 8 ft long. How tall is Niko?  $6\frac{2}{3}$ ft or 6 ft 8 in.

**3.** A 15.5-ft tall tree casts a shadow 25 ft long. At the same time, another tree casts a shadow that is 18 ft long. How tall is the other tree?  11.16 ft

**4.** Jana places a mirror on the ground 36 ft from the base of a building. She then stands 5 ft from the mirror so that he can see the top of the building. If Jana is 5.2 ft tall, how tall is the building?  37.44 ft

**5.** A 15-ft ladder is leaning against a wall. A rung that is 3 ft from the bottom of the ladder is 2 ft above the ground. How far above the ground does the top of the ladder touch the wall?  10 ft

**6.** Kira places a mirror 40 ft from a 60-ft tall tree. If Kira is standing 48 ft from the base of the tree and can see the top of the tree in the mirror, how tall is Kira?  12 ft

**7.** A 42-m tall tree casts shadow 40 m long. At the same time, a flag pole casts a shadow 24 m long. How tall is the flag pole?  25.2 m

**8.** A 5.8-ft tall person casts a shadow 8 ft long. At the same time, a dog casts a shadow that is 3 ft long. How tall is the dog?  2.175 ft

**9.** A telephone pole casts a shadow 21 ft long. At the same time, a 6-ft tall bush casts a shadow 9 ft long. How tall is the telephone pole?  14 ft

**10.** The ratio of the length of Tia's shadow to the length of Trevor's shadow at the same time of day is 2 : 3. If Tia is 4.9 ft tall, how tall is Trevor?  7.35 ft

**11.** Rhonda stands 8 m from a mirror she has placed on the ground to measure the height of light pole. If the mirror is 24 m from the light pole and Rhonda is 4 m tall, how tall is the light pole?  12 m

### Enrichment Worksheet 11-2

Name _____  Date _____

ENRICHMENT  **11-2**
**THE TRIANGULOMETER**

Sometimes it is difficult to take indirect measurements to find a height—the sun may not be shining, for example. What you need is a triangulometer.

**How to make a triangulometer**

**a.** Draw a right triangle with sides of 6 in., 8 in. and 10 in. on a stiff piece of cardboard. Cut it out carefully.

**b.** Use tape to attach one end of a short length of string (about 1 ft) to the vertex of the 6-in. leg and the hypotenuse. Tie a small weight, such as a washer, to the other end of the string.

10 in.  6 in.  8 in.

**How to use a triangulometer**

**a.** Make sure that the 6-in. leg is vertical by lining up the string and the edge of the triangle.

**b.** "Aim" the hypotenuse of the triangulometer at the top of the object you want to measure. Move around until you find a suitable position.

**c.** Measure the distance between your position and the base of the object.

☑ **EXERCISES**

**1.** Write a proportion that you could use to find the value of *m* on the diagram above.  $\frac{6}{8} = \frac{m}{l}$

**2.** Express the value of *m* in terms of *l*.  $m = \left(\frac{3}{4}\right)l$

**3.** Express the value of *h* in terms of *l* and *t*.  $h = \left(\frac{3}{4}\right)l + t$

**4.** Find the value of *t* if you were using the triangulometer.  distance of student's eye level from the floor

## Vocabulary Review

**Lesson 11-1**
similar figures

**Lesson 11-2**
indirect measurement

## ASSIGNMENT GUIDE

All students: 1–14

## Chalkboard Examples

**Lesson 11-1**
Determine if the triangles are similar.

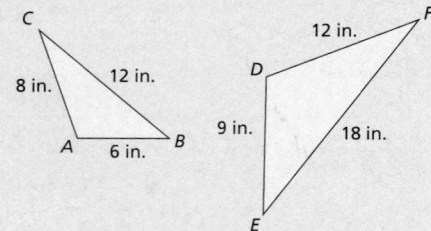

$$\frac{ED}{AB} = \frac{9}{6} = \frac{3}{2} \qquad \frac{DF}{AC} = \frac{12}{8} = \frac{3}{2}$$

$$\frac{FE}{CB} = \frac{18}{12} = \frac{3}{2}$$

The ratios are equivalent. So, corresponding sides are in proportion, and $\triangle ABC \sim \triangle DEF$.

**Lesson 11-2**
To find the width $DC$ of an impassable stretch of marshland, a surveyor has laid out this diagram.

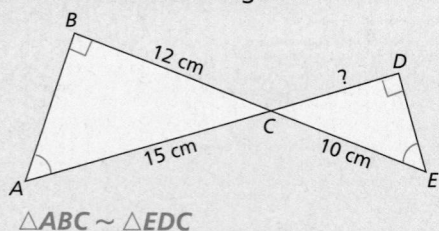

$$\triangle ABC \sim \triangle EDC$$

$$\frac{BC}{DC} = \frac{AC}{EC}$$

$$\frac{12}{DC} = \frac{15}{10}$$

$$15(DC) = 12(10)$$

$$DC = 8 \text{ cm}$$

### PRACTICE ■ LESSON 11-1

**Determine if each pair of triangles is similar.**

**1.**
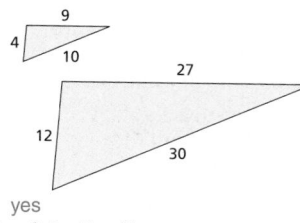
yes

**2.**
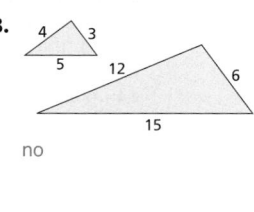
yes

**3.**

no

**Find the length of $\overline{AB}$ in each pair of similar figures.**

**4.**
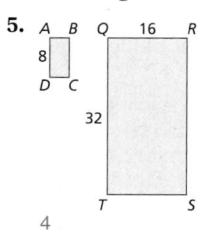
49

**5.**

4

**6.**
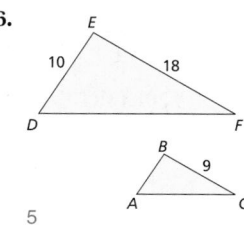
5

**Find $m\angle B$ in each pair of similar polygons.**

**7.**
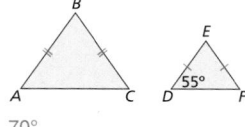
70°

**8.**
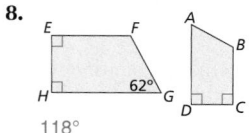
118°

**9.**
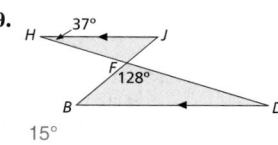
15°

### PRACTICE ■ LESSON 11-2

**Use indirect measurement to find the unknown length $x$.**

**10.**
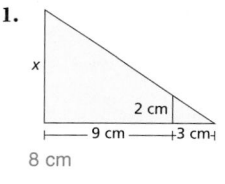
37 m

**11.**
8 cm

**12.**
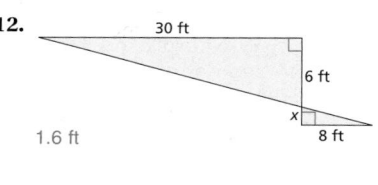
1.6 ft

**13.** A tree casts a 20 m shadow while at the same time a 1.5 m person casts a shadow that is 1.2 m long. How tall is the tree? 25 m

**14.** If a person who is 2 m tall casts a 5 m shadow at 7 P.M., how long should the shadow of the 445 m tall Sears Tower be at the same time? 1112.5 m

## Teaching Tip

In the Chalkboard Example from Lesson 11-2, students see one possible proportion, $\frac{BC}{DC} = \frac{AC}{EC}$. In this case, the ratios are written from large triangle to small triangle.

Have students write other possible proportions, explaining the order in which they worked. For example, the proportion shown at the right works within the large triangle and then within the small triangle.

$$\frac{BC}{AC} = \frac{DC}{CE}$$

Have students compare the proportions, $\frac{BC}{DC} = \frac{AC}{CE}$ and $\frac{BC}{AC} = \frac{DC}{CE}$, noting that the means have been interchanged, which yields the same cross-products.

# MathWorks | Career – Aerial Photographer
### Workplace Knowhow

**A**erial photographs are useful in many professions such as real estate development, transportation planning, construction and cartography. These photographs are used to design a new neighborhood, determine the necessity and size of new roads, as well as the development of new maps. Three different techniques are used to take aerial photographs.

**High Oblique Technique**

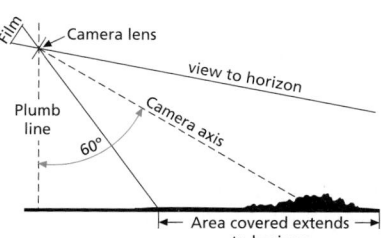

**Vertical Technique**

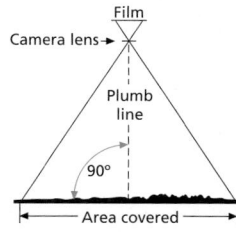

**Low Oblique Technique**

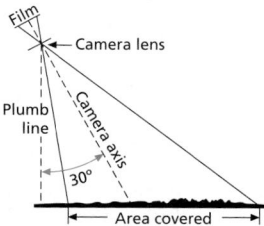

**Use the three techniques, Figure A, and Figure B for Exercises 1–3.**

1. Figure A is a sketch of an aerial view of a city street and a skyscraper ($\overline{FD}$) that is positioned along a street. The height of the skyscraper is 933 ft. The camera lens is located at point *A*. A portion of the road between points *C* and *D* must be resurfaced. Using similar triangles, determine the length of the section of the road that must be repaired. ≈ 801 ft

2. The vertical technique, in Figure B, uses two similar triangles. Name the triangles and explain why they are similar. △*MNP* ≈ △*QSP*; all corresponding angles are congruent.

3. If the width of the film ($\overline{MN}$) in Figure B is 35 mm and the distance from the center of the film to the camera lens is 100 mm, determine the width of the area covered in the photograph. Assume that the camera lens is 500 m above the ground. 175 m

**Figure B**

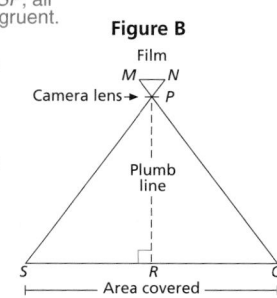

**Figure A**

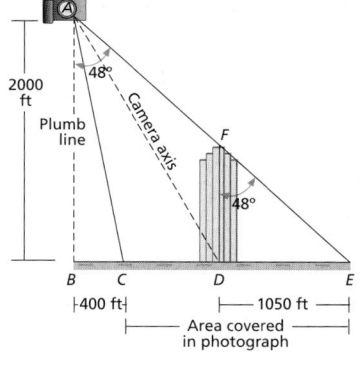

## MathWorks

Surveyors, architects, civil engineers, tax assessors, naturalists, and military strategists are some of the many professionals who use aerial photographs in their work. Aerial photographs can provide a current pictorial view of a region and can show features that do not appear on maps.

Students should answer Questions 1–3 to better understand how indirect measure can be accomplished from aerial photographs.

Have students investigate the advantages and disadvantages of the three types of aerial photographs. Ask students to find out what each type of aerial photo is used for and when one would be preferred over another.

*Photogrammetry* is the science of making reliable measurements by the use of photographs. Geologists, for example, use aerial photography and satellite imagery to map the movements of ancient glaciers. Ask students to find out how the work of an aerial photographer might be applied to a particular profession.

Students who are interested in learning more about this career choice can go to mathmatters2.com/mathworks. School Guidance Counselors are another resource for information about training requirements and appropriate schools.

## Teaching Tip

In preparation for Exercises 1–3, remind students that to determine similar triangles, it is necessary to show only two pairs of congruent angles; but, equivalent ratios must be checked for all three pairs of corresponding sides. When students are using proportions to find a length, as in Exercises 4–6 or 10–12, remind them that they can work between figures to set up the ratios or they can stay within a figure to set up each ratio. Emphasize that whatever order is chosen, it is essential to maintain the same order for both ratios.

### Vocabulary

hypotenuse
legs of right triangle
Pythagorean Theorem

### Tools/Materials Needed

calculator
scissors
centimeter grid paper

### Lesson Resources

Warm-up Transparency 45
Transparency RF-56
Reteaching 11-3
Extra Practice 11-3
Enrichment 11-3
Technology Activity 11-3

## Getting Started

### 5-Minute Warm-Up

Evaluate each expression.
1. $9^2 + 12^2$  225    2. $13^2 - 5^2$  144
3. $\sqrt{961}$  31      4. $\sqrt{112.36}$  10.6

### Introduction to Lesson 11-3

After students have grasped the proof shown in the diagrams, have them verify it for themselves. Have them cut four congruent right triangles from centimeter grid paper (suggest sides of 3 cm, 4 cm, and 5 cm, or 5 cm, 12 cm, and 13 cm), and superimpose them on a separate sheet of grid paper in the arrrangements shown in the diagrams.

See the Teaching Tip at the bottom of this page for another diagrammatic view of the Pythagorean Theorem.

---

# 11-3 The Pythagorean Theorem

**Goals** ■ Use the Pythagorean Theorem to find unknown lengths.

**Applications** Fitness, Recreation, Sports, Hobbies, Photography

**HISTORY** An ancient Chinese mathematical manuscript called the Zhoubi is between 2000 and 3000 years old. The manuscript includes an illustration similar to Figure 1. The figure is a square that encloses four congruent triangles and a smaller square.

**Figure 1**
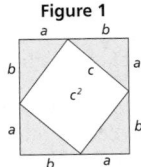

1. The triangles can be rearranged as shown in Figure 2. How do the areas of Figure 1 and Figure 2 compare?
They are equal.

2. How do the areas of the unshaded regions of the two figures compare?  They are equal.

**Figure 2**
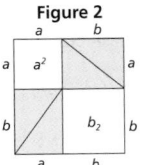

3. How do the unshaded regions relate to the length of the triangle sides? Their areas are the squares of the side lengths of the triangle.

## ▧ BUILD UNDERSTANDING

In a right triangle, the side opposite the right angle is the **hypotenuse**. The other two sides are the **legs**. About 2500 years ago, a Greek mathematician named Pythagoras proved a property about the hypotenuse and legs of a right triangle. This property is called the **Pythagorean Theorem**.

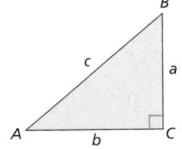

| Pythagorean Theorem | $c^2 = a^2 + b^2$ <br> In any right triangle, the square of the hypotenuse ($c^2$) is equal to the sum of the squares of the legs ($a^2 + b^2$). |
|---|---|

### Example 1

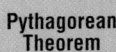

**Find the length of the hypotenuse of triangle *ABC*.**

**Solution**

$$c^2 = a^2 + b^2 \qquad \text{Use the Pythagorean Theorem.}$$
$$c^2 = 8^2 + 15^2 \qquad \text{Substitute 8 for } a \text{ and 15 for } b.$$
$$c^2 = 64 + 225$$
$$c^2 = 289$$
$$\sqrt{c^2} = \sqrt{289} \qquad \text{Take the square root of each side.}$$
$$c = 17$$

The length of the hypotenuse is 17 cm.

### Math: Who, Where, When

A 1940's collection of 370 different proofs of the Pythagorean Theorem includes work by the 12th century Hindu Bhaskara, the 15th century Italian Da Vinci, and the 19th century American James Garfield, the 20th U.S. president.

---

## Differentiated Instruction

**VISUAL LEARNERS** Another diagrammatic view of the Pythagorean Theorem is shown at the right. A corresponding statement of the theorem is that the square *on* the hypotenuse is equal to the sum of the squares *on* the legs.

## Example 2

**Find the length of $\overline{MO}$ to the nearest tenth.**

### Solution

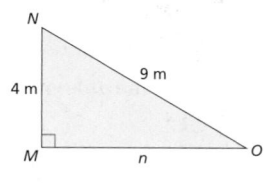

$$9^2 = 4^2 + n^2 \qquad c^2 = a^2 + b^2$$
$$81 = 16 + n^2$$
$$65 = n^2 \qquad \text{Subtract 16 from both sides.}$$
$$\sqrt{65} = \sqrt{n^2} \qquad \text{Take the square root of both sides.}$$
$$8.062 \approx n$$

The length of $\overline{MO}$ is approximately 8.1 m.

## Example 3

**RECREATION** The longest side of a right triangular sail measures 6 m, and the base of the sail measures 3 m. What is the minimum height of the mast to the nearest tenth?

### Solution

Draw a diagram of the problem. The triangle is a right triangle, and the longest side is the hypotenuse.

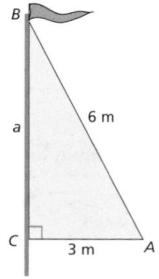

$$c^2 = a^2 + b^2$$
$$6^2 = a^2 + 3^2 \qquad \text{Substitute 6 for } c \text{ and 3 for } b.$$
$$36 = a^2 + 9$$
$$27 = a^2 \qquad \text{Subtract 9 from both sides.}$$
$$\sqrt{27} = \sqrt{a^2}$$
$$5.196 \approx a$$

The height of the mast must be at least 5.2 m.

## Example 4

**What is the length of the diagonal of rectangle $ABCD$?**

### Solution

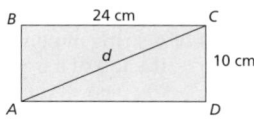

Since the diagonal forms the hypotenuse of a right triangle, the Pythagorean Theorem can be used to solve the problem.

$$d^2 = 10^2 + 24^2$$
$$d^2 = 100 + 576$$
$$\sqrt{d^2} = \sqrt{676}$$
$$d = 26$$

The length of the diagonal of rectangle $ABCD$ is 26 cm.

> ### Check Understanding
> Use the Pythagorean Theorem to write expressions for $a^2$ and $b^2$.
>
> $a^2 = c^2 - b^2; b^2 = c^2 - a^2$

 **Math Online** mathmatters2.com/extra_examples

Lesson 11-3 **The Pythagorean Theorem** | 485

# Chalkboard Examples

### Supplementary Example 1
The hypotenuse of a right triangle measures 17 cm and one leg measures 15 cm. Find the measure of the other leg.

$$\text{hypotenuse}^2 = \text{leg}^2 + \text{leg}^2$$
$$17^2 = 15^2 + x^2$$
$$289 = 225 + x^2$$
$$64 = x^2$$
$$\sqrt{64} = \sqrt{x^2}$$
$$8 = x$$

So, the measure of the other leg is 8 cm.

### Supplementary Example 2
**CONSTRUCTION** The Ruiz family is having new siding put on the exterior walls of their house. For stability, a worker places the foot of his 17-ft ladder 4 ft from the house. How far up the side of the house will the ladder reach?

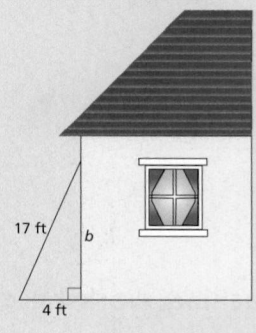

$$c^2 = a^2 + b^2$$
$$17^2 = 4^2 + b^2$$
$$289 = 16 + b^2$$
$$273 = b^2$$
$$\sqrt{273} = \sqrt{b^2}$$
$$16.5 \approx b$$

So, the ladder will reach about 16.5 ft up the side of the house.

## Extend the Lesson

From the Exercises, students see that applying the Pythagorean Theorem sometimes results in three integers for the lengths of the sides of a right triangle. More often, not all three sides are integers. Three integers that are connected by the Pythagorean Theorem, such as 3, 4, 5, are called *Pythagorean Triples*. This particular triple is commonly used and is worth committing to memory. In addition, recognizing multiples of this triple can save calculations. For example, if you know that the legs of a right triangle measure 6 cm and 8 cm, then the hypotenuse must measure 10 cm (these numbers are twice the 3, 4, 5 triple). Be sure students understand that if the legs of a right triangle are 3 cm and 5 cm, then the hypotenuse cannot be 4 cm.

### QUICK ASSESSMENT

Ask the following questions to determine if students understand the context presented in this lesson.

1. What is the only type of triangle to which the Pythagorean Relation applies?   a right triangle

### ASSIGNMENT GUIDE

**Basic:** 1–24, 30–45
**Enriched:** 1–45

---

### Reteaching Worksheet 11-3

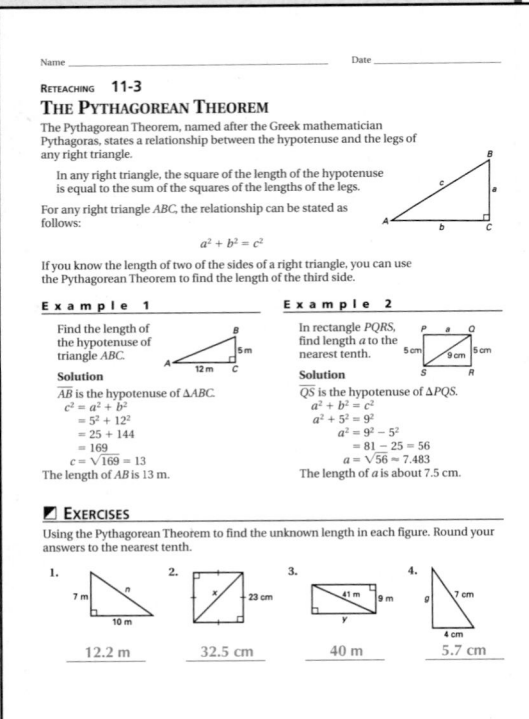

Name _____ Date _____

RETEACHING  **11-3**

**THE PYTHAGOREAN THEOREM**

The Pythagorean Theorem, named after the Greek mathematician Pythagoras, states a relationship between the hypotenuse and the legs of any right triangle.

In any right triangle, the square of the length of the hypotenuse is equal to the sum of the squares of the lengths of the legs.

For any right triangle $ABC$, the relationship can be stated as follows:

$$a^2 + b^2 = c^2$$

If you know the length of two of the sides of a right triangle, you can use the Pythagorean Theorem to find the length of the third side.

**Example 1**

Find the length of the hypotenuse of triangle $ABC$.

**Solution**

$\overline{AB}$ is the hypotenuse of $\triangle ABC$.
$c^2 = a^2 + b^2$
$= 5^2 + 12^2$
$= 25 + 144$
$= 169$
$c = \sqrt{169} = 13$
The length of $AB$ is 13 m.

**Example 2**

In rectangle $PQRS$, find length $a$ to the nearest tenth.

**Solution**

$\overline{QS}$ is the hypotenuse of $\triangle PQS$.
$a^2 + b^2 = c^2$
$a^2 + 5^2 = 9^2$
$a^2 = 9^2 - 5^2$
$= 81 - 25 = 56$
$a = \sqrt{56} \approx 7.483$
The length of $a$ is about 7.5 cm.

**EXERCISES**

Using the Pythagorean Theorem to find the unknown length in each figure. Round your answers to the nearest tenth.

1.   12.2 m
2.   32.5 cm
3.   40 m
4.   5.7 cm

---

## TRY THESE EXERCISES

Find the unknown length. Round to the nearest tenth.

1.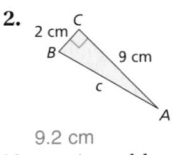
9.4 m

2.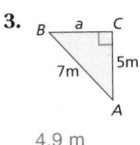
9.2 cm

3.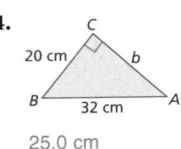
4.9 m

4.
25.0 cm

5. A flagpole is supported by a wire cable connected to its highest point. The cable is 40 ft long and is attached to the ground 15 ft from the base of the pole. How tall is the flagpole? Round to the nearest foot.  37 ft

6. How long is the diagonal of a square with sides of 4 cm? Round to the nearest tenth.
5.7 cm

7. What is the length of a rectangle that has a diagonal of 16 ft and width 7 ft?  14.4 ft

8. **WRITING MATH**  Explain how you could find the perimeter of a rhombus whose diagonals measure 12 m and 16 m. Find the perimeter.
See additional answers.

## PRACTICE EXERCISES  •  For Extra Practice, see page 621.

Find the length of each hypotenuse. Round to the nearest tenth.

9.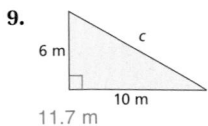
11.7 m

10.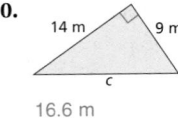
16.6 m

11.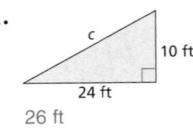
26 ft

Find the unknown length. Round to the nearest tenth.

12.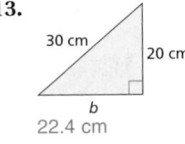
8.9 cm

13.
22.4 cm

14.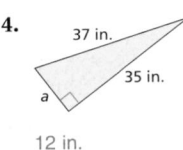
12 in.

15. What is the length of the diagonal of a rectangle with sides 40 ft and 9 ft?  41 ft

16. How wide is a rectangle that is 20 in. long and has a diagonal of length 25 in.?  15 in.

17. A string of pennants is 65 ft long. It is stretched from the top of a tree to a point on the ground 39 ft from the base of the tree. How tall is the tree?  52 ft

18. **FITNESS**  A rectangular swimming pool is 48 ft long and 14 ft wide. A life preserver must be located nearby and have a rope at least as long as the diagonal of the pool. What is the minimum length of the rope?  50 ft

19. **SPORTS**  A baseball diamond is a square with 90-ft sides. To the nearest foot, what is the approximate distance a catcher must throw from home plate to second base? (Hint: Find the length of a diagonal of the square.)  127 ft

## ADDITIONAL ANSWERS

8. The diagonals of a rhombus divide it into four right triangles. Recall that the diagonals are perpendicular and bisect each other. Since they bisect, each side of each of the four right triangles is either 6 m or 8 m. By the Pythagorean Theorem each hypotenuse is 10 m. The rhombus is composed by the four hypotenuse. So the perimeter of the hypotenuse is 4 · 10 m or 40 m.

**20.** A rectangular park is 1384 ft long and 1293 ft wide. To the nearest foot, how long is the walk from one corner of the park to the opposite corner? If Leya walks at an average rate of 264 ft/min, approximately how long will it take her to make this walk? Round to the nearest minute.  1894 ft; 7 min

**21. HOBBIES** Sarah is embroidering a square design in an embroidery hoop with a 6-in. diameter. How long are the sides of the largest square that will fit in the hoop? Round to the nearest tenth.  4.2 in.

**Find the unknown length in each figure. Round to the nearest tenth.**

**22.**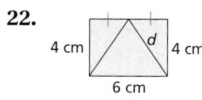
4 cm  $d$  4 cm
6 cm
5 cm

**23.**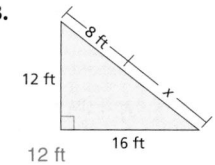
8 ft
12 ft
$x$
16 ft
12 ft

**24.**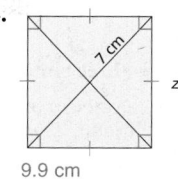
7 cm
$z$
9.9 cm

## ■ EXTENDED PRACTICE EXERCISES

**25.** The sloping sides of the triangular front of a tent are 7 ft long from the peak to the ground. If the base of the tent is 6 ft wide, how tall is the tent? Round to the nearest tenth.  6.3 ft

**26. DATA FILE** Refer to the data on the planet's heart on page 565. If the earth is cut in half at the equator and the cross section is divided into 4 equal sectors of 90°, how long would the chord of a sector be? Round to the nearest mile.  5605 mi

**27.** A lumber mill is cutting lengths of wood with square crosssections that have 12-in. sides. What is the minimum diameter of the tree trunks that the lumber mill can use? Round to the nearest tenth.  17 in.

**28. CRITICAL THINKING** Evaluate the expressions $2n$, $n^2 - 1$ and $n^2 + 1$ for the values $n = 2, 3, 4$ and 8. Study the three numbers you obtained for each value of $n$. What do you notice? How can each set of three numbers be related to the Pythagorean Theorem?  They are the lengths of the sides of a right triangle.

**29. PHOTOGRAPHY** A photographer takes a picture of the Washington Monument for a magazine. He stands 1000 ft away from the base of the monument, and the distance from this point to the peak is 1143.7 ft. How tall is the Washington Monument? Round to the nearest foot.  555 ft

## ■ MIXED REVIEW EXERCISES

**Solve each system of equations. Check the solution.** (Lesson 8-4)

**30.** $3x - y = 3$  (2, 3)
$5x - y = 7$

**31.** $2x + 2y = 10$  (4, 1)
$2x - y = 7$

**32.** $3x + 4y = 5$
$x + 4y = -1$  (3, −1)

**33.** $2x - 3y = -14$  (−1, 4)
$5x - 3y = -17$

**34.** $2x + 2y = -8$
$6x + 2y = -16$
(−2, −2)

**35.** $4x - 2y = -16$
$4x + 6y = 0$
(−3, 2)

**36.** $x + 3y = 16$
$2x - y = -3$
(1, 5)

**37.** $2x - 4y = 20$  (2, −4)
$3x + 2y = -2$

**Determine whether the graph of the inequality has a dashed or solid boundary. Tell whether to shade above or below the boundary.** (Lesson 6-4)

**38.** $y > 3x - 4$
dashed, above

**39.** $y < 2x + 8$
dashed, below

**40.** $y \leq 5x - 7$
solid, below

**41.** $y > 2x - 5$
dashed, above

**42.** $y \geq x + 5$
solid, above

**43.** $y \leq -3x - 6$
solid, below

**44.** $y < 4x + 2$
dashed, below

**45.** $y \geq x + 13$
solid, above

## Extend the Lesson

**CHALLENGE** Patterns can be used to generate more *Pythagorean triples*. Ask students to make an observation about the numbers in the *a*-column of the table.  consecutive odd integers

How are the numbers in the *c*-column related to the numbers in the *b*-column?  $c = b + 1$

Do this calculation for each row of numbers:
row × *a* + row  Example: 1 × 3 + 1

Compare results to the numbers in the columns; draw a conclusion.
row × *a* + row = *b*

Write the numbers for row 6.  13, 84, 85

|       | a  | b  | c  |
|-------|----|----|----|
| row 1 | 3  | 4  | 5  |
| row 2 | 5  | 12 | 13 |
| row 3 | 7  | 24 | 25 |
| row 4 | 9  | 40 | 41 |
| row 5 | 11 | 60 | 61 |

### Vocabulary

trigonometric ratios:
   sine
   cosine
   tangent

### Tools/Materials Needed

ruler
calculator

### Lesson Resources

Warm-up Transparency 45
Transparency RF-57
Reteaching 11-4
Extra Practice 11-4
Enrichment 11-4

## Getting Started

### 5-MINUTE WARM-UP

**Find each value of *x*, rounded to the nearest tenth.**
1. $x = 180 - 31$    **149**
2. $x = 9 \div 26$    **0.3**
3. $x^2 = 6^2 + 4^2$    **7.2**

### Introduction to Lesson 11-4
After students have discovered the relationship between the sides of similar right triangles, you may have them create right triangles of different shapes, given the lengths of the hypotenuse and one leg or the lengths of two legs. Students can use straws, pipe cleaners, or thin paper strips. Students should be able to reaffirm that the ratios for a given angle are constant.

See the Teaching Tip at the bottom of this page for an extension of this activity, which will show limiting values for sine and cosine.

---

# 11-4   Sine, Cosine, and Tangent Ratios

**Goals**
- Identify the sine, cosine, and tangent ratios in a right triangle.
- Compute the sine, cosine, and tangent ratios for different angles.

**Applications**   Travel, Photography, Navigation

---

**Use the three similar triangles shown to answer the questions.**

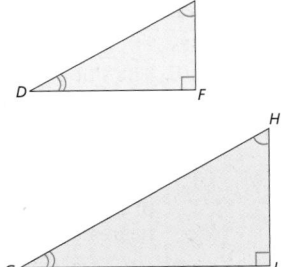

1. Use a ruler to measure the sides of each triangle to the nearest millimeter.   See additional answers.

2. Find each ratio to the nearest hundredth.
   See additional answers.
   **a.** $\dfrac{BC}{AB}$, $\dfrac{EF}{DE}$, and $\dfrac{HI}{GH}$    **b.** $\dfrac{AC}{AB}$, $\dfrac{DF}{DE}$, and $\dfrac{GI}{GH}$    **c.** $\dfrac{BC}{AC}$, $\dfrac{EF}{DF}$, and $\dfrac{HI}{GI}$

3. What can you conclude about the ratio of the length of one leg of a right triangle to its hypotenuse as compared to the ratio of the length of the corresponding leg and hypotenuse of a similar triangle?   They are equal.

4. What can you conclude about the ratio of the lengths of the legs of one right triangle as compared to the ratio of the lengths of the corresponding legs of a similar right triangle? They are equal.

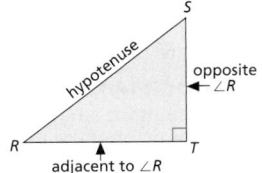

### ■ BUILD UNDERSTANDING

The legs of a right triangle are often described by relating them to one of the acute angles of the triangle. In relation to $\angle R$, $\overline{RT}$ is the leg *adjacent* to $\angle R$ and $\overline{ST}$ is the leg *opposite* $\angle R$.

For any right triangle, there are three **trigonometric ratios** of the lengths of the sides of the triangle. These ratios are the same for all congruent angles in right triangles even though the side lengths of the triangles may be different.

The trigonometric ratios for right triangle *ABC* are summarized in the chart.

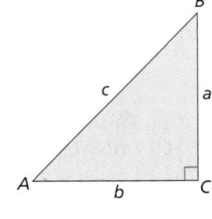

**Trigonometric Ratios**

| Name of ratio | Abbreviation | Ratio |
|---|---|---|
| **sine** of $\angle A$ | sin A | $\dfrac{\text{length of leg opposite } \angle A}{\text{hypotenuse}}$ or $\dfrac{a}{c}$ |
| **cosine** of $\angle A$ | cos A | $\dfrac{\text{length of leg adjacent to } \angle A}{\text{hypotenuse}}$ or $\dfrac{b}{c}$ |
| **tangent** of $\angle A$ | tan A | $\dfrac{\text{length of leg opposite } \angle A}{\text{length of leg adjacent to } \angle A}$ or $\dfrac{a}{b}$ |

---

## Extend the Lesson

**Have students copy this diagram and complete this table.**

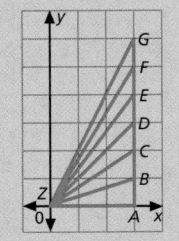

| | length of vertical leg / length of hypotenuse | length of horizontal leg / length of hypotenuse |
|---|---|---|
| $\triangle AZB$ | 0.32 | 0.95 |
| $\triangle AZC$ | 0.55 | 0.83 |
| $\triangle AZD$ | 0.71 | 0.71 |
| $\triangle AZE$ | 0.80 | 0.60 |
| $\triangle AZF$ | 0.86 | 0.51 |
| $\triangle AZG$ | 0.89 | 0.45 |

As the measure of the angle with vertex at *Z* increases, what happens to the ratios? vertical/hypotenuse increases and approaches 1; horizontal/hypotenuse decreases, with minimum value of 0

## Example 1

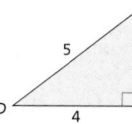

Find sin D, cos D, and tan D.

### Solution

$$\sin D = \frac{\text{length of leg opposite } \angle D}{\text{hypotenuse}} = \frac{3}{5}$$

$$\cos D = \frac{\text{length of leg adjacent to } \angle D}{\text{hypotenuse}} = \frac{4}{5}$$

$$\tan D = \frac{\text{length of leg opposite } \angle D}{\text{length of leg adjacent to } \angle D} = \frac{3}{4}$$

## Example 2

In right triangle PQR, if sin $P = \frac{12}{13}$, find cos P and tan P.

### Solution

Make a diagram of $\triangle PQR$.

$$\sin P = \frac{\text{length of leg opposite } \angle P}{\text{hypotenuse}} = \frac{12}{13}$$

Find the length of $q$, the side adjacent to $\angle P$.

$$12^2 + q^2 = 13^2 \qquad \text{Use the Pythagorean Theorem.}$$
$$144 + q^2 = 169$$
$$q^2 = 25 \qquad \text{Subtract 144 from both sides.}$$
$$\sqrt{q^2} = \sqrt{25}$$
$$q = 5$$

So the length of the side adjacent to $\angle P$ is 5. Therefore,

$$\cos P = \frac{\text{length of leg adjacent to } \angle P}{\text{hypotenuse}} = \frac{5}{13}$$

$$\tan P = \frac{\text{length of leg opposite } \angle P}{\text{length of leg adjacent to } \angle P} = \frac{12}{5}$$

When right triangles are similar, corresponding angles are congruent and the ratios of the lengths of corresponding sides are equal. This means that the trigonometric ratios for corresponding angles are the same. Because these ratios are the same, scientific calculators have sine, cosine and tangent keys, which store the values of these ratios for every possible angle measure.

 **Math Online** mathmatters2.com/extra_examples

Lesson 11-4 **Sine, Cosine, and Tangent Ratios** | **489**

# Chalkboard Examples

## Supplementary Example 1
Find the values of the three trigonometric ratios of $\angle X$.

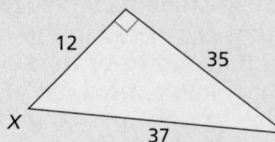

Mark the positions of the sides of the triangle with respect to $\angle X$.

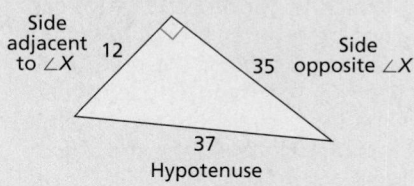

$$\sin X = \frac{\text{length of leg opposite } \angle X}{\text{length of hypotenuse}} = \frac{35}{37}$$

$$\cos X = \frac{\text{length of leg adjacent to } \angle X}{\text{length of hypotenuse}} = \frac{12}{37}$$

$$\tan X = \frac{\text{length of leg opposite } \angle X}{\text{length of side adjacent to } \angle X} = \frac{35}{12}$$

## Supplementary Example 2
In right triangle MNO, if cos $O = \frac{24}{25}$, find sin O and tan O.

$$\cos O = \frac{\text{length of leg adjacent to } \angle O}{\text{hypotenuse}} = \frac{24}{25}$$

Use this information to draw a diagram.
Then apply the Pythagorean Theorem to find the length o, the leg opposite $\angle O$.

$$o^2 + 24^2 = 25^2$$
$$o^2 + 576 = 625$$
$$o^2 = 49$$
$$\sqrt{o^2} = \sqrt{49}$$
$$o = 7$$

Use the length of the leg opposite $\angle O$ to write the values of sin O and tan O.

$$\sin O = \frac{\text{length of leg opposite } \angle O}{\text{hypotenuse}} = \frac{7}{25}$$

$$\tan O = \frac{\text{length of leg opposite } \angle O}{\text{length of leg adjacent to } \angle O} = \frac{7}{24}$$

## ADDITIONAL ANSWERS

1. $AB = 17$ mm, $BC = 8$ mm, $AC = 15$ mm; $DE = 34$ mm, $EF = 16$ mm, $DF = 30$ mm; $GH = 51$ mm, $HI = 24$ mm, $GI = 45$ mm

2. a. $\frac{BC}{AB} = \frac{EF}{DE} = \frac{HI}{GH} \approx 0.47$

   b. $\frac{AC}{AB} = \frac{DF}{DE} = \frac{GI}{GH} \approx 0.88$

   c. $\frac{BC}{AC} = \frac{EF}{DF} = \frac{HI}{GI} \approx 0.53$

## Teaching Tip

**ESL/LEP** These students may benefit from copying the diagram on page 488 that identifies the sides opposite and adjacent angle R. Students can refer to the drawing while working the exercises for this lesson.

## QUICK ASSESSMENT

Ask the following questions to determine if students understand the content presented in this lesson.

1. Given the lengths of the sides of a right triangle, how can you find the sine, cosine, and tangent for each angle?  Use the ratios: $\sin = \frac{\text{opp}}{\text{hyp}}$, $\cos = \frac{\text{adj}}{\text{hyp}}$, $\tan = \frac{\text{opp}}{\text{adj}}$

2. Which trigonometric ratios cannot be greater than 1? Explain. Sine and cosine; the divisor of each is the hypotenuse, which is the longest side of the triangle—making these values fractions less than 1.

3. What is the least number of lengths needed to find all the trigonometric ratios for the acute angles of a right triangle?  two

## ASSIGNMENT GUIDE

**Basic:** 1–35, 44–58
**Enriched:** 1–58

### Reteaching Worksheet 11-4

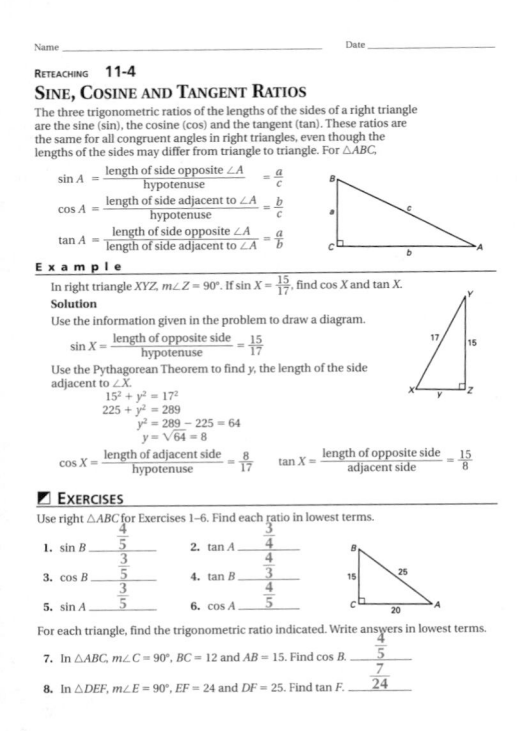

Name _____  Date _____

RETEACHING **11-4**
**SINE, COSINE AND TANGENT RATIOS**
The three trigonometric ratios of the lengths of the sides of a right triangle are the sine (sin), the cosine (cos) and the tangent (tan). These ratios are the same for all congruent angles in right triangles, even though the lengths of the sides may differ from triangle to triangle. For △ABC,

$\sin A = \frac{\text{length of side opposite } \angle A}{\text{hypotenuse}} = \frac{a}{c}$

$\cos A = \frac{\text{length of side adjacent to } \angle A}{\text{hypotenuse}} = \frac{b}{c}$

$\tan A = \frac{\text{length of side opposite } \angle A}{\text{length of side adjacent to } \angle A} = \frac{a}{b}$

**Example**
In right triangle XYZ, $m\angle Z = 90°$. If $\sin X = \frac{15}{17}$, find $\cos X$ and $\tan X$.
**Solution**
Use the information given in the problem to draw a diagram.
$\sin X = \frac{\text{length of opposite side}}{\text{hypotenuse}} = \frac{15}{17}$
Use the Pythagorean Theorem to find y, the length of the side adjacent to $\angle X$.
$15^2 + y^2 = 17^2$
$225 + y^2 = 289$
$y^2 = 289 - 225 = 64$
$y = \sqrt{64} = 8$
$\cos X = \frac{\text{length of adjacent side}}{\text{hypotenuse}} = \frac{8}{17}$   $\tan X = \frac{\text{length of opposite side}}{\text{adjacent side}} = \frac{15}{8}$

**EXERCISES**
Use right △ABC for Exercises 1–6. Find each ratio in lowest terms.
1. $\sin B$ $\frac{4}{5}$   2. $\tan A$ $\frac{3}{4}$
3. $\cos B$ $\frac{3}{5}$   4. $\tan B$ $\frac{4}{3}$
5. $\sin A$ $\frac{3}{5}$   6. $\cos A$ $\frac{4}{5}$
For each triangle, find the trigonometric ratio indicated. Write answers in lowest terms.
7. In △ABC, $m\angle C = 90°$, $BC = 12$ and $AB = 15$. Find $\cos B$. $\frac{4}{5}$
8. In △DEF, $m\angle E = 90°$, $EF = 24$ and $DF = 25$. Find $\tan F$. $\frac{7}{24}$

---

# Example 3

**CALCULATOR** Use a calculator to find sin 35°, cos 35°, and tan 35° to four decimal places.

## Solution

Use the key sequence required by your calculator. Be sure the calculator is set in degree mode.

$\sin 35° \approx 0.5736$       $\cos 35° \approx 0.8192$       $\tan 35° \approx 0.7002$

## TRY THESE EXERCISES

**In △JKL, find each trigonometric ratio.**

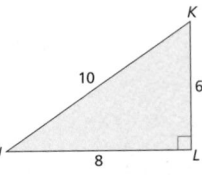

1. $\sin J$ $\frac{3}{5}$   2. $\sin K$ $\frac{4}{5}$
3. $\cos K$ $\frac{3}{5}$   4. $\tan J$ $\frac{3}{4}$
5. $\tan K$ $\frac{4}{3}$   6. $\cos J$ $\frac{4}{5}$

**In △XYZ, $\angle Z$ is a right angle. If $\cos Y = \frac{8}{10}$, find these ratios.**

7. $\sin Y$ $\frac{3}{5}$       8. $\tan Y$ $\frac{3}{4}$       9. $\cos X$ $\frac{3}{5}$

 **CALCULATOR** Use a calculator to find each ratio to four decimal places.

10. $\sin 60°$ 0.8660       11. $\cos 42°$ 0.7431       12. $\tan 65°$ 2.1445

## PRACTICE EXERCISES • For Extra Practice, see page 621.

**In △TVW, find each trigonometric ratio in lowest terms.**

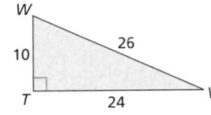

13. $\sin V$ $\frac{5}{13}$   14. $\cos V$ $\frac{12}{13}$
15. $\cos W$ $\frac{5}{13}$   16. $\sin W$ $\frac{12}{13}$
17. $\tan W$ $\frac{12}{5}$   18. $\tan V$ $\frac{5}{12}$

 **CALCULATOR** Use a calculator to find each ratio to four decimal places.

19. $\cos 52°$ 0.6157   20. $\tan 17°$ 0.3057   21. $\tan 85°$ 11.4301   22. $\sin 45°$ 0.7071
23. $\sin 81°$ 0.9877   24. $\tan 58°$ 1.6003   25. $\cos 33°$ 0.8387   26. $\cos 76°$ 0.2419

27. **PHOTOGRAPHY** For his photography class, Mike takes a picture of an oak tree during autumn. Mike stands 75 ft from the base of the tree and 139 ft from the top of the tree. What is the cosine of the angle formed by the base of the tree, Mike's position and the top of the tree?  ≈ 0.5396

 28. **WRITING MATH** Restate in your own words the definition of the sine ratio, the cosine ratio and the tangent ratio.  Answers will vary. Check students' work.

29. In right triangle EFG, if sin E is greater than sin F, which side of the triangle is longer, $\overline{EF}$ or $\overline{FG}$? Drawing a picture and selecting some values for the lengths of the sides may help you solve the problem.  $\overline{FG}$

**490**   Chapter 11  **Right Triangle Trigonometry**

---

## Teaching Tip

In Example 2, note with students that when applying the information $\sin P = \frac{12}{13}$ to drawing a diagram, the actual lengths of the side opposite $\angle P$ and the hypotenuse need not be 12 and 13, respectively. But, the lengths of these sides have to be in the ratio 12 : 13. This information is sufficient to determine the corresponding third value, 5. Now, have students suggest other side lengths for a triangle that satisfies this information.  any multiple of 5, 12, 13—for example, 10, 24, 26

**For each right triangle, find the trigonometric ratio in lowest terms.**

30. In $\triangle ABC$, $m\angle C = 90°$, $BC = 6$ and $AC = 8$. Find $\cos A$. $\frac{4}{5}$

31. In $\triangle DEF$, $m\angle F = 90°$, $EF = 15$ and $DE = 25$. Find $\sin E$. $\frac{4}{5}$

32. In $\triangle MAT$, $m\angle A = 90°$, $MT = 10$ and $AT = 8$. Find $\tan T$. $\frac{3}{4}$

33. **NAVIGATION** A ship returning from sea is 295 m from the base of a lighthouse on the beach. If the lighthouse is 82 m tall, what are the sine, cosine, and tangent of the angle formed by the base of the lighthouse, the ship, and the top of the lighthouse? $\sin \approx 0.2678$, $\cos \approx 0.9635$, $\tan \approx 0.2780$

34. **ERROR ALERT** In $\triangle JKL$, $\angle L$ is a right angle, $\tan J = \frac{9}{40}$ and $\sin J = \frac{9}{41}$. Jim says this means that $KL = 9$, $JL = 40$ and $JK = 41$. Do you agree with Jim's reasoning? Explain why or why not. See additional answers.

35. **TRAVEL** An airplane travels down a 2200-ft runway to takeoff. By the time the plane reaches the end of the runway, it is 310 ft above the ground. What is the tangent of the angle formed by the end of the runway, the plane's starting position and the plane's current position? What is the cosine of the angle? $\tan \approx 0.1409$, $\cos \approx 0.9902$

## ■ EXTENDED PRACTICE EXERCISES

36. **CRITICAL THINKING** If the tangent of an angle is greater than 1, which side of the triangle is longer, the leg adjacent to the angle or the leg opposite the angle? opposite side

**CALCULATOR** Determine how each ratio changes as an angle increases from 0° to 90°.

37. sine  increases

38. cosine  decreases

39. tangent  increases

**Tell whether each statement is *true* or *false* for $\triangle ABC$.**

40. $\sin A = \cos B$  true

41. $\cos A = \frac{1}{\sin A}$  false

42. $\tan A = (\sin A)(\cos A)$  false

43. $\tan A = \frac{\sin A}{\cos A}$  true

## ■ MIXED REVIEW EXERCISES

**Simplify.** (Lesson 9-4)

44. $4k(6k + 2p)$  $24k^2 + 8kp$

45. $3r(6r^2 + 8)$  $18r^3 + 24r$

46. $6st(4s + 7t)$  $24s^2t + 42st^2$

47. $6p(4p^2 - 3) + 7p(3p^2 - 5)$  $45p^3 - 53p$

48. $2a^2(a - b) + 5b^2(a + b)$  $2a^3 - 2a^2b + 5ab^2 + 5b^3$

49. $4g^2h(6h - 3g + 5h^2)$  $24g^2h^2 - 12g^3h + 20g^2h^3$

**Solve each equation. Check the solution.** (Lesson 3-4)

50. $7z + 4 = 25$  3

51. $\frac{x}{4} - 8 = 6$  56

52. $6b - 18 = 0$  3

53. $5 = \frac{2}{3}k + 3$  3

54. $4y - 3 = 7.8$  2.7

55. $\frac{1}{3}(g + 12) = 9$  15

56. $-6b + 5 = -8$  $\frac{13}{6}$

57. $3x + 2.8 = -3.2$  $-2$

58. $4b - 27 - 2b = 14$  $\frac{41}{2}$

Math Online  mathmatters2.com/self_check_quiz

**Lesson 11-4** **Sine, Cosine and Tangent Ratios** | **491**

## ADDITIONAL ANSWERS

34. Jim is correct if there has been no reducing of fractions. That is, if the dimensions of the triangle are 9, 40, and 41. But it is possible that the dimensions may have been reduced to the tangent and sine given. That is, they could be some factor times 9, 40, and 41. For example: 18, 80, and 82.

---

### Extra Practice Worksheet 11-4

Name _____  Date _____

**EXTRA PRACTICE  11-4**
**SINE, COSINE AND TANGENT RATIOS**

☑ **EXERCISES**

In $\triangle MNP$, find each trigonometric ratio.

1. $\sin M$ $\frac{12}{13}$
2. $\cos M$ $\frac{5}{13}$
3. $\tan N$ $\frac{5}{12}$
4. $\sin N$ $\frac{5}{13}$
5. $\tan M$ $\frac{12}{5}$
6. $\cos N$ $\frac{12}{13}$

In $\triangle ABC$, $\angle C$ is a right angle. If $\sin B = \frac{8}{17}$, find these ratios.

7. $\cos B$ $\frac{15}{17}$
8. $\sin A$ $\frac{15}{17}$
9. $\tan B$ $\frac{8}{15}$
10. $\tan A$ $\frac{15}{8}$
11. $\cos A$ $\frac{8}{17}$

Use a calculator to find each ratio to four decimal places.

12. $\sin 48°$ 0.7431
13. $\tan 82°$ 7.1154
14. $\cos 34°$ 0.8290
15. $\sin 86°$ 0.9976
16. $\cos 19°$ 0.9455
17. $\tan 53°$ 1.3270
18. $\sin 24°$ 0.4067
19. $\cos 65°$ 0.4226

For each right triangle, find the trigonometric ratio in lowest terms.

20. In $\triangle DEF$, $m\angle F = 90°$, $DE = 5$ and $EF = 4$. Find $\sin E$. $\frac{3}{5}$
21. In $\triangle RST$, $m\angle S = 90°$, $RS = 9$ and $ST = 40$. Find $\cos T$. $\frac{40}{41}$
22. In $\triangle MNP$, $m\angle N = 90°$, $MP = 26$ and $NP = 10$. Find $\tan P$. $\frac{12}{5}$

---

### Enrichment Worksheet 11-4

Name _____  Date _____

**ENRICHMENT  11-4**
**RECIPROCAL RATIOS**

In addition to the sine, cosine and tangent, there are three other trigonometric ratios that are the reciprocals of the sine, cosine, and tangent.

cotangent $A = \dfrac{\text{side adjacent to } \angle A}{\text{side opposite } \angle A}$   $\cot A = \dfrac{b}{a}$

secant $A = \dfrac{\text{hypotenuse}}{\text{side adjacent to } \angle A}$   $\sec A = \dfrac{c}{b}$

cosecant $A = \dfrac{\text{hypotenuse}}{\text{side opposite } \angle A}$   $\csc A = \dfrac{c}{a}$

**Example**

If $\sin D = \frac{12}{13}$, find the other five trigonometric function values for $\angle D$.

**Solution**

Use the Pythagorean Theorem to find the adjacent side.
$$DE^2 + FE^2 = FD^2$$
$$DE^2 + 12^2 = 13^2$$
$$DE^2 + 144 = 169$$
$$DE^2 = 169 - 144 = 25$$
$$DE = \sqrt{25} = 5$$

Therefore,

$\sin D = \frac{12}{13}$   $\csc D = \frac{13}{12}$
$\cos D = \frac{5}{13}$   $\sec D = \frac{13}{5}$
$\tan D = \frac{12}{5}$   $\cot D = \frac{5}{12}$

☑ **EXERCISES**

If $\cos B = \frac{8}{17}$, find the other five trigonometric function values for $\angle B$. Refer to the triangle shown at the right.

1. $b = \frac{15}{17}$
2. $\sin B = \frac{15}{17}$
3. $\tan B = \frac{15}{8}$
4. $\csc B = \frac{17}{15}$
5. $\sec B = \frac{17}{8}$
6. $\cot B = \frac{8}{15}$

If $\tan Q = \frac{7}{24}$, find the other five trigonometric function values for $\angle Q$. Refer to the triangle shown at the right.

7. $r = 25$
8. $\sin Q = \frac{7}{25}$
9. $\cos Q = \frac{24}{25}$
10. $\csc Q = \frac{25}{7}$
11. $\sec Q = \frac{25}{24}$
12. $\cot Q = \frac{24}{7}$

## ASSIGNMENT GUIDE

**All students:** 1–34

## Chalkboard Examples

**Lesson 11-3**
**ENGINEERING** A truck driver uses a 13-ft-long conveyor belt to unload cartons to a loading dock that is 5 ft above the truck bed. How far does the conveyor belt extend into the truck?

$$c^2 = a^2 + b^2$$
$$13^2 = 5^2 + b^2$$
$$169 = 25 + b^2$$
$$144 = b^2$$
$$\sqrt{144} = \sqrt{b^2}$$
$$12 = b$$

So, the conveyor belt extends 12 ft into the truck.

---

**PRACTICE** ■ **LESSON 11-3**

Find the unknown length. Round to the nearest tenth.

**1.**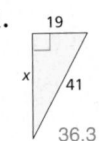
19
x
41
36.3

**2.**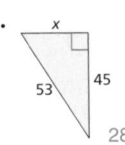
x
53   45
28

**3.**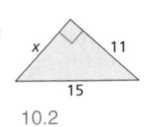
x   11
15
10.2

Find the length of each hypotenuse. Round to the nearest tenth.

**4.**
27   x
36
45

**5.**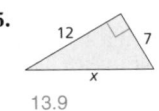
12   7
x
13.9

**6.**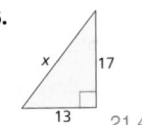
x   17
13   21.4

**7.** How long is the diagonal of a square with 5-in. sides?   7.1 in.

**PRACTICE** ■ **LESSON 11-4**

In △XYZ, find each trigonometric ratio in lowest terms.

**8.** sin X  $\frac{15}{17}$          **9.** tan Z  $\frac{8}{15}$

**10.** cos X  $\frac{8}{17}$          **11.** cos Z  $\frac{15}{17}$

**12.** sin Z  $\frac{8}{17}$          **13.** tan X  $\frac{15}{8}$

X
17   8
Z   15   Y

In △ABC, ∠B is a right angle. If sin $C = \frac{12}{15}$, find these ratios.

**14.** cos A  $\frac{4}{5}$

**15.** cos C  $\frac{3}{5}$

**16.** tan C  $\frac{4}{3}$

 **CALCULATOR** Use a calculator to find each ratio to four decimal places.

**17.** cos 30°  0.8660          **18.** sin 60°  0.8660

**19.** sin 30°  0.5          **20.** cos 60°  0.5

**21.** sin 81°  0.9877          **22.** cos 9°  0.9877

**23.** cos 45°  0.7071          **24.** sin 45°  0.7071

**25.** What do you notice about the sine and cosine of two pairs of complementary angles in Exercises 17–24?
The sine of an acute angle is equal to the cosine of its complement.

In △MNO, ∠N is a right angle. If sin $M = \frac{3}{5}$, find these ratios.

**26.** cos M  $\frac{4}{5}$          **27.** sin O  $\frac{4}{5}$          **28.** tan O  $\frac{4}{3}$

**492**   Chapter 11  **Right Triangle Trigonometry**

---

## Teaching Tip

After students have completed Exercise 31, discuss the methods they used to decide if the two equilateral triangles are similar. Note that similarity can be established either by:
   *side length*—the lengths of the sides of all equilateral triangles are in the ratio 1:1, which makes all equilateral triangles similar, or by
   *angle measure*—the measure of each of the three angles of all equilateral triangles is 60°, which makes all equilateral triangles similar.
Students can extend this thinking to conclude that all squares are similar, and that regular polygons of the same number of sides are similar.

**Determine if the figures are similar.** (Lesson 11-1)

**29.**

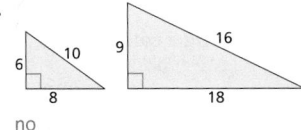

no

**30.**

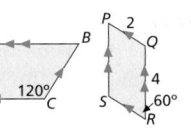

yes

**31.**

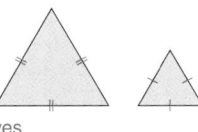

yes

**Find the unknown length. Round to the nearest tenth.** (Lesson 11-3)

**32.**

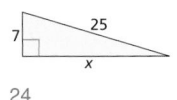

24

**33.**

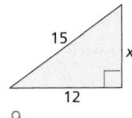

9

**34.**

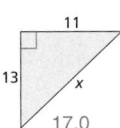

17.0

# Mid-Chapter Quiz

**Determine if each pair of polygons is similar.** (Lesson 11-1)

**1.**

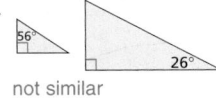

not similar

**2.**

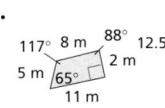 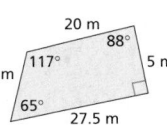

similar

**Use indirect measurement to find the length of x.** (Lesson 11-2)

**3.**

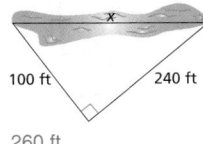

100 ft 240 ft

260 ft

**4.**

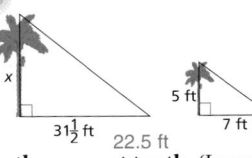

x  5 ft

$31\frac{1}{2}$ ft  7 ft

22.5 ft

**5.**

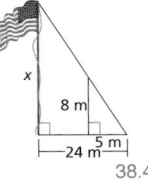

x  8 m

24 m  5 m

38.4 m

**Find the unknown length. Round to the nearest tenth.** (Lesson 11-3)

**6.**

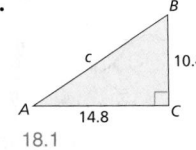

c  10.4

A  14.8  C

18.1

**7.**

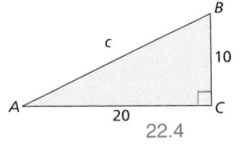

c  10

A  20  C

22.4

**8.**

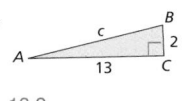

A  c  B  2  C

13

13.2

**In △FGH, find each trigonometric ratio.** (Lesson 11-4)

F  13  G
5  12  H

**9.** $\sin F$  $\frac{12}{13}$

**10.** $\sin G$  $\frac{5}{13}$

**11.** $\cos G$  $\frac{12}{13}$

**12.** $\tan G$  $\frac{5}{12}$

**13.** $\cos F$  $\frac{5}{13}$

**14.** $\tan F$  $\frac{12}{5}$

Chapter 11 **Review and Practice Your Skills** | 493

**Lesson 11-4**

In right triangle *RST*, if $\tan T = \frac{9}{40}$, find sin *T* and cos *T*.

$\tan T = \frac{\text{length of leg opposite } \angle T}{\text{length of leg adjacent to } \angle T} = \frac{9}{40}$

Use this information to draw a diagram.

T  s  R  9  S  40

Then apply the Pythagorean Theorem to find the length *s*, the hypotenuse.

$s^2 = 9^2 + 40^2$
$s^2 = 81 + 1600$
$s^2 = 1681$
$\sqrt{s^2} = \sqrt{1681}$
$s = 41$

Use the length of the hypotenuse to write the values of sin *T* and cos *T*.

$\sin T = \frac{\text{length of leg opposite } \angle T}{\text{length of hypotenuse}} = \frac{9}{41}$

$\cos T = \frac{\text{length of leg adjacent to } \angle T}{\text{length of hypotenuse}} = \frac{40}{41}$

## Teaching Tip

In preparation for Exercises 32–34, suggest that some students may find it easier to remember the Pythagorean Theorem as leg² + leg² = hypotenuse², so that there is no confusion as to appropriate letters.

### NCTM Standards/Strands
- Measurement
- Geometry
- Connections
- Algebra

### Tools/Materials Needed

calculator

### Lesson Resources

Warm-up Transparency 46
Reteaching 11-5
Extra Practice 11-5
Enrichment 11-5
Technology Activity 11-5

## Getting Started

### 5-MINUTE WARM-UP

**Find each value of x, rounded to the nearest tenth.**

1. $1.7321 = \frac{x}{31}$   53.7

2. $\frac{15}{x} = 0.2924$   51.3

3. $0.8746 = \frac{x}{11}$   9.6

4. $0.6157 = \frac{22}{x}$   35.7

### Introduction to Lesson 11-5

In preparation for Questions 1–3, note with students that an equation involving any of the trigonometric ratios has three quantities: the function of the angle and the lengths of two sides of the right triangle. The given equations all have the measure of the angle given; so, students can find the value of the indicated trigonometric function from a calculator.

There is not enough information initially from the diagram to solve Equation 3. However, after solving Equation 1 (or Equation 2), that information could then be used to solve Equation 3.

---

# 11-5 Find Lengths of Sides in Right Triangles

**Goals** ■ Use trigonometric ratios to find the lengths of sides in right triangles.

**Applications**  Engineering, Construction, Photography, Archaeology

**For each equation, decide if you can substitute two values using a calculator and the figure shown. If so, show the substitution.**  For 1–5, see additional answers.

1. $\sin 40° = \frac{\text{opposite}}{\text{hypotenuse}}$

2. $\cos 40° = \frac{\text{adjacent}}{\text{hypotenuse}}$

3. $\tan 40° = \frac{\text{opposite}}{\text{adjacent}}$

4. Solve the equations for which you are able to find two substitutions in Questions 1 through 3. Find the unknown lengths of the triangle. Round to the nearest tenth.

5. Use the Pythagorean Theorem to verify your answers.

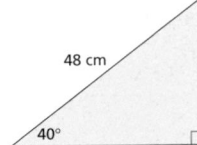

### ◀ BUILD UNDERSTANDING

Recall that the trigonometric ratios for any given acute angle are the same for any right triangle. If you know the measures of one acute angle and one side of a right triangle, you can find the lengths of the triangle's other sides.

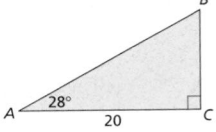

#### Example 1

**In △ABC, find AB to the nearest tenth.**

**Solution**

Decide which trigonometric ratio relates the unknown side to the known angle and the known side. $\overline{AC}$ is *adjacent* to ∠A. $\overline{AB}$ is the *hypotenuse*. The ratio that relates an adjacent leg to the hypotenuse is the cosine ratio.

Write and solve an equation involving the trigonometric ratio and the known values. Use a calculator to approximate cos 28°.

$$\cos 28° = \frac{AC}{AB} \qquad \frac{\text{adjacent leg}}{\text{hypotenuse}}$$

$$0.8829 \approx \frac{20}{AB}$$

$$0.8829 \cdot AB \approx 20 \qquad \text{Find the cross-products.}$$

$$\frac{0.8829AB}{0.8829} \approx \frac{20}{0.8829} \qquad \text{Divide both sides by 0.8829.}$$

$$AB \approx 22.7$$

The length of $\overline{AB}$ is approximately 22.7.

> **Check Understanding**
>
> What trigonometric ratio would you use to find the length of $\overline{BC}$ in △ABC of Example 1?
>
> tangent

---

### Teaching Tip

Once students understand how the substitutions are made in an equation involving a trigonometric ratio, you may wish to encourage them to do more with the calculator than just obtain the value of the trigonometric ratio. They can do the entire calculation on the calculator, as shown below.

$\sin 42° = \frac{x}{12}$

  $x = 12(\sin 42°)$   Solve for x and then do the calculation.

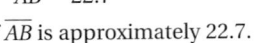

Guide students through a "calculator version" of Example 1, in which they solve for AB without substituting for cos 28°.

## Example 2

**ENGINEERING** A bridge engineer surveys a completed bridge from a distance of 106.5 m from the center of the bridge's base. She looks up at an angle of 32° to see the top of the bridge. How tall is the bridge?

### Solution

Draw a picture of the bridge, and label the picture with the given information to decide which trigonometric ratio to use.

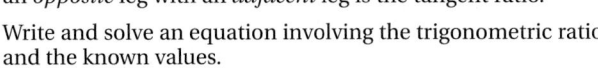

$\overline{YZ}$ is opposite of $\angle X$. $\overline{XZ}$ is adjacent of $\angle X$. The ratio that relates an *opposite* leg with an *adjacent* leg is the tangent ratio.

Write and solve an equation involving the trigonometric ratio and the known values.

$$\tan 32° = \frac{YZ}{106.5} \quad \frac{\text{opposite leg}}{\text{adjacent leg}}$$

$$0.6249 \approx \frac{YZ}{106.5}$$

$$0.6249 \cdot 106.5 \approx YZ \quad \text{Find the cross-products.}$$

$$66.6 \approx YZ$$

The height of the bridge is approximately 66.6 m.

## Example 3

**Find the value of *x* in the figure shown.**

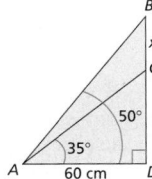

### Solution

Use trigonometric ratios to find *BD* and *CD*.

| | |
|---|---|
| $\tan 50° = \dfrac{BD}{60}$ | $\tan 35° = \dfrac{CD}{60}$ |
| $1.1918 \approx \dfrac{BD}{60}$ | $0.7002 \approx \dfrac{CD}{60}$ |
| $1.1918 \cdot 60 \approx BD$ | $0.7002 \cdot 60 \approx CD$ |
| $71.508 \approx BD$ | $42.012 \approx CD$ |

Subtract *CD* from *BD* to find *x*, the length of *BC*.

$$71.508 - 42.012 = 29.496$$

So *x* is approximately 29.5 cm.

### Math: Who, Where, When

The Hindu mathematician Aryabhata first tabulated sines of angles around the year 500 A.D.

## ▨ TRY THESE EXERCISES

**Find each length to the nearest tenth.**

1. *DF*
   14.3
2. *EF*
   20.5
3. *AB*
   31.9
4. *BC*
   33.8

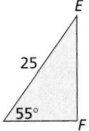

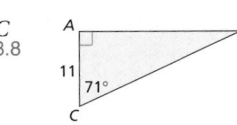

### Supplementary Example 1

Find, to the nearest tenth, the length of the side whose measure is represented by *x*.

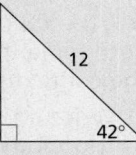

Identify the placement of the sides of the right triangle with respect to the given angle so that you can choose the appropriate trigonometric ratio.

$$\sin \angle = \frac{\text{opposite}}{\text{hypotenuse}}$$

$$\sin 42° = \frac{x}{12}$$

$$0.6691 \approx \frac{x}{12}$$

$$x \approx 12(0.6691)$$

$$x \approx 8.0$$

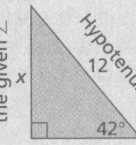

### Supplementary Example 2

Find the length of $\overline{BC}$ to the nearest hundredth.

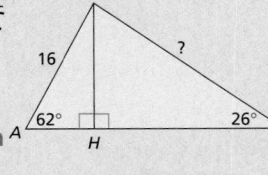

First work in right triangle *ACH* to obtain *CH*, which can then be used in right triangle *BCH*.

$$\sin 62° = \frac{CH}{CA}$$

$$\sin 62° = \frac{CH}{16}$$

$$CH = 16(\sin 62°)$$

$$CH \approx 16(0.8829)$$

$$CH \approx 14.126$$

$$\sin 26° = \frac{CH}{BC}$$

$$BC(\sin 26°) = CH$$

$$BC = \frac{CH}{\sin 26°}$$

$$BC \approx \frac{14.126}{0.4384}$$

$$BC \approx 32.22$$

## ADDITIONAL ANSWERS

1. $0.6428 \approx \dfrac{\text{opposite}}{48}$

2. $0.7660 \approx \dfrac{\text{adjacent}}{48}$

3. Two substitutions cannot be made directly from the information given.

4. opposite ≈ 30.8538
   adjacent ≈ 36.7001

5. $(30.8538)^2 + (36.7701)^2 \stackrel{?}{\approx} 48^2$
   $2303.997228 \approx 2304$

## QUICK ASSESSMENT

Ask the following questions to determine if students understand the context presented in this lesson.

1. Write an equation involving a trigonometric ratio that can be used to find the value of $x$.

$$\tan 22° = \frac{x}{16}$$

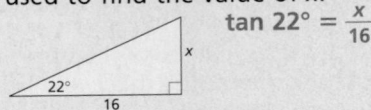

2. Given the measure of one of the acute angles of a right triangle and the length of one side, explain how you would find the measures of all angles and all sides.   **The second acute angle is the complement of the first. With one side and one angle, use the appropriate trigonometric ratio and find a second side. With two sides, use the Pythagorean Theorem to find the third side.**

## ASSIGNMENT GUIDE

**Basic:** 1–24, 29–40
**Enriched:** 1–40

### Reteaching Worksheet 11-5

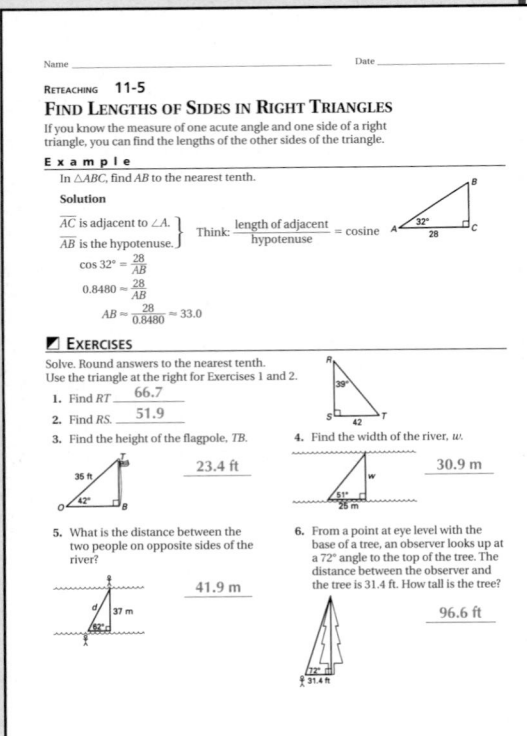

---

5. **CONSTRUCTION** A guy wire is secured near the top of a television transmitting tower. The guy wire meets the ground at an angle of 48°. If the height of the tower is 32 m, how far from the base of the tower is the guy wire secured? Round to the nearest tenth.  28.8 m

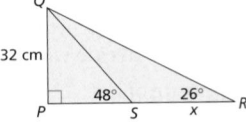

6. An angle of a right triangle measures 75°. If the length of the side opposite this angle is 27 ft, what are the lengths of the two other sides?   ≈ 7.23 ft, ≈ 28.0 ft

7. Find the value of $x$ in the figure shown.   ≈ 36.8 cm

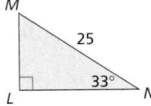

8. **WRITING MATH** Explain how you would find the length of $\overline{AC}$ in isosceles triangle $ABC$, where $m\angle C = 90°$ and $\overline{AB}$ measures 10 cm.
   See additional answers.

### ◼ PRACTICE EXERCISES   •   For Extra Practice, see page 622.

**Find each length to the nearest tenth.**

9. $PQ$   52.3   10. $PR$   38.9

11. $ML$   13.6   12. $LN$   21.0

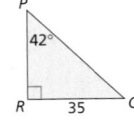

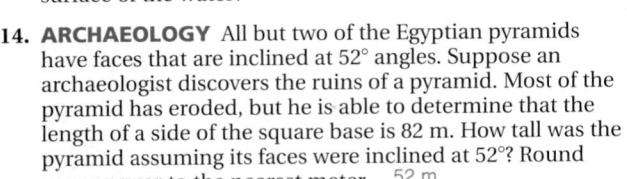

13. **RECREATION** A parasailor is being towed behind a boat on a 250-ft rope. If the parasailor is being towed at an angle of elevation of 32°, approximately how high is he above the surface of the water?   132.5 ft

14. **ARCHAEOLOGY** All but two of the Egyptian pyramids have faces that are inclined at 52° angles. Suppose an archaeologist discovers the ruins of a pyramid. Most of the pyramid has eroded, but he is able to determine that the length of a side of the square base is 82 m. How tall was the pyramid assuming its faces were inclined at 52°? Round your answer to the nearest meter.   52 m

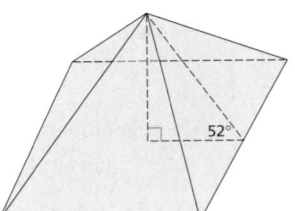

15. An angle of a right triangle measures 39°. If the length of the leg adjacent to this angle is 6 m, what are the lengths of the other two sides?   4.9 m, 7.7 m

16. An angle of a right triangle measures 58°. If the length of the hypotenuse is 40 cm, what are the lengths of the other two sides of the triangle?
    ≈ 33.9 cm, ≈ 21.2 cm

17. The tailgate of a truck is 1.12 m from the ground. How long should a ramp be so that the incline from the ground up to the tailgate is 9.5°? Round your answer to the nearest tenth.   6.8 m

**Find the area of each figure. Round to the nearest tenth.**

18. 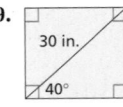   146.7 cm²

19.   443.2 in.²

20. 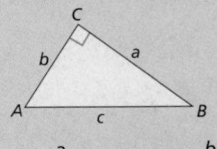   36.8 mm²

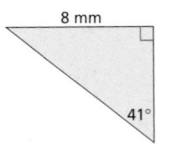

---

## Extend the Lesson

From this diagram, note with students the three trigonometric functions of $\angle A$ and $\angle B$.
Elicit that $\angle A$ and $\angle B$ are complementary angles.
Ask students to make observations about the relationships between the trigonometric functions of the complementary angles, noting that $\sin A = \cos B$, $\cos A = \sin B$, and that $\tan A$ and $\tan B$ are reciprocals. Have students use a calculator to verify these relationships—for example: $\sin 20° = \cos 70°$ and $\tan 20° \cdot \tan 70° = 1$

$$\sin A = \frac{a}{c} \qquad \sin B = \frac{b}{c}$$
$$\cos A = \frac{b}{c} \qquad \cos B = \frac{a}{c}$$
$$\tan A = \frac{a}{b} \qquad \tan B = \frac{b}{a}$$

**21. PHOTOGRAPHY** An aerial photographer takes pictures of two remote islands in the Pacific Ocean. The islands are 6 mi apart. When the plane is directly above Island 1, the line of sight of the plane from Island 1 to Island 2 forms a 54° angle. How high above Island 1 is the plane? Round to the nearest tenth of a mile. 4.4 mi

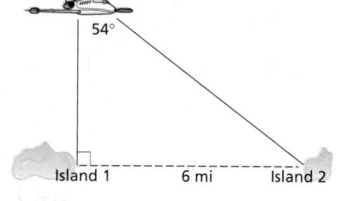
54°
Island 1    6 mi    Island 2

**22. WRITING MATH** If the measure of an acute angle of a right triangle and the length of its opposite side are given, explain how to find the measures of the other two sides. See additional answers.

**23.** A 15-ft ladder leaning against a wall makes a 53° angle between the ground and the ladder. To the nearest foot, how far up the wall does the ladder reach? 12 ft

**24. DATA FILE** Refer to the data on the size and weight of balls used in sports on page 572. If the sun's rays make an angle of 28° with the ground, how long is the shadow of a soccer ball? a large softball? a croquet ball? Round to the nearest tenth. 41.4 cm, 24.4 cm, 16.2 cm

## ■ EXTENDED PRACTICE EXERCISES

**25. GEOMETRY SOFTWARE** Use geometry software to draw an equilateral triangle that has sides of length 5 cm. What is the area of this triangle? (Hint: Use the software to draw an altitude of the triangle, which is a segment perpendicular to a side from one of the vertices.) Round to the nearest centimeter. 11 cm²

**26. CRITICAL THINKING** Jamaal is facing north when he sees an airplane. The angle that his line of sight makes with the ground is 62° when he looks up. At the same time, Jill is standing 10 mi away and also facing north. Her line of sight makes an angle of 26° with the ground when she looks up. What is the altitude of the airplane in feet? 34,769 ft

**27. MODELING** On grid paper, draw three different right triangles for which the tangent of one of the acute angles is 0.8. What is the tangent of the other acute angle of each triangle? Explain how you arrived at the three right triangles you have drawn. Triangles will vary. The tangents are 1.25.

**28. CHAPTER INVESTIGATION** In your diagram, label the right angle, the legs of the right triangle and the angle of the camera. What trigonometric ratio will you use to find the distance the photographer is from the subject? Answers will vary. Use sine or cosine.

## ■ MIXED REVIEW EXERCISES

For 29–32, check students' drawings. The number of lines of symmetry is given.

**Trace each figure. Draw all the lines of symmetry, or write *none*.** (Lesson 7-4)

**29.** B
1 line

**30.** H
2 lines

**31.** G
none

**32.** M
1 line

**Evaluate each expression when** $a = -2$ **and** $b = 3$. (Lessons 2-7 and 2-8)

**33.** $a^2$  4

**34.** $b^2$  9

**35.** $a^3$  −8

**36.** $b^3$  27

**37.** $(a^2 + 5)^2$  81

**38.** $(a^2 - b)^2$  1

**39.** $(b^2)^2$  81

**40.** $(a - b^2)^3$  −1331

**Math Online** mathmatters2.com/self_check_quiz    Lesson 11-5 **Find Lengths of Sides in Right Triangles**    **497**

## ADDITIONAL ANSWERS

**8.** $\overline{AB}$ is the hypotenuse of △ABC. Let *x* equal the length of the two equal sides and use the Pythagorean Theorem to find *x*.
$$x^2 + x^2 = 10^2$$
$$2x^2 = 100$$
$$x = \sqrt{50}$$
$$x \approx 7.1 \text{ cm}$$

**22.** To find the length of the other leg, divide the length of the given side by the tangent of the given acute angle.

To find the length of the hypoteneuse, divide the length of the given side by the sine of the given angle.

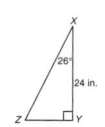
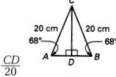

### Tools/Materials Needed

protractor
calculator

### Lesson Resources

Warm-up Transparency 46
Reteaching 11-6
Extra Practice 11-6
Enrichment 11-6

## Getting Started

### 5-Minute Warm-Up

**Find each value of x rounded to four decimal places.**

**1.** $x = \frac{17}{24}$    0.7083

**2.** $x = \frac{94}{78}$    1.2051

**3.** $x = \frac{11}{37}$    0.2973

**4.** $x = \frac{193}{17}$    11.3529

### Introduction to Lesson 11-6

After students have read Question 2, have them explain what tan $E \approx$ 1.3764 tells them about the lengths of the legs of triangle $EFG$. The length of $FG$ is about 1.3764 times the length of $EG$.

---

# 11-6 Find Measures of Angles in Right Triangles

**Goals**   ■ Use trigonometric ratios to find the measures of angles in a right triangle.

**Applications**   Travel, Safety, Photography, Astronomy

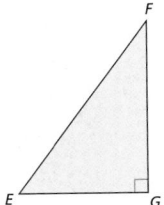

**Use △EFG for Questions 1–3.**

1. Given that the tan $E \approx 1.3764$ and $EG = 8$, find all measures of the triangle that you can determine.   $EF \approx 13.6105$, $FG \approx 11.0112$

2. Use your measures from Question 1 to verify that tan $E \approx 1.3764$, then find the sine of $\angle E$ and the cosine of $\angle E$.
$\tan E \approx 1.3764$, $\sin E \approx 0.8090$, $\cos E \approx 0.5878$

3. Using the information you found in Questions 1 and 2, can you find $m\angle E$? If so, state the $m\angle E$ and explain how you found it. If not, what information is missing to determine the $m\angle E$?
Students may not be able to find $m\angle E$ since they have not studied inverse trigonometric functions introduced in this lesson. ($m\angle E \approx 54°$)

## ■ BUILD UNDERSTANDING

If you know the sine, cosine, or tangent of an angle in a right triangle, you can find the measure of the angle.

In addition to having keys for the sine, cosine, and tangent functions, calculators also have keys for the inverses of each of these functions. They are symbolized $\sin^{-1}$, $\cos^{-1}$, and $\tan^{-1}$. These inverse functions "undo" the sine, cosine, and tangent functions. So if you know that the sine of an angle is 0.7071067812, the inverse sine key on a calculator shows that the angle is about 45°.

### Reading Math

Read "$\sin^{-1}(0.75)$" as "the angle whose sine is 0.75."

### Example 1

**CALCULATOR** Use a calculator to find what angles have the given trigonometric ratios. Round to the nearest degree.

   **a.** $\sin A = 0.866025$     **b.** $\cos B = 0.087156$     **c.** $\tan C = 0.344327$

### Solution

Use the key sequence required by your calculator. Be sure the calculator is set in degree mode.

   **a.** $\sin^{-1}(0.866025) \approx 60$

     $m\angle A \approx 60°$        Press [2nd] [sin⁻¹] 0.866025 [)] [ENTER].

   **b.** $\cos^{-1}(0.087156) \approx 85$

     $m\angle B \approx 85°$        Press [2nd] [cos⁻¹] 0.087156 [)] [ENTER].

   **c.** $\tan^{-1}(0.344327) \approx 19$

     $m\angle C \approx 19°$        Press [2nd] [tan⁻¹] 0.344327 [)] [ENTER].

---

## Differentiated Instruction

**VISUAL LEARNERS** To assist students who have difficulty grasping that the relationships between the angles and lengths of the sides of a right triangle must be constant, use the "as-the-crow-flies" paths on a street map of city blocks to show in real-life terms how the angles in similar triangles must be congruent.

Sometimes instead of being given one of the trigonometric ratios of an angle, you may be given the lengths of two sides of a right triangle. You can use this information to write a trigonometric ratio and, in turn, use the ratio to find the measure of the angle.

## Example 2

**Find $m\angle M$ in the right triangle.**

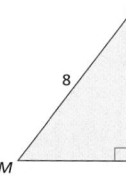

### Solution

Decide which trigonometric ratio relates the angle whose measure you want to find and the sides whose lengths are known. $\overline{NP}$ is the leg opposite $\angle M$. $\overline{MN}$ is the hypotenuse of the triangle. The ratio that relates an opposite leg with the hypotenuse is the sine ratio.

Write and solve an equation involving the sine ratio and the given values.

$$\sin M = \frac{NP}{MN} \qquad \frac{\text{opposite leg}}{\text{hypotenuse}}$$

$$\sin M = \frac{6}{8} \qquad \text{Substitute the known values.}$$

$$\sin M = 0.75$$

Use a calculator to find the inverse sine of 0.75.

In the triangle, $m\angle M \approx 49°$.

Sometimes you need to combine your knowledge of trigonometric ratios with other geometric concepts to find the measure of an angle.

## Example 3

**In the figure $\overleftrightarrow{AD} \parallel \overleftrightarrow{BC}$. Find $m\angle DAC$.**

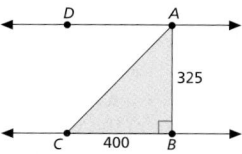

### Solution

Note that $\angle DAC$ and $\angle ACB$ are alternate interior angles of two parallel lines cut by a transversal, so they are congruent. Use the inverse tangent function.

$$\tan \angle ACB = \frac{325}{400} \qquad \frac{\text{opposite leg}}{\text{adjacent leg}}$$

$$\tan \angle ACB = 0.8125$$

Using a calculator, $m\angle ACB \approx 39°$. Since $\angle DAC \cong \angle ACB$, $m\angle DAC \approx 39°$.

###  TRY THESE EXERCISES

 **CALCULATOR** Use a calculator to find what angles have the given trigonometric ratios. Round to the nearest degree.

**1.** $\sin A = 0.345$  20°  **2.** $\tan Q = 1.15036$  49°  **3.** $\cos P = 0.93358$  21°  **4.** $\cos U = 0.43837$  64°

**5.** $\tan H = 0.4592$  25°  **6.** $\sin I = 0.5$  30°   **7.** $\cos Y = 0.1$  84°    **8.** $\tan E = 0.265$  15°

Math Online mathmatters2.com/extra_examples    Lesson 11-6  **Find Measures of Angles in Right Triangles**  |  **499**

---

## Teaching Tip

Students may also find an angle measure on a calculator directly from a trigonometric ratio that is expressed as a fraction. Re-examine with students the calculation for Example 2. Students can find the measure of the angle whose sine is $\frac{6}{8}$ by using the key sequence that follows.

[2nd] [SIN] 6 [÷] 8 [ ) ] [ENTER]

---

## Chalkboard Examples

### Supplementary Example 1

**HISTORY** It is said that the physicist Galileo dropped objects off a tower in Pisa, Italy to disprove Aristotle's claim that objects fall at speeds proportional to their weight.

Use the diagram to find at what angle from the vertical this now-famous tower of Pisa leans.

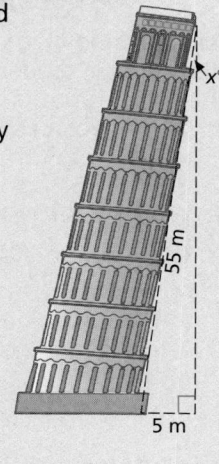

Write an equation involving a trigonometric ratio.

$$\sin x = \frac{5}{55}$$

Use a calculator to find the measure of the angle whose sine is $\frac{5}{55}$.

[2nd] [SIN] 5 [÷] 55 [ ) ] [ENTER]

On some calculators, the inverse key is used after the given value is entered.

So, the tower of Pisa leans at about 5° from the vertical.
Note: The lean is said to be increasing at a rate of about 1 mm per year.

### Supplementary Example 2

The diagonals of a rhombus measure 6 cm and 8 cm. Find the measure of the acute angle of the rhombus that is bisected by the longer diagonal.
The diagonals of a rhombus are the perpendicular bisectors of each other. To find $m\angle BCD$, first find $x$ by writing an equation involving a trigonometric ratio.

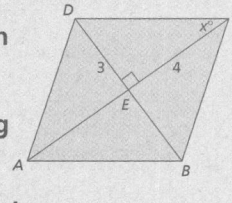

$$\tan x = \frac{3}{4}$$

$$x = \tan^{-1}\left(\frac{3}{4}\right)$$

$$x \approx 36.9°$$

So, $m\angle BCD \approx 2(36.9°) \approx 74°$

Ask the following questions to determine if students understand the content presented in this lesson.

1. What does $x$ represent in the equation $\sin x = 0.5$?  the measure of the angle whose sine is 0.5

2. What does $x$ represent in the equation $\sin 30° = \frac{x}{10}$?  the length of the side opposite the 30°-angle in a right triangle whose hypotenuse measures 10 units

### ASSIGNMENT GUIDE

**Basic:** 1–34, 39–44
**Enriched:** 1–44

### Reteaching Worksheet 11-6

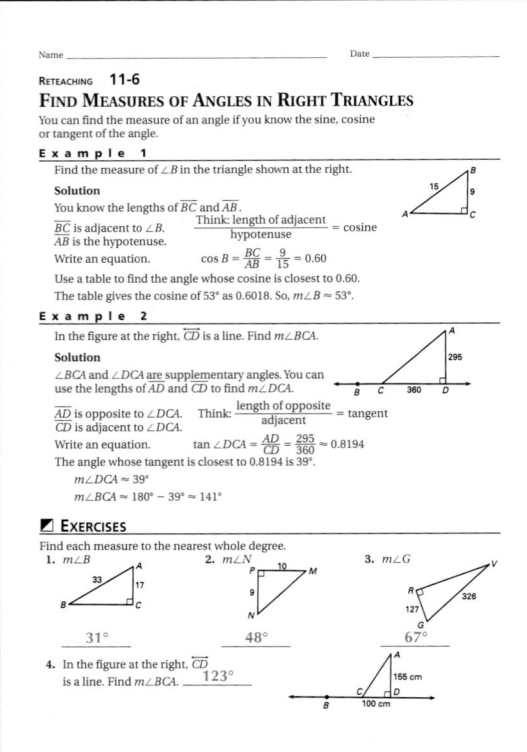

9. Find $m\angle A$ in the right triangle shown.  ≈ 5°

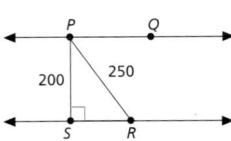

10. In right triangle $XYZ$, $\cos Z = 0.4848$. Find $m\angle Z$.  ≈ 61°

11. In the figure, $\overrightarrow{PQ} \parallel \overrightarrow{SR}$. Find $m\angle QPR$.  ≈ 53°

12. **WRITING MATH** Explain how you might find the angles in a right triangle whose sides measure 5 m, 12 m, and 13 m.
See additional answers.

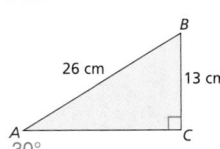

## PRACTICE EXERCISES • For Extra Practice, see page 622.

**CALCULATOR** Use a calculator to find what angles have the given trigonometric ratios. Round to the nearest degree.

13. $\tan N = 0.895$   42°
14. $\cos W = 0.69753$   46°
15. $\cos Q = 0.2323$   77°
16. $\sin K = 0.5612$   34°
17. $\sin T = 0.54321$   33°
18. $\cos D = 0.9$   26°
19. $\sin B = 0.3816$   22°
20. $\tan G = 1.9$   62°

**Find each measure to the nearest whole degree.**

21. $m\angle A$

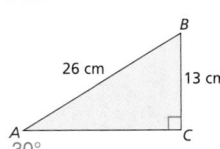
B, 26 cm, 13 cm, A 30°, C

22. $m\angle S$

451, T, W, 250, S 61°

23. $m\angle G$

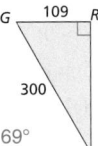
G 109 R, 300, 69°, V

24. An airplane takes off from an airport and flies due south. When it has reached a ground distance of 1500 m from its starting point, it is 970 m above the ground. What angle does the plane's path make with the ground?  ≈ 33°

25. **TRAVEL** San Francisco's Filbert Street is the steepest street in the world. It rises 1 ft for every 3.17 ft of horizontal distance. Find the angle at which Filbert Street rises.  ≈ 18°

26. The Chamonix Line of the French National Railroad is the steepest climbing train track in the world. It ascends 1 ft for every 11 ft of horizontal distance. Find the angle at which the Chamonix Line rises.  ≈ 5°

Filbert Street, San Francisco

**SAFETY** In order to prevent ladders from accidentally slipping off of a wall, many construction companies follow the rule that the measure of the angle that an unsecured ladder makes with the ground should not be less than 75°. Determine if each ladder is safe to use.

27. The base of an 8-m ladder is 1.5 m away from the wall.  safe, ≈ 79°

28. A ladder's base is 6.9 yd away from the wall and touches 4.7 yd up the wall.  not safe, ≈ 34°

29. The base of a 3.6-m ladder is 0.8 m away from the wall.  safe, ≈ 77°

500 | Chapter 11 **Right Triangle Trigonometry**

### ADDITIONAL ANSWERS

12. To find one of the acute angles, find the inverse sine of $\frac{12}{13}$, which is about 67°. The other acute angle has a measure of about 90° − 67°, or 23°. The third angle is the right angle, which has a measure of 90°.

38. $\sin 15° = \frac{5.5}{x}$; 21 ft

$\sin 28° = \frac{5.5}{x}$; 12 ft

$\sin 35° = \frac{5.5}{x}$; 10 ft

**30. PHOTOGRAPHY** A reporter photographs a firefighter fighting a fire on the fourth floor of a burning building. The photographer is 60 ft away from the bottom of the building, and the second floor window is 48 ft above the ground. At what angle does the photographer hold her camera? ≈ 39°

**31.** Without using a table of trigonometric values or a calculator, find the angles of a right triangle with two sides measuring 17.5 m. (Hint: Drawing a picture may help solve the problem.) ≈ 45°

**32.** When is the cosine of an angle greater than the sine of the angle as the angle varies from 0° to 90°? Use a calculator to experiment with several different angles to solve the problem. 0° < x < 45°

**33. ASTRONOMY** A large telescope is being used to track an object circling the earth. If the distance between the telescope and the object is 1400 mi and the object is 610 mi above the surface of the earth, at what angle is the telescope raised? ≈ 26°

**34. WRITING MATH** Explain why your answer in Exercise 33 is an approximation and cannot be precise. Both distances given in the exercises are themselves approximations.

## ■ EXTENDED PRACTICE EXERCISES

**35.** One leg of a right triangle is twice as long as the other leg. To the nearest whole degree, what are the measures of the acute angles of the triangle? 27°, 63°

**36. TRAVEL** A commercial jet is flying at a height of 2.8 km, and the ground distance between the plane and the point of takeoff is 6 km. To the nearest degree, what is the angle of the plane's path with the ground? 25°

**37. CRITICAL THINKING** A circle has a radius of 22.4 mm. What is the measure of the central angle that determines a chord of length 16.8 mm? Round to the nearest degree. 44°

**38. CHAPTER INVESTIGATION** Suppose the subject is 5.5 ft from the ground. Use a trigonometric ratio to write an equation for each degree: 15°, 28° and 35°. For each angle measure, write the distance to the nearest foot that the photographer needs to be from the subject. See additional answers.

## ■ MIXED REVIEW EXERCISES

**Find the surface area of each figure. Use 3.14 for π. Round to the nearest tenth.** (Lesson 10-3)

**39.**
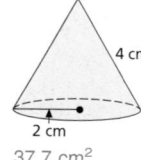
37.7 cm²

**40.**
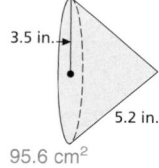
95.6 cm²

**41.**
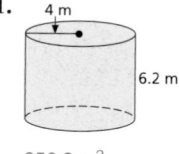
256.2 m²

**Factor each polynomial.** (Lesson 9-7)

**42.** $12p^2 + 8p^3$  $4p^2(3 + 2p)$

**43.** $12f^4 + 6f^3 + 18f^2$  $6f^2(2f^2 + f + 3)$

**44.** $24x^3 - 32x^4 + 40x^3$  $8x^3(8 - 4x)$

---

## Extend the Lesson

**CHALLENGE** Tell students that an *identity* is an equation that is true for all replacements of the variable(s). For example, $(a + b)^2 = a^2 + 2ab + b^2$ is an identity because it is true for all values of $a$ and $b$.
Have students find the value of each of the following.
$(\sin 20°)^2 + (\cos 20°)^2$   $(\sin 38°)^2 + (\cos 38°)^2$   $(\sin 62°)^2 + (\cos 62°)^2$
Ask students to write a general statement, based on their findings, that appears to be an identity.   $(\sin x)^2 + (\cos x)^2 = 1$

---

 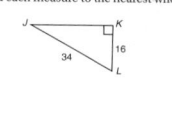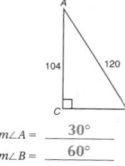
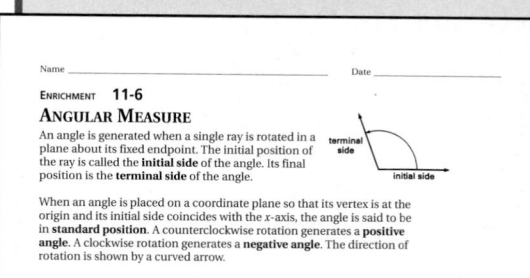 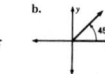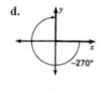

## Chalkboard Examples

### Lesson 11-5

**AGRICULTURE** Mr. Ash needs to buy a conveyor belt to haul bales of hay to the loft of his barn, which is 15 ft above ground. One conveyor he is considering has legs that sets it 3 ft above the ground and can be raised to a maximum angle of 35°. Can this conveyor reach his loft? Explain.

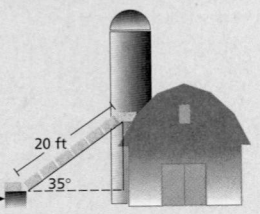

Use the sine ratio to find the length of the vertical leg of the right triangle. Add on the 3ft-height that the conveyor is above ground:

$\sin 35° = \frac{x}{20}$

$x = 20(\sin 35°)$

$x \approx 20(0.5736)$

$x \approx 11.5$

$11.5 + 3 = 14.5$ ft

which will not reach the 15-ft loft.

### Lesson 11-6

Find, to the nearest degree, the value of x in the right triangle.

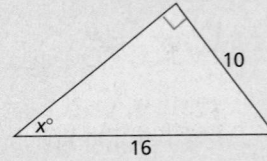

Write an equation involving a trigonometric ratio.

$\sin \angle = \frac{\text{opposite}}{\text{hypotenuse}}$

$\sin x° = \frac{10}{16}$

Use a calculator to find the angle whose sine is $\frac{10}{16}$.

| 2nd | SIN | 10 | ÷ | 16 | ) | ENTER |

On some calculators, the inverse key is entered after the value. So, $x \approx 39°$.

# Review and Practice Your Skills

## PRACTICE ◼ LESSON 11-5

Find the value of *y* rounded to the nearest hundredth. State whether you used sine, cosine, or tangent to solve each exercise.

**1.**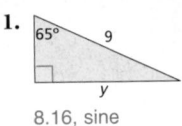

8.16, sine

**2.**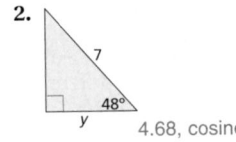

4.68, cosine

**3.**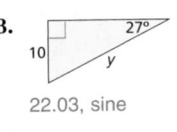

22.03, sine

Find the value of *y* to the nearest hundredth.

**4.**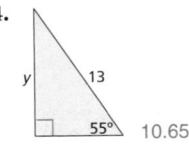

10.65

**5.**

2.12

**6.**

15.89

**7.**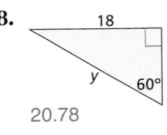

7.37

**8.**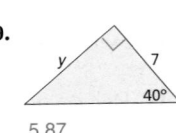

20.78

**9.**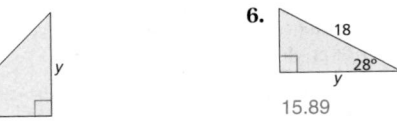

5.87

## PRACTICE ◼ LESSON 11-6

Find $m\angle A$ rounded to the nearest degree.

**10.** $\sin A = 0.05463$  3°

**11.** $\cos A = 0.2318$  77°

**12.** $\cos A = \frac{5}{9}$  56°

**13.** $\sin A = 0.16$  10°

**14.** $\tan A = \frac{5}{3}$  59°

**15.** $\sin A = \frac{1}{2}$  30°

Find $m\angle B$ rounded to the nearest degree.

**16.**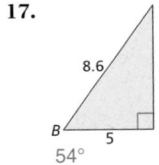

37°

**17.**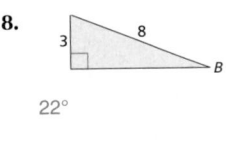

54°

**18.**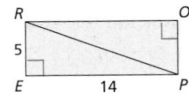

22°

**19.**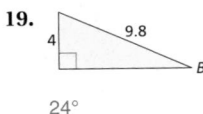

24°

**20.**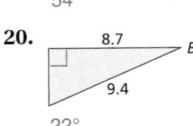

22°

**21.**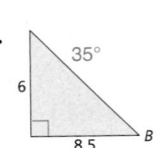

**22.** In the rectangle shown, what is the measure of $\angle RPE$?  ≈ 19.65°

## Teaching Tip

For Exercises 12, 14, and 15, remind students that they need not first change the fraction to a decimal. They can enter the fraction directly onto the calculator, being careful to use appropriate parentheses. Key sequences for Exercise 12 are shown below, for both a calculator that requires the $\cos^{-1}$ key to be entered first (graphing calculator) and for a calculator that requires the $\cos^{-1}$ key to be entered after the value (scientific calculator).

| 2nd | COS | 5 | ÷ | 9 | ) | ENTER |

The TI-84 Plus calculator supplies the opening parentheses.

| ( | 5 | ÷ | 9 | ) | cos⁻¹ | = |

Student must enter both parts of the parentheses.

**Find the unknown length. Round to the nearest tenth.** (Lesson 11-3)

23.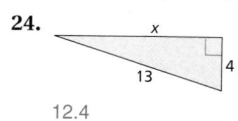
5   11
x
9.8

24.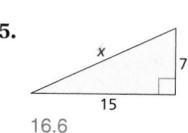
x
13   4
12.4

25.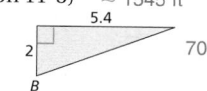
x   7
15
16.6

**In $\triangle CDE$, $\angle D$ is a right angle and $\sin C = \frac{7}{25}$. Find these ratios.** (Lesson 11-4)

26. $\tan E$  $\frac{24}{7}$

27. $\cos C$  $\frac{24}{25}$

28. $\tan C$  $\frac{7}{24}$

29. After taking off, an airplane climbs at a steady 18° angle for 5000 ft of air distance. How far above the ground is the plane? (Lesson 11-5)  $\approx 1545$ ft

30. Find the $m\angle B$ to the nearest degree. (Lesson 11-6)

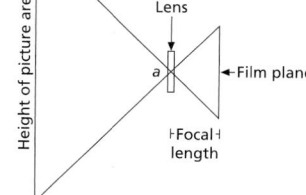
5.4
2    70°
B

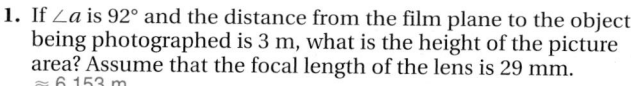 **Career – Camera Designer**

**A**lthough cameras are very complicated and intricate, the basic functioning can be explained in general terms. Light from an object is focused on a film plane through a lens. The size of the image produced on a photograph is affected by several parameters, one of which is the focal length. The focal length is the distance from the front of the lens to the film plane. In general, as the focal length increases, the size of the picture area decreases.

1. If $\angle a$ is 92° and the distance from the film plane to the object being photographed is 3 m, what is the height of the picture area? Assume that the focal length of the lens is 29 mm.
$\approx 6.153$ m

2. If the focal length of the lens doubles from 40 mm to 80 mm, what do you predict will happen to the size of $\angle a$? What will happen to the height of the picture area? Assume that the distance from the film plane to the object remains the same.
See additional answers.

3. Comment on the validity of your conjecture about $\angle a$ in Exercise 2 after calculating $m\angle a$ for the following focal lengths. Assume that the film plane is 6 cm high.

   **a.** 40 mm  73.7°     **b.** 80 mm  41.1°
   When the focal length doubles $\angle a$ is slightly more than half its original value.

4. Using the two values of $\angle a$ calculated in Exercise 3, determine the heights of the picture areas that may be photographed for the following focal lengths. Assume that the object remains 3 m from the film. Does this confirm your prediction in Exercise 3 concerning the heights of the picture areas?

   **a.** 40 mm  $\approx 443.7$ cm     **b.** 80 mm  $\approx 219.0$ cm
   When the focal length doubles, the height is halved.

Lens

a   ←Film plane

⊢Focal⊣
length

Height of picture area

 **mathmatters2.com/mathworks**

Chapter 11  **Review and Practice Your Skills**  **503**

## MathWorks

Today's cameras all derive from the 16th-century *camera obscura*. The earliest form of this device was a darkened room with a tiny hole in one wall. Light entered the room through this hole and projected an upside-down image of the subject onto the opposite wall. Over the course of three centuries, the camera obscura evolved into a hand-held box with a lens replacing the pinhole and an angled mirror at the back. The mirror reflected an image onto a ground-glass viewing screen on the top of the box. Long before film was invented, artists used this device to help them draw more accurately. They placed thin paper onto the viewing screen and could easily trace the reflected image.

Students should answer Questions 1–4 to better understand how angle measure is used in determining focal lengths.

Have students investigate the evolution of advancements made in camera design, reporting especially on the range of automated features that greatly simplify picture taking and reduce the likelihood of error.

Students who are interested in learning more about this career choice can go to mathmatters2.com/mathworks. School Guidance Counselors are another resource for information about training requirements and appropriate schools.

### ADDITIONAL ANSWERS

2. Answers will vary. A likely answer may be that $\angle a$ will be half the size and the object will be half the size of the original values.

## Teaching Tip

For Exercises 16–21 and 30, encourage students to check that their results are reasonable. Discuss various methods that can be used to check that would be independent of the way the problem was originally solved. For example, in Exercise 16, suppose students used an incorrect trigonometric ratio instead of sine. Say, students used $\cos B = \frac{6}{10}$, which would result in $m\angle B \approx 53°$. If they simply reverse their procedure, they will see that $\cos 53° \approx 0.6$, and they will think their answer is correct. A different approach will point out that their answer is incorrect. By their result, the measure of the other acute angle = 37°. But, this would not be reasonable since, by the Pythagorean Theorem, the other leg is 8 units, and the incorrect result is not placing the longer leg opposite the greater acute angle.

### NCTM Standards/Strands
- Measurement
- Geometry
- Connections
- Algebra

### Vocabulary

30°-60°-90° right triangle
45°-45°-90° right triangle

### Tools/Materials Needed

ruler            protractor
calculator       grid paper
dot paper

### Lesson Resources

Warm-up Transparency 47
Transparency TK-9, 15, RF-59
Reteaching 11-7
Extra Practice 11-7
Enrichment 11-7

## Getting Started

### 5-MINUTE WARM-UP

**Write each square in simplest form.**

1. $4^2$  16          2. $(1 + 3)^2$  16
3. $(2 \cdot 2)^2$  16     4. $\left(\frac{8}{2}\right)^2$  16

### Introduction to Lesson 11-7

In answer to Question 3, students will get $\sqrt{8}$. Based on previous experience with factoring whole numbers, note with students that $\sqrt{8} = \sqrt{4} \cdot \sqrt{2}$, which can then be written as $\sqrt{8} = 2\sqrt{2}$.

Note also that *squaring* and *taking a square root* are inverse operations.
$(\sqrt{2})^2 = 2$   $(\sqrt{3})^2 = 3$
$(\sqrt{x})^2 = x, x \geq 0$

---

# 11-7

# Special Right Triangles

**Goals**
- Explore the relationships in 30°-60°-90° right triangles.
- Explore the relationships in 45°-45°-90° right triangles.

**Applications**   Architecture, Entertainment, Photography, Sports, Nature

**Use a ruler and a protractor.**

1. Draw a 2-in. square and its diagonal. Cut along the diagonal.
   Observe students' work.
2. Measure each angle and the legs of one of the triangles formed by the halves of the square. Record these on the triangle.
   45°, 45°, 90°; 2 in., 2 in.
3. Use the Pythagorean Theorem to find the measure of the hypotenuse of the triangle. Express this measure as a square root, and record it on the triangle.  $2\sqrt{2}$
4. How do the measures of the legs of a right triangle with a 45° angle compare?   They are equal.
5. How does the measure of the hypotenuse of a right triangle with a 45° angle compare to the measure of its legs?
   $\sqrt{2}$ time greater

## BUILD UNDERSTANDING

Many engineers, draftspeople, architects and designers use right triangles to maintain drawing proportions. These include two special forms of right triangles. The triangles are a **30°-60°-90° right triangle** and a **45°-45°-90° right triangle**.

These special right triangles can be used to solve problems in a manner similar to using trigonometric ratios. The special geometric properties of 30°-60°-90° right triangles and 45°-45°-90° right triangles are summarized in the table.

| 30°-60°-90° right triangles | 45°-45°-90° right triangles |
|---|---|
| Length of side opposite 30° angle: $x$ | Length of each leg: $x$ |
| Length of side opposite 60° angle: $x\sqrt{3}$ | Length of hypotenuse: $x\sqrt{2}$ |
| Length of hypotenuse: $2x$ | |

### Problem Solving Tip

Use this memory device to help you remember which triangle uses $\sqrt{2}$ and which uses $\sqrt{3}$.

There are two different side lengths in a 45°-45°-90° right triangle, so it uses $\sqrt{2}$.

There are three different side lengths in the 30°-60°-90° right triangle, so it uses $\sqrt{3}$.

### Example 1

**Find *MP* and *NP* in the triangle.**

**Solution**

Triangle *MNP* is a 45°-45°-90° triangle, and $\overline{MP}$ is the hypotenuse.

$$MP = MN\sqrt{2} = 20\sqrt{2}$$

Since the legs are congruent, $NP = 20$.

## Differentiated Instruction

**VISUAL LEARNERS** To assist students in further visualizing the relationships in the 45°-45°-90° right triangle, you may have them draw a series of similar 45°-45°-90° right triangles on graph paper, as shown below. Using the relationships in $\triangle XYZ$, ask students to find:

GH  $\sqrt{2}$        EF  $2\sqrt{2}$
CD  $3\sqrt{2}$        AB  $4\sqrt{2}$

For an analogous experience with the 30°-60°-90° right triangle, see Differentiated Instruction at the bottom of page 505.

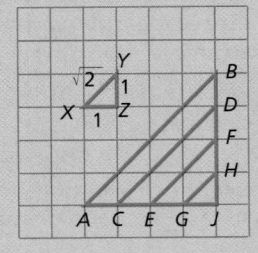

## Example 2

**Find *BC* and *AC* in the triangle.**

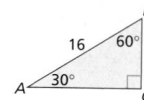

### Solution

Triangle *ABC* is a 30°-60°-90° triangle, and $\overline{AB}$ is the hypotenuse.

Leg $\overline{BC}$ is the side opposite the 30° angle.

$$AB = 2 \cdot BC$$
$$16 = 2 \cdot BC \qquad \text{Divide both sides by 2.}$$
$$8 = BC$$

Leg $\overline{AC}$ is the side opposite the 60° angle.

$$AC = BC \cdot \sqrt{3}$$
$$AC = 8\sqrt{3}$$

## Example 3

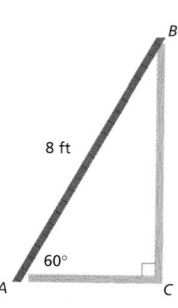

**ARCHITECTURE** The angle formed by the roof of a monument measures 60°. Since this is such a steep angle, an architect places a support beam at a slant distance of 8 ft along the roof from the corner. How tall is the support beam to the nearest tenth?

### Solution

Let the distance from the corner to the support beam equal *x*. Triangle *ABC* is a 30°-60°-90° right triangle. Since $\overline{AB}$ is the hypotenuse, 8 ft = 2*x*. Solve for *x*.

$$2x = 8$$
$$x = \frac{8}{2} = 4$$

Leg $\overline{BC}$, the height of the support beam, is the side opposite the 60° angle.

$$BC = x\sqrt{3}$$
$$BC = 4\sqrt{3}$$
$$BC \approx 4 \cdot 1.7321$$
$$BC \approx 6.9284$$

So the height of the support beam is approximately 6.9 ft.

---

> ### Check Understanding
> When is it necessary to convert square roots into their approximate decimal equivalents?
>
> when you need concrete answers, such as with measurements

---

### ◤ TRY THESE EXERCISES

**Find each length. Approximate any square roots with decimals.**

**1.** *RS* 10   **2.** *QR* 8.7

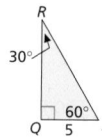

**3.** *GF* 17.0   **4.** *GH* 17.0

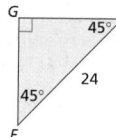

Math Online mathmatters2.com/extra_examples

---

## Chalkboard Examples

### Supplementary Example 1
Find the area of a square whose diagonal measures $10\sqrt{2}$ cm.

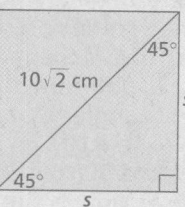

To find the area of a square, you need to know the length of the side of the square. A diagonal divides a square into two 45°-45°-90° right triangles, where the diagonal is the hypotenuse. Work backwards: since the hypotenuse of this 45°-45°-90° right triangle is $10\sqrt{2}$ cm, each leg of this special right triangle is 10 cm.

$$A = s^2$$
$$A = 10^2 \text{ or } 100$$

So, the area of the square is 100 cm².

### Supplementary Example 2
Find the length of the altitude of an equilateral triangle whose sides measure 10 cm.

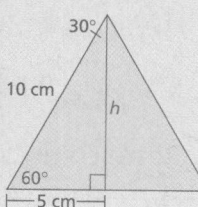

Each altitude of an equilateral triangle is the perpendicular bisector of the side to which it is drawn, and it bisects the vertex angle from which it is drawn. Thus, an altitude divides an equilateral triangle into two 30°-60°-90° right triangles.

In one of these special right triangles, a side of the equilateral triangle is the hypotenuse, and the altitude of the equilateral triangle is the leg opposite the 60°-angle.

$$h = \frac{1}{2} \text{ hypotenuse} \cdot \sqrt{3}$$
$$h = \frac{1}{2}(10)\sqrt{3}$$
$$h = 5\sqrt{3}$$

So, the measure of the altitude of the equilateral triangle is $5\sqrt{3}$ cm.

---

## Differentiated Instruction

**VISUAL LEARNERS** To assist students in further visualizing the relationships in the 30°-60°-90° right triangle, you may have them draw a series of similar 30°-60°-90° right triangles on isometric dot paper, as shown at the right. Using the relationships in △*XYZ*, ask students to find:

| | |
|---|---|
| *GH* $\sqrt{3}$ | *EF* $2\sqrt{3}$ |
| *CD* $3\sqrt{3}$ | *AB* $4\sqrt{3}$ |

Ask the following questions to determine if students understand the content presented in this lesson.

1. How is the measure of the hypotenuse of an isosceles right triangle related to the measure of a leg?   hypotenuse = leg $\sqrt{2}$

2. In a 30°-60°-90° right triangle:
   a. How is the measure of the side opposite the 30°-angle related to the measure of the hypotenuse?   side opposite 30° $\angle = \frac{1}{2}$ hypotenuse
   b. How is the measure of the side opposite the 60°-angle related to the measure of the hypotenuse?   side opposite 60° $\angle = \frac{1}{2}$ hypotenuse $\sqrt{3}$

## ASSIGNMENT GUIDE

**Basic:** 1–26, 33–38
**Enriched:** 1–38

### Reteaching Worksheet 11-7

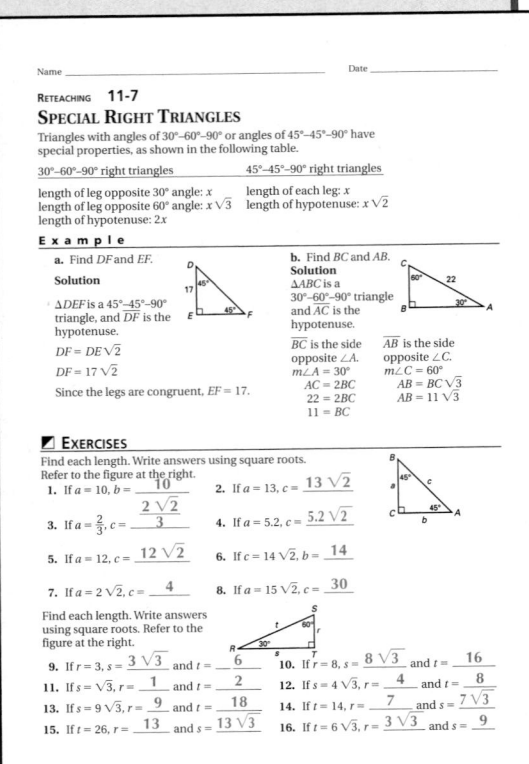

5. **ENTERTAINMENT** Jeff is flying his kite in an open, flat field. He lets out 840 ft of taut string, which forms an angle of 60° with the ground. How high above the ground is the kite? Round to the nearest tenth of a foot.   727.5 ft

6. An isosceles triangle has a right angle and a hypotenuse of length 20.8 cm. Find the lengths of the other two sides of the triangle. Round to the nearest tenth.   14.7 cm

7. The shortest side of a right triangle with a 60° angle is 10 m. Find the lengths of the other two sides of the triangle. Leave your answers in square root form.   $10\sqrt{3}$ m, 20 m

8. The legs of a 45°-45°-90° triangle each measure 2 in. How long is the hypotenuse of the triangle? Round to the nearest tenth.   2.8 in.

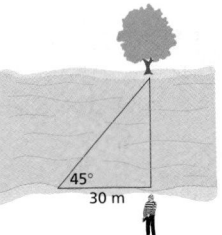

## PRACTICE EXERCISES  •  For Extra Practice, see page 623.

**Find each length. Leave your answers in square root form.**

9. $BC$   16

10. $AC$   $16\sqrt{2}$

11. $NP$   19

12. $MN$   $19\sqrt{3}$

13. $GH$   $\frac{3\sqrt{2}}{2}$

14. $GK$   $\frac{3\sqrt{2}}{2}$

15. $VW$   $\frac{14\sqrt{3}}{3}$

16. $SW$   $\frac{28\sqrt{3}}{3}$

17. **PHOTOGRAPHY** A reconnaissance aircraft flies at an elevation of 30,000 ft and takes pictures of the terrain below. The camera mounted on the bottom of the jet points downward to form an angle of 60° with the bottom of the plane. How far in front of the jet does the reconnaissance camera point? Round to the nearest foot.   17,321 ft

18. A 4.2-m ladder leaning against a wall makes a 75° angle with the ground. How far from the wall is the foot of the ladder? Round to the nearest tenth.   1.1 m

19. How far up the wall is the top of the ladder in Exercise 18? Find a decimal value to the nearest tenth.   4.1 m

20. When the sun is at an angle of 30°, a tree casts a 90-ft shadow. Find a decimal value for the height of the tree. Round to the nearest tenth.   52.0 ft

21. **NATURE** Pearl and Joey use a directional compass to find the distance across a river. They select an object directly across the river and take a compass reading to that object. Pearl then walks along the river in a direction perpendicular to her original line of sight until the compass reading has changed by 45°. Joey measures the distance Pearl walked as 30 m. What is the width of the river?   30 m

22. **SPORTS** A professional baseball diamond is a square with sides that are 90 ft long. Find the distance from first base to third base to the nearest foot.   127 ft

**506** | Chapter 11  **Right Triangle Trigonometry**

## ADDITIONAL ANSWERS

23. **Answers will vary.** One possible explanation follows: The octagon is composed of four rectangles, four triangles and one square. Let $x$ represent the length of each side of the octagon. This $x$ also represents the length of the hypotenuse of each 45°–45°–90° right triangle, the length of each side of the square, and the length of the two longer sides of the rectangles. The length of each leg of the triangles, which is also the length

of the shorter sides of the rectangles is $\frac{x\sqrt{2}}{2}$. Now we have all the dimensions of the figure and can compute the area of the regions.

$$\text{area of the triangles} + \text{area of rectangles} + \text{area of square}$$

$$= 4 \cdot \frac{1}{2}\left(\frac{x\sqrt{2}}{2}\right)\left(\frac{x\sqrt{2}}{2}\right) + 4 \cdot (x)\left(\frac{x\sqrt{2}}{2}\right) + x \cdot x$$

$$= x^2 + 2\sqrt{2}x^2 + x^2$$

$$= 2x^2 + 2x^2\sqrt{2}$$

$$= x^2(2 + 2\sqrt{2}) \approx 4.83x^2$$

**23.** The figure is a regular octagon divided into several non-overlapping regions. Explain how you can use these regions to find the area of the octagon. See additional answers.

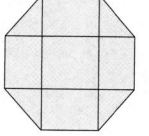

**24.** If the length of a side of the regular octagon described in Exercise 23 is 5 cm, what is the area of the octagon? 120.7 cm²

**25.** A swimmer tries to swim across a river from point $K$ to point $M$. Because of the current, the swimmer reaches point $L$ instead. How far does the swimmer travel? Find a decimal value to the nearest tenth. 106.1 ft

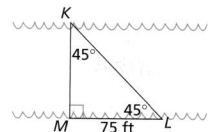

**26. WRITING MATH** Are all right isosceles triangles similar? Explain.
All corresponding angles are always congruent with measures of 45°, 45° and 90°. Corresponding sides are always proportional.

## ■ EXTENDED PRACTICE EXERCISES

**27.** Find the measures of the other sides of the triangles shown. Use these measures to complete the table. Leave your answers in square root form.
See additional answers.

| | Sine | Cosine | Tangent |
|---|---|---|---|
| 30° | | | |
| 45° | | | |
| 60° | | | |

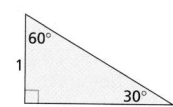

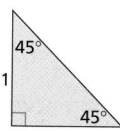

**28. CALCULATOR** Use a calculator to rewrite the table in Exercise 27 with decimal values rounded to four places. See additional answers.

**Write an expression that represents each of the following.**

**29.** The area of a right triangle with a 30° angle and shortest side of length $x$. $\frac{\sqrt{3}}{2}x^2$

**30.** The area of a right triangle with a 45° angle and legs of length $x$. $\frac{1}{2}x^2$

**31.** The area of a rectangle whose diagonal forms two triangles, each having a 60° angle and whose shorter legs measure $x$. $\sqrt{3}x^2$

**32. DATA FILE** Refer to the data on road congestion at ten major U.S. cities on page 575. Use an atlas, a ruler and a protractor to find three cities that approximately form a 45°-45°-90° or 30°-60°-90° right triangle.
Answers will vary. Check students' work.

## ■ MIXED REVIEW EXERCISES

**Find the volume of each figure. Use 3.14 for $\pi$. Round to the nearest tenth.** (Lesson 10-7)

**33.**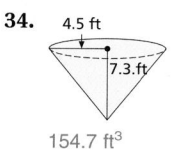
3 cm
6 cm
169.6 cm³

**34.**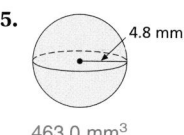
4.5 ft
7.3 ft
154.7 ft³

**35.**
4.8 mm
463.0 mm³

**On grid paper, graph each figure and its image under the given rotation.** (Lesson 7-3)

**36.** $A(2, 3)$, $B(8, 3)$, $C(8, 7)$; 90° clockwise around $(0, 0)$   For 36–38, see additional answers.

**37.** $A(-9, 5)$, $B(-3, 5)$, $C(6, -5)$, $D(1, -5)$; 180° clockwise around $(0, 0)$

**38.** $A(2, -2)$, $B((3, -5)$, $C(8, -5)$; 360° clockwise around $(0, 0)$

Math Online mathmatters2.com/self_check_quiz

**27.**

| | sine | cosine | tangent |
|---|---|---|---|
| 30° | $\frac{1}{2}$ | $\frac{\sqrt{3}}{2}$ | $\frac{\sqrt{3}}{3}$ |
| 45° | $\frac{\sqrt{2}}{2}$ | $\frac{\sqrt{2}}{2}$ | 1 |
| 60° | $\frac{\sqrt{3}}{2}$ | $\frac{1}{2}$ | $\sqrt{3}$ |

**28.**

| | sine | cosine | tangent |
|---|---|---|---|
| 30° | 0.5 | 0.8660 | 0.5774 |
| 45° | 0.7071 | 0.7071 | 1 |
| 60° | 0.8660 | 0.5 | 1.7321 |

**36.**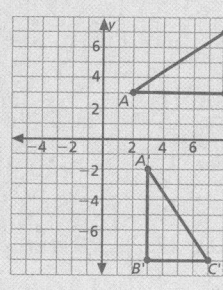

**37.**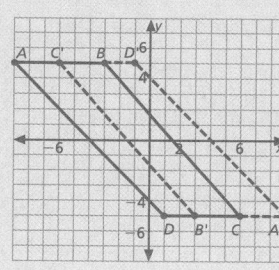

**38.**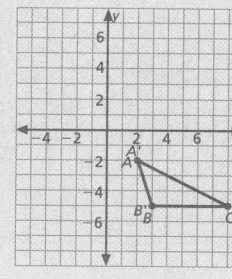

---

## Extra Practice Worksheet 11-7

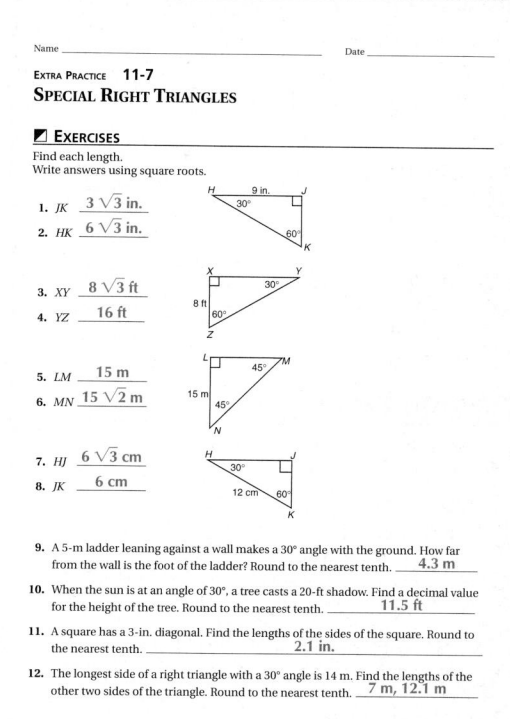

Name _____ Date _____

EXTRA PRACTICE **11-7**
**SPECIAL RIGHT TRIANGLES**

**☑ EXERCISES**
Find each length.
Write answers using square roots.

1. $JK$ ___3 √3 in.___
2. $HK$ ___6 √3 in.___

3. $XY$ ___8 √3 ft___
4. $YZ$ ___16 ft___

5. $LM$ ___15 m___
6. $MN$ ___15 √2 m___

7. $HJ$ ___6 √3 cm___
8. $JK$ ___6 cm___

9. A 5-m ladder leaning against a wall makes a 30° angle with the ground. How far from the wall is the foot of the ladder? Round to the nearest tenth. ___4.3 m___

10. When the sun is at an angle of 30°, a tree casts a 20-ft shadow. Find a decimal value for the height of the tree. Round to the nearest tenth. ___11.5 ft___

11. A square has a 3-in. diagonal. Find the lengths of the sides of the square. Round to the nearest tenth. ___2.1 in.___

12. The longest side of a right triangle with a 30° angle is 14 m. Find the lengths of the other two sides of the triangle. Round to the nearest tenth. ___7 m, 12.1 m___

---

## Enrichment Worksheet 11-7

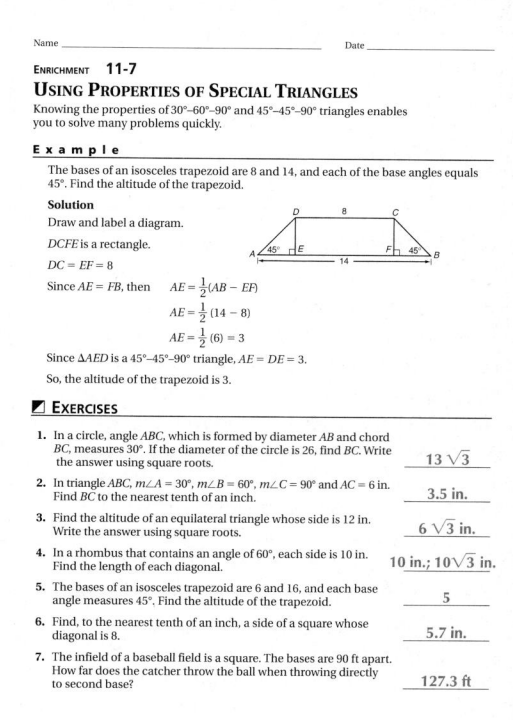

Name _____ Date _____

ENRICHMENT **11-7**
**USING PROPERTIES OF SPECIAL TRIANGLES**
Knowing the properties of 30°-60°-90° and 45°-45°-90° triangles enables you to solve many problems quickly.

**Example**
The bases of an isosceles trapezoid are 8 and 14, and each of the base angles equals 45°. Find the altitude of the trapezoid.

**Solution**
Draw and label a diagram.
$DCFE$ is a rectangle.
$DC = EF = 8$
Since $AE = FB$, then    $AE = \frac{1}{2}(AB - EF)$
$AE = \frac{1}{2}(14 - 8)$
$AE = \frac{1}{2}(6) = 3$
Since $\triangle AED$ is a 45°-45°-90° triangle, $AE = DE = 3$.
So, the altitude of the trapezoid is 3.

**☑ EXERCISES**

1. In a circle, angle $ABC$, which is formed by diameter $AB$ and chord $BC$, measures 30°. If the diameter of the circle is 26, find $BC$. Write the answer using square roots. ___13 √3___

2. In triangle $ABC$, $m\angle A = 30°$, $m\angle B = 60°$, $m\angle C = 90°$ and $AC = 6$ in. Find $BC$ to the nearest tenth of an inch. ___3.5 in.___

3. Find the altitude of an equilateral triangle whose side is 12 in. Write the answer using square roots. ___6 √3 in.___

4. In a rhombus that contains an angle of 60°, each side is 10 in. Find the length of each diagonal. ___10 in.; 10√3 in.___

5. The bases of an isosceles trapezoid are 6 and 16, and each base angle measures 45°. Find the altitude of the trapezoid. ___5___

6. Find, to the nearest tenth of an inch, a side of a square whose diagonal is 8. ___5.7 in.___

7. The infield of a baseball field is a square. The bases are 90 ft apart. How far does the catcher throw the ball when throwing directly to second base? ___127.3 ft___

## Lesson Planning

### NCTM Standards/Strands
- ■ Problem Solving
- ■ Measurement
- ■ Representation
- ■ Number & Operations

### Vocabulary
eliminate possibilities

### Tools/Materials Needed
calculator

### Lesson Resources
Warm-up Transparency 47
Transparency RF-1
Reteaching 11-8
Extra Practice 11-8
Enrichment 11-8

### ASSIGNMENT GUIDE
**Basic:** 1–16
**Enriched:** 1–16

## Getting Started

### 5-MINUTE WARM-UP
Determine the most reasonable answer for each trigonometric ratio.
1. sin 30°  **C**
   A. 1  B. −1  C. 0.5  D. 0.9
2. tan 45°  **B**
   A. −1  B. 1  C. 0.5  D. −0.5

**THE FIVE-STEP PLAN Read**—ask questions to help students understand the problem. **Plan**—guide students to related problems and previously mastered skills and strategies. **Solve**—students solve problem on their own. **Answer**—write the solution in a format that answers the question. **Check**—review work, check for reasonableness, and review strategy used.
**THE STRATEGY** *Eliminate possibilities*—in this strategy, students make judgments about potential answers, discarding those that are not reasonable in light of known information about the problem situation.

---

When you solve a multistep problem or a problem that requires logical reasoning, you need to examine all possibilities and combinations. One strategy, **eliminate possibilities**, is often used to search for reasonable solutions. With this strategy, all possible solutions to a problem are considered. Then they are tested and either dismissed as impossible or accepted as reasonable.

> **Problem Solving Strategies**
> Guess and check
> Look for a pattern
> Solve a simpler problem
> Make a table, chart or list
> Use a picture, diagram or model
> Act it out
> Work backwards
> ✓ Eliminate possibilities
> Use an equation or formula

### Problem

**FITNESS** Sam, Queisha and Carlos climb Mt. Everest, which has an elevation of 29,028 ft. They take a break at 25,740 ft. Sam tells the group that they have approximately 3200 ft left to climb to the top. Queisha disagrees, saying that they have approximately 9000 ft left to climb. Carlos thinks that they have approximately 7500 ft left to climb. They use surveying instruments to find that the angle of elevation to the peak is 20.5°. Use trigonometry to determine which hiker has the most reasonable answer.

### Solve the Problem

Draw a diagram of the situation.

First find *a*, the difference between the top of Mt. Everest and where the group is now.

$$29{,}028 - 25{,}740 = 3288$$

Sam's estimate of 3200 ft can be eliminated because the distance left to climb is the hypotenuse shown in the diagram, not *a*.

Use a trigonometric ratio to find *x*, the remaining distance to the top.

$$\sin 20.5° = \frac{3288}{x}$$
$$0.3502 \approx \frac{3288}{x}$$
$$0.3502 \cdot x \approx 3288$$
$$\frac{0.3502x}{0.3502} \approx \frac{3288}{0.3502}$$
$$x \approx 9388.9$$

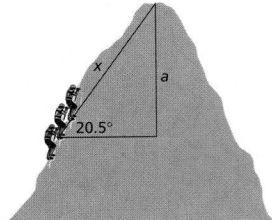

The distance left to climb is approximately 9388.9 ft, so Carlos' estimate can also be eliminated. Queisha's estimate of approximately 9000 ft is close to the actual answer, so her answer is the most reasonable.

## Extend the Lesson

**REAL WORLD CONNECTION** Note with students that since *elevation* implies a height, an observer is looking up at an object to create an of *angle of elevation*.
Ask students to discuss what happens to the size of the angle of elevation as the observer gets closer to the object.  measure of angle increases  Have students imagine getting closer to the screen in a movie theater.

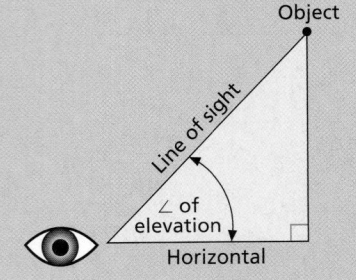

## TRY THESE EXERCISES

**Use trigonometry to find the most reasonable answer.**

**Five-step Plan**
1 Read
2 Plan
3 Solve
4 Answer
5 Check

1. If $m\angle A = 40°$ and $AC = 12.4$, is $BC \approx 9.4$, 10.4, or 11.4? 10.4

2. If $m\angle B = 42°$ and $AC = 9.3$, is $AB \approx 8.7$, 6.9, or 13.9? 13.9

3. **YOU MAKE THE CALL** Emma knows that $m\angle A = 54°$ and $AC = 13$ cm in right triangle $ABC$. She reasons that $m\angle B = 36°$ and, using trigonometric ratios, that $AB \approx 17.9$ and $BC \approx 10.5$. Are her answers reasonable? Explain.
no; $BC \approx 17.9$ and $AB \approx 22.1$

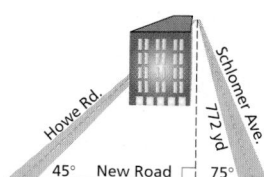

## PRACTICE EXERCISES

**Use trigonometry and the figure for Exercises 1 and 2 to find the most reasonable answer.**

4. If $m\angle A = 12°$ and $AC = 8.5$, is $AB \approx 7.9$, 10.1, or 8.7? 8.7

5. If $m\angle B = 63°$ and $BC = 6.9$, is $AB \approx 12.6$, 15.2, or 19.3? 15.2

6. **BUSINESS** A business developer plans to construct an office near the intersection of Howe Rd. and Schlomer Ave. The two streets will be connected. Is it reasonable for the new road to be 200 yd, 750 yd, or 950 yd? 950 yd

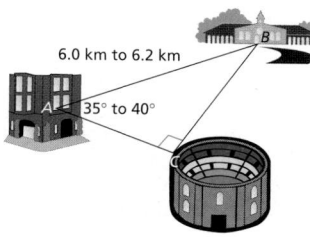

**GEOGRAPHY** Ricki is certain that $\triangle ABC$, whose vertices are an office building, a school, and a stadium, is a right triangle. Her best estimate for $AB$ is between 6.0 km and 6.2 km and between 35° and 40° inclusive for $\angle A$.

7. If Ricki uses 35° for $m\angle A$ and 6.0 for $AB$, is it reasonable to expect that she will get the smallest estimate of $BC$? yes

8. If she uses 40° for $m\angle A$ and 6.2 for $AB$, is it reasonable to expect that she will get the largest estimate of $BC$? yes

9. Estimate $BC$ using each set of measurements in Exercises 7 and 8. 3.4 km, 4.0 km

10. If Ricki estimates $BC$ using $m\angle A = 37.58$ and $AB = 6.1$, is it reasonable to assume her answer will be between the two estimates in Exercise 9? Explain. Estimate $BC$ using these measurements to verify your answer.
Yes; the two estimates used are between the given parameters. 3.7 km

## MIXED REVIEW EXERCISES

**Factor each polynomial, if possible.** (Lesson 9-8)

11. $d^2 - 12d + 36$  $(d - 6)^2$     12. $r^2 + 8r + 16$  $(r + 4)^2$     13. $p^2 - 36$  $(p - 6)(p + 6)$

**Find the sum of the interior angles of each convex polygon.** (Lesson 5-7)

14. 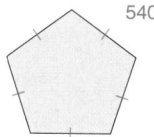 540°     15. 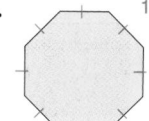 1080°     16. 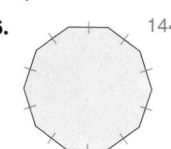 1440°

---

## Chalkboard Examples

### Supplementary Problem

**SPORTS** Sy, Eli, and Al have a map with data about an off-shore island ($P$). Figuring that they can swim at about 3.5 mi/h, Sy thinks it would take about 5 min to swim to the island from point $B$, Eli says 2 min, and Al says 10 min. Who has the most reasonable estimate?

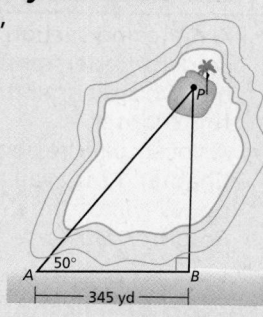

$PB$ represents the shortest distance. At 3.5 mi/h, they could swim about 100 yd/min. Since , $m\angle APB = 40°$, $PB > 345$ yd. So, Eli's estimate is not reasonable.

$$\tan 50° = \frac{PB}{AB} = \frac{PB}{345}$$
$$PB = 345(\tan 50°) \approx 411 \text{ yd}$$

They would need a little more than 4 min. Sy's estimate is the most reasonable.

## Lesson Wrap-up

### QUICK ASSESSMENT

Ask the following question to determine if students understand the contents presented in this lesson.

If you know the measure of one acute angle of a right triangle, how can you tell which is the shortest side of the triangle?   Subtract the known acute angle's measure from 90° to find the other acute angle's measure. The shortest side of the triangle is opposite the smaller acute angle.

---

## Alternative Assessment

**MATH JOURNAL** Have students tell how they would measure the disance from point $P$ to line $\ell$.
Lay a ruler down from $P$ to $\ell$ so that the edge of the ruler is perpendicular to $\ell$.
Note with students that the perpendicular between the point and the line represents the *shortest distance*.

### Vocabulary Assessment

- A matching section checks for student understanding of the new vocabulary introduced in this chapter.
- A vocabulary review/test for Chapter 11 is available on pp. vii–viii of the *Chapter 11 Resource Masters*.

### Lesson-by-Lesson Review

For each lesson,

- the main ideas are summarized, and
- practice exercises are provided.

## EXAMVIEW® PRO

Use the networkable **ExamView® Pro** to:

- Create **multiple versions** of tests.
- Create **modified** tests for *inclusion* students.
- **Edit** existing questions and **add** your own questions.
- Use built-in **state curriculum correlations** to create tests aligned with state standards.
- Change **English** tests to **Spanish** and vice versa.

# Chapter 11 Review

## VOCABULARY

**Choose the word from the list that best completes each statement.**

1. In △*ABC*, *m*∠*C* = 90°. The __?__ of ∠*A* is the ratio of the length of the leg adjacent to ∠*A* to the length of the hypotenuse.  b

2. The __?__ is a method of indirect measuring that is useful on a cloudy day when there are no shadows.  g

3. In △*ABC*, *m*∠*C* = 90°. The __?__ of ∠*A* is the ratio of the length of the leg opposite to ∠*A* to the length of the leg adjacent to ∠*A*.  k

4. In a right triangle, the side opposite the right angle is the __?__.  d

5. __?__ have the same shape, but not necessarily the same size.  i

6. In a right triangle, the sides that form the right angle are called __?__.  f

7. The __?__ relates the lengths of all three sides of right triangles.  h

8. In △*ABC*, *m*∠*C* = 90°. The __?__ of ∠*A* is the ratio of the length of the side opposite to ∠*A* to the length of the hypotenuse.  j

9. Three __?__ are sine, cosine, and tangent.  l

10. Determining a length by using similar triangles is an example of __?__ measurement.  e

| | |
|---|---|
| **a.** | congruent figures |
| **b.** | cosine |
| **c.** | direct |
| **d.** | hypotenuse |
| **e.** | indirect |
| **f.** | legs |
| **g.** | mirror method |
| **h.** | Pythagorean Theorem |
| **i.** | similar figures |
| **j.** | sine |
| **k.** | tangent |
| **l.** | trigonometric ratios |

## LESSON 11-1 ■ Similar Polygons, p. 474

▶ In **similar polygons**, vertices can be matched so that pairs of corresponding angles are congruent and all pairs of corresponding sides are in proportion.

**Determine if each pair of polygons is similar.**

11. 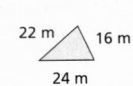 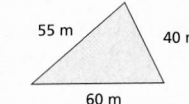  similar

12. 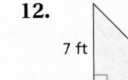 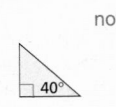  not similar

## LESSON 11-2 ■ Indirect Measurement, p. 478

▶ An indirect measurement is one in which you take other measurements that allow you to calculate the required measurement.

**Use indirect measurement to find the unknown length x.**

13. 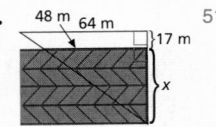  224 ft

14. 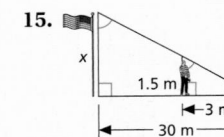  51 m

15. 15 m

## Alternative Assessment

**STUDENT PORTFOLIO** In preparation for this review, suggest that students create their own study aids to organize the information, methods, and formulas given in this chapter. For example, on one side of an index card, students might write a term (such as *sine*) and its definition or formula; on the other side of the card, students can make notes or show examples of when and how the concept is applied.

# LESSON 11-3 ■ The Pythagorean Theorem, p. 484

▶ The **Pythagorean Theorem** states that in any right triangle, the square of the **hypotenuse** is equal to the sum of the squares of the **legs**. In right triangle $ABC$, this property can be stated as $c^2 = a^2 + b^2$.

**Find the unknown length. Round to the nearest tenth.**

16.  15 m, $c$, 9 m, 12 m

17. 35.7 ft, 40 ft, 18 ft, $a$

18. 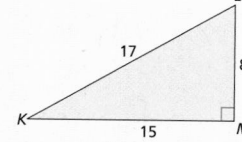 27.5 m, 30 m, 12 m, $b$

19. What is the length of the hypotenuse of a right triangle whose legs measure 13 cm and 6 cm? Round to the nearest tenth. 14.3 cm

# LESSON 11-4 ■ Sine, Cosine and Tangent Ratios, p. 488

▶ For each acute angle in a right triangle, the lengths of the sides can be used to form **trigonometric ratios: sine, cosine,** and **tangent**.

**In △KLM, find each trigonometric ratio.**

20. $\sin K$  $\frac{8}{17}$

21. $\cos L$  $\frac{8}{17}$

22. $\tan L$  $\frac{15}{8}$

23. $\cos K$  $\frac{15}{17}$

24. $\sin L$  $\frac{15}{17}$

25. $\tan K$  $\frac{8}{15}$

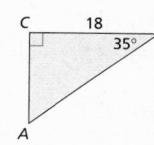

L, 17, 8, K, 15, M

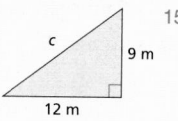 **CALCULATOR** Use a calculator to find each ratio to four decimal places.

26. $\sin 42°$  0.6691

27. $\cos 53°$  0.6018

28. $\tan 22°$  0.4040

# LESSON 11-5 ■ Find Lengths of Sides in Right Triangles, p. 494

▶ If you know the measure of one acute angle and the measure of one side of a right triangle, you can use trigonometric ratios to find the lengths of the other two sides.

**Find each length to the nearest tenth.**

29. $ST$  20.0

30. $SU$  12.1

31. $AB$  22.0

32. $AC$  12.6

T, 37°, 16, S, U

C, 18, B, 35°, A

33. To guard against a fall, a ladder should make an angle of 75° or less with the ground. What is the maximum height that a 20-ft ladder can reach safely?  ≈ 19.3 ft

34. The angle that a wheelchair ramp forms with the ground is 6°. What is the height of the ramp if it is 20 ft long?  ≈ 2.1 ft

## Teaching Tip

In preparation for Exercise 11, elicit that students can write a proportion either by working between triangles for each ratio or working within each triangle for each ratio. Suggest that students first write a word pattern for a proportion, such as:

$$\frac{\text{longest side of small triangle}}{\text{longest side of large triangle}} = \frac{\text{shortest side of small triangle}}{\text{shortest side of large triangle}}$$

Also, remind students that to determine similarity, all three pairs of corresponding sides must have the same ratio.

## LESSON 11-6 ◼ Find Measures of Angles in Right Triangles, p. 498

▶ If you know the sine, cosine or tangent of an angle in a right triangle, you can find the measure of the angle.

**35.** In right triangle *DEF*, cos *D* = 0.25. Find *m∠D*.  ≈ 75.5°

**36.** In right triangle *RST*, tan *S* = 0.7265. Find *m∠S*.  36.0°

**37.** In △*WXY*, *m∠W* = 90°, leg *WX* is 14 in., and hypotenuse *XY* is 20 in. Find *m∠X*.  45.6°

**38.** In △*LMN*, *m∠L* = 90°, leg *LM* is 5 ft, and hypotenuse *MN* is 8 ft. Find *m∠N*.  38.7°

**39.** In △*HIJ*, *m∠H* = 90°, leg *HI* is 22 cm, and leg *HJ* is 9 cm. Find *m∠I*.  ≈ 22.2°

## LESSON 11-7 ◼ Special Right Triangles, p. 504

▶ Sometimes it is easier to use the special geometric properties of a **30°-60°-90° right triangle** or a **45°-45°-90° right triangle** to solve problems than to use trigonometric ratios.

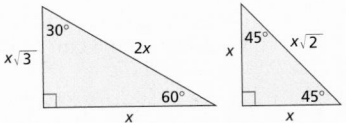

**Find each length. Leave your answer in square root form.**

**40.** *MP* 7    **41.** *MN* 7√2    **42.** *EF* 9    **43.** *DF* 9√3

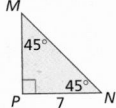
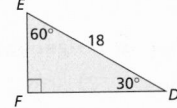

**44.** The length of the hypotenuse of a 30°-60°-90° right triangle is 7.5 m. Find the length of the side opposite the 30° angle.  3.75 m

**45.** The length of one of the legs of a 45°-45°-90° right triangle is 6.5 in. Find the lengths of the other sides.  6.5 in., 6.5√2 or about 9.2 in.

## LESSON 11-8 ◼ Problem Solving Skills: Reasonable Solutions, p. 508

▶ One strategy for solving problems is to **eliminate possibilities**.

**Use trigonometry to find the most reasonable answer.**

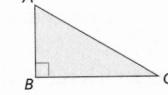

**46.** If *m∠A* = 20° and *AB* = 5.6, is *BC* ≈ 2.04 , 5.9, or 8.7?  2.04

**47.** If *m∠C* = 36° and *AB* = 15.9, is *AC* ≈ 11.2 , 21.9, or 27.1?  27.1

**48.** If *m∠A* = 55° and *AC* = 7.5, is *AB* ≈ 4.3, 8.0, or 13.1?  4.3

**49.** If *m∠C* = 28° and *BC* = 12.3, is *AC* ≈ 5.8, 10.9, or 13.9?  13.9

**50.** If *m∠C* = 26° and *BC* = 26.2, is *AB* ≈ 12.8, 25.4, or 53.7?  12.8

### CHAPTER INVESTIGATION

**EXTENSION** Since most amateur photographers do not carry a tape measure to mark distances, estimating is necessary. Use a yardstick to measure in feet the length of your stride. Take this measurement four times and find the average length of your stride to the nearest quarter foot. Once you know the length of your stride, estimate the number of steps you would take to shoot pictures at the angles of 15°, 28°, and 35°.

---

### THEME: Photography

The benchmarks and expectations for this extension are as follows.
- Students begin a right-triangle diagram to represent a photographer shooting a subject from an upward angle, using the distance between the subject and the ground as one leg of the right triangle.
- Students determine the trigonometric ratio they will use to find the distance between the photographer and the subject.
- Students write and solve trig equations, determining the distance between the photographer and the subject for each angle measure.
- Students use a yardstick to measure the length of their stride, doing this four times and getting an average. Then they estimate the number of steps they would take to shoot pictures at the three different measures.

# Chapter 11 Assessment

**Find the unknown measure in each pair of similar polygons.**

**1.**

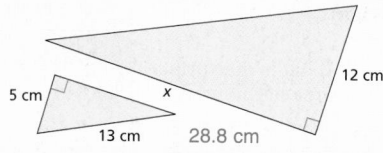

**2.**

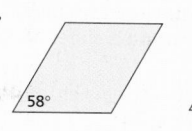

**3.** A flagpole casts a shadow 49.2 m long, while Joe, who is 1.8 m tall, casts a shadow 2.4 m long. How tall is the flagpole?   36.9 m

**Find each unknown measure. Round to the nearest tenth.**

**4.**

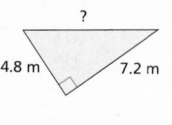

**5.**

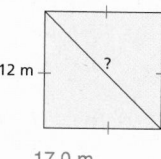

**6.**

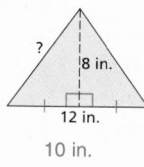

**7.**

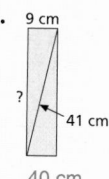

**In △QRS, find each trigonometric ratio.**

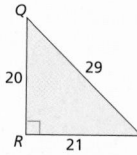

**8.** $\cos S$   $\dfrac{21}{29}$

**9.** $\tan Q$   $\dfrac{21}{20}$

**10.** $\sin Q$   $\dfrac{21}{29}$

**Use a calculator to find each value to four decimal places.**

**11.** $KL$   27.0459

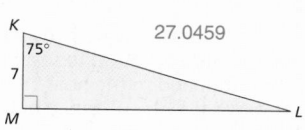

**12.** $m\angle C$   50.1944°

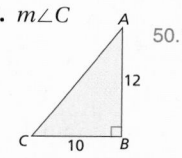

**Find each length. Leave your answer in square root form.**

**13.** $AB$ and $CB$   $5\sqrt{2}$ and 5

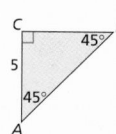

**14.** $YZ$ and $XZ$   $8\sqrt{3}$ and 16

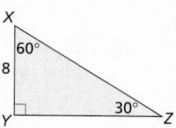

**15.** The length of a kite string fastened to the ground is 86 m. The vertical height of the kite is 52 m. Find the angle that the string makes with the ground. Round to the nearest degree.   37°

**16.** A guy wire is anchored to the ground 95.6 m from the base of a transmitting tower. If it forms a 62.5° angle with the ground, how long is the wire? Round to the nearest tenth.   207.0 m

 **Math Online** mathmatters2.com/chapter_assessment

## Assessment Options

Chapter 11 Test A, pages 373–374
Chapter 11 Test B, pages 375–376

## ALTERNATIVE ASSESSMENT

**HEIGHTS** Have students work in small groups to locate and identify five tall nearby structures or trees. Students should use trigonometry to calculate the heights of these objects. Have students report their findings and an explanation of their calculations.

**RUBRIC** The following rubric is a sample scoring guide.

| Points | Description |
|---|---|
| 4 | Designs a method for measuring heights using the principles of the chapter, and **accurately** applies this method to finding the heights of five tall objects. |
| 3 | Designs a method for measuring heights using the principles of the chapter, and, **with minor errors**, applies this method to finding the heights of five tall objects. |
| 2 | Designs a method for measuring heights using the principles of the chapter, and, **with several errors**, applies this method to finding the heights of fewer than five tall objects. |
| 1 | Attempts to design a method for measuring heights using the principles of the chapter, but **does not apply** it. |
| 0 | Makes **no attempt** to design a method of measuring tall objects. |

## Teaching Tip

In preparation for Exercises 15 and 16, where students have to draw their own diagrams to represent the problem situation, elicit that the basic diagram is a right triangle. Remind students that heights are represented on the vertical leg of the right triangle. In the given situations, the length of the kite string or the guy wire are represented as the length of the hypotenuse.

**Standardized Test Practice**

These two pages contain practice questions in the various formats that can be found on the most frequently given standardized tests.

A student recording sheet for these two pages can be found on p. A1 of the *Chapter 11 Resource Masters*.

## Standardized Test Practice Student Recording Sheet

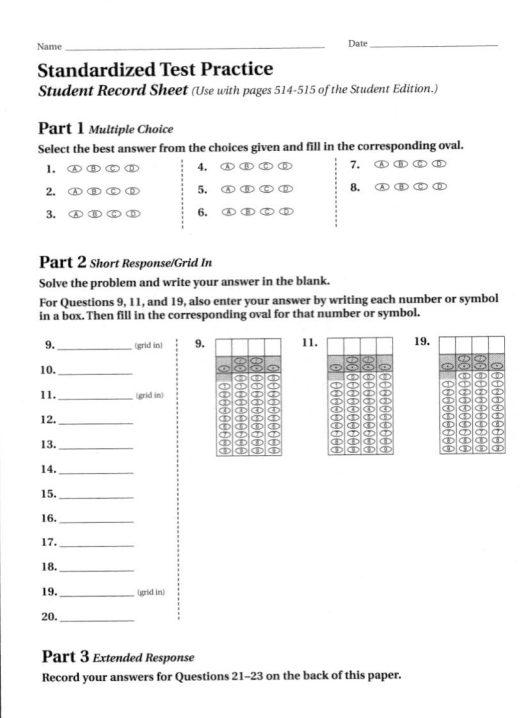

### Additional Practice

See pp. 377–379 in the *Chapter 11 Resource Masters* for additional standardized test practice.

# Standardized Test Practice

| Part 1 | Multiple Choice |
|---|---|

**Record your answers on the answer sheet provided by your teacher or on a sheet of paper.**

1. The high temperature of twelve cities one day in March were 40°F, 72°F, 74°F, 35°F, 58°F, 64°F, 40°F, 67°F, 40°F, 75°F, 68°F, and 51°F. What is the range of the data? (Lesson 1-2) C
   - (A) 75°F
   - (B) 51°F
   - (C) 40°F
   - (D) 11°F

2. Which angle is *not* congruent to ∠1? (Lesson 5-3) C

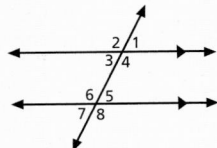

   - (A) ∠3
   - (B) ∠5
   - (C) ∠6
   - (D) ∠7

3. Which graph is the solution of $y > 2x + 1$? (Lesson 6-4) B

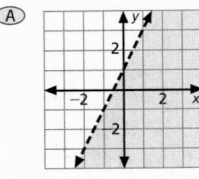 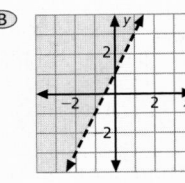

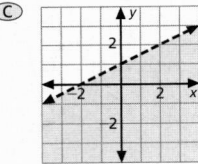 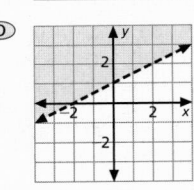

4. If $-5xy + 2x^2y - xy^2 + 4$ is multiplied by $3x^2y$, what is the coefficient of the $x^2y$ term? (Lesson 9-1) D
   - (A) $-15$
   - (B) $-3$
   - (C) 6
   - (D) 12

For Exercises 5 and 6, use the prism at the right.

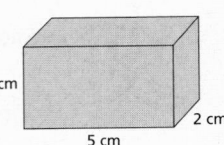

5. What is the surface area of the prism? (Lesson 10-3) D
   - (A) 25 cm²
   - (B) 31 cm²
   - (C) 50 cm²
   - (D) 62 cm²

6. What is the volume of the prism? (Lesson 10-7) B
   - (A) 15 cm³
   - (B) 30 cm³
   - (C) 50 cm³
   - (D) 60 cm³

7. In △PQR, what is the value of tan R? (Lesson 11-4) D

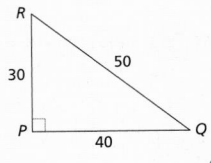

   - (A) $\dfrac{3}{4}$
   - (B) $\dfrac{4}{5}$
   - (C) $\dfrac{5}{4}$
   - (D) $\dfrac{4}{3}$

8. A pole is supported with a guy wire. The wire is secured at the ground to form an angle of 75°. It is attached to the pole 15 ft above the ground. What is the distance between the pole and the place where the guy wire is secured to the ground? (Lesson 11-8) A
   - (A) 4.0 ft
   - (B) 5.6 ft
   - (C) 6.1 ft
   - (D) 15.5 ft

---

**Test-Taking Tip**
(A) (B) (C) (D)

**Question 8**
You can often eliminate incorrect answers. In Question 8, you know that the side opposite the 75° angle must be longer than the side opposite the 15° angle. So you can eliminate answer choice D from consideration since 15.5 ft > 15 ft.

Preparing for Standardized Tests
For test-taking strategies and more
practice, see pages 627–644.

## Part 2 | Short Response/Grid In

Record your answers on the answer sheet
provided by your teacher or on a sheet of paper.

**9.** What is the value of $12(9 + 5) - 6 \cdot 3$?
(Lesson 2-2)  150

The formula $T = 40 + \frac{c}{4}$ shows the relationship
between $T$, the temperature in degrees Fahrenheit,
and $c$, the number of cricket chirps per minute.
Use the formula for Questions 10 and 11.

**10.** If the number of cricket chirps in 1 min is 88,
what is the approximate temperature?
(Lesson 3-1)  62°F

**11.** If the temperature is 75°F, how many cricket
chirps would you expect to hear in 1 min?
(Lesson 3-4)  140 chirps

In a lottery, the jackpot is won by choosing four
numbers between 1 and 50 in the correct order.
Numbers cannot be repeated. Use this
information for Questions 12 and 13.

**12.** How many permutations of the numbers can
be chosen?  (Lesson 4-6)  5,527,200

**13.** A smaller prize can be won if you choose the
4 correct numbers in any order. How many
combinations can be chosen? (Lesson 4-7)
230,300

**14.** The circumference of a circle varies directly
as the length of the diameter. What is the
constant of variation? (Lesson 6-8)  $\pi$

**15.** What is the slope of a line perpendicular to
the graph of $4x - 2y = 2$? (Lesson 8-1)  $-\frac{1}{2}$

**16.** The sum of two numbers is 2. Twice the first
number minus three times the second is -11.
What are the numbers? (Lesson 8-4)  $-1, 3$

**17.** Evaluate the determinant of $\begin{bmatrix} -2 & 3 \\ -1 & 5 \end{bmatrix}$.
(Lesson 8-5)  $-7$

 **Math Online** mathmatters2.com/standardized_test

**18.** In a blueprint, 1 in. represents an actual
length of 16 ft. If the dimensions of the living
room are $1\frac{1}{4}$ in.-by-$1\frac{1}{2}$ in. on the blueprint,
what are the actual dimensions of the room?
(Lesson 11-1)  20 ft by 24 ft

**19.** Find the height of
the lamppost.  (Lesson
11-2)  15 ft
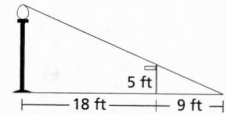

**20.** If the hypotenuse of a 30°-60°-90° right
triangle is 60 cm long, what is the length of
the shorter leg of the triangle? (Lesson 11-7)
30 cm

## Part 3 | Extended Response

Record your answers on a sheet of paper. Show
your work.

**21.** Two cars leave at the same time and both
drive to Nashville. The cars' distance from
Knoxville, in miles, can be represented by
the two equations below, where $t$ respresents
time in hours. (Lessons 6-2 and 9-1)
Car A: $A = 65t + 10$   Car B: $B = 55t + 20$

**a.** Which car is faster? Explain. Car A is faster
because it has a greater speed (slope).

**b.** How far did Car B travel after 2 h? 130 mi

**c.** Find an expression that models the
distance between the two cars. $10t - 10$

**22.** Diego hikes 4 mi north, 5 mi west, and then
6 mi north again. Draw a diagram showing
the direction and distance of each segment of
Diego's hike. At the end of his hike, how far is
Diego from his starting point? Explain how
you determined this distance.  (Lesson 11-3)
See additional answers.

**23.** Explain how you could find the area of the
parallelogram. (Lesson 11-5)  See additional
answers.
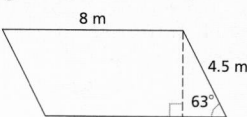

Chapter 11 **Standardized Test Practice** | **515**

## Rubrics

The following rubrics are sample
scoring guides for short response
and extended response questions.

### Short Response

| Points | Description |
| --- | --- |
| 2 | The student demonstrates a **thorough understanding** of the mathematics of the task. The response may contain minor flaws that do not detract from the demonstration of a thorough understanding. |
| 1 | The student has provided a response that is only **partially correct**. |
| 0 | The student has provided a **completely incorrect** solution or no response at all. |

### Extended Response

| Points | Description |
| --- | --- |
| 4 | The student demonstrates a **thorough understanding** of the mathematics of the task. The response contains minor flaws that do not detract from the demonstration of a thorough understanding. |
| 3 | The student demonstrates an **understanding** of the mathematics of the task. The response is essentially correct and demonstrates an essential but less than thorough understanding of the mathematics. |
| 2 | The student has demonstrated only a **partial understanding** of the mathematics of the task. Although the student may have used the correct approach to a solution or may have provided a correct solution, the work lacks an essential understanding of the underlying mathematical concepts. |
| 1 | The student has demonstrated a **very limited understanding** of the mathematics of the task. The response is incomplete and exhibits many flaws. |
| 0 | The student has provided a **completely incorrect** solution or no response at all. |

## ADDITIONAL ANSWERS

**22.**
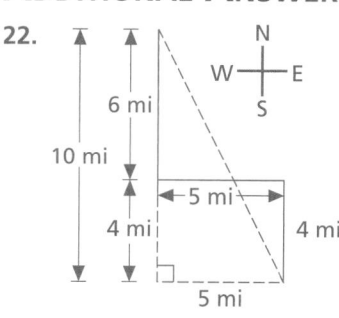

Diego is about 11.2 mi from his starting point. You can
draw a right triangle with legs 5 mi and 6 + 4 or 10 mi
long. You can use the Pythagorean Theorem to find the
hypotenuse. The length of the hypotenuse is Diego's
distance from his starting point.

**23.** Use sin 63° and the right triangle to find the height of
the parallelogram. Multiply the height by the base 8.
The area is about 32.1 m².

## Logic and Sets

**CHAPTER 12**

| Lesson | Lesson Objectives | Pacing (days) | NCTM Standards | State/Local Objectives |
|--------|-------------------|---------------|----------------|------------------------|
| 12-1 | **Properties of Sets** *(pp. 520–523)*<br>• Define sets using different notations.<br>• Explore and use properties of sets. | 1 | 7, 9, 10 | |
| 12-2 | **Union and Intersection of Sets** *(pp. 524–527)*<br>• Find the complement of a set.<br>• Find the union and the intersection of two sets. | 1 | 7, 9, 10 | |
| 12-3 | **Problem Solving Skills: Conditional Statements** *(pp. 530–531)*<br>• Solve a problem using conditional statements. | 1 | 6, 8, 9, 10 | |
| 12-4 | **Converse, Inverse, and Contrapositive** *(pp. 532–535)*<br>• Compare the converse, inverse, and contrapositive of conditional statements.<br>• Determine if conditional statements are true or false. | 2 | 8, 9 10 | |
| 12-5 | **Inductive and Deductive Reasoning** *(pp. 538–541)*<br>• Identify and use inductive reasoning.<br>• Identify and use deductive reasoning. | 2 | 7, 8, 9, 10 | |
| 12-6 | **Patterns of Deductive Reasoning** *(pp. 542–545)*<br>• Identify arguments as valid or invalid. | 2 | 7, 8, 9, 10 | |
| 12-7 | **Logical Reasoning and Proof** *(pp. 548–551)*<br>• Use logical reasoning to prove algebraic statements.<br>• Use logical reasoning to prove geometric statements. | 2 | 7, 8, 9, 10 | |
| Review | | 1 | | |
| Testing | | 1 | | |

**Key to NCTM Standards:**

*1=Number & Operations, 2=Algebra, 3=Geometry,*
*4=Measurement, 5=Data Analysis & Probability,*
*6=Problem Solving, 7=Reasoning & Proof,*
*8=Communication, 9=Connections, 10=Representation*

**Pacing:** Suggestions for the year can be found on page xvi.

# Chapter Resource Manager

**Chapter 12 Resource Masters**

| Reteaching Activities | Extra Practice | Enrichment | Assessment | Basic Mathematics Review | Study Skills Activities | Lesson Warm-Ups Transparencies | Teaching Transparencies | Technology Activities | Materials Needed |
|---|---|---|---|---|---|---|---|---|---|
| 381 | 382 | 383 | | | | 48 | | | slips of paper, bag or box |
| 384 | 385 | 386 | | | | 48 | RF-15 | 12-2 | |
| 387 | 388 | 389 | | | 34 | 49 | RF-1, RF-59 | | |
| 390 | 391 | 392 | | | | 49 | RF-59 | 12-4 | |
| 393 | 394 | 395 | | | | 50 | | 12-5 | calculator |
| 396 | 397 | 398 | | | | 50 | RF-60 | | |
| 399 | 400 | 401 | 405–411 | | | 51 | | | |

**Quick Review Math Handbook, Book 2**

*hot words* *hot topics*

| MathMatters 1 Lesson(s) | Hot Topic Lesson(s) |
|---|---|
| 12-1, 12-2, 12-3 | 5-3 |
| 12-4 | 5-1, 5-2 |
| 12-5, 12-6, 12-7 | 5-1, 5-2, 5-3 |

# Content and Connections

## Connections to the Past

**MM1 (Ch. 3):** Categorize numbers according to sets.

**MM1 (Ch. 5):** Use the additive inverse to solve equations.

**MM1 (Ch. 11):** Draw and use Venn diagrams to solve problems.

**MM1 (Ch. 11):** Write conditional statements and identify them as true or false.

**MM1 (Ch. 11):** Determine the truth value of statements.

**MM1 (Ch. 11):** Use inductive reasoning to make and test conjectures.

**MM1 (Ch. 11):** Identify valid and invalid deductive arguments.

**MM1 (Ch. 11):** Solve non-routine problems involving multiple steps.

## MathMatters 2 Chapter 12 Highlights

Explore and use properties of sets. (12-1)

Find the complement of a set. (12-2)

Find the union and the intersection of two sets. (12-2)

Solve a problem using conditional statements. (12-3)

Determine if conditional statements are true or false. (12-4)

Identify and use inductive reasoning. (12-5)

Identify arguments as valid or invalid. (12-6)

Use logic to prove algebraic and geometric statements. (12-7)

## Connections to the Future

**MM3 (Ch. 1):** Use mathematical symbols to describe sets.

**MM3 (Ch. 1):** Describe relationships among sets and elements of sets.

**MM3 (Ch. 1):** Identify union and intersection of sets.

**MM3 (Ch. 3):** Identify and evaluate conditional statements.

**MM3 (Ch. 3):** Identify and evaluate conditional statements.

**MM3 (Ch. 3):** Use inductive reasoning to complete patterns.

**MM3 (Ch. 3):** Solve a problem using logical reasoning.

**MM3 (Ch. 3):** Write geometric proofs in two-column format.

### Key

PC = Previous Course
MM1 = *MathMatters 1*
MM2 = *MathMatters 2*
MM3 = *MathMatters 3*

### Connecting the Strands

| NCTM Strand | Lesson(s) |
|---|---|
| Problem Solving | 12-3 |
| Reasoning & Proof | 12-1, 12-2, 12-5, 12-6, 12-7 |
| Communication | 12-3, 12-4 |
| Connections | 12-1, 12-2, 12-3, 12-4, 12-5, 12-6, 12-7 |
| Representation | 12-1, 12-2, 12-3, 12-4, 12-5, 12-6, 12-7 |

# Ongoing Assessment and Intervention

| | Type | Student Edition | Teacher Resources | Technology/Internet |
|---|---|---|---|---|
| **INTERVENTION** | Ongoing | Are You Ready?, pp. 518–519<br>Check Understanding, pp. 520, 539, 549<br>Review and Practice Your Skills, pp. 528–529, 536–537, 546–547<br>Mid-Chapter Quiz, p. 537 | Lesson Warm-Ups Transparencies, pp. WU-48, WU-47, WU-49, WU-50, WU-51<br>Quick Assessment, *ATE* pp. 519, 522, 526, 531, 534, 540, 544, 550 | mathmatters2.com/extra_ examples<br>mathmatters2.com/self_check_quiz |
| | Mixed Review | pp. 523, 527, 531, 535, 541, 545, 551 | | |
| | Error Analysis | You Make the Call, p. 541<br>Error Alert, p. 523 | | |
| **ASSESSMENT** | Standardized Test Practice | pp. 556–557<br>Preparing for Standardized Tests, pp. 627–644 | Standardized Test Practice, *CRM* pp. 409–411 | mathmatters2.com/standardized_test |
| | Open-Ended Assessment | Chapter Investigation, pp. 517, 523, 527, 535, 551, 554 | Chapter Investigation, *ATE* p. 554<br>Alternative Assessment, *ATE* p. 555 | |
| | Chapter Assessment | Chapter Review, pp. 552–554<br>Chapter Assessment, p. 555 | Multiple-Choice Tests (Forms A and B), *CRM* pp. 405–408 | mathmatters2.com/chapter_assessment |

**Key to Abbreviations:** *ATE* = Annotated Teacher's Edition, *CRM* = Chapter Resource Masters

## Additional Intervention

***Basic Mathematics Review*** includes 80 lessons, consisting of an instructional page and a test page. This workbook also features a pretest, posttest, table of measurement equivalents, and calculator appendices.

## ExamView® Pro

Use ExamView® Pro Testmaker CD-ROM to:
- Create **multiple versions** of tests.
- Create **modified** tests for *inclusion* students with one mouse click.
- **Edit** existing questions and **add** your own questions.
- Build tests aligned with **state standards** using built-in **state curriculum correlations**.
- Change **English** tests to **Spanish** with one mouse click and vice versa.

# Logic and Sets

## THEME: Music

## NCTM Standards/Strands
- Data Analysis & Probability
- Connections

## Vocabulary

sets        logic

## Theme Connections
A *set* is a collection of items that have some common attribute. Sets offer a way to categorize items in order to think logically about them. Logic provides a way to state relationships between sets. Sets in the field of music to which logic would be applied are: notes to make an arrangement, arrangements to make a concert, and instruments to make a musical ensemble.

## Career Opportunities
Many careers require understanding of the principles of sets and logic. Two such careers are highlighted in the MathWorks features. Others include: detective, computer progammer, meteorologist, musicologist, mechanical engineer, systems analyst, game designer, military strategist.
- Symphony orchestra conductor, page 529
- Professor of music history, page 547

## Internet Connection

### Theme Activities
Mathmatters2.com/chapter_theme provides links to the Internet that will help students gather information about the use of math in the real world, particularly data and measures. To search for additional addresses, begin a search of *music*. Then within that search, use key words that will call up types of music, such as *jazz* or *country/western*; or types of musical ensembles, such as *symphony orchestra*; or particular instruments, such as *violin* or *piano*; or famous concert halls, such as *Carnegie Hall*. In groups, students can brainstorm other key words.

In everyday life, you encounter many types of groups that are arranged in sets. For example, the nutrition that you receive each day comes from food groups consumed in meals and snacks. The music you listen to each day brings together groups of instruments and recording artists to create a pleasing sound.

You can group almost all musical components into sets and arrangements. Notes must be arranged using properties of sets and logic to create a song. The voice ranges in a choir are grouped to produce the perfect sounds. Instruments in a band are arranged so that the sounds complement those instruments in the same area.

- **Symphony orchestra conductors** (page 529) combine subsets of range, sound, and intensity to produce harmonious music.

- A **professor of music history** (page 547) uses sets and logic to teach the timeline of the development of musical instruments.

### Math Online
mathmatters2.com/chapter_theme

## Chapter Investigation
Use the Internet and other resources to locate additional information about musical composers.

## As a Chapter Project
The goal of this project is for students to make a Venn diagram of the musical time period of various composers. Students can use the Group Project Planner on page 403 and the Project Planning Calendar on page 404 in the *Chapter 12 Resource Masters* to complete the project. Benchmarks **a**, **b**, **c**, and **d** should be completed after the lesson listed in parentheses has been studied. Benchmark **e** should be completed at the end of the chapter.

## Range of Frequencies for Selected Instruments and Voices

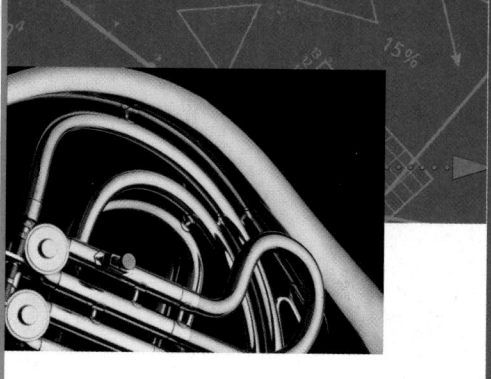

| Instrument | Frequency range (Hz) | Voice | Frequency range (Hz) |
|---|---|---|---|
| Flute | 256-2304 | Soprano | 240-1365 |
| Clarinet | 160-1536 | Alto | 171-683 |
| French horn | 106-853 | Tenor | 128-683 |
| Trombone | 80-840 | Baritone | 96-384 |
| Tuba | 43-341 | Bass | 80-341 |
| Violin | 192-3072 | | |
| Cello | 64-683 | | |
| Double bass | 40-240 | | |

### Data Activity: Range of Frequencies for Selected Instruments and Voices

**Use the table for Questions 1–5.**

1. Which instruments or types of voice are able to produce sounds with a frequency of 950 Hz?   flute, clarinet, violin, soprano

2. Which instrument has the widest frequency range? Which has the narrowest range?   violin; double bass

3. Which voice has the widest frequency range? Which has the narrowest range?   soprano; bass

4. Name an instrument and voice that have the same highest frequency. Which instrument and voice have the same lowest frequency?   cello and alto, cello and tenor, tuba and bass; trombone and bass

5. How could you use frequencies to create new groupings of instruments?   Answers will vary.

### CHAPTER INVESTIGATION

Western music is divided into time periods or eras. Each musical era has specific characteristics of style, theme and genre. The eras include the Middle Ages, the Renaissance, the Baroque Age, the Classical Period, the Romantic Era and the Twentieth Century. Each of these eras and their composers constitute a set. Musical styles gradually change from one era to the next. Cross-over artists are musicians that show characteristics of more than one era in their compositions.

#### *Working Together*

Make a Venn diagram of composers from the Baroque Age, Classical Period and Romantic Era, including crossover composers from each time period. Use the Chapter Investigation icons to guide your group's progress.

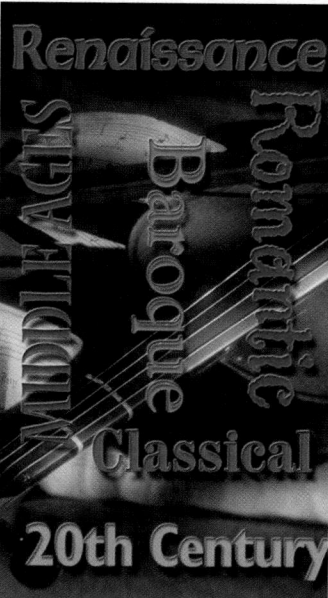

Chapter 12 **Logic and Sets**  517

### Project Planning Calendar

Name _____  Date _____

CHAPTER 12 PROJECT PLANNING CALENDAR

Benchmarks
a. Find and list five composers from the Baroque Age. *(Lesson 12–1)*
b. Find and list five composers from the Classical Period. *(Lesson 12–2)*
c. Find and list five composers from the Romantic Age. *(Lesson 12–4)*
d. Which composer(s) is a cross-over from Baroque to Classical? Which composer(s) is a cross-over from Classical to Romantic? Create a Venn diagram of the composers from these three eras. *(Lesson 12-7)*
e. Find composers from the Renaissance (the time period before the Baroque Age) and the _____ two time periods _____

PROJECT GOAL
To make a Venn diagram of the musical time period of various composers.

### Group Project Planner

Name _____  Date _____

CHAPTER 12 GROUP PROJECT PLANNER

Assignment _____  Objective _____
_____  _____
_____  _____

Group Members          Assigned Roles
1) _____     _____
2) _____     _____
3) _____     _____
4) _____     _____
5) _____     _____

          _____dlines       Done

## Data Activity

Sound is measured in *frequencies*, the number of wave vibrations per second required to produce the sound. Students should answer Questions 1–4 to get a sense of the range of frequencies of selected instruments and voices. Have students consider which professionals associated with the field of music might need this type of information in order to make decisions.   **Possible answers: composers, arrangers, orchestrators, orchestral and choral conductors, instrument makers, music teachers, singers, instrumentalists**

### Extend the Data Activity
**Student Portfolio** Students can research the various categories of musical instruments, identifying the instruments that fall into each category. Or students can find out about such electronic devices as synthesizers. Or students can research the impact of computer technology on such aspects of music as composition and arrangement.

## Chapter Investigation

### As an Overarching Problem
Display information about the different periods of music in the Western World. Discuss differences and similarities about the music from each period. Students will continue to work on the Investigation as they complete the exercises identified by the Chapter Investigation icon that is found throughout the chapter. These exercises will guide students through the tasks described in *Working Together*. Encourage students to keep all of their work on the Investigation together. Have students use the suggestions in the Chapter Investigation Extension to summarize their work.

See page 516 for Chapter Investigation As a Chapter Project.

## Refresher Skills

The skills on these two pages are skills that have been presented in earlier chapters of this book or in previous math courses. Continuous review of basic math skills will make stronger math students. These skills are identified as necessary to be successful in Chapter 12.

### Skills Correlation Chart

| Skill | Lesson Number |
|-------|---------------|
| Venn Diagrams | 12-1, 12-2 |
| Logical Reasoning | 12-3, 12-4, 12-5, 12-6, 12-7 |
| Non-Routine Problem Solving | 12-5, 12-6 |

### Vocabulary

Venn diagrams
logical reasoning
non-routine problem solving

## Chalkboard Examples

### Venn Diagrams

In a Math-Science Honors Program, a school has 25 students studying Calculus, 23 studying Chemistry, and 28 studying Physics. Of these, 4 students are taking all three courses, 5 are studying Chemistry and Physics but not Calculus, 8 are studying only Calculus, and 11 are studying only Physics. How many students are in the program?

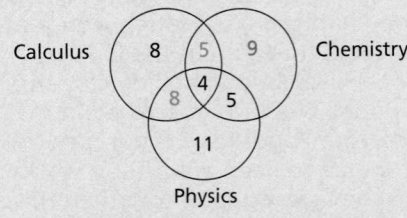

The data shown in black can be filled in directly from the given.
**To fill in Physics:**
$28 - (11 + 4 + 5) = 8$
**To fill in Calculus:**
$25 - (8 + 8 + 4) = 5$
**To fill in Chemistry:**
$23 - (5 + 4 + 5) = 9$
Counting numbers in intersections only once, there are 50 students in all.

The skills on these two pages are ones you have already learned. Use the examples to refresh your memory and complete the exercises. For additional practice on these and more prerequisite skills, see pages 576–584.

## VENN DIAGRAMS

Some problems are more easily solved if you can see a picture of the problem. Venn diagrams provide a clear organized picture of information.

**Example** Of the 30 students on the field trip, 14 ordered pasta salad with their lunch and 22 ordered potato salad. Four students ordered neither pasta salad nor potato salad. How many students ordered both pasta salad and potato salad?

Draw a Venn diagram to help solve the problem.

The diagram shows that 10 students ordered both pasta salad and potato salad.

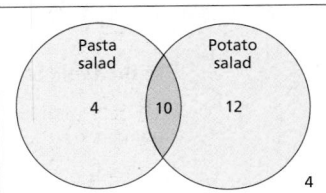

**Use the Venn diagram for Exercises 1–4.**

1. How many students prefer apples over oranges?   36

2. How many students prefer both apples and oranges?   12

3. How many students do not prefer apples or oranges?   8

4. How many students are represented in the Venn diagram?   100

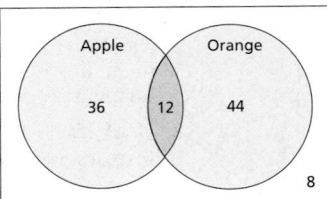

Students' Fruit Preference

**Use the Venn diagram for Exercises 5–9.**

5. How many people have driven a dozer and a forklift, but not a loader?   17

6. How many people have driven a loader and a dozer, but not a forklift?   20

7. How many people have driven only a dozer?   52

8. How many people have driven all three machines?   7

9. How many people have driven none of machines?   12

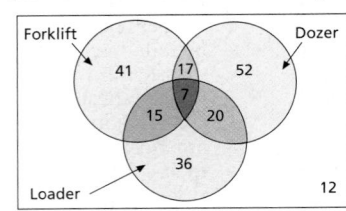

Experience on Heavy Equipment
(Zoo Construction Workers Surveyed)

10. Make a Venn diagram to show the following information. Of 100 people surveyed, 10 like only country music, 8 like only opera and 26 like only rock. Six like country and opera, but not rock. Twelve like rock and country, but not opera. Eighteen like rock and opera, but not country. Twenty people like all three kinds of music.   See additional answers.

## Teaching Tip

Note with students that certain generalizations about logical reasoning can be made and then applied to all cases of that type in a true/false mode. For example, in Exercises 7 and 8, an *or*-statement consisting of two possibilities is given as true. Then, information is given to "discredit" or rule out one of the possibilities. Thus, the other possibility must be the one that is correct.

## LOGICAL REASONING

Logical reasoning involves examining facts and drawing conclusions from the facts.

**Example**   Three cars entered the race: Car 1, Car 2 and Car 3. The drivers in no special order were Karl, Taro and Melinda. At the 100-mi mark, Taro was ahead of Car 3 and behind Melinda. Karl could see Car 2 and Melinda ahead. Who drove each car?

| **Fact** | **Conclusion** |
| --- | --- |
| Taro was ahead of Car 3. | Taro was not driving Car 3. |
| Taro was behind Melinda. | Melinda was not driving Car 3. |
| | **Therefore, Karl was driving Car 3.** |
| Karl could see Car 2. | Karl was not driving Car 2. |
| Karl could see Melinda ahead. | Melinda was not driving Car 2. |
| | **Therefore, Taro was driving Car 2.** |
| | **Therefore, Melinda was driving Car 1.** |

**Draw a conclusion from the following sets of facts.**

11. Miguel has either gym class or chemistry class fourth period. He does not need to change his clothes for his fourth period class.   Miguel has chemistry class fourth period.

12. Natalie will watch one of two movies tonight: Creature From the Slime Pit or Poodles on Parade. She does not like scary movies.   Natalie will watch Poodles on Parade.

13. We have a Dalmatian, a long-haired cat, and a short-haired cat. Pealer does not have long hair, but he barks. Spats has white feet. Trophy sheds long hair. What is the name of each animal?   Dalmation: Pealer; long-haired cat: Trophy; short-haired cat: Spats

14. The Blue Sox baseball team has three men on base. Willie batted first of the three. Gerry's walk on balls forced Juan to move up one base. Which man is on which base?   first base: Gerry; second base: Juan; third base: Willie

## NON-ROUTINE PROBLEM SOLVING

Some problems require you to think logically to determine the correct answer.

**Solve.**

15. Mrs. Miller wants to put up a clothes line 250-ft long. The line requires a pole to support it every 5 ft. How many poles will she need?   51

16. A hat and matching scarf and gloves cost $49 altogether. The hat costs $3 more than the scarf and $2 more than the gloves. What is the cost of each item?   hat: $18; scarf: $15; gloves: $16

17. A target has areas worth 13, 15, 17, 19, 21 and 26 points. Raymond scored exactly 100 points with 5 darts. Which areas did he hit?   Answers will vary. One example is 21, 19, 26, 21, 13.

18. Charlene's piggy bank contains $12.95 in quarters and dimes. There are 95 coins in all. How many of each coin are in the bank?   23 quarters, 72 dimes

Chapter 12   **Are You Ready?**   519

### QUICK ASSESSMENT

Ask the following questions to determine if students have mastered the basic skills reviewed on these pages.

**Draw a conclusion from each set of facts.**

1. Tom or Joe is going to take Sue to the prom. Joe has to be away on the night of the prom.   **Tom is taking Sue to the prom.**

2. All birds have two feet. A toucan is a bird.   **A toucan has two feet.**

**Use logical reasoning to solve each problem.**

3. A 1-mi-long train travels through a 1-mi-long tunnel at a rate of 1 mph. How long will it take the train to pass through the tunnel?   **2 hr; the front of the train emerges from the tunnel in 1 hr, but it takes another hour for the end of the train to emerge from the tunnel**

4. What digit does each letter represent?   S = 9, E = 5, N = 6, D = 7, M = 1, O = 0, R = 8, Y = 2

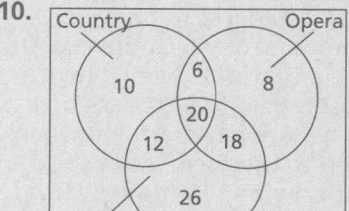

```
  S E N D
+ M O R E
---------
M O N E Y
```

### ADDITIONAL PRACTICE

Refer to the Prerequisite Skills lessons beginning on page 576 for more practice.

### ADDITIONAL ANSWERS

10.

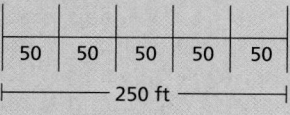

Country    Opera   10   6   8   20   12   18   26   Rock

## Differentiated Instruction

**VISUAL LEARNERS** In Exercise 15, a usual—but incorrect—reaction is to divide 250 by 5, concluding that 50 poles are needed. Point out how effective thinking with a diagram in a simpler case be. Suppose the poles were to be every 50 ft. Then a diagram shows that 6 poles are needed, since one pole is needed at the beginning. Extending this thinking to the larger problems, 51 poles are needed.

| 50 | 50 | 50 | 50 | 50 |
| --- | --- | --- | --- | --- |

⊢————— 250 ft —————⊣

### NCTM Standards/Strands
- Representation
- Connections
- Reasoning & Proof

### Vocabulary

set
element (member) of a set
∈ means *is an element of*
∉ means *is not an element of*
notations: description, roster,
  set-builder
infinite set          finite set
equal sets            equivalent sets
subset, ⊆ or ⊂
empy set (null set), ∅ or { }

### Tools/Materials Needed

slips of paper      bag or box

### Lesson Resources

Warm-up Transparency 48
Reteaching 12-1
Extra Practice 12-1
Enrichment 12-1

## Getting Started

### 5-MINUTE WARM-UP

**Give the next term in each sequence.**
1. 1, 4, 7, 10, . . .   **13**
2. 2, 1, 0, −1, . . .   **−2**
3. 1, 4, 9, 16, . . .   **25**
4. 3, 5, 8, 13, . . .   **21**

### Introduction to Lesson 12-1
Encourage students to be creative in naming sets to which the chosen items belong—for example, pens and erasers belong to the set of things that are never around when you need to use them; eraser and protractor belong to the set of objects whose English names have three syllables.

# 12-1

# Properties of Sets

**Goals**
- Define sets using different notations.
- Explore and use properties of sets.

**Applications**  History, Food service, Music

**Work in groups of four or five students.**
For 1–3, observe students' work.
1. Have each member of the group write the names of two classroom objects, such as eraser and pen, on slips of paper.

2. Put the slips of paper in a bag, and mix them well. Then have each member draw two slips from the bag and describe how the objects are related.

3. After you have finished, put all the slips back into the bag and begin again. This time have each student draw three slips.

### ▨ BUILD UNDERSTANDING

A **set** is a well-defined collection of items. Each item is called an **element**, or a **member**, of the set. A set is usually named with a capital letter and may be defined in three ways.

**Description notation** describes the set.

$W$ = the set of whole numbers

$S$ = the set of even whole numbers less than 20

**Roster notation** lists the elements of the set.

$W = \{0, 1, 2, 3, . . .\}$

$S = \{0, 2, 4, 6, 8, 10, 12, 14, 16, 18\}$

**Set-builder notation** gives the rule that defines each element.

$W = \{x \mid x \text{ is a whole number}\}$

$S = \{x \mid x \text{ is an even whole number less than 20}\}$

A set whose elements cannot be counted or listed is called an **infinite set**. If all of the elements of a set can be counted or listed, the set is called a **finite set**.

**Reading Math**

Braces are used to enclose the elements of a set.

Three dots, or an ellipsis, indicate that the pattern of a set continues.

In set-builder notation, {x|x is a whole number} is read as "the set of all numbers x such that x is a whole number."

### Example 1

**Define each set in roster notation and in set-builder notation. Then determine whether the set is finite or infinite.**

a. $Z$, the set of integers

b. $P$, the set of odd whole numbers less than 10

## Extend the Lesson

**CONNECTING TO PRIOR KNOWLEDGE** Students have been aware of the basic term *set* since their early studies in mathematics. In this text, material on sets has already been integrated where useful—for example, in Chapter 2, the real number system is described in terms of a series of subsets; in Chapter 4, sets appear in the context of probability; in Are Your Ready for Chapter 12, Venn diagrams have been used for problem solving.

## Solution

**a.** Roster notation: $Z = \{\ldots, -3, -2, -1, 0, 1, 2, 3, \ldots\}$

Set-builder notation: $Z = \{x \mid x$ is an integer$\}$

The ellipsis indicates that all the elements cannot be listed, so $Z$ is infinite.

**b.** Roster notation: $P = \{1, 3, 5, 7, 9\}$

Set-builder notation: $P = \{x \mid x$ is an odd whole number less than 10$\}$

All the elements in the set are listed, so $P$ is a finite set.

To show that 5 is an element of the set $\{1, 3, 5\}$, write $5 \in \{1, 3, 5\}$.

To show that 7 is not an element of the set $\{1, 3, 5\}$, write $7 \notin \{1, 3, 5\}$.

### Example 2

**Use set notation to write the following.**

**a.** 5 is an element of $\{0, 1, 2, 3, 4, 5\}$.

**b.** The letter $e$ is not an element of the letters in "banana."

**Math: Who, Where, When**

Georg Cantor (1845-1918) is credited with being the first to develop set theory as a separate branch of mathematical logic.

### Solution

**a.** $5 \in \{0, 1, 2, 3, 4, 5\}$     **b.** $e \notin \{b, a, n\}$

Two sets $A$ and $B$ are **equal sets** (written $A = B$) if they contain the same members. The members of the sets do not necessarily have to be in the same order. Two sets are **equivalent sets** if they contain the same number of elements.

### Example 3

**Determine whether the following sets are *equal* or *equivalent*.**

$S = \{E, G, B, D, F\}$, $T = \{F, B, D, G, E\}$, $Q = \{3, 7, 11, 5, 9\}$

### Solution

Sets $S$, $T$, and $Q$ each contain five elements, so they are equivalent sets. Also, each set is equivalent to itself. Since $S$ and $T$ have exactly the same elements, $S = T$.

If every element of set $A$ is also an element of set $B$, then $A$ is called a **subset** of $B$. Read $A \subseteq B$ as "$A$ is a subset of $B$." Consider the sets $X = \{1, 2\}$, $Y = \{1, 2, 3\}$ and $Z = \{1, 3, 5\}$. All of the elements of $X$ are also elements of $Y$, so $X$ is a subset of $Y$, or $X \subseteq Y$. Not all of the elements of $X$ are elements of $Z$, so $X$ is not a subset of $Z$, or $X \nsubseteq Z$.

Any set is equal to itself. For set $Y$, $\{1, 2, 3\} = \{1, 2, 3\}$, or $Y = Y$. For this reason, every set is a subset of itself. So $Y \subseteq Y$.

Consider $W$, weeks containing eight days. Since no week contains eight days, $W$ has no elements. A set having no elements is called an **empty set**, or the **null set**. To indicate that $W$ is an empty set, write either $W = \{\ \}$ or $W = \varnothing$. The null set is a subset of every set.

 **Math Online** mathmatters2.com/extra_examples

Lesson 12-1 **Properties of Sets** 521

## Chalkboard Examples

**Supplementary Example 1**
Tell whether each sentence is *true* or *false*. Explain your answer.
**a.** 4 is an element of {14, 24, 34, 44} false; all the elements of the set are two-digit numbers
**b.** ● ∈ {○, ◐, ◑, ◒, ◓, ○} false; ● is not one of the elements in this set of symbols
**c.** rhombus ∉ {types of regular polygons} true; a rhombus is not a regular polygon since its angles are not congruent
**d.** $0 \in \{n \mid n$ is a whole number$\}$ true; 0 is a whole number

**Supplementary Example 2**
Tell which of the given sets A–F are equal and which are equivalent.
$A = \{$the sum of 1 and 2$\}$
$B = \{3, 6, 9\}$
$C = \{x \mid x$ is a letter of PEEK$\}$
$D = \{3\}$
$E = \{\triangle, \square, \bigcirc\}$
$F = \{\blacktriangle, \square, \bigcirc\}$

Sets $A$ and $D$ are equal since they consist of the same member. Sets $A$ and $D$ are also equivalent. Sets $B$, $C$, $E$, $F$ are equivalent since each set has three elements.

**Supplementary Example 3**
Draw a Venn diagram to illustrate the following statement.

$A \subseteq C$ and $B \subseteq C$, but $A \nsubseteq B$ and $B \nsubseteq A$.

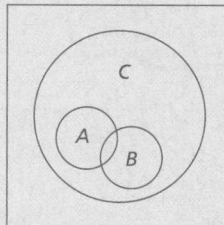

### Teaching Tip

Students should be aware of when the different set notations are useful. For example, to name the set of even numbers from 1 through 1000, it is more desirable to write a description than to write 500 numbers. However, in this case, roster notation can be used if the *ellipsis* . . . is included: { 2, 4, 6, 8, . . . , 1000}. Set-builder notation is useful in writing the solution of an inequality; for example, $\{x \mid x < 7\}$ denotes the solution set of the inequality $2x - 3 < 11$.

## Example 4

**HISTORY** List all of the subsets of the set {World War II, Independence Day}.

### Solution

Each single-element set that uses an element of a set is a subset of that set. Also, the set itself is a subset, and the null set is a subset. So there are four subsets: {World War II}, {Independence Day}, {World War II, Independence Day}, ∅.

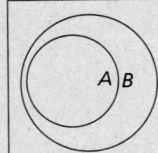
### TRY THESE EXERCISES

**Define each set in roster notation and in set-builder notation. Then determine whether the set is finite or infinite.**   For 1–4, see additional answers.

1. $L$, the set of whole numbers less than 7
2. $W$, the set of whole numbers
3. $P$, the set of positive integers less than 22
4. $R$, the set of negative integers

**Use set notation to write the following.**

5. 3 is an element of $\{3, 6, 9, 12, \ldots\}$.
   $3 \in \{3, 6, 9, 12, \ldots\}$

6. $m$ is not an element of $\{a, e, i, o, u\}$.
   $m \notin \{a, e, i, o, u\}$

7. Determine whether the sets are *equal* or *equivalent*.
   $P = \{1, 3, 5, 7\}$, $Q = \{3, 7, 1, 4\}$, $R = \{1, 7, 3, 4\}$   P, Q, and R are equivalent.
   Q and R are equal and equivalent.

8. List all of the subsets of $\{a, c, t\}$.
   $\emptyset, \{a\}, \{c\}, \{t\}, \{a, c\}, \{a, t\}, \{c, t\}, \{a, c, t\}$

### PRACTICE EXERCISES • For Extra Practice, see page 623.

**Define each set in roster notation and in set-builder notation. Then determine whether the set is finite or infinite.**   For 9–14, see additional answers.

9. $U$, the set of whole numbers less than 15
10. $GL$, the set of the Great Lakes
11. $M$, the set of months having 32 days
12. $V$, the set of vowels in *Figueroa*
13. $K$, the set of integers greater than $-4$
14. $J$, the set of whole numbers greater than 3

**Use set notation to write the following.**

15. 4 is an element of $\{4, 6, 8, 10\}$.
    $4 \in \{4, 6, 8, 10\}$
16. Set $N$ is not a subset of set $M$.   $N \nsubseteq M$
17. The null set is a subset of set $B$.   $\emptyset \subseteq B$
18. Set $R$ has no elements.   $R = \{ \ \}$ or $R = \emptyset$

**Determine if the following sets are *equal* or *not equal*.**

19. $\{r, o, v, e\}$ and $\{o, v, e, r\}$   equal

20. $\{a, b, c, d, e\}$ and $\{c, d, e, 1, 2\}$   not equal

21. Write a set that is equivalent to the pair of sets in Exercise 19.
    Answers will vary but set must have four elements.
22. Write a set that is equivalent to the pair of sets in Exercise 20.
    Answers will vary but set must have five elements.
23. **MUSIC** List all subsets of the set of musical instruments {cello, harp, flute}.
    See additional answers.
24. **WRITING MATH** Explain why the null set is a subset of every set.
    Answers will vary.

**522**   Chapter 12 **Logic and Sets**

## ADDITIONAL ANSWERS

1. Roster notation: $L = \{0, 1, 2, 3, 4, 5, 6\}$
   Set-builder notation: $L = \{x \mid x \text{ is a whole number less than 7}\}$
   finite set
2. Roster notation: $W = \{0, 1, 2, 3, 4, 5, 6, \ldots\}$
   Set-builder notation: $W = \{x \mid x \text{ is a whole number}\}$
   infinite set
3. Roster notation: $P = \{1, 2, 3, 4, 5, \ldots, 21\}$

Set-builder notation: $P = \{x \mid x \text{ is a positive integer less than 22}\}$
   finite set
4. Roster notation: $R = \{\ldots, -5, -4, -3, -2, -1\}$
   Set-builder notation: $R = \{x \mid x \text{ is a negative integer}\}$
   infinite set
9. Roster: $U = \{0, 1, 2, 3, \ldots, 14\}$
   Set-builder: $U = \{x \mid x \text{ is a whole number less than 15}\}$
   finite set

**Determine if each statement is *true* or *false*. If *false*, explain why.**

**25.** $2 \in \{x \mid x \text{ is a whole number}\}$ true

**26.** $8 \in \{1, 3, 5, 7, \ldots\}$
False; 8 is not an odd number.

**27.** $\{8, 12, 16\} \subseteq \{4, 16, 12, 8\}$ true

**28.** $\{x \mid x \text{ is a square}\} \subseteq \{x \mid x \text{ is a rectangle}\}$
true

**29.** If two sets are equal, then they are equivalent.
true

**30.** The empty set is a subset of itself.
true

**31.** If two sets are equivalent, then they are equal.
False; equivalent sets may not be equal.

**32.** The set $\{1\}$ is a subset of $\varnothing$.
False; 1 is an element of $\varnothing$.

 **33. ERROR ALERT** To indicate that 5 is an element of $\{5, 10, 15, 20\}$, Marcellus writes $\{5\} \in \{5, 10, 15, 20\}$. What mistake has Marcellus made? How should he correct it? Marcellus has put brackets around the 5. He should delete the brackets.

**34. FOOD SERVICE** Determine if the sets of lunch specials offered in the cafeteria are *equal* or *equivalent*. $A = \{\text{pizza, meatloaf, lasagna}\}$; $B = \{\text{meatloaf, lasagna, pizza}\}$; $C = \{\text{lasagna, hamburger, pizza}\}$ $A$, $B$ and $C$ are equivalent. $A$ and $B$ are equal.

**Write all the subsets of each set.**

**35.** $\{1\}$ $\varnothing$, $\{1\}$

**36.** $\{8, 9\}$
$\varnothing$, $\{8\}$, $\{9\}$, $\{8, 9\}$

**37.** $\{m, a, t\}$
See additional answers.

**38.** $\{\}$ $\varnothing$

## ◼ EXTENDED PRACTICE EXERCISES

**Determine the number of subsets for each set.**

**39.** $\{1\}$ 2

**40.** $\{1, 2\}$ 4

**41.** $\{1, 2, 3\}$ 8

**42.** $\{1, 2, 3, 4\}$ 16

**43. CRITICAL THINKING** How many subsets does a set of five elements have? How many subsets does a set of six elements have? How many subsets does the null set have? 32; 64; 1

**44. WRITING MATH** Write a rule or definition that expresses the relationship between the number of elements in a set and its number of subsets. If a set has $x$ elements, then it has $2^x$ subsets.

**45. CHAPTER INVESTIGATION** Find and list five composers from the Baroque Age. Answers will vary.

## ◼ MIXED REVIEW EXERCISES

**Find the number of possible outcomes.** (Lesson 4-6)

**46.** Nick has 6 pairs of jeans, 2 pairs of sneakers and 5 T-shirts. From these clothes, how many different outfits can he make? 60

**47.** For lunch, the cafeteria offers 3 entrees, 6 side dishes, 2 salads and 5 drinks. How many different meals are possible? 180

**48.** A new car comes in 7 colors, 4 body styles, with 3 engines and 4 kinds of tires. How many different cars can be ordered? 336

**Use the distance formula to find the distance between the points. Round answers to the nearest tenth.** (Lesson 6-1)

**49.** $A = (5, 3)$, $B = (4, -2)$ 5.1

**50.** $C = (6, -2)$, $D = (4, 3)$ 5.4

**51.** $E = (-4, 3)$, $F = (2, -5)$ 10

**52.** $G = (6, 4)$, $H = (-3, 2)$ 9.2

**53.** $I = (-1, 3)$, $J = (2, -5)$ 8.5

**54.** $K = (-5, 4)$, $L = (4, -5)$ 12.7

**Math Online** mathmatters2.com/self_check_quiz

Lesson 12-1 **Properties of Sets** 523

Lesson 12-1 **Properties of Sets** 523

---

---

**10.** Roster: $GL = \{\text{Michigan, Superior, Erie, Huron, Ontario}\}$
Set-builder: $GL = \{x \mid x \text{ is one of the Great Lakes}\}$
finite set

**11.** Roster: $M = \{ \}$
Set-builder: $M = \{x \mid x \text{ is a month having 32 days}\}$
finite set

**12.** Roster: $V = \{i, u, e, o, a\}$
Set-builder: $V = \{x \mid x \text{ is a vowel in Figueroa}\}$
finite set

**13.** Roster: $K = \{-3, -2, -1, 0, 1, \ldots\}$
Set-builder: $K = \{x \mid x \text{ is an integer greater than } -4\}$
infinite set

**14.** Roster: $J = \{4, 5, 6, 7, \ldots\}$
Set-builder: $J = \{x \mid x \text{ is a whole number greater than 3}\}$
infinite set

**23.** $\varnothing$, $\{\text{cello}\}$, $\{\text{harp}\}$, $\{\text{flute}\}$, $\{\text{cello, harp}\}$, $\{\text{cello, flute}\}$, $\{\text{harp, flute}\}$, $\{\text{cello, harp, flute}\}$

**37.** $\varnothing$, $\{m\}$, $\{a\}$, $\{t\}$, $\{m, a\}$, $\{m, t\}$, $\{a, t\}$, $\{m, a, t\}$

### Vocabulary

universal set
complement of a set
union of sets
intersection of sets
disjoint sets

### Lesson Resources

Warm-up Transparency 48
Transparency RF-15
Reteaching 12-2
Extra Practice 12-2
Enrichment 12-2
Technology Activity 12-2

## Getting Started

### 5-Minute Warm-up

**Tell whether the sets in each pair are equal, equivalent, or neither.**
1. {2, 4, 6, 8}; {8, 6, 3, 2}
   equivalent
2. {s, t, a, r}; {r, a, t, s}   equal and
   equivalent
3. {0}; ∅   neither

### Introduction to Lesson 12-2
From the Venn diagram, emphasize that the 4 students who are in both band and choir are to be counted only once.

## Additional Answers

1.

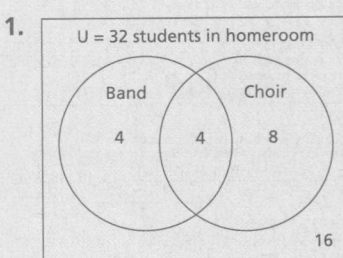

---

# 12-2 Union and Intersection of Sets

**Goals**
■ Find the complement of a set.
■ Find the union and the intersection of two sets.

**Applications**   Biology, Machinery, Cooking, Music

**HOBBIES**  Suppose there are 32 students in your homeroom. Of the 32 students, 8 play in the band, 12 sing in the choir and 4 are in both band and choir.

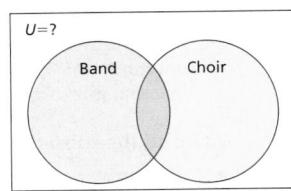

1. Copy and complete the Venn diagram.
   See additional answers.
2. How many students are in band only?   4
3. How many students are in choir only?   8
4. How many of the 32 students are in neither group?   16

### ▨ Build Understanding

In working with sets, you must define the general set of elements being discussed. The set of all such elements is the **universal set**. The universal set ($U$) can be an infinite set, such as the set of whole numbers or the set of real numbers. It can be a finite set, such as {a, e, i, o, u}.

From the universal set, several subsets can be formed.

If $U = \{0, 1, 2, 3, 4, 5, 6, 7, 8, 9\}$, then one possible subset is $A = \{2, 4, 6, 8\}$.

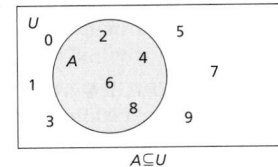

Another subset contains all elements of $U$ that are *not* elements of $A$. This subset is the **complement** of $A$, symbolized as $A'$.

In the universal set above, $A' = \{0, 1, 3, 5, 7, 9\}$.

In set-builder notation, $A' = \{x \mid x \in U \text{ and } x \notin A\}$.

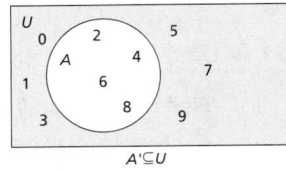

### Example 1

**Use roster notation to represent each complement.**

$U = \{0, 1, 2, 3, 4, 5, 6, 7, 8\}$     $A = \{0, 2, 4, 6, 8\}$     $B = \{1, 3, 5\}$

**a.** $A'$

**b.** $B'$

### Solution

**a.** $A'$ is the set of elements in $U$ that are not in $A$.
   $A' = \{1, 3, 5, 7\}$

**b.** $B'$ is the set of elements in $U$ that are not in $B$.
   $B' = \{0, 2, 4, 6, 7, 8\}$

**524**   Chapter 12  **Logic and Sets**

---

## Extend the Lesson

**CONNECTING TO PRIOR KNOWLEDGE**  Guide students into connecting the concept of *complementary sets* to probability. Ask students for the probability of getting a 4 in one roll of a number cube.  $\frac{1}{6}$

Then ask what a probability of $\frac{5}{6}$ would represent in this context.  the probability of not getting a 4
Have students draw a Venn diagram to represent the situation.

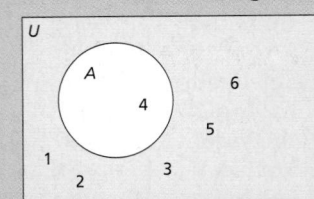

---

Two or more sets can be combined to form new sets. The **union** of any two sets, $A$ and $B$, is symbolized as $A \cup B$ and read as "$A$ union $B$."

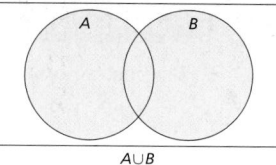

$A \cup B$

The set $A \cup B$ contains all the elements that are in $A$, in $B$, or in both, as shown in the Venn diagram of $A \cup B$.

$$A \cup B = \{x \mid x \in A \text{ or } x \in B\}$$

The **intersection** of two sets, $A$ and $B$, is symbolized by $A \cap B$ and read as "$A$ intersect $B$."

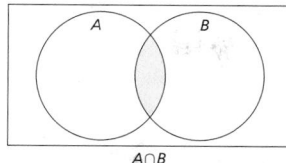

$A \cap B$

The set $A \cap B$ contains the elements that are common to both $A$ and $B$, as shown in the Venn diagram of $A \cap B$.

$$A \cap B = \{x \mid x \in A \text{ and } x \in B\}$$

### Example 2

List the members of each set.

**a.** $C \cup D$

**b.** $C \cap D$

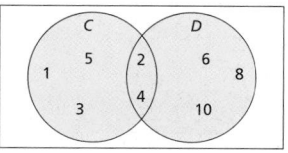

#### Solution

**a.** $C \cup D$ is the set of those elements that are in $C$, in $D$, or in both.

$C = \{1, 2, 3, 4, 5\}$ and $D = \{2, 4, 6, 8, 10\}$

$C \cup D = \{1, 2, 3, 4, 5\} \cup \{2, 4, 6, 8, 10\}$

$C \cup D = \{1, 2, 3, 4, 5, 6, 8, 10\}$

**b.** $C \cap D$ is the set of elements common to both $C$ and $D$.

$C \cap D = \{1, 2, 3, 4, 5\} \cap \{2, 4, 6, 8, 10\}$

$C \cap D = \{2, 4\}$

> **Problem Solving Tip**
>
> The beginning sound of "union" and "intersection" can help you remember what symbol to use.
>
> "U"nion – $\cup$
>
> "In"tersection – $\cap$

If two sets have no elements in common, their intersection will be the empty set, $\varnothing$. Two sets whose intersection is the empty set are called **disjoint sets**.

### Example 3

**BIOLOGY** On a hiking trip, Team A collected the objects indicated by the set $A = \{\text{maple leaves, soil, tree sap}\}$. Team B collected the objects indicated by the set $B = \{\text{river water, flower pollen, oak leaves}\}$. Find $A \cap B$.

#### Solution

No item was collected by both teams, so the two sets are disjoint. Therefore, $A \cap B = \varnothing$.

 **Math Online** mathmatters2.com/extra_examples

Lesson 12-2 **Union and Intersection of Sets** 525

## Chalkboard Examples

### Supplementary Examples 1 and 2

Use roster notation to represent each set.
$U = \{1, 2, 3, 4, 5, 6, 7, 8, 9, 10, 11\}$
$P = \{1, 4, 7, 10\}$
$Q = \{3, 4, 5, 6, 7, 8, 9, 10\}$
**a.** $P'$ $\{2, 3, 5, 6, 8, 9, 11\}$
**b.** $Q'$ $\{1, 2, 11\}$
**c.** $P \cup Q$ $\{1, 3, 4, 5, 6, 7, 8, 9, 10\}$
**d.** $P \cap Q$ $\{4, 7, 10\}$

### Supplementary Example 3

**CRAFTS** In the diagram, $U$ is the set of 9 craft supplies needed to make crafts $A$, $B$, and $C$.

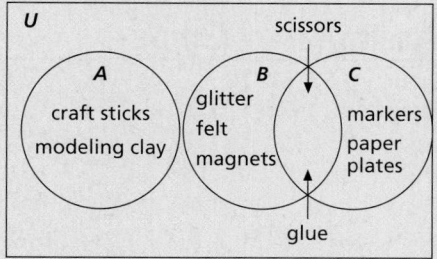

Name each set.
**a.** $B \cup C$ {glitter, felt, magnets, scissors, glue, markers, paper plates}
**b.** $B \cap C$ {scissors, glue}
**c.** $A \cap C$ $\varnothing$
**d.** $A \cup B'$ {craft sticks, modeling clay, markers, paper plates}

## Extend the Lesson

**REAL WORLD CONNECTION** The idea of sets, subsets, unions, intersections, and complements is used often in the life sciences.
Have students research characteristics of groups such as fish, reptiles, and mammals, and then display the relationships among the groups using set notation and symbols.

## Lesson Wrap-up

### QUICK ASSESSMENT

Ask the following questions to determine if students understand the content presented in this lesson.

1. What set will always be a subset of an intersection of two sets?
   **the null set**

2. Can an element of set $A'$ be an element of $A \cap B$? Explain. **No; any element of $A \cap B$ must be an element of $A$.**

3. If $A$ and $B$ are disjoint sets, what can you tell about $A' \cup B'$?
   **$A' \cup B' = U$**

### ASSIGNMENT GUIDE

**Basic:** 1–57, 67–76
**Enriched:** 1–76

---

## Reteaching Worksheet 12-2

Name _____ Date _____

RETEACHING  **12-2**
### UNION AND INTERSECTION OF SETS

If every element of a set $A$ is also an element of $B$, then $A$ is called a **subset** of $B$. The set of all elements considered in a discussion is the universal set, $U$. Suppose that $U = \{2, 4, 6, 8, 10\}$. One possible subset of $U$ is $A = \{2, 4\}$. The set of all elements of $U$ that are not members of $A$ is called the **complement** of $A$, written $A'$.

$$A' = \{6, 8, 10\} \text{ or } A' = \{x \mid x \underset{\text{Read "is an element of."}}{\in} U \text{ and } x \notin A\}$$

**Example 1**
Use roster notation to represent the sets named, given the following.
$U = \{1, 2, 3, 4, 5, 6, 7, 8\}, A = \{2, 4, 6, 8\}, B = \{1, 3, 5\}$
**a.** $A'$    **b.** $B'$
**Solution**
**a.** $A'$ is the set of all elements in $U$ that are not in $A$. So, $A' = \{1, 3, 5, 7\}$.
**b.** $B' = \{2, 4, 6, 7, 8\}$

For any two sets $A$ and $B$, the set of all elements that are elements of $A$, of $B$, or of both is called the **union** of sets $A$ and $B$, symbolized as $A \cup B$.

For any two sets $A$ and $B$, the sets of all elements that are elements of $A$ and also elements of $B$ is called the **intersection** of sets $A$ and $B$, symbolized as $A \cap B$.

**Example 2**
Let $C = \{2, 3, 4, 5, 6, 7\}$ and $D = \{1, 3, 5, 7, 8, 9\}$
**a.** Find $C \cup D$.    **b.** Find $C \cap D$.
**Solution**
**a.** $C \cup D = \{1, 2, 3, 4, 5, 6, 7, 8, 9\}$
**b.** Elements that are members of both sets are 3, 5, and 7. So, $C \cap D = 3, 5, 7$.

**■ EXERCISES**
Let $U = \{1, 2, 3, \ldots, 11, 12\}, A = \{3, 5, 7, 9\}, B = \{2, 4, 6, 8, 10\}, C = \{1, 2, 3, 4\}$, and $D = \emptyset$. Use roster notation to represent the following sets.

1. $A'$ _{1, 2, 4, 6, 8, 10, 11, 12}_   2. $B'$ _{1, 3, 5, 7, 9, 11, 12}_
3. $C'$ _{5, 6, 7, 8, 9, 10, 11, 12}_   4. $D'$ _{1, 2, 3, …, 11, 12} or U_
5. $A \cup B$ _{2, 3, 4, 5, 6, 7, 8, 9, 10}_   6. $A' \cup B'$ _{1, 2, 3, …, 11, 12} or U_
7. $A \cap B$ _∅_   8. $A' \cap B'$ _{1, 11, 12}_
9. $C \cap D$ _∅_   10. $C \cap D$ _∅_
11. $B \cup D$ _{2, 4, 6, 8, 10}_   12. $A' \cap D$ _∅_

**526**  Chapter 12  **Logic and Sets**

---

## ▮ TRY THESE EXERCISES

**Use roster notation to represent each set.**

$U = \{1, 2, 4, 6, 8, 9\}$   $A = \{1, 2, 4\}$   $B = \{4, 6, 9\}$   $C = \{1, 2\}$

1. $A'$  {6, 8, 9}
2. $B'$  {1, 2, 8}
3. $C'$  {4, 6, 8, 9}
4. $A \cup B$  {1, 2, 4, 6, 9}
5. $B \cup C$  {1, 2, 4, 6, 9}
6. $A \cap C$  {1, 2}
7. $B \cap C$  ∅
8. $A \cup C$  {1, 2, 4}

**Find each set by listing the members.**

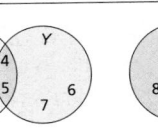

9. $X \cup Y$
   {1, 2, 3, 4, 5, 6, 7}
10. $Y \cup Z$
    {4, 5, 6, 7, 8, 9}
11. $X \cap Y$
    {4, 5}
12. $Y \cap Z$  ∅
13. $X \cap Z$  ∅
14. $X \cup Z$
    {1, 2, 3, 4, 5, 8, 9}

15. **WRITING MATH** Explain how drawing a diagram to represent data can be helpful in naming unions, intersections and complements of sets.
    Answers will vary.

## ▮ PRACTICE EXERCISES  •  For Extra Practice, see page 624.

**Use roster notation to represent each set.**

$U = \{-3, -2, -1, 0, 2, 4, 8\}$   $A = \{0, 2, 8\}$   $B = \{-3, -2, 2\}$   $C = \{-2, -1, 4, 8\}$

16. $A'$  {-3, -2, -1, 4}
17. $B'$  {-1, 0, 4, 8}
18. $C'$  {-3, 0, 2}
19. $A \cup B$  {-3, -2, 0, 2, 8}
20. $B \cup C$
    {-3, -2, -1, 2, 4, 8}
21. $A \cap C$  {8}
22. $B \cap C$  {-2}
23. $A \cup C$  {-2, -1, 0, 2, 4, 8}

**MACHINERY** Find each set by listing the members. Making a diagram may help.
$A = \{$chain saw, tractor, lawn mower$\}$
$B = \{$tractor, table saw, edger, backhoe, chain saw$\}$
$C = \{$hedge trimmer, forklift$\}$
For 24–29, see additional answers.

24. $A \cup B$
25. $A \cap B$
26. $A \cup C$
27. $A \cap C$
28. $B \cap C$
29. $B \cup C$

30. Let $A = \{f, l, o, a, t\}$ and $B = \{b, r, o, t, h\}$. Find $A \cap B$.  {o, t}

31. Let $C = \{2, 4, 8, 16\}$ and $D = \{3, 9, 27\}$. Find $C \cap D$.  ∅

**Use roster notation to represent each set.**

$U = \{1, 2, 3, 4, 5, 6, 7, 8, 9\}$   $E = \{3, 5, 7\}$   $F = \{4, 6\}$   $G = \{2, 4, 6, 8\}$

32. $E' \cap F'$  {1, 2, 8, 9}
33. $E \cap F$  ∅
34. $E' \cap F$  {4, 6}
35. $E \cup F'$  {1, 2, 3, 5, 7, 8, 9}
36. $G \cap E'$  {2, 4, 6, 8}
37. $(G \cup F)'$  {1, 3, 5, 7, 9}

**COOKING** $U$ is the set of eight baking ingredients shown in the diagram. Name each set.
For 38–45, see additional answers.

38. $A \cup B$
39. $A \cap C$
40. $B' \cap A$
41. $C \cup A'$
42. $(C \cup A)'$
43. $(C \cap A)'$
44. $A' \cap B$
45. $(C' \cup A')'$

$U$

| | sugar | |
|---|---|---|
| A milk water oil | B vanilla | C eggs chocolate |
| | flour | |

**526**  Chapter 12  **Logic and Sets**

---

## ADDITIONAL ANSWERS

24. {chain saw, tractor, lawn mower, table saw, edger, backhoe}
25. {chain saw, tractor}
26. {chain saw, tractor, lawn mower, hedge trimmer, forklift}
27. ∅
28. ∅
29. {tractor, table saw, edger, backhoe, chain saw, hedge trimmer, forklift}

38. {milk, water, oil, sugar, flour, vanilla}
39. ∅
40. {milk, water, oil}
41. {eggs, chocolate, vanilla}
42. {vanilla}
43. {milk, water, oil, sugar, flour, vanilla, eggs, chocolate}
44. {vanilla}
45. ∅
46. {1, 4, 6, 8, 9, 10, 12, 14, 15, 16, 18, 20}
47. {6, 7, 8, 9, 10, 11, 12, 13, 14, 15, 16, 17, 18, 19, 20}

**Use roster notation to represent each set.**

$U = \{1, 2, 3, \ldots, 19, 20\}$    $A = \{2, 3, 5, 7, 11, 13, 17, 19\}$    $B = \{2, 4, 6, 8, \ldots, 18\}$

$C = \{1, 2, 3, 4, 5\}$    $D = \varnothing$

For 46–53, see additional answers.

**46.** $A'$          **47.** $C'$          **48.** $B'$          **49.** $D'$

**50.** $A \cap B$    **51.** $C \cup D$    **52.** $B \cap C$    **53.** $A \cup C$

**Let $A = \{x \mid x$ is a real number and $x > -1\}$ and $B = \{x \mid x$ is a real number and $x < 3\}$.**

**54.** On two separate number lines, graph $A$ and $B$.
See additional answers.

**55.** Use set-builder notation to describe $A \cup B$.
$A \cup B = \{x \mid x$ is a real number$\}$

**56.** Use set-builder notation to describe $A \cap B$.
$A \cap B = \{x \mid x > -1$ and $x < 3\}$

**57.** **WRITING MATH** Describe the complement of the complement of a set. Given a set $A$, describe $(A')'$.
$(A')' = A$

## ■ EXTENDED PRACTICE EXERCISES

**MUSIC** Let $A = \{$flute, drums, cymbals, french horn, tuba, saxophone, oboe$\}$; $B = \{$flute, guitar, piccolo, violin, tuba, keyboard$\}$; $C = \{$flute, guitar, tuba, violin, tamborine$\}$; $D = \varnothing$. List the members of each set.
For 58–61, see additional answers.

**58.** $B \cap (C \cap D)$          **59.** $B \cup (C \cap D)$

**60.** $A \cap (B \cup C)$          **61.** $C \cup (B \cap A)$

**CRITICAL THINKING** Determine whether each statement is *true* or *false*. If *false*, provide the correct answer.

$U = \{$whole numbers$\}$    $S = \{0, 2, 4, 6, 8, \ldots\}$    $R = \{1, 3, 5, 7, \ldots\}$    $T = \{1, 2, 3, 4, \ldots\}$

**62.** $R' \cup S = S$  true          **63.** $R \cap S = \varnothing$  true

**64.** $S \cup T = T$  false; $S \cup T = U$          **65.** $R \cup S = S$  false; $R \cup S = U$

**66.** **CHAPTER INVESTIGATION** Find and list five composers from the Classical Period.  Answers will vary.

## ■ MIXED REVIEW EXERCISES

**State whether it is possible to have a triangle with sides of the given lengths.**
(Lesson 5-4)

**67.** 12, 8, 6  yes    **68.** 14, 7, 7  no    **69.** 15, 8, 9  yes    **70.** 9, 5, 5  yes

**71.** 3, 4, 9  no    **72.** 5, 8, 17  no    **73.** 3, 4, 5  yes    **74.** 2, 9, 10  yes

**Find the unknown angle measures in each figure.** (Lesson 5-4)

**75.**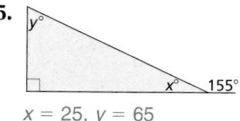
$x = 25, y = 65$

**76.**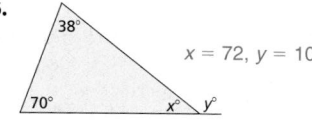
$x = 72, y = 108$

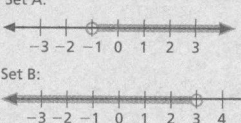

---

## ADDITIONAL ANSWERS

**48.** $\{1, 3, 5, 7, 9, 11, 13, 15, 17, 19, 20\}$

**49.** $\{1, 2, 3, 4, 5, 6, 7, 8, 9, 10, 11, 12, 13, 14, 15, 16, 17, 18, 19, 20\}$

**50.** $\{2\}$

**51.** $\{1, 2, 3, 4, 5\}$

**52.** $\{2, 4\}$

**53.** $\{1, 2, 3, 4, 5, 7, 11, 13, 17, 19\}$

**54.** Set A:

Set B:

**58.** $\varnothing$

**59.** $\{$flute, guitar, piccolo, violin, tuba, keyboard$\}$

**60.** $\{$flute, tuba$\}$

**61.** $\{$flute, guitar, tuba, violin, tamborine$\}$

---

### Extra Practice Worksheet 12-2

Name _____    Date _____

EXTRA PRACTICE   **12-2**
**UNION AND INTERSECTION OF SETS**

✓ **EXERCISES**

Use roster notation to represent each set.

$U = \{-4, -2, 0, 2, 4, 6\}$    $A = \{0, 2\}$    $B = \{-4, 4, 6\}$    $C = \{-2, 0, 2\}$

**1.** $A'$  $\{-4, -2, 4, 6\}$    **2.** $B'$  $\{-2, 0, 2\}$

**3.** $C'$  $\{-4, 4, 6\}$    **4.** $B \cup C$  $\{-4, -2, 0, 2, 4, 6\}$

**5.** $A \cup C$  $\{-2, 0, 2\}$    **6.** $A \cup B$  $\{-4, 0, 2, 4, 6\}$

**7.** $A \cap B$  $\varnothing$    **8.** $B \cap C$  $\varnothing$

**9.** $A \cup C'$  $\{-4, 0, 2, 4, 6\}$    **10.** $B' \cap C$  $\varnothing$

**11.** $A' \cap B$  $\{-4, 4, 6\}$    **12.** $B' \cup C'$  $\{-4, -2, 0, 2, 4, 6\}$

**13.** $(A \cup C)'$  $\{-4, 4, 6\}$    **14.** $(B \cap C)'$  $\{-4, -2, 0, 2, 4, 6\}$

Find each set by listing the members.

**15.** $M \cup P$  $\{0, 1, 2, 3, 4, 5, 6\}$

**16.** $M \cup N$  $\{2, 3, 4, 5, 6, 7, 8, 9\}$

**17.** $M \cap P$  $\varnothing$

**18.** $M \cap N$  $\{5, 6\}$

**19.** $N \cap P$  $\varnothing$

**20.** $(M \cup P)'$  $\{7, 8, 9\}$

**21.** $M' \cap N$  $\{7, 8, 9\}$

**22.** $N' \cap P'$  $\{2, 3, 4\}$

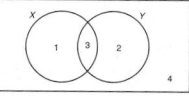

**23.** Let $X = \{c, o, m, p, u, t, e, r\}$ and $Y = \{d, i, s, k\}$. Find $X \cap Y$.  $\varnothing$

Let $A = \{x \mid x$ is a real number and $x < 4\}$ and $B = \{x \mid x$ is a real number and $x > -5\}$.

**24.** On two separate number lines, graph $A$ and $B$. Use your own paper.  Check students' graphs.

**25.** Use set builder notation to describe $A \cup B$.  $\{x \mid x$ is a real number$\}$

**26.** Use set builder notation to describe $A \cap B$.  $\{x \mid x$ is a real number and $-5 < x < 4\}$

---

### Enrichment Worksheet 12-2

Name _____    Date _____

ENRICHMENT   **12-2**
**VENN DIAGRAMS AND OPERATIONS WITH SETS**

Venn diagrams are a useful way to visualize the union and intersection of sets and their complements. The diagram at the right can be used to represent the union and intersection of two sets, $X$ and $Y$. Circle $X$ represents set $X$. Circle $Y$ represents set $Y$. Region 1 represents elements that are members only of set $X$. Region 2 represents elements that are members only of set $Y$.

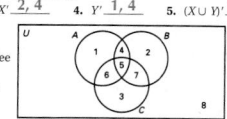

✓ **EXERCISES**

Name the region or regions that represent the following.

**1.** $X \cap Y$  3    **2.** $X \cup Y$  1, 2, 3    **3.** $X'$  2, 4    **4.** $Y'$  1, 4    **5.** $(X \cup Y)'$  4

The diagram at the right can be used to represent the union and intersection of three sets, $A$, $B$, and $C$. Notice that the three sets create 8 regions. Region 1 includes elements that are members only of set $A$.

**6.** What region represents elements that are members only of $B$?  2

**7.** What region represents elements that are members only of $C$?  3

Name the region or regions that represent the following.

**8.** $A \cup B$  1, 2, 4, 5, 6, 7    **9.** $A \cup C$  1, 3, 4, 5, 6, 7    **10.** $A \cap B$  4, 5

**11.** $A \cap C$  5, 6    **12.** $A \cap B \cap C$  5    **13.** $A \cup B \cup C$  1, 2, 3, 4, 5, 6, 7

**14.** $A'$  2, 3, 7, 8    **15.** $B'$  1, 3, 6, 8    **16.** $A' \cap B$  2, 7

Use the eight regions of the second diagram to show that the following properties of sets are true.

**17.** $A \cup B = B \cup A$  1, 2, 4, 5, 6, 7 = 1, 2, 4, 5, 6, 7    **18.** $A \cap B = B \cap A$  4, 5 = 4, 5

**19.** $A \cup (B \cup C) = (A \cup B) \cup C$  1, 2, 3, 4, 5, 6, 7 = 1, 2, 3, 4, 5, 6, 7

**20.** $A \cap (B \cap C) = (A \cap B) \cap C$  5 = 5

**21.** $A \cap (B \cup C) = (A \cap B) \cup (A \cap C)$  4, 5, 6 = 4, 5, 6

**22.** $A \cup (B \cap C) = (A \cup B) \cap (A \cup C)$  1, 4, 5, 6, 7 = 1, 4, 5, 6, 7

## Vocabulary Review

**Lesson 12-1**
set
element (member) of a set
$\in$ means *is an element of*
$\notin$ means *is not an element of*
notations: description, roster,
  set-builder
infinite set        finite set
equal sets          equivalent sets
subset, $\subseteq$ or $\supseteq$
empy set (null set), $\varnothing$ or { }

**Lesson 12-2**
universal set
complement of a set
union of sets
intersection of sets
disjoint sets

## ASSIGNMENT GUIDE

All students: 1–34

## Chalkboard Examples

### Lesson 12-1
Draw a Venn diagram to illustrate
the following statement.
$$A \subseteq B \subseteq C$$

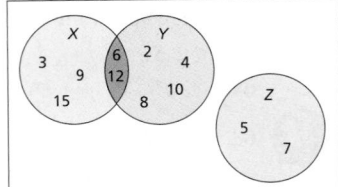

### Lesson 12-2
**Write the complement of each set.**
a. $U = $ {multiples of 3 between 10
   and 30} with $A = $ {12, 30}
   $A' = $ **{15, 18, 21, 24, 27}**
b. $U = $ {integers} with $S = $ {negative
   integers}  $S' = $ **{nonnegative
   integers}**
c. $U = $ {types of regular quadrilater-
   als} with $B = $ {square}  $B' = \varnothing$

---

# Review and Practice Your Skills

## PRACTICE ◼ LESSON 12-1

**Define each set in roster notation and in set-builder notation. Then determine whether the set is finite or infinite.**
For 1–6, see additional answers.

1. $M$, the set of months having 30 days
2. $C$, the set of consonants in *achieve*
3. $S$, the set of integers greater than $-10$
4. $T$, the set of whole numbers greater than 3
5. $P$, the set of positive integers less than 18
6. $O$, the set of odd one-digit numbers

**Use set notation to write the following.**

7. $C$ is a subset of $E$.  $C \subseteq E$
8. $e$ is not an element of {$a, b, c, d$}.
   $e \notin \{a, b, c, d\}$
9. Set $M$ has no elements.  $M = \{ \}$
10. 5 is an element of {5, 10, 15, 20, . . .}.
    $5 \in \{5, 10, 15, 20, . . .\}$
11. List all of the subsets of {$e, f, g$}.
    $\varnothing$, {$e$}, {$f$}, {$g$}, {$e, f$}, {$e, g$}, {$f, g$}, {$e, f, g$}

## PRACTICE ◼ LESSON 12-2

**Use roster notation to represent each set.**

$U = \{-5, -3, -1, 0, 1, 3, 5\}, A = \{1, 3, 5\}, B = \{-5, -3, -1\}, C = \{0, 1\}$

12. $A'$  {$-5, -3, -1, 0$}
13. $B'$  {$0, 1, 3, 5$}
14. $C'$  {$-5, -3, -1, 3, 5$}
15. $A \cup B$  {$-5, -3, -1, 1, 3, 5$}
16. $B \cup C$  {$-5, -3, -1, 0, 1$}
17. $A \cap C$  {1}
18. $B \cap C$  $\varnothing$
19. $A \cup C$  {$0, 1, 3, 5$}

**Find each set by listing the members.**

20. $X \cup Y$  {2, 3, 4, 6, 8, 9, 10, 12, 15}
21. $Y \cup Z$  {2, 4, 5, 6, 7, 8, 10, 12}
22. $X \cap Y$  {6, 12}
23. $Y \cap Z$  $\varnothing$
24. $X \cap Z$  $\varnothing$
25. $X \cup Z$  {3, 5, 6, 7, 9, 12, 15}

26. Let $A = $ {f, l, o, w, e, r} and $B = $ {r, o, s, e}. Find $A \cap B$.
    {o, e, r}
27. Let $C = $ {0, 3, 6, 9} and $T = $ {2, 4, 6, 8}. Find $C \cup T$.
    {0, 2, 3, 4, 6, 8, 9}

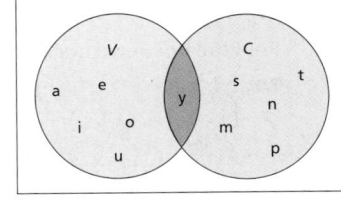

## PRACTICE ◼ LESSON 12-1–LESSON 12-2

**Use set notation to write the following.** (Lesson 12-1)

28. 6 is an element of {2, 4, 6, 8, . . .}
    $6 \in \{2, 4, 6, 8, . . .\}$
29. Set $D$ is a subset of set $E$  $D \subseteq E$
30. Set $M$ has no elements.
    $M = \{ \}$

**Find each set by listing the members.** (Lesson 12-2)

31. $V$  {a, e, i, o, u, y}
32. $V'$  {m, n, p, s, t}
33. $V \cup C$
    {a, e, i, o, u, y, m, n, p, s, t}
34. $V \cap C$  {y}

---

## Extend the Lesson

**CHALLENGE** For Exercise 1–6, for each given set, ask students to name a subset and a *superset* of which the given set is a subset. Set $A$ is a superset of set $B$ if every element of $B$ is in $A$.

**Example** In Exercise 1, $M = $ {months having 30 days}.
{months having 30 days that end in *ber*} is a subset of $M$.
$M$ is a subset of {12 months of the year}.

## MathWorks — Career – Symphony Orchestra Conductor
### Workplace Knowhow

A symphony orchestra is composed of instruments grouped into four subsets: woodwinds, brass, percussion and strings. A conductor directs the tempo of a musical piece and cues the musicians. They must also understand the range, sound, and intensity of each instrument in order to produce harmony among them. An orchestra conductor must sometimes arrange subsets of the full orchestra to perform for private or community events.

#### Subsets of a Full Symphony Orchestra

| Woodwinds | Brass | Percussion | Strings |
|---|---|---|---|
| Clarinet | Trumpet | Timpani | Violin |
| Bass Clarinet | Trombone | Snare drum | Viola |
| Bassoon | Tuba | Glockenspiel | Cello |
| Contrabassoon | Horn | Bass drum | Bass |
| Flute | | Triangle | Harp |
| Oboe | | Cymbals | |
| Piccolo | | Celesta | |
| English horn | | Piano | |

**Use the information in the table for Exercises 1 and 2.**
For 1–3, see additional answers.
1. A couple would like a chamber group to perform during a wedding ceremony. They would like the group to consist of two different brass instruments and three different string instruments. List two possible configurations for the chamber group.

2. For the opening of the new civic center, the city would like a quartet of four woodwind players to perform. Two of the four instruments must be the same and the remaining two should be different. List three possible groups using all of the instruments from the woodwind subset of the orchestra.

During the summer months, a Pops orchestra is formed using the same instruments as a full symphony, but composed of performers from a variety of backgrounds. Some instrumentalists perform only during the summer with the Pops. Others participate in the Pops as well as the symphony.

3. If the "universe" (in mathematical terms) is considered all the performers in the Pops or the Symphony Orchestra, draw a Venn diagram representing these two groups.

4. When both the Pops and the Symphony Orchestra perform together, this is considered the __?__ of these two sets. When only the members belonging to both groups perform together, this is considered the __?__ of the two sets.
union; intersection

Math Online mathmatters2.com/mathworks

### MathWorks

The development and standardization of the modern orchestra took place between about 1600 and about 1750. The New York Philharmonic, founded in 1842, is the oldest symphony orchestra in the United States. Its home is at New York City's Lincoln Center for the Performing Arts and it has more than 100 members.

Students should answer Questions 1–4 to better understand how sets that categorize musical instruments can be used to form musical ensembles.

Although orchestras in their earliest years were anonymous entities, in the mid-19th and 20th centuries, they became associated with the strong personalities of the conductors.

Students might research and report on some famous conductors, such as Leonard Bernstein or Arturo Toscanini.

Students who are interested in learning more about this career choice can go to mathmatters2.com/mathworks. School Guidance Counselors are another resource for information about training requirements and appropriate schools.

### MATHWORKS

1. Sample answer: trumpet, trombone, violin, viola, cello; tuba, trombone, violin, bass, cello
2. Sample answer: clarinet, flute, flute, English horn; bassoon, clarinet, clarinet, oboe; bass clarinet, English horn, English horn, flute

3.
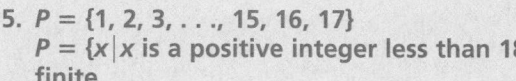
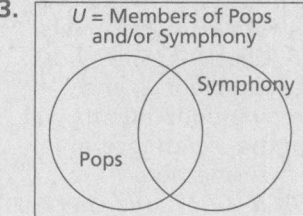
U = Members of Pops and/or Symphony

Symphony

Pops

1. $M$ = {April, June, September, November}
   $M = \{x \mid x$ is a month having 30 days}
   finite
2. $C = \{c, h, v\}$
   $C = \{x \mid x$ is a consonant in *achieve*}
   finite
3. $S = \{-9, -8, -7, \ldots\}$
   $S = \{x \mid x$ is an integer greater than $-10\}$
   infinite
4. $T = \{4, 5, 6, \ldots\}$
   $T = \{x \mid x$ is a whole number greater than 3}
   infinite

5. $P = \{1, 2, 3, \ldots, 15, 16, 17\}$
   $P = \{x \mid x$ is a positive integer less than 18}
   finite
6. $O = \{1, 3, 5, 7, 9\}$
   $O = \{x \mid x$ is an odd one-digit number}
   finite

## Lesson Planning

### NCTM Standards/Strands
- Problem Solving
- Representation
- Connections
- Communication

### Vocabulary
conditional statement (if-then)
converse          counterexample
guess and check

### Lesson Resources
Warm-up Transparency 47
Transparency RF-1, 59
Reteaching 12-3
Extra Practice 12-3
Enrichment 12-3

## ASSIGNMENT GUIDE
**Basic:** 1–20
**Enriched:** 1–20

## Getting Started

### 5-MINUTE WARM-UP
**Tell if each statement is *true* or *false*.**
1. If $2x + 3 = 11$, then $x = 7$.
   false
2. If a triangle is equilateral, then
   it is equiangular.   true
3. If a quadrilateral is equilateral,
   then it is equiangular.   false

**THE FIVE-STEP PLAN** Read—ask
questions to help students understand the problem. **Plan**—guide
students to related problems and
previously mastered skills and strategies. **Solve**—students solve problem
on their own. **Answer**—write the
solution in a format that answers
the question. **Check**—review work,
check for reasonableness, and
review strategy used. Students will
benefit from the experience of
verbalizing their methods.
**THE STRATEGY** *Guess and check*—
finding a counterexample, one
that satisfies the hypothesis of a
conditional statement but not the
conclusion, enables students to
determine that a conditional
statement is false.

**530**   Chapter 12   **Logic and Sets**

---

An *if-then* statement is called a **conditional statement**. Conditional
statements have two parts, a *hypothesis* and a *conclusion*. Statements
that are not in the form of conditional statements can sometimes be
rephrased as *if-then* statements.

hypothesis                              conclusion

If **two lines are perpendicular**, then **the lines form four right angles**.

Another conditional statement can be formed by interchanging the
hypothesis and conclusion of the original statement. The second
statement is called the **converse** of the original.

hypothesis                              conclusion

If **two lines form four right angles**, then **the lines are perpendicular**.

A conditional statement may be either true or false. To show that a
conditional statement is false, find a **counterexample**. This is an
instance that satisfies the hypothesis but not the conclusion. Just one
counterexample proves that the conditional statement is false.

Finding a counterexample is a way of guessing an answer and then
checking it. Determining the truth of a conditional statement is a form
of the **guess and check** problem solving strategy.

### Problem

**Refer to the following statement.**

Two right angles are congruent.

a. Rephrase the statement as an *if-then* statement.

b. Write the converse.

c. Determine if the statement and its converse are *true* or *false*.
   If *false*, give a counterexample.

### Solve the Problem

a. If two angles are right angles, then the angles are congruent.

b. *Converse:* If two angles are congruent, then the angles are
   right angles.

c. The original statement is true since all right angles measure
   90°. The converse, however, is false. A counterexample would
   be two angles that both measure 30°. They are two congruent
   angles, but they are not right angles.

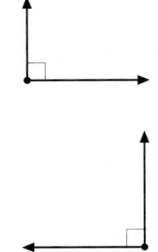

**530**   Chapter 12   **Logic and Sets**

---

## ADDITIONAL ANSWERS

1. If the product of two numbers is positive,
   then the two numbers are negative.
   (Converse)
   Statement: true
   Converse: false; Example: $3 \cdot 4 = 12$
2. If there is a cloud in the sky, then it is
   raining. (Converse)
   Statement: true
   Converse: false; It can be a cloudy day
   without any rainfall.

3. If a triangle is isosceles, then it has two
   congruent sides. (Converse)
   Statement: true
   Converse: true
4. If the sum of two numbers is even, then
   the two numbers are even.
5. If an object is thrown into the air, then it
   will fall back down to the ground.
6. If $a$ does not equal zero, then $a$ is a negative number. (Converse)
   Statement: true
   Converse: false; Example $a = 7$

Write the converse of each statement. Then determine whether the statement and its converse are *true* or *false*. If *false*, give a counterexample.
For 1–3, see additional answers.

1. If two numbers are negative, then their product is positive.

2. If it is raining, then there is a cloud in the sky.

3. If a triangle has two congruent sides, then it is isosceles.

**Rephrase each statement as an *if-then* statement.**
For 4–5, see additional answers.

4. **NUMBER SENSE** Two numbers whose sum is even are even.

5. **PHYSICS** All objects thrown into the air will fall back to the ground.

**Five-step Plan**
1 Read
2 Plan
3 Solve
4 Answer
5 Check

■ PRACTICE EXERCISES

Write the converse of each statement. Then determine whether the statement and its converse are *true* or *false*. If *false*, give a counterexample.
For 6–8, see additional answers.

6. If $a$ is a negative number, then $a$ does not equal zero.

7. If $3b + 7 = 25$, then $b = 6$.

8. If the only factors of a positive number are 1 and itself, then the number is prime.

**Rephrase each statement as an *if-then* statement.**
For 9–12, see additional answers.

9. All squares are rectangles.

10. Paintings by Monet are masterpieces.

11. To climb the wall you need a ladder.

12. Toothbrushing prevents cavities.

13. **WRITING MATH** Describe the relationship between a conditional statement and its converse. If a statement is true, is the converse necessarily true?
See additional answers.

**DATA FILE** For Exercises 14 and 15, refer to the data on audible frequency ranges on page 561. Use this information to complete the conditional statements.

14. If a dog is able to hear a noise, then the noise is at least __?__ Hz.
15

15. If a noise is emitted at 235 Hz, then it will sound as loud as __?__.
a human

■ MIXED REVIEW EXERCISES

16. There are 7 horses in the parade. If they march single file, how many possible ways can they be ordered? (Lesson 4-6)  5040

17. Of the 14 students trying out for volleyball, only 5 will be selected to join the team. How many groups of students can be selected? (Lesson 4-6)  2002

**Solve each system of equations.** (Lesson 8-2–Lesson 8-4)

18. $y = 3x - 9$  (2, −3)
$y = -x - 1$

19. $y = 2x - 5$  (4, 3)
$y = 3x - 9$

20. $y = -x - 3$  (−5, 2)
$y = 2x + 12$

## Chalkboard Examples

### Supplementary Problem
Refer to the following statement.

People living in Iowa live in the U.S.

a. Rephrase the statement as an if-then statement.  **If a person lives in Iowa, then that person lives in the USA.**

b. Write the converse of the statement.  **If a person lives in the USA, then that person lives in Iowa.**

c. Determine if the statement and its converse are true or false. If false, give a counterexample.  **The statement is true, but the converse is false. Counterexample: the person could live in California**

## Lesson Wrap-up

### QUICK ASSESSMENT
Ask the following questions to determine if students understand the contents presented in this lesson.

**Identify the hypothesis and conclusion in each statement.**

1. I will carry my umbrella if it is raining.  **hypothesis: it is raining  conclusion: I will carry my umbrella**

2. The legs of an isosceles triangle are congruent.  **hypothesis: a triangle is isosceles  conclusion: the triangle has congruent legs**

## Teaching Tip

**ESL/LEP** The statements in this lesson and in the remaining lessons in this chapter involve vocabulary that may be difficult for these students. You may want to have these students work with others who can help them to understand the meaning of the statements before they begin.

7. If $b = 6$, then $3b + 7 = 25$. (Converse)
Statement: true   Converse: true

8. If a positive number is prime, then the only factors of the number are 1 and itself. (Converse)
Statement: true   Converse: true

9. If a figure is a square, then it is a rectangle.

10. If a painting is a work of Monet's, then it is a masterpiece.

11. If you intend to climb the wall, then you will need a ladder.

12. If you will brush your teeth, then you will prevent cavities.

13. A conditional statement has a hypothesis and a conclusion. The converse of the original statement interchanges the conclusion and the hypothesis. If a statement is true, the converse is not necessarily true.

# 12-4 Converse, Inverse, and Contrapositive

**Goals**
- Compare the converse, inverse, and contrapositive of conditional statements.
- Determine if conditional statements are true or false.

**Applications**   Advertising, Weather, Music, Geography

**Read each pair of statements.**

**a.** If the instrument is a guitar, then it has strings.
If the instrument has strings, then it is a guitar.

**b.** If the instrument is a guitar, then it has strings.
If the instrument is not a guitar, then it does not have strings.

**c.** If the instrument is a guitar, then it has strings.
If the instrument does not have strings, then it is not a guitar.

1. In which pair(s) are both statements true?   c

2. In which pair(s) is only one statement true?   a, b

## ▨ BUILD UNDERSTANDING

Any statement can be negated. To write the **negation** of a statement, add "not" to the statement or add the words "It is not the case that..."

*Statement*  The instrument is a guitar.
*Negation*  The instrument is not a guitar.
*Negation*  It is not the case that the instrument is a guitar.

In logic, the letters *p* and *q* are often used to symbolize statements. The negation can then be symbolized as ~*p* or ~*q*, read "not *p*" or "not *q*." If a statement is true, its negation is false. If a statement is false, then its negation is true.

### Problem Solving Tip

The negation of a negative statement is a positive statement.

For example, the negation of "It is not raining," is "It is raining."

### Example 1

**Write the negation of the statement two ways.**

*Statement*  The instrument has strings.

### Solution

*Negation*  The instrument does **not** have strings.
*Negation*  **It is not the case that** the instrument has strings.

Three related conditional statements can be made from a given statement. Consider the statement: *If you are in Chicago, then you are in Illinois.*
  Let *p* stand for the hypothesis, *you are in Chicago.*
  Let *q* stand for the conclusion, *you are in Illinois.*
  Use the symbol → to represent the *if-then* relationship.

**532**  Chapter 12 **Logic and Sets**

---

**ADDITIONAL ANSWERS** (Exercises beginning on page 534)

1. The trumpet is not a brass instrument. It is not the case that the trumpet is a brass instrument.
2. The number 14 is not divisible by 3. It is not the case that the number 14 is divisible by 3
3. Cars do not all have four wheels. It is not the case that all cars have four wheels.
4. Baseball is not America's favorite pasttime. It is not the case that baseball is America's favorite pasttime.
5. Converse: If a plant has leaves, then it is a tree; false; counterexample: geranium.
Inverse: If a plant is not a tree, then it does not have leaves; false; counterexample: fern.
Contrapositive: If a plant does not have leaves, then it is not a tree; false; counterexample: pine tree.

**Statement**  If you are in Chicago, then you are in Illinois.
     If $p$, then $q$.          $p \rightarrow q$

**Converse**  If you are in Illinois, then you are in Chicago.
     If $q$, then $p$.          $q \rightarrow p$

**Inverse**  If you are not in Chicago, then you are not in Illinois.
     If $\sim p$, then $\sim q$.       $\sim p \rightarrow \sim q$

**Contrapositive**  If you are not in Illinois, then you are not in Chicago.
     If $\sim q$, then $\sim p$.       $\sim q \rightarrow \sim p$

Recall that the converse of a true conditional statement is not necessarily true.

## Example 2

**WEATHER** Write the inverse of the statement, and tell whether it is *true* or *false*. Explain.

*Statement*  If it is raining, then there is a cloud in the sky.

### Solution

*Inverse*  If it is not raining, then there is not a cloud in the sky.

The original statement is true, but the inverse is false. This is because it is possible to not have rain even though there is a cloud in the sky.

If a conditional statement is true, its contrapositive is also true. If a conditional statement is false, its contrapositive is also false.

## Example 3

**Find the contrapositive of each statement. Tell whether each statement and its contrapositive are *true* or *false*. Explain.**

**a.** *Statement*  If a figure is a rectangle, then the figure is a polygon.

**b.** *Statement*  If a figure is a rectangle, then it is a square.

### Solution

**a.** *Contrapositive*  If a figure is not a polygon, then the figure is not a rectangle.

The statement is true. A rectangle is a type of polygon. The contrapositive is also true. If a figure is not a polygon, then it cannot be a special polygon such as a rectangle.

**b.** *Contrapositive*  If a figure is not a square, then the figure is not a rectangle.

The statement is false. A figure may be a rectangle but not necessarily a square. Its contrapositive is also false. A figure may not be a square, but it might be a rectangle.

 **Math**
**Online**  mathmatters2.com/extra_examples

Lesson 12-4 **Converse, Inverse, and Contrapositive**  |  **533**

6. Converse: If a number is greater than 15, then the number is greater than 25; false; counterexample: 17.
Inverse: If a number is not greater than 25, then it is not greater than 15; false; counterexample: 20.
Contrapositive: If a number is not greater than 15, then it is not greater than 25; true.

7. Converse: If you play a stringed instrument, then you play the violin; false; counterexample: viola.
Inverse: If you do not play the violin, then you do not play a stringed instrument; false; counterexample: cello.
Contrapositive: If you do not play a stringed instrument, then you do not play a violin; true.

## TRY THESE EXERCISES

**Write the negation of each statement two ways.**
For 1–4, see additional answers.

1. The trumpet is a brass instrument.
2. The number 14 is divisible by 3.
3. All cars have four wheels.
4. Baseball is America's favorite pastime.

**Write the converse, inverse, and contrapositive of each statement. Determine if each is *true* or *false*. If *false*, give a counterexample to explain why.**
For 5–8, see additional answers. Counterexamples will vary.

5. If a plant is a tree, then it has leaves.
6. If a number is greater than 25, then that number is greater than 15.
7. If you play the violin, then you play a stringed instrument.
8. **GEOGRAPHY** If you live in Colorado, then you live in Denver.

## PRACTICE EXERCISES • For Extra Practice, see page 624.

**Write the negation of each statement two ways.**
For 9–12, see additional answers.

9. History is Jasmine's favorite subject.
10. Tomorrow is Wednesday.
11. The factory recycles unused paper.
12. The house is made out of wood.

**Write the converse, inverse, and contrapositive of each statement. Determine if each is *true* or *false*. If *false*, give a counterexample to explain why.**
For 13–16, see additional answers. Counterexamples will vary.

13. If the object is an airplane, then it has wings.
14. If you are studying geometry, then you are studying mathematics.
15. If two lines intersect, then they are not parallel to each other.
16. If a triangle is acute, then all its angles are less than 90°.

17. **WRITING MATH** Choose a conditional statement, and draw the corresponding Venn diagram. Describe how the Venn Diagram would be different for the contrapositive of the statement.   Answers will vary.

**ADVERTISING** For Exercises 18–22, refer to the following statement:
*Those who wear Swift shoes run fast.*

18. Rewrite the statement as a conditional statement.
If you wear Swift shoes, then you run fast.
19. Identify the hypothesis and conclusion of the statement.
hypothesis: You wear Swift shoes. conclusion: You run fast.
20. Write the converse of the statement. Is it necessarily true? Explain.
See additional answers.
21. Write the inverse of the statement. Is it necessarily true? Explain.
See additional answers.
22. Write the contrapositive of the statement. Is it necessarily true? Explain.   See additional answers.

23. **DATA FILE** Refer to the data on calories used per minute by people of different body weights on page 568 . Using the chart, write an if-then statement. Then write its converse, inverse, and contrapositive.   Answers will vary.

**MUSIC** For Exercises 24–28, refer to the following statement:
*Those who play the french horn play a brass instrument.*

**24.** Rewrite the statement as a conditional statement.
   If you play the french horn, then you play a brass instrument.
**25.** Identify the hypothesis and conclusion of the conditional statement.
   hypothesis: You play the french horn. conclusion: You play a brass instrument.
**26.** Write the converse of the statement. Is it necessarily true? Explain.
   See additional answers.
**27.** Write the inverse of the statement. Is it necessarily true? Explain.
   See additional answers.
**28.** Write the contrapositive of the statement. Is it necessarily true? Explain.
   See additional answers.

**Write the negation of each statement.**

**29.** My car is not a convertible.
   My car is a convertible.
**31.** The bananas are not ripe.
   The bananas are ripe.

**30.** There is no snow on the ground.
   There is snow on the ground.
**32.** The tent is not torn.
   The tent is torn.

**Write the inverse and contrapositive of each statement.**
For 33–35, see additional answers.
**33.** If the bill is not paid, then the phone service will be turned off.

**34.** If the bus arrives on time, then we will not miss our plane.

**35.** If Akiko does not study, then he will not pass the test.

## ■ EXTENDED PRACTICE EXERCISES

**Complete each statement with *converse, inverse,* or *contrapositive*.**

**36.** The inverse of the converse of a conditional statement is the __?__. contrapositive

**37.** The contrapositive of the converse of a conditional statement is the __?__. inverse

**38.** The converse of the inverse of a conditional statement is the __?__. contrapositive

**39.** The converse of the contrapositive of a conditional statement is the __?__. inverse

**40. CRITICAL THINKING** Write a conditional statement for which the converse, inverse and contrapositive are all true. Answers will vary.

**41. CHAPTER INVESTIGATION** List five composers from the Romantic Era.
   Answers will vary.

## ■ MIXED REVIEW EXERCISES

**State whether each pair of triangles is congruent by SAS, ASA, or SSS.** (Lesson 5-5)

**42.**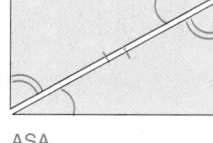
ASA

**43.**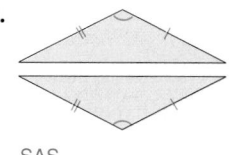
SAS

**44.**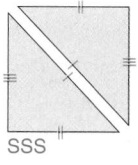
SSS

**Find the range of each function using the given domain.** (Lesson 6-5)

**45.** $y = 5x - 3$, when the domain is $\{-3, -2, -1, 0, 1, 2, 3\}$ $\{-18, -13, -8, -3, 2, 7, 12\}$

**46.** $y = x + 6$, when the domain is $\{-5, -4, -3, -2, -1, 0\}$ $\{1, 2, 3, 4, 5, 6\}$

**47.** $y = 3x - 7$, when the domain is $\{-3, -2, -1, 0, 1, 2, 3\}$ $\{-16, -13, -10, -7, -4, -1, 2\}$

**48.** $y = x^2 - 4$, when the domain is $\{1, 2, 3, 4, 5, 6\}$ $\{-3, 0, 5, 12, 21, 32\}$

---

Name _____ Date _____

EXTRA PRACTICE **12-4**
**CONVERSE, INVERSE, AND CONTRAPOSITIVE**

**☑ EXERCISES**

Write the negation of each statement two ways.

**1.** The clarinet is a woodwind instrument. The clarinet is not a woodwind instrument. It is not the case that the clarinet is a woodwind instrument.

**2.** All dogs bark. All dogs do not bark. It is not the case that all dogs bark.

Write the converse, inverse, and contrapositive of each statement. Determine if each is *true* or *false*. If false, give a counterexample to explain why.

**3.** If a tree is an apple tree, then it will produce apples. Converse: If a tree produces apples, then it is an apple tree. Inverse: If a tree is not an apple tree, then it will not produce apples. Contrapositive: If a tree will not produce apples, then it is not an apple tree.

**4.** If a triangle is isosceles, then it has two equal angles. Converse: If a triangle has two equal angles, then it is isosceles. Inverse: If a triangle is not isosceles, then it does not have two equal angles. Contrapositive: If a triangle does not have two equal angles, then it is not isosceles.

For Exercises 5–9, refer to the statement *All pansies are flowers.*

**5.** Rewrite the statement as a conditional statement. If a plant is a pansy, then it is a flower

**6.** Identify the hypothesis and conclusion of the conditional statement. Hypothesis: a plant is a pansy; conclusion: it is a flower

**7.** Write the converse of the statement. Is it necessarily true? Explain. If a plant is a flower, then it is a pansy.; no; There are flowers that are not pansies.

**8.** Write the inverse of the statement. Is it necessarily true? Explain. If a plant is not a pansy, then it is not a flower.; no; There are flowers that are not pansies.

**9.** Write the contrapositive of the statement. Is it necessarily true? Explain. If a plant is not a flower, then it is not a pansy.; yes; A plant has to be a flower to be a pansy.

---

**26. Converse:** If you play a brass instrument, then you play the french horn; false; counterexample: trumpet.

**27. Inverse:** If you do not play the french horn, then you do not play a brass instrument; false; counterexample: trombone.

**28. Contrapositive:** If you do not play a brass instrument, then you do not play the french horn; true.

**33. Inverse:** If the bill is paid, then the phone service will not be turned off.
**Contrapositive:** If the phone service is not turned off, then the bill is paid.

**34. Inverse:** If the bus does not arrive on time, then we will miss our plane.
**Contrapositive:** If we will miss our plane, then the bus does not arrive on time.

**35. Inverse:** If Akiko studies, then he will pass the test.
**Contrapositive:** If Akiko will pass the test, then he will study.

---

**16. Converse:** If all of the angles of a triangle are less than 90°, then the triangle is acute; true.
**Inverse:** If a triangle is not acute, then not all its angles are less than 90°; false; counterexample:

**Contrapositive:** If not all of the angles of a triangle are not less than 90°, then the triangle is not acute; true.

**20. Converse:** If you run fast, then you wear Swift shoes; this statement is not necessarily true since you may wear another brand of shoes and run fast.

**21. Inverse:** If you do not wear Swift shoes, then you do not run fast; this statement is not necessarily true, as you may wear another brand of shoes and run fast.

**22. Contrapositive:** If you do not run fast, then you do not wear Swift shoes; this statement is not necessarily true since you may wear Swift shoes and still run slowly.

**Lesson 12-3**
conditional statement (if-then)
converse          counterexample
guess and check

**Lesson 12-4**
negation          converse
inverse          contrapositive

## ASSIGNMENT GUIDE

All students: 1–26

## Chalkboard Examples

**Lesson 12-3**
**Rewrite each statement in if-then form, and then write the converse of the statement.**
a. Even integers are multiples of 2.
   Statement: If an integer is even, then it is a multiple of 2.
   Converse: if an integer is a multiple of 2, then it is even.
b. The sum of the measures of two supplementary angles is 180°.
   Statement: If two angles are supplementary, then the sum of their measures is 180°.
   Converse: If the sum of the measures of two angles is 180°, then the angles are supplementary.

# Review and Practice Your Skills

## PRACTICE ◼ LESSON 12-3

**Write the converse of each statement. Then determine whether the statement and its converse are *true* or *false*. If *false*, give a counterexample.**

1. If Mahala lives in Alabama, then he lives south of Canada.   See additional answers.
2. If $6x = 24$, then $x = 4$.   If $x = 4$, then $6x = 24$ ; true; true.
3. If a triangle has 3 congruent angles, then it has 3 congruent sides.   See additional answers.
4. If $x = 6$, then $x^2 = 36$.   If $x^2 = 36$, then $x = 6$; true; false, counterexample $x = -6$.

**Rephrase each statement as an *if-then* statement.**
For 5–10, see additional answers.
5. All squares are rhombuses.
6. To drive a car you need a license.
7. Music composed by Mozart is classical.
8. In bad weather your mom drives you to school.
9. To get an A for the semester, Adam must get a 95% on the final exam.
10. Plastic bottles are recyclable.

## PRACTICE ◼ LESSON 12-4

**Write the negation of each statement.**
11. The house is made of brick.   The house is not made of brick.
12. The flute is wooden.   The flute is not wooden.
13. Soccer is a popular sport in Brazil.   Soccer is not a popular sport in Brazil.
14. The car is not red.   The car is red.

**Refer to the following statement for Exercises 15–20.**
   *Those who play the oboe play a wind instrument.*
15. Rewrite the statement as a conditional statement.
    If you play the oboe, then you play a wind instrument.
16. Identify the hypothesis of the statement.   You play the oboe.
17. Identify the conclusion of the statement.   You play a wind instrument.
18. Write the converse of the statement. Is it *true* or *false*? If *false*, give a counterexample.   See additional answers.
19. Write the inverse of the statement. Is it *true* or *false*? If *false*, give a counterexample.   See additional answers.
20. Write the contrapositive of the statement. Is it *true* or *false*? If *false*, give a counterexample.   See additional answers.

## ADDITIONAL ANSWERS

1. If Mahala lives south of Canada, then he lives in Alabama; true; false; counterexample: Kansas.
3. If a triangle has 3 congruent sides, then it has 3 congruent angles; true.
5. If a quadrilateral is a square, then it is a rhombus.
6. If you drive a car, then you need a license.
7. If the music is composed by Mozart, then it is classical.
8. If the weather is bad, then your mom drives you to school.
9. If Adam is to get an A for the semester, then he must get 95% on the final exam.
10. If the bottle is plastic, then it is recyclable.
18. If you play a wind instrument, then you play the oboe; false; counterexample: flute.
19. If you do not play the oboe, then you do not play a wind instrument; false; counterexample: saxophone.
20. If you do not play a wind instrument, then you do not play the oboe; true.

Use the set $M = \{g, l, o, v, e\}$ for Exercises 21 and 22. (Lessons 12-1)

21. Write a set that is equal to set $M$.
Answers will vary. example: $N = \{g, l, o, v, e\}$

22. Write a set that is equivalent to set $M$.
Answers will vary. example: $O = \{a, b, c, d, e\}$

23. Rephrase the following statement as an if-then statement: *All parallelograms have interior angles whose measures have a sum of 360°.* (Lesson 12-3)
If a figure is a parallelogram, then the sum of the measures of the interior angles is 360°.

24. Write the converse of the statement in Exercise 23. (Lesson 12-4)
If the sum of the measures of the interior angles of a figure is 360°, then the figure is a parallelogram.

**Tell whether each statement is *true* or *false*. Then tell if the converse is *true* or *false*.** (Lessons 12-3 and 12-4)

25. If today is Monday, then tomorrow is Tuesday.   Bowzer is a canine.

26. If $y > 0$, then $y^2 > 0$.   true; false

# Mid-Chapter Quiz

**Define each set in roster notation and set-builder notation. Then determine whether the set is finite or infinite.** (Lesson 12-1)   See additional answers.

1. $D$, the set of odd integers less than 100

2. $N$, the set of natural numbers

3. $S$, the set of seasons in a year

4. $T$, the set of positive three-digit numbers

**Use set notation to write the following.** (Lesson 12-1)

5. $B$ is the set of blue apples.
$B = \{\ \}$ or $B = \varnothing$

6. $-5$ is not an element of $\{-6, -4, -2\}$.
$-5 \notin \{-6, -4, -2\}$

7. The null set is a subset of the universal set.
$\varnothing \subseteq U$

8. Set $Q$ has no elements.
$Q = \{\ \}$ or $Q = \varnothing$

**Use roster notation to represent each set.** (Lesson 12-2)

$U = \{10, 11, 12, \ldots, 18\}$, $A = \{10, 12, 14, 16, 18\}$, $B = \{10, 11, 12\}$, $C = \{15, 17\}$

9. $A \cup B$
$\{10, 11, 12, 14, 16, 18\}$

10. $A'$
$\{11, 13, 15, 17\}$

11. $A' \cap B$
$\{11\}$

12. $B \cup C$
$\{10, 11, 12, 15, 17\}$

13. $B \cap C$
$\varnothing$

14. $A \cap B$
$\{10, 12\}$

15. $A \cup C$
$\{10, 12, 14, 15, 16, 17, 18\}$

16. $B' \cap C'$
$\{13, 14, 16, 18\}$

**Write the converse, inverse and contrapositive of each statement. Determine if each is *true* or *false*. If *false*, give a counterexample.** (Lesson 12-4)
See additional answers.

17. If you are in Tokyo, then you are in Japan.

18. If $n$ is a whole number, then $n$ is a natural number.

19. If two lines are parallel, then they do not intersect.

20. If the weather is foggy, then driving visibility is low.

**Lesson 12-4**
Write the converse, inverse, and contrapositive of the conditional statement and tell whether the statement and related conditionals are true or false.
Statement: If an angle measures 30°, then it is an acute angle.

Converse: If an angle is acute, then it measures 30°; false.

Inverse: If an angle does not measure 30°, then it is not an acute angle; false.

Contrapositive: If an angle is not acute, then it does not measure 30°; true.

**MID-CHAPTER QUIZ**

1. $D = \{\ldots, -5, -3, -1, 1, 3, \ldots, 95, 97, 99\}$
$D = \{x \mid x$ is an odd integer less than 100$\}$
infinite

2. $N = \{1, 2, 3, \ldots\}$
$N = \{x \mid x$ is a natural number$\}$
infinite

3. $S = \{$spring, summer, fall, winter$\}$
$S = \{x \mid x$ is a season of the year$\}$
finite

4. $T = \{100, 101, 102, \ldots, 997, 998, 999\}$
$T = \{x \mid x$ is a positive three-digit number$\}$
finite

17. Converse: If you are in Japan, then you are in Tokyo; false; counterexample: in Osaka.
Inverse: If you are not in Tokyo, then you are not in Japan; false; counterexample: in Osaka.
Contrapositive: If you are not in Japan, then you are not in Tokyo; true.

18. Converse: If $n$ is a natural number, then $n$ is a whole number; true.
Inverse: If $n$ is not a whole number, then $n$ is not a natural number; true.
Contrapositive: If $n$ is not a natural number, then $n$ is not a whole number; false; counterexample: 0.

19. Converse: If two lines do not intersect, then they are parallel; false; counterexample: skew.
Inverse: If two lines are not parallel, then they do intersect; false; counterexample: skew.

Contrapositive: If two lines do intersect, then they are not parallel; true.

20. Converse: If driving visibility is low, then the weather is foggy; false; counterexample: blizzard.
Inverse: If the weather is not foggy, then driving visibility is not low; false; counterexample: blizzard.
Contrapositive: If driving visibility is not low, then the weather is not foggy; true.

# 12-5 Inductive and Deductive Reasoning

**Goals**
- Identify and use inductive reasoning.
- Identify and use deductive reasoning.

**Applications**   Number theory, Biology, Music, Food service, Travel

**Suppose you are drawing marbles from a bag. There are exactly 15 marbles in the bag. The first marble you draw is green, as are the next four marbles.**

1. If you know the bag contains an equal number of red, green and white marbles. What can you conclude with certainty about the next marble you will draw?   It will not be green.

2. Suppose you have been told nothing about the color of the marbles in the bag. You draw five more marbles, and they are all green. What might you conclude about the color of the next marble you will draw? Can you make this conclusion with certainty?
It will be green. No.

### ■ BUILD UNDERSTANDING

When you examine individual instances of an event and then make a conjecture that is supposed to apply to all such events, you use **inductive reasoning**. The greater the number of instances that support a conclusion, the greater the experimental probability that the conclusion is correct.

You cannot be sure, however, since you cannot test all possible instances. So you cannot know that an inductive conclusion is true beyond a doubt.

### Example 1

**Find a pattern for the sum of the first $n$ odd integers.**

$$1 = 1 = 1^2$$
$$1 + 3 = 4 = 2^2$$
$$1 + 3 + 5 = 9 = 3^2$$

$$1 + 3 + 5 + 7 = 16 = 4^2$$
$$1 + 3 + 5 + 7 + 9 = 25 = 5^2$$
$$1 + 3 + 5 + 7 + 9 + 11 = 36 = 6^2$$

**Solution**

Let $n =$ the number of odd numbers added together. The series of statements suggests the following conjecture.

*Conjecture* The sum of the first $n$ odd whole numbers equals $n^2$.

Test the conjecture. Shown are the next two sums in the series.

$$1 + 3 + 5 + 7 + 9 + 11 + 13 = 49 = 7^2$$
$$1 + 3 + 5 + 7 + 9 + 11 + 13 + 15 = 64 = 8^2$$

The conjecture that the sum of the first $n$ odd whole numbers probably equals $n^2$ seems to be true.

■

### Teaching Tip

Use Example 1 to note that since there are an infinite number of cases, there is no way to test every case. Students might try another test case with a higher number, such as 20. Elicit that a computer program or an electronic spreadsheet could easily test many cases.

Inductive reasoning can lead to conclusions that are true, but since every instance cannot be tested, inductive reasoning alone cannot make the conclusions certain.

**Deductive reasoning** begins with a set of statements, called **premises**, that are accepted as true. The **conclusion** of a deductive argument follows from the premises and is implied by them. Together the premises and conclusion make up an **argument**.

In a deductive argument, the premises themselves lead logically to the conclusion. If the logic used to reach a conclusion is sound, it can be accepted as true, since the premises are true.

## Example 2

**MUSIC** Complete the deductive argument by writing the conclusion that follows from the premises.

*Premise 1* If a student is a member of the school orchestra, then the student plays a musical instrument.

*Premise 2* Francine is a member of the school orchestra.

### Solution

Francine is a member of the school orchestra, so she fits the condition stated in Premise 1. Given these premises, the following conclusion is certain.

*Conclusion* Francine plays a musical instrument.

## Example 3

**Tell whether the reasoning is *inductive* or *deductive*.**

**a.** Frank finds that on five different Friday evenings before the basketball game, a coffee and dessert cart is outside the gymnasium. He concludes that the cart is outside the gymnasium every night before a basketball game.

**b.** Kolene uses the definition of a square (a rectangle with four congruent sides) and of perimeter (the sum of the lengths of the sides of a figure) to conclude that the perimeter of any square is equal to 4 times the length of a side.

> ### Check Understanding
>
> Which type of reasoning involves drawing a conclusion based on a pattern of examples?
>
> Which type of reasoning involves drawing conclusions based on a set of definitions or premises?
>
> inductive; deductive

### Solution

**a.** Frank draws a conclusion about the coffee and dessert cart from evidence about five Friday evenings. He reasons from evidence of a few instances to a conclusion about every instance. The reasoning is inductive.

**b.** Kolene reasons from the definition of a square and the definition of perimeter to a conclusion about the perimeter of a square. The conclusion follows logically from the premises. The reasoning is deductive.

**Math Online** mathmatters2.com/extra_examples          Lesson 12-5  **Inductive and Deductive Reasoning**  |  **539**

### Supplementary Example 1
**Predict the next number in each pattern.**
a. 1, −3, 9, −27, ? 81
b. $3^2 = 9$, $33^2 = 1089$, $333^2 = 110889$, $3333^2 = 11108889$, $33333^2 = ?$ 1111088889
c. 0, 2, 6, 12, 20, 30, ? 42

### Supplementary Example 2
**MUSIC** Complete the deductive argument by writing the conclusion that follows from the premises.
*Premise 1* If Ken does not get to sing in the choir, then he will try out for the school band.
*Premise 2* Ken does not get to sing in the choir.
*Conclusion* Ken will try out for the school band.

### Supplementary Example 3
**Tell whether the reasoning is *inductive* or *deductive*.**
a. Harvey uses the definition of perpendiculars and the definition of complementary angles to conclude that $\angle 1 \cong \angle 3$ **deductive reasoning**

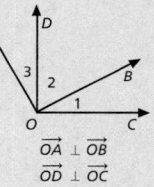

$\overrightarrow{OA} \perp \overrightarrow{OB}$
$\overrightarrow{OD} \perp \overrightarrow{OC}$

b. For two hours, an alien from Mars observes that when the traffic light at the intersection of Main and Fifth turns red, the Earthlings stop their cars. So, the alien concludes that all the Earthlings that come to the intersection of Main and Fifth in a car will stop when the traffic light turns red. **inductive reasoning**

## Teaching Tip

Use Example 2 to guide students into a general rule.
In words: If a conditional statement is true and its hypothesis is true, then its conclusion is true.
In symbols:
| Premises | If $p$, then $q$. | Remind students that a *premise* means |
| | $p$ | a statement assumed to be true. |
| Conclusion | $q$ | |

This generalization is one of the laws of inference, known as the Law of Detachment. This law and another will be introduced in Lesson 12-6.

## QUICK ASSESSMENT

Ask the following questions to determine if students understand the content presented in this lesson.

1. What is a *conjecture*? **An assumption based on some examples.**
2. What is a *premise*? **A statement that is taken as true in a logical argument.**
3. Given some premises and that the steps of an argument are logically correct, which type of reasoning will always give a valid conclusion? **deductive reasoning**

## ASSIGNMENT GUIDE

**Basic:** 1–25, 29–35
**Enriched:** 1–35

### Reteaching Worksheet 12-5

Name _____ Date _____

RETEACHING **12-5**

#### INDUCTIVE AND DEDUCTIVE REASONING

Examining a number of individual events to make a conjecture about all such events is an example of **inductive reasoning**. No inductive conclusion is true beyond a doubt, because you cannot test all possible instances. In a **deductive argument**, one set of statements, called **premises**, leads logically to another statement, called a **conclusion**, implied by those premises.

**Example 1**

Complete the deductive argument by writing the conclusion that follows from the premises.

**Premise 1:** If Carlo passes his tests, then Carlo can graduate.
**Premise 2:** Carlo passes his tests.

**Solution**

Carlo has passed all his tests. So, he fits the conditions stated in Premise 1. Given these premises, only one conclusion follows. **Conclusion:** Carlo may graduate.

**Example 2**

Tell whether the reasoning is *inductive* or *deductive*.

George notices that on the second Monday of September, October, and November, a sign was posted announcing the science club meeting. George concludes that the club has regular monthly meetings on the second Monday of every month.

**Solution**

George makes a conjecture about all the monthly meetings of the science club on the basis of evidence about three Mondays. He reasons from a few instances to a conclusion about every instance. The reasoning is inductive.

#### ✎ EXERCISES

Complete the deductive argument by writing the conclusion that follows from the premises.

1. **Premise 1:** If the figure is a pentagon, then the figure is a polygon.
   **Premise 2:** The figure is a pentagon.
   **Conclusion:** _____ The figure is a polygon

Tell whether the reasoning is *inductive* or *deductive*.

2. Whenever Vera sees Frankie, Frankie always has a new magic trick to show her. Vera concludes that Frankie is learning to do magic tricks. _____ Inductive

3. Bernie reasons from the side-angle-side congruence postulate and the fact that two sides and an included angle of triangle *ABC* are congruent to two sides and an included angle of triangle *DEF* that triangles *ABC* and *DEF* are congruent. _____ Deductive

---

### TRY THESE EXERCISES

**Predict the next number in each pattern.**

1. $1 \cdot 1 = 1$; $11 \cdot 11 = 121$; $111 \cdot 111 = 12{,}321$; $1111 \cdot 1111 = $ __?__   1,234,321

2. 4, 12, 36, 108, __?__   324    **3.** 1, 1, 2, 3, 5, 8, 13, __?__   21    **4.** 18, 6, −6, −18, __?__   −30

**Complete each argument by drawing a conclusion.**

5. *Premise 1* If you are 16 years old or older, you may apply for a driver's license.
   *Premise 2* Ramon is 17 years old.    Ramon may apply for a driver's license.

6. *Premise 1* If the animal is a spaniel, then it is a canine.
   *Premise 2* Bowzer is a spaniel.
   Bowzer is a canine

**Tell whether the reasoning is *inductive* or *deductive*.**

7. Whenever Damica enters a room where there is a vase of roses, her eyes water and she begins to sneeze. So she must be allergic to roses.   inductive

8. Tomás knows that to be in the school choir, you must be able to read music. Mark is a member of the choir. Tomás concludes that Mark can read music.
   deductive

### PRACTICE EXERCISES • For Extra Practice, see page 625.

**Predict the next number in each pattern.**

9. 3, 6, 12, 24, __?__   48      **10.** 2, 4, 7, 11, 16, __?__   22

11. 10, 1, 0.1, 0.01, __?__   0.001      **12.** $12, 3, \frac{3}{4},$ __?__   $\frac{3}{16}$

**Complete each argument by drawing a conclusion.**

13. *Premise 1* If Alita finishes her homework, then she will join us for dinner.
    *Premise 2* Alita has finished her homework.
    Alita will join us for dinner.

14. *Premise 1* All parallelograms have two pairs of parallel sides.
    *Premise 2* A rectangle is a parallelogram.
    A rectangle has two pairs of parallel sides.

15. *Premise 1* If the electricity is off, then our appliances do not work.
    *Premise 2* There is a storm and our electricity is off.
    Our appliances do not work.

**Tell whether the reasoning is *inductive* or *deductive*.**

16. **FOOD SERVICE** Marcia notices that pizza has been on the cafeteria menu every Friday for the past six weeks. She reasons that the cafeteria always serves pizza on Fridays.   inductive

17. **BIOLOGY** Albert knows that the Earth's nitrogen, oxygen and water are all necessary for life. He reasons that evidence of nitrogen, oxygen and water on a planet means that life must be present.   inductive

18. If *x* is greater than *y* and *y* is greater than *z*, what conclusion can be drawn about the relationship between *x* and *z*? What type of reasoning did you use to draw your conclusion?   $x > z$; deductive

## ADDITIONAL ANSWERS

19. **Red sports cars are often stopped and given speeding tickets.**
20. **No. The officers can see the big picture. They know that all types of cars get speeding tickets.**
21. **He could check police records.**
22. **He may have been more inclined to speed in his new car.**

**TRAVEL** When Reshad turned 24 years old, he bought a new red sports car. He had never gotten a speeding ticket before that time. During the first six months after buying the car, Reshad got four speeding tickets. For 19–22, answers will vary.
See additional answers for possible answers.

**19.** What conjecture might Reshad make about red sports cars?

**20.** Are the officers who issued the tickets likely to make the same conjecture? Why or why not?

**21.** What observations might Reshad make to test his conjecture?

**22.** Could Reshad's behavior have changed after he bought the car? Explain.

**23. WRITING MATH** Explain the similarities and differences between inductive and deductive reasoning. Give an example of each type.   Answers will vary.

**Draw a conclusion if possible. If not, write _no conclusion_.**

**24.** Kelly is older than Franchesca.
Franchesca is older than Megan.
Kelly is older than Megan.

**25.** Kendall is taller than Doug.
Hoshiko is taller than Doug.
no conclusion

## ■ EXTENDED PRACTICE EXERCISES

**26. YOU MAKE THE CALL** Ron notices a pattern in the whole numbers shown. He conjectures that every whole number can be written as the sum of consecutive whole numbers. Is he correct? Test his conjecture to find a counterexample, if possible.   no; counterexample: 4

$$5 = 2 + 3 \qquad\qquad 6 = 1 + 2 + 3 \qquad\qquad 9 = 2 + 3 + 4$$
$$15 = 1 + 2 + 3 + 4 + 5 \qquad 42 = 9 + 10 + 11 + 12 \qquad 51 = 16 + 17 + 18$$

**27. CRITICAL THINKING** If Chloe is taking French III, then she will be able to translate the passage. Chloe is able to translate the passage. Can a conclusion be drawn from these premises? Explain why or why not.   No. Chloe could be a native of France and did not need to take the class to translate the passage.

**28.** Suppose that you are taking a quiz. You know that if the first answer is true, then the next answer is false. The last answer is the same as the first answer. The second answer is true. How can you show that the last answer on the quiz is false? (Hint: Assume that the last answer on the quiz is true.)
See additional answers.

## ■ MIXED REVIEW EXERCISES

**Use the table for Exercises 29–31.** (Lesson 4-1)

**Jolly Trolley Riders**

| Age group | 21-30 yr | 31-40 yr | 41-50 yr | 51-60 yr |
|-----------|----------|----------|----------|----------|
| Monday | 123 | 256 | 304 | 193 |
| Tuesday | 204 | 372 | 302 | 188 |
| Wednesday | 251 | 400 | 255 | 194 |
| Thursday | 294 | 415 | 278 | 253 |
| Friday | 309 | 420 | 391 | 266 |
| Saturday | 422 | 518 | 476 | 283 |

**29.** What is the probability of a Thursday rider being in the 31–40 age range?   ≈ 0.33

**30.** What is the probability of a rider in the 41–50 age range riding on a Monday?   ≈ 0.15

**31.** What is the probability of any rider riding on a Tuesday?   ≈ 0.14

**Write the polynomial in standard form.** (Lesson 9-1)

**32.** $8x + 4x^2 - 3$   $4x^2 + 8x - 3$

**33.** $3y - 2y^2 + 6 + 2y^4$   $2y^4 - 2y^2 + 3y + 6$

**34.** $3x^4 + 2x - 3x^2 + 4$   $3x^4 - 3x^2 + 2x + 4$

**35.** $5x^2 + x^5 - 3x^2 + 4x + x^4$   $x^5 + x^4 + 2x^2 + 4x$

 mathmatters2.com/self_check_quiz

---

## Extend the Lesson

**CHALLENGE** Have students work in pairs to find a pattern for the sum of the first $n$ even integers, not including zero.

$2 + 4 + 6 + 8 \ldots + n = n(n + 1)$
or $n^2 + n$

## ADDITIONAL ANSWERS

**28.** Assume the last answer on the quiz is true. Therefore the first answer is true. So the second answer is false. This is a contradiction to the given statement that the second answer is true. So the first assumption was incorrect. Therefore the last answer must be false.

---

### Extra Practice Worksheet 12-5

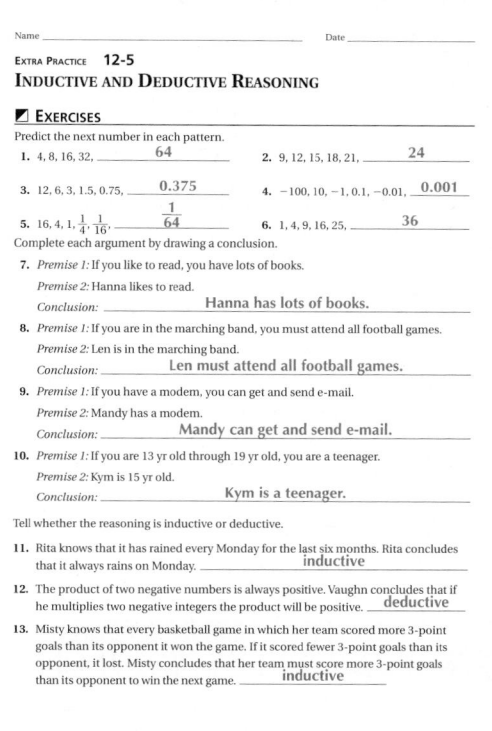

### Enrichment Worksheet 12-5

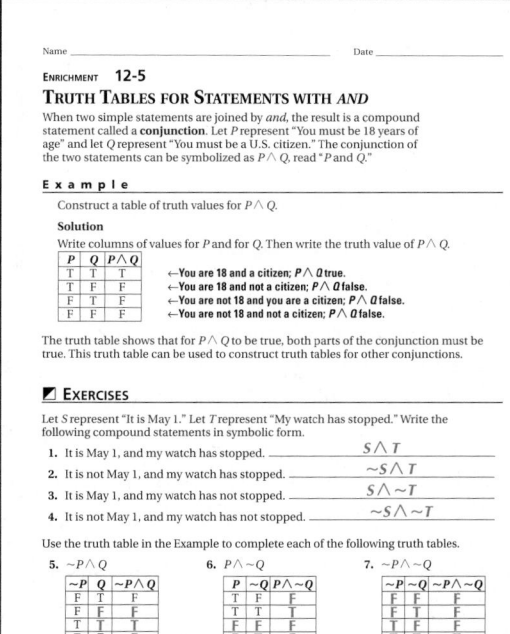

## NCTM Standards/Strands
- Reasoning & Proof
- Representation
- Connections
- Communication

## Vocabulary

valid argument    invalid argument
sound argument
unsound argument
Law of Detachment
Law of the Contrapositive

## Lesson Resources

Warm-up Transparency 50
Transparency RF-60
Reteaching 12-6
Extra Practice 12-6
Enrichment 12-6

---

## Getting Started

### 5-MINUTE WARM-UP

Write the converse, inverse, and contrapositive of the conditional statement, and tell whether each statement is *true* or *false*.

If $x = 5$, then
$x$ is an odd number.

**Converse:** If $x$ is an odd number, then $x = 5$; false.
**Inverse:** If $x \neq 5$, then $x$ is not an odd number; false.
**Contrapositive:** If $x$ is not an odd number, then $x \neq 5$; true.

### Introduction to Lesson 12-6

Because of their familiarity with cities and states, students are likely to recognize that Arguments 3 and 4 are not logical. Have students write the converse, inverse, and contrapositive of the statement "If you live in San Francico, then you live in California" and note that Argument 3 is reasoning by the converse and Argument 4 is reasoning by the inverse. Argument 2 is reasoning by the contrapositive.

---

# 12-6 Patterns of Deductive Reasoning

**Goals**
- Identify arguments as valid or invalid.
- Identify arguments as sound or unsound.

**Applications** Number sense, Music, Horticulture, Retail, Advertising

**Read the arguments and answer the questions.**

*Argument 1* If you live in San Francisco, then you live in California. You live in San Francisco. Therefore, you live in California.

*Argument 2* If you live in San Francisco, then you live in California. You do not live in California. Therefore, you do not live in San Francisco.

*Argument 3* If you live in San Francisco, then you live in California. You live in California. Therefore, you live in San Francisco.

*Argument 4* If you live in San Francisco, then you live in California. You do not live in San Francisco. Therefore, you do not live in California.

San Francisco, California

1. In which arguments does the conclusion follow logically from the premises?  1, 2

2. In which arguments does the conclusion not follow from the premises?  3, 4

---

### ▶ BUILD UNDERSTANDING

An argument may be valid or invalid depending on the relationship between the premises and the conclusion. In a **valid argument**, if the premises are true, then the conclusion must be true.

One valid argument form is the **Law of Detachment**, or *modus ponens*. This says that given a premise $p \rightarrow q$, if $p$ is affirmed, then $q$ logically follows.

> *Premise* 1  If an animal is a dog, then it has four legs. ($p \rightarrow q$)
> *Premise* 2  Clarence is a dog. ($p$)
> *Conclusion*  Therefore, Clarence has four legs. ($q$)

Another valid argument form is the **Law of the Contrapositive**, or *modus tollens*. In this form, when given a premise $p \rightarrow q$, if $q$ is denied, then the negation of $p$ logically follows.

> *Premise* 1  If an animal is a dog, then it has four legs. ($p \rightarrow q$)
> *Premise* 2  Polly does not have four legs. ($\sim q$)
> *Conclusion*  Therefore, Polly is not a dog. ($\sim p$)

**Reading Math**

Latin phrases are sometimes used in mathematics. They are understood even though most people don't know the Latin language.

**Valid Argument Forms**

| *Law of Detachment* | *Law of the Contrapositive* |
|---|---|
| Premise 1 $p \rightarrow q$ | Premise 1 $p \rightarrow q$ |
| Premise 2 $p$ | Premise 2 $\sim q$ |
| Conclusion $q$ | Conclusion $\sim p$ |

---

### Teaching Tip

Use the warm-up and the opening activity to emphasize with students that a conditional statement and its contrapositive always have the same truth values (are *logically equivalent*).

However, the converse and inverse need not have the same truth value as the original conditional statement.

So, one of the laws of logic is the Law of the Contrapositive, while reasoning by a converse or an inverse are not valid argument forms.

In an **invalid argument**, even if the premises are true, the conclusion does not logically follow. Given a premise $p \rightarrow q$, an invalid argument occurs when $q$ is affirmed or when $p$ is denied.

> *Premise* 1 If an animal is a dog, then it has four legs. $(p \rightarrow q)$
> *Premise* 2 Fifi has four legs. $(q)$
> *Conclusion* Therefore, Fifi is a dog. $(p)$

> *Premise* 1 If an animal is a dog, then it has four legs. $(p \rightarrow q)$
> *Premise* 2 Sam is not a dog. $(\sim p)$
> *Conclusion* Therefore, Sam does not have four legs. $(\sim q)$

## Example 1

**Determine by form whether the arguments are *valid* or *invalid*.**

**a.** If $2x = 4$, then $x = 2$. $2x = 4$. Therefore, $x = 2$.

**b.** If a polygon is a square, then the measures of its angles total 360°. This polygon is not a square. Therefore, the measures of its angles do not total 360°.

### Solution

**a.** Let $p$ represent "$2x = 4$" and $q$ represent "$x = 2$." The argument has premises $p \rightarrow q$ and $p$ and conclusion $q$. This is the valid form of the Law of Detachment.

**b.** Let $p$ represent "this polygon is a square" and $q$ represent "the measures of its angles total 360°." The argument has premises $p \rightarrow q$ and $\sim p$ and conclusion $\sim q$. This argument form is invalid. Both premises can be true without the conclusion necessarily being true. The polygon could be any nonsquare quadrilateral.

The validity of an argument does not depend on the truth or falsity of the statements in it. Validity is concerned only with the form of an argument.

A valid argument form guarantees that *if* the premises are true, then the conclusion *must* be true. A deductive argument whose form is valid and whose premises are true is called a **sound argument**. A deductive argument whose form is valid but contains at least one false premise is an **unsound argument**.

## Example 2

**HORTICULTURE** Determine the validity and soundness of the argument.

If a flower has red petals, then it is a rose.
This flower has red petals.
Therefore, this flower is a rose.

### Solution

Let $p$ represent "a flower has red petals" and $q$ represent "it is a rose." The argument has premises $p \rightarrow q$ and $p$ and conclusion $q$. So the argument form is Law of Detachment, which is valid. However, the first premise is not true. There are many different types of flowers with red petals, such as a carnation or a tulip.

So the argument is unsound. It is valid because of its form, but it is unsound because its first premise is false.

mathmatters2.com/extra_examples

Lesson 12-6 **Patterns of Deductive Reasoning** **543**

---

## Chalkboard Examples

### Supplementary Example 1
Determine by form whether the argument is valid or invalid.
**a.** *Premise* 1 $r \rightarrow \sim s$
*Premise* 2 $r$
*Conclusion* $\sim s$ valid, Law of Detachment
**b.** *Premise* 1 $\sim m \rightarrow t$
*Premise* 2 $m$
*Conclusion* $\sim t$ invalid, reasoning by inverse
**c.** *Premise* 1 $g \rightarrow \sim h$
*Premise* 2 $h$
*Conclusion* $\sim g$ valid, Law of Contrapositive
**d.** *Premise* 1 $\sim a \rightarrow \sim b$
*Premise* 2 $\sim b$
*Conclusion* $\sim a$ invalid, reasoning by converse

### Supplementary Example 2
**SCIENCE** Determine the validity and soundness of the following argument.

If a scientist discovered radioactivity, the scientist is famous.
Newton discovered radioactivity.
Therefore, Newton is famous.

Let $p$ = discovered radioactivity and $q$ = is famous. In symbolic form, the given argument is:
> *Premise 1* $p \rightarrow q$
> *Premise 2* $p$
> *Conclusion* $q$

So the argument form is Law of Detachment, which is valid.

---

## Teaching Tip

From Example 2 and Supplementary Example 2, note with students how important it is to examine the truth value of given conditions and to be on the lookout for hidden assumptions.
Emphasize that soundness of an argument depends on the premises being true, while validity depends on a logical conclusion to the premises—true or not.

### QUICK ASSESSMENT

1. What does it mean to say that an argument is *valid*?  **The laws of reasoning have been applied correctly to a set of premises.**
2. If an argument is valid, when must the conclusion be true?  **If the original assumptions (the premises) are true.**

### ASSIGNMENT GUIDE

Basic: 1–18, 25–32
Enriched: 1–32

### ADDITIONAL ANSWERS

6. No. The form of the argument may be valid. Such an argument is valid even though the conclusion may not be true in reality. A valid argument containing a conclusion that is not true in reality also contains at least one premise that is not true in reality. The argument is valid, but it is unsound.

### Reteaching Worksheet 12-6

Name _____ Date _____

RETEACHING  **12-6**

**PATTERNS OF DEDUCTIVE REASONING**

A deductive argument may be valid or invalid. A valid argument has a form such that, if the premises are true, then the conclusion *must* be true. Some examples of valid and invalid argument forms are the following.

|  Valid  |  |  Invalid  |  |
|---|---|---|---|
| $p \to q$ | $p \to q$ | $p \to q$ | $p \to q$ |
| $\dfrac{p}{q}$ | $\dfrac{\sim q}{\sim p}$ | $\dfrac{q}{p}$ | $\dfrac{\sim p}{\sim q}$ |

**Example**

Determine by form whether the arguments are *valid* or *invalid*.
a. If the figure is a cube, then the figure has six sides.
   The figure does not have six sides.
   The figure is not a cube.
b. If the animal is a horse, then the animal is a mammal
   The animal is a mammal.
   The animal is a horse.

**Solution**

a. Let $p$ = "The figure is a cube" and $q$ = "The figure has six sides." The premises of the argument assert $p \to q$ and $\sim q$. The argument form is valid.
b. Let $p$ = "The animal is a horse" and $q$ = "The animal is a mammal." The premises of the argument assert $p \to q$ and $q$. The argument is invalid.

**EXERCISES**

Determine whether each argument is *valid* or *invalid*.

1. If you play a French horn, then you play a valved instrument.
   You play a valved instrument.
   You play the French horn.    invalid
2. If you speak Spanish, then you know the meaning of *adios*.
   You do not speak Spanish.
   You do not know the meaning of *adios*.    invalid
3. If the weather is rainy, then the humidity is high.
   It is raining.
   The humidity is high.    valid

Write a minor premise and a conclusion for an invalid argument, using the given premise.

4. If the figure is a trapezoid, then the figure is a quadrilateral.
   Answers may vary.

---

### ◼ TRY THESE EXERCISES

**Determine by form whether the arguments are *valid* or *invalid*. If *valid*, name the argument form.**

1. If $3b = 12$, then $b = 4$. $3b = 12$. Therefore, $b = 4$.    valid; Law of Detachment

2. If it rains, then our picnic will be canceled. Our picnic will be canceled. Therefore, it must have rained.    invalid

3. If you like to eat tacos, then you will like Taco Joe's. You like Taco Joe's. Therefore, you like to eat tacos.    invalid

**Determine the validity of each argument. If valid, name the argument form and determine its soundness.**

4. **NUMBER SENSE** If a number is not a whole number, then it is not greater than zero. The number 1.2 is greater than zero, so it must be a whole number.
   valid; Law of the Contrapositive; unsound

5. If the bulb is burned out, then the lamp will not light. The lamp does not light. Therefore, the bulb is burned out.    invalid

6. **WRITING MATH** If the conclusion of an argument is untrue, must the argument necessarily be invalid? Explain.    See additional answers.

### ◼ PRACTICE EXERCISES • For Extra Practice, see page 625.

**Determine by form whether the arguments are *valid* or *invalid*. If *valid*, name the argument form.**

7. **MUSIC** If you dedicate years to learning how to play the guitar, then you will be a talented player. Natasha has not dedicated years to learning how to play the guitar, so Natasha will not be a talented guitar player.    invalid

8. If the animal is a whale, then it is a mammal. The animal is a whale. Therefore, the animal is a mammal.    valid; Law of Detachment

9. If two coplanar lines intersect, then they intersect at one point. These two coplanar lines intersect, so their intersection is a point.    valid; Law of Detachment

**Determine the validity of each argument. If valid, name the argument form and determine its soundness.**

10. If the food is an apple, then it is a vegetable. This food is not an apple. So this food is not a vegetable.
    invalid

11. **RETAIL** If a customer buys two sweaters at regular price, then the third sweater is 50% off. Suppose the customer does not receive 50% off the price of a third sweater. Therefore, the customer has not purchased two sweaters at regular price.    valid: Law of the Contrapositive; sound

12. If a number is greater than zero, then it is an integer. The number 23.49 is greater than zero, so it must be an integer.    valid; Law of Detachment; unsound

13. If a number is prime, then its only factors are 1 and itself. The number 4 has factors 1, 2 and 4. Therefore, the number 4 is not prime.
    valid; Law of the Contrapositive; sound

---

For 19–22, the unstated key premise may be given in one of two ways depending on if the stated premise is taken to be the affirmation of $p$ or the denial of $q$.

19. If you feel tired, then you should eat Pep Crackles for breakfast.
   If you eat Pep Crackles for breakfast, then you won't feel tired.

20. If you are not a fool, then you will buy Springsole running shoes.
   If you don't buy Springsole running shoes, then you are a fool.

21. If you don't like rich coffee flavor, then don't buy Golden Bean coffee.

If you buy Golden Bean coffee, you like rich coffee flavor.

22. If you don't have life insurance, you can't feel secure about your future.
   If you feel secure about your future, then you have life insurance.

24. Assume: $2x$ is not odd, it is even.
   $(2x)^2 = 4x^2 = 2(2x^2)$
   Because the square of $2x$ takes the form 2 times a number, the square of $2x$ is also even.
   Therefore, the contrapositive is true.
   If the contrapositive is true, then the original conditional statement is true.

**14. DATA FILE** Refer to the data on music media and the year they were introduced on page 563. Use the information to complete the argument. Then determine its validity and soundness.

If ___?___ was introduced before 1982, then it does not play CDs. *a music medium*
The ___?___ was invented in 1979. *Walkman*
Therefore, ___?___. *The Walkman does not play CDs.*
*valid; Law of Detachment; sound*

**Determine the validity. If valid name the argument form and determine its soundness.**

**15.** If a basketball player is fouled while taking a three-point shot, then he shoots three free throws. John shoots three free throws, so he must have been fouled while taking a three-point shot. *invalid*

**16.** All humans are mammals. Terrance's dog is a mammal. Therefore, Terrance's dog is a human. *invalid*

**17.** If dogs were cats, pigs would whistle. Pigs whistle. Dogs are cats. *invalid*

**18.** If a number is a whole number, it is a perfect square. The number 14.5 is not a perfect square. So the number 14.5 is not a whole number. *valid; Law of the Contrapositive; unsound*

## ▮ EXTENDED PRACTICE EXERCISES

**ADVERTISING** Many advertisements are actually arguments in which only a premise and a conclusion are stated. This often leads to invalid arguments. Determine the unstated key premise in each argument.
*For 19–22, see additional answers.*

**19.** Feeling tired? Eat Pep Crackles for breakfast.

**20.** Don't be a fool. Buy the best—Springsole running shoes!

**21.** Don't like rich coffee flavor? Then don't buy Golden Bean coffee.

**22.** Without life insurance, you can't feel secure about your future.

**23. WRITING MATH** Write an example of an invalid argument in advertising. Explain why a certain conclusion cannot be drawn from such an argument.
*Answers will vary.*

**24. CRITICAL THINKING** Show that if the square of a number is odd, then the number is odd. (Hint: Show that the contrapositive is true. Show that if a number is not odd, then the square of the number is not odd. Use $2x$ to represent any even number.) *See additional answers.*

## ▮ MIXED REVIEW EXERCISES

**Find the surface area of each figure.** (Lesson 10-3)

**25.**
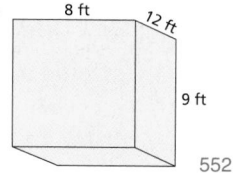
8 ft · 12 ft · 9 ft
552 ft²

**26.**
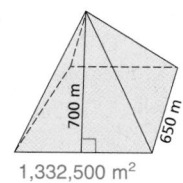
700 m · 650 m
1,332,500 m²

**Find the trigonometric ratios in lowest terms.** (Lesson 11-4)

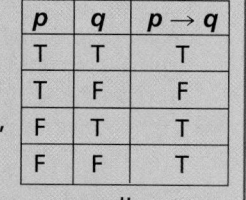
R · 16 · 20 · T · 12 · S

**27.** sin $R$ $\frac{3}{5}$
**28.** tan $R$ $\frac{3}{4}$
**29.** cos $R$ $\frac{4}{5}$
**30.** cos $S$ $\frac{3}{5}$
**31.** sin $S$ $\frac{4}{5}$
**32.** tan $S$ $\frac{4}{3}$

Math Online mathmatters2.com/self_check_quiz

---

# Extend the Lesson

**CONNECTING TO PRIOR KNOWLEDGE** Have students determine the various possibilities for the truth value of two statements $p$ and $q$, and summarize the possibilities in a table. Then give students a symbolic representation for three statements: Let $m$ = Tuesday follows Monday, $w$ = There are 7 days in one week, and $h$ = There are 40 h in one day. Determine the truth values of various conditionals: $m \rightarrow w$ (T → T is T), $w \rightarrow h$ (T → F is F), $\sim m \rightarrow \sim w$ (F → F is T), $\sim w \rightarrow m$ (F → T is true). Enter these results in a third column of the *truth table,* indicating the possibilities for the truth value of a conditional statement corresponding to the four cases that are possibilities for the individual statements.

| $p$ | $q$ | $p \rightarrow q$ |
|---|---|---|
| T | T | T |
| T | F | F |
| F | T | T |
| F | F | T |

---

## Extra Practice Worksheet 12-6

Name _____ Date _____

EXTRA PRACTICE **12-6**
**PATTERNS OF DEDUCTIVE REASONING**

**✔ EXERCISES**

Determine by form whether the arguments are valid or invalid. If valid, name the argument form.

**1.** If you practice shooting the basketball every day for a year, then you will make the basketball team. Yolanda did not practice shooting the basketball every day for a year so she did not make the basketball team. *invalid*

**2.** If it snows more than 8 inches, school will be canceled. School was not canceled on Monday, so it did not snow more than 8 inches on Monday. *valid: Law of Contrapositive*

**3.** If Juanita earns at least $10 babysitting, she will go to the movies with her friends. Juanita earned $12 babysitting. Therefore, she will go to the movies with her friends. *valid; Law of Detachment*

**4.** If you live in Chicago, then you live in Illinois. Gwen lives in Illinois, so she lives in Chicago. *invalid*

Determine the validity and soundness of each argument. If valid, name the argument form.

**5.** If the food is a tomato, then it is a fruit. The food is a fruit. So, this food is a tomato. *This argument is invalid*

**6.** If a person eats bran cereal everyday, they will have normal blood pressure. Lyle eats bran cereal everyday. So, Lyle has low blood pressure. *The argument is valid by the Law of Detachment, but is not sound.*

**7.** If a car is white, it will not be hot inside in the summer. Alyn's car is hot inside in the summer. So, Alyn's car is not white. *This argument is valid by the Law of the Contrapositive, but is not sound.*

**8.** If a number is an integer, it is a rational number. The number $\sqrt{2}$ is not a rational number. Therefore, $\sqrt{2}$ is not an integer. *This argument is valid by the Law of the Contrapositive and is sound.*

---

## Enrichment Worksheet 12-6

Name _____ Date _____

ENRICHMENT **12-6**
**TAUTOLOGIES AND CONTRADICTIONS**

A compound statement that is true for *any* combination of truth values of the simple statements it contains is called a **tautology.** A statement that is false for any combination of truth values of the statements it contains is called a **contradiction.**

**E x a m p l e**

Determine whether the statement is a *tautology* or a *contradiction*.
 **a.** Today is Saturday and today is not Saturday.
 **b.** If today is Tuesday, then today is Tuesday or the roses are pink.

**Solution**

**a.** Let $P$ represent "Today is Saturday." The compound statement has the form $P \wedge \sim P$. Construct a truth table for this conjunction.

| $P$ | $\sim P$ | $P \wedge \sim P$ |
|---|---|---|
| T | F | F |
| F | T | F |

$P \wedge \sim P$ is false, regardless of the truth values of $P$ and $\sim P$.

The statement is a contradiction.

**b.** Let $P$ be "Today is Tuesday." Let $Q$ be "The roses are pink." The conditional can be symbolized as $P \rightarrow (P \vee Q)$. Construct a truth table for the statement.

| $P$ | $Q$ | $P \vee Q$ | $P \rightarrow (P \vee Q)$ |
|---|---|---|---|
| T | T | T | T |
| T | F | T | T |
| F | T | T | T |
| F | F | F | T |

The statement is true for all combinations of truth values of $P$ and $Q$.

The statement is a tautology.

**✔ EXERCISES**

Write each statement symbolically and indicate whether it is a tautology or a contradiction.

**1.** If today is Saturday, then today is Saturday and tomorrow is Sunday.
 $P \rightarrow (P \vee Q)$; tautology

**2.** The sun is a star and the sun is not a star.
 $P \wedge \sim P$; contradiction

**3.** Write the following statement symbolically and construct a truth table to determine whether it is a tautology or a contradiction. If the sun is a star, then $2 + 2 \neq 4$, or the sun is a star.

| $P$ | $Q$ | $\sim Q \vee P$ | $P \rightarrow (\sim Q \vee P)$ |
|---|---|---|---|
| T | T | T | T |
| T | F | T | T |
| F | T | F | T |
| F | F | T | T |

## Chalkboard Examples

**Lesson 12-5**
Find a pattern for the sum of the first $n$ integers.

$$1 = \frac{1 \cdot 2}{2}$$

$$1 + 2 = 3 = \frac{2 \cdot 3}{2}$$

$$1 + 2 + 3 = 6 = \frac{3 \cdot 4}{2}$$

$$1 + 2 + 3 + 4 = 10 = \frac{4 \cdot 5}{2}$$

$$1 + 2 + 3 + 4 + 5 = 15 = \frac{5 \cdot 6}{2}$$

$$1 + 2 + 3 + 4 + 5 + 6 = 21 = \frac{6 \cdot 7}{2}$$

Let $n$ = the number of consecutive integers in the sum. The series of statements suggests:
*Conjecture*

$$1 + 2 + 3 + \ldots + n = \frac{n(n + 1)}{2}$$

Test the conjecture for the sum of the first say 10 consecutive integers.

$$1 + 2 + 3 + 4 + 5 + 6 + 7$$
$$+ 8 + 9 + 10 = \frac{10(10 + 1)}{2}$$
$$55 = 55 \checkmark$$

So, it seems that the sum of the first $n$ consecutive integers is $\frac{n(n + 1)}{2}$.

# Review and Practice Your Skills

## PRACTICE ■ LESSON 12-5

**Predict the next number in each pattern.**

1. 1, 4, 16, 64, __?__    256

2. 10, 5, 0, __?__    −5

3. 3, 30, 15, 150, 75, __?__
750

**Complete each argument by drawing a conclusion.**

4. *Premise 1* All rhombuses have diagonals that are perpendicular.
   *Premise 2* A square is a rhombus.
   A square has diagonals that are perpendicular.

5. *Premise 1* Courtney is older than Lamar.
   *Premise 2* Lamar is older than Al.
   Courtney is older than Al.

6. *Premise 1* If the electricity is out, our cordless phone does not work.
   *Premise 2* The flood caused the power to go out.
   Our cordless phone does not work.

7. *Premise 1* If you are over 12 years old, you can babysit.
   *Premise 2* Sakima is 13 years old.
   Sakima can babysit.

## PRACTICE ■ LESSON 12-6

**Determine by form whether the arguments are *valid* or *invalid*. If *valid*, name the argument form.**

8. If Shantel gets home early, then she will play tennis.
   Shantel got home early. Therefore, she will play tennis.
   valid; Law of Detachment

9. If the animal is a kangaroo, it is a mammal. The animal is not a mammal.
   Therefore, the animal is not a kangaroo.
   valid; Law of the Contrapositive

10. If an animal is a horse, it has a mane.
    Shadow has a mane. Therefore, Shadow is a horse.
    invalid

11. If the temperature is 28°F, then water freezes.
    The water is frozen. Therefore, the temperature is 28°F.
    invalid

12. If the figure is a triangle, then the figure is a polygon.
    The figure is not a polygon. Therefore, the figure is not a triangle.
    valid; Law of the Contrapositive

## PRACTICE ■ LESSON 12-1–LESSON 12-6

**Write each statement in if-then form. Then write its converse. Determine if the converse is *true* or *false*.** (Lessons 12-3 and 12-4)   For 13–14, see additional answers.

13. The angles in a linear pair are supplementary.

14. The secretary is in a bad mood when it rains.

**Predict the next two numbers in the pattern.** (Lesson 12-5)

15. 7, 9, 11, 13, __?__, __?__   15, 17

16. $\frac{1}{32}, \frac{1}{16}, \frac{1}{8}$, __?__, __?__   $\frac{1}{4}, \frac{1}{2}$

**Let $A = \{f, o, t, b, a, l\}$ and $B = \{b, a, s, l\}$.** (Lesson 12-2)

17. Find $A \cup B$.  {f, o, t, b, a, l, s}

18. Find $A \cap B$.  {b, a, l}

## Extend the Lesson

After students have completed Exercises 1–3, ask them to try to generalize some of the pattern characteristics observed. For example:
A pattern may involve a single operation that works on preceding terms to produce successive terms, as in the sequences of Exercise 1 and Exercise 2.
A pattern may involve pairs of successive terms, as in the sequence of Exercise 3.

# MathWorks Career – Professor of Music History
**Workplace Knowhow**

In the process of studying the development of music in any culture, a professor of music history examines a broad spectrum of topics relating to music, from the basic construction of musical instruments to the role it plays in cultural development. Professors teach courses, maintain grades, advise students, conduct research and write for scholarly journals.

For 1–3, see additional answers.

1. A *box zither*, native to the Middle East, is a rectangular- or trapezoidal-shaped box with strings that lie parallel to and stretch the length of the resonating box. The strings are either struck with light hammers or plucked. Construct an argument using deductive reasoning that explains why the box zither is not a percussion instrument. Begin by assuming that the box zither is a percussion instrument.

box zither

2. The *English horn* is a woodwind instrument utilizing two thin reeds that are connected laterally and vibrate jointly. However, the following argument could be made regarding the English horn. **If an instrument is a type of horn, then it must be a brass instrument. The English horn is a type of horn. Therefore, it must be a brass instrument.** Evaluate the validity and soundness of this argument.

3. The *alphorn*, a long horn used by Alpine herdsman and villagers, is carved or bored in wood and covered with bark from a birch tree. On a two-week visit to Switzerland, a music professor observed that the instrument was played in a village at noon and 1:00 P.M. each day. She also noticed that within five minutes after the horn was sounded at noon, all of the village farmers gathered in the town hall for a meal. She reasoned that the sound of the alphorn signaled the beginning and end of the daily "lunch hour." What type of reasoning was the professor applying? Justify your answer.

4. The *jew's harp*, a percussion instrument played in many Southeast Asian countries, is commonly used during courtship rituals. While observing these rituals in Bali, a professor determined that if the jew's harp were played by a man three consecutive nights in front of the home of an unwed woman, then he was seeking her hand in marriage. Hayak had stated that he was not yet prepared to enter into a marriage relationship with Maya. Therefore, one can conclude that Hayak had not played the jew's harp for three consecutive nights in front of Maya's home. What valid argument form is used to draw this conclusion? Law of the Contrapositive

**Math Online** mathmatters2.com/mathworks

---

## Lesson 12-6
**Determine by form whether the argument is valid or invalid.**

a. *Premise 1* $\sim a \rightarrow \sim b$
   *Premise 2* $\sim b$
   *Conclusion* $\sim a$   invalid, reasoning by converse

b. *Premise 1* $\sim c \rightarrow d$
   *Premise 2* $c$
   *Conclusion* $\sim d$   invalid, reasoning by inverse

c. *Premise 1* $\sim r \rightarrow \sim s$
   *Premise 2* $\sim r$
   *Conclusion* $\sim s$   valid, Law of Detachment

d. *Premise 1* $\sim j \rightarrow \sim k$
   *Premise 2* $k$
   *Conclusion* $j$   valid, Law of Contrapositive

## MathWorks

Music, which can be thought of as an artful arrangement of sounds, is part of virtually every culture on Earth; but it varies widely among cultures in style and structure. Throughout the world, musical instruments vary greatly in purpose and design, from natural, uncrafted objects to complicated products of industrial technology.

Students should answer Questions 1–4 to better understand how logical arguments can be applied to categorize musical instruments.

Many professors of music are themselves accomplished on one or more musical instruments.

Students who are interested in learning more about this career choice can go to mathmatters2.com/mathworks. School Guidance Counselors are another resource for information about training requirements and appropriate schools.

---

## MATHWORKS

1. *Assume:* Box zither is a percussion instrument.
   *Therefore:* Box zither has either a stretched membrane that vibrates or the instrument as a whole vibrates to produce a sound.
   The preceding statement is false because only the strings of the box zither vibrate to produce a sound.
   *Therefore:* The box zither is not a percussion instrument.

2. The argument is valid and makes use of the Law of Detachment. However, the argument is not sound because the first premise is false. That is, not all horns are classified as brass instruments.

3. The professor was using inductive reasoning. She had observed several instances of a particular repetitive behavior and drew her conclusion from those observations.

## ADDITIONAL ANSWERS

13. If angles are a linear pair, then they are supplementary.
    Converse: If angles are supplementary, then they are a linear pair; false

14. If it rains, then the secretary is in a bad mood.
    Converse: If the secretary is in a bad mood, then it rains; false

## NCTM Standards/Strands
- Reasoning & Proof
- Representation
- Connections
- Communication

## Lesson Resources

Warm-up Transparency 51
Reteaching 12-7
Extra Practice 12-7
Enrichment 12-7

## Getting Started

### 5-MINUTE WARM-UP

Solve for $x$.
1. $x = 5(7 - 3) + 12$   **32**
2. $x + 25 = 2x - 4$   **29**
3. $48 = 6(x + 5)$   **3**

### Introduction to Lesson 12-7

In conjunction with Question 2, note with students that the Addition Property they applied to equations (for example: if $x - 2 = 7$, then $x - 2 + 2 = 7 + 2$) is applicable in geometric situations.

As an extension of the activity, you may ask students to consider a situation in which the line segments are not all on the same line.

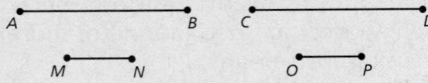

If $\overline{AB} \cong \overline{CD}$ and $\overline{MN} \cong \overline{OP}$, ask students what conclusions can be drawn and how they can be certain about those conclusions.
$AB + MN = CD + OP$ and $AB - MN = CD - OP$

Students should be aware that if definitions or properties that are known to be true are used as reasons in a valid argument, then the argument will be sound.

---

# 12-7 Logical Reasoning and Proof

**Goals**
- Use logical reasoning to prove algebraic statements.
- Use logical reasoning to prove geometric statements.

**Applications** Travel, Number theory, Landscaping, Safety, Music

**Refer to line segment $AD$.**

A    B        C    D

1. Suppose $\overline{AB}$ and $\overline{CD}$ have the same length. What conclusion can be drawn about the lengths of $\overline{AC}$ and $\overline{BD}$?
   *AC and BD also have the same lengths.*
2. Describe how you can be certain about your conclusion from Question 1.   Answers will vary. See additional answers.

3. Do you need to know the length of $\overline{BC}$ to draw this conclusion? Explain.   no; reflexive and commutative properties

4. Suppose you know that $\overline{AC}$ and $\overline{BD}$ have the same measure. Could you conclude from this information that $\overline{AB} \cong \overline{CD}$? Explain.   See additional answers.

## BUILD UNDERSTANDING

Deductive reasoning is important in mathematics. In geometry you use true premises, including definitions and postulates, to reach true conclusions. In algebra you use properties and laws to simplify algebraic expressions and to solve equations. Knowing which facts to use and how to organize your argument logically is an important part of solving problems successfully.

### Example 1

Show that $m\angle a = m\angle b$ in the figure shown. Present your reasons in a logical order.

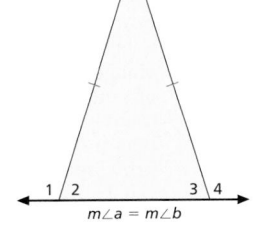

#### Solution

Since the triangle is isosceles, its base angles are congruent, or So, $m\angle 2 = m\angle 3$. Also, angles 1 and 2 and angles 3 and 4 are supplementary.

Therefore, $m\angle 1 + m\angle 2 = 180°$ and $m\angle 3 + m\angle 4 = 180°$. Use these facts from geometry and the laws of algebra to reach the desired conclusion.

$m\angle 2 = 180° - m\angle 1$
$m\angle 3 = 180° - m\angle 4$
$180° - m\angle 1 = 180° - m\angle 4$
$m\angle 1 = m\angle 4$

Example 1 is a deductive proof in which definitions and rules are applied in order to arrive at a new conclusion.

---

## Differentiated Instruction

**VISUAL LEARNERS** To assist students in understanding the proof of Example 1, you may wish to set up a numbered list of statements and reasons, stressing logical order and noting options in order. The beginning of the proof is given. Steps 4–6 are not shown.

| Statements | Reasons |
|---|---|
| 1. $m\angle 1 + m\angle a = 180°$<br>   $m\angle 2 + m\angle b = 180°$ | 1. Definition: Supplementary Angles. |
| 2. $m\angle 1 = 180° - m\angle a$<br>   $m\angle 2 = 180° - m\angle b$ | 2. Subtraction Property of Equality |
| 3. The triangle is isosceles. | 3. Given |

## Example 2

**Prove that the statement below is true.**

*Statement* The sum of an odd integer and an even interger is an odd integer.

### Solution

Use a deductive argument to show that the statement is true.

Let $n$ be any integer. Then any odd integer can be represented by the expression $2n + 1$. Then any even integer can be represented by the expression $2m$, where $m$ is an integer.

Use these expressions to represent the sum of any odd integer and any even integer.

$$(2n + 1) + 2m = (2n + 2m) + 1$$
$$= 2(n + m) + 1$$

The expression $2(n + m) + 1$ is in the form of an odd integer. So the statement is true for any odd and any even integer.

Example 2 considers the general case of odd and even integers. Any value can be selected for $n$ and $m$ and the result will still hold true. Therefore, we can be certain that the statement is true for *all* odd and even integers.

> ### Check Understanding
>
> Why do the expressions $2n + 1$ and $2m$ represent any odd and even number, respectively?
>
> Find the values of $n$ and $m$ that result in the numbers 23, $-56$, 1, 120 and 45.
>
> See additional answers.

## Example 3

**TRAVEL** A plane leaves airport A and flies 240 mi northeast. Another plane leaves airport B and flies 240 mi southwest. Show that $m\angle 1 = m\angle 2$.

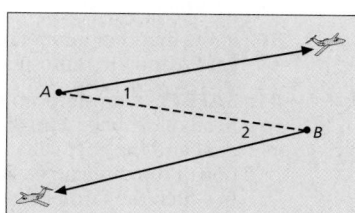

### Solution

Since the two airplanes are flying in opposite directions, their flight routes are parallel to each other. This means that $\overline{AB}$ is a transversal cutting the two parallel lines formed by the airplanes. Since $\angle 1$ and $\angle 2$ are alternate interior angles of the two parallel lines cut by a transversal, they are congruent to each other.

## ▇ TRY THESE EXERCISES

**Show that the conclusion given is true. Present your argument in a logical order.** For 1–2, see additional answers.

**1.** $a° + b° = 180°$

**2.** $a° = b° = 45°$

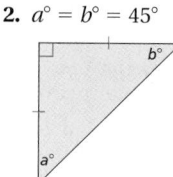

Math**O**nline mathmatters2.com/extra_examples

Lesson 12-7 **Logical Reasoning and Proof** 549

---

## Chalkboard Examples

### Supplementary Example 1 and 2

Prove that a diagonal of a parallelogram divides the parallelogram into two congruent triangles.

Draw and label a diagram. Use the labels of the diagram to express what is given and what you have to prove.

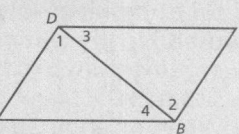

*Given ABCD* is a parallelogram.
*Prove* $\triangle ABD \cong \triangle CDB$
*Argument* By the definition of parallelogram, both pairs of opposite sides are parallel. Each pair of parallel sides yields a pair of congruent alternate interior angles. So, from $AD \parallel CB$, $\angle 1 \cong \angle 2$ and from $AB \parallel CD$, $\angle 3 \cong \angle 4$. Thus, two pairs of corresponding angles of the triangles are congruent. In each triangle, diagonal $BD$ is the side included between the two pairs of angles. Therefore, $\triangle ABD \cong \triangle CDB$ by the Angle-Side-Angle Postulate.

### Reteaching Worksheet 12-7

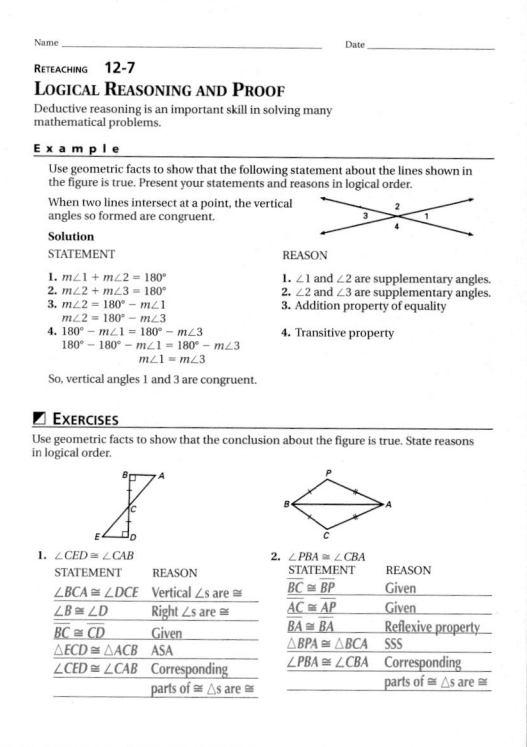

---

## ADDITIONAL ANSWERS

### Introduction

**2.**

| | |
|---|---|
| $AB = CD$ | given |
| $BC = BC$ | reflexive property |
| $AB + BC = CD + BC$ | addition property of equality |
| $AC = BD$ | substitution |

**4.**

| | |
|---|---|
| $AC = BD$ | given |
| $BC = BC$ | reflexive property |
| $AC - BC = BD - BC$ | subtraction property of equality |
| $AB = CD$ | substitution |

### Check Understanding

$2m$ must be an even number because it is a multiple of 2. One more than a multiple of 2 is an odd number. So $2n + 1$ must be odd.

$23 \rightarrow n = 11$    $-56 \rightarrow m = -28$    $1 \rightarrow n = 0$
$120 \rightarrow m = 60$    $45 \rightarrow n = 22$

Lesson 12-7 **Logical Reasoning and Proof** 549

## QUICK ASSESSMENT

Ask the following questions to determine if students understand the content presented in this lesson.

1. What problem-solving strategy is useful in presenting a logical argument involving a geometric situation?  **Draw a diagram.**

2. When offering an argument for a geometric proof, what is crucial in the presentation? Give an example.  **You must follow logical order. Example: To say that the base angles of an isosceles triangle are congruent, you must first establish that you have an isosceles triangle.**

## ASSIGNMENT GUIDE

**Basic:** 1–19, 24–38
**Enriched:** 1–38

## ADDITIONAL ANSWERS

1. $\angle a$ and $\angle b$ are supplementary angles. $m\angle a + m\angle b = 180°$
   $a + b = 180°$

2. $a° + b° + 90° = 180°$  the sum of angles in a triangle is 180°
   $a° = b°$        isosceles triangle
   $a° + b° = 90°$  subtraction
   $a° + a° = 90°$  substitution
   $2a° = 90°$      combine like terms
   $a° = 45°$       division
   $b° = 45°$

3. $2n + 1 + 2m + 1 = 2n + 2m + 2$
   $= 2(n + m + 1)$
   The sum is even since it is a multiple of 2.

4. $(2n + 1)(2m + 1) = 4nm + 2n + 2m + 1 = 2(2nm + n + m) + 1$
   general form of an odd number

5. $\angle A \cong \angle B$  given
   $\angle C$ is supplement of $\angle A$;
   $\angle D$ is supplement of $\angle B$  given
   $m\angle A + m\angle C = 180°$;
   $m\angle B + m\angle D = 180°$  definition of supplementary angles
   $m\angle A + m\angle C = m\angle B + m\angle D$
   transitive property
   $m\angle C = m\angle D$  subtraction property
   $\angle C \cong \angle D$  definition of congruent angles

---

3. **NUMBER THEORY** Show that the sum of any two odd numbers is even. Let $2n + 1$ and $2m + 1$ represent any two odd numbers.  See additional answers.

4. Show that the product of two odd numbers is odd. Let $2n + 1$ and $2m + 1$ represent any two odd numbers.  See additional answers.

5. Show that the supplements of two congruent angles are congruent to each other.  See additional answers.

6. **LANDSCAPING** Find the measure of each angle in the four-sided garden shown in the figure.
   $5x + 10 = 95°; 7x - 6 = 113°; 4x + 2 = 70°; 6x - 20 = 82°$

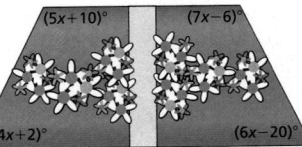

■ **PRACTICE EXERCISES** • For Extra Practice, see page 626.

**Show that the conclusion given is true. Present your argument in a logical order.**  For 7–8, see additional answers.

7. $m\angle 2 = 32°$

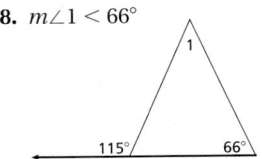

8. $m\angle 1 < 66°$

9. Show that the difference of two even numbers is another even number. Let $2n$ and $2m$ represent any two even numbers.
   See additional answers.

10. Show that the product of two even numbers is an even number. Let $2n$ and $2m$ represent any two even numbers.
    See additional answers.

11. **SAFETY** A farmer wants to safely transport a wolf, a goat and a head of cabbage across a river. If left alone, the wolf will eat the goat and the goat will eat the cabbage. The farmer can take only one of the three on each trip. Use logical reasoning to list the order in which the farmer needs to escort the wolf, goat and cabbage across the river so that they all arrive safely.  See additional answers.

12. Use the diagram of the river and its banks to find the width of the river. Give geometric reasons in a logical order to support your answer.  See additional answers.

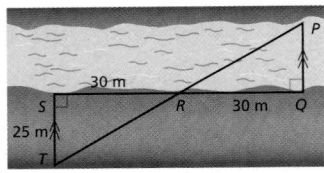

13. **MODELING** Draw a Venn diagram to justify the following statement: *If A is a subset of B and B is a subset of C, then A is a subset of C.*  See additional answers.

14. Show that the difference of two odd numbers is an even number. Let $2n + 1$ and $2m + 1$ represent any two odd numbers.  See additional answers.

15. The angles of a hexagon have measures $10x°$, $(7x + 25)°$, $(12x - 5)°$, $(11x - 20)°$, $(12x + 5)°$, and $(9x + 65)°$. Find the measure of each angle of the hexagon.
    $100°, 95°, 115°, 130°, 125°, 155°$

---

7. $m\angle 2 + 148° = 180° \rightarrow m\angle 2 = 32°$

8. $m\angle 1 + 66° = 115° \rightarrow m\angle 1 = 49°$, and $49° < 66°$.

9. $2n - 2m = 2(n - m)$, and $2(n - m)$ is a multiple of 2

10. $2n \cdot 2m = 4nm = 2(2nm)$, and $2(2nm)$ is a multiple of 2

11. 1st trip across river: take goat across, leaving wolf and cabbage on 1st bank
    1st trip back: go back across river alone

2nd trip across: take cabbage across, leaving wolf on 1st bank
2nd trip back: leave cabbage on 2nd bank, but bring goat back to 1st bank
3rd trip across: take wolf across, leaving goat on 1st bank
3rd trip back: go back across river alone
4th trip across: take goat across
Now all three have been transported across without leaving goat and wolf alone or goat and cabbage alone.

**16. MUSIC** Use deductive reasoning to arrange the statements in a logical order.
   a. Pam sits closer to the conductor than Smitty.
   b. Smitty plays either a woodwind or a percussion instrument.
   c. Pam does not play a percussion instrument.
   d. All woodwind players are seated closer to the conductor than the percussion players.   Answers will vary.

**17.** Write the conclusion that follows from the statements in Exercise 16.   Answers will vary.

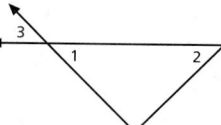

**18.** In the figure, show that if $\angle 1 \cong \angle 2$, then $\angle 2 \cong \angle 3$.
See additional answers.

**19. GEOMETRY SOFTWARE** Use geometry software to show that the sum of the angles of a triangle is 180°. Draw several different types and sizes of triangles, and measure the angles. Is this an example of inductive or deductive reasoning? Explain.   Inductive. The conclusion is based on a pattern of examples.

## ■ EXTENDED PRACTICE EXERCISES

**20.** Show that the product of two rational numbers is a rational number. (Hint: Let $\frac{a}{b}$ and $\frac{c}{d}$ represent any two rational numbers, where $a$, $b$, $c$ and $d$ are integers and $b$ and $d$ are not zero.)   See additional answers.

**21. CRITICAL THINKING** Do you think the quotient of two rational numbers is a rational number? Use algebraic facts to prove this statement, or find a counterexample that disproves it.   See additional answers.

**22. WRITING MATH** Explain the different ways that a rational number can be expressed.   Answers will vary, but may include fractions, repeating decimals and terminating decimals.

**23. CHAPTER INVESTIGATION** Which composer(s) is a crossover from Baroque to Classical? Which composer(s) is a crossover from Classical to Romantic? Create a Venn diagram of the composers from these three eras.
See additional answers.

## ■ MIXED REVIEW EXERCISES

**Find each product.** (Lesson 9-5)

**24.** $(x + 4)(x + 5)$  $x^2 + 9x + 20$     **25.** $(x + 1)(x + 3)$  $x^2 + 4x + 3$

**26.** $(x + 2)(x - 4)$  $x^2 - 2x - 8$     **27.** $(x + 3)^2$  $x^2 + 6x + 9$

**28.** $(x - 4)^2$  $x^2 - 8x + 16$     **29.** $(x - 5)(x + 5)$  $x^2 - 25$

**30.** $(2x + 5)(x - 3)$  $2x^2 - x - 15$     **31.** $(3x - 4)(2x + 1)$  $6x^2 - 5x - 4$

**32.** $(5x - 7)(2x - 3)$  $10x^2 - 29x + 21$     **33.** $(4x + 2)^2$  $16x^2 + 16x + 4$

**34.** $(3x - 8)^2$  $9x^2 - 48x + 64$     **35.** $(3x + 3)^2$  $9x^2 + 18x + 9$

**Find the volume of each solid.** (Lesson 10-7)

**36.**
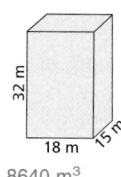
18 m   32 m   15 m
8640 m³

**37.**
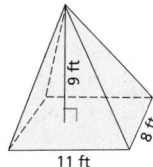
9 ft   8 ft   11 ft
264 ft³

**38.**
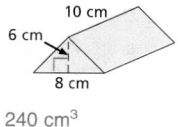
10 cm   6 cm   8 cm
240 cm³

---

**12.** $m\angle S = m\angle Q$   right angles are congruent
$m\angle SRT = m\angle QRP$   vertical angles have equal measure
$SR \cong QR$   line segments with equal measure are congruent
$\triangle TSR \cong \triangle PQR$   angle-side-angle theorem
$\overline{PQ} \cong \overline{TS}$   corresponding parts of congruent triangles are congruent
$PQ = 25$ m   substitution or transitive property

**13.**
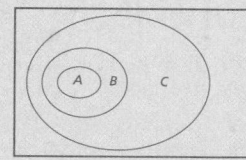

**14.** $(2n + 1) - (2m + 1) = 2n + 1 - 2m - 1 = 2n - 2m = 2(n - m)$, and $2(n - m)$ has the form of an even number.

**18.** $\angle 1 \cong \angle 2$   given
$\angle 1 \cong \angle 3$   vertical angles are congruent
$\angle 2 \cong \angle 3$   transitive property

---

Name _____   Date _____

EXTRA PRACTICE   **12-7**
**LOGICAL REASONING AND PROOF**

### ■ EXERCISES
Show that the conclusion given is true. Present your argument in a logical order.

**1.** $m\angle 1 + m\angle 2 = 90°$
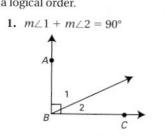

Since $\angle ABC$ is a right angle, its measure is 90°. Also, $m\angle 1 + m\angle 2 = m\angle ABC$. By substitution, $m\angle 1 + m\angle 2 = 90°$.

**2.** $m\angle 1 = m\angle 8$
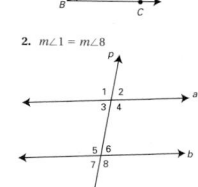

Since $a \parallel b$, $\angle 1$ and $\angle 5$ are congruent because they are corresponding angles. $\angle 5$ and $\angle 8$ are congruent because they are vertical angles. So $\angle 1$ and $\angle 8$ are congruent by the Transitive Property of Congruence, and $m\angle 1 = m\angle 8$.

**3.** Show that the sum of any two consecutive integers is an odd number. Let $n$ and $n + 1$ represent any two consecutive integers.   Suppose $(n) + (n + 1) = 2n + 1$. Since 2 times any number is always even, adding 1 makes it odd. So $2n + 1$ is odd and thus the sum of any two consecutive integers is odd.

**4.** Show that the complements of two congruent angles are congruent to each other. Suppose that $\angle 1$ and $\angle 2$ are both complements of $\angle 3$. So, $m\angle 1 + m\angle 3 = 90°$ and $m\angle 2 + m\angle 3 = 90°$. By substitution, $m\angle 1 + m\angle 3 = m\angle 2 + m\angle 3$. Subtracting $m\angle 3$ from both sides, $m\angle 1 = m\angle 2$. So, the complements of two congruent angles are congruent to each other.

---

**20.** $\frac{a}{b} \cdot \frac{c}{d} = \frac{a \cdot c}{b \cdot d} = \frac{ac}{bd}$, and $\frac{ac}{bd}$ has the form of a rational number.

**21.** Yes; $\frac{a}{b} \div \frac{c}{d} = \frac{a}{b} \cdot \frac{d}{c} = \frac{ad}{bc}$, assuming $c \neq 0$, and $\frac{ad}{bc}$ has the form of a rational number.

**23.** Answers will vary, but possible answers are listed.

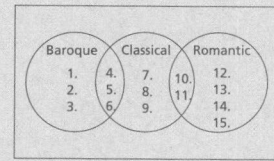

1. Henry Purcell
2. Monteverdi
3. Johann Sebastian Bach
4. Georg Philipp Telemann
5. George Frideric Handel
6. Carl Philip Emmanuel Bach
7. Joseph Haydn
8. Wolfgang Amadeus Mozart
9. Christoph Willibald Gluck
10. Ludwig van Beethoven
11. Felix Mendelssohn
12. Peter Tchaikovsky
13. Johannes Brahms
14. Gustav Mahler
15. Richard Strauss

### Vocabulary Assessment

- A matching section checks for student understanding of the new vocabulary introduced in this chapter.
- A vocabulary review/test for Chapter 12 is available on pp. vii–viii of the *Chapter 12 Resource Masters*.

### Lesson-by-Lesson Review

For each lesson,

- the main ideas are summarized, and
- practice exercises are provided.

## EXAMVIEW® PRO

Use the networkable **ExamView® Pro** to:

- Create **multiple versions** of tests.
- Create **modified** tests for *inclusion* students.
- **Edit** existing questions and **add** your own questions.
- Use built-in **state curriculum correlations** to create tests aligned with state standards.
- Change **English** tests to **Spanish** and vice versa.

# Chapter 12 Review

## VOCABULARY ◼

**Choose the word from the list that best completes each statement.**

1. Two sets $A$ and $B$ are __?__ if they contain the same members. c
2. Two sets are __?__ if they contain the same number of elements. d
3. Two sets whose intersection is the empty set are called __?__. b
4. To write the __?__ of a statement, add "not" to the statement. i
5. In a deductive argument, the __?__ themselves lead logically to the conclusion. k
6. If a set of statements is accepted as true, you are using __?__. a
7. A set that contains no elements is called a(n) __?__ j
8. Given the statement $p \rightarrow q$, if $p$ is true then $q$ is also true. This is an example of the __?__. g
9. The set of integers is a __?__ of the set of whole numbers. l
10. A set that contains elements common to two other sets is the __?__ of the two sets. f

| | |
|---|---|
| **a.** | deductive reasoning |
| **b.** | disjoint sets |
| **c.** | equal sets |
| **d.** | equivalent sets |
| **e.** | inductive reasoning |
| **f.** | intersection |
| **g.** | Law of Detachment |
| **h.** | Law of the Contrapositive |
| **i.** | negation |
| **j.** | null set |
| **k.** | premises |
| **l.** | subset |

## LESSON 12-1 ◼ Properties of Sets, p. 520

▶ **Description notation** describes the set; **roster notation** lists the elements of the set; and **set-builder notation** gives the rule that defines each element.

**Define each set in roster notation and in set-builder notation. Then determine whether the set is finite or infinite.**
For 11 and 12, see additional answers.

11. $A$, the set of whole numbers less than 5
12. $B$, the set of negative integers less than $-3$.
13. $C$, the set of whole numbers greater than $-8$  $C = \{-7, -6, -5, ...\}$; $C = \{x \mid x$ is a whole number $> -8\}$; infinite
14. $D$, the set of positive integers  $D = \{1, 2, 3, ...\}$; $D = \{x \mid x$ is a positive integer$\}$; infinite
15. $R$, the set of negative integers greater than $-100$  $R = \{-99, -98, -97, ..., -1\}$; $R = \{x \mid x$ is a negative integer $> -100\}$; infinite
16. $S$, the set of natural numbers less than or equal to 100  $S = \{1, 2, 3, ..., 100\}$; $S = \{x \mid x$ is a natural number $\leq 100\}$; infinite

**Use set notation to write the following.**

17. 5 is an element of $\{5, 10, 15, 20, 25, ...\}$
    $5 \in \{5, 10, 15, 20, 25, ...\}$
18. 8 is an element of $\{2, 4, 6, 8, ...\}$
    $8 \in \{2, 4, 6, 8, ...\}$

## LESSON 12-2 ◼ Union and Intersection of Sets, p. 524

▶ If $A$ is a subset of $U$ then the **complement** of $A$, $A'$, is the subset containing all elements of $U$ that are not elements of $A$.

▶ The **union** of two sets $A$ and $B$ is the set of all elements that are in $A$, in $B$, or in both $A$ and $B$. The **intersection** of two sets $A$ and $B$ is the set of all elements that are elements of $A$ and elements of $B$.

**552** | Chapter 12 **Logic and Sets**

## ADDITIONAL ANSWERS

11. $A = \{0, 1, 2, 3, 4\}$; $A = \{x \mid x$ is a whole number less than 5$\}$; finite
12. $B = \{-4, -5, -6, ...\}$; $B = \{x \mid x$ is a negative integer less than $-3\}$; infinite
29. If a figure is a rectangle, then it is a quadrilateral.

**Let $U = \{1, 2, 3, 4, \ldots, 12\}$, $A = \{1, 2, 3, 4\}$ and $B = \{3, 6, 9, 12\}$. Find the following.**

**19.** $A'$  {5, 6, 7, 8, 9, 10, 11, 12}  **20.** $A \cup B$ {1, 2, 3, 4, 6, 9, 12}  **21.** $A \cap B$ {3}

**22.** $B'$
{1, 2, 4, 5, 7, 8, 10, 11}  **23.** $A' \cap B$
{6, 9, 12}  **24.** $A' \cup B$
{3, 5, 6, 7, 8, 9, 10, 11, 12}

**List the members of each set.**

**25.** $R \cup S$ {1, 2, 3, 4, 5, 7, 9, 10}  **26.** $R \cap S$ {1, 3}

**27.** $S \cap T$ {9}  **28.** $R \cup T$
{1, 2, 3, 5, 7, 6, 8, 9, 11}

# LESSON 12-3 ■ Problem Solving: Conditional Statements, p. 530

▶ An *if-then* statement is called a **conditional statement**.

▶ Interchanging the hypothesis and conclusion of a conditional statement results in the **converse** of the original statement.

**Refer to the following statement:** *All rectangles are quadrilaterals.*
For 29–31, see additional answers.

**29.** Rephrase the statement as an *if-then* statement.  **30.** Write the converse.

**31.** Determine if the statement and its converse are *true* or *false*. If *false*, give a counterexample.

**Refer to the following statement:** *When it's raining people use umbrellas.*

**32.** Rephrase the statement as an *if-then* statement.  **33.** Write the converse.

**34.** Determine if the statement and its converse are *true* or *false*. If *false*, give a counterexample.
For 32–37, see additional answers.
**Refer to the following statement:** *All figures that are rhombi have perpendicular diagonals.*

**35.** Rephrase the statement as an *if-then* statement.  **36.** Write the converse.

**37.** Determine if the statement and its converse are *true* or *false*. If *false*, give a counterexample.

# LESSON 12-4 ■ Converse, Inverse and Contrapositive, p. 532

▶ The **converse** and **inverse** of a true conditional statement are not necessarily true.

▶ A conditional statement and its **contrapositive** are either both true or both false.

**Refer to the following statement:** *If you are studying Russian, then you are studying a foreign language.*

**38.** Write the converse of the statement. If you are studying a foreign language, then you are studying Russian.

**39.** Write the inverse of the statement. If you're not studying Russian, then you are not studying a foreign language.

**40.** Write the contrapositive of the statement. If you're not studying a foreign language, then you are not studying Russian.

**Refer to the following statement:** *If you like vegetables then you like broccoli.*

**41.** Write the converse of the statement. If you like broccoli then you like vegetables.

**42.** Write the inverse of the statement. If you don't like vegetables, then you don't like broccoli.

**43.** Write the contrapositive of the statement. If you don't like broccoli, then you don't like vegetables.

Chapter 12 **Review** | 553

**50.** $x + 3x + 50 + 2x + 4 = 360$
(The sum of the measures of the interior angles of a quadrilateral is 360°.)
$6x + 54 = 360$ (simplify)
$6x = 306$ (subtraction property)
$x = 51$ (division property)
Therefore, $m\angle A = 51°$.

**51.** Since the sum of the interior angles of a triangle equal 180°, $a° + b° + c° = 180°$. Since the triangle is an equiangular triangle it is also equilateral. Therefore, $a° = b° = c°$. By substitution, $3a° = 180$. By the division property, $a° = 60°$. Therefore, $a° = b° = c° = 60°$.

## LESSON 12-5 ◾ Inductive and Deductive Reasoning, p. 538

▶ In **inductive reasoning**, a limited number of individual instances provide evidence for a conjecture about all instances of something.

▶ In **deductive reasoning**, a conclusion is drawn from premises that are accepted as true.

**Complete each argument by drawing a conclusion.**

**44.** *Premise 1* If the animal is a lion, then it has a mane.
*Premise 2* Elsa is a lion.
Elsa has a mane.

**45.** *Premise 1* If you live in Chicago, then you live in Illinois.
*Premise 2* Jacquie lives in Chicago.
Jacquie lives in Illinois.

**46.** *Premise 1* Green leafy vegetables are a good source of calcium.
*Premise 2* Spinach is a green leafy vegetable.
Spinach is a good source of calcium.

## LESSON 12-6 ◾ Patterns of Deductive Reasoning, p. 542

▶ In a **valid argument**, if the premises are true then the conclusion must be true.

**Determine by form whether the argument is *valid* or *invalid*. If *valid*, name the argument form.**

**47.** If the bird is a canary, then the bird is not a macaw.
My bird Chatter is a macaw.
Therefore, my bird is not a canary.  valid; Law of the Contrapositive

**48.** If you earn an A on the test, then you studied.
Abby earned an A on the test.
Therefore she studied for the test.  valid; Law of Detachment

**49.** If your pet swims, then it is a fish.
Fluffy doesn't swim.
Therefore, Fluffy is not a fish.  invalid

## LESSON 12-7 ◾ Logical Reasoning and Proof, p. 548

▶ Knowing which facts to use and how to organize your argument logically is an important part of solving problems successfully.

**Show that the conclusion given is true. Present your argument in a logical order.**
For 50 and 51, see additional answers.

**50.** $m\angle A = 51°$

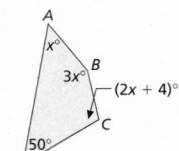

**51.** $a° = b° = c° = 60°$

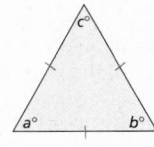

## CHAPTER INVESTIGATION

**EXTENSION** Find composers from the Renaissance, the time period before the Baroque Age, and the Twentieth Century. Add these two time periods to your Venn Diagram.

## THEME: Music

The benchmarks and expectations for this extension are as follows.
• Students find and list five composers from the Baroque Age.
• Students find and list five composers from the Classical Period.
• Students find and list five composers from the Romantic Age.
• Students determine which composer(s) is a cross-over from Baroque to Classical and from Classical to Romantic. They create a Venn diagram of the composers from these eras.
• Students find composers from the Renaissance and the Twentieth Century. They add these two time periods to their Venn diagram.

# Chapter 12 Assessment

1. Determine which sets are *equal* and which are *equivalent*.
   A, B and C are equivalent; A = B
   $A = \{9, 3, 1, 7, 11\}$      $B = \{11, 7, 1, 9, 3\}$      $C = \{7, 1, 5, 9, 4\}$

Let $U = \{t, i, m, e, s\}$, $P = \{t, i, m, e\}$ and $Q = \{s, i, t, e\}$. Find the following.

2. $P' \cup Q'$   $\{s, m\}$
3. $(P \cup Q)'$   $\varnothing$
4. $P' \cap Q'$   $\varnothing$

**Write the converse, inverse, and contrapositive of each statement. Determine whether each statement is *true* or *false*. If *false*, give a counterexample.**
For 5–7, see additional answers.

5. If a triangle is equilateral, then each angle of the triangle has a measure of 60°.

6. If a number is a member of the set $\{1, 3, 5, 7, 11\}$, then the number is prime.

7. If a plant is a tree, then it has roots.

8. Write the following statement in if-then form. Our collie Max barks whenever he hears a knock at the door.   If our collie Max hears a knock at the door, then he barks.

**Write the negation of each statement two ways.**
For 9 and 10, see additional answers.

9. The young man is entering college in the fall.

10. Mia is building her science project out of mylar.

**Tell whether the reasoning used is inductive or deductive.**

11. Ravi measured 12 pairs of alternate interior angles formed by parallel lines and transversals. He then concluded that alternate interior angles have the same measure.   inductive

12. Harry used the definitions of a square and of the area of a rectangle to conclude that the area of a square with sides of length $x$ is equal to $x^2$.   deductive

**Determine by form whether the arguments are *valid* or *invalid*. If *valid*, name the argument form.**

13. If a number is odd, then the square of the number is odd. The number 7 is odd. Therefore, the square of 7 is odd.   valid; Law of Detachment

14. If the figure is a pentagon, then the figure is a polygon. The figure is not a pentagon. Therefore, the figure is not a polygon.   invalid

**Show that the conclusion given is true. Present your argument in a logical order.**   For 15–16, see additional answers.

15. $AB = 5$ cm

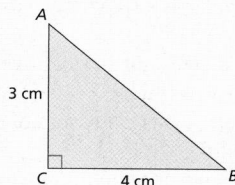

16. The slope of $\overline{AB} = \frac{4}{5}$.

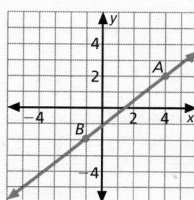

## ADDITIONAL ANSWERS

5. If each angle of a triangle has a measure of 60°, then the triangle is equilateral. True.
   If a triangle is not equilateral, then not all of its angles have a measure of 60°. True.
   If it is not the case that all angles of a triangle have a measure of 60°, then the triangle is not equilateral. True.

6. If a number is prime, then the number is a member of the set $\{1, 3, 5, 7, 11\}$. False. 2 is prime.

If a number is not a member of the set $\{1, 3, 5, 7, 11\}$, then the number is not prime. False, 2 is prime.
If a number is not prime, then the number is not a member of the set $\{1, 3, 5, 7, 11\}$. True.

7. If a plant has roots, then the plant is a tree. False. Grass has roots, but is not a tree.
   If a plant is not a tree, then it does not have roots. False. Grass has roots, but is not a tree.
   If a plant does not have roots, then the plant is not a tree. True.

Additional answers continued on page 556.

---

## Assessment Options

Chapter 12 Test A, pages 405–406
Chapter 12 Test B, pages 407–408

## ALTERNATIVE ASSESSMENT

**LOGICAL JEOPARDY** Prior to class, make up 3 sets of 6 *if-then* statements that vary in difficulty. Assign the statements in each set a point value: 100, 200, 300, 400, 500, or 1000, with no repetition. Write the inverse, converse, and contrapositive of each statement on an index card and its point value on the opposite side. Display the cards on a chalkboard as follows.

| Inverse | Converse | Contrapositive |
|---------|----------|----------------|
| 100 | 100 | 100 |
| 200 | 200 | 200 |
| 300 | 300 | 300 |
| 400 | 400 | 400 |
| 500 | 500 | 500 |
| 1000 | 1000 | 1000 |

Divide the class into two teams, A and B. Team A selects a category and point value. After you read the corresponding *if-then* statement, select a member of Team A to write the appropriate statement on the chalkboard. (Be sure to select each team member at least twice.) If Team A's response is correct, they get the points. If not, any member of Team B is given the chance to win the points by answering correctly. Teams take turns selecting and responding. The team with the highest score at the end of the game is the winner.

**RUBRIC** The following rubric is a sample scoring guide.

| Points | Description |
|--------|-------------|
| 4 | Fully participates in the game, and offers **consistently correct** responses. |
| 3 | Fully participates in the game, but offers only **one correct** response. |
| 2 | Fully participates in the game, but offers **no correct** responses. |
| 1 | Only **somewhat participates** in the game, and offers no correct responses. |
| 0 | **Does not participate** in the game. |

## Standardized Test Practice

These two pages contain practice questions in the various formats that can be found on the most frequently given standardized tests.

A student recording sheet for these two pages can be found on p. A1 of the *Chapter 12 Resource Masters*.

### Standardized Test Practice Student Recording Sheet

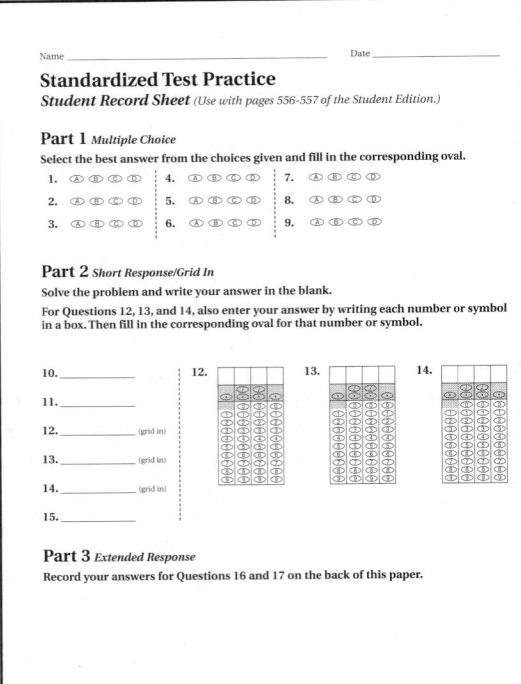

### Additional Practice

See pp. 409–411 in the *Chapter 12 Resource Masters* for additional standardized test practice.

# Standardized Test Practice

**Record your answers on the answer sheet provided by your teacher or on a sheet of paper.**

1. Simplify: $\frac{x^2 y^{-3}}{x^{-2} y^2}$. (Lesson 2-8)  D

   Ⓐ $\frac{1}{y^5}$   Ⓑ $x^4$   Ⓒ $\frac{x^2}{y^6}$   Ⓓ $\frac{x^4}{y^5}$

2. A die is rolled, and the spinner shown is spun. What is the probability of rolling a 3 and spinning the letter D? (Lesson 4-4)  D

   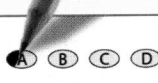

   Ⓐ $\frac{1}{5}$   Ⓑ $\frac{1}{6}$   Ⓒ $\frac{1}{11}$   Ⓓ $\frac{1}{30}$

3. The coordinates of the vertices of $\triangle RST$ are $R(3, 3)$, $S(5, 4)$, and $T(4, -3)$. If the triangle is reflected over the $x$-axis, what are the coordinates of $S'$? (Lesson 7-2)  B

   Ⓐ $(-5, -4)$   Ⓑ $(5, -4)$
   Ⓒ $(-5, 4)$   Ⓓ $(4, 5)$

4. When solving the system of equations, which expression could be substituted for $x$? (Lesson 8-3)  C

   $$x + 4y = 1$$
   $$2x - 3y = -9$$

   Ⓐ $4y - 1$   Ⓑ $3y - 9$
   Ⓒ $1 - 4y$   Ⓓ $-9 - 3y$

5. What is the determinant of matrix $M$? (Lesson 8-5)  B

   $$M = \begin{bmatrix} -3 & 2 \\ 0 & 8 \end{bmatrix}$$

   Ⓐ $-26$   Ⓑ $-24$   Ⓒ $0$   Ⓓ $22$

**Test-Taking Tip**

Ⓐ Ⓑ Ⓒ Ⓓ

**Question 1**
When answering a multiple-choice question, first find an answer on your own. Then, compare your answer to the answer choices given in the item. If your answer does not match any of the answer choices, check your calculations.

6. What is the distance from one corner of the rectangular garden to the opposite corner? (Lesson 11-3)  A

   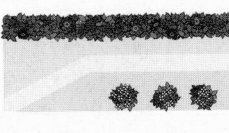
   5 yd
   12 yd

   Ⓐ 13 yd
   Ⓑ 14 yd
   Ⓒ 15 yd
   Ⓓ 17 yd

7. Which of the following represents the union of $X$ and $Y$? (Lesson 12-2)  A

   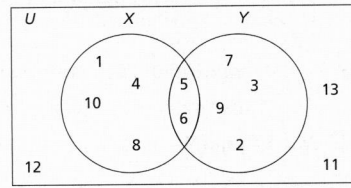

   Ⓐ $\{1, 2, 3, 4, 5, 6, 7, 8, 9, 10\}$
   Ⓑ $\{1, 2, 3, 4, 5, 6, 7, 8, 9, 10, 11, 12, 13\}$
   Ⓒ $\{5, 6\}$
   Ⓓ $\{11, 12, 13\}$

8. Which of the following is a counterexample to the statement: *If Eric did not eat lunch, then he must not feel well?* (Lesson 12-3)  A

   Ⓐ Eric was not hungry.
   Ⓑ Eric ate lunch so he must feel fine.
   Ⓒ Eric ate at a deli.
   Ⓓ Eric does not feel well.

9. Which of the following is the converse of the statement: *All right angles measure 90°?* (Lesson 12-4)  C

   Ⓐ If an angle is a right angle, then its measure is 90°.
   Ⓑ If an angle is not a right angle, then its measure is not 90°.
   Ⓒ If an angle has a measure of 90°, then it is a right angle.
   Ⓓ If an angle does not have a measure of 90°, then it is not a right angle.

## ADDITIONAL ANSWERS

(continued from page 555)

9. The young man is not entering college in the fall. It is not the case that the young man is entering college in the fall.

10. Mia is not building her science project out of mylar. It is not the case that Mia is building her science project out of mylar.

15. Triangle $ABC$ is a right triangle, therefore the length of its hypotenuse, $AB$, is the square root of the sum of the squares of each of its leg lengths. $3^2 + 4^2 = 25$. Square root of 25 is 5. Therefore $AB = 5$ cm.

16. Since the slope of a line is the ratio of the difference of the $y$-values of two points on the line to the difference of two $x$-values of the same two points, then $\frac{2 - (-2)}{4 - (-1)} = \frac{4}{5}$.

## Part 2  Short Response/Grid In

Record your answers on the answer sheet provided by your teacher or on a sheet of paper.

10. Solve the system of equations. (Lesson 8-3)  $(-3, 8)$

$$x + 2y = 13$$
$$-2x - 3y = -18$$

11. What polynomial expression describes the area of the rectangle shown? (Lesson 9-5)  $3x^2 + 26x + 48$

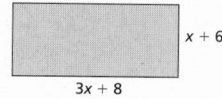

$x + 6$

$3x + 8$

12. Shelly bought a triangular prism at the science museum. The bases of the prism are equilateral triangles with side lengths of 2 cm. The height of the prism is 4 cm. What is the surface area of Shelly's prism? Round to the nearest square centimeter? (Lesson 10-3)  27 cm²

13. Allison is 5 ft tall. She is standing next to a tree with a shadow that is 22.5 ft long. If her shadow is 11 ft long, how tall in feet is the tree? Round to the nearest tenth of a foot. (Lesson 11-2)  10.2 ft

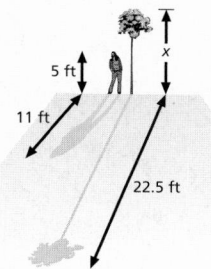

5 ft

11 ft

$x$

22.5 ft

14. A 17-ft ladder is propped against a window ledge. If the top of the ladder is 8 ft above ground, how far away from the building is the base of the ladder? (Lesson 11-3)  15 ft

**Math Online**  mathmatters2.com/standardized_test

15. What is the length of $\overline{RT}$? Round to the nearest tenth. (Lesson 11-7)  7.1 cm

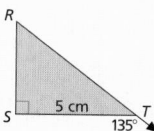

R

S   5 cm   T   135°

## Part 3  Extended Response

Record your answers on a sheet of paper. Show your work.

16. A movie theatre concession is ordering cones for popcorn. There are two sizes available. (Lesson 10-8)

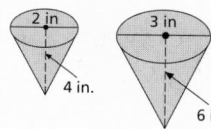

2 in   3 in

4 in.   6 in.

a. What is the volume of each cone? Use 3.14 for π and round to the nearest tenth.  16.7 in.³, 56.5 in.³

b. What is the ratio of the height of the larger cone to the height of the smaller cone?  1.5

c. What is the ratio of the volume of the larger cone to the volume of the smaller cone?  3.375

17. Miguel hikes 3 mi north, 7 mi east, and then 6 mi north again. (Lesson 11-3)

a. Draw a diagram showing the direction and distance of each segment of Miguel's hike. Label the starting point, ending point, and the distance in miles of each segment of his hike.  See additional answers.

b. To the nearest tenth of a mile, how far is Miguel from his starting point?  11.4 mi

c. How did your diagram help you find Miguel's distance from his starting point? See additional answers.

**Chapter 12  Standardized Test Practice  557**

17a.

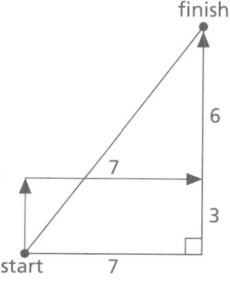

finish

6

7

3

start   7

17c. **The diagram shows that there are two right triangles. The distance is equal to the sum of the measure of the hypotenuse of each triangle.**

## Rubrics

The following rubrics are sample scoring guides for short response and extended response questions.

### Short Response

| Points | Description |
|---|---|
| 2 | The student demonstrates a **thorough understanding** of the mathematics of the task. The response may contain minor flaws that do not detract from the demonstration of a thorough understanding. |
| 1 | The student has provided a response that is only **partially correct.** |
| 0 | The student has provided a **completely incorrect** solution or no response at all. |

### Extended Response

| Points | Description |
|---|---|
| 4 | The student demonstrates a **thorough understanding** of the mathematics of the task. The response contains minor flaws that do not detract from the demonstration of a thorough understanding. |
| 3 | The student demonstrates an **understanding** of the mathematics of the task. The response is essentially correct and demonstrates an essential but less than thorough understanding of the mathematics. |
| 2 | The student has demonstrated only a **partial understanding** of the mathematics of the task. Although the student may have used the correct approach to a solution or may have provided a correct solution, the work lacks an essential understanding of the underlying mathematical concepts. |
| 1 | The student has demonstrated a **very limited understanding** of the mathematics of the task. The response is incomplete and exhibits many flaws. |
| 0 | The student has provided a **completely incorrect** solution or no response at all. |

# Student Handbook

## Data File

Animals ..................................................................560

Arts & Entertainment ....................................562

Earth Science ....................................................564

Environment ......................................................566

Health & Fitness ..............................................568

Leisure ................................................................570

Travel & Transportation ..............................572

United States of America ............................574

## Prerequisite Skills ....................................576

## Extra Practice ............................................585

## Preparing for Standardized Tests ......627

## Technology Reference Guide ................646

## English-Spanish Glossary ....................650

## Selected Answers ....................................672

## Photo Credits ............................................699

## Index ............................................................700

# Data File

## Animals

### How Big is a Bird Egg?

| Type of Bird Egg | Length (centimeters) | Mass (grams) |
|---|---|---|
| Arctic Tern | 4.0 | 19 |
| Barn Owl | 3.9 | 20.7 |
| Chicken (extra large) | 6.3 | 63.8 |
| Chicken (small) | 5.3 | 42.5 |
| Grey Heron | 6.0 | 60 |
| Hummingbird | Less than 1.25 | Less than 0.5 |
| Louisiana Egret | 4.5 | 27.5 |
| Partridge | 3.6 | 14 |
| Swallow | 1.9 | 2 |
| Swift | 2.5 | 3.6 |
| Turtledove | 3.1 | 9 |

### American Pet Ownership

| Pet | Millions of U.S. Households |
|---|---|
| Dogs | 34.6 |
| Cats | 29.2 |
| Birds | 5.4 |
| Fish | 2.7 |
| Rabbits | 2.3 |
| Horses | 1.9 |
| Rodents | 1.4 |
| Reptiles | 0.9 |

### Cricket Chirps Per Minute in Relation to Temperature

| Temperature (°F) | Chirps/Minute |
|---|---|
| 50 | 40 |
| 52 | 48 |
| 55 | 60 |
| 56 | 64 |
| 58 | 76 |
| 60 | 80 |
| 64 | 98 |
| 68 | 116 |
| 72 | 125 |
| 73 | 135 |
| 75 | 140 |
| 80 | 160 |

## Percent of Americans Owning a Pet for Particular Reasons

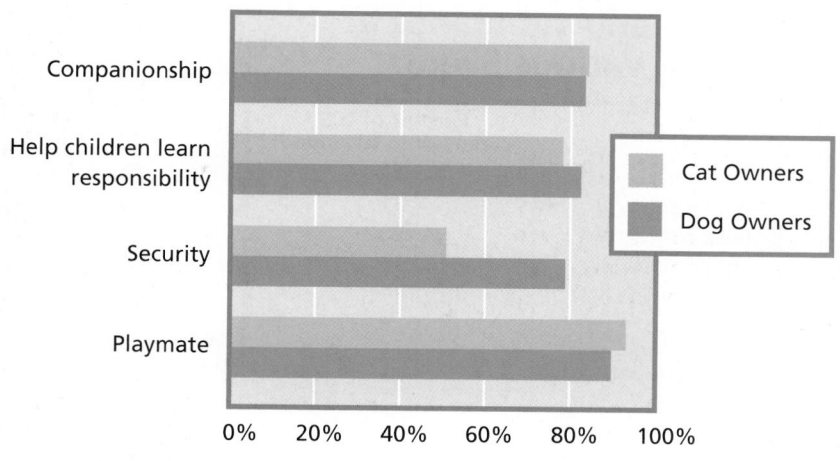

Companionship

Help children learn responsibility

Security

Playmate

0%  20%  40%  60%  80%  100%

Cat Owners

Dog Owners

## Audible Frequency Ranges

| Animal | Emission (Hertz: vibrations/second) | | Reception (Hertz: vibrations/second) | |
|---|---|---|---|---|
| | Minimum | Maximum | Minimum | Maximum |
| Bats | 10,000 | 120,000 | 1,000 | 120,000 |
| Cats | 760 | 1,520 | 60 | 65,000 |
| Dogs | 452 | 1,080 | 15 | 50,000 |
| Dolphins | 7,000 | 120,000 | 150 | 150,000 |
| Grasshoppers | 7,000 | 100,000 | 100 | 15,000 |
| Humans | 85 | 1,100 | 20 | 20,000 |

## Sleep Times

| Creature | Average hours/day |
|---|---|
| Armadillo | 19 |
| Cow | 7 |
| Elephant | 3 |
| Giraffe | 4 |
| Horse | 5 |
| Human adult | 8 |
| Human child | 10-12 |
| Jaguar | 11 |
| Mole | 8 |
| Mountain Beaver | 14 |
| Pig | 13 |
| Rabbit | 10 |
| Sheep | 6 |
| Shrew | Less than 1 |
| Two-toed Sloth | 20 |

# Arts & Entertainment

## Teen Attendance at Various Events

| Event | Percent of U.S. Teens Who Attended |
|---|---|
| Pro sports | 44 |
| Art museum | 31 |
| Rock concert | 28 |
| Other museum | 26 |
| Symphony concert | 11 |
| Ballet | 7 |
| Opera | 4 |

## Popular Symphony Orchestras

| Instrument | Orchestra Members | | |
|---|---|---|---|
| | Boston Symphony Orchestra | Japan Philharmonic Symphony Orchestra | Tenerife Symphony Orchestra |
| | Boston, Massachusetts | Tokyo, Japan | Canary Islands, Spain |
| Violins | 25 | 24 | 26 |
| Violas | 11 | 9 | 10 |
| Cellos | 11 | 9 | 9 |
| Basses | 9 | 6 | 7 |
| Flutes | 3 | 4 | 3 |
| Piccolo | 1 | 0 | 2 |
| Oboes | 3 | 4 | 3 |
| English horn | 1 | 0 | 2 |
| Clarinets | 4 | 4 | 6 |
| Bassoons | 3 | 4 | 3 |
| Contrabassoon | 1 | 0 | 1 |
| Horns | 6 | 6 | 5 |
| Trumpets | 3 | 4 | 2 |
| Trombones | 3 | 4 | 2 |
| Tuba | 1 | 1 | 1 |
| Timpani & Percussion | 5 | 4 | 3 |
| Harps | 1 | 1 | 1 |

## Music Media and Year Introduced

| Music Type | Year Introduced |
|---|---|
| Record player | 1877 |
| 33-RPM records | 1948 |
| 45-RPM records | 1949 |
| Transistor radio | 1957 |
| Audio cassette | 1965 |
| Walkman | 1979 |
| CD's | 1982 |
| CD walkman | 1986 |
| MP3 player | 1997 |

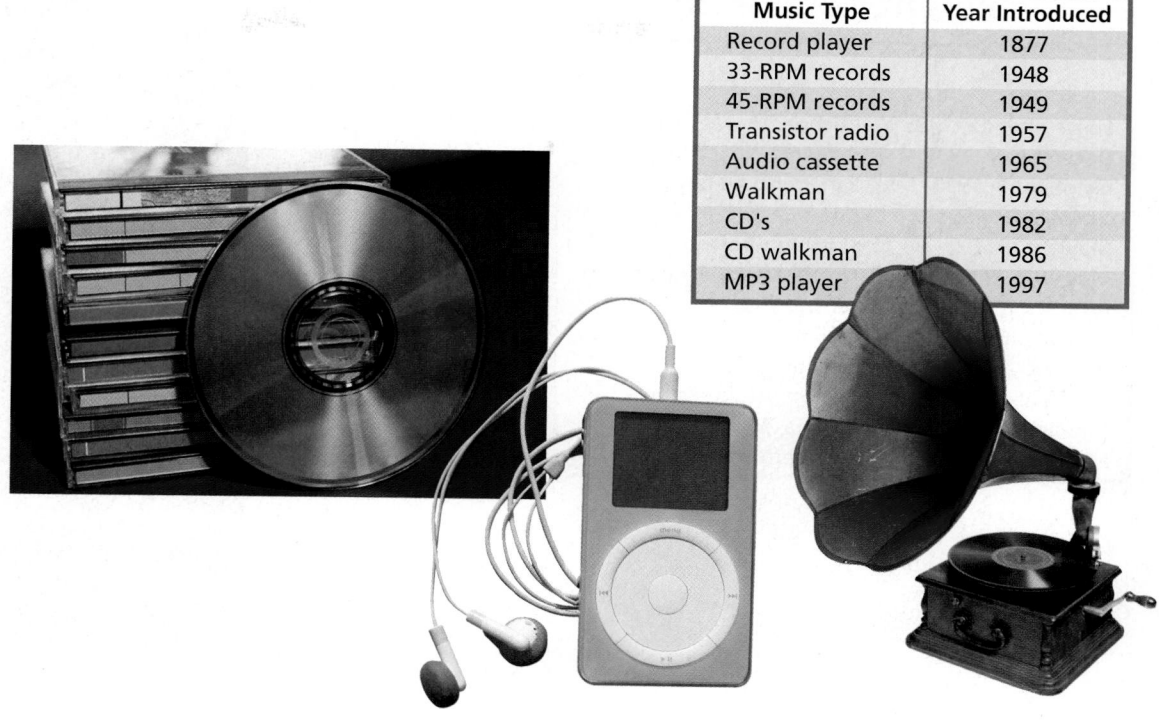

## Top Concert Tours

| Rank | Performer | Year | Gross revenues |
|---|---|---|---|
| 1 | The Rolling Stones | 1994 | $121,200,000 |
| 2 | U2 | 2001 | $109,700,000 |
| 3 | Pink Floyd | 1994 | $103,500,000 |
| 4 | Paul McCartney | 2002 | $103,300,000 |
| 5 | The Rolling Stones | 1989 | $98,000,000 |
| 6 | The Rolling Stones | 1997 | $89,300,000 |
| 7 | The Rolling Stones | 2002 | $87,900,000 |
| 8 | 'N Sync | 2001 | $86,800,000 |
| 9 | Backstreet Boys | 2001 | $82,100,000 |
| 10 | Tina Turner | 2000 | $80,200,000 |
| 11 | U2 | 1997 | $79,900,000 |
| 12 | The Eagles | 1994 | $79,400,000 |
| 13 | 'N Sync | 2000 | $76,400,000 |
| 14 | The New Kids on the Block | 1990 | $74,100,000 |
| 15 | Cher | 2002 | $73,600,000 |
| 16 | Dave Matthews Band | 2000 | $68,200,000 |
| 17 | U2 | 1992 | $67,000,000 |
| 18 | Billy Joel/Elton John | 2002 | $65,500,000 |
| 19 | The Rolling Stones | 1999 | $64,700,000 |
| 20 | The Eagles | 1995 | $63,300,000 |

# Earth Science

## Recent Notable Earthquakes

| Date | Place | Magnitude (Richter Scale) |
|------|-------|---------------------------|
| September 19, 1985 | Michoacan, Mexico | 8.1 |
| December 7, 1988 | Armenia | 7.0 |
| October 17, 1989 | San Francisco Bay Area, CA | 7.1 |
| January 16, 1995 | Kobe, Japan | 6.9 |
| May 10, 1997 | Northern Iran | 7.5 |
| May 30, 1998 | Northeastern Afghanistan | 6.9 |
| August 17, 1999 | Western Turkey | 7.4 |
| January 26, 2001 | Gujarat, India | 7.9 |
| June 23, 2001 | Arequipa, Peru | 8.1 |
| March 25–26, 2002 | Nahrin, Afghanistan | 6.1 |
| January 22, 2003 | Colima, Mexico | 7.6 |
| May 21, 2003 | Northern Algeria | 6.8 |

## The Planet's Heart

**Crust:** average depth is 19-22 mi (30-35 km)

**Mantle:** total depth is 1780 mi (2870 km)

**Outer core:** 1300 mi (2100 km) of molten iron

**Inner core:** solid, mostly iron ball, 1700 mi (2740 km) thick

HOW BIG IT IS
Diameter at poles: 7,900 mi (12,713 km).
Diameter at equator: 7,926 mi (12,756 km).
Surface area: 196,885,000 square mi (510,066,000 km²).
Land area: 57,294,000 square mi (148,429,000 km²).
Sea area: 139,591,000 square mi (361,637,000 km²).

## Measuring Earthquakes

| Richter Scale | Description |
|---------------|-------------|
| 2.5 | Generally not felt, but recorded on seismometers. |
| 3.5 | Felt by many people. |
| 4.5 | Some local damage may occur. |
| 6.0 | A destructive earthquake. |
| 7.0 | A major earthquake. |
| 8.0 and above | Great earthquakes. |

The energy of an earthquake is generally reported using the Richter scale, a system developed by American geologist Charles Richter in 1935, based on measuring the heights of wave measurements on a seismograph. On the Richter scale, each single-integer increase represents 10 times more ground movement and 30 times more energy released. The change in magnitude between numbers on the scale can be represented by $10^x$ and $30^x$, where $x$ represents the change in the Richter scale measure. Therefore, a 3.0 earthquake has 100 times more ground movement and 900 times more energy released than a 1.0 earthquake.

## How Often Quakes Occur

| Richter Scale | World-wide Occurrence |
|---------------|------------------------|
| 8 and higher | 1 per year |
| 7.0-7.9 | 18 per year |
| 6.0-6.9 | 120 per year |
| 5.0-5.9 | 800 per year |
| 4.9 or less | 9150 per year |

## 10 Largest Lakes of the World

| Name and Location | Area | | Length | | Maximum Depth | |
|---|---|---|---|---|---|---|
| | square miles | square kilometers | miles | kilometers | feet | meters |
| Caspian Sea, Azerbaijan-Russian-Kazakhstan-Turkmenistan-Iran | 152,239 | 394,299 | 745 | 1199 | 3104 | 946 |
| Superior, U.S.- Canada | 31,820 | 82,414 | 383 | 616 | 1333 | 406 |
| Victoria, Tanzania-Uganda | 26,828 | 69,485 | 200 | 322 | 270 | 82 |
| Aral, Kazakhstan-Uzbekistan | 25,659 | 66,457 | 266 | 428 | 223 | 68 |
| Huron, U.S.-Canada | 23,010 | 59,596 | 247 | 397 | 750 | 229 |
| Michigan, U.S. | 22,400 | 58,016 | 321 | 517 | 923 | 281 |
| Tanganyika, Tanzania-Congo | 12,700 | 32,893 | 420 | 676 | 4708 | 1435 |
| Baikal, Russia | 12,162 | 31,500 | 395 | 636 | 5712 | 1741 |
| Great Bear, Canada | 12,000 | 31,080 | 232 | 373 | 270 | 82 |
| Nyasa, Malawi-Mozambique-Tanzania | 11,600 | 30,044 | 360 | 579 | 2316 | 706 |

Lake Michigan

## Wind Speeds

| Beaufort Scale Number | Miles per Hour | Beaufort Scale Number | Miles per Hour | Beaufort Scale Number | Miles per Hour |
|---|---|---|---|---|---|
| 1 | 1–3 | 5 | 19–24 | 9 | 47–54 |
| 2 | 4–7 | 6 | 25–31 | 10 | 55–63 |
| 3 | 8–12 | 7 | 32–38 | 11 | 64–75 |
| 4 | 13–18 | 8 | 39–46 | 12 | greater than 75 |

# Environment

## Largest National Parks, in Acreage

| National park | Location | Acreage (millions) |
|---|---|---|
| Wrangell-St. Elias | Alaska | 7.6 |
| Gates of the Arctic | Alaska | 7.0 |
| Denali | Alaska | 4.7 |
| Katmai | Alaska | 3.5 |
| Glacier Bay | Alaska | 3.2 |
| Lake Clark | Alaska | 2.5 |
| Yellowstone | Montana/Wyoming | 2.2 |
| Koouk Valley | Alaska | 1.7 |
| Everglades | Florida | 1.4 |
| Grand Canyon | Arizona | 1.2 |

Yellowstone National Park
Montana/Wyoming

## Most Visited Sites in the National Park System, 2002

| Site (Location) | Recreation Visits |
|---|---|
| Blue Ridge Parkway (NC & VA) | 21,538,760 |
| Golden Gate National Recreation Area (CA) | 13,961,267 |
| Great Smoky Mountains National Park (NC & TN) | 9,316,420 |
| Gateway National Recreation Area (NJ & NY) | 9,014,438 |
| Lake Mead National Recreation Area (AZ & NV) | 7,550,284 |
| George Washington Memorial Parkway (VA, MD, and D.C.) | 7,419,375 |
| Natchez Trace Parkway (MS, AL, & TN) | 5,643,170 |
| Delaware Water Gap National Recreation Area (NJ & PA) | 5,165,415 |
| Gulf Islands National Seashore (FL & MS) | 4,561,862 |
| Cape Cod National Seashore (MA) | 4,455,931 |

Cape Cod

## Threatened and Endangered Species

| Group | Endangered[1] | | Threatened[2] | |
|---|---|---|---|---|
| | U.S. | Foreign | U.S. | Foreign |
| Mammals | 56 | 252 | 7 | 16 |
| Birds | 75 | 178 | 15 | 6 |
| Reptiles | 14 | 65 | 18 | 14 |
| Amphibians | 9 | 8 | 7 | 1 |
| Fishes | 65 | 11 | 40 | 0 |
| Snails | 15 | 1 | 7 | 0 |
| Clams | 56 | 2 | 6 | 0 |
| Crustaceans | 15 | 0 | 3 | 0 |
| Insects | 24 | 4 | 9 | 0 |
| Arachnids | 5 | 0 | 0 | 0 |
| Flowering plants | 500 | 1 | 111 | 0 |
| Conifers | 2 | 0 | 0 | 2 |
| Ferns & others | 26 | 0 | 2 | 0 |
| **Total** | **862** | **522** | **225** | **39** |

1. Endangered species are those in danger of extinction.
2. Threatened species are those likely to become an endangered species within the foreseeable future.

## Where the Water Goes for a Family of Four in the U.S.

| Usage | Gallons/Day |
|---|---|
| Toilet flushing | 100 |
| Shower and bathing | 80 |
| Laundry | 35 |
| Dishwashing | 15 |
| Other | 13 |

## What Creates Solid Waste?

37.5%
17.9%
14.6%
8.3%
6.7%
6.7%
8.3%

- ■ Paper and paperboard
- ■ Yard wastes
- ■ Rubber, leather, textile, wood, other
- □ Metals
- ■ Plastics
- ■ Food wastes
- □ Glass

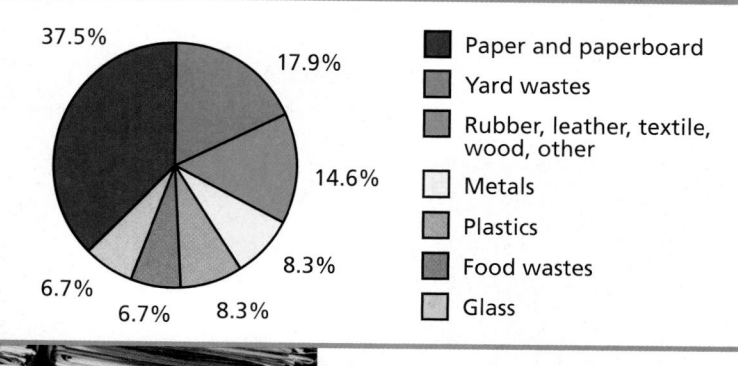

# Health & Fitness

## Physicians' Office Visits

| Specialist Visited | Percent of all Visits |
|---|---|
| General & Family Practice | 29.8 |
| Pediatrics | 12.6 |
| Internal Medicine | 11.4 |
| Obstetrics & Gynecology | 8.4 |
| Opthalmology | 5.6 |
| Orthopedic Surgery | 5.1 |
| Dermatology | 3.8 |
| General Surgery | 3.7 |
| Psychiatry | 2.4 |
| Otolaryngology | 2.3 |
| Cardiovascular Disease | 1.6 |
| Urological Survey | 1.5 |
| Neurology | 0.9 |
| All other specialists | 11.0 |

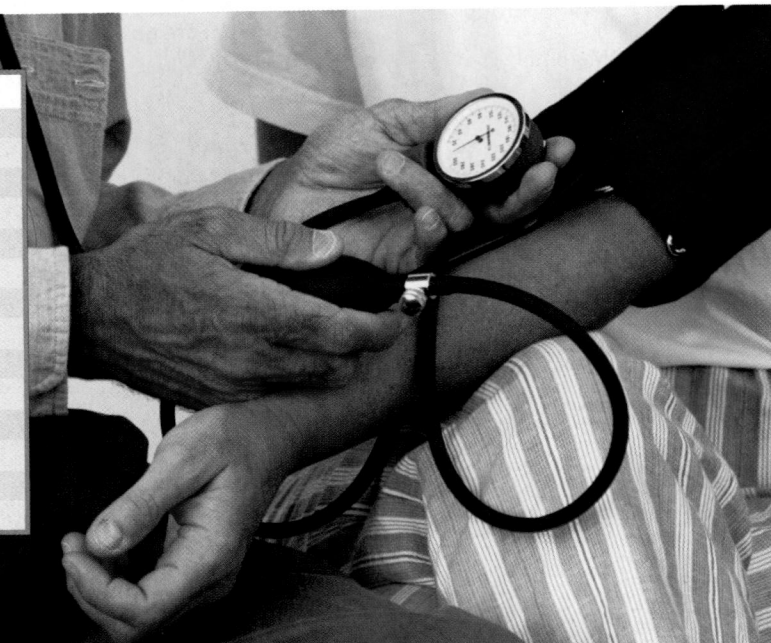

## Pizza Toppings

| Topping | Calories | Fat Grams |
|---|---|---|
| Bacon | 110 | 9 |
| Black olives | 56 | 5 |
| Extra cheese | 168 | 8 |
| Green peppers | 5 | 0 |
| Ham | 41 | 2 |
| Mushrooms | 5 | 0 |
| Onions | 11 | Less than 1 |
| Pepperoni | 80 | 7 |
| Sausage | 97 | 8 |

## Calories Used Per Minute by People of Different Body Weights

| Activity | 100 lb | 120 lb | 150 lb | 200 lb |
|---|---|---|---|---|
| Volleyball | 2.3 | 2.7 | 3.4 | 4.6 |
| Walking (3 mi/h) | 2.7 | 3.2 | 4.0 | 5.4 |
| Tennis | 4.5 | 5.4 | 6.8 | 9.1 |
| Swimming (crawl) | 5.8 | 6.9 | 8.7 | 11.6 |
| Skiing (cross-country) | 7.2 | 8.7 | 10.8 | 14.5 |

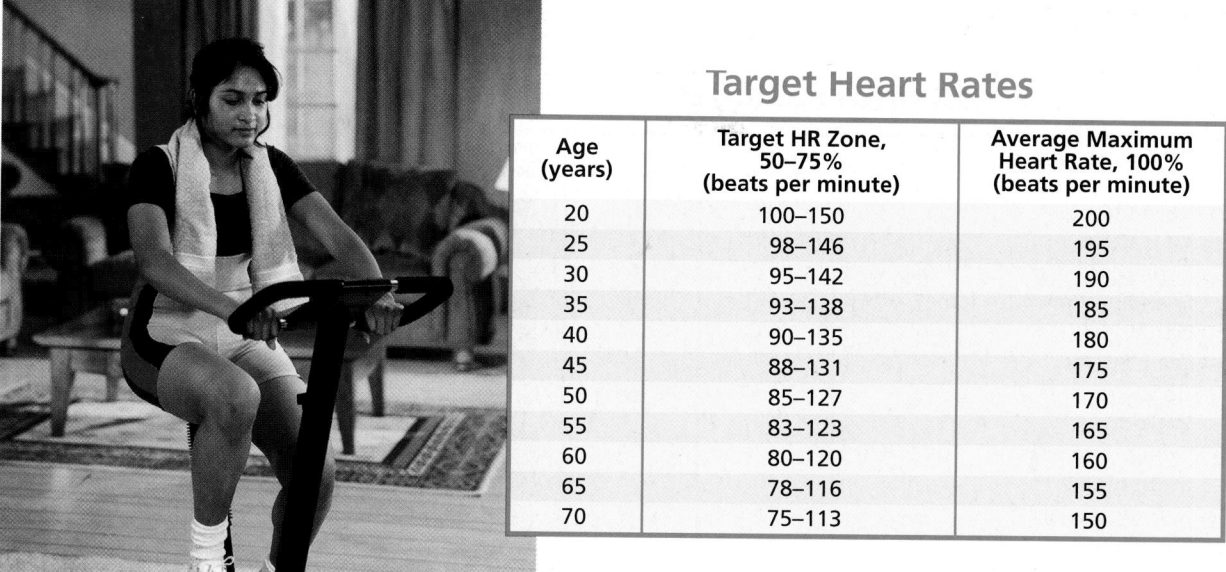

## Target Heart Rates

| Age (years) | Target HR Zone, 50–75% (beats per minute) | Average Maximum Heart Rate, 100% (beats per minute) |
|---|---|---|
| 20 | 100–150 | 200 |
| 25 | 98–146 | 195 |
| 30 | 95–142 | 190 |
| 35 | 93–138 | 185 |
| 40 | 90–135 | 180 |
| 45 | 88–131 | 175 |
| 50 | 85–127 | 170 |
| 55 | 83–123 | 165 |
| 60 | 80–120 | 160 |
| 65 | 78–116 | 155 |
| 70 | 75–113 | 150 |

## Leading Causes of Death for Men and Women in the U.S., 2000

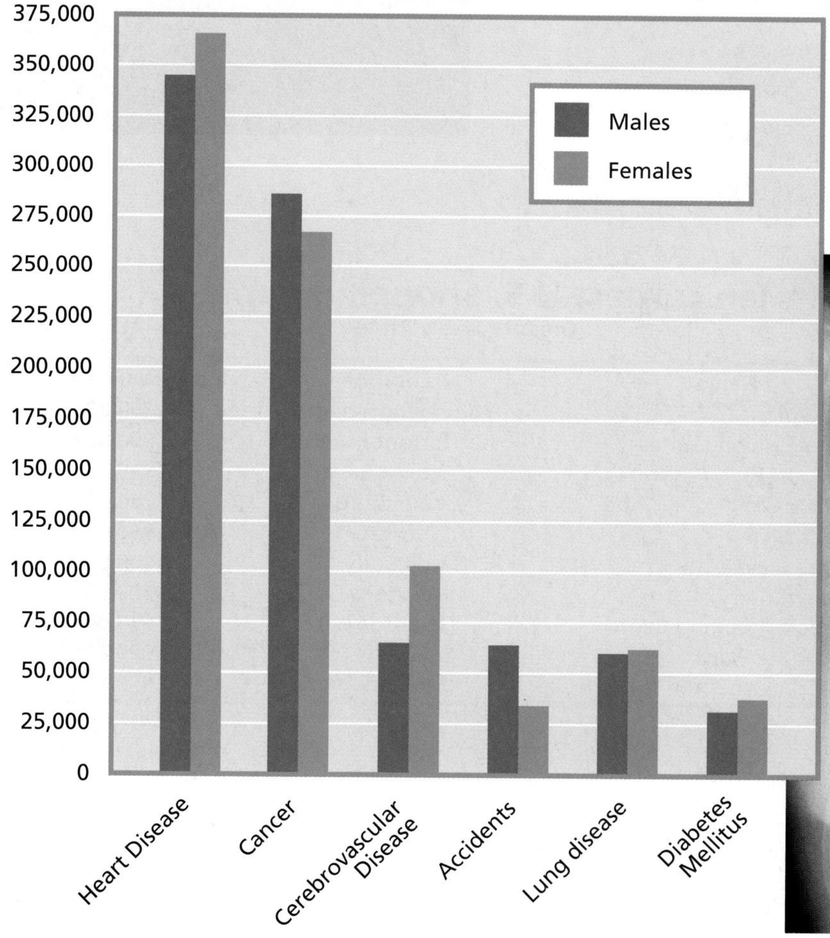

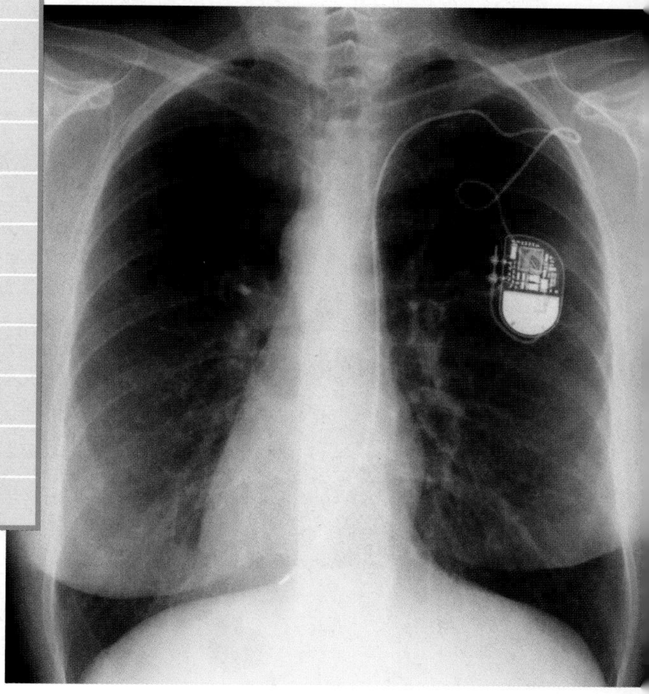

Males
Females

# Leisure

## Favorite Pastimes

| Activity | All Adults (percent) | Men (percent) | Women (percent) |
|---|---|---|---|
| Reading | 28 | 15 | 41 |
| TV watching | 19 | 19 | 20 |
| Fishing | 12 | 21 | 4 |
| Spending time with family/kids | 12 | 13 | 12 |
| Gardening | 11 | 8 | 13 |
| Team Sports | 9 | 15 | 4 |
| Golf | 8 | 14 | 2 |
| Walking | 8 | 6 | 10 |
| Going to movies | 7 | 4 | 9 |
| Swimming | 6 | 6 | 6 |
| Renting movies | 5 | 6 | 5 |
| Traveling | 5 | 4 | 5 |
| Sewing/crocheting | 4 | - | 8 |
| Exercise | 4 | 4 | 4 |
| Hunting | 4 | 7 | - |
| Church/church activities | 4 | 3 | 5 |

## Ten Largest U.S. Shopping Centers
### (Gross Leasable Area)

| Name | Location | Size (square feet) |
|---|---|---|
| Mall of America | Bloomington, MN | 4,200,000 |
| Del Amo Fashion Center | Torrance, CA | 3,000,000 |
| South Coast Plaza/Crystal Court | Costa Mesa, CA | 2,918,236 |
| Woodfield Mall | Schaumburg, IL | 2,700,000 |
| Sawgrass Mills | Sunrise, FL | 2,350,000 |
| Roosevelt Field Mall | Garden City, NY | 2,100,000 |
| The Galleria | Houston, TX | 2,100,000 |
| Oak Brook Shopping Center | Oak Brook, IL | 2,013,000 |
| Garden State Plaza | Paramus, NJ | 1,909,804 |
| Tysons Corner Center | McLean, VA | 1,900,000 |

## Sizes and Weights of Balls Used in Various Sports

| Type | Diameter (centimeters) | Average Weight (grams) |
|---|---|---|
| Baseball | 7.6 | 145 |
| Basketball | 24.0 | 596 |
| Croquet ball | 8.6 | 340 |
| Field hockey ball | 7.6 | 160 |
| Golf ball | 4.3 | 46 |
| Handball | 4.8 | 65 |
| Soccer ball | 22.0 | 425 |
| Softball (large) | 13.0 | 279 |
| Softball (small) | 9.8 | 187 |
| Table tennis ball | 3.7 | 2 |
| Tennis ball | 6.5 | 57 |
| Volleyball | 21.9 | 256 |

## Shopping Day Preference

| Day | Percent U.S. Shoppers |
|---|---|
| Sunday | 7 |
| Monday | 4 |
| Tuesday | 5 |
| Wednesday | 12 |
| Thursday | 13 |
| Friday | 17 |
| Saturday | 29 |
| No preference | 13 |

## Age of Internet Users

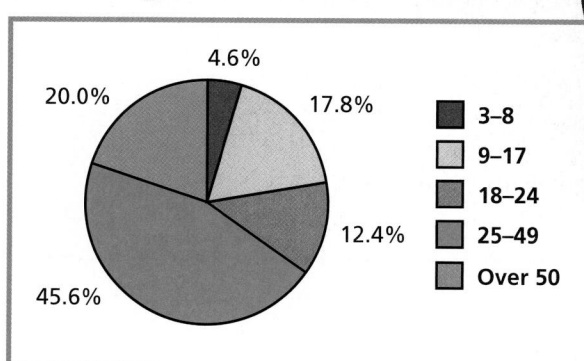

- 3–8
- 9–17
- 18–24
- 25–49
- Over 50

4.6%
17.8%
20.0%
12.4%
45.6%

# Travel & Transportation

## Trips to Foreign Destinations from the U.S.

| Destinations | Number (thousands) | Percent |
|---|---|---|
| All trips to foreign destinations | 41,295 | 100.0 |
| Canada | 11,534 | 27.9 |
| Mexico | 9,579 | 23.2 |
| Central America | 857 | 2.1 |
| Caribbean | 4,470 | 10.8 |
| South America | 1,016 | 2.5 |
| Europe | 7,305 | 17.7 |
| Africa | 508 | 1.2 |
| Asia | 3,312 | 8.0 |
| Pacific | 443 | 1.1 |
| All other foreign destinations | 2,271 | 5.5 |

## Weekly Time Spent Traveling by Trip Purpose of Persons Age 16 and Older

| Trip Purpose | Time Spent (hours) |
|---|---|
| To or from work | 1.76 |
| Work-related business | 0.16 |
| Shopping | 0.85 |
| Other family of personal business | 1.30 |
| School/church | 0.36 |
| Doctor/dentist | 0.08 |
| Vacation | 0.12 |
| Visiting friends/relatives | 0.70 |
| Pleasure driving | 0.05 |
| Other social and recreational | 1.04 |
| Other | 0.05 |
| Total time per week | 6.47 |

## Ways People Get to Work
## (workers 16 years and older)

| Method | Amount | Percent |
|---|---|---|
| Car, truck, or van-drive alone | 97,102,050 | 75.7 |
| Car, truck, or van-carpool | 15,634,051 | 12.2 |
| Public transportation (including taxicab) | 6,067,703 | 4.7 |
| Walked | 3,758,982 | 2.9 |
| Other means | 1,532,219 | 1.2 |
| Worked at home | 4,184,223 | 3.3 |

## Record Transportation Speeds

| Type of Transportation | Record Speed (mi/h) |
|---|---|
| Steam locomotive | 126 |
| Magnetic levitation train (with passengers) | 321.2 |
| Supersonic transport (SST) (Concorde) | 1,037.5 |
| Combat jet fighter | 2,110 |
| Unmanned monorail | 3,090 |
| Fixed wing aircraft | 4,534 |
| Unmanned rocket sled (railed) | 6,121 |
| Apollo command module | 24,791 |

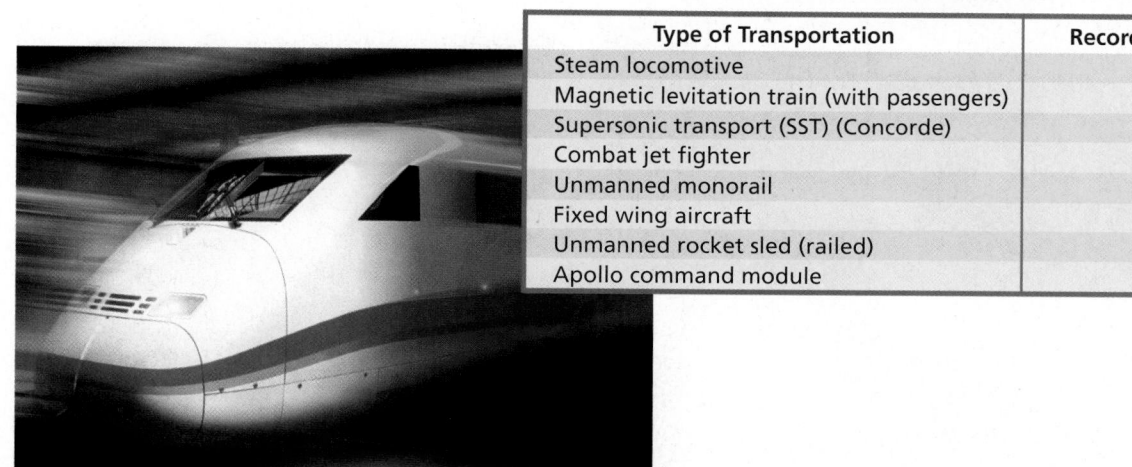

## Road Congestion at 10 Major U.S. Cities

| | Daily Vehicle Miles (thousands) | Vehicle Hours of Delay (thousands) | Delay and Fuel Cost (millions of dollars) |
|---|---|---|---|
| New York, NY | 101,295 | 400,115 | 7660 |
| Boston, MA | 22,890 | 84,845 | 1595 |
| Cincinnati, OH | 15,745 | 25,385 | 505 |
| St. Louis, MO | 25,740 | 41,690 | 805 |
| Atlanta, GA | 42,940 | 97,245 | 1885 |
| Miami, FL | 13,585 | 74,850 | 1365 |
| Dallas, TX | 48,700 | 141,125 | 2640 |
| Phoenix, AZ | 19,425 | 72,590 | 1360 |
| Los Angeles, CA | 126,495 | 791,970 | 14,635 |
| Seattle, WA | 22,455 | 67,550 | 1315 |

# United States of America

## U.S. Population

| Year | Population (thousands) | Year | Population (thousands) | Year | Population (thousands) | Year | Population (thousands) |
|---|---|---|---|---|---|---|---|
| 1950 | 152,271 | 1964 | 191,889 | 1978 | 222,585 | 1992 | 256,894 |
| 1951 | 154,878 | 1965 | 194,303 | 1979 | 225,055 | 1993 | 260,255 |
| 1952 | 157,553 | 1966 | 196,560 | 1980 | 227,726 | 1994 | 263,436 |
| 1953 | 160,184 | 1967 | 198,712 | 1981 | 229,966 | 1995 | 266,557 |
| 1954 | 163,026 | 1968 | 200,706 | 1982 | 232,188 | 1996 | 269,667 |
| 1955 | 165,931 | 1969 | 202,677 | 1983 | 234,307 | 1997 | 272,912 |
| 1956 | 168,903 | 1970 | 205,052 | 1984 | 236,348 | 1998 | 276,115 |
| 1957 | 171,984 | 1971 | 207,661 | 1985 | 238,466 | 1999 | 279,295 |
| 1958 | 174,882 | 1972 | 209,896 | 1986 | 240,651 | 2000 | 282,434 |
| 1959 | 177,830 | 1973 | 211,909 | 1987 | 242,804 | 2001 | 285,545 |
| 1960 | 180,671 | 1974 | 213,854 | 1988 | 245,021 | 2002 | 288,600 |
| 1961 | 183,691 | 1975 | 215,973 | 1989 | 247,342 | 2003 | 290,810 |
| 1962 | 186,538 | 1976 | 218,035 | 1990 | 250,132 | | |
| 1963 | 189,242 | 1977 | 220,239 | 1991 | 253,493 | | |

## Top 10 Coldest U.S. Temperatures on Record

| Location | Date | Temperature (°F) |
|---|---|---|
| Prospect Creek Camp, AK | January 23, 1971 | −80 |
| Rogers Pass, MT | January 20, 1954 | −70 |
| Peter's Sink, UT | February 1, 1985 | −69 |
| Moran, WY | February 9, 1933 | −63 |
| Maybell, CO | February 1, 1985 | −61 |
| Island Park Dam, ID | January 18, 1943 | −60 |
| Parshall, ND | February 15, 1936 | −60 |
| Pokegama Dam, MN | February 16, 1903 | −59 |
| McIntosh, SD | February 17, 1936 | −58 |
| Seneca, OR | February 10, 1933 | −54 |

## Birth Years of the States

| State | Date | State | Date | State | Date |
|---|---|---|---|---|---|
| AL | 1819 | LA | 1812 | OH | 1803 |
| AK | 1959 | ME | 1820 | OK | 1907 |
| AZ | 1912 | MD | 1788 | OR | 1859 |
| AR | 1836 | MA | 1788 | PA | 1787 |
| CA | 1850 | MI | 1837 | RI | 1790 |
| CO | 1876 | MN | 1858 | SC | 1788 |
| CT | 1788 | MS | 1817 | SD | 1889 |
| DE | 1787 | MO | 1821 | TN | 1796 |
| FL | 1845 | MT | 1889 | TX | 1845 |
| GA | 1788 | NE | 1867 | UT | 1896 |
| HI | 1959 | NV | 1864 | VT | 1791 |
| ID | 1890 | NH | 1788 | VA | 1788 |
| IL | 1818 | NJ | 1787 | WA | 1889 |
| IN | 1816 | NM | 1912 | WV | 1863 |
| IA | 1846 | NY | 1788 | WI | 1848 |
| KS | 1861 | NC | 1789 | WY | 1890 |
| KY | 1792 | ND | 1889 | | |

## 10 Windiest U.S. Cities

| City | Mean Speed (mi/h) |
|---|---|
| Blue Hill, MA | 15.4 |
| Dodge City, KS | 13.9 |
| Amarillo, TX | 13.5 |
| Rochester, MN | 13.1 |
| Cheyenne, WY | 12.9 |
| Casper, WY | 12.8 |
| Great Falls, MT | 12.6 |
| Goodland, KS | 12.5 |
| Boston, MA | 12.5 |
| Lubbock, TX | 12.4 |

## Top 10 Hottest U.S. Temperatures on Record

| Location | Date | Temperature (°F) |
|---|---|---|
| Greenland Ranch, CA | July 10, 1913 | 134 |
| Parker, AZ | July 7, 1905 | 127 |
| Laughlin, NV | June 26, 1990 | 122 |
| Alton, KS | July 24, 1936 | 121 |
| Steele, ND | July 6, 1936 | 121 |
| Gannvalley, SD | July 5, 1936 | 120 |
| Ozark, AK | August 10, 1936 | 120 |
| Seymour, TX | August 12, 1936 | 120 |
| Tishmomingo, OK | July 26, 1943 | 120 |
| Pendleton, OR | August 10, 1898 | 119 |

# Prerequisite Skills

## ❶ Place Value and Order

### Example 1

**Write 2,345,678.9123 in words.**

**Solution**

The place value chart shows the value of each digit. The value of each place is ten times the place to the right.

| millions | hundred thousands | ten thousands | thousands | hundreds | tens | ones | . | tenths | hundredths | thousandths | ten thousandths |
|---|---|---|---|---|---|---|---|---|---|---|---|
| 2 | 3 | 4 | 5 | 6 | 7 | 8 | . | 9 | 1 | 2 | 3 |

*The number shown is two million, three hundred forty-five thousand, six hundred seventy-eight and nine thousand one hundred twenty-three ten-thousandths.*

### Example 2

**Use < or > to make this sentence true.**        **6 ■ 2**

**Solution**

Remember, < means "less than" and > means "greater than." So, 6 > 2.

### ■ EXTRA PRACTICE EXERCISES

**Write each number in words.**

**1.** 3647   three thousand, six hundred forty-seven

**2.** 6,004,300.002   six million, four thousand, three hundred and two thousandths

**3.** 0.9001   nine thousand one ten-thousandths

**Write each of the following as a number.**

**4.** two million, one hundred fifty thousand, four hundred seventeen   2,150,417

**5.** five thousand, one hundred twenty and five hundred two thousandths   5120.502

**6.** nine million, ninety thousand, nine hundred and ninety-nine ten-thousandths   9,090,900.0099

**Use < or > to make each sentence true.**

**7.** 9 ■ 8   >

**8.** 164 ■ 246   <

**9.** 63,475 ■ 6,435   >

**10.** 52 ■ 50   >

**11.** 5.39 ■ 9.02   <

**12.** 43.94 ■ 53.69   <

# ❷ Add and Subtract Whole Numbers and Decimals

To add or subtract whole numbers and decimals, write the digits so the place values line up. Add from right to left, renaming when necessary. When adding or subtracting decimals, be sure to place the decimal point directly below the aligned decimals in the problem.

## Example 1

**Add 0.058, 25.39, 6346, and 1.57. The answer is called the *sum*.**

### Solution

$$\begin{array}{r} 0.058 \\ 25.39 \\ 6346. \\ +\quad 1.57 \\ \hline 6373.018 \end{array}$$

The zero to the left of the decimal point is used to show there are no ones.

The decimal point is at the end of whole numbers.

Add from right to left.

## Example 2

**Subtract 6.37 from 27. The smaller number is subtracted from the larger number. The answer is called the *difference*.**

### Solution

$$\begin{array}{r} 27.00 \\ -\quad 6.37 \\ \hline 20.63 \end{array}$$

Add zeros if that helps you complete the subtraction.

## ■ EXTRA PRACTICE EXERCISES

**Add or subtract.**

1. $23.146 - 17.215$  5.931
2. $46.48 - 6.57$  39.91
3. $52 - 1.95$  50.05
4. $0.86 + 0.75$  1.61
5. $83 - 82.743$  0.257
6. $9.45 + 13.2$  22.65
7. $14.5 - 9.684$  4.816
8. $913.03 - 79$  834.03
9. $0.8523 - 0.794$  0.0583
10. $30,000 - 1237.64$  28,762.36
11. $45.3 + 160.09$  205.39
12. $6000 - 4362$  1638
13. $462.09 + 32.7$  494.79
14. $78,850 - 56,176.8$  22,673.2
15. $3160.915 + 1920.03$  5080.945
16. $17,347.85 - 12,516.90$  4830.95
17. $107,285 - 61,500.25$  45,784.75
18. $6.4 + 54.2 + 938.05 + 3.7 + 47.3$  1049.65
19. $1765.36 + 1587.50 + 1400$  4752.86
20. $51,876.36 + 48,156.95 + 1417.86$  101,451.17
21. $76.2 + 80 + 56 + 9.321$  221.521
22. $567.1 + 6 + 13.452 + 100$  686.552
23. $5.93 + 0.06 + 96.021 + 0.0378$  102.0488
24. $51.5 + 87 + 68.2$  206.7
25. $6532.03 + 861.006 + 3170.95$  10,563.986

# ③ Multiply Whole Numbers and Decimals

To multiply whole numbers, find each partial product and then add.

When multiplying decimals, locate the decimal point in the product so that there are as many decimal places in the product as the total number of decimal places in the factors.

## Example 1

**Multiply 2.6394 by 3000.**

### Solution

$$\begin{array}{r} 2.6394 \\ \times\ \ 3000 \\ \hline 7918.2000 \end{array}$$ or 7918.2

Zeros after the decimal point can be dropped because they are not significant digits.

## Example 2

**Multiply 3.92 by 0.023.**

### Solution

$$\begin{array}{rl} 3.92 & \text{2 decimal places} \\ \times\ 0.023 & \text{+ 3 decimal places} \\ \hline 1176 & \\ +\ 7840 & \\ \hline 0.09016 & \text{5 decimal places} \end{array}$$

The zero is added before the nine, so that the product will have five decimal places.

## ◼ EXTRA PRACTICE EXERCISES

**Multiply.**

**1.** $36 \times 45$  1620

**2.** $500 \times 30$  15,000

**3.** $17,000 \times 230$  3,910,000

**4.** $6.2 \times 8$  49.6

**5.** $950 \times 1.6$  1520

**6.** $3.652 \times 20$  73.04

**7.** $179 \times 83$  14,857

**8.** $257 \times 320$  82,240

**9.** $8560 \times 275$  2,354,000

**10.** $467 \times 0.3$  140.1

**11.** $2.63 \times 183$  481.29

**12.** $0.758 \times 321.8$  243.9244

**13.** $49.3 \times 1.6$  78.88

**14.** $6.859 \times 7.9$  54.1861

**15.** $794.4 \times 321.8$
255,637.9181

**16.** $0.08 \times 4$  0.32

**17.** $0.062 \times 0.5$  0.031

**18.** $0.0135 \times 0.003$  0.0000405

**19.** $21.6 \times 3.1$  66.96

**20.** $8.76 \times 0.005$  0.0438

**21.** $5.521 \times 3.642$  20.107482

**22.** $5.749 \times 3.008$  17.292992

**23.** $8.09 \times 0.18$  1.4562

**24.** $89,946 \times 2.85$  256,346.1

**25.** $6.31 \times 908$  5729.48

**26.** $391.05 \times 25$  9776.25

**27.** $35,021 \times 76.34$
2,673,503.14

# ❹ Divide Whole Numbers and Decimals

Dividing whole numbers and decimals involves a repetitive process of estimating a quotient, multiplying and subtracting.

$$
\begin{array}{r}
34 \quad \leftarrow \text{quotient} \\
\text{divisor} \rightarrow 7)\overline{239} \quad \leftarrow \text{dividend} \\
\underline{21}\!\downarrow \quad \leftarrow 3 \times 7 \\
29 \quad \leftarrow \text{Subtract. Bring down the 9.} \\
\underline{28} \quad \leftarrow 4 \times 7 \\
1 \quad \leftarrow \text{remainder}
\end{array}
$$

## Example 1

**Find: 283.86 ÷ 5.7**

### Solution

When dividing decimals, move the decimal point in the divisor to the right until it is a whole number. Move the decimal point the same number of places in the dividend. Then place the decimal point in the answer directly above the new location of the decimal point in the dividend.

If answers do not have a remainder of 0, you can add 0's after the last digit of the dividend and continue dividing.

$$
5.7)\overline{283.8.6} \quad \rightarrow \quad
\begin{array}{r}
49.8 \\
57)\overline{2838.6} \\
\underline{228} \\
558 \\
\underline{513} \\
45\ 6 \\
\underline{45\ 6} \\
0
\end{array}
$$

## ◢ EXTRA PRACTICE EXERCISES

**Divide.**

1. 72 ÷ 6  12
2. 6000 ÷ 20  300
3. 26,568 ÷ 8  3321
4. 5.6 ÷ 7  0.8
5. 120 ÷ 0.4  300
6. 936 ÷ 12  78
7. 3.28 ÷ 4  0.82
8. 0.1960 ÷ 5  0.0392
9. 1968 ÷ 0.08  24,600
10. 16 ÷ 0.04  400
11. 1525 ÷ 0.05  30,500
12. 109.94 ÷ 0.23  478
13. 0.6 ÷ 24  0.025
14. 7.924 ÷ 0.28  28.3
15. 32.6417 ÷ 9.1  3.587
16. 24 ÷ 0.6  40
17. 1784.75 ÷ 29.5  60.5
18. 0.01998 ÷ 0.37  0.054
19. 7.8 ÷ 0.3  26
20. 12,000 ÷ 0.04  300,000
21. 820.94 ÷ 0.02  41,047
22. 89,946 ÷ 28.5  3156
23. 15 ÷ 0.75  20
24. 7.56 ÷ 2.25  3.36
25. 0.19176 ÷ 68  0.00282
26. 0.168 ÷ 0.48  0.35
27. 5.1 ÷ 0.006  850
28. 55,673 ÷ 0.05  1,113,460
29. 84.536 ÷ 4  21.134
30. 261.18 ÷ 10  26.118
31. 134,554 ÷ 0.14  961,100
32. 90,294 ÷ 7.85  11,502.42038
33. 59,368 ÷ 47.3  1255.137421
34. 11,633.5 ÷ 439  26.5
35. 28.098 ÷ 14  2.007
36. 16.309 ÷ 0.09  181.2$\overline{1}$
37. 55.26 ÷ 1.8  30.7
38. 8276 ÷ 0.627  13,199.36204
39. 10,693 ÷ 92.8  115.2262931
40. 48.8 ÷ 1.6  30.5
41. 27,268 ÷ 34  802
42. 546.702 ÷ 0.078  7009

# ⑤ Multiply and Divide Fractions

To multiply fractions, multiply the numerators and then multiply the denominators. Write the answer in simplest form.

## Example 1

Multiply $\frac{2}{5}$ and $\frac{7}{8}$.

### Solution

$$\frac{2}{5} \times \frac{7}{8} = \frac{2 \times 7}{5 \times 8} = \frac{14}{40} = \frac{7}{20}$$

To divide by a fraction, multiply by the reciprocal of that fraction. To find the reciprocal of a fraction, invert the fraction (turn upside down). The product of a fraction and its reciprocal is 1. Since $\frac{2}{3} \times \frac{3}{2} = \frac{6}{6}$ or 1, $\frac{2}{3}$ and $\frac{3}{2}$ are reciprocals of each other.

## Example 2

Divide $1\frac{1}{5}$ by $\frac{2}{3}$.

### Solution

$$1\frac{1}{5} \div \frac{2}{3} = \frac{6}{5} \div \frac{2}{3} = \frac{6}{5} \times \frac{3}{2} = \frac{6 \times 3}{5 \times 2} = \frac{18}{10}, \text{ or } 1\frac{4}{5}$$

## ◾ EXTRA PRACTICE EXERCISES

**Multiply or divide. Write each answer in simplest form.**

1. $\frac{2}{3} \div \frac{5}{6}$   $\frac{4}{5}$

2. $\frac{3}{5} \times \frac{10}{12}$   $\frac{1}{2}$

3. $\frac{5}{8} \div \frac{1}{4}$   $2\frac{1}{2}$

4. $\frac{1}{2} \times \frac{2}{3}$   $\frac{1}{3}$

5. $\frac{2}{3} \times \frac{1}{2}$   $\frac{1}{3}$

6. $\frac{3}{4} \times \frac{5}{8}$   $\frac{15}{32}$

7. $\frac{1}{2} \div \frac{2}{3}$   $\frac{3}{4}$

8. $\frac{2}{3} \div \frac{1}{2}$   $1\frac{1}{3}$

9. $\frac{3}{4} \div \frac{5}{8}$   $1\frac{1}{5}$

10. $2\frac{2}{3} \div 1\frac{3}{5}$   $1\frac{2}{3}$

11. $1\frac{1}{5} \times 2\frac{1}{4}$   $2\frac{7}{10}$

12. $3\frac{1}{3} \times 1\frac{1}{10}$   $3\frac{2}{3}$

13. $5\frac{2}{5} \div 2\frac{4}{7}$   $2\frac{1}{10}$

14. $2\frac{4}{7} \div 5\frac{2}{5}$   $\frac{10}{21}$

15. $2\frac{4}{7} \times 5\frac{2}{5}$   $13\frac{31}{35}$

16. $1\frac{7}{8} \div 1\frac{7}{8}$   $1$

17. $\frac{3}{4} \times \frac{2}{3} \times 1\frac{5}{8} \times 2\frac{2}{3}$   $2\frac{1}{6}$

18. $7\frac{1}{2} \div 2\frac{1}{4}$   $3\frac{1}{3}$

19. $6\frac{2}{3} \times 4\frac{1}{2} \times 5\frac{3}{8}$   $161\frac{1}{4}$

20. $11\frac{5}{9} \times 6\frac{1}{12}$   $70\frac{8}{27}$

21. $\frac{25}{42} \div \frac{5}{21}$   $2\frac{1}{2}$

22. $\frac{13}{18} \div \frac{8}{9}$   $\frac{13}{16}$

23. $\frac{3}{8} \times \frac{11}{12} \times \frac{16}{33}$   $\frac{1}{6}$

24. $\frac{51}{56} \div \frac{17}{24}$   $1\frac{2}{7}$

# ⑥ Add and Subtract Fractions

To add and subtract fractions, you need to find a common denominator and then add or subtract, renaming as necessary.

## Example 1

Add $\frac{3}{4}$ and $\frac{5}{6}$.

### Solution

$$\frac{3}{4} = \frac{3}{4} \times \frac{3}{3} = \frac{9}{12}$$
$$+\frac{5}{5} = \frac{5}{6} \times \frac{2}{2} = +\frac{10}{12}$$
$$\frac{19}{12}$$

Add the numerators and use the common denominator.

Then simplify. $\frac{19}{12} = 1\frac{7}{12}$

## Example 2

Subtract $1\frac{3}{5}$ from $5\frac{1}{2}$.

### Solution

$$5\frac{1}{2} = \quad 5\frac{5}{10} = \quad 4\frac{15}{10}$$
$$-1\frac{3}{5} = -1\frac{6}{10} = -1\frac{6}{10}$$
$$3\frac{9}{10}$$

You cannot subtract $\frac{6}{10}$ from $\frac{5}{10}$, so rename again.

## ■ EXTRA PRACTICE EXERCISES

**Add or subtract.**

1. $\frac{1}{5} + \frac{1}{10}$    $\frac{3}{10}$

2. $\frac{2}{3} + \frac{1}{3}$    $1$

3. $\frac{5}{8} + \frac{3}{4}$    $1\frac{3}{8}$

4. $\frac{6}{7} - \frac{2}{7}$    $\frac{4}{7}$

5. $\frac{3}{4} - \frac{1}{3}$    $\frac{5}{12}$

6. $\frac{5}{8} - \frac{1}{4}$    $\frac{3}{8}$

7. $2\frac{1}{2} + 3\frac{1}{2}$    $6$

8. $6\frac{5}{8} + 3\frac{7}{8}$    $10\frac{1}{2}$

9. $3\frac{2}{3} + 4\frac{1}{2}$    $8\frac{1}{6}$

10. $2\frac{3}{4} - 1\frac{1}{4}$    $1\frac{1}{2}$

11. $5\frac{1}{8} - 3\frac{7}{8}$    $1\frac{1}{4}$

12. $1\frac{1}{3} - \frac{2}{3}$    $\frac{2}{3}$

13. $6\frac{1}{2} + 5\frac{7}{9}$    $12\frac{5}{18}$

14. $9\frac{2}{5} - 1\frac{1}{8}$    $8\frac{11}{40}$

15. $7\frac{2}{3} + 6\frac{1}{5}$    $13\frac{13}{15}$

16. $8\frac{1}{10} - 5\frac{2}{3}$    $2\frac{13}{30}$

17. $6\frac{1}{2} - 5\frac{3}{5}$    $\frac{9}{10}$

18. $10\frac{5}{8} - 9\frac{3}{4}$    $\frac{7}{8}$

19. $1\frac{1}{5} + 2\frac{1}{3} + 5\frac{1}{4}$    $8\frac{47}{60}$

20. $9\frac{2}{3} + 4\frac{3}{5} + 6\frac{1}{2}$    $20\frac{23}{30}$

21. $10\frac{7}{8} + 3\frac{3}{4} + 6\frac{1}{2} + 2\frac{5}{8}$    $23\frac{3}{4}$

# ❼ Fractions, Decimals and Percents

Percent means per hundred. Therefore, 35% means 35 out of 100. Percents can be written as equivalent decimals and fractions.

$$35\% = 0.35$$       Move the decimal point two places to the left.

$$= \frac{35}{100}$$       Write the fraction with a denominator of 100.

$$= \frac{7}{20}$$       Then simplify.

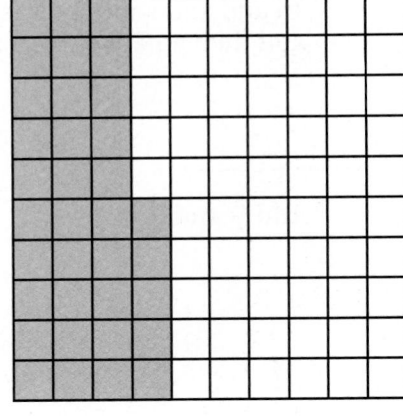

## Example 1

Write $\frac{3}{8}$ as a decimal and as a percent.

### Solution

$\frac{3}{8} = 0.375$       Divide to change a fraction to a decimal.

$0.375 = 37.5\%$       To change a decimal to a percent move the decimal point two places to the right and insert the percent symbol.

Percents greater than 100% represent whole numbers or mixed numbers.

$$200\% = 2 \text{ or } 2.00 \qquad\qquad 350\% = 3.5 \text{ or } 3\frac{1}{2}$$

## ■ EXTRA PRACTICE EXERCISES

**Write each fraction as a decimal and as a percent.**

1. $\frac{1}{2}$   0.5; 50%

2. $\frac{1}{4}$   0.25; 25%

3. $\frac{3}{4}$   0.75; 75%

4. $\frac{9}{10}$   0.9; 90%

5. $\frac{3}{10}$   0.3; 30%

6. $\frac{1}{25}$   0.04; 4%

7. $3\frac{7}{8}$   3.875; 387.5%

8. $1\frac{1}{5}$   1.2; 120%

9. $\frac{13}{25}$   0.52; 52%

**Write each decimal as a fraction and as a percent.**

10. 0.63   $\frac{63}{100}$; 63%

11. 0.15   $\frac{3}{20}$; 15%

12. 0.4   $\frac{2}{5}$; 40%

13. 2.35   $2\frac{7}{20}$; 235%

14. 10.125   $10\frac{1}{8}$; 1012.5%

15. 0.625   $\frac{5}{8}$; 62.5%

16. 0.05   $\frac{1}{20}$; 5%

17. 0.125   $\frac{1}{8}$; 12.5%

18. 0.3125   $\frac{5}{16}$; 31.25%

**Write each percent as a decimal and as a fraction.**

19. 10%   0.10; $\frac{1}{10}$

20. 12%   0.12; $\frac{3}{25}$

21. 100%   1; 1

22. 150%   1.5; $1\frac{1}{2}$

23. 160%   1.6; $1\frac{3}{5}$

24. 75%   0.75; $\frac{3}{4}$

25. 8%   0.08; $\frac{2}{25}$

26. 87.5%   0.875; $\frac{7}{8}$

27. 0.35%   0.0035; $\frac{7}{2000}$

# ⑧ Multiply and Divide by Powers of Ten

To multiply a number by a power of 10, move the decimal point to the right. To multiply by 100 means to multiply by 10 two times. Each multiplication by 10 moves the decimal point one place to the right.

To divide a number by a power of 10, move the decimal point to the left. To divide by 1000 means to divide by 10 three times. Each division by 10 moves the decimal point one place to the right.

## Example 1

**Multiply 21 by 10,000.**

### Solution

$21 \times 10,000 = 210,000$    The decimal point moves four places to the right.

## Example 2

**Find 145 ÷ 500.**

### Solution

$145 \div 500 = 145 \div 5 \div 100$

$\qquad\qquad = 29 \div 100$

$\qquad\qquad = 0.29$    The decimal point moves two places to the left.

## ◣ EXTRA PRACTICE EXERCISES

**Multiply or divide.**

1. $15 \times 100$  1500
2. $96 \times 10,000$  960,000
3. $1296 \div 100$  12.96
4. $9687.03 \div 1000$  9.68703
5. $36 \times 20,000$  720,000
6. $7500 \div 3000$  2.5
7. $9 \times 30$  270
8. $94 \times 6000$  564,000
9. $561 \div 30$  18.7
10. $1505 \div 500$  3.01
11. $71 \times 90,000$  6,390,000
12. $9 \times 120,000$  1,080,000
13. $3159 \div 10,000$  0.3159
14. $1,000,000 \times 0.79$  790,000
15. $601 \times 30,000$  18,030,000
16. $75 \div 300$  0.25
17. $4000 \times 12$  48,000
18. $14 \times 7,000,000$  98,000,000
19. $49,000 \div 7000$  7
20. $980 \div 10,000$  0.098
21. $216 \div 2000$  0.108
22. $108,000 \div 900$  120
23. $72 \times 10,000,000$  720,000,000
24. $953.16 \div 10,000$  0.095316
25. $1472 \div 8000$  0.184
26. $490,000 \div 700$  700
27. $80 \times 90,000$  7,200,000
28. $8001 \div 90$  88.9
29. $50 \times 6000$  300,000
30. $950,000 \div 50,000$  19
31. $81,000 \times 5$  405,000
32. $1458 \times 30,000$  43,740,000
33. $452.3 \div 10$  45.23
34. $986,856.008 \div 10,000$  98.6856008
35. $316 \times 70,000$  22,120,000
36. $60 \div 1200$  0.05

# ⑨ Round and Order Decimals

To round a number, follow these rules:

1. Underline the digit in the specified place. This is the place digit. The digit to the immediate right of the place digit is the test digit.

2. If the test digit is 5 or larger, add 1 to the place digit and substitute zeros for all digits to its right.

3. If the test digit is 4 or smaller, substitute zeros for it and all digits to the right.

## Example 1

**Round 4826 to the nearest hundred.**

### Solution

| | |
|---|---|
| 4826 | Underline the place digit. |
| 4800 | Since the test digit is 2, and 2 is less than 5, substitute zeros for 2 and all digits to the right. |

To place decimals in ascending order, write them in order from least to greatest.

## Example 2

**Place in ascending order: 0.34, 0.33, 0.39.**

### Solution

Compare the first decimal place, then compare the second decimal place.

0.33 (least), 0.34, 0.39 (greatest)

## ■ EXTRA PRACTICE EXERCISES

**Round each number to the place indicated.**

1. 367 to the nearest ten  370

2. 961 to the nearest ten  960

3. 7200 to the nearest thousand  7000

4. 3070 to the nearest hundred  3100

5. 41,440 to the nearest hundred  41,400

6. 34,254 to the nearest thousand  34,000

7. 208,395 to the nearest thousand  208,000

8. 654,837 to the nearest ten thousand  650,000

**Write the decimals in ascending order.**

9. 0.29, 0.82, 0.35  0.29, 0.35, 0.82

10. 1.8, 1.4, 1.5  1.4, 1.5, 1.8

11. 0.567, 0.579, 0.505, 0.542
0.505, 0.542, 0.567, 0.579

12. 0.54, 0.45, 4.5, 5.4  0.45, 0.54, 4.5, 5.4

13. 0.0802, 0.0822, 0.00222
0.00222, 0.0802, 0.0822

14. 6.204, 6.206, 6.205, 6.203
6.203, 6.204, 6.205, 6.206

15. 88.2, 88.1, 8.80, 8.82
8.80, 8.82, 88.1, 88.2

16. 0.007, 7.0, 0.7, 0.07  0.007, 0.07, 0.7, 7.0

# Extra Practice

## Chapter 1

**RETAIL** The owners of a new music store want to survey local residents to find out what kinds of music they prefer. What kind of sampling method is represented by each of these possibilities that the owners have considered using?

1. Ask every tenth customer who enters the store on a certain day. systematic

2. Ask all people who enter the store between 2:00 P.M. and 5:00 P.M. convenience

3. Send a survey form to people listed in the telephone directory whose telephone numbers end with the digit 7. systematic

4. Ask all customers who were checked out at a certain cash register chosen at random. cluster

**NUTRITION** Heather is preparing a report on nutrition for health class and she wants to find out the favorite vegetable among teenagers in her school. Name the sampling method represented by each of the following. Then give one reason why the findings that would result from each method could be biased. For 5–8, see additional answers.

5. Ask every tenth teenager who enters a fast-food restaurant.

6. Ask ten teenagers whose names are drawn at random from the names of all students in your school.

7. Ask ten students in another health class.

8. Ask the first ten students who arrive at a health fair.

**For Exercises 1–5, use the following ages of students in a theater club. If necessary, round your answers to the nearest tenth.**

13  18  14  15  14  17  17  16  13  16  17  17  18  5  13

1. Find the mean. 14.9
2. Find the median. 16
3. Find the mode. 17
4. Find the range. 13

5. Which measure of central tendency is the best indicator of the age of a member of the club? mean, median or mode

**Use the table for Exercises 6–10. If necessary, round your answers to the nearest tenth.**

6. Find the mean. 4.1
7. Find the median. 4
8. Find the mode. 4
9. Find the range. 7

10. Which measure of central tendency is the best indicator of the number of hours per week spent engaging in aerobic exercise? median

### Hours of Aerobic Exercise Per Week

| Number of hours | Frequency |
| --- | --- |
| 0 | 4 |
| 1 | 5 |
| 2 | 5 |
| 3 | 19 |
| 4 | 27 |
| 5 | 16 |
| 6 | 14 |
| 7 | 10 |

**Extra Practice**

---

**ADDITIONAL ANSWERS**

**Extra Practice 1-1**
**For 5–8, reasons will vary.**

5. Systematic; Teens may favor potatoes because french fries are often served at fast-food restaurants.

6. Random; The response may be affected by the season or by the availability of certain produce.

7. Convenience; In health class students may name the most healthful vegetable rather than their favorite.

8. Convenience; Students at a health fair may be predisposed to name a healthful vegetable rather than their favorite.

## Extra Practice 1-3

**1.**

### Push-Ups by Students in One Minute

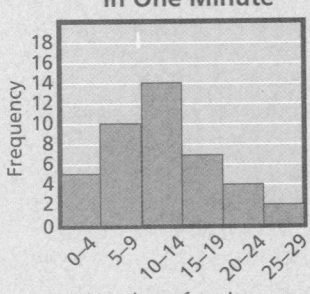

**7. Number of Book Covers Sold Daily**

| 5  | 7       |
|----|---------|
| 9  | 2 3 3 3 |
| 10 | 4       |
| 11 | 0 5 6 7 8 |
| 12 | 1 9     |
| 17 | 0 1 4 4 7 |
| 18 | 2 3 4 5 |
| 25 | 1       |

5 | 7 represents 57 book covers.

---

Extra Practice 1–3 • Histograms and Stem-and-Leaf Plots • pages 16–19

**For Exercises 1–6, use the following number of push-ups by students in 1 min.**

| 18 | 18 | 0  | 15 | 1  | 3  | 4  |
|----|----|----|----|----|----|----|
| 2  | 25 | 29 | 5  | 6  | 7  | 15 |
| 12 | 10 | 9  | 8  | 10 | 15 | 7  |
| 8  | 16 | 18 | 5  | 6  | 12 | 10 |
| 9  | 14 | 14 | 11 | 20 | 21 | 14 |
| 13 | 22 | 24 | 12 | 14 | 13 | 13 |

1. Use a frequency table to make a histogram of the data. See additional answers

2. How many students are there in the data? 42

3. How many students did from 10 to 14 push-ups? 14

4. How many students were unable to do as many as 15 push-ups? 29

5. How many students did 20 or more push-ups? 6

6. Which number of push-ups were performed least frequently? 25–29

**For Exercises 7–10, use the following number of book covers sold each day at a school store.**

| 104 | 121 | 182 | 170 | 185 | 93  | 251 | 177 | 93  | 57  | 93  | 115 |
|-----|-----|-----|-----|-----|-----|-----|-----|-----|-----|-----|-----|
| 184 | 92  | 117 | 110 | 174 | 118 | 183 | 116 | 171 | 129 | 174 |     |

7. Organize the data into a stem-and-leaf plot. See additional answers.

8. On how many days were at least 170 book covers sold? 10

9. What is the median number of book covers sold? 121

10. Find the mode of the set of data. 93

Extra Practice 1–4 • Scatter Plots and Lines of Best Fit • pages 20–23

**Use the scatter plot for Exercises 1–9.**

1. How many students were surveyed if no two students answered in exactly the same way? 13

2. What is the range of hours spent watching television? 16 h

3. What is the range of hours spent exercising? 14 h

4. Find the mode(s) of the hours spent watching television. 4, 9

5. Find the mode(s) of the number of hours spent exercising. 12 h

6. Predict the weekly number of hours of television watching of students who exercise 8 h per week. 10.5 h

7. One student watches television 12 h per week. How many more hours is this than the median number of hours of television watching? 3 h

8. Which point lies farthest from the trend line? What could account for this? (2, 10); Answers will vary.

9. Is there a positive or negative correlation between watching television and exercising? negative

**TV Watching And Exercise**

**For each set of data, find the first quartile, the median, and the third quartile.**

1. 47  70  47  63  52  55  62  59  62  $Q_1$ = 49.5; median = 59; $Q_3$ = 62.5

2. 13  10  15  19  12  17  10  14  11  13  18  15  $Q_1$ = 11.5; median = 13.5; $Q_3$ = 16

3. Make a box-and-whisker plot for the following scores on a math achievement test.

8  6  7  9  5  4  8  3  6  3  5  8  6

See additional answers.

**This box-and-whisker plot shows the results of a survey on the amount of money families budgeted for vacations. Use the plot for Exercises 6–8.**

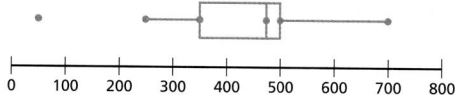

4. What are the least and greatest amounts reported? $50, $700

5. What percent of those surveyed budgeted $450 or more? 50%

6. In which interval are the data most closely clustered? The most spread out? 450–500, 500–700

7. On a test, Erica has the 8th highest test score. If 28 students took the test, what is Erica's percentile rank? 75th

8. Nick scored in the 80th percentile on a test, how many people scored above him out of 40 students? 8

**REAL ESTATE** A real-estate broker sold eight houses last month for $90,000, $75,000, $150,000, $80,000, $140,000, $80,000, $100,000 and $95,000. For 1 and 2, see additional answers.

1. Which measure of central tendency might the broker use to tell homeowners the average selling price in order to encourage them to want to sell their houses? Explain.

2. Which measure of central tendency should the broker use to describe the average selling price to people looking for a house? Explain.

**FOOD SERVICE** A school cafeteria charges $3 for the daily lunch special. The manager is considering raising the price and asked 25 students to name the greatest amount they would be willing to pay for the lunch special. The results are shown in the table.

3. In order to justify a large increase in the lunch price, which measure of central tendency might the manager use? Explain. See additional answers.

4. If students that buy their lunch saw this survey, which measures of central tendency might they point out to the manager to keep the price increase low? Explain. Mode; it is the lowest of the three measures.

**Greatest Amount People Would Pay For The Daily Lunch Special**

| Amount (dollars) | Frequency |
| --- | --- |
| 6.00 | 3 |
| 5.00 | 4 |
| 4.50 | 3 |
| 4.00 | 5 |
| 3.75 | 7 |
| 3.50 | 1 |
| 3.00 | 1 |
| 2.00 | 1 |

Extra Practice | **587**

---

## ADDITIONAL ANSWERS

**Extra Practice 1-6**

3.

Scores on a Math Achievement Test

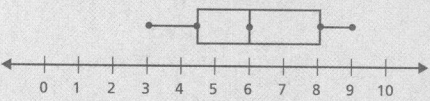

**Extra Practice 1-7**

1. Mean; It is greater ($101,250) than the median ($92,500) and mode ($80,000). Most people selling their houses would like to make as much money on the sale as possible.

2. Mode; Potential buyers are interested in saving money.

3. Mean; The mean ($4.25) is higher than the median ($4.00) and the mode ($3.75).

Extra Practice

## Extra Practice 1-8

1. $\begin{bmatrix} 8 & 3 & 9 & 2 \\ 6 & 5 & 0 & 4 \\ 8 & 7 & 6 & 5 \end{bmatrix}$  $3 \times 4$

2. $\begin{bmatrix} 200 & 321 \\ 218 & 282 \\ 135 & 129 \end{bmatrix}$  $3 \times 2$

3. $\begin{bmatrix} 6 & 0 & 5 & 9 & 2 \\ 3 & 9 & 4 & 0 & 7 \end{bmatrix}$  $2 \times 5$

6. $\begin{bmatrix} 9 & 5 & 6 \\ 2 & 5 & 0 \\ 7 & 10 & 5 \end{bmatrix}$  7. $\begin{bmatrix} 9 & 5 & 6 \\ 2 & 5 & 0 \\ 7 & 10 & 5 \end{bmatrix}$

8. $\begin{bmatrix} -3 & 3 & 0 \\ 0 & -3 & 4 \\ -3 & 4 & 7 \end{bmatrix}$  9. $\begin{bmatrix} 3 & -3 & 0 \\ 0 & 3 & -4 \\ 3 & -4 & -7 \end{bmatrix}$

10. $\begin{bmatrix} 13 & 4 & 9 \\ 5 & 3 & 0 \\ 2 & 18 & 8 \end{bmatrix}$

11. $\begin{bmatrix} 1 & 2 & 3 \\ 3 & -5 & 4 \\ -8 & 12 & 10 \end{bmatrix}$

12. $G + H = \begin{bmatrix} 48 & 106 \\ 52 & 119 \\ 110 & -65 \end{bmatrix}$

$G - H = \begin{bmatrix} 116 & -60 \\ -2 & 13 \\ -84 & -29 \end{bmatrix}$

## Extra Practice 2-1

1. ![number line from -3 to 4]
   $-3 \ -2 \ -1 \ \ 0 \ \ 1 \ \ 2 \ \ 3 \ \ 4$

2. ![number line from -6 to 8]
   $-6 \ -4 \ -2 \ \ 0 \ \ 2 \ \ 4 \ \ 6 \ \ 8$

3. ![number line from -6 to 8]
   $-6 \ -4 \ -2 \ \ 0 \ \ 2 \ \ 4 \ \ 6 \ \ 8$

4. ![number line from -12 to 2]
   $-12 \ -10 \ -8 \ -6 \ -4 \ -2 \ \ 0 \ \ 2$

5. ![number line from -1 to 6]
   $-1 \ \ 0 \ \ 1 \ \ 2 \ \ 3 \ \ 4 \ \ 5 \ \ 6$

6. ![number line from -6 to 1]
   $-6 \ -5 \ -4 \ -3 \ -2 \ -1 \ \ 0 \ \ 1$

7. ![number line from -3 to 4]
   $-3 \ -2 \ -1 \ \ 0 \ \ 1 \ \ 2 \ \ 3 \ \ 4$

8. ![number line from 0 to 7]
   $0 \ \ 1 \ \ 2 \ \ 3 \ \ 4 \ \ 5 \ \ 6 \ \ 7$

9. ![number line from -6 to 1]
   $-6 \ -5 \ -4 \ -3 \ -2 \ -1 \ \ 0 \ \ 1$

10. ![number line from -10 to -3]
    $-10 \ -9 \ -8 \ -7 \ -6 \ -5 \ -4 \ -3$

---

**Write each set of data as a matrix. Name its dimensions.**  For 1–3, see additional answers.

1. 
| | A | B | C | D |
|---|---|---|---|---|
| 1 | Age | | | |
| 2 | 0-3 | 8 | 3 | 9 | 2 |
| 3 | 4-7 | 6 | 5 | 0 | 4 |
| 4 | 8-11 | 8 | 7 | 6 | 5 |

2. 
| | A | B | C |
|---|---|---|---|
| 1 | | Male | Female |
| 2 | Monday | 200 | 321 |
| 3 | Tuesday | 218 | 282 |
| 4 | Wednesday | 135 | 129 |

3. 
| | A | B | C | D | E | F |
|---|---|---|---|---|---|---|
| 1 | | Jan | Feb | Mar | Apr | May |
| 2 | Paid | 6 | 0 | 5 | 9 | 2 |
| 3 | Unpaid | 3 | 9 | 4 | 0 | 7 |

For 6–11, see additional answers.

**Use matrices *A–D* for Exercises 4–11.**

4. Give the elements of *A*. 3, 4, 3, 1, 1, 2, 2, 7, 6

5. Name the dimensions of *D*.  $3 \times 2$

$A = \begin{bmatrix} 3 & 4 & 3 \\ 1 & 1 & 2 \\ 2 & 7 & 6 \end{bmatrix}$  $B = \begin{bmatrix} 4 & -1 & 3 \\ 3 & -2 & 0 \\ -5 & 8 & 3 \end{bmatrix}$

6. Find $A + C$.  7. Find $C + A$.

8. Find $A - C$.  9. Find $C - A$.

10. Find $A + C + B$.  11. Find $A + B - C$.

$C = \begin{bmatrix} 6 & 1 & 3 \\ 1 & 4 & -2 \\ 5 & 3 & -1 \end{bmatrix}$  $D = \begin{bmatrix} 4 & -5 \\ 2 & 0 \\ -7 & 6 \end{bmatrix}$

12. Use a graphing calculator to find the sum and difference of matrices *G* and *H*.
    See additional answers.

$G = \begin{bmatrix} 82 & 23 \\ 25 & 66 \\ 13 & -47 \end{bmatrix}$  $H = \begin{bmatrix} -34 & 83 \\ 27 & 53 \\ 97 & -18 \end{bmatrix}$

## Chapter 2

**Extra Practice 2–1 • Real Numbers • pages 52–55**  For 1–10, see additional answers.

**Graph each set of numbers on a number line.**

1. $\left\{ -3, -2.5, -\dfrac{1}{2}, 2, 3.6 \right\}$

2. $\{-3, -2, 0, 2.9, 5\}$

3. the integers from $-5$ to 3

4. the integers from $-5$ to $-12$

5. all real numbers less than 4

6. all real numbers less than or equal to $-4$

7. all real numbers greater than $-3$

8. all real numbers less than or equal to 5

9. all real numbers greater than or equal to $-4$

10. integers from $-3$ to $-8$

**Evaluate each expression.**

11. $-x$, when $x = -2.4$  2.4

12. $|n|$, when $n = -3$  3

13. $-|-n|$, when $n = 2$  $-2$

14. $-|x|$, when $x = -4$  $-4$

15. $-|f|$, when $f = -5.3$  $-5.3$

16. $-b$, when $b = 4.78$  $-4.78$

17. $-\left(\dfrac{b}{c}\right)$, when $b = 2$ and $c = -4$  $\dfrac{1}{2}$

18. Which depth is closer to sea level, a depth of $-1689$ ft or a depth of $-3792$ ft?  $-1689$ ft

**Simplify each numerical expression.**

1. $3 \cdot 8 - 2 + 6$  28
2. $(30 + 5) \div (5 \cdot 3)$  $2\frac{1}{3}$
3. $4 \cdot 9 - 7$  29
4. $3^2 + 8$  17
5. $(31 - 7) \div 6 \cdot 9$  36
6. $9.4 - 1.2 \cdot 18 \div 9$  7
7. $\frac{1}{4}\left(\frac{1}{4} + \frac{3}{8}\right)$  $\frac{5}{32}$
8. $\frac{1}{3}\left(\frac{1}{2} + \frac{4}{5}\right)$  $\frac{13}{30}$
9. $(16 - 5) \cdot 2 + 2^3$  30

**Evaluate each variable expression when $n = 12$.**

10. $20 - n$  8
11. $\frac{1}{2}n$  6
12. $n + 6$  18
13. $n \div 4$  3
14. $4n - 18$  30
15. $\frac{60}{n}$  5
16. $n + 3n$  48
17. $\frac{2}{3}n + 7$  15
18. $5n + 36 \div 3^2$  64

19. Write a variable expression for the phrase: multiply a number $n$ by 3 and then add 2.  $3n + 2$

20. Ben charges \$4/h to babysit. He charges an extra \$3 if he babysits on a Friday night. Write and simplify a numerical expression for the amount Ben charges to babysit for 5 h on a Friday night.  $5 \cdot 4 + 3 = 23$

**Write each phrase as a variable expression.**

1. the sum of five and a number  $5 + n$
2. the quotient of a number and 30  $n \div 30$
3. negative two times a number  $-2n$
4. twice a number decreased by 11  $2n - 11$
5. a number decreased by eight  $n - 8$
6. negative eight times a number  $-8n$
7. twice a number divided by negative four  $\frac{2n}{-4}$
8. the quotient of one and twice a number  $\frac{1}{2n}$
9. nine less than the sum of five and a number  $(5 + n) - 9$
10. the quotient of twice a number and three  $\frac{2n}{3}$
11. negative one-third times a number  $-\frac{1}{3}n$
12. the difference of nine and a number  $n - 9$
13. a number less 18  $n - 18$
14. twice a number multiplied by three  $(2n)3$
15. the difference of one and a number  $1 - n$
16. the sum of one and twice a number  $1 + 2n$

**Translate each variable expression into a word phrase.**  For 17–28, see additional answers.

17. $8 + t$
18. $\frac{x}{2}$
19. $-4p$
20. $3n - 2$
21. $\frac{1}{2}g$
22. $-\frac{14}{2y}$
23. $12s - 4$
24. $6x + 10$
25. $-\frac{y}{2}$
26. $h^2 - 12$
27. $0.4 - 7j$
28. $22 + \frac{1}{3}n$

29. When water freezes, its volume increases. The volume of ice equals the sum of the volume of water and the product of one-eleventh and the volume of water. If $x$ cm$^3$ of water is frozen, write an expression for the volume of the ice that is formed.  $x + \frac{1}{11}x$

**Extra Practice** | **589**

**Extra Practice**

**Simplify.**

1. $4x + 9x$  $13x$

2. $6n - 9n$  $-3n$

3. $-5ab + 6ab$  $ab$

4. $4s + 4s - 3m$  $8s - 3m$

5. $6j + (-j) + 9j$  $14j$

6. $3jk + (-jk) + 7j$  $2jk + 7j$

7. $\frac{1}{3}a + \frac{1}{4}a$  $\frac{7}{12}a$

8. $-3w + 6w + (-w)$  $2w$

9. $-5d - (2d + d)$  $-8d$

10. $2g - (-g) + 4 - 3g$  $4$

11. $-6e - 4 + 3e - e$  $-4e - 4$

12. $3r + 9pq + 6r - 3pq$  $9r + 6pq$

13. $3x + (-9x)$  $-6x$

14. $6n + 9n + 3mn - 8mn$  $15n - 5mn$

15. $\frac{1}{4}ab + \frac{3}{4}ab - \frac{5}{6}b + \frac{1}{6}a$  $ab - \frac{5}{6}b + \frac{1}{6}a$

16. $4mn + 4m - 3mn$  $mn + 4m$

17. $-j + (-4j) - 6j$  $-11j$

18. $0.13jk + (-0.5jk) + 1.2jk$  $0.83jk$

19. $\frac{1}{8}xy + \frac{1}{4}xy + \frac{1}{2}xy$  $\frac{7}{8}xy$

20. $-\frac{3}{7}w - \frac{6}{7}w + \left(-\frac{1}{7}w\right)$  $-\frac{10}{7}w$

21. $-5de + 2d + de - de$  $-4de - 2$  $-9de + 2d - 2$

22. $2g + (-g) - 4 + 3g$  $4g - 4$

23. $-6e + 4 - 3e + e$  $-8e + 4$

24. $-3rs + (-2rs) - 6r + 6s$  $-5rs - 6r + 6s$

**Evaluate each expression when $a = -3$ and $b = 10$.**

25. $a - 3a$  $6$

26. $-b + 4b$  $30$

27. $a - b + 3a - 9b$  $-112$

28. $\frac{1}{3}a - \frac{1}{5}b$  $-3$

29. $-2a - (-3a)$  $-3$

30. $3ab - ab + 2ab$  $-120$

31. $4a + 4b - 6a - 6b$  $-14$

32. $\frac{3}{5}ab + \frac{2}{3}ab - b$  $-48$

33. $3a + 4b + 2b - 5a$  $66$

34. Theresa sold $20x$ sweaters on Tuesday. On Wednesday she sold $8x$ sweaters fewer than on Tuesday. Write and simplify an expression for the number of sweaters Theresa sold on Wednesday.  $20x - 8x = 12x$

**Simplify.**

1. $5(3a + 2a)$  $25a$

2. $-(3z + x)$  $-3z - x$

3. $-3(4b + 9b)$  $-39b$

4. $-8(x - y)$  $-8x + 8y$

5. $\frac{1}{3}(6a + 12ab - 21a)$  $-5a + 4ab$

6. $4(5 - z)$  $20 - 4z$

7. $-2(e + 3)$  $-2e - 6$

8. $\frac{1}{5}(10f - 5)$  $2f - 1$

9. $-3(-n + 9)$  $3n - 27$

10. $\frac{-6p + 4}{-2}$  $3p - 2$

11. $\frac{5g - 10}{5}$  $g - 2$

12. $\frac{-14v - 7}{-2}$  $7v + \frac{7}{2}$

13. $\frac{12 - 36d}{4}$  $3 - 9d$

14. $\frac{3.9 + 4.5h}{0.3}$  $13 + 15h$

15. $\frac{225r + 30}{-15}$  $-15r - 2$

16. $\frac{6t + 12st - 21s}{3}$  $2t + 4st - 7s$

17. $\frac{10n + 5}{-5}$  $-2n - 1$

18. $\frac{3a + (-6)}{-3}$  $-a + 2$

**Evaluate each expression when $a = \frac{1}{2}$, $b = -2$, and $c = 10$.**

19. $-4(a - 22)$  $86$

20. $6(-b - 8)$  $-36$

21. $\frac{c - 24}{7}$  $-2$

22. $c(8 + b)$  $60$

23. $\frac{-10a + 12b}{-2}$  $\frac{29}{2}$

24. $\frac{3c - 2b}{17}$  $2$

25. A piece of wood measures $(6a + 3b)$ in. long. Write and simplify an expression for the length of a piece of wood 6 times as long.  $36a + 18b$

**Simplify.** For 1–18, see additional answers.

1. $4(n + 3s) - 6s$
2. $-8(b - 5c) + 10c$
3. $(9a - 3b) - (4a + 6b)$
4. $-\frac{1}{2}(4m - 5n) - \frac{1}{2}n$
5. $4(5f - 2g) - (2f + 3g)$
6. $1.5(3b + 4c) - 3(2.5b + 5c)$
7. $5(3b - 4c) - 3(5b - 5c)$
8. $(3x + 2y) - 3(2x - y)$
9. $-2(3m + n) - 2(2m + 7n)$
10. $6(-2b - 3c) + 3(2b + 3c)$
11. $\frac{1}{2}(4p + 8q) - \frac{3}{4}(8p + 4q)$
12. $15(3b + 3) - 19$
13. $-(2x - 4y) - 6(x - 5y)$
14. $7\left(\frac{1}{7}b + \frac{1}{7}c\right) + 6\left(\frac{1}{3}b + \frac{2}{3}c\right)$
15. $1.2(5f - 20g) - 5.2(5f + 30g)$
16. $13(3s + 4t) - 3(15t)$
17. $17(3m + 4n) - 17(3m + 4n)$
18. $9(-a + b) - 3(-a - 5c)$

19. Heta wrapped 6 gifts for a birthday party. Some of the gifts were wrapped in green paper and the rest in blue paper. It cost $1.25 for each sheet of green paper and $0.75 for each sheet of blue paper. Write and simplify a variable expression for the total amount Heta spent on $x$ sheets of wrapping paper. $x(1.25) + (6 - x)0.75 = 0.5x + 4.5$

20. Michael bought 8 paperback books. Some of the books were mysteries and the rest were science fiction. The mystery books cost $4.95 and the science fiction books were on sale for $2.95. Write and simplify a variable expression for the total amount Michael spent on $x$ books. $x(4.95) + (8 - x)2.95 = 2x + 23.6$

**Evaluate each expression when $m = 5$ and $n = -2$.**

1. $n^2$  4
2. $m^2 + n^3$  17
3. $(m + n)^2$  9
4. $3mn^2$  60
5. $4(n + 3)^2$  4
6. $(m - n)^2$  49
7. $6(2 + n)^2$ 0
8. $\frac{m^3}{m^2}$  5
9. $(1 - m)^2$  16
10. $(n^2 - 5)^2$  1
11. $8(m - 1)^2$  128
12. $\left(\frac{n}{4}\right)^2$  $\frac{1}{4}$
13. $(n^2 - 3)^2$  1
14. $\left(\frac{m}{2}\right)^2$  6.25
15. $\frac{n^8}{n^7}$  $-2$
16. $4n^2 + m$  21

**Simplify.**

17. $c \cdot c^3$  $c^4$
18. $(m^2)^3$  $m^6$
19. $4(b^2)^3$  $4b^6$
20. $x^9 \cdot x^3$  $x^{12}$
21. $\frac{y^3}{y}, y \neq 0$  $y^2$
22. $\left(\frac{1}{z}\right)^3, z \neq 0$  $\frac{1}{z^3}$
23. $(x^2)^2$  $x^4$
24. $4(a^3)^3$  $4a^9$
25. $\left(\frac{y}{3}\right)^3$  $\frac{y^3}{27}$
26. $\frac{18n^8}{3n^3}, n \neq 0$  $6n^5$
27. $m^2 \cdot m \cdot m^3$  $m^6$
28. $3(x^2)^4$  $3x^8$
29. $t^{15} \cdot t^8$  $t^{23}$
30. $\left(\frac{1}{d}\right)^{11}, d \neq 0$  $\frac{1}{d^{11}}$
31. $(2yx^3)^3$  $8y^3x^9$
32. $(r^2)(r^5)(r^3)$  $r^{10}$

33. A piece of wood $x^4$ in. long is to be cut into pieces $x^2$ in. long. How many pieces will there be?  $x^2$

34. If the value of $x$ in Exercise 33 is 6, how long would each piece be?  36 in.

35. A piece of string $x^5$ in. long is to be cut into $x^2$ pieces. How long will each piece be?  $x^3$ in.

**ADDITIONAL ANSWERS**

**Extra Practice 2-6**
1. $4n + 6s$
2. $-8b + 50c$
3. $5a - 9b$
4. $-2m + 2n$
5. $18f - 11g$
6. $-3b - 9c$
7. $-5c$
8. $5y - 3x$
9. $-10m - 16n$
10. $-6b - 9c$
11. $q - 4p$
12. $45b + 26$
13. $34y - 8x$
14. $3b + 5c$
15. $-20f - 180q$
16. $39s + 7t$
17. 0
18. $-6a + 9b + 15c$

**Simplify.**

1. $a^2 \cdot a^{-4}$   $a^{-2}$
2. $b^3 \div b^{-2}$   $b^5$
3. $3a^2 \cdot 5a^{-2}$   15
4. $x^2 \div x^5$   $x^{-3}$
5. $(m^2)^{-1}$   $m^{-2}$
6. $x^{-4} \cdot x^{-3}$   $x^{-7}$
7. $a^{-3} \div a^3$   $a^{-6}$
8. $(x^3)^{-2}$   $x^{-6}$

**Evaluate each expression when $x = -2$ and $y = 3$.**

9. $x^3$   $-8$
10. $x^3 \cdot x^{-2}$   $-2$
11. $(xy)^{-3}$   $-\frac{1}{216}$
12. $x^2 \cdot y^{-2}$   $\frac{4}{9}$
13. $(y - x)^{-2}$   $\frac{1}{25}$
14. $(x^3 - y)^2$   121
15. $y^3 \div y^2$   3
16. $(xy)^{-3}$   $-\frac{1}{216}$

**Write each number in scientific notation.**

17. 9560   $9.56 \cdot 10^3$
18. 0.0598   $5.98 \cdot 10^{-2}$
19. 3450   $3.45 \cdot 10^3$
20. 34,900   $3.49 \cdot 10^4$
21. 0.0096   $9.6 \cdot 10^{-3}$
22. 0.0000007   $7 \cdot 10^{-7}$

**Write each number in standard form.**

23. $3.75 \cdot 10^{-2}$   0.0375
24. $1.9 \cdot 10^5$   190,000
25. $1.23 \cdot 10^{-3}$   0.00123
26. $6.3 \cdot 10^{-8}$   0.000000063
27. $2.590 \cdot 10^{-4}$   0.000259
28. $1.095 \cdot 10^6$   1,095,000
29. $4.5 \cdot 10^{-4}$   0.00045
30. $5.890 \cdot 10^3$   5890
31. $9.65 \cdot 10^{-5}$   0.0000965

32. A mid-western state spends $1,900,000 annually on books for its libraries. At that rate, how much would it spend in eight years? Write the number in scientific notation.   $1.52 \cdot 10^7$

## Chapter 3

**Which of the given values is a solution of the equation?**

1. $a + 5 = 3; 8, -8, -2$   $-2$
2. $-4n - 7 = 1; 2, -2, -3$   $-2$
3. $12 + w = 9; -3, -9, 9$   $-3$
4. $15 + 3n = 3; 3, 4, -4$   $-4$

**Use mental math to solve each equation.**

5. $m - 12 = 32$   44
6. $-4 + x = -8$   $-4$
7. $21 = 3 + t$   18
8. $\frac{1}{3}x = 15$   45
9. $7t = 4.9$   0.7
10. $n - 7.6 = 0$   7.6
11. $-4 = \frac{1}{2}x$   $-8$
12. $-5 - x = 1$   $-6$
13. $y + 6 = 21$   15

**Find the unknown measure of each triangle. Use the formula $A = \frac{1}{2}bh$.**

14. The area of the triangle is 32 ft$^2$ and the height is 8 ft. Find the base.   8 ft

15. The area of the triangle is 50 m$^2$ and the base is 25 m. Find the height.   4 m

16. The height of the triangle is 46 cm and the base is 11 cm. Find the area.   253 cm$^2$

**Solve each equation. Check the solution.**

1. $3x = 48$   16
2. $1.5 = n - 3$   4.5
3. $11 - m = -8.7$   19.7
4. $\frac{2}{7}p = 4$   14
5. $5 - b = 6$   −1
6. $-3w = 1$   $-\frac{1}{3}$
7. $\frac{5}{6}a = 5$   6
8. $-4p = 80$   −20
9. $-\frac{n}{5} = -4$   20
10. $-85 = 17r$   −5
11. $1.4x = 8.4$   6
12. $5.6 = 7 + n$   −1.4
13. $\frac{n}{6} = 5$   30
14. $\frac{7}{8} = \frac{1}{4} + t$   $\frac{5}{8}$
15. $50b = -20$   $-\frac{2}{5}$
16. $j - 4.7 = 12$   16.7
17. $n + 13 = 7$   −6
18. $2.4g = 6$   2.5
19. $\frac{5}{6}s = -10$   −12
20. $-6d = 40$   $-6\frac{2}{3}$
21. $18x = -12$   $-\frac{2}{3}$

22. During a 4-wk period Makota ran a total of 196 mi. To show the situation, he let $n$ equal "the average number of miles run per week" and wrote the equation as $4n = 196$. What was the average number of miles Makota ran each week?   49 mi/wk

23. Twelve times a certain number equals −4. To model the situation, Elaine let $x$ equal "a certain number." Then she wrote the equation $12x = -4$. What was the original number?   $-\frac{1}{3}$

**Solve each equation. Check the solution.**

1. $4x - 2x + 3 = 27$   12
2. $4b - 7 = 0$   $\frac{7}{4}$
3. $16 = -2 - 3w$   −6
4. $\frac{4}{5}d + 7 = 19$   15
5. $\frac{n}{4} + 3 = 15$   48
6. $2d + 4d - 2 = -14$   −2
7. $-y - y + 7 = -1$   4
8. $3x - 2.7 = 5.1$   2.6
9. $3(a + 4) = 21$   3
10. $-6a + 4 + 2a + 1 = 13$   −2
11. $5.1x - 4 = 31.7$   7
12. $7(t - 2) = 21$   5
13. $5z + 4 = z + \frac{16}{5}$   $-\frac{1}{5}$
14. $4(2x + 3) = 52$   5
15. $6y - 5 + y + 2 = 11.7$   2.1
16. $3(a + 2) = -2(a - 13)$   4
17. $7(12 - x) = -14$   14
18. $\frac{1}{4}(6r - 2) = \frac{1}{4}$   0.5

19. Find $m\angle YXZ$ and $m\angle XZY$ in the figure below.

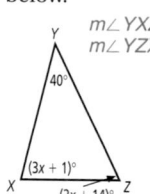

$m\angle YXZ = 76°$
$m\angle YZX = 64°$

20. Find $m\angle CDB$ and $m\angle CDA$ in the figure below.

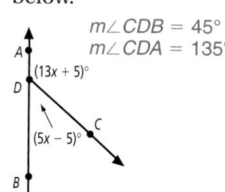

$m\angle CDB = 45°$
$m\angle CDA = 135°$

21. Find $m\angle AYD$ and $m\angle CYB$ in the figure below.

$m\angle AYD = 60°$
$m\angle CYB = 60°$

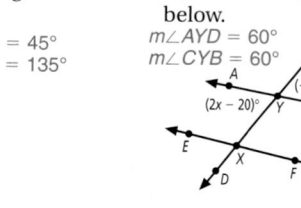

22. Twice a number decreased by 7 is the same as four times the number decreased by 23. Find the number.   8

## ADDITIONAL ANSWERS

**Extra Practice 3-6**

1.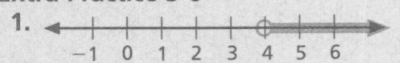

(number line graphs 1-18 for Extra Practice 3-6)

---

Extra Practice 3–5 • Proportions • pages 122–125

**Solve each proportion. Check the solution.**

1. $\frac{5}{3} = \frac{a}{9}$   15

2. $\frac{33}{z} = \frac{15}{10}$   22

3. $\frac{-36}{b} = \frac{24}{16}$   $-24$

4. $18 : x = 20 : 60$   54

5. $14 : 16 = 35 : a$   40

6. 15 is to $z$ as 21 is to 14   10

7. $\frac{e + 3}{5} = 8$   37

8. $\frac{8}{f - 5} = \frac{1}{2}$   21

9. $\frac{n - 9}{6} = 4$   33

10. $\frac{p + 9}{p} = \frac{2}{-3}$   $-11$

11. $\frac{g - 7}{-3} = \frac{g}{4}$   4

12. $\frac{3v - 7}{5} = v + 3$   $-11$

13. $\frac{2 - d}{7} = \frac{2 + d}{3}$   $-\frac{4}{5}$

14. $\frac{9 + h}{h} = \frac{4}{5}$   $-45$

15. $\frac{5r + 3}{9} = \frac{r - 1}{2}$   $-15$

16. $\frac{6t + 1}{2} = \frac{t - 1}{5}$   $-\frac{1}{4}$

17. $\frac{3n + 5}{7} = \frac{1 - 3n}{5}$   $-\frac{1}{2}$

18. $\frac{3}{7} = \frac{a + 6}{3a + 2}$   18

19. A company produces 1450 tires. Of these, 12% are for recreational vehicles. How many tires are for recreational vehicles?   174 tires

20. For one year, a company's income was $620,980. The company's expenses for that year were $496,784. What percent of the company's income was profit? (Hint: income − expenses = profit)   20%

21. Of all the employees at a company, 15% have reported in sick in the last month. There are 560 employees at this company. How many reported in sick last month?   84 employees

Extra Practice 3–6 • Graph Inequalities on a Number Line • pages 126–129

**Graph the solutions of each inequality on a number line.** For 1–18, see additional answers.

1. $b > 4$

2. $x < 5$

3. $4 > f$

4. $b \geq 4$

5. $n > 0$

6. $x \leq 5$

7. $-4 \geq c$

8. $4 \leq f$

9. $x \geq 5$

10. $x > 3$

11. $1.5 > f$

12. $-1 \leq h$

13. $n < 2$

14. $m < -2$

15. $b > -4$

16. $j \leq 18$

17. $0 > k$

18. $2.5 \geq t$

**State the inequality that is represented on each number line.**

19. $x < 1$

20. $x \geq 1$

22. $x > -5$

23. $x \leq 0$

Extra Practice

**Solve and graph each inequality.** For 1–16, see additional answers.

**1.** $4x - 2 < 22$  $x < 6$

**2.** $4 - r > 12$  $r < -8$

**3.** $4 \leq \frac{1}{5}y$  $y \geq 20$

**4.** $5m + 2 \geq -3$  $m \geq -1$

**5.** $3r + 2 > -7$  $r > -3$

**6.** $7 + 2a < 19$  $a < 6$

**7.** $15 < 3n + 21$  $n > -2$

**8.** $8 - 2m > 14$  $m < -3$

**9.** $12 \geq -3n + 5$  $n \geq -\frac{7}{3}$

**10.** $\frac{1}{4}d - 2 \leq 1$  $d \leq 12$

**11.** $20 \leq -3n + 5$  $n \leq -5$

**12.** $0.4p - 3 \leq -1$  $p \leq 5$

**13.** $8 - 4a > 12$  $a < -1$

**14.** $5 - \frac{1}{2}w \geq 6$  $w \leq -2$

**15.** $18 \leq 3 - 5x$  $x \leq -3$

**16.** $0.3x - 4 > 0.2$  $x > 14$

**17.** Pablo wants to get a grade of at least 95 in math this semester. So far he has test scores of 89, 98, 97 and 92. He will take his last test on Friday. What is the lowest grade he can get on the test and still get a 95 this semester? 99

**18.** Ellie can lift a maximum of 225 lb. The bar already has 105 lb of weights on it. She wants to add more weight. Each disk weighs 20 lb. How many disks can she add to the bar so that she can lift her maximum weight? 6

**Solve each equation. Check the solutions.**

**1.** $x^2 = 121$  $\pm 11$

**2.** $b^2 = \frac{25}{64}$  $\pm\frac{5}{8}$

**3.** $n^2 = 81$  $\pm 9$

**4.** $x^2 = 1.44$  $\pm 1.2$

**5.** $\sqrt{f} = \frac{1}{10}$  $\frac{1}{100}$

**6.** $\sqrt{x + 3} = 1$  $-2$

**7.** $\sqrt{x} = 3$  9

**8.** $\sqrt{y} = 0.5$  0.25

**9.** $\sqrt{v - 5} = 8$  69

**10.** $\sqrt{4 + x} = 4$  12

**11.** $3 = \sqrt{x} - 7$  100

**12.** $8\sqrt{x} = 24$  9

**13.** $\sqrt{3r} - 2 = 7$  27

**14.** $7x^2 = 210$  $\pm\sqrt{30}$

**15.** $8 + 3n^2 = 83$  $\pm 5$

**16.** $6 = \sqrt{2(x + 4)}$  14

**17.** $\sqrt{5h} = \frac{1}{5}$  $\frac{1}{125}$

**18.** $\sqrt{6y - 7} = 2\frac{11}{6}$

**19.** $4t^2 = 9$  $\pm\frac{3}{2}$

**20.** $r^2 + 8 = 908$  $\pm 30$

**21.** $12 = \sqrt{x + 3} - 8$  397

**22.** The formula $d = 16t^2$ gives the distance $d$ in feet traveled by an object dropped from a resting position and allowed to fall freely. The variable $t$ represents the time of the fall in seconds. If you dropped an object from a height of 1024 ft above the ground, how long would it take to land on the ground? 8 sec

**23.** Payton will place 4 square tiles over a floorboard with a total area of 576 cm². Each of the tiles has the same dimensions and when placed together fit exactly over the floorboard. Write and solve an equation to find the dimensions of each tile. 12 cm

Extra Practice

**1.**

**2.**

**3.**

**4.**

**5.**

**6.**

**7.**

**8.**

**9.**

**10.**

**11.**

**12.**

**13.**

**14.**

**15.**

**16.**

**Extra Practice 4-3**

1. (red, heads), (red, tails), (blue, heads), (blue, tails), (green, heads), (green, tails), (yellow, heads), (yellow, tails)

**Coin Marble Outcomes**

$$H\begin{cases} R \to HR \\ B \to HB \\ G \to HG \\ Y \to HY \end{cases} \quad T\begin{cases} R \to TR \\ B \to TB \\ G \to TG \\ Y \to TY \end{cases}$$

2. (A, heads), (A, tails), (B, heads), (B, tails), (C, heads), (C, tails), (D, heads), (D, tails), (E, heads), (E, tails), (F, heads), (F, tails)

**Spinner Coin Outcomes**

$$A\begin{cases} H \to AH \\ T \to AT \end{cases}$$
$$B\begin{cases} H \to BH \\ T \to BT \end{cases}$$
$$C\begin{cases} H \to CH \\ T \to CT \end{cases}$$
$$D\begin{cases} H \to DH \\ T \to DT \end{cases}$$
$$E\begin{cases} H \to EH \\ T \to ET \end{cases}$$
$$F\begin{cases} H \to FH \\ T \to FT \end{cases}$$

## Chapter 4

Extra Practice 4–1 • Experiments and Probabilities • pages 150–153

**Use the table for Exercises 1–5.**

**Science Fair Attendance**

|           | 10th graders | 11th graders | 12th graders | Teachers | Students' family |
|-----------|--------------|--------------|--------------|----------|------------------|
| Wednesday | 162          | 129          | 135          | 27       | 87               |
| Thursday  | 336          | 180          | 144          | 24       | 36               |
| Friday    | 288          | 240          | 179          | 144      | 109              |

1. Find the probability that a person at the fair on Wednesday is a 10th grader. 0.3

2. Find the probability that a person at the fair on Wednesday is a teacher. 0.05

3. Find the probability that a person at the fair on Thursday is an 11th grader. 0.25

4. Find the probability that a person at the fair on Thursday is a 12th grader. 0.20

5. Find the probability that a person at the fair on Friday is a family member. ≈ 0.114

**SPORTS** On a particular day at a ski resort, 19 people skied on the beginner slope, 123 people skied on the intermediate slope and 58 skied on the advanced slope. Find the probability that a skier used the following slope.

6. intermediate slope ≈ 0.615    7. beginner slope 0.095    8. advanced slope 0.29

Extra Practice 4–3 • Sample Spaces and Theoretical Probability • pages 158–161

1. A coin is tossed and a marble drawn from a bag that contains 1 red marble, 1 blue marble, 1 green marble, and 1 yellow marble. Show the sample space using ordered pairs. Then show the sample space using a tree diagram. See additional answers

2. A spinner with six equal sectors labeled A through F is spun and a coin is tossed. Show the sample space using ordered pairs. Then show the sample space using a tree diagram. See additional answers.

3. **SPORTS** At a baseball tryout there were 3 candidates for pitcher, 5 candidates for catcher and 7 candidates for shortstop. How many different ways can these positions be filled? 105

**The spinners shown are both spun for Exercises 4–10.**

4. How many possible outcomes are there? 48

5. Find $P$(letter before F in the alphabet, odd number) $\frac{5}{12}$

6. Find $P$(C, 4) $\frac{1}{48}$

7. Find $P$(D, multiple of 3) $\frac{1}{24}$

8. Find $P$(F, odd number) $\frac{1}{12}$

9. Find $P$(vowel, number less than 3) $\frac{1}{12}$

10. Find $P$(consonant, prime number) $\frac{1}{3}$

1. Two number cubes are rolled. Find the probability that the sum of the numbers is 3 or 4. $\frac{5}{36}$

2. A card is drawn at random from a standard deck of 52 cards. Find the probability that the card is a 7 or a queen. $\frac{2}{13}$

3. Two number cubes are rolled. Find the probability that the sum of the numbers is even and greater than 9. $\frac{1}{9}$

4. A card is drawn at random from a standard deck of 52 cards. Find the probability that the card is a club or a king. $\frac{4}{13}$

**The spinner shown is spun one time. Use the diagram of the spinner to solve Exercises 5–16. Find each probability.**

5. $P$(green or 5) $\frac{1}{2}$

6. $P$(green or even) $\frac{3}{4}$

7. $P$(blue or yellow) $\frac{5}{8}$

8. $P$(green or less than 5) $\frac{1}{2}$

9. $P$(blue or prime) $\frac{3}{4}$

10. $P$(yellow or less than 4) $\frac{1}{2}$

11. $P$(blue and odd) $\frac{1}{4}$

12. $P$(green and even) $\frac{1}{8}$

13. $P$(green and prime) $\frac{1}{4}$

14. $P$(green and a multiple of 3) $\frac{1}{2}$

15. $P$(green or yellow) $\frac{1}{8}$

16. $P$(yellow and even) $\frac{1}{8}$

17. A card is drawn at random from a standard deck of 52 cards. Find the probability that the card is a diamond or a multiple of 3. $\frac{11}{26}$

18. Four coins are tossed. Find the probability that the coins show 2 heads or 2 tails. 0.375

**A group of numbered cards contains one 1, two 2s, four 3s, five 4s and six 5s. Cards are picked, one at a time, then replaced. Find each probability.**

1. $P$(1, then 2) $\frac{1}{162}$

2. $P$(1, then 3) $\frac{1}{81}$

3. $P$(1, then 4) $\frac{5}{324}$

4. $P$(2, then 3) $\frac{2}{81}$

5. $P$(2, then 4) $\frac{5}{162}$

6. $P$(2, then 2) $\frac{1}{81}$

7. $P$(1, then 5) $\frac{1}{54}$

8. $P$(3, then 5) $\frac{2}{27}$

9. $P$(4, then 5) $\frac{5}{54}$

**A bag contains 4 red, 5 blue, and 6 green marbles. Marbles are taken at random and not replaced. Find each probability.**

10. $P$(red, then blue) $\frac{2}{21}$

11. $P$(red, then green) $\frac{4}{35}$

12. $P$(red, then red) $\frac{2}{35}$

13. $P$(blue, then red) $\frac{2}{21}$

14. $P$(green, then green) $\frac{1}{7}$

15. $P$(blue, then green) $\frac{1}{7}$

**As a result of a storm, a sign reading NO SWIMMING lost three of its letters.**

16. What is the probability that the letters were all vowels? $\frac{1}{120}$

17. What is the probability that the letters were not vowels? $\frac{7}{24}$

18. What is the probability that the letters were lost in this order: O, S, M? $\frac{1}{360}$

Extra Practice 4–6 • Permutations of a Set • pages 172–175

1. In how many different ways can a teacher arrange 6 students in a row of seats? 720

2. From 8 candidates, a committee of judges must choose 5 candidates and rank them. In how many ways can this be done? 6720

3. A radio disc jockey has a set of 12 songs to play. In how many different ways can the disc jockey play the next 3 songs? 1320

4. A video store owner wants to display 7 different video boxes in a row on a shelf. In how many ways can this be done? 5040

5. How many different 5-digit numbers can be formed from the digits 1, 2, 3, 4 and 5 if each digit can be used only once? 120

6. Find the number of 5-letter "words" that can be formed from the letters of the word "chair"? 120

7. The class offices of president, vice president and secretary are to be filled. There are 20 candidates. In how many ways can the positions be filled? 6840

**Calculate each of the following permutations.**

**8.** $_4P_0$ 1      **9.** $_6P_3$ 120      **10.** $_3P_3$ 6      **11.** $_{10}P_6$ 151,200    **12.** $_7P_2$ 42

Extra Practice 4–7 • Combinations of a Set • pages 178–181

1. There are 8 one-liter cans each containing a different fruit juice. How many different types of fruit juice can be obtained by mixing 3 full containers of juice together? 56

2. A deck of 26 cards, marked A through Z, is shuffled and 3 cards are dealt. What is the probability that the cards are A, B and C in any order? $\frac{1}{2600}$

3. Alana, Gina and Lenisa are among 20 candidates competing for 3 open positions on the track team. What is the probability that they will be the 3 who are selected? $\frac{1}{1140}$

4. A taco restaurant offers 10 different fillings for tacos. If you were to choose 3 fillings, how many different tacos could you order? 120

5. How many "words" can be made with the letters, $a, c, e, g, i, k$ and $m$ if only three different letters are used in each word? 35

6. A random drawing is held to determine which 2 of the 8 members of the chorus will be sent to a district competition. How many different pairs of 2 could be sent to the competition? 28

7. How many different ways can a 4-person committee be chosen from 10 people if there are no restrictions? 210

**Calculate each of the following combinations.**

**8.** $_4C_0$ 1      **9.** $_6C_3$ 20      **10.** $_3C_3$ 1      **11.** $_{10}C_6$ 210    **12.** $_7C_2$ 21

# Chapter 5

### Extra Practice 5–1 • Elements of Geometry • pages 192–195

**State whether each statements is *true* or *false*.**

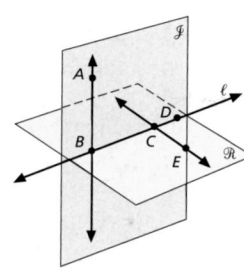

1. $B$, $C$ and $D$ lie in plane $\mathcal{J}$.  true
2. $A$, $B$ and $C$ line in plane $\mathcal{R}$.  false
3. Planes $\mathcal{J}$ and $\mathcal{R}$ intersect in line $\ell$.  true
4. Exactly one line contains $C$ and $E$.  true
5. $D$ does not lie in plane $\mathcal{R}$.  false
6. $\overleftrightarrow{AB}$ lies on plane $\mathcal{J}$.  true
7. $\overleftrightarrow{CE}$ lies on plane $\mathcal{J}$ and plane $\mathcal{R}$.  false

**Identify the points in each figure as *collinear* or *noncollinear* and *coplanar* or *noncoplanar*.**

8.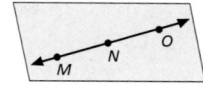

collinear, coplanar

9.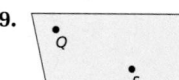

noncollinear, coplanar

10.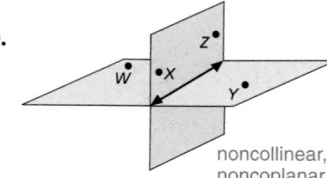

noncollinear, noncoplanar

### Extra Practice 5–2 • Angles and Perpendicular Lines • pages 196–199

**Find the measure of a complement and supplement of each angle.**

1. $m\angle X = 18°$  72°, 162°
2. $m\angle Y = 60°$  30°, 120°
3. $m\angle Z = 20°$  70°, 160°
4. $m\angle M = 8°$  82°, 172°
5. $m\angle N = 85°$  5°, 95°
6. $m\angle O = 50°$  40°, 130°

**In the figure shown, $\overline{AD} \perp \overline{XC}$.**

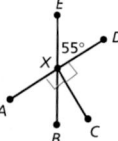

7. Name all right angles.  $\angle AXC$, $\angle CXD$
8. Name a pair of vertical angles.  Sample answer: $\angle EXD$ and $\angle AXB$
9. Name two adjacent complementary angles.  $\angle AXB$ and $\angle BXC$
10. Find $m\angle BXC$.  35°
11. Find $m\angle BXD$.  125°

**For Exercises 12 and 13, use the figure shown.**

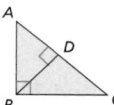

12. Name all pairs of perpendicular lines.  $\overleftrightarrow{AC} \perp \overleftrightarrow{BD}$, $\overleftrightarrow{AB} \perp \overleftrightarrow{BC}$
13. Name two angles that are congruent to $\angle ADB$.  $\angle BDC$ and $\angle ABC$

14. Write a rule for finding the supplement of any angle.  $180 - x$

## Extra Practice 5–3 • Parallel Lines and Transversals • pages 202–205

**Refer to the figure to classify each pair of angles.**

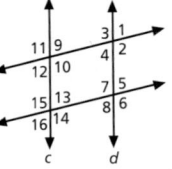

1. ∠8 and ∠13   alternate interior
2. ∠11 and ∠15   corresponding
3. ∠6 and ∠15   alternate exterior
4. ∠4 and ∠9   alternate interior
5. ∠12 and ∠16   corresponding
6. ∠4 and ∠10   same-side interior

**In the figure, $\overrightarrow{AB} \parallel \overrightarrow{CD}$. Find each measure.**

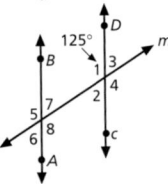

7. $m\angle 5$   125°
8. $m\angle 6$   55°
9. $m\angle 7$   55°
10. $m\angle 8$   125°
11. $m\angle 2$   55°
12. $m\angle 3$   55°

**State whether the lines cut by the transversal are parallel or not.**

13.
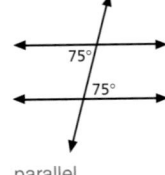
75°
75°
parallel

14.
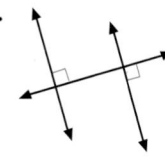
parallel

15.

95°
93°
not parallel

## Extra Practice 5–4 • Properties of Triangles • pages 206–209

**State whether it is possible to have a triangle with sides of the given lengths.**

1. 11, 8, 3   no
2. 15, 8, 8   yes
3. 4, 5, 6   yes
4. 100, 150, 160   yes

**Use the figure to classify each triangle by its sides.**

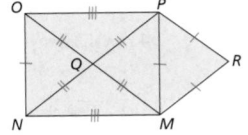

5. △OQN   isosceles
6. △MPQ   isosceles
7. △MPR   equilateral

**In the figure $\overrightarrow{WX} \parallel \overrightarrow{YZ}$ and $\overrightarrow{WZ} \perp \overrightarrow{VX}$ find each measure.**

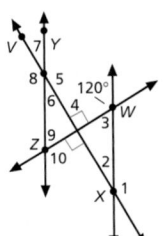

8. $m\angle 1$   150°
9. $m\angle 2$   30°
10. $m\angle 3$   60°
11. $m\angle 4$   90°
12. $m\angle 5$   150°
13. $m\angle 6$   30°
14. $m\angle 7$   30°
15. $m\angle 10$   120°

**Find the unknown angle measures in each figure.**

16.
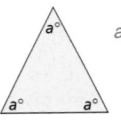
$a° = 60°$

17.
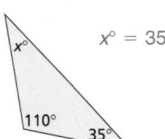
$x° = 35°$
110°
35°

18.
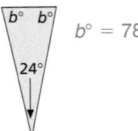
$b° = 78°$
24°

**For Exercises 1–5 use △XYZ.**

1. Which angle is included between $\overline{XY}$ and $\overline{YZ}$? ∠Y

2. Which angle is included between $\overline{YX}$ and $\overline{XZ}$? ∠X

3. Which side is included between ∠X and ∠Y? $\overline{XY}$

4. Which side is included between ∠Y and ∠Z? $\overline{YZ}$

5. Which side is included between ∠X and ∠Z? $\overline{XZ}$

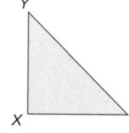

**State whether the pair of triangles is congruent by SAS, ASA, or SSS.**

6. 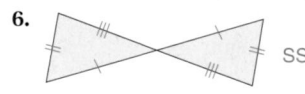 SSS

7. 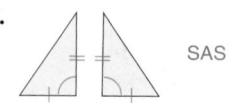 SAS

8. 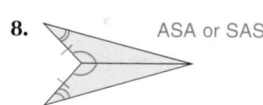 ASA or SAS

9. 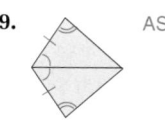 ASA or SAS

10. 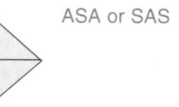 SSS

11. 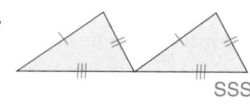 SAS

12. Can you show that two triangles are congruent if two of their corresponding parts are congruent? Why or why not? No; two isosceles triangles could have their legs congruent but have an acute included angle in one triangle and an obtuse included angle in the other triangle.

**Match the property named with all the quadrilaterals listed that have that property: *parallelogram, rectangle, rhombus, square*.**

1. Consecutive angles are supplementary. all

2. The sum of the angle measure is 360°. all

3. Four sides are congruent. rhombus, square

4. All four angles are right angles. rectangle, square

5. The diagonals are perpendicular. rhombus, square

6. The diagonals are congruent. rectangle, square

**Find the unknown angle measure in each parallelogram.**

7. $m\angle Q$ 148°

8. $m\angle R$ 32°

9. $m\angle S$ 148°

10. $m\angle Y$ 49°

11. $m\angle X$ 131°

12. $m\angle W$ 49°

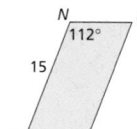

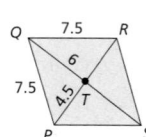

**Find each unknown measure in each parallelogram.**

13. $m\angle P$ 112°

14. $NO$ 8

15. $m\angle M$ 68°

16. $OP$ 15

17. $m\angle O$ 68°

18. $PS$ 7.5

19. $RS$ 7.5

20. $QS$ 12

21. $RT$ 4.5

22. $PR$ 9

**Classify each polygon by its number of sides. Tell whether it is *convex* or *concave*, *regular* or *not regular*.**

1. 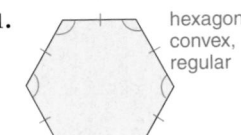 hexagon, convex, regular

2. 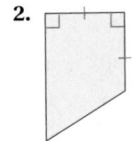 quadrilateral, convex, not regular

3.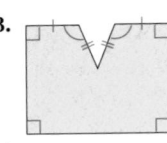

heptagon, concave, not regular

**Find the sum of the interior angles of each convex polygon.**

4. heptagon
900°

5. nonagon
1260°

6. decagon
1440°

7. quadrilateral
360°

8. 16-gon
2520°

9. 18-gon
2880°

10. pentagon
540°

11. octagon
1080°

**Find the measure of an interior angle of each regular polygon.**

12. pentagon  108°

13. hexagon  120°

14. octagon  135°

15. What is the number of sides of a regular polygon in which each interior angle measures 168°?  30 sides

16. What is the measure of each interior angle of a convex 90-gon?  176°

In ⊙$T$, $m\angle BXC = 90°$ and $m\angle AXB = 45°$. Find each measure.

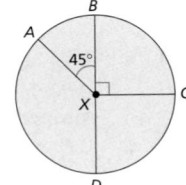

1. $m\angle \widehat{DC}$  90°

2. $m\angle \widehat{DA}$  135°

3. $m\angle \widehat{ABC}$  135°

4. $m\angle \widehat{ADC}$  225°

In ⊙$T$, $\overline{NQ}$, $\overline{PS}$, and $\overline{OR}$ are diameters. Use ⊙$T$ for Exercises 5–10.

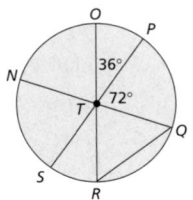

5. Name four semicircles.  Sample answer: $\widehat{NOQ}$, $\widehat{OQR}$, $\widehat{RSO}$, $\widehat{QRN}$

6. Name two inscribed angles.  $\angle NQR$, $\angle ORQ$

7. Find the measure of $\widehat{SR}$.  36°

8. Find the measure of $\widehat{SNO}$.  144°

9. If $\overline{NT}$ has a length of 5, what is the length of $\overline{TQ}$?  5

10. Name two chords that are twice the length of $\overline{RT}$.  $\overline{RO}$, $\overline{NQ}$, or $\overline{PS}$

**State whether each of the following statements is *true* or *false*.**

11. A central angle is an angle whose vertex lies on the circle.  false

12. A radius is a chord.  false

13. A diameter is a chord.  true

14. The measure of a minor arc is always less than 180°.  true

## Chapter 6

Extra Practice 6–1 • Distance in the Coordinate Plane • pages 244–247

**Use the graph to calculate the length of each segment.**

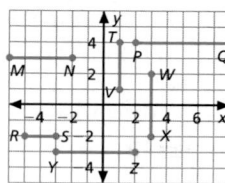

1. $\overline{RS}$  2
2. $\overline{TV}$  3
3. $\overline{WX}$  4
4. $\overline{YZ}$  5
5. $\overline{MN}$  5
6. $\overline{PQ}$  6

**Find the distance between the points. Round to the nearest tenth.**

7. $A(2, 3)$, $B(-4, 3)$  6
8. $A(2, 3)$, $D(2, -2)$  5
9. $B(-4, 3)$, $E(-4, 0)$  3
10. $D(2, -2)$, $F(-1, -2)$  3
11. $E(-4, 0)$, $G(0, 0)$  4
12. $H(5, 0)$, $E(-4, 0)$  9

**Use the given endpoints of each circle's diameter. Find each circle's center and the lengths of its diameter and radius. Round to the nearest tenth, if necessary.**
For 13–18, see additional answers.

13. $A(-1, 2)$, $B(-3, -4)$
14. $A(3, 4)$, $D(6, 9)$
15. $B(5, 1)$, $E(6, -2)$
16. $D(-5, 9)$, $F(-2, 0)$
17. $A(6, 1)$, $B(-4, 5)$
18. $A(2, 3)$, $B(-4, 5)$

Extra Practice 6–2 • Slope of a Line • pages 248–251

**Find the slope of each line segment shown.**

1. $\overline{AB}$  $-\dfrac{3}{4}$
2. $\overline{CD}$  3
3. $\overline{EF}$  $-2$
4. $\overline{GH}$  $\dfrac{2}{5}$
5. $\overline{IJ}$  $\dfrac{3}{2}$
6. $\overline{KL}$  4
7. $\overline{MN}$  $\dfrac{1}{3}$
8. $\overline{OP}$  $-2$
9. $\overline{QR}$  1
10. $\overline{ST}$  $-7$
11. $\overline{UV}$  $-\dfrac{3}{4}$
12. $\overline{WX}$  $\dfrac{1}{5}$

**Graph the line that passes through the given point and has the given slope.** For 13–20, see additional answers.

13. $(-1, 2)$, $m = \dfrac{1}{5}$
14. $(0, -3)$, $m = -\dfrac{1}{2}$
15. $(1, 4)$, $m = 3$
16. $(3, -2)$, $m = -\dfrac{5}{2}$
17. $(-2, -2)$, $m = \dfrac{1}{4}$
18. $(4, 0)$, $m = -2$
19. $(-1, 2)$, $m$ is undefined
20. $(-4, -5)$, $m = 0$

**Find the slope of the line containing the given points. Name any vertical or horizontal lines.**

21. $(1, 1)$, $(0, 4)$  $-3$
22. $(-5, 2)$, $(9, 0)$  $-\dfrac{1}{7}$
23. $(5, -3)$, $(5, 8)$  undefined, vertical line
24. $(-2, 0)$, $(0, -4)$  $-2$
25. $(5, 8)$, $(3, -2)$  5
26. $(4, -3)$, $(8, -21)$  $-4.5$
27. $(8, 8)$, $(2, 5)$  $\dfrac{1}{2}$
28. $(3, 7)$, $(-3, -8)$  $\dfrac{5}{2}$

**Extra Practice 6-1**
13. $C(-2, -1)$; $d \approx 6.3$; $r \approx 3.2$
14. $C(4.5, 6.5)$; $d \approx 5.8$; $r \approx 2.9$
15. $C(5.5, -0.5)$; $d \approx 3.2$; $r \approx 1.6$
16. $(-3.5, 4.5)$; $d \approx 9.5$; $r \approx 4.7$
17. $C(1, 3)$; $d \approx 10.8$; $r \approx 5.4$
18. $C(-1, 4)$; $d \approx 6.3$; $r \approx 3.2$

**Extra Practice 6-2**

13.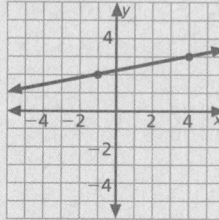

14.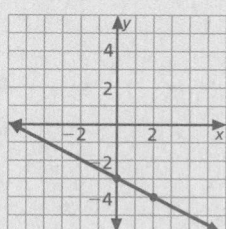

15.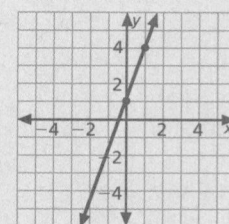

16.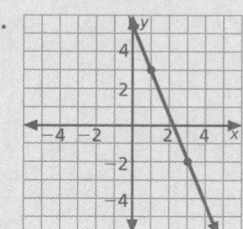

17.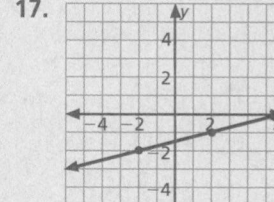

18.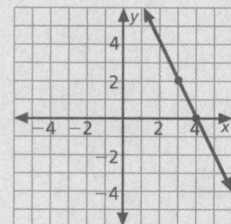

19.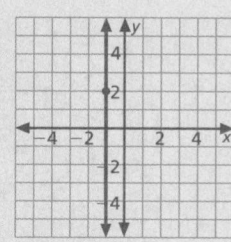

20.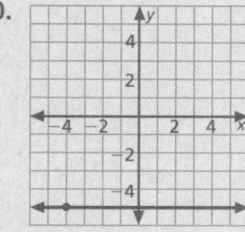

**Extra Practice 6-3**

**5.**
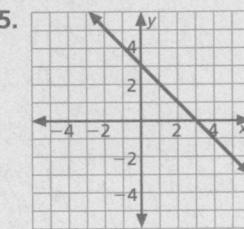

**6.**
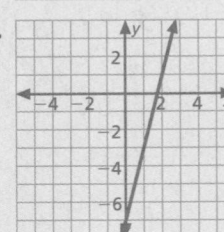

**7.**
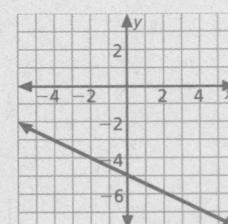

**8.**
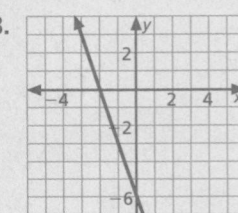

**9.**
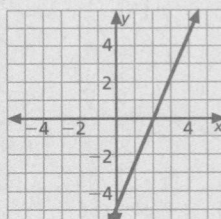

**10.**
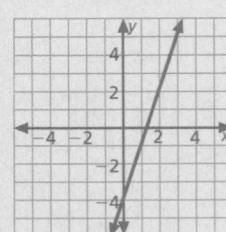

**Extra Practice 6-4**

**13.**
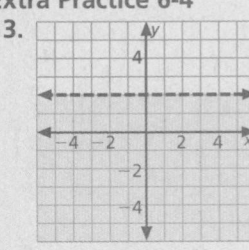

Extra Practice 6–3 • Write and Graph Linear Equations • pages 254–257

**Identify the slope and the $y$-intercept for each line.**

**1.** $y = \frac{1}{2}x + 5$   $m = \frac{1}{2};\ b = 5$

**2.** $y = 3x - 4$   $m = 3;\ b = -4$

**3.** $y = -7$   $m = 0;\ b = -7$

**4.** $-2x - 4y = 8$   $m = -\frac{1}{2};\ b = -2$

**Graph each line.** For 5–10, see additional answers.

**5.** $y = -x + 3$

**6.** $y = 4x - 7$

**7.** $y = -\frac{1}{2}x - 5$

**8.** $-3x - y = 6$

**9.** $5x - 2y = 10$

**10.** $y = 3x - 4$

**Write an equation of each line using the given information.**

**11.** $m = 2,\ b = -1$   $y = 2x - 1$

**12.** $(1, -1), (-2, -4)$   $y = x - 2$

**13.** $m = -3,\ (5, -2)$   $y = -3x + 13$

**14.** $m = -2,\ (3, -1)$   $y = -2x + 5$

**15.** $m = -\frac{3}{2},\ b = 0$   $y = -\frac{3}{2}x$

**16.** $m = \frac{1}{2},\ (-8, 4)$   $y = \frac{1}{2}x + 8$

**17.** $(1, 3), (2, -2)$   $y = -5x + 8$

**18.** $(-1, 4), (-3, -2)$   $y = 3x + 7$

**19.** $m = 10,\ b = \frac{1}{2}$   $y = 10x + \frac{1}{2}$

**Write an equation of each line whose graph is shown below.**

**20.**
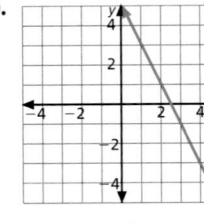
$y = -2x + 5$

**21.**
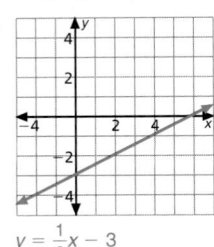
$y = \frac{1}{2}x - 3$

**22.**
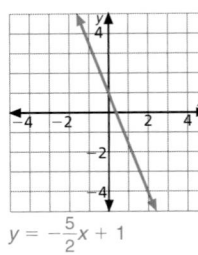
$y = -\frac{5}{2}x + 1$

Extra Practice 6–4 • Write and Graph Linear Inequalities • pages 258–261

**State whether the graph of each inequality has a *dashed* or *solid* line.**

**1.** $y > x + 3$ dashed

**2.** $y \le 2x - 5$ solid

**3.** $y \ge 4$ solid

**4.** $x - 2y < 4$ dashed

**Determine whether solutions of the inequality are *above* or *below* the boundary. State if the boundary line is included.**

**5.** $y + 2x > 5$ above, not included

**6.** $y - 2x > 5$ above, not included

**7.** $y \le x - 4$ below, included

**8.** $y < -3$ below, not included

**9.** $-y < 3$ above, not included

**10.** $x - y > 2$ below, not included

**11.** $-2y > 8$ below, not included

**12.** $4x + y \le 6$ below, included

**Graph each inequality.** For 13–20, see additional answers.

**13.** $y < 2$

**14.** $y \ge 3$

**15.** $x \ge 2$

**16.** $x < -1$

**17.** $y > -x$

**18.** $y \le -x + 1$

**19.** $y > 2 - x$

**20.** $y \le 3 - 2x$

**21.** Write and graph an inequality that describes the set of points for which the $y$-coordinate is greater than or equal to the $x$-coordinate decreased by 2.
$y \ge x - 2$. See additional answers.

**22.** Write and graph an inequality that describes the set of points for which the sum of the $y$-coordinate and twice the $x$-coordinate is less than 5.
$y + 2x < 5$. See additional answers.

**14.**
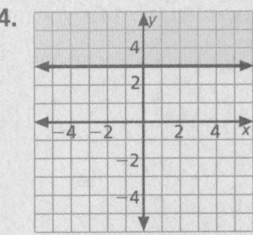

**15.**
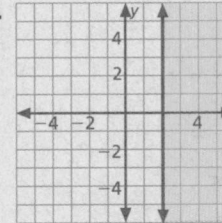

**16.**
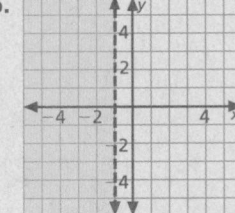

**17.**
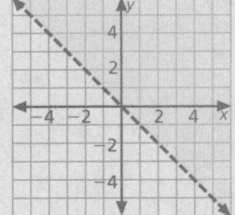

## Extra Practice 6–5 • Linear and Nonlinear Functions • pages 264–267

**Determine if each graph represents a function. Explain.**

**1.**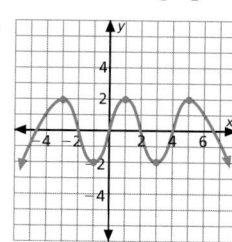

**2.**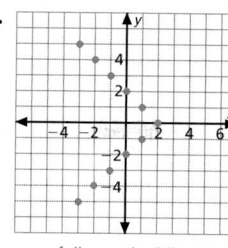

**3.**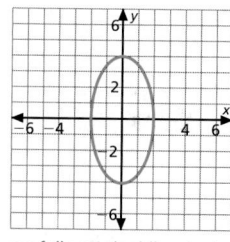

yes; passes vertical line test

no; fails vertical line test

no; fails vertical line test

**Graph each function for the given domain.** For 4–7, see additional answers.

**4.** $y = 4x + 1$, $\{-2, -1, 0, \frac{1}{2}, 1\}$

**5.** $y = 3x - 2$, $\{-3, -1, 0, 2, 4\}$

**6.** $y = 3x + 1$, {all real numbers}

**7.** $y = -2x$, {all real numbers}

**Graph each function when the domain is $\{-2, -1, 0, 1, 2\}$.** For 8–10, see additional answers.

**8.** $y = 4x - 1$

**9.** $y = -x - 1$

**10.** $y = 3$

**11.** If a car is moving at a constant speed of 40 mi/h, then the distance it covers is a function of the amount of time it is moving. Let $y$ be the distance in miles and let $x$ be the time in hours. Then the distance function is $y = 40x$. Graph the function when the domain is $\left\{\frac{1}{4}, \frac{1}{2}, 1, 1\frac{1}{2}, 1\frac{3}{4}\right\}$. See additional answers.

## Extra Practice 6–6 • Graph Quadratic Functions • pages 268–271

**Graph each function for the domain of real numbers.** For 1–4, see additional answers.

**1.** $y = x^2 - 1$

**2.** $y = 3x^2$

**3.** $y = 2x^2 + 1$

**4.** $y = 2x^2 - 4$

**PHYSICS** The equation for the height of an object shot straight up into the air from ground level at a velocity of 64 ft/sec is $y = -16t^2 + 64t$, where $y$ is the height of the object in feet and $t$ is the time in seconds.

**5.** Graph the function for the domain of real numbers from $t = 0$ through $t = 4$. See additional answers.

**6.** What is the maximum height the object reaches? 64 ft

**7.** How long does it take the object to reach the maximum height? 2 sec

**8.** At what time(s) is the object 48 ft above the ground? 1 sec and 3 sec

**9.** At what time does the object return to the ground? 4 sec

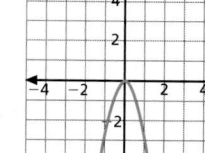

**Complete each ordered pair so that it corresponds to a point on the graph.**

**10.** $(0, ?)$ 0

**11.** $(?, -3)$ 1 or $-1$

**12.** $(-1, ?)$ $-3$

**18.**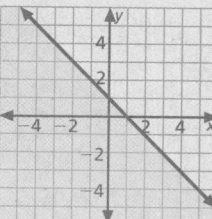

**19.**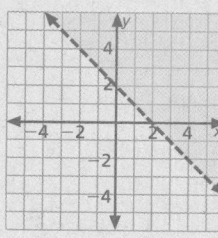

**20.**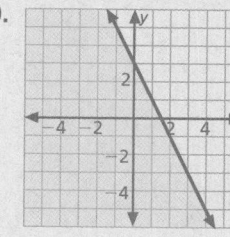

**21.**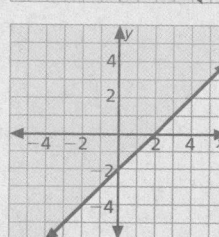

**22.**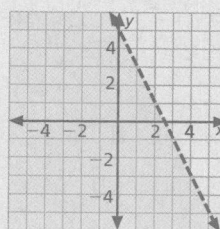

### Extra Practice 6-5

**4.**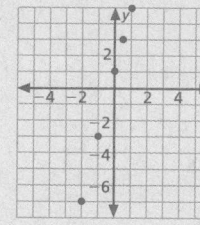

**Extra Practice**

**Extra Practice** | **605**

**5.**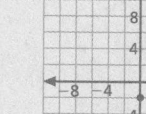

**6.**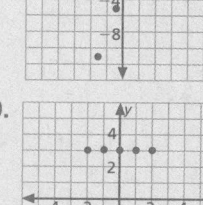

**7.**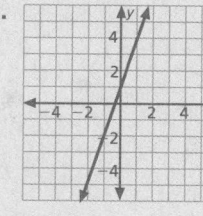

**8.**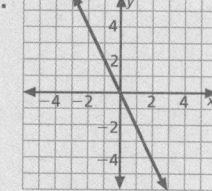

**9.**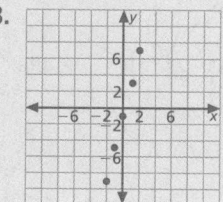

**10.**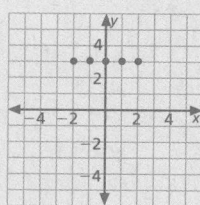

**11.**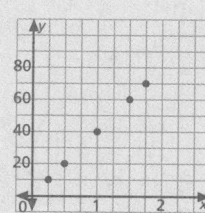

See page 632 for additional answers for Extra Practice 6-6.

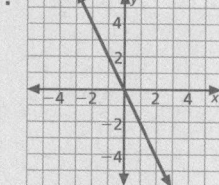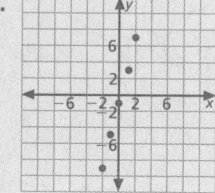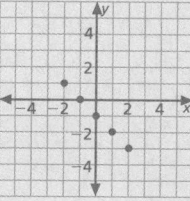

**Extra Practice 6-6**

1.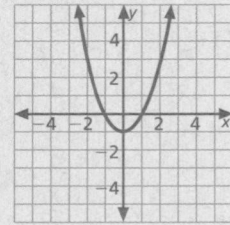

2.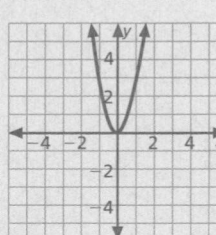

3.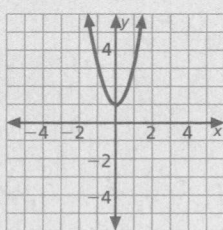

4.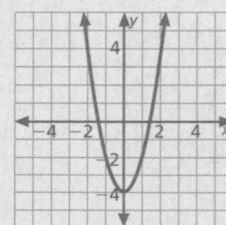

5.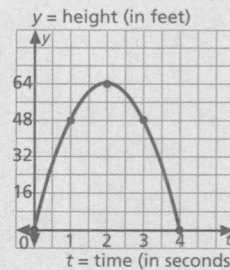

$y$ = height (in feet)

$t$ = time (in seconds)

**Extra Practice 6–8 • Direct Variation • pages 276–279**

1. Assume that $y$ varies directly as $x$. When $x = 15$, $y = 20$. Find $y$ when $x = 36$. 48

2. Assume that $y$ varies directly as $x$. When $x = 10$, $y = 4$. Find $x$ when $y = 8$. 20

3. Assume that $y$ varies directly as $x$. When $x = 4$, $y = 3$. Find $y$ when $x = 5$. $\frac{15}{4}$

4. Assume that $y$ varies directly as $x$. When $x = 3$, $y = 5$. Find $y$ when $x = 6$. 10

5. The annual simple interest on a loan varies directly as the amount of the loan. The interest on a $1000 loan is $65. Find the interest on an $800 loan. $52

6. If you drop an object out of a window, the distance that it falls varies directly as the square of the amount of time it is falling. If an object falls 64 ft in 2 sec, how far will it fall in 5 sec? 400 ft

7. The distance a spring stretches varies directly as the weight attached to it. If a 15-kg weight stretches the spring 24 cm, how many centimeters will a 20-kg weight stretch it? 32 cm

8. The distance an object rolls down a slope varies directly as the square of the time it rolls. A ball rolls 80 ft down the slope in 5 sec. How far will it roll in 10 sec? 320 ft

**Extra Practice 6–9 • Inverse Variation • pages 282–285**

1. Assume that $y$ varies inversely as $x$. When $x = 8$, $y = 12$. Find $y$ when $x = 2$. 48

2. Assume that $y$ varies inversely as $x$. When $x = 3$, $y = 7$. Find $y$ when $x = 5$. 4.2

3. Assume that $y$ varies inversely as $x$. When $x = 45$, $y = 20$. Find $y$ when $x = 60$. 15

4. Assume that $y$ varies inversely as $x$. When $x = 9$, $y = 30$. Find $y$ when $x = 10$. 27

5. Assume that $y$ varies inversely as $x$. When $x = 3$, $y = 4$. Find $y$ when $x = 2$. 6

6. Assume that $y$ varies inversely as $x$. When $x = 12$, $y = 3$. Find $y$ when $x = 4$. 9

7. The time it takes to fill a water tank varies inversely as the square of the diameter of the pipe used to fill it. A pipe with a diameter of 3 cm takes 8 min to fill the tank. How long would it take to fill the tank with a pipe having a diameter of 5 cm? 2.88 min

8. The amount paid by each member of a group chartering a bus varies inversely as the number of people in the group. When there are 24 people in the group, the cost is $35. What is the cost per person when there are 32 people in the group? $26.25

**Identify each relationship as a *direct variation* or an *inverse variation*.**

9. the surface area of a sphere and its radius   direct

10. the speed of a train and the time it takes to travel 10 mi   inverse

11. the weight of a steel rod and the length of the rod   direct

12. the intensity of light and the distance from the light source   inverse

**Extra Practice**

606 | **Extra Practice**

## Chapter 7

Extra Practice 7–1 • Translations in the Coordinate Plane • pages 296–299

**On a coordinate plane, graph △MNP with vertices M(2, 2), N(1, −2) and P(−2, −1). Then graph its image under each translation from the original position.** For 1–3, see additional answers.

**1.** 2 units up

**2.** 3 units right

**3.** 4 units left and 2 units down

**On a coordinate plane, graph trapezoid RSTV with vertices R(−5, 1), S(−2, 4), T(−1, 2) and U(−3, 0). Then graph its image under each translation from the original position.** For 4–6, see additional answers.

**4.** 5 units down

**5.** 3 units right

**6.** 1 unit left and 3 units up

**Write the rule that describes each translation.**

**7.**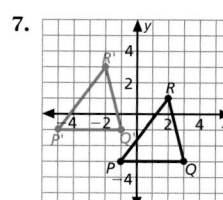

$(x, y) \rightarrow (x − 4, y + 2)$

**8.**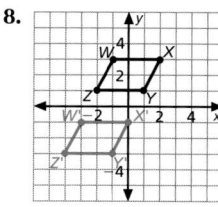

$(x, y) \rightarrow (x − 2, y − 4)$

**9.**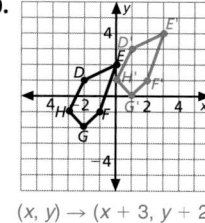

$(x, y) \rightarrow (x + 3, y + 2)$

**10.** The coordinates of a point after a translation of 7 units left and 7 units down are (4, −2). Find the coordinates of the point in its original position. (11, 5)

Extra Practice 7–2 • Reflections in the Coordinate Plane • pages 300–303

**Give the coordinates of the image of each point under a reflection across the given line.**

**1.** (−4, 3); $x$-axis
(−4, −3)

**2.** (6, 2); $y$-axis (−6, 2)

**3.** (−2, 0); $y$-axis
(2, 0)

**4.** (−5, 7); $y = x$
(7, −5)

**5.** (−4, 4); $y = −x$
(−4, 4)

**6.** (4, −6); $y = −x$
(6, −4)

**7.** (4, 0); $x = 1$
(−2, 0)

**8.** (3, 5); $y = 1$
(3, −3)

**Copy each figure on a coordinate plane. Then graph its image under a reflection across the given line.** For 9–11, see additional answers.

**9.** $y = x$

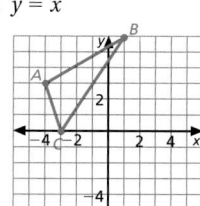

**10.** $y = −x$

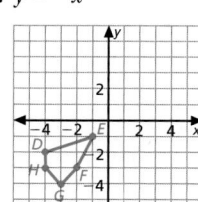

**11.** $y = 1$

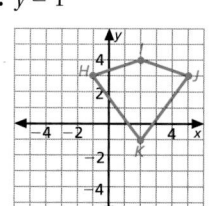

**1, 2, 3.**

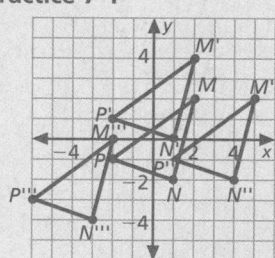

**4, 5, 6.**

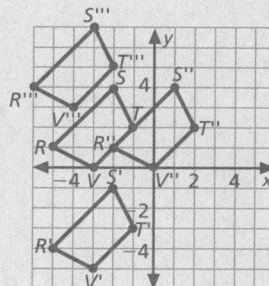

### Extra Practice 7-2

**9.**

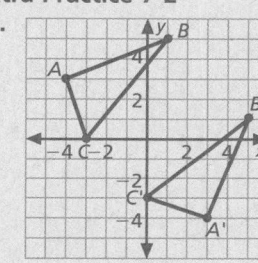

**10.**

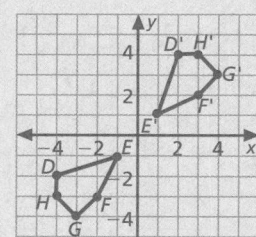

**11.**

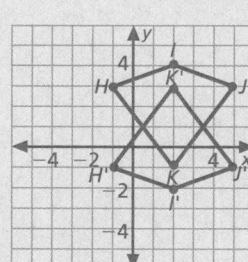

**Extra Practice 7-3**

**1.**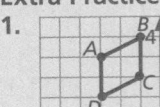

**2.**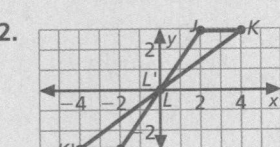

**3.**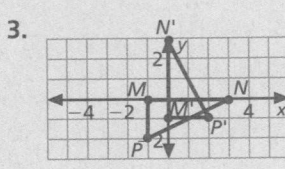

**4.**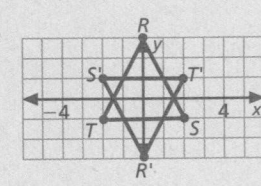

**5.**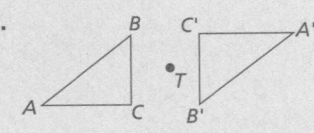

**6.**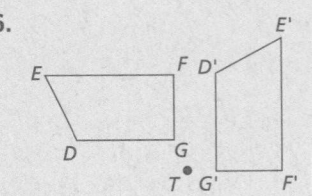

**7.**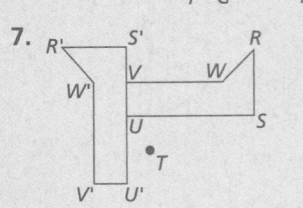

---

Extra Practice 7–3 • Rotations in the Coordinate Plane • pages 306–309

**Copy each figure on a coordinate plane. Then graph its image after each rotation about the origin.** For 1–4, see additional answers.

**1.** 90° clockwise

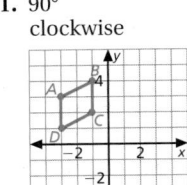

**2.** 180° clockwise

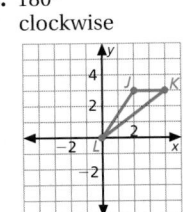

**3.** 90° counterclockwise

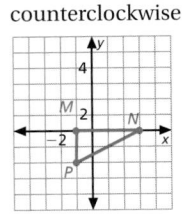

**4.** 180° counterclockwise

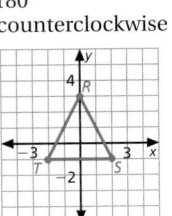

**Trace each figure and its rotated image. Identify the center of rotation, the angle of rotation and the direction of rotation.** For 5–7, see additional answers for the location of the center of rotation.

**5.**

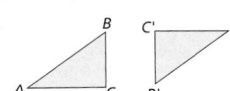

180° clockwise or counterclockwise about T

**6.**

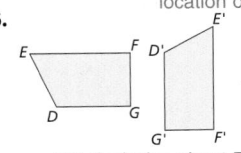

90° clockwise about T

**7.**

90° counterclockwise about T

**Give the coordinates of the image of A(5, 2) after each rotation about the origin.**

**8.** 90° counterclockwise
(−2, 5)

**9.** 90° clockwise
(2, −5)

**10.** 180° counterclockwise
(−5, −2)

**11.** 180° clockwise
(−5, −2)

Extra Practice 7–4 • Line Symmetry and Rotational Symmetry • pages 310–313

**Tell whether each dashed line is a line of symmetry. If not, trace the line and one side of the figure. Complete the drawing so that it has line symmetry.**

**1.**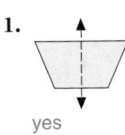

yes

**2.**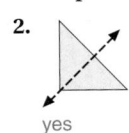

yes

**3.**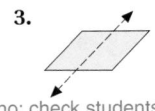

no; check students' drawings

**4.**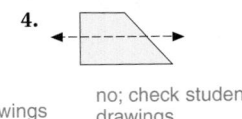

no; check students' drawings

**Give the order of rotational symmetry for each figure.**

**5.**

4

**6.**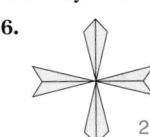

2

**7.**

5

**8.**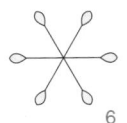

6

**Draw a figure with the given number of lines of symmetry.**

**9.** 0
**10.** 1
**11.** 2
**12.** 3
**13.** infinite

For 9–13, answers will vary. Check students' drawings.

Extra Practice 7–5 • Dilations in the Coordinate Plane • pages 316–319

**Copy △PQR on grid paper. Draw each dilation.** For 1–3, see additional answers.

1. scale factor: 2, center (0, 0)

2. scale factor: $\frac{1}{2}$, center (0, 0)

3. scale factor: 1.5, center (0, 0)

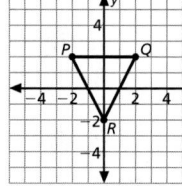

**Copy rectangle ABCD on grid paper. Draw each dilation.**

4. scale factor: 3, center (0, 0) For 4–5, see additional answers.

5. scale factor: $\frac{1}{3}$, center (0, 0)

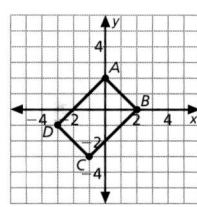

**Give the scale factor and center for each dilation.**

6. Triangle ABC has vertices A(3, 1), B(6, −1) and C(7, 6). Its dilated image is △A′B′C′ with vertices A′(6, 2), B′(12, −2) and C′(14, 12).  2, (0, 0)

7. Quadrilateral LMNO has vertices L(6, 0), M(−8, −2), N(−4, 4) and O(8, 6). Its dilated image is quadrilateral L′M′N′O′ with vertices L′(3, 0), M′(−4, −1), N′(−2, 2) and O′(4, 3).  $\frac{1}{2}$, (0, 0)

## Chapter 8

Extra Practice 8–1 • Parallel and Perpendicular Lines • pages 334–337

**For each line identified by two points, state the slope of a line parallel and the slope of a line perpendicular to it.**

1. A(3, 1) and B(6, 10)  3; $-\frac{1}{3}$

2. C(−1, −4) and D(−5, −5)  $\frac{1}{4}$; −4

3. E(0, −2) and F(−5, 6)  $-\frac{8}{5}$; $\frac{5}{8}$

4. G(6, 0) and H(0, 6)  −1; 1

5. J(−2, 3) and K(−5, 7)  $-\frac{4}{3}$; $\frac{3}{4}$

6. L(−3, −5) and M(2, −2)  $\frac{3}{5}$; $-\frac{5}{3}$

**Determine if the graphs will show parallel or perpendicular lines, or neither.**

7. $y = -3x + 4$
   $y = \frac{1}{3}x - 1$  perpendicular

8. $y = 2x + 6$
   $y = -2x$  neither

9. $y = -\frac{1}{4}x - 1$
   $y = 4x + 10$  perpendicular

10. $x + 2y = 12$
    $3x + 6y = 3$  parallel

11. $2x + y = -7$
    $2x + y = 0$  parallel

12. $3x - y = 5$
    $3x + y = -10$  neither

**Write an equation in slope-intercept form of a line passing through the given point and parallel to the given line.**

13. (3, 4); $y = -3x + 4$
    $y = -3x + 13$

14. (4, −2); $2x + y = 7$
    $y = -2x + 6$

15. (3, −2); $y = -2x + 5$
    $y = -2x + 4$

**Write an equation in slope-intercept form of a line passing through the given point and perpendicular to the given line.**

16. (4, −2); $y = -\frac{1}{2}x + 5$
    $y = 2x - 10$

17. (3, −2); $y = -\frac{2}{3}x + 5$
    $y = \frac{3}{2}x - \frac{13}{2}$

18. (−3, −2); $y = 2x + 5$
    $y = -\frac{1}{2}x - \frac{7}{2}$

1, 2, 3.

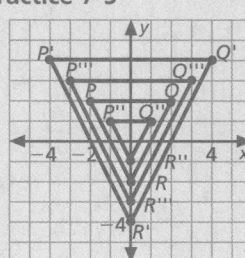

4, 5.

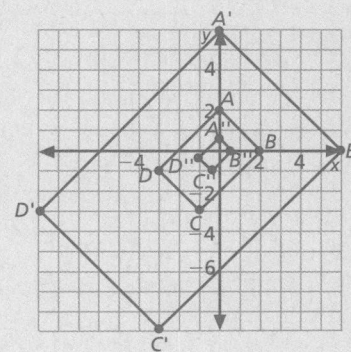

**7.**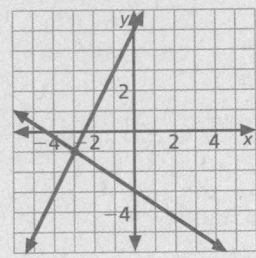

**8.**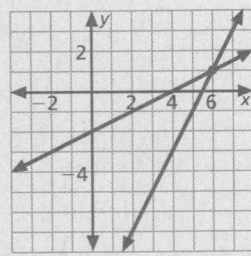

**9.**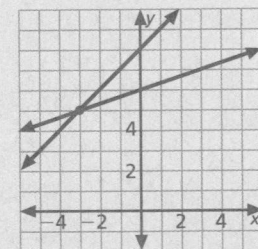

**10.**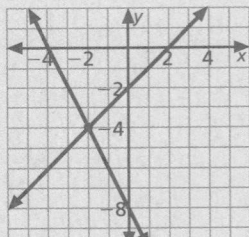

**11.**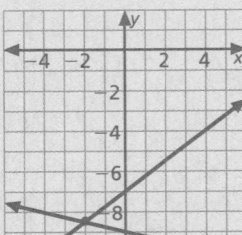

**12.**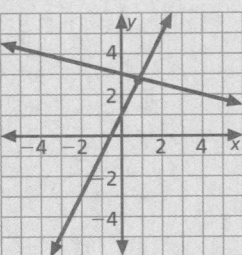

---

Extra Practice 8–2 • Solve Systems of Equations Graphically • pages 338–341

**Determine if the given ordered pair is a solution of the system of equations.**

**1.** $(3, 1)$; $3x + y = 10$
$x - y = -1$   no

**2.** $(-2, -5)$; $6x - 2y = -2$
$2x + y = -9$   yes

**3.** $(6, 0)$; $x + 5y = 12$
$2x + 2y = 6$   no

**4.** $(-1, 2)$; $-x + 2y = 5$
$4x - 3y = -10$   yes

**5.** $(2, 1)$; $-2x + 3y = -1$
$5x + y = 11$   yes

**6.** $(0, 4)$; $4x - 2y = -8$
$-3x + y = -4$   no

**Solve each system of equations graphically. Check the solution.**   For 7–12, see additional answers.

**7.** $y = 2x + 5$
$y = -\frac{2}{3}x - 3$  $(-3, -1)$

**8.** $y = \frac{1}{2}x - 2$
$y = 2x - 11$   $(6, 1)$

**9.** $y = \frac{1}{3}x + 6$
$y = x + 8$   $(-3, 5)$

**10.** $y = x - 2$
$y = -2x - 8$   $(-2, -4)$

**11.** $y = \frac{3}{4}x - 7$
$y = -\frac{1}{4}x - 9$   $\left(-2, -\frac{17}{2}\right)$

**12.** $y = 2x + 1$
$2y = -\frac{1}{2}x + 6$   $\left(\frac{8}{9}, \frac{25}{9}\right)$

 **GRAPHING**   Use a graphing calculator to solve each system of equations.

**13.** $-3x + y = 28$
$3x + y = -14$
$(-7, 7)$

**14.** $x + 6y = 42$
$-x + 2y = 6$
$(6, 6)$

**15.** $5x + 6y = 0$
$-x + 3y = -21$
$(6, -5)$

Extra Practice 8–3 • Solve Systems by Substitution • pages 344–347

**Solve each system of equations. Check the solution.**

**1.** $2x + 3y = 18$
$-x + 4y = 13$  $(3, 4)$

**2.** $5x - y = -10$
$5x + y = 0$  $(-1, 5)$

**3.** $4x - 2y = 14$
$x + 8y = 12$  $(4, 1)$

**4.** $3x - 9y = 15$
$x - 3y = 5$   infinitely many solutions

**5.** $-x - y = 2$
$3x + y = 2$   $(2, -4)$

**6.** $5x - 4y = -19$
$x + 2y = -1$  $(-3, 1)$

**7.** $-x + 4y = -23$
$-2x - y = 17$   $(-5, -7)$

**8.** $7x - 3y = -20$
$-2x + y = 16$   $(28, 72)$

**9.** $3x + 3y = -12$
$5x - 2y = 22$  $(2, -6)$

**10.** $4x + y = 6$
$-x + 2y = -15$  $(3, -6)$

**11.** $-3x + 2y = 8$
$-7x + 4y = 20$ $(-4, -2)$

**12.** $-x + 3y = -11$
$2x + 7y = 9$ $(8, -1)$

**13.** $9x - 2y = -5$
$5x + y = 12$   $(1, 7)$

**14.** $4x + 4y = 15$
$-x - y = 5$   no solutions

**15.** $7x + y = -1$
$-10x - 2y = -2$
$(-1, 6)$

**16.** $3x - 4y = 5$
$-x + y = -10$ $(35, 25)$

**17.** $-2x + 8y = -18$
$-x - 2y = -9$   $(9, 0)$

**18.** $5x + 2y = -1$
$-3x - y = 2$
$(-3, 7)$

**19.** The schoolyard has 12 trees. The number of maple trees is 3 less than twice the number of oak trees. How many maple trees are there in the schoolyard?   7

**20.** At the farm market, Jed bought 4 lb of apples and 6 lb of peaches for $18. Maria bought 2 lb of apples and 10 lb of peaches for $23. Find the cost per pound of the apples and peaches. apples: $1.50; peaches: $2.00

**Extra Practice**

**Solve each system of equations. Check the solutions.**

1. $x + 2y = 5$ (1, 2)
   $-x + 2y = 3$

2. $2x - 3y = 9$ (3, −1)
   $3x + 3y = 6$

3. $2x - y = -3$ (−1, 1)
   $5x + y = -4$

4. $4x - y = 5$ (2, 3)
   $-4x + 2y = -2$

5. $-x - 3y = 2$ (4, −2)
   $5x + 3y = 14$

6. $2x + y = -4$ (−3, 2)
   $-2x - 6y = -6$

7. $3x + 4y = 1$ (−5, 4)
   $3x + 2y = -7$

8. $6x - y = 2$ (1, 4)
   $5x - y = 1$

9. $x - 3y = -16$ (−1, 5)
   $x + 2y = 9$

10. $-x + 4y = -6$ (2, −1)
    $2x - 6y = 10$

11. $2x - y = 2$ (−3, −8)
    $3x + 3y = -33$

12. $4x - 8y = 8$ (6, 2)
    $x - y = 4$

13. $3x + 2y = -2$ (−4, 5)
    $5x - y = -25$

14. $5x + y = 11$ (1, 6)
    $10x - 3y = -8$

15. $x + 7y = 18$ (−3, 3)
    $-4x - 4y = 0$

16. $3x - 4y = 7$ (5, 2)
    $-2x + 2y = -6$

17. $-x + 8y = -17$ (9, −1)
    $3x + 9y = 18$

18. $5x - 8y = 3$ (−1, −1)
    $-x + y = 0$

19. Taylor has 25 coins made up of quarters and dimes. The value of the coins is $3.55. How many of each coin does she have?   7 quarters and 18 dimes

20. Evan has 50 coins made up nickels and dimes. The value of the coins is $4.20. How many of each coin does he have?   16 nickels and 34 dimes

**Evaluate each determinant.**

1. $\begin{vmatrix} 0 & 3 \\ -1 & 4 \end{vmatrix}$ 3

2. $\begin{vmatrix} -6 & 6 \\ 4 & -4 \end{vmatrix}$ 0

3. $\begin{vmatrix} 3.1 & -2.4 \\ 0.2 & -2.5 \end{vmatrix}$ −7.27

4. $\begin{vmatrix} 5 & -1 \\ 4 & 0 \end{vmatrix}$ 4

5. $\begin{vmatrix} 3 & 0 \\ 0 & -3 \end{vmatrix}$ −9

6. $\begin{vmatrix} 4 & -3 \\ 5 & 3 \end{vmatrix}$ 27

7. $\begin{vmatrix} 6 & 6 \\ 6 & 6 \end{vmatrix}$ 0

8. $\begin{vmatrix} 2 & 3 \\ 4 & 8 \end{vmatrix}$ 4

**Solve each system of equations using the method of determinants. Round to the nearest thousandth, if necessary.**

9. $-3x + y = 14$ (4.429, 0.714)
   $x + 2y = -3$

10. $6x + y = 2$ (1, −4)
    $5x - y = 9$

11. $x - 3y = -7$ (−4, 1)
    $x + 2y = -2$

12. $-5x + 4y = -5$ (1, 0)
    $2x - 7y = 2$

13. $2x - 4y = -6$ (3, 3)
    $3x + 3y = 18$

14. $5x - y = -17$ (−2, 7)
    $x - 3y = -2$

15. $3x + 4y = 17$ (−17, 17)
    $x + 2y = 17$

16. $3x - 5y = 12$ (7.929, 2.357)
    $5x + y = 42$

17. $x - 2y = 11$
    $5x + y = 9$
    (2.636, −4.182)

18. $-x + 4y = 21$ (5.483, 6.621)
    $9x - 7y = 3$

19. $2x - 9y = 22$ (6.787, −0.936)
    $5x + y = 33$

20. $14x - 6y = 23$
    $11x - 7y = 46$
    (−3.594, −12.219)

**7.**

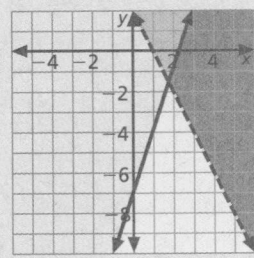

**8.**

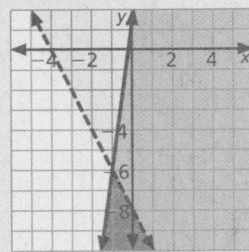

**9.**

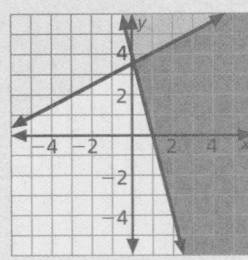

**10.**

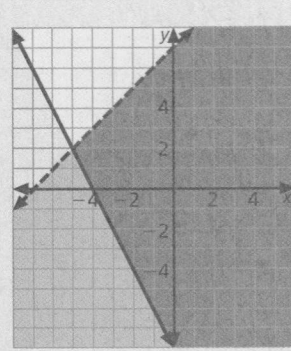

Extra Practice 8–7 • Systems of Inequalities • pages 362–365

**Write a system of linear inequalities for each graph.**

**1.**

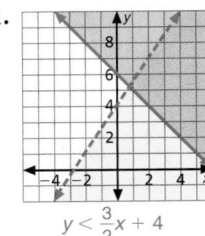

$y < \frac{3}{2}x + 4$
$y \geq -x + 6$

**2.**

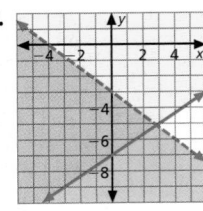

$y < -\frac{3}{4}x - 3$
$y \geq \frac{3}{5}x - 7$

**3.**

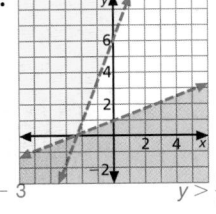

$y > \frac{8}{3}x + 6$
$y < \frac{2}{5}x + 1$

**4.**

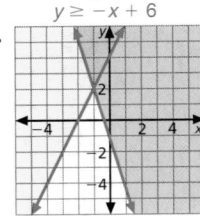

$y \geq 2x + 4$
$y \geq -3x - 1$

**5.**

$y \geq -3x - 7$
$y < 4x$

**6.**

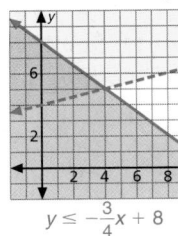

$y \leq -\frac{3}{4}x + 8$
$y > \frac{1}{4}x + 4$

**Graph the solution set of each system of inequalities.**

For 7–10, see additional answers.

**7.** $2x + y > 2$
$-3x + y \leq -7$

**8.** $7x - y \geq -1$
$2x + y < -8$

**9.** $4x + y \geq 4$
$-x + 2y \leq 7$

**10.** $-x + y < 7$
$-2x - y \leq 8$

## Chapter 9

Extra Practice 9–1 • Add and Subtract Polynomials • pages 376–379

**Write each polynomial in standard form for the variable $x$.**

**1.** $5 + x^2 + 3x + x^3$   $x^3 + x^2 + 3x + 5$

**2.** $x^2 + x^4 + 4x + 2x^3$   $x^4 + 2x^3 + x^2 + 4x$

**3.** $2x^3 + 3x^5 + 5x - x^4$   $3x^5 - x^4 + 2x^3 + 5x$

**4.** $1 - 4x - x^2 - 3x^3$   $-3x^3 - x^2 - 4x + 1$

**5.** $-2x^2 + 3 - x^5 + 6x$   $-x^5 - 2x^2 + 6x + 3$

**6.** $3x^3 - 2x^7 - 2 + 5x^4$
  $-2x^7 + 5x^4 + 3x^3 - 2$

**Simplify.**

**7.** $6k - k$   $5k$

**8.** $10m - 15m$   $-5m$

**9.** $3h - 4h + 8h - 5h$   $2h$

**10.** $4t^2 + 5t^2 - 9t^2$   $0$

**11.** $x + 3y - 4x + 6y$   $-3x + 9y$

**12.** $5 - 2z + 4z^2 - 3z$   $4z^2 - 5z + 5$

**13.** $6w - 3 + 4v + w + 6$   $7w + 4v + 3$

**14.** $10mn + 2m^2 - 4mn + 2n$   $2m^2 + 6mn + 2n$

**15.** $(4a - 6) + (3a - 1)$   $7a - 7$

**16.** $(3b + 4c) - (8c - 5b)$   $8b - 4c$

**17.** $(4r^2 - 2r + 3) + (2r^2 - 6r - 9)$   $6r^2 - 8r - 6$

**18.** $(w^2 + 5w + 8) - (w^2 + 6w + 12)$   $-w - 4$

**19.** $(6s + 4st - t) + (-3s - 6st + 7t)$
  $3s - 2st + 6t$

**20.** $(4d^2 + de - e^2) - (d^2 + 3de + 8e^2)$
  $3d^2 - 2de - 9e^2$

**Extra Practice**

**Simplify.**

1. $(2a)(6b)$  $12ab$

2. $(4xy)(-5y)$  $-20xy^2$

3. $(-10c)(-3d)$  $30cd$

4. $(ab)(-4d)$  $-4abd$

5. $-5(12x)$  $-60x$

6. $(3d)\left(\dfrac{1}{3}e\right)$  $de$

7. $\left(\dfrac{1}{2}w\right)(12v)$  $6wv$

8. $15(3z)$  $45z$

9. $(-3x^2)(4y^3)$  $-12x^2y^3$

10. $(5j^2)(4k^2)$  $20j^2k^2$

11. $(-m^4)(2n^2)$  $-2m^4n^2$

12. $(c^3d^2)(e^5d^3)$  $c^3d^5e^5$

13. $(m^2n^3p^3)(m^2n^2p^3)$  $m^4n^5p^6$

14. $(-2de)(9de)$  $-18d^2e^2$

15. $(8f)(-3f^2)$  $-24f^3$

16. $(5a^2b)(-b)$  $-5a^2b^2$

17. $(2.5r)(0.3r^2)$  $0.75r^3$

18. $\left(\dfrac{5}{6}gh^2\right)\left(-\dfrac{12}{25}h\right)$  $-\dfrac{2}{5}gh^3$

19. $(4w)^2$  $16w^2$

20. $(-3x)^2$  $9x^2$

21. $(2k)^3$  $8k^3$

22. $(3st^2)^3$  $27s^3t^6$

23. $(x^2y^3z)^4$  $x^8y^{12}z^4$

24. $(-de^2f^3)^3$  $-d^3e^6f^9$

**Write and simplify an expression for the area of each figure.**

25.
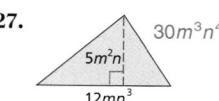
$6xy^2$ (top), $6xy^2$ (side)   $36x^2y^4$

26. $3d^2$ (top), $5de$ (side)   $15d^3e$

27.

$5m^2n$ (height), $12mn^3$ (base)   $30m^3n^4$

**Simplify.**

1. $\dfrac{6n^3}{3n}$  $2n^2$

2. $\dfrac{14x^5}{2x}$  $7x^4$

3. $\dfrac{8h^2}{-8h}$  $-h$

4. $\dfrac{18f}{2f}$  $9$

5. $\dfrac{3x}{9xz}$  $\dfrac{1}{3z}$

6. $\dfrac{100a^2b^2}{10ab^2}$  $10a$

7. $\dfrac{22e^2f}{11e^2}$  $2f$

8. $\dfrac{-32j^4k^2}{-4j^3k^2}$  $8j$

9. $\dfrac{49f^3gh^2}{7fh}$  $7f^2gh$

10. $\dfrac{35a^8b^7}{21a^3b^5}$  $\dfrac{5}{3}a^5b^2$

11. $\dfrac{6x+18}{6}$  $x+3$

12. $\dfrac{10y-50}{2}$  $5y-25$

13. $\dfrac{42j^3+28j^2}{7j}$  $6j^2+4j$

14. $\dfrac{22k^4+44k^5}{11k^2}$  $2k^2+4k^3$

15. $\dfrac{100s^5-50s^7}{25s^4}$  $4s-2s^3$

16. $\dfrac{d^5-5d^4+3d^3}{d}$  $d^4-5d^3+3d^2$

17. $\dfrac{3e^4+12e^3-9e}{3e}$  $e^3+4e^2-3$

18. $\dfrac{4r^2st+9rs^2t-rst^2}{rst}$  $4r+9s-t$

19. $\dfrac{v^3w^2x^3+2v^2w^3x^4+6vw^4x^4}{vwx^2}$  $v^2wx+2vw^2x^2+6w^3x^2$

20. $\dfrac{8cd-12c^2d+10cd^2-6c^2d^2}{-2cd}$  $-4+6c-5d+3cd$

21. The area of a rectangle is $24x^2y^3$ ft$^2$ and the length is $6x^2y$ ft. Find the width.   $4y^2$ ft

22. The area of a rectangle is $150a^4b^2c^3$ yd$^2$ and the width is $10ab^2c$ yd. Find the length.   $15a^3c^2$ yd

Extra Practice

**Simplify.**

1. $x(3x + 4y)$   $3x^2 + 4xy$

2. $2a(5a + 3b)$   $10a^2 + 6ab$

3. $8m(2m - n)$   $16s^2 - 12s$

4. $4s(4s - 3)$   $16m^2 - 8mn$

5. $6j(j + 9)$   $6j^2 + 54j$

6. $3k(-k + 7)$   $-3k^2 + 21k$

7. $3a(4a + 5a^2)$   $12a^2 + 15a^3$

8. $w(w^4 - w^3)$   $w^5 - w^4$

9. $-5d(2d - d^2)$   $-10d^2 + 5d^3$

10. $2g(-g^3 + 4g^2 - 3)$   $-2g^4 + 8g^3 - 6g$

11. $-6e(4 + 3e^3 + e^5)$   $-24e - 18e^4 - 6e^6$

12. $\frac{1}{3}f(9f^2 + 6f - 3)$   $3f^3 + 2f^2 - f$

13. $4v\left(\frac{1}{2}v + \frac{1}{4}v^2\right)$   $2v^2 + v^3$

14. $7x(2x^2 - x^3 + 4x^5)$   $14x^3 - 7x^4 + 28x^6$

15. $-3m(4m^2 + 6mn + 2n^2)$
    $-12m^3 - 18m^2n - 6mn^2$

16. $4(t^2 - 2) + 2(-t^2 + 1)$   $2t^2 - 6$

17. $5(2z + 3) - 3(4z - 5)$   $-2z + 30$

18. $7w(3w + 3) - 6w(4w + 5)$   $-3w^2 - 9w$

19. $6v(2v - 2) + 5v(4v - 8)$   $32v^2 - 52v$

20. $\frac{1}{3}a(9a^3 - 12a^2 + 15a)$   $3a^4 - 4a^3 + 5a^2$

21. $(c^4 - 3.5c^3 - 2.5c^2)1.6c$   $1.6c^5 - 5.6c^4 - 4c^3$

22. $5z^2(3 - 6z + 8z^2)$   $15z^2 - 30z^3 + 40z^4$

23. Jessica's weekly salary can be represented by the formula $S = 50 + 3n$ where $n$ is the number of widgets she makes in one week. Write and simplify an expression for her salary for two weeks if she made $d$ widgets the first week and $2d$ widgets the second week.   $100 + 9d$

24. Last week Chiko mowed 12 lawns at $25.00 per lawn. This week, he mowed an additional $k$ lawns. Write a variable expression in simplest form that represents the total amount Chiko was paid last week and this week.   $300 + 25k$

**Find each product.**

1. $(x + 2)(x + 1)$
   $x^2 + 3x + 2$

2. $(b - 3)(b + 2)$
   $b^2 - b - 6$

3. $(y - 5)(y - 2)$
   $y^2 - 7y + 10$

4. $(c + 3)(c - 1)$
   $c^2 + 2c - 3$

5. $(4 - a)(3 - a)$
   $12 - 7a + a^2$

6. $(5 - z)(1 + z)$
   $5 + 4z - z^2$

7. $(e + 3)^2$
   $e^2 + 6e + 9$

8. $(f - 5)^2$
   $f^2 - 10f + 25$

9. $(n + 9)(n - 3)$
   $n^2 + 6n - 27$

10. $(p + 4)(p - 6)$
    $p^2 - 2p - 24$

11. $(g + 10)^2$
    $g^2 + 20g + 100$

12. $(v - 7)(v - 6)$
    $v^2 - 13v + 42$

13. $(12 - d)(-1 + d)$
    $-12 + 13d - d^2$

14. $(3 + h)(9 - h)$
    $27 + 6h - h^2$

15. $(r + 3)(r - 3)$
    $r^2 - 9$

**Simplify.**

16. $2(n + 2)(n - 4)$
    $2n^2 - 4n - 16$

17. $3(a + 3)(a + 8)$
    $3a^2 + 33a + 72$

18. $k(k - 2)(k + 1)$
    $k^3 - k^2 - 2k$

19. $j(j - 3)(j - 5)$
    $j^3 - 8j^2 + 15j$

20. $(v + 4)(v - 5) - (v + 6)(v + 8)$
    $-15v - 68$

21. $(d + 6)(d - 3) + (d + 5)(d - 8)$
    $2d^2 - 58$

22. $5(x + 3)(x - 3) + 3(x - 1)(x + 7)$
    $8x^2 + 18x - 66$

23. $2(y + 3)(y + 1) - 3(y + 2)(y + 1)$
    $-y^2 - y$

24. Write an expression for the area of a square if the measure of each side is $(s + 7)$ in.   $(s^2 + 14s + 49)$ in.$^2$

**Factor each polynomial.**

1. $8x - 4$  $4(2x - 1)$
2. $6xy - 6xz$  $6x(y - z)$
3. $15m + 5$  $5(3m + 1)$
4. $14c - 21$  $7(2c - 3)$
5. $-3d + 18$  $-3(d - 6)$
6. $16k - 14$  $2(8k - 7)$
7. $8f^3 + 24f$  $8f(f^2 + 3)$
8. $4g^4 - 16g^2$  $4g^2(g^2 - 4)$
9. $7h^3 + 35h$  $7h(h^2 + 5)$
10. $ab + b^2$  $b(a + b)$
11. $s^2t^3 + st^4$  $st^3(s + t)$
12. $wv^3 - w^2v^5$  $wv^3(1 - wv^2)$
13. $10m^5 - 15m^3$  $5m^3(2m^2 - 3)$
14. $8n^3 + 6n$  $2n(4n^2 + 3)$
15. $z^8 - z^5$  $z^5(z^3 - 1)$
16. $120d - 80$  $40(3d - 2)$
17. $20x^2y - 4xy^2$  $4xy(5x - y)$
18. $-3ef^2 + 24e^3g$  $-3e(f^2 - 8e^2g)$
19. $x^4 - 2x^3 + 3x^2$  $x^2(x^2 - 2x + 3)$
20. $5y^5 + y^4 - 2y^3$  $y^3(5y^2 + y - 2)$
21. $4n^2 - 8n + 20$  $4(n^2 - 2n + 5)$
22. $12b^4 + 6b^3 - 9$  $3(4b^4 + 2b^3 - 3)$
23. $3de + 5de^2 + 4e$  $e(3d + 5de + 4)$
24. $r^3s^2t + r^2s^3v + r^2s^2w$  $r^2s^2(rt + sv + w)$
25. $35c^2 + 14cd + 21cd^2$  $7c(5c + 2d + 3d^2)$
26. $15jk^3 - 15jk + 10j^3k$  $5jk(3k^2 - 3 + 2j^2)$
27. $4x^2y^2 - x^4y^2 + 2xy^2z$  $xy^2(4x - x^3 + 2z)$
28. $g^3h^3 + 3g^4h^2 - 5g^5h$  $g^3h(h^2 + 3gh - 5g^2)$
29. $2m^3n^2 - m^3n^3 - 4m^4n^2$  $m^3n^2(2 - n - 4m)$
30. $p^2q^3 + 9p^4 - 8p^3q^2$  $p^2(q^3 + 9p^2 - 8pq^2)$

**Evaluate each expression. Let $x = 2$ and $y = -2$.**

31. $4xy^3 + 2x^2y$  $-80$
32. $2xy(2y^2 + x)$  $-80$

**Rewrite each formula by factoring.**

33. $C = 3r + 6s + 3t$  $C = 3(r + 2s + t)$
34. $A = 10d + 35d^2$  $A = 5d(2 + 7d)$

**Tell whether the trinomial is a perfect square trinomial.**

1. $x^2 + 4x + 4$ yes
2. $y^2 + 25y + 50$ no
3. $k^2 + 20k + 121$ no
4. $a^2 + 12a + 36$ yes
5. $e^2 + 16e + 81$ no
6. $d^2 + 16d + 64$ yes
7. $m^2 + 30m + 150$ no
8. $t^2 + 26t + 169$ yes

**Factor each polynomial if possible.**

9. $s^2 + 14s + 49$  $(s + 7)^2$
10. $p^2 - 60p + 90$ not factorable
11. $n^2 - 16n + 64$  $(n - 8)^2$
12. $j^2 + 8j + 16$  $(j + 4)^2$
13. $b^2 + 14b + 144$ not factorable
14. $f^2 - 2f + 1$  $(f - 1)^2$
15. $t^2 + 60t + 900$  $(t + 30)^2$
16. $a^2 + 12a + 38$ not factorable
17. $k^2 - 36$  $(k + 6)(k - 6)$
18. $c^2 - 64$  $(c + 8)(c - 8)$
19. $x^2 - 10$ not factorable
20. $z^2 - 49$  $(z + 7)(z - 7)$
21. $w^2 - 81$  $(w + 9)(w - 9)$
22. $d^2 - 96$ not factorable
23. $t^2 - 49$  $(t + 7)(t - 7)$
24. $v^2 - 75$ not factorable
25. $g^2 - 25$  $(g + 5)(g - 5)$
26. $a^2 - 16$  $(a + 4)(a - 4)$
27. $c^2 - 1$  $(c + 1)(c - 1)$
28. $h^2 - 9$  $(h + 3)(h - 3)$
29. $q^2 - 40$ not factorable
30. $r^2 - 100$  $(r + 10)(r - 10)$
31. $n^2 - 225$  $(n + 15)(n - 15)$
32. $x^2 + 12x + 36$  $(x + 6)^2$
33. $y^2 - 256$  $(y + 16)(y - 16)$
34. $b^2 - 7b + 49$ not factorable
35. $k^2 - 100$ $(k + 10)(k - 10)$
36. $2x^2 + 32x + 128$  $2(x + 8)^2$
37. $y^2 + 16$ not factorable
38. $6b^2 - 600b$  $6b(b - 100)$

**Extra Practice**

## Extra Practice 10-1

**10.**

**11.**

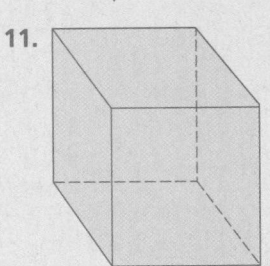

**12.** 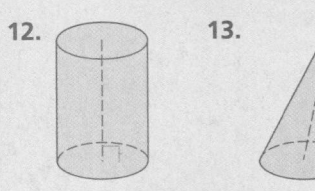     **13.**

**14.** 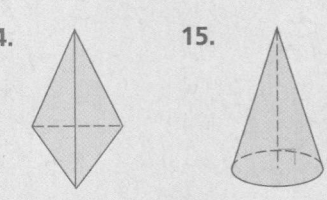     **15.**

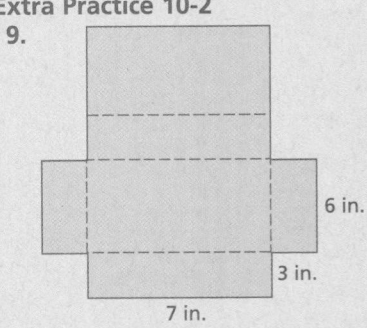

## Extra Practice 10-2

**9.**

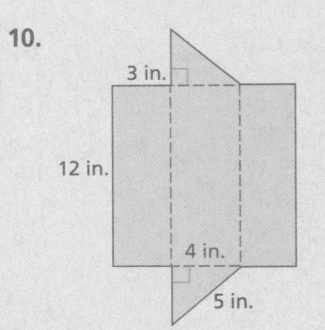

6 in.

3 in.

7 in.

**10.**

3 in.

12 in.

4 in.

5 in.

# Chapter 10

**Extra Practice 10–1** • Visualize and Represent Solids • pages 422–425

### Identify each figure and name its base(s).

**1.** 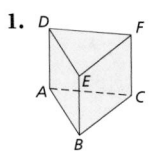 triangular prism; △DEF and △ABC

**2.** 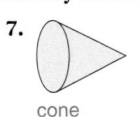 triangular pyramid; △ABC

**3.** 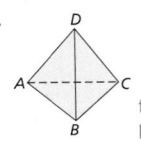 pentagonal prism: ABCDE and FGHIJ

### Identify a pair of parallel edges, intersecting faces, and intersecting edges for each figure. For 4–6, answers will vary. Possible answers given.

**4.** the figure in Exercise 1
$\overline{EF}$ and $\overline{BC}$; △ABC and BCFE; $\overline{DE}$ and $\overline{EF}$

**5.** the figure in Exercise 2
none; △ABC and △BCD; $\overline{BC}$ and $\overline{DC}$

**6.** the figure in Exercise 3
$\overline{EI}$ and $\overline{DH}$; ABCDE and DEIH; $\overline{ED}$ and $\overline{DH}$

### Identify each figure.

**7.** 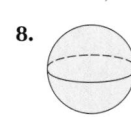 cone

**8.**  sphere

**9.** 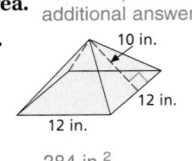 cylinder

**Draw each figure.** For 10–15, see additional answers.

**10.** right triangular prism    **11.** cube    **12.** right cylinder

**13.** oblique cone    **14.** triangular pyramid    **15.** right cone

**Extra Practice 10–2** • Nets and Surface Area • pages 426–429

### Identify the three-dimensional figure for each net.

**1.** 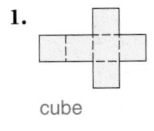 cube

**2.** 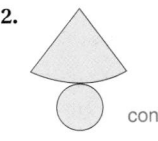 cone

**3.** 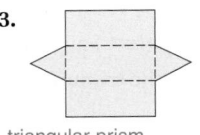 triangular prism

**4.** 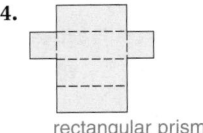 rectangular prism

**5.** 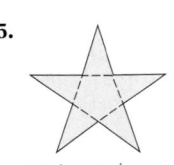 pentagonal pyramid

**6.** 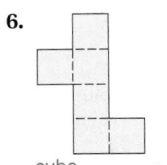 cube

**7.**  pentagonal prism

**8.** 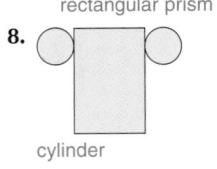 cylinder

**Draw a net for each figure. Then find the surface area.** For 9–12, see additional answers.

**9.** 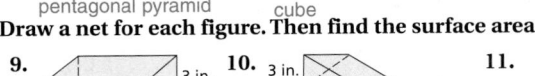 3 in. 6 in. 7 in.
162 in.²

**10.** 3 in. 12 in. 4 in. 5 in.
156 in.²

**11.** 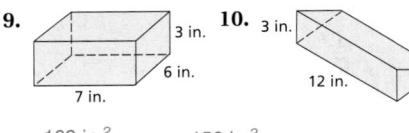 10 in. 12 in. 12 in.
384 in.²

**12.** 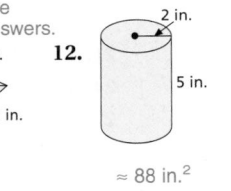 2 in. 5 in.
≈ 88 in.²

**11.**

12 in.

10 in.

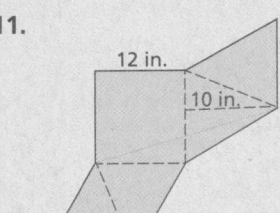

**12.**

2 in.

5 in.

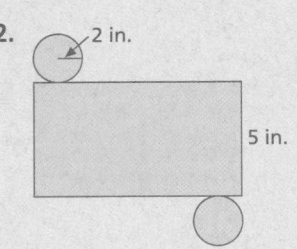

**Find the surface area of each figure. Use 3.14 for π. If necessary, round to the nearest tenth.**

**1.**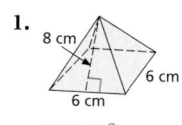
8 cm
6 cm
6 cm
132 cm²

**2.**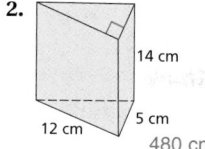
14 cm
5 cm
12 cm
480 cm²

**3.**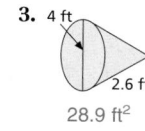
4 ft
2.6 ft
28.9 ft²

**4.**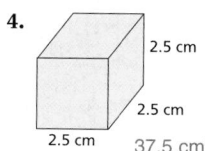
2.5 cm
2.5 cm
2.5 cm
37.5 cm²

**5.**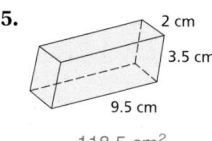
2 cm
3.5 cm
9.5 cm
118.5 cm²

**6.**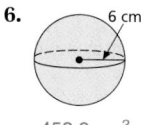
6 cm
452.2 cm²

**7.**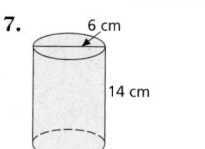
6 cm
14 cm
320.3 cm²

**8.**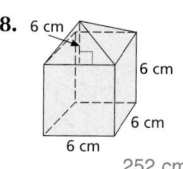
6 cm
6 cm
6 cm
6 cm
252 cm²

**9.**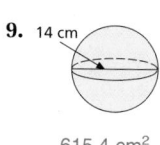
14 cm
615.4 cm²

**10.**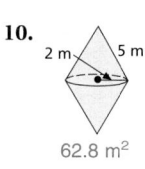
2 m
5 m
62.8 m²

**11.**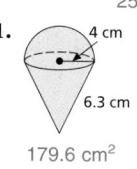
4 cm
6.3 cm
179.6 cm²

**12.**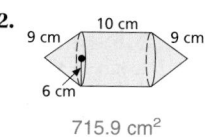
9 cm
10 cm
9 cm
6 cm
715.9 cm²

**13.** A metal cylinder has a radius of $\frac{1}{2}$ ft and a surface area of 30 ft². What is the height of the cylinder to the nearest whole number?  9 ft

**Sketch each object in one-point perspective.** For 1–3, see additional answers.

**1.** a three-dimensional letter F

**2.** a pentagonal prism

**3.** a flat envelope

**Sketch each object in two-point perspective.** For 4–6, see additional answers.

**4.** a triangular prism

**5.** an open book

**6.** a computer screen

**Use each perspective drawing to locate the vanishing point(s).**

**7.**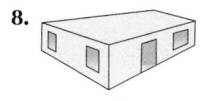

**8.**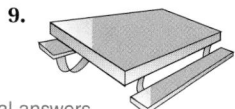

**9.**

For 7–9, see additional answers.

**Extra Practice**

**1.**

**2.**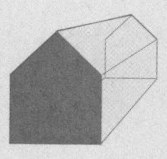

**3.**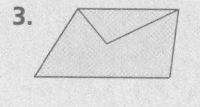

**4.**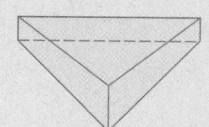

**5.**

**6.**

**7.**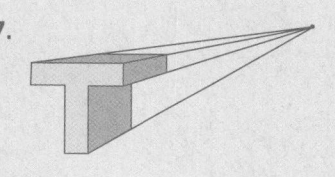

**8.**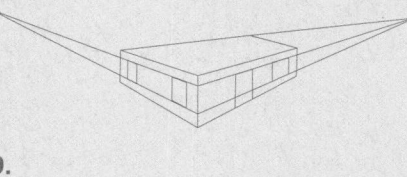

**9.**

## Extra Practice 10-5

**1.**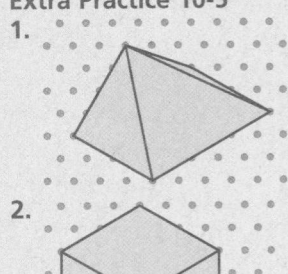

**2.**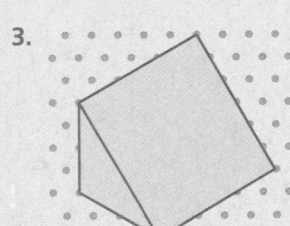

**3.**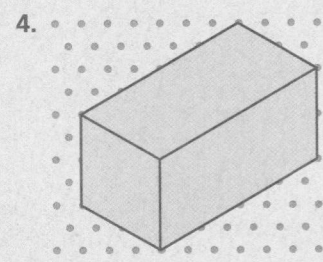

**4.**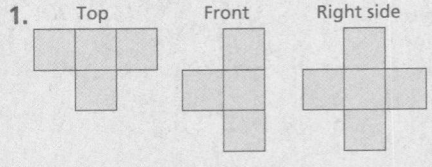

## Extra Practice 10-6

**1.** Top   Front   Right side

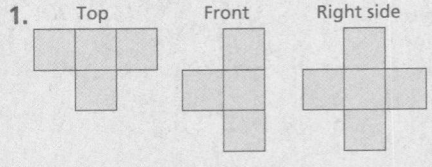

**2.** Top   Front   Right side

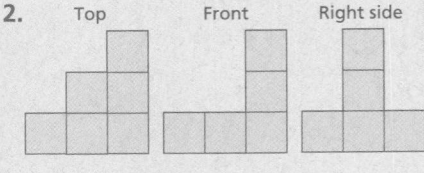

**3.** Top   Front   Right side

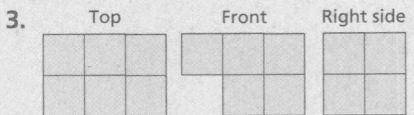

Extra Practice 10–5 • Isometric Drawings • pages 442–445

**Create an isometric drawing of each figure.** For 1–4, see additional answers.

1. a rectangular pyramid
2. a right triangular prism
3. a 2-unit cube
4. a 2-unit by 4-unit rectangular prism

**Use the isometric drawing for Exercises 5–7.**

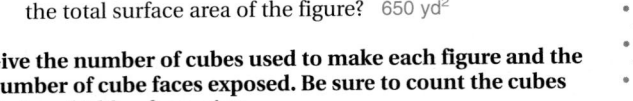

5. How many cubes are used in the drawing?   6
6. How many cube faces are exposed in the figure?   26
7. If the length of an edge of one of the cubes is 5 yd, what is the total surface area of the figure?   650 yd$^2$

**Give the number of cubes used to make each figure and the number of cube faces exposed. Be sure to count the cubes that are hidden from view.**

**8.**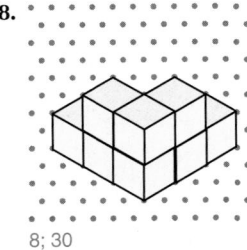

**9.**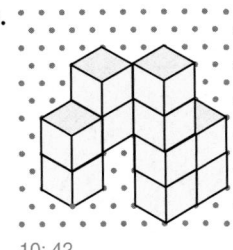

**10.**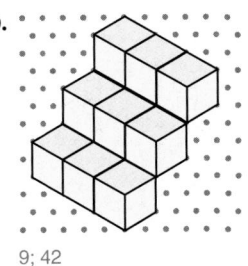

8; 30          10; 42          9; 42

Extra Practice 10–6 • Orthogonal Drawings • pages 446–449

**Make an orthogonal drawing labeling the front, top and right-side views.**
For 1–3, see additional answers.

**1.** 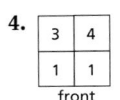 front

**2.** 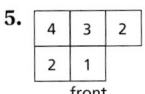 front

**3.** 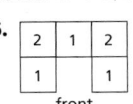 front

**For each foundation drawing, sketch a figure composed of cubes.** For 4–6, see additional answers.

**4.**

| 3 | 4 |
|---|---|
| 1 | 1 |
front

**5.**

| 4 | 3 | 2 |
|---|---|---|
| 2 | 1 | |
front

**6.**

| 2 | 1 | 2 |
|---|---|---|
| 1 | | 1 |
front

**4.**

**5.**

**6.**

**Create a foundation drawing for each figure.** For 7–9, see additional answers.

**7.**

**8.**
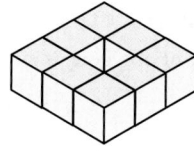

**9.**
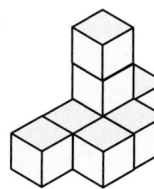

**7.**

| 2 | 1 | 1 |
|---|---|---|
| 1 |   | 3 |

**8.**

| 1 | 1 | 1 |
|---|---|---|
| 1 | 0 | 1 |
| 1 | 1 | 1 |

**9.**

| 1 | 1 | 3 | 1 |
|---|---|---|---|
|   | 1 | 1 |   |

**Extra Practice 10–7 •** Volume of Prisms and Pyramids • pages 452–455

**Find the volume of each figure.**

**1.**
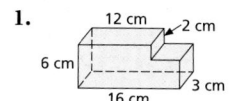
12 cm, 2 cm, 6 cm, 16 cm, 3 cm
264 cm³

**2.**
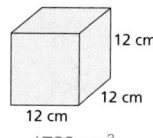
12 cm, 12 cm, 12 cm, 12 cm
1728 cm³

**3.**
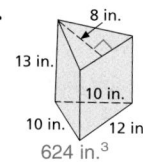
8 in., 13 in., 10 in., 10 in., 12 in.
624 in.³

**4.**
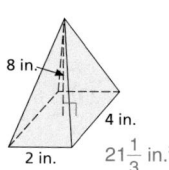
8 in., 4 in., 2 in.
$21\frac{1}{3}$ in.³

**5.**
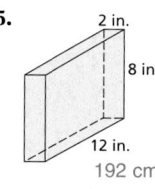
2 in., 8 in., 12 in.
192 cm³

**6.**
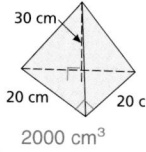
30 cm, 20 cm, 20 cm
2000 cm³

**7.**
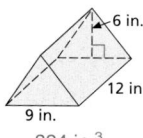
6 in., 12 in., 9 in.
324 in.³

**8.**
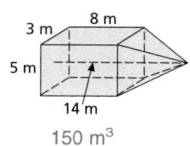
3 m, 8 m, 5 m, 14 m
150 m³

**9.** A crate is 1.5 ft long, 2.5 ft wide and 15 in. high. What is the volume of the crate? Round your answer to the nearest tenth.   4.7 ft³

**Extra Practice 10–8 •** Volume of Cylinders, Cones and Spheres • pages 456–459

**Find the volume of each figure. Use 3.14 for π. Round to the nearest whole number.**

**1.**
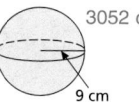
3052 cm³
9 cm

**2.**

9 cm
3306 cm³
13 cm

**3.**
5 in.   314 in.³
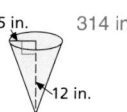
12 in.

**4.**
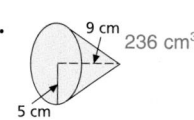
9 cm   236 cm³
5 cm

**5.**

1583 cm³
6 cm
10 cm

**6.**
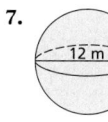
273 in.³
13 in.   8 in.
3 in.

**7.**
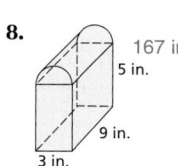
904 m³
12 m

**8.**
167 in.³
5 in.
9 in.
3 in.

**9.** A water tank in the shape of a sphere has a diameter of 50 ft. How many cubic feet of water, to the nearest whole number, can the tank hold? Use 3.14 for π. ≈ 65,417 ft³

## Chapter 11

Extra Practice 11–1 • Similar Polygons • pages 474–477

**Determine if each pair of polygons is similar.**

1.  yes
    80° 45° / 80° 55°

2.  no
    50° / 60°

3.  no
    12 cm / 15 cm
    8 cm / 12 cm

**Find the length of $\overline{AB}$ in each pair of similar figures.**

4.  27 m B
    C A
    36 m E
    F 20 m
    15 m D

5.  A D
    16 in.
    B C  H 15 in. E
    20 in. / 15 in.
    G F
    12 in.

6.  B 8 cm C
    A D  F 12 cm G
    E H  6 cm
    4 cm

**Find the $m\angle A$ in each pair of similar polygons.**

7.  68°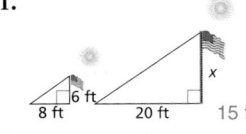
    B
    A C
    E
    D 22° F

8.  55°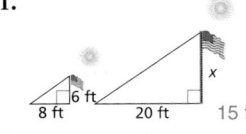
    F
    B 55°
    E D
    A C

9.  145°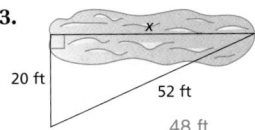
    E
    D A  35°
    C B
    G F

10. Triangle *ABC* and △*DEF* are similar triangles. If $m\angle A = 30°$ and $m\angle F = 50°$, what are the measures of $\angle D$ and $\angle E$?  $m\angle D = 30°; m\angle E = 100°$

Extra Practice 11–2 • Indirect Measurement • pages 478–481

**Use indirect measurement to find the unknown length *x*.**

1.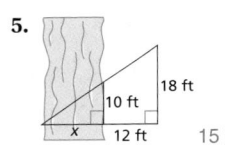
    6 ft x
    8 ft  20 ft  15 ft

2.  x
    21 m  3 m  9 m
    10 m

3.  x
    20 ft  52 ft
    48 ft

4.  x
    12 m  4 m  3 m
    9 m

5.  18 ft
    10 ft
    x  12 ft  15 ft

6.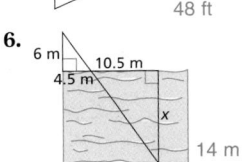
    6 m  10.5 m
    4.5 m
    x
    14 m

7.  Brian uses the mirror method to find the height of a tree. He places the mirror 30 ft from the tree's base and he stands 5 ft from the mirror. Brian is 4.5-ft tall. Find the height of the tree.  27 ft

8.  A 1-m stick casts a 0.8-m shadow. At the same time, a flagpole casts a 4.8-m shadow. How tall is the flagpole?  6 m

**Extra Practice**

**Find the length of each hypotenuse. Round to the nearest tenth.**

1.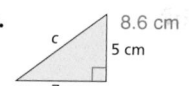
10 m
8 m  c
6 m

2.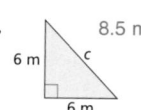
7.2 cm
4 cm  c
6 cm

3.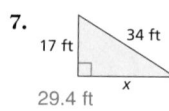
8.6 cm
c  5 cm
7 cm

4.
8.5 m
6 m  c
6 m

**Find the unknown length. Round to the nearest tenth.**

5.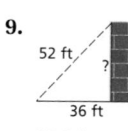
39 ft
15 ft
x
36 ft

6.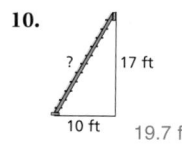
25 in.
x
24 in.
7 in.

7.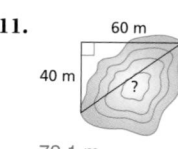
34 ft
17 ft
x
29.4 ft

8.
18 yd
8 yd
x
16.1 yd

**Find each unknown measurement. Round to the nearest tenth.**

9.
52 ft
?
36 ft
37.5 ft

10.
?  17 ft
10 ft
19.7 ft

11.
60 m
40 m
?
72.1 m

12. If you traveled 36 mi south and then 48 mi east, what is the shortest distance you could travel to return to your starting point? 60 mi

**In △RST, find each ratio in lowest terms.**

1. sin T $\frac{15}{17}$

2. tan S $\frac{8}{15}$

3. cos T $\frac{8}{17}$

4. tan T $\frac{15}{8}$

5. cos S $\frac{15}{17}$

6. sin S $\frac{8}{17}$

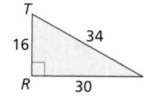
T
16  34
R  30  S

**For each triangle, use the information given to find the trigonometric ratio indicated. Write the answer in lowest terms.**

7. In △ABC, m∠B = 90°, AB = 12, and BC = 9. Find cos C. $\frac{3}{5}$

8. In △DEF, m∠F = 90°, FE = 24, and DE = 26. Find cos E. $\frac{12}{13}$

9. In △JKL, m∠L = 90°, JL = 10, and JK = 26. Find cos J. $\frac{5}{13}$

10. In △PQV, m∠Q = 90°, PV = 34, and QV = 30. Find cos P. $\frac{8}{17}$

11. In △TAG, m∠G = 90°, TA = 39, and TG = 15. Find cos T. $\frac{5}{13}$

12. In △HOP, m∠O = 90°, OP = 36, and HO = 15. Find cos P. $\frac{12}{13}$

**CALCULATOR** Use a calculator to find each ratio to four decimal places.

13. cos 50° 0.6428

14. tan 20° 0.3640

15. cos 37° 0.7986

16. sin 74° 0.9613

17. tan 51° 1.2349

18. sin 15° 0.2588

19. tan 8° 0.1405

20. tan 82° 7.1154

21. sin 44° 0.6947

22. cos 45° 0.7071

23. sin 50° 0.7660

24. cos 25° 0.9063

**Find each length to the nearest tenth.**

**1.** *AB*  5.7   **2.** *BC*  14.9   **3.** *RP*  6.6   **4.** *MP*  5.5

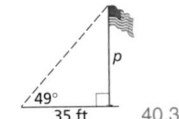

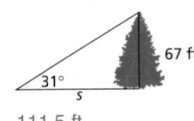

**5.** Find the height of the flagpole, *p*.

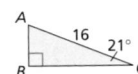

40.3 ft

**6.** Find the length of the tree's shadow, *s*.

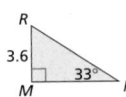

111.5 ft

**In the figure shown, find the value of *x* to the nearest tenth.**

**7.**

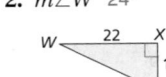

48.1 cm

**8.**

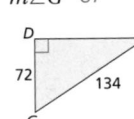

80.4 m

**Find each measure to the nearest whole degree.**

**1.** *m∠B*  39°   **2.** *m∠W*  24°   **3.** *m∠B*  34°   **4.** *m∠G*  57°

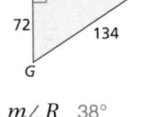

**5.** *m∠R*  67°   **6.** *m∠T*  44°   **7.** *m∠H*  26°   **8.** *m∠R*  38°

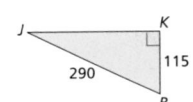

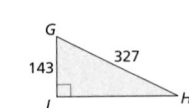

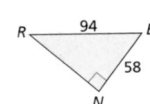

**9.** When a certain airplane has reached a ground distance of 1800 ft from its lift-off point, it is 1050 ft above the ground. To the nearest whole degree, what angle does the plane's path make with the ground?  30°

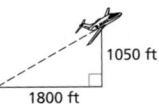

1050 ft

1800 ft

**10.** The base of a ladder is 32 in. from a wall. The top of the ladder is touching the wall at a place that is 132 in. from the ground. To the nearest degree, what is the measure of the angle formed by the ladder and the wall?  14°

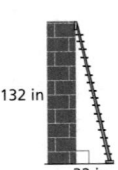

132 in

32 in

**Use △ABC for Exercises 1–6. Leave your answers in square root form.**

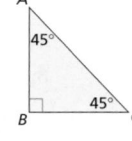

1. If $AB = 9$, find $BC$ and $AC$.  9; 9√2
2. If $AB = 15$, find $BC$ and $AC$.  15; 15√2
3. If $BC = 4$, find $AB$ and $AC$.  4; 4√2
4. If $BC = 12$, find $AB$ and $AC$.  12; 12√2
5. If $AC = 27$, find $AB$ and $BC$. $\frac{27\sqrt{2}}{2}$, $\frac{27\sqrt{2}}{2}$
6. If $AC = 2$, find $AB$ and $BC$.  √2; √2

**Use △XYZ for Exercises 7–12. Leave your answers in square root form.**

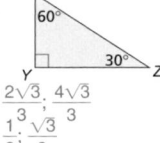

7. If $XY = 4$, find $YZ$ and $XZ$.  4√3; 8
8. If $XY = 7$, find $YZ$ and $XZ$.  7√3; 14
9. If $YZ = 18$, find $XY$ and $XZ$.  6√3; 12√3
10. If $YZ = 2$, find $XY$ and $XZ$.  $\frac{2\sqrt{3}}{3}$, $\frac{4\sqrt{3}}{3}$
11. If $XZ = 24$, find $XY$ and $YZ$.  12; 12√3
12. If $XZ = 1$, find $XY$ and $YZ$.  $\frac{1}{2}$; $\frac{\sqrt{3}}{2}$

**A 300-ft guy wire that supports an antenna makes a 60° angle with the ground.**

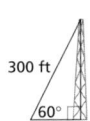

300 ft

13. How far is the bottom of the guy wire from the bottom of the antenna?  150 ft
14. How tall is the antenna? Round to the nearest tenth.  259.8 ft

# Chapter 12

**Define each set in roster notation and in set-builder notation. Then determine whether the set is finite or infinite.** For 1–6, see additional answers.

1. $W$, the set of whole numbers less than 6
2. $D$, the set of letters in *dinosaur*
3. $N$, the set of the odd whole numbers
4. $V$, the set of vowels
5. $F$, the set of whole number factors of 12
6. $M$, the set of multiples of 5 less than 30

**Write a set equivalent to each set.** For 7–9, answers will vary. Possible answer is given.

7. $\left\{\frac{1}{2}, 1, \frac{3}{2}, 2\right\}$  $\left\{\frac{5}{2}, 5, \frac{15}{2}, 10\right\}$
8. $\{d, z, m, h, v, q\}$  $\{a, b, c, d, e, f\}$
9. $\{4, 12, 24, 48\}$  $\{2, 4, 6, 8\}$

**Determine if the sets are *equal or not equal*.**

10. $\{c, x, k, r, g\}$ and $\{k, x, g, r, c\}$  equal
11. $\{5, 31, 7, 27, 9, 53\}$ and $\{7, 9, 37, 53, 5, 29\}$  not equal
12. $\{t, j, a, w, n, f\}$ and $\{a, n, f, v, t, w\}$  not equal
13. $\{18, 33, 79, 57, 82\}$ and $\{57, 18, 79, 82, 33\}$  equal

**Determine if each statement is *true* or *false*.**

14. $62 \in \{0, 2, 4, 6, \ldots\}$  true
15. $34 \in \{4, 8, 12, 16, \ldots, 48\}$  false
16. $\{30, 40\} \subseteq \{3, 6, 9, 12, \ldots\}$  false
17. $\{d, m\} \subseteq \{a, s, j, m, y, c, n, d, f\}$  true
18. $\{x | x$ is a parallelogram$\} \subseteq \{x | x$ is a quadrilateral$\}$  true

**Write the subsets of each set.** For 19–22, see additional answers.

19. $\{3, 6, 9\}$
20. $\{a, b\}$
21. $\{15, 30\}$
22. $\{d, e, n\}$

1. $\{0, 1, 2, 3, 4, 5\}$; $\{x | x < 6$ where $x$ is a whole number$\}$; finite
2. $\{d, i, n, o, s, a, u, r\}$; $\{x | x$ is a letter in the word *dinosaur*$\}$; finite
3. $\{1, 3, 5, 7, \ldots\}$; $\{x | x$ is an odd whole number$\}$; infinite
4. $\{A, E, I, O, U\}$; $\{x | x$ is a vowel$\}$; finite
5. $\{1, 2, 3, 4, 6, 12\}$; $\{x | x$ is a whole number factor of 12$\}$; finite
6. $\{5, 10, 15, 20, 25\}$; $\{x | x$ is a multiple of 5 less than 30$\}$; finite
19. $\{3\}$, $\{6\}$, $\{9\}$, $\{3, 6\}$, $\{3, 9\}$, $\{6, 9\}$, $\{3, 6, 9\}$, ∅
20. $\{a\}$, $\{b\}$, $\{a, b\}$, ∅
21. $\{15\}$, $\{30\}$, $\{15, 30\}$, ∅
22. $\{d\}$, $\{e\}$, $\{n\}$, $\{d, e\}$, $\{d, n\}$, $\{e, n\}$, $\{d, e, n\}$, ∅

## Extra Practice 12-4

1. Converse: If an animal has paws, then it is a cat; false. A dog has paws. Inverse: If an animal is not a cat, then it does not have paws; false. A dog is not a cat, but has paws. Contrapositive: If an animal does not have paws, then it is not a cat; true.

2. Converse: If a figure has four sides, then it is a square; false. A rectangle has four sides. Inverse: If a figure is not a square, then it does not have four sides; false. A concave quadrilateral is not a square and it has four sides. Contrapositive: If a figure does not have four sides, then it is not a square. True.

3. Converse: If an angle measures greater than 90°, then it is obtuse; true. Inverse: If an angle is not obtuse, then its measurement is not greater than 90°; true. Contrapositive: If an angle measurement is not greater than 90°, then it is not obtuse; true.

4. Converse: If a vehicle has four wheels, then it is a station wagon; false. A truck has four wheels. Inverse: If a vehicle is not a station wagon, then it does not have four wheels; false. A truck has four wheels. Contrapositive: If a vehicle does not have four wheels, then it is not a station wagon; true.

5. Converse: If you have a pet, then you have a dog; false. A cat is a pet. Inverse: If you do not have a dog, then you do not have a pet; false. A cat is a pet. Contrapositive: If you do not have a pet, then you do not have a dog; true.

6. Converse: If a figure has a diameter, then it is a circle; true. Inverse: If a figure is not a circle, then it does not have a diameter; true. Contrapositive: If a figure does not have a diameter, then it is not a circle; true.

7. Converse: If a number is greater than 50, then the number is greater than 100; false. 80 is greater than 50. Inverse: If a number is not greater than 100, then the number is not greater than 50; false. 80 is not greater than 100. Contrapositive: If a number is not greater than 50,

---

### Extra Practice 12–2 • Union and Intersection of Sets • pages 524–527

**Find each set by listing the members.**

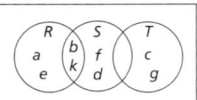

1. $R \cup S$ {a, b, d, e, f, k}
2. $R \cup T$ {a, b, c, e, g, k}
3. $R \cap S$ {b, k}
4. $S \cap T$ ∅

**Let $U = \{s, t, r, i, p, e\}$, $B = \{t, r, i, p\}$ and $C = \{p, i, t\}$. Find each union.**

5. $B' \cup C'$ {s, r, e}
6. $B' \cup C$ {s, e, p, i, t}
7. $B \cup C'$ {t, r, i, p, s, e}

**Let $U = \{q, t, f, j, b, w\}$, $R = \{t, j, w\}$ and $S = \{q, j, b\}$. Find each union.**

8. $R \cup S'$ {w, f, t, j}
9. $R' \cup S$ {q, j, b, f}
10. $R' \cup S'$ {q, f, b, t, w}

11. Let $M = \{t, r, u, c, k\}$ and $N = \{c, h, a, r, t\}$. Find $M \cap N$. {t, r, c}
12. Let $F = \{6, 12, 24, 48\}$ and $G = \{8, 12, 48\}$. Find $F \cap G$. {12, 48}

**Use roster notation to represent each set.**

$U = \{2, 4, 6, 8, 10, 12, 14, 16, 18\}$   $A = \{6, 10, 16\}$   $B = \{4, 12, 18\}$   $C = \{4, 8, 12, 14\}$

13. $A' \cap B$ {4, 12, 18}
14. $A \cap C'$ {6, 10, 16}
15. $A \cap B$ ∅
16. $B \cap C$ {4, 12}
17. $B' \cap C$ {8, 14}
18. $A' \cap C'$ {2, 18}

---

### Extra Practice 12–4 • Converse, Inverse and Contrapositive • pages 532–535

**Write the converse, inverse and contrapositive of each statement. Determine if each is *true* or *false*. If *false*, give a counterexample to explain why.**

For 1–13, answers will vary. See additional answers for possible answers.

1. If an animal is a cat, then it has paws.
2. If a figure is a square, then it has four sides.
3. If an angle is obtuse, then its measure is greater than 90°.
4. If a vehicle is a station wagon, then it has four wheels.
5. If you have a dog, then you have a pet.
6. If a figure is a circle, then it has a diameter.
7. If a number is greater than 100, then the number is greater than 50.
8. If you vacation in Paris, then you vacation in France.
9. If an object is a baseball, then it is round.
10. If a whole number is even, then it is divisible by two.
11. If you are studying Italian, then you are studying a foreign language.
12. If a set contains all the factors of 48, then one element in that set is 8.
13. If two sides of a triangle are congruent, then the angles opposites those sides are congruent.

---

then the number is not greater than 100; true.

8. Converse: If you vacation in France, then you vacation in Paris; false. Normandy is in France. Inverse: If you do not vacation in Paris, then you do not vacation in France; false. Normandy is in France. Contrapositive: If you do not vacation in France, then you do not vacation in Paris; true.

9. Converse: If an object is round, then it is a baseball; false. A basketball is round. Inverse: If an object is not a baseball, then it is not round; false. A basketball is round. Contrapositive: If an object is not round, then it is not a baseball; true.

10. Converse: If a whole number is divisible by two, then it is an even number; true. Inverse: If a whole number is not even, then it is not divisible by two; true. Contrapositive: If a whole number is not divisible by two, then it is not an even number; true.

11. Converse: If you are studying a foreign language, then you are studying Italian; false. French is a foreign language. Inverse: If you are not studying Italian, then you are not studying a foreign lan-

**Predict the next number in each pattern.**

1. 5, 15, 35, 65, 105, __?__  155

2. 1, 2, 4, 8, 16, 32, __?__  64

3. 50, 10, 2, $\frac{2}{5}$, __?__  $\frac{2}{25}$

4. 30, 25, 21, 18, 16, __?__  15

5. 3, 6, 18, 72, __?__  360

6. 24, 12, 6, 3, __?__  $\frac{3}{2}$

**Complete each argument by drawing a conclusion.**

7. *Premise 1* All A+ students are on the High Honor Roll.
   *Premise 2* Kim is an A+ student.  Kim is on the High Honor Roll.

8. *Premise 1* If the Rams win the basketball game, they are the conference champions.
   *Premise 2* The Rams win the basketball game.  The Rams are the conference champs.

9. *Premise 1* All four-year olds may register for story-time at the Library.
   *Premise 2* Mike is four years old.  Mike may register for story-time at the library.

**Tell whether the reasoning is *inductive* or *deductive*.**

10. The football team has been undefeated for the past three years. Since the coach is the same this year the team should be undefeated this year as well.  inductive

11. The swim club requires lifeguards to be at least 18 years old. Sam is working as a lifeguard at the swim club, so he must be at least 18 years old.  deductive

12. If $x$ is one more than $y$ and $y$ is two more than $z$, what conclusion can be drawn about the relationship between $x$ and $z$? What type of reasoning did you use to draw your conclusion?  $x$ is 3 more than $z$; deductive reasoning

**Determine by form whether the arguments are *valid* or *invalid*. If *valid*, name the argument form.**

1. If an animal is a cat, then it has a tail. Fluffy is a cat. Therefore Fluffy has a tail.  valid; Law of Detachment

2. If my bicycle is broken, then I cannot exercise. I cannot exercise. Therefore, my bicycle is broken.  invalid

3. If a number is a multiple of ten, then it is an even number. The number is not an even number. Therefore, the number is not a multiple of ten.  valid; Law of Contrapositive

4. If Julie becomes a cheerleader, then she will go to all the soccer games. Julie does not become a cheerleader. Therefore, Julie does not go to all the soccer games.  invalid

5. If you are a member of Lake City Swim Club, then you are a resident of Lake City. You are not a resident of Lake City. Therefore, you are not a member of Lake City Swim Club.  valid; Law of Contrapositive

6. If a rectangle has a width of $m$ and a length of $n$, then its area is $mn$. The area of a rectangle is $mn$. Therefore, the rectangle has a width of $m$ and a length of $n$.  invalid

Extra Practice

Extra Practice | **625**

guage; false. French is a foreign language. Contrapositive: If you are not studying a foreign language, then you are not studying Italian; true.

12. Converse: If 8 is one element in a set, then that set contains all factors of 48; false. {8, 10} does not contain all factors of 48. Inverse: If a set does not contain all the factors of 48, then 8 is not one element in that set; false. {2, 8} contains 8. Contrapositive: If 8 is not one element in a set, then that set does not contain all factors of 48; true.

13. Converse: If the angles opposite two sides of a triangle are congruent, then those sides of the triangle are congruent; true. Inverse: If two sides of a triangle are not congruent, then the angles opposite those sides are not congruent; true. Contrapositive: If the angles opposite two sides are not congruent, then those sides of the triangle are not congruent; true.

**Show that the conclusion given is true. Present your argument in a logical order.** For 1–4, see additional answers.

1. $a° + b° = 100°$

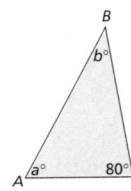

2. $m\angle 1 + m\angle 2 = 180°$

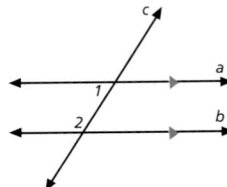

3. $m\angle 1 = 60°$

4. $w = 50$ in.

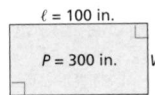

5. Find the measure of each central angle in circle $E$.
   $m\angle 1 = 35°$, $m\angle 2 = 145°$; $m\angle 3 = 35°$

6. The exterior angles of a pentagon have measures $5x°$, $3x°$, $(2x + 7)°$, $(3x - 1)°$, and $(5x - 6)°$. Find the measure of each interior angle. 80°, 120°, 133°, 121°, 86°

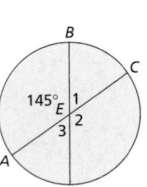

7. Show that when the square of a number is cubed, the result is the same as that number to the sixth power. Let $n$ represent the number. $(n^2)^3 = n^2 \cdot n^2 \cdot n^2 = n^{2+2+2} = n^6$

8. Show that 2 less than any even integer is an even integer. Let $n$ be any integer. See additional answers.

# Preparing for Standardized Tests

## Becoming a Better Test-Taker

Ⓐ Ⓑ Ⓒ Ⓓ

At some time in your life, you will probably have to take a standardized test. Sometimes this test may determine if you go on to the next grade or course, or even if you will graduate from high school. This section of your textbook is dedicated to making you a better test-taker.

**TYPES OF TEST QUESTIONS** In the following pages, you will see examples of four types of questions commonly seen on standardized tests. A description of each type of question is shown in the table below.

| Type of Question | Description | See Pages |
|---|---|---|
| multiple choice | 4 or 5 possible answer choices are given from which you choose the best answer. | 628–631 |
| gridded response | You solve the problem. Then you enter the answer in a special grid and shade in the corresponding circles. | 632–635 |
| short response | You solve the problem, showing your work and/or explaining your reasoning. | 636–639 |
| extended response | You solve a multi-part problem, showing your work and/or explaining your reasoning. | 640–644 |

**PRACTICE** After being introduced to each type of question, you can practice that type of question. Each set of practice questions is divided into five sections that represent the concepts most commonly assessed on standardized tests.

- Number and Operations
- Algebra
- Geometry
- Measurement
- Data Analysis and Probability

**USING A CALCULATOR** On some tests, you are permitted to use a calculator. You should check with your teacher to determine if calculator use is permitted on the test you will be taking, and if so, what type of calculator can be used.

**TEST-TAKING TIPS** In addition to Test-Taking Tips like the one shown at the right, here are some additional thoughts that might help you.

- Get a good night's rest before the test. Cramming the night before does not improve your results.
- Budget your time when taking a test. Don't dwell on problems that you cannot solve. Just make sure to leave that question blank on your answer sheet.
- Watch for key words like NOT and EXCEPT. Also look for order words like LEAST, GREATEST, FIRST, and LAST.

> **Test-Taking Tip**
>
> If you are allowed to use a calculator, make sure you are familiar with how it works so that you won't waste time trying to figure out the calculator when taking the test.

# Multiple-Choice Questions

Multiple-choice questions are the most common type of questions on standardized tests. These questions are sometimes called *selected-response questions*. You are asked to choose the best answer from four or five possible answers.

To record a multiple-choice answer, you may be asked to shade in a bubble that is a circle or an oval, or to just write the letter of your choice. Always make sure that your shading is dark enough and completely covers the bubble.

The answer to a multiple-choice question is usually not immediately obvious from the choices, but you may be able to eliminate some of the possibilities by using your knowledge of mathematics. Another answer choice might be that the correct answer is not given.

Incomplete Shading
Ⓐ Ⓑ Ⓒ Ⓓ
Too light shading
Ⓐ Ⓑ Ⓒ Ⓓ
Correct shading
Ⓐ Ⓑ Ⓒ Ⓓ

## Example 1

A storm signal flag is used to warn small craft of wind speeds that are greater than 38 miles per hour. The length of the square flag is always three times the length of the side of the black square. If $y$ is the area of the black square and $x$ is the length of the side of the flag, which equation describes the relationship between $x$ and $y$?

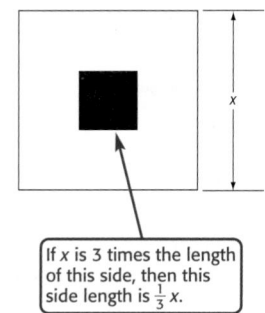

If $x$ is 3 times the length of this side, then this side length is $\frac{1}{3}x$.

Ⓐ $y = \frac{1}{3}x^2$

Ⓑ $y = \frac{1}{9}x^2$

Ⓒ $y = x^2 - 1$

Ⓓ $y = 3x$

Ⓔ $y = 9x$

For the area of a square, $A = s^2$. So, $A = x \cdot x$ or $x^2$.

The area of the black square is part of the area of the flag, which is $x^2$. Eliminate choices D and E because they do not include $x^2$.

$A = \left(\frac{1}{3}x\right)^2$ or $\frac{1}{9}x^2$ square units

So, $y = \frac{1}{9}x^2$. This is choice B.

Use some random numbers to check your choice.

Multiples of 3 make calculations easier.

| Length of Flag ($x$) | Length of Black Square | Area of Black Square | Area = $\frac{1}{9}x^2$ |
|---|---|---|---|
| 12 | 4 | 16 | $16 \stackrel{?}{=} \frac{1}{9}(12^2)$ ✓ |
| 27 | 9 | 81 | $81 \stackrel{?}{=} \frac{1}{9}(27^2)$ ✓ |
| 60 | 20 | 400 | $400 \stackrel{?}{=} \frac{1}{9}(60^2)$ ✓ |

Many multiple-choice questions are actually two- or three-step problems. If you do not read the question carefully, you may select a choice that is an intermediate step instead of the correct final answer.

## Example 2

**Barrington can skateboard down a hill five times as fast as he can walk up the hill. If it takes 9 min to walk up the hill and skateboard back down, how many minutes does it take him to walk up the hill?**

   F  1.5 min     G  4.5 min     H  7.2 min     J  7.5 min

Before involving any algebra, let's think about the problem using random numbers.

Skating is five times as fast as walking, so walking time equals 5 times the skate time. Use a table to find a pattern

| Skate Time | Skate Time × 5 = Walk Time |
|------------|-----------------------------|
| 6 min | $6 \cdot 5 = 30$ min |
| 3 min | $3 \cdot 5 = 15$ min |
| 2 min | $2 \cdot 5 = 10$ min |
| $x$ min | $x \cdot 5 = 5x$ min |

> Use the pattern to find a general expression for walk time given any skate time.

The problem states that the walk time and the skate time total 9 min.

> Use the expression to write an equation for the problem.

$$x + 5x = 9 \qquad \text{skate time + walk time = 9 min}$$
$$6x = 9 \qquad \text{Add like terms.}$$
$$x = 1.5 \qquad \text{Divide each side by 6.}$$

Looking at the choices, you might think that choice F is the correct answer. But what does $x$ represent, and what is the problem asking?

The problem asks for the time it takes to walk up the hill, but the value of $x$ is the time it takes to skateboard. So, the actual answer is found using $5x$ or $5(1.5)$, which is 7.5 min.

The correct choice is J.

## Example 3

**The Band Boosters are making ice cream to sell at an Open House. Each batch of ice cream calls for 5 c of milk. They plan to make 20 batches. How many gallons of milk do they need?**

   A  800     B  100     C  25     D  12.5     E  6.25

The Band Boosters need $5 \times 20$ or 100 c of milk. However, choice B is not the correct answer. The question asks for *gallons* of milk.

4 c = 1 qt and 4 qt = 1 gal, so 1 gal = $4 \times 4$ or 16 c.

$100 \, \cancel{c} \times \dfrac{1 \text{ gal}}{16 \, \cancel{c}} = 6.25$ gal, which is choice E.

# Multiple Choice Practice

**Choose the best answer.**

## Number and Operations

1. One mile on land is 5280 ft, while one nautical mile is 6076 ft. What is the ratio of the length of a nautical mile to the length of a land mile as a decimal rounded to the nearest hundredth? C
   - (A) 0.87
   - (B) 1.01
   - (C) 1.15
   - (D) 5.68

2. The star Proxima Centauri is 24,792,500 million mi from Earth. The star Epsilon Eridani is $6.345 \times 10^{13}$ mi from Earth. In scientific notation, how much farther from Earth is Epsilon Eridani than Proxima Centauri? B
   - (A) $0.697 \times 10^{14}$ mi
   - (B) $3.866 \times 10^{13}$ mi
   - (C) $6.097 \times 10^{13}$ mi
   - (D) $38.658 \times 10^{12}$ mi

3. In 1976, the cost per gallon for regular unleaded gasoline was 61 cents. In 2002, the cost was $1.29 per gal. To the nearest percent, what was the percent of increase in the cost per gallon of gas from 1976 to 2002? D
   - (A) 1%
   - (B) 53%
   - (C) 95%
   - (D) 111%

4. The serial numbers on a particular model of personal data assistant (PDA) consist of two letters followed by five digits. How many serial numbers are possible if any letter of the alphabet and any digit 0–9 can be used in any position in the serial number? B
   - (A) 676,000,000
   - (B) 67,600,000
   - (C) 6,760,000
   - (D) 676,000

## Algebra

5. The graph shows the approximate relationship between the latitude of a location in the Northern Hemisphere and its distance in miles from the equator. If $y$ represents the distance of a location from the equator and $x$ represents the measure of latitude, which equation describes the relationship between $x$ and $y$? C
   - (A) $y = x + 69$
   - (B) $y = x + 690$
   - (C) $y = 69x$
   - (D) $y = 10x$

6. A particular prepaid phone card can be used from a pay phone. The charge is 30 cents to connect and then 4.5 cents per minute. If $y$ is the total cost of a call in cents where $x$ is the number of minutes, which equation describes the relation between $x$ and $y$? A
   - (A) $y = 4.5x + 30$
   - (B) $y = 30x + 4.5$
   - (C) $y = 0.45x + 0.30$
   - (D) $y = 0.30x + 0.45$

7. Katie drove to the lake for a weekend outing. The lake is 100 mi from her home. On the trip back, she drove for an hour, stopped for lunch for an hour, and then finished the trip home. Which graph best represents her trip home and the distance from her home at various times? B
   - (A)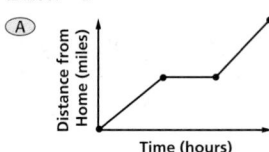
   - (B)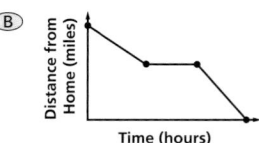
   - (C)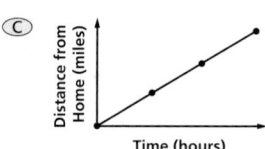
   - (D)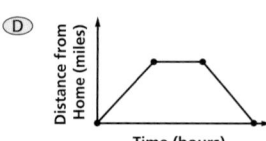

8. Temperature can be given in degrees Fahrenheit or degrees Celsius. The formula $F = \frac{9}{5}C + 32$ can be used to change any temperature given in degrees Celsius to degrees Fahrenheit. Solve the formula for $C$. A
   - (A) $C = \frac{5}{9}(F - 32)$
   - (B) $C = F + 32 - \frac{9}{5}$
   - (C) $C = \frac{5}{9}F - 32$
   - (D) $C = \frac{9}{5}(F - 32)$

## Geometry

**9.** Which of the following statements are true about the 4-in. quilt square? **E**

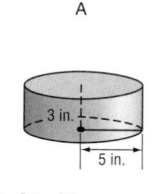

R 2 in.
2 in.
U · V · S
X · T · W

&#9398; *VSWT* is a square.

&#9399; *UVTX* ≅ *VSWT*

&#9400; Four right angles are formed at *V*.

&#9401; Only A and B are true.

&#9402; A, B, and C are true.

**10.** At the Daniels County Fair, the carnival rides are positioned as shown. What is the value of *x*? **A**

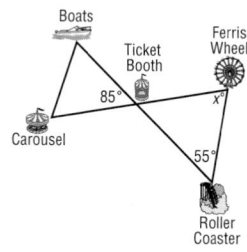

Boats
Ticket Booth    Ferris Wheel
85°         *x*°
Carousel
55°
Roller Coaster

&#9398; 40     &#9399; 47.5

&#9400; 55     &#9401; 70

&#9402; 85

**11.** The diagram shows a map of the Clearwater Wilderness hiking area. To the nearest tenth of a mile, what is the distance from the Parking Lot to Bear Ridge using the most direct route? **A**

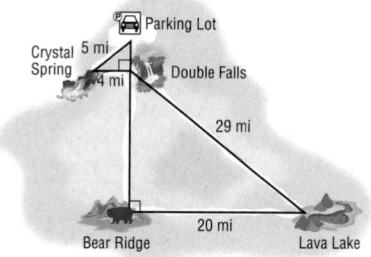

Parking Lot
Crystal Spring  5 mi
4 mi   Double Falls
29 mi
20 mi
Bear Ridge        Lava Lake

&#9398; 24 mi     &#9399; 25.5 mi

&#9400; 26 mi     &#9401; 30.4 mi

## Measurement

**12.** Laura expects about 60 people to attend a party. She estimates that she will need one quart of punch for every two people. How many gallons of punch should she prepare? **A**

&#9398; 7.5

&#9399; 15

&#9400; 30

&#9401; 34

**13.** Stone Mountain Manufacturers are designing two sizes of cylindrical cans below. What is the ratio of the volume of can A to the volume of can B? **D**

A           B

3 in.       5 in.
5 in.       3 in.

&#9398; 9 to 25     &#9399; 25 to 3

&#9400; 3 to 5     &#9401; 5 to 3

## Data Analysis and Probability

**14.** The 2000 populations of the five least-populated U.S. states are shown in the table. Which statement is true about this set of data? **E**

| State | Population |
|---|---|
| Alaska | 626,932 |
| North Dakota | 642,200 |
| South Dakota | 754,844 |
| Vermont | 608,827 |
| Wyoming | 493,782 |

&#9398; The mode of the data set is 642,200.

&#9399; The median of the data set is 626,932.

&#9400; The mean of the data set is 625,317.

&#9401; A and C are true.

&#9402; B and C are true.

# Gridded-Response Questions

Gridded-response questions are other types of questions on standardized tests. These questions are sometimes called *student-produced responses* or *grid-ins,* because you must create the answer yourself, not just choose from four or five possible answers.

For gridded response, you must mark your answer on a grid printed on an answer sheet. The grid contains a row of four or five boxes at the top, two rows of ovals or circles with decimal and fraction symbols, and four or five columns of ovals, numbered 0–9. Since there is no negative symbol on the grid, answers are never negative. At the right is an example of a grid from an answer sheet.

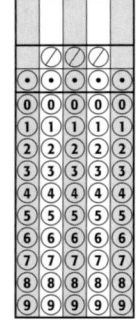

## Example 1

**Diego drove 174 mi to his grandmother's house. He made the drive in 3 h without any stops. At this rate, how far in miles can Diego drive in 5 h?**

*What value do you need to find?*

You need to find the number of miles Diego can drive in 5 h.

Write a proportion for the problem. Let $m$ represent the number of miles.

$$\text{miles} \longrightarrow \frac{174}{3} = \frac{m}{5} \longleftarrow \text{miles}$$
$$\text{hours} \longrightarrow \qquad\qquad \longleftarrow \text{hours}$$

Solve the proportion.

$\dfrac{174}{3} = \dfrac{m}{5}$  Original proportion

$870 = 3m$  Find the cross products.

$290 = m$  Divide each side by 3.

*How do you fill in the grid for the answer?*

- Write your answer in the answer boxes.

- Write only one digit or symbol in each answer box.

- Do not write any digits or symbols outside the answer boxes.

- You may write your answer with the first digit in the left answer box, or with the last digit in the right answer box. You may leave blank any boxes you do not need on the right or the left side of your answer.

- Fill in only one bubble for every answer box that you have written in. Be sure not to fill in a bubble under a blank answer box.

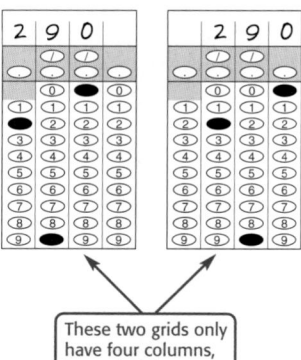

These two grids only have four columns, instead of five.

Many gridded response questions result in an answer that is a fraction or a decimal. These values can also be filled in on the grid.

## Example 2

**What is the slope of the line that passes through $(-2, 3)$ and $(2, 4)$?**

Let $(-2, 3) = (x_1, y_1)$ and $(2, 4) = (x_2, y_2)$.

$$m = \frac{y_2 - y_1}{x_2 - x_1}$$   Slope formula

$$= \frac{4 - 3}{2 - (-2)} \text{ or } \frac{1}{4}$$   Substitute and simplify.

*How do you grid the answer?*

You can either grid the fraction $\frac{1}{4}$, or rewrite it as 0.25 and grid the decimal.

Be sure to write the decimal point or fraction bar in the answer box. The following are acceptable answer responses that represent $\frac{1}{4}$ and 0.25.

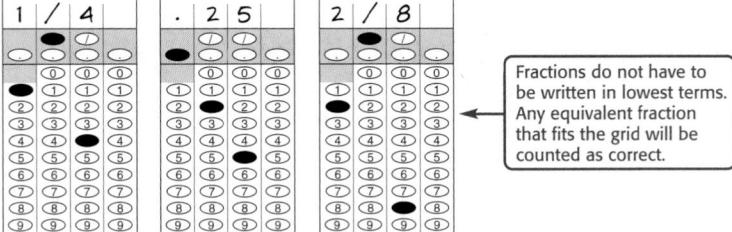

Fractions do not have to be written in lowest terms. Any equivalent fraction that fits the grid will be counted as correct.

Some problems may result in an answer that is a mixed number. Before filling in the grid, change the mixed number to an equivalent improper fraction or decimal. For example, if the answer is $1\frac{1}{2}$, do not enter 11/2 as this will be interpreted as $\frac{11}{2}$. Instead, either enter 3/2 or 1.5.

## Example 3

**Amber's cookie recipe calls for $1\frac{1}{3}$ c of coconut. If Amber plans to make 4 batches of cookies, how much coconut does she need?**

Find the amount of coconut needed using a proportion.

coconut → $\dfrac{1\frac{1}{3}}{1} = \dfrac{x}{4}$ ← batches

$$4\left(1\frac{1}{3}\right) = 1x$$

$$4\left(\frac{4}{3}\right) = x$$

$$\frac{16}{3} = x$$

Do not leave a blank answer box in the middle of an answer.

Leave the answer as the improper fraction $\frac{16}{3}$, as you cannot correctly grid $5\frac{1}{3}$.

# Gridded-Response Practice

Solve each problem. Then copy and complete a grid like the one shown on page 632.

## Number and Operations

1. China has the most days of school per year for children with 251 days. If there are 365 days in a year, what percent of the days of the year do Chinese students spend in school? Round to the nearest tenth of a percent.   68.8

2. Charles is building a deck and wants to buy some long boards that he can cut into various lengths without wasting any lumber. He would like to cut any board into all lengths of 24 in., 48 in., or 60 in. In feet, what is the shortest length of boards that he can buy?   20

3. At a sale, an item was discounted 20%. After several weeks, the sale price was discounted an additional 25%. What was the total percent discount from the original price of the item?  40

4. The Andromeda Spiral galaxy is $2.2 \times 10^6$ light-years from Earth. The Ursa Minor dwarf is $2.5 \times 10^5$ light-years from Earth. How many times as far is the Andromeda Spiral as Ursa Minor dwarf from Earth?   8.8

5. Twenty students want to attend the World Language Convention. The school budget will only allow for four students to attend. In how many ways can four students be chosen from the twenty students to attend the convention? 4845

## Algebra

6. Find the $y$-intercept of the graph of the equation $3x + 4y - 5 = 0$.  5/4 or 1.25

7. Name the $x$-coordinate of the solution of the system of equations $2x - y = 7$ and $3x + 2y = 7$. 3

8. Solve $2b - 2(3b - 5) = 8(b - 7)$ for $b$. 11/2 or 5.5

9. Kersi read 36 pages of a novel in 2 h. Find the number of hours it will take him to read the remaining 135 pages if he reads them at the same rate?   15/2 or 7.5

10. The endpoints of a segment are $(-5, 7)$ and $(-2, 9)$. Find the length to the nearest tenth. 3.6

11. Ms. Blackwell needs to rent a car for her family vacation. She has found a company that offers the following two options.

| Plan | Flat Rate | Cost per Mile |
|------|-----------|---------------|
| Option A | $40 | $0.25 |
| Option B | $30 | $0.35 |

How many miles must the Blackwells drive for the plans to cost the same?   100

## Geometry

12. Triangle $MNP$ is reflected over the $x$-axis. What is the $x$-coordinate of the image of point $N$?   2

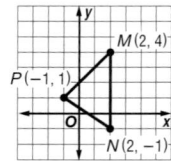

13. The pattern for the square tile shown in the diagram is to be enlarged so that it will measure 15 in. on a side. By what scale factor must the pattern be enlarged?   24

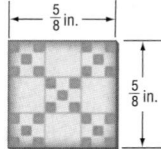

14. Find the measure of $\angle A$ to the nearest degree. 56

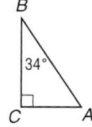

### Test-Taking Tip

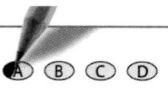

**Question 14**
Remember that the hypotenuse of a right triangle is always opposite the right angle.

**15.** ∠KLM and ∠XYZ are complementary. If m∠KLM = 3x − 1 and m∠XYZ = x + 7, find the measure of the larger angle.  62

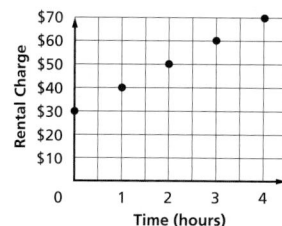

**16.** A triangle has a perimeter of 96 cm. The ratio of measures of its three sides is 6:8:10. Find the length of the longest side in centimeters.  40

**17.** The scale on a map of Texas is 0.75 in. = 5 mi. The distance on the map from San Antonio to Dallas is 8.25 in. What is the actual distance from San Antonio to Dallas in miles?  275

## Measurement

**18.** Pluto is the farthest planet from the Sun in this solar system at 2756 million mi. If light travels at 186,000 mi/sec, how many minutes does it take for a particular ray of light to reach Pluto from the Sun? Round to the nearest minute.  247

**19.** Noah drove 342 mi and used 12 gal of gas. At this same rate, how many gallons of gas will he use on his entire trip of 1140 mi?  40

**20.** The jumping surface of a trampoline is shaped like a circle with a diameter of 14 ft. Find the area of the jumping surface. Use 3.14 for π and round to the nearest square foot.  154

**21.** A cone is drilled out of a cylinder of wood. If the cone and cylinder have the same base and height, find the volume of the remaining wood. Use 3.14 for π and round to the nearest cubic inch.  1055

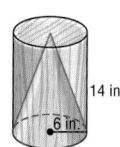

**22.** Chi-Yo wants to make a quilt pattern using similar triangles as shown. What is the length of the third side of the larger triangle?  7.5

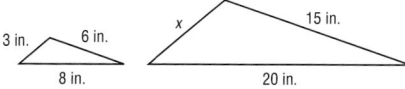

## Data Analysis and Probability

**23.** The table shows the average size in acres of farms in the six states with the largest farms. Find the median of the farm data in acres.  2600

| Average Size of Farms for 2001 | |
|---|---|
| **State** | **Acres per Farm** |
| Alaska | 1586 |
| Arizona | 3644 |
| Montana | 2124 |
| Nevada | 2267 |
| New Mexico | 2933 |
| Wyoming | 3761 |

**24.** The Lindley Park Pavilion is available to rent for parties. There is a fee to rent the pavilion and then a charge per hour. The graph shows the total amount you would pay to rent the pavilion for various numbers of hours. If a function is written to model the charge to rent the pavilion, where x is the number of hours and y is the total charge, what is the slope of the function?  10

**25.** A particular game is played by rolling three tetrahedral (4-sided) dice. The faces of each die are numbered with the digits 1–4. How many outcomes are in the sample space for the event of rolling the three dice once?  64

**26.** In a carnival game, the blindfolded contestant draws two toy ducks from a pond without replacement. The pond contains 2 yellow ducks, 10 black ducks, 22 white ducks, and 8 red ducks. The best prize is won by drawing two yellow ducks. What is the probability of drawing two yellow ducks? Write your answer as a percent rounded to the nearest tenth of a percent.  0.1

# Short-Response Questions

Short-response questions require you to provide a solution to the problem, as well as any method, explanation, and/or justification you used to arrive at the solution. These are sometimes called *constructed-response, open-response, open-ended, free-response,* or *student-produced questions.* The following is a sample rubric, or scoring guide, for scoring short-response questions.

| Credit | Score | Criteria |
|--------|-------|----------|
| Full | 2 | Full credit: The answer is correct and a full explanation is provided that shows each step in arriving at the final answer. |
| Partial | 1 | Partial credit: There are two different ways to receive partial credit.<br>• The answer is correct, but the explanation provided is incomplete or incorrect.<br>• The answer is incorrect, but the explanation and method of solving the problem is correct. |
| None | 0 | No credit: Either an answer is not provided or the answer does not make sense. |

On some standardized tests, no credit is given for a correct answer if your work is not shown.

## Example

Susana is painting two large rooms at her art studio. She has calculated that each room has 4000 ft$^2$ to be painted. It says on the can of paint that one gallon covers 300 ft$^2$ of smooth surface for one coat and that two coats should be applied for best results. What is the minimum number of 5-gal cans of paint Susana needs to buy to apply two coats in the two rooms of her studio?

**FULL CREDIT SOLUTION**

First find the total number of square feet to be painted.
$$4000 \times 2 = 8000 \text{ ft}^2$$
Since 1 gal covers 300 ft$^2$, multiply 8000 ft$^2$ by the unit rate $\frac{1 \text{ gal}}{300 \text{ ft}^2}$.
$$8000 \text{ ft}^2 \times \frac{1 \text{ gal}}{300 \text{ ft}^2} = \frac{8000}{300} \text{ gal}$$
$$= 26\frac{2}{3} \text{ gal}$$
Each can of paint contains 5 gal, so divide $26\frac{2}{3}$ gal by 5 gal.
$$26\frac{2}{3} \div 5 = \frac{80}{3} \div 5 = \frac{\overset{16}{\cancel{80}}}{3} \times \frac{1}{\underset{1}{\cancel{5}}} = \frac{16}{3} = 5\frac{1}{3}$$
Since Susana cannot buy a fraction of a can of paint, she needs to but 6 cans of paint.

The steps, calculations, and reasoning are clearly stated.

The solution of the problem is clearly stated.

## PARTIAL CREDIT SOLUTION

In this sample solution, the answer is correct; however there is no justification for any of the calculations.

There is no explanation of how $26\frac{2}{3}$ was obtained.

$$26\frac{2}{3} \div 5 = \frac{80}{3} \div 5$$

$$= \frac{\overset{16}{\cancel{80}}}{3} \times \frac{1}{\underset{1}{\cancel{5}}}$$

$$= \frac{16}{3}$$

$$= 5\frac{1}{3}$$

Susana will need to buy 6 cans of paint.

## PARTIAL CREDIT SOLUTION

In this sample solution, the answer is incorrect. However, after the first statement, all of the calculations and reasoning are correct.

There are 4000 ft² to be painted and one gallon of paint covers 300 ft².

$$4000\,ft^2 \times \frac{1\,gal}{300\,ft^2} = \frac{4000}{300}\,gal$$

$$= 13\frac{1}{3}\,gal$$

The first step of doubling the square footage for painting the second room was left out.

Each can of paint contains five gallons. So 2 cans would contain 10 gal, which is not enough. Three cans of paint would contain 15 gal which is enough.

Therefore, Susana will need to buy 3 cans of paint.

## NO CREDIT SOLUTION

The wrong operations are used, so the answer is incorrect. Also, there are no units of measure given with any of the calculations.

$300 \times 2 = 600$

$600 \div 5 = 120$

$4000 \div 120 = 33\frac{1}{3}$

Susana will need 34 cans of paint.

# Short-Response Practice

**Solve each problem. Show all your work.**

## Number and Operations

1. The world's slowest fish is the sea horse. The average speed of a sea horse is 0.001 mi/h. What is the rate of speed of a sea horse in feet per minute?   0.088 ft/min

2. Two buses arrive at the Central Avenue bus stop at 8 A.M. The route for the City Loop bus takes 35 min, while the route for the By-Pass bus takes 20 min. What is the next time that the two buses will both be at the Central Avenue bus stop?   10:20 A.M.

3. Toya's Clothing World purchased some denim jackets for $35. The jackets are marked up 40%. Later in the season, the jackets are discounted 25%. How much does the store lose or gain on the sale of one jacket at the discounted price?   gain of $1.75

4. A femtosecond is $10^{-15}$ sec, and a millisecond is $10^{-3}$ sec. How many times faster is a millisecond than a femtosecond?
$10^{12}$ times greater

5. Find the next three terms in the sequence.
$$1, 3, 9, 27, \ldots \quad 81, 243, 729$$

## Algebra

6. Find the slope of the graph of $5x - 2y + 1 = 0.$   $\frac{5}{2}$ or 2.5

7. Simplify $5 + x(1 - x) + 3x.$ Write the result in the form $ax^2 + bx + c.$   $-x^2 + 4x + 5$

8. Solve $17 - 3x \geq 23.$   $x \leq -2$

9. The table shows what Gerardo charges in dollars for his consulting services for various numbers of hours. Write an equation that can be used to find the charge for any amount of time, where $y$ is the total charge in dollars and $x$ is the number of hours.   $y = 25 + 15x$

| Hours | Charge | Hours | Charge |
|-------|--------|-------|--------|
| 0     | $25    | 2     | $55    |
| 1     | $40    | 3     | $70    |

10. The population of Clark County, Nevada, was 1,375,765 in 2000 and 1,464,653 in 2001. Let $x$ represent the years since 2000 and $y$ represent the total population of Clark County. Suppose the county continues to increase at the same rate. Write an equation that represents the population of the county for any year after 2000.   $y = 88{,}888x + 1{,}375{,}765$

## Geometry

11. Triangle $ABC$ is dilated with scale factor 2.5. Find the coordinates of dilated $\triangle A'B'C'.$
$A'(2.5, 2.5), B'(5, -5), C'(-5, -2.5)$

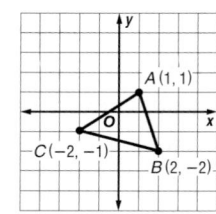

12. At a particular time in its flight, a plane is 10,000 ft above a lake. The distance from the lake to the airport is 5 mi. Find the distance in feet from the plane to the airport.
about 28,230 ft

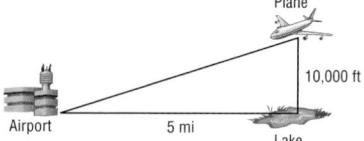

13. Refer to the diagram of the two similar triangles below. Find the value of $a.$   61.5

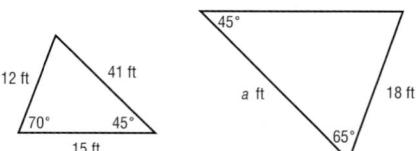

14. The vertices of two triangles are $P(3, 3),$ $Q(7, 3), R(3, 10),$ and $S(-1, 4), T(3, 4),$ $U(-1, 11).$ Which transformation moves $\triangle PQR$ to $\triangle STU?$   translation $(x - 4), (y + 1)$

**15.** Find the coordinates of the vertices of quadrilateral $G'H'I'J'$ after a reflection of quadrilateral $GHIJ$ across the $x$-axis.

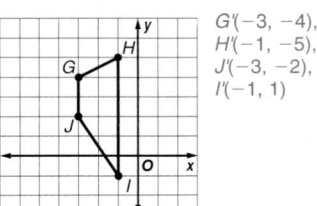

$G'(-3, -4),$
$H'(-1, -5),$
$J'(-3, -2),$
$I'(-1, 1)$

**20.** A child's portable swimming pool is 6 ft across and is filled to a depth of 8 in. One gallon of water is 231 in.³. What is the volume of water in the pool in gallons? Use 3.14 as an approximation for $\pi$ and round to the nearest gallon.   141 gal

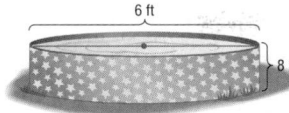

6 ft

8 in.

---

## Measurement

**16.** One inch is equivalent to approximately 2.54 cm. Nikki is 61 in. tall. What is her height in centimeters?   154.94 cm

**17.** During the holidays, Evan works at Cheese Haus. He packages gift baskets containing a variety of cheeses and sausages. During one four-hour shift, he packaged 20 baskets. At this rate, how many baskets will he package if he works 26 h in one week?   130 baskets

**18.** Ms. Ortega built a box for her garden and placed a round barrel inside to be used for a fountain in the center of the box. The barrel touches the box at its sides as shown. She wants to put potting soil in the shaded corners of the box at a depth of 6 in. How many cubic feet of soil will she need? Use 3.14 for $\pi$ and round to the nearest tenth of a cubic foot.   1.7 ft³

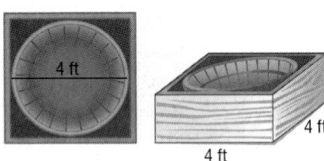

4 ft

4 ft

4 ft

**19.** A line segment has its midpoint located at $(1, -5)$ and one endpoint at $(-2, -7)$. Find the length of the line to the nearest tenth.   7.2

---

### Test-Taking Tip

Ⓐ Ⓑ Ⓒ Ⓓ

**Question 20**

Most standardized tests will include any commonly used formulas at the front of the test booklet. Quickly review the list before you begin so that you know what formulas are available.

---

## Data Analysis and Probability

**21.** The table shows the five lowest recorded temperatures on Earth. Find the mean of the temperatures.   $-108.16°F$

| Location | Temperature (°F) |
|---|---|
| Vostok, Antarctica | −138.6 |
| Plateau Station, Antarctica | −129.2 |
| Oymyakon, Russia | −96.0 |
| Verkhoyansk, Russia | −90.0 |
| Northice, Greenland | −87.0 |

**22.** Two six-sided dice are rolled. The sum of the numbers of dots on the faces of the two dice is recorded. What is the probability that the sum is 10?   $\frac{1}{12}$

**23.** The table shows the amount of a particular chemical that is needed to treat various sizes of swimming pools. Write the equation for a line to model the data. Let $x$ represent the capacity of the pool in gallons and $y$ represent the amount of the chemical in ounces.   $y = 0.003x$

| Pool Capacity (gal) | Amount of Chemical (oz) |
|---|---|
| 5000 | 15 |
| 10,000 | 30 |
| 15,000 | 45 |
| 20,000 | 60 |
| 25,000 | 75 |

**24.** Fifty balls are placed in a bin. They are labeled from 1 through 50. Two balls are drawn without replacement. What is the probability that both balls show an even number?   $\frac{12}{49}$

# Extended-Response Questions

Extended-response questions are often called *open-ended* or *constructed-response questions*. Most extended-response questions have multiple parts. You must answer all parts correctly to receive full credit.

Extended-response questions are similar to short-response questions in that you must show all of your work in solving the problem, and a rubric is used to determine whether you receive full, partial, or no credit. The following is a sample rubric for scoring extended-response questions.

| Credit | Score | Criteria |
|--------|-------|----------|
| Full | 4 | A correct solution is given that is supported by well-developed, accurate explanations. |
| Partial | 3, 2, 1 | A generally correct solution is given that may contain minor flaws in reasoning or computation or an incomplete solution. The more correct the solution, the greater the score. |
| None | 0 | An incorrect solution is given indicating no mathematical understanding of the concept, or no solution is given. |

On some standardized tests, no credit is given for a correct answer if your work is not shown.

Make sure that when the problem says to *Show your work,* show every aspect of your solution including figures, sketches of graphing calculator screens, or reasoning behind computations.

## Example 1

The table shows the population density in the United States on April 1 in each decade of the 20th century.

**a.** Make a scatter plot of the data.

**b.** Alaska and Hawaii became states in the same year. Between what two census dates do you think this happened. Why did you choose those years?

**c.** Use the data and your graph to predict the population density in 2010. Explain your reasoning.

| U.S. Population Density | |
|---|---|
| Year | People Per Square Mile |
| 1910 | 31.0 |
| 1920 | 35.6 |
| 1930 | 41.2 |
| 1940 | 44.2 |
| 1950 | 50.7 |
| 1960 | 50.6 |
| 1970 | 57.4 |
| 1980 | 64.0 |
| 1990 | 70.3 |
| 2000 | 79.6 |

**FULL CREDIT SOLUTION**

**Part a** A complete scatter plot includes a title for the graph, appropriate scales and labels for the axes, and correctly graphed points.

- The student should determine that the year data should go on the $x$-axis while the people per square mile data should go on the $y$-axis.

- On the $x$-axis, each square should represent 10 years.

- The $y$-axis could start at 0, or it could show data starting at 30 with a broken line to indicate that some of the scale is missing.

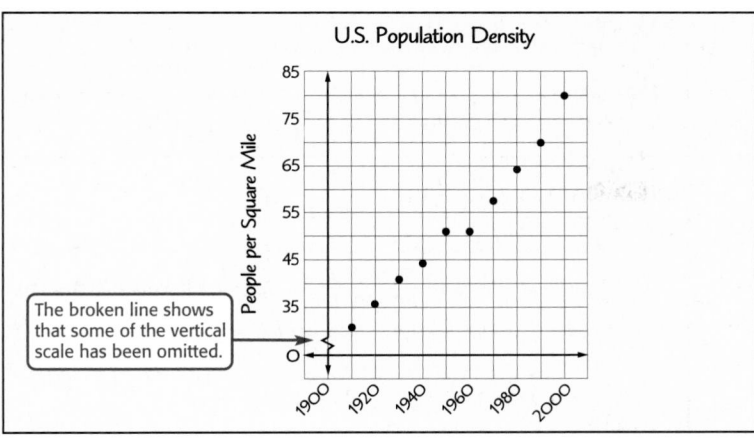

U.S. Population Density

People per Square Mile

The broken line shows that some of the vertical scale has been omitted.

You might know when Alaska became a state. So, another acceptable reason is that both Alaska and Hawaii became states in 1959.

**Part b**

1950–1960 because when Alaska became a state it added little population but a lot of land, which made the people per square mile ratio less.

**Part c**

About 85.0, because the population per square mile would probably get larger so I connected the first point and the last point. The rate of change for each year was $\frac{79.6 - 31.0}{2000 - 1910}$ or about 0.54. I added $10 \times 0.54$, or 5.4 to 79.6 to get the next 10-year point.

Actually, any estimate from 84 to 86 might be acceptable. You could also use different points to find the equation for a line of best fit for the data, and then find the corresponding $y$ value for $x = 2010$.

### PARTIAL CREDIT SOLUTION

**Part a** This sample answer includes no labels for the graph or the axes and one of the points is not graphed correctly.

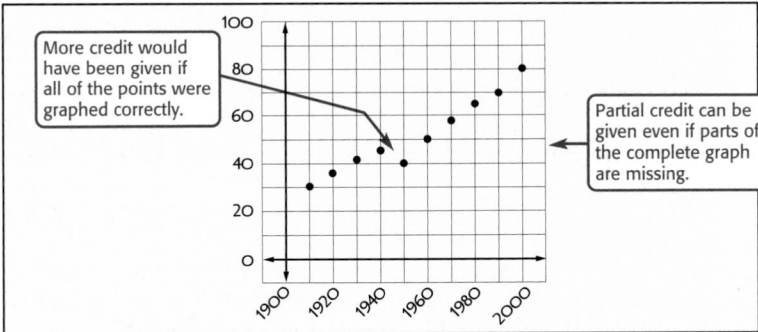

More credit would have been given if all of the points were graphed correctly.

Partial credit can be given even if parts of the complete graph are missing.

**Part b** Partial credit is given because the reasoning is correct, but the reasoning was based on the incorrect graph in Part a.

> 1940–1950, because when Alaska became a state it added little population but a lot of land, which made the people per square mile ratio less.

**Part c** Full credit is given for Part c.

> Suppose I draw a line of best fit through points (1910, 31.0) and (1990, 70.3). The slope would be $\frac{70.3-31.0}{1990-1910}$ or about 0.49. Now use the slope and one of the points to find the y-intercept.
>
> $y = mx + b$   So an equation of my
> $70.3 = 0.49(1990) + b$   line of best fit is
> $-904.8 = b$   $y = 0.49x - 904.8$.
>
> If $x = 2010$, then $y = 0.49(2010) - 904.8$ or about 80.1 people per square mile in the year 2010.

This sample answer might have received a score of 2 or 1. Had the student graphed all points correctly and gotten Part B correct, the score would probably have been a 3.

### NO CREDIT SOLUTION

**Part a**

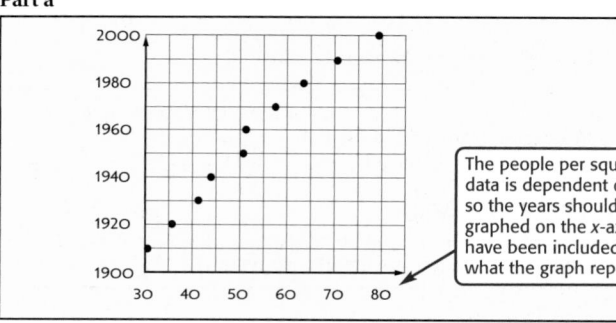

The people per square mile data is dependent on the year, so the years should have been graphed on the x-axis. No labels have been included to identify what the graph represents.

**Part b**

> I have no idea.

**Part c**

> 85, because it is the next grid line.

In this sample answer, the student does not understand how to represent data on a graph or how to interpret the data after the points are graphed.

# Extended Response Practice

Solve each problem. Show all your work.

## Number and Operations

1. The table shows what one dollar in U.S. money was worth in five countries in 1970 and in 2001. a–c. See margin.

| Money Equivalent to One U.S. Dollar | | |
|---|---|---|
| Country | 1970 Value | 2001 Value |
| France | 5.5 francs | 7 francs |
| Germany | 3.6 marks | 2 marks |
| Great Britain | 0.4 pounds | 0.67 pounds |
| Italy | 623 lire | 2040 lire |
| Japan | 358 yen | 117 yen |

a. For which country was the percent of increase or decrease in the number of units of currency that was equivalent to $1 the greatest from 1970 to 2001?

b. Suppose a U.S. citizen traveled to Germany in 1970 and in 2001. In which year would the traveler receive a better value for their money? Explain.

c. In 2001, what was the value of one franc in yen?

2. The table shows some data about the planets and the Sun. The radius is given in miles and the volume, mass, and gravity quantities are related to the volume and mass of Earth, which has a value of 1. a–c. See margin.

| | Volume | Mass | Density | Radius | Gravity |
|---|---|---|---|---|---|
| Sun | 1,304,000 | 332,950 | 0.26 | 434,474 | 28 |
| Mercury | 0.056 | 0.0553 | 0.98 | 1516 | 0.38 |
| Venus | 0.857 | 0.815 | 0.95 | 3760 | 0.91 |
| Moon | 0.0203 | 0.0123 | 0.61 | 1079 | 0.17 |
| Mars | 0.151 | 0.107 | 0.71 | 2106 | 0.38 |
| Jupiter | 1321 | 317.83 | 0.24 | 43,441 | 2.36 |
| Saturn | 764 | 95.16 | 0.12 | 36,184 | 0.92 |
| Uranus | 63 | 14.54 | 0.23 | 15,759 | 0.89 |
| Neptune | 58 | 17.15 | 0.30 | 15,301 | 1.12 |
| Pluto | 0.007 | 0.0021 | 0.32 | 743 | 0.06 |

a. Make and test a conjecture relating volume, mass, and density.

b. Describe the relationship between radius and gravity.

c. Can you be sure that the relationship in part b holds true for all planets? Explain.

## Algebra

3. The graph shows the altitude of a glider during various times of his flight after being released from a tow plane. a–e. See margin.

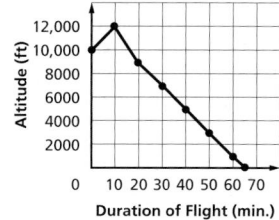

a. What point on the graph represents the moment the glider was released from the tow plane? Explain the meaning of this point in terms of altitude.

b. During which time period did the greatest rate of descent of the glider take place? Explain your reasoning.

c. How long did it take the glider to reach an altitude of 0 ft? Where is this point on the graph?

d. What is the equation of a line that represents the glider's altitude $y$ as the time increased from 20 to 60 min?

e. Explain what the slope of the line in part d represents?

4. John has just received his learner's permit which allows him to practice driving with a licensed driver. His mother has agreed to take him driving every day for two weeks. On the first day, John will drive for 20 min. Each day after that, John's mother has agreed he can drive 15 min more than the day before. b–c. See margin.

a. Describe the pattern.

b. For how many minutes will John drive on the last day? Show how you found the number of minutes.

c. John's driver's education teacher requires that each student drive for 30 h with an adult outside of class. Will John fulfill this requirement? Explain.

4a. The first term is 20. Add 15 to each consecutive term.

## ADDITIONAL ANSWERS

1a. Italy had a 227% increase.

1b. 1970; you could get more marks for every U.S. dollar and buy more merchandise.

1c. There were about 16.7 yen for 1 franc.

2a. Sample answer: In each case, mass ÷ volume is approximately equal to the density.

2b. Sample answer: The greater the radius, the greater the gravity. However, the relationship does not look like it is strictly linear.

2c. Sample answer: No, you would need to examine the similar statistics for all the planets.

3a. The glider was released when $x = 0$. The altitude of 10,000 feet is the altitude of the glider upon release.

3b. During 10 to 20 minutes after release, the rate of descent was greatest as the slope of the line is greatest and the line is steepest.

3c. It appears to have taken about 65 minutes. It is the $x$-intercept, where the altitude $y$ is 0.

3d. $y = -200x + 13,000$

3e. The slope is the rate of descent of the glider, which is 200 feet per minute.

4a. $a_n = 5 + 15n$; If $x$ represents the days and $y$ represents the number of minutes, Anna will drive 20 minutes on the first day (1, 20) and 35 minutes on the second day (2, 35). Using these points, I found the point-slope form of the equation to be $y = 15x + 5$. Then, I changed the equation into the formula with variables $a_n$ and $n$.

4b. $a_{14} = 5 + 15(14)$ or 215 minutes; sample answer: I substituted $n = 14$ days into the formula.

4c. No; the total of all the minutes for 14 days is only 1645 minutes while 30 hours is 1800 minutes. He will be short 155 minutes.

## ADDITIONAL ANSWERS

**5a.** $Q'(-2, 3)$, $U'(-2, -2)$, $A'(4, -3)$, $D'(1, 2)$; sample answer: Since the reflection occurred over the $y$-axis, I found the opposite of the $x$-coordinate for each point.

**5b.** $(-a, b)$

**5c.** A reflection over the $x$-axis will make the polygon look "upside down." The coordinates of the vertices will be $Q'(2, -3)$, $U'(2, 2)$, $A'(-4, 3)$, $D'(-1, -2)$.

**6a.** The ratio is 4 to 3.

**6b.** The ratio is 1 to 1.

**6c.** Sample answer: $r = a$; $h = 4a$

**7a.** The distance is 105 kilometers. Sample answer: I set up the proportion $\frac{2\,cm}{30\,km} = \frac{7\,cm}{x\,cm}$; $x = 105$.

**7b.** The distance is 74.4 miles.

**7c.** She will need about 20 gallons. Sample answer: I found 54 cm = 810 km = 502.2 mi. Then I divided 25 mi/gal into 502.2 mi to get 20.088 gal.

**8a.** The area of region 6 is about 12.4 in².

**8b.** The area of region 1 is about 2.4 in².

**8c.** $\frac{\pi}{25}$; Sample answer: The area of region 5 is $\frac{1}{4}\pi 2^2$, or $\pi$ in². The area of the square is $5^2$ or 25, so the ratio is $\pi$ to 25 of $\frac{\pi}{25}$.

**9a.**
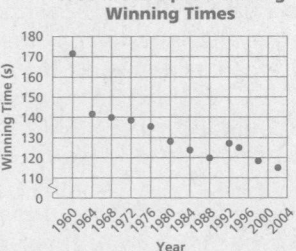
1500-Meter Speed Skating Winning Times

**9b.** Sample answer: In recent years, the times have decreased by 4 seconds every 4 years. Since 2010 is 8 years from 2002, the winning time in 2010 will be $114 - 2(4)$ or 106 seconds.

**10a.** There are 12 students on the debate team because there are $12 \cdot 11 \cdot 10$ or 1320 ways for three students to win the top three places during the debate.

**10b.** $\frac{\text{ways to come in the first 3 places}}{\text{number of students}} =$

$\frac{3}{20}$ or 15%

**10c.** $\frac{2}{19}$ or about 10.5%

## Geometry

**5.** Polygon *QUAD* is shown on a coordinate plane.

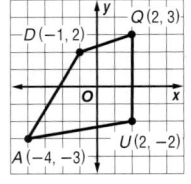

**a.** Find the coordinates of the vertices of $Q'U'A'D'$, which is the image of *QUAD* after a reflection over the $y$-axis. Explain.

**b.** Suppose point $M(a, b)$ is reflected over the $y$-axis. What will be the coordinates of the image $M'$?   a–c. See margin.

**c.** Describe a reflection that will make *QUAD* look "upside down." What will be the coordinates of the vertices of the image?

**6.** The diagram shows a sphere with a radius of $a$ and a cylinder with a radius and a height of $a$.
a–c. See margin.

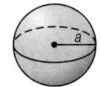 

**a.** What is the ratio of the volume of the sphere to the volume of the cylinder?

**b.** What is the ratio of the surface area of the sphere to the surface area of the cylinder?

**c.** The ratio of the volume of another cylinder is 3 times the volume of the sphere shown. Give one possible set of measures for the radius and height of the cylinder in terms of $a$.

## Measurement

**7.** Alexis is using a map of the province of Saskatchewan in Canada. The scale for the map shows that 2 cm on the map is 30 km in actual distance. a–c. See margin.

**a.** The distance on the map between two cities measures 7 cm. What is the actual distance between the two cities in kilometers? Show how you found the distance.

### Test-Taking Tip

Ⓐ Ⓑ Ⓒ Ⓓ

**Question 5**
In a reflection over the $x$-axis, the $x$-coordinate remains the same, and the $y$-coordinate changes its sign. In a reflection over the $y$-axis, the $y$-coordinate remains the same, and the $x$-coordinate changes its sign.

**b.** Alexis is more familiar with distances in miles. The distance between two other cities is 8 cm. If one kilometer is about 0.62 mi, what is the distance in miles?

**c.** Alexis' entire trip measures 54 cm. If her car averages 25 mi/gal of gasoline, how many gallons will she need to complete the trip? Round to the nearest gallon. Explain.

**8.** The diagram shows a pattern for a quilt square called Colorful Fan.

**a.** What is the area of region 6? Explain.

**b.** What is the area of region 1? Explain.   a–c. See margin.

**c.** What is the ratio of the area of region 5 to the area of the entire square? Show how you found the ratio. Leave the ratio in terms of $\pi$.

## Data Analysis and Probability

**9.** The table shows the Olympics winning times in the women's 1500-meter speed skating event. The times are to the nearest second.

| Year | Time (s) | Year | Time (s) |
|------|----------|------|----------|
| 1960 | 172 | 1984 | 124 |
| 1964 | 143 | 1988 | 121 |
| 1968 | 142 | 1992 | 126 |
| 1972 | 141 | 1994 | 122 |
| 1976 | 137 | 1998 | 118 |
| 1980 | 131 | 2002 | 114 |

**a.** Make a scatter plot of the data.   a–b. See margin.

**b.** Use the data and your graph to predict the winning time in 2010.

**10.** There are 1320 ways for three students to win first, second, and third place during a debate.
a–c. See margin.

**a.** How many students are on the debate team?

**b.** What is the probability that a student will come in one of the first three places if each student has an equal chance of succeeding?

**c.** If the teacher announces the third place winner, what is the probability that one particular other student will win first or second place?

# Technology Reference Guide

## Graphing Calculator Overview

This section summarizes some of the graphing calculator skills you might use in your mathematics classes using the TI-83 Plus or TI-84 Plus.

### General Information

- Any yellow commands written above the calculator keys are accessed with the 2nd key, which is also yellow. Similarly, any green characters or commands above the keys are accessed with the ALPHA key, which is also green. In this text, commands that are accessed by the 2nd and ALPHA keys are shown in brackets. For example, 2nd **[QUIT]** means to press the 2nd key followed by the key below the yellow **[QUIT]** command.
- 2nd **[ENTRY]** copies the previous calculation so it can be edited or reused.
- 2nd **[ANS]** copies the previous answer so it can be used in another calculation.
- 2nd **[QUIT]** will return you to the home (or text) screen.
- 2nd **[A-LOCK]** allows you to use the green characters above the keys without pressing ALPHA before typing each letter.
- Negative numbers are entered using the (−) key, not the minus sign, − .
- The variable $x$ can be entered using the X,T,θ,$n$ key, rather than using ALPHA **[X]**.
- 2nd **[OFF]** turns the calculator off.

---

### Key Skills

Use this section as a reference for further instruction. For additional features, consult the TI-83 Plus or TI-84 Plus user's manual.

#### ENTERING AND GRAPHING EQUATIONS

Press Y= . Use the X,T,θ,$n$ key to enter *any* variable for your equation. To see a graph of the equation, press GRAPH .

#### SETTING YOUR VIEWING WINDOW

Press WINDOW . Use the arrow or ENTER keys to move the cursor and edit the window settings. Xmin and Xmax represent the minimum and maximum values along the $x$-axis. Similarly, Ymin and Ymax represent the minimum and maximum values along the $y$-axis. Xscl and Yscl refer to the spacing between tick marks placed on the $x$- and $y$-axes. Suppose Xscl = 1. Then the numbers along the $x$-axis progress by 1 unit. Set Xres to 1.

#### THE STANDARD VIEWING WINDOW

A good window to start with to graph an equation is the **standard viewing window.** It appears in the WINDOW screen as follows.

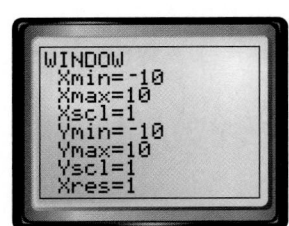

To easily set the values for the standard viewing window, press ZOOM 6.

#### ZOOM FEATURES

To easily access a viewing window that shows only integer coordinates, press ZOOM 8 ENTER .

To easily access a viewing window for statistical graphs of data you have entered, press ZOOM 9.

### USING THE TRACE FEATURE

To trace a graph, press TRACE . A flashing cursor appears on a point of your graph. At the bottom of the screen, *x*- and *y*-coordinates for the point are shown. At the top left of the screen, the equation of the graph is shown. Use the left and right arrow keys to move the cursor along the graph. Notice how the coordinates change as the cursor moves from one point to the next. If more than one equation is graphed, use the up and down arrow keys to move from one graph to another.

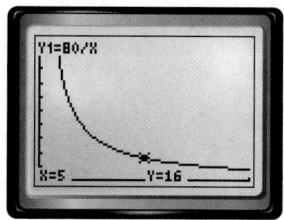

### SETTING OR MAKING A TABLE

Press 2nd [TBLSET]. Use the arrow or ENTER keys to move the cursor and edit the table settings. Indpnt represents the *x*-variable in your equation. Set Indpnt to *Ask* so that you may enter any value for *x* into your table. Depend represents the *y*-variable in your equation. Set Depend to *Auto* so that the calculator will find *y* for any value of *x*.

### USING THE TABLE

Before using the table, you must enter at least one equation in the Y= screen. Then press 2nd [TABLE]. Enter any value for *x* as shown at the bottom of the screen. The function entered as Y1 will be evaluated at this value for *x*. In the two columns labeled X and Y1, you will see the values for *x* that you entered and the resulting *y*-values.

### PROGRAMMING ON THE TI–83 PLUS

When you press PRGM , you see three menus: EXEC, EDIT, and NEW. EXEC allows you to execute a stored program by selecting the name of the program from the menu. EDIT allows you to edit or change an existing program. NEW allows you to create a new program. For additional programming features, consult the TI–83 Plus or TI–84 Plus user's manual.

### ENTERING INEQUALITIES

Press 2nd [TEST]. From this menu, you can enter the $=$, $\neq$, $>$, $\geq$, $<$, and $\leq$ symbols.

### ENTERING AND DELETING LISTS

Press STAT ENTER. Under L1, enter your list of numerical data. To delete the data in the list, use your arrow keys to highlight L1. Press CLEAR ENTER. Remember to clear all lists before entering a new set of data.

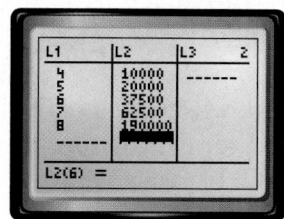

### PLOTTING STATISTICAL DATA IN LISTS

Press Y= . If appropriate, clear equations. Use the arrow keys until Plot1 is highlighted. Plot1 represents a Stat Plot, which enables you to graph the numerical data in the lists. Press ENTER to turn the Stat Plot on and off. You may need to display different types of statistical graphs. To see the details of a Stat Plot, press 2nd [STAT PLOT] ENTER. A screen like the one below appears.

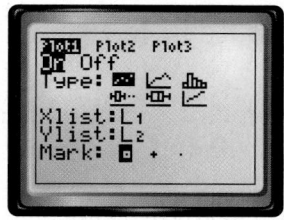

At the top of the screen, you can choose from one of three plots to store settings. The second line allows you to turn a Stat Plot on and off. Then you may select the type of plot: scatter plot, line plot, histogram, two types of box-and-whisker plots, or a normal probability plot. Next, choose which lists of data you would like to display along the *x*- and *y*-axes. Finally, choose the symbol that will represent each data point.

# Cabri Jr. Overview

Cabri Junior for the TI-83 Plus and TI-84 Plus is a geometry application that is designed to reproduce the look and feel of a computer on a handheld device.

## General Information

***Starting Cabri Jr.*** To start Cabri Jr., press APPS and choose Cabri Jr. Press any key to continue. If you have not run the program on your calculator before, the F1 menu will be displayed. To leave the menu and obtain a blank screen, press CLEAR. If you have run the program before, the last screen that was in the program before it was turned off will appear. See Quitting Cabri Jr. for instructions on clearing this screen to obtain a blank screen.

In Cabri Jr., the four arrow keys (◀, ▶, ▼, ▲), along with ENTER, operate as a mouse would on a computer. The arrows simulate moving a mouse, and ENTER simulates a left click on a mouse. For example, when you are to select an item, use the arrow keys to point to the selected item and then press ENTER. You will know you are accurately pointing to the selected item when the item, such as a point or line, is blinking.

***Quitting Cabri Jr.*** To quit Cabri Jr., press 2nd [QUIT], or [OFF] to completely shut off the calculator. Leaving the calculator unattended for approximately 4 minutes will trigger the automatic power down. After the calculator has been turned off, pressing ON will result in the calculator turning on, but not Cabri Jr. You will need to press APPS and choose Cabri Jr. Cabri Jr. will then restart with the most current figure in its most recent state.

As Cabri Jr. resembles a computer, it also has dropdown menus that simulate the menus in many computer programs. There are five menus, F1 through F5.

***Navigating Menus*** To navigate each menu, press the appropriate key for F1 through F5. The arrow keys will then allow you to navigate within each menu. The ▲ and ▼ keys allow you to move within the menu items. The ▶ and ◀ keys allow you to access a submenu of an item. If an item has an arrow to the right, this indicates there is a submenu. Although not displayed, the menu items are numbered. You can also select a menu item by pressing the number that corresponds to each item. For example, to select the fourth menu item in the list, press [4]. If you press a number greater than the number of items in the list, the last item will be selected. If you press [0], you will leave the menu without selecting an item. This is the same as pressing CLEAR.

# Key Skills

Use this section as a reference for further instruction. For additional features, consult the TI-84 Plus user's manual.

## [F1] MANAGING FIGURES

The menu below provides the basic operations when working in Cabri Jr. These are commands normally found in menus within computer applications.

## [F2] CREATING OBJECTS

This menu provides the basic tools for creating geometric figures. You can create points in three different ways, a line and line segment by selecting two points, a circle by defining the center and radius, a triangle by finding three vertices, and a quadrilateral by finding four vertices.

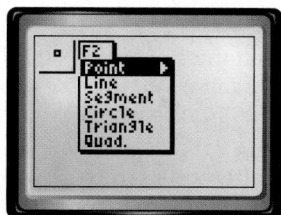

## [F3] CONSTRUCTING OBJECTS

This menu provides the tools to construct new objects from existing objects. You can construct perpendicular and parallel lines, a perpendicular bisector of a segment, an angle bisector, a midpoint of a line segment, a circle using the center and a point on the circle, and a locus.

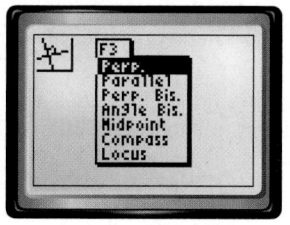

## [F4] TRANSFORMING OBJECTS

This menu provides the tools to transform geometric figures. Using figures that are already created, you can access this menu to create figures that are symmetrical to other figures, reflect figures over a line of reflection, translate figures using a line segment or two points that define the translation, rotate figures by defining the center of rotation and angle of rotation, and dilate figures using the center of the dilation and a scale factor.

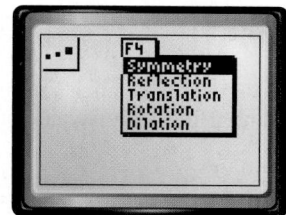

## [F5] COMPUTING OBJECTS

This menu provides the tools for displaying, labeling, measuring, and computing. You can make an object visible or invisible, label points on figures, alter the way objects are displayed, measure length, area, and angle measures, display coordinates of points and equations of lines, make calculations, and delete objects from the screen.

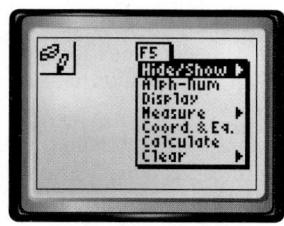

While a graphing calculator cannot do everything, it can make some tasks easier. To prepare for whatever lies ahead, you should try to learn as much as you can about the technology. The future will definitely involve technology and the people who are comfortable with it will be successful. Using a graphing calculator is a good start toward becoming familiar with technology.

# Glossary/Glosario

A mathematics multilingual glossary is available at
**www.math.glencoe.com/multilingual_glossary**.
The glossary is available in the following languages.

Arabic     English          Korean    Tagalog
Bengali    Haitian Creole   Russian   Urdu
Cantonese  Hmong            Spanish   Vietnamese

## English                                    ## Español

### ▪ A ▪

**absolute value** (p. 54) The distance a number is from zero on a number line. The absolute value of an integer, *a*, is written as $|a|$.

**valor absoluto** (p. 54) Valor que tiene una cifra por su figura, por ejemplo, en el número 592 el valor absoluto de 5 es 5.

**acute angle** (p. 196) An angle measuring less than 90°.

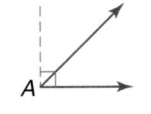

$0° < m\angle A < 90°$

**ángulo agudo** (p. 196) Ángulo que mide menos de 90°.

**acute triangle** (p. 206) A triangle with three acute angles.

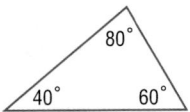

three acute angles
*tres ángulos agudos*

**triángulo acutángulo** (p. 206) Triángulo que sus tres ángulos son agudos.

**adjacent angles** (p. 197) Two angles that have a common vertex and a common side, but no interior points in common.

**ángulos adyacentes** (p. 197) Dos ángulos que tienen el mismo vértice y un lado común pero no comparten ningún punto interior.

**alternate exterior angles** (p. 202) In the figure, transversal *t* intersects lines *l* and *m*. $\angle 5$ and $\angle 3$, and $\angle 6$ and $\angle 4$ are alternate exterior angles.

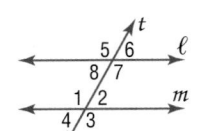

**ángulos alternos-externos** (p. 202) En la figura, la transversal *t* intersec las rectas *l* y *m*. $\angle 5$ y $\angle 3$, $\angle 6$ y $\angle 4$ son ángulos alternos enternos.

**alternate interior angles** (p. 202) In the figure, transversal *t* intersects lines *l* and *m*. $\angle 1$ and $\angle 7$, and $\angle 2$ and $\angle 8$ are alternate interior angles.

**ángulos alternos-internos** (p. 202) En a figura, la transversal *t* intersec las rectas *l* y *m*. $\angle 1$ y $\angle 7$, y $\angle 2$ y $\angle 8$ son ángulos alternos internos.

**angle** (pp. 196, 206) The figure formed by two rays that have a common endpoint.

**ángulo** (pp. 196, 206) Figura formada por dos rayos o líneas rectas que parten del mismo vértice.

**angle of rotation** (p. 306) The amount of turn of a rotation expressed as a fractional part of a whole turn or in degrees.

**ángulo de rotación** (p. 306) Cantidad de un movimiento de rotación que se expresa ya sea como parte fraccional de una rotación completa o en grados.

**Angle-Side-Angle Postulate (ASA)** (p. 213) If two angles and the included side of one triangle are congruent to two corresponding angles and the included side of another triangle, then the triangles are congruent.

**Postulado de ángulo-lado-ángulo (ALA)** (p. 213) Si dos ángulos y el lado incluido de un triángulo son congruentes a dos ángulos y al lado incluido de otro triángulo, entonces los triángulos son congruentes.

**arc** (p. 227) A section of the circumference of the circle.

**arco** (pp. 227) Porción de una circunferencia o de un círculo.

**area** (p. 418) The number of square units needed to fill a two-dimensional space.

**área** (p. 418) El número de unidades al cuadrado que se necesitan para llenar una figura bidimensional.

# English

# Español

## ■ B ■

**bar graph** (p. 2) A means of displaying statistical information in which horizontal or vertical bars are used to compare quantities.

**gráfica de barra** (p. 2) Representación gráfica de una serie de datos valiéndose de barras horizontales o verticales.

**base (of an exponent)** (p. 82) The factor being multiplied in a number written in exponential form. For example, in $b^2$, $b$ is the base.

**base (de un exponente)** (p. 82) Factor que es afectado por el exponente en una potencia. Por ejemplo, en $b^2$ la base es $b$.

**base angle** (p. 207) For an isosceles triangle, the two congruent angles opposite the congruent sides.

**base angular** (p. 207) En un triángulo isósceles, el lado que se opone a los dos ángulos congruentes.

**biased** (p. 7) The characteristic of a survey whose findings are not truly representative of the entire population.

**tendencioso** (p. 7) Característica de una encuesta que no representa el total de una población.

**binomial** (p. 376) A polynomial with two terms.

**binomio** (p. 376) Polinomio formado por dos términos.

**bisector (of an angle)** (p. 197) A ray that divides the angle into two congruent adjacent angles.

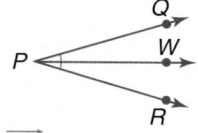

**bisectriz (de un ángulo)** (p. 197) Rayo o línea recta que divide un ángulo en dos ángulos iguales y adyacentes.

$\overrightarrow{PW}$ is the bisector of $\angle P$.
$\overrightarrow{PW}$ es la bisectriz del $\angle P$.

**bisector (of a segment)** (p. 193) Any line, segment, ray or plane that intersects the segment at its midpoint.

**bisectriz (de un segmento o de una recta)** (p. 193) Cualquier línea, segmento, rayo o plano que interseque a una recta en su punto medio.

**box-and-whisker plot** (p. 29) A method of displaying data that uses quartiles to draw a box to illustrate the interquartile range and to draw whiskers to illustrate data values outside the interquartile range.

**diagrama de bloque** (p. 29) Representación gráfica que identifica tendencias y síntesis informativas mostrando la distribución de datos dividida en cuatro partes iguales, de las cuales las dos interiores se representan con una caja y las dos exteriores con pelo.

## ■ C ■

**center of dilation** (p. 316) The point of which the distance between it and every point on the image is equal to the distance between it and every corresponding point on the preimage times the scale factor.

**centro de homotecia** (p. 316) Punto donde se intersecan las líneas que parten de los vértices de la primera figura y pasan por los vértices correspondientes de la figura o las figuras homólogas hechas a escala.

**center of rotation** (p. 306) The point about which the figure is rotated in a rotation.

**centro de rotación** (p. 306) Punto donde se apoya la rotación de una figura.

**central angle (of a circle)** (p. 227) An angle with its vertex at the center of a circle. The measure of a central angle is always less than 180°.

**ángulo central (de un círculo)** (p. 227) Ángulo cuyo vértice es el centro del círculo. La medida de un ángulo central es siempre menor de 180 grados.

**chord** (p. 226) A segment with both endpoints on the circle.

**cuerda** (p. 226) Recta o segmento de línea en la que ambos polos son puntos de la circunferencia.

**circle** (p. 226) In a plane, the set of all points that are a given distance for a fixed point. That fixed point is the center of the circle.

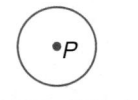

**círculo** (p. 226) En un plano, el conjunto de todos los puntos a una distancia dada de un punto fijo. El punto fijo es el centro del círculo.

$P$ is the center of the circle.
$P$ es el centro del círculo.

**circle graph** (p. 232) A means of displaying data where items are represented as parts of the whole circle. Each part, or percent of the data, is represented by a *sector*.

**gráfica dentro del círculo o diagrama de sectores** (p. 232) Representación gráfica en la cual los datos se muestran como porciones de un todo representado por un círculo. Cada porción o porcentaje representa un *sector*.

# English

# Español

**closed half-plane**  (p. 259)  The region that is a solution of an inequality that includes the solid line.

**cluster sampling**  (p. 6)  A sampling method in which the members of the population are randomly selected from particular parts of the population and then surveyed in clusters.

**coefficient**  (p. 376)  The numerical part of a monomial.

**coefficient of correlation**  (p. 26)  A statistical measure, *r*, between 1 and −1, that tells if a correlation is positive or negative, strong or weak.

**collinear points**  (p. 192)  Points that lie on the same line.

*P, Q,* and *R* are collinear.
*P, Q y R son colineales.*

**combination**  (p. 178)  A set of items in which order is not important. For example, *acb* and *bac* are both combinations of the letters *a*, *b*, and *c*. The number of combinations of *n* items taken *r* items at a time is written

$$_nC_r = \frac{n!}{(n-r)!\, r!}.$$

**complement (of an event)**  (p. 165)  The complement of event *A* is the event *not A*.

**complement (of a set)**  (pp. 147, 524)  If *A* is a subset of *U*, then the subset of all elements of *U* that are not elements of *A* is called the complement of *A*, symbolized as *A'*.

**complementary angles**  (p. 196)  Two angles whose measures have a sum of 90°.

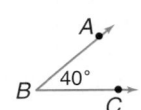 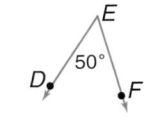

$m\angle ABC + m\angle DEF = 90°$

**compound event**  (p. 162)  An event made up of two or more simple events.

**concave polygon**  (p. 222)  A polygon is concave if a line that contains a side of the polygon also contains a point in its interior.

**conclusion**  (p. 539)  That which logically follows the premises of a deductive argument.

**conditional statement**  (p. 530)  An *if-then* statement having two parts, a hypothesis and a conclusion, symbolized *p → q*.

**cone**  (p. 422)  A three-dimensional figure with a curved surface and one circular base. The *axis* is a segment that joins the vertex to the center of the base. If the axis forms a right angle with the base, it is a *right* cone. Otherwise it is an *oblique* cone.

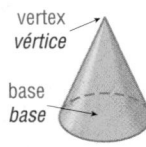

vertex
*vértice*

base
*base*

**congruent angles**  (pp. 197, 206)  Angles that have the same measure.

**congruent line segments**  (p. 193)  Line segments that have the same measure.

**medio plano cerrado**  (p. 259)  Región que es una solución de una desigualdad que incluye la línea sólida.

**muestra por conglomerado**  (p. 6)  De una parte de la población se escogen algunos miembros al azar y luego se les registra como conglomerado, no como individuos.

**coeficiente**  (p. 376)  Parte numérica de un monomio.

**coeficiente de correlación**  (p. 26)  Medida estadística, *r*, entre 1 y −1, que señala si una relación es positiva o negativa.

**puntos colineales**  (p. 192)  Dos o más puntos que forman parte de la misma línea.

**combinación**  (p. 178)  Conjuntos de artículos en que el orden no es importante. Por ejemplo, *acb* y *bac* son ambas combinaciones de las letras *a*, *b*, y *c*. El número de combinaciones de *n* artículos tomados *r* a la vez se escribe $_nC_r = \frac{n!}{(n-r)!\, r!}.$

**suceso de complemento**  (p. 165)  El complemento del evento *A* es el evento *no A*.

**conjunto de complemento**  (pp. 147, 524)  Si *A* es un subconjunto de *U*, entonces el subconjunto de todos los elementos que no forman parte de *A* sería el complemento de *A*, simbolizado como *A'*.

**ángulos complementarios**  (p. 196)  Dos ángulos cuyas medidas al sumarse dan como resultado 90°.

**evento compuesto**  (p. 162)  Evento que está compuesto por dos o más eventos simples.

**polígono cóncavo**  (p. 222)  Un polígono es cóncavo si una línea que contiene un lado del polígono además contiene un punto de su interior.

**conclusión**  (p. 539)  Lo que se desprende lógicamente de las premisas de un argumento deductivo.

**declaración condicional**  (p. 530)  Declaración compuesta por dos partes, *si* y *entonces*, llamadas respectivamente *premisa* o *antecedente*, y *conclusión* o *consecuente*. Se representa *p → q*.

**cono**  (p. 422)  Figura tridimensional con una base circular y un vértice. La línea perpendicular a la base que inicia en el vértice viene siendo la *altura*. Si el punto extremo opuesto al vértice es el centro de la base, entonces será un *cono regular*. De otra manera será un cono *oblicuo*.

**ángulos congruentes**  (pp. 197, 206)  Ángulos que tienen la misma medida.

**rectas o segmentos congruentes**  (p. 193)  recta o segmento de línea que tienen la misma medida.

## English

## Español

**congruent triangles**   (p. 212) Triangles whose vertices can be matched so that corresponding parts of the triangle are congruent.

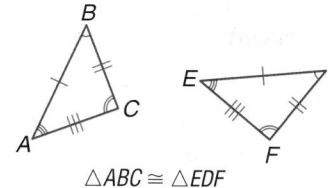

$\triangle ABC \cong \triangle EDF$

**triángulos congruentes**   (p. 212) Triángulos cuyos tres vértices se corresponden.

**constant**   (p. 376) A monomial that has no variables.

**constante**   (p. 376) Monomio que no contiene variables.

**continuous**   (p. 265) A characteristic of a function in which the domain is all real numbers and the function is defined for all values of the domain.

**continuo**   (p. 265) Característica de una función en la cual el dominio está compuesto por números reales y los valores de dominio definen la función.

**contrapositive**   (p. 533) A conditional statement formed by interchanging and negating the hypothesis and conclusion of the original conditional statement, symbolized $\sim q \Rightarrow \sim p$. A statement and its contrapositive are either both true or both false.

**contrapuesto**   (p. 533) Declaración condicional en la que se niegan tanto las premisas o hipótesis como la conclusión de una declaración condicional antes expuesta. Se simboliza $\sim q \Rightarrow \sim p$. Una declaración y su contrapuesto pueden ser ambas verdaderas o ambas falsas.

**convenience sampling**   (p. 6) A sampling method is which members of a population are selected because they are readily available, and all are surveyed.

**muestra por conveniencia**   (p. 6) Método de muestreo en el cual los miembros de una Población son escogidos sólo porque están disponible o porque ya han sido encuestados.

**converse**   (p. 530) A conditional statement formed by interchanging the hypothesis and conclusion of the original conditional statement, symbolized $q \to p$. The converse of a true statement is not necessarily true.

**converso**   (p. 530) Declaración condicional en la que se intercambian la premisa o hipótesis por la conclusión. Se simboliza $q \Rightarrow p$. El opuesto de una declaración verdadera no es necesariamente verdadero.

**convex polygon**   (p. 222) A polygon is convex if each line containing a side has no points in the interior of the polygon.

**polígono convexo**   (p. 222) Un polígono es convexo si cada línea que contiene un lado no tiene puntos al interior del polígono.

**coordinate plane**   (p. 244) A mathematical system in which two number lines are drawn perpendicular to each other and form four quadrants. The horizontal number line is called the $x$-axis. The vertical number line is called the $y$-axis.

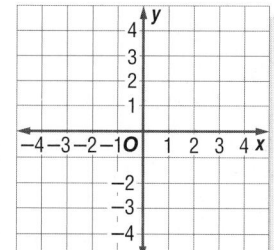

**plano de coordenadas o plano cartesiano** (p. 244)  Dos rectas numéricas perpendiculares que forman una cuadrícula. La recta numérica horizontal se llama eje $x$, y la vertical se llama eje $y$.

**coplanar points**   (p. 192) Points that lie in the same plane.

**puntos coplanares**   (p. 192) Puntos que forman parte del mismo plano.

**corresponding angles**   (p. 202) Two angles in corresponding positions relative to two lines cut by a transversal. Also, angles in the same position in congruent or similar polygons.

**ángulos correspondientes**   (p. 202) Ángulos que están en la misma posición con relación a la secante y a las líneas paralelas. También los ángulos que se encuentran en la misma posición en polígonos congruentes o iguales.

**cosine**   (p. 488) The trigonometric ratio of an $\angle A$, abbreviated cos $A$, of the length of the leg adjacent to $\angle A$ to the length of the hypotenuse.

**coseno**   (p. 488) Razón trigonométrica del $\angle A$, se abrevia cos $A$, y se define como el cociente del cateto adyacente del $\angle A$, sobre la hipotenusa.

**counterexample**   (p. 530) An instance that satisfies the hypothesis, but not the conclusion of the conditional statement. A single counterexample proves that the conditional statement is false.

**contraejemplo**   (p. 530) Instancia que satisface la hipótesis o la premisa, pero no la conclusión de la declaración condicional. Un contraejemplo prueba que la conjetura no es válida.

**cross-products**   (p. 122) The cross-products of $\frac{a}{b} = \frac{c}{d}$ are $ad$ and $bc$. In a proportion, the cross-product of the means is equal to the cross product of the extremes.

**productos cruzados**   (p. 122) Para $\frac{a}{b}$ y $\frac{c}{d}$, los productos cruzados son $ad$ y $bc$. En una proporción los productos cruzados son iguales.

# English

**cylinder** (p. 422) A three-dimensional figure made up of a curved quadrilateral region and two congruent circular bases that lie in parallel planes. The *axis* is a segment that joins the centers of the bases. If the axis forms a right angle with the bases it is a *right* cylinder. Otherwise it is an *oblique* cylinder.

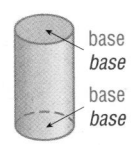

# Español

**cilindro** (p. 422) Figura tridimensional que esta compuesta por una superficie curva, cuadrilátera y cerrada, además de dos bases circulares las cuales son paralelas. El *eje* es una recta o segmento que unifica los centros de cada base. Si el eje forma un ángulo recto con ambas bases, será un cilindro *regular*. De otra manera será un cilindro *oblicuo*.

base
*base*
base
*base*

## ■ D ■

**deductive reasoning** (p. 539) A process in which a conclusion is reasoned based on a set of premises. The conclusion necessarily follows from the premises.

**dependent events** (p. 169) If the result of the second event is affected by the result of the first event, the second event is dependent on the first event. If event $B$ is dependent on event $A$, then $P(A \text{ and } B) = P(A) \cdot P(B, \text{given } A)$.

**description notation** (p.520) Set notation that describes the set.

**determinant** (p. 354) The difference of the products of the diagonal entries of a $2 \times 2$ square matrix. The determinant of a matrix $A$, named det $A$, is symbolized by using vertical bars in place of matrix brackets:

$$\det A = \begin{vmatrix} a & b \\ c & d \end{vmatrix} = ad - bc.$$

**diagonal** (p. 223) A segment that joins two vertices of a polygon but is not a side. Diagonals separate the interior of the polygon into nonoverlapping triangular regions.

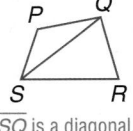

$\overline{SQ}$ is a diagonal.
$\overline{SQ}$ *es una diagonal.*

**diameter** (p. 226) A chord that passes through the center of a circle and has endpoints on the circle. The diameter is equal to twice the measure of the radius.

**dilation** (p. 316) A transformation that produces an image that is the same shape as the original figure but a different size.

**directed graph** (p. 358) A geometrical representation of a map that shows locations as points and roads as lines. Connections may be possible in only one direction on some paths and in both directions on other paths. Directed graphs can be analyzed by using matrices.

**direct square variation** (p. 277) A function that can be written in the form $y = kx^2$, where $k$ is a nonzero constant.

**direct variation** (p. 276) A function that can be written in the form $y = kx$, where $k$ is a nonzero constant.

**disjoint sets** (p. 525) Two sets whose intersection is the empty set.

**razonamiento deductivo** (p. 539) Razonamiento donde la conclusión se deduce de las premisas. La conclusión necesariamente se desprende de las premisas.

**eventos dependientes** (p. 169) Dos eventos en los que el resultado del primero afecta el resultado del segundo y viceversa. Si el evento $B$ depende del evento $A$, entonces $P(A \text{ y } B) = P(A) \cdot P(B, \text{dado a } A)$.

**notación descriptiva** (p. 520) Notación del conjunto que describe al mismo conjunto.

**determinado** (p. 354) Diferencia de los productos de las notaciones diagonales $2 \times 2$ matriz cuadrada. Lo determinado de la matriz $A$, llamado det $A$, se simboliza usando barras verticales en lugar de llaves:

$$A = \begin{vmatrix} a & b \\ c & d \end{vmatrix} = ad - bc.$$

**diagonal** (p. 223) Recta o segmento de línea que conecta dos vértices de un polígono pero que no es un lado. Las diagonales dividen el interior del polígono en una región triangular no superpuesta.

**diámetro** (p. 226) Línea recta que pasa por el centro del círculo y que sus puntos extremos se localizan en la circunferencia. El diámetro está formado por dos radios.

**homótecia** (p. 316) Transformación que da como resultado una imagen que tiene la misma forma de la figura original pero de diferente tamaño.

**gráfica directa** (p. 358) representación geométrica de un mapa en el que las localidades se señalan con puntos y las caminos con líneas. Las conexiones serán posibles en un sentido en algunos senderos, pero en otros serán posibles en doble sentido. Las gráficas directas se pueden analizar usando matrices.

**variación cuadrada directa** (p. 277) Función que se puede escribir en la forma $y = kx^2$, donde $k$ es una constante que no es igual a cero.

**variación directa** (p. 276) Función que se puede escribir en la forma $y = kx$, donde $k$ es una constante que no es igual a cero.

**conjuntos disyuntivos** (p. 525) Dos conjuntos en los que su intersección es el conjunto vacío.

# English

**distance formula**   (p. 245)  For any points $P_1(x_1, y_1)$ and $P_2(x_2, y_2)$, the distance between $P_1$ and $P_2$ is given by the formula $P_1P_2 = \sqrt{(x_2 - x_1)^2 + (y_2 - y_1)^2}$.

**distributive property**   (p. 390)  Each factor outside parentheses can be used to multiply each term within the parentheses. $a(b + c) = ab + ac$.

**division property of inequality**   (p. 133)  If you divide each side of an inequality by the same positive number, the order of the inequality remains the same. If you divide each side of an inequality by the same negative number, the order of the inequality is reversed.

**domain**   (p. 264)  The set of all possible values of $x$ for the function $y = f(x)$.

# Español

**fórmula de la distancia**   (p. 245)  Para cualquier par de puntos $P_1(x_1, y_1)$ y $P_2(x_2, y_2)$, la distancia entre $P_1$ y $P_2$ es dada por la fórmula $P_1P_2 = \sqrt{(x_2 - x_1)^2 = (y_2 - y_1)^2}$.

**propiedad distributiva**   (p. 390)  Cada factor fuera del paréntesis puede multiplicarse con cada término dentro del paréntesis. $a(a + c) = ab + ac$.

**propiedad de la división en la desigualdad**   (p. 133)  Si se dividen ambos lados de una desigualdad entre el mismo número positivo, la desigualdad proporcional seguirá siendo la misma. Si se dividen ambos lados de una desigualdad entre el mismo número negativo, la desigualdad proporcional será la opuesta.

**dominio**   (p. 264)  Conjunto de todos los valores posibles de $x$ para la función $y = f(x)$.

## ■ E ■

**edge**   (p. 422)  The intersection of the faces of a polygon.

**element**   (pp. 38, 520)  A member of a set or a number in a matrix.

**enlargement**   (p. 316)  A dilation that creates an image that is larger than the preimage.

**equal sets**   (p. 521)  Sets that contain the same members, written $A = B$.

**equation**   (p. 104)  A statement in which two numbers or expressions are equal.

**equiangular triangle**   (p. 206)  A triangle with all three angles congruent.

**equilateral triangle**   (p. 206)  A triangle with all three sides congruent.

**arista**   (p. 422)  La intersección de las caras de un *poliedro*.

**elemento**   (pp. 38, 520)  Miembro de un conjunto o un número en una matriz.

**ampliación**   (p. 316)  Dilatación que crea una figura más grande que la figura original.

**conjuntos iguales**   (p. 521)  Conjuntos que contienen los mismos elementos, se escribe $A = B$.

**ecuación**   (p. 104)  Planteamiento matemático donde dos números o expresiones algebraicas son iguales.

**triángulo equiangular**   (p. 206)  Triángulo que tiene sus tres ángulos iguales.

**triángulo equilátero**   (p. 206)  Triángulo que tiene sus tres lados iguales.

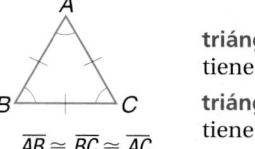

$$\overline{AB} \cong \overline{BC} \cong \overline{AC}$$
$$\angle A \cong \angle B \cong \angle C$$

**equivalent sets**   (p. 521)  Sets that contain the same number of elements.

**event**   (p. 158)  Any one of the possible outcomes or combination of possible outcomes of an experiment.

**experiment**   (p. 150)  An activity that is used to produce data that can be observed and recorded.

**experimental probability**   (p. 150)  The probability of an event based on the results of an experiment in which the number of favorable observations is divided by the total number of observations.

**exponent**   (pp. 57, 82)  A number showing how many times the base is used as a factor. For example, in $b^x$ the exponent is $x$.

**exterior angle (of a triangle)**   (p. 207)  The angle formed by extending one of the sides of a triangle and that is equal to the two remote interior angles of the triangle.

$\angle 1$ is an exterior angle.
$\angle 1$ *es un ángulo externo.*

**conjuntos equivalentes**   (p. 521)  Conjuntos que contienen el mismo número de elementos.

**evento**   (p. 158)  Resultado o la combinación de varios resultados de un experimento.

**experimento**   (p. 150)  Actividad que se usa para producir datos que pueden ser observados y grabados.

**probabilidad experimental**   (p. 150)  La probabilidad de un evento basándose en los resultados de un experimento en el cual el número de observaciones favorables se divide entre el número total de observaciones.

**exponente**   (pp. 57, 82 )  Número que muestra las veces que la base se usa como factor. Por ejemplo, en $b^x$ el exponente es $x$.

**ángulo exterior (de un triángulo)**   (p. 207)  Ángulo que se forma al extender uno de los lados de un triángulo y su medida será igual a la suma de los dos ángulos interiores que no le sean adyacentes.

# English

# Español

**exterior angles (of a transversal system)**  (p. 202)  The four angles formed by a transversal and the two lines it intersects that are outside the two lines.

**ángulos exteriores (de un sistema transversal)**  (p. 202)  Los cuatro ángulos exteriores que se forman en los puntos de intersección de la secante o transversal con las dos líneas paralelas.

■ **F** ■

**face**  (p. 422)  A polygonal surface of a polyhedron.

**factor**  (p. 404)  Any number or polynomial multiplied by another to produce a product.

**factorial**  (p. 172)  The product of all whole numbers from $n$ to 1. The factorial function is used to compute the number of permutations of $n$ different items, $n(n - 1(n - 2) \ldots (2)(1)$ and is written as $n!$.

**factoring**  (p. 404)  To express a number or polynomial as a product of numbers or polynomials.

**Fibonacci sequence**  (p. 93)  A sequence in which each term is the sum of the previous two terms.

**finite set**  (p. 520)  A set whose elements can all be counted or listed.

**FOIL**  (p. 397)  An acronym and memory device used to remember the order to multiply binomials (*first, outer, inner, last*).

**formula**  (p. 105)  An equation stating a relationship between two or more quantities.

**foundation drawing**  (p. 447)  A drawing that shows the base of a structure and the height of each part.

**frequency table**  (p. 16)  A method of recording data that shows how often an item appears in a set of data.

**front-end estimation**  (p. 3)  A method of estimating in which only initial digits, or *front-end* digits, are used. This method results in a simpler computation but also in a less precise estimation.

**function**  (p. 264)  An equation in two variables that has a relationship where each $x$-coordinate is paired with exactly one $y$-coordinate.

**function notation**  (p. 264)  Writing a function as equal to $f(x)$ in contrast to writing it as equal to $y$.

**fundamental counting principle**  (p. 159)  If there are two or more stages of an activity, the total number of possible outcomes is the product of the number of possible outcomes for each stage of the activity.

**cara**  (p. 422)  Superficie poligonal de un poliedro.

**factor**  (p. 404)  Cualquier número o polinomio multiplicado por otro número que da como resultado un producto.

**factorial**  (p. 172)  Producto de todos los números enteros de $n$ a 1. La función factorial se usa para ordenar el número de permutaciones de $n$ cifras diferentes, $n(n - 1)(n - 2)...(2)(1)$ y se escribe como $n$.

**factorizar**  (p. 404)  Expresar un número o polinomio como un producto de otros números o polinomios.

**secuencia fibonacci**  (p. 93)  Secuencia en la cual cada término es la suma de los dos términos previos.

**conjunto finito**  (p. 520)  Conjunto en el que todos sus elementos se pueden contar o enlistar.

**PFDU**  (p. 397)  Siglas y ardid memorístico que se usa para recordar los pasos para multiplicar binomios (*Primero, Fuera, Dentro, Último*).

**fórmula**  (p. 105)  Ecuación que determina las relaciones entre dos o más cantidades o variables.

**dibujo de cimientos**  (p. 447)  Dibujo que muestra la base de una estructura y la longitud de cada parte.

**tabla de frecuencia**  (p. 16)  Método de recopilación de datos que muestra la frecuencia con que un dato aparece en un conjunto de datos.

**estimación de digitos en los extremos delanteros**  (p. 3)  Método de estimación en el que se usan sólo los dígitos iniciales o de los *extremos delanteros*. Este método da como resultado una manera más simple de ordenar aunque la estimación es menos precisa.

**función**  (p. 264)  Ecuación en dos variables en la que se da una relación donde cada coordenada de $x$ se aparea con una de la coordenada $y$.

**notación de la función**  (p. 264)  Descripción de una función como igual a $f(x)$ en contraste con la descripción de que ésta es igual a $y$.

**principio fundamental de conteo**  (p. 159)  Si hay dos o más etapas en una actividad, el número total de resultados posibles es el producto del número de resultados posibles por cada etapa de la actividad.

■ **G** ■

**geometry**  (p. 192)  The study of points in space (from the Greek *geo*, meaning "earth" and *metria* meaning "measurement").

**graph of an equation**  (p. 254)  The set of all points whose coordinates are solutions of an equation.

**geometría**  (p. 192)  Estudio de los puntos en el espacio (viene de las raíces griegas *geo*, que significa tierra; y *metro*, que significa "medida").

**gráfica de una ecuación**  (p. 254)  Conjunto de puntos cuyas coordenadas son las soluciones de una ecuación.

Glossary/Glosario

# English

**graph of a number** (p. 52) The point that corresponds to a number and is indicated on the number line by a solid dot.

**graph of an inequality** (p. 258) A graph on the coordinate plane that includes a boundary, either a solid line or dashed line, and a shaded region.

**greatest common factor (GCF)** (p. 404) The greatest expression that is a factor of two or more expressions.

# Español

**gráfica de una desigualdad** (p. 52) Gráfica en el plano de coordenadas que incluye un límite representado ya sea por una línea cerrada o fragmentada.

**gráfica de un número** (p. 258) Punto que corresponde a un número; se indica en la recta numérica con un punto cerrado.

**máximo factor común (MFC)** (p. 404) La expresión mayor que es factor de dos o más expresiones.

## ■ H ■

**histogram** (p. 16) A type of bar graph used to show frequencies in which no space is between the bars and the bars usually represent grouped intervals of numbers.

**histograma** (p. 16) Tipo de gráfica de barras que se usa para mostrar frecuencias en las cuales no hay espacio entre las barras, y las barras por lo general representan intervalos agrupados de números.

**hypotenuse** (p. 484) The side opposite the right angle in a right triangle.

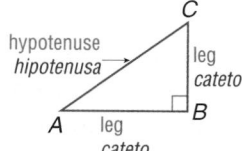

**hipotenusa** (p. 484) Lado opuesto al ángulo recto en un triángulo rectángulo.

## ■ I ■

**image** (p. 296) The new figure that results from a transformation of the original figure.

**independent events** (p. 168) If the result of the second event is not affected by the result of the first event, the second event is independent of the first. If $A$ and $B$ are independent events, $P(A \text{ and } B) = P(A) \cdot P(B)$.

**indirect measurement** (p. 478) A measurement that is made in situations where it is impossible or impractical to find a length by measuring the actual distance (direct measurement). Using similar triangles, by means of shadows or mirrors, is one method of indirect measurement.

**inductive reasoning** (p. 538) A process in which a conclusion is reasoned based on the examination of a pattern of instances of an event. The conclusion is called a *conjecture* and cannot be known to be true beyond a doubt.

**inequality** (p. 126) A mathematical sentence that contains one of the symbols $\neq, <, >, \leq,$ or $\geq$.

**infinite set** (p. 520) A set whose elements cannot be counted or listed.

**inscribed angle** (p. 228) An angle whose vertex lies on the circle and whose sides contain chords of the circle. The measure of an inscribed angle is one-half the measure of the arc it intercepts.

**integers** (p. 52) The set of whole numbers and their opposites.

**imagen** (p. 296) Nueva figura que resulta de una transformación.

**eventos independientes** (p. 168) Si el resultado de un evento no es afectado por el resultado del primero, el segundo evento es independiente del primero. Si $A$ y $B$ son eventos independientes, $P(A \text{ y } B) = P(A) \cdot P(B)$.

**medida indirecta** (p. 478) Cálculo de una medida que se hace en situaciones donde es imposible o impráctico encontrar la longitud midiendo la distancia real (medida directa). El uso de triángulos similares por medio de sombras y espejos, es un método de medida indirecta.

**razonamiento inductivo** (p. 538) Proceso lógico donde una conclusión se desprende del examen de un conjunto de eventos específicos. La conclusión es llamada conjetura y no puede ser aceptada si hay por lo menos una duda.

**desigualdad** (p. 126) Declaración matemática que usa uno de los símbolos $\neq, <, >, \leq,$ o $\geq$.

**conjunto infinito** (p. 520) Conjunto en el cual sus elementos no se pueden contar o enlistar.

**ángulo inscrito** (p. 228) Ángulo que su vértice recae en el círculo y cuyos lados vienen a ser cuerdas del mismo. La medida de un ángulo inscrito es la mitad de lo que mide el arco que lo intercepta.

**enteros** (p. 52) Conjunto de los números enteros y sus opuestos.

# English

**interior angles** (p. 202) The four angles formed by a transversal and the two lines it intersects that are inside the two lines. ∠1, ∠2, ∠7, and ∠8 are interior angles.

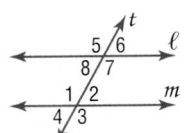

**interquartile range** (p. 28) The difference between the values of the first and third quartiles.

**intersection (of two sets)** (pp. 147, 525) The intersection of two sets, $A$ and $B$, symbolized $A \cap B$, contains all the elements that are common in both $A$ and $B$.

**invalid argument** (p. 543) A deductive argument such that even if the premises are true, the conclusion does not logically follow.

**inverse (of a statement)** (p. 533) A conditional statement formed by negating the hypothesis and conclusion of the original conditional statement, symbolized $\sim p \rightarrow \sim q$. The inverse of a true statement is not necessarily true.

**inverse square variation** (p. 283) A function that can be written in the form $y = \frac{k}{x^2}$ or $x^2 y = k$, where $k$ is a nonzero constant.

**inverse trigonometric functions** (p. 498) Functions $\sin^{-1}$, $\cos^{-1}$ and $\tan^{-1}$ that "undo" the sin, cos and tan functions and are useful in finding measures of angles in right triangles when only the length of the sides is known.

**inverse variation** (p. 282) A function that can be written in the form $y = \frac{k}{x}$, where $k$ is a nonzero constant.

**irrational numbers** (p. 52) Numbers that are non-terminating and non-repeating decimals, such as $\pi$ and $\sqrt{2}$.

**isometric drawing** (p. 442) A drawing of a three-dimensional object in such a way that all lines are drawn to scale, all parallel edges of the structure are drawn parallel, but all perpendicular lines are not necessarily drawn perpendicular.

**isosceles triangle** (p. 206) A triangle with at least two congruent sides and angles.

**legs** (p. 484) In a right triangle, the two sides that are not the hypotenuse.

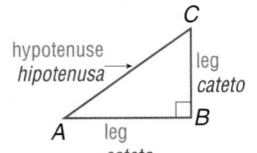

# Español

**ángulos interiores** (p. 202) Los cuatro ángulos interiores formados por las intersecciones de la secante o transversal y las dos líneas paralelas. ∠1, ∠2, ∠7, y ∠8 son ángulos interiores.

**alcance intercuartil** (p. 28) Diferencia entre los valores del primero y del tercer cuartil.

**intersección (de dos conjuntos)** (pp. 147, 525) La intersección de dos conjuntos, $A$ intersección $B$, simbolizado $A \cap B$, contiene todos los elementos que ambos conjuntos tienen en común.

**razonamiento inválido** (p. 543) Razonamiento deductivo que incluso si las premisas son verdaderas, la conclusión es ilógica.

**opuesto (de una declaración)** (p. 533) Declaración condicional formada por la negación de la hipótesis o antecedente y de la conclusión o consecuente de la declaración condicional original, se simboliza $\sim p \Rightarrow \sim q$, el opuesto de una declaración verdadera no es necesariamente falso.

**variación cuadrada inversa** (p. 283) Función que puede escribirse en la forma $y = \frac{k}{x^2}$ o $x^2 y = k$, donde $k$ no es igual a cero.

**función trigonométrica inversa** (p. 498) Las funciones $sen^{-1}$, $\cos^{-1}$ y $\tan^{-1}$ que "deshacen" las funciones sen, cos y tan, y son prácticas para encontrar medidas de ángulos en triángulos rectángulos cuando sólo las medidas de los lados se conocen.

**variación inversa** (p. 282) Función que puede escribirse en la forma $y = \frac{k}{x}$, donde $k$ es una constante que no es igual a cero.

**número irracional** (p. 52) Números con decimales como $\pi$ y (raíz cuadrada de 2) que no terminan y que además no llegan a una cifra que se repita.

**dibujo isométrico** (p. 442) Dibujo de un cuerpo tridimensional que se hace de tal forma que todas las rectas se dibujan a escala, todas las aristas paralelas de la estructura se dibujan paralelas, pero no todas las rectas perpendiculares se dibujan de forma perpendicular necesariamente.

**triángulo isósceles** (p. 206) Triángulo que tiene dos lados y dos ángulos iguales y un lado y un ángulo desigual.

**catetos** (p. 484) En el triángulo rectángulo, los dos lados que no son la hipotenusa.

### ■ L ■

**like terms**   (pp. 66, 377)  Terms that have identical variable parts, or in other words, monomials that differ only in their coefficients.

**line**   (p. 192)  A set of points that extends infinitely in two opposite directions.

**linear equation**   (pp. 254, 257)  An equation for which the graph is a line. The *standard form* of a linear equation is written $Ax + By = C$ where $A$, $B$ and $C$ are real numbers and $A$ and $B$ are not both zero.

**line graph**   (p. 3)  A means of displaying data using points and line segments to show changes in data over periods of time.

**line of best fit or trend line**   (p. 21)  A line that can be drawn near most of the points on a scatter plot. A trend line that slopes upward to the right indicates a *positive correlation* between the sets of data. A trend line that slopes downward to the right indicates a *negative correlation*.

**line of symmetry**   (p. 310)  A line on which a figure can be folded so that when one half is reflected over that line it matches the other part exactly.

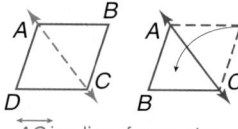

$\overleftrightarrow{AC}$ is a line of symmetry.
$\overleftrightarrow{AC}$ es un eje de simetría.

**line segment**   (p. 193)  Part of a line consisting of two endpoints and all points that lie between these two endpoints.

**términos comunes**   (pp. 66, 377)  Términos que tienen las mismas variables, o en otras palabras, términos que sólo difieren en sus coeficientes.

**línea**   (p. 192)  Conjunto infinito de puntos que se extiende en dos direcciones opuestas.

**ecuación lineal**   (pp. 254, 257)  Ecuación que representa una función lineal. La forma estándar de una ecuación lineal se escribe $Ax + By = C$ donde $A$, $B$ y $C$ son números reales y $A$ y $B$ no son ambos igual a cero.

**gráfica de línea**   (p. 3)  Representación gráfica de datos valiéndose de puntos y rectas o segmentos de línea para mostrar los cambios de datos en un periodo de tiempo.

**línea más apropiada o línea de tendencia**   (p. 21)  Línea que se puede dibujar cerca de casi todos los puntos en un diagrama disperso. Una línea de tendencia que suba hacia la derecha indica una *correlación positiva* entre el conjunto de datos. Una línea de tendencia que baje hacia la derecha indica una *correlación negativa*.

**línea simétrica**   (p. 310)  Línea que divide a una figura en dos parte de tal manera que al doblarse una mitad es exactamente igual a la otra.

**recta o segmento de línea**   (p.193)  Conjunto infinito de puntos que apuntan hacia la misma dirección contenidos entre dos puntos extremos.

### ■ M ■

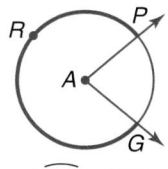

$m\overset{\frown}{PRG} > 180°$

**major arc**   (p. 227)  An arc that is larger than a semicircle.

**matrix**   (pp. 38, 354)  A rectangular array of data in rows and columns and enclosed by brackets. The number of rows and columns in a matrix determine its dimensions. When two matrices have equal dimensions, corresponding elements are elements in the same position of each matrix.

**mean,** or *arithmetic average*   (p. 10)  The sum of the values in a data set divided by the number of data.

**arco mayor**   (p. 227)  Arco que es más largo que un semicírculo.

**matriz**   (pp. 38, 354)  Formación rectangular de datos en filas y en columnas enmarcadas por llaves. El número de filas y de columnas en una matriz determina sus dimensiones. Cuando dos matrices tienen las mismas dimensiones, Los elementos que se corresponden están en la misma posición en cada matriz.

**media** o *promedio aritmético*   (p. 10)  La suma de un conjunto de números dividida entre la cantidad de números que forman el conjunto.

# English

**measures of central tendency**   (p. 10)  Statistical values mean, median and mode that represent a central, or middle, value of a data set.

**median**   (p. 10)  The middle value of a data set when the data are arranged in numerical order.

**midpoint**   (p. 193)  The point that divides the segment into two congruent segments.

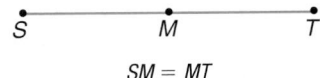

$SM = MT$

**midpoint formula**   (p. 245)  For any points $P_1$ and $P_2$, the midpoint between $P_1$ and $P_2$ is given by the formula $\left( \dfrac{x_1 + x_2}{2}, \dfrac{y_1 + y_2}{2} \right)$.

**minor arc**   (p. 227)  An arc that is smaller than a semicircle.

**misleading data**   (p. 34)  Data that leads to a false perception.

**mode**   (p. 10)  The value that occurs most often in a set of data.

**model**   (p. 114)  A physical or numerical representation of a real-life situation.

**monomial**   (p. 376)  An expression that is a number, variable, or product of a number and one or more variables with whole number exponents.

**multiplication property of equality**   (p. 108)  When two expressions are equal, you can multiply each expression by the same number and the resulting products will be equal. If $a = b$, then $a \cdot c = b \cdot c$ and $c \cdot a = c \cdot b$.

**multiplication property of inequality**   (p. 133)  If you multiply each side of an inequality by the same positive number, the order of the inequality remains the same. If you multiply each side of an inequality by the same negative number, the order of the inequality is reversed.

**mutually exclusive**   (p. 162)  Events that cannot occur at the same time are mutually exclusive. If $A$ and $B$ are mutually exclusive events, then $P(A \text{ or } B) = P(A) + P(B)$. If $A$ and $B$ are not mutually exclusive, then $P(A \text{ or } B) = P(A) + P(B) - P(A \text{ and } B)$.

# Español

**medidas de tendencia central**   (p. 10)  Medidas que se usan en la estadística para analizar datos. Estas medidas son la *media*, la *mediana* y la *moda*.

**mediana**   (p. 10)  El valor que queda en el medio al ordenarse los datos de menor a mayor. Si quedaran dos valores, la mediana sería el promedio de ambos.

**punto medio**   (p. 193)  Punto que divide a una recta en dos rectas de igual medida.

**fórmula del punto medio**   (p. 245)  Para dos puntos $P_1$ y $P_2$, el punto medio entre $P_1$ y $P_2$ es dado por la fórmula $\left( \dfrac{x_1 + x_2}{2}, \dfrac{y_1 + y_2}{2} \right)$.

**arco menor**   (p. 227)  Arco que es más pequeño que el semicírculo.

**datos engañosos**   (p. 34)  Datos que te llevan a una falsa percepción.

**moda**   (p. 10)  Número o artículo que se da con más frecuencia en un conjunto de datos.

**modelo**   (p. 114)  Representación física o numérica de una situación de la vida real.

**monomio**   (p. 376)  Expresión que puede ser un número, una variable o el producto de un número y de una o más variables con números enteros como exponentes.

**propiedad en la multiplicación de la igualdad**   (p. 108)  Cuando dos expresiones son iguales, se puede multiplicar cada expresión por el mismo número y los resultados serán iguales. Si $a = b$, entonces $ac = bc$ y $ca = cb$.

**propiedad en la multiplicación de la desigualdad**   (p. 133)  Si multiplicas ambos lados de una desigualdad por el mismo número positivo, la proporción de la desigualdad seguirá siendo la misma. Si multiplicas ambos lados de una desigualdad por el mismo número negativo, la proporción seguirá siendo la misma pero opuestas.

**mutuamente exclusivo**   (p. 162)  Eventos que no pueden ocurrir a la vez son mutuamente exclusivos. Si $A$ y $B$ son eventos mutuamente exclusivos, entonces $P(A \text{ o } B) = P(A) + P(B)$. Si $A$ y $B$ no son mutuamente exclusivos, entonces $P(A \text{ o } B) = P(A) + P(B) - P(A \text{ y } B)$.

# N

**negation**   (p. 532)  To write the negation of a statement, add "not" to the statement or add the words "it is not the case that." The symbol for negation is $\sim$.

**negative correlation**   (p. 21)  A relationship between the sets of data on a scatter plot such that the slope of the line of best fit is down and to the right, or in other words, as the horizontal axis value increases, the vertical axis value decreases.

**negative reciprocals**   (p. 334)  Two numbers that have a product of $-1$.

**negación**   (p. 532)  Para señalar la negación de una declaración se le añade "no" o la frase "no se da el caso de que". El símbolo de la negación es $\sim$.

**correlación negativa**   (p. 21)  Relación tal entre los conjuntos de datos en un diagrama disperso que la inclinación de la línea más apropiada es hacia abajo y a la derecha, o en otras palabras, cuando el valor del eje horizontal aumenta y el valor del eje vertical disminuye.

**recíprocos negativos**   (p. 334)  Dos números cuyo producto es igual a $-1$.

# English        # Español

**net**   (p. 426) A two-dimensional pattern that can be folded to form a three-dimensional figure. A three-dimensional figure can have more than one net.

**noncollinear points**   (p. 192) Points that do not lie on the same line.

**noncoplanar points**   (p. 192) Points that do not lie in the same plane.

**null set**   (p. 521) A set having no elements. The symbol for the null set is ∅ or { }.

**numerical expression**   (p. 56) An expression that contains two or more numbers joined by operations.

**red**   (p. 426) Patrón dimensional que, cuando se dobla, forma una figura tridimensional. Una figura tridimensional puede tener más de una red.

**puntos no colineales**   (p. 192) Puntos que no forman parte de la misma línea.

**puntos no coplanares**   (p. 192) Puntos que no forman parte del mismo plano.

**conjunto nulo**   (p. 521) Conjunto que no tiene ningún elemento. El símbolo para el conjunto vacío es ∅ o { }.

**expresión numérica**   (p. 56) Expresión que contiene dos o más números conectados por una operación.

## ■ O ■

**obtuse angle**   (p. 196) An angle whose measure is greater than 90° but less than 180°.

**obtuse triangle**   (p. 206) A triangle that has one obtuse angle.

one obtuse angle
un ángulo obtuso

**ángulo obtuso**   (p. 196) Cualquier triángulo que tiene un ángulo obtuso.

**triángulo obtuso**   (p. 206) Triángulo que tiene un ángulo obtuso.

**one-point perspective**   (p. 436) A perspective drawing that has one vanishing point.

**open half-plane**   (p. 258) The region on either side of a line on a coordinate plane. The line separating the half-planes forms the boundary, or edge, of each half-plane.

**opposite rays**   (p. 196) Rays that extend in opposite directions.

**opposites**   (p. 52) Numbers that are the same distance from zero on a number line but in the opposite direction.

**ordered pair**   (p. 244) A point in the coordinate plane stated as $(x, y)$.

**order of operations**   (p. 56) A set of rules that specify which operations must precede other operations in order to properly evaluate expressions.

**order of rotational symmetry**   (p. 311) The number of times a figure fits exactly over its original position when the figure is being turned about a point during a complete rotation.

**origin**   (p. 244) The point (0, 0) of intersection of the $x$-axis and $y$-axis in a coordinate plane.

**orthogonal drawing or orthographic drawing**   (p. 446) A drawing of the top, front and side views of a three dimensional figure as seen from a "straight on" viewpoint.

**outliers**   (pp. 17, 19, 29) Specifically, any data value that is less than the median of the lower half of data minus 1.5 times the interquartile range or greater than the median of the upper half of the data plus 1.5 times the interquartile range. Generally, see *stem-and-leaf plot*.

**punto de perspectiva**   (p. 436) Dibujo a perspectiva que tiene un punto de fuga.

**medio plano abierto**   (p. 258) Región en cualquier lado de una línea en un plano de coordenadas. La línea que separa los medios planos forma un límite o borde de cada medio plano.

**rayos o líneas opuestas**   (p. 196) Rayos o líneas que se extienden en direcciones opuestas.

**opuestos**   (p. 52) Números que están a la misma distancia del cero pero en direcciones opuestas.

**par ordenado**   (p. 244) Punto en un plano de coordenadas establecido como $(x, y)$.

**orden de las operaciones**   (p. 56) Conjunto de pasos que especifican cuales operaciones deben de preceder a otras operaciones para evaluar expresiones correctamente.

**orden de simetría en rotación**   (p. 311) Número de veces que una figura cabe exactamente sobre su posición original cuando la figura gira alrededor de un punto durante una rotación completa.

**origen**   (p. 244) El punto (0, 0) de intersección del eje $x$ y del eje $y$ en un plano coordenado o cartesiano.

**dibujo ortogonal o proyección ortogonal**   (p. 446) Vista tridimensional de un objeto en el cual desde uno de los "vértices superiores" se muestran las aristas de una figura sin distorsionar las dimensiones de la misma.

**datos extremos**   (pp. 17, 19, 29) Específicamente, cualquier valor que sea menor que la mediana de la mitad más baja de los datos menores 1.5 veces al alcance intercuartil o mayor que la mediana más alta de los datos positivos mayores 1.5 veces al alcance intercuartil. Generalmente, véase *diagrama de tallo y hoja*.

# English

# Español

## ■ P ■

**palindrome**  (pp. 175, 313)  A number or word that reads the same backward or forward.

**parabola**  (p. 268)  A curve that is the graph of a quadratic function. Not all parabolas represent functions.

**parallel lines**  (pp. 202, 334)  Coplanar lines that do not intersect. Parallel lines have equal slopes.

$$\overleftrightarrow{AB} \parallel \overleftrightarrow{CD}$$

**parallelogram**  (p. 216)  A quadrilateral with two pairs of parallel sides.

**percentile**  (p. 30)  A measure of a rank, or standing, within a group. A percentile divides a group of data into two parts, those at or below a certain score and those above. The percentile represents the percent of scores at or below a particular score by dividing the number of scores less than or equal to a given score by the total number of scores.

**perfect number**  (p. 93)  A number equal to the sum of its factors, excluding the number itself.

**perfect square**  (p. 373)  An integer whose square roots are integers.

**perimeter**  (p. 418)  The number of units needed to go around a two-dimensional space.

**permutation**  (p. 172)  An arrangement of items in a particular order. The number of permutations of $n$ different items is $n!$. The number of permutations of $n$ different items taken $r$ items at a time and with no repetitions is $_nP_r = \frac{n!}{(n-r)!}$.

**perpendicular lines**  (pp. 197, 334)  Two lines that intersect to form right angles. The slopes of perpendicular lines have a product of $-1$.

line $m \perp$ line $n$
recta $m \perp$ recta $n$

**perspective drawing**  (p. 436)  A drawing of a three-dimensional object in such a way that parallel lines that extend into the distance are not actually drawn parallel but instead are drawn toward a *vanishing point*.

**pictograph**  (p. 2)  A means of displaying data that uses pictures or symbols to represent data. The key identifies the number of data items represented by each symbol.

**plane**  (p. 192)  A flat surface that exists without end in all directions.

**point**  (p. 192)  A location in space having no dimensions.

**palíndromo**  (pp. 175, 313)  Número o palabra que dice lo mismo al leerse desde el principio o desde el final.

**parábola**  (p. 268)  Curva que viene a ser la gráfica de una función cuadrática. No todas las parábolas representan funciones.

**rectas paralelas**  (pp. 202, 334)  rectas coplanares que no se intersecan. Las rectas paralelas tienen la misma inclinación.

**paralelogramo**  (p. 216)  Cuadrilátero con dos pares de lados paralelos.

**porcentil (alcance)**  (p. 30)  Medida de un alcance o categoría dentro de un grupo. Un porcentil divide un grupo de datos en dos partes, Aquellos que están por debajo de una cierta puntuación y aquellos que están por encima. El porcentil representa el por ciento de posiciones debajo de una posición particular y resulta al dividir el número de posiciones menores o iguales que la posición dada entre el total de posiciones.

**números perfectos**  (p. 93)  Número igual a la suma de sus factores, excluyendo el número mismo.

**cuadrado perfecto**  (p. 373)  Número cuya raíz cuadrada es un entero.

**perímetro**  (p. 418)  Distancia alrededor de una figura de dos dimensiones.

**permutación**  (p. 172)  Arreglo de objetos en un orden particular. El número de permutaciones de diferentes objetos $n$ se denomina $n!$. El número de permutaciones de diferentes artículos n que toma un artículo $r$ sólo una vez se lee $_nP_r = \frac{n!}{(n-r)!}$.

**rectas perpendiculares**  (pp. 197, 334)  Dos rectas que se intersecan para formar ángulos rectos. Las pendientes de las rectas perpendiculares tienen un producto de $-1$.

**dibujo en perspectiva**  (p. 436)  Dibujo de un objeto de tres dimensiones en el que las líneas paralelas no se dibujan en realidad en forma paralela sino que son dirigidas hacia un *punto de fuga*.

**pictografía**  (p. 2)  Gráfica que usa figuras o símbolos para representar datos. La clave identifica el número de datos representados por cada símbolo.

**plano**  (p. 192)  Superficie llana que se extiende sin fin en todas direcciones.

**punto**  (p. 192)  Lugar específico en el espacio que no tiene dimensiones.

# English

**polygon** (p. 222) A closed plane figure formed by joining three or more line segments at their endpoints. Each segment, or *side* of the polygon, intersects exactly two other segments, one at each endpoint. The point at which the endpoints meet is called a *vertex*.

**polyhedron** (p. 422) A closed, three-dimensional figure made of polygons. The polygonal surfaces are called *faces*. Two faces meet, or intersect, to form an *edge*. The point at which three or more edges intersect is called a *vertex*.

**polynomial** (p. 376) The sum or difference of monomials. Each monomial is called a *term* of the polynomial. A polynomial is in *standard form* when its terms are ordered from the greatest to the least powers of one of the variables.

**population** (p. 6) The entire set or group of individuals from which a sample is taken.

**postulate** (p. 193) A hypothesis that is assumed to be true.

**power of a product rule** (p. 83) A property of exponents which states that when factors of a product are raised to an exponent, the power of each factor is that exponent. For all real numbers $a$ and $b$, if $m$ and $n$ are integers, then $(ab)^m = a^m b^m$.

**power of a quotient rule** (p. 83) A property of exponents which states that when factors of a quotient are raised to an exponent, the power of each factor is that exponent. For all real numbers $a$ and $b$, if $m$ and $n$ are integers, then $\left(\dfrac{a}{b}\right)^m = \dfrac{a^m}{b^m}$ if $b \neq 0$.

**power rule** (p. 83) A property of exponents which states that when a number in exponential form is raised to an exponent, the power of the base is the product of the exponents. For all real numbers $a$ and $b$, if $m$ and $n$ are integers, then $(a^m)^n = a^{mn}$.

**preimage** (p. 296) The original figure of the image that resulted from a transformation.

**premises** (p. 539) A set of statements accepted as true and from which a conclusion is drawn in deductive arguments.

**prism** (p. 422) A polyhedron with two identical parallel faces called *bases*. The other faces are parallelograms. A prism is named according to the shape of its bases.

# Español

**polígono** (p. 222) Figura plana y cerrada que se forma al conectarse tres o más líneas rectas en sus puntos extremos. Cada *lado* del polígono se interseca exactamente con otros dos, uno en cada extremo. El punto en el que unen los lados se llama *vértice*.

**poliedro** (p. 422) Figura cerrada tridimensional formada por polígonos. Cada polígono recibe el nombre de *cara*. Dos caras se unen, o se intersecan, para formar una línea de encuentro que se llama *arista*. El punto de encuentro de tres o más aristas se llama *vértice*.

**polinomio** (p. 376) Suma o resta de dos o más monomios. Cada monomio es un *término* del polinomio. Un polinomio se halla en su *forma estándar* cuando sus términos se encuentran ordenados de la mayor a la menor potencia de una de sus variables.

**población** (p. 6) Totalidad de un conjunto o grupo de individuos que son tomados de una muestra.

**postulado** (p. 193) Hipótesis que se asume como cierta.

**regla de la potencia de un producto** (p. 83) Propiedad de los exponentes que establece que cuando los factores de un producto son elevados, el poder de dicho factor es ese exponente. Para todos los números reales $a$ y $b$, si $m$ y $n$ son números enteros, entonces $(ab)^m = a^m b^m$.

**potencia de la regla del cociente** (p. 83) Propiedad de los exponentes que establece que cuando los factores de un cociente elevados a un exponente, la potencia de cada factor es ese exponente. Para todos los números reales $a$ y $b$, si $m$ y $n$ son números enteros, entonces $\left(\dfrac{a}{b}\right)^m = \dfrac{a^m}{b^m}$, si $b$ es desigual a 0.

**regla de la potencia** (p. 83) Propiedad de los exponentes que establece que cuando un número en forma exponencial es elevado al valor de un exponente, la potencia de la base es el producto de los exponentes. Para todos los números reales $a$ y $b$, si $m$ y $n$ son números enteros, entonces $(a^m)^n = a^{mn}$.

**pre-imagen** (p. 296) Figura original que resulta de una transformación.

**premisas** (p. 539) Conjunto de afirmaciones que se aceptan como ciertas y del que se llega a conclusiones por medio de argumentos deductivos.

**prisma** (p. 422) Poliedro con dos caras paralelas idénticas llamadas *bases*. Las otras caras son paralelogramos. Los prismas reciben su nombre a partir de la forma de sus bases.

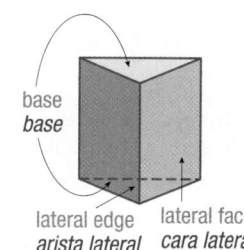

base
*base*

lateral edge  lateral face
*arista lateral*  *cara lateral*

triangular prism
*prisma triangular*

# English

**probability**   (p. 148)  The chance or likelihood that an event will occur, written $P(E)$. An impossible event has a probability of 0. A certain event has a probability of 1.

**property of negative exponents**   (p. 86)  For any nonzero real number $a$, if $n$ is a positive integer, $a^{-n} = \frac{1}{a^n}$.

**proportion**   (p. 122)  An equation stating that two ratios are equal. A proportion can be written as *a is to b as c is to d*, $a : b = c : d$, or $\frac{a}{b} = \frac{c}{d}$. In any of these forms, $b$ and $c$ are called the *means* of the proportion, and $a$ and $d$ are called the *extremes*.

vertex
*vértice*

lateral face
*cara lateral*

base
*base*

rectangular pyramid
*pirámide rectangular*

**pyramid**   (p. 422)  A polyhedron with only one base. The other faces are triangles that meet at a vertex. A pyramid is named by the shape of its base.

**Pythagorean theorem**   (p. 484)  In any right triangle, the square of the length of the hypotenuse $c$ is equal to the sum of the squares of the lengths of the legs $a$ and $b$. The Pythagorean theorem is expressed as $c^2 = a^2 + b^2$.

# Español

**probabilidad**   (p. 148)  Posibilidad de que ocurra un evento y que se lee $P(E)$. Un evento imposible tiene una probabilidad de 0. Un evento que es cierto tiene una probabilidad de 1.

**propiedad de exponentes negativos**
(p. 86)  Para cualquier número real que no sea cero $a$, si $n$ es un número entero positivo, $a^{-n} = \frac{1}{a^n}$.

**proporción**   (p. 122)  Ecuación que establece que dos razones son equivalentes. Una proporción puede ser escrita de la siguiente manera: *a es a b como c es a d*, $a : b = c : d$, o $\frac{a}{b} = \frac{c}{d}$. En cualquiera de estas formas, $b$ y $c$ se denominan *medios* de la proporción, y $a$ y $d$ se denominan *extremos*.

**pirámide**   (p. 422)  Poliedro con una sola base. Las otras caras son triángulos. Una pirámide recibe el nombre de acuerdo a la forma de su base.

**teorema de Pitágoras**   (p. 484)  En un triángulo rectángulo, la suma de los cuadrados de las longitudes de los catetos $a$ y $b$ es igual al cuadrado de la longitud de la hipotenusa $c$. El Teorema de Pitágoras se expresa así: $c^2 = a^2 + b^2$.

## ■ Q ■

**quadrant**   (p. 244)  One of the four regions formed by the axes of the coordinate plane.

**quadratic equation**   (p. 268)  An equation of the form $Ax^2 + Bx + C = 0$, where $A$, $B$ and $C$ are real numbers and $A$ is not zero.

**quadrilateral**   (p. 216)  A closed plane figure that has four sides.

**quartiles**   (p. 28)  The three values which divide an ordered set of data into four equal parts. The *first quartile* is the median of the lower half of the data. The *third quartile* is the median of the upper half. The *second quartile* is another name for the median of the entire set of data.

**cuadrante**   (p. 244)  Una de las cuatro regiones formadas por los ejes del plano de coordenadas.

**ecuación cuadrática**   (p. 268)  Ecuación de la forma $Ax^2 + Bx + C = 0$, donde $A$, $B$ y $C$ son números reales y $A$ no es cero.

**cuadrilátero**   (p. 216)  Polígono que tiene cuatro lados.

**cuartiles**   (p. 28)  Se refiere a los tres valores que dividen un conjunto ordenado de datos en cuatro partes iguales. El *primer cuartil* es la mediana de la mitad inferior de los datos. El *tercer cuartil* es la mediana de la mitad superior. El *segundo cuartil* es otro nombre para la mediana del conjunto entero de datos.

## ■ R ■

**radical**   (p. 136)  An expression in the form $\sqrt{a}$, where $\sqrt{\phantom{a}}$ is called the radical symbol and $a$ is called the radicand.

**radius**   (p. 226)  A line segment that has one endpoint at the center of the circle and the other endpoint on the circle.

**radical**   (p. 136)  Expresión en la forma $\sqrt{a}$ donde $\sqrt{\phantom{a}}$ se llama símbolo radical y $a$ es el radicando.

**radio**   (p. 226)  Distancia que hay entre el centro del círculo y cualquier punto de la circunferencia.

Glossary/Glosario

# English

# Español

**random sampling**   (p. 6)  A sampling method in which each member of the population has an equal chance of being selected.

**muestra aleatoria**   (p. 6)  Cada miembro de una población tiene la misma posibilidad de ser seleccionado.

**range**   (p. 11)  The difference between the greatest and least values in a set of data.

**alcance**   (p. 11)  Diferencia entre el número mayor y el menor en un conjunto de datos.

**range (of a function)**   (p. 264)  The set of all possible values of $y$ for the function $y = f(x)$.

**alcance (de una función)**   (p. 264)  Conjunto de todos los valores posibles de $y$ para la función $y = f(x)$.

**rate**   (p. 101)  A ratio that compares different units.

**tasa**   (p. 101)  Razón que compara diferentes tipos de unidades.

**ratio**   (p. 100)  A comparison of two quantities represented in one of the following ways: $a{:}b$, $\frac{a}{b}$, $a$ to $b$.

**razón**   (p. 100)  Comparación de un número con otro que se representa de las tres siguientes formas: $a{:}b$, $\frac{a}{b}$, $a$ es a $b$.

**rational number**   (p. 52)  A number that can be expressed as a ratio of two numbers $a$ and $b$, where $b$ is not equal to zero. This is written $\frac{a}{b}$, $b \neq 0$.

**número racional**   (p. 52)  Cualquier número que pueda ser expresado en forma $\frac{a}{b}$, donde a es cualquier entero y $b$ es también cualquier entero excepto 0. Se escribe $\frac{a}{b}$, $b$ no es igual a $b$.

**ray**   (p. 196)  Part of a line that starts at one endpoint and extends without end in one direction.

**rayo o línea recta**   (p. 196)  Parte de una línea que tiene un punto extremo y se extiende sin fin en una dirección.

**real numbers**   (p. 52)  The set of rational and irrational numbers.

**números reales**   (p. 52)  Conjunto formado por los números racionales e irracionales.

**reciprocals**   (p. 334)  Two numbers that have a product of 1. To find the reciprocal of a number, switch the numerator and the denominator.

**recíprocos**   (p. 334)  Dos números son recíprocos cuando su producto es 1. Para encontrar el recíproco de un número intercambie el numerador por el denominador.

**rectangle**   (p. 216)  A parallelogram that has four right angles.

**rectángulo**   (p. 216)  Paralelogramo que tiene cuatro ángulo rectos.

**reflection**   (p. 300)  A transformation in which a figure is reflected, or flipped, across a line of reflection. A reflection image is congruent to the preimage but oriented in the opposite direction.

**reflexión**   (p. 300)  Transformación en la cual una figura se voltea o se refleja sobre una línea de reflejo. La reflexión de una imagen es congruente con la pre-imagen pero orientada en dirección opuesta.

**regular polygon**   (p. 222)  A polygon that has all sides congruent and all angles congruent.

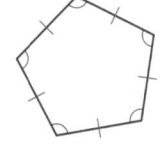

regular pentagon
*pentágono regular*

**polígono regular**   (p. 222)  Polígono que tiene todos sus lados y sus ángulo congruentes.

**relative frequency**   (p. 150)  A comparison of the number of times a particular outcome occurs to the total number of observations.

**frecuencia relativa**   (p. 150)  Comparación del número de veces que un resultado particular ocurre con el número total de observaciones.

**repeating decimal**   (p. 52)  A decimal in which a digit or group of digits repeats. A bar above the group of repeating digits is used to express the repeating decimal.

**decimal periódico**   (p. 52)  Decimal en donde un dígito o grupo de dígitos se repiten. Se usa una barra encima del grupo de dígitos que se repite para expresar el decimal periódico.

**rhombus**   (p. 216)  A parallelogram that has four congruent sides.

**rombo**   (p. 216)  Paralelogramo que tiene sus cuatro lados iguales.

**right angle**   (p. 196)  An angle measuring exactly 90°.

**ángulo recto**   (p. 196)  Ángulo que mide exactamente 90°.

# English

**right triangle**   (p. 206)  A triangle having one right angle.

**roster notation**   (p. 520)  Set notation that lists the elements of the set.

**rotation**   (p. 306)  A transformation in which a figure is rotated, or turned, about a point.

**rotational symmetry**   (p. 311)  A figure has rotational symmetry if it fits exactly over its original position at least once during a complete rotation about a point.

# Español

**triángulo rectángulo**   (p. 206)  Triángulo que tiene un ángulo recto.

**lista de anotaciones**   (p. 520)  Conjunto de anotaciones que ponen en una lista de determinados elementos.

**rotación**   (p. 306)  Transformación en la que una figura gira o rota sobre un punto.

**simetría rotacional**   (p. 311)  Propiedad de una figura que puede quedar exactamente en su posición original después de haber rotado una vez.

## ■ S ■

**sample**   (p. 6)  A representative part of a population.

**sample space**   (p. 158)  The set of all possible outcomes of an experiment.

**scale drawing**   (p. 122)  A drawing that represents an object. All lengths in the drawing are proportional to actual lengths in the object. The *scale* of the drawing is the ratio of the size of the drawing to the actual size of the object.

**scale factor**   (p. 316)  The number that is multiplied by the length of each side of a figure to create an altered image in a dilation.

**scalene triangle**   (p. 206)  A triangle with no congruent sides and no congruent angles.

**scatter plot**   (p. 20)  A method of displaying the relationship between two sets of data in which the data are represented as ordered pairs and graphed as unconnected points.

**scientific notation**   (p. 87)  A notation for writing a number as the product of a factor that is greater than or equal to 1 and less than 10 and a second factor that is a power of 10.

**sector**   (p. 232)  A part of a circle graph formed by a central angle.

**semicircle**   (p. 227)  An arc of a circle with endpoints that are the endpoints of a diameter.

**sequence**   (p. 92)  A set of numbers that is arranged according to a pattern. Each number is a *term* of the sequence.

**muestra**   (p. 6)  Parte representativa de una población.

**espacio de muestra**   (p. 158)  El conjunto de todos los resultados posibles en un experimento.

**dibujo a escala**   (p. 122)  Dibujo que representa un objeto. Todas las longitudes en el dibujo son proporcionales a las longitudes reales del objeto. La *escala* del dibujo es la razón del tamaño del dibujo al tamaño del objeto real.

**factor escala**   (p. 316)  Número que se multiplica por la longitud de cada uno de los lados de una figura para crear una imagen alterada a través de una dilatación.

**triángulo escaleno**   (p. 206)  Triángulo que tiene tanto sus lados como sus ángulos desiguales.

**diagrama disperso**   (p. 20)  Representación gráfica que muestra la relación entre dos conjuntos de datos en los cuales los datos se representan como pares ordenados y también como puntos sin conexión.

**notación científica**   (p. 87)  Notación de un número como el producto de un primer factor que es igual o mayor que 1 y menor que 10 y un segundo factor que es una potencia de 10.

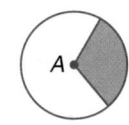

**sector**   (p. 232)  Parte de una gráfica dentro del círculo formada por un ángulo central.

The shaded region is a sector of ⊙*A*.
*La región sombreada es un sector de ⊙A.*

**semicírculo**   (p. 227)  Arco de un círculo cuyos puntos extremos son también los puntos extremos del diámetro.

**secuencia**   (p. 92)  Conjunto de números que se ordena de acuerdo a un patrón. Cada número es un *término* de la secuencia.

# English

**set** (p. 520) A well-defined collection of items. Each item is called an *element*, or *member*, of the set. A set is usually named with a capital letter.

**set-builder notation** (p. 520) Set notation that gives a rule that defines each element in the set.

**side** (pp. 206, 222) A line segment that joins the vertices of a two-dimensional figure or a plane that joins the edges of a three-dimensional figure.

**Side-Angle-Side Postulate (SAS)** (p. 213) If two sides and the included angle of one triangle are congruent to two corresponding sides and the included angle of another triangle, then the triangles are congruent.

**Side-Side-Side Postulate (SSS)** (p. 213) If three sides of one triangle are congruent to three corresponding sides of another triangle, then the triangles are congruent.

**similar figures** (p. 474) Figures that have the same shape but not necessarily the same size, indicated by the symbol ~. In *similar polygons*, all pairs of corresponding angles are congruent and all pairs of corresponding sides are in proportion.

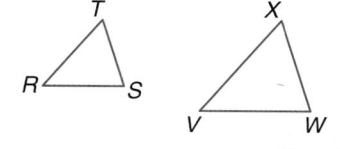

$\angle T \cong \angle X$, $\angle S \cong \angle W$, $\angle R \cong \angle V$; $\frac{RT}{VX} = \frac{ST}{WX} = \frac{RS}{VW}$

**simplify** (pp. 56, 66) To find the value of a numerical expression or to perform as many of the indicated operations as possible in a variable expression.

**simulation** (p. 154) A model of a situation in which you carry out trials, collect data and calculate probabilities. The model is used because it is easier to implement than the actual problem.

**sine** (p. 488) The trigonometric ratio of an $\angle A$, abbreviated sin $A$, of the length of the leg opposite $\angle A$ to the length of the hypotenuse.

**skew lines** (p. 202) Noncoplanar lines that do not intersect and are not parallel.

**slant height** (p. 433) The slant height of a cone is the length of a line drawn from its vertex to its base along the side of the cone. The slant height of a pyramid is the height of a face.

**slope** (p. 248) The ratio of a line segment's change in vertical distance compared to its change in horizontal distance, given by the formula $m = \frac{y_2 - y_1}{x_2 - x_1}$.

**slope-intercept form** (p. 254) A linear equation in the form $y = mx + b$ where $m$ is the slope of the graph of the equation and $b$ is the $y$-intercept.

**space** (p. 192) The set of all points.

# Español

**conjunto** (p. 520) Colección bien definida de datos. Cada dato recibe el nombre de *elemento* o *miembro* de el conjunto. A un conjunto por lo general se le define con una letra mayúscula

**notación de un conjunto construido** (p. 520) Notación de un conjunto que da la pauta que define a cada elemento del conjunto.

**lado** (pp. 206, 222) Recta o segmento de línea que comparte los vértices ya sea de una figura bimensional o de un plano que comparte las aristas de una figura tridimensional.

**Postulado de lado-ángulo-lado (LAL)** (p. 213) Si dos lados y el ángulo contenido de un triángulo se corresponden con los lados y el ángulo de otro triángulo, entonces los triángulos son congruentes.

**Postulado de lado-lado-lado** (p. 213) Si tres lados de un triángulo son congruentes con los lados correspondientes de otro triángulo, entonces los triángulos son congruentes.

**figuras similares** (p. 474) Figuras que tienen la misma forma pero no necesariamente el mismo tamaño, indicado con el símbolo ~. En polígonos similares, todos los pares de ángulos correspondientes son congruentes y todos los pares de lados correspondientes son proporcionales.

**simplificar** (pp. 56, 66) Encontrar el valor de una expresión numérica o hacer todas las operaciones indicadas que sean posibles.

**simulación** (p. 154) Modelo de una situación en la cual realizas pruebas, recolectas datos y calculas probabilidades. El modelo se usa porque es más fácil de implementar que el problema real.

**seno** (p. 488) Razón geométrica de un $\angle A$, se abrevia sen $A$, que es el cociente del cateto opuesto al ángulo en cuestión, sobre la hipotenusa.

**líneas oblicuas** (p. 202) Líneas que no son coplanares, que no se intersecan y tampoco son paralelas.

**altura diagonal** (p. 433) La altura diagonal de un cono es la longitud de la recta que sale del vértice de su punta y baja por todo lo largo de su lado. La altura diagonal de una pirámide es la altura de una de sus caras.

**pendiente** (p. 248) La razón de cambio de una recta en distancia vertical comparada a su cambio en distancia horizontal, es dada por la fórmula $m = \frac{y_2 - y_1}{x_2 - x_1}$.

**forma de pendiente e intersección** (p. 254) Ecuación lineal en forma de $y = mx + b$ donde $m$ es la pendiente de la gráfica de la ecuación y $b$ es el interceptor en $y$.

**espacio** (p. 192) Conjunto de todos los puntos.

# English

**sphere** (p. 422) The set of all points in space that are a given distance from a given point, called the *center* of the sphere.

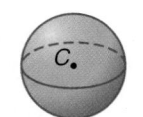

*C* is the center of the sphere.
*C es el centro de la esfera.*

**square** (p. 136) A factor multiplied by itself, or in other words, a number raised to the second power.

**square** (p. 216) A parallelogram that has four right angles and four congruent sides.

**square matrix** (pp. 39, 354) A square matrix is a matrix that has the same number of rows and columns.

**square root** (p. 136) A number, *a*, is a square root of another number, *b*, if $a^2 = b$. A square root is one of two equal factors of a number.

**stem-and-leaf plot** (p. 17) A method of displaying data in which certain digits are used as *stems* and the remaining digits are used as *leaves*. *Outliers* are data values that are much greater than or much less than most of the other values. *Clusters* are isolated groups of values. *Gaps* are large spaces between values.

**straight angle** (p. 196) An angle measuring 180°.

**subset** (p. 521) If every element of set *A* is also an element of set *B*, then *A* is called a subset of *B*, written $A \subseteq B$.

**substitution method** (p. 345) A method of solving systems of equations algebraically. Solve one of the equations for one variable, and substitute that expression in the other equation and solve.

**supplementary angles** (p. 196) Two angles whose measures have a sum of 180°.

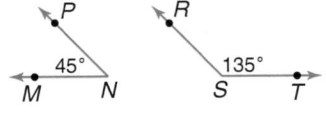

$m\angle MNP + m\angle RST = 180°$

**surface area** (p. 427) The sum of the areas of all the faces and bases of a three-dimensional figure.

**systematic sampling** (p. 6) A method of sampling in which members of a population that have been ordered in some way are selected according to a pattern.

**system of linear equations** (p. 338) Two or more linear equations with the same two variables. The *solution of a system* of linear equations is the ordered pair that makes both equations true.

# Español

**esfera** (p. 422) Figura tridimensional formada por puntos que están a la misma distancia de un punto dado llamado el centro de la esfera.

**cuadrado** (p. 136) Factor multiplicado por sí mismo, o en otras palabras, un número elevado a la segunda potencia.

**cuadrado** (p. 216) Paralelogramo con cuatro ángulos rectos y todos los lados iguales.

**matriz cuadrada** (pp. 39, 354) Es una matriz que tiene el mismo número de filas y de columnas.

**raíz cuadrada** (p. 136) Un número, *a*, es la raíz cuadrada de otro número, *b*, si $a^2 = b$. Una raíz cuadrada es uno de los dos factores iguales de un número.

**diagrama de tallo y hoja** (p. 17) Representación gráfica donde se organizan y se muestran datos donde algunos dígitos se usan como tallos, y otros como hojas. Los datos extremos son valores que son mucho más grandes o mucho más pequeños que los otros valores. Los datos extremos son grupos de valores aislados. Las separaciones son largos espacios entre los valores.

**ángulo recto** (p. 196) Ángulo que mide 180°.

**subconjunto** (p. 493) Si cada elemento del conjunto *A* es también un elemento del conjunto *B*, entonces *A* es subconjunto de *B*, se escribe $A \subseteq B$.

**método de substitución** (p. 345) Método para resolver sistemas de ecuaciones algebraicas. Se resuelve una ecuación por una variable, y se substituye esa expresión en la otra ecuación y se resuelve.

**ángulos suplementarios** (p. 196) Dos ángulos cuya suma de sus medidas es igual a 180°.

**superficie del área** (p. 427) La suma de las superficies de todas las caras y bases de una figura tridimensional.

**muestra sistemática** (p. 6) Después de que una población se ordena de algún modo, los miembros de la población se eligen de acuerdo a un patrón.

**sistema de ecuaciones lineales** (p. 338) Dos o más ecuaciones con las mismas variables. La solución de un sistema de ecuaciones lineales es el par ordenado que hace a ambas ecuaciones verdaderas.

■ **T** ■

**tangent** (p. 488) The trigonometric ratio of an $\angle A$, abbreviated tan *A*, of the length of the leg opposite $\angle A$ to the length of the leg adjacent to $\angle A$.

**tangente** (p. 488) Razón trigonométrica de un $\angle A$, se abrevia tan *A*, que es el cociente del cateto opuesto sobre el cateto adyacente al ángulo en cuestión.

# English

## Español

**terminating decimal** (p. 52) A decimal in which the only repeating digit is 0.

**decimal terminal** (p. 52) Decimal en donde el único dígito que se repite es 0.

**terms** (pp. 66, 376) The parts of a variable expression or polynomial that are separated by addition or subtraction signs. Terms that have identical variable parts are called *like terms*. Terms that have different variable parts are called *unlike terms*.

**términos** (pp. 66, 376) Partes de una expresión algebraica separadas por el signo de la suma o de la resta. Los términos que tienen variables idénticas se llaman *términos semejantes*. Los términos que tienen variables diferentes se llaman *términos diferentes*.

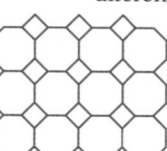

**tessellation** (p. 320) A repeating pattern of figures that completely covers a plane without gaps or overlaps.

**mosaico** (p. 320) Patrón de una figura en donde copias idénticas caben sin dejar huecos y sin sobrepasar los bordes.

**theoretical probability** (p. 159) The probability of an event based on the value of a mathematical formula in which the number of favorable outcomes is divided by the total number of possible outcomes.

**probabilidad teórica** (p. 159) Probabilidad de un evento basado en el valor de una fórmula matemática en la cual el número de resultados favorabes se divide entre el número total de resultados posibles.

**transformation** (p. 296) A way of moving or changing the size of a geometric figure in the coordinate plane by translation, reflection, rotation or dilation. The new figure is referred to as the *image* of the original figure, and the original is referred to as the *preimage* of the new.

**transformación** (p. 296) Movimiento de una figura ya sea por traslación, reflexión o rotación. La nueva figura recibe el nombre de *imagen* del original, y al original se le llama *pre-imagen* de la nueva.

**translation** (p. 296) A transformation in which a figure is slid to produce a new figure exactly like the original. Imagine all the points of the figure sliding along a plane at once in the same direction and for the same distance. A translation image is congruent to the preimage.

**traslación** (p. 296) Transformación en la cual todos los puntos de una figura se deslizan hacia la misma dirección produciendo una nueva figura idéntica a la original. Imagina los puntos de una figura deslizándose a lo largo de un plano a la vez en la misma dirección y a la misma distancia. Una imagen de traslación es congruente con la pre-imagen.

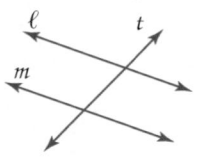

**transversal** (p. 202) A line that intersects each of two other coplanar lines in different points to produce interior and exterior angles.

Line *t* is a transversal.
*La recta t es una transversal.*

**transversal** (p. 202) Línea que interseca dos o más líneas en puntos distintos de un plano para producir ángulos interiores y exteriores.

**trapezoid** (p. 216) A quadrilateral that has exactly one pair of parallel sides.

**trapezoide** (p. 216) Cuadrilátero que tiene solamente un par de lados paralelos.

**tree diagram** (p. 158) A diagram that shows all the possible outcomes in a sample space.

**diagrama de árbol** (p. 158) Diagrama que muestra todos los resultados posibles en un espacio de muestra.

**triangle** (p. 206) The closed plane figure formed by three line segments joining three noncollinear points. Each point is called a *vertex*. Each vertex names an *angle* of the triangle. Each of the line segments that joins the vertices is called a *side*. The sum of the angles is 180°.

**triángulo** (p. 206) Polígono que tiene tres lados y tres puntos no colineales. Cada punto se llama *vértice*. Cada vértice determina un *ángulo* del triángulo. Cada línea que une a los vértices se conoce como *lado*. La suma de los ángulos es igual a 180 grados.

**trinomial** (p. 376) A polynomial with three terms.

**trinomio** (p. 376) Polinomio compuesto por tres términos.

**two-point perspective** (p. 436) A perspective drawing that has two vanishing points.

**perspectiva de dos puntos** (p. 436) Dibujo en perspectiva que muestra dos puntos de fuga.

**two-step equations** (p. 116) Equations involving two operations. To solve, use the correct order of operations.

**ecuaciones en dos pasos** (p. 116) Ecuaciones que encierran dos operaciones. Para resolverlas, es necesario usar las operaciones en el orden correcto.

Glossary/Glosario

# English        Español

## ■ U ■

**union (of two sets)** (pp. 147, 525) The union of two sets, *A* and *B*, symbolized $A \cup B$, contains all the elements that are in *A*, in *B*, or in both.

**unit rate** (p. 101) A rate that is a comparison to 1 unit.

**universal set** (p. 524) The general set of all elements being considered in a discussion. The universal set, *U*, can be an infinite set or a finite set.

**unlike terms** (p. 66) See *terms*.

**unsound argument** (p. 543) A deductive argument whose form is valid but contains at least one false premise.

**unión (de dos conjuntos)** (pp. 147, 525) Unión de dos conjuntos, *A* y *B*, simbolizados como $A \cup B$. Esta unión contiene todos los elementos que hay en *A*, en *B* o en ambos.

**tasa de unidad** (p. 101) Valor que tiene un denominador de una sola unidad.

**conjunto universal** (p. 524) Conjunto general de todos los elementos que se consideran en una discusión. El conjunto Universal se simboliza con *U* y se puede referir a conjuntos infinitos y finitos.

**términos diferentes** (p. 66) Véase *términos*.

**razonamiento inestable** (p. 543) Razonamiento deductivo cuya forma es válida pero contiene por lo menos una premisa falsa.

## ■ V ■

**valid argument** (p. 542) A deductive argument such that if the premises are true, then the conclusion must be true. In other words, the premises are assumed or known to be true and the conclusion logically follows.

**value** (p. 56) The number represented by a numerical expression.

**vanishing point** (p. 436) A point on the horizon line where parallel lines appear to come together.

**variable** (p. 54) A symbol used to represent a number.

**variable expression** (p. 57) An expression that contains one or more variables.

**Venn diagram** (pp. 147, 516) A diagram that can help you see sets and their relationships more clearly. The diagram is composed of a rectangle that represents the universal set and one or more circles that represent sets within the universe.

**vertex** (pp. 196, 206, 222, 422) The common endpoint of two rays that form an angle or of two sides of a polygon. The rays are called the *sides* of the angle or polygon.

**razonamiento válido** (p. 542) Razonamiento deductivo cuyas premisas son verdaderas y por lo tanto la conclusión también es verdadera. En otras palabras, si las premisas se asumen como verdaderas, la conclusión por lógica también lo es.

**valor** (p. 56) Número asignado a una expresión numérica.

**punto de fuga** (p. 436) Punto en el cual las líneas paralelas parecen hacer intersección pero que en un dibujo a perspectiva tiende a desaparecer.

**variable** (p. 54) Símbolo que se usa para representar un número.

**expresión variable** (p. 57) Expresión que contiene por lo menos una variable.

**diagrama de Venn** (pp. 147, 516) Diagrama en el cual un conjunto de datos se representan. En un diagrama de Venn cada cosa se representa por una región circular dentro de un rectángulo. El rectángulo se llama el *conjunto universal*.

**vértice** (pp. 196, 206, 222, 422) Punto donde se intersecan dos lados para formar un ángulo o donde se unen dos lados de un polígono. Los rayos se consideran lados de un ángulo o de un polígono.

**vertical angles** (p. 197) The angles that are not adjacent to each other when two lines intersect. Vertical angles are congruent.

∠1 and ∠3 are vertical angles.
∠2 and ∠4 are vertical angles.
*∠1 y ∠3 son ángulos opuestos por el vértice.*
*∠2 y ∠4 son ángulos opuestos por el vértice.*

**ángulos verticales** (p. 197) Ángulos de la misma medida formados por dos líneas que se intersecan. Los ángulos verticales son congruentes.

**vertical line test** (p. 265) If a vertical line drawn anywhere on the graph does not cross the graph more than one time, then the graph represents a function.

**prueba de la línea vertical** (p. 265) Si cualquier línea vertical pasa a través de la gráfica diagramada más de una vez, entonces la relación no es una función.

# English

**vital capacity**   (p. 456)  The measure of the volume of air in a person's full lungs.

**volume**   (p. 452)  The number of cube units needed to fill a three-dimensional space.

## ■ W ■

**weighted mean**   (p. 13)  A mean in which certain data values are given different degrees of emphasis by multiplying them by a variable factor called the *weight* of the data value.

**whiskers**   (p. 29)  Lines that are drawn from the sides of the box in the box-and-whisker plot.

**whole numbers**   (p. 52)  The set of natural numbers and zero.

## ■ X ■

**x-axis**   (p. 244)  The horizontal number line of the coordinate plane.

## ■ Y ■

**y-axis**   (p. 244)  The vertical number line of the coordinate plane.

**y-intercept**   (p. 254)  The y-coordinates of the point (or points) where the graph intersects the y-axis, represented by the variable b in the equation $y = mx + b$.

## ■ Z ■

**zero pairs**   (p. 67)  Of Algeblocks, when equal numbers of the same block are on opposite sides of the mat. To simplify an expression using Algeblocks, remove zero pairs from the mat.

**zero property of exponents**   (p. 86)  For any nonzero real number $a$, $a^0 = 1$.

# Español

**capacidad vital**   (p. 456)  Medida del mayor volumen de aire en los pulmones de una persona.

**volumen**   (p. 452)  Número de unidades cúbicas que se necesita para llenar un objeto tridimensional.

## ■ W ■

**media cargada**   (p. 13)  Media en que a los valores de ciertos datos se les dan diferentes grados de importancia al multiplicarlos por una variable llamada el *peso* de los datos.

**pelos**   (p. 29)  Líneas que se dibujan a los lados de un diagrama de bloque.

**números enteros**   (p. 52)  Conjunto de los números naturales que incluye al cero.

## ■ X ■

**eje x o de las abscisas**   (p. 244)  Recta numérica horizontal en un plano cartesiano.

## ■ Y ■

**eje y o de las ordenadas**   (p. 244)  Recta numérica vertical en un plano cartesiano.

**intersección en y**   (p. 254)  Véase *intersección*.

## ■ Z ■

**pares de cero**   (p. 67)  Es cuando los números iguales de un mismo bloque se encuentran en lados opuestos en los bloques algebraicos.

**propiedad cero de los exponentes**   (p. 86)  Se refiere a cualquier número real que no sea cero, $a$, $a^0 = 1$

# Selected Answers

## Chapter 1: Sample and Display Data

### Lesson 1-1, pages 6–9

1. systematic   3. cluster   5. convenience   7. Answers will vary, but a possible answer is to ask every fifth teenager in line at the cafeteria.   9. Systematic. People who attend a sporting event usually have a greater interest in that sport than another.   11. Convenience. Teenagers at the same party are most likely friends, and a common interest of friends can be the sport they participate in or enjoy watching.   13. Convenience. Only people with a strong opinion are likely to call in.   15. Random. The people may not be home or may not eat pizza.   17. Answers will vary.   19. Answers will vary.   21. convenience   23. A possible method is to survey fifty people at a recycling center.   25. Answers will vary.   27. A possible method is to survey all citizens whose phone number ends with a particular digit.   29. Answers will vary.   31. 5983   33. 656.23   35. 11,873   37. 1440.444   39. 1471   41. 5465   43. 451   45. 2108

### Lesson 1-2, pages 10–13

1. mean = 15.3 mi; median = 13.15 mi; no mode; range = 15.7 mi   3. mean   5. Removing the $15.87 meal will affect the measures of central tendency except for the mode, since in this case there is no mode. The mean decreases by $1.09, the median decreases by $0.51, and the range decreases by $5.87.   7. 4.5   9. 4   11. Answers will vary. Have students experiment with their grades. Different students' grades will benefit from different measures.   13. 93   15. Mean. Some animals hibernate or are more dormant at certain times of the year than they are at other times.   17. 13   19. always   21. Sometimes; change 1 to 4 in 1, 1, 2, 4.   23. No. She needs to average all test scores, not just the previous average. Her average is 86.7.   25. 800   27. 70   29. 21,576   31. 40,194   33. 12,155   35. 14,990.112   37. 178.577   39. 122.133   41. 116.279   43. 39.484

### Review and Practice Your Skills, pages 14–15

1. systematic   3. convenience   5. cluster   7. convenience   9. mean = $27,285.70; median = $27,000; mode = $22,000; range = $13,000   11. mean = $95.70; median = $89; mode = $105; range = $90   13. mean = $315; median = $305; no mode; range = $150   15. 57   17. 225   19. Sample answer: Send a survey to 50 random addresses of one neighborhood within the community.   21. Sample answer: Send a survey in every tenth water bill, with a total of 50 surveys sent in all.   23. mean = 6.6 mi; median = 6.2 mi; mode = 6; range = 4 mi

### Lesson 1-3, pages 16–19

1. 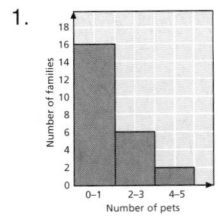   3. 2   5. median = 1; mode = 1; range = 5   7. outlier: 520; clusters: 146–189, 229–305, 412–427; gaps: 189–229, 305–366, 367–412, 427–520   9. 253

11.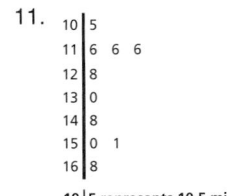

10|5 represents 10.5 mi

13. 120–129   15. 100–109, 110–119, 120–129, 130–139, 140–149

17.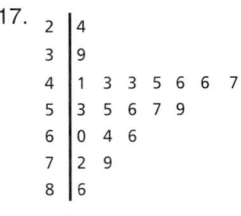

2|4 represents 24%

19. 6   21. The mean and median are almost equal in this case.   23. Answers will vary.

25.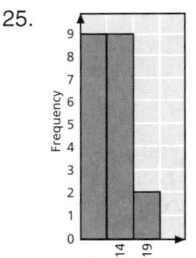

27. The data has no outliers.   29. $18   31. 80,238 people

### Lesson 1-4, pages 20–23

1. 8   3. 7   5. Answers will vary.   7. 72   9. There are two points that are farthest from the trendline. One point reflects that the student only watched one hour of TV, but scored only a 50. This suggests that perhaps the student participates in other activities that take away from study time. The other point reflects that a student did not watch any TV, but only scored a 64. Answers will vary as to why for both points.   11. positive   13. Answers will vary.   15. Answers will vary.   17. 4000   19. 15   21. 2000   23. 2000   25. 30   27. 6

## Review and Practice Your Skills, pages 24–25

1.
| 2 | 3 7 9 |
|---|---|
| 3 | 1 4 5 8 |
| 4 | 2 |

2|3 represents 23

3.
| 4 | 8 9 |
|---|---|
| 5 | 0 1 4 7 7 7 7 8 |
| 6 | 1 1 4 5 8 |

4|8 represents 48

5. 57

7.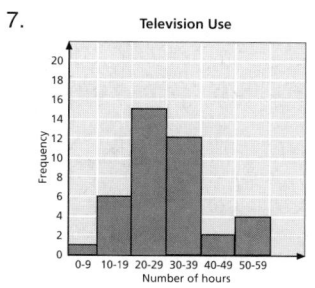
Television Use

9. 50–59   11. 10
13. positive   15. none
17. yes   19. 80
21. 6.9, 8.1   23. 7.2
25. 23.5

## Lesson 1-5, pages 26–27

1. B; negative   3. C; no correlation   5. $r = -0.996$
7. Negative. As temperature rises, snow ski sales will fall.
9. Negative. In general, as a car experiences wear and tear, gas mileage will suffer.   11. $\frac{1}{4}, \frac{2}{8}, \frac{4}{16}$

13. $\frac{4}{5}, \frac{8}{10}, \frac{12}{15}$   15. $\frac{14}{16}, \frac{21}{24}, \frac{28}{32}$   17. 14   19. $-12$
21. 7   23. 10   25. 4

## Lesson 1-6, pages 28–31

1. $Q_3 - Q_1$   3.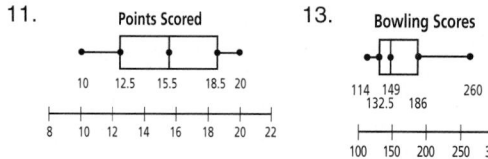
Science Test Scores
63  73.5  80  87  94

5. 2   7. 12.5, 15.5, 18.5   9. 132.5, 149, 186

11.
Points Scored
10  12.5  15.5  18.5  20

13.
Bowling Scores
114  149  260
132.5  186

15. The range for Mario's scores was less than the range for Shannon's scores. However, the interquartile range was greater for Mario than Shannon.   17. 95th   19. 55th
21. 45th   23. If Bly ranked 19th in the class then 18 students scored higher and 13 scored lower on the history exam. The percentile rank is the number of scores less than or equal to Bly's, 14, divided by the total number of students, 32. His percentile rank is 44. The information about his score of 27 out of 50 is not needed.   25. To be ranked in the 90th percentile means that 90% of the scores were equal or less than yours. To be ranked in the 10th percentile means that 90% of the scores were greater than yours.   27. 75th   29. Answers will vary.   31. $-12$
33. $-91$   35. $-9$   37. 48

## Review and Practice Your Skills, pages 32–33

1. positive; $r = 0.991$   3. negative: $r \approx -0.99$
5. negative   7. 20.5, 29.5, 31.5

9.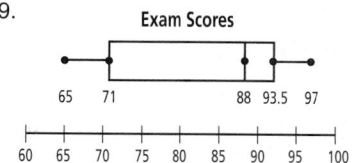
Exam Scores
65  71  88  93.5  97
60  65  70  75  80  85  90  95  100

10–13.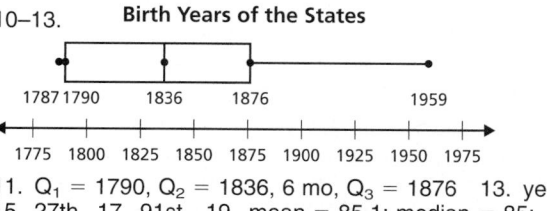
Birth Years of the States
1787 1790  1836  1876  1959
1775  1800  1825  1850  1875  1900  1925  1950  1975

11. $Q_1 = 1790$, $Q_2 = 1836$, 6 mo, $Q_3 = 1876$   13. yes
15. 27th   17. 91st   19. mean = 85.1; median = 85; mode = 76, 90   21. Mr. Pascal's

## Lesson 1-7, pages 34–37

1. No. By tripling the diameter, the area is increased 9 times.   3. median   5. The mean would be a little better (12); however, since the data varies greatly, only the summer month data should be used.

7.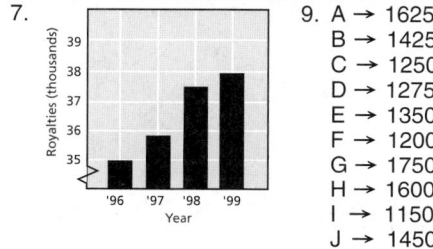

9. A → 1625
   B → 1425
   C → 1250
   D → 1275
   E → 1350
   F → 1200
   G → 1750
   H → 1600
   I → 1150
   J → 1450

11. Only positions of the complete bars are shown.
13. He should use the mean to justify the largest increase.
15. Yes. Answers will vary.   17. Answers will vary.
19. A marketer may use the first graph to advertise for a potential new trend to fad buyers. The second graph could be used to advertise the reliability and consistency of its product line.   21. 16 ft   23. 14 m   25. false   27. true
29. false   31. false

## Lesson 1-8, pages 38–41

1. $\begin{bmatrix} 106 & 255 \\ 348 & 491 \\ 196 & 304 \end{bmatrix}$ $3 \times 2$

3. $\begin{bmatrix} 390 & 1 \\ 400 & 5 \\ 402 & 1 \\ 404 & 3 \\ 410 & 3 \\ 440 & 1 \end{bmatrix}$ $6 \times 2$

7. $2 \times 2$   9. $\begin{bmatrix} 35 & 19 \\ 17 & 12 \\ 21 & 32 \end{bmatrix}$   11. $\begin{bmatrix} 23 & 10 \\ 9 & 6 \\ 1 & 19 \end{bmatrix}$   13. $\begin{bmatrix} 38 & 35 \\ 25 & 40 \end{bmatrix}$

15. $\begin{bmatrix} 142 & 114 \\ 110 & 125 \end{bmatrix}$   17. 1916   19. $\begin{bmatrix} 992 & 1008 & 960 \\ 888 & 912 & 920 \\ 1184 & 1128 & 1152 \\ 816 & 872 & 824 \end{bmatrix}$

21. $\begin{bmatrix} 11 & 15 & 24 \\ 19 & 31 & 28 \end{bmatrix}$   23. Yes. Addition of each element is commutative.

25. 1.96 ft² 27.

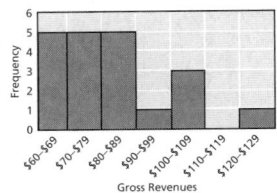

## Chapter 1 Review, pages 42–44

1. h 3. c 5. d 7. f 9. l 11. convenience
13. mean = $39.69; median = $38; mode = $34;
range = $24 15.

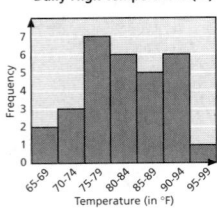

17. between 92 and 99 19. positive 21. 25 23. negative;
$r = -0.83$ 25. negative 27. 12.5 29. mode 31. 3, 10, 5,
6, 11, 4, 8, 1, 0, 5

33. $\begin{bmatrix} 10 & 23 \\ 11 & 12 \\ 20 & 6 \\ 8 & 4 \\ 7 & 7 \end{bmatrix}$

# Chapter 2: Foundations of Algebra

## Lesson 2-1, pages 52–55

1.

3. 5. <

7. 9.

11. 0 13. −3 15. $\frac{3}{4}$

17.

19. 21.

23. Fairbanks; $-10°F > -13°F$ 25. = 27. < 29. <
31. $-2\frac{1}{2}$ 33. −4 35. 20 37. −80

39.

41.

43.

45. False; there are no integers between 3 and 4.
47. false; $-\pi$ 49. convenience sampling

## Lesson 2-2, pages 56–59

1. 2 3. 3.3 5. 7 7. 29 9. 255 11. Answers will
vary depending on calculator function. 13. 34 15. 11
17. 0.5 19. 61 21. 21 23. 263 25. 32
27. $15 + (15 - 6) = 24$ mi 29. $(x + y +\_z) ÷ 3$
31. $x^2 + 3$; 7 33. $y - 5x$; −6 35. 0.283
37. 53.04 39. $\frac{17}{18}$ 41. 15.6 43. Answers will vary.
45. $\approx 86$

## Review and Practice Your Skills, pages 60–61

1. 3.

5. 7. > 9. <

11. <

13. 15.

17. 19. 17 21. 111 23. −4

25. 27 27. 4 29. 71 31. 6 33. 73 35. 10 37. 3
39. 21 41. 27 43. 40 45. 152 47. 36
49. < 51. > 53. =
55.

57. 59. 2 61. 54 63. 3

## Lesson 2-3, pages 62–65

1. $7x$ 3. $-2 + x$ 5. $x - 22$ 7. the product of eight
and a number 9. the quotient of −20 and a number
11. half of a number 13. 9 sec before blastoff
15. $x - 101$ 17. $\frac{-6}{x}$ 19. $32 + 2x$ 21. $16x$
23. $\frac{5}{10} + x$ 25. $-4 - x$ 27. $8 - x$ 29. $\frac{30x}{-62}$
31. six decreased by a number 33. the sum of one-half
and a number 35. a number divided by 25 37. −21
divided by three times a number 39. 12 less than three
times a number 41. the quotient of negative five times
a number and negative 11 43. the product of a number
and three 45. $n + 1,000,000$, a number increased
by one million 47. $n + 200,000$, a number increased
by 200 thousand 49. $\frac{1}{2}x + 2$ 51. $2x - 101,000$
53. $180(n - 2)$ For 55–57, answers will vary. 59. −12
multiplied by the sum of three times a number and nine

61.

| 2 | 2 6 6 |
|---|---|
| 3 | 3 5 9 9 |
| 4 | 1 2 3 5 8 8 |
| 5 | 2 6 8 |
| 6 | 4 5 7 8 |

**3 | 5 represents 35.**

63. 20

## Lesson 2-4, pages 66–69

1. $7t$ 3. $-12t$ 5. $\frac{1}{2}x + \frac{1}{5}y$ 7. $8ab - 9ac$ 9. 20

11. 43   13.

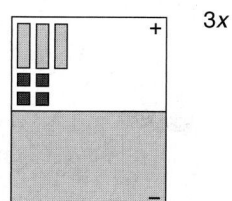

$3x + 4$

15. $14s$   17. $-7k$   19. $\frac{1}{9}m$   21. $7c$   23. $8xy + x$
25. $18a - 8b$   27. $\frac{1}{6}d$   29. $8.7st - 0.4t$   31. $-6b$
33. $\frac{13}{8}xy - \frac{1}{4}x$   35. $6wz + 15w$   37. $-30$   39. 41
41. $-16$   43. 68   45. Answers will vary.   47. 160.847 cm
49.

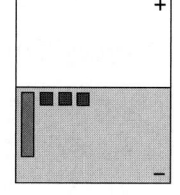

$-y - 3$   51. $x - 5$   53. $x - 2$
55. $4x + 9$   57. $6a - 9b$

59.

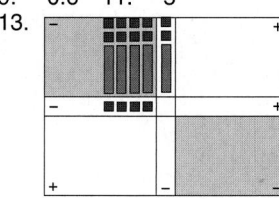

## Review and Practice Your Skills, pages 70–71

1. $8 + x$   3. $x - 5$   5. $8y$   7. $4x - 7$   9. $\frac{1}{2}x + 6$
11. $\frac{2}{3}x - 14$   13. the difference of a number and six
15. negative four decreased by a number   17. the product of negative seven and a number   19. the product of five and a number divided by ten   21. six times a number decreased by 11   23. the sum of a number and $-15$   25. twice a number decreased by seven   27. a product of five and two other numbers   29. $2x$   31. $-2y$
33. $11c$   35. $\frac{5}{4}t$   37. $2xy + 4x$   39. $2.1r + 7.5t$
41. $-8y$   43. $3cd - 3d$   45. $3n - 3m$   47. $7\frac{2}{3}a - \frac{1}{3}b$
49. $1.6x + 2.2t$   51. $2.4j - 9.1k$   53. $-25$   55. $-2$
57. 37   59. 16   61. $-6$   63. 7   65. 20   67. $4\frac{1}{2}$
69. 2   71. $5 + 2x$   73. $\frac{12}{y}$   75. the difference of 8.7 and a number   77. the quotient of a number and three
79. $5x$   81. 0   83. $15 + 13z$   85. 29   87. 4   89. 43

## Lesson 2-5, pages 72–75

1. $10 + 2s$   3. $18.6 - 24b$   5. $d - 3$   7. $-6w - 5$
9. $-0.6$   11. $-5$
13.

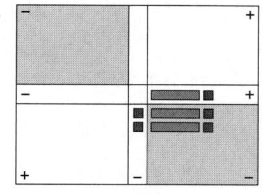

15. Answers will vary but may include to distribute $-7$ over the expression $(x + 4)$.
17. $-5m - 15$
19. $-9 - \frac{1}{4}x$
21. $0.32h - 0.24k$
23. $9q + 12r$

25. $-56q - 49r$

27. $14c - 35d$   29. $-6b - 2$   31. $7 - 8p$   33. $4m - 10n$
35. $3q - 3r$   37. $2d + g$   39. $\frac{-169}{11}w + \frac{39}{11}v$
41. $-8$   43. 8   45. 8.5   47. 4
49.

$-2y - 2$

51.

$-2x - 3$   53. 627 ft$^2$
55. A2 · 21   57. $2667
59. No; he did not multiply $-5$ and $4xy$ and he combined unlike terms $-10x$ and $15y$.
61. $-369a + 1025b - 41c + 492d$   63. 9184 m$^3$
65. Answers will vary.   67. 58–62

## Lesson 2-6, pages 76–79

1. $-9x + 21$   3. $-6n + 6m$   5. $4c - 84$
7. $-0.5a - 1.5b - 2$   9. $25x + 8y - 21$
11. $83x + 56(15 - x) = 27x + 840$ or $56x + 83(15 - x) = 1245 - 27x$   13. $6m - 5$   15. $-3x + 12$   17. $4x + 24$
19. $3d + 4.3$   21. $15x + 30$   23. $3\frac{1}{2}y - 9$   25. $32f - 148$
27. $-47t + 58$   29. $20 - 11w$   31. $-p + 14q$
33. $-9r - 8s$   35. $-16c - 5cd - 12d$   37. $18x + 21(200 - x) = 4200 - 3x$ or $21x + 18(200 - x) = 3x + 3600$
39. e   41. a   43. d   45. $14.9a + 2.5b$   47. $-88a + 32b$
49. $-2ab + 65a - 83b$   51. $-24x - 24$   53. 41
55. positive   57. 61–70

## Review and Practice Your Skills, pages 80–81

1. $-6c + d$   3. $\frac{3}{2}y + 8$   5. $10e - 30f$   7. $x - 2$
9. $-a - 2b$   11. $-18bc + 21$   13. $-4s - 6t$
15. $11c - 5$   17. 67   19. 9   21. 4   23. $-31$   25. 9
27. $-5$   29. $7x + 16y$   31. $15a + 40$   33. $9b - 4a + 35$
35. $-6x + 2y$   37. $-1.3x - 8.4$   39. $13x + 7$
41. $-2a + b$   43. $\left(2\frac{1}{2}x + 11\frac{1}{3}z\right)$ cm   45. d   47. a
49. $-2x + 5$   51. $3r - 11$   53. 0   55. $-3x + 21$
57. $16t + 24$   59. $10ab - 1$   61. $-7$   63. $\frac{9}{2}$   65. 30

## Lesson 2-7, pages 82–85

1. 4   3. $-50$   5. $c^{11}$   7. $d^{10}$   9. $v^4$   11. $z^4$   13. It is impossible to divide by 0.   15. $-7$   17. $\frac{16}{49}$
19. 3   21. 16   23. $x^{15}$   25. $g^6$   27. $j^{12}$   29. 0
31. $5w^2$   33. $d^9$   35. 819,200 bytes   37. $2^{10}$ or 1024 times   39. $x^{18}$   41. $fg^2$   43. $\frac{r^5}{s^{10}}$   45. $v^4$
47. 271 million   49. 4   51. 12   53. true   55. 3
57. 38.4   59. 10

61.

## Lesson 2-8, pages 86–89

1. $x^{-3}$ or $\frac{1}{x^3}$  3. $w^{-20}$ or $\frac{1}{w^{20}}$  5. $\frac{1}{16}$  7. $\frac{1}{25}$  9. $2.9 \cdot 10^7$

11. $8.08 \cdot 10^{-5}$  13. $0.0095$  15. $2.7 \cdot 10^7$

17. $y^{-10}$ or $\frac{1}{y^{10}}$  19. $a^0 = 1$  21. $b^0 = 1$  23. $\frac{1}{a^{12}}$ or $a^{-12}$

25. $\frac{1}{1024}$  27. 16  29. $\frac{1}{16}$  31. $-1$  33. $4.658 \cdot 10^{-2}$

35. $1.5 \cdot 10^7$  37. $3.658 \cdot 10^6$  39. $530,000,000$
41. $3907$  43. $60,046,000$  45. $3.46 \cdot 10^7$
47. $123,840,000$ km $= 1.2384 \cdot 10^8$ km

49. $(6 \cdot 3)^0$, $2^3 \cdot 2^{-2}$, $\left(\frac{1}{3}\right)^{-1}$  51. $4$; $a^n$  53. $\frac{y^2}{x^2}$

55. $\frac{1}{m^7 n^3}$  57. $-5v - 2w$  59. $-11tw - 6w$

61. $-6r + 12$  63. $-8.5v + 4$  65. $2x - \frac{3}{2}y + 3$

### Review and Practice Your Skills, pages 90–91

1. $144$  3. $\frac{9}{16}$  5. $73$  7. $2$  9. $\frac{8}{9}$  11. $18$  13. $a^7$

15. $c^8 d^2$  17. $4x^6$  19. $\frac{16}{y^4}$  21. $x^2$  23. $m^8$

25. $a^9$  27. $64x^6$  29. $-3d^6 e^3$  31. $y^{-8}$ or $\frac{1}{y^8}$

33. $b^{-2}$ or $\frac{1}{b^2}$  35. $m^{-5}$ or $\frac{1}{m^5}$  37. $\frac{1}{16}$  39. $8$

41. $\frac{1}{16}$  43. $1 \cdot 10^6$  45. $3.334 \cdot 10^3$  47. $1.3 \cdot 10^{-4}$

49. $0.0072$  51. $0.000012$  53. $55,000$

55. 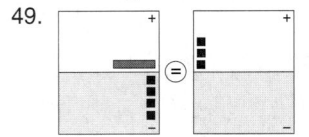  57.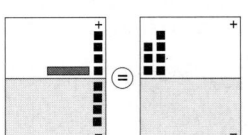

59. 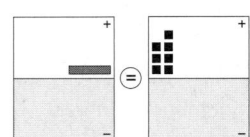  61. $5$  63. $11\frac{1}{2}$

65. $32$  67. the sum of a number and seven
69. the product of negative three and a number
71. $-0.5$ decreased by a number  73. $2b$  75. $2a^3 b^2$
77. $2x + 6$  79. $-3a - 8$  81. $32$  83. $8a^6 b^3$
85. $-17x - 73$  87. false  89. false  91. true  93. true
95. false  97. true  99. $31$  101. $18$  103. $-11$

105. $18$  107. $\frac{1}{2}$  109. $8.9$  111. $72$

### Lesson 2-9, pages 92–93

1. $12, 19, 26, 33, 40$  3. $-20, -\frac{20}{3}, -\frac{20}{9}, -\frac{20}{27}, -\frac{20}{81}$
5. $3x + 2, 4x + 7, 5x + 12, 6x + 17, 7x + 22$  7. $2323,$
$2424, 2525, 2626, 2727$  9. $11,109, 22,218, 33,327,$
$44,436, 55,545$
11.

Increase the number of rows and columns of dots by 1.

13. add $2, 3, 4, \ldots$ ; $21, 28, 36$  15. divide by 3; $1, \frac{1}{3}, \frac{1}{9}$

17. $\$588$  19. 1: 5%; 2: 10%; 3: 15%; 4: 20%;
5: 25%; 6: 30%; 7: 35%; 8: 40%  21. $\$1687.50$
23. yes; $28 = 1 + 2 + 4 + 7 + 14$  25. $8, 13, 21, 34, 55,$
$89$  27. $>$  29. $-25°F$  31. $-18$

## Chapter 2 Review, pages 94–96

1. f  3. a  5. e  7. d  9. k  11. [number line with open circle at 1, arrows, marks $-2 -1\ 0\ 1\ 2$]  13. $<$  15. $>$

17. $12$  19. $17$  21. $65$  23. $144$  25. $n - 9$  27. $4 - 2n$
29. the quotient of a number and three  31. one less than
sixteen times a number  33. $2.2mn + 1$  35. $-2xy - x$
37. $-10$  39. $17$  41. $-c - 3d$  43. $-6y + 12x$  45. $3y - 3x$

47. $2x + \frac{1}{2}y$  49. $14x - 3$  51. $3x - 8$  53. $6x + 18$

55. $-x + 16$  57. $(6x - 8)$ in.  59. $33$  61. $20$  63. $a^8$

65. $9w^4$  67. $\frac{1}{4}$  69. $\frac{1}{8}$  71. $0.00075$  73. $5.46 \cdot 10^{-5}$

75. $\frac{1}{81}, \frac{1}{243}, \frac{1}{729}$  77. $36, 34, 45$

## Chapter 3: Equations and Inequalities

### Lesson 3-1, pages 104–107

1. $-1$  3. $1$  5. $6$  7. $0.6$ m  9. $27$ mi/h  11. $3$  13. $\frac{3}{4}$

15. $35$  17. $0$  19. $-4, 4$  21. $2.5$  23. $-6$  25. $13.3°C$
27. $17.8°C$  29. $63$ ft  31. $154$ ft  33. $8, -8$  35. $\varnothing$,
absolute value is positive.  37. $0.22$ kWh  39. Answers
will vary.  41. irrational  43. rational  45. $58$  47. $34$
49. $4$  51. $8.5$

### Lesson 3-2, pages 108–111

1. divide by 3  3. multiply by 8  5. subtract 3  7. $12$
9. $4.6$  11. $-\frac{17}{30}$  13. $s = \frac{P}{4}$  15. $r = \frac{I}{pt}$  17. $21$

19. $-0.9$  21. $0.12$  23. $-9$  25. $13.5$  27. $-4$

29. $-\frac{25}{2}$  31. $-2.5$  33. $-6\frac{1}{2}$  35. $-2.5$  37. $65$

39. $-20$  41. $-\frac{14}{15}$  45. No; He needs to multiply both

sides by $-\frac{5}{2}$.  47. $6.5\%$

49.

49. $y = 7$  51. $x + 6 = 10$; $4$
53. $\frac{1}{3}x = 24$; $72$

55. $20$  57. The value of $x$ decreases.  59. $-28$
61. $16–25$ and $36–45$; $26–35$ and $46–55$  63. $4$
65. $3.8$  67. $85$

### Review and Practice Your Skills, pages 112–113

1. $-2$  3. $-6, 6$  5. $11\frac{3}{4}$  7. $0$  9. $4$ in.  11. $6$ ft

13. $2$  15. $\frac{1}{7}$  17. $12$  19. $9$  21. $-7$  23. $-32$  25. $1$

27. $-11$  29. $\frac{16}{25}$  31. $-90$  33. $36$  35. $32$  37. $-\frac{1}{32}$

39. $2.2$  41. $\frac{1}{2}$  43. $-\frac{2}{3}$  45. $-7$  47. $-5$  49. $t = \frac{I}{pr}$

51. $7x = -35$; $-5$  53. $10 + x = 27$; $17$  55. $5$  57. $-5$
59. $-27$  61. $r = \frac{C}{2\pi}$  63. $C = A - B - D$  65. $10$

## Lesson 3-3, pages 114–115

1.  3.

5.

| Weight on Earth | 100 | 125 | 150 | 175 | 200 |
|---|---|---|---|---|---|
| Weight on Pluto | 4 | 5 | 6 | 7 | 8 |

7. $P = \frac{1}{25}E$

9.

| Week | 1 | 2 | 3 | 4 | 5 | 6 | 7 |
|---|---|---|---|---|---|---|---|
| Distance of run (miles) | 1 | $1\frac{1}{2}$ | 2 | $2\frac{1}{2}$ | 3 | $3\frac{1}{2}$ | 4 |

$1 + \frac{1}{2}w(w-1)$, $d = 1 + \frac{1}{2}(w-1)$

11.

| Week | 1 | 3 | 5 | 7 | 9 | 11 |
|---|---|---|---|---|---|---|
| Amount in savings account | $300 | $350 | $400 | $450 | $500 | $550 |

$300 + 50w$, $A = 300 + 50w$

13.

| Number of children at camp | 1 | 2 | 3 | 4 | 5 |
|---|---|---|---|---|---|
| Total cost | $20 | $25 | $30 | $35 | $40 |

15. $C = 15 + 5n$   17. $45 + 5n$   19. Answers will vary, but should include a discussion of the flat rate and cost per child.
21. $8a$   23. $14k$   25. $\frac{11}{24}b$   27. $1.3g + 3.9h$   29. $3t - s$
31. $h^{12}$   33. $2f^{21}$   35. $m^5$

## Lesson 3-4, pages 116–119

1. 4   3. 16   5. 7   7. 17   9. $x = \frac{y - b}{m}$   11. $n + 16 +$
$n + 32 + 34 = 100$; $n = 9$, $n + 16 = 25$   13. 4   15. 9
17. $-5$   19. $-4$   21. $-1$   23. 2.2   25. $-11$   27. $-2$
29. 1   31. $-\frac{6}{7}$   33. 2   35. $r = \frac{8}{7}(p - 20)$
37. $C = \frac{5}{9}(F - 32)$   39. 27.8°C

41.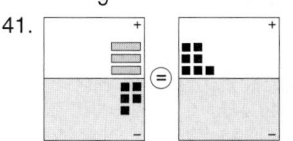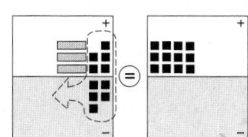

$x = 4$

43.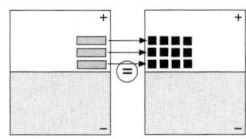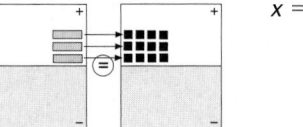

$x = -3$

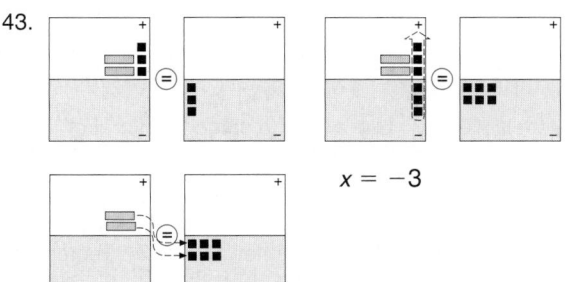

45. $m\angle EFG = 51°$, $m\angle GFH = 39°$   47. $l = 120$ yd,
$w = 53$ yd   49. $\frac{1}{2}x - 5 = -12$, $x = -14$   51. 24°, 54°, 102°

53. 0   55. 5   57. 43, 45, 50, 129   59. clusters: high 80s/low 90s; gaps: 50–82, 108–129   61. 86

## Review and Practice Your Skills, pages 120–121

1.

| Week | 1 | 2 | 3 | 4 | 5 | 6 |
|---|---|---|---|---|---|---|
| Amount in bank | $120 | $150 | $180 | $210 | $240 | $270 |

3. $A = 90 + 30w$

5.

| Miles | 100 | 200 | 300 | 400 | 500 | 600 |
|---|---|---|---|---|---|---|
| Charge per day | $47 | $59 | $71 | $83 | $95 | $107 |

7. $35 + 0.12m$   9. $B = 35 + 0.12m$   11. 3   13. $-\frac{19}{2}$
15. $-4$   17. 5   19. 12.5   21. 117   23. 4   25. $-28$
27. $\frac{3}{4}x + 2 = 8$, $x = 8$   29. $5x - 10 = 0$, $x = 2$   31. 30
33. $-3.1$   35. $-8$

37.

| Week | 1 | 2 | 3 | 4 | 5 | 6 |
|---|---|---|---|---|---|---|
| Amount in savings account | $250 | $300 | $350 | $400 | $450 | $500 |

$200 + 50w$, $A = 200 + 50w$   39. 30   41. 4   43. 2
45. $-4$

## Lesson 3-5, pages 122–125

1. 12   3. 33   5. $-54$   7. 3   9. 12   11. 39   13. 32
15. 17   17. 16   19. 44   21. 37.5   23. 51   25. 5
27. 25   29. $-3$   31. $\frac{1}{2}$   33. 5   35. $\frac{34}{25}$   37. Jenisa;
Erica added 8 to $-18$ and received an answer of 10.
Dividing 2 into 10 resulted in 5.   39. 8%   41. $\frac{part}{whole} = \frac{x}{100}$   43. about 47%   45. 3 m   47. 7   49. $-33$
51. 4.5%

53.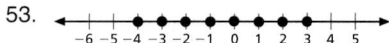

55.

57.   59.

## Lesson 3-6, pages 126–129

1. $y < 2.8$   3. $y = 2.8$
5.   7.

9. $x > 0$   11. $p \geq 13$   13. $d < -\frac{1}{3}$   15. $d = -\frac{1}{3}$
17. substitution and number line

19.   21.

23.   25.

27.   29.

31.   33.

35. $x < 13$   37. $x \leq \frac{2}{3}$   39. $x < 212$

41.   43. $x < 1199$

45. always   47. sometimes; true when $a = b$

49. terminating   51. terminating   53. repeating
55. terminating   57. $z^{-3}$   59. $r^2$   61. $p$   63. $v^{-25}$
65. 93 min

## Review and Practice Your Skills, pages 130–131

1. 14   3. 14   5. 12   7. 81   9. 49   11. 11   13. 7
15. $15\frac{2}{3}$   17. 31   19. 0   21. 3   23. 20%

25.   27.

29.   31.

33.   35.

37. $x > -8$   39. 30   41. 4.5   43. $\frac{7}{20}$   45. 10   47. 14

49.

## Lesson 3-7, pages 132–135

1.   $z \le 2$

3.   $y < -6$

5.   $t \ge 12$

7.   $n < -4$

9.   $w \le 18$

11. He can consume at most 675 calories.

13.   $x \ge -4$

15.   $x \ge 3$   17.   $h \le -8$

19.   $r \le -\frac{7}{2}$   21.   $k \ge -2$

23.   $y < 8$   25.   $q < -3$

27.   $b \le 6$   29.   $x \le 9$

31.   $a \le -8$   33.   $x \le -4$

35.   $p < -5.2$   37.   $x \ge -1$

39. 28   41. $-6 < 18x,\ x > -\frac{1}{3}$   43. $8 + 4x \le -12,\ x \le -5$

45. 12.5 yd   47. $a < 8\frac{1}{3}$   49. Sometimes; for example if
$a = 0$, $b = 2$, $c = 4$, and $d = 1$, then $2 > 1$, or if $a = 1$,
$b = 0$, $c = 4$, and $d = 1$, then $-3c - 1$.   51. 7.382047 ·
$10^6$   53. $3.84719 \cdot 10^7$   55. 0.0005697   57. $10z + 40$
59. $f - 3g$   61. $-2a - 6$

## Lesson 3-8, pages 136–139

1. $\pm 5$   3. $\pm \sqrt{7}$   5. $\pm \frac{7}{10}$   7. 1   9. $\pm 12$   11. 0   13. In
Exercise 7 the entire expression $d + 3$ is under the radical
and both sides of the equation can be easily squared
immediately. In Exercise 12 add 3 to both sides before

squaring them.   15. 81   17. $\pm 8$   19. 4
21. $\pm \sqrt{59}$   23. $\varnothing$   25. $\pm 4$   27. $\pm 16$   29. 36   31. 72
33. $\pm \sqrt{50}$   35. 10   37. $\pm \sqrt{105}$   39. 40 mi/h
41. $3x^2 = 588$, $x = 14$ in.; 14 in. by 14 in.   43. $\left(\frac{T}{2\pi}\right)^2 \cdot$

$981 = L$   45. $\pm 0.12$   47. $\pm 0.5$   49. $\pm 9.055$   51. $\pm 4.583$
53. 13   55. 576 lb   57. No. No.  An object's velocity

increases the further it falls.   59. $x + 7$   61. $\frac{5x}{-12}$

63. 4   65. $-6$

## Chapter 3 Review, pages 140–142

1. 1   3. g   5. f   7. c   9. d   11. 7   13. 12
15. 282.7 cm$^3$   17. $-4$   19. 9   21. $\frac{1}{4}x = -15$, $x = -60$

23.

| Age of alligator (years) | 0 | 1 | 2 | 3 | 4 | 5 |
|---|---|---|---|---|---|---|
| Length of alligator (inches) | 8 | 20 | 32 | 44 | 56 | 68 |

Let $a$ = age in years; $8 + 12a$. Let $l$ = length of alligator;
$l = 8 + 12a$.

25.

| Days overdue | 0 | 1 | 2 | 3 | 4 | 5 |
|---|---|---|---|---|---|---|
| Amount owed | $1.80 | $2.10 | $2.40 | $2.70 | $3.00 | $3.30 |

Let $d$ = days overdue; $1.80 + 0.30d$. Let $a$ = amount
owed; $a = 1.80 + 0.30d$.

27. 0.5   29. $-56$   31. 3   33. 10   35. 10 gal

37.   39.

41.   43.   $z > 2$

45.   $t > 5$   47.   $s < 11$

49. 625   51. 64   53. $\pm 6$   55. 1.8 h

# Chapter 4: Probability

## Lesson 4-1, pages 150–153

1. $\approx 0.66$   3. 0.4, 0.6   5. 0.71   7. 0.31   9. 0.25
11. Answers will vary.   13. 0.12   15. $\approx 0.06$   17. 0.16
19. $\approx 0.41$   21. $\approx 0.19$   23. 0.004   25.

**Wind Speeds**

| Miles per hour | Tally | Frequency |
|---|---|---|
| 1-3 | l | 1 |
| 4-7 | ll | 4 |
| 8-12 | llll | 8 |
| 13-18 | ll | 3 |
| 19-24 | l | 2 |
| 25-31 | l | 1 |
| 32-38 | ll | 3 |
| 39-46 | | 0 |
| 47-54 | l | 2 |
| 55-63 | | 0 |
| 64-75 | | 0 |
| 75+ | | 0 |

## Lesson 4-2, pages 154–155

1. Models will vary. Use a coin to model gender. Let
heads represent a girl and tails represent a boy. Since the
family is planning to have 4 children, flip 4 coins at a time.
3. Answers will vary.   5. Models and experimental
probabilities will vary. Use a number cube to model the
chance for a cure. Let the outcomes 1, 3, and 5 represent
that the drug works. Let the outcomes 2 and 4 represent
that the drug does not work. Disregard the outcome
6. Toss 2 number cubes at a time to represent the 2
patients chosen randomly   7. Models and experimental
probabilities will vary. Use a spinner divided into three

equal sections labeled 1, 2, and 3. Let 1 and 2 represent a made free throw and 3 represent a missed free throw. Spin 5 spinners at a time to model 5 free throws shot by Tia.   9. Jolon is correct. Any device, such as a number cube, that has an even number of outcomes can be used since the outcomes can be separated into two equal categories.   11. $-8$   13. $0.8\overline{8}$   15. $-3$   17. $-\dfrac{8}{3}$
19. 40,800   21. 0.0000917   23. 3,298,700
25. 0.000659

## Review and Practice Your Skills, pages 156–157

1. 0.75   3. 0.84   5. $\approx 0.48$   7. $\approx 0.46$   9. $\approx 0.24$
For 11–13, models and experimental probabilities will vary.
11. Use a number cube with each number representing a different baseball card. Roll 6 cubes at once to represent 6 boxes.   13. Use a coin to model gender. Let heads represent a girl and tails represent a boy. Since the family wants to have 3 children, flip 3 coins at a time.
15. $\approx 0.94$   17. $\approx 0.79$   19. 60   21. 0.90

## Lesson 4-3, pages 158–161

1. 24
3.

5. $\dfrac{1}{24}$   7. $\dfrac{1}{4}$   9. 160   11. 64   13. $\dfrac{3}{64}$   15. $\dfrac{1}{16}$
17. 30   19. $\dfrac{5}{13}$   21. 72   23. $\dfrac{1}{216}$   25. $\dfrac{125}{216}$
27. $\dfrac{1}{9}$   29. 7   31. $-6$   33. 2   35. 10   37. 0.6   39. 2

## Lesson 4-4, pages 162–165

1. $\dfrac{1}{2}$   3. $\dfrac{2}{9}$   5. $\dfrac{3}{26}$   7. $\dfrac{3}{4}$   9. $\dfrac{1}{4}$   11. $\dfrac{1}{6}$   13. $\dfrac{5}{8}$   15. $\dfrac{7}{8}$
17. $\dfrac{5}{6}$   19.

$\dfrac{1}{4}$

21. $\dfrac{4}{5}$   23. $\dfrac{1}{5}$   25. Mary is probably incorrect because the results of the survey are most likely not mutually exclusive. In other words, just because a voter lies about voting on one county position does not exclude them from lying about voting for the other position.   27. 40   29. Yes. They are mutually exclusive.   31. $\dfrac{4}{9}$   33. mean: 1.8; median: 2; mode: 2   35. mean: 8.7; median: 8; mode: 6, 12   37. 32   39. 7

41. 98   43. $-4$   45. $0.8\overline{8}$   47. 4.76

## Review and Practice Your Skills, pages 166–167

1. 30   3. $\dfrac{1}{10}$   5. $\dfrac{1}{5}$   7. $\dfrac{1}{26}$
9.

11. $\dfrac{1}{36}$   13. $\dfrac{25}{36}$
15. $\dfrac{11}{26}$   17. $\dfrac{4}{5}$   19. $\dfrac{4}{15}$   21. $\dfrac{1}{12}$   23. $\dfrac{1}{9}$   25. 0.81
27. (dime, nickel) → (H, H), (H, T), (T, H), (T, T)   29. $\dfrac{4}{5}$

## Lesson 4-5, pages 168–171

1. $\dfrac{1}{10}$   3. $\dfrac{1}{25}$   5. $\dfrac{1}{15}$   7. $\dfrac{5}{12}$   9. $\dfrac{1}{50}$   11. $\dfrac{4}{25}$
13. $\dfrac{868}{43,500} \approx 0.02$   15. $\dfrac{4}{91}$   17. 0.1024   19. 0.2105
21. Independent events are events whose outcomes do not affect one another. For example, when a card is drawn from a deck of cards it is then replaced and reshuffled before drawing the second card. Dependent events are events for which the outcome of one can affect the other. When a card is drawn from a deck of cards and not replaced, the probability of the next card drawn is different than if the card were replaced and the deck reshuffled.
23. 0.013   25. $\dfrac{25}{1352}$   27. 3; $\dfrac{8}{81}$   29. No; there are 12 ways to get a multiple of 3 and 9 ways to get a multiple of 4.   31. 9   33. 52   35. $-8$   37. 9   39. $\dfrac{81}{4}$
41. $-4ab - 4a$   43. $3k - 3m$   45. $-11c + b$

## Lesson 4-6, pages 172–175

1. 20   3. 4   5. 720   7. 120   9. 30   11. 1   13. 60
15. 24   17. 5040   19. 35   21. 3125; 120   23. 5040
25. 72   27. 24   29. $\dfrac{24}{625}$   31. 48
33.

35.

37.

39.

41.

43.

45. $x \geq 4$   47. $r < 8$   49. $f < 2$   51. $r \leq 3$   53. $s \leq 50$
55. $a < 4$

## Review and Practice Your Skills, pages 176–177

1. $\dfrac{5}{36}$   3. $\dfrac{5}{48}$   5. $\dfrac{25}{144}$   7. $\dfrac{3}{26}$   9. $\dfrac{1}{13}$   11. $\dfrac{1}{26}$   13. $\dfrac{5}{51}$
15. $\dfrac{2}{51}$   17. $\dfrac{28}{153}$   19. 210   21. 20   23. 504   25. 5

27. 332,640  29. 5040  31. 210  33. 48  35. $\frac{1}{8}$  37. $\frac{5}{48}$
39. $\frac{11}{26}$  41. $\frac{1}{24}$  43. 120  45. 12

### Lesson 4-7, pages 178–181

1. 10  3. 1  5. $\frac{1}{36}$  7. 20  9. 165  11. 1  13. $\frac{1}{325}$
15. 252  17. 38,760  19. Answers will vary. An insightful answer will note that a combination is equal to the permutation divided by $r!$  21. 1140  23. $\frac{1}{20,825}$
25. 7315  27. $\frac{1}{120}$  29. Answers will vary.  31. 20
33. 2.5  35. 7  37. $\pm5\sqrt{3}$  39. 36  41. $\frac{33}{4}$
43. $t = 190p$

### Chapter 4 Review, pages 182–184

1. g  3. k  5. d  7. e  9. h  11. ≈ 0.21  13. 0.23  15. Answers will vary. Sample answer: Use the numbers 1 and 2 on a number cube to represent whole wheat bread. Use heads on a coin to represent bread dated to be sold by the middle of the week. Roll the number cube and flip the coin. Record whether or not the number cube shows 1 or 2 and the coin shows heads. Repeat the simulation 30 times and determine the experimental probability.  17. Answers will vary. Sample answer: Let 1 and 2 represent one action figure, 3 and 4 represent another action figure, and 5 and 6 represent the third action figure. Roll a number cube five times and record the result. Determine whether all 3 action figures are represented. Repeat the simulation 30 times and determine the experimental probability.  19. 32 cars  21. $\frac{1}{4}$  23. $\frac{2}{3}$
25. $\frac{1}{10}$  27. $\frac{1}{3}$  29. 24  31. 378  33. 70

# Chapter 5: Logic and Geometry

### Lesson 5-1, pages 192–195

1. any three of $A$, $B$, $X$ and $Y$  3. 1  5. neither
7. 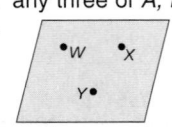  9.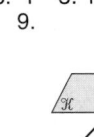

11. $X$ and $Y$  13. line $\ell$  15. true  17. true  19. true
21. Postulate 1  23. Postulate 2  25. Postulate 3
27. $U$  29. $\overline{LB}, \overline{LC}, \overline{LU}, \overline{LN}, \overline{LP}$  31. It would most likely be a point, but it could be a line.  33. Atlanta, New York, Boston  35. 24  37. 4

### Lesson 5-2, pages 196–199

1. 76°, 166°  3. 60°, 150°  5. $\angle BGC$, $\angle CGE$, $\angle EGF$, $\angle FGB$  7. 70°  9. 37° since the two angles are complementary and 90° − 53° = 37°.  11. 90° since the supplement of a right angle is a right angle.  13. $\overline{TO} \perp \overline{RO}$; $\overline{TO} \perp \overline{OS}$  15. $\angle ROP$ and $\angle QOS$, $\angle ROQ$ and $\angle POS$  17. 87°

19.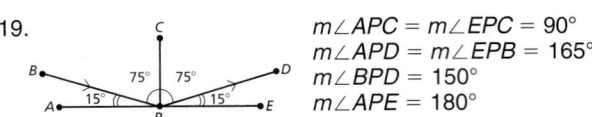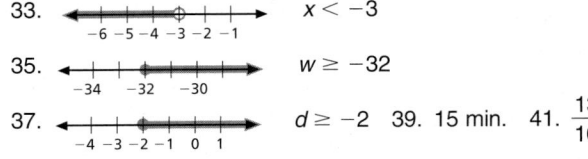

$m\angle APC = m\angle EPC = 90°$
$m\angle APD = m\angle EPB = 165°$
$m\angle BPD = 150°$
$m\angle APE = 180°$

21. 72°  23. the bisector of the angle  25. 90°  27. lowered
29. $m\angle 4 = 45°$, $m\angle 1 = 45°$, $m\angle 3 = 45°$  31. False; the complement of an acute angle is an acute angle.
33. 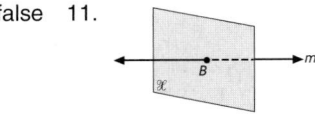  $x < -3$

35. [number line] $w \geq -32$

37. [number line] $d \geq -2$  39. 15 min.  41. $\frac{13}{10}$

### Review and Practice Your Skills, pages 200–201

1. 3  3. $F$ and $C$  5. $\overleftrightarrow{DE}, \overleftrightarrow{EF}, \overleftrightarrow{DF}$ or line $\ell$  7. true
9. false  11.

[figure showing plane with point B and line m]

13. 70°  15. none  17. 40°  19. 13°, 103°  21. 31°, 121°  23. 30°, 120°  25. 45°, 135°  27. 59°, 149°
29. 85°, 175°  31. b  33. c  35. 131°, supplementary
37. 30°, complementary

### Lesson 5-3, pages 202–205

1. $\angle 6$ and $\angle 3$, $\angle 5$ and $\angle 4$  3. $\angle 5$ and $\angle 3$, $\angle 6$ and $\angle 4$
5. corresponding  7. alternate interior  9. 120°  11. 60°
13. corresponding  15. corresponding  17. alternate exterior  19. alternate exterior  21. 105°  23. 105°
25. 75°  27. parallel by alternate interior angles
29. parallel by alternate exterior angle  31. Answers will vary.  33. $m\angle 1 = 58°$; $m\angle 3 = 58°$; $(9x - 13)° = 122°$; $(7x + 17)° = 122°$  35. Skew  37. They are parallel.
39. alternate interior angles  41. False; by definition, skew lines do not lie in the same plane.  43. Answers will vary, but one idea is parallel lines in poetry.  45. $\frac{1}{66}$
47. $P$(white or blue or green or red)

### Lesson 5-4, pages 206–209

1. yes  3. yes  5. $x = 35$  7. $x = 64$, $y = 58$, $z = 122$
9. no  11. yes  13. scalene  15. equilateral  17. $3p = 54$; $2p = 36$  19. $y = 99$  21. 123°; The sum of angles is 180°.  23. 40°  25. 90°  27. 40°  29. 140°  33. Yes. The angles opposite of congruent sides are congruent.
35. equilateral; interior angles: 60°; exterior angle: 120°
37. sometimes  41. $35t^5$  43. $5s^2 - 25s$  45. $-7st + 12$  47. $-x^4 + 3x^2$

### Review and Practice Your Skills, pages 210–211

1. vertical  3. alternate, interior  5. corresponding
7. supplementary, same-side interior  9. alternate, exterior
11. 60°  13. 60°  15. 120°  17. parallel by corresponding angles  19. not enough information  21. yes  23. no
25. no  27. 65°  29. 50°  31. 65°  33. 115°

**35.**  **37.**

**39.** true  **41.** 49°, 139°  **43.** 76°, 166°  **45.** 8°, 98°
**47.** a = 70°, b = 70°, c = 110°  **49.** a = 80°, b = 80°

## Lesson 5-5, pages 212–215

**1.** $\overline{AB} \cong \overline{DE}$, $\overline{AC} \cong \overline{DF}$, $\overline{BC} \cong \overline{EF}$, $\angle A \cong \angle D$, $\angle B \cong \angle E$, $\angle C \cong \angle F$  **3.** $\triangle USR \cong \triangle UST$ by SSS  **5.** $\angle B$  **7.** $\overline{AB}$
**9.** $\overline{RS} \cong \overline{XY}$, $\overline{ST} \cong \overline{YZ}$, $\overline{RT} \cong \overline{XZ}$, $\angle R \cong \angle X$, $\angle S \cong \angle Y$, $\angle T \cong \angle Z$  **11.** SAS  **13.** SAS or ASA  **15.** $\angle R$  **17.** $\overline{RU}$  **19.** yes; by SSS  **21.** yes; by SAS, SSS and ASA
**23.** 6  **25.** Latravis is correct. Since two angles of one triangle are congruent to two angles of another triangle, their third angles must also be congruent. This is because the sum of the angles in every triangle is 180°. The triangles then are congruent by ASA.  **27.** No. The sides of the two triangles are not necessarily congruent.
**29.** Rochester, MN  **31.** −15,625, 78,125, −390,625
**33.** 8, 13, 21  **35.** 34, 43, 53  **37.** $\frac{1}{100}$

## Lesson 5-6, pages 216–219

**1.** 138°  **3.** 138°  **5.** 10  **7.** 8  **9.** 6  **11.** 122°
**13.** 122°  **15.** 58°  **17.** 18  **19.** 106°  **21.** 106°
**23.** rectangle, square  **25.** parallelogram, rectangle, rhombus, square  **27.** rhombus, square  **29.** rectangle, square  **31.** 59°, 59°, 121°  **33.** 10  **35.** 111°  **37.** false
**39.** false  **41.** true  **43.** false  **45.** 360°; Turn U will be more difficult because it is a sharper turn.  **47.** a quadrilateral has two pairs of parallel sides  **49.** The legs represent the diagonals of a quadrilateral where $\overline{AB}$ and $\overline{DC}$ are opposite sides. Since $\overline{AO} \cong \overline{OC}$ and $\overline{BO} \cong \overline{OD}$, these diagonals bisect each other. Thus, the quadrilateral $ABCD$ is a parallelogram and $\overline{AB} \parallel \overline{DC}$.  **51.** $\frac{47}{4}$  **53.** 25
**55.** 2  **57.** 10  **59.** 48  **61.** −3.2

## Review and Practice Your Skills, pages 220–221

**1.** ASA  **3.** SSS or SAS  **5.** ASA  **7.** $\angle S$  **9.** $\angle T$  **11.** $\overline{TU}$  **13.** 8  **15.** 81°  **17.** 128°  **19.** 52°  **21.** $\overline{DN}$  **23.** $\angle NIF$  **25.** ASA  **27.** not necessarily congruent  **29.** 82°
**31.** 82°  **33.** 82°

## Lesson 5-7, pages 222–225

**1.** convex; regular pentagon  **3.** concave; not regular hexagon  **5.** 1440°  **7.** 1980°  **9.** 144°  **11.** 156°
**13.** 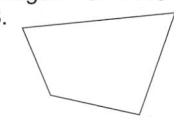  **15.** 360°  **17.** 3240°  **19.** 165°
**21.** convex, not regular, 12-gon
**23.** quadrilateral, yes
**25.** octagon, yes  **27.** false; the sum is 1620°  **29.** true

**31.** 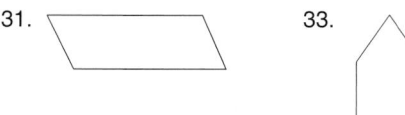  **33.**

**35.** (sum of interior angles) + (sum of exterior angles) = n(180°) the sum of interior angles = (n − 2)180°. So, (n − 2)180° + (sum of exterior angles) = n(180°)

(180°n − 360°) + (sum of exterior angles) = 180°n sum of exterior angles = 360°  **37.** 30  **39.** 21  **41.** $\frac{1}{7}$

## Lesson 5-8, pages 226–229

**1.** $\overline{LP}$, $\overline{LN}$, $\overline{LM}$  **3.** $\overarc{PMN}$, $\overarc{PNM}$, $\overarc{NOP}$, $\overarc{MPO}$, $\overarc{PNO}$  **5.** 180°
**7.** 263°  **9.** $\angle MNO$  **11.** 60°  **13.** 105°  **15.** $\overarc{POQ}$, $\overarc{PNQ}$, $\overarc{NQO}$, $\overarc{OPN}$  **17.** 110°  **19.** Both are radii.  **21.** Answers will vary.  **23.** 60°  **25.** True; the measure of a radius is one half the measure of a diameter.  **29.** 160°  **31.** 26.4 ft
**33.** $\frac{1}{16}$  **35.** $\frac{1}{8}$  **37.** $\frac{1}{12}$

## Review and Practice Your Skills, pages 230–231

**1.** 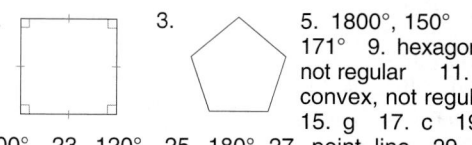  **3.**  **5.** 1800°, 150°  **7.** 6840°, 171°  **9.** hexagon, concave, not regular  **11.** rectangle, convex, not regular  **13.** b  **15.** g  **17.** c  **19.** f  **21.** 300°  **23.** 120°  **25.** 180°  **27.** point, line  **29.** congruent
**31.** congruent  **33.** supplementary  **35.** neither  **37.** yes
**39.** yes  **41.** no  **43.** 30°  **45.** ASA  **47.** SSS  **49.** false  **51.** true  **53.** true

## Lesson 5-9, pages 232–233

**1.** 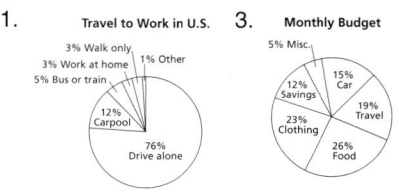  **3.**
**5.** 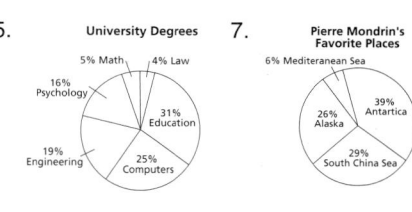  **7.**
**9.** 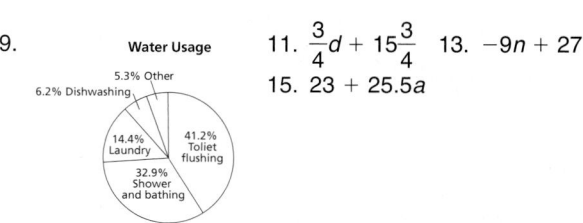  **11.** $\frac{3}{4}d + 15\frac{3}{4}$  **13.** −9n + 27
**15.** 23 + 25.5a

## Chapter 5 Review, pages 234–236

**1.** h  **3.** 1  **5.** c  **7.** b  **9.** i  **15.** Answers will vary. Sample answer: the floor and the ceiling  **17.** 41°, 131°
**19.** 78°, 168°  **21.** $\angle 1$ and $\angle 5$; $\angle 2$ and $\angle 6$; $\angle 3$ and $\angle 7$; $\angle 4$ and $\angle 8$  **23.** $\angle 1$ and $\angle 8$; $\angle 2$ and $\angle 7$  **25.** The lines are parallel because the angles are alternate exterior angles.  **27.** no  **29.** x = 30  **31.** x = 60, y = 70, z = 50  **33.** cannot be determined  **35.** 10  **37.** 100°  **39.** false
**41.** 1620°  **43.** 135°  **45.** $\angle KML$  **47.** $\overline{KL}$, $\overline{KM}$  **49.** $\overline{KL}$, $\overline{KM}$

**Ocean Surface Areas**

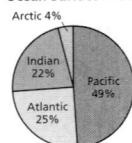

Arctic 4%

Indian 22%

Pacific 49%

Atlantic 25%

# Chapter 6: Graphing Functions

## Lesson 6-1, pages 244–247

1. 8   3. 13   5. (−2, −0.5)   7. 7.2; 3.6; (7, 9)
9. (3.5, 5); (6.5, 5); (5, 3)   11. 10   13. 7   15. (−2, 2)
17. (3, 3.5)   19. 3.2   21. 13   23. 3.2   25. 2.2
27. 1.0   29. C(9, −5); d ≈ 6.3; r ≈ 3.2   31. C(4, 0.5);
d = 15; r = 7.5   33. C(6, −6); d ≈ 12.8; r ≈ 6.4
35. 136.5 mi²   37. (−146.75, 43), (−103.5, 39),
(−60.25, 35)   39. (−8, 14)

41. **Shopping Day Preference**

43. −3   45. −1

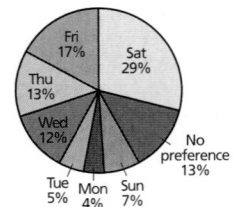

Fri 17%   Sat 29%
Thu 13%
Wed 12%
No preference 13%
Tue 5%   Mon 4%   Sun 7%

## Lesson 6-2, pages 248–251

1. $m_a = -\frac{5}{9}$; $m_b = \frac{1}{2}$   3. $m_l = -\frac{1}{3}$; $m_m = \frac{1}{6}$

5. 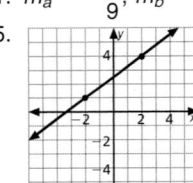   7.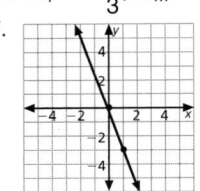

9. 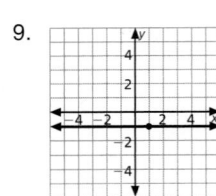   11. $-\frac{3}{4}$
13. $\frac{2}{5}$   15. $\frac{2}{5}$   17. −2
19. $\frac{2}{3}$

21. 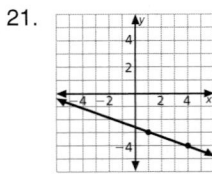   23.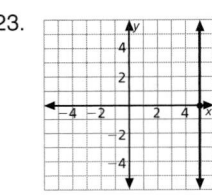

25. 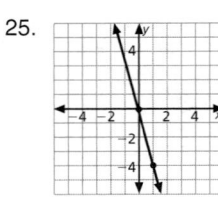   27.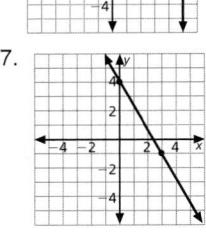

29. 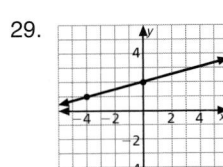   31. x = 4   33. The coordinates
have the same x- or y-value.
35. −2   37. 40 mph; 60 mph
39. returning home   41. 12   43. 6

## Review and Practice Your Skills, pages 252–253

1. 13   3. 16.3   5. 15   7. $\left(1, -3\frac{1}{2}\right)$   9. $\left(4, -1\frac{1}{2}\right)$
11. $\left(5\frac{1}{2}, -3\right)$   13. 11.3   15. 8   17. (2, 0)
19. (−2, 0)   21. C(3, 5); d = 14, r = 7   23. C(0, 2);
d ≈ 8.9; r ≈ 4.5   25. $C\left(5, 1\frac{1}{2}\right)$; d = 9; r = $4\frac{1}{2}$
27. $m_a = 0$; $m_b$ = undefined

29. 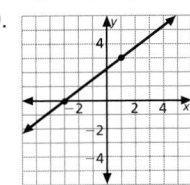   31.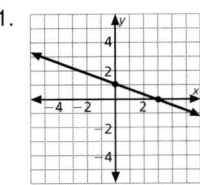

33. 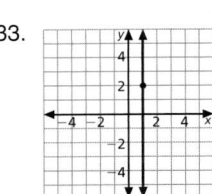   35. $\frac{6}{7}$   37. y = 4   39. $C\left(\frac{1}{4}, -\frac{1}{3}\right)$;
$d = \frac{5}{6}$; $r = \frac{5}{12}$   41. $C\left(-1\frac{1}{2}, -1\frac{1}{2}\right)$;
$d ≈ 11.0$;   r = 5.5
43. $C\left(-7\frac{1}{2}, 4\right)$; d ≈ 2.2; r ≈ 1.1

45. 18.8   47. 2.8   49. 17.2

51. 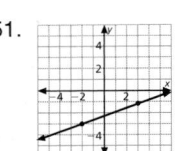   53. 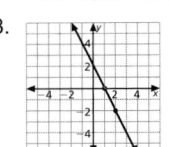   55.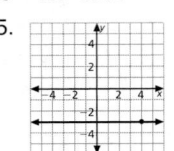

## Lesson 6-3, pages 254–257

1. $y = \frac{1}{2}x - 2$   3. $y = -\frac{1}{3}x + 5$
5. y = −x   7. 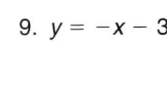   9. y = −x − 3

11. 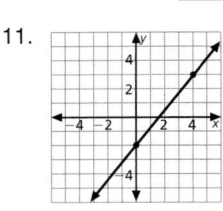   13.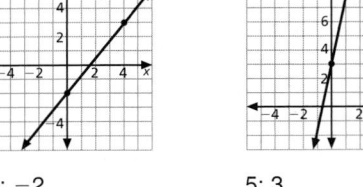

$\frac{5}{4}$; −2   5; 3

15. First, plot the *y*-intercept. Then use the slope to locate one or more other points. Next draw the line. If $ax + by = c$ is the form, first solve for *y*.

17. $y = \frac{5}{11}x - \frac{12}{11}$  19. $y = -\frac{1}{4}x + \frac{29}{4}$  21. $x = 0$

23. $y = -x - 1$  25. $y = -x + 6$  27. $y = -4$

29. $y = -x - 3$  31. $y = \frac{1}{2}x - 6$  33. $y = \frac{5}{2}x - 3$

35. The change in barometric pressure.

Pressure decreases as altitude increases.  37. $-13.5$ mm

39. $y = -\frac{A}{B}x + \frac{C}{B}$; $m = -\frac{A}{B}$; *y*-int $= \frac{C}{B}$

41. 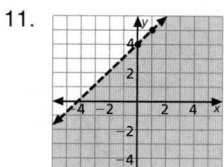  43.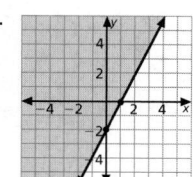

45. 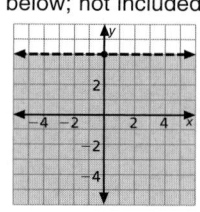  47.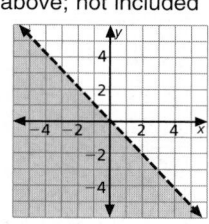

49. $72°$, $162°$  51. $7°$, $97°$

## Lesson 6-4, pages 258–261

1. yes  3. no  5. below; not included  7. below; included  9. above; included

11. 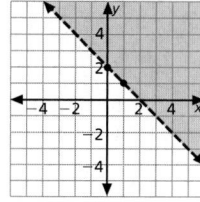  13.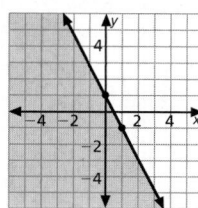

15. below; not included  17. above; not included

19. 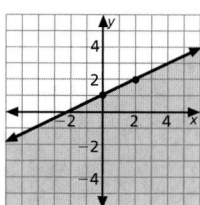  21.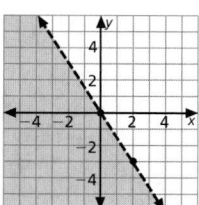

23. 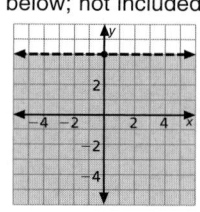  25.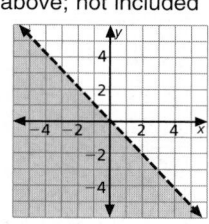

27. 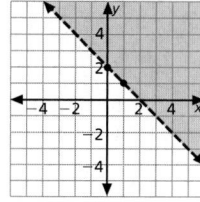  29.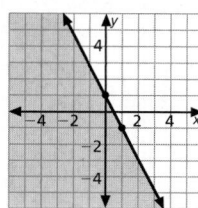

31. 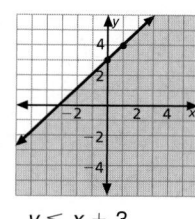  33.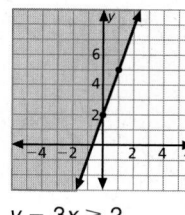

$y \leq x + 3$   $y - 3x \geq 2$

35. $y < x + 1$

37.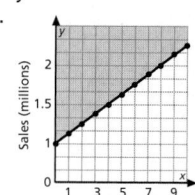

$y \geq 125,000x + 1,000,000$

39. 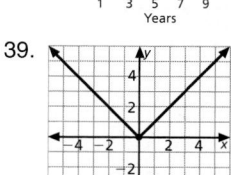  41. yes  43. yes

45. Answers will vary.

47. $\frac{1}{50}$  49. $p^9$  51. $m^4$

53. $f$  55. $\frac{1}{r^8}$ or $r^{-8}$

## Review and Practice Your Skills, pages 262–263

1. 1; 2  3. 2; 0  5. 5; $-6$  7. $y = \frac{2}{3}x + 4$

9. $y = -\frac{4}{3}x + \frac{2}{3}$  11. $y = -\frac{1}{2}x + \frac{3}{2}$  13. $y = x - 8$

15. $y = 6x - 1$  17. $y = 5$  19. $y = x + 4$

21. $y = \frac{1}{3}x - 4$  23. $y = -x - 5$  25. $y = -\frac{5}{3}x + 18$

27. $y = -\frac{1}{2}x - 1$  29. no  31. yes  33. yes

35. above; included  37. above; included

39. below; included

41. 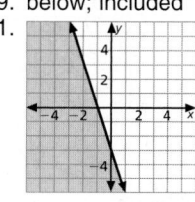  43.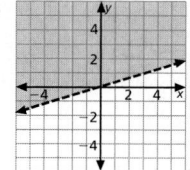

45. 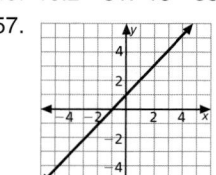  47. $y \geq -x - 3$

49. 10.2  51. 13  53. $y = -2x + 2$  55. $y = -5x - 6$

57. 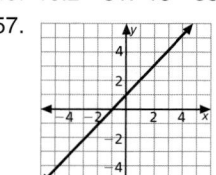  1; 1  59.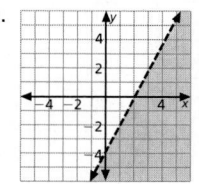

**61.** 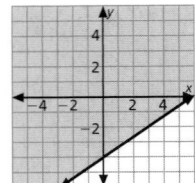  **63.** 6.3  **65.** isosceles

## Lesson 6-5, pages 264–267

**1.** no  **3.** no  **5.** yes

**7.** 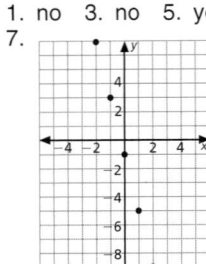  **9.**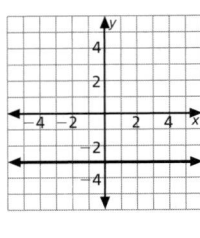

**11.** no; vertical line test fails
**13.** yes; vertical line test passes

**15.** 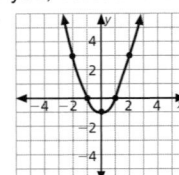  **17.**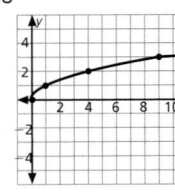

**19.** 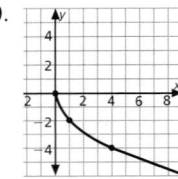  **21.**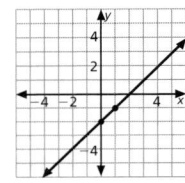

**23.** $c = 12t + 20$; linear function  **25.** 13 mL  **27.** $-3$
**29.** $-4, 4$  **31.** $z < 6$  **33.** $a \le -6$  **35.** $r < \dfrac{11}{2}$

## Lesson 6-6, pages 268–271

**1.** 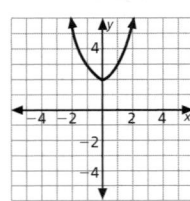  **3.**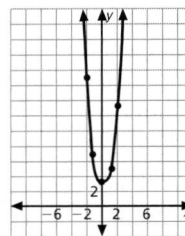

**5.** 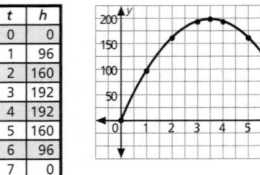  **7.** 3.5 sec  **9.** 2
**11.** 0

**13.** 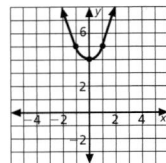  **15.**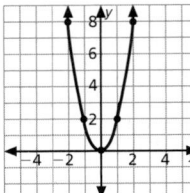

**17.** 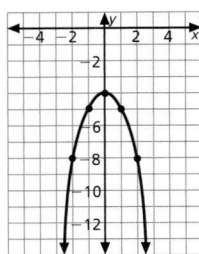  **19.** Answers will vary but may include $25 \times 25$, $30 \times 20$, $35 \times 15$, $40 \times 10$, etc.

**21.** 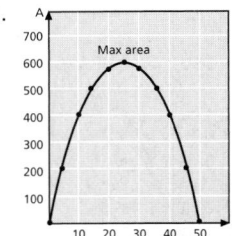  **23.** 625 ft²  **25.** $-2$
**27.** 1 or $-1$  **29.** 2.5 sec
**33.** $y = x^2 + 10$; $y = x^2 - 10$
**35.** Yes; changing the term shifts the graph horizontally.
**39.** Yes. If $a$ is between 0 and 1 the parabola opens wider than the graph of $y = x^2$. It is narrower if $a$ is greater than 1.

**41.** 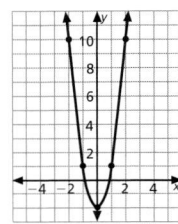  **43.**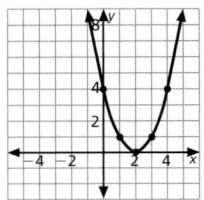

**45.** 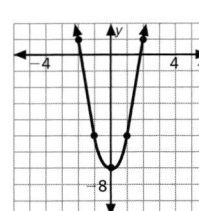  **47.**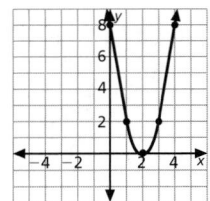

**49.** $\left(\dfrac{-b}{2a}, c - \dfrac{b^2}{4a}\right)$  **51.** 128°  **53.** 128°  **55.** 113°
**57.** $27x$  **59.** $13x$

## Review and Practice Your Skills, pages 272–273

**1.** 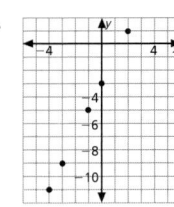  **3.**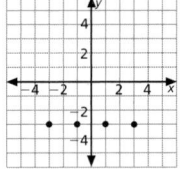

**5.** yes  **7.** yes

**9.** 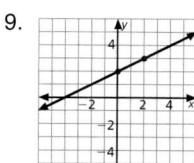 **11.**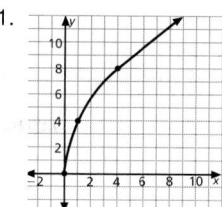

**13.**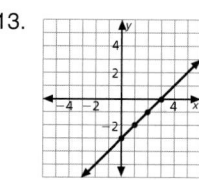

**15.** 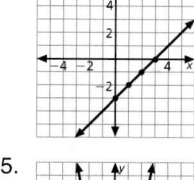 **17.**

**19.**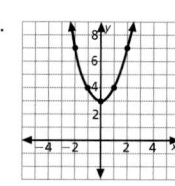

**21.** 1  **23.** −2 or 2  **25.** 2 sec
**27.** Above. Although *h* is negative at *t* = 3 sec, we know from experience that balls bounce.
**29.** $\left(2\frac{1}{16}, -2\frac{3}{4}\right)$  **31.** −1; 0
**33.** 2; −4  **35.** $y < \frac{3}{2}x - 2$
**37.** $y \le -\frac{2}{3}x + 2$

## Lesson 6-7, pages 274–275

**1.** c  **3.** (4, 7), (−2, −5), (0, −1), (1, 1), (2, 3)  **5.** $y = \sqrt{x}$
**7.**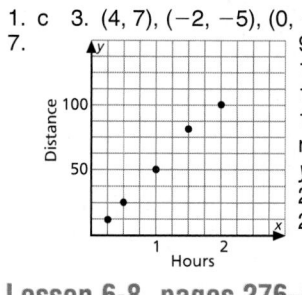

**9.** $x \ge 0$  **11.** all real numbers
**13.** Answers will vary.
**15.** $C(x) = 1.5 + 0.75(x - 1)$
**17.** If the domain is the set of natural numbers, there is no *y*-intercept.  **19.** 23 hr
**21.** 665,280  **23.** 336
**25.** 36  **27.** ±7

## Lesson 6-8, pages 276–279

**1.** 28  **3.** $91  **5.** 10  **7.** 50  **9.** 66  **11.** 7  **13.** 1760
**15.** 18.2 lb  **17.** 78 m  **19.** Answers will vary.  **21.** direct
**23.** neither  **25.** *y* is quadrupled; *y* is multiplied by 9
**27.** $\frac{y}{x} = \frac{a}{b}$; *by* = *ax*; *by* + *xy* = *ax* + *xy*; *y*(*b* + *x*) = *x*(*a* + *y*); $\frac{y}{x} = \frac{a + y}{b + x}$  **29.** increases  **31.** decreases
**33.**

| 0 | 4 8 |
|---|---|
| 1 | 2 5 7 8 8 9 9 |
| 2 | 0 4 7 7 9 |
| 3 | 1 |

0|4 represents 4 calls

**35.** −3*b* − 12  **37.** 8*c* − 2*d*
**39.** 4.5  **41.** $-\frac{3}{2}$

## Review and Practice Your Skills, pages 280–281

**1.** c  **3.** b  **5.** (−4, −9), (−2, −7), (0, −5), (5, 0), (10, 5)  **7.** (−6, −4), (−3, −1), (0, 2), (3, −1), (6, −4)
**9.** $f(x) = 3x$  **11.** $f(x) = |x|$  **13.** 24  **15.** 39  **17.** −4

**19.** $15.84  **21.** b  **23.** d  **25.** yes  **27.** yes
**29.**

| x | 2 | 4 | 6 | 8 |
|---|---|---|---|---|
| y | 4 | 5 | 6 | 7 |

**31.** $C\left(\frac{3}{2}, 2\right)$; $d \approx 11.2$; $r \approx 5.6$  **33.** $C\left(\frac{3}{2}, \frac{17}{2}\right)$; $d \approx 17.3$; $r \approx 8.6$

## Lesson 6-9, pages 282–285

**1.** 6  **3.** increase  **5.** 5 yd/sec  **7.** inverse variation
**9.** 320  **11.** 2.5  **13.** 1.6 min  **15.** $24  **17.** inverse
**19.** inverse  **21.** 1 newton  **23.** 500  **25.** 0.8  **27.** *y* varies directly as $z^2$  **29.** $h = \frac{132}{\pi r^2}$  **31.** 42°  **33.** 117°
**35.** 70°  **37.** 33°  **39.** 19°

## Chapter 6 Review, pages 286–288

**1.** i  **3.** f  **5.** l  **7.** k  **9.** h  **11.** 1  **13.** 5  **15.** 2  **17.** 4.5
**19.** 2.2  **21.** $\left(-1\frac{1}{2}, 0\right)$  **23.** −4  **25.** 6  **27.** $\frac{5}{3}$  **29.** undefined
**31.** $y = -\frac{2}{5}x + 3$  **33.** $y = x + 7$  **35.** $y = x + 4$  **37.** $y = -2x + 11$  **39.** $y = -\frac{1}{2}x + 2$  **41.** $y = \frac{2}{3}x + 4$  **43.** yes
**45.** no  **47.** $y \ge -2x + 2$  **49.**

**51.** No; vertical line test fails.  **53.** Yes; vertical line test passes.  **55.** 0  **57.** (−3, −7), (−2, −6), (0, −4), (1, −3), (2, −2)  **59.** $y = 2x^2$  **61.** 15  **63.** 14  **65.** 7.5  **67.** $\frac{1}{4}$

# Chapter 7: Coordinate Graphing and Transformations

## Lesson 7-1, pages 296–299

**1.** 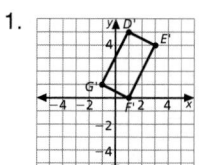  **3.**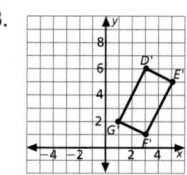

**5.** $D'(-560, -154)$, $E'(-558, -155)$, $F'(-560, -159)$, $G'(-562, -158)$  **7.** $(x, y) \rightarrow (x + 6, y - 1)$
**9.**  **11.**

**13.**  **15.** No; angles are not all congruent, sides are not all congruent.  **17.** $(x, y) \rightarrow (x + 5, y - 2)$  **19.** The image should be translated right and up.
**21.** The sliding door moves horizontally the appropriate number of units to open the door

wide enough for a person to access the deck. A move to the right or left depending on the position of the door is a translation.   23. Mandy translated the preimage 4 units up and 2 units right. The correct vertices are $A(1, 4) \rightarrow A'(1 + 4, 4 + 2) = A'(5, 6)$; $B(4, -2) \rightarrow B'(4 + 4, -2 + 2) = B'(8, 0)$; $C(7, 9) \rightarrow C'(7 + 4, 9 + 2) = C'(11, 11)$
25. No; the vertices did not all move the same number of units to the right.   27. Answers will vary.   29. $\frac{4}{13}$
31. 4  33. 12  35. 8  37. $-3.5$  39. 14  41. 6

## Lesson 7-2, pages 300–303

1. 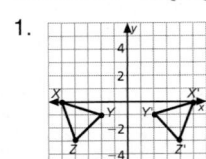   3.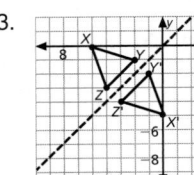

5. 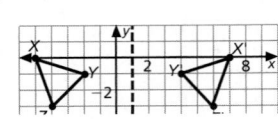   7. $y = -x + 1$
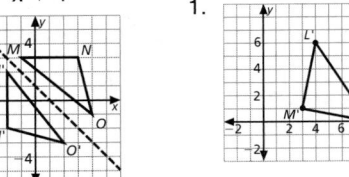

9. $(x, y) \rightarrow (x, -y)$; Quadrant I
11. 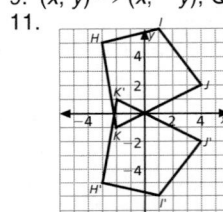   13.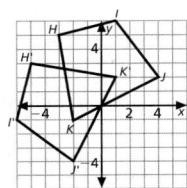

15. 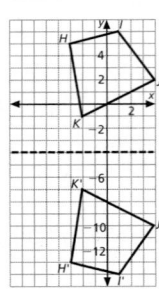   17. (0, -4)
19. (8, -6)
21. (3, -3)
23. $y = x + 2$

25. Draw a horizontal line at least twice the distance from $A$ to line $m$ from point $A$ through the line $m$. Measure the distance from line $m$ to point $A$. Locate point $A'$ which is to the right of line $m$ by measuring this distance from line $m$. Repeat for vertices $B'$ and $C'$. Connect the points $A'$, $B'$, and $C'$.

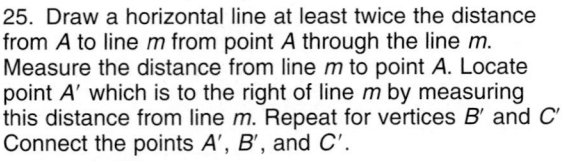
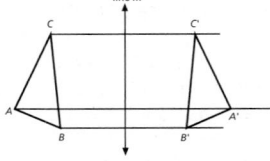

27. 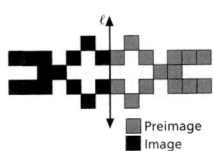   29. $(-10, 0) \rightarrow (8, 0)$
$(-5, 0) \rightarrow (3, 0)$
$(-10, 11) \rightarrow (8, 11)$
$(-5, 11) \rightarrow (3, 11)$
$(-7.5, 14) \rightarrow (5.5, 14)$

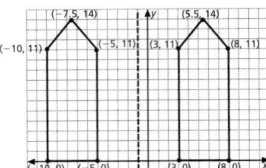

31. It is the same as $\triangle ABC$.   33. mean = 152; median = 152; mode = 145, 152; range = 118   35. mean = 32.1; median = 32; mode = 32; range = 32   37. 59°, 149°
39. 11°, 101°   41. 68°, 158°   43. 6°, 96°

## Review and Practice Your Skills, pages 304–305

1. 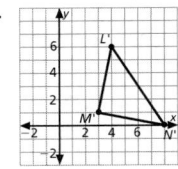   3.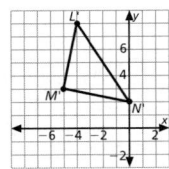

5. $(x, y) \rightarrow (x + 2, y - 4)$   7. $(x, y) \rightarrow (x - 3, y + 2)$
9. $A'(-2, 3)$, $B'(-1, 2)$, $C'(-3, -1)$   11. $A'(2, -8)$, $B'(3, -9)$, $C'(1, -12)$
13. 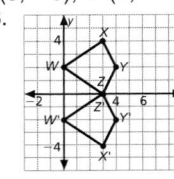   15.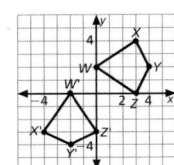

17. 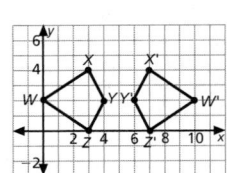   19. (4, 4)   21. (-6, -1)
23. (3, 0)
25. $(x, y) \rightarrow (x + 3, y - 4)$
27. (5, -4)   29. (6, 0)
31. (0, -1)

## Lesson 7-3, pages 306–309

1. 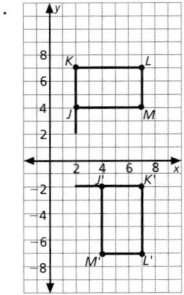   3.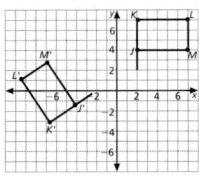

5. Draw a line segment connecting any two corresponding vertices between the image and the preimage. Construct the perpendicular bisector of the line segment. Repeat for two other corresponding vertices. The intersection of these perpendicular bisectors is the center of rotation.   7. 90° clockwise or 270° counterclockwise

9. 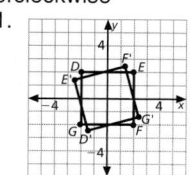   11.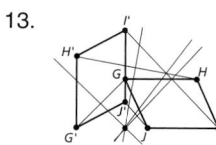

13. 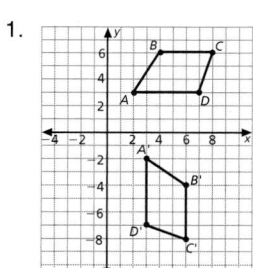   90° counterclockwise or 270° clockwise

15.
$L(0, 500) \to L'(500, 0)$
$C(100, 200) \to C'(200, -100)$
$E(400, 200) \to E'(200, -400)$
$K(200, 0) \to K'(0, -200)$
$O(0, 0) \to O'(0, 0)$

17. F   19. H
21. counterclockwise
23. ASA   25. not congruent   27. 3.6

## Lesson 7-4, pages 310–313

1. 1 line   3. none   5. 8   7. Yes. Answers will vary but Exercise 4 is one example.   9. yes   11. 3   13. 5   15. Any line through the center of the circle is a line of symmetry. Since a person can draw an infinite number of lines through a point, a circle would have an infinite number of lines of symmetry.   17. Answers will vary. Any palindrome which uses the digits 0, 1, 3 and 8 has line symmetry. A palindrome which uses the digits 0, 1, or 8 has rotational symmetry of order 2.   19. There are 6 lines of symmetry. This figure has order 6 rotational symmetry. 21. Each of the letters B, C, D, E, H, I, K, O and X has one horizontal line of symmetry. Each of the letters A, H, I, M, O, T, U, V, W, X and Y has one vertical line of symmetry.   23. Answers will vary.   25. Answers will vary.   27. Answers will vary.   29. Answers will vary. 31. n   33. 35   35. 495   37. 56   39. 108°   41. 60°

## Review and Practice Your Skills, pages 314–315

1. 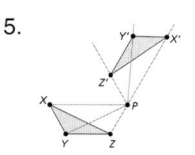   3.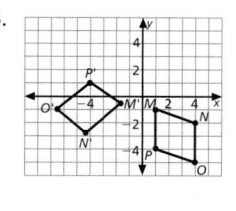

5. 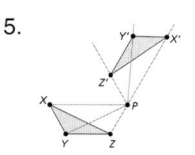   7. 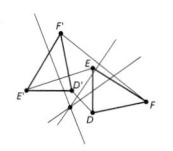   90° counterclockwise or 270° clockwise

9. 2 lines   11. 1 line   13. none   15. 4   17. 6   19. 4 21. 2   23. none

## Lesson 7-5, pages 316–319

1. 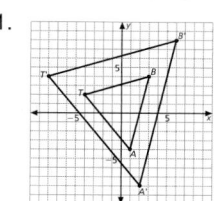   3. 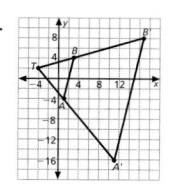   5. 3; (0, 0)
7. 2; (0, 0)

9. 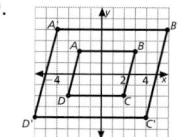   11.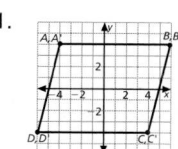

13. 13.8   15. ≈ 342.86   17. A dilation changes each figure into a similar figure not necessarily congruent to the original figure, while translations, reflections, and rotations change each figure into a congruent figure. All corresponding angles are equal in translations, reflections, rotations, and dilations. Dilations and translations have parallel corresponding sides between the preimage and the image.   19. $\frac{1}{3}$; (0, 0)
21. $5\frac{1}{3}$ in.   23. Answers will vary. Possible solution: Translation to the left 3 and up 2. Then use a dilation with center $(-1, 1)$ and a scale factor of 2.   25. 9 square units; 36 square units; 2.25 square units   27. tennis ball: 292.5 cm ≈ 3 m; baseball: 343 cm ≈ 3.43 m; basketball: 1080 cm ≈ 10.8 m   29. −5   31. 9 33. 22.5   35. −45   37. −16   39. 3; 5   41. 1; −4 43. $-\frac{5}{2}$; 3   45. $\frac{1}{2}$; 5

## Lesson 7-6, pages 320–321

1. yes   3. yes   7. Sample answer:

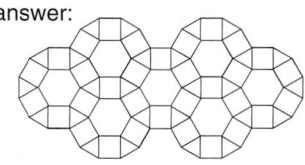

9. yes   11. yes   13. Answers will vary.
15. 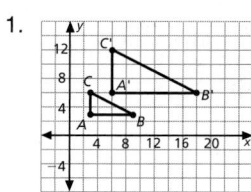   17. tessellating rhombuses and four-pointed stars.   19. Answers will vary.   21. 28   23. $\frac{13}{5}$ 25. 3   27. $\frac{25}{6}$   29. $\frac{16}{37}$

## Review and Practice Your Skills, pages 322–323

1. 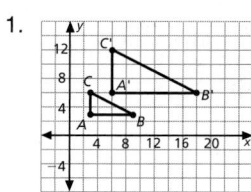   3.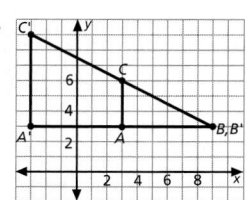

5. $G'(4,12)$, $H'(16,4)$, $I'(4,4)$   7. $N'(-12,0)$, $O'(0,0)$, $P'(0,-6)$, $Q'(-12,-6)$   9. yes   11. yes

13. yes

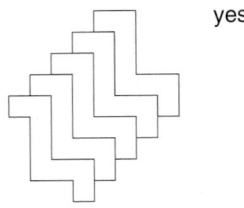

15.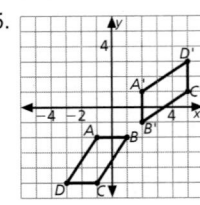

17. 2 lines
19. 1 line

## Chapter 7 Review, pages 324–326

1. f   3. a   5. l   7. j   9. i   11.

13. $(x, y) \rightarrow (x - 5, y - 3)$

15.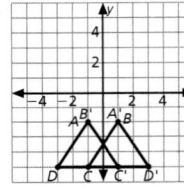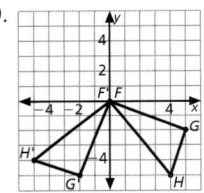

17. 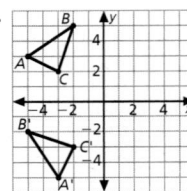   19.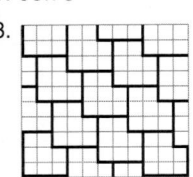

21.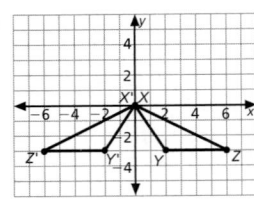

23. 2 lines   25. 6   27. 2

29. $(x, y) \rightarrow (x - 5, y - 3)$

31. 93.75

33.

# Chapter 8: Systems of Equations and Inequalities

## Lesson 8-1, pages 334–337

1. $-\dfrac{5}{2}, \dfrac{2}{5}$   3. 1, −1   5. neither   7. $y = 3x - 13$

9. $y = \dfrac{5}{7}x - \dfrac{17}{7}$   11. $y = -\dfrac{4}{3}x + 11$   13. $-\dfrac{1}{2}, 2$

15. $-\dfrac{7}{5}, \dfrac{5}{7}$   17. undefined, 0   19. If the line is a horizontal line, then the $y$-coordinates will be the same in each point. If the line is a vertical line, then the $x$-coordinates will be the same in each point.   21. perpendicular   23. parallel

25. neither   27. $y = -\dfrac{2}{3}x - \dfrac{44}{3}$   29. $y = 7x - 6$

31. $y = -\dfrac{5}{3}x - 3$   33. $y = -\dfrac{1}{5}x - 1$   35. $y = \dfrac{7}{2}x + 14$

37. $y = \dfrac{3}{2}x + \dfrac{3}{2}$

39. 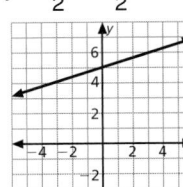   No. The planes will not crash since their paths are parallel.

41. $y = -\dfrac{2}{3}x + 3$

43. 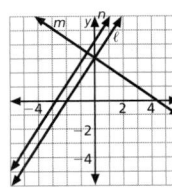   slope of $\overline{AD} = -\dfrac{5}{4}$, slope of $\overline{AC} = 0$, slope of $\overline{BD}$ is undefined Opposite sides are parallel. Diagonals are perpendicular. The quadrilateral is a rhombus.

45. 14   47. 71°

## Lesson 8-2, pages 338–341

1. no   3. yes

5. 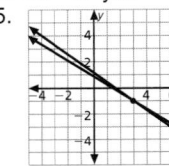   (3, −1)
7. Julian: $d = 8t$;
Leticia: $d = 12t - 10$
9. no   11. yes   13. no

15. 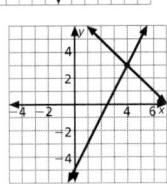   (4, 3)   17. 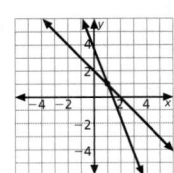   (1, 1)

19. 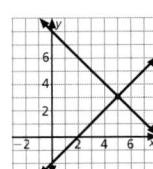   (5, 3)   21. 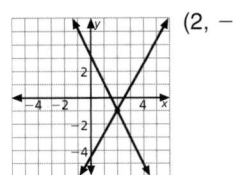   (2, −1)

23. no solution   25. (8.14, −0.29)   27. c, the police car
29. 1 solution   31. no solution
33. $y = -x + 7$         $m_1 = -1, b_1 = 7$
$y = 2x - 5$         $m_2 = 2, b_2 = -5$
$x = \dfrac{b_2 - b_1}{m_1 - m_2}$
$x = \dfrac{-5 - 7}{-1 - 2} = \dfrac{-12}{-3} = 4$
35. 9.2   37. 11.2

## Review and Practice Your Skills, pages 342–343

1. $\frac{5}{4}$, $-\frac{4}{5}$  3. $-\frac{2}{3}$, $\frac{3}{2}$  5. $\frac{3}{7}$, $-\frac{7}{3}$  7. neither  9. parallel
11. neither  13. $y = 3x - 11$  15. $y = 2x + 5$
17. $y = -3x + 6$  19. no  21. yes  23. no

25. 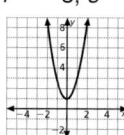 (3, 1)  27. 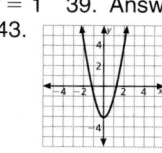 (4, 2)

29. 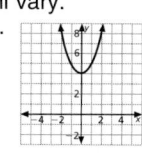 (0, 3)  31. (4, 3)
33. (1, 1)  35. no

37. (2, 3)  39. (1, −1)

41. $y = x + 1$  43. $y = -\frac{2}{3}x + 2$  45. $y = -3x + 5$

## Lesson 8-3, pages 344–347

1. (7, 0)  3. (4, 3)  5. $\left(-\frac{1}{4}, \frac{5}{4}\right)$  7. A hotdog cost $2
and a drink costs $1.  9. (0, 1)  11. (3, 1)  13. no
solution  15. (4, 1)  17. (−1, 2)  19. (2, 1)  21. (9, 15)
23. Answers will vary.  25. 1500 men  27. infinitely many
solutions  29. no solution  35. $x = 2$, $y = -1$, $z = 5$
37. $r = -3$, $s = 2$, $t = 1$  39. Answers will vary.
41.  43.  45.

47. 924

## Lesson 8-4, pages 348–351

1. (4, −3)  3. (−4, 6)  5. (1, 3)  7. length = 6 m;
width = 10 m  9. (0, −1)  11. (5, −3)  13. infinitely
many solutions  15. (1, 0)  17. (8, −1)  19. $\left(\frac{29}{10}, \frac{-2}{15}\right)$
21. (−9, −5)  23. Answers will vary.  25. 41 hits
27. 3 pepperoni and 2 extra cheese  29. infinitely many
solutions  31. One equation is a multiple of the other.
These are infinitely many solutions in each case.
33. Answers will vary.  35. 5  37. $\frac{5}{8}$  39. $\frac{5}{3}$  41. 138°
43. 42°  45. 42°

## Review and Practice Your Skills, pages 352–353

1. (2, 4)  3. $\left(3, \frac{3}{2}\right)$  5. (2, 3)  7. (2, −3)  9. $\left(\frac{1}{2}, -1\right)$
11. (0, 3)  13. (3, 2)  15. no solution  17. (−1, 1)

19. (4, 3)  21. $\left(0, \frac{1}{9}\right)$  23. (−2, 4)  25. (2, 2)  27. (2, −2)
29. (10, 6)  31. $\left(4, \frac{18}{5}\right)$  33. 55°, 125°  35. $y = 3x + 1$
37. (3, 2)  39. (2, 5)  41. (4, −2)  43. (2, 0)  45. (1, 5)

## Lesson 8-5, pages 354–357

1. 8  3. −4.65  5. (−3, −2)  7. (−62, 39)  9. (−1, 4)
11. 35 female members  13. 32  15. −171  17. $\left(4, \frac{18}{5}\right)$
19. (−3.5, 2.5)  21. (5, −2)  23. (−4, −2)  25. (2, 3)
27. (−4, −1)  29. The congruent sides are each 10 m.
The third side is 15 m.  31. tennis: 50 min, swimming:
20 min  33. Answers will vary.  35.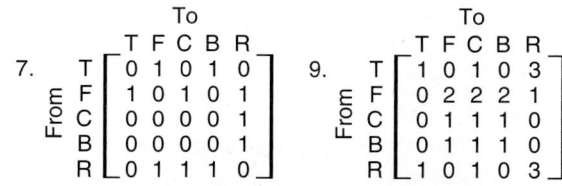

37. 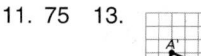 $c > -6$

39. 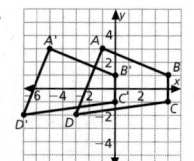 $g \leq 1$

41.  $d > 6$

45. 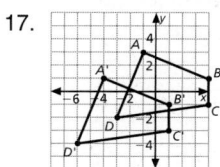 $a \geq \frac{8}{3}$

## Lesson 8-6, pages 358–359

1.
$$\begin{array}{c} \\ \text{From} \end{array} \begin{array}{c} \\ A \\ B \\ C \\ D \end{array} \overset{\text{To}}{\begin{array}{cccc} A & B & C & D \\ \left[\,0 \right. & 1 & 1 & \left. 1\,\right] \\ 1 & 0 & 0 & 1 \\ 1 & 0 & 0 & 1 \\ 0 & 1 & 0 & 0 \end{array}}$$

3.
$$\begin{array}{c} \\ \text{From} \end{array} \begin{array}{c} \\ A \\ B \\ C \\ D \end{array} \overset{\text{To}}{\begin{array}{cccc} A & B & C & D \\ \left[\,2 \right. & 1 & 0 & \left. 2\,\right] \\ 0 & 2 & 1 & 1 \\ 0 & 2 & 1 & 1 \\ 1 & 0 & 0 & 1 \end{array}}$$

5. 34

7.
$$\begin{array}{c} \\ \text{From} \end{array} \begin{array}{c} \\ T \\ F \\ C \\ B \\ R \end{array} \overset{\text{To}}{\begin{array}{ccccc} T & F & C & B & R \\ \left[\,0 \right. & 1 & 0 & 1 & \left. 0\,\right] \\ 1 & 0 & 1 & 0 & 1 \\ 0 & 0 & 0 & 0 & 1 \\ 0 & 0 & 0 & 0 & 1 \\ 0 & 1 & 1 & 1 & 0 \end{array}}$$

9.
$$\begin{array}{c} \\ \text{From} \end{array} \begin{array}{c} \\ T \\ F \\ C \\ B \\ R \end{array} \overset{\text{To}}{\begin{array}{ccccc} T & F & C & B & R \\ \left[\,1 \right. & 0 & 1 & 0 & \left. 3\,\right] \\ 0 & 2 & 2 & 2 & 1 \\ 0 & 1 & 1 & 1 & 0 \\ 0 & 1 & 1 & 1 & 0 \\ 1 & 0 & 1 & 0 & 3 \end{array}}$$

T represents Towertop Restaurant
F represents Forest Theater
C represents Cascade Falls Water Ride
B represents Bootjack Camp Museum
R represents Redwood Rodeo

11. 75  13.  15.

17.

## Review and Practice Your Skills, pages 360–361

1. 2   3. −31   5. −44   7. 47   9. (3, −1)   11. (−1, 3)
13. (7, −1)   15. (1, 1)   17. (1, −2)   19. (−2, 2)

21.

|       | To A | B | C | D | E |
|-------|------|---|---|---|---|
| **From** A | 0 | 0 | 1 | 0 | 1 |
| B | 1 | 0 | 1 | 0 | 0 |
| C | 0 | 1 | 0 | 1 | 1 |
| D | 0 | 1 | 0 | 0 | 0 |
| E | 0 | 0 | 1 | 1 | 0 |

23.

|       | To A | B | C | D | E |
|-------|------|---|---|---|---|
| **From** A | 0 | 1 | 1 | 2 | 1 |
| B | 0 | 1 | 1 | 1 | 2 |
| C | 1 | 1 | 2 | 1 | 0 |
| D | 1 | 0 | 1 | 0 | 0 |
| E | 0 | 2 | 0 | 1 | 1 |

25. Denver and Philadelphia   27. $-\frac{1}{2}$, 2   29. $-\frac{3}{4}, \frac{4}{3}$

31. 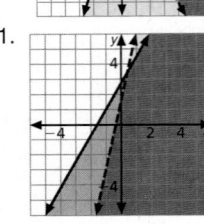   (−2, −4)   33. (2, 3)   35. (8, −7)

## Lesson 8-7, pages 362–365

1. $y \le -3x + 2; y > \frac{1}{3}x - 1$   3. $y < 2x + 2; y > -\frac{1}{2}x + 1$   7. Answers will vary, but a possible answer follows. Choose a point above or below the line. Usually choosing the origin is a good point. Substitute the $x$ and $y$ values of the coordinate into the original inequality. If it is a true statement, shade the area that includes the point. If it is a false statement, shade on the other side of the line. To check the solution, choose another point in the shaded area to verify that it results in a true statement.

5. 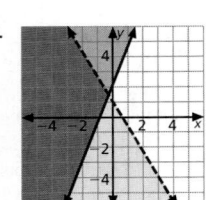   9. $y \ge -4x + 2; y \le -x - 2$

11. 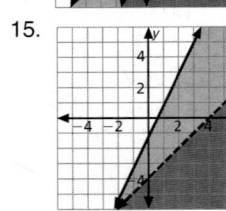   13.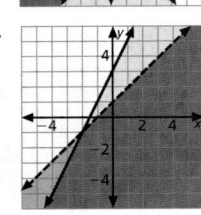

15. 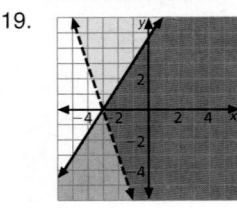   17.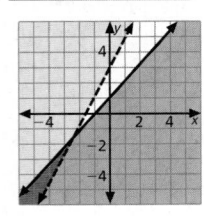

19. 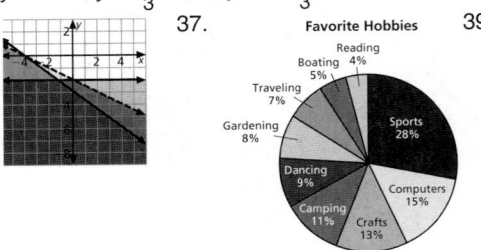   21.

23. $x + y > 10; 10x + 15y < 200$   25. Answers will vary, but a possible answer follows. A coordinate that satisfies the inequalities is (3, 9). A coordinate that does not satisfy the inequality is (5, 3). Jill can buy three $10 CD's and nine $15 CD's.   27. $x + y \le 2000; 0.05x + 0.10y > 150$
29. (400, 1400); (1000, 600)   31. $x > -2; x < 5$
33. $y \ge -3; y \le \frac{2}{3}x - 2; y > -\frac{1}{3}x + 3$

35. 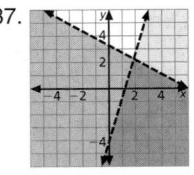   37.

**Favorite Hobbies**   39. 4.6 T

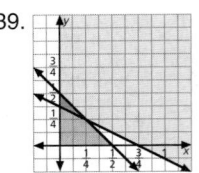

Reading 4%
Boating 5%
Traveling 7%
Gardening 8%
Dancing 9%
Camping 11%
Crafts 13%
Computers 15%
Sports 28%

## Chapter 8 Review, pages 366–368

1. f   3. h   5. a   7. k   9. i   11. perpendicular
13. $y = 2x - 5$   15.   (3, 3)
17. (−3, −1)   19. (0, 5)
21. (2, 1)   23. (7, 4)
25. (2, −1)   27. −6   29. −7
31. 30 CDs, 10 videos   33. 1
35. $y < x + 1, y \le -x + 1$

37.   39.

# Chapter 9: Polynomials

## Lesson 9-1, pages 376–379

1. $3x^3 + 9x^2 - 2x + 4$   3. $x^2y^2 - xy^3$   5. $-k^3 + k^2 - k$   7. $11h^2 + 3h$   9. $-7jk^2 + 3jk$   11. $8x + 5$   13. $2x^4 + 3x^3 + x^2 + x$   15. $-5x^3 - 3x^2y + 2xy^2 + y^3$

17. $x^3y + x^2y^2 + xy^4$   19. $\frac{19}{28}x^2$   21. $6y^3 - 4y^2$

23. $2x^3 + 11x$   25. $4n^2 + 8n$   27. $4.6x - 2.2$
29. $6hk + 10k$   31. $12x^2y + 10xy - 6$   33. $-1.9m + 11.6n - 2.3$   35. $x - 2.4$   37. $15r + 46t$   39. $(3x^2 - 22y - 71)$ ft   41. $16x - 10$   43. $b^3 + 4a^2b^2 - 4$

45. Answers will vary.   47. 9 in.   49. $y = 3x - \frac{5}{2}$

51. $y = -3x + 9$   53. $y = 6x + 21$

## Lesson 9-2, pages 380–383

1. $27ef$   3. $-8abc$   5. $-\frac{4}{15}y^7$   7. $16p^{20}$   9. $64a^9b^6c^{15}$

11. $2x(-y - x)$   13. Both monomials involve exponents. The monomial $a^m \cdot a^n$ calls for the use of the product rule for exponents where $m$ and $n$ are added to form $a^{m+n}$. The monomial $(a^m)^n$ calls for the use of the power rule for exponents where $m$ and $n$ are multiplied to form $a^{mn}$. The difference to note is that in one case $m$ and $n$ are added and in the other case they are multiplied.   15. $-8ab$

17. $5hkxy$   19. $12tw$   21. $10a^5b^6$   23. $-24x^2y^2$
25. $2.58xy^6$   27. $15x^7y^3$   29. $-a^2b^2c^2$   31. $-\frac{3}{8}p^3q^3$
33. $8h^9$   35. $25x^4y^2$   37. $a^6b^6c^{12}$   39. $8a^{16}$   41. $-40x^{11}$
43. $-a^{18}b^9$   45. $128h^{13}$   47. $6a^2b^3$   49. $30x^2$   51. $3x + x = 4x$   53. $100x^4$ ft$^2$   55. $2a^3b, 3ab$   57. $(2x^2)(3y^2) - (2x)(2xy) = 6x^2y^2 - 4x^2y$   59. $32a^4b^3$   61. 3   63. $16a^4b^8$
65a. $1.5x$ mi   b. $2.5x$ mi   c. $2x$ mi   d. $3x$ mi   e. $2.5x$ mi
f. $2x$ mi   67. mean = 41.9, median = 40, mode = 35
69.

### Review and Practice Your Skills, pages 384–385

1. $5x^3 + 2x^2 + 4$   3. $-3x^3 + 7x^2y - xy + y^3$   5. $6x^3 - 4x^2 + 9x - 10$   7. $5c$   9. $4m$   11. $5b + 4d$   13. $-k^2 + 4k$   15. $2a^2$   17. $5.3x - 9$   19. $2x - 7$   21. $2ab^2 - 7ab + 6$   23. $36ab$   25. $-9cb$   27. $8b^4c^8$   29. $-2s^2t^2u^2$
31. $10g^7$   33. $125g^6$   35. $x^{10}$   37. $e^4f^8g^4$   39. $675h^{14}$
41. $81p^{12}$   43. $x^4y^8z^4$   45. $-18a^6b^6$   47. $72n^5$ ft$^2$
49. $\frac{27}{2}x^3$ m$^2$   51. $4t - 10$   53. $a - 9b$   55. $-27x^3y^9$
57. $31p^7$   59. $-a^6$   61. $6b^3c^5$

### Lesson 9-3, pages 386–389

1. $-3a$   3. $\frac{-3yz}{4}$   5. $p - 2r$   7. $2k^2m - 1$
9. $-3c^2d^2 + d - 2$   11. $\frac{2xy - 6x}{2x}$   13. $4x$   15. $-\frac{10}{7}$
17. $\frac{b}{2c}$   19. $15xy$   21. $11abc^3$   23. 3   25. $-6b^4$
27. $a + 5$   29. $3a - 2$   31. $2 - 3x$   33. $1 - 3a^2 + 5a^4$
35. $5w^2 - 3w - 6$   37. $-5ab^2 + 2a^2b^3 - b$   39. $3x - 4y + 2z - 1$   41. $6p$

43.

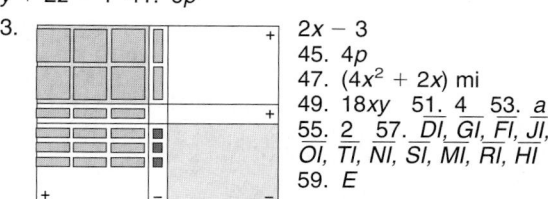

2x – 3
45. $4p$
47. $(4x^2 + 2x)$ mi
49. $18xy$   51. $\underline{4}$   53. $\underline{a}$
55. $\underline{2}$   57. $\overline{DI}, \overline{GI}, \overline{FI}, \overline{JI},$
$\overline{OI}, \overline{TI}, \overline{NI}, \overline{SI}, \overline{MI}, \overline{RI}, \overline{HI}$
59. $E$

### Lesson 9-4, pages 390–393

1. $6x^2 + 24x$   3. $12k^5 + 12k^7 + 36k^3$
5. $-4p^3 + 8p^2 - 20p$   7. $-3a^2b^2 - 4a^6b$
9. $21a^2 - 18a$   11. $d = 5(56 - m)$
13. $6m^2 + 3mn$   15. $6a^2 + 8a$   17. $24p^3 - 88p^2$
19. $15x^2 + 10x^3$   21. $-33n^{10} - 132n^8$
23. $27c^2 + 9c^3 + 54c^4$   25. $7x^3 + 14x^2 + 7x$
27. $-28r^4 + 8r^2 - 40r$   29. $-24x^3y^3 + 12xy^4$
31. $12k^7 - 3k^6 + k^5$   33. $3.51c^7 + 1.17c^6 - 4.42c^5$
35. $-96t^3 - 40t^4 + 8t^9$   37. $24m^3 + 12m^2n + 4mn^2$
39. $5h^2 + 4$   41. $10x - 15$   43. $5w^2 - 20$
45. $26x^2y + 6xy^2$   47. $16(8.50 + d) = 136 + 16d$ dollars
49. $w(2w - 40) = (2w^2 - 40w)$ m$^2$   51. \$14

---

53. $48x^3 - 20x^2$   55.

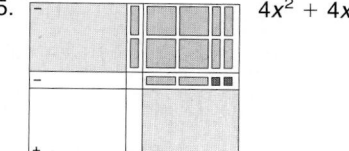

$4x^2 + 4x$

57.

$3xy + 3x$

59. $2.5x^5 - 23x^4 - 11.5x^3$   61. $-5x^6y^6 - 10x^9y^4 + 5x^3y^6 - 15x^4y^3$   63. $12(16 + n) = (192 + 12n)$ in.$^2$
65. $13.5x$ mi   67. 192   69. $\frac{1}{3}$   71. 9   73. 36   75. 18

### Review and Practice Your Skills, pages 394–395

1. $4b$   3. $\frac{7}{4}$   5. $12x^2 - 9x + 6$   7. $12x^5yz^2$   9. $-7a + 4$   11. $9xy$   13. $\frac{-e^2 + 6e + 4}{e}$   15. $w^2$   17. $4q$

19. $18a^2 + 6ab$   21. $-28b^2 + 35bd^2$   23. $7v^5 + 4v^4$
25. $3xy^3 - 9x^2y + 3xy$   27. $10m^3 + 2m^2n - 8mn^2$
29. $\frac{2}{3}d^4 + \frac{1}{10}d^3 + \frac{3}{2}d^2$   31. $10b + 35$   33. $13r^2s - 4rs^2$   35. $-12x^4 + 24x^3 - 96x^2 + 84x$   37. $63n + 36$
39. $21b^2 - 18b$   41. $18x^2 + 54x$   43. $12y^3 + 2y^2$
45. $2a^2b$   47. $15a^3b + 3a^2b^2$   49. $27x^3y^9$   51. $-5b^2 + 6b$   53. $3h - 7$

### Lesson 9-5, pages 396–399

1. $x^2 + 7x + 10$   3. $p^2 - 36$   5. $y^2 + 23y + 132$
7. $p^2 + 11p - 42$   9. $7y^2 + 35y + 36$
11. $(x + 3)(1 - 2x) = -2x^2 - 5x + 3$   13. $a^2 + 5a + 6$
15. $p^2 - 2p - 3$   17. $h^2 + 4h - 21$   19. $x^2 - 8x + 15$
21. $c^2 - 25$   23. $k^2 - 18k + 81$   25. $-x^2 + 36$   27. $t^2 + 19t + 84$   29. $w^2 - 17w + 72$   31. $10p^2 + 38p - 60$
33. $x^2 + 16x - 80$   35. $16k^2 + 32k + 16$   37. $49y^2 - 7y - 12$   39. $30x^2 + 61x + 30$   41. Yes, she is correct.
43. $x^3 - 2x^2 - 3x$   45. $25n^3 - 42n^2 - 102n$   47. $(5 - v)^2 = 25 - 10v + v^2$   49. 12 in. by 18 in.   51. $5k^2 + 3k - 2$
53. $x^3 + 3x^2 + 3x + 1$   55. \$1123.60
57. $\left(\frac{3}{2}, 5\right)$   59. $(33, -42)$

### Lesson 9-6, pages 400–401

1. 13   3. \$12.60   5. 1545 mi$^2$   7. 7:00 A.M.
9. Allegheny   11. 13.5 ft   13. $x, 5$   15. $c^2, 3c, 6$
17. $4w^2y, 5wk^2, 1$   19. $7x$   21. 180   23. $-336x^3z^2$
25. $-4xz$

### Review and Practice Your Skills, pages 402–403

1. $x^2 + 8x + 15$   3. $m^2 - 4m - 21$   5. $n^2 + 5n + 6$
7. $8x^2 - 9x - 14$   9. $20x^2 - 22x + 6$   11. $9x^2 + 18x + 9$
13. $25y^2 - 120y + 144$   15. $30a^3 - 38a^2 + 12a$
17. $11x^2 - 47x + 1$   19. $n^3 - 3n^2 - 10n$   21. $b^4 + 7b^3 - 30b^2$   23. $4y^2 + 32y - 596$   25. 150   27. 333

29. $b, a$  31. $3c^2, 9c, 1$  33. $4xy^2, 3xy, 1$  35. $125a^6b^3$
37. $\dfrac{9x^2 - 1}{y}$  39. $30m^2 - 18m$  41. $y^2 - 16y + 64$
43. $3c^2 - 22c - 16$  45. $4x^2 + 2x + \dfrac{1}{4}$

## Lesson 9-7, pages 404–407

1. $7(w - 3)$  3. $3a(3a - 2)$  5. $9ab(5a - 3b)$
7. $A = P(1 + r)$  9. $P = 2(l + w)$  11. $3(4k + 5)$
13. $7e(e + 3)$  15. $x(x - y)$  17. $5y^3(y - 4)$  19. $100(c - 2)$
21. $7x(y - 8z)$  23. $5(n^3 - 6m^2 - 3)$  25. $x(y + z + 2)$
27. $2xy(a - 2b + 3c)$  29. $8(h^2 - 2h + 3)$
31. $5ab(3a^2 + 4a - 2)$  33. $m^2n^2(6mn + 3m + 1)$
35. 90  37. Exercise 35  39. $D = \dfrac{1}{2}n(n - 3)$
41. $\dfrac{1}{2}(Z - N)$

43. 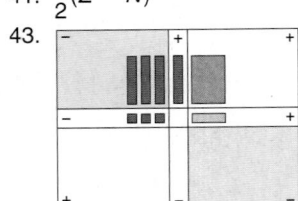  $y(x - 3)$  45. $9m^2n(2mn + 5n^2 + 3m^2 - 6n)$
47. $4ab(12 - 10a^2b + 6ab^2 + 7ab)$  49. $16n + 6$; $2(8n + 3)$  51. $16c^2d + 10cd^2$; $2cd(8c + 5d)$  53. no
55. no  57. no  59. $x^2 - 25$
61. $p^2 - 16$  63. $y^2 - 121$
65. $(v + 3)(v - 3)$  67. $(m + 6)(m - 6)$  69. $(2x + 5)(2x - 5)$  71. 2  73. $-1$  75. 1  77. $x + (x + 2) + (x + 4) = -54$; $-20, -18, -16$

## Lesson 9-8, pages 408–411

1. no  3. yes  5. $(m + 9)^2$  7. not factorable
9. not factorable  11. $x^2 - 8x + 16 = (x - 4)^2$  13. yes
15. no  17. no  19. $(k - 9)^2$  21. $(x + 8)(x - 8)$
23. $(h + 15)(h - 15)$  25. $(y + 1)(y - 1)$  27. $(e - 3)^2$
29. $(p + 16)(p - 16)$  31. no  33. $(h + 12)^2$
35. $(p + 12)(p - 12)$  37. no  39. $(c - 4)^2$  41. no
43. $(b + 13)^2$  45. no, $(x + 3)^2$  47. $3(m + 3)(m - 3)$
49. $2(m + 8)^2$  51. $3a(k + 10)(k - 10)$
53. 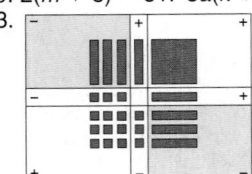  $(y - 3)^2$
55. Sumi is correct. It is a perfect square trinomial.
57. $\dfrac{(x - 6)5 + 30}{x}$
59. $(2n + 5)(2n - 5)$
61. $(3m + 5)^2$  63. $(5x - 4)^2$
65. 7.5 mi  67. $\approx 6.2$ mi
69. $36\dfrac{2}{3}$ yd$^2$  71. $-99n^3 + 27n^2$  73. $12x^3y - 16xy^2$
75. $27a - 39b$

## Chapter 9 Review, pages 412–414

1. g  3. f  5. a  7. e  9. d  11. $x^4 + 2x^2 - 6$
13. $5x^7 - 10x^6 + 3wx^2 + 6w^3x$  15. $4k^2 + 3k$
17. $-6m^3n$  19. $-6a^3b^7c$  21. $-20x^4y^3$  23. $\dfrac{3y^2}{4}$
25. $p^3 + 4p^2q + 5p$  27. $5y^3 + 4xy^2 - x^2z$  29. $3x^2y$
31. $2x^2 + 4$  33. $3w^2 - 108$  35. $-2d^2 + 19d$
37. $-6c^3 - 19c^2 - 8$  39. $160 - 0.02x$  41. $2t^2 - 6t + 4$
43. $e^2 + 10e + 21$  45. $4y + 108$  47. 16  49. 7:40 A.M.
51. $4(3x - 4)$  53. $3m^2n(8 - m + 5m^2n^2)$  55. $5x(x^2y^2 + 2xy + 5)$  57. 42  59. 72  61. $-50$  63. $(k + 6)^2$
65. $(x - 8)(x + 8)$  67. $(m - 5)^2$

# Chapter 10: Three-Dimensional Geometry

## Lesson 10-1, pages 422–425

1. Right rectangular prism; any face can be considered a base  3. Answers will vary.  5. 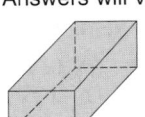  7.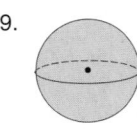

9. right square pyramid; square $DFGH$  11. right hexagonal prism; hexagons $ABCDEF$ and $GHIJKL$
13. Answers will vary.
15. 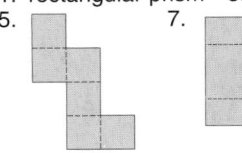  19.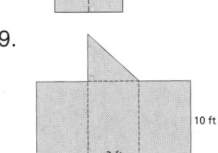

21. Prisms and pyramids are both polyhedrons and are both named by the shape of their base. However, prisms have two parallel bases and pyramids have one base. The lateral faces of a prism are parallelograms and the faces of a pyramid are triangles.  23. cube or rectangular prism; 6 faces, 8 vertices, and 12 edges  25. right cone; no faces, vertices or edges  27. right square pyramid; 5 faces, 5 vertices, and 8 edges  29. cylinder
31. cone with cut-off tip  33. True. A cube is a closed three-dimensional figure made up of square faces.
35. False. The faces must be polygonal.  37. Yes. Every face is a polygon.  39. Yes. Every face is a polygon.
41. 6, 8, 12; 2  43. 6, 6, 10; 2  45. The number of edges in a polyhedron is two less than the sum of faces and
vertices.  47. $-\dfrac{1}{2}$  49. $\dfrac{5}{3}$  51. vertical line;
undefined  53. 0; horizontal line  55. 80°  57. 100°
59. 100°

## Lesson 10-2, pages 426–429

1. rectangular prism  3. square pyramid
5. 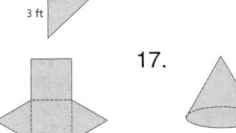  7.

9. 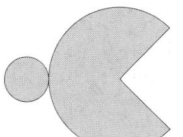  111.4 ft$^2$  11. rectangular prism
13. hexagonal prism

15.  17.

19. 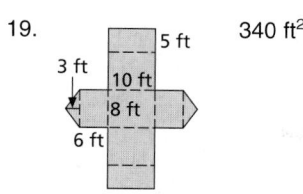 340 ft²

21. 164.9 ft²  23. Nets help you visualize the three-dimensional object in two dimensions. Nets also help you account for every part of a three-dimensional figure, especially figures with curved surfaces. Nets can transform some curved surfaces into flat surfaces.  25. 84 m²
27. 113 ft²  29. Answers will vary.  31. 61  33. 13
35. 8  37. 57  39. 350  41. $24r^5g^2$  43. $10c^4d^5$
45. $-18s^4t^5q$

## Review and Practice Your Skills, pages 430–431

1. d  3. b  5. f  7. square pyramid; 5, 5, 8
9. pentagonal pyramid; 6, 6, 10  11. cone
13.  15.  17. 156 cm²

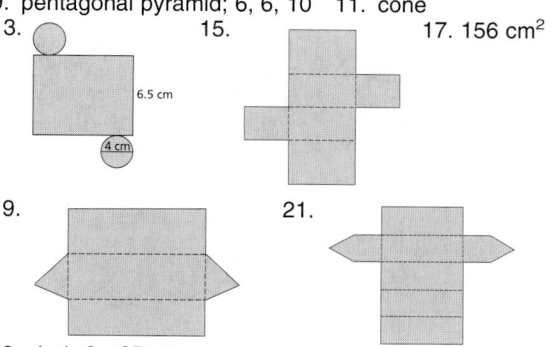

19.  21.

23. 4, 4, 6  25. a

## Lesson 10-3, pages 432–435

1. 572 ft²  3. 1752.12 ft²  5. 1631.25 ft²  7. 10.88 cm²
9. 71.22 m²  11. 3.19 m²  13. 406.19 m²  15. 251.2 m²
17. 279 in.²  19. Wrapping a gift requires more paper than just the surface area of the box.  21. 282.6 cm²;
678.24 cm²;1808.64 cm²; 5425.92 cm²  23. 112 m²
25. 336 m²  27. 115 cm²  29. $y = 3x + 1$  31. $y = 2x + 3$
33. $r^2 - r - 12$  35. $b^2 - 8b + 16$  37. $v^2 - 4v - 32$
39. $6k^2 + 10k - 4$

## Lesson 10-4, pages 436–439

1.  3.  5. Answers will vary.

7.  9.  11.

13.  15.  17.

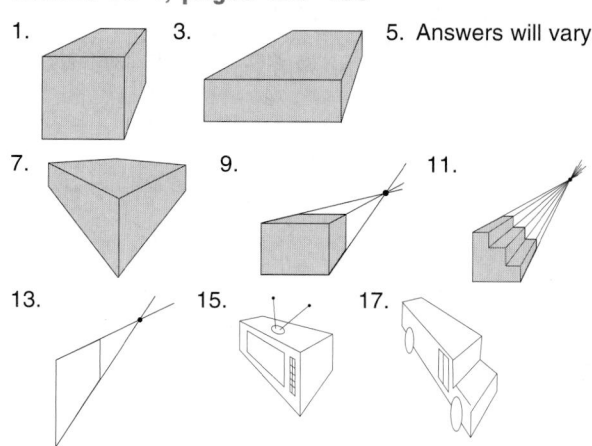

19. 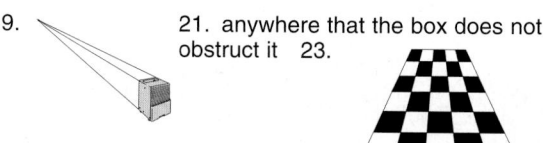  21. anywhere that the box does not obstruct it  23.

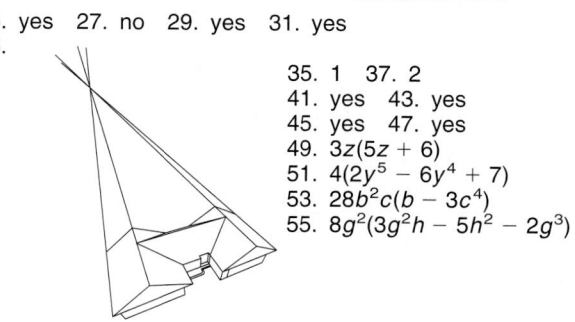

25. yes  27. no  29. yes  31. yes
33.

35. 1  37. 2
41. yes  43. yes
45. yes  47. yes
49. $3z(5z + 6)$
51. $4(2y^5 - 6y^4 + 7)$
53. $28b^2c(b - 3c^4)$
55. $8g^2(3g^2h - 5h^2 - 2g^3)$

## Review and Practice Your Skills, pages 440–441

1. 192 m²  3. 175.84 mm²  5. 72 m²  7. 360 cm²
9.  11.  13.  15.

17.  19.  21.

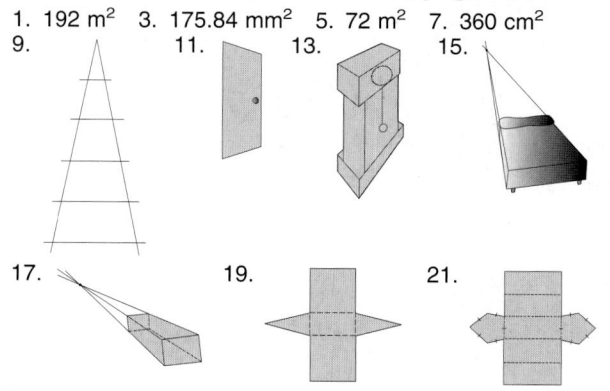

23. 7

## Lesson 10-5, pages 442–445

1.  3.  5.

7. 9; 2  9. 32 yd²
11.  13.  15.

17.  27.  29.

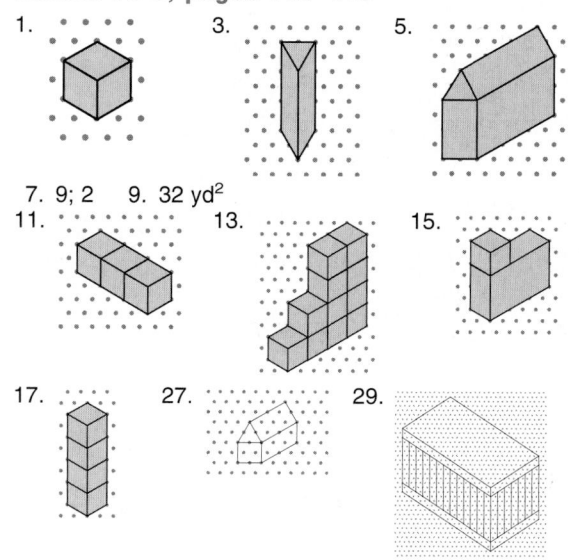

19. 34  21. 8; 24  23. 6; 22  25. 5; 22  31. 60
33. 72  35. (3, −1)  37. (−3, 5)  39. (2, 3)  41. HH,
HT, TH, TT  43. 11, 12, 13, 14, 15, 21, 22, 23, 24, 25, 31,
32, 33, 34, 35, 41, 42, 43, 44, 45, 51, 52, 53, 54, 55, 61,
62, 63, 64, 65

## Lesson 10-6, pages 446–449

**1.**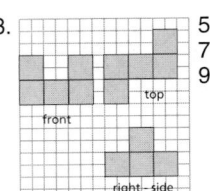

**3.**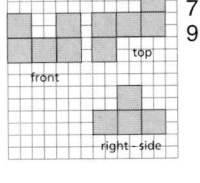

**5.** right-side
**7.** front
**9.**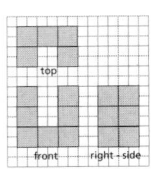

**11.**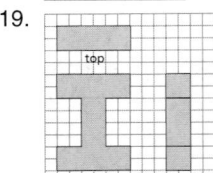

**13.**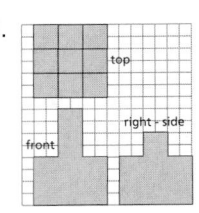

**15.**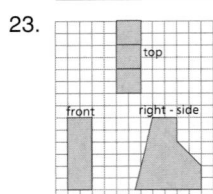

**17.** Answers will vary.

**19.**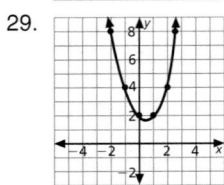

**21.**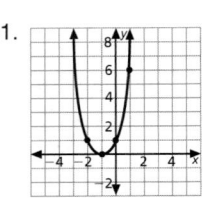

**23.**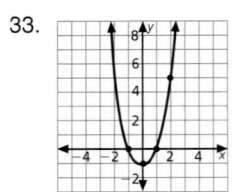

**25.** Answers will vary.
**27.** 1280 in.$^2$

**29.**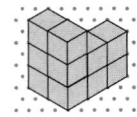

**31.**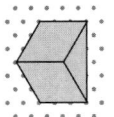

**33.**

**35.**

**37.** $\dfrac{6x}{3}$
**39.** $12n + 2$
**41.** $x - 9$

## Review and Practice Your Skills, pages 450–451

**1.** 12   **3.** 313.6 in.$^2$   **5.** 

**7.** 

**9.**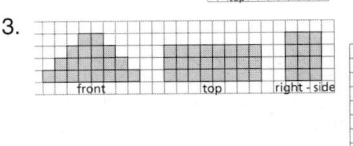

**11.**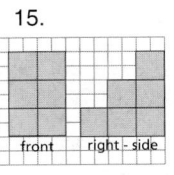

**13.**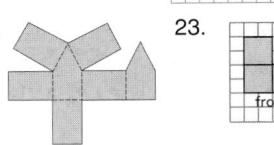

**15.**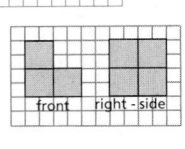

**17.** 5   **19.** 1   **21.** 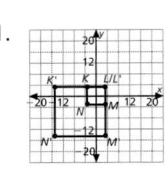   **23.**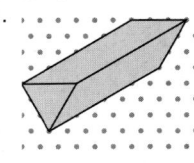

## Lesson 10-7, pages 452–455

**1.** 552 m$^3$   **3.** 1078 m$^3$   **5.** 6 in.   **7.** 4.5 cm
**9.** 658.8 m$^3$   **11.** 29,791 cm$^3$   **13.** 1122 ft$^3$   **15.** 480 m$^3$
**17.** Answers will vary.   **19.** 5625 cm$^3$   **21.** $288
**23.** 99,944 m$^3$   **25.** 1976 cm$^3$   **27.** 330 in.$^3$   **29.** 469 in.$^3$
**31.** $8z^2 + 2zw$   **33.** $15r^2s - 20rs^2$   **35.** $43p^2 - 34pr$
**37.** $16y^2z - 4yz^2$
**39.** 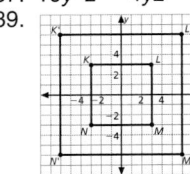   **41.**

## Lesson 10-8, pages 456–459

**1.** 3151 m$^3$   **3.** 816 cm$^3$   **5.** 5 cm   **7.** 117,750 lb
**9.** 7235 m$^3$   **11.** 1417 m$^3$   **13.** 1884 ft$^3$   **15.** 2 in.
**17.** 359.0 cm$^3$   **19.** 489.8 cm$^3$   **21.** approximate volume
of Earth $\approx$ 1,086,230,341,000 $\approx$ 1.086 $\cdot$ 10$^{12}$ early
astronomers' estimate $\approx$ 588,678,827 $\approx$ 5.887 $\cdot$ 10$^8$
The early astronomers were not even close.   **23.** 15 cm
**25.** 41.6 cm$^3$   **27.** 332.9 cm$^3$   **29.** a and b
**31.**

| radii | volume |
|-------|--------|
| 2 m | 33.49 m$^3$ |
| 4 m | 267.95 m$^3$ |
| 8 m | 2143.57 m$^3$ |
| 16 m | 17,148.59 m$^3$ |

When the radius is increased by a factor of 2, the
volume is increased by a factor of 8.
**33.** 21   **35.** 112   **37.** 6   **39.** 18   **41.** 3   **43.** 35°   **45.** 270°

## Review and Practice Your Skills, pages 460–461

**1.** 90 m$^3$   **3.** 390 m$^3$   **5.** 208 m$^3$   **7.** 216 cm$^3$   **9.** 540 cm$^3$
**11.** 2512 m$^3$   **13.** 4924 in.$^3$   **15.** 707 m$^3$   **17.** 16 mm
**19.** 17 ft$^2$
**21.**

**23.** 1205.8 in.$^2$; 2411.5 in.$^3$
**25.** 456 m$^2$; 408 m$^3$
**27.** 74.4 ft$^2$; 37.4 ft$^3$
**29.** square pyramid; 5, 5, 8
**31.** triangular prism; 5, 6, 9

33.

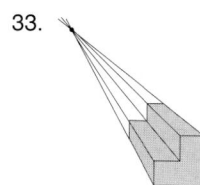

## Lesson 10-9, pages 462–463

1. 168.0 ft   3. 98.9 in.²   5. 7 lb   7. 907.5 ft³   9. Answers
will vary.   11. 7*b*   13. 3*g*²   15. $\frac{7}{2}$   17. 20   19. 151,200
21. 19,958,400   23. 720   25. 990

## Chapter 10 Review, pages 464–466

1. g   3. h   5. k   7. j   9. d   11. right triangular prism
13. rectangles *ACFD*, *BCFE*, and *ABED*   15. 9 edges
17.

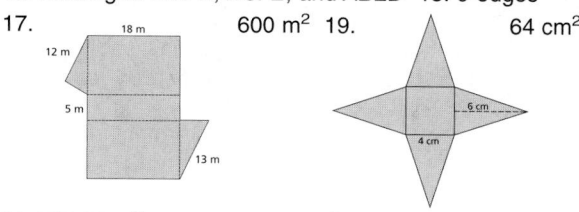

600 m²   19.   64 cm²

21. 703.38 m²   23. ≈ 270.43 cm²
25.

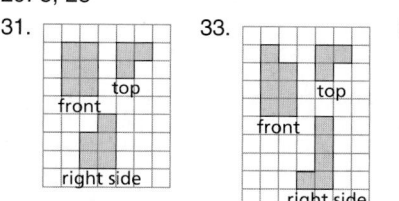

27.

29. 8; 28
31.    33.    35.

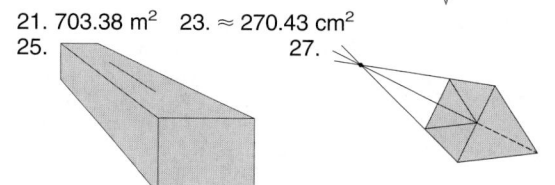

37. 1725 cm³   39. the rectangular pan   41. 203.1 cm³
43. 392.5 in.³   45. 2 gal   47. ≈ 91,394,008 ft³

# Chapter 11: Right Triangle Trigonometry

## Lesson 11-1, pages 474–477

1. yes   3. no   5. 7 in.   7. Answers will vary.   9. yes
11. yes   13. 24 m   15. 30°   17. 132°   19. 28 in.
21. *AB* : *DE*, *BC* : *EF*, *CA* : *FD*   23. Matt; △*ABC* ~ △*DBE*
25. always   27. sometimes   29. 675 cm²   31. 64
33. 42   35. SSS

## Lesson 11-2, pages 478–481

1. 35 ft   3. 250 ft   5. 70.8 ft   7. 30 ft   9. 30 ft   11. 60 m
13. ≈ 6.7 m   15. 4.5 ft   17. 139.5 ft   19. 8 : 7; Yes. This
ratio will not exist if the sun is directly over either or both
objects or if the sun is not shining.   21. ≈ 17.3 m

23. (−4, 6)   25. (−3, −7)   27. $\frac{1}{2}$

## Review and Practice Your Skills, pages 482–483

1. yes   3. no   5. 4   7. 70°   9. 15°   11. 8 cm   13. 25 m

## Lesson 11-3, pages 484–487

1. 9.4 m   3. 4.9 m   5. 37 ft   7. 14.4 ft   9. 11.7 m
11. 26 ft   13. 22.4 cm   15. 41 ft   17. 52 ft   19. 127 ft
21. 4.2 in.   23. 12 ft   25. 6.3 ft   27. 17 in.   29. 555 ft
31. (4, 1)   33. (−1, 4)   35. (−3, 2)   37. (2, −4)
39. dashed, below   41. dashed, above   43. solid, below
45. solid, above

## Lesson 11-4, pages 488–491

1. $\frac{3}{5}$   3. $\frac{3}{5}$   5. $\frac{4}{3}$   7. $\frac{3}{5}$   9. $\frac{3}{5}$   11. 0.7431   13. $\frac{5}{13}$
15. $\frac{5}{13}$   17. $\frac{12}{5}$   19. 0.6157   21. 11.4301
23. 0.9877   25. 0.8387   27. ≈ 0.5396   29. $\overline{FG}$   31. $\frac{4}{5}$
33. sin ≈ 0.2678, cos ≈ 0.9635, tan ≈ 0.2780
35. tan ≈ 0.1409, cos ≈ 0.9902   37. increases
39. increases   41. false   43. true   45. 18*r*³ + 24*r*
47. 45*p*³ − 53*p*   49. 24*g*²*h*² − 12*g*³*h* + 20*g*²*h*³
51. 56   53. 3   55. 15   57. −2

## Review and Practice Your Skills, pages 492–493

1. 36.3   3. 10.2   5. 13.9   7. 7.1 in.   9. $\frac{8}{15}$   11. $\frac{15}{17}$
13. $\frac{15}{8}$   15. $\frac{3}{5}$   17. 0.8660   19. 0.5   21. 0.9877
23. 0.7071   25. The sine of an acute angle is equal to the
cosine of its complement.   27. $\frac{4}{5}$   29. no   31. yes   33. 9

## Lesson 11-5, pages 494–497

1. 14.3   3. 31.9   5. 28.8 m   7. ≈ 36.8 cm   9. 52.3
11. 13.6   13. 132.5 ft   15. 4.9 m, 7.7 m   17. 6.8 m
19. 443.2 in.²   21. 4.4 mi   23. 12 ft   25. 11 cm²
27. Triangles will vary. The tangents are 1.25.   29. 1 line
31. none   33. 4   35. −8   37. 81   39. 81

## Lesson 11-6, pages 498–501

1. 20°   3. 21°   5. 25°   7. 84°   9. ≈ 5°   11. ≈ 53°
13. 42°   15. 77°   17. 33°   19. 22°   21. 30°   23. 69°
25. ≈ 18°   27. safe, ≈ 79°   29. safe, ≈ 77°   31. 45°
33. ≈ 26°   35. 27°, 63°   37. 44°   39. 37.7 cm²
41. 256.4 m²   43. 6*f*²(2*f*² + *f* + 3)

## Review and Practice Your Skills, pages 502–503

1. 8.16, sine   3. 22.03, sine   5. 2.12   7. 7.37   9. 5.87
11. 77°   13. 10°   15. 30°   17. 54°   19. 24°   21. 35°
23. 9.8   25. 16.6   27. $\frac{24}{25}$   29. ≈ 1545 ft

## Lesson 11-7, pages 504–507

1. 10   3. 17.0   5. 727.5 ft   7. 10√3 m, 20 m   9. 16
11. 19   13. $\frac{3\sqrt{2}}{2}$   15. $\frac{14\sqrt{3}}{3}$   17. 17,321 ft   19. 4.1 m
21. 30 m   23. Answers will vary. One possible explanation
follows: The octagon is composed of four rectangles, four
triangles and one square. Let *x* represent the length of
each side of the octagon. This *x* also represents the length
of the hypotenuse of each 45°-45°-90° right triangle, the

length of each side of the square, and the length of the two longer sides of the rectangles. The length of each leg of the triangles, which is also the length of the shorter sides of the rectangles is $\frac{x\sqrt{2}}{2}$. Now we have all the dimensions of the figure and can compute the area of the regions.

$$\underset{\substack{\text{area of the}\\\text{triangles}}}{} + \underset{\substack{\text{area of}\\\text{rectangles}}}{} + \underset{\substack{\text{area of}\\\text{square}}}{}$$

$$4 \cdot \frac{1}{2}\left(\frac{x\sqrt{2}}{2}\right)\left(\frac{x\sqrt{2}}{2}\right) + 4 \cdot (x)\left(\frac{x\sqrt{2}}{2}\right) + x \cdot x$$

$$= x^2 + 2\sqrt{2}x^2 + x^2$$
$$= 2x^2 + 2x^2\sqrt{2} = x^2(2 + 2\sqrt{2}) \approx 4.83x^2$$

25. 106.1 ft

27.

| | sine | cosine | tangent |
|------|------|--------|---------|
| 30° | $\frac{1}{2}$ | $\frac{\sqrt{3}}{2}$ | $\frac{\sqrt{3}}{3}$ |
| 45° | $\frac{\sqrt{2}}{2}$ | $\frac{\sqrt{2}}{2}$ | 1 |
| 60° | $\frac{\sqrt{3}}{2}$ | $\frac{1}{2}$ | $\sqrt{3}$ |

29. $\frac{\sqrt{3}}{2}x^2$

31. $\sqrt{3}\,x^2$

33. 169.6 cm³ 35. 463.0 mm³ 37.

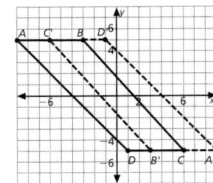

## Lesson 11-8, pages 508–509

1. 10.4  3. no; $BC \approx 17.9$ and $AB \approx 22.1$
5. 15.2  7. yes  9. 3.4 km, 4.0 km  11. $(d - 6)^2$
13. $(p - 6)(p + 6)$  15. 1080°

## Chapter 11 Review, pages 510–512

1. b  3. k  5. i  7. h  9. l  11. similar  13. 224 ft
15. 15 m  17. 35.7 ft  19. 14.3 cm  21. $\frac{8}{17}$  23. $\frac{15}{17}$
25. $\frac{8}{15}$  27. 0.6018  29. 20.0  31. 22.0  33. ≈ 19.3 ft
35. ≈ 75.5°  37. 45.6°  39. ≈ 22.2°  41. $7\sqrt{2}$  43. $9\sqrt{3}$
45. 6.5 in., $6.5\sqrt{2}$ or about 9.2 in.  47. 27.1  49. 13.9

# Chapter 12: Logic and Sets

## Lesson 12-1, pages 520–523

1. Roster notation: $L = \{0, 1, 2, 3, 4, 5, 6\}$; Set-builder notation: $L = \{x \mid x$ is a whole number less than 7$\}$ finite set
3. Roster notation: $P = \{1, 2, 3, 4, 5, \ldots, 21\}$; Set-builder notation: $P = \{x \mid x$ is a positive integer less than 22$\}$ finite set  5. $3 \in \{3, 6, 9, 12, \ldots\}$  7. $P$, $Q$, and $R$ are equivalent. $Q$ and $R$ are equal and equivalent.
9. Roster: $U = \{0, 1, 2, 3, \ldots, 14\}$; Set-builder: $U = \{x \mid x$ is a whole number less than 15$\}$; finite set  11. Roster: $M = \{ \}$ Set-builder: $M = \{x \mid x$ is a month having 32 days$\}$ finite set  13. Roster: $K = \{-3, -2, -1, 0, 1, \ldots\}$
Set-builder: $K = \{x \mid x$ is an integer greater than $-4\}$ infinite set  15. $4 \in \{4, 6, 8, 10\}$  17. $\varnothing \subseteq B$  19. equal
21. Answers will vary but set must have four elements.
23. $\varnothing$, {cello}, {harp}, {flute}, {cello, harp}, {cello, flute}, {harp, flute}, {cello, harp, flute}  25. true  27. true
29. true  31. False; equivalent sets may not be equal.

33. Marcellus has put brackets around the 5. He should delete the brackets.  35. $\varnothing$, {1}  37. $\varnothing$, {$m$}, {$a$}, {$t$}, {$m$, $a$}, {$m$, $t$}, {$a$, $t$}, {$m$, $a$, $t$}  39. 2  41. 8  43. 32; 64; 1  45. Answers will vary.  47. 180  49. 5.1
51. 10  53. 8.5

## Lesson 12-2, pages 524–527

1. {6, 8, 9}  3. {4, 6, 8, 9}  5. {1, 2, 4, 6, 9}  7. $\varnothing$  9. {1, 2, 3, 4, 5, 6, 7}  11. {4, 5}  13. $\varnothing$  15. Answers will vary.
17. {−1, 0, 4, 8}  19. {−3, −2, 0, 2, 8}  21. {8}  23. {−2, −1, 0, 2, 4, 8}  25. {chain saw, tractor}  27. $\varnothing$
29. {tractor, table saw, edger, backhoe, chain saw, hedge trimmer, forklift}  31. $\varnothing$  33. $\varnothing$  35. {1, 2, 3, 5, 7, 8, 9}
37. {1, 3, 5, 7, 9}  39. $\varnothing$  41. {eggs, chocolate, vanilla}
43. {milk, water, oil, sugar, flour, vanilla, eggs, chocolate}
45. $\varnothing$  47. {6, 7, 8, 9, 10, 11, 12, 13, 14, 15, 16, 17, 18, 19, 20}  49. {1, 2, 3, 4, 5, 6, 7, 8, 9, 10, 11, 12, 13, 14, 15, 16, 17, 18, 19, 20}  51. {1, 2, 3, 4, 5}  53. {1, 2, 3, 4, 5, 7, 11, 13, 17, 19}  55. $A \cup B = \{x \mid x$ is a real number$\}$
57. $(A')' = A$  59. {flute, guitar, piccolo, violin, tuba, keyboard}  61. {flute, guitar, tuba, violin, tamborine}
63. true  65. false; $R \cup S = U$  67. yes  69. yes
71. no  73. yes  75. $x = 25°$, $y = 65°$

## Review and Practice Your Skills, pages 528–529

1. $M = \{$April, June, September, November$\}$ $M = \{x \mid x$ is a month having 30 days$\}$; finite  3. $S = \{-9, -8, -7, \ldots\}$ $S = \{x \mid x$ is an integer greater than $-10\}$ infinite  5. $P = \{1, 2, 3, \ldots, 15, 16, 17\}$; $P = \{x \mid x$ is a positive integer less than 18$\}$ finite  7. $C \subseteq E$  9. $M = \{ \}$  11. $\varnothing$, {$e$}, {$f$}, {$g$}, {$e$, $f$}, {$e$, $g$}, {$f$, $g$}, {$e$, $f$, $g$}  13. {0, 1, 3, 5}  15. {−5, −3, −1, 1, 3, 5}  17. {1}  19. {0, 1, 3, 5}  21. {2, 4, 5, 6, 7, 8, 10, 12}  23. $\varnothing$  25. {3, 5, 6, 7, 9, 12, 15}  27. {0, 2, 3, 4, 6, 8, 9}  29. $D \subseteq E$  31. {a, e, i, o, u, y}  33. {a, e, i, o, u, y, m, n, p, s, t}

## Lesson 12-3, pages 530–531

1. If the product of two numbers is positive, then the two numbers are negative. (Converse); Statement: true; Converse: false; Example: $3 \cdot 4 = 12$  3. If a triangle is isosceles, then it has two congruent sides. (Converse); Statement: true; Converse: true  5. If an object is thrown into the air, then it will fall back down to the ground.
7. If $b = 6$, then $3b + 7 = 25$. (Converse); Statement: true; Converse: true  9. If a figure is a square, then it is a rectangle.  11. If you intend to climb the wall, then you will need a ladder.  13. A conditional statement has a hypothesis and a conclusion. The converse of the original statement interchanges the conclusion and the hypothesis. If a statement is true, the converse is not necessarily true.
15. a human  17. 2002  19. (4, 3)

## Lesson 12-4, pages 532–535

1. The trumpet is not a brass instrument. It is not the case that the trumpet is a brass instrument.  3. Cars do not all have 4 wheels. It is not the case that all cars have four wheels.  5. Converse:  If a plant has leaves, then it is a tree. false; Counterexample: geranium; Inverse:  If a plant is not a tree, then it does not have leaves.  false; Counterexample: fern Contrapositive: If a plant does not have leaves, then it is not a tree. false; Counterexample: pine tree  7. Converse:  If you play a stringed instrument, then you play the violin. false;

Counterexample: viola Inverse: If you do not play the violin, then you do not play a stringed instrument. false; Counterexample: cello Contrapositive: If you do not play a stringed instrument, then you do not play a violin. true  9. History is not Jasmine's favorite subject. It is not the case that history is Jasmine's favorite subject.  11. The factory does not recycle unused paper. It is not the case that the factory recycles unused paper.  13. Converse: If the object has wings, then it is an airplane. false; Counterexample: bird; Inverse: If the object is not an airplane, then it does not have wings. false; Counterexample: wasp Contrapositive: If an object does not have wings then it is not an airplane. true  15. Converse: If two lines are not parallel to each other, then they intersect. false; Counterexample: skew lines Inverse: If two lines do not intersect, then they are parallel to each other. false; Counterexample: skew lines Contrapositive: If two lines are parallel to each other, then they do not intersect. true  17. Answers will vary.  19. hypothesis: You wear Swift shoes. conclusion: You run fast.
21. Inverse:  If you do not wear Swift shoes, then you do not run fast. This statement is not necessarily true, as you may wear another brand of shoes and run fast.
23. Answers will vary.  25. hypothesis: You play the french horn. conclusion: You play a brass instrument.
27. Inverse:  If you do not play the french horn, then you do not play a brass instrument. false; Counterexample: trombone  29. My car is a convertible.  31. The bananas are ripe.  33. Inverse:  If the bill is paid, then the phone service will not be turned off. Contrapositive: If the phone service is not turned off, then the bill is paid.  35. Inverse: If Akiko studies, then he will pass the test. Contrapositive: If Akiko will pass the test, then he will study.  37. inverse
39. inverse  41. Answers will vary.  43. SAS  45. {−18, −13, −8, −3, 2, 7, 12}  47. {−16, −13, −10, −7, −4, −1, 2}

### Review and Practice Your Skills, pages 536–537

1. If Mahala lives south of Canada, then he lives in Alabama; true; false; Counterexample: Kansas  3. If a triangle has 3 congruent sides, then it has 3 congruent angles.  true  5. If a quadrilateral is a square, then it is a rhombus.  7. If the music is composed by Mozart, then it is classical. 9. If Adam is to get an A for the semester, then he must get 95% on the final exam.  11. The house is not made of brick. 13. Soccer is not a popular sport in Brazil.  15. If you play the oboe, then you play a wind instrument.  17. You play a wind instrument.  19. If you do not play the oboe, then you do not play a wind instrument. false; Counterexample: saxophone  21. Answers will vary. example: $N = \{g, l, o, v, e\}$  23. If a figure is a parallelogram, then the sum of the measures of the interior angles is 360°.  25. true; true

### Lesson 12-5, pages 538–541

1. 1234321  3. 21  5. Ramon may apply for a driver's license.  7. inductive  9. 48  11. 0.001  13. Alita will join us for dinner.  15. Our appliances do not work.
17. inductive  19. Red sports cars are often stopped and given speeding tickets.  21. He could check police records. 23. Answers will vary.  25. no conclusion  27. No. Chloe could be a native of France and did not need to take the class to translate the passage.  29. ≈ 0.33  31. 0.14  33. $2y^4 − 2y^2 + 3y + 6$  35. $x^5 + x^4 + 2x^2 + 4x$

### Lesson 12-6, pages 542–545

1. valid; Law of Detachment  3. invalid  5. invalid  7. invalid  9. valid; Law of Detachment  11. valid: Law of the Contrapositive; sound  13. valid; Law of the Contrapositive; sound  15. invalid  17. invalid  For 19–22, the unstated key premise may be given in one of two ways depending on if the stated premise is taken to be the affirmation of $p$ or the denial of $q$.  19. If you feel tired, then you should eat Pep Crackles for breakfast. If you eat Pep Crackles for breakfast, then you won't feel tired.  21. If you don't like rich coffee flavor, then don't buy Golden Bean coffee. If you buy Golden Bean coffee, you like rich coffee flavor.  23. Answers will vary.  25. 552 ft²
27. $\frac{3}{5}$  29. $\frac{4}{5}$  31. $\frac{4}{5}$

### Review and Practice Your Skills, pages 546–547

1. 256  3. 750  5. Courtney is older than Al.
7. Sakima can babysit.  9. valid; Law of the Contrapositive  11. invalid  13. If angles are a linear pair, then they are supplementary. Converse: If angles are supplementary, then they are a linear pair. false
15. 15, 17  17. {f, o, t, b, a, l, s}

### Lesson 12-7, pages 548–551

1. $\angle a$ and $\angle b$ are supplementary angles.
$m\angle a + m\angle b = 180°$   $a + b = 180°$
3. $2n + 1 + 2m + 1 = 2n + 2m + 2$
$\qquad\qquad\qquad\quad = 2(n + m + 1)$
This sum is even since it is a multiple of 2.
5. $\angle A \cong \angle B$   given
$\quad \angle C$ is supplement of $\angle A$;
$\quad \angle D$ is supplement of $\angle B$   given
$\quad m\angle A + m\angle C = 180°$;
$\quad m\angle B + m\angle D = 180°$  definition of supplementary angles
$\quad m\angle A + m\angle C = m\angle B + m\angle D$
$\quad$ transitive property
$\quad m\angle C = m\angle D$   subtraction property
$\quad \angle C \cong \angle D$   definition of congruent angles
7. $m\angle 2 + 148° = 180° \rightarrow m\angle 2 = 32°$
$m\angle 1 = m\angle 2 = 32°$  9. $2n − 2m = 2(n − m)$, and $2(n − m)$ is a multiple of 2.  11. 1st trip across river: take goat across, leaving wolf and cabbage on 1st bank; 1st trip back: go back across river alone; 2nd trip across: take cabbage across, leaving wolf on 1st bank; 2nd trip back: leave cabbage on 2nd bank, but bring goat back to 1st bank; 3rd trip across: take wolf across, leaving goat on 1st bank; 3rd trip back: go back across river alone; 4th trip across: take goat across; Now all three have been transported across without leaving goat and wolf alone or goat and cabbage alone.  13.

15. 100°, 95°, 115°, 130°, 125°, 155°  17. Answers will vary.  19. Inductive. The conclusion is based on a pattern of examples.  21. yes; $\frac{a}{b} \div \frac{c}{d} = \frac{a}{b} \cdot \frac{d}{c} = \frac{ad}{bc}$, assuming $c \neq 0$, and $\frac{ad}{bc}$ has the form of a rational number.

23. Answers will vary, but possible answers are listed.

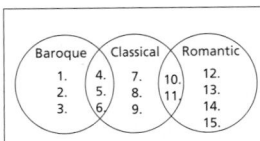

1. Henry Purcell
2. Monte Verdi
3. Johann Sebastian Bach
4. George Philipp Telemann
5. George Frideric Handel
6. Carl Philip Emmanuel Bach
7. Joseph Haydn
8. Wolfgang Amadeus
9. Christoph Willibald Gluck
10. Ludwig van Beethoven
11. Felix Mendelssohn
12. Peter Tchaikovsky
13. Johannes Brahms
14. Gustav Mahler
15. Richard Strauss

25. $x^2 + 4x + 3$    27. $x^2 + 6x + 9$    29. $x^2 - 25$
31. $6x^2 - 5x - 4$    33. $16x^2 + 16x + 4$    35. $9x^2 + 18x + 9$    37. 264 ft$^3$

## Chapter 12 Review, pages 552–554

1. c    3. b    5. k    7. j    9. l    11. $A = \{0, 1, 2, 3, 4\}$;
$A = \{x|x$ is a whole number less than 5\}; finite
13. $C = \{-7, -6, -5, ...\}$; $C = \{x|x$ is a whole number $>$
$-8\}$; infinite    15. $R = \{-99, -98, -97, ..., -1\}$;
$R = \{x|x$ is a negative integer $> -100\}$; infinite
17. $5 \in \{5, 10, 15, 20, 25, ...\}$    19. $\{5, 6, 7, 8, 9, 10, 11, 12\}$
21. $\{3\}$    23. $\{6, 9, 12\}$    25. $\{1, 2, 3, 4, 5, 7, 9, 10\}$    27. $\{9\}$
29. If a figure is a rectangle, then it is a quadrilateral.
31. The statement is true. The converse is false. A
counterexample would be any concave quadrilateral.
33. If people are using umbrellas, then it is raining.    35. If a
figure is a rhombus, then it has perpendicular diagonals.
37. The statement is true. The converse is false. A kite
has perpendicular diagonals and is not a rhombus.    39. If
you're not studying Russian, then you are not studying a
foreign language.    41. If you like broccoli then you like
vegetables.    43. If you don't like broccoli, then you don't
like vegetables.    45. Jacquine lives in Illinois.    47. valid;
Law of Contrapositive    49. invalid    51. Since the sum of
the interior angles of a triangle equal 180°, $a° + b° + c° =$
180°. Since the triangle is an equiangular triangle it is also
equilateral. Therefore, $a° = b° = c°$. By subsitituion, $3a° =$
60°. Therefore, $a° = b° = c° = 60°$.

# Photo Credits

**Cover** (tl)MTPA Stock/Masterfile, (tr)Jim Cummings/ Getty Images, (bl)Stewart Cohen/Getty Images, (br)Mark Adams/Getty Images; **Endsheet** File photo; **iv** File photo; **vii** Aaron Haupt; **viii** CORBIS; **ix** Getty Images; **x** Mark Ransom; **xi** Getty Images; **xii** CORBIS; **xiii through xviii** Getty Images; **1** Mark Ransom; **2** Aaron Haupt; **3** (tl)Aaron Haupt, (tr)Mark Burnett, (c)Getty Images, (b)CORBIS; **6 7** Getty Images; **8** (t)Mark Ransom, (b)Getty Images; **9 12 15** Getty Images; **16** File photo; **18 20** Getty Images; **22** CORBIS; **31** Getty Images; **36** CORBIS; **37** File photo; **48** Getty Images; **49** (t)Getty Images, (b)CORBIS; **55** Getty Images; **56** Aaron Haupt; **59** MAK-1; **61** Getty Images; **63** Laura Sifferlin; **65 66 69** Getty Images; **73** Geoff Butler; **77 78** Getty Images; **81** Cessna Aircraft Co.; **85 through 101** Getty Images; **104** Ryan J. Hulvat; **111 113** Getty Images; **115** Masterfile; **125 127 129** Getty Images; **131** Doug Martin; **135 138** Getty Images; **146** (t)Getty Images, (b)Doug Martin; **147 through 157** Getty Images; **161** Mark Ransom; **164** Getty Images; **169** Light Source; **170** CORBIS; **172** Mark Ransom; **174** Stephen Webster; **177 through 189** Getty Images; **192** Ryan J. Hulvat; **194 197** Getty Images; **205** CORBIS; **209 215** Getty Images; **225** Skip Comer; **240 245** Getty Images; **247** Laura Sifferlin; **257** Getty Images; **268** Mark Ransom; **270** Getty Images; **273** CORBIS; **275 276** Getty Images; **277** CORBIS; **278** Courtesy of Tiara Observatory; **279 through 312** Getty Images; **317** Mark Steinmetz; **318 through 331** Getty Images; **334** Images 100; **340 343 345** Getty Images; **347** CORBIS; **351 356** Getty Images; **361** Tim Fuller; **362** Getty Images; **363** Mark Steinmetz; **365 372 379** Getty Images; **380** Ryan J. Hulvat; **385 389** Getty Images; **390** Ryan J. Hulvat; **392** Getty Images; **396** Mark Ransom; **406 411 418** Getty Images; **419** Library of Congress; **427** Getty Images; **429** Dynamic Graphics, Inc.; **431** CORBIS; **432** Matt Meadows; **433 through 453** Getty Images; **454** Elaine Shay; **456 457 459 462** Getty Images; **463** Tom Stack; **470** (l)Skip Comer, (r)Getty Images; **471** Getty Images; **477** CORBIS; **478 through 500** Getty Images; **501** CORBIS; **503** Getty Images; **504** File photo; **506** CORBIS; **508 516 517 520** Getty Images; **523** Aaron Haupt; **525 through 561** Getty Images; **562** (t)Getty Images (c)Aaron Haupt, (b)Geoff Butler; **563** (tr, tl, b)Getty Images, (tc)Jone Mason; **564** Getty Images; **565** (l)Tim Courlas, (r)Getty Images **566 567 568** Getty Images; **569** (t)Mullinix/KS Studio, (b)Getty Images; **570** (t)Tim Fuller (b)Getty Images; **571** (t)Getty Images, (b)Geoff Butler; **572** Getty Images; **573** (t)Masterfile, (b)Getty Images; **574 575** Getty Images; **2A** Aaron Haupt; **48A** CORBIS; **100A** Getty Images; **146A** Mark Ransom; **188A** Getty Images; **240A** CORBIS; **292A** Getty Images; **330A** Getty Images; **372A** Getty Images; **418A** Getty Images; **470A** Getty Images; **516A** Getty Images.

# Index

## ■ A ■

Absolute values, 51, 54
Acute angles, 196
Acute triangles, 188, 206
Addition
  of decimals, 51
  of fractions, 50
  of integers, 51
  of opposites, changing subtraction to, 67
  of polynomials, 376–379
  solving systems of equations by, 348–351
  subtraction as opposite operation for, 109
  of variable expressions, 66–69
  word phrases for, 62
Addition property
  of equality, 108
  of inequality, 132
Adjacent angles, 197
Algeblocks, 57–59, 64, 67–69, 72, 74, 108, 111, 114, 118, 376, 379, 381, 382, 388, 390, 391, 393, 396, 405, 406, 407, 408, 411
Algebra, 48–145, 240–291, 372–417
  absolute values, 49, 54
  addition property of equality, 108
  addition property of inequality, 132
  binomials, 396–399
  coefficients, 376
  difference of squares, 409
  direct variations, 276–359
  division property of inequality, 133
  equations, 104–125, 136–139, 241, 254–257, 331, 338–353, 355–357, 471
  expressions, 56–57, 62–69, 72–79, 240
  factoring, 404–407, 409–411
  foundations of, 48–99
  functions, 242–285, 498
  greatest integer function, 267
  inequalities, 126–135, 258, 331, 362–365
  inverse variations, 282–285
  like terms, 66, 373, 377–378
  linear equations, 254–257, 265
  linear inequalities, 258–261
  model, 114–115
  monomials, 376–383, 386–393

  multiplication property of equality, 108
  multiplication property of inequality, 133
  order of operations, 56–59, 76
  patterns and functions, 274–275
  perfect square trinomials, 408–411
  polynomials, 374–411
  properties of exponents, 82–86, 380–381, 386
  proportions, 101, 122–125
  quadratic equations, 268–271
  radical equations, 471
  solutions, 104–113, 116–126, 258, 338–353, 355–357, 508–509
  systems of equations, 338–353, 355–357
  systems of inequalities, 362–365
  terms, 66, 376
  variables, 54
Algebraic models, 114
Alternate exterior angles, 202
Alternate interior angles, 202
Angle measures of regular polygons, 223
Angles, 592
  acute, 196
  adjacent, 197
  alternate exterior, 202
  alternate interior, 202
  base, 207
  bisectors of, 197
  central, 227
  complementary, 196
  congruent, 197, 206
  consecutive, 216
  corresponding, 202
  defined, 196
  degrees of, 196
  drawing, 295
  exterior, 202, 207
    of triangles, 207
  included, 213
  inscribed, 228
  interior, 202
  measuring, 295
  obtuse, 196
  opposite, 216
  perpendicular lines and, 196–199
  of polygons, 222–225
  right, 196
  in right triangles, finding measures of, 498–501

  of rotations, 306
  same-side interior, 202
  straight, 196
  sum of, in triangles, 191
  supplementary, 196
    of triangles, 206
  vertical, 197
Angle-Side-Angle Postulate (ASA), 213
Angle sums of polygons, 223
Applications, Real World
  Advertising, 35, 93, 480, 534, 545
  Agriculture, 270, 278
  Archaeology, 496
  Architecture, 294, 299, 303, 309, 312, 318, 428, 437, 439, 443, 476, 505
  Art, 122, 195, 215, 229, 301, 309, 313, 321, 445, 477
  Astronomy, 89, 457, 501
  Biology, 82, 525, 540
  Business, 34, 40, 41, 124, 126, 130, 135, 242, 260, 261, 267, 275, 285, 358, 509
  Business Travel, 251
  Chemistry, 267, 459
  Civil Engineering, 218
  Communication, 89
  Communications, 132
  Community Service, 247
  Computers, 85
  Construction, 194, 204, 217, 345, 351, 357, 462, 496
  Consumer Topics
    banking, 115, 125
    cost, 77, 78, 89, 115, 119, 132, 245, 257, 267, 274, 275, 284, 346, 351, 352, 363, 364, 388, 391, 392
    discounts, 93, 125, 219
    home ownership, 463
    income, 58, 63, 93, 115, 124, 135, 273, 278, 341, 351, 379, 392, 406
    inflation, 275
    interest, 111, 125, 365, 399
    investments, 78, 92, 93, 111, 115, 125, 365, 393, 399, 406
    rent, 65, 391
    retail, 8, 17, 26, 41, 78, 125, 159, 219, 257, 346, 364, 388, 427, 534, 544, 545
    savings, 115, 125

stocks, 78, 393

taxes, 260

vehicle ownership, 41, 119, 275, 385

Cooking, 173, 526

Data File, 9, 12, 13, 19, 23, 25, 31, 32, 41, 65, 69, 79, 89, 107, 125, 129, 153, 161, 164, 171, 174, 181, 195, 215, 233, 247, 275, 303, 319, 347, 351, 357, 365, 379, 435, 459, 487, 497, 507, 531, 534, 545

Detective Work, 69

Earth Science, 455, 481

Economics, 23, 275, 341

Education, 11, 12, 16, 28, 30

Engineering, 75, 139, 214, 284, 447, 495, 513

Entertainment, 7, 18, 37, 41, 59, 115, 174, 181, 232, 318, 359, 363, 506

Fashion, 78

Finance, 78, 84, 92, 93, 120, 278, 365, 393, 399, 406

Fitness, 17, 58, 59, 115, 134, 456, 486, 508

Food Service, 8, 36, 159, 228, 435, 523, 540

Games, 148, 161, 163, 164, 171, 175, 180

Gardening, 319

Geography, 129, 244, 374, 379, 382, 389, 393, 399, 401, 406, 411, 433, 509, 534

Government, 127, 170

Health, 134, 170, 181, 199, 478

History, 62, 420, 425, 428, 435, 438, 445, 449, 455, 459, 522

Hobbies, 65, 135, 224, 321, 455, 487, 524

Horticulture, 458, 543

Industry, 65, 233, 284, 311

Interior Design, 209, 389, 438, 449

Landscaping, 180, 303, 350, 388, 463, 550

Machinery, 123, 307, 424, 429, 455, 526

Manufacturing, 7, 124, 383

Market Research, 4, 19, 23, 36, 151, 227, 245, 261

Mechanics, 119, 139

Medicine, 21, 155, 171

Money, 40

Movies, 356

Music, 11, 36, 121, 153, 160, 174, 205, 282, 284, 298, 518, 522, 527, 535, 539, 544, 551

Nature, 224, 320, 478, 506

Navigation, 190, 194, 199, 205, 209, 219, 229, 233, 302, 491

Number Sense, 93, 164, 275, 348, 411, 531, 544

Number Theory, 161, 313, 550

Packaging, 111, 423, 435, 454, 463

Part–Time Job, 58, 63, 73, 74, 93, 115, 154, 278, 379, 392

Photography, 65, 78, 194, 299, 317, 318, 383, 399, 472, 477, 481, 487, 490, 497, 501, 506, 513

Physics, 88, 89, 107, 110, 114, 119, 125, 129, 136, 138, 198, 269, 270, 272, 276, 277, 278, 283, 285, 401, 406, 531

Political Science, 9, 25

Population, 50, 55, 59, 65, 69, 79, 85, 88, 153

Recreation, 8, 41, 214, 229, 264, 346, 398, 424, 444, 453, 480, 485, 496

Recycling, 55, 69, 365

Research, 439

Retail, 8, 17, 26, 41, 125, 130, 152, 159, 219, 257, 364, 388, 427, 544

Safety, 107, 135, 138, 180, 205, 224, 341, 449, 500, 550

Science, 257

Space Science, 64, 278

Sports, 19, 31, 55, 68, 77, 79, 119, 128, 155, 160, 171, 174, 180, 270, 297, 332, 337, 340, 347, 351, 356, 357, 362, 382, 392, 458, 475, 486, 506

Statistics, 152

Transportation, 89, 120, 344, 359, 360

Travel, 106, 129, 164, 174, 208, 284, 337, 360, 379, 391, 392, 401, 411, 491, 500, 501, 541, 549

Weather, 31, 36, 54, 74, 93, 153, 312, 533

Arcs, 227

Area formulas, 420

Area models, 151

Areas, 148

of parallelograms, 420

of rectangles, 420

of squares, 420

surface, *see* Surface areas

of triangles, 420

volumes and lengths and, 462–463

Arguments, 539

invalid, 543

sound, 543

unsound, 543

valid, 542

Arithmetic average, 10

Aryabhata, 495

ASA (Angle-Side-Angle Postulate), 213

Assessment xii, 2D, 48D, 100D, 146D, 188D, 240D, 292D, 330D, 372D, 418D, 470D, 516D

Alternative Assessment,

Math Journal, 34, 84, 197, 246, 264, 279, 356, 389, 401, 474, 509

Student Portfolio, 10, 59, 88, 153, 208, 426, 510

Quick Assessment, 5, 8, 12, 18, 22, 27, 30, 36, 40, 51, 54, 58, 64, 68, 74, 78, 84, 88, 93, 103, 106, 110, 115, 118, 124, 128, 134, 138, 149, 152, 155, 160, 164, 170, 174, 180, 191, 194, 198, 204, 208, 214, 218, 224, 228, 233, 243, 246, 250, 256, 260, 266, 270, 275, 278, 284, 295, 298, 302, 308, 312, 318, 321, 333, 336, 340, 346, 350, 356, 359, 364, 375, 378, 382, 388, 392, 398, 401, 406, 410, 421, 424, 428, 434, 438, 444, 448, 454, 458, 463, 473, 476, 480, 486, 490, 496, 500, 506, 509, 522, 526, 531, 534, 540, 544, 550

Chapter, 45, 97, 143, 185, 237, 289, 327, 369, 415, 467, 513, 555

Standardized Test Practice, 46–47, 98–99, 144–145, 186–187, 238–239, 290–291, 328–329, 370–371, 416–417, 468–469, 514–515, 556–557

Auditory Learning Style,

*see* Differentiated Instruction

Average

arithmetic, 10

using word, 35

Axis, 422

## ■ B ■

Bar graphs, 4, 36

Base angles, 207

Bases

of exponents, 82

of prisms, 422

of pyramids, 422

Bhaskara, 484

Biased surveys, 7, 376

Binomials

multiplication of, 396–399

Bisectors
  of angles, 197
  of segments, 193
Boundary of half-planes, 258
Box-and-whisker plot, 29–31
Boxplot, 29

## ■ C ■

Calculators, 10, 11, 16, 21, 58, 88, 92,
    129, 139, 155, 172, 173, 178, 226,
    268, 490, 491, 492, 494, 498, 499,
    500, 501, 507
Cantor, Georg, 521
Careers
  Aerial Photographer, 483
  Air Traffic Controller, 403
  Architect, 323
  Automobile Designer, 131
  Baseball Player, 157
  Camera Designer, 503
  Campus Facilities Manager, 305
  Cattle Rancher, 201
  Coach, 361
  Commercial Aircraft Designer, 81
  Concession Stand Operator, 61
  Exhibit Designer, 451
  Game Board Designer, 177
  Market Researcher, 33
  Mechanical Engineer, 113
  Music Store Owner, 253
  Product Tester, 15
  Professor of Music History, 547
  Restaurateur, 273
  Runner, 343
  Ship Captain, 221
  Symphony Orchestra Conductor,
    529
  Truck Driver, 385
  Urban Planner, 431
Carroll, Lewis, 555
Caveat emptor, 35
Cayley, Arthur, 39
Celsius temperature, 74
Centers
  of circles, 226
  of dilations, 316
  of rotations, 306
  of spheres, 422
Central angles of circles, 227
Central tendency, measures of, see
    Measures of central tendency
Challenge, see Extend the Lesson
Chapter Assessment, 45, 97, 143, 185,
    237, 289, 327, 367, 415, 467, 513,
    555

Chapter Investigation
    3, 9, 31, 37, 44, 49, 59, 75, 89, 96,
    101, 107, 119, 139, 142, 147, 161,
    171, 181, 184, 189, 195, 209, 229,
    236, 241, 247, 257, 261, 271, 279,
    285, 288, 293, 299, 313, 319, 326,
    331, 347, 351, 357, 368, 373, 383,
    393, 411, 414, 423, 439, 455, 466,
    471, 481, 497, 501, 512, 517, 523,
    527, 535, 551, 554
Chapter Review, 42–44, 94–96,
    140–142, 182–184, 234–236,
    286–288, 324–326, 366–368,
    412–414, 464–466, 510–512,
    552–554
Check Understanding, 7, 11, 29, 63,
    67, 104, 122, 133, 137, 151, 159,
    163, 169, 193, 207, 222, 245, 248,
    283, 300, 301, 306, 307, 310, 317,
    339, 345, 346, 348, 349, 377, 381,
    386, 397, 404, 409, 423, 427, 432,
    456, 475, 479, 485, 494, 505, 539,
    549
Chords, 226
Circle graphs, 4, 232–233
  defined, 232
Circles
  areas of, 148
  centers of, 226
  central angles of, 227
  circumferences of, 226
  properties of, 226–229
Circumferences of circles, 226
Classifying triangles, 190
Closed half-planes, 259
Clusters, 17
Cluster sampling, 6
Coefficient of correlation, 26–27
Coefficients, 376
Collinear points, 192
Combinations, 178–181
Combining like terms, 66, 373
Compass, magnetic, 191
Complementary angles, 196
Complements
  of events, 165
  of sets, 147, 524
Complete turns, 306
Compound events
  defined, 162
  probabilities of, 162–165
Computer Aided Drafting (CAD)
    program, 327
Concave polygons, 222
Conclusion, 530, 539
Conditional statements, 530–531
  defined, 530

Cones, 422
  slant heights of, 433
  surface areas of, 433
  volumes of, 456–459
Congruent angles, 197, 206
Congruent line segments, 193
Congruent sides, 206
Congruent triangles, 212–215
Connecting to Prior Knowledge,
    see Extend the Lesson
Consecutive angles, 216
Consecutive sides, 216
Constant
  of proportionality, 276
  of variation, 276
Constants, 376
Consumer topics, see Applications
Content and Connections, 2C, 48C,
    100C, 146C, 188C, 240C, 292C,
    330C, 372C, 418C, 470C, 516C
Continuous graphs, 265
Contrapositive, 533
  converse and inverse and, 532–535
  Law of the, 542
Convenience sampling, 6
Converse, 530
  inverse and contrapositive and,
    532–535
Convex polygons, 222
Coordinate graphing,
    transformations and, 294–329
Coordinate planes, 242
  defined, 244
  dilations in, 316–319
  distances in, 244–247
  graphing on, 294
  reflections in, 300–303
  rotations in, 306–309
  translations in, 296–299
Coordinates of points, 52, 242
Coplanar lines, 202
Coplanar points, 192
Correlation, 21
  coefficient of, see Coefficient of
    correlation
  degree of, 26
  negative, 21
  positive, 21
Corresponding angles, 202
Corresponding elements, 39
Cosine ratios, 488–491
Counterexample, 530
Course Planning Guide, see Pacing
Cramer, Gabriel, 355
Cramer's rule, 355
Critical Thinking, 9, 13, 19, 31, 37, 41,
    55, 65, 69, 75, 79, 85, 89, 111, 129,

135, 139, 161, 165, 171, 175, 181,
195, 199, 209, 215, 219, 225, 229,
247, 251, 257, 271, 279, 285, 299,
303, 309, 313, 319, 321, 337, 341,
347, 351, 365, 379, 383, 389, 407,
411, 429, 435, 439, 449, 455, 459,
463, 477, 481, 487, 491, 497, 501,
523, 527, 535, 541, 545, 551
Cross–products, 122
Cubes, 423
   volumes of, 453
Cylinders, 422
   surface areas of, 433
   volumes of, 456–459

### ■ D ■

Daily Intervention, *see* Intervention
Data, 4
   display, *see* Display data
   misleading, 34
   presented, 34
   using matrices to organize, 38–41
Data Activity
   Area and Population of Ten
     Countries, 49
   Events in the History of
     Photography, 471
   Extreme Points in the U.S., 373
   Mathematicians throughout
     History, 419
   Nested Shapes, 147
   Participation in Leisure Activities, 3
   Planet Table, 101
   Range of Frequencies for Selected
     Instruments and Voices, 517
   Sales of Cars in the U.S.,
     1995–2004, 241
   United States, 189
   Winter Olympics Medal Standings,
     331
   World's Ten Highest Dams, 293
Data File, 9, 12, 13, 19, 23, 31, 32, 65,
   69, 79, 89, 107, 125, 129, 153, 161,
   164, 171, 174, 195, 215, 233, 247,
   275, 303, 319, 347, 351, 357, 365,
   379, 435, 459, 487, 497, 507, 531,
   534, 545
Da Vinci, 484
Decagons, 222
Decimals
   operations with, 51
   repeating, 52
   terminating, 52
Deductive reasoning
   defined, 539
   inductive reasoning and, 538–541

patterns of, 542–545
Degree of correlation, 26
Degrees of angles, 196
Density, population, 51, 75, 89, 97
Dependent events, 168–171
Descending order for polynomials,
   376
Description notation, 520
Detachment, Law of, 542
Determinants
   defined, 354
   matrices and, 354–357
Diagonals
   of parallelograms, 217
   of polygons, 222–225
Diameters, 226
Difference of squares
   defined, 409
   perfect squares and, 408–411
Differentiated Instruction, x, xi
   Auditory, 32, 77, 150
   Tactile/Kinesthetic, 20, 316, 396,
     408, 432
   Visual, 116, 136, 148, 191, 203, 204,
     212, 381, 384, 386, 411, 479,
     484, 498, 504, 505, 519, 548
Dilations, 316
   centers of, 316
   in coordinate planes, 316–319
Diophantus of Alexandria, 62
Directed graphs, 358–359
Direct square variation, 277
Direct variation, 276–279
Disjoint sets, 525
Display data, samples and, 2–47
Distance formula, 245
Distances in coordinate planes,
   244–247
Distributive property, 66, 72, 375, 390
Division
   exponents for, properties of, 83–84
   of fractions, 50
   of integers, 51
   by monomials, 386–389
   multiplication as opposite
     operation for, 109
   of polynomials by polynomials, 389
   of signed numbers, 73
   solving equations by using, 243
   of variable expressions, 72–75
   word phrases for, 62
Division property of inequality, 133
Domains of functions, 264
Drawing angles, 293
Drawings
   foundation, 447
   isometric, *see* Isometric drawings

orthogonal, *see* Orthogonal
   drawings
orthographic, 446
perspective, *see* Perspective
   drawings
scale, 122, 467

### ■ E ■

Edges
   lateral, 423
   of polyhedra, 422
   skew, 423
Elements
   of matrices, 38
   of sets, 53, 520
Ellipsis, 520
Empty set, 521
English as a Second
   Language/Limited English
   Proficiency (ESL/LEP),
   *see* Teaching Tip
Enlargements, 316
Entries of matrices, 38
Equality
   addition property of, 108
   multiplication property of, 108
Equal sets, 521
Equations
   defined, 104
   formulas and, 104–107
   graphing, 333
   inequalities and, 102–145
   linear, *see* Linear equations
   one-step, 108–111
   quadratic, 268
   radical, solving, 471
   solutions of, 104
   solving, *see* Solving equations
   with squares and square roots,
     136–139
   systems of, *see* Systems of
     equations
   with two or more operations,
     116–119
   two-step, 116
Equiangular triangles, 206
Equilateral triangles, 188, 206
Equivalent ratios, 473
Equivalent sets, 521
Error Alert, 75, 175, 224, 299, 382, 491,
   523
   Talk About It, 9
   You Make the Call, 13, 79, 111, 124,
     155, 165, 181, 215, 218, 246, 341,
     357, 399, 411, 424, 445, 477, 509,
     541

Index

Estimation, 5
Evaluating
expressions, 242
variable expressions, 57
Evaluation, *see* Assessment
Events, 158
complements of, 165
compound, *see* Compound events
dependent, *see* Dependent events
independent, *see* Independent events
mutually exclusive, 162
ExamView® Pro, 2D, 42, 48D, 94, 100D, 140, 146D, 182, 188D, 236, 240D, 286, 292D, 324, 330D, 366, 372D, 412, 418D, 464, 470D, 510, 516D, 552
Experimental probabilities, 150
Experiments
defined, 150
probabilities and, 150–153
Exponential form, 82
Exponents, 57, 82
bases of, 82
for division, properties of, 83–84
for multiplication, properties of, 83
negative, *see* Negative exponents
power of a product rule for, 83, 381
power of a quotient rule for, 83
power rule for, 83, 381
product rule for, 83, 380
properties of, 82–85
quotient rule for, 83, 386
using, 374
of zero, 86–89
zero property of, 86
Expressions
evaluating, 242
numerical, 56
simplifying, 56
variable, *see* Variable expressions
Extended Response, 47, 99, 145, 187, 239, 291, 329, 371, 417, 469, 515, 557
Extend the Lesson, 117, 167, 216, 300, 310, 311, 355, 376, 398, 480, 485, 488, 496, 546
Challenge, 5, 11, 57, 79, 138, 163, 169, 180, 181, 202, 219, 223, 301, 346, 350, 363, 409, 443, 476, 486, 501, 528, 541
Connecting to Prior Knowledge, 51, 106, 179, 209, 214, 226, 228, 245, 255, 258, 276, 297, 307, 336, 380, 382, 395, 434, 458, 520, 524, 545
Historical Note, 227

Interdisciplinary Connection, 35, 107
Real World Connection, 7, 21, 27, 29, 39, 192, 42, 132, 206, 244, 277, 284, 285, 306, 312, 436, 481, 508, 525
Exterior angles
of transversal systems, 202
of triangles, 207
Extremes of proportions, 122

■ **F** ■

5-step problem solving plan, 27, 93, 115, 155, 233, 275, 321, 359, 401, 463, 509, 531
45°-45°-90° right triangles, 504
Faces
lateral, 423
of polyhedra, 422
Factorial, 172–173
Factoring
defined, 404
using greatest common factor, 404–407
Fahrenheit temperature, 74
False equations, 104
False inequalities, 126
Fibonacci sequence, 93
Figures
geometric solid, 593
intersection of, 193
similar, 474
three-dimensional, surface areas of, 432–435
Finite sets, 520
First quartile, 28
Flexible Grouping, 58, 351, 435, 446
Flips, 300
FOIL acronym, 397
Formulas
defined, 105
equations and, 104–107
Foundation drawings, 447
Fractions
addition of, 50
division of, 50
multiplication of, 48
reducing, 148
subtraction of, 50
Frequency, relative, 150
Frequency charts, 145
Frequency tables, 16, 195
Function notation, 264
Function rules, 274
Functions, 264
domains of, 264

graphing, 242–291
inverse trigonometric, 498
linear, *see* Linear functions
nonlinear, *see* Nonlinear functions
patterns and, 274–275
quadratic, *see* Quadratic functions
range of, 264
Function table, 264
Fundamental counting principle, 159

■ **G** ■

Gaps, 17
Garfield, James, 484
GCF, *see* Greatest common factor
Geometry, 190–237, 294–369, 420–513
angles, 196–221, 223–225, 227–232, 293, 306, 498–501
Angle-Side-Angle Postulate, 213
arcs, 227
area, 146, 418
bases, 422
bisectors, 193, 197
centers, 226, 306, 316, 422
chords, 226
circles, 226–229
complementary angles, 196
concave, 222
cones, 422, 433–434, 456–458
congruent triangles, 212–215
convex, 222
cubes, 423, 453
cylinders, 422, 433–435, 456–459
decagons, 222
degrees, 196
diagonals, 217, 222–225
diameters, 226
dilations, 316–319
edges, 422–423
faces, 422–423
foundation drawings, 447–448
half planes, 258–259
heptagons, 222
hexagons, 222
hypotenuse, 484
images, 296
indirect measurement, 478–481
isometric drawings, 442–445
legs, 484
lines, 192, 202–205, 249, 300, 310, 334–337
logic and, 190–237
midpoints, 193, 245, 293
nets, 426–429
*n*–gons, 222
nonagons, 222
octagons, 222

orthogonal drawings, 446–449
parallel lines, 202–205, 334–337
parallelograms, 216–219
pentagons, 222
perimeters, 418
perpendicular lines, 197–198, 334–337
perspective drawings, 436–439
planes, 192, 202
points, 52, 192, 240, 436
polygons, 222–225, 418, 474–477
polyhedra, 422
preimages, 296
prisms, 422–432, 452–455
pyramids, 422–429, 453–455
Pythagorean theorem, 484–487
quadrilaterals, 216–219, 222
radii, 226
rays, 196
rectangles, 146, 189, 216
reflections, 300–303
rhombus, 189, 216
right triangles, 188, 206, 478–509
rotations, 306–309
scale drawings, 122
segments, 193
Side-Angle-Side Postulate, 213
sides, 206, 222, 494–497
Side-Side-Side Postulate, 213
similar figures, 474–477
skew lines, 202, 423
slant heights, 433
space, 192
spheres, 422, 457–459
squares, 101, 146, 189, 216, 418
supplementary angles, 196
surface area, 427–429, 432–435
symmetry, 310–313
tessellations, 320–321
three-dimensional, 420–467
transformations, 294–309, 316–319
translations, 296–299
transversals, 202–205
trapezoids, 216
triangles, 146, 188–189, 206–215, 222, 470, 478–509
trigonometry, 488–509
vanishing points, 436
vertex, 196, 206, 222, 422
volume, 419, 452–459, 462–463
Graphically solving systems of equations, 338–341
Graphing
coordinate, *see* Coordinate graphing
on coordinate planes, 294
equations, 333

functions, 242–291
inequalities, 331
on number lines, 126–129
linear equations, 254–257, 687
linear inequalities, 258–261
quadratic functions, 268–271
Graphs, 243
bar, 4, 36
circle, *see* Circle graphs
continuous, 265
directed, *see* Directed graphs
of inequalities, 258
line, 5, 34–35
misleading, *see* Misleading graphs
of numbers, 52
pictographs, 4, 36
reading, 4
Greatest common factor (GCF), 146, 374
factoring using, 404–407
Greatest integer function, 267
Grid In, 47, 99, 145, 187, 239, 291, 329, 371, 417, 469, 515, 557
Grid paper, 86, 282, 292, 295, 296, 300, 426, 449, 455, 507
Group work, 3, 38, 49, 52, 101, 147, 178, 189, 241, 293, 331, 373, 419, 471, 517, 518

■ **H** ■

Half-planes
boundary of, 258
closed, 259
open, 258
Half turns, 306
Heptagons, 222
Hexagons, 222
Histograms, 75, 111, 251
defined, 16
stem-and-leaf plots and, 16–19
Historical Notes,
*see* Extend the Lesson
Horizontal lines, 249
Hypotenuse of right triangle, 484
Hypothesis, 530

■ **I** ■

*if-then* relationship symbol (*p*), 532
*if-then* statements, 530
Images, 296
Included angles, 213
Included sides, 213
Independent events, 168–171
Indirect measurements, 478–481

Inductive reasoning
deductive reasoning and, 538–541
Inequality(ies)
addition property of, 132
defined, 126
division property of, 133
equations and, 102–145
graphing, 333
on number lines, 126–129
graphs of, 258
linear, *see* Linear inequalities
multiplication property of, 133
solutions of, 126, 258
solving, 132–135
systems of, 362–365
systems of equations and, 332–371
Infinite sets, 520
Inscribed angles, 228
Instructional Strategies, vii-ix
Integers, 51, 52
Interdisciplinary Connection, *see* Extend the Lesson
Interior angles, 202
Internet, 59, 243, 327, viii, ix, xi, 2D, 48D, 100D, 146D, 188D, 240D, 292D, 330D, 372D, 418D, 470D, 516D
Interquartile range, 28
Intersection
of figures, 193
of sets, 147, 524–527
Intersection symbol (∩), 525
Intervention, xi
Quick Assessment, *see* Assessment
Interviews, 6–9
Invalid arguments, 543
Inverse
contrapositive and converse and, 532–535
Inverse cosine, 498
Inverse sine, 498
Inverses of matrices, 356
Inverse tangent, 498
Inverse trigonometric functions, 498
Inverse variation, 282–285
Inverse square variation, 283
Irrational numbers, 52
Is an element of symbol (∈), 147
Is a subset of symbol (⊆), 147
Is not an element of symbol (∉), 147
Is not a subset of symbol (⊄), 147
Is not equal to symbol (≠), 52
Isometric drawings, 442–445
Isosceles triangles, 188, 206

## ■ L ■

Lateral edges, 423
Lateral faces, 423
Law of Detachment, 542
Law of the Contrapositive, 542
Learning Styles, *see* Differentiated
    Instruction
Legs of right triangles, 484
Lengths
    areas and volumes and, 462–463
    of sides in right triangles, finding,
      494–497
Lesson Objectives, 2A, 48A, 100A,
    146A, 188A, 240A, 292A, 330A,
    372A, 418A, 470A, 516A
Less than or equal to symbol ($\leq$), 126
Less than symbol ($<$), 126
Like terms, 66, 375
    combining, 66
    defined, 377
Linear equations
    defined, 254
    graphing, 254–257
    writing, 254–257
Linear functions
    defined, 265
    nonlinear functions and, 264–267
Linear inequalities
    defined, 258
    graphing, 258–261
    writing, 258–261
Linear regression, 21
Line graphs, 5, 34–35
Lines, 192
    of best fit, 21
    defined, 21
    scatter plots and, 20–23
    coplanar, 202
    horizontal, 249
    number, *see* Number lines
    parallel, *see* Parallel lines
    perpendicular, *see* Perpendicular
      lines
    of reflections, 300
    skew, 202
    slopes of, *see* Slopes of lines
    of symmetry, 310
    vertical, 249
Line segments, 193
    congruent, 193
Line symmetry
    defined, 310
    rotational symmetry and, 310–313
Logic
    geometry and, 190–239
    sets and, 518–557

Logical reasoning, 518–519
    proof and, 548–551
Looking for patterns, 92

## ■ M ■

Major arcs, 227, 688
Manipulatives
    Algeblocks, 57–59, 64, 67–69, 72, 74,
      108, 111, 114, 118, 376, 379,
      381, 382, 388, 390, 391, 393,
      396, 405, 406, 407, 408, 411,
      415
    Cardboard patterns, 467
    Cards, 45, 158, 163, 164, 168, 170,
      261
    Coins, 150, 158, 172
    Compass, 222, 226, 232, 295
    Compass, magnetic, 191
    Cubes, 442, 446
    Dried beans, 452
    Expression cards, 104
    Grid paper, 86, 282, 292, 295, 296,
      300, 426, 449, 455, 507
    Isometric grid paper, 443
    Marbles, 168–170, 538
    Miras, 585
    Mirror, 310
    Modeling, 58, 59, 64, 68, 69, 74,
      111, 114, 118, 119, 139, 195,
      321, 359, 379, 381, 382, 388,
      392, 393, 398, 399, 405, 406,
      407, 410, 411, 497, 550
    Number cards, 104
    Number cubes, 154, 158, 160, 161,
      162–165, 229
    Paper folding, 199, 426
    Patty paper, 321
    Protractor, 206, 216, 222, 232, 293,
      504
    Ruler, 226, 296, 300, 504
    Scissors, 296, 310, 422, 426
    Sheets of heavy paper, 452
    Spinners, 160, 164, 229
Map, 237, 244, 289, 344, 375
Mapping, 264
Market, 4
Math Journal, *see* Alternative
    Assessment
Math: Who, Where, When, 35, 39,
    355, 437, 484, 495, 521
Mathematical models, 114
MathWorks, 15, 33, 61, 81, 113, 131,
    157, 177, 201, 221, 253, 273, 305,
    323, 343, 361, 385, 403, 431, 451,
    483, 503, 529, 547

Matrices
    capital letters naming, 38
    columns in, 38, 354
    defined, 38, 354
    determinants and, 354–357
    elements of, 38
    entries of, 38
    inverses of, 356
    rows in, 38, 354
    square, 39, 354
    using, to organize data, 38–41
Mean, 10, 13
Means of proportions, 122
Measurements, indirect, *see* Indirect
    measurements
Measures of angles in right triangles,
    finding, 498–501
Measures of central tendency
    defined, 10
    range and, 10–13
Measuring
    angles, 293
    triangles, 470
Median, 10, 28
Members of sets, 53, 520
Mental Mathematics, 105, 106, 107
Mental Math Tip, 87
Mid Chapter Quiz, 25, 71, 121, 167, 211,
    263, 315, 353, 395, 441, 493, 537
Midpoint formula, 245, 295
Midpoints of segments, 193
Minor arcs, 227
Mirror method, 479
Misleading data, 34
Misleading graphs, statistics and,
    34–37
Mixed Review Exercises, 9, 13, 19, 23,
    27, 31, 37, 41, 55, 59, 65, 69, 75,
    79, 85, 89, 93, 107, 111, 115, 119,
    125, 129, 135, 139, 153, 155, 161,
    165, 171, 175, 181, 195, 199, 205,
    209, 215, 219, 225, 229, 233, 247,
    251, 257, 261, 267, 271, 275, 279,
    285, 299, 303, 309, 313, 319, 321,
    337, 341, 347, 351, 357, 359, 365,
    379, 383, 389, 393, 399, 401, 407,
    411, 425, 429, 435, 439, 445, 449,
    455, 459, 463, 477, 481, 487, 491,
    497, 501, 507, 509, 523, 527, 531,
    535, 541, 545, 551
Mode, 10, 596
Model algebra, 114–115
Modeling, 58, 59, 64, 68, 69, 74, 111,
    114, 118, 119, 139, 195, 321, 359,
    379, 381, 382, 388, 392, 393, 398,
    399, 405, 406, 407, 410, 411, 497,
    550

Models
  area, 151
  mathematical, 114
*Modus ponens*, 542
*Modus tollens*, 542
Monomials, 376
  division by, 386–389
  multiplication of, 380–383
  multiplication of polynomials by,
    390–393
Multiple Choice, 46, 98, 144, 186, 238,
    290, 328, 370, 416, 468, 514, 556
Multiplication
  of binomials, 396–399
  exponents for, properties of, 83
  of fractions, 50
  of integers, 51
  of monomials, 380–383
  of polynomials by monomials,
    390–393
  solving equations by using, 243
  solving systems of equations by,
    348–351
  of variable expressions, 72–75
  word phrases for, 62
Multiplication property
  of equality, 108
  of inequality, 133
Mutually exclusive events, 162

## ■ N ■

Natural numbers, 52
NCTM Principles and Standards, 2A,
    48A, 100A, 146A, 188A, 240A, 292A,
    330A, 372A, 418A, 470A, 516A
Negation, 532
Negative correlation, 21
Negative exponents, 86–89
Negative reciprocals, 334
Nets
  defined, 426
  surface areas and, 426–429
*n* factorial, 172–173
*n*-gons, 222
Nonagons, 222
Noncollinear points, 192
Noncoplanar points, 192
Nonlinear functions
  defined, 265
  linear functions and, 264–267
Not symbol (~), 532
Null set, 521
Null set symbol (∅), 147
Number lines, 52
  graphing inequalities on, 126–129

Numbers
  absolute values of, 49, 54
  graphs of, 52
  irrational, 52
  natural, 52
  perfect, 93
  rational, 52
  real, *see* Real numbers
  signed, *see* Signed numbers
  squares of, *see* Squares of numbers
Numerical expressions, 56

## ■ O ■

Oblique cones, 422
Oblique cylinders, 422
Oblique rectangular prisms, 423
Oblique square pyramids, 423
Obtuse angles, 196
Obtuse triangles, 188, 206
Octagons, 222
One-point perspective, 436
One-step equations, 108–111
Open dots on number lines, 127
Open half-planes, 258
Open sentences, 104, 126
Operating costs, 243
Operations
  with decimals, 51
  equations with two or more,
    116–119
  with integers, 51
  order of, *see* Order of operations
Opposite angles, 216
Opposite rays, 196
Opposites, 49, 52
  addition of, changing subtraction
    to, 67
  of opposites, 54
  of sums, property of, 72
Opposite sides, 216
Ordered pairs, 21, 244
Order of operations, 56–59, 76
Order of rotational symmetry, 311
Origin, 244
Orthogonal drawings, 446–449
Orthographic drawings, 446
Outliers, 17, 19, 29

## ■ P ■

Pacing, xvi
Palindromes, 175, 313
Parabolas, 268
Parallel line postulates, 203

Parallel lines
  defined, 202
  perpendicular lines and, 334–337
  transversals and, 202–205
Parallelograms, 191, 216
  areas of, 148
  diagonals of, 217
  properties of, 216
  quadrilaterals and, 216–219
Parallelogram symbol (▱), 217
Parallel planes, 202
Patterns
  of deductive reasoning, 542–545
  finding, 92–93
  functions and, 274–275
  looking for, 92
  series and, 243
Pentagonal prisms, 422
Pentagons, 222
Percentiles
  defined, 30
  quartiles and, 28–31
Perfect numbers, 93
Perfect squares, 375, 408
  difference of squares and,
    408–411
Perfect square trinomials, 408
Perimeter formulas, 420
Perimeters, 420
Permutations
  defined, 172
  of sets, 172–175
Perpendicular lines
  angles and, 196–199
  defined, 197
  parallel lines and, 334–337
Perspective
  one–point, 436
  two–point, 436–437
Perspective drawings, 436–439, 467
Pictographs, 4, 36
Planes, 192
  coordinate, *see* Coordinate planes
  parallel, 202
Planning Guide, *see* Pacing
Point, line and plane postulates,
    193
Points, 192,
  collinear, 192
  coordinates of, 52, 240
  coplanar, 192
  noncollinear, 192
  noncoplanar, 192
  vanishing, 436
Point-slope form, 256
Polygons
  angles of, 222–225

angle sums of, 223
concave, 222
convex, 222
defined, 222
diagonals of, 222–225
names of, 222
perimeters of, 418
regular, 222
angle measures of, 223
similar, *see* Similar polygons
Polyhedra, 422
Polynomials, 374–417
addition of, 376–379
descending order for, 376
division of polynomials by, 389
multiplication of, by monomials, 390–393
relatively prime, 407
in standard form, 376
subtraction of, 376–379
Population, 6
Population density, 51, 75, 89, 97
Positive correlation, 21
Positive integers, 52
Postulates, 193
Power of a product rule for exponents, 83, 381
Power of a quotient rule for exponents, 83
Power rule for exponents, 83, 381
Predictable Error, 62, 83, 123, 491
Prediction, 22, 23, 26, 27, 32, 82, 334
Preimages, 296
Premises, 539
Prerequisite Skills, xi
Prisms, 422
volumes of, 452–455
Probability, 146–187
combinations, 178–181
complements of events, 165
of compound events, 162–165
dependent events, 169–171
events, 158, 162–163, 165, 168–169
experimental, 150–155
fundamental counting principle, 159
independent events, 168–171
mutually exclusive events, 162
permutations, 172–175
sample spaces, 158
theoretical, 158–171
tree diagrams, 158–159
Problem Solving Skills
circle graphs, 232–233
coefficient of correlation, 26–27
conditional statements, 530–531
directed graphs, 358–359

finding patterns, 92–93
lengths, areas and volumes, 462–463
model algebra, 114–115
patterns and functions, 274–275
reasonable solutions, 508–509
simulations, 154–155
tessellations, 320–321
work backwards, 400–401
Problem Solving Strategies
Act it out, 154
Eliminate possibilities, 508
Guess and check, 26, 530
Look for a pattern, 320
Make a table, chart or list, 92, 274
Use an equation or formula, 462
Use a picture, diagram or model, 114, 232, 358
Work backwards, 400
Problem Solving Tip, 123, 160, 163, 212, 249, 255, 266, 344, 356, 363, 376, 378, 391, 427, 453, 479, 489, 504, 525, 532
Product rule for exponents, 83, 380
Proof, logical reasoning and, 548–551
Property
of negative exponents, 86
of opposites of sums, 72
Proportionality, constant of, 276
Proportions, 103, 122–125
Pyramids, 422
regular square, 433
volumes of, 452–455
Pythagorean theorem, 484–487

### ■ Q ■

Quadrants, 240, 244
Quadratic equations, 268
Quadratic functions
defined, 268
graphing, 268–271
Quadrilaterals, 222
defined, 216
parallelograms and, 216–219
Quarter turns, 306
Quartiles
defined, 28
percentiles and, 28–31
Questionnaires, 6–9
Quick Review Math Handbook: Hot Words, Hot Topics, 2B, 48B, 100B, 146B, 188B, 240B, 292B, 330B, 372B, 418B, 470B, 516B
Quotient rule for exponents, 83, 386

### ■ R ■

Radical equations, solving, 473
Radicals, 136
Radicands, 136
Radius, 226
Random sampling, 6
Range
defined, 11
of function, 264
interquartile, 28
measures of central tendency and, 10–13
Ranking, *see* percentile
Rates, 103
unit, 103
Rational numbers, 52
Ratios, 102
equivalent, 472
trigonometric, 488
Rays, 196
opposite, 196
Readiness, 4–5, 50–51, 102–103, 148–149, 190–191, 242–243, 294–295, 332–333, 374–375, 420–421, 472–473, 518-519
Reading graphs, 2
Reading Math, 28, 38, 53, 57, 82, 126, 127, 179, 217, 226, 297, 390, 498, 520, 542
Real numbers, 52–55
Real World Connection, *see* Extend the Lesson
Reasonable solutions, 508–509
Reasoning
deductive, *see* Deductive reasoning
inductive, *see* Inductive reasoning
logical, *see* Logical reasoning
Resources for Teachers, xiii, 2B, 48B, 100B, 146B, 188B, 240B, 292B, 330B, 372B, 418B, 470B, 516B
Reciprocals, 332
negative, 334
Records of events, 6–9
Rectangles, 191, 216
areas of, 148, 420
perimeters of, 420
Rectangular prisms, 423
volumes of, 421, 453
Reducing fractions, 148
Reductions, 316
Reflections,
defined, 300
in coordinate planes, 300–303
lines of, 300
Reflection symmetry, 310
Regular polygons, 222

Regular square pyramids, 433
Relative frequency, 150
Relatively prime polynomials, 407
Repeating decimals, 52
Representing solids, 422–425
Review and Practice Your Skills,
    14–15, 24–25, 32–33, 60–61,
    70–71, 80–81, 90–91, 112–113,
    120–121, 130–131, 156–157,
    166–167, 176–177, 200–201,
    210–211, 220–221, 230–231,
    252–253, 262–263, 272–273,
    280–281, 304–305, 314–315,
    322–323, 342–343, 352–353,
    360–361, 384–385, 394–395,
    402–403, 430–431, 440–441,
    450–451, 460–461, 482, 492–493,
    502–503, 528, 536–537, 546
Rhombus, 191, 216, 695
Right angles, 196
Right cones, 422
Right cylinders, 422
Right rectangular prisms, 423
Right square pyramids, 423
Right triangles, 188, 206
    angles in, finding measures of,
        498–501
    finding lengths of sides in, 494–497
    legs of, 484
    special, 504–507
Right triangle trigonometry, 472–515
Rise on line, 248
Roster notation, 520
Roster notation symbol ({}), 147
Rotational symmetry
    defined, 311
    line symmetry and, 310–313
    order of, 311
Rotations
    angles of, 306
    centers of, 306
    in coordinate planes, 306–309
    defined, 306
Rows in matrices, 38, 354
Rules, 114
Rubrics, 47, 99, 145, 187, 291, 329,
    371, 417, 469, 515
Run on line, 248

■ S ■

Sales revenue, 243
Same-side interior angles, 202
Samples, 6
    display data and, 2–47
Sample spaces
    defined, 158

theoretical probability and,
        158–161
Sampling
    cluster, 6
    convenience, 6
    random, 6
    systematic, 6
Sampling methods, surveys and, 6–9
SAS (Side-Angle-Side Postulate), 213
Scale, 122
Scale drawings, 122
Scale factors, 316
Scalene triangles, 188, 206
Scatter plots, 79, 144
    defined, 20
    lines of best fit and, 20–23
Scientific notation, 87
Second quartile, 28
Sectors, 232
Segments
    bisectors of, 193
    midpoints of, 193
Semicircles, 227
Sentences, open, 104, 126
Sequences, 92
Series, patterns and, 241
Set-builder notation, 520
Sets, 53, 149
    combinations of, 178–181
    complements of, 149, 524
    defined, 520
    disjoint, 525
    elements of, 53, 520
    empty, 521
    equal, 521
    equivalent, 521
    finite, 520
    infinite, 520
    intersection of, 147, 524–527
    logic and, 518–557
    null, 521
    permutations of, 172–175
    properties of, 520–523
    union of, 147, 524–527
    universal, 524
Short Response, 47, 99, 145, 187, 239,
    291, 329, 371, 417, 469, 515, 557
Side–Angle–Side Postulate (SAS), 213
Sides
    congruent, 206
    of polygons, 222
    of right triangles, finding lengths
        of, 494–497
    of triangles, 206
Side-Side-Side Postulate (SSS), 213
Similar figures, 474
Similar polygons, 474–477

defined, 474
Simplifying
    expressions, 56
    variable expressions, 66, 76–79
Simulations, 154–155
Sine ratios, 488–491
Skew edges, 423
Skew lines, 202
Slant heights, 433
Slides, 296
Slope–intercept form, 254
Slopes of lines, 248–251, 332
SOH CAH TOA acronym, 489
Solid dots on number lines, 127
Solids
    representing, 422–425
    visualizing, 422–425
Solutions
    of equations, 104
    of inequalities, 126, 258
    reasonable, 508–509
    of systems of equations, 338
Solving
    equations, 105
    by using multiplication and
        division, 241
    inequalities, 132–135
    radical equations, 471
    systems of equations by addition,
        subtraction and
        multiplication, 348–351
    graphically, 338–341
    by substitution, 344–347
Sound arguments, 543
Space, 192
Special right triangles, 504–507
Spheres, 422
    centers of, 422
    volumes of, 456–459
Spreadsheets, 38, 40, 75, 248, 425,
    435, 459
Square matrices, 39, 354
Square pyramids, 423
Square roots, 103
    equations with, 136–139
Squares, 103, 191, 216
    areas of, 148, 420
    perimeters of, 420
Squares of numbers
    difference of, see Difference of
        squares
    equations with, 136–139
    perfect, 373, 408, 415
SSS (Side–Side–Side Postulate), 213
Standard form, 87
    polynomials in, 376
Standardized Test Practice, 46–47,

98–99, 144–145, 186–187, 238–239, 290–291, 328–329, 370–371, 416–417, 468–469, 514–515, 556–557

Extended Response, 47, 99, 145, 187, 239, 291, 329, 371, 417, 469, 515, 557

Grid In, 47, 99, 145, 187, 239, 291, 329, 371, 417, 469, 515, 557

Multiple Choice, 46, 98, 144, 186, 238, 290, 328, 370, 416, 468, 514, 556

Short Response, 47, 99, 145, 187, 239, 291, 329, 371, 417, 469, 515, 557

Statements, conditional, *see* Conditional statements

Statistics, 4–45
  bar graphs, 2, 36
  biased, 7–8
  box-and-whisker plots, 29–31
  circle graphs, 2, 232–233
  clusters, 17–18
  cluster samplings, 6–8
  convenience samplings, 6–8
  correlations, 21, 26–27
  data, 4, 34, 38–41
  frequency tables, 16–18, 195
  gaps, 17–18
  graphs, 2, 34–36, 232–233
  histograms, 16–17, 75, 111, 251
  interquartile range, 28–30
  interviews, 6–9
  linear regression, 21
  lines of best fit, 21–23
  matrices, 38–41
  means, 10–13, 35
  measures of central tendencies, 10–13, 35–37
  medians, 10–13, 35
  misleading, 34–37
  modes, 10–13, 35
  outliers, 17, 19, 29
  percentiles, 30–31
  pictographs, 2, 36
  populations, 6
  predictions, 22–23, 26–27
  quartiles, 28–30
  random samplings, 6–8
  range, 11–13
  relative frequency, 150
  samples, 6–9
  scatter plots, 20–23, 79
  spreadsheets, 38, 40, 75, 248, 425, 435, 459
  stem–and–leaf plots, 17–19

surveys, 6–9
  systematic samplings, 6–8
  trend lines, 21
Stem, 17
Stem–and–leaf plots
  defined, 17
  histograms and, 16–19
Straight angles, 196
Student Portfolio, *see* Alternative Assessment
Subsets, 521
Substitution method
  defined, 344
  solving systems of equations by, 344–347
Subtraction
  addition as opposite operation for, 109
  changing, to addition of opposites, 67
  of fractions, 48
  of integers, 49
  of polynomials, 376–379
  solving systems of equations by, 348–351
  of variable expressions, 66–69
  of whole numbers, 603
  word phrases for, 62
Sums, property of opposites of, 72
Supplementary angles, 196
Surface areas
  of cones, 433
  of cylinders, 433
  defined, 427
  nets and, 426–429
  of three-dimensional figures, 432–435
Surveys, 5
  biased, 7
  preference, 45
  sampling methods and, 6–9
Sylvester, James, 39
Symmetry
  line, *see* Line symmetry
  lines of, 310
  reflection, 310
  rotational, *see* Rotational symmetry
Systematic sampling, 6
Systems
  of equations
    defined, 338, 344
    inequalities and, 332–371
    solutions of, 338
    solving, *see* Solving systems of equations
  of inequalities, 362–365

■ T ■

30°-60°-90° right triangles, 504
Tactical/Kinesthetic Learning Style, *see* Differentiated Instruction
Tangent ratios, 488–491
TeacherWorks, xiii
Teaching Tip, 4, 6, 12, 15, 16, 24, 26, 38, 42, 50, 51, 52, 53, 56, 60, 66, 67, 68, 70, 72, 76, 80, 81, 82, 86, 90, 91, 95, 102, 103, 105, 112, 113, 120, 122, 124, 127, 126, 130, 144, 151, 158, 161, 166, 172, 173, 176, 178, 182, 190, 196, 200, 201, 207, 210, 211, 213, 217, 220, 221, 230, 231, 243, 248, 254, 259, 265, 281, 282, 294, 334, 335, 338, 339, 342, 344, 345, 348, 349, 352, 353, 354, 362, 366, 378, 385, 387, 388, 391, 394, 403, 404, 405, 422, 423, 427, 433, 452, 453, 456, 460, 462, 463, 472, 473, 475, 478, 482, 483, 490, 492, 493, 494, 499, 502, 503, 511, 513, 518, 521, 538, 539, 542, 543
ESL/LEP, 28, 63, 170, 193, 235, 242, 296, 489, 531
Technology, 97, 555, x, xi, xii, xiii
  Calculators, 11, 16, 21, 58, 88, 92, 129, 139, 155, 172, 173, 178, 226, 490, 491, 492, 494, 498, 499, 500, 501, 507
  Geometry software, 197, 205, 215, 229, 299, 303, 319, 439, 477, 497, 551
  Graphing calculator, 16, 21, 22, 26, 29, 39, 45, 260, 266, 268, 269, 270, 271, 334, 335, 340, 341, 347, 353, 356, 357, 392, 410
  Matrices, *see* Matrices
  Spreadsheets, 38, 40, 75, 248, 425, 435, 459
  Statistics, 34–37
Technology Note, 10, 11, 29, 88, 172, 173, 178, 269, 335
Temperatures, Celsius and Fahrenheit, 74
Terms
  like, *see* Like terms
  of polynomials, 376
  in sequences, 92
  of variable expressions, 66
Tessellations, 320–321
Test points, 259
Test Software, *see* ExamView® Pro
Theme Activities, 2, 48, 100, 146, 188, 240, 292, 330, 372, 418, 470, 516

Index

Theoretical probability
    defined, 159
    sample spaces and, 158–161
Think Back, 66, 73, 76, 108, 136, 137,
    196, 206, 264, 387, 408
Third quartile, 28
Three–dimensional figures, surface
    areas of, 432–435
Three-dimensional geometry,
    420–469
Three dots, 520
Tilings, 320
Transformations
    coordinate graphing and, 294–329
    defined, 296
Translations
    in coordinate planes, 296–299
    defined, 296
Transversals
    defined, 202
    parallel lines and, 202–205
Transversal systems, exterior angles
    of, 202
Trapezoids, 216
    isosceles, 595
Tree diagrams, 158–159
Trend lines, 21
Triangles, 222
    acute, 188, 206
    areas of, 148, 420
    classifying, 190
    congruent, *see* Congruent triangles
    equiangular, 206
    equilateral, 188, 206
    exterior angles of, 207
    isosceles, 188, 206
    measuring, 472
    obtuse, 188, 206
    properties of, 206–209
    right, *see* Right triangle *entries*
    scalene, 188, 206
    sum of angles in, 189
Triangular prisms, volumes of, 421
Triangular pyramids, 422
Trigonometric functions, inverse, 498
Trigonometric ratios, 488
Trigonometry, right triangle, 472–515
Trinomials, 376
    perfect square, 408
True equations, 104
True inequalities, 126
Turns, 306
Two-point perspective, 436–437
Two-step equations, 116

## ■ U ■

Union of sets, 147, 524–527

Union symbol (∪), 525
Unit rates, 103
Universal set, 524
Universal set symbol (U), 147
Unlike terms, 66
Unsound arguments, 543
Using exponents, 372

## ■ V ■

Valid argument forms, 542
Valid arguments, 542
Values, 56
    absolute, 49, 54
Vanishing points, 436
Variable expressions
    addition of, 66–69
    defined, 57
    division of, 72–75
    evaluating, 57
    multiplication of, 72–75
    simplifying, 66, 76–79
    subtraction of, 66–69
    terms of, 66
    writing, 62–65
Variables, 54
Variation
    constant of, 276
    direct, *see* Direct variation
    direct square, 277
    inverse, *see* Inverse variation
    inverse square, 283
Venn diagrams, 149, 162, 518
Vertex
    of angle, 196
    of polygon, 222
    of polyhedron, 422
    of pyramid, 422
    of triangle, 206
Vertical angles, 197
Vertical lines, 249
Vertical line test, 265
Vertically, lining up like terms, 378
Vertical translations, 597
Videos. *See* What's Math Got To Do
    With It? Real-Life Math Videos
Visualizing solids, 422–425
Visual Learning Style.
    *See* Differentiated Instruction
Vital capacity, 456
Vocabulary, 42, 94, 140, 182, 234, 286,
    324, 366, 412, 464, 510, 552
Volume formulas, 421
Volumes
    of cones, 456–459
    of cubes, 453
    of cylinders, 456–459
    defined, 452

lengths and areas and, 462–463
    of prisms, 452–455
    of pyramids, 452–455
    of rectangular prisms, 421, 453
    of spheres, 456–459
    of triangular prisms, 421

## ■ W ■

Weighted mean, 13
*What's Math Got To Do With It?*
    Real-Life Math Videos, 100A,
    146A, 240A, 330A
Whiskers, 29
Workplace Knowhow, *see* MathWorks
Writing
    linear equations, 254–257
    linear inequalities, 258–261
    variable expressions, 62–65
Writing Math, 9, 12, 18, 19, 23, 27, 31,
    37, 40, 41, 54, 58, 65, 69, 74, 78,
    84, 93, 106, 110, 115, 118, 124,
    125, 128, 134, 135, 138, 152, 153,
    155, 161, 164, 165, 170, 171, 175,
    180, 195, 199, 204, 208, 209, 215,
    218, 225, 228, 233, 247, 251, 256,
    261, 267, 269, 275, 278, 279, 284,
    298, 302, 308, 312, 318, 321, 336,
    341, 347, 351, 357, 359, 364, 378,
    382, 392, 399, 401, 406, 410, 424,
    429, 435, 438, 444, 448, 449, 454,
    458, 463, 476, 477, 480, 486, 490,
    496, 497, 500, 501, 507, 522, 523,
    526, 527, 531, 534, 541, 544, 545,
    551

## ■ X ■

*x*-axis, 244
*x*-coordinates, 244

## ■ Y ■

*y*-axis, 244
*y*-coordinates, 244
*y*-intercept, 254

## ■ Z ■

Zero, 52
    exponents of, 86–89
    factorial, 173
Zero pairs, 67, 396
Zero property of exponents, 86